MAGAZINES FOR LIBRARIES

SECOND EDITION

MAGAZINES FOR LIBRARIES

Second Edition

For the general reader,
and school, junior college,
college, and public libraries

BILL KATZ
and Berry Gargal, Science Editor

R.R. BOWKER COMPANY
NEW YORK & LONDON, 1972
A XEROX EDUCATION COMPANY

XEROX

Published by R. R. Bowker Co. (a Xerox company)
1180 Avenue of the Americas, New York, N.Y. 10036

Printed and bound in the United States of America

Library of Congress Cataloging in Publication Data

Katz, William Armstrong, 1924–
  Magazines for libraries.

  Bibliography: p.
  1. Periodicals—Bibliography. I. Title.
Z6941.K2 1972   016.05   72–6607
ISBN 0–8352–0554–1

For Linda (partner); Janet (daughter); Randy (son); and
for students and librarians (friends).

CONTENTS

PREFACE

Anyone who considers a second edition of a reference work has to answer a single basic question: Will the revision be different enough from the first edition to warrant consideration by potential users? Yes, this second edition of *Magazines for Libraries* is different—primarily in scope and updated information. It is not different in terms of purpose. As the first edition, the second is put together to help guide the librarian, teacher, and layman through the mass of magazines. There are now some 50,000 titles listed in the fourteenth edition of *Ulrich's International Periodicals Directory*. Hopefully, this guide will make it possible for the librarian to at least select the basic magazines from the 50,000.

The approach and philosophy, as outlined in the first edition, remain the same. It is redundant to repeat it all here, and those who are curious will find most of the first preface reprinted below. What though, are the real differences?

Over 4,500 titles are annotated in this edition, compared to approximately 2,400 last time. Unless out of business, all magazines included in the first edition are included in the second with updated information. Cessations and title changes are indicated also.

There are more subjects covered, and those used in the last edition were modified to keep up with current trends. There are now subject headings for everything from the counterculture to women's liberation and the environment, and even one on witchcraft. A few subjects, such as accounting, printing, and office and secretarial practices have been deleted, or incorporated into larger headings. Where possible, the subjects employed in *Ulrich's* are used here as well.

All data on the price, publisher, address, etc., has been checked and revised as necessary. The greatest amount of revision was the single item—price. Yes, they have gone up, up, and up. Comparison with the 1969 prices shows them up by as much as 30 percent—sometimes even higher. This goes a long way toward explaining why a selection guide is needed. As prices increase the need for more cautious selection becomes more apparent.

Most annotations in the first edition were carefully checked with the editor and/or publisher for accuracy and fairness. The editor was asked also to comment on the evaluative or descriptive statements. His or her comments were or were not followed depending on the opinion of the compiler. Conversely, all statements of factual changes were verified and included. The result is that each and every annotation from the first edition has been carefully examined. Some, although not all, were rewritten. If the information remained the same, the annotation is practically as it was.

The selection and description of scientific journals and abstracts is, once again, the work of Berry Gargal, librarian, Mart Science and Engineering Library, associate librarian, Lehigh University. However, in addition, the second edition represents the work and opinion of numerous contributors, all experts in their fields. Contributors' annotations are acknowledged by their initials appearing after the annotation. (Unsigned annotations are written by the co-editors.) Most of the contributors looked over the annotations in the previous edition, and although they did not always rewrite or revise them, their overview was another check for accuracy. It seems redundant to add that we are grateful for the work of all the contributors and advisers.

A major advantage of increasing the size of the second edition was that selection became much easier for the editors and contributors, who were able to choose from a broader base, and therefore were less likely to make the error of excluding a first-rate title. We can say, with some assurance, that in most cases the resulting selection represents the "best" basic titles in each of the fields.

One problem that will result from the increased number of titles, is that as the size of the list grows, the librarian's selection problems increase as well. There is more to select from, requiring more time, with probably not much more budget or staff. In order to help, each of the sections begins with a list of Basic Periodicals, divided by audience and type of library. In the previous edition there were lists in the back of the book, but this proved less than satisfactory. The present approach, suggested by a number of librarians, is more inclusive, and hopefully, more helpful. These lists represent the core of the selection process, and are based on numerous surveys, conversations, use studies, and just plain personal opinion.

In addition to these changes, there are several other new features. Where possible the word "Sample" is included in the bibliographic information—this is to assist the librarian who wishes to know whether the publisher will send a free sample, or a bill. To assist

ix

the binder, the date when the publisher ends a volume is also given. Another change is the inclusion of the term "Refereed," primarily to alert librarians to journals which have exhibited attempts at sustaining reliable publications. Refereeing, particularly important in the sciences, is a method of evaluating articles submitted to a publication by having them scrutinized by authoritative specialists, sometimes called an editorial board. The referees apparently assure a better chance that the final product will be a contribution to knowledge.

Selection of Scientific and Engineering Journals

The library literature has well described the proliferation of science and engineering periodicals in the past three decades, and the corresponding rises in costs. (See *Bibliography* for recent selected references.) Today, most scientific journals are so highly specialized that it is difficult to recommend many that would warrant inclusion in the collections of general libraries. The problem is even greater than that of layman vs. specialist. In the case of school and academic libraries, periodicals can be selected for student vs. faculty use or general science journals vs. research journals, depending on the needs of the faculty and the level of sophistication of the institution.

It is emphasized that little value judgment can be made by the nonspecialist on periodicals which primarily are publications of learned societies or academic institutions, and whose purpose is to promote understanding and to disseminate research results among the scientists of the world. Many of these journals, to assure quality of publication, have consistently had a policy of refereeing. Of course, lack of refereeing, in the case of commercial trade journals or news organs of societies, should not imply that these periodicals do not merit a place on the shelves. Obviously, they fill an entirely different need—one of alerting the profession to announcements of interest, and of providing tutorials in fields wherein technical obsolescence can be a fearful certainty.

Interdisciplinary journals are now the trend in all the sciences. An added problem has been the "labeling" of these publications for one field or another. The emergence of new societies and new periodicals representing these cross disciplines has, in some instances, adumbrated many of the journals of the past which were once considered vital for any research library. A number of these have been included in the second edition. Yet, one can scarcely ignore the periodicals which contributed enormously to the growth of science in the nineteenth century, which still continue to publish high-quality papers, and which still will appear in most collections of quality. A few selected titles have also been added. With the translation efforts of many scientific and commercial organizations, much important literature has become accessible from the

USSR and Asian countries. These, too, cannot be overlooked, and some representative selections have been made.

The annotations included in the second edition do not, by any means, represent the full scope of research publications available for specialized collections. Rather, based on selected citation studies, we have attempted to show, by discipline: (1) some of the periodicals available to interested laymen or nonspecialists; (2) the main research journals sponsored by distinguished scientific societies in the U.S., Canada, and Great Britain; (3) some high-quality, commercial publications most commonly found in academic libraries. In a few instances, namely new fields in which the literature has sprouted weed-like within a short period, titles have been included whose reputations are not, and may never be, well established. In part, this has been to clarify contents, particularly when several periodicals are similar in title, and to indicate at least the flavor of the publication.

Selection of Scientific Abstracts and Indexes

At this juncture in the state of the ever-expanding literature (nearly 40,000 sci-tech publications at last count), and the concomitant increase in number of specialized abstracts, libraries must begin to take a realistic look at costs. The decisions are not only whether they can afford to support the smaller indexing services (some, admittedly, timelier and more specific) as opposed to the major abstracting services, but also how far the library is willing to secure secondary material at the price of sacrificing primary publications. Larger installations, with a computer and supporting staff, face the choice of putting their money into a few magnetic tape subscriptions, and abandoning all those services which overlap. Despite genuine strides by such groups as the National Federation of Science Abstracting and Indexing Services, this overlap still exists in high degree.

The trend with the major abstracting services continues to be the repackaging of information in a variety of formats: microform; magnetic tape; selective dissemination of information (SDI) via card or computer; or simply the sale of custom-prepared searches.

The only caveat emptor which bears repeating is that coverage of titles should be thoroughly checked in each service, and the number of redundancies considered. With so many commercial organizations as well as information centers selling computerized information retrieval services, smaller libraries may be well advised to consider the economics of purchasing custom packages from these organizations, rather than to try and support subscriptions which may severely drain their resources.

In addition to the main indexes and abstracts for each scientific subject, we have also added annotations on most abstracting services sold in machine-readable form or those which provide services in custom packages.

Our particular thanks to Madeline Miele, editor extraordinary for R. R. Bowker. Due to her knowledge, skill, patience and imagination this compilation has come to a successful conclusion. She and her fellow editors have truly brought order out of chaos. Thanks to the librarians (and reviewers) who so kindly accepted the first edition, the second is now possible.

We would hope to go on with a third, perhaps in another three years. And as one attempts to improve with each time out, we invite individual librarians to send their comments and suggestions. Thanks to several of you, this edition is much improved (in all modesty) over the first. The third should be even better.

BILL KATZ AND BERRY GARGAL

FROM THE *PREFACE* TO THE FIRST EDITION

This is a classified, annotated guide to magazines in major, and a few minor subject areas. It represents the views and experiences of the compiler, his science editor, librarians, teachers, subject specialists, students and informed magazine readers. Its purpose is to suggest to the general reader and the librarian the titles best suited for his individual needs. Hopefully, it will introduce him to periodicals which will be stimulating, pleasant and helpful in his quest for knowledge.

The guide is purposefully compiled for all types of readers and libraries. The only exceptions are that it will be of limited use to the specialist in his particular field, and to the librarian building a large, specialized collection.

Emphasis is on the magazine first, the reader second, and the library last. It is a case of the last really being first. This emphasis is believed to be the greatest service to the library in that it gives the librarian the widest base of selection, and does not limit him or her to the necessary qualifications imposed on a list devised for a single type of library. Lists which are put together for a given size, or library type suffer from a major fault—they must by their very nature include or exclude titles which do or do not meet the nebulous needs of what the compiler, no matter how well intentioned or informed, believes is that library's audience. Yet, no library serves a single public, and it would seem most logical to offer a wider choice of magazines, and thereby a less restricted view of the world.

Thus, while each of the periodical entries is keyed for particular types of libraries, the key is only suggestive. There are enough alternatives to offer the librarian a wide choice, a choice which may very well eschew the compiler's notion of what is best suited for this or that type of library. . . .

In a word, this guide offers the widest possible latitude to reader and librarian. By so doing, the compiler hopes to avoid the necessity of running up the warning flag, i.e., any list of periodicals must be considered from the viewpoint of the community it serves. The

compiler has worked on this premise from the first, and while there inevitably will be some titles not included which some reader thinks essential (particularly true of regional magazines), at least the main titles have been annotated.

The compiler is suspicious of any "best" list, particularly for use by librarians and library users. The typical library client, after all, does not require to be told that this or that title is best; he simply wants to know the alternatives within certain limits of value. Conversely, he does require something more than a union list or a bibliography of say, 1,200 titles in one area. In a word, a guide to the field is required. Therefore, the number of titles is purposefully large (although not large enough, and given another edition, the number will be increased).

Finally, despite a consensus of experts, the inclusions or exclusions are admittedly subjective. They can be no other way, for as a wise consultant noted:

"You will do well to recognize that there is *none* of this which is not subjective, and to declare, in the description of your book, that it is directed primarily to librarians seeking *subjective* information for the purchase of periodicals. I naively imagine that they can, with little effort, find all the *objective* information from the dealers with whom they deal."

Selection

Anyone remotely familiar with the magazine world recognizes that no one is quite certain how many titles are now available, but world-wide the number is variously estimated at between 60,000 and 100,000. . . . Approximately 16,000 magazines are published in the United States, and about one half are company magazines or house organs. Still closer to the average library situation, the various American Library Association standards call for from 75 to 150 titles in a small public library; 125 to 175 in a senior high school. Junior colleges, universities and colleges set no particular number, but a collection of 400 to 1,000 titles is considered respectable. Large, special, state university and urban public libraries have holdings in excess of 5,000 titles, but these are the glorious exceptions, not the dismal rule. The check for most small and medium-sized libraries is the *Readers' Guide to Periodical Literature,* which now lists 158 magazines, many of a general or popular nature. It requires no survey, of course, to realize that in the vast majority of libraries—regardless of type—the magazine collection does not measure up even to the limited listing of the *Readers' Guide to Periodical Literature,* and certainly not to A.L.A. standards. Fortunately, matters seem to be improving, but until they do the titles in the average library require particular care in selection. They also require something more than a single index, but that is another story.

Considering what is available (almost infinite) and what the average library purchases (frequently finite) selection was made for this work as follows:

(1) The major point of departure consisted of polling experts—librarians, teachers, professionals, students, laymen and magazine readers. Each consultant was asked to check a basic list, add and delete. While this procedure was not considered necessary for all areas, it was employed for the major subjects.

(2) Within each subject category, consultants were asked to select titles which were both the "best," and the most often used by the greatest number of their fellow experts. This was not always possible, but it at least eliminated a number of the more esoteric magazines.

(3) Before and after the tentative lists were returned by the consultants, each of the subject areas was checked against previous bibliographies, holdings of representative libraries, use studies, and other standard lists and articles about specific categories. The basic indexes were examined. A list of the other works consulted will be found in the bibliography to this book.

(4) Emphasis is on American magazines with some, but admittedly not enough, attention to Canadian and British publications. A few foreign titles are included, but only in those areas where they are of such importance that exclusion would constitute total provincialism.

(5) The number of titles within each subject area is dictated by the relative number of publications in the area and, more important, by the relative weight (let it be noted, not importance) of the subject in the curricula and day-by-day workings of the average public school, junior college and college and university library. This required eliminating many long, carefully thought out lists submitted by experts, but again, this was necessary to keep the total within balance.

(6) Finally, certain subjects were not included, or only in a representative way because they were considered too specialized for this type of general list; e.g., law, medicine, dentistry, at one extreme and at the other, astrology, apparel, building, etc.

HOW TO USE THIS BOOK

TITLE. DATE FOUNDED. *FREQUENCY. *PRICE. EDITOR.
PUBLISHER AND ADDRESS. ILLUSTRATIONS, INDEX,
ADVERTISING. CIRCULATION. *SAMPLE. *DATE VOLUME
ENDS. REFEREED. *MICROFORM. *REPRINT. *INDEXED.
*BOOK REVIEWS. *AUDIENCE. *JUDGMENT VALUE.

The magazines in this book are listed alphabetically, by title, under the subjects given in the Contents. All subject classifications used, as well as variations in wording of subject headings, and as many additional subject cross-references as the authors expected would be useful, are listed in the Index.

The bibliographic form of each entry is shown above, and additional explanation follows for items preceded by an asterisk. The Abbreviations section below lists the general abbreviations found in the bibliographic information, and the acronyms used for the microform and reprint companies, and abstracts and indexes. The names of the contributors whose initials are at the end of many of the annotations are also listed in the Abbreviations section.

Frequency and Price

The frequency is given immediately after the founding date, and the symbols used are explained in the General Abbreviations section. The price quoted is the annual subscription rate given by the publisher, usually as of the end of 1971 or early 1972. Since the prices of periodical subscriptions are continually rising, all prices are subject to change. Furthermore, the devaluation of the dollar makes the prices of foreign magazines even more relative.

Sample

Publishers were asked whether or not they will send a free copy of their magazine to a library if requested. Those who replied favorably are indicated by the single word "sample." The request should be by the head of the library, or by the head of the serials department, and on official stationery. The indication that a publisher is willing to send samples to institutions does not mean he is necessarily interested in sending them to individual subscribers.

Date Volume Ends

Several librarians indicated it would be helpful to know when a publisher ends a volume—obviously for purposes of binding. The information provided is from the publisher.

Microform, Reprint, Indexed

Companies providing microform and reprint runs of magazines are indicated, and information concerning where each title is abstracted or indexed is listed also. See the Abbreviations section for explanation of acronyms and addresses. (The word "index" as used in the bibliographic entry means that the publication provides its own index.)

Book Reviews

Information given refers to the approximate number of reviews which appear in a typical issue of the periodical, the average length, and whether or not they are signed.

Audience

Each magazine has an indication of audience or type of library for which it is suited. The scale is specific, but as most magazines are for more than one audience, several audience levels are usually given for each title. Periodicals for elementary and junior high school students (Ejh) are not separated because it is often difficult to draw the line between these two age groups. The titles and descriptive annotations leave little doubt as to the level of maturity for which the magazine is intended. The high school level (Hs) includes readers in grades 10–12, who are 16 to 18 years old. Magazines suitable for public libraries, and college and university library reading rooms are rated General Adult (Ga). The abbreviation Jc (Junior College) is used only in the basic lists of recommendations before each section. However, publications designated Academic Audience (Ac) should also be considered for junior colleges. Magazines rated Special Adult (Sa) are for specialized audiences and will be read by few people other than professionals or students of a particular subject.

In this edition the terms Ht (high school teacher) and Et (elementary school teacher) have been eliminated. Magazines suitable for teachers are so indicated in the annotation, and the simple designation Hs or Ejh indicates the level.

It is assumed that the audience symbols are only guides, not designations for type of library. Which is to say that the symbol Ga does not mean the magazine is only limited to public libraries, any more than Ac means a magazine is only for academic libraries. Ob-

viously the choice should be made by the librarian, and this will depend on his or her assessment of the audience to be served. Public libraries will often include many of the same magazines found in all other libraries.

Judgment Value

In this edition only two symbols are used to rank magazines: V for the exceptional ones, and C for those which are unexceptional, or below average. In the previous edition several ranking symbols were used and the result was not entirely satisfactory—to say the least. This time around we tried to simplify matters. The vast majority of titles are between this radical V–C scale, and as such, no value judgment is attempted. The editors and contributors have only indicated extremes. Hopefully this will assist the librarian, particularly the one with a limited budget who must be highly selective in given subject areas. Where no symbol of judgment is employed, the magazine is acceptable and choice should be based entirely on what is needed for the particular library audience.

ABBREVIATIONS

GENERAL ABBREVIATIONS

a.	Annual
Ac	Academic Audience
Aud	Audience
bi-m.	Every two months
bi-w.	Every two weeks
d.	Daily
Ejh	Elementary and Junior High School
Ga	General Adult
Hs	High School
irreg.	Irregular
Jc	Junior College
Jv	Judgment Value
m.	Monthly
q.	Quarterly
Sa	Special Adult
s-a.	Twice annually
s-m.	Twice monthly
s-w.	Twice weekly
3/yr.	Three per year, m., w., etc.
w.	Weekly

MICROFORM AND REPRINT COMPANIES

ACRPP	ACRPP, 4 rue Louvois, Paris 2e, France
AMC	American Chemical Society, 1155 16th St., N.W., Washington, D.C. 20036
AMS	AMS Press Inc., 56 E. 13th St., New York, N.Y. 10003
Abrahams	Abrahams Magazine Service, 56 E. 13th St., New York, N.Y. 10003
B&H	Bell & Howell, Microphoto Division, Old Mansfield Rd., Wooster, Ohio 44691
Canner	J. S. Canner & Co., 49–65 Lansdowne St., Boston, Mass. 02215
Carrolton	Carrolton Press, Inc., 1647 Wisconsin Ave., N.W., Washington, D.C. 20007
Dawson	William Dawson & Sons, Ltd., 16 West St., Farham, Surrey, England

Johnson	Johnson Reprint Corp., 111 Fifth Ave., New York, N.Y. 10003
Kraus	Kraus Reprint Co., 16 E. 46th St., New York, N.Y. 10017
MCA	Microfilming Corporation of America, 21 Harristown Rd., Glen Road, N.J. 07452
MF	Microcard Editions, Inc., 901 26th St., N.W., Washington, D.C. 20037
MR	Maxwell Reprint Co., Fairview Park, Elmsford, N.Y. 10523
NYPL	New York Public Library, Photographic Service, New York, N.Y. 10018
Niemeyer Verlag	Niemeyer Verlag, Pfrondorferstrasse 4, Tubingen, W. Germany
PMC	Princeton Microfilm Corporation, Box 235, Princeton, N.J. 08550
Swets & Zeitlinger	Keizersgracht, 847 Amsterdam, The Netherlands
UM	University Microfilms, 300 N. Zeeb Rd., Ann Arbor, Michigan 48106
UnivChicago	University of Chicago Library, Photoduplication Dept., Chicago, Ill. 60637

ABSTRACTS AND INDEXES

ABCPolSci	ABC Pol Sci
API	Alternative Press Index
ASTI	Applied Science and Technology Index
AbAn	Abstracts in Anthropology
AbEnSt	Abstracts of English Studies
AbFolkSt	Abstracts of Folklore Studies
AbMilt	Abstracts of Military Bibliography
AbPhoto	Abstracts of Photographic Science and Engineering Literature
AbSocWk	Abstracts for Social Workers
AbVoc	Abstracts of Research and Related Materials in Vocational and Technical Education
AbrIMed	Abridged Index Medicus
AbrRG	Abridged Readers' Guide

AfrAb	African Abstracts	EdAb	Education Abstracts
AirPolAb	Air Pollution Abstracts	EdAd	Educational Administration Abstracts
AirUnLibI	Air University Library Index to Military Periodicals	EdI	Education Index
		EmAb	Employment Relations Abstracts
AmerH	America: History and Life	EngI	Engineering Index
AmerLitAb	American Literature Abstracts	Env	Environment Information Access
AntroI	Anthropological Index	EnvI	Environment Index
ApMec	Applied Mechanics Review	ExChAb	Exceptional Child Education Abstracts
AquaBiolAb	Aquatic Biology Abstracts (title changed to: *Aquatic Sciences and Fisheries Abstracts*)	GInd	Guide to Indian Periodical Literature
		GPerfArts	Guide to Performing Arts
		GeoAb	Geographical Abstracts
ArmC	Arms Control and Disarmament	HistAb	Historical Abstracts
ArtArch	Art and Archaeology Technical Abstracts	HorsAb	Horseman's Abstracts
		HospAb	Hospital Abstracts
ArtI	Art Index	HousP	Housing and Planning References
Ast&AstroAb	Astronomy and Astrophysics Abstracts	HwyResAb	Highway Research Abstracts
BibAg	Bibliography of Agriculture	IBZ	Internationale Bibliographie der Zeitschriften-literatur
BibI	Bibliographic Index		
BibIGeo	Bibliography and Index of Geology	ICLM	Index to Commonwealth Little Magazines
BioAb	Biological Abstracts		
BioAg	Biological and Agricultural Index	IBk	Index to Book Reviews in the Humanities
BioI	Biography Index	IChildMag	Subject Index to Children's Magazines
BoAb	Boating Abstracts (ceased)	IEc	Index of Economic Articles
BoRv	Book Review Digest	IIn	Index India
BritArchAb	British Archaeological Abstracts	IJewAr	Index of Articles on Jewish Studies
BritEdI	British Education Index	IJewPer	Index to Jewish Periodicals
BritHum	British Humanities Index	IMed	Index Medicus
BritTechI	British Technology Index	INeg	Index to Periodicals by and about Negroes
BusI	Business Periodicals Index		
CIJE	Current Index to Journals in Education	InfP	Information Processing Journal
CINL	Cumulative Index to Nursing Literature	InfSciAb	Information Science Abstracts
CISI	CIS Index	IntAe	International Aerospace Abstracts
CanEdI	Canadian Education Index	IntGuC	International Guide to Classical Studies
CanI	Canadian Periodical Index	IntNurI	International Nursing Index
CathI	Catholic Periodical and Literature Index	IntPolSc	International Political Science Abstracts
ChemAb	Chemical Abstracts	JEconLit	Journal of Economic Literature
ChemTitles	Chemical Titles	LMags	Index to Little Magazines
ChildDevAb	Child Development Abstracts	LangAb	Language and Language Behavior Abstracts
ColStuAb	College Student Personnel Abstracts		
ComAb	Computer Abstracts	LangTAb	Language Teaching Abstracts
ComRev	Computing Reviews	LatAm	Index to Latin American Periodicals
CrimAb	Abstracts on Criminology and Penology	LegPer	Index to Legal Periodicals
CurrCont	Current Contents	LibLit	Library Literature
Dsh	DSH Abstracts	LibSciAb	Library and Information Science Abstracts
EKI	Ekistic Index		
EconAb	Economic Abstracts	MLA	Modern Language Association. International Bibliography
EconCont	Contents of Recent Economics Journals		

MathR	Mathematical Reviews
MedS	Medical Socioeconomic Research Sources
MetAb	Metals Abstracts
Met&GeoAb	Meteorological and Geoastrophysical Abstracts
MusicI	Music Index
NucSciAb	Nuclear Science Abstracts
NutrAb	Nutrition Abstracts
OceanAb	Oceanic Abstracts
PAIS	Public Affairs Information Service
PHRA	Poverty and Human Resources Abstracts
PeaceResAb	Peace Research Abstracts
PerManAb	Personal Management Abstracts
PhAb	Photographic Abstracts
PhilosI	Philosopher's Index
PolAb	Pollution Abstracts
PsyAb	Psychological Abstracts
QBib	Quarterly Bibliography of Computers and Data Processing
RAND	Selected Rand Abstracts
RG	Readers' Guide to Periodical Literature
RILM	RILM Abstracts of Music Literature
RelAb	Religious and Theological Abstracts
RelPer	Index to Religious Periodical Literature
RelPerI	Religious Periodicals Index
RepBibPhil	Repertoire Bibliographique de la Philosophie
ResEduc	Research in Education
SCI	Science Citation Index
STAR	Scientific and Technical Aerospace Reports
SciAb	Science Abstracts
SelEnv	Selected References on Environment Quality
SocAb	Sociological Abstracts
SSHum	Social Sciences and Humanities Index
THB	Today's Housing Briefs
WatPolAb	Water Pollution Abstracts
WatResAb	Water Resources Abstracts

CONTRIBUTORS AND ADVISERS

A.L.	Anne Leibl, Univ. of Toronto (Counterculture, Underground Newspapers)
A.P.	Ann Prentice, SUNY, Albany, Library School Faculty
A.S.	Adeline Smith, Hoosic Valley Central School Library, Schaghticoke, N.Y. (Free Magazines)
A.T.	Alice Tillman, SUNY, Albany, Library School (Art)
B.A.	Barbara Abrash, Empire State College, SUNY, Albany (Africa)
B.B.	Barbara Brenner, SUNY, Albany, Library School (Psychology)
B.G.	Barbara Guay, SUNY, Albany, Library School (Aging)
C.B.	Christine Bulson, SUNY, Oneonta (Theater, Travel)
C.B.	Carol Brannan, SUNY, Albany, Library School (Occupations)
C.D.	Clover Drinkwater, SUNY, Albany, Library School (Art)
C.F.	Carol Fleishauer, Univ. of Wisconsin Library, Madison (Hobbies)
C.W.	Celeste West, Editor, *Synergy*, San Francisco (Wine)
D.D.	Don Dorrance, South Milwaukee Public Library, Wis. (Little Mags, Poetry)
D.D.	Douglas DeLong, Illinois State Univ., Normal (Geography, Newspapers)
D.L.	Dorothy Lutz, SUNY, Albany, Library School (Criminology)
D.S.	Donna Sopalsky, SUNY, Albany, Library School (China & Asia)
D.V.	David Voorhees, Kent State Univ., Ohio (City Mags)
E.L.	Eta Lustig, SUNY, New Paltz (USSR)
E.W.	Earl Wilcox, Winthrop College, Rock Hill, S.C. (Literature/Author Newsletters)
F.A.	Fred Abrams, Univ. of Texas, Medical Branch Library, Galveston (Health, Medicine)
F.B.	Freida Bregger, Univ. of Wisconsin, Madison (Hobbies)
F.B.	Frank Brandon, SUNY, Albany, Library School (Linguistics)
F.L.	Frank London, Tulane Univ., New Orleans, La. (Radio, Television)
F.M.	Fred MacFadden, Coppin State College, Baltimore (Folklore)
F.P.	Frederick Patten, Los Angeles Science Fantasy Society (Comics)
F.S.	Fran Seaholm, SUNY, New Paltz (USSR)
G.L.	Gary Lenox, Univ. of Wisconsin, Rock County (Hobbies)
G.M.	Gerald Melton, SUNY, Albany, Library School (Anthropology)
G.S.	Gerta Steuer, SUNY Library, Albany (French, Italian)

G.S.	Gordon Stevens, SUNY, Albany, Library School Faculty (Music)
G.S.	Grant T. Skelley, Univ. of Washington, Seattle, Library School Faculty (Magazine Bibliography)
H.B.	Harry Broussard, Tulane University, New Orleans (Automobiles)
H.D.	Harold Diamond, Lehman College, Bronx, N.Y. (Art, Literature)
I.G.	Irma Garlick, SUNY, Albany, Library School (Indians)
J.A.	John K. Amrhein, Kutztown State College, Pa. (Philosophy)
J.B.	John Berger, Alternative Feature Service, Berkeley, Calif.
J.C.	Jeff Cannel, Skidmore College, Saratoga, N.Y. (Hobbies/Models)
J.G.	John Greene, SUNY, Albany (Blacks)
J.J.	Josephy Judy, U.S. Dept. of Agriculture Library, Wash, D.C. (Agriculture)
J.L.	John Liberty, Sacramento State College, Calif. (Counterculture, News and Opinion)
J.M.	Jane Maloney, SUNY, Albany, Library School (Interior Design & Decoration)
J.M.	Joe Morehead, SUNY, Albany, Library School Faculty (Government Magazines)
J.M.	Joe McDonald, State College, West Chester, Pa. (Health)
J.N.	Joan Nethercott, SUNY, Albany, Library School (Environment)
J.W.	J. B. Wood, California State College, Los Angeles (Chicano)
K.R.	Keith Revelle, Oakland Public Library, Calif. (Spanish)
L.A.	Lee Ash, New Haven, Conn. (Ornithology)
L.G.	Linda Greene, University of Pittsburgh (Women/Teenage; Counterculture)
L.H.	Lillian Hecht, SUNY, New Paltz (USSR)
L.O.	Lillian Orsini, SUNY, Albany, Library School Faculty (Children)
L.T.	Lorna Tracy, co-editor, *Stand* (Poetry, Little Magazines)
M.A.	Mary Anderson, SUNY, Albany Library School (Sports)
M.B.	Melissa Bradley, Univ. of Denver (Boats)
M.D.	Merle Downing, University of California, Riverside (Urban Studies)
M.E.	Michael Esposito, New York State Library, Albany (Men's Magazines)
M.M.	Mary McKenney, St. Mary's College, Maryland
M.S.	Mike Shannon, Lehman College, Bronx, N.Y. (Law, Political Science)
M.W.	Murray Wortzel, Lehman College, Bronx, N.Y. (Sociology)
N.B.	Neil Barron, Baker & Taylor, Somerville, N.J. (Science Fiction)
N.E.	Neal Edgar, Kent State Univ., Ohio (Labor)
N.H.	Nancy Heller, SUNY, Albany (Spanish)
N.H.	Norman Horrocks, Dalhousie Univ., Halifax, Library School Faculty
N.P.	Nancy Putman, SUNY, Albany, Library School (Archaeology)
P.B.	Peter Betz, SUNY, Johnstown (Fishing, Hunting)
P.G.	Peter Gellatly, Univ. of Washington Library, Seattle
P.M.	Patricia Majestic, SUNY, Albany, Library School (Pets)
P.S.	Paula Strain, Mitre Corp., Mclean, Va., Librarian (Mountaineering)
P.V.	Paul Vesenyi, Lehman College, Bronx, N.Y. (Abstracts and Indexes)
P.W.F.	P. William Filby, Maryland Historical Soc., Baltimore (Genealogy)
R.B.	Robert Burgess, SUNY, Albany, Library School Faculty (Business/Banking and Finance; Investments)
R.C.	Robert Chatterton, SUNY, Albany, Library
R.C.	Ronald Colman, SUNY, Albany, Library School (Journalism)
R.S.	Richard Seidel, Newberry Library, Chicago (Architecture, History)
R.T.	Ruth Tronik, Jewish National Univ. Library, Jerusalem (Israeli Magazines)
S.B.	Sanford Berman, Univ. of Uganda (Africa, Blacks)
S.G.	Sheryl Griffith, SUNY, Albany, Library School (Linguistics)
S.W.	Susan Walch, SUNY, Albany, Library School (Books & Book Reviews)
W.H.	Walter Hagen, SUNY, Albany, Library School (Business, Communications, Radio)
W.D.	William J. Demo, SUNY, Albany, Library School (Motion Pictures)

MAGAZINES FOR LIBRARIES

SECOND EDITION

MAGAZINES FOR LIBRARIES

ABSTRACTS AND INDEXES

Basic Abstracts and Indexes

Ejh: *Readers' Guide to Periodical Literature, Education Index, Subject Index to Children's Magazines, Index to Periodicals By and About Negroes.* Hs: *Readers' Guide to Periodical Literature, Education Index, Index to Periodicals By and About Negroes, Current Index to Journals in Education, Social Sciences and Humanities Index*—other subject and special indexes as needed. Ga: *Readers' Guide to Periodical Literature, Social Sciences and Humanities Index, Applied Science and Technology Index, Index to Periodicals By and About Negroes, Public Affairs Information Service*—other subject and special indexes as needed. Jc: Same as for public library, i.e., Ga., but with special attention to needs of the curriculum in terms of special subject abstracts and indexes. Ac: Same as for public library, i.e., Ga, but with special attention to special subject abstracts and indexes. Ideally, the academic library should have all abstracts and indexes listed here.

See Newspapers Section for individual newspaper indexes, e.g., *New York Times Index, Christian Science Monitor Index,* etc.

Cessations

Book Review Index, Abstracts of North American Geology, Boating Abstracts, Geophysical Abstracts.

ABC Pol Sci: Advance bibliography of contents, political science and government. 1969. 9/yr. Service basis $43 to $93 (individuals $10). ABC–Clio, Inc., Riviera Campus, 2040 Alameda Padre Serra, Santa Barbara, Calif. 93103. Circ: 1,600. Sample. Vol. ends: Dec.

This bibliography presents information gathered from the tables of contents of various magazines. It provides a subject, author, and title approach to articles in the field of political science. (One presumes that the editors will have examined the contents of the articles themselves, in order to provide a detailed subject analysis.) The great benefit of this bibliography lies in its currency (faster than most published indexes) and scope. Some 300 journals from 30 countries are covered. Its format is clear and easy to read, an improvement over *Current Contents*. Numbers 1 through 8 appear with a separately bound index arranged by subject, law, cases, and authors. A list of periodicals

included appears in issues 1, 5, and 9. Number 9 is the annual cumulative index. There is also an article copying service available to subscribers, at five cents a page. This can be of use in nearly all larger research collections with concentrations in the social sciences. It can be particularly helpful in tracking down elusive, foreign titles. Smaller libraries with access to larger collections may also be interested. (M.S.)

Abridged Index Medicus. 1970. m. $12. National Library of Medicine. Subs. to: Supt. of Documents, U.S. Govt. Printing Office, Washington, D.C. 20402.

The *Abridged Index Medicus* is designed to afford rapid access to selected biomedical journal literature of immediate interest to the practicing physician. Each issue contains citations from 100 English-language journals, representing one month's input into the National Library of Medicine's computer-based MEDLARS (Medical Literature Analysis and Retrieval System). The selection of the journals was made by the library with the guidance from an advisory committee of physicians, medical editors, and medical librarians. Consideration was given to the quality of the journals, usefulness of journal content for the medical practioner, and the need for providing coverage of all fields of clinical medicine. In some fields, where there are more high-quality journals than could be included in the bibliography, consideration was given to the availability of the journals to the American practitioner. In limiting the size of *Abridged Index Medicus*, it was necessary to omit many excellent publications. The list of journals indexed will be reviewed periodically and is subject to change. (F.A.)

Abridged Readers' Guide to Periodical Literature. 1935. m. (except June, July, Aug.). $14. Zada Limerick. H.W. Wilson Co., 950 Univ. Ave., Bronx, N.Y. 10452. Circ: 25,886. Sample. Vol. ends: May.

A cutdown version of the *Readers' Guide to Periodical Literature.* Indexes 44 magazines, all of which appear in the larger version. Although the price is less than one half that of the unabridged work, it is not recommended. With the increase in duplicating services, interlibrary loans and cooperation between libraries, the user should have access to the full index. Magazines not carried by the library may be borrowed or, at best, the user may find the material he needs and go to a larger library. See also *Readers' Guide to Periodical Literature.*

1

Abstracts in Anthropology. 1970. q. $20. M. Estellie Smith. Eastern New Mexico University, Portales, N. Mex. Greenwood Periodicals, Inc., 51 Riverside Ave. Westport, Conn. 06880. Vol. ends: November.

Bk. rev: various number.

This journal presents unsigned abstracts on all four subfields of anthropology, arranged in the same classes, Ethnology, Linguistics, Archaeology, and Physical Anthropology. The abstracts are taken from over 40 professional journals, and some from papers presented at learned societies. The scope is international. A few extensive book reviews are also published unsigned. An elaborate cross index helps orientation, but for author entries a cumulated index is offered only in the last issue of the volume. Nevertheless, this publication is a valuable research instrument in the field of anthropology, complementing Wilson's *Social Sciences & Humanities Index* and the *Abstracts of Folklore Studies.* (P.V.)

Abstracts on Criminology and Penology (Formerly: *Excerpta Criminologica).* 1961. bi-m. $45. Ed. bd. Kluwer. Polstraat 10, Deventer, Netherlands. Circ: 1,150. Sample. Vol ends: No. 6.

"An international abstracting service covering the etiology of crime and juvenile delinquency." It uses broad classifications with subject and author index; annual cumulation. Some 2,000 abstracts a year from around the world, but the vast majority from United States and United Kingdom periodicals.

Abstracts of English Studies. 1958. 10/yr. (Sept.–June). John B. Shipley. National Council of Teachers of English, 1111 Kenyon Rd., Urbana, Ill. 61801. Index, adv. Circ: 3,645. Sample. Vol. ends: June. Microform: UM. Reprint: AMS.

Summarizes numerous monographs and scholarly articles from more than 1,100 journals in the subject areas of literature (by period and genre), general studies and language (history, linguistics, Celtic, etc.), English and American literature, and world literature in English. Journals searched include many outside the normal scrutiny of English scholars. (The annual index, ordered by year—1958 to present—is $1.00 each, $1.50 for institutions.)

Abstracts of Folklore Studies. 1963. q. $5. Richard E. Buehler. Published for the American Folklore Society by the Univ. of Texas Press, Box 7819, Austin, Tex. 78712. Circ: 2,200. Vol. ends: Winter. Reprint: Kraus.

Presents signed abstracts taken from about 160 journals from all parts of the world, in the fields of folklore studies, ethnology, ethnomusicology, and related areas. There are 800 to 1000 entries per year. The arrangement is by journal titles in alphabetical order. Under each entry abstracts are listed in chronological order as the articles appeared in the journal. Subject approach is through the Name–Subject Index which is cumulated annually. A valuable feature of this publication is the *Bibliographical Notes* which survey the literature not published in periodicals. Combined with the Ethnology section of *Abstracts in Anthropology,* this service is indispensable for the specialized reader of folklore. (P.V.)

Abstracts of Military Bibliography/ Resumenes Analiticos de Bibliografia Militar. 1967. q. $25. Ruben A. Ramirez Mitchell. National Security Council, Esmeralda 356 Buenos Aires, Argentina. Circ: 5,000. Sample.

A 75 to 100 page quarterly abstracting service, arranged by some 50 broad subject headings, of materials found worldwide on the military. Periodicals, books, reports, and monographs are considered. Some 100 magazines and journals are analyzed—interestingly enough the greatest number come from the United States, followed by Germany, Argentina, and Great Britain. The Soviet Union is represented by only one title, and China not at all. Articles are fully abstracted in both Spanish and English. The abstracts are quite long, analytical, and well written.

Abstracts of Photographic Science & Engineering Literature. 1962. m. $300 ($120 to educational and public libraries). Thomas T. Hill. Soc. of Photographic Scientists & Engineers, 1330 Massachusetts Ave., N.W., Washington, D.C. 20005. Circ: 1,000. Sample. Vol. ends: Dec.

Abstracts the significant technical literature related to photography, including its physics and chemistry, photographic theory and materials, photographic apparatus, and applied photography. Over 3,000 informative abstracts are published annually, and over 300 international journals are screened. The literature covered is predominantly from periodicals and patents. Entries are arranged under four broad classifications subdivided by a large number of specific subject headings. In addition to full bibliographic citation, each entry contains descriptors which further delineate the subject matter. Cross-references appear under each classification. Each issue contains an author and patent index. An annual index is issued with each volume, but multivolume indexes must be purchased separately. Academic and special libraries concentrating in this field will need both this and the older *Photographic Abstracts.*

Abstracts of Research and Related Materials in Vocational and Technical Education. 1967. q. $11. Robert E. Taylor. ERIC Clearinghouse, Center for Vocational and Technical Education, Ohio State Univ., 1900 Kenny Rd., Columbus, Ohio 43210. Microform: UM.

While an abstracting service of basic research in

vocational education, this must be used via the major ERIC index, i.e., *Research in Education*.

Abstracts for Social Workers. 1965. q. $20. Inez L. Speer. National Assn. of Social Workers, 2 Park Ave., New York, N.Y. 10016. Circ: 8,000. Sample. Vol. ends: Winter. Microform: UM.

Classified arrangement of abstracts of articles in social work and allied areas. Author and subject indexes.

African Abstracts/Analyses Africanistes; a quarterly review of ethnographic, social, and linguistic studies appearing in current periodicals. 1950. q. $7 (French edition, F32). International African Institute, 10/11 Fetter Lane, London EC 4, England. (French edition: Editions Mouton et Cie, 45 rue de Lille, Paris, France.) Circ: 1,000. Microform: MF. Reprint: Wm. Dawson.

Available in both French and English (the two editions are identical, except for language), this summarizes articles which appear in African periodicals, no matter where they are published. Coverage is explained in the subtitle. There is an annual cumulation with author and periodical indexes.

Air Pollution Abstracts. 1970. m. $22. Air Pollution Technical Information Center, Research Triangle Park, N.C. Subs. to: Supt. of Documents, U.S. Govt. Printing Office, Washington, D.C. 20402.

Produced by the Air Pollution Technical Information Center (APTIC) of the Environmental Protection Agency (EPA), the journal is an outgrowth of *NAPCA Abstract Bulletin*. Presently, it serves as a current awareness and abstracting service to EPA and others, for the in-house literature accessioned by APTIC. As would be expected, its scope is broad, going from emission sources (whether caused by industry, processes, or materials), to control and measurement methods; through air quality, atmospheric interactions, basic science, and on to effects on plants, animals, and materials. Also included are sections on legislation, air quality standards, and economic and social aspects. Entries are arranged by accession number under the general headings mentioned above. Abstracts are not restricted to the journal literature; books, conference proceedings, technical reports, patents, and some translations and theses are reviewed as well. Each issue carries author-subject indexes, with cumulative indexes published periodically. Since this is at present the only abstracting service dedicated exclusively to air pollution, it would seem essential for any library supporting research in the field. The timeliness of entries may be erratic, however, probably because the abstracts are of documents as received at APTIC. For academic libraries. (B.G.)

Air University Library Index to Military Periodicals; a subject index to significant articles, news items and editorials appearing in 65 military and aeronautical periodicals not indexed in readily available commercial indexing services. 1949. q. Exchange. Frances B. Rucks. Air Univ. Library, Maxwell Air Force Base, Ala. 36112.

The subhead is descriptive of the scope, purpose, and contents of the index which can be as valuable to the sociologist, historian, and generalist as to the military man or woman.

Alternative Press Index. 1969. q. $6/individual; $10/movement groups; $15/high schools; $30/libraries and educational institutions; $60/military and corporate institutions. Radical Research Center, Bag Service 2500, Postal Station E, Toronto, Ont. (formerly located at Carleton College, Northfield, Minn).

The only index to alternative and underground periodicals. It covers approximately 120 publications, ranging from *Center Magazine* and the *New York Review of Books* to *Akwesasne Notes, Gay, Every Woman*, and the *Berkeley Tribe*. Several Canadian and English-language papers are included. Papers indexed include local newspapers, plus papers and magazines dealing exclusively with women's liberation, gay liberation, educational alternatives, the Native American movement, radical professionals, liberation struggles in foreign countries, and the back-to-the-earth movement. The *Index* is a subject index using a subject heading list developed at the Center. Indexing is done by a network of volunteers in the United States and Canada. Includes only liberal and left papers; conservative and right wing papers not included.

America: History and Life; a guide to periodical literature. 1964. q. Service basis, $44 to $192. Eric H. Boehm. Amer. Bibliographical Center, Clio Press, 2040 Alameda Padre Serra, Santa Barbara, Calif. 93103. Circ: 2400.

Contains abstracts of some 800 American and Canadian, and 1,400 foreign periodicals, covering all aspects of the nation's history and life from earliest times to current events. It employs a classified arrangement—Canada represented by a separate section. Annual subject and personal name indexes are published. A major reference aid. See also *Historical Abstracts*, which covers history other than American and Canadian.

American Literature Abstracts; a review of current scholarship in the field of American literature. 1967. s-a. $4. James K. Brown, Dept. of English, San Jose State College, San Jose, Calif. 95114. Circ: 500.

Full abstracts of periodical articles which cover all aspects of criticism in American literature. It also includes book reviews in the field, and an author-subject index. A useful, although not necessary, index for larger academic collections.

Anthropological Index to Current Periodicals in the Library of the Royal Anthropological Institute. 1963. q. $9. Ed. bd. Royal Anthropological Inst., 21 Bedford Sq., London WC 1, England. Circ: 370.

A quarterly index to the basic international journals in the field of anthropology and related sciences. There is a cumulative author-subject index to vol. 1–5 (1963–1967) in preparation.

Applied Mechanics Reviews. 1948. m. $125 ($115 to ASME members). Stephen Juhasz. American Society of Mechanical Engineers, 345 East 47th St., New York, N.Y. 10017. Circ: 5,000. Vol. ends: December. Microform: UM. Reprint: Johnson.

The ASME's excellent journal is not an abstracting service in the usual sense; rather, it supplies critiques of the literature of applied mechanics. Prescreening and value judgments of books, articles, and some technical reports by authoritative, international experts cull out the truly significant works in the field. Subjects encompassed within the scope of the journal include rational mechanics and mathematical methods and also analog and digital computations, mechanics of solids, mechanics of fluids, heat, and miscellaneous fields such as aeronautics, fluid and plasma dynamics, acoustics, and physical oceanography. Over 1,000 journals on a worldwide basis are searched for references. Entries are arranged under subjects, then by accession numbers. Reviews range from two-line summaries to over 500 words. Every issue has an author index, and cumulative author-subject indexes are available on an annual basis. An interesting feature is the occasional appearance of a lead review paper on some timely and broadly significant topic. The scope of this publication is so wide, with applications to aeronautical, mechanical, civil, and chemical engineering, and applied mathematics, that no technical library supporting these areas should be without it. (B.G.)

Applied Science and Technology Index. 1913. m. (except Aug.). $30; also service basis. Elsa Toom. H.W. Wilson Company, 950 University Ave., Bronx, N.Y. 10452. Circ: 4,560. Sample. Vol. ends: Dec.

Following the format of the other well-known Wilson indexes, the publication is an alphabetical subject index to about 225 periodicals in the applied physical and engineering sciences—from aeronautics through transportation. Formerly called the *Industrial Arts Index,* the publication presently emphasizes the applied literature of the foregoing soup-to-nuts listing. Journals primarily represent U.S. periodicals, although a fair percentage of titles are international in scope, including some coverage of Canadian and British periodicals. Entries represent books, articles, and some pamphlets. Indexing of articles takes place, on the whole, six months after publication of the original material. Cumulative indexes are available every three months, and a bound, annual volume is also published. With-

out proceeding on a discussion of some of the jarring inconsistencies in the Index, one must state that it is a necessary addition for most technical libraries. One wonders, however, about selection of fields, as well as individual titles chosen for indexing. Newer fields (pollution technology and oceanography, to name but two) seem overlooked; older technologies seem overloaded; and rapidly moving areas, such as the computing sciences, seem skimpy in terms of U.S. coverage. (Why the theoretical *J. Association for Computing Machinery* and not also its excellent *Communications of the ACM* and *Computing Surveys?*) Regarding title selection, a number of fine, albeit highly theoretical periodicals, indeed beyond the purported scope of the service, are included. Yet a large body of the publications of one of our most important engineering societies is ignored. Admittedly, title selection is based on committee work (ALA and SLA supported), but one hopes that eventually these groups will show some sensitivity to changing technologies. Again, for the base price, the publication is a first-choice selection for any library needing some index to the technical literature, but not requiring the exhaustive bibliographic control supplied by the more sophisticated abstracting journals. (B.G.)

Aquatic Sciences and Fisheries Abstracts. 1969. m. $150. E. S. Krudy, Information Retrieval, Ltd., 1 Falconberg Court, London W1V 5FG, England.

The three-year history of this abstracting journal is rather complicated. Originally produced by Information Retrieval, Ltd., as *Aquatic Biology Abstracts,* the publication changed title when it joined forces with *Current Bibliography for Aquatic Sciences and Fisheries* (Food and Agriculture Org. of the U.N. and published by Taylor & Francis, London). Further mergers are planned with the Institut für Dokumentationswesen (Frankfurt), and the data base of this service will probably be in machine-readable form by 1973. At the moment, the publication abstracts significant papers in related fields such as physical and chemical oceanography and limnology, all aspects of aquatic biology, ecology, and pollution related to marine sciences, and fisheries. About 3,000 journals are culled for references; 15,000 abstracts are produced annually. Reviews of articles, books, and some technical reports are included. Entries are grouped under broad subject headings, then listed by abstract number. Author, taxonomic, and geographic indexes are produced for each issue, and cumulative author indexes are issued semiannually. The question immediately arises: why another abstracting service which clearly duplicates such a major tool as *Biological Abstracts?* One reason, of course, is that with today's concerns with environmental crises, particularly in water pollution, the field is more in demand than ever before. Libraries catering to interests in the marine sciences may find its specialty useful; and subscribers to the former *Current Bibliography for Aquatic Sciences and Fisheries* will undoubtedly need it, since its new coverage has been expanded. (Note: Information Retrieval, Ltd., also puts out other abstracting journals, including *Calcified Tissue Abstracts, Entomology Abstracts, Genetics Abstracts, Microbiology Abstracts, Nucleic Acids Abstracts* and *Virology Abstracts*.) (B.G.)

Arms Control and Disarmament; a quarterly bibliography with abstracts and annotations. 1964. q. $2.50. Supt. of Documents, U.S. Government Printing Office, Washington, D.C. 20402. Vol. ends: Fall. Microform: UM.

Covering all publications and over 1,700 English, French, German, and Russian journals, this is a major bibliography and aid for anyone seriously concerned with the subject. There are approximately 400 to 500 detailed abstracts and annotations in each issue, and a full author-subject index. English translations are given for all foreign titles, and all annotations are in English. The material is relatively up-to-date, although a few abstracts may be printed 6 to 18 months from time of original issue. While primarily for the academic library, the bibliography's low price puts it well within the grasp of public and high school collections. The journals may not be readily available, but the abstracts and annotations are so full as to give the user a solid idea of activities in the whole field. The bibliography is compiled at the Library of Congress, and is divided by major subject fields, such as war, peace, weaponry, and the "international political environment." (M.S.)

Art and Archaeology Technical Abstracts; abstracts of the technical literature on archaeology and the fine arts. (Formerly: *ICC Abstracts*). 1955. bi-a. $20. Ed. bd. New York Univ., Conservation Center of the Inst. of Fine Arts, 1 East 78th St., New York, N.Y. 10021. Circ: 2,200. Sample. Vol. ends: No. 2.

Covers material found in reports, magazines, newspapers, books, and monographs which deal "specifically with the technical examination, investigation, analysis, restoration, preservation, and technical documentation of objects and monuments having historic or artistic significance." It is organized under subject headings with author index. A highly technical approach; only for large, specialized collections.

Art Index; a cumulative author and subject index to fine arts periodicals and museum bulletins covering archaeology, architecture, arts and crafts, ceramics, decorations, and ornaments. 1929. q. Service basis. David Patten. H. W. Wilson Co., 950 Univ. Ave., Bronx, N.Y. 10452. Circ: 2,391. Sample. Vol. ends: Oct.

Author-subject index which analyzes contents of 150 periodicals and museum bulletins. Coverage is international and wider than the title indicates. "Subject areas indexed include archaeology, architecture,

art history, arts and crafts, city planning, fine arts, graphic arts, industrial design, landscape design, photography and films, and related fields." A basic reference aid in all university, college, junior college, and medium to large-sized high school and public libraries.

Astronomy and Astrophysics Abstracts. 1969. s-a. $19.50/v. ($39.60/yr.) Ed. bd. Springer-Verlag, Heidelberger Platz 3, 1000 Berlin 33, W. Germany and 175 Fifth Ave., New York, N.Y. 10010.

The Astronomisches Rechen-Institut, Heidelberg, for whom these abstracts are published (under the aegis of the International Astronomical Union), were also the producers of the fine *Astronomischer Jahresbericht*, which covered the astronomical literature for 68 years (1900–1968). More or less a refurbished resurrection and extension of *Jahresbericht*, the *Abstracts* document the literature in all fields of astronomy and astrophysics. (Falling within its scope are applied mathematics, instrumentation, celestial mechanics, space research, planetary systems, stellar systems, interstellar matter, etc.) Hardbound volumes appearing twice annually abstract the literature for that calendar year. The editors' *apologia* for this periodicity, as opposed to the usual monthly issues, is that six-month cumulations (with a subject index) are more useful to the researcher, and that generally their abstracts appear in eight months or less of original publication. Their point is well taken, particularly from the stand that the literature of astronomy is not so overwhelming as that of some of the other sciences. About 415 serials are screened for input; in addition, books, proceedings of symposia, and observatory reports are also recorded. Entries are arranged under 108 subject categories, and then by accession number. Usually, the authors' own abstracts are used, and these are predominantly in English. Each volume has its own subject-author indexes. Considering that the other major abstracting tools in the field necessitate knowledge of French or Russian (i.e., *Bulletin signaletique—Section Astronomie, Astrophysique, Physique du Globe*, and *Referativnyi Zhurnal*), any academic library requiring bibliographic control of the astronomical/astrophysical literature would be well advised to purchase a subscription. (B.G.)

Avery Index to Architectural Periodicals. 1963. a. $65. G.K. Hall & Co., 70 Lincoln St., Boston, Mass. 02111.

Since the publication of the 12-volume set in 1963 ($745), there have been annual supplements. This indexes all major architectural periodicals found in the Columbia University Avery Architectural Library. It is particularly useful as it includes other major disciplines: art, furniture, city planning, landscape architecture, etc. Should be purchased by any large library interested in the arts, if only to supplement the *Art Index*.

BA Previews. See *Biological Abstracts*.

✓*Bibliographic Index.* 1937. 3/yr. Service basis. Marga Franck. H. W. Wilson Co., 950 Univ. Ave., Bronx, N.Y. 10452. Circ: 2,536. Sample. Vol. ends: Dec.

The basic index to bibliographies, not to articles per se. The editor searches some 1,900 periodicals for bibliographic material, and lists by subject all bibliographic lists "containing forty or more citations." In addition, it includes bibliographies from books and pamphlets. An invaluable reference aid for any library.

Bibliography of Agriculture. 1942. m. $85. CCM Information Corporation, 909 Third Ave., New York, N.Y. 10022. Circ: 2,500. Vol. ends: Dec. Microform: UM.

A comprehensive index of agricultural and agriculturally related publications received in the National Agricultural Library. Published by the Library until December 1969. Beginning January 1970 it has been published by the CCM Information Corporation. Issues are arranged in a main entry section, a subject index and an author index. The main entry section provides full bibliographic information for each item and is divided into broad subject categories such as agricultural economics, agricultural products, forestry, plant science, entomology, natural resources, pesticides, etc. Within each section, items are arranged alphabetically by journal citation, to allow the reader to scan a given journal which is known to be relevant to his interests. All titles are given in English with the original language indicated by a language code. The subject index is entirely computer-produced and resembles a KWIC index. All subject entries are chosen by the computer from the title but words having the same or similiar meanings are grouped together under a single subject heading. An annual cumulated index is sold separately and is not included in the subscription price.

While both the *Bibliography of Agriculture* and the Wilson *Biological and Agricultural Index* cover the same subject areas, the *Bibliography of Agriculture* provides much more extensive coverage, not only for English-language materials, but foreign publications as well. The National Agricultural Library reviews and indexes over 8,000 titles in more than 40 languages as compared to the 189 titles indexed by the Wilson publication. An important index for any large library and for any library with a collection in agriculture, the life sciences, natural resources, plant science, and entomology. (J.J.)

Bibliography and Index of Geology. 1934. m. $250. Geological Society of America, Colorado Bldg., P.O. Box 1719, Boulder, Colo. 80302. Circ: 900.

Since its title change in 1969 (formerly called *Bibliography and Index of Geology Exclusive of North America*), the publication has been considerably expanded. The *Bibliography* is produced in cooperation with the American Geological Institute. Moreover,

bibliographic information is coordinated with the use of the AGI's magnetic tape file, GEO-REF (Geological Reference File), custom searches of which are also sold. All fields of the geological sciences are covered by 21 subject categories, and over 36,000 citations are produced annually. Although no abstracts are given, entries, arranged sequentially by accession number, do supply brief descriptors or phrases for each publication cited. In addition to culling a large number of serials, the *Bibliography* includes in its listings maps, books, reports, and a few dissertations. Citations of original source material appear as quickly as three months after original publication. Author-subject indexes are available in each issue, and cumulative indexes are published annually. With the demise of the U.S. Geological Survey's *Abstracts of North American Geology* and *Geophysical Abstracts* in 1971, this index is the only major U.S. source giving some type of timely access to the literature. Necessary for any academic library with a good geology collection. (B.G.)

✓*Biography Index; a quarterly index to biographical material in books and magazines.* 1946. q. $23. H. W. Wilson Co., 950 Univ. Ave., Bronx, N.Y. 10452. Circ: 6,641. Sample. Vol. ends: Aug.

An index to biographical material in the some 1,900 magazines indexed elsewhere by Wilson, and to collective biography and individual volumes as published. Obituaries as reported in the *New York Times* are included. Each entry indicates illustrations, bibliographies, and portraits when they appear with the indexed piece. The whole is arranged alphabetically by name with a useful professions and occupations index. Quarterly issues are cumulated annually and then every three years.

Although considered reference sources issued serially rather than magazines, there are two basic biographical serials for all types and sizes of libraries. (No magazine per se is devoted solely to biography, genealogical magazines excepted.)

✓ *Current Biography.* (1940. m. (Sept.–July). $12. H. W. Wilson Co.) The monthly issues, cumulated annually and sold as separate *Yearbooks* for $10, include some 30 to 40 biographies of approximately two pages each. An effort is made to feature personalities from all walks of life who are currently in the news. The sketches are objective, usually in a style within the grasp of anyone from junior high school to adult. Basic data for each entry include sources of information, pronunciation of the name, date of birth, occupation, and address. The whole is arranged alphabetically with an index by occupation.

Contemporary Authors. (1962. s-a. $25. Gale Research Co., Book Tower, Detroit, Mich. 48226.) Brief sketches of some 2,000 authors a year in almost every field from technical books to fiction. In addition to background information the work includes: a list of writings completed, works in progress, and other biographical sources where available. In view of its wide scope it often is the single source for information about a little known or new writer. Should be found in all libraries from junior high through university.

Biological Abstracts. 1926. s-m. $1,000 ($800 to qualified institutions or individuals). P. V. Parkins. BioSciences Information Service of Biological Abstracts, 2100 Arch St., Philadelphia, Pa. 19103. Microform: Biosis. Reprint: Johnson.

The major abstracting service for the biological sciences also includes coverage of the literature on agriculture, behavioral sciences, basic medicine, and veterinary science. Approximately 8,000 serials, as well as books, government reports, and proceedings of symposia, are screened annually to produce 140,000 abstracts. Entries are arranged under general headings, with many specific subdivisions, by accession numbers. Titles of citations appear both in original language and in translation.

Biological Abstracts have probably the most elegantly indexed issues of all the major services. In addition to an author index and an alphabetical list of subject headings used, each issue contains the following: (1) A "Biosystematic Index" coordinates abstracts under lists of taxonomic categories. Along with the name of the organism, additional abbreviations (based on subject headings) appear; these terms delineate the exact nature of the study. (2) A "CROSS Index" (Computer Rearrangement of Subject Specialties) comprises an alphabetical list of subject headings under which pertinent abstract numbers have been posted in ten columns. (Column location is determined by the last digit of the abstract number.) Since most entries will appear under as many subject headings as are necessary, this index is used as a coordinating tool (particularly in combination with the Biosystematic Index and "B.A.S.I.C.") to locate subject material as broadly or as narrowly as required. All indexes are composed by computer.

The main subject index to *Biological Abstracts* is B.A.S.I.C. (Biological Abstracts Subjects in Context), included within each issue or sold separately ($15/yr.). B.A.S.I.C. consists of a computer-produced keyword index, arranged alphabetically and expanded editorially to accommodate subject words both preceding and following the keyword.

The total subscription price to *Biological Abstracts* includes a second publication, *BioResearch Index,* which provides access to some 100,000 research papers not covered in *Biological Abstracts.* (If, for example, the proceedings of a symposium is cited in *Biological Abstracts,* the papers presented at that meeting are included in *BioResearch Index.)* Citations appear in an alphabetically permuted subject index with, again, expanded titles. All the elements used in *Biological Abstracts* are employed here as well: author index, Biosystematic Index, and CROSS Index. A large and important Bibliography section lists the title of each publication reviewed and its complete table of contents.

Cumulative indexes to *Biological Abstracts* (including B.A.S.I.C., Author, Biosystematic, and CROSS) must be purchased separately ($400; $320 to educational institutions), as must the cumulative index to *BioResearch Index* ($200, $160).

Small libraries will probably find *Biological and Agricultural Index* adequate for their requirements. Nonetheless, *Biological Abstracts* is still the most important bibliographic tool in the field. In fact, the entire spectrum of BIOSIS services has provided a distinguished asset to the biological sciences community. Magnetic tapes are available *(BA Previews);* a variety of custom searches may be purchased; and their latest publications include *Abstracts of Entomology, Abstracts of Mycology,* and *Abstracts on Health Effects of Environmental Pollutants* (1972). (B.G.)

Biological and Agricultural Index. 1916. m. (except Aug.). Service basis. Florence Arnold. H. W. Wilson Co., 950 Univ. Ave., Bronx, N.Y. 10452. Circ: 1,514. Sample. Vol. ends: July.

A subject index to approximately 189 magazines. While many of the periodicals are highly specialized, a number in the areas of agriculture, biology, botany, forestry and conservation, ecology, nutrition, and soil sciences have a wider appeal. It is recommended where the subject matter is an important part of the curriculum or the library is in a predominately agrarian area. May be used profitably by large high school libraries.

BioResearch Index. See *Biological Abstracts.*

Book Review Digest. 1905. m. (except Feb. and July). Service basis. Josephine Samudio. H. W. Wilson Co., 950 Univ. Ave., Bronx, N.Y. 10452. Circ: 13,695. Sample. Vol. ends: Feb. Microform: Canner.

An index to reviews which have appeared in some 70 English and American periodicals. It is arranged alphabetically by author with a subject-title index; cumulated annually, with a cumulative index every five years. Probably more important for most libraries, *Book Review Digest* includes excerpts from enough reviews to give a balanced opinion of the book. Approximately 6,000 titles—primarily of a general nature—are listed each year. As the United States alone is now publishing over 25,000 titles a year, the index is highly selective.

British Archaeological Abstracts. 1968. s-a. $12. Cherry Lavell. Published by the Council for British Archaeology, 8 St. Andrew's Place, London, NW 1, England. Vol. ends: Oct.

International coverage. Presents abstracts of over 100 British and Irish, and 50 foreign, periodicals on various topics of archaeology with special emphasis on preservation. The list of journals consulted is based on the Council's *Archaeological Bibliography*. Only important contributions are abstracted. Minor investigations and small finds are not included, but they are recorded in the *Bibliography*. Long book review articles in which the reviewer comments extensively on the text are abstracted. Classified by archaeological periods, author-subject index appears in the October issue. Five-year index cumulations are planned. A significant scholarly publication with an accent on Great Britain's and Ireland's archaeology. (P.V.)

British Education Index. 1961. 3/yr. $26.50 for 6 nos. and cumulation. British National Bibliography, 7–9 Rathbone St., London W1P 2AL England.

A subject approach to some 100 British periodicals in education. An average 60-page issue is cumulated every two years.

British Humanities Index. 1962, q. $40. Betty King. Library Assn., 7 Ridgmount St., Store St., London WCIE 7AE, England. Circ: 1,350. Sample.

Somewhat equivalent in Britain to our *Readers' Guide to Periodical Literature*. The scope is now narrower than the earlier work, *Subject Index to Periodicals* (1915–1961,) but the quarterly issues cover "all materials relating to the arts and politics." The quarterly numbers are by subject only, but there is an author index to the annual cumulations. Some 396 magazines are included.

British Technology Index. 1962. m. $65. Library Assn., 7 Ridgmount St., Store St., London WC1E 7AE, England.

Comparable in scope to *Applied Science and Technology Index*, the publication is a straight subject guide to about 350 journals in various technologies and engineering. Within its framework are also some periodicals in the basic physical sciences. Journals selected for inclusion are ones published exclusively in Great Britain, although a number of these are actually international publications. Without elaborating on its careful scheme of indexing, suffice it to say that the *B.T.I.* is noted for its abundance of cross-references, and for an index which permits a high degree of specificity in searching. Over 30,000 entries are produced annually; these are arranged under very detailed alphabetical subject headings. The price of a subscription includes an annual, bound volume. Technical libraries will find it useful, particularly for retrieval from British trade journal literature, and for narrowing subject searches on articles which emphasize applications and processes. Since its coverage of the literature is confined to British periodicals, smaller libraries in the United States would probably find their needs better served by *Applied Science and Technology Index*. (Note: Magnetic tapes of the *B.T.I.* have been for sale since 1971.) (B.G.)

Business Periodicals Index; a cumulative subject index to the fields of accounting, advertising, banking & finance, general business, insurance, labor & management. 1958. m. (except Aug.). Service basis. Elizabeth E. Pingree. H. W. Wilson Co., 950 Univ. Ave., Bronx, N.Y. 10452. Circ: 4,554. Sample. Vol. ends: July.

A subject index to some 170 magazines in business and related fields, e.g., advertising and public relations, automation, economics, applied engineering, etc. Because of its wide scope it is useful for considerably more than either business or economics.

Business Precis; the best in print. 1971. m. $25. Robert H. Tissot. Quiddity Press, Waccabuc Road, Goldens Bridge, N.Y. 10526.

A 35-page abstracting service "to make available to the business community (and others) selected articles from the many academic and specialty journals of the social sciences." Under a dozen or so subject headings—from management and marketing to history and education—the editor gives long, often detailed reports on pertinent articles. "The style," he notes, "is meant to be readable and incisive beyond the normal abstract." There is a four-page center section, "news tally," which is a summary of major events. The idea is good enough, and as a type of current awareness service it is useful for libraries. It has limited value, though, as an index or regular abstracting service, and the price is too high for any library except the largest. It is meant more for the individual reader with time to browse through its pages. If libraries cannot afford the service, librarians might bring it to the attention of businessmen.

CALL (Current Awareness—Library Literature). 1972. bi-m. $25. Samuel Goldstein. 35 Whittemore Rd., Framington, Mass. 01701.

The idea—as the editor/publisher is at some pains to explain—is not new. In some 47 out of 64 pages he prints the content pages of basic library literature periodicals and magazines in related fields. The purpose, of course, is "to enable librarians to browse the contents of their professional literature." The first issue is to be commended for its timeliness: some of the content pages go back to mid-1971, but most are representative of copy to be found in late 1971 or early 1972. Apparently the editor will not fall victim to the major fault with the current content approach, i.e., the only thing current is the content journal. Here the contents pages are from yesterday's magazines, not from those published years ago. All major English-language publications are covered, including Canada, England, and Australia. There are even entries from Nigeria and Sweden. Other pages are given to a lengthy editorial on the purpose of the effort, a history of the table of contents approach to library literature from 1914 to the present, a review of new periodicals, a profile of a deceased library periodical (Garfield's *Contents in Advance*), and three pages of abstracts of current literature. It all winds up with an index to periodical titles. The editorial material is interesting enough, but it might be better to give the space to content pages—or cut back the size of the effort, and lower the price. (The price is high, although for what is involved it probably is no higher than necessary for the publisher to survive.) How valuable this is depends on where you stand. As an aid to librarians who are eager to keep up with current events in the field, it is first rate. As an index, it is next to worthless. The whole current contents approach is up for debate, and there isn't space here for the inevitable pro and con arguments. (The editor gives a few in his introductory remarks.) For most libraries this new reference aid will be a frill—useful enough, but only after the basic indexes from *Library Literature* to *Library and Information Science Abstracts* and *Information Science Abstracts* are in the house. Meanwhile, what the publisher has done, he has done extremely well and for those who like this approach it can be recommended without hesitation.

This could also be compared with the "In the Literature" section of *Information–News/Sources/Profiles* which includes contents pages from library journals too. *Information*, however, limits itself to a handful of titles, and there is simply no comparison. Both in purpose and scope the two approaches are quite different. The only thing they have in common is the subscription price.

CIS Index; congressional information service/index to publications of the United States Congress. 1969. m. Service basis. ($95 to $395). James B. Adler. CIS, 600 Montgomery Blvd., Washington, D.C. 20014. Circ: 1,000.

An index to the 400,000 plus pages of hearings, reports, committee prints, and other documents produced yearly by the U.S. Congress. Published monthly, there are quarterly and annual cumulations. The testimony of every witness at every hearing is summarized in brief, sharply descriptive, abstracts. Page references to the original document are clearly indicated. The extensive index utilizes every conceivable access point—from witness names and affiliations to the numbers and popular names of pending bills. Subject cross-references are numerous and helpful. The journal's straightforward system of organizing Congressional documents by committee lends itself to ready use as a rapid classification scheme. It is, in fact, a comprehensive catalog, an analytic index, an announcement service, and a shelf list, all in one. It is indispensable to every library with a U.S. documents collection, and is strongly recommended for any reference or research facility with a stake in current public issues.

COMPENDEX. See *Engineering Index.*

Canadian Education Index/Repertoire Canadien sur l'Education. 1965. 3/yr. $25. Gary J. Sirois. Canadian Council for Research in Education, 265 Elgin St., Ottawa 4, Ont., Canada. Circ: 350.

A subject index to close to 150 Canadian periodicals and newsletters in the field of education. The 90 pages are arranged by subject and are extremely useful for any large library in Canada or the United States.

Canadian Periodical Index. 1948. m. Rates on request. Canadian Library Assn., 151 Sparks St., Ottawa, Ont. KIP 5E3, Canada. Circ: 1,350. Sample. Vol. ends: Dec.

An author-subject index to some 90 Canadian magazines, 15 in French, this is the Canadian equivalent of the *Readers' Guide to Periodical Literature*. An earlier version (by the same name) ran from 1928 to 1947, when the name was changed to *Canadian Index to Periodicals and Documentary Films*. In 1964, the name was changed back to the current one. An annual cumulation is available.

The Catholic Periodical and Literature Index. 1930. bi-m. Service basis. Catherine M. Pilley. Catholic Library Assn., 461 W. Lancaster Ave., Haverford, Pa. 19041. Circ: 1,988. Sample. Vol. ends: Nov/Dec.

According to the editor, this publication "provides a broad Christian approach to currently significant subjects. It is an author-subject index to 121 Catholic periodicals, published here and abroad, of which 75 are uniquely indexed and 96 are unique in American indices, and an author-subject-title bibliography of adult books by Catholics, with a selection of Catholic-interest books by other authors. Other features: book reviews are indexed, and papal and conciliar documents, in all languages, including commentaries and excerpts are completely indexed."

Chemical Abstracts. 1907. w. $2,400 with indexes; $2,250 without indexes. Chemical Abstracts Service, Ohio State Univ., Columbus, Ohio 43210. Microform: AMC.

Unquestionably, this is the world's most important abstracting service. Librarians who can recall the slim, monthly issues of two decades ago marvel at its presently *weekly* size of over 1 inch. Moreover, the publication now culls some 13,000 journals, covering 50 languages, as well as patents from 25 countries, and includes a large number of books, conference proceedings, theses, and technical reports. Its output is fast approaching nearly 330,000 abstracts per year. The scope, of course, is not confined to chemistry, but extends to all the scientific and technical literature which involves some chemical or chemical engineering aspect of study. Abstracts can be extremely detailed. Its present format is to publish, in even-numbered issues, abstracts on macromolecular chemistry, applied chemistry, chemical engineering, and physical and analytical chemistry, including nuclear phenomena.

Odd-numbered issues are devoted entirely to biochemistry and organic chemistry. Each issue of the journal contains (1) a keyword index, with entries derived from both text and titles; (2) a patent index and concordance; and (3) an author index.

The heart of this service is in its elaborately structured indexing program. Complicated as the system can be, *CA* produces an indispensable Index Guide, compiling collections of cross-references, heading notes, synonyms, and an index guide to ring systems. Each volume (2 v./yr.) produces its own author-subject indexes, formula, patent, and HAIC (Hetero-Atom-In-Context) indexes. An Index of Ring Systems and a Registry Index are also published. Collective indexes (through 1971) may be purchased separately.

Selective sections of the *Abstracts* can be obtained, if the entire service is not desired. *CA* is also available on 16mm cartridge microfilm. In combination with a reader-printer, this medium provides a facile method for conducting literature searches.

Of course, an even faster search can be performed by the variety of magnetic tape services offered by this organization. The range is from *CA Condensates* (the full service, minus abstracts, through *BJA (Basic Journal Abstracts)*, *CBAC (Chemical-Biological Activities)*, and *POST (Polymer Science and Technology)*, all containing selected abstracts in their fields of specialization. Prices vary from over $4,000 to around $6,500. Custom computer searches will also be performed.

Another invaluable reference tool sold in conjunction with *CA* is the *CAS Source Index* ($100), which is updated by quarterlies ($75/yr.). These provide over 60 years of cumulative listings of all periodicals abstracted, including title changes and locations of the journals in the world's major research libraries.

No scientific research library can survive without some features of *CA*, despite the cost.

Chemical Titles. 1961. bi-w. $60 ($30 to ACS members). Russell J. Rowlett, Jr., Chemical Abstracts Service, Ohio State Univ., Columbus, Ohio 43210. Subs. to: American Chemical Soc., 1155 16th St., N.W., Washington, D.C. 20036.

Acting as a current awareness service to the chemical and chemical engineering community, the publication is actually a keyword-in-context index to significant research papers appearing in about 700 international journals. There are three points of access to the publication: (1) the keyword index, a concordance to the titles of the papers, (2) a bibliography section, and (3) an author index. Keywords, arranged alphabetically in the center of the page, include additional words preceding and following them, to further delineate the meaning of the terms; and reference codes refer to the appropriate citation in the bibliography section. (Note: a stoplist ignores trivial words or those of no subject interest.) The bibliography section, in alphabetical order by title of journal, can be used

for scanning tables of contents. The author index refers, again, to references in the bibliography section. Timeliness of the twice-monthly service is excellent, since many publishers supply proofs of their tables of contents prior to publication. Each issue carries about 5,000 titles. Coverage is also broad enough to include selected journals from the biological, agricultural, engineering and physical sciences. Vital for any research collection, the publication would also give some access to the chemical literature for libraries which cannot afford *Chemical Abstracts*. It is emphasized, however, that this is a current awareness service, and there are no cumulative indexes for retrospective searching. For libraries with affluence, computers, and staff to supply the software, *Chemical Titles* is also available on magnetic tape at a cost of $1,700 per year. (B.G.)

Child Development Abstracts and Bibliography. 1927. 3/yr. $10. Dale Harris. Univ. of Chicago Press, 5750 S. Ellis Ave., Chicago, Ill. 60637. Index. Circ: 3,922. Reprint: Kraus.

Another publication of the Society of Research in Child Development (see *Child Development*). Lists abstracts of articles which have appeared in psychological, educational, medical, and other kinds of journals which have any relationship to the study of children. Also includes notices of new books, pamphlets and periodicals in the field. An invaluable research tool for anyone involved in this field. Should be in all larger collections.

College Student Personnel Abstracts. 1965. q. $20. Emily A. Starr. Claremont Graduate School, Claremont, Calif. 91711. Circ: 1,700. Sample. Vol. ends: Summer.

Abstracts of articles concerning college students and their problems largely from the point of view of college administrators. Accent is on student services such as counseling and housing. It is broken up into general subject categories such as admission, college environment, and student behavior. Main entry within a category is alphabetical by author. Author and subject indexes are included.

Computer Abstracts. 1957. $96. B. A. Fancourt. Technical Information Company, Martins Bank Chambers, P.O. Box 59, St. Helier, Jersey, British Channel Islands.

Although the publication does only about 4,000 abstracts per year, coverage of the computer literature ranges over the whole field—science, ancillary fields, spinoff specialties, mathematics, programming, specific hardware, and specific applications. In addition to the journal literature, the abstracts also include conference proceedings, technical reports (mainly United States), and patents, both British and United States. Entries are arranged by accession number under the classified sections indicated above, and adequate cross-references are made to other sections. Timeliness of entries is standard, ranging from three to six months. Each issue has its own author, subject and patent indexes; cumulative indexes are also provided annually. Pages are printed on one side to facilitate clipping of abstracts. Overshadowed by the INSPEC publication, *Computer & Control Abstracts,* whose output is much fuller, the periodical is still a useful tool for academic libraries with strong collections in the computing sciences.

Included with the subscription and appearing as an insert in each issue is a four-page addition, *Computer News,* which spotlights current developments in markets, hardware, contracts, etc., both in Great Britain and elsewhere. (B.G.)

Computer & Control Abstracts. See *Science Abstracts, Section C: Computer & Control Abstracts.*

Computer and Information Systems. 1962. 10/vol. $130. Cambridge Scientific Abstracts, Inc., Suite 437, 6611 Kenilworth Ave., Riverdale, Md. 20840.

Formerly called *Information Processing Journal.* About 12,000 abstracts from the world's literature on computing sciences appear in one volume of ten issues. It is difficult to determine the periodicity of the publication, however, since issues are not dated, and the lag between issues seems fairly erratic. Short abstracts deal with facets of software, hardware, applications to other disciplines, and electronics, as well as the mathematics of computation. Books, symposia, patents and technical reports are culled for abstracts. Entries are arranged under general subject headings. Delay between date of original publication and inclusion in the journal can be as late as one year. (Note: in a recent issue bibliographic citations of the entries were sloppy, with a number of typos and little regard for consistency in references—apparently its editorial board never consulted its own list of abbreviations.) Each issue carries an author, subject, and source index, the source comprised of a list of journals covered in that issue. Although three times the size of *Computer Abstracts,* and somewhat smaller than *Computer & Control Abstracts,* the publication does not approach the timeliness of either service. For the same price range, *Computer & Control Abstracts* is the better buy. (Note: The publishers also supply a number of other services, including *Solid State Abstracts Journal, Electronics Abstracts Journal, Theoretical Physics Journal.*) (B.G.)

Computer Program Abstracts. See *Scientific and Technical Aerospace Reports (STAR).*

Computing Reviews. 1960. m. $25 (members $12.50). Michael A. Duggan. Assn. for Computing Machinery, 1133 Avenue of the Americas, New York, N.Y. 10036. Circ: 12,000. Reprint: Johnson.

One of the most prominent publications in the computing sciences, the journal produces critical reviews, not merely abstracts, in all branches of the literature. Within the scope of these reviews are books, articles (selected from over 230 journals), conference proceedings, selected theses, or anything which the editorial board considers significant for its readership. A few abstracts may be pulled from other services, such as *Referativnyi Zhurnal* (USSR). Signed reviews, prepared by knowledgeable specialists, may range from four lines to 1,500 words. Authors and reviewers alike are allowed rebuttal in the journal. Entries are arranged sequentially under broad headings of software, hardware, engineering, mathematics, applications in the social, behavioral, and physical sciences. Author indexes are included in each issue; a cumulative index, *Bibliography and KWIC Subject and Permuted Index to Computing Reviews,* must be purchased separately ($25). Although the emphasis is on *reviewing,* and not timely documentation of the literature, the periodical is an excellent one and should be a first-choice selection for every academic library developing a collection in the computing sciences. (B.G.)

Contents of Contemporary Mathematical Journals and New Publications. See *Mathematical Reviews.*

Contents of Recent Economics Journals. 1971. w. $17.50. Dept. of Trade and Industry, Library Services, Her Majesty's Stationery Office, P.O. Box 569, London SE1, England.

A current awareness service which concentrates on the familiar approach of printing the contents page of journals. Some 200 publications are considered either in total or selectively. Early issues are confined to journals written solely or partly in the English language which cover all aspects of theoretical and applied economics—"including finance, taxation and agriculture, labour, regional and business economics." Emphasis is on English and western European publications, with a few basic American entries. The idea is neither new nor novel, but the coverage is unique, and it will be of value to larger economics and business collections.

Cumulated Index Medicus. See *Index Medicus.*

Cumulative Index to Nursing Literature. 1961. 5 bi-m. suppl. and 1 cum. $25. Mildred Grandbois. Glendale Adventist Hospital Publns. Service, P.O. Box 871, Glendale, Calif. 91209.

Indexes book reviews, pamphlets, illustrated materials, films, filmstrips, and recordings as well as journals. Coverage is exclusively of English-language publications, and journals which are ancillary to nursing are selectively indexed. Arrangement is by subject and author. (F.A.)

Current Abstracts of Chemistry and Index Chemicus. See *Science Citation Index.*

Current Bibliography for Aquatic Sciences and Fisheries. See *Aquatic Biology Abstracts.*

Current Contents

Agricultural, Food & Veterinary Sciences. 1970. w. $75.

Behavior, Social & Educational Sciences. 1969. w. $75.

Engineering & Technology. 1970. w. $75.

Life Sciences. 1958. w. $75.

Physical & Chemical Sciences. 1961. w. $75.
Eugene Garfield. Institute for Scientific Information, 325 Chestnut St., Philadelphia, Pa. 19106. Illus., index, adv. Sample.

A table of contents approach, each weekly issue simply reprints the contents of the journals indexed. An average issue in each area will cover some 150–200 journals per week—and over a year's time (because the journals, obviously, are not all issued weekly) the publisher claims to index over 1,000 titles in each of the fields covered. Effective use of the service depends on the user's knowledge of the magazine containing material he is interested in, or his knowledge of authors in his field. The contents pages are reproduced by subject, in no particular order. Each issue features an author index, but there is no subject index—at least as of late 1971. A subject approach for *Life Sciences* was to begin in 1972. There is a tri-annual cumulation, but in the meantime the user must go through a maximum of some 18 individual issues. (The firm, which publishes *Science Citation Index,* offers a number of services—at additional cost—such as tearsheets of articles and a personalized alerting system.) While this may have some advantage in technical fields, many of the journals covered are now indexed elsewhere. Lacking a subject approach, and considering the high price, most libraries can skip this one.

Current Index to Journals in Education (CIJE). 1969. $39 ($74 for m., s-a., a.cum.). Lee G. Burchinal. CCM Information Corporation, 866 Third Ave., New York, N.Y. 10022. Vol. ends: Jan.

A very thorough indexing service with numerous subject approaches and author entries. Indexes over 230 English language journals in the field of education and peripheral literature. It is a monthly companion piece to *Research in Education,* the U.S. Office of Education publication that announces new and unpublished reports. *CIJE's* chief advantage over Wilson Company's *Education Index* is that it has short annotations referring to the contents of the articles. Otherwise it is more cumbersome to use, because of its division into three parts. The three sections of the journal are (1) Main Entry Section (arranged by broad subject categories), (2) Subject Index, and (3) Author Index. (P.V.)

Current Papers on Computers & Control. See *Science Abstracts.*

Current Papers in Electrical & Electronics Engineering. See *Science Abstracts.*

Current Papers in Physics. See *Science Abstracts.*

Current Physics Advance Abstracts. See *Current Physics Information* in Physics Section.

Current Physics Titles. See *Current Physics Information* in Physics Section.

d s h Abstracts (Deafness Speech and Hearing Abstracts). 1960. $13. Jesse J. Villarreal. Published by Deafness Speech and Hearing Publications, Inc., Gallaudet College, Washington, D.C. 20002. Vol. ends: Oct.

From educational, medical, psychological, and social aspects this is the most prominent instrument for the periodical literature on deafness and speech disorders. It is international in scope and covers over 350 periodicals and a few monographs. About 2,000 signed informative abstracts appear per year. The length of the abstracts varies from 40 to 200 words. The periodical literature searched is summarized annually. Material is classified in five broad subject areas: Hearing, Hearing disorders, Speech, Speech disorders, General. Annual author and subject indexes appear in the October issue. This publication might be especially useful for the educational curricula of colleges and universities. (P.V.)

Deep-Sea Research and Oceanographic Abstracts. See Oceanography Section.

Documentation Abstracts. See *Information Science Abstracts.*

Economic Abstracts. 1953. s-a. $10. Martinus Nijhoff, 9–11 Lange Voorhout, The Hague, Netherlands.

The work of the three Netherlands libraries. Includes abstracts of both books and magazine articles in Dutch, English, French, and German. There is a detailed subject and an author index. An invaluable aid for the large economic or business library.

Education Abstracts. 1963. m. Contr. circ. Brent Breedin. American College Public Relations Assn., One Dupont Circle, N.W., Suite 600, Washington, D.C. 20036. Circ: 4,500.

An informal, usually topical, survey of basic journals and books in American education. No substitute for other education indexes, it is extremely useful because of the abstracts, and because it is selective. Libraries should request copies, which are free.

Education Index. 1929. m. (Sept.–June). Service basis. Julia Enrenreich. H. W. Wilson Co., 950 Univ. Ave., Bronx, N.Y. 10452. Circ: 5,472. Sample. Vol. ends: June.

A subject approach to not only magazines, but yearbooks, bulletins, and monographs in education, which covers the United States, Canada, and Great Britain. Every aspect of education from adult to international education is indexed, as well as from elementary grades through graduate study. An absolute necessity in any large public or college library, and highly desirable in the medium to large-sized elementary and high school library.

Educational Administration Abstracts. 1966. 3/yr. $12.50. W. D. Knill. Pub. under the sponsorship of the Univ. Council for Educational Adm. by School of Education, Univ. of North Carolina, Chapel Hill, N.C. 27514. Vol. ends: Winter.

Publishes signed 100–200 word abstracts from 90 English-language journals in the field of educational administration, i.e., organization, administrative processes, societal factors influencing education, and programs for educational administrators. A classified arrangement in four main classes and many subdivisions is used. At every subject entry references are given to related abstracts published under different headings. Author and journal index appears in every issue. Since *Education Abstracts* ceased publication in 1965 this is the best collection of abstracts dealing with practical events in school and campus. (P.V.)

Ekistic Index. 1968. m. $60. J. Tyrwhitt. Athens Center of Ekistics of the Athens Technological Org., Box 471, Athens 136, Greece. s-a. cums. Sample.

Indexes a wide variety of publications from popular to scholarly, from many disciplines and from many countries, about ekistics, the science of human settlements. Selection is based on interest to planners, architects, social scientists, and others concerned with developments in the field of ekistics. Articles are indexed in one alphabet by author and subject, with up to four key word subjects used. If the country or region dealt with in the article is of importance, it too is indexed. The permuted entries also include codes for type of illustrations, economic level of the country, and the basic geographical region of which they are a part. CODEN periodical abbreviations are used. Of most use to academic collections since a large proportion of the journals are foreign. (M.D.)

Electrical & Electronics Abstracts. See *Science Abstracts, Section B: Electrical & Electronics Abstracts.*

Employment Relations Abstracts. 1951. s-m. $70. Florence Kretzschmar. Information Coordinators, 1435 Randolph Street, Detroit, Mich. 48226. Vol. ends: Dec.

In 1960 changed title from *Labor–Personnel Index.* Each volume is divided into twenty sections treating such topics as: Employee–Management Relations; Industrial and Human Engineering; Planning and Computer Systems; Labor Economics; Wages, Salaries, Income, and Fringe Benefits; Laws and Legislation; Legal Decisions; and Labor Organizations.

Index refers to section and abstract number, and is composed of generally applicable subject headings as well as catchwords from titles. Some searching is necessary. Over 100 current publications from management, union, and professional sources, as well as those published by schools of industrial relations in the United States and Canada, are "scanned" regularly. Titles are of high caliber and include many viewpoints.

Publication is looseleaf and issued semimonthly for currency. It seems fairly well up-to-date. Some overlap with other indexing and abstracting services, but generally an excellent source for material in a fairly narrow field. (N.E.)

Engineering Index. (Various formats and prices—see below). Engineering Index, Inc., 345 E. 47th St., New York, N.Y. 10017. Microform: Engineering Index. Reprint: Johnson; Western Periodicals.

The world's leading service for all the engineering sciences is now packaged into a number of formats to suit the requirements of its users. All branches of engineering (chemical, civil, electrical, industrial, mechanical, metallurgical), technology, and ancillary fields are represented by about 85,000 abstracts culled from over 3,500 international journals. In addition to papers, books, and conference proceedings, technical reports are frequently included. Patents are not within the scope of the service, however.

Engineering Index Monthly. 1962. m. $450/yr. Furnishes about 7,000 monthly abstracts. The journal proper is the subject index, and entries are arranged first by broad subject heading, further with additional subdivisions, and then alphabetically by title. Cross references are liberal. An author index is included with each issue.

Engineering Index Annual. 1884. $250/yr. Contains the year's cumulation of abstracts, following the same format as mentioned for the *Monthly.* (Note: Combination rate for *Monthly* and *Annual* is $560.) In 1972, a microform edition will be sold for the previous year's *Annual.*

Also available to affluent customers at $6,500/year is *COMPENDEX* (*Comp*uterized *En*gineering Ind*ex*). The full 7,000 abstracts which appear in the *Monthly* are on 7- or 9-track magnetic tape. Software is not provided in the base price, however.

Useful for selective dissemination of information (SDI), particularly for users not wishing the full series, is a CARD-A-LERT service. Pertinent abstracts are printed on cards and distributed by 167 divisions. (Price varies from $50 to $75 per section, and $1,500 for the whole series.)

All engineering libraries need at least the *Monthly;* the *Annual* too if they can afford both. (B.G.)

English-Teaching Abstracts. See *Language-Teaching Abstracts.*

Environment Index. 1972. a. $50. Environment Information Center, 124 E. 39th St., New York, N.Y. 10016.

The editors describe: "This 600-page volume is a multiple entry index to the key environmental literature of 1971. Lists 42,000 entries representing coverage from scientific, technical trade and general magazines, government reports, conference papers and proceedings, nationally read newspapers, books, and films. Each entry is indexed by subject, industry (according to Standard Industrial Classifications), and author. The multiple entry indexing provides title, source, date, volume, number, page number, and length in full-page equivalents, and accession number. The accession is a cross-reference to abstracts of each item as published in EIC's monthly journal *Environment Information Access.*"

Environment Information Access. 1971. m. $100. Ed. bd. Environment Information Center, 124 E. 39th St., New York, N.Y. 10016.

Covers all major areas of environment, i.e., air pollution, environmental education, land use, solid waste, transportation, wildlife, etc. It includes abstracts from some 700 magazines, government reports, conference papers and proceedings, newspapers, and even films. There is an annual *Environment Index* (may be purchased separately for $50) which covers the same 42,000 citations in the cumulated monthly service.

Exceptional Child Education Abstracts. 1968. q. $50. Carl F. Oldsen. The Council for Exceptional Children, 1411 S. Jefferson Davis Highway, Jefferson Plaza, Suite 900, Arlington, Va. 22202.

The sponsor functions as the clearinghouse for ERIC programs in the area of exceptional children. The term takes in the handicapped slow learner and the bright child. Well over 225 journals are examined, as well as reports, surveys, and texts. Abstracts are arranged in numerical order as they are entered; reason is restored by a computerized author, subject, and title index. The latter covers some 10 pages, and is nicely broken down. Only a few subjects list more than four or five abstract numbers. The abstracts are keyed so the user can readily find the cost of obtaining either hardcopy reprints or microfiche reproductions which are available for most of the material abstracted. The abstracts lag by three to six months, but certainly cover the whole field. An average issue runs to 150 pages, with seven to ten abstracts per page. The price is right, the whole is easy enough to use with a bit of practice, and the format is excellent.

Excerpta Criminologica. See *Abstracts on Criminology and Penology.*

GEO-REF. See *Bibliography and Index of Geology.*

Genealogical Periodical Annual Index. 1962. a. $5.50. George Ely Russell, 2906 Stonybrook Drive, Bowie, Md. 20715. Adv. Circ: 500. Vol. ends: Spring.

Donald Lines Jacobus first thought of a cumulative index of articles and reference material contained in genealogical and historical journals in 1932, and by 1953 he had produced three volumes containing an index covering 1858–1952. (These have been reprinted by the Genealogical Publ. Co., Baltimore.) In 1962 Mrs. Rogers of Bladensburg, Maryland, restarted the index, and in 1966 Mr. Russell, the present editor, continued it. Thus the period 1953–1961 still remains to be covered. The latest volume (7; 1968) lists 133 periodicals and another 60 family or surname periodicals. There are 4,000 individual entries. Items are listed in topical, subject, surname, location, and author indexes, and it is the only journal which covers genealogical literature, records, and book reviews published each year in American, Canadian and British genealogical and historical periodicals. Although there are only 60 quarto pages annually it is the only one of its type, and is an essential tool. Unfortunately, for various reasons not the fault of the editor, the annual volume appears two years after the year being indexed. (P.W.F.)

Geographical Abstracts A-F. 1966. bi-m. $7.50. H. D. Clout. Geo Abstracts, Univ. of East Anglia, Norwich, NOR 886, England.

A rapidly developing abstract journal for geography. It is divided into six sections: Section A—Geomorphology; B—Biogeography and Climatology; C—Economic Geography; D—Social Geography and Cartography; E—Sedimentology; F—Regional and Community Planning. All six are available individually for $7.50 each, or as a unit. Each section is divided by subject, with a full citation and brief signed abstract. Indexes for the individual sections are published in the last number for each year, and a comprehensive annual index for all six sections is also issued—several years later. Beginning in 1972, the publisher promised a comprehensive author-subject index annually for Sections A, B, E; and another similar index for Sections C, D, F. The title is essential for all meaningful geography collections. (D.D.)

Government Reports Announcements. 1938. s-m. $52.50 (Combination rate with Index, $125). National Technical Information Service, U.S. Dept. of Commerce, Springfield, Va. 22151. Index. Circ: 7,000. Microform: PMC.

Issued under a variety of titles and agencies since its inception in the late thirties (its last being *U.S. Government Research and Development Reports*), the publication has settled, temporarily, on the above. The journal abstracts recently issued scientific and technical reports (and some documents in the social and behavioral sciences), produced under the sponsorship of over 225 Government organizations, and for sale to the public. In addition, cross-references are made to reports abstracted in *Nuclear Science Abstracts* (NSA) of the Atomic Energy Commission and *Scientific and Technical Aerospace Reports* (STAR) of NASA. (See separate annotations in this section for NSA and STAR.) About 50,000 abstracts are produced annually. All fields of science and engineering are covered, and entries are made under 22 major subject categories, with further subdivisions into groups. Reports may sometimes represent reprints from the technical literature, or translations, or foreign documents, if the above have been supported by Government sponsorship. Entries carry full bibliographic citation, indicative abstracts, and descriptors, which further delineate the subject matter and aid in compilations of subject indexes. Cross-referencing of entries is more than adequate. Information on the availability of documents and ordering procedures is also provided. Each issue has a *Report Locator* (by AD number), and a handy edge index for subject fields.

Its indispensable sister publication, *Government Reports Index* (s-m. $57.50), includes subject, personal and corporate author, contract number, and accession/report indexes. Annual cumulative indexes may be purchased either individually or as a complete set at various prices.

Microfilm editions of *GRA*, including index, are available from Princeton Microfilm at $80/year; moreover, the entire NTIS Abstract Reference File since 1964 (some 240,000 abstracts) will be available from them in reel or cartridge during 1972. Magnetic tapes of same can be obtained from NTIS at $1,500/year.

With a data base of over 630,000 titles, NTIS has also repackaged its information in a variety of ways. A large number of custom-designed services and computer searches can be purchased from them at reasonable costs and are well worth investigating. (See, for example, their Fast Announcements and Topical Announcements.) The primary journals, however, should be available in any library (including public) which supports science and engineering clientele. (B.G.)

Guide to Indian Periodical Literature. 1964. q. $45. Vijay Jain. Indian Documentation Service, Gurgaon, Haryana, India.

An author-subject index to articles, research papers, etc., from about 300 Indian journals in social sciences and humanities as well as significant articles from the daily *Times of India*. It is much like the standard Wilson indexes, with an annual cumulation.

Guide to the Performing Arts. 1960. a. Price varies. S. Yancey Belknap, Comp. Scarecrow Press, Metuchen, N.J.

This is a subject and name index to periodical articles in the field of the performing arts, including drama, music, dance, moving pictures, television, opera, and theatre in general. Some educational material concerning the above fields is also covered. About 50 periodicals, a few of them foreign, are scanned. The

time lag between the original appearance of the article and its publication in the guide is 2–3 years. The first edition, 1960, covers literature from 1957. (P.V.)

Highway Research Abstracts. 1931. m. $5. Stephen Montgomery. Highway Research Board, National Academy of Sciences, 2101 Constitution Ave. N.W., Washington, D.C. 20418. Index. Circ: 7,000. Vol. ends: Dec.

Its stated purpose is to "provide the highway administrator and engineer with timely and significant information in capsule form from the current literature. Spanning the interest of those engaged in or concerned with highway transportation and related subjects . . ., reports of research developments, practices and procedures from the United States and around the world have been incorporated. The arrangement is by subject, titles of abstracts being listed chronologically under the subjects." Ordering information for each article is given as well as abstracts and an order form for new publications of the Highway Research Board. The December issue contains a program of the annual (January) meeting, and the journal is of use only to special and academic collections that emphasize civil engineering. The HRB also publishes a house organ, *Highway Research News* (1963. q. $5. Hugh M. Gillespie. Circ: 7,000), and *Highway Research Reports*, an irregular but frequent series with each issue devoted to papers on a particular theme. (H.B.)

Historical Abstracts; bibliography of the world's periodical literature, 1775 to present. 1955. q. Service basis, $75–$350. Erich H. Boehm. Amer. Bibliographic Center, Clio Press, 2040 Alameda Padre Serra, Santa Barbara, Calif. 93103. Circ: 1,500. Sample. Vol. ends: Winter.

The companion to the firm's *America: History and Life*, this includes worldwide material not indexed in the American–Canadian index. Beginning with volume 17 (1971), it comes in two parts: Part A, modern history abstracts 1775–1914; and Part B, twentieth century abstracts 1914 to the present. (The subscription price includes both parts.) Some 2,200 periodicals covering all aspects of world history are examined. Arrangement is classified, and there is an annual subject index for each part. Five year cumulations. An absolute necessity for any medium to large-sized world history collection.

Horseman's Abstracts. 1969. q. $20. Joan Ingalls. Leisure Abstracts, 5852 Stow Canyon Rd., Goleta, Calif. 93017.

Covers all aspects of horses and breeding. Abstracts from major English language periodicals, with emphasis on American-based magazines. Each issue is indexed, with an annual cumulative index. While this is primarily for the professional, it has definite meaning and importance for any library where the horse is a major consideration—and this includes a number of elementary, junior high, and high school libraries.

Hospital Abstracts. 1961. m. $13.92 (£ 5.70). Her Majesty's Stationery Office, P.O. Box 569, London SE1, England. Vol. ends: Dec.

This covers the field of hospitals only from the aspects of administration, planning, and technology. Medical and related professional matters are excluded, though hygiene and sterilization are covered. The scope is international. It presents informative abstracts of periodical articles and a few books. Entries number about 2,000 per year, arranged by a minutely elaborate classification scheme. It is a valuable companion in studies in nursing and managing health institutions. The publishers announced photocopy service of the abstracted papers for five pence per page. (P.V.).

Housing and Planning References. 1965. bi-m. Free to libraries. Library of the U.S. Dept. of Housing and Urban Development (HUD), 7th and D Sts., Washington, D.C. 20410. Circ: 2,000. Vol. ends: Nov./Dec.

Consults about 1,200 periodicals regularly received in the HUD library. The scope is international. All aspects of urban affairs are represented, including the technical, environmental, and social branches of the field. New books are also listed. This is a subject index with a wide variety of entries, providing also short annotations concerning the contents of the indexed item. Author and geographical indexes are in every issue. The list of periodicals is published separately at irregular intervals in "Periodicals received in the Housing and Urban Development Library." (P.V.)

Hydata. See *Water Resources Abstracts.*

ICC Abstracts. See *Art and Archaeology Technical Abstracts.*

INSPEC. See *Science Abstracts.*

Index of Articles on Jewish Studies. 1969. a. $5. Issachar Joel. Magnes Press, Jewish National and University Library, Hebrew University, Jerusalem, Israel. Circ: 1,000.

Since 1969 the editorial board of Kirjath Sepher has also published a classified list of articles, culled from about 7,000 periodicals in Hebrew and other languages. The subjects covered include: bibliography, Old Testament and Dead Sea Scrolls, Jewish philosophy, mysticism, religion, liturgy, Hebrew and Yiddish language and literature, Jewish history, cultural life, Palestine, Zionism and the State of Israel. There are indexes of author names, and of places and persons. Publications began in 1969 covering material for 1966. The plan is to reduce the lag between publication date and appearance in the *Index* to one year. The material presented is similar to that in the Periodicals section of Kirjath Sepher; but there it is listed under the name of the periodical and scattered over 4 issues; here the presentation is by subject and in annual cumulation. The appearance of the *Index* was greeted warmly by Israeli students and scholars since they had deplored the lack of this kind of index. It was also well accepted by scholars of Jewish subjects abroad. (R.T.)

Index to Book Reviews in the Humanities. 1960. a. $15. Phillip Thomson, Williamston, Michigan.

Lists book reviews published in English–language periodicals of various countries. The number of periodicals consulted varies yearly between 150 and 500. The subject coverage extends over the disciplines of arts and humanities and includes also some areas of social sciences. From 1968 the following subject fields are considered: art and architecture, biography, drama and dance, folklore, history, language, literature, music, philosophy, travel and adventure. Religion and theology are not included. The index is arranged in one alphabet by authors; subject and title approach not offered. It is a worthy addition to *Book Review Digest* and particularly useful in some special areas, such as history and biography. (P.V.)

Index to Commonwealth Little Magazines. 1964. Various publishers. Apparently discontinued.

Before cessation (hopefully only temporarily), the annual index covered from 40 to 60 little magazines published in the English Commonwealth. Compiled by Stephen Goode, the index has covered the years 1964 through 1967. See also *Index to Little Magazines.*

Index of Economic Articles (Formerly: **Index of Economic Journals**). 1961. a. $5. Richard Ruggles. Under the Auspices of the American Economic Assn. Richard D. Irwin, Inc. Homewood, Ill.

Lists by author and subject English language articles in major professional economic journals published during the period from 1886 to date. About 150 journals are scanned from all parts of the world. After volume 7, published in 1967 (covering 1964–1965), volume 7/a was published in 1969 listing articles in collective volumes published during the period of 1964–1965. It was designed to blend with the original index, and vol. 8 was published under the present title covering for the first time journals along with collective volumes. The lag between the appearance of the original article and the index is about 3 years. (P.V.)

Index India. 1967. q. $50. N. N. Gidwani. Rajasthan Univ. Library, Jaipur, India. Vol. ends: Dec.

One of the most comprehensive periodical indexes in the English language. It consults about 1,200 periodicals and 300 composite books of various countries in all subject fields, including science, technology, medicine, social sciences, and humanities. Among the nationalities of the journals, 600 are Indian, 250 American, the rest British and others, yielding 50,000 entries per year. In the selection, specific Indian problems are emphasized, which makes the publication the most convenient research tool for Indian and Asian affairs. Arranged by subject classes; book reviews are not included. (P.V.)

Index to Jewish Periodicals. 1963. s–a. $35. Miriam Leikind. Cleveland College of Jewish Studies, 2030 S. Taylor Rd., Cleveland, Ohio 44118.

The basic index to Jewish-oriented magazines. Indexes magazines published by and for Jews in all parts of the world, but more particularly those issued in the United States or Israel.

Index to Latin American Periodicals. 1961. q. $25. Pan American Union. Scarecrow Press, Inc. Box 656, Metuchen, N.J. 08840.

A selective guide to articles which appear in Latin American magazines—primarily in the social sciences and the humanities. Well over 300 titles are indexed, but few of them thoroughly. It is the best index available for this area, and a required item where the library takes more than a token number of Spanish language magazines from Latin America.

Index to Legal Periodicals. 1908. m. (Oct.–Aug.). Service basis. Grace Meyer. H. W. Wilson Co., 950 Univ. Ave., Bronx, N.Y. 10452. Circ: 2,636. Sample. Vol. ends: Aug.

The basic law index to some 333 periodicals, journals of bar associations, and journals of judicial councils. It features a three-part arrangement: subject and author index, table of cases, and book reviews. Annual and three year cumulations.

Index to Little Magazines. a. $7.50. Swallow Press Inc., 1139 S. Wabash Ave., Chicago, Ill. 60605.

Primarily an author (with some subject) approach to 40 to 50 little magazines. Most are published in the United States. The annual volumes now cover 1943–1969. A primary difficulty is that the indexes are currently three years behind issues, i.e., the last index, covering 1968 to 1969, was issued in 1972. Be that as it may, it is an invaluable service, and the only one currently available. See also *Index to Commonwealth Little Magazines.*

Index Medicus. 1960. m. $63. National Library of Medicine. 8600 Rockville Pike, Bethesda, Md. Subs. to: Supt. of Documents, U.S. Govt. Printing Office, Washington, D.C. 20402. Circ: 6,000 Microform: UM.

Encompassing the world's biomedical literature, the *Index* is produced by the National Library of Medicine's MEDLARS (Medical Literature Analysis and Retrieval System), a computer-based system screening nearly 3,000 journals and consisting of about 200,000 citations annually. Computer-produced issues include the *Index* proper, namely a subject-author section, and the "Bibliography of Medical Reviews Subject-Author" sections (also sold separately), which survey the current

biomedical field. The scope of the journal is limited to the periodical literature; symposia, congresses, etc., are not included unless the proceedings have been published in the actual journals. Interesting features of the entries are the handling of foreign literature: a foreign title is translated into English in the subject section, but appears in its original language in the author index; also, citations in the same field are grouped by the language of the text (with English first), then alphabetically by language, and finally alphabetically by title of journal. "Medical Subject Headings," the subject authority list which controls the vocabulary and subject access to MEDLARS, as well as a complete list of journals indexed, appear in the January issue, Part 2 (also sold separately). The *Cumulated Index Medicus,* an annual compilation, is not part of the subscription price and must be purchased separately. Any library with concentration on the biomedical literature will need it. Small libraries can now purchase an *Abridged Index Medicus,* annotated above, which should be an adequate tool for modest bibliographic needs. (Note: The MEDLARS system, and its regional centers, supply many additional bibliographic services for researchers and practitioners, including computer-produced literature searches.) (B.G.)

Index to Periodical Articles By and About Negroes (Formerly: *Index to Selected Periodicals*). 1950. a. $13. G. K. Hall & Co., 70 Lincoln St., Boston, Mass. 02111.

About 20 black interest magazines are indexed, primarily by subject and author. The majority are not indexed elsewhere. A one-volume decennial cumulation for 1950–1959 is available ($40). An absolute necessity for any library serving a Black community.

Index to Religious Periodical Literature. 1949. $40. G. Fay Dickenson. Amer. Theological Library Assn., 800 W. Belden Ave., Chicago, Ill. 60614. Circ: 800. Sample. Vol. ends: July and Dec. Cum. vol. every 2nd yr.

Primarily an index to theology, church history, and biblical literature, with some history of religions, archaeology, religion, and personality. It is international in scope, analyzing some 135 periodicals. Separate book review section is included. Useful, too, for indexing in related fields, i.e., literature and religion.

Index to Selected Periodicals. See *Index to Periodical Articles By and About Negroes.*

Information Processing Journal. See *Computer and Information Systems.*

Information Science Abstracts. 1966. bi-m. $40 (individuals $25). Ben–Ami Lipetz. Documentation Abstracts, Inc., P.O. Box 8510, Philadelphia, Pa. 19101. Circ: 1,200.

A continuation of *Documentation Abstracts,* published by the former American Documentation Institute. Today, the journal is under the general sponsorship of the American Society for Information Science, the American Chemical Society, Div. of Chem. Lit., and the Special Libraries Association. Any facet of the broad term "information" is covered: its generation, publication, collection, identification, documentation, translation, storage, retrieval, and dissemination. Research in other fields, e.g., the computing sciences, is also within its scope. Books, journal literature, selected theses and selected reports all fall within its coverage. Both technical and some popular items are noted. Arrangement is classified, with an author index, and an annual subject index is provided. Certainly, every practitioner needs access to this thorough, international, and comprehensive service. A valuable addition for the larger libraries. (B.G.)

International Aerospace Abstracts. 1961. s-m. $110 (Cum. index $75). John J. Glennon. AIAA Technical Information Service, 750 Third Ave., New York, N.Y. 10017.

Sponsored by the American Institute of Aeronautics and Astronautics, this service provides informative abstracts of the published literature relating to the space sciences and technology (including aeronautics). Coverage is international and includes books, periodicals, conference proceedings, and translations. (Note: abstracts of the technical report literature are available through a companion publication, STAR, *Scientific and Technical Aerospace Reports*, published by NASA.) Entries, carrying full bibliographic citation, are arranged by accession number under broad subject categories. Each issue has its own subject index, as well as personal, corporate author, contract number, meeting paper or report number, and accession number indexes. Cumulated indexes must be purchased separately. The publication is essential for anyone dealing largely with the aerospace literature. Its scope is so broad, however (including basic sciences such as physics, chemistry, mathematics, life sciences), that its usefulness should extend to many more academic libraries, as well. (B.G.)

International Guide to Classical Studies; a quarterly subject index to periodical literature. 1963. q. $30. American Bibliographic Service, Darien, Conn. 06820.

A subject index to articles in western languages, published throughout the world, concerned with any aspect of classical studies, i.e., archeology, epigraphy, language and literature, science, arts and crafts, religion and philosophy, social, economic, and political life. "Classical" is meant here as the period between the early Aegean civilizations and the decline of the Roman Empire. The subject index is cumulated annually.

The same firm issues two similar indexes: *International Guide to Medieval Studies* (1961. q. $35); and *International Guide to Indic Studies* (1963. q. $30). These are similar in approach to the classical studies index, the only difference being that the Indic studies includes an index of current book reviews germane to the field.

International Mathematics Abstracts. See *SIAM Review* in Mathematics Section.

International Nursing Index. 1966. q. $25 ($20 annual cumulation only). Lucille E. Notter, R. N. International Nursing Index, 10 Columbus Circle, New York, N.Y. 10019. Circ: 1,600.

"Over 200 nursing journals received from all over the world are indexed, as well as all nursing articles in more than 2,300 non-nursing journals currently indexed in *Index Medicus*. It is arranged in two main sections: (1) a Subject Section, and (2) a Name Section. The Index also includes lists of nursing periodicals and serials indexed, current nursing publications of organizations and agencies, and nursing books published [during the year]." Preface. (F.A.)

International Political Science Abstracts. Documentation Politique Internationale. 1952. q. $10. Serge Hurtig. International Political Science Association in co-operation with the International Committee for Social Sciences Documentation; with the support of UNESCO. Basil Blackwell, 49 Broad St., Oxford, England.

A bilingual publication with international coverage. Presents abstracts of about 250 periodicals on political science (in general), political theory, methods, processes, government, and international relations. Over 40 of the periodicals consulted are indexed in Wilson's *Social Sciences and Humanities Index*. As a rule the non-English literature is abstracted in French. One of the main advantages of this publication is the relatively short time lag (sometimes 6–7 months) between the appearance of the original article and the abstract. A subject index goes with every issue, cumulated annually. Author index is in the last issue of the volume. (P.V.)

Internationale Bibliographie der Zeitschriften Literatur Aus Allen Gebieten des Wissens. 1965. 2 vols/yr. $603. Felix D. Verlag, Jahnstr. 15, 45 Osnabruck, Germany.

The largest of all the general indexing services. There are some 30 parts a year (which are cumulated semiannually), and they take over 8,000 periodicals from all parts of the world. Arrangement is by subject. English and French references assist the user who does not know German. The index is an invaluable aid in any large research library, but it does presuppose the user is going to be familiar with several languages and that the library has the magazine indexed. Along with the price, these factors limit this index to large public and academic libraries.

Journal of Economic Literature (Formerly: *Journal of Economic Abstracts*). 1963. q. $6. Mark Perlman.

American Economic Assn., 1313 21st Ave., S., Nashville, Tenn. 37212.

A two-part abstracting service. The first section includes the contents pages of some 35 to 50 journals. Part two consists of the rather long abstracts arranged by subject. There is an annual author index. Only for large academic collections—the more popular economic journals are included in the standard indexes.

Language and Language Behavior Abstracts. (LLBA). 1967. q. $45. Frank M. Koen. University of Michigan. LLBA, Suite 256, City Center Building, 220 East Huron, Ann Arbor, Mich. 48108. Vol. ends: October.

In the early issues 500, now over 1,000, journals in some thirty-two languages are regularly screened on linguistics, psycholinguistics, psychology, educational psychology, phonetics, hearing pathology, communication sciences, and some other related areas. The abstracts are informative, their length ranging from 50 to 300 words. This is a partially computerized research instrument, perspicuously arranged in 25 subject classes. Author index and cumulative author-subject indexes for complete volumes are available. The editors offer a reprint service for about 100 journals.

Language-Teaching Abstracts. 1968. $6.75. Ed. jointly by the English-Teaching Information Centre and the Centre for Information on Language Teaching. Cambridge Univ. Press, American Branch: 32 E. 57th St., New York, N.Y. 10022. Vol. ends: Oct.

International coverage. Presents informative abstracts of periodical articles in the field of teaching modern languages, including English as a second language. It covers also "relevant works in psychology, linguistics, language studies, teaching methodology and technology, and experimental teaching" (Ed.). Over 300 periodicals are scanned resulting in about 90 abstracts per issue. The abstracts are not signed. There is a classified arrangement with a cumulative subject index in the last issue of the year. This is the continuation of *English-Teaching Abstracts* published by the English-Teaching Information Centre from 1961 to 1967. (P.V.)

Library & Information Science Abstracts (LISA). 1969. bi-m. $27. Tom Edwards. Library Assn., 7 Ridgmount St., Store St., London, WC1E 7AE, England. Vol. ends: Nov./Dec.

Supersedes *Library Science Abstracts*. This is a well-organized reference tool, covering about 200 professional journals of various countries in the field of library science and technology. It uses an elaborate classification scheme with letter symbols. The outline of classification was extended and rearranged in 1971, and in addition, many important areas, like professional education, have been enlarged. Author-subject index on tinted paper is placed in the middle of the bimonthly copies. Despite its complicated arrangement

it is perspicuous and easy to use. Photocopies of the material abstracted are available from the libraries of *Aslib* and the Library Association for five new pence per sheet. (P.V.)

Library Literature; an author and subject index to selected material on library science and librarianship. 1933. bi-m. Service basis. Jane Stevens. H. W. Wilson Co., 950 Univ. Ave., Bronx, N.Y. 10452. Circ: 2,927. Sample. Vol. ends: Dec.

Close to 240 periodicals, concerned directly or indirectly with library science, are indexed. Also includes films, filmstrips, microcards, library school theses, and "all books and pamphlets dealing with libraries and librarianship that come to the attention of the editor." The emphasis is on American publications, although major foreign works are included. There are bound annuals, permanent two–year cumulations. Only for library schools and large libraries.

Library Science Abstracts. See *Library & Information Science Abstracts.*

MLA International Bibliography of Books and Articles on Modern Languages and Literature. 1922. a. $32 (Members $16). Harrison T. Meserole. Modern Language Assn. of America, 62 Fifth Ave., New York, N.Y. 10011. Circ: 30,000.

An annual bibliography, in four volumes, and issued separately from *PMLA*, the parent journal. While each volume is available separately, most libraries will want them all. The compilation is based on articles found in over 1,500 journals and magazines, as well as some books. The first volume: general, English, American, medieval and Latin, and Celtic literature; the second: European, Asian, African and neo-Latin literatures; the third: linguistics; the fourth: teaching of modern foreign languages.

Mathematical Reviews; a reviewing journal covering the world literature of mathematical research. 1940. m. $320. Ed. bd. Amer. Mathematical Soc., P.O. Box 6248, Providence, R.I. 02904. Circ: 6,000.

Essential for any good mathematics collection, *Reviews* publishes abstracts and reviews of mathematical literature comprising nearly 1,200 journals and books, conference proceedings, and translations. Sponsored by some of the world's leading mathematical societies, the publication is international in scope and is the most comprehensive source for reviews in this field. Reviews are signed, critical, and range in length from short abstracts to excellent 1,000-word essays; many appear in French and German, as well as English. Entries are grouped under general subject headings, and an author index is provided for each issue. Cumulative author and subject heading indexes are published twice a year, but detailed subject indexes are not supplied.

Medical Socioeconomic Research Sources. 1971. m. $20. Susan Crawford. American Medical Assn., 535 N. Dearborn St., Chicago, Ill. 60610.

Indexes events and developments in the sociology and economics of medicine as they appear in some 4,000 journals. It is arranged by broad subject headings, with an author index. There is an annual cumulation. The purpose of the index is to reflect the medical profession's concern with "the objectives of the health sciences, in the nature of the institutions which the profession has built, and in the responsiveness of health care organizations to the community at large." Much, if not all, of the material is of value to the student of sociology, political science, and economics.

Metals Abstracts. 1968. m. $325 ($145 to academic or public libraries). T. Graff and H. D. Chafe. Metals Abstracts Trust, Metals Park, Ohio. Circ: 1,500.

Formed by the marriage of *Metallurgical Abstracts* (Institute of Metals, London) and the *Review of Metal Literature* (American Society for Metals), the publication now represents a powerful tool for searching the world's metallurgical literature. Informative abstracts are grouped under seven main sections, representing all branches of metals science, engineering, and technology, for easy scanning. Journals, books, conference proceedings, and translations are included. Timeliness of abstracts varies from five months and later from original date of publication. Its monthly companion, the essential *Metals Abstracts Index* (sold separately for $130) contains the computer-generated subject and author indexes to the *Metals Abstracts* proper. The subject index, based on the *ASM Thesaurus of Metallurgical Terms,* is well organized. (Note: magnetic tapes of the *Index* are available for $1,500/year.) A set of hardbound cumulative volumes, collated by subject, with appropriate indexes, is also sold annually ($455 to monthly subscribers; $220 to libraries). The combined forces of two of the world's leading metals societies make at least the monthly issues a necessary acquisition for technical libraries with heavy concentration in the field. (B.G.)

Meteorological and Geoastrophysical Abstracts. 1950. m. $400 ($200 to educational institutions and public libraries). Malcolm Rigby. American Meteorological Society, 45 Beacon St., Boston, Mass. 02108.

The major abstracting service for the atmospheric sciences (e.g., meteorology, climatology, planetary atmospheres, etc.). Its scope includes ancillary fields such as astrophysics, radio astronomy, hydrology, glaciology, physical oceanography, and some general references in the environmental sciences as related to atmospheric problems. Coverage of the literature is worldwide; some 300 serials from 135 countries are culled, and over 10,000 indicative abstracts of articles, books, conference proceedings, selected technical reports, patents, and citations of maps, are produced

annually. Entries are arranged first under broad subject headings, and then by accession number. Author, subject, and geographic indexes are available in every issue. Cumulative indexes are also published. (Note: The G. K. Hall Co., Boston, Mass., has recently released a Cumulative Bibliography and classified subject-author index, 1950–1969, to these *Abstracts.*) A necessary bibliographic tool for libraries involved in the atmospheric sciences. (B.G.)

Mineralogical Abstracts. See *Mineralogical Magazine* in Earth Sciences Section.

Music Index. 1949. m. $275. Florence Kretzschmar. Information Coordinators, Inc., 1435 Randolph St., Detroit, Mich. 48226. Circ: 600.

Indexes approximately 270 periodicals from all English speaking countries and 19 non-English speaking nations. Entries from the latter are generally in the language of the country in which they originated. Author-subject approach, and includes obituaries, first performances and music reviews.

NAPCA Abstract Bulletin. See *Air Pollution Abstracts.*

Nuclear Science Abstracts. 1948. s-m. $42. U.S. Atomic Energy Commission, Div. of Technical Information, P.O. Box 62, Oak Ridge, Tenn. 37830. Subs. to: Supt. of Documents, U.S. Govt. Printing Office, Washington, D.C. 20402. Circ: 7,500. Microform: Canner; Princeton; UM. Reprint: Johnson.

With the intent of providing comprehensive coverage of the world literature on nuclear science and technology, the service encompasses the following fields: chemistry, physics, earth sciences, life sciences, engineering, instrumentation, metallurgy. The periodical not only abstracts the technical report literature for research reports sponsored by the AEC, but also pertinent reports of other government agencies, universities, and foreign research establishments. Books, journal articles, conference proceedings, and patents also fall within its scope. Entries are arranged by accession numbers under subject categories. Each issue contains corporate author, personal author, subject and report indexes; cumulative indexes must be purchased separately ($38/yr.) and five-year indexes are also published. Since this is the only service which draws together nuclear studies concerned with all the basic sciences and engineering, and includes both published literature and technical reports, it is a valuable abstracting journal for any kind of scientific research library. (B.G.)

Oceanic Abstracts. 1964. bi-m. $300 (2 copies with indexes); $95 without indexes. William C. Farmer. Pollution Abstracts, Inc., 6811 La Jolla Blvd. P.O. Box 2369, La Jolla, Calif. 92037.

The basic abstracting service for "oceanics." The scope of the service is broad, and the subject divisions under which entries appear bear repeating to indicate coverage: biology/fisheries; geology/meteorology/oceanography; acoustics/optics/positioning/remote sensing; desalination/pollution/engineering/materials; diving/offshore/deep sea; ships/submersibles/buoys. About 10,000 entries appear annually; over 2,000 serials are searched on a worldwide basis for references. Books, periodicals, and technical reports are culled for references. In addition to full bibliographic description, entries include keyterms and descriptors. Abstracts, many of them informative, are both author-prepared and staff-produced. Indexes bound within each issue are: author and "keytalpha" (alphabetical keyterm) permuted index. A short, well-illustrated feature article on some recent development in the field appears in each issue. A nice touch: for fillers at the end of subject divisions there are photos of oceanographic interest. An essential bibliographic tool for biological, geological, and physical oceanography, and ocean engineering collections. (B.G.)

PANDEX Current Index of Scientific and Technical Literature. 1969. CCM Information Corp., Crowell, Collier and Macmillan, Inc., 909 Third Ave., New York, N.Y. 10022.

As of this writing, PANDEX in hard copy format has been discontinued. The publisher is still selling magnetic tapes of the Index, however ($6,500/yr.). Briefly, the service comprised a bi-weekly guide to the literature of all science and engineering. About 2,000 journals, presumably those most prominent in each field, were screened for input. Subjects covered were physical, mathematical, biological, selected behavioral, and engineering sciences. Author-subject indexes were supplied, subject indexes being formed from the keywords taken from titles. The service does not produce abstracts, only citations. (B.G.)

Peace Research Abstracts Journal. 1964. m. $70. Alan and Hanna Newcombe. Canadian Peace Research Inst., Oakville, Ont., Canada. Vol. ends: Dec.

This publication is a product of scientists, Quakers, and World Federalists, directed to researchers, with the aim of preventing a third World War. The coverage is international. About 800 abstracts are presented in every monthly issue, taken from periodicals and books in the field of foreign affairs, international law, arms limitations, etc. The abstracts are informative, without intended evaluative notes. Most of them are signed. A good aid in the study of international relations but only for those who do not mind the long time lag (often two years) between the appearance of the original paper and the abstract. (P.V.)

Personnel Management Abstracts. 1955. q. $15. Gloria Jean Reo. Bureau of Industrial Relations, Grad. Sch. of Business Admin., Univ. of Michigan, Ann Arbor, Mich. 48104. Illus., adv. Circ: 7,000. Sample. Vol. ends: Winter.

An index to periodical literature in the areas of management, personnel policies, manpower, and industrial relations. Approximately 80 magazines are indexed, and there are 15 to 20 abstracts of current books.

The Philosopher's Index; an international index to philosophical periodicals. 1967. q. $20 (Individuals $10). Hardbound a. cum. ed. $25 (Individuals $15). Richard H. Lineback. Bowling Green Univ., Bowling Green, Ohio 43402. Circ: 1,650. Sample. Vol. ends: Winter.

An up-to-date index of articles from over 175 major philosophy periodicals and related interdisciplinary journals. Though international in scope, more than half the publications indexed are in English. Articles are indexed by subject and author. Most subject headings are key words drawn from titles, but these are supplemented by more descriptive terms where necessary. Abstracts of the articles are published in each issue and are generally written by the authors of the articles. A separate book review index is included. Though not nearly so complete as the *Répertoire Bibliographique de la Philosophie,* and considerably more expensive, it is easier to use. Any library serving people doing serious work in philosophy should have both tools. However, if the library can afford only one, the *Répertoire* is probably the better value. (J.A.)

Photographic Abstracts. 1921. bi-m. $48. D. H. O. John. Scientific and Technical Group of the Royal Photographic Society of Great Britain, 14 South Audley Street, London, W1Y 5 DP, England. Vol. ends: 7th issue.

Arranged by the Universal Decimal Classification system with author, patent, and subject index. Contains abstracts of the whole of the world's literature, including patents, on the science and technology of photography, and its numerous applications in industry, medicine, and commerce. Emphasis is placed on original material, and elementary articles on familiar topics are excluded. Not to be confused with *Abstracts of Photographic Science and Engineering Literature,* an American publication by the Society of Photographic Scientists and Engineers.

Physics Abstracts. See *Science Abstracts, Section A: Physics Abstracts.*

Pollution Abstracts. 1970. bi-m. $70. W. C. Farmer. P.O. Box 2369, La Jolla, Calif., 92037. Illus., adv. Circ: 1,800. Sample. Vol. ends: No. 6.

This covers well over 2,000 American and foreign journals, technical reports, newspapers, government documents, and symposia. The subject matter is limited to environmental pollution, but this is interpreted broadly and takes in material of interest to the modern day ecologist, planner, and layman. There is a cumulative annual and two year index. A typical issue includes a number of general articles, abstracts; author, organization, products/services, and subject index; and an appendix which lists new books, journals, and special publications and includes a calendar of events. An excellent service worth consideration by any large library.

Poverty & Human Resources Abstracts. 1966. bi-m. $40 (Faculty $10; students $8.50). Louis A. Ferman. Inst. of Labor & Industrial Relations, Univ. of Michigan–Wayne State Univ., Box 1567, Ann Arbor, Mich. 48106. Circ: 1,500.

Includes abstracts of periodicals, books, pamphlets, reports, and just about anything the editors can find which deals with poverty and human resources in the United States. (There are some international articles, too.) Thanks to the interest in environment, ecology, and human development in all areas, the abstracts have taken on new importance for the 1970s. Should be in any library interested in vital questions not only of poverty, but the whole condition of man and his government and surroundings.

Psychological Abstracts. 1927. m. $130. Harold P. Vancott. American Psychological Assn., Inc. 1200 17th St., N.W., Washington, D.C. 20036. Circ: 10,000. Microform: UM.

Covers the world's literature in psychology and related fields. Foreign language articles are abstracted in English. There is an author index for each monthly issue, which is arranged by subject, and a combined author-subject index semiannually and annually. Basic for any medium to large-sized collection.

Public Affairs Information Service. Bulletin. 1915. w. (no issues last two weeks of each quarter). $100. W. and cum. *Bulletins* (5/yr), one of which is an a. cum. Cum. *Bulletins* including a. $75. A. cum. *Bulletin* $40. Robert S. Wilson. Public Affairs Information Service, Inc. 11 W. 40th St., New York, N.Y. 10018. Circ: 3,200. Sample. Vol. ends: Sept.

This side of the *Readers' Guide to Periodical Literature* and the *Social Sciences and Humanities Index,* this is the best basic index for most libraries. Indexes magazines, books, pamphlets, documents, and other materials related to the social sciences, i.e., economics, political science, government, sociology, etc. Libraries may purchase the weekly, monthly, or annual service separately.

Public Affairs Information Service. Foreign Language Index. 1972. q. $100. Robert S. Wilson. Public Affairs Information Service, Inc. 11 W. 40th St., New York, N.Y. 10018. Sample.

PAIS now also issues a second quarterly index which does much the same as the *Bulletin.* The primary difference, as suggested in the title, is that the index considers the same materials in foreign journals, books, pamphlets, etc. This would be required only in large

research libraries. The quarterly is cumulated annually.

Quarterly Bibliography of Computers and Data Processing. 1971. q. $29.50. Applied Computer Research, 8900 N. Central Ave., Suite 208, Phoenix, Ariz. 85020.

Some 50 periodicals are analyzed—plus "all the major books"—for this index "designed specifically for the practicing computer and data processing professional." Perhaps they will have the patience to use its muddled approach: instead of having "see" and "see also" references in the body of the index, one must go back to the glossary and subject guide to discover the allied subject headings. For example, a definition is given of Analog computers, followed by "See also, Hybrid computers; process control." There is no "hybrid computer" subject heading in the main body of the work, but "process control" is there. Then there's a subject called "Used computers" in the main index, but no reference to it anywhere else. A first class mess, which is a fine argument against, not for, computerized indexes. On the plus side, abstracts are given for periodical articles, and for books—but no price stated for books analyzed. Considering the high price, libraries are advised to wait until the publisher's computer is better programmed.

Quarterly Check-list of Literary History; international index of current books, monographs, brochures and separates. 1958. q. $11. Stanford Becker. Amer. Bibliographic Service, Darien, Conn. 06820.

An author listing of books and monographs published on American, English, German, and French literature. There are no annotations, but complete bibliographic data is provided, including a list of publishers. The fourth issue of each year gives a cumulative author, translator, and editor index. While other than western language works are listed, emphasis is on material in these areas. An annual run covers some 1,000 titles, often not found in regular reviewing sources. The lack of annotations is a handicap for the novice, but the author approach makes the listing useful for the knowledgeable professor trying to keep up with his field. Should be found in all larger academic collections.

The American Bibliographic Service issues similar checklists in a variety of subjects: *Quarterly Check List of: Biblical Studies* (1958. q. $5.50) *Classical Studies* (1958. q. $8); *Economics and Political Science* (1958. q. $10.50); *Ethnology & Sociology* (1958. q. $5); *Linguistics* (1958. q. $5); *Medievalia* (1958. q. $9); *Musicology* (1959. q. $5); *Oriental Studies* (1959. q. $9.50); *Psychology* (1961. q. $4.50); *Renaissance Studies* (1959. q. $5). The approach is similar in all, again with emphasis on western language books, and monographs.

R I L M Abstracts. Repertoire International de Litterature Musicale. 1968. q. $24. Barry S. Brook. Intl. Musicological Soc. and the Intl. Assn. of Music Libraries with the support of the American Council of Learned

Societies, at the City Univ. of New York, 33 West 42nd St., New York, N.Y. 10036.

An international instrument for musicological documentation. It presents signed abstracts of all significant literature in music that has appeared since January 1, 1967. The abstracts are in English with explanatory notes in French and German. About 160 periodicals are consulted. It is classified by nine basic subject areas with many subdivisions. In 1970 the publication fell behind; subsequent issues were delayed. Nevertheless it is a very ambitious reference work covering more literature and providing more information in the field of music than any other index. If the editors make up for the time lapse it will also be the most important one. (P.V.)

Readers' Guide to Periodical Literature. 1900. s-m. (Sept.–June). m. (July–Aug.). $35. Zada Limerick. H. W. Wilson Co., 950 Univ. Ave., Bronx, N.Y. 10452. Circ: 22,232. Sample. Vol. ends: Feb. 10.

The basic periodical index in any library. The author-subject approach to 160 magazines serves as the primary key to current materials for everyone from the elementary school student to the graduate student. Magazines are selected for indexing by librarians. Titles represent the best (and some of the worst) magazines published in America. Emphasis is on popular, consumer magazines. There is a decided de-emphasis on controversial materials. The index cumulates quarterly and has a permanent bound annual.

Religious Periodicals Index. 1970. q. $15. Philip Deemer. Jarrow Press, 1556 Third Ave., New York, N.Y. 10028.

There have been two basic indexes to religious magazines: *Index to Religious Periodical Literature* which has been published since 1949 as an annual by the American Theological Library Association; and *Religious and Theological Abstracts,* a quarterly published since 1958. This newest one covers more American religious magazines than either of its predecessors. All major faiths are represented, as are divisions in those faiths. It is organized in two main parts: author, with unsigned articles given by title and documents and official statements listed separately. Each is numbered. Then comes the subject approach, the less successful in that under every subject the reader is referred back to the author for the main entry. Thus, under "Ecology" are some 30 author numbers, forcing the user to check back and forth 30 times. Perhaps the main entry under author is the way most specialists approach the area, but for anyone else the arrangement is a first class headache. A final section is given to book reviews, arranged by the author and title of the book reviewed. In view of the emphasis on 211 American magazines, and the need for such an index, it will prove useful, albeit a terror for researchers.

Hopefully, the editor will take a second look at his approach.

Religious and Theological Abstracts. 1958. q. $20 (Individuals $15). J. Creighton Christman, 121 S. College St., Myerstown, Pa. 17067. Circ: 1,000. Sample. Vol. ends: Winter.

International in scope, this is the basic abstracting service in the area. It is nonsectarian, abstracting from Christian, Jewish, and Muslim journals. All abstracts are in English. Abstracts appear about six months following publication of article. Author, subject, and biblical index.

Répertoire Bibliographique de la Philosophie. 1949. q. Issued as a supplement to *Revue Philosophique de Louvain* (q., $14) or separately for $9. Georges Van Riet. Editions Nauwelaerts, Mgr. Ladeuzeplein 2, B-3000, Louvain, Belgium. Circ: 2,000. Vol. ends: Nov.

This is the successor to the *Répertoire Bibliographique* which appeared between 1934–1948 as a supplement to the *Revue Néoscholastique de Louvain.* The February, May, and August numbers contain references to books and articles, while the November issue includes a list of book reviews and a general index of names. Exhaustive coverage of philosophic literature in Dutch, English, French, German, Italian, Latin, Portuguese, Spanish, and Catalan is attempted. Some works published in other languages are also included. Over 350 periodicals are regularly indexed. The bibliography of books and articles is in a classified arrangement; the list of book reviews is alphabetical. The index of names brings together under an author's name all the publications which he has signed, translated, or edited, all those titles which cite his name, and the book reviews which he has signed. Although the *Philosopher's Index* is somewhat easier to use than the *Répertoire,* and might be preferred by some because of its abstracts, the *Répertoire* must be acknowledged the more valuable of the two, simply on the grounds of comprehensiveness. (J.A.)

Research in Education. 1966. m. $22. Educational Resources Information Center (ERIC). Subs. to: Supt. of Documents, U.S. Govt. Printing Office, Washington, D.C. 20402 (SDC: HE 5.77) Vol. ends: Dec.

This monthly abstract journal is published by the Educational Resources Information Center (ERIC) of the Office of Education. The abstracts cover all OE project reports and other relevant documents prepared in ERIC's several clearinghouses, including the CLIS, the Clearinghouse on Library and Information Science. The product thus offered is designed to keep teachers, administrators, librarians, research specialists, and others informed of the latest significant findings from educational research. The semi-annual and annual indexes are not included as part of the subscription service but are sold separately. Subscribers are notified when the indexes are published.

The publication is organized as follows: A document section contains abstract resumes that include descriptors as well as all pertinent bibliographic information. A sample entry is given in each issue. This section has a separate subject, author (or investigator) and institution index. An accession numbers section provides a cross-reference from the ERIC clearinghouse number to the Document (ED) number for the resumes. There was a Project Section on current research, but it was dropped as of the January 1971 issue. In February of that year, Leasco Information Products, Inc., began to provide ERIC document reproductions in microfiche and hard copy.

The journal is designed for machine searching. Descriptors published are incomplete, and to retrieve a title under all headings requires the use of ERIC tapes. This in turn requires one to use the *Thesaurus of ERIC Descriptors,* a GPO publication available from the Superintendent of Documents. A feature titled "How To Order ERIC Publications" is included in each issue.

Libraries having (or having access to) the tapes might find this a useful journal, though presently the value is more potential than actual. Definitely not a panacea. (J.M.)

Review of Metal Literature. See *Metal Abstracts.*

SPIN: (Searchable Physics Information Notes) See *Current Physics Information* in Physics Section.

Science Abstracts. 1898. Institution of Electrical Engineers, Savoy Pl., London WC2R OBL, England. Microform: Institution of Electrical Engineers.

A brief review of this old and highly important abstracting service is in order. Originally issued in two sections, Series A: *Physics,* and Series B: *Electrical and Electronics,* the publication added a third section, Series C: *Computer and Control,* in 1966. These are now all part of the INSPEC system (Information Service in Physics, Electrotechnical and Control), supported also by the American Institute of Physics and Physical Society, London, the Institute of Electrical and Electronics Engineers (U.S.), the Institution of Electronic and Radio Engineers (London), and the International Federation of Automatic Control. The format of these three abstracting journals (also sold separately) is the same: indicative abstracts are provided, accommodations are made for liberal cross-references between the overlapping fields, and semiannual author-subject indexes are available for each. Microfiche editions are also published. Magnetic tapes, SDI services, card services, and three current-awareness publications fall within the purview of INSPEC. Most technical collections will have all or one of these services, depending on needs.

The three companion INSPEC publications providing fast, current-awareness services are as follows: *Current Papers in Physics* (s-m., $34.) lists titles of significant research papers; *Current Papers in Electrical and Electronics Engineering* (m., $34.) supplies important references in electrical engineering and related fields; and *Current Papers on Computers and Control* (m., $30.) disseminates titles on new research in these areas. Titles appear under the same classification scheme as provided by the respective sections of *Science Abstracts.*

Series A: *Physics Abstracts.* 1898. bi-w. $290. Institution of Electrical Engineers, Savoy Pl., London, WC2R OBL, England. U.S. Subs. to: Amer. Inst. of Physics, 335 E. 45th St., New York, N.Y. 10017.

The major abstracting journal for physics. Subjects include such overlapping fields as mathematical physics, quantum electronics, physical chemistry, geophysics, astrophysics, and biophysics, as well as the more traditional divisions of physics. About 85,000 entries are included annually, as obtained from such sources as journals, books, conference proceedings, patents, and selected technical reports. Each issue contains its own author index and a subject index to the classification scheme; more detailed subject indexes are published semiannually. All physics collections will need this section.

Series B: *Electrical and Electronics Abstracts.* 1898. m. $240. Institution of Electrical Engineers, Savoy Pl., London, WC2R OBL, England. U.S. Subs. to: Inst. of Electrical & Electronics Engineers, 345 E. 47th St., New York, N.Y. 10017.

Provides coverage in such fields as circuits, electron devices and materials, electromagnetics and communications, instrumentation, and power and industry, as well as general electronics. About 40,000 abstracts appear annually. Patents and technical reports, as well as books, journals, and conference proceedings, fall within its scope. A major abstracting tool for electrical engineering collections.

Series C: *Computer and Control Abstracts.* 1966. m. $120. Institution of Electrical Engineers, Savoy Pl., London, WC2R OBL, England. U.S. Subs. to: Inst. of Electrical & Electronics Engineers, 345 E. 47th St., New York, N.Y. 10017.

Entries which, in previous years, had been incorporated in Series B, were provided with a separate and expanded publication in 1966. Its present coverage takes in systems and control theory, including cybernetics; control technology, including equipment and applications; computer programming and applications, including information science and documentation, and programming systems and languages; data processing; other computer applications; and computer systems and equipment. Over 24,000 abstracts are issued annually. In addition to the journal literature, books, symposia, patents, and technical reports are also included. This service gives the most comprehensive coverage in its field.

Science Citation Index. 1963. q. $1,950 ($1,250 to educational institutions). Eugene Garfield. Institute for Scientific Information, 325 Chestnut St., Philadelphia, Pa. 19106.

The *SCI*, first initiated as an experimental project and later sold on a regular subscription basis since the early sixties, has been described and discussed in the literature in elegant detail. (For a comprehensive review on the subject, see M. Weinstock, "Citation Indexes," *Encyclopedia of Library and Information Science*, vol. 5, N.Y., Marcel Dekker, 1971. pp. 16–40.) Very briefly, it consists of the following. It is a computer-produced index, issued quarterly and cumulated annually, to some 2,500 source journals in the mathematical, natural, physical, and behavioral sciences, and to cited U.S. and foreign patents. (A five-year index, 1965–1969, is also available.) Counted among the components of the *SCI* are: (1) the "Citation" Index proper, arranged by author; (2) the "Source" Index, which gives full bibliographic details of source items listed in the Citation Index; and (3) a "Permuter" Index, which provides a subject approach through keywords of titles. Included as well are a "Corporate" Index gleaned from affiliations of authors; "Patent" Index, source journal lists, delineated also by subject and geography.

The uniqueness of the *SCI*, as opposed to other retrieval schemes, is that it is a network of connections between authors citing the same papers during a current year. In other words, if, in searching for particular subject matter, one has a key paper or review article in the field, or even an author's name, one consults the *Citation Index* by author. Beneath his name will be listed in chronological order *any* of his publications cited during a particular year, together with the *citing* authors (source items) who have referred to his work. If one continues to check the citing authors in the Citation Index, a cyclical process takes place, often with mushrooming results. The Source Index is then used to establish the full bibliographic reference to the citing author.

Another subject approach is the "Permuterm" Subject Index, an alphabetically arranged subject index derived from words appearing in the titles of the source articles. Each significant word has been precoordinated with other terms to produce all possible permutations of terms.

The following is not a discussion of approach, history, concepts. methodology, or coverage. Suffice it to say that the multidisciplinary *SCI* covers the main research journals of every aspect of science and technology, and produces about 4 million citations as culled from 341,000 source items annually. Rather, this emphasizes its practical utility for a librarian. Since cost is clearly a prohibitive factor, the SCI will hardly be a first-choice selection for a librarian whose research/reference work is minimal and for whom the standard indexes are perfectly adequate. But if speed

and currency of search are vital, seven points can be made.

(1) At some time or other everyone searches the literature backward by the citation principle; the SCI allows one to move *forward* in time, for the current year. (2) Frequently, several abstracting journals must be consulted; by coordinating references, the SCI often reduces this need. (3) Since usage of the index is not dependent on knowledge of the proper terminology, the onerous task of searching for appropriate synonym, related term, etc. is eliminated. (4) In the case of prolific writers or authors who cite themselves regularly, it provides a quick bibliography of one author's work. (5) Current references appear frequently before they have been picked up by the standard abstracting services. (6) Its pyramidal effect can be huge; relevancy of citations is large. (7) Most importantly, it can give a lead into the literature in a few minutes—the amount of time it takes to check an author's name and to scan the column.

It seems evident, then, that this very clever and powerful bibliographic tool should be an absolute necessity in every institution in which scientific research is being conducted.

The Institute for Scientific Information also supplies the SCI on magnetic tape and provides other publications and custom alerting services. *ASCA* (Automatic Subject Citation Alert), a weekly service, gives citations based on user-profiles. *Current Contents*, available for chemical and physical, life, engineering and technology, behavioral, social and educational sciences; agricultural, food, and veterinary sciences, provides weekly tables of contents of pertinent journals (see *Current Contents* annotation for further information).

Current Abstracts of Chemistry and Index Chemicus, a weekly indexing-abstracting journal, also contains graphic data on new chemical compounds, many of which have not yet been listed by the other abstracting services. And *Chemical Substructure Index*, another computer-produced index featuring Wiswesser Notation to delineate chemical structure, is particularly useful for organic and pharmaceutical chemists. (B.G.)

Scientific and Technical Aerospace Reports (STAR).

1963. s-m. $54. National Aeronautics and Space Administration, Scientific and Technical Information Office, Washington, D.C. Subs. to: Supt. of Documents, U.S. Govt. Printing Office, Washington, D.C. 20402. Circ: 8,000.

With a large percentage of the aerospace literature released as technical reports, NASA's abstracting and indexing service, *STAR*, performs a useful function. There are presently in its total data base over 1,000,000 entries, covering, on a worldwide basis, the report literature on aeronautics, astronautics, the basic physical and biological sciences related to the space effort, and supporting technologies such as electronics, communications, etc. Reports abstracted are those produced by NASA, NASA-funded contractors and grantees, as well as other government agencies here and abroad. A few theses, patents, and translations also appear. (Note: Some reports are picked up from *Nuclear Science Abstracts* and *Government Reports Announcements*, if related to aerospace.) Entries are arranged sequentially under 34 subject categories; cross references are liberal; and information about availability of documents is also provided. Every issue contains 5 indexes: author, corporate-source, subject, contract number and report/accession. Cumulative indexes are also published (purchased separately for $23). *STAR*, coupled with its sister publication, *International Aerospace Abstracts*, listed above, which documents the journal literature, would be first-choice purchases for every library supporting a strong aerospace collection.

Another interesting and nominally priced NASA-sponsored publication is *Computer Program Abstracts* (1969, q., $1). Briefly, it gives documented computer programs in the subject categories noted for *STAR*, which have been prepared under NASA funding and which are for sale. Programs described are not restricted to sci-tech fields alone, but include under a "general" slot, such items as vendor analysis systems, library automation, and the like. For a dollar, useful for any institution with a computer. (B.G.)

Selected RAND Abstracts. 1963. q. Free to agencies of the government, academic and public libraries, and to nonprofit research organizations; others $15. Rand Corp., Reports Dept., 1700 Main St., Santa Monica, Calif., 90406.

The nonprofit research organization, RAND Corporation, needs little introduction. These abstracts serve as a guide to the unclassified publications produced by this firm which, in large part, performs public interest research with large application government policy. Not restricted to any field, subjects range from economic, political, and military studies, to mathematics (mainly mathematical models of problems) and science and engineering reports. Three sections make up each issue: subject and author indexes lead to an abstract section arranged by accession number. The unclassified publications range from short memoranda, reports, papers, to scholarly monographs; many of these are available in the published literature. The diversity of material, representing both social and physical sciences, makes this a worthwhile service for any academic institution, many of whom will also obtain subscriptions to the RAND unclassified publications themselves. (B.G.)

Selected References on Environment Quality as it Relates to Health. 1971. m. $4. National Library of Medicine, 8600 Rockville Pike, Bethesda, Md. 20014. Subs. to: Supt. of Documents, U.S. Govt. Printing Office, Washington, D.C. 20402.

This indexing service is directed to those who are interested in the quality of our environment but are not versant in using *Index Medicus* or other specialized products of the National Library of Medicine (NLM). The subject entries are selected to cover the area indicated in the title, produced by the same computer-based analysis and retrieval system as *Index Medicus*. It is, however, much easier to use because of its defined, perspicuous organization. The monthly issues are divided into a subject and an author section. Cross-references are rather scarce. (For instance there is no such entry as *Pollution*. The topic is covered under Air–Water, etc. without a general entry which refers to specific ones.) Otherwise it is a truly international service, providing short notes about the contents in case of foreign titles. In regard to the rising interest in the quality of our environment, this instrument is welcomed by all major public and academic libraries. (P.V.)

Selected Water Resources Abstracts. 1968. s-m. $22. Water Resources Scientific Information Service, Office of Water Resources Research, U.S. Dept. of the Interior, Washington, D.C. 20240; Subs. to: National Technical Information Service, Springfield, Va. 22151.

Produced also with the cooperation of selected organizations which supply the input to the Water Resources Sci-Info service, the publication covers the following areas in water study: water cycle, properties of water, its conservation, quantity and quality, resources, engineering, as well as some general categories, including legislation. Books, journals, reports, are all within the scope of the publication. Each issue has its own subject-author, organization, and accession number indexes. With all the research centers acting as information gathering units, the coverage is comprehensive. The service immediately invites comparison with AWRA's *Water Resources Abstracts*. Although the intent of WRA is different, the coverage of abstracts in *Selected Water Resources Abstracts* is broader, searching is facilitated by subject-author indexes in each issue, and the price is significantly cheaper (1/5 the cost of WRA). Recommended for any technical library investigating the water literature. (B.G.)

Social Sciences and Humanities Index (Formerly: *International Index.* 1907). 1965. q. Service basis. J. Doris Dart. H. W. Wilson Co., 950 Univ. Ave., Bronx, N.Y. 10452. Circ: 4,122. Sample. Vol. ends: March.

Next to the *Readers' Guide to Periodical Literature*, this is the closest thing to a general periodical index. It should be included in most libraries because of its broad coverage—202 English language periodicals—in many fields: anthropology, archaeology, classical and area studies, economics, folklore, geography, history, language and literature, music, philosophy, political science, religion and theology, sociology and theatre arts, plus many periodicals of general scholarly interest.

Sociological Abstracts. 1952. 7/yr. $100. Leo P. Chall. Sociological Abstracts, Inc., 73 Eighth Ave., Brooklyn, N.Y. 11215. Adv. Circ: 1,800. Sample.

An international approach to journals in sociology and related fields. Abstracts from 19 languages, although many are in English—not because of any bias, but because "it is a temporary fortuitous fact that English is lingua franca of sociology." Coverage is exhaustive, and the abstracting service is a must for any library with an interest in sociology and related areas.

Subject Index to Children's Magazines. 1949. m. (except June and July). $10.50. Gladys Cavanah, 2223 Chamberlain Ave., Madison, Wis. 53705. Circ: 5,000. Sample. Vol. ends: Aug.

The only index devoted solely to children's magazines (primarily, but not exclusively, grades 1–8). Some 50 magazines are analyzed under subject headings familiar to teachers and librarians, as well as most students. Titles range over those suitable for elementary through senior high school. Unfortunately, several of the magazines, including *Popular Mechanics, Popular Science,* etc., are also indexed in the *Readers' Guide to Periodical Literature.* Nevertheless, the index is an absolute must in any school, at least for elementary grades. For high schools the unabridged *Readers' Guide* is preferable.

Technical Book Review Index. 1935. m. (Sept.–June). $15. Albert Kamper. Special Libraries Assn., 235 Park Ave. So., New York, N.Y. 10003. Circ: 2,015.

Somewhat the technical book equivalent of *Book Review Digest,* i.e., it prints excerpts from reviews which have appeared in scientific and trade periodicals. A lag of 6 to 9 months is usual between the time the review appeared and the time it is indexed. Nevertheless, a valuable service for all libraries with more than average involvement in reviews of science books.

Today's Housing Briefs. 1971. bi-m. $90. F. S. Gospodarek. Information Planning Associates, Inc., 310 Maple Drive, Rockville, Md. 20850. Illus.

An abstracting service, this surveys some 60 journals, magazines, and government reports for material on the low and moderate income housing field. There are eight major subject divisions, an author-subject index, and a list of publishers. Noncomputerized, the 50-page service is well printed, easy enough to read. The subject index identifies the articles by a code number, and as the subjects are broken down sufficiently, only a few items (industrialized housing, financing, building codes, etc.) list more than six or seven articles. This eliminates fruitless back and forth searching for items identified only by broad subject classification. Most of the material is current. The abstracts, of 150 to 250 words, are clear and well within the understanding of either the layman or expert. Se-

lection seems to bear out the editor's contention that every effort is given to be objective; present all sides of controversial issues. Aside from the obvious audience, the abstracts will be of interest to environment and urban problem groups. The irony, to be sure, is the price, which is not out-of-line, for an abstracting service but is for most small to medium sized libraries serving low income and moderate income families.

U.S. Government Research and Development Reports. See *Government Reports Announcements.*

Water Pollution Abstracts. 1927. m. £ 4.25. Her Majesty's Stationery Office, P.O. Box 569, London, SE1, England; for sale in U.S. by British Information Services, 845 Third Avenue, New York, N.Y.

Well-established for many years, the publication is produced by the Water Pollution Research Staff of the Department of Environment (Great Britain). The scope of the service is not in the least restricted to the waters of the British Isles, and coverage is fully international. Included on a worldwide basis are monographs, journal literature, conference proceedings, and technical reports. Fields covered encompass water conservation, analysis, sewage, wastewater, and effects of pollution. Cross references are extensive within the body of informative abstracts. Reviews of conference proceedings are particularly detailed. An annual author-subject index is supplied with the cost of a subscription. Although the range of subject matter covered in the U.S. *Selected Water Resources Abstracts* has far more breadth, these abstracts are nonetheless extremely useful and highly recommended for technical libraries focusing on water pollution. (B.G.)

Water Resources Abstracts. 1968. m. $120 ($180 on heavy perforated paper). American Water Resources Assn., 905 West Fairview Ave., Urbana, Ill. 61801.

In keeping with AWRA's concern to collect and disseminate information in such an interdisciplinary area as the water literature, the society puts out about 2,000 informative abstracts annually. Grouped under 46 categories, with about 150 entries in each section, the abstracts, emphasizing resources, cover such subjects as water properties, conservation, ground water pollution, limnology and hydrobiology, as well as water quality, wastewater, and water management. Journal and report literature, books and conference proceedings are reviewed. In loose-leaf binder format, about 3 abstracts appear on each page, printed on one side to facilitate clipping. Entries also contain keyterms, taken from *Water Resources Thesaurus.* The only index available is one which shows the number of entries published in each category. Each section, incidentally, may be purchased separately; at $5.00 per category for individual subscribers, the abstracts are a bargain. For libraries relying solely on the loose-leaf format, however, the lack of author-subject indexes makes retrospective searching nearly impossible. Their needs would be better served (at a considerably cheaper price) by *Selected Water Resources Abstracts.* AWRA also issues a current awareness bulletin, *Hydata* (m., 1965, $25) which not only supplies tables of contents of the significant journals in the field, but also includes timely information on report titles, selected monographs, etc. (B.G.)

Women Studies Abstracts. 1972. q. $10 (Individuals $7.50; students $5). Sara S. Whaley, Box 1, Rush, N.Y. 14543.

This is an abstracting service that no library can afford to miss. It is both unique and useful. The 75-page pocket-sized offset service is put together to serve and support women and their relationship to the world. "Hopefully," the editor notes, "it will help some men to see the why and wherefore of the movement in order that they examine their own attitudes and prejudices towards women. Above all, it should help women examine themselves." The issue examined included abstracts of articles under eight subject headings from education to family, and women in history and literature. Another section was a listing of articles which could not be abstracted, but which the editor considered important. There was also an index to book reviews of books about women, and a good subject index to the 200 numbered abstracts. The abstracts are written by the editor and volunteers, and hopefully more will be included in subsequent issues. Meanwhile, they are models of their kind. Articles are drawn from all types and varieties of magazines (some 2,000 were examined) and the largest problem seemed to be deciding what to exclude. The editor has done rather well, and there is little here which should not be considered. Apparently this is a nonprofit-making effort, and it is one of the few recent abstracting services which is not first and foremost another way of ripping off the library budget. Not only is the approach excellent, but the price is modest enough to warrant support by most libraries, certainly all the medium to large ones.

AERONAUTICS AND SPACE SCIENCE

Basic Periodicals

Hs: *Flying; Space World;* Ga: *Flying, Aviation Week and Space Technology; Space World;* Ac: (Nonspecialist) *Astronautics and Aeronautics; Aeronautical Journal; Aviation Week and Space Technology; Spaceflight;* (Research/Engineering) *AIAA Journal; Aeronautical Quarterly; Astronautica Acta; Journal of Aircraft; Journal of Spacecraft and Rockets; Space Science Reviews.*

Basic Abstracts and Indexes

International Aerospace Abstracts; Engineering Index; Scientific and Technical Aerospace Reports.

Introduction

Included here are selections from the popular, business, and technical literature on sports flying, general aviation, aeronautical science and engineering, astronautical science and engineering, and the physics of space. Periodicals represent both American and British efforts, in most cases. Although no attempt has been made to suggest a first-class research collection, the few journals which have been named do represent high-quality publications. (See also sections on Astronomy and Atmospheric Sciences.)

AIAA Bulletin. 1964. m. $10 (members $2). American Inst. of Aeronautics and Astronautics, Inc., 1290 Ave. of the Americas, New York, N.Y. 10019. Index. Circ: 37,800. Vol. ends: Dec.

Aud: Sa, Ac.

The official announcement publication and news organ of the AIAA. Issues take in meeting schedules, calls for papers, abstracts of papers presented at conferences of the society, and miscellaneous reports. Most academic libraries subscribing to the main technical journal of the society, *AIAA Journal* (see below) would be likely to get the *Bulletin* for its news and abstracts.

AIAA Journal. 1963. m. $60 (members $14). George W. Sutton. American Inst. of Aeronautics and Astronautics, 1290 Ave. of the Americas, New York, N.Y. 10019. Illus., index. Circ: 9,000. Sample. Vol. ends: Dec. Refereed. Microform: UM.

Indexed: ChemAb, EngI, IntA, MathR, SCI. *Aud:* Sa, Ac.

Dedicated to the advancement of astronautics and aeronautics, the basic research journal of the AIAA was formed by a merger of the *ARS Journal* (American Rocket Society) and *Journal of the Aerospace Sciences* (Institute of the Aerospace Sciences). Original and high quality research papers report on fields such as rocket propulsion, space and atmospheric flight, guidance and flight control systems, fluid mechanics, and some papers on space physics. In addition to full-length papers and short technical notes, a new feature, "synoptics," (i.e. technical papers described briefly in 1 to 2 pages) has been added in the last few years. The full-length papers of the "synoptics" are on file with AIAA and may be purchased for those desiring detailed information. An excellent and first-choice selection for aerospace libraries.

The society also puts out a nonspecialist publication, *Astronautics and Aeronautics,* and three highly specialized journals: *Journal of Aircraft, Journal of Spacecraft and Rockets,* and *Journal of Hydronautics* (see Oceanography). These are dedicated to systems and craft, rather than the basic science of the field.

AIAA Student Journal. 1963. q. $4. P. M. Sforza. American Inst. of Aeronautics and Astronautics, 1290

Ave. of the Americas, New York, N.Y. 10019. Illus., index. Circ: 7,000. Sample. Vol. ends: Dec. Refereed. *Bk. rev:* 1–2, 1,000–2,000 words, signed. *Aud:* Ac. Sa.

Contributions to this student-oriented periodical border on the general and philosophical, i.e., contemplations of technology, the draft and the engineering student, etc. Historical articles appear frequently, as well as news of educational programs, design projects, educational experiments, news of the student organization. An important supplement for students, published periodically, is one which contains information on employment opportunities. Readable and professionally oriented, the magazine will appeal to budding engineers and to faculty interested in new teaching methods. For academic libraries.

AOPA Pilot. 1958. m. $10 (membership). Max Karant. Aircraft Owners and Pilots Assn., Box 5800, Washington, D.C. 20014. Illus., index, adv. Circ: 160,000. Sample. Vol. ends: Dec.

Bk. rev: 1,500 words, signed. *Aud:* Sa, Ga.

The magazine for pilots—amateurs and professionals, as well as members of the AOPA. Long, well-illustrated articles contain information on general aviation, the latest models and developments in aircraft, air traffic systems, radar and communications equipment, landing strips, and legislation pertaining to air regulations. Emphasis is on airmanship and flight safety. Travel tips are frequently included. Any academic or public library supporting active flying clubs will surely want it.

Aerojet-General Booster. See Free Magazines Section.

Aeronautical Journal. 1897. m. $15.75. G. R. Wrixon. Royal Aeronautical Soc., 4 Hamilton Place, London W1V OBQ, England. Illus., index, adv. Circ: 12,000. Vol. ends: Dec. Refereed. Microform: UM. Reprint: Dawson.

Indexed: BritTechI, EngI. *Bk. rev:* 3, 300–500 words, signed. *Aud:* Sa, Ac.

The Royal Aeronautical Society, now incorporating the Institution of Aeronautical Engineers and the Helicopter Association of Gt. Brit., is one of the foremost scientific organizations dedicated to aeronautical studies (counterpart to the American Institute of Aeronautics and Astronautics). Its *Journal,* formerly called *Royal Aeronautical Society Journal,* is both a nonspecialist and a technical publication. For general interest appeal, feature articles review trends and developments, speculate on the future, or step backward into the past through reminiscences by one-time flying greats. On the engineering side, a few short technical notes are published, plus "Supplementary Papers," frequently representing papers presented at special symposia. Brief reports and news of the membership at large are also included. The bulk of research papers will appear in the Society's *Aeronautical Quarterly,* a high

quality publication. Both journals are excellent and would be necessary for good aeronautics collections in university libraries.

Aeronautical Quarterly. 1949. q. $12 (membership). E. C. Pike. Royal Aeronautical Soc., 4 Hamilton Place, London, W1V OBQ, England, Illus., index. Sample. Vol. ends: Nov. Refereed. Microform: UM. Reprint: Dawson.

Indexed: BritTechI, EngI, MathR, SCI. *Aud:* Sa, Ac.

Specializing in sophisticated technical papers in aeronautics, the chief journal of the RAS covers topics such as aerodynamics, aeroelasticity, astronautics, instruments, heat transfer, fatigue mechanics, solid mechanics, and the like. Reports are both theoretical and experimental. A leading publication for any research aeronautical collection. (See also *Aeronautical Journal.*)

Aerospace (English). m. Free. G. R. Wrixon. Royal Aeronautical Soc., 4 Hamilton Place, London W1V OBQ, England. Illus., adv. Circ: 38,000.

Indexed: ASTI. *Bk. rev:* 3–4, 100–300 words, signed.

The newspaper of the Royal Aeronautical Society. In tabloid format, the RAS reports on international news, mergers, markets, contracts, airships, products, components, tests, sales, interviews, and new books, letters, personalia, and classified. Quick to be scanned, and just as quick to be tossed out, more societies ought to publish their ephemera and news bits in just this format. Academic libraries with aerospace collections will probably want to get on the mailing list.

Aerospace Medicine. 1930. m. $18. John P. Marbarger. Aerospace Medical Assn., Washington National Airport, Washington, D.C. 20001. Illus., index, adv. Sample. Vol. ends: Dec. Refereed. Microform: Microcard Editions. Reprint: Johnson.

Indexed: BioAb, ChemAb, IMed, PsyAb. *Aud:* Sa, Ac.

Although a specialized medical periodical (formerly called *Journal of Aviation Medicine*), the publication contains enough information on the physiology, psychology, safety survival of travel by air and space flight to make it interesting to a wide host of scientists and to round out an aerospace collection. Titles such as "Aircraft noise and the community," "Effects of simulated sonic booms," "Sensitivity to rotation of pilots and nonpilots" indicate the scope. Clinical and research-type studies are published. Well-organized monthly departments include Association and other news, abstracts of current literature, and an FAA question-answer section. The December issue consists entirely of a Directory of Members and index. Biomedical as well as aerospace collections will want it.

Aircraft Engineering. 1929. m. $13.50. Harry Stone. Bunhill Publns. Ltd., 4 Ludgate Circus, London EC4, England. Illus., index, adv. Vol. ends: Dec. Microform: UM.

Indexed: ASTI, BritTechI, EngI, SCI. *Bk. rev:* 3–4, 200 words, staff. *Aud:* Sa, Ac.

Not merely a technical journal, the publication also reviews markets, supporting equipment, materials, tools, and anything else concerned with aircraft systems. Noted particularly for its well-illustrated and diagrammed engineering features on new aircraft, the periodical supplies one or two technical articles per issue, plus staff-written reviews. Departments turn out fairly thorough coverage of international news, although some concentration centers on the U.K. A good choice for a general aviation publication for engineering collections.

Airman. 1957. m. $7. Supt. of Documents, U.S. Govt. Printing Office, Washington, D.C. 20402. Illus. Circ: 175,000. Vol. ends: Dec.

Aud: Ga.

Produced by the Information Division of the U.S. Air Force, the magazine is the "official organ of the USAF published for the enlightenment and the building of morale of all AF personnel." The blurb gives an indication of its general content and level. Articles, photos, etc. are contributed by members of the Air Force at all hierarchical levels; the editorial staff puts out the rest. Issues are given to the usual amateur vignette, profile, short story, but may contain features on technical activities going on in Air Force installations throughout the world. Personalia are also included. Stylistically simplistic, it may be of possible interest to service-oriented youth, as well as to Air Force men and women in need of a morale boost.

Air Transport World. 1964. m. $8. Joseph S. Murphy. World Aviation Publns, 333 Shoreham Bldg., Washington, D.C. Illus., index, adv. Circ: 43,000. Sample. Vol. ends: Dec.

Aud: Sa, Ac.

Business-oriented, the emphasis in this periodical is on transport—its legislation, carriers, routes, pilots, passengers, markets, sales, economics, etc. News and features discuss activities of major airlines, airports, and trade policies. Monthly departments also supply regular information on new products, airline statistics, calendars and personalia. From time to time special issues provide state-of-the-art reports on topics such as airline electronics, air cargo, etc. The statistical data on airline operations and the broad feature articles assure a wider audience than airline management.

Astronautica Acta. 1954. bi-m. $50. Martin Summerfield. Pergamon Press, Maxwell House, Fairview Park, Elmsford, N.Y. 10523. Illus., index, adv. Sample. Vol. ends: No. 6. Refereed. Microform: Maxwell. Reprint: Maxwell.

Indexed: ChemAb, EngI, MathR, SCI, IntAe. *Aud:* Sa, Ac.

The celebrated Wernher von Braun, a member of the first editorial board, commented that the time will come when "it will no longer be respectable to raise doubt at the feasibility of astronautics." Nearly 20 years later, with the feasibility of the field now a commonplace matter, this archival journal still continues to publish high-quality research papers in all areas of the discipline. As the official organ also of the International Academy of Astronautics (a division of the International Astronautical Federation), papers explore such topics as astrodynamics, gas dynamics, propulsion, guidance, spaceflight, and the physics of space. An authoritative source for literature on astronautics. Principally for university libraries.

Astronautics & Aeronautics. 1957. m. $20 (membership). John Newbauer. American Inst. of Aeronautics and Astronautics, 1290 Ave. of the Americas, New York, N.Y. 10036. Illus., index, adv. Circ: 40,415. Vol. ends: Dec. Microform: UM.

Indexed: ChemAb, EngI, SCI. *Bk. rev:* 3–4, 200–500 words, signed. *Aud:* Sa, Ac, Ga.

Intended for a broad spectrum of readers, the periodical represents the AIAA's news organ and nonspecialist publication, focusing on interpretive reviews, surveys, and trends in the fields of aeronautics, spaceflight, hydronautics, and rocketry. (See also *AIAA Journal.*) Well-illustrated feature articles may also serve as tutorials or provide biographical sketches and other general material intelligible to laymen. Aerospace news, as well as that of the profession, is amply covered by monthly sections, including a well-written "National Scene." A noteworthy department, "In the Journals," culls new research as reported in the more specialized journals and discusses these papers in one evaluative essay. While one of the best general aeronautics publications, it does require technical knowledge for full use and is highly recommended for engineering collections. On a more popular level, a magazine such as *Space World,* or for a business slant, *Aviation Week and Space Technology,* might be more appropriate.

Astrophysics and Space Science. See Astronomy Section for this title and other journals related to space science.

Aviation Week and Space Technology. 1916. w. $15. Robert B. Hotz. McGraw-Hill, Inc., 330 W. 42nd St., New York, N.Y. 10036. Illus., adv. Circ: 108,000. Sample. Vol. ends: No. 52. Microform: UM.

Indexed: BusI, RG. *Aud:* Sa, Ac, Ga.

Drawing upon the prodigious resources of the McGraw research staff, this publication represents the most comprehensive news magazine for the aviation, aerospace, and allied industries. Articles are short, crisp, factual, with occasional, reliable, in-depth reports on special topics, such as the aerospace budget.

Developments reviewed weekly are space technology, air transport, management, aeronautical engineering, and avionics. Weekly departments round up events, both from industry and the government, people, calendar, and some international news bits. A useful, special marketing directory is issued annually. With the emphasis on the pulse of business, the magazine is still suitable for both those connected with industry and the interested general reader. Its high factual content makes it a valuable choice for public and academic libraries.

British Interplanetary Society. Journal. 1934. m. $25. G. V. Groves. British Interplanetary Soc., 12 Bessborough Gardens, London, SW1, England. Illus., index. Circ: 1,500. Vol. ends: Dec. Refereed. Microform: Datamics. Reprint: Kraus.

Indexed: EngI. *Aud:* Sa, Ac.

When the probability of interplanetary travel was only a sci-fi concept, this interesting society first formed the hard core of British interest in rocketry in the early thirties. Despite the skepticism of the overwhelming majority, the organization, dedicating itself to stimulating public interest in space science, drew support on an international basis. Advancing from an early article by Willy Ley on rocketry in Germany, to an article, 40 years later, on aeronautical satellites, the journal is concerned with technical papers on propulsion systems, lunar and planetary research, navigation, materials, extraterrestrial life, space medicine and law, etc. For engineering collections of university libraries. (Note: Still intent on disseminating information to the public, the society issues a fine, popular periodical, *Spaceflight,* listed below.)

Business/Commercial Aviation. 1958. m. $15. James Holahan. Ziff Davis Publishing Co., 1 Park Ave., New York, N.Y. 10016. Illus., adv. Circ: 60,000. Sample. Vol. ends: Dec.

Bk. rev: 2, 50–200 words, signed. *Aud:* Sa, Ga.

Reviews the latest developments in aircraft fleets acquired by corporations and commercial airlines. Although the periodical is mainly directed toward pilots, airport management, and the aviation departments in industry, articles (written mostly by staff editors) do discuss general topics such as air legislation, practical features on piloting, design and performance of aircraft, problems associated with airports, and the like. Public libraries will find more popular appeal in another Ziff Davis publication, *Flying,* listed below. Nonetheless, the magazine's tips on piloting, and other tutorial features, are excellent, and its audience could extend to anyone with flying blood.

Comments on Astrophysics and Space Physics. See Astronomy Section for this title and others in space physics.

Flight International. 1909. w. $18. J. M. Ramsden. Iliffe Transport Publns. Ltd., Dorset House, Stamford St., London, SE1, England. Illus., index, adv. Circ: 40,000. Sample. Vol. ends: Dec. Microform: UM.

Indexed: BritTechI, EngI. *Aud:* Sa, Ac, Ga.

Billed as the "First aeronautical weekly in the world," the magazine is also the official voice of the United Service and Royal Aero Club. (Note: former title *Flight and Aircraft Engineer.*) In terms of aircraft and airlines, the magazine probably gives as much concise international information as any other publication along these lines. Feature articles review new developments in aircraft (e.g., "World Aero Engines"), and regular monthly departments cull the news from air transport, private flying, light commercial and business planes, defense aircraft, and spaceflight. Another useful feature is a periodic directory of airlines. Although more sophisticated than *Flying,* and written with a slant toward British aerospace, the magazine is appropriate for any library and would be thoroughly appreciated by flying buffs.

Flying. 1927. m. $7. Robert B. Parke. Ziff Davis Publishing Co., 1 Park Ave., New York, N.Y. 10016. Illus., index. adv. Circ: 231,000. Sample. Vol. ends: Dec. Microform: UM.

Indexed: AbrRG, RG. *Bk. rev:* 5, 200 words, signed. *Aud:* Ga, Hs, Ac.

Justifiably so, the periodical boasts the largest circulation of the popular sports flying magazines. Heavily illustrated features focus on light craft (new models shown in color centerfold)—their design and construction, performance, auxiliary equipment, etc. Emphasis is also on pilot safety: tips on flying, air routes, FAA regulations, new products and equipment. Pros, beginners, weekend pilots, or anyone who just likes planes will find something at his level of interest. A separate publication, *Flying Annual,* is a comprehensive, authoritative reference tool which includes a directory and reviews of aircraft during the past year. A good package for $1.50. Both publications are recommended for any type of library.

Flying Review International. See *Interavia.*

Historic Aviation. 1968. m. $5. K. W. Charles, P.O. Box 2037, Kansas City, Kans. 66110. Illus., adv. Circ: 8,000. Vol. ends: Dec.

Bk. rev: 4, 40 words, signed. *Aud:* Ga, Hs.

Devoted to the history of early flying. Besides the historical aspects, it promotes the upholding of old ideas in modeling, ballooning, and gliding. A collection of articles, photos, drawings, and plans is presented monthly for enthusiasts of the romantic saga of man's attempts to fly. The interest in the field is such that the editor reports a growing international circulation. Should be as much of interest to the historian as to the aviation enthusiast, but will be particularly welcome in school and public libraries.

IEEE Transactions on Aerospace and Electronic Systems. 1952. bi-m. $24. Harry R. Mimno. Inst. of Electrical and Electronics Engineers, Inc., 345 E. 47th St., New York, N.Y. 10017. Illus., index. Sample. Vol. ends: No. 6. Refereed. Microform: IEEE.

Indexed: ASTI, ChemAb, EngI, MathR, SciAb. *Aud:* Sa, Ac.

Supportive electronic and communications equipment have always been an integral part of airborne and spaceflight systems. This journal, a special publication from the IEEE group on Aerospace and Electronics, concerns itself with studies on radar/sonar, long-range navigational systems, instrumentation, energy conversion systems, command, control and communications systems, etc. Research-type papers deal not only with equipment but also discuss procedures and techniques. An important journal for both aerospace collections and for technical libraries with electrical engineering interests.

Interavia. 1946. m. $17. K. Regelin, 86 av. Louis Casai, 1216 Cointrin-Geneva, Switzerland. Illus., index, adv. Vol. ends: Dec. Microform: UM.

Bk. rev: 1–2, 200 words, unsigned. *Aud:* Sa, Ac.

Subtitled a "world review of aviation-astronautics-avionics" (and incorporating the old *Flying Review International*), the periodical offers a miscellany of views, reviews and factual material on international aerospace developments. Feature articles, mostly staff-produced and elegantly illustrated, discuss in nontechnical language commercial, private, and military aircraft, as well as spacecraft, and their systems, components, equipment, tests, and performance. The slightly oversize magazine is available in four languages: English, French, Spanish, German. A handsomely produced addition for any aerospace collection desiring well-documented, worldwide coverage of the field. (Note: For another $200/yr. libraries requiring day-by-day coverage of the international marketing scene may subscribe to *Interavia Air Letter*, a service aimed mostly at management, rather than technical staff.)

Journal of Aircraft. 1964. m. $50. Carl F. Schmidt. American Inst. of Aeronautics and Astronautics, 1290 Ave. of the Americas, New York, N.Y. 10019. Illus., index. Sample. Vol. ends: No. 12. Refereed.

Indexed: IntAe. *Aud:* Sa, Ac.

A specialty journal of the AIAA. Rigorously refereed technical papers concentrate on aspects of airborne flight, including aircraft design, flight mechanics, flight testing, navigation systems, development of engines. (Note: More theoretical studies of airborne flight are included in the *AIAA Journal*, listed above.) Both full-length papers and shorter notes are published. This and the other AIAA research publications should

be first-choice selections for any collection in aeronautical engineering.

Journal of the Astronautical Sciences. 1954. bi-m. $12. R. M. L. Baker. American Astronautical Soc., 815 15th St., N.W., Suite 800, Washington, D.C. 20005. Illus., index. Circ: 2,500. Vol. ends: No. 6. Refereed.

Bk. rev: 5, 300 words, signed. *Aud:* Sa, Ac.

The official organ of the AAS, a society dedicated to advances in the astronautical sciences. Technical papers and notes revolve around the general areas of guidance and control systems, orbit analysis, satellite systems, thermonuclear propulsion, etc. Studies might be of considerable length. Although the journal does not have the visibility of some of the publications of the American Institute of Astronautics and Aeronautics, it is, nonetheless, a valuable one for research collections.

Journal of Aviation Medicine. See *Aerospace Medicine.*

Journal of Spacecraft and Rockets. 1964. m. $50. Ralph R. Ragan, American Inst. of Aeronautics and Astronautics, 1290 Ave. of the Americas, New York, N.Y. 10019. Illus., index. Circ: 6,000. Sample. Vol. ends: Dec. Refereed.

Indexed: IntAe. *Aud:* Sa, Ac.

As its cousin publication, *Journal of Aircraft,* centers around airborne flight, this technical journal concentrates on spaceflight. Original papers and engineering notes discuss the design, development and systems of spacecraft, their missions, propulsion, launch vehicles, flight operation, and ground support equipment. Some survey articles or papers presented at specialist meetings appear now and then. Along with the other AIAA technical publications, the journal is an important one for aerospace collections.

Planetary and Space Science. See Astronomy Section for this title and others in space science.

Rotorways. See Free Magazines Section.

Sikorsky News. See Free Magazines Section.

Skyline. See Free Magazines Section.

Spaceflight. 1956. m. $11. Kenneth W. Gatland. British Interplanetary Soc., 12 Bessborough Gardens, London, SW1, England. Illus., index, adv. Circ: 4,500. Vol. ends: Dec. Refereed. Microform: UM. Reprint: Swets & Zeitlinger.

Indexed: BritTechI, ChemAb, EngI. *Bk. rev:* 7–8, 300–600 words, signed. *Aud:* Sa, Ac, Ga.

With a visioned eye into the future of space science, this "popular" periodical of the British Interplanetary Society speculates on subjects such as "signals from other worlds, extra-terrestrial intelligence," and other curious phenomena. Although many articles require technical expertise, the magazine has, nonetheless, a good deal of material for laymen, including vignettes of early space pioneers. Emphasis is on an overview of astronautics: space propulsion; space exploration, both by manned and unmanned vehicles; or anything which relates to research and development in the field. Several excellent departments note milestones in space history, provide a satellite digest, and review ancillary fields, e.g., astronomy. An interesting and informative publication, recommended for academic libraries or large public libraries serving a semi-technical readership. (Note: Highly technical papers appear in the Society's other periodical, *British Interplanetary Society. Journal,* listed above.)

Space Science Reviews. 1962. 9/yr. $57.35/vol. C. De Jager. D. Reidel Publishing Co., Box 17, Dordrecht, Netherlands. Illus., index, adv. Sample. Vol. ends: June, Dec. Refereed.

Indexed: ChemAb, IntAe, Met&GeoAb, NuSciAb, SciAb, SCI. *Bk. rev:* 20, 50–1000 words, signed. *Aud:* Sa, Ac.

Synthesizing common elements in astronautics, astronomy, astrophysics, and the physics of space into one total picture, the journal gives an overview of the field. Review papers are invited from international authorities in any country engaged in space research. Subjects cover areas such as ionospheric investigations, interplanetary matter as observed from rocket-propelled vehicles, etc. Material might be as lengthy as 120 pages, and corresponding bibliographies tend to be exhaustive. The common language of the publication is English; should the surveys appear in another language, English abstracts are long and detailed. An excellent and important reviewing medium for university collections in astronomy and atmospheric sciences, as well as astronautics.

Space World. 1962. m. $8. Ray Palmer. Palmer Publns, Inc. Amherst, Wis. 54406. Illus., adv. Circ: 25,000. Vol. ends: Dec. Microform: UM.

Indexed: RG. *Bk. rev:* 1–2, 300 words. *Aud:* Hs, Ga.

Collected here, in modest format, are reprints from other publications, digests or reviews spanning advances in space research, its technology, spacecraft, mission accomplishments, reports on astronauts, etc. The technicalities and jargon of the specialty and trade journals have been shaken loose, and reinterpreted to serve the needs of the layman. Well-illustrated features are either by authorities or staff-produced. Monthly departments sort the significant news from NASA, from Russia, and also include reports on satellites, contract awards, etc. Of the numerous space magazines available, this periodical is especially commendable to high school and public libraries for its popular approach.

AFRICA

Basic Periodicals

Ejh: *African Arts;* Hs: *Africa Report, African Arts;* Ga: *Africa Report, Africa and the World, African Arts;* Jc: *Africa Report, Africa and the World, Ufahamu, African Arts;* Ac: *Africa Report, African Arts; Africa and the World, Journal of Modern African Studies, Africa, Ufahamu.*

Library and Teaching Aids

African Image, Africana Library Journal, Current Bibliography on African Affairs.

Basic Abstracts and Indexes

African Abstracts.

Cessations

African Forum, The Jewel of Africa.

Abbia; revue culturelle Camerounaise. 1963. q. $5. Bernard Fonlon. Centre de Littérature Evangelique, B. P. 4048, Yaounde, Cameroon. Circ: 500.

Indexed: AfrAb. *Aud:* Ac.

"Not merely to recount what has been, but to share in moulding what should be." That is the motto for Cameroon's finely-produced, French-English "cultural review." And it's no mere slogan. Each issue, in fact, fuses the old and the new, tradition and modernity. Material ranges from studies on "superstition," local archaeology, and diverse elements of the Cameroonian heritage—folklore, music, dance, speech, customary social organization, law—to essay-probes on the "staffing dilemmas of African universities," and black literary giants like Aime Cesaire and Amos Tutuola. Also, there's a pleasing admixture of poetry, plays, and graphics. (SB)

Africa; journal of the International African Institute. 1928. q. $9.90 individuals; $12.30 institutions. Daryll Forde. International African Institute, 10/11 Fetter Lane, London EC4A, England. Adv. Circ: 2,700. Vol. ends: Oct. Microform: Micro-Methods Ltd.

Indexed: AfrAb, MLA, PAIS. *Bk. rev:* 20, length varies, signed. *Aud:* Ac, Ga.

A scholarly journal of African ethnology, sociology, linguistics, and history with articles in French and English. A typical issue carries three or four 20 page articles on such topics as "Medicines and Fetishes in Igala," "Ibibio Drama," and "African Conversion," plus a six to ten page notes and news section, and book reviews. A bibliography of current publications on Africa, formerly part of the journal itself, is now a separate publication.

The notes and news section surveys African studies programs, research in progress, bibliographic aids, and new journals in all parts of the world. (It is also available by separate subscription.) There are descriptive and discerning reviews in each issue. The reviews and news and notes sections alone make this an important tool for librarians. This journal should be in all libraries with an interest in Africana. (B.A.)

Africa Confidential. 1960. bi-w. $25. Godfrey Morrison, Flat 5, 33 Rutland Gate, London SW7, England. Circ: 2,500. Vol. ends: Dec.

Aud: Ac.

Concise analysis of current affairs in Africa, designed for diplomats, students of Africa, business concerns, banks, etc. Six to eight pages. (B.A.)

Africa Quarterly; a journal of African affairs. 1961. $5. Asoka Mehta. Indian Council for Africa, 5, Balvantray Mehta Lane, New Delhi, India. Illus., index, adv. Circ: 3,000.

Indexed: PAIS. *Bk. rev:* 5–10, length varies, signed. *Aud:* Ac, Ga.

"Devoted to a study and objective understanding of African affairs," the quarterly—whose Editorial Board includes journalist/historian Basil Davidson and *Le Monde* correspondent/*Mois en Afrique* editor Philippe Decraene—"publishes contributions from outstanding writers, experts, and specialists on various political, economic, social, cultural and literary subjects of interest to the people of Africa."

This is at once a distinctive and significant medium on several grounds: (1) It views African developments from a shared Third World orientation (e.g., "nonalignment" as a fundamental tenet of foreign policy). Moreover, India—and Indians—have been deeply involved in Africa for centuries, but *not* (unlike the British, French, Italians, Germans, Spanish, Dutch, Portuguese, and Belgians) as slavers or colonialists. Indeed, Indians now constitute fairly large minorities in much of East, Central, and South Africa, in the latter area forming an historically active segment of the broad underclass. (2) It elaborates, more extensively than any other source, India's continuing ties with the continent (political, commercial, etc.), as well as investigating the mutual relevance of African and Indian experience in fields like economic and educational planning. (Commented Editor Mehta in 1970: "Both of us, Africans and Indians, have complex problems to overcome. We can be comrades-in-arms against want.") (3) Each issue contains a "Quarterly chronicle," reprinting widely-gathered news excerpts under such rubrics as "India and Africa," "African unity," and "Economic cooperation in Africa," followed by specific regional and country coverage, the whole representing a capsule history of the quarter. Further, a "Documentation" section publishes the complete texts of contemporary Africa-related treaties, manifestoes, diplomatic statements, and U.N. resolutions (e.g., the principal speeches and declarations from the Third

Non-Aligned Nations Conference in Lusaka, 1970). An essential title, no less for Africana than Asian studies, Third World, and international affairs collections. (S.B.)

Africa Report. 1956. 9/yr. (Oct.–Aug.), $9. Aaron Segal, 530 Dupont Circle Building, Washington, D.C. 20036. Illus., adv. Circ: 10,000 Sample. Vol. ends: Dec.

Indexed: AfrAb, ABC Pol.Sci, MLA, PAIS, SSHum. *Bk. rev:* 6, length varies, signed. *Aud:* Ga, Ac, Hs. *Jv:* V.

One of the few objective current news magazines on Africa, this is closer to a popularized political science journal than an average popularized news periodical. Still, it can be recommended highly for its month-by-month coverage of events on the whole African continent. Often the reports differ sharply from those found in magazines of a wider circulation. Averaging 42 pages, it includes articles by experts, firsthand reports from correspondents, notes on major economic and political developments, and some outstanding biographies of leading Africans, both black and white. The book reviews should serve any small to medium–sized library which is seeking material in this important area.

Africa Today. 1965. q. $6.50. John Marcum, exec. ed. G. W. Shepherd, Ezekiel Mphahlele, T. LeMelle, eds. Center for International Race Relations, Univ. of Denver, University Park Campus, Denver, Colo. 80210. Adv. Circ: 3,000. Sample. Vol. ends: Dec. Microform: UM. Reprint: Johnson.

Indexed: PAIS. *Bk. rev:* length varies, signed. *Aud:* Ac, Ga.

This publication offers intelligent background and analysis of academic, economic, and political issues relating to Africa and the Third World and U.S. relations with Africa. There is a black American–African focus.

Africa Today has recently changed its format. Each issue has a central theme, e.g., Africanists and academic research, China and Africa, and offers in-depth articles by African and non-African academics. There are review essays covering several important new books at once. A section on publications includes references to scarce ephemera, especially dealing with U.S.–African relations and southern African issues.

Of interest to anyone concerned with contemporary Africa, and recommended for academic libraries. (B.A.)

Africa and the World. 1964. m. $2.50. Douglas G. Rogers, 89 Fleet St., London EC4, England. Illus., adv.

Indexed: AfrAb, AntroI, BritHum. *Bk. rev:* Various number, length. *Aud:* Ac, Ga, Ha. *Jv:* V.

The purpose of this magazine is to promote a radical Pan-Africanism, both supra-national and socialist, much as conceived and espoused by Ghana's coup–

deposed President, Kwame Nkrumah. Apart from its uncompromisingly proliberation, anti-imperialist stance and often vitriolic prose, what makes the magazine noteworthy is that it is one of the rare publications to openly criticize the "feudal," "bourgeois," or "sell-out" elites and personalities that rule ostensibly "free" and "independent" black states like Malawi, Kenya, Ghana, Lesotho, and Ethiopia, countries which popular mythology has rendered almost sacrosanct and unassailable. Little wonder, then, that the magazine has been regularly banned, for instance, in Kenya, a favorite target for both its editorial and feature writers. Conversely, much material of a laudatory sort appears on Tanzania's Ujamaa village campaign, the increasing nationalization—e.g., in Uganda and Zambia—of "foreign—owned firms." and Nkrumah's accomplishments while in power (though these paeans to the Ghanaian leader tend to become monotonously repetitive and nearly devotional). Particularly relevant to an American audience is the frequent "Africa Miscellany" column, prepared by the Africa Research Group, based in Cambridge, Massachusetts, which reports—in the best muckraking tradition—on U.S. governmental and business activities throughout the continent. For all Africana and Third World collections, while other libraries—whose coverage of Africa may be limited to quasi-official, respectably "objective," or stuffily academic journals—could well consider it a consistently intemperate, albeit readable and stereotype-mashing leaven. (S.B.)

African Affairs. 1901. q. $5.50. Alison Smith and Anthony Atmore. Royal African Society, 18 Northumberland Ave., London, England. Subs. to: Oxford Univ. Press, Press Road, Neasden, London 10, England. Index, adv. Circ: 2,300. Vol. ends: Oct. Refereed. Microform: Micro-Methods, Ltd. Reprint: Kraus.

Indexed: AfrAb, BritHum, SSHum. *Bk. rev:* 20–30, 500–600 words, signed. *Aud:* Ac.

Primarily academic in character, this journal also reflects the world of politics, administration, and business. Intended for readers in universities, research institutions, and government, *African Affairs* deals with modern political, economic, and social affairs on a continent-wide basis. Each issue has about three scholarly essays, followed by a section of short articles, talks, and notes. Especially valuable to librarians and researchers are the book reviews—approximately 30 titles per issue—and bibliographies of current books and journal articles. (B.A.)

African Arts. 1967. q. $10. Paul O. Proehl and John F. Povey. Univ. of California at Los Angeles, Los Angeles, Calif. 90024. Illus., index, adv. Circ: 5,000. Vol. ends: Summer.

Indexed: AntroI, ArtI. *Bk. rev:* 4, 1,500 words, signed. *Aud:* Ga, Ac, Hs, Ejh. *Jv:* V.

A beautifully produced, richly illustrated glossy magazine with a scholarly soul. It covers sculpture, dance, traditional and contemporary art, film, literature, music. As part of its effort to stimulate new talent, *African Arts* each year conducts a competition—this year in literature and in graphic and plastic arts.

Articles are authoritative, well written, and do not require expertise on the part of the reader. Each is accompanied generously by illustrations (many in color) which make this an excellent resource for teachers. Subjects in a recent issue typically include articles on Liberian ballet, dance in Mali, recent acquisitions of African art at the Art Institute of Chicago, the decorative arts in Rwanda and Burundi, African puppet theatre, a new gallery in Kampala, as well as some folk tales, an essay on the black man and art, and book reviews. Stories, poems, and listings of exhibitions, festivals and other current events appear in each issue.

This is a unique magazine, and it belongs in all libraries. (B.A.)

African Historical Studies. 1968. 3/yr. $9. Norman R. Bennett. African Studies Center of Boston Univ., 10 Lenox St., Brookline, Mass. 02146. Sample.

Bk. rev: 50, 2–5 pages, signed. *Aud:* Ac.

Drawing upon university departments of history and anthropology for its authors, this 250-page journal is made up of six or seven major articles, review articles, notes and documents, and first-rate book reviews (approximately 50 titles are reviewed in each issue). The focus is on all aspects of African history, including archeology, and on relations between Africa and black America. The material is well documented, represents original research, and is intended for experts in the field.

Librarians will probably find the book reviews most helpful, especially since many titles examined here rarely find their way into normal review media. For this reason, this journal is a required item in academic libraries with an interest in Africa. (B.A.)

African Image. 1969. 9/yr. $9. Daniel A. Okoronkwo. Center for Advanced African Understanding Inc., 1400 Lincoln Hwy., East Chicago Hts., Ill. 60411. Illus., adv.

Aud: Ac, Hs, Ejh.

The nonprofit center which sponsors this magazine is primarily concerned with making Africa better known to Americans. In order to achieve this, the editor presents outlines, bibliographies, and course material useful in all aspects of teaching about Africa, e.g., articles move from politics and government to music and art. Outlines are given for lectures which may be used at almost any level from the elementary school through the university. An extremely useful magazine for the teacher who is involved with bringing Africa to his or her students.

African Literature Today. 1968. a. $8. Eldred D. Jones. Africana Publishing Co., 101 Fifth Ave., New York, N.Y. 10003. Adv.

Indexed: MLA. *Bk. rev:* various number, 750 words, signed. *Aud:* Ga, Ac.

Formerly a semi-annual publication, in 1971 *ALT* became a hardcover publication of approximately 175 pages, published annually in October or November. It is devoted to the examination of the literature and writers of Africa, each volume centering on one subject, e.g., "The Novel." There are perceptive book reviews of novels, poetry, and drama by African authors, and of critical works. A uniquely valuable feature for libraries is a bibliography of books and periodical articles dealing with African literature, which picks up items issued in Africa and England, as well as the United States. (B.A.)

African Music. 1954. a. $4. Hugh Tracey. African Music Soc., P.O. Box 138, Roodepoort, Transvaal, South Africa. Illus., index. Circ: 500.

Bk. rev: 5–6, 500 words, signed. *Aud:* Ac, Ga, Hs.

Any library, academic or public, interested in resources for African studies programs has only one central, continuing, major source for solid research in the vast areas of African music: Hugh Tracey's *African Music*, which is the organ of the African Music Society which he founded. Tracey is one of the world's leading experts on African music. His journal has contributions from leading scholars throughout the world (but most of the articles are in English). The articles are technical with many musical illustrations and photographs of instruments and musicians. Some recent articles were: "Takada Drumming," "The Music of Zumaile Village, Zambia," "Ganda Zylophone Music." This is for the serious student of African music and presupposes a basic musical vocabulary. The book and record reviews are thorough and scholarly. "Note and News" reports on African music studies throughout the world. Basic to all African and Afro-American studies programs and to public libraries serving any groups interested in Africa and African roots. (G.S.)

African Opinion; journal of independent thoughts and expressions. 1961. bi-m. $1.50. J. L. Brown. African Picture & Information Service, 8 W. 117th St., New York, N.Y. 10026. Illus., adv.

Aud: Ga, Ac.

Attempts to keep Afro–Americans informed about developments in Africa. Although this magazine is published in the United States, the articles appearing in it are focused heavily on the struggles, customs, and traditions of the black African states. Unfortunately, some of the articles are not as effective as they might be; however, useful features are to be found in the magazine's advertisement of economy excursions to parts of Africa, and its publishing of names, addresses, and dates for readers interested in those associations, conferences, and committees devoted to promoting Pan-Africanism. Suitable for most public and college libraries. (J.G.)

African Studies Bulletin. See *African Studies Review.*

African Studies Review. 1957. 3/yr. $25 Libraries ($18 Individuals). John P. Henderson. Brandeis Univ., Room 205, Shiffman Humanities Center, Waltham, Mass. 02154. Vol. ends: Dec.

Indexed: AfrAb. *Bk. rev:* 10–12, lengthy, signed. *Aud:* Ac.

Formerly the *African Studies Bulletin*, this journal changed its name in 1970. It is the official publication of the African Studies Association, and serves as a line of communication for professional American Africanists. Each issue includes several scholarly articles and bibliographic essays. The book reviews and review articles are of special interest to libraries and Africanists. (B.A.)

Africana Bulletin. 1964. s-a. $6. Bogodar Winid. Center of African Studies, Univ. of Warsaw, ul. Krakowskie-Przedimiescie, Nr. 26/28, Warsaw 64, Poland. Illus.

Bk. rev: various number, length. *Aud:* Ac.

A scholarly vehicle for Polish Africanists, with articles, dissertation abstracts, book reviews, and "short notices" appearing in either French or English. The subject content ranges from art and archaeology, e.g., "Polish excavations in Egypt and the Sudan, 1968–69," to linguistics and economics analysis, e.g., "Input-output flows in Nigeria," problems of agricultural development, and the contemporary socio-political situation. Drawings, photos, tables, and diagrams figure prominently in each issue. A useful title for academic collections, reflecting high standards of East European research and non- (if not anti-) capitalist perspective, yet rarely or obtrusively "ideological" in tone. (S.B.)

Africana Library Journal; a quarterly bibliography and news bulletin. 1970. q. $20 ($13.50 individuals). John B. Webster. Africana Publishing Corp., 101 Fifth Ave., New York, N.Y. 10003. Adv. Circ: 600. Sample. Vol. ends: Dec.

Bk. rev: 4–8, 400–800 words, signed. *Aud:* Ac, Sa.

Intended for librarians, documentalists, and researchers, this journal is an invaluable guide to the acquisition of Africana, and serves also as a forum for all those concerned with problems of African bibliography. A major portion of each issue consists of comprehensive and current bibliographic listings of new Africana material in English and foreign languages. Entries are classified by subject and geographic area, with author, subject, and key-word indexes.

Features include a checklist of periodicals, a news and notes section, and guides to the acquisition of Africana, including audiovisual material. Each issue features an article by a specialist on a subject such as bibliography, documents acquisition, etc. (The Spring, 1971 issue, for instance, has a four-page article on "The Bibliography of the Countries of French-speaking Black Africa.")

There are excellent book reviews of new reference works. (B.A.)

Afro-American Studies. See Blacks Section.

Afro-Asian Writings. See *Lotus.*

Asian and African Studies. See China and Asia/Asia Section.

✓ *Black Orpheus.* 1957. $2.82. Patrick Ugbomah. Daily Times of Nigeria Ltd. P.O. Box 139, Lagos, Nigeria. Illus., adv. Reprint: Kraus.

Indexed: MLA. *Bk. rev:* various number, length. *Aud:* Ac, Ga.

Begun in 1957 by Ulli Beier, to promote and encourage black writers, *Black Orpheus* has played an important role in the development of African literature in English. Stories and poetry by authors from the West Indies, America, and francophone Africa appear in its pages, but it was the work of young West African and South African writers in English that distinguished *Black Orpheus* as a showcase of a new, vital literature in the sixties.

Contributors are drawn from all over the world. Along with fiction and poetry, *Black Orpheus* includes critical articles and book reviews of great interest, as well as articles on traditional literature and on contemporary and traditional art.

There have been several changes in the editorship—at various times writers Ezekiel Mphahlele, Wole Soyinka, and J. P. Clark have been on the editorial board—and publication has recently been irregular. A new series has begun, and regular publication will be resumed. (B.A.)

Bulletin of African Studies. See *The Canadian Journal of African Studies.*

Busara (Formerly *Nexus*). 1968. q. $5. Student editor (changes each yr.). East African Literature Bureau, Univ. of Nairobi, Box 30197, Nairobi, Kenya. Index, adv. Circ: 2,000.

Aud: Ac.

This "lively little magazine"—with an emotive "shouting mask" as its cover design—"provides a unique forum for creative writing and literary criticism in East Africa." The contents: half a dozen critical eassays (e.g., on Peter Abrahams, Gabriel Okara, and "neo-African literature"), a short (usually pungent) play, three or four stories, and sundry poems. (S.B.)

✓ *The Canadian Journal of African Studies/La Revue Canadienne des Etudes Africaines.* 1967. 3/yr. $9. Myron J. Echenberg and Alf Schwarz. Department of Geography, Carleton University, Ottawa, Canada.

Adv. Circ: 1,000. Vol. ends: Autumn. Reprints: Pub.

Bk. rev: various number, length, signed. *Aud:* Ac.

A publication of the Committee on Africa Studies in Canada, it replaces the Committee's earlier *Bulletin of African Studies.* According to an editorial statement in the journal, African studies need more attention than they have been getting, and the hope is that the *Canadian Journal* will help both to stimulate studies on Africa and its problems and to facilitate the exchange of information between Africanists everywhere. Contains a number of substantial articles—some in English, some in French—on such diverse subjects as family planning in Ghana and the return of Brazilian freedmen to Africa in the eighteenth and nineteenth centuries. There are also lengthy book reviews and several sections of notes on happenings of interest to Africanists.

Conch; a sociological journal of African cultures and literatures. 1969. 2/yr. $5.50. Sunday O. Anozie, Dept. of English, Univ. of Texas, Austin, Tex. 78712. Index, adv. Circ: 1,000. Vol. ends: Sept.

Indexed: AbEnSt, MLA. *Bk. rev:* 3–4, 600 words, signed. *Aud:* Ac.

Conch is a scholarly journal dedicated to the development of interdisciplinary research techniques with a strong emphasis on structural analysis in the social sciences and humanities. It carries five or six essays on linguistics, literature, and sociology, as well as poems and book reviews. Originally subtitled "A Biafran Journal of Literary and Cultural Analysis," it changed its name with Volume 2. Special issues have dealt with Ibo traditional life, culture, and literature, and structuralism and African folklore. Emphasis is on African literature, contemporary and traditional, and on methods of analysis. For specialists.

Cultural Events in Africa. 1964. m. $30. Maxine Lautre. Transcription Centre, 6 Paddington St., London W1, England. Illus. Circ: 500. Vol. ends: Dec. Reprint: Pub.

Bk. rev: 6–8, 6–10 lines, unsigned. *Aud:* Ac.

A six to ten page newsletter about plays, films, art, dance, music, and literature by Africans in Africa and all over the world. Performances, broadcasts, publications, and exhibitions are announced and described. The contents of current magazines are often reported. Interviews with African writers and artists are a regular feature. Excellent for those who want to keep up with African culture as it is happening. (B.A.)

✓ *A Current Bibliography on African Affairs.* 1962. bi-m. $25. Daniel G. Matthews. African Bibliographic Center, Box 13096, Washington, D.C. 20009. Adv. Circ: 800. Sample. Vol. ends: Dec. Reprint: Pub.

Indexed: MLA. *Bk. rev:* 7–8, 500 words, signed. *Aud:* Sa.

This is primarily a guide to current books and

magazine articles concerning Africa and the black world. Divided into three parts, it begins with two or three bibliographic articles, review essays and annotated book reviews, moves on to a bibliographic listing of material under general subjects and concludes with a geographic section. There is an author index. Full bibliographic description is given for each work in the language of the issuing country (all languages are included except for Arabic and Oriental languages). A 15 to 30 word content summary is given in English for major listings. Includes a section on juvenile literature and K-12 instructional materials. The best single guide of its type now available.

East Africa Journal. 1964. m. $10. Alan Bethwell Ogot and Richard Carl Ntiru, Uniafric House, Koinange St., Box 30571, Nairobi, Kenya. Adv. Circ: 3,000. Vol. ends: Dec. Reprint: Pub.

Indexed: AfrAb, MLA. *Bk. rev:* 3, 800 words, signed. *Aud:* Ga. Ac.

An articulate and alive magazine of opinion on political, economic, social, and cultural development in East and Central Africa. Articles on current issues (law reform, economic problems, literature, the role of the university, etc.) are informative, well written, and often controversial. A typical 40 page issue includes five or six articles, a vigorous editorial statement, poetry, and book reviews. A literary issue, *Ghala,* published in January and July, consists of short stories, poems, book reviews, and articles.

It is the editorial style of the magazine to encourage response from readers, and one gets a sense of an ongoing dialogue among concerned people. It should be available to all readers with an interest in present-day Africa. (B.A.)

Geneva-Africa/Geneve-Afrique; acta africana. 1962. s-a. $6.30. Pierre Bungener. Institut Africain de Geneve, 2–4 route de Drize, 1227 Carouge-Geneve, Switzerland. Circ: 550. Reprint: SZ.

Bk. rev: 40, length varies, signed. *Aud:* Ac.

A majority of contributors to this social science-oriented vehicle are themselves African, exploring matters like nation-building and "Humanism" in Zambia, the relationship between Third World countries and the International Monetary Fund, recent Dahomean history, and Nigerian industrial relations, while their European, Indian, and American colleagues discuss such questions as U.S. policy toward Southern Africa, the "myth and reality of ethnocentrism," and the U.N.'s role on the continent. Apart from the usual excellence and depth of its typically 20-page essays, what makes the bilingual (English/French) magazine particularly valuable for research and academic libraries is its bibliographic dimension. Each issue ordinarily carries not only 40 or more evaluative reviews of new Africana titles, but also a major bibliographic study (e.g., "Critique of official documents as

source material for West African history," "La Croix Rouge et l'Afrique," "L'U.R.S.S., la Chine Populaire, et l'Afrique," and "Contribution à la bibliographie des ouvrages relatifs au Burundi"), as well as a discursive "Review of reviews," highlighting and often summarizing "worthwhile reading matter in recent issues of Africanist journals." (S.B.)

Grass Curtain. 1970. q. $5. E. M. De Garang. Southern Sudan Assn., Ltd., Room 19, 29 Ludgate Hill, London EC4, England.

Aud: Ac.

For 15 years some four million black Southern Sudanese have "been fighting for survival" against the Arab-dominated Khartoum government. *Grass Curtain* is easily the most accessible and authentic fount of information on that bitter struggle (which has already resulted in either the death or flight of nearly one million persons), faithfully enunciating the "separatist" viewpoint of the Southern Sudan Liberation Movement, outlining the activities of its military wing, the Anya–Nya ("Scorpion"), commenting astringently on Sudanese politics (e.g., coup, counter–coup, and imminent membership in the "Federation of Arab Republics"), and reporting in detail on both the seriously mounting refugee problem and alleged persecution of southerners. Photos and occasional verse further illumine the "rebels'" intensely-felt cause. (S.B.)

Habari. 1969. m. $25 (individuals, $10). J. T. Winch. Washington Task Force on African Affairs, Box 13033, Washington, D.C. 20009. Illus.

Aud: Ac.

A newsletter whose object is to furnish "informational, educational, education, research, and monitoring services on African affairs with an activist orientation," contributing to the "establishment of an informed constituency for Africa in the United States." Of special note is the continuing survey feature, "Towards a racist press," which critically examines Africa reportage in the American mass media. A calendar of Africa-connected activities in the Greater Washington area also appears regularly, together with current information on Black Studies programs and reviews of "radical literature." Subscriber-members additionally receive WTFAF "Policy papers" issued once or twice monthly and dealing, e.g., with "Institutional racism in African Studies and U.S.-African relations," "U.S. investments in Africa," and "Foreign assistance to Africa." (S.B.)

Journal of African History. 1960. q. $17 ($13 to individuals). R. A. Oliver, J. D. Fage, J. R. Gray, and Shula Marks. Cambridge Univ. Press, 32 East 57th St., New York, N.Y. 10022. Illus., adv. Circ: 2,400. Sample. Vol. ends: Oct. Microform: UM. Reprint: Pub.

Indexed: AfrAb, AntroI, BritHum, HistAb, SSHum. *Bk. rev:* 10–15, 1½–2 pages, signed. *Aud:* Ac, Ga.

Features scholarly articles on all phases of African history from the Stone Age to present times. The journal attempts to portray African history as a whole rather than merely to describe the last few centuries in which European exploration and settlement took place. The articles frequently are concerned with the history and culture of native races and dynasties. Some pictures and illustrations are used and the text is in both English and French. Several excellent book reviews appear in each issue. While this is a scholarly journal, it should be available to all those interested in African history. (B.A.)

Journal of Asian and African Studies. See China and Asia/Asia Section.

Journal of Modern African Studies. 1963. q. $12.50. David and Helen Kimble. Cambridge Univ. Press, 32 East 57th St., New York, N.Y. 10022. Adv. Circ: 2,400. Vol. ends: Dec. Reprint: Pub.

Indexed: ABC Pol.Sci., AfrAb, BritHum MLA, PAIS, SSHum. *Bk. rev:* 10–15, 2–3 pages, signed. *Aud:* Ac. *Jv:* V.

"The Journal offers a quarterly survey of politics, economics, and related topics in contemporary Africa," and seeks to "promote a deeper understanding of what is happening in Africa today" by selecting authorities from various fields, especially scholars working in both African and Western universities.

To keep scholars and librarians up-to-date, a section entitled "Africane" publishes resumes of the work of institutes and centers for African studies. The critical book reviews are selective and within the scope of the journal's purpose. With its stress upon human and current problems, it is an outstanding choice in academic libraries.

Legon Observer. 1966. bi-w. $23. K. A. B. Jones-Quartey. Legon Society on National Affairs, Box 11, Legon, Ghana.

Aud: Ac.

Sponsored by the Legon Society on National Affairs, the *Observer* ordinarily presents some six articles, sober and outspoken, under rubrics like Law, Politics, Administration, Education, and Social Problems, together with readers' letters, editorials, and reviews. "Highly recommended," says Kwama Avafia, a Ghanian colleague. (S.B.)

London University. School of Oriental and African Studies. Bulletin. See China and Asia/Asia Section.

Lotus; Afro-Asian writings. (Formerly: *Afro-Asian Writings*). 1968. q. Inquire. Youssef El Sebai. Permanent Bureau of Afro-Asian Writers, 104 Kasr El-Amin St., Cairo, U.A.R. Illus.

Aud: Ac.

Confected by the Permanent Bureau of Afro-Asian

Writers and dedicated to the "emancipation of Afro-Asian culture from colonialist and neocolonialist chains" as well as the "promotion of Afro-Asian literature and presentation of its new and genuine elements," this is a highly attractive, fully engrossing compend of art, literature, and opinion. Thus far there have been contributions—variously bitter, comic, enraged, and lyric—from Turkey, Zambia, Ivory Coast, Madagascar, Senegal, the U.A.R., Vietnam, Guinea, South Africa, Ceylon, Sudan, Ghana, Angola, Palestine, and ten more countries. Subjects span African masks, the Ashanti Adaekesee festival, Patrice Lumumba, the Senegalese legend of Silamakan, romance-by-telephone and Burmese rice-pounding songs. (S.B.)

Mazungumzo; student journal of African studies. 1970. q. Free. Chui Karega. African Studies Center, Michigan State Univ., East Lansing, Mich. 48823.

Aud: Ac.

Meaning "dialogue" in Swahili, *Mazungumzo* aims not only to "expose the myths about Africa as myths," but also to "educate the unaware world to the traditional greatness of Africa and its people." Occasional poetry and a lively letter column complement full length articles like Kojo Yankah's "Congo—not yet free"; a scathing analysis of "Ethnocentrism in four contemporary general works on Africa," by Hayden Jones; and Delisle Worrell's "Agricultural classes and a national development policy for the Caribbean." Eminently quotable (and representative) in the Spring 1971 issue (vol. 1, no. 3) is Maina-wa-Kinyatti's advice to a correspondent regarding "racist terms": "You must understand that the white man is clever with words. In many cases he uses some words to 'divide and conquer' us. Such words as 'native,' 'bantu,' 'tribesmen,' 'negro,' 'nigger,' 'kaffir,' 'colored,' etc., are racist words used to degrade and divide the African race."

The journal also reports news on the Black Liberation Front International (headquartered in East Lansing at P.O. Box 1554, 448823), which—among other pursuits—has lately created a "Political Prisoners Library Fund" to "facilitate the development of black political prisoners by supplying them with as much literature and information as possible." (S.B.)

Moto. 1969. m. Rhod. $0.45. Mambo Press, Box 779, Gwelo, Rhodesia.

Aud: Ac.

Issued under Catholic auspices, bilingual (English-Shona), tabloid in format, and committed to electoral rather than revolutionary politics, *Moto* may well be the solitary voice of African dissent inside Rhodesia. It surely enjoys the distinction of being one of the few, if not the only, general circulation newspapers published in Baaskap lands between the Cape and Zambezi whose photos and ads display black faces. Apart from local and Africa-wide news, the paper carries consistently tough-minded editorials, as well as a sprightly double column, "We cheer/We chide." (S.B.)

Mozambique Revolution. 1965. m. Postage only. Dept. of Information, FRELIMO, Box 15274, Dar es Salaam, Tanzania.

Aud: Ac.

"Five years ago on the Makonde highlands, the first guerrilla units attacked the Portuguese and our armed struggle began." Thus starts the 68-page 40th issue, dated Sept. 25, 1969, marking the fifth anniversary of the revolt, led by the Mozambique Liberation Front, against Portuguese dominion. This number alone, studded with Grosz-like cartoons and on-the-spot photos, could well serve as a handbook to the Mozambique war. It blisteringly details Portuguese colonial policy, denounces Western (including U.S.) support for the "Fascist clique," minutely reviews FRELIMO military progress, proudly tells of "national reconstruction" in the three liberated provinces (population: 1,000,000), and in a final section, "Plunder in Mozambique," dissects the country's classically exploitative economy.

This mimeographed report records an arduous, dramatic, and nearly victorious surge toward freedom. Heroic, too, in the fullest sense. (S.B.)

Namibia News. 1967. 56s. South West African People's Organization, Provisional Headquarters, Box 2604, Dar es Salaam, Tanzania.

Aud: Ac.

"We are doing it! We can free our country. From London or New York it may seem hard. But from what we have seen with our own eyes: We are doing it!" So declared a SWAPO fact-finding mission (Jan.–Mar. 1969) after a visit to the "battlefields" of northern Namibia, where in late 1968 guerrilla action provoked "atrocious retaliations" by the South African Government. Each number describes and analyzes conditions in the one-time UN Trust Territory annexed by South Africa, relates progress in the growing war for independence, enunciates SWAPO goals, and terminates with "News in Brief," a topical digest culled from the South African and international press. (S.B.)

Nexus. See *Busara.*

Nigeria: Bulletin on Foreign Affairs. 1971. q. $8. Nigerian Institute of International Affairs, Kofo Abayomi Rd., Victoria Island, G.P.O. Box 1727, Lagos, Nigeria. Sample.

A collection of primary documents which covers the international affairs of Nigeria and Africa, this 48-page magazine is divided into three sections: "Commentaries," one or two short articles on recent significant events; "Events," containing brief reports and news items; and "Documents," which supports much of what is found in the first two categories. The last section makes up a good half of the journal. The magazine is carefully edited, well written, and should prove of invaluable aid to the specialist in Nigerian-African historical, political, social, and even cultural affairs.

Pan-African Journal. 1968. q. $15. M. D. Kagombe. 675 West End Ave. Suite 2D, New York, N.Y. 10025. Adv. Circ: 5,000. Sample. Vol. ends: Fall. Microform: UM.

Bk. rev: various number, length. *Aud:* Ac, Ga.

Published largely by African students, this journal serves "as a platform where students, scholars, and statesmen can enter into academic dialogue." There is a strong emphasis on African political issues, the study of African political society, Pan-Africanism, and black studies. Each well-printed issue contains about six essays—thoughtful, lively, and diverse—by African and non-African contributors. Poetry is a regular feature.

While much of the material is scholarly in nature, it is presented in a popular, readable style. The journal will have particular appeal to young college students, both Afro-American and white, as well as the interested layman. (B.A.)

The People. 1969. m. $5. Olu Akinsanya. Box 3121, Lagos, Nigeria. Illus., adv. Sample.

Aud: Ac, Ga.

A 40-page magazine of opinion and politics published in Nigeria for Nigerians. The writing is exceptionally lucid, the material of interest to many blacks outside of the country, e.g., a series on how a correspondent views the progress of American blacks. Some problems are universal. This is demonstrated in a long editorial on poor health service and even poorer doctors in the August 1971 issue. Poetry and prose are included, but emphasis is on politics. A useful and fascinating magazine for medium to large collections.

Research in African Literatures. 1970. 2/yr. Free; available to libraries on exchange. Bernth Lindfors, 2609 Univ. Ave., Room 314, Univ. of Texas, Austin, Tex. 78712. Circ: 1,500. Vol. ends: Fall.

Bk. rev: 6, 2–3 pages, signed. *Aud:* Sa.

The official organ of the African Studies Association Literature Committee and the African Literatures Seminar of the Modern Language Association, this journal provides "an international, interdisciplinary forum for all students and teachers of the literatures of Africa." Each issue of approximately 100 pages includes scholarly articles, news of current research, and book reviews. It is rich in bibliographic information. Abstracts of theses and papers, reports from libraries and archives, announcements of new publications, and reports of conferences are regular features. (B.A.)

Sechaba. 1967. m. $6. M. P. Naicker. African National Congress of South Africa, 49 Rathbone St., London W1A 4NL, England. Illus. Circ: 25,000.

Aud: Ac, Ga.

"Be up-to-date with the struggle in South Africa—read *Sechaba!*" So the advertisements proclaim. And it's true. Although printed in the German Democratic Republic and distributed from London, this "official organ" of the 56-year-old African National Congress, banned in South Africa itself, is a genuinely *African* product. Mixing polemic with reportage, it is probably the most significant single source of views and information not only on the situation south of the Limpopo but also in the several other regions not yet freed from alien overlordship: Angola, Mozambique, Guinea-Bissau, Namibia, and Zimbabwe. Well illustrated, *Sechaba* explores the South African scene in full-scale articles, announces ANC programs, and chronicles the worldwide drive against apartheid, together with events in sister liberation movements. The frequent reports on the U.S./apartheid axis may be of particular interest to stateside readers, e.g. the May 1971 report on American workers against the Polaroid Corporation's operations in South Africa. (S.B.)

South African Panorama. See Free Magazines Section.

South African Scope. See Free Magazines Section.

Tarikh. 1967. 2/yr. $2. Obaro Ikime and Segun Osoba. Humanities Press, 303 Park Ave. S., New York, N.Y. 10010. Illus., adv. Sample.

Aud: Ac, Hs.

Tarikh, in Arabic, means "written history." This attractively produced periodical presents historical research in clear, readable form, especially for high school and first year college students. Each issue focuses on a single theme (such as indirect rule, early Christianity in Africa, modernizers in Africa, etc.) and includes about a half dozen short essays, 10 to 15 pages long. Bibliographies, maps, and glossaries accompany each article. (B.A.)

Transafrican Journal of History. 1969. s–a. $6. B. A. Ogot. Subscriptions Dept., East African Publishing House, Box 30571, Nairobi, Kenya. Circ: 2,000.

Bk. rev: various number, length. *Aud:* Ac.

Issued on behalf of the University History Departments at Makerere, Nairobi, Dar es Salaam, Zambia, and Malawi, the journal commonly includes three to six main articles, together with genuinely exciting (in fact, frequently devastating) book reviews and an occasional review article, e.g., T. O. Ranger's "Historiography of Southern Rhodesia," v. 1, no. 2. Unsurprisingly, the geographical compass seems to be East and Central Africa, thus far embracing topics as varied and engrossing as "Christian villages in northeastern Tanzania," conflict among Chewa Kingdom rulers, Harry Thuku and the emergence of Kenyan nationalism, "war and land in Rhodesia," firearms in pre-1900 Zambia, and the calamitous failure of interwarring Mahdists and Ethiopians to jointly resist Italian invaders in the late 1890s. Because of its unimpeachable quality, refreshing readability, and African base, might well be preferred—where an either/or choice must be made, and despite its present area limitation—over the more venerable but duller and extracontinental *Journal of African History.* (S.B.)

Transition. 1961. bi–m. $6.60. Rajat Neogy. P.O. Box 9063, Accra (A), Ghana. Illus., adv. Circ: 15,000. Reprint: Kraus; Johnson.

Bk. rev: 5, 1,200 words, signed. *Aud:* Ga, Ac, Hs.

This distinguished magazine, originally published in Uganda, became a forum for intellectual discussion in politics, literature, economics, and the arts under the bold editorship of Rajat Neogy. Contributors represented all shades of opinion and all parts of the world. Articles by African leaders, such as Julius Nyerere and Kenneth Kaunda, and prominent African literary figures appeared regularly. Special issues dealt with violence in Africa, sex, student unrest, and contemporary African literature.

Transition temporarily ceased publication in 1968 when Neogy was imprisoned on charges of sedition—specifically for publishing a letter suggesting that Ugandan courts should be independent of the views of the ruling party. Neogy is resuming publication in Accra.

For all public and academic libraries, and high schools with an interest in African studies. (B.A.)

Ufahamu; journal of the African Activist Association. 1970. 3/yr. $7 (individuals, $3). Renee Poussaint. African Studies Center, Univ. of Calif., 405 Hilgard Ave., Los Angeles, Calif. 90024. Circ: 5,000.

Aud: Ac, Ga. *Jv:* V.

Like *Mazungumzo, Ufahamu* (Swahili for "understanding") gestated in the aftermath of the African Studies Association's tumultuous October 1969 meeting. As the editors stated in the first issue, that landmark conference "pointed out the need for Africanists to become more responsive to the pressing social and political issues facing Africa and Africans." Accordingly, the editorial board's policy is "to solicit articles that reflect new and often controversial approaches to African Studies." Interdisciplinary in scope, militant in mood, agnostic vis-a-vis orthodox dicta in African Studies, the journal has already published a rich variety of material, much of a uniquely firsthand, documentary sort; e.g., a forthright, fact-filled interview with Gil Fernandez, Cairo representative of the PAIGC (African Independence Party of Guinea and Cape Verde Islands); Fritz Pointer's acid "Appeal to African writers to be African"; studies of "Arts in a changing society: Northern Sudan," and the "Post-independence literature of Kenya and Uganda;" an evaluation of Marxist models in teaching and writing African history; fine graphics by Sudanese and Ugandan artists; a personal account of the 1964 political upheavals in Malawi by Henry B. M. Chipembere, exiled former cabinet minister under President Banda; a lengthy conversation with sociologist Ben Magubane, accenting his own bitter experiences within South Africa and later as a passportless refugee. Other articles have covered the South African liberation scene and Africa/Black America nexus; Amilcar Cabral's full testimony, including questions and answers, before the House Committee on Foreign Affairs in early 1970; a heated exchange between S. Goujon and Basil Davidson on the freedom fight in Angola; Stephanie A. Williams' "Black talk: creative communication" (in which she holds that "one of the most damaging results of the removal of Africans from the mother country to America was the loss of the mother tongue—damaging in that Africans had English forced on them, a language filled with dehumanizing and demoralizing definitions of themselves"); "Resistance and the Africanization of African history," by Ali A. Ner-i, a Somalian, who concludes: "One asks not *how* resistance can be studied, but *why* it has not attracted the attention of scholars before?"; and an appreciative, socio-cultural essay on a complex topic, "Chokwe art." Elinor Wadlow, appraising *Ufahamu* in *Geneva-Africa* (v. 10, no. 1), says that it "is addressed, of course, to the left and far left, but those whose opinions are nearer the center—and even the silent majority—will find it informative, both in content and in what it reveals of the thinking of an important, vociferous Africanist minority." In sum, a solid choice for libraries of all sizes. (S.B.)

West Africa. 1917. w. $13. Overseas Newspapers Ltd. 9 New Fetter Lane, London EC4, England. Illus., adv. Reprint: Microcard Editions.

Indexed: AfrAb. *Bk. rev:* various number, length. *Aud:* Ac.

A very good source of information on current political, economic, and social developments in West Africa, with an emphasis on Nigeria and Ghana. Desirable for anyone who wants to keep up with contemporary events in Africa. (B.A.)

Z Magazine. 1969. m. $1.67. David Simpson. Zambia Information Services, Box RW 20, Ridgeway, Lusaka, Zambia. Illus. Circ: 10,000. Sample.

Aud: Ga, Hs.

A chamber of commerce effort for Zambia, and within the bounds of its purpose, the 32-page, nicely illustrated magazine is well worth considering. An average issue features material on the history and geography of the country, one or two personalities, sports, the arts, and some politics. A debate between the Prime Minister of South Africa and Zambia's president was printed in a special supplement. Considering the low price and the good format, this is a good addition for any library from high school up.

Zimbabwe Review. 1969. bi-m. 6s. Publicity Bureau, Zimbabwe African People's Union, Box 1657, Lusaka, Zambia. Illus.

Aud: Ac.

Published wholly in English, this 16 page illustrated magazine features in-depth analyses of the Rhodesian (Zimbabwe) scene. It attempts to give the Black's side of the current controversy, a controversy which seems to be intensifying each year. In addition to the bi-monthly publication, the same Bureau issues an identically titled weekly mimeographed report ($10 airmail). Edited by Saul Gwakuba Ndlovu, this warns against "imaginary and cowardly" reliance on the UN—itself subservient to Big Powers who are "allies and trading partners of the colonizers"—to end oppression, and unflinchingly advocates massive "armed struggle" as the only effective means to "throw out the racist regime." The magazine is probably more suitable for small and general libraries than the weekly 5-page newsletter, which reports essentially topical material in English, Shona, and Sindebele. However, both editions—identically titled but distinct in content—are recommended for university and Africana collections. (S.B.)

Zuka; a journal of East African creative writing. 1967. $1.50. Jonathan Kariara. Oxford Univ. Press, East Africa Branch, Box 12532, Nairobi, Kenya. Adv. Circ: 2,000. Sample.

Bk. rev: 1, 1,000 words, signed. *Aud:* Ac, Ga.

The editors point out that the title is a Swahili word meaning "emerge," and the contents of a typical well-printed 72 page issue feature emerging new writers as well as established ones, including a few from outside East Africa. Short stories, poems, critical essays and book reviews are included. The level of both subject matter and style is exceptionally high for what is essentially a little magazine. The American reader will find that the contributors give an accurate picture of an Africa somehow passed over in many learned journals. Equally important, not one of the items is dull. A good representative African literary magazine, and at a price almost any library can afford.

AGING

Basic Periodicals

Ga: *Modern Maturity, Harvest Years, Aging;* Jc and Ac: *Aging, Geriatrics, Journal of Gerontology.*

AARP News Bulletin. 1958. m. Membership. $2. Lloyd Wright. Amer. Assn. of Retired Persons, 1225

Connecticut Ave. N.W., Washington D.C. 20036. Sample.

Aud: Ga.

An 8-page tabloid which reports objectively and with no little persuasion the problems of growing old in America. The Association publishes two regular magazines, *Modern Maturity* and *Dynamic Maturity.* The bulletin comes out more often, keeps members advised of political and legislative actions. Incidentally, the bulletin is published in large type. Should be in just about any public library, if for no other reason than to alert older readers to the *AARP.*

√*Aging.* See Government Magazines/United States Section.

Aging & Human Development. 1970. q. $20. Robert J. Kastenbaum. Greenwood Periodicals Co., 51 Riverside Ave., Westport, Conn. 06680. Illus., index, adv. Circ: 500. Sample.

Bk. rev: 2, lengthy, signed. *Aud:* Ac.

This journal treats the social and financial aspects of aging in a scholarly manner, with exhaustive documentation. The long list of bibliographic references is rather impressive. There is a wide variety of papers from "Models for Organization of Services to the Aging," to "Etiquette of Filial Behavior." The editors are soliciting manuscripts that illuminate psychological aspects of aging and the aged. This is a thoroughly technical publication, by no means a duplication of the Department of Health, Education, and Welfare's *Aging.* Recommended for public, municipal, and academic libraries and for all those who are interested in analytical essays on sociology and community life. (P.V.)

√*American Geriatrics Society. Journal.* 1953. m. $15. Edward Henderson. Amer. Geriatrics Soc., 10 Columbus Circle, New York, N.Y. 10010. Illus., index, adv. Circ: 9,420.

Indexed: BioAb, ChemAb, IMed. *Bk. rev:* Notes. *Aud:* Ac.

Being the "official journal" of the American Geriatrics Society, an organization "open to all physicians who are members in good standing of their state or provincial medical societies . . .," this journal emphasizes the geriatric patient rather than the elderly person. Thus, many of the articles are studies of medical management or institutional care. Although this is basically for the professional practitioner the style employed is not esoteric and it should be found in any medium to large academic library. (B.Guay)

Dynamic Maturity. 1965. bi-m. $2. Hubert C. Pryor. Amer. Assn. of Retired Persons, 215 Long Beach Blvd., Long Beach, Calif. 90802. Illus., index. Circ: 50,000.

Aud: Ga.

The kid brother of *Modern Maturity* in size as well as age, the articles are similar in content and it likewise lacks advertisement. The major difference is format. *Dynamic Maturity* is not so luxurious—no lovely colored photos or special game sections. Then too, this is aimed at the person preparing for retirement whereas its older brother is a magazine for the retired person. Recommended for any public library having clientele in the preretirement or retirement age brackets. (B. Guay)

√*Geriatrics; devoted to diseases and processes of aging.* 1946. m. $21. John F. Briggs. 4015 W. 65th St., Minneapolis, Minn. 55435. Illus., index, adv. Circ: 51,000.

Indexed: BioAb, ChemAb, IMed, PsyAb. *Aud:* Ac.

A medical journal whose subtitle states the purpose. Occasionally an article will be outside the realm of medicine, e.g., "Creative Retirement." As with most medical journals today it contains far too many advertisements, mainly for drugs. A typical issue will contain seven to nine major articles of five to ten pages each. These, plus five one or two page departments, and a "geriatrics abstracts" section (varying greatly in length) produce a 130 to 200 page issue each month. The complaint about the ads is not meant to belie the quality of the articles or esteem of the authors and the magazine should be in any medium to large-sized academic library. (B.Guay)

Geriatrics Digest; a summary of the world's literature on preventive geriatrics. 1968. m. $17.50. Walter M. Bortz. Medical Digest Group, 445 Central Ave., Northfield, Ill. 60093. Illus., index, adv. Circ: 15,000.

Bk. rev: Various number, length. *Aud:* Ac.

Primarily, although not exclusively, an abstracting service which alerts members of the American Geriatrics Society to articles published in medical, neurology, psychiatry, sociomedical, etc. journals. Aside from this survey, the journal publishes a few original articles, editorials, book reviews, etc. It is controlled circulation, i.e., almost all its circulation represents free copies sent to those dealing with geriatrics.

√*Gerontologist.* 1961. q. $10. Jerome Kaplan. Gerontological. Soc., 1 Dupont Circle, No. 520, Washington, D.C. 20036. Illus., index, adv. Circ: 4,200.

Indexed: BioAb, ChemAb, SocAb. *Bk. rev:* 3, 2 pages, signed. *Aud:* Ac.

Each issue is about 75 to 100 pages long with articles averaging four to eight pages in length and two to four broad topics are dealt with per issue. The magazine is published specifically for the "professional practitioner" but the articles are brief enough and readable enough for any college educated person. Although a quarterly journal, the issues are generally published in two separate parts. Part I in each instance continues the format of former volumes while Part II is completely flexible in format and content. Appropriate in any large public library or medium-sized academic library. (B.Guay)

Harvest Years; the magazine for successful retirement. 1960. m. $6. Peter Dickinson. Harvest Years Publishing Co., 104 E. 40th St., New York, N.Y. 10016. Illus., adv. Circ: 103,000. Sample.

Bk. rev: Notes. *Aud:* Ga.

One of the few general circulation magazines specifically edited for the man or woman who is planning to retire, or who is retired. It is the work of a private publisher, and therefore differs from the more objective publications of the American Association of Retired Persons, i.e., *Modern Maturity* and *Dynamic Maturity.* Most of the articles are of a how-to-do-it nature, i.e., where to retire, how to manage on a limited budget, how to take care of medical expenses, what hobbies to pursue, etc. Advice is given by experts, and while it is accurate enough it does tend to be a bit on the rah rah side. The journal includes some undistinguished fiction and poetry. A second choice after the AARP publications.

Industrial Gerontology. 1969. q. Free. Irma R. Withers. National Council on the Aging. 1828 L St., N.W., Washington, D.C. 20036. Index.

Bk. rev: Notes. *Aud:* Ac. Ga.

An objective examination of the employment and retirement problems of middle-aged workers, information on job counseling, vocational training and placement is reported. The journal is concerned with the transition from employment to retirement and retirement stages of the aged. It draws upon economics, psychology, medicine, sociology, adult education, industrial and labor relations, and management science.

Journal of Gerontology. 1946. q. $26. James E. Birren. Gerontological Soc., 1 Dupont Circle, No. 520, Washington, D.C. 20036. Illus., index, adv. Circ: 4,100.

Indexed: BioAb, ChemAb, IMed, PAIS, PsyAb. *Bk. rev:* 3–5, 200–800 words, signed. *Aud:* Ac.

As the title indicates, this is a scholarly journal and it deals with the problems of aging from the fields of natural and social sciences. Since the Gerontological Society is "A Society Devoted to Research on Aging," all of the articles are reports of research in the field and as such often include tables and occasionally photographs. Incidentally, the studies are not limited to the aging of the human species. An invaluable feature of the *Journal* is "Current Publications in Gerontology and Geriatrics," by Nathan W. Shock, which occupies the final 20 or so pages of each issue. Besides the index to the volume, the final issue each year (volume) contains an author index to the "Current Publications . . ." listed that year. While the magazine is specifically for the specialist in geriatrics, any library which looks upon itself as providing reference in either the biological or social sciences should have it. (B.Guay)

Mature Years. 1954. q. $2. Daisy D. Warren. Methodist Publishing House, 201 Eighth Ave., S. Nashville,

Tenn. 37203. Illus., index, adv. Circ: 175,000. Sample.

Bk. rev: Notes. *Aud:* Ga.

Published by the Methodists, this is typical of a number of religious publications, i.e., it is expressly directed to the retired or older person who is of like religious persuasion. It enjoys a rather healthy circulation, and serves its purpose well enough. It is better than most in that considerable emphasis is on how the elderly can serve the community, not simply how they can serve themselves. Usually each issue has one or two articles on individual and group projects which have aided neighborhoods or cities. Some fiction is included. Of questionable value for libraries.

Modern Maturity. 1958. bi-m. Membership (Nonmembers, $2). Hubert C. Pryor. Amer. Assn. of Retired Persons, 215 Long Beach Blvd., Long Beach, Calif. 90802. Illus. Circ: 2,000,000.

Aud: Ga.

While not a magazine likely to be used for research, this is by far the most popular of the periodicals for and/or about the aging. Articles are quite short, contain photographs or drawings, and are usually human interest in nature. Some news stories and practical "how-to" articles such as "Fix Your own Plumbing" and "How to Get a Husband After 50" in the June/July 1971 issue. Because it is an association publication it also gives AARP reports from time to time. Special features include "Fun-Fare"—two pages of crossword puzzles, cryptograms, etc.—and a centerfold and front and back cover of outstanding pastoral photographs. There are no advertisements except to encourage membership in the AARP. Highly recommended for any library that has users over 60. (B.Guay)

NRTA Journal. 1950. bi-m. Membership. Hubert Pryor. National Retired Teachers Assn., 215 Long Beach Blvd., Long Beach, Calif. 90802. Illus. Circ: 200,000. Sample.

Aud: Ga.

Typical of a number of journals, bulletins, and magazines published by various organizations which are directed at retired members. This one is for teachers, and is associated with the more general American Association of Retired Persons. There are articles on all aspects of retirement from income and health to personal experiences. In format and approach it somewhat resembles *Modern Maturity,* and while directed at teachers will be of interest to anyone with an above average education. Some good to excellent photographs are offered plus the usual features.

Retirement Life. 1954. m. Membership (Nonmembers $4.) John E. Worden, Jr., National Assn. of Retired Civil Employees, 1909 Q St., N.W., Washington, D.C. 20009. Illus., adv. Circ: 100,000.

Aud: Ga.

A similar approach as *NRTA Journal,* for a different

group, is offered by *Retirement Life*. Directed to anyone who is drawing federal civil service employee retirement benefits, this is considerably narrower in scope than the *NRTA Journal*. Most of the material deals directly with laws, legislation, programs, etc., which govern annuitants and their survivors. It includes some articles of a broader nature on the aged and the aging, and a few pieces are directed to social workers. Because of the influence of federal retirement benefits on the country, the magazine can be recommended for larger collections.

AGRICULTURE

Basic Periodicals

Ejh: *National 4-H News;* Hs: *National Future Farmer;* Ga: *Farm Journal, Successful Farming, Farm Quarterly;* Jc: *Farm Journal, Successful Farming, Agricultural Science Review;* Ac: *Farm Journal, Successful Farming, Agricultural Science Review, Crops & Soils, Agricultural History, Farm Quarterly.*

Library and Teaching Aids

Agricultural Education Magazine.

Basic Abstracts and Indexes

Biological and Agricultural Index, Bibliography of Agriculture, Biological Abstracts.

Agricultural Economics Research. 1949. q. $1. E. Lane & A. B. Paul. Economic Research Service, Dept. of Agriculture, Supt. of Documents, U.S. Govt. Printing Office, Washington. D.C. 20402. Illus., index. Circ: 2,500. Vol. ends: Oct. Microform: UM. Reprint: Johnson, Abrahams.

Indexed: BibAg, BioAb, BioAg, ChemAb, JEconLit, PAIS. *Aud:* Ac, Sa.

A basic government publication in the area of agricultural economics. Each issue gives technical information based upon research and findings of a number of government divisions and departments on various aspects of agricultural economics, e.g., prices, statistics, marketing, methodology, etc. While primarily for the professional, it has some value for both the student of agriculture and the economist.

The Agricultural Education Magazine. 1929. m. $3. Harry Kitts. Lawhead Press, 900 East State St., Athens, Ohio 45701. Illus., index. Circ: 9,000. Vol. ends: June. Reprint: Johnson, Abrahams.

Indexed: BibAg, CIJE, EdI. *Bk. rev:* 3, 300 words, signed. *Aud:* Hs, Ejh, Ac.

Intended primarily for anyone involved with practical aspects of teaching agriculture and especially the high school vocational agricultural teacher. Each issue normally is devoted to one particular area of the subject, and there are some 8 to 12 supporting articles on

research, education, practice, etc. The book reviews and abstracts are an excellent way for the teacher to keep up with additional current thinking in the field. While of limited interest to anyone but the teacher of agriculture, it should be in any public or school library where agricultural courses are important.

Agricultural Engineering. 1920. m. $12. James Basselman. Amer. Soc. of Agricultural Engineers, 2950 Niles Rd., St. Joseph, Mich. 49085. Illus. Circ: 9,636. Vol. ends: Dec. Microform: UM. Reprint: Johnson.

Indexed: BibAg, BioAg, ChemAb, EngI. *Aud:* Ac, Sa.

Features articles describing research carried out by agricultural engineers working at universities, private industry and in government. Topics are mostly on new agricultural applications of instruments and controls, experimental farm systems, structures and machinery, and new methods and ideas for teaching agricultural engineering in universities and colleges. Lists of new books and recently published bulletins in the field are included in each issue along with the usual news and notes on the doings of the American Society of Agricultural Engineers and its members. (J.J.)

Agricultural History. 1927. q. Membership (Nonmembers $5). James H. Shideler. Periodicals Dept., Univ. of California Press, Berkeley, Calif. 94720. Illus., index, adv. Circ: 1,520. Sample. Vol. ends: Oct. Microform: UM. Reprint: AMS.

Indexed: BibAg, BioAb, BioAg. *Bk. rev:* 10–20, approx. one page, signed. *Aud:* Ga, Ac. *Jv:* V.

Features historical articles on agriculture, which extend to all areas of the world, but the emphasis is on the United States. It usually contains five or six scholarly monographs and a section giving news and notes on the Agricultural History Society's activities and members. Because of its wide scope it is useful to the student of both social and historical problems.

Agricultural Meteorology. 1964. bi–m. $20. W. Baier. Elsevier Publishing Co., P.O. Box 211, Amsterdam, The Netherlands. Illus., index. Vol. ends: Nov.

Indexed: BibAg, BioAb, BioAg. *Bk. rev:* 1–2, 300–500 words, signed. *Aud:* Ac.

An important international journal that reports on research into all atmospheric factors that influence plant growth and plant communities. Articles appear in English, French, and German and are either reviews of current research or reports on original research work performed anywhere in the world. An important feature in each issue is an extensive bibliography of 450 to 500 citations of recent papers in the field that have been published in other journals. (J.J.)

Agricultural Science Review. 1963. q. $1.25. Ward W. Konkle. Cooperative State Research Service, Dept. of Agriculture, Supt. of Documents, U.S. Govt. Printing Office, Washington, D.C. 20402. Illus., index. Circ: 6,000. Vol. ends: 4th quarter. Microform: UM.

Indexed: BibAg, BioAb, BioAg. *Aud:* Ga, Ac, Hs. *Jv:*V.

A critical review journal that publishes articles and commentary on the current state of agricultural research. Agricultural research encompasses a wide range of subjects and articles range from discussions on the corn leaf blight to commentary on the consumer behavior of young adults; from the problems of cattle feedlot pollution to reports on a new Australian milk biscuit. The articles are not primary research papers but are informative, well written, and in a style that is easily understood. Recommended for school libraries from the high school level up, and for any public library. (J.J.)

Agronomy Journal. 1907. bi-m. $22. Matthias Stelly. Amer. Soc. of Agronomy, 677 Segoe Rd., Madison, Wis. 53711. Illus., adv. Circ: 6,000. Vol. ends: Dec. Microform: UM. Reprint: Abrahams.

Indexed: BibAg, BioAg, ChemAb. *Aud:* Ac.

A technical journal for the scientist and teacher which is made up primarily of research papers by members of the American Society of Agronomy. The articles touch on all aspects related to the production and growing of field crops. For large research libraries.

Agway Cooperator. See Free Magazines Section.

American Agriculturist And The Rural New Yorker. 1842. m. $2. Gordon L. Conklin. A. James Hall, Savings Bank Bldg., Ithaca, N.Y. 14850. Illus., adv. Circ: 180,204. Sample. Vol. ends: Dec. Microform: UM.

Aud: Ga.

For 125 years a welcome visitor in country homes throughout the Northeast, this journal offers practical suggestions on how to raise profits in commercial farming. Content is divided between various types of farming from dairy and poultry to field crops. In addition to research, production, and marketing, the magazine also contains articles of interest to women. It is a general agricultural magazine which would be a first or second choice in the Northeastern states for all public libraries.

This is only one example of a general, regional farm magazine. Others which tend to stress particular problems and types of farming or ranching in a given area range from the *Alabama Farmer* to *Wisconsin Agriculturist* and *Wyoming Stockman-Farmer*. Obviously both public and academic libraries in these areas should check for the regional publication of interest to them, all listed in *Ulrich's International Periodicals Directory*.

American Journal of Agricultural Economics. 1919. 5/yr. Membership (Nonmembers $25). Varden Fuller. Amer. Agricultural Economics Association, John C. Redman, Dept. of Agricultural Economics, Univ. of Kentucky, Lexington, Ky. 40506. Circ: 6,850. Vol. ends: Dec. Microform: UM.

Indexed: BibAg, BioAg, JEconLit, PAIS *Bk. rev:* 8–15, 800 words, signed. *Aud:* Ac.

Contains articles in the area of general agricultural economics and specialized research papers. Featured also are the proceedings of annual AAEA meetings, short articles on current topics under research, and news of people in the field. Contains more articles and special features than does the USDA publication *Agricultural Economics Research* but both are important journals for the student and professional not only in agriculture but in economics as well. (J.J.)

American Journal of Veterinary Research. 1920. bi-m. $30. Donald A. Price. Amer. Veterinary Medical Assn., 600 S. Michigan Ave., Chicago, Ill. 60605. Illus., index, adv. Circ: 4,500 Microform: Canner, UM. Reprint: Johnson, Abrahams.

Indexed: BibAg, BioAb, BioAg, ChemAb, IMed. *Aud:* Ac, Sa.

Primarily interested in reporting original research in veterinary medicine and related areas such as agriculture and biomedicine. Authors generally are scholars or teachers working in the field, universities, and state extension services. The journal takes on an added dimension in that it not only reports on work in America, but from major countries abroad. A basic periodical for large research-oriented libraries, in both veterinary science and agriculture.

The Cattleman. 1914. m. $5. Don C. King. Texas and Southwestern Cattle Raisers Assn., Inc., 410 East Weatherford, Fort Worth, Tex. 76102. Illus., index, adv. Vol. ends: May. Microform: UM.

Indexed: BibAg. *Aud:* Ga, Ac.

Emphasis is on cattle raising in the great Southwest, but this magazine has a popular following among cattlemen from all areas of the country. The articles are short, easy to read and contain practical advice for every cattleman. Subjects range from descriptions of successful beef cattle operations, to articles on new pasture grasses, veterinary care, cattle breeding, cutting horses, etc. The majority of space in each issue is advertising, but this advertising is more interesting and important than most, especially the notices of production sales and sales of beef cattle bulls. Special features include news of coming events of interest to cattlemen in the Southwest, a sales calendar and news from the Texas and Southwestern Cattle Raisers Association. (J.J.)

Ceres. See Government Magazines/United Nations and Selected Foreign Section.

Country Guide. 1882. m. $2. Don Baron. The Public Press, Ltd., 1760 Ellice Ave., Winnipeg 21, Manitoba, Canada. Illus., adv. Circ: 300,000. Vol. ends: Dec.

Indexed: BibAg. *Aud:* Ga, Ac.

Directed to the interests of the Canadian farmer, providing him with information on improved methods, market forecasts, and problems of an agricultural nature of the various regions of Canada. Ten to twelve feature articles, one to three pages in length, are written in direct, concise style, and are largely the work of field editors of the magazine. A very occasional piece of fiction with regional or topical interest is included. Regular features include sections on beef, hogs, dairy, poultry, and soils and crops, with successful practices reported and new methods suggested. A full page is devoted to a weather forecast for the succeeding month, dividing Canada by provinces and giving weekly prognostications for each. Advertising features farm and household products. While directed mainly to Canada's farm population, there is much to commend this for any rural area where livestock is raised, or to schools and colleges with agricultural courses.

Crops and Soils. 1948. 9/yr. $3. William R. Luellen. Amer. Soc. of Agronomy, 677 S. Segoe Rd., Madison, Wis. 53711. Illus., index, adv. Circ: 23,225. Sample. Vol. ends: Aug–Sept. Refereed.

Indexed: BibAg, BioAb, BioAg. *Aud:* Ga, Ac. *Jv:* V.

This slim, attractive periodical features articles which are highly specialized, yet written in a readable style, stressing practical applications of farm research. They are written by extension agronomists, agronomy specialists, and professors in agricultural colleges. An interesting and unusual feature is a box on the title page giving the botanical names of all plants mentioned in the issue. Useful in the high school library as well as in colleges.

√*Farm Index.* See Government Magazines/United States Section.

Farm Journal. 1877. m. $2. Lane Palmer. Farm Journal, Inc., 230 W. Washington Sq., Philadelphia, Pa. 19105. Illus., adv. Circ: 2,300,000. Vol. ends: Dec. Microform: MF, UM. Reprint: Johnson, Abrahams.

Indexed: RG. *Aud:* Ga, Hs, Ac. *Jv:* V.

Boasting the largest circulation of any general farm magazine, indexed in *Readers' Guide,* and directed to almost every interest of the farmer and his family, this is probably the best known magazine of its type in America. Approximately two thirds of each well-illustrated number is devoted to business advice on farm production and management. It rightfully claims to be "the business magazine of farming," and differs from its competitors in the attention it gives to economics as contrasted with the how-to-do-it aspects of other journals. Each issue features material on business forecasts, late Washington news, and the trade involved with farming. Much emphasis is placed on the role of the woman as a business partner in management of the farm with additional articles written for the homemaker only. Useful in all public and high school libraries where agriculture and/or home economics is a major interest.

Farm Quarterly. 1946. 6/yr. $2. Bill Barksdale. F&W Publishing Corp., 22 E. 12th St., Cincinnati, Ohio 45210. Illus., index, adv. Circ: 315,000. Vol. ends: Nov. Microform: UM.

Indexed: BibAg, BioAg. *Bk. rev:* 2, 500 words, signed. *Aud:* Ga, Hs, Ac.

The glamor and business magazine of agriculture. Its attractive format and striking color photography will captivate the general adult reader as well as the high school student. In a field as specialized as agriculture, it is difficult to find a magazine with so wide an appeal. The articles are authoritative and constructive, with emphasis on management problems that are common to farmers everywhere. Though *Farm Quarterly* has regional editions for its advertisements, it has retained its national approach editorially. It is the only farm magazine today covering the nation with a single editorial edition—the concept being that farmers can profit from studying farm practices of regions other than their own. This magazine and *Farm Journal* should be in most public and many high school and academic libraries.

Farmer's Digest. 1937. m. (Oct–May), bi-m. (June–Sept.). $4. H. Lee Schwanz. Farmer's Digest, Inc., Box 363 Brookfield, Wis. 53005. Index, adv. Circ: 45,000. Sample. Vol. ends: Apr. Microform: UM.

Aud: Ga, Ejh. *Jv:* C.

Similiar in format to more familiar digests, this little magazine serves the same purpose for the busy farmer—a brief overview of current thought in his field. The 25 or so condensed articles are selected from as many periodicals to cover all phases of farm operations. They vary in length from 500 to 2,500 words. Interspersed with them are short comments by experts in farm management. The articles selected are highly practical and are easy to read. A useful, albeit far from necessary, acquisition for larger public library collections.

The Fence Rider. See Free Magazines Section.

√*Foreign Agriculture.* 1937. w. $10. Kay Owsley Patterson. Dept. of Agriculture, Supt. of Documents, U.S. Govt. Printing Office, Washington, D.C. 20402. Illus., index. Circ: 8,500. Microform: UM. Reprint: Johnson, Abrahams.

Indexed: BibAg, BioAb, BioAg, ChemAb, PAIS. *Aud:* Ga, Ac.

Usually about 16 pages of tightly packed information, this government publication features brief, signed articles written in a popular style. Its purpose is to examine U.S. agricultural export trade, overseas markets, competitive foreign production and trade, and U.S. and world farm trade policy. Regular features include "Crops and Markets Short" and a "Crop and Market Index." Not only a useful reference on world agricultural trade, but can be used effectively in political and economics classes from senior high school through college and university levels.

Hoard's Dairyman; the national dairy farm magazine. 1885. s-m. $3. W. D. Knox. W. D. Hoard & Sons Co., 28 Milwaukee Ave. W, Fort Atkinson, Wis. 53538. Illus., index, adv. Circ: 358,254. Sample. Vol. ends: Dec. Microform: UM.

Indexed: BibAg, BioAg. *Aud:* Ga, Ac.

Every article is aimed at helping the farmer get the most out of every hour of labor and dollar spent. The material is written by experts such as agricultural engineers and university professors. A page called "Young Dairymen" offers advice to 4–H members and Future Farmers. The percentage of advertising seems overwhelming, but one subscriber protested, "but we want the ads, too." Tabloid format is used. The practical approach to problems makes it a must for the libraries of all country areas.

International Harvester Farm. See Free Magazines Section.

Journal of Agricultural and Food Chemistry. 1953. bi–m. Membership $10 (Nonmembers $20). Philip K. Bates. Amer. Chemical Soc., 1155 16th. St., N.W., Washington, D.C. 20036. Illus. Circ: 4,892. Vol. ends: Nov./Dec. Microform: ACS.

Indexed: BibAg, BioAb, BioAg, ChemAb. *Aud:* Ac.

Reports results of original research in the broad field of agricultural and food processing chemistry. This area includes research on pesticides (their mode of action and residue analysis), plant nutrients and regulators, chemistry of food processing, the chemistry of flavors, biochemistry of nutrition, and the nature and identity of food additives.

The articles are of a highly technical nature and useful either to the specialist or student in the fields of chemistry, chemical engineering, agronomy, entomology, and nutrition. (J.J.)

Journal of Dairy Science. 1917. m. $20. E. O. Herried. Amer. Dairy Science Assn., 113 N. Neil St., Champaign, Ill. 61820. Illus., index, adv. Circ: 5,300. Sample. Vol. ends: Dec. Microform: PMC. Reprint: Johnson.

Indexed: BibAg, BioAb, BioAg, ChemAb. *Aud:* Ac, Sa.

A source of research papers on the dairy industry as a whole, and on specific problems of manufacturing and production. Although the articles are scholarly, usually representing original research, they tend to be more pragmatic in nature than those found in most scientific journals. Hence, the publication is not only of value to the teacher, but to the practicing farmer, at least the one with a better than average education. Some space in each issue is given to developments in teaching and education, and there are the usual news items about personalities and business of the American Dairy Science Association. A basic journal for larger libraries.

National 4-H News. 1923. m. (June/July combined) $3. Gordon Bieberle. National 4-H Committee, Inc., 59 E. Van Buren St., Chicago, Ill. 60605. Illus., index, adv. Circ: 115,000. Sample. Vol. ends: Dec.

Bk. rev: 2, 150 words. *Aud:* Ga, Ejh, Hs.

Published for adults and teens who lead 4-H clubs, helping youngsters between 9 and 19 from inner city, suburbia or farms have fun learning about all kinds of things ranging from aerospace and rocketry to photography or art or clothing or veterinary science or any one of nearly 50 other subjects. Articles, ranging from one to five magazine pages, tell what's happening in 4-H throughout the country, and suggest how leaders anywhere might adapt new ideas to their own 4-H programs. Graphic design, including four–color cover, informal page design and modern type faces, reflect 4-H's expanded youth education programs. This and/or the *National Future Farmer* should be in all junior and senior high school collections in rural and urban areas as well.

The National Future Farmer. 1952. bi-m. $1. Wilson W. Carnes. Future Farmers of Amer., Box 15130, Alexandria, Va. 22309. Illus., adv. Circ: 460,000. Sample. Vol. ends: Aug/Sept.

Aud: Ga, Hs.

Directed to the 14 to 21 year-old students of vocational agriculture who are members of the Future Farmers of America (FFA) organization. The editorial policy is to encourage these students to seek a career in agribusiness and to develop their abilities in leadership and citizenship. There are a number of cartoons, one or two stories, and a few articles of general interest—particularly in the area of outdoor sports. The style is at times oversimplified, but the approach is definitely adult and there is no talking down to the reader. Although primarily for members of the FFA, it will be of interest to many urban readers who are interested in agriculture and youth.

Poultry Science. 1908. bi–m. Membership (Nonmembers $30). H. D. Branion. Poultry Science Assn., Texas A & M Univ., College Station, Tex. 77843. Illus., index. Circ: 3,700 Vol. ends: Nov. Microform: UM.

Indexed: BibAg, BioAb, BioAg, ChemAb. *Bk. rev:* 5, 200–800 words., signed. *Aud:* Ac, Sa.

The most important U.S. journal reporting on current poultry research. Articles cover all aspects of poultry—anatomy, physiology, embryology, nutrition, housing, etc. This journal is designed primarily for the poultry researcher in universities, colleges, and private industry and contains little of practical use to the poultry farmer or commercial poultry raiser.

Special features include abstracts of papers presented at annual Poultry Science Association meetings, notes on current research topics, and news of Association members and activities. (J.J.)

Progressive Farmer. 1886. m. $3 in Southern States; $5 elsewhere. Hal Johnson. Progressive Farmer Co., 821 N. 19th St., Birmingham, Ala. 35203. Illus., adv. Circ: 1,100,000. Vol. ends: Dec.

Aud: Ga.

A regional, general farm magazine which is primarily concerned with agriculture in the South and Southwest. Emphasis is on practical matters of machinery, crops, livestock, and the economics of farming. Articles tend to be short, informative, and for the practical farmer. A home section, "Southern Farm Living," makes up about one third of each issue and is devoted to matters of interest to women and children. The projects for children are excellent and have wider appeal than most of the magazine. Published in five regional editions, it enjoys a circulation second only to *Farm Journal* and *Successful Farming.* A first choice for a general agricultural publication in all libraries south of the Mason Dixon line; but for others, of limited interest.

Soil Conservation. See Government Magazines/United States Section.

Soil Science. 1916. m. $18. John C. F. Tedrow. The Williams & Wilkins Co., 428 E. Preston St., Baltimore, Md. 21202. Illus., index. Circ: 2,527. Vol. ends: June and Dec. Microform: AMC, PMC, UM. Reprint: Johnson.

Indexed: BibAg, BioAg, ChemAb. *Bk. rev:* 8–10, 100–200 words, signed. *Aud:* Ac.

Contains papers representing original research in soils and in soil-plant problems written by researchers from around the world. An important journal on the subject since it presents contributions from scientists from various countries reporting on soil research that is as varied as the soils that make up the earth's crust. For larger research libraries. (J.J.)

Successful Farming; the magazine of farm management. 1902. m. $2. Dick Hanson. Meredith Publishing Co., 1716 Locust St., Des Moines, Iowa 50303. Illus., adv. Circ: 1,000,000. Sample. Vol. ends: Nov./Dec. Microform: UM.

Indexed: BibAg, BioAb, RG. *Aud:* Ga, Ac, Hs.

In many ways this is very similar to *Farm Journal.* It professes to emphasize economics as much as its rival, is national in scope, and covers much the same material. Format, writing style, and editorial approach are similiar. Finally, it too is indexed by *Readers' Guide.* Apparently it enjoys many of the same readers as *Farm Journal.*

The articles are practical and informative, and deal with problems solved on working farms. A choice between this and *Farm Journal* is more a matter of personal taste than anything else. Should be in most public and high school libraries.

Veterinary Medicine/Small Animal Clinician. 1905. m. $15. Carlos M. Cooper. Veterinary Medicine Publishing Co., 144 N. Nettleton, Bonner Springs, Kan. 66012. Illus., index, adv. Circ: 14,250. Vol. ends: Dec. Microform: UM. Reprint: Abrahams.

Indexed: BibAg, BioAb, BioAg, ChemAb, IMed. *Bk. rev:* 2, 400 words. *Aud:* Ac, Sa.

Covers all aspects of veterinary medicine for the specialist and the advanced student, e.g., articles on treatment of cattle, horses, dogs, cats, etc. As this is for the practicing veterinarian, about one quarter of each issue is given over to management of a vet hospital or clinic, personalities, new products, and news of the field. There are many useful features including bibliographies, abstracts, and case histories submitted by readers. Hardly for the amateur, but a necessary addition for any large agricultural or animal collection.

World Crops. 1949. bi-m. $10. K. W. Bean. The S. Bayard Co., Inc., 20 Vesey St., New York, N.Y. Illus., index, adv. Vol. ends: Nov./Dec. Microform: UM.

Indexed: BibAg, BioAg, ChemAb. *Aud:* Ga, Ac.

Contains short three or four page articles written by agriculturists from all over the world. The articles usually discuss developments in crop production, plant propagation, plant protection, and recent agricultural techniques introduced in the developing countries of Southeast Asia, Africa, and Latin America. Included also are short news notes, commodity reports, special research reports, and short papers on new agricultural implements and machinery.

This is but one of several journals concerned with agriculture in the developing nations. Others include *World Agriculture,* published quarterly by the International Federation of Agricultural Producers, *World Farming,* published monthly by Intertec Publishing Corp. of Kansas City, Mo., and *Ceres,* which also covers the broader subject of general economic development in the Third World. It is published by the Food and Agriculture Organization of the United Nations. *World Crops* is a good first choice for libraries that want a magazine covering international agricultural development, but any of the others would be useful as well. (J.J.)

ANTHROPOLOGY

Basic Periodicals

Hs: *Plains Anthropologist;* Ga: *Current Anthropology, Anthropological Journal of Canada;* Jc: *Current An-*

thropology, *American Anthropologist, Southwestern Journal of Anthropology;* Ac: *American Anthropologist, Current Anthropology, Southwestern Journal of Anthropology, Anthropological Journal of Canada, Plains Anthropologist, Human Organization.*

Basic Abstracts and Indexes

Abstracts in Anthropology, Anthropological Index.

American Anthropologist. 1888. bi-m. Membership (Nonmembers, $25). Laura Bohannan. Amer. Anthropological Assn., 1703 New Hampshire Ave., N.W., Washington, D.C. 20009. Illus., index, adv. Circ: 6,000. Microform: UM, B&H, Canner. Reprint: Kraus.

Indexed: AbAn, SSHum. *Bk. rev:* 50–60, 250–800 words, signed. *Aud:* Ac, Sa. *Jv:* V.

The major American anthropological journal, this is intended primarily for the teacher, advanced student and professional. Articles, which vary from short pieces to those of monographic length, cover all aspects of anthropology, both here and abroad. The five to seven entries represent basic research, and are often rather technical. Most writers deal with physical and cultural anthropology, but there are some who are involved with ethnology. The journal is particularly valuable to librarians because of the numerous book reviews, which vary from essays to notes. There are also, from time to time, reviews of films and recordings. A basic choice for all public and academic libraries, and might be considered for a few professional collections in high schools.

The same association issues: *AAA Newsletter* (1947. 10/yr. $3) and an *AAA Bulletin* (1968. q. $5). The former is a short tabloid report on persons and activities of the Association; the latter goes into more detail, but is essentially an enlarged newsletter.

American Journal of Physical Anthropology. 1919. bi-m. $42. William S. Pollitzer. Wistar Inst. of Anatomy and Biology, 36th St. at Spruce, Philadelphia, Pa. 19104. Illus., index, adv. Circ: 1,730.

Indexed: AbAn, BioAb, ChemAb, IMed. *Bk. rev:* 6–10, 500–1,000 words, signed. *Aud:* Ac.

This journal employs a scholarly, technical approach to the following: comparative human and primate morphology, physiology, and genetics, human evolution and fossil man, and techniques and methods employed in physical anthropology. There are excellent photographs. Only for large collections.

Anthropologica. 1959. s-a. $8. St. Paul University, Canadian Research Centre for Anthropology, 223 Main St., Ottawa 1, Ont. Illus. index. Circ: 500. Sample. Reprint: Swets and Zeitlinger N.V.

Indexed: BioAb. *Bk. rev:* 5, 500 words, signed. *Aud:* Ac.

A scholarly journal published in Canada, but worldwide in scope. A few articles may have appeal for students and involved laymen, but on the whole it is for the teacher and expert. Articles and book reviews both in French and English.

Anthropological Journal of Canada. 1963. q. $5. Thomas E. Lee. Anthropological Assn. of Canada, 1575 Forlan Dr., Ottawa, Ont. K2C OR8. Illus. Sample. Vol. ends: Oct.

Indexed: AbAn. *Bk. rev:* 1–2, 500–3,000 words, signed. *Aud:* Ga, Ac, Hs. *Jv:* V.

A 32 to 56 page pocket-sized journal which features one long article and several shorter pieces. Its primary attraction for the nonspecialist is that the writers include both scholars and amateurs, and often the articles are nontechnical, enthusiastic, and purposefully written for the interested layman, e.g., an illustrated article on the history of salt. There is equal emphasis on anthropology and archaeology, and material is not limited to Canada, but takes in the entire world. In view of the style, it is quite suitable for high schools and for many public libraries, as well as for the college and university.

Anthropological Linguistics. 1959. 9/yr. $3.50. Florence M. Voegelin. Indiana University, Archives of Languages of the World, Anthropology Dept., Rawles Hall 108, Bloomington, Ind. 47401. Illus. Reprint: Kraus.

Indexed: AbAn, MLA. *Aud:* Ac.

A highly individual periodical designed primarily, but not exclusively, for the immediate publication of sophisticated papers containing linguistic data. Each study has attestation available in the form of tape recordings on deposit in the Archives of Languages of the World. Contributors are not restricted to scholars working in the archives; attestations and papers from scholars elsewhere are copied and returned to the collectors. Most heavily exemplified papers in the form of preliminary or final statements deal with phonology, morphology, syntax, and comparative grammar. Occasionally, theoretical and methodological papers in areas central to linguistics, and in the overlapping areas of ethnolinguistics, ethnoscience, ethnography, psycholinguistics, and sociolinguistics are published. Examples of studies are: (1) Samoan Color Terminology: A Note on the Universality and Evolutionary Ordering of Color Terms; (2) A Semantic Characterization of Kusaren Pronouns; (3) A Partial Investigation of the Spatial Forms of Some Tuomatuan Dialects. Illustrations are detailed and qualitative. Excellent bibliography. Sixty pages of ecstasy for the *true* philologist. (G.M.)

Anthropological Quarterly. 1928. q. $6. Michael Kenny. Catholic Univ. of America Press, 620 Michigan Ave., N.E., Washington, D.C. 20017. Illus., index, adv. Circ: 860. Microform: UM.

Indexed: AbAn, CathI. *Bk. rev:* Various number, length. *Aud:* Ac.

Devoted to ethnographic treatment of nonwestern societies. Technical language is defined and used sparingly. Each article is followed by excellent references for further reading. Illustrations are few, and are just acceptable qualitatively. Authors are professional anthropologists who are in university residence or practicing in the field. Primarily for the subject specialist, but suitable for professional collections in the high school or public library with a strong demand in this area. (G.M.)

Anthropos; international review of ethnology and linguistics. 1906. 3/yr. $28. Anthropos-Institut, D-5205 St. Augustin, Switzerland. Josef Franz Thiel. Editions St.-Paul, 40 Pérdles, CH–1700 Fribourg. Subs. to: Stechert-Hafner, 31 E. 10th St., New York, N.Y. 10003. Illus., index. Circ: 1,000. Reprint: Johnson.

Indexed: AntroI, MLA. *Bk. rev:* 50, signed. *Aud:* Ac.

Covers ethnography, anthropology, ethnology, linguistics, and history of religions in Europe, Asia, Africa, the Americas, and Oceania. Each issue is a collection of monographs by the world's leaders in the field. (Material is published in the language of the author, preferably English, French, or German.) Generally it is well illustrated. There are extensive book reviews, plus shorter notes and information on current periodical articles. The 1,000 or more pages of the volume add up to an impressive, major journal which is basic in any medium to large-sized academic library.

Arctic Anthropology. 1965. s–a. $15 (Individuals $10). C. S. Chard. Journals Dept., Univ. of Wisconsin Press, Box 1379, Madison, Wis. Illus. Circ: 800. Sample. Vol. ends: Winter. Microform: UM.

Bk. rev: various number, length. *Aud:* Ac.

A handsome, 150-page, illustrated journal which concentrates "in all fields of anthropology dealing with northern Eurasia and northern North America." Contributors are international scholars, but all articles appear in English. Archaeological aspects are treated as well. Most of the material is monographic, technical, and primarily for the expert.

Canadian Review of Sociology and Anthropology. See Sociology/General Section.

Current Anthropology; world journal of the sciences of man. 1960. 5/yr. $21.00. Sol Tax. Univ. of Chicago, 1126 E. 59th St., Chicago, Ill. 60637. Illus., index. Circ: 7,500. Vol. ends: Dec. Microform: UM. Reprint: Johnson.

Indexed: AbAn, SSHum. *Bk. rev:* 2 per year, 14 pages, signed. *Aud:* Ac, Ga. *Jv:* V.

A general approach to anthropology, supervised by a worldwide community of individual scholars who participate in a continuous exchange of ideas. It serves

as a clearinghouse for new ideas and as an indicator of trends in the profession. The editor encourages and builds a broad, interdisciplinary knowledge base for the study of all aspects of man by choosing topics "relevant to the sciences of man" which are "broad in scope, thoroughly documented and clearly delimited in terms of time, available data and methodology." The format is unusual; each scholarly presentation is accompanied by two or more critical comments by other subject experts which provide insight regarding the article's accuracy and importance. There are three or four articles per issue averaging 10 to 15 pages with another 8 to 14 pages devoted to comments and a reply by the author. There is a series of regular features of value to people in the field. The journal is of great value to anthropologists and college students. As one of the few general approaches to anthropology, this is basic to all academic and larger public libraries. While a bit advanced for most high schools, it is worth considering where there is a major emphasis on this area in the curriculum.

Expedition. See Archaeology Section.

Florida Anthropologist. 1948. q. $4 (Students, $2). Sara B. Benson, 3400 East Grant Ave., Orlando, Fla. 32806. Illus., index. Circ: 518. Reprint: Johnson.

Indexed: AbAn. *Bk. rev:* Notes. *Aud:* Ac, Ga.

Some 40 pages carry research in all subfields of anthropology with an emphasis on archaeology. Articles from allied disciplines dealing with anthropological problems appear frequently. Geographic scope of this journal is limited; in order of importance, it includes: (1) Florida; (2) Southwestern United States; (3) Caribbean and related regions. The language is relatively nontechnical. Articles are written by professional anthropologists or affiliates of research organizations active in the field. Useful to laymen as well as scholars. (G.M.)

Human Organization. 1941. q. $18 (Individuals, $8). Deward E. Walker, Jr., Inst. of Behavioral Science, Univ. of Colorado, Boulder, Colo. 80302. Illus., index. Circ: 3,500. Reprint: Johnson.

Indexed: AbAn, SSHum. *Aud:* Ac.

The purpose of this journal is to report on new findings which help to explain human behavior in community situations. The authors consider not only anthropology, but matters of interest to sociologists and anyone working directly with community organizations. The articles focus on original research which studies and promotes relations between peoples. As a broad interdisciplinary journal, it can be recommended for all academic libraries. It is a trifle too technical for the average public library collection.

Journal of Anthropological Society of Nippon. 1886. q. Free to academic libraries. Jus Ikeda. Anthropological Soc. of Nippon, Dept. of Anthropology, Univ. of Tokyo, Hong 731, Bunkyo-ku, Tokyo, Japan.

Indexed: AntroI. *Aud:* Ac.

A highly technical scholarly publication dealing with physical anthropology. All articles are in English and are written by professional anthropologists who are members of the Society of Nippon. Strong emphasis is placed on human evolution and ecology. Includes excellent illustrations and bibliography, papers presented at meetings of the Society and its proceedings. (G.M.)

Man. 1966. q. $14. I. M. Lewis. Royal Anthropological Inst., 21 Bedford Sq., London WC1B 3HH. Illus., index, adv. Circ: 3,000. Vol. ends: Dec. Microform: MF.

Indexed: BioAb, BritHum. *Bk. rev:* 60, 400 words, signed. *Aud:* Ac.

A general anthropological magazine which covers the activities of scientists throughout the world. Articles are scholarly, well documented, and usually illustrated. They are technical, meant primarily for the expert. A basic journal for large collections, but too limited in interest for the average library.

Mankind. 1931. s-a. Membership (Nonmembers, $5.70). L. Hiatt & R. Jones. Anthropological Soc. of N.S.W. Subs. to: Dept. of Anthropology, Univ. of Sydney, Sydney, Australia. Illus., index. Circ: 750.

Indexed: PAIS. *Bk. rev:* various number, length. *Aud:* Ac, Ga.

The official organ of the Anthropological Societies of Australia. Its 80 pages focus on Australian ethnographic studies and analytical classification of anthropometric data. Authors are professors of anthropology at the University of Sydney, and occasionally articles are contributed by their colleagues abroad. Its definitive, easily understood language, excellent illustrations, critical reviews of quality books, and appended bibliography will be attractive to the educated layman or subject specialist. It deserves strong consideration in any library with such an audience. (G.M.)

Masterkey; for Indian lore and history. 1927. q. Membership (Nonmembers, $3.50). Bruce Bryan. Southwest Museum, Highland Park, Los Angeles, Calif. 90042. Illus., index. Circ: 800. Sample.

Indexed: AmerH, HistAb. *Bk. rev:* Various number, length. *Aud:* Ac, Ga, Hs.

An anthropology magazine which is primarily concerned with the Indians of the Southwest, this journal includes illustrated articles on all aspects of their history and culture. While the articles are written by experts, most are quite within the grasp of the interested layman. Somewhat on the order of the *Plains Anthropologist,* and just as suitable for teen-agers.

Na'pao; a Saskatchewan anthropology journal. 1968. irreg. $3 (Students $1.00). Dept. of Anthropology and Archaeology, Univ. of Saskatchewan, Saskatoon, Saskatchewan. Illus. Circ: 500. Sample. Vol. ends: 2nd issue.

Indexed: AbAn, AntroI. *Bk. rev:* 2–3, 500 words, signed. *Aud:* Ga, Ac, Hs.

A processed 80 to 100 page student journal of anthropology whose aim is "to help all interested persons to achieve . . . deeper understanding of aboriginal and nonaboriginal peoples, present and past, in Saskatchewan and in adjacent areas." The eight to ten articles are particularly well written, and easily within the grasp of the layman or high school student. As might be expected, most of the material concerns the Indians of the area, although other articles touch on all aspects of related interdisciplinary subjects. As the editor points out, a journal of anthropology of this type "is rather uncommon," and particularly in Canada where the number of anthropological journals is extremely limited. Anyone who enjoys the *Plains Anthropologist* will welcome this publication as well.

Oceania; devoted to the study of the native peoples of Australia, New Guinea and the Islands of the Pacific Ocean. 1930. q. $11. A. P. Elkin. Univ. of Sydney, New South Wales, Australia. Illus., index, adv. Circ: 1,400. Vol. ends: June.

Indexed: PAIS. *Bk. rev:* 10, 300 words, signed. *Aud:* Ac.

Features four to five technical articles in each issue. The material is fairly well illustrated, and there are a number of worthwhile book reviews. From time to time the publishers issue *Oceania Monographs,* which are listed in each number. Primarily for the professional anthropologist and anyone seriously interested in ethnology.

Plains Anthropologist. q. $6. Alfred E. Johnson. Museum of Anthropology, Univ. of Kansas, Lawrence, Kans. 66044. Illus. Circ: 750. Sample. Vol. ends: Nov.

Indexed: AbAn. *Bk. rev:* 5, 250–750 words, signed. *Aud:* Ga, Ac, Hs. *Jv:* V.

One of the more fascinating anthropology journals which deserves a much wider audience than its circulation indicates. Concerned as it is with the Plains area of the United States, the majority of articles are involved with some aspect of the Indian and his life and habits. Articles, by scholars who write extremely well, touch on everything from Indian wars to burial mounds, arrowheads, and various other artifacts. The whole is adequately illustrated with black and white photographs, maps, charts, and diagrams. Although a good part of the information is technical, it is within the grasp of any interested high school student, and much of it may be used by teachers in even lower grades. Laymen who are interested in Indian or American history will welcome an introduction to this magazine.

Practical Anthropology. 1953. bi-m. $3. Charles R. Taber. Box 1041, New Canaan, Conn. 06840. Index. Circ: 3,250. Microform: UM. Reprint: Johnson.

Indexed: AbAn, Re1Ab, Re1Per. *Bk. rev:* Various number, length. *Aud:* Ga.

This 45-page magazine has a serious religious orientation. It assimilates in a nontechnical but creative style the resources of Christians and others involved in a cross-cultural view of man and society. The sole purpose is the development of more effective worldwide Christianity by the investigation, interpretation, and dissemination of the practical implications of anthropology and other culturally oriented studies. Its articles are by theologians and diverse dedicated professionals in the social sciences. (G.M.)

Southwestern Journal of Anthropology. 1945. q. $7. Harry W. Basehart, ed., Stanley Newman and Bruce Rigsby, co–editors, Univ. of New Mexico, Albuquerque, N.M. 87106. Illus., Index. Circ: 2,800. Vol. ends: Winter. Microform: UM. Reprint: Kraus.

Indexed: AbAn, BioAb, PsyAb, SocAb, SSHum. *Aud:* Ga, Ac, Hs. *Jv:* V.

Designed to include articles on all branches of anthropology relating to peoples and cultures, past and present, in any region of the world. Authors are professors or researchers associated with museums and there are generally five to six articles per issue averaging from 15 to 30 pages. They deal primarily with social and cultural anthropology. Some attention is given to archaeology, linguistics, and physical anthropology. Necessary for most libraries because of its general coverage of the field and a "must" in larger and specialized collections, as well as in many high school teachers' collections.

University of Alaska. Anthropological Papers. 1952. s-a. $4. John P. Cook. Dept. of Anthropology, Univ. of Alaska, College, Alaska 99701. Illus. Circ: 750. Sample.

Indexed: AntroI. *Bk. rev:* 1–2, 2 pages, signed. *Aud:* Ac, Sa.

An 80 to 100 page scholarly, well illustrated approach to Alaskan anthropology. According to the editor, "The areal scope is usually limited to Alaska and the Yukon Territory. Subject matter includes cultural and social anthropology, and archeology. Sometimes, geological, polynological, and paleontological data are presented. The articles can be either synthetic or a presentation of field or laboratory data." The journal is well written, equally well documented, and can be recommended for larger collections.

ARCHAEOLOGY

Basic Periodicals

Hs: *Expedition, Archaeology;* Ga: *Archaeology, Expedition, Antiquity;* Jc: *American Journal of Archaeology,*

Archaeology, American Antiquity Ac: *American Journal of Archaeology, Archaeology, Expedition, American Antiquity, Biblical Archaeologist, Antiquity.*

Basic Abstracts and Indexes

Abstracts in Anthropology, Art and Archaeology Technical Abstracts, Art Index, British Archaeological Abstracts.

ANES; a journal of the Ancient Near Eastern Society of Columbia University. 1968. bi-a. $6. The Society, 614 Kent Hall, Columbia Univ., New York, N.Y. 10027. Illus., index, adv. Circ: 500. Sample. Vol. ends: Summer.

Bk. rev: 1–2, 1,200–2,000 words, signed. *Aud:* Ac.

Published and written by a small group of students who are interested in various aspects of the ancient Near East, this offset journal of some 70 pages covers a variety of topics. There usually are six to seven articles on archaeology, language and culture, art, economics, history, religion, etc. It is scholarly, if not always lively. Since our first review of this publication, it has improved considerably. The editors claim "major scholars in the field have been quite favorably impressed." It deserves a wider circulation, particularly among students.

American Antiquity. 1879. q. $20. Edwin N. Wilmsen. Soc. for Amer. Archaeology, 1703 New Hampshire Ave. N.W., Washington, D.C. 20009. Illus., index, adv. Circ: 4,125. Vol. ends: Oct. Reprint: Kraus.

Indexed: AbAn. *Bk. rev:* 15, 300–500 words, signed. *Aud:* Ac, Hs, Ga.

The publication of the Society for American Archaeology covers archaeology of the Western hemisphere, and related areas of significance to American archaeologists. In addition to scholarly papers, there are detailed obituaries of notable archaeologists, a section called "Facts and Comments" contributed by readers and authors, "Current Research," and a book review section. Primarily for the scholar and the college student, but the general coverage of the field makes it suitable for professional collections in more advanced high schools.

American Journal of Archaeology. 1885. q. $15. Richard Stillwell. Archaeological Inst. of America, 260 W. Broadway, New York, N.Y. 10003. Illus., index. Circ: 4,500. Vol. ends: Oct. Microform: UM.

Indexed: ChemAb, SSHum, ArtI. *Bk. rev:* Approx. 25, 1 page, signed. *Aud:* Ac, Ga. *Jv:* V.

Contains scholarly articles written by American and European archaeologists about excavations in the Near East, Greece, Egypt, and the Mediterranean area. Excellent plates illustrating artifacts and excavations are grouped at the end of the journal. Short notes of progress of digs and special studies are included. Abstracts of papers presented at annual general meetings of AIA appear each April. Of special interest to students in the fields of archaeology, history, and art. Because of its relatively wide coverage and overlapping areas of interest, this should be considered for medium to large-sized public libraries, and certainly for all junior college to graduate university collections. See also *Archaeology.*

American Schools of Oriental Research. Bulletin. 1919. q. $6. Delbert Hillers. Amer. Schools of Oriental Research. 126 Inman St., Cambridge, Mass. 02139. Illus., index. Circ: 5,000. Sample. Vol. ends: Dec. Microform: UM.

Indexed: SSHum. *Aud:* Ac.

"Generally recognized as among the most creative, original and important single journals dealing with both epigraphic and non-epicgraphic discoveries in the ancient Near East." Pocket sized, heavily illustrated with charts and photographs, averaging some 40 to 50 pages, it reports on various excavations. The style is scholarly, yet always clear, and fascinating to the individual who finds excitement in discovery. Like the organization's *Biblical Archaeologist,* a basic journal for any archaeology collection.

Antike Kunst. 1958. s-a. $11.60. Ed. bd. Francke Verlag, Postfach, CH-3000 Bern 26, Switzerland. Illus., index, adv. Circ: 1,200.

Indexed: IBZ. *Aud:* Ac, Ga.

One of the few journals written for both the expert and amateur archaeologist. It is published by the Society of Friends of Antique Art, is international in scope, and articles appear in English, French and German. Scholars publish information on previously unknown works from public and private collections, and there are more general articles illustrating and commenting on the latest archaeological findings. It is all adequately illustrated. While of rather specialized interest, librarians who don't have the funds for its purchase might mention it to interested laymen.

Antiquaries Journal. the journal of the Society of Antiquaries of London. 1921. s-a. $9.50. Oxford Univ. Press, Press Rd., Neasden, London NW 10, England. Illus., index. Circ: 600. Sample.

Indexed: BritArchAb, BritHum, IBZ. *Bk. rev:* Various number, length. *Aud:* Ac.

A technical approach to archaeology and antiquarian subjects. Articles tend to be monographic, scholarly, and tedious unless one happens to be an expert in the field. The journal is valuable to librarians for the excellent book reviews and for its classified bibliography of publications as well as listing of articles dealing with archaeology. This bibliographic, index-abstract side to the journal gives it importance for large collections.

Antiquity; a quarterly review of archaeology. 1927. q. $8. Glyn Daniel. Antiquity Publns. Ltd., Heffer & Sons

Ltd., St. John's College, Cambridge, England. Illus., index, adv. Circ: 3,500. Sample. Vol. ends: Dec. Reprint: Johnson.

Indexed: AbAn, ArtI, BritArchAb, BritHum, IBZ, MLA. *Bk. rev:* 16–20, 700 words, signed. *Aud:* Ga, Ac, Hs. *Jv:* V.

A highly readable British quarterly review of the latest archaeological discoveries in ancient lands, Europe, and the British Isles. Documented articles on digs, historic monuments, history, and pro and con discussions on the use or meaning of archaeological finds. "News and Notes" section covers a wide field. Good black and white plates depict the artifacts, excavations, and wall drawings. Articles are written by esteemed archaeologists. The journal is of value to students of world archaeology and allied fields, and to the interested layman. It differs from the *American Journal of Archaeology* in its style, which is a bit more popular; hence, of the two, better suited for the general reading collection and the layman. See also *Archaeology.*

Archaeological Reports for 19--. a. $2.00. Council of the Soc. for the Promotion of Hellenic Studies, 31–34 Gordon Sq., London, WC1H OPP England. Sample.

Indexed: ArtI. BritArchAb. *Aud:* Ga, Ac, Hs.

An annual 50 to 60 page report on basic archaeological activities, primarily in the Mediterranean area, for the previous year, e.g., "Archaeology in Cyprus, 1966–69," "Archaeology in Greece in 1969–70." The reports are extremely well illustrated with black and white photographs. Most of the material is understandable to the layman. This is an excellent, inexpensive magazine. The illustrations make it a first choice for the popular reading collection in public and academic libraries.

Archaeology; a magazine dealing with the antiquity of the world. 1948. q. $8.50. Anna S. Benjamin. Archaeological Inst. of America, 260 W. Broadway, New York, N.Y. 10003. Illus., index, adv. Circ: 14,000. Vol. ends: Oct.

Indexed: AbAn, ArtI. *Bk. rev:* 55, 150–200 words. *Aud:* Ga, Ac, Hs. *Jv:* V.

The best general archaeology magazine for the non-expert and the interested layman. (The Institute also publishes a scholarly journal. See *American Journal of Archaeology.*) The articles are short and written in semipopular language for a widespread appeal. Articles about excavations and their revealed treasures in the Old World, the New World, and the Orient are by well-known authorities and experts. There is also a news section with brief notes of activities in the field, museum exhibitions and collections, and new finds. Given a choice between this and other titles mentioned in this section, *Archaeology* would be first for most medium to large-sized public libraries, and about the only one suitable for almost all high schools.

It would, however, be less appealing to the scholar and graduate student, and a second or third choice in larger academic libraries.

Archaeometry. 1958. bi-a. $9.50. E. T. Hall & M. J. Atiken. Cambridge Univ. Press, 32 East 57th St., New York, N.Y. 10022. Illus., index, adv. Sample.

Indexed: BritArchAb. *Aud:* Ac.

A multidisciplinary approach to archaeology, this is the scholarly bulletin of the Oxford University Research Laboratory for Archaeology. Coverage is worldwide, but the journal differs in that contributors range from chemists to art historians. Each expert writes on the application of his knowledge to a given aspect of archaeology. And while the approach requires knowledge of the subject, the authorities from different fields write in a style which should be readily grasped by the interested layman or student of archaeology.

Arkansas Archeologist. See *Field Notes.*

Art and Archaeology Newsletter. 1965. q. $3.50. Otto F. Reiss. 243 E. 39th St., New York, N.Y. 10016. Illus., index, adv. Circ: 1,000 Sample.

Bk. rev: 8-10, 50-100 words. *Aud:* Ga, Ac, Hs.

A highly personalized, lighthearted, yet authoritative report of some 15 to 20 pages on primarily ancient Greek and Roman archaeology. The editor writes the copy and turns out the small, offset publication on his own. He notes that *The Newsletter* frequently publishes discoveries that you cannot find anywhere else. Example: the observation that modern Albanian skirts resemble the Minoan costumes of 3500 years ago." Meant for the interested layman of all ages, it is a bit slight in size, but packed with fascinating information.

Artibus Asiae. See China and Asia/Asia Section.

Biblical Archaeologist. 1938. q. $5. Edward F. Campbell. Amer. Schools of Oriental Research, 126 Inman St., Cambridge, Mass. 02139. Illus., index. Circ: 6,500. Sample. Vol. ends: Dec. Microform: UM.

Indexed: ArtI, RelAb, RelPer. *Aud:* Ac, Ga.

A pocket-sized 20 to 30 page report on current activities whose importance is considerably greater than its format. "Its purpose is to supply reliable information in an area where unreliability seems almost the rule and 'biblical' in the title means the whole ancient world." There are usually four or five brief, illustrated articles, usually by Harvard faculty. The style is lucid, and will interest anyone involved with the area. Again, it is small in size, but basic. See also *American Schools of Oriental Research. Bulletin.*

Ethnohistory; devoted to the original research in the documentary history of the culture and movements of primitive peoples and related problems of broader scope. 1954. q. $10 ($6 individual). Bernard L. Fontana. Amer. Soc. for Ethnohistory. Arizona State Museum, The Univ. of Arizona, Tucson, Arizona 85721. Illus. Circ: 650. Sample. Vol. ends: Fall.

Indexed: AbFolkSt. *Bk. rev:* 4-10, 400-600 words, signed. *Aud:* Ac.

Directed to the scholar and layman interested in the history and culture of American Indian tribes. Includes also material on peoples throughout the world at all levels of socio-cultural organization, including primitives and peasantries. The two to four articles are thoroughly documented and contain references to additional sources of information. In addition to reviews there are "Book Notes" which list additional titles in the field, a general discussion about 400 words long. Only for large academic collections.

Expedition—The Magazine of Archaeology/Anthropology. 1958. q. $6.50. Erle Leichty. Univ. Museum of the Univ. of Pennsylvania, 33rd and Spruce Sts., Philadelphia, Pa. 19104. Illus., index. Circ: 6,500. Sample. Vol. ends: Summer.

Indexed: ArtI. *Aud:* Ga, Ac, Hs.

Articles of current interest by world's foremost scholars and field workers, reporting on recent excavations, discoveries, and anthropological studies; written for the interested layman as well as the professional specialist. The journal is profusely and handsomely illustrated. The University Museum, by virtue of its leading position among American institutions in the field, produces a unique publication, covering the world scope of these twin disciplines. Included are exploration, dating techniques, preservation and restoration, underwater archaeology, physical and cultural anthropology, etc. Should be in all medium to large collections.

Field Notes. (Including *Arkansas Archeologist*) 1965. m. $4. Hester A. Davis, Arkansas Archeological Soc., Central Office, Univ. of Arkansas Museum, Fayetteville, Ark., 72701. Illus. Circ: 600.

Bk. rev: Notes. *Aud:* Ac.

A few chatty mimeographed pages of news about the latest local digs and archaeological meetings, this is the newsletter of the Arkansas Archeological Society. Local devotees will no doubt appreciate learning about the locations, discoverers, and preliminary reports of findings of new Arkansas sites. Apart from an occasional book review or informal personal narrative, however, this is of little interest to those outside the Society. (N.P.)

Greek, Roman and Byzantine Studies. 1958. q. $10. William H. Willis. Duke Univ., Box 4715 Duke Station, Durham, N.C. 27706. Subs. to: Box 144, Cambridge, Mass. 02138. Circ: 700. Sample. Vol. ends: Winter. Refereed.

Bk. rev: 1-2 per volume, 12-15 pages. *Aud:* Ac, Ga.

A general journal of the classics but differs from others in that it contains a fair amount of material on the Byzantine Empire. Each issue presents seven to ten long articles, some with illustrations, on any subject of classical Greek or Byzantine interest. The tone is learned, but not formidable. Any reader of cultivated taste is bound to find articles here that catch his attention. Some recent articles are concerned with Mycenaean amber, new texts, first translations and new interpretations of Greek literature, the religion of Alexander the Great, and Byzantine relations with Islam. Recommended for large public and academic libraries.

Hesperia. 1932. q. $10. Lucy Shoe Meritt. Amer. School of Classical Studies at Athens. Subs. to: Inst. for Advanced Study, Princeton, N.J. 08540. Illus., index. Circ: 900. Reprint: Swets & Zeitlinger.

Indexed: ArtI. *Aud:* Ac.

Includes highly technical and detailed reports of findings by scholars and students. The text is primarily English with some ancient Greek. Illustrations, which are together at the end of the journal, usually run to about 30 pages and represent one quarter of the total content. However, photo quality is somewhat lower than *Artibus Asiae,* and subjects are of limited general interest because of their tendency to emphasize technical details. (N.P.)

Industrial Archaeology. See History/General Section.

Israel Exploration Journal. 1950/1. q. $6. M. Avi-Yonah, Israel Exploration Soc., Box 7041, Jerusalem, Israel. Illus., index. Circ: 1,350. Sample. Microform: UM.

Indexed: BritArchAb. *Bk. rev:* 12–13, lengthy, signed. *Aud:* Ac, Ga.

Features papers in English and occasionally in French on ancient as well as more recent history and archaeology of Israel and the Near East. Articles, mainly written by Israeli scholars, cover geography, geology, and natural history. There are maps and black and white pictures to elucidate the text. In view of the attention given to exploration in this area, the journal will have more than average interest for interested laymen as well as scholars.

Journal of Egyptian Archaeology. 1914. a. $12. J. Gwyn Griffiths. Egypt Exploration Soc., 3 Doughty Mews, London, WC1 England. Illus. Circ: 1,400.

Indexed: ArtI, BritHum, IBZ. *Bk. rev:* 20, 1,000 words, signed. *Aud:* Ac.

Concerned with all aspects of Ancient Egypt, Graeco-Roman Egypt, and Christian Egypt in its earliest phases; also, the Sudan in so far as that country is considered a sphere of Egyptian interest. The journal features reports of current fieldwork carried out by the Society. The book reviews are long, critical and among the best in the field. Only for specialized collections.

Journal of Near Eastern Studies. 1884. q. $8. Keith C. Seele. Univ. of Chicago Press, 5801 Ellis Ave., Chicago, Ill. 60637. Illus., index, adv. Circ: 2,063. Sample. Vol. ends: Oct. Microform: UM. Reprint: Johnson.

Indexed: SSHum. *Bk. rev:* 8–10, lengthy, signed. *Aud:* Ac.

A learned journal concerned with translations of inscriptions of ancient manuscripts and artifacts discovered in archaeological excavations in Western Asia and the Near East. Lengthy studies (10 to 20 pages) are written by well-known scholars of the Oriental Institute of the University of Chicago. Linguistic analyses and translations and results of recent archaeological discoveries are frequently published. Original research covers: literature, history, religion, linguistics, art, architecture, and archaeology. Larger academic libraries will want, but others can pass.

Journal of Roman Studies. 1911. s-a. $9.27. M. W. Frederiksen. Soc. for the Promotion of Roman Studies, 31–34 Gordon Square, London WC1, England. Illus., index.

Indexed: SSHum. *Bk. rev:* 40, length varies. *Aud:* Ac.

A scholarly approach to the history, archaeology, literature, and art of Rome, Italy and the Roman empire to about 700 A.D. There are usually 15 or so articles which cover every aspect of Roman studies, e.g., a study of the Treaty of Apamea to air reconnaissance in Britain. Particularly useful for libraries because of the extensive book review section, it is a basic acquisition for classic collections.

Palacio. 1913. q. $6. Carl E. Rosnik. Museum of New Mexico, Publns. Division, Box 2087, Santa Fe, N.M. 87501. Illus., index. Circ: 1,200. Sample. Vol. ends: No. 4.

Indexed: AbAn. *Bk. rev:* various number, length. *Aud:* Ac, Ga, Hs.

The archaeologists and their techniques as well as archaeological findings in New Mexico provide the subject material for this layman–oriented journal. Articles, primarily by students and amateur archaeologists, range from how-to-do-it discussions—e.g., "How to Make Rubbings"—to human interest stories on New Mexican Indians. Supplemental illustrations are provided. Highly recommended for general collections. (N.P.)

Pennsylvania Archaeologist. 1930. 3/yr. Membership (Nonmembers $6). P. Schuyler Miller. Soc. for Pennsylvania Archaeology, Box 368, Aliquippa, Pa. 15001. Illus., index.

Indexed: AbAn. *Bk. rev:* various number, length. *Aud:* Ac.

Contrary to expectations implied by the title, this journal presents reports of discoveries in several states located in the mid-Atlantic and Ohio Valley regions. Although the reports are often quite technical, the familiarity of the sites may be enough to keep the interest of the local layman. (N.P.)

World Archaeology. 1969. 3/yr. $11. Colin Platt. Routledge & Kegan Paul Ltd., 68–74 Carter Lane, London, EC4, England. Illus., adv.

Indexed: AbAn. *Aud:* Ac.

An international journal devoted to "a fresh generation of professional archaeologists," each issue usually planned around a central theme. The first 145-page issue of ten articles is devoted to "recent work and new approaches," and moves from East African culture to statistics. Nicely printed, well illustrated, it is primarily for the serious student and professional. Its unique contribution is its worldwide scope. The papers come from all geographic points, and reflect a high level of scholarship.

ARCHITECTURE

Basic Periodicals

Hs: *Architectural Record, Historic Preservation;* Ga: *Architectural Record, Architectural Forum, Historic Preservation;* Jc: *Progressive Architecture, Architectural Record, Domus;* Ac: *Progressive Architecture, Architectural Record, Architectural Forum, Domus, Architectural Review, Historic Preservation.*

Basic Abstracts and Indexes

Art Index, Ekistic Index, Housing and Planning References, Today's Housing Briefs.

Cessations

American Builder

AIA Journal (Formerly: *American Institute of Architects. Journal.*) 1900. m. $5 (Qualified subscribers). Robert E. Koehler. The American Inst. of Architects, 1785 Massachusetts Ave., N.W., Washington, D.C. 20036. Illus., index, adv. Circ: 30,000. Microform: UM.

Indexed: ArtI. *Bk. rev:* 7–8, full column, signed and unsigned. *Aud:* Sa, Ac.

A professional journal for architects, with articles written by well-known architects and related professionals which reflect the contemporary architect's concern with the building as an integral part of the total environment. This is a specialized journal which is recommended only for architectural collections. (R.S.)

American Institute of Architects. Journal. See *AIA Journal.*

Architect's Journal. 1895. w. $28.80. D.A.C.A. Boyne. Architectural Press Ltd., 9 Queen Anne's Gate, London SW 1, England. Illus., index, adv. Circ: 22,000.

Indexed: BritHum, BritTechI, IBZ. *Bk. rev:* Various number, length, signed. *Aud:* Ac, Sa.

A British weekly which reports on all matters of current interest to architects, builders, planners, etc. In addition to the ephemeral news items there are usually several articles on broader aspects of the art. While of limited use in American libraries, it is the basic weekly for English libraries in this subject area. See also *Architectural Review.*

Architectural Forum. 1892. 10/yr. $12 ($6 to students and faculty members of accredited schools of architecture). Peter Blake. Whitney Publns. Inc., 130 E. 59th St., New York, N.Y. 10022. Illus., index, adv. Circ: 40,000. Vol. ends: June, Dec. Microform: UM. Reprint: Johnson, Abrahams.

Indexed: ArtI, ASTI, CIJE, PAIS, RG. *Bk. rev:* 5–6, lengthy, signed. *Aud:* Ga, Ac. *Jv:* V.

This well-illustrated publication focuses interest on the physical aspects of buildings as part of the whole community, rather than on the individual, isolated structure. It relates architecture to human needs for housing, work, recreation, public places, education, and institutions. It examines the social, political and economic forces bearing on buildings. Highly readable articles occasionally compare the problems of ancient buildings and villages to modern concepts. The monthly review of notable buildings and a review of events and ideas are regular features. One of three basic architecture magazines for public and academic libraries. See concluding note for *Architectural Record.* (R.S.)

Architectural History; journal of the Society of Architectural Historians of Great Britain. 1958. a. $9.55. The Society, 8 Belmont Ave., Melton Park, Newcastle upon Tyne, NE3 5QD, England. Illus.

Indexed: BritHum. *Aud:* Ac, Ga.

This is somewhat the British equivalent to the American *Society of Architectural Historians Journal.* It differs in that it is an annual, and the average issue is more in the nature of an 80 to 100 page book than a magazine. There are original, sometimes fascinating, always dependable articles on all aspects of British architecture. It seems too little known in America.

Architectural News. (Formerly: *Architectural Products*). 1966. m. Request. Peter Cockshaw. Gordon Publns., 20 Community Pl., Morristown, N.J. 07960. Illus., adv. Circ: 50,000.

Aud: Ac, Sa.

A controlled circulation, i.e., free, tabloid magazine which is sent to engineers and registered architects. The material is of two types: (1) current news about contracts, specifications, personnel, labor, new products, etc.; (2) heavy advertising. While of limited use to nonprofessionals, it is of some interest to those involved with both residential and commercial construction.

This is one of a good many controlled circulation magazines in this field—most of which are available upon request by a library. Some charge subscription rates for so-called nonqualified readers, but most libraries can obtain them without charge. Two examples: *Architectural and Engineering News* (1958. m. Chilton Co., 56 & Chestnut Streets, Philadelphia, Pa. 19139) and *Building Design & Construction* (1958. m. $10 if not qualified. Keith Ray. Industrial Publications, 5 S. Wabash, Chicago, Ill. 60603).

Architectural Products. See *Architectural News.*

Architectural Record. 1891. m. $20 (For architects & engineers, $7.50). Walter F. Wagner. McGraw-Hill, Inc., Box 430, Hightstown, N.J. 08520. Illus., index, adv. Circ: 52,000. Microform: UM. Reprint: Abrahams.

Indexed: ArtI, ASTI, CIJE, EngI, RG. *Bk. rev:* 2–3, brief, signed. *Aud:* Ga, Ac, Hs. *Jv:* V.

While this is primarily for architects and engineers, the abundant illustrations, the frequent emphasis on homes, and the well-written articles make it an ideal introduction to architecture for interested laymen. It is well illustrated and contains news and features on building design and technology covering all types of buildings, the latest construction methods and materials, as well as techniques of managing and professional practice. Two thirds of each issue is composed of advertisements for building materials and building services. *Architectural Record, Architectural Forum,* and *Progressive Architecture* are three general architecture magazines for all medium to large-sized public and academic libraries. Each fills a different role, with *Architectural Record* being the most general of the trio, hence the most suitable for the average library which can take only one or two magazines in the area. Given this limited choice, the librarian might well consider a more specialized type such as *Domus* (see Europe/Italian section), for a second acquisition.

The Architectural Review. 1896. m. $15. D.A.C.A. Boyne, Chairman of Eds. Architectural Press, 9–13 Queen Anne's Gate, London SW1, England. Illus., index, adv. Circ: 12,275. Microform: UM.

Indexed: ArtI, BritHum, BritTech, CIJE. *Bk. rev:* Various number, length, signed. *Aud:* Ga, Ac. *Jv:* V.

One of the world's leading architectural magazines, of particular value for its stress on modern, often avant-garde trends. While directed to the professional architect and student, the excellent illustrations and text give it an added dimension for the interested layman. The scope is international, although there is considerable emphasis on English building, landscape architecture, and interior design. Also, each issue usually features one or two articles on modern painting and sculpture and furniture, particularly as related to trends in architecture. Occasional issues on special subjects give it particularly high reference value. Definitely a second or third choice in larger academic and junior college libraries, and a first where there is any effort to have a representative architectural collection. The same firm issues *The Architect's Journal* (see above), which provides up-to-date news, reviews, and comments on more professionally oriented architectural matters. The *Architectural Review* is particularly valuable for the technical information section with its detailed cost analyses and studies of specific buildings. The *Journal,* being a more technical approach, is only for the large architecture collection.

Architecture Canada. 1924. m. $10. Annabel Slaight. Greey DePencier Publns., 56 Esplanade St., E., Toronto 1, Canada. Illus., index, adv. Circ: 5,548.

Indexed: ArtI, CanI. *Bk. rev:* 2,500 words, signed. *Aud:* Ga, Ac.

This journal of the Royal Architectural Institute of Canada averages 40 pages and features articles on the arts allied to architecture, i.e., sculpture, murals, glass, etc. There are review sections on national and international architecture, text and illustrated sections on housing, planning, schools, etc. Work related to schools and Canadian architecture is reported. Although of primary interest to the professional architect, the coverage of related fields gives this an added dimension for general art collections. Should be in all Canadian academic libraries and many medium to large-sized collections in the United States. See also *Canadian Architect.*

Architecture d'aujourd hui. See Europe and Middle East/French Language Section.

Canadian Architect. 1956. m. $12. James A. Murray. Southam Business Publns., Ltd., 1450 Don Mills Rd., Don Mills, Ont., Canada. Illus., index, adv. Circ: 5,500.

Indexed: CanI. *Aud:* Ga, Ac.

Somewhat similar to the *Architectural Forum,* i.e., the emphasis is on urban planning; development of the environment in terms of creative and imaginative architecture is a major consideration. It differs from *Architecture Canada* in that there seems to be more interest in progressive, avant-garde design, and this has the more attractive format with many photographs and illustrations. Edited for the architect, the magazine is a bit too technical for the average reader, but should be required reading in any school of architecture.

Creative Ideas in Glass. See Free Magazines Section.

Design & Environment. 1970. q. $11. Ann Ferebee. R. C. Publns., 6400 Goldsboro Rd., N.W., Washington, D.C. 20034. Illus., index, adv. Circ: 11,000. Sample.

Bk. rev: various number, length, signed. *Aud:* Ac, Ga, Hs. *Jv:* V.

An important environmental magazine for both the architect and the layman or expert. Although primarily involved with architecture, this semipopular journal treats all aspects of the many problems connected with environmental design. The purpose is to show that the same technology and imagination which wrecks the environment can be reversed and harnessed to improve man's way. There are, also, related articles on all aspects of environmental concern, i.e., there are articles on everything from graphic design to methods of improving the interior of a house or factory. Along with *Landscape* this is one of the growing number of architectural and building magazines which look at how to save rather than exploit the environment. Of the two, this would be a first choice for the general collection. It is broader in its outlook than *Landscape*, although both are equally good. The reading level does require some knowledge of architecture, city planning, etc. Still, most of the material is within the grasp of the interested layman. High school students, too, will find much here of interest.

Domus. See Europe and Middle East/Italian Language Section.

Form and Function. See Free Magazines Section.

Historic Preservation. 1949. q. Membership ($5 to libraries). Mrs. Terry B. Morton. National Trust for Historic Preservation, 740 Jackson Pl. N.W., Washington, D.C. 20006. Illus., index. Circ: 25,000.

Indexed: ArtI. *Aud:* Ga, Hs, Ac.

A publication of the National Trust for Historic Preservation, chartered by an Act of Congress "to facilitate public participation in the preservation of sites, buildings, and objects of national significance by providing a national trust for historic preservation." Each issue contains 9 to 10 well-illustrated, brief essays on the preservation or restoration of historic landmarks or natural sites, and presents their historic background in a well-written and readable style. Of interest to general adult students and instructors of architecture and history. See also *Society of Architectural Historians. Journal.*

House and Home. 1952. m. $9. John F. Goldsmith. McGraw-Hill, Inc., 330 W. 42nd St. New York, N.Y. 10036. Illus., index, adv. Circ: 115,000. Vol. ends: Dec. Microform: UM. Reprint: Abrahams.

Aud: Ga, Ac. *Jv:* C.

The marketing and management publication of the housing industry, this is a large, glossy, photograph-filled periodical designed to describe and illustrate trends in housing. Builders, investors, realtors, mortgage lenders, and community planners will find the articles readable. Ideas and advice are offered about planning, building, and financing of individual homes and housing developments. Building successes as well as failures are frequent subject matter. Advertisements are numerous and offer information about new building materials and products. For large business and architecture collections.

The Japan Architect. 1925. m. $21. Shozo Baba. Yasugoro Yoshioka, Shinkenchiku-Sha Co., Ltd., 31–2, Yushima 2-chome, Bunkyo-ku, Tokyo, Japan. Illus., adv. Circ: 15,260. Vol. ends: Dec.

Indexed: ArtI. *Bk. rev:* 1–6, 1–3 pages. signed. *Aud:* Ga, Ac.

Introduces the imaginative and exciting architecture of modern Japan. Individual homes, housing complexes, industrial, office, ecclesiastic, and national buildings are described in detail and photographed from all ele-

vations. The articles are usually long (10 to 20 pages) and the illustrations are generous and excellent. There are fewer advertisements than found in American magazines of this type. The publisher holds an annual competition for superior designs in building (the "ideal home" was the subject assigned in 1967). Text is in English with summaries in Spanish. Along with *Domus* (see Europe/Italian section), an excellent second or third choice for the library which is not specialized, but which wishes to break out of the limits of general American architectural magazines. A necessary addition for all medium to large-sized architecture collections.

Landscape. 1951. 3/yr. $6 (Libraries: $9). Blair M. Boyd, Box 7177, Landscape Station, Berkeley, Calif. 94707. Illus. Circ: 2,000. Reprint: Johnson. Microform: UM.

Indexed: ArtI. *Bk. rev:* 6–15, 300–500 words, some brief annotations, signed. *Aud:* Ac, Ga, Hs.

Although superficially a journal devoted to landscape architecture, it does, in actuality, bear on many aspects of environmental quality and deals with all aspects of man's physical and cultural relationship with his environment. In this respect, it can be recommended to architects, geographers, city and regional planners, industrial designers, biologists, etc. Emphasis is on current urban problems and a sampling of recent issues includes such topics as: "The Urban Homestead Act; a proposal for America's cities," "Crowding in the city, the Japanese solution," and "Heating, lighting, plumbing, and human relations." This magazine is particularly recommended for large college and university collections. (R.S.)

Landscape Architecture. 1910. q. $8.50. Grady Clay. Publications Board, American Soc. of Landscape Architects, Schuster Bldg., 1500 Bardstown Rd., Louisville, Ky. 40205. Illus., adv. Circ: 8,300. Reprint: Johnson.

Indexed: ArtI, CIJE, PAIS. *Bk. rev:* 5, length varies, signed. *Aud:* Ga, Ac.

Devoted to all aspects of landscape architecture from national park planning to private gardens. The some 15 articles per issue cover land improvement, city planning, park and natural resource design, and gardens about the home. Emphasis is on the larger municipal and national developments, and the whole is primarily for the professional, whether he be a landscape architect, city planner, or private developer. Because of the many excellent illustrations, it will have some interest for the conservationist and the enthusiastic gardener. Regular departments include book reviews, people, new products, and critiques of recent work in the field. A useful addition for business, conservation, architecture, and some gardening collections in medium to large-sized public and academic libraries. (R.S.)

Prairie School Review. 1963. q. $10. W. R. Hasbrouck. The Prairie School Press, Inc., 12509. S. 89th Ave., Palos Park, Ill. 60464. Illus., adv.

Indexed: ArtI. *Bk. rev:* 2–3, 250–1,000 words, signed. *Aud:* Ac.

The three to four articles in each issue are devoted solely to the "Prairie School" of architecture which originated in Chicago, but has left its mark throughout the Midwest. It includes among its ranks not only such giants as Louis H. Sullivan and Frank Lloyd Wright, but also their followers, especially Hugh Garden, Walter Burley Griffin, William Drummond, and George Grant Elmslie, among others. This journal has played no small part in bringing recognition to these lesser lights of the Chicago school. Its high standards of design, line cuts, and sharp photographs make it particularly attractive. Albeit a specialized periodical for historians of modern architecture, particularly in one region, it is recommended for all academic libraries interested in architectural history. (R.S.)

Progressive Architecture. 1920. m. $6. Burton H. Holmes. Reinhold Publishing Corp., 25 Sullivan St., Westwood, N.J. 07695. Illus., adv. Circ: 65,000. Microform: UM.

Indexed: ASTI, ArtI. CIJE, EngI. *Bk rev:* 3–4, ½ to full-page. *Aud:* Ga, Ac, Hs. *Jv:* V.

Progressive Architecture, Architectural Forum, and *Architectural Record* represent the three general magazines in this field. Many architects and even lay readers prefer *Progressive Architecture* because of its emphasis on modern work (as the title implies) and the international scene. The articles tend to be technical, but are well illustrated, and this latter feature gives the journal particular value for the interested layman. There is some emphasis, too, on the social and ethical responsibilities of the architect and the builder. All aspects are covered from private homes to large industrial complexes and schools. Although written for the professional architect and the student, it should be considered for general collections in medium to large-sized public and academic libraries. See concluding comments in annotation for *Architectural Record.*

RIBA Journal. 1879. m. $11. Royal Inst. of British Architects, 66 Portland Pl., London WIN 4AD, England. Illus., index, adv. Circ: 30,000. Microform: UM.

Indexed: ArtI, BritHum, BritTechI, IBZ. *Bk. rev:* Essays & notes, signed. *Aud:* Ac, Sa.

The British counterpart of the AIA, the RIBA has a similar journal. It reports on activities of the membership, and has a number of rather technical articles— some of monographic length—on aspects of British architecture and planning. It is heavy with advertising, and an average issue will have more advertising copy than editorial material. Be that as it may, it is an important journal for larger architectural collections.

RIBA Library Bulletin. 1946. q. $6. D. E. Dean. Royal Inst. of British Architects. 66 Portland Pl., London WIN, 4AD, England.

An average 30 to 40 page issue is, among other things, a bibliographic guide to the literature. There are abstracts, short reviews, notes, and, to be sure, articles of value to anyone involved with an architectural library. Possibly of more interest to American librarians than *RIBA Journal.*

Society of Architectual Historians. Journal. 1940. q. $15 (Membership). Osmund Overby. Executive Secretary, S.A.H., Room 716, 1700 Walnut St., Philadelphia, Pa. 19103. Illus., index, adv. Circ: 3,800. Sample. Vol. ends: Dec. Microform: UM. Reprint: Johnson.

Indexed: ArtI. *Bk. rev:* 5–6, full page, signed. *Aud:* Ac, Ga.

Membership in the Society is open to all who are interested in furthering the study, enjoyment, and preservation of architecture and its related arts. There are well-illustrated, scholarly, but readable articles (both brief and lengthy) devoted to architectural history, theory, and aesthetics of extant architecture in Europe and America. An allied journal is *Historic Preservation.* Both will be needed in large architectural and historical collections, but of the two, *Historic Preservation* probably will be of most interest to the average layman; therefore, it should be considered by any size or type library where there is an interest in the field.

Transactions of the Ancient Monuments Society. 1925. a. $3. The Society, 12 Edwards Square, London W 8, England.

Indexed: BritHum. *Aud:* Ac, Ga.

An average issue of some 150 to 175 pages includes monographs, short articles, and news items. The name of the Society is meant to include anything worth saving from historic buildings to whole areas and regions. The approach therefore, is somewhat similar to *Historic Preservation.* The articles are delightful, usually clear, concise and well within the understanding of the interested layman.

ART

Basic Periodicals

Hs: *Art in America, Artforum;* Ga: *Art in America, Art News, Artforum;* Jc: *Artforum, Art in America, Art International;* Ac: *Artforum, Art in America, Art News, Art International, Graphis, Arts Canada.*

Library and Teaching Aids

Arts and Activities, School Arts, Design (U.S.), Art Education, Art and Craft in Education.

Basic Abstracts and Indexes

Art Index.

Cessations

Art and Literature, Art Scene, Aspen, Sculpture International, Art & Auction, S.M.S.

African Art. See Africa Section.

The American Art Journal. 1969. $10. Kennedy Galleries/Da Capo Press, 20 East 56 St., New York, N.Y. 10022. Illus. Circ: 2,000. Sample. Vol. ends: Fall. Refereed.

Indexed: ArtI. *Bk. rev:* 5,300 words. *Aud:* Ac, Ga.

Well-documented articles on a wide range of topics relating to American art, supported by an attractive format, make this periodical a pleasure to absorb on two levels: reading in depth, or leafing through the illustrations. Though all the illustrations are in black and white, they are well selected for interest and are grouped for optimum page composition. The content of the periodical is quite broad and often treats its focal subject of American art in its historical, literary, or social context. Therefore, the appeal of this journal will extend beyond the subject of art. It is published on excellent heavy duty paper and is, in all respects, a welcome addition to the field. (H.D.)

American Artist. 1937. m. (Sept.–June) $10. Susan E. Meyer. Billboard Publishing Co., Inc., 165 W. 46th St., New York, N.Y. 10036. Illus., index, adv. Circ: 10,000. Sample. Vol. ends: Dec. Microform: UM. Reprint: Abrahams.

Indexed: ArtI, PAIS, RG. *Bk. rev:* 18, short, signed. *Aud:* Hs, Ejh.

A how-to-do-it magazine primarily for teachers and students in elementary through high school. Most emphasis is on material for the teacher. Articles run the gamut from early to contemporary American artists and describe their subject matter, style, and technique. The essays are written by contributors to the magazine, or by the artists, and are informal and descriptive rather than critical. The illustrations are clear and adequate to elucidate the topic and there are frequent profiles of past and present American artists. News of art competitions and scholarships should interest art students. The advertisements are not excessive and are a good source of information about art materials. A useful second choice in elementary through high school professional collections, but way down the list for general art collections in public or academic libraries. See also concluding remarks in annotation for *Art Education.*

American Journal of Art Therapy; art in education, rehabilitation and psychotherapy (Formerly: **Bulletin of Art Therapy**). 1961. q. $6.50. Elinor Ulman, Box 4918, Washington, D.C. 20008. Illus., index. Circ: 1,500. Sample. Vol. ends: July. Microform: UM.

Indexed: ArtI, IMed, PsyAb. *Bk. rev:* 6, 1000 words, signed. *Aud:* Ac, Hs, Ejh.

A forum for professional art therapists, teachers, psychologists, psychiatrists, and others interested in art and its place in the rehabilitation of adults and children. While a highly specialized journal, it offers a new avenue to understanding for both elementary and secondary school art teachers. The two to four articles "include new theoretical formulations, reports of research, descriptions of actual programs, news of opportunities for training and international developments in the field." Material is concerned with all of the visual arts. A required magazine for larger libraries, and well worth trying in the professional school collection.

Apollo; the international magazine of art and antiques. 1925. q. $32. Denys Sutton, 22 Davies St., London W1Y 1LH, England. Subs. to: 551 Fifth Ave., New York, N.Y. 10017. Illus., index, adv. Circ: 14,000. Sample. Microform: UM.

Indexed: ArtI, BritHum, IB2. *Bk. rev:* 5–7, full page, signed. *Aud:* Ac.

This British magazine is an essential and expanding encyclopedia for collectors and connoisseurs of art and antiques of all periods throughout the world. Magnificently illustrated biographical essays and criticism about artists and their works, pieces on individual works of art, exhibitions, museums, and collections are written by experts in their fields. Notes on sales and auctions are included. Advertisements of galleries, auctioneers, and art dealers account for half of the magazine's bulk, 180 to 200 pages in each issue. See also *The Connoisseur.*

Art and Craft in Education. 1946. m. $9. Henry Pluckrose. Evans Bros. Ltd., Montague House, Russell Sq., London WC1B 5BX, England. Illus., adv. Circ: 22,000. Sample.

Aud: Ac, Hs, Ejh.

Roughly the English equivalent to *Arts and Activities, Design,* etc. "All that the child learns should have personal relevance and be understood as contributing to the great creative business of being alive," says one contributor, and this quite well expresses the purpose of each 30 or so page issue. Diagrams and illustrations punctuate the short how-to-do-it articles. The writing is clear, the notations imaginative. It is written primarily for the elementary and junior high level. The English base does make for some differences, but the material is good enough to warrant consideration by any teacher looking for new approaches.

Art and Man (Incorporating: **Artist Junior**). 1970. m. 8/yr. $3 (lower group rates). Gray Williams, Jr., Scholastic Magazines, 50 W. 44th St., New York, N.Y. 10036. Illus.

Aud: Ejh, Hs.

An inexpensive classroom teaching aid—primarily for junior and senior high schools. Each issue is given over to rather good, although hardly outstanding, reproductions of art work which carry out the month's theme, e.g., American Indian art, African sculpture, etc. There are the usual gimmicks which accompany the thin textual matter, i.e., slides, recordings, and other guides. This may be of some assistance to teachers who have never studied art, but it will be superficial for most. It definitely should not be used as an art magazine for young people. The illustrations help, of course, but several more sophisticated, adult efforts will do better. A nonessential item for teachers. (See also Scholastic Magazines in Education section.)

Art Bulletin. 1912. q. Membership. John R. Martin. College Art Assn. of America, 432 Park Ave. S., New York, N.Y. 10016. Illus., index. Circ: 5,700. Vol. ends: Dec. Microform: UM. Reprint: Kraus.

Indexed: ArtI. *Bk. rev:* various number, length, signed. *Aud:* Ac.

A controlled circulation magazine for members of the College Art Association of America. Brings serious, learned articles written by faculty members of the Association to students of art history. Its scope includes all facets and periods of the fine arts, from the most esoteric subjects to architecture. The articles are long and well-documented studies of aesthetics and theory, with excellent illustrations and drawings. This and *Art Quarterly* are the two major magazines devoted to art history in America, and one or both should be found in larger art collections. See also *Art Journal.*

Art Direction; the magazine of visual communication, serves the field of advertising art, photography, typography and related graphic arts field. 1950. m. $9.50. Myles Eric Ludwig. Advertising Trade Publns., 19 W. 44th St., New York, N.Y. 10036. Illus., adv. Circ: 13,000. Sample. Vol. ends: Dec. Microform: UM.

Bk. rev: 6,150 words. *Aud:* Ac, Ga.

A basic magazine for anyone involved with advertising art. A typical issue includes some 300 pictures and editorial material on every aspect of the subject from illustration, typography, and photography to design of posters, television commercials, packaging, direct mail pieces, etc. Special departments (taxes, business activity, accounting, legal advice, news of people and events) are directed at the professional.

Art Education. 1948. 9/yr. Membership (Nonmembers $6). John Mahlman. National Art Education Assn., 1201 16th St., N.W., Washington, D.C. 20036. Illus., adv. Circ: 10,000. Sample. Vol. ends: Dec. Reprint: Kraus.

Indexed: CIJE, EdI. *Bk. rev:* 8,350 words, signed. *Aud:* Ac, Hs, Ejh.

Since the last edition, the editor reports, "our journal has been expanded in range of interest and audience reached." Whereas before the primary audience was the elementary and high school teachers, college teachers and students of art are now considered within the scope of editorial purpose. The magazine is now concerned with "museum art education, as well as supervision and administration in art education." A typical issue does reflect this change, although the primary audience remains those involved with art from the elementary through the high school. The material tends to be scholarly, albeit well within the grasp of the average teacher. Its particular value is for its studies of the psychology of art in relation to children and for its attention to aesthetics and the theory of art. There are illustrations both of children's work and of work by recognized artists. All schools should include this in their professional collections, and schools of education in junior colleges and universities will also want to subscribe.

At the more practical, how-to-do-it level, a second or first choice (depending upon need) would be *Arts and Activities, School Arts Magazine* or possibly *Design* and *Art and Man. Everyday Art* is slight, yet a useful secondary consideration, and *American Artist, Art Journal* and *American Journal of Art Therapy* are for more specialized situations. It cannot be emphasized too strongly that all of these are for teachers and adults, not for the students who should be given an opportunity to meet art through the better illustrated, more meaningful adult magazines such as *Art in America.* Granted, the text may be over their heads, but is art a matter of reading or of seeing?

Art in America. 1913. bi-m. $15. Brian O'Doherty. Art in America, Inc., 150 E. 58th St., New York, N.Y. 10022. Illus., adv. Circ: 50,694. Sample. Vol. ends: Nov/Dec. Microform: UM. Reprint: AMS, Abrahams.

Indexed: ArtI, RG. *Bk. rev:* 1, 3–4 pages, signed. *Aud:* Ac, Ga, Hs, Ejh. *Jv:* V.

This remains the single best general art magazine for American libraries. In a trifle more specialized way, *Artforum* would be a close second, followed by *Art Now* and *Art International. Art in America* is primarily concerned with the visual arts. It is international in scope, and while there are selected retrospective and historical articles, the emphasis is on contemporary art. Each number, from 128 to 144 pages, features an average of 25 full color plates and scores of black and white reproductions and photographs. Printed on high grade paper, the format is as outstanding as the contents. Painting, sculpture, architecture, design, and photography are the magazine's main concerns, and the critics writing on these subjects are among the best in the world—Harold Rosenberg, Elizabeth Hardwick, John Canaday, Brian O'Doherty, Barbara Rose. The style is imaginative, intellectual, and always challenging.

High school libraries (not to mention elementary school libraries) should consider *Art in America,* if only for the illustrations, as a first choice. What follows depends upon curriculum, but hopefully the selection will be broader than the standard educational art magazines such as *School Arts*.

Art International. 1956. 10/yr. $18. James Fitzsimmons, Via Maraini 17-A, Lugano, Switzerland. Illus., index, adv. Circ: 25,000. Sample. Vol. ends: Dec. Microform: UM.

Indexed: ArtI. *Bk. rev:* Various number, length. *Aud:* Ac, Ga. *Jv:* V.

The basic international, general art magazine which should be found in most American libraries. Text is in English, French, German, and Italian. The reproductions are superb—witness the fact that it is published in Switzerland, long the home of superior art printing. And while the articles represent a high level of scholarship, they are jargon free, often penetrating, and easily understood by the interested layman. Coverage is of the world's art scene. Since the last edition, the magazine has expanded its scope to include regular features and articles dealing with other arts, i.e., literature, music, film, and even poetry. While continuing to emphasize the visual arts, the purpose of the change is to explore the larger cultural aspects of art.

Art Journal. 1912. q. $5. Henry R. Hope. College Art Assn. of America, 432 Park Ave. S., New York, N.Y. 10019. Illus., index, adv. Circ: 9,000. Vol. ends: Summer. Microform: UM.

Indexed: ArtI. *Bk. rev:* 5, one half to full page, signed. *Aud:* Ac.

The sister publication of *Art Bulletin*, but available via subscription—which explains, in part, a circulation of almost twice that of the *Bulletin*. Brings news of exhibitions, recent acquisitions, and new art buildings on American college and university campuses. Articles consider some of the problems of teaching art in higher education. Several serious, scholarly pieces on aesthetics and criticism are included and black and white photographs illustrate the points of interest.

Art News. 1902. m. (Sept.–May); q. (June–Aug.). $13. Thomas B. Hess. Newsweek, Inc., 444 Madison Ave., New York, N.Y. 10022. Illus., adv. Circ: 38,000. Sample. Vol. ends: Feb. Microform: UM.

Indexed: ArtI, RG. *Aud:* Ga, Ac, Hs. *Jv:* V.

Neither as spectacular as *Art in America*, nor as daring as *Artforum*, this remains a basic art magazine for most libraries. Because of its longevity, and because it has been indexed in *Readers' Guide* for many years, it is often the only art magazine in the smaller library. Readers deserve something more (see comments for *Art in America*). However, it does include serious, well-written criticism of art movements, works of individual artists, special collections, and exhibitions of interest to the art collector, as well as to artists and to students. Illustrations are in black and white and color. A good exhibition calendar lists exhibits by artist's

names. News of important auctions of art collections, and notes on art from London, Paris, Rome, Chicago, Los Angeles, and New York are given. Information on competitions and scholarships, on where and when to exhibit, and on new materials is of special concern to the art student. The *Art News Annual*, usually available around Christmas time, is a separate publication devoted to a variety of art topics. At $7.95 the issue, it is a sound investment for any library. (The *Annual* and the magazine may be purchased for a combined price of $18.95.)

Art Now: New York. 1969. q. $15. Ward Jackson, Paul Katz. Univ. Galleries, Inc., 520 Fifth Ave., New York, N.Y. 10036. Illus., index. Circ: 1,000. Sample. Vol. ends: 4th issue.

Aud: Ac, Ga, Hs. *Jv:* V.

A unique periodical which requires the attention of anyone interested in the current art scene and the avant-garde. Each edition consists of expert reproductions of art works by eight artists being exhibited in major and minor galleries in New York City. Texts of varying length and depth by the artists themselves accompany the color plates. The background of this indispensable quarterly portfolio is held in this excerpt from one of the editor's letters: "*Art Now: New York* started out with the thought of bridging the gap—in a unique way—between the New York art world, its exciting exhibitions of new and important contemporary art, and all of those people (especially students and art teachers) who are interested in seeing and experiencing these exhibitions, but are unable to do so primarily because they live or study too far from New York. The folio format (with separate color reproductions) was decided upon so that the plates could be displayed along with the text, providing a focus for classroom discussions or library exhibition. It is significantly different from other art publications in that its text is principally comprised of original statements by the artists. Thus, the artist is provided with an opportunity of expressing himself in writing concerning his ideas and methods. Our publication is not involved with critical analysis, but prefers to be wholly objective, letting the artist speak for himself. This, of course, permits the viewer an insight into the artist's thinking and objectives." *Art Now: New York* should be in the collections of all liberal arts and fine arts libraries, public, academic, and, where possible, high school libraries.

The Art Quarterly. 1938. q. $12. Jerrold Lanes. The Founders Soc., Detroit Inst. of Arts, 5200 Woodward Ave., Detroit, Mich. 48202. Illus., adv. Microform: UM. Reprint: Johnson.

Indexed: ArtI. *Bk. rev:* 12–13, brief, signed. *Aud:* Sa, Ac.

Contains lengthy, historical articles on art of all periods, well documented and well illustrated. The magazine has a "Consultative Committee" of some of the most esteemed art scholars in the country. Regular checklist, notes, and illustrations about recent acquisitions of American and Canadian museums and universities offer scholarly comment for art historians, museum curators, dealers, and galleries. Only for larger art collections, but should be a dual selection with *Art Bulletin*.

Art Voices; an independent art magazine, voicing news, views and opinions on art. 1962. q. $9.25. Joseph James Akston. Art Voices, Inc., 23 E. 26th St., New York, N.Y. 10010. Illus.

Bk. rev: various number, length. *Aud:* Ac.

An independent art journal which stresses developments in the avant-garde, prides itself on original, nonacademic criticism, and has excellent reproductions. In addition to the sometimes controversial views, there is news of modern art and artists, book reviews, and short notes. A good magazine to balance any collection which is top heavy with academic-based journals.

L'Arte. 1968. q. $16.50. Enio Sindona. Pennsylvania State Univ. Press, 215 Wagner Bldg., Univ. Park, Pa. 16802. Illus. Circ: 1,000. Sample. Vol. ends: Dec.

Bk. rev: 1, 8–10 pages, signed. *Aud:* Ac.

An art history magazine which is published in Milan and has most of its articles in Italian, but with adequate summaries in English, French, and German. Each of the eight to ten articles is liberally illustrated with black and white and some colored plates. The 140 pages are printed on glossy stock, and the format is good, if not impressive. Articles presuppose a knowledge of art, are by authorities, and vary in style from good to excellent. A basic journal in large art collections, but it is a trifle too esoteric for smaller libraries.

Artes de Mexico. See Latin American and Chicano/Spanish Language Section.

Artforum. 1962. m. $22.50. John Coplans. Charles Cowles, 667 Madison Ave., New York, N.Y. 10021. Illus., index, adv. Circ: 20,000. Vol. ends: June.

Indexed: ArtI. *Aud:* Ga, Ac, Hs. *Jv:* V.

The leading avant-garde art magazine in America, and in many ways one of the better written and illustrated. In fact, the format is superb. There are numerous colored plates, and the black and white photographs are excellent. And while confined to art, the editors do move about a bit, e.g., one issue was given over to the film in America. This is the only popular magazine to devote so much space to profound discussions of aesthetics and theory. The articles are by well-known young critics. The attention to younger artists and current movements makes this particularly suitable for high school students with a serious interest in art. Among the first choices for any kind of library.

Artibus Asiae. See China and Asia/Asia Section.

The Artist. 1931. m. $8. Frederick Parkinson, Dist. by: Artist Publishing Corp., 155 W. 15th St., New York, N.Y. 10011. Illus., index, adv. Circ: 27,000. Sample. Vol. ends: Sept. & March. Microform: UM. Reprint: Abrahams.

Aud: Hs, Ejh. *Jv:* C.

Published in England, this is the English counterpart of *Art Education*, *Arts & Activities*, etc. It gives practical advice on technique, composition, use of media, color mixing, and other information of interest to amateurs and elementary and high school teachers. It is well illustrated, and there are articles by artists and teachers. While of some value for American libraries, it would be among the last choices.

Artist Junior. See *Art and Man*.

Artist's Proof. 1961. a. $15 (Members $12.50). Fritz Eichenberg. Pratt Graphics Center, in association with New York Graphic Soc., Ltd., 831 Broadway, New York, N.Y. 10003. Illus., index, adv. Circ: 5,000. Microform: UM.

Indexed: ArtI. *Bk. rev:* 2–3, 250 words, signed. *Aud:* Ac, Hs, Ejh.

Edited by one of the world's finest graphic artists, this annual volume is the "only existing publication devoted exclusively to the contemporary print and to its creators." It is definitely aimed at the serious student and not the dabbler. The scope is international, the emphasis is progressive, and contemporary trends are favored. The novel feature is that it allows artists to speak for themselves rather than to be interpreted by critics or art historians. The reproductions are excellent. Recommended for elementary and high school teachers, high school students, and academic libraries. Public libraries, too, will find a ready audience for this work.

Arts and Activities; creative activities for the classroom. 1937. m. (Sept.–June). $7. Mary C. Emerson. Publisher's Development Corp., 8150 N. Central Park Blvd., Skokie, Ill. 60076. Illus., index., adv. Circ: 35,000. Sample. Vol. ends: Jan. & June. Microform: UM.

Indexed: EdI. *Bk. rev:* 5,250 words, signed. *Aud:* Ac, Ejh, Hs. *Jv:* V.

Along with *Design* and *School Arts*, one of the basic do-it-yourself arts magazines for teachers in elementary and junior high schools. It is particularly useful at the elementary level. Although the only one of the three not indexed in *Readers' Guide*, it is a first choice for teachers, particularly those without formal art training. The eight to ten articles are well illustrated, usually with children's art; the ideas for classroom activities seem to be a trifle more imaginative than found in the competitors; and the emphasis is on the average, not the ideal, classroom situation, where there is often a lack of space, equipment, and even encouragement. There are the usual articles on art education—although not so many as found in *School Arts*—news of the profession, new products, and audiovisual aids. The book reviews tend to be short notes, although from time to time there are longer reviews. A regular department includes outstanding child art. Primarily a magazine to be used by the teacher with the students.

Arts Canada. 1943. bi-m. $10 ($12 foreign). Anne Brodzky, 129 Adelaide St., W., Toronto 1, Ont. Canada. Illus., index, adv. Circ: 8,000.

Indexed: ArtI, CanI. *Bk. rev:* various number, length, signed. *Aud:* Ac, Ga, Hs. *Jv:* V.

The Canadian equivalent of *Art in America*. An average issue of 100 or so pages includes articles on painting, sculpture, architecture, archaeology, etc. There is often material on the film, poetry, photographic essays, and, of course, news of exhibitions and artists. The emphasis tends to be on Canadian modern art and crafts. Articles are by authorities, and are usually well written and clear enough for the reader from high school up. The reproductions, many in full color, are superb—and the magazine can be enjoyed as much for the illustrations as for the editorial material. On occasion there is a double number, e.g., December/January 1972 was devoted to the "Eskimo World" and included an outstanding survey of Eskimo art. Should be found in all Canadian libraries, and certainly in most American collections too.

Arts Magazine. 1926. m. (Nov.–June); bi-m. (Sept./Oct., Dec./Jan.). $11.20 (including *Arts Yearbook*, $22.95). Gregorie Muller. Art Digest, Inc., 23 E. 26th St., Room 1012, New York, N.Y. 10010. Illus., adv. Circ: 25,000. Sample.

Indexed: ArtI. *Bk. rev:* 9, length varies. *Aud:* Ac, Ga.

One of the basic magazines for coverage of modern and avant-garde art. Articles tend to be a bit more reserved and scholarly than found in its rival *Artforum*, but the plates (both in color and black and white) are equally good. Articles consider artists, movements, and art shows. There is some attention given to traditional art, but this seems to be changing in favor of on-the-spot reports of modern trends and figures. Regular departments cover shows at museums and galleries, and a directory for artists seeking a place to show. Since the previous edition, this magazine has improved considerably and it can now be recommended as equal to, if not sometimes better than, *Artforum*—at any rate, both should be considered where there is any interest in modern art. The illustrations, if not always the articles, make it a good choice for high school and medium-sized public libraries, as well, of course, as for larger collections. The annual yearbook should be part of any subscription.

Auction. 1967. m. (Sept.–June). $15. Linda Rosenkrantz. Auction Communications Inc., 200 W. 57th St., New York, N.Y. 10019. Illus., adv. Circ: 13,000. Sample. Vol. ends: June.

Bk. rev: 5, 300 words, signed. *Aud:* Ac, Ga.

While this began as a $2 a year magazine it has expanded in size and scope to a $15 item. The jump in cost is almost worth it because of the increase in illustrations and pages; but with this new price it is primarily for the private collector. Generally highlights coming and past auctions at Parke-Bernet and its English partner, Sotheby's of London. Each issue features several articles, frequently documented, on antiques, art, books, furniture, and other matters of interest to the rich collector. Book reviews cover the latest works on antiques, art, and book collecting.

Avalanche. 1970. q. $7. Uza Bean. Willoughby Sharp, 204 E. 20th St., New York, N.Y. 10003. Illus., adv. Circ: 10,000.

Aud: Ac, Ga.

This striking art magazine is devoted to the international avant-garde. The black and white illustrated numbers feature short news items on artists and shows, interviews, and portraits of artists. Earth sculpture to body works are considered. While not all of the text will be meaningful to laymen, the handsome layout and well-chosen illustrations should impress anyone remotely involved with today's art. The price is modest enough. Recommended without reservation for any medium to large-sized art collection.

Boston Museum Bulletin. 1903. q. $4. Carl F. Zahn. Museum of Fine Arts, Boston, Mass. 02115. Illus., index. Circ: 11,500. Sample. Vol. ends: Winter. Microform: UM.

Indexed: ArtI. *Aud:* Ac, Ga, Hs.

A nicely illustrated and produced art bulletin of some 48 pages. The articles are written by the curatorial staff and other scholars on works of art in the collection. It also includes shorter items on exhibits and related activities, and is particularly strong in Egyptian and classical art. The writing style is a bit ponderous. All of the material is fully documented. It may be beyond the average layman or high school student, although it is suitable for larger high school and public libraries. Required in academic art collections.

Bulletin of Art Therapy. See *American Journal of Art Therapy.*

The Burlington Magazine. 1903. m. $24. Benedict Nicolson. Burlington Magazine Publns. Ltd., 49 Park Lane, London, W1, England. Illus., index, adv. Vol. ends: Dec. Reprint: Kraus—Thomson.

Index: ArtI, BritHum, IBZ. *Bk. rev:* 6–8, 1,000 words, signed. *Aud:* Ac, Ga.

One of the basic magazines in the antique-artist-collector circle. The others: *Apollo, Connoisseur,* and lately, *Auction.* All are costly, all are published for the collector, private or institutional, and all feature marvelous illustrations, right down to the advertisements. *The Burlington* features news of recent museum acquisitions, and current and forthcoming international exhibitions. The worldwide emphasis makes this one of the standard art magazines in the field, but the high price and English base of publication somewhat limits its use in all but the larger academic art collections.

Classical America. 1971. 2/yr. $7.50 (Membership $15). Henry Hope Reed. Classical American Society, Inc., 10–41 51st Ave., Long Island City, New York, 11101. Illus. Sample ($2 each).

Bk. rev: 2–3, 750–1,000 words, signed, group reviews. *Aud:* Ac.

Editor Reed advises that "It is safe to boast that the society is probably the only one of its kind in the world, namely an organization dedicated to promoting the classical tradition in the arts." The nicely-printed 60-page magazine supports the society's purpose by featuring some 10 well-written articles—several with black and white illustrations—which point up the necessity of preserving what is left of classical American art and architecture. Reed's article, for example, is a survey of city planning, or the lack of, in New York City. Other writers examine the meaning of classicism in terms of life, literature, and music; current building styles; and the necessity to return to the classical pattern in architecture. Although the society has a bit of an axe to grind, the grinding is not offensive, and much can be learned. A good addition for both art and urban and city planning collections. Note: subscribers receive a newsletter, issued irregularly, called *Classical Forum.*

Cleveland Museum of Art. Bulletin. 1914. m. (Sept–June). Membership (Nonmembers $6). Merald E. Wrolstad, 11150 E. Blvd., Cleveland, Ohio 44160. Illus., index. Circ: 11,000. Microform: UM.

Indexed: ArtI. *Aud:* Ga, Ac.

A scholarly bulletin from one of the finest museums in the country. Each issue, which runs about 30 pages, has two lead articles written by museum staff about pieces in the museum's collection. Often these pieces are recent acquisitions. The articles are well illustrated with black and white photographs. One issue each year is devoted to an annual report. Should be in any large art collection, because the articles are often the only detailed discussions available of the individual works of art. (H.D.)

Connaissance des Arts. See Europe and Middle East/French Language Section.

The Connoisseur. 1901. m. $30. L.G. G. Ramsey. National Magazine Co., Ltd., Chestergate House, Vanxall Bridge Rd., London SW 1, England. Illus., adv. Microform: MF.

Indexed: ArtI, BritHum. *Bk. rev:* 8–10, length varies, signed. *Aud:* Ga, Ac.

Connoisseurs and collectors of international works of arts of all periods, antique furniture, silver, porcelain, and paintings will be interested in this magazine. It contains authoritative articles, illustrated in color and monochrome, on individual works of arts, special collections, biographies of artists, and contemporary art. More than half of each issue is composed of advertisements of art dealers and galleries, European and American. Includes sales news and exhibition news. There is a special section on exhibitions and recent acquisitions by American museums. While written for the wealthy collector, the illustrations and advertisements make this useful for both dreamer and art enthusiast. See also, *Apollo.*

Critica d'Arte. See Europe and Middle East/Italian Language Section.

Design. 1949. m. $10. C. H. Stanton. Council of Industrial Design, The Design Center, 28 Haymarket, London SW 1, England. Illus., index, adv. Microform: UM.

Indexed: ArtI, BritTech. *Aud:* Sa, Ac.

Not to be confused with the American magazine of the same name. It aims to promote excellence of design in everything produced by industry, from jewelry to the most mundane household objects. The magazine consists mainly of photographs and descriptions of products which have been chosen for their superior design. Short profiles of industrial designers and articles about special aspects of business are written by experts in design and industry. Of interest to designers, manufacturers, and students in this field.

Design; the magazine of creative art, for teachers, artists & craftsmen. 1899. bi-m. $4.50. Rita A. Cooper. Reviews Publishing Co., Inc., 1100 Waterway Blvd., Indianapolis, Ind. 46207. Illus., adv. Circ: 11,000. Microform: UM.

Indexed: RG. *Bk. rev:* Notes. *Aud:* Ac, Hs, Ejh.

A useful magazine of practical suggestions for teachers of art, from elementary school through college, interested in pottery, glass, textiles, painting, and sculpture. Deals with art appreciation, instructions, and hints on how to improve techniques and skills used in various crafts. Announcements of forthcoming art exhibits and competition news are included. Emphasis is on teaching and differs from the publisher's other magazine *Craft Horizons* (see Hobbies/Arts & Crafts section), which is primarily for the student. Next to *School Arts Magazine,* a useful secondary purchase for elementary and secondary schools, and should be in all school of education collections.

Design News; the design engineers's idea magazine. 1946. s-m. $20. K. F. Kircher. William M. Platt, Philadelphia, Pa. Subs. to: 270 St. Paul St., Denver, Colorado. 80206. Illus., index, adv. Circ: 106,000. Sample. Vol. ends: Dec.

Aud: Ac.

Primarily for the professional design engineer. Covers every aspect of design from small items to complete machinery. Averaging some 48 short articles per issue, the magazine "provides a wide range of proven design ideas in a concise, graphic form." All articles are illustrated, with four colors used for "perspective" pieces and "special reports." Only for specialized collections.

Design Quarterly. 1946. q. $5. Mildred Friedman. Walker Art Center, Vineland Pl., Minneapolis, Minn. 55403. Illus., index. Circ: 7,000. Vol. ends: Summer. Microform: UM.

Indexed: ArtI. *Aud:* Ga, Ac, Hs, Ejh.

Thanks to illustrations, this is one of the few art magazines which may be used profitably by almost any size or type of library. The low cost helps, too. Each issue presents a symposium upon a given theme from the design field. "The subject is previously agreed upon by the writer and editor and written especially for our publication." Writers are authorities in the field. The magazine is particularly valuable for its black and white illustrations—between 55 and 90 in a single number, even more in double issues. It averages 32 to 36 pages (48 to 64 for a double number) and does not include advertisements.

Detroit Institute of Arts. Bulletin. 1913. q. $3. 5200 Woodward Ave., Detroit, Mich. 48202. Illus., index. Circ: 10,000. Microform: UM. Reprint: Johnson.

Indexed: ArtI. *Aud:* Ga, Ac.

A handsomely printed and illustrated 40 to 50 page report of the Detroit Institute of Art, this covers all phases of the subject from the traditional to the modern. There are usually one or two major acquisition articles. Issues are occasionally devoted to exhibitions which are primarily concerned with the permanent collections. Specialists will want this along with the many other bulletins and programs issued by leading museums, while the numerous black and white illustrations will interest both the layman and the student. One of many museum bulletins, it ranks somewhat behind the *Metropolitan Museum of Art. Bulletin,* yet is among the best in the field. See also *Philadelphia Museum of Art. Bulletin.* A check of *Ulrich's International Periodicals Directory* will show which museums in the library's immediate area issue bulletins; these, of course, should be included in most local or regional collections. Incidentally, those indexed in *Art Index* tend to be better, but this is not always true and each should be checked individually.

Everyday Art. 1922. 3/yr. $1.25. Edward Mattil. American Crayon Co., Box 2067, Sandusky, Ohio

44870. Illus. Circ: 20,000. Sample. Vol. ends: Spring. Microform: UM.

Aud: Hs, Ejh.

A trade publication which features pictorial essays on the beauty of the color, forms, and structures found in nature and in everyday surroundings. Colors are related to designs in buildings, bridges, and motifs frequently used by adults and by children in art work. Would be welcomed by art teachers, elementary school teachers, and children.

Gebrauchsgraphik. See Europe and Middle East/German Language Section.

Goya. See Latin American and Chicano/Spanish Language Section.

Graphic Arts Monthly and the Printing Industry. 1929. m. $10. J. Hartsuch. Graphic Arts Publishing Co., 7373 N. Lincoln Ave., Chicago, Ill. 60646. Illus., adv. Circ: 61,000. Microform: UM.

Indexed: BusI, PhotoAb. *Aud:* Sa, Ac.

Illustrated news stories on new developments, techniques, and management procedures range from short, explanatory paragraphs to 1,000 to 1,500 word features. Nearly sixty-five percent of the magazine is devoted to advertising. Both the technical and management fields of the various areas of graphic arts are covered for management and supervisory personnel and craftsmen. Graphic arts students will also find the magazine of value.

Graphic Arts Progress. 1954. m. $18. Graphic Arts Research Center, Rochester Inst. of Technology, Rochester, New York 14623. Circ: 1,500.

Aud: Sa, Ac.

Important to libraries because of the "Graphic Arts Index," which closely analyzes the contents of some 150 periodicals under ten major headings, from the printing industry to education. It has a limited number of articles. This is a major contribution to bibliographic control and, as such, should be in every library with more than a minor interest in the graphic arts, printing, and publishing.

Graphis; international journal of graphic art and applied art. 1944. bi-m. $23.50. Walter Herdeg. Graphis Press, 45, Nuschelestr., 8001 Zurich, Switzerland. Illus., index, adv. Circ: 23,000. Sample.

Indexed: ArtI. *Bk. rev:* 3, 350 words. *Aud:* Ac, Ga. *Jv:* V.

Published in Switzerland in English, French, and German, this is the best known of all graphic arts periodicals. Each issue is literally a work of art in itself, and the reproductions are among the finest printed in any magazine. All articles are lavishly illustrated, often to the point that it is difficult to concentrate on the text. Coverage extends from exhibitions, artists, and awards, to typography, posters, advertising, and package design. Although directed to the graphic artist, it will be enjoyed by anyone in the arts. A required item in large academic and special libraries, and in any type or size library where there is a call for graphic arts material.

Illustrator Magazine. 1916. q. $3. Don L. Jardine. Art Instruction Schools, 500 S. Fourth St., Minneapolis, Minn. 55415. Illus., adv. Circ: 70,300. Sample.

Bk. rev: Notes. *Aud:* Ga, Hs.

Primarily for students in commercial art schools, but of some value for high schools, this magazine is in tabloid format. Editorial material concerns commercial art and related fields. Ideas, trends, and techniques are featured in the articles.

Industrial Design; designing for industry. 1954. 10/yr. $10. J. Roger Guilfoyle. Whitney Publns., 130 E. 59th St., New York, N.Y. 10012. Illus., adv. Circ: 13,000. Microform: UM.

Index: ArtI. *Bk. rev:* Notes. *Aud:* Ac, Hs.

Although a trade magazine, this has added dimension for the layman involved with good design. Every product from a can opener to an automobile is considered. Averaging some 100 pages, it is beautifully illustrated with photographs and line drawings, features short expository articles on all aspects of design. There are special issues, but the one of most interest to the layman (and many high school students) is the annual automotive number. Experts critically look at both the good and bad features in American and foreign car design. Other articles and sections touch on the bathroom, furniture for the average home, and specifications for new ideas in packaging and graphics. A good item for both the art and the general collection in larger libraries.

Italimuse Italic News. 1969. irreg. $1 per issue. Fred & Joanne Eager, Italimus, Inc., Grand Island, N.Y. 14072. Illus. Sample.

Bk. rev: 2–4, column. *Aud:* Ac, Ga, Hs.

Until 1969 there had been no regular magazine on calligraphy published in America. The Society of Italic Handwriting published a journal in London, but Italimus, Inc. issues a very useful journal for American calligraphy and especially italic devotees. Each issue has a biography of a well-known calligrapher with illustrations of his work, book reviews, information on writing implements, and useful tips for would-be italicists. (P.W.F.)

Italix, the Calligraphic Quarterly. 1971. q. $10. Haywood House, Box 279, Fair Lawn, N.J. 07410. Illus.

Bk. rev: Various number, length, signed. *Aud:* Ac, Ga.

Devoted to samples of writing, caligraphic implements, biographies, and book reviews. It is calligraphed throughout. The purpose is to support the art of calligraphy, indicate means and methods of teaching, and

show the benefits of a major art form. While particularly suited to calligraphers—especially those interested in chancery cursive—it will be of interest to a general audience as well as teachers responsible for any aspect of penmanship. (P.W.F.)

Journal of Glass Studies. 1959. a. $7. Paul N. Perrot. Journal of Glass Studies, The Corning Museum of Glass, Corning Glass Center, Corning, N.Y. 14830. Illus. Circ: 800–1,000.

Bk. rev: 2–3, lengthy, signed. *Aud:* Ac.

A learned annual journal devoted to the study of the art and history of glass from prehistoric to present times. The writers are curators, archaeologists, art historians and other experts from the diversified fields which are concerned with glass. A 25–page (average length) bibliography of the previous year's publications of books and articles on glass is of major importance for any library in this or allied fields. Of interest to anyone involved with the art and design of glass, as well as to the serious collector.

Marsyas. 1940. a. $5. J. J. Augustin, Locust Valley, N.Y. 11560. Illus. Circ: 500. Sample.

Index: ArtI. *Aud:* Ac.

A scholarly annual devoted to "studies in the history of art" and published by the Fine Arts Department of New York University. It frequently includes masters' theses among its well-documented articles. There are numerous black and white illustrations. Several abstracts of unpublished theses appear at the end of each issue. Only for large art collections.

Master Drawings; devoted exclusively to the study and illustration of drawings. 1963. q. $20. Felice Stampfle. Master Drawings Assn., Inc., 33 E. 36th St., New York, N.Y. 10016. Illus., index, adv. Circ: 950. Vol. ends: Winter.

Index: ArtI. *Bk. rev:* 2–3, lengthy, signed. *Aud:* Ac.

On the same high plane as the *Journal of Aesthetics and Art Criticism*, but concerned solely with drawings. There are one or two long (10 to 20 pages), well-documented articles devoted to the study of the drawings and cartoons of an individual artist, a specific collection, etc. Annotated lists of recent publications in the field appear in each issue. In addition, there are about six "notes" (4 to 5 pages each) dealing with the works of an artist, or with a single project or work of art. Its beautiful typography, good paper, attractive layout, and 50 to 60 splendid reproductions of drawings make it a quality publication suitable for any library. (See Cultural-Social Studies section for *Journal of Aesthetics*.)

Metro. See Europe and Middle East/Italian Language Section.

Metropolitan Museum of Art. Bulletin, N.S. 1942. 6/yr. Membership (Nonmembers, $7.50). Katharine H. B. Stoddert. Metropolitan Museum of Art, Fifth Ave.

and 82nd St., New York, N.Y. 10028. Illus., index. Circ: 42,000. Sample. Vol. ends: June. Microform: UM.

Indexed: ArtI. *Aud:* Ga, Ac, Hs.

One of the best art museum bulletins, this contains articles about the museum's own holdings, its activities, news of exhibitions, and special events in the art world. Most articles are too short for reference, but frequently one finds here the only published discussion of the material. The *Bulletin* is never dull and gives an intimate glimpse of what goes on behind the scenes of the nation's largest and richest museum of art. A secondary, important aspect, for high school libraries and up, is the fine illustrations and drawings supplementing the text.

Mid-Atlantic Graphic Arts Review. 1938. m. $7. Philip Katcher. North American Publishing Co., 134 N. 13th St., Philadelphia, Pa. 19107. Illus., adv. Circ: 5,000.

Aud: Sa.

This review has in-depth reports on printing markets and how to reach them, creative uses of paper and inks, printing direct mail promotion, profiles of firms and individuals, as well as industry and association news. Edited for readers in the various graphic arts trade services in the middle-Atlantic region exclusively.

Mobilia; for furniture, art handicraft, art and architecture. 1955. m. $25. Mette Bratvold, 3070 Snekkersten, Denmark. Illus., adv. Circ: 6,000. Vol. ends: Dec.

Aud: Ac.

A Danish magazine with text in four languages, including English, this is probably the world's leading journal for new concepts in the design of furniture, handicrafts, and materials used in day-to-day living. Also includes sections on art and architecture. It is a visual delight, as much care going into the design of the multi-colored illustrations and layouts as into the preparation of the articles. The photography is a study in itself. In that the format is almost as important as the contents, this can be compared favorably with *Graphis* as an outstanding example of the graphic arts. A necessity in any medium to large-sized art or advanced home economics or design collection.

Museum. See Free Magazines Section.

Museum News. 1952. m. (Sept.–June). $15. Michael W. Robbins, Roberta Faul. Amer. Assn. of Museums, 2306 Massachusetts Ave., N.W., Washington, D.C. 20008. Illus., index, adv. Circ: 5,500. Vol. ends: June.

Bk. rev: 1, 1,000 words, signed. *Aud:* Ac.

Similar to the British *Museums Journal* in its purpose and scope. It is intended for the museum profession, but has a wide lay readership. Information retrieval, recruitment of staff, education and the museum appear to be universal topics. This magazine offers additional information on aesthetics and solutions to problems of displays and exhibitions with "Technical Supplements" that discuss various problems in museology. There are many illustrations. Features include announcements of current exhibitions and lists of publications by American museums.

Museums Journal. 1901. q. $7.35. Colin Sizer. The Museums Assn., 87 Charlotte St., London W1P 2BX, England. Illus., index, adv. Circ: 2,200. Sample. Vol. ends: March.

Indexed: ArtI. *Bk. rev:* 8–12, 500–1,000 words, signed. *Aud:* Ac.

Presents an exchange of ideas and information among members of the museum profession both in Great Britain and in other countries. Subjects discussed include: information retrieval, education, various newly built—or redesigned—museums or art galleries, problems of display, and preservation, management, etc. Of value to museum and art gallery personnel, specialist and university libraries.

National Sculpture Review. 1951. q. $4. Adolph Block, National Sculpture Soc., 250 E. 51st St., New York, N.Y. 10012. Illus., adv. Circ: 6,000. Sample. Vol. ends: Winter. Microform: MF.

Indexed: ArtI. *Bk. rev:* 4, 150 words, signed. *Aud:* Ga, Ac.

One of the few periodicals devoted solely to sculpture, meant to spread the knowledge of good sculpture. Each issue reviews work in a particular field or technique. Many high quality photographs and articles are included. The *Review* features news of exhibitions and award-winning examples of sculpture. Primarily for medium to large public and academic collections.

Oeil. See Europe and Middle East/French Language Section.

Oriental Art; devoted to the study of all forms of Oriental art. N.S. 1955. q. $3. Mary Tregear. Oriental Art Magazine Ltd., 12 Ennerdale Rd., Richmond, Surrey, England. Illus., index, adv. Vol. ends: Winter.

Indexed: ArtI. *Bk. rev:* 3–4, length varies. *Aud:* Ac.

Scholarly articles about individual works of art, history, and legends are written by specialists, and illustrated with black and white plates. A bibliography section lists books and periodicals by geographic areas of the Orient. Well-written essays review exhibitions.

Pantheon. See Europe and Middle East/German Language Section.

Philadelphia Museum of Art. Bulletin. 1903. q. $4. George H. Marcus. The Museum, Box 7646, Philadelphia, Pa. 19101. Illus. Circ: 13,000. Microform: UM.

Indexed: ArtI. *Aud:* Ga, Ac.

Concentrating on a show, artist, period, etc., each issue features one main article with two or three related pieces. Illustrated with 50 to 100 black and white reproductions. The low price, and the in-depth coverage, assure a place for the *Bulletin* in any medium to large-sized art collection. Art teachers, too, will find the illustrations extremely useful for class work.

Pictures on Exhibit; world wide reviews of the art shows. 1937. m. (Oct.–June). $5. Charles Z. Offin. Pictures Publishing Co., 30 E. 60th St., New York, N.Y. 10022. Illus., adv. Circ: 24,000.

Aud: Ga, Ac.

Primarily a monthly report and criticism of art exhibitions both here and abroad this journal is profusely illustrated with black and white photographs. The illustrations serve to introduce both the student and the general reader to some of the world's finest art. Articles are staff-written, objective and considered quite accurate. A useful addition for any library where art is of particular interest.

Print. 1939. bi-m. $12.50. Robert Cadel, President. RC Publns., Inc., 19 W. 44 St., New York, N.Y. 10036. Illus., index, adv. Vol. ends: Dec.

Indexed: ArtI. *Aud:* Ac, Ga.

Though the central theme of this excellent magazine is graphic design in all its applications, there is decided emphasis on the role of art in advertising. Just leafing through any given issue is a lesson on how profoundly this use of art has penetrated our minds, largely owing to television. In this sense, this very specialized publication has broad appeal. Techniques of graphic design and photography are discussed in a way that is accessible to the layman as well as informative to the professional. However, in spite of the journal's specialized focus, the range of topics covered outside the field of advertising seems to be unlimited. Here are some of the topics encountered at random: "The New American Heritage Dictionary," (its use of words with pictures), the creative potential of computers, (computer-made drawings, etc.), signs and posters in relation to the urban environment, and McLuhan on printed versus electronic media. The advertising in the magazine itself is handled the way one might expect from a publication concerned with the subject of advertising. That is, the advertisements become an integral part of the magazine's layout. There are annotations of books in the field, though they may not be termed reviews. This is certainly a leading journal in its field and is highly recommended for academic and large public libraries. (H.D.)

Print Collector's Newsletter. 1970. bi-m. $12. Judith Goldman. Print Collector's Newsletter, Inc., 205 E. 78 St., New York, N.Y., 10021. Illus. Sample. Vol. ends: Jan./Feb.

Bk. rev: 4–5, 800–1,500 words. *Aud:* Ga, Ac. *Jv:* V.

As noted in its title, this is a newsletter, in looseleaf format, punched for a three-ring notebook. Quality and quantity are packed into 24 pages. There are several articles. Usually one is an interview with a contemporary artist, but on occasion attention is given to a historical figure. The May/June 1971 issue, for example, featured Albrecht Durer. There was an article on "Durer's Representation of 'Christ in Limbo'," a brief biography of the artist, a discussion of his work, material about museum shows featuring Durer's work, and an annotated exhibition calendar. Regular features are "International Auction Review," "Prints and Portfolios Published," "News of the Print World," and about four to five detailed book reviews. If the price can be justified, it is highly recommended for all but the smaller libraries. (F.B.)

Prisme International. 1968. bi-m. $20. Overseas Publishers' Representatives, 424 Madison Ave., New York, N.Y. 10017. Illus., adv. Reprint: Kraus.

Aud: Ac, Sa.

A 72 to 80 page graphic arts French publication with text in French, German, and English. But the text is of little importance, as most of each issue is given over to black and white (and some colored) illustrations of materials used in advertising posters, packages, typography, logotypes, etc. The scope is international and its primary interest to Americans will be the coverage of European trends. While it does not measure up to the luxurious approach of *Graphis*, it is an excellent second choice for large academic and specialized libraries.

Revue de L'Art. See Europe and Middle East/French Language Section.

School Arts Magazine; the magazine for art education. 1901. m. 10/yr. $8. George F. Horn. Davis Publns., Inc., Printers Bldg., Worcester, Mass. 01608. Illus., adv. Circ: 32,000. Microform: UM. Reprint: Abrahams.

Indexed: EdI, RG. *Bk. rev:* Notes. *Aud:* Hs, Ejh.

Primarily valuable to elementary and secondary school teachers as a source of inspiration for creative art projects. The 10 to 12 articles describe a great variety of art techniques and suggest means of presenting them to classes. An occasional piece discusses curriculum or educational philosophy. Contributors are drawn from art faculty and museum staff members. General format is pleasing, with each article accompanied by many well-reproduced illustrations consisting of photos and art reproductions in black and white. A yearly buyers' guide of supplies and tools and a directory of suppliers appear in the February issue. A first or second purchase in all elementary and secondary schools' professional collections, and equally important in schools of education.

Stained Glass; devoted to the craft of painted and stained glass. 1906. q. $5. J. G. Lloyd. Stained Glass

Assn. of America, 3600 University Dr., Fairfax, Va. 22030. Illus., index, adv. Circ: 2,100. Sample. Vol. ends: Winter.

Bk. rev: 1, 1 page, signed. *Aud:* Ac.

The only popular periodical devoted exclusively to the ancient craft of stained glass and related topics. There are brief articles about craftsmen and outstanding examples of ancient and contemporary work. Illustrations are good to excellent. Advertisements of suppliers to the trade and a convenient list of sources of supplies are given, as are announcements of competitions and scholarship news. Will be of some interest to antique collectors, but primarily for specialized collections. See also *Journal of Glass Studies.*

Studies in Art Education; a journal of issues and research in art education. 1959. 3/yr. $4.50. Mary Rouse. National Art Education Assn., 1201 16th St., N.W., Washington, D.C. 20036. Illus., adv. Circ: 2,800. Reprint: Kraus.

Indexed: CIJE, EdI. *Bk. rev:* Various number, length. *Aud:* Ac, Hs, Ejh.

Of interest to all art educators from the elementary schools through the university. Content concentrates mostly on issues and research in art education. Research studies on important topics of concern to teachers of art are discussed at length. Advertising includes various art supplies available and schools of art. To be used mainly by an instructor.

Studio International. 1893. m. $23. Peter Townsend. W&J Mackay & Co., 37 Museum St., London W6 1, England. Subs. to: Eastern News, 155 W. 15th St., New York, N.Y. 10011. Illus., index, adv. Circ: 12,500. Sample. Vol. ends: June, Dec. Microform: UM.

Indexed: Art I, IBZ. *Bk. rev:* 3, 750 words, signed. *Aud:* Ga, Ac.

A well-balanced general art magazine which has a number of useful features for any library: (1) there are three supplements per year which consider new books in the field; (2) every six months there is a prints and lithographs supplement; (3) there are some 60 black and white illustrations per issue, as well as numerous color plates. Although published in England, it features American and European critics as well as British writers. Emphasis is on the twentieth century, but there are a number of background articles which focus on the heritage of the past in sculpture, painting, criticism, education, etc. Regular departments include reviews of exhibitions, news of sales, personal notes, and quarterly supplements which cover new art books, prints, graphic design, and the like. The style of writing is much above average for an art magazine—i.e., a minimum of jargon and a clarity of thought not often associated with modern art criticism. A worthwhile addition for any medium to large-sized art collection in a public or academic library.

ASTROLOGY

American Astrology. 1933. m. $7. Joanne Clancy. Clancy Publns., Inc., 2505 N. Alvernon Way, Tucson, Ariz. 85712. Illus., index, adv. Circ: 130,000. Sample. Vol. ends: Feb.

Bk. rev: Occasional, 1,500 words, signed. *Aud:* Ga.

A general approach to astrology, meant for both the student of the age of Aquarius and the average reader. If the reader is a believer, this is his or her first choice. And even those who fail to take astrology seriously will find much in a 112-page issue to interest them. There are a number of well-written articles. Departments and, of course, monthly guides for the various signs are included. Advertising is kept to a minimum. Such short items as "astro weight hints" and "fishing by moon signs" indicate that the editor carefully tries to have something for everyone. This certainly can be recommended for most public libraries as a fun or serious item, depending on where you stand.

And in case you think this is a joke or a come-on, be sure to read Sylvia Carroll's article, "Astrology's Comeback" in the November, 1971 issue.

American Federation of Astrologers. Bulletin. 1932. m. Membership (Libraries, $15). AFA, 6 Library Court, S.E., Washington, D.C. 20003.

Bk. rev: Various number, length, signed. *Aud:* Sa.

A report and a constant source of book reviews on all aspects of astrology. The sponsoring organization is made up of professional astrologers. The result is a magazine which is strong on technical data quite beyond the average reader. Book reviews tend to concentrate on esoteric items which are as involved as the journal's writers. The result is a publication which should be taken by a library with a serious interest in astrology. Others should bypass.

The Aquarian Agent; for the contemporary astrologer. 1970. m. $6. Henry Weingarten. N.Y. Astrology Center, 306 E. 6th St., New York, N.Y. 10003. Illus. Sample.

Bk. rev: 2–5, 150–250 words, signed. *Aud:* Ga.

Comparatively speaking, this is the "little magazine" of the astrology world. Its 45 or so pages feature such items as "astrology and literature;" an astrologer's song by Rudyard Kipling; a long, detailed dissertation on Neptune; a column on handwriting analysis; a bibliography of medical astrology; and other items guaranteed to delight the intelligent man or woman. It is not for the reader who wants to know his immediate fortune or misfortune for the days ahead. This nicely edited, relatively well-printed magazine should be an answer for libraries who want something in this area, but hesitate to take on the more popular magazines such as *Horoscope.* Suitable too, for advanced high schools.

Astrological Index. 1970. bi-a. $2.50. Mildred E. Kettell, 153 Main St., Yarmouth Port, Mass. 02675.

While not properly a magazine, this is included here because of its high interest for anyone who follows astrology, more particularly material in *Horoscope* (1954–1962) and *American Astrology* (1956–1959). The compiler and publisher of the 40 to 50 page mimeographed index points out that the next issue will cover other years and other journals. Arrangement is chronological with an author-subject index. While far from professional, this is an indexing effort which might be brought to the attention of individuals where the library does not want to buy.

Astrology; the astrologer's quarterly. 1926. $5. R. C. Davison. Theosophical Soc. in England, Astrological Lodge, 50 Gloucester Pl., London W.1, England. Illus., index, adv. Circ: 600. Sample.

Bk. rev: 1–2, 150–200 words, signed. *Aud:* Ga.

The basic "little magazine" of scientific astrology in England. Tied as it is to the Theosophical Society, it is a serious, scientific effort to harness astrology for man's spiritual betterment. It has enjoyed a rather long life and a limited audience, but exercised a major influence on the astrologers of the western world. An important item for larger collections.

Horoscope. 1935. m. $6. Edward A. Wagner. Dell Publishing Co., Inc., 750 Third Ave., New York, N.Y. 10017. Illus., index, adv. Circ: 225,000. Sample. Vol. ends: Dec.

Aud: Ga.

Along with *American Astrology*, the basic popular astrology magazine in the United States. The two look alike, right down to using newsprint paper and the same general-sized format. Astrology fans, however, tend to favor one over the other. *Horoscope* seems to be a little more orderly, a trifle more geared to the reader who takes his or her astrology seriously. The writing style, though, is about the same as *American Astrology*, requiring no great degree of sophistication or education to grasp. However, let it be said that both magazines do require some knowledge of astrology—at least for the articles. When it comes to such things as the daily guides it is a matter of faith. *Horoscope*, for example, gives a summary of each of the signs, then a facing "daily activity guide." Of the two it is difficult to say which would be better for a library. It is a matter of personal preference, and I would send for samples before entering subscriptions.

Kosmos. 1968. m. Membership $15. Julienne P. Sturm. Intl. Soc. for Astrological Research, 89 Clinton Ave., Montclair, N.J. 07042. Illus., index, adv. Circ: 500. Sample. Vol. ends: Aug.

Bk. rev: 1, 2 pages, signed. *Aud:* Ga.

A serious scientific effort to get to the meaning of astrology on an international basis. Contributors are from all parts of the world, and each 40 page offset issue features four or five articles. The editor states: "Its major function is to promote and facilitate serious research in the field. It publishes not only reports of projects sponsored by the Society's International Research Council, but news of all studies in the discipline which come to the attention of its editorial staff." Each issue features a list of conferences to be held by the ISAR. A major addition for the person who takes astrology seriously, or the library which is seeking a balance of materials.

Sybil Leek's Astrology. 1942. m. $7. Sybil Leek. Twin World Publns., Inc. 155 E. 55th St., New York, N.Y. 10022. Illus.

Bk. rev: Notes. *Aud:* Ga.

One of the better popular astrology journals. The editor covers all aspects of the science from daily horoscopes to ideal recipes for health and for the sign under which the reader was born. A good deal of the material depends upon some knowledge of astrology, but there are simplified instructions too. Some claim this is the best of its type—at least in terms of offering almost everything of interest to the astrology fan.

ASTRONOMY

Basic Periodicals:

Hs: *Sky and Telescope;* Ga: *Sky and Telescope* (Note: Large public libraries should also consider *Mercury* and *Astronomy and Space*.) Jc: *Sky and Telescope; Mercury;* Ac: *Astronomical Journal; Astrophysical Journal; Astronomical Society of the Pacific. Publications.*

Basic Abstracts and Indexes

Astronomy and Astrophysics Abstracts

Introduction

Viewed with the naked eye or elaborate telescopic equipment, celestial objects have been the study of amateurs since the history of mankind. Moreover, astronomy is probably the only science left in which amateurs can and do make some contributions to the field.

The range of periodicals in this section extends from popular to more sophisticated publications still within the purview of the amateur, to a sampling of research journals for academic collections. Of necessity titles have been restricted to those available in English. Thus, a corpus of fine, foreign publications has been omitted: the German *Die Sterne* and French *l'Astronomie*, both nonspecialist periodicals, usually deserve a place in academic libraries. Similarly, research journals such as the venerable *Astronomische Nachrichten* (first published in 1821), to name but one, would most likely be found in good research libraries. Reports from observatories were considered beyond the scope of this collection and have also been omitted.

American Astronomical Society. Bulletin. 1969. q. $8. H. M. Gurin. American Inst. of Physics (for the American Astronomical Soc.), 335 East 45th St., New York, N.Y. 10017. Index. Sample. Vol. ends: Dec.

Indexed: Ast&AstroAb. *Aud:* Sa, Ac.

Prior to 1969, much of the material in this bulletin appeared in the *Astronomical Journal* (see below). Due to increased publication and space requirements, an entire journal has now been dedicated to the abstracts of papers presented at meetings of the Society and its divisions, reports of observatories, and miscellaneous news and notes of professional interest. Since a number of the papers given at these symposia may never achieve full-blown publication, or may experience delays of years before they appear in print, the *Bulletin* would be a necessary acquisition for university libraries supporting research in the field. Note: members of the Society receive it gratis.

Annales d'Astrophysique. See *Astronomy and Astrophysics.*

Astronomical Institutes of the Netherlands. Bulletin. See *Astronomy and Astrophysics.*

Astronomical Journal. 1849. m. 10/yr. $40. L. Woltjer and N. H. Baker. American Inst. of Physics (for the American Astronomical Society), 335 E. 45th St., New York, N.Y. 10017. Illus., index. Circ: 2,200. Sample. Vol. ends: Dec. Refereed. Reprint: Johnson.

Indexed: Ast&AstroAb, ChemAb, MathR, Met&GeoAb, SCI. *Aud:* Sa, Ac.

Founded by the eminent nineteenth century astronomer, B. A. Gould, and sponsored by a highly distinguished society, the journal is one of the world's leading astronomical publications. Its range is broad and original research reports cover both theoretical and observational work. Contributions appear in all branches of the science, e.g., asteroids and meteorites, astrometry, celestial mechanics, comets, cosmology, galactic structures, instrumentation, and radio astronomy. (Note: Papers devoted to studies in astrophysics generally come out in the other major U.S. research journal, *Astrophysical Journal,* annotated below.) A first-choice research selection for the development of any academic collection.

Astronomical Society of the Pacific. Publications. 1889. bi-m. $12. D. H. McNamara. Astronomical Soc. of the Pacific, N. Amer. Hall, California Academy of Sciences, San Francisco, Calif. 94118. Illus., index. Circ: 2,000. Sample. Vol. ends: no. 6. Refereed. Reprint: Kraus.

Indexed: Ast&AstroAb, ChemAb, MathR, SciAb, SCI. *Aud:* Sa, Ac.

In the past few years, this journal, breaking with

over 80 years of tradition, has restyled and restructured its *Publications* to elevate the periodical to the ranks of a scholarly journal featuring refereed articles on original research in the astronomical sciences. All branches of the field are considered. In addition to observational reports on astronomy, papers are published on astrophysics, radio astronomy, solar atmospheres, cosmology, galaxies, and the like. Invited review papers, by well-known authorities on subjects of topical importance, are also carried. Selected issues contain, as well, abstracts of papers presented at meetings of the association, plus some comet notes. Nonspecialist material, which formerly appeared in the *Publications,* is now contained in *Mercury* (see below), the new, nontechnical periodical of this organization. Most academic libraries will want to subscribe to this authoritative research journal of an old and prominent astronomical association.

Astronomy and Astrophysics. 1969. m. 6v/yr. $231. S. R. Pottasch. Springer-Verlag, 175 Fifth Ave., New York, N.Y. 10010. Illus., index, adv. Sample. Refereed.

Indexed: Ast&AstroAb, ChemAb, MathR, Met&GeoAb, SCI, SciAb. *Aud:* Sa, Ac.

Under the aegis of the European Southern Observatory (ESO) and a number of other European scientific organizations, the journal was formed by the merger of five excellent research publications: *Annales d'Astrophysique* (France), *Astronomical Institutes of the Netherlands. Bulletin, Bulletin Astronomique* (France), *Journal des Observateurs* (France), and *Zeitschrift für Astrophysik* (Germany). Research papers, covering all aspects of astronomy and astrophysics, are subdivided into such areas as stars, galactic structures, cosmology, the Sun, plasmas, planetary systems, celestial mechanics, and instruments and data processing. Theoretical, observational, and instrumental papers are published. The common language for the journal is English, although some papers may appear in French or German. Representing a powerful, international amalgmate of research organizations, the journal is an important acquisition for all research collections of university libraries.

For a small additional sum, subscribers may also obtain *Astronomy and Astrophysics Supplement Series* (m., Springer-Verlag, $15), which contains lengthy and highly specialized reports, frequently with considerable tabular material or observational data.

Astronomy and Astrophysics Abstracts. See Abstracts and Indexes Section.

Astronomy and Space. 1971. q. £2.50. Patrick Moore. David and Charles, S. Devon House, Newton Abbot, Devon, England. Illus., index. Circ: 2,000. Sample. Vol. ends: no. 4. Refereed.

Bk. rev: 6,100 words, signed. *Aud:* Sa, Ac, Ga.

The prodigiously prolific Patrick Moore, well known

for his popularizations of advances in astronomy and space (including a successful BBC series), has launched a new quarterly on this same subject. The thrust of the periodical is toward the amateur astronomer, yet the contents are not the garden variety, tips-for-amateurs type. Rather, its focus is on long reviews, and treatment of topics in depth, all of which are contributed by authorities in the field. The first volume's subject matter varied from a review of space research to "Simple Mathematics for Astronomy Exams," and a technical description of the world's largest telescope. One issue also carried a translation by Mr. Moore of part of an out-of-print monograph. Features vary in length from 6 to 20 pages; photos are black and white. News, notes, and an evening sky map also make up part of each issue. The periodical's tutorial aspects seem excellent, and the publication appears to rest in a category between a somewhat popular, yet scholarly periodical, and the highly technical review journal. Recommended for all types of academic libraries, and large public libraries supporting a clientele of amateur astronomers.

Astrophysical Journal. 1895. s–m. $65. Helmut A. Abt (Part I) and Donald Osterbook (Part II). Univ. of Chicago Press, 5801 Ellis Ave., Chicago, Ill. 60637. Illus., index. Circ: 1,489. Sample. Vol. ends: Dec. Refereed. Microform: UM. Reprint: Johnson.

Indexed: Ast&AstroAb, ChemAb, MathR, Met& GeoAb, SCI, SciAb. *Aud:* Sa, Ac.

Published with the collaboration of the American Astronomical Society, the journal is one of the foremost in its field. Research reports encompass the entire spectrum of astrophysics, with emphasis on spectroscopy, cosmology, nuclear physics, solar physics, galactic structure, stellar and planetary atmospheres, and theoretical astronomy. Two parts appear semi-monthly: Part I, the journal proper, contains full-length research papers; Part II, "Letters to the Editor," consists of urgent communications in need of quick dissemination. Still a third publication, the *Astrophysical Journal Supplement Series* (irreg., $16/yr., Univ. Chicago Press), produces papers too lengthy to appear in the *Journal.* Frequently one paper of monographic length comprises an entire issue. *Astrophysical Journal,* in combination with the excellent *Astronomical Journal,* would indeed be the basis of any beginning research collection in this field.

Astrophysical Letters. 1967. m. $21/v.; $8.50/v. for individuals. Alan Maxwell and Evry Schatzman. Gordon and Breach Science Publishers, 440 Park Ave. S., New York, N.Y. 10016. Illus., index. Sample. Vol. ends: June, Dec. Refereed. Microform: Gordon and Breach.

Indexed: Ast&AstroAb; SCI. *Aud:* Sa, Ac.

The general field of astrophisics has undergone enormous advances in the last two decades, and this express, letter-type journal attempts to publish noteworthy research in progress within four to six weeks after receipt of manuscript. All areas of astrophysics are covered; communications are either theoretical or observational. Mainly for research libraries. Note: not to be confused with the "letters" portion of *Astrophysical Journal,* generally cited as *Astrophys. J. Letters.*

Astrophysics and Space Science. 1968. m. 5v./yr. $36.12/v. Zdenek Kopal. D. Reidel Publishing Co., P.O. Box 17, Dordrecht, Holland. Illus., index, adv. Sample. Refereed.

Indexed: Ast&AstrAb, ChemAb, Met&GeoAb, NuclSciAb, SCI, SciAb. *Bk. rev:* 6–7, 100–200 words, signed. *Aud:* Sa, Ac.

Research papers which appear in this authoritative, international journal are dedicated to the entire field of astrophysics (stellar, galactic, extragalactic), particularly in those areas which have been enhanced by other investigations in space research, e.g., satellite astronomy. Excluded from the journal are papers dealing with the Sun and Moon. These subjects are covered by two other Reidel publications discussed below, *The Moon* and *Solar Physics.* Important for space science collections, as well as astrophysics, in university libraries.

British Astronomical Association. Journal. 1890. 6/yr. $10. Colin Ronan. British Astronomical Assn., Burlington House, Piccadilly, London W1 VONL, England. Illus., index, adv. Circ: 6,000. Vol. ends: October. Refereed.

Indexed: SciAb. *Bk. rev:* 5–6, 300–700 words, signed. *Aud:* Sa, Ac.

Sponsored by an association fostering "popular interest in astronomy," the official publication of the Society caters to the needs of its membership at all levels of sophistication. Issues offer a good blend of technical and nontechnical material, including well-written historical essays, discussions of instrumentation, tutorials for beginners, and observational sections reporting on the Moon, meteors, radio astronomy, etc. An interesting department, "Notes from Other Journals," culls significant papers from the sophisticated research periodicals and digests these for the membership. Of course, issues also contain news of the association. Well within the technical grasp of amateur astronomers, the periodical would be a valuable choice for academic libraries supporting undergraduate interests.

Bulletin Astronomique. See *Astronomy and Astrophysics.*

Comments on Astrophysics and Space Physics. 1969. bi–m. $35. A. G. W. Cameron. Gordon and Breach Science Publishers, Inc., 440 Park Ave. S., New York, N.Y. 10016. Illus., index. Sample. Vol. ends: Nov/Dec. Refereed.

Indexed: Ast&AstroAb. *Aud:* Sa, Ac.

Part C of the series *Comments on Modern Physics*, critical reviews of trends in present-day physics research. (See Physics section for other titles in this series.) In essence, the periodical consists of five or six short articles contributed by a regular board of "correspondents," i.e., prominent, international authorities representing all areas of astro- or space physics. The authors (frequently discussing their own research) not only review the current literature, but raise questions concerning further work or comment on ambiguous evidence. Topics chosen for discussion, e.g., pulsar theory, cosmic rays, are usually those of timely interest to a wide readership. Bibliographies, although brief, do pinpoint key papers in the field. Serving as an excellent point of departure for students, the publication also provides a tutorial-type review for professionals. These *Comments*, and the entire series, are highly recommended for academic libraries interested in this field.

Icarus. 1962. bi-m. 2v./yr. $30/v. Carl Sagan. Academic Press, Inc., 111 Fifth Ave., New York, N.Y. 10003. Illus., index, adv. Sample. Refereed.

Indexed: Ast&AstroAb, ChemAb, SCI, SciAb. *Bk. rev:* 3–5, 500–1,000 words, signed. *Aud:* Sa, Ac.

Having selected a single theme, the journal attempts to draw together scientific works on the subject: in chemistry, physics, geology, or any other technical area contributing to the knowledge of our solar system. Research papers deal with topics such as the chemical classification of meteorites, study of the atmosphere of Jupiter, the topography of Mars, analysis of Apollo samples from the Moon, etc. In addition to scholarly contributions, the periodical carries two regular departments: (1) scientific meetings are reviewed by lengthy and informative accounts, and (2) running bibliographies are produced of the literature; some of these are supplied by the Air Force Cambridge Research Labs., and others indicate research activities in the USSR. An important research journal for university collections.

Journal des Observateur. See *Astronomy and Astrophysics.*

Journal for the History of Astronomy. 1970. q. $25. M. A. Hoskin. Science History Publns., c/o M. A. Hoskin, Churchill College, Cambridge Univ., Cambridge, CB3 OD5, England. Dist. by: Neale W. Watson, Academic Publications, 21 West St., New York, N.Y. 10016. Illus., index, adv. Circ: 2,000. Sample. Refereed.

Indexed: Ast&AstroAb. *Bk. rev:* 5, 500–1,000 words, signed. *Aud:* Sa, Ac.

Although snatches of the history of astronomy are published in a large number of periodicals, this is still the first scholarly publication devoted exclusively to the field. The journal includes papers on astrophysics and cosmology, the ancillary fields of navigation, time-keeping, and geography. A distinguished editorial advisory board, well represented by international authorities, has provided an auspicious beginning for the publication. There are no restrictions on time periods, and contributions range from earliest civilization to the present. Included in each issue is a section on source or other archival material invaluable to researchers. Good and lengthy book reviews are an important feature, too. Necessary for any history of science collection, the periodical is also recommended for the astronomy collections of academic libraries.

Mercury. 1972. bi-m. $6.50. D. H. McNamara. Astronomical Soc. of the Pacific, N. Amer. Hall, California Academy of Sciences, San Francisco, Calif. 94118. Illus., index. Sample. Vol. ends: no. 6. Refereed.

Bk. rev: 2, 250 words, signed. *Aud:* Sa, Ac, Ga, Hs.

With the cessation, in 1971, of *Astronomical Society of the Pacific. Leaflets,* dedicated to promoting interest in and interpreting progress in the astronomical sciences on a popular level, the Society has issued this new title to supplant material formerly carried by the *Leaflets.* Issues provide a mixture of authoritative feature articles by specialists on some area of astronomical work (toned down for laymen and students), or history of astronomy, along with announcements of professional interest, news of its organization, selected teaching aids, and personal notes. Added extras for observers are "aspects of heavens" and an evening sky map, both useful guides for amateur astronomers. The Astronomical Society of the Pacific has carried on a long tradition of disseminating information regarding advances in the field, both through lectures, films, and published material. Its present publication, though not having quite the scope of *Sky and Telescope,* deserves the support of both academic and public libraries. Amateur astronomy clubs will be particularly happy to welcome another periodical to the fold. (See also *Astronomical Society of the Pacific. Publications,* for the technical journal of the Society.)

Moon. 1969. q. $37.20. H. Alfven, Z. Kopal, and H. C. Urey. D. Reidel Publishing Co., P.O. Box 17, Dordrecht, Holland. Illus., index, adv. Sample. Vol. ends: No. 4. Refereed.

Indexed: Ast&AstroAb, ChemAb, IntAe, Met&GeoAb, NucSciAb, SciAb. *Bk. rev:* Occasional, signed. *Aud:* Sa, Ac.

The memorable mission of Apollo 11 spawned this research publication, devoted exclusively to lunar investigations. Despite its "selenophilic" specialty, the journal is interdisciplinary enough and reports on research not only in optical and radio astronomy, and astronautics, but also on the chemistry, geology and space physics of the Moon. Observational studies are both ground-based and spacecraft oriented. An important feature of the publication is a bibliography section which draws together related literature on the subject. An authoritative, international editorial board assures equal numbers of U.S. and USSR contributions. For university libraries.

Observatory. 1877. bi-m. $9. Ed.Bd. Royal Greenwich Observatory, Herstmonceux Castle, Halsham, Sussex, England. Illus., index, adv. Sample. Vol. ends: Dec. Refereed.

Indexed: Ast&AstroAb, ChemAb, Met&GeoAb, SciAb. *Bk. rev:* 4–5, 200–450 words, signed. *Aud:* Sa, Ac.

One of the older astronomical periodicals, the publication currently provides an overview of recent research and development in astronomy and related fields. About two to three short technical articles appear in each slim issue, followed by brief notes from observatories, scientific correspondence, and a book review section. The magazine also makes a full report on papers read at meetings of the Royal Astronomical Society and the discussions thereon. Reviews of other symposia are also included from time to time. Although not of the sophistication of some of the other research journals, the publication is nonetheless valuable to academic libraries for its reports of current developments.

Royal Astronomical Journal of Canada. 1907. bi-m. $12. Ian Halliday. Royal Astronomical Soc. of Canada, 252 College St., Toronto 2B, Ont., Canada. Illus., index. Circ: 3,000. Vol. ends: no. 6. Refereed.

Indexed: Ast&AstroAb, ChemAb, SciAb, SCI. *Bk. rev:* 3–4, 400–500 words, signed. *Aud:* Sa, Ac.

Available through membership to the Society (which is open to anyone interested in astronomy), the journal provides a good blend of articles and reports, varying in technicality, for students, specialists, and amateurs. Lead articles, contributed by authorities, report on current advances, supply historical essays, or provide technical papers and tutorial reviews of major developments in the astronomical sciences. Monthly departments, again directed toward amateurs and professionals, carry notes from planetaria and observatories, Variable Star Notes (supplied by the American Association of Variable Star Observers), and notes from Canadian scientists, as well as information for amateurs. Selected abstracts of the proceedings of the Society are also published. A useful *Observer's Handbook,* particularly good for amateur astronomers, is also supplied with the subscription. Canadian libraries will certainly need it as the chief publication for astronomical reports on Canadian skies. U.S. collections will benefit from its review features, general information for amateurs, and published reports from Canadian observatories.

Royal Astronomical Society. Monthly Notices. 1827. m. 6v./yr. $37.50/v. Ed. Bd. Blackwell Scientific Publns., 5 Alfred St., Oxford, England. Illus., index. Circ: 1,600. Sample. Refereed. Microform: UM.

Indexed: Ast&AstroAb, ChemAb, MathR, Met&GeoAb, SCI, SciAb. *Aud:* Sa, Ac.

The prestigious and very old Royal Astronomical Society puts out some excellent, authoritative publications which should be found in any astronomical research collection. Its main journal, *Monthly Notices* (and the foremost astronomical publication in the British Commonwealth), consists of original investigations in "astronomy, astrophysics, radio astronomy, cosmology, space research and design of astronomical instruments." In addition to full-length papers, a small, separate section contains short communications of research in progress. Both papers and brief reports first are communicated to the Society by a Fellow and then subjected to further refereeing.

Included with a subscription price to the *Monthly Notices* are issues of its *Memoirs* and *Quarterly Journal* (annotated below). The *Memoirs,* published in larger format to accommodate the considerable tabular material contained therein, are comprised of long, highly specialized monographic type papers. Interestingly enough, the Society also puts out a *Geophysical Journal* (see Earth Sciences), issued for many years as a supplement to *Monthly Notices.* All of the above are important for any good university collection.

Royal Astronomical Society. Quarterly Journal. 1960. q. $12. (Free to subscribers of *Royal Astronomical Society Monthly Notices.*) Ed.Bd., Blackwell Scientific Publns., Ltd., 5 Alfred St., Oxford, England. Illus., index. Circ: 3,261. Sample. Vol. ends: Dec. Refereed.

Indexed: Ast&AstroAb, MathR, SCI. *Aud:* Sa, Ac.

Available with a subscription to *Monthly Notices* (see above), the publication has many nonspecialist features of interest to the librarian who may not wish to receive the entire technical output of the RAS. In addition to the usual news of the society, their calendar, etc., issues contain general and not too technical review articles on facets of astronomical research, history of astronomy, etc. Reports from observatories and reviews of astronomical observations for the calendar year are also published. A library accessions list serves as an excellent and comprehensive check for research collections. Invaluable tools such as "Catalogue of Reproductions of Astronomical Photographs," available from the RAS, also appear irregularly. Recommended for academic collections.

Sky and Telescope. 1941. m. $8. Charles A. Federer, Jr. Sky Pub. Corp., 49–51 Bay State Rd., Cambridge, Mass. 02138. Illus., index, adv. Circ: 38,000. Sample. Vol. ends: Dec. Refereed. Microform: UM. Reprint: Johnson.

Indexed: Met&GeoAb, RG. *Bk. rev:* 1–3, 1,000–2,000 words, signed. *Aud:* Ga, Sa, Ac, Hs. *Jv:* V.

In every discipline there occurs a fine publication deserving of notice by amateurs and professionals alike. *Sky and Telescope* has been successfully interpreting advances in the astronomical sciences to laymen for over 30 years. Well-illustrated feature articles (some with color photos) vary from purely descriptive works to reports requiring technical background. Also reviewed are activities of observatories and new developments in instrumentation. Contributors are authoritative, international experts. Regular departments include reports on amateur astronomers, an observer's page, monthly evening sky map, and tutorial information for amateurs. An excellent publication for public, high school, and academic libraries.

Solar Physics. 1967. m. $253.50. C. De Jager and Z. Svestka. D. Reidel Publishing Co., P.O. Box 17, Dordrecht, Holland. Illus., index. Sample. Vol. ends: 6v./yr. Refereed.

Indexed: Ast&AstroAb, ChemAb, IntAe, Met&GeoAb, NucSciAb, SciAb, SCI. *Bk. rev:* occasional, 300 words, signed. *Aud:* Sa, Ac.

With the subtitle "a journal for solar research and the study of solar terrestrial physics," the publication provides a communications outlet for research papers which hitherto had been scattered in the astrophysical, geophysical, and space science literature. Studies embrace the entire solar spectrum: solar physics, the solar interior, corona, solar activity, solar magnetic field, and the like. As a further aid in drawing together the publications in this area, the periodical has, from time to time, provided bibliographic information from other journals, or contributed reports from observatories. As the focus on solar studies increases with more sophisticated means of space travel, this publication becomes an important specialty journal for good collections in the astronomical, atmospheric, and space sciences.

Soviet Astronomy. 1957. bi-m. $65. Ed.Bd., American Inst. of Physics, 335 E. 45th St., New York, N.Y. 10017. Illus., index, adv. Circ: 617. Sample. Vol. ends: May/June. Refereed.

Indexed: Ast&AstroAb, ChemAb, MathR, Met& GeoAb, SCI, SciAb. *Bk. rev:* Occasional. *Aud:* Sa, Ac.

Prior to the Sputnik era, relatively little attention was given to translations of the Russian literature. This journal, one of the early translations undertaken by the program of the American Institute of Physics, is a cover-to-cover translation of *Astronomicheskii Zhurnal,* the leading astronomical journal of the USSR (and a product of their Academy of Sciences). Comparable in quality and stature to *Astronomical Journal* (see above), the periodical covers all fields of astronomical research (including astrophysics, radio astronomy, cosmology, stellar spectroscopy, astrometry). The time delay in publication of the translation is about six months. As well as full length articles, issues also carry brief communications and, occasionally, reports on symposia and book reviews. The latter two are particularly important to librarians, since they point out

little-publicized literature emanating from the USSR. For university libraries.

Strolling Astronomer. 1947. bi-m. Walter H. Hass. Assn. of Lunar and Planetary Observers, 3AZ Univ. Pk., New Mexico 88001. Illus., index, adv. Circ: 850. Sample. Refereed.

Bk. rev: 2–3, 200–400 words, signed. *Aud:* Hs, Ga, Ac.

The Association of Lunar and Planetary Observers, a loosely structured international organization of amateur and professional astronomers, publishes this periodical as their official organ. Open for membership to anyone, from high school upward, the society also supplies tutelage to beginners, and their journal is mainly the reportings of amateur astronomers. Monthly observational information, organized by sections, is contained in each 30-page issue, along with some pertinent book reviews and news/announcements. Contributions are of course, augmented from time to time by those of professionals. Not necessarily of the tutorial or popular appeal of other magazines in this section, the periodical nonetheless offers an opportunity for any amateur to record publicly his observations and, when qualified, to amplify with interpretations. A subscription to the magazine implies membership in the organization, a bonus, since a number of benefits are available. For any library supporting amateur astronomy clubs.

Zeitschrift für Astrophysik. See *Astronomy and Astrophysics.*

ATMOSPHERIC SCIENCES

See also Aeronautics and Space Science, Astronomy, Earth Sciences, and Environmental Sciences Sections.

Basic Periodicals

Hs: *Weatherwise;* Ga: *Weatherwise, Weather;* Jc: *Weatherwise, Weather, American Meteorological Society, Bulletin;* Ac: *American Meteorological Society. Bulletin, Journal of Applied Meteorology, Journal of the Atmospheric Sciences, Monthly Weather Review, Weatherwise, Weather.*

Basic Abstracts and Indexes

Meteorological and Geoastrophysical Abstracts.

Introduction

Recent advances in the atmospheric sciences, coupled with strong support from the Federal Government in space exploration and the focus of ancillary disciplines, e.g., environmental and physical oceanographic studies, on the atmosphere, have made this field more active and interdisciplinary than ever before.

The following suggests some basic journals in the fields of meteorology, climatology, and weather, along with a few popular titles dealing with these subjects.

As noted in "Selection of Scientific Journals" in the Introduction to this book, the publications described below do not purport to comprise a full listing of research resources, and have been restricted to English-language periodicals. Strong academic collections would most assuredly carry such fine and well-recognized foreign titles as *Archiv für Meteorologie, Geophysik und Bioklimatologie, Météorologie, Meteorologische Rundschau,* to name but a few.

✓ *American Meteorological Society. Bulletin.* 1920. m. $15. Kenneth C. Spengler. American Meteorological Soc., 45 Beacon St., Boston, Mass. 02108. Illus., index, adv. Circ: 12,000. Vol. ends: Dec. Refereed.

Indexed: BioAb, Met&GeoAb, SCI, SciAb. *Bk. rev:* 5–6, 500–1,000 words, signed. *Aud:* Sa, Ac.

Serving as the official journal of the Society and as its news medium, the publication offers timely and interesting information to a wide span of professionals, nonspecialists, and amateur meteorologists. Monthly issues contain two to three feature articles, mostly in the way of survey material or state-of-art, a historical piece now and then, and some reviews of fields related to meteorology. Abundant with coming events, programs of meetings, professional and membership notes, the periodical runs special sections on reviews of conferences and also carries abstracts of papers presented at symposia organized by the Society. A first-choice acquisition as a nonspecialist publication and news organ for the development of any meteorology collection. The Society also published two valuable research journals, *Journal of Applied Meteorology* and *Journal of the Atmospheric Sciences,* and a popular weather magazine, *Weatherwise,* discussed below.

Atmosphere. 1963. q. $10 (free to members). E. J. Truhler. Canadian Meteorological Soc., P.O. Box 41, Willowdale, Ont., Canada; Dist. by; Univ. of Toronto Press, Front Campus, Univ. of Toronto, Toronto 181, Canada. Illus., index, adv. Circ: 640. Sample. Vol. ends: Nov. Refereed.

Indexed: Met&GeoAb. *Bk. rev:* 1–2, 300–500 words, signed. *Aud:* Sa, Ac.

The official journal of the Canadian Meteorological Society. The one or two scientific papers in each issue feature, but are not restricted to, the atmosphere of Canada. Historical or nontechnical contributions also appear from time to time. In addition to technical reports, education notes, announcements of local and international meetings, news of the Society is included. Canadian libraries will need it; other academic libraries may be particularly interested in facets of its specialty, such as arctic and subarctic climatology, polar studies, and the like.

Atmospheric Environment. See Environmental Sciences Section.

Average Monthly Weather Outlook. See Government Magazines/United States Section.

Boundary-Layer Meteorology. 1970. q. $49.50 (Individuals $15.35). R. E. Munn. D. Reidel Publishing Co., P.O. Box 17, Dordrecht, Holland. Illus., index, adv. Sample. Refereed.

Indexed: BioAb, Met&GeoAb, SciAb. *Bk. rev:* occasional, 1,000 words, signed. *Aud:* Sa, Ac.

The atmospheric boundary layer is the lowest 1,000 meters of air in which most life exists. Theoretical and experimental investigations in this interdisciplinary research journal explore this level of atmosphere, and report on such subjects as heat processes and heat transfer, humidity transport over land, the structure of turbulence, air-sea interactions, effect of wind on tall structures, urban meteorology. Papers in the biological sciences are supposed to be included, but the first volume comprised only physical studies. Useful not only to meteorologists, but also to environmentalists, physical oceanographers, applied mathematicians, civil engineers, and presumably biologists. For university libraries.

✓ *Journal of Applied Meteorology.* 1952. bi-m. $30 (Members $15). Edward S. Epstein and Glenn R. Hilst. American Meteorological Soc., 45 Beacon St., Boston, Mass. 02108. Illus., index. Vol. ends: Dec. Refereed.

Indexed: BioAb, ChemAb, EngI, Met&GeoAb. *Aud:* Sa, Ac.

Of the two excellent research journals published by the American Meteorological Society, one of the world's leading organizations in the field, this journal, as its title indicates, is concerned with the practical aspects of the atmospheric sciences. (See *Journal of the Atmospheric Sciences* for more theoretical reports.) Papers and short notes, as well as a very few survey articles, consider applications of meteorology to such related topics as air pollution, ocean measurements, cloud seeding, airport safety, etc.—in short, studies affecting the safety and health of the population, industrial applications, and pertinent instrumentation. A first-choice selection for any research collection in meteorology.

✓ *Journal of the Atmospheric Sciences.* 1944. 8/yr. $40 (Members $20). Robert Jastrow and S. I. Rasool. American Meteorological Soc., 45 Beacon St., Boston, Mass. 02108. Illus., index. Vol. ends: Nov. Refereed.

Indexed: BioAb, ChemAb, EngI, MathR, Met&GeoAb, SCI, SciAb. *Aud:* Sa, Ac.

Formerly called *Journal of Meteorology,* the publication is the "knowledge-oriented," or more theoretical journal of the American Meteorological Society (see also *Journal of Applied Meteorology*). In the last ten years, the journal has shown a shift from a preoccupation with the physics of processes going on in the upper atmosphere to investigations of other planets, i.e., Martian and Venusian atmospheres. The trend will obviously continue, particularly with the availability of data through "on-site" explorations. (Recent issues carried some papers by Russian scientists discussing the USSR flight to Venus.) An important theoretical journal, the publication is necessary not only to meteorologists, but to researchers in astronomy and space sciences as well. First-choice for research meteorology collections.

Journal of Atmospheric and Terrestrial Physics. 1950. m. $125. J. A. Ratcliffe. Pergamon Press, Maxwell House, Fairview Pk., Elmsford, N.Y. 10523. Illus., index, adv. Vol. ends: Dec. Microform: Maxwell.

Indexed: ChemAb, Met&GeoAb, SCI, SciAb. *Bk. rev:* 3, 500 words, signed. *Aud:* Sa, Ac.

Subjects generally discussed in this scholarly journal include (upper atmosphere) the physics of the magnetosphere or ionosphere, aeronomy, aurora, airglow and radiowave propagation, and (lower atmosphere) thunderstorm electricity and electric fields near the earth. Theoretical papers stress basic physics. In addition to full-length studies, short papers and an occasional review are also published. Of interest to physicists, geophysicists, as well as meteorologists. For university libraries.

Journal of Meteorology. See *Journal of the Atmospheric Sciences.*

Meteorological Magazine. 1866. m. $10. Meteorological Office, London Rd., Bracknell, Berkshire RG 12 252, England. Subs. to: H.M.S.O., Atlantic House, Holborn Viaduct, London, England. Illus., index, adv. Circ: 2,000. Vol. ends: no. 12. Refereed. Microform: UM. Reprint: Johnson.

Indexed: Met&GeoAb, SCI. *Bk. rev:* 2–3, 300 words, signed. *Aud:* Sa, Ac.

The scope of this well-known publication is rather broad. Authoritative papers and short notes cover most areas in the atmospheric sciences, and extend from some theoretical studies and laboratory accounts, to methodology and applications of meteorology (including industry, aviation, hydrology, agriculture), and instrumentation, and descriptions of meteorological phenomena. Generally, contributions are from members of the Meteorological Office. News and notes of interest to the profession are also included. Although U.S. publications will still be first-choice for small, academic libraries, nonetheless collections in the atmospheric sciences will find this periodical valuable.

Monthly Weather Review. 1872. m. $10.50. Harold A. Corzine. National Oceanic and Atmospheric Administration, Rockville, Md.; Subs. to: Supt. of Documents, U.S. Govt. Printing Office, Washington, D.C. 20402. Illus., index. Circ: 3,000. Vol. ends: Dec. Refereed. Microform: UM.

Indexed: ChemAb, Met&GeoAb, SCI. *Aud:* Sa, Ac.

For a century, the periodical has been contributing original research papers to the meteorological literature. Its present attention focuses on such areas as numerical weather forecasting, satellite meteorology, physical meteorology, atmospheric turbulence, etc. Some articles are topical, e.g., tornadoes over southern Florida; others are more generalized, e.g., air pollution, instrumentation for the collection of meteorological data. Contributions are not restricted to those from U.S. agencies, and foreign authors are well represented. Features include a review of weather and circulation for the third month preceding the current issue, and a "picture of the month," usually a satellite photo. A basic publication for the beginning of any meteorology collection.

It is appropriate to note here some of the other valuable publications sold through the Government Printing Office which supply the raw data to the meteorological literature.

Average Monthly Weather Outlook. See Government Magazines/United States Section.

Climatological Data (m. $2.50) is sold by sections (states) and contains observational data within a section.

Climatological Data, National Summary (m. $2.50) gives a condensation of data by states (also Pacific area and West Indies), along with various charts, flood data, upper air information.

Daily Weather Maps, Weekly Series ($7.50) publishes for each day a weather map of the U.S. showing conditions observed throughout the nation, along with other miscellaneous information.

Local Climatological Data (m. $1.00) are issued for about 287 major U.S. cities or airports where Weather Bureau offices are located.

Monthly Climatic Data for the World (m. $2.75) features data for selected world cities (temperature, humidity, etc.).

Ionospheric Data (m. $1.50) records data measured in the upper atmosphere.

Storm Data (m. $1.50) describes unusual weather phenomena.

Royal Meteorological Society. Quarterly Journal. 1871. q. $36.60. R. C. Sutcliffe. Royal Meteorological Soc., 49 Cromwell Rd., London, England. Illus., index. Circ: 4,500. Vol. ends: no. 4. Refereed. Reprint: Johnson.

Indexed: Met&GeoAb, SciAb, SCI. *Aud:* Sa, Ac.

The Royal Meteorological Society has long maintained prominence as one of the learned scientific societies in its field. Its *Quarterly Journal* is dedicated to high quality and authoritative research papers in most branches of the atmospheric sciences, including studies in geomagnetism, aeronomy, cosmic relationships, as well as general meteorology. Some news of the Society is also provided. An excellent and important publication for all good research collections in the atmospheric sciences. (For a more popular periodical in the field, see *Weather*, listed below.)

Space Science Review. See Aeronautics and Space Science Section.

WMO Bulletin. 1952. q. $6. Oliver M. Ashford. World Meteorological Organization, Case postale no. 1, CH-1211, Geneva 20, Switzerland; distributed by Unipub, Inc., P. O. Box 433, New York, N.Y. 10016. Illus., index, adv. Circ: 5,000. Vol. ends: no. 4. Sample.

Indexed: Met&GeoAb. *Bk. rev:* 12, 400 words, signed. *Aud:* Sa, Ac, Ga.

The official organ of the World Meteorological Organization. Available in four language editions (English, French, Spanish, Russian), the focus of the publication is on activities of the WMO, including applications of meteorology for the betterment of mankind. Well-illustrated features describe, on a general and nontechnical level, such topics as meteorological aspects of air pollution, effects of air pollution on agriculture, research trends in different countries, weather modification. The net effect is that the reader gets an overview not only of current scientific endeavors in the atmospheric sciences on a worldwide scale, but also the extent of the complexities and cooperation required to support the collection of reliable meteorological data. General news and notes of the organization are also included. For any type of library.

Weather. 1946. m. $2.25. D. E. Pedgley. Royal Meteorological Soc., Cromwell Houce, High St., Bracknell, Berks RG12 IDP, England. Illus., index, adv. Circ: 5,500. Vol. ends: Dec. Refereed.

Indexed: Met&GeoAb. *Bk. rev:* 2–3, 400–600 words, signed. *Aud:* Sa, Ac.

Somewhat the British counterpart to *Weatherwise* (see below), although more technical in tone, is the excellently-produced magazine of the Royal Meteorological Society. Short articles, well embellished with photos, report, interpret, and review recent advances in the science of weather and meteorology for both nonspecialists and members of the Society. Although some of the material centers around the atmospheric phenomena of the British Isles, the periodical is by no means local, and contributions are international. A regular insert, "Weather Log," records the weather of two months past and includes Daily Weather maps for that period. The publication also carries some professional news. Although small libraries may find their popular needs best served by the U.S. *Weatherwise,* the periodical deserves the attention of every academic library developing a meteorology collection.

Weatherwise. 1948. bi-m. $8. David M. Ludlum. American Meteorological Soc., 45 Beacon St. Boston, Mass. 02108. Illus., adv. Circ: 11,631. Vol. ends: Dec. Microform: UM.

Indexed: ChemAb, Met&GeoAb, RG. *Aud:* Ga, Hs, Ac. *Jv:* V.

Styled for a wide audience, the magazine features popularly written articles which acquaint and interpret to its readership the science of meteorology, climatology, and weather. Issues carry material both timely and historical and are nicely illustrated. Regular sections include "Weatherwatch," a review of weather events for preceding months, as well as daily weather maps for that period. The February number, an almanac issue, covers records for the previous year. An excellent guide for librarians is the "Bibliography and Film Guide Issue," published biannually, which provides information on both popular and specialist works. Highly recommended as a general publication in the field for public, high school and academic libraries alike.

AUTOMOBILES

Basic Periodicals

GENERAL. Hs: *Hot Rod, Motor Trend;* Ga: *Motor Trend, Car and Driver, Road and Track;* Ac: *Road and Track, Car and Driver.*

MOTORCYCLES. All libraries: *Cycle.*

Cessations

Auto Topics

Introduction

Safety, environment, population, and economic factors may have already caused the nation to turn the corner on the concept of motor vehicles as devices for pleasure and transportation. However, we are still enjoying vast automotive personal freedom, and increasing leisure time, coupled with a need to examine the motor vehicle critically and exhaustively has often been met with inadequate resources. Whereas patron needs may have been satisfied in the past with one or two general car magazines, it now often becomes necessary to provide current, detailed information on such disparate subjects as all-terrain vehicles, emissions control, automobile repairing, and even highway and traffic engineering. Thus the following sections on automobiles and motorcycles are intended to serve two purposes: to help a library fill general readership interests, and to help the librarian select the occasional special-interest periodical required to meet a local need. (H.B.)

General

The Air Force Driver Magazine. (Formerly: ***Driver***). 1967. m. $2. Capt. Tobias van Rossum Daum. IGDSED, Norton AFB, Calif. 92409. Dist. by: U.S. Supt. of Documents., U.S. Govt. Printing Office,

Washington, D.C. 20402. Illus., index. Circ: 78,000. Vol. ends: May. Sample.

Aud: Ga, Hs, Ac.

A quality magazine, and as obscure as most government publications. Appearance differs from other auto magazines due to lack of advertisements and a less expensive color process, but at an average of 28 pages, it is the equal of many general car journals twice its size. Each issue highlights a theme, e.g., winterizing, stock car racing, driving in Germany, in addition to regular features. Billed as the "Traffic Safety Magazine of the United States Air Force," its emphasis on common sense safety and courtesy has earned it the Alfred P. Sloan Award for 1971. Second priority in content goes to maintenance and mechanics since servicemen are notorious do-it-yourselfers, but driving techniques, racing news, motorcycles and legislation are among its many concerns. Except for the comparative lack of eye appeal on the rack it is a worthy beginning to a car magazines collection. (H.B.)

American Youth. See Free Magazines Section.

Antique Automobile. 1947. bi-m. $5. William E. Bomgardner. Antique Automobile Club of America, Inc., 501 W. Governor Rd., Hershey, Pa. 17033. Illus., index, adv. Circ: 29,000. Vol. ends: Dec.

Bk. rev: 4, 300 words, signed. *Aud:* Ga, Hs, Ac.

Primarily devoted to reporting winners and showing pictures of show class winners at various competitions of the club, and information about its activities and members. Some issues feature articles on the history of a particular automobile manufacturer or on restoration. Other articles note the going market price for antique cars. The magazine provides a good place to advertise and exchange cars, parts, and information. It is reasonably valuable for the history of various cars with minimal emphasis on restoration and mechanical repair. A useful, if nonessential magazine for both adult and high school students, not to mention a few college professors. Compare with *Automobile Quarterly.* (H.B.)

Autocar. 1895. w. $27.50. Peter Garnier. IPC Transport Press Ltd., Dorset House, Stamford St., London SE1, England. Dist. by: Eastern News Distributors, 155 W. 15th St., New York, N.Y. 10011. Illus., index, adv. Circ: 107,469. Microform: UM.

Indexed: BritTech. *Aud:* Ga, Hs, Ac. *Jv:* V.

Typical British concern for detail and their genuine love of driving make this the best foreign car magazine currently available. It is recommended as a source of accurate, unbiased information by *Consumer Bulletin,* and the American who has any question regarding the performance and overall quality of a foreign car should turn here first. It has the distinct advantage of appearing weekly and so is able to carry

more road tests than its American counterparts *Road & Track* and *Car and Driver.* In addition to the appraisal of new cars, each issue contains information of particular interest to the racing fan and those who look upon cars as a serious hobby. Special numbers are given over to large automobile shows, and once a year the London Show number covers almost every new development in the industry. Each car studied gets a complete physical, complete with cutaway drawings showing all significant dimensions. Despite its price it is highly recommended for any type of library where there is an interest in foreign automobiles and racing. (H.B.)

Automobile Quarterly. 1962. q. $22.50. Don Vorderman. Automobile Quarterly, Inc., 40 E. 49th St., New York, N.Y. 10022. Illus., index. Circ: 35,000. Sample. Vol. ends: Oct.

Aud: Ga, Hs, Ac. *Jv:* V.

This is to the automobile fan what *American Heritage* (see History/American section), is to the amateur historian, i.e., a hardbound collection, without advertisements, of both black and white and color illustrations fitted into a series of nontechnical articles on automobiles. Emphasis is historical, and each issue usually features one manufacturer or type of car from yesteryear. This is balanced with data on new, superior cars in terms of design and individuality. The writing is as sound as the marvelous illustrations. It will be welcomed by anyone who looks to a car for more than simple transportation, and the pictures make it suitable for enthusiasts from junior high up. Although the price is a bit high, a run virtually constitutes an on-going history of automobiles, and many librarians simply catalog each issue as a book. By and large the best of its type, it should be in most school, public, college and university libraries. (H.B.)

Automotive Information. See Free Magazines Section.

Car. 1962. m. $8. Ian Fraser. National Magazine Co., Chestergate House, Vauxall Bridge Rd., London SW1, England. Illus., adv. Circ: 60,000.

Aud: Ga.

A monthly from England which is somewhat similar to the weekly English *Autocar,* i.e., it is primarily a device for analyzing new cars and keeping up with sport car news. The consumer information is as reliable as *Autocar,* sometimes even more detailed. Often an issue will emphasize a single car, such as a new Jaguar or a new Citroen. The machine is then analyzed from almost every angle, including historical background and technical data. Other numbers will discuss cars from different nations, e.g., April 1972 had road tests of German cars. Has a car-of-the-year award and a number of running features. The editing is excellent. In many ways it compares favorably with *Road and Track,* and has much of the same elan. A useful, downright fascinating magazine for the sport car fan, and of some use to anyone who is simply considering a foreign car purchase.

Car Craft. 1953. m. $5. Terry Cook. Peterson Publishing Co., 8490 Sunset Blvd., Los Angeles, Calif. 90069. Illus., adv. Circ: 300,000. Vol. ends: Dec. Microform: UM.

Aud: Ga, Hs.

A drag racing magazine containing a basketfull of regular columns (including ones for motorcycles and VW's), in addition to features on modifying engines and suspensions, on prominent mechanics or drivers and their cars, and information on the latest performance cars and options from Detroit. (Road tests, however, are not performed regularly, and the general car journals do this quite adequately.) Articles are detailed, cleverly written and rather short, although there is much to read each month. Only the more important drag events are covered. While this has many enthusiastic readers in the younger set (and not a few adults), it would be a second or third choice for public or school libraries. *Hot Rod Magazine* is adequate for most situations. (H.B.)

Car and Driver. 1956. m. $7. Bob Brown. Ziff Davis Publishing Co., 1 Park Ave., New York, N.Y. 10016. Illus., adv. Circ: 600,000. Vol ends: June & Dec. Microform: UM.

Aud: Ga, Hs, Ac. *Jv:* V.

Competes with *Road & Track* as the best general automotive magazine in America. Written for foreign car and high performance American car enthusiasts, it is generally anti-Detroit in tone, and editorials show interest in promoting car racing into a major league sport. Most of the articles are written by the staff with an occasional guest expert. Results of their own road tests are reported in detail. An occasional article appears on a personality in the racing field. Special monthly departments give information on new cars and related products, short, belated, detailed results of races, and a racing calendar listing important worldwide events. There are many fine black and white photographs and occasional color ones. *Car and Driver* issues a yearbook, not included in the subscription price, which is capricious in its coverage. A third choice for school and public libraries after *Road & Track* and *Motor Trend*. (H.B.)

Car Life. See *Motor Trend*.

Competition Press and Autoweek. 1958. w. $12. Competition Press, Inc., Autoweek Bldg., Lafayette, Calif. 94549. Illus., adv. Circ: 98,100.

Aud: Ga, Hs, Ac.

A lively weekly for car race fans in the vein of *National Speed Sport News*. However *Autoweek* goes a step further in providing excellent coverage of interna-

tional events. Sports and foreign cars are not adequately covered by *Speed Sport News*. *Autoweek* contains the usual events calendar and classified ads as well as late news headlines and feature articles on specific models and general news. Although younger than its competition, *Autoweek* numbers several well-known automotive journalists among its contributing editors, and by-lines are happily more frequent. Occasional use of color is also a welcome sight. In sum this tabloid is less exhaustive but better balanced and more sophisticated, and is favored over *National Speed Sport News* where newspaper timeliness is desired. (H.B.)

Corvette News. See Free Magazines Section.

Driver. See *Air Force Driver Magazine*.

Ford Truck Times. See Free Magazines Section.

Foreign Car Guide. See *World Car Guide*.

Hot Rod Magazine. 1948. m. $7.50. A. B. Shuman. Peterson Publishing Co., 8490 Sunset Blvd., Los Angeles, Calif. 90069. Illus., index, adv. Circ: 850,000. Vol. ends: Dec. Microform: UM, MF.

Indexed: AbrRg, RG. *Aud:* Ga, Hs, Ac. *Jv:* V.

The king of the performance car magazines has gathered *Rod & Custom* within its pages, adding to its reputation as the most popular wellspring of tuning and modifying information for drag racer, mechanic, and customizer. Technical articles lean toward describing speed tricks and products, and feature articles typically cover national drag meets as well as other important news. A separate section is devoted to individual customized cars. Color is used generously here and is really necessary to portray accurately the exotic paint jobs. The entire magazine emphasizes the feats of individual mechanics, body craftsmen, and racing personalities, and speaks to a young adult audience. The editors frequently publish monographs on a single theme, partially gleaned from the monthly issues. *Hot Rod's* rival is *Car Craft*, but as a standard for the sport this one should be acquired first. (H.B.)

Motor Trend. 1949. m. $5. Eric Dahlquist. Peterson Publishing Co., 8490 Sunset Blvd., Los Angeles, Calif. 90069. Illus., index, adv. Circ: 640,000. Vol. ends: Dec. Microform: UM, MF.

Indexed: RG. *Aud:* Ga, Hs, Ac. *Jv:* V.

This family favorite has traditionally been bullish on the American philosophy of automobiles, i.e., style, modernity, comfort, size. It still is, but has recently gained the staffs of *Car Life* and *Sports Car Graphic*. Both were enthusiast magazines of a European bent, i.e., handling, engineering, compactness, durability. The merger has resulted in excellent coverage of foreign cars, bringing it into more direct rivalry with *Car and Driver* and *Road & Track*. And it is still the best journal for coverage of Detroit's bread-and-butter models. Besides road tests, *Motor Trend* touches on antiques, international developments, racing, and technical subjects. Articles are well written and color is used quite frequently. Highly recommended. (H.B.)

Motor Trend World Automotive Yearbook. 1954. a. $2. Peterson Publishing Co., 8490 Sunset Blvd., Los Angeles, Calif. 90069. Dist. by: Curtis Circ. Co. Independence Sq., Philadelphia, Pa. 19105. Illus., adv. Sample. Microform: UM.

Aud: Ga, Hs.

Organized by manufacturer, with U.S. cars listed first. Each section for the "big four" introduces the reader to Detroit changes in general. This is followed by chart comparisons of car dimensions, options, engine availability and specifications, and body style availability. Next, each model (or group of similar models) is given a page or two of text and pictures, plus a box containing basic data. The descriptions are objective, laden with more facts and figures, and they heavily emphasize style. Next, recreational vehicles (RV's) are described, including pickups, vans and four-wheel-drives. Imports are treated last and have neither charts nor box specifications. Interspersed throughout the issue are short articles on safety, prices, styling, etc. In summation, a reader can find and compare specifications for a car that he is interested in, but (except for the imports section) the yearbook will not give him an evaluation of the car, and he will have to consult another source (such as *Car and Driver* or *Road & Track*) if he wants to know how well it handles, or if the air conditioner blows ashes out of the ash tray. Although *Car and Driver* also publishes an annual, this is far better. (H.B.)

National Speed Sport News. 1932. w. $7. Chris Economaki. Kay Publishing Co., Box 608, Ridgewood, N.J. 07451. Illus., adv. Circ: 63,300. Sample. Vol. ends: Dec.

Bk. rev: Irreg. *Aud:* Ga, Hs.

Hard core car racing coverage in tabloid format. Chris Economaki has a solid reputation as a sportscaster for ABC, and as both editor and publisher here he puts his aggression to good use. The paper reports on all professional races in the U.S. (except drag competition) as well as people on the scene, and describes new designs and speed tricks. International racing is reported to a far lesser degree. A classified ads section is included as is an events calendar, and the commercial advertisements plug upcoming events, parts, and services. The editor's column is crisp and informative and the letters column allows readers to blow off steam. While of some merit in a racing conscious town, it can be ignored elsewhere. (H.B.)

Road & Track. 1947. m. $7. James T. Crow. 1499 Monrovia Ave., Newport Beach, Calif. 92663. Illus.,

index, adv. Circ: 300,000. Vol. ends: August: Refereed.

Aud: Ga, Hs, Ac. *Jv:* V.

One of the best automobile magazines for people who are seriously concerned with driving and cars. It has appeal both for the well educated and for those who can hardly read a road sign. Emphasis is on foreign-made cars, particularly the sports models. Every issue gives detailed road test results on at least two cars. There is generally an article on a personality in the racing field. Regular departments present nontechnical information about the motor industry, a calendar of motor sports events and technical advice to those readers who write for help. Black and white and some color photographs are used. The editors issue an annual which includes all road tests for the year. Both this and *Car and Driver* as a second choice, should be in every library where there is an automobile enthusiast about. (Of course, the Detroit minded readers should be equally served with *Motor Trend.*) (H.B.)

Road Test. 1963. m. $6. Don MacDonald. Motorsport Publns., Inc., 6675 E. 26th St., Los Angeles, Calif. 90040. Illus., adv. Circ: 100,000. Vol. ends: Dec.

Aud: Ga. *Jv:* C.

Devoted to presentation of facts about cars, accessories and automotive products. Industry highlights from around the world, readers' problems and opinions, and simple maintenance tricks all receive regular attention. There is very little advertising, and the bulk of the journal is given over to model testing and evaluation. The tests are really not up to par, however. Both U.S. and foreign models are considered, and the magazine does not cover all important models adequately. The reports also do not always analyze the cars logically, and the result is an occasional goulash of whatever facts and comments the editors were able to lay their hands on. The writing style lacks the elan of *Road & Track* and *Car and Driver.* It is more comparable to *Motor Trend*, but should be considered merely as adjunctive to a car collection. (H.B.)

Rockwell Standard News. See Free Magazines Section.

Rod & Custom. See *Hot Rod.*

Sports Car Graphic. See *Sports Cars of the World.*

Sports Cars of the World. 1971. q. $3.95. Robert T. Kovacik. Peterson Publishing Co., 8490 Sunset Blvd., Los Angeles, Calif. 90069. Dist. by: Curtis Circ. Co., Independence Sq., Philadelphia, Pa. 19105. Illus. Circ: 50,000.

Aud: Ga, Hs, Ac.

Sports Car Graphic was possibly the finest racing-enthusiast magazine published anywhere, and its transition to this quarterly, guide-type publication is unfortunate. It is still undergoing an identity crisis, with a substantial portion of the staff now writing for

Motor Trend, and frequency, price, and content may vacillate some more in the near future. The magazine (judging from the first issue) now concentrates on the history, development, and performance of classic and antique sports cars worldwide (making it tangentially competitive to *Antique Automobile* and *Automobile Quarterly*), and the best of corporate litters are photographed, drawn and described eloquently. Scattered articles also describe great races, profile famous drivers, guess at future styling, and initiate the new owner to the dimensions of the sport. Although the quality of coverage has not diminished, a library might do well to let the journal find its footing before deciding to subscribe. (H.B.)

Super Stock & Drag Illustrated. 1964. m. $5. Jim McGraw. Eastern Publishing Co., 522 North Pitt St., Alexandria, Va. 22314. Illus., adv. Circ: 118,109. Vol. ends: Oct.

Aud: Ga, Hs. *Jv:* C.

Covers individual races more than *Hot Rod* or *Car Craft.* The journal is studious in featuring fancy super cars (often including a full page color photo) and in helping the younger person to hop up his machine. There is more news here of the two major U.S. drag organizations, the American Hot Road Association and the National Hot Rod Association. The mechanical articles are slightly inferior to those in either of the competitors mentioned above. (H.B.)

World Car Guide (Formerly: **Foreign Car Guide**). 1955. m. $6. Joe Wherry, Hal Schell. Rajo Publns., 319 Miller Ave., Mill Valley, Calif. 94941. Illus., adv. Circ: 32,000.

Aud: Ga, *Jv:* C.

Primarily of interest to Volkswagen owners, as many of the articles are devoted to simple repairs and additions for that car. Under a new editor (and a new name) the magazine has spread a bit, and now takes in information on smaller cars from the American to the foreign variety. Considerable information on conversion to dune buggies, snowmobiles, camping etc., is given, and the illustrations are fair to good. In trying to be something for everyone, this is not too successful, but it does have appeal for Volkswagen owners and for those who prize small cars. The publisher also issues an annual at $1 called the *Volkswagen Owners Annual,* an interesting, although not overly thoughtful, publication.

Motorcycles

AMA News. 1947. m. $3. Alton Ismon Jr., American Motorcycle Assn., Box 231, Worthington, Ohio 43085. Illus., index, adv. Circ: 18,000.

Aud: Ga, Hs.

Primarily a news magazine of interest to members of the American Motorcycle Association—a member-

ship which the editor claims is primarily age 30 and in a middle income tax group. Most of the material concerns events and personalities. There are no road tests. Apparently the primary purpose of the Association is to give motorcycle operators a better name. There is emphasis on the clean-cut, all American type and his activities. This drive towards public relations will have some appeal, but limits the journal's use in libraries.

Cycle. 1950. m. $6. Cook Neilson. Ziff Davis Publishing Co., One Park Ave., New York, N.Y. 10016. Illus., index, adv. Circ: 312,964. Sample. Vol. ends: Dec.

Bk. rev: Irreg. *Aud:* Ga, Hs, Ac. *Jv:* V.

Regarding writing style, *Cycle* may be the *Esquire* of motorcycle magazines. The articles are longer and fewer than in the others, and the tests are knowledgeable, critical and quite professionally handled. In addition, test reports of new models appear earlier than in other magazines except *Cycle Guide,* which competes for the same market. (Occasionally a price or other specification is not yet available at the time of writing.) *Cycle* is very weak on maintenance and technical articles, and is not thorough in its coverage of competition, so serious patron interest here would have to be met either by a second journal (such as *Modern Cycle*), or by one of the news magazines (see *Cycle News*). The editors also publish an annual called *Cycle Buyers Guide.* It is surprisingly mediocre—only about twenty five percent of the guide is devoted to listing the models and accessories, and the balance consists of articles introducing the reader to motorcycles, their joys and accoutrements, and a list of suppliers. Fortunately, if great need for this type of work is noticed the editors say they will provide a free issue on request. (H.B.)

Cycle Guide. 1967. m. $6. Bob Braverman. Cycle Guide Publns., P.O. Box 267, Mt. Morris, Ill. 61054. Illus., adv. Circ: 91,915. Vol. ends: Dec.

Aud: Ga, Hs.

A competitor to *Cycle.* Both use color lavishly, both place less emphasis on racing, and both take road tests seriously. *Cycle Guide's* reports are short, well written, and critical, but they lack the performance and in-depth personal evaluation to be found in *Cycle.* Slightly more space is devoted to maintenance, and commercial advertising is the most extensive of any cycle magazine. (H.B.)

Cycle News/Eastern Edition. 1968. bi-w. $6. Tod Rafferty. C & S Publishing Co., Box 133, Avon, Ohio 44011. Illus., adv. Sample. Vol. ends: Dec.

Bk. rev: Irreg., 100 words, signed. *Aud:* Ga.

This newspaper is action packed and competition oriented. There are features and advertisements concerning upcoming events and reports of past ones, and the paper abounds in dramatic photographs of motorcycle racers in action. It is also published in two other editions, *Cycle News/West* and *Dixie Cycle News.*

Combined circulation is 60,000, and the Eastern edition includes Canada. All editions share multiple-part series, regular by-lined columns and nationally important news, as well as the best regional news available. An alternative would be *Motorcycle Weekly* where absolute completeness is not mandatory. (H.B.)

Cycle News/West. 1965. w. $9. John Bethea, P.O. Box 498, Long Beach, Calif. 90801. Illus., adv. Sample. Vol. ends: Dec.

Bk. rev: Infrequent, 100 words, signed. *Aud:* Ga.

See *Cycle News/Eastern Edition.*

Dixie Cycle News. 1970. bi-w. $6. Don Woods. C & S Publishing Co., 4190 First Ave., Tucker, Ga. 30084. Illus., adv. Sample. Vol. ends: Dec.

Bk. rev: Irreg., 100 words, signed. *Aud:* Ga.

See *Cycle News/Eastern Edition.*

Dune Buggies and Hot VWs. See *Off-Road Vehicles Magazine.*

Mini-Bike Guide. 1969. m. $7.50. Patrick J. Mackie. Century Publns., Inc., 11044 McCormick St., North Hollywood, Calif. 91603. Illus., adv. Vol. ends: Dec.

Aud: Ga, Ejh, Hs.

Monthly coverage of one of America's latest pastimes. It is a full scale enthusiast magazine written for both kids and their parents, since the participating age seems limited only by the age of reason. Typical feature articles may cover youth races, tests of bikes and equipment, and do-it-yourself projects for everyone. Regular departments include a letters' page, technical tips, a column on go-karts and an advertisers' index. Buy where needed. (H.B.)

Modern Cycle Magazine. 1966. m. $7.50. Dave Ekins. Modern Cycle Publishing Co., 7950 Deering Ave., Canoga Park, Calif. 91304. Dist. by: Publishers Distributing Corp., 401 Park Ave. S., New York, N.Y. 10016. Illus., index, adv. Circ: 165,000. Sample. Vol. ends: Dec.

Aud: Ga, Ejh, Hs. *Jv:* V.

By far the journal most devoted to maintenance, repair, technical, and driving aspects, it is also the one displaying most concern for safety and the image of motorcycling, including a respect for environment. *Cycle* is the only magazine to speak up defensively for cyclists' rights. Extensive racing coverage is another strong point. This is the most "popular" of the motorcycle magazines. A biker friend of this compiler, who used to ride with the Hells Angels, was asked to rate the five, and he gave this one the trophy. His evaluation, in a few words: "Rougher; *Modern Screen* type (the two are *not* related); better gut technical and racing coverage, especially for up-and-coming racers." He reserved second row seats for *Motor Cyclist Magazine* and *Motorcycle World* ("more conservative"), and con-

signed *Cycle* and *Cycle Guide* "to the trash heap." And his view is sound, placing the action-oriented veteran (and perhaps younger, less conservative, less affluent), at one end and the verbal-oriented initiate (the opposite), at the other. (H.B.)

Motor Cycle. 1903. w. $12.50. Norman Sharpe. IPC Specialist and Professional Press Ltd., 161–166 Fleet St., London EC4P 4AA, England. Dist. by: IPC Business Press Ltd., 40 Bowling Green Lane, London EC1P 1DB, England. Illus., adv. Circ: 88,881. Sample. Vol. ends: Dec. Microform: UM.

Indexed: BritTech. *Bk. rev:* 1, 100 words. *Aud:* Ga. *Jv:* C.

A British weekly tabloid covering motorcycle news and major sporting events from all parts of the world. Informative articles with expert commentary provide up-to-date accounts of new machines, technical developments, and famous personalities in the cycling world. It includes many practical hints for the enthusiast, plus a hefty classified section, and is liberally illustrated with dramatic action photographs in black and white, including an occasional cartoon. Especially interesting for the young adult group, as is *Motor Cycle News*, but in America it is less helpful than *Motorcycle Weekly*. (H.B.)

Motor Cycle News. 1955. w. $7.80. Robin Miller. East Midland Allied Press Ltd., Park House, 117 Park Road, Peterborough, England. Illus., adv. Circ: 103,538. Sample. Vol. ends: Dec.

Bk. rev: Approx. 12/yr., 250–500 words, signed. *Aud:* Ga. *Jv:* C.

Another British weekly which deals with all aspects of motorcycles, and emphasizes the sporting side. It, too, is in newspaper form, and covers current motorcycling activity throughout the world. Road tests on new models and equipment are reported; latest technical developments related; readers' technical queries answered. Geared to the young adult audience, it employs a liberal use of action photographs in black and white, a semi-regular photo contest, and a large classified advertisement section. Either this or *Motor Cycle* is useful where good foreign coverage is important, but most libraries would sooner require a U.S. publication such as *Cycle News*. (H.B.)

Motor Cyclist Magazine. 1912. m. $6. William M. Bagnall. The Bagnall Publishing Co., P.O. Box 638, Sierra Madre, Calif. 91024. Dist. by: Curtis Cir. Co., Independence Sq., Philadelphia, Pa. 19105. Illus., index, adv. Circ: 95,000. Sample. Vol. ends: Dec.

Bk. rev: Irreg., 175 words. *Aud:* Ga, Ejh, Hs.

More outdoors emphasis (travel, camping) than the other magazines reviewed, it also describes heritage and development more consistently. It is more international than *Modern Cycle* and its tests are somewhat better, being more detailed and thorough, and with more attention to engineering, although *Motorcycle World* rates slightly higher in the test department. Each of these three employs a chart to summarize impressions of the bike being tested, while *Cycle* and *Cycle Guide* limit their evaluations to textual description—and comparing different models is faster using charts. Racing is covered less here than in *Modern Cycle*, although specific race reports are more complete, and result charts are always presented. Generally, its closest competitor in quality and scope is probably *Motorcycle World*. (H.B.)

The Motorcycle Enthusiast. See Free Magazines Section.

Motorcycle Weekly. 1969, w. $9. John Weed. Presswork Publishing Co., 15740 Paramount Blvd., Paramount, Calif. 90723. Illus., adv. Vol. ends: Dec.

Aud: Ga, Hs, Ac.

Tabloid format, international but with strong U.S. emphasis, and somewhat more conservative than *Cycle News*. Prominent competition is reported in detail, and photographs are included. In addition to racing and personality features there is a smattering of non-racing articles, such as a profile of a company's new models, an article on a custom bike, or a review of new products. Classified advertisements and a calendar of events complete the picture. *Motorcycle Weekly* is most useful where a library requires broad, timely racing news. (H.B.)

Motorcycle World. 1967. bi-m. $4.50. Gregory Gore. Countrywide Publns., Inc., 222 Park Ave. S., New York, N.Y. 10003. Illus., adv. Circ: 115,000. Vol. ends: Dec. odd years.

Bk. rev: Irreg. *Aud:* Ga, Ejh, Hs.

Less affluent and literate than *Cycle*, this one should appeal to a younger audience, and is a nicely balanced general magazine. Racing and European travels are adequately covered. *Motor Cyclist Magazine*, its chief rival, handles racing news somewhat better, but the cycle tests are more thorough here. Both of these two "middle ground" magazines have more technical articles than either *Cycle* or *Cycle Guide*, but fewer than *Modern Cycle*. The editors also publish *Cycle Illustrated*, a specialty magazine geared to dirt bikes and off-road competition. (H.B.)

Off-Road Vehicles Magazine. bi-m. $3.50. Donald Edgington. Argus Publishers Corp., 131 S. Barrington Pl., Los Angeles, Calif. 90049. Illus., adv. Vol. ends: Dec.

Aud: Ga, Hs.

Competition is the keynote here, and the magazine tries to provide something for everyone interested in avoiding pavement as much as possible. Car and engine modifications are depicted and races are covered. There is usually something for the motorcycle set, as well as a camping trip or similar adventure. Most off-road publications do not seem to have a firm hold on the market, and this is no exception. Compare with *Four Wheeler* (see Automobiles/Trailers section), before you buy, since there is more than one attitude among off-roaders. *Dune Buggies and Hot VW's* (Parkhurst Publg. Co., Box 1757, Newport Beach, Ca. 92663) used to be excellent for this type of competition and for modifying the Volkswagen, but it has been whittled down from monthly to quarterly, and its value may be only marginal in this fast-changing field. (H.B.)

Special and Technical

American Car Prices Magazine. 1966. bi-m. $8. Lou Kjose. JEK Publishing, Inc., 1680 North Vine St., Hollywood, Calif. 90028. Dist. by: Kable News Co., 777 3rd Ave., New York, N.Y. 10017. Illus., adv. Circ: 60,000. Sample. Vol. ends: May.

Aud: Ga, Ac.

Preferable to both the *NADA Official Used Car Guide* (the "blue book'), and the *Red Book Official Used Car Valuations* because of its wider scope, this periodical consists of three parts. The first (66 pages), is a journal geared to the enthusiast. The articles examine exotic machinery, test and critically compare new models, discuss safety, and delve into technical subjects. Although they are well researched, the level of writing is checkered and often substandard, and the many grammatical, spelling, and typographical errors must be charged to very poor editorship. The second part contains new car, truck, and accessory prices, both U.S. and foreign. Two prices for each item are given, the "dealer's cost" and the "window sticker retail." The last part gives used car and truck wholesale and retail price (same scope) for the four major market areas of the U.S. Where accessories affect a used car's value this too is noted. Despite poor journalism *Car Prices* is uniquely useful for the patron about to buy or trade, and for diachronic price analysis. (H.B.)

For those needing the information for the "blue book" and the "red book," the *NADA Official Used Car Guide* (1917. m. $12.) is available from National Automobile Dealers Used Car Guide Co., 2000 K St., N.W., Washington, D.C. 20006. The *Red Book Official Used Car Valuations* (8/yr. $10.) is available from National Market Report, 900 S. Wabash Ave., Chicago, Ill. 60605.

Autobody and the Reconditioned Car. 1922. m. $3. Richard S. Broshar. Spokesman Publishing Co., 1103 First National Bank Bldg., Cincinnati, Ohio 45202. Illus., adv. Circ: 40,000.

Aud: Ga, Hs.

A trade journal for automobile body shops and anyone involved with repairing automobiles. A good one half of the editorial content is how-to-do-it information on putting a wrecked or damaged machine back on the road. Articles move from major body work to methods of painting and replacing glass. There is little or no emphasis on mechanics. Departments cover latest news of productions, personalities, and general trade developments. While intended primarily for the adult employed in the field, its direct, well-illustrated approach gives it a particular value for the teenager working on his own car or in a vocational school. A good bet for any library where there is an interest in automobile repair. (H.B.)

Automobile Facts and Figures. 1919. a. Automobile Manufacturers Assn., 310 New Center Bldg., Detroit, Mich. 48202. Illus., index. Sample.

Aud: Sa, Hs, Ac. *Jv:* V.

Superior source of statistics for automotive and related industries, this contains data on production, sales, imports, mileage traveled, tax revenues, drivers, parts, etc. International in scope, this annual brings together statistics from many sources, including the U.S. Departments of Commerce and Transportation, and many foreign sources. Often the figures show comparisons between states, countries, or years, and may be displayed in chart, pie, or graph fashion. Valuable for most types of libraries since it will support term papers, debates, or plain curiosity. (H.B.)

Automotive Industries. 1899. s-m. $5. Richard H. Groves. Automotive Industries, Chestnut & 56th Sts., Philadelphia, Pa. 19139. Illus., index, adv. Circ: 45,319. Microform: UM.

Indexed: ASTI, BusI, EngI. *Aud:* Ac, Sa.

For students of engineering, vehicle design, management, and production in the automotive industry. A large number of articles written by the staff review design and engineering trends in the industry—new models, assembly line techniques, quality control, etc. It includes many advertisements by suppliers to the automotive industry, with an index to advertisers. Definitely pro-Detroit; only for specialized collections. (H.B.)

Automotive News; engineering, manufacturing, merchandising, servicing. 1925. w. $12. R. M. Finlay. Marketing Services Inc., 965 E. Jefferson, Detroit, Mich. 48207. Illus., adv. Circ: 45,000. Sample. Vol. ends: 3rd issue in Aug.

Bk. rev: Notes. *Aud:* Sa.

A 30-page tabloid which reports on all aspects of the automotive industry but stresses the economic and business side. A front page is designed like a newspaper; includes such stories as: "Progress on clean air coming up for scrutiny" and "Japanese move past Germans in U.S. Import sales." Most emphasis is on the business, not the technical side, although there is a complete monthly section on "Service management"

which discusses shop work. Regular features include a "truck industry news," classified advertisements, and reports on upcoming events. Larger public libraries will want it for the business collection. Of some interest, also, for larger academic collections.

Behavioral Research in Highway Safety. 1970. q. $20 (Individuals, $12). Theodore Kolehd. Behavioral Publns., 2852 Broadway, New York, N.Y. 10025. Adv. Circ: 700. Sample. Vol. ends: Oct.

Bk. rev: 1,500 words, signed. *Aud:* Ac.

Here is one of the most fortunate encounters of behavioral sciences with the practical aspects of life. Highway safety in a professional context is a rather new formulation which opens the door to an interdisciplinary dialogue on the pages of this journal. Its articles include a great variety of topics. Analytic approach to the driving task, administrative and research problems, emotional stress, characteristics of drinking drivers, improving driver licensing programs, suicidal gestures, and other subjects are covered in the first issues. According to the editors, priority is given to reports on research and evaluation, new theoretical constructs, and program developments where they are concerned with behavior, human factors, and education. Professionality and competence seem to be decisive in the selection.

Chilton's Auto Repair Manual. 1926. a. $11. John Milton. Chilton Book Co., 401 Walnut St., Philadelphia, Pa. 19106. Illus.

Aud: Ga.

An inferior alternative to *Motor's Auto Repair Manual.* Its arrangement and scope are essentially the same; however, descriptions of specific operations are not nearly as detailed here, and figures are not linked to the text with numbers, as in *Motor's.* Caution notes and other special notes are also much less prevalent. The mechanic is often given the number of a special factory tool used to simplify an operation—a minor advantage only, since infrequent use seldom justifies purchase. On the positive side, *Chilton's* boasts a Time Saver feature, a quicker method of performing some tasks. These are repeated throughout the manual as needed. Some are completely novel and others are common sense shortcuts that the amateur might otherwise forget in the heat of frustration. There is a section on trouble shooting but it is overly organized, and not really helpful in starting a stalled car. Despite its many comparative defects, *Chilton's* is far from useless, for even good pictures and text can confuse one on a project, and another book is often the equivalent of a friend showing up with an entirely different and simpler explanation. Hard covers. (In late 1971 the firm also introduced two similar annuals: *Chilton's Foreign Car Repair Manual,* which covers German, Swedish and Italian cars, $14.50; and *Chilton's Truck Repair Manual* at $18.) (H.B.)

Fleet Owner. 1928. m. $3. Robert M. Saxton. Mc-Graw-Hill, Inc., 330 W. 42nd St., New York, N.Y. 10036. Illus., adv. Microform: UM.

Indexed: BusI. *Aud:* Sa.

Supplies information, opinion, news and know-how service to managers who administer, operate, and maintain motor vehicle fleets. It covers all aspects of operating a fleet of trucks or autos, and articles deal with management, operations, maintenance, and safety. Occasionally there is an article on related businesses like air transport. Well illustrated with many black and white photos and advertisements. Only for specialized and business collections.

High Speed Ground Transportation Journal. 1967. 3/yr. $45. James T. Murray. Planning-Transport Associates, Inc., P.O. Box 4824, Duke Station, Durham, N.C. 27706. Illus. Circ: 1,000. Vol. ends: Fall.

Indexed: EngI, HwyResAb. *Bk. rev:* Irreg. *Aud:* Ac, Sa.

One nice thing about academic journals is that their title is often the best description of their contents. This specialty item (only for research and engineering libraries), covers transit problems and systems worldwide, their history, current development, and future prospects. In addition to original reports, books and papers are occasionally reviewed. U.S. Department of Transportation activities are also closely followed. (See also *Public Roads, A Journal of Highway Research.*) The tables of contents for each volume are repeated in back of the number three issue.

Highway Research Abstracts. See Abstracts and Indexes Section.

Motor; the automotive business magazine. 1903. m. $5. William Wolfe. Hearst Corp., 250 W. 55th St., New York, N.Y. 10019. Illus., index, adv. Circ: 140,000. Microform: UM.

Aud: Sa.

A trade magazine for service station owners or students of automobile mechanics. About one half of the articles are devoted to technical information and tips on servicing cars. The rest of given over to management information for the individual service station owner or for the larger service operation employing many mechanics. Some of the monthly features include: "What Detroit Is Thinking," rumors and statements about future automobiles; "Engineers at Work," new design ideas; "New Products," a survey of new products; and "New Literature," brief descriptions of new service charts, parts catalogs, handbooks, etc. Many advertisements and black and white pictures and cartoons are included. A valuable source of information to the mechanic who needs to become familiar with various models of cars and special problems encountered in certain makes and models, it can also be of great value to the do-it-yourself home mechanic, and should be in larger public libraries, certainly in all technical and specialized collections. (H.B.)

Motor's Auto Repair Manual. 1920. a. $10.95. Louis C. Forier. Motor Book Dept., 250 W. 55th St., New York, N.Y. 10019. Illus. Approval copy.

Aud: Ga, Hs, Ac. *Jv:* V.

The most authoritative general repair manual on the market. Mechanical specifications and service procedures for the last seven years are covered, with a panoply of charts, pictures, diagrams and step-by-step instructions to help even the novice forge ahead. A section on trouble shooting and general information is followed by sections covering the unique problems of each U.S. model, plus the VW. A series of charts is included with information such as tune-up data for the twenty years prior to the main coverage, tire wear and conversion charts, foreign car tune-up data, and tap and drill sizes. The manual is in hard covers but heavy usage might require rebinding to library standards. *Chilton's Auto Repair Manual* is also available, but this is better, and is strongly recommended for all public libraries and for large high school and academic collections. In addition to these general manuals, specific books for almost every U.S. model are available from the manufacturer. (H.B.)

Public Roads. See Government Magazines/United States Section.

SAE Journal of Automotive Engineering. 1917. m. $12. Otto W. Vathke. Society of Automotive Engineers, Dept. 7, 2 Pennsylvania Plaza, New York, N.Y. 10001. Illus., index, adv. Circ: 40,000. Vol. ends: Dec. Microform: UM.

Indexed: ASTI, EngI, MetAb. *Aud:* Sa, Ac.

SAE is a highly respected organization. Their standards and reports are definitive for the automobile and combustion engine industries, and the technical or academic library with even minimal engineering emphasis should consider this acquisition as a cost of doing business. Current research and development in both fields is detailed each month, from tire tread design to antenna installation. New publications and products, people, current events, standards, and legislation are regularly covered. Even a collection including materials production information or car safety design and experimentation data might benefit from a subscription. (H.B.)

Speed & Custom Equipment Directory. 1963. $2. Noel Carpenter. Noel Carpenter & Associates, 10347 Calvin Ave., Los Angeles, Calif. 90025. Illus., adv. Circ: 5,000. Sample. Refereed.

Aud: Ga, Hs, Ac.

The specialty equipment market for automobiles and motorcycles continues to expand, largely in response to increasing owner interest in modifying their own vehicles, and in exotic new machinery. If magazines cannot fill patron needs for sources of high performance or customizing equipment and services, then this is a good reference tool to acquire. It lists most

U.S. manufacturers, distributors and dealers ("speed shops"), and service companies (publishers, racing associations, machine shops, etc.). Firms are listed alphabetically and contain, in addition to address and phone number, the officers of the company plus a brief description of the business. In addition there are geographic and subject indexes. The latter are not complete, but nevertheless useful when the reader knows only the type of part or service he wants. (H.B.)

Traffic Safety. 1927. m. $5.60. Angela Maher. National Safety Council, Inc., 425 N. Michigan Ave., Chicago, Ill. 60611. Illus., index, adv. Circ: 20,000. Sample. Vol. ends: Dec. Microform: UM.

Indexed: PsyAb. *Bk. rev:* Irreg., ¾ column, signed. *Aud:* Hs, Ac.

Issued by the National Safety Council for the purpose of bringing together the latest information on accident prevention. The journal is not for the layman, but primarily for the educator, traffic specialist, and police officer. Articles are geared to the expert, moving from traffic control methods to safety devices. Particularly useful is the 30 to 40 page "Research Review" which summarizes all activity in this field. Teachers of driver education will find articles of value. The National Education Association and its American Driver and Traffic Safety Education Division issues *Safety—Administration, Instruction, Protection* for members. It is free, and reports on safety instruction at the secondary school level. (H.B.)

Traffic World; a working tool for traffic and transportation men. 1907. w. $48. J. C. Scheleen. Traffic Service Corp., Washington Bldg., Washington, D.C. 20005. Illus., index, adv. Circ: 11,500. Sample. Vol. ends: Dec. 31. Microform: UM.

Aud: Sa.

Directed to transportation managers in the manufacturing industries, and to water, motor, rail, and air carriers. Articles give worldwide coverage to all aspects relating to the movement of goods. Regular features include ICC decisions, applications, petitions, and hearings, CAB News, Maritime Commission News, Court News, international transportation, legislative news, statistics, etc. There are some black and white pictures and many advertisements. While a specialized trade journal, the scope is wide enough to warrant consideration in many large public and academic libraries.

Ward's Auto World. 1964. m. $15. David C. Smith. Ward's Communications, 28 W. Adams, Detroit, Mich. 48226. Illus., adv. Circ: 30,000. Sample. Vol. ends: Dec. Refereed.

Aud: Ga, Ac.

Economics and the automotive industry's viewpoint are the mainstays of this controlled circulation journal, formerly called *Ward's Quarterly.* Regular departments deal with new products, people in the news,

trucks, technical advances, labor, imports, etc. Feature articles continue the theme, and may analyze the effects of wage and price controls, or describe the history of a car or company, or honor a prominent person in the field. While the pulse of automobile manufacturing is a minute and specialized concern, a library with a strong business collection may be required to cover this area as well, and either this or *Automotive Industries* is a good way to get one's feet wet. Ward's Communications also publishes *Ward's Automotive Reports* and *Ward's Automotive Yearbook.* (H.B.)

Ward's Quarterly. See *Ward's Auto World.*

Trailers

Camper Coachman. See *Motorhome Life.*

Camping and Trailering Guide. See Environment and Conservation/Camping Section.

Family Motorcoaching. 1964. bi-m. $5. Joe Martens. Family Motor Coach Assn., Box 44144, Cincinnati, Ohio 45244. Illus., index, adv. Circ: 15,000. Sample. Vol. ends: Nov/Dec.

Aud: Ga.

A 100 or so page plea for the good life via an expensive motorhome. The first part of each issue is given to news of local chapters of the Family Motor Coach Association. There are then some ten articles on travel, equipment, highways, and the "coach of the month," a type of consumer report. It is more folksy and involved with new products than *Motorhome Life.* (Also, part of the circulation is controlled.)

Four Wheeler. 1962. m. $6. Bill Sanders. Nationwide Publishing, Inc., P.O. Box 8617, La Crescenta, Calif. 91214. Illus., adv. Circ: 40,000 Vol. ends: Dec.

Aud: Ga, Hs, Ac.

One of the better known off-road magazines, this has recently undergone changes in ownership and format and now uses four color process. Information on vehicles, accessories, places to go, and hints on camping and maintenance can be found in a typical issue. Regular columns report on off-roading in other states and answer readers' questions. Articles are brief and plainly written and are aimed at the family man (rather than the race fan) with a four-wheel-drive vehicle. *Four Wheeler* is similar to *Wheels Afield,* but the emphasis is on the vehicle itself rather than on outdoor living and its associated equipment. If there is interest in other off-road vehicles or in competition either *Modern Cycle,* for motorcycle racing, or *Off-Road Vehicles Magazine,* for general off-road competition, should be remembered. (H.B.)

Motorhome Life. 1968. bi-m. $5. Arthur J. Rouse. Trailer Life Publishing Co., 10148 Riverside Drive, North Hollywood, Calif. 91203. Illus., adv. Circ: 32,000. Sample.

Aud: Ga.

A special magazine for the affluent or the relatively rich retired who can afford a motorhome, i.e., a self-propelled recreational vehicle which may run from $10,000 to well over $50,000. (It has some value, too, for the dreamer who may now only own a second hand car and a sleeping bag.) Particularly useful for reliable consumer information on the various types of motorhomes, it is way down the list for most libraries, but see the same publisher's *Trailer Life* for a better all around approach.

There are a number of other acceptable to good special magazines in this same field which libraries might wish to consider. One is *Camper Coachman*. 1963. m. $5. (by the same publisher as *Motorhome Life*). Illus., adv. Circ: 60,000. Here the emphasis is on the pickup-type camper. The magazine has appeal for younger readers, particularly for campers and sportsmen.

Trailer Life. 1941. m. $6.50. Arthur J. Rouse. Trailer Life Publishing Co., 10148 Riverside Dr., North Hollywood, Calif. 91602. Illus., adv. Circ: 200,000. Sample.

Aud: Ga. *Jv:* V.

The most popular of the many trailering magazines. It is generally the most diversified in its coverage. Features numerous short articles and features on all types of trailers from the simple travel variety to pickup campers and motorhomes. It addition to considerable advertising, there are short travel articles, and regular departments which consider club and caravan news. It not only covers trailers, but most allied fields from camping and fishing to hiking and boating. The photographs are fair, and even the less then enchanted trailer fan will enjoy the travel bits. The magazine is particularly good for its how-to-do-it approach, the critical analysis of various types of equipment, and the full reports on prices and facilities, and tips for the economy minded. This is very much a middle income type magazine with attention given as much to saving as to spending. Will have wide appeal for everyone interested in the subject, and despite the quantity of advertisements, a first choice in most libraries.

Trailering Guide. 1962. q. $2. George S. Wells. Rajo Publns., Inc., 4110 E. Van Buren St., Phoenix, Ariz. 85008. Illus., adv.

Aud: Ga. *Jv:* C.

Edited for owners or prospective owners of travel trailers, pickup truck campers, and motor homes. Also includes helpful information on travel. Articles, written by the staff and contributors, draw on people's experiences in building and living in trailers. There is at least one how-to-do-it article for trailer owners. Regular monthly features are "Meals on Wheels," recipes and tips for trailer cooks; "Technical Tips," answers to readers' problems; "Calendar of Events," a listing of shows, rallies, and caravans; "Rolling Along," news of new products. The many black and white pictures

help make this quick and easy to read. For public libraries where demand warrants—others can pass. See also *Wheels Afield.* (H.B.)

Western Mobile News. 1951. w. $3. Opal Calliham. Edwin W. Dean, Jr., 4043 Irving Pl., Culver City, Calif. 90230. Illus., index, adv. Circ: 30,000. Sample. Vol. ends: June.

Bk. rev: 1, length varies, signed. *Aud:* Ga.

Primarily for dealers of mobile homes in the seven western states, this is a tabloid weekly which reports on all aspects of the business. About one quarter to one third of each number is of interest to the mobile home owner. However, the stress is on the trade, covering everything from personalities and trailer parks to the stock market and legislation. Useful for the business collection, but of limited value for the layman.

Wheels Afield. 1967. m. $7.50. Ken Fermoyle. Peterson Pub. Co., 8490 Sunset Blvd., Los Angeles, Calif. 90069. Dist., by: Curtis Circ. Co., Independence Sq., Philadelphia, Pa. 19105. Illus., index, adv. Circ: 100,000. Sample. Vol. ends: Dec.

Aud: Ga.

Comprehensive coverage of the field of recreational vehicles, including motor homes, travel trailers (small mobile homes), camping trailers (the collapsible, tent type), and pickup campers. Generous supply of regular departments, including "Woman's Angle," "Meals Afield," "Campground Reports," and "Trouble Shooting." The features concentrate on product information (often comparing the specifications of several brands in chart form) and on how-to projects to improve both safety and convenience. New trucks, camping units and accessories are evaluated as they appear, and the emphasis is more on description than on criticism. Laws governing speeds, licensing, and overnight parking are explicated. Approximately half of the journal is advertising so this is a good place for the novice to become familiar with different types and brands of camping units. *Wheels Afield* is geared to the middle class camping family (often retired), and the library with this type of clientele will get most mileage from the magazine. See also *Trailering Guide.* (H.B.)

Woodall's Trailer Travel Magazine. 1935. m. $6. Paul Foght. Woodall Publishing Co., 500 Hyacinth Pl., Highland Park, Ill. 60035. Illus., adv. Circ: 142,000. Sample.

Aud: Ga.

Somewhat similar in scope and purpose to *Trailer Life*, this differs in that there is more emphasis on camping grounds and trailer parks than on associated activities. Still, what it does it does well enough, and the equipment reports are up to those found in *Trailer Life*. The prospective buyer should examine both, and anyone who is going to live in a trailer for more than a weekend will want to consider both, too. Libraries will probably wish this as a third or fourth choice after the same publisher's more general *Better Camping* (see Environment & Conservation/Camping section).

Woodall's Trailering Parks and Campgrounds. See Environment and Conservation/Camping Section.

BIBLIOGRAPHY

Basic Periodicals

Ga: *American Book Collector;* Jc: *Bibliographical Society of America. Papers, Book Collector;* Ac: *Bibliographical Society of America. Papers, Book Collector, Bulletin of Bibliography.*

American Book Collector. 1950. m. (Sept.-June). $7.40. W. B. Thorsen, 1822 School St., Chicago, Ill. 60657. Illus., index, adv. Circ: 2,000. Sample.

Bk. rev: Numerous, length varies. *Aud:* Ac, Ga.

Essentially of interest to book collectors, librarians, and members of the antiquarian trade, the contents reflect a wide variety of articles of special concern to printers, publishers, and illustrators as well. Everything of interest to the bookman is here: critical book reviews, articles on authors, special collections, bookbinders, illustrators, etc. Regular features include extensive personal bibliographies of collected authors or illustrators, summary reviews of the auction sales, lists of dealers' catalogs recently published, etc. Advertisements of interest to the bibliographer, collector, and dealer are a special attraction. There is a five year cumulated index. (L. A.)

Bibliographical Society of America. Papers. 1904. q. Membership $10. William B. Todd. P. O. Box 397, Grand Central Station, New York, N.Y. 10017. Illus., index, adv. Circ: 1,600. Vol. ends: No 4. Reprint: Kraus.

Indexed: LibLit, LibSciAb, SSHum. *Bk. rev:* 10–20 500–2,000 words, signed. *Aud:* Ac. *Jv:* V.

The major voice of the dedicated bibliographer and book collector in America, this features such articles as G. Thomas Tanselle's "Textual Study and Literary Judgement," or a biographical sketch of "Thomas W. Streeter, Collector," by Howell J. Heaney. Each issue contains four to five articles by experts on various aspects of bibliography, both analytical and historical. While the contributions tend to be a trifle esoteric, there are usually one or two items of interest to anyone remotely involved with books and publishing. The book reviews are the best available in this field, and following the lengthy critical remarks there are extensive notes by the review editor, Lawrence S. Thompson. Averaging some 150 to 200 pages, the whole boasts a pleasing format. A required item in all larger academic and public libraries.

Bibliography, Documentation Terminology. 1960. bi-m. Free. UNESCO, Place de Fontenoy, Paris, 7e., France. Circ.: 8,000. Sample. Vol. ends: Dec.

Aud: Ac.

An alerting service for bibliographic information, i.e., each 45 to 50 page bulletin reports on new bibliographies available, steps towards bibliographic control, and international bibliographic activities. Specific information is given about available titles, and the newsletter serves as a good source for ordering new material. Primarily for large academic and public libraries, special libraries, and scientific and technical information centers. Note: available in English, French, Spanish and Russian.

Book Collecting & Library Monthly. 1968. $5. B. Hutchison, 42 Trafalgar St., Brighton, England. Circ: 2,000.

Aud: Ga, Ac.

Roughly the British equivalent of the *American Book Collector,* this publishes both long and short articles on all aspects of books, collecting, and libraries. There are usually one or two long articles per issue, along with notes, news, and biographical sketches. A chatty, informative, important, well-written magazine for larger libraries or for individuals "hooked" on collecting.

The Book Collector. 1952. q. $10. Nicholas Barker. Collector Ltd., 58 Frith St., London W1V 6BY, England. Illus., index, adv. Reprint: Kraus-Thomson.

Indexed: BritHum, LibLit, LibSciAb. *Bk. rev:* 5–10, 240–1,000 words, signed. *Aud:* Ac. *Jv:* V.

Somewhat of a British cross between the *Papers of the Bibliographical Society of America* and the *American Book Collector.* It is unique in that it is one of the few collector's magazines left which caters to both the sophisticated bibliographer and the amateur. Articles range from sophisticated and esoteric research on various "points" in analytical bibliography to general comments on collectors and libraries. There are excellent, witty, and always informative introductory remarks by the editor. The whole concludes with reviews of books concerning bibliography, printing, and publishing. Should be in almost any library, if only for the joy and edification of the book-loving librarian.

British Printer; leading technical journal of the printing industry. 1888. m. $10. Maclean-Hunter Ltd., 30 Old Burlington St., London W1, England. Illus., adv. Circ: 11,000.

Indexed: BritTech. *Bk. rev:* 4,200 words. *Aud:* Sa, Ac.

A magazine of equal interest to the collector, bibliographer and printer. Many of the articles are on machinery, techniques, design, and history of the book. From time to time particular attention is given to some historical aspect of printing and typefounding. Considered the leading technical journal for printers in Europe, this should be in every large American collection.

Bulletin of Bibliography and Magazine Notes. 1897. q. $10. Walter T. Dziura. F. W. Faxon Co., 15 Southwest Park, Westwood, Mass. 02090. Index., adv. Circ: 1,200. Microform: UM. Reprint: Johnson.

Indexed: LibLit, LibSciAb. *Aud:* Ac, Ga.

Important on two counts. First, although it only is some 30 to 40 pages long, each issue contains a bibliography of an author, a critical literary study and bibliographic notes. The second part is "Births, deaths and magazine notes," which records new and changed titles and deaths in the periodical world. This includes some short book reviews and, from time to time, reading lists. From a pragmatic point of view, most valuable to larger libraries for the notes on magazines.

Cambridge Bibliographical Society. Transactions. 1949. a. $6.50. J. R. Harrison. Cambridge Univ. Press, 32 E. 57th St., New York, N.Y. 10022.

Indexed: BritHum. *Aud:* Ac.

Unlike other bibliographic society publications, emphasis here is almost exclusively on esoteric bibliographic research which has limited appeal except for the subject expert. One of five parts is issued each year, the volume cumulating at the end of the fifth year. Only for large collections.

Journal of Typographic Research. See *Visible Language,* Library Periodicals Section.

Kirjath Sepher; bibliographical quarterly of the Jewish National and University Library. 1924. q. $10. J. Orman, Magnes Press, Jewish National and Univ. Library, P.O.B. 503, Jerusalem, Israel, Circ: 1,000.

Bk. rev: 2–4, lengthy, signed. *Aud.* Ga, Ac.

The Jewish National and University Library is the national library of the State of Israel and the national library of the Jewish people. It acquires all materials concerning the Jewish people, Jewish culture, and the State of Israel, and its collection on Judaica is the largest in the world. The library publishes the bibliographic quarterly *Kirjath Sepher* which contains articles and book reviews in Hebrew and a multilingual bibliography. The bibliography has two divisions: "Israel Publications" and "Hebraica and Judaica." The first lists Israeli publications (mostly in Hebrew), received by the Jewish National and University Library as deposit copies and in fact constitutes the Israel national bibliography. "Hebraica and Judaica" is multilingual and lists new books and periodicals published outside of Israel on the following subjects: Biblical studies including Dead Sea Scrolls, Talmud and Rabbinic literature, Jewish philosophy and religion, history of the Jewish people, Palestine and Zionism, the State of Israel, Hebrew and Yiddish literature, literature in other languages on Jewish themes. Each issue

also offers a selection of articles from Israeli and non-Israeli periodicals on the aforementioned subjects. Since these articles are listed solely under the name of the periodical, and not by subject, they are useful only for current awareness (see also *Index of Articles on Jewish Studies,* in Abstracts and Indexes section).

Kirjath Sepher is distinguished for its detailed and reliable bibliographic descriptions. It gives also the advantages of a broad, international bibliography on Judaica. It is a useful reference source for librarians, bibliographers, students, and scholars. The principal difficulty is the lack of any cumulation, even annual. However, there is an annual index of author names and titles. (R.J.)

Library. 1899. q. Membership (Nonmembers $14). Peter Davison. Dept. of English, Univ. of Birmingham. Subs. to: Oxford Univ. Press, Oxford, England. Illus., index, adv. Circ: 1,700. Sample. Vol. ends: Dec. Refereed. Microform: UM. Reprint: Kraus.

Indexed: LibLit, LibSciAb. *Bk. rev:* 8–10, 600–700 words, signed. *Aud:* Ac.

In many ways this is the equivalent in Great Britain to the American *Papers of the Bibliographical Society of America*. The journal consists of the transactions of The Bibliographical Society. (The editor observes that the Society requires no additional identification. Which is to say, it has a position much like that of England's *Who's Who,* where it is felt that anyone "who is who" must be English and it is redundant to add "England.") This pleasant touch will not add to its value for most Americans, but regardless of title or subtitle it is a second choice after the American *Papers*. Emphasis here is on all aspects of not only English, but international history of books, publishing, printing, libraries, and book collecting. The articles are scholarly, yet boast a quite pleasant style. The book reviews, while limited in number, are excellent.

Private Library. 1957. q. Membership (Libraries $8.50). John Cotton. Private Libraries Assn., 41 Cuckoo Hill Rd., Pinner, Middlesex, England. Illus., index, adv. Circ: 1,000.

Indexed: LibLit, LibSciAb. *Bk. rev:* 5–10, length varies. *Aud:* Ac, Ga.

A somewhat more popular version of the *Book Collector,* i.e., the articles are less esoteric, more inclined to point up the basic joys of book collecting without too much emphasis on bibliographic detail. The journal is unique, too, in that it puts particular stress on the work of private presses, both in England and abroad. (An annual checklist of titles, *Private Press Books,* is published by the Association annually, and constitutes the best current source of information in this field). Although rarely more than 50 pages, the magazine is nicely printed and edited, and a joy to read. Again, as much for the library as for the private collector.

Studies in Bibliography and Booklore; devoted to research in the field of Jewish bibliography. 1953. 2/yr. $7.50 (for 4 nos.). Herbert Zafren. Library of Hebrew Union College, Jewish Inst. of Religion, Cincinnati, Ohio 54220. Illus. Circ: 1,600. Sample. Vol. ends: No. 4. Reprint: Johnson.

Indexed: IJewPer. *Bk. rev:* 1–2, 800 words, signed. *Aud:* Ac.

A scholarly journal devoted primarily to Jewish bibliography, publishing, bookselling, etc. While most of the articles are in English, many references are made in Hebrew. Issues tend to concentrate on a given area, e.g., Jewish-Persian studies. There are numerous black and white illustrations. A superior bibliographic journal for the specialist and for all large collections.

BIOLOGICAL SCIENCES

Basic Periodicals

Hs: *American Biology Teacher, BioScience.* Ga: *BioScience* (for large public libraries); see also Zoos in Zoology Section. Ac: *American Journal of Botany, American Zoologist, Biological Bulletin, Ecology, Genetics, Journal of Bacteriology, Journal of Experimental Biology, Journal of Experimental Zoology, Physiological Reviews* Jc: *BioScience, American Biology Teacher.*

Basic Abstracts and Indexes

Biological Abstracts, Biological and Agricultural Index.

Introduction

The biological sciences probably contain more areas of specialization than any other science. Research developments in the last twenty years have so altered the emphasis in the study of modern biology that sharp delineations can no longer be made between subfields. Journals included in this section have been grouped into six areas. (1) General, covering more than one subfield and including a sampling of publications on ecology, evolution, cytology, developmental biology, etc.; (2) Biochemistry and Biophysics; (3) Botany; (4) Microbiology and Genetics; (5) Physiology; and (6) Zoology. Selections of research journals for academic libraries have been severely limited, mostly to U.S. publications. Unless noted otherwise, these represent authoritative, high quality publications of distinguished scientific societies and well-known commercial publishers. Moreover, each research report submitted for publication is usually reviewed critically by one or two referees. Thus, the annotations which follow are brief, general descriptions of the periodicals, rather than evaluative ones, which only subject specialists are qualified to make. The American Institute of Biological Sciences Subcommittee on Facilities and Standards published a list of first-choice journals for biology libraries (*BioScience*, v. 13, no. 6, 1963, pp.

14–19). Their basic selection of essential periodicals is listed above under Basic Periodicals for academic libraries. Several additional journals, many of which have been included here, were also suggested for possible academic choices. See also Environment and Conservation, Oceanography, Environmental Sciences, and Ornithology Sections.

General

Academy of Sciences of the USSR. Proceedings. Biological Sciences Section. bi-m. $125. Consultants Bureau, 227 W. 17th St., New York, N.Y. 10011. Illus., index. Sample. Vol. ends: 1v./issue. Refereed.

Indexed: BioAb, ChemAb, SCI *Aud:* Sa, Ac.

The well-known *Proceedings of the Academy of Sciences of the USSR* represent some of the best and most important studies in Russian research. *Doklady Biological Sciences*, as this journal is commonly called, is a cover-to-cover translation of the biological portions of the *Proceedings*, and contains the cumulated research reports of such areas as: anatomy, cytology, ecology, embryology, endocrinology, evolutionary morphology, genetics, histology, immunology, microbiology, morphology, parasitology, physiology, virology, zoology, etc. Each issue represents one volume (of six issues) of the Russian text. Generally, the translation appears six months after publication of the original Russian. An important periodical for strong research collections in university libraries.

In complementary fields, and following the same general publications format as the *Doklady Biological Sciences*, are three other journals in translation also put out by Consultants Bureau. *Doklady Biochemistry* covers research reports in biochemistry; *Doklady Biophysics* is devoted exclusively to biophysical work; and *Doklady Botanical Sciences* incorporates research on botany, phytopathology, plant anatomy, plant ecology, plant embryology, plant morphology, and plant physiology.

American Biology Teacher. 1938. m. $10. Jack Carter. National Assn. of Biology Teachers, 1420 N St., N.W., Washington, D.C. 20005. Illus., index, adv. Circ: 13,500. Sample. Vol. ends: Dec. Refereed. Microform: UM, Canner.

Indexed: BioAb, EdI. *Bk. rev:* 5–10, 500 words, signed. *Aud:* Sa, Ac, Hs.

The professional journal for high school teachers or anyone teaching undergraduate courses at a beginning level. Articles, written both by educators and scientists, are concerned with new teaching methods, aids and demonstrations in the classroom and laboratory, as well as interpretations of new research and technologies. A basic item for high school libraries and college libraries focusing on undergraduate education. See also *Journal of Biological Education.*

American Midland Naturalist. 1909. q. $15. Robert P. McIntosh. Univ. of Notre Dame, Notre Dame, Ind. 46556. Illus., index. Circ: 1,500. Vol. ends: no. 4. Refereed. Microform: UM, Canner. Reprint: Johnson.

Indexed: BioAb, BioAg, ChemAb, SCI. *Aud:* Sa, Ac.

A well-established general biological journal concentrating mostly on the natural history of the Midwest. Ecological studies of plant and animal life are frequently stressed, although occasional critical papers on selected topics such as morphology, physiology, and taxonomy are also included. A good, all-encompassing natural history periodical for academic collections.

American Naturalist. 1867. bi-m. $12.50. Robert Sokal and Lawrence Slobodkin. Univ. of Chicago Press, 5801 Ellis Ave., Chicago, Ill. 60637. Illus., index. Circ: 2,600. Sample. Vol. ends: no. 6. Refereed. Microform: UM, Canner, Princeton. Reprint: Johnson.

Indexed: BioAb, BioAg, ChemAb, SCI. *Aud:* Sa, Ac.

For over a century, the official organ of the American Society of Naturalists has been emphasizing broad biological studies of flora and fauna and a "view of organic evolution." Papers and short, scientific letters to the editors discuss such fields as population genetics and selection, ecosystems, evolution, geographic distributions, and other areas of interest in natural history. A good first choice for undergraduate collections, the journal is an authoritative and excellent one for any academic library.

Biological Bulletin. 1898. bi-m. $28. W. D. Russell-Hunter. Marine Biological Laboratory, Woods Hole, Mass. 02543. Illus., index. Circ: 3,100. Sample. Vol. ends: no. 3; 2v/yr. Refereed. Microform: Canner, Princeton.

Indexed: BioAb, BioAg, ChemAb, PsyAb, SCI. *Aud:* Sa, Ac.

A fine, general biological publication, produced by the well-known Woods Hole Marine Biological Laboratory. Specializing in studies on marine biology, original research articles report on any aspect of aquatic plant and animal life, biochemical through physiological. Papers represent fairly comprehensive work. On occasion, reports of the Marine Biological Lab are carried, as well as abstracts of special symposia organized by them. Particularly recommended as a publication for undergraduate libraries, the journal is a first-choice selection for any academic collection.

BioScience. 1951. m. $24. John A. Behnke. Amer. Inst. of Biological Sciences, 3900 Wisconsin Ave., N.W., Washington, D.C. 20016. Illus., index, adv. Vol. ends: no. 12. Refereed.

Indexed: BioAb, ChemAb, SCI. *Bk. rev:* 6–8, 500–700 words, signed. *Aud:* Sa, Ac, Hs.

About the best nonspecialist periodical interpreting advances in the biological, medical, and agricultural sciences. Starting out as a fledgling newsletter devoted to news and editorials of the American Institute of Biological Sciences (AIBS), the publication now carries features, reports, and news on contemporary problems in the biological sciences, both from a research standpoint and an educational overview. For the student and informed layman, feature articles provide a basis for keeping informed on developments in the field; for the specialist and educator, research reports, about one to two pages in length, discuss on-going activities in the laboratory; and for the librarian, the book review section concentrates far less on the specialized monograph and more on the type of literature required by the general academic collection. Recommended for any type of library, including larger public libraries which seek more than a general science periodical.

Cambridge Philosophical Society. Biological Reviews. 1923. q. $26.50. E. N. Willmer. Cambridge Univ. Press, 32 E. 57th St., New York, N.Y. 10022. Illus., index. Circ: 1,700. Sample. Vol. ends: no. 4. Refereed.

Indexed: BioAb, ChemAb, IMed, SCI. *Aud:* Sa, Ac.

Specializes in the long, authoritative and scholarly review article on specific topics in the biological sciences. Each issue contains three to four lengthy papers which, although constituting a high degree of specialization, are still styled as tutorials for the nonspecialist biologist. The spread of subjects is quite diversified, however, and is not limited to any one section of the biological sciences. Reviews, contributed by prominent scientists, also contain detailed tables of contents, excellent bibliographies, and resumes (not merely short abstracts), which detail the main facts and conclusions of the paper. Small academic libraries may find their needs for a review journal adequately served by *Quarterly Review of Biology*, but every research-oriented and university collection will need this.

Developmental Biology. 1959. m. $30./v. 3v./yr. Elizabeth D. Hay. Academic Press, 111 Fifth Ave., New York, N.Y. 10003. Illus., index. Sample. Vol. ends: 3v./yr. Refereed.

Indexed: BioAb, BioAg, ChemAb, IMed, SCI. *Aud:* Sa, Ac.

An international publication, and also the official organ of the Society for Developmental Biology, the journal draws together related papers from both botanical and zoological fields, and focuses on current research in the broad area of development. Original research articles deal with "embryonic and post-embryonic development, growth, regeneration, tissue repair of plants and animals," and may be studied from a biochemical, cytological, genetic standpoint, etc. Included in each issue is also a section on news and editorial or reader opinion, as well as a bibliography, "Current Literature," covering relevant publications in development biology. The field represents an important facet of the biological sciences, and the journal offers authoritative studies for research-oriented biological collections.

Ecology. 1920. bi-m. $24. Alton A. Lindsey. Duke Univ. Press, Box 6697, College Station, Durham, N.C. 27708. Illus., index. Circ: 7,000. Vol. ends: no. 6. Refereed. Microform: Princeton.

Indexed: BioAb, BioAg, ChemAb, SCI. *Bk. rev:* 5–8, 500 words, signed. *Aud:* Sa, Ac.

The burst of interest in this field has also shot up the circulation of this journal by over 30 percent in the last few years. Notwithstanding current concern of scientists and laymen, the publication is, and always has been, a basic journal for every biological collection. Published for the Ecological Society of America, the periodical considers some of the fundamental biological problems of the interrelationship of organisms and their environments. Both plant and animal ecology is studied. Articles branch from general principles of ecology, ecosystems, to population studies, mathematical modeling of ecological processes, environmental control, biogeography, and the like. Papers are usually restricted to 20 pages in length. Longer research papers are published in the Society's other journal, *Ecological Monographs* (1931, q. $14.). Papers, on general ecological subjects of both plant and animal life, are authoritative, comprehensive studies. Both journals are necessary for good, academic collections. For libraries with miniscule budgets, *Ecology* would be first choice. See Environmental Sciences Section for related titles in this field.

Evolution. 1947. q. $17. Robert F. Inger. Soc. for the Study of Evolution, c/o R. E. Beer, Entomology Dept., Univ. of Kans., Lawrence, Kans. 66044. Illus., index. Circ: 3,000. Vol. ends: no. 4, December. Refereed. Microform: UM.

Indexed: BioAb, ChemAb, SCI. *Bk. rev:* 1–2, 500–700 words, signed. *Aud:* Sa, Ac.

Papers in this publication deal with the broad area of evolution, and cover a wide biological spectrum of both plants and animals. Genetic, ecological, morphological, and physiological studies, as related to evolutionary biology, are all within its scope. Typical of its contents are such titles as "Group Selection and the Evolution of Dispersal" and "Dinosaur Physiology and the Origin of Mammals." An authoritative, international journal of "organic evolution" for academic libraries.

Experimental Cell Research. 1950. m. $32./v. 5v./yr. Ed. bd. Academic Press, 111 Fifth Ave., New York, N.Y. 10003. Illus., index. Sample. Vol. ends: 5v./yr. Refereed.

Indexed: BioAb, ChemAb, IMed, SCI. *Aud:* Sa, Ac.

Published under the auspices of the International Society for Cell Biology. Original research reports and preliminary notes of on-going investigations are dedicated to studies of the structure, behavior, growth and general operation of the cell, and the chemistry and function of cell components. More specifically, papers deal with the physical and chemical aspects of cellular and intercellular structure; environmental relations and adaptation of the cell; biosynthesis with reference to cell growth; subcellular particles, etc. A representative, high quality journal in cytology, and an important publication for research-oriented university collections.

Federation of American Societies for Experimental Biology. Federation Proceedings. 1942. bi-m. $25. Lorin J. Mullins. Federation of Amer. Societies for Experimental Biology, 9650 Rockville Pike, Bethesda, Md. 20014. Illus., index, adv. Circ: 15,000. Sample. Vol. ends: no. 6 (Nov./Dec.). Refereed. Microform: UM.

Indexed: BioAb, ChemAb, SCI. *Aud:* Sa, Ac.

The Federation is comprised of the following prominent scientific societies: American Physiological Society, American Society of Biological Chemists, American Society for Pharmacology and Experimental Therapeutics, American Institute of Nutrition, and American Association of Immunologists. *Federation Proceedings,* reflecting their combined research interests, consists of papers presented as special symposia organized as part of the group's annual meetings. One issue (March-April) is devoted to abstracts of papers presented at these sessions. Papers generally center around themes of wide interest, e.g., "Developmental Pharmacology," etc. Some news and announcements are also included in each issue. A broad-based journal for research-oriented biological collections.

Human Biology. 1929. q. $8. Gabriel W. Lasker. Wayne State Univ. Press, Detroit, Mich. 48202. Illus., index. Vol. ends: no. 4. Refereed. Microform: UM. Reprint: Kraus.

Indexed: BioAb, BioAg, ChemAb, PsyAb, SCI. *Bk. rev:* 6, 200–500 words, signed. *Aud:* Sa, Ac.

The official journal of the Society for Human Biology. Studies are generally concerned with human variation and the underlying factors, whether genetic, environmental, etc., which have caused these variants. Both present and past populations are concerned. Titles such as "Height of 7-Year Old Children," and "Genetically Contrasted Groups in the Near East," indicate its scope. Papers embrace such fields as demography and physical anthropology, as well as evolution, genetics, and human biology. In addition to critical reviews, the book review section contains a useful and lengthy list of recent publications in the field. A good, authoritative, supportive journal for biological collections.

Journal of Biological Education. 1967. 6/yr. $10. Ed. bd. Academic Press, 111 Fifth Ave., New York, N.Y. 10003. Illus., index, adv. Vol. ends: no. 6. Sample. Refereed.

Indexed: ChemAb. *Bk. rev:* 12, 250–350 words, signed. *Aud:* Hs, Sa, Ac.

Published for the Institute of Biology, London. Somewhat the British counterpart to *American Biology Teacher,* issues discuss biological education at all levels, secondary through undergraduate. The focus is not only on course development, instructional aids, and apparatus equipment for laboratories, but also takes in experimentation suitable for lab work. A section on reviews takes in film reviews, as well as books. First-choice for U.S. libraries will naturally be *American Biology Teacher,* but the publication is well worth the subscription for larger libraries which can broaden their scope to instructional methods in other countries.

Journal of Experimental Biology. 1923. bi-m. (2v./yr.) $19.50/v. Vincent Wigglesworth and J. A. Ramsay. Cambridge Univ. Press, 32 E. 57th St., New York, N.Y. 10022. Illus., index. Sample. Vol. ends: no. 3, 2v./yr. Refereed. Reprint: Johnson.

Indexed: BioAb, BioAg, ChemAb, IMed, PsyAb, SCI. *Aud:* Sa, Ac.

A well-known and authoritative journal published for the Company of Biologists, Ltd. Research reports deal in good measure with invertebrates, although the range includes marine biology, neurophysiology, and entomology, as related to experimental zoology, physiology and biochemistry. A prominent, international publication, and because of its broad scope, should be a first-choice selection for academic libraries.

Journal of Natural History. 1967. bi-m. $52.34. Ed. bd. Taylor & Francis, Ltd., Cannon House, Macklin St., London, WC2, England. Illus., index, adv. Vol. ends: no. 6. Sample. Refereed. Reprint: Dawson.

Indexed: BioAb. *Bk. rev:* 3, 600 words, signed. *Aud:* Sa, Ac.

Formerly the *Annals and Magazine of Natural History.* The journal is primarily a publication dedicated to papers on taxonomy, and includes studies of classifications of both plants and animals. Occasionally some work on ecology as related to taxonomy, and paleontology, as well as general biology papers, are also included. Both originals research articles and reviews are published. The scope is not limited to the flora and fauna of the British Isles, but is international. A useful taxonomic journal for academic collections.

Life Sciences. 1962. s.-m. $100., combined edition; $55. per part. C. Matsumoto. Pergamon Press, Inc., Maxwell House, Fairview Park, Elmsford, N. Y. Illus., index. Sample. Vol. ends: no. 24. Refereed. Microform: Maxwell. Reprint: Maxwell.

Indexed: BioAb, ChemAb, IMed, PsyAb, SCI. *Aud:* Sa, Ac.

A journal devoted to short research papers discussing on-going research in the fields of biochemistry, molecular biology, physiology, and pharmacology. Communications generally represent important results in these fields and are reproduced from manuscript copy to ensure early publication. Available in two parts (each of which may be purchased separately): Part I, appearing on the first and fifteenth of each month, is dedicated to physiology and pharmacology; Part 2, issued on the eighth and twenty-second of the month, contains reports on biochemistry, and general and molecular biology. International in scope, papers may appear in French and German, as well as English. Individual researchers in the field and large collections will need it, although it may be too specialized and expensive for small academic libraries.

Linnean Society. Biological Journal. 1969. 4/yr. $24. Doris M. Kermack. Academic Press, 111 Fifth Ave., New York, New York 10003. Illus., index. Circ: 1,500. Vol. ends: no. 4. Sample. Refereed.

Indexed: BioAb. *Aud:* Sa, Ac.

The Linnean Society of London, named in honor of the famed Swedish naturalist Carl Linnaeus (creator of a binomial system of nomenclature for plants and animals), was first established in 1788. A series of prominent publications since that time have marked the progress of taxonomy in the annals of the biological literature. The present journal continues the Society's *Proceedings,* published since the nineteenth century. Original papers are again concerned primarily with taxonomy, but articles of general biological interest are also carried (e.g., a recent issue discussed biological information retrieval services). Reports of the meetings of the Society are sometimes included.

Two other well-known publications of the Society are its *Botanical Journal* and *Zoological Journal,* in print since the mid 1800s and formerly called *Linnean Society of London. Botany* and *Zoology,* respectively. Since the Society restructured its publications, these have also been issued quarterly ($24/yr., Academic Press). The journals are characterized, as before, by scholarly papers on taxonomic classification both of plants and animals. All three periodicals are authoritative additions to academic libraries interested in their field of specialization.

Quarterly Review of Biology. 1926. q. $10. Bentley Glass and Frank C. Erk. Stony Brook Foundation, Inc., State Univ. of N.Y., Stony Brook, N.Y. 11790. Illus., index. Circ: 3,100. Vol. ends: no. 4 (Dec.). Refereed. Microform: UM, Princeton. Reprint: Johnson.

Indexed: BioAb, BioAg, ChemAb, IMed, PsyAb, SCI. *Bk. rev:* 2–3, major; 50–60 brief, signed. *Aud:* Sa, Ac.

Addressed to both researcher, general biologist, and student, the journal publishes about two to three lengthy critical review articles on any timely and current research topic in the biological sciences. Reviews are highly authoritative, often of monographic length, and generally contain enough of background or historical material to be of tutorial value to students. A section on "New Biological Books," which often comprises half the journal, constitutes a comprehensive overview of new publications. One or two reviews may be critical, essay type, and the remainder are brief notices classified by field of specialization. An excellent and first-choice review publication for every academic library.

Royal Society. Philosophical Transactions. Series B, Biological Sciences. See Science/General Section.

Royal Society. Proceedings. Series B, Biological Sciences. See Science/General Section.

Society for Experimental Biology and Medicine. Proceedings. 1903. m. (11/yr.). $25. L. J. Cizek. Academic Press, 111 Fifth Ave., New York, N.Y. 10003. Illus., index. Circ: 7,740. Vol. ends: Irreg. Microform: Princeton. Reprint: Johnson.

Indexed: BioAb, ChemAb, IMed, PsyAb, SCI. *Aud:* Sa, Ac.

Specializes in short, timely research reports which emphasize the experimental method of investigation in the biological or medical sciences. Papers deal with such subjects as biochemistry, enzymology, microbiology, nutrition, pathology, physiology, tissue culture, virology, etc. A valuable journal for biomedical research collections.

Stain Technology. 1925. bi-m. $10. H. A. Davenport. Williams & Wilkins Co., 428 E. Preston St., Baltimore, Md. 21202. Illus., index, adv. Circ: 3,400. Sample. Vol. ends: no. 6. Refereed. Microform: UM, Princeton. Reprint: Johnson.

Indexed: BioAb, ChemAb, IMed. *Bk. rev:* 1-2, 400 words, signed. *Aud:* Sa, Ac.

An international "journal for microtechnic and histochemistry" and the official organ of the Biological Stain Commission. Original articles relate to the nature and use of staining agents in the studies of microscopic structure of tissues of organisms, and other histological techniques. A section on "Notes of Technics," consists of short reports, less than two pages, also concerned with the use of dyes in biological research. The periodical is a particularly important one for undergraduate laboratory training, and is recommended for academic collections.

Biochemistry and Biophysics

Archives of Biochemistry and Biophysics. 1942. m. (5v./yr.). $29./v. Ed.bd. Academic Press, Inc., 111 Fifth Ave., New York, N.Y. 10003. Illus., index. Sample. Vol. ends: 5v./yr. Refereed.

Indexed: BioAb, ChemAb, IMed, SCI. *Aud:* Sa, Ac.

The journal publishes scholarly research papers on current biochemical and biophysical problems underlying aspects of biological processes in plant and animal systems. Recent studies have been concerned with such topics as protein synthesis, nucleic acids, metabolic reactions, enzymes, etc. A significant and authoritative journal for biological research collections in university libraries.

Biochemical and Biophysical Research Communications. 1959. s-m. (4v./yr.). $25./v. Ed.bd. Academic Press, 111 Fifth Ave., New York, N.Y. 10003. Illus., index. Sample. Vol. ends: 4v./yr. Refereed.

Indexed: BioAb, ChemAb, IMed, SCI. *Aud:* Sa, Ac.

To accommodate the rapid dissemination of short communications, this journal, devoted to "modern experimental biology," reproduces its manuscripts by offset printing. Research studies are concerned with work on proteins, DNA, enzymology, membrane processes, nucleic acids, etc. An important publication for researchers requiring the latest developments in their field. See also *Archives of Biochemistry and Biophysics* for a corollary Academic Press publication in the field.

Biochemical Journal. 1906. s-m. $112. D. G. Walker. Biochemical Soc., 7 Warwick Court, London, WC1R 5DP, England. Illus., index. Sample. Vol. ends: 5v./yr. Refereed. Microform: MF, PMC. Reprint: Dawson, Johnson.

Indexed: BioAb, ChemAb, IMed, SCI. *Aud:* Sa, Ac.

This journal is the official organ of the prestigious Biochemical Society (London). Papers and short communications deal with fundamental studies on chemical and physicochemical aspects of life processes, and some methodological studies related to biochemistry. Topics under investigation have centered around carbohydrates, lipids, proteins, enzymes, energy metabolism, etc. Included in the journal are also the *Proceedings of the Biochemical Society,* short, extended abstracts of papers presented at meetings of the organization. One of the earliest, and most authoritative scholarly journals in the field. Necessary for research collections.

Biochemistry. 1962. s-m. $60. Hans Neurath. Amer. Chemical Soc., 1155 16th St., N.W., Washington, D.C. 20036. Illus., index. Circ: 5,400. Sample. Vol. ends: no. 26. Refereed. Microform: Amer. Chemical Soc.

Indexed: ChemAb, SCI. *Aud:* Sa, Ac.

All areas of fundamental research in biochemistry are explored in this high quality journal. Emphasis is placed on the chemical aspects of biochemical processes, and the relationship of chemistry to the biological sciences. Research papers investigate enzymes, proteins, lipids, nucleic acids, etc. In addition to tables and charts, the journal has been illustrated with some excellent color stereophotography. An important, authoritative research journal for both chemical and biological collections in academic libraries. (Note: A similar title, *Biochemistry,* published by Consultants Bureau, is the English translation of the Russian journal, *Biokhimiya.*)

Biochimica et Biophysica Acta. 1947. w. $766.10. E. C. Slater. Elsevier Publishing Co., Box 211, Amsterdam, Netherlands. Illus., index, adv. Circ: 4,500. Sample. Vol. ends: 33v./yr. Refereed. Reprint: Johnson.

Indexed: BioAb, ChemAb, IMed, SCI. *Aud:* Sa, Ac.

An authoritative, international journal dedicated to all areas of biochemical and biophysical research. At its current subscription price, the budget-minded research librarian can only wince. Luckily, however, the journal is published in several sections and each part may be purchased separately, according to the following breakdown: (1) Nucleic Acids and Protein Synthesis; (2) Lipids and Lipid Metabolism; (3) Enzymology; (4) Protein Structure; (5) BioEnergetics; (6) Biomembranes; (7) General. Each section contains the usual research papers and shorter communications. For affluent university collections.

Biophysical Journal. 1960. m. $35. Max A. Lauffer, Rockefeller Univ. Press, 66th St. and York Ave., New York, N.Y. 10021. Illus., index. Circ: 2,000. Sample. Vol. ends: Dec. Refereed.

Indexed: BioAb, ChemAb, IMed, SCI. *Aud:* Sa, Ac.

Research papers of the official journal of the Biphysical Society are concerned with physical studies of processes in living organisms, and the methodology of physics in these processes. Authoritative studies include both work in molecular biology and theoretical biophysics, i.e., mathematical models of life processes. Titles of papers such as "Muscle Energetics," and "Red Blood Cell Damage by Shear Stress" are indicative of its research scope. A basic journal in the field for both physics and biological collections in academic libraries. (More specialized collections would also be interested in two other authoritative publications: *Biophysik*, published by Springer-Verlag; and *Biophysics*, a translation of *Biofizika* (USSR), put out by Pergamon.)

Doklady Biochemistry. See *Academy of Sciences of the USSR. Proceedings. Biological Sciences Section.* Biological Sciences/General Section.

Doklady Biophysics. See *Academy of Sciences of the USSR. Proceedings. Biological Sciences Section.* Biological Sciences/General Section.

Journal of Biological Chemistry. 1905. s.-m. $75. Herbert Tabor. Amer. Soc. of Biological Chemists, 428 E. Preston St., Baltimore, Md. Illus., index. Vol. ends: no. 24. Refereed. Microform: UM. Reprint: Johnson.

Indexed: BioAb, ChemAb, IMed, SCI. *Aud:* Sa, Ac.

One of the oldest publications devoted exclusively to chemical problems in the life sciences. Research articles contribute to the literature of such fields as the chemistry and metabolism of macromolecules; the chemistry and metabolism of substances of low molecular weight; oxidation-reduction processes and bio-

energetics; enzymology; and control mechanisms and biochemical genetics. This prominent and authoritative publication, plus *Biochemistry,* published by the American Chemical Society, would make first-choice selections for the development of any biochemical collection. For academic libraries.

Journal of Molecular Biology. 1959. s.-m. $242. J. C. Kendrew. Academic Press, 111 Fifth Ave., New York, N.Y. Illus., index. Sample. Vol. ends: 8v./yr. Refereed.

Indexed: BioAb, ChemAb, IMed. *Aud:* Sa, Ac.

Since 1945, the field of molecular biology has been the motivating force in current biological research. This English-based research journal contains papers and short communications concerning the nature, production, and replication of biological structure at the molecular level. Studies under investigation have included the molecular structure of muscle, nerve, and other tissues; structure of proteins, nucleic acids, lipids, and carbohydrates; structure of viruses, and molecular genetics. A scholarly journal for biological research collections.

Quarterly Reviews of Biophysics. 1968. q. $22.50. Arne Engstrom. Cambridge Univ. Press, 32 E. 57th St., New York, N.Y. 10002. Illus., index, adv. Circ: 1,200. Vol. ends: no. 4. Sample. Refereed.

Indexed: BioAb, ChemAb. *Aud:* Sa, Ac.

Published for the International Union for Pure and Applied Biophysics. The journal is comprised of authoritative and lengthy, critical review papers on all areas of biophysics. Generally, topics selected are those covering fields of greatest biophysical interest. Recent papers have discussed such areas as physical principles underlying biological phenomena, physical measurements and techniques used in biological research, and sophisticated instrumentation used to carry out biological investigations. Papers are usually invited from specialists, and frequently represent the invited papers presented at meetings organized by IUPAB. About two to five reviews appear in each issue; some are as lengthy as 100 pages. An authoritative and important reviewing medium for collections in the biological sciences; certainly all good biophysical collections will need it.

Botany

American Journal of Botany. 1914. 10/yr. $21.50. Norman H. Boke. Allen Press, Inc., 1041 New Hampshire St., Lawrence, Kans. Subs. to: Lawrence J. Crockett, City College, City Univ. of New York, New York, N.Y. 10031. Illus., index. Vol. ends: Nov/Dec. Refereed. Reprint: Johnson.

Indexed: BioAb, BioAg, ChemAb, SCI. *Aud:* Sa, Ac.

The official journal of the Botanical Society of America, the leading society of the United States, which also includes the Society for Plant Morphology and Physiology and the American Mycological Society within its association. Issues are devoted entirely to authoritative research papers on "all aspects of plant science," including such areas as plant morphology, physiology, pathology, microbiology as related to plant science, etc. A first-choice selection for every collection in the biological sciences.

Annals of Botany. 1887. 5/yr. $25. J. F. Sutcliffe. Oxford Univ. Press, Ely House, 37 Dover St., London, England. Illus., index. Circ: 2,000. Sample. Vol. ends: no. 5. Refereed. Microform: Princeton. Reprint: Dawson.

Indexed: BioAb, BioAg, ChemAb, SCI. *Aud:* Sa, Ac.

A leading research journal in the botanical sciences. Scholarly investigations study such fields as plant embryology, plant genetics, cell structure, plant pathology, etc. A fine, and long-established journal for botanical collections, although small academic libraries might find a publication such as the *American Journal of Botany* sufficient for their needs.

Botanical Gazette. 1875. q. $15. Taylor A. Steeves. Univ. of Chicago Press, 5801 Ellis Ave., Chicago, Ill. 60637. Illus., index. Circ: 1,750. Vol. ends: no. 4 (Dec.). Microform: UM, Canner. Reprint: Johnson.

Indexed: BioAb, BioAg, ChemAb, SCI. *Aud:* Sa, Ac.

One of the oldest botanical research journals in the United States, and a quality publication for any research library. Articles cover all aspects of the plant sciences, including some works on paleobotany and plant ecology, as well as the usual plant morphology, plant physiology, taxonomy, and the like. A valuable choice for academic collections supporting the botanical sciences.

Botanical Review. 1935. q. $12. Arthur Cronquist. New York Botanical Garden, Bronx, N. Y. 10458. Illus., index. Circ: 2,500. Vol. ends: no. 4. Refereed. Microform: UM, Canner, Princeton. Reprint: Johnson.

Indexed: BioAb, BioAg, ChemAb, SCI. *Aud:* Sa, Ac.

"Interpreting botanical progress," the journal acts as a forum for reviews of the latest achievements in botanical research. All facets of the fields are explored. Usually, articles are invited from leading authorities, who present an overview of the subject and include enough background and bibliography for the nonspecialist botanist or advanced student. Important for research collections and most academic libraries, particularly undergraduate ones.

Canadian Journal of Botany. 1929. m. $24. Michael Shaw. National Research Council of Canada, Ottawa 7, Canada. Illus., index. Circ: 2,200. Sample. Vol. ends: Dec. Refereed. Microform: Princeton.

Indexed: BioAb, BioAg, ChemAb, SCI. *Aud:* Sa, Ac.

Supersedes Part C of the original *Canadian Journal of Research.* Original research papers report the results of studies in most fields of botany, including morphology, physiology, pathology, and cell structure of plants. In large part contributions originate from Canadian institutions, but reports do not necessarily center around Canadian flora. A reputable and established research journal for academic collections. (Note: *Canadian Journal of Plant Science,* a complementary publication, is given over to more applied studies including reports on agronomy.)

Doklady Botanical Sciences. See *Academy of Sciences of the USSR. Proceedings. Biological Sciences Section.* Biological Sciences/General Section.

Economic Botany. 1947. q. $15. Richard E. Schultes. New York Botanical Garden, Bronx, N. Y. 10458. Illus., index. Circ: 2,000. Vol. ends: no. 4. Refereed. Microform: UM.

Indexed: BioAb, BioAg, ChemAb, SCI. *Bk. rev:* 7–8, 100–800 words, signed. *Aud:* Sa, Ac.

On a more applied level, the official journal of the Society for Economic Botany pursues studies on utilization of plant species—their origin, uses, etc.—and applications of principles of botanical research. Although some papers are highly scientific, a good portion of contributions represent ethnobotanical studies, e.g., relationships between primitive societies and their cultures, ethnomedicine, folk uses of plants, and some articles bordering on economic studies, e.g., olive production in Greece. Less technical than most botanical journals, the publication should be within the subject scope of undergraduates. Recommended for academic libraries.

Journal of Experimental Botany. 1950. 4/yr. $35. L. J. Andus. Oxford Univ. Press, Ely House, Dover St., London, W1X 4AH, England, Illus., index. Circ: 1,800. Sample. Vol. ends: no. 4. (Nov.). Refereed. Microform: UM.

Indexed: BioAb, BioAg, ChemAg, SCI. *Aud:* Sa, Ac.

Sponsored by the Society for Experimental Biology. Quarterly issues are dedicated to research papers on plant physiology, plant biochemistry and biophysics, as well as some studies on experimental agronomy. A good, scholarly journal, important for research collections, but probably too sophisticated for the small academic library.

Linnean Society. Botanical Journal. See *Linnean Society. Biological Journal.* Biological Sciences/General Section.

Phytopathology. 1911. m. $40. Robert Aycock. Amer. Phytopathological Soc., 3340 Pilot Knob Rd., St. Paul, Minn. 55121. Illus., index. Vol. ends: Dec. Refereed. Microform: UM.

Indexed: BioAb, BioAg, ChemAb. *Aud:* Sa, Ac.

The official journal of the Society. Original research papers are devoted to studies of diseases affecting plants. All branches of the field are covered, e.g., disease physiology, biochemical factors associated with infection, genetics with respect to disease physiology, host parasites, and plant disease control. A section on "Phytopathological News" describes either short studies on research or descriptive reports on techniques. The journal is particularly important with regard to agricultural applications, and should be useful to university libraries with botanical collections.

Plant Physiology. 1926. m. (2v./yr.). $35./v. Martin Gibbs. Amer. Soc. of Plant Physiologists, Box 5706, Bethesda, Md. Circ: 5,000. Vol. ends: June and Dec. Microform: Canner.

Indexed: BioAb, BioAg, ChemAb, SCI. *Aud:* Sa, Ac.

The journal investigates the fundamental physiological processes and constituents of plants and plant cells. Papers delineate, for example, the metabolic pathways of cells, the enzyme activity controlling these processes, their mechanism of respiration, mineral nutrition, general areas of plant growth, as well as studies on the basic chemical and physical principles which control these processes. An important research journal for botanical collections in academic libraries.

Torrey Botanical Club. Bulletin. 1870. bi-m. $12. Gily E. Bard. Subs. to: Dr. Gary Smith, New York Botanical Garden, Bronx, N.Y. 10458. Illus., index, adv. Circ: 1,400. Vol. ends: no. 6; Nov./Dec. Refereed. Reprint: Johnson. Microform: UM; Canner.

Indexed: BioAb, BioAg, ChemAb. *Bk. rev:* 2, 400 words, signed. *Aud:* Sa, Ac.

The publication boasts of being the "oldest botanical journal of this hemisphere, founded by W. H. Leggett." There are several features of this periodical of interest to librarians. The *Bulletin* proper contains research-type papers. All areas of the plant sciences are included: general botany, paleobotany, genetics, ecology and plant geography, morphology, etc. *"Torreya,"* also included in each issue was really the mother publication of the *Bulletin*. Today, it is given over to short papers, interesting notes on flora within the range of the Club's activities, biographical sketches, reports of field trips, news and reviews. Also taking up a portion of the journal is an "Index to American Botanical Literature," an invaluable classified list of recent botanical publications. Past volumes have also carried annotated bibliographies of the floristic publications of New Jersey covering the years 1753–1965 (published 1944 and 1966). A good general botanical journal for academic libraries.

Genetics

Behavior Genetics. 1970. q. $30. S. G. Vandenberg and John C. Defries. Greenwood Periodicals, Inc., 51 Riv-

erside Ave., Westport, Conn. 06880. Illus., index. Circ: 550. Sample. Vol. ends: no. 4. Refereed.

Indexed: BioAb. *Aud:* Sa, Ac.

A specialty journal concentrating on the "inheritance of behavior in animal and man." Research in this field in hybrid, drawing on elements from biology, psychology, ecology, sociology, evolution, etc. Papers and short communications in the first volume were as varied as a mathematical analysis of genetic variance, to psychological studies on timidity of mice, to IQ's of identical twins. The range is broad, the list of editors and advisors to the editorial board impressive, and the quality of the first volume good. A valuable journal for psychology and biology collections interested in this area of research.

Biochemical Genetics. 1967. 8/yr. (2v./yr.). $24./v. Hugh S. Forrest, Robert P. Wagner and Forbes Robertson. Plenum Publishing Corp., 227 W. 17th St., New York, N.Y. 10011. Illus., index. Sample. Vol. ends: no. 4 (2v./yr.). Refereed.

Aud: Sa, Ac.

An international publication dedicated to studies on the chemical processes undergone during biological inheritance. Any type of organism is considered, "from virus to man." Representative topics handled by research papers in the journal include the molecular genetics of genetic variation, mutation, gene action, nucleic acid function in heredity, and the like. A research journal for both biochemists and geneticists. For university libraries.

Canadian Journal of Genetics and Cytology. 1959. q. $20. A. Wilkes. Genetics Soc. of Canada, c/o H. Baenziger, Forage Section, Ottawa Research Station, Central Experimental Farm, Ottawa, Ontario, Canada, Illus., index. Circ: 1,000. Vol. ends: no. 4; (Dec). Refereed. Microform: Princeton.

Indexed: BioAb, BioAg, ChemAb, IMed. *Bk. rev:* 3, 300 words, signed. *Aud:* Sa, Ac.

The official organ of the Genetics Society of Canada. Research papers deal with both the various aspects of genetics and the genetics of cell biology. A large part of the journal is devoted to plant breeding (e.g., effects of mutation, genetic variation in wheat, soybeans, etc.). Since much of the work borders on applied studies, the journal would be of interest to agricultural collections as well as biological collections.

Genetical Research. 1960. bi-m. (2v./yr.) $19.50/v. C. H. Waddington. Cambridge Univ. Press, 32 E. 57th St., New York, N.Y. 10022. Illus., index. Circ: 1,140. Sample. Vol. ends: no. 3 (2v./yr.). Refereed. Microform: UM.

Indexed: BioAb, BioAg, MathR. *Aud:* Sa, Ac.

An authoritative international journal covering all

aspects of genetics and concerned with any type of organism. Research papers explore the nature and behavior of genes, molecular genetics, mechanisms of heredity, population genetics, mathematical studies of genetic variability, and the like. A valuable, scholarly publication under the aegis of a distinguished editorial board. For biological research collections.

Genetics. 1916. m. $29. Ernest W. Caspari. Business Manager, Genetics, Drawer U, Univ. Station, Austin, Tex. 78712. Illus., index. Circ: 4,500. Vol. ends: Dec. Refereed. Microform: Princeton.

Indexed: BioAb, BioAg, ChemAb, IMed. *Aud:* Sa, Ac.

A fine, general genetics journal, and the official organ of the Genetics Society of America. Research articles and short reports are dedicated to studies in such representative fields as genetic variation and evolution, natural selection, mutation, cytogenetics, population genetics, and some molecular genetics. Generally, the tenor of the publication is not too sophisticated nor too specialized to be inappropriate for the undergraduate collection. Since the entire field of genetics underlies many of the other subfields in the biological sciences, the journal would be a first-choice selection for any academic library.

Heredity. 1947. bi-m. $24. Ed. bd. Longmans Group, Tweedale Ct., Edinburgh, Scotland. Illus., index, adv. Circ: 1,350. Sample. Vol. ends: no. 6. Refereed.

Indexed: BioAb, BioAg, ChemAb, IMed, SCI. *Bk. rev:* 5–6, lengthy, signed. *Aud:* Sa, Ac.

The various aspects of genetics included in this publication cover fields of experimental breeding, cytology, statistical and biochemical genetics, evolutionary theory, etc. Also published are abstracts of papers read at meetings of the Genetical Society (United Kingdom). An authoritative research journal for good biological collections. Small academic libraries will probably find their needs served adequately enough by *Genetics* and *Journal of Heredity.*

Journal of Heredity. 1910. bi-m. $15. Barbara Kuhn. Amer. Genetic Assn., 32nd St. and Elm Ave., Baltimore, Md. 21211. Illus., index, adv. Circ: 4,300. Vol. ends: no. 6. Refereed. Microform: UM, Canner, Microcard, Princeton. Reprint: Swets & Zeitlinger.

Indexed: BioAb, BioAg, ChemAb, IMed, PsyAb, SCI. *Bk. rev:* 1, occasional, 300 words, signed. *Aud:* Sa, Ac.

A product of the American Genetic Association, promoting "laws of heredity and their application to the improvement of plants, animals, and human welfare." Focus in this excellent publication is on aspects of plant breeding, animal breeding, and eugenics. In addition to six to seven research-type articles, a section on news and notes carries short technical reports in the field, as well as news of the organization and profession. A good, broad-based publication, applica-

ble to undergraduate libraries, and recommended also for agricultural, as well as biological collections.

Microbiology

Applied Microbiology. 1953. m. $40. Marvin P. Bryant. Amer. Soc. for Microbiology, 1913 I St., N.W., Washington, D.C. 20006. Nonmenber subs. to: Williams & Wilkins Co., 428 E. Preston St., Baltimore, Md. 21202. Illus., index, adv. Sample. Vol. ends: 2v./yr. Refereed. Microform: UM. Reprint: Johnson.

Indexed: BioAb, BioAg, ChemAb, IMed. *Aud:* Sa, Ac.

The research journal of the Society dedicated to applied studies of microorganisms. (More fundamental studies appear in its *Journal of Bacteriology.*) Topics by authorities discuss such fields as clinical microbiology, virology, immunology (papers on oral immunization, disease virus, etc); food microbiology and toxicology (e.g., "Bacteriological surveys of pork sausage); ecology and taxonomy (papers on soil microorganisms, and growth and isolation of bacteria); and metabolism and products. An important journal particularly for its applications of principles of microbiology, and a valuable one for public health collections, as well as biological collections.

Bacteriological Reviews. 1937. q. $10. R. G. E. Murray. Amer. Soc. for Microbiology, 1913 I St., N.W., Washington, D.C. 20006. Illus., index. Circ: 16,000. Vol. ends: no. 4. Refereed. Microform: UM. Reprint: Johnson.

Indexed: BioAb, BioAg, ChemAb, IMed, SCI. *Aud:* Sa, Ac.

The journal contains authoritative and critical review papers on the current state of research in all areas of microbiology, including studies of protozoa, algae, fungi, bacteria, viruses, rickettsiae. Historical analyses may appear occasionally. Articles range in number from three to eight, and vary considerably in length, i.e., from ten to 100 pages. A fine review journal in the field, and recommended for most academic libraries.

CRC Critical Reviews in Microbiology. 1971. q. $56. Allen I. Laskin and Hubert Lechevalier. CRC Press, 18901 Cranwood Pkwy., Cleveland, Ohio 44128. Illus., index. Sample. Vol. ends: no. 4. Refereed.

Indexed: BioAb. *Aud:* Sa, Ac.

Focuses its attention on recent and significant developments in the field of microbiology, including bacteria, viruses, algae, fungi, and protozoa. Prominent authorities are invited to produce in-depth critical reviews, and generally these scientists are authors who have contributed heavily to the literature themselves. Each issue carries about four articles, 50 pages in length, and generally centers around one topic, e.g., bacterial membrane. An important review publication for research collections. First choice for smaller academic libraries would still be *Bacteriological Reviews,* however.

Canadian Journal of Microbiology. 1954. m. $24. A. C. Blackwood. National Research Council of Canada, Ottawa 7, Canada. Illus., index. Circ: 2,700. Sample. Vol. ends: Dec. Refereed. Microform: Princeton.

Indexed: BioAb, ChemAb, IMed, SCI. *Aud:* Sa, Ac.

A good, all-encompassing general microbiology journal, and part of the Canadian Journals of Research series. Papers on microorganisms consider their general environment (i.e., bacterial colonies; growth of cultures); infection and immunity (isolation and characterization of bacteria); physiology (mutations of micoorganisms); and virology, molecular biology, and genetics. A fine, authoritative publication for biological research collections.

Journal of Bacteriology. 1916. m. $52. L. Leon Campbell. Amer. Soc. for Microbiology, 1913 I. St., N.W., Washington, D.C. 20006. Nonmember subs. to: Williams & Wilkins Co., 428 E. Preston St., Baltimore, Md. 21202. Illus., index, adv. Circ: 12,000. Sample. Vol. ends: 4v./yr. Refereed. Microform: UM, Microcard, Princeton. Reprint: Johnson.

Indexed: BioAb, BioAg, ChemAb, IMed, SCI. *Aud:* Sa, Ac.

The main journal of the Society, concerned with general, fundamental reports on microorganisms. (See also *Applied Microbiology* and *Bacteriological Reviews.*) Studies by authoritative specialists deal with any type of microorganism, e.g., bacteria, protozoa, algae, fungi, and report on their taxonomy and ecology, morphology and ultrastructure, genetics and molecular biology, physiology and metabolism, and enzymology. In recent years, the section on viruses in this journal splintered off and formed a separate publication, *Journal of Virology* (1967, m., $40.). The explorations of microorganisms for their disease-producing roles, and of microbes in maintaining the ecocycle, or industrially, in food technology, etc., have long been of prominence in biological studies. This journal, the leading one in the United States, should be of interest to a wide variety of scientific libraries, and should certainly be a basic one in every biological collection.

Journal of General Microbiology. 1947. 5v./yr. $30./v. Ed. bd. Cambridge Univ. Press, 32 E. 57th St., New York, N.Y. 10022. Illus., index. Circ: 5,000. Sample. Vol. ends: no. 3 (5v./yr.). Refereed.

Indexed: BioAb, BioAg, ChemAb, IMed, SCI. *Aud:* Sa, Ac.

Produced for the Society for General Microbiology, the leading society in its field in the United Kingdom. The journal, an authoritative and high quality one, concerns itself with more fundamental studies on microfungi, bacteria, microscopic algae, etc. Reports discuss the development and structure of microorganisms, their physiology and growth, biochemistry, genetics, ecology, and some papers on medical microbiology. This is a prominent publication for academic collections. Research libraries will need it; smaller libraries will look first to the publications of the American Society for Microbiology.

Physiology

American Journal of Physiology. 1898. m. $60. Ed. bd. Amer. Physiological Soc., 9650 Rockville Pike, Bethesda, Md. 20014. Illus., index, adv. Circ: 4,655. Vol. ends: 2v./yr (June/Dec.). Refereed. Microform: UM, Canner, Princeton.

Indexed: BioAb, BioAg, ChemAb, IMed, PsyAb, SCI. *Aud:* Sa, Ac.

The American Physiological Society is the leading U.S. association in its field, and publisher of a number of high quality journals in addition to this title: *Journal of Applied Physiology, Journal of Neurophysiology,* and *Physiological Reviews.* Research papers in this journal represent scholarly and fundamental studies, and report on all areas of physiological work. Fields include circulation, respiration, renal and electrolyte physiology, endocrinology and metabolism, environmental physiology, comparative and general physiology, neurobiology and muscle studies. A valuable, authoritative journal for any biological research collection.

Canadian Journal of Physiology and Pharmacology. 1929. m. $20. F. C. MacIntosh. National Research Council of Canada, Ottawa 7, Ontario, Canada. Illus., index. Circ: 1,600. Sample. Vol. ends: Dec. Refereed. Microform: Princeton.

Indexed: BioAb, ChemAb, IMed, SCI. *Aud:* Sa, Ac.

Part of the Canadian Journals of Research group. Scholarly contributions to the journal cover work on pharmacology, as well as all areas of physiology, including muscle studies, neurophysiology, environmental physiology, metabolism, etc. An authoritative publication for any research collection.

Journal of Applied Physiology. 1948. m. $45. Ed. bd. Amer. Physiological Soc., 9650 Rockville Pike, Bethesda, Md. 20014. Illus., index, adv. Circ: 3,900. Vol. ends: 2v./yr. Refereed. Microform: UM, Canner. Reprint: Johnson.

Indexed: BioAb, BioAg, ChemAb, IMed, PsyAb, SCI. *Aud:* Sa, Ac.

Less fundamental than the Society's *American Journal of Physiology,* it considers the applications of physiological principles in all areas of the subject. Special emphasis is given, yet by no means restricted to, circulatory, environmental, respiratory, and muscle physiology. Titles such as "Respiratory Weight Losses during Exercise," and "Airways Resistance in Man," indicate the type of article. An excellent journal representing applied research in the field. For biological research collections.

Journal of Cellular and Comparative Physiology. See *Journal of Cellular Physiology.*

Journal of Cellular Physiology (Formerly: *Journal of Cellular and Comparative Physiology*). 1932. bi-m. $48. Vittorio Defendi. Wister Inst. Press, 36th at Spruce St., Philadelphia, Pa. 19104. Illus., index. Circ: 2,000. Sample. Vol. ends: 3v./yr. Refereed. Microform: Princeton. Reprint: Johnson.

Indexed: BioAb, ChemAb, IMed, SCI. *Aud:* Sa, Ac.

The specialty of this research journal is oriented around the physiology of the cell: the biochemical and biophysical phenomena and mechanisms which regulate growth, reproduction, and other functions on a cellular level. Both full-length articles and short communications are published. An important journal for every physiology collection, and for rounding out good collections in the biological sciences.

Journal of General Physiology. 1918. m. $50. Paul F. Cranefield. Rockefeller Univ. Press, P.O. Box 5108, Church St. Station, New York, N.Y. 10008. Illus., index. Circ: 2,300. Sample. Vol. ends: 2v./yr. Microform: UM. Reprint: Johnson.

Indexed: BioAb, BioAg, ChemAb, IMed, SciAb, SCI. *Aud:* Sa, Ac.

The official organ of the Society of General Physiologists. The high quality research papers in this journal revolve around the experimental studies of physical and chemical phenomena that characterize functions in living organisms, rather than applied work. Subjects such as oxidations, reductions, membranes, etc., are all within its scope (e.g. "Calcium Ion Uptake of Red Blood Cell Membranes."). A sophisticated and authoritative journal for any research collection.

Journal of Physiology. 1878. s-m. $156. W. F. Widdas. Cambridge Univ. Press, 32 E. 57th St., New York, N.Y. 10022. Illus., index. Circ: 3,560. Sample. Vol. ends: Irreg. Refereed. Microform: UM, Microcard, Princeton. Reprint: Dawson.

Indexed: BioAb, ChemAb, IMed, PsyAb, SciAb, SCI. *Aud:* Sa, Ac.

Edited for the prominent Physiological Society (United Kingdom). Highly authoritative papers explore all areas of physiological research, from the cell to man. Studies include work on neurophysiology, general physiology, cellular physiology, and the like. The journal has been a basic research publication in the field since the nineteenth century and continues to be essential for every good collection in the biological sciences. Small academic libraries should look first to the publications of the American Physiological Society, such as *Physiological Reviews.*

Physiological Reviews. 1921. q. $20. J. R. Brobeck. Amer. Physiological Soc., 9650 Rockville Pike, Bethes-da, Md. 20014. Illus., index. Circ: 5,600. Vol. ends: no. 4. Refereed. Microform: Canner, UM, Microcard, Princeton. Reprint: Johnson.

Publishes critical, comprehensive review articles on timely and active research topics by scientists prominent in their fields. Each issue contains three to five lengthy (20–50 pages) reviews. Bibliographies are exhaustive, and each article has a prefatory outline and a detailed and informative summary. Titles such as "Thirst," with a bibliography of over 450 references, represent, in fact, authoritative monographs. An excellent periodical and a first-choice selection for every academic library.

Zoology

American Journal of Anatomy. 1901. m. $60. Burton Baker. Wistar Inst. Press, 36th at Spruce St., Philadelphia, Pa. 19104. Illus., index, adv. Circ: 1,500. Sample. Vol. ends: 3v./yr. Refereed. Reprint: Swets & Zeitlinger.

Indexed: BioAb, BioAg, IMed, SCI. *Aud:* Sa, Ac.

One of the primary anatomical research journals in the United States dedicated to reports on experimental and descriptive vertebrate anatomy. Some histological and embryological studies are included. The intent of the journal is to provide fairly long and comprehensive papers, but included in recent issues are "zipgrams," short and rapidly published communications. An important periodical for research-oriented biological collections. See also *Anatomical Record.*

American Zoologist. 1961. q. $15 (Members free). Joseph T. Bagnara. Amer. Soc. of Zoologists, Business Office, Box 2739, California Lutheran College, Thousand Oaks, Calif. 91360. Illus., index, adv. Circ: 5,100. Vol. ends: no. 4. Refereed. Microform: UM.

Indexed: BioAb, BioAg. *Aud:* Sa, Ac.

The official journal of the American Society of Zoologists, publishing research reports and reviews in all areas of animal biology. Two issues each year are devoted exclusively to research papers centering around one specialized and timely topic (usually papers presented at a symposium organized by the Society). The other two issues contain the entire programs and abstracts of papers given at annual and summer meetings of the Society, as well as short reports on a special symposium. (Note: prior to 1961, abstracts originally appeared as a supplement to *Anatomical Record.*) Papers represent authoritative work by specialists (e.g., an entire issue devoted to an expedition to the Galapagos Archipelago) and are generally solicited by the editorial board. A first-choice selection for every academic collection in the biological sciences.

Anatomical Record. 1906. m. $60. Aaron J. Ladman. Wistar Inst. Press, 36th at Spruce St., Philadelphia, Pa. 19104. Illus., index, adv. Circ: 1,700. Sample. Vol. ends: 3v./yr. Refereed. Reprint: Swets & Zeitlinger.

Indexed: BioAb, ChemAb, IMed, SCI. *Aud:* Sa, Ac.

Published, also, as the official journal of the American Association of Anatomists, the periodical's broad domain is research in the anatomical sciences, with emphasis on "biological structure of vertebrate anatomy." Papers are less than 20 pages; if longer and more comprehensive, studies generally appear in the *American Journal of Anatomy*. Brief communications are also included, as well as an occasional review paper. Abstracts and programs of meetings of the Association are also presented. The leading anatomical journal for biological collections.

Animal Behaviour. 1953. q. $28. D. J. McFarland and J. Hirsch. Bailliere, Tindall and Cassell, Ltd., 7–8 Henrietta St., London WC2 8QE, England. Illus., index, adv. Sample. Vol. ends: no. 4. Refereed.

Indexed: BioAb, IMed, PsyAb, SCI. *Bk. rev:* 4–6, 500 words, signed. *Aud:* Sa, Ac.

Sponsored also by the Association for the Study of Animal Behaviour (United Kingdom) and the Animal Behavior Society (United States), the journal publishes scholarly reports on biological studies of animal behavior. Some ecological and zoological studies are included. Topics such as vertebrate social stystems, and titles such as "Competition in Frogs," indicate the scope. Available to subscribers are *Animal Behaviour Monographs* ($10.), dealing with specialized topics in the habits and behavior of animals. An important journal in the field not only for zoologists, but psychologists and ecologists as well.

Canadian Journal of Zoology. 1929. m. $24. W. S. Hoar. National Research Council of Canada, Ottawa 7, Canada. Illus., index. Circ: 2,500. Sample. Vol. ends: Dec. Refereed.

Indexed: BioAb, BioAg, IMed, SCI. *Aud:* Sa, Ac.

One of the Canadian Journals of Research series. A good, general zoological journal discussing all aspects of animal biology, including their behavior, ecology, genetics, biochemistry and physiology, morphology and ultrastructure, parasitology and pathology, systematics and evolution. In large measure, studies reflect Canadian research interests. An authoritative publication for well-rounded university collections. Canadian libraries will certainly want it for reports of fauna in that country. (Note: a complementary periodical, *Canadian Journal of Animal Science*, studies more applied areas such as animal production, and should be of interest to agricultural collections.)

Journal of Experimental Biology. See Biological Sciences/General Section.

Journal of Experimental Zoology. 1904. m. $64. Clement L. Markert and Edgar J. Boell. Wister Inst. Press, 36th at Spruce St., Philadelphia, Pa. 19104. Illus., index, adv. Circ: 2,000. Sample. Vol. ends: 3v./yr. Refereed. Reprint: Swets & Zeitlinger.

Indexed: BioAb, BioAg, ChemAb, IMed, SCI. *Aud:* Sa, Ac.

Under the sponorship of the American Society of Zoologists, the journal investigates biological organization of animals at any level, from the molecular upward. Studies may be either analytical or experimental, and embrace such areas as animal physiology, morphology, ultrastructure, biochemistry as related to organisms, genetics and embryology, etc. It is a first-rate zoological research journal. Most academic collections will need this plus the other journal of the Society, *American Zoologist*.

Journal of Mammalogy. 1919. q. J. Knox Jones, Jr. Allen Press, Lawrence, Kans. 66044. Illus., index. Circ: 6,400. Vol. ends: no. 4 (Nov.). Refereed. Microform: UM, Microcard, Princeton. Reprint: Johnson.

Indexed: BioAb, SCI. *Bk. rev:* 4, 1,000 words, signed. *Aud:* Sa, Ac.

Published for the American Society of Mammalogists. The journal concentrates exclusively on mammalian biology. Studies may range over the broadest spectrum, i.e., their anatomy, behavior, conservation, disease, distribution, ecology, evolution, genetics, physiology, and taxonomy. A good portion of the periodical is dedicated to "general notes"—short reports—rather than full-blown articles on the above subjects. "Comments and News" provides timely information to mammalogists on professional meetings, personalia, etc. Of interest to librarians is an excellent book review section which supplies critical, essay-type reviews. Also published as a separate, offset supplement is "Recent Literature of Mammalogy," covering books, articles, and proceedings of symposia on a worldwide basis. Most zoological collections will need the journal. Moreover, articles on zoogeography, etc., are generally on a level which can be handled by the undergraduate.

Journal of Morphology. 1887. m. $60. Carl Gans. Wistar Inst. Press, 36th at Spruce St., Philadelphia, Pa. 19104. Illus., index, adv. Circ: 1,300. Sample. Vol. ends: 3v./yr. Refereed. Microform: Princeton. Reprint: Swets & Zeitlinger.

Indexed: BioAb, ChemAb, IMed, SCI. *Aud:* Sa, Ac.

The publication is dedicated to original research articles on shapes, structures, and spatial relations in biological systems. Included in the realm of the journal are studies on the structure of cells, protozoa, and embryos. Authoritative work by specialists is of high quality. Important for anatomists and zoologists, the journal would be an excellent choice for any good academic library.

Journal of Wildlife Management. See Environment and Conservation/Special Interest Section.

Physiological Zoology. 1928. q. $12. Thomas Park. Univ. of Chicago Press, 5750 Ellis Ave., Chicago, Ill. 60637. Illus., index, adv. Circ: 1,300. Sample. Vol. ends: no. 4. Refereed. Microform: UM, Princeton, Canner.

Indexed: BioAb, BioAg, ChemAb, SCI. *Bk. rev:* 1–2, 500 words, signed. *Aud:* Sa, Ac.

The quarterly specializes in research papers on physiological zoology, including the physiology of development, physiology of the cell, physiology of nervous systems, genetics, etc. Titles such as "Metabolism of Chorus Frogs," and "Water Balance in Desert Insects," characterize the scope. Articles represent authoritative and fairly comprehensive studies. A valuable publication both for physiologists and zoologists; recommended for academic collections.

Systematic Zoology. 1952. q. $12. Albert J. Rowell. Allen Press, Lawrence, Kans. 66044. Illus., index, adv. Circ: 2,600. Vol. ends: no. 4 (Dec.). Refereed. Reprint: Swets & Zeitlinger.

Indexed: BioAb, BioAg, SCI. *Bk. rev:* 1–2, 500 words, signed. *Aud:* Sa, Ac.

Published for the Society of Systematic Zoology. The journal takes in that branch of zoology concerned with the principles or methodology of animal classification. Within the range of these interests, papers are also included on evolution, morphology, population aspects of species, and genetics. A small section called "Points of View" provides a vehicle for discussion or rebuttal, either on papers published in the journal or elsewhere in the literature. Since taxonomic studies are fundamental to the zoological literature, the publication, good for undergraduate collections, is an important one for zoological collections.

zoos. There are a number of popular titles, well written and well illustrated, which are sponsored by our country's zoos, friends of the zoo, or local zoological societies. Generally, the price is modest ($2.–$5.), the contents lively, and the appeal wide, particularly for public libraries and school libraries with zoos available within their state. A few of these are: ***America's First Zoo*** (produced by the Philadelphia Zoological Garden and sponsored by the Zoological Society of Philadelphia); ***Animal Kingdom*** (sponsored by the New York Zoological Society); ***Spots and Stripes*** (put out by the Friends of the National Zoo, Washington); ***Zoonooz*** (issued by the Zoological Society of San Diego); ***Zoo's Letter*** (produced by the Indianapolis Zoological Society).

BLACKS

See also Africa Section.

Basic Periodicals

Ejh: *Ebony.* (As of early 1972 there was no magazine specifically edited for black children); Hs: *Ebony, Black World;* Ga: *Black World, Ebony, Essence, Journal of Negro History;* Jc: *Black World, Journal of Negro History, Journal of Black Poetry, Ebony;* Ac: *Black World, Liberator, Journal of Black Poetry, Journal of Negro History, Ebony, Essence.*

Library and Teaching Aids

Bibliographical Survey: The Negro in Print, Journal of Negro Education, Journal of Black Studies, Afro-American Studies.

Basic Abstracts and Indexes

Index to Periodical Articles By and About Negroes.

Cessations

Corelator, The Hustler, Quarterly Review of Higher Education Among Negroes.

AIM. 1969. bi-a. $3. T. J. Reddy. Aim Publns., P.O. Box 1915, Charlotte, N.C. 28201. Illus., index. Circ: 1,200. Sample.

Aud: Ga, Ac, Hs.

This is one of the few black little magazines. Aproximately half of the contributors are under 30 and black—a few are under 12. The 50-page issue is impressive, and the editors pretty much carry out their intent of providing a forum for black "people to make creativity a challenge and worth pursuing."

Afro-American Studies; and interdisciplinary journal. 1970. q. $41 (Individuals $11). Richard D. Trent. Gordon and Breach, Science Publishers, Inc., 440 Park Ave. S., New York, N.Y. 10016. Sample.

Bk. rev: 1–2, essays, notes. *Aud:* Ac, Hs.

Specifically for "educators and professionals in colleges and other educational institutions initiating and developing curricula, programs, institutes and faculties in Black Studies." The editor is at Medgar Evers College of the City University of New York, and while this is published by an English publisher, the scope and purpose is almost exculsively American. It contains approximately 75 pages of five to eight scholarly articles on all aspects of the Black from music and literature to politics. The material is documented, clearly written, and usually of exceptional interest. Emphasis is on the American Black, but there is some African material. One quarter of each issue is given over to "Documents," which print verbatim important items relating to Blacks, e.g., "Senate Hearings on Equal Educational Opportunity." This is a high price for a worthwhile journal which should be available in all libraries involved with black studies from high school up.

Amistad; writings on black history and culture. 1970. s-a. $1.95/no. John A. Williams & Charles F. Harris. Random House, Inc., 201 E. 50th St., New York, N.Y. 10022. Illus. Circ: 50,000.

Aud: Ac, Ga, Hs.

Following the familiar paperback format of *New American Review,* this has emerged as an important voice of the third world philosophy. (Supported by Random House, the format is supposed to assure its use as a supplement to texts in schools.) Averaging some 300 pages, its essays, prose, and poetry are a balanced combination of literature, scholarship, and rhetoric. The contributors (John Williams, Chester Himes, Ishmael Reed, etc.), are articulate, and are obviously directing their efforts at the young—primarily at the college level—but also aim to appeal to high school students. The first issues struck a balance between material on history, sociology, and current affairs along with stories and graphics. This approach will be as instructive to whites as to blacks. For a similar effort, see *Black Review*.

Amsterdam News. See Newspapers/U.S. National Section.

Beau-Cocoa. 1958. q. $3.75. Lloyd Addison, P.O. Box 409, New York, N.Y. 10035.

Aud: Ac.

The most unusual item in this list, *Beau-Cocoa* passes for a literary periodical. Most of the works are unsigned, but seem to be the work of one man—Lloyd Addison. Apparently, Addison has selected long poems, fiction, philosophical essays, and other material from his own heretofore unpublished, rejected works for appearance in this journal. Employing extremely personal writing, meaning is often further obscured by the writer's use of involved, archaic syntax, and esoteric rhythms. The editor feels that the elegance of *Beau-Cocoa* should appeal to those who are a little weary of the black and "funky" literary publications. Black studies' groups will not like this one, but they should have a chance to criticize it. (J.G.)

Bibliographic Survey: the Negro in print. 1965. 5/yr. $11. Beatrice M. Murphy. Negro Bibliographic & Research Center, Inc., 117 R St., N.E., Washington, D.C. 20002. Index. Vol. ends: March.

Aud: Ga, Ac, Hs, Ejh. *Jv:* V.

The best single source of information on books, periodicals, and paperbacks concerned with the Black. Each issue lists titles for adults, teen-agers, and children. Full bibliographic information is given, yet more important are the descriptive (not evaluative) annotations which give the reader or librarian an excellent notion as to content, slant, and any particular biases. While most of the information is on recently published works, some issues are devoted to areas such as history and civil rights, which contain a good deal of retrospective material. As all aspects of history are considered, and as this is for all ages, it should be an essential book buying tool in any library.

Bi-Monthly Booklist. Free. Liberation Bookstore, 421 Lenox Ave., New York, N.Y. 10037.

A typical issue of the *Booklist* consists of approximately three mimeographed pages of books available at the Liberation Bookstore in Harlem. The books are loosely listed under such headings as "Recommendations," "New Books," "Know Your Enemy" (black liberation materials), "Children's Books," "Novels,"

"Current Events and World Affairs," "Reference Books," etc. Periodicals are not listed, although the Liberation Bookstore does stock many of the newer, militant publications. Book selectors in all types of libraries will find this list of some use. Not all listings are annotated. (J.G.)

Black Academy Review: quarterly of the black world. 1970. q. $7. S. Okechukwu Mezu. Black Academy Press, Inc., 135 Univ. Ave., Buffalo, N.Y. 14214. Adv. Circ: 5,000. Sample. Vol. ends: Winter. Microform: UM.

Bk. rev: 2–4, 2–4 pages, signed. *Aud:* Ac, Ga, Hs.

Designed for students, high school teachers, and adults with an interest in "black civilization in all its dimensions and variations." Essays of high quality deal with literary, social, and political concerns of black people here and in Africa and the West Indies. Each issue runs about 75 pages, with six essays on such subjects as black studies, education for the disadvantaged, and poetry and revolution in modern Africa. A recent typical issue has articles on Azikiwe, Martin Luther King, Richard Wright, and on the crisis in African studies, as well as a book review article on the works of three black poets. Special issues focus on major events or outstanding individuals. (B.A.)

Black Books Bulletin. 1971. q. $8. Don Lee. Inst. of Positive Education, 7850 S. Ellis Ave., Chicago, Ill. 60619. Illus., index, adv. Sample.

Bk. rev: 10–12, 250–500 words, signed. *Aud:* Ga, Ac, Hs, Ejh.

A 60-page magazine devoted to a quarterly survey of publishing and publishers of black materials. One issue included two articles on writers and music, an interview with the editor of *Black World*, and reviews of some 12 titles. There is also a "continuing bibliography of books published by and about blacks" which is divided by subject. In the issue examined it covered some ten pages. The choices seem good, but the bibliographic information is incomplete. Conversely the four- to six-word summaries are excellent. The magazine ends with "news from the publishers," i.e., notes from five presses which concentrate on black titles. The strongest parts of the magazine are the first rate reviews; the weakest the bibliography. And somewhere in between is the other material. The idea is good but it lacks direction, and while the publisher says it is a periodical "with various topics of interest to Black people," the interests are almost too diverse. Still, it is a beginning, and not really that bad. With time the nonprofit organization and publisher of the *BBB* should get it into better shape. Meanwhile, though, it supplements but in no way replaces the more conventional and thorough *Bibliographic Survey: The Negro in Print.*

Black Careers; guidelines to equal opportunity. 1967. bi-m. $6. E. W. Washington. Project Magazines, Inc.,

Box 8214, Philadelphia, Pa. 19101. Illus., adv. Circ: 93,000. Sample.

Aud: Ga, Ac, Hs.

Primarily for the black college student or graduate, this gives detailed reports on opportunities in business, industry, and government. Careers the humanities and the sciences are also covered in depth. Its primary value is to alert the reader (which includes a good number of high school advisors as well as counselors in colleges and universities) to changes which spell new horizons for Blacks. The articles are written by both staff and experts who are working in the fields they describe. Regular departments update information on everything from law to economics. The style is popular, the information factual and sound. A basic magazine for guidance. See also *Equal Opportunity.*

Black Caucus. 1968. s-a. $2 per no. Charles Sanders. Assn. of Black Social Workers, 2008 Madison Ave., New York, N.Y. 10027. Adv.

Bk. rev: Notes. *Aud:* Ac, Ga.

According to the editors, "the aim of the journal is to further the purposes of the Association of Black Social Workers . . . it aims to provide a creative literary, journalistic outlet for its members and others involved with the black community on issues significant to the fields of social work and the social sciences." *Black Caucus* is one of the more sober and scholarly black periodicals that should appeal to the black professional in particular, regardless of his profession. Articles are written by both new militant professionals and members of the old guard. This periodical should be found in both public and academic libraries. (J.G.)

Black Culture Weekly. 1968. w. $7. G. L. Sherman. Afro-Arts, Inc., 433 W. 21st St., New York, N.Y. 10011.

Aud: Ga, Ac.

BCW is primarily a listing of plays, films, music, dance, benefits, and exhibits offered in the New York City area that should be of special interest to Blacks. Future issues of *BCW* promise book reviews, theater critiques, recommended reading lists, short-short stories, poems, and some original music scores. Should be suitable for public and college libraries located within easy access to the New York City area. (J.G.)

Black Dialogue. 1965. q. $3.50. Edward Springs, Box 1019, New York, N.Y. 10027.

Aud: Ac, Ga.

Black Dialogue was started as an off-campus publication by a few San Francisco State College students as a "meeting place for the voices of the black community, wherever that community may exist." The magazine contains poems, fiction, essays, reviews, plays, drawings, and photographs—the most impressive features of the journal. One of the better publications, it should be found in most college and public libraries. (J.G.)

Black Enterprise. 1970. m. $7.50. Pat Patterson. Earl G. Graves Publishing Co., Inc., 295 Madison Ave., New York, N.Y. 10017. Illus., index, adv. Circ: 110,000. Sample.

Indexed: BusI. *Bk. rev:* 6–10, 150 words. *Aud:* Ga, Ac, Hs.

Julian Bond, Edward Brooke, and Shirley Chisholm are on the board of advisors for this effort to advise black businessmen and would-be businessmen on activities and career opportunities in both black and non-black companies and organizations. Averaging some 75 pages on slick paper, it has a professional format, a progressive outlook, and is one of the best of its type available. The editor tends to zero in on particular issues, e.g., the past and present hopes in various careers are analyzed in one issue. The approach is objective, the style is popular, yet sound. Articles are primarily staff written and well researched. And while for adults, it would serve to introduce senior high school students to some definite possibilities for their futures.

Black News. 1969. w. $3.50. Jim Williams, 10 Claver Pl., Brooklyn, N.Y. 11238. Illus.

Aud: Ac, Ga.

Black News, which has an attractive but unpretentious format, aims to "agitate, educate, and organize" the black community. A single issue consists of approximately ten pages, rendered in a terse, interesting, and earthy journalistic style. Many of the topics discussed are current, local issues rife in the New York City area that are of special interest to the black community, but there are paternal chidings here that Blacks anywhere ought to ponder. Each issue contains some striking, illustrative material that strives to make a political or social point. Future issues promise a new feature: "What's On?" For the success of this new column, the editors have requested the cooperation of black organizations in the New York area to submit notices to *Black News* of their planned special events and programs. Although this publication is often uncomplimentary to both the black and white establishment, it is a very worthwhile little publication, and should be included in most public and college libraries. (J.G.)

Black Panther. See Newspapers/Special Interest Section.

The Black Politician; a journal of current political thought. 1969. q. $4. Mervyn M. Dymally and Lynne B. Bennett. Center on Urban and Minority Affairs, 955 S. Western Ave., Los Angeles, Calif. 90006. Circ: 4,000. Sample. Vol. ends: Spring.

Bk. rev: 5, 50 words. *Aud:* Ac, Ga. *Jv:* V.

Black power is an entity that defies ready definition, but that it is a meaningful and growing force in American life is beyond question. This journal attempts to show what strides the black community is making on the political scene. The emphasis is of course on the work of prominent Blacks, politicians or not. One issue, for instance, contained articles on Mayor Hatcher of Gary, Indiana, and Congresswoman Chisholm of Brooklyn, a speech by Martin Luther King, and an interview held with Eldridge Cleaver before his departure for Cuba. Other things appear also, among them an assessment of the political swat of Americans of Mexican origin and a discussion of the problems of credit-buying. This is a solid and even-toned publication, one that is both informative and readable. Extremist Blacks may not care for it. (P.G.)

Black Politics. 1968. bi-m. $3. Richard Assegai. Box 1233, Berkeley, Calif. 94701. Adv.

Bk. rev: Various number, length. *Aud:* Ac, Ga.

Dedicated to the politics of revolution, the editors and contributors are able students of guerrilla warfare. The articles found here often discuss disruptive strategies in their historical aspects, suggesting how strategies used in the past—both in the United States and elsewhere—could or could not be adaptable to the third world liberation struggle. *Black Politics* is somewhat like a manual on guerrilla warfare, giving detailed formulas for making molotov cocktails and other explosives, and sketching diagrammatic characteristics of certain guns and other artillery, as well as other points that lead to effective guerrilla warfare. Many of the articles are interesting, and the editors are to be taken seriously. (J.G.)

The Black Position. 1971. irreg. $1/issue. Gwendolyn Brooks. Broadside Press, 15205 Livernois, Detroit, Mich., 48238.

Aud: Ga, Ac.

Edited by poet Gwendolyn Brooks, published by the nation's leading black press, this 16-pager features some eight short articles on all aspects of black culture. The first issue, for example, had a lead article on white reviewers of black books (hardly favorable), a plea for black community unity, the failure of black studies, and shorter editorial pieces. Most of the writers are from the Broadside Press group, and are as lucid as they are sometimes angry. The price is a bit steep, but perhaps the journal will expand its pages in issues to come.

Black Review. 1971. s-a. $2.95 per. no. Mel Watkins. William Morrow & Co., 105 Madison Ave., New York, N.Y. 10016. Illus.

Aud: Ac, Ga.

Similar in format and approach to *Amistad,* this is a magazine in paperback format. The content value, as high as *Amistad,* includes graphics, poetry, prose, essays, and criticism. It differs in two ways: it is more general in scope, and less ideologically black than *Amistad.* There is more emphasis on literary diversity, and a real effort is made to present both sides of an opinion and viewpoint that may exist in the black community. Among contributors are Ed Bullins, Julius Lester, Nikki Giovanni, and other well known names. Of the two magazines, this will have a wider appeal among the less revolutionary, more middle-of-the-road audience. And like *Amistad,* it can be recommended for senior high school students.

Black Scholar; a journal of black studies and research. 1969. m. $10. Robert Chrisman. Nathan Hare, Box 908, Sausalito, Calif. 95965. Index, adv. Circ: 18,000.

Indexed: CIJE. *Bk. rev:* Various number, length. *Aud:* Ac, Ga.

Devoted to a nice balance between academic interests and black revolution, this is a serious effort to unite the black intellectual and the street radical. In one issue a Folsom Prison inmate reported on the success of the magazine: "It is an especial comfort to know that the academy has truly joined the street in a relevant unification and will continue to point the way." In addition to documented, scholarly articles there are a few poems, some prose, and regular book reviews. The magazine defies the usual categorization, and for this very reason has a wide appeal.

Black Sports. 1970. m. $6. Sheila F. Younge. Allan P. Barron, Black Sports, Inc., 386 Park Ave. S., New York, N.Y. 10016.

Aud: Ga, Hs.

A magazine that all dedicated sports fans will enjoy, no matter what their ethnic background. The black stars of football, baseball, track, basketball, and tennis come to life on its pages. The sport in season gets the best coverage, of course, but not to the exclusion of the others. The staff-written articles cover the players' personal lives and team issues. Medicine, profiles of college and high school athletes, players in history, and athletes-turned-businessmen are the subjects of the magazine's regular features. Articles are well illustrated with some color photos. Medium to large-sized public libraries would do well to subscribe. (M.A.)

Black Theatre. 1968. 3/yr. $2.50 for 6 issues. Ed Bullins. Black Theatre, Rm. 103, 200 W. 135th St., New York, N.Y. 10030. Illus., adv. Circ: 3,000. Sample. Vol. ends: 6th issue.

Bk. rev: 1, 700 words, signed. *Aud:* Ac, Ga.

A periodical of the black theater movement, it surveys the activity of black, experimental community workshops in major cities throughout the country. Articles strongly support the idea of a Black National Theatre in search of positive black identity and black aesthetics, which would search for new forms and techniques unhampered by Western traditions. The journal includes some scripts of new, unpublished plays and scenarios, interviews, critiques, and reviews. Recommended for most public and college libraries. (J.G.)

Black World (Formerly: **Negro Digest**). 1942/1970. m. $5. John H. Johnson. Johnson Publishing Co., 1820 S. Michigan Ave., Chicago, Ill. 60616. Illus., index. Circ: 80,000. Sample. Vol. ends: Oct.

Indexed: CIJE, INeg. *Bk. rev:* 4–5, 500 words, signed. *Aud:* Ga, Ac, Hs. *Jv:* V.

The only member of the Johnson publishing family which can be said to reflect accurately and objectively the militant black attitude in America. It has been consistently open to agitation and has maintained a considerably better literary and artistic style than *Ebony, Jet,* or *Tan.* Contains about four to eight signed articles, plays, short stories, and poetry concerning the Black. Features book reviews, cartoons and "Letters to the Editor Not Printed There," which is a column of opinions rejected by other major publications. One recent issue was devoted to drama, and another to poetry. A creatively edited periodical that has a place in all libraries.

Broadside Series. 1970. m. $.50 ea. Dudley Randall. Broadside Press, 12651 Old Mill Pl., Detroit, Mich. 48238. Sample.

Aud: Ac, Ga, Hs.

In addition to publishing paperbacks, hardbound books, and tapes of poetry, essays, and other nonfiction by and about black people, Broadside Press puts out a series of poems by black poets. Called simply Broadside Series, they are printed on a single sheet of stiff, poster-like paper (broadside fashion), and feature a single poet each month. A sample is sent free, single copies are $.50, and enlargements of some of the numbers are sold in poster form for $1. or $1.50.

The broadside has a very impressive appearance: each poem is illustrated by drawings or photographs, and the printing is letterpress. A brochure listing all the back numbers by poet and title is sent with the single free copy.

Sample poems in the series are "For Black Poets Who Think of Suicide," by Etheridge Knight, "Liberation Poem," by Sonia Sanchez, "A Poem for Black Hearts," LeRoi Jones, and "Booker T. and W.E.B.," by the editor of the series, Dudley Randall. (M.W.).

CLA Journal. 1957. q. $6. Therman B. O'Daniel. College Language Assn., Morgan State College, Baltimore, Md. 21239. Index, adv. Circ: 900. Vol. ends: June.

Indexed: AbEnSt, INeg. *Bk. rev:* 4–6, 1–3 pages, signed. *Aud:* Ac, Hs.

Although a language and linguistics publication, emphasis has been on work by and about scholars relating to the black in American literature, and this is one of the few scholarly journals devoted to the area. Conversely, it also includes a wide variety of material (with the text in the language of the author) on all aspects of language and literature. Each issue contains some eight to ten articles, book reviews, and a limited amount of business news about the College Language Association. It is a required item in any academic library where black literature and linguistics are a consideration, and it will be of value to high school libraries which have programs in this area.

Community. 1941. q. $2. Ann Stull. Friendship House, 21 E. Van Buren St., Chicago, Ill. 60605. Illus. Circ: 2,500.

Indexed: INeg. *Bk. rev:* Notes. *Aud:* Ga, Ac.

A general newsletter on activities at Friendship House, an interracial center in Chicago, which reports on work-study programs in interracial affairs, and usually has one or two longer articles on some current issues. A good part of the magazine is devoted to the particular problems of whites and Afro-Americans. While centered in Chicago, the various reports are national and international in scope. The periodical is particularly suited to the lay group which is endeavoring to find nontechnical means of improving interracial harmony in a community. This should be found in all academic libraries and high school and public libraries where useful.

Cricket. 1969. bi-m. $2. Ed. bd. Box 663. Newark, N.J. 07101.

Aud: Ac, Ga, Hs.

The editors of the *Cricket* have taken it upon themselves to see that black music is used to further black nationalistic goals, "to uplift the morale of black musicians, and to guide black musicians and people in a positive direction." Many accusations are made in the articles against racist, white musicians' unions; against black musicians who have sold out to white audiences for financial security, a drain that impoverishes black communities musically. The magazine would like to see self-supporting black institutions created to allow the gifted black musician to be heard without having to compromise his art to accommodate white tastes. However, it seems that when the *Cricket* speaks of black music, it is talking mainly in terms of jazz. The magazine is a valuable source of reference to little-known jazz musicians struggling to lift black jazz from a state of quiescence. Recommended for college and public libraries. (J.G.)

Crisis. 1910. m. $3.50. Henry Lee Moon. National Assn. for the Advancement of Colored People. 1790 Broadway, New York, N.Y. 10019. Illus. Circ: 115,000. Sample. Microform: UM. Reprint: NUP.

Indexed: INeg. *Bk. rev:* 1–2, 250–1,500 words, signed. *Aud:* Ga, Ac, Hs.

With a newsmagazine-sized format (it is no longer in the pocket-sized version), this takes a rather moderate social position in its articles and editorials. It is a 50 to 60 page magazine which features four to six articles that touch on all aspects of black culture, politics, history, and activities of the National Association for the Advancement of Colored People (NAACP). The style of writing is popular, and the message is clearly middle-of-the-road. About one half of each issue is devoted to civil rights actions, and there are a number of shorter items, and letters to the editor which give a representative overview of the NAACP position. A basic, although sometimes not overly exciting, magazine for all libraries from high school through the university.

Ebony. 1945. m. $5. John Johnson. Johnson Publishing Co., Inc., 1820 S. Michigan Ave., Chicago, Ill. 60616. Illus., index, adv. Circ: 1,250,000. Sample. Vol. ends: Oct. Microform: UM.

Indexed: INeg, RG. *Aud:* Ga, Ac, Hs, Ejh.

The best known, most widely circulated of all the black magazines, this is roughly comparable to *Life.* In the last edition it was noted *Ebony* was "less sophisticated" than its counterpart. The evaluation is withdrawn, for as more than one reader has pointed out: "perhaps to black readers it is decidedly more sophisticated." And in view of what has been happening to *Life,* there can be no argument on that score. In fact, aside from its obvious interest for Blacks, this 150 to 200 page monthly affords honest insights into another culture for nonblack readers. Although the emphasis is on photographs, there are many articles which focus on all aspects of the current scene. Writers discuss everything from politics to sports, art to civil rights. No other black magazine, in fact, has such a wide, general scope. Issued by the Johnson Publishing Company, this is only one of several general black magazines put out by the firm. See also *Jet, Tan,* and *Black World* (formerly *Negro Digest*). Johnson was among the first to recognize the importance of separate magazines for a public long overlooked by the white press, and he has done much to build his magazine in a middle-of-the-road, respectable voice for Blacks. While in most ways no better or worse than other mass circulation magazines, it is at least relevant to the audience it serves. As such, it should be in all libraries, regardless of type or size.

Equal Opportunity. See Occupations and Employment Section.

Essence. 1970. m. $6. Marcie Gillespie. The Hollingsworth Group, Inc., 102 E. 30th Street, New York, N.Y. 10016. Illus., adv. Circ: 150,000.

Bk. rev: 2–3, 500 words, signed. *Aud:* Ga, Ac.

Nothing exposes the fatuousness of this society like the advertising in a black magazine. The familiar advertisements that make those all-too-familiar claims ("You've come a long way baby") appear even more ludicrous than usual when the smiling faces and cavorting figures are black instead of white. A black women's magazine that patterns itself after a white middle-class publication seems just as incongruous. The "essence" of black womanhood is clearly not fashion, dieting, home furnishings, and male attention.

Admittedly, there is more to *Essence* than this. More space is given to the search for (black) identity, and to political and educational questions in general, than in white women's magazines. The politics is moderate with a healthy touch of militancy; for middle-class readers it may even be instructive. But for the majority of the black women it really has little of consequence to say. Better to have it than not, probably, but surely someone can do better. (M.M.)

Freedomways; a quarterly review of the freedom movement. 1961. q. $4.50. Esther Jackson. Freedomways Associates, Inc., Suite 544, 799 Broadway, New York, N.Y. 10003. Illus., adv. Circ: 10,000. Sample. Vol. ends: 4th quarter. Microform: UM. Reprint: Kraus.

Indexed: INeg. *Bk. rev:* 7–10, 1–3 pages, signed. *Aud:* Ga, Ac, Hs.

A quarterly collection of poetry, fiction, art, and nonfiction concerning the black freedom movement, primarily in the United States. Articles are generally 10 to 12 pages long. Regular features are an editorial, "Readers' Forum," and "Book Reviews and Recent Books." All books mentioned in "Book Reviews and Recent Books" cover some facet of black life, either in America or abroad. The book reviews are detailed and critical; the recent books are given brief bibliographic listings. One of the best black periodicals, and for most libraries.

Harvard Journal of Afro-American Affairs (Formerly: *Harvard Journal of Negro Affairs*). 1965. s-a. $2.50. Lee A. Daniels. Harvard Journal of Afro-American Affairs, 20 Sacramento St., Cambridge, Mass. 02138. Adv. Circ: 3,000.

Aud: Ac.

Objective, often scholarly and well-documented articles on all aspects of Africa and the Black in America are featured in this journal. Contributors are students, teachers, or subject experts. The content is a trifle uneven, particularly the student efforts. It is refreshing in that the supporting organization (Association of African and African-American Students) has no real axe to grind, and within its pages one can find diametrically opposed viewpoints fully aired. A useful magazine for large collections, particularly in academic libraries.

Harvard Journal of Negro Affairs. See *Harvard Journal of Afro-American Affairs.*

Interracial Review. 1934. m. $4. Arthur D. Wright. Catholic Interracial Council of New York, 55 Liberty St., New York, N.Y. 10007. Illus. Circ.: 4,000. Sample. Vol. ends: Winter. Microform: GW. Reprint: GNR.

Indexed: CathI. *Bk. rev:* 6, 300 words, signed. *Aud:* Ac.

The emphasis in this magazine is on relating Catholic ideas and doctrine to present trends in the civil rights movement. However, each issue will also contain articles on such general subjects as union discrimination and black "subculture," which do not necessarily advance the Catholic viewpoint. Editorials discuss civil rights, poverty, and Catholic social action. A rather specialized work for large libraries and most medium to large-sized Catholic collections.

Jet. 1952. w. $12. John H. Johnson. Johnson Publishing Co., Inc., 1820 S. Michigan Ave., Chicago, Ill. 60616. Illus., adv. Circ: 403,000. Sample.

Bk. rev: Notes. *Aud:* Ga, Ac, Hs.

A five-by-eight-inch black newsmagazine "to provide blacks with a convenient-sized magazine summarizing the week's biggest black news in a well-organized, easy-to-read format." A sister of *Ebony* and *Tan*, the magazine can be deceptive. Many of the articles have sensational titles and photos, but along with that is hard, solid reporting. The editor has come down heavily on injustices to blacks, and has run a number of exclusive news stories. All in all, the reporting is some of the best in the country, certainly up to the level of the better-known white publications such as *Time* and *Newsweek*. In addition to the news, there are countless special features including a listing of black performers on television for the week, and columns on sports, fashion, books, music, religion, etc. As the nation's only black news weekly this should be found in all libraries. In the last edition the annotation wasn't as favorable, but the magazine has come a long way since then. It is now highly recommended.

Journal of Black Poetry. 1966. q. $5. Joe Goncalves. 922-5 Haight St., San Francisco, Calif. 94117. Illus. Circ: 500. Sample.

Bk. rev: 3-4, 150-200 words, signed. *Aud:* Ga, Ac, Hs. *Jv:* V.

A descriptive title. The content is rough, frequently angry, and always authentic. There is a general news section, with book reviews and notes. Should be considered essential for any school, college or university with more than one black student. (D.D.)

Journal of Black Studies. 1970. q. $15 (Individuals $10). Arthur L. Smith. Sage Publns. Inc., 275 S. Beverly Dr., Beverly Hills, Calif. 90212. Index, adv.

Indexed: CIJE. *Bk. rev:* Essays, notes. *Aud:* Ac, Hs.

Edited by the director of the Afro-American Studies Center at UCLA, this journal publishes scholarly original research on social, economic, political, philosophical, literary, and historical issues. The first issue included the following: "The Significance and Challenge of Afro-American Studies," by Boniface Obichere of UCLA and "Black Persuaders in the Anti-salvery Movement," by Patrick C. Kennicott of the University of Maryland.

Journal of Human Relations. 1952. q. $4. Don Werkheiser. Central State Univ., Wilberforce, Ohio 45384. Microform: UM. Reprint: Johnson.

Indexed: INeg, PAIS, PsyAb, Curr. Cont. *Bk. rev:* 7-10, 400-1,000 words, signed. *Aud:* Ga, Ac.

Approaches human relations from all disciplines in the belief "that the human conditions require the light of every science in order to increase social awareness and to establish more meaningful practical relationships." There are usually eight nontechnical articles, of 10 to 12 pages, written by professors and laymen in the fields of literature, philosophy, education, sociology, and the other social sciences. Authors have dealt with the necessity of identifying and constructing meaningful national goals, the philosophical basis for a democracy, human goals, and the psychological factors inducing warfare. Occasionally, several articles will present a symposium on various aspects of a topic such as poverty. Of use to laymen, students and scholars.

The Journal of Negro Education; a quarterly review of problems incident to the education of Negroes. 1932. q. $5. Walter G. Daniel, Howard Univ., Washington, D.C. 20001. Index. Circ: 3,000. Sample. Vol. ends: Fall. Microform: UM. Reprint: Kraus.

Indexed: CIJE, EdI, INeg, PAIS, PsyAb. *Bk. rev:* 3-5, 500-1,000 words, signed. *Aud:* Ga, Ac, Hs, Ejh. *Jv:* V.

Perhaps the best-respected and established journal in this field, the editors express three goals: the collection and dissemination of facts, the presentation of critical appraisals of these facts and discussion based on them, and the stimulation and sponsorship of research and investigation in the field. The articles cover all levels and all tangents of education. Viewpoints range through the historical, legal, sociological, psychological, and political. An average issue has seven to eight long articles and five shorter ones, usually on a variety of subjects. Articles are documented. The third (summer) issue of the year is the *Yearbook of Negro Education*, giving extensive coverage to a single topic which has been of particular note or concern that year. Essential in college and university libraries, and in elementary and secondary schools with black students.

Journal of Negro History. 1916. q. $7. W. Augustus Low. Assn. for the Study of Negro Life and History, Inc., 1401 14th St., N.W., Washington, D.C. 20005. Index, adv. Circ: 5,600. Sample. Microform: PMC, UM. Reprint: UPC.

Indexed: EdI, MLA, INeg, PAIS, PsyAb. *Bk. rev:* 3-5, 500-1,000 words, signed. *Aud:* Ac, Ga. *Jv:* V.

Intended for the scholar of black history, this is one of the oldest, most prestigious (certainly best-indexed) journals in the field. Of the four to six long articles in each issue, most are concerned with the biography of a Black in the United States. In addition to retrospective figures, the magazine also considers current Blacks who are making their place in American history. There is an excellent section of book reviews, notes on meetings and events, and brief news items. See also the organization's publication for schools, the *Negro History Bulletin.*

Liberator. 1961. m. $4. Daniel H. Watts, Afro-American Research Inst., Inc., 244 E. 46th St., New York, N.Y. 10017. Illus., adv. Circ: 20,000.

Aud: Ga, Ac, Hs.

A type of black *Nation* or *New Republic,* this is a militant voice for such things as civil rights, housing, education, and employment. A good part of each issue is devoted to political and social reporting, but it is unique, too, for its fine movie, television, and theater reviews. In addition, it publishes original poetry and prose, and some photographs. The editor often comments on the white press, pointing up discrepancies and unfair reporting. While the tone is definitely militant, it is equally intelligent and generally fair. A good basic black magazine for almost any public or academic library.

Muhammad Speaks. See Newspapers/Special Interest Section.

Negro American Literature Forum for School and University Teachers. 1967. q. $4. John F. Bayliss. Dept. of English, Indiana State Univ., Terre Haute, Ind. 47809. Illus. Circ: 800. Sample. Vol. ends: Winter.

Indexed: CIJE, MLA. *Bk. rev:* 2, 1 page, signed. *Aud:* Ac, Ga, Hs, Ejh.

An overview of black literature, from all periods. "Editorial policy is to run the possible gamut in the subject, from kindergarten to university material." A typical offset issue of 36 pages includes a general article on black literature, a biographical sketch of an author, methods of working with black students, reports on various teaching projects, book reviews, and general news notes. The magazine is one of the few ideally suited for the teacher interested in integrating black material into school programs. Should be in elementary, high school, and all academic libraries.

Negro Book Club Newsletter. 1960. 8–10/yr. Free to members. Negro Book Club, Inc., 160 W. 85th St., New York, N.Y. 10024. Illus. Circ: 60,000.

Aud: Ac, Ga, Hs, Ejh.

The *Newsletter* opens each issue with evaluative comments on its book-of-the-month selection. The remaining pages are devoted to annotated lists of books available through the Negro Book Club, loosely arranged under such subject headings as "Reference Books," "Pictorial History Books," "Slavery," "Education" (subdivided into Juvenile Selections, with suggested grade levels indicated; and Visual Aid Material, including maps and power posters). Although a typical issue consists of only approximately eight well-spaced pages, the selections are diverse enough to be of interest to both school and academic librarians and their

clients. The *Newsletter* is a membership service only. (J.G.)

Negro Braille Magazine. 1952. q. Free. Mrs. E. R. Merrick. Amer. Printing House for the Blind, 1839 Frankfort Ave., Louisville, Ky. 40206. Circ: 300.

Aud: Ga, Hs.

A 78-page quarterly which extracts material from leading black periodicals, i.e., *Black World, Ebony, Jet,* etc. The material is suitable for young adults and adults. The magazine is free to the blind, being financed by gifts and the time of its editor. Hopefully, libraries which have a need for this worthwhile publication will donate something to the cause. Obviously, it is the only magazine for the library serving Blacks who are in need of such a service.

Negro Digest. See *Black World.*

Negro Educational Review. 1950. q. $5. R. Grann Lloyd, Nashville, Tenn. 37202. Index, adv.

Indexed: EdI. *Aud:* Ac, Hs, Ejh.

Primarily of interest to teachers, this presents articles and research reports on all aspects of education and the Black. Contributions move from the elementary through the academic level. Articles are primarily by administrators and teachers who have faced the problems they discuss. It is a bit uneven, and is not up to the level of *The Journal of Negro Education.*

Negro History Bulletin. 1937. m. (Sept.–May). $3.50. Charles H. Wesley. Assn. for the Study of Negro Life and History, 1538 9th St., N.W., Washington, D.C. 20001. Illus., index, adv. Circ: 22,000. Sample. Vol. ends: Dec. Microform: UM.

Indexed: INeg, RG. *Bk. rev:* 2–5, one page, signed. *Aud:* Ga, Ac, Hs.

The purpose of this 24 to 30 page magazine is "to promote an appreciation of the life and history of the Negro, to encourage an understanding of his present status and to enrich the promise of the future." Articles are written in readable style, often with photos and illustrations. Among its regular features are the monthly "Current History," poems, and chapter news. Biographical material on famous Blacks is also featured. The book reviews are critical, written by experts in the field. Most books reviewed cover some facet of black life.

Negro Traveler & Conventioneer. 1942. m. $6. C. M. Markham, Jr. Travelers' Research Publishing Co., Inc., 8034 S. Prairie Ave., Chicago, Ill. 60619. Illus., adv. Circ: 72,000. Sample.

Aud: Ga.

A travel magazine for the middle-and upper-income Black. Editorial material is primarily concerned with basic travel information, transportation, and conventions. There are updated guides to restaurants and hotels, and a good deal of advertising. Originally, this magazine was geared for black travel agencies and for administrators planning conventions. In recent years it has become more of a general travel magazine and has branched out to include European trips. It has a long way to go to compete with such titles as *Holiday* or *Travel,* but it is a fine item for communities serving Blacks.

Neighbors. See Urban Studies Section.

New Lady; reflecting a greater way of living. 1966. m. $5. Edward N. Evans. Mecco Enterprises Inc., Box 6125, Hayward, Calif. 94545.

Aud: Ga, Hs.

The first of two magazines directed explicitly to the black woman reader, this has basically the same approach as the newer *Essence.* It is neither as slick, nor as cleverly edited, but the subject approach is pretty much the same. Most of the articles are pleasant subjects: an interview with a successful career girl, a feature on a personality, and similar subjects. In addition to regular columns on foods, health, fashions, homemaking, and fiction, there is a children's page. Of the two *Essence* is better, but *New Lady* can be recommended as a second, particularly in a community serving a middle-class black audience. (J.G.)

New South. q. $3. Robert E. Anderson, Jr. Southern Regional Council, 5 Forsyth St., N.W., Atlanta, Ga. 30303. Illus., index. Circ: 3,500. Sample. Vol. ends: Fall. Microform: UM.

Indexed: INeg, PAIS. *Aud:* Ga, Ac.

The focus here is on economic, political, and social problems of the southern Black. Articles document what some (mostly white) Southerners are doing to alleviate these problems, the success they have had and the resistance they have encountered. The publication sometimes devotes a whole issue to a single topic such as school desegregation, poverty, voter registrations, etc. The writing is effective and photographs are used for maximum emotional impact. A magazine for all Southern public and high school libraries, as well as a good many of those north of the Mason-Dixon line. As a source of social documentation, it should be found in larger academic libraries.

Nommo. 1969. q. $4. Hoyt W. Fuller. Organization of Black Amer. Culture, Writers' Workshop, 77 E. 35th St., Chicago, Ill. 60616. Illus.

Aud: Ac, Ga.

Nommo is a publication of the Organization of Black American Culture's Writers' Workshop. The creators tell us that the aim of this publication is to approach "the realities of the everyday cultural life of black people, as well as the development of a special set of standards with which to interpret and evaluate . . . it is necessary to establish a new positive accep-

tance of our cultural resources. . . ." The great bulk of *Nommo* consists of poetry, but the essay and the short story are also represented. Some of the creations in this magazine are basically good in idea, but what one wishes for, at times, is greater subtlety in treatment. Suitable for the college and large public library. (J.G.)

Phylon; the Atlanta University review of race and culture. 1940. q. $4.50. Tilman C. Cothran. Atlanta Univ., 223 Chestnut St., Atlanta, Ga. 30314. Index. Circ: 2,200. Microform: UM. Reprint: Kraus.

Indexed: CIJE, INeg, PsyAb, PAIS, SSHum. *Bk. rev:* 4–5, 500–1,000 words, signed. *Aud:* Ac, Ga.

Founded by W. E. B. DuBois, this is a scholarly journal which considers in its seven to nine articles almost every aspect of the Black in America. Contributions are divided between historical and social studies. The style is rather good, certainly within the grasp of anyone who is interested in the subject matter. And as a good deal of the material is timely, it serves as a solid balance for discussion which may arise from less thoughtful articles in the popular press. There are excellent book reviews and, on occasion, poetry and a short story. A basic magazine for both the general and specialized collection.

Race Relations Reporter (Formerly: *Southern Education Report*). 1970. bi-w. $10. Jim Leeson. Race Relations Information Center, Box 6156, Nashville, Tenn. 37212. Sample. Microform: UM.

Indexed: INeg. *Aud:* Ga, Ac.

A 12-page newsletter which reports on race relationships between all minority groups and the establishment, not just Blacks and whites. The sponsoring group is a private, nonprofit organization supported mainly by a grant from the Ford Foundation. "The Center is the successor to Southern Education Reporting Service, which reported for 15 years on school segregation in the Southern and border states." The reporting is objective, cool, and professional. Each issue begins with five or six brief items in the news, followed by a biographical sketch, commentaries, and shorter articles on various activities. Despite the wide scope, most of the material does concern the Black, particularly in the South. The publisher offers a number of special reports from time to time on all aspects of the question from the Black Muslims to the American Indian in revolt. (Note: apparently libraries may receive the newsletter free for the asking. The $10 subscription price assures receipt of the special reports as issued.)

Rights & Reviews. 1964. irreg. $2. Doris Innis, National CORE, 200 W. 135th St., New York, N.Y. 10030. Illus. Circ: 3,000. Sample. Microform: UM.

Bk. rev: 2, 3 pages, signed. *Aud:* Ac, Ga, Hs.

A magazine of the Black Power movement, this is devoted both to the activities of CORE and to the "Movement" in general. It has been supported by such writers as LeRoi Jones, Julian Bond, and Floyd McKissick, and represents a factual account of things as they are from the black man's side of the city and the world. There are photographs, cartoons, and book reviews. One of the best of its type, this journal can be read profitably by anyone from the high school student to the graduate student—not to mention those now actively working for change.

Sepia. 1954. m. $6. Ben Burns. Good Publishing Co., 1220 Harding St., Fort Worth, Tex. 76102. Illus., adv. Circ: 52,000. Sample.

Indexed: INeg. *Aud:* Ga.

This, a *Life*-like general magazine for Blacks, boasts an average of 80 to 100 pages and many photographs. In September 1971 the editorial offices for *Sepia* were moved to Chicago. With the change came a revamping of policy. What was once a bland general magazine now addresses itself to "outstanding writing, exciting photography, and a positive view of the black man's role in his native land." Despite this claim, the magazine has a long way to go to catch up with *Ebony* in either circulation or positive social dedication. Still, the white-owned *Sepia* seems to be making the effort, e.g., with such articles as "The Crisis in Medical Care," and "Is Baseball Ready for a Black Manager?" On the other hand, an article such as "Blacks who Turned White" may turn off a good number of more serious, less sensationally minded readers. And the advertisements are atrocious. It remains a second choice after *Ebony* and *Jet* and way down the list if the library is subscribing to more than general black magazines.

Soul. 1967. bi-w. $2.50. Ken Jones. 8271 Melrose Ave., Suite 208, Los Angeles, Calif. 90046. Circ: 150,000.

Aud: Ga.

In tabloid newspaper format, this is something like *Variety.* It attempts to report the latest happenings on the soul scene. *Soul* includes short, readable, entertaining articles—replete with photographs—about black performers of soul music (in this case, jazz, blues, rock, and gospel). Among those columns appearing regularly is Walter Burrell's "Hollywood," which gossips about the professional and personal successes and failures of these artists. Other regular columns are the "Jazz Scene," and the "Glorybound Train," a column on gospel music; the section "Sounds" gives a critical, annotated list of new LP releases, selecting from jazz, rock, blues, and gospel. This should be suitable for public and undergraduate college libraries whose clients have some interest in soul music. (J.G.)

Soul: Illustrated. 1968. bi-m. $3. 8271 Melrose Ave., Los Angeles, Calif. 90046. Illus., adv. Circ: 250,000. Sample.

Aud: Ga.

A sister publication of *Soul,* this is a general man's magazine which looks a bit like *Playboy,* but without the pressure of the centerfold. Emphasis is on the Black in the world of entertainment. The majority of articles tell how this or that performer made it in the world. There is material on sports, books, records, movies, and other features. The style is obviously geared to the male reader and any library trying to reach out for the average man is advised to send for a sample copy.

Soulbook. 1965. q. $3. Ed. bd. Soulbook, Inc., Box 1097, Berkeley, Calif. 94701. Illus., adv.

Bk. rev: Various number, length. *Aud:* Ga, Ac.

A militant publication, *Soulbook* is greatly concerned with the politics of revolution, and the evils of modern-day imperialism. Articles reflect favor with that which is innovative in black economics, literature, and music. It contains book reviews and a poetry section: "Reject Notes." As militant as *Black Politics,* *Soulbook* is more varied in subject material. There are articles in Spanish and French. Recommended for most college libraries and the large public library. (J.G.)

Southern Education Report. See *Race Relations Reporter.*

Studies in Black Literature. 1970. 3/yr. $4. Raman K. Singh. Dept. of English, Mary Washington College, Fredericksburg, Va. 22401.

Bk. rev: 4–6, 500–1,500 words, signed. *Aud:* Ac.

An 80 or so page mimeographed journal "devoted to the critical study of Afro-American and African literatures." The issue examined (Vol. 1, no. 2) included an article on the thrillers of Chester Himes by Edward Margolies, a critical piece on LeRoi Jones, two other shorter articles, essay book reviews, and a 35-page unannotated "Bibliography of Afro-American Fiction (1853–1970)." The articles are jargon free, clear, and perceptive, and the bibliography seems objective enough. A good addition for any academic library.

Tan. 1950. m. $5. Mrs. Ariel P. Strong. Johnson Publishing Co., Inc., 1820 S. Michigan Ave., Chicago, Ill. 60616. Illus., adv. Circ: 126,000. Sample.

Aud: Ga.

Although this started out as a confessional magazine, and still has a sensational quality, the Johnson Publishing Company has brought it more in line with its other publications, i.e., *Ebony, Jet,* and *Black World.* It is now a rather honest effort to be a black woman's general magazine. Emphasis is still on the confessional, but this is balanced with articles on the home, fashions, food, and child raising. There are a number of biographical sketches and regular features on stretching the budget. It is not, in any way, the editorial equal of *Essence* or *New Lady,* but with these two new competitors Johnson may bring it up to the times. Meanwhile, it stands as a fair bet for a library serving the less well educated; but is still far down the list. It can be recommended only for the large black collection.

Uptown Beat. 1968. q. $3.50 (8 issues/$.50 ea.). Ed. comm. E. Harlem Writing Center, Box 24, Hellgate Station, New York, N.Y. 10029. Illus. Circ: 500. Vol. ends: 1st quarter.

Aud: Ac, Ga, Hs.

They're black, white, and brown. Men and women. They live in the big-city streets, in ghetto tenements, in therapeutic junkie communities. Their ages range from teens to sixties. They meet weekly to generate poems, stories, and essays, and to rap about each other's work. They're the East Harlem Writing Center: an emotive, truth–hunting, life–grappling bunch who speak a language lightyears distant from the anemic, "proper" patois of, say, Boston Brahmins, or the phony, trivial patter of chrome-brained suburbanites. The word–truths of their dreams, disappointments, discoveries, and daily reality appear in *Uptown Beat.* Much of it is not polished. Some of it does not click. But nearly every line is honest, direct. And the variety staggers: collective verse-collages and improvisations, finger-snapping "rocks," prose-bits, poems—rhymed as well as free-style—cryptic and expansive, and amazing, magnificent graphics: charcoals, line drawings, photos, calligraphy. An "off beat" item for almost any library, particularly the one who cares about blacks. (S.B.)

Vibrations. See Little Magazines Section.

WCLC Newsletter. 1965. m. Contributions. Western Christian Leadership Conference, 4802 McKinley, Los Angeles, Calif. 90011. Illus., adv.

Aud: Ac, Ga.

A reporting device for activities of both the Western and the Southern Christian Leadership Conferences. The organization is involved with assisting the black wherever he may be, and in helping him to help himself. And while of no great physical size, the newsletter is of major importance for anyone interested in civil rights.

BOOKS AND BOOK REVIEWS

Basic Periodicals

Ejh: *School Library Journal, Hornbook, Center for Children's Books* (Note: All titles are for the librarian–teacher, not for the child.); Hs: *New York Times Book Review, New York Review of Books;* Ga: *New York Times Book Review, New York Review of Books, Saturday Review;* Jc: *New York Review of Books, New York Times Book Review, San Francisco Book Review, Saturday Review;* Ac: *New York Review of Books, New York Times Book Review, San Francisco Book Review, Times Literary Supplement, Scholarly Books in America, Saturday Review.*

Book Selection Aids

Library Journal, Choice, Kirkus, Publisher's Weekly, AB Bookman's Weekly.

Basic Abstracts and Indexes

Book Review Digest, Technical Book Review Index.

Cessations

Books, Book Buyer's Guide, Book World.

AB Bookman's Weekly; the specialist book trade weekly. 1948. w. $13.50. Sol M. Malkin, 240 Mulberry St., Newark, N.J. 07102. Illus., index, adv. Circ: 5,500.

Indexed: LibLit. *Bk. rev:* 10–30, 50 words. *Aud:* Ga, Ac. *Jv:* V.

While directed to the antiquarian and used-book dealer, this is very much a part of any librarian's reading. Why? Because the first part, usually 10 to 30 pages, is composed of articles, notes, and news items on every facet of the antiquarian book trade. Also, from time to time there is material on libraries and their acquisitions. The second part, which makes up most of every issue, consists of lists of books wanted by various dealers, and books for sale. There is an annual *Bookman's Yearbook* (included in the subscription price). This consists of advertisements from the world's used-book dealers, nicely indexed by subjects. Also, a part of each yearbook is devoted to a bibliographic subject. The magazine continues to be the work of Sol Malkin and his wife, who write most of the copy. It is now an institution among bookmen and women in America—a required item in any library where books are important. Incidentally, from time to time, libraries seeking hard-to-get titles run advertisements in the magazine too.

ASLIB Book List; a monthly list of recommended scientific and technical books. 1935. m. $12.10. Ms. D.A.R. Solwiej. Aslib, 3 Belgrave Sq., London SW1X 8PL, England. Index. Circ: 3,250. Sample. Vol. ends: Dec.

Aud: Ac.

Concise, critical reviews of some 50 titles per issue. Most of the technical and scientific books are from English or continental publishers. They are recommended by Aslib. What it comes down to is an English equivalent of *New Technical Books*, and, as such, of value to the library that takes the American publication.

Appraisal; children's science books. 1967. 3/yr. $4. Frances Doughty. Children's Science Book Review Committee, Longfellow Hall, Appian Way, Cambridge, Mass. 02138. Index. Circ: 750.

Aud: Ejh, Hs.

Supported by the Harvard Graduate School of Education and New England libraries, this is an objective book review service. It offers a rating system for science books which qualify for inclusion in elementary through high school collections. Some 50 to 75 books are analyzed in each issue. A dual approach is usually offered, i.e., first a subject expert places the work within his area; second, a librarian describes how it will fit into the total collection. The two 50 to 100 word descriptions are used to give the book a rating from "Excellent" to "Unsatisfactory." This is far superior to most services for children's and teenagers' books, and deserves wider backing than it is now getting.

Best Sellers; the semi-monthly review. 1941. s–m. $7. William B. Hill. Univ. of Scranton, Scranton, Pa. 18510. Index. Circ: 3,000.

Indexed: CathI.

A book review service which is primarily aimed at the religious library. All types of books are examined, not just religious titles. However, an effort is made to point up what is good or bad about them, in terms of moral and other values, as seen by the reviewers and editor. The service is biased, intentionally so, and should not be used outside of the context of its purpose. Within that purpose it is fine.

Bestsellers. 1946. m. $3. Vera Haldy. North Amer. Publishing Co., 134 N. 13th St., Philadelphia, Pa. 19107. Illus., adv. Circ: 40,000.

Aud: Ga.

While this is a guide for wholesale and retail paperback book and magazine stores, it is of some help to both laymen and librarians. Each month there are a number of articles on paperbacks and periodicals, somewhat along the order of *Publishers' Weekly.* Most of this is concerned with how to merchandise the books and magazines, but some of it deals with readership, sales data of given titles, etc. The letters column, which tells readers' likes or dislikes in paperbacks and magazines, affords librarians an informal view of reading habits. Hardly a necessary item, yet useful—and too little known—for libraries.

Black Books Bulletin. See Blacks Section.

Bookbird; literature for children and young people, news from all over the world, recommendations for translation. 1963. q. $5. Richard Bamberger. Verlag fuer Jugend und Volk Tiefer Graben 7–9, Vienna, 1, Austria. Illus., index. Circ: 2,000.

Indexed: LibLit. *Aud:* Ejh, Hs.

The subtitle explains the content and purpose. This is primarily a news magazine to inform readers about what is going on in the world of children's and teen-age books. There are book reviews and notes on what the editors and contributors think should be translated. It is useful because of its international coverage, and while most of the emphasis is on titles for younger people, it can be valuable in high schools.

The magazine is in English, is sponsored by the nonprofit International Board on Books for Young People and the International Institute for Children's Juvenile and Popular Literature. In a word, it is authoritative.

Booklist (Formerly: *Booklist and Subscription Books Bulletin*). 1905. s–m. $12. Edna Vanek. Amer. Library Assn., 50 E. Huron St., Chicago, Ill. 60611. Index, adv. Circ: 35,000. Microform: UM.

Aud: Ga, Ejh, Hs. *Jv:* C.

Made up of 50- to 150-word descriptive, sometimes analytical reviews of current books and nonprint material for adults, children, and young people. The usual issue gives full bibliographic information on some 150 titles. Over the years this has developed a reputation of being the bastion for conservative, middle-of-the-road reviews. The result? It enjoys (or enjoyed) a healthy circulation among libraries, particularly school libraries where some 25,000 of the 35,000 issues go twice each month. Another 7,000 copies go to small and medium-sized public libraries. Even college libraries are included, but here the subscription is primarily for the front material, i.e., "Reference and Subscription Book Reviews," which analyze one to three basic reference books and encyclopedias in each issue. The difficulty is that success has spoiled the reviewing service, and more and more librarians are calling out for a more meaningful, unique approach. (Much of what is found here is found earlier and in a better fashion in *Library Journal* and *School Library Journal,* and even, to a lesser degree, in the ALA's own *Choice.*) In an effort to diversify, the magazine has taken on the periodic reviewing of nonprint materials from filmstrips to recordings, and twice a year, notes on new magazines. All of the services are useful, although usually done better somewhere else. The book reviews, prepared by staff reviewers, are colorless but objective. Also, there is no denying that the reviews of children's and young adult books are well done. The trouble? Almost total lack of excitement or a willingness to recommend anything which sparks controversy. What is needed is a new approach to the purpose of the service. In attempting to serve all libraries, it seems to serve none well. In attempting to be noncontroversial, it seems to be continuing the bland, nonmeaningful collection. Except for the reference book reviews, which remain the best anywhere, the service cannot be recommended. And for those who do insist on continuing, it is hoped they will at least subscribe to one or two other major review services.

Booklist and Subscription Books, Bulletin. See *Booklist.*

Book News. 1940. m. $7.50. Jessie Kitching. Book News Publishing Co. (Sub of Bro-Dart, Inc.), 1609 Memorial Ave., Williamsport, Pa. 17701. Illus., index, adv. Circ: 20,000. Sample. Microform: AA.

Aud: Ga, Ejh, Hs.

One of a decreasing number of magazines put out by book jobbers, this one by Bro-Dart. The purpose is to announce what titles are going to be published, or have just been published. The information is of interest to public and school librarians. The reviews are descriptive, but obviously not analytical other than in terms of extremes. About 15 to 20 titles are given added coverage, i.e., are included in "An Expert Makes His Choice" column. How reliable is all of this? Fair to good, but the purpose of the publisher is to sell books, not to be a critical reviewer. Keeping that in mind, the service does have a useful alerting purpose. The magazine is usually sent free to libraries dealing with Bro-Dart.

The expense of this type of publicity (or service) is severely limiting the genre. At one time almost every jobber had his own magazine. This is no longer so, which is just as well. Too many unsophisticated librarians were depending on them for reviews and collection building.

Book-of-the-Month Club News. 1927. 15/yr. Membership. Ralph Thompson. Book-of-the-Month Club, 280 Park Ave., New York, N.Y. 10017. Illus. Circ: 1,000,000.

Aud: Ga.

The best known and longest lived of the scores of book clubs, the Book-of-the-Month Club has been issuing a newsletter and "little" magazine since its inception. Each issue highlights the month's choice with information on the book and its author. There are also alternative selections which are usually annotated and otherwise described. Obviously this is not one most libraries will need to take, but it is useful to have access to the newsletter, if only to know the titles members or nonmembers are going to request; and later, quite probably, donate to the library.

Others of this same genre are: *Literary Guild.* (1927. m. Membership. Margon Bockus. Literary Guild of America, Inc., 501 Franklin Ave., Garden City, N.Y. 11531); *Doubleday Bargain Book Club.* (m. Membership. The Club, Garden City, N.Y. 11530); *History Book Club Review.* (m. Membership. Marilyn H. Shenton. History Book Club, Inc., 40 Guernsey St., Stamford, Conn. 06904); plus scores, if not hundreds, more. See also *Junior Literary Guild.*

Book Production Industry. 1924. m. $10. Paul D. Doebler. Penton Publishing Co., 1213 W. 3rd St., Cleveland, Ohio 44113. Illus., index, adv. Circ: 12,500. Microform: UM.

Bk rev: Notes. *Aud:* Sa, Ac.

Covers all phases of book and magazine design, publication, and manufacturing. It includes areas of research and new developments and trends, and is well illustrated with charts and diagrams. Only for specialized collections or where curriculum demands.

Books Abroad; an international literary quarterly. 1927. q. $4. Ivar Ivask. Univ. of Okla. Press, 1005 Asp Ave., Norman, Okla. 73069. Illus., index, adv. Circ: 3,000. Sample. Vol. ends: Winter.

Indexed: SSHum. *Aud:* Ac.

In two parts: the first devoted to articles about foreign publishing, writers, and movements; the second to 200 to 300 word reviews of new original works published abroad. Emphasis is on the review of literary and liberal arts titles, and they are representative of all nations. The editor reports that in the past years his publication has followed "belles-lettres in some 60 languages." Reviews are by scholars and subject experts, and in English. A minor criticism is that most of the comments are favorable, the less acceptable titles not being considered. As a current source of information on international literature this has no equal, at least in the number of titles covered. A necessity for large academic and public libraries.

Books and Bookmen. 1955. m. $8.25. James Gordon. Hansom Books, Artillery Mansions, 75 Victoria St., London SW1, England. Illus., index, adv. Circ: 18,000. Sample.

Bk. rev: Various number, length. *Aud:* Ac, Ga.

An English magazine by the publisher who puts out *Films and Filming, Dance and Dancers,* etc. The format and approach are basically the same here, i.e., emphasis on pictures, notes, and articles directed to the layman, librarian, and bookseller. The whole is chatty, lucid, and of value to anyone dealing with British book dealers. There are usually one or two major articles, but a good deal of every issue is devoted to book reviews. These will vary from one or two essays built around several related books to short notes. About 100 titles are mentioned in each issue. It in no way replaces *The Bookseller,* but the library taking one will want to take both.

Books in Canada. 1971. 18/yr. $9.95. Val Clery. Canadian Review of Books Ltd., 6 Charles St. E., Suite 219, Toronto, Ont., Canada. Illus., adv. Circ: 40,000.

Aud: Ac, Ga.

A tabloid, 24 to 32 page general reviewing service "to stimulate popular awareness of contemporary Canadian writing and books." It concentrates on reviewing books published in Canada about Canada, and has editorials, interviews, and features. Reviews of children's titles and small press books, and advertising of Canadian books, are included. There is a short biographical sketch of each reviewer. The whole thing is professional and neat, almost too neat. It comes close to being a gentleman's *Saturday Review of Literature* of old, i.e., sans the added features. It is unquestionably helpful to Canadians, and to larger American libraries. As Mordecai Richler puts it, the magazine "seems (on the evidence of two issues) to be suing for the shallow, folksy office of old *John O'London's* rather than the *New York Review of Books.* It is also fiercely nationalistic."

The Bookseller; the organ of the book trade. 1858. w. $16. Philothea Thompson. J. Whitaker & Sons, Ltd., 13 Bedford Sq., London, WC1, England. Illus., adv. Circ: 14,000. Sample. Vol. ends: Dec.

Indexed: BritHum. *Aud:* Ac, Ga.

Somewhat the English equivalent of *Publishers' Weekly (PW)*, this covers news of the booktrade, publishing, and libraries, and lists all new British books each week. The weekly lists are cumulated in *Whitaker's Books of the Month & Books to Come* and in *Whitaker's Cumulative Book List*, i.e., the cousins of the *American Book Publishing Record* and its annual volume. Advertising, as in *PW*, composes a large part of each issue, and there are special features such as "Under Review," which quotes from and digests reviews of new titles. A required item in any medium to large-sized academic or public library.

✓ *Braille Book Review.* 1932. bi-m. Free. Claire Holcomb. Amer. Foundation for the Blind. Subs. to: Div. for the Blind, Library of Congress, 1291 Taylor St., N.W., Washington D.C. 20542. Illus., index. Circ: 10,500 (Braille ed.); 11,100 (Inkprint ed.).

Aud: Ga, Ac, Hs, Ejh.

In some 20 pages, current books available in braille are briefly annotated. (All titles are free for loan from cooperating libraries.) There are adult fiction and nonfiction sections as well as children's titles. The type is purposefully large for the near blind, and there is a braille edition. Includes items and announcements of interest to those who are blind or are working with the handicapped. An obvious choice for any library serving the blind or the physically handicapped, and it should be brought to the attention of individuals who may receive it free as well. See also *Talking Book Topics*.

British Book News; a guide to new books. 1940. m. $6. Gillian Dickinson. British Council, 59 New Oxford St., London WC1A 1BP, England. Index, adv. Circ: 10,000. Sample. Vol. ends: Dec.

Indexed: BritHum, LibSciAb. *Aud:* Ac, Ga, Hs.

Small in format, and lacking a good deal of the advertising, this still is the closest England comes to America's *Choice*. It offers some 230 to 250 critical reviews of adult, university level books published the previous month(s) in the British Commonwealth. The annotations average 200 words, and are written by experts whose names are never given, but whose ability and opinions are not difficult to ascertain. Some of the reviews are negative, but as the service is monthly, most of the bad titles have been eliminated by the editor. Special sections include a title listing of forthcoming books, a half dozen titles for younger readers, a list of paperbacks, and usually a lead article on some aspect of selection. International Standard Book numbers (ISBNs) are given, and the whole is arranged by

Dewey. The result is a general reviewing service, with emphasis on academic titles, which can be recommended to any imaginative library.

Catholic Bookseller & Librarian. See *Religious Book Guide.*

✓ *Center for Children's Books. Bulletin.* 1945. m. (Sept.–July). $6. Zena Sutherland. Univ. of Chicago Press, 5801 Ellis Ave., Chicago, Ill. 60637. Index. Circ: 9,000. Sample. Vol. ends: July.

Aud: Ejh, Hs. *Jv:* V.

The single best source for reviews of children's books, this publication covers some 60 to 70 titles per issue. While material for readers from primary through twelfth grades is included, the main emphasis is on the elementary and junior high school levels. The reviews follow a definite pattern: each title is rated in terms of reading level, the importance within the field, and its usefulness for both the child and the library or classroom situation. Editor Sutherland, who edits a children's books column in *Saturday Review*, includes both recommended and not recommended works. A helpful feature is the bibliography of suggested readings for teachers and librarians which is usually included in each issue. In view of the high critical standards, the succinct, literate reviews, and the degree of coverage, this should be the first choice in any library dealing with younger readers. *Horn Book* or *School Library Journal* would be a second choice, *Booklist* a third.

✓ *Choice.* 1964. 11/yr. $20. Amer. Library Assn., 50 E. Huron St., Chicago, Ill. 60611. Index, adv. Circ: 6,200. Sample. Vol. ends: Feb.

Indexed: BoRv, LibLit. *Aud:* Ac, Ga. *Jv:* V.

This and *Library Journal* are the two leading basic book review media for public, college, university, and, to a degree, high school libraries. While the primary emphasis is on scholarly titles for college libraries, a good number of the titles are useful in larger public libraries, certainly for curriculum and teacher support in many high schools. There are some 30 subject categories, and approximately 500 to 700 American-based books are reviewed in each issue. The annotations, written by teachers and subject experts, are from 75 to 150 words in length. On the whole, they are much more critical than those found in other media. As there are over 3,000 reviewers from whom the editor chooses, the reviews vary in style and content. None are signed, although a full list of the issue's contributors is given in the back of each issue. Another useful feature is the 10 to 30 page front matter which usually includes one or two timely and discursive bibliographies on everything from religion to "skin" books. These are signed.

Christian Bookseller; the business magazine of church supply stories. 1955. m. $6. Robert C. Hill. Christian

Life Publications, Inc., Tundersen and Schmale, Wheaton, Ill. 60187. Illus., index, adv. Circ: 7,100. Sample.

Indexed: RelPer. *Aud:* Ga. *Jv:* C.

Primarily a business magazine for Protestant church supply stores. Only a little more then one third of each issue is given to news and material on books. The remainder is devoted to telling readers how to make sales in every department from church robes to filmstrips. The difference in emphasis is important because the magazine in no way replaces or is a substitute for *Religious Book Guide.* Most of the circulation is controlled, i.e., free.

Contemporary Psychology; a journal of reviews. See Psychology Section.

Diplomatic Bookshelf. 1964. m. $2.50. Arthur H. Thrower. 44–46 South Ealing Road, London, W5, England. Charts, illus.

Aud: Ac. *JV:* C.

Published as a supplement to *Diplomat's Annual,* this is the last source one would consult for book reviews, even if—or especially if—you were connected with the diplomatic service. The reviews by editor Thrower appear to have been thrown in for fillers at the last minute before publication. Actually, titles are not reviewed as such. They are simply accompanied by a spew of words such as "charming," "delightful," or "absolutely indispensable." As a reviewing medium, *Diplomatic Bookshelf* is dispensable. However, diplomats would find other features, such as the list of diplomatic arrivals and departures, or notices of diplomatic receptions and parties, useful. One might suggest that Mr. Thrower change his title from *Diplomatic Bookshelf,* incorporating diplomatic and consular list of arrivals and departures, to *Diplomatic and Consular List of Arrivals and Departures,* incorporating diplomatic bookshelf. (S.W.)

Educational Studies; a journal of book reviews in the foundations of education. 1970. q. $6. (Member $5). John A. Laska. Subs. to: School of Education, Univ. of Va., Charlottesville, Va. 22903.

Index: EdI. *Aud:* Ac, Hs, Ga.

Published by the American Educational Studies Association, this 50-page journal is devoted to reviewing current American books in education. (Foreign titles distributed here are included, and the editor hopes at some time to extend coverage to include other foreign books.) The 200 to 500 word signed reviews cover some 70 to 90 titles, are written primarily by professors of education, and are generally free of jargon. Most of the books are specialized, although a few would be of interest to laymen. The reviews are duly indexed and broken down by broad subjects from research and history of education to systems and policy

issues. Ease of use is matched only by timeliness—the majority of reviewed titles appeared within the previous one to three months. A cursory check indicates the reviewers are relatively objective; more important, critical. Of some 15 reviews read, only half were totally favorable, and the other half were downright caustic. An aid for all libraries where educational collections are a consideration.

Hebrew Book Review. 1965. s-a. $1. Reuven Ben-Yosef. Inst. for the Translation of Hebrew Literature, 3 Modigliani St., Tel-Aviv, Israel. Illus.

Bk. rev: 10–20, lengthy, signed. *Aud:* Ga, Ac.

The Institute for the Translation of Hebrew Literature promotes the translation of Hebrew literature into foreign languages. One of their publications is this small but useful magazine. Each issue contains 10 to 20 book reviews dealing with fiction, drama, poetry, and essays. The reviews are of an informative nature and tend to be noncritical; in addition to a description of content, a review also gives details on previous works of the author and his place in contemporary Hebrew literature. Poetry is given a prominent place. Poetry reviews always contain one or two passages translated into English as the best way of presenting the author to an English reader. At the end of each issue there are a few lines of biographical information on the authors reviewed. Recent translations into Hebrew are also announced. This is a modest but useful publication for librarians responsible for acquiring foreign literature, and for students and general readers interested in Hebrew literature. (R.T.)

Horn Book Magazine; about children's books and reading. 1924. bi-m. $7.50. Paul Heins. Horn Book Inc., 585 Boylston St., Boston, Mass. 02116. Illus., index, adv. Circ: 27,500. Sample. Microform: UM. Reprint: AMS.

Indexed: IChildMags, LibLit, RG. *Aud:* Ejh. *Jv:* V.

Combines four or five articles per issue with 75 to 100 reviews of children's books, i.e., those for preschool through junior high. The articles are by experts, and are well written. They touch on everything from the history of children's books and illustrators to current trends and biases. The reviews are grouped by age interest, run from 75 to 200 words each, and are critical as well as descriptive. Usually only recommended titles are listed. Recordings are sometimes reviewed, as are books of interest to adults working with children. The total impression is one of professionalism, plus courage and conviction. It is as imaginative as it is realistic about children's reading needs. A basic magazine for school libraries and public libraries serving this age group.

In Review. 1967. q. $3. for 3 yrs. Irma McDonough. Provincial Library Service, 14th Fl., Mowat Block, Queen's Park, Toronto, 182, Ont., Canada. Illus., index, adv. Circ: 7,800. Sample. Vol. ends: Autumn. *Aud:* Ejh, Hs.

Critical, signed reviews of Canadian books, pamphlets, and even documents suitable for children. Also, some short articles on Canadian literature and profiles of authors are included. The 70 to 80 critical appraisals in each issue are by librarians and specialists, are signed, and usually run from 150 to 300 words. The reviewer clearly indicates whether he or she thinks the book should be purchased. The writing is good to excellent, the criticism just that, and the total effect is a profit to just about any librarian, in or out of Canada. In my opinion, the reviews are equal to anything found in the three American favorites, i.e.: *Horn Book*, *School Library Journal*, and *Center for Children's Books Bulletin*. While free to Ontario libraries, a modest fee is charged to others.

International P.E.N. Bulletin of Selected Books. 1950. q. $2.60. Kathleen Nott. Intl. P.E.N., 62 Glebe Pl., London SW3, England. Illus., adv. Circ: 2,500. Sample. Vol. ends: Winter.

Aud: Ac.

Since books published in France, Britian, and the United States are excluded from consideration, the scope of this publication is distinctly different from that of most popular reviewing media. Each issue is devoted exclusively to recent literary accomplishments of a country which is not noted for its publishing industry. A critical history of the current literary developments in the country precedes the reviews. This appraisal is written by a literary scholar of the country and is printed in both English and French. Approximately 10 to 15 novels, poems, or essays are selected for review in each issue. Although most of the items are recent, a few earlier works may sometimes be included. Reviews, varying from 200 to 300 words in length, are primarily focused on the literary value of each work, and the language employed is fairly scholarly. With the current stress on non-Western cultures in our educational institutions, this publication with its emphasis on lesser-known literature is useful. Unfortunately, bibliographic information is scanty. Frequently only the author, title, and date of publication are listed. (S.W.)

Junior Bookshelf. 1936. 6/yr. $4.25. D. J. Morrell. Marsh Hall, Thurstonland, Huddersfield HD4 6XB, Yorkshire, England. Illus., index, adv. Microform: UM.

Indexed: LibLit, LibSciAb. *Aud:* Ejh.

An English magazine which reviews some 125 to 150 children's books (i.e., preschool through about the 8th grade). The reviews are well written, critical, and descriptive. Most, although not all, titles are published in England. There are excellent articles on all aspects of children's reading and books. Obviously this is of limited use to most American libraries, but it should

be of interest to libraries with larger collections. Also, it is worth taking to see how a good review should be written.

Junior Literary Guild. bi-m. Free. Doubleday & Co., Garden City, N.Y. Illus., adv.

Aud: Ejh. *JV:* C.

Limited in scope to selections chosen by the Junior Literary Guild editorial board, reviews are aimed at school librarians. Books are arranged by reading level and age group. Reviews are unsigned and consist of three parts: a brief plot summary, biography of the author, and "curriculum indications." Plot summaries provide only a "bare-bones" view of the work. Little attempt is made to evaluate the literary merits of the book. Extensive treatment is given to chatty and personal biographies of authors, complete with photograph. "Curriculum Indications," devoid of inspiration or innovation, suggests traditional classroom uses for the book. For the librarian, Dewey classification and subject headings are provided. Unless one happens to be a subscriber to Junior Literary Guild and needs the catalog for ordering purposes, this should not be used as a selection tool. (S.W.)

Kirkus Reviews. 1933. s-m. $30. to $96. (Rates set according to book budget.) Alice Wolff and Kenneth Kister. Kirkus Service, Inc., 60 W. 13th St., New York, N.Y. 10011. Index. Sample.

Aud: Ga, Hs, Ejh.

In the last edition this was given a low rating, but it has since been purchased by *The New York Review of Books*, employed a former librarian and professor of library science (Ken Kister), and moved rapidly into a new approach. While the looseleaf service remains independent of *NYRB*, it is not injured by the association. What was once rather a vapid, cautious approach has been replaced by forthright, realistic reviewing. (The "Q" designation for controversial titles is no more.) It has two primary advantages over all other reviewing media: (a) it usually reports on titles a good six to eight months ahead of publishing date; (b) the reviews are somewhat longer, detailed, and more critical than those found in similar media. And while geared primarily for public and school libraries, it should be seriously considered by an academic library with a general reading collection. Some 4,000 to 5,000 books are covered annually. Each issue is divided into sections covering fiction, nonfiction, and books for younger readers, with seasonal supplements on religious books. It is indexed, with quarterly and semiannual cumulative indexes. Reviews are unsigned, written by staff members, with highly qualified outside reviewers used in special areas such as science, political science, and poetry. The style of the reviews assumes a literate, liberal, and well-educated reader. They are extremely clever, informative, and particularly good in terms of evaluating fiction. The minus side is the indexing—with only a quarterly service, the librarian must check back through a number of issues to find what is needed. Hopefully, one day the service will include a cumulative index with each issue. (Of course, the indexing is no better in other reviewing media, but—for large libraries, at least—the asking price isn't quite as high, either.) All in all, a much improved service which can be heartily recommended.

Kliatt Paperback Book Guide; selected, annotated list of current paperback books. 1967. q. $12. Doris Hiatt and Celeste Klein, 6 Crocker Circle, W. Newton, Mass. 02165.

Aud: Hs, Ga.

A looseleaf quarterly service which primarily reviews paperback books for high school students. As the range of high school is wide—taking in both adult and junior high interest titles—the service is of considerable help for both public libraries and high schools, and possibly junior colleges. It is not, however, for elementary grades. The reviews are both descriptive and critical, and the editors are librarians who know of what they write. Also, they have an advisory board made up of equally well-trained librarians. As good paperback reviews are difficult, if not downright impossible to find, this is as unique as it is valuable. All in all a most useful service which should be widely supported.

Library Journal. See Library Periodicals Section.

Microform Review. 1972. q. $20. Allen B. Veaner. Microform Review, Rogues Ridge, Weston, Conn. 06880. Illus., adv. Sample. Vol. ends: Oct. Microform: Publisher.

Aud: Ac, Hs.

Here, at last, is a major reviewing medium for all types of microform. About one half of this new magazine is devoted to reviews. The remainder is made up of articles on various aspects of microform, comments on the passing scene, and short news items. While the articles are timely, interesting, and informative, the reviews are the primary value of what is an expensive journal ($20 comes out to $4 per 80-page issue). The reviews, which hopefully will be expanded in later issues, more than justify the price. They are written by experts who not only evaluate their intrinsic worth, but consider the technical and financial aspects in a very specific and exact sequence. How good, for example, is the picture quality? As most of these collections run from several hundred to many thousands of dollars, and as they are rarely evaluated elsewhere, the reviews represent a major new service. Most reviews are critical. In evaluating Research Publications' city directories project (which retails at $3,600) the reviewer notes: "I have but one objection to it: the format. Microfiche is utterly unsuited to sustained use of serial publications such as city directories."

Other features include a listing of "simultaneous publications," i.e., journals and books available in microform and print simultaneously, and a list of articles on micropublishing. A necessary purchasing aid for any medium to large library.

There are a number of publishers who issue free bulletins, magazines, and newsletters about microform. Among the better known are: University Microfilms, 300 N. Zeeb Rd., Ann Arbor, Mich. 48106: *Microcosm.* 1955. q.; NCR Microcard Editions, 901 26th St., N.W., Washington, D.C. 20037: *Microcard Bulletin.* 1948; Bell & Howell, Old Mansfield Rd., Wooster, Ohio 44691: *Micropublisher.* 1958. 3/yr.

New Book Review. 1966. q. $2 (Free to libraries). Maureen Sullivan. Herder and Herder, 232 Madison Ave., New York, N.Y. 10016. Illus., adv. Circ: 62,000.

Aud: Ga.

Another example of a magazine put out primarily to advertise a firm, this time a publisher, not a jobber. (See *Book News*). The controlled-circulation magazine is free to libraries. It reviews some 200 to 250 religious titles each year, and the reviews, which run from notes to essays, are rather perceptive and critical. The exception? Books published by Herder & Herder, which somehow are always good. Still, a useful enough service, particularly as it is free. How much longer the publisher will supply this magazine remains to be seen.

New Technical Books. 1915. m. (except Aug. & Sept.). $7.50. Arnold Sadow. New York Public Library, Fifth Ave & 42nd St., New York, N.Y. 10018. Index. Circ: 1,580. Sample. Vol. ends: Dec.

Aud: Ac, Ga.

The primary source of current reviews of English language books in physical sciences, mathematics, and engineering. Biological and medical titles are not included. According to the editor: "The annotations are, mainly, descriptive with recommendations of reader or library suitability. Critical notes on the literary quality and treatment may also be given, including evaluations of the bibliography, references, illustrations and index." Arrangement is by the Dewey Decimal Classification, and along with the usual bibliographic data, the table of contents is published in full. Annotations are written by the New York Public Library staff, and usually appear within two to four months after the title is released. Most of the books are too technical for the average library, but the reviewing service is a major aid for special and larger libraries. See also *Technical Book Review Index* and *Aslib Book List.*

New York Review of Books. 1963. bi-w. $10. Robert B. Silvers & Barbara Epstein. N.Y. Review, Inc., 250 West 57th St., New York, N.Y. 10019. Subs. to: Box

1162, Ansonia Sta., New York, N.Y. 10023. Illus., index, adv. Circ: 89,000. Sample. Vol. ends: Jan & July.

Indexed: CIJE. *Aud:* Ac, Ga. *Jv:* V.

A poll of what American intellectuals read (see introduction to General Magazines section) gives this title the first place. It is by far the most important major reviewing service in America, and for that matter, anywhere. The 10 to 15 reviews are often long essays, the book under question serving as a springboard for the thoughts of the reviewer. Usually, too, there are one or two essays on some aspect of the current political or social scene. Among the distinguished corps of writers from the literary establishment are Mary McCarthy, Edmund Wilson, W. H. Auden, and Dwight Macdonald. The letters to the editor easily rival those found in the English counterpart, *The Times Literary Supplement.* Readers who are accustomed to short, snappy, journalistic review notes are often confused by the more scholarly, throughful style of the *New York Review of Books.* In a word, this is for the reader with an above-average education, an appreciation of literary style, left to radical left politics, and some background in literature and the arts. A must for all medium to large-sized libraries, and not a few high school libraries.

Since the death of *I.F. Stone's Bi-Weekly* in 1971, the *NYRB* has picked up the subscribers to that noteworthy news magazine. Its editor, Stone, has become an *NYRB* contributing editor, and each issue now features a lead story by Stone. One more point: the *NYRB* represents the wing of the more progressive literary intellectuals. It is opposed by *Commentary.* The "battle" which has raged for the past two years may be of some interest to those who follow such matters. It has been written about in many places, c.f. Merle Miller's "Why Norman and Jason Aren't Talking," *New York Times Magazine,* March 26, 1972, p. 34.

New York Times Book Review. 1896. w. $13. John Leonard. New York Times Co., Times Sq., New York, N.Y. 10036. Illus., index, adv.

Indexed: BoRv. *Aud:* Ac, Ga, Hs.

A general service which has relatively long reviews of some 20 to 30 titles, and notes on about as many more. Reviewers are authors and scholars, write well, and can be counted upon for a point of view. All interests are considered, and there is a children's and teen-ager section. Under a new editor, John Leonard, the old face of this best-known book review in America has changed. How drastically is a matter much in debate, see for example, comments by Richard Kostelanetz in the *San Francisco Book Review,* December (Vol. 9, no. 1, 1971), and Harry Smith in *The Newsletter on the State of the Culture* (July 30, 1971)—to name two critics. The charge, so familiar to the 1950s and 1960s, that the editor was controlled by the advertisers and by friendship as much as by real criticism, is heard again. Still, the tone is much more liberal than in the past, the reviews more representative of current trends in taste and needs. If still connected to advertising and to log rolling, it is not so obvious as in the past. In fact, it is much improved and at least Leonard is making an effort to give it a personality and some direction. Regardless of what one may think, it is a major reviewing service, and one which should be found in every library, particularly larger ones and all within subscription range of the daily and Sunday *New York Times.*

Publishers' Weekly; the book industry journal. 1872. w. $18.50. Arnold Ehrlich. R. R. Bowker Co., 1180 Ave. of the Americas, New York, N.Y. 10036. Illus., index, adv. Circ: 28,885. Microform: UM.

Indexed: BusI, LibLit, RG. *Bk. rev:* 75–85, 90–120 words. *Aud:* Ac, Ga, Hs, Ejh. *Jv:* V.

The basic American book trade journal, *PW* features news of publishers and booksellers, lists of new and forthcoming American publications, and editorials and articles which concentrate on the business activities of the book world. Important to all libraries for two reasons. First, the "Weekly Record," an alphabetical listing by authors of books published the previous week in America, gives full bibliographic data for each title, plus (often) a short descriptive note. The "Weekly Record" becomes the base of the major American trade bibliography which cumulates monthly as a separate publication, *The American Book Publishing Record,* and in an annual volume. The second reason for having *PW* in all libraries is that it is the only publication which gives complete information on the book-trade from statistics to a monthly feature devoted to book design and production.

Adjacent features in each issue include: "PW Forecasts," detailed, often critical reviews of forthcoming fiction, nonfiction, children's books, and paperbacks. There are, also, announcement issues for the spring and fall which give detailed information on publishers' lists of forthcoming works. Every number features several articles on publishing, book selling, and related topics. Of lesser interest to libraries are regular departments on personnel changes, tips on sales, and brief news notes. In addition to seasonal announcement numbers there are special issues devoted to children's books, religion, and scientific and technical works, and an annual summary number of statistics, trends, and awards. Should be in every library regardless of size or type.

Quinzaine Litteraire. See Europe and Middle East/French Language Section.

Religious Book Guide for Booksellers and Librarians (Formerly: *Catholic Bookseller & Librarian*). 1959. 5/yr. $5. Charles A. Roth. 200 Sunrise Highway, Rockville Centre, Long Island, N. Y., 11570. Illus., index, adv. Circ: 10,000. Sample. Vol. ends: Sept./Oct.

Aud: Ga, Ac, Hs, Ejh.

This is a nondenominational type of *Publisher's Weekly* for religious books. As it is objective, and as it does cover all faiths, it differs radically from flyers and book dealer catalogues. The 65-page journal features pertinent articles on authors, collections, publishers, etc., by booksellers and librarians. In terms of reviews it has two departments: "Advance News of New Religious Books," and "Subject Guide to New Religious Books." Titles are briefly annotated (50 to 150 words), and the annotations are more descriptive than critical. Should be invaluable to libraries with significant collections in this area.

Reprint-Bulletin—Book Reviews. 1955. bi-m. $12.50. Sam P. Williams, Oceana Publns. Inc., Dobbs Ferry, N.Y. 10522. Index, adv. Circ: 850.

Aud: Ac, Ga.

Review of out-of-print scholarly titles are the special focus of this periodical. Titles reviewed and listed would be primarily of interest to scholars, librarians, or persons interested in some aspect of the past. Each review is accompanied by a complete bibliographic citation including the original as well as the reprint publisher and date. The brief scholarly appraisals concentrate on edition, added features, and contemporary significance of each reprint book. Reviews appear alphabetically by book author and are unsigned. However, reviews are written by 48 consultants, nearly all university professors, whose names and subject fields are listed in each issue. "Current and Available Reprints," another feature of this bulletin, lists books according to Dewey classification. An author-title index also makes it easy to locate specific titles. Current happenings in the reprint publishing business are briefly reported. A valuable service for most libraries. (S.W.)

The San Francisco Book Review. 1969. m. (except July & Feb.). $4. Jay Bail. J. B. Goncharsky, P.O. Box 14143, San Francisco, Calif. 94114. Illus., index, adv. Circ: 2,000. Vol. ends: Dec.

Aud: Ga, Ac, Hs. *Jv:* V.

One of the best alternative book review sources, this is a refreshing change from the commercial, establishment approach. The 40-page offset newsprint format has improved since its founding, and in appearance it is quite acceptable. There are usually 8 to 10 basic reviews of 2 to 3,000 words which cover a number of titles in a given area from ecology and the occult to literature. Diversity seems to be an editorial policy. The reviews are lively, perceptive, and always informative. They are geared as much for the high school–college group as for the adult who wants to keep up with the counterculture. Between reviews are articles on everything from the poor quality of *The New York Review of Books* to critical notes on art books. Poetry is handled deftly by Richard Morris. Librarians who think *The New York Times* is the end

will not understand this review, but others will subscribe for its iconoclastic approach.

Saturday Review. See General Magazines Section.

Scholarly Books in America. 1959. q. Free. Constance B. Levinson. Amer. Univ. Press Services, Inc., 1 Park Ave., New York, N.Y. 10016. Circ: 70,000. Vol. ends: April.

Aud: Ac, Ga.

A free, useful, annotated listing of publications of the American University Press Service membership, this includes books, journals, and serials. Arrangement is by broad subject classification, and the annotations are descriptive rather than critical. Also, there are usually one or two articles of general interest. As the organization includes almost all university presses (and includes nonmember scholarly publications as well), this title should be an automatic request by all academic, and larger public libraries.

Scholarly Publishing. 1969. q. $10. Eleanor Harman. Univ. of Toronto Press, Toronto 181, Ont., Canada. Illus., index, adv. Circ: 1,350 Sample. Vol. ends: July.

Indexed: CurrCont. *Bk. rev:* 2–3, 100–500 words, signed. *Aud:* Ac, Ga.

Includes scholarly articles and studies of all aspects of university press and other scholarly publishing, emphasizing but not limited to the North American trade. It covers problems of editorial content and editing, typography, physical design, publishing, promotion, sales, copyright, etc. Includes book reviews and news notes relative to the field. (L.A.)

School Librarian. 1937. q. Membership (Nonmembers $7.20). School Library Assn., 150 Southampton Row, London WC1, England. Index, adv. Circ: 7,000.

Indexed: BritEdI, LibLit, LibSciAb. *Bk. rev:* Numerous, 125–175 words, signed. *Aud:* Hs, Ejh.

Although this publication is the journal of the English School Library Association, between 60 and 70 pages of each issue are devoted to book reviews. Geared for librarians, the signed reviews are well written, descriptive, evaluative, and often critical. Emphasis is placed on British books for children and young adults, but several books on librarianship and new reference materials are also included. Reviews are grouped by subject and by age level. Bibliographic references—author, title, publisher, price, date, pagination, and special features—are supplied for each review item. An index, arranged alphabetically by author, facilitates the search for a particular selection. For quality, reviews offered in *School Librarian* are on a par with those found in *Hornbook, Center for Children's Books. Bulletin,* and *School Library Journal.* (S.W.)

School Library Journal. See Library Periodicals Section.

✓*Science Books: A Quarterly Review.* 1965. q. $6.50. American Assn. for the Advancement of Science, 1515 Massachusetts Ave., N.W., Washington, D.C. 20005. Index. Circ: 6,000. Sample. Vol. ends: March.

Aud: Ga, Ac, Hs, Ejh.

Approximately 250 relatively popular science books are reviewed in each issue, including both recommended and not recommended titles. The selection and the reviews are purposefully directed to the layman, not the specialist. Titles for all ages, from preschool through professional, are considered, and a series of symbols indicates the various age levels. This is one of a number of works issued by the American Association for the Advancement of Science (AAAS), and librarians who need assistance in this area should write for the complete listing of the AAAS services. *Science Books* would be a first choice for most small to medium–sized libraries, while *New Technical Books* would be first choice in larger libraries.

Select; Philippine publications for college use. 1971. q. $20. Maria S. Q. Luspo Xavier University Library, Cagayan de Oro City, Philippines.

Aud: Ac.

This is an effort to devote a magazine exclusively to the review of "materials about the Philippines, or about the rest of the world from a Philippine view–written by Filipino authors—or, at least, by persons familiar with the Philippines." The target audience for the 50-page magazine is the country's 600 colleges and universities. The pilot number included 14 pages of general information on education and publishing, 16 pages of annotated reviews, a title listing of newspapers and magazines issued in the Philippines, and an author and title index. The unsigned 150-word reviews are arranged under broad subject headings, and in this first number are more retrospective than current, i.e., some imprints date back to 1967. A worthwhile effort and libraries that have the interest, and the funds, are urged to support the venture.

✓*Stechert-Hafner Book News.* 1946. m. (Sept.–May). Free. Christine M. Smith. Stechert-Hafner, Inc., 31 E. 10th St., New York, N.Y. 10003. Illus. Circ: 5,000. Sample. Vol. ends: May. Microform: UM.

Aud: Ac, Ga.

Although this has undergone some changes (the lead essay has been dropped), it remains one of the few advertising media which has a sound, solid, and intelligent approach to reviews and acquisitions. There is a lead section of notes on books, libraries, and people. This is now followed by special bibliographies such as "Children and young adult books in foreign languages," or "Soviet Magazines in foreign languages." However, the primary value is the up-to-date information on new books and periodicals which "is compiled from advance bibliographical data gathered from a global network of branch offices and agents." Emphasis is on foreign periodicals and books in all languages and subject areas. Most of the titles are briefly annotated and by the close of 1971 many of the annotations had taken on a mildly critical as well as a descriptive note. Of particular value to large academic and public libraries.

✓*Talking Book Topics.* 1935. bi–m. Free. Claire Holcomb. Amer. Foundation for the Blind. Subs. to: Div. for the Blind, Library of Congress, 1291 Taylor St., N.W., Washington D.C. 20542. Illus., index. Circ: 174,500 (inkprint ed.).

Aud: Ga, Ac, Hs, Ejh.

An annotated list of new titles on tape and/or record available for the blind or physically handicapped. The approach is similar to the *Braille Book Review.* For those unable to read, a record is inserted which includes all of the annotations. The publication is free to libraries and to individuals and, of course, the material is free on loan from libraries.

✓*The Times Literary Supplement.* 1902. w. $18. A. C. W. Crook. Times Newspapers of Great Britain, Inc., 201 E. 42nd St., New York, N.Y. 10017. Illus., index., adv. Circ: 44,500. Sample. Vol. ends: Dec. 31. Microform: Recordak. Reprint: Bowker.

Indexed: BritHum, SSHum. *Aud:* Ga, Ac. *Jv:* V.

Probably the best single review medium in the English language, the *TLS* sets standards for excellence considerably ahead of most of its American counterparts. (*The New York Review of Books* is an exception.) The writing is scholarly, yet well within the grasp of any educated man or woman; the style is both varied and lively. Major books in every language are considered, and it is in no way limited to British publishers. In fact, some of the best reviews of major American titles will be found here. In addition to the lead essay article, there is a leader column devoted to a current event, and letters to the editor which are as fascinating as they are informative. Irregular columns appear on little magazines, paperbacks, and items of literary or historical importance. Usually, too, one page is devoted to important reference and bibliographic titles. Several issues a year are devoted to special topics, and in these there are long, signed articles by some of the world's leading scholars. Yet, one major criticism of the *TLS* is that none of the reviews are signed, and it is a guessing game as to who either tore a book apart or did a bit of log rolling for the author. Often, too, the fiction reviews are much too brief and the treatment of American scholarship tends to be a trifle less than sacred. The overall level of sophistication is high, and quite a pleasant shock for the reader who equates reviews with *The New York Times* or *Saturday Review.* While of limited value for small or medium-sized libraries seeking advice on new titles, it should be found in all libraries as a source of information and intellectual stimulation for readers.

Zwillingsbruder Book Notes. 1971. irreg. Free. Box 4509, Berkeley, Calif. 94704.

Aud: Ga, Ac.

An eight-page newsletter which is primarily made up of as many book reviews. The selection is catholic enough. The January 19, 1972 number, for example, included unsigned reviews of Norman MacKenzie's *Dreams and Dreaming*, *The Germans* by Adolph Schalk, and Randall's *Dukedom Large Enough*. Immediacy seems to be of no real concern, and the approach is casual. It is, also, highly personal. In a letter signed "Windcatcher," the editor-publisher notes: "The publication is one of the projects of a parent organization, which is a private library, of, curiously enough, antiquities." Well, that may or may not be an explanation. Still, it is free, and worth considering.

BUSINESS

See also Economics and Free Magazines Sections.

Basic Periodicals

The basic list represents titles found in the general section. The subsequent sections are too specialized for basic selection and no recommendations are offered.

GENERAL Hs: *Fortune, From Nine to Five;* Ga: *Business Week, Fortune, Forbes;* Jc: *Business Week, Fortune, Forbes, Business & Society Review;* Ac: *Fortune, Economist, Business Week, Business & Society Review, Harvard Business Review, Nation's Business.*

Basic Abstracts and Indexes

Business Index, Personnel Management Abstracts, Public Affairs Information Service.

Cessations

African World, American Pressman, Business World, Commerce, Junior Secretary, Media/Scope, Printing Magazine.

General

American Import and Export Bulletin. 1934. m. $5. John F. Budd Pubns., Inc., 80 Wall St., New York, N.Y. 10005. Illus., index, adv. Circ: 5,460. Microform: UM.

Aud: Sa, Ac.

Includes statistical information on trade and tariffs, government activities, personalities in the import-export field, and port and railroad activities. This is a useful addition for both business and political science collections in large academic and public libraries.

The Appalachian Financial Review. 1966. s-a. $10 (Individuals $5). Albert G. Sweetser, School of Business, State Univ. of N.Y. at Albany, Albany, N.Y. 12203. Circ: 1,000. Microform: UM.

Bk. rev: 6, short, signed. *Aud:* Ac.

This is not about the poverty belt. The name comes from the 14-state area where members of the Appalachian Finance Association work, including the four eastern provinces of Canada. The teaching of banking and finance is the topic of one article in most issues. Articles are scholarly, well documented, and very much down-to-business. Should be in all medium to large-sized business collections and might be considered by other libraries because of the wide scope of the articles.

Barclays Overseas Review. 1968. m. Free. Barclays Bank DCO, 54 Lombard Street, London EC3P 3 AH, England.

Indexed: PAIS. *Aud:* Ac, Sa.

"An economic and trade review." This is useful as a source of economic information on little-known countries. Profiles of countries are featured, giving a thumbnail sketch of the country's economy at present: prices, food situation, resources, weather, etc. It covers about 35 countries, those in which there are Barclay banks. One recent article, unsigned, "Britain in the EEC—For and Against" shows the very thorough coverage of this journal. "Talking Point" discusses current economic problems, such as the international monetary crisis. "Market Report" selects a country to examine as to trade possibilities; "Commodity News" covers a certain commodity such as sisal or vegetable oil as to quotas, sources, and trends in the market. Though useful to investors and economists the appeal is limited mainly to research libraries, but other librarians should be aware of this periodical. (R.B.)

Barrons. See Newspapers/Special Interest Section.

Black Enterprise. See Blacks Section.

Business Abroad; the international trade review. 1919. m. $10. John M. Roach. Reuben H. Donnelley Corp., 466 Lexington Ave., New York, N.Y. 10017. Illus., adv. Circ: 12,113.

Indexed: BusI, CurrCont. *Bk. rev:* Notes. *Aud:* Sa, Ac.

For students of international trade and investment. In addition to articles there are special sections on new developments, personnel news, and news from Washington concerning international trade and tariffs. One especially valuable yearly feature is the "World Trade Data Yearbook" which gives foreign exchange rates, trade rates, and other statistical data. A useful addition to the government's *Commerce Today*, but only for relatively specialized collections in economics and political science. (R.B.)

Business Conditions Digest. 1961. m. $15. Feliks Tamm. U. S. Dept. of Commerce, Washington, D.C. 20402. Subs. to: Supt. of Documents, U.S. Govt. Printing Office, Washington, D.C. 20402. Illus., index. Circ: 8,000.

Indexed: PAIS. *Aud:* Ac, Ga, Sa.

Brings together many of the more useful U.S. government statistics. It contains gross national income and product changes, anticipations and intentions in foreign trade, balance of payments, analytical measures such as actual and potential gross national product, and some international comparisons. Most statistics are shown both in chart and table form. For the specialist who needs up-to-date, accurate information, and basic in any business or economics library.

Business History Review. 1926. q. $10. Glenn Porter. Harvard Univ., Grad. School of Business Admin., 214–16 Baker Library, Soldiers Field, Boston, Mass. 02163. Illus., index, adv. Circ: 2,200. Sample. Vol. ends: Winter. Microform: UM. Reprint: Kraus.

Indexed: BusI, PAIS. *Bk. rev:* 28, 800 words, signed. *Aud:* Ac.

Features scholarly articles, of interest to both students of business and history, on the historical evolution of business in the United States and abroad. Current events are noted in the "Editor's Corner." An added value for libraries is the book review section. All reviews are by experts and are critical. Not an essential magazine, but one for larger collections.

Business Horizons. 1958. bi-m. $8. William G. Ryan. School of Business, Indiana Univ., Bloomington, Ind. 47481. Illus., index, adv. Circ: 10,000. Sample. Vol. ends: Dec. Refereed. Microform: UM.

Indexed: BusI, PAIS. *Bk. rev:* 3, 120 words, signed. *Aud:* Ac, Ga.

One of the more readable publications from a graduate school of business, primarily because many of the articles are written by businessmen as well as by professors. The journal covers approaches to management and marketing, studies of the business stituation in specific countries, accounting, banking, business education, unions, and corporation mergers. Little emphasis is placed upon foreign and governmental topics. Of special note is the regular feature "Research Clearinghouse," which indicates current research projects that are of interest to business executives. A useful addition for most medium to large-sized academic and public business libraries.

Business International. Complete service, library rate $970. Business Intl. Corp., 757 Third Ave., New York, N. Y. 10017.

Indexed: Master Key Index, published by Business Intl. *Aud:* Ac., Sa. *Jv:* V.

These publications are expensive, but valuable to the businessman or researcher interested in any of the areas covered. As indicated, they may be purchased separately or as a unit at considerable saving.

Business International. w. $198. Looseleaf format—binder furnished.

"Written and edited for managers of worldwide operations, this weekly provides current information and sales-producing ideas in the form of news, analysis and actual corporate experience. *Business International* interprets developments in international management, marketing, finance, licensing, exporting, taxation, law, accounting, personnel, planning, government, and public relations."

Business Asia. w. $198. Looseleaf format—binder furnished.

This is "for the whole of the Asian and the Pacific market. Published in Hong Kong, it provides up-to-the-minute information on what is happening throughout Asia. Coverage includes trading opportunities with mainland China and progress toward regional cooperation in Southeast Asia."

Business Europe. w. $198. Looseleaf format—binder furnished.

"Provides management information for European, African and Middle Eastern operations. *Business Europe* brings in-depth reporting and analysis of EEC and EFTA developments, as well as country-by-country information on finance, marketing, taxation, personnel, organization, politics and actual corporate experience."

Business Latin America. w. $198. Looseleaf format—binder furnished.

Provides information "for operations throughout the region or in any Latin American nation. *Business Latin America* interprets the new opportunities and obstacles being created by LAFTA and CACM, as well as reporting political, economic and corporate trends and events in every country."

Financing Foreign Operations. m. $198. Looseleaf format—binder furnished.

"Up-to-date guide to sources of capital and credit throughout the world. Country-by-country and institution-by-institution, it locates money sources and shows how they can be tapped.

"Its three main sections are: international financing; cross-border financing; and domestic financing in 24 major markets—general climate, monetary and banking systems, sales and consumer financing, short-, medium- and long-term credit, capital incentives, stock and bond financing, export credit and insurance, factoring, leasing."

Investing, Licensing and Trading Conditions Abroad. m. $240. Looseleaf format—binder furnished.

"Designed as a daily reference for companies operating abroad, *ILT* answers questions ranging from the latest GNP of a given market to interpretations of the laws, rules and regulations governing establishment of new industrial enterprises, local financing, limitations on foreign ownership and management, transfer of profits and repatriation of capital, tax and other incentives, personal and corporate tax rates, marketing practices, labor conditions, import controls and export incentives."

Management Monographs. irreg. (about 3/yr.). $15 each.

"These are brief analyses of how companies solve some of the most vexing problems of doing business abroad. They draw on the experience of many corporations that have faced and solved similar problems." Titles include: *The New Yugoslavia, Developing Distribution in Europe, The European Communities,* etc.

Master Key Index. q. $40.

Covers all publications listed above and is cumulated quarterly for the 12 months ending on date of issue. Annual year-end index should be retained.

Research Reports. irreg. (about 3/yr.) $20–$75 each (mostly $40–$50).

Titles include *Central American Common Market, Organizing for Latin American Operations, Prospects for Business in Developing Africa, Organizing the Worldwide Corporation, Solving International Accounting Problems,* etc.

Business Quarterly. 1934. q. $8. Ms. Doreen Sanders. School of Business Administration, Univ. of Western Ontario, London 72, Ont., Canada. Illus., adv. Circ: 6,000. Sample. Vol. ends: Winter.

Indexed: CanI, CurrCont, PAIS. *Bk. rev:* 1–2, essays, signed. *Aud:* Ac, Sa.

A technical, not a popular, magazine of business, this is edited primarily for Canadian business executives, top and middle management in commerce, industry, and finance. It will be of some value to American business schools because of its articles which deal as much with theory as with the nuts and bolts of business, e.g., the Autumn 1971 number featured articles on management information systems, cost-effectiveness in budget planning, and a check on the performance of Canadian mutual funds. There are, too, regular features including a Washington letter. An average issue of 120 pages is well edited and carefully printed. An important magazine for larger business or economics collections.

Business Service Checklist. See Government Magazines/United States Section.

Business and Society Review. 1972. q. $24. Theodore Cross. Warren, Gorham & Lamont, 89 Beach St., Boston, Mass. 02111. Circ: 15,000.

Aud: Ga, Ac. *Jv:* V.

Something different, but possibly indicative of what may happen to many business magazines in the seventies. This one's primary purpose is to convey a message of social concern to businessmen. The first issue contained articles by various economists with many viewpoints, e.g., Milton Friedman equating social responsibility with suicide; Paul Samuelson "cheerfully predicting unprecedented constraints for business," and J. Kenneth Galbraith arguing for "public ownership of large companies." Other articles moved from the responsibilities of big companies for city improvement to considering social issues when rounding out an investment portfolio. There is no advertising—although there may be by 1973. (The *Review* is published by the same firm which issues *Bankers Magazine* and *Real Estate Review.*) See also *MBA* in the Management, Administration, Personnel section.

Business Today. 1968. q. $6. Ed. Bd. Princeton Business Review Publishing Co., 171 Broadmend Rd., Princeton, N.J. 08554. Illus., adv. Circ: 200,000. Microform: UM.

Bk. rev: 1–3, 250 words, signed. *Aud:* Ac, Ga.

Written for students, this is circulated free to most business schools. The 10 to 12 articles are by businessmen and educators, normally trying to explain their interests to students and laymen. There are a number of editorials, reports on trends in finance, communication, advertising, etc. Almost every economic and business interest is considered, usually on a more long-range basis than found in commercial journals of this type.

Business Week. 1929. w. $12. Louis Young. McGraw-Hill, Inc., 330 W. 42nd St., New York, N.Y. 10036. Illus., index, adv. Circ: 729,000. Microform: UM. Reprint: Abrahams.

Indexed: BusI, PAIS, RG. *Aud:* Ga, Ac, Hs. *Jv:* V.

A first choice among general business magazines for most libraries. It is one of three basic, general business magazines for libraries. (The others are *Forbes* and *Fortune.*) Like its cousins, *Business Week* is conservative yet objective and reasonable when it comes to anything which deals with the dollar. The underlying premise is that what is good for business is good for the country. American and foreign items are included, with increasing emphasis on those that have the greatest effect on worldwide business. Regular departments, edited by experts in the field, investigate the significant developments and outlooks in labor, production, marketing research, finance, foreign business, and other allied areas. The articles covering the whole area of general business are up-to-date, concise, and well written in terms easily understood by the informed layman. Illustrations, graphs, charts, and statistical tables are graphically clear and well placed. As the most general of the three, it is the business magazine for all libraries from senior high school through the university. A second choice would be *Fortune,* followed by *Forbes.*

Canada Commerce (Formerly: *Foreign Trade*). 1904. m. $5 ($7 abroad). W. H. Lambton. Dept. of Industry, Trade and Commerce, 112 Kent St., Ottawa, Ont. K1A OH5, Canada. Illus., index. Circ: 17,500. Sample. Vol. ends: Dec.

Aud: Sa.

A general business magazine to acquaint businessmen of market possibilities outside of Canada. An average 50-page issue includes four or five survey articles on exports to everywhere, from the Caribbean to Ireland, departments, and directories. An official government publication, it is particularly useful as it prints reports by Canadian Trade Commissioners on aspects of trade. A basic business magazine for Canadian libraries (who might be able to get it free of charge), but of limited interest to others.

Canadian Business: the magazine for management. 1930. m. $9. Howard Gamble. CB Media Ltd., 1080 Beaver Hall Hill, Montreal 128, Que., Canada. Illus., adv. Circ: 42,000. Vol. ends: Dec.

Indexed: CanI, PAIS. *Aud:* Ac, Ga.

For the Canadian businessman or the man with financial interests in Canada, this has a variety of articles about such diverse subjects as computers, motivation, women and their pay, politics, etc. Also, it has an investment newsletter, national report, and a "how's business" among its departments. A service of selected reprints from the magazine is offered. Belongs on the shelves of most university or public libraries with marketing or economics clientele.

Columbia Journal of World Business. 1965. bi-m. $20. George James. Columbia Business School. Subs. to: Maxwell House, Fairview Park, Elmsford, N.Y. 19523. Illus., index. Vol. ends: Nov./Dec. Microform: MR.

Indexed: BusI. *Bk. rev:* 2–3, essay length. *Aud:* Ac.

Serves as a means of communication between the university and the practical world, and has the subsidiary purpose of keeping business executives abreast of important advances in their field. Its ten to twelve articles cover the world both geographically and topically. The journal has investigated such topics as investment, transportation, agriculture, computers, steel, leasing, and inflation. The book reviews are critical and quite lengthy. Belongs in every academic and large public library.

Commerce Today: coming developments in business and technology (Formerly: *International Commerce*). 1970. bi-w. $20. U.S. Dept. of Commerce. Supt. of Documents. U.S. Govt. Printing Office, Washington, D.C. 20402. Illus. Circ: 8,000 (Non-paid 6,425). Microform: UM.

Indexed: BusI. *Aud:* Sa, Ac.

Supersedes and includes *International Commerce*, so covers both domestic and international business. This is an excellent business news magazine with high reference value. Recent issues included articles on an EDA program involving Indians, simplifying red tape for government aid to businesses, trademark protection, so the journal has popular appeal.

Regular features include "Economic Highlights"—state of the U.S. economy plus graphs; "Domestic Business Report"—a variety of news shorts; "Science & Technology Report"—including "Patents of Special Interest," an informative feature and a listing of "New Publications" of the U.S. Government for business and technology. The "International Commerce" feature includes a "Foreign Trade Opportunities" section listing products wanted for direct purchases or agency agreements. Excellent for public and academic libraries for a broad audience. (R.B.)

Conference Board Record. 1964. m. $30 (Members and academic subscribers $15). W. Jerome Arnold. Conference Board, Inc., 845 Third Ave., New York, N.Y. 10022. Illus., index, adv. Circ: 34,000. Sample. Vol. ends: Dec.

Indexed: BusI, PAIS. *Aud:* Ac, Ga.

An objective report of original research in the fields of business management and economics. There is little or no bias, a somewhat unique feature for a journal which is primarily read by business executives and professional economists. Hence, it is ideal for the student seeking basic information on a variety of topics from antitrust and consumer economics to employment and economic trends. There are usually some 12 articles per 64-page issue, and in 1971 approximately one half the material was staff written. All material is supported by documentation, charts, and statistics. A basic journal for larger business and economics collections.

Dun's (Formerly: *Dun's Review*). 1893. m. $7. Raymond Brady. Dun & Bradstreet Publns. Corp., 466 Lexington Ave., New York, N.Y. 10017. Illus., index, adv. Circ: 200,000 Microform: UM. Reprint: Abrahams.

Indexed: BusI, RG. *Bk. rev:* 1–2, 1 column, signed. *Aud:* Sa, Ac.

Once you have made it to the top you read *Dun's.* It is not a general business magazine; it is an executive's approach to life. (Why is it indexed in *Reader's Guide?*) Management, marketing, accounting, specific industries and positions, labor, employee relations, investment advice, and new techniques in industry are discussed in the longer articles. Regular features include: "The Economy," which reports on the strength of business, effect of government spending and activities; "Business Failures," which gives the number of failures and the size of the debts, with an accompanying article on various aspects of business failures; "The Washington Desk," which supplies brief reports on the Administration's economic decisions. Only for large, special collections.

Economist. 1843. w. $48. J. W. A. Burnet, 25 St. James St., London SW1A, England. Illus., adv. Circ: 102,551. Sample. Vol. ends: Dec. Microform: UM, MF.

Indexed: BritHum, BusI, PAIS SSHum. *Bk. rev:* 10, 400 words, signed. *Aud:* Ga, Ac. *Jv:* V.

A long-lived, distinguished English business and economics magazine which enjoys an international reputation. While its primary importance is to the businessman and investor, it is read by many others for its excellent coverage of the world's economic, political, and social news. (In this respect, it is somewhat like the *Wall Street Journal,* i.e., both a specialized and a general source of clear, objective information.) British trade and industry are reviewed, as are the business conditions of various countries and regions. The "American Survey" offers a look at ourselves as others see us. Statistics concerning production, products, and earnings are published, though a knowledge of the British monetary system is often required to understand the charts and graphs. Should appear on the shelves of all medium to large-sized college, university, and public libraries.

Forbes. 1917. s-m. $9.50. James Michaels. Forbes Inc., 60 Fifth Ave., New York, N.Y. 10011. Illus., index, adv. Circ: 625,00. Microform: UM.

Indexed: BusI, RG. *Aud:* Ga, Ac. *Jv:* V.

A basic, well written and concerned business and investment magazine. Most readers are involved with the financial bases it covers, and it is a well-known aid to anyone playing the stock market. The political slant, when it shows, is reasonably conservative, but the editors are never above looking behind the public relations' face of business. In fact, it is one of the few general business magazines which cuts through the news releases and gets down to the essential facts about operations, executives, and general practices. Particularly noteworthy for personal profiles and candid business case histories, this is a good magazine for both the specialist and the reader who has only a peripheral interest in the world of business. After *Fortune,* an excellent choice for the general public and academic collection.

Fortune. 1930. 14/yr. $16 (Libraries $10.50). Robert Lubar. Time, Inc., Time-Life Bldg., New York, N.Y. 10020. Illus., adv. Circ: 580,000. Vol. ends: Dec. Microform: UM. Reprint: Johnson.

Indexed: BusI, PAIS, RG. *Bk. rev:* 1, 2 pages, signed. *Aud:* Ga, Ac, Hs. *Jv:* V.

The most ambitious of all business periodicals, dealing with business and general interest topics on a grand scale. It is designed to appeal to students, top management, and those on the way up, analyzing news from a broader point of view than the strictly business scene. World affairs, political questions, new industries and products are discussed. Biographies presented in "Businessmen in the News" are valuable, supplying facts that cannot be found anyplace else. Social, economic, and political aspects of industries, regions and countries are traced and forecasts attempted. The material is presented in a vivid manner, making use of colorful illustrations and easily read graphs and charts. This journal supplies the background material which can be used with factual statistics and data discovered in more technical magazines. *Fortune* is relatively objective and demonstrates only a mildly conservative bias. Recommended for all types of libraries.

From Nine to Five. 1960. s-m. $9.50. Anne Montgomery. Dartnell Corp., 4660 Ravenswood Ave., Chicago, Ill. 60640. Illus. Circ: 25,000. Sample. Vol. ends: Dec. 31. Microform: UM.

Aud: Ga, Hs. *Jv:* V.

This bulletin-type magazine offers general interest reading to inspire and inform secretaries and other office personnel. Some issues contain biographical sketches of individuals ranging from secretaries to famous people. Its "Problem Clinic" sometimes raises a lively discussion among readers which points out the importance of personality and good human relations in any organization. Also included are suggestions for better work habits and procedures, proper office dress, poise, office etiquette, new products, and news of professional organizations like The National Secretaries Association and the associations of legal, medical, and educational secretaries. Should be of interest to any school where secretarial practices are taught, and to many public libraries.

Harvard Business Review. 1922. bi-m. $12. Ralph F. Lewis. Harvard Univ., Grad. School of Business Admin., Soldiers Field, Boston, Mass. 02163. Illus., index, adv. Circ: 135,000. Sample. Vol. ends: Nov./Dec. Microform: UM. Reprint: Kraus.

Indexed: BusI, PAIS, RG. *Aud:* Ac, Ga. *Jv:* V.

Lengthy articles concern trends, predictions, and developments in all phases of business, as well as political, social, and economic developments which affect business. Primarily written by scholars, the articles are the result of extensive research. The authors, unbaised by ties to a certain industry or company, are able to give an objective analysis of the problems researched. It includes such feature items as "Thinking Ahead," which lists and discusses future outlooks for a specific industry, and "Keeping Informed," notes on new publications. The prestigious reputation is well earned, but this is not the type of magazine the layman is apt to read. It is primarily for the better educated executive, graduate student and professor. There are more acceptable, if not better, journals for the average small to medium-sized library—and these, despite the indexing of the Harvard entry in *Reader's Guide*—should be given first consideration. In larger libraries, of course, this is a must. Note: This annotation was revised in early 1972, but it may need even more revision by 1973. The new editor, R. F. Lewis, hopes to double the size of the subscription list by making the magazine broader in scope and interest. In an interview in the *New York Times* (Dec. 22, 1971, p. 61) he observed, "I'll try to make the magazine easier to get into, it's been a little forbidding; try to add a little more four color and we'll have no more algebraic formulae. If a guy can't say it in English, we won't print it."

International Commerce. See *Commerce Today.*

Journal of Business. 1928. q. $12 (Individuals $8). Irving Schweiger & Winfield Smith. Univ. of Chicago Press, 5801 Ellis Ave., Chicago, Ill. 60637. Illus., index, adv. Circ: 4,000. Microform: UM, Canner. Reprint: Johnson.

Indexed: BusI, JEconLit, PAIS. *Bk. rev:* 15–20, essays, signed. *Aud:* Ac.

A scholarly, research-oriented approach to both economics and business. The four or five articles are highly technical, require a solid understanding of statistical and economic procedures. Articles deal with both current and historical questions. There are excellent book reviews. Where there is a need for a theoretical journal of business, this is one of the best.

Journal of Common Market Studies. 1962. q. $10 (Individuals $7.50). U. W. Kitzinger. Basil Blackwell, Broad St., Oxford, England. Index, adv. Circ: 1,200. Sample. Vol. ends: June.

Indexed: PAIS. *Bk. rev:* Various number, length. *Aud:* Ac.

An English journal for specialists of the European Common Market, as well as other regional economic trading groups. The average four articles per number deal with social and political issues within the Common Market, and trade in general; there is a register of current research being done in the field. Primarily for large academic libraries.

Just Between Office Girls. 1950. s–m. $6. Irene Stone. Bureau of Business Practice, 681 Fifth Ave., New York, N.Y. 10022. Illus. Circ: 36,000. Sample. Vol. ends: Dec.

Bk. Rev: Notes. *Aud:* Ga, Hs.

An attractive, pocket-sized brochure which is aimed at the general secretary, stenographer, and office girl. The articles, which emphasize the importance of good interpersonal relationships, are chatty and filled with bits of useful information. Regular features include vocabulary quizzes, grammar notes, and typing tips. Useful in high schools or anywhere where commercial office courses are taught; and, to be sure, in the office.

The same firm issues somewhat similar brochures for more advanced groups: *P.S. For Private Secretaries* (1960. s–m. $15. Irene Stone. Sample.) and *M.S. for Medical Secretaries* (1964, s–m. $15. Sample). These brochures average 8 to 16 pocket-sized pages, and while the information is practical—ranging from how to save on telegrams to fashions—the price is a bit steep for libraries. Still, a worthwhile investment for offices, and businessmen and secretaries might appreciate your calling this to their attention.

Kiplinger Washington Letter. 1923. $28. Austin H. Kiplinger. Kiplinger Washington Eds., Inc., 1729 H St., N.W., Washington, D.C. 20006. Sample. Vol. ends: Dec.

Aud: Ga, Ac.

A weekly four-page business newsletter on current activities in Congress and government. It is written in a staccato fashion to keep the businessman up-to-date on bills before Congress, new rules and regulations, tax changes and proposals, contracts, etc. The facts are accurate enough, but the editorial line is definitely conservative. Political views aside, the newsletter is valuable for its currency and inside information on personalities and matters which rarely make the average newspaper. It is of interest to both the businessman and the general student of government. The firm, best known for *Changing Times* (see Consumer Services section), also issues a number of other newsletters, i.e., *Kiplinger Agricultural Letter, Florida Letter, California Letters, Tax Letter*. Only for large business collections in public and academic libraries.

Knowledge Industry Report. See Communications and Media Section.

MSU Business Topics. 1953. q. Free. Mary Lu Hough. 5–7 Berkey Hall, Div. of Research, Grad. School of Business Admin., Michigan State Univ., E. Lansing, Mich. 48823. Illus., index. Vol. ends: Autumn. Microform: UM.

Indexed: BusI, PAIS. *Aud:* Ac, Sa.

For all those who are interested in business or economics. The editor shows a wide tolerance for disparate views so long as they are within the current economic system. About one fourth of the material is either from graduates of or professors at Michigan State University. In about ten articles authors investigate such topics as discounts, morals in advertising, customer costs in product failure, poverty, how to get a corporate image, and the role of management in crisis. The articles are well thought out and well written. It is much the same as the *Michigan Business Review*, but longer and more interesting. Recommended for universities with marketing, economics, or any courses leading to management. The larger public libraries would also do well to include this.

Michigan Business Review. 1949. bi–m. Free. J. Philip Wernette, Grad. School of Business Admin., Univ. of Michigan, Ann Arbor, Mich. 48104. Illus., index. Circ: 26,000. Vol. ends: Nov. Microform: UM. Reprint: Johnson.

Indexed: BusI, PAIS. *Aud:* Ac.

Covers topics ranging from inflation and insurance in Chile to nuclear power, from the European Common Market to the discovery of real estate by big business. The articles are by such authors as James M. Roche and Glenn Seaborg. The journal is for the generalist, and belongs on the shelves of larger academic and public libraries. Not quite so good as *MSU Business Topics*.

Modern Office Procedures. 1956. m. $12. John B. Dykeman. Industrial Publishing Co., 614 Superior Ave., W., Cleveland, Ohio 44113. Illus., adv. Circ: 120,000. Microform: UM.

Bk. rev: Notes. *Aud:* Ga, Hs.

To be read by anyone involved in office operations. Articles stress the techniques and technology of modern office operation, i.e., strong emphasis on data processing and systems. Practical information is given for both the office manager and the office employee. A useful, if not essential, magazine for business and secretarial courses. Most copies sent free to regular readers.

Nation's Business. 1912. m. $9. Jack Wooldridge. Chamber of Commerce of the United States, 1615 H St., N.W., Washington, D.C. 20006. Illus., index, adv. Circ: 895,000. Microdorm: UM, MF.

Indexed: BusI, RG. *Aud:* Ga, Ac.

Claiming to be "the largest and most efficient business magazine in the world," this is the voice of the conservative business lobby in Washington, D.C.— better known as the Chamber of Commerce of the United States. As a frankly conservative voice its target audience is the industrialist and businessman. It gives monthly reports on economics, politics, legislative issues, and international activities. The stock villains in the magazine's columns are government and labor. As a frankly biased report the magazine has a given amount of interest, particularly as it is extremely well edited and written. But it should be understood that it is no more objective in its reporting than *National Review*, or, for that matter, *New Republic* and *Nation*. A library wishing a somewhat more direct approach to business is advised to consider *Business Week* and *Fortune* first. (When sent a questionnaire with the last edition's annotation, Mr. Wooldridge replied: "I am returning your questionnaire without any information since we do not choose to be listed in your new edition.") Fair enough, but before librarians choose *Nation's Business*, I strongly suggest they look at a sample copy.

New York University. Graduate School of Business Administration. Institute of Finance. Bulletin. 1926. 4–6/yr. $5 (Teachers $3). The Bulletin. 100 Trinity Place, New York, N.Y. 10006.

Aud: Ac, Sa.

Approximately five to six monographs (or Bulletins as they are called) are issued every year from NYU's Institute of Finance. Prepared by various experts, the 50 to 100 page reports represent a consensus of thinking on questions which interest economists and business leaders. For example in the 1972/1973 academic year such topics as automation of the stock market, the necessity of bank examinations, and the "exchange risk under fixed and flexible exchange rate system," are to be considered. The language is technical, although clear enough to the professional economist or serious businessman. Each bulletin, under the editorship of a recognized scolar, offers a reliable introduction to an important financial or economic area. A run of the bulletins is essential for any medium to large-sized academic or public collection.

The Office. 1935. m. $6. William R. Schulhof. Office Publns., Inc., 1200 Summer St., Stamford, Conn. 06904. Illus., charts, diagrams, adv. Circ: 110,000. Sample. Vol. ends: June and Dec. *Microform:* UM.

Indexed: BPI. *Bk. rev:* 12, 100 words. *Aud:* Sa.

Good coverage of many aspects of office practice and management for both corporate executive and office manager. Articles on systems analysis, computer programing, equipment, buildings, and employee relations. Recently it has emphasized computer applications in quite technical language. It has good descriptions of office equipment including a Readers' Service Card feature which provides for mailing further information on products advertised and books reviewed. This makes it valuable to business managers at all levels. Occasionally an issue will be devoted to one aspect of office practice, e.g., hospital offices.

The Secretary. 1942. m. (Sept.–June). $5. Shirley S. Englund. National Secretaries' Assn., 616 E. 63rd St., Kansas City, Mo. 64110. Illus., adv. Circ: 57,000. Sample. Vol. ends: Dec.

Bk. rev: Notes. *Aud:* Ga, Hs.

Edited for the career secretary with articles on all aspects of management, personnel, and operational skills. Good information on the latest office equipment. Primarily a how-to-do-it magazine for the Institute for Certifying Secretaries, a department of The National Secretaries Association (International). Sometimes the whole issue is devoted to a special feature such as libraries, equipment purchase, or the male secretary. Male secretaries have been accepted for membership, and NSA avoids the slant towards the office "girl" usually found in this type of periodical. A basic magazine in the field.

Survey of Current Business. See Government Magazines/United States Section.

Today's Secretary. 1898. m. $5. Donna Zack. Gregg Division of McGraw–Hill, 330 W. 42nd St., New York, N.Y. 10036. Illus., adv. Circ: 60,000. Sample. Vol. ends: May. Microform: UM.

Bk. rev: Notes. *Aud:* Hs.

Directed to the student preparing for a secretarial career. Several articles in each issue stress the importance of developing and improving skills; in several others guidance is given on requirements and attributes of various secretarial career areas. Specific experiences are sometimes related to illustrate unusual job opportunities. Tips on grooming, including beauty, dress, and speech are suggested. An extensive "Skill Building" section includes material for practice in Gregg, Diamond Jubilee shorthand, transcription, typing speed tests, and vocabulary, spelling, grammar, and usage suggestions. Several regular single column or one page departments follow this general theme. The 32-page format includes black and white photos and drawings, and a moderate amount of appropriate advertising. A teacher's edition is also available. Used widely in high school and post-high school business education departments and in business schools.

Wall Street Journal. See Newspapers/Special Interest Section.

Wall Street Transcript. See Newspapers/Special Interest Section.

Accounting and Taxation

Abacus; a journal of accounting and business studies. 1965. s–a. $3.40. R. J. Chambers. Sydney Univ. Press, Univ. of Sydney, Sydney 20006, Australia. Illus., index, adv. Circ: 1,000. Sample. Vol. ends: Dec.

Bk. Rev: 5, 300 words, signed. *Aud:* Ac.

Has as its objective the publication "of exploratory, constructive and critical articles on all aspects of accounting. Also, covers phases of the theory and administration of organizations and of economic behaviour related to accounting and finance." Articles are theoretical, and assume special knowledge on the part of the reader. Only for large academic collections.

Accountancy. 1889. m. $8. Walter Taplin. Inst. of Chartered Accountants in England and Wales, 26–34 Old Street, London EC1, England. Illus., index, adv. Circ: 33,000. Microform: UM.

Bk. rev: Essays, notes. *Aud:* Ac, Sa.

The English equivalent of *Journal of Accountancy,* this publishes technical articles of interest to accountants, lawyers, and businessmen. Emphasis is on accounting, with material on general finanace and business. Regular departments report news which affects the profession, parliamentary reports, personnel, etc. Some of the articles will run as much as 10,000 words, and are monographic in length and purpose. A highly specialized journal for only the largest collections.

Accounting Review. 1926. q. $15. Eldon Hendriksen. American Accounting Assn., Paul L. Gerhardt, 1507 Chicago Ave., Evanston, Ill. 60201. Illus., index, adv. Circ: 18,500. Reprint: Kraus.

Indexed: BusI. *Bk. rev:* 15–20, essays and notes, signed. *Aud:* Ac, Hs.

A professional magazine for the teacher of accounting at the high school through university level. Usually four to five well documented articles on methodology of teaching, developments in the field, controversial legislation, etc. There are several regular departments; best are the book reviews which are relatively current but, more important, as inclusive as any in the field. A basic choice for high school professional collections, and for college and university teachers. Working accountants will want *Journal of Accountancy* as a first choice, and it would be an equal consideration in most universities and colleges.

Canadian Chartered Accountant. 1911. m. $9. L. J. Reesor. FCA Canadian Inst. of Chartered Accountants, 250 Bloor St., E., Toronto 5, Canada. Illus., index, adv. Circ: 28,500.

Indexed: CanI, PAIS. *Bk. rev:* Various number and length. *Aud:* Ac, Sa.

The Canadian equivalent of the American *Journal of Accountancy.* The majority of articles are technical, involved with the finer points of accounting, and presume considerable knowledge by the reader. The whole field from small business problems to national taxation is considered. Regular features keep readers posted on new developments and legislation. A required item for any Canadian library with an interest in this area, but a third or fourth choice for most American collections.

Cost and Management. 1926. bi-m. Membership (Nonmembers $7.50). O. E. Dickman. Soc. of Industrial Accountants of Canada, 154 Main St., E. Hamilton, Ont., Canada. Illus., index adv. Circ: 20,000.

Bk. rev: 2–3, 500 words, signed. *Aud:* Ac, Sa.

Along with *Canadian Chartered Accountant,* a basic choice for Canadian libraries with an interest in the field. Differs from the other magazine in that the emphasis is of a specialized area, i.e., industrial accounting, and there is considerable writing about economics and business. Most of the articles are in English, but some editorials and other pieces are in French.

Journal of Accountancy. 1905. m. $10. William O. Doherty. American Inst. of Certified Public Accountants, 666 Fifth Ave., New York, N.Y. 10019. Illus., index, adv. Circ: 132,000.

Indexed: BusI, PAIS. *Bk. rev:* 4–5, length varies, signed. *Aud:* Ac, Sa. *Jv:* V.

The basic accounting magazine for any library with an interest in the subject. As the official organ of the American Institute of Certified Public Accountants, it enjoys the largest readership of a magazine of this type. Articles report on the most important developments in the field, but also include: taxation, management, business interests, industrial practices, government legislation, etc. Most articles are by CPAs or businessmen. Regular departments include: current accounting and auditing problems, taxation management, current reading, practitioners forum, etc. The material is too technical for the general reader or businessman, but is extremely informative. See also *Tax Adviser*. Many states have their own CPA chapters and magazines, for example: *Maryland CPA, Connecticut CPA*, and *West Virginia CPA*. Larger libraries will want to subscribe to these as well. The majority, although not all, are listed in the 14th edition of *Ulrich's International Periodicals Directory*.

Journal of Accounting Research. 1963. s-a $7.50 (Students $5). Nicholas Dopuch. Inst. of Professional Accounting, Grad. School of Business, Univ. of Chicago, Chicago, Ill. 60637. Illus., index. Circ: 2,300.

Bk. rev: Essays, signed. *Aud:* Ac.

One of the best scholarly journals in accounting. As such it is fairly esoteric, intended primarily for the teacher and advanced student, not necessarily for the practicing accountant. There is both current and historical material, and most of the writing is by professors. Included in the subscription price is the annual separate: *Empirical Research in Accounting, Selected Studies 19–*, which offers research reports followed by discussion by two or more experts.

√*Journal of the American Statistical Association.* 1888. q. $15. Robert Ferber. American Statistical Assn., 806 15th St., N.W., Washington, D.C. 20005. Illus., index, adv. Circ: 13,500. Vol. ends: Dec.

Indexed: BusI, BioAb, PsyAb. *Bk. rev:* 12–15, essay length. *Aud:* Ac, Sa.

A highly thought-of magazine, written for those who are interested in the marriage of statistical methods to practical problems. The problems may be practical, but the articles are quite complex. At least one half of the magazine is taken up with theory and methods; the other half with applications. There are about 40 articles in each issue. Only for the specialist or advanced student of statistics.

√*Management Accounting.* 1921. m. Membership $10. Stephen Landekich. National Assn. of Accountants, 919 Third Ave., New York, N.Y. 10022. Illus., index, adv. Circ: 69,000.

Indexed: BusI, EngI, PAIS. *Bk. rev:* Notes. *Aud:* Sa, Ac.

Edited and written for professional accountants (not necessarily CPAs, it should be noted), businessmen, and managers. It is a less technical version of the CPA's *Journal of Accountancy*. The primary source of manuscripts are members of the sponsoring organization—the editor has a type of contest going to bring in acceptable material. Most of the articles are concerned with the problems of day-to-day activities which range from computers and business machines to handling simple or advanced financial systems. This is

a good, basic magazine for both the business and specialized collections in large public libraries. Of less interest, though, to universities.

National Tax Journal. 1948. q. Membership (Nonmembers $13.) Daniel M. Holland. National Tax Assn., 21 E. State St., Columbus, Ohio 43215. Illus., index. Circ: 3,200. Sample. Vol. ends: Dec. Microform: UM. Reprint: Kraus.

Indexed: BusI, LegPer, PAI . *Aud:* Ac, Sa.

Although the primary emphasis is on taxes, the authors frequently touch on aspects of economic and business theory. The articles are scholarly, usually technical, and cover private and public finance at both national and international levels. Accountants will consider this a basic journal, but it should be brought to the attention of all teachers of economics and business. And, as many journals in this section, it will be of considerable interest to attorneys who practice in this field. Only for large academic business and legal libraries and a few public libraries.

New York Certified Public Accountant. 1930. m. $10. Max Block. N. Y. State Soc. of Certified Public Accountants, 355 Lexington Ave., New York, N.Y. 10017. Index, adv. Circ: 20,000. Microform: UM.

Indexed: BusI, PAIS. *Bk. rev:* 1–2, 1 page, signed. *Aud:* Ac, Sa.

Offers excellent insights into professional problems faced by public and private accountants, financial analysts, and credit grantors. The 70 pages are written in shop jargon by CPAs/PhDs. The emphasis is on accounting technique, taxes, management, estate planning, and systems book reviews. Opinions are those of the authors and not promulgations of the society. All material is fresh and crucial knowledge to all desiring the latest information on new tax legislation or insolvency procedures. The classified section is very useful to people entering or seeking mobility in the field. Most appropriate for professional collections. (G.M.)

Tax Adviser. 1970. m. $25. Gilbert Simonetti. American Inst. of Certified Public Accountants, 666 Fifth Ave., New York, N.Y. 10019. Illus., index. Circ: 15,000.

Indexed: BusI. *Aud:* Ac, Sa.

The technical tax journal published by the same organization responsible for the related *Journal of Accountancy*. Less popular than *Taxes*, it is primarily intended to keep the CPA and lawyer advised as to the latest developments in the tax laws. Regular features include: Tax Trends, Estate Planning Techniques, Working with the Internal Revenue Service, Washington Report, Tax Practices Management. Only for professionals and advanced students.

Taxes, the tax magazine. 1923. m. $11. Allen E. Schecter. Commerce Clearing House, Inc., 4025 W.

Peterson Ave., Chicago, Ill. 60646. Illus., index, adv. Circ: 17,300. Microform: UM. Reprint: Kraus.

Indexed: BusI, LegPer, PAIS. *Bk. rev:* Notes. *Aud:* Ac, Sa, Ga. *Jv:* V.

A semipopular approach to a far from popular subject. Articles are written in a journalistic, easy to understand style, and the editor attempts to keep as much technical jargon out of the magazine as possible. Often a single issue is devoted to a report on a conference or some major development in taxation such as the so-called "added value" question. All issues cover the major news and legislative developments of the previous month. Thanks to its style, it can be recommended as the tax magazine for most general collections, as well as for special situations.

Advertising and Marketing

See also Communications and Media Section.

✓*Advertising Age.* See Newspapers/Special Interest.

Advertising and Sales Promotion. 1953. m. $7. Louis J. Haugh. Crain Communications, Inc., 740 Rush St., Chicago, Ill. 60611. Illus., adv. Circ: 25,500. Vol. ends: Dec. Microform: UM.

Bk. rev: 1, 250 words, signed. *Aud:* Ac, Ga.

A carefully edited, well written and illustrated effort to tell readers how to promote almost any conceivable item. Articles discuss direct mail, packaging, photography, displays, management techniques, public relations, etc. There is quite an emphasis on business meetings, how and where to hold them. Some biographical material. The approach is pretty much down to earth, obviously prepared for men and women who want facts. The primary emphasis is on promotion, not advertising per se. But, understandably, between the articles there is a considerable amount of advertising. A good solid magazine for special collections at both the public and academic level.

Industrial Marketing; selling and advertising to business and industry. 1915. $7. Crain Communications, Inc., 740 Rush St., Chicago, Ill. 60611. Illus., adv. Circ: 23,000. Vol. ends: Dec. Microform: UM.

Indexed: BusI. *Bk. rev:* Notes. *Aud:* Ac, Sa.

Deals with all phases of marketing, advertising, and sales promotion, in the industrial field. Overall business trends and activities and governmental regulations affecting business are discussed. Problems of specific companies and reports of their results with advertising are included. Departments include: "Factfile," advertising volume in business publications, managing market information, and marketing meetings; "Association of Industrial Advertisers Newsletter"; "Washington Report"; and "Market Guide Information," where to locate specific information pamphlets. Considerably more general than *Journal of*

Marketing or *Journal of Marketing Research,* and a first choice for libraries, where there is an audience for this type of material.

Journal of Advertising Research. 1960. q. $15. Charles K. Ramond. Advertising Research Foundation, 3 E. 54th St., New York, N.Y. 10022. Circ: 3,000. Microform: UM.

Indexed: BusI. *Aud:* Ac, Ga.

An examination of advertising and its impact on the individual and society. The journal is prepared by and for teachers of advertising, psychologists, and businessmen. Articles examine advertising and its long-range promise or nightmare. Some case histories and regular features deal with federal and state regulations. The *Journal* is biased in favor of the advertising world, but in spite of that (or because of it), it affords a good balance for collections heavy with the Ralph Nader variety of material.

✓*Journal of Marketing.* 1936. q. $14. Eugene J. Kelly. Amer. Marketing Assn., 230 N. Michigan Ave., Chicago, Ill. 60601. Index, adv. Circ: 26,000. Vol. ends: Oct. Microform: UM. Reprint: Kraus.

Indexed: BusI, PAIS. *Bk. rev:* 8, 500 words, signed. *Aud:* Ac, Sa.

Concerned with international marketing facts and the impact of government policy on the field. Scholarly articles, also, suggest improved theories and techniques, and study the ethical and historical facets of marketing. Special sections give information on current marketing questions, leaders in marketing, and legal developments. All material presented in an extremely well-written and interesting manner. A good item for large public and academic business collections.

Journal of Marketing Research. 1964. q. $14. Ralph Day. Amer. Marketing Assn., 230 N. Michigan Ave., Chicago, Ill., 60601. Index, adv. Circ: 13,000. Vol. ends: Nov. Microform: UM.

Indexed: BusI, PAIS. *Bk. rev:* 8, 500 words, signed. *Aud:* Ac., Sa.

Offers sophisticated papers describing the latest marketing research. It is considerably more technical than its sister publication, *Journal of Marketing,* and readers must have a good basic knowledge of research methods as well as marketing principles. The contributions discuss new methods of research, systems of evaluation, and comparisons of marketing and research methods. Also included are studies of current trends, review articles on different aspects of marketing research, and experiments in social psychology and other behavioral sciences relating to marketing. Only for special collections.

Journal of Purchasing. 1965. q. $6. Harold E. Fearon. National Assn. of Purchasing Management. Arizona

State Univ., Tempe, Arizona 85281. Illus., index. Circ: 4,500. Vol. ends: Nov. Microform: UM.

Bk. rev: 2–3, 300 words. *Aud:* Sa.

Presents articles from the fields of business, statistics, economics, engineering, and behavioral science which relate to purchasing or management. This may range from philosophies to theories, from economic issues to legal or social issues. The six articles are quite scholarly.

Marketing. 1923. m. Membership. (Nonmembers $12.60). Michael Rines. Haymarket Publishing Ltd., Gillow House, 5 Winsley St., London W1, England. Illus., index, adv. Circ: 18,000. Sample. Vol. ends: Dec. Microform: UM.

Bk. rev: 2, 400 words, signed. *Aud:* Ac, Sa.

The official journal of the United Kingdom Institute of Marketing—and not to be confused with journals of the same name coming from Brazil and Canada. It has several purposes: "to promote the adoption of the marketing concept; to improve knowledge of marketing techniques; and to provide news of important marketing events." An average issue features six to seven articles and a number of departments. Particularly impressive because of the clarity of expression and attractive format. A useful addition for larger public and academic business collections.

Marketing/Communications (Formerly: *Printer's Ink*). 1888. m. $10. Decker Communications, Inc., 501 Madison Ave., New York, N.Y. 10022. Illus., Adv. Circ: 41,546. Microform: UM.

Indexed: BusI, PAIS. *Bk. rev:* Notes. *Aud:* Sa, Ac.

Directed to the individual buying advertising and those seeking the best method to plug their products, discussing packaging, the advantage or disadvantage of a given type of media for advertising, and methods of merchandising. Legislation which affects advertisers is considered. Book reviews are short, but good.

Public Relations Journal; a journal of opinion in the field of public relations practice. 1945. m. $9. Reed Trask. Public Relations Soc. of Amer., Inc., 845 Third Ave., New York, N.Y. 10022. Illus., index., adv. Circ: 9,600. Sample. Vol. ends: Dec. Reprint: Kraus.

Indexed: BusI, PAIS. *Aud:* Ga, Ac.

Deals with the wider aspects, trends, and policies of public relations in all fields. Articles, written by active businessmen, are timely and literate, containing very few statistics and charts. Problems in all areas are discussed and possible solutions offered. Most of the articles are specific, exemplified by actual cases rather than theoretical studies. National agencies, federal regulations, and current news are given in the regular feature, "Washington Focus." Other material supplied by the magazine are new devices, progress reports, and news of conferences and symposiums. A specialized periodical for larger collections.

Public Relations Quarterly. 1957. q. $8. Howard P. Hudson. Richard Toohey, Public Relations Aids, Inc., 305 E. 45th St., New York, N.Y. 10017. Circ: 5,000. Sample. Vol. ends: July.

Bk. rev: 4, 500 words, signed. *Aud:* Ac, Ga.

The leading semi-scholarly magazine in the field. Each issue includes not only pragmatic examples of successful public relations, but contributions from teachers, sociologists, and psychologists on various aspects of what constitutes a viable method of winning or losing public approval. Much of the material is of value to the student of the behavioral sciences. Good book reviews, and features on current trends, programs, and the like.

Purchasing. 1915. bi-m. $25. Walter E. Willets. C-M Business Publns. Inc., Conover-Mast Bldg., 205 E. 42nd St., New York, N.Y. 10017. Illus., adv. Circ: 71,000. Vol. ends: March.

Indexed: BusI, EngInd. *Bk. rev:* Various numbers and lengths. *Aud:* Ac, Sa.

The editor tries to take the reader inside the plant where the actual buying decision is made, and give the purchasing agent information so as to buy better for all departments. Features special issues in distributors, transportation, etc. Regular departments cover market trends, purchasing ideas, and Washington reports, among others.

Sales Management; the magazine of marketing. 1918. bi-w. $15. Robert H. Albert. Sales Management, Inc., 630 Third Ave., New York, N.Y. 10017. Illus., index, adv. Circ: 41,000. Sample. Vol. ends: June & Dec. Microform: UM.

Indexed: BusI, PAIS. *Aud:* Ac, Sa.

Offers information on all phases of the marketing process. Unsurpassed in its field, it concentrates on the strategies and the tactics of marketing; including the research and evaluation of markets for products and services, the operations involved in bringing them to the consumer, and the building of effective sales teams. Most of the articles are short reports of developments in business and selling, or descriptions of individual campaigns, selling techniques, and the use of media. Of particular note is the annual service issue, *Survey of Buying Power,* which factually and statistically reports the current estimated figures in buying power, showing population, sales and income changes. Definitions, descriptions, sources, methods, and application of the data are also supplied. This enables the reader to use the facts for his own specific needs. Although specialized, it will be useful in most public and academic libraries.

Banking and Finance

Magazines in this section are directed toward people having a professional interest in some aspect of finance, either through involvement in banking, in corporate finance, or in the teaching of finance. The liquidity crises faced by many firms in the early 1970s have made it essential for controllers and treasurers to keep current in finance in a much broader way than formerly, through such journals as *Financial Executive.* American bankers have had to increase the scope of their reading in several directions as the impact of federal financial policy has become more direct, as banks have become involved in overseas operations, as many have reorganized as holding companies, and as some have moved into a variety of non–banking activities.

None of the magazines included are designed for general readership, so consideration of these titles is suggested for university libraries serving schools of business and larger public libraries serving clientele needing collections with some depth in economics, domestic and international finance, and banking. (R.B.)

American Banker. 1836. 5/wk. $150. Willard C. Rappleye, Jr. American Banker Inc., 525 W. 42nd St., New York, N.Y. 10036. Illus., index, adv. Circ: 13,692.

Aud: Ac, Sa.

Calls itself "the only daily banking newpaper." It emphasizes United States banking news mainly but does include "Foreign File," "Foreign Finance," and a section called "International Banker." Most of its features are not daily; some are special, such as texts of addresses by experts in banking, and "Required Reading," opinions voiced by experts. These have high reference value. Many features are directed to the investment field: "Bank Stocks," "Securities," "Portfolio Management," "Offerings," "Municipal Investor," "The Markets." Others would interest bankers primarily: "Housing Market Memo Pad," listing buildings available, "Mortgages," "Calendars of Events," "Executive Changes," listed by state, "Legal Notices." The editorials are liberal in tone. Columns such as "Speaking of Governments" and "Inside the Economy" are signed; these would also serve economists. While this newspaper is comprehensible to the novice, only specialized collections would justify the subscription price. (R.B.)

Bank of England Quarterly Bulletin. 1960. q. Free to libraries, financial institutions, economists, etc. Economic Intelligence Dept., Bank of England, London EC2R 8AH, England. Index. Circ.: 10,000.

Indexed: PAIS. *Aud:* Ac, Sa.

An invaluable guide to the British banking scene, and the British economy as a whole. At the beginning of each issue, there is a fairly lengthy commentary section, which reviews the British economy during the preceding three months. A specialized journal for large academic libraries, although it may be useful in other situations where there is a particular interest in the politics and economics of Britain. (R.B.)

Bank of Israel Bulletin. See *Economic Review.*

The Banker. 1926. m. $11. Michael Green. The Banker Ltd., Bracken House, 10 Cannon St., London, EC4P 4BY, England. Illus., index, adv. Vol. ends: Dec. Microform: UM.

Indexed: BusI, BritHum, PAIS. *Bk. Rev:* 5–10, length varies. *Aud:* Ac, Sa.

This is for the international banker or someone who wishes an international view of what is happening in the world of banking. It includes among its five plus articles one or two on banking in the United States. It usually zeroes in on one country or sector of a country and does an in-depth appraisal of its banking problems and successes. The journal regularly features columns on legal decisions and international reviews of the financial community and financial statistics. It summarizes significant articles which have appeared in other banking magazines. Recommended for large libraries with economics, business, banking, or marketing interests. (R.B.)

The Bankers' Magazine. 1844. m. $8. G. W. Maynard. Waterlow & Sons Ltd., Waterlow House, Worship St., London, EC2, England. Illus., index, adv. Circ: 5,566. Microform: UM.

Indexed: BusI, PAIS. *Bk. rev:* 2–4, short, signed. *Aud:* Ac, Sa.

The British counterpart of the American journal of the same name. Articles cover every aspect of British money, finance, banking, and the economy in general. Material tends to be technical and presupposes at least a basic knowledge of the field. American students will profit from the section which gives model answers for the bank examination. Only for large business collections. (R.B.)

Bankers Magazine. 1846. q. $28. Theodore L. Gross. Warren, Gorham & Lamont, Inc., 89 Beach St., Boston, Mass. 02111. Illus., adv. Microform: UM.

Indexed: BusI, PAIS. *Bk. rev:* 20–25, short, signed. *Aud:* Ac, Sa.

One of the oldest professional journals in America devoted to aspects of banking such as planning, economics, business trends, and current problems of banking, e.g., robbers. The articles are scholarly, prepared by professors, accountants, and lawyers with banking background. Government officials and bankers also contribute. While highly specialized, from time to time it publishes articles of more general interest in the fields of economics and history. Primarily for business collections and academic libraries, where there is a major business school. (R.B.)

Bankers Monthly, national magazine of banking investments. 1884. m. $9. Alvin M. Younquist, Jr., 1528 Skokie Blvd., Northbrook, Ill. 69962. Illus., adv. Circ: 29,549.

Indexed: BusI. *Aud:* Ac, Sa.

Prepared for top management in banks and investment houses, this is primarily concerned with how money is invested. Interestingly enough, the writing style is good to excellent, and the otherwise technical material relatively easy to understand for a student of economics. Serious investors will find it of value for the advice on stocks and bonds. There is an annual report on finance companies, and a section giving brief comments about people in the profession. Obviously not everyone's reading matter, but an important item in business collections and schools of business. (R.B.)

Banking. 1907. m. $8. Harry L. Waddell. Simmons-Boardman Publ. Corp., 350 Broadway, New York, N.Y. 10013. Illus., index, adv. Circ: 42,082.

Indexed: BusI, PAIS. *Aud:* Ac, Sa. *Bk. rev:* 200–300 words, signed.

This Journal of the American Bankers Association is more of a trade publication—sixty percent advertisements with the advertisers indexed in the back. Number of articles range from 6 to 16, those issues devoted to a special report such as bank automation running longer. The short articles have practical appeal; many are on the legal aspects of banking, such as equal pay for women, the bank reform bill, fair credit reporting act. The signed book reviews, which appear on an irregular basis, are useful critical evaluations from a popular viewpoint. "Communications Clinic" and "Idea Exchange" feature banks' innovations in reaching their public. This journal functions to keep bankers aware of the latest products and services available, through the advertisements and the "New Products" column. Since it would have narrow appeal, only special banking and finance collections or large university libraries should consider it. (R.B.)

Banking Law Journal. 1889. m. $34. M. W. Kimball. Warren, Gorham & Lamont, Inc., 89 Beach Street, Boston, Mass. 02111. Illus. Circ: 5,000. Microform: UM.

Indexed: CurrCont. *Bk. rev.:* 3–4, 300 words, unsigned. *Aud:* Ac, Sa.

Since bankers are very much concerned with law, this journal is a good choice for a large university or special library. It features one or two signed banking law articles on subjects such as savings association legislation and litigation, or state laws on branch banking. Offers a section on current Federal and state legal decisions affecting banking, "The Law of Banking and Negotiable Instruments." Regular features include "Banking Briefs" from the field of commercial banking, "Trust Decisions," and "Trust and Estate Tax Decisions." Signed columns featured are "Investment and Finance" and "Legislative Developments." "Books For Bankers" reviews two books in law or business. Aimed toward "bankers, bank counsel, the depositor and the bank student seeking advancement." (R.B.)

Burroughs Clearing House; for bank and financial officers. 1916. m. Controlled circ. Harry V. Odle. Box 299, Detroit, Mich. 48232. Illus., index, adv. Circ: 85,000. Microform: UM.

Indexed: BusI. *Aud:* Ac, Ga, Sa.

A controlled circulation, i.e., free, magazine which goes primarily to officers and executives of banks. Articles offer pragmatic solutions to everything from complex managerial problems to personnel systems. Most of the material is staff written, but based on actual experience. There are numerous departments: Investment Banking Developments, The Booklet Counter, Letters, Washington Developments, etc. Some light humor appears too. Since the magazine is free, and the advice is solid enough for any executive, larger libraries might wish to ask for copies.

Canadian Banker. 1893. s-m. $3. Pamela Arnould. Canadian Bankers Assn., P.O. Box 282, Royal Trust Tower, Toronto Dominion Centre, Toronto 11, Ont. Illus., index, adv. Circ: 12,000.

Indexed: CanI, PAIS. *Bk. rev:* 1–3, medium length, signed. *Aud:* Ac, Sa.

The Canadian equivalent to *Banking,* covering much the same type of material and interests. Most articles are in English, with occasional contributions in French. There are sections on foreign banking, "Banking Is News," giving news events in the banking profession, and a section on legal decisions that affect banking in Canada. Only for the special or large business collections. (R.B.)

Commercial and Financial Chronicle. See Newspapers/Special Interest Section.

Economic Review (Formerly: **Bank of Israel Bulletin**). 1955. irreg. Free. Bank of Israel Research Dept., Mitzpe Bldg., Jerusalem, Israel. Circ: 1,800. Sample.

Indexed: PAIS. *Aud:* Ac.

The Bank of Israel is the Central Bank of the State; it was founded in 1954 in order to administrate, regulate, and direct the currency system in Israel in accordance with the economic policy of the Government and the provisions of the law. This review covers problems such as national budget, public finance, movements in prices, industrial development, and investments, all in relation to the Israeli economy. Each contribution is documented and generally supported by tables and statistical data. Apart from the articles, the Review contains announcements on banking legislation, regulations, and Bank of Israel directives. Each issue also contains "Statistical Tables" dealing with specific financial data: currency, assets and liabilities of the Bank of Israel and other banks, credit, trade balance, etc. It is an important journal, of interest to the specialist. (R.T.)

Federal Reserve Bank of New York. Monthly Review. 1919. m. Free. Public Information Dept., Federal Reserve Bank of N. Y., 33 Liberty St., New York, N.Y. 10005. Circ: 56,000. Microform: UM.

Indexed: BusI, PAIS. *Aud:* Sa, Ac.

This short periodical is of importance primarily because it is the voice of the Federal Reserve Bank of New York, one of twelve regional member banks. It normally contains three or four articles, reviews current domestic and international economic and financial developments, with occasional articles on select subjects in banking and finance. Charts and tables often accompany the text. The *Review* is intended for economists, bankers, businessmen, and teachers and students of economics and banking. It often includes the texts of major addresses by top officials of the Reserve Bank. Regular features are "The Business Situation" and "The Money and Bond Markets," reviewing the prior month. The other eleven regional banks also publish free periodicals. These periodicals are invaluable in giving a picture of U.S. banking as well as the entire U.S. economy. All are useful additions to the *Federal Reserve Bulletin,* and should be found in large reference collections. (R.B.)

Federal Reserve Bulletin. See Government Magazines/ United States Section.

Finance; the magazine of money. 1941. m. $35. James P. Roscow. Box G, Lenox Hill Sta., New York, N.Y. 10021. Illus., adv. Circ: 52,295. Microform: MF.

Indexed: PAIS. *Aud:* Ga, Ac.

A well-edited, expensive looking journal, aimed at trust officers, investment bankers, security analysts and corporate officers. Lengthy profiles of innovative leaders of finance feature portraits by Yousuf Karsh. Articles provide background and understanding rather than news and tips. (Examples: Peking's Banking System, Free Enterprise as a Social Force.) This is recommended for large libraries and special collections in economics and banking. A subscription includes two yearbooks of reference value: *Investments Banker—Broker Almanac* and *International Almanac of Finance and Business,* both directories of addresses. (R.B.)

Finance and Development. 1964, q. Free. J. D. Scott, Intl. Monetary Fund & World Bank Group, 19th & H St., N.W., Washington, D.C. 20431. Illus., index. Circ: 65,000. Microform: UM.

Indexed: BusI, CurrCont, PAIS. *Bk. rev:* 10, 200–800 words, signed. *Aud:* Ga, Ac.

Despite the sponsor and title, the editors assert this is not for the specialist, but for a wider audience. The seven to eight articles are purposefully written for the layman who is seeking knowledge of activities of the International Monetary Fund and the World Bank. The authors presuppose some knowledge of business and finance, but manage to avoid jargon. Material covers such things as business in Europe, the problems of new nations, worldwide inflation, sales taxes—and almost anything concerned with international finance and development. Features include a summary of recent activities of the International Bank for Reconstruction and Development and the International Monetary Fund. Since the magazine is free and the scope is wide, it should be found in both academic and public libraries. (R.B.)

International Monetary Fund Staff Papers. 1950. 3/yr. $6 (Universities $3). Norman K. Humphreys. Intl. Monetary Fund, 19th & H Sts., N.W., Washington, D.C. 20431. Microform: UM.

Indexed: BusI, CurrCont, JEconLit, PAIS. *Aud:* Ac, Sa.

A well-written collection of papers by the staff of the International Monetary Fund concerned with world monetary policies in regard to international trade, exchange rates, balance of payments, and inflation. Many of the staff members are foreign nationals working in the Washington bank, thus adding variety to the viewpoints expressed. Only for large collections. (R.B.)

The Journal of Commercial Bank Lending. 1918. m. $10. Clarence R. Reed. Robert Morris Associates, 1432 Philadelphia National Bank Bldg., Broad at Chestnut Sts., Philadelphia, Pa. 19107. Illus., index, adv. Circ: 10,000. Vol. ends: Aug.

Indexed: BusI, CurrCont. *Aud:* Ac, Sa.

Appealing to the bank officer, this does a fine job handling a great variety of banking subjects. It includes about eight feature-length articles per issue, and an interesting column "Associates Will be Interested In," which gives news briefs. It covers some foreign problems but with a domestic bias. For the specialist. (R.B.)

Treasury Bulletin. See Government Magazines/United States Section.

Commerce, Industry, and Trade

There are several thousand journals and periodicals in this area. What follows is a list of the more general ones, i.e., those most likely to be found in large academic and/or public libraries. The list is representative, not exhaustive or even highly selective.

Aerosol Age. 1956. m. $7. Joseph M. Pedersen. Industry Publns. Inc., 200 Commerce Rd., Cedar Grove, N.J. 07009. Illus., adv. Circ: 5,280. Vol. ends: Dec. Microform: UM.

Indexed: BusI, ChemAb. *Aud:* Sa.

Pressure-packed cosmetics, chemicals, paints, automotive products, foods, etc.—all are considered in this basic business magazine for the aerosol manufacturer. Some four to six articles consider all problems from marketing abroad to safety, labeling, and ecology and environment. For the specialist, although of some interest to students of packaging. (W.H.)

Air Conditioning, Heating and Refrigeration News. 1926. w. $8. John O. Sweet. Business News Publishing

Co.; Box 6000, 700 E. Maple, Birmingham, Mich. 48102. Illus., index, adv. Circ: 29,000. Vol. ends: Dec. Microform: UM.

Indexed: BusI. *Aud:* Sa.

A weekly covering all news in the areas of air conditioning, heating, and refrigeration. Newspaper style and format are employed, with many feature articles, a continuing series, patents, a technical column, and a what's new in the industry section. The last issue in December is a directory containing associations, exporters, manufacturers, products, and wholesalers. Large public, and most university libraries with engineering and architecture courses in this area will wish to subscribe. (W.H.)

Airline Management and Marketing Including American Aviation. m. $12. Eric Bramley. Ziff Davis Aviation Division, 1156 15th St., N.W., Washington, D.C. 10005. Subs. to: Box 517, Neptune, N.J. 07753. Illus., adv. Circ: 43,000. Vol. ends: Dec.

Indexed: BusI. *Aud:* Ac, Ga.

An airline news magazine with many timely features such as mail delivery, charters, foreign airlines, and safety. Emphasis is on information vital to management or marketing decisions. The journal features columns on predictions of management, reports on traffic, finances, and new products. Enough general information is included to make it a consideration for large public libraries, and for any university with flight engineering management, marketing, or economic courses.

American Aviation. See *Airline Management and Marketing Including American Aviation.*

American Druggist. 1871. bi-w. $11. Stanley Siegelman. Hearst Corp., 224 W. 57th St., New York, N.Y. 10019. Illus., adv. Circ: 68,000.

Aud: Sa, Ac.

One of America's oldest business trade magazines. While of special interest to the druggist, it is of some value to laymen looking into consumer activities, i.e., there is considerable material here on product development and advertising. As Americans spend as much on drugs and cosmetics as anything except food and shelter, the trade magazine is closer to home than many suspect.

American Machinist. 1877. bi-w. $25 (Free to qualified personnel). Anderson Ashburn. McGraw-Hill, 330 W. 42nd St., New York, N.Y. 10036. Illus., index, adv. Circ: 69,000. Sample. Vol. ends: Dec. Microform: UM.

Indexed: ASTI. *Bk. rev:* 2, notes. *Aud:* Ga, Sa.

One of America's oldest trade journals, *American Machinist* "is edited to provide men responsible for planning and operating manufacturing operations in the metal working industries with timely information

on developments that will affect their work." Articles tend to concentrate on innovations in equipment, methods, and materials, but attention is given to law, finance, economics, and social issues. And there are numerous regular departments and features which touch on everything from legislation to spot news. This journal is primarily for the businessman or technologist, not for the average worker. (As this is a controlled-circulation magazine, it is heavy on advertising—something like 60 percent of each issue.) (W.H.)

Apparel Manufacturer. 1932. m. $8. Don S. Johnson. Forge Assn. Publns., Inc., 1075 Post Rd., Riverside, Conn. 06878. Illus., adv. Circ: 8,000. Sample. Vol. ends: Dec.

Aud: Sa, Ac.

Illustrated with line drawings and photographs, this is a 60 or so page magazine geared for management in apparel manufacturing. (It will be of incidental interest to others, i.e., the fashion notes are often a bit ahead of the popular magazines in this area.) The journal covers management techniques, new manufacturing approaches, corporate and financial areas, employee incentives, plus effects of various governmental policies, impact of imports on domestic production, etc. Only for special collections. (W.H.)

The Appraisal Journal. 1932. q. $10. Paul Fullerton. American Inst. of Real Estate Appraisers of the National Assn. of Real Estate Boards, 155 E. Superior St., Chicago, Ill. 60611. Illus., index. Circ: 18,500. Sample. Vol. ends: Oct.

Indexed: BusI. *Bk. rev:* Occasional, length varies. *Aud:* Ac, Sa.

Covers all areas of land appraisal, e.g., such divergent topics as condominiums, recreational land, condemnation, financing, easements, computers, mobile homes, and airspace problems. The tables and photographs are especially valuable. Includes as regular features: dissertation abstracts, legal ramifications, and building cost trends. Belongs in any large business library. (W.H.)

Bell Laboratories Record. 1925. m. $5. L. A. Howard, Jr. Bell Telephone Laboratories, Inc., 600 Mountain Ave., Murray Hill, N.J. 07974. Illus., Index. Circ: 33,000 Sample. Vol. ends: Dec. Microform: UM.

Aud: Ac.

Covers research, equipment development, and systems engineering in the broad field of communications. Each issue contains four or more substantial articles by Bell Laboratories scientists and engineers. Topics range from purely scientific to those showing practical applications and improvement of components of communications systems. Presentation is thorough and detailed, and is further clarified by many diagrams and some good quality photos. "Development News Briefs," a regular feature, devotes a page to shorter items of news related to research and development. Other regular features are pages on "40 & 20 Years Ago in *The Record,*" and short sketches on the authors. Editorial comment in each issue helps to interpret company and industry policy relating to the broad field of communications. For large public and specialized libraries. (A.S.)

C. L. U. Journal. 1946. q. $6. Kenneth Black, Jr. Amer. Soc. of Chartered Life Underwriters, 270 Bryn Mawr Ave., Bryn Mawr, Pa. 19010. Illus., index, adv. Circ: 24,000. Sample. Vol. ends: Oct.

Bk. Rev: 6, 50–200 words. *Aud:* Ac, Sa.

A substantial, specialized magazine for the health and life insurance industry. Authoritative articles deal with trusts, management, estate planning, business insurance, psychology and human relations, taxes, personnel selection and training. Only for large libraries. (W.H.)

Canadian Forest Industries. 1880. m. $8. Steve Trower. Southam Business Publns. Ltd., 1450 Don Mills Rd., Don Mills, Ont., Canada. Illus., index, adv. Circ: 12,000. Sample. Vol. ends: Dec.

Indexed: CanI. *Bk. rev:* Various number, length. *Aud:* Sa, Ac.

A working man's magazine, i.e., the 50-page monthly is published for "field, operating and administrative management in the logging and sawmilling and related wood products industries." The five or six articles usually are concerned with equipment and techniques—both of which are as applicable in other countries as in Canada. Some short notes on personnel organizational meetings, etc., are included. A well-edited, informative magazine for any library with an interest in forestry. (W.H.)

Chain Store Age: Executives Edition. 1927. m. $4. James Tolman. Lebhar-Friedman Inc., 2 Park Ave., New York, N.Y. 10016. Illus., adv. Circ: 117,000. Vol. ends: Dec.

Indexed: BusI. *Aud:* Sa.

Edited for everyone interested in the local chain store or shopping center. This includes executives of chain stores, developers, builders, and architects. It has as regular departments sections on legal problems, remodeling, and new products. Special issues deal almost entirely with interests such as remodeling and forecasts of construction. Some of the topics discussed include television advertising, non-foods, toys, image, and security. Any library with a clientele interested in marketing or economics will want this publication. (W.H.)

Commerce Today. See Government Magazines/United States Section.

Construction Review. 1955. m. $6.50. Aaron Sabghr. U.S. Dept. of Commerce. Subs. to: Supt. of Docu-

ments, U.S. Govt. Printing Office, Washington, D.C. 20402. Illus., index. Circ: 3,000. Vol. ends: Dec.

Indexed: BusI, PAIS. *Aud:* Sa, Ac.

This is a summary of the major construction statistics for the nearest preceding month. It also includes articles and statistics on some special feature of construction, such as residential siding products. Covers new construction, housing, building permits, contract awards, costs, prices, construction materials, and employment. Few charts. (W.H.)

Continental Franchise Review. 1968. 26/yr. $52. Thomas H. Murphy. Continental Reports, Inc., P.O. Box 6360. Denver, Colo. 80260. Vol. ends: Jan. and July.

Aud: Sa.

Included in the subscription are semi-annual hardbound cumulations completely indexed. The 26 issues are in looseleaf format—binder included. At the moment this is the only periodical covering the burgeoning franchise market with a general approach. Most other trade magazines cover only their individual industry—such as *Softdrink* for the bottling companies. An increasing number of calls can be expected for this type of material. (W.H.)

Cornell Hotel & Restaurant Administration Quarterly. 1960. q. $5. Helen J. Recknagel. Cornell Univ., School of Hotel Administration, Ithaca, N.Y. 14850. Illus., index. Circ: 5,000. Vol. ends: Feb. Microform: UM.

Indexed: PAIS. *Bk. rev:* 12, 100 words, signed. *Aud:* Ac, Sa.

One of the few, if not the only, scholarly journal in the hotel and restaurant area. It comes from the major university in the country offering a degree in the field. While a good many of the readers are students, even more are administrators and executives in the food and lodging industry, investors, lending institutions, government—in the U.S. and in foreign countries. An average 100-page issue is noteworthy for its wide coverage. Given its scope, and because this is the only magazine in the field which is indexed properly, it can be recommended for larger business collections. See also *Hotel & Motel Management,* and *Nation's Restaurant News.* (W.H.)

Distribution World Wide. 1901. m. $11. James M. Dixon. Chilton Company, 1 Decker Sq., Bala-Cynwyd, Pa. 19004. Illus., index, adv. Circ: 40,000. Vol. ends: Dec.

Indexed: BusI. *Aud:* Sa.

Devoted to highway carriers, railroads, airplanes, and public warehousing. In its seven to ten articles each month, it considers such innovations as air trucking, containerization, mergers, etc. Columns regularly cover Washington and international news. For the specialist. (W.H.)

Drug and Cosmetic Industry. 1914. m. $7. Donald A. Davis. Drug Markets Inc., 101 W. 31st St., New York, N.Y. 10001. Illus., index, adv. Circ: 6,000. Vol. ends: June and Dec. Microform: UM.

Indexed: BioAb, ChemAb. *Bk. rev:* Various number, length. *Aud:* Ac, Sa.

Considers raw materials, production, packaging, and sale of cosmetics and drugs. There are numerous articles on the ethics of the industry, e.g., consumerism, quality in drugs and cosmetics, and drug stability. Departments include news from the industry, Washington outlook, production and engineering, a perfumers' and compounders' corner. The book reviews tend to be critical. A magazine for the specialist, this is vital for a school offering cosmetology, pharmacy, or marketing degrees. (W.H.)

Electronic News. 1957. w. $5. James J. Lydon. Fairchild Publns. Inc., 7 E. 12th St., New York, N.Y. 10003. Illus., adv. Circ: 72,000.

Aud: Sa, Ac.

A weekly, printed in tabloid format. Columns report the technical and financial news in the governmental, industrial, consumer, and commercial electronic markets. This newspaper covers just about everything in the world of electronics within its forty to fifty pages, and has a special section on computer news. (W.H.)

Factory. See *Modern Manufacturing.*

Forest Industries. 1889. m. $10 (Free to personnel in the industry). David A. Pease. Forest Industries, 500 Howard St., San Francisco, Calif. 94105. Illus., adv. Circ: 23,500. Vol. ends: Dec. Microform: UM.

Indexed: BioAg. *Aud:* Ac, Sa.

Aimed at those who are in the business of forestry or engaged in the manufacture of any wood products. It speaks to management, the logging and forestry sections of the industry, as well as manufacturers. The articles are wide ranging in content, from forward-looking ones on the position of wood in tomorrow's market, to today's pollution, to computer applications within the logging mill. It has monthly sections on security prices, a news column, and one on the usual new products. The May issue is an annual buyers guide/yearbook. (W.H.)

Hotel & Motel Management. 1957. m. Free to qualified personnel. Robert C. Freeman. Clissold Publishing Co., Rm. 534, Sun Times Bldg., 401 N. Wabash Ave., Chicago, Ill. 60611. Illus., adv., index. Circ: 25,000. Microform: UM.

A general trade magazine which touches on all pragmatic matters of interest to the hotel or motel operator, e.g., rooms, food, personnel, furnishings, management, etc. Controlled circulation, i.e., free to qualified personnel. (W.H.)

Industrial Development and Manufacturers Record. 1954. bi-m. $18. Linda L. Liston. Conway Research Inc., 2600 Apple Valley Rd., N.E., Atlanta, Ga. 30319. Illus. Vol. ends: Nov./Dec. Microform: UM.

Indexed: BusI, PAIS. *Aud:* Ac, Sa.

Aimed at the professional, this magazine examines every type of large-scale development. It has special notes and analyses on the ecological and environmental effects that are taking more and more of a developer's time. In the past it has featured such articles as automated site selection, air pollution, and cash flow analysis in industrial parks. For the specialist but of some interest to anyone involved in ecology. (W.H.)

Industrial Engineering (Supersedes: *Journal of Industrial Engineering*). 1969. m. $20. Jim F. Wolbrink. American Inst. of Industrial Engineers, 345 E. 47th St., New York, N.Y. 10017. Illus., index, adv. Circ: 26,000. Sample. Vol. ends: Dec. Refereed. Microform: UM. Reprint: Kraus.

Bk. rev: 3, 300 words, signed. *Aud:* Ac, Sa.

A technical journal which features 8 to 10 articles for professional industrial engineers and others in allied fields. Topics covered include engineering economy, facilities planning, human factors, production and inventory control, labor relations, motivation and wage incentives, organization theory, quality control, queueing theory, simulation, work measurement, and other subjects pertinent to the field. There is considerable dependence on technical language, charts, etc. Only for large specialized collections.

The Institute also publishes *AIIE Transactions* (1968. q. $30. American Inst. of Industrial Engineers. Illus., index. Circ: 5,000. Sample. Vol. ends: Dec. Refereed. Microform: UM). This is "devoted primarily to the publication of new developments and research in industrial engineering." Again, highly technical. (W.H.)

Industrial Research. 1959. 13/yr. $14. T. F. Sinclair. Industrial Research Inc., Beverly Shores, Ind. 46301. Illus., index, adv. Circ: 90,000. Vol. ends: Dec. Microform: UM.

Indexed: ChemAb, CurrCont, EngI. *Aud:* Ac, Sa.

This interdisciplinary publication is for the applied scientist. Its news stories contain significant laboratory advances and techniques. The subscriber has three options to chose from: the vacuum and cryogenics, the laser and electro-optics, or the chromatography editions. In 1971 issues it had articles ranging from vacuum gauges to gas chromatography to semiconductors. Its news section runs even further afield. It is, as it states, the "News of the $28 billion research industry." Belongs in every large library. (W.H.)

Industry Week (Formerly: *Steel*). 1882. w. $25 (Free to qualified personnel). Penton Publishing Co., 1213 W. 3rd St., Cleveland, Ohio 44113. Illus., index, adv. Circ: 168,000. Sample. Vol. ends: Jan. and July. Microform: UM.

Indexed: ASTI, BusI, EngI. *Aud:* Ac, Sa.

A controlled circulation weekly, i.e., free to qualified

personnel, this touches on almost all business bases, i.e., production engineering, purchasing, administration, and marketing. It is primarily of value for up-to-date reports on trends, technology, personnel, and developments of interest to industrial management. Especially useful are the production indexes, trends, and outlooks. Labor problems and government activities round out the information. It is of considerable value to the library with a large business clientele, and will be equally useful to academic libraries with business schools. (W.H.)

Inland Printer/American Lithographer. 1883. m. $12. Wayne V. Harsha. Maclean-Hunter Publishing Corp., 300 W. Adams St., Chicago, Ill. 60606. Illus., adv. Circ: 18,182. Microform: UM.

Indexed: ASTI, BusI, PhotoAb. *Bk. rev:* 6–8, 50–150 words, signed. *Aud:* Sa, Ac.

This pioneer magazine deals with current problems and possible solutions in all aspects of printing. The approximately eight well-written, technical articles cover the small shop as well as the large. An annual "Buyer's Reference Guide and Directory" for the forthcoming year is included in the December issue. Useful in university and certain special libraries, and public libraries in areas where printing plants are located.

International Railway Journal. 1950. m. $9. 350 Broadway, New York, N.Y. 10013. Illus., adv. Circ: 11,000.

Aud: Sa.

Written to keep railroad management abreast of what is new and what is planned in railroad construction around the world. Articles all have brief abstracts in French, German, and Spanish, and are generously illustrated with maps and pictures. Regular monthly features are "World Market," "World Report," and "New Products." Only for large collections, *Railway Age* being a better choice for small libraries. (W.H.)

Journal of Industrial Engineering. See *Industrial Engineering.*

Modern Lithography. 1934. m. $4. Hamilton C. Carson. Modern Lithography, Inc., 4 Second Ave., Denville, N.J. 07834. Illus., adv. Circ: 10,000. Microform: UM.

Indexed: ChemAb, PAIS. *Bk. rev:* Notes. *Aud:* Sa.

Two to nine articles of 1,000 to 3,000 words by staff and professionals cover all aspects of the industry. Many black and white illustrations are used. Several issues have carried a special report in one area: color proofing, litho blankets, a history of the National Association of Litho Clubs, etc., with reprints in pamphlet form available. Primarily for personnel in the offset-lithographing industry.

Modern Manufacturing (Formerly: *Factory*). 1891. m. $10. Herbert Lund. McGraw-Hill Inc., 330 W. 42nd St., New York, N.Y. 10036. Illus., index, adv. Circ: 92,000. Microform: UM.

Indexed: BusI, ChemAb, EngI. *Aud:* Ac, Ga, Sa.

A practical approach to the business, engineering, and maintenance needs in industrial plants. Articles discuss improved techniques, latest data, and comprehensive surveys of the manufacturing world. Newsletters report recent developments, legislation, seminars, and conferences. Cost indexes suggest the latest prices of facilities, materials, labor, and equipment. Ten "Casebooks" present the specific ideas of the month including practical views on troublesome problems, helpful pamphlets, and new techniques. A basic item for all large business collections.

Nation's Restaurant News; the newspaper of the food service industry. 1967. bi-w. $3. Michael J. Whiteman. Lebhar-Griedman Publns. Inc., 2 Park Ave., New York, N.Y. 10016. Illus., adv. Circ: 48,000.

A tabloid newspaper which reports on the business side of restaurants. Includes short articles and some features on personnel, legislation, equipment, commodities, etc. (W.H.)

National Petroleum News. 1909. 13/yr. $12. Frank Breese. McGraw-Hill Inc., Box 430, Hightstown, N.J. 02850. Illus., adv. Circ: 22,000. Vol. ends: Dec. Microform: UM.

Indexed: BusI, ChemAb. *Aud:* Sa, Ac.

Edited for the service station managers and executives of the major oil companies, this focuses upon the profitable marketing of petroleum products. Includes all operations from refinery to consumer sales. Covers diverse topics from crime to adding groceries to service stations, from the four-day week to fiberglass tanks. Special sections take up such diverse but important items as mutual funds and college drop outs. Its May Factbook issue includes acquisitions, mergers, additives, pollution information, annual reports of the larger oil companies, antitrust cases, and information on everything about automobiles from air conditioning to warranties. For the marketing man, with possible uses in public or academic libraries which have a clientele composed of economics, marketing, or engineering students. (W.H.)

Oil & Gas Journal. 1902. w. $10. George Weber. Petroleum Publishing Co., 211 S. Cheyenne, Tulsa, Okla. 74101. Illus., adv. Circ: 47,500. Microform: UM.

Indexed: ASTI, ChemAb, EngI. *Bk. rev:* various number, length. *Aud:* Ac, Sa.

Covers just about everything on oil, its by-products, and its problems, e.g., drilling, production, processing, transportation, and exploration. Departments include an up-to-the-moment newsletter, oilfield discoveries, statistics, a look at the international scene, watching Washington and the world. The approach to ecology is moderate. Writers feel that we need the energy produced by oil and therefore some damage to the landscape will result, but nowhere near the degree that is pictured by the environmentalists. Libraries will find it useful, if for no other reason than to let their patrons discover there is another side to the ecology issue. (W.H.)

Oil, Paint and Drug Reporter; the chemical marketing newspaper. 1871. w. $10. Arthur R. Kavaler. Schnell Publishing Co., Inc., 100 Church St., New York, N.Y. 10007. Illus., adv. Circ: 15,000.

Indexed: BusI, ChemAb. *Aud:* Ac, Sa.

A newspaper devoted to those who buy or sell oil, chemicals, or drugs in large volume. It includes current prices, new plant facilities, legislation, mergers, market reports, and special reports on supply and demand relationships. Each week there is a profile of a chemical compound including supply, demand, growth, price, uses, strengths, weaknesses, and market outlook of the chemical. The basic paper for this field. (W.H.)

Paper Trade Journal. 1872. w. $5. John C. W. Evans. Lockwood Trade Journal Co., 551 Fifth Avenue., New York, N.Y. 10017. Illus., index, adv. Circ: 3,000. Vol. ends: Dec. Microform: UM.

Indexed: BioAb, BusI, ChemAb, EngI. *Aud:* Ac, Sa.

Edited primarily for the supervisory personnel in the paper trade and converting industry. A large percentage of the articles is devoted to technical procedures and production. Occasionally there is a feature on the problems or successes of the paper industry as a whole, and prospects for the future. Departments include a trends column, news of the week, supplier news, new products and literature, and prices of pulp and wastepaper. (W.H.)

Printing and Publishing. 1958. q. $1. Printing & Publishing Industries Div., U.S. Dept. of Commerce. Supt. of Documents, U.S. Govt. Printing Office, Washington, D.C. 20402. Circ: 1,080.

Aud: Sa.

A 16 to 20 page publication with emphasis on statistics of printing and publishing, from photo engraving to imports and exports. Several short articles are supported by lengthy statistical tables and data. Of primary value for the student or expert in economics and the printing and publishing industry.

Progressive Grocer; the magazine of super marketing. 1922. m. $15. Robert E. O'Neill, 708 Third Avenue, New York, N.Y. 10017. Illus., adv. Circ: 78,500. Vol. ends: Dec.

Indexed: BusI. *Aud:* Sa.

Edited for executives in the retail food industry who control buying, merchandising, administrating, and operating of supermarkets. Articles cover trends in the field, and case histories of successful merchandising and operating activities. Designed to make more money for supermarkets through "how to" informa-

tion, it has special quarterly merchandising reviews, and a store-of-the-month column. It has many idea departments such as "Profit Talk" and "Pointers on Perishables." The articles are well written. (W.H.)

Pulp and Paper. 1927. m. $10. Charles W. Heckroth. Miller Freeman Publns., Inc., 370 Lexington Ave., New York, N.Y. 10017. Subs. to: 500 Howard St., San Francisco, Calif. 94105. Illus., adv. Circ: 16,000.

Aud: Sa, Ac.

The basic paper magazine which is free to people in the field. It contains brief news items on paper from the United States and Canada, plus five or six technical articles by both staff and professionals. Tables, charts or graphs accompany many of the reports of mill operations, production, management, training, and research features. The "Annual World Review" in July is a definitive report on the pulp and paper industry in every country in the world.

Quick Frozen Foods. 1938. m. $8 (Free to qualified personnel). Conover–Mast Publns., Div. of Cahner Publishing Co., 205 E. 42nd St., New York, N.Y. 10017. Illus., adv. Circ: 50,000. Vol. ends: July.

Indexed: BusI, BioAb, PAIS. *Bk. rev:* Various number, length. *Aud:* Sa.

Written for those involved in the various aspects of the frozen food industry, i.e., retail merchants to wholesalers and packaging experts. Content moves from initial processing to transportation and sales. Regular features cover developments in warehousing and transportation, primary packing items for that month, prices, markets, etc. The basic magazine in this field. There is, also, an annual directory of frozen food processors, and an international edition of this trade journal. (W.H.)

Railway Age. 1856. w. $6. Luther S. Miller. Simmons-Boardman Publishing Corp., 350 Broadway, New York, N.Y. 10013. Illus., index, adv. Circ: 14,000. Microform: UM.

Indexed: BusI, EngI, PAIS. *Aud:* Ac, Sa.

Articles written by the staff discuss problems in railway operations and management, urban rapid transit, new diesel designs, use of computers, railroad communications, etc. Most issues are devoted to a special area like freight traffic, railway engineering, transit, or special reports to management. Regular features: "New Products Report," "People in the News," "Market Outlook"—sales information and statistics—and "Lines on Labor." Many black and white pictures and indexed advertisements. (W.H.)

Share Your Knowledge Review. 1919. m. Membership (Nonmembers $4). John A. Davies. Intl. Assn., of Printing House Craftsmen, Inc., 7599 Kenwood Rd., Cincinnati, Ohio 45236. Illus. Circ: 16,900.

Aud: Sa, Ac.

The official monthly publication of the International Association of Printing House Craftsmen, Inc., combined with Craftsmen's Technical Digest. Two to six technical articles are reprints from a number of periodicals. Often an overall theme unites them. News and views of local clubs, and the president's message complete this 16 to 20 page magazine.

Stores. 1918. m. $8. John S. Kelly. National Retail Merchants Assn., 100 W. 31st St., New York, N.Y. 10001. Illus., adv. Circ: 13,000.

Indexed: BusI, PAIS. *Aud:* Sa, Ac.

Provides association news, merchandising information, and financial and political news of interest to retailers. Regular features supply comments on current marketing and retailing practices, governmental trends, statistics, and congressional activities. Hearings and regulations of the Federal Trade Commission are reported and discussed and the economy as it concerns retailers is carefully analyzed. Only for specialized collections.

World Oil. 1916. m. $14. Robert W. Scott, 3301 Allen Parkway, Houston, Tex. 77001. Subs. to: Box 2608, Houston, Tex. 77001. Illus., index, adv. Circ: 28,000. Vol. ends: June and Dec. Microform: UM.

Indexed: BusI, ChemAb, EngI. *Aud:* Ac, Sa.

Edited specifically for the oil and gas exploration, drilling, and production business. It includes "how we did it here" type articles in about one half of the magazine; economic and management of oil wells, about one fifth; and international developments, one seventh. In 1971 it featured articles on sand control, geology, Soviet and Mideast oil, and new techniques for locating oil. Two special issues: August 15, an annual "International Outlook Issue" covering in depth the whole free world's oil; February 15, a forecast and review issue. (W.H.)

Investments

Books, periodicals, and advisory services about the stock market and other avenues for investing are among the most intensely-used library materials. The magazines listed here are directed both at the knowledgeable amateur and the professional, but will be used principally by the former, since the professional often has access to a special library. In addition to these magazines, many more general periodicals carry valuable sections on investments—*Fortune, Medical Economics, Forbes, Changing Times,* to cite just a few. (R.B.)

American Investor. 1956. 10/year. $5. Robert M. Keane. American Stock Exchange Bldg., 86 Trinity Pl., New York, N.Y. 10006. Illus., index. Circ: 55,000.

Aud: Ga, Ac.

"The magazine of the American Stock Exchange."

This is a short news magazine for the field, giving run-downs on current activities of investment companies, complete with illustrations, graphs and tables. "It is an educational publication, not an advisory service." The journal contains about three short articles on events of interest to private investors. The feature "New Listing" gives information on possibilities for investment. A graph of American Stock Exchange price change index weekly for the current year is furnished. Includes such articles as "Securities Industry Weighs Future of Stock Certificate," "Exchange Realigns Staff Responsibilities," and others on Exchange officers and news of "general interest." (R.B.)

Bank and Quotation Record. 1928. m. $75. George J. Morrissey. Claude D. Seibert, 25 Park Pl., New York, NY. 10007. Circ: 1,500. Adv. Microform: UM.

Aud: Ac, Sa.

This publication is a monthly record of prices of stocks, bonds, and money, and statistics of varying sorts.

Stock exchange quotations are for the seven principle United States stock exchanges. Figures include volume of sales for the month of issue and cumulative for the calendar year; opening bid and ask or sale for the calendar year as well as first and last days of month of issue; high and low sales for month of issue and the calendar year to the date of issue. For the New York Stock Exchange, figures are given for bonds as well as stocks.

Bid and ask quotations are given for important over-the-counter securities as of the last business day of the month of issue.

Additional statistical information includes: money rates, foreign exchange, and quotations of memberships including the latest sale in the important United States stock and commodity exchanges.

Value of the periodical obviously depends upon the individual library's need for this type of material. Usefulness is limited to students of market trends constructing charts, and to those who may need a record of the price of a security during a given period for tax purposes. Only for the largest libraries serving a clientele doing investment research. (R.B.)

Better Investing. 1951. m. $4. Thomas E. O'Hara. National Assn. of Investment Clubs, 1515 E. Eleven Mile Rd., Royal Oak, Michigan 48067. Index, adv. Circ: 156,897. Microform: UM.

Aud: Ga.

The official publication of the National Association of Investment Clubs and Member of World Federation of Investment Clubs. There are many advice columns but it is noted that "companies mentioned in *Better Investing* are used as illustrations or suggestions for study . . ." Features include "Stock to Study," description of possible investments, also a follow-up of the previous year's choices; "Undervalued Stock";

"Repair Shop," prescriptions for ailing portfolios; "Unproven Growth Company, featuring different companies monthly; "Challenge Tree," questions and answers; "For Women Only," advice for any investor. It is designed to appeal to a popular, not a scholarly audience. Public libraries would find this magazine suitable for the largest audience of investors. (R.B.)

Commodities; the magazine of futures trading. 1972. m. $28. Investor Publns. Inc., 1000 Century Plaza, Columbia, Md. 21043. Illus., adv.

Aud: Sa, Ga.

Futures trading volume is enjoying enormous growth, both from those whose interest is commercial and protective (producers and major users), and those whose interest is speculative. The higher leverage involved in futures trading is attracting speculation from the stock market, and there is a widespread need for sound information. This journal tries to supply it, and it should receive wide acceptance. The editors have recruited a distinguished set of columnists and writers, who (we judge) initially are to perform a teaching function, introducing the basis of fundamental approaches (e.g., effect of future prospects on prices) as well as the technical approach to speculation profits (charting, etc.). Any library in which material in the stock market is heavily used would probably want this journal too. (R.B.)

Exchange. 1939. m. $2.50. Edward Kulkosky. N.Y. Stock Exchange, 11 Wall St., New York, N.Y. 10005. Illus. Circ: 122,000. Reprint: Johnson.

Indexed: PAIS. *Aud:* Ga, Ac.

A small magazine written in a popular style for the "amateur" as well as for the "pro" in the market. The five articles per issue range from industry surveys to economic forecasts, discussions of industries of the future, far-out scientific developments, portofolio analysis, trends in dividends, stock splits, odd lots. Features "News on the Big Board," and sketches companies newly listed on the stock exchange. Considering the low subscription price, a good investment/business magazine for almost any library.

Most periodicals in this section are primarily for the specialist, and aside from *Exchange,* the average public, junior or college library will probably only be interested in magazines of wider scope. Although each has a particular audience and purpose, the three more generalized finance magazines are *Finance, Financial World,* and *Magazine of Wall Street.* The last-named, along with *Exchange,* is probably the most helpful for the private investor; the first two are for the average businessman. (R.B.)

Finance; the magazine of money. 1941. m. $25. James P. Roscow, Box G, Lennox Hill Sta., New York, N.Y. 10021. Illus., index, adv. Circ: 58,000.

Indexed: PAIS. *Aud:* Ga, Ac.

A magazine of finance and investment for executives, not for the average laymen. The articles, which tend to be technical, are directed to heads of banks, institutional fund directors, and professional finance experts. Most of the material is statistical, and includes summaries and interpretations of data on various aspects of the U.S. economy, i.e., bank credit, mortgage and consumer credit, government and corporate finance, etc. There is an annual rating by net worth of the leading investment brokerage firms and banks. (And while this listing is often reported in more general magazines, it is good to know its original source.) The ranking can sometimes be important to private investors of limited means. There is also an annual directory of individuals and banks and financial concerns operating here and abroad. A basic magazine for large collections, but a bit too involved for the average library.

Financial Analysts Journal. 1945. bi-m. $12. Jack L. Treynor. Financial Analysts Federation, 219 E. 42nd St., New York, N.Y. 10017. Index, adv. Circ: 21,000.

Indexed: BusI. *Bk. rev:* 2-3, 150 words, signed. *Aud:* Ga, Ac.

For fund managers and teachers of finance, and of some interest to the private investor. The strength of the magazine is in its unbiased reports on the corporate and economic outlook and techniques of money management. Other articles cover a wide range of topics from foreign investments to an overview of investment literature (an excellent feature for large business libraries), and short book reviews. The analyses of various industries may make it a worthwhile addition for any size or type library where there is more than passing interest in the stock market, but in general, it is only for large libraries and academic business collections. (R.B.)

Financial Executive. 1932. m. $12.50. Ben Makela. Financial Executives Inst., 50 W. 44th St., New York, N.Y. 10036. Illus., index, adv. Circ: 13,175. Microform: UM.

Indexed: BusI, CurrCont. *Aud:* Ac, Sa.

As the title of the magazine (and its former title of "Controller") suggests, it is aimed at top corporate financial executives and managers of pension funds. There is an average of four to six articles per issue, and the editorial material is written almost entirely by financial executives. Features information on taxes, quality of annual reports, accounting methods, corporate financial reporting, and principles of portfolio management. Graphs and charts are used extensively. Only for large business libraries. (R.B.)

Financial World. 1902. w. $28. R. J. Stinson. Guenter Publishing Corp., 17 Battery Pl., New York, N.Y. 10004. Illus., index, adv. Circ: 57,310. Microform: UM.

Indexed: BusI. *Aud:* Ga, Ac.

A weekly which is directed primarily toward the private investor, and is a basic magazine (along with *Exchange* and *The Magazine of Wall Street*) in this area. Each issue includes "Special Studies" of topics of interest in the field, reviews of industries with trend forecasts, as well as profiles of specific companies. In the first issue of each month there is a section rating up to 1,900 stock issues. Once a quarter, data on convertible preferred and mutual funds are added. Two special features of note: "Selected Issues," a portfolio selection guide, and "Focus on Funds," with news and data on mutuals. Graphs and charts are used extensively. The periodical has a definite conservative editorial policy. For all academic business collections, and for medium to large-sized public libraries. (R.B.)

Institutional Investor. 1967. m. $30. George J. W. Goodman. Institutional Investor Systems, Inc., 140 Cedar St., New York, N.Y. 10006.

Indexed: PAIS. *Aud:* Sa, Ac.

Institutions are now the largest factor in securities transactions. This magazine is directed toward the informational needs of managers and decision makers for mutual funds, pension funds, endowment funds, bank trust departments, and other institutions with large sums to invest. Not technical, and of interest to many individual investors who will have to depend on libraries, since individual subscribers are usually persons employed full-time in the investment field. A typical issue features several general articles, e.g., "Do institutional investors have a social responsibility?", a biography of someone prominent in investing, an industry review, and two regular features, "Regulation" and "Fund Performance." Any library with an avid investor-reader clientele should try to subscribe to this journal. (R.B.)

Investors Chronicle and Stock Exchange Gazette. 1967. w. 14/yr. A. Whittam Smith. Throgmorton Publns., Ltd., 30 Finsbury Sq., London EC 2, England. Circ: 50,025.

Indexed: PAIS. *Aud:* Ac, Sa.

Good overall coverage of the British investment scene with features comparable to those in several popular American investment journals such as *Financial World*. It surveys and interprets the general investment climate in Great Britain, the Commonwealth, and the world, through the reports of a worldwide network of correspondents, and through one or more general articles in each issue ("Surcharge Impact on Importers"). In addition, it supplies the raw material for specific investment decisions by printing recommendations of brokers, write-ups of industries and individual companies by the magazine's research staff, the formalized advertising of companies (called "Chairmen's Statements"), and columns on various categories of investments, including one on investment trusts (mutual funds). It also gives selected weekly price data

from various stock markets. For those who want more specific advice, a model portfolio is maintained.

Obviously only for the largest libraries, and special libraries needing coverage of the British investment field. (R.B.)

Journal of Finance. 1946. 5/yr. $10. Alexander A. Robichek. Robert A. Kavesh, Grad. School of Business, N. Y. Univ., 100 Trinity Pl., New York, N.Y. 10006. Index, adv. Circ: 6,000. Reprint: Kraus.

Indexed: BusI, CurrCont, JEconLit, PAIS. *Bk. rev:* 20, 1000 words, signed. *Aud:* Ac, Sa.

This scholarly journal of the American Finance Association is aimed at teachers, as well as the professional financier. Articles touch on every aspect of finance from international banking to consumer credit. The book reviews give a relatively current check on new works in the field. Dissertation abstracts and proceedings of the annual meeting are published. A basic magazine for schools of business at all academic levels, and for large public libraries. (R.B.)

Journal of Financial and Quantitative Analysis. 1966. 5/yr. $7. Charles A. D'Ambrosio, Grad. School of Business Admin., U. of Washington, Seattle, Wash. 98105. Index, adv. Circ: 1,310.

Indexed: CurrCont, JEconLit. *Aud:* Ac, Sa.

A joint publication of the Western Finance Association and UW's Graduate School of Business Administration, this specializes in the uneasy art of predicting stock market trends. More, however, than merely a handbook for market buffs, it contains much general information on the market, finance, and banking. The publication's tone is, on the whole, heavily learned, and even at times esoteric. Yet for those with the right vocabulary, it is not likely to prove oppressive. Recent articles include reports on discount rate problem in capital rationing, short-run earnings, fluctuation bias, and the risk-return hypothesis using common stock portfolios of life insurance companies. (R.B.)

The Magazine of Wall Street. 1907. bi-w. $25. Arthur J. Gaines. Hornbeam Corp., 425 E. 53rd St., New York, N.Y. 10022. Illus., index, adv. Circ: 10,000.

Indexed: BusI. *Aud:* Ga, Ac.

Quite successfully fulfulls its editorial policy: "to provide a publication written and produced by the experts in their fields but presented in such a way to make it useful to the average investor as well as the professional." The average eight unsigned articles per issue will be readable by the layman and are concerned primarily with the investment scene. There are also sections devoted to "Inside News" of Washington and Wall Street, as well as columns of analysis and information on investments. This magazine has long featured graphic presentation of economic data; a new addition is "Stockmap," a colored visualization of major trends of big board stocks. A good and necessary purchase for larger business collections in both public and academic libraries. (R.B.)

Management, Administration, and Personnel

Academy of Management Journal. 1958. q. $10. William G. Scott. Grad. School of Business Admin., Univ. of Washington, Seattle, Wash. 98105. Illus., adv. Circ: 3,000. Vol. ends: Dec. Refereed. Microform: UM.

Indexed: BusI, PAIS. *Bk. rev:* Essays. *Aud:* Ac.

A scholarly publication covering research, organization theory, and administration in an era of technological change. The approach is often psychological and sociological with such articles as "Risk, Fate, Conciliation and Trust," "An International Study of Attitudinal Differences Among Executives," "Technology and Organization," and "An Empirical Analysis of Organizational Effectiveness." Only for specialized collections.

Administrative Management; the magazine of methods, personnel and equipment. 1940. m. $7. Walter A. Kleinschrod. Geyer-McAllister Publns., 51 Madison Ave., New York, N.Y. 10010. Illus., adv. Circ: 55,000. Vol. ends: Dec. Microform: UM. Reprint: Abrahams.

Indexed: BusI. *Bk. rev:* 4–5, short, unsigned. *Aud:* Ac, Sa.

As the title suggests, focus is primarily upon personnel and systems management. It is particularly valuable for libraries because of the emphasis on electronic data processing, office equipment, furniture, and supplies. Most of this is carefully analyzed in terms of its use (or non-use) in the average business firm. Because of equipment purchase and use coverage, this magazine should be in the libraries of junior colleges and secretarial schools training office workers, as well as those libraries with a management clientele.

Administrative Science Quarterly. 1956. q. $20. W. H. Starbuck. Grad. School of Business and Public Admin., Cornell Univ., Ithaca, N.Y. 14850. Illus., index, adv. Circ: 4,500.

Indexed: BusI, PAIS, PsyAb, SocAb. *Bk. rev:* 8–9, 1–3 pages. *Aud:* Sa, Ac.

"Dedicated to advancing the understanding of administration through empirical investigation and theoretical analysis." Besides the rather lengthy book reviews, a listing of publications received and abstracts of relevant publications are included. Primarily for the advanced administrator and graduate students.

Advanced Management Journal. 1936. q. $8. William Mumpower. Soc. for Advancement of Management, 1472 Broadway, New York, N.Y. 10036. Illus., index, adv. Circ: 20,000. Sample. Vol. ends: Oct. Microform: UM. Reprint: Abrahams, AMS.

Indexed: BusI. *Bk. rev:* 8, short notes. *Aud:* Ac, Sa.

A source of management advice from outstanding and successful managers. Contributors are business and corporate executives who offer many "how to" suggestions for new techniques and innovations in business administration. Although the articles are short and practical rather than scholarly, this periodical is valuable both in university business schools and in public libraries for the working administrator.

Business Management. 1951. m. $12. Lawrence Bernard. CCM Professional Magazines Inc., 22 W. Putnam Ave., Greenwich, Conn. 06830. Illus., adv. Circ: 200,000. Microform: UM.

Indexed: BusI. *Aud:* Ga, Ac.

Appealing to the general executive, this is far ranging within its field. About ten articles appear each month. Covers personnel ¹and business techniques. Regular departments are devoted to thought starters, staying healthy, what's new, and investor insights. For both the specialist and the generalist, e.g., the average college graduate with just a passing interest in management, it belongs in all but the smallest libraries.

California Management Review. 1958. q. $7.50. Robert N. Katz. Grad. School of Business Admin., Univ. of Calif., 350 Barrows Hall, Berkeley, Calif. 94720. Index, adv. Circ: 5,000. Sample. Vol. ends: Summer. Microform: UM. Reprint: Abrahams.

Indexed: BusI, PAIS. *Aud:* Ac, Sa.

Despite the title, this does not draw exclusively from California writers, nor does it limit itself to the Pacific scene. Under a new editorial policy it has become general in scope, and contributors represent all aspects of management. The primary audience is businessmen, teachers, and scholars. It will be of as much value in a general business library collection as in the specialized academic library.

The Director. 1947. m. $30. George Bull. Director Publns. Ltd. 10 Belgrave Sq., London SWI, England. Illus., adv. Circ: 44,000. Vol. ends: June and Dec. Microform: UM.

Indexed: PAIS. *Bk. rev:* Number varies, 100–200 words, signed. *Aud:* Ac, Sa.

Aimed at the directors of British business, but deserves to get into U.S. public libraries because it includes general articles on inflation, unemployment, the space race, how to do business with the Russians, the Penn Central affair, the art of communication, etc. Provides an interesting look, from the British point of view, of English business. This is one of those rare magazines which is for both the specialist who has investments or companies in England and the generalist who is just interested in how the British look at things. Every university library with a course in comparative economics or marketing should have this title, as should larger public libraries.

Human Resource Management. 1961. q. $10. Gloria Reo. Bureau of Industrial Relations, Univ. of Michigan, 703 Haven St., Ann Arbor, Mich. 48104. Circ: 7,200. Sample. Vol. ends: Dec.

Aud: Ac.

Focuses upon the development of practices to effectively utilize the human resources of an organization. The journal is involved with the application rather than the development of theory. It takes theories which have been tested and activates them with case studies and research reports which give the link that is often missing—the sense of how to apply the theory. Useful to libraries whose clientele includes management level people from a wide variety of organizations and to academic libraries.

The Journal of Management Studies. 1964. 3/yr. $5. T. Lupton, Basil Blackwell, Broad St., Oxford, England. Illus. Circ: 1,400. Vol. ends: Oct.

Bk. rev: 10, essay length, signed. *Aud:* Ac.

Articles in the fields of organizational structure, delegation of authority, and decision making. The majority of the experience is in Great Britain. Book reviews are quite critical. Definitely for the specialist.

Journal of Systems Management. 1950. m. $15. John W. Haslett. Assn. for Systems Management, 24587 Bagley Rd., Cleveland, Ohio 44138. Illus., index, adv. Circ: 14,000. Vol. ends: Dec. Microform: UM.

Indexed: BusI. *Aud:* Ac, Ga.

Edited for executives, with emphasis on the latest developments in administrative planning and management. About one fourth of each issue is on data processing, one fifth on techniques, and office records and facilities occupy about two fifths. Articles have considered such topics as work measurement and environment, prisoners, inventories, the post office, and even the ordering of periodicals. A regular feature is information on other magazines and articles which the editors feel are worth reading. Useful to anyone with managerial responsibilities, and with an interest in data processing and systems.

MBA: the magazine of management education for the masters in business administration. 1966. m. $8. Bartlett R. Rhoades, MBA Enterprises, Inc., 373 Fifth Ave., New York, N.Y. 10016. Illus., index, adv. Circ: 31,000. Sample.

Bk. rev: Various number, length. *Aud:* Ac, Ga, Sa. *Jv:* V.

Directed primarily to students and younger professional men, this is one of the few magazines devoted almost entirely in editorial policy to a sense of social responsibility for business. (See also *Business & Society Review.*) While the articles cover all aspects of business and management, the focal point is usually the same: what can business do for the society and the community? There is, for example, an annual issue on the problems of environment and the cities; another

on black management. There is hard information on current salaries, openings, opportunities, etc.—precisely the type of information needed by students and younger men in the field. And there are features ranging from activities on Wall Street to sports. Note: the magazine's circulation is controlled, and most of the subscriptions are free. It is supported by advertisers who are primarily recruiting for business.

The firm in 1972 announced similar free magazines for three more specific fields: law, *Juris Doctor;* engineering, *New Engineer;* and medicine, *Medical Dimensions.*

Management Decision; the Bradford Review of Management Technology. 3/yr. $20. David Ashton. MCB, 200 Keighley Rd., Bradford BD9 4J2, Yorkshire, England. Illus., index, adv. Circ: 5,000. Vol. ends: Dec.

Bk. rev: 8, 150–200 words, signed. *Aud:* Ac, Ga. *Jv:* V.

With such articles as "The pathology of success," "Investing the future," and "Computer aided management," the editor puts together a magazine well above the average. It is directed to businessmen and management, but the material will interest anyone involved in the daily process of trying to organize his or her own life, and/or the lives of others. The articles are written by experts (both in universities and in business), have a distinctive literary style (no less), and are mercifully free of cloudy, jargon-ridden thoughts. The book reviews are equally good. One of the few titles in this field which can be read with pleasure by the curious as well as the dedicated manager. The British base does not detract from the general conclusions, although admittedly a few articles about specific English firms are a bit thick.

Management of Personnel Quarterly. 1961. q. $6.50. Thomas K. Connellan. Bureau of Industrial Relations, Grad. School of Business Admin., Univ. of Michigan, Ann Arbor, Mich. 48104. Illus., adv. Circ: 8,200. Microform: UM.

Indexed: PerManAb. *Bk. rev:* 3, 300 words, signed. *Aud:* Sa, Ac.

A practical source of information for managers of industrial personnel, with some emphasis on the sociology of manufacturing organizations. Articles (about 2,500 words in length), are nicely balanced between academic and industrial contributors. There is a concerted (and usually successful) effort to make the articles both readable and scholarly. Useful to academic libraries serving schools of business administration and industrial relations.

Management Review. 1923. m. Members $7.50 (Nonmembers $15). Edmond M. Rosenthal. Management Assn. Inc., 135 W. 50th St., New York, N.Y. 10020. Illus., index. Circ: 61,000. Vol. ends: Dec. Microform: UM. Reprint: Kraus.

Indexed: BusI, PsyAb. *Bk. rev:* 1, 500 words, signed. *Aud:* Ac, Ga.

A type of *Reader's Digest* approach which provides a quick overview of current management literature for both students and businessmen. A typical issue condenses and/or revises a number of articles which have appeared in major business magazines. Also, some 15 to 20 articles are capsulated in short summaries. This approach will not appeal to all, but it has a definite place in small and medium-sized libraries where subscriptions are limited to a few titles in the management field.

Management Science. 1954. m. $25. Martin K. Starr. Inst. of Management Sciences, 146 Westminister St., Providence, R.I. 02904. Subs. to: Institute of Management Sciences, Box 6112, Providence, R.I. 02904. Illus., index, adv. Circ: 20,000. Refereed. Microform: UM.

Aud: Ac, Sa.

Edited for managers who wish to apply the methods and results of science to the business of managerial decision making. Two sections are published in alternate months: the theory series, of interest to scientists; and the applications series, which is of interest to both scientists and managers. The ten or so articles cover the fields of operations research, systems, and behavioral science. The theory section is very complex and can only be understood by a person trained in that field. The application section is just as complex, but discusses real problems as opposed to the theoretical approach. Highly recommended for the university with higher mathematics courses or masters degrees in management science.

Management Services; a magazine of planning, systems and controls. 1964. bi-m. $12.50. Robert Smith. Amer. Inst. of Certified Public Accountants, 666 Fifth Ave., New York, N.Y. 10019. Illus., index, adv. Circ: 20,000. Sample. Vol. ends: Dec. Microform: UM.

Indexed: PAIS. *Bk. rev:* 3–10, notes. *Aud:* Sa, Ac.

Interdisciplinary coverage of accounting and management, of value in both business and academic situations. Contributors are practicing accountants, managers, or teachers. Thus, the numerous scholarly articles are balanced with some of general appeal. "People, Events, Techniques" is a valuable section to keep the administrator up-to-date on news in the field. This journal makes an effort to review periodical literature through use of PhD candidates in fifteen universities who scan the literature and present five to ten of the best articles in 100 to 300 word summaries. The latter services give it added reference value for larger academic and public business collections.

✓*Operational Research Quarterly.* 1949. q. (plus a special conference issue). $20. R. A. Cuningham Green. Pergamon Press, Fairview Park, Elmsford, N.Y. 10523. Illus., index, adv. Circ: 4,300. Vol. ends: Dec.

Indexed: BusI, BritTech. *Bk. rev:* 10, 1 page. *Aud:* Sa.

This magazine shows what progress has been made and is being made in fitting man into his managerial and technological environment. It includes studies of management and administration, economics, accounting, work flow and measurement. Within those confines it tries to be as pragmatic as possible with actual case histories. It will consider any article which has to do with the theory, practice, history, or methodology of OR. Its book reviews are critical and good. It is published on behalf of the Operational Research Society Limited by Pergamon. Obviously for the specialist, and a second choice after *Operations Research.*

Operations Research. 1952. 7/yr. $20. Hugh J. Miser. Operations Research Soc. of Amer., 428 E. Preston St., Baltimore, Md. 21202. Illus., index, adv. Circ: 15,000. Vol. ends: Nov/Dec. Reprint: Kraus.

Indexed: ASTI, BusI, ChemAb, PsyAb. *Bk. rev:* 5, 1 page. *Aud:* Ac, Sa.

Covers the field of operations research from the military to stock transactions, from airline operations to chances of biological extraterritorial contamination. The illustrations and derivations add much to the clarification of the problems. Occasionally an entire issue is devoted to one facet of OR such as the military or guidelines for OR. These all have to do with the interface of man and machine which operations research tries to describe or predict. This is for the specialist, especially within the large university. The finest of its type.

✓*Personnel Administration; the journal of the Society for Personnel Administration.* 1938. bi-m. $10. Fred Peterson. The Society for Personnel Admin. Suites 485–487, National Press Bldg., 529 14th St., N.W., Washington, D.C. 20004. Illus., index. Circ: 5,800. Vol. ends: Nov/Dec. Microform: UM. Reprint: Kraus.

Indexed: BusI, PAIS, PsyAb. *Bk. rev:* Various number, length. *Aud:* Ac, Ga.

A mildly conservative journal, addressed to getting and keeping personnel on the job. Articles cover such topics as productivity, motivation, teamwork, business ethics, management's responsibility to society, the generation gap, sensitivity training, and labor turnover. For the specialist and the larger universities with graduate degrees in personnel administration.

The Personnel Administrator. 1948. bi-m. Membership (Nonmembers $10). Robert Truscello. Amer. Soc. for Personnel Admin., 19 Church St., Berea, Ohio 44017. Illus., index, adv. Circ: 10,000. Sample. Vol. ends: Nov/Dec. Microform: UM.

Indexed: PAIS, PsyAb. *Bk. rev:* 1, one page, signed. *Aud:* Ac, Sa.

Covering almost every aspect of personnel work in business, government, and education, it features six or seven well-documented articles. Among a wide variety of topics, authors consider recruitment, training and development, employer-employee relations, communications, and (inevitably) automation and computerization of records. There are regular "opinion" and "comment" sections devoted to current problems. While of primary interest to the professional administrator, it has some value for guidance counselors.

Personnel and Guidance Journal. 1952. m. (Sept.-June). Membership (Nonmembers $15). Leo Goldman. Amer. Personnel and Guidance Assn., 1607 New Hampshire Ave., N.W., Washington, D.C. 20009. Illus., index, adv. Circ: 32,000. Vol. ends: June. Microform: UM. Reprint: Johnson.

Indexed: EdI, PHRA, PsyAb. *Bk. rev:* 8, 600 words, signed. *Aud:* Sa, Ac, Hs.

Published by the American Personnel and Guidance Association, this is for the practicing counselor in school, college, and agency. Articles emphasize new ideas and practices, ethical problems, and interpretations of theory and research. Examples: "The Counselor as Specialist in Psychological Education," "The Counselor and Civil Liberties," and "Dimensions of Counseling for Career Development."

Personnel Journal; the magazine of industrial relations and personnel management. 1922. m. $12. Arthur C. Croft. The Personnel Journal, Inc., Box 239, Swarthmore, Pa. 19081. Adv. Circ: 14,000. Sample. Vol. ends: Dec. Microform: UM. Reprint: Kraus.

Indexed: BusI, PsyAb. *Bk. rev:* 1-2, 500 words, signed, and notes. *Aud:* Sa, Ac.

The best known of the many personnel journals (and one of the best indexed) this is a primary choice for any library with interest in the subject. Articles covering every aspect of personnel management, are both scholarly and popular in style and content. Contributors range from professors to people actively working in the field. The target audience, however, is the individual charged with personnel practices, not the teacher of the subject. Its book reviews, complete conference calendar, and general coverage make it a must for anyone in personnel work.

Professional Management Bulletin. 1960. m. Membership (Nonmembers $10). K. H. Kostenbader. Administrative Management Soc., Willow Grove, Pa., 19090. Illus. Circ: 15,000. Sample. Vol. ends: June.

Aud: Ac, Sa.

A small, 24-page magazine which offers managers useable information regarding current trends and methods and new developments in the administrative management field. Articles cover all management disciplines with special emphasis on personnel management, finance, administrative services, and systems and information management. Although the information is good, the slight size and the high price rule it out except for larger libraries.

Research Management. 1958. bi-m. $14. Henry R. Clauser. Industrial Research Institute, 100 Park Ave., New York, N.Y. 10017. Subs. to: Box 51, Red Bank, N.J. 07701. Illus., index. Vol. ends: Nov.

Indexed: EngInd. *Bk. rev:* 5-10, 50-150 words. *Aud:* Ac, Sa.

Published by the Industrial Research Institute, which is made up of the largest and most influential industrial research and development corporations in the United States. The editor tries quite successfully to foster improved communication between research and other corporate activities. About six articles per issue range from stories about a humanistic technology to current project selection practices, from Russia's and China's research and development to motivation. Its book reviews are critical and quite to the point. Another section reviews articles which have appeared in other journals which might be of interest to the researcher. Although a magazine for the specialist, this is general enough in its coverage of research, business, and management to be of interest to every academic and most larger public libraries.

SAM Advanced Management Journal. 1935. q. $8. William Mumpower. Society for Advancement of Management, 1472 Broadway, New York, N.Y. 10036. Illus., index, adv. Circ: 10,000. Sample. Vol. ends: Oct. Refereed. Microform: UM.

Indexed: BusI. *Bk. rev:* 4-5, notes. *Aud:* Ac, Sa.

Devoted to problems of top management but of equal value to almost anyone involved in business. Articles consider everything from computers and education to planning and personnel. Authors are professors and, more often, chairmen of American corporations. Interestingly enough, the material is just as often concerned with practical social issues and politics as with technical matters. And there is a good deal of emphasis on communication. The writing is realistic, even liberal, and often of a higher caliber than found in average business magazines.

Supervisory Management. 1955. m. $14. Thomasine Rendero. American Management Assn., 135 W. 50th Street, New York, N.Y. 10020. Illus., index. Circ: 47,000. Microform: UM. Reprint: Kraus.

Indexed: BusI. *Aud:* Ac, Sa.

A "better your performance" manual for supervisors and managers in the plant or office. Its 50 pages offer expert advice on key problems concerning budget, personnel training, delegation of responsibility, and better human relations. Case studies are written by practicing professionals focusing on variations of the theme "tough situations faced." Articles are easily read and accompanied by quality illustrations. (G.M.)

CHEMISTRY

Most of the periodicals represented in this section are research journals appropriate for academic libraries. As is usually the case with scholarly publications of scientific societies or well-established commercial research journals, editorial boards consist of prominent specialists in the field, and the contributions are generally high-quality studies. Moreover, in every journal listed herein which reports on original research, each paper has been submitted to the scrutiny of one or two subject specialists who determine the caliber of the research effort according to their respective fields. No attempt has been made to incorporate the vast number of periodicals necessary for a good research library, nor to include those covering the more specialized branches of chemistry. Rather, we have tried to select (1) titles available in English of some of the highly distinguished general chemistry journals; (2) the important review journals; (3) a representative sampling of periodicals available in analytical, inorganic, organic, and physical chemistry; (4) a few foreign titles of historical importance; (5) and some magazines or trade publications of interest to students and laymen. Most academic libraries will carry several of the important publications of the American Chemical Society, the number depending on the size of the library, the curriculum offered by their institution, and the specific needs of their faculty. Libraries supporting full research programs would naturally subscribe to many more titles, including the prestigious publications of foreign chemical societies, such as *Acta Chemica Scandinavica, Bulletin de la Société de France, Helvetica Chimica Acta, Recueil des Travaux Chimique des Pays-Bas,* and *Bulletin of the Chemical Society of Japan,* to name a very few.

Basic Periodicals

Hs: *Chemistry;* Ga: *Chemistry;* Jc: *Journal of Chemical Education;* Ac: See Introduction above. Generally, academic libraries supporting a chemistry curriculum will have all of the publications of the American Chemical Society (see text below for details).

Basic Abstracts and Indexes

Chemical Abstracts

Accounts of Chemical Research. 1968. m. $10. J. F. Bunnett. Amer. Chemical Soc., 1155 16th St., N.W., Washington, D.C. 20036. Illus., index. Sample. Vol. ends: Dec. Refereed. Microform: AMC.

Indexed: ChemAb, SCI. *Aud:* Sa, Ac.

Reporting on work being carried out at the very "frontiers of chemical research," the journal publishes short, critical review articles. All branches of chemistry are represented, although the emphasis is on fundamental studies, rather than on applied research. Reviews are generally about five to six pages; though not of the exhaustive nature associated with the broad survey, bibliographies may be fairly comprehensive. Contributions by specialists have frequently been at the invitation of the editorial board. It is a valuable,

authoritative journal covering short reviews on specialized subjects. For academic collections.

American Chemical Society. Journal. 1879. s-m. $66. Martin Styles. Amer. Chemical Soc., 1155 16th St., N.W., Washington, D.C. 20036. Illus., index, adv. Circ: 16,000. Sample. Vol. ends: no. 24. Refereed. Microform: Amer. Chemical Soc., UM, MF, PMC. Reprint: Johnson.

Indexed: ASTI, BioAb, ChemAb, EngI, MetAb, SciAb, SCI. *Bk. rev:* 3–4, 400 words, signed. *Aud:* Sa, Ac.

With a membership of over 110,000 strong, the American Chemical Society is one of our leading scientific societies and one of the foremost scientific publishers in the United States. In the last three decades, *JACS,* the oldest publication of the Society, has emerged as one of the world's most important chemical periodicals, ranking second on the *Chemical Abstracts* list of 1,000 most frequently cited journals. Significant research papers report on all branches of fundamental chemistry; rigorously refereed articles are selected on the basis of broad chemical interest, and papers which merely report routine measurements are avoided. Fields covered include physical, inorganic, organic, and biological chemistry. A large section of "Communications" consists of short, preliminary studies of importance and timeliness. Some book reviews are essay-type and excellent. A primary publication for every academic collection.

Analyst. 1876. m. $80.40. J. B. Attrill. Soc. for Analytical Chemistry, 9/10 Savile Row, London, England. Subs. to: Chemical Soc., Blackhorse Rd., Letchworth, Herts, England. Illus., index, adv. Circ: 7,138. Sample. Vol. ends: Dec. Refereed. Microform: UM; PMC. Reprint: Johnson.

Indexed: BioAb, BritTechI, ChemAb, SCI. *Bk. rev:* 5–6, 300–500 words, signed. *Aud:* Sa, Ac.

Published by the Society for Analytical Chemistry (U.K.), the journal is one of the earliest periodicals dedicated exclusively to all branches of analytical chemistry (predated by *Fresenius' Zeitschrift für Analytische Chemie*). Research papers range from general, analytical procedures through inorganic, organic, biochemical, and pharmaceutical analyses to papers on techniques and apparatus. An occasional, authoritative review paper appears, with the usual, lengthy, supportive bibliography. Short, urgent communications are also included from time to time. The journal is international, and papers are not restricted to members of the Society. Necessary for any library supporting research in analytical chemistry, small academic libraries will probably find their needs sufficiently served by the American *Analytical Chemistry.*

Of course, the journal is *not* available without a subscription to *Analytical Abstracts,* and subscribers to the *Abstracts* may avail themselves of a number of packaged deals, including the *Analyst* and *Proceedings of the Society for Analytical Chemistry,* for varying amounts. Despite the fact that the Society is assuring itself of a built-in audience, the combination deal is itself a bargain at the price. *Analytical Abstracts*, as may be expected, covers the world's literature in the main fields of analytical chemistry from some 360 journals. About 25,000 abstracts are issued annually. Short, signed, indicative abstracts appear about six months after the original papers, but coverage of East European and Russian literature is particularly good. The *Proceedings of the Society for Analytical Chemistry* contains, in the main, news of the organization, reports of technical meetings, and some prior announcements of papers accepted for publication in the *Analyst*.

Analytical Chemistry. 1929. m. $7. Herbert A. Laitinen. Amer. Chemical Soc., 1155 16th St., N.W., Washington, D.C. 20036. Illus., index, adv. Circ: 36,000. Sample. Vol. ends: Dec. Refereed. Microform: AMC.

Indexed: ASTI, BioAb, ChemAb, EngI, SciAb, SCI. *Bk. rev:* 7, 300 words, signed. *Aud:* Sa, Ac.

All aspects of analytical chemistry are represented in this publication. Research-type papers and reports, bearing on both the theoretical and methodological, range from studies of procedures, instrumentation, measurements, to aids for analytical chemists. Very thorough news coverage of research, product developments, chemicals, and professional activities is given. Two special issues appear annually: an April supplement provides excellent, comprehensive, and authoritative reviews of the literature; and a laboratory guide, issued in July, gives detailed information on new services, equipment, and the like. This is the best source for authoritative and comprehensive information on analytical chemistry. Recommended for every academic collection.

Libraries with strong interest in analytical chemistry will, of course, support a large number of international journals with research scope, such as the *Analyst* (see above), *Analytica Chimica Acta*, published by Elsevier, and *Talanta*, put out by Pergamon, as well as specialty journals within the field of analytical chemistry.

Angewandte Chemie. International Edition. 1962. m. $49. H. Grunewald. Academic Press, 111 Fifth Ave., New York, N.Y. 10003. Illus., index, adv. Circ: 4,000. Sample. Vol. ends: Dec. Refereed.

Indexed: ChemAb, SCI. *Bk. rev:* 7, 250 words, signed. *Aud:* Sa, Ac.

The International Edition, sponsored by the Gesellschaft Deutscher Chemiker and published jointly with Verlag-Chemie, Weinheim, is a translation of the German edition which first originated in 1888. The journal features about four to five extended, authoritative review articles, covering all facets of chemistry, including applied research, chemical technology, etc. A very important section is "Communications," devoted to brief research reports; many of these communications are in the fields of organic chemistry and biochemistry. Other monthly departments include conference reports, selected abstracts, and book reviews. These latter sections are particularly useful, since they provide a current awareness program of unpublished results presented at European conferences, and announcements of new chemical texts appearing abroad. For academic collections.

Biochemical Journal. See Biological Sciences/Biochemistry and Biophysics Section.

Biochemistry. See Biological Sciences/Biochemistry and Biophysics Section.

CRC Critical Reviews in Analytical Chemistry. 1970. q. $56. Louis Meites. CRC Press. Chemical Rubber Co., 18901 Cranwood Parkway, Cleveland, Ohio 44128. Illus., index. Sample. Vol. ends: no. 4. Refereed.

A new and authoritative critical review journal, publishing lengthy survey papers with extended bibliographies. The aim of the publication is to highlight the timeliest and most important areas of research currently being conducted in all phases of analytical chemistry—concepts, methodology, and experimentation. Scholarly articles are generally invited by the editorial board from specialists in the field. The publisher, well known for an array of miscellaneous handbooks, has added a large selection of review journals to its lengthy publications slate. This periodical will provide great support for all good collections in analytical chemistry.

Canadian Journal of Chemistry. 1929. s-m. $48. J. W. ApSimon, K. O. Kutschke, and A. M. Eastham. National Research Council of Canada, Ottawa 7, Ontario. Illus., index. Circ: 4,000. Vol. ends: Dec., no. 24. Microform: PMC.

Indexed: BioAb, ChemAb, SCI. *Aud:* Sa, Ac.

Part of the Canadian Journals of Research series. The journal covers all areas of chemical research, including organic, inorganic, physical, analytical, and biochemical work. Papers are given over to studies of chemical synthesis, chemical dynamics, molecular structure and properties, etc. About one very short communication is also carried in each issue. Contributions are, in large part, from Canadian universities and research establishments, A good, general, and authoritative publication in chemistry. For academic libraries.

Chemical and Engineering News. 1923. w. $8. Patrick P. McCurdy. Amer. Chemical Soc., 1155 Sixteenth St., N.W., Washington, D.C. 20036. Illus., index, adv. Circ: 134,200. Sample. Vol. ends: Dec. Microform: AMC.

Indexed: ASTI, BioAb, ChemAb. *Aud:* Sa, Ac.

Viewed from any aspect—government, industry, science, technology, education—*C&E News* supplies the best current coverage of weekly news for both professionals affiliated with the ACS or anyone concerned with recent developments in the chemical field. Special features and reports (often reprinted separately) provide an overview of rapidly advancing technologies, trends in federal support, and chemical market surveys. Regular departments highlight activities in business, academia, government. Useful for professionals are frequently published surveys on salaries, schools, chemical stocks, calendar of events, and full programs of ACS meetings. Good reference tools are two supplementary issues: "Facts & Figures," appearing in September, lists statistical information on the chemical industry; an extra issue in April is given over to a buyer's guide of chemical products and services. Both academic and large public libraries can profitably use subscriptions; moreover, a must for every collection in chemistry.

Chemical Instrumentation. 1968. 4/yr. $35. Clemens Auerbach. Marcel Dekker, Inc., 95 Madison Ave., New York, N.Y. 10016. Illus., index. Sample. Vol. ends: no. 4. Refereed.

Aud: Sa, Ac.

Although research-type papers on instrumentation appear in a wide variety of journals, and there are entire publications dedicated solely to scientific instruments, this recent periodical concerns itself exclusively with the apparatus, methodology, and experimentation for chemical and biochemical research. Instrumentation is interpreted broadly to include computers and their applications; in fact, a number of issues have been dedicated to the proceedings of symposia on this subject. Recent issues have also carried a New Products section. This specialty publication will hardly be a first choice for every academic library; yet the journal will be welcomed for libraries of institutions actively engaged in chemical research.

Chemical Reviews. 1924. bi-m. $39. Harold Hart. Amer. Chemical Soc., 1155 16th St., N.W., Washington, D.C. 20036. Illus., index. Circ: 6,100. Sample. Vol. ends: no. 6. Referred. Microform: AMC. Reprint: Johnson.

Indexed: BioAb, ChemAb, SciAb, SCI. *Aud:* Sa, Ac.

"Authoritative, critical reviews and comprehensive summaries of recent research in theoretical chemistry" are contributed by distinguished scientists (frequently at the invitation of the editor) in areas representing all branches of chemistry. Generally, the topics under discussion have not been reviewed in a readily available publication for at least five years, although exceptions are made if developments in a field have been particularly rapid, or if new insight can be achieved through further evaluation of a subject. The timely articles, averaging 10–20 pages in length, and their exhaustive bibliographies make the journal an excellent, invaluable reference for both advanced students and researchers. For every academic library.

Chemical Society, London. Journal. 1848. $420. Ed. bd. Chemical Soc., Burlington House, London W1V OBN, England. Illus., index. Microform: UM, MF, PMC. Reprint: Johnson.

Indexed: ChemAb, SCI. *Aud:* Sa, Ac.

The Chemical Society, London, is one of the earliest extant organizations, and one of the most prominent, in the advancement of chemical science. Following a recent merger with the Royal Institute of Chemistry (U.K.), the Faraday Society, and the Society for Analytical Chemistry (U.K.), the Society has also revamped in 1972 all its publications, including an assimilation of some of the journals of its sister associations, within the generic title *Journal of the Chemical Society.* Delineated below are the various parts of the journal, each of which may be purchased separately. Certainly all research libraries will need the six sections of this powerful amalgamate of outstanding contributions to chemical research. Smaller institutions will, because of the price, look to the interests of their faculty for selected sections. Included in the full subscription price are *Chemistry in Britain* and the *Faraday Discussions* (see below).

J.C.S. Chemical Communications. 24/yr. $72. Covers urgent communications of about one printed page in length. All branches of chemistry are included. (Supersedes the former *Chemical Communications.*)

J.C.S. Dalton Transactions. 24/yr. $96. Dedicated to papers on inorganic compounds. Studies cover structures, reaction kinetics, equilibria, crystallographic investigations, etc. (Supersedes, in part, *Journal of the Chemical Society, Part A.*)

J.C.S. Faraday Transactions. Part I. Physical Chemistry. 12/yr. $43.20. Includes such topics as electrochemistry, radiation chemistry, surface chemistry, polymers, catalysis, etc. (Supersedes, in part, the former *Transactions of the Faraday Society*, and some of the papers which used to appear in *Journal of the Chemical Society, Part A.*)

J.C.S. Faraday Transactions. Part II. Chemical Physics. 12/yr. $28.80. Can be considered a new journal. Contains theoretical studies on quantum theory, valence, statistical mechanics, intermolecular forces, spectroscopic studies, etc.

Faraday Discussions (2/yr, $19.20) and *Faraday Symposia,* (1/yr, $9.60), containing papers presented at symposia organized by the former Faraday Society, are still published; *Discussions* is included in the package deal, and *Symposia* must be purchased separately.)

J.C.S. Perkin Transactions. Part I. Organic Chemistry. 24/yr. $100.80. Given over to papers on natural products, including bioorganic chemistry, and aliphatic, alicyclic, aromatic, carbocyclic, heterocyclic compounds, etc. (Supersedes *Journal of the Chemical Society. Part C.*)

J.C.S. Perkin Transactions. Part II. Physical Organic Chemistry. 15/yr. $60. Specializes in papers on reaction kinetics and mechanisms of organic systems, use of physicochemical techniques in organic chemistry, etc. (Supersedes *Journal of the Chemical Society, Part B.*)

✓ *Chemical Society Reviews.* 1972. q. $19.20. Ed. bd. Chemical Soc., Burlington House, London, W1V OBN, England. Illus., index. Sample. Vol. ends: no. 4. Refereed.

Indexed: ChemAb, SCI. *Aud:* Sa, Ac.

A new publication formed by the merger of the Chemical Society's *Quarterly Reviews* and the Royal Institute of Chemistry's *RIC Reviews.* In-depth review articles cover all fields of chemistry and "its interfaces with other disciplines." As has been the case with its predecessors, the *Reviews* articles are not merely specialist-oriented, but discuss topics of current chemical interest for a wide readership. Generally, articles are invited from authorities in the field by the editorial board. Because of its excellent tutorial features, the publication should be available in most chemistry collections.

Chemical Technology. 1971. m. $18 (free to members). B. J. Luberoff. Amer. Chemical Soc., 1155 Sixteenth St., N.W. Washington, D.C. 20036. Illus., index, adv. Circ: 100,000. Sample. Vol. ends: no. 12. Refereed. Microform: AMC.

Indexed: ChemAb. *Bk. rev:* 3–4, 200 words, signed. *Aud:* Ac, Sa.

The newest in the long line of ACS publications. Subtitled "The Innovator's Magazine," the periodical aims at generating interaction and collaboration among the many separate disciplines pertinent to chemistry and chemical engineering, and at promoting the application of chemistry to the achievement of economic and social goals. Contributions include reports of original work, state-of-the-art surveys, and critical discussions of technical and nontechnical subjects that impinge on the industrial practice of chemistry and chemical engineering. Also included are special departments, such as "Brownstein's Closet," which culls new developments from the chemical and patent literature, and "The Last Word," a regular page for women. The makeup of the Advisory Panel for this periodical gives a good indication of the breadth of material which can be expected in future volumes: representatives from Divisions of the ACS on plastics, fertilizer and soil chemistry, polymers, cellulose, wood and fiber chemistry, chemical marketing, fuel chemistry, microbial chemistry, water, air and waste chemistry, rubber chemistry, and analytical chemistry. A comprehensive, interdisciplinary, and nonspecialist publication for every academic library.

Chemical Titles. See Abstracts and Indexes Section.

Chemical Week. 1914. w. $9. Ralph R. Schultz. McGraw-Hill, Inc., 330 W. 42nd St., New York, N.Y. 10036. Illus., index, adv. Circ: 60,000. Sample. Vol. ends: Dec. Microform: UM.

Indexed: BusI. *Aud:* Sa, Ac.

A trade journal which spots the news: in legislation emerging from Washington; from high-level executive suites; from production lines and research laboratories; from corporate battles in court to pickets on streets. Primarily directed toward professionals in the chemical process industries, the scope of the magazine is still broad enough to be of interest to laymen concerned with this field. Some issues feature special reports—comprehensive resumés of state-of-art—on topics ranging from plant sites to pollution control. Regular departments cover business (sales, mergers); international activities; technology (new products); marketing (including price indexes and surveys); and people (profiles of executives). A buyers' guide is issued annually. Indispensable for the desktops of investors or sales executives for its news and statistics, it may also serve business-oriented clientele of public libraries.

Chemische Berichte. 1868. m. DM.330. Ed. bd. Verlag Chemie GmbH, Pappelallee 3, Weinheim/Bergstr., W. Germany. Ills., index, adv. Circ: 3,600. Sample. Refereed. Microform: UM, MF. Reprint: Johnson.

Indexed: BioAb, ChemAb, SCI. *Aud:* Sa, Ac.

The publication is a continuation of the very renowned *Berichte der Deutschen Chemischen Gesellschaft* which, prior to 1945, had established itself as one of the giants in the field of chemical literature. Currently, high-quality research papers are concerned with both inorganic and organic chemistry, although in recent years, it has leaned heavily toward studies in organic research. Still a prestigious item for academic libraries interested in its present research emphasis.

✓ *Chemistry.* 1927. m. $6. O. Theodor Benfey. Amer. Chemical Soc., 1155 16th St., N.W., Washington, D.C. 20036. Illus., index, adv. Circ: 34,000. Microform: AMC, UM.

Indexed: ChemAb, RG. *Bk. rev:* 2, 300–500 words, signed. *Aud:* Hs, Ga, Ac.

"How were the elements named?" is the type of question answered on a nontechnical level in this periodical directed at introducing chemistry to beginning students at any level. The three to four features in each issue probe into such areas as the application of chemical research in our daily lives, supply historical or biographical notes from the annals of chemistry, and explore and interpret new research. Articles, usually by highly distinguished scientists, are written in general, readable prose, lavishly illustrated with good photography, and make entertaining as well as informative reading. To further its educational aim, special tutorial departments are included, some of which describe experiments which have been, and can be, undertaken at the high school level. An exceptional title for high school libraries and worthwhile for any public library seeking more than a general science periodical. Academic libraries will want it as one title which can be read by undergraduates.

Chemistry in Britain. 1965. m. $24. P. J. Farago. Chemical Soc., Burlington House, London W1V OBN, England. Illus., index, adv. Circ: 48,000. Sample. Vol. ends: Dec.

Indexed: BritTech, ChemAb. *Bk. rev:* 12–13, 150–250 words, signed. *Aud:* Sa, Ac.

The nonspecialist publication of the Chemical Society, incorporating the *Journal of the Royal Institute of Chemistry* and some elements of the former *Proceedings of the Chemical Society.* The periodical supplies the majority of British chemists with the "raw gossip" of their profession—personalia, salaries, news bits, calendar, etc. Some worthwhile features of interest to any libraries are its articles discussing trends in research, education, government, and industry. Contributions, often by specialists, as well as editorial board, supply excellent tutorials in their area of research. And since many of the reports are written in fairly nonspecialist language, the publication should be quite useful to undergraduates. Occasional, essay-type book reviews (500–600 words) are excellent; the short reviews also provide a good checklist of available literature, particularly from the United Kingdom. For academic libraries.

Chemistry and Industry. 1881. s-m. $28.80. T. F. West. Soc. of Chemical Industry, 14 Belgrave Sq., London, SW1X 8PS. Illus., index, adv. Circ: 10,171. Sample. Vol. ends: no. 24. Refereed.

Indexed: ASTI, BioAb, BritTech, ChemAb, SCI. *Bk. rev:* 9–10, 100–200 words, signed. *Aud:* Sa, Ac.

Serves as the news organ for the Society, as well as supplying essay reviews, short accounts of methods and apparatus in product and process developments, resumés of current literature, and personalia. A small section on "Communications to the Editor" publishes short research reports, the bulk of which fall in the category of organic chemistry. Prior to the restructuring of the publications of the Society, the section on "Communications" used to occupy a prominent portion of the journal, formerly published on a weekly basis. At present, only about five to six 500-word reports are given in the section. Included with the subscription is a comprehensive buyers' guide to chemicals and equipment (issued annually). For academic libraries.

Electrochemical Society. Journal. 1948. m. $40. Norman Hackerman. Electrochemical Soc., Inc., P.O. Box 2071, Princeton, New Jersey 08540. Illus., index, adv.

Circ: 7,500. Sample. Vol. ends: Dec. Refereed. Microform: UM. Reprint: Johnson.

Indexed: ASTI, ChemAb, EngI, MetAb, SciAb, SCI. *Bk. rev:* 1–2, 250 words, signed. *Aud:* Sa, Ac.

Although directed toward the specialist, this important journal, which publishes both fundamental and applied research in electrochemistry, is interdisciplinary in character and incorporates papers from all the sciences concerned with electrochemical phenomena. Divided into three sections of "Electrochemical Science and Technology," "Solid-State Science and Technology," and "Reviews and News," the publication reports on work in the areas of corrosion, dielectrics and insulation, electrodeposition, batteries, electronics, as related to chemical research, electrothermics and metallurgy, industrial electrolytic processes, fundamental physical electrochemistry, and the like. "Reviews" publishes both invited and contributed papers summarizing current problems in chemistry, physics, electronics, metallurgy, and medicine, as they relate to electrochemistry. Also included in this section twice annually are abstracts of papers presented at meetings of the Society, as well as news, personalia, book reviews, etc. Most academic libraries will need it.

Faraday Transactions. See *Chemical Society, London. Journal/J.C.S. Faraday Transactions.*

Industrial and Engineering Chemistry. Quarterlies. See *Chemical Engineering* in Engineering and Technology Section.

Inorganic Chemistry. 1962. m. $54. M. Frederick Hawthorne. Amer. Chemical Soc., 1155 16th St., N.W., Washington, D.C. 20036. Illus., index, adv. Circ: 6,000. Sample. Vol. ends: Dec. Refereed. Microform: AMC.

Indexed: ChemAb, EngI, MetAb. *Aud:* Sa, Ac.

Both experimental and theoretical research papers are published in this journal devoted exclusively to all phases of inorganic chemistry. Authoritative studies cover such areas as synthesis of new compounds, their properties, reaction mechanisms, quantitative investigations of structures, and thermodynamics. In addition to full-length papers, some brief notes describing research of a more limited scope are also carried. Since the periodical is a primary medium for reporting new results in inorganic chemistry, it is an important addition for academic libraries supporting curricula in this field, and an essential item in any research collection.

Journal of Applied Chemistry and Biotechnology (Formerly: *Journal of Applied Chemistry*). 1951. m. $48. Ed. bd. Soc. of Chemical Industry, 14 Belgrave Sq. London, England. Subs. to: Chemical Soc. Publns., Sales Office, Blackhorse Rd., Letchworth, Hertfordshire, England. Illus., index. Circ: 4,000. Sample. Vol. ends: no. 12. Refereed.

Indexed: ASTI, BritTech, ChemAb, EngI, MetAb, SCI. *Aud:* Sa, Ac.

Reorganized in 1971, the base of this journal has been strengthened by the addition of papers on industrial biology, including the areas of fermentation technology, enzymic processes, and biodegradation. Its traditional concern with other applied chemical sciences, including chemical processing and materials, continues. Generally, papers do not cover the fields of polymers and food and agriculture, since these are handled by two specialty publications of the Society of Chemical Industry, *Journal of the Science of Food and Agriculture,* and *British Polymer Journal.* The *Abstracts,* issued as part of the publication, were dropped as of December 1971. The journal is a valuable one, both for chemistry collections and chemical engineering, and materials science libraries.

✓ *Journal of Biological Chemistry.* See Biological Sciences/Biochemistry and Biophysics Section.

Journal of Chemical Documentation. 1961. q. $21. Herman Skolnik. Amer. Chemical Soc., 1155 16th St., N.W., Washington, D.C. 20036. Illus., index. Circ: 2,000. Sample. Vol. ends: no. 4. Refereed. Microform: AMC.

Indexed: ChemAb, SCI. *Bk. rev:* 2–3, 250 words, signed. *Aud:* Sa, Ac.

Dealing with far more than the problems of handling the chemical literature, the journal publishes studies of subjects concerned with the science of documentation, its results and methodology. Papers, varying in levels of sophistication, cover such topics as classification systems, indexing, abstracting, chemical nomenclature, information processing, storage and retrieval systems, machine translations, technical writing, etc. Frequently, contributions are based on papers presented at the American Chemical Society's Division of Chemical Literature, for which the journal is the official publication. Because of the broad variety of subject matter, the journal belongs on the professional reading list of any information scientist and librarian concerned with the above subjects.

✓ *Journal of Chemical Education.* 1924. m. $6. W. T. Lippincott. 441 Lexington Ave., New York, N.Y. 10017. Illus., index, adv. Circ: 25,000. Sample. Vol. ends: Dec. Refereed. Reprint: Johnson.

Indexed: BioAb, ChemAb, SCI. *Bk. rev:* 10, 300–400 words, signed. *Aud:* Sa, Ac, Hs.

Perhaps every chemistry library and every chemical educator is a subscriber, but this is one publication which ought to find its way into the hands of high school educators, as well. Papers encompass the full range of chemistry—ideas, theory, method, laboratory experimentation, philosophy, and history. Levels of sophistication vary; articles are useful to both students and teachers. Reports covering the technical problems

of teaching—administration, curricula, lecture demonstrations, and methods of presentation—are featured regularly. Several monthly departments review new instruments, chemicals, products, safety in the laboratory. Appearing each September is a comprehensive, classified checklist of new technical books. An excellent journal for every academic library.

Journal of Chemical and Engineering Data. 1959. q. $45. Bruno Zwolinski. Amer. Chemical Soc., 1155 16th St., N.W., Washington, D.C. 20036. Illus., index. Circ: 2,064. Sample. Vol. ends: no. 4. Refereed. Microform: AMC.

Indexed: ChemAb, EngI. *Aud:* Sa, Ac.

When the journal was founded 15 years ago, it became the first publication dedicated exclusively to numerical data in chemical and chemical engineering sciences. Others have subsequently joined this class; see, for example. *Journal of Physical and Chemical Reference Data.* The usefulness of such publications to any scientists is that they draw together accurate experimental data, plus the method by which these data have been generated, evaluated, and correlated. Titles such as "Thermodynamic Properties of Binary Liquid Mixtures" and "Molecular Weights and Conductivities" indicate the scope. For any chemical and chemical engineering research collection.

✓ *Journal of Chemical Physics.* See Physics Section.

Journal of General Chemistry of the USSR. 1949. m. $210. Consultants Bureau, 227 W. 17th St., New York, N.Y. 10011. Illus., index. Sample. Refereed. Microform: Consultants Bureau.

Indexed: ChemAb, SCI. *Aud:* Sa, Ac.

The journal is a complete translation of *Zhurnal Obshchei Khimii,* the leading chemical journal of the USSR, and a publication of their well-known Academy of Sciences. Comparable in scope and quality to *Journal of the American Chemical Society,* the periodical reflects the current chemical interests of reputable Russian scientists. Research papers deal with all branches of chemistry and include studies on analytical, biochemical, inorganic, organic, and physical chemistry. (Note: Consultants Bureau publishes in translation a large number of journals pertinent to chemical interests. This title was selected as a representative, authoritative publication from the USSR.)

✓ *Journal of Inorganic and Nuclear Chemistry.* 1955. m. $190. Ed. bd. Pergamon Press, Fairview Pk., Elmsford, N.Y. 10523. Illus., index. Sample. Vol. ends: no. 12. Refereed. Microform: Maxwell. Reprint: Maxwell.

Indexed: ChemAb, MetAb, SCI. *Aud:* Sa, Ac.

A well-established international publication, this journal has taken a prominent role in the literature of both nuclear and inorganic chemistry. Research reports published therein include studies of synthesis of new compounds and their reactions, structures, mechanisms, solution complexes, and work on stable and radioactive isotopes. Short, research communications in need of faster publication may appear in its monthly, letter-type, sister journal, *Inorganic and Nuclear Chemistry Letters* (m., $70). The papers are high quality and the editorial boards represent a distinguished body of international specialists. Both *Journal* and *Letters* would be necessary for any library focusing on research in inorganic chemistry. Small, cost-minded academic libraries will find the publication of the American Chemical Society, *Inorganic Chemistry*, adequate for a selection in this field.

Journal of Organic Chemistry. 1936. m. $60. Frederick D. Greene. Amer. Chemical Soc., 1155 16th St., N.W., Washington, D.C. 20036. Illus., index, adv. Circ: 10,400. Sample. Vol. ends: no. 24. Refereed. Microform: AMC. UM. Reprint: Johnson.

Indexed: BioAb, ChemAb, SCI. *Aud:* Sa, Ac.

Devoted to "original contributions on fundamental research in all branches of the theory and practice of organic chemistry." The journal publishes both comprehensive research papers and shorter notes on investigations of organic reactions, mechanisms, natural products, synthesis of new compounds, theoretical organic chemistry, and some aspects of spectroscopy related to organic chemistry. A prominent and authoritative publication in the field. If a library is limited to a single publication on organic chemistry, this journal would be the first choice.

Journal of Physical and Chemical Reference Data. See Physics Section.

Journal of Physical Chemistry. 1896. s-m. $60. Bryce Crawford, Jr. Amer. Chemical Soc., 1155 16th St., N.W., Washington, D.C. 20036. Illus., index. Circ: 6,400. Sample. Vol. ends: no. 24. Refereed. Microform: AMC, UM, MF. Reprint: Johnson.

Indexed: ChemAb, EngI, MetAb, SciAb, SCI. *Aud:* Sa, Ac.

The journal is one of the foremost in its field, dealing with "fundamental aspects of physical chemistry." High-quality papers represent thorough and complete studies on such subjects as atomic and molecular phenomena, quantum mechanical calculations, magnetic resonance spectroscopy, and molecular electronic spectroscopy. On occasion, short communications also appear. There are a number of other journals, also high quality, which would be necessary for strong collections in physical chemistry, including the well-known *Zeitschrift für Physikalische Chemie* (both Frankfurt and Leipzig editions), as well as some of the specialty journals within the field of physical chemistry, e.g., *Journal of Colloid and Interface Science, Journal of Polymer Science, Journal of Catalysis*, to name but a few. This publication, however, would be essen-

tial to any academic library supporting either a graduate or undergraduate chemistry program.

Justus Liebigs Annalen der Chemie. 1832. irreg. approx. 10 v./yr. DM. 27/v. Ed.bd. Verlag Chemie GmbH, Pappelallee 3, Weinheim/Bergstr., W. Germany. Illus., index, adv. Circ: 2,450. Sample. Refereed. Microform: UM, MF. Reprint: Johnson.

Indexed: ChemAb, SCI. *Aud:* Sa, Ac.

Published in the days when a journal was known by the name of its founder, *Annalen* is one of the oldest chemical journals still in print. Through a series of highly distinguished editors, and other scientists, the publication made some of the most valuable contributions to the development of chemistry in the nineteenth century. Originally an outgrowth of two pharmaceutical journals, it expanded its scope to all phases of chemistry, with a strong emphasis on organic chemistry. Today, the journal is devoted exclusively to organic chemistry, including natural products, and though it may be equalled in quality and content by many other research publications, it is still a distinguished addition to academic libraries.

Pure and Applied Chemistry. 1960. irreg. $36/v. B. C. L. Weedon. Butterworth & Co., Ltd., 88 Kingway, London, SC2, England. Illus., index. Circ: 2,000. Sample. Vol. ends: no. 4. Refereed.

Indexed: BioAb, ChemAb, EngI. *Aud:* Sa, Ac.

The journal is the official organ of the International Union of Pure and Applied Chemistry. Papers are given over entirely to those presented at symposia organized by IUPAC, and usually these center around one theme, e.g., macromolecules. Contributions are international, authoritative, and text may be in English, French, or German. Frequently, separate issues representing proceedings of entire congresses are reprinted in book form. Recommended for libraries with heavy chemical interests, particularly since the issues of the journal predate the publication of the proceedings of the symposia by a considerable period of time.

Russian Chemical Reviews. 1960. m. $79.20. Ed. bd. Chemical Soc., Burlington House, London, W1V OBN, England. Illus., index. Circ: 820. Vol. ends: no. 12. Refereed.

Indexed: ChemAb, SCI. *Aud:* Sa, Ac.

With the exception of a few articles, the journal is a cover-to-cover translation of *Uspekhi Khimii*, a monthly publication of the Academy of Sciences of the USSR. Comparable in scope and purpose to *Chemical Reviews*, it publishes review papers by leading Russian scientists in all branches of current chemical research. The few exceptions which have not been translated are papers which originally appeared in other review journals (e.g., *Angewandte Chemie*) and were subsequently translated into Russian. Reviews are authoritative and critical, and cover selected topics in inorganic, analytical, physical, and organic chemistry, with some biochemical studies included. The time lag in translation is about standard, i.e., six months. An important feature of this journal for research libraries is that the comprehensive bibliographies frequently bring to light little-known publications from the USSR. Note: The Chemical Society of London also sponsors two other translations of specialized journals: *Russian Journal of Inorganic Chemistry (Zhurnal Neorganicheskoi Khimii)* and *Russian Journal of Physical Chemistry (Zhurnal Fizicheskoi Khimii.)* For large academic collections.

Tetrahedron. 1957. s-m. $240. T. Stephen. Pergamon Press, Fairview Park, Elmsford, New York 10523. Illus., index, adv. Circ: 3,500. Sample. Vol. ends: no. 24. Refereed. Microform: Maxwell. Reprint: Maxwell.

Indexed: BioAb, ChemAb, SCI. *Aud:* Sa, Ac.

An international journal dealing exclusively with research papers on organic chemistry. Comprehensive studies cover topics on organic reactions, natural products, studies of mechanism, and spectroscopy. Short reports of on-going research appear in its supplement, *Tetrahedron Letters,* a letter-type journal produced by photo-offset (52/yr, $187.50). Both journals are high-quality publications with distinguished editorial boards, and provide the forum in which some of the best organic research is reported. The cost of these publications, however, is clearly a prohibitive factor for small, academic libraries, whose needs may be best served by the ACS periodical *Journal of Organic Chemistry.* Nevertheless, the journals are essential for any institution with an active research program in organic chemistry.

U.S. National Bureau of Standards. Journal of Research. Section A: Physics and Chemistry. See Science Section.

CHILDREN

See also Education/Educational Aids Section.

Basic Periodicals

FOR CHILDREN. All titles can be considered for use at the primary, elementary, junior high (and sometimes high school) levels, or age groups. There are too few basic children's magazines of any type. The result is that libraries tend to take almost all of them. A "V" rating, of course, indicates favorites.

ABOUT CHILDREN. All libraries: *Children, Exceptional Children, Child Welfare.*

Basic Abstracts and Indexes

Child Development Abstracts, Current Index to Journals in Education, Education Index, Exceptional Child Education Abstracts, Subject Index to Children's Magazines.

Cessations

Catholic Boy, Hi-Venture, My Baby, Your New Baby.

For Children

American Girl. 1917. m. $5.00. Pat di Sernia. Girl Scouts of the U.S.A., 830 Third Ave., New York, N.Y. 10022. Illus., index, adv. Circ: 800,000. Sample. Vol. ends: Dec.

Indexed: IChildMag. *Bk. rev:* Short notices. *Aud:* Ejh.

A compact, low-keyed magazine designed for the young girl. Officially an organ of the Girl Scouts of America, some regular features are so oriented, but the publication is not limited in scope. Articles emphasize hostess hints, fashion, movie and record news. Special reports range from studies of Vista to careers. Two or three stories help span the age range by including material of interest for the preteen and older girl. Advertising is tasteful and appropriate to the group it serves. (L.O.)

American Red Cross Youth News (Formerly: *American Junior Red Cross News*). 1919. m. (Oct.-May, except Jan.) $1.50. James C. Lee. Amer. National Red Cross, 18th & D Sts., N.W., Washington, D.C. 20006. Illus. Circ: 300,000. Sample. Vol. ends: May.

Indexed: IChildMag. *Aud:* Ejh. *Jv:* V.

Intended to be used by elementary school Red Cross youth volunteers, this is useful also as a classroom supplement in the areas of science and social studies. Reports of successful projects are presented as suggestions for action by other youngsters. General interest articles and good stories with world interest encourage concern for others in this country and throughout the world. These are written by qualified people. Each issue contains a "Primary Graders' Book" about three pages in length, illustrated, and set in type somewhat larger than that of the rest of the magazine. Excellent articles on science are usually included, written and illustrated for elementary grades. An occasional skit on the topic of one of the articles makes an interesting way of making the topic more meaningful in the elementary classroom. Some verse by contributors in grades 4 to 6, a fun page, and a classroom calendar of notable dates are other features. The format is appealing, from the well-designed, colorful cover to the good, clear type and the photos and drawings illustrating the contents. (L.O.)

Badger History. See History/States and Provinces Section.

Boys' Life. 1911. m. $4. Robert Hood. Boy Scouts of America, U.S. Highway No.1, New Brunswick, N.J. 08903. Illus., index, adv. Circ: 2,410,000. Sample. Vol. ends: Dec.

Indexed: IChild Mag. *Aud:* Ejh. *Jv:* V.

The best all-around magazine published for the adolescent male. It is not, however, recommended for advanced or sophisticated boys, although even they may find sections of interest. Boy Scout–oriented, it ranges far afield from prosaic camping advice to articles on ecology and vocations. Regular features include a hobby column, patrol ideas, stamp and coin collecting and a full page of jokes. Special features offer well-written, signed articles on nature, chess, autos, and even tips on getting along with girls. Essays vary in reading level and interest and include something for everyone from 9 to 16. Two or three stories are included. The advertising is in good taste, and the color and black and white photographs and illustrations enhance this attractive periodical. (L.O.)

Calling All Girls. See *Young Miss.*

Child Life. 1921. m. $6. B. R. SerVaas, 1100 Waterway Blvd., Indianapolis, Ind. 46202. Illus. Circ. 210,000. Sample. Vol. ends: Dec.

Indexed: IChildMag. *Aud:* Ejh.

A magazine created for children from pre-readers to sixth graders. Equally divided among fiction, arts, crafts, and miscellanea, it features poems, letters to the editor, jokes, riddles, and activity pages. Inside each cover, a well-known encyclopedia publisher features learning units, such as "Trees—Their Products and Uses." Each issue is done in two colors with a white background. Generally appealing to elementary school children. (L.O.)

Children's Digest. 1950. m. (except June and Aug.). $5.95. Elizabeth R. Mattheos. Parents' Magazine Enterprises, Inc., 52 Vanderbilt Ave., New York, N.Y. 10017. Illus., index, adv. Circ: 850,000. Sample. Vol. ends: Dec.

Indexed: IChildMag. *Bk. rev:* 6–8, short, signed. *Aud:* Ejh.

Presents, in conventional digest format of 100 pages, material from a variety of sources for children ages 7 to 12. Old and new fiction (reprints and excerpts) accounts for the bulk of each issue, plus some articles on science, nature, and history. Authors of classic works for children, such as Kipling, Stevenson, Milne and others, are represented, along with some of the leading present-day writers. A current picture book (using all of text and 90 percent of art) is reprinted monthly, and covers 19 to 21 pages. Book reviews are especially well done for the age group intended, and should tempt young readers to explore some of the new books. Short features of one to two pages include games, hobbies, play activities, puzzles and jokes. All material is well illustrated, in one color, and in some cases illustrations are reproduced from the original book. The digest format includes dull paper with a light green "eye ease" tint, and a specially designed binding which is intended to lie flat when open. Advertising in limited amounts is chiefly confined to offerings of Parents' Magazine Press. (L.O.)

Children's Playmate. 1929. 10/yr. $6. Rita A. Cooper. Children's Playmate Magazine, 1100 Waterway Blvd., Indianapolis, Ind. 46207. Illus., adv. Circ: 250,000. Vol. ends. Apr.

Indexed: IChildMag. *Aud:* Ejh.

Directed to ages 3 to 8, features the usual type of illustrated stories, poems and articles. There are games, and things to make and do, with some material submitted by young readers. The two–color illustrations are mediocre and show little or no relationship to what has come to be known as imaginative work for children. In no way a competitor to *Jack and Jill*, it is a fair second choice in school libraries. (L.O.)

Elizabethan. 1947. m. $6. Lewis Sheringham, Ashford Rd., Box 7, Staines, Middlesex, England. Illus., adv. Circ: 20,000. Sample. Vol. ends: Dec.

Indexed: IChildMag. *Aud:* Ejh.

A general English magazine for girls ages 10 to 17, it has definitely more possibilities for the girls in the lower age bracket. Anyone over 13 who reads *Seventeen* or any of the American teen magazines will find it uninteresting. Using somewhat the same approach as *American Girl*, it pays considerably more attention to current events than most periodicals of this type. The format is good; the writing style good to excellent. The problem for American girls is to relate to the material which is often entirely English-centered, right down to the vernacular and personalities. Only for large collections. (L.O.)

Golden Magazine. 1964. m. $6. Beth Thomas. Review Publishing Co., 1100 Waterway Blvd., Indianapolis, Ind. 46202. Illus. index, adv.

Indexed: IChildMag. *Aud:* Ejh.

Now a member of the *Child Life* and *Children's Playmate* group. Much improved for the change but it remains a cheerful magazine published for the sole purpose of providing a special form of reading matter for boys and girls from ages 9 to 13. It emphasizes different types of material: fiction, history, adventure, science, geography, things-to-do, and jokes and games. Colorful sketches by well-known illustrators enhance the pages. The "How-To" section runs the gamut from cooking fun to first lessons in French.

Gopher Historian. See History/States and Provinces Section.

Highlights for Children. 1946. 11/yr. $7.95. Dr. & Mrs. Garry C. Myers and Dr. Walter B. Barbe, 2300 W. Fifth Ave., Columbus, Ohio 43216. Index. Circ: 1,000,000. Sample. Vol. ends: Dec. 15.

Indexed: IChildMag. *Aud:* Ejh. *Jv:* V.

Edited by leading child specialists, educators, and scientists, this is to assist the preschool and elementary child to "gain in creativeness, ability to think and reason and to learn worthy ways of living." There is reading material suitable for all elementary levels in a wide variety of subject areas, including social studies, biographies, science, and literature. Games, tricks and teasers, word fun, party and craft ideas are aimed at stimulating thinking. Signed, informative articles by eminent scientists such as Dr. Donald Menzel of the Harvard College Observatory, Dr. Jack Myers of the University of Texas and Dr. Joel Hildebrand of the University of California; by prominent leaders such as Supreme Court Justice William Douglas and news commentator Walter Cronkite; and by educators such as Dr. Paul Witty make *Highlights* an up-to-date authoritative source of valuable information. There is no paid advertising. A reading guide for parents and teachers is an added feature. The Resource/Index issue (11th issue) contains special and regular editorial features, plus a pictured index to the calendar year. The sturdy format makes it a prime candidate for circulation, and the contents recommend it to most school libraries. (L.O.)

Humpty Dumpty's Magazine; magazine for little children. 1952. m. (except June and Aug.). $6. Thomas Roberts. Parents' Magazine Enterprises, 52 Vanderbilt Ave., New York, N.Y. 10017. Illus., adv. Circ: 1,379,111. Sample. Vol. ends: Dec.

Indexed: IChildMag. *Bk. rev:* 3–4, 500 words. *Aud:* Ejh.

Written and illustrated for children from 3 to 7 years of age, many consider this the best of the children's magazines primarily because it is a sincere effort to both entertain and educate. Stories, articles, and features are written to develop reading and vocabulary. Three to four book reviews averaging 500 words are done by Ingeborg Boudreau. Although printed on "eye ease" paper, the format is reminiscent of yesterday's newspaper; the illustrations are no better. On the plus side, the large type, the lack of advertisements (except for the publisher's products), and the pocket size make it attractive for the younger set. Content, though, is nothing more than can be found in most good children's story books readily available in libraries. A second choice for most libraries. (L.O.)

Illinois History. See History/States and Provinces Section.

Jack and Jill Magazine. 1938. m. $5.95. Nelle K. Bell. Jack and Jill Publishing Co., 1100 Waterway Blvd., Indianapolis, Ind. 46202. Illus., adv. Circ: 700,000. Sample. Vol. ends: Dec.

Indexed: IChildMag. *Aud:* Ejh.

A variety magazine with material presented on various levels to suit the reading ability and interests of children ages 5 to 12. Each issue contains six or seven stories and an equal number of articles, with a variation in type size and reading level from grades 1 to 6. Many single page items are included in each issue. Games, riddles and puzzles, projects, pictures features, jokes and contests serve the purpose of providing individual and group amusement. Some simple recipes are

usually included, perhaps suggested by the theme of one of the articles or stories. "Let's Discover America" is one of the best features, and describes points of interest which families might visit. Color photos for these articles are good, and well chosen. The series "My Father Is" and "My Mother Is" helps young boys and girls understand the finer facets of the American way of life. There are no book reviews. Illustrations throughout the magazine consist mainly of drawings and are colorful, generally good, and well arranged. (L.O.)

Kids. 1970. 10/yr. $5. Valentine Smith Co., Dept TB-1, 777 Third Ave., New York, N.Y. 10017. Illus. Sample.

Aud: Ejh. *Jv:* V.

A magazine written and illustrated by children, aged 5 to 13, from all over the country, for each other. Issues examined included original fiction, poetry, plays, and articles ranging in subject matter from hobbies to pollution. There are sections on things to make and do. Illustrations are reproduced in black and white and full color, many are full page. The magazine is printed on dull white paper with easy-to-read type. An exciting new addition to the children's magazine field. It is just what a magazine for children ought to be! A must for libraries. (Note: The original editors, Robinson and Kahn, in late 1971 sold the magazine to Valentine Smith Co. The new firm has decided to accept advertising, but promises not to touch the original format idea.) (L.O.)

The Open Home. 1971. m. $5.95. Sara Stein. C. Carter Smith, Jr., Media Projects Inc., 159 W. 53rd St., New York, N.Y. 10019. Illus., index. Vol. ends: Dec.

Aud: Ejh (to be used by parents with children).

This "mini-magazine" consisting of six pages is the creation of Media Projects Incorporated, a workshop of educators, writers, and designers specializing in preschool education. It is a learning package for children, newborn to six years old, and their parents. Each issue offers articles, activities, and a picture game. Every other month, the package will include a seven-inch LP record, a poster or a fold-out game. An index accompanies issue No. 12, and slipcases for storage purposes will be available for $1.00. The articles are written in an easy to understand style, and the activities are fun, requiring no special skills or equipment—just willingness.

Carter Smith, the publisher, believes that ". . . the home should benefit from the same open concept that is employed in Open Classrooms—learning by discovery rather than rote, being aware of a child's particular interest, adjusting to his pace." The issues examined reflect this philosophy. Not only parents but anyone working with preschool children and their parents should find this mini-magazine quite helpful. (L.O.)

Plays. See Theater Section.

Ranger Rick's Nature Magazine. 1967. 10/yr. Membership, $6. Trudy Dye Farrand. National Wildlife Federation, 1412 16th St., N.W., Washington, D.C. 20036. Illus., adv. Circ: 400,000. Sample. Vol. ends: Dec.

Indexed: IChildMag. *Bk. rev:* 4, 150 words. *Aud:* Ejh. *Jv:* V.

The children's version of *National Wildlife* designed to give boys and girls a program of activities, adventures, and knowledge which will help them appreciate and enjoy nature. The color photography and illustrations draw the eye to the information-packed pages. Stories and articles, games and puzzles are of graded difficulty and interest levels. The type sizes are also adjusted to the age of the reader. "Ranger Rick's Book Nook" selects and reviews books each month which may be purchased through the magazine at a discount from publishers' list prices. These too are chosen with differing ages and reading abilities in mind. A good magazine for elementary schools and children in that age group.

Sesame Street. 1970. m. 10/yr. $3. Jane O'Connor. Children's Television Workshop, 1 Lincoln Plaza, New York, N.Y. 10023. Illus., Index. Circ: 650,000. Sample. Vol. ends: July.

Aud: Ejh.

Intended for the preschool child, the magazine has the same educational goals as the Sesame Street television program and features characters such as Big Bird, teaching the same things being taught on the show. Each issue has a big four-color fold-out poster, stories, activities, and a parents' guide section. The text is in English and Spanish. Since the format of the magazine encourages children to learn by writing, coloring, or cutting, it is best for home or classroom use. (L.O.)

Texas Historian. See History/States and Provinces Section.

Vacation Fun; summer magazine for leisure reading and for pleasure. 1961. w. (June–Aug). $1. Linda Beech. Scholastic Magazines Inc., 50 W. 44th St., New York, N.Y. 10036. Illus. Circ: 100,000.

Aud: Ejh.

One of three summer magazines issued by Scholastic, this is a 16-page periodical for grades 3 and 4 and includes the usual type of material featured in classroom newspapers published by the same firm. More emphasis is placed on "fun," less on learning, but the style, format, and approach are about the same. The magazine does have useful games, a few rather pedestrian stories, and suggestions on where and what to do around the home.

Two other periodicals of the same type are published by Scholastic for the summer months: *Merry-Go-Round,* for grades 1 to 2, and *Summertime,* for grades 5 to 7. Parents may be grateful to be introduced to one more ploy to keep the children happy during the long summer, but librarians can skip with ease. (See also Scholastic Magazines entry in Education/Elementary and Secondary Section).

Wee Wisdom. 1893. m. $4. Thomas Hopper. Unity School of Christianity, Unity Village, Mo. 64063. Illus. Circ: 135,000. Sample. Vol. ends: July. *Microform:* UM.

Indexed: IChildMag. *Aud:* Ejh.

While the magazine is subtitled "a character-building magazine" and is issued by a religious organization, there is a minimum of moralizing and religious teaching. Format and content are focused on the third grade reading level with subject matter that will appeal to both younger and slightly older children. It is one of the better children's magazines, combining four to six stories, poems, and various things to do in a single issue. The illustrations done in two colors are fair, but no worse than most in this genre. Braille subscriptions are sent free to the blind.

Weewish Tree. See Indians (American) Section.

World Traveler. 1969. 12 issues, Oct.–May (2 issues Oct., Nov., Feb., and Mar.). $2.50. Bettie Loux Donley. Alexander Graham Bell Assn. for the Deaf, Inc., 1537 35th St, N.W., Washington, D.C. 20007. Illus. Sample.

Aud: Ga, Hs, Ejh. *Jv:* V.

A brightly colored, well-illustrated new kind of publication designed for "teenagers with language handicaps who are reading at about the third grade level." Text and illustrations adapted from the *National Geographic School Bulletin* and *National Geographic Magazine.* Each issue is devoted to one subject with a crossword puzzle comprehension quiz at the end. An important contribution to the disadvantaged reader.

The Yorker. See History/States and Provinces Section.

Young Miss (Formerly: *Calling All Girls*). 1955. 10/yr. $6. Rubie Saunders. Parents' Magazine Enterprises, Inc., 52 Vanderbilt Ave., New York, N.Y. 10017. Illus., adv. Circ: 500,000. Sample. Vol. ends: Dec.

Indexed: IChildMag. *Bk. rev:* 4–10, 500 words. *Aud:* Ejh.

A compact, low keyed magazine for girls up to 14. Regular features include fashions, food, beauty tips, personality articles, and a fiction novelette. There are also articles on careers, self-help (getting along with siblings, parents, etc.), and parties. "Letters to the Editor" is a popular column in which the reader tells her problem and a possible solution is given. Four to ten book reviews, averaging 500 words, are done by Ingeborg Boudreau. There are also movie reviews. Advertising is tasteful and oriented to the group it serves. (L.O.)

RELIGIOUS MAGAZINES FOR THE CHILD. Some of the largest circulation children's magazines in America are published by various religious groups. Few if any of these find their way into a public or school library. The desire to separate state from church is commendable, but there seems no reason not to have some of the better magazines in a library—particularly when an effort is made to strike a balance between faiths. The lack of really first rate children's magazines in the private sector, coupled with an increased interest of some teenagers in the Jesus Movement, would warrant serious consideration of a few of the better religious children's magazines in a collection.

The outlook is obviously biased, but more often than not, it is equally sophisticated. These days there is considerably more emphasis on the good life via intellectual growth and imagination than blind, fundamental acceptance. This shows in the articles and stories. As the managing editor of *Friend* put it, her magazine "emphasizes wholesome virtues, but avoids preachiness. The magazine includes games and activities, book reviews, stories, and poems . . . We are happy to receive and publish contributions from children regardless of their church affiliations, and welcome manuscripts from all writers." Much the same is true of other magazines. What follows, in alphabetical order by title, is a list of some of the better magazines. All publishers are willing to send samples, and it is strongly suggested that a library ask for sample copies before coming to any decision.

Adventure. 1962. w. $2.75. Muriel F. Blackwell. Southern Baptist Convention, Sunday School Board, 127 Ninth Ave., N. Nashville, Tenn. 37203. Circ: 212,000.

Baptist. Ages 9–12. A tabloid. Articles, short stories, poetry; all at a realistic level with little emphasis on religion per se. Some photos and line drawings. Good to excellent writing.

Climb. 1938. w. $2.25. William A. White. Warner Press, Box 2499, Anderson, Ind. 46011. Circ: 19,000.

General Christian. Ages 10–12. Articles, some short stories, poetry. Photos. Strong on Christian living as found in sports, home, and school. Fair writing.

Explore. 1969. w. $1.85. Rosalie Logan. Christian Board of Publications, Box 179, St. Louis, Mo. 63166. Circ: 20,000.

General Christian. Ages 6–8. Articles on how-to-do-it, humor. Some stories, poetry. Fair to good writing.

Five/Six. 1964. w. $2.50. Martha Wagner. Methodist Publishing House, 201 Eighth Ave. S., Nashville, Tenn. 37203. Circ: 350,000.

Methodist. Grades 5–6. More of a religious overtone than in the others. Good articles and fiction. Some biography. Writing is fair.

Friend. 1971. m. $3. Lucile C. Reading. Church of Jesus Christ of Latter-Day Saints, 79 S. State St., Salt Lake City, Utah. 84111. Circ: 175,000.

Mormon. Ages 4–12. Articles and stories. Good format and illustrations. Some articles on Church history. Writing good to excellent.

Junior Trails. 1926. w. $1.25. Dorothy B. Morris. General Council of the Assemblies of God, 1445 Boonville, Springfield, Mo. 65802. Circ: 123,700.

General Christian. Grades 4–6. Articles, fiction, some photographs. Tends to moralize a bit more than others. Writing style is fair.

Young Judaean. 1910. m. (Nov.-June). $1.75. Doris B. Gold. National Young Judaea, 116 W. 14th St., New York, N.Y. 10011. Circ: 8,500.

Jewish. Ages 8–13. Strong on modern nonpolitical Israeli features. Some fiction and poetry. Text in English, Hebrew and Yiddish. Writing good.

About Children

Academic Therapy. 1965. q. $6. John I. Arena. Academic Therapy Publications, Inc. 1549 Fourth St., San Rafael, Calif., 94901. Illus., adv. Circ: 6,000. Sample. Vol. ends: Summer.

Bk. rev: 2, 1½ pages, signed. *Aud:* Ac, Hs, Ejh.

Directed to an understanding of children who have problems with reading, learning, and communication. "Attention is focused on the inefficient learner who, although intellectually capable, is unable to achieve academically by traditional educational methods." The authors are psychologists, doctors, and teachers. Each 100 or so page issue is divided into three parts: four or five scholarly articles, about as many practical ideas from the field, and a number of departments. The Fall 1971 issue had an article on the school library. For classroom and special teachers, parents, and educational therapists.

Adolescence. 1966. q. $10. William Kroll. Libra Publns., Inc., Box 165, 391 Willets Rd., Roslyn Heights, L.I., N.Y. 11577. Illus., adv. Circ: 3,500. Sample. Vol. ends: Winter. Microform: UM.

Bk. rev: 20, 250 words. *Aud:* Ac, Sa.

Primarily directed to the experienced psychologist, psychiatrist, and sociologist who is involved with the education and the problems of adolescents. Articles are well documented, for the most part represent original research or observation, and are usually illustrated with necessary charts. While an interdisciplinary journal for the specialist, the better educated parent and the interested teacher will find much here of value. The wide scope guarantees an interest in this unique periodical in larger psychology, sociology and education collections of academic libraries.

Baby Talk. 1935. m. $4. Eve Hammerschmidt. Leam Corp., 149 Madison Ave., New York, N.Y. 10016. Illus., adv. Circ: 1,100,000.

Aud: Ga.

One of some half dozen baby magazines, but differs from them all in that it is the only one with a paid circulation. All others, from *Mothers-to-be* to *Young Mother*, are free, usually sent to mothers in the mail or via the doctor's office. *Baby Talk* is a regular magazine, not simply an advertising vehicle. It includes informative, accurate, and well–written articles for parents of babies and children up to three years of age. Also, of course, there are articles for the expectant mother. Many photographs, short features, and even reports of material published in pediatric journals are included. All in all, the best of its type. See also *Mothers-to-be* for more information on this genre.

Child Development. 1930. q. $25. W. E. Jeffrey. Univ. of Chicago Press, 5801 Ellis Ave., Chicago, Ill. 60637. Circ: 6,000. Sample. Vol. ends: Dec. Reprint: Kraus.

Indexed: BioAb, EdI, IMed, PsyAb. *Aud:* Ac, Sa.

The basic scholarly journal in the field of children, this is issued by the Society for Research in Child Development, Inc. It is devoted to publishing original research articles which are well documented, often rather technical. The authors come from the fields of sociology, medicine, psychology, and psychiatry. The result is an impressive journal, but only for the advanced student and professional.

Child Psychiatry and Human Development. 1970. q. $20 (Individuals $15). John C. Duffy. Behavioral Publns., 2852 Broadway, New York, N.Y. 10025. Illus., adv. Circ: 1,000. Sample. Vol. ends: Summer. Refereed.

Bk. rev: 3, 250 words, signed. *Aud:* Ac, Sa.

A technical journal for specialists in child psychiatry, pediatrics, psychology, social science, and human development. Such articles as "Maternal perception of the neonate as related to development," or the "Hyperkinetic Syndrome" indicate the reader must have command of a special vocabulary to get through the 58 or so pages.

Child Welfare. 1920. m. (Oct–July). $6 (Students $4). Carl Schoenberg. Child Welfare League of America, 67 Irving Place, New York, N.Y. 10003. Adv., index. Circ: 9,000. Sample. Vol. ends: Dec. Microform: UM. Reprint: Kraus, Abrahams.

Bk. rev: 2–3, 2–3 pages, signed. *Aud:* Ac, Ga.

Concerned with the welfare of children; with practice methods, research, and education as they relate to child welfare services; and with issues of social policy that have bearing on them. Its purpose is to extend knowledge on the welfare of children and to give information for the improvement of practice and services for children. Each issue contains a variety of articles written by social workers, psychiatrists, and social scientists. In addition, there are editorials, book reviews, reports on agencies' practices throughout the country, classified personnel openings, and letters from readers.

Childhood Education. 1924. m. (Oct.–May). $12. Monroe D. Cohen. Assn. for Childhood Education Intl., 3615 Wisconsin Ave., N.W., Washington, D.C. 20016. Illus., index, adv. Circ: 50,000. Sample. Vol. ends: May. Microform: UM. Reprint: Johnson.

Indexed: CIJE, EdI. *Bk. rev:* 15–20, 200 words, signed. *Aud:* Ga, Ac, Ejh. *Jv:* V.

Directed to both parent and teacher of the child from pre-nursery school through the elementary grades (i.e. infancy through early adolescence) and written in language understandable by layman and professional alike. Generally each issue is devoted in part to a single theme, e.g., Head Start, Outdoor Education, Parents and Educators. The tone is liberal, the style relatively popular, the content accurate and pragmatic. As the emphasis is on child development, equal attention is given to problems faced daily by the teacher or parent either in the classroom or in the home. Yet it is not parochial, and a major asset of the magazine is proper emphasis on international developments in education. Including short book reviews for children and adults and data on magazine articles, it is an ideal all around education/childhood magazine for almost any size or type of library.

Children. See Government Magazines/United Nations and Selected Foreign Section.

Exceptional Children. 1934. m. (Oct.–May). $10. Grace T. Warfield. Council for Exceptional Children, 1411 S. Jefferson Davis Highway, Jefferson Plaza Bldg., Suite 900, Arlington, Va. 22202. Illus., index, adv. Circ: 45,000. Sample. Vol. ends: May. Reprint: Abrahams.

Indexed: EdI, PsyAb. *Bk. rev:* 5–8, 500 words, signed. *Aud:* Ac, Hs, Ejh.

Covers not only the bright child and his educational problems, but is concerned with any exceptional child, i.e., handicapped psychologically or physiologically. Experienced educators and teachers contribute articles on planning curriculum, classroom hints, organization of programs, and report on current developments in all areas; also included is information on new teaching aids, news notes, a calendar of events, and some book reviews. While primarily for the educator, the journal should be introduced to parents of above average education who have exceptional children of one type or another. See also *Teaching Exceptional Children.*

The Exceptional Parent. 1971. bi-m. $12. Ed. bd., Box 101, Back Bay Annex, Boston, Mass. 02117. Illus. Sample.

Aud: Ga, Ac.

Subtitled "practical guidance for the parents of exceptional children," this is a handsome, professionally edited 40-page information bulletin. As "an estimated 10 to 20 percent of all children in this country suffer from chronic handicapping conditions," the magazine has a wide audience. (Exceptional in this case means handicapped, not genius.) In an early editorial the purpose of the magazine was outlined: "We will provide a wide range of practical information about the human day-to-day problems you face as well as the long range issues that arise in planning for the future life of your child and family—issues ranging from how to buy shoes to how to plan your estate; from how to deal with bruises and cuts to how to select and work with the most specialized experts. Our challenge is to provide you with useful information. We are aware that each article will not be relevant to each of you. However, we believe that parents of children with widely different disabilities have a great deal in common. Nonetheless, we will try to balance each issue of the magazine with a wide range of subjects."

The purpose is more than fulfilled, and the magazine is well worth the price. It should be found in almost every public and academic library—certainly should be brought to the attention of parents with exceptional children.

√ *Gifted Child Quarterly.* 1957. q. $20. Ann F. Issacs. National Assn. for Gifted Children, 8080 Springvalley Dr., Cincinnati, Ohio 45236. Illus., index, adv. Circ: 3,000.

Indexed: EdI, PsyAb. *Aud:* Ac, Hs, Ejh.

A scholarly approach to the gifted child, i.e., of above-average intelligence, imagination, etc. The well-documented articles explore current activities in the field, putting particular emphasis on how to develop new teaching techniques. While of value to teachers in elementary through high schools, it is more appropriately defined in terms of psychologists and teachers of education.

√ *International Journal of Early Childhood.* 1969. bi-a. Membership (Nonmembers $5.50). Anne McKenna. Universitetsforlaget, Blindern, Oslo 3, Norway. Circ: 1,500. Sample.

Bk. rev: Various number, length. *Aud:* Ac.

A publication of OMEP—Organisation Mondiale pour l'Education Prescolaire. "Its purpose is to publish in popularized, readable form the results of research and experiences in child psychology, preschool education, medical and social work for preschool children, architecture, town planning, etc." In fact, it covers every aspect of children. And while a good deal of the material is technical, it is certainly of interest and value to anyone involved with young children (preschool and elementary school age). Should be considered for the professional collection in elementary school libraries, and is a must in academic schools of education and academic centers of psychology, social planning, etc.

Mothers-to-be/American Baby. 1960. m. Free. Judith Nolte. American Baby, Inc., 10 E. 52nd St., New York, N.Y. 10022. Illus., adv. Circ: 1,083,000.

Bk. rev: Notes. *Aud:* Ga.

One of the controlled circulation (i.e., free) baby magazines. It is edited by a woman, has four or five basic articles on baby care, two or three pieces on fashions, and a number of features and departments from question and answer columns to notes on new booklets. The advertising is not objectionable, and the format is quite acceptable. As it is free (copies are sent mothers by direct mail) a library might try a few copies.

Others in this field include: *Mother's Manual* (1939. bi-m. $2. Free to most. Box 243, Franklin Lakes, N.J. 07417. Circ: 900,000); *Baby Care; Expecting* (1940. 1967. q. Free. Both published by Parents' Magazine Enterprises, Inc., 52 Vanderbilt Ave., New York, N.Y. 10017. Circ. for each: 700,000 to 800,000); *Redbook's Young Mother* (1968. a. Free. McCall Publishing Co., 230 Park Ave., New York, N.Y. 10017. Circ: 3,100,000). While not all of these are suitable for a library, they are of interest to any parent or expectant parent. As they are free, they might be called to the attention of mothers and fathers, particularly in so-called disadvantaged neighborhoods.

√ *Teaching Exceptional Children.* 1968. q. $5. Council for Exceptional Children, Jefferson Plaza, Suite 900, 1411 S. Jefferson Davis Highway, Arlington, Va. 22202.

Indexed: CIJE, ExChAb. *Aud:* Ac, Hs, Ejh.

Primarily a journal for the teacher of the gifted or handicapped. Articles are technical, well documented and deal with teacher-oriented aspects of the subject, from diagnostic techniques to instructional methods and materials. Several features are devoted to the exchange of ideas and questions and answers by teachers.

CHINA AND ASIA

Basic Periodicals

CHINA. Ejh: *China Pictorial;* Hs: *Understanding China Newsletter, China Pictorial;* Ga: *Understanding China Newsletter, Peking Review;* Jc: *Understanding China Newsletter, China Quarterly;* Ac: *China Quarterly, Asia Translation Series, Clearinghouse Translation Series, Peking Review, Understanding China Newsletter.*

ASIA. Ejh: *Japan Illustrated;* Hs: *Japan Illustrated, Orientations;* Ga: *Japan Illustrated, Orientations;* Jc: *Asia, Bulletin of Concerned Asian Scholars;* Ac: *Asia, Bulletin of Concerned Asian Scholars, Pacific Research.*

China

In view of America's recognition of the People's Republic of China, the following is a special section to help libraries do much of the same for their users. The need for accurate information on China is often expressed, but perhaps no better than in an article by Benjamin Weiner in The *New York Times* on October 31, 1971 (F-5): "A complaint voiced frequently by United States corporations taking their first serious look at . . . China is that there is hardly any information available that permits them to decide whether there is a potential for their products and services. In fact, there is a wealth of material available directly from China and elsewhere that will allow most companies to come to a valid decision as to whether there are realistic and immediate markets for them in the People's Republic." Well, what is good enough for American business, should be good enough for the conservative (possibly a businessman, himself) who may complain about a special section for China.

The other China, on Taiwan, is included here. Most of the magazines from Peking may be ordered through a jobber. Those who have problems may wish to contact China Books & Periodicals, 2929 24th St., San Francisco, Calif. 94110. They seem to handle the Peking subscriptions directly. The store also will send libraries a free copy of *Imported Books from China in English, 1970–1971.* Under broad subject headings, it includes hundreds of titles, most of which are briefly annotated. There is, also, a short list of periodicals and recordings. All items, unless noted, are published by the Foreign Language Press of Peking.

Asian Translation Series (Journals of translations). International Arts and Science Press, Inc. 901 N. Broadway, White Plains, N.Y. 10603. (Publisher will send sample copies.)

Chinese Economic Studies. 1967. q. $60 ($15 to individuals). George C. Wang.

Chinese Education. 1967. q. $60 ($15 to individuals). Ursula K. Springer.

Chinese Law and Government. 1967. q. $60 ($15 to individuals). James D. Seymour.

Chinese Sociology and Anthropology. 1968. q. $60 ($15 to individuals). Signey L. Greenblatt.

Chinese Studies in History. 1967. q. $60 ($15 to individuals). Li Yu-nig.

Chinese Studies in Philosophy. 1970. q. $60 ($15 to individuals). Chung-ying Cheng.

Averaging 75 to 100 pages and four to five articles translated from Chinese mainland journals, newspapers, and collections of articles in book form, the object of this translation service is "to present the more important Chinese studies . . . in the light of the interest of those who are professionally concerned with it." The translations are accurate, free of any tampering or bias. The selection seems objective, and an effort is made to devote a given issue to a central problem, i.e., the whole of one number of the philosophy translation journal is turned over to "On Kuan Chung's System of Thought." While timeliness is not a major concern, it is considered. In the education issue examined, the translations are from current sources. Conversely, in other journals the translations may go back as far as 1928 and the early 1950s and 1960s. The emphasis is on translation of material which has lasting value for research, not necessarily for current ephemeral discussions. The library subscribing to any of these in hopes of keeping posted on day-to-day activities in China will be disappointed. The format is good, and original sources are clearly designated. The institutional price is high, automatically putting it in a category for only large research libraries. Libraries with limited budgets might care to bring this series to the attention of concerned individuals who can subscribe for much less. See also *Clearinghouse Translation series.*

Bridge Magazine. 1971. bi-m. $10 (Individuals $5). Frank Ching, Margarett Loke. Basement Workshop Inc., 54 Elizabeth St., New York, N.Y. 10013. Illus.

Bk. rev: 1–2, 250–500 words, signed. *Aud:* Ga, Ac, Hs.

Following the path of several Asian "little" magazines and newspapers (e.g., *Gidra, Getting Together,* and *Literature East/West,* to name three), this is a new effort to "bridge" the Western and Asian cultures. Primarily put together for and by young people, it is published and "written by an independent, nonprofit organization of Chinese professionals and students on the East Coast." The coverage is universal, e.g., articles have discussed the Chinese community in Britain, the reaction of Far Eastern students to life in America, and the life and times of the overseas Chinese. Most of the emphasis is on the young Chinese-American student—particularly as expressed in his own poetry, art, and short miscellaneous prose pieces. The magazine appears to avoid politics, to concentrate on cultural and social activities. The supporters are activists in the sense that they are pushing Asian-American programs in the schools. There are some excellent book and magazine reviews. A good magazine for almost any library, particularly one where there is an interest in China and the Chinese-American.

China Journal. 1969. m. $42. East Asia Publns., 711 Regent House, Queen's Rd., Central, Hong Kong.

Aud: Ac. Jv: C.

A processed 40 to 50 page report on current activities in the People's Republic prepared in Hong Kong by unidentified editors. The operation is definitely pro Mao, and while articles are signed they represent more propaganda than fact, at least in historical and social items. Where the mimeographed magazine is useful is in its economic and trade reports. It is not worth $42, and it would be at the bottom of most acquisition lists.

China News Analysis. 1953. w. $80. Box 13225, Hong Kong. Index.

Aud: Ac.

Hong Kong is the place where the Western world listens in on Communist China, and one of the products of this activity is *China News Analysis.* It is a brief weekly newsletter—only about seven pages long—which contains one or more unsigned articles based on Communist Chinese sources. The articles may be on any aspect of China—political, cultural, economic, etc.—or on other areas where China has an interest, such as North Vietnam. They are well written and well documented, and should be of interest to anyone concerned with China. The usefulness of this newsletter to students is greatly increased by a subject and name index which appears in every twenty-fifth issue. (A.M.)

China Notes. 1962. q. $2. Donald E. MacInnis. China Program, East Asia Dept, Div. of Overseas Ministries, National Council of Churches, 475 Riverside Dr., New York, N.Y. 10027. Index. Microform: UM.

Bk. rev: Notes. *Aud:* Ac, Ga.

Primarily reports on the missions and missionaries who carried on Protestant teachings in the People's Republic. Also involved with problems of religion in China, particularly in relation to religious freedom. The book reviews are brief but critical, and there is some reviewing of films and recordings. The editors take a remarkably objective viewpoint, and the whole can be recommended for not only the large religious collection, but for anyone attempting to understand all sides of China.

China Pictorial. 1951. m. $3. Guozi Shudian, Box 399 Hsitan Bldg., Peking, People's Republic of China. Illus.

Aud: Ac, Ga, Hs.

China produces a number of magazines aimed at foreign consumption, and this is the major one. Each issue is approximately 50 pages long, with about 15 short articles. The focus is mainly on China, but there are also some articles on people and events in other Communist countries, such as North Vietnam. But it is the illustrations which are the really important part of this magazine. They are large, they are numerous, and some are in color. Since it is intended for a general foreign audience, the content tends to be nonscholarly and very favorable to China. A sample of the contents of a typical issue includes: "Photographs by Revolutionary Amateurs," "Women Bridge Builders," and "The North Vietnamese Army and People Are Fighting Valiantly." The information content of this magazine may not be great, but is one of the few

sources available for recent pictures of life in mainland China. (A.M.)

China Quarterly. 1960. q. $10 (Students $5). David Wilson. Contemporary China Inst. of the School of Oriental and African Studies, London Univ. Subs. to: Research Publns. Ltd., Victoria Hall, East Greenwich, London SE10 ORF, England. Index, adv. Circ: 5,000. Sample. Vol. ends: Oct./Dec.

Indexed: PAIS. *Bk. rev:* 10–15, 500–750 words, signed. *Aud:* Ac, Ga. *Jv:* V.

An international journal for the study of contemporary China. The bulk of each issue contains academic articles by China scholars, but, reflecting greater interest in travel opportunities to China, it also carries first-hand Reports from China, of interest to the general reader. Almost all new publications about China are reviewed in the book section, including some Soviet titles and (in a new feature) books published in the People's Republic of China. The final section, the Quarterly Chronicle and Documentation, consists of an account of domestic developments and China's foreign relations over the previous three-month period, mainly based on Chinese reports.

China Reconstructs. 1952. m. $3. Ed. bd. Guozi Shudian, Box 399, Hsitan Bldg., Peking 37, People's Republic of China. Illus.

Aud: Ga, Ac, Hs, Ejh.

Another of the illustrated monthlies (cf. *China Pictorial*) which attempts to literally illustrate the path of progress in China. It has a more political overtone then *China Pictorial*, yet takes the same general approach. There are stories on industry, schools, the arts, even the army. But all are on a relatively superficial level. The primary interest is in the pictures which are good to excellent. *China Pictorial* is preferable, although larger libraries will want both. Note: With some explanation this might be used in grade schools and high schools. The English is simple, the type large, and the pictures suitable. Even a child with an elementary reading ability should be able to handle it.

China Trade and Economic Newsletter. 1955. m. $24. British Council for the Promotion of Intl. Trade, Monitor Consultants, 35 John St., London, WC1, England.

Bk. rev: Notes. *Aud:* Ga, Ac.

A 12 to 16 page newsletter which is of primary interest to British businessmen and economists. It publishes articles on trade with Mainland China in terms of British experience, particularly as reported by businessmen dealing with the Chinese. Statistics, views and comments are quite objective. One of the best, although costly, reports on doing business with China.

China Trade Report. 1963. m. $50. P. H. M. Jones. Kayser Sung, Far Eastern Economic Review, Box 160, Hong Kong.

Aud: Ac, Ga. *Jv:* C.

Another processed Hong Kong monthly similar to *China Journal*. The point of view is considerably more objective, but the amount of actual information is almost as limited. It is a roundup of statistics and data from Mainland sources for the purpose of assisting businessmen in trading with China. From time to time some valuable information is given, but it is not worth $50.

China's Foreign Trade. 1966. bi-m. $3. China Council for the Promotion of Intl. Trade. Guozi Shudian, Box 399, Hisitan Bldg., Peking 37, People's Republic of China. Illus., adv.

Aud: Ga.

An official government publication which points up the benefits of trading with the People's Republic. Unlike many of the other government-sponsored magazines, this is relatively free of propaganda. It is useful for current background information on standard trade matters and has some reports on industrial development. Note: Query the publisher before subscribing. By early 1972 rumored change in title and purpose.

China's Medicine (Formerly: ***Chinese Medical Journal***). 1966. m. $11. Guozi Shudian, Box 399, Hisitan Bldg., Peking 37, People's Republic of China.

Aud: Ac.

In view of aroused interest in all aspects of Chinese medicine, this is a particularly valuable English language journal from Peking. The articles, by experienced doctors and teachers, are at two levels: (1) those dealing with the social aspects of bringing medicine to all people; (2) those dealing with techniques and findings in medical sciences. Most emphasis, though, is on the first purpose. The articles tend to report on health work and advances in medical services delivered to the countryside. Given this dimension, the magazine is as much of interest to the socially aware layman as to the professional doctor. There is considerable propaganda here for the works of Mao, but above and beyond that the material is useful.

Chinese Culture. 1957. q. $7. Chang Chi-yun. Inst. for Advanced Chinese Studies, Box 12, Yang Ming Shan, Taiwan. Index, adv.

Aud: Ac.

Published in English, a Taiwan-based literary magazine of some 120 poorly printed pages. Contributors are mostly from Taiwan University; a few are American based. Coverage moves from religion and art to fiction and poetry. There is a minimum of political material. On the whole a scholarly, esoteric magazine for the subject specialist.

Chinese Literature. Litterature Chinoise. 1951. m. $3. Mao Tun. Guozi Shudian, Box 399, Hisitan Bldg., Peking 37, People's Republic of China.

Aud: Ac, Ga.

A general cultural magazine, not one limited to literature. It seems about equally divided between creative writing (stories, poems, and criticism) and reports on the benefits of the Cultural Revolution. The material tends to be semipopular. As the publisher puts it "articles on the experience of China's worker-peasant-soldier writers and artists and literary and art workers in putting into practice Mao Tse-tung's thought on literature and art." The news notes which report on current activities in Chinese art and literature are excellent, and some of the historical pieces are fine. The drawback is the heavy reliance on spreading cheer and good faith via the arts, i.e., somewhat analogous to *Partisan Review* having a free hand, but ultimately being under the supervision of a Vice President Agnew. (*Note:* The magazine appears as a quarterly in French, but this is essentially the same as the monthly English edition, only a trifle larger.)

Clearinghouse Translations Series. Clearinghouse for Federal Scientific and Technical Information, U.S. Dept. of Commerce, Springfield, Va. 22151.

> *Translations from China Mainland Press.* 1970. w. $130. *Translations of Political and Sociological Information on Communist China; Translations on Communist China's Food and Agriculture; Translations on Communist China's Industry and Materials; Translations on Communist China's Management, Trade and Finance; Translations from Hung-Ch'i (Red Flag).*

The U.S. government supplies a number of excellent translation services of the People's Republic of China's newspapers, magazines, and documents. These vary in price, frequency, and operational procedures. The most useful for the general large academic or public library collection is the first, i.e., *Translations from China Mainland Press*, which consists of numerous parts (a) weekly selection from various daily newspapers; (b) a monthly selection of articles from nontechnical magazines; (c) monographs based on research into given subject areas in the Chinese press; and (d) a quarterly subject index. Interested libraries are advised to write the Clearinghouse for details. (Price, frequency, and items were in a state of change in early 1972, and there is some indication the service is to be considerably expanded.)

Current Scene; developments in Mainland China. 2–3/month. Price not given. Chung Shun Bldg. 13 Gordon Rd., Hong Kong.

Aud: Ac, Ga. *Jv:* V.

A newsletter of 24 to 30 pages which includes a lead article, usually by a scholar, and brief reports on activities in Mainland China, e.g., "Chinese Communist party provincial committees," "New Policy on popular books," and a "Chronolog" which outlines major events of the previous month. The reports have tended to be a trifle biased against the Communists, but no more so than what one might find about the liberals in, say, *U.S. News and World Report*. An apparent honest effort is made to report all sides. Topics covered range from history and politics to economics and philosophy. Of the newsletters coming out of Hong Kong this is one of the best, one of the more reliable. (No price is given, but apparently it is modest.)

Getting Together/Wor Kuen. 1970. m. $5. Chicago and East: 24 Market St., New York, N.Y. 10002. West of Chicago: 850 Kearny St., San Francisco, Calif. 94108. Illus., adv.

A militant Chinese-American tabloid which represents the young American-born Chinese in New York, San Francisco, and points between. The paper is opposed to the Vietnam war, is for child care centers, health care housing, and a fair shake for all, but particularly for the Chinese and those who are members of, or related to, the third world movement. Closely allied with other groups such as the Black Panthers and the Young Lords, it supports close alliance with the Chinese Communist Party. The tone is militant, the format fair to good, but the spirit is all together. One half of each issue is in English, the other half (apparently a repeat of most of the English material) is in Chinese. As the first of its kind in this country, the paper deserves support from libraries serving the Chinese, or for that matter any minority group.

Gidra: monthly of the Asian American community. 1969. m. $5 (individuals $2.50). Box 18046, Los Angeles, Calif. 90018. Illus. Sample.

Bk. rev: Various number, length. *Aud:* Ac, Ga.

Like blacks, Chicanos, Indians, and other ethnic minorities, Asian-Americans have abundant reason to proclaim and revitalize their identity, to assail a system that has sought to emasculate if not destroy them. This tabloid effectively voices their new consciousness, simultaneously uncovering a century of wrongs committed by the white majority and enunciating a determination to make the future at once different from and better than the past. A "People's Page" prints original verse by Asians sensitively probing both their heritage and present situation; feature articles variously limn aspects of Ameriasian history (e.g., "Atrocities against Chinese amerikans," "Anti-Asian legislations"), explore contemporary problems (e.g., drug abuse, suicide, the corporate-military stranglehold on Hawaii, ghettoization, sweat shops, unemployment, self–hate), and chronicle developments within the momentous "Amerasian Movement": community organization, social programs, political action, legal aid, Asian Studies, employment counseling, etc. Photos and drawings visually interpret the Amerasian scene. Because of demography, the focus is on the Western states and Hawaii, but much of the material is of general interest and relevance. For all Asian and ethnic studies collections, every library serving Amerasian communities, and public as well as university facilities attempting to fairly represent all segments of the U.S. population. (S.B.)

Issues and Studies; a monthly journal of Communist problems and world affairs. 1964. m. $12. Ed. Bd. Wu Chen-Tsai, Box 1189, Taipei, Taiwan, Republic of China.

Indexed: CurrCont. *Bk. rev:* 1, length varies. *Aud:* Ac, Ga.

Essentially this is a reflection of Nationalist China's preoccupation with Communist China, and it shows the Nationalists' anti–Communist point of view. There are five or six articles in each issue concerning various aspects of Communist China past and present—the Communist party, social policies, foreign affairs, economic developments, etc. The articles are more or less scholarly, and are often written by professors. In each issue there is also a "Chronicle of Events" section which briefly lists recent events in Communist China, and a "Current Affairs" section which contains five or six short articles dealing with significant recent events. A typical issue also includes: a translation of an address by Chiang Kai-shek, a book review, and a short biographical article on a prominent Chinese Communist. Any library that intends to have a collection on China should consider this magazine. (A.M.)

Peking Review. 1958. w. $4. Pai Wan Chuang. Guozi Shudian, Box 399 Hsitan Bldg. Peking 37, People's Republic of China.

Indexed: PAIS. *Aud:* Ac, Ga, Hs.

For foreigners who prefer more reading material and fewer pictures than in *China Pictorial*, Peking has thoughtfully provided this weekly journal. It is about 25 pages long and contains six to eight articles and translations of documents, plus a number of shorter items. These are divided into three sections: "The Week," "Round the World," and "Socialist China in Progress," which include more or less newsworthy items on current events, political developments in other countries, and China's economic and other successes. The longer articles deal with a variety of topics concerning both China and the rest of the world. Examples: "In a Regiment Party Committee: A Discussion on Party Democratic Centralism," and "Latin America: Mounting Struggle to Defend National Independence and State Sovereignty." Some readers may find the writing style a bit heavy handed, especially in the political articles, but that is a matter of taste. This could be a valuable addition to any library, provided that everyone keeps in mind that it is not and never was intended to be unbiased. (A.M.)

Philosophy East and West. See Philosophy Section.

Understanding China Newsletter. 1964. bi-m. $3. Louise Bennett. AFSC. Box 203, Ann Arbor, Mich. 48107. Illus. Microform: Publisher, vol. 1–7.

Bk. rev: 2–3, 500–1,000 words, signed. *Aud:* Ac, Ga, Hs. *Jv:* V.

A modest, but fact-filled 8-page newsletter from the American Friends Service Committee, a group dedicated to getting objective, unvarnished facts about China to the American people. The editors hope "to improve relations between the United States and the People's Republic of China." Various points of view are aired, and within the limits of its purpose the writing is objective. For example, the issue examined includes a lead article by Senator George McGovern on "Five Steps Toward a New U.S.–China policy," an editorial plugging Asian studies, a review of U.S.–China relations and an article on Maoist economics. There are two long book reviews and a new map of China. Considering the sponsors, it is difficult to imagine anyone but the hard rock Taiwan group objecting to the newsletter. In view of its objectivity, modest price, and bibliographical services, it is highly recommended for all libraries.

Asia

American Oriental Society. Journal. 1843. q. $17.25. Ernest Bender. The Society, 329 Sterling Memorial Library, Yale Station, New Haven, Conn. 06520. Illus., index. Circ: 2,400. Vol. ends: Oct./Dec. Microform: UM.

Bk. rev: Various number, length. *Aud:* Ac.

The basic journal in Oriental studies. Promotes scholarly research in Oriental languages, literature, and cultures. The articles presuppose considerable knowledge of archaeology, literature, religion, and history. "The Soma of the Rig Veda: What was It?" is a typical enough title. Interestingly enough, the author claims the soma was the mushroom. The article was well illustrated with colored plates. About one half of each number is devoted to book reviews, and about one third of these deal with foreign titles. A necessary acquisition where there is any interest in the area.

Artibus Asiae; quarterly of Asian art and archaeology for scholars and connoisseurs. 1925. q. $18. Alexander C. Soper, 6612 Ascona, Switzerland. Subs. to: Inst. of Fine Arts, New York Univ., 1 E. 78th St., New York, N.Y. 10021. Illus., index. Reprint: Johnson.

Indexed: ArtI. *Bk. rev:* 10–15, 750–1,500 words, signed. *Aud:* Ac.

An oversized, 130 page (i.e., for double issues) journal which features four or five scholarly articles, book reviews, and numerous black and white photographs of art objects. The writing is for the dedicated scholar (who may happen to be a connoisseur, but this is not the same connoisseur such magazines as *Apollo* have in mind). There is no advertising. The articles cover art in the Near East, India and Southeast Asia, and the Far East, including China. Most of the material appears in English, but a bit (i.e., reviews and some shorter articles) are in French or German. An impressive art and archaeology magazine for larger, specialized collections.

Asia; a journal published by the Asia Society, New York. 1964. q. $6. Maggie Brown. 112 E. 64th St.,

New York, N.Y. Illus. Circ: 3,500. Sample. Microform: UM.

Indexed: ABCPolSci, PAIS. *Aud:* Ga, Ac. *Jv:* V.

A pocket-sized semipopular magazine published by the Asia Society, "a nonprofit, nonpolitical organization founded for greater knowledge of Asia in the United States and for a better understanding between Americans and the peoples of Asia. A major activity of the Society is to provide its members and friends a wide range of information on Asia by means of lectures and conferences focused on various Asian countries. This publication consists of articles on various aspects of life in Asia drawn principally from these lectures and selected to provide representative geographical and topical coverage." The journal takes an uncluttered, nonspecialist approach in its articles, for the most part without sacrificing academic rigor. Each issue is devoted solely to five to eight long articles, usually on a number of different subjects, such as politics, family life, social organization, industrialization, some point of history, etc. An occasional issue narrows the spread to a specific country or topic, such as modern China. Worthwhile in both public and academic libraries.

Asian and African Studies. 1965. a. $6. Gabriel Baer. The Israel Oriental Soc., c/o Hebrew Univ. of Jerusalem, Jerusalem, Israel. Circ: 2,000.

Indexed: IJewAr. *Aud:* Ga, Ac.

The material included deals with a variety of subjects related to Asia and Africa with the accent on the Middle East. This scholarly journal presents long, scientific and well-documented articles on politics ("The Military in Burma"), history ("The Governor-General of the Sudan and his Relations with the British Consuls-General in Egypt, 1899–1916"), literature ("The Influence of Western Poetry and Particularly T. S. Eliot on Modern Arabic Poetry"). Almost every issue includes articles dealing with social and political life in Israel and Israel–Arab relations. The articles are signed by Israeli and foreign contributors, most of them from the staff of the Israeli universities. The majority of articles are translated from the journal *Hamizrah Hehadash (The Near East)*, the Hebrew language quarterly of the Israel Oriental Society. Biographical details on the authors of the articles are given at the end of each issue. (R.T.)

Asian Recorder; a weekly digest of outstanding Asian events. 1955. w. $31.50. M. Henry Samuel, C-I 9, Tilak Marg, Box 595, New Delhi, 1, India. Index. Circ: 2,500. Sample. Vol. ends: Dec. 31.

Bk. rev: 1, 200 words, signed. *Aud:* Ac, Ga.

A type of *Facts on File* of activities in Asia. The weekly service is loose leaf, consists of 10 to 16 pages, and is divided by countries, i.e., India, Indonesia, Iran, China, Israel, etc. Under each of the nations are summary reports concerned with commerce, legislation, foreign relations, finance, etc. The reporting is unbiased, objective, and timely. (Timely when it comes out in India, but it may take weeks to reach here.) There are good quarterly and annual indexes. While most of the major items will be in *Facts on File* or the *N.Y. Times Index*, the service is extremely useful for the lesser-known bits of information, particularly on Asian countries rarely noted in the American press.

Asian Survey. 1961. m. $10. Robert A. Scalapino. Univ. of California Press, 2223 Fulton St., Berkeley, Calif. 94720. Circ: 3,000. Sample. Vol. ends: Dec.

Indexed: PAIS, SSHum. *Aud:* Ac, Ga.

Leading American monthly devoted to current political, economic, and social developments in Asia. Five or six scholarly articles appear in each issue, frequently accompanied by charts and tables. As a regular feature, two structured issues are published in January and February surveying major trends for the previous year in eighteen Asian countries. For any public or academic library where there is a need for current information on Asia.

Bulletin of Concerned Asian Scholars. 1968. q. $10 (Individuals $6). Mark Selden & Perry Link. The Bulletin, 9 Sutter St., Rm. 300, San Francisco, Calif. 94104. Illus., index, adv. Circ: 4,000. Sample. Vol. ends: Fall.

Bk. rev: 2, 5 pages, signed. *Aud:* Ga, Ac. *Jv:* V.

An offset 80 or so page magazine which is one of the most important now published for an understanding of China and Asia. As such, the writers, many of whom have lived in Asia, discuss the matters of Asian policy much more frankly, and to a degree much more objectively, than those who write in magazines or newspapers. Most supporters are university teachers from UCLA, Columbia, MIT, Stanford, and the various schools and universities in Hong Kong. For example, a 1971 double issue of 170 pages was devoted entirely to China, included a long interview with Chou En-lai by members of the magazine staff and contributors. The articles definitely have a point of view, but one which apparently is being shared by the Nixon Administration as of early 1972. It will not, however, appeal to the conservative or Taiwan lobby. The journal covers not only China, but also all of Asia. Articles and book reviews deal with Indochina, Philippines, Japan, India, etc. Membership in the Committee of Concerned Asian Scholars, also brings the *CCAS Newsletter*, a monthly "newsheet with organizational and topical news." The organization has a sister group in England, the Association for Radical East Asian Studies.

East. 1963. m. $5.90. Tohru Morita. The East Publns., Inc., 10-5, Roppongi 3, Minato-ku, Tokyo, Japan. Illus., adv. Circ: 65,000. Sample. Vol. ends: Dec.

Aud: Ga, Hs.

A general magazine which covers Japan and some countries in the Far East. Most of the emphasis is on Japanese culture, business, literature, and just about any topic which would be of passing interest to the traveler, actual or armchair. The illustrations are good, the style clear, and the whole is quite suitable for a general public or high school collection. Its reference value is limited because, as is usual in this type of publication, there is little or no material given to controversial topics, i.e., politics and social issues.

Far East Trade and Development. 1946. m. $9.60. Laurence G. French. Laurence French Publns., Ltd., 3 Belsize Crescent, London NW3 5QZ, England. Illus., index, adv. Circ: 10,000.

Bk. rev: Various number, length. *Aud:* Ac, Ga. *Jv:* V.

A basic business and economics magazine which covers the Third World and the Far East. It is a down-to-earth report on markets, business activities, opportunities for trade, information on contracts, fluctuations in the tariff and monetary schedules, etc. The journal also includes short articles on new products, methods of dealing with various governmental agencies, business operation, and techniques for advertising and merchandising. Although published in English, its readers are as apt to be British, European, Chinese, and Russian. The audience is primarily executives in industry and business, but it can be studied by anyone involved in Far East affairs. There is an annual "China Review" in October and an "Indian Review" in January. One of the best, objective, and nonpartisan business journals in this area. Should be a first choice for most libraries.

Harvard Journal of Asiatic Studies. 1936. a. $10/v. John L. Bishop. Harvard-Yenching Inst., 2 Divinity Ave., Cambridge, Mass. 02138. Circ: 1,200. Microform: B&H, UM. Reprint: Johnson.

Indexed: SSHum. *Bk. rev:* 10–12, 1,000–1,500 words, signed. *Aud:* Ac.

Published under the auspices of the Harvard-Yenching Institute, the pioneer in the field of Chinese studies, the journal is edited by experts in the field of Asiatic studies, and written by those most conversant with and knowledgeable in that subject. Bibliographic material is prolific. Six to nine long articles appear in each issue, followed by the reviews and five or six lengthy notices of other publications. For large research collections.

Japan Illustrated. q. $4. Mitsuo Suzuki. Japan Times, Ltd. 5–4 Shibaura 4 Chrome, Minato-ku, Tokyo, Japan. Illus., adv.

Aud: Ga, Hs, Ejh.

A sometimes fascinating pictorial view of Japan by the Japanese. The chamber of commerce approach is never too intrusive, and most of the material is imaginative, intelligent, and thoughtfully put together. There is some descriptive matter, but most of the emphasis is on pictures. All areas are covered, and examination of two or three issues gives the reader the quite natural impression that Japan is a delightful place to visit, to live, or to do business with. Nothing overly serious; an idea magazine for the browser or the teacher trying to bring home the less controversial aspects of the country.

Journal of Asian and African Studies. 1966. q. Approx. $16. K. Ishwaran. E. J. Brill Publishers, Leiden, The Netherlands.

Bk. rev: 10–15, 500 words, signed. *Aud:* Ac.

Although issued quarterly, practice has been to publish double numbers of some 160 pages twice a year. Issues center on specific subjects of interest to any scholar involved with man and society in developing nations of Asia and Africa. Emphasis is on sociology, but contributors come from other disciplines such as political science, history, anthropology, and related social science areas. The material represents original research, is well documented, and is an excellent source of reference for the specialist.

Journal of Asian History. 1967. s-a. $10.30. Denis Sinor. Otto Harrassowitz, Postfach 349, Wiesbaden, West Germany. Illus., index, adv. Circ: 2,000.

Indexed: HistAb. *Bk. rev:* 10–12, 500 words, signed. *Aud:* Ac.

Covers historical research largely from the Middle Ages to the present with some emphasis on the nineteenth and early twentieth centuries for all regions of Asia, with the exception of the Ancient Near East. The majority of the articles are in English, but a few have appeared in German or the language of the author. The book reviews tend to emphasize books which have appeared in the English language. The three to four articles which appear in each issue are universal in scope, ranging from a well-illustrated monograph on Asian Elephants in Renaissance Europe, to Soviet-Japanese Confrontations in Outer Mongolia. This is a specialized journal for scholars and graduate students who have any interest in Asia, historical or otherwise.

Journal of Asian Studies. 1941. 5/yr. $15. John A. Harrison. Subs. to: Secretary, Assn. for Asian Studies, Inc., 48 Lane Hall, Univ. of Michigan, Ann Arbor, Mich. 48104. Adv. Circ: 2,000. Vol. ends: Sept. Refereed.

Indexed: AmerH, HistAb. PAIS., SSHum. *Bk. rev:* 5, 200 to 300 words, signed. *Aud:* Ac, Ga.

At $15 per year, this is a real bargain. The annual bibliography alone should justify a subscription. This lists both books and periodical articles from the previous year, arranged by country or area and then by broad subjects (politics, religion, economics, literature, science, etc.) within each country. The area covered includes all of Southeast Asia, both Chinas, India,

Pakistan, Japan, Korea, Mongolia, Tibet, Central Asia, and the Soviet Far East. The journal itself is also excellent. Each issue contains 8 to 10 articles, scholarly in style and content, on a variety of topics concerning Asia and its peoples. Sometimes a symposium is presented, with several articles on the same general topic. College and university libraries should have this, and the larger public libraries might also find it useful. (A.M.)

Journal of Contemporary Asia. 1971. q. $8. Ed. bd. Box 49010, Stockholm 49, Sweden.

Aud: Ac.

A scholarly international English-language journal which has among its editors Peter Weiss, Noam Chomsky, and Jean Chesneaux. The 124-page journal covers all parts of Asia; considers a wide variety of interests. Articles "in the first two issues discussed the agrarian structure of southeast Asia, Laotian politics, technology and the Vietnam war, Philippines education, and the like," reports Gabriel Kolko of the editorial board. It also contains some original documents. A basic journal for medium to larger-sized collections.

Journal of Southeast Asian Studies (Formerly: ***Journal of Southeast Asian History***). 1970. s-a. $8.50 per copy. Png Poh-seng. McGraw-Hill Far Eastern Publishers Ltd., Jalan Boon Lay, Jurong, Singapore 22. Circ: 1,700.

Indexed: HistAb, SSHum. *Bk. rev:* 14–15, 500–600 words, signed. *Aud:* Ac, Ga.

A multidisciplinary approach is applied to the region of Southeast Asia in order to better understand its past and the interaction of current forces at work in this area of the world. Emphasis is placed upon nineteenth and twentieth century events with many contributions stemming from the social sciences, especially anthropology, philology, sociology, economics, and social psychology. It makes available data which is available in few other sources, at least to the Westerner. This is a significant publication when one considers the need for objective understanding of this area of the world. An obvious must for college and university libraries, it is also suitable for large public library collections.

Literature East & West. 1953. q. $12. Roy E. Teele, Box 8107, Univ. Station, Austin, Tex. 78712. Index. Circ: 1,000.

Bk. rev: 35–40, notes or 500–1,000 words, signed. *Aud:* Ac, Ga.

An official publication of the Oriental–Western Literary Relations Group of the Modern Language Association of America. Usually each issue is devoted to the works of a single country, and in addition to critical essays there are excerpts from books and poetry. The book reviews are usually grouped by subject, i.e., two or three titles of a similar nature considered by the same reviewer, and afford the librarian one of the best single sources of information in this area. A secondary purpose is to "encourage the greater use of non-Western literature in Western classrooms," and the adventuresome high school teacher will find something of value here for his or her classes.

Mahfil; a quarterly of South Asian literature. 1965. q. $5. Carlo Coppola, Surjit Dulai, C. M. Naim. Asian Studies Center, 101 Center for Intl. Programs, Michigan State Univ., East Lansing, Mich. 48823. Index. Circ: 200. Sample. Vol. ends: Winter.

Bk. rev: 6–8, 3–4 pages, signed. *Aud:* Ac.

Focuses on the contemporary literary scene; includes examples of prose, poetry and songs, but tends to stress criticism. Special numbers are devoted to a single subject or author (e.g., Vol. 5, No. 3 is given to the work of Amrita Pritam, Indian poet and writer, who deserves more attention in America; another, Vol. 5, No. 4 to the Urdu genius, Ghalib). Most contributions are within the grasp of the interested student. An important magazine which deserves wider support than it seems to be getting.

Modern Asian Studies. 1967. q. $17. (Individuals $13). G. Johnson. Cambridge Univ. Press, 32 E. 57th St., New York, N.Y. 10022. Circ: 1,200. Sample.

Indexed: HistAb. *Bk. rev:* 7–10, 500–1,500 words, signed. *Aud:* Ac.

Concerned "with the history, geography, politics, sociology, literature, economics and social anthropology of South Asia, South-East Asia, China and Japan." The monographic articles—usually four to five in each 100 page issue—are by experts, well documented, and meaningful to fellow scholars in the field. It is a little too complicated and involved for the casual student. The reviews are strong on British titles, but do include publications from other countries. Only for large academic libraries.

Orientations. 1970. m. $20. J. T. Gatbonton. Pacific Communications Ltd., Asia House, 1 Hennessy Rd., Hong Kong. Illus., adv. Vol. ends: Dec.

Aud: Ga, Ac, Hs.

As one reader observes, "this is a cross between *Holiday* and *Horizon* with an Oriental flavor." The 95 glossy pages bear out the initial impression. Moving from Saigon to Singapore, the 10 to 12 well-illustrated articles cover every aspect of the Orient. The thrust is towards the traveler, and one section features guidelines on new places to visit. There is a dash of history, art, fashion, food, and you name it—just about anything of interest to the general reader except controversy and politics. The articles are well written, nontechnical, and as suitable for adults as for children at the junior high or high school level. The full-page colored illustrations will be of special value to vertical file freaks who may want to cut and snip. This should

have wide interest for the general reader, and can be recommended, even at the relatively high price.

Pacific Affairs. 1928. q. $7. William L. Holland. Univ. of British Columbia, Vancouver, 8, B.C., Canada. Index, adv. Circ: 3,260. Vol. ends: Winter. Microform: UM.

Indexed: HistAb, PAIS, SSHum. *Bk. rev:* 75, 350 words, signed. *Aud:* Sa, Ac.

A scholarly magazine concerned with political, economic, social, and diplomatic relations of the countries of eastern and southern Asia and the Pacific area. Primarily for the social scientist, the journal touches on all related issues such as economics, sociology, and personalities. The articles are objective, and where a controversial point of view is introduced every effort is made to indicate both sides of the issue. There are excellent book reviews and shorter items of interest to students of the area. While primarily for the specialist, this is still a basic magazine for the college student studying any area touched on by the magazine. Should be in all medium to large-sized collections.

Pacific Research and World Empire Telegram. 1969. bi-m. $15 (Individuals $5). Pacific Studies Center, 1963 Univ. Ave., East Palo Alto, Calif. 94303. Illus., index. Circ: 800. Sample. Vol. ends: Sept./Oct.

Aud: Ac, Ga.

A 15 to 20 page magazine on newsprint, this is the publication of a "non-profit, cooperative radical research center," which, among other things, "maintains a storefront library and resource center for the use of the local community." Each issue is devoted to one or two subjects which have some bearing on the Pacific rim countries, e.g., "Vietnam's Electronic Battlefield," "Rebellion in Bangla Desh," "Inside the World Bank." Articles are by experts, well documented and footnoted, and written in a straightforward fashion without an obtrusive viewpoint. Granted, the sponsor is liberal, but the reporting is such that the magazine will be of interest to students and scholars of the Pacific countries, as well as to political activists. It is this informative reporting, difficult enough to find for the area, that gives it a peculiar and important position in any academic or public library with interest in the Pacific rim.

School of Oriental and African Studies. Bulletin (University of London). 1917. 3/yr. $12. Edward Ullendorf (Chairman of the Ed. bd.). Luzac & Co., Ltd., 46 Gt. Russell St., London WC1, England. Illus., index, adv.

Indexed: BritHum, HistAb. *Bk. rev:* 80, 100–500 words, signed. *Aud:* Ac.

Concerned with both modern and ancient history, art and archaeology, this is a highly considered journal for experts in Orientalia covering religion, literature, anthropology, etc. The five to eight technical articles are all by scholars, primarily British. The primary use of the journal for the librarian and nonexpert is found in the book review section. Here, some 80 to 100 titles are noted each issue, and the signed reviews are both descriptive and critical.

CITY MAGAZINES

See also Travel and Regional/State and Regional Section.

Basic Periodicals

First choice for all libraries is obviously your city, or the magazine originating from the largest city in your state or region.

After that, the order of preference for all libraries is: *Philadelphia, Los Angeles, Chicago, Atlanta, San Francisco, Washington.* See also *New York Magazine,* General Magazines Section.

Atlanta. 1961. m. $8. Norman Shavin. Atlanta Chamber of Commerce, 1104 Commerce Bldg., Atlanta, Ga. 30303. Illus., index, adv. Circ: 20,000. Vol. ends: April. Microform: UM.

Bk. rev: 5, 150 words, signed. *Aud:* Ac, Ga, Hs. *Jv:* V.

One of the major city magazines, both in terms of content and size. An average 120-page number is as professionally put together as *New York* or any general magazine. (And the amount of advertising, which is substantial, makes it the envy of better known titles.) The target audience is Atlanta, Georgia, and the South with regular columns on personalities, politics, restaurants, etc. Still, there is much here which will interest the average reader. For example, there are travel pieces, movie and book reviews, and features which range from humor to serious studies of social change. The editors frequently are involved with less than popular issues from race relations to the economy. A solid and necessary acquisition for any Southern library, and a good number of larger libraries in the North, particularly those dealing with history, political science, and sociology.

Baltimore Magazine. 1907. m. $6. Chamber of Commerce of Metroplitan Baltimore, 22 Light St., Baltimore, Md. 21202. Illus., adv. Circ: 9,000. Sample. Vol. ends: Dec.

Aud: Ga, Ac, Hs. *Jv:* V.

A three-time winner of the American Association of Commerce publications "best in its field" award. One of the oldest general city magazines, it has a broad base of interest from sports to Maryland history. Editorial emphasis shifted from business community features to some of the unpleasant problems of city life such as "Skid Row Blood" and "Adopting the Unwanted." The lead article is usually an interview with a person active in current affairs and not restricted to the Baltimore region. Articles are open-minded and useful for current material on the city and state. Departments on films, restuarants, and the environment are included. Note: the hazards of editing a magazine of this type were demonstrated on February 12, 1972 when the *New York Times* reported Stump had been fired as editor. Why? Because "he was not in a position to go along with the policies of the chamber." Controversy can bring dismissal, and libraries checking out city magazines would do well to see first if the magazine is privately published, or under the control of a chamber of commerce. If the latter, it will probably be considerably more conservative, attentive to the status quo, than if published privately.

Beacon: magazine of Hawaii. 1957. m. $10. Bob Maxwell. W. G. Sturgis, 537 Ahui St., Honolulu, Hawaii 96813. Illus., adv. Circ: 16,000. Sample. Vol. ends: Dec.

Aud: Ga. *Jv:* C.

One of two city mags published in Hawaii—the other is *Honolulu.* Both are primarily controlled circulation, i.e., free to local residents. (Those outside the state must pay the $10 fee.) Of the two, *Beacon* is more folksy, less sophisticated, but tends to cover the same general territory, i.e., one or two feature articles on noncontroversial items from bike races to ships, current events, pets, crossword puzzles, and the whole "let's enjoy ourselves" syndrome. The writing is sometimes embarrassingly cute—in fact so much so that given a choice between the two magazines, *Honolulu* would be first without even a second thought.

Birmingham. 1960. m. $6. Donald A. Brown. Birmingham Area Chamber of Commerce, 1914 Sixth Ave., N., Birmingham, Ala. 35203. Illus., adv. Circ: 8,000.

Bk. rev: Notes. *Aud:* Ga.

A rather good, typical chamber of commerce effort. Most of the material is directed at the convinced reader who wants to support his staying in Birmingham (a natural enough policy for any magazine of this type, not just this one). Its primary function, though, is to report on activities (drama, art, music, etc.), assign praise to well-known personalities, and boost the community. It covers not only Birmingham, but a good part of Alabama; is carefully edited, fairly well illustrated, and has a passable format. What it does, it does well enough and should be in libraries in Alabama and surrounding states.

Boston Magazine. 1911. m. $7. Nancy Love. Municipal Publns., 38 Newbury St., Boston, Mass. 02116. Illus., index, adv. Circ: 22,000. Microform: UM. Vol. ends: Dec. Sample. *Aud:* Ga.

A general magazine which carries authoritative articles on current events in Boston and the immediate area with the usual attention to the arts. It is particularly good for objective articles about the joys and dangers of urban living. Herbert Lipson, owner of *Philadelphia Magazine*, recently bought *Boston Magazine;* thus it will probably continue to be one of the better-written liberal city magazines. Directed towards the successful middle-aged audience. (D.V.)

Cambridge. 1970. bi-m. $2. Bernadine McLeod. Cambridge Chamber of Commerce, 69 Rogers St., Cambridge, Mass. Illus., adv. Circ: 1,700. Vol. ends: Dec./Jan. Sample.

Aud: Ga.

Cambridge is in a unique situation. It is published by the Chamber of Commerce in a relatively small city, 40 percent of whose population is between 20 and 34 years of age. It is directly across the river from the City of Boston and the relatively ancient *Boston Magazine.* Two of the most prestigious universities in the world are within its borders. It is trying to present a fairminded business view of the social and economic problems of a rapidly and radically changing city. If *Cambridge* survives, look for it to be a leader in the area of Town–Gown relations. (D.V.)

Chicago Magazine. 1964. bi-m. $5. Richard Frisvie. New Chicago Foundation, 110 S. Dearborn St., Chicago, Ill. 60603. Illus., adv. Circ: 50,000. Sample. Vol. ends: Nov./Dec.

Aud: Ga, Ac, Hs. *Jv:* V.

Directed to the upper income groups in the greater Chicago area. Editorial emphasis is on art, culture, biographical sketches, and general business and economic news. There is little controversial material, e.g., concerning the good mayor, Richard Daley, and his regime. The level of writing is high, the format is excellent, and the whole will be of interest to anyone living in the Chicago area.

Anyone who has lived in or near Chicago also knows the FM station, WFMT. The station publishes *The Chicago Guide* (1970. m. $5. Allen H. Kelson. WFMT, Inc., 500 N. Michigan Ave., Chicago, Ill. 60611. Illus., adv. Circ: 58,000). This is primarily a guide to the radio and public television in the area, but it does include timely articles, movie reviews, and notes on cultural events. It, too, is directed to a better-educated audience.

Cincinnati. 1967. m. $8. Richard L. Gordon. Greater Cincinnati Chamber of Commerce, 309 Vine St., Cincinnati, Ohio 45202. Illus., adv. Circ: 12,500. Sample. Vol. ends: Dec.

Aud: Ga.

A 60 to 70 page chamber of commerce–sponsored effort which is heavy on advertising, boasts a handsome format, and features four to five general articles, plus a number of features: music, theatre, galleries, films, sports, etc. Its primary value seems to be the up-to-date information on current activities. The articles are long on photographs and illustrations, well

written, and noncontroversial. They will rarely interest anyone outside Cincinnati or Ohio. The editor says: "Our audience consists of people who are average or above in education, income and community involvement." Most emphasis is on that "involvement." The magazine is useful only to libraries in the greater Cincinnati area.

Dallas. 1922. m. Members $6 (Nonmembers $10). Lucille Enix. Dallas Chamber of Commerce, 1507 Pacific Ave., Dallas, Tex. 75201. Illus., index, adv. Circ: 12,000. Sample. Vol. ends: Dec. Microform: UM.

Indexed: PAIS. *Bk. rev:* 2, 1,500 words, signed. *Aud:* Ga.

In the November 1971 issue, three feature articles: "Creating the Dallas Dress," "Dallas' Air Harbor," and "Herman Lay's Quest for Life"; a number of departments: civic and cultural affairs, business briefs, convention calendar. There is considerable advertising. This adds up to a competent 72-page noncontroversial magazine whose primary purpose "is to assist the people of Dallas achieve a sense of unity and cooperation." The writing style is good, the information sure to interest anyone living in or around Dallas. But outside of the immediate area it will be of limited use for libraries.

Dayton U.S.A. 1964. bi-m. $4. Kathleen Tuiner. Dayton Area Chamber of Commerce, 210 N. Main St., Dayton, Ohio 45402. Illus., adv. Circ: 10,000. Sample. Vol. ends: Oct.

Aud. Ga.

Directed primarily to the business community of the Dayton area. Articles are generally noncontroversial, touching on industry, education, government, entertainment and prominent civic leaders. A good example of a smaller city magazine with average editorial skill evident in its format and content. Chamber of Commerce optimism is balanced by occasional articles on Dayton's urban problems. (D.V.)

Honolulu Magazine. 1966. m. $10. David Eyre. Joseph Mrantz, Box 80, Honolulu, Hawaii, 96810. Illus., index, adv. Circ: 20,500. Sample. Vol. ends: June.

Aud: Ga.

A semisophisticated city magazine which takes in all of Hawaii. While apparently not rushing into controversy, it does have a number of human interest articles which are far and above those found in similar magazines, e.g., an interview with the Amy Vanderbilt of Japan, and how to hold a household together without a job. The editorial comment is honest and forthright, even down to admitting "there are no letters to the editor in this month's issue" (June, 1971). The format is good, if not exciting. And there are the usual commentaries on restaurants, films, shows, etc. This is of interest only to those living in Hawaii, or planning a visit. However, the editor points out, there is a special November issue "which is largely aimed at tourists and is habitually bought by local residents to send to Mainland friends and family as a Christmas gift." That one might be worth buying, even for those in distant places. Note: Most of the 20,500 subscribers represent controlled circulation, i.e., free distribution, and, hopefully, libraries in Hawaii will be on the free list.

Houston Magazine. 1930. m. $7.35. Mary M. Midkiff. Houston Chamber of Commerce, Box 53600, Houston, Tex. 77052. Illus., adv. Circ: 15,000. Sample. Vol. ends: Dec.

Aud: Ga.

Primarily a business magazine for the upper echelon managers. Emphasis is on industry, commerce, finance, construction, and general business news in the greater Houston area. It has an excellent format. This is a good example of a city magazine adhering to the Chamber of Commerce line. Consequently, this side of the greater Houston area has limited appeal for anyone except the business executive. (D.V.)

Hudson Valley Profile; the involvement magazine. 1971. m. $6. Enn Lepist. Leap Enterprises, Inc., 2 LaGrange Ave., Poughkeepsie, N.Y. 12601. Illus., adv. Sample. Vol. ends: Sept.

Aud: Ac, Ga, Hs.

A new city magazine which extends its range beyond IBM's Poughkeepsie to the whole surrounding Hudson Valley region. Well-illustrated articles touch all bases from art and ecology to industry and fashion. In the initial issue the editor states "We do not intend to become controversial or sensational. We want to be involved." The paradox of the statement apparently has not struck home, but in the meantime the nicely produced 65-page journal offers a little something for everyone—particularly those living in the region. Others can skip, or at least until such time as the editorial policy is a bit better defined. Right now it is a controlled circulation magazine, which means it comes free to many. A library might try for a free subscription.

Los Angeles Magazine. 1960. m. $8. David R. Brown. Pacific West Publishing Co., 342 N. Rodeo Dr., Beverly Hills, Calif. 90210. Illus., index, adv. Circ: 73,000. Vol. ends: Dec. Sample.

Aud: Ga, Ac, Hs. *Bk. rev:* 3, 300 words, signed. *Jv:* V.

Despite the title, of interest to other than Los Angeles readers. Directed to all Southern Californians, it covers the broad spectrum of urban problems, California politics, culture, travel, and personalities. Total effect is often controversial, relatively sophisticated, and much above the average for this type of magazine. The "Departments" are particularly strong in breadth and depth of coverage. It continues to enjoy a large circulation because the editor intentionally attempts to touch on materials which will be of interest to any Californian or anyone interested in the area. One of the five best city magazines, and should be a major consideration for all medium to large-sized western libraries. (D.V.)

Louisville Magazine. 1950. m. $6.50. Betty Lou Amster. Louisville Area Chamber of Commerce, 300 W. Liberty St., Louisville, Ky. 40202. Illus., adv. Circ: 9,500. Sample. Vol. ends: Dec.

Aud. Ga.

A general business magazine with emphasis on trends, economics, and industry of the Louisville region. Some historical and current events articles are included, especially at Kentucky Derby time. Although an essential item in Kentucky libraries, its business orientation will be of little interest outside the state. (D.V.)

Miamian. 1920. m. $9. Michael J. Lee. Greater Miami Chamber of Commerce. 1434 Brickell Ave., Miami, Fla. 33131. Illus., adv. Circ: 37,000. Vol. ends: Dec.

Aud: Ga.

Lacks the polish and slick format of some of the other city magazines, yet manages to make its point well enough. It covers Miami, Florida, and the Caribbean with six to seven illustrated articles, and has the usual features from restaurant guide to historical notes. The writing is fair to good, and the editor's style is fine. Developments, sports, education, etc., are subjects of most interest. There is little or no controversial material. Primarily of value to libraries in and around Miami.

Milwaukee. 1955. $7.50. Frederick G. Schmidt. Schmidt Publns., 735 W. Wisconsin Ave., Milwaukee, Wis., 53233. Illus., adv. Circ: 15,000. Sample. Vol. ends: Dec.

Aud: Ga.

A personalized approach to Milwaukee, i.e., the editor takes an active voice in commenting on just about anything of interest. In his column he is not above pointing out faults in the city. Usually two or three major articles, which tend to be of the chamber of commerce variety—differing from most because of excellent photography. There are the usual columns on coming and current events, restaurants, sports, etc. The magazine is well made up, and while a bit lighter on editorial content than others of this genre, it is a required item in the greater Milwaukee area.

New York. See General Magazines Section.

Palm Springs Life. 1946. m. (Sept.–June). $8. Milton W. Jones. 250 E. Palm Canyon Dr., Palm Springs, Calif. 92202. Illus., adv. Circ: 25,000. Sample. Vol. ends: June.

Bk. rev: Various number, length. *Aud:* Ga.

One of the most handsome and one of the oldest city magazines. It is edited for a rather high income group, i.e., those who permanently live in, or visit, the resort area of Palm Springs. Considerable emphasis is placed on cultural activities, social life and sports—particularly golf. The format is noteworthy for clever use of photography. The articles are professional, often mildly controversial, and touch on all subjects. Regular departments include travel, restaurants, local business news, etc. A good general magazine for anyone living in southern California, and of some interest to western libraries.

Philadelphia Magazine. 1908. m. $8. Alan Halpern. Municipal Publns., Inc., 1500 Walnut St., Philadelphia, Pa. 19102. Illus., index, adv. Circ: 90,000. Sample. Vol. ends: Dec.

Aud: Ga, Ac, Hs. *Bk. rev:* 1-2, 2,000 words, signed. *Jv:* V.

Aggressively points out the faults of the community as well as its glories. The reporting is good to excellent, coverage includes every aspect of city life from slums to the suburbs. Various issues have considered such subjects as blockbusting in Wynnefield (a suburb), analysis of rape statistics, the Philadelphia jet set, and the evils of graffiti. This type of coverage is better than that found in many American general magazines. The whole is professionally edited, the format is good and an average issue will run to some 200 to 250 pages. A must magazine for any library in the greater Philadelphia area and one of the best in the United States for almost any library. (D.V.)

Portland. 1894. m. $5. (Members $2.50). Rolv H. Schillios. Portland Chamber of Commerce, 824 S.W. Fifth Ave., Portland, Ore., 97204. Illus., index, adv. Circ: 6,000. Vol. ends: Dec.

Bk. rev: 3, length varies. *Aud:* Ga.

Short articles on business, commerce and industry are of primary interest. The usual reader departments such as calendar of events, business roundup, and some book reviews. An average 60 to 72 page issue has a solid look which indicates that its purpose is to plug Portland. Little or no controversial matters are covered. As far as it goes, fine. But outside of Portland and Oregon, of limited interest.

Raleigh Magazine. 1969. bi-m. $2.25. Robert W. Jones. Raleigh Publishing Co., 201 New Bern Ave., Raleigh, N.C. 27601. Illus., adv. Circ: 15,000. Sample. Vol. ends: Dec.

Aud: Ga.

An aggressive young entry in the genre of city magazines. It promotes Raleigh and the "Capital City area" as a nice place to live with the usual broad spectrum of articles about Raleigh people, business, and culture. The editors maintain credibility with articles such as what the poor black man is thinking, discrimi-

nation against women in Raleigh, pornography, and the perennial North Carolina legislative battle to have liquor sold by the drink. Individually owned, it does have some tie-ins with the local Chamber of Commerce but apparently maintains an independent editorial policy. "Our Past on Parade" Department is especially well done by Elizabeth Reid, a local historian. As a city magazine for a small city, *Raleigh* is crisp, friendly and making it. Of interest to all North Carolina libraries. (D.V.)

St. Louis Commerce. 1927. m. Membership (Nonmembers $6). Robert E. Hannon. Chamber of Commerce, 224 N. Broadway, St. Louis, Mo. 63102. Illus., adv. Circ: 6,000. Sample. Vol. ends: Dec.

Indexed: PAIS. *Aud:* Ga.

A city magazine of the standard, older variety, i.e., it is published by the St. Louis Chamber of Commerce to plug the city and its business. It employs a good format, and some interesting reports. Solid main street talk for anyone interested in business and industry.

San Diego Magazine. 1948. m. $6. Edwin F. Self. San Diego Magazine Co., 5254 Rosecrans St., San Diego, Calif. 92110. Illus., index, adv. Circ: 20,000. Sample. Vol. ends: Dec.

Aud: Ga. *Bk. rev:* Occasional; various number, length.

Of more than local interest when it features travel articles on Mexico, Central America, and the Pacific. Sophisticated writing on culture, sports, and amusements of the area, it can also be hard hitting in features about city planning, business elites, and local politics. It has done much to balance a somewhat reactionary press in conservative Southern California where it is considered a liberal magazine. Any library which subscribes to *Los Angeles Magazine* will want to consider this one too although its appeal is directed to the upper middle class. It definitely should be included in all libraries in and around San Diego. (D.V.)

San Francisco. 1963. m. $6. Geoffrey Link. San Francisco Magazine, 120 Green St., San Francisco, Calif. 94111. Illus., adv. Circ: 33,000. Sample. Vol. ends: Dec.

Bk. rev: 1-2, 1 page, signed. *Aud:* Ga, Ac, Hs. *Jv:* V.

Pros and cons of high rises, alpha waves, pot smoking, con games people play, historical sketches—all of these are topics in this sophisticated approach to life and the San Francisco/California scene. Over the past two or three years the magazine has improved considerably, now offers material of enough general interest to involve any educated reader—and this means outside of the target area. The style equals anything found in *New York*, lacking, though, the biting social satire and muckracking. For those living in the immediate area there are the usual departments on music, books, restaurants, etc. One bonus for everyone is a general essay on American life in each issue by

Kenneth Rexroth. A good acquisition for just about any general library collection, in or out of California.

Texas Metro; magazine of north central Texas. 1965. m. $5. Dona Strother. Lester Strother, Drawer 5566, Arlington, Tex. 76011. Illus., adv. Circ: 7,500. Sample. Vol. ends: Dec.

Aud: Ga.

Edited for the Dallas–Fort Worth metropolitan region, a 10-county area known as North Central Texas. Other than reaching a wider area than most metropolitan magazines, the approach is about the same. There are usually five or six short feature articles, then regular departments on recreation and travel, the home, business, the arts, restaurants, etc. The format is adequate, and an average 52-page issue will be of value to anyone living in the area. The editor claims it features travel articles on six additional states, i.e., Louisiana, Arkansas, Missouri, Oklahoma, New Mexico, and Colorado, and there is even some material on Europe. Libraries in these states might find it of interest, and surely should send for a sample copy.

Tulsa. 1959. m. $7.50 (Members $5). Larry Silvey. Metropolitan Tulsa Chamber of Commerce, 616 S. Boston, Tulsa, Okla. 74119. Illus., index, adv. Circ: 6,000. Sample. Vol. ends: Dec.

Aud: Ga.

Dedicated to tell the Tulsa story, truthfully, without bias, and with every effort made in the primary feature stories to eliminate typical Chamber propaganda. And it pretty well brings it off. Thanks to some brilliant cartoons by one D. Varmecky, and hard hitting stories on government, personalities (J. Paul Getty), and good photo essays, this proves to be one of the better Chamber of Commerce efforts. Somehow it escapes the curse of being a Chamber child, and is apparently given freedom of expression beyond the norm. Departments, are good too, from the arts to films. Of more interest than just to Tulsa, and can be recommended for all libraries in the region, as well as larger public and academic libraries everywhere.

Washingtonian Magazine. 1965. m. $7. Laughlin Phillips. Washington Magazine Inc., 1218 Connecticut Ave., Washington, D.C. 20036. Illus., adv. Circ: 40,000. Vol. ends Dec.

Aud: Ga.

In a sense the city magazine with the widest appeal because it concerns our nation's capitol. Feature articles, 8 to 10 in each issue, have touched upon federal treasury mismanagement, Washington lawyers, and runaway kids. Other feature subjects have been hair and hairdressers, how to buy eyeglasses, and the family fight over Drew Pearson's estate. The reporting is professional with follow-ups of previous features. The style is good with as broad appeal as *Atlanta Magazine* or *Philadelphia Magazine*. There are regular columns on entertainment, restaurants, fashion, etc. One of the nation's five best and a consideration for any library regardless of location. (D.V.)

CIVIL LIBERTIES

Basic Periodicals

Hs: *Free Speech, Civil Liberties;* Ga: *Free Speech, Civil Liberties, Civil Rights Digest;* Jc: *Free Speech, Civil Liberties, Civil Rights Court Digest;* Ac: All titles listed in this section.

Library and Teaching aids

Newsletter on Intellectual Freedom, National Decency Reporter.

Cessations

Censorship Today, Tangents.

Civil Liberties. 1931. m. Membership (Subscriptions $10 & up). Claire Cooper. American Civil Liberties Union, 156 Fifth Ave., New York, N.Y. 10010. Illus., adv., Circ: 150,000. Sample. Vol. ends: Dec.

Aud: Ga, Ac.

The national 8 to 12 page tabloid of the American Civil Liberties Union which keeps members up-to-date on activities of the ACLU. More important, there are succinct reports on court cases, rulings, legislative action, and official pronouncements which either advance or threaten civil liberties.

Civil Liberties in New York. 1953. m. Membership (Subscriptions $10 & up.) Kenneth P. Norwick, Ellen Azoom. New York Civil Liberties Union, 84 Fifth Ave., New York, N.Y. 10011. Illus. Circ: 30,000. Sample.

Aud: Ga, Ac.

There are a number of ACLU state publications which augment the national paper. This is one of the more outstanding, certainly boasts the largest circulation. The 6 to 8 pages cover the national scene, but concentrate on activities affecting New York State—everything from voter registration for 18 year olds to the Attica prison riots. There are occasional signed book reviews. ACLU members in New York receive both papers with a single membership, while members in other states receive *Civil Liberties* and their local ACLU newsletter, if any.

Civil Rights Court Digest. 1968. m. $15. Emanuel Bund. Juridical Digests Inst., 1860 Broadway, Suite 1110, New York, N.Y. 10023. Index. Sample. Vol. ends: Dec.

Aud: Ac.

A six-page summary report of major national cases in civil rights. A case is cited with a one paragraph,

150-word summary of the judgment. Reporting is about five to six months after the decision, although a few in the sample copy examined were published only two months after the decision. Grouping decisions in this manner may be useful, but the publisher's price is high for material which can be found in more detail and more promptly elsewhere, i.e., The *New York Times* and its index, to cite only one popular source. There are eight other such reports issued by the same firm. Prices are apparently the same for: *Administrative Court Digest, Conservation Court Digest, Ecclesiastical Court Digest, Education Court Digest, Mental Health Court Digest, Public Health Court Digest, The Sex Problems Court Digest, The Social Welfare Court Digest.* Send for a sample before taking any of them.

✓ Civil Rights Digest. 1968. q. $.35/copy. Joe Mancias, Jr. U.S. Commission on Civil Rights, 1405 T St., N.W., Washington, D.C. Subs. to: Supt. of Documents, U.S. Govt. Printing Office, Washington, D.C. 20402. Illus. Sample (from the U.S. Commission on Civil Rights). Vol. ends: Fall.

Bk. rev: 2, 500–1,000 words, signed. *Aud:* Ga, Ejh, Hs, Ac.

Short, general articles are presented on matters affecting the civil rights of Americans of all races. Since this is a magazine published by the Commission on Civil Rights, the matters discussed for the most part relate to existing Federal legislation. Articles have appeared on media exaggeration of violence, housing, and desegregation of schools. The material is not technical, and can be recommended for the average reader, the social worker, teachers, and high school students.

Free Speech. 1962. 3/yr. (Nov., Feb., May). Request. H. A. Bosmajian. Newsletter of the Committee on Freedom of Speech, Speech Communication Assn. Subs. to: Dept. of Speech, Univ. of Washington, Seattle, Wash. 98105. Circ: 270.

Aud: Ac, Ga, Hs. *Jv:* V.

A mimeographed 24-page newsletter which is too little known. It should have a much larger circulation, because each number is concerned with legal decisions, social activities, political moves, and any events which have occurred during the previous four months which threaten or support freedom of speech. It has many bibliographic notes on articles which have appeared in various places regarding freedom of speech. "Some issues are devoted almost exclusively to specific freedom of speech controversies. One past number contained much material related to college and university policies regarding outside speakers; another issue dealt with loyalty oaths and their First Amendment implications. Short essays on freedom of speech occasionally are included. Free speech incidents and controversies, along with excerpts from court decisions, make up the bulk of the publication." The whole seems to be put together as the items come to the attention of the editor, and while it lacks a given amount of organization and continuity, it jumps with interest. The editor's writing style is more than equal to his material, and the journal compares favorably with others in this field. In fact, it should be required reading for all librarians, not to mention journalists and students of the passing scene. Highly recommended.

Harvard Civil Rights–Civil Liberties Law Review. 1966. 3/yr. $6.50 (Students $4.50). Eric E. Van Loon. Langdell Hall, Harvard Law School, Cambridge, Mass. 02138. Circ: 1,800.

Indexed: LegPer, PHRA. *Aud:* Ga, Ac.

Devoted to the legal frontiers in the fields of civil rights, liberties, poverty, draft and consumer law, and urban legal problems, i.e., the emphasis is on the great social problems of the time. It has featured essays on legal actions against pollution, the legal rights of students, and the right to housing. The style of writing is one of substance and detail, and the material is directed to the serious and legally astute reader. All problems are approached from a national perspective.

National Decency Reporter. 1962. m. $4. Citizens for Decent Literature, Inc., 5670 Wilshire Blvd., Suite 1670, Los Angeles, Calif. 90036. Circ: 8,000.

Aud: Ga.

The verso of *Newsletter on Intellectual Freedom,* i.e., the sponsors are eager and anxious to curb certain types of publications which they deem pornographic. A typical 16-page offset issue includes information on the latest crackdowns by police on so-called "porno publishers," court actions, and shorter notes on events in various states. Activities of members are noted. This is particularly recommended because it gives the censor's viewpoint in an undiluted fashion—and, along with that is the frequent claim that the sponsoring group does not believe in censorship.

Newsletter on Intellectual Freedom. 1952. bi-m. $5. Judith F. Krug and James A. Harvey. American Library Assn., 50 E. Huron, Chicago, Ill. 60611. Illus., index. Circ: 2,900. Sample. Vol. ends: Nov.

Aud: Ga, Ac, Hs, Ejh. *Jv:* V.

A 20-page newsletter which attempts to give objective current information on censorship. There are usually one or two introductory articles, and then "Censorship Dateline" which traces activities in various regions and states. "From the Bench" gives current legal opinions; followed by "Is it Legal?" and "Success Stories." There is a minimum of ALA business. Unfortunately, this does not enjoy a wide circulation. It should be brought to the attention of nonlibrarians, and certainly is a required item in any library, regardless of size, type, or location.

COMICS

See also Counterculture/Underground Comix Section.

Basic Periodicals

Here divisions and choice are such that the adventuresome may make their own basic selection in terms of what they are trying to do with the collection.

Introduction

If "the child is father of the man" (Wordsworth), then it is important for libraries to take note of the literature that influences childhood. This certainly includes comic books. Whatever their faults, whatever children may be told to read instead, comic books continue to have a tremendous circulation among children at their most impressionable and formative ages. Many children, especially those in disadvantaged circumstances, may find little else to read. Among children who have the advantages of a wider range of literary resources, comic books are still popular because of their bright, attention-holding images and because of their rapid pacing, which makes them quickly read relaxation pleasure when one has no time to settle down with a richer book that requires more leisurely and thoughtful reading.

Comic books can be worthwhile acquisitions for libraries working with school-age children, especially the slow learners and those with reading problems, as aids to teach and encourage regular reading. The trend to "relevant" treatment of modern social problems (the depiction of the consequences of pollution, racial prejudice, school vandalism, etc.) may be of help in enabling teachers to discuss these matters with students not yet prepared to be introduced to them in more serious literature. The presence of comics in libraries can lead to a more friendly, informal atmosphere, encouraging the greater use of libraries among children who tend to think of them as dull places of no interest. Libraries should also make comic books available to scholars of children's literature and of popular literature, and to educators studying effective ways to present knowledge to students. (The comic book format is being used to teach English to children of a foreign-language background in some schools' texts; and some state governmental offices have commissioned special public-service comics for distribution in schools to promote mental health, dental care, etc.) A case can even be made for the preservation for archival purposes of the most worthless and lurid comic books by university research libraries, for the benefit of future analysts of today's society.

The comic books reviewed here are among the most popular currently available in the different plot categories—funny animal, romance, western war adventure, superhero, etc. This is meant primarily to serve as a representative list of what today's children and young adults are reading, rather than as a guide to recommended titles, though recommendations are present where they are felt to be merited. The suggested reading ages are for the benefit of libraries desiring to buy titles for use with a particular age group or with children with special interests or reading problems.

The major event in the comic magazine field during 1971 was undoubtedly the death of most 15¢ comic books. Inflation, and rising printing costs in particular, simply made the price impossible to maintain. While some companies merely raised their prices to 20¢, others raised them to 25¢ and added extra pages (usually reprints of old stories). The change also occasioned the deaths of some titles that had been only marginally successful. Experiments with 64-page 35¢ titles and 96-page 50¢ titles appeared, and one publisher was reported to be considering a 500-page $2 "special" (all reprints). The situation is in flux, and the future of some of these titles is uncertain.

ORDERING INFORMATION. Unless otherwise noted, the following addresses, sizes, prices, and ordering information will apply to all titles reviewed here issued by their respective publishing companies.

Archie Comic Publications, Inc., 1116 First Ave., New York, N.Y. 10021. Prices given with reviews. 32-page titles contain 24 features, 8 of advertising (give or take a page or two from issue to issue).

Harvey Comic Publications, Inc., 1860 Broadway, New York, N.Y. 10023. 25¢ per issue; no subscriptions. 48 pages; 40 of features, 8 of advertising.

Marvel Comic Group: Magazine Management Co., 625 Madison Ave., New York, N.Y. 10022. 20¢ per issue; $2.75 for 12 issues. 32 pages; 21 of features, 11 of advertising.

National Comic Periodical Publications, Inc., Box 1047, Flushing, N.Y. 11352. 25¢ per issue; $3 for 12 issues. 48 pages; 39 of features, 9 of advertising.

Gold Key: Western Publishing Co., Inc., North Road, Poughkeepsie, N.Y. 12602. 15¢ per issue; no subscriptions (exceptions are noted in reviews). 32 pages; 26 of features, 6 of advertising. (F.P.)

Magazines about Comics

Cartoonist Profiles. q. $8.00. Cartoonist Profiles, Inc., P. O. Box 325, Fairfield, Conn. 06430.

This 88-page magazine about cartoonists seems to have the support of the National Cartoonists Society, the guild of professional cartoonists. It contains articles by and about many popular comic strip, political, and sports cartoonists, including many photographs of them, their studios, and their work. Among those included in recent issues are Stan Lynde ("Rick O'Shay"), Leonard Starr ("Mary Perkins—On Stage"), Chon Day (*New Yorker* cartoonist), John Fischetti (Pulitzer Prize winning political cartoonist), Mort Walker ("Beatle Bailey," "Hi and Lois"), Dan DeCarlo (the anonymous artist for the Archie comic books), and most of the *Mad* magazine staff. The articles are extremely heavily weighted toward the technical side—how the artists work; what kinds of pens, brushes, and inks they use; whether they recommend the use of shadows or highlights; how they develop and use a research "morgue" of art (Hal Foster describes his vacations to Europe to take photos of real castles that later appear in "Prince Valiant"); etc. There are also nostalgic articles on famous strips and cartoonists of the 1910s and 1920s. A large amount of advertising from art supply manufacturers and from the newspaper comic strip distribution syndicates indicates a large readership among the cartoonists and newspaper editors themselves. This magazine is of interest to all who enjoy reading about comic strips, and especially invaluable to high school and college graphic arts and journalism classes. (F.P.)

Funnyworld. irreg. but about 3/yr. $4.50 (4 issues). Mike Barrier, Box 5229, Brady Station, Little Rock, Ark. 72205.

"*Funnyworld* is an amateur, nonprofit magazine devoted to comic books, comic strips and animated cartoons," especially those involving cartoon or "funny animal" characters. Each issue is 56 pages, professionally typeset and printed, well laid out and profusely illustrated. The current issue (no.13) includes: Lengthy and highly critical reviews of three recent major animated films (Disney's *The Aristocats*, the "Peanuts" special, and MGM's cartoon version of Juster's *The Phantom Tollbooth*). Two interviews with Chuck Jones (former director of the Warner Brothers cartoon department) and Carl Stalling (composer of musical scores for hundreds of Disney and Warner Brothers cartoons), who describe conversationally but with a wealth of historical and technical information how their studios grew during the 1930s and how such cartoon stars as Bugs Bunny and "The Three Little Pigs" were created and filmed. (Many original sketches, old studio publicity photos, and model sheets are reproduced here.) Two articles on "underground/radical" comic books and a report on new developments in animated filmmaking are included. Also in this issue part of a continuing bibliography of the works of Carl Barks, who wrote and drew the Donald Duck comic books for decades and created most of the now-popular supporting characters such as Uncle Scrooge, and other features. This magazine is both enjoyable reading for fans of "the funnies" and an extremely valuable acquisition for libraries wanting materials for the history and study of popular literature and entertainment, and for cinema and art classes. (F.P.)

Graphic Story Magazine. irreg. but about 3/yr. $4.00 (4 issues). Bill Spicer, 329 North Avenue 66, Los Angeles, Calif. 90042.

The circumstances of the publication of Spicer's

GSM are similar to those of Barrier's *Funnyworld*, but *GSM* is more oriented toward the action and fantasy comic books and newspaper strips. The current issue contains a moderately good amateur comic book adaptation of a famous pulp-adventure SF story, Eando Binder's "Adam Link's Vengeance;" plus a lengthy interview with John Severin, an old professional comic book artist, who describes his own career and gives a good view of the production end of the mass-produced adventure comic books of the 1950s and 1960s; plus other features. The previous issue told the career of another old pro, Basil Wolverton, who was around when comic books were first created in the 1930s. The issue before that was devoted to the history of the popular newspaper detective strip of the thirties, "Red Barry," but it was really the strip's author's autobiography, a fascinating account of breaking into the newspapers in the 1920s, covering sports events, rubbing shoulders with Prohibition-era crime bosses, and the like. Again, an engrossing magazine for the comic strip fan and the student of modern popular culture, and probably a valuable study aid for journalism classes as well. (F.P.)

Graphic Story World. bi-m. $2.00. Richard Kyle, P. O. Box 16168, Long Beach, Calif. 90806.

If *Graphic Story World* is unfortunately similar in title to *Graphic Story Magazine*, it may be because editors Kyle and Spicer are fellow hobbyists, and *World* is intended in part to complement *Magazine*. Spicer is publishing an irregular magazine with lengthy and timeless features devoted to comic art and cartoonists of the past. Kyle is publishing a rigidly bimonthly, attractively offset, illustrated newsmagazine covering the latest information in the field. It has support from a number of professional cartoonists and editors who supply it with news. The report of the forthcoming change in publishers and format for the *Tarzan* comic book, five months in advance of the event, is taken from *GSW*. It also features reports on professional and fan conventions and awards within the field, and critical reviews of new comic-art books as soon as possible after their publication. Studies of the past are limited to brief "where are they now" reports on old-time cartoonists. *GSW* is attempting to obtain coverage of the whole world, and already has hobbyist/correspondents throughout Western Europe and in Japan reporting on new developments in comic magazines in their countries. An important feature is the editor's insistence on carrying full ordering information wherever possible, so that readers know how to obtain any of the books reviewed, American or foreign. (F.P.)

Phenix. q. $7. Dist. by: Fred Patten, 11863 W. Jefferson Blvd., Apt. 1, Culver City, Calif. 90230.

This 100-page magazine for serious students of comic art is the French equivalent of *Graphic Story*

Magazine or *Cartoonist Profiles*. It features biographical articles and lengthy interviews of leading cartoonists in America, Belgium, France, and Italy, profusely illustrated with photographs of the cartoonists and samples of their work. American cartoonists so studied have included Neal Adams, Milton Caniff, Rube Goldberg, Burne Hogarth, Carmine Infantino, and Joe Kubert. The editors of *Phenix* are active in arranging and attending exhibitions of comic art in museums and art salons throughout Europe, all of which are reported with extensive photographic coverage of the displays and prominent attendees. There is also a book department in each issue that notes the publication of scholarly studies of comic art around the world. (F.P.)

Boys and Girls: Elementary and Junior High

Archie. $1.35 yr. (9 issues). 32 pp. Archie Comic Publns., Inc. *Archie and Me.* $1.05 yr. (7 issues). 48 pp. *Archie's Joke Book Magazine.* $1.80 yr. (12 issues). 32 pp. *Archie's T.V. Laugh-out.* $1.25 yr. (5 issues). 48 pp. *Everything's Archie.* $1.50 yr. (6 issues). 48 pp. *Life with Archie.* $1.80 yr. (12 issues). 32 pp. *Little Archie.* $1.50 yr. (6 issues). 48 pp.

Archie Andrews and his friends at Riverdale High—Betty, Veronica, Jughead, and Reggie—are old enough to be American institutions. Unlike the newspaper comic strip, which features humor about teen-agers natural to a high school setting and written for the adults who buy newspapers, these comic books feature more juvenile plots with lots of simplistic action and even pure fantasy. In one story, a confidence man passes himself off as the manager of a famous singer and tricks our heroes into helping him sell tickets for a promised personal appearance, whereupon he skips town with the money and leaves the kids to face the angry townsfolk. But Sabrina, the teen-age witch, casts a spell to bring him back to town to be caught. In another story, Archie and his friends have their own rock group and find themselves fighting two dishonest hippies named Freek and Weerdo who try to keep them from winning a music contest. *Little Archie* features the same fivesome when they were about eight years old, having adventures like exploring haunted houses and discovering counterfeiters. The *Laugh-out* and *Joke Book* titles feature short gag strips rather than adventure stories. All these work in public-message plots about such things as pollution and school vandalism, and the supporting cast of Archie's schoolmates is well integrated. Though the stories are *about* teen-agers, the level of the plotting and the fantasy element make these titles more suitable for elementary school and lower junior high grades, or for slow readers. (F.P.)

Bugs Bunny. bi-m. $1.00 yr. Gold Key: Western Publishing Co., Inc.

Bugs Bunny is a favorite cartoon character with younger children. In this magazine he takes them on simple fantasy adventures. In one story, he idly carves holes in a carrot and makes a magic flute that attracts all the girl bunnies. But their boy friends are irate, so Bugs runs away and becomes the first mate on Yosemite Sam's pirate ship to escape. They go looking for buried treasure and Sam wants to make Bugs do all the digging, but Bugs uses his flute to call the native girl bunnies to do it for him. The treasure turns out to be a chest full of old pennies. In another story Bugs goes treasure hunting again, this time with his friend Elmer Fudd and an old sea captain. A treasure map leads them to an unexplored island with a large rock of solid gold in the center. But the rock is surrounded by Biting Begonias (pictured as piranha-like pansies), and our friends have to escape before they are eaten. Bugs is ready for new adventures, but Elmer is tired of trouble and ready to return home. (Time for his nap?) Other stories (often old reprints, but the characters and formula haven't changed in decades) feature other familiar Warner Brothers cartoon stars, such as Porky and Petunia Pig, Pepe le Pew the debonair skunk, Sylvester P. Pussycat, or Tweety Pie ("I tot I taw a Puddy Tat!") the canary. (F.P.)

Casper, the Friendly Ghost. m. $2.00 (10 issues). 32 pp. Harvey Comic Publns., Inc. *Casper and Nightmare.* bi-m. $.25 (no subscription). 48 pp. *Casper's Ghostland.* bi-m. $.25 (no subscription). 48 pp. *TV Casper and Company.* q. $.25 (no subscription). 48 pp.

Casper the friendly ghost, and his friends such as Wendy the good little witch, may be outcasts among their own scary fellows but they have lots of fun playing with real children and woodland animals. Casper often uses his ghostly abilities to scare away criminals and teach bullies it is no fun to be picked on by someone whom they cannot fight back. Casper teaches a bit of the Horatio Alger message to the youngest readers: he's always cheerful and ready to lend a friendly helping hand, and he shows strength of character in resisting the urgings of bad companions (his fellow ghosts) to do what he knows is wrong. Unlike the fantasy characters of a number of comics for youngest readers, who cause their adventures by acting sillily and illogically, Casper is always very practical and reasonable. The magazines have recently begun integrating the supporting characters, showing Negro children in prominent and favorable roles. These are popular titles with youngest readers, both boys and girls. (F.P.)

The Little Monsters. q. Gold Key: Western Publishing Co., Inc.

Monsters can be fun! Hollywood thought so a few years back when it unleashed *The Munsters* and *The Addams Family* as wholesome situation comedies. *The Little Monsters* is in the same vein. 'Orrible Orvie and Awful Annie are preteen Frankenstein's monsters, living in a bat-filled castle where they have lots of fun scaring the mailman, setting booby traps for pesky salesmen, romping with their pet weremonster, and so on. On the debit side, this comic is filled with "rubber-skulled violence"—bashing people over the head or dropping them through trapdoors into pits is shown as good, clean fun that couldn't really *hurt* anybody. On the credit side, it helps teach young readers that the monsters of horror movies and nightmares are just pretend and nothing to be really frightened of. (F.P.)

O. G. Whiz. q. Gold Key: Western Publishing Co., Inc.

Every little boy has wanted to (a) have all the toys he can possibly play with, and (b) be able to tell grown-ups what to do. Shoeshine boy Orvie Whiz finds himself in this position when a fluke makes him president of the moribund Tikkletoy Company, and he uses childhood common sense and rapport with the product's customers to put new life into the doddering firm. The Board of Directors is at his feet ("You're right again, O. G.!"), but the great-grandson of the original president feels he should have inherited the post and constantly tries to sabotage Orvie's position. The humor is broad enough to amuse both younger children and their parents—in one story, when a dissatisfied customer stalks in threatening to perform mayhem upon O. G., his office secretary muses, "I'd really like to warn O. G. the creep is back, but it is my lunch hour. . . ." The anonymous author is apparently also amusing himself by adding obscure references that readers are not supposed to spot but that may be an extra bonus if they do. The August 1971 issue has a variant on the "Prince and the Pauper" plot involving O. G. and a boy king, named Simeon II, of a mythical European kingdom. Is it only a coincidence that the last Tsar of Bulgaria, who abdicated in 1946 at the age of nine, also happens to have been named Simeon II? A child who collects postage stamps might get the reference. (F.P.)

Sad Sack Comics. bi-m. **Sad Sack and the Sarge.** bi-m. **Sad, Sad Sack.** q. **Sad Sack's Army Life Parade.** q. Harvey Comic Publns., Inc.

The Sad Sack started out as a World War II Army humor cartoon for the GIs. The Army boot camp setting is the same today, but Sack and his friends now appear in several comic books for younger readers. The humor has necessarily become much gentler and simplified, but there is still a lot of satire that even young readers will recognize. The Sad Sack is always trying to outwit his friendly enemy, the Sarge, to get out of KP or some other dirty job. Though the Sarge tries hard, fate is always on the side of the GIs. A lot of the humor is basic trainee wish-fulfillment; Sack is always "accidentally" blowing up the Sarge or knocking him into mud puddles, without any repercussions against himself or any damage to the invulnerable Sarge. Fun is also poked at the brass hat mentality of the commissioned officers. In one story, Sack inadver-

tently gets in the way of a publicity news photo being taken of Gen. Rockjaw endorsing a Senatorial candidate. The photo is published, and rather than admit that he was involved in a mistake, Gen. Rockjaw insists that Sack really run for the Senate. Despite the military setting, violence (other than the fantasy wish-fulfillment) never enters these comic books, which seem most suitable for little boys who like to play soldier. (Or possibly for basic trainees looking for speedily read relaxation during their brief rest moments?) (F.P.)

Walt Disney's Comics and Stories. m. $2.00 yr. Gold Key: Western Publishing Co., Inc.

The Walt Disney characters need no introduction. This magazine is a collection of three main stories and some minor features. First are Donald Duck and his nephews and friends. Donald's humorous misadventures are among the best writing and drawing in comic book literature. Always well motivated, with witty dialog and characterization, they have been enjoyed by young children and parents alike for 25 years. In fact, the publisher has given up trying to replace staff author-artist Carl Barks since his retirement a few years ago and is now simply reprinting the same timeless stories that earlier generations of children loved. Last is a Mickey Mouse adventure, an installment of a two- or three-part serial in which Mickey and Goofy go exploring or help the police capture spies, or do something similarly exciting. In between is a story featuring characters from whatever Disney feature-length animated film has most recently been released—at the moment, it's *The Aristocats*. In comparison with most other funny animal comics, the Disney titles feature intelligent characters who have fast-paced adventures with a minimum of violence. This is one of the best comic books available for young children through the elementary school grades. (F.P.)

Young Women: Adventure and Romance

The Dark Mansion of Forbidden Love. bi-m. **The Sinister House of Secret Love.** bi-m. National Comic Periodical Publns., Inc.

It was only a matter of time before the Gothic mystery romance came to comic books. To quote the splash panel from the October 1971 issue *Dark Mansion,* "Who killed Bettina? Was it the cruel old woman who ruled the Langfrey family? Was it Francesca, who roamed the house at night, singing to herself? Was it the family lawyer, suave and sinister? Was it handsome, brooding Michael, who attracted and yet repelled young Laura? *The dreadful answer lay hidden somewhere in the crumbling old mansion.*" The climax is straight out of Du Maurier's *Rebecca.* As in the old fairy tales, the heroine is a young girl who blunders through evil and deadly dangers, protected from all harm by her purity and innocence, and at the end finds her Prince Charming to live with happily ever after, their true love all the more surely proven by the peril they endured together. This will appeal to teenage girls who like more melodrama in their romance than the usual high school prom settings. (F.P.)

Lois Lane, Superman's Girl Friend. m. National Comic Periodical Publns., Inc.

Lois Lane seems to be a transitional comic for young women getting too old to read the boys' Superman titles, but not quite ready for the straight romance titles. Lois is the eternal, unofficial fiancée of the Man of Steel, but he doesn't dare marry her for fear of making her a target for revenge by his superenemies. In some issues, Lois tries scientifically to make herself superpowerful so she will be a fit mate for Superman. In others, she tries to forget him in the arms of another man, handsome, talented, and kind. But always she returns to wait, hoping that someday, someday. . . . Recent issues have mixed social relevancy with the romance. In one, Lois uses a superscientific device to turn herself into a Negro for a day to get a news story on ghetto conditions, and learns first hand about prejudice. (Shades of John Howard Griffin.) In another, she takes charge of a cute Indian infant until its real father can be found, but a snide gossip columnist spreads the rumor that she does not really care about the baby but only wants a good news story, making her a target for indignant social protestors. Good for girls up to the junior high school level. (F.P.)

Wonder Woman. bi-m. National Comic Periodical Publns., Inc.

Wonder Woman is one of the oldest comic magazines in existence, but its attempt to appeal to both boys and the more adventure-loving younger teen girls has never made it a big seller. After 25 years as a superheroine with magic powers from the Greek goddesses and a skimpy but patriotic costume, she was almost killed by falling sales. In a recent drastic format change, Wonder Woman has surrendered all this. She now lives solely in her mortal secret identity as Diana Prince, stripped of superpowers, her star-spangled red-white-blue outfit replaced by a mod white buckskin jacket and matching pants suit. She hasn't given up crime fighting, though. A kindly Oriental mentor, I Ching, has taught her the secrets of bodily self-defense, and she is now a sort of free-lance secret agent, a female James Bond, battling international criminal organizations, political assassins, and the like. There's a bit of romance in it, a bit of Women's Lib, and a touch of the supernatural, but mostly lots of action involving karate and judo against underworld hoods. As with a number of this publisher's titles, the economic state of the industry makes it impossible to fill the issue with all new stories, so the back half consists of a "classic reprint" showing Wonder Woman in her old superheroine mode. (F.P.)

Young Romance. m. *Girls' Love Stories.* m. National Comic Periodical Publns., Inc.

These similar magazines contain four to six short stories each. One issue of *Young Romance,* for example, tells the story of attractive Donna, who feels sorry for her plain sister and insists that Jeff get one of his friends to double-date so Eileen won't have to stay home alone, then feels betrayed when Jeff himself falls in love with her. But then Donna realizes that it is really Jeff's friend that she loves, so all ends in a double wedding. In another story, Janie is worried that she may not really love Peter because she can't get as excited over him as Cynthia is over her boy friend. But when she sees Cynthia get just as thrilled over next week's date, she realizes that her calm, steady love is more lasting than flighty emotionalism. There is a reprint of a "classic love story . . . your mothers read 20 years ago," and readers are asked at the conclusion if they would like to see more such reprints, "old-fashioned clothes and all." The issue also contains dating hints and a simplified advice to the lovelorn column. The dating counselor, Page Peterson, could be called a token Black; the stories themselves all feature the romantic problems of teen-age, middle-class, Caucasian girls. Implied or stated ages are usually 17 or older; settings are high school and junior college campuses; but the situations described are more applicable to girls just going out on their first dates. Such comics may help such girls to realize that their emotions and doubts are not unique. However, the happy endings in which a true, undying love is always achieved in a matter of days or weeks may give some immature readers the impression that they should be able to find and recognize a lifelong mate all too easily. (F.P.)

Costumed Heros

Batman. m. National Comic Periodical Publns., Inc.

The Batman is still running around Gotham City in those night-colored leotards, but not much else is the same in this 31-year-old title. In an attempt to make the character more salesworthy to modern teen-agers, the old superhero and "camp" humor story lines have given way to one more like that of the famous crime fighter of the 1930s, The Shadow. Where the Batman used to rely upon Batmobiles, Batcomputers, and a whole Batcaveful of scientific gimmicks, he now gets by on Sherlock Holmes–type deduction. Where he used to trade quips as he battled improbably garbed supervillains, he is now a grim, silent figure of the night as he swoops down upon gangsters and other more plausible baddies. In his alter ego as Bruce Wayne, millionaire, the old guise of an idle young playboy has been replaced by that of a concerned philanthropist, using his money to help the needy. The biggest change has been Batman's separation from Robin, his boy companion from time immemorial. The Boy Wonder has finally grown old enough to go to college and now has a separate story in the comic, set on the campus of the college he attends as Dick Grayson, where he helps break up juvenile delinquency and expose off-campus rabble rousers stirring up malicious student protest violence. For those who preferred the old formula, there are "classic reprints" in each issue. The publisher is trying to appeal to boys over a wide age group. (F.P.)

The Brave and the Bold. bi-m. **World's Finest Comics.** bi-m. National Comic Periodical Publns., Inc.

The unique feature of these two superhero comics is that both are "team-up" titles, featuring one of DC's most popular heroes co-starring with a less popular one. In *Brave and the Bold* the lead star is always the Batman, and in *World's Finest* it is always Superman. The guest stars are usually heroes whose own comics need a sales boost, or whose own comics have disappeared and whose return appearance is a special occasion not to be missed by their fans. The backup features in both titles are reprints of stories featuring long-forgotten minor heroes and villains from the forties and fifties, identified in an introductory bibliographic note as to their special powers or gimmicks, their first and last appearances, and the title and date from which this particular sample is reprinted. Since this is much more information than the normal comic book reader will care for, it looks like both these titles are being assembled with an eye toward the teen-age collector of comic books and connoisseur of costumed heroes. Additional evidence is provided in the letter columns, where readers request guest appearances of their favorite heroes, many of whom are so old that only collectors would still remember them. Many go out of their way to cite their status as college undergraduates, and in *Brave and the Bold,* no. 99, a USC reader writes, "Now that you're reaching out to grab us college kids as readers . . .," indicating a growing cliqueishness among the readership. As to the quality of the stories in these two comics, neither the editorial staff nor the readers seem to care for anything more than making sure that all costumes are displayed with maximum visibility. (F.P.)

Daredevil. m. Marvel Comic Group: Magazine Management Co.

Daredevil (subtitle: *The Man Without Fear!*) is one of the few traditional superhero comics holding out against the trend to relevancy. His particular gimmick is that he is blind but he has a radar sense that nobody else knows about, so the world little suspects that the helpless young lawyer, Matt Murdock, is in reality the dashing Daredevil! That is incidental, though. This comic is for the younger teens who like lots of action, especially spectacular slug-fests with grotesque monsters or fearsomely costumed supervillains with names like the Man-Bull, the Assassin, or the Gladiator. Wisecracks and repartee ("I wuz just gonna BEAT you to a pulp . . . now I'm gonna MURDER yuh!" "All by your little LONESOME?!") fly thicker than the fists. Marvel Comics is long on soap-opera plotting, and the constant subplot is that Daredevil is on the verge of losing his girl friend who cannot take the emotional strain of loving someone who lives as recklessly as he does. He also worries if there isn't something a bit abnormal in his compulsion to go running through downtown Manhattan is his bright red skin-tight suit. But every time he resolves to give up his secret identity and begin leading a normal life, he happens upon another bank robbery or skyjacking which only he can prevent, and he is off again. Long-time readers are beginning to yawn, but apparently the turnover in comic book readership is so rapid that this is always fresh to the majority of the readers, provided it doesn't happen more often than once in a dozen issues. (F.P.)

Fantastic Four. m. $3/13 issues. Marvel Comic Group: Magazine Management Co.

This is the oldest of the "new" or "realistic" super hero comics. The characters themselves are even more fantastic than most: Mr. Fantastic (Reed Richards) can stretch his body to unbelievable lengths; the Invisible Girl (Sue Storm Richards) can turn invisible; the Human Torch (Johnny Storm) is a teen-ager who can burst into flame and fly; and the Thing (Ben Grimm) is an ugly orange granite-complexioned monster with tremendous strength. Their reality is in their emotions and character development. Richards is the liberal-intellectual who leads them; Grimm has a hard-hat political philosophy (they're always arguing); the Torch is interested in sports cars and prone to leave in a huff if he thinks the others aren't treating him like an adult. After a romance lasting dozens of issues, Reed and Sue got married and now have a son. They live in New York City, not some mythical metropolis, and their dialogue is phonetically spelled dialect. Their real identities are not secret, and they suffer all the annoyances of any celebrity, not to mention attempted suits for false arrest from the villains they capture and public indignation when they are not able to stop a monster before it destroys property. United in their freakdom as the result of one of Richards' early experiments gone wrong, they are willing to try to turn their disabilities into assets and do the best they can to improve America by working within the system. A good magazine for boys from junior high school on up. (F.P.)

Justice League of America. m. National Comic Periodical Publns., Inc.

The JLA is a society of super do-gooders composed of almost every costumed hero published by this company: Superman, Batman, Flash, Green Lantern, Hawkman, Atom, Aquaman, and several others. Its raison d'etre is the hope that fans of any one hero will buy this magazine as well, and possibly also the individual comics of the other heroes they meet here. This is one of the titles that has recently become "relevant." One story shows the heroes lamenting that with all their powers, they cannot increase the amount of food available for an earth rapidly becoming overpopulated. Another shows the heroes being battled to a standstill by an alien menace, while ordinary people— a Vietnamese peasant, an Arab merchant, and an American hippie—stumble onto the Achilles' heel that destroys it, all presumably symbolizing that one does not have to have superpowers to stand tall as a human being. Unfortunately, with 8 or 12 heroes to share the action, the stories are all much too fast-paced and shallow. However, many young teens buy for the maximum number of colorful costumes available for their quarter, rather than for literary value, and this is a popular title with them. Backup reprints include old SF stories or short tales featuring adventures of individual JLA'ers. (F.P.)

The New Gods. bi-m. ***Mister Miracle.*** bi-m. ***The Forever People,*** bi-m. ***Superman's Pal, Jimmy Olsen,*** m. National Comic Periodical Publns., Inc.

Jack "King" Kirby has been designing and drawing superhero comics since 1940, and today he has a fanatical following among the comic book collectors and "intellectuals." His publisher has given him free rein to create, write, and draw his own series of three interlocking comics, plus the poorest-selling of the "Superman family" titles, gambling that Kirby's name alone on the cover can make them successes. Early sales reports indicated that it has worked; one Hollywood newsstand reported selling over 500 copies of one issue in a week. In five issues of each title examined all that was evident was a bewildering farrago of grotesquely costumed heroes and villains from two opposed superworlds, using Earth as a battleground, with lots of hints of dire revelations to unfold in forthcoming issues. The good guys, from New Genesis, include Orion, Lightray, Metron, Mark Moonrider, Beautiful Dreamer, and all their friends. The bad guys, from Apokolips, are DeSaad, Dr. Bedlam, Kalibak the Cruel, Steel Hand, a pseudo-Mafia called Inter-Gang, and a number of other henchmen all controlled by deadly Darkseid. Half of each issue is devoted to a "classic reprint" of an early forties Kirby story. High school and college boys are grabbing them up. (F.P.)

Superboy. m. National Comic Periodical Publns., Inc.

Every American child must know the Superman legend—how he was sent as a baby from the exploding planet Krypton to Earth, was adopted by kindly Mr. and Mrs. Kent, and was raised as a rural Midwestern youth in Smallville, U.S.A., until he grew up and moved to the big city of Metropolis. By editorial fiat announced in the January 1971 issue, in these tales of Superman's youth he will remain eternally 14 years old in stories set 15 years prior to the current date. *Superboy* is also showing signs of relevancy (one re-

cent issue had him battling insensitive industrialists polluting the sea), but on the whole the stories maintain the old traditions. The superyouth plays with Krypto, his superpooch, patrols Smallville to keep it safe from supervillains and menaces from outer space, and tries to keep his secret identity safe from Lana Lang, that pesky girl next door. A backup feature in each issue is "The Legion of Super-Heroes," a story featuring a whole club of costumed teenagers with different spectacular powers living in the thirtieth century. Superboy often flies into the future to join their adventures. Though Superboy himself may be 14, the comic appears more suitable for boys a few years younger than that, and for slow readers. (F.P.)

Superman. m. National Periodical Publns., Inc.

Superman founded the superhero industry in 1938, and by now he is universally recognized as the invulnerable symbol for "truth, justice, and the American way." All during 1971, however, the character has been undergoing a major renovation to make him more popular with today's youth. This includes stripping him of the more fantastic abilities bestowed upon him by various writers during his career, to the point of making him so impregnable and virtuous as to be positively boring. His mild-mannered alter-ego, Clark Kent, has also been updated, leaving his reporter's job at the *Daily Planet* to become a TV newscaster. His old pals Jimmy Olsen, Lois Lane, and Perry White are still around but are in the background at the moment. The traditional self-contained stories have been replaced by an interminable serial, science-fictional in nature but with a menace as yet undefined, which may be confusing to new readers entering in mid-tale. But *Superman* is still this publisher's main comic and biggest seller, and if there is any basic superhero magazine, this is it! Good for boys of all ages. (F.P.)

Thor. m. Marvel Comic Group: Magazine Management Co.

This is a superhero comic with the trappings of Norse mythology. The hero is Thor, Storm God and son of Odin. Supporting characters include other genuine deities, such as Balder, Heimdall, and evil Loki (Thor's archenemy, naturally); various editorially created noble warriors, like Hogun the Grim or Fandral the Flashing (an Errol Flynn type); and more standard comic book menaces, such as giant robots, monsters from outer space, supercriminals, etc. In early issues, Thor used to spend most of his time on Earth (where he has the meek alter-ego of Don Blake, surgeon) fighting Communists and mundane monsters. But the readers apparently prefer the mythology because these days most of the action is against the Trolls, Frost Giants, and other dooms from the old legends, usually under Loki's control. Everybody has a colorful superhero's costume, and Asgard/Valhalla looks like a cross between Disneyland and Rockefeller Center. The dialogue is Brooklyn dialect when on Earth, and a pseudomedieval English most of the rest of the time. It canst but drive thy true scholar up the walls, but thine high school students seemest to diggest it the most. This must be where "camp" has gone. (F.P.)

Westerns

All-Star Western. bi-m. National Comic Periodical Publns., Inc. (DC Comics)

The casualty rate among Western comics has been high recently. DC has decided to concentrate all its efforts on one new title, and that appears to be just barely hanging on. A perusal of the ten issues to date indicates that DC is not quite sure what it is doing. There have been a number of "different" stars, most of whom have disappeared after two or three trial stories. One was Billy the Kid—not the real one, but a young girl, Billy Jo, impersonating the famous boyish gunslinger to gain entry into unsavory circles to look for her father's killers. The latest is Jonah Hex, a disfigured (physically and emotionally), rather pathetic bounty hunter. The art (Tony De Zuñiga) and scripts (John Albano) are quite good; it is unfortunate that the Western stereotype is so hackneyed today that they have to stretch the limits of credibility in their attempts to create original characters. For fans of formula Western heroes, there's El Diablo, a copy of Zorro superbly drawn by Gray Morrow but incredibly poorly written by Robert Kanigher. The dialogue is banal even for a comic book, and El Diablo seems unable to win against his foes without the aid of such dei ex machina as convenient avalanches or pools of quicksand that inexplicably appear beneath their feet. There are also reprints from DC's various past Western titles, most of which are at least adequate. The overall quality is varied but generally high enough to make this a good title for boys throughout their teens. (F.P.)

Kid Colt, Outlaw. bi-m. **Outlaw Kid.** bi-m. **Rawhide Kid.** m. **Ringo Kid.** bi-m. **Two-Gun Kid.** bi-m. Marvel Comics Group: Magazine Management Co.

These titles from the same publisher are so identical that they can be covered by the same review. Each is an epitome of the hack formula Western. The Kid is a young loner, a modern Robin Hood, the fastest gun and the surest shot in the West, sometimes falsely believed to be an outlaw and unable to prove his innocence. He never settles down, stopping in a town just long enough to catch some bank robbers or expose a crooked banker or whip a gunslinger terrorizing the peaceful townfolks before riding on again. Occasionally there is an attempt to mix historical fact with the fiction, and the Kid will be just too late to prevent the massacre at the Alamo or the Little Big Horn (40 years apart in actual fact). The magazines are almost all reprints of stories written in the 1950s, and it is

almost impossible to tell the stories apart aside from the costumes of the different Kids. (Not costumes in the costumed-hero sense, but none of them have changed their clothes since their magazines began.) For younger boys or slow readers, who like simple and short stories with nothing but lots of predictable action. (F.P.)

War

Our Army at War. m. National Comic Periodical Publns., Inc.

Sgt. Rock and his veterans of Easy Co. have been pushing the Nazis back across France for years now. Though Rock always manages to win handily, the comic has moved away from the old flag-waving formula in which the GI superman faced hordes of sadistic swastikaed demons with a wisecrack on his lips. The war is shown as a dirty one; a hammering away at a faceless gray mass. Though Easy's morale is good, the men are tired and there's no glamour. Rock is the father-figure who looks after his men, who eases fresh recruits through the shock of battle into the small brotherhood, not without lengthy thought-balloon soliloquies (behind his impassive front) in which he worries about the responsibilities of leadership. The emotional problems he faces are stereotyped but not unreal—the kid who feels that every enemy bullet has his name on it, the kid who is overconfident and who has to be taught caution, the kid who is worried that he will not be able to pull his weight among his new buddies. Recently the trend to "relevancy" has brought less savory types through Easy, such as one who sees each Nazi as a potential source of war souvenirs to impress his pals back home, or (in the June 1971 issue, which appeared during the height of the My Lai publicity) a soldier who could not see any difference between an enemy combatant and an enemy civilian and who killed all indiscriminately. (He was finally killed himself, simplistically solving Rock's problem of what to do about him.) Each story in this magazine, and in all this publisher's war comics, carries a small circled message in the final panel: "Make War No More." A good title for junior high and high school boys. (F.P.)

Star Spangled War Stories. bi-m. National Comic Periodical Publns., Inc.

This war comic features two rather different series characters. The Unknown Soldier is a World War II U.S. Army secret agent, a master of disguise who gets sent behind enemy lines to smuggle Resistance fighters out of Nazi concentration camps or perform similar feats of one-man derring-do. The Enemy Ace is a German World War I aerial fighter, obviously patterned after Richthofen, shown as a sensitive, deeply philosophical man fighting for his homeland, stoically expecting his own death with each new mission. The letter column of the September 1971 issue contains several protests that Enemy Ace has been relegated to the back of the book, and the editor replies, "But all the acclamation via letters and cards did *not* make up for the lack of market sales," which have begun rising again now that they have returned to featuring the Invulnerable GI versus Nasty Nazi formula, so it is better to keep Enemy Ace alive as a backup feature than to have poor sales kill the comic altogether. Editor Joe Kubert (who also draws both series) seems to have a genuine concern for his work, and the stories avoid the hack formulas as much as he can manage—more so than is good for sales, apparently. A few old reprints pad out the issue. A good title for boys in the upper teens. (F.P.)

Weird Fantasy

The Phantom Stranger. bi-m. National Comic Periodical Publns., Inc.

The Phantom Stranger is a weird/occult superhero. Most comic book superheroes have a pseudoscientific explanation for their powers, and battle science-fictional mad scientists or menaces from outer space. The Phantom Stranger is an ageless, modern-garbed white warlock who struggles against evil sorcerers, supernatural forces, and demons as close to Satan himself as the Comics Code Authority will permit. It is a very current blend of the old superhero formula and the modern fad among the older teens in astrology and *Rosemary's Baby*-type urban black magic. It seems to have a small but enthusiastic readership among fans of both sexes, and artist Jim Aparo's drawings are consistently praised in the letter column. The backup features in each issue is an adventure of Dr. Terry Thirteen, an intellectual detective who specializes in investigating supposedly supernatural crimes and disasters, usually to reveal a human agent behind them. (F.P.)

The Twilight Zone. Boris Karloff Tales of Mystery. Both bi-m. $1.00 yr. Gold Key: Western Publishing Co., Inc.

The Twilight Zone, Rod Serling's 1959 sophisticated fantasy television series, disappeared from the TV screens years ago, but its associational comic book lives on. Each issue contains three or four short stories, introduced in the large introductory panel by Serling himself. The stories are all fantasies in modern settings, with such plots as department store mannequins who come to life to foil a nighttime burglar, or a man who tries to outwit the Grim Reaper by attempting to stay away from the Empire State Building where he's fated to die, or an explorer who scoffs at a native curse only to have it befall him. Another title from this publisher is *Boris Karloff Tales of Mystery*, the last remnant of Karloff's short-lived TV series of the early sixties. The stories in the two comics are so alike as to be interchangeable; the only difference is that it is Karloff who is depicted as the m.c. in the latter title

rather than Serling. Despite their trappings of colorful fantasy, the stories are all rather shallow and lifeless, making these magazines most suitable for uncritical readers in the 10 to 14 year-old age group who have a taste for the eerie, but nothing *too* scary. (F.P.)

The Witching Hour. bi-m. *The Unexpected.* m. *House of Secrets.* bi-m. *House of Mystery.* m. National Comic Periodical Publns., Inc.

The weird-fantasy comics were among the first to die under the attacks of Dr. Wertham and the purity censors of the 1950s, but today, after the popularity of such films as *Rosemary's Baby* and such TV series as *Dark Shadows*, they've risen from the grave. Usual plots concern shiftless relatives who murder wealthy aunts or uncles for their inheritance, or jealous lovers who rid themselves of rivals, and the ghostly way in which the culprit is punished. Deals with the devil, in which the bargainer tries to cheat the devil but always fails, are also popular. There are plenty of witches, demons, and other bogies, but evil always fails to prosper, though the stories often imply that the villains are so clever that it is only through the supernatural that they can be punished. Some of the stories are imaginative and told with a dash of sardonic humor (endings are ironic whenever possible), though the majority are formula. The stories are most distinctly successful in their artwork, with each story drawn by a different illustrator in an individualistic style. The art is signed, and the readers have their favorite artists whom they request more of in the letter columns. These titles present weird-fantasy with some originality, and are most popular with older teens who appreciate and comment on the quality of the writing and art beneath the surface of the stories. (F.P.)

Fantasy Adventure

Amazing Spider-Man. m. $3/13 issues. Marvel Comic Group: Magazine Management Co.

Spider-Man continues to be "the comic book for every red-blooded teen-age introvert." Bookish Peter Parker, who was bitten by a radioactive spider and given super powers, is now a college student. But his life is still as confused as ever: he is constantly on the verge of flunking because his crime fighting leaves too little time for homework, and losing his girl friends because they can sense he is keeping secrets he will not trust them with, and fearful that aged Aunt May will learn of his double life and die of shock; and hounded and despised by the public who (thanks to J. Jonah Jameson's yellow-journalistic newspaper articles) see him only as a supershowoff and dynamic delinquent. In other words, his super powers do not solve his adolescent growing problems; they magnify them; and high school and college readers really identify with him. Despite flamboyant battles with some of the most grotesque supervillains in the trade, the title is one of the most "relevant" of all comic magazines, thanks to realistic dialogue and vocabulary, plus up-to-the-minute story hooks such as ghetto racial unrest, the need for prison reform, Women's Lib, campus violence, the Viet Nam war, and others presenting these problems in an honest light and offering no simplistic solutions. (F.P.)

From Beyond the Unknown. bi-m. ***Strange Adventures.*** bi-m. National Comic Periodical Publns., Inc.

These are collections (currently all reprints of stories written in the 1950s and early 1960s) of standard juvenile science fiction, mostly of the space opera variety. Space explorers encounter fantastic beasts and exotic civilizations while discovering new planets. The space police match wits and rayguns with Martian criminals. Alien invaders menace Earth until a handsome young scientist finds the flaw in their superscientific armor. Jungle explorers discover the ruins of a prehistoric city or a crashed spaceship that contains unknown scientific devices which almost destroy Earth when carelessly meddled with. An ugly alien monster driven away with atomic bombs was really an emissary from an advanced world coming to bring mankind a cure for all diseases. There are one or two continuing spacemen-heroes in all this, but most stories are unrelated and only 8 to 10 pages in length. Many revolve around a particular simple scientific fact that is explained to the reader in a footnote. This is pure Buck Rogers–type fiction, aimed at boys just entering their teens. (F.P.)

Conan the Barbarian. m. Marvel Comic Group: Magazine Management Co.

In the early 1930s, in the pulp magazine *Weird Tales,* a young author named Robert Howard created a new school of swashbuckling fantasy with his tales of Conan the Cimmerian, a brawny warrior living in a past age in which prehistoric monsters still lived and the science of sorcery had not yet been lost. The series was immensely popular, and the stories are all still in print today, three decades after Howard's death. Last year Roy Thomas, a young Conan fan and an English teacher turned comic book scenarist, persuaded his employers to experiment with a Conan comic book. In these adaptations of Howard's original stories, and Thomas's new pastiches of them, the brooding, sullen Conan once more strides across the map of Earth's first forgotten civilizations, slaying dragons, cheating corrupt noblemen, battling evil wizards, adventuring as a mercenary or a pirate, and heading toward his unsuspecting destiny as usurper of the throne of Aquilonia. Thomas affects a flowery, pseudo-Victorian style of writing that enhances the aura of antiquity and primitive, barbaric splendor that has made the magazine an instant success with older boys. The letter column often shows addresses at several colleges. (F.P.)

Creatures on the Loose. bi-m. ***Monsters on the Prowl.*** bi-m. ***Where Monsters Dwell.*** bi-m. Marvel Comic Group: Magazine Management Co.

These comic books are for monster fans. The stories are virtually all reprints from the early 1960s when the flood of Japanese monster movies was at its height. A grotesquely huge ant or a blob or a tentacled "thing" lands from outer space or is awakened in an ancient Egyptian tomb, and proceeds to conquer Earth. Jet fighters, atomic bombs, nothing can stop it. "Puny humans, your infantile weapons are insignificant against the might of *Kragoom the Conqueror!!!!*" But an average citizen, usually the poor sap who unknowingly turned the monster loose in the first place, gets a simple idea that has occurred to nobody else in the world, and tricks the creature into fleeing back into outer space. Other stories are "anti-science fiction," of the "things man was never meant to know" variety. Editor Stan Lee has publicly admitted that these are the stories he was bored with and sick of grinding out when he created the "different" Fantastic Four. However, kids to whom a "sci-fi classic" means an old monster movie on TV still go for this. Can these titles survive the publisher's using up of its backlog of reprint material? (F.P.)

Tarzan. m. ***Korak.*** bi-m. National Comic Periodical Publns., Inc.

Tarzan of the Apes is another character who needs no introduction to the public. Thanks to the paperback reprinting of the entire series in the early 1960s, most people are now aware that the Jungle Lord is an intelligent and well-educated gentleman-adventurer, despite his unusual upbringing, and not the "Me Tarzan, you Jane" apeman created by Hollywood. For the last 30 years Tarzan has also had his own comic book, based more on the movie stereotype than on the novels and was generally shallow and insipid. News releases received just as this book was going to press promised a change. "The December *Tarzan of the Apes* will be the last issue published by Gold Key comics. Long dissatisfied with Gold Key's presentation . . . Edgar Rice Burroughs, Inc. has ended its contract with Western Publishing Company . . ." The new publisher will be National Periodical Publications, the first issues were due in March 1972. There will be two titles, *Tarzan* and *Korak,* the latter featuring Tarzan's teen-age son (a minor character in Burroughs' books). In addition both comics will contain back-up stories starring Burroughs' other famous pulp heroes, John Carter of Mars, Carson Napier of Venus, and David Innes of Pellucidar. The stories will be adaptations of the originals or new tales adhering faithfully to these, in collaboration with the Burroughs estate. The company is assigning its top artists and writers to these; Tarzan's own adventures will be drawn by their designer-editor Joe Kubert. Burroughs' adventurous fantasies pitting clean-cut heroes against lost civilizations and prehistoric monsters in the jungles of Africa, Venus, or the center of the Earth have always been popular with teen-age boys (he reportedly claimed he was trying to write the kind of stories that Boy Scouts would find clean, exciting reading around the campfire), and the new *Tarzan* sounds like it should be a success. (F.P.)

Foreign Language Comics

European comic magazines can be valuable aids for libraries in schools with active foreign language programs. The stories are often more exciting than those in textbooks, the dialogue shows how the speech is in current usage, and the individual word balloons are small enough to make translating seem less of a chore. It is educational to see the cultural differences in stories set in Europe. But the most popular feature many stories set in America (there are more Westerns than any other single plot category), and it is especially educational to study the stereotyped view of American culture presented to European youth by European writers. Some are painstakingly accurate; others have gross errors. Many are much more critical of the seamier aspects of American history, such as racial prejudice, than any American comics have dared to be until the "relevancy" fad of last year.

The best magazines are originated in the French language, in France and Belgium. The common practice is to publish weekly magazines of 60 or so pages in full color on high-quality paper, containing numerous comic strips, puzzle pages, and popularized articles on such subjects as sports cars, natural history, or famous battles. The result is rather like a combination of American Sunday newspaper comic-strip supplements and youth magazines such as *Boys' Life*. The most important features are the comic strips, which appear in a variety of styles. There are numerous one-page humor strips, and a few 6- or 8-page complete adventures, but most of the strips are serialized at a rate of a couple of pages per issue for half a year or so. In addition, the most popular of the serialized comics are later reprinted in stiff-backed book form as complete adventures of 48 or 64 pages. The really popular adventures may stay in print for years; one of the earliest volumes in the "Tintin" series, *Tintin en Amerique*, which is still available, has topical allusions to the Volstead Act, the Lindbergh Kidnapping, and Al Capone. Because a popular strip may keep earning money for years, and because European cartoonists retain a larger financial interest in their creations than do American cartoonists (who usually must sell all rights to their comic book publishers or newspaper syndicates), much more care and effort is put into these French strips than into American comic books designed to be casually read once and then discarded. The result is a much superior product by almost any literary standards.

These French strips are popular enough that they are reprinted around the world. A few short-lived attempts were made to introduce some of the most popular reprint volumes into America, but due to printing costs in this country they had to be marketed at $3 each, and the public simply will not pay $3 for a comic book. Some of these French magazines have foreign-language editions in Greece, Portugal, and Scandinavian nations, the Netherlands, and others. Some countries have their own weekly magazines that contain a mixture of original strips and selections from among all the French journals. These annotations will concentrate on those magazines known to accept American subscriptions and to accept checks in American currency in payment.

Warning to serials departments: because of the vagaries of boat mail delivery from Europe, it is not unusual to receive issues of a weekly magazine in an order of, say, 1, 4, 3, 2, 5, or to go three weeks without receiving any and then get four issues at once. Issues seldom arrive sooner than a month and a half after cover date, and may be as much as two and a half months late. Discretion should therefore be exercised in claiming apparently missing issues. (F.P.)

Bang! irreg. $9 U.S. (6 issues, plus 12 issues of the informative bulletin). *Bang!* Apartado de Correos 9331, Barcelona, España.

Bang! (Información y estudios sobre la historieta) is Spain's magazine of serious appreciation of comic art. The 68-page regular magazine features one long illustrated section per issue, usually a lengthy episode of a famous strip or a work by a cartoonist studied in that issue. The remainder of the issue consists of numerous short editorials, interviews with Spanish cartoonists and bibliographic checklists of their work with a few sample illustrations, and book reviews. The informative bulletins are 12 or 14 page mimeographed newsletters carrying readers' letters, answers to questions, a collectors wants and sales column, and current news and reviews of a minor nature. *Bang!* exists in fits and starts; after a period of excessive activity between Summer 1970 and Spring 1971 it appears to have fallen into a slumber again. (F.P.)

Charlie. m. 36 French francs ($6.48 U.S.) for 12 issues. *Charlie*, Editions du Square, 35 Rue Montholon, Paris 9e, France.

Charlie is not exactly an underground comic but it certainly is full of political and black humor. It contains three or four new strips of its own, and a number of reprints of American and Italian strips. It specializes in showing off the work of famous American cartoonists from the superreactionary Al Capp and the superconservative Charles Schulz to the superradical Gilbert Shelton. American reprints in various issues have included complete episodes of "Li'l Abner" and "Fearless Fosdick," Shelton's "Wonder Wart–Hog," long selections from "Peanuts" and "Krazy Kat," several pages of old "Betty Boop" daily strips from the thirties to demonstrate how standards of the shockingly sexy in comic art have changed, and an anonymous superpatriotic comic book story dating from World War II as an example of monumental bad taste. There have also been selected examples of the work of such morbid cartoonists as Goya, Heinrich Kley, and Edward Gorey.

Charlie's editor affects the air of a jaded dilettante but he appears to know his stuff. (F.P.)

Corriere dei Ragazzi. (Formerly: *Corriere dei Piccoli.*) w. annual subscription L9,750 ($16.50 U.S.). *Corriere dei Ragazzi,* 20100 Milano, Via Solferino 28, Italy.

Possibly the oldest existing childrens' magazine in the world, Italy's *Corriere dei Ragazzi* has been appearing since 1908. Until recently it was titled *Corriere dei Piccoli,* but a market study showed that its evolution to a comic-art magazine has brought it a readership of older children and young adults, and the *Piccoli* (infants) in the title was possibly creating some sales resistance. An examination of a current 68-page issue shows 42 pages of comic art (mostly realistic adventure strips) of which 25 pages are original, 15 are translations from the French-language *Spirou* and *Tintin* magazines, and two are translations of U.S. newspaper comic strips. The remaining 16 pages consist of puzzles and games, a short story and an installment of a serialized novel, a two-page summary of children in current news around the world, pop record reviews, a school fasion department for girls, and lots of advertising. This issue contains an insert, *Corriere bis Ragazzi,* a small 16-page black-and-white booklet reprinting U.S. Sunday newspaper comic strips of a family situation–comedy nature, such as "Hi and Lois" and "Pony." The publisher's colophon lists the magazine's price in 36 different currencies (U.S., $.35), with one overall annual foreign subscription rate. It is cited in *Ulrich's International Periodicals Directory* as having a circulation of 300,000. (F.P.)

Pilote. w. 2 French francs (36¢ U.S.) per issue; 55 F ($9.90) for 6 months; 100 F ($18.00) for 1 year; 190 F ($34.20) for 2 years. Subs. to: Dargaud Editeur, Service des Abonnements, 12 Rue Blaise Pascal, 92 Neuilly-sur-Seine, France. Make checks payable in U.S. currency to: Dargaud Editeur, C.C.P. Paris 14420–20.

This 60-page magazine for older teens is considered the most intellectual of the comics. It is divided into two halves, the colored half containing the comic strips and the bland-and-white half containing a selection of "current event" satires a la *Mad* Magazine. (*Pilote's* artistic staff exhibits a thorough familiarity with the work of such *Mad* artists as Jack Davis, Mort Drucker, and George Woodbridge.) The strips include a number that have been made into animated films or live-action TV adventure shows in France. Among these are "Asterix," a humorous fantasy whose Popeye-like hero is a Gallic warrior living in the days of Caesar's conquests; "Lieutenant Blueberry," the most authentic of the Westerns ("blueberry" was an old slang term for a blue-jacketed Cavalryman); "Michel Tanguy," a realistic Air Force adventure strip similar to Caniff's "Steve Canyon" but with a greater emphasis on French Air Force technology and operations; "Valerian," a semi-cartoon science-fiction strip in the grand space opera tradition; "Lucky Luke," a hilarious cartoon Western fantasy that satirizes every grade-B movie cliche in existence; "Lone Sloane," a science-fictional tour de force of surrealistic art; and numerous others. Not all these strips appear every week; there are usually gaps of several issues between episodes. But there are always a number of good strips in each issue. (F.P.)

Ran Tan Plan. q. single issues 110 FB ($2.20 U.S.); annual subscription 400 FB ($8.00 U.S.) *Ran Tan Plan,* Andre Leborgne, Avenue Van Volxem 435, B-1060 Bruxelles, Belgium.

Ran Tan Plan is one of the leading French-language scholarly comic-art magazines, progressing over 20 issues from mimeography to a professionally offset, illustrated format. It features news of current developments in comic art throughout Europe and in America, as well as articles on popular works of the past. The emphasis is on European material, though. Where most serious comic-art magazines study strips and artists individually, *Ran Tan Plan* has been studying them from the point of view of the magazines they appear in. It ran a lengthy series on French youth journals of the 1930s and early 1940s, trying to establish their fates following the German lightning invasion of 1940. (Some were caught with issues printed that could never be distributed; others managed to survive haphazardly for varying amounts of time until circulation impossibilities and wartime paper shortages eventually killed them.) The current issue has a photo-report on a comic-art convention in Brussels; a lengthy article and checklist on the new Italian vogue of "exotic" mens' comics; and an introduction and sampler of the work of one of the more graphically dynamic modern American comic book cartoonists, Jim Steranko. (F.P.)

Spirou. w. 15 FB (30¢ U.S.) per issue; 468 FB ($9.36) for 6 months; 936 FB ($18.72) for 1 year. Subs. to: *Spirou,* Editions J. Dupuis, Fils & Cie., Rue Destrée 39, 6001 Marcinelle-Charleroi, Belgium. Make checks payable in U.S. currency to: Editions J. Dupuis, C.C.P. 3621–59.

Spirou is the oldest of the French-language weeklies, dating from April 1938. It contains the usual mixture but for a slightly younger age group, about 8 to 14. The emphasis is more on funny animal and light fantasy strips and less on realistic adventures. The historic research in *Spirou's* Westerns leaves a bit to be desired; one running early in 1971 showed an immaculately uniformed General Grant taking command of the Union armies within days of the fall of Fort Sumter. (To be fair, there have been American Western comics with even more glaring errors.) *Spirou* is also available in a Dutch-language edition, *Robbedoes,* for the same price. (F.P.)

Tintin. w. 15 Belgian francs (30¢ U.S.) per issue; 450 FB ($9.00) for 6 months; 870 FB ($17.40) for 1 year; 1,710

FB ($34.20) for 2 years for intl. ed. Subs. to: *Tintin*, Editions du Lombard, Service des abonnements, Avenue P.–H. Spaak 1 á 11, 1070 Bruxelles, Belgium. Make checks payable in U.S. currency to: Tintin-Bruxelles, C.C.P. 1909.16.

The slogan of the 64-page *Tintin* is "The weekly of super-youth from 7 to 77 years." It is designed for a wide range of readers, but mostly for the teen-age range from 13 to 19. Its strips include the usual wide assortment of Westerns, funny animals, detectives and secret agents, science fiction, historical strips of a wide range from caveman to modern times, and others. It has an auto-racing strip, "Michel Vaillant," that has been turned into a live-action TV adventure series. It has one of the few strips that seems designed primarily for girls, "Les Panthéres," about three young girls trying to break into show business. Strangely, one of the few heroes that can no longer be found in *Tintin* magazine is Tintin himself. When the journal was founded in 1946, it became the home of its famous namesake who had already become a popular comic strip star in European youth journals in the 1930s and 1940s. But author/artist Hergé has since retired. He is reportedly working on one special return appearance to celebrate the magazine's twenty-fifth anniversary, but the last regular adventure of Tintin ended in 1967. However, an animation studio in Brussels has just begun a new series of feature-length Tintin animated films, so the character will continue to live in the present. *Tintin* is also available in a Dutch-language edition, *Kuifje*, for the same price. (F.P.)

COMMUNICATIONS AND MEDIA

See also Business/Advertising and Marketing, Journalism, Motion Pictures, and Music/Counterculture Sections.

Basic Periodicals

Ejh: *K-Eight*; Hs: *Media & Methods, Radical Software*; Ga: *Media & Methods, Media Industry Newsletter*; Jc: *Media Industry Newsletter, Journal of Communication*; Ac: *Public Opinion Quarterly, Media Industry Newsletter, Journal of Communication, AV Communication Review, Broadcasting, Radical Software*.

Library and Teaching Aids

Media & Methods, Audiovisual Instruction, Educational Screen and AV Guide.

AV Communication Review. 1953. q. $13. 1201 16th St., N.W., Washington, D.C. 20036. Illus., index, adv. Circ: 7,000. Vol. ends: Winter. Microform: UM.

Bk. rev: 10, 1,200 words, signed. *Aud:* Ac.

A journal devoted to theoretical aspects of the instructional technology field. Not for the average teacher, but for the administrator, behavioral scientist, and school of education professor. Librarians who direct audiovisual programs will find it of some value. Rather technical articles deal with theory, research, and development related to technological processes in education with emphasis on teaching-learning behavior. Features include book reviews and abstracts of research.

Audiovisual Instruction. 1956. 10/yr. $6. Anna L. Hyer. Dept. of Audiovisual Instruction, National Education Assn., 1201 16th St., N.W., Washington, D.C. 20036. Illus., index, adv. Circ: 21,000. Sample. Vol. ends: Dec. Microform: UM.

Indexed: EdI. *Bk. rev:* 2, 1 column, signed. *Aud:* Ac, Ejh, Hs.

Concerned with educational technology for teachers and media specialists. Ten or twelve articles of varying length give practical information about instructional media and its development and use. Recent issues have included monthly themes such as Educational Consumerism, Instructional Development, Visual Literacy and Telecommunications. It includes notes about recent materials, equipment, and techniques, along with news items in the field. One of its best features is an index to audiovisual reviews in other publications. A good general addition for the primary and secondary school's professional collection, and for schools of education. Lacks the liveliness of *Media and Methods*, the editorial forthrightness of *Educational Screen and AV Guide*. Still, any library with an active media program should subscribe to all three with *Media and Methods* a first, the other two tied for second, choice.

Broadcasting. 1931. w. $14. Sol Taishoff. Broadcasting Publns., Inc., 1735 Desales St., N.W., Washington, D.C. 20036. Illus., adv. Circ: 40,000. Vol. ends: June and Dec. Microform: UM.

Indexed: BusI. *Aud:* Ga, Ac. *Jv:* V.

All-inclusive business newsweekly of the television and radio broadcasting profession. This journal is staff-written and edited to serve national and regional advertisers and their agencies; networks; stations; equipment manufacturers; sales representatives; research organizations; and those who write, report, analyze, and broadcast news for TV and radio. News of interest to programmers, journalists, engineers, and managers is included. Completely reports the Federal Communications Commission's regulations, hearings, and legal procedures, discussing all legislation affecting broadcasting. The latest trends, statistics, and developments in the field of communications are reported and analyzed for the media and advertising executive. A required magazine where radio and television courses are given, and good for large business collections. The *Broadcasting Yearbook* (each January. $13.50), includes basic economic, technical, and business facts relating to the profession in the United States and abroad, especially Canada. This almanac of broadcasting provides a state-by-state description of all commercial and educational radio and television stations in the nation. Typical data includes year of commission, power, frequency or channel allocation, call letters, mailing address, ownership information, and names of key personnel of each station. This handy reference compendium contains a directory of radio and TV representatives, executives, attorneys, and advertising agencies. It is an up-to-date source of information on the National Association of Broadcasters (NAB) radio and TV codes. (F.L.)

CTVD: Cinema-TV-Digest; a quarterly review of the serious foreign language cinema-tv-press. 1961. q. $3. Ben Hamilton. Hampton Books, Rt. 1, Box 76, Newberry, S.C. 29108. Illus., adv. Sample. Vol. ends: no. 4.
Aud: Ac.

Some 32 to 40 pages of articles from foreign journals, plus original reports from abroad on developments in cinema and television. It includes an occasional interview. The approach is conversational, i.e., after one or two pages of notes by the editor, there are discursive bits on films and television. A few specific films are reviewed, but the editor notes that "general principles rather than specific instances are emphasized." As a world overview it has some merit, and considering the small price and the delight it brings any film buff, it should be considered for purchase for medium to large–sized collections.

Central States Speech Journal. 1949. q. Membership. $6 (Students $3.50). James W. Gibson. Subs. to: Kenneth E. Anderson, Dept. of Speech, Univ. of Illinois, Urbana, Ill. 61801. Illus., index; adv. Circ: 2,000. Sample. Vol. ends: Winter.
Indexed: PsyAb. *Aud:* Ac.

A well-edited, regional speech journal which has more than its average of original articles. Material ranges from the technical, e.g., "An analysis of psychophysiological research in communication" to the topical, "Freedom of speech and the new left: a response." Authors are usually professors, members of the association, and write no better or no worse than others. Special reports on current attitudes, news notes, and other features round out each issue. The approach is for the speech teacher at the university level. Others can bypass.

Educational Broadcasting International (Formerly ***Educational Television International***). 1967. q. £5. F. Marriott, Wynn Williams (Publishers) Ltd., Centenary Bldgs., King St., Wrexham, England; Headington Hill Hall, Oxford OX3 OBW, England. Illus., adv.
Aud: Ac.

Includes articles and film reviews on educational TV in such places as Hawaii, Norway, Singapore, and Plymouth, by the Centre for Educational Television Overseas. Features range from production notes to bibliographies. Primarily for the expert, this is an intelligent international approach to an increasingly important area. Again, a basic magazine for academic libraries supporting educational television curricula, and large public libraries. (F.L.)

Educational Broadcasting Review (Formerly ***NAEB Journal***). 1941. bi–m. $1.50. Dr. A. Edward Foote. National Assn. of Educational Broadcasters, Ohio State Univ., 2470 N. Star Rd., Columbus, Ohio 43321. Adv. Circ: 5,000. Microform: UM. Vol. ends: Dec.
Indexed: CurrCont. *Aud:* Ga, Ac, Hs.

One of the few objective sources of news and developments in an ever important area of education—educational television and radio. This keeps the reader advised about government financing and activities in the field, and includes theoretical as well as pragmatic articles for the teacher who is using educational television, and also for directors of such programs. Schools without educational television facilities should subscribe too, if only to indicate to administrative officials and teachers what is going on in this particular field of education. (F.L.)

Educational Screen and AV Guide. 1922. m. $5. Henry C. Ruark, Jr. Educational Screen, Inc., 434 S. Wabash, Chicago, Ill., 60605. Illus., index, adv. Circ: 12,000. Sample. Vol. ends: Dec. Microform: UM.
Indexed: EdI. *Bk. rev:* Notes. *Aud:* Hs, Ejh.

Geared to the practical, not the technical, this is a how-to-do-it approach for the media expert in elementary through high schools. As an independent journal, edited by an even more independent editor, it has taken a consistently firm stand on strengthening media in the American educational system. There are frequent in-depth articles and features, and in 1971 there were more than 25 special information series on everything from how to organize and operate an instructional media center to CATV developments. Regular features include film, filmstrip, audiovisual, and television evaluations. An annual "Blue Book" issue (usually in August) lists new products with necessary purchasing data. In the previous edition, it was recommended as second to *Audiovisual Instruction.* Several critics point out it should be first because it does represent the voice of independent elementary and secondary educators. Conversely, *Audiovisual Instruction* would probably be preferred for education departments in many colleges and universities. Hopefully, libraries with media programs will take both.

Educational Television International. See *Educational Broadcasting International.*

Educator's Guide to Media and Methods. See *Media & Methods.*

Gallagher Report; a confidential letter to advertising, marketing, and media executives. 1950. q. $36. Bernard P. Gallagher. 230 Park Ave., New York, N.Y. 10017. Index.

Aud: Ac, Ga.

One of the more famous weekly newsletters in the advertising/communications world. The editor, writer, and owner, Bernard P. Gallagher, has gained fame for his rapid, colorful style of reporting about individuals, business, and industrial planning. As Gallagher himself puts it, the newsletter "keeps its readers abreast of upheavals in advertising, the media, retailing. It features case histories—with names, figures and no punches pulled. It prepares exclusive compilations of advertising pages and revenue in magazines, annual consumer and industrial advertising budgets, circulation of leading consumer publications, salaries of top media and agency executives." Many consider Gallagher one of the most influential men in the communications industry, and, for that reason alone, subscribe to his publication. However, it is highly controversial, e.g., Chris Welles' "Bernard Gallagher's Report: Is the magic gone?" (*Columbia Journalism Review,* December 1971). Welles documents a case for proof that "much of the information . . . was exaggerated, twisted, or simply wrong."

Be that as it may, Gallagher's report is necessary for any meaningful advertising or communications collection. What is more, he puts out several other newsletters (usually edited by others, if Welles is correct) which librarians might consider.

✓ *Gallup Opinion Index.* 1965. m. $28. John O. Davies. Gallop Opinion Index, 53 Bank St., Princeton, N.J. Illus (charts). Circ: 1,000.

Aud: Ac.

Gives the findings of research surveys conducted by the nationally known Gallup organization. Plotted are the political, social, and economic trends in public attitudes, nationwide. Some articles are standard in each month's issues, such as those which gage voter preference for Presidential candidates. On the other hand, further articles present the public's views on changing problems, such as the China situation, Vietnam, inflation, and smoking. Numerous charts are resorted to. This service is a must for any research collection having an interest in sociology and current political attitudes.

Gazette; international journal for mass communications studies. 1955. q. $10. A. E. Kluwer, N.V., Polstraat 10, Deventer, Netherlands. Illus., index, adv.

Indexed: PAIS. *Bk. rev:* various number, length. *Aud:* Ac.

Devoted to all aspects of communications. Its primary value for an American audience is the record of research it offers through good bibliographies, both separately published and with articles. Social scientists and psychologists will find it useful for the study of propaganda. Published in English, French, and German editions.

Information Processing Letters. 1971. bi-m. $25. North-Holland Publishing Co., P.O. Box 3489, Amsterdam, The Netherlands. Charts, diagrams, adv.

Aud: Ac.

The 35 pages are "devoted to the rapid publication of short contributions in the field of information processing." The issue examined featured nine articles, for the most part built around system architecture and application programs. The authors are primarily concerned with reporting on their current work. Canada, Austria, and the United States are heavily represented. The price is much too high, and the content much too technical for all but the largest library.

Information Retrieval and Library Automation Letter. 1970. m. $24. Lowell H. Hattery. Lomond Systems, Inc. Mt. Airy, Md. 21771. Sample.

Aud: Ac, Ga.

It is too bad the price is so high—$24 seems a bit steep for a year's subscription to a 12-page newsletter. Too bad because the information is current, coverage relatively complete, and the succinct reporting a joy to read in a field notorious for jargon and verbiage. Of particular value is the section on "literature" which alerts the librarian to manuals, reports, and books in the field. Coverage is primarily limited to America, but some effort is made to touch on international highpoints. The note headings may give the reader a better idea of content: "Microfiche Camera Processor for the Office," "Laser Beam Carried Information," "Subject Headings for Engineering." Send for a sample copy. The currency and coverage may be more important to your library than the price.

✓ *Journal of Broadcasting.* 1956/57. q. $8. John M. Kittross. Assn. for Professional Broadcasting Education, Temple Univ., Philadelphia, Pa. 19122. Illus., index. Circ: 1,600.

Indexed: PAIS, SocAb. *Bk. rev:* various number, length. *Aud:* Ad, Ga.

The only reference periodical published in the United States devoted exclusively to all facets of broadcasting. It serves the common interests of broadcasters, teachers, researchers, and students of broadcasting, integrating the classroom and the broadcasting industry. Regular departments cover broadcasting, communications law, media research, education for broadcasting, and broadcasting literature. Most articles are 6 to 16 pages in length. The source of most articles is the academic community. (R.C.)

✓ *Journal of Communication.* 1951. q. $15. Paul Holtzman. Intl. Communication Assn., Center for Communication Studies, Ohio Univ., Athens, Ohio 45701. Illus., index, adv. Circ: 3,000.

Bk. rev: 8–10, 500–1,000 words; notes. *Aud:* Ac, Ga. *Jv:* V.

Devoted to research and theory in communication (a multidisciplinary enterprise) the editors define "communication" as "all the processes of interaction which lead to changes in the participants, whether those participants are humans and human institutions, other animals, or machines." Articles provide analyses or syntheses which promise to advance development of communication theory. Contribution of articles dealing with communication practices divorced from their significance for communication theory and articles of interest only to specialized disciplines is discouraged. Most articles are 10 to 20 pages long and are written almost exclusively by college professors in a variety of disciplines (speech, journalism, education, psychology, environmental studies, communication, and medicine were all represented in a recent issue), though authors specializing in speech and communication appear more often. The publisher calls itself the "International" Communication Association, but 11 of the officers are employed by American universities or companies as are all 18 editors and associate editors. Contributors also appear to be exclusively American. (R.C.)

K-Eight. (Formerly: *Modern Media Teacher.*) 1969. bi-m. $5. Murray Suid. North American Publishing Co., 134 N. 13th St., Philadelphia, Pa. 19107. Illus., index, adv. Circ: 50,000. Sample.

Bk. rev: Various number, length. *Aud:* Ejh.

The approximate equivalent for the elementary grades of *Media and Methods.* Put out by the same publisher, it follows the pattern of the better known, older magazine. There is the usual audiovisual material, with due emphasis on books, new teaching methods, etc. In fact, it is an extended version of *Media and Methods,* and adds up to an interesting magazine for any elementary and junior high school collection. However, until the editorial policy is better established, would advise schools to take *Media and Methods* first. (As of late 1971 *K-Eight* was a controlled circulation, i.e., free magazine, but the publisher was seeking to change it over to a subscription magazine.)

Knowledge Industry Report; a businessman's newsletter on the knowledge industry. 1967. s-m. $60. Efrem Sigel. Knowledge Industry Publns., Inc., Tiffany Towers, White Plains, N.Y. 10602. Sample. Vol. ends: May 15.

Aud: Ac, Ga.

A 6 to 8 page newsletter whose primary function is to report on educational developments which are likely to influence investment. Short items touch on cable television, magazines, mergers, and the closing list of stocks. Some issues apparently give in-depth analysis of prospects for various companies. The non-investor will be interested in brief reports on personnel, legislation, inventions, company shifts and changes, etc. In a word, the editor attempts to keep ahead of the daily papers in reporting activities in education. He generally succeeds. Hence, it has an added dimension for education collections. But while it may be worth the stiff price to the individual, it is overpriced for most libraries.

Tapping this same market, the firm publishes two related newsletters. Both are similar in format and approach, differing only in areas covered.

The Educational Marketer; a newsletter for sales, marketing and advertising executives in educational publishing, materials and equipment companies. (1969. s-m. $36. E. A. Minsker. Sample. Vol. ends: Sept. 15.)

The Video Publisher; a newsletter for executives who produce, distribute, advertise in or broadcast programming for cable, cartridge, closed circuit, subscription and local television. (1971. s-m. $75. Bill Donnelly. Sample. Vol. ends: April 24.)

There is no denying that all of these are of considerable interest to investors and speculators who may use your library. The newsletters may be worth the price for larger business and economics collections. Suggest anyone in doubt send for sample copies.

Media Decisions. 1966. m. $10 (Controlled circulation). Norman R. Glenn. Glenn Publications Inc., 342 Madison Ave., New York, N.Y. 10017. Illus., index, adv. Circ: 22,000.

Aud: Ga.

A controlled circulation magazine, i.e., it is sent free to top advertising agencies and agency people. Its purpose, according to the publisher, is to "search out the in-depth meaning behind the news. We concern ourselves with the entire spectrum of media: TV, radio, newspapers, magazines, business papers, outdoor, transit. *Media Decisions* is for in-depth interpretation of the news." Six to eight articles follow the month's past developments, and there are regular columns on the media. Primarily for special libraries and those serving people in advertising.

Media Industry Newsletter. 1947. w. $35. Leon Garry. Business Magazines, Inc., 150 E. 52nd St., New York, N.Y. 10022. Index. Circ: 5,000. Sample. Vol. ends: Dec. 31.

Aud: Ga, Ac. Jv: V.

A 12 to 16 page newsletter which is essential for anyone attempting to keep up with the activities of the media, i.e., magazines, newspapers, recordings, motion pictures, television, book publishing, etc. Each issue consists of succinct articles (250–500 words) on current activities, and briefs on everything from changes in personnel and stock market reports to new magazine titles, equipment, and speculation on what happens next. The material is accurate, timely, and well written. The audience is not only the businessman, but the librarian—particularly the librarian anxious to know about pending media activities.

Media & Methods: exploration in education. (Also called: *Educator's Guide to Media and Methods.*)

1965. m. (Sept.–May). $7. Frank McLaughlin. North American Publishing Co., 134 N. 13th St., Philadelphia, Pa. 19107. Illus., index, adv. Circ: 45,000. Sample. *Bk. rev:* 3–5, 750–1,000 words, signed. *Aud:* Hs, Ejh. *Jv:* V.

The best, and by far the most imaginative, magazine in the middle and secondary school, audiovisual field. It is a first choice for any library, and while of primary interest to the schools, should be considered by public libraries too. Teachers are primary contributors, tend to write articles which shakeup the established view of education. There is a great emphasis on new approaches to learning. And while a good deal of the material covers films, video, television, etc., there are usually one or two articles on the book. In fact, the book is never forgotten, and what makes this magazine fascinating is that it can stress audiovisual without resorting to dumping everything for the machine. Nor is it all pie in the sky. The articles tend to be practical, give down to earth hints on materials, methods, and practices. There are regular departments which review both feature and educational films, television programs, recordings, tapes, books, etc. A required item. Note: At one time this was a controlled circulation, i.e. free magazine. This is no longer true, although about one half of the circulation is still controlled. (The equivalent to this for elementary grades is *K-Eight.*)

Media Mix Newsletter. 1969. 8/yr. (Oct.–May). $5. Jeffrey Schrank. Media Mix, Box 5139, Chicago, Ill. 60680. Illus. Circ: 1,200.

Aud: Ac, Hs, Ejh. *Jv:* C.

An eight page offset newsletter. The issue for November 1971 includes: a one-page lecture on improving group discussion; a page of reviews of new short films; capsule reviews of paperbacks; a two-page film-available chart, which lists major distributors and prices for renting "the most used quality short films of the early 1970's"; an article on alternatives in education; and television previews. It is worth the $5 only when all the standard magazines are on the racks and there is nothing left to do with an extra $5.

Modern Media Teacher. See *K-Eight.*

NAEB Journal. See *Educational Broadcasting Review.*

Pepper & Salt. 1969. bi-m. $2. Frank Blake. 210 Fifth Ave., New York, N.Y. 10010. Illus. Circ: 2,000. Vol. ends: Dec. 31.

Aud: Ac, Hs.

One man's view of the politics, social system, and workings of the world. His audience is the younger generation; the content is in the form of a newsletter and ranges from an interview on VD—which is excellent in terms of needed information for many people these days—to a critical look at shopping centers. While

pretty slim in terms of coverage, it is heavy in terms of relevance.

Public Opinion Quarterly. 1937. q. $8.50. W. Phillips Davidson. Columbia Univ. Press, 136 S. Broadway, Irvington-on-Hudson, N.Y. 10533. Adv. Circ: 4,643. Vol. ends: Winter. Microform: UM. Reprint: Johnson. *Indexed:* PAIS, PsyAb, SSHum. *Bk. rev:* 20, 1,000 words, signed. *Aud:* Ac. *Jv:* V.

Reports on all aspects of how media affect or fail to affect public. According to the editors, it is "hospitable to all points of view, provided only that the material presented will help readers gain insight into the problems of public opinion." Aside from the lengthy and scholarly articles, there is a section entitled "Current Research" for briefer reports such as case histories and hypotheses. "News and Notes" lists news about professional organizations, awards and grants and personnel and personal notes. "The Polls" reprints current poll results which have significance in public opinion. A basic magazine wherever a sociology, political science, or communication course is taught. Should be in all larger public libraries as well.

Quarterly Journal of Speech. 1915. q. $15.00. Robert L. Scott. Speech Communication Assn., William Work, Secy., Statler Hilton Hotel, New York, N.Y. 10001. Circ: 7,500. Sample. Vol. ends: Dec. Microform: UM. Reprint: Johnson.

Indexed: EdI. *Bk. rev:* 8, 750 words. *Aud:* Ac.

Contains essays, research reports, and book reviews relating to all areas of the speech communication arts and sciences including forensics, instructional development, interpersonal and small group interaction, oral interpretation, mass communication, public address, rhetorical and communication theory, speech sciences, and theatre. An excellent resource not only for teachers and researchers in higher education, but valuable as well for secondary school teachers wishing to keep abreast of latest developments in the field. A first for colleges and universities, a second for secondary schools, where *The Speech Teacher* would be generally more useful.

Radical Software. 1971. $3 issue. Beryl Korot & Megan Williams. 8 E. 12th St., New York, N.Y. 10003. Illus.

Aud: Ac, Ga, Hs.

With the sixth issue, the editors plan to change the format rather drastically—they are switching from the magazine/newsprint approach to videotape. And while the first numbers look like a fatter than usual underground newspaper, even that is deceptive. Inside are articles on every aspect of television from videotape to alternative television networks. The target audience is just about anyone involved with video both as a communication and art form, and there is a grand mixture of theory (beyond all but the true believer's comprehension) with nuts and bolts information on equipment. If this isn't unique enough, there are special sections such as "Canadian Content," which report on activities and thought north of the border. The editorial pitch seems to be that public television and developments in low cost portable videotape equipment will open up a whole new communications field based on traditional television. This is supported by articles and an information exchange between people involved with do-it-yourself television. Whether or not this publication is the key to the new world is debatable, but it is a step toward understanding an important part of the future. It should be a must in all media collections, regardless of size or type, and librarians are advised to write asking about past issues and plans for the future. Again, forget this format, and get to the content before reaching any judgment.

Screen (Formerly: *Screen Education*). 1959. q. $6.50. Sam Rohdie. Soc. for Education in Film and Television, 81 Dean St., London, Wl, Eng aud. Illus., adv.

Bk. rev: various number, length; signed. *Aud:* Ac, Hs.

Directed to the film educator, and primarily devoted to a discussion of film. Only a small section discusses television. Heavy on theory, it seeks to develop an aesthetics of film and to integrate film and film education into their proper place among other academic and artistic disciplines as well as into a broad sociological, political, and cultural context. The three to five documented articles—some of which are reprinted from other respected film journals such as *Cahiers du Cinema*—have such titles as "Sociology and the Cinema" and "Cinema/Ideology/Criticism." The book reviews often provide lengthy critical commentary on the various schools of thought in film, film criticism, and film education. A new feature is "Education Notes" which provides practical information on such topics as film distribution and acquisition and methods of film use in the classroom. Primarily for the education collection in college or high school. (W.D.)

Screen Education. See *Screen.*

See. 1968. 5/yr. $5. Sal Giarrizzo. Film Education Resources Corp., 1825 Willow Rd., Northfield, Ill. 60093. Illus., adv. Circ: 1,500. Vol. ends: May.

Bk. rev: 3–4, 250–700 words, signed. *Aud:* Hs, Ejh.

The voice of the Screen Educators' Society. Film study, reviews, and forums on all aspects of the flick are included. Writers tend to be educators. The 32-page issue examined included an interview with Stanley Kauffman. While no *Media and Methods,* it certainly is a fine contribution to the field. Particularly useful in elementary and high schools. (A sample copy is available at a service charge of $1.)

Sightlines. 1967. bi-m. Membership (Nonmembers $8). Esme J. Dick. Educational Film Library Assn. Inc., 17 W. 60th St., New York, N.Y. 10023. Illus., adv. Circ: 5,000. Sample.

Aud: Ga, Hs, Ejh.

Covers all aspects of the film, video, and audiovisual world. Usually opens with one or two articles on the use of film in educational film making, filmographies. The body of the 32-page magazine consists of reviews and notes on 8mm and 18mm films for use by schools and libraries. For example, one issue includes an annotated listing of "Films for Now" covering adult films for social change. A regular feature is "The Film-list"—a listing with short unevaluative descriptors of new films and filmstrips. Also features: "Film Review Digest," with quotes from film reviews from many sources: "Who's Who in Filmmaking," profiles of nontheatrical film producers.

The Educational Film Library Association also publishes *Film Evaluation Guide.* This is a compilation of 4,500 critical film reviews covering films released from 1946 to 1964. A Supplement carries it up to 1967. Thereafter, EFLA Evaluations are available on 3 by 5 in. cards (36 per month.)

Speech Monographs. 1934. q. $15. Thomas Scheidel. Speech Communication Assn., Statler Hilton Hotel, 33rd St. & Seventh Ave., New York, N.Y. 10001. Circ: 2,500. Sample. Vol. ends: Nov.

Indexed: EdI, PsyAb. *Aud:* Ac.

Provides a vehicle for in-depth reports of research in all areas of the speech communication arts and sciences. Includes rhetorical and communication theory, interpersonal and small group interaction, mass communication, public address, speech science, oral interpretation of literature, and theatre. Particularly useful for researchers and teachers in higher education.

The Speech Teacher. 1952. q. Membership (Nonmembers $15). Frank E. Dance. Speech Communication Assn., Statler Hilton Hotel, New York, N.Y. 10001. Illus., index, adv. Circ: 4,000. Sample. Vol. ends: Nov.

Indexed: EdI, PsyAb. *Bk. rev:* 6,500 words, signed. *Aud:* Hs, Ejh.

Another journal of the Speech Communication Association of America (see *Speech Monographs* and *Quarterly Journal of Speech*) more directed to the teaching of the subject than to research. Articles tend to be methodological, giving information on debate, rhetoric, and general communication. The journal includes book reviews which relate to the subject of teaching speech. Some of the articles will be of interest to high school students. A basic journal in the field for elementary and secondary school professional collections.

Straus Editor's Report. 1969. w. $34 ($68 to individuals & business). Walt Wurfel. R. Peter Straus, 1211 Connecticut Ave., N.W., Washington, D.C. 20036. Index. Circ: 4,500. Sample.

Bk. rev: 1, 100 words. *Aud:* Ac, Ga.

A Washington newsletter designed for editors, publishers, and broadcasting and television executives. The four pages report on happenings which in some way will influence the media, and while directed to those actively engaged in the news, it has definite interest for journalism courses. Short items cover the successes and failures of the press, report on current activities of the media, and offer an ongoing commentary of how to improve services. Supplements, but does not replace, a similar newsletter—*Media Industry Newsletter*. Of the two, the latter will be of more interest to general collections: although universities building large communication and journalism collections should subscribe to both.

Today's Speech. 1953. q. Membership (Nonmembers $10). Eugene Vasilew, State Univ. of New York, Binghamton, N.Y. 13401. Subs. to: William Price, Dept. of Speech, Univ. of Mass., Amherst, Mass. 01002. Index, adv. Circ: 2,600. Sample. Vol. ends: Fall. Refereed. Microform: UM.

Bk. rev: 4–5, 350 words, signed. *Aud:* Ac, Hs.

According to the editor, the magazine touches on "all phases of speech-communication (the new name for this discipline). Among these are: pedagogy, public speaking, rhetoric, theatre, communication, public address, speech therapy and speech science." A policy has developed whereby each issue is devoted to a single theme, e.g., "Speech Communication as an Art," or "Black Language, Literature, Rhetoric, and Communication." Usually four or five articles support the central issue, with two or three others on more diverse topics. The writing, primarily by teachers, is scholarly yet manages to avoid the ponderous. There is some rough in-fighting. For example, in the Summer 1971 issue the editor prints a critical letter about an earlier article carefully retaining all of the writer's spelling errors with the usual "sic". This type of thing may have wide appeal for the fighters, but is a bit petty. Still, the journal remains one of the best in its field, certainly is livelier and better written then *Speech Teacher* or *Quarterly Journal of Speech*. A first choice for both academic and high school libraries serving speech departments.

University Film Association Journal. 1943. q. Membership (Nonmembers $6). Robert W. Wagner. Ohio State Univ., Dept. of Photography & Cinema, 156 W. 19th Ave., Columbus, Ohio 43310. Illus., index. Circ: 1,000. Sample. Vol. ends: 4th issue.

Bk. rev: 3–4, 75–500 words, signed. *Aud:* Ac, Hs.

As the title suggests, this is a professional magazine for film teachers at the college level. However, there is enough here to warrant serious consideration by high school teachers. The normal issue touches on film production, cinematography, and photography. Articles are written by those with experience, and in a style which is generally down to earth. Topics range from the history of the film and its social implications to technical pieces on the media. Regular features include coverage of meetings and conferences, projects of university film units, and hints on instruction and work with students. It should enjoy a higher circulation than it now has. It is a basic magazine in schools where film courses are taught.

Videorecord World; the magazine of cartridge TV, videocassettes, and videodiscs. 1971. m. $18. Patrick McNulty. Playback Publishing Ltd., Box A-Z, Irvine, Calif. 93664. Illus., adv. Sample.

Aud: Ac, Ga.

On the cover of the March 1971 issue a quote: "There is no quick money to be made in videorecords." No, but there may be in a magazine geared for businessmen and investors willing to pay $18 a year for 28 pages of news, views, and reports on a glamour industry. In the issue examined there was a short interview, an article on the use of videocassettes in training personnel, news notes, and short pieces on producers, teachers, agencies, writers, and cable television. All of this seems pretty slim for the steep price, and until such time as the subscriptions come down or the quality goes up, libraries can avoid without loss.

COMPUTERS AND AUTOMATION

Basic Periodicals

Ga: *Computers and Automation* (for large public libraries); Ac: *Computers and the Humanities, Computers and Automation*, (Technical) *Association of Computing Machinery. Journal, Communications of the ACM, Computing Surveys;* Jc: *Computing Surveys, Datamation, Computers and Automation.*

Basic Abstracts and Indexes

Computing Reviews, Science Abstracts, Section C: Computer and Control Abstracts.

Introduction

Arbitrarily grouped under this one heading are publications falling under the ill-defined categories of "information processing," including the more restrictive "data processing," and "automation," which includes automatic control. Offered, too, in this section, are a miscellany of interdisciplinary publications on simulation and systems science. The bulk of the periodicals is appropriate for good, well-rounded collections in the computing sciences, i.e., interdisciplinary, research-oriented collections embracing supportive elements from mathematics and mathematical logic, and electrical engineering. Thus, publications deal primarily with computers, their hardware, software, and applications, and range from the general to the highly specialized within an already highly specialized field. In a field where technology advances so rapidly, trade journals play an important role. Listed here are a number of the more popular trade journals; no attempt has been made to be comprehensive. See the Mathematics Section for journals on the mathematics of computation. Similarly, see the Library Periodicals Section for journals covering library automation.

Acta Informatica. 1971. q. $29.70. Ed. bd. Springer-Verlag, 175 Fifth Ave., New York, N.Y. 10010. Illus., index. Sample. Vol. ends: no. 4. Refereed.

Aud: Sa, Ac.

Broader in scope than its mathematical cousin, *Computing,* the journal encompasses many of the major elements of the information sciences: design of systems, hardware-software interface, software engineering, and on a more theoretical level, information theory, theory of formal languages, etc. An international publication, papers my appear in English, French, or German, with English summaries. A new research journal which will strengthen large collections in the computing sciences.

Artificial Intelligence. 1970. q. $27.30. Bernard Meltzer. Amer. Elsevier Publishing Co., Inc., 52 Vanderbilt Ave., New York, N.Y. 10017. Illus., index. Sample. Vol. ends: no. 4. Refereed.

Indexed: ComAb, EngI, MathR, PsychAb. *Aud:* Sa, Ac.

With the hard edge between disciplines blurred, this international research publication spreads over a large number of fields. Its main concern is to draw together studies on the simulation of "intelligent behavior," by theory and applications of computer programs or other practices. Thus, papers discuss such topics as the design of question-answering systems, automatic theorem-proving by computer, algorithms for searching graphs, interrelations between philosophy and artificial intelligence, and logic by machine. In large part mathematically oriented, the journal will be of considerable interest not only to computing scientists, but also to mathematicians, logicians, and psychologists. For university libraries.

Association for Computing Machinery. Journal. 1954. q. $25 (Members $7). Raymond E. Miller. Assn. for Computing Machinery, 1133 Ave. of the Americas, New York, N.Y. 10036. Illus., index. Circ: 14,232. Vol. ends: Oct. Refereed. Reprint: Johnson.

Indexed: ASTI, BPI, EngI, MathR, SCI. *Aud:* Sa, Ac.

The overall intent of the Association for Computing Machinery, the leading computer society in the United States, is to promote advances in the sciences and arts of information processing. The corpus of high quality papers by authoritative specialists makes its *Journal* one of the world's foremost periodicals in the computing sciences, particularly in the mathematical theory of computing. Scholarly studies appear in such fields as automata theory, formal languages, graph theory, numerical mathematics, pattern recognition, operations research, etc. Less theoretical work is pub-

lished in the ACM's other periodicals, *Communications of the ACM,* and *Computing Surveys.* An excellent and primary journal for all sophisticated collections in the computing sciences.

Automatica. 1963. bi-m. $50. George S. Axelby. Pergamon Press, Maxwell House, Fairview Park, Elmsford, N.Y. 10523. Illus., index. Sample. Vol. ends: no. 6. Refereed. Microform: Maxwell. Reprint: Maxwell.

Indexed: SciAb, SCI. *Bk. rev:* 1–2, 400 words, signed. *Aud:* Sa, Ac.

The official organ also of the International Federation of Automatic Control. Research papers are dedicated to all aspects of control theory and systems, including the design of systems, their reliability, and applications (e.g., industrial process control), and effects of instrumentation in operations involving automatic control. An authoritative, scholarly journal representing the international interests of the association. For university libraries.

Automation. 1954. m. $12 (Free to qualified personnel). James C. Keebler. Penton Publishing Co., Penton Building, Cleveland, Ohio 44113. Illus., index, adv. Circ: 46,000. Sample. Vol. ends: Dec. Microform: UM. Reprint: Johnson.

Indexed: ASTI, EngI. *Aud:* Sa, Ac.

The emphasis in this periodical is on the engineering and manufacturing aspects of automated equipment and systems. Articles include expositions on automatic techniques vs. traditional methods, reviews on pertinent technology from related sciences, and the economics of automation. Written in a style that is comprehensible to the nonspecialist, the magazine would be particularly useful to those concerned with clarification of problems or advantages connected with automation in particular fields. For technical libraries.

Business Automation. 1958. s-m. $25 (Controlled circulation). Arnold E. Keller. Hitchcock Publishing Co., 288 Park Ave. W., Elmhurst, Ill. 60126. Illus., index, adv. Circ: 90,000. Sample. Microform: UM.

Indexed: PAIS. *Aud:* Sa, Ac.

A trade journal directed toward business and management interested in information processing systems. About two feature articles, contributed both by specialists and editorial staff, are prepared for each issue of about 40 pages. The remainder of the issue consists of a good-sized spread of departments, furnishing notes about industrial trends, news briefs, new products, etc. Features profile not only the use of data processing equipment for business applications (management decisions, personnel records, sales, etc.), but also novel usage of computing equipment tailored to individual organizations. Published in December is an annual hardware specifications and purchasing guide (also available separately for $10.). Despite the fact that the cost is steep for libraries having to pay the full subscription price, the magazine is useful to the clientele to whom it is directed.

Communications of the ACM. 1958. m. $25. M. Stuart Lynn. Assn. for Computing Machinery, 1133 Ave. of the Americas, New York, N.Y. 10036. Illus., index, adv. Circ: 32,000. Vol. ends: Dec. Refereed. Reprint: Johnson.

Indexed: ComRev, SciAb. *Aud:* Sa, Ac.

Spanning the spectrum of the computing sciences, the *Communications* acts as a technical forum for reflecting the current trends in research and development in all areas of information processing. Papers deal with the subjects of computer systems, operating systems, programming techniques, management/data base systems, computational linguistics, information retrieval, graphics and image processing, scientific applications, and education. (Mathematically or theoretically oriented papers usually appear in the *Journal of the ACM.*) Regular departments review ACM and other professional and industrial activities. The high quality of the papers and the diversity of topics make this one of the leading journals in the field. For libraries supporting instruction in the computer sciences, this, plus the three other major publications of the ACM, its *Journal, Computing Reviews* and *Computing Surveys,* form the nucleus for a basic, technical collection.

Computer (Formerly: *IEEE Computer Group News*). 1966. bi-m. $6. Robert A. Short. Computer Soc. of IEEE. 8949 Reseda Blvd., Suite 202, Northridge, Calif. 91324. Illus., index, adv. Circ: 17,000. Sample. Vol. ends: no. 6. Microform: IEEE.

Aud: Sa, Ac.

This magazine has come to full flower as the voice of the IEEE Computer Society (formerly IEEE Group on Computers). Issued gratis with the excellent and highly technical *IEEE Transactions on Computers* (see below), the periodical specializes on two or three general interest articles, mostly on computer system design. Some of these are tutorials or simply reviews of ancillary fields. New and recent, too, are "social implications" interests, e.g., articles on "computers and autistic children." Of reference value are abstracts of technical papers, hitherto unpublished, residing in the IEEE Computer Society Repository. Product information, coming events, and news of the IEEE are also included in every issue. An interesting and imaginatively illustrated periodical for technical libraries.

Computer Bulletin. 1957. m. 90s. T. F. Goodwin. British Computer Soc., 29 Portland Place, London, W1, England. Illus., index, adv. Circ: 20,000. Vol. ends: Dec. Refereed. Reprint: Dawson.

Indexed: BritTech, MathR, SCI. *Bk. rev:* 10, 100–500 words, signed. *Aud:* Sa, Ac, Ga.

Reflecting the interests of the British Computer So-

ciety (the leading organization in the United Kingdom), the periodical serves as news organ for the Society and reviews trends and developments in the computing sciences. Much of its material has a non-technical tone, and general articles on topics such as the computer and society, or computer applications to other disciplines would be of interest to and within the grasp of the interested layman. Departments include reports on equipment, new products, etc., with emphasis on British industry. An insert, *Computer Bulletin Supplement,* covers stop-press items, conferences, recruitments, etc. Small academic libraries will undoubtedly concentrate first on U.S. publications, but larger collections will want both this and the technical journal of the Society, *Computer Journal.*

Computer Decisions. 1969. m. $15. Robert C. Haavind. Hayden Publishing Co., 50 Essex St., Rochelle Park, N.J. Illus., adv. Circ: 89,250. Sample. Vol. ends: Dec.

Bk. rev: 1–2, 300–500 words, signed. *Aud:* Sa, Ac.

Another trade publication available as controlled circulation. Directed toward managers who use computers, the accent in this magazine is on the decision maker, and feature articles deal with systems, information processing, and practical problem solving (e.g., "Planning for your New Computer."). As usual, a good portion focuses on the news bit: "we hear" departments, grapevine from Washington, etc. New product announcements are developed in a section divided by systems, peripherals, accessories, software, and services. Written in simple, down-to-earth language, the whole tone of the magazine is geared for busy people who can flip through quickly, select whatever is timely, and pass it on.

Computer Design. 1962. m. $15 (Controlled circulation). John A. Camuso. Computer Design Publishing Corp., 221 Baker Ave., Concord, Mass. 01743. Illus., index, adv. Circ: 50,000. Sample. Vol. ends: Dec.

Indexed: ASTI. *Aud:* Sa, Ac.

Orientation in this trade publication is around digital control systems: their design and applications. Feature articles cover such areas as computer organization, computer-aided design, data communications, network control, etc. Aimed at the electronics engineer, articles are written simply enough, or are tutorial in nature, to find an audience in anyone knowledgeable in the computing sciences. A major portion of the magazine is dedicated to industry notes, applications briefs, new products and literature.

Computer and Information Systems. See Abstracts and Indexes Section.

Computer Journal. 1958. q. $12.60. P. Hammersley. British Computer Soc., 29 Portland Place, London W1, England. Illus., index, adv. Circ: 10,000. Vol. ends: no. 4. Refereed. Reprint: Dawson.

Indexed: BritTech, MathR, SciAb, SCI. *Bk. rev:* 5, 300–500 words, signed. *Aud:* Sa, Ac.

Authoritative, research-level papers on every facet of the computing sciences appear in the leading technical journal from the United Kingdom. Studies are not restricted to theoretical investigations, but include engineering reports and practical applications. Essays on such general topics as computers and the law are also provided regularly. On occasion, an algorithms supplement, which has been compiled from references appearing elsewhere in the literature, is published. With its coverage of computer science theory, hardware design, advanced programming, and business applications, the journal is a valuable addition to every good collection in the computing sciences.

Computer News. See Abstracts and Indexes/*Computer Abstracts* Section.

Computer Studies in the Humanities and Verbal Behavior. 1968. q. Floyd R. Horowitz and Sally Y. Sedelow. Mouton & Co., Box 482, The Hague, Netherlands. Illus., index. Vol. ends: no. 4.

Bk. rev: 3, 700 words, signed. *Aud:* Sa, Ac.

In the same vein as *Computers and the Humanities,* this periodical, sponsored also by the University of Kansas, gives voice to computer applications in the creative arts, literature, history, music, philosophy, etc. Contributions are generally by scholars in those fields. Emphasis in articles is placed on word usage ("Content Analysis by Computer"; "Platonic Prose Rhythm"), although an essay on "Computer Choreography—Dance and Computer" indicates the breadth of the publication. A fundamental knowledge of computers is desirable, since articles tend to vary in their mathematical or technical sophistication. Although *Computers and the Humanities* has extra dividends by way of abstracts, bibliographies, and directories, both journals should certainly be available in academic libraries supporting research programs in the humanities.

Computers and Automation. 1951. m, $18.50. Edmund C. Berkeley. Berkeley Enterprises, Inc., 815 Washington St., Newtonville, Mass. 02160. Illus., index, adv. Circ: 9,000. Vol. ends: Dec. Refereed.

Indexed: BPI. *Bk. rev:* 10, 100 words, unsigned. *Aud:* Sa, Ac, Ga.

The periodical has the distinction of being the oldest magazine in the field. After two decades, it has the further distinction of being one of the best sources for topical, timely, useful, nonspecialist information about computers. Features are written in such understandable language that even a general readership can follow (glossaries for the uninitiated are often included). Articles focus less on hardware and software and more on applications—the computer and: education, law, science, business, transportation, and even art produced by computers. Following a recent edito-

rial bent to raise our consciousness levels, the shift has now veered to computers and societal problems, e.g., privacy, human values. An interesting addition has been a section on computers and assassinations ("How Many Coincidences Make a Plot?"). Regular monthly departments let the facts speak for themselves; news briefs on applications, products, services, installations, and new contracts; a monthly computer census which tells who bought what. Moreover, the June issue (in two parts; comprises a valuable *Computer Directory and Buyers' Guide* (sold separately $17.). Just for fun, games and puzzles are offered monthly, and in "Golden Trumpet," voicing the opinion of the readership, the editor even invites polemics. A useful magazine for both public and academic libraries. Highly recommended.

Computers and the Humanities. 1966. bi-m. $20. Joseph Raben. Queens College Press, Queens College, Flushing, N.Y. 11367. Illus., index. Circ: 2,000. Vol. ends: no. 6. Refereed. Microform: UM.

Indexed: HistAb, SCI. *Bk. rev:* 1–3, 700 words, signed. *Aud:* Sa, Ac.

Articles written for and by scholars in history, literature, music, visual arts, and the social sciences, all concerned with uses of computers in their fields of interest. The editors presuppose some basic knowledge of computers, but require neither the technical jargon nor the mathematical background necessary for understanding most computer/automation journals. Material tends to stress the use of computers for bibliographies, compilation of indexes, concordances, etc. Articles such as "Computer Study of Medieval German Poetry" indicate the scope. In addition to book reviews, each issue abstracts a number of articles from books and periodicals in the area; an annual bibliography, directory of scholars in the field, and an annual listing of literary materials in machine-readable form is also produced. An extremely useful journal for almost any scholar who is actively engaged in research. Should be found in most academic libraries, and the wise librarian will do well to scan each issue for developments which may influence the library.

Computerworld. 1967. w. $9. Robert M. Patterson. Computerworld, Inc., 60 Austin St., Newton, Mass. 02160. Illus., adv. Circ: 45,000. Sample. Vol. ends: Dec.

Aud: Sa, Ac.

Somewhat the *Wall Street Journal* of the computer industry, the newspaper sniffs out major activities in finance, corporate organization, societies, education, government, etc. Financial sections include full information on acquisitions, mergers, contracts, and also include stock trading surveys. Special reports on companies, products, users, systems, and editorials interpret trends. Reporting seems to be accurate and timely. Well worth the subscription price, the newspaper is recommended for any library which needs up-to-the-minute information on sales, finance, or latest developments in computers and peripheral equipment and services.

Computing; archives for electronic computing. 1966. 2v./yr. (4 nos./vol.). $35.70/vol. Ed. bd. Springer-Verlag, 175 Fifth Ave., New York, N.Y. 10010. Illus., index, adv. Sample. Vol. ends: no. 4. Refereed.

Indexed: SciAb. *Bk. rev:* 3, 200–800 words, signed. *Aud:* Sa, Ac.

A research journal, the publication stresses the application of mathematics as related to the theory and analysis of computation. A large number of papers focus around numerical analysis, and some studies deal with applications, e.g., mathematical models for special industries. Papers appear both in German and English, although in a recent count, the German outweighed the English. A few algorithms are also published. A high quality, theoretical journal of sophisticated collections in university libraries.

√ ***Computing Report in Science and Engineering.*** 1965. q. Free (Controlled circulation). Donald T. Sanders. Data Processing Division, IBM Corp., 1133 Westchester Ave., White Plains, N.Y. 10604. Illus., index. Circ: 50,000. Sample. Vol. ends: no. 4.

Aud: Sa, Ac.

A promotional publication issued by IBM sales offices. The 20-page magazine describes in two to three-page sections how IBM installations are used in industry, government, universities, etc. An extra section details, briefly, new products and services. For librarians, an extremely useful department is "For Further Reference," which lists reports, programs, bibliographies, and other unpublished material available from their sales offices. Features are varied enough to be of general interest for any type of library, and a number of reports and bibliographies are library oriented. Technical readers will find more to their interests IBM's the *IBM Technical Disclosure Bulletin*, and *IBM Systems Journal*.

Computing Reviews. See Abstracts and Indexes Section.

√ ***Computing Surveys; the survey and tutorial journal of the ACM.*** 1969. q. $25 (ACM Members $7). William S. Dorn. Ass. for Computing Machinery, 1133 Ave. of the Americas, New York, N.Y. 10036. Illus., index. Vol. ends: no. 4. Refereed.

Indexed: ComRev. *Aud:* Sa, Ac.

As its subtitle indicates, the journal is the general review publication of the Association for Computing Machinery (ACM). About two to three papers in every issue survey subjects of more than topical interest to a wide clientele (e.g., "Computers in the Humanities and Fine Arts."). And tutorial articles elucidate well-known theories or applications of an old subject (e.g., on flowcharting). Contributors to the journal are well-known specialists. A fine publication for both specialist and nonspecialist, and particularly recommended for those libraries which do not require the sophistication of the more theoretical journals in the field such as the *Journal of the ACM*.

Control Engineering. 1954. m. $10. Byron K. Ledgerwood. Reuben H. Donnelly Corp., 466 Lexington Ave., New York, N.Y. 10017. Illus., index, adv. Microform: UM. Reprint: Johnson.

Indexed: ASTI, EngI, SciAb, SCI. *Bk. rev:* 2, 100 words, signed. *Aud:* Sa, Ac.

Circulated without charge to technical personnel responsibile for the "design, application and testing of automatic control systems," the trade journal is replete with ads, photos, and short announcements of new products and installations. Its two or three general interest articles view the computer technology field broadly, in terms of automation in factories, transportation, education, and the economics of such systems. Features are aimed at the nonspecialist and frequently are tutorial in nature. A good, trade publication centering around control systems for any technical library.

Data Management (Formerly: ***Journal of Data Management).*** 1964. m. $5. Don Young. Data Processing Management Assn., 505 Busse Highway, Park Ridge, Ill. 60068. Illus., index, adv. Circ: 50,000. Vol. ends: Dec. Microform: UM.

Bk. rev: 2, 200 words, signed. *Aud:* Sa, Ac.

Formerly called *Journal of Data Management*, the publication is the official journal of the Association, and is aimed at the management-level user. General articles review hardware and software developments in all areas of data processing, with special emphasis on applications to auditing, banking, education, insurance, publishing, retailing, and transportation. (Titles such as "Where to get Data Processing Help" are typical.) Monthly departments review news from Washington, the industry, the Association, new products, and the like. For the subscription price the periodical is meaty enough to fill a need for the special applications groups mentioned above. For academic libraries.

Data Processing Digest. 1955. m. $51. Margaret Milligan. Data Processing Digest, Inc., 6820 La Tijera Blvd., Los Angeles, Calif. 90045. Index. Circ: 4,500. Sample. Vol. ends: no. 12. Microform: UM.

Bk. rev: 2, 200 words, signed. *Aud:* Sa, Ac.

It is difficult to evaluate a digest service, since what might be ephemeral to one library might prove to be solid gold to another. This publication, now approaching its second decade, is one of the better services and was selected as a representative title of the genre. Generally, the digest focuses each issue on one topic (e.g., data management systems) and discusses and evaluates suppliers, costs, and other comparative features. The remainder of the issue, published in looseleaf format, contains news briefs gleaned from other sources: journals, trade magazines, product development releases, etc. The pitch is to data processing managers and other executives. Happily, the service also provides an index. Again, whether libraries need to spend money on evaluative digests or on the primary sources themselves remains the decision of the individual librarian for the clientele served.

Datamation. 1957. $25 (Qualified personnel free). Robert B. Forest. Technical Publishing Co., 1301 S. Grove Ave., Barrington, Ill. Illus., index, adv. Circ: 110,000. Sample. Microform: UM. Reprint: Swets.

Indexed: SCI. *Bk. rev:* Occasional, 250–500 words, signed. *Aud:* Sa, Ac.

The popularity of this magazine among those associated with computer technology is well deserved; yet its scope is broad enough to be informative and interesting to any nonspecialist wishing details on the intricacies of information processing. Feature articles range from the economics and history of computers, to reviews on programming languages, algorithms, systems, etc. Market coverage, both U.S. and foreign, is exhaustive; technical meetings are also reported in detail. Contributions by the editorial staff are evaluative, rather than expressive of the platitudes of the trade, and the prose is often lively. News briefs, products information, gossip of the trade, and personalia comprise a good part of each issue. This should be a good choice for a trade journal dealing with hardware and software, business and science, and may also be valuable for high schools in which a data processing curriculum has been established.

EDP Analyzer. 1963. m. $36. Richard G. Canning. Canning Publns., Inc., 925 Anza Ave., Vista, Calif. 92083. Index. Sample. Vol. ends: no. 12. Microform: Canning.

Aud: Sa, Ac.

The approach of this service is somewhat different from other digest-type services. In one evaluative essay, of about 14 pages, the editor explores, analyzes critically, in-depth, and supports with an accompanying bibliography, selected and timely topics in the field: "Security of the Computer Center"; "Intelligent Terminals"; "Programmer-Operations Interface." The emphasis is on the evaluation, rather than the straight chart–graph–figure marketing survey, or new product development. A useful service, particularly for business libraries concerned with electronic data processing or other applications of computers. Also serves as a good foundation for student term papers.

IBM Journal of Research and Development. See Science/General Section

IBM Systems Journal. 1962. q. $3. H. E. Mehring. Intl. Business Machines Corp., Armonk, N.Y. 10504. Illus., index. Sample. Vol. ends: no. 4. Refereed. Microform: UM. Reprint: Maxwell.

Indexed: ChemAb, EngI, MathR, Sciab, SCI. *Aud:* Sa, Ac.

Contributions to this journal come from the scientific staff of the various divisions of the IBM complex. Refereed papers include investigations on all aspects of system design, including computer systems, mathematical programming techniques, formal language design, control systems, simulation, etc. Issues also contain relevant abstracts of recent papers (published elsewhere) by other IBM authors. Since IBM still reigns as king of computers, most collections in the computing sciences will want it.

IEEE Computer Group News. See *Computer.*

IEEE Transactions on Automatic Control. 1952. bi-m. $24. José B. Cruz, Jr. Inst. of Electrical and Electronics Engineers, 345 E. 47th St., New York, N.Y. 10017. Illus., index. Sample. Vol. ends: no. 6. Refereed. Microform: IEEE.

Indexed: ASTI, ChemAb, EngI, MathR, SciAb, SCI. *Bk. rev:* 5–6, 300–1,000 words, signed. *Aud:* Sa, Ac.

The major articles, short notes, and brief technical correspondence in this research journal are concerned with the "theory, design, and application of control systems." Thus, subjects of interest include the fields of optimization, adaptation, modeling, design of components, self-organization, and application to physical systems. On occasion, an entire issue may be dedicated to tutorial papers or reviews of the state of the art. The journal, a product of the IEEE Control Systems Society, is another example of the high quality, albeit specialized, technical *Transactions* published by the IEEE. All good collections on automatic control will need this publication, as will most electrical engineering collections.

IEEE Transactions on Computers. 1952. m. $42 (including *Computer*). Robert A. Short. Inst. of Electrical and Electronics Engineers, 345 E. 47th St., New York, N.Y. 10017. Illus., index. Sample. Vol. ends: Dec. Refereed. Microform: IEEE.

Indexed: ASTI, ChemAb, EngI, MathR, SciAb, SCI. *Bk. rev:* 3, 300 words, signed. *Aud:* Sa, Ac.

Directed toward engineers, these transactions contribute to the research literature on theory, design, and applications of digital, analog, and special-duty computers. Articles cover such topics as hardware, logic design, fault-tolerant machines, simulation, switching theory, artifical intelligence, pattern recognition, and applications. Included with most issues are abstracts of current computer literature, prepared by the Cambridge Communications Corporation (producers of several abstracting journals). An authoritative and important research journal for any collection in the computing sciences supporting electrical engineering interests. (Note: nonspecialist review-type articles and news of the IEEE Computer Society are incorporated in *Computer.*)

IEEE Transactions on Information Theory. 1952. bi-m. $24. G. D. Forney, Jr. Inst. of Electrical and Electronics Engineers, 345 E. 47th St., New York, N.Y. 10017. Illus., index. Sample. Vol. ends: Nov. Microform: IEEE.

Indexed: ASTI, ChemAb, EngI, MathR, SciAb, SCI. *Bk. rev:* 2–3,300–600 words, signed. *Aud:* Sa, Ac.

Of high quality and theoretical, the journal is dedicated to mathematical principles governing systems designed to transmit, manipulate, or utilize information. Within the scope of its research papers are such topics as communication, coding, signal processing, stochastic processes, pattern recognition, and learning. Essential for communications engineers, the journal is also an authoritative source for theoretical papers related to the computing sciences. For university libraries.

IEEE Transactions on Systems Science and Cybernetics. 1952. q. $18. Inst. of Electrical and Electronics Engineers, 345 E. 47th St., New York, N.Y. 10017. Illus., index. Sample. Vol. ends: no. 4. Refereed. Microform: IEEE.

Indexed: ASTI, ChemAb, EngI, MathR, SciAb, SCI. *Aud:* Sa, Ac.

Both theoretical and practical, the scope of this interdisciplinary publication covers systems science and engineering, and cybernetics. Research papers on systems science discuss large technological systems (e.g., whole factories, complete transportation systems) and include studies on the economics, operation and utilization of the system, as well as its engineering design. Investigations are frequently carried out by use of computers. Contributions on cybernetics stress the methodology of these technological systems to biological, behavioral, sociological, political, legal, and economic systems. The applications to other fields make it a valuable research journal for university libraries.

Information and Control. 1957. 10/yr. $24/vol. Murray Eden. Academic Press, 111 Fifth Ave., New York, N.Y. 10003. Illus., index. Sample. Vol. ends: no. 10. Refereed.

Indexed: ChemAb, EngI, MathR, SciAb, SCI. *Bk. rev:* Occasional, 1,000–2,000 words, signed. *Aud:* Sa, Ac.

One of the early scholarly journals to appear in the literature of the computing sciences, the journal has remained a high quality publication with a distinguished editorial board. Original research papers appear in "theories of communication, computers, and auto-

matic control;" studies are included on automata, codes, grammars, formal languages, etc. An important publication, particularly for electrical engineers interested in communication theory and automatic control theory. For technical and university libraries.

Information Processing Letters. 1971. bi-m. $25. Ed. bd. North-Holland Publishing Co.; U.S. sub to: Amer. Elsevier Publishing Co., 52 Vanderbilt Ave., New York, N.Y. 10017. Illus., index. Sample. Vol. ends: no. 4. Refereed.

Aud: Sa, Ac.

The aim of this research-oriented publication is to disseminate short reports on such topics as theory of computer programming, including analysis of algorithms, automata theory, formal languages, and numerical mathematics; the structure of systems and systems programming, including file processing, simulation, and software engineering; and applications of information processing in such fields as artificial intelligence, information retrieval, pattern recognition, etc. Some prominent names in the computing sciences appear on the first editorial board of the journal, and its first volume has an impressive array of papers by well-known specialists in the field. A sophisticated journal for university collections.

Information Sciences. 1969. q. $30. John M. Richardson. American Elsevier Publishing Co. 52 Vanderbilt Ave., New York, N.Y. 10017. Illus., index, adv. Circ: 660. Sample. Vol. ends: no. 4. Refereed.

Indexed: ComAb. *Aud:* Sa, Ac.

With an orientation toward mathematics and engineering, the journal publishes research and expository papers on such areas as information theory, communication theory, pattern recognition, coding theory, adaptive control, stochastic processes, identifications of systems. A prominent and international editorial board selects high quality papers, also with an international spread. An authoritative and relevant journal for engineering collections as well as those in the computing sciences.

Information Storage and Retrieval. 1963. bi-m. $40. Bernard M. Fry. Pergamon Press, Maxwell House, Fairview Park, Elmsford, N.Y. 10523. Illus., index. Sample. Vol. ends: no. 6. Refereed. Microform: Maxwell. Reprint: Maxwell.

Indexed: LibSciAb, MathR. *Bk. rev:* 3, 500 words, signed. *Aud:* Sa, Ac.

This journal studies storage and retrieval of information from its generation, through processing and retrieval, to its effective use as an end product. Typical papers (both research-type or simply descriptive articles) may report on mathematical models of information sources; thesauri development; computer-assisted indexing; statistical analyses of documents files; file searches; evaluation of retrieval searches, etc. Some issues are entirely dedicated to papers presented at conferences. Reflecting the international character of the publication, papers may appear in French, German, Italian, as well as English. Issues may also carry abstracts of selected reports and theses in relevant areas. Indispensable for the information scientist, the journal is an authoritative and high quality publication for anyone interested in this field.

International Journal of Man-Machine Studies. 1969. q. $24. G. B. B. Chaplin, Academic Press, 111 Fifth Ave., New York, N.Y. 10003. Illus., index. Sample. Vol. ends: no. 4. Refereed.

Bk. rev: Occasional, 500 words, signed. *Aud:* Sa, Ac.

It is difficult to classify such an interesting interdisciplinary journal, which rests between engineering and mathematical considerations in the study of man (quantifying human behavior), and biological considerations of machines (neurophysiology, pattern recognition). At any rate, the English-originated journal publishes scholarly papers on "man-machine interaction," and the "man-machine interface," and covers topics such as computer-assisted instruction, communication with machines in natural language, systems theory, control strategy, etc. Heavily computer oriented, the publication also carries articles on simulation and modeling of human behavior and thought processes. A valuable publication for large academic libraries supporting research in the computing sciences.

Journal of Chemical Documentation. See Chemistry Section.

Journal of Computer and System Sciences. 1967. bi-m. $32. E. K. Blum. Academic Press, 111 Fifth Ave., New York, N.Y. Illus., index. Sample. Vol. ends: Dec. Refereed.

Indexed: SciAb. *Aud:* Sa, Ac.

A well-known editorial board of mathematicians and computing scientists has established the journal's reputation as one of the quality publications in the field. Emphasis is on the mathematical research report in the fields of automata theory, theory of formal languages, algorithms, computer programming, as well as theory of systems and applications of mathematics to systems. Too sophisticated for the small college library (unless of interest to the math dept.), the journal will enhance university collections in the computing sciences.

Journal of Data Management. See *Data Management*.

SIAM Journal on Computing. See Mathematics Section.

Simulation. 1963. $32. John H. McLeod. Simulation Councils, Inc., P. O. Box 2228, La Jolla, Calif. 92037. Illus., index, adv. Circ: 3,090. Microform: Simulation Councils, Inc.

Indexed: ComRev. EngI, SciAb, SCI. *Bk. rev:* 2–3, 100 words, unsigned. *Aud:* Sa, Ac.

The journal considers simulation of systems by the use of mathematical or physical analogies performed by computers or other devices. Research papers, and review or tutorial articles thus cover both the theory, design and construction of these computing devices, their applications to simulation systems, and techniques suitable for simulation. Special departments include notes on techniques, educational demonstrations, reviews of meetings, informal news of the society, etc. An excellent corollary publication for collections in the computing sciences.

Software Age. 1967. m. $10 (Free to qualified subscribers). John F. Sikora. Press-Tech, Inc., 2211 Fordem Ave., Madison, Wis. 53701. Illus., index, adv. Circ: 140,000. Sample. Vol. ends: no. 12.

Aud: Sa, Ac.

A trade journal comprised of the usual short, feature articles describing computer power, systems, the software industry, programming language development, and monthly departments for new product listings, etc. The unique aspect of the magazine is that it runs a swapshop for software programs, the abstracts of which are published. Any type of program will be listed: scientific, engineering, management, systems, applications. Libraries may welcome it as a giveaway, but the subscription price is too steep for a trade magazine.

Software: Practice & Experience. 1971. q. $20. D. W. Barron and C. A. Lang. John Wiley & Sons, Baffins Lane, Chichester, Sussex, England. Illus., index. Circ: 700. Sample. Vol. ends: no. 4. Refereed.

Aud: Sa, Ac.

The editors of this British-based journal have aptly expressed the present state of the software industry as one comparable to "cottage industry: labour-intensive, producing a product of variable quality by methods that are unbelievably unsophisticated by comparison with the best of the products themselves." To alleviate some of the problems besetting the profession, this journal has been set up especially for software writers and managers, to provide a medium for exchange of practical experience in the field. Both "applications" and "systems" software papers are considered, for either batch, interactive, multi-access, or real-time systems. Case studies and some tutorial studies are also published. Highly theoretical or mathematical papers are generally avoided. The first volume looks promising; topics range from an empirical study of FORTRAN, to an overview of software architecture for this decade, through a number of case studies and selected articles on software design. Issues also contain a regular series, "Computer Recreations," describing games which can be played with computers. Contributors to the first volume also represented several highly prominent names in the field both from the U.K. and the U.S. Definitely should be a worthwhile and authoritative addition to collections in the computing sciences.

CONSUMER SERVICES

Basic Periodicals

Hs: Consumer Reports, Can; Ga: *Consumer Reports, Can, Consumer Bulletin;* Jc: *Consumer Reports, Can, International Consumer;* Ac: *Consumer Reports, Can, Consumer Bulletin, International Consumer, Consumers Voice, Consumer Price Index.*

Note: for information on automobile purchases, see the Automobile section. *Road and Track* in America, and several excellent guides in England have information on new and used automobiles. See also the Counterculture section.

ACCI Newsletter. See *Journal of Consumer Affairs.*

Can; consumer action now. 1970. m. $5. Hildy Johnson. Consumer Action Now, 815 Park Ave., New York, N.Y. Illus. Sample.

Aud: Ac, Ga, Hs. *Jv:* V.

One of the best volunteer efforts to win change. The four page newsletter is published by a nonprofit organization made up of women. They are intent on bringing honesty to consumer advertising and improving manufactured products of both small and giant corporations. The whole operation is volunteer, and extremely effective in that the advice, notes, articles, and analysis of various aspects of everyday living are first rate. The women reporters, drawing on documents, interviews, clippings, and just plain common sense, have written about pollution, phosphates, bread, pesticides, foods, etc. As "a do-it-yourself newspaper," this is well worth the modest price. It is in no way provincial. (The women workers have been on several national "Talk shows," and won support from consumers all over the country.) It is of value to every consumer in or out of the New York area. Should be in all libraries.

The Capitalist Reporter. 1971. m. $9. Patrick Garrard. The Reporter, 150 Fifth Ave., New York, N.Y. 10011. Illus., adv.

Aud: Ga. *Jv:* C.

A 64-page tabloid, well-illustrated newspaper which tells the reader how he or she can make money. Most of it is sensational, badly documented, and aimed at the greedy. A good deal of the material is written by someone with a product to push or an idea to plug, and it is a far cry from the consumer-type magazines which are to protect the reader. There are articles such as "Beware of New Mexico Land Promoters," but at the same time "Santa Fe Real Estate Bonanza.

Some property is increasing in value 50% a year." Then there are such items as how to "pyramid 10 grand into $856,025," or how to make $2,000 a month writing patent licenses, or how to invest in Alaska oil. Between these bits of information there is much advertising trying to take, rather than raise, the income of the reader. It's all fun enough, and it makes grand browsing for anyone who doesn't take it seriously. Here and there are even a few worthwhile tips, but on the whole it is questionable. Not recommended, particularly where there is an unsophisticated, trusting audience.

Caveat Emptor. 1971. m. $5.95. Robert L. Berko. 556 U.S. Highway 22, Hillside, N.J. 07205. Illus., adv.

Bk. rev: 1–2, 500 words. *Aud:* Ga.

A 24-page approach to "facts, opinions and consumer information for anyone wishing to keep abreast of the developments in the consumer action movement." The relatively low price is due to the format—it is produced on cheap newsprint in regular magazine size. Even so, the content is hardly worth it. Some material is reprinted from standard sources—including other consumer magazines and government documents. The rest is in the form of notes the editor apparently has rewritten from newspapers, magazines, and reports. The whole is useful enough, but hardly new or revealing. Way down the list for most libraries.

Changing Times; the Kiplinger magazine. 1947. m. $6. Robert W. Harvey. Kiplinger Washington Editors, Inc. 1729 H St., N.W., Washington, D.C. 20006. Illus., index, adv. Circ: 1,400,000. Sample. Vol. ends: Dec. Microform: UM. Reprint: Abrahams.

Indexed: AbrRG, PAIS, RG. *Bk. rev:* 35, 50 words. *Aud:* Ga, Ac, Hs.

This side of *Consumer Reports* and the equally as well advertised *Moneysworth,* this is the best known of the consumer-type magazines. In fact, Kiplinger pioneered the popular, somewhat "gee-whiz, look what you can save" approach to the market. In spite of, or possibly because of, the free and easy style, the magazine enjoys a healthy circulation. Much of this is well deserved. The short advice articles are accurate, although sometimes a bit exaggerated. New research and activities in education, science, medicine, and the arts are reported. Concise discussions of current business developments enable the consumer to stay aware of the latest events. Also included are practical articles concerning ways to earn, buy, and save. Simple graphs, charts, and statistics are provided to clarify and illustrate the more difficult topics discussed. Capsule news items and fresh ideas are supplied each issue in a regular section "The Months Ahead" to act as a guide for families in planning their future budgets. This may not be the best of the consumer-oriented magazines, but it certainly is one of the most popular. As such, should be found in most libraries.

Choice. 1960. m. Membership. $6. The Secretary, Australian Consumers' Assn., 28 Queen St., Chippendale, N.S.W. 2008, Australia. Illus., index. Circ: 125,000. Sample. Vol. ends: Dec.

Aud: Ga.

The Australian 32-page version of *Consumer Reports.* As a publication of a nonprofit member of the International Organization of Consumer Unions, the magazine carries no advertising, represents a disinterested and objective view of consumer goods. The material is familiar enough, e.g., the January 1972 issue evaluated the cost of air travel, home freezers, freezer food plans, etc. Previous issues considered power mowers, door locks, dinner sets, car theft devices, etc. The reports tend to be somewhat longer and more detailed than those found in other consumer magazines. And while primarily for Australians, let it be noted that many of the brands are international, e.g., Sunbeam, General Electric, Norge, etc., and much of the advice is as applicable to United States consumers as to Australians. In addition to *Choice,* the organization publishes: *Car Magazine* (1965. q. $3. Illus., index. Circ: 100,000 Sample). At one time this was published as a supplement to *Choice,* but is now a separate quarterly. Usually one or two cars are considered in great detail. And as most of the cars are imported from England, the United States or Europe, the tests tend to be as applicable here as in Australia. An excellent backstop for the English and American magazine, in this area.

Consumer Alert. 1971. m. free. SDC: FT 1.24/2. Office of Public Information, Federal Trade Commission, 6th St. and Pennsylvania Ave., N.W., Washington, D.C. 20580. Vol. ends: Dec.

Aud: Ga, Ac, Hs.

The Federal Trade Commission underwent internal reorganization in the summer of 1970, secured a get-things-done chief, and became a tiger. Acting more vigorously on its mandate to prevent and curtail illegal business practices, it has rapidly expanded its consumer protection capability. As part of this stepped–up activity, it issued an awareness service, a four page newsletter, and the first issue was published in February 1971.

The newsletter discusses subjects of current and practical interest to the buying public. Topics include everything that the FTC is empowered to regulate pursuant to the laws: common deceptions such as mailing unordered merchandise, confidentiality of consumer credit reports, packaging deceptions, wool and fur labeling, and a host of other problems.

Since this is free, it is a useful publication for all academic, business, and public libraries, and for high school collections. The FTC urges media representatives, consumer organizations, and consumer educators to relay the contents of this newsletter to their audiences—in print, on the air, or through other channels available to them. Regular Features include listings of a series of "Buyer's Guides" issued by the FTC Division of Consumer Education and sent free to persons and institutions upon request; and a column called "Consumer Briefs," short notes on actions and activities of FTC that are designed to be used as newspaper filler or radio/TV spots.

Although news of watchdog activities of government in this crucial area appears in the media, and detailed rulings are published in the *Federal Register* (q.v.), there is a need for an expanded popular publication in this field. Meanwhile, this slim newsletter will have to do. (J.M.)

Consumer Bulletin (and Consumer Bulletin Annual). 1927. m. $8. F. J. Schlink, Consumers' Research, Inc., Washington, N.J. 07882. Illus., index. Circ: 100,000. Sample. Vol. ends: Dec. Microform: Mc, UM.

Indexed: RG. *Aud:* Ga, Ac, Hs. *Jv:* V.

The oldest of the consumer product test magazines. It reports ratings on tested brand name products. Ratings of recommended, intermediate, and not recommended are applied to hundreds of items which have been laboratory tested or, in some cases, judged by qualified experts. The research involved is highly impartial and results are reported accurately; simple enough for understanding by the novice, yet with enough further technical information to satisfy the more informed reader. Products tested include a wide range of household appliances and supplies, floor coverings, clothing and textiles, musical instruments, automobiles, radio, television, hi-fi's, cameras, precautions for safety in the home, and many other categories. Regular departments include editorials, reviews of classical and popular recordings, motion picture recommendations and ratings based on motion picture reviews in 14 periodicals. There are also news items of special interest to the consumer, and to teachers in their work with classes on consumer problems, and other business and science education subjects. Short articles provide information concerning nutrition, health, chemical food additives and food adulteration, appliance hazards, and descriptive recommendations of new products considered as meriting special attention by consumers. In the previous edition this was noted as a second choice after *Consumer Reports,* but due to increased interest in the whole field, the average library is strongly advised to consider them both equally. (The subscription price now includes the annual, published in September.)

Consumer Education Forum. See *Journal of Consumer Affairs.*

Consumer Newsweek (Formerly: *U.S. Consumer*). 1967. w. $15. Arthur E. Rowse. Consumer News Inc., 813 National Press Bldg., Washington, D.C. 20004. Circ: 1,500. Sample. Vol. ends: Mid–Oct.

Bk. rev: Notes. *Aud:* Ac, Ga.

A four-page, reasonably priced newsletter which covers all aspects of consumer problems likely to interest the involved consumer group advocates. It has considerable material on health, law, standards, etc. Much of the reporting concerns activities in Washington which relate to the consumer, e.g., a feature on "big business control of farming." And there is a regular column "Washington highlights." Because of the emphasis on social and political involvement, it is a newsletter more likely to appeal to the socially involved than to the average man or woman who wants to know how to save a dollar. It is by far one of the better, more serious approaches to the consumer and American industry, and seems particularly suited for academic and larger public libraries.

Consumer Price Index. 1940. m. free. SDC: L 2.38/3. Office of Information 14th St. and Constitution Ave., N.W. Washington, D.C. 20210. Charts, index.

Aud: Ga, Ac, Hs.

The publication, whose title is a household word for the adult public, measures average changes in prices of goods and services usually bought by urban wage earners and clerical workers, both families and single persons living alone. It is based on prices of about 400 items which were selected to represent the movement of prices of all goods and services purchased by these two categories of employees. Prices for items are obtained in urban portions of 39 Standard Metropolitan Statistical Areas (SMSA's) and 17 smaller cities chosen as a sample to represent the universe of urban United States (including Alaska and Hawaii). They are collected from grocery and department stores, hospitals, filling stations, and other types of stores and service establishments which wage earners and clerical workers patronize.

Every month prices of foods, fuels, and a few other items are obtained in all 56 locations. Prices of most other commodities and services are collected every month in the five largest SMSA's and every quarter in other SMSA's and cities. With these figures, a narative profile of the month precedes the tabular data. It begins invariably with the ominous phrase "The Consumer Price Index rose . . .," the verb by any other name inducing resignation if not despair in the hearts of consumers. The report is divided into three categories: food, commodities other than food (apparel, auto, housing, etc.), and services (Maintenance, transportation, medical, etc.). Following this analysis are the tables.

Because the results of the CPI seem as politically potent as the Nielsen ratings are for TV, the methodology is critical. Mail questionnaires are used to obtain local transit fares, public utility rates, newspaper prices, fuel prices, and certain other items which change in price relatively infrequently. Prices of most other goods and services are obtained by personal visits of the highly trained and indefatigable agents of the Bureau of Labor Statistics. The third cover has a useful list of BLS regional offices, with name of director, address, and phone number.

Comparison of indexes for individual SMSA's show only that prices in one location changed more or less than in another. The indexes cannot be used to measure differences in price levels or in living costs between areas. Reliability of percent changes is crucial, and each issue gives a table of average standard errors of percent changes by month, quarter, and annually for large components based on previous year's data. Replicated samples introduced into the index structure in 1964 permit a more precise estimate of sampling error for the data.

Most tables in this publication appear later in the *Monthly Labor Review* (q.v.), and advance notice may be found in the daily *News, U.S. Department of Labor* (which, like the CPI, is free to libraries and individuals). Also free is the pamphlet *The Consumer Price Index, A Short Description,* which may be obtained by writing to the Bureau of Labor Statistics, Washington, D.C. 20212 or any of the regional offices. Also useful is an article on the method of deriving estimates of sampling error published by Marvin Wilkerson in the *Journal of the American Statistical Association,* September 1967.

Senior high school libraries as well as all academic and public libraries should find this publication a worthwile addition to their collections. (J.M.)

Consumer Reports. 1936. m. $8. Consumers Union of U.S., Inc. 256 Washington St., Mount Vernon, N.Y. 10550. Illus., index. Circ: 2,000,000. Microform: UM.

Indexed: AbrRG, PAIS, RG. *Bk. rev:* Notes, signed. *Aud:* Ga, Ac. *Jv:* V.

The best known, best all around general consumer magazine for the average American. The nonprofit organization which sponsors the magazine provides consumer information on goods and services through ratings of brand name products which have been laboratory and use tested as well as expertly inspected. Estimated overall quality is either judged acceptable, with variations from good to poor, or not acceptable. Products which have a high overall quality coupled with a low price are judged best buys. The testing is thorough and qualitative with the results reported impartially. A regular feature comments on news items, prices, products, advertising, and recommendations for the best use of certain products. Other columns report government actions to enforce consumer protection laws and discuss government legislation and judical decisions which have a healthy or unhealthy effect on the consumer economy. Articles are as technically accurate as *Consumer Bulletin,* but have a more diversified appeal. Broader topics are discussed in an informative manner conducive to reading for pleasure. A first choice for all sizes and types of libraries. Subscription price includes annual *Buying Guide,* a compilation of findings over the previous year.

Consumers Voice; let the seller beware. 1966. m. $3. Max Weiner. CEPA Intl Inc., 6048 Ogontz Ave., Philadelphia, Pa. 19126. Illus. Circ: 5,000. Sample. Vol. ends: Dec.

Aud: Ga.

A militant approach to the problem of the consumer vs. the faceless business or manufacturer which seems to be working. A national nonprofit voluntary organization, CEPA is Consumer Education and Protective Association. Its major publication is this four-page tabloid newspaper. News is about equally divided between national and Philadelphia interests, e.g., a typical front page includes a story on a Washington, D.C. court approving consumer picketing and one about a local automobile dealer buying back a "lemon" car. The whole paper leans towards a militant consumer drive for fair play at both the local and the national level. (According to a columnist, it is the only one of seven organizations in the eastern states which uses the picketing technique for getting attention, i.e., the organization throws pickets around a business that has been unfair to a consumer.) It might be a model for others trying to start such a paper. Should be in all Pennsylvania libraries, and purchased by any consumer group or library.

Council for Family Financial Education. 1110 Fidler La., Suite 1616, Twin Towers, Silver Spring, Md. 20910

This is an organization, not a magazine, but it is of sufficient importance to list here. The "council was established in 1969 as an independent, nonprofit educational corporation to assist schools, colleges and other institutions in the development and implementation of programs in consumer education as a vital aspect of a national instructional need." The organization offers three publications" which are available at cost, and will be of interest to anyone who turned to this section. The publications are:

Teaching Consumer Education and Financial Planning. $6.

A 170 page resource manual for school and classroom use for grades K through 12. Built around 6 major themes of planning, buying, borrowing, protecting, investing, and sharing, and features extensive use and suggestions for such teaching techniques as role playing, visuals, student self evaluations, and discussions.

Family Financial Education for Adults. $4.

This adult education handbook of 116 pages provides a step-by-step approach for providing content and method in 14 areas of financial decision making.

New elements of the revised handbook include sections on "conducting a financial council" and "the consumer and the law."

Free and Inexpensive Material. $1.

A highly selective bibliography for reaching consumer education and financial planning. This 92-page listing of books, publications, films, and filmstrips covers all aspects of consumer education and consumer interest. Also contains a listing of supplemental classroom materials and their sources.

F.D.A. Papers. 1967. m. (10/yr.) bi-m. (July/Aug., Dec./Jan.). $3.50. Howard C. Hopkins. Supt. of Documents, U.S. Govt. Printing Office, Washington, D.C. 20402. (Depository) SDC HE: 20.4010. Illus. Vol. ends: Dec./Jan.

Indexed: PAIS. *Aud:* Ga, Ac.

This is the official magazine of the Food and Drug Administration. Under the provisions of Section 705 of the Food, Drug, and Cosmetic Act, the publication is used as the vehicle for disseminating information regarding food, drugs, devices, or cosmetics in situations involving imminent danger to health or gross deception of the consumer. The first part contains approximately five or six articles written by FDA employees. The authors are professional scientific, legal, and medical specialists, yet the articles are eminently readable for the informed layman. Topics include a spectrum of the current problems in consumer education and information: dangerous drugs, activities of the FDA in assuring surveillance of the food and drug scene, and legislation affecting consumer products.

Part two consists of six sections of regular features. These are: "Field Reports," a compilation of investigatory activity of the Administration arranged by major city, with the action FDA took pursuant to its enforcement powers; "Product Safety Report," a statistical study of a specific product causing injury or death; "News Highlights," notes and comments on functions of the FDA and its several divisions in their watchdog activities; "State Actions," brief reports on activities of State agencies in this field; "Seizures and Post Office Cases," violations of the Food, Drug, and Cosmetic Act, and the Hazardous Substances Act are published in this section when they are reported by the FDA District Offices; "Notices of Judgment," reports of cases involving seizure, criminal and injunction proceedings against firms or individuals charged responsible for violations. Arranged by broad subject areas and alphabetically by product, decisions rendered have the force of law. A worthy publication for all college, university and public libraries. (J.M.)

Family Economics Review. q. Free. Consumer and Food Economics Research Div., Agricultural Research Service, U.S., Dept. of Agriculture, Washington, D.C. 20250.

Aud: Ga.

A government publication directed primarily to home demonstration agents and specialists, but of some use to the layman. There are succinct reports on the past quarter's or year's activities in such diverse matters as cost of living and its effect on home economics, food prices and distribution, etc. The numerous charts and the direct, easy-to-understand style give it relevance for many consumers.

International Consumer. 1960. q. Membership $10. John Calascione. Intl. Organization of Consumers Unions, 9, Emmastraat, The Hague, Netherlands. Illus., index. Circ: 1,000. Sample. Vol. ends: Winter.

Bk. rev: Various number, length. *Aud:* Ga, Ac. *Jv:* V.

An important magazine, which is too little known. It is only one of several publications by this international group. The journal is the official voice of the International Organization of Consumers Unions (IOCU), "an independent, non-profit and non-political foundation. It promotes worldwide cooperation in the comparative testing of consumer goods and services, and in all other aspects of consumer information, education and protection." Founded in 1960, it now has members from 35 countries—including government-financed consumer councils. And while it was originally set up as a clearinghouse for information (and remains that today), it also represents consumer interests in international agencies, such as UNESCO, UNICEF, and FAO.

The magazine averages some 28 pages, deals primarily with material regarding consumer education and practices. It is not a testing publication. Articles represent an active political and social interest in consumer education leadership. A good amount of each number is given to international news and events, particularly in developing countries. The articles are by experts, often teachers. The issue ends with brief news items, and a one page summary in French of the English text.

The IOCU also publishes the following services. *IOCU Newsletter*—a monthly publication which goes to all members. It is primarily a report of events in international agencies. Free to members. *Consumer Review*—a bi-monthly abstracting service. This abstracts journals, technical reports, legislative documents, books, etc. An annual subscription is $50, and well worth the price where there is an active interest in the wider, international implications of consumer protection. *Consumer Directory*—an annual 112 page paperback directory, by country, of consumer organizations. Includes address, officers, main activities, and lists of publications. The directory lists all members of the IOCU, and many who are not members. The price is $5.

From time to time the organization issues monographs, e.g., "Knowledge is Power," the proceedings of the 1970 sixth IOCU world conference.

Journal of Consumer Affairs. 1967. s-a. $10 (Includes sub. to the ***ACCI Newsletter*** and ***Consumer Education Forum***). Gordon E. Bivens. American Council on Consumer Interests, 238 Stanley Hall, Univ. of Missouri, Columbia, Mo. 65201. Illus., adv. Circ: 3,200. Sample. Vol. ends: Winter. Refereed.

Bk. rev: 8–10, ½-1 page, signed. *Aud:* Ac, Ga.

A nonprofit, academic organization which aims "to stimulate an exchange of ideas among consumer groups; to contribute more effective research and fact finding; and to disseminate information on consumer problems." Directed to the teacher, student, and, to a degree, the interested layman. The 150 pages are divided among five or six articles, shorter pieces and news notes, and book reviews. Written by professors of sociology, business, home economics, etc., the articles vary from technical to relatively easily understood overviews of everything from wages, food prices, and financing to trading stamps. The discussions are both practical and theoretical. The objective treatment of matters concerning almost every American product gives it an added dimension for the lay reader who wants to go beyond the standard *Consumer Reports* or *Consumer Bulletin*. A good bet for all academic libraries, and a number of public libraries. (The *ACCI Newsletter* comes out 9 times a year; and the *Consumer Education Forum*, three times a year. Each acts to update the semi-annual journal.)

Journal of Retailing. 1925. q. $7. Sallie W. Sewell. New York Univ., Inst. of Retail Management, Commerce Bldg., Washington Sq., New York, N.Y. 10003. Illus., index. Circ: 3,000. Sample. Vol. ends: Winter. Refereed. Microform: UM. Reprint: Kraus, Abrahams.

Indexed: BusI, PAIS. *Bk. rev:* 6–8, 500 words, signed. *Aud:* Ga, Ac.

While this is primarily for the man or woman actively involved with the study of retailing practices in America, the contents are of equal interest to the average consumer. (It is somewhat similar to a man reading a good woman's magazine to find out what it's all about with women, or vice versa.) This "back door" approach to consumerism should be brought to the attention of anyone involved seriously with the process. Analyzing the broad aspects of retailing and current developments, the scholarly studies are designed for students and teachers of retailing, and managers in chain, department, and specialty shops. Articles concern shopper habits, price strategies, trends in stores, and the labor market. Factual and readable studies of the trading stamp mystery, the decline of department stores, and why the check-out woman in the food market seldom lasts more than a month. Articles are not overburdened with statistics and are, on the whole, fascinating. One of the few technical journals which deserves a wider, general reading public.

Money Doctor. 1969. q. $5. Willodean Vance. 5050 Clairemont Mesa Blvd., Suite 10, San Diego, Calif. 92117. Illus., index. Circ: 50,000. Sample. Vol. ends: Dec.

Aud: Ga.

This is a "common sense solution to financial and consumer problems" for the average American. A cross between *Consumer Reports* and *Changing Times,* the close to 100 advertisement-free pages feature tips on investment, employment, travel, housing, retirement, and almost anything which will interest the consumer. Articles, primarily by staffers and free lancers, are followed by extensive questions and answers, the queries beginning with "Dear Doctor." The replies are sensible, informative, and, as far as can be ascertained, accurate. Unlike *Changing Times* (which if you are short of money I'd drop in favor of this one) or the newer *Moneysworth,* the material is refreshingly free of the slick "how I'm going to save you money" approach. The clear down-to-earth style and usually well-documented information, lead the reader to think the editor is personally involved with helping him. There are literally hundreds of bits of valuable information in each issue, but it is not always easy to find without a thorough reading. (If there is a serious fault, it is the organization, which is too broad for the amount of material covered.) Highly recommended for most libraries.

Moneysworth. 1970. s-m. $5. Ralph Ginzburg. 110 W. 40th St., New York, N.Y. 10018. Illus. Sample.

Aud: Ga.

A four-page newsletter on what to, and what not to buy, with generous tips and evaluations of everything from best sellers and cameras to automobiles ·and life insurance. The main editorial push is to touch on items every consumer is interested in, and the editor pretty well succeeds. And while in four pages this is not a *Consumer Reports,* or, for that matter, a *Changing Times,* it manages to cover much the same territory in a briefer, usually satisfactory way. The whole is particularly well written, factual, and considerably better than several other Ginzburg children, i.e., *Fact* and *Avant Garde.* Trying to hold on to these slim publications is not easy, but it can be recommended for most libraries. (And if 1971 is any example, there is sure to be a call for it—the advertising which plugs the newsletter appeared in every major magazine.)

National Consumer League Bulletin. 1972. bi-m. Membership. Donation. Sarah H. Newman. National Consumer League, 1029 Vermont Ave., N.W., Washington, D.C. 20005. Circ: 2,000. Sample. Vol. ends: Dec.

Bk. rev: Notes. *Aud:* Ga, Ac.

Although the four-page newsletter is relatively new, the NCL came into being in 1899; has had such officers as Mrs. Eleanor Roosevelt, Louis D. Brandeis and Felix Frankfurter. The group is a lobbying organization "frankly committed to legislative action, as well as to research and public education." The newsletter has some 20 to 30 brief reports on government action, or lack thereof, in the consumer field, e.g., the December 1971 issue had items on such things as poultry ruling, dangerous toys, lead paint ban, school lunch bill signed, coal mine benefits, meals for the elderly, etc. It does not include specific information on products, although it does report on findings of the Public Health Service and the Federal Trade Commission. There apparently is no set price, but interested libraries should inquire. The bulletin is invaluable in the area of consumer legislation.

Of Consuming Interest. 1967. bi-w. $24. Jane S. Wilson. Federal State Reports, 2201 Wilson Blvd., Arlington, Va. 22201. Sample. Vol. ends: Sept.

Primarily for the manufacturer and supplier, not the lay consumer. Given this viewpoint, the four-page newsletter "covers Federal and State consumer legislation, consumer groups and their influence on Congress, and a plethora of related information from Federal agencies, the White House, and business sources." The approach is somewhat similar to the *National Consumer League Bulletin,* i.e., short news items of interest to readers. The essential difference is that the publisher is involved with information for businessmen, not with proposing reform or legislation. The reports are objective and the difference in audience is more of emphasis on material, than on the way the material is treated. Only for large business collections.

Service; USDA's report to consumers. 1963. m. Free. Lillie Vincent. U.S. Dept. of Agriculture, Washington, D.C. 20250. Circ: 8,000. Vol. ends: Nov.

Aud: Ac, Ga, Hs.

A four-page newsletter which gives accurate, unbiased information on all aspects of the consumer's life style. One issue, for example, opened with a warning about the dangers of cold turkey, gave information on a USDA pamphlet on environment, a page on best buys in the food market for the winter, a piece on how to winterize plants, safety tips, and advice on basting a turkey. The editor states that "other monthly letters report on films, nutrition, gardening, and recreation; relate case histories and stories that explain to consumers rather than to individuals." A good supplement, by the way, for home economics classes.

U.S. Consumer. See *Consumer Newsweek.*

Which? 1957. m. $6. Peter Goldman. Consumer's Assn., 14 Buckingham St., London WC2N 6DS, England. Illus., index. Circ: 610,000. Sample.

Aud: Ga.

The English equivalent of *Consumer Reports.* The

supporting nonprofit organization was founded in 1957 "and learnt almost everything about comparative testing, in the early days, from CU." It follows much the same procedure as its American counterpart, i.e., there are tests of every conceivable consumer product from dishwashers and tea-maker alarms to automobiles. Even the format is somewhat similar to *Consumer Reports*, and there are the usual "extras" including articles on all aspects of health, consumer protection, etc. While many of the products will be unfamiliar to Americans, there are reports on a few which make it worthwhile for larger collections, e.g., automobiles. The group has tested almost all English and European makes. There are a number of supplements to *Which*, costing a bit more. The interested library should send for a sample and request information on the other material available.

In addition to Consumers' Association and its affiliate, National Federation of Consumer Groups, there are two other major consumer protection groups in the United Kingdom. The Research Institute for Consumer Affairs (43 Villiers St., London WC2N 6NE) was founded in 1963, and has infrequent publications, but no magazine. The Women's Advisory Committee of the British Standards Institution has a quarterly publication: *Consumer Report* (2 Park St., London W1A 2BS) and issues a number of free leaflets on British Standards.

COUNTERCULTURE

See also Astrology, Education, Environment and Conservation, Health, Humor, Little Magazines, Library Periodicals, Music, Occult and Witchcraft, Parapsychology, Peace, Poetry, Religion and Theology, Women and Teenage/Women's Liberation Sections.

Basic Periodicals

ALTERNATIVE LIVING. Ejh: *Foxfire, Full Circle;* Hs: *Foxfire, Natural Life Styles, Ecology Action, Alternatives/The Modern Utopian;* Ga: *Mother Earth News, Foxfire, Earth, Natural Life Styles;* Jc: *Mother Earth News, Earth, Big Rock Candy Mountain, Ecology Action;* Ac: *Ecology Action, Mother Earth News, Big Rock Candy Mountain, Earth, Canadian Whole Earth Catalog, Source Catalog, Alternatives/Modern Utopian.*

SOCIAL AND POLITICAL CHANGE. Hs: *Other Scenes;* Ga: *Radical America, New Guard;* Jc: *Other Scenes, Radical America, New Guard;* Ac: *Other Scenes, Radical America, New Guard; Two, Three, Many . . .; Expatriate Review.*

UNDERGROUND COMIX. All libraries: *Zap Comix.*

UNDERGROUND NEWSPAPERS. Hs: *Phoenix, Berkeley Tribe;* Ga: *Berkeley Barb, Los Angeles Free Press;*

Jc: *Berkeley Tribe, Phoenix;* Ac: *Phoenix, Berkeley Tribe, Chicago Seed, IT, Georgia Straight.* All libraries: the underground paper closest to the library.

Basic Abstracts and Indexes

Alternate Press Index, Index to Little Magazines, Environment Index, Environment Information Access.

Cessations

East Village Other, Rags.

Introduction

Here "counterculture" means challenge.

The challenge is by young people, and not a few older ones, too. They are questioning established ways of doing things, established values; the whole establishment.

The expression comes out in many directions. Education and law have their own built in counterculture activities, as do libraries and children's centers; not to mention doctors and even psychologists. Here, though, the listing is primarily limited to three types: the environment, "let's change our way of living" magazine; the social and political magazine; and finally, the underground newspaper and its offshoot, the underground comic. Another major expression—in fact, the outstanding and obvious one—is in music, i.e., such magazines as *Rolling Stone.*

This section replaces the traditional "teenager" section. A look at the first edition shows that almost all so called teen-age magazines are for women—and they are so located in this edition. A few of the more general variety will be found here and in other sections.

Alternative Living

Alternatives/The Modern Utopian. 1966. irreg. $10. Alternatives Foundation, P.O. Drawer A Diamond Hgts. Sta., San Francisco, Calif. 94131. Circ: 5,000.

Indexed: API. *Bk. rev:* 3–4, 200 words. *Aud:* Hs, Ga, Ac. *Jv:* V.

According to a publicity flyer, this outfit consists "of only two of us working full time on this project." The two appear to be Dick Fairfield and Consuelo Sandoval. Alternatives is a publishing firm of sorts. For the $10 subscription, the library gets the following: *The Modern Utopian*, an annual; *Alternatives Newsletter*, a bi–monthly report on alternative life styles; and the *People Directory.*

The Modern Utopian (Vol. 5, nos. 5 & 6) came out in late 1971. It is titled "Modern Man in Search of Utopia," and consists of 195 pages. Volume 5 (nos. 1 & 2) appeared late 1970, and was titled "Communes, U.S.A." The annuals have two claims to a place in a library. First and foremost, they give accurate information on the problems and joys of commune living, and will be welcomed by most young people from high school through university. Second, they serve as a directory of communes. Unfortunately, addresses are not always given, although a bibliography of newsletters issued by the communes will serve to assist the reader trying to make a contact. And, obviously, a query to the publisher will serve equally well where additional information is wanted. The format is offset, yet easy to read; and there are a number of illustrations. The language is sincere, honest, but not delicate. The viewpoint is, to say the least, liberal and a far cry from those who see life as a matter of settling down in the suburbs. The best overall view of the movement is written by the movement, and it should be in all libraries.

Alternatives; perspectives on society and environment. 1971. q. $4. Collective. c/o Trent Univ., Peterborough, Ont., Canada. Illus.

Aud: Ga, Ac.

An offset 38-page journal put out by "a group of faculty and students," who believe the eventual solution to environmental problems will involve basic social change as much as technological innovations. The issue examined included articles by teachers both in Canada and the United States, and a multidisciplinary view of change by a teacher of economics at an English university. The politics of ecology is the basic concern, and future issues seem to promise the same, e.g., "An issue dealing with case law and legislation in several countries" is planned. The Canadian publishing in no way limits the journal's universal message and content.

Big Rock Candy Mountain. Education and Consciousness. 1969. q. $8. Samuel Yanes, Portola Inst., 1115 Merill St., Menlo Park, Calif. 94025. Subs. to: Small Publisher's Co., Elm. St., Millerton, N.Y. 12546; Libraries west of the Mississippi to: Book People, 2940 Seventh St., Berkeley, Calif. 94710. Illus. Circ: 15,000. Sample. Vol. ends: Spring.

Bk. rev: 20, 1,000 words, signed. *Aud:* Ga, Ac, Hs. *Jv:* V.

An oversized (10″x13″) 95 to 100 page well-printed and illustrated journal which since its inception has undergone many changes, but now touches all bases from yoga and zen to communes, food, and ecology. The publisher, a nonprofit, tax-exempt corporation, is set up "to encourage innovative educational projects . . . aimed at making education more holistic, more humanistic, and more responsive to social values." About one third to one half of each issue is given to perceptive reviews of books, monographs and sometimes magazines which are of interest to the counterculture. (Most titles are new, but in an essay on a given topic they may be retrospective, too. Hence, the reviews serve as both a current awareness and basic selection aid.) The tone of the contributors, who range

from young people to experts in a given field, is sane, informative, and balanced. Usually a bit of poetry and prose—which is a trifle uneven—is included. Of the best in its field, and suitable for advanced high schools, public, college, and university libraries.

Black Bart Brigade; the outlaw magazine. 1971. bi-m. Donation. Irv Thomas, Box 84, Canyon, Calif. 94516. Illus., adv. Sample.

Aud: Ga.

Here is a great switch. This is an alternative, serious little magazine for people over 30. It is pocket sized, printed on newsprint, carefully edited, and has some illustrations. The format is not important, but the message will appeal to anyone who is dragging a bit. Articles offer ways of living besides an 8 to 5 job. As the editor carefully explains, "The use of the word outlaw refers to anyone who has learned how to pursue life outside the confines of the system, and has opened his or her perspective to all the rewards and possibilities that are inherent in that condition." And six or seven articles away there is a letter column which really tells you what it is all about—"Is there a commune or collective anywhere with space for a 33 year old woman and four sons?" Or, "We have been tropical homesteaders for twelve years now . . . we are a three day's journey on foot or mule to the nearest road . . . any pioneers left in America?" Which all adds up to a magazine to bring older people together for the purpose of discovering themselves again. There is nothing new in magazines of this sort; what is new is the proposed audience, i.e., adults who have been through the muck and want out. (One article is by a 65 year old who just now changed his life style.) "The fact is that many men and women, not only in their 30s and 40s, but well into the 50s and beyond, have discovered they were on a treadmill to a rather hollow old age security. . . ." The articles are serious, sincere, and helpful. Not much pie in the sky, but a good deal of hard thinking. Send for a sample, and send a dollar or two as a donation.

Canadian Whole Earth Almanac. 1970. q. $9. Ken Coupland, Box 6, 341 Bloor St., West, Toronto, Canada. Illus., index. Circ: 25,000.

Bk. rev: Numerous, length varies. *Aud:* Ac, Ga, Hs. *Jv:* V.

A junior version (150 pages, 7 × 10 inch format) of the *Whole Earth Catalog;* published in Canada, and still coming out regularly every quarter. Contents are pretty much the same as the American cousin. Special issues on health, shelter, environment, etc. Organized by broad subject headings, the directory offers advice on where to purchase almost anything, and how to make things. Extensive book reviews: up to 100 in some issues and each about 250 words long. It is a how-to-do-it bible, better organized than the American version, and now comes with full index. A run of this is as important to a library as the *World Almanac* or the encyclopedia . . . at least if the library is serving anyone this side of a geriatric ward, and even there interest will be shown by dreamers. The American complement to this now seems to be *Source*.

Clear Creek. 1970. m. $7.50. Pennfield Jensen. Clear Creek, 1 South Park, San Francisco, Calif. 94107. Illus., adv. Circ: 30,000. Sample. Microform: B & H.

Aud: Ac, Ga, Hs.

One of the better, certainly one of the more lively alternate culture-environment oriented magazines. (It began as a tabloid, but by early 1972 became a 72 to 100 page magazine.) A good layout carries the message of a counter revolution which will "be a reassertion of community control over community resources." There are several feature stories, including historical background and biographical sketches. Other articles discuss various activities of communes and individuals. Sections are included on environmental education and organic living. The importance of the magazine lies in its practical approach to change. Apparently the editors and the writers believe in using the system for their own ends, and rather than trying to destroy it, ask only to work from within it to change matters. Several articles and features give practical advice on how this can be done. An impressive approach to environmental control, and the alternative culture, the magazine seems to come from the heart, and is not a commercial rip-off. It can be recommended for anyone involved in this subject, from high school on.

Dear Earth. 1971. m. $4. Gayle and Michael Atherton, 1452 Pennsylvania, Suite 21, Denver, Colo. 80203. Illus., adv. Sample.

Bk. rev: 2–3, 150 words, signed. *Aud:* Ga, Hs.

A Colorado based, nonprofit, environment mag. A good part of the material is local, i.e., involved with the Denver or the Colorado scene. The 24-page format opens with a calendar and directory, moves to short news notes and editorials, and winds up with two or three articles (usually from the national media). The articles cover all aspects of the environment from phosphates to cars and noise pollution. An interesting, sincere effort which should be supported locally, and by all larger collections in the U.S.

Earth. 1970. m. $8. James Goode. Earthe Publishing Corp., Agriculture Building, Embarcadero at Mission, San Francisco, Calif. 94105. Illus., adv. Circ: 200,000. Sample. Vol. ends: Dec.

Bk. rev: 7,500 words, signed. *Aud:* Ga, Ac, Hs. *Jv:* V.

Among the more general, popular, environmental magazines now on the newsstands, this is not pure ecol-

ogy, but rather a commercial mix of pop art, rock, the underground, and the modern scene. Put together by a former *Life* correspondent, the 80 pages are professional, a bit slick, and heavy on both color and black–and–white photographs. The target audience is the young who dig rock festivals, street people, and the less scientific, political aspects of ecology. Opening with a calendar of events and book reviews there are usually four to five well illustrated articles which cover everything from the new politics to music. There are usually excellent bibliographies, e.g., a 13-page Indian guide in the August 1971 issue. These are annotated listings of almost every aspect of the field from books and magazines to organizations involved with the topic of the bibliography. In themselves they are invaluable. Among the authors: Paul Goodman, Robert Sherrill, Alan Watts, David Brower, and even Fellini. An excellent all around magazine for young people from junior high through college. A few oldsters will enjoy, too.

Ecology Action; the journal of cultural transformation. 1969. q. $5. Mary P. Humphrey and Ted Radke, Ecology Actional Educational Inst., Box 3895, Modesto, Calif. 95352. Illus. Circ: 2,000. Sample. Vol. ends: Spring.

Aud: Ac, Ga, Hs, Ejh.

A 30 to 40 page journal which covers all aspects of ecology at a popular, easy to understand level of style and content. Food, population, politics, advertising—any aspect of what it takes to make or break the land—constitute the material for articles. Authors are sometimes a bit more fervent than scholarly, but the general material seems accurate enough. As a good, all around approach this is hard to beat, especially for the generalist and the high school student. The format is particularly attractive as it includes drawings and a number of photographs, all of which are related to the articles. (The publishers also put out a number of pamphlets and posters—all at reasonable prices—which are particularly geared for elementary schools and teachers. And while the magazine is a bit advanced for elementary school students, there is much here which can be used by the teacher.)

Ecology Center. 1971. m. Membership $6. Marc Monaghan. Ecology Center, 2179 Allston Way, Berkeley, Calif. 94704. Illus. Circ: 300. Sample. Vol. ends: Dec.

Bk. rev: 1–2, 500 words, signed. *Aud:* Ga, Hs.

A 20-page mimeographed report to members of the Berkeley ecology group. This is of more than local interest because it has short articles on all aspects of ecology and environment, i.e., pollutants, detection of oil spill, etc. However, most of the bulletin is given over to the local group and a calendar of events. Primarily for the Bay area.

Foxfire. 1967. q. $3. B. Eliot Wigginton. Rabun Gap School, Rabun Gap, Ga. 30568. Illus. Circ: 5,000. Sample. Vol. ends: Winter.

Indexed: AbFolkSt. *Bk. rev:* 2, 1 page, signed. *Aud:* Ga, Ac, Hs, Ejh. *Jv:* V.

The editor, an M.A. from Cornell, started *Foxfire* while teaching high school in the Rabun Gap Nacoochie school district. It was by way of preserving a whole culture which surrounded the school. The preservation was to be done by the natives, who contributed practical ideas, and the students who put the 70 to 80 page magazine together. A well-illustrated copy includes such material as: how to make an ox yoke, how to wash clothes in an iron pot, two new folk songs, mountain recipes, midwives and granny women, and poetry and short prose pieces. All of this, by the way, has been collected into an excellent book, *The Foxfire Book* (Doubleday, 1972) which is some 384 pages from earlier copies of the magazine. Unlike other magazines of this type, the editor has no axe to grind, no way of life to support. All the editor and his students and contributors try to do is to show authentic bits of rapidly passing American life. They succeed remarkably well, and in the process offer material of vast interest to just about anyone who has more than an urban approach to existence.

Full Circle. 1968. irreg. $1.98 to $4.95 per issue. Robert J. Fox. Full Circle Associates, Inc., 436 E. 119th St., New York, N.Y. 10035.

Aud: Ac, Ga, Hs, Ejh. *Jv:* V.

The issues are primarily posters. They are in a removable binder, and can be used for display. An average issue of 20 to 30 colorful posters is either of circular size or about 8 by 12 inches. Each poster features photographs, art work, and pertinent quotes. A playbook ($3.95) offers a discussion activity resource guide for the series. Beverly Sparling, who is one of the group, explains the purpose of the project: "These anthologies are a response to the many experiences of persons who have had the eyes to see not only the despair and sorrows of the inner city but also the hopes, joys and life that's to be found there. It challenges all of society to a new way of seeing beyond the seemingly apparent to the deeply human. The artistic conception and the dramatic and beautiful design are by Sister Judith Savard. Some of the quotes and ideas come from Monsignor Robert Fox, the creator and director of our program, some of them are from people on the streets and some from writers as varied as Albert Camus and John Lennon. The photographs come from both professional and inner city photographers. The sum of the magazine is to make the ordinary extraordinary. . . . At a time when most people are viewing the city as a place of depression, hopelessness and meanness, *Full Circle* says something challenging yet positive about the possibilities for a

rich full life there." *Full Circle* is unique, and deserves a place in any library. If particularly suited for schools, it will be equally enjoyed and used in public, university, and college libraries. Get a couple of copies—one for "reading," the other for display.

The Green Revolution. 1962. m. $4. Collective. Brookshires, King St., Lancaster, Pa. Subs. to: Rt. 1, Box 129, Freeland, Md., 21053. Illus., index, adv. Circ: 2,600. Sample. Vol. ends: Dec.

Bk. rev: 1–2, 300–500 words, signed. *Aud:* Ga, Hs, Ac.

An eight-page tabloid newspaper with a basic message: the right life style consists of a philosophy "centered in the organic and creative rather than the mechanical aspects of life," and can be found primarily through "the modern homestead, intentional communities and decentralization." Articles are written by commune members; consider such things as the economy of the land, recycling garbage, lessons from small farming, and childhood in an Indian village. There is considerable emphasis on the "how-to-do-it," and most of this comes from actual experience in everything from meditation to gardening. The style is folksy, relaxed and, noncombative, i.e., read and enjoy, accept or reject, it is all the same to the writers. Still, it is precisely this easy approach which gives this journal a peculiar place in the literature: it is so relaxing as to be quite acceptable to even the most cynical; and it certainly will have wide appeal among sympathizers. A good addition for any library, particularly high schools and colleges. (The group publishes a descriptive directory of intentional communities which should be of considerable interest to many. Only 50 cents.)

The Mother Earth News. 1970. bi-m $6. John Shuttleworth, P.O. Box 38, Madison, Ohio 44057. Illus., adv. Circ: 60,000. Sample. Vol. ends: Nov/Dec.

Bk. rev: Various number, length. *Aud:* Ga, Ac, Hs. *Jv:* V.

Now that *The Whole Earth Catalog* is no more, this is one of its better, logical replacements. Primarily a "how-to-do-it" approach to environment and the new life style, articles are written by both the young and old who have experience of what they write. A typical 124-page newsprint magazine issue covers a variety of material from diet tips and cooking to communal living. The style is lively, informative, and generally accurate. Where matters of health are concerned, the pieces are usually supported by evidence from authorities. But the primary interest for young and old is the material on how to get by with a minimum of money and a maximum of imagination. Even establishment members will profit from the practical articles on building anything from a simple shelter to a log cabin—great for vacations, if nothing else. Little politics, little rough language, this should be acceptable and welcome in almost any type or size library.

Mountain Life & Work; the magazine of the Appalachian South. 1925. 8/yr. $5. Council of the Southwest Mountains, Box 2307, Berea, Ky. 40403. Illus., index. Circ: 3,272. Sample. Vol. ends: Winter.

Bk. rev: 1,500 words, signed. *Aud:* Ac, Ga.

With newspaper tabloid format of some 24 to 36 pages, this long-lived modest magazine has a major message: "the effect of organization in the rebuilding of Appalachia." The nonprofit sponsor is a group of "vigorous, experienced, south Appalachian folk. It publishes a magazine that shouts Appalachian self determination and solidarity from the housetops." A typical issue features articles by laymen, politicians, students, and just about anyone interested in the area. They cover topics from education to mining, health to the environment. This is definitely an activist approach, and one which seems to be working. Hence, the magazine is not only appealing to the region it covers, but will be of value to any group who looks for a way out of old community habits, seeks to beautify the land, and give new hope to the people.

Natural Life Styles. 1971. q. $3. Sally Freeman. Isabelle and Bob Liiakala, 5–C Tillson Road, Tillson, N.Y. 12486. Illus., index, adv. Circ: 95,000. Sample. Vol. ends: No. 4. Microform: B & H.

Bk. rev: Various number, length. *Aud:* Ac, Ga, Hs. *Jv:* V.

An oversized (11 × 17 inch), 90 or so page approach to natural cooking, acupuncture, vitamins, rock climbing, dandruff, kiln building, real food restaurants, flying swami, natural cosmetics, good food suppliers, farmsteading, grain grinding etc., etc. All of these items are considered, along with many more, in the third issue. The articles are by professionals and amateurs who write from experience or considerable research or both. There are line drawings or photographs on almost every page, and where needed charts and diagrams help the reader through an article. The format seems purposely arranged by tossing various sheets of carefully composed script and seeing where they land. What is on each page is clear enough, but what comes next may be a surprise. For example, "How to read a label" is followed by an article on how to build "A Better Mousetrap." (By the way, a major aid for the reader who does not want to ramble through the pages, is an accurate subject index.) The material is practical, and apparently accurate. It is difficult to imagine anyone who enjoyed the *Whole Earth Catalog* not appreciating this too. One difference though: there is much more here on diet and natural foods, less on communes and building per se. Among the many imitators of the *Whole Earth Catalog* this seems to be among the best; would be a first choice in all libraries—primarily because of its diversity. P.S. There is nothing here to offend anyone; no reason to keep it out of the library.

Omen. 1970. irreg. 9 issues/$8. Walter H. Bowart. Omen Press, Box 12457, Tucson, Ariz. 85711. Illus., adv. Circ: 700. Sample

Bk. rev: 1, 500–2,000 words, signed.

A little magazine which touches all bases from ecology and revolution to transcendence. Each issue centers about a given theme, and tends to anthologize better articles in that area. It is large (10″ × 15″) and printed on quality paper, but the most striking thing about its appearance is the artistic use of color. Some of the articles are printed on brightly colored pages; the cover is so attractive it is suitable for framing; and the interior of the magazine contains full–color reproductions of art work, charts, designs, line engravings, and some interesting photography. The editor's purpose is to "note change, make prophecy, set criteria." The editors intend that *Omen* will illuminate the causes which create change. "We will show from where the next change will come and how particular, exemplary individuals have scratched, made changes, and adapted to the demands of a new and changing world." A vastly interesting magazine for any library where the aspects of change are important.

Organic Gardening and Farming. 1942. m. $5.85. Robert Rodale. Rodale Press, 33 E. Minor St., Emmaus, Pa. 18049. Illus., adv. Circ: 350,000. Sample. Vol. ends: Dec.

Indexed: BioAg. *Aud:* Ga, Hs, Ejh.

Ecology is the message, chemicals the villain, and the result is a how-to-do-it approach to gardening which has vast appeal. The editor/owner stresses the natural maintenance of nutrients in the soil by careful use of organic wastes for compost, cover crops, and the like. Emphasis is on the garden and the small farm. Even those who fail to go all the way with the editor's viewpoint will find much of value in suggestions on how to garden. Advertisements and illustrations round out the message. As another critic wisely points out: "It might have particular usefulness in disadvantaged areas, since some of the suggested activities involve little economic investment." And, one might add, among young people—particularly those dedicated to living off the land with occasional trips to the health food store. (The publisher has gained national recognition for being a pioneer in this, and the do–it–yourself health field. Complimentary magazines, sure to interest anyone who reads *Organic Gardening*, are issued by the same firm. See *Fitness for Living* and *Prevention* in the Health section.)

Source Catalog. 1971. irreg. $1.50 per copy. Ed. collective. U.S. National Student Assn., Inc. Center for Educational Reform, 2115 S St. N.W., Washington, D.C. 20008. Subs. to: Swallow Press, 1139 S. Wabash Ave., Chicago, Ill. 60605. Illus., index.

Aud: Ga, Ac, Hs.

Put together by the nonprofit Center for Educational Reform, a student group in Washington D.C. dedicated to revitalizing American educational processes, *Source Catalog* is a bibliographer's approach to communication. It is, in fact, on the order of the *Last Whole Earth Catalog*, the notable exception being that the content concerns audio, film, books, pamphlets, and magazines. There is no rapid "how-to-do-it" thing here, but there is enough bibliographic information to delight the librarian who has been fighting for attention. Each title, or bit of information, is adequately annotated, fitted into some category which relates to the "communication process" (an undefined term which seems to mean anything which brings people closer together). *Source* "is designed to put people in touch with projects and resources and to encourage the building of creative, new working relationships among people." And the philosophy behind it is to help the movement "to build the support networks needed to liberate this country and ourselves." The table of contents in the first 118-page paperbound issue begins with mass media and art, ends with libraries and community communications. Under each section there is a well-defined approach: (a) a directory of individuals, organizations, and sources where the reader can get further information; (b) books, pamphlets, magazines, and films; sometimes even recordings; (c) scattered comments by the compilers and others on almost every aspect of communication. It all adds up to some of the best browsing in years. Each entry is fully annotated. Complete, usually accurate information is given about price, names, and addresses. The organization leaves much to be desired, yet anyone who has gone through the *Last Whole Earth Catalog* will more than appreciate that the effort here is more important than the appearance or ease of use, and there is a fairly good index. Meanwhile, let every librarian be advised to order a personal copy, as well as one for the library. There is so much here to order, to consider, that it will be well worth having an extra one to mark.

For the future? The ambitious editors and compilers hope to bring out issues with information on communities, economics, justice, food, environment, etc. Cut it anyway you like, but it may just be possible that the young people can make bibliography (which this essentially is) popular and, let it be hoped, meaningful for all concerned.

Travelers' Directory. 1960. bi-a. $3. Peter Kacalanos. 51–02 39th Ave., Woodstock, N.Y.

Aud: Ac, Hs.

The young and not-so-young looking for a place to "crash" find this 130-page listing of some 12,000 people who will put them up without charge a basic necessity. It gives places in the United States and throughout the world. In addition to the listing, there is a short descriptive biography of the individual(s) offering the free lodging. Those listed submit their own information. According to a feature article in the *New York Times* (Nov. 14, 1971, Sect. 10, p. 1), the publisher does the whole thing at a bit of a financial loss. The *Directory* is clearly a labor of love, and those who have used it, or been listed, find it first rate. There is one major catch for libraries; you cannot get a subscription unless you agree to list yourself in it, thus offering your own hospitality to strangers. And while this pretty well cuts it out as a regular library subscription, more imaginative (and adventuresome) librarians might take a try at an individual subscription. Certainly many will be interested in this unique venture.

P.S. According to the *Times*, the editor issues two other publications: A newsletter, *The Anemic Traveler: the newsletter with poor circulation,* and a magazine, *Trips.* Both are published irregularly and are free to *Directory* listees.

University Review. 1969. 8/yr. $4. Ed. Bd. Entelechy Press, 2929 Broadway, New York, N.Y. 10025. Illus., adv. Circ: 200,000. Sample.

Bk. rev: 5, 1200 words, signed. *Aud:* Ac.

A counterculture tabloid of some 50 or so pages which resembles a cross between the *New York Review of Books* and the *Village Voice.* It is neither, of course, and emerges as a unique, interesting magazine which "publishes feature articles and interviews concerned with cultural and political life in America today." Issue No. 22, for example, included an article on "Coming through the 60's," by a movement leader; a report on Attica; the moving introduction from a book *Letters from Attica;* short notes on the media (which are by way of reviews of magazines, newsletters, etc. of interest to movement people); and then lengthy reviews of books, films, and recordings. This particular number also had a special section on "Technology and revolution." And it all ended with an interview with Brigitte Bardot. The whole is professionally edited, and "is directed primarily at college and university audiences, though it appeals to socially and politically conscious people of all ages and occupations." The editor is quite right. It is recommended for all academic and many public libraries.

Vocations for Social Change. See Occupations and Employment Section.

Whole Earth Catalog. 1969. bi-m. $8. Stewart Brand. Portola Institute, 558 Santa Cruz Ave., Menlo Park, Calif. 94025.

With the spring of 1971 this mother of the ecology-environment movement ceased publication. *The Last Whole Earth Catalog* became so famous it made the best seller list for weeks, and even won a National Book Award. As a guide to a new way of living, the

Catalog was a catch-all of information about everything from pup tents to diet, a veritable library of facts and data, a bibliography, if you will, for the alternative life style. Since its death, there are many imitators, some fair to good. Among those listed here, among those suggested for libraries who want something close to the *Whole Earth Catalog*, the following are recommended —and are annotated in this section: *Natural Life Styles, Source, Woodstock Journal, Clear Creek, Canadian Whole Earth Almanac,* and *Mother Earth News.*

For other possible replacements, see Johanna Goldschmid's "After the Whole Earth," in *Synergy* (Winter 1971, no. 35).

Woodstock Aquarian. 1970. q. $7.50. Allen Gordon. Great Turtle Enterprises, Inc., Box 401, Woodstock, N.Y., 12498. Illus., adv. Microform: B & H.

Bk. rev: Various number, length. *Aud:* Ac, Ga, Hs.

A large format (11″×17″) with an even larger message—the burden and the joy of the Woodstock spirit. The editor notes the purpose is to spread the word about "group consciousness, tribal consciousness, spaceship earth. . . . We'd like to think everything in this publication is part of a wheel. The content is many faceted . . . like the spokes of the wheel." Well, he is trying to take the magazine out of "the realm of religious morbidity and mystical hocus pocus," but articles of some length on the Hopi, Meditation, Tarot, Karma, and Reincarnation pretty well tell the reader where it's at in different ways. The format is good; the material, if the reader enjoys this kind of thing, is equally good. Of all the magazines, this is the most honest effort to carry on the Woodstock spirit. Aside from the mystic and spiritual material, there are numerous articles on health, food, farming, communes, etc. However, the primary emphasis is on the philosophy rather than the pragmatics of the alternative life style. It should be found in all libraries serving young people, particularly in high schools. Once again, nothing here should offend a parent, no matter how straight; but much to puzzle him.

Social and Political Change

Advocate; the newspaper of America's homophile community. 1967. bi-w. $7.50. Dick Michaels. Advocate Publications Inc., Box 74695, Los Angeles, Calif. 90004. Illus., index adv. Circ: 40,000. Sample. Microform: UM.

Aud: Ga.

The editor claims this is "the oldest largest and most comprehensive of all newspapers published for the homophile (i.e. homosexual) community in the entire world. We are proud that our reputation is one founded on presenting the news in an unbiased manner, and in good taste." A look at two tabloid issues, which average about 40 illustrated, well-printed pages,

seems to bear out the editor's claim. Each issue begins with news stories, e.g. "Top demos give note to gay rights," or "ACLU blasts Los Angeles Police Department complaint probe figures." A good deal of material concerns Los Angeles and west coast activities, and is is definitely male oriented. Still, the features will be of interest to anyone who follows the gay movement. There is a regular column on food and cooking, body building advice column, film and theatre reviews, editorials, etc. Some of the advertising and the cartoons are out of step with the serious editorial content, and often downright foolish and sophomoric. But this aside, the paper is one of the few which offers a sane, balanced approach to the gay male movement. Now that *Transactions* is dead, *The Advocate* is a possible replacement for a library seeking a balanced collection in this area.

The American Exile in Canada. See *Amex/Canada.*

Amex/Canada; The American Expatriate in Canada (Formerly: *The American Exile in Canada*). 1968. bi-m. $3.25/9 issues. Stan Pietlock, Jr. Amex, P.O. Box 187, Station D. Toronto 165, Ont., Canada. Illus., index, adv. Circ: 3,800. Sample. Vol. ends: every 8 issues.

Indexed: API. *Bk. rev:* 4, 1500 words, signed. *Aud:* Ga, Ac, Hs.

A news magazine by and for United States political exiles in Canada. While *Amex* started as a one sheet newsletter, it has grown to a well-printed 48-page magazine—and has every indication of staying power. The cover of one issue reproduces, with typical irony, an 1898 cartoon in which Uncle Sam is shaking hands with Jack Canuck and saying "I hate to see any of the folks leaving home, but when they do go I like to see 'em go to Canada." The main article, "Getting American teachers-training recognized by Ontario Department of Education," shows the exiles' concern for bread-and-butter issues, one of the best features of their magazine. Useful addresses are listed in Canada and England. Besides the lengthy "Trans-Canada Report" on what Amexiles in various Canadian cities are doing, every issue carries commentary on Canada by exiles, cartoons, book reviews, and what has been called the "best letters to the editor section in Canada." (A.L.)

Black & Red. 1968. irreg. $10/10 issues. Box 9546, Detroit, Mich., 48202. Illus. Circ: 2,000.

Aud: Ac.

An 84-page mimeographed, pocket-sized magazine devoted, as the editors claim, "to create at long last a situation which goes beyond the point of no return." It is primarily student oriented, e.g., such items as "The struggle for self-expression," or "The University is a provocation." The enemy seems to be the university establishment, teachers not excepted. The cause: liberation of the student, Vietnam, and reports on international student activities. The writing style moves from sophomoric diatribes to really thoughtful analyses ("If You Make A Social Revolution, Do It For Fun") of a situation which the writers apparently believe can be remedied only by a revolution. Sometimes the problem is more evident than the solution. Still, the whole represents an extremely lively, current and sincere approach to an important segment of student thought. Should be in the reading collection of socially oriented and lively libraries.

Despite Everything. 1964. q. $2. P. S. MacDougal and Alan Dutscher. 1937½ Russell St., Berkeley, Calif. 94703 Illus. Circ: 1,000. Microform: UM.

Aud: Ac, Hs.

A "little magazine" of the movement. However, the editors are independent of any organization or group, and their publication—a 30 to 54 page offset—has the format and approach of most little literary magazines. When it comes to a political doctrine or philosophy, the writers tend to follow Marx. However, material is of a broader nature—includes action pieces on everything from women's liberation to getting out of Vietnam. The writers continue to be young people with more than a little intellectual ability. And if the editors grow older, their fervor remains. One of the best of its type, and particularly good in a library where the voice of the younger generation is heard.

The Expatriate Review. 1971. bi-a. $2.50. Roger W. Gaess and Wyatt James. Box D, Staten Island, New York, N.Y. 10301.

Aud: Ac.

"Dedicated to creative American expatriates who, . . . have chosen to leave the country . . . *ER* will attempt to function as a meeting ground of some sort for current (or prospective) expatriates." This is done in a 44-page poetry and prose magazine whose editors and contributors seem to be primarily editors in larger firms. (The stated purpose, unless something escapes me entirely, is more romantic than is warranted by any of the contributors or their works. In fact, this side of Lowenfeld, it is difficult to trace any movement away from American shores. A small point, still . . . .) The first half of the issue in the summer of 1971 was turned over to an extract from Walter Lowenfeld's autobiography, i.e., his years in Paris. The six poets, including the two editors, are all professionals and extremely effective. Between Lowenfeld's memoirs and the poets, this can be recommended for just about any collection.

Fag Rag. 1971. irreg. 30¢/issue. Red Book Store, 91 River St., Cambridge, Mass. 02139. Illus., adv.

Aud: Ga, Ac.

Following the familiar format of the underground magazine, this 18-page tabloid is devoted to bringing news of gay male liberation to its readers. The articles are well written, relatively objective, and tied in with the third world revolution. Men kissing may upset some, but aside from that the illustrations and advertisements are all right. The subscription information is a bit difficult to verify, and interested librarians should write the dealer before entering a subscription. Samples appear to be available.

Gay Sunshine. 1969. m. $3.75. P.O. Box 40397, San Francisco, Calif. 94140. Illus., adv.

Aud: Ga.

A 16-page activitist newspaper dedicated to the gay liberation movement, this isn't much on format, but it is good in content. Now in its second year, the paper's editorial policy is explained in the issue reviewed. It is "an open forum for the Gay Community, providing a place for all ideas to be expressed without fear of censorship. Although the Collective takes the radical perspective on Gay Oppression, we do not see ourselves as the arbiters of who is revolutionary and who is not. Material of both local significance and also of relevance to the wider community is to be accepted." It gives a variety of viewpoints from both men and women, and includes a useful national list of other groups. While primarily a news and opinion medium, the editors welcome poetry and graphics. There is a minimum of advertising, and unless one objects strenuously to the basic purpose it is difficult to find anything to offend. The writing style is a bit uneven; the purpose is serious enough.

The New Guard. 1961. m. (except June and Aug.) $4. Jerry Norton. Young Americans for Freedom, Inc., 1221 Massachusetts Ave., N.W., Washington, D.C. 20005. Illus., adv. Circ: 15,000. Sample. Vol. ends: Dec. Microform: UM.

Bk. rev: 5, 500 words, signed. *Aud:* Ga, Hs.

Representing the younger element of the conservative philosophy, *New Guard*, to quote a contributor, seeks to "resist the collectivism and statism that emanate from indigenous Liberalism and simultaneously to repel and overcome the Communist attack upon Western civilization." Oriented toward the Conservative (i.e., Buckley–Regan) wing of the Republican Party, the magazine lauds broadcasters M. Stanton Evans and William F. Buckley, maintains that former Alabama Governor George Wallace "simply does not qualify as a Conservative, but rather as a Populist–Segregationist," has published essays on the distinction between "traditionalist" and "libertarian" Conservatives, cautions against American universities becoming "havens for revolutionaries and subversives," hails the growth of a two-party system in the South, encourages "a strong foreign policy for the United States," and advocates "private enterprise" plus "individual responsibility." Current contributors include David Brudnoy, a

National Review associate; Will Herberg, a professor at Drew and a leading theologian; and M. Stanton Evans. Representing as it does the voice of conservative young people, as opposed to the sometimes more vocal, better known followers of the New Left, this is a good bet for public, academic and even high school libraries where balance is sought. (S.B.)

Other Scenes. 1967. q. $6. John Wilcock. Box 8, Village Station, New York, N.Y. 10014. Illus. Circ: 10,000. Sample.

Index: API. *Aud:* Ac, Ga. *Jv:* V.

This unpaged (100 or so) newsprint blast at society is the work of John Wilcock. That alone assures it a place in any library where the underground press, the little magazine, or just plain satire is important. It also marks it as the curse of librarians who live in mortal fear of words, pictures, and comments guaranteed to bring out radical elements of the PTA, DAR, and the American Legion. The co-founder of the *Village Voice, Los Angeles Free Press,* and *East Village Other* (to name a few), Wilcock is author of several of those $5 a day travel tomes read like the *Bible* by travelers who would drop from sheer surprise to realize their guide is the king of the underground press. (The guides authored by Wilcock are far and above the best in the series.) *Other Scenes* takes on a new dimension. There are the obvious and the not so obvious slams at our current shams, primarily done up in a package which is meant to shock—even frighten—the so called establishment. One issue, for example, starts off with a bit on the English royal comic opera (a blast at the monarchy), goes on to several essays on witchcraft, breaks in the middle with an intelligent article on hip capitalism, features an interview with Andy Warhol (now John Doe), and ends with astrology notes. There is a minimum of such things as "Thoughts about pubic hair," and "Prostitution in Nevada," but that minimum will do it for too many libraries. On balance, this, along with *The Realist,* is the most important underground, little magazine now being published on social issues. Enough, or probably too much, said.

Our Generation. 1961. 4/yr. $5. Cooperative bd. Our Generation, 3934 rue St. Urbain, Montreal, 131, Que., Canada. Illus., index, adv. Circ: 6,000. Sample.

Indexed: API. *Bk. rev:* 2–6, 1–10 pages, signed. *Aud:* Ac, Ga, Hs. *Jv:* V.

As the title suggests, this is written and edited for the young who seek change. It is a well-printed journal of 120 to 175 pages which claims it has the largest circulation of any magazine of dissent in Canada. A typical issue features four to five editorials, as many articles, and perceptive book reviews. The writers are lucid, and committed to a "nonviolent revolution to replace the system of violence." The editors condemn the terrorism of more rabid American and Canadian factions, and call for such things as jobs for all, better housing, freedom of political prisoners, and an end to war. While a good deal of the material is involved with Canada, much of it also concerns the United States and the world. Given a conservative base, one might consider this radical; but the average liberal reader will discover much to agree with here, and will find the magazine particularly useful for its critical treatment of where the Movement is at, and where it is going. One of the best magazines of its type, and an excellent choice for public, academic, and advanced high schools both here and in Canada.

Radical America. 1967. bi-m. $5. Ed. bd. Radical America, 1878 Massachusetts Ave., Cambridge, Mass. 02140. Illus., index, adv. Circ: 4,000. Sample. Vol. ends: Nov/Dec.

Index: API. *Bk. rev:* 3, 1,000 words, signed. *Aud:* Ac, Ga.

This began as a voice of the SDS (Students for a Democratic Society), but this affiliation no longer holds. Having broken with the student group, the editorial board now concentrates "on a Marxist overview of the development of American society, particularly of the working class." An average 70-page issue contains articles, bibliographic studies, letters, and book reviews. The emphasis is on change (with historical pieces too) and on differentiation between views held by the traditional Left (now considered conservative) and those championed by the American New Left. The tone, within the editorial framework, is scholarly, calm, and objective. In fact, this is one of the best of its type, and can be recommended for any library seeking representative magazines in the area of the radical left.

Two, Three, Many . . . 1970. q. $5. Comm. of Returned Volunteers, 840 West Oakdale Ave., Chicago, Ill. 60657. Illus. Sample.

Aud: Ga, Ac, Hs.

A 32-page effort to give voice to the "women and men who have served overseas as volunteer teachers, community developers . . . and have seen the effect of U.S. policies in the countries of Asia, Africa and Latin America." The six articles, which move from Palestine to Vietnam, indicate that the volunteers do not think much of United States policies. But it is not all polemics. The articles are well documented and show a professional approach. The credibility of the whole is high, particularly as the writers have lived abroad and experienced much of what they claim is the negative influence of American presence overseas. Conservatives will not care for the approach, but objective middle-of-the roaders and liberals will find much of value. A sound, intellectual, and serious effort which deserves support by libraries.

Youth and Society. 1969. q. $15 ($10 to professionals; $7.50 to students). A. W. McEachern. Sage Publications, Inc., 275 So. Beverly Drive, Beverly Hills, Calif. 90212. Illus., adv. Circ: 1,000. Sample. Vol. ends: June, Refereed.

Bk. rev: 1–2, 500–700 words, signed. *Aud:* Ac.

"An interdisciplinary journal concerned with the social and political implications of youth culture and development. Concentrates primarily on the age span from mid-adolescence through young adulthood— bringing together significant empirical and theoretical studies relevant to the processes of youth development, political socialization, the impact of youth culture on society, and patterns of acquisition of adult roles." Articles concern the generation gap, hippie values, racial minorities, etc. Will interest those concerned with youth in various social and behavioral contexts.

Underground Comix

The underground comics (or "comix" as some insist on spelling it to distinguish their work from the bland, censored Establishment product) are *not for children.* They are for *adults only.* They are worth acquiring by university research libraries with broad collections documenting the present hippie and radical youth cultures, and libraries with specialized collections of contemporary youth-oriented literary and art forms such as Beat poetry and pop-art posters. For linguists, they are one of the best literary sources of current slang and street speech patterns from about 1967 to the present.

Underground comix are produced by members of the under-30 generation as a medium of unsuppressed self expression. Many are deliberately designed to be offensive to the "repressive American Establishment mentality" by spectacularly breaking every taboo possible. (One carries an indicium, "Printed in the Peoples' Republic of America," but its contents would earn its producers long prison terms for moral offensiveness from any Communist government in existence.) Others are not interested in shock for shock's sake, but feel that their work is a healthy step forward in the natural social evolution away from the stifling hypocrisy of Victorian prudity. The keynote is natural realism. War stories are full of blood and sadism. Romance stories show what happens when a boy and girl go all the way. Contemporary hippie community scenes show all the dirt, the casual acceptance of pot and nudity, the locker-room dialogue, the contempt for established authority. The producers of comix see themselves as the harbingers of a new, honest American society of 5, 10, or 15 years from now. Their antagonists see them as the product of a morally sick subculture that has already reached a dead end, or—at best—a shrill new form of the natural but meaningless tendency of youth to protest the traditional values of society. If the former is true, these comix will ob-viously have literary importance in helping to bring on a major cultural adjustment. If the latter is true, these booklets may contain the early art of young rebels who will settle down to become the important names in commercial and fine art and social satire of the next decade—the new Peter Maxes, Andy Warhols, Al Capps, or Art Buchwalds. In any case, their content in today's society, their advocacy of radical politics and illegal drugs, their scoffing at sacred values, their graphically obscene or pornographic portrayal of nudi-ty, cunnilingus, cannibalism, sado-masochism, and bod-ily elimination, will make them controversial acquisi-tions for many libraries. Handle with care.

The publishing mechanics of comix are more akin to those of paperback books than periodicals. Though some are issued as consecutively numbered issues of a single series, many more are one-shot titles. Most of the popular ones have gone into several printings by now. Because of this it is virtually impossible to sub-scribe to comix; titles should be bought individually. An additional reason is that the publishers are often semi-amateur businessmen whose bookkeeping is not the best in the world. An order that can be filled immediately is safe, but sending advance money for material to be published in the indefinite future is risky. The following is quoted with gratitude from a mimeographed newsletter published by Don and Maggie Thompson (8786 Hendricks Road, Mentor, Ohio 44060), two collectors trying to compile a biblio-graphically complete listing of underground comix: "Underground comics go in and out of print with daz-zling rapidity and a given title might be unavailable one day and common the next, or one dealer may be out while another is being crowded out with unsold comix. So we list a bunch of dealers and suggest that you write for catalogs (send a dime or a stamped ad-dressed envelope). . . . Most underground comix cost 50¢, some go quite a bit higher; most mailorder deal-ers add a dime or 15¢ per copy (you can check the "hippie hangouts" if your city has any and pick up some at cover price). We recommend all of the follow-ing:

Krupp Comic Works Inc., 2560–A No. Frederick Ave., Milwaukee, Wis. 53211.

Bob Sidebottom, 58 E. San Fernando, San Jose, Calif. 95113.

Bud Plant, 4160 Holly Drive, San Jose, Calif. 95127.

Rip Off Press, Box 14158. San Francisco, Calif. 94114.

Eric Fromm, P.O. Box 31075, Diamond Heights, San Francisco, Calif. 94131.

Print Mint, 830 Folger Ave., Berkeley, Calif. 94710." (F.P.)

Air Pirates Funnies. Issues 1 and 2, 50¢. Hell Comics, P.O. Box 40219, San Francisco, Calif.

The purpose of *Air Pirates Funnies* is to present profane, pornographic cartoons featuring Mickey

Mouse, Donald Duck, and all the Walt Disney characters. Its creators are the Disney Liberation Front: Li'l Bobby London, Ted Richards, Gary "Ha-Ha" Halgren, and their leader, Dan O'Neill. In an article in the *Los Angeles Free Press* (Aug. 13, 1971), O'Neill spoke impassionedly about how Disney has brainwashed generations of children without their knowledge or consent. "We're outraged at what Disney has done to our heads and right now we're getting it all out. Disney is our springboard and we're using him as a jumping off point to get us into some serious drawing. This is our last defense against schizophrenia." Unauthorized pornographic comics featuring popular comic strip characters are nothing new, but this is the first time that anybody has gone about it publicly for therapeutic motives, with an attitude of righteous indignation. Needless to say, Walt Disney Productions does not appreciate this point of view and is countersuing to stop production. A great deal of care is being taken to lampoon the old Disney style correctly. The stories feature early Disney cartoon characters and are drawn in the appropriate style of the period. Back in the thirties Disney staff artist Floyd Gottfriedson was drawing the "Mickey Mouse" newspaper strip as an adventure serial, and the Air Pirates turn out to be all his old enemies: Sylvester Shyster, Pegleg Pete, the Phantom Blot, and others. Even the "Hell Comic" trademark is a burlesque of the "Dell Comic" trademark of the forties under which Disney's comics were distributed. The most impressive work is that of Bobby London, who for unexplained reasons draws in an imitation of George Herriman's art style which he captures superbly. All this makes *Air Pirates Funnies* the propaganda outlet of a highly unusual revolutionary movement designed to destroy the Disney morality. (See *Dan O'Neill's Comics and Stories* below.) (F.P.)

Bijou Funnies. Issues 1 through 6, 50¢. Krupp Comic Works, Inc.

After *Zap*, the title with the greatest variety, longevity, and appeal is probably *Bijou Funnies*. *Bijou* also contains work by R. Crumb, but for the most part it features its own staff including Skip Williamson, Jayzey Lynch, Justin Green, Jay Kinney, and Kim Deitch. The two most popular continuing features are those by Lynch and Williamson. Lynch's "Nard 'n Pat," about a dumb man and his smart kitty-kat, satirizes common wish-fulfillment fantasies with a strong cinematic orientation, such as private eyes (be tuff an' have the broads chasin' after ya), invisible men (be able to sneak into the ladies' locker room and peek), and werewolves (have everybody in terror of you). Williamson's "Snappy Sammy Smoot" and "Ragtime Billy" are more politically oriented. Snappy Sammy is the eternally good-natured innocent who is always glad to do people a favor, such as delivering a package (ticking) to the local draft board. Ragtime Billy is a

parody of the 103 percent All–American patriotic bigot. Williamson also does short strips with titles like "Class War Comix" and "Racist Pig Comix." On the whole the stories in *Bijou Funnies* are more concerned with humor, political satire, and intelligible plots than are those in the more shockingly revolutionary *Zap*. (F.P.)

Dan O'Neill's Comics and Stories. 50¢. Co. & Sons; no address.

This and the annotation for *Air Pirates Funnies* give an unusual view of the evolution of one particular author/artist. The interior of this magazine, titled "The Blasphemy of Fred," is an arrangement of a selection of O'Neill's straight newspaper strip "Odd Bodkins," which appeared in the *San Francisco Chronicle* off and on during the late 1960s. It was a weird, surrealistic strip featuring strange animals and people wandering across an abstract landscape, making commentaries on the current social and political scene. (It was finally dropped when the *Chronicle* objected to the taste of a sequence inspired by the Marin County Courthouse shootings, and O'Neill refused to accept the censorship.) These particular sequences comment on the presence of atheists in foxholes, the evolution of baboons (in 40,000 years they will be taking over), and Fred's theory that American industry is controlled by Martians who are trying to convert the atmosphere of Earth into smog, which is what they breathe. It should be enjoyed by anyone who appreciates the "Pogo" strip. The title is an exact pastiche of *Walt Disney's Comics and Stories;* the cover carries a spurious "January 1948" date, and its layout is like that of a Disney comic of that period. The illustrations go farther than Disney ever did, though. The front cover shows Practical Pig blowing the Big Bad Wolf's head off, while the interior covers feature a minor Disney comic book character of the forties, Bucky Bug, in a dialogue laced with profanity. (F.P.)

Fabulous Furry Freak Brothers. 50¢. Rip Off Press.

This 52-page *Collected Adventures of the Fabulous Furry Freak Brothers* gathers together the best episodes of one of the most popular underground strips. Some are reprints from other comix, but most originally appeared as a syndicated strip by Gilbert Shelton in the *Los Angeles Free Press* and other underground newspapers. Freewheelin' Franklin, Phineas, and Fat Freddie are three potheads living in the hippie community of a large city. The strips (mostly one page each) chronicle their escapades in trying to score pot without getting busted by the cops, in trying to get past the border guards into Tijuana and Disneyland, Fat Freddie's brief fling into campus radicalism, their experience as peace marchers, and the like. On one level, it is a pro-marijuana, radical strip. On a deeper level, it is as merciless a study of the Haight-Ashbury subculture as any parody that Al Capp has ever drawn. Most of the hippies are shown as jargon-quoting, empty-headed, self-centered, totally naive youths. The Freak brothers are as worried about being ripped off by their friends and neighbors or being burned on phoney grass as they are about being hassled by the pigs. Shelton's depiction of the police as Neanderthal subhumans is as much a lampoon of the radical's stereotyped distrust of all symbols of Establishment authority as it is a lampoon of police mentality itself. ("Rookies: When dealing with hippies, radicals, and Niggers, shoot first and ask questions later. Above all, don't let them get to their Jewish lawyers.") This is one of the most valuable of the comix because of its genuine humor and its light-hearted but revealing picture of the modern dropout world. (F.P.)

Feds 'n' Heads Comics. 50¢. Print Mint.

One of the oldest and most popular of all the comix, the copies currently on sale state, "Copyright © 1968 by Gilbert Shelton; Fourth printing—7/70." It is entirely the work of Shelton, one of the funniest and most imaginative of all underground cartoonists. The booklet is a potpourri of his different themes and strips, including "Wonder Wart-Hog," his parody of super-hero comics; "Those Fabulous Furry Freak Brothers," a look at the hippie-pot culture; numerous illustrated poems starring "Oat Willie," including some traditional schoolyard verses ("Nobody loves us, Everybody hates us, Let's go out and eat some worms . . ."); and a radical-youth lampoon of comic book advertisements for cheap mail-order magic tricks ("Dissolving cigarette papers! When someone licks the gummed paper, it completely dissolves, dropping contents of reefer into victim's lap! Many laughs.") When popular magazines such as *Playboy* run articles about the new comix, an excerpt from *Feds 'n' Heads* is often selected as an illustration. (F.P.)

Legion of Charlies. 50¢. Last Gasp Eco–Funnies Co., P.O. Box 212, Berkeley, Calif. 94704.

This disturbing political fantasy by Tom Veitch and Greg Irons is "respectfully dedicated to the brave veterans who turned in their medals in Washington D.C., Memorial Day, 1971." It draws some ugly parallels between the 1968 My Lai massacre in Vietnam and the 1969 Sharon Tate murders in Hollywood, adds the philosophical message of Robert Heinlein's prize-winning science fiction novel *Stranger In a Strange Land* as misinterpreted by Charles Manson, and predicts a new cannibalistic religion. It also makes the interesting equation, Calley = Kali (Hindu goddess of death and destruction). Paranoia is love! (F.P.)

Moondog #1 & 2. 50¢ each. Print Mint.

Not all underground cartoonists are out to shock or advocate social revolution. *Moondog* is simply George Metzger's attempt to tell a science fiction story. It could appear in a regular commercial comic book except that Metzger's highly individualistic art style does not have the polish of the professional comics, and he presumably does not want to relinquish editorial control of his creation. He also works much too slowly for the professionals; *Moondog* #1 came out in 1969, and #2 did not appear until two years later. The story is laid in an after-the-bomb America, where Moondog and his companions journey among the ruins of the old civilization and combat the petty despots ruling individual townships who try to prevent the rebuilding of the land. A separate feature at the end of each issue is an attempt to tell a different tale in a wordless and more experimental artistic manner. Metzger's artistic style is interesting and not unattractive. Though there are a few bare breasts, *Moondog* is one of the least offensive of all underground comix, and a good example of how the medium may be used to present a one-man literary and art show. (F.P.)

New Adventures of Jesus. $1, 1st printing; 50¢, 2nd printing (new format). *Jesus meets the Armed Services.* 50¢. Rip Off Press.

These two titles by Foolbert Sturgeon are humorous extrapolations of one of the basic convictions of liberal youths: that the "straights" are so close-mindedly biased against all things youth-oriented or differing from the status quo that if Jesus Christ Himself were to come to America today He would be persecuted by the police and the pillars of society as a filthy, long-haired, Commie hippie, His message of brotherly love would get Him accused of homosexuality, and so on. *The New Adventures of Jesus* tells of His first experiences with both the straight and hippie societies and ends with His becoming a pot-smoking flower child. There is a lot of sardonic commentary about modern, complacent established religions and their perversion of His original teachings. *Jesus Meets the Armed Services* (the funnier of the two) describes Jesus' encounter with a local draft board and His inability to prove Himself a pacifist according to the official rules. (F.P.)

Rowlf. 50¢. Rip Off Press.

Rowlf is another one-man showcase. Richard Corben is the artist of this bloody adventure fantasy. A medieval kingdom is invaded by cannibalistic demons employing vaguely Afrika Korps-ish uniforms and weaponry. Princess Maryara is captured, and the only witness to her abduction is her faithful wolfdog, Rowlf. A wizard attempts to transform Rowlf into a man so that he can speak and tell what happened, but the spell is botched and Rowlf emerges a sort of were-human. Still devoted to his mistress, the wolf-man breaks loose and sets out on a lone commando mission to rescue her, combining his new human intelligence with his feral lupine instincts to counter anything that the unprepared demons can throw at him. This title exemplifies many of the positive and negative points of the underground comix.

The story is powerful, devoting realistic attention to profanity, brutality, gore, sadism, and the unclothed state of the heroine, who is ravished by the chief of the demon warriors. It's consistent and well developed. It shows several touches of imagination, such as having the demons speak Esperanto. (Reportedly, in the U.S. Army's war training games, Esperanto is often used as the language of the "enemy aggressor nation.") The art is strong but raw, lacking what might be called a professional finish. The text is studded with remarkably amateurish errors such as "it's" for "its" and other simple spelling mistakes (as though the author checked all the difficult words in the dictionary but could not be bothered to check the simple ones) and abrupt shifts in tense within the same passage. There are any number of paperback novels in supermarket racks across the nation that describe as much violence, sex, and nudity, but only in the underground comix can you get away with showing this in pictures. (F.P.)

Up From the Deep. $1. Rip Off Press.

Zap Comix introduced the concept of do-it-yourself comic book publishing to the hippie community, and for four years numerous cheap titles have been produced on basement presses. With *Up from the Deep* in 1971, interior color pages entered the medium. This 52 page title contains six stories, the center two of which are in bright colors on stiff white paper—a higher quality of printing than that employed in the commercial comics. Since this time there have been other comix with colored sections, and the full-color comix have recently appeared. *Up from the Deep* is recommended, though, partly because it was the historic "first" and partly because of the quality of the material in it. It features the work of Jaxon, Corben, Irons and Deitch, four of the top names in the comix field. They are good as stories, and good as representative samples of the work of these particular artists. (F.P.)

Zap Comix. Issues 0 & 1, 35¢; 2 through 5, 50¢. Apex Novelties; no address.

Zap Comix is the prototype of all underground comix, and its history is a history in minature of the whole field. It is also the most commonly cited example in general media coverage of the comix, and therefore the most famous. *Zap* #1 was the first of all to appear, back in November 1967, from the Haight-Ashbury headquarters of hippiedom. It was solely the work of an unknown young cartoonist named Robert Crumb, and is positively innocuous by today's standards. What made it popular was its rough, non-Establishment, labor-of-love look. Its speech was natural–sounding, full of lower–class crudities and dialect. Its characters were concerned with their own personal hangups and endless daily routine totally unimportant to anyone else. It satirized conventional comic book artificiality, it was "real," and it was the right message for a readership that has its own hangups about avoiding hypocrisy and stultifying middle class morality. It popularized the spelling of "comix" and introduced hippiedom to the concept of the comic book as an individual art form and medium of self expression. Some of its characters such as Mr. Natural have gone on to stardom in the world of comix. *Zap* #1 was quickly followed by *Zap* #0, which Crumb had actually written first but, which was stolen before it could be printed. (Crumb had to re-ink his file photocopies of the art.) *Zap* #2 went considerably farther in breaking established taboos. It also introduced other artists such as Rick Griffin and Victor Moscoso, who specialize in incomprehensible almost wordless stories filled with swirling geometric shapes, and the notorious S. Clay Wilson, whose work has since come to be almost unanimously agreed to be the most shocking and revolting in the whole field. His debut here included a story of two homosexual pirates, one of whom cuts off and eats his friend's penis. *Zap* #3 was about the same except for the addition of Gilbert Shelton to the staff. *Zap* #4 resulted in the immediate arrests on obscenity charges of the printer and booksellers across the nation. The main objection was to a story by Crumb that cheerfully advocates incest. One of these cases, the arrest and conviction of a bookstore clerk in New York in October 1970, has become mildly famous as the "Zap Comix Case" (New York vs. Kirkpatrick); the Freedom to Read Committee of the Association of American Publishers has reportedly filed an *amicus* brief in Mr. Kirkpatrick's behalf during the appeal. Whatever troubles *Zap* #4 may be having elsewhere, it is openly on sale for the moment in Hollywood and around UCLA. *Zap* # 5 has apparently avoided any legal problems, though it contains what may be Wilson's most nauseating piece to date, as well as what may be Shelton's most brilliant political satire to date. *Zap* #6 should be out by the time this book is in print. The quality of these issues is highly mixed, but *Zap* #1 is surely important if only for what it started—a whole new field of underground literature. (F.P.)

Underground Newspapers

All You Can Eat. 1970. m. $5. Committee. New Brunswick Free Community, 5 Railroad Plaza, New Brunswick, N.J. 08903. Illus., adv. Circ: 20,000. Sample. Vol. ends: July.

Bk. rev: 1–2, ¼ page. *Aud:* Ga, Ac.

A radical member of the underground press, featuring 24 well-edited tabloid pages of news and views on the Movement. Most of the copy concerns Rutgers University and the state of politics in New Jersey, particularly in the New Brunswick–Newark area. The primary drive is political, i.e., articles and short pieces revolve around the Movement, women's liberation,

Blacks, etc. There is little or no film, art, or theatre criticism. An interesting feature is "ruling class comix" which follows the European pattern of using photographs of individuals with words penned in by the author. A good example of this was the introduction to readers to the Johnson & Johnson Board of Directors—which, by the way, includes not one woman. What strikes the reader immediately is the professional editing and the format which would do any editor proud. And while primarily for New Jersey it can be recommended for all larger collections.

Ann Arbor Argus. 1969. bi–m. $5. White Panther Party, Ann Arbor Chapter, 708 Arch St., Ann Arbor, Mich. 48104. Illus., adv. Circ: 16,000. Sample. Microform: B & H.

Indexed: API. *Bk. rev:* various number, length. *Aud:* Ac, Ga.

National; political. Counterculture as the voice of the revolutionary movement at the University of Michigan, and more specifically that of the White Panther Party, the *Argus* has a national status. By late 1971 it was best known for its campaign to free John Sinclair, and for coming down on Ann Arbor politics. The political tone is militant, the stories primarily local (although local news at Ann Arbor tends to take on a national character, thanks to the size of the university and the fact that many movement members call Ann Arbor home. An average 36 to 40 page tabloid is illustrated with photos and line drawings—some of which may still shock a few conservatives—and boasts a fair to excellent layout. It includes material on the counterculture, and some particularly good record and book reviews, as well as interviews with leaders in the culture movement. A basic undergound paper for any medium to large collection.

Astral Projection. 1968. q. $5/10 nos. Felipe Galdon. Astral Projection, Box 4383, Albuquerque, N.M. 87106. Illus., adv. Circ: 15,000. Sample. Microform: B & H.

Aud: Ac, Ga, Hs.

Rolling Stone magazine/newspaper format, although the make up and typography are a bit on the sloppy side. It's planned that way, primarily because the contents of a 32-page issue is made up of what readers send to the editor. This covers all topics of interest, e.g., music, ecology, astrology, politics, films, photography. A late 1971 issue featured three pages of photographs of young people, a short piece on environment, notes on Albuquerque, record reviews, some book notes, and a long article on space astrology. A few pages are in Spanish, although they are so few as to make it meaningless for a Spanish language collection. A note at the beginning of the issue examined read: "The *Astral Projection* needs your help. We are over $3,200 in debt." Hopefully, the money was raised.

Meanwhile, the paper is of considerable interest to New Mexico, but of limited value to other libraries.

Berkeley Barb. 1964. w. $6. Marx Scherr, Box 1247, Berkeley, Calif. 94701. Illus., adv. Circ: 30,000. Sample. Vol. ends: Last Friday in Dec. Microform: B & H. *Aud:* Ga, Ac.

National, political, and sexist. One of the oldest, best known of the undergrounds which reached a peak in influence during the University of California uprisings in the late sixties. From its beginning the editor was in the forefront for ending the war in Vietnam, championing the Chicanos and other minority groups. The paper, doing well enough, lost many of its readers in 1969. This was after the squabble by the staff regarding the *Barb's* financing. The staff split, one part starting the *Berkeley Tribe.* Today the *Barb's* national interest is involved primarily with its leadership in the fight for prison reform, black freedom, and some involvement with educational change. The style of writing is good, the 20 to 24 page format terrible, and the stories tend to be shorter than those found in most underground papers (news items are more important than features). The level of satirical writing about everything from politics to ecology remains high, if not high as before. But, this is a large "but," the essential weakness of the paper is its continued emphasis on erotic advertising, lurid classifieds, and general sexism which is a bit old fashioned. About 8 of the 24 pages contains sexist junk. This may give it added appeal for oldsters, but it does not do much for the young. (Of course, it does much for the financial well being of the publisher. The advertisements have made the *Barb* one of the most profitable of the undergrounds, and the argument goes that the sexist material helps carry the worthwhile message.)

Between it and the *Berkeley Tribe,* the *Tribe* would be a first choice, at least for a beginning. But if the library has been taking the *Barb,* keep it up. It may change again, and its life story is somewhat like the story of the whole underground. It remains important if for no other reason than that it was germinal to the movement.

Berkeley Tribe. 1969. w. $6. Collective. Red Mountain Tribe Inc., Box 9043, Berkeley, Calif. 94709. Illus., adv. Circ: 30,000. Microform: B & H.

Indexed: API. *Aud:* Ga, Ac, Hs. *Jv:* V.

National politics. Having split from the *Barb,* the tabloid *Tribe* is what the *Barb* was a number of years back, i.e., there is considerable emphasis on national and local politics. The tone is radical, the mood cooperative, and one gets the impression of a closely knit group working together to make the paper succeed. The writing is good to excellent, although the passionate politics may turn off the older readers. The sexist advertising is minimal. The usual book, film, and record reviews, although in these departments the coverage of the *Barb* is often better. If a library had to choose between this and the *Barb*, I'd go for the *Tribe*, because it now seems less commercial, more dedicated to the notions of the radical young. Conversely, someone who wants a slightly better balanced coverage might prefer the *Barb*. For someone in California, both are required.

Blue-Tail Fly. 1969. m. 25¢/issue. Guy Mendes, P.O. Box 7304, Lexington, Ky. 40506.

When the University of Kentucky was considered a country club, this 20-page under, above, and around campus newspaper would never have made it past the board of regents. But things change, and now that the University is very much a part of the activist world, the editor's only real problem is not censorship, but funds. Financed out of their own pockets and from subscriptions (apparently the University allows distribution, but not much financing), the editors attempt to zero in on political, social, and artistic problems of the area. The issue examined has a long piece on the Hurricane Creek coal mine disaster and seriously questions some of the politicians who otherwise support the University, a raft of first rate poems by Captain Kentucky, and the usual music notes. It is a fine newspaper which certainly deserves support from Kentucky libraries, and those in surrounding areas.

Chicago Seed. 1967. bi-m. $12 (Individuals $6). Collective. Seed Publishing Co., 950 West Wrightwood, Chicago, Ill. 60614. Illus., adv. Circ: 40,000. Microform: B & H.

Indexed: API. *Aud:* Ac, Ga. *Jv:* V.

National. General. A 32-page tabloid, loaded with multi-colored drawings and photographs. But unlike some technicolor efforts of this type, it is quite readable. The issue examined included rules on hitchhiking, letters concerning the Gay Liberation movement, an article on an Indian commune, poetry, a piece on failure to end the Vietnam war, and regular features which cover theatre, record reviews, happenings in Chicago, ecology, etc. The primary drive seems to be towards a redefinition of politics and culture in terms of revolution and youth. There is more of the counterculture than new left politics per se. Heavy on satire, it also has some cartoons. The writing style is good, and most of its seems to be local, although the paper does have several national press stories. One of the better general papers.

Chinook. 1969. w. $7. Collective. Joy Publns., Inc. 1458 Pennsylvania St., Denver, Colo., 80203. Illus., adv. Circ: 12,000. Sample. Vol. ends: Dec. 31.

Index: API. *Aud:* Ga, Ac, Hs.

One of the few general underground newspapers, this runs an average of 12 to 20 pages, is well printed, easy to read, and operates in a very business like man-

ner, i.e., your subscription will be honored. While published out of Denver, most of the news is national in scope, e.g., an interview with Dan Ellsberg, a study of the professional secretary, an analysis of inflation, etc. Features from the Alternative Features Service and UPS are balanced with local material on music, art, ecology, and politics. Some cartoons are used. Illustrations and advertisements are pretty calm compared to many of this genre. An obvious first bet for libraries in the Denver vicinty, and a solid contribution to any medium to large-sized library with an interest in the underground.

The Drummer. 1967. w. $7. Don Demaio. Tixeon Inc., 169 Pine St., Philadelphia, Pa. 19103. Illus., adv. Circ: 10,000 paid (40,000 free).

Bk. rev: 1,700 words, signed. *Aud:* Ga, Ac.

A kind of cross between the former *East Village Other* and *The Village Voice* in content and tone. A much better print job than *EVO* had and not as sloppy in appearance, but it has much of the same type of art work as both *EVO* and *The Voice*—rather pointed political cartoons, less than flattering pictures of Nixon. It also runs some of the same kind of "personal" ads that *EVO* was noted for. It functions for Philadelphia in the same way that *The Voice* does for New York in that it lists showings of underground films, reviews plays, and advertises meetings of encounter groups, etc.

The articles seem to be very well written and informative and cover a wide range of topics, from astrological birth control to Nixon's visit to San Jose, California ("Nixon Wasn't Stoned," a reprint of a *Voice* article). There are numerous advertisements and announcements, book and record reviews, and an interesting letters to the editor column. Information concerning abortion counseling is provided in the form of an announcement for the Abortion Referral Service. A typical advertisement is one for "A Fake Marijuana Plant with a Real Purpose." (Proceeds of sales go to the Marijuana Civil Liberties Project to help legalize pot.) All in all, *Drummer* makes extremely interesting reading (the advertisements, announcements, fillers, and letters, as well as the full length articles), even for those who do not live in the Philadelphia area.

Fifth Estate. 1965. bi-w. $3.75. Collective staff. 4403 Second, Detroit, Mich. 48201. Illus., adv. Circ: 12,500. Sample. Vol. ends: No. 26. Microform: B & H.

Indexed: API. *Aud:* Ga, Ac.

Local, political, counterculture. A 24-page tabloid with a fine makeup (one of the easiest to read in the whole group). Good local reporting on politics, suppression of rights, student activities, etc. Tries to relate national issues such as women's liberation and prison reform to the Detroit scene. After the first half of the the paper, which covers the political ins and outs of the community, the editors turn to music, film, and record reviews. The level of writing is good to excellent, and most of it is original, i.e., there is little reliance on national press services. This represents a radical change from a few years back when a good deal of the copy was LNS. One of the better local papers, and a good bet for Detroit and anyone living in the greater Michigan area.

Freedom News. 1967. m. $3.50. M. H. Segal. Freedom News Inc., Box 1087, Richmond, Calif. 94802. Illus., adv. Circ: 8,000. Sample. Vol. ends: Dec. Microform: B & H.

Aud: Ac, Ga.

Political, national. A professional liberal approach to reporting on national and local (i.e. California) events. The 36-page tabloid is carefully edited, and the format is good. Almost all material concerns the alternative culture in terms of politics, education, etc. For example, the October 1971 issue included editorials, letters to the editor, considerable material on George Jackson and prison reform, draft resistance, national political commentary, and articles on education, busing, abortion, equal rights for women, etc. The editor tends to concentrate on a given subject in each issue—health, employment, reform, etc. The style of writing is as professional as the total approach. This is a far cry from the normal underground newspaper. A good bet for almost any library, particularly in the West.

Fusion. 1970. bi-w. $6. Robert Somma. New England Scenes Pub., 909 Beacon St., Boston, Mass. 02215. Illus., adv. Microform: B & H.

Aud: Ac.

National, counterculture, music. The Boston replacement for the deceased *Avatar* (1968). (Incidentally, a complete story on the history and activities of *Avatar,* one of the best of the American underground newspapers is found in the April 16, 1971 issue of *Fusion.*) The essential difference between *Fusion* and other underground papers, including *Avatar,* is that the emphasis is on music, literature, and film. Culture takes up about three quarters of each issue. Most of the criticism, reports, and views are by staffers. The level of evaluation is high. What politics there is concerns national issues from prison reform to ending the war. Advertising is primarily for recordings. A sophisticated, much above average 28-page newspaper which can be enjoyed as much for its counterculture criticism as for its political and social concern.

Georgia Straight. 1967. s-w. $13. Dan McLeod. Georgia Straight Publishing Ltd., 56A Powell St., Vancouver 4 B.C. Canada. Illus., adv. Circ: 17,000. Microform: B & H.

Aud: Ac, Ga, Hs.

National, covering politics, environment, counterculture. This is the best known of several Canadian underground newspapers. The other four or five Canadian undergrounds of considerable circulation and reputation are: *Harbinger* of Toronto; *Logos* of Montreal; *Octopus* of Ottawa; and the *Omphalos* of Winnipeg. In the beginning the *Straight* won a national, indeed an international, reputation for being busted more often by the establishment than any paper in Canada. Since 1970 the government has retreated a bit as have the editors, who now make less of the startling, more of local, solid reporting. A 24-page tabloid issue is about evenly divided between local and national politics, and reports of efforts to live off the land and save the natural beauty of Northwestern Canada. Some film, record, and book reviews. The format is adequate. Most of the material is staff written and there is little dependence upon press syndicate. One of the better features is the lively letter to the editors column. Some cartoons are used. There is little sex, and a good deal of anti-drug material. Down on the cops, who in Vancouver give the younger generation a particularly difficult time. A good choice for most Canadian libraries and for libraries in the Northwestern states.

Good Times (Formerly: *San Francisco Express Times).* 1968. w. $6. 2377 Bush St., San Francisco, Calif. 94103. Illus., adv. Microform: B & H.

Indexed: API. *Aud:* Ac, Ga, Hs.

National, covering alternative life styles, politics. It follows the format of the *Berkeley Barb* and *The Tribe,* concentrating on the San Francisco scene. It does considerably more which gives it a unique reputation. After two or three pages of local news, the editors move into good natured satire of the American scene, for example, "Jesus Saves, but Billy Prophets," a spoof on Nixon's spiritual adviser; a cartoon feature on the Platypus party—a comic political group; an interview from the San Francisco Women's Media center, etc. The paper often gives short, practical tips to its younger readers on everything from how to avoid jail to poor travel agencies. Then there are short movie reviews, health tips, recipes, theatre, etc. But there is no sexist advertising. The tone is not only professional, it is often sardonic and humorous. And the politics are genuine Movement stuff, but seem more down to earth, less wrapped up in ego trips. Given this set of standards, the 28-page journal is, in many ways, more interesting, more national then either the better known *Barb* or *Tribe.* A first choice over both, and, for that matter, ahead of both Los Angeles papers, too. The title *Good Times* seems apt for the 1970s.

Great Speckled Bird. 1967. w. $6. Collective. Cooperative Atlanta News Project Inc., 253 North Ave. N.E., Atlanta, Ga. 30308. Illus., adv. Sample. Microform: B & H.

Aud: Ac, Ga.

National, covering, racial equality and politics. This

is one of the leaders of the underground movement in the continuing battle for racial equality, not only in the south, but in the north. About one half of each issue is given to stories involving racial matters, in politics, housing, health, etc. And while most of the material is centered around Atlanta and Georgia, it is equally applicable to other areas. The tone is confident, intelligent, and remarkably cool. There is little of the harried, sometimes frantic tone found in other politically oriented papers. The editorial policy is to report what happens, call for action, and do its thing without fuss—only firmness. Aside from the fight for racial equality, the paper is for women's liberation programs, ecology and environment, and makes some effort at record and book reviews. In fact, the record music reviews are some of the best found in any of the undergrounds. The format is good, with no objectionable advertising. James Ridgeway ("The New Journalism," *American Libraries*, June 1971, p. 587) makes an observation about southern underground papers: "Many of the most interesting and most enduring papers are southern. They have an easy native populist-radical quality which other papers strive to imitate but somehow fail to achieve. It should be supported by all libraries, but most certainly by southern libraries—although let it be noted the political tone is revolutionary, even for a southern Republican."

Harbinger. 1968. bi-w. $4. Box 571, Station F, Toronto, 5 Canada. Illus., adv. Circ: 10,000. Microform: B & H.

Aud: Ac, Ga.

Local, counterculture, political. Similar in format and approach to the *Georgia Straight*, it emphasizes the Toronto counterculture scene. Although politics is an item, and the writers are quick to lead the liberal movements, the primary interest of the paper is its reporting of what is going on with the alternative life styles. The format is fair, but the reporting is often excellent, particularly in terms of notes on the local scene. There is a bit too much reliance on the press services for national items, but it is fine for record, film, and music reviews. And the calendar of events, at least as the editors choose to report it, makes the paper pretty much required reading for anyone in the Toronto area. Apparently it has had no trouble with local authorities, and Ann Leibl says its "staff attributes this to the fact that the Establishment is either dead from the neck up, or not able to read, or both."

IT (Formerly: *International Times*). 1966. bi-w. $7.50. Paul Lewis and Joy Farren. Bloom Ltd., 11A Berwick St., London W 1, England. Illus., adv. Circ: 35,000. Microform: B & H.

Aud: Ac, Ga. Jv:V.

English, general. Along with *Oz* one of the two basic underground English based newspapers. *IT*, or the *International Times*, has been around a long time,

closed down, raided and taken to court year in and year out. But it survives, even seems to grow. A 24-page issue is in technicolor, although generally readable. Material covers everything from politics to drugs and music. Some rather modified sex advertising, but on the whole the language is conservative. In America this paper would have had troubles finding someone to take it to court. Of primary importance in this country for its record, theatre, and film reviews—not to mention feature stories which give insight into how the fringe groups are living and prospering in England and Europe. It often has useful information on life styles and travel of interest to Americans. A basic paper for larger collections.

International Times. See IT.

Kaleidoscope. 1967. bi-w. $5. Dennis M. Gull. Kaleidoscope Publishing, Box 90526, Milwaukee, Wis. Illus., adv. Circ: 10,000. Sample. Vol. ends: Dec. 31. Microform: B & H.

Indexed: API. *Aud:* Ac, Ga.

Local, political, counterculture. The primary push here is heavy, radical politics, somewhat like the *Berkeley Tribe*. The editors come down on the local scene more than the *Tribe*, and feature a good deal of counterculture material from commune news to music and nutrition. The tone is sometimes a bit stringent, but the writing is much above average. In fact, this is one of the better locally–produced underground papers in the United States. Even the format is exceptional. A good subscription for any library in the middle–west, certainly for the greater Chicago–Milwaukee–Madison area. Note: Different versions of this, with the same basic center fold but with changes in local reporting, are issued from both Milwaukee and Madison. Libraries can contact either one through the Milwaukee address.

Kudzu. 1968. irreg. (every 2–4 weeks). $4 for 18 nos. Box 22502, Jackson, Miss. 39205. Circ: 10,000. Sample. Microform: B & H.

Indexed: API. *Aud:* Ac, Ga, Hs.

Local, political, counterculture. It is primarily a vehicle for telling the southern college students and anyone else who will read it what the Movement is all about. While neither as ambitious nor as well known as the *Great Speckled Bird*, it is gutsy. Note the place of publication—which does not mean all that much now, but in 1968 was no mean trick. The paper has reported on overzealous police, racial persecution, bad local politics, etc. A typical 10 to 16 page tabloid issue covers the local scene, has material on ending the war, drugs, etc. The format is adequate. Some reviews, but best known for the sensitive and perceptive notes and reviews of current popular music. The circulation indicates the paper is having an influence. It should be found in all southern libraries, and in larger northern ones, too.

The Literary Times. 1961. m. $3. Jay R. Nash. Box 4327, Chicago, Ill. 60680. Illus. Circ: 38,000.

Bk. rev: Critical notes. *Aud:* Ac.

A great grab-bag of information on new writers, magazines, and news of the literary scenes. Interviews with writers, critics, and musicians are featured, as well as poetry and fiction of high quality. It is Chicago-oriented, but the many columns by contributors keep readers informed both nationally and internationally. The editor writes highly opinioned and interesting comments. One of the best magazines available to those seeking to keep up with poetry and small press publishing in the U.S. Newspaper format. (D.D.)

Logos. 1967. m. $3. Collective. Fip Publishing Co., Box 782, Montreal 101, Que., Canada. Illus., index, adv. Circ: 30,000. Sample. Microform: B & H.

Aud: Ac.

National, political, counterculture. In format, more like the familiar American underground press than other Canadian papers, i.e., strong on illustrations, color, and satirical pieces directed at the national government. Some of it still continues to shock, but over the years it has tamed a bit. The style of writing is excellent, the reporting often superior, and the balance between the political scene and the cultural quite well done. In fact, the reports on film, recordings, etc. are some of the best in Canada. This enjoys a much larger circulation than any of the Canadian underground papers helped by the local authorities' efforts at censorship. Probably the most original and shocking of the Canadian underground.

Long Beach Sunset Press (Formerly: **Long Beach Free Press**). 1969. bi-w. $6/25 issues. 1255 E. 10th St., Long Beach, Calif. 90813. Illus., adv.

Indexed: API. *Aud:* Ac, Ga.

A colorful, unorganized 28-page tabloid which is strong on the legalization of marijuana. There is a considerable amount of advertising and most of the editorial material is from one of the underground press services. In the issue examined (September 1971) there was little local material. Neither the advertisements nor the editorial matter will be offensive, unless one is long gone on the conservative trip. Conversely, from the single number checked, it is probably passable in Long Beach, but it will not be of much interest anywhere else.

Los Angeles Free Press. 1964. w. $8. Art Kunkin. New Way, 6013 Hollywood Blvd., Los Angeles, Calif. 90029. Illus., index, adv. Circ: 95,000. Sample. Vol. ends: Dec. 31. Microform: B & H.

Indexed: API. *Aud:* Ac, Ga. *Jv:* V.

National, general. Modeled after the *Village Voice*, and the second oldest underground newspaper in America, the "Freep" is considered to be the most successful of the lot. (*The Village Voice* is no longer considered a member of the underground, and for that matter, many believe this to be equally true of the *Free Press.* Circulation, profit, and style are such that both papers are quite beyond the pattern of the average, or even above-average underground newspaper.) From its beginnings the *Free Press* helped to define a good deal of the style for the underground, and while closely tied to local issues it then, as now, concerned itself with national problems. The reporters are first rate writers and observers, better, in fact, than those found on many large daily newspapers. Politically, the columns are liberal, although no longer liberal enough for some who claim the paper has gone the way of *The Village Voice*, i.e., has become a national institution for the genteel liberal factions. This may well be. An average tabloid issue of 48 to 60 pages covers the local and national news in some four or five pages, and then turns to features and theatre, film, and music reviews. On balance, the editor touches on every conceivable interest of his readers from health and ecology to television and art. The style of writing is professional and opinioned. There is no effort at so called objectivity. This is a paper where personalized journalism reigns. Along with the *Berkeley Barb* it continues to run sexist classified and display advertising, but much less than in former years. Such advertising is still objectionable, although it probably pays a good many printing bills.

As financial success spells trouble, the *Free Press,* as with the *Barb* earlier, had its schism. In 1971 the staff split, some organizing a counter underground paper called *The Staff.* The latter is an interesting, much above average paper, but no more replaces the *"Freep"* than *EVO* replaced the *Village Voice.* The *Free Press* is a required item in any library west of the Mississippi, and should be, along with the *Voice,* in almost any library from high school up. However, it should be noted: it is no more for the little old man in knickers than the *Voice.*

Mobster Times. See *Screw.*

Nola Express. 1968. bi-w. $5. Robert Head and Darlene Fife. Box 2342, New Orleans, La. 70116. Illus., adv. Microform: B & H.

Indexed: API. *Aud:* Ac, Ga.

National, counterculture. A tabloid of some 24 pages which is in and out of censorship trouble a good deal of the time. The reason is heavy satire, often using sexual images, against the local political establishments. Poetry and prose, sometimes by leaders in the little magazine/underground movement, make up most of the contents. *Nola* is good on music reviews, particularly of new records and the New Orleans jazz scene. The makeup is fair. Because of its strong interest in the stuff of the counterculture, it comes closer to being a little magazine in its intention than most of the underground papers. In fact, it is noted as much for its literary and artistic content as for its satirical jabs. It is strong on local campuses. Some sexist advertising, but nothing near the *Berkeley Barb* variety. Good paper for most larger libraries, and for any library near the New Orleans sphere of influence.

Northwest Passage. 1969. bi-w. $6. Mary K. Becker. Frank Kathman, Box 105, S. Bellingham Sta., Bellingham, Wash. 98225. Illus., adv. Circ: 6,000. Sample. Microform: B & H.

Indexed: API. *Aud:* Ac, Ga, Hs.

National. Contents cover ecology, environment, counterculture issues. The 28-page tabloid is issued from the Northwest corner of the United States, the heart of America's natural wonderland. The reporting is in depth, and most of the paper depends upon the local staff, not the national news services. Each number, too, tends to specialize in a given area of interest, e.g., issues have covered natural childbirth, organic gardening, and even astrology. There is some direct political coverage, particularly in terms of cartoons and comics. A small part of each issue is given over to record, film, and book reviews. Some classified advertising is included. On balance, this is one of the better of the underground/counterculture newspapers. It is professionally edited, the writing is good to excellent, and the material will appeal to a wider audience than just Washington state.

Octopus. 1967. m. $4.50. Steve Harris. Box 1259, Sta. B, Ottawa, Ont., Canada. Illus., adv. Circ: 4,000. Microform: B & H.

Indexed: API. *Aud:* Ac, Ga.

Local, political, counterculture. Primarily reports on activities from the Ottawa viewpoint, but not necessarily from the same point of view as that of the national government. The politics are liberal, but not fanatical. Does a good to excellent job reporting on local activities, or lack of activities in such areas as housing, jobs, discrimination. Tends to include more poetry and prose than most papers of this type—and it is not always a fortunate selection. Some material is in French, but on the whole an English presentation. Format is good; writing style is uneven, but generally acceptable. Libraries in and around Ottawa should take this because of the coverage of local cultural events, and the fine reviews.

Old Mole; a radical bi-weekly. 1968. bi-w. $5/20 nos. (Students $3). 2 Brookline St., Cambridge, Mass. 02139. Illus., adv. Circ: 9,000. Microform: B & H.

Indexed: API. *Aud:* Ac, Ga.

Local, political. One of the more popular of the Boston-Cambridge undergrounds, differing from others because of a strong emphasis on radical politics. While a good deal of the copy concerns the national/inter-national scene, more is involved with changes locally—particularly in terms of the meaning and direction of student activities. It has become a semi–official Harvard newspaper. (And gained some national attention in 1968 when it reprinted material found by the SDS in Harvard administration buildings.) Format is fair to good. Some excellent reviews and feature stories of the passing cultural scene are included. Less culture-directed than *Fusion*, more politically aware than *Phoenix*, it is primarily for libraries in the Boston area.

Omphalos. 1969. bi-w. $5. Collective. Territories Publishing Co., 971 Sherbrook St., Winnipeg, 2, Man., Canada. Illus., adv. Circ: 10,000. Microform: B & H.

Aud: Ac.

Local, political, social issues. The title is the Greek for navel, i.e., the editors believe Winnipeg to be the navel of Canada. The pretentious title does not do justice to content which is sometimes lively, always radical, and impressive. The tabloid tends to concentrate on given cultural and social issues, exploring them in depth, e.g., it has given over a total issue to faults in local education. Writers are both students and teachers. The format is fair. A good, although not absolutely necessary underground paper for medium to larger collections—and, it goes without saying, for all libraries near greater Winnipeg.

Organ. 1970. m. $5. Gerard Van der Leun, Box 4520 Berkeley, Calif. 94704. Illus., adv.

Aud: Ga, Ac.

Influenced by the success and the format of such magazines as *Rolling Stone* and *Rag*, the old underground press is going through a number of changes. The papers which make it are the ones which pay attention to format (you have to be able to read it), special features, and reporting in some detail on current fads and fashions. *Organ* hits all three bases, and comes nicely home. One issue, for example, had a special report on the "motorcycle consciousness," traced the history of the bike, its social and even political significance. The series was followed by interviews with musicians, and articles on everything from sensitivity training to analysis of H. P. Lovecraft. There are cartoons, photos, and poetry, but all is at a professional, fairly high stylistic level. Most of the material is national in scope, although a given number of items relate closely to the Berkeley University of California syndrome. Even so, the Berkeley group exerts such an influence, and is of wide enough interest, that the paper is in no way provincial. The usual four letter words, slams at censors, and words on drugs make the scene but at nowhere near the high saturation of a few years back. The shift from radical politics to real politics, from sex to ecology, and from drugs to community concern is apparent in this and many other underground newspapers. (The legalization of marijuana is still a major issue, but the door has been slammed on hard drugs. The July 1971 number has a full report on heroin in the military. It is not sympathetic, although certainly more objective than most such studies.) Which is not to say that politics, sex, and drugs are absent, but the mixture is changing (for better or worse, depending on how you view it). Editors seem to realize, or at least the editor of *Organ* has the message, that the old shock and sock treatment is just that—old. Younger readers want something less shocking, more meaningful, more related to their daily lives. And that is what this 36 to 50 page paper is about. It promises to stay, and it can be recommended for libraries which are looking for the better underground/rapidly moving above ground magazine-newspaper.

Phoenix. 1969. w. $7. Harper Barnes. Richard Missner, 12 Arrow St., Cambridge, Mass. 02138. Illus., adv. Circ: 60,000. Vol. ends: Oct. 9. Microform: B & H.

Indexed: API. *Bk. rev:* Various number, length. *Aud:* Ac, Ga, Hs. *Jv:* V.

National, general. The closest thing going to *The Village Voice*, i.e., this is something more than an underground or alternate culture newspaper—it is a Boston metropolitan weekly trying to cover what is not covered in regular Boston papers. It has a large local staff, draws upon professionals for feature articles, cartoons, and photos, and stresses articles which have a local interest. There are long, objective reports on politics, education, and even national events which touch Boston. Most issues include feature stories on sports, science, and personalities. The format is clean, undistinguished, but easy to read. An average tabloid issue may go as high as 60 pages. The editorial policy is as liberal as *The Voice*. Despite the Boston focal point, about half of every issue follows *The Voice* technique, i.e., it is turned over to reviews of recordings, theatre, books, etc. The essential difference is that what opens in Boston may not be opening anywhere else, and Boston is not New York. In other words, the *Phoenix* lacks the pull of the *Voice*, but more because of its location than any lack of editorial skill. Again, this is not a typical underground newspaper. It comes closer to being a metropolitan weekly, differing from 99 percent of the breed in that it is liberal, sophisticated, and obviously written for a public with an above average education and income. It is a required item in and around Boston (the calendar of events is enough to make it so), and should be considered by medium and larger-sized libraries after the *Village Voice*.

Quicksilver Times. 1969. bi-w. $8. Collective. Quicksilver Times Inc., 1736 R St. N.W., Washington D.C. 20009. Illus, index, adv. Circ: 20,000. Sample. Vol. ends: Dec. 15. Microform: B & H.

Aud: Ac, Ga.

National, political. By the end of 1971 the paper was having financial difficulties—might not survive. If it continues, it is particularly valuable for Washington coverage as seen from the point of view of radicals. An average 24-page issue is given almost entirely to factual and satirical reports on everything from the FBI to the President. The revolutionaries look at the gay liberation movement, women's liberation, the draft, the war, consumers, etc. There is a given amount of local coverage. The format is fair, strong on photographs and line drawings, but weak on typography. The stories are primarily written by local staff; are good to excellent. Many short items, a few longer features are included. One of the best radical political underground newspapers for most academic and some high school and public libraries.

Rag. 1966. w. $7.50. Collective. 2330 Guadalupe, Austin, Tex., 78705. Illus., index, adv. Circ: 7,000. Sample. Vol. ends: Oct. 10. Microform: B & H.

Indexed: API. *Aud:* Ga, Ac.

Local, covering politics, ecology, counterculture. One of the oldest of the underground newspapers, and the first to be founded in the South, it began after a battle between school editors and regents at the University of Texas. In 1971 the battle still raged, with a good deal of the circulation for the paper coming from university students. The format of the 16 to 18 page tabloid is bad, although readable. Though chiefly involved with local politics—both town and school, it includes good local and national reporting on everything from environment and race to recipes. Primarily for the community in and around Austin.

Red Notes. 1969. m. $2.40. Collective. Agitprop, 248 Bethnal Green Rd., London, E2, England. Illus. Circ: 5,000. Sample.

Bk. rev: 6–7, short. *Aud:* Ac.

A combination little magazine and underground newspaper which is issued "usually monthly" out of London by Agitprop, a collective of activists. The group publishes a number of booklets, pamphlets, and posters. It is dedicated to such things as an end to racism, liberation of women, improved education, and "non–exploitative children's books." The magazine reflects all of these interests. The tone is stringent, and the whole represents one of the better vehicles for finding out what is going on within the movement in England. Admittedly of limited interest to most Americans, it will have considerable appeal for sympathizers, i.e., for students in many college and university libraries.

San Francisco Bay Guardian. 1966. m. $5 for 24 nos. Bruce B. Brugmann. 1070 Bryant St., San Francisco, Calif. 94103. Illus., index, adv. Circ: 30,000. Microform: B & H.

Indexed: API. *Bk. rev:* Various number, length. *Aud:* Ac, Ga.

A combination watch on the local newspapers and a traditional political muckraking magazine/newspaper. It is primarily concerned with the San Francisco Bay area. The editors are professional newspaper reporters, as are the writers. The topics vary from ecology and housing to monopolies by various industries. A typical 16-page tabloid issue covers the local and regional news and offers some excellent reviews of plays and films. Because of the focus on the Bay Area, this will have limited interest elsewhere.

San Francisco Express Times. See *Good Times.*

Screw; the sex review. 1968. w. $20. James Buckley and Al Goldstein. Milky Way Productions Inc., Box 432, Old Chelsea Sta., New York, N.Y. 10011. Illus., adv. Circ: 110,000. Microform: B & H.

Aud: Ga.

The first of the blatant sex underground magazine/newspapers. It was started to channel off some of the sex material and advertising found in many of the politically-oriented underground newspapers, e.g., *East Village Other, Rat,* etc. The tabloid publishes blatant pornography. There is just enough of the "social redeeming factor" to keep it sometimes free of the courts, where the editors appear regularly.

A typical issue includes articles, stories, film reviews (which, by the way, are some of the best going for the type of film reviewed), and photographs which leave absolutely nothing to the imagination. The paper's editors, while freely admitting it is a money concern take a certain wry pleasure in their contention that the whole thing is a sardonic putdown. Readers, both by law and by inclination, seem to be middle-aged, relatively well off middle class American men—the same men who often come down on the side of the censor.

The paper might have a place in a library (see discussion in the introduction to the Underground Comix section), but for most public and academic libraries it probably is best left alone. Trying to keep it on the racks is difficult enough, and there is even some question whether it would get past the librarians to the racks. (The men would read, and the women's liberation members, quite correctly, would ban.) Still, it seems worthwhile mentioning in a compilation of this type. Note the circulation. Other "reviews", literary and political, consider themselves fortunate to have circulations of over 10,000.

Meanwhile, for the interested, it should be noted the same publisher brings out other newspaper/magazines of the same variety, e.g., *Gay.* And there are countless copies of the original from *Kiss* to *Pleasure.*

By early 1972 the two publishers of *Screw* announced an even more daring venture. This is the *Mobster Times* (bi-m. $6. Box 431, Old Chelsea Sta., New York, N.Y. 10011). The *Life*-sized monthly magazine is devoted to the thesis that crime does pay and glorifies criminals who gain from their crimes. It is also a running, satirical commentary on violence in America.

Well, between this and *Screw* and the countless copies, it is all a matter of honesty rather than hypocrisy, a recognition that some people, at any rate, do enjoy reading what most librarians think they should not. And depending on your point of view, one (e.g., *Readers' Digest*) variety, is not better (or worse) than the other (e.g., *Screw*), variety. 'Tis all a matter of taste, or lack of. . . .

Second City. 1968. m. $2.50. Collective. Guild Cooperative Fellowship, 1155 W. Webster, Chicago, Ill. 60614. Illus., index, adv. Circ: 15,000. Sample. Vol. ends: No. 12. Microform: B & H.

Indexed: API. *Aud:* Ac, Ga.

National, political. The voice of the Chicago radical movement, this 16 to 20 page tabloid features stories on racism, welfare, civil rights, and local politics. There is considerable emphasis on the development of black consciousness and on ending the war. Included are frequent articles on how business is ripping off America, some book reviews, and a calendar of local events. The format is poor to fair; utilizes many illustrations and photographs. What sets this off from most papers is the definite radical, no–holds–barred reporting. In fact, it is probably one of the more radical of the underground papers—an understandable condition in view of the control of Chicago by the movement's arch foe, Mayor Daley. Anyone interested in the movement will find much here of value.

Space City. 1969. w. $7.50. Collective. Houston Media Project Inc., 1217 Wichita, Houston, Tex. 77004. Illus., adv. Circ: 8,000. Microform: B & H.

Indexed: API. *Aud:* Ac, Ga.

Local, covering racial equality, politics. It is somewhat similar to the *Great Speckled Bird,* i.e., a strong emphasis on stories which bear down on local officials who do not observe racial equality. Stories have covered the local police and the Klu Klux Klan, the activities of the space center in the larger context of the war and the American budget, as well as national news. But the emphasis is primarily populist, local, and hard hitting. There is some cultural material ranging from book reviews to notes on concerts and records. The format is good, the writing good to excellent, and the approach cool but firm. A fine paper, right up there with the other major undergrounds, both north and south.

Staff. 1971. w. $8. Brian Kirby. 7617½ Milrose Ave., Los Angeles, Calif. 90046. Illus., adv. Microform: B & H.

Aud: Ac, Ga.

National, general. This is produced by former staff

members of the *Los Angeles Free Press*, who quit the parent paper for a number of reasons; but primarily because they wanted a more radical editorial policy and more relevant local reporting. (And a number of women objected to the "Freep's" continued use of sexism in advertising.) By late 1971 it seemed touch and go whether the paper would survive. However, the 32-page tabloid deserves to make it. It is strong on covering local material which has more than local interest; has good critical reviews of music, theatre, and films; and publishes a number of feature stories on all aspects of modern living. (Interestingly enough, some of the sexist classifieds made it from the *Free Press* to the *Staff*.) Of the two papers, the *Staff* is livelier, the *Free Press* more professional; the *Staff* digs deeper, seems to be more involved with radical politics, but the *Free Press* has a balanced view which is hardly "soft" on the establishment. Anyone living in California will want both; those outside may want to stick to the *Free Press* until such time as the *Staff* demonstrates staying power. (Conversely, younger readers will enjoy the *Staff* more, and if it is a matter of serving age groups it comes before the *Free Press* for the teenager-early twenties group.)

G.I. UNDERGROUNDS IN THE UNITED STATES

The following is not complete, but it does give an idea of how many papers are involved with the "new" army. The list is from the Radical Research Center, when it was located at Carleton College.

Alabama. *Left Face*, Box 1595, Anniston, 36201. *Our Thing*, Box 853, Huntsville, 35804.

Alaska. *Green Machine*, Box 2697, Fairbanks, 97701.

California. *All Ready on the Left*, Box 1356, Vista 92038. *The Ally*, Box 9276, Berkeley 94709. *As You Were*, Box 1062, Monterey 93940. *Black Unity*, Box 1356, Vista 92083. *Duck Power*, Box 3552, San Diego 92103. *Final Flight*, 2214 Grove St., Berkeley 94704. *Now Hear This*, 1812 Anaheim St., Long Beach 90813. *Pay Back*, Box 11354, Santa Ana 92711. *Pentagon GI Coffeehouse Newsletter*, 690 7th St., Oakland 94607. *Redline*, Box 4398, Berkeley 94704. *Snorton Bird*, Box 225, San Bernadino 92409. *Spaced Sentinel*, Box 2045, Marysville 95901. *Truth Instead*, Box 31387, San Francisco 94131. *Up Against the Bulkhead*, 968 Valencia, San Francisco 94110.

Colorado. *Aboveground Press Service*, Box 2255, Colorado Springs 80901. *Counter Attack*, 318 E. Pikes Peak, Colorado Springs 80901.

District of Columbia. *Common Sense*, Box 21073, Kalorama Station, Washington, D.C. 20004. *GI Press Service*, 1029 Vermont Ave., N.W., 8th Floor, Wash., D.C. 20005. *Open Sights*, c/o Berrigan House, 1132 22nd St., N.W., Washington, D.C. 20037.

Georgia. *Last Harass*, Box 2994, Hill Station, Augusta 30904. *Rap!*, Box 894, Main P.O., Columbus, 31902.

Hawaii. *C.O.M. Newsletter*, 2223 Komo Mai Drive,

Pearl City 96782. *The O.D.*, 1434 Makaloa St., Rm 9, Honolulu 96814.

Illinois. *Camp News*, 2214 Halsted St., Chicago 60614. *Dull Brass*, Box 4598, Chicago 60680. *Navy Times Are Changin'*, Box 164, North Chicago 60664. *Veterans Stars & Stripes For Peace*, Box 4598, Chicago 60680. *Vietnam GI*, Box 9273, Chicago 60690.

Kentucky. *Fun, Travel & Adventure*, Box 336, Louisville 40201.

Louisiana. *G.A.F.*, 525 Wichita, Shreveport 71101.

Maryland. *The Pawn*, c/o GIs United, Box 1438, Frederick 21701

Massachusetts. *Catharsis*, Box 881, JFK Station, Boston 02114. *Morning Report*, Box 359, Groton 01450. *Raw Truth*, 65 A Winthrop St., Cambridge 02138.

Michigan. *Broken Arrow*, Box 471. Mt. Clemens 48043.

Missouri. *Underwood*, c/o GI Committee, St. Louis Peace Info. Center, 6244 Delmar, St. Louis 63130.

New Jersey. *Shakedown*, Box 68, Wrightstown, 08562.

New York. *The Bond*, Rm 633, 156 Fifth Ave., NYC 10010. *Bragg Briefs*, c/o GIs United, Box 437, Spring Lake 28390. *Potemkin*, ASU, Rm 633, 156 Fifth Ave., NYC 10010. *S P D News*, c/o ASU, Rm 633, 156 Fifth Ave., NYC 10010. *X-Press*, Box 11, St. George Station, Staten Island 10301.

North Carolina. *The Other Side*, c/o COM Bragg, Box 5424, Fayetteville 28303.

Ohio. *Star Spangled Banner*, c/o GIs United, Box 700, Fairborn 45324.

Pennsylvania. *The Destroyer*, c/o Box Y, 9th & Chestnut Sts. Philadelphia 19107.

Rhode Island. *All Hands Abandon Ship*, c/o Potemkin Book Shop, 126 Broadway, Newport 02840.

Texas. *Gigline*, Box 31094, Summit Hts. Station, El Paso 79931. *Napalm*, Box 44, Clarksville 75426. *Your Military Left*, Box 561, San Antonio 78206.

Virginia. *On the Beach*, c/o Dennis Nicholas, Box 85, Norfolk 23501.

Washington. *Counterpoint*, 515 20th St., Seattle 98102. *Fed Up!*, Box 414, Tacoma 98409. *Lewis-Mc Chord Free Press*, Box 421, Tacoma 98401.

G.I. UNDERGROUNDS ABROAD

England. *PEACE*, 3 Round Church St., Cambridge.

France. *Act* and *Baumholder Gig Sheet*, c/o Miss Rita, 10 Passage du Chantier, Paris XIIe.

Germany. *About Face*, c/o Politische Buchhandlung, Schiffgasse 3, 69 Heidelberg. *Call Up*, J. Burkhardt, c/o Politische Buchhandlung, Schiffgasse 3, 69 Heidelberg. *Graffiti*, c/o Politische Buchhandlung, Schiffgasse 3, 69 Heidelberg. *The Next Step*, c/o S.C., Box 2441, 6Ffm. *The Proper Gander*, c/o Politische Buchhandlung, Schiffgasse 3, 69 Heidelberg. *Up Against the Wall*, c/o Karin Rohrbein, 1 Berlin 15, Ludwigskirch Str. 4. *Venceremos*, c/o S.C., Box 2441, 6 Ffm. *We Got the Brass*, c/o S.C., Box 2441, 6 Ffm.

Japan. *Demand for Freedom,* c/o Ishii Bldg. 6–44, Kagurazaka, Shinjiku-Ku, Tokyo. *Fall In at Ease,* c/o Ishii Bldg. 6–44, Kagurazaka, Shinjiku-Ku, Tokyo. *Freedom Rings,* c/o Ishii Bldg. 6–44, Kagurazaka, Shinjiku-Ku, Tokyo. *Kill For Peace,* c/o Beheiren, Ishii Bldg. 6–44, Kagurazaka, Shinjiku-Ku, Tokyo. *Semper Fi,* Box 86, Chuo Post Office, Hiroshima City. *Stars-N-Bars,* c/o Semper Fi, Box 86, Chuo Post Office, Hiroshima City. *Y.A.N.D.,* Box 12, Haka-ta-Kuyoku, Fukuoka. *Yokosuka David,* c/o Ishii Bldg. 6–44, Kagurazaka, Shinjiku-Ku, Tokyo.

Korea. *Korea Free Press,* Box 94, Elmhurst, Ill. 60126.

Philippines. *Below Decks,* 272 Harrison St., Ashland Ore. 97520. *The Whig,* c/o John Hancock, 26–E La-Salle St., Cubao, Quezon City.

Sweden. *Paper Grenade,* c/o Sundstrom, Hogs-bergsgaten 46B/IoG, 116 20 Stockholm.

UNDERGROUND PRESS SERVICES

Alternative press services appear almost as quickly as the newspapers and little magazines they serve. And while of primary value to editors who depend upon them for national and international fuel for their publications, they are of considerable interest to libraries. A library which may not be able to take the majority of the underground papers can soon build a viable file of material useful for research and as a running social-political commentary on today's world as viewed by the young. Librarians might bring a few of these services to the attention of campus and high school editors, not to mention laymen who are starting or are developing local magazines and newspapers.

Alternative Features Service. m. & w. $15 and $125. P.O. Box 2250, Berkeley, Calif. 94702.

John Berger explains that the packet contains original feature news stories, commentaries, columns, cartoons, graphics, book and record reviews, "And whatever else of clear social importance has come along." It is primarily geared for college newspapers and radio stations whose audience is "students who haven't decided what they want to do with their lives or who are disenchanted with the jobs the establishment offers." The August 13, 1971 packet includes book and film reviews, comments on the "war" against pot, a political essay on American Asian policies, record reviews, etc. The writing is much above average, and the reviews considerably better than those found in many traditional sources. Contributors have been associated with such mags and newspapers as *Crawdaddy, Rolling Stone, The Realist,* and *Suppository.* All in all a professional approach.

College Press Service. bi-w. Inquire. 2064 E. York St., Denver, Colo. 80210.

Puts out general information of interest to college newspapers.

Cooperative High School Independent Press Syndicate. CHIPS & News Service for High School Underground (FPS). 1970. John Challer, 3210 Grace St., N.W., Washington, D.C. *American Press Syndicate* P.O. Box 5175, Beverly Hills, Calif. 90210. Microform: B & H.

The basic services for high school underground newspapers. The first service, now defunct, began in 1968 as the *High School Independent Press Service* (HIPS), a part of the Liberation News Service. The Student Information Center, affiliated with *CHIPS* and *FPS,* gives information on the high school underground. *CHIPS* issues a directory of high school papers and a bi–weekly packet of articles, graphics, and information for progressive high school papers. (Of particular interest is a pamphlet, "How to start a high school underground," which sells for 50 cents, and will be of some interest to journalism students and young activists. The west coast, the *American Press Syndicate,* group is similar to *CHIPS* and gives press and information service.

Information on the high school press is found from time to time in various publications. See, for example, *Media Industry Newsletter,* Sept. 16, 1971, p. 9 for an account of the press near the end of 1971; and *New Schools Exchange Newsletter* No. 54 for a list, with addresses, of high school papers.

Liberation News Service. 1967. bi-w. $100-$240 (inquire). 160 Claremont, New York, N.Y. 10027. Microform: B & H.

Founded in 1967 by Ray Mungo and Marshall Bloom, this is the most famous and the most radical of the underground press services. The emphasis is on the Movement. At one time it was heavily tied into the SDS. Now its staff writes material to bring an end to the war, raise employment, assure racial and sexual equality, and, to a degree, revolution. It delivers packets of materials to the papers (and to libraries) which includes everything from cartoons and short fillers to feature stories.

Pacific News Service. Price: inquire. Suite 300, 9 Sutter St., San Francisco, Calif. 94104.

This specializes in coverage of the Far East for both over and underground media. John Berger says: "Their correspondents are often Asian experts with facility in Chinese, Vietnamese and other languages." In addition, the organization has an extensive file of materials and offers current research in areas requested. Even librarians with no interest in the underground, but with a strong Far East department, should make inquiries.

Underground Press Syndicate. 1966. $25. Box 26, Village Station, New York, N.Y. 10014. Microform: B & H.

The first underground press service started by the staff of the *East Village Other* and, of course, John

Wilcock. While it began as a regular press service, it developed into a cooperative effort to pool experience and to draw advertising for members. It is now a clearing house for information on the underground press, sets up collective subscription and advertising contracts, and is more like the traditional magazine jobber. It lists UPS papers, gives information on starting underground papers, and generally is the best single contact for libraries seeking current information on the underground. In fact, any library remotely interested in the new media is advised to write the syndicate and inquire for information about their services.

CRIMINOLOGY AND LAW ENFORCEMENT

Basic Periodicals

Ga: *Journal of Criminal Law, Prisoners' Rights Newsletter;* Jc: *Journal of Criminal Law, The Criminologist, Prisoners' Rights;* Ac: *Journal of Criminal Law, British Journal of Criminology, The Criminologist, International Police Academy Review, Prisoners' Rights Newsletter.*

Basic Abstracts and Indexes

Abstracts on Criminology & Penology, Index to Legal Periodicals, Abstracts for Social Workers.

American Journal of Correction. 1920. bi-m. $4. Roberts J. Wright. Amer. Correctional Assn., 2642 University Ave., St. Paul, Minn. 55114. Illus., index, adv. Circ: 7,685. Reprint: Kraus.

Indexed: PAIS. *Bk. rev:* Various number, length. *Aud:* Ac, Ga.

The official publication of several organizations dealing with prisons and prisoners (National Jail Association, etc.). Contributors are actively engaged in prison work. The emphasis is decidedly progressive with a good part of each issue going to innovations and new programs for rehabilitation. Of considerable value to the serious student and one of the most reliable sources of information in this field.

American Journal of Police Science. See *Journal of Criminal Law, Criminology, and Police Science.*

Australian and New Zealand Journal of Criminology. 1968. q. $7. A. A. Bartholomew. Australian and New Zealand Soc. of Criminology, c/o Univ. of Melbourne, Melbourne, Victoria, Australia.

Indexed: CrimAb. *Bk. rev:* Various number, length. *Aud:* Ac.

While reporting on the developments in criminal law, cases, and corrections practices found in Australia and New Zealand, this journal also includes a myriad of articles of international interest. Covers questions of psychiatric determinations in law, studies of the characteristics of various types of offenders, and theoretical discussions on correctional practice, administration, and the relationship between crime, the penal system, and society. Case reports on important events in the Australian and New Zealand legal proceedings are included. Book reviews and abstracts are found in every issue. (D.L.).

BNDD Bulletin. See U.S. Government and United Nations/United States Section.

British Journal of Criminology; delinquency and deviant social behavior. 1950. q. $15. Edward Glover, J. E. Hall Williams, Peter D. Scott. The Inst. for the Study and Treatment of Delinquency, 11 New Fetter Lane, London, EC4, England. Illus., index, adv. Circ: 1,500. Sample. Vol. ends: No. 4.

Indexed: BritHum, CrimAb, PAIS, PsyAb. *Bk. rev:* 7, 500 words, signed. *Aud:* Ac, Ga. *Jv:* V.

Drawing upon all fields, but particularly psychology and sociology, authors in this distinguished British journal make a strong case for reform in treatment of juvenile delinquency. There are enough general approaches to give it considerable value for American libraries. In fact, it is outstanding for its view of the international situation in this area. Social and cultural differences are duly considered, and there is an invaluable section: "Current Survey: Research and Methodology," which will be of vital concern to anyone involved in criminology. Should be considered by all larger academic and public libraries.

Canadian Journal of Criminology and Corrections (Formerly: **Canadian Journal of Corrections**). 1958. q. $10. Social Development, Canadian Criminology and Corrections Assn., 55 Parkdale Ave., Ottawa K1Y 1E5 Ont., Canada. Circ: 900. Vol. ends: Oct. Microform: UM.

Indexed: AbSocWk, CanI. *Bk. rev:* Various number, length. *Aud:* Ac.

The major emphasis of this journal is on two related but distinct topics. One area, the psychological and sociological studies of criminal behavior, would be of use to anyone studying criminology. The other area comments specifically on Canadian laws and practices and would be of use only to those interested in the Canadian legal system. A drawback is that articles are published in either French or English with no summary statements in the other language. Each issue has several extensive and well-written book reviews with shorter capsule summaries of other pertinent books plus a list of books received but not reviewed. Reviews of Canadian films on criminology are included. The first issue of every volume contains a useful list of research projects in progress, their scope, sponsors, and funding. (D.L.).

Criminal Justice Newsletter. 1970. bi-w. $48. Robert D. Lipscher. Institute of Judicial Admin. 33 Washington Sq. W., New York, N.Y. 10011.

Aud: Ac.

An eight-page reporting service which alerts attorneys and public officials to current activities of law enforcement planning, legislatures, the courts, planning, police, statistics, and a variety of matters which the publishers feel are of major importance. The style is factual and free of jargon. Effort is made to be objective, although each issue features a special report which gives pros and cons of an issue, i.e., problems in work release, criminal justice coordinating councils. A worthwhile alerting service whose primary audience is lawyers, although it will be of value to anyone deeply involved with crime. Primarily for the special collection.

Criminal Law Bulletin. 1965. 10/yr. $24. Fred Cohen. Warren, Gorham and Lamont, Inc., 89 Beach St., Boston, Mass. 02111.

Indexed: LegPer. *Bk. rev:* Numerous; length varies. *Aud:* Ac.

Devoted to the rehabilitation of the offender and the rights of the individual, this journal comments strongly on the injustices of the American legal system and correctional practices. Whole issues are often given to one aspect of criminal justice such as juvenile delinquency. Articles on the sociological and psychological sources of criminal behavior and its implications for society are regular features. Each issue contains a complete listing of U.S. Supreme Court Decisions plus significant decisions in other federal and state courts. The book reviews reflect the editorial beliefs of the journal and consequently cover many books dealing with aspects of society not included in the more legalistic journals. The "From Legal Literature" section reviews important publications not in monograph form. (D.L.)

Criminal Law Quarterly. 1958. q. $18.75. Alan W. Mewett. Canada Law Book Co., Ltd. 80 Cowdray Court, Agincourt, Ont., Canada. Circ: 1,200.

Indexed: CrimAb.

The chief use of this journal to those not engaged in Canadian criminal proceedings will be the listing of Criminal Proceedings in the Canadian Supreme Court and the Decisions on Sentencing. A small number of articles of sociological importance in understanding the Canadian problems in criminology are included in each issue along with listings of important cases and decisions in the lower Canadian courts. (D.L.)

Criminologica. See *Criminology.*

The Criminologist. 1956. q. $8. Nigel Morland. Forensic Publishing Co., 9 Old Bailey, London, EC4, En-

gland. Illus., index, adv. Circ: 10,000. Sample. Vol. ends: Nov.

Indexed: CrimAb. *Bk. rev:* 18–20, 80–100 words, signed. *Aud:* Ga, Ac.

"The views and the experiences of the world's leading authorities on all matters relating to crime." Features some 14 articles by scholars who write with verve and style. The editor strikes a nice balance between professional interests and matters fascinating to any detective story fan, e.g., the articles "Anatomy of the Lock" (a combination history and advisory piece) and "Post Mortem Fingerprinting" (certain problems after rigor mortis). Correspondence and book reviews round out the British journal. An invaluable publication for experts as well as mystery fans.

Criminology; an interdisciplinary journal (Formerly: *Criminologica*). 1963. q. $15. C. Ray Jeffrey. American Soc. of Criminology. Sage Publns., 275 S. Beverly Drive, Beverly Hills, Calif. Circ: 600.

Indexed: CrimAb. *Aud:* Ac.

"Devoted to crime and deviant behavior, as found in sociology, psychology, psychiatry, law, and social work." This quote from the editorial policy of *Criminology* best defines the scope of this journal. Articles are usually the result of original empirical research concerned with providing an understanding of crime and society. The "Across the Desk" section gives compact summaries of reports by various crime agencies and new trends in the field. (D.L.)

Enforcement Journal. 1962. bi-m. $12. Frank J. Shira. National Police Officers Assn. of Amer. 2801 E. Oakland Park Blvd., Ft. Lauderdale, Fla. 33306. Illus., index, adv. Circ: 17,000.

Aud: Ga.

The basic police journal in this field. Most copies go directly to administrative officers and policemen—including sheriffs and private police. It is the cousin of the other large organization's journal, *The National Sheriff,* but both share much in common. Here the emphasis is on how to get along as a police officer, i.e., public relations activities and familiarization with the law are almost as important as new equipment and techniques. The tone is sane, the information accurate, and the approach objective.

FBI Law Enforcement Bulletin. 1931. m. Free to qualified personnel. Federal Bureau of Investigation, U.S. Dept. of Justice, Washington, D.C. 20535. Illus.

Aud: Ac.

Before J. Edgar Hoover's death, this bulletin contained both a bit of propaganda for the Bureau chief and a statistical analysis of crime in the United States. Each issue featured a message from the FBI chief, along with short articles on all aspects of the current criminal scene as viewed by the FBI. Needless to say, the FBI always looks good. This was an interesting item for the statistical data, for understanding Hoover's patterns, and sometimes for objective information. Apparently it can be obtained by academic and large public libraries, but Hoover had no desire to have it in high schools. A letter from him to a New York high school librarian, dated April 20, 1970, noted that: "Because of the nature of the contents of the Bulletin, we have adopted a policy of not placing it in high school libraries. I regret it will not be possible to furnish you copies." Apparently high school students should rely on the papers and television for their version of the FBI. Watch this one, as well as the FBI, for changes under new leadership.

Federal Probation. See U.S. Government and United Nations/United States Section.

International Journal of Offender Therapy (Formerly: *Journal of Offender Therapy*). 1956. 3/yr. Membership. Ed. Bd. Assn. for Psychiatric Treatment of Offenders, 162–17 73rd Ave., Flushing, N.Y. 11366. Circ: 650.

Indexed: CrimAb, PsyAb, IMed. *Aud:* Ac.

The significant stress of this journal is on the role of psychiatry and various mental health programs in the rehabilitation of the offender. Articles include not only reports on the results of various therapies but also theoretical discourses on types of therapies and their uses. Articles on crime and sociological and psychological studies of specific cases of abnormal behavior or social phenomena are also included. Book reviews appear sporadically but appear to cover only the most important additions to the field. (D.L.)

International Police Academy Review. 1967. q. Free. Office of Public Safety, Agency of Intl. Development, Dept. of State, Washington, D.C. 20523. Illus. Circ: 4,000.

Aud: Ac.

According to Thomas M. Finn, chief of the training division of the office of public safety, this is "distributed to graduates of the International Police Academy. In some instances, where a need has been indicated, the *Review* has been sent to government agencies and other institutions for research. It is not available to others." University and special libraries will have to decide if they qualify for this journal which is devoted to international aspects of criminal control. In the previous edition it was recommended for larger collections, but Mr. Finn's letter obviously poses problems for all but the most determined.

Issues in Criminology. 1965. bi-a. $4. Frances S. Coles. School of Criminology, 101 Haviland Hall, Univ. of California, Berkeley, Calif. 94720. Adv. Circ: 1,100. Sample. Vol. ends: Summer.

Indexed: CrimAb. *Bk. rev:* 3–4, lengthy, signed. *Aud:* Ac.

A behavioral science journal produced by the graduate students of the School of Criminology at the University of California, Berkeley aiming to cover "Criminology as a Discipline," "Juvenile Delinquency and the Juvenile Court," "The Criminal Self and Criminal Careers," "Comparative Criminology," and the "Criminal Justice System." Includes historical papers, philosophical discussions of modern jurisprudence, and emphasizes abnormal behavior. Primarily for the special collection in this area.

Journal of Criminal Law, Criminology, and Police Science. 1910. q. $15. Jon E. Steffesen. Williams & Wilkins Co., 428 E. Preston St., Baltimore, Md. 21202. Circ: 4,186.

Indexed: ChemAb, CrimAb, LegPer, PAIS, PsyAb. *Bk. rev:* Various number, length. *Aud:* Ac.

Actually three journals in one, each topic in the title—criminal law, criminology, and police science—is a separate section. The criminal law section deals specifically with questions pertaining to confusing or controversial applications of the law and means of utilizing this law. Extremely legalistic, this section would be of use only to lawyers or people with a strong background in law. Not quite so oriented to the legal profession, the criminology section comments on studies relating to the social implications of criminology. The police science section incorporates the former *American Journal of Police Science* and deals with scientific advances in crime detection and evidence gathering. Some articles cover the sociological aspects of the role and concept of crime agencies in society. The criminology and police science sections contain excellent book reviews. "Recent trends in criminal law" in the criminal law section provides coverage of new interpretations of laws and court rulings while the "Police science technical abstracts and notes" supplies news on all the various advances in police science work. (D.L.)

Journal of Offender Therapy. See *International Journal of Offender Therapy.*

Juvenile Court Digest. 1971. bi-m. $8. National Council of Juvenile Court Judges, P.O. Box 8978, University Station, Reno, Nevada, 89507.

Indexed: CrimAb. *Aud:* Ac.

The publishers of the quarterly *Juvenile Court Journal* augment that service with this 16-page newsletter. Each issue begins with a brief summary of important rulings, followed by 15 pages of digests of the facts and details of each case. The arrangement is under broad subject heading with state subheadings, i.e., Adoption, Maryland to School Regulations, Texas. The language is nontechnical, does not require more than a basic understanding of law to follow. A useful reference tool.

Law and Order; for all concerned with the business of law enforcement. 1953. m. $4. Frank G. MacAloon. Copp Organization, Inc., 37 W. 38th St., New York, N.Y. 10018. Illus., index, adv. Circ: 23,000. Microform: UM.

Bk. rev: Notes. *Aud:* Ga.

Methods of keeping law and order—from a gun to a technique for mob control—make up the content of this magazine. It is directed to policemen, but more particularly to administrators and officers. The emphasis on the "how-to-do-it" approach should interest anyone who is: (a) involved with police work or (b) involved with fighting for better police work. The articles are written by experts and by men on the street, cover all topics from drugs and traffic violations to interrogation and photography. Over the past year or so the editor has tended to focus on one or more subjects in each issue. Some fascinating photographs.

NCCD News; on delinquency and crime prevention control. 1921. 5/yr. $2.25. Matt Matlin. National Council on Crime and Delinquency, 44 E. 23rd St., New York, N.Y. 10010. Circ: 11,300.

Indexed: CrimAb. *Aud:* Ac.

A newsletter, *NCCD News* is a reference source of information on federal grants, crime statistics, major court rulings, and programs relating to crime control and rehabilitation along with the usual "Names in the news" and obituaries. (D.L.)

National Sheriff. 1948. bi-m. Membership (Nonmembers $7.50). Ferris E. Lucas. National Sheriff's Assn., Inc., 1250 Connecticut Ave., N.W., Washington, D.C. 20036. Illus., index, adv. Circ: 21,022.

Aud: Ac, Ga. *Jv:* C.

The type of professional journal rarely seen by laymen, but of interest because of its position on issues. It seeks to instill in its readers the viewpoint that the individual who commits a crime should be punished for that crime, and tends to look askance at sociological and psychological theories which would absolve the criminal of his guilt. Summed-up by the editor: "While the root causes of crime may someday be eliminated from society, until then the suggestion of Messrs. Gilbert and Sullivan that the punishment fit the crime may have to suffer." Presentation is direct, honest, and of value for anyone who seeks a broader understanding of law enforcement.

Police Chief. 1934. m. $7.50. Quinn Tamm. Intl. Assn. of Chiefs of Police, Inc. 11 Firstfield Rd., Gaithersburg, Md. 20760. Illus., index, adv. Circ: 14,500.

Aud: Ac, Ga.

While edited particularly for chiefs of police, much of the magazine will interest any law enforcement officer. Each issue is concerned with the administrative and personnel factors involved with running a

department or a section—and, as such, is more concerned with public policy and administration than any of the others in the field. There is, too, stress on equipment, methods of handling safety and education programs, etc. The tone favors fairly rigid practices, and it is all a bit conservative. This probably comes from the fact that most of the material is written by and for men on the job.

Prison Service Journal. See U.S. Government and United Nations/United States Section.

Prisoners' Rights Newsletter. 1971. 8/yr. Free. National Committee for Prisoners' Rights, 77 West Eagle St., Buffalo, N.Y. 14202.

Aud: Ac, Ga.

A jointly sponsored publication of the National Committee for Prisoner's Rights and the American Civil Liberties Union Foundation, this began shortly after the Attica, New York tragedy. Its purpose is to keep readers aware of current news on prison reform, prison life, and legislation which may affect prisoners and their families. The organizations, also, will assist prisoners in efforts they make towards litigation. Editorials suggest needed changes and reform. The whole is written objectively and the factual material is invaluable to any library interested in this area.

Another similar is *Connections* (3189 16th St., San Francisco, Calif 94103). It apparently is free, began publication in 1971, and covers much of the same ground—although not as thoroughly as the *Prisoners' Rights Newsletter.*

CULTURAL-SOCIAL STUDIES

See also Sociology section.

Basic Periodicals

Hs: *Society;* Ga: *Society, Journal Social Issues;* Jc: *Society, Journal of Social Issues, Newsletter on the State of the Culture;.* Ac: *Society, Journal of Social Issues, Newsletter on the State of the Culture, Journal of Popular Culture, Arts in Society, International Social Science Journal.*

Basic Abstracts and Indexes

Social Science & Humanities Index.

American Quarterly. 1949. q. (1 supplement/yr) $8. Murray G. Murphy. Box 30, Bennett Hall, Univ. of Pa., Philadelphia, Pa. 19104. Illus., adv. Circ: 4,000. Sample. Vol. ends: Dec. Refereed. Microform: UM.

Indexed: MLA, SSHum. *Bk. rev:* 3–5, 1,000 words, signed. *Aud:* Ac.

As the journal of the American Studies Association, features scholarly articles on American politics, society, history, art, belles-lettres, etc. Supplement contains a selected, annotated interdisciplinary bibliography of current articles on American Studies, dissertations in progress, writings on the theory and teaching of American Studies, a list of college and university programs in American Studies, financial aid available to graduate students, and a membership directory. Supplement also contains year's list of short reviews, descriptive in nature, approximately 175 words in length, and signed.

Arion; a quarterly journal of classical culture and the humanities. 1962. q. $6. Donald Carne-Ross. Univ. of Texas Press, Austin, Tex. 78712. Illus., index. Circ: 800.

Indexed: SSHum. *Aud:* Ac.

Interested in items with an interdisciplinary appeal, and while not ignoring what it refers to as the "specialisms" of philology and criticism, it attempts to display these subjects in the broadest possible context. The usual items of textual and historical criticism appear, but there are many more philosophical and literary items here than in other publications. There are also original literary works—but, of course, with a classical content. Only for large university libraries.

✓ ***Arts in Society.*** 1958. 3/yr. $5.50. Edward L. Kamarck. Univ. Extension, Univ. of Wisconsin, 738 Lowell Hall, 610 Langdon St., Madison, Wisconsin, 53706. Illus., index, adv. Circ: 5,000. Sample. Vol. ends: Winter. Microform: UM. Reprint: Johnson.

Indexed: LMags, CurrCont, PAIS, SocAb. *Bk. rev:* 2–3, 2,500–3,500 words, signed. *Aud:* Ac, Ga, Hs. *Jv:* V.

A general art magazine which views art as just about every one of man's activities short of filling in a tax return. The magazine stresses arts in relation to particular social concerns; and contributors represent a variety of fields ranging from aesthetics to psychiatry. Each 150 to 170 page issue is devoted to a major theme, e.g., the issue at hand is "Sounds and Events of Today's Music," and past numbers have considered everything from censorship in the arts to mass culture. Contributors represent major voices in the field, and the whole is tastefully illustrated with photographs and line drawings. And while this is published by the University of Wisconsin, the editor has a free hand, demonstrates professional and always superb taste, and puts out a magazine any commercial firm would be proud to claim. An index in every third number is a great help in terms of reference. Between the copy and the pictures this should be useful in all libraries from high school up.

Carnegie Magazine; dedicated to literature, science, art and music. 1927. 10/yr. $3. James M. Walton. Carnegie Inst. and Carnegie Library of Pittsburgh, 4400 Forbes Ave., Pittsburgh, Pa. 15213. Illus., index, adv. Circ: 10,000. Sample. Vol. ends: Dec.

Aud: Ga, Ac.

"Dedicated to literature, science, art and music," this is designed to extend the program of its two parent bodies. Each issue includes about 15 articles on topics in the areas of interest of the Institute and the Library. Holdings of the museum in the field of art form the basis for some articles, in which historical and other background material is included. Exhibits, festivals, and items of civic improvement and local history, and of cultural importance are often included. Contributors represent the editorial and Institute staff and other experts. This is nicely illustrated, and some advertising is included, always tastefully and cleverly related to the general theme of the magazine.

Charioteer. 1960. a. $3. Andonis Decavalles and Bebe Spanos. Parnassos, Greek Cultural Soc. of N.Y., 2928 Grand Central Station, New York, N.Y. 10017. Illus., adv. Circ: 1,500.

Bk. rev: 5, 1–2 pages, signed. *Aud:* Ga, Ac.

An annual anthology of modern Greek literature and the arts. All material is in English and there are numerous illustrations of Greek painting, drawing, and sculpture. Past issues have included such things as poems by George Seferis, sculpture by Christos Kapralos, Cavafy's Ars Poetica, etc. There is no political material. As a well-balanced approach to Greek humanism, this is a fine annual addition for larger arts and sciences collections.

✓ ***Comparative Studies in Society and History: an international quarterly.*** 1958. q. $8.50. Sylvia L. Thrupp and Eric R. Wolf. Cambridge Univ. Press, 32 E. 57 St., New York, N.Y. 10022. Illus., index, adv. Circ: 2,000.

Indexed: HistAb, SSHum, SocAb. *Aud:* Ac.

Features articles on problems in history and related fields such as sociology, economics, and psychology. Interest is demonstrated in social organization, the structure of society, and explanations of stability change. The articles are scholarly and include theoretical debate. In view of its close relations to other academic fields, it should be considered a basic addition to all large research libraries.

Cultural Affairs. 1967. q. $5. Peter Spackman. Associated Council of the Arts, 1564 Broadway, New York, N.Y. 10036. Illus.

Aud: Ac, Ga.

A general magazine of the arts written for the better educated layman. It is not for the professional. Articles consider music, drama, literature, dance, painting, education, even environment and money. The writers have included Jacques Barzun, Allan Kaprow, Clive Barnes, Isaac Stern, Agnes DeMille, and, to be sure, some lesser known but also excellent writers. Published by the Associated Council of the Arts (a nonprofit organization), the driving purpose of the magazine is to arouse enough interest in the arts to gain them the support they need. (Useful reference material on grants, community activities, education, cultural changes etc.) A basic cultural magazine for almost all libraries.

The Futurist. 1966. bi-m. $7.50. Edward Cornish. World Future Soc., P.O. Box 19285, 20th St. Sta., Washington, D.C. 20036. Illus., index. Circ: 9,000. Sample. Vol. ends: Dec.

Bk. rev: 2, 1000 words, signed. *Aud:* Ac, Ga.

What does the future hold? This nonprofit, nonpolitical society tries to give the answer in terms of objective reports by scientists, educators, political scientists, and industrial leaders. For example, one issue examined had articles from an official at General Electric, a teacher at the University of Pittsburgh and a New Left historian. The 40 pages are not always comfortable, but are provocative. The style is generally nontechnical, but presupposes a genuine interest in aspects of future developments both here and abroad.

Impact of Science on Society. 1950. q. $3.50. Bruno Friedman. United Nations Educational, Scientific and Cultural Organization. Subs. to: UNESCO Publns. Center, P.O. Box 433, New York, N.Y. 10016.

Indexed: BioAb, ChemAb, CurrCont, PAIS. *Aud:* Ga, Ac.

This journal examines and concerns itself with the effects of technology on society. Issues generally contain articles directed toward a predetermined central theme. The April/June 1970 issue, for example, was on the theme "The Scientists Riposte," concerning scientists's views of the impact of technology: "Science in the Unity of Culture;" and "Fragmentation in Science and Culture." Features include a "Letterbox," and notes on contributors. This is an interesting, topical publication with which to enlarge a basic collection, but is by no means indispensable. (M.W.)

Journal of Aesthetic Education. 1966. q. $7.50. Ralph A. Smith. Univ of Illinois Press, Urbana, Ill. 61801. Illus., index, adv. Circ: 1,200.

Indexed: EdI, PhilosI, SSHum. *Bk. rev:* Various number, length. *Aud:* Ac.

Features scholarly articles on the arts environment and the mass media. In some respects it is a combination of the *Journal of Popular Culture* and *Journal of Aesthetics and Art Criticism,* but differs from both in that it is more general, more concerned with the broader implications of teaching and learning about aesthetics at every level. For example, one issue may be devoted entirely to the film, another to music, etc. A required item, particularly for libraries which subscribe to the aforementioned journals. And while primarily for the academic researcher, of some interest to any involved high school teacher.

Journal of Aesthetics and Art Criticism. 1941. q. Membership. (Nonmembers $15). Herbert M. Schueller. Wayne State Univ. Press, 5980 Cass Ave., Room 205, Detroit, Mich., 48202. Illus., index, adv. Circ: 2,650. Sample. Vol. ends: Summer. Microform: UM. Reprint: AMS, Abrahams.

Indexed: ArtI, MusicI, PsyAb. *Bk. Rev:* 15, 50–500 words, signed. *Aud:* Ac.

Published by the American Society for Aesthetics to "promote study, research, discussion, and publication in aesthetics." The Society is supported by the major art galleries and universities in America. Long, well-documented articles on the theory of art and literature are written by recognized experts in the field and individual issues are sometimes given over to a single topic. An excellent 25-page (average length) bibliography, arranged by subject, of the previous year's publications in aesthetics and related fields appears in the summer issue. An invaluable study aid and source of reference to students of the arts and related disciplines, from a philosophical, scientific, or theoretical standpoint. A useful addition for medium to large-sized academic libraries, particularly as its scope is so broad it can be used in programs other than art.

Journal of the History of Ideas; a quarterly devoted to cultural and intellectual history. 1940. q. $7.50 (Libraries $10). Philip P. Wiener. City Univ. of New York, Graduate Center, 33 W. 42d St., New York, N.Y. 10036. Index, adv. Circ: 3,500. Vol. ends: Oct. Microform: Publisher. Reprint: Johnson.

Indexed: HistAb, PhilosI, SSHum. *Aud:* Ac, Ga.

Contributors to this journal, professionals in their fields, seek to isolate and explain the germinal ideas behind significant intellectual movements. Many articles are concerned with showing the influences of one important figure or school of thought upon another. Devoted to "cultural and intellectual history," the journal usually contains eight or ten contributions dealing with the history of philosophy, of literature and the arts, of the natural and social sciences, of religion, and political and social movements. The editorial board includes such distinguished scholars as George Boas, Peter Gay, Jack H. Hexter, Paul O. Kristeller, and Harry Levin. Not only of value to the student of intellectual history, but to anyone seeking to understand current developments in the theoretical basis of an academic discipline. It is for the educated general reader as well as the student.

Journal of Popular Culture. 1967. q. $8 (Students $4). Ray B. Browne. Bowling Green Univ., Bowling Green, Ohio. 43402. Illus., adv. Circ: 2,000. Microform: UM.

Indexed: MLA. *Bk. rev:* 10–15, 800 words, signed. *Aud:* Ga, Ac. *Jv:* V.

Good short articles (about six to ten) on popular culture, including folklore, in each issue. Sample titles: "The Film and the Folk: Authentic Nostalgia" and "The American Western: Myth and Anti-Myth." Usual departments: "In-Depth," treating a particular subject, such as "Black Popular Culture" or "The Western" in from about five to ten short articles; and "The Film: A Supplement," in which five or six brief articles treat diverse facets of film art. The "Review Essays" department appears regularly. It consists of four or five long book reviews running from about eight to ten pages in length. "The editorial policy of the *Journal of Popular Culture* is dedicated to 'Popular Culture' in the broadest sense of the term." Areas include both the general and the special, e.g., folklore, Black Culture, football, bibliography in the field of science fiction, movies, western literature, baseball, discography (at times a department), popular music, and sociology. This journal has wide applicability and high interest value, both in scholarship and teaching, as well as in pure entertainment. (F.M.)

Journal of Popular Film. 1972. q. $4. Samuel Grogg, Jr. Bowling Green Popular Press, 101 Univ. Hall, Bowling Green State Univ., Bowling Green, Ohio 43403. Illus., index, adv. Sample. Vol. ends: Fall. Refereed.

Bk. rev: 5–10, 500 words, signed. *Aud:* Ac, Ga.

A nice addition from the university which started it all with the *Journal of Popular Culture.* Here the approach is pretty much the same, the difference being that the scope is narrowed to film. Critics, who are primarily from university campuses, take a careful look at films made for people who only saw a university through those same films. Most, although not all, of the studies are historical, e.g., "Hollywood and World War I," or "Monster Movies: They Came From Beneath the Fifties." Usually some book reviews and bibliographies are included. The advisory board is impressive—Andrew Sarris and Otto Preminger, to name two. The journal is just beginning, but as a study of movies and how they reflect our culture, the magazine will please almost any movie buff and serious student of the cultural scene.

Journal of Value Inquiry. 1967. q. $9. Ed. bd. Martinus Nijhoff N.V., Lange Voorhout 9-11 Vox 269, The Hague, Netherlands. Index, adv.

Bk. rev: 5–6, essays, signed. *Aud:* Ac, Ga.

A philosophical journal which should have a wider readership, particularly among informed laymen who may have little basic interest in philosophy. The two to three articles and the panel discussions are conducted by some of the world's leading thinkers, and, more important, they are involved with questions concerning everyday value judgments. More specifically, the contributors consider "the nature, origin, experi-

ence and scope of value in general, as well as . . . problems of values in ethics, social and legal theory and practice, science, aesthetics and methodology. The journal is committed to no position or program." Such articles as: "One being morally justified," or "Aspects of contemporary nihilism" indicate the scope. The articles are usually written clearly enough to be understood by the educated layman. The book reviews are excellent. A major philosophical and interdisciplinary journal for larger public and academic libraries.

Journal of World History. 1935. q. $15. Guy S. Metraux. UNESCO, Editions de la Baconniere S.A., Neuchatel, Switzerland. Index, adv. Circ: 1,500. Microform: UM.

Indexed: HistAb, SSHum. *Aud:* Ac.

Published by UNESCO's International Commission for a History of Scientific and Cultural Development of Humanity. Articles are by scholars from many countries. The text is primarily in English and French with some Spanish. Emphasis is on cultural history in the broadest sense of the word, especially the history and evolution of culture, contacts between cultures, the history of ideas, and cultural creativity. In view of its broad scope, it is particularly well suited for both undergraduate and graduate study. In most cases, however, the *Journal of the History of Ideas* will meet the needs of the average library.

The New Scholar; a journal of graduate studies in the social sciences. 1969. bi-a. $5.50. Bernon H. Kjonegaard. College of Arts and Letters, San Diego State College, San Diego, Calif. 92115. Illus., index, adv. Circ: 800. Sample. Vol. ends: Spring. Refereed.

Bk. rev: 10–12, 1500 words, signed. *Aud:* Ac.

Directed to social scientists and graduate students in the field, this is a forum of opinion on everything from primitive warfare to comments on job discrimination. The 100 or so pages will fascinate anyone who enjoys *The Journal of Popular Culture,* i.e., where else can you find an article like "A structural analysis of an American family's annual group deer hunt?" As the editor points out, "there is less an emphasis on jargon" than in most journals of this type, and even the layman will enjoy the well-written articles. Each issue features extensive book reviews and bibliographies. An off-beat magazine which deserves wider attention.

The Newsletter on the State of the Culture. 1968. m. (Sept–June). $10. Harry Smith. 5 Beekman St., New York, N.Y. 10038. Illus. Circ: 2,500. Sample. Vol. ends: Dec.

Aud: Ga, Ac. *Jv:* V.

A very specialized monthly report on culture as applied to the literary scene and little magazine publishing, by the editor of a top-quality magazine, *The Smith.* Librarians responsible for magazine acquisitions should subscribe, if only for name changes, new magazines, and cessations. Colleges and universities with creative writing courses should also have this, both for the news and the gossip. This goes along with the *Small Press Review*. (D.D.)

Washington International Arts Letter. 1962. 10/yr. $21.60. Allied Business Consultants, 115 Fifth St., S.E., Washington, D.C 20003. Illus. Circ: 17,000. Sample.

Aud: Ac, Ga.

An eight-page newsletter at a steep price—but it may be worth it to some libraries. The editors cover "the practical aspects of grants and other forms of assistance to the arts and cites names and addresses of those who are doing things." In a word, the data is invaluable for anyone seeking up-to-date information on where to apply for money. Short items trace the progress of congressional bills likely to provide funds, and there is a state-by-state report on prizes, state aid, grants, etc. which are available. In a way, this is a handy supplement to the *Foundation Guide* for the man or woman interested in literature and the arts. Send for a sample.

DANCE

Basic Periodicals

Ejh: Dance Magazine; Hs: *Dance Magazine, Dance and Dancers;* Ga: *Dance Magazine, Dance and Dancers, Square Dancing;* Jc: *Dance Magazine, Dance and Dancers, Dance Perspectives;* Ac: *Dance Perspectives, Dance Magazine, Dance and Dancers.*

Basic Abstracts and Indexes

Music Index.

Cessations

Ballroom Dance Magazine, Ballet Today, Balletopics.

Country Dance and Song. 1968. a./supplementary newsletters. $5 (Libraries, educational organizations and undergraduates $3). John Dunn. The Secretary, Country Dance and Song Society of America, 55 Christopher St., New York, N.Y. 10014. Illus.

Bk. rev: Various numbers, length. *Aud:* Ga, Hs, Ejh.

Departments of this fifty-some-page publication, with examples, are as follows: Articles—"Folk Dance in the Western World," Dances—"I Care not for These Ladies," "The Busy Body," and reviews of books and records. Short featurettes include such disarming titles as "The Lasciviousness of Country Dancing," "The Philadelphia Mummers," and "The Broccoli Tradition." Occasional poems are used. Photo reproduction quality is high. Noteworthy events and coming attractions in the field are included. (F.M.)

Dance and Dancers. 1950. m. $11.20. Peter Williams. Hansom Books, Artillery Mansions, 75 Victoria St.,

London, SW1H, England, OJQ. Illus., adv. Circ: 19,000. Sample. Vol. ends: Dec.

Aud: Ac, Hs, Ga.

A nicely illustrated magazine, issued in England but international in its coverage of ballet and modern dance. Excellent reviews of recitals, articles on dance and dancers, education, and all topics of interest to both the professional dancer and the viewer. Particularly useful for the many illustrations, usually photographs, which make up a good part of the content. News notes, record reviews and some general gossip are included. In view of its scope, of interest to students and laymen alike, and a good acquisition for medium to large-sized public and academic libraries.

Dance Magazine. 1926. m. $10. William Como. Danad Publishing Co., Inc., 10 Columbus Circle, New York, N.Y. 10019. Illus., adv. Circ: 80,000. Sample. Vol. ends: Dec. Microform: UM.

Indexed: RG. *Bk. rev:* 5, length varies, signed. *Aud:* Ga, Ac, Hs, Ejh.

A general dance magazine which covers all aspects of the subject from ballet to biography both on a national and international scale. The brief articles move from traditional to modern, from theory to practice. The editor claims the magazine "expands dance perspectives geographically, intellectually and visually." There is little argument with that, particularly the visual—the numerous photographs are excellent. Regular features include information on tours, schools, costumes, dance companies, etc. There is an annual directory of dancers, choreographers, and dance features. Suitable for adults and children from junior high on.

Dance News. 1942. m. $4.50. Mrs. Helen V. Atlas. 119 W. 57th St., New York, N.Y. 10019. Illus., adv. Circ: 13,500. Sample. Vol. ends: June.

Aud: Ga, Ac.

A tabloid newspaper which offers international coverage of the current dance scene. Comprehensive news concerning performances, dancers, choreographers, schools, colleges, and companies and other related items of interest to dance fans is presented. The paper, which runs approximately sixteen pages, also contains evaluative reviews of performances. An excellent source for dance news, and should be in all larger academic and public library collections.

Dance Perspectives. 1959. q. $8. Selma J. Cohen. Dance Perspectives Foundation. 29 E. 9th St., New York, N.Y. 10003. Illus. Circ: 2,000. Sample. Vol. ends: Winter.

Indexed: MusicI. *Aud:* Ac.

Publishes critical and historical monographs or symposia. An entire issue is devoted to a single topic treated by several authors, or often a single author writes the entire issue except for an introduction. The authors are notable people in the dance or related fields—including designers, musicians, anthropologists, and sociologists. Frequently, the author discusses and explains his own work. The cover design, illustrations, typography, etc. are arranged with care to produce a handsome format.

English Dance & Song. 1936. q. $2.40. Tony Wales. English Folk Dance and Song Soc., Cecil Sharp House, 2 Regents Park Rd., London NW1, England. Illus., adv. Circ: 12,000.

Indexed: MusicI. *Bk. rev:* Various number, length. *Aud:* Ga, Hs, Ejh.

A small-print slick with diminutive, medium-quality photos. The few "Songs and Dances," including musical scores, are valuable inclusions. "Reviews" is divided into "Bookshelf," "Record Rack" (a sizeable selection, about six to ten albums), and "Live Folk," which deals with folk concerts. Six to eight brief articles of about three or four pages each make up the first half of *English Dance & Song.* Style, both editorial and reader, is light and witty. Crossword puzzles, letters, and various notes round out the contents. Articles are newsy and fit in with notes, puzzles, and cartoons. Features interspersed among the articles are much more valuable. These include "Between the Grooves," "for which readers are asked to provide queries, comments and answers to previous queries, on folk music records—past and present;" and "Songs under the Microscope," "for which readers are asked to provide queries on songs, tunes, dances or folklore, and answers or comments on previous queries." At heart, *English Dance & Song* exists for the enjoyment of its subscribers and for the furtherance of active participation in the field. (F.M.)

Northern Junket. 1950. bi-m. $3 for 12 nos. Ralph G. Page. 117 Washington St., Keene, N.H. 03431. Circ: 1,000.

Aud: Ga.

Directed to New England callers and square dancers, this is a typical local publication for dance groups. It presents approximately 40 pages of news, articles, dances, and calls and even anecdotes and a few recipes. Usually included are two or three, five or six page articles related to square dancing. Hardly essential for most libraries, it serves to indicate the type of material which may be available in the region.

Sets in Order. See *Square Dancing.*

Square Dance. 1945. $5. Stan and Cathie Burdick. Box 788, Sandusky, Ohio 44870. Illus., index, adv. Circ: 10,000. Sample. Vol. ends: Dec.

Aud: Ga, Hs.

Since the last edition of this book, the magazine has undergone a number of changes—all to the good. The 62-page pocket-sized title includes numerous short articles on all aspects of the art from leadership, round and square dancing, to teaching tips and equipment reports. The tone is chatty, folksy and, at times, humorous. It is strong on features which include record reviews, book notes, news of events, editorials, letters, etc. A regular feature: calls and dances for various levels of skill. The magazine fits the needs of all square dance fans: teachers, leaders, callers, and dancers. Will be of as much interest to teenagers as to adults. See also *Square Dancing*—a competitor which was earlier known as *Sets in Order.*

Square Dancing: the official magazine of the sets in order American Square Dance Society (Formerly: *Sets in Order*). 1948. m. $5. Bob Osgood. 462 North Robertson Blvd., Los Angeles, Calif. 90048. Illus., adv. Circ: 22,463. Sample. Vol. ends: Dec.

Aud: Ga, Hs, Ejh.

Published "for and by square dancers and for the general enjoyment of all." Each issue contains approximately 15 articles on subjects pertaining to: training for callers and teachers, party ideas, club organization, and national and international news. The editorial aim is the promotion, protection, and perpetuation of the activity. Regular features include dances and calls, record reviews, fashions, and caller of the month and paging the round dancers. Should have a place in public and school libraries where there is an interest in the subject. Other publications include *Caller/Teacher Manuals* and a yearbook containing dances presented in *Square Dancing.*

EARTH SCIENCES

Basic Periodicals

(Note: Titles mentioned below for the General Adult or High School are of a nontechnical level appropriate for some, but not every public and high school library. Please see annotations for details.)

Ga: *Earth Science, Mineral Digest, Mineralogical Record, Rocks and Minerals;* Hs: *Geotimes, Earth Science, Rocks and Minerals;* Jc: *Geotimes, Journal of Geological Education;* Ac: *American Association of Petroleum Geologists. Bulletin, Geological Society of America Bulletin, Journal of Geophysical Research.* (See text below for large range of important subfields in the geological sciences.)

Basic Abstracts and Indexes

Bibliography and Index of Geology

Introduction

The periodicals in this section are mainly research journals found in most academic libraries. Concentration has been largely on high quality U.S. publications covering aspects of geology, geochemistry, geophysics, mineralogy, paleontology, petrology, and petroleum geology, sedimentology, and seismology. Journals on oceanography are listed in a separate section. The selections are but a sampling of the distinguished journals required by sizable research libraries. A few titles of a less technical nature, or of popular interest have also been included. (See also Atmospheric Sciences and Oceanography Sections.)

American Association of Petroleum Geologists. Bulletin. 1917. m. $45. Frank E. Kottlowski. Amer. Assn. of Petroleum Geologists, 1444 S. Boulder Ave., Box 979, Tulsa, Okla. 74101. Illus., index, adv. Circ: 16,000. Sample. Vol. ends: no. 12. Refereed. Microform: Canner; UM. Reprint: Johnson.

Indexed: ASTI, BioAb, ChemAb, EngI, SCI. *Bk. rev:* 5–6, 500 words, signed. *Aud:* Sa, Ac.

The AAPG is the largest geological society in the world; moreover, half the geologists in the U.S. are members. The range of topics presented in its *Bulletin* is impressive. Primarily directed at petroleum geologists, a major focus of the journal is, and always has been, exploration geology, which is concerned with finding deposits of oil and gas. Nonetheless, its scope is by no means restricted to these minerals, but includes uranium, water, coal, other ores related to sedimentary rocks, as well. Similarly, further subject areas extend to sedimentology, stratigraphy, reservoirs, drifting continents, etc. Selected issues (June and August) annually publish statistical data pertinent to the oil and gas industry, exclusively for North America. Research papers can be lengthy, and shorter investigations appear as geological notes. Noteworthy departments include "Association Round Tables," which features abstracts of papers presented at various meetings, as well as the Proceedings of the AAPG. Also published are news items of professional interest, calendars, and personalia. The book review section frequently contains a long checklist, by country, of recent publications. An authoritative and basic journal for geological collections.

American Geophysical Union. Transactions. 1919. m. $5. A. F. Spilhaus, Jr. Amer. Geophysical Union, 1707 L St., N.W., Washington, D. C. 20036. Illus., index, adv. Circ: 10,500. Sample. Vol. ends: no. 12. Microform: MF. Reprint: Johnson.

Indexed: BioAb, EngI, Met&GeoAb. *Bk. rev:* 6, 450–500 words, signed. *Aud:* Sa, Ac.

This is the nonspecialist publication of the American Geophysical Union, well known for a number of excellent and authoritative research journals (see for example, *Journal of Geophysical Research*). The periodical is concerned with the "interface of all aspects of geophysics with society, and of semitechnical reviews of currently exciting areas of geophysics." About

one or two feature articles lead off each issue, on such subjects as geodesy, seismology, planetology, oceanography, hydrogology, and tectonophysics. Frequently, conferences of interest to the AGU are reviewed in detail. The remainder of each issue carries news, both of the organization and its membership, as well as international developments, calendar, etc. A recent department, "Geophysical Abstracts in Press," contains abstracts of papers to appear in forthcoming issues of other journals published by the AGU. This section, plus tables of contents of selected Russian journals translated by the AGU, are most useful to librarians. A good book review section is fairly comprehensive. The publication provides, in nonspecialist terms, a good overview of trends and events in geophysical research. For academic libraries.

American Journal of Science. 1818. m. (except July and Sept.) $15. Ed. bd. Kline Geology Lab., Yale Univ., Box 2161 Yale Station, New Haven, Conn. 06520. Illus., index. Circ: 2,900. Vol. ends: Dec. Refereed. Microform: UM, Princeton, Canner. Reprint: Johnson.

Indexed: BioAb, ChemAb, EngI, SCI. *Bk. rev:* 1–3, 500–1000 words, signed. *Aud:* Sa, Ac.

Originally entitled *Silliman's Journal*, the publication has the distinction of being the first scientific journal published in the United States. Although it had a brief career as a general science periodical, this path was short-lived, however, and it has been a general geological journal for most of the duration. Today, papers report on original research in most branches of the geological sciences. This is an old and authoritative journal for any academic collection. Libraries having vol. 1 have a prestige item on their hands. (Note: Since 1959, the same journal has been publishing *Radiocarbon* (s-a, $30.), devoted, in part, to tabular data on radiocarbon dating.)

American Mineralogist. 1916. bi-m. $40. William T. Holser. Mineralogical Soc. of America, 2201 M St., N.W., Washington, D.C. 20037. Illus., index, adv. Circ: 4,200. Vol. ends: no. 6. Refereed. Microform: Microcard, Princeton. Reprint: Kraus.

Indexed: ASTI, ChemAb, EngI, MetAb, SCI. *Bk. rev:* 3–4, 250–300 words, signed. *Aud:* Sa, Ac.

One of the leading journals in the field and the official journal of the Mineralogical Society. Original contributions are published in such areas as crystallography, petrology, and some geochemistry, as well as mineralogy, including the descriptive science, properties of minerals, mineral occurrence and deposits, apparatus and equipment pertinent to the field, etc. Special departments in each issue are worth mentioning. "Mineralogical Notes" contains short reports, generally on new data of known minerals. "New Mineral Names" gives brief summaries of new minerals as reported elsewhere in the literature, and includes discredited names. Also included are news and notices for the profession. A first-choice selection for any collection in the geological sciences. The Mineralogical Society of America, in cooperation with the Mineralogical Society (United Kingdom) is one of the sponsors of *Mineralogical Abstracts*, an important abstracting service in the field. See *Mineralogical Magazine* for details.

Bibliography and Index of Geology. See Abstracts and Indexes Section.

Canadian Journal of Earth Sciences. 1964. m. $24. J. W. Ambrose. National Research Council of Canada, Ottawa 7, Canada. Illus., index. Circ: 3,200. Sample. Vol. ends: Dec. Refereed.

Indexed: ChemAb, Bibl.&Ind.Geol., Sci. *Aud:* Sa, Ac.

Part of the Canadian Journals of Research group. A broadly based publication representing many of the geological sciences. Research papers and short notes deal with such subjects as geophysics, mineralogy, paleontology, stratigraphy, geochemistry, sedimentology, petrology, etc. Since much of the fieldwork for these investigations has taken place in North America and Canada, in particular, Canadian libraries will certainly want it. A good, authoritative publication for any academic library.

Comments on Earth Sciences: Geophysics. 1970. bi-m. $35. Peter J. Smith and J. A. Jacobs. Gordon and Breach Science Publishers, Inc., 440 Park Ave. S., New York, N.Y. Illus. Sample. Vol. ends: no. 6. Refereed.

Aud: Sa, Ac.

In a new concept of the review journal, the publication offers critical discussion of recent advances in geophysics, as shown through the published literature. Contributors do not submit manuscripts to the journals. Rather, a select group of "correspondents"—some with well-established reputations, others, active young scientists chosen by the editors (coordinators)—regularly review in short articles the significant literature in the field. Frequently, their own research may be included. All fields of the subject are represented, as well as related disciplines such as geochemistry, physical oceanography, seismology, etc. Attendant bibliographies may be fairly lengthy. A good, tutorial-type publication, particularly for undergraduates and nonspecialists, and is recommended for academic libraries supporting the area of the geological sciences.

Earth and Extraterrestrial Sciences. 1969. irreg. $53. A. G. W. Cameron. Gordon and Breach Science Publishers, Inc., 150 Fifth Ave., New York, N.Y. 10011. Illus. Circ: 300. Vol. ends: irreg. Microform: Gordon & Breach.

Bk. rev: irreg., 100–150 words, signed. *Aud:* Sa, Ac.

The publication reports on conferences, symposia, etc., and news in the field of the geological, astronomical, atmospheric, oceanographic, and space sciences. Going beyond straight reporting, issues frequently include introductory progress reports on the literature of the topics under review. Frequently, reports are published before the official proceedings are relased, and may contain lengthy bibliographies. The intent of the journal is laudable, i.e., to get research results to the user as quickly as possible, and to serve both specialist and nonspecialist alike. But the price to libraries (particularly when its periodicity is not well established) makes the publication far more of a luxury than any kind of necessity.

Earth Science. 1946. bi-m. $3. Mary G. Cornwell. Midwest Federation of Mineralogical Societies, Earth Science Publishing Co., Box 550, Downers Grove, Ill. 60515. Illus., index, adv. Circ: 5,500. Vol. ends: no. 6. Microform: UM. Reprint: Johnson.

Bk. rev: 5–8, 100–200 words. *Aud:* Ga, Ac, Hs.

According to the editors, about 20 percent of the subscribers to this popular rockhound magazine are universities, colleges, and senior and junior high schools. Whether for educator, student, or hobbyist, the magazine serves as a good point of departure for nontechnical articles on timely aspects of earth science, plus the usual curiosa of gems, fossils, etc. Well-illustrated articles are frequently contributed by specialists. Of special interest to the hobbyists are the pages on club news, notices, etc., although admittedly regionalized. Good for schools with earth science clubs, plus interested public libraries with rockhound clientele. (See also *Rocks and Minerals*.)

Earth Science Reviews. 1966. q. $21. Elsevier Publishing Co., Box 211, Amsterdam, The Netherlands. Illus., index, adv. Sample. Vol. ends: no. 4. Refereed.

Indexed: SCI. *Bk. rev:* 7, 250–500 words, signed. *Aud:* Sa, Ac.

Subtitled the "international magazine for geoscientists," the publication sweeps over a large number of fields, and employs the term "reviews" in a two-fold sense. The first section of the journal is dedicated to the standard type of critical, comprehensive review paper contributed by authorities in the field. Topics reviewed in recent volumes have included mineralogy, geochemistry, petrology, stratigraphy, geophysics, volcanology, geotectonics, glaciology, sedimentology, paleontology, historical geology, geomorphology, economic geology, engineering geology, soil science, and climatology. About two to three major papers appear in each issue. The reviewing, in the news sense, consists of forthcoming events, new books, a general interest article, contents of recent journals (drawn from other Elsevier publications), as well as professional news. A comprehensive publication for academic libraries.

Earthquake Information. See Government Magazines/ United States Section.

Economic Geology and the Bulletin of the Society of Economic Geologists. 1905. 8/yr. $15. Brian J. Skinner. Economic Geology, c/o J. Kalliokowski, Business Ed., Box 74, Mich. Technological Univ., Houghton, Mich. 49931. Illus., index, adv. Circ: 6,000. Vol. ends: no. 8. Refereed. Microform: UM. Reprint: Johnson.

Indexed: ASTI, ChemAb, EngI, SCI. *Bk. rev:* 5, 150–200 words, signed. *Aud:* Sa, Ac.

On a less theoretical level, the journal is devoted to technical papers concerned with the application of geological principles to exploiting the Earth's resources, including selected studies on mining. A major portion of recent issues deal with mineral deposits: their genesis, classification, determination in environment, etc. The publication is, as well, the official organ of the Society and contains a number of departments of interest to the membership. In addition to "Scientific News and Notes," and a book review section which includes a lengthy checklist of books received, the journal also publishes selected tables of contents, in part, of journals of general geologic interest. An excellent, applied journal for any collection in the geological sciences interested in this field.

Engineering Geology. 1965. 4/yr. $18.75. Ed. bd. Elsevier Publishing Co., Box 211, Amsterdam, The Netherlands. Illus., index. Vol. ends: no. 4. Refereed.

Indexed: SCI. *Bk. rev:* 5–6, 300 words, signed. *Aud:* Sa, Ac.

Large engineering endeavors have always been intimately associated with principles and methodologies in the geological sciences, e.g., drilling for oil; building power stations beneath ground surfaces; using radioactive tracers to uncover leaks in dams, etc. This title forges a closer link between two related fields, by drawing together papers from both engineering and geology, with particular emphasis on geotechnical studies. The journal carries not only research reports, but also selected review articles. A valuable, authoritative, international publication for civil engineering, as well as geology collections.

Geochimica et Cosmochimica Acta. 1950. m. $75. D. M. Shaw. Pergamon Press, Maxwell House, Fairview Pk., Elmsford, N.Y. 10523. Illus., index, adv. Sample. Vol. ends: Dec. Refereed. Microform: Maxwell. Reprint: Maxwell.

Indexed: ChemAb, SCI. *Bk. rev:* 1–3, 400 words, signed. *Aud:* Sa, Ac.

A publication of both the international Geochemical Society and the Meteoritical Society. High quality papers by authorities report on all aspects of geochemistry, including studies of meteorites, and the chemical composition of extraterrestrial matter, as well as

the Earth. Both full-length articles and communications of smaller scope are published. A prominent, interdisciplinary publication sponsored by two important societies. For academic libraries.

Of course, strong collections in the geological sciences will need more than one representative title in the geochemical field. Attention is drawn to three other well-known publications, *Chemical Geology*, published by Elsevier, *Geochemical Journal*, sponsored by the Geochemical Society of Japan, as well as *Geochemistry International*, the English translation of *Geokhimiya*, put out by the American Geological Institute.

Geological Magazine. 1864. bi-m. $24. Ed. bd. Cambridge Univ. Press, 32 E. 57th St., New York, N.Y. 10022. Illus., index, adv. Sample. Vol. ends: no. 6. Refereed. Reprint: Dawson.

Indexed: BioAb, BritTech, ChemAb, EngI, SCI. *Bk. rev:* 5–6, 400 words, signed. *Aud:* Sa, Ac.

Published by Cambridge University Press since 1970, the journal is one of the oldest geological periodicals still in existence, and has incorporated *The Geologist*, founded in 1858. The present editorial practice is to embrace all fields of earth science (including, for example, marine geology, palaeontology, and the like), although papers lean toward descriptive geology. Articles are shorter than comprehensive, scholarly studies, to permit enough diversity of material in each issue. Similarly, papers are not restricted to regional studies, but are international in scope. Book reviews are either essay type (frequently involving one long, critical essay) or short reports. A checklist of recent literature supplies a good source for acquisitions in this field. A well-known, well-rounded, authoritative and diversified periodical for academic collections in geology.

Geological Society. Journal. (Formerly: ***Geological Society of London. Quarterly Journal***). 1845. q. $23.25. Ed. bd. Scottish Academic Press, 25 Petrth St., Edinburgh, EH3 SDW, Scotland. Illus., index. Vol. ends: no. 4. Refereed. Reprint: Kraus.

Indexed: BioAb, EngI. *Aud:* Sa, Ac.

Formerly called *Geological Society of London. Quarterly Journal.* The venerable Geological Society, London, was one of the leading scientific societies in the nineteenth century. Its journal is not only the oldest extant general geological periodical in the United Kingdom, but also its most prominent. High quality and authoritative papers explore all areas of geology, including paleontology, stratigraphy, and sedimentology. An important and distinguished acquisition for any collection in the geological sciences.

Geological Society of America. Bulletin. 1888. m. $50. Bennie W. Troxel. Geological Soc. of America, P.O. Box 1719, Boulder, Colo. 80302. Illus., index. Circ:

8,500. Sample. Vol. ends: Dec. Refereed. Microform: Canner, Princeton. Reprint: Carrolton (indexes only).

Indexed: ASTI, BioAb, ChemAb, EngI, SCI. *Aud:* Sa, Ac.

The Society's official publication is one of the most prestigious general journals in the geological sciences, certainly in this country and probably throughout the world. Papers are representative of any branch of the science, including such fields as geophysics, geochemistry, stratigraphy, and sedimentology. A good balance of subject matter is maintained; and studies are not particularly regionalized. Both full-length papers and short notes and "discussions" are included in each issue. Issues also carry advance abstracts of forthcoming papers. The *Bulletin,* imperative for every academic collection, is the basis for every geology library. A number of other publications of the GSA are also important and most academic collections will probably subscribe to some of these as well. Whereas the *Bulletin* publishes papers of a certain length, longer papers appear in the Society's *Memoirs* and *Special Papers* series; indeed, many of the papers appearing in either one of these may really comprise a long, detailed monograph, treating one subject exhaustively. Issued since 1969 have been the GSA's *Abstracts with Programs,* consisting of abstracts of papers given at meetings organized by the Society, and detailed advance programs of these symposia.

Geological Society of London. Quarterly Journal. See *Geological Society. Journal.*

Geophysical Journal of the Royal Astronomical Society. 1958. irreg. $37.50/v. Blackwell Scientific Publns., Ltd., Osney Mead, Oxford OX 2 OEL, England. Illus., index. Circ: 1,500. Sample. Vol. ends: no. 5; 3–4 v./yr. Refereed. Microform: UM.

Indexed: ChemAb, Met&GeoAb, SciAb, SCI. *Aud:* Sa, Ac.

It is not usually common for astronomical societies to publish geophysical journals. This periodical, however, is the extension of the *Geophysical Supplement to the Monthly Notices of the Royal Astronomical Society.* The journal covers all aspects of the physics of the Earth, including "geophysics at sea; work on the upper atmosphere," as related to atmospheric conditions of the Earth. Some studies on palaeomagnetism are also included. Generally, research articles and short letters are published, although some review papers appear from time to time. In the fifteen years that *Geophysical Journal* has been in existence as a periodical in its own right, the publication has achieved prominence as an authoritative research journal. For all good collections in the geological sciences.

Geophysics. 1936. bi-m. $15. Thomas R. Lafehr. Soc. of Exploration Geophysicists, Box 3098, Tulsa, Okla. 74101. Illus., index, adv. Circ: 9,000. Sample. Vol.

ends: Dec. Refereed. Microform: UM, Soc. of Exploration Geophysicists.

Indexed: ASTI, BioAb, ChemAb, EngI, SciAb, SCI. *Bk. rev:* 5–6, 300 words, signed. *Aud:* Sa, Ac.

Now approaching its fourth decade, this official journal of the Society publishes technical papers both on the various areas of geophysics and the more applied art of geophysical prospecting. Articles and short notes report on such subjects as marine operations, gravity, geomagnetism, seismic theory, mining geophysics, and computer techniques for manipulating geophysical data. A fair portion of the periodical is dedicated to miscellaneous departments, including abstracts of the literature from selected geophysical journals, patent abstracts, new products, news of the Society, and personalia. A good, authoritative publication covering both scientific and applied aspects of the field. Recommended for most academic libraries.

Geotimes. 1956. m. $4. Wendell Cochran. Amer. Geological Inst., 2201 M St., N.W., Washington, D.C. 20037. Illus., index, adv. Circ: 40,000. Sample. Vol. ends: no. 12. Reprint: Johnson.

Bk. rev: 3, 250–400 words, signed. *Aud:* Sa, Ac, Hs.

Published as a service to the 18 supporting societies of the American Geological Institute, the magazine supplies general information and interpretations on latest research activities and society-sponsored events for the geological community. Its subject range is as broad as the interests of the supporting societies—paleontology to information science—and touches on aspects of government, legislation, education, and industry. Articles are both staff-written and contributed by well-known specialists; the tone is nontechnical. Also included are the usual calendars, news bits, personalia, and classifieds. A useful, nonspecialist magazine for geology collections, high school through academic.

International Association for Mathematical Geology. Journal. 1969. q. $35. D. M. Merriam. Plenum Publishing Corp., 227 W. 17th St., New York, N.Y. 10011. Illus., index. Sample. Vol. ends: no. 4. Refereed.

Bk. rev: 6, 600 words, signed. *Aud:* Sa, Ac.

In recent years a trend toward publication of research papers in mathematical or statistical geology has come to the fore. This journal, official organ also of the Association, attempts to draw together under a common title papers dealing with the application of mathematics to the geological sciences. Titles such as "Review of Data Processing in the Earth Sciences," or "Statistical Analysis of Tectonic Patterns" are indicative of the scope. For research collections.

International Geology Review. 1959. m. $150. Ed. bd. Amer. Geological Inst., 2201 M St., N.W., Washington, D.C. 20037. Illus., index. Circ: 700. Vol. ends: Dec. Refereed.

Indexed: ChemAb. *Aud:* Sa, Ac.

A translation journal of some of the significant Russian literature in all phases of the geological sciences. About 15 papers, representing a wide sampling of journals from the USSR, are translated in each issue. Occasionally, a chapter of a monograph also appears. A monthly feature of this journal is the prepublication announcement of new geologic works, taken from the weekly bibliographic periodical, *Novye Knigi* (New Books). Russian titles therein have been translated, and a brief summary of the publication given. The price will be a deterrent to small academic libraries, but research collections will certainly need it.

Journal of Atmospheric and Terrestrial Physics. See Atmospheric Sciences Section.

Journal of Geological Education. 1951. 5/yr. $10. Joseph L. Weitz. National Assn. of Geology Teachers, 2201 M St., N.W., Washington, D.C. 20037. Illus., index. Circ: 4,000. Sample. Vol. ends: no. 5 (Nov.).

Bk. rev: 8–10, 300–600 words, signed. *Aud:* Ejh, Hs, Ac.

Primarily for earth science teachers or professional educators from the junior high through college levels. Each issue has about four or five features, many of which are short review articles appropriate for study by students, as well as educators, on items of current geologic interest. Articles on improvements in teaching, guides, classroom projects, and laboratory and field work techniques are also contributed. Short reports are dedicated exclusively to teaching methodology. Both books and films are reviewed. Some news of the NAGT is also communicated from time to time. For every school library or institution supporting a curriculum in earth science.

Journal of Geophysical Research. 1896. 36/yr. $75. Ed. bd. Amer. Geophysical Union, 2100 Pennsylvania Ave., N.W., Washington, D.C. 20037. Illus., index, adv. Circ: 9,500. Sample. Vol. ends: Dec. Refereed. Reprint: Johnson.

Indexed: BioAb, ChemAb, EngI, Meteor&GeoastAb, SciAb, SCI. *Aud:* Sa, Ac.

The journal is one of the world's leading publications of geophysical research, devoted to the "full spectrum of the physics of the Earth and its environment in space." Papers represent comprehensive and authoritative studies by specialists. Three issues appear monthly. On the first of the month, the issue is devoted entirely to space physics (including solar physics), and the physics of planetary atmospheres. Papers appearing on the tenth of the month center around the physics and chemistry of solid earth, the geophysics of other planets, and materials related to geo-

physical problems. The last issue, published on the twentieth, concerns the physics and chemistry of our atmosphere, oceans and ocean basins, and air-sea interactions. An important and primary publication for every geological collection.

Journal of Paleontology. 1927. bi-m. $38. Ed. bd. Allen Press, Lawrence, Kan. 66044. Illus., index. Circ: 3,200. Sample. Vol. ends: no. 6. Refereed. Microform: UM, Canner. Reprint: Johnson.

Indexed: BioAb, ChemAb. *Bk. rev:* 5, 400–700 words, signed. *Aud:* Sa, Ac.

The publication is sponsored jointly by the Paleontological Society (Jan., May, Sept. issues) and the Society of Economic Paleontologists and Mineralogists (Mar., July, Nov. issues). Research papers touch on most branches of paleontology and include studies on both vertebrates and invertebrates, micropaleontology, paleobotany, stratigraphic paleontology, paleoecology, and paleobiogeography. Occasional review papers, items on nomenclature, and notes and announcements are included. Illustrations are superior. The journal is an excellent vehicle for publications concerning the occurrence, relationship, and evolutionary development of organisms through geologic times. For every biological and geological collection. Another excellent and authoritative publication in the field is the British journal *Paleontology*, sponsored by the Paleontological Society, United Kingdom. Good collections will need both journals.

Journal of Petrology. 1960. 3/yr. $19. Ed. bd. Oxford Univ. Press, Ely House, London, England. Illus., index. Circ: 1,800. Sample. Vol. ends: no. 3. Refereed. Reprint: Dawson.

Indexed: ChemAb, SCI. *Aud:* Sa, Ac.

Scholarly, authoritative, and strengthened by an international advisory board, the journal publishes research papers on such topics as the origin, classification, and occurrence of rocks, the physics and chemistry of rocks and minerals (including lunar rocks), the studies of rock-forming minerals, and anything else which would fit under the broad term "petrology." Mostly fundamental studies are included; regional studies are published if they enhance or elaborate on a basic problem in petrology. The leading journal in its field, the publication belongs in any collection in the geological sciences.

Journal of Sedimentary Petrology. 1931. q. $22. Donn S. Gorsline. Soc. of Economic Paleontologists and Mineralogists, Box 4756, Tulsa, Okla. 74104. Illus., index. Circ: 4,700. Sample. Vol. ends: no. 4. Refereed. Microform: UM, Canner, Princeton. Reprint: Johnson.

Indexed: BioAb, ChemAb, SCI. *Bk. rev:* 3–4, 500 words, signed. *Aud:* Sa, Ac.

Developing from the needs of the petroleum industry for research on sedimentary rocks, the Society early voiced an interest in the science of stratigraphy through investigations in sedimentary petrology. After joining forces with the Paleontological Society of America to produce the *Journal of Paleontology*, the organization spun off its papers on sedimentology, a few years later, to produce this journal. Today, the publication includes, in addition to authoritative studies in this field, selected papers on mineralogy and marine geology. Some professional notes and news are also included. A leading journal for every collection in the geological sciences.

Mineral Digest. 1970. q. $16. Louis Zara. Mineral Digest, Ltd., P.O. Box 341, Murray Hill Station, New York, N.Y. 10016. Illus., index, adv. Vol. ends: no. 4. *Aud:* Ga, Sa, Ac.

A slightly oversized, high gloss publication representing a minor miracle of photography, a lush feast of gems and minerals glinting on paper. It is enough to pore over the elegant gallery of photos, and even tasteful and beautifully executed ads, without troubling about the content. But for those who are word oriented, the magazine is a potpourri of articles centering around minerals of the world, their history and origins, gems for investment, mineral collections of musea, and short stories (one issue containing an old Maugham piece). Some articles are by scientists; some by artists; all are for laymen. Emphasis is on a photographic treatment of minerals as "things" in jewel cases, which indeed they are. Of course, it's expensive. Librarians, splurge!

Mineralogical Magazine. 1876. q. $26. M. H. Hey. Mineralogical Soc., 41 Queen's Gate, London, SW, England. Illus., index. Circ: 2,000. Vol. ends: no. 4. Refereed. Reprint: Dawson.

Indexed: ChemAb, SCI. *Bk. rev:* 7–8, 500–800 words, signed. *Aud:* Sa, Ac.

A widely known, highly authoritative publication of the Mineralogical Society (United Kingdom), comparable in stature to the Mineralogical Society of America. Research articles and short communications span the field and take in studies on the genesis and occurrence of deposits, discoveries of new minerals, physicochemical properties, and crystallography, to name but a few topics. It is an important journal for collections in the geological sciences. Small libraries, restricted in funds, would undoubtedly select *American Mineralogist* first. Nonetheless, this journal, plus *American Mineralogist* would make the foundation for a basic, technical mineralogy collection.

The Society, with the cooperation of the Mineralogical Society of America, has also produced *Mineralogical Abstracts*, the basic abstracting service in this specialized field. Abstracts are indicative; literature is culled on a worldwide basis and includes abstracts of

related fields. (Note: the Mineralogical Society also published *Clay Minerals Bulletin*, dedicated to that specialty.)

Mineralogical Record. 1970. bi-m. $6. John S. White, Jr. Box 783, Bowie, Md. 20715. Illus., index, adv. Circ: 2,000. Sample. Vol. ends: no. 6. Refereed.

Indexed: Mineralogical Abstracts. *Bk. rev:* 3, 400 words, signed. *Aud:* Ga, Sa, Hs, Ac.

Somewhat of a crossbreed between a technical journal and the nonspecialist or hobbyist publication, dedicated exclusively to minerals and collecting. "Affiliated with the Friends of Mineralogy" and now in its third season of publication, the periodical specializes in the tutorial-type feature article reviewing mineralogy of specific regions, or providing state-of-art reports on some ancillary field, such as crystal growth. Articles are well illustrated, including stereo pair photos. (Note: color covers are extraordinary.) The regular departments contain the practical, how-to-do-it sections: questions-answers from readership; "Friends of Mineralogy" notices and news; new mineral notes, advice to collectors, swap column, etc. It is refreshing to find a publication, suitable for any type of library, which forms the link between the scholarly journal of the learned society and the amateur news of the rockhound magazines. Publications of this type should be supported and the model noted for other fields, as well. Highly recommended for academic libraries, and, with some reservations, interested public libraries and enthusiastic and sophisticated high school libraries.

Modern Geology. 1970. q. $41. Luciano B. Ronca. Gordon and Breach Science Publishers, 150 Fifth Ave., New York, N.Y. 10011. Illus., index. Sample. Vol. ends: no. 4. Refereed.

Aud: Sa, Ac.

Veering from the traditional areas of geological study, the journal concentrates on theoretical or experimental research papers in such fields as lunar and planetary geology, new approaches to geochemical and geophysical studies, such as thermoluminescent studies, remote sensing, nuclear geology, radiation damage, and some papers on mathematical or statistical geolgy. An international publication, the first volume had wide representation from foreign contributors, including the USSR. Papers all appear in English. For research collections.

Reviews of Geophysics and Space Physics. 1963. q. $15. Ed. bd. Amer. Geophysical Union, 2100 Pennsylvania Ave., N.W., Washington, D.C. 20037. Illus., index. Circ: 5,200. Vol. ends: no. 4. Refereed.

Indexed: SciAb, SCI. *Aud:* Sa, Ac.

Critical and comprehensive, the journal is dedicated to review articles giving an overview of current research in all fields of geophysics. Papers by authorities fall under such broad subject areas as atmospheres, oceans, solid earth and planets, and space physics. Contributions may be as lengthy as over 80 pages, or may be "topical reviews," five to six descriptive pages of on-going research or introductions to doctoral dissertations. Generally, reviews contain the necessary background material and bibliographies to be meaningful to both nonspecialist and advanced student. An excellent and authoritative review-type publication for academic libraries.

Rocks and Minerals. 1926. m. $4. James and Winifred Bourne. Rocks and Minerals, Box 29, Peeksill, N.Y. Illus., adv. Circ: 12,000. Sample. Vol. ends: Dec.

Indexed: ChemAb. *Bk. rev:* 3–4, 100 words, unsigned. *Aud:* Ga, Hs, Ac.

"America's oldest and most versatile magazine for the mineralogist, geologist, lapidary." Official journal, too, of the Rocks and Minerals Association, as well as the Eastern Federation of Mineralogical and Lapidary Societies. The magazine carries a miscellany of informally written articles in these areas. Some features represent small tutorials by those knowledgeable in the field; others may be notes on equipment; some contain histories of gems; and yet others may be chatty reports on field trips, etc. Departments include current events, bits from club bulletins, a swap column, information on mineral localities, new equipment, and a variety of personals, ads, or comments from readers. A good choice for schools with mineral or geology clubs, and also popular enough in tone to be appropriate for any interested public library. See also *Earth Science,* for the organ of the Midwest Federation of Mineralogical Societies.

Sedimentology. 1962. 8/yr. 2v./yr. $34. H. Fuchtbauer. Elsevier Publishing Co., Box 211, Amsterdam, The Netherlands. Illus., index, adv. Sample. Vol. ends: no. 4; 2v./yr. Refereed.

Indexed: SCI. *Bk. rev:* 6–8, 500 words, signed. *Aud:* Sa, Ac.

Official journal of the International Association of Sedimentologists. In each issue, about five research papers discuss current investigations in such areas as the origin, chemical and mineral composition of sediments, fossil organisms in sediments, the weathering and physical processes taking place, transportation, and deposition into its sedimentary environment. "Clay Mineralogy of Black Sea Sediments" is a typical title. An authoritative publication for academic collections interested in these fields. (Note: Elsevier puts out a companion journal. *Sedimentary Geology,* concentrating on applied, geological aspects of sedimentology, including marine sediments, near-shore processes, etc.)

Seismological Society of America. Bulletin. 1911. bi-m. $36. Otto W. Nuttli. Seismological Soc., c/o William

K. Cloud, Secretary, Seismographic Station, Dept. of Geology and Geophysics, Univ. of Calif., Berkeley, Calif. 94720. Illus., index. Circ: 2,000. Vol. ends: no. 6. Refereed.

Indexed: SciAb, SCI. *Bk. rev:* 3, 200 words, signed. *Aud:* Sa, Ac.

The official organ of the Society, dedicated to technical studies on such subjects as the causes, distribution, and occurrence of earthquakes. Analyses of historical, as well as recent, seismic activity are frequently included. In addition to research papers and short, technical notes, a monthly department, "Seismological Notes," records data on shocks reported in any area of the world. Some professional news of seismological interest and news of the society are also given. Because of the scope of the publication, i.e., its impact on economic and societal development, the journal's studies would be of interest to a number of technical and engineering groups, for example, in the design of tall buildings in urban areas, design of nuclear power plants, and the like. For academic libraries.

Tectonophysics. 1964. m. $48. Ed. bd. Elsevier Publishing Co., Box 211, Amsterdam, The Netherlands. Illus., index, adv. Circ: 1,000. Sample. Vol. ends no. 12. Refereed.

Indexed: ChemAb, SCI. *Bk. rev:* 3–4, 250 words, signed. *Aud:* Sa, Ac.

The literature in this specialty journal is concerned with the science of the physical processes involved in forming geologic structures, i.e., large structural units of the Earth's crust, as well as studies of the physics of the interior of the Earth. Both original research papers and occasional review articles are published. Some issues are devoted entirely to special symposia like "Global Tectonics and Sea-Floor Spreading." The journal is typical of a large number of other authoritative specialty, research-type journals in the geological sciences, all published by Elsevier, some of which have been included in this section. Usually, acquisition of these publications would depend on faculty interest in academic libraries.

ECONOMICS

Basic Periodicals

Ga: *American Economic Review, American Journal of Economics and Sociology;* Jc: *American Economic Review, Economic Journal, American Journal of Economics and Sociology;* Ac: *American Economic Review, Economic Journal, American Journal of Economics and Sociology, Brookings Papers, Canadian Journal of Economics.*

Basic Abstracts and Indexes

Business Periodicals Index, Current Contents, Journal

of Economic Literature, Economic Abstracts, Contents of Recent Economic Journals.

Cessations

Challenge, The Magazine of Economic Affairs, Yale Economic Essays.

American Economic Review. 1911. 5/yr. Membership (Nonmembers $20). G. H. Borts. Amer. Economic Assn., Brown Univ., Robinson Hall, Providence, R.I. 02912. Index, adv. Circ: 26,000. Microform: UM. Reprint: Johnson.

Indexed: PAIS, SSHum. *Bk. rev:* 50–75, one to two pages, signed. *Aud:* Ac, Ga. *Jv:* V.

Outstanding both for its extensive book reviews and its forthright articles. The reviews, which take up a good half of the magazine, are arranged under economics subject headings, e.g., methodology, price and allocation theory, history, statistical methods, etc. In addition, there is usually a listing of 250 to 300 new books in the field and notes on periodicals. Articles, often with bibliographies, range from wages and employment to marketing and welfare. Comments and letters make up a good part of each issue, and there is an annual list of doctoral dissertations. Appointments, research grants, deaths, and promotions are noted. A basic journal for any collection in this area.

American Journal of Economics and Sociology. 1941. q. $8. Will Lissner. Amer. Journal of Economics and Sociology, Inc., 50 E. 69th St., New York, N.Y. 10021. Illus., index. Circ: 1,062. Sample. Vol. ends: Oct. Refereed. Microform: UM, Canner. Reprint: Abrahams, Kraus.

Indexed: CurrCont, PAIS, SSHum, SocAb. *Bk. rev:* 1–2, lengthy, signed. *Aud:* Ac, Ga.

Aims at a "constructive synthesis in the social sciences" through the reporting of the results of original research aimed at achieving an understanding of contemporary economic and social processes. It could be used effectively by the scholar, college student, or interested layman who is seeking analysis of economic problems and situations; or by one who is seeking studies of the interrelationships between economics and sociology, history, and political science. Two important areas covered are the sociological aspects of economic institutions and the economic aspects of social and political institutions. Besides studies of the United States, material concerns foreign situations. While the articles are thoroughly documented, the style is nontechnical. Authors are professors and government officials. Each issue contains one or more lengthy reviews of important recent works along with briefer book notices.

Applied Economics. 1969. q. $25.60. Michael A. Crew and Ralph Day. Chapman and Hall, 11 New Fetter Lane, London, EC4P 4EE, England. (Subs to: Periodicals Department, A.P.B., North Way, Andover, Hampshire, United Kingdom). Illus. Vol. ends: Dec. Refereed.

Indexed: CurrCont, PAIS. *Bk. rev:* 4–5, 200 words, signed. *Aud:* Ac.

A general economics magazine. Articles range from a discussion of discounting public investments to the relationship of hospital costs to prices. There are many charts and derivations. The book reviews are concise and critical. For the specialist in the field of economics, but contains material which would well be worthwhile for the generalist.

Australian Economic Papers. 1962. bi-a. $5. K. J. Hancock and G. C. Harcourt. Economics Dept., Univ. of Adelaide, Adelaide, Australia. Illus., index, adv. Circ: 1,000. Sample. Vol. ends: Dec. Refereed.

Indexed: EconLit. *Aud:* Ac.

A scholarly journal which concentrates primarily on Australian economics. Some theoretical material of a wider scope on applied economics, economic history and accounting is included. Only for large, specialized collections.

Brookings Papers on Economic Activity. 1970. 3/yr. $6. Arthur M. Okun and George L. Perry. Brookings Institution, 1775 Massachusetts Ave., N.W., Washington, D.C. 20036.

Indexed: PAIS. *Aud:* Ac.

A series on various aspects of the national and international economic condition. Usually each issue centers around a topic, then builds opinion, pro and con, with five to seven contributors. The papers are inevitably by experts, sometimes by the editors who are renowned economists in their own right. In addition to the main theme, there are longer papers on various current matters such as the corporate bond market, the capacity of the homebuilding industry to expand, and long term trends in United States foreign trade. Although basically conservative, there is an honest effort to present various sides of controversial issues. Note: The Brookings Institute issues a number of pamphlets, newsletters, etc. during the year, has a joint subscription price for the whole. Interested libraries should write the Institute for current offerings and prices, which tend to change frequently.

Canadian Journal of Economics. 1968. q. Membership. $15 (Individuals $13). A. Asimakopulos. Univ. of Toronto Press, Front Campus, Toronto, 181 Ont. Index, adv. Circ: 3,500. Sample. Vol. ends: Nov.

Indexed: CanI, CurrCont, PAIS, SSHum. *Bk. rev:* 12, 750 words, signed. *Aud:* Ac.

A publication of some 150 pages, articles are primarily concerned with general economic issues written by economists and teachers. They appear in French and English. Material more relevant to the

Canadian scene appears in shorter items as notes. There is usually a bibliographic article and the whole is the best approach to the subject available in Canada.

Econometrica. 1933. bi-m. $26. Franklin Fisher. J. W. Arrowsmith Ltd., Winterstoke Rd., Bristol, BS 3 2NT, England. Illus., index, adv. Circ: 7,200. Sample. Vol. ends: Nov.

Indexed: CurrCont, SSHum. *Aud:* Ac.

A highly specialized and scholarly journal "for the advancement of economic theory in its relation to statistics and mathematics." The articles are written mainly by faculty members of American universities. Material is technical, and would have interest only for the expert.

Economic Development and Cultural Change. 1952. q. $8. Bert F. Hoselitz. Research Center in Economic Development and Cultural Change, Univ. of Chicago. Subs. to: Univ. of Chicago Press, 5801 S. Ellis Ave., Chicago, Ill. 60637. Index, adv. Circ: 3,300. Sample. Vol. ends: July. Refereed. Microform: UM, Canner. Reprint: Johnson.

Indexed: CurrCont, PAIS. *Bk. rev:* 4, 5 pages, signed. *Aud:* Ac.

A well-written journal primarily concerned with developments in the emerging nations of the world. Economic, political, and cultural activities are examined, and an effort is made to link all factors relevant to development. The material is technical, but because it covers such a wide range of social and political issues, it will be of interest to a great number of scholars and graduate students. Should be in most medium to large-sized economics, sociology, and political science collections.

Economic Geography. See Geography Section.

Economic Indicators. See Government Magazines/ United States Section.

Economic Journal. 1891. q. $15.50. W. B. Reddaway, D. G. Champernowne and Phyllis Deane. Macmillan Journals Ltd., 4 Little Essex St., London WC 2 England. Index, adv. Circ: 10,000. Vol. ends: Dec. Refereed. Microform: UM. Reprint: Carrollton, Wm. Dawson.

Indexed: BritHum, CIJE, PAIS, SSHum. *Bk. rev:* 35–40, 800 words, signed. *Aud:* Ac, Ga. *Jv:* V.

Sponsored by the Royal Economic Society at Cambridge, this scholarly journal features articles by faculty members of British, American, and Canadian universities. Most of the material is of interest only to the professional economist and university teacher. However, the excellent book reviews offer libraries one of the best means of keeping up with current titles in the field—particularly those issued in England and in Europe. For this reason it should be found in any large library where an effort is made to have a substantial economics collection.

Economic Priorities Report. 1971. $25 (Students $7.50). Council on Economic Priorities, 1028 Connecticut Ave., N.W., Suite 926, Washington, D.C. 20036.

Indexed: PAIS. *Aud:* Ac, Ga.

Organized to remind corporations of their social responsibilities, the Council on Economic Priorities supports the reminder with considerable clout. The principal weapon of the nonprofit group is the 50 or so page monthly off-set report. This is supported and backed by irregular studies such as the Council's in-depth study: *Paper Profits: Pollution in the Pulp and Paper Industry* (480p. $50 a copy from the Council). A summary of this report is found in the issue under review. The material is primary, well documented, and objective. The reporters study the situation, give all the raw data, and suggest methods of cleaning up the pollution. The effectiveness of the approach has been commented on widely from *Time* to the *Wall Street Journal.* Students will find the *Report* a vital research source, and community groups involved with ecology and pollution will discover an approach here which might be applicable to individual community situations. In addition to pollution control, the group takes a good hard look at minority hiring practices, foreign investments and munitions manufacturing. Accountability is the theme, research is the method, and the result is the type of material which should be available in any library. The price is steep, but in view of the effort and the results—highly recommended for all libraries.

Economica. 1921. q. $9. B. S. Yamey. London School of Economics and Political Science, Economica Publ. Off., Houghton St., Aldwych, London WC2, England. Index, adv. Circ: 4,000. Vol. ends: Nov. Reprint: Wm. Dawson.

Indexed: BritHum, CurrCont, PAIS, SSHum. *Bk. rev:* 20, 150 words, signed. *Aud:* Ac.

Limited to "economics, economic history, statistics and closely related problems." Approximately half of the articles are written by non-British faculty members, primarily Americans. Since the subject matter is theoretical and universal, there is no special emphasis on the British economy. There is an extensive bibliography in each issue giving a list of the new books in the field. Primarily for graduate students and scholars.

Inter-American Economic Affairs. 1947. q. $10. Simon G. Hanson. Box 181, Washington, D.C. 20044. Index. Sample. Vol. ends: Spring.

Indexed: PAIS, SSHum. *Bk. rev:* Long, signed review article. *Aud:* Ac, Ga.

Inter-American political and economic agreements, governmental regulations and practices, political elections and activities, credit programs, and the development of specific companies are discussed. Many of the papers are historical and theoretical rather than practical studies. Some issues present several articles (or the entire issue) devoted to the various economic aspects of a single country or field. Primarily for large business and economics collections.

International Development Review. 1959. q. Membership (Libraries $7.50). Andrew E. Rice. Soc. for Intl. Development, 1346 Connecticut Ave., N.W. Washington, D. C. 20036. Adv. Circ: 7,200. Microform: UM. Reprint: Johnson.

Indexed: PAIS. Bk. rev: 15, 200 words, signed. Aud: Ac.

A well-written, readable journal devoted to the economic development of the emerging nations. Articles are practical, documented, and usually in English. Those in French or Spanish have English abstracts. News of the United Nations, film reviews, and short, perceptive book reviews round out the average issue. Valuable for difficult-to-find information on smaller nations.

International Economic Review. 1960. 3/yr. $13. P. J. Dhrymes. Kansai Economic Federation, Shin-Osaka Bldg., Dojima-Hamadori, Kita-ku, Osaka, Japan. Index, adv. Circ: 1,500.

Indexed: PAIS. Aud: Ac.

Published in Japan with the text in English. The emphasis is primarily on quanitative economics. Over half of the average seven articles per issue are written by American university faculty members. Only for large libraries.

International Monetary Fund Staff Papers. 1950. 3/yr. $6. Norman K. Humphreys. Intl. Monetary Fund, 19th and H Streets, N.W., Washington, D.C. 20431. Illus. Circ: 2,500. Vol. ends: Nov. Microform: UM.

Indexed: BusI, PAIS. Aud: Ac.

Acts as an exchange medium for information on international monetary and financial problems. Contains resumés of each article in both French and Spanish along with the English text. Illustrations and derivations add much to this publication. In the past it has included such subjects as discussions on the balance of payments, special drawing rights, interest rates, East-West trade, the effects of re-evaluation, and an in-depth analysis of the economies of various countries. One of the best magazines in its field.

The Israel Economist (Formerly: **The Palestine Economist**). 1945. m. $12.50. Y. Ramati. 6 Hazanovitch St., POB, 7052, Jerusalem, Israel. Illus., adv. Circ: 12,000. Sample.

Indexed: PAIS. Bk. rev: 2–3, 600–1000 words. Aud: Ga, Hs, Ac.

As the name indicates, it is in a more modest format the Israeli equivalent of the British *Economist* (see Business/General section) and covers political and economic news from Israel and from the international news scene related to Israel. Arranged in sections, "Notes of the Month" report political and socio-economic news, "Comments" feature government policies, regulations, labor relations, currency reserves, "Company Interviews" briefly show the activities of local firms. An occasional supplement devoted to a special subject reports more extensively on, e.g., an economic branch, "Agriculture in Judea and Samaria," or on a firm, its activities and executives, e.g., EL-AL.

It is useful to students, businessmen wishing to get acquainted with Israeli business and industry, and to the general reader interested in keeping up to date on economic life in Israel. (R.T.)

The Journal of Developing Areas. 1966. q. $8 (Individuals $6). Spencer H. Brown. Western Illinois Univ. Press, 900 W. Adams St., Macomb, Ill. 61455. Illus., index, adv. Circ: 1,500. Sample. Vol. ends: July. Refereed.

Indexed: CurrCont, HistAb. Bk. rev: 15, 500 words, signed. Aud: Ac.

Concerned with the problems of underdeveloped countries, this journal takes more of an interest in the general type of development problems than in the problems of particular countries. The approach is not purely economic but attempts to deal with all potentially relevant aspects of changing societies, from tangible variables such as wage structures, schools, the military, unions, and trade to intangible ones such as goal orientation and values in their relations to change. There is much data given on many different areas and a regular news and notes section.

Journal of Economic History. 1941. q. $15. Robert Gallman. Grad. Sch. of Business Admin., New York Univ., 100 Trinity Pl., New York, N.Y. 10006. Index, adv. Circ: 3,300. Vol. ends: Dec. Refereed. Microform: UM, Canner. Reprint: Kraus.

Indexed: JEconLit, PAIS, SSHum. Bk. rev: 20–25, 1 page, signed. Aud: Ac, Ga.

The journal of the Economic History Association, this is devoted to articles on the history of economic life in all its phases. The articles are not confined to any one country or period of history, and cover such subjects as transportation, taxation, investment, and the history of business and industry. The book reviews are critical and a particularly excellent guide for librarians. Although an academic journal, the material is broad enough in scope to be of interest to teachers or graduate students in economics, history, sociology, and related areas. A basic journal for medium to large-sized academic and public library economics collections.

Journal of Economic Issues. 1967. q. Membership (Nonmembers $8.50). Warren J. Samuels. Dept. of Economics, Michigan State Univ., East Lansing, Mich. 48864. Index, adv. Circ: 1,450. Sample. Vol. ends: Dec.

Indexed: PAIS. *Bk. rev:* 8–10, 750 words, signed. *Aud:* Ac.

Written by and primarily for professors of economics, each issue includes some six or seven articles on a variety of issues, e.g., the gold-dollar problem, the political economy of poverty, wages in historical context. There are comments of a shorter nature, and critical book reviews, as well as a listing of new books received. Emphasis tends to be on general economics, and the magazine unquestionably has a wide appeal for anyone who teaches the subject or for graduate students.

The Journal of Industrial Economics. 1952. 3/yr. $5.40. Basil Blackwell Publishers, 49 Broad St., Oxford, England. Illus. Circ: 1,492. Vol. ends: July. Microform: UM. Reprint: Kraus.

Indexed: BritHum, BusI, JEconLit, PAIS. *Aud:* Ac.

Explores the many problems facing modern industry. The relationship of the individual company to the whole economy is of paramount concern. What will happen if a company raises or lowers its prices or output or decides to change locations? How will the economy react to these influences? This concentration on definitive companies or industries makes it a very pragmatic magazine. In 1971 it looked at the American brewing industry, the sausage industry, African businessmen, labor, supermarkets, communications, and the machine tool industry to name only a few. Liberal use of diagrams and occasional derivations helps a great deal in understanding the articles. This is one of the best magazines around for the businessman and economist.

Journal of International Economics. 1971. q. $25 (Individuals $10). Jagdish Bhagwati. North-Holland Publishing Co., Box 3489, Amsterdam, Netherlands. Illus., adv.

Bk. rev: 3–5, 500–1500 words, signed. *Aud:* Ac.

"Designed to serve as the principle outlet for analytical work in the pure theory of international trade and in balance of payment analysis . . ." In a word, technical, jargon and equation prone, and only for the professional economist. The first number included seven articles, and the publisher says four issues will come to approximately 400 pages. The editor is with MIT, and the contributors and editorial board have equally impressive credentials. Unfortunately, the in-bred message is quite beyond the people affected.

Journal of Political Economy. 1892. bi-m. $15. Ed. Bd. Univ. of Chicago Press, 5801 S. Ellis Ave., Chica-

go, Ill. 60637. Index, adv. Circ: 6,000. Sample. Vol. ends: Dec. Refereed. Microform: UM, Canner. Reprint: Johnson, Abrahams.

Indexed: CurrCont, JEconLit, PAIS, SSHum. *Bk. rev:* 2, 2 pages, signed. *Aud:* Ac.

Written primarily for professional economists. The average ten articles per number are written almost exclusively by faculty members of various universities. There are occasional review articles as well as periodic supplementary issues devoted to one topic—usually one discussed at a conference. For large academic collections.

The Journal of Taxation. 1954. m. $34. William S. Papworth. Tax Research Group, Inc., 512 North Florida Ave., Tampa, Fla. 33602. Index, adv. Circ: 15,600. Vol. ends: Dec.

Indexed: BusI, CurrCont. *Aud:* Ac.

Current news and commentary for tax advisors, and a bit cheaper than (although not as up to date as) the various services of Prentice Hall. This covers much the same ground as P-H, but with much more depth and analysis. It regularly includes departments on accounting, compensation, corporations, estates, exempt institutions, fraud, international trade, oil and gas, partnership, payroll, personal procedures, real estate, and a general catch-all called shop talk. Written by tax men for tax men, it deserves a place in every special library.

Kyklos, international Zeitschrift fur Sozialwissenshaften. 1948. q. $7.50. Bruno S. Frey. Kyklos-Verlag, Postfach 524, Ch 4000, Basen 2, Switzerland. Index, adv. Circ: 4,000. Sample. Vol. ends: Winter. Refereed. Reprint: Johnston, Abrahams.

Indexed: PAIS. *Bk. rev:* 25, 750 words, signed. *Aud:* Ac.

An international review of the social sciences, specializing in economics, yet giving weight to the interdisciplinary aspects of both fields. The text is in English, French, and German, but most of the seven to eight articles per issue appear in English. In view of its international scope, its scholarly contributors, extensive book reviews, and its professional approach to both the social sciences and economics, it is a major consideration for any academic library.

Land Economics. See Urban Studies Section.

Mergers & Acquisitions. 1965. bi-m. $35. S. F. Reed. Mergers & Acquisitions, Inc., 1725 K St., N.W., Washington, D.C. 20006. Illus., index. Circ: 8,000. Sample. Vol. ends: Winter.

Indexed: PAIS. *Bk. rev:* 1, length varies, signed. *Aud:* Ac, Ga.

Lengthy feature articles offer well-documented essays concerning the history and current development of mergers, practices of American investors, government agencies, and regulations relating to the subject. Articles include many charts, graphs, and photocopies of pertinent material. Actual techniques of specific companies are analyzed and evaluated.

National Institute Economic Review. 1959. q. $10. M. J. Artis. National Institute of Economic and Social Research, 2 Dean Trench St., Smith Square, London, SW1, England. Illus. Circ: 4,500. Vol. ends: Nov. Reprint: Wm. Dawson.

Indexed: BusI, PAIS. *Aud:* Ac.

Designed to be of service to those in business who need to look at the general economic situation and its prospects. Each issue contains figures on the British economy, covers the balance of payments, output, demand, a forecast of industrial production, and the implications of each of these. The same approach is taken for the rest of the world, but without as much detail. Every large academic library should subscribe.

OECD Main Economic Indicators. 1960. m. $18. Organization for Economic Cooperation and Development Publications Center, Suite 1305, 1750 Pennsylvania Ave., N.W., Washington, D.C. 20006. Vol. ends: Dec.

Aud: Ac.

This bulletin is intended to serve both as a rapid guide to recent economic developments and as a basic source of international statistical data. In order to meet these needs, the bulletin has been divided into the following parts. "Indicators By Country" consists of indexes for the 12 OECD member countries and Yugoslavia, selected as the most important indicators with business cycle significance. "Indicators By Subject" consists of industrial production, consumer prices, official gold and foreign exchange holdings and imports and exports. "Foreign Trade Indicators" consists of tables giving a detailed regional analysis of the trade of the main country grouping in the OECD area; a set of tables organized by subject for each individual country, its total trade, and a standard breakdown of trade flows by major areas. "Main Economic Indicators" consists entirely of charts and tables without commentary.

OECD Observer. 1962. bi-m. $3.50. Anker Randsholt, Organization for Economic Cooperation and Development Information Service, Chateau de la Muette, 2 rue Andre Pascal, F75, Paris 16ᵉ France. Illus., index. Circ: 25,000. Vol. ends: Dec.

Indexed: BusI, CurrCont, PAIS. *Bk. rev:* short, number varies. *Aud:* Ac.

The *Observer* is the official medium of information exchange for the Organization for Economic Cooperation and Development. It covers a multitude of problems within the OECD, e.g., such diverse topics as the environment and the need for intragovernmental

cooperation to clean it up, implications of higher education, foreign investment, road research, retirement age, inflation, and energy. Most articles are by OECD staff members or committees. For the person interested in foreign investments, marketing or economics.

Oxford Economic Papers. 1937. 3/yr. $7. J. F. Wright. Oxford Univ. Press, Press Rd., Neasden, London NW 10, England. Circ: 2,250. Microform: UM.

Indexed: BritHum, PAIS. *Aud:* Ac.

A general review of economics, primarily for the professional and graduate student. The material shows a definite sophistication. Coverage is universal, both in terms of country and time. The six to eight articles frequently include a long book review, although there is no book review section. Only for the large library.

The Palestine Economist. See *The Israel Economist.*

Quarterly Journal of Economics. 1886. q. $8. Richard Musgrave. Harvard Univ. Press, 79 Garden St., Cambridge, Mass. 02138. Adv. Circ: 5,700. Microform: UM. Reprint: Kraus.

Indexed: PAIS, SSHum. *Aud:* Ac.

Authoritative articles tend to examine the implications of the long rather than the short movements in prices, labor, public finance, and industrial development. Coverage is international, and while no particular theory of economics is championed, the tone is definitely liberal, at all times free of either national or political overtones. Its wide scope gives it a place of importance in any library serving the teacher, professional economist, or graduate student.

Quarterly Review of Economics and Business. 1961. q. $6 (Organizations $8). Joseph D. Phillips. Bureau of Economic and Business Research, Urbana, Ill. 61801. Circ: 1,500. Sample. Vol. ends: Winter. Refereed. Microform: UM. Reprint: Johnson.

Indexed: BusI, CurrCont, JEconLit, PAIS, SSHum. *Bk. rev:* 3–4, 500–750 words, signed. *Aud:* Ac.

The seven or eight articles emphasize business in practice as much as in theory. There is a good deal of original research and theoretical material on economics, usually related to contemporary problems. The book reviews are excellent, and on the whole it is a much above-average journal for the medium to large business and economics collection.

Review of Economic Studies. 1933. q. $12.50. G. M. Heal and D. F. Hendry. Longman Group Ltd., Journals Division, 33 Montgomery St., Edinburgh, EH7 5JX, Scotland. Illus., index, adv. Circ: 3,000. Vol. ends: Oct. Refereed. Microform: UM. Reprint: Kraus, Abrahams.

Indexed: BritHum, JEconLit, PAIS, SSHum. *Aud:* Ac.

Originally founded by a group of young British and American economists, the Economic Study Society encourages research in theoretical and applied economics. Although now older, the magazine still encourages work from younger men. There are an average of nine articles per issue, and each contribution is documented and usually supported by extensive graphs and charts. Emphasis tends to be international. A useful journal for medium to large academic and public business and economics collections.

Review of Economics and Statistics. 1919. q. $12. Otto Ekstein. Harvard Univ. Press, 79 Garden St., Cambridge, Mass. 02138. Illus., index, adv. Circ: 4,900. Reprint: Johnson.

Indexed: BusI, PAIS. *Bk. rev:* Lengthy, number varies. *Aud:* Ac.

Concentrates on economic analysis with particular reference to issues of public policy. Content is made up of symposia by economists on various issues of the day. There is a bibliography of books that have been received, and a few lengthy critical reviews. Primarily for the large, specialized business and economics collection.

Review of Social Economy. 1944. s-a. Membership (Nonmembers $8). William R. Waters. Assn. for Social Economics, De Paul University, 2323 N. Seminary Ave., Chicago, Ill. 60614. Adv. Circ: 800. Sample. Vol. ends: Sept. Refereed.

Indexed: CathI, PAIS. *Bk. rev:* 5, 500 words, signed. *Aud:* Ac.

Combines a concern for economics with the interests of society. A recent issue on the overall theme of "Economic Priorities in the 1970's" included articles on planning, concentrated power, the social role of the business organization, "Psychological Counterpart Analyses," "Consumer Freedom of Choice and Social Needs," and "Racial Discrimination, Productivity, and Negro-White Male Income." An extremely interesting and scholarly publication which university libraries and those serving readers concerned with socioeconomic matters will wish to consider.

Southern Economic Journal. 1933. q. $10. Vincent J. Tarascio. Southern Economic Assn., Univ. of North Carolina, Carroll Hall, Chapel Hill, N.C. 27514. Illus., adv. Circ: 3,300. Vol. ends: July. Refereed. Microform: UM. Reprint. Kraus.

Indexed: PAIS, SSHum. *Bk. rev:* 5, 750 words, signed. *Aud:* Ac.

Emphasis is on applied and theoretical economics. Contributions cover both national and international problems. Contents are not concerned with the South alone, or written from a Southern viewpoint. Occasionally there are review articles of previously written papers. An extensive list of new books in the field and short book previews are included. Only for larger academic and public libraries.

EDUCATION

See also Foreign Language Teaching and Sports/Physical Education and School Sports Sections.

Basic Periodicals

(Note: The majority of magazines in this section are written for and by teachers. Selection in education is too individualized to permit any more than general recommendations.)

GENERAL. Ga: *Education Digest, Education Summary;* Jc: *Harvard Educational Review, Education Digest, Education Summary;* Ac: *Teachers College Record, Harvard Educational Review, Education Summary, Educational Studies, Educational Products Report, Education Digest.*

COUNTERCULTURE. All libraries: *Integrated Education, This Magazine is About Schools.*

ELEMENTARY AND SECONDARY EDUCATION. Ejh: *Grade Teacher, Instructor;* Hs: *Clearing House, Today's Education;* Ga: *PTA Magazine, Today's Education.*

HIGHER EDUCATION. Jc: *College and University, Chronicle of Higher Education;* Ac: *Chronicle of Higher Education, College and University, Improving College and University Teaching.*

Basic Abstracts and Indexes

Education Index, Research in Education (ERIC), Current Index to Journals in Education, State Education Journal Index, British Education Journal Index, Canadian Education Index.

Cessations

Catholic Education Review, Catholic School Journal, National Catholic Education Association Bulletin, English, Literature Criticism, Teaching, English Progress.

General

AEDS Journal. 1967. q. Membership (Nonmembers $10). Bruce K. Alcorn. Assn. for Educational Data Systems, 1201 16th St., N.W., Washington, D.C. 20036. Illus., index, adv. Circ: 2,500. Sample. Vol. ends: June. Refereed.

Indexed: CIJE. *Bk. rev:* 1, ½ page, signed. *Aud:* Ac.

The computer and the school is the primary thrust here. The 20 to 30 page journal features short articles on the use of data systems for everything from record keeping to simulated teaching. Most of it is for the elementary and high school level. The authors presuppose knowledge on the part of readers about computers. Only for the expert and near expert.

The same nonprofit organization issues: *AEDS Moni-*

tor (1962. m. $15. Dean D. Crocker) which is a bit more involved with news about data processing, less with research articles. Aside from describing applications of computers and data processing, it reports on Association activities, employment opportunities, etc.

ARGR Journal. 1959. s-a. $1. Richard Clark and Gerald Wohlfred. Dept. of Education, Kingston, R.I. 02881. Sample. Vol. ends: April.

Indexed: CIJE. *Bk. rev:* 2–3, 2–3 pages, signed. *Aud:* Ac.

A processed publication of the Association for Research in Growth Relationship. Translated, this comes down to a number of papers on research in education as it relates to human growth and development. Articles move from child development and psychology to common problems of education. The tone is progressive, and of value to anyone who is looking for new directions in teaching.

Adult Education (British). 1926. bi-m. $6. A. K. Stock. National Inst. of Adult Education, 35 Queen Anne St., London W1M OBL, England. Index, adv. Circ: 2,500. Sample. Vol. ends: March.

Indexed: BritEdI, PAIS. *Bk. rev:* 5, 500 words, signed. *Aud:* Ac.

An English approach to adult education in some 50 pages. Usually four to five articles, often a symposium, reviews, and notes. One issue, for example, had a series of articles on training personnel for adult education work, and a piece on discrimination against women in top jobs. While the nitty gritty examples apply only to England, much of the theory and the solutions to general problems is useful for Americans and anyone dealing with adult education. The style of writing is much above average, the material well documented without being stuffy. An interesting and valuable addition for larger collections.

Adult Education (U.S.). 1950. q. Membership (Nonmembers $10). Dwight Rhyne. Adult Education Assn. of the United States of America, 810 18th St., N.W., Washington, D.C. 20006. Index, adv. Circ: 5,200. Sample. Vol. ends: Summer. Microform: UM.

Indexed: BritEdI, EdI, *Bk. rev:* 3, 2 pages, signed. *Aud:* Ac.

Reports research and provides news and views of interest to adult education administrators. There are usually about five articles which range in length from 2 to 18 pages. The writing style is semipopular to scholarly. Primarily for academic and large public libraries.

Agricultural Education Magazine. See Agriculture Section.

Alberta Journal of Educational Research. 1955. q. $5. E. Miklos. Faculty of Education, Univ. of Alberta, Edmonton, 7, Alta., Canada. Illus., index, adv. Circ: 700. Sample. Vol. ends: Dec.

Indexed: PsyAb. *Bk. rev:*3–4, 500 words, signed. *Aud:* Ac.

Primarily concerned with the theory and methods of teaching at the elementary and high school levels. Articles tend to be by professors and those involved in research. Little or no so-called "practical" information. The editor sees his journal as "devoted to the dissemination, criticism, interpretation, and encouragement of all forms of systematic enquiry into education and fields related to or associated with education." Only for large education collections.

American Education. See Government Magazines/ United States Section.

American School & University. 1928. m. $8. James E. Talbot. North American Publishing Co., 41 E. 42nd St., New York, N.Y. 10017. Illus., adv. Circ: 40,000. Vol. ends: Aug. Microform: UM.

Indexed: EdI. *Aud:* Ac.

The journal for the executives and the administrators in American elementary, secondary, and university systems. Articles pertain to planning, construction, furnishings, equipment, maintenance, audiovisual systems. Also included is information about the latest products of use in administration or maintenance of school. Under a new publisher (who also issues *Media & Methods* and *Audio,* to name two), the magazine has improved considerably since last written of here. Unfortunately, the publisher will not send samples, but librarians might try to examine it elsewhere.

American Teacher. 1972. m. (Sept.–June). Membership (Nonmembers $5). David Elsila. American Federation of Teachers, AFL-CIO, 1012 14th St., N.W., Washington, D.C. 20005. Illus., adv. Circ: 275,000. Sample. Vol. ends: June.

Bk. rev: 2, 250–500 words, signed. *Aud:* Ac, Hs, Ejh.

A 20 to 32 page tabloid newspaper which represents the official voice of an ever-growing group, i.e., teachers aligned with the American Federation of Teachers. The tone is militant, the feeling one of action, and the articles, news items, and editorials, push the drive to organize. At one time this was limited to elementary and high school teachers, but it has been extended to include a good many college and university professors. Hence, the articles touch on all aspects of American education. Not all the emphasis is on better working conditions. There is an equal amount of space given to problems of academic freedom, school finance, teaching methods, and administration. There are regular departments on teacher rights, civil rights, national affairs, international news, and other areas. Even those who have little sympathy with the union will find much of interest—and this seems particularly true of parents. While members will receive on membership, libraries where there is no member willing to give up his or her copy should subscribe. (See also *Changing Education*.)

Art Education. See Art Section.

Business Education Forum. 1947. m. (Oct.–May). $15. National Business Education Assn., 1201 16th St., N.W., Washington, D.C. 20636. Circ: 16,000.

Indexed: EdI. *Aud:* Hs, Ac.

Both a voice for high school teachers of business and for business teachers in colleges and universities. (At one time the two were separate, but by 1970 the *BEF* had incorporated the college journal, i.e., the former *National Business Education Quarterly*.) Each issue includes information on instruction of various business courses, plus more philosophical and scholarly articles dealing with various aspects of the profession. Primarily for the school of education and the high school professional collection.

Business Education World. See Free Magazines.

Canadian Education and Research Digest. See *Education Canada* in Education/Elementary and Secondary Education Section.

Catholic Counselor. See *National Catholic Guidance Conference Journal.*

Changing Education. 1967. q. $5. David Elsila. Amer. Federation of Teachers, AFL-CIO, 1012 14th St., N.W., Washington, D.C. 20005. Illus., adv. Circ: 250,000. Microform: UM.

Bk. rev: 1–2, lengthy, signed. *Aud:* Ac, Hs, Ejh.

Whereas the *American Teacher* is a monthly "battle" report on issues of interest to the teachers' union, this quarterly sets a more leisurely, cool-headed pace. Longer-range concerns are examined. A good part is both informative and persuasive propaganda, yet is never dull or pedantic. It has wider implications for all those involved or interested in education. As it comes with a subscription to *American Teacher,* the reader or librarian actually has two magazines for the price of one. They are both well worth the subscription.

The Classical Bulletin. 1925. m. (Nov.–Apr.). $2. John J. Welch. Dept. of Classical Languages. St. Louis Univ., 221 N. Grand, St. Louis, Mo. 63103. Index, adv. Circ: 1,750. Sample. Vol. ends: Apr. Microform: UM.

Indexed: CathI. *Aud:* Ac.

A 16-page report on activities in Latin and Greek classical studies, i.e. literature, language, history, and culture. Usually two to three articles, such as "Ancient myth and modern play," or "Children in the Media." Brief notes. Despite its small size, it is one of the more important periodicals in this field, and should be in all larger academic collections.

Classical Journal. 1905. bi-m. $8. W. Robert Jones. Classical Assn. of the Middle West and South, Inc. Subs. to: Galen O. Rowe, Dept. of Classics, Univ. of Iowa, Iowa City, Iowa 52240. Illus., index., adv. Circ: 5,000. Microform: UM. Reprint: Johnson.

Indexed: EdI. *Bk. rev:* 8–12, 1,300 words, signed. *Aud:* Ac, Ga, Hs.

The best general classical journal in the field for teachers. In addition to the usual two to four articles, there are notes of the Association, and the "Forum," a source of helpful hints for teachers in secondary schools. An annual feature, "From Other Journals," constitutes a survey of articles which have appeared on classical subjects. It is invaluable for the teacher as well as the student, and is a handy checklist for the librarian attempting to build a meaningful periodical collection in this area. The book reviews by distinguished classical scholars are authoritative, critical, and detailed. A first choice for most school, academic, and public libraries. See also *Classical World.*

Classical Outlook. 1936. m. (Sept.–June). $5. Konrad Gries. Amer. Classical League, Queens College, Flushing, N.Y. 11367. Subs. to: Edna Cunningham, Miami Univ., Oxford, Ohio 45056. Index, adv. Circ: 5,000. Sample. Vol. ends: June.

Bk. rev: 11, 300 words, signed. *Aud:* Ac, Hs.

A professional magazine for the college and high school teacher of classics. (See also *Classical World,* the publication of the Classical Association of the Atlantic states.) Text is in English and, occasionally, Latin. It features news of the American Classical League, as well as of the Junior and Senior Classical Leagues. Special features: an annual listing (December) of scholarships for summer study available to teachers; an annual listing (December) of financial assistance available to undergraduates and graduate students of the classics; an annual listing (April) of summer courses and workshops; placement service; and a service bureau which offers for sale materials such as posters, tapes, stationery, etc. Membership in the American Classical League includes a subscription. A basic, extremely useful journal in any high school or college where the classics are taught.

Classical Review. 1886. 3/yr. $7.25. C. J. Fordyce and J. S. Morrison. Oxford Univ. Press, Ely House, Dover St., London W1, England. Index. Circ: 1,378. Sample. Microform: UM. Reprint: Johnson.

Indexed: BritHum, IBZ, SSHum. *Bk. rev:* Numerous, length varies, signed. *Aud:* Ac.

The second of two journals published under the auspices of the Classical Association and the Oxford and Philological Societies. The other is *Classical Quar-*

terly. The *Review* differs from the *Quarterly* in terms of emphasis. Most of the journal is composed of signed, often essay-length reviews of some 40 to 60 titles per issue. About as many shorter notices are also included. Living up to the best British tradition, the comments are detailed, comparative, extremely well written, and rarely superfluous. Although many of the titles represent English publishers, an equal number are from American and continental presses. While for the average library the book reviews in the *Classical Journal* will be sufficient—and usually more current—*The Classical Review* is a basic selection medium in larger, specialized libraries.

Classical World. 1907. m. (Sept.–June). $5.25. Joseph A. Maurer. Classical Assn. of the Atlantic States, Lehigh Univ., 246 Mayinnes Hall, Bethlehem, Pa. 18015. Index, adv. Circ: 3,200. Microform: UM. Reprint: Kraus.

Bk. rev: 16–22, 250 words, signed. *Aud:* Ac, Hs.

The eastern seaboard equivalent of *Classical Journal*. It features brief, signed, scholarly articles, with useful bibliographies. An annual aid is the list of audiovisual materials, Greek and Latin college textbooks, and inexpensive titles for the teaching of the classics. High school teachers find the occasional list of historical fiction with classical themes for young adults particularly helpful. This is a useful item wherever the classics constitute a part of the curriculum. While required in most eastern libraries, a second choice for others, after the more scholarly *Classical Journal*.

Comparative Education Review. 1956. 3/yr. $10. Andreas Kazamais. Comparative and International Education Soc., Univ. of Wisconsin, Madison, Wis. 53706. Circ: 3,000. Sample. Vol. ends: Oct. Reprint: Johnson.

Indexed: EdI. *Bk. rev:* 12, 800 words, signed. *Aud:* Ac, Sa.

A basic journal in comparative and international education. Each number averages 10 to 15 articles of both a descriptive and analytical nature. The level of scholarship is high, the style relatively difficult. As the magazine stresses international coverage, it has some interest for political scientists and sociologists, but the primary audience is the professional educator. Only for large collections.

Contemporary Education. 1929. 6/yr. Free. Dale Baughman, 217 Alumni Center, Indiana State Univ., Terre Haute, Ind. 47809. Illus., index. Circ: 3,500. Vol. ends: May. Refereed. Microform: UM.

Indexed: CIJE, CurrCont, EdI. *Bk. rev:* 1–2, 400 words, signed. *Aud:* Ac, Hs, Ejh.

"Presents competent discussions of professional problems in education and toward this end usually restricts its contributing personnel to those of training

and experience in the field." About one half of the issue concentrates on a theme: Teacher education: Pressure and Problems; Education for Peace. In view of its content and the fact that it is free it is certainly worth trying in almost any library.

Counselor Education and Supervision. 1961. q. $6. Edwin L. Herr. American Personnel and Guidance Assn., 1607 New Hampshire Ave., N.W., Washington, D.C. 20009. Index, adv. Circ: 4,000. Vol. ends: June. Refereed. Microform: UM.

Aud: Ac, Hs.

A basic journal for those teaching personnel and guidance work. (It is not for the student seeking personnel or guidance counseling.) The articles are by professionals, range from elementary school guidance through formal training in a university. As a journal for those who guide the guides, it will be of interest to only the large academic library.

Dramatics. See Theater Section.

Epie Forum. See *Educational Product Report*.

Education Digest. 1935. m. (Sept.–May). $6. Lawrence Prakken, Prakken Publns., Inc., 416 Longshore Dr., Ann Arbor, Mich. 48107. Index, adv. Circ: 49,000. Microform: UM. Reprint: Abrahams.

Indexed: CIJE, EdI, RG. *Bk. rev:* 5, 120 words. *Aud:* Ga, Ac, Hs, Ejh.

Drawing upon what the editors consider to be the best and most representative articles on education, this magazine condenses or publishes in full some 15 to 20 contributions each month. The scope is broad, moving through the elementary grades to graduate school, and the magazine is purposefully geared for the generalist. The articles average two to four pages in length, and the style of writing depends to a degree upon the original source. The editors claim they research some 300 magazines a month for articles. Regular features include: "With Education in Washington," "Education Briefs," "Dates of the Month," "New Educational Materials" and a limited number of short book reviews. This is primarily for the library with little demand for educational news and research. It will not satisfy the professional educator or the serious student, but admittedly is a handy overview of more important educational issues.

Education Summary; a bi-weekly analysis of new developments, trends, ideas and research in education. 1947. bi-w. $25. James Bolyer. Croft Educational Services, 100 Garfield Ave., New London, Conn. 06320. Circ: 18,000.

Bk. rev: Various number, length. *Aud:* Ac, Ga.

A looseleaf newsletter issued semimonthly to keep subscribers advised of latest developments in elementary, secondary, and higher education. The service is particularly useful for keeping up with current federal and state activities, and is good as an up-to-date reference source. Not only for education collections, but for any medium to large-sized reference department where there are recurrent questions in the area. (A bit expensive, though, for most libraries.)

Education and Urban Society. 1968. q. $15 (Individuals $10). Louis H. Masotti. Sage Publications Inc., 275 South Beverly Dr., Beverly Hills, Calif. 90212. Illus., index, adv. Sample. Vol. ends: August.

Bk. rev: Group essays, lengthy, signed. *Aud:* Ac.

The sociologists look at urban elementary and secondary education in some six or seven articles and come up with pretty much the same set of conclusions. It is hopeless, but the child will get through. There is much here on finance, politics, and such jargon as "factorial structure of self-concept and sense of control attitudes." Clear it away, and a good deal of the material will help the student to understand current urban education problems. A bigger help: the long and numerous book reviews—they make up about one quarter of each issue.

Educational Product Report (Formerly: *Epie Forum*). 1967. m. (Oct.–June). $35. Educational Products Information Exchange Inst., 386 Park Ave. S., New York, N.Y. 10016. Index. Circ: 3,500. Vol. ends: June.

Indexed: CIJE. *Aud:* Ac, Hs, Ejh.

A consumer's report for the administrator and teacher who must select equipment and materials for schools from the elementary through high school. (Some of the equipment, however, is used in colleges and universities—particularly schools of education—and therefore the magazine is almost as valuable at this level.) Issues have dealt with programmed instruction, science kits, 8mm projectors, study carrels, textbooks, and the like. Comparative data is given for price, grade level, content or design, and producer's warrantees in a self-contained section. Informative articles, interviews, analyses, and guidelines are presented in the main portion of each issue. A required magazine for almost every situation where a decision must be made regarding the purchase of materials for education.

Educational Record. 1920. q. $10. C. G. Dobbins. Amer. Council on Education. One Dupont Circle, Washington, D.C. 20036. Illus. Circ: 9,500. Microform: UM.

Indexed: CIJE, EdI, PAIS, PsyAb. *Bk. rev:* 15 (Fall and Summer Issues), 500–2,500 words. *Aud:* Ac.

Covering the general education field, emphasis is on material of interest to the college and university administrator, school of education personnel and, to a limited extent, faculty. The content and style are scholarly, yet pragmatic in that specific suggestions are often given on everything from legal and governmental regulations to how to train the junior college teacher. The importance of the American Council on Education gives the *Record* added interest, since the activities of the Council are reported in full. Only for larger libraries.

Educational Studies; a journal of book reviews in the foundations of education. 1970. q. Membership. $6. John A. Laska. American Educational Studies Assn. Subs. to: Peter Hackett, School of Education, Univ. of Virginia, Charlottesville, Va. 22903. Index, adv. Circ: 1,500. Sample. Vol. ends: Winter.

Bk. rev: 250–300, 200–400 words. *Aud:* Ac, Ga, Hs, Ejh.

As the subtitle indicates, the complete journal is composed of reviews of books in education. The 250 to 300 titles examined are arranged under broad subject headings, apply to teachers and students from elementary school through graduate school. The signed reviews are from 200 to 400 words long, critical, and generally descriptive of content, purpose, and scope. Reviewers primarily are university teachers in the field of education. Most titles are recent, or none more than six months to a year old. There is an author and reviewers index, but no subject index—a badly needed feature. As a basic review medium, this should be found in all professional educational collections, and in any library buying books in the area. It is not only timely and authoritative, it is reasonably priced.

Educational Theory; a medium of expression for the John Dewey Society and the Philosophy of Education Society. 1961. q. Membership (Nonmembers $6). Joe R. Burnett. Education Bldg., Univ. of Illinois, Urbana, Ill. 61801. Index, adv. Circ: 2,100. Sample. Vol. ends: No. 4. Refereed. Microform: UM. Reprint: Johnson.

Indexed: CIJE, CurrCont, EdI, PhilosI. *Bk. rev:* 2, 2,000 to 4,000 words, signed. *Aud:* Ac.

"The general purposes of this journal are to foster the continuing development of educational theory and to encourage wide and effective discussion of theoretical problems within the education profession." Scholarly articles further this end, and material covered will be of interest to any student of the history, theory, or practical application of educational philosophy. Primarily for graduate students in schools of education, and definitely for those interested in the theoretical and historical aspects of education.

Greece and Rome. 1931. s-a. $4. P. Walcot and E. R. A. Sewter. Oxford Univ. Press, Ely House, Dover St. London W1, England. Illus., adv. Circ: 2,000. Sample. Microform: UM. Reprint: Johnson, Abrahams.

Indexed: BritHum, IBZ. *Bk. rev:* 40, short, signed. *Aud:* Ac, Hs.

Whereas the Classical Association's *Classical Review* is for the scholar, this is the review medium for the teacher at the high school and beginning college level. The reviews rate books according to four categories: "Recommended for school libraries," "For advanced students," "For non-Greek readers," and "Include bibliographies." Each note gives a concise and useful evaluation. There is a limited amount of textual material and some fine art. For reviewing purposes, a third or fourth choice in most American libraries.

Harvard Educational Review. 1931. q. $10. Harvard Univ., Graduate School of Education, Longfellow Hall, 13 Appian Way, Cambridge, Mass. 02138. Index, adv. Circ: 14,000. Sample. Vol. ends: Nov. Microform: UM. Reprint: Johnson.

Indexed: CIJE, EdI, PAIS, PsyAb, SocAb. *Bk. rev:* 8–10, 3–6 pages; 1–2, long essays, signed. *Aud:* Ac. *Jv:* V.

The intellectual teacher's quarterly, certainly the basic journal for anyone even remotely connected with educational policy or the education and supervision of teachers. Here, as in the less ambitious *Educational Theory*, the emphasis is on theoretical, long-range topics that concern not only education but also the relationship of education to the larger society. Many of the contributors are distinguished in fields outside of education. The tone is scholarly, always critical, always challenging, and rarely dull. A major journal for all medium to large-sized libraries where education and its many facets are of interest.

Interchange: a journal of educational studies. 1970. q. $7 (Individuals $5). Andrew Effrat. Ontario Institute for studies in Education, 252 Bloor St. W., Toronto, 5, Ont., Canada. Adv. Sample.

Indexed: CIJE, CanEdI, CurrCont, PsyAb. *Bk. rev:* 6–8, essays, signed. *Aud:* Ac.

While *Orbit,* a publication of the same organization, is geared for teachers, laymen and students, *Interchange* is for the professor in schools of education. One supposes this audience will consider, but the 120 pages are pretty rough going for anyone but the dedicated. The style is scholarly, material is documented, and topics are to the point, e.g., "What is Individualized Instruction?" and "Games and Learning." A film review of Frederick Wiseman's *High School* is about the shortest and easiest to read piece in the issue examined. Well, one does need this type of journal, but considering the purpose and drive of *Orbit* why is it not 120 pages and *Interchange*, which offers no more than found in scores of other scholarly publications, cut down to an essential 30 pages?

International Review of Education. 1955. q. $10. Martinus Nijhoff, Lange Voorhout 9-11, The Hague, Netherlands. Index, Circ: 2,000. Sample. Vol. ends: No. 4.

Indexed: CIJE, EdI, BritEdI, CurrCont. *Bk. rev:* 20, 500–1,500 words, signed. *Aud:* Ac.

Edited on behalf of the UNESCO Institute for Education under the direction of an international independent Board of Editors, with articles in German, French, and English, and summaries in the three languages. Articles cover all aspects of education. The *Review* has excellent book reviews of titles not often found in American journals. It is primarily for the teacher of education, the educational planner and administrator, and those doing graduate study in related fields such as sociology and political science.

Jewish Education. 1929. q. $5. Alvin Schith. National Council for Jewish Education, 101 Fifth Ave., New York, N.Y. 10003. Index, adv.

Indexed: PsyAb. *Bk. rev:* 8, 50–75 words, signed. *Aud:* Ac, Hs, Ejh.

Deals exclusively with the problems and directions of Jewish education in America and abroad. Most emphasis is on the early years of education. Periodically, there is an added section for preschoolers. A required item in large school of education collections, and will be appreciated in any community with a large Jewish population.

Journal of American Indian Education. See Indians (American) Section.

Journal of Creative Behavior. 1967. q. $8. Angelo M. Biondi. Creative Education Foundation, State University of New York at Buffalo, 1300 Elmwood Ave., Buffalo, N.Y. 14222. Adv. Circ: 5,000. Vol. ends: 4th quarter.

Indexed: CIJE. *Aud:* Ac, Hs, Ejh.

Although the subject scope here is limited to "the general area of creativity, intelligence and problem-solving," the magazine has wide appeal for teachers sharing interdisciplinary interests. The six to eight articles, reports on various research activities, bibliographic services, etc., are well within the grasp of the more involved elementary, secondary, or university teacher, the researcher and scholar. Well worth a subscription in more advanced school libraries and in all larger schools of education.

Journal of Education. 1875. q. $3. Adolph Manoil. Boston Univ. School of Education, 765 Commonwealth Ave., Boston, Mass. 02116. Illus. Circ: 2,500. Sample. Vol. ends: April. Microform: UM. Reprint: Johnson.

Indexed: CIJE, EdI. *Aud:* Ac, Hs, Ejh.

Devoted to the in-service education of school teachers. Each issue focuses on a particular theme. There are usually five well-documented articles, but each issue is almost a book in itself. Noted for the practical nature of its articles, this a must for any library concerned with elementary or secondary education.

Journal of Educational Psychology. 1910. bi-m. $10. Raymond G. Kuhlen. Amer. Psychological Assn., Inc., 1200 17th St., N.W., Washington, D.C. 20036. Illus., index, adv. Circ: 8,325. Microform: UM. Reprint: AMS, Abrahams.

Indexed: BioAb, EdI, PsyAb. *Aud:* Ac.

"Publishes original investigations and theoretical papers dealing with problems of learning, teaching, and the psychological development, relationships, and adjustment of the individual." The editors give preference "to studies of the more complex types of behavior, especially in or relating to educational settings." The articles "concern all levels of education and all age groups." The style of writing is scholarly, and requires a solid background in psychology.

The Journal of Educational Research. 1920. 10/yr. $10. Wilson Thiede. Dembar Educational Research Services, Inc., Box 1605, Madison, Wis. 53701. Illus., index, adv. Circ: 6,800. Microform: UM, Canner. Reprint: AMS.

Indexed: EdI, PsyAb. *Bk. rev:* 1–2, 500–1,500 words, signed. *Aud:* Ac, Hs, Ejh.

An overall view for anyone seriously involved with educational research. Short reports move from elementary school problems through graduate study. Each article is well documented, normally accompanied by useful charts, tables, and graphs. This is the basic journal in this field, and, as such, should be found in all large libraries and schools of education. Progressive elementary and secondary school libraries will also wish to subscribe. See also the same publisher's *Journal of Experimental Education.*

Journal of Experimental Education. 1932. q. $10. John Schmid. Dembar Educational Research Services, Inc., Box 1605, Madison, Wis. 53701. Illus., index, adv. Circ: 2,000. Microform: UM, Canner. Reprint: AMS.

Indexed: EdI. *Aud:* Ac.

Similar to *Journal of Educational Research* in scope, but more esoteric. Emphasis is upon new and experimental tests and procedures. Articles are for and by teachers of education at all levels. Extensive use is made in the articles of graphs, charts, and statistics. Only for the largest colleges having teacher education programs.

Journal of Industrial Arts Education. See Man/Society/Technology.

Journal of Learning Disabilities. 1967. m. $10. P. E. Lane. Professional Press, 5 N. Wabash Ave., Chicago, Ill. 60602. Illus., index, adv. Circ: 12,000. Sample. Vol. ends: Dec. Refereed.

Indexed: CIJE, PsyAb. *Bk. rev:* 2–3, 500 words, signed. *Aud:* Ac, Hs, Ejh.

"Our purpose is to serve as an unbiased forum of exchange and rebuttal for qualified research, new developments and advances in the many disciplines concerned with learning disabilities." The journal represents 24 disciplines, from anthropology to speech. Each is supported by a member of a large editorial advisory board, primarily made up of professors and doctors. The four to five articles touch every level, from adult education to techniques used in diagnosing a learning disability in a child. Obviously for the professional educator and specialist, yet will have considerable interest for the average elementary school through college teacher who works in this area.

Journal of Negro Education. See Blacks Section.

Journal of Research and Development in Education. 1967. q. $7. Ms. E. J. Blewett, College of Education, Univ. of Georgia, 175 W. Wievca Rd. N. E., Atlanta, Ga. 30342. Illus., index. Circ: 5,000. Vol. ends: Summer. Microform: UM.

Aud: Ac, Hs, Ejh.

Each issue of the 132-page journal is devoted to the treatment of a central theme. Subjects are selected from proposals submitted by members of the education profession who serve in the capacity of Advisory or Guest Editor, if their theme is accepted. Contributors of articles do so by invitation. Detailed references accompany each article. The journal is used extensively for pre-service and in-service teacher training. Teachers and administrators at all levels of education may find it of interest.

Journal of Research in Mathematics Education. See Mathematics Section.

Journal of Teacher-Education. 1950. q. $8. D. D. Darland. National Education Assn., Div. of Instruction and Professional Development, 1201 16th St., N. W., Washington, D. C. 20036. Index, adv. Circ: 9,000. Sample. Vol. ends: Winter. Microform: UM. Reprint: Kraus.

Indexed: CIJE, EdI, PsyAb. *Bk. rev:* 8–10, 500–1,000 words, signed. *Aud:* Ac.

Devoted exclusively to teacher education. Usually contains 12 to 15 signed monographs from professional contributors. Frequently a single current problem or question is considered. The articles are scholarly and primarily geared for schools of education. Regular features: "With the Researchers," "ERIC Clearinghouse on Teacher Education," "They Said This," "Browsing Through the Bookshelves." An essential magazine for universities or junior colleges with any type of teacher education program.

Lighting. 1934. bi-m. $2. Edward A. Campbell. Better Light/Better Sight Bureau, 90 Park Ave., New York, NY. 10016. Illus. Index. Circ: 20,000. Vol. ends: July/Aug. Sample.

Aud: Ga, Ac.

The sponsoring body states its purpose as being "to foster through educational means a better understanding of the relationship of light and sight." Subject matter covers distinctive examples of lighting design in a variety of buildings including schools, municipal buildings, office complexes, factories, and industrial showrooms, whose lighting has been conceived as a part of the structural or decorative design, as well as being functional. There is some emphasis on school facilities such as libraries and auditoriums, and occasionally an article describes an innovative school building or complex, highlighting the desirability of electric features which it incorporates. This may be useful in the school field for administrators contemplating building or renovation projects, as well as those concerned with the planning of lighting for other types of buildings. There may also be some small value in an introductory study of the aesthetics of architecture. Nicely illustrated, and adequately presenting its material for the intended readership. (Formerly published as *BLBS News.*) (A.S.)

Lovejoy's Guidance Digest. 1947. 10/yr. $15. Clarence E. Lovejoy's Guidance Services, 443 Broad St., Red Bank, N.J. 07701. Index, adv. Circ: 4,000. Sample.

Aud: Ac, Hs, Ga.

This monthly supplement to Lovejoy's familiar *College Guide* provides up-to-date news of colleges and schools to prospective students, their parents, and guidance counselors. Its 20 pages contain newsy short articles concerning scholarship information, innovations in colleges and education, how to get into college, and a great deal of advertising from colleges and prep schools. There are two regular monthly features of interest to students: "Career Corner," a description of a specific occupation, and "New Programs," a listing of new majors offered by colleges and private schools.

Man/Society/Technology; a journal of industrial arts education (Formerly: *Journal of Industrial Arts Education*). 1941. 8/yr. $9 (Individual membership $15; students $7.50). Edward Kabakjian. Amer. Industrial Arts Assn., 1201 16th St., N.W., Washington, D.C. 20036. Illus., index, adv. Circ: 10,000. Vol. ends: May/June. Refereed. Microform: UM.

Indexed: CIJE, CurrCont, EdI. *Bk. rev:* 3, 200 words, signed. *Aud:* Ga, Hs.

Covers all aspects of industrial arts education, and is particularly valuable for teachers in technical schools, high schools, and community colleges. An average 30 to 40 page issue is directed towards discussion of developments in technology as they are (or should be) reflected in education; teaching methods, employment opportunities, personalities, etc. On occasion a number is given over to a single topic, e.g., January 1972 fea-

tures seven articles on communications, from the visual and graphic to organizing a course. Authors tend to give practical advice, limit themselves to short pieces, and are wonderfully free of jargon. Most of the material is well illustrated with photographs or diagrams and charts. A regular feature is "The Researcher's Index"—an author-title listing of two or three pages of dissertations. A basic magazine in this area.

Mathematical Gazette. See Mathematics Section.

The Mathematics Teacher. See Mathematics Section.

Media & Methods. See Communications and Media Section.

Modern Schools. 1955. 9/yr. (Sept.—May). $2.50. Marcella M. Koch. Electrical Information Publns., 2132 Fordem Ave., P.O. Box 1648, Madison, Wis. 53701. Illus. Index. Circ: 40,000. Adv. Vol. ends: Dec. Sample.

Aud: Ga, Ac.

This 16-page magazine is intended primarily to promote the use of electric power in schools, and may prove helpful to administrators looking for ideas to be used in building remodeling, or in selection of equipment. Articles are divided between the presentation of new "all electric" schools, and the showing of various ways in which electrically powered equipment can improve various facilities of school plant operation, such as heating and cooling, water heating, food service, and teaching equipment. School food service directors may be interested as well in the recipes and menus suggested for school cafeterias. A customer service "mailer" is included in each issue, to be used for further information on any of the installations described. Adequate format. (A.S.)

National Business Education Quarterly. See *Business Education Forum.*

National Catholic Guidance Conference Journal (Formerly: *Catholic Counselor*). 1956. q. $5. Donald Briggs, Univ. of Minnesota, 332 Walter Library, Minneapolis, Minn. 55455. Illus., index, adv.

Indexed: CathI. *Aud:* Ac, Hs.

Geared to the practice and theory of guidance and related areas, specifically to Catholic schools and colleges, or to Catholic students in other institutions. Articles appear to be fairly scholarly and are written by members of the association. (C.B.)

Negro Education Review. See Blacks Section.

Phoenix. 1947. q. $10. Classical Assn. of Canada, Univ. of Toronto Press, Toronto, Ont., Canada. Illus., index, adv. Circ: 1,100. Sample. Vol. ends: Winter. Refereed.

Bk. rev: 15, 750 words, signed. *Aud:* Ac.

Features articles on philology, literature, philosophy, archaeology, and history. The interdisciplinary approach gives it added interest, but as all contributors are scholars writing for their fellows, it is difficult reading. And while the official voice of the Classical Association of Canada, contributors are international and the amount of news notes and material for teachers is limited. The book reviews cover much the same ground as *Classical Journal* and *The Classical Review*. Articles are in either French or English. A basic acquisition for Canadian academic libraries, but only for large American collections.

Prospects in Education. See Government Magazines/ United States Section.

Review of Educational Research. 1931. q. Membership (Nonmembers $10). Sam Messick. American Educational Research Assn., 1126 16th St., N.W., Washington, D.C. 20036. Adv. Circ: 10,000. Vol. ends: Fall. Microform: UM. Reprint: AMS.

Indexed: CIJE, EdI, PsyAb. *Aud:* Ac.

The basic journal for the national organization of educators and behavioral scientists "who have a vital interest in basic research in education and the improvement, development and application of that research to education problems." Beginning in 1970 the policy of publishing solicited manuscripts around a single subject changed to a more general approach. The magazine now publishes not only reviews of educational research, but those in the social and behavioral sciences, management, and humanities, so long as they bear on educational issues. The papers tend to be technical, rather heavy going. It is primarily for professional schools of education at the academic level.

Scholastic Coach. See Sports/Physical Education and School Sports Section.

School Business Affairs. 1936. m. Membership (Nonmembers $30; college and univ. libraries $15). Charles W. Fostern. Assn. of School Business Officials, 2424 W. Lawrence Ave., Chicago, Ill. 60625. Illus., index, adv. Circ: 5,000.

Bk. rev: 20, notes, signed. *Aud:* Ejh, Hs, Ac.

Geared for the dollars and cents activities of education from the elementary through the junior college level. A 20 to 26 page issue includes news of the parent organization, personalities, and four to five articles, as well as shorter news briefs. The material includes "accounting, finance, budgeting, insurance, maintenance & operations, management, personnel, office management, food service, transportation, book stores, data processing, purchasing school buildings, etc." A stiff price for other than members (who get it with their membership) although large academic schools of education might want it at the reduced rate.

School Product News. See Free Magazines.

School Review; a journal for research, theory and philosophical inquiry in education and related disciplines. 1893. 4/yr. $8 (Students $4). Benjamin D. Wright. Univ. of Chicago Press, 5801 Ellis Ave., Chicago, Ill. 60637. Illus., adv. Circ: 4,000. Sample. Vol. ends: Aug. Microform: UM.

Indexed: CIJE, EdI. *Bk. rev:* 3-4, 3-15 pages, signed. *Aud:* Ac, Hs.

Authors consider philosophical and pragmatic approaches to educational practice and theory. Most, although not all, emphasis is on secondary education. The result is a forum for the intellectual aspects of education. As the authors are varied in opinion and experience, the articles are uneven. Some are sparkling, innovative; others are speculative and dull. But the overall mix is good to excellent, and it is the type of journal which has won general respect from its readers. A required item in schools of education, and welcome in any secondary school professional collection.

School and Society. 1915. s-m. (Oct.–May). $10.75. William W. Brickman. Soc. for the Advancement of Education, 1860 Broadway, New York, N.Y. 10023. Index, adv. Circ: 8,300. Microform: UM. Reprint: Johnson.

Indexed: EdI, PsyAb, RG. *Aud:* Ac, Hs, Ejh.

A somewhat jargon-ridden approach to the topics of current secondary and higher education, although the coverage is broad enough to overcome the style. Articles cover every conceivable facet of current secondary and advanced education. The six to eight contributions are semipopular and the journal has expanded news coverage in education, including pictorial reporting. Special departments: events, special book preview (excerpts from forthcoming books). Way down the list, except for the large school of education or general professional collection.

Sociology of Education. 1927. q. $9. Charles E. Bidwell. Amer. Sociological Assn., 1001 Connecticut Ave., N.W., Washington, D. C. 20036. Illus., index., adv. Circ: 2,400. Microform: UM.

Indexed: EdI, PAIS, PsyAb. *Aud:* Ac.

An international and interdisciplinary journal. The presentations use the perspectives of history, anthropology, education, political science, psychology, and sociology to analyze educational institutions. The four 15 to 25 page articles are research studies on such subjects as investment in education and economic growth; teacher attitudes toward academic freeedom; the relation of education, mobility, social values, and expectations. A specialized magazine for schools of education and larger school professional collections.

Southern Education Report. See *Race Relations Reporter* in Blacks Section.

Studies in Art Education. See Art Section.

Studies in Philosophy and Education. 1960. irreg. $6. Francis T. Villemain. Southern Illinois University, Edwardsville, Ill. 62025. Index, adv. Circ: 1,000. Sample. Vol. ends: Nov.

Indexed: CIJE. *Aud:* Ac.

One of the few education journals given entirely to the theoretical aspects of education and society. It enjoys a small circulation which deserves to be larger, and certainly should be supported by schools of education.

Teachers College Record: a professional journal of ideas, research and informed opinion. 1900. m. (Sept.–May). $10.00. Frank G. Jennings. Teachers College, Columbia Univ., 525 W. 120th St., New York, N.Y. 10027. Index, adv. Circ: 7,300. Vol. ends: May. Microform: UM.

Indexed: CIJE, EdI, HistAb, PsyAb. *Bk. rev:* 8, 800 words, signed. *Aud:* Ac, Hs, Ejh. *Jv:* V.

An excellent magazine on the philosophy and methodology of education. It has appeal for students and teachers at all levels. As the editors explain, "It is a forum for articulate discussion by those engaged in the teaching activity." There are usually about ten articles, which survey current opinions, as well as a wide-ranging book review section concentrating on books of both general and specialized interest to the educator. A good deal of emphasis is placed on the humanities and the behavioral sciences, hence giving it a considerably broader appeal than the related *Journal of Teacher-Education.* While this may be relatively difficult going for the average reader, it is among the best of its kind for the involved educator—therefore the high rating and the recommendation that it be in all school libraries.

Teaching Adults. 1966. q. $2.50. Arthur Stock. National Inst. of Adult Education, 35 Queen Anne St., London W1M OBL, England. Circ: 10,000. Sample. Vol. ends: April.

Aud: Ac.

Differs from the British *Adult Education* in that emphasis is on current news and short articles which cover research, organization, and personnel. Valuable equipment evaluation is done. The journal frequently has short notes on new magazines. Only for large, comprehensive collections.

Technical Education News. See Free Magazines Section.

Theory Into Practice. 1962. 5/yr. $5. Jack R. Frymier. College of Education, Arps Hall, Ohio State Univ., 1945 N. High St., Columbus, Ohio 43210. Circ: 3,700. Sample. Vol. ends: Dec. Reprint: Kraus. Microform: UM.

Indexed: CIJE. *Bk. rev:* 2–3, 100–900 words, signed. *Aud:* Ac, Hs, Ejh.

"Committed to the point of view that there is an integral relationship between educational theory and practice." Each issue focuses on a specific theme, e.g., research, independent study, planning for education change. The format is above average, and the general style of writing and research makes it a worthy addition for all school of education libraries and large elementary and high school teachers' libraries.

Unesco Courier. See Government Magazines/United Nations and Selected Foreign.

Western European Education. 1969. q. $50 (Individuals $10). Ursula Springer. International Arts & Science Press, Inc., 901 N. Broadway, White Plains, N.Y. 10603. Index, adv. Sample. Vol. ends: Winter.

Index: CurrCont. *Aud:* Ac.

After launching *Soviet Education* in 1958 and *Chinese Education* in 1968, the publishers finally turned to what remained from Europe after World War II. One might meditate on the principles of priority, but let us settle for "better late than never." The new publication presents unabridged translations of articles from leading journals and some abridged research reports and documents from research centers of western European countries. Publishers focus every issue on a particular topic. It is a well-selected collection and an important contribution to the scholarly studies of comparative education.

State Education Association Publications

Every state except Rhode Island issues publications from the state education association. Most are concerned only with local issues, and while important to the area library, of limited interest to others. All of the magazines here listed are indexed in: *State Education Journal Index.* Those indexed and/or abstracted elsewhere are so indicated.

Alabama Education Assn., 422 Dexter Ave., Box 4177, Montgomery, Ala. 36104. *Alabama School Journal.* 1921. m. (Sept.–May). Membership (Nonmembers $4). Paul R. Hubbert. Illus., index, adv. Circ: 40,000.

Alaska Education Assn., Room 207, Seward Bldg., Juneau, Alaska. 99801. *Alaska Teacher.* 1953. 7/yr. Membership (Nonmembers $5). Illus., adv. Circ: 4,000. Bk. rev.

Arizona Education Assn., 2102 W. Indian School Rd., Phoenix, Ariz. 85015. *Arizona Teacher.* 1914. 5/yr. $2. Romona Weeks. Ed. bd. Illus., index, adv. Circ: 15,500. *Indexed:* EdI.

California Teachers Assn., 1705 Murchison Dr., Burlingame, Calif. 94011. *California Journal of Educational Research.* 1950. 5/yr. $10. Garford C. Gordon. Index. Circ: 1,374. *Indexed:* EdI, PsyAb. Bk. rev.

Colorado Education Assn., 5200 S. Quebec St., Englewood, Colo. 80110. *Colorado School Journal*. 1885. 19/yr. $5. Randall Lemond. Illus., adv. Circ: 28,000. Bk. rev.

Connecticut Education Assn., 21 Oak St., Hartford, Conn. 06106. *Connecticut Teacher*. 1932. m. (Oct.–May). Membership (Nonmembers $2.50). Norman E. Delisle. Illus., adv. Circ: 28,000. Bk. rev.

Florida Education Assn., 208 W. Pensacola St., Tallahassee, Fla. 32034. *Florida Education*. 1923. q. $3. Chuck Cook. Illus., adv. Circ: 50,000. Bk. rev.

Georgia Assn. of Educators, G.E.A. Bldg., 197 Central Ave., S.W., Atlanta, Ga. 30334. *Georgia Educator*. 1970. m. (Sept.–May). $8. Margaret B. Jones. Illus., adv. Circ: 27,361.

Hawaii Education Assn., 1649 Kalakaua Ave., Honolulu, Hawaii 96814. *HEA News Flash*. 1939. w. Membership. Mrs. Gardiner B. Jones. Circ: 10,500.

Idaho Education Assn., Inc., Box 2638, Boise, Idaho 83701. *Idaho Education News*. 1926. m. (Sept.–May). $1.75. Donovan van Douglas. Illus., adv. Circ: 8,500.

Illinois Education Assn., 100 E. Edwards St., Springfield, Ill. 62704. *Illinois Librarian*. 1855. q. $2. Francine Richard. Illus., adv. Circ: 80,000. *Indexed*: EdI. Bk. rev.

Indiana State Teachers Assn., 150 W. Market St., Indianapolis, Ind. 46204. *Indiana Teacher*. 1856. q. Membership. Lowell C. Rose. Illus. Circ: 42,000.

Kansas State Teachers Assn., 715 W. 10th St., Topeka, Kans. 66612. *Kansas Teacher*. 1914. m. (Sept.–May); s-m. (Oct.). $3. Anna M. Murphy. Illus., adv. Circ: 40,000.

Kentucky Education Assn., 101 W. Walnut St., Louisville, Ky. 40202. *Kentucky School Journal*. 1922. m. (Sept.–May). Membership (Nonmembers $2). Gerald Jaggers. Illus., adv. Circ: 34,000. *Indexed*: EdI. Bk. rev.

Louisiana Teachers Assn., 1755 Nicholson Dr., Box 1906, Baton Rouge, La. 70821. *Louisiana Schools*. 1923. m. (Sept.–May). $3. Illus., adv. Circ: 25,000.

Maine Teachers Assn., 184 State St., Augusta, Me. 04330. *Maine Teacher*. 1940. 9/yr. Membership (Nonmembers $3). John H. Marvin. Illus., adv. Circ: 12,000.

Maryland State Teachers Assn., Inc., 344 N. Charles St., Baltimore, Md. 21201. *Maryland Teacher*. 1944. q. Membership (Nonmembers $3). Milson C. Raver. Illus., adv. Circ: 28,000. *Indexed*: EdI. Bk. rev.

Massachusetts Teachers Assn., 20 Ashburn Pl., Boston, Mass. 02108. *Massachusetts Teacher*. 1914. m. (Sept.–May). Membership (Nonmembers, $2.25). Russell P. Burbank. Illus., adv. Circ: 49,500.

Minnesota Education Assn., 41 Sherburne Ave., St. Paul, Minn. 55103. *Minnesota Journal of Education*. 1920. 4/yr. $3.50. Donald N. Nelson. Illus., index, adv. Circ: 40,000. *Indexed*: EdI. Bk. rev.

Mississippi Education Assn., 219 N. President St., Drawer 22529, Jackson, Miss. 39205. *Mississippi Educational Advance*. 1911. m. (Oct.–May). Membership

(Nonmembers $2). C. A. Johnson. Illus., adv. Circ: 17,500.

Missouri State Teachers Assn., Teachers Bldg., Columbia, Mo. 65201. *School and Community*. 1915. m. (Sept.–May). $4.50. Inks Franklin. Illus., index, adv. Circ: 51,063. *Indexed*: EdI. Bk. rev.

Montana Education Assn., 1232 E. Sixth Ave., Box 1690, Helena, Mont. 59601. *Montana Education*. 1924. m. Membership. (Nonmembers $4). Illus., index, adv. Circ: 9,500.

Nebraska State Education Assn., 94846 Statehouse, Lincoln, Nebra. 68509. *Nebraska Education News* 1946. w. (Sept.–May). Membership (Nonmembers $2). Conrad Good. Illus., adv. Circ: 20,000.

Nevada State Education Assn., 151 Park St., Carson City, Nev. 89701. *Nevada Education Journal*. 1966. q. Membership (Nonmembers $4). Pat Stevenson. Illus., adv. Circ: 6,500. Bk. rev.

New Hampshire Education Assn., 103 N. State St., Box 800, Concord, N.H. 03301. *New Hampshire Educator*. 1920. 2/yr. Membership (Nonmembers $2). John B. Tucken. Illus., adv. Circ: 7,500. Bk. rev.

New Mexico Educational Assn., Box 729, Santa Fe, N.M. 87501. *New Mexico School Review*. 1921. q. Membership (Nonmembers $2). James W. Green. Illus., adv. Circ: 13,884. Bk. rev.

New York State Teachers Assn., 152 Washington Ave., Albany, N.Y. 12210. *New York State Education*. 1914. m. (Oct.–May). Membership (Nonmembers $2). Matthew F. Doherty. Illus., adv. Circ: 120,000. *Indexed*: EdI, PsyAb. Bk. rev.

North Carolina Education Assn., Box 27347, Raleigh, N.C. 27611. *North Carolina Education*. 1906. m. $2. Glenn Keever. Index, adv. Circ: 55,000. Bk. rev.

North Dakota Education Assn., Box J, Bismarck, N.D. 58501. *North Dakota Journal of Education*. 1959. 5/yr. Membership only. Richard J. Palmer. Illus., adv. Circ: 9,000. Bk. rev.

Ohio Education Assn., 225 E. Broad St., Columbus, Ohio 43215, *Ohio Schools*. 1923. s-m. (Sept.–May). Membership (Nonmembers $7.50). William E. Henry. Illus., adv. Circ: 95,000. *Indexed*: EdI.

Oklahoma Education Assn., 323 E. Madison, Oklahoma City, Okla. 73105. *Oklahoma Teacher*. 1919. m. (Sept.–May). Membership (Nonmembers $4). Illus., index, adv. Circ: 42,000. Bk. rev.

Oregon Education Assn., 1 Plaza Southwest, 6900 S.W. Haines Rd., Tigard, Ore. 97225. *Oregon Education*. 1926. s-m. (Sept.–May); (m. Dec.). Membership (Nonmembers $3). Richard H. Barss. Illus., adv. Circ: 22,000. Bk. rev.

Pennsylvania State Education Assn., 400 N. Third St., Harrisburg, Pa. 17101. *Pennsylvania School Journal*. 1852. q. Membership (Nonmembers $3.50). Barbara J. Stevens. Illus., adv. Circ: 95,000. *Indexed*: EdI. Bk. rev.

South Carolina Education Assn., 421 Zimalcrest Dr., Columbia, S.C. 29210. *South Carolina Education Jour-*

nal. 1966. 8/yr. Membership (Nonmembers $3). Patsy Oliver. Illus., index, adv. Circ: 29,000. Bk. rev.

South Dakota Education Assn., Box 939, Pierre, S.D. 57501. *Educators' Advocate.* 1961. 14/yr. $3.50. Clarence Drenkhahn. Illus., adv. Circ: 10,286.

Tennessee Education Assn., 598 James Robertson Parkway, Nashville, Tenn. 37219. *Tennessee Teacher.* 1934. m. (Sept.–May); s.m. (Oct.). Membership (Nonmembers $1.50). Sara S. Nolan. Illus., adv. Circ: 40,000. Bk. rev.

Texas State Teachers Assn., Inc., 316 W. 12th St., Austin, Tex. 78701. *Texas Outlook.* 1917. m. Membership (Nonmembers $4). L. P. Sturgeon. Illus., index, adv. Circ: 136,198. Bk. rev.

Vermont Education Assn., 138 Main St., Montpelier, Vt. 05602. *The Vermont Blackboard.* 1933. m. (Sept.–June). $4.50. Circ: 5,000.

Virginia Education Assn., 116 S. 3rd St., Richmond, Va. 23219. *Virginia Journal of Education.* 1907. m. (Sept.–May). Membership only. Phyllis G. Brown, Illus., index, adv. Circ: 52,500. *Indexed:* EdI. Bk. rev.

Washington Education Assn., 910 Fifth Ave., Seattle, Wash. 98104. *Washington Education.* 1889. m. (Oct.–May). $3.50 (Available only with joint subscription to *WEA Action;* combined cost, $5). Barbara Krohn. Index, adv. Circ: 40,465.

West Virginia Education Assn., 1558 Quarrier St., Charleston, W. Va. 25311. *West Virginia School Journal.* 1881. m. (Sept.–May). Membership (Nonmembers $2). Illus., index, adv. Circ: 21,500. Bk. rev.

Wisconsin Education Assn., Insurance Bldg., 119 Monona Ave., Madison, Wis. 53703. *Wisconsin Journal of Education.* 1856. m. Membership (Nonmembers $3). Arlene Tobias. Illus., adv. Circ: 44,500. *Indexed:* EdI.

Wyoming Education Assn., 115 E. 22nd St., Cheyenne, Wyo. 82001. *Wyoming Education News.* 1935. m. (Sept.–May). $2. Illus., adv. Circ: 6,649.

Counterculture

√**Change Magazine** (Formerly: **Change in Higher Education**). 1969. m. $10. George W. Bonham. Science and Univ. Affairs, N.B.W. Tower, New Rochelle, N.Y. 10801. Sample. Vol. ends: Dec.

Bk. rev: 30, notes, signed. *Aud:* Ac.

To say that we are living in a time of change is to state in black-and-white terms a truth that obviously deserves the benefit of some living color. Change is rampant everywhere. Its effects, however, are felt most noticeably in the city and on the campus. This magazine, which is one of commentary and criticism, devotes itself to an interpretation of the "sweep and drama of higher education in flux." It examines "higher education's present delicate state of nerves," and attempts to prescribe for these nerves. Contributors include educators and students (usually of the dissident variety), and what they contribute are essays on such subjects as the political mood on campus, student targets in the confrontation game, and the Berkeley heritage. A carefully edited magazine that puts campus growth in proper perspective.

EdCentric; a journal of educational change. 1968. 9/yr. $5. Bill Anderson. United States National Student Assn., Inc., Center for Educational Reform, 2115 S St., N.W., Washington, D.C. 20008. Illus., index. Sample.

Indexed: CIJE. *Bk. rev:* 2–3, 1,000 words, signed. *Aud:* Ac, Hs, Ejh.

For the past few years the Center for Educational Reform has tried to change education. One method is this 35 to 40 page broadside at the present educational system. Most attention is given to higher education, but there is plenty left over for the elementary and high schools. The writing is free of jargon, forthright, and usually as imaginative as it is intelligent. The writers "are students and recent students who recognize that to be worthwhile, education must meet the needs of all people and oppress no people." Articles discuss everything from texts and tenure to Vietnam and guerilla tactics for the public school teacher. Excellent book reviews. An activist magazine to liven up any education collection at any level—and, hopefully, it will get to schools of education as well as into elementary and high school libraries. The nonprofit sponsoring organization issues a number of pamphlets, directories, and bibliographies. Most are usually listed in the last pages of the magazine. Of major interest to any library is The Directory of Free Universities and Experimental Colleges.

An outgrowth of the Centers' Educational Liberation Front is the Source coalition which, with a little help from Swallow Press, issues the *Source Catalog.*

√**Independent School Bulletin.** 1941. q. $6. Esther Osgood. National Association of Independent Schools, 4 Liberty Square, Boston, Mass., 02109. Illus., index, adv. Circ: 9,500. Vol. ends: May.

Aud: Ac, Hs, Ejh.

By independent school, the association does not mean the free school, but rather the privately sponsored organization. An important distinction in terms of content, although even here there is a good deal of information of interest to those involved with experimental efforts. Directed to elementary and secondary school teachers and administrators, this stresses the peculiar benefits, and a few of the drawbacks, of a private or independent school education. The writing is lively, often controversial. A greater emphasis is found here on creative teaching and thinking than in many other formal educational publications. Obviously for all libraries serving this type of school, and for larger education collections.

√**Integrated Education; a report on race and schools.** 1963. bi-m. $8. Meyer Weinberg. Integrated Education Associates, 343 S. Dearborn St., Chicago, Ill. 60604. Illus., index, adv. Circ: 4,000. Sample. Vol. ends: Nov/Dec.

Indexed: CIJE, EdI, INeg, PAIS. *Bk. rev:* 5, length varies, signed. *Aud:* Ac, Hs, Ejh, Ga.

A nonpartisan 80 to 100 page report on developments in the integration of the nation's schools. Each issue includes a bibliography of current books and articles on the subject, and the ten pages or so arranged under 16 subject headings are an invaluable guide to integration and related topics. The bibliography is preceded by articles, a chronicle of race and schools on a state by state basis, and pertinent court decisions and documents. The July/August 1971 issue featured such articles as: "Testing and the educational power struggle," "Opportunities for blacks in engineering." A basic journal for almost all libraries.

New Schools Exchange Newsletter. 1969. bi-w. $10. Kate Marin. New Schools Exchange, 701B. Anacapa, Santa Barbara, Calif., 93101. Illus., index. Circ: 5,000. Sample.

Aud: Ac, Ga, Hs, Ejh.

A 16 to 20 page magazine which has two major missions. The first is to collect and offer information on elementary through high school educational experiments and patterns which try to break the traditional forms. This is achieved by regular departments: "Schools," which lists alternative schools and briefly explains what each is trying to accomplish; "People Seeking Places," advertisements for teachers and parents seeking new schools; "Places Seeking People," a listing of schools looking for pupils or teachers. The second mission, which now takes up about one half of the magazine, is to publish articles about specific schools, and ways of restoring vitality and meaning to education. Also, there are articles on parents, for as the editor points out: "We cannot learn what we owe the young, or even what the young are without first understanding what is going on in our own lives." This is rapidly becoming a major voice for the counterculture educational advocates, and of considerable interest to all teachers and many parents. Should be in teacher collections, and certainly in public and academic libraries.

Orbit; the journal for ideas about teaching and learning. 1970. 5/yr. $3. Hugh Oliver. Ontario Institute for Studies in Education. Publication Sales, OISE, 252 Bloor St. West, Toronto, 5, Ont., Canada. Illus.

Indexed: CanEdI. *Aud:* Hs, Ejh.

The Canadian teachers seem to have more than a slight edge on innovative, interesting educational magazines. First, *This Magazine Is About Schools* began publication; now a smaller but equally fascinating effort from Ontario: OISE. Averaging some 25 to 30 pages, the imaginatively edited and illustrated maga-

zine covers everything from micro-teaching to criticism of teacher education. The editors say this is for "everybody involved in or concerned with education," and adds it is "not written for students, but we foresee no harm if copies fall into their hands—on the contrary." Well, an article entitled "Kids Deserve a Natural Hi," a proposal for new approaches in education, seems to indicate the editors speak the same language as their charges.

Rank and File. 1968. 5/yr. $2.40. Ed. bd. 28 Manor Rd., London N16, England. Illus. Circ: 5,000. Vol. ends: Nov.

Bk. rev: 3, 500 words, signed. *Aud:* Ac, Hs, Ejh.

Nearly everybody complains about school: taxpayers, lawmakers, students, parents—teachers, too. And perhaps nowhere on either side of the Atlantic are these complaints more militant and solidly documented, nor coupled with such compellingly sensible proposals for righting what is wrong, than in *Rank and File.* Produced by "left-wing teachers within the NUT (National Union of Teachers) who believe the union should be the most effective factor in forcing change and progress, both in the general educational field and in the struggle for better salaries and conditions," it squarely attacks child-maiming evils like racism and caning, and aggressively argues for thorough-going democracy in education, smaller classes, an end to "streaming," improved wages, heightened professional recruitment, and—as the means to attain these ends should persuasion fail—strikes. For all labor and education collections: first, as an example of gutsier, more highly politicized teacher-union journalism than the AFT's *Changing Education* and *American Teacher;* second, as a suitable shelfmate to nonauthoritarian, Friedenbert–Kozol–Goodmanesque tradition-mashing titles like *This Magazine is About Schools* and *New Directions in Teaching.*

Summerhill Society Bulletin. 1960. bi-m. Membership. $3. 137a W. 14 St., New York, N.Y. 10011. Illus. Circ: 700.

Aud: Ga, Ejh.

The April/May 1971 processed 26-page issue featured the results of a questionnaire of 30 free schools, i.e., staff responses to childrens' activities, decision making in the schools, etc. This is typical of the material found in a bulletin dedicated to the Summerhill notion of change and consciousness raising in education. Most of the articles are based on experience, written by those involved, and pragmatic, e.g., how to start a free school, laws and regulations governing schools, reactions of parents and teachers to the kids etc., etc. It will offer the regular teacher some valuable hints, and suggests, as it is meant to do, viable alternatives. Most of the material is involved with the elementary grade level.

This Magazine Is About Schools. 1967. q. $4 ($3.50 Canadian). George Martell. 56 Esplanade St. E., No. 401 Toronto, Ont., Canada. Illus., adv. Circ: 10,000. Sample. Vol. ends: Fall. Microform: UM.

Indexed: API, CIJE. *Bk. rev:* Number varies, essay length. *Aud:* Ac, Ga, Hs, Ejh. *Jv:* V.

One of the more imaginative and fascinating approaches to elementary and high school education is offered in understandable prose. This is a nice switch from the jargon mill, and a switch which has won the magazine a fervent following. (The circulation, still far from impressive, has tripled in the past three years.) Although published in Canada, the material is useful to anyone involved with elementary and secondary education: parent, teacher, or administrator. The tone is progressive, and the emphasis is on innovation and improvement. There are usually 10 to 12 articles per 150-page issue, as well as poetry, provocative letters and short notes, and essays on controversial books, magazine articles, and public pronouncements by educators. Authors vary from a professor of religion and a freelance photographer to a music expert and a professor of English at Columbia. Material ranges from a study of films in schools to the meaning and use of rock music in education. The emphasis on media uses shows the strong influence of the best of McLuhan. Highly recommended not only for educators, but also for their brighter charges in high school.

Elementary and Secondary Education

American School Board Journal; a periodical of school administration. 1891. m. $8.00. James Betchkal. National School Boards Assn., State National Bank Plaza, Evanston, Ill. 60201. Illus., adv. Circ: 55,000. Microform: UM.

Indexed: EdI, PAIS. *Bk. rev:* 5–8, short to 1,500 words. *Aud:* Hs, Ejh.

Contains "articles on the work of boards of education and on problems of school administration, school business, fiscal and architectural subjects." It is a "market place for the objective examination of the significant issues, innovations, problems and points of view dealing with education today. The constant purpose of the *Journal* has always been the promotion of the efficiency of local public schools through the betterment of the work of school boards and their professional staffs." The style of writing is semipopular. Articles are written by and for professional educators, administrators and school board members at the primary and secondary levels. For large collections, but should be brought to the attention of administrators and board of education members in even the smallest community.

B. C. Teacher. 1921. m. (Oct.–May). $3.50. K. M. Aitchison. British Columbia Teachers' Federation, 105-2235 Burrard St., Vancouver 180, B.C., Canada. Illus., index, adv. Circ: 27,000. Sample. Vol. ends: May.

Indexed: CanEdI, CanI. *Bk. rev:* 6–8, length varies, signed. *Aud:* Hs, Ejh.

A well-edited 40 to 50 page magazine which represents the British Columbia Teachers' Federation, and in so doing offers articles of interest to any elementary or secondary school teacher. Issues examined seem to stress material for the secondary level. Articles, by teachers, administrators and professors of education, touch on all topics from audiovisual aids to philosophical questions concerning education, to teacher salaries. Thanks to a good deal of general material, the magazine will be of interest to many teachers outside of British Columbia, particularly in Canada.

CSSEDC Newsletter. 1970. 3/yr. Membership. $3. Thomas D. Ragan. National Council of Teachers of English, 1111 Kenyon Rd., Urbana, Ill. 61801. Circ: 600. Sample. Vol. ends: May.

Bk. rev: 8, notes. *Aud:* Hs.

A publication of the newly formed Conference for Secondary School English Department Chairmen (CSSEDC). "Articles intended to keep English department chairmen and others with comparable responsibilities alert to the role of the English department chairman and its relationship to the study and improvement of the teaching of English."

Canadian Education and Research Digest. See *Education Canada.*

Clearing House; a journal for modern junior and senior high faculties. 1920. m. (Sept.–May). $5. Joseph Green. Fairleigh Dickinson Univ., Teaneck, N.J. 07666. Index, adv. Circ: 9,200. Sample. Vol. ends: May. Microform: UM.

Indexed: CIJE, EdI, RG. *Bk. rev:* 3, 250 words, signed. *Aud:* Hs.

Articles, principally by college professors, offer the latest trends and developments in curriculum practices. Experiments, research findings and new slants on persistent problems in education are reported. Unburdened by statistical formulas and complicated charts and tables, the articles are concise and easily read. The emphasis is upon practical application to problems in courses of study, teaching methods, student activities, the library, guidance work, and other areas relating to programs, services, and personnel. Regular departments offer current information in the fields of the Humanities and instructional media. For teachers, guidance counselors, and administrators working in secondary schools.

Education Canada (Supersedes: *Canadian Education and Research Digest*). 1969. q. Membership (Nonmembers $5). Harriet Goldsborough. Canadian Education Assn., 252 Bloor St., W. Toronto, 5, Ont., Canada. Illus., index, adv. Circ: 5,500. Sample. Vol. ends: Dec.

Indexed: CanEdI, CanI, CurrCont, EdI. *Bk. rev:* 6–10, notes. *Aud:* Hs, Ejh.

The "official" journal for teachers and administrators in Canadian primary and secondary schools. Usually has five to seven articles which vary from the innovative to the pedestrian. The Canadian Education Association is not precisely the most adventuresome of its type, somewhat equivalent to the National Education Association in America before the NEA discovered unions. As a result the tone of the articles is not always up to some of the more advanced Canadian education journals. And yet, with that reservation, the magazine is important and does have a distinct voice. Addressed to "senior persons responsible for policy and administration," it manages to face practical problems with practical solutions. The writing style is good to excellent, and the editorial control quite adequate. In addition to the articles, which may be written by both those in the field and professors in schools of education, there is a brief listing of books. One or two articles in French, but the emphasis is on English.

The CEA also issues: *CEA Newsletter* (1945. 9/yr. Illus. Circ: 7,000. Sample. Vol. ends: May/June). This is a six-page report on CEA events, new programs, appointments and changes in legislation. It has a calendar of events, and a short booklist.

Educational Leadership. 1943. m. (Oct.–May). $6.50. Robert R. Leeper. Assn. for Supervision and Curriculum Development, NEA, 1201 16th St., N.W., Washington, D.C. 20036. Illus., adv. Circ: 18,573. Sample. Vol. ends: May. Microform: UM.

Indexed: CIJE EdI. *Bk. rev:* 8, 400 words, signed. *Aud:* Hs, Ejh.

Curriculum and all its implications are involved here and concern is with an administrative, professional educator, or teacher's view of curriculum in elementary and secondary schools. Usually an issue is given to a single major theme with an occasional general piece on education. Regular departments touch most bases from research to innovations in education. The whole is a trifle dull, yet as the voice of a major affiliate of the NEA well deserves a place in larger school and education collections.

Edvance. 1971. 5/yr. (Sept.–June). $3. Helen Scott. Combined Motivation Education Systems, 6300 River Rd., Rosemont, Ill. 60018. Illus. Sample.

Aud: Hs, Ejh.

A six-page, moderately priced newsletter which presents articles, curriculum materials, news notes, and practical classroom suggestions to help teachers provide meaningful effective experiences for their students. There is usually a long lead article on such sub-

jects as the search for values, or training parents and teachers in new ways of talking to kids. This is followed by short items, some of them reprints, and notes on new books, articles, films, etc. The whole has a chatty, informal character which should be of value to most teachers. Send for a sample.

Elementary English; a magazine of the language arts. 1924. 8/yr. (Oct.–May). Membership. $12. Rodney P. Smith. National Council of Teachers of English, 1111 Kenyon Rd., Urbana, Ill. 61801. Index, adv. Circ: 28,000. Sample. Vol. ends: Dec. Microform: UM. Reprint: Kraus.

Indexed: CIJE, CurrCont. EdI. *Bk. rev:* 25, 100–2,000 words, signed. *Aud:* Ejh.

Written for the teacher of English at the elementary and junior high school level. "Devoted to encouraging better teaching in the elementary language arts, this magazine contains practical, lively articles on reading, grammar, spelling, creative writing, and children's authors, as well as audiovisual developments, and news of the profession. The book reviews are in two sections. The professional section includes some seven new titles in long reviews of 1,000 to 2,000 words. The children's section considers some 18 titles in 100 to 300 word reviews. A required item in any school library.

Elementary School Journal. 1900. m. (Oct.–May). $6. Kenneth Rehage. Univ. of Chicago Press, 5750 S. Ellis Ave., Chicago, Ill. 60637. Index, adv. Circ: 19,500. Microform: UM.

Indexed: AbSocWk, CurrCont, EdI, PsyAb. *Bk. rev:* Occasional. *Aud:* Ac, Ejh.

Strives to keep elementary school educators abreast of new developments and provide them with practical in-service education. Generally its scope emphasizes what should go on in the classroom, but occasionally there are other types of articles. Each issue contains approximately 8 to 10 articles. It is more scholarly than *Childhood Education,* and some of the writers have a tendency to lapse into an educational jargon which is rather stiff, even for professional educators. A basic journal for almost all education school libraries, but others are better served by *Childhood Education* (see Children section).

English Journal. 1912. 9/yr. Membership. $12. Richard S. Alm. National Council of Teachers of English, 1111 Kenyon Rd., Urbana, Ill. 61801. Index, adv. Circ: 51,000. Sample. Vol. ends: Dec. Microform: UM. Reprint: Kraus.

Indexed: CIJE, CurrCont, EdI. *Bk. rev:* 13, 200–1,000 words, signed. *Aud:* Hs, Ejh.

The high school (and junior high) equivalent of *Elementary English,* i.e., a journal devoted to teachers of English at the secondary school level. It brings together articles on language, literature, and composition, ranging in subject from *Beowulf* through *Easy Rider* and the *Dictionary of American Regional English* to surveys of research. Occasionally a special issue presents scholarly appraisals of major literary works, or a study of important trends in English teaching. Columns include "Professional Publications," reviews; "The Scene," reports on non-text and non-classroom materials; "Book Marks," reviews of junior-senior high fiction and nonfiction; "This World of English," pertinent quotes from other journals; and others. A basic magazine for any high school library.

The English Record. 1950. q. $4. Daniel J. Casey. Univ. College, Oneonta, N.Y. 13820. Index, adv.

Bk. rev: 1–2, 500–1,000 words, signed. *Aud:* Ac, Hs.

Published by the New York State English Council, this journal presents the study of literature with a view toward teaching it in the classroom. The scope is wide, ranging from preschool to college-oriented topics. For instance, one article is titled "Stimulating Oral Expression with Preschool Children" and another "Eugene O'Neill and the Creative Process." Some original poetry and fiction by teachers and new writers are featured. All in all, it is a journal mainly of interest to teachers of high school English. Recommended primarily for high school libraries, though of some interest to colleges and universities. (H.D.)

Grade Teacher. 1882. m. (Sept.–May). $8. Harold Littledale. CCM: Professional Magazines Inc., 22 W. Putnam Ave., Greenwich, Conn. 06830. Illus., index, adv. Circ: 308,000. Vol. ends: May.

Indexed: EdI. *Bk. rev:* 10, 75–100 words, signed. *Aud:* Ejh.

Provides practical "how-to" articles for the elementary school teacher, and an occasional inspirational article which calls on teachers to take the lead in improving their schools. The magazine covers all subjects and activities of the elementary school program. The 15 to 26 articles are semipopular in style. There are some 22 departments which range from authoritative reviews of textbooks to guides in the new math. A good half of each issue is advertising. A useful, if not exciting, addition for school libraries.

Industrial Arts and Vocational Education; the shop teacher's professional magazine. 1914. m. (Sept.–June). $7. John L. Feirer and Howard E. Smith. CCM: Professional Magazines, Inc., 22 W. Putnam Ave., Greenwich, Conn. 06830. Illus., index, adv. Circ: 32,000. Sample. Vol. ends: Dec. Microform: UM.

Indexed: EdI. *Bk. rev:* 14–16, 100 words. *Aud:* Hs, Ejh.

The professional magazine for the instructor at the advanced vocational, high school, and elementary school levels. Articles support the need for industrial and vocational courses and give specific advice of a how-to-do-it nature. There is emphasis, too, on how to assist young boys, unique tools and methods, and a number of departments: equipment, news in the field, and book reviews. A must in any school with an industrial arts program.

Instructor. 1891. m. $8. Ernest Hilton. Instructor Publns., Inc., Instructor Park, Dansville, N.Y. 14437. Illus., index, adv. Circ: 310,000. Sample. Vol. ends: June/July. Microform: UM.

Indexed: EdI. *Bk. rev:* Various number, length. *Aud:* Ejh.

Directed primarily to the elementary school teacher, principal, and special staff. The large, colorful format is familiar to almost any librarian or teacher. Each issue includes articles "dealing with trends in educational theory and practice, and sections on arts and crafts and teaching suggestions for all subjects." Each area is supplemented with diagrams, illustrations, and photographs. There is a considerable amount of advertising (about 50 per cent of each number). There is very little difference between this and its rival, *Grade Teacher*. (The editor of *Instructor* would hardly agree, points out that his magazine reaches "a substantially wider circulation"—*Instructor's* 310,000 vs. *Grade Teacher's* 308,000.) It is a matter of taste, the reviewer preferring *Instructor* because the writing style is better and there is more emphasis on social and education issues than on *Grade Teacher's* familiar how-to-do-it approach. Both enjoy a healthy circulation, are useful, and should be considered by all elementary school libraries. Still, this reviewer would put *Instructor* first, *Grade Teacher* second, and neither ahead of different approaches such as *This Magazine is About Schools*.

Journal of English Teaching Techniques. 1968. q. $3. P. J. Hickerson. American Language Skills Program and the Educational Research and Development Council, Southwest Minnesota State College, Marshall, Minnesota. 56258.

Bk. rev: Various number, length. *Aud:* Ac, Hs.

Here is a pragmatic approach to teaching English by English teachers. There is theory, but in every case the theory is grounded in what the teacher does or does not do in the classroom. Articles tend to stress the high school and junior college situation, but some attention is given to lower grades, and most of the techniques would be applicable anywhere. The journal deals with all areas of English, is extremely well edited, and the writing is first rate.

Journal of Reading. 1968. 8/yr. Membership (Institutions $15). Lloyd W. Kline. International Reading Assn., Six Tyre Ave., Newark, Del. 19711. Illus., index, adv. Circ: 14,000. Sample. Vol. ends: May. Microform: UM. Reprint: Johnson.

Indexed: EdI, PsyAb. *Bk. rev:* 6–12, 400 words, signed. *Aud:* Hs Ac.

Features suggestions for the improvement of reading in high school, college, and adult programs. Members of the International Reading Association have the option of receiving either this or *The Reading Teacher,* which emphasizes reading in the elementary schools, or *Reading Research Quarterly.* Each issue contains signed articles, which range in length from five to ten pages. Special departments: "Viewpoint," "Open to Suggestion," "Study Sheet," "Reviews," "ERIC/CRIER" and "IRA Clipboard." A required journal for most schools of education and for high school teachers in the area of reading development and improvement.

Momentum. 1970. 5/yr. $7. Carl Balcerak. National Catholic Education Assn. Suite 350, I Dupont Circle, Washington, D.C. 20036. Illus., index. Circ: 17,500. Sample. Vol. ends: Dec.

Indexed: CathI, CIJE, CurrCont, EdI. *Bk. rev:* 2, 1,500 words, signed. *Aud:* Hs, Ejh.

The basic educational journal for Catholic elementary and secondary schools. The 48-page, nicely illustrated and professionally put together magazine features five or six in depth articles, and a number of features. An examination of four issues indicates the emphasis is on the liberal Catholic approach to education—which represents quite a change from past years. "There is no general theme per issue other than innovative programs. However, we have published issues that focus on one particular aspect of Catholic education, e.g., the December 1971 number was completely devoted to religious education." Now that most of the Catholic education journals are dead, e.g., *Catholic Educational Review, Catholic School Journal, National Catholic Educational Assn. Bulletin, Momentum* is required in all Catholic schools. Also, because of its coverage and approach, it should be represented in larger academic education collections.

NEA Journal. See *Today's Education.*

NEA Research Bulletin. 1923. q. $2. Beatrice C. Lee. National Education Association, Research Division, 1201 16th St., N.W., Washington, D.C. 20036. Illus., index. Circ: 140,000. Sample. Vol. ends: Dec. Microform: UM.

Indexed: EdI, PAIS. *Aud:* Hs, Ejh.

A semipopular, well-written report on new education data, news, and events. Material touches all aspects of problems and discussions in current education. The concise nature of the reports makes it a useful addition for most school libraries; also for medium to large-sized public libraries, because it is particularly helpful in answering queries from the lay community.

National Association of Secondary-School Principals. Bulletin. 1926. m. (Oct.–May). $15. Thomas F. Ko-

erner. The Association. 1201 16th St., N.W., Washington, D.C. 20036. Adv. Circ: 35,000. Vol. ends: Dec. Microform: UM. Reprint: Kraus.

Indexed: CIJE, EdI. *Bk. rev:* 2–4, 2–4 pages, signed. *Aud:* Hs.

The *Bulletin* presents indexed articles on current issues concerning educators generally and school principals particularly. Content includes articles focusing on theme subjects as well as on individual topics. Articles are written by professional educators in a serious style. Larger school libraries will want, but in many cases the principal can well subscribe to this item himself.

National Elementary Principal. 1921. 6/yr. Membership. $20. Paul L. Houts. National Assn. of Elementary School Principals, 1201 16th St., N.W., Washington, D.C. 20036. Illus., index, adv. Circ: 27,000. Sample. Vol. ends: April.

Indexed: CIJE, EdI. *Bk. rev:* 2, 1,300 words, signed. *Aud:* Ejh.

Graphically, an impressive, fat (120 to 140 pages) magazine which tries to tell elementary school principals the answers to their numerous problems. It poses a few questions, too. There are usually four or five general articles, a special section given over to a central topic such as staffing, and a number of features which range from commentary by Jacques Barzun to letters and news about the NAESP. Articles are by both principals and professors, tend to be a bit esoteric at times, yet are grounded in experience. It is not the kind of magazine the layman is apt to sit down and enjoy, but it is a first choice for principals—and for elementary school teachers who are directly affected by decisions principals make. The graphics and layout are really outstanding. Whoever put this together should be applauded for its exciting look.

Nation's Schools; the magazine of better school administration. 1928. m. $15. L. C. Hickman. McGraw-Hill Publns., Circ. Dept., 230 W. Monroe, Chicago, Ill. 60606. Illus., index, adv. Circ: 48,000. Vol. ends: Dec. Microform: UM.

Indexed: CIJE, EdI. *Aud:* Hs, Ejh.

Concentration is on personnel, finance, equipment, and buildings in a journal for administrators from elementary through high school. Articles of a wider scope are usually connected with the curriculum, and normally involve innovations which call for new equipment or teaching methods. Regular reports are included on activities out of Washington and in the courts which have a direct effect on education. A required item for most school libraries, and should be distributed to teachers as well as administrators.

The PTA Magazine. 1906. m. (Sept.–June). $2.50. Eva H. Grant. 700 N. Rush St., Chicago, Ill. 60611. Illus., index, adv. Circ: 150,000. Sample. Vol. ends: June. Microform: UM.

Indexed: CIJE, EdI, RG. *Bk. rev:* 4, ½ page, signed. *Aud:* Hs, Ejh, Ga.

A sounding board for anyone involved with the PTA. All aspects of elementary and secondary education are considered in a semipopular style. Features include: Our Life and Times, Happenings in Education, The President's Message, Child's Health, TV and motion picture reviews, PTA—Where the Action Is, and Parents Keep Pace with Change (a discussion section). Although it is not *the* source for educational information, it is useful to active parents and teachers.

Phi Delta Kappa. 1916. m. (Sept.-June). $6.50. Stanley Elam. Phi Delta Kappa, Inc. Eighth St. and Union Ave., Bloomington, Ind. 47401. Illus., index, adv. Circ: 93,000. Vol. ends: June. Microform: UM. Reprint: Kraus.

Indexed: CIJE, EdI. *Bk. rev:* 6, 750 words, signed. *Aud:* Hs, Ejh.

Published by the professional fraternity for men in education. The emphasis is on research and public schools, elementary and secondary. The level of the 10 to 12 articles is consistently high, not loaded with the educationist's jargon. A good, solid addition for most professional libraries.

Planning & Changing; a journal for school administrators. 1970. q. $6. Leo O. Garber. Dept. of Educational Administration, Illinois State Univ. Normal, Ill. 61761. Sample. Refereed.

Indexed: CIJE. *Bk. rev:* 2, 500 words, signed. *Aud:* Hs, Ejh.

Features four to five articles on various aspects of primary and secondary school administration by both professors and those working in the field. The material is a mixture of pragmatic advice and theoretical planning. There is heavy emphasis on politics and money. A special section, "Reports from the states," covers reports issued by various state agencies. A down-to-earth approach which will be of value to managers dealing with the daily problems of running a school; others can pass.

Reading Improvement. 1963. 3/yr. $5. Allen Berger. Box 125, Oshkosh, Wis. 54901. Index, adv. Circ: 1,500. Sample. Vol. ends: Winter.

Bk. rev: Notes. *Aud:* Ac, Hs. *Jv:* V.

"Devoted to the idea that English teaching in high school and college is essentially the teaching of reading, since the act of reading underlies nearly all learning in composition and literature." The material covers all aspects of reading from censorship to initiating a reading program. Each issue contains about six articles which range in length from 2 to 5 pages, and are written in a semipopular style. Special departments:

"Selected Abstracts from Current Literature," "New Materials for Reading Improvement." Differs from *College English, English Journal* and *Journal of Reading* in that it has a wider scope and a somewhat more interesting method of presentation. As such, it is useful in all types of school libraries, schools of education, and might be considered in larger public libraries.

The Reading Teacher. 1947. 8/yr. Membership (Institutions $15). Lloyd W. Kline. International Reading Assn., 5 Tyre Ave., Newark, Del. 19711. Illus., index, adv. Circ: 44,000. Sample. Vol. ends: May. Microform: UM. Reprint: AMS.

Indexed: EdI. *Bk. rev:* 6–12, 400 words, signed. *Aud:* Ejh, Hs.

Deals with all aspects of the teaching of elementary and secondary reading, but concentrates on the elementary level. Each issue carries signed articles which range from scholarly studies of reading habits to semipopular contributions on the woes and joys of teaching the subject. Regular departments include notes on current research, magazine articles and books worth examining, a list of materials particularly suited for children, "Crossfire," "Interchange," "Critically Speaking," "ERIC/CRIER" and "The Membership Card." Particularly useful for the teacher who is searching for new methods of improving reading. See also *Journal of Reading* and *Reading Research Quarterly*.

Research in the Teaching of English. 1967. s-a. $3. Richard Braddock. National Council of Teachers of English, 1111 Kenyon Rd., Urbana, Ill. 61801. Adv. Circ: 2,913. Sample. Vol. ends: No. 2.

Indexed: CIJE, CurrCont, EdI. *Bk. rev:* 1, essay, signed. *Aud:* Ac, Hs, Ejh.

A journal addressed to research in the teaching of English at all levels from elementary through university. Its obvious first audience, however, is the university teacher in a college of education. Subjects include language development, reading, writing, attempts to measure quality of response to literature, and other problems of English teaching at all levels. Each issue features a "roundtable review" on a recent report of research and "notes and comment" about recent developments relevant to research in the teaching of English. There is a comprehensive bibliography of research in each issue.

The School Review. 1893. q. $8. Univ. of Chicago Press, 5750 S. Ellis Ave., Chicago, Ill. 60637. Index, adv. Circ: 4,000. Microform: UM.

Indexed: EdI, PsyAb, SocAb. *Aud:* Hs, Ejh.

"The purpose of *The School Review* is to encourage reflection and discussion by all persons who are interested in or concerned about education." This the journal does, and it has become, through time and reputation, the bastion of scholarship for articles on secondary education and education in general. The writing style varies from pompous to excellent, the content from the theoretical to the practical. Considerably above the average educational journal, this should be in all schools of education and read by teachers.

School Safety. 1965. q. $3.60. Lindy Buck. National Safety Council, 425 N. Michigan Ave., Chicago, Ill. 60611. Illus., index. Circ: 17,000. Sample. Vol. ends: March/April.

Indexed: EdI. *Aud:* Ejh.

Issued by the National Safety Council as a teaching aid in the elementary schools. It features articles, simplified instructional materials, and hints on how to instill the importance of safety in youngsters. Useful as an added magazine for health and safety classes, but not essential.

School Science and Mathematics; journal for all science and mathematical teachers. 1901. m. (Oct.–June). $10. George G. Mallinson. School Science and Mathematics Assn., Inc., Box 246, Bloomington, Ind. 47401. Illus., index, adv. Circ: 7,500.

Indexed: ChemAb, CIJE, EdI. *Bk. rev:* 6–10, 100–250 words. *Aud:* Hs, Ejh.

Pocket sized, 80 to 100 pages, and features 10 to 20 articles on the teaching of mathematics and science at the elementary and high school level. Articles are primarily by teachers and concentrate on methodology and the psychology of dealing with students. The book reviews are short, yet critical. The journal has considerable merit in that the material is easy to understand, often well written, and based on practical experience. A must for any science or math teacher in the primary and secondary schools.

School Shop; for industrial education teachers. 1942. m. (Sept.–June). $5. L. W. Prakken, Prakken Publns., 416 Longshore Dr., Ann Arbor, Mich. 48107. Illus., index, adv. Circ: 44,000. Microform: UM.

Indexed: EdI. *Bk. rev:* Notes. *Aud:* Hs.

A magazine of hints, suggestions, and some inspiration to shop teachers at the secondary and vocational school level. It is primarily given to articles on teaching techniques and detailed reports of successful projects. News items on Washington legislative action affecting vocational training, new products, and personnel and the profession are included. A basic periodical for most secondary and vocational schools.

Social Education. 1937. m. $10. Daniel Roselle. National Council for the Social Studies, 1201 16th St., N.W., Washington, D.C. 20036. Illus., adv. Circ: 23,000. Sample. Vol. ends: Dec. Microform: UM.

Indexed: EdI. *Bk. rev:* 6, 500 words, signed. *Aud:* Hs, Ejh.

The professional magazine for social studies teachers

and social studies educators at all grade levels. It contains articles on social studies subject matter, teaching problems, methods, and the curriculum. Authors are teachers, supervisors, professors of education, and social scientists from all over the country. Regular features include the following: reviews of books, instructional media, and pamphlets; what research says to the classroom teacher; sources and resources; elementary education supplement; and research supplement.

Social Studies. 1909. m. (Oct.–Apr.). $6. Leonard B. Irwin. McKinley Publishing Co., 112 S. New Broadway, Brooklawn, N.J. 08030. Index, adv. Circ: 6,500. Sample. Vol. ends: Dec. Microform: UM.

Indexed: CIJE, EdI, PAIS. *Bk. rev:* 10–15, ½–1 page, signed. *Aud:* Hs, Ejh.

An independent publication which, despite the title, concentrates primarily upon the teaching of history and current affairs in junior high and high school. The articles are well written, generally free of jargon. The journal is particularly useful for the book reviews and for critical notes on films and records. In the previous edition it was suggested that this come after a subscription to *Social Education.* The editor of *Social Studies* says the comparison is not fair because the competitor "represents the National Council for the Social Studies and *Social Studies* is an entirely independent magazine." More to the point, though, *Social Studies* has a stronger concentration on history—and in this area would definitely be a first choice. Otherwise, *Social Education* still a first choice.

Today's Education: NEA journal. 1913. m. (Sept.–May) Membership (Nonmembers $7). Mildred S. Fenner. National Education Assn. of the U.S., 1201 16th St., N.W., Washington, D.C. 20036. Illus., adv. Circ: 1,300,000. Sample. Vol. ends: Dec. Microform: UM.

Indexed: AbrRg, CIJE, EdI, PsyAb, RG. *Aud:* Ga, Hs, Ejh.

The official journal of the largest educational association in the United States, this is directed to public school teachers and administrators. Included are articles of a general interest within the education profession. New developments in education and news of the National Education Association are featured. Some issues focus on special subjects. A list of new NEA publications is included. Laymen who are interested or involved with education will find it almost as much of value as the teacher. It belongs in every school library, and in medium to large-sized public libraries.

Educational Aids

There are a number of school papers which are oriented to the curriculum, but are to be read—and supposedly enjoyed—by the children. The more important ones are listed below.

American Education Publications. w. or bi-m. 70¢ to $1.90 (school year). David Peck. AEP, 245 Long Hill Rd., Middletown, Conn. 06457. Sample.

Indexed: The following are indexed in IChildMag: *My Weekly Reader, News Parade, World Parade, Senior Weekly Reader. Aud:* Ejh, Hs.

GRADE	TITLE	CIRCULATION
K	*My Weekly Reader Surprise.* 1959.	1,634,000
1	*My Weekly Reader Picture Reader.* 1930.	2,077,000
2	*My Weekly Reader News Reader.* 1934.	2,286,000
3	*My Weekly Reader News Story.* 1929.	2,136,000
4	*My Weekly Reader News Parade.* 1928.	1,864,000
5	*My Weekly Reader World Parade.* 1930.	1,451,000
6	*Senior Weekly Reader.* 1947.	1,106,000
7–8	*Current Events.* 1902.	1,052,264
7–10	*Urban World.* 1970.	142,221
9–12	*Issues Today.* 1970.	182,632

The largest single curriculum-oriented news magazine publisher in the United States, American Education Publications began as the child of a nonprofit university—Wesleyan. It is now a subsidiary of the Xerox Corporation. While it publishes only a limited number of magazines other than those listed here (*Current Science, Read,* and *Science & Math Weekly*), it exceeds in total circulation almost all of the Scholastic Magazines publications. The reasons are twofold—first it got off to an earlier start, and, second, the prestigious backing of Wesleyan University created a favorable climate among educators.

Although the two companies are rivals for teachers' goodwill, it is sometimes difficult to tell the products apart. The *My Weekly Reader* series seems to have an edge in the number of pictures and guides it employs for helping the student to build vocabulary and critical thinking, and on the whole the format tends to be a trifle more appealing. There are usually one or two feature articles geared for the interest and reading level of the grade, and a number of special sections on everything from science and social studies to art and literature. In the more advanced papers, e.g., *Urban World* and *Issues Today*, a serious effort is made to present controversial issues, more so than in the Scholastic group. That they often contain fewer features and articles is balanced by somewhat better coverage. Finally, unlike its competitor, this series carries no advertising. In that most of the papers are intentionally classroom oriented, they are of dubious value for the average school or public library.

Civic Education Service. 1733 K St., N.W., Washington, D.C. 20006.

Since the last edition, the three class magazines published by this firm are now published by Scholastic, e.g., *Junior Review* was merged with *Junior Scholastic; Weekly News Review* merged with *American Observer.* Civic Education Service "now produces visuals for the U.S. history classroom and for black studies."

Literary Cavalcade. 1948. m. (8/yr.). $1.50. Jerome Brondfield. Scholastic Magazines, Inc., 50 W. 44th St., New York, N.Y. 10036. Illus. Circ: 350,000. Sample.

Bk. rev: Notes. *Aud:* Hs.

A 40-page Scholastic publication which serves the dual purpose of assisting the senior high school English teacher (grades 10 to 12) and introducing modern writers to students. Examples of drama, fiction, and poetry are offered with a detailed analysis of techniques, social meaning, and biographical information on authors. The selections are good, sometimes notable, but always "safe" in that they are devoid of violence, sex, and politics. It also features student writing, and guidance for those interested in attending college. One issue a year, usually in May, features student award winners of Scholastic-sponsored contests in art, photography, and writing. Useful, short book reviews, particularly of paperbacks. Primarily for classroom use.

Read Magazine. 1951. s–m (during school year). $1.50. Edwin A. Hoey. American Education Publications, Xerox Education Group, Education Center, Columbus, Ohio 43216. Illus. Circ: 400,000. Sample.

Aud: Ejh.

Primarily for English classes in grades 6 to 9, this familiar, pocket-sized, 32-page magazine comes on newsprint without advertising. Thanks to an imaginative editorial policy, the material is current, usually intelligent. It follows a prescribed approach of a short piece on current events, biography, fiction, etc. There are the usual word puzzles, tips on creative writing, and items to help the student learn as painlessly as possible something about the language. It is not the type of magazine the average student is going to read on his own, but for the genre it is good enough. Hopefully teachers will augment it with current general and special magazines. Only for the classroom.

Scholastic Magazines, Inc. w. (30–32 issues), except where noted below. 60¢ to $2. 50 W. 44th St., New York, N.Y. 10036.

Indexed: Most are indexed in IChildMag, except *Senior Scholastic*, which is indexed in RG.

GRADE	TITLE	CIRCULATION
K	*Let's Find Out*. 1966. m. (8).	
1	*Scholastic News Pilot*. 1960.	720,000
2	*Scholastic News Ranger*. 1960.	740,000
3	*News Trails*. 1960.	1,100,000
4	*News Explorer*. 1957.	1,100,000
5	*Young Citizen*. 1940.	401,000
6	*Newstime*. 1952.	1,250,000
7	*Junior Scholastic*. 1937.	1,800,000
8–10	*World Week*. 1942.	500,000
9–12	*Scholastic Voice*, 1946.	350,000
8–12	*Co-ed*. 1956.	1,000,000
8–12	*Science World*. 1959.	620,000
8–12	*Scholastic Scope*. 1964.	940,000
10–12	*Senior Scholastic*. 1920.	450,000

The second giant in the educational newspaper field. The publisher issues over two dozen classroom aids and magazines, including foreign language magazines; not to mention numerous publications for the teacher, e.g., *Scholastic Coach, Scholastic Teacher*. It differs from its primary competitor, American Educational Publications in one important way and that is advertising, and Scholastic pushes it for all the unwary teacher or parent is likely to take. Advertising is sought for: *Senior Scholastic, World Week, Junior Scholastic, Science World, Scholastic Scope, Scholastic Voice*, and *Newstime*. Apparently the editors do not feel the advertising is worth while in magazines below grade five. Somewhat sensitive to the fact that they are plugging products as well as education, the magazine came out with a full page advertisement in *The New York Times* (Nov. 4, 1971, p. 68). After admitting "the model of the average consumer a generation ago is gone," the magazine called for more subtle approaches. It all ended with a statement that "teachers want to see more ads in the classroom that can be used as teaching aids." Well, with about 70 percent editorial matter and about 30 percent advertising, the corporation is doing its bit. Fortunately, the editorial matter is fairly good. Each of the various-sized magazines is edited for a specific reading or grade level. The editors know what they are about, and while never controversial, the information is at least accurate and relatively objective in its "give 'em both sides" approach. The magazines seem to be doing relatively well in the lower and middle grades, but with more sophisticated teenagers (not to mention teachers), the old standbys such as *Senior Scholastic* are suffering. Any conscientious teacher, parent, or librarian might question the advisability of introducing youth to a series of classroom papers which seem more involved with the product and the advertiser than with education. If subscriptions are to be placed for Scholastic classroom magazines choose the non-advertising ones, and let the others go.

Scholastic Scope. 1964. w. (Sept.–May). $1.85. Katherine Robinson. Scholastic Magazines, Inc., 50 W. 44th St., New York, N.Y. 10036. Illus., adv. Circ: 1,070,000. Vol. ends: May.

Aud: Hs, Ejh.

Of particular value to reading teachers in junior and senior high schools because the 20 plus page magazine is primarily aimed at reaching the reluctant or slow teenage reader. Somewhat along the lines of Scholastic's *Literary Cavalcade*, but with definite attention given to publishing poetry, fiction, drama, and articles on current topics which have a reading level of the fourth to sixth grade. The attention level is through senior high school. This latter feat is carried off by subtle editing and features such as careers, profiles of successful teenagers, word games, fashions, etc. While of primary interest to the classroom teacher, the publication can be considered for public libraries who are serving the so-called disadvantaged teenage reader.

Higher Education

AAUP Bulletin. 1915. q. Membership (Nonmembers $4.50). Amer. Assn. of Univ. Professors, 1 Dupont Circle, N.W., Washington, D.C. 20036. Circ: 96,000. Microform: UM.

Indexed: CIJE, CurrCont, EdI, PAIS. *Aud:* Ac.

This journal has three main features. First, it includes four to six articles per issue on various aspects of the profession and teaching; second, it documents cases against censured college and university administrations, and gives the present standing of such censure; finally, the summer issue is devoted primarily to a detailed analysis of faculty salaries and compensation. While the latter item is of limited interest to laymen, the forthright reports on education and matters of academic freedom make it an invaluable aid for anyone interested in or involved with the field. Should be in all college and university libraries.

AAUW Journal. 1882. 7/yr. Membership (Nonmembers $3). American Assn. of Univ. Women, 2401 Virginia Ave., N.W., Washington, D.C. 20037. Illus., index, adv. Circ: 175,000. Sample. Vol. ends: Summer.

Indexed: PAIS. *Aud:* Ac.

One of the earliest women's magazines devoted entirely to education, community, and cultural affairs without a whisper of home economics or fashions. Each issue of the semiannual magazine includes material on the education of women, their social and economic problems, and their progress and regression in making a way in the world. While not precisely militant, it is a champion of the second sex, and men are advised to give this a closer look for a better understanding of the aspirations of the modern woman. Should be in most education collections, and in general collections. (While the magazine comes out twice a year, the Association issues news and notes in a supplementary newspaper which is issued 5 times a year. The subscription price covers both.)

ADE Bulletin. 1964. q. $6. Michael F. Shugrue. Assn. of Depts. of English, 62 Fifth Ave., New York, N.Y. Circ: 1,000. Sample. Vol. ends: May. Refereed.

Bk. rev: 2–3, length varies, signed. *Aud:* Ac.

A 36-page bulletin with six to eight short articles on all aspects of the English profession, e.g., "Soliloquy in an Academic Cloister," and "The D. A. and the Future of the Doctorate." As membership is made up of chairmen of English departments, the writing is lucid—and sometimes entertaining, always informative. In addition to articles, there are news notes and brief bibliographies. While chairmen may know about this, it will be of equal interest to anyone considering a future in teaching English at the college or university level.

American Educational Research Journal. q. $8. Richard L. Turner. American Educational Research Assn., 1126 16th St., N.W., Washington, D.C. 20036. Adv. Circ: 10,000. Vol. ends: Fall. Microform: UM.

Bk. rev: 5–9 in a single essay, signed. *Aud:* Ac.

No longer associated with the National Education Association, the American Educational Research Association is made up of "administrators and faculty in universities and colleges all over the world . . . and a growing number of graduate students. The Association serves as a second home to many scholars whose research activities embrace education: historians, sociologists, political scientists, etc." The 85-page journal reflects the interests of this audience, publishes original research, both empirical and theoretical. The five to six articles are technical, usually clear and well documented. The focus, unlike the earlier efforts under the NEA, is now more specific and predictable. A basic journal for all schools of education, but too involved for high schools or elementary schools.

The Association publishes also: *Education Researcher* (1964. m. $5. William Wolf, Jr. Circ: 10,000.), a monthly, processed, short report on research activities. This has the same basic purpose and audience as the *Journal.* See also *Review of Educational Research.*

CEA Critic. 1939. bi-m. (Nov.–May). Membership. $10 (Individual $8). Earle Labor. College English Assn., Centenary College of Louisiana, Shreveport, La. 71104. Illus., index, adv. Circ: 3,000. Sample. Vol. ends: May.

Indexed: AbEnSt. *Bk. rev:* 6, 1 page, signed. *Aud:* Ac.

One of two magazines included in the $10 subscription price. Each 45 or so page issue features 5 to 6 articles (normally by association members) which discuss aspects of the teaching of English. Usually one or two poems, a short story, good book reviews, and, of course, association business and personal items are included. An interesting point about all of this is that the editor attempts to avoid jargon, calls for articles which are distinguished "by lucidity, wit, and grace of style"—and no footnotes. He does not always succeed, but does so often enough to warrant careful reading.

CEA Forum. 1970. q. Earle Labor. College English Association, Centenary College of Louisiana, Shreveport, La. 71104. Circ: 3,000. Sample.

Indexed: AbEnSt. *Bk. rev:* Various number, length; signed. *Aud:* Ac.

This is a relatively new journal which is part of the *CEA Critic* subscription. (The two may be subscribed to separately, although to take one without the other is pointless.) The *Forum* is somewhat like the *Critic,* has the same editor, and serves pretty much the same purpose.

The Chronicle of Higher Education. 1966. w. (38/yr.) $20. Corbin Gwaltney. 1717 Massachusetts Ave., N.W., Washington, D.C. 20036. Illus., adv. Circ: 25,000. Sample. Vol. ends: Aug. Microform: UM.

Indexed: CIJE, EdI. *Bk. Rev.* 10–20, notes. *Aud:* Ac. *Jv:* V.

Reports on events, trends, reforms, speeches, meetings, government actions, legislation, polls, and studies dealing with higher education. There is special concern with student, faculty, and administrative reform movements. The standard issue is in newspaper format, with a number of signed articles and regular features such as books, deaths, promotions, and appointments, and a calendar of coming events. Necessary in the college and university library, and recommended in any library which meets needs of users interested in higher education.

College and University. 1925. q. $6. Robert E. Mahn. American Assn. of Collegiate Registrars & Admissions Officers. 1 Dupont Circle, N.W., Suite 330, Washington, D.C. 20036. Illus., index. Circ: 67,000. Sample. Vol. ends: Summer. Microform: UM. Reprint: Johnson.

Indexed: CIJE, CurrCont, EdI. *Bk. rev:* 8, 1/2 page, signed. *Aud:* Ac.

Contains many articles of general interest to anyone concerned with higher education. In addition to statistical and research data in the field of the Association's interest, there is material on the average type of college student, problems of enrollment, difficulties of securing top-rated students, what to do with dropouts, etc. Proceedings of the organization are included in the summer issue.

College and University Journal; devoted to the advancement of higher education. 1962. bi-m. Membership. (Nonmembers $9.50). Amer. College Public Relations Assn., 1 Dupont Circle, N.W., Washington, D.C. 20036. Illus., index, adv. Circ: 4,300. Microform: UM.

Indexed: PAIS. *Aud:* Ac.

Not to be confused with *College and University,* this is, nevertheless, a magazine for administrators and, more particularly, the public relations experts who are fundamental in raising funds for the schools. A good three quarters of the space is devoted to some aspect of money. The remainder is turned over to everything from publicity for the cafeteria to how to get along with college trustees and presidents. Of limited use in most libraries, although it gives a side of administration rarely covered in other educational journals.

College Board Review. 1947. q. $4. David Coleman. College Entrance Examination Board, 808 Seventh Ave., New York, N.Y. 10019. Illus., index. Circ: 22,000. Sample. Vol. ends: Summer. Microform: Kraus. Reprint: Johnson.

Indexed: PAIS, PsyAb. *Aud:* Ac, Hs.

The major focus is on the transition from high school to post secondary stages of education. The magazine also reports on other diverse subjects such as junior high student decision making, aspects of continuing education, access to education for minority/poverty students, and other current issues of concern in American education. The *Review* is of special interest to guidance counselors, admissions officers, administrators, teachers, psychologists, and other persons concerned with learning today. It is also a useful research tool for those interested in the various activities and programs of the College Entrance Examination Board.

College Composition and Communication. 1950. 5/yr. Membership. $3. William F. Irmscher. National Council of Teachers of English, 1111 Kenyon Rd., Urbana, Ill. 61801. Index, adv. Circ: 5,114. Sample. Vol. ends: Dec. Microform: UM.

Indexed: CIJE, CurrCont. *Bk. rev:* 77, 300–500 words, signed. *Aud:* Ac.

One of eight publications by the National Council of Teachers of English. See also: *Abstracts of English Studies, College English, CSSEDC Newsletter, English Education, Elementary English, English Journal,* and *Research in the Teaching of English.* Emphasis here is on basic composition at the college level. "A typical issue might contain studies of semantics, the teaching and analysis of style, preparing junior college teachers, pidgins, prewriting, film as a method of teaching composition, and an annotated bibliography on heuristics. Counterstatement, a regular feature, presents comment and rebuttal. Staffroom Interchange collects short papers on subjects of current interest." The extensive book reviews are found in the February issue. Useful for high school teachers as well as college and university teachers.

College English. 1939. 8/yr. (Oct.–May). Membership. $12. Richard Ohmann. National Council of Teachers

of English, 1111 Kenyon Rd., Urbana, Ill. 61801. Index, adv. Circ: 13,646. Sample. Vol. ends: May. Microform: UM.

Indexed: CIJE, CurrCont, EdI. *Bk. rev:* 2, 3,000 words, signed. *Aud:* Ac.

A journal for the teachers of English at the college and university level. The style is fair to good, and while a good deal of the material is only for college teachers, some of it is applicable at the high school level too. Articles cover the working concepts of criticism; the nature of critical and scholarly reasoning; the structure of the field; relevant work in other fields; curriculum, pedagogy, and educational theory; practical affairs in the profession; and scholarly books, textbooks, and journals. (*College English* no longer publishes critical articles or explications, except those which have a quite general significance.) Also includes a comments and rebuttal section.

College Management. 1966. m. $15. Campbell Geeslin. CCM: Professional Magazines, Inc., 22 W. Putnam Ave., Greenwich, Conn. 06830. Illus., adv. Circ: 19,000. Microform: UM.

Aud: Ac.

An administration magazine to give college officials information on how to run their schools effectively. Experts write on such things as budgets, personnel, buildings, business and finance, and, of course, student activities. The administrative side of curriculum is considered too. Considerable emphasis is placed on mechanical innovations. An esoteric journal for large education collections.

College Student Journal; an interdisciplinary journal of attitude research (Formerly: *College Student Survey*). 1967. q. $7.50. R. N. Cassel and R. E. Hoye. Project Education, Box 5504, Milwaukee, Wis. 53211. Illus., index, adv. Circ: 1,000. Sample. Vol. ends: Dec.

Bk. rev: 10, length varies, signed. *Aud:* Ac.

What does the average college student think? How does he vote, how does he pick a program, a wife? What are the roles of women in education? These and scores of other questions are answered in this journal which is given over to "factual information about college student attitudes, values and opinions." While primarily for the teacher in the school of education, it has a good deal to offer anyone who is involved with current education and students.

Continuing Education. 1968. q. $15. Peggy Corwin. Data Bases, 101 North 33rd St., Philadelphia, Pa. 19104. Illus., adv. Circ: 1,000. Sample. Vol. ends: Oct. Microform: UM.

Indexed: CIJE, CurrCont. *Bk. rev:* 12, 200 words. *Aud:* Ac.

A combination magazine and directory which features some five or six articles and 50 pages of advanced education directory information. A complex approach is used for the directory which locates courses by place they are given and by subject—the latter identified by code numbers which must be referred to in a schedule at the beginning of the book. Courses cover science, technology, management, medicine, law, and government. They are for the professional looking for a seminar or short course; not for laymen seeking new departures in education. The articles are short pieces on subjects of interest to adult education teachers and directors.

Continuous Learning. 1962. bi-m. $6. N. High. Canadian Assn. for Adult Education, 238 St. George St., Toronto, 5, Ont., Canada. Index, adv. Circ: 2,100. Vol. ends: Nov./Dec.

Indexed: CanI, PAIS. *Bk. rev:* 2, 750 words, signed. *Aud:* Ac.

"Excerpts from a learner's diary," "An experiment with electronic correspondence," and "Toward a learning society" are examples of articles found in an average 45-page issue, and if the titles do not indicate the style, let it be noted that it can be read with ease by anyone interested in adult education. It has a Canadian bias, but most of the material is applicable in any program. And it is mercifully free of jargon and the calls from the mountain top to change the world without telling quite how. A first-class magazine of its type.

Education. 1880. q. $7.50. R. E. Hoye. Project Education, Box 5504, Milwaukee, Wis. 53211. Illus., index, adv. Sample.

Indexed: CIJE, EdI, PsyAb. *Bk. rev:* Number varies, 100 words. *Aud:* Ac.

The sponsor represents "a group of university professors interested in improved sharing of worthwhile ideas related to learning." This comes out as a 120 to 150 page journal with some 30 reports, articles, studies, etc., on all aspects of education. Many of the articles are concerned with education at the college and university level and discuss everything from the use of computers in instruction to "Considerations in serving black college students on university campuses." However, the journal is not limited to higher education, and there are research reports by various teachers of education on methods of improving reading instruction, taxes and the public schools, curriculum changes, etc. Book reviews are scattered through each issue. A good basic journal for larger education collections, particularly at the school of education level.

Educational Administration Quarterly. 1964. 3/yr. $7.50. Van Miller. Univ. Council for Educational Admin., Ohio State Univ., 29 W. Woodruff Ave., Columbus, Ohio 43210. Index. Circ: 2,000. Sample. Vol. ends: Autumn.

Bk. rev: 2, length varies, signed. *Aud:* Ac.

A journal of administrative woes and delights at the college and university level. While a number of the contributions are of a practical nature, some, from those both in and outside the administrative framework, are theoretical and concerned with larger problems of education from student revolt in secondary schools to the future of colleges. Serious students of education will find much here not otherwise touched on by other journals, and a given amount of frankness which is enlightening.

English Education. 1969. 3/yr. Membership. $5. Oscar M. Haugh. National Council of Teachers of English, 1111 Kenyon Rd., Urbana, Ill. 61801. Index, adv. Circ: 1,941. Sample. Vol. ends: Spring.

Indexed: CIJE, CurrCont. *Aud:* Ac.

A journal for those who teach the teaching of English to future teachers. "Short, incisive articles on problems related to the preparation of English teachers are included. Material is of interest to members of English education departments and others who prepare English teachers, to supervisors, and to those engaged in curriculum preparation."

Higher Education. 1972. q. $22 (Individuals $12). Ed. bd. Elsevier Publishing Co., Box 211, Amsterdam, The Netherlands. Sample.

Bk. rev: Various number, lengthy, signed. *Aud:* Ac.

An international journal which considers all aspects of higher education from finance and teaching to technological innovations. The editorial and advisory boards are composed of leading educators from a number of countries, including Japan. Each issue is given to four or five long articles, reports, information notes, and essay type book reviews. As one of the few systematic efforts to look at higher education from a world view, this will be a required item in larger academic libraries.

IIE Report. 1967. 3–4/yr. Free. Mary Louise Taylor. Institute of International Education, 809 United Nations Plaza, New York, N.Y. 10017. Illus. Circ: 14,000,000. Sample.

Bk. rev: 3–5, notes. *Aud:* Ac.

A six-page newsletter which reports on foreign students in United States higher education institutions (some 145,000 in 1971) and Americans studying abroad. It is particularly useful for listings of opportunities for scholarships and foreign study. The organization publishes an annual report *Open Doors* ($3) which provides a comprehensive compilation of current data on the international exchange of students, scholars, and faculty members.

Improving College and University Teaching; international quarterly journal. 1953. q. $6. Delmer M.

Goode. Oregon State Univ., 101 Waldo Hall, Corvallis, Ore. 97331. Illus., index, adv. Circ: 3,000. Sample. Vol. ends: Autumn.

Indexed: CIJE, EdI. *Bk. rev:* Various number, length. *Aud:* Ac. *Jv:* V.

A major journal for the teacher at the junior college, college, or university level. As the title indicates, the emphasis is pragmatic, the articles usually reflecting practical experience, ideas, problems, and suggestions for improvement of teaching. While there are longer articles on ongoing research, most of the 30 or so contributions are relatively brief. Teachers of many subjects report on successes and failures in classroom procedures. Reports come from various types and sizes of schools from all parts of the United States, Canada and, recently, the world. An issue rarely goes by in which the teacher cannot find at least two or three items to help him with his classes. The book reviews, too, represent the best single source for locating material in this field. (The winter issues concentrate on books, e.g., Winter 1972 previewed or annotated 150 new titles.) As one fan puts it, the magazine "promotes a continuous awareness of the need for constant self-evaluation, reappraisal . . . and innovation which characterizes the effective teacher." It hardly holds all the answers, but faculty members will thank the librarian who brings it to their attention.

JGE; Journal of General Education. 1946. q. $7.50. Henry W. Sams. Pennsylvania State Univ. Press, Univ. Park, Pa. 16802. Adv. Circ: 2,100. Sample. Vol. ends: Jan. Reprint: Kraus.

Indexed: CIJE, EdI. *Bk. rev:* 3, 3 pages, signed. *Aud:* Ac.

Primarily a journal for teachers of undergraduates in colleges and universities, each issue features five to eight scholarly, sometimes theoretical, articles on a wide variety of subjects of interest to professional educators. Emphasis is on the humanities, albeit articles such as "Larger Implications of Computerization" and "Anthropology and Afro-American Studies" broach all fields. Faculty will welcome librarians bringing this to their attention.

Journal of College Student Personnel. 1959. bi-m. $12.50. D. Robert Callis. American College Personnel Assn. 1605 New Hampshire Ave., N.W., Washington, D.C. 20009. Index.

Indexed: CIJE, EdI. *Aud:* Ac.

The 10 to 15 articles, averaging four to six pages in length, emphasize research. This journal is the primary reference for research in the student personnel field. Articles cover such things as due process, education orientation programs, minority education, and so on. Each issue has a section of abstracts of pertinent writings which have appeared in other journals. (C.B.)

Journal of Higher Education. 1930. m. (Oct.–June). $10 (Individuals $8). Robert J. Silverman. Ohio State Univ. Press, 2070 Neil Ave., Columbus, Ohio 43210. Index, adv. Circ: 6,000. Sample. Vol. ends: Dec.

Indexed: AbSocWk, ChemAb, CIJE, EdI, PsyAb (plus many more). *Bk. rev:* 6, 500 words, signed. *Aud:* Ac.

Primarily for college and university faculty and administrators. The purpose as the editor defines it: this is a "leading medium for the transmission of ideas, opinion, and reports on topics which deal with the implications of research studies on higher education, discuss emerging policy problems and issues, examine existing concepts and analyze concepts that seem to be outmoded, and report on case studies which have significant implications subject to generalization. In addition to full-length articles, it carries special departments on different aspects of higher education." The articles take strong stands on issues, there is a minimum of jargon, and the whole is one of the better journals for this area. Somewhat more limited in coverage than either the *AAUP* Bulletin or the administration-directed *Educational Record,* but a strong contender for just about any college or university collection.

Junior College Journal. 1930. m. $5. Roger Yarrington. American Assn. of Junior Colleges, One Dupont Circle, N.W., Washington, D.C. 20036. Illus., index, adv. Circ: 43,000. Sample. Vol. ends: June. Microform: UM. Reprint: Johnson.

Indexed: CIJE, EdI. *Aud:* Ac.

Limited to interests of faculty and administrators in junior colleges. A typical issue will discuss music, art, the library, salaries, administrative problems, research, and general teaching concerns. Articles are sound, yet semipopular in style. A useful feature is the report on dissertations in progress, or completed, which have anything to do with junior colleges. A basic journal for all two-year colleges.

Reading Research Quarterly. 1965. q. Membership (Institutions $15). International Reading Assn., 6 Tyre Ave., Newark, Del. 19711. Illus., index, adv. Circ: 45,000. Sample. Microform: UM.

Indexed: EdI. *Aud:* Ac.

A scholarly 140-page journal which features two to three documented articles on research in teaching and understanding the reading process. Abstracts are given in English, French, and Spanish, but the basic material is in English. Primarily for the academic library, although it may have some value in high schools where the staff is deeply involved with the theoretical aspects of the subject.

University Today. 1971. bi-w. $15. M. Meyer, P.O. Box 7092, St. Louis, Mo. 63177.

Aud: Ac.

A six-page tightly-packed newsletter. It is heavy in quotes from previously published articles and reports; has little original material. Pulling all the information together results in a twice monthly overview of trends in administration, student outlook, and politics. The editor notes subscribers include administrators, public relations officers and college news directors, as well as parents. A lively, useful summary which should have appeal for the rushed university leader, student, or executive. Price is about right.

ENGINEERING AND TECHNOLOGY

Basic Periodicals

Ac: Most of the periodicals listed under the subfields of engineering (chemical, civil, etc.) are basic to any collection concerned with these specialties.

Basic Abstracts and Indexes

Engineering Index

Introduction

It would be difficult to include, within the scope of this section, even a minimum selection of journals in a field which not only consists of applications of other sciences, e.g., mathematics, physics, chemistry, but which, by itself, contains many specialties, such as navigational, marine, and materials engineering, to name a few. Moreover, with the exception of technical institutes, many college libraries do not support engineering curricula. The following, then, simply provides a small sampling of periodicals in general, chemical, civil, electrical, and mechanical engineering, most of which are the publications of U.S. technical societies, as well as a few general engineering magazines which cross over into all these areas. There are a number of periodicals which, in interpreting scientific and technological advances to the layman, include some aspects of engineering in their scope. These have been discussed in the Science/General section.

General

Engineer. 1856. w. £12. J. Mortimer. Morgan-Grampian, Ltd., 28 Essex St., Strand, London WC2, England. Illus., index, adv. Circ: 28,300. Sample. Microform: UM.

Indexed: ASTI, BritTech, EngI, SciAb. *Aud:* Sa, Ac.

The weekly has been interpreting technological progress since the mid-nineteenth century when the sophistication of the general field was a far cry from its present state-of-art. It continues to interpret developments in applied fields for everyone involved in engineering—"technologist, technician, inventor, design-er, research worker, executive, applied scientist,"—and in terminology available to all. Most fields of engineering are covered, as well as those closely allied to engineering problems, and industrial advances are comprehensively reviewed. The emphasis is on the news development, rather than the lengthy tutorial. Although a great deal involves British engineering and industry, European and U.S. coverage is more than adequate. Probably should be considered the granddad of all technical trade journals. For engineering collections.

Engineering. 1866. m. £3.30. Roy D. Cullum. IPC Industrial Press, Ltd., 33–40 Bowling Green Lane, London EC 1R ONE, England. Illus., index, adv. Circ: 9,033. Sample. Vol. ends: no. 12. Microform: UM.

Indexed: ASTI, BritTech, EngI, MetAb, SciAb. *Bk. rev:* 4–5, 50 words, unsigned. *Aud:* Sa, Ac.

With the switch in publisher, and accompanying change in periodicity, format, and focus, the magazine has turned into a reviewing medium for all the applied sciences and branches of engineering, aeronautical through telecommunications. Three to four feature articles supply the in-depth coverage and broad-based reviews; and regular departments, in spot-news format, report on the timely developments of the month. Features are contributed by both specialists and staff. Although the scope of the periodical is international, surveys emphasize British engineering. For engineering collections.

Engineering Geology. See Earth Sciences Section.

International Journal of Engineering Science. 1963. m. $100. A. C. Eringen. Pergamon Press, Maxwell House, Fairview Pk., Elmsford, N.Y. 10523. Illus., index. Sample. Vol. ends: no. 12. Refereed. Microform: Maxwell. Reprint: Maxwell.

Indexed: EngI, MathR. *Aud:* Sa, Ac.

An interdisciplinary-type publication devoted to the application of physical, chemical, and mathematical sciences to several of the engineering disciplines. Both theoretical and experimental papers register new research activities in cross fields involving mechanics, electricity, magnetism, thermodynamics; continuum mechanics is stressed. From time to time a review paper may appear. A sophisticated, highly theoretical publication for good university research collections. To appear in 1972 is a companion letters-type journal, *Engineering and Applied Science Letters,* which will involve short reports in the above fields.

Technology and Culture. 1960. q. $12. Melvin Kranzberg. Univ. of Chicago Press, 5750 Ellis Ave., Chicago, Ill. 60637. Illus., index, adv. Circ: 1,600. Sample. Vol. ends: no. 4. Refereed. Microform: Univ. of Chicago.

Bk. rev: 20, 500–600 words, signed. *Aud:* Sa, Ac.

Published for the Society for the History of Technology, the journal is concerned with the history of technological devices or processes and their relations to any aspect of society: politics, economics, humanities, etc. Long, scholarly articles and research notes range in epoch and culture from Greek catapults and early electric motors in India to a study of the first skyscraper and a review of the space program. Although the research investigations by distinguished historians and specialists are clearly not intended for breezy reading, the journal provides fascinating material for those with a historical bent and a respect for the technical contributions of the past. Organizational notes and announcements are also included in each issue. Excellent book reviews comprise a good portion of the periodical. An authoritative source in the field for both scholars and students, it is highly recommended for academic collections.

Technology Review. See Science/General Section.

Chemical Engineering

AIChE Journal. 1955. bi-m. $50. R. C. Reid. Amer. Inst. of Chemical Engineers, 345 E. 47th St., New York, N.Y. 10017. Illus., index, adv. Circ: 7,000. Sample. Vol. ends: no. 6. Refereed. Reprint: Johnson.

Indexed: ASTI, ChemAb, EngI, SCI. *Aud:* Sa, Ac.

The American Institute of Chemical Engineers is the chief society in the United States dedicated to advancement of chemical engineering sciences. Well known, also, for its high-quality publications output, the organization offers a number of "publications packages" for the interested technical librarian. *AIChE Journal,* the main research journal of the Institute, and one of the leading publications in its field, is devoted to fundamental studies in all areas of chemical engineering. Subjects under investigation have included fluid mechanics, chemical thermodynamics, reaction kinetics, heat and mass transfer, and process control, to name a few. A basic and authoritative periodical for every collection in chemical engineering. See also *Chemical Engineering Progress* and *International Chemical Engineering* for its two other journals.

Chemical and Engineering News. See Chemistry Section.

Chemical Engineering. 1902. fortn. $5. Calvin S. Cronan. McGraw-Hill, Inc., 330 W. 42nd St., New York, N.Y. 10036. Illus., index, adv. Circ: 70,000. Sample. Vol. ends: no. 12. Microform: UM, Microcard. Reprint: Johnson.

Indexed: ASTI, ChemAb, EngI, MetAb, SCI. *Bk. rev:* 1 major, 300 words, signed; 20 short, 50 words, unsigned. *Aud:* Sa, Ac.

McGraw's trade journal for the chemical process industry covers not only the latest technical achievements from industry, academia, and government, but also provides political, social, and economic comment. Feature reports investigate special aspects of chemical engineering and constitute excellent tutorials for the less-than-recent graduate, as do the shorter articles. Articles are both staff produced and contributed by leading industrialists or specialists. Many issues also carry reports on professionalism (how to get ahead, salary schedules), as well as an abundance of news coverage. The balance of the magazine is good—extending from highly technical papers, to practical engineering tips, management essays, market studies, and news flashes. New product coverage is particularly thorough, both through special departments and more than liberal advertising. The basic trade journal for the field, it should be in every technical library.

Chemical Engineering Progress. 1947. m. $25. Larry Resen. Amer. Inst. of Chemical Engineers, 345 E. 47th St., New York, N.Y. 10017. Illus., index, adv. Sample. Vol. ends: no. 12. Refereed. Microform: Canner, UM, Princeton. Reprint: Johnson.

Indexed: ASTI, ChemAb, EngI, SCI. *Aud:* Sa, Ac.

Issued as the general organ of the AIChE to its membership. The journal supplies interpretive news and reviews of the latest developments in chemical engineering and peripheral disciplines. Each issue contains its quota of review or tutorial papers, contributed by specialists, which cover timely topics of research; frequently a body of papers will investigate a subject from various viewpoints (e.g., engineering aspects of air pollution). Regular features include: a professional interest section; industrial developments; and a wealth of announcements concerning new publications, activities of all sections of the society, forthcoming meetings, etc. Of particular note are lists of PhD theses in chemical engineering, or notes on research in progress. Every collection in chemical engineering needs the periodical.

Chemical Engineering Science. 1951. m. $120. Ed. bd. Pergamon Press, Maxwell House, Fairview Pk., Elmsford, N.Y. 10523. Illus., index. Sample. Vol. ends: no. 12. Refereed. Microform: Maxwell. Reprint: Maxwell.

Indexed: BritTech, ChemAb, EngI. *Bk. rev:* 2–3, 400 words, signed. *Aud:* Sa, Ac.

An international research journal dealing with applications of the basic sciences, mathematics, physics, and chemistry, to chemical engineering. Authoritative papers and short communications cover ground from general theoretical principles to the more applied and newer chemical processes, plant design, and some specific processes related to industry. The editorial board is well represented with some prominent names in chemical engineering. A good journal for research-oriented technical collections.

Chemical Technology. See Chemistry Section.

Chemical Week. See Chemistry Section.

Chemistry and Industry. See Chemistry Section.

IBM Journal of Research and Development. See Science/General Section.

Industrial and Engineering Chemistry. Quarterlies. Amer. Chemical Soc., 1155 16th St., N.W., Washington, D.C. 20036. Illus., index. Sample. Refereed. Microform: Amer. Chemical Soc. Reprint: Johnson.

Indexed: ASTI, ChemAb, EngI, SciAb, SCI. *Aud:* Sa, Ac.

For many years *I & E Chemistry* served as the vehicle for providing the chemical engineer and chemist both technical papers and surveys of current research in applied chemistry and chemical engineering. In 1962, the publication was fragmented into four parts: a general nonspecialist periodical; and three quarterlies, specialized and research oriented. In the last few years, the nonspecialist publication ceased. The quarterlies continue and are discussed below. Most chemistry and chemical engineering collections will need the entire series.

Industrial and Engineering Chemistry. Fundamentals. 1962. q. $21. Robert L. Pigford. Amer. Chemical Soc., 1155 16th St., N.W., Washington, D.C. 20036. Circ: 10,000. Microform: Amer. Chemical Soc.

This is the most theoretical of the three publications. Original research papers are concerned with such fields as theory of fluidization, kinetic reactions, chemical thermodynamics, heat transfer, etc. Short communications on new laboratory apparatus and procedures are also published in a section called "Experimental Technique."

Industrial and Engineering Chemistry. Process Design and Development. 1962. q. $14. Hugh M. Hulburt. Amer. Chemical Soc., 1155 16th St., N.W., Washington, D.C. 20036. Circ: 9,166. Microform: Amer. Chemical Soc.

The focus in this research-oriented quarterly centers on the development and design of process equipment: computer control of processes, integrations of systems analysis, determination of design parameters, etc., are all within the scope.

Industrial and Engineering Chemistry. Product Research and Development. 1962. q. $21. Howard L. Gerhart. Amer. Chemical Soc., 1155 16th St., N.W., Washington, D.C. 20036. Circ: 11,000. Microform: Amer. Chemical Soc.

Emphasis here is on the mechanisms and reactions involved in the preparation of chemicals, as well as their properties. The journal is divided into a number of sections. "Plenary Accounts" are review-type papers frequently invited by the editors. "Technical or Product Reviews" also supply an overview of a se-

lected subject. The body of the publication is devoted to technical articles, including a "Catalyst" section, with "Signals of Science" discussing possible trends in a particular field.

International Chemical Engineering. 1961. q. $125. Waldo Hoffman. Amer. Inst. of Chemical Engineers, 345 E. 47th St., New York, N.Y. 10017. Illus., index. Sample. Vol. ends: no. 4. Refereed.

Indexed: EngI, MetAb, SCI. *Aud:* Sa, Ac.

A translation of important technical articles gleaned from the chemical engineering journals of the USSR, Eastern Europe, and Asia (mostly Japan). Although the journal does not provide the cover-to-cover capability available in other translation journals, it does give an overview of trends in foreign research. A good balance of subjects is maintained. Research collections will need it, though smaller academic libraries may find the other two journals of the AIChE sufficient for their needs. (See *AIChE Journal* and *Chemical Engineering Progress.*)

Journal of Chemical and Engineering Data. See Chemistry Section.

Journal of Physical and Chemical Reference Data. See Chemistry Section.

Civil Engineering

American Society of Civil Engineers. Proceedings. 1873. Price varies. Robert D. Walker. Amer. Soc. of Civil Engineers, 345 E. 47th St., New York, N.Y. 10017. Illus., index. Circ: 105,000. (Total journals) Refereed. Microform: UM.

Indexed: ASTI, ChemAb, EngI, SCI. *Aud:* Sa, Ac.

The scope of the ASCE's interest is enormous and, indeed, reflects the variety of technical endeavor being carried out under the broad phrase "civil engineering." Each specialty division of this association publishes its own research journal and, frequently, a newsletter. Too numerous to cite here, the journals overlap into other fields of engineering, e.g., mechanics, ocean engineering, and power engineering. Generally, each publication contains original research papers and important discussions of current papers. Reference "cards" for each article, containing keywords and abstracts, are also included. Periodicity and price vary from journal to journal. Fields represented by these publications are: construction, engineering mechanics, hydraulics, irrigation and drainage, power, sanitary engineering, soil mechanics and foundations, structures, surveying and mapping, transportation engineering, urban planning and development, waterways and harbors, and professional activities. Most civil engineering collections will need several of the specialized journals, if not all of them. The key to these ASCE papers and discussions rests with *ASCE Publications*

Abstracts (bi-m., $25), which is dedicated exclusively to informative abstracts of all material in the *ASCE Proceedings*, plus *Civil Engineering*, the nonspecialist publication of the society.

Civil Engineering. 1930. m. $7. Kneeland A. Godfrey. Amer. Soc. of Civil Engineers, 345 E. 47th St., New York, N.Y. 10017. Illus., index, adv. Circ: 69,000. Sample. Vol. ends: Dec. Refereed. Microform: UM, Microcard.

Indexed: ASTI, ChemAb, EngI, MetAb. *Bk. rev:* 12, 50 words, signed. *Aud:* Sa, Ac.

Twofold in purpose, the ASCE's general nonspecialist publication puts out both review papers to supply civil engineers with the latest technical developments in and out of their fields, and current-awareness articles on activities in the profession and the Society. Feature articles extend their subject matter from goals in professional cooperation to construction details of buildings. Frequently, applications of civil engineering to other technologies are stressed. Liberal coverage is given to new products and materials, engineering education, and spot news of the industry. For every technical library seeking a broad-based, nonspecialist publication in this field.

Engineering News Record. 1874. w. $10. Arthur J. Fox, Jr. McGraw-Hill, Inc., 330 W. 42nd St., New York, N.Y. 10036. Illus., index, adv. Circ: 117,346. Sample. Microform: UM.

Indexed: ASTI, BusI, EngI, SciAb. *Bk. rev:* 1, 200 words, signed. *Aud:* Sa, Ac.

The publication is the chief announcement bulletin in the United States for the construction and related industries. Brief reports highlight latest developments in business, labor, and engineering. A significant portion of the weekly is devoted to contract statistics, i.e., highway contracts awarded, or announcements of large construction programs in the planning and bidding stages. Materials, equipment, and new product briefs also receive ample coverage. Most technical and business libraries interested in this field will need it for its accurate, factual reports.

Electrical Engineering

Bell System Technical Journal. 1922. 10/yr. $10. G. E. Schindler. Bell Telephone Laboratories, Inc., Mountain Ave., Murray Hill, N.J. 07974. Illus., index. Circ: 14,000. Sample. Vol. ends: no. 10. Refereed.

Indexed: ASTI, ChemAb, EngI, MathR, MetAb, PsyAb, SciAb, SCI. *Aud:* Sa, Ac.

Although a large bulk of the research papers reported in this journal fall under the realm of electrical engineering, studies include any of the sciences and technologies related to electrical communication, such as applied physics, mathematics, the computing sci-

ences, and others. Contributors are all from the vast complex of the Bell System, and papers represent the research and engineering efforts explored in their laboratories and concerned with their products and systems. Studies can be very comprehensive, in-depth reports (up to 50 pages), and represent high quality investigations. A distinguished publication which belongs in every technical library.

The Bell System publishes another periodical, *Bell Laboratories Record*, described elsewhere in this book, which reviews, in less specialized language, the current research activities and technological advances in the Bell Laboratories.

Electronics. 1930. fortn. $8. Kemp Anderson. McGraw-Hill, Inc., 330 W. 42nd St., New York, N.Y. 10036. Illus., index, adv. Circ: 30,000. Microform: Canner. Reprint: Kraus, Johnson.

Indexed: ASTI, BioAb, ChemAb, EngI, SciAb, SCI. *Bk. rev:* 4, 200 words, signed. *Aud:* Sa, Ac.

One of the best periodicals for supplying concise, yet thorough and worldwide coverage of the news of the electronics industry. Authoritative, yet nonspecialist, interpretations of developments in electronics technology include articles on application to other sciences. Technical articles, review papers, and tutorials range from advanced circuit design, to tips for professional development, electronics in avionics, space, communications, computers, and consumer usage in TV and appliances. Marketing statistics, frequently supplied, are comprehensive and reputable, as gleaned by the widespread research bureaus of the McGraw complex. The prose is informal, extremely readable, and well illustrated by graphic techniques. New products and processes are particularly well represented by excellent color photographs. Departments cover, on a monthly basis, the usual news from government, business, and laboratories. A large buyers' guide, issued annually, is a valuable reference source for information on electronic components and services. Necessary for electronics engineers and interested special libraries, the magazine may also be a welcome choice for faculty of vocational schools or public libraries serving a technical clientele.

IEEE Proceedings. 1913. m. $36. Joseph E. Rowe. Inst. of Electrical and Electronics Engineers, Inc., 345 E. 47th St., New York, N.Y. 10017. Illus., index. Circ: 45,000. Sample. Vol. ends: Dec. Refereed. Microform: IEEE.

Indexed: ASTI, ChemAb, EngI, MathR, SciAb, SCI. *Aud:* Sa, Ac.

The *Proceedings* of this professional society are devoted to research papers deemed of broad applicability or interest to the membership. Invited and excellent review papers or surveys by specialists are also published. Frequently, an entire issue will investigate one special topic, e.g., transportation, and the research or review papers will explore particular facets of the field as related to engineering. The journal also carries "Letters," or brief reports of timely and important research. These fall under such categories as: circuit theory and design, electromagnetics; electronic devices; communications theory and technology; computers. A few departments report briefly on association meetings. A basic journal for every electrical engineering collection.

IEEE Spectrum. 1964. m. $24. J. J. G. McCue. Inst. of Electrical and Electronics Engineers, Inc., 345 E. 47th St., New York, N.Y. 10017. Illus., index, adv. Sample. Vol. ends: no. 12. Refereed. Microform: IEEE.

Indexed: ChemAb, EngI, SciAb, SCI. *Bk. rev:* 3–4, 250–350 words, signed. *Aud:* Sa, Ac.

The periodical is as fine a publication as that offered by any technical society as a news medium to its general membership. Whether the emphasis lies on relating scientific developments in electrical engineering to other fields (sonar for exploration of oceans), relating technology to culture (electronics and urban crises), or providing historical essays and tutorial articles on specialty fields, the approach is always creative, informative, and well written. Contributions are usually by distinguished specialists. Useful, and informative departments supply a variety of professional news, and also cover advance abstracts of research papers to appear in the IEEE's other technical journals (*Proceedings* and *Transactions*) plus several foreign journals published in translation by the Institute. A section called "Scanning the Issues" gives longer reviews of significant papers that have already appeared in these journals. Members of the IEEE probably make the publication cover-to-cover reading, but the audience for this journal should extend much further than its membership. An excellent nonspecialist periodical for every technical library.

IEEE Transactions. 1952. Inst. of Electrical and Electronics Engineers, 345 E. 47th St., New York, N.Y. 10017. Illus., index. Sample. Refereed. Microform: IEEE.

Indexed: ASTI, ChemAb, EngI, MathR, SciAb, SCI. *Aud:* Sa, Ac.

In addition to the *IEEE Proceedings* and *Spectrum*, which serve the interests of the entire membership, the IEEE also publishes 31 *Transactions* and two other research journals which reflect the specialized interests of their 31 professional groups. The publications range from such a high degree of technicality as antennas to more general ones concerned with management. Periodicity, price and format vary according to journal; some carry a few notes on the professional group, occasional book reviews, entire proceedings of special symposia, or even abstracts of the pertinent literature;

others are devoted exclusively to research papers. The fields covered by these specialty periodicals are listed here to indicate the breadth of IEEE interests: aerospace and electronic systems; antennas and propagation; audio and electroacoustics; automatic control; biomedical engineering, broadcast and television receivers; broadcasting; circuit theory; communication technology; computers; education; electrical insulation; electromagnetic compatibility; electron devices; engineering management; engineering writing and speech; geoscience electronics; industrial electronics and control instrumentation; industry and general applications; information theory; instrumentation and measurement; magnetics; microwave theory and techniques; nuclear science; parts, materials, and packaging; power apparatus and systems; reliability; quantum electronics; sonics and ultrasonics; solid state circuits; systems, man and cybernetics; vehicular technology. Many technical libraries subscribe to all; most engineering libraries will need a portion.

RCA Review. 1936. q. $6. Ralph F. Ciafone. RCA Laboratories, Princeton, N.J. 08540. Illus., index. Circ: 7,500. Sample. Vol. ends: no. 4. Refereed. Microform: UM. Reprint: Johnson.

Indexed: ASTI, ChemAb, EngI, MathR, SciAb, SCI. *Aud:* Sa, Ac.

Contributions to this journal emanate from the various divisions of the Radio Corporation of America. Research reports cover all branches of the applied sciences and engineering, and emphasize solid state electronics. Papers are of the high caliber usually associated with the scholarly journals and studies may be detailed works as lengthy as 50 pages. Each issue also contains an index of technical publications by the RCA staff which have appeared in other journals. Electrical engineering collections will need it; and since many of the investigations fall under the category of applied physics, the quarterly is also a valuable choice for academic libraries interested in the applied sciences and their relation to engineering.

Also of interest to engineering collections is *RCA Engineer,* put out by the RCA Corporate Engineering Services, Camden, New Jersey. Primarily published to stimulate discourse and disseminate information among the various technical groups of RCA, the magazine reviews RCA developments in avionic, microelectronics, computers, ordnance, TV systems, etc.

Mechanical Engineering

American Society of Mechanical Engineers. Transactions. 1880. Amer. Soc. of Mechanical Engineers, 345 E. 47th St., New York, N.Y. 10017. Illus., index. Microform: Microcard, Princeton.

For many years the *Transactions* have been published in separate journals, representing the diversified interests of the ASME. Available in six series, the titles are listed here and annotated elsewhere in this section. *Series A: Journal of Engineering for Power; Series B: Journal of Engineering for Industry; Series C: Journal of Heat Transfer; Series D: Journal of Basic Engineering; Series E: Journal of Applied Mechanics; Series F: Journal of Lubrication Technology.* The newest in the series is, beginning 1972, *Journal of Dynamic Systems, Measurement and Control.* Packaged deals are available on any and all of these publications. All seven journals are basic to any good mechanical engineering collection.

Applied Mechanics Reviews. See Abstracts and Indexes Section.

Chartered Mechanical Engineer. 1954. m. (Except Aug.) $10. D. J. Sinden. Institution of Mechanical Engineers, 1 Birdcage Walk, Westminster, London, England. Illus., index, adv. Circ: 73,922. Vol. ends: Dec. Refereed.

Indexed: BritTech, ChemAb, EngI. *Aud:* Sa, Ac.

More than simply a review of the society's news, the publication discusses any topics which concern the scientific community, as well as recent advances in mechanical engineering. Feature articles delve into the general areas of creativity, science teaching, education, and similar concerns. Many articles are topical: e.g., Britain's weather, patent system, but on the whole, its focus is not regionalized. Occasional essays on the history of engineering, for example, are excellent. For its membership, the periodical attempts to view the field from several sites: management, materials, design and development, education and training, as well as world news. A good, nonspecialist publication for engineering collections. As first choice for small libraries, however, the ASME's *Mechanical Engineering* would take priority.

Journal of Applied Mathematics and Mechanics. 1958. m. $90. Ed. bd. Pergamon Press, Maxwell House, Fairview Pk., Elmsford, N.Y. 10523. Illus., index. Sample. Vol. ends: No. 12. Refereed. Microform: Maxwell. Reprint: Maxwell.

Indexed: ASTI, EngI, MathR, SciAb, SCI. *Aud:* Sa, Ac.

PMM, as the publication is commonly called, is an English translation of the leading Russian periodical in the field of mechanics, *Prikladnaia Matematika i Mekhanika.* Despite the fact that it is an expensive translation, it is, nonetheless, one of the most important journals in this area, and no good research library can afford to be without it. Papers, emphasizing the research thrust of Soviet investigations, include studies on structural mechanics, soil mechanics, fluid mechanics, and some work on rocket propulsion. A prominent, authoritative, and high quality publication for university collections.

Journal of Applied Mechanics. 1935. q. $30. J. J. Jaklitsch, Jr. Amer. Soc. of Mechanical Engineers, 345 E. 47th St., New York, N.Y. 10017. Illus., index. Sample. Vol. ends: Dec. Refereed. Microform: Microcard, Princeton.

Indexed: ASTI, ChemAb, EngI, SCI. *Aud:* Sa, Ac.

Series E of the ASME Transactions. An authoritative research publication, and a fundamental one for any mechanical engineering collection. Papers cover topics on elasticity, flow and fracture, hydraulics, stress analysis, and thermodynamics, to name a few. For all engineering libraries.

Journal of Basic Engineering. q. $30. J. J. Jaklitsch, Jr. Amer. Soc. of Mechanical Engineers, 345 E. 47th St., New York, N.Y. 10017. Illus., index. Sample. Vol. ends: Dec. Refereed. Microform: Microcard, Princeton.

Indexed: ChemAb, EngI, MetAb, SCI. *Aud:* Sa, Ac.

Series D of the ASME Transactions. The research papers contained in this quarterly deal with the fields of fluid mechanics, flow measurement, hydrodynamics, cavitation, fracture in metals, and other related topics. Authoritative and of high quality, the journal is a fundamental one for mechanical engineering collections.

Journal of Dynamic Systems, Measurement and Control. 1972. q. $30. J. J. Jaklitsch, Jr. Amer. Soc. of Mechanical Engineers, 345 E. 47th St., New York, N. Y. 10017. Illus., index. Sample. Vol. ends: Dec. Refereed.

Indexed: EngI. *Aud:* Sa, Ac.

The latest in the series of *ASME Transactions.* The full scope of this technical journal is difficult to define, since it is in its infancy. It purportedly will be concerned with such fields as fluidics and fluidic power control; control system components; economic system dynamics; applications of optimization techniques; power systems; machine tool and production control; and process control. Also included will be selected papers on transportation engineering and bioengineering.

Journal of Engineering for Industry. q. $30. J. J. Jaklitsch, Jr. Amer. Soc. of Mechanical Engineers, 345 E. 47th St., New York, N.Y. 10017. Illus., index. Sample. Vol. ends: Nov. Refereed. Microform: Microcard, Princeton.

Indexed: ASTI, ChemAb, EngI, SCI. *Aud:* Sa, Ac.

Series B of ASME Transactions. More general in scope than the other transactions, the journal is devoted to articles and technical reports in such areas as management, plant engineering, machine design, materials handling, and the process industries. A broad-based publication for any mechanical engineering collection.

Journal of Engineering for Power. q. $30. J. J. Jaklitsch, Jr. Amer. Soc. of Mechanical Engineers, 345 E. 47th St., New York, N.Y. 10017. Illus., index. Sample. Vol. ends: Oct. Refereed. Microform: Microcard, Princeton.

Indexed: ASTI, ChemAb, EngI, SCI. *Aud:* Sa, Ac.

Series A of ASME Transactions. Technical papers in this research journal are concerned with the conversion of energy from fuels, gas turbines, nuclear energy, solar energy, and general power generation. Similarly, in light of environmental concern, the scope of the publication extends to air pollution, products from burning, and similar topics. For most technical collections.

Journal of Heat Transfer. q. $30. J. J. Jaklitsch, Jr. Amer. Soc. of Mechanical Engineers, 345 E. 47th St., New York, N.Y. 10017. Illus., index. Sample. Vol. ends: Nov. Refereed. Microform: Microcard, Princeton.

Indexed: ASTI, ChemAb, EngI, SCI. *Aud:* Sa, Ac.

Research papers in this field have application to a number of other engineering sciences, including chemical engineering. Technical reports deal with such areas as thermophysical properties, heat exchangers, insulation, phase changes and phase mixtures, and thermometry. As *Series C of the ASME Transactions,* the journal is a basic one for collections in the mechanical engineering sciences.

Journal of Lubrication Technology. 1967. q. $30. Amer. Soc. of Mechanical Engineers, 345 E. 47th St., New York, N.Y. 10017. Illus., index. Circ: 3,547. Sample. Vol. ends: Oct. Refereed.

Indexed: ASTI, ChemAb, EngI, MetAb, SCI. *Aud:* Sa, Ac.

Series F of ASME Transactions, covering lubrication and lubricants. Technical papers discuss investigations on bearing technology, friction and wear, seals, dry and solid lubricants, and nuclear lubrication, for example. Applications to other applied sciences are many, and the journal is an important one for technical libraries interested in this field.

Mechanical Engineering. 1906. m. $10. J. J. Jaklitsch, Jr. Amer. Soc. of Mechanical Engineers, 345 E. 47th St., New York, N.Y. 10017. Illus., index, adv. Circ: 65,400. Sample. Vol. ends: Dec. Refereed. Microform: Microcard, UM.

Indexed: ASTI, ChemAb, EngI, MetAb, SciAb, SCI. *Bk. rev:* 1, 250 words, signed. *Aud:* Sa, Ac.

The ASME's general, nonspecialist periodical, and a good medium for surveys of trends and developments in both mechanical engineering and related sciences. Features include tutorials in special aspects of the discipline, as well as some general articles on management, economics, education, and other related disciplines. Its special departments provide exhaustive coverage of news and literature: abstracts of recent ASME meetings, digests of the current technical literature; briefs on engineering developments, both U.S. and foreign; programs of meetings; Society personalia, etc. An informative and useful periodical for every mechanical engineering collection.

ENVIRONMENT AND CONSERVATION

See also Counterculture/Alternative Living Section.

Basic Periodicals

GENERAL. *Ejh: Awareness, Ranger Rick's Nature Magazine; Hs: Environment, National Wildlife; Ga: Environment, Environmental Quality Magazine, National Parks and Conservation Magazine, National Wildlife; Jc: Ecologist, Environment, Environmental Quality Magazine, Sierra Club Bulletin; Ac: Ecologist, Environment, Environmental Quality Magazine, International Wildlife, National Wildlife, Sierra Club Bulletin.*

CAMPING. *Ga: Better Camping, Camping and Trailering Guide, Wilderness Camping.*

MOUNTAINEERING AND TRAILS. *All libraries: American Alpine Journal,* in addition to the magazine of the library's state or region.

ORNITHOLOGY. *American Birds, Audubon Magazine, The Auk, Wilson Bulletin.*

Basic Abstracts and Indexes

Ekistic Index, Environment Index, Environment Information Access, Pollution Abstracts, Poverty and Human Resources Abstracts, Selected References on Environmental Quality, Water Pollution Abstracts, Water Resources Abstracts.

General

Adirondack Life. 1969. q. $4. Lionel A. Stwill. Willsboro, N.Y. 12996. Illus. Sample. Vol. ends: Fall.

Indexed: Env. *Aud:* Hs, Ga, Ac.

Supported entirely by subscriptions, this beautifully illustrated 55-page ecology-nature magazine will delight youngster and adult alike. While the subject matter is fairly well limited to the wilds of New York State, the problems and solutions to preserving those wilds are universal enough to capture the attention of a national audience. Furthermore, the photographs, many in full color, capture the joy of outdoor living no matter where the reader is located. Not all articles are limited to nature—there is material on hobbies, cooking, medicine, and art. The writers tend to be professionals and the editing is first rate. A required item for

New York and adjoining states, and of considerable interest for all others.

Alternatives. See Counterculture/Alternative Living Section.

Animals. 1920. m. $9. Nigel Sitwell, Ltd., 21–22 Great Castle Street, London, WC 1, England.

Indexed: Env. *Bk. rev:* 5–10, 100–250 words. *Aud:* Ga, Ac, Hs.

Although published in England, this has considerable interest and value for any layman interested in animal life and conservation. The editor-publisher champions saving animals which are almost extinct, and over the years has run an outstanding campaign in this area. The magazine tends to emphasize world wildlife as much as British, and an average well-illustrated number will range from Africa to Florida. Among the regular features are a guide to world zoos, short book reviews, and news notes on personalities and events. Should be useful, but in view of the English base probably a second choice for most libraries.

Archives of Environmental Health. See Health Section.

Awareness. 1971. m. $3. Paul E. Goff, 4031 Royer Rd. Apt. 209, Toledo, Ohio 43623. Illus.

Indexed: Env. *Aud:* Ejh, Ha, Ga.

A 15-page, pocket-sized magazine which is nicely printed and illustrated. It offers personalized yet accurate nature studies. The scope is broad. One issue, for example, is given to such items as searching for fox fire, camouflage used by animals, designs and patterns in plant life, etc. In addition, the author-editor offers suggestions and hints about how to get the most out of a nature walk. The style is authoritative, charming, and respectful of the reader's intelligence. Articles are directed both to the child and the teacher or adult who supervises nature studies. As a guide for adults involving upper elementary and lower high school groups with the joys of nature, it is perfectly marvelous. Furthermore, the information is presented in such a way as to interest any adult who has the vaguest love affair with the out-of-doors. There is an appreciation of life here which is rarely found in more professional magazines. A naturalist with vast experience, Mr. Goff knows how to translate his knowledge into an even more meaningful experience for the reader. He deserves wide support by all librarians.

√ **CF Letter: a report on environmental issues.** 1966. m. $6. Rice Odell. The Conservation Foundation, 1717 Massachusetts Ave., N.W., Washington, D.C. 20036. Circ: 5,000. Sample. Vol. ends: Dec.

Indexed: Env. *Aud:* Ga, Ac.

Now that environmental abuse is monumental and rampant, more attention is being paid to ways of un-

doing the damage that has occurred and of preventing more of it from occurring in the future. The Conservation Foundation dedicates itself to sustaining and enriching life on earth, and it seeks to do this by encouraging wise use of the earth's resources. It conducts surveys and educational programs, and engages in a considerable publishing program. Most of its publications are free, but some of the larger ones are issued commercially. The *CF Letter* is a looseleaf item. Each issue has about a dozen pages in it, and each is usually concerned with one specific problem. One issue, for instance, was given over to a discussion of what is happening to San Francisco Bay. An important publication, and one that most libraries will want.

The Conservationist. 1946. bi-m. $2. Alvin Flick. New York Environmental Conservation Dept., 50 Wolf Rd., Albany, N.Y. 12201. Illus., index. Circ: 145,000. Sample. Vol. ends: June/July.

Indexed: BioAb, Env., RG. *Aud:* Ga, Hs, Ejh.

A conservation-environment–oriented magazine with a national approach to current problems in these areas. Although published in New York, the scope is wide enough to warrant a subscription by most libraries. It is particularly outstanding for its color photography—a centerfold is devoted in each issue to some environmental aspect. Pond fish, edible wild plants, and winter birds have been typical subjects. The articles, bibliographies, and the general approach will make it particularly useful in schools.

Cry California. 1955. q. Membership. $9. California Tomorrow, 681 Market St., San Francisco, Calif. 94105. Illus. Circ: 7,300. Vol. ends: Fall.

Aud: Ga.

Somewhat similar to the Sierra Club, this nonprofit organization is not as old, but just as dedicated. Their 40-page magazine includes four to five articles on various aspects of California (and national) conservation. Authors' occupations range from city planners and professors to students and laymen. The articles, usually illustrated with black and white photographs, are written for the nonspecialist. The tone is militant, demanding more meaningful steps to save the environment. While this is not up to the *Sierra Club Bulletin*, it is gaining. It is well worth the subscription price for larger libraries, and for all libraries in California.

Dear Earth. See Counterculture/Alternative Living Section.

Defenders of Wildlife News. 1964. q. $5. Mary Hazell Harris. Defenders of Wildlife, 2000 N St., N.W., Washington, D.C. 20036. Illus., index. Circ: 30,000.

Indexed: Env. *Bk. rev:* 10–12, 500 words, signed. *Aud:* Ga, Hs.

Dedicated to the preservation of all forms of wildlife. Articles and comments are slanted towards environment and ecology control. They are written by experts in language any high school student can understand. Writers deal with factual material and proposed legislation, and support their material with bibliographies. Special articles often deal with various endangered species. Occasional poetry is included. Primarily for the dedicated conservationist. While the message is worthwhile, it would be a third or fourth choice in most general school and public library collections.

Ecologist. 1970. m. $8. Darby House. Blechingley Rd., Merstham, Redhill, Currey, England. Illus., index, adv. Circ: 45,000.

Indexed: Env. *Bk. rev:* Various number, length. *Aud:* Ac, Ga. *Jv:* V.

The leading British magazine on ecology. In 1972 the journal published "Blueprint for Survival," a measure supported by 33 leading British scientists to save the environment. The Blueprint caused a national debate. *Nature,* for example, questioned the conclusions, while 187 other scientists supported the views of the *Ecologist.* This single example points up the fact that the magazine is a leader in its field, publishes not only long, detailed reports, but shorter items by distinguished writers on aspects of British ecology and environment. While a good deal of this is useful only in England, some can be carried to America—particularly the tactics of the environmentalists. An important addition for any medium to large-sized collection.

Ecology Action. See Counterculture/Alternative Living Section.

Environment (Formerly: *Science & Citizen*). 1958. m. (except Jan.). $8.50. Sheldon Novick. Committee for Environmental Information, 438 N. Skinker Blvd., St. Louis, Mo. 63130. Illus., index. Circ: 25,000. Sample. Vol. ends: Dec. Microform: UM.

Indexed: Env, EnvI, RG. *Bk. rev:* 1, 1 page, signed. *Aud:* Ga, Ac, Hs. *Jv:* V.

Published by a nonprofit group, and limiting itself to problems of the environment, this magazine is among the best in its field. Fortunately, it is indexed in *Readers' Guide,* so the librarian who buys blindly anything indexed in *RG* is safe. An average 50 or 60 page issue features five to six articles, short news notes, a book review, editorial comments, etc. Articles are by authorities, yet are written purposefully for the layman. Most can be understood by the attentive high school student, although the journal is not written for the younger set. The illustrations are adequate, as is the format. The magazine has a relatively long publishing history and enjoys a well-earned reputation. Should be in all libraries.

Environmental Quality Magazine. 1970. bi-m. $5.50. Richard Cramer, 6464 Canoga Ave., Woodland Hills, Calif. 91364. Illus., adv. Circ: 115,000. Sample. Vol. ends: Dec.

Indexed: Env. *Bk. rev:* 3, 300 words. *Aud:* Ga, Ac, Hs. *Jv:* V.

Supported by a nonprofit, student-oriented group this is an 80-page, well illustrated weapon in the fight for the environment. Supported by such diverse figures as Edmund Muskie and Barry Goldwater, Jr., the magazine represents an effort to cut the strings with commercialism and tell the truth as dedicated lovers of mother earth. It is a refreshing middle-ground between the mass media latching onto a profitable idea and the esoteric scientific efforts of specialists. Authors represented include Ralph Nader, Paul Ehrlich, Ray Bradbury, and a number of lesser-known writers, who may not have quite the style, but make up for it with vim, vigor, and dedication. There have been interviews with Sen. Gaylord Nelson and Cleveland Amory; articles on strip mining, the Lear steam car, the Santa Barbara oil slicks, etc. All bases are covered, from how advertising affects ecology to an action guide telling the reader what he can do as an individual. A well-balanced presentation for almost all libraries.

The Explorer; a magazine of the natural sciences. 1938. q. Membership (Nonmembers $5). Joann Scheele. Cleveland Museum of Natural History, 10600 East Blvd., University Circle, Cleveland, Ohio 44106. Illus., index. Circ: 13,000. Sample.

Indexed: Env. *Bk. rev:* 2–3, 250 words, signed. *Aud:* Ac, Ga, Hs.

Touching on every aspect of natural science and ecology from birds in your back yard to the stars, this is an above average museum magazine. The articles, often by staff members, are geared for the layman (including high school students), and never assume he or she knows more than a college graduate in the subject under discussion. Each of the 6 to 10 articles is well illustrated, and the scope of the material goes considerably beyond any local boundary. This should have wide appeal among teachers, students, and ecologists—expert or amateur. It deserves a much wider audience. A sample copy will make the point.

Fields Within Fields . . . Within Fields. 1967. irreg. $1 per issue. World Institute Council, 777 United Nations Plaza, New York, N.Y. 10017. Illus. Sample.

Aud: Ac.

Published by a nonprofit research institution, past issues have covered such things as economic fluctuations, man's emergent evolution, and aspects of human ecology. The one examined is devoted in 86 well-printed pages to such articles as Abraham H. Maslow's "Toward an Humanistic Biology," Ervin Laszlo's "Reverence for Natural Systems," and Robert Smith's "Synergistic Organizations." While a trifle technical for the casual reader, it is an excellent source for those devoted to improving man's lot.

Idaho Wildlife. See Free Magazines Section.

International Wildlife. 1971. bi-m. Membership. $6.50. John Strohm. National Wildlife Foundation, 1412 16th St., N.W., Washington, D.C. 20036. Illus., adv. Circ: 125,000. Sample. Vol. ends: Nov/Dec.

Indexed: Env. *Bk. rev:* Notes. *Aud:* Ga, Ac, Hs, Ejh.

This serves the same purpose as the organization's other adult publication, *National Wildlife*—but with one important difference. The focus is worldwide, not limited to the United States. There are numerous articles on wildlife from Tasmania to Switzerland, discussions of pollution, ecology, and every aspect of the environment—again, by experts. Given the difference, the annotation for this might read the same as for *National Wildlife*, i.e., the purpose and audience are very much the same, and the layout is identical. (In fact, at first glance it is difficult to tell the two magazines apart.) If a choice had to be made between the coverage of the international scene and the American scene, the latter would win, but, hopefully, the library that subscribes to one will subscribe to both.

Land Economics. See Urban Studies Section.

Landscape. See Architecture Section.

The Living Wilderness. 1935. q. $7.50. Richard C. Olson. The Wilderness Society, 729 15th St., N.W., Washington, D.C. 20005. Illus. Circ: 70,000. Sample. Vol. ends: Winter.

Indexed: Env, RG. *Bk. rev:* 5, 600 words, signed. *Aud:* Ga, Hs, Ejh. *Jv:* V.

Next to *National Wildlife* probably the best general conservation magazine for teenagers and adults. Its major views are: (a) the need to preserve national, state, and local wilderness areas; (b) encouraging public support for such preservation; and (c) the necessity for scientific studies concerning the wilderness. Although the editorials and articles are slanted in accordance with the Society's policies and aims, news, forthcoming legislation, and the pros and cons of various issues are objectively presented. Reports of citizen-conservationist studies and opinions as well as government authorized studies on national forests, parks, and wildlife refuges as they are affected by the proposed inroads of civilization upon wild lands are interspersed with narrative articles, wilderness experience essays, occasional poetry and future activities of the Society. The format is enhanced by clear maps and artistic photographs. A useful magazine for all libraries from junior high school up.

Maine Times. See Newspapers/Special Interest Section.

Mother Earth News. See Counterculture/Alternative Living Section.

National Maple Syrup Digest. 1961. q. $2. Lloyd H. Sipple, R.D. No. 2, Bainbridge, N.Y. 13733. Illus., adv. Sample.

Aud: Ga, Ac, Hs.

"As I sit and gaze out of the office window . . . my thoughts are on the maple tree, and what is going to happen come syruping time." So begins a letter in a recent issue of this 24 to 36 page magazine, and it quite well sums up the purpose and audience. Articles tell expert and amateur syrup enthusiasts what to do and what not to do when the time to make maple syrup comes around. The information is down-to-earth, sometimes colorful, and even of interest to the man or woman who simply dreams about the process. The advertising is almost as enlightening.

National Parks & Conservation Magazine. 1919. m. $10. Eugenia H. Connally. National Parks Assn., 1701 18th St., N.W., Washington, D.C. 20009. Illus., index, adv. Circ: 50,000.

Indexed: BioAb, Env, RG. *Bk. rev:* 1–5, 300–1,000 words, signed. *Aud:* Ga, Ac, Hs, Ejh. *Jv:* V.

Since the National Parks Association is a completely independent, private, nonprofit, public-service organization, it can and does offer constructive criticism of government and private agencies. The Association's primary aim is to protect the great national parks and monuments of America, but its interests extend to the protection of the natural environment generally, including work in watershed management and river basin planning. Each issue carries beautifully illustrated stories of famous parks, little known beauty spots, and areas of special natural interest, some of which lie within easy traveling distance of our cities. A feature is the "Conservation Docket" which lists bills relating to conservation in the legislatures and official government actions. Editorials comment on current national conservation issues, and "News and Commentary" relates news items. In view of format, content and non-partisan sponsorship, this is an excellent magazine for almost all libraries.

National Wildlife. 1962. bi-m. $6.50. John Strohm. National Wildlife Federation, Inc., 1412 16th St., N.W., Washington, D.C. 20036. Illus., adv. Circ: 600,000. Sample. Vol. ends: Oct./Nov.

Indexed: Env, RG. *Bk. rev:* Notes. *Aud:* Ga, Ac, Hs, Ejh. *Jv:* V.

Although at one time this was primarily concerned with wildlife conservation, in recent years it has broadened its scope considerably. It is now the best known, best general magazine devoted to the preservation of the environment. The six to ten articles support the editorial creed, i.e., "to create and encourage an awareness among the people of this nation for wise use and proper management of those resources of the earth upon which the lives and welfare of men depend: the soil, the water, the forests, the minerals, the plant life, and the wildlife." All topics mentioned in the creed are considered in most issues. An interesting annual feature is the Environmental Quality yardstick (usually published in the Oct./Nov. issue) which measures the quality of national environment, i.e., indicates just how dirty the air is, the level of water pollution, etc. While emphasis is on the interdependence of mankind and earth's resources, there is a given amount of material on how to camp, photograph animals, etc. All articles are beautifully illustrated both in color and black and white. Regular features include current views on conservation, legislation at the national and state levels, and the Washington Report on aspects of conservation. The tone, while factual and objective, is popular and intentionally at the level of the interested layman. The approach is suitable for all libraries regardless of size or type. The publisher also issues *Ranger Rick's Nature Magazine,* for elementary grades, and *International Wildlife.*

O-I Outlook. See Free Magazines Section.

Organic Gardening and Farming. See Counterculture/Alternative Living Section.

Our Public Lands. See Government Magazines/United States Section.

Outdoor World. 1968. bi-m. $6. Robert L. Polley. Country Beautiful Corp., 24198 W. Bluemound Rd., Waukesha, Wis. 53186. Illus., adv. Circ: 40,000. Sample. Vol. ends: Nov./Dec.

Indexed: Env. *Bk. rev:* 6, 100–300 words, signed. *Aud:* Ga, Hs, Ejh.

A conservation-environment magazine with a wide appeal for all ages and interests. The 34 to 40 page magazine touches on all aspects of outdoor life from canoeing to desert plants and mushrooms. It differs from its competitors primarily in that its scope is much wider, and it focuses on nature in all countries, not only America. It rightfully claims to use some of the best outdoor writers, photographers, and artists. The text accompanying the pictures (many in excellent color) is purposefully written for the layman, and most of it will be understood by the youngster from junior high school age up. Some issues feature an insert such as a brief guide to hiking, canoeing, outdoor photography, etc., which is separately bound and paged so it may be removed for use in a vertical file. One of the better magazines which should be found in most general library collections.

Oxycat. See Free Magazines Section.

Ranger Rick's Nature Magazine. See Children/For Children Section.

Reclamation Era. See Government Magazines/United States Section.

Science & Citizen. See *Environment.*

Sierra Club Bulletin. 1893. m. Membership. (Nonmembers $5). James Ramsey. Sierra Club, 1050 Mills Tower, San Francisco, Calif. 94104. Circ: 110,000

Indexed: Env, SelEnv. *Aud:* Ga, Ac, Hs. *Jv:* V.

The Sierra Club is the premier outdoors club and environment champion in the United States. Its *Bulletin* edited first by John Muir, the Club's founder, is beyond question among the finest such publications anywhere. Each issue, which is from 20 to 50 large, glossy pages long, is made up of articles, many illustrated, on matters of concern to people interested in preserving America's remaining wilderness and in keeping naturally beautiful areas beautiful. It is a first choice in almost any library.

The Totem. See Free Magazines Section.

Washington Wildlife. See Free Magazines Section.

Weyerhaeuser World. See Free Magazines Section.

World Wildlife Illustrated. 1966. bi-m. $5. Michael J. Urslin. World Wildlife Publishing Co., 221 Baker Ave., Concord, Mass. 01742. Illus., Circ: 10,000.

Aud: Ga, Hs, Ejh.

About one half of this 25 to 30 page magazine is devoted exclusively to black and white or color photographs of animals. The articles, for the most part staff written, are short, popular in style and concentrate on habits and physical aspects of animals. Several pieces have a boxed summary of the animal features, i.e., common name, scientific name, feeding habits, coloration, etc. No advertising. After *Ranger Rick's Nature Magazine,* probably a first choice at the elementary school level, not so much for the text as the pictures.

Yankee. See Travel/State and Regional Section.

Camping

Better Camping. 1960. m. $6. Katie McMullen. Woodall Publishing Co., 500 Hyacinth Place, Highland Park, Ill. 60035. Illus., adv. Circ: 62,000. Sample. Vol. ends: Dec.

Aud: Ga, Hs.

Judging by the number of camping vehicles on the highways, this type of travel magazine will become more and more popular. The well-illustrated articles discuss recreational areas in this country and Europe, different types of camping equipment, and the art of camp cookery. There is a strong emphasis on conservation throughout the magazine. In the column "Wilderness Getaway" campers are reminded that hiking is as pleasant as driving. Other monthly features include a basic guide to camping equipment and a section on new camping equipment. A campground directory and coming events for campers are also listed monthly. This is an excellent magazine for the camping enthusiast. It is very similar to *Camping and Trailering Guide* and it becomes the choice of the librarian or patron as to which is preferred. Certainly both are not needed. See also the publisher's annual: *Woodall's Trailering Parks & Campgrounds*, and *Woodall's Trailer Travel Magazine* (Automobiles/Trailers Section). (C.B.)

Camping Journal. 1960. m. $6. Fred Sturges. Davis Publns. Inc., 229 Park Ave. S., New York, N.Y. 10003. Illus., adv. Circ: 258,000. Sample.

Aud: Ga.

A popular camping magazine, and a wiser choice for libraries than the *Readers' Guide* item, i.e., *Camping Magazine*. It is for the outdoor man, woman, or teenager who enjoys reading about every aspect of camping. Articles, which are usually adequately illustrated, touch on all aspects of the sport; boating, tenting, treks, trailers, pack horses, camping equipment, personal experiences, camping grounds, parks, etc. There is some attention given to evaluation of trips, better than average places to stay, and the how-to-do-it approach. The magazine is written for the middle-income American and costs are duly considered. One of the better, general camping magazines for most public and some academic libraries.

Camping Magazine. 1926. m. (Jan.–June); bi-m. (Sept.–Dec.). Membership (Nonmembers $9). Howard Galloway. Galloway Corp., 5 Mountain Ave., N. Plainfield, N.J. 07060. Illus., adv. Circ: 11,000. Sample. Vol. ends: Nov/Dec. Microform: UM.

Indexed: RG. *Bk. rev:* 4–6, 50–100 words. *Aud:* Hs, Ejh.

Although indexed in *Readers Guide*, this is not a general, family camping magazine. Published by the American Camping Association, it is primarily directed to administrators and staffs of professional camps, particularly those for children. In that a number of articles are devoted to various outdoor activities, e.g., sports, drama, crafts, it has some value for high school and elementary school teachers. The writing style is popular, the material authoritative, and the ideas imaginative, if not always original. On the whole, the material is for the camp director who is involved with such things as supervision, administration, purchasing, and insurance.

Camping and Trailering Guide. 1959. m. $5. George S. Wells. Rajo Publications, 319 Miller Ave., Mill Valley, Calif. 94941. Illus., adv. Circ: 100,000. Sample. Vol. ends: Dec.

Aud: Ga, Hs.

With *Motor Coach Travel* as a supplement, the title of *Camping Guide* has been lengthened. It covers auto, trailer, boat, and pack camping. Articles, illustrated with black and white photographs, tell where

to go, how to do it, and what to buy. There are monthly features on camping in Mexico and Europe, a travel trailer answer man, a column for canvas campers, and a directory of private campgrounds and trailer parks. Three or four pages of each issue are devoted to the National Campers and Hikers Association which is a nonprofit group with the motto "the friendliest people in the world." Choosing between this and *Better Camping* is up to the patron or librarian (C.B.)

Motor Coach Travel. See *Camping and Trailering Guide.*

Wilderness Camping. 1971. bi-m. $3. John R. Fitzgerald. Fitzgerald Communications, Inc., 1654 Central Ave., Albany, N.Y. 12205. Illus., adv. Circ: 10,000. Sample.

Bk. rev: 1–2, 750 words, signed. *Aud:* Ga, Ac, Hs.

A general camping magazine for "the self-propelled wilderness enthusiast," this is as much involved with how to do it as with how to save it. As the editor points out, "A personal wilderness ethic is not developed by reading trail signs and top maps, but it can be nurtured in these pages by the prevailing attitude of our writers." It all adds up to an individualistic approach to the wilderness which involves hiking, camping, and survival; not automobiles, trailers, and snowmobiles. The six to eight articles are concerned with camping in all regions of the United States and Canada, not just New York. Authors usually speak from personal experience and conviction. Particularly useful are the general trail maps. There are good black and white illustrations, and topical information on camping equipment. All in all, one of the better camping magazines for the ecology minded.

Woodall's Trailering Parks & Campgrounds. 1967. a. $5.95. Curtin F. Fuller. Woodall Publishing Co., 500 Hyacinth Pl., Highland Park. Ill. 60035. Illus., adv. Circ: 250,000.

Aud: Ga.

One of the better annuals which attempts to advise readers on where to camp. The company has a rating system which covers 65 different items (from bath facilities to availability of stores). Private, state, federal, county, and municipal parks and camping grounds are evaluated in the United States, Canada, and Mexico. The whole is keyed to a map section. While most travelers will probably want to buy this for personal use, it makes an excellent reference and general circulation item in libraries. It usually is revised and out by the first part of February or March. The same publisher issues: *Woodall's Mobile Home Directory* (1917 a. $5.95. Circ: 32,000), which rates trailer homesites for campers who want to avoid the trailer grounds. Another equally excellent annual guide is *Rand McNally*

Campground and Trailer Park Guide. (1960. a. $4.95. Rand McNally, Box 728, Skokie, Ill. 60076. Illus., adv. Circ: 288,500.)

Mountaineering and Trails

AAC News. 1948. 5/yr. $2.50. (Subs. must begin with Sept.) American Alpine Club, 113 E. 90th St., New York, N.Y. 10038.

Aud: Ga.

A four to six page newspaper reporting briefly on club activities, climbs, and expeditions scheduled or underway; conservation, and other mountaineering news. (P.S.)

Adirondac. 1937. bi-m. Membership (Nonmembers $3). Ms. John F. Brown. Adirondack Mountain Club Inc., RD 1, Ridge Rd., Glens Falls, N.Y. 12801. Illus., adv. Circ: 3,600. Sample. Vol. ends: Nov./Dec.

Bk. rev: 3, 200 words, signed. *Aud:* Ga.

A pocket-sized, nicely printed 20 to 30 page bulletin. The editor notes: "It is designed (1) to inform the membership of matters involving conservation and the environment and wild-forest recreation, particularly in the Adirondacks, and of Club positions taken in respect thereto; (2) to enable members to share with others their outdoor experiences in the Adirondacks and elsewhere; and (3) to offer members articles of general Adirondack interest." The ecology and general Adirondack interest make up most of each bulletin. Recommended for any library in the area.

The American Alpine Journal. 1902. a. $5. H. Adams Carter. Amer. Alpine Club, 113 E. 90th St., New York, N.Y. 10028. Illus., index. Circ: 4,000.

Bk. rev: 10, 100–500 words, signed. *Aud:* Ga. *Jv:* V.

The major annual mountaineering publication of the United States. Articles report on mountaineering activity all over the world, with many illustrative photographs and sketches. Three short sections on: scientific research funded by the club; Alpine Club activities; and activities of mountaineering clubs throughout the United States, whether affiliated with the Alpine Club or not.

Another annual is *Accidents in North American Mountaineering.* (1902. a. 75¢.) This cheerful report represents the work of the AAC's safety committee. See also *AAC News.*

Appalachia. 1876. m. $8. Lyle M. Richardson. Appalachian Mountain Club, 5 Joy St., Boston, Mass. 02108. Illus., index, adv. Circ: 10,000.

Indexed: BioAb. *Bk. rev:* 18–20, 50–600 words, signed. *Aud:* Ga.

For the mountain climbing and hiking enthusiast of all age levels. Long articles, well-illustrated and written by club members, detail climbing adventures in the United States, Canada, and around the world. Great emphasis is placed on conservation of natural resources and the preservation of the wilderness. The journal contains many suggestions for new trail cutting and the maintenance and care of existing ones; includes tips on safety precautions for climbing and hiking, and reports on the condition of various trails. Most suitable for eastern libraries.

Appalachian Trailway News. 1939. 3/yr. $2. Florence Nichol. Appalachian Trail Conference, 1718 N St., N.W., Washington, D.C. Illus. Circ: 7,000. Sample. Vol. ends: Dec.

Bk. rev: Occasional, 100–300 words. *Aud:* Ga.

Carries news of the Appalachian Trail, Appalachian Trail Conference Clubs and their trail-related activities, and information on backpacking, long-distance hiking, and trails elsewhere in the world. (P.S.)

Bruce Trail News. 1963. q. Membership only. $6. Douglas Brown. 75 Paisley Blvd., W. Cooksville, Ont., Canada. Vol. ends: Dec.

Bk. rev: 50–75 words. *Aud:* Ga.

An excellent source of information on trail activities and interests in Canada, though it concentrates on Bruce Trail in Ontario. (P.S.)

Canadian Alpine Journal. 1917. q. Inquire. Andrew Gruft, 4630 W. 5th Ave., Vancouver 5, B. C. Canadian Alpine Club, Box 1026, Banff, Alta. Illus. Vol. ends: Dec.

Bk. rev: 200–500 words, signed. *Aud:* Ga.

An annual through 1970, the latest volume is being issued more frequently (on a quarterly basis?) in a larger size. Mountaineering and technical climbing of the "how we did it" type makes up most of text, though some conservation material included. Book reviews include some Canadian items not noticed elsewhere. Well illustrated. (P.S.)

Finger Lakes Trail News. 1962. 3/yr. Membership $1. Robert L. LaBelle. Finger Lakes Trail Conference, Rochester Museum of Science, Rochester, N.Y. Illus. Circ: 450. Sample. Vol. ends: No 3.

Aud: Ga, Hs.

A 10-page mimeographed letter which reports on activities of the sponsoring group—a group whose purpose is "to promote, construct, and preserve a continuous east-west public footpath across New York State." The report discusses this project, other trails, and gives short notes on people, new publications, and environment. A folksy, refreshing approach for anyone in the New York state region.

The Long Trail News. 1940. q. Inquire (Club members and exchange only). Margaret M. Pons. Green Mountain Club, 45 Part St., Rutland, Vt. 05701. Circ: 2,000. Vol. ends: Dec.

Aud: Ga.

Reports news of the Long Trail and the Green Mountains and activities of the Green Mountain Club in and out of Vermont. (P.S.)

Mazama. 1918. 13/yr. $2.50 (13th issue Annual, $3.50 extra). Elizabeth Ann Wendlandt. The Mazamas, 909 N. W. 19th Ave., Portland, Ore. 97309. Illus. Circ: 2,000. Sample. Vol. ends: Dec.

Bk. rev: 1, 200 words, infrequent. *Aud:* Ga.

Monthly issues (eight to ten pages letterpress) list scheduled club events, report news of activities of club committees and special projects, and club's relations with government organizations for trail and wilderness matters. The annual issue runs 100 to 150 letterpress pages, containing photographs and maps. It has articles on mountain trips, conservation problems, and the annual reports of club officers and committees. Annuals have been issued since 1896. (P.S.)

The Mountaineer. 1922. m. (s-m. June and July). The Mountaineers, P.O. Box 122, Seattle, Washington 98111. Circ: 6,000. Sample. Vol. ends: Dec.

Aud: Ga.

Monthly issues are six to eight pages letterpress, listing club programs in many areas (hiking, climbing, snowshoeing, skiing, folk dancing, etc.) and with short review articles on conservation legislation, etc. An annual issue of 120 to 150 pages carries articles on mountain trips, natural history, conservation, and annual reports of club officers and activities. Photographs and maps. (P.S.)

Potomac Appalachian Trail Club. Bulletin. 1931. q. $3. Jack Neal and David Heinly. Potomac Appalachian Trail Club, 1718 N St., N. W., Washington, D.C. 20036. Illus. Circ: 2,000. Sample. Vol. ends: Dec.

Bk. rev: 1, 300 words, signed. *Aud:* Ga.

Articles on mountain trips, problems of conservation, reports on natural areas especially in the mid-Atlantic region, natural and local history usually of places within a 300 mile radius of Washington, D.C., Club activities and general information on hiking, backpacking, mountaineering, etc. (P.S.)

Prairie Club Bulletin. 1910. m. (Sept.–June). Membership. (Nonmembers $4). Prairie Club, Rm. 900, 28 E. Jackson Blvd., Chicago, Ill. 60604. Sample. Vol. ends: Dec.

Aud: Ga.

Subtitled "for the promotion of outdoor recreation in the form of walks, outings, camping and canoeing," this is an 8-12 letterpress page bulletin. It gives programs and outings planned by club, with brief notes on club activities and conservation problems. (P.S.)

Summit; a mountaineering magazine. 1955. m. $7. J. M. Crenshaw, 44 Mill Creek Rd., Big Bear Lake, Calif. 92315. Illus., index, adv. Circ: 7,500. Sample.

Aud: Ac, Ga, Hs.

This is for the man or woman who looks at a mountain as a challenge for climbing. There are usually one or two articles on just plain hiking, but the emphasis is on piton, axe, and crampon. Coverage is international with emphasis on American peaks and trails. Feature pieces tell how this or that slope was navigated, and include all of the excitement and thrills of a first rate story. There are some fair to excellent photographs and line drawings. While primarily for the involved climber, it will have equal appeal for the armchair expert.

The Trail Walker: News of Hiking and Conservation. 1963. bi-m. $1. Richard Goldin. New York–New Jersey Trail Conference, Box 2250, New York, N.Y. 10001. Sample. Vol. ends: July/August.

Bk. rev: 1, 200 words. *Aud:* Ga.

Reports news of foot-trails and hiking in a 200 mile radius of New York City, and includes major news of trails in other areas. It is also concerned with developments in natural areas, parks, and conservation. (P.S.)

Ornithology

American Birds; devoted to reporting the distribution, migration and abundance of North American Birds. (Incorporating: *Audubon Field Notes*). 1947. bi-m. $6. Robert S. Arbib, Jr. National Audubon Society, 950 Third Ave., New York, N.Y. 10028. Illus., index. Circ: 46,000.

Indexed: BioAb. *Aud:* Ac, Ga, Hs. *Jv:* V.

Devoted to the birds of North America, this journal includes feature articles and photographs. Special issues on the Christmas Bird Count (April), Fall Migration (February), Winter Season and Winter Bird Population Study (June), Spring Migration (August), Nesting Season (October), Breeding Bird Census (December). Each issue reports on regional observations of birds, etc. Very popular with ardent, confirmed birdwatchers. (L.A.)

American Cage-Bird Magazine. 1928. m. $3. Grace K. Gloster, A. J. Petrando. 3449 N. Western Ave., Chicago, Ill. 60618. Illus., adv. Circ: 6,100.

Bk. rev: Various number, length. *Aud:* Ga, Hs.

A great variety of articles on the care and feeding of birds in captivity. There are highly personalized articles describing individuals' experiences, specialists' recommendations, etc. Purpose is "to create greater interest in cage birds," to educate the public, and enlarge cooperation among breeders and fanciers. Numerous pertinent advertisements about equipment, feeds, birds for sale, etc. (L.A.)

Audubon Field Notes. See *American Birds.*

✓*Audubon Magazine.* 1899. $8.50. Les Line. National Audubon Soc., 1130 Fifth Ave., New York, N.Y. 10028. Illus., index, adv. Circ: 145,000. Microform: Princeton, UM.

Indexed: BioAb, RG. *Bk. rev:* 5–19, 100–550 words. *Aud:* Ga, Ac, Hs, Ejh. *Jv:* V.

Since its beginnings, *Audubon's* primary interest has been the preservation of bird life. But with the ecology/environmental drive, the magazine is now putting equal emphasis on preservation of all wildlife, plant life, and our natural resources. *Audubon* commands an outstanding place in the ornithology and conservation fields. Articles are written by some of the best-known names in the field of nature literature, and are authoritative without being stuffy. The color photography is outstanding, and this, along with the black and white photographs, gives it an added dimension for use in the elementary grades. Because of the National Audubon Society's fight for the preservation of our natural resources, it often finds itself at odds with landowners, industry, and government agencies. Thus, the magazine does not present an unbiased viewpoint, but still manages to stay on the side of the angels.

The Auk; a journal of ornithology. 1884. q. Membership (Nonmembers $12). Oliver Austin. Amer. Ornithologists' Union, Box 23447, Anchorage, Ky. 40223. Illus., index, adv. Circ: 4,200. Microform: Princeton.

Indexed: BioAb. *Bk. rev:* Various number, length. *Aud:* Ac, Ga.

Outstanding for its book reviews and original articles containing significant new knowledge. The language is highly technical and the material authoritative. In a section called "Recent Literature," articles in other journals are cited and the book reviews are the best available in this field. As much a magazine for the serious bird watcher as for the professional ornithologist, this is a basic item for larger public and academic library collections.

Bird-Banding; journal of ornithological investigation. 1930. q. $5. E. Alexander Bergstrom. Northeastern Bird Banding Assn., S. Londondery, Vt., 05155. Illus., index.

Indexed: BioAb. *Bk. rev:* Notes. *Aud:* Ac, Ga, Hs.

Features articles on scientific observations, General Notes (largely concerning the Northeastern states), Recent Literature (abstracts of articles in the current literature), NEBBA News, Notes and News, etc. This will be of special interest to the general bird person and to the New England Region. (L.A.)

Birding. bi-m. $5. American Birding Assn., Box 4335, Austin, Tex. 78751.

Aud: Ga, Hs.

"Devoted to the hobby and sport of birding," this relatively new periodical (acquired by Association membership only) is written at a semipopular level and includes articles of all kinds. A particular feature is the "Inserts," attached for permanancy but perforated for easy removal if desired, each page devoted to a different bird. (L.A.)

California Birds; journal of California field ornithologists. 1970. q. $5. Box 369, Del Mar, Calif. 92014.

Bk. rev: Notes. *Aud:* Ga.

Containing fairly scientific articles of a (western) regional nature. Book reviews, regional birds notes, etc. (L.A.)

Canadian Audubon. 1939. bi-m. $3. Canadian Audubon Soc., 46 St. Clair Ave., E. Toronto 7, Ont. Illus., adv. Circ: 12,192.

Indexed: CanI, IChildMag. *Bk. rev:* 1–2, one page. *Aud:* Ga, Hs, Ejh.

The counterpart in Canada of the *Audubon Magazine,* this features five or six articles on conservation and natural resources. It is well illustrated, and the material is suitable for students in junior high as well as adults. Particular attention is given to younger readers. While the American version is more elaborate, and to be preferred in most schools, *Canadian Audubon* is excellent where a second choice is advisable.

The Colorado Field Ornithologist. 1967. s-a. $1.50. Colorado Field Ornithologist, 220 31st St., Boulder, Colo. 80303. Illus.

Indexed: BioAb. *Bk. rev:* 1–2, short. *Aud:* Ga, Ac.

A small, 22-page, offset magazine with some line drawings, this packs a good deal of information in a little space. Not a necessary purchase, but should be considered by any library in or near Colorado.

Condor. 1899. q. Membership (Nonmembers $10). Ralph J. Raitt. New Mexico State Univ., Dept. of Biology, Las Cruces, N.M. 88001. Illus., index, adv. Circ: 3,000.

Indexed: BioAb. *Aud:* Ac, Ga.

A professional ornithology magazine, and the leading source of information on birds of the Pacific and the West. The scholarly papers appeal primarily to the specialist and the advanced student. All libraries in the West, regardless of type, will want a subscription. In other parts of the country will only be for large collections.

Ducks Unlimited Magazine. 1938. q. Membership. Ducks Unlimited Inc., Box 66300, Chicago, Ill. 60666. Illus., adv. Circ: 45,000.

Bk. rev: Notes. *Aud:* Ga, Ac, Hs.

Publication of a private, nonprofit membership organization dedicated to the conservation and propagation of North American waterfowl as a natural resource, and rehabilitation of Wetland areas on the Canadian prairie breeding grounds, which produce the majority of continental waterfowl. It is popular and of general interest, including news notes, legislation, etc. Considerable advertising of equipment decoys, etc. (L.A.)

EBBA News. 1924. bi-m. $4. Frederick S. Schaeffer. Eastern Bird Banding Assn., Box 3295 Grand Central Sta., New York, N.Y. 10017. Illus., index. Circ: 800.

Bk. rev: Notes. *Aud:* Ga, Hs.

News and studies of the entire eastern regional bird family, bird banding, and matters of conservation, bird-banding techniques, etc. (L.A.)

Kingbird. 1950. 4/yr. Membership (Nonmembers $5). Joseph W. Taylor. Federation of N.Y. State Bird Clubs, Inc., 20 Parish Rd., Honeoye Falls, N.Y. 14472. Illus., adv.

Bk. rev: Notes. *Aud:* Ga, Hs.

Devoted largely to birds and conservation problems of the State of New York and contiguous regions. (L.A.)

Massachusetts Audubon. 1917. q. Membership $7. Wayne Hanley, Massachusetts Audubon Soc., Lincoln, Mass. 01773. Illus., adv. Circ: 18,000. Microform: UM.

Bk. rev: Notes. *Aud:* Ga, Hs.

This slim quarterly has an important place in the ornithology literature. While it is directed to New England readers, the articles will interest those who are far from the Atlantic coast. Contributors are generally well-known New England naturalists and enthusiastic amateurs, but many articles are published by nationally known or even foreign writers. Should be on every high school periodical list, and is recommended for most libraries.

Raven. 1930. 4/yr. $3. F. R. Scott, Virginia Soc. of Ornithology, 115 Kennondale Lane, Richmond, Va. 23226. Illus., index. Circ: 600.

Bk. rev: Notes. *Aud:* Ga.

Refers largely to the birds of Virginia and the neighboring Central Atlantic states, and concerns itself with birds and the conservation of wildlife and other natural resources. News and Notes refers to sightings of different species. (L.A.)

Redstart. 1934. q. $5. G. F. Hurley. Brooks Bird Club, 707 Warwood Ave., Wheeling, W. Va. 26003. Illus., index. Circ: 350.

Indexed: BioAb. *Bk. rev:* Notes. *Aud:* Ac, Ga.

Brief miscellaneous articles, field notes, etc.; largely, but not exclusively, related to the West Virginia area. (L.A.)

Wilson Bulletin; a quarterly magazine of ornithology. 1889. q. $10. George A. Hall. Wilson Ornithological Soc., 2140 Lewis Drive, Lakewood, Ohio 44107. Illus., index. Circ: 2,000.

Indexed: BioAb. *Bk. rev:* Various number, length. *Aud:* Ac, Ga, Hs. *Jv:* V.

One of the finest periodicals in the field (along with *The Auk, American Birds,* and *The Condor*), containing specialized, scientific articles on the observations of birds of the world. Each issue contains articles, ornithological news, a survey and reviews of the current literature, publication notes, etc. Particularly noteworthy for the excellent reviews of bird books. (L.A.)

Special Interest

American Forests. 1895. m. $6. James B. Craig. Amer. Forestry Assn., 919 17th St., N.W., Washington, D.C. 20006. Illus., index, adv. Circ: 75,000. Microform: UM.

Indexed: BioAb, PAIS, RG. *Bk. rev:* 5–6, 500 words. *Aud:* Ga, Ac.

Important: although indexed in *Reader's Guide,* this is not an objective conservation magazine. Quite the contrary. It represents the voice of the American Forestry Association, an organization dedicated to making a healthy living from forestry. The result is that articles are purposefully in favor of legislative action first guaranteed to protect the men who capitalize on the forests. Which, of course, is not to say this is a bad magazine. Once the bias is understood, the magazine is quite fine. An honest effort is made to consider how to conserve the woodlands, and there is general material on outdoor activities. Much of the material on how to best conserve and use the forests is suitable for the nonexpert, and the illustrations and photographs give it an added dimension for high school students. Not an essential purchase, but a useful one for any type of library serving forestry and conservation interests.

California Fish and Game. 1914. q. $2. Garol M. Ferrel. Calif. Dept. of Fish and Game, 987 Jedsmith Drive, Sacramento, Calif. 95819. Subs. to: Office of Procurement, Box 20191, Sacramento, Calif. 95820. Illus., index. Circ: 5,300. Sample. Vol. ends: Oct.

Indexed: BioAb, ChemAb. *Bk. rev:* 5–10, 150–200 words, signed. *Aud:* Ac, Ga.

One of the oldest of the state fish and game reports, and one of the best. Articles are by experts, usually quite technical, cover all aspects of fish and game in California. This is not for the average reader. Most emphasis is on the conservation element in terms of specialized definitions and background, e.g., "Harvest and Survival of Rainbow Trout Infected with Sanguiniscola davisi Wales." The book reviews cover more popular conservation titles. Only for larger libraries, although medium-sized public and academic libraries in California would find it well worthwhile.

Canadian Field-Naturalist. 1879. q. Membership. (Nonmembers $10). Theodore Mosquin. Ottawa Field-Naturalists' Club, Box 3264, Postal Station C, Ottawa, Canada K1Y, 4J5. Illus., index. Circ: 1,600. Sample. Refereed.

Indexed: BioAb. *Aud:* Ac.

Canada's leading scientific journal in the field of natural history, and, today, in ecology and environment. Articles are prepared by experts, but the style is free and most can be understood by an interested layman. There are a few charts and graphs, and some photographs. Only a small part is too technical. The balance between the scientific and the popular is such that the magazine should enjoy a much wider audience—particularly in the United States. The material is limited to Canada, and, more particularly, to Ontario, but all of it is of interest to people involved with environment. Each issue features notes, letters, and columns which are fascinating to read. All in all one of the best of its kind.

Ecolog. 1971. w. $200. John S. Hoyt, P.O. Box 184, Oyster Bay, N.Y. 11771.

Aud: Ga, Ac.

A four-page newsletter, which under a variety of subject headings from International and The Washington Scene to Technology and Economics, reports on ecology events. The timely summary statements are accurate and factual. Given an index, this would be an extremely useful reference aid. Subtitled "The common sense bridge between business and environment," it includes supplements which report on federal contract activities, how congressman vote, etc. The primary target is apparently business. The price puts it out of reach for many libraries, and the lack of a cumulative index makes it a luxury item for even larger libraries.

Forests and People. 1951. q. $2. Robert W. Dardenne, Jr. Louisiana Forestry Assn., Box 5067, Alexandria, La., 71301. Illus., index, adv. Circ: 10,000. Sample. Vol. ends: No. 4.

Aud: Ga.

The official publication of this "state-wide organization of landowners, foresters and friends of forestry, interested in the intelligent management of forests and forest lands. Its purpose is to promote public appreciation of these resources and their contribution to Louisiana's economic life." This appreciation is fostered by the presentation of a range of material including all of the forestry-related forces at work in the state. The viewpoint of the forest industry is presented, as well as views on existing or desirable legislation related to the conservation of all natural resources. Programs de-

signed to boost conservation education are regularly included, along with types of organized youth programs which benefit both the participants and the environment. Some articles on wood frame dwellings, noteworthy new designs, renovation of older houses, and prize competitions for students emphasize the desirable qualities of wood as a building material. The recreational possibilities of well-managed forested land, accounts of some smaller-scale tree farming operations, and some interesting sidelights on local history and unique Louisiana plant and wildlife round out the subject matter. Most material is written on the popular level, with a majority of the articles signed and credited to qualified writers in the field of forestry and journalism. The pleasing 48-page format is composed of 8 to 10 articles, adequately illustrated with mostly black and white and two-tone photos of fair to good quality. An acceptable addition where material on reforestation and conservation is needed, with much of it applicable also to areas other than the deep South. (A.S.)

IUCN Bulletin. 1961. m. $5. Robert Standish. Intl. Union for Conservation of Nature and Natural Resources, 1110 Morges, Geneva, Switzerland. Illus., index. Circ: 2,500. Sample. Vol. ends: Dec.

Bk. rev: 3, 400 words, signed. *Aud:* Ga, Ac.

A four-page report on activities of the IUCN, a Unesco supported organization which works towards worldwide conservation. A typical issue gives information on major conservation activities throughout the world, and reports on the Union's program, plans, and accomplishments, and its long term objectives. The editor notes that "periodically, a larger issue will contain longer articles and special material." An important addition for larger collections.

International Journal of Environmental Studies. 1970. q. $41 (Individuals $14.50). J. Rose. Gordon & Breach Science Publishers Ltd. Subs. to: Box 1305, Long Island City, N.Y. 11101. Vol. ends: Oct. Refereed.

Bk. rev: 1–3, 750–1,000 words, signed. *Aud:* Ac.

Published in England, edited by the principal of the College of Technology and Design in Blackburn, this 85-page journal serves "as a vehicle for an interdisciplinary environmental science." It is international, relatively technical, and authoritative. The eight to ten articles range from the effects of irrigation on mosquitoes to cancer and the environment. The first issue featured a well-written piece on future social repercussions of computers. A solid addition for large, special collections.

Journal of Forestry; a journal reporting on all phases of professional forestry. 1902. m. $18. H. R. Glascock. Soc. of Amer. Foresters, 1010 16th St., N.W., Washington, D.C. 20036. Illus., adv. Circ: 19,000.

Indexed: BioAb, BioAg, ChemAb, PAIS. *Bk. rev:* Various number, length. *Aud:* Ac.

The basic, scholarly journal in the field of forestry. Emphasis is on technical aspects of conservation, timberlands, lumbering, land management, etc. Articles, by educators, researchers, and professional foresters, tend to stress long range planning, economic and scientific problems. Here it differs from the more commercially oriented *American Forests,* which is primarily geared for the man working in the field. It is particularly useful to librarians because of the departments which cover all major new books in the area, monographs, and other literature of forestry. A required item in any academic library where there is an interest in the subject. Conversely, *American Forests* would be a first in more business-oriented collections.

Journal of Remote Sensing. 1970. bi-m. Free (Individuals $15). A. J. Simmons International Remote Sensing Inst., 6151 Freeport Blvd. Sacramento, Calif. 95882. Illus., index, adv. Circ: 7,000. Sample.

Aud: Ac, Ga, Hs.

The institute publishing this journal is engaged in remote sensing application for resources inventory, land use, air and water pollution, and regional planning. The remote sensing is applied mainly by photographic means, and this journal offers a well-edited collection of aerial photographs and their analysis. The presentation of mapping water pollution, for instance, is very instructive. The analyses are not too technical and so are intelligible to the layman. This is a particularly useful tool for classroom demonstrations in all environmental studies. Recommended for school, municipal, and some special libraries.

Journal of Soil and Water Conservation. 1946. bi-m. Membership (Libraries $10). Max Schnepf, 7515 N.E. Ankeny Rd., Ankeny, Iowa 50021. Illus., index, adv. Circ: 14,000. Sample. Vol. ends: Nov/Dec. Reprint: Abrahams.

Indexed: BioAb, BioAg. *Aud:* Ac, Ga, Hs.

Issued by the Soil Conservation Society of America, and useful in high school, public, and academic libraries as a source of supplementary material in the field of ecology and conservation. It covers such subjects as the sources of soil and water pollution and the steps being taken by public and private agencies to abate the destruction of our natural resources. Although the articles are written by experts, they are popular in approach and are well illustrated. Film reviews are a distinctive feature, and will interest librarians in instructional materials centers.

Journal of Wildlife Management. 1937. q. $20. Glen C. Sanderson. Wildlife Society, Suite 3900 S-176 Wisconsin Ave., N.W., Washington, D.C. 20016. Illus., index. Circ: 7,500. Vol. ends: Oct. Microform: UM. Reprint: Johnson.

Indexed: BioAb, BioAg, ChemAb, SCI. *Bk. rev:* 2–5, 350 words, signed. *Aud:* Ac.

A publication of an international professional organization which reflects a high level of scholarship. The subjects covered include habitat management, the effects of various toxic agents on plants and animals, and studies of animal behavior and life histories. The detailed charts and graphs, as well as the few photographs, enrich and clarify the material. Each article is signed and accompanied by an extensive bibliography. In addition to the critical book reviews, there are some two pages devoted to listings of recently published books in the field. The Society also issues occasional lengthy papers in the *Wildlife Monographs* and current events in the bimonthly *Wildlife Society News.*

Land Economics; a quarterly journal devoted to the study of economic and social institutions. 1928. q. $15 (Individuals $10). Mary A. Lescohier. Subs. to: Univ. of Wisconsin Press, 817 W. Dayton, Madison, Wis. 53706. Index. Circ: 4,000. Sample. Vol. ends: Nov. Microform: UM. Reprint: Kraus.

Indexed: BusI, PAIS. *Aud:* Ac, Ga.

"Reflects the growing emphasis on planning for the wise use of urban and rural land to meet the needs of an expanding population." It usually contains about 15 articles on such topics as housing, air and water use, and land reform. Emphasis is on public action. Of interest to public service-minded citizens as well as to public officials.

New York Fish and Game Journal. 1954. s-a. $1.50. R. W. Darrow, New York Dept. of Environmental Conservation, Albany, N.Y. 12201. Illus. Circ: 1,300.

Aud: Ga, Hs.

A fine journal for the scientifically minded or the serious student of wildlife conservation. It is not directed toward the sportsman. Each issue contains about four long articles and a section called "General Notes." Articles deal mainly with research done in New York State on animals, plants, and other elements of natural environment. Members of the Conservation Department and professors of biological, agricultural, and other sciences are the major contributors. Illustrations are mainly photographs, graphs, and charts. Good for science, academic, and research libraries.

Outdoor California. 1940. bi-m. $2. Ray Chapman. California Dept. of Fish and Game, 1416 9th St., Sacramento, Calif. 45814.

Aud: Ga, Hs.

Published by the California Department of Fish and Game this periodical offers articles on the wildlife of the California area and on the work of the department in conservation efforts. About eight articles, written by the department staff, are included in each issue. The presentation is directed toward the general public and offers a clear picture of what one state has in terms of conservation programs. The articles are generally two to three pages long, show the sportsman where his money is going.

Outdoor Recreation Action. 1966. q. $2. Bureau of Outdoor Recreation. Supt. of Documents, U.S. Government Printing Office, Washington, D.C. 20402.

Aud: Ac, Ga.

Mainly for the public official or layman who wants to keep up-to-date on federal, state, local, and private outdoor recreation actions. It is filled with short, staff-written news items on financing, organization and administration, research, conferences, planning, and judicial actions. Some issues also have longer articles on items of more general interest, e.g., the federal Summer Recreation Support Program, which are well illustrated with black and white photographs. Recommended for the academic library, but it may also be of use in the public library. (M.A.)

ENVIRONMENTAL SCIENCES

See also Counterculture/Alternative Living and Environment and Conservation Sections.

The majority of titles mentioned in this section are periodicals predominantly of a scientific or engineering nature, of interest to technical libraries and science collections of academic libraries. A few are appropriate for public library purchase.

The spate of publications appearing in the last few years on the environmental sciences presents a problematic area for the librarian interested in spending the dollar wisely. Of the 100-odd entries listed in the 14th edition of *Ulrich's International Periodicals Directory,* well over 50 percent of them have been published since 1967. Even the phrase "environmental sciences" is ill defined, since it appears to include the entire spectrum of air, water, land, noise, and odor pollution; conservation; ecology; chemical, physical, biological, medical, geological studies thereon; technological journals dealing with apparatus, facilities and processes for pollution control; newsletters concerned with federal, state, and municipal legislation; publications devoted to studies on human ecology; and periodicals reporting on the activities of an aroused citizenry alarmed at the disturbance of the ecocycle. Misleading, too, are the titles of a number of these journals, many of which have been in existence for decades, and have more appropriately been located in public health, water research and engineering, sanitary engineering collections, but which have modified their scope slightly and adapted to the current vogue by the inclusion or substitution of such words as "environment" or "pollution" on the title page.

How many of these new ones will last or will have significant value during the next decade depends on a large number of variables, not the least of which is how successful the editors of the research journals can be in drawing "names" in the field to publish their best work in a new journal, rather than releasing it to the well-established periodicals.

Air Pollution Control Association. Journal. 1907. m. $75. Harold M. Englund. Air Pollution Control Assn., 4400 Fifth Ave., Pittsburgh, Pa. 15213. Illus., index, adv. Sample. Vol. ends: Dec. Refereed.

Indexed: ChemAb, EngI, IMed. *Bk. rev:* 7, 300 words, unsigned. *Aud:* Sa, Ac.

For sixty-five years, this organization has been the spokesman for clean air, its management, and standards thereon, in the United States. Its journal, issued under the present title since 1951, is both a technical publication and the news and tutorial medium for its membership. Within the range of subject matter fall such topics as ambient air and source measurements, atmospheric reactions, control equipment, discharges of motor vehicles, fuels and power, medical and biological effects, meteorological problems, waste disposal, and lastly, legislation and standards. About half of each issue is given to three or four technical papers, and the other half to nonspecialist or review material. A new series called "Pollution Control Progress" contains industrial case studies. Issues are liberally provided with new product and equipment briefs. An authoritative and long-established technical journal for science and engineering collections.

Air and Water News. 1967. w. $145. McGraw-Hill, Inc., 330 W. 42nd St., New York, N.Y. 10036. Index. Sample. Vol. ends: no. 52.

A weekly newsletter in loose-leaf format, covering current events on environmental and pollution problems. Reports review legislative activities on a Federal, state, and local level, as well as developments in governmental agencies, industrial laboratories, and other organizations. The publication also contains short summaries of technical advances, some marketing information, and the like. The McGraw complex is vast, and their factual reporting accurate; this newsletter generally follows their high standards. Frequent references are made to earlier issues of the letter, thus affording some continuity in terms of new developments and outcomes of legislative action. Occasional references are made to the original sources, and the technical section includes some citations to literature available. Three-month indexes are published for accessibility to the information. A useful newsletter in culling out the major happenings in the environmental crisis. The price is steep (something over $2.75 per 8-page issue), but large libraries ought to have it.

Ambio. 1972. bi-m. $13. Eric Dyring. Universitets-forlaget, P. O. Box 142, Boston, Mass. 02113. Illus., index. Sample. Vol. ends: no. 6. Refereed.

Aud: Sa, Ac.

It is appropriate that the country which hosted the United Nations Conference on the Human Environment, Stockholm, June 1972, has now put out a "journal of the human environment." Published for the distinguished Royal Swedish Academy of Sciences, the periodical is intended for an international nonspecialist, as well as specialist, audience. English is its common language. About half of the first issue was dedicated to feature articles, and the remainder, to technical reports. Contents deal with both international problems ("Changing Chemistry of the Ocean," "Global Consensus or Global Catastrophe") to the examination of pollution relating to all Scandinavian countries ("Sulphur Pollution across National Boundaries") and those typically Swedish ("Gradual Destruction of Sweden's Lakes"). Articles are all by prominent authorities. A few international news briefs are also included. The format is good and well illustrated, particularly with color photos, charts and figures. From a preview of the first volume, the journal promises to be an important and authoritative publication, branching into all areas of environmental research. Academic libraries should certainly investigate it.

Atmospheric Environment. 1967. bi-m. $65. James P. Lodge, Jr. Pergamon Press, Inc., Maxwell House, Fairview Pk., Elmsford, N.Y. 10523. Illus., index. Sample. Vol. ends: Dec. Refereed. Microform: Maxwell. Reprint: Maxwell.

Bk. rev: 3–4, 300–500 words, signed. *Aud:* Sa, Ac.

An interdisciplinary journal, the periodical is concerned with research investigations on air pollution, e.g., control and measurements of emissions, transport of pollutants, etc. Since many of the problems of airborne pollutants are intimately related to atmospheric conditions, meteorological and some climatological studies are also published, as well as papers on evaporation, aerosols, etc. Titles such as "Urban Climate and Day of Week," "Influence of Vertical Wind Profile on Dust Deposition," "Determination of Airborne Matter by X-ray Fluorescence," are typical. Included with full-length papers are short technical notes, and discussions of papers. A review article, frequently a literature-survey type of paper, is published from time to time, as well as a "news" section. The "News" also incorporates titles of timely and significant papers appearing in the recent literature. For collections in the atmospheric sciences, as well as those concerned with air pollution research.

CRC Critical Reviews in Environmental Control. 1970. q. $56. Richard G. Bond and Conrad P. Straub. Chemical Rubber Co., 18901 Cranwood Parkway, Cleveland, Ohio 44128. Illus., index. Sample. Vol. ends: no. 4. Refereed.

Aud: Sa, Ac.

Published by the CRC Press, producers of a number of indispensable scientific handbooks, including the ubiquitous *Handbook of Chemistry and Physics,* the journal is a reputable and reliable source for critical reviews of significant topics in environmental science and technology, and the only scholarly review journal currently in print in this field. Authoritative studies by specialists sweep over a wide range of subjects: communicable diseases, radiation pollution, air and water pollutants, fluoridation, and instrumentation for pollution abatement, etc. Recent papers tend to favor biological and medical reports, rather than engineering studies. About four lengthy papers, well documented with comprehensive bibliographies, appear in each issue. On occasion, the publisher reprints papers of broad appeal in book form, which fact alone may warrant a subscription. Recommended for any technical library supporting some aspect of environmental research.

Clean Air. 1971. q. $3.50 P. G. Sharp. National Soc. for Clean Air, 134/137 North Street, Brighton, BN1 1RG, England. Illus., index, adv. Circ: 6,500. Sample. Vol. ends: no. 4.

Indexed: BritTech. *Bk. rev:* 7, 50–250 words, signed. *Aud:* Sa, Ac.

In existence since 1929 under the title *Smokeless Air,* the periodical is the official voice of the National Society for Clean Air. The publication rightly calls itself "Britain's leading air pollution journal" since it was one of the first to trumpet the cause of environmental hazards due to air pollution. Indeed, it was organizations like the NSCA, and its parents, the Coal Smoke Abatement Society (1899) and the Smoke Abatement League of Gt. Brit. (1909), which, through the creation of an informed public opinion and encouragement into investigations of atmospheric pollution, helped clean up the London fog. Today, its semitechnical journal still champions environmental causes. Much of the information is topical, but the review articles and international news should be of interest to technical libraries. Also included in each issue are "Air Pollution Abstracts," covering the pertinent literature.

Clean Air and Water News. 1967. w. $100. Commerce Clearing House, Inc., 4025 W. Peterson Ave., Chicago, Ill. 60646. Index. Sample. Vol. ends: no. 52.

Aud: Sa, Ga, Ac.

Considered a topical law newsletter, in loose-leaf format, covering recent legislation and other developments in air and water pollution, and related environmental problems. Similar in scope and format to other well-known publications of the CCH, the newsletter focuses on Federal, state, and municipal legislation, international agreements, activities and actions of governmental agencies, and industry. Compared to a newsletter such as McGraw's *Air and Water News*, the emphasis here, as mentioned before, is on the legal aspects of the field, although news, developments, and publications announcements from EPA and other agencies are well advanced. An excellent three-month index includes subjects (with cross-references by states, as well as government agency), list of acronyms used (a nuisance factor nicely solved here), and a useful Directory of Federal and State Agencies concerned with pollution, plus tables citing cases reported in the publication. A good newsletter for isolating the laws, actions, agreements, etc., issued by the multiplicity of agencies currently involved in the environmental crisis. Large libraries should have it.

Ecology. See Biological Sciences Section.

Environment Reporter. 1970. $340. John D. Stewart. Bureau of National Affairs, 1231 25th St., N.W., Washington, D.C. 20037. Index.

Aud: Sa, Ac.

BNA publications need little introduction to reference librarians. Here, in looseleaf format, and for libraries which can afford it, is a monumental effort dedicated to "weekly review of pollution control and related environmental management problems." Issued in sections, the service breaks down into the following components. (1) Current Developments. Reviews any news development considered pertinent to the field, as well as full text of selected documents (e.g., EPA Performance Standards), or background information leading to legislation. (2) Federal Laws. Covers policies, standards, criteria, enforcement, programs, directories, and actual statutes and orders. (3) Decisions. Gives full coverage of all Supreme Court decisions on environmental law. (4) Federal Regulations. Covers grants on air, water, pesticides, and radiation. (5) State Laws. Includes solid waste and land use, state air laws, state water laws. In addition, selected monographs, developed by the BNA staff, review such areas as federal aid for water pollution control, noise pollution, etc. Best of all, each section has an index. No other service matches it (particularly noteworthy is the advantage of having full text of decisions), and the publication certainly belongs in any scholarly collection concerned with environmental law.

Environmental Letters. 1971. 8/yr. $40. James W. Robinson. Marcel Dekker, Inc., 95 Madison Ave., New York, N.Y. 10016. Illus. Sample. Vol. ends: no. 4 (2v/yr). Refereed.

Aud: Sa, Ac.

Generally a letters-type journal is used as a vehicle to disseminate research results quickly, and usually the reports are no longer than two to three pages. This publication, produced by a photo offset process, does,

indeed, contain new research discoveries, largely in the fields of chemical analysis and chemical engineering. But it carries, as well, a curious combination of studies from an essay on engineering ecology, to a 30-page legal study of nerve gas, to a 3-page product report from a manufacturer (billed as a "letter"). The intent of the publisher is to draw together related works in any field involving the contamination of our environment, and other problems. From a review of vol. 1, however, the scope of the publication (e.g., technical vs. nonspecialist; research vs. survey-type paper) has not yet been defined.

Environmental Research. 1967. bi-m. $30. I. J. Selikoff. Academic Press, Inc., 111 Fifth Ave., New York, N.Y. 10003. Illus., index. Sample. Vol. ends: no. 6. Refereed.

Aud: Sa, Ac.

The scope of this journal is loosely defined as "original research in any of the disciplines now concerned with man-environment relationships." Research studies generally emphasize broad problems in environmental biology and medicine, such as toxicity of materials to humans, the effect of nuclear weapons testing on life, air pollution and mortality rates, survival of humans at extreme temperatures. Issues may also include clinical studies. Recommended for medical libraries, academic libraries with strong biological collections and interest in medicine and ancillary fields.

Environmental Science and Technology. 1967. m. $9. James J. Morgan. Amer. Chemical Soc., 1155 16th St., N.W., Washington, D.C. 20036. Illus., index, adv. Circ: 30,000. Sample. Vol. ends: no. 12. Refereed. Microform: Amer. Chemical Soc.

Indexed: ChemAb. *Bk. rev:* 1–2, 600 words, signed. *Aud:* Sa, Ac.

"Emphasizing water, air, and waste chemistry," the publication nonetheless contains a good deal of nonspecialist information for interested citizenry concerned with clean water, clean air, and other environmental improvements. About half of each issue is spent on discussions of current activities along these lines—in the government, in industry, in universities—and the one or two feature articles interpret, in general language, some new facet of environmental research. The remaining sections of each issue are devoted mainly to specialized research reports, new product briefs, and meeting announcements. An authoritative and important publication for most technical collections, if not all.

International Journal of Environmental Studies. 1970. q. $41. J. Rose. Gordon and Breach Science Publishers, Inc., 440 Park Ave. S., New York, N.Y. 10016. Illus., index. Sample. Vol. ends: no. 4. Refereed.

Indexed: ChemAb, SciAb. *Bk. rev:* 3, 800–1,000 words, signed. *Aud:* Sa, Ac.

A journal on human ecology, emphasizing the "relationship between man and his environment." Papers focus more on reviews of recent research than on original investigations themselves. The view is broad, sweeping from the physical and biological sciences through behavioral and educational studies. In one issue, for example, the subjects ranged from a study of cancer and its environmental causes, through interaction of weather and air pollution, on to British medicine at the turn of the twentieth century, to an essay on education and our environment. Articles vary in level of technicality, but generally are comprehensible to the nonspecialist. Special sections of the journal are devoted to news, editorial opinion, and conference reports. An international editorial board contains some prominent names in their listing. Recommended for academic libraries as a good, multidisciplinary and authoritative publication in the field.

Journal of Environmental Sciences. 1958. bi-m. $12. T. W. H. Miller. Inst. of Environmental Sciences, 940 E. Northwest Highway, Mt. Prospect, Ill. 60056. Illus., index, adv. Sample. Vol. ends: no. 6. Refereed. Microform: UM.

The Institute of Environmental Sciences is a society of "professional engineers and scientists simulating and testing in the environments of earth and space." Now in its second decade, the journal publishes technical papers varying from studies on space vacuum, ultra high temperatures, nuclear radiation, solar radiation, shock and vibration, electromagnetics, instrument metrology, marine technology, acoustics, corrosion, and environmental pollution. Titles such as "Nuclear Environment Against Which Equipment Must Be Hardened," and "Comparison of Lunar Orbiter Vibration Responses with Calculations Based on Mathematical Models," indicate the type of material. About five or six technical articles appear in each issue, and the rest of the material covers organizational news, exhibits, meetings, etc. A good environmental engineering journal for technical libraries interested in this field.

Journal of Environmental Systems. 1971(?) q. $28. Paul R. De Cicco. Baywood Publishing Co., Inc., Box A-114, Wantagh, N.Y. 11793. Illus., index. Sample. Vol. ends: no. 4. Refereed.

Aud: Sa, Ac.

Emphasis in this new journal is on the interface of large, complex systems in our total societal environment, and the interdisciplinary approaches which can be taken to analyze, design, and manage them. Thus, the journal draws on studies from engineering, systems analysis, economics, computing sciences, law, operations research, and other related fields. Titles such as "Comprehensive Modeling of the Urban Housing Problem," "Comprehensive Community Analysis and Planning," and "Education of Urban Systems Analysts" are indicative of its scope. A good, interdisci-

plinary publication for academic libraries. Particularly recommended for urban studies programs, management engineering courses, etc.

Marine Pollution Bulletin. See Oceanography Section.

Pesticides Monitoring Journal. See Government Magazines/United States Section.

Pollution Engineering. 1969. bi-m. $12. (controlled circulation) Richard A. Young. Technical Publishing Co., Thompson Div., 35 Mason St., Greenwich, Conn. 06830. Illus., index, adv. Circ: 39,000. Sample. Vol. ends: no. 6.

Aud: Sa, Ac.

A trade journal for the "pollution engineer." Brief, 2-page reports review aspects of air, water, solid waste, and noise and odor pollution problems. Occasional special reports supply in-depth coverage on specific topics, or reviews of meetings. The remainder of the periodical is largely taken by new product information and ads. The money for a subscription is certainly better spent elsewhere, but perhaps technical libraries can wheedle some free copies.

Water, Air, and Soil Pollution. 1971. q. $43.95. B. M. McCormac. D. Reidel Publishing Co., P.O. Box 17, Dordrecht, Holland. Illus., index. Sample. Vol. ends: no. 4. Refereed.

Aud: Sa, Ac.

Spanning several fields, the quarterly is a multidisciplinary research journal covering the major elements of environmental pollution, as indicated by its title. Studies cross the boundaries of atmospheric, chemical, engineering, geological, and biological sciences. Subjects such as chemical analyses of water; investigations of atmospheric aerosols; biological studies of species diversity and water quality; engineering considerations of pollution caused by offshore mining, indicate the diversity. Although the majority of contributors from the issues reviewed are from the United States, the journal is an international publication and supported by an authoritative, worldwide, editorial board. A broad-based research journal for technical collections interested in the above aspects of pollution.

Water Pollution Control Federation. Journal. 1928. m. $30. Bob G. Rogers. Water Pollution Control Federation, 3900 Wisconsin Ave., N.W., Washington, D.C. 20016. Illus., index, adv. Circ: 22,000. Sample. Vol. ends: Dec. Refereed. Microform: UM.

Indexed: ASTI, BioAb, ChemAb, EngI. *Bk. rev:* 4–5, 350 words, signed. *Aud:* Sa, Ac.

Formerly called *Sewage Works Journal* and *Sewage and Industrial Wastes*, the official journal of the Federation changed its title in 1950 to accommodate a broader purpose. The bulk of the material in the present publication is dedicated to technical papers dealing with wastewater collection and disposal; wastewater treatment processes, both domestic and industrial; and the construction and management of such facilities. Articles on water quality standards, effluent quality control, wastewater reuse, microorganisms in wastewater, sludge pumping, are typical of the content. Each issue includes abstracts of the published papers with keyword information; and multilingual abstracts are also provided. News, notices, and product information also appear monthly. An annual *Yearbook,* published as part of the journal, gives organizational information and a buyers' guide for new products and processes. Necessary for sanitary engineering collections, the journal would also be useful for any technical library supporting work on chemical and biological treatment of water. (Note: The Federation also issues a monthly *Water Pollution Control Federation Highlights,* which is their newsletter to the membership.)

Water Research. 1967. m. $100. W. W. Eckenfelder, Jr. Pergamon Press, Maxwell House, Fairview Pk., Elmsford, N.Y. 10523. Illus., index. Sample. Vol. ends: no. 12 (Dec.). Refereed. Microform: Maxwell. Reprint: Maxwell.

Indexed: BioAb, ChemAb, EngI. *Aud:* Sa, Ac.

The official journal of the International Association on Water Pollution Research. Original research papers are published on any aspect of water quality, including chemical and biological studies, and engineering or technological developments in water and wastewater treatments. Papers reflect diverse treatments of these fields, such as chemical or microbiological analyses; new techniques in instrumentation; treatment of municipal sewage and industrial wastes; effects of water discharges into inland, coastal or tidal waters, and related topics. A few review papers may be published, as well as an occasional short note. An authoritative, international journal and an important one for any library supporting water pollution research in the physical and biological sciences, or sanitary engineering.

Water Resources Bulletin. 1965. bi-m. $20. A. I. Kashef. Amer. Water Resources Assn., 206 E. University Ave., Urbana, Ill. Illus., index. Circ: 2,000. Vol. ends: no. 6. Refereed.

Indexed: BioAb. *Bk. rev:* 1–2, 250 words, signed. *Aud:* Sa, Ac.

The official Journal of the American Water Resources Association, as subtitled, links together research efforts in the physical, biological, and engineering sciences, with studies in the social sciences, to bring out a total picture of water resources—their quality, pollution, management, etc. Articles may be as varied in field and approach as from technical papers on hydrology and hydrodynamics, chemical analyses of water quality, or statistical methods for predicting pollutants in rivers, to legal studies on ground water rights, or

historical essays on water resources of the past. Emphasis is on the technical—on hydrology and U.S. waters. Issues also include *Water Resources Newsletter,* providing the latest in information on research, development, state and regional news, international trends, comments, and discussions. Necessary for all engineering collections in hydrology, the publication would be a valuable and authoritative choice for academic libraries supporting research interests in water resources.

Two other publications of the AWRA merit attention, namely *Hydata,* a current-awareness periodical, and *Water Resources Abstracts,* its abstracting service (see *Abstracts and Indexes*).

Water Resources Research. 1965. bi-m. $20. Walter B. Langbein and Charles W. Howe. Amer. Geophysical Union, 2100 Pennyslvania Ave. N.W., Washington, D.C. 20037. Illus., index. Circ: 4,500. Sample. Vol. ends: no. 6. Refereed. Microform: Amer. Geophysical Union.

Indexed: SCI. *Aud:* Sa, Ac.

Founded by the section of Hydrology of the American Geophysical Union, this "journal of the sciences of water" goes far beyond the scope originally envisioned, and offers an interesting combination of papers from the physical, biological, and social sciences. Contributions are published from such areas as hydrology, fluid mechanics, geochemistry, economics, and water law, and blend such studies as thermal pollution of river ice, with biological investigations of water, and economic analyses of lakeshore properties. Papers are authoritative and scholarly. A valuable journal for any academic library involved with research on environmental studies, as well as hydrology, and geological sciences.

NEWSLETTERS. There are a number of weekly newsletters, too numerous to treat here, which are similar in scope and replete with redundancies. Three services have been mentioned in this chapter . . . the most expensive ones: *Air and Water News* (McGraw); *Clean Air and Water News* (Commerce Clearing House), and *Environment Report* (Bureau of National Affairs). For the record, these others, some newcomers to the field, are listed below. Prices vary from $60 to $90. The only suggestion that one makes is to write for a sample and check the index (if there is any) before purchase.

Air/Water Pollution Report (Eiserer); *Clean Water Report* (Eiserer); *Environment Report* (Trends); *Ecolert; Ecolog; Environment Quality Report; New Pollution Technology; Special Report Ecology; Washington Environmental Protection Report.*

EUROPE AND MIDDLE EAST

See also Foreign Language Teaching and Motion Pictures/Foreign Language Sections.

Basic Periodicals

ENGLISH LANGUAGE GENERAL. Hs: *Realities, European Studies Review, Europa;* Jc: *European Studies Review, Europa, Realities;* Ac: *European Studies Review, Journal of European Studies, Realities, Middle Eastern Studies, International Journal of Middle East Studies, Europa.*

FRENCH LANGUAGE. Hs: *Marie-France, L'Auberge de la Jeunesse;* Ga: *Paris-Match, Marie France, Touring Club of France;* Jc: *Paris-Match, Africasia;* Ac: *Le Figaro, Paris-Match, Africasia.*

GERMAN LANGUAGE. Hs: *Scala International;* Ga: *Spiegel, Scala International, Stern;* Jc: *Spiegel, Stern;* Ac: *Spiegel, Frankfurter Hefte, Merkur.*

ITALIAN LANGUAGE. Hs: *Epoca;* Ga: *Epoca, L'Europeo. Rivista Mensile del Club Alpino Italian;* Jc: *L'Europeo, Epoca;* Ac: *L'Europeo, Mondo, Epoca.*

Cessations

Monat, Monatpost, Table Ronde.

English Language General

American-German Review. 1934. bi-m. $5. National Carl Schurz Assn., Inc., 339 Walnut St., Philadelphia, Pa. 19106. Illus., index, adv. Circ: 7,500. Microform: UM.

Bk. rev: Various number, length. *Aud:* Ga.

A general cultural magazine which is out to prove the benefits of working and living with Western Germans. Articles range from the historical to the survey of current artistic movements. There is some German-Language material, but almost all is in English. Illustrations are good to excellent. The magazine tends to be a bit bland, yet no worse or no better than most of this type. A useful, but not necessary, acquisition for larger libraries, and smaller ones serving a German-oriented community.

American-Scandinavian Review. 1913. $7.50. Erik J. Friis. American-Scandinavian Foundation, 127 E. 73rd St., New York, N.Y. 10021. Illus., index, adv. Circ: 7,000. Sample. Vol. ends: Dec. Microform: UM.

Indexed: PAIS. *Bk. rev:* 5–6, 300–600 words, signed. *Aud:* Ga, Hs.

Well-illustrated accounts of cultural and political life in Denmark, Finland, Iceland, Norway, and Sweden. Scandinavian poetry and short stories are printed in translation. The style is popular and the magazine will be of interest to travelers, and to anyone studying the Scandinavian countries.

Arab World. See Free Magazines Section.

Aramco World. See Free Magazines Section.

Ararat. q. $6. David Kherdian. Armenian General Benevolent Union of America, Inc., 109 East 40th St., New York, N.Y. 10016. Illus. Vol. ends: Fall.

Bk. rev: 3–5, 250–1,500 words, signed. *Aud:* Ga.

In 1971 this ethnic group magazine got a new editor, a face-lift and, fittingly enough, published a lead article by the best known Armenian-American of them all, William Saroyan. Dedicated to the future as well as the past history of Armenians, the nicely printed 50 to 60 page illustrated magazine covers a variety of topics from poetry and prose to book reviews and notes on Armenian activities both here and abroad. There are interviews, bibliographies, and regular departments. The literary quality is exceptionally high and of broad enough interest to capture the attention of most laymen.

Ariel; a quarterly of arts and letters in Israel. 1962. q. $6. Yehuda Hanegbi. Ministry for Foreign Affairs, Cultural and Scientific Relations Div., Jerusalem, Israel. Illus. Circ: 6,100. Sample.

Indexed: IJewAr. *Bk. rev:* 3–20, 100–700 words. *Aud:* Ga, Hs, Ac.

An abundantly illustrated literary and art magazine covering every aspect of cultural life in Israel, its purpose is to present to readers abroad Israeli painters, sculptors, theater people, and writers and Israeli achievements in humanities and science. It features articles from 5 to 20 pages on a variety of subjects such as archaeology, history, and education. The accent however is on the plastic arts with the help of many reproductions in color and black and white. The section "Arts and Science" presents brief informative articles on cultural events such as recent archaeological excavations, scientific activities of research institutions, and international meetings held in Israel. From time to time special issues are devoted to one subject, e.g., "The Revival of the Hebrew Language," "The Writer S.Y. Agnon," which are very useful to high school and college students. Articles are written by well-known specialists, but are popular in style and destined to reach a wide public. *Ariel* is not directed toward the specialist. Book reviews cover Israeli imprints in Hebrew, English, and French, and foreign imprints on Jewish subjects. They are very short, dated, and feature subjects much more specialized than this general periodical warrants. (R.T.)

Central European History. 1968. q. $10 (Institutions $15). Douglas A. Unfug. Emory Univ., Atlanta, Ga. 30322. Index, adv. Circ: 1,200. Sample. Vol. ends: Dec.

Indexed: HistAb. *Bk. rev:* 2–3, 2–3 pages, signed. *Aud:* Ac.

Sponsored by the Conference Group for Central European History of the American Historical Association, this is a scholarly journal with two to three articles based on original research on central Europe, especially the old German and Austro-Hungarian empires. The editorial board includes the major figures in the field. Occasional bibliographical articles and extensive notes are also published. This is a publication for the specialist in central European history and is recommended for large university and research libraries. (R.S.)

Dimension; contemporary German arts and letters. 1968. 3/yr. $7.50. A. Leslie Willson. Dept. of Germanic Languages, Univ. of Texas, P.O. Box 7939, Austin, Tex. 78712. Illus., index. Circ: 550. Vol. ends: No. 3. Microform: UM.

Indexed: MLA. *Aud:* Ac.

Averaging some 200 well-printed pages, this is an outstanding journal of current German thought and will be useful for both the student and the specialist in German literature. Each issue offers contributors in German with the English translation and the German original printed side by side. Material varies from poetry to critical comments on current writers, political events, and social developments. A good one half of each issue includes material heretofore not published elsewhere. The critical style is definitely academic (poetry and prose aside), but the wide selection of current German writings makes it a suitable addition for any type of library where there is more than passing interest in the country or its writers.

Eire-Ireland; a journal of Irish Studies. 1966. q. $10. Lawrence O'Shaughnessy and Eoin McKiernan. Irish American Cultural Inst., Box 5026, College of St. Thomas, St. Paul, Minn. 55101. Adv. Circ: 3,000. Vol. ends: Dec.

Indexed: AbEnSt. *Bk. rev:* 10–12, 500–1,500 words, signed. *Aud:* Ga, Ac.

The editor claims, probably rightfully, that this is "the only intelligent Irish magazine published in the United States." In that it is free of wild stories and worship of the old country, he is quite correct. In fact, the contributors are teachers, authors, and historians who give an unbiased account of everything from the Irish theatre to the Irish revolt. The writing style is easily within the grasp of the average layman, and the scope is wide enough to appeal to anyone remotely interested in Irish culture. Emphasis is on history, literature, and the arts, particularly in the critical book reviews, notes, queries, and bibliographies. A good acquisition for the general or fine arts collection in most medium to large-sized public and academic collections.

L'Esprit Createur; a critical quarterly of French literature. 1961. q. $4. John D. Erickson, Box 222, Lawrence, Kans. 66044. Illus., index, adv. Circ: 1,100. Microform: UM.

Bk. rev: 3–8, 700 words, signed. *Aud:* Ac.

Interested in the interpretation of French literature. Each issue presents five to eight 4,000-word critical analyses of different aspects of the literary production of one author, or of a movement. Most of the material is in English, but often with extensive quotes in French, and a knowledge of French is helpful. Covers all periods of French literature. See also *Yale French Studies.*

Europa; the Newsmagazine of Europe. 1971. m. $10. Jean Jacques van Belle. Europa, 59 Rue du Prince Royal, Brussels, 5, Belgium. Illus., index, adv. Sample.

Bk. rev: 5–7, 500–1,500 words, signed. *Aud:* Ga, Ac, Hs.

The ghost of Henry Luce may never be put to rest. Here, for example, his spirit is resurrected in the format, approach, and style of *Time.* Divided into two parts, the magazine whips through the top European news stories of the month, then gets on to music, art, movies, books, and even gourmet notes. A heading such as "And now the Ironical Curtain," would make Henry moan, but he would quite understand the professional approach of the editors who tend to treat the news as a short story. They are all professionals, and know how to hold the attention of readers (a plus, for high school teachers trying to introduce current affairs to reluctant students, but a pain for the mature adult seeking hardrock information). The political bias, if any, is not evident. Writers tend to put more stock in the snide fast remark than the objective statement. As in *Time,* the back of the book is well worth reading. The criticism is first rate. Ilustrations are good—some in color—and the layout is excellent. Still, one wonders who will bother to read it. European news is covered in our news magazines, and in a month's time they probably carry as much as this monthly effort. Europe watchers will be involved with more serious magazines. It is fun, but does not add up to much.

European Community. 1954. m. Free. Kathleen Lynch. European Community Information Service, Suite 707, 2100 M Street, N.W., Washington, D.C. 20007. Illus., index. Circ: 35,000.

Indexed: PAIS. *Bk. rev:* Number varies, short. *Aud:* Ga, Ac.

Covers the affairs of the European Economic Community (Common Market), the European Coal and Steel Community (ECSC), and the European Atomic Energy Community (Euratom). Includes discussions on tariffs, agriculture, customs, social developments, monetary and economic union, harmonization of law, trade, and relations with the rest of the world. Some political concerns are mentioned, but politics is not stressed. The editorial treatment is semipopular. As the publication is free, it is worth trying.

European studies review. 1971. q. $9.25 J. H. Shennon. Macmillan Journals, Ltd., Subscription Dept., Brunel Rd., Basingstoke, Hamps., England. adv.

Bk. rev: 4–7, 750–2,000 words, signed. *Aud:* Ac, Ga. *Jv:* V.

The four to five articles per issue, together with occasional review articles which trace trends in historical studies of an interdisciplinary nature, makes this one of the leading contenders in the field of interdisciplinary studies. It covers all aspects of European history and literature from about 1500 through 1945. Manuscripts are accepted in any European language, although most are translated into English. Book reviews stress books published in European languages other than English. A special feature is the critical *résumés* (in English) of important articles which have appeared abroad. Although essentially a publication based at the University of Lancaster, the Advisory Board is international in scope and includes such doyens as: A.P. d'Entrèves (Turin), Golo Mann (Zurich), R. R. Palmer (Yale), Michael Oakeshott (London), P. Renouvin (Paris), J. Caro Broja (Madrid) and I. Schöffer (Leiden). Given the increasing emphasis on interdisciplinary studies, this publication is a must for all academic libraries. (R.S.)

France Actuelle. 1952. s-m. $6 (Academic use $3). France Actuelle, 1001 Connecticut Ave., N.W., Suite 828, Washington, D.C. 20036. Illus., index. Circ: 20,000. Sample. Vol. ends: Dec. 15.

Aud: Ac, Ga.

France Actuelle is sponsored by the Comité France Actuelle, a private association of French businessmen, and the purpose of their well-illustrated magazine is to promote French society and industry in the United States. It is an attempt to win both approval and investments. A section in each issue is devoted to current notes on French internal and external economics. While geared for the businessman, it is quite suitable for general adult use. It is in English and usually runs 8 to 12 pages.

French Historical Studies. 1958. s-a. $8. David H. Pinkney. George T. Matthews, Treasurer, Soc. for French Historical Studies, Dept. of History, Oakland University, Rochester, Mich. 48063. Index. Vol. ends: Sept. (2 yrs. per vol.).

Indexed: HistAb. *Aud:* Ac. *Jv:* V.

With text in English or French, each issue contains some four or six articles on all aspects of French history. Other features include "Notes and Suggestions" which often explores archival and documentary materials which are available to the historian interested in French history, as "The Dépot in Aix and Archival Sources for France Outre-Mer." From time to time, the holdings of an outstanding library, such as the Newberry in Chicago, are described for the reader. Although *French Historical Studies* does not have a book review section, each issue does contain a list of

"Recent Books on French History," which is arranged chronologically by period. (R.S.)

French News. 1957. 5/yr. Free. Cultural Services of the French Embassy, 972 Fifth Ave., New York, N.Y. 10021. Illus. Circ: 15,000.

Aud: Ga, Hs, Ejh.

A pleasant, illustrated, primarily English-language introduction to French culture, history, and people. As a propaganda effort of the French government it is rather good. Its purpose, of course, is to lure travelers and to build up feelings of good will for the French and their products. A calendar of events makes it most useful. As it is free, it is certainly worth a request by libraries.

French Studies; a quarterly review. q. $10.80. L. J. Austin. Basil Blackewell & Mott Ltd., 108 Cowley Rd., Oxford OX 4, 1JF, England. Illus., index, adv. Circ: 1,475. Sample. Vol. ends: Oct.

Indexed: BritHum. *Bk. rev:* 30, 750–1,000 words, signed. *Aud:* Ac.

A 100 to 125 page journal which represents the findings of members of England's Society for French Studies. The material is usually in French, consists of four or five articles on somewhat esoteric points about French literature and language. There are extensive book reviews. A major item for larger academic collections.

German Economic Review; an English language quarterly on German economic research and current developments. 1963. q. $7.40. Dieter Held. Wissenschaftliche Verlagsgesellschaft mbH, Postfach 40, Stuttgart, W. Germany. Index, adv. Circ: 4,750. Sample. Vol. ends: Dec.

Indexed: CurrCont, JEconLit, PAIS. *Bk. rev:* 15–20, ½–3 pages, signed. *Aud:* Ac.

The audience for this English-language quarterly is primarily professional economists. The average of two articles per number are translations of papers written by faculty members of German universities and there are reviews of German books and abstracts of material from various German periodicals. There is also a selected bibliography of books and periodicals on various aspects of economics, and a section devoted to reports and news of economic developments in Germany.

German Life and Letters. 1936. q. $7.20. L. W. Forster. Basil Blackwell & Mott Ltd. 108 Cowley Rd., Oxford OX4 IJF, England. Index, adv. Circ: 1,100. Sample. Vol. ends: July.

Indexed: BritHum. *Bk. rev:* 15–36, 500 words, signed. *Aud:* Ac.

A general German literature magazine, published with both English and German texts. It is primarily for the scholar. Of considerable value to larger libraries because of the extensive book review section which covers all aspects of German and European literature. Some material on German intellectual history is included. For all academic libraries. The *American-German Review* is a better choice for most public libraries.

Germanic Notes. 1970. 8/yr. $4. Wayne Wonderley and Lawrence Thompson. Erasmus Press Inc., 225 Culpepper, Lexington, Ky. 40502. Circ: 400. Sample. Vol. ends: No. 8.

Aud: Ac.

Devoted to studies in Germanic languages, each issue, according to editor Wayne Wonderly, is divided into the following sections: (1) a note of 1,000–3,000 words; (2) queries, in the style of Notes and Queries, and answers; (3) one or two longer critical reviews of major contributions to Germanic studies, ranging up to 2,000 words; and (4) a short annotated list of major current titles in the broad fields covered by the journal, with special emphasis on reference books and essential titles for a research library, in other words, a book selection tool. The notes (item 1) are refereed by competent readers, whose identity will not be revealed without permission.

Germanic Review: devoted to studies dealing with the Germanic languages and literatures. 1926. q. $7.50. Joseph Bauke. Columbia Univ. Press, 562 West 113th St., New York, N.Y. 10025. Adv. Circ: 1,100. Sample. Vol. ends: Nov. Microform: UM.

Indexed: SSHum. *Bk. rev:* 6, 1,000 words, signed. *Aud:* Ac.

Features long, detailed and documented articles on German literature and language. Book reviews are excellent. The authors focus on all German literatures and consider all fields from the history of ideas to criticism. Primarily for the academic library. See also *Romanic Review*, a similar approach in the Romanic languages.

International Journal of Middle East Studies. 1970. q. $12.50. Stanford J. Shaw. Cambridge University Press, 32 E. 57th St., New York, N. Y. 10022. Ilus., index, adv. Circ: 1,400.

Indexed: HistAb. *Bk. rev:* 6–8, 2–3 pages, also short notices of ½ page, signed. *Aud:* Ac.

A publication sponsored by the Middle East Studies Association of North America, Inc., which stresses the history, political science, economics, anthropology, sociology, philology and literature, folklore, comparative religion and theology, law, and philosophy of the area encompassing Iran, Turkey, Afghanistan, Israel, Pakistan, and the countries of the Arab world from the seventh century to modern times. Spain, Southeastern Europe, and the Soviet Union also are included for the periods in which their territories were parts of Middle Eastern empires or were under the influence of Middle Eastern civilization. Special features include reports on archives and other source materials, as well as news and short notices of interest to scholars in the field. (R.S.)

International Problems. 1963. q. $6. M. Mushkat. Israeli Inst. of Intl. Affairs, Political Doctrine and Problems of Developing Countries, POB 17027, Tel-Aviv, Israel. Index, adv.

Indexed: IJewAr, PAIS. *Bk. rev* 1–2, lengthy, signed. *Aud:* Ga, Ac.

The subjects covered in this quarterly include international relations (e.g., "Ceylon and the Middle East"), international law ("Recrudescence of the 'Bellum Justum et Pium' Controversy and Israel's Reunification of Jerusalem"), problems related to developing countries ("African Socialism—An Instrument to Promote Economic Progress and National Sovereignty"), problems concerning the Arab-Israel conflict ("The Soviet-Egyptian 'Solution' to the Israel Problem"), and current Israeli political and social issues ("The Impact of Immigration on Israel's Development"). In recent issues, the journal has devoted more and more space to problems of peace research. Theoretical problems such as ideology and political doctrine are also treated (e.g., "Ideology and International Communications"; "Security: the Use and Abuse of a Concept"). Each number is divided into two non-identical parts: one in Hebrew and another, larger, in English. The Hebrew articles are summarized in English. The contributions, presented with clarity and simplicity, are signed by statesmen, political figures, and researchers. It should be noted that Israeli scholars writing on foreign countries often have a personal knowledge of these countries and their languages and have access to primary sources of documentation. (R.T.)

Israel Magazine. 1967. m. $12. Howard Blake. Spotlight Publns., Ltd. 88 Hahashmonaim St., Tel Aviv, Israel. Subs. to: 110 E. 59th St., New York, N.Y. 10022. Illus., index, adv.

Indexed: IJewPer. *Aud:* Ga, Ac, Hs.

A general magazine of Israeli art, culture, social and political life. It is published in Israel, and rather naturally does not offer a completely objective view of the political scene. Still, within its limitations, the magazine is a good introduction to Israel. It serves to keep readers advised of current affairs, changes and developments in education, and personalities. In fact, there are some excellent interviews, and many of the better articles are written by public figures. A little poetry and fiction is included. One of the better, general national magazines, and useful in any library where there is an interest in Israel.

Italian Quarterly. 1957. q. $6. Carlo L. Golino. Vice Chancellor–Academic Affairs. Univ. of California, Riverside, Calif. 92592. Illus., index. Circ: 650. Sample. Vol. ends: Winter

Bk. rev: 4, 2–3 pages, signed. *Aud:* Ac.

A literary quarterly covering the entire spectrum of Italian literature and culture. Occasional issues with color illustrations are devoted to important literary figures. A regular feature is "Trends," which deals with the current Italian scene. There are critical reviews of books about Italian literature, art, and politics, and "Items," an eclectic list of brief news items about Italy and Italians. A useful journal not only for language and linguistics purposes, but for social and historical reasons. Should be in most medium to large-sized academic libraries.

Journal of European Studies. 1971. q. $12.25. J. E. Flower. Seminar Press, Inc., 111 Fifth Ave., New York, N.Y. 10003. Vol. ends: Dec.

Bk. rev: 10–15 review notices, 300 words, signed. *Aud:* Ac.

The three to four articles in each issue are often interdisciplinary in nature and relate to the history, literature, and thought of Europe. Each issue also contains several review essays of 4,000 to 5,000 words which discuss books "which highlight trends in recent research or stimulate discussions of interdisciplinary and comparative approaches." The editors promise that emphasis will also be given to bibliographical articles on major figures, movements, key works, and topics wherein they relate to European affairs. (R.S.)

The Middle East Journal. 1947. q. $10.00. William Sands. Middle East Inst., 1761 N St., N.W., Washington, D.C. 20036. Illus., index, adv. Circ: 4,000. Sample. Vol. ends: Autumn. Refereed. Microform: UM.

Indexed: PAIS, SSHum. *Bk. rev:* 20, 500 words, signed. *Aud:* Ac, Ga.

"Designed to develop among the American people an interest in the Middle East and an appreciation of its history, culture and political and economic affairs." In achieving these ends the nonprofit Institute takes no editorial stand on problems, but seeks only to give accurate and objective information. Four to five ten-page articles dealing with all possible facets of the Middle East, written by Middle East specialists, make this a must for research in international political science. "Recent Publications," arranged by country and topic, and a "Bibliography of Periodical Literature," list magazine articles dealing with the Middle East. Because of its objective treatment of a major crisis point in the world, this can be recommended for all medium to large-sized academic and public libraries.

Middle Eastern Affairs. 1950. m. (Oct.–May); bi-m. (June–Sept.). $6. Council for Middle Eastern Affairs, 2061 Belmont Ave., Elmont, N.Y.

Bk. rev: 5, 300–500 words, signed. *Aud:* Ac. *Jv:* C.

This journal, published under a respectable Editorial Advisory Board, covers both international relations and the affairs of individual Middle Eastern governments. The articles can be absorbed by the average reader, and special features cover the chronology of Middle Eastern affairs, present the text of important documents, or consist of an occasional bibliography. (M.S.)

Middle Eastern Studies. 1964. 3/yr. $12.50. Elie Kedouri. Subs. to: Frank Cass & Co., Ltd., 67 Great Russell St., London WC1B 3 BT, England.

Bk. rev: 6–8 , essays, signed. *Aud:* Ac.

The leading journal in the international field of studies concerned with the Middle East, this covers the Arabic speaking countries of Southwest Asia and North Africa, together with Iran, Turkey, and Israel. An average 120-page issue features six to eight articles in English on history, economics, politics, religion, social elements, linguistics, and literature. A trifle esoteric for general collections, but a required item in large, special collections.

Near East Report. 1957. w. $7. I. L. Kenen, 1341 G St., N.W., Washington, D.C. 20005. Circ: 27,000. Sample. Vol. ends: Last week Dec.

Aud: Ac.

A pro-Israel newsletter. The four pages give a definite point of view, but are quite accurate factually. As the editor notes: "We are frankly partisan. But in this respect I do think we fill a need. Over the years the various Arab embassies and propaganda agencies have flooded libraries with pro-Arab pamphlets and publications. We have always felt there was a need to provide the answers." A department, "Viewing the News," touches on aspects of Jewry in other parts of the world, primarily Russia. The growing interest in the Near East situation dictates that this be found in medium to large university and public libraries.

New Outlook; Middle East monthly. 1957. m. $7.50. Tazpioth Ltd., 8 Karl Netter St., POB 11269, Tel Aviv, Israel. Subs. to: 150 5th Ave., New York, N.Y. 10011. Circ: 4,000. Sample.

Indexed: PAIS, IJewAr. *Bk. rev:* 2–4, lengthy, signed. *Aud:* Ga, Ac.

This monthly was created for the clarification of problems concerning peace and cooperation among all the peoples of the Middle East. The journal describes economic, political, and social problems of the Middle East by publishing articles on all aspects of life in the area, e.g., "Middle East in Transition," "The King [of Jordan], the Palestinians and Ourselves." Much importance is given to Israeli problems: "The Search for a New Society and the Kibbutz Experiment," to the Israel–Arab conflict, and to relations between the Jewish and Arab populations in the country. The tone of the articles is not academic and does not require a specialized background from the reader. Members of the Editorial Board comprise a cross section of views, Jewish and Arab, and are known for their dove-like attitude toward the Arab–Israeli conflict. (R.T.)

Realities. 1946. m. $25. Société d'Etudes et de Publications Economiques, 13 rue Saint-George, Paris 9e, France. Illus., adv. Circ: 187,000 (French and English editions). Sample. Vol. ends: Dec. Microform: UM.

Indexed: PAIS. *Aud:* Ac, Ga, Hs. *Jv:* V.

The best known general French magazine in this country, as much because of its relatively high quality as because of its extensive advertising campaign. The writers are some of the leading figures in France. It is similar to other general magazines in that a single issue will touch on almost every interest from sports and travel to cooking and art. It differs on two counts: there is considerably more emphasis placed upon cultural activities, and the illustrations and format are superior. Many of the photographs and reproductions are in striking color. In fact, the illustrations alone make a subscription worthwhile for any library that can afford the high price. Available in both a French and English edition—the former being ideal for advanced French courses.

Romanic Review. 1910. q. $7.50. Michael Riffaterre. Columbia Univ. Press, 562 West 113th St., New York, N.Y. 10025. Adv. Circ: 900. Sample. Vol. ends: Dec. Microform: UM. Reprint: Kraus.

Indexed: SSHum. *Bk. rev:* 6, 1,000 words, signed. *Aud:* Ac.

A scholarly approach to almost every aspect of Romance language literature. The text is in several languages. About one quarter to one third of each issue is given over to book and general review articles. Primarily for university teachers of Romanic literature. A similar effort from the same University is *Germanic Review.*

Sweden Now. 1967. 6/yr. $9. Helene Türk-modin. Ingenjörsforlaget AB, Box 40058, S-103, Stockholm, Sweden. Illus., index, adv. Circ: 30,000. Sample. Vol. ends: Nov.

Aud: Ga, Ac, Hs.

A general magazine which is somewhat oriented to business interests, but in the past few years has changed to concern with travel, history, art, etc. It is now more of a well-rounded approach to Sweden and surrounding areas. Thanks to the illustrations and the semipopular writing style, the whole will be of interest to both laymen and businessmen alike. Not an essential item, but worthwhile for general collections in larger libraries. (Available also in German and Italian.)

Yale French Studies. 1948. s-a. $3. Ray Ortali. W. L. Harkness Hall, Yale Univ., New Haven, Conn. 06520. Circ: 3,000. Microform: UM. Reprint: Kraus.

Indexed: SSHum. *Aud:* Ac.

A basic journal. It is well edited and carefully structured to bring original research to bear on all aspects of French literature and criticism. Every number is built around a single theme or subject, e.g., "Image and symbol in the Renaissance," or "Valery." All articles are in English and while written for the specialist, are usually literate, free of jargon, and relatively easy to follow for the advanced student of French culture. Although not a popular journal, it is supported widely enough to warrant careful consideration by any medium to large-sized academic library.

French Language

Africasia. 1969. bi-m. $15. Ed. board. Société Africasia Presse Editions S.A.R.L., 68 Champs Elysées, Paris 8e, France. Illus., adv. Circ: 170,000.

Aud: Ga, Ac. *Bk. rev:* 3–4, 200–300 words, signed.

The French-language *Africasia* styles itself a journal of information, opinion, and analysis. It is indeed informative, but its opinion is outspokenly anti-European and anti-American. Nonetheless the very broad coverage of political and other news of African, Asian and Latin American countries will make it a valuable addition to all periodical collections. A weekly column, called "Dossier," brings objectively reported, well researched and documented articles about slavery in Mauritania and other unusual topics. Another authoritative reportage describes torturing methods of political prisoners in Brazil. The book reviews consider publications related to third world interests. A regular feature, "Culture," in one of the issues examined, analyzes at length a Parisian production of plays by José Triana and Carlos Fuentes. Because of news items seldom found in such concentration in other similar periodicals (e.g., *Time, Newsweek, L'Express*) *Africasia* should be added to general and academic collections. (G.S.)

Annales de Géographie. 1891. bi-m. $11.20. Librairie Armond Colin, 103 bd. St.-Michel, Paris 5e, France. Vol. ends: Dec. Reprint: Kraus.

Bk. rev: 7–10, various lengths, signed. *Aud:* Ac.

One of the leading French language geographical journals, this scholarly publication covers not only France and the French-speaking world, but other areas as well. The book reviews are quite extensive, and deal with non-French materials as well as French. The magazine does not have English language abstracts. Should be in any academic library with an active program in Geography. (D.D.)

L'Architecture d'aujourd'hui. 1930. 6/yr. $22.50. Marc Emery. 5 rue Bartholdi, 92 Boulogne-sur-Seine, France. Illus., adv.

Indexed: ArtI. *Aud:* Ac.

A glossy, well-illustrated journal which is, perhaps, the leading French vehicle of architectural expression. Each issue is usually devoted to a particular topic or architectural problem, such as "Aéroports," "La ville," "Le design," or "L'Architecture et l'enfance." Although there is a decidedly French emphasis, this publication covers all aspects of world architecture. Regular features include professional news, new products, new buildings, etc. Articles are summarized in English. It is recommended for all architectural collections. (R.S.)

Astrado Prouvencalo; revue bilingue de Provence. 1965. bi-a. $5. Astrado Prouvencalo, 2 rue Vincent-Allegre, 83 Toulon, France. Illus. Circ: 1,000.

Bk. rev: Various number, length. *Aud:* Ac.

A bilingual journal, i.e., both in French and Provençal. All of the articles in Provençal have an accompanying translation in modern French. An average 150 to 200 page issue, well illustrated, is primarily given over to the study of the literature of Provence. The purpose of the journal is to justify the study of the secondary language. While this has some interest in France, its primary audience is in the academic community where there is a specialized study in Provençal literature and/or the French language.

L'Auberge de la Jeunesse; Organe officielle de la Ligue Française pour les Auberges de la Jeunesse. 1932. 2.50F. m. (10/yr.). Pierre Mulet (Rédacteur en chef). L'Auberge de la Jeunesse, 38 Bd. Raspail, Paris 7e, France. Illus. Sample. Vol. ends: Dec.

Aud: Ga, Ejh, Hs.

For the benefit of our peripatetic youth this is an indispensable publication. It costs less than one dollar for a year's subscription and brings invaluable information to those who are fond of travelling with minimal expenses. All the facilities and the numerous and varied programs of the organization, summer and winter, are listed. For admission to the hostels, membership in either the International Youth Hostels Federation (I.Y.H.F.) or American Youth Hostels, Inc. (20 West 17th St, N.Y., N.Y. 10011—an affiliate of the I.Y.H.F.) is necessary. Boys and girls not less than 15 or more than 30 years of age will be admitted. Parental authorization for minors is obligatory. The publishers will send upon request not only sample issues of the periodical, but also additional documentation of great value, including a sizable booklet listing all youth hostels in France with a map showing the locations. (G.S.)

Avant Scene du Theatre. 1949. $16. bi-w. 27 rue St. Andre des Arts, Paris 6, France. Subs. to: R. A. Reagan, Box 215, Cathedral Station, New York, N.Y. 10025. Illus. Sample.

Aud: Ga, Ac.

Each issue is the complete script of a modern play. The plays are in French, represent leading European playwrights from Arrabal to Ionesco. There are short comments on the actors, playwrights, theatre, etc.; good photographs. Of somewhat less interest than the publisher's other magazine, *Avant Scene du Cinema,* but equally important for large theatre collections.

Cahiers Pédagogiques. 1946. m. (Sept.–June). $3.90. Jean Delannoy. Sevpen, 13 rue de Four, Paris 6e, France. Adv. Circ: 20,000. Sample. Vol. ends: June.

Bk. rev: 8–10, essay, signed. *Aud:* Ga, Ac.

Though published since 1964 by the Institut Pédagogique National this is not an official publication, but is owned and edited by an educational research and action movement (Féderation des Circles de Recherche et d'Action Pédagogique). The 1,500 groups forming the federation participate in the preparation of the "Cahiers," compile questionnaires, organize discussion groups and interviews, distribute leaflets and the publication to their fellow-teachers. "Our aim is to have a chapter in every school." The general tendency of the publication is progressive, promoting new teaching ideas and critical of the establishment. Every issue is devoted in its entirety to one particular topic, e.g.: "An examination of examinations," "Theatre," and "Teachers' formative experiences." A few significant passages in translation, taken from the lead article of the November 1970 issue, illustrate the purpose, the trend, the high standards, and the depth of the varied investigations. "Our double inquiry demonstrates how rarely young students visit the theatre and how unaware they are of theatrical facts. The investigation also shows that teachers themselves are conscious of their own lack of experience . . . that they are awaiting the necessary means enabling them to bring about a change. The most significant of all these efforts is, without a doubt, the decision of teachers and actors to work together. . . . Finally teachers' training in dramatics is discussed, followed by reports dealing with two workshops offered at the meeting of C.R.A.P. at Avignon: Epic Theatre and Education in physical expression." This lively and interesting publication is recommended for students of education, as well as of psychology. (G.S.)

Canard Enchaine; journal satirique paraissant le mercredi. 1915. w. $10. A. Ribaud. 2 rue des Petits-Peres, Paris 2e, France. Illus. Circ: 400,000.

Aud: Ga, Ac.

A satirical magazine which is to France what *Krokodil* is to the USSR, and *Mad* and *The Realist* are to the United States. Published every Wednesday, the tabloid newspaper format is familiar to any European who keeps up with satire and political humor. It gained particular fame early in 1972 for its publication of Premier Jacques Chaban-Delma's tax returns.

Through cartoons and hard hitting features it seeks to deflate politics and politicians. It generally succeeds. Incidentally the name means chained duck, duck being a slang term for newspaper in France. Requires an excellent understanding of French, and is of limited use for anyone who is not up on French expressions and political affairs.

Connaissance des Arts. 1952. m. $30. Francis Spar. Société d'Etudes et de Publications Artistiques (S.E.P.A.) 13 rue Saint-Georges, Paris 9e, France. Illus., adv. Circ: 81,000. Sample.

Indexed: ArtI. *Aud:* Ga, Ac.

An excellent art magazine, beautifully illustrated, and written by experts who are well known for their specialties and unencumbered by technical jargon. The short essays on eastern and western, old and contemporary art will appeal to the layman as well as to the scholar. The many pages of advertisement are an asset, not a nuisance, since they are informative, and handsomely illustrated. There is a buyer's guide for those with means, detailing the criteria concerning style, period, subject, and conservation of the objects on the market. A special feature is "Encyclopédie de la Connaissance des Arts." One to three detachable pages range over a great variety of topics interesting to collectors. (G.S.)

Ecrits de Paris; revue des questions actuelles. 1944. m. $12. Madeleine Malliavin. Société Parisienne d'Edition et de Publication. 354 rue Saint-Honoré, Paris 1e, France. Circ: 30,000. Sample.

Bk. rev: Essay, 5–6 pages concerned with trends. *Aud:* Ga, Ac.

Recommended for mature, well-informed readers. This is a conservative magazine comparable to Buckley's *National Review,* and enjoyable reading for those who indulge in witty and educated controversy. It is devoted to articles debating current (less often historical) events in France and the world. Regular columns discuss new books, visual arts, music theatre, motion pictures, and foreign literature. The writers select consistently controversial works well suited for the display of their biting criticism. (G.S.)

Elle. 1945. w. $20. Helene Gordon-Lazareff. France Editions et Publications, 100 rue Reaumur, Paris 2e, France. Illus., adv. Circ: 600,000.

Bk. rev: Notes. *Aud:* Ga, Ac.

A French-language periodical somewhat the equivalent of *Cosmopolitan, Good Housekeeping* and *Glamour.* This is to say that its range covers fashions, cooking, interior decorating, needlework, gardens, travel, one or two short stories or excerpts from novels, and a few articles on various aspects of French life. The audience is the teenager and the young married. Primarily of interest to American high school girls and women for the illustrations and information it gives on the average French counterpart. Interestingly enough, the fashions are not always as "high" as those found in many American magazines. Depending upon the views of the teacher this might be used in advanced French classes. It is a luxury item for libraries in a non-French community. (M.M.)

Express. 1957. w. $26. ($42/air). Pierre Barret. S. A. Express Union, 25 rue de Berri, Paris 8e, France. Illus., adv. Circ: 700,000.

Aud: Ga, Ac, Hs. *Jv:* V.

The outstanding news magazine of France, this was founded by Jean-Jacques Servan-Schreiber. In appearance it follows the familiar *Time* format. In content it is much more liberal. Considerably better edited, *L'Express* covers Europe in depth, and pays a lesser amount of attention to the rest of the world. It is as aggressive in its criticism of the government as its counterpart in Germany, *Spiegel,* and it·has wide appeal for its excellent coverage of the arts, film, theatre, sports, etc. A basic magazine in the news world, and an excellent choice where French teachers are trying to make the language meaningful to Americans.

Le Figaro Littéraire; lettres, arts, spectacles, sciences, enquetes, loisirs. 1946. w. $17. Michel Droit. Le Figaro. 14 Rond-Point des Champs-Elysées, Paris 8e, France. Illus., adv. Sample.

Bk. rev: 8, lengthy, signed. *Aud:* Ga, Ac. *Jv:* V.

Periodicals reporting political, literary, artistic, and other news are so numerous in France that it is difficult to make a choice. One of the richest in variety, least controversial, middle-of-the-road, and very authoritative is the weekly *Figaro Littéraire.* For libraries with limited budgets for foreign books, this journal serves competently and adequately as a book selection tool. For those who like to keep up with the news of the literary and artistic world it provides easy, enjoyable reading. The excellence of this publication and the standards of its contributors are unquestionable. (G.S.)

Gazette des Beaux-Arts. 1859. m. $24. Daniel Wildenstein. Presses Universitaires de France, Département des Périodiques, 12 rue Jean-de-Beauvais, Paris 5e, France. Illus. Vol. ends: Dec. Microform: MF. Reprint: Kraus.

Indexed: ArtArch, ArtI. *Aud:* Ac, Ga.

One of the most sumptuous journals ever devoted to art. Some articles are in French, others in English. However, the journal's worth may be realized on the level of its treatment of pictorial content alone. Lavishly illustrated on heavy calendar paper, its impeccable taste is in evidence on every page. Its directors include Sir John Pope-Hennessy, Jacques Maritain, Sir Kenneth Clark, Sir Anthony Blunt, Helen C. Frick (of the Frick Collection), and Alfred H. Barr. It is a giant in its field and a decided must for academic art libraries and large public libraries with adequate art collections. (H.D.)

Jardin des Modes. 1921. m. $10. Pierre Lazareff. France Editions et Publications, S.A.R.L., 100 rue Reaumur, Paris 2e, France. Illus., adv. Circ: 139,400. Sample.

Aud: Ga.

An outstanding fashion magazine, richly and beautifully illustrated. The largest part is naturally devoted to haute couture. Regular columns deal with skin care and hair styles, knitting and needle work. Special sewing and knitting patterns are available from the magazine. Well known French authors contribute articles about new fiction, poetry, the visual arts, musical events, the cinema, and television. The issue distributed in English-speaking countries includes a digest of the main feature-articles in English. Special issues are devoted to the culinary arts, knitting, and layettes. (A "coupled" subscription will consist of 12 regular monthly issues and five special issues giving the newest fashion trends in knitting, all about cooking, and new styles in baby things. This will cost $17 per year.) (G.S.)

Jeune Afrique L'Hebdomadire international de l'Afrique. 1960. w. $30. Bechir Ben Yahmed. Presse Africaine Associée, 51 Avenue des Ternes, Paris 17e, France. Illus., adv. Circ: 84,865. Sample.

Bk. rev: 5, 150 words. *Aud:* Ga, Ac, Hs.

Strong emphasis on current events in and relative to Africa. Format, style of writing and makeup closely resemble *Time* and *Newsweek*. This fairly impartial weekly is regularly cited on "World Press in Review," a weekly presentation of the Public Broadcasting Service. The book reviews do not necessarily cover new publications and are only vaguely relevant to the students of the African scene. The Notebook (Carnet) reports new nominations of diplomatic personnel, changes in industrial management, obituaries, etc. Useful in all types of libraries from junior high to academic institutions. (G.S.)

Lectures pour Tous. 1898. m. Willy Saphir, 100 Avenue Raymond Poincare, Paris 16e, France. Illus., adv. Circ: 220,000.

Aud: Ga, Hs.

A general interest magazine with appeal for adults and high school students whose interests are somewhat less than sophisticated. Almost every base is covered, usually in a journalistic, relatively simplistic style. For example, various issues have included such articles as: "Maillol: the Reign of the Robust Nymph," "Confessions of a Clairvoyant," "The Young Leftists," "In Search of the Relics of Saint Peter," "Common

Errors Made in the French Language," "About the French Winner of the Nobel Prize in Science," "Women's Liberation," "Karl Marx in Love," "23 Days as Prisoner of the Palestinian Guerillas," a long article about the Mafia, an American funeral home, Theodore Rousseau, or the rustic life at Barbizon. Regular features: Puzzles, Science for Everybody, Who said this? Very good illustrations. (G.S.)

Marie-France. 1944. m. $5.10. Jean Sangnier. Société de Presse et d'edition Féminine, 14 Champs-Elysées, Paris 8e, France. Illus., adv. Circ: 746,467. Sample.

Bk. rev: Various number. *Aud:* Ga, Hs.

Nothing more needs to be said than that this publication resembles closely our *Good Housekeeping.* The 100 or so pages are richly filled with news of fashions, beauty care, knitting, interior decorating, cooking, book and record reviews, ideas for entertaining children during vacation, etc. In addition to the profusion of advice and helpful hints there are short stories, biographical sketches of personalities in the news, and readers' letters of the "Dear Abby" type. (G.S.)

Oeil; revue d'art. 1955. m. (double no. in summer). $25. Georges Bernier. Sedo S. A., 33 Ave. de la Gare, Lausanne, Switzerland. Illus., adv. Circ: 40,000.

Indexed: ArtI. *Aud:* Ac.

The outstanding French art magazine, with articles in French. Still of some value to non-French readers because of the colored illustrations and its international coverage. Articles are by well-known critics. Both the articles and illustrations touch on all periods and all types of art from painting and sculpture to architecture. There is a considerable amount of advertising. Only for large collections.

Officiel de la Photographie et du Cinema. 1952. m. Charles Vandamme, 22 rue Paul Valery, Paris 16e, France. Illus., index, adv. Circ: 15,000.

Bk. rev: 5–6, 250 words, signed. *Aud:* Sa.

Emphasis upon photography both as an art and as a technical skill. Articles deal especially with coverage of the two professional societies, "Federation française de la Photographie" and "Federation Nationale des Sociétés Photographiques de France." Particularly pleasing are the striking, double-page spreads of photos selected for the annual international contest. Sometimes there is a portfolio of photos with accompanying poems. Too specialized except for large public and academic libraries.

Paris-Match. 1949. w. $20. Jean Prouvost. 51 rue Pierre-Charron, Paris 8e, France. Illus., adv. Circ: 1,400,000.

Aud: Ga.

A popular low to middle brow illustrated news and current events magazine. The format and approach is familiar, i.e., the typical *Life/Look* syndrome worked into a French motif. Features: personalities, scandals, new products, and anything to catch the eye, if not always the brain. It is entertaining enough, even informative for those who want to see what a good deal of the French public reads—the circulation is one of the highest of all French magazines. It is also useful in classrooms where middle to advanced French is taught. And, of course, it is a good enough choice where there is a large French-reading community.

Photo-Cine-Review. 1888. m. $7. Vincent Robert. Editions de Francia, 118 rue d'Assas, Paris 6e, France. Illus., index, adv. Circ: 40,000.

Indexed: ChemAb. *Bk. rev:* Occasional, short. *Aud:* Sa.

Directed to much the same audience as *Officiel de la Photographie et Du Cinema*, this emphasizes the technical aspects of photography. Articles often pertain to the audiovisual and the photographic reportage of events. There are instructional articles of interest to the amateur film-maker–photographer. A substantial portion is devoted to photographs of high artistic quality accompanied by text and criticism.

Présence Africaine; revue culturelle du monde noir. 1947. q. $5.10. Alioune Diop. 25 bis, rue des Ecoles, Paris 5e; France. Adv. Circ: 5,000. Vol. ends: Dec.

Indexed: AfrAb, MLA. *Bk. rev:* several, length varies, signed. *Aud:* Ac, Ga.

Formerly available both in a French and an English edition, and now a single bilingual publication, this is a basic journal for study of African literature and culture. The review is published by Africans, and is intended for all with an interest in the "striking evolution" of the African continent. Its aim is to contribute to the defining of "African originality." While the review has a literary tone—essays, short stories, poems, and reviews appear prominently—it is more broadly devoted to a study of African society, with articles on politics, economics, and culture. Thus one finds in recent issues (each about 200 pages long) articles on apartheid, African religion, negritude, economic development, jazz, and literature. Separately priced monographs are issued under the imprint "Editions Présence Africaine." This review and its monographs constitute a good source of information on contemporary African culture, and, to a lesser extent, on social and political events in Africa. (B.A.)

Quinzaine Littéraire. 1966. s-m. $14. Francois Erval and Maurice Nadeau. 22 rue de Grenelle, Paris 7e, France. Illus., index, adv. Circ: 50,000.

Aud: Ac.

A French *New York Times Book Review*, but having no connection with a daily newspaper. As a newspaper itself, it is the only one put out in France that is devoted exclusively to literary criticism and informa-

tion about new books. Although a large part of its space is given over to critical articles on new books, it also contains: interviews with authors; articles on writers and painters; poems; lists of best-sellers; recommended books and new books in general. Nicely produced on improved, white, newspaper stock, with many illustrations and the occasional use of colored type.

Réeducation. Revue Française de l'Enfance Delinquante Deficiente et en Danger Moral. 1945. m. (10/yr.). $7.10. P. Lutz, 25 rue des Ecoles, Paris 5e, France. Sample. Vol. ends: Dec.

Aud: Ac.

An important publication which serves all professionals dedicated to the rehabilitation of delinquent, scholastically and emotionally maladjusted young people. The contributors are university teachers, ranking officials of various social agencies, correction officers, judges, physicians, and lawyers with considerable experience in dealing with the troubles and problems of youth. An impressive variety of topics is authoritatively discussed in the four to five articles in every 60 to 90 page issue. There are no regular special features, but infrequent annotated bibliographies and announcements of forthcoming conferences, conventions, and professional vacancies. Because of its specialized nature and its scholarly approach, this publication is primarily recommended to academic and special professional libraries, but will also attract the socially concerned educated reader. (G.S.)

Revue de l'Art. 1968. q. $23. Francis Bouvet. Librairie E. Flammarion, 26 rue Racine, 75 Paris 6e, France. Illus.

Bk. rev: various number, length. *Aud:* Ga, Ac.

Less stuffy than the *Gazette des Beaux Arts*, this provides important contributions to the study of art history. Its format is lively with large glossy pages and excellent color plates. The editors prove that a pleasing format can contain genuine scholarship, and the magazine's three lead articles (always in French, but with summaries in English and German) are written by scholars from all over the world. Each issue also contains a section of brief notes and documents, book reviews, notices of exhibitions, and a few advertisements. Unlike the *Gazette* this magazine is willing to entertain articles on modern art. Should be ordered by any library which takes the *Gazette*, and because of its excellent plates should be considered a possibility for more general college collections. (C.D.)

Revue Française de Sociologie. 1960. 5/yr. $8.50. Jean Stoetzel. Centre National de la Recherche Scientifique, Centre, d'Etudes Sociologiques, 15 Quai Antole-France, Paris 7e, France. Adv. Circ: 3,000. Vol. ends: Dec. Refereed.

Bk. rev: 11, 350 words, signed. *Aud:* Ac.

Issued with the cooperation of the Centre d'Études Sociologiques. It covers a broad selection of sociological issues and includes articles on such topics as research on the evolution of criminality, industrial sociology, perceptions of class by manual workers, spatial proximity and social distance, Swedish professors, and percption of identity by North American Jews repatriated to France. The language used in most of the text is French, summaries of the articles are given in English, German, Russian, and Spanish. Features include critical notes, research notes, list of books received, bibliography (book reviews), "Review of Reviews" (contents of related journals in sociology and social psychology). Useful for scholarly research of an international nature. (M.W.)

La Revue de Géographie de Montréal. 1947. $12. Les Presses de l'Université de Montréal, Box 6128, Montréal 101, Que., Canada. Vol. ends: Oct.

Indexed: CanI. *Bk. rev:* 7–12, lengthy, signed. *Aud:* Ac.

One of the leading Canadian geographical journals. Subject matter, beginning 1972, will be limited to human geography—city, transport, and communication; and physical geography—cold environment. Articles are usually in French, with abstracts in French, English and a third language of the author's choice. Book reviews are arranged by subject. A scholarly journal; important for Canadian academic libraries, and for comprehensive collections elsewhere. (D.D.)

Revue d' Histoire de l'Amerique Française. 1947. q. $15 (In Canada $13). Institut d'Histoire de l'Amerique Francaise, 261 Bloomfield Ave., Montreal 153, Que., Canada. Illus., index, adv. Circ: 1,700. Sample. Vol. ends: March. Microform: UM.

Indexed: CanI, HistAb. *Bk. rev:* 20, length varies, signed. *Aud:* Ac.

A French-language journal dedicated to the study of French civilization in America. An average 150-page issue contains three to four articles, research notes, detailed and critical book reviews, heretofore unpublished documents, news of the Institute, and a running bibliography of publications concerning French America. The writing is lucid, scholarly, and primarily of appeal to the expert, i.e., teacher or graduate student. A good item for many larger Canadian and American academic libraries, but of limited use in the average public library.

Revue d'Histoire Littéraire de La France. 1894. bi-m. $10.10. Rene Pameau, Librairie Armand Colin, 103 bd. St.-Michel, Paris 5e, France. Index. Circ: 2,500. Microform: Microcard. Reprint: Johnson.

Bk. rev: 30–40, 500 words, signed. *Aud:* Ac. Jv:V.

Covers all periods of French literature, and at least once a year an entire issue is given to a series of articles on one literary figure. It includes an extensive book review section, with titles primarily from French and other continental presses. The "Bibliography" section is a subject list of books and articles on French literature. While of particular interest in larger academic libraries, the book reviews make it of some value to smaller and medium-sized libraries.

Revue d'Histoire Moderne et Contemporaine. 1954. q. $7. Jean-Baptiste Duroselle. Librairie Armand Colin, 103 bd. Saint-Michel, Paris 5e, France. Index, adv. Vol. ends: Oct.

Indexed: HistAb. *Bk. rev:* 6–8, 2–5 pages, signed. *Aud:* Ac.

This publication of La Société d'Histoire Moderne contains seven to eight articles per issue on all periods, areas, and regions of modern history from the Renaissance to the present. There is special emphasis on studies pertaining to the nineteenth and early twentieth centuries. The lengthy, substantive book reviews make this journal particularly noteworthy. It is especially recommended for college and university libraries with large historical collections. (R.S.)

Revue Historique. 1876. q. $13. Pierre Renouvin. Presses Universitaires de France, Services des Périodiques, 12 rue Jean-de-Beauvais, 75 Paris 5e, France. Index, adv. Vol. ends: Oct. Reprint: Kraus.

Indexed: HistAb. *Bk. rev:* 25–30, 2–30 pages, signed. *Aud:* Ac.

The five to ten articles cover all areas and periods of history, but with a French emphasis. This journal is especially important for book selectors who must keep abreast of current French scholarship. It often contains bibliographic articles of special interest, such as: "Histoire de l'Espagne au moyen age, publications des années 1948–1969," "La Grande-Bretagne au xviiie siecle," and "Histoire de l'Allemagne (1789–1914)," which review recent scholarship in these areas. Other features include the "Bulletin Historique" which lists new French historical publications, and lists of important journal articles. This is perhaps the leading French historical journal and should be a standard item for inclusion in college and university periodical lists. (R.S.)

Revue Philosophique de Louvain. 1894. q. $14. Institut Supérieur de Philosophie Editions, Kardinal Mercierplein 2, Louvain, Belgium. Circ: 1,800.

Indexed: CathI, PhilosI. *Bk. rev:* 24, 400 words, signed. *Aud:* Sa, Ac.

A periodical largely of interest to followers of Roman Catholic neo-realism. Presents papers in French by professional philosophers concerning questions of epistemology, ontology, atheism, ethics, and other questions of philosophical import. Of especial interest to the student are the many historical essays concerned with classical and modern philosophers and the great Church metaphysicians. Included in the subscription price is the quarterly supplement, *Repertoire Bibliographique de la Philosophie*, a very valuable bibliography of publications in philosophy and philosophical psychology in all Western languages. The bibliography may be subscribed to separately at $10 per year. The *Revue* is of value mainly to students of philosophy, while the librarian and bibliographer will find the supplementary bibliography of great reference value.

Touring Club de France; Revue Mensuelle. 1890. m. 45f. Bernard Hennequin. Touring Club de France, 65 Avenue de la Grande-Armeé, Paris 16e, France. Illus., adv. Sample.

Bk. rev: 10–16, short, descriptive. *Aud:* Ac, Ga.

This very moderately priced membership publication is designed to help all who are planning their vacation trips, by car, boat, or any other kind of conveyance. A good part of the review is devoted to the many and varied regions of France, but other countries and continents are considered. Many good illustrations are used, mostly black and white with a few in color. Car, boating, camping, and photography fans will find useful advice and information about French and foreign products of interest to them. The many advertisements, as expected in this kind of publication, are helpful for tourists and vacationists in search of ideas. All aspects of conservation are given competent coverage. From elementary through high school classrooms, this periodical can be put to many uses. (G.S.)

German Language

√ *Anglia; Zeitschrift fur englische Philologie.* 1878. q. $22.95. Ed. bd. Max Niemeyer Verlag, Pfrondorfer Str. 4, Turbingen 74, F Germany. Circ: 750. Microform: MF.

Bk. rev: 20, 500 words, signed. *Aud:* Ac.

A German journal (text in German and English) of English studies, presenting the results of scholarly investigation in the English and American languages and literatures. Includes criticism, interpretation, textual studies, literary sources and traditions, and linguistics. All periods from Old English to the twentieth century are represented, and emphasis is on examination of original or newly discovered works and manuscripts. Only for large academic libraries.

√ *Archiv fur das Studium der Neuren Sprachen und Literaturen.* 1849. bi-m. $16.60. Ed. bd. George Westermann Verlag, Georg-Westermann-Allee 66, Braunschweig, Germany. Index, adv. Circ: 800. Sample. Vol. ends: No. 2.

Bk. rev: 10–15, 500 words, signed. *Aud:* Ac.

Devoted to the study of the Germanic, Romance, and Slavic languages and literatures on an advanced level of scholarship. Emphasis is on criticism and interpretation. Articles are generally long, averaging from 7,000 to 9,000 words, and the text is in English, French, German, Italian, and Spanish. While extremely esoteric in terms of a general collection, this is a superior journal for graduate study.

Die Erde. 1959. q. $17.50. Drs. Frido Bader and Dietrich O. Müller, Gesellschaft fur Erdkunde zu Berlin, 1 Berlin 41, Arno-Holz Strasse 14, W. Germany. Illus.

Bk. rev: 40–50, length varies, signed. *Aud:* Ac.

A scholarly journal in the European sense, with few photographs but long, well-documented articles. It is worldwide in interest—not limited to Germany or Europe. Articles are normally in German, with an English summary. Most issues include an aerial photograph, with an interpretive diagram detailing the important features in the photograph. An important journal, particularly for schools offering extensive work in geography. (D.D.)

Erdkunde. 1947. q. $15.70. Dr. Helmut Hahn. Ferd. Dümmlers Verlag, 53 Bonn, Kaiserstrasse 33, W. Germany. Illus. Vol. ends: Dec.

Bk. rev: 20, 400 words, signed. *Aud:* Ac.

Another leading German geographical journal concerned more with the human aspects of geography. Articles are in German or English, with summaries in the other language. This magazine might be of more value than *Die Erde* because the summaries are more extensive and articles are oriented more toward economic and social geography. (D.D.)

Frankfurter Hefte; Zeitschrift fuer kultur und politik. 1946. m. $12. Hubert Habicht and Walter Dirks. Eugen Kogon, Leipzigerstr 18, 6000 Frankfurt/Main, W. Germany. Illus., index, adv. Circ: 7,000.

Bk. rev: 4–7, length varies, signed. *Aud:* Ac.

An independent political/literary magazine which appears in a format similar to *Encounter.* Unlike the relatively middle-of-the-road *Monat,* (ceased), this is liberal to left. It covers current German social, political, and cultural activities. Writers may not be quite so popular as those that were found in *Monat,* but the message is sure, the commitment to ideals obvious. Continues to be an important literary/political magazine, and should be found in any medium to large-sized German-language collection.

Gebrauchsgraphik/International Advertising Art. 1924. m. $25.15. Erhardt D. Stiebner and Hans Kuh. F. Bruckmann KG, Nymphenburger Str. 86, 8000 Munich 2, W. Germany. Illus., adv. Circ: 13,000.

Indexed: ArtI. *Bk. rev:* Various number, length. *Aud:* Ga, Ac.

A publication of great interest to students and commercial artists, *Gebrauchsgraphik* concerns itself with "presenting a variety of international model solutions of certain problems of graphic art." The German title should not deter the reader: all explanatory material is in German, English, and French, and a Spanish translation is provided at the back of the issue. The layout is primarily pictorial; pictures are small, usually black and white, many to a page. (A.T.)

Historische Zeitschrift. 1859. 6/yr. $26.50. Theodor Schieder and Theodor Schieffer. R. Oldenbourg Verlag, Rosenheimer Strasse 145, München 80, W. Germany. Index, adv. Circ: 2,400. Vol. ends: July & Dec. (2 vols. per yr.). Reprint: Johnson.

Indexed: HistAb. *Bk. rev:* 90–110, 1–3 pages signed. *Aud:* Ac.

With a pedigree which stretches back to Heinrich von Treitschke and Friedrich Meinecke, both of whom served as editors, and even further back to Leopold von Ranke, who presided at its birth, *Historische Zeitschrift* was the first journal to expound the principles of scientific historiography. In this respect, it has also influenced other "national" journals such as *Revue Historique* and *The English Historical Review.* Each issue includes some three to five scholarly articles on all aspects of history, but of particular importance are the book reviews which comprise fifty percent of each issue. The journal reviews books in all languages but is especially important as a means of keeping abreast of recent German historical scholarship. In addition, this periodical lists some 100 to 125 titles of new books received and indexes pertinent journal articles which have appeared in German magazines. This journal is recommended for all university libraries. (R.S.)

Merkur; Deutsche zeitschrift fuer europaeisches denken. 1947. m. $13. Hans Paeschke. Ernst K. Verlag, Postfach 568, 8 Munich 13, W. Germany. Illus., index, adv. Circ: 5,200.

Bk. rev: Various number, length; signed. *Aud:* Ac.

Somewhat along the same lines as the ceased *Monat,* but considerably more esoteric and intellectual. It also emphasizes the current socio-political scene. The difference is that here the focus is more international, more dependent upon influences of literature, social and political philosophy, and a number of intellectual factors which the magazine is famous for in its explanation of trends and activities in Germany and throughout Europe. Some excellent book and film reviews are included. Requires an excellent understanding of German. Only for larger libraries.

Monatshefte Fuer Deutschen Unterricht. 1899. q. $10 (Individuals $7.50). J. D. Workman, Univ. of Wisconsin Press, Box 1379, Madison, Wis. 53706. Index, adv. Circ: 1,472. Microform: UM. Reprint: Kraus.

Bk. rev: 20, 400 words, signed. *Aud:* Ac.

Along with the *Journal of English and Germanic Philology,* one of the oldest German journals in America. But the two differ considerably in purpose. *Monatshefte,* as the title indicates, is for the German teacher. (It differs, too, from the *German Quarterly,* in that it is for the teacher at the college level.) Articles (which are in both English and German) deal with all aspects of the German language and literature, are usually rather short, and better written than found in most journals of this type. Some articles are included on theories of teaching, organizational problems of German departments, etc. There is an annual listing of members of the German departments of United States colleges and universities, and a listing of dissertations in the Fall number. A basic journal for all academic libraries.

Neue Rundschau. 1890. q. $5.70. Ed. bd. S. Fischer Verlag, Mainzer Landstr. 10–12 Frankfurt am Main, W. Germany. Index., adv. Circ: 8,000.

Bk. rev: Various number, length; signed. *Aud:* Ac.

One of the oldest literary reviews in Germany, and it continues to enjoy a rather respectable, although not always innovative, reputation. Emphasis is on the literary essay, but in addition there are fiction, poetry, and drama. During its long history it has published every major European writer, and a run of the magazine is an absolute must for any medium to large-sized academic collection. Its present status is debatable, but it remains a major voice among German intellectuals.

Pantheon; internationale Zeitschrift fuer Kunst. 1928. bi-m. $27.19. Theodor Muller. Verlag F. Bruckmann Kg. 8 Munich, 2, W. Germany. Illus., index, adv. Circ: 1,500.

Indexed: ArtI. *Bk. rev:* number varies, notes, essays. *Aud:* Ac.

An international art journal with many advertisements, impressive color plates, and excellent articles. The collections of different art galleries and museums are frequently considered. Among its features are book reviews, abstracts, a bibliography, illustrations, and an index. The text is in original languages with summaries in English or German. Geared to those with a multilingual background, and only for large libraries.

Scala International. 1961. m. $4. Werner Wirthle. Veraghshaus Frankfurter Societaets-Druckerei, Frankenallee 71–81, Frankfurt Am Main, W. Germany. Illus., index, adv. Circ: 400,000. Vol. ends: Nov.

Aud: Ga, Hs.

This is published in a number of languages throughout Europe, and attempts to be a type of European *Life.* Its relatively large circulation attests to its popularity, although it should be noted this is spread throughout Europe, not limited to Germany. It has one major advantage over *Stern*—it is a trifle more intellectual, a trifle less involved with German politics. Furthermore, it is independent, i.e., not a part of the impressive Gruner/Jahr chain. Still, it would be way down the list for representative popular German magazines.

Spiegel. 1947. w. $27 (air $47). Rudolf Augstein. Spiegel-Verlag, 2 Hamburg 11, Brandstwiete 19/Ost-West-Strasse. Illus., index, adv. Circ: 1,100,000. Sample. Vol. ends: Last wk. Dec.

Bk. rev: 3–5, 200 words. *Aud:* Ga, Ac. *Jv:* V.

An independent hard hitting news magazine, often called the *Time, Newsweek,* and *U.S. News and World Report* of West Germany. (East Germany does not have an equivalent.) A glance at the circulation and beginning date of publication shows that this is one of the great success stories of publishing in Germany after the end of World War II. No magazine is better known. The typical 240-page issue is loaded with advertising, photographs, and news stories. It tends to be middle-of-the-road to liberal, and for the first time was supporting the German government in 1972. (Rudolf Augstein has long been a member of the Free Democratic Party which supports, of course, Willy Brandt.) While the magazine follows the familiar American format, its content is way ahead of all three American news magazines. Over the years it has built a reputation for not only well-written articles, but ones which are investigatory in nature. Many consider it the best news weekly in Europe, and it should be in all American libraries where readers can handle German. *Note:* In the previous edition *Spiegel* was erroneously given as a member of the Axel Springer holdings. It is not, never has been, and is not likely to be. In fact, *Spiegel* has consistently fought the monopolistic holdings of Springer, and the two are deadly enemies, c.f. *Spiegel,* March 9, 1970, for its analysis of how Springer and the Bertelsmann group virtually control the mass German press. For those who caught the error, thanks. For those who did not—apologies.

Stern. 1947. w. $17. Henri Nannen. Gruner and Jahr. CmbH and Co., Pressehaus, 200 Hamburg 1, W. Germany. Illus., index, adv. Circ: 1,600,000.

Aud: Ga.

The German *Life,* and along with *Spiegel* one of the largest circulation magazines in West Germany. (It is also a key member of a large publishing chain which is connected with the Springer newspaper group.) The publisher, who is no friend of *Spiegel,* claims that one in four Germans reads his illustrated magazine. The formula is familiar to anyone in America: a mixture of comments and pictures on current affairs, mixed up with consumer-type stories. Violence on one page, a marriage on the next. Henry Luce did it all in *Life*

many years before. There are, though, several major differences. *Stern* has considerably more sex, and what might be considered bad taste in an American family magazine is given full vent here. Also there is more concern with politics, and longer stories on the activities of the German government. Hardly an inspiring magazine, but an interesting one as it reflects the current taste of many middle to lower class Germans. Also, by the way, because of the pictures and photographs and relatively unsophisticated text, a good magazine for middle to advanced German classes. (See also *Scala International.*) In terms of mass circulation magazines, *Stern* is one of the leaders. But close behind, as one might suspect, is no other than America's contribution to literature, *Reader's Digest.* Its German edition (*Das Beste Selections* from *RD*) has a circulation of 1,250,000.

Zietschrift für Deutsche Philologie. 1869. q. $15. Hugo Moser and Benno Von Wiese. Erich Schmidt Verlag, Berlin 30, Genthiner Str. 30g, Germany. Index., adv. Circ: 900. Vol. ends: No. 4. Reprint: Johnson.

Bk. rev: 5–10, 1,000 words, signed. *Aud:* Ac.

The primary German publication devoted to studies of the Germanic languages and literature. Intended for the advanced student and the scholar, it features technical writing on specialized problems of language and interpretation, with emphasis on the examination of original texts and manuscripts. Articles include critical discussions of theory and history of criticism, analysis of literary forms and periods, biography and history, textual studies—especially those dealing with literary provenance and newly discovered texts—and structural linguistics. The text is in German, and the articles are of medium length, averaging 3,500 words.

Italian Language

Critica d'Arte. 1935. bi-m. $18. Carlo L. Ragghianti, Casa Editrice Vallecchi, Via Gino Capponi 26, 50121 Florence, Italy. Illus., index, adv. Circ: 2,000. Sample.

Bk. rev: various number, length. *Aud:* Ac.

An important and highly respected review which publishes critical and analytical studies dealing with the history of art. Every issue devotes an extensive essay to a contemporary artist, e.g., one issue is wholly dedicated to the futurist painter Gino Severini. Besides the numerous illustrations demonstrating the stylistic development of the artist, it also prints heretofore unpublished correspondence of the artist with other famous writers and artists. At intervals the periodical devotes several pages to book reviews with many illustrations from the books discussed. Other occasional valuable features are detailed and richly illustrated reports about lesser known museums. *Critica d'Arte* concentrates on Italian art in general. In three issues examined only one essay about a French artist was found. Articles are often continued in two and three parts in consecutive issues. (G.S.)

Domus; architettura arredamento arte. 1928. m. $30. Gio Ponti. Editoriale Domus, Via Monte di Pieta 15, 20121 Milan, Italy. Illus., index, adv. Circ: 34,000. Vol. ends: Dec.

Indexed: ArtI. *Bk. rev:* 1–2, 250–500 words. *Aud:* Ac, Ga. *Jv:* V.

Covers architecture, interior decoration, and art, and is one of the world's leading magazines in this area. Each 60 to 100 page illustrated issue features a number of short articles on *avant garde* material which may not appear in America for months or years. Most of the articles are in Italian, but some are in English, French, and German. For the convenience of all, digests of the important texts are translated into English, French, and German and inserted in separate sheets. A calendar of architectural and design competitions, as well as of congresses and important exhibitions, is included. Unquestionably a first choice in larger academic libraries, and public libraries where the price is not prohibitive should seriously consider, too. The illustrations, alone, will give the layman some startling new notions about interiors. (G.S.)

Economia e Storia; rivista Italiana di storia politica e sociale. 1954. q. $9.70. Gino Barbieri. Casa Editrice Dott. A. Giuffre, Via Statuto 2, 20121 Milan, Italy. Illus., index, adv. Circ: 2,200 Vol. ends: Oct.

Indexed: HistAb. *Bk. rev:* various number, length. *Aud:* Ac.

An Italian historical journal, but with summaries in English and French, which includes the work of American historians and scholars. Emphasis is on the Mediterranean region, and this journal is considered by authorities to be one of the best for the area. It is especially recommended for large college and university collections.

Epoca. 1950. w. $25. Giovanni Cavallotti. Arnoldo Mondadori Editore. Via Bianca di Savoia 20, 20122. Milan, Italy. Illus., index, adv. Circ: 350,000.

Bk. rev: 1–2, 1 page. *Aud:* Ga, Ac, Hs. *Jv:* V.

Italy's *Life* and *London Illustrated News*, but on a grander scale. There are 100 or more pages, excellent illustrations (many in color), and the magazine is outstanding for its high quality reporting. This independent journal covers a wide range of topics and summarily reports on the week's national and international activities. The stories are in depth, sometimes running over a number of issues, e.g., Walter Bonati tells of his expedition to the remote natural wonders of Chile and Bolivia. Emphasis is on matters of general cultural and scientific interest for educated readers. In addition to

book reviews, films, music, and theatre are covered. The best all-around general magazine for a library with an Italian interest, and can be used for more advanced Italian classes in high schools. (G.S.)

L'Europeo. Settimanale politico d'attualita. 1945. w. $22. Tommaso Giglo. Rizzoli Editore. Via Civitavecchia 102, 20132 Milan, Italy. Illus., adv. Circ: 220,000.

Bk. rev: various number, length. *Aud:* Ac, Ga. *Jv:* V.

Somewhat similar in appearance to *Epoca,* this tends to cover much of the same ground. The difference is that it stresses both Italian and international politics more than cultural matters. It has a considerable following among the better educated, boasts Luigi Barzini as a regular contributor. There are good book, film, and even television reviews. American readers of Italian will find its primary value in its relaxed, journalistic style. The illustrations, many in color, are excellent. If it comes to a matter of choice, this would be somewhat more limited in interest than *Epoca,* but certainly of the same quality. (G.S.)

F.I./Forum Italicum. 1967. q. $4. M. Ricciardelli. State Univ. of N.Y. at Buffalo, Dept. of Italian, Spanish, and Portuguese, Buffalo, N.Y. 14214. Index.

Indexed: MLA. *Bk. rev:* 15–20, 1–20 pages, signed. *Aud:* Ac.

Describes itself as ". . . a meeting-place where scholars, critics and teachers can present their views on the language, literature and culture of Italy . . ." An issue totals about 170 pages, and contains five to seven scholarly articles of 5 to 20 pages apiece. As authors are mostly Italian, usually not more than one or two articles are in English. Each issue also contains selections of poetry with critical introductions, one or two translations into English of poems or passages from works in Italian, and a short work of fiction. The journal lists recent publications in Italian and English, and gives notices of prizes and honors received, new journals, biographical information on outstanding authors, etc. Suitable for college and university libraries, or perhaps larger public libraries serving an educated Italian-speaking population. (S.G.)

Filosofia. 1950. q. $8. Augusto Guzzo. Filosofia, Piazza Statuto 26, 10144 Turin, Italy. Index. Circ: 1,500.

Bk. rev: 6–8, 1–10 pages, signed. *Aud:* Ac.

Concerned with current trends of philosophical thought, as well as with the history of philosophy of all ages. In one of the four issues examined there was an important bibliographic essay devoted to the history and philosophy of nonviolence. In another issue an extensive essay, quasi-bibliographic, deals with the new polemic Spinoza literature. Several pages are reserved for periodicals received from all continents; notable articles of these periodicals are listed. See also *Studi Internazionali di Filosofia.* (G.S.)

Giornale della Libreria. 1888. m. L: 10,000. Frederico Elmo. Giornale della Libreria, Foro Buonaparte 24, 20121 Milan, Italy. Adv. Circ: 3,500.

Aud: Ac, Ga, Hs.

The Italian equivalent of our *Publishers' Weekly* and, as such, a required item in any library, regardless of type or size, where Italian language titles are a consideration. Publications issued during the current month are classified by subject, publishers, and authors. For those who do not wish to take the monthly, there are quarterly issues available. If a library does not subscribe, the librarian might consider *Rassegna . . .* as a possible substitute. (G.S.)

Lettere Italiane. 1949. q. $14. Vittore Branca & Giovanni Getto. Leo S. Olschki, Casella Postale 295, 50100 Florence, Italy. Index, adv.

Bk. rev: essays, signed. *Aud:* Ac.

Published by the Instituto della Letteratura Italiana of the universities of Padova and Turino, this is one of Italy's major literary journals. Emphasis is on Italian literary history, articles tend to be technical, and it is roughly equivalent to our more esoteric literary journals. The essay length book reviews are written in Italian and French and cover major European publications. Aside from the basic essays, the reviews are of primary importance to any library building a collection in Italian literature. (G.S.)

Metro. 1961. s-a. $20. Ed. bd. Edizioni d'Arte Alfieri, S. Marco 2291, Venice, Italy. Subs. to: Wittenborn & Co., 1019 Madison Ave., New York, N.Y. 10031. Illus., adv.

Indexed: ArtI. *Aud:* Ac.

An international magazine in English and Italian about contemporary painting and sculpture with an emphasis on the latest trends and avant garde movements. Includes articles on the recent work of artists, important art exhibitions, critical examinations of new movements and their place in art history. Caters to the more affluent who can afford to take advantage of what is offered and advertised.

Mondo. 1948. w. $24. Gianni Mazzocchi. Editoriale Domus, Via Monte di Pieta 15, 20121 Milan, Italy. Illus., adv.

Bk. rev: 5–7, 100–200 words. *Aud:* Ga. Ac.

This independent and progressively oriented weekly is the most refined of the Italian weeklies. Although a magazine, it is issued in large newspaper format, is well printed, and with an elegant layout. True to its title, it covers in detail and without sensationalism, politics, economics, and cultural events around the world. In the issue of October 17, 1971, six columns were devoted to an Italian writer's encounters with Ezra Pound. In the same issue a full-page article told the story of Cyrus the Great, the founder of the Per-

sian Empire. In another long piece the return of paintings spirited out of Italy during the German occupation is told. The book reviews are less significant. Theatre, music, cinema, and television are given broad coverage. (G.S.)

La Rassegna della Letteratura Italiana. 1898. 3/yr. L. 7000. Walter Binni. Casa Editrice G. C. Sansoni, Viale Mazzini 46, 50121 Florence, Italy. Index; adv. Circ: 1,000.

Aud: Ac.

Published by the Istituto di Filologia Moderna della Facolta di Lettere, Università di Roma, this is some 300 pages, of which one third are devoted to bibliographies of books and periodicals. All periods of Italian literary history are covered and articles are based on original research. The bibliographies are critical, annotated, and arranged by centuries or significant periods, or movements. An annual index is appended to the first issue of the new year. Particularly recommended as a selection tool, and definitely a first choice for libraries which do not subscribe to a regular reviewing service, e.g., see *Giornale della Libreria.* (G.S.)

Rivista Italiana di Musicologia. 1966. s-a. $9.50. Ed. comm. Casa Editrice Leo S. Olschki, Casa Postale 295, 50100 Florence, Italy. Illus., adv.

Bk. rev: 6, various length, signed. *Aud:* Ac.

A scholarly musical journal which has well-documented articles, e.g., one issue is given to four lengthy pieces on musical composition of the fifteenth through eighteenth centuries. The book reviews discuss recent subject literature published in Italy, Germany, Poland, the United States, and Scandinavia. The reviews afford the knowledgeable reader a good general idea of contents. All articles and reviews are illustrated with musical examples. The department entitled "Notiziaro" informs the reader of coming events and their detailed programs, i.e., congresses, meetings, and conventions of interest to the musicologists. It is not uncommon that such scholarly publications are far behind publishing schedule. It may sound paradoxical, but Vol. 3 No. 2, 1968 reports in the past tense events which took place in 1969. A subscription is easily justified, because musicologists and readers interested in the field are usually familiar with the language. (G.S.)

Rivista Mensile del Club Alpino Italiano. 1879. m. L.3600. Giovanni Bertoglio. Club Alpino Italiano, Via U. Foscolo 3, 20121 Milan, Italy. Illus., index, adv. Circ: 70,000.

Bk. rev: various number, length. *Aud:* Ac, Ga, Hs.

The passion and popular interest of the young and not so young for skiing and mountain climbing well justifies this addition to a library collection. Even if the potential reader does not master the Italian language he can enjoy the illustrations. This should not be considered a sports magazine in the usual sense of the term. It publishes scientific, historic, artistic, and literary articles related to the mountains; reports on expeditions in Europe and other parts of the world; and all aspects of conservation are of concern to the editors. A good part of the journal is devoted to climbing and skiing techniques. Under the heading of Bibliography new publications and maps are announced and briefly reviewed. There is an elaborate yearly index which, among other features, lists separately new accommodations (Refugio) at high altitudes for the sportsman. (G.S.)

Rivista Storica Italiana. 1884. q. $14.60. Guido d'Agostino, Gabriella Mortarotto, and Narciso Nada. Edizioni Scientifiche Italiane, Via Carducci 29, 80121 Naples, Italy. Illus., adv. Circ: 2,000 Vol. ends: Dec.

Indexed: HistAb. *Bk. rev:* 12–15, 250–750 words, signed; also, 8–10 longer reviews (2–8 pages). *Aud:* Ac.

Rivista storica italiana is among the more important foreign publications and belongs in any historical collection which purports to cover all the modern languages of scholarship. The three to four articles cover all aspects of history, although with something of an Italian emphasis. Approximately half of each issue is devoted to book reviews, not only of Italian publications, but those appearing in English, French, and German. (R.S.)

Societa Geografica Italiana. Bollettino. 1868. m. L.2500. Ferdinando Gzibandi. Societa Geografica Italiana, Via della Navicella 12, Rome, Italy. Illus., index. Circ: 2,000.

Bk. rev: 10–14, lengthy, signed. *Aud:* Ac.

The publication of the Italian Geographical Society, this journal is general in scope, with only the expected emphasis on Italy and the Mediterranean area. All articles have an English-language summary. Maps as well as books and articles are reviewed. A scholarly publication for comprehensive collections. (D.D.)

Studi Internazionali di Filosofia. 1970. a. $5. Augusto Guzzo, Piazza Statuto 26, 10144 Turin, Italy.

Bk. rev: 6–8, 1–3 pages, signed. *Aud:* Ac.

This is an annual supplement to *Filosofia* (same publisher, same editor). The articles are issued in the language of the author, e.g. Italian, French, English, German. It is primarily a report of meetings and congresses around the world. The book reviews are in the language of the reviewer. (A combined subscription to this and *Filosofia* is $10.) (G.S.)

Studi Storici. 1959. q. $13.60. Ed. comm. S.G.R.A., Via dei Frentani 4, 0185 Rome, Italy. Index; adv. Circ: 11,800.

Bk. rev: 5, 2–5 pages, signed. *Aud:* Ac.

An explicitly Marxist oriented journal of cultural history. In spite of the ideological bias this is a very scholarly review. To illustrate the variety of topics treated and the unquestionably scientific quality of the review it is sufficient to list some titles. In number four of 1970 under the heading of research problems: "The Origins of 17th Century Reactionary Catholicism" and "The Italian Army on the Eve of World War I"; under the heading of opinions and debates in the same issue a 40-page article: "The Late Victorian Imperialism: Continuity or Qualitative Change." The signed book reviews are specific in their analysis and written by specialists in the respective fields. (G.S.)

Vita e Pensiero; rassegna italiana di cultura. 1914. m. $8. Vincenzo Cesareo. Societa Editrica Vita e Pensiero. Pubblicazioni dell'Universita Cattolica del Sacro Cuore, Largo Gemelli 1, 20123 Milan, Italy. Adv. Circ: 3,500. Sample.

Bk. rev: 6–8, essay length, signed. *Aud:* Ac, Ga.

This stimulating and scholarly review is the voice of the Catholic University of the Sacred Heart in Milan. All issues (often double) are monographic and deal with the controversial questions of contemporary culture: literature, politics, cinema, church, and problems of the city. The double issue for January/February 1971 was devoted to all aspects of the Italian theatre. The March issue, entitled "The city and its territory" dealt with urban problems. All topics are explored from a Catholic point of view. Every issue offers an extensive, critical, annotated bibliography of basic older and recent publications (books and periodical articles) related to the particular theme. Because of the unquestionably high standards of scholarship, the great variety of topics dealing with pressing problems, the high reference value of book reviews and bibliographies, this publication is highly recommended. (G.S.)

FICTION

Basic Periodicals

GENERAL. All libraries: *Fiction.*

SCIENCE FICTION. All libraries: *Analog, Extrapolation.*

General

Alfred Hitchcock's Mystery Magazine. 1956. m. $7. Ernest M. Hutter. HSD Publns., Inc., 2241 Beach Ct., Riviera Beach, Fla. 33404. Illus., adv. Circ: 150,000.

Aud: Ga.

The story with the trick-O'Henry-ending is favored. The style is violent, yet not bloody. The subject and background can be anything from a golf course to a bathroom, as long as it is in good taste and offends no individual or minority group. Some of the stories tend to take off into the supernatural, even the world of science fiction, but most are based on everyday events. The writing is extremely uneven. Some is exceptionally good; some equally bad. On balance, though, it is one of the better of this genre. For the most imaginative, somewhat preferable to the predictable, sometimes pedestrian Ellery Queen entry.

Armchair Detective; a quarterly journal devoted to the appreciation of mystery, detective and suspense fiction. 1967. q. $4. Allen J. Hubin, 3656 Midland, White Bear Lake, Minn. 55110. Circ: 500.

Aud: Ga, Ac.

A processed fanzine for the detective and mystery story. The editor covers all points: from authors, to the story of a given fictional detective, to the fate of the genre in America, to reviews. It is a product of love, and of considerable interest (and value) to any mystery fan or librarian trying to keep up on developments. The editor puts out an annual bibliography and checklists which will help any librarian keep his or her collection up-to-date.

Baker Street Journal; a quarterly of Sherlockiana. 1964. 4/yr. $4. Julian Wolff. Baker Street Irregulars, 33 Riverside Dr., New York, N.Y. 10023. Illus., index. Circ: 900.

Aud: Ga.

The basic journal to keep up with the activities of Sherlock Holmes and his many friends, not to mention a few enemies. Straight articles, prose and even some verse are included, but the primary interest is in critical, exegetical and chronological analyses of the Holmes work. A serious approach, it is for lovers of mystery and personality. See *Sherlock Holmes Journal* for the English equivalent of this magazine.

Ellery Queen's Mystery Magazine. 1941. m. $9. Eleanor Sullivan. David Publns., Inc., 229 Park Ave. S., New York, N.Y. 10003. Illus., adv. Circ: 250,000.

Bk. rev: 10–20, notes, signed. *Aud:* Ga.

Somehow in the past three years the magazine has slipped a bit, or the formula grows old. At any rate, while still good enough for what it does, the master mind of money and mystery isn't up to former years. The format remains the same, the number of stories (about 150–175 a year) about the same, and the approach the same. There are some top stories, usually by someone besides Ellery Queen, by the way; and the magazine has not sold out to violence and sensationalism. It can be recommended for just about any reader who enjoys a less sophisticated type of mystery yarn. All in all, it is pretty harmless. The plus side for librarians is the book review section by John Dickson Carr—some of the best reviews in the field.

Fiction. 1972. 3/yr. $2. Mark Mirsky, 513 E. 13th St., New York, N.Y. 10009. Illus., adv. Circ: 5,000.

Aud: Ga, Ac.

A 24-page tabloid-type magazine which features short stories, impressions and bits from novels. It is a little magazine in a different format. It has one major claim to fame: the contributors represent some of the best-known writers in America. Heading the list are Donald Bartheleme, John Hawkes, Stanley Elkin, and James Kempton. Bartheleme did the layout and apparently got the authors to contribute the stories, as well as putting up speculative money to get out the first issue. The material is, at best, medicore. The magazine has a long way to go to catch up with the better little magazines, more or less *The New Yorker, Harper's, The Atlantic* and others, which the editor hopes eventually to supplement. Despite the rather weak beginning, the notion deserves support from libraries. It is reasonably priced, the effort is commendable, and the need for more fiction outlets is certainly obvious. The second and third issues should improve. In the meantime it is worth the modest $2. (Not to be confused with *Fiction Magazine*, a new enterprise by Richard Wallace out of Suffern, New York. This has yet to be seen, but it is quite different from *Fiction.*)

Mike Shayne Mystery Magazine. 1956. m. $7. Cylvia Kleinman. Renown Publns. Inc., 56 W. 45th St., New York, N.Y. 10036. Illus., adv. Sample.

Aud: Ga.

Formatwise this resembles the familiar Alfred Hitchcock and Ellery Queen approach, i.e., pocket-sized, 124 pages, with some line illustrations, on newsprint. Each issue features an original Brett Halliday story on Shayne (usually about one third of each number), and then five to eight short suspense, mystery tales by other writers. The style is tight, usually with more violence than is found in competitors, but the violence is kept in hand, and the yarns are usually creditable. Between this and its two primary cousins, it is simply a matter of personal taste. All three are newsstand items for quick reading and to be just as easily forgotten. Of special value, though, for the library trying to encourage readers who find other magazines too square or too difficult.

The Mystery Reader's Newsletter (Formerly: *Mystery Lovers' Newsletter*). 1967. bi-m. $3. Lianne Carline, P.O. Box 113, Melrose, Mass. 02176. Illus., adv. Circ: 300. Sample.

Bk. rev: 30–50, 200 words. *Aud:* Ga; Hs.

This is worth a subscription by almost any public or school library where the mystery story is a minor focus. In some 40 mimeographed pages the editor includes articles, information on prices for collectors, a section of comments and queries for and by the reader, a directory of collectors, and ten or more pages of annotated book reviews. The latter feature makes it most valuable for librarians, particularly as the signed

200-word reviews are about as critical as will be found this side of *The New Yorker* or *The New York Times Book Review*. Despite the format, the approach is professional, the information valuable, and the tone just right for the subject matter. A copy around the library will be of equal interest to mystery fans.

Panache. 1965. a. $1. R. B. Frank. Subs to: Eighth Street Bookstore, 17 W. 8th St., New York, N.Y. 10014.

Indexed: LMags. *Bk. rev:* 6–7, 500 words, signed. *Aud:* Ac, Ga.

Primarily a vehicle for publishing the Frances Steloff prize short story. In addition, there are four to six runner-ups. Rounded out by articles and book reviews, the 64 pages is well worth the modest subscription price.

Sherlock Holmes Journal. 1952. s-a. $3. Marquis of Donegall, Sherlock Holmes Soc. of London, The Studio, 39 Clabon Mews, London SW1, England. Illus., index.

Aud: Ga.

A trifle more dignified, and stuffy, than the American counterpart, but equally valid. The material and approach is similar, although at times the British turn up some really startling bits of information not available to Americans.

This Issue; the magazine book for stories. 1970. bi-m. $6. Mel McKee, Box 15247, Emory Univ. Sta., Atlanta, Ga. 30333. Illus., index. Circ: 20,000. Sample.

Bk. rev: Notes. *Aud:* Ga, Hs.

This 40-page magazine features short stories, poems, essays and photographs. Most of the yarns are for undemanding adults and teen-agers. In an effort to eliminate stories which feature "a patchwork of symbols, stream of consciousness, character sketches, Kafkian obscurity, or four-letter words," the editor ends up with pretty tame and dull material. He has an editorial advisory board with such names as James Dickey, Richard Eberhart and Jesse Stuart. Where they are when the stories come up for review is anyone's guess. Having said all of that, if one grants that there is a large audience for fairly simplistic short stories, the magazine serves a solid enough purpose in public libraries and many high schools. Its limited appeal to sophisticated readers will make it all that more popular among those who want a "good, clean and not-too-disturbing" title. It depends on your audience whether or not you order, but it may be just the kind of magazine you and your library have been looking for.

Tolkien Journal. 1964. q. $2. Edmund R. Meskys. Tolkien Soc. of America, Belknap College, Center Harbor, N.H. 03226. Illus., index, adv. Circ: 2,000.

Indexed: AbEnS. *Bk. rev:* Notes. *Aud:* Ac, Ga, Hs.

One of the few of this genre which has a wide popular circulation, and can be recommended for high schools as well as colleges and universities. The books of Tolkien, i.e., *Lord of the Rings*, are treated as true history and analyzed as such. There is a given amount of serious consideration to J.R.R. Tolkien, the author, but the primary interest is with his imaginative world. The closest thing around for older readers is the papers devoted to Sherlock Holmes, e.g., *Baker Street Journal*.

Science Fiction

Modern science fiction (SF) is sometimes dated from the founding of *Amazing Stories* in 1926, edited by Hugo Gernsback (1884–1967), for whom the major science fiction literary award, the Hugo, is named. Although a substantial number of what were then called scientific romances had appeared in magazine form since the late 1800s, notably in the Munsey pulps, *Amazing* is generally considered to be the first magazine devoted wholly to science fiction. (For the earlier periods, see the detailed accounts by Sam Moskowitz, in *Under the Moons of Mars*, Holt, Rinehart & Winston, 1970, and *Science Fiction by Gaslight*, World, 1968.)

The thirties saw a large increase in the number of titles, which reached a peak during the 1950s. In spite of the present widespread acceptance of SF, however, the number of professional (paying) SF magazines now published is relatively small, a situation caused largely by economic and distribution problems, and the growth of paperback publishing.

The four professional magazines listed, *Amazing, Analog, Galaxy, Magazine of Fantasy and Science Fiction*, and dozens of others, have been indexed as follows: Donald B. Day's *Index to the Science Fiction Magazines, 1926–1950* (1952; available from F & SF Book Co., PO Box 415, Staten Island, N.Y. 10302, $10., hardbound); *MIT Science Fiction Society's Index to the S-F Magazines, 1951–1965* (1966; available from the New England SF Association, Box G, MIT Branch PO, Cambridge, Mass. 02139, $8., hardbound) or Norman Metcalf's *Index of Science Fiction Magazines, 1951–1965* (1968; available from J. Ben Stark, Box 261, Fairmount Station, El Cerrito, Calif. 94530, $8.50, soft cover); and *Index to the Science Fiction Magazines, 1966–1970* (1971; same source as MIT index, $5., hardbound). Reviews of science fiction adult and juvenile books in eight professional SF magazines, seven fanzines, *Library Journal*, and *Publishers Weekly* were indexed in what will hopefully be an annual. The *Science Fiction Book Review Index* for 1970 is a mimeographed booklet available for $1. from its compiler, Hal Hall, 3608 Meadow Oaks Lane, Bryan, Texas 77801. No professional SF magazines are currently available in reprint form or microform, although a very large percentage of the better material has appeared in anthologies, short story collections, and novels in both hard and soft cover format. Frederick Siemon's *Science Fiction Story Index* (American Library Association, 1971) indexes approximately 2500 short stories and some novels appearing in book form, most of which appeared earlier in the SF pulps.

Supplementing the well-established paying magazines are amateur fanzines, usually mimeographed or offset, in which the early work of many subsequently well-known writers has appeared. Their short life spans make the compilation of a directory impossible. Listed below are four which are likely to be of more general interest and of some research value. Sample copies of both professional and amateur magazines are available from the editors and could be used for a display to gauge reader interest. Back issues are often not available. Prepayment of fanzine subscriptions is recommended. (N.B.)

Amazing Stories. 1926. bi-m. $3. Ted White, ed. Ultimate Pub. Co., Box 7, Flushing, N.Y. 11364. Illus., adv. Circ: 30,000.

Bk rev: 0–5, 100–500 words, signed. *Aud:* Ga, Hs, Ejh.

Each 130-page issue contains about 85 percent new material, with the balance devoted to a "classic" reprinted from *Amazing's* earlier years. Features include "The Clubhouse," devoted to fanzine reviews and fan activities, and a science article. The quality of writing is still reminiscent of an earlier period, and the letters to the editor suggest a somewhat less knowledgeable and younger readership than that of *Analog* or *Galaxy*. (N.B.)

Analog Science Fiction/Science Fact. 1930. m. $6. Box 5205, Boulder, Colo. 80302. Illus., adv. Circ: 109,000.

Bk. rev: 8–10, 150–400 words, signed. *Aud:* Ga, Ac, Hs. *Jv:* V.

Under the leadership of John W. Campbell, who became editor in 1937, the magazine veteran readers know as *Astounding* (the present name dates from 1965) quickly became the leading SF magazine, a position it held for over two decades. Rejecting the emphasis on gimmicks, bug-eyed monsters, and "space opera" characteristic of the pulps of the period, Campbell insisted on logic and at least some scientific rigor underlying the stories. While Campbell himself sometimes pushed pseudoscientific ideas (dianetics and psi-machines, for example), virtually every major SF writer's works appeared in the pages of *Astounding*, which was heavily mined for the dozens of anthologies published during the 1950s. (See especially the Modern Library Giant, *Famous Science-Fiction Stories*, edited by Raymond J. Healy and J. Francis McComas, for a generous sampling from the magazine's "golden age.") Recent years have seen an increasing element of social criticism in the stories. The editorials and letters are often relatively technical and provocative. P. Schuyler Miller's reviews of books and the SF scene

are balanced and useful. The deaths of Campbell and August Derleth, head of Arkham House, in July 1971, only a week apart, marked the passing of two of the most influential figures in science fiction and fantasy. (N.B.)

Extrapolation: A Journal of Science Fiction and Fantasy. 1959. s-a. $3. Thomas D. Clareson. Box 3186, College of Wooster, Wooster, Ohio 44691.

Bk rev: 2–4, 100–400 words, signed. *Aud:* Ac, Ga, Sa. *Jv:* V.

Originally the *Newsletter of the Modern Language Association Seminar in Science Fiction*, this 80-page journal is now jointly sponsored by the MLA and the Science Fiction Research Association. Its contributors are usually academics and its audience is literary scholars, critics, and historians of science, although regular SF readers would find many articles of great interest. It is strong on bibliography, history, and criticism, and of permanent value. Volumes 1–10 (1959–1969) have been reprinted in one paperback volume by Johnson Reprint for $20. (N.B.)

Galaxy Magazine. 1950. irreg. $9./12 issues. Ejlet Jakobbsen, 235 E. 45th St., New York, N.Y. 10017. Illus., adv. Circ: 43,000.

Bk. rev: 5–8, 150–500 words, signed. *Aud:* Ga, Ac, Sa.

Under the editorship of H. L. Gold in the early 1950s, *Galaxy* began to challenge *Analog* as the most distinguished SF magazine and still retains a large readership. The usual mixture of serialized novels and shorter stories, it is much closer to *Analog* than to *Amazing* in quality, and, with the former, is one of the two major SF magazines. Also available in French, German, Italian, Japanese and Spanish editions, in Braille, and on tape (inquire for details). (N.B.)

Locus. 1968. irreg. (about 36/yr.) $8.50/yr. Charles N. Brown, 2078 Anthony Ave., Bronx, N.Y. 10457. Illus., adv. Circ: 1,100. Sample.

Bk. rev: 10–15, 100–300 words, signed. *Aud:* Ga.

Each ten-page issue, a combination of mimeo and offset, goes to over 1,000 subscribers, a large circulation in this field. Called a "newszine" by fans, it provides the most comprehensive news of the SF field of any single fanzine. Short columns are complemented at irregular intervals by book and occasional film reviews, publishing and market reports, convention and other fan activity accounts, with frequent contributions from foreign readers. Particularly thorough coverage of other fanzines is included, should you wish to expand your subscription list. A good introduction for the neophyte reader, with some value for retrospective research as well. Hugo award, best fanzine, for 1970. (N.B.)

Luna Monthly. 1969. m. $5. Franklin Dietz and Ann F. Dietz, 655 Orchard St., Oradell, N.J. 07649. Illus., adv.

Bk. rev: 20–30 adult, 5–10 juvenile, 50–300 words, signed. *Aud:* Ac, Ga.

When the *Science Fiction Times*, listed in the first edition of this directory, folded in 1969, many of its readers turned to *Luna Monthly*, whose audience overlaps that of *Locus*. Almost a third of each 32-page issue is devoted to book reviews. Like too many reviews in specialty SF publications, they lean heavily on plot summaries with little real criticism or depth. The reviews and the "New Books" listings, which include British and American works, will help you monitor SF book output. The "Have You Read?" bibliography lists articles and reviews dealing with SF in a wide variety of sources often not otherwise indexed. Regular contributors from abroad cover the foreign scene. The "Coming Events" department provides a calendar of fan meetings and conventions throughout the U.S. Probably the best general interest fanzine for a public library, and useful for academic libraries supporting courses in this area. (N.B.)

Magazine of Fantasy and Science Fiction. 1950. m. $8.50. Edward L. Ferman. Mercury Press, Inc., Box 56, Cornwall, Conn. 06753. Illus., adv. Circ: 46,000.

Bk. rev: 6–10, 150–300 words, signed. *Aud:* Ga.

Under the original editorial direction of J. Francis McComas and the late Anthony Boucher, this achieved a reputation among regular critics—such as Clifton Fadiman—for a more polished literary quality than was common in such writing. Present day quality is more uneven. James Blish (William Atheling) is the ascerbic book reviewer. The prolific Isaac Asimov contributes interesting if lightweight science articles. (N.B.)

Riverside Quarterly. 1964. s-a. $2./4 issues. Leland Sapiro, ed. Box 40, Univ. Station, Regina, Canada. Illus.

Bk. rev: 2–3, 800–3,000 words, signed. *Aud:* Ac, Ga.

Each 80-page issue consists of several articles (Alexei Panshin's *Heinlein in Dimension*, Advent, 1968, originally appeared in its pages), several essay book and film reviews, occasional poetry and fiction, and a generous assortment of letters. Contributors are often professional SF writers and editors. While no less scholarly than *Extrapolation*, its appeal is somewhat broader and the letters provide some spirited discussion. (N.B.)

FOLKLORE

Basic Periodicals

Hs: *Western Folklore;* Ga: *Journal of American Folklore, Western Folklore;* Jc & Ac: *Journal of American Folklore, Western Folklore, Folklore Institute. Journal.*

Basic Abstracts and Indexes

Music Index, Abstracts of Folklore Studies.

F F Communications (Folklore Fellows Communications). 1910. 2–5/yr. Price varies per no. Prof. Dr. L. Honko. Suomalainen Tiedeakatemia, Academia Scientiarum Fennica, Snellmanenkatu, 9–11, Helsinki 17, Finland. Illus. Circ: 500–600. Vol. ends: Dec.

Indexed: AbFolkSt, MLA. *Aud:* Ac.

Issues vary in format and language (English, French, German). A number may consist of a single monograph on, for example, African proverbs, or it may be a series of short articles built around a single theme, such as Finnic-Slavic folk relations. Discussions are highly developed and technical. Scope of topics, whether collaborated on or handled by individual scholars, may be narrow or broad as need occasions. Withal, certain of the contributions are highly readable, considering the difficulty of their subject matter. The value of such articles as "Balder und Die Mistel" and "The Flemish Popular Tale" (in French) cannot be overestimated, and *F F Communications* could well be considered to the field of folklore what the scholarly *Encyclopaedia Britannica* is to the field of general knowledge. (F.M.)

Folklore (England). 1878. q. $9. Christina Hole. Folk-Lore Soc., c/o Univ. College of London, Gower St., London WC1E. 6BT, England. Vol. ends: Dec. Microform: UM.

Indexed: AbFolkSt, BritHum. *Bk. rev:* 5–10, 500–800 words, signed. *Aud:* Ac.

Somewhat recondite and frequently more narrow in its interests than *F F Communications, Folklore,* nevertheless, provides a truly valuable source of good book reviews, and some articles are of a high content quality. The style of the journal is, in the best tradition, illustrious. Departments include Folklore Notes and Society Notes, filled with many useful announcements and memorabilia. Issues also include Society obituaries, notices of meetings, and letters to the editor. This journal was started so long ago that one member of the society, W. J. Thoms, actually originated the term "Folk-Lore." Since the beginning it has maintained an overall high quality of production. (F.M.)

Folklore (India). 1956. m. $7.50. Senkar Sen Gupta. Indian Publns., 3 British Indian St., Calcutta 1, India. Illus., adv. Circ: 6,800. Sample. Vol. ends: Dec.

Indexed: AbFolkSt, MLA. *Bk. rev:* 1–5, 100–300 words, signed. *Aud:* Ga, Ac.

Contains editorials, from time to time "Books Received," and new book annotations in addition to the short reviews; also miscellaneous "Notices," quite useful, scholarly bibliographies on Asiatic folklore, and many sound general articles on folklore topics of worldwide interest. A short, for the most part English-language publication, *Folklore* (India) makes many solid theoretical and quantitative gains for the field. This must weigh heavily in its favor against a style which is frequently awkward or downright careless and ungrammatical, in addition to being rather heavily larded with well-nigh impossible transliterations of Indian proper nouns. (F.M.)

Folklore Institute. Journal. 1964. 3/yr. $4. Fellows of the Folklore Inst., Mouton & Co., Herderstract 5, The Hague, Netherlands. Illus., adv. Circ: 1,000. Sample. Vol. ends: Dec. Microform: UM.

Indexed: AbFolkSt. *Aud:* Ac.

Entitled *Midwest Folklore* until 1964. Coverage has been broadened to take in the whole subject field. Topics on which various facets of folklore have a bearing are picked. Particular features and the general state of folklore studies are also treated. Articles are written by those engaging in actual fieldwork. Issues have included such topics as Indo-European subgroup relations, Celtic life-style since antiquity, and culture myths in relation to folkways of various regions. (F.M.)

✓ ***Journal of American Folklore.*** 1888. q. Membership (Nonmembers, $3. per no.). Americo Paredes. Amer. Folklore Soc., Univ. of Texas Press, Box 7819, Austin, Tex. 78712. Illus., index, adv. Circ: 2,000. Sample. Vol. ends: Dec. Microform: UM. Reprint: Kraus.

Indexed: AbFolkSt, MusicI, SSHum. *Bk. rev:* 15–20, 500–800 words, signed. *Aud:* Ga, Ac, Hs. *Jv:* V.

The most important publication in the field, it should be in all library collections from college through high school. The style of articles is colloquial and with broad appeal. Coverage includes the entire spectrum of folk dance and music, local color biography, traditions and mores, and folk literature and art. Some of the subject matter is technical: comparisons are made between oral transmission, thematics, commercial adaptations, belletristic transformations, and textual references. Notes and queries, short selected subjects, recent research, and editorial opinions help to vary the format. Book reviews do not shun value judgment, and are topically arranged. Sections devoted to new editions of key studies, as well as notices and reviews of reprints, keep the reader up to date on the cumulative body of permanent contributions. "Folklore Bibliography" is a yearly feature. It covers recent articles and books in a highly usable format, including author, title, and a subject index broken down by types of tales and by regional and ethnic groups, incidents, and characters. (F.M.)

Kentucky Folklore Record. 1955. q. $3. Charles S. Guthrie. Kentucky Folklore Soc. & Western Kentucky Univ., Bowling Green, Ky. 42101. Circ: 450. Reprint: Johnson.

Indexed: AbFolkSt, HistAb, MLA, MusicI. *Bk. rev:* 2–4, 400 words, signed. *Aud:* Ga, Ac.

Like a good many of the small regional folklore journals. There are four or five articles to an issue, on such topics as famous events, folk language, topical and local folk songs, and legends and beliefs of Kentucky. Reviews of books, announcements of meetings, and "News and Notes" appear regularly. Area music on various new LPs is reviewed from time to time. Contributions may be submitted by both amateur and professional writers in the field. An annual bibliography of Kentucky folklore includes "Discography," a section on important records. (F.M.)

New York Folklore Quarterly. 1945. q. Membership (Nonmembers, $5). Roderick J. Roberts. New York Folklore Soc., c/o Betty Morris, The Farmers Museum, Cooperstown, N.Y. 13326. Illus., index, adv. Circ: 650. Sample. Vol. ends: Dec. Microform: UM.

Indexed: AbFolkSt, MusicI. *Bk. rev:* 20–30, 150 words, signed. *Aud:* Ga, Ac.

A journal for the general reader, though many of the articles pertain to New York State. NYFQ is helpful down through junior high school. The editors are interested in customs, festivals, songs, ballads, folk music, art, proverbs, superstitions, ghost stories, witchcraft, the history of place names, local customs, architecture, homemaking and cooking, Indian lore, frontier and rural life and folkways, and the contributions of the foreign born to New York's folk heritage. Reviews of books give excellent information about New York State coverage and meet the demands of the journal for flexible interests, including customs of early American and pioneer life. (F.M.)

North Carolina Folklore. 1954. s-a. $2. (Students, $1.) Leonidas Betts & Guy Owens, North Carolina Folklore Soc. Dept. of English, N.C. State Univ., Box 5308, Raleigh, N.C. 27607. Illus., index. Circ: 700.

Indexed: AbFolkSt. *Bk. rev:* 3–4, 150–250 words, signed. *Aud:* Ac, Ga, Hs.

A nicely illustrated offset journal which publishes folklore stories and yarns. The November 1971 issue, for example, consisted primarily of some 60 pages of short articles on Christmas customs and beliefs in North Carolina. Most of the material is local, and written by both amateur and professional folklorists. It is highly readable. A useful magazine in almost any library, particularly in North Carolina and the southern and border states; it is certainly required for larger collections. (Beginning with the end of 1971, the editor reports a change in equipment which will allow the staff to get out a "more professional" looking magazine. Well, it's not bad now.) (F.M.)

Northwest Folklore. 1965. s-a. $2.50. J. Barre Toeklen. Univ. of Oregon Publns., Friendly Hall, Eugene, Oreg. 97403. Circ: 750.

Indexed: AbFolkSt. *Aud:* Ga, Ac.

Replacing the smaller, mimeographed *Oregon Folklore Bulletin*, this journal publishes the "raw materials of folklore . . . the actual collected superstitions, tales, songs, etc., of oral traditions in the Northwest." Brief research inquiries, critical discussions, and short monographs on Northwest folklore appear. Early issues are concerned with an Idaho analogue to Baron Munchausen, beliefs and superstitions of military flyers, and sources for children's songs. An excellent, vital journal, it serves to maintain the growing body of miscellaneous humor and quaintness hidden here and there throughout the region. (F.M.)

Southern Folklore Quarterly. 1937. q. $5.50. Edwin C. Kirkland. Univ. of Florida in cooperation with the South Atlantic Modern Language Assn., Gainesville, Fla. 32601. Circ: 800. Microform: UM.

Indexed: AbFolkSt, MLA, MusicI, SSHum. *Bk. rev:* 2–3, 500 words, signed. *Aud:* Ac.

Of international application. Concerned with the theoretical and descriptive history of folklore, the magazine's main interests include historical and literary discussions of folk literature, both written and oral; also the replications of theme, beginnings, structure, and motifs of various regions. In addition, the journal values the study of literature to reveal the sociology of folk history. Numerous folklore specimens serve as illustrative examples in analyzing an author's work. Books and articles from the previous year are listed in an annual "Folklore Bibliography." (F.M.)

Tennessee Folklore Society Bulletin. 1935. q. $2. Tennessee Folklore Soc., Middle Tennessee State Univ., Box 234, Murfreesboro, Tenn. 37130. Index. Circ: 246.

Indexed: AbFolkSt, MusicI. *Bk. rev:* 5–7, 40 words, signed. *Aud:* Ac.

Up to four articles per issue dealing for the most part with Tennessee-Kentucky regional materials. A few articles on other parts of the world, such as Asia, central Europe, and the South Seas are featured. Reviews of books cover the entire field of folklore. Reviews of country music albums appear from time to time. "Tales and Superstitions" and "Events and Comments" make up regular departments. (F.M.)

Viltis. 1942. bi-m. $5. V. F. Beliajus, Box 1226, Denver, Colo. 80201. Illus., adv. Vol. ends: Dec.

Indexed: AbFolkSt. *Bk. rev:* 3–5, 50–100 words, unsigned. *Aud:* Ga.

"*Viltis* means hope," we are told. The magazine actually caters to three categories of readers: folk dancers, ethnics, and "Ole Time Friends of Byts" [the editor]. The majority of the readers would appear to be folk dance enthusiasts, judging from the prolific and very well done black and white photographs. "Five

sizeable groups" are represented: Lithuanians, Poles, Jews, Yugoslavs, and Irish, but many other ethnic groups are found in the journal. At least half the departments are of the newsy variety. Also, we find "Foreign Cuisine," "Dance Selection" (a set of directions for doing one of a particular kind of dance), "Latest Books," and "Latest Records," and such articles as "Art of Waking the Irish Dead or the Gentle Art of Burying the Irish," "The Waste of Our Linguistic Resources," and "Teaching Folk Dancing to Children." Musical scores appear. "As for Myself" is the editor's own column. Style is popular and familiar. A good general purpose slick which meets many needs. (F.M.)

Western Folklore (California Folklore Soc.) 1942. q. $5. Albert B. Friedman. Univ. of California Press, Berkeley, Calif. 94720. Adv. Circ: 900. Microform: UM. Reprint: AMS.

Indexed: AbFolkSt, MusicI. *Bk. rev:* 20, 300–500 words, signed. *Aud:* Ga, Ac, Hs. *Jv:* V.

Published by the California Folklore Society, this journal encompasses a broad spectrum of interest and practical use. Because of its wide appeal and its readable style, it should be acquired by most libraries. Between five and seven articles deal with any facet of folklore, including popular characters from folklore, folk beliefs and superstitions, comparisons and source-tracings between folk material and sophisticated literature, musicology, colloquial expressions, news and history of folklore organizations, and intercultural comparisons of all folklore characteristics. A fine series of regular features includes "Notes and Queries," a column by Peter Tamony on western folk etymology, and "Folklore and Folklorists," which gives news of folklore work. Book reviews are arranged topically and give well-considered evaluations. There are five or six pages of record release coverage, mainly concerned with genre music and individual artists. (F.M.)

FOREIGN LANGUAGE TEACHING

See also Europe and Middle East, Latin America and Chicano, and USSR and East Europe sections.

Basic Periodicals

Ejh: *Foreign Language Review* (For teachers, not general readers); Hs, Ga, Jc: *Quinto Lingo, Foreign Language Review.*

Foreign Language Review. 1958. q. $1.50. Maxine Ferris. Foreign Language Review, Inc., 200 Park Ave. S., New York, N.Y. 10003. Illus., adv. Circ: 32,000.

Bk. rev: 5–6, 100–150 words. *Aud:* Ac, Hs, Ejh.

A review of various languages, and as such it is useful for the adult who wishes to brush up on a language, or for the student from high school through college. It covers current news events of human interest type from around the world, with corresponding articles in French, German, Latin, and Spanish. Quotes by famous persons are given in the five languages (including, of course, English) and there is a section of questions in each language. Book reviews are in English. Illustrations are of places within the countries discussed in each issue. See also the more general *Quinto Lingo.*

Le Français dans le Monde. 1961. 8/yr. $6.50. Andre Reboullet. Librairies Hachette and Larousse. 79 Blvd. Saint-Germain, Paris 6e, France. Subs. to: European Publishers, 36 W. 61st St., New York, N.Y. 10023. Illus., adv. Circ: 20,000.

Indexed: CIJE. *Bk. rev:* 4–5, essay, signed. *Aud:* Ga, Ac, Hs. *Jv:* V.

Written by teachers for teachers of French as foreign language, this is an eminently scholarly and practical journal. No teacher of French can afford to be without it, regardless of the age-group he teaches. It is obvious that most of the contributors favor the methods of the structuralist linguists. Always with the classroom teachers in mind, examples and innovative exercises are provided, linguistic and grammatical problems are interpreted, commented on, and criticized. In every issue at least one important work of a modern or contemporary author is explained and analyzed in detail, not unlike in the time-honored French method of "Explication des Textes." All aspects of French daily life, politics, economics, etc., are the subject of essays enriched with documents, dialogues, and examples for class use. A recording supplementing the texts is enclosed in every other issue of the journal. The newest findings of educational research and their application are reported by specialists and teachers. Ways and means to improve foreign language teaching are discussed. The high standards of this journal are complemented by a very attractive layout and good printing. (G.S.)

French Review. 1927. 6/yr. $8. Jacques Hardré. Amer. Assn. of Teachers of French. F. W. Nachtmann, 59 E. Armory Ave., Champaign, Ill. 61820. Index, adv. Circ: 13,400. Sample. Vol. ends: May. Microform: PMC. Reprint: AATF, Johnson.

Indexed: CIJE, EdI. *Bk. rev:* 50, 600 words, signed. *Aud:* Ac, Hs.

Publishes articles of interest to teachers and students of French on the secondary and college level. Literary students include critical analyses of literary works and historical and scholarly studies of all periods. Studies of the French language, linguistics, methods of teaching French, and articles of professional interest also appear. Articles in both French and English are of medium length, averaging 10–12 per issue.

Regular features are professional notes, including lists of dissertations in progress, and society notices and news. The numerous book reviews cover every aspect of the language from textbooks to creative works. A required magazine for most professional collections in secondary schools, and for all academic libraries.

German Quarterly. 1928. 4/yr. Membership (Nonmembers, $7.50). William A. Little, Subs. to: Van Rooy Printing Co., S. Memorial Dr., Appleton, Wis. 54911. Illus., index, adv. Circ: 5,200.

Indexed: EdI. *Bk. rev:* 20, 600 words, signed. *Aud:* Ac, Hs, Ejh.

The official voice of teachers of German at all levels from secondary through college, it is sponsored by the American Association of Teachers of German. It has articles associated with this type of journal, i.e., those which give hard advice on how to teach, and those which deal with the theoretical aspects of the language, culture, and literature. More emphasis is on the latter than the former, although in this case both types are given equal opportunity. The normal departments, features, etc., are included. Also, the subscription price includes a membership directory issue.

Hispania; a journal devoted to the interests of the teaching of Spanish and Portuguese. 1919. q. $8. Irving P. Rothberg. Amer. Assn. of Teachers of Spanish & Portuguese. Subs. to: Eugene Saraiano, Wichita State Univ., Wichita, Kans. 66608. Index, adv. Circ: 15,500. Sample. Vol ends: Dec. Refereed. Microform: B&H, UM. Reprint: Kraus.

Indexed: CIJE, EdI. *Bk. rev:* 35, 500 words, signed. *Aud:* Ac, Hs.

Devoted to the teaching of Hispanic languages from the elementary to graduate levels. It functions both as a scholarly journal for the advancement of literary and language studies and as a professional bulletin for the diffusion of language instruction methods. The text is in English, Portuguese, and Spanish, and includes professional and pedagogical departments. Of special interest is the May issue listing of dissertations in the Hispanic languages and literatures. The Spanish teacher's equivalent to the *French Review,* and just as necessary in all secondary and academic libraries.

Italica. 1924. q. $8. Alga Ragusa. Amer. Assn. of Teachers of Italian. Dept. of Romance Languages, Rutgers Univ., New Brunswick, N.J. 08903. Adv. Circ: 1,800. Sample. Vol. ends: Winter. Microform: UM. Reprint: Johnson.

Bk. rev: 4–6, ½ page, signed. *Aud:* Ac, Hs.

A scholarly magazine for teachers of Italian at the secondary and academic levels. Articles are discussions of Italian literature, covering all periods, but with emphasis on the Renaissance. Critical articles appear occasionally, as do articles on Italian history and art and on linguistics and language teaching. Generally six to eight articles, averaging 3,500 words, appear in each issue. Regular features are the *A.A.T.I. Newsletter* and a "Bibliography of Italian Studies in America." Text is in English and Italian.

Journal des Instituteurs et des Institutrices; un guide de la vie scolaire et administrative. m. (Sept.–June). $5.25. G. Duchateau. Fernand Nathan & Cie, 9 Rue Méchain, Paris 14e, France. Illus., adv. Sample. Vol ends: June.

Bk. rev: 3–5, 250–500 words. *Aud:* Ac.

Issued in loose-leaf form and directed to teachers of age-groups about five to 15 years old. This is a gold mine of ideas for lessons in all subjects and all grade levels. It is especially useful for teachers of French as a foreign language. It must be kept in mind that there are considerable differences of structure and curriculum between compulsory public education in France and the United States. However, the imaginative teacher will have no difficulty in adapting the information for use in American schools. The articles seldom exceed two pages and are written in simple language understandable to everyone with a reading knowledge of French. All issues show the same pattern of presentation: an editorial, two to three short reviews of juvenile literature, another page reviewing professional and adult literature, detailed information and sample questions of promotional and competitive examinations for instructors, and suggested questions for students preparing for final achievement tests leading up to their graduation diploma. (G.S.)

Lingua Nostra. 1939. q. $4.90. Bruno Migliorini. C. C. Sansoni, Viale Mazzini 46, Florence, 50132, Italy. Index. Circ: 1,500.

Bk. rev: 3–4, length varies. *Aud:* Ac.

Promotes the study and the love of the Italian language, its history, and its linguistic problems. Among the topics discussed by specialists are the terminology of sciences and technology, stylistic analyses, problems of vocabulary, regional dialects, and the Italian language in countries outside the homeland. Other interesting studies are devoted to the correct usage of the language, teaching experiences, and criteria for translating. The book review segment calls attention also to significant articles in scholarly periodicals. The great value of this publication cannot be judged by its moderate size, i.e., about 130 pages for the four issues per volume. Recommended for teachers of Italian as foreign language and for advanced students. (G.S.)

Quinto Lingo. 1964. m. $7. Rita Reemer. Rodale Press, Inc., 33 E. Minor St., Emmaus, Pa. 18049. Illus., adv. Circ: 85,000. Sample.

Aud: Ga. *Jv:* V.

A general magazine for the adult or secondary school student wishing to improve his reading skills in the modern languages. The unique format features four columns of identical text, short articles and anecdotes, in German, Spanish, French, and English. The Russian and Italian languages appear in separate departments, each with a column of text and its English translation. Helpful language notes are given for Russian. All articles relate to a monthly topic. The magazine does a good job in presenting vocabulary and grammar in an easily understood manner. The translations are skillfully done, with each of the languages rendered freely and yet parallel to the others. Among the regular features are: Aesop's Fables in the six languages, with grammatical instruction based on the text; travel; word puzzles in different languages; and special articles. Because of the magazine's limited purpose and the fact that the intrinsic interest of both the articles and the departments lies in the languages, their intellectual content is kept on a superficial level. Nevertheless, this is a basic magazine for almost any beginning language study and it is recommended for all libraries.

Russian Language Journal. 1947. q. $6. Vladimir I. Grebenschikov. Michigan State Univ., East Lansing, Mich. 48823. Index. Circ: 500. Microform: UM.

Bk rev: 4–8, 400 words, signed. *Aud:* Ac, Hs.

Intended exclusively for teachers of Russian in secondary schools and colleges. Articles concentrate on teaching problems, training, professional matters, and linguistics. Some comparative studies, with emphasis on the Russian language, are presented. Articles are in Russian and English.

Russkii Iazyk za Rubezhom (Russian Language Abroad) 1967. q. $3.60. L. S. Alekseeva. Moscow Univ., ul. Gertsena, 5/7, Moscow, K-9 USSR. (In U.S.: Four Continent Book Corp., 156 Fifth Ave., New York, N.Y.) Illus.

Bk. rev: 3–4. *Aud:* Ac, Hs.

An excellent teaching aid, this journal is a must wherever Russian is taught at the university level. Combining scientific approach with specific examples, the writers cover all aspects of the language, including phonetics and intonation, which are demonstrated on accompanying records. Various teaching devices such as dialogues, riddles, and cartoons are used, and Soviet culture and literature is presented in poetry, satires, and entertaining articles. Book reviews present a critical analysis and evaluation of language study material published abroad. News of international language conferences and developments of Russian language education appear regularly. There are also announcements of correspondence courses, including a description of materials. Illustrations consist of photos, sketches, and drawings, in black and white, of fair quality. Print and paper are of mediocre quality, and the layout appears congested. But these are minor flaws in this otherwise well-organized and comprehensive magazine. (E.L.)

Russkii Iazyk v Shkole (Russian in the Classroom). 1936. bi-m. $2.40. N. M. Shanski. "Prosveshchenie" 3-i proezd Mar'inoi roshchi, d. 41, Moscow, GSP-110, USSR. Illus. Circ: 300,000.

Aud: Hs, Ac.

A methodological journal published by the Ministry of Education of the Russian Republic, designed for teachers of Russian in the primary and secondary schools. All aspects of language instruction are covered by specialists, with particular attention to the classroom. A whole page under the heading "Konsultatsiia" (consultation) offers guidelines and text for teachers of Russian in various grades. Articles on linguistics and literature appear regularly, as do profiles on distinguished philologists and educators. In each issue a teacher of Russian is singled out for outstanding performance, with a detailed evaluation of his or her work included. Book reviews represent lengthy critical analyses of scientific publications (mostly government sponsored) on the Russian language. The American teacher of Russian will find interesting and useful material in this periodical if he is willing to put up with the dry, laborious style of writing, the orthodox ideological editorials, and the poor quality of print. Illustrations are sparse and consist of portraits of linguists or teachers. (E.L.)

Scholastic Magazines. 50 W. 44th St., New York, N.Y. 10036. Various dates. m. (during school year). $1.–$1.50. Sample.

	LANGUAGE LEVEL	INTEREST LEVEL	CIRCULATION
French			
Bonjour	1	E	120,000
Ca Va	1–2	Jh, Sh	42,000
Chez Nous	2–3	Jh, Sh	63,000
German			
Das Rad	1–2	E, Jh	37,000
Schuss	2	Jh, Sh	15,000
Der Roller	2–4	Sh	21,000
Spanish			
Sol, El	1–2	Jh, Sh	90,000
Hoy Dia	2–4	Sh	41,000

(Discontinued: *Kometa* and *Loisirs*)

All of the Scholastic foreign-language classroom magazines follow a definite pattern. First and foremost, they are prepared by Mary Glasgow & Baker, Ltd., an outstanding British publisher. Working with American specialists, the firm has developed an eight-page format which is geared specifically to the needs and curricula of schools. The format and content are equally attractive. An effort is made to familiarize the student, via the short conversations, exposi-

tory material, cartoons, crossword puzzles and games, with the French, German, and Spanish people. The material is quite understandably noncontroversial, but honest in that the approach is imaginative and intelligent. The many photographs and line drawings show an appreciation for aesthetics, as well as for education, on the part of the editors.

A particularly good feature in each issue is the vocabulary page. Here, the foreign word is given with the English translation on a page-by-page basis as found in the magazine. The vocabulary becomes progressively more difficult with each issue in the series.

Unlike many of the Scholastic classroom papers, the language papers are uniformly excellent, always at the top of most recommended lists. It is doubtful whether they would be of much use in a library, but they should certainly be considered by any language teacher in elementary through high school.

Taking full advantage of the situation, the firm also issues phonograph records of most of their magazines' contents. A monthly teacher edition includes the student edition plus a two- or four-page supplement with background on the major articles, questions, crossword puzzle solutions, etc.

The Slavic and East European Journal. 1943. q. Membership (Nonmembers, $17.50). Frank Gladney. Wisconsin Press, Journals Dept., Box 1379, Madison, Wis. 53701. Index, adv. Circ: 2,500.

Bk rev: 15–25, 600 words, signed. *Aud:* Ac.

Devoted to research in language, linguistics, and literature, and to pedagogy. Each issue contains six or eight full-scale articles, a large review section and a section of news and notes concerning AATSEEL matters, i.e., American Association of Teachers of Slavic and East European Languages, an affiliate of the Modern Language Association and the Canadian Association of Slavists and East European Specialists. The journal's appeal is mainly to literature and language specialists.

Unsere Zeitung. m. (school year). $4.50. German News Co., 218 E. 86th St., New York, N.Y. 10028.

Aud: Hs.

A six-page tabloid teaching aid for advanced high school students of German (levels 4–6). It has an attractive format, with translations of more difficult words in English, French and Spanish. The content is fair to good. Compares well with the *Scholastic Magazine* efforts.

FREE MAGAZINES

Basic Periodicals

Ejh: *Marathon World;* Hs: *Grace Log, Marathon World;* Ga: *Kaiser News, Compass, Marathon*

World; Jc: *Compass, Kaiser News, Surveyor, Arab World;* Ac: *Arab World, Kaiser News, Compass, Surveyor, Norelco Reporter, Grace Log.*

Introduction

This section consists of a sampling of "house magazines" and others which are available to libraries on a complimentary basis. Editors of all magazines listed in this section have been contacted directly, and approval has been given for their listing. The number of entries offered in this second edition has more than doubled the number in the first edition.

A house magazine is generally construed to mean a publication of a company or commercial establishment, or of an association, commercial or otherwise. These are issued on some regular basis and are generally free to employees, stockholders, prospective customers and, in some cases, to the general public. Their main purpose is to promote the interests of the sponsor. Very little, if any, advertising is included.

The usefulness of this type of publication to libraries has been increased in the past decade by a change in general approach, from the frankly promotional, one-sided, and sometimes exaggerated picture of the company, to a more factual presentation based on the policy that public relations value is increased by giving a broader picture of the company, including its history, projections for the future, and its relationship to a much broader field such as public service. In his *Gebbie House Magazine Directory,* editor Bill Penkert analyzes recent trends in house magazines as follows: "The last years of the 1960s and the first of the 1970s saw sweeping social changes: integration, ecology, drugs, violence. The house magazine editor was caught up in the sociological changes as were his company and its officers. No longer could the company ignore the black problem or the pollution being caused by its smokestacks. The wise editor used the pages of his house organ—and many of them—to tell of his company's position on the problems of the day . . . Today's alert editor realizes that unless his publication has something to say about the problems of the day, he will lose his readership . . . More and more publications are drawing strength from a mixture of let's-put-the-facts-on-the-table approach and an honest desire to forward the interests of both the company and the employee." (Seventh ed. Sioux City, Iowa, House Magazine Publishing Co., 1971. p. 452.)

Included here are representatives of this very broad field. (Estimates vary, up to the tens of thousands, of the number of house magazines being published in the United States and Canada.) Variety is shown not only in the industries and interests represented, but also in the format, quality, and level of presentation. Some are published for the general reader, some for specialized economic groups, and some for a scholarly audience.

In compiling this list, a large percentage of the selections were chosen from *Gebbie House Magazine Directory,* which is the most comprehensive source. Those listed here have a substantial circulation. The cooperation of the editor of *Gebbie,* as well as the editors of all magazines listed, is gratefully acknowledged. (A.S.)

Aerojet-General Booster. 1952. m. free. Bill Hessel. Aerojet-General Corp., 9100 E. Flair Dr., El Monte, Calif. 91734. Illus. Circ: 10,000. Sample. Vol. ends: June.

Aud: Ac.

This corporation, concerned with space, defense, and commercial research, development, and production, uses the *Booster* to report on its current programs, products and concepts. Five to six short articles are included in each issue of this four-page leaflet. Many of its products are developed and manufactured for NASA, and applications and successful results of these items are explained. One page of "Technology" explains by text and pictures the technical operation of some piece of equipment or system, ranging from service propulsion system engines for Apollo spacecraft to new and better water desalination processes. A full-page illustration used for the cover is related to one of the articles, and illustrations for other articles consist of photos, diagrams, and drawings. Of use where there is interest in the technology of these specialized subjects. (A.S.)

Agway Cooperator. 1925. m. 10/yr. free. James E. Hurley. Agway Inc., Box 1333, Syracuse, N.Y. 13201. Illus., adv. (this company's products). Circ: 125,000. Sample. Vol. ends: Dec.

Aud: Ga.

A cooperative serving northeastern agricultuure, Agway "publishes this magazine to provide information about its operations in purchasing supplies and marketing products for farmers . . . and to report research developments and other information to help them farm better and more profitably." This service is performed by bringing to farmers in the designated area, news relating to agricultural products and practices. Each issue includes six or seven articles, written by Agway staff and experts from its various divisions. "Farm Diary," one of two or three regular features, presents some excellent writing in the form of commentary on changing seasons and the joys of rural life as they progress throughout the year. Format is well suited to the purpose and audience. Black and white photos are used for illustration, with eye-catching color photos used for covers. (A.S.)

Alcan News. 1960. m. free. George Hancocks. Alcan Canada Products, Box 269, Toronto-Dominion Centre, Toronto 111, Ontario, Canada. Illus., index. Circ: 25,500 English (9,000 French). Sample. Vol. ends: Dec.

Aud: Ga, Hs.

Published "as a continuing source of information about developments in the aluminum industry," this eight to 12-page magazine is confined to products and processes manufactured in Canada, while uses of such products may extend around the world. The rather short, staff-written articles describe a diversity of subjects, including uses of aluminum by transportation industries, housing and other construction, descriptions of appliances and other consumer goods, and accounts of some manufacturing plants and processes. Enough detailed description is given to interest potential users, while still serving the purpose of informing the general public. Writing style is popular, and does not require scientific background. Illustrated with vividly reproduced color photos, well selected, it is noteworthy for its pleasing experiments in page layout, some showing unusual combinations of pictures and text. Useful for additional material on general interest level. (A.S.)

American Investor. 1955. 10/yr. free. Robert Keane. Amer. Stock Exchange, 86 Trinity Place, New York, N.Y. 10006. Illus., index. Circ: 55,000. Sample. Vol. ends: Nov./Dec.

Aud: Ga, Ac (Restricted to college, public, and business libraries.)

This, the magazine of the American Stock Exchange, makes the declaration that "articles appearing in this publication are selected for their news content and general interest. It is an educational publication, not an advisory service." The two to four articles of each issue will be of interest primarily to the brokerage industry, to serious investors, and to students of investment or finance, as well as to the interested adult nonspecialist. Staff-written articles remain within the gamut of the stock market and the investment field at large, and are designed to broaden the reader's knowledge of their functioning. Occasionally an article touches on the history of the parent body, the American Stock Exchange. Each issue includes several pages of "New Listings" in which descriptions of newly listed companies are given, as well as sales, earnings, and other financial data for the last several years. It is illustrated with well-presented graphs, detailed charts, and some pertinent photos. Covers in a single color are appropriate and carry out the reserved, dignified tone of the magazine. Would be improved by the addition of a table of contents. (A.S.)

American Youth. 1960. q. free. Robert M. Girling. Ceco Publishing Co., 17390 W. Eight Mile Rd., Southfield, Mich. 48075. Illus. Circ: 2,000,000. Vol. ends: Nov./Dec.

Aud: Hs.

"General Motors sends *American Youth* to newly licensed young drivers with the hope that its articles on driving safety will help to develop further their driving skills." Each issue of this 24-page magazine contains several articles on driving safety and automobile construction features and equipment. Other articles reflect the concerns of today's youth, and salute young Americans who have achieved beyond the average. Projects dealing with the selection of a career, viewpoints of youth from minority groups, and advice aimed at helping youth to assume roles as social beings in an increasingly crowded world, are all written in a style geared to modern youth without resorting to slang or the vernacular. Format and arrangement are tasteful and pleasing, with an adequate number of good illustrations in various media. (A.S.)

The Arab World. 1949. bi-m. free. Randa Khalidi El-Futtal. Arab Information Center, 405 Lexington Ave., Suite 3711, New York, N.Y. 10017. Illus., index. Circ: 30,000. Sample. Vol. ends: Nov./Dec.

Indexed: PAIS. *Bk rev:* 1 (some issues); 300 words. *Aud:* Ga, Ac, Hs. *Jv:* V.

An editorial statement of late 1970 competently presents the viewpoint: "Prior to 1967 [the publication] was mostly of a touristic, cultural nature, the purpose being to avoid entering into controversial issues that require a great deal of diplomacy." It further states: "It is our belief that the 1967 aggression and its aftermath have demonstrated the necessity to re-examine the fundamentals which underlie the existing relationship between the Americans and the Arabs in all fourteen independent states . . . Since 1967, we have doubled our efforts to examine the issues at stake in their political context, and have tried to dispel some of the distortions and lies that have been disseminated by the organized enemies of the Arab peoples on this vast continent." This viewpoint is based on the premise that an enormous amount of bias exists in this country's attitude toward the Arab-Israeli conflict in general. The Arab countries, and possibly a large part of the world, consider that Americans identify almost exclusively with the Israeli position. Scholarly, documented articles examine individual subjects or areas of conflicting opinion, where the Arab side of the question has been either little known or seemingly disregarded, and competently report what appears to be a thoroughly researched presentation. Cultural material continues to be presented, with tourism largely deleted. Works in English translation, by some outstanding Arab literary figures, are presented, often with an appreciation or critique of the author. Authors of material presented are drawn from qualified writers with extensive experience in the Near East, and/or extended education and research in this area of study, and represent both Arabic and Western nationalities. Authors' backgrounds and qualifications are always noted. A substantial book review appears in some issues, on subjects which hopefully will assist the reader and the historian alike in their endeavor to assess the situation in the Near East. All are signed, written with objectivity within the framework of the magazine's avowed purpose. The 24-page format includes some illustrations. This is an offering which should be made available by libraries which serve an adult clientele, as well as by educational institutions from secondary school level up, where it is important to combat bias by showing an outstanding example of a means of presenting a minority point of view. (A.S.)

Aramco World. 1949. bi-m. free. Paul F. Hoye. Arabian Amer. Oil Co., A Corporation, 1345 Sixth Ave., New York, N.Y. 10019. Illus. Circ: 100,000. Sample. Vol. ends: Nov./Dec.

Indexed: PAIS. *Aud:* Ga, Hs, Ac. *Jv:* V.

Does a nice colorful job of interpreting the Near East, and the role of the Arabian American Oil Co. there, to the American public. Confined to this locale, its articles cover historical background material including archaeology, exploration, architecture, etc., in about equal proportion to current descriptive matter such as social customs, the impact of western civilization on the natives of Near Eastern countries, technology (oil), and various aspects of science. All material in its 32 to 36 pages is presented objectively, but has been selected to show assets and accomplishments of the area, and of course, material related to petroleum interests shows this industry to advantage. Articles are generally substantial, some qualifying as really excellent studies. All are signed and many are written by authorities in a given field, many who are, or have been, correspondents for some of the leading magazines, newspapers or news services. Staff writers of the Arabian American Oil Co. cover the technological subjects relating to petroleum. Many superb quality color photographs are included, as well as black and white photos and other illustrations. This is an excellent source of historical, geographical, cultural and social material on the Arab countries and surrounding locale. (A.S.)

Architectural News. See Architecture Section.

Asphalt. 1949. q. free. Richard C. Dresser. The Asphalt Institute, Asphalt Institute Bldg., College Park, Md. 20740. Illus. Circ: 50,000. Sample. Vol. ends: Oct.

Aud: Ga.

Published by ". . . an international, nonprofit association sponsored by the members of the petroleum asphalt industry to serve both users and producers of asphaltic materials through programs of engineering service, research and education." The 7 to 9 articles, in keeping with the stated purpose, present by means of interesting text and good illustrations, examples of the use of asphalt for paving highways, airstrips and other off-highway areas, stressing its desirable qualities for these uses. Road maintenance by means of various repair techniques using asphalt is fully explained. Featured also is information regarding availability of the Institute's publications, both print and audiovisual, for use in design and installation of asphalt for its generally accepted uses. Primarily for those concerned with the decision-making level in the use of paving materials, yet much of the information presented is within the grasp of the interested adult reader. (A.S.)

The Attack on Narcotic Addiction and Drug Abuse. 1967. q. free. Warren W. Stout. New York State Narcotic Addiction Control Commis., Executive Park South, Albany, N.Y. 12203. Illus. Circ: 125,000 controlled free mailing and up to 150,000 free bulk. Sample. Vol. ends: Dec.

Aud: Ga, Hs.

"Available for individuals who want to know more about the Narcotic Addiction Control Commission and what it is doing about the drug problem in N.Y. State." The commission has indicated that requests for subscriptions will be welcomed from outside N.Y. State, and even internationally. News articles of varying length fill the 8–12 pages of this tabloid-size magazine. They cover this commission's education program, with news of community narcotic education centers set up throughout the state by this agency, descriptions of rehabilitation programs being carried on by its centers, and drug education programs which have been successful in schools and with all types of youth groups. Descriptive material on individual drugs is extremely useful. Sources, use patterns, users' reactions and dangerous effects are well covered, as well as the nicknames in common usage. Withdrawal effects and cure methods are thoroughly explored. Articles are illustrated with photographs and are written in good journalistic style. This should be useful to parallel agencies in other states, as well as to students from high school up, interested in the topic and its current implications. (A.S.)

Automotive Information. 1963. q. free. Philip Liburdi. Automobile Manufacturers Assn., Inc., 320 New Center Bldg., Detroit, Mich. 48202. Illus. Circ: 30,000. Sample. Vol. ends: No. 4.

Aud: Ga.

This is not, as might seem the case at first glance, another item to placate the hot rod set, but rather an overall look at the interests of the automotive industry. Its eight pages, illustrated with two-tone photos, include solid but nontechnical articles covering subjects such as highways, vehicle safety, vehicle-oriented outdoor recreation, automotive advances which affect the consumer, etc. Some more technical articles look into the prospects for the internal combustion engine, explain research being done, and discuss improvements already in use to combat air pollution. "Motor Milestones," appearing in each issue, is an interesting vignette with cartoon-type illustration, of an early model or sidelight on early auto transportation for the historical auto buff. Can have some tie-in with social studies courses where these economic factors are studied in a sociological context, as well as being useful for the general reader in most libraries. (A.S.)

BSCS Newsletter. 1959. 4/yr. (Sept., Nov., Feb., Apr.) free. George M. Clark. The Biological Sciences Curriculum Study, P.O. Box 930, Boulder, Colo. 80302. Illus. Circ: 40,000. Sample. Vol. ends: Apr.

Aud: Ga, Ac.

This organization, located at the University of Colorado, reports activities for the improvement of the curriculum in the biological sciences in this newsletter of 18–32 pages. Each issue generally follows a theme, with several related articles of interest to those concerned with the teaching of any area of the biological sciences on secondary school level. Material relates to methods of presenting new curricula, use of new teaching materials, and reports of successful innovative programs being conducted by secondary schools. Research into the biological curriculum is conducted and reported according to established research procedures. Signed articles are credited to staff consultants and school and college faculty and experts in this field. BSCS publications available through commercial distribution and from BSCS are listed for the convenience of biology teachers. Photos, diagrams, charts, and drawings are used for illustration. (A.S.)

Baby Care. See Children/About Children Section.

Bank of England Quarterly Bulletin. See Business/Banking and Finance Section.

Barclays Overseas Review. See Business/General Section.

Better Nutrition. See Health Section.

Bi-Monthly Booklist. See Blacks Section.

Blue Cross Reports Research Series. 1963. 3 or 4/yr. free. Antone G. Singsen, Vice Pres., R&D, Betsy Buckley, Manag. Ed., Blue Cross Assn., 840 N. Lake Shore Dr., Chicago, Ill. 60611. Circ: 5,500. Sample. Reports arranged in series, not by vol.

Aud: Ac.

This series "publishes articles pertinent to the Blue Cross System . . . prepared by the Association's division of Research and Development staff and by authors outside of the Blue Cross System." It is a monograph series consisting of a substantial, definitive report comprising each issue. Topics, all relating to our national health care picture, include hospital care utilization patterns, medical expense payment studies, preventive health care programs and similar areas of exploration. In 8 to 16 pages, articles summarize findings of studies

which have been conducted according to established research techniques. The presentation is further clarified by generous use of data in tabulated form. Material has been prepared by health care professionals for health care professionals, and will be useful in public and specialized libraries where scholarly material on health care services and financing is available. (A.S.)

Blue Print for Health. 1947. usually ann. free. Duane R. Carlson, Exec. ed., Susan C. Restea, Manag. ed. Blue Cross Assn., available only from local Blue Cross Plan offices. Illus. Circ: 750,000 and reprints up to 2,250,000. Samples only at the discretion of local offices. Vol. ends: not specified.

Aud: Ac, Ga, Hs. *Jv:* V.

Each digest-size issue is a popularly written study on a matter of current concern in the health care field. Depending on the theme, some issues are arranged as a collection of essays reflecting the opinions of several authors, such as the issue entitled, "Adolescence for Adults," while others are structured as a well-organized development of the subject, as "The Hospital People," a description of hospital personnel and their functions, with some emphasis on recruitment. Authors are well-qualified persons, either on the magazine staff, members of the medical professions, or, in some cases, others who are not so closely related to the health care field. Some pieces are excerpted from works of well-known writers, from Margaret Mead and Pearl S. Buck, in the issue on "The Modern Baby." The cover bears the title of the report, plus "A Report by Blue Cross," with the magazine name, *Blue Print for Health* appearing only in the publishing statement. Illustrations, consisting mostly of good quality color photos, are well chosen. Designed to be distributed as single issues to individuals and groups where material on such subjects is needed, this will be found useful by schools, public libraries, and all institutions responsible for training professionals and supporting personnel, as well as hospitals and health care units. (A.S.)

Brazilian Bulletin. 1945. m. free. Editor not given. Brazilian Govt. Trade Bureau, 551 Fifth Ave., New York, N.Y. 10017. Illus. Circ: 16,000. Sample. Vol. ends: Dec.

Aud: Ga.

"The aim is to publish objective, impartial facts, mainly of a self-explanatory economic nature, not subjective impressions," was the response given to a query regarding the lack of political news published in the *Bulletin.* Current items and events relating directly to the economic picture in Brazil are presented in journalistic style, on popular level. An occasional investor's page gives straightforward information on trends of interest to outside investors possibly considering Brazil, current facts about regulations and status of the investment potential, and even tips on whom to see in Brazil. Tourism, as an economic factor, is not overlooked, and items about the attractions and accommodations of specific areas of interest to tourists are listed. Short news squibs report activities of successful artists, performers and sports figures at home and abroad. The eight-page newspaper format, with some black and white photos, carries out the purpose of the magazine. Of interest to the business community, as well as to students of any course related to the economics of Latin America. (A.S.)

Bulletin. 1913. q. free. John A. Hildreth. Standard Oil Co. of California, 225 Bush St., San Francisco, Calif. 94120. Illus. Circ: 320,000. Sample. Vol. ends: Fall.

Aud: Ga.

Responding to what the oil industry considers "the incredible growth of man's need for energy, and his ever-increasing dependency on petroleum . . .," *Bulletin* selects facets of this challenge and presents them in well-composed and well-illustrated articles. All items have some bearing on the oil industry's concern for providing petroleum-based fuel, which indisputably will be required by advances in present day technology, and on the need for agricultural chemicals, with what this industry considers to be due regard for the environment. Each issue includes one or more articles on oil-producing localities throughout the world. Excellent color photos accompanying articles help to show the changes which oil production has made in the life of the native populations. Some articles consists of reports of research being done in pollution control. Perceptive editorials by the chairman of the board of Standard Oil of California explore some of the problems facing a technological society, and express a broad-minded viewpoint regarding the position of the petroleum industry in its attempt to meet the problems of escalating worldwide energy requirements. Cover art is produced in varied media, some innovative, all excellent. General format is aesthetically pleasing. Of interest to the general reader, and of some use for secondary school level social studies reading. (A.S.)

Bulletin, National Tuberculosis and Respiratory Disease Association. 1914. m. 10/yr. Free from state and local tuberculosis and respiratory disease associations. Miss Lucille Fisher. National Tuberculosis and Respiratory Disease Assn., 1740 Broadway, New York, N.Y. 10019. Illus., index. Circ: 46,000. Sample. Vol. ends: Dec.

Aud: Ga, Ac.

Published "for persons interested in public health and administrative aspects of tuberculosis and respiratory disease control . . ." One of the main concerns of this group, reflected in its *Bulletin,* that of the provision for adequate health services for all, is discussed in light of sociological factors affecting public health.

Subjects include environmental factors affecting health, especially those related to respiratory diseases, patterns of urban growth and population shifts, and the impact of poverty, among others. Other subjects covered include the changing climate of cigarette smoking, treatment of people with emphysema and other serious respiratory diseases, and the role of volunteers in this work. This organization proposes that one factor of control which is within the realm of associations, local or state, is the molding, or changing, of public attitude. The magazine serves as the vehicle for presenting sound reasoning on various levels of comprehension, which associations may provide to the public to help make the necessary changes. Research material included seems to be authoritative and well supported. In the aim of this group toward the molding of public opinion, where facts are used to support the reasoning, they are used in a straightforward manner. Authors of articles are members of the medical profession and others holding responsible positions in the health care field. Format is adequate, with well-related photos, and some statistical information. (A.S.)

Business in Brief. 1956. bi-m. free. Richard W. Everett. Chase Manhattan Bank, N. A., 1 Chase Manhattan Plaza, New York, N.Y. 10015. Illus. Circ: 145,000. Sample. Vol. ends: Dec.

Aud: Ga, Ac.

Published by the Economic Research Division of this large banking institution to help business in general, and its financial backers, to keep abreast of some of the factors which tend to influence the economic status. The first page of each issue consists of a summary of trends, percentage comparisons, and effects of legislation and political policy on business and finance for a seasonal or a yearly period. Occasional articles attempt to explain to the practicing financier (banker) some principles of economics and finance which may have been newly formulated, or are receiving emphasis in a new manner. In some issues, a two-page article presents, in text and graphs, the economic perspective and outlook of a single large industry. A series, "Improving the Quality of Life," in several parts, has appeared in recent issues, each part consisting of two pages of interpreted statistics on one phase of the environmental condition. An interest and some background knowledge in economics and finance are assumed. This consists of an eight-page newsletter format on high quality paper. Well-conceived graphs in two colors assist in the comprehension of the factual material presented. (A.S.)

Business Conditions. 1917. m. free. Editor not given. Research Dept., Federal Reserve Bank of Chicago, P.O. Box 834, Chicago, Ill. 60690. Illus., index. Circ: 42,000. Sample. Vol. ends: Dec.

Indexed: PAIS. *Aud:* Ga.

Designed to serve the five states of the Seventh Federal Reserve District: Illinois, Indiana, Iowa, Michigan, and Wisconsin. Its 16 pages are devoted to two or three articles consisting of reports of recent activities, forecasts, and the interpretation of trends of broad areas of trade and economy, together with discussions of these. Banking and all forms of financial transaction and interaction, both national and international, are included. Aimed at the reader with an interest in banking and finance, it assumes some knowledge of financial and economic principles. Investors, the business community, those engaged in banking or other financial pursuits, and students of subjects related to any area of these will find this a useful additional source. Compact arrangement, easy-to-read double column page layout, and graphs using tones of a color in addition to black, make the format well suited to carry out the purpose of the magazine. (A.S.)

Business Education World. 1920. bi-m except July/Aug. free. Marianne Oustecky. Don M. Weaver, Gregg Division, McGraw-Hill Book Co., 330 W. 42nd St., New York, N.Y. 10036. Illus., index. Circ: 103,000. Sample. Vol. ends: May/June.

Indexed: BusI. *Aud:* Ac.

Published "as a service to business educators," and presented in a form interesting to, and on a level useful to, secondary school business educators. Feature articles consist of reports of research being done in teaching all business subjects which normally are offered in the secondary school curriculum. Emphasis is on new methods to make the subject matter more interesting and relevant, and thereby to render the learning process more permanent, and the skills more proficient. Some articles are based on a theoretical approach, while others are specific examples of successful approaches to problems of teaching in the field of business. Several regular columns give news and opinions on some specialized fields, such as consumer education, continuing education, vocational education, and others, and also give tips and tricks of the trade for the business education teacher. Some advertising of Gregg texts and instructional materials. Authors are drawn from teaching and other personnel in colleges and universities, business teachers on the secondary school level, and Gregg personnel of its various related divisions. Writing is authoritative, and some articles are documented. (A.S.)

CU Voice. See Library Perodicals Section.

The Cameo Newsletter. 1962. 3 or 4/yr. free. James J. O'Malley, Acting Director. New York Executive Dept., Office for the Aging, 855 Central Ave., Albany, N.Y. 12206. Illus. Circ: 30,000. Sample. Vol. ends: Fall or early Winter.

Aud: Ga, Ac.

Published as a newsletter devoted to the aging and those concerned with the aging. "Its purpose is to serve as a central source of information on programs and services available to the older citizens of N. Y. State." News as reported falls into two categories, consisting of what is being done for the aging, and what they themselves are doing. State and federal legislation designed specifically to aid this age-group is reported, together with implications for them of other programs whose provisions reach a broader section of the populace. News of the projects of young people, and of other groups designed to serve senior citizens, are reported, as well as programs carried out by the senior citizens themselves, and accounts of volunteer workers from among older people who have found rewarding experiences in helping others. Rounding out the subjects covered are reports of studies being made on needs of the aging, building programs, homes for the aged, and news of appointees and the work they are doing in the Office for the Aging. This should be in all public libraries in N.Y. State, in schools where sociology is included in the curriculum, and can serve in other states as a source of ideas for possible programs and as a tool for comparison. Adequate format with some appropriate black and white illustrations; lacks a table of contents. (A.S.)

Canadian Weekly Bulletin. 1945. w. free. Mrs. M. B. Sheldon. Information Division, Department of External Affairs, Ottawa, Canada K1A, OG2. Illus. Circ: 5,000 English, 1,000 French (not distributed in Canada). Sample. Vol. ends: Dec. 31.

Aud: Ga, Hs.

A six-page, stapled newsletter which could serve admirably as a digest of current affairs for Canada. While not designed to replace a daily newspaper or extensive news magazine, it should serve to keep readers who are not in a position to read that extensively on Canada, abreast of current developments in a broad variety of subject areas. News of government includes new legislation, personnel changes, work of committees and commissions under government sponsorship, and international affairs and alliances. Material on the economics field includes all phases of production within the country, international trade, and government programs designed to boost the economic picture. Plans and programs for humanitarian concerns such as housing, public health, youth and minority groups such as the Eskimo, are reported. Canada's current interest in the arts is reflected in reports of cultural events, especially in the field of the performing arts, as well as fine arts, together with sports and recreational activities. Developments in the fields of science and technology round out the list of subjects. A few photos are used for illustration in most issues. This should be a very useful addition to the holdings of any library from secondary school level up, where there is an interest in Canada, or where a course in Canadian studies is taught. (A.S.)

Carnation. 1920. q. free. Marilyn C. Smith. Carnation Co., 5045 Wilshire Blvd., Los Angeles, CA 90036. Illus. Circ: 17,000. Sample. Vol. ends: Winter.

Aud: Ga, Hs.

The public relations organ of Carnation Co., whose interests include, in addition to dairy products, a line of pet foods and a diversified line of convenience foods, leans somewhat toward the "hard-sell" approach. One or more articles in each issue cover some specific product or special division of the company, giving a substantial but nontechnical account of manufacture, marketing, and advertising promotion. Others cover expansion, new products, and occasionally a feature on a company official who has been outstanding in his outside activities as well as in his position with the company. Some human interest material related to employees, their families, or former employees tells of some noteworthy social service projects. In the same vein, space is given to accounts of scholarships and philanthropic causes supported by the company, incentive awards, prizes, etc., which Carnation supports in generous number. Also of interest to students of television advertising will be the accounts of the making of Carnation television commercials. These include the specific qualities of the product which are being promoted as well as the staging and technical information on the filming, etc. Incorporated in some of these is material related to salesmanship, training of Carnation salesmen and their indoctrination in promotion of the specific product. A double-page spread of recipes for some unusual foods using Carnation evaporated milk or other products appears in most issues. (A.S.)

Carolina Highways. See Travel/State and Regional Section.

Collins Signal. 1933. s.-a. free. Bob Knott. Collins Radio Co., Dallas, Tex. 75207. Illus. Circ: 20,000. Sample. Vol. ends: Fall/Winter.

Aud: Ac.

The Collins motto, "Communication/Computation/Control," indicates the scope of subject matter covered. Directed to an audience of engineers and sales directors, the range extends over Collins avionics used on military aircraft, Collins communication systems on private and commercial planes, commercial satellite communication, to descriptions of specific corporations using this company's equipment and systems, their installation, purpose and operation. Some articles are primarily theoretical studies which require knowledge of communications engineering and will be of interest only to those with this background. Other articles are concerned with events where communications have played an important part, such as the voyage of the S.S. *Manhattan* through the Northwest Passage, and are of more interest to the general reader. Most articles relate theory to practical applications. A minority of the articles are signed, usually credited to personnel of the various company divisions, and all are documented where pertinent. The general high-quality format includes illustrations consisting of black and white and color photos, and sophisticated charts, diagrams, and drawings accompanying the more technical articles. (A.S.)

The Compass. 1953. s.-a. free. Marine Office, Appleton & Cox Corp., 123 William St., New York, N.Y. 10038. Illus. Circ: 11,000. Sample. Vol. ends: Fall/Winter.

Aud: Ga, Hs.

Published by an underwriter of all classes of inland and ocean marine insurance ". . . in the interests of its personnel, its member companies, its assureds, and the agents and brokers serving the marine insurance industry." Fairly long articles are comprehensive in treatment, yet geared to the general reader. Often the historical aspect of the subject is incorporated if it has a bearing. Subjects covered include the many aspects of shipping, with emphasis on unusual cargoes and the solutions to problems presented by handling them. Other topics include shipping routes, agencies concerned with, and practices being carried out to increase, safety at sea, training and certification of merchant seamen and officers, and marine museums. The problems of underwriting, as well as the advice and assistance given by the insuring agency, are incorporated in articles where they apply. Editorial comment on maritime issues is unusually good, in that all aspects of the issue are discussed, and usually a straightforward course of action suggested, which will have maximum benefit to the parties involved. Some articles are signed, and a contributor to each issue is Commander Arthur E. Wills, retired naval officer, who travels extensively to cover stories for *The Compass* as well as other marine publications. Format is pleasing, with good type and a triple column arrangement which is easy to read. Illustrations are appropriate, consisting of photos together with some sketches showing an interesting pen technique. Cover photos in full color are excellent in terms of subject matter presented. Will be of interest to anyone concerned with marine shipping and to the general reader who has an interest in the sea. (A.S.)

The Compass. 1920. q. free. K. V. W. Lawrence. Mobil Sales & Supply Corp., 150 E. 42nd St., New York, N.Y. 10017. Illus. Circ: 20,000. Sample. Vol. ends: Fall.

Aud: Ga, Ac, Hs. *Jv:* V.

Characterizes itself as a "mature magazine aimed at the international marine trade and . . . customer oriented." Because of the high quality, demand for *The Compass* is high, and publishers wish it known that distribution is perforce limited. To such libraries as qualify by virtue of marine-shipping-oriented clientele, it will be of great value. Its two primary objectives are to give readers a first-class "Magazine of the Sea," through creative design and varied story content. Stories cover many phases of the maritime world, ranging from the historical to the current, all the way from fiction to the technical aspects of a fascinating business. Subjects include ports of the world, history of the sea, new and innovative ships and marine services, operational components such as power systems, shipbuilding facilities of note, and interesting places connected with the waterways of the world. An occasional piece of fiction is directed to the interest of the seafaring man, and holds a vestige of the superstitious belief in powers of the supernatural long associated with the sea. Signed articles are substantial in length and content, authoritative and, as stated, are prepared for a mature readership. Format is exceptional. Quality of color photos is superb, both in composition and in fidelity of reproduction. Some maps are included, and the centerfold is often a reproduction of a painting or print of a historic ship. Covers open to a double-page spread consisting of a panoramic aerial photo of a port where Mobil marine fuels and lubricants are available. (A.S.)

Computing Report in Science and Engineering. 1965. 5/yr. free. Donald T. Sanders. IBM Corp., Data Processing Div., 1133 Westchester Ave., White Plains, N.Y. 10604. Illus., index. Circ: 49,000. Sample. Vol. ends: Oct. or Nov.

Aud: Ac.

The publishing statement, "distributed through IBM sales offices to persons interested in scientific and engineering applications of data processing," indicates the specialized readership for which this is intended. Each issue is composed of eight to ten articles, staff written, varying from one to four pages. Subjects selected show applications of data processing to such problems as construction, geologic investigation, meteorology, and biologic subjects, as well as the more generally known uses involving statistics and record keeping in business and education. Emphasis, of course, is on the new and extremely sophisticated systems now being developed by IBM. Illustrated with charts and diagrams where applicable, and some fine quality black and white photos. Pleasing format on quality paper, with appropriate cover designs. (A.S.)

Connchord. 1958. q. free. H. Brooks Dawson. C. G. Conn, Ltd., 616 Enterprise Dr., Oak Brook, Ill. 60521. Illus. Circ: 60,000. Sample. Vol. ends: Oct.

Aud: Ac, Hs.

Connchord is, by its stated purpose "dedicated to the advancement of music education." Its 32 pages contain several articles and features which help to promote music in general, with emphasis on public school band participation and instrumental technique. Related material includes a few historical sketches, the position of band music in the national image, proposed legislation, and the position of the adult amateur. A series, "Profiles in Music," presents a one-page biographical sketch of a prominent personality in the field of music management, performance, education or composition. Some articles are contributed by music educators, others are staff written, and average two to four pages. "News Briefs" brings to the attention of readers events, scholarships, and competitions in which teachers and students will have an interest. Music educators contribute opinions in their letters in "Sounding Board." Illustrations are adequate, size is slightly larger than digest, format is generally pleasing with some of the pages printed on colored or tinted paper. Useful in secondary schools, and in colleges training prospective music teachers. (A.S.)

Consol News. 1962. bi-m. free. Leonard S. Gross. Consolidation Coal Co., 407 Monongahela Bldg., Morgantown, W.Va. 26505. Illus. Circ: 20,500. Sample. Vol. ends: Nov./Dec.

Aud: Ga.

Serves both as an employee news source, and as a source of general information on coal mining and related industries. News of the various mines and divisions of this rapidly expanding company accounts for at least half of the magazine content, and here the emphasis is on development of new facilities and improvement of others, and on personnnel changes, awards, etc. Other articles, of interest to the general reader, show the endeavors of the coal industry to sponsor research, to promote utilization of its waste products, and to combat pollution problems. Safety is often stressed. Also reported are the activities of the Consolidation Coal Co. in the field of vocational, technical, and mining engineering education, such as scholarships for higher education in the Appalachian area, the company's training program, and its active recruitment of personnel. Illustrations are mostly black and white photos, and while there are some in which the personalities are dominant, there are also some good quality shots showing industrial plants, mine operations, etc. This will be of interest where material showing various phases of coal and related industries is needed. (A.S.)

Consumer Alert. See Consumer Services.

Consumer Price Index. See Consumer Services.

Contemporary Education. See Education/General Section.

Cooperation. 1914. q. free. G. J. Bayles. Kimberly-Clark Corp. Main Office, Neenah, Wis. 54956. Illus. Circ: 24,000. Sample. Vol. ends: Fall.

Aud: Ga, Hs.

A general-interest magazine, primarily internal, but

designed to help tell the story of this large manufacturer of paper and paper products. Service-related and human interest articles are included with those describing processes and products, and general industrial management problems and procedures. Subjects have ranged from industrial concern for drug use among workers to development of genetically superior trees for society and industry, and from the development of a new line of packaging for Kleenex tissues to Mayan artifacts found on the site of a new Kimberly-Clark factory in El Salvador. Emphasis is placed on people and activities in communities where Kimberly-Clark factories are located, especially the youthful segment of the population. Staff-written articles are illustrated with good photos and sketches. Each issue includes 10–14 pages of "Highlights" of the activities of people in or connected with the company. In addition to general interest reading, material will be most useful in showing the many and varied aspects of a large industrial concern. (A.S.)

Corvette News. 1957. bi-m. free (pub. may see fit to restrict number of free subscriptions, if excessive). J. P. Pike. Chevrolet Motor Division, General Motors Bldg., Detroit, Mich. 48202. Illus. Circ: 118,000. Sample. Vol. ends: no. 6.

Aud: Ga, Hs.

Published "for Corvette enthusiasts," and generally distributed by Corvette dealers to customers. Its 32 pages are entirely devoted to articles on racing, meets, customizing, adaptations, specifications, personalities, and news relating to this sports car and its owner. Staff-written articles vary in length, are profusely illustrated with photos and diagrams, in a single color plus black. The breezy style and esoteric vocabulary suggest the "hot rod set" and the specialized subject matter limits the appeal to this group. Included in each issue is a Corvette Club directory, with names and addresses of officers of the National Council of Corvette Clubs, Inc., and officers and addresses of local clubs listed by states. (A.S.)

Creative Ideas in Glass. 1966. q. free. W. K. Clark. ASG Industries, Inc., P.O. Box 929, Kingsport, Tenn. 37662. Illus. Circ: 23,000. Sample. Vol. ends: Fall.

Aud: Ga, Ac.

A promotional publication issued primarily for distribution to architects and specifiers. Since libraries number among their patrons a segment whose interest is in the many areas of planning buildings, the ideas included here may well be of interest in some public libraries for groups or individuals looking for ideas for new concepts in building. It may be used, as well, by colleges and schools of various sorts with responsibility for training architects and others in a position to suggest and specify types of construction. Each issue consists of five presentations of examples of new buildings featuring glass by ASG Industries. A full-page color photo for each is faced by a page with several additional views, brief description of the general features, and some detail on specific glass used and type of installation. The cover opens to a double-spread color photo of the building described in the first article in the issue. Included are commercial and municipal buildings, schools and colleges, and multiple and single unit dwellings. In addition to its value in the field of architecture, the excellent quality of the color photos and the artistic and aesthetic qualities of their composition may be useful in the study of photographic composition. Would be improved by the addition of a table of contents. (A.S.)

Dodge News Magazine. 1935. m. free. William Hinds. Dodge News Magazine, P.O. Box 7687. Detroit, Mich. 48209. Illus. Circ: 900,000. Sample. Vol. ends: Dec.

Aud: Ga, Hs.

A general-interest magazine distributed by Dodge dealers to their customers. Some very worthwhile subjects are selected for the three to four main articles in each issue. Interest range is very broad, and includes travel, sports, science, ecology and natural resource conservation, and personalities, among others. Dodge trucks and Dodge-mounted recreational vehicles are featured, with suggestions of places to see and tips for successful vacationing. Material presented is of greatest interest to active young adults, but is not confined too closely to this age bracket. Main articles are signed, well written, and nicely illustrated with many color and black and white photos. Most issues include a double-page spread on food or fashions, both interestingly presented. Regular features included in each issue are the "Views & Clues" puzzle or quiz, the "What's Your Verdict?" legal problem and decision, letters from readers, and the editor's column. The general-interest level of presentation makes this suitable for secondary schools and public libraries where additional broadly varied reading material is needed. (A.S.)

EPF Newsletter. See Religion and Theology/Counterculture Section.

Economic Review. See Business/Banking and Finance Section.

European Community. 1954. m. free. Kathleen Lynch. European Community Information Service, 2100 M Street, N.W., Washington, D.C. 20037. Illus., index. Circ: 35,000. Sample. Vol. ends: Dec.

Indexed: PAIS. *Aud:* Ga, Hs, Sa. *Bk rev:* 6–8, 75–100 words.

Taking its name from the organization whose activities it reports, *European Community* is published to help the serious, rather than the casual, reader to keep abreast of the programs of its various branches, and of the problems which stand in the way of the goal, set by the six member governments, of full economic and monetary union by 1980. Discussed in substantial, well-written articles are such subjects as status of special segments of the population, encouragement of educational cooperation across national frontiers, the role of design centers in raising standards of industrial aesthetics in production of consumer goods, among many others, both sociological and economic. Authors of articles which are signed are mostly editors and special correspondents of other leading newspapers and news magazines. "The Year in Brief," in the February issue, gives a very helpful chronological resume of events pertinent to the European Community and its member states. Included in most issues are a number of short reviews of new books "dealing with Community and Atlantic topics." Complete bibliographic information is included, together with descriptive rather 'than evaluative annotations. Adequate format with newsworthy photos in black and white and excellently presented graphs and charts. (A.S.)

Expecting. See Children/About Children Section.

FBI Law Enforcement Bulletin. See Criminology Section.

FMC Progress. 1951. 3/yr. free. George Lajeunesse. FMC Corp., P.O. Box 760, San Jose, Calif. 95106. Illus. Circ: 110,000. Sample. Vol. ends: Fall.

Aud: Ga, Hs.

"Published to create a broader understanding of how FMC Corporation serves nearly everyone in some way every day by putting ideas to work in machinery, chemicals, fibers and films, and defense." Fairly short articles, some 500 words or less, cover an exceptionally wide range of subjects. Each is related to the use of some product of this large and diverse corporation. Interest is achieved through selection of topics as widely separated as a special ingredient in vinyl padding that helps reduce sports injuries, machinery operating a new pineapple cannery in the Philippines, problems involved in producing printed circuits, and innovations in decompression chambers for Navy deep diving. Copy is divided between a general interest description of the project, and a fairly simple explanation of the machinery and/or processes involved, indicating the part played by FMC products, for promotional purposes. High quality, mostly colored photos form an integral part of the descriptions in all articles, and excellent cover photos relate to a subject in the issue. Useful where there is a need for short general-interest articles on unusual topics, and may serve some community groups with suggestions for improvements in some services. (A.S.)

Family Economic Review. See Consumer Services Section.

Federal Reserve Bank of N.Y. See Business/Banking and Finance Section.

The Fence Rider. 1937. q. free. J. W. Campbell. Armco Steel Corp., 7000 Roberts St., Kansas City, Mo. 64125. Illus. Circ: 50,000+. Sample. Vol. ends: Nov./Dec.

Aud: Ga, Hs.

"Published in the interest of good fencing," for stock farmers in the Midwest, this presents material which may be of interest to those engaged in other types of farming operations and in other geographic areas also. Articles of fairly short length present, in journalistic style, items of current interest, often with references to the successful use of various types of Sheffield fencing. Longer articles often consist of a detailed account of noteworthy livestock farming operations, describing procedures and equipment used, and sometimes some human-interest material about the owners and operators. Reports of research carried on at Midwest colleges of agriculture which have resulted in improved livestock breeding, superior strains of feed crops, etc., should prove beneficial to farmers in many areas. Short news items cover facts of interest and helpful how-to tips. Farmers in other areas may be interested to note that there is a growing interest in Oklahoma in a new livestock venture, namely, commercial catfish production. Illustrated with photos well coordinated with the text, this eight-page tabloid-size offering will be of interest to beginning agriculture students also. (A.S.)

Finance and Development. See Business/Banking and Finance Section.

Finance Facts. 1958. m. free. Dr. S. Lees Booth. National Consumer Finance Assn., 1000 16th St., N.W., Washington, D.C. 20036. Illus. Circ: 62,980. Sample. Not arranged by vol.

Aud: Ga.

This four-page newsletter, "provided as a public service by the finance and loan companies of the U.S.," summarizes and comments briefly on the current financial picture. Such subjects as young adults' income and purchasing power, school enrollment, and personal income by regions are typical of the areas explored. Figures are given in many instances, and comments made on trends, both past and future. Small but readable graphs present a wealth of material in concise form. This is a good source of up-to-date information on the finance picture as related mainly to consumer buying power. Newsletter format includes punching for use in standard ring binder. For public and all school libraries where summarized and tabulated information will supplement other sources offered. (A.S.)

Focus. 1964. m. free to libraries which are Associates of The Conference Board. (No editor given.) The Conference Board, 845 Third Ave., New York, N.Y. 10022. Illus. Circ: 36,000. Sample. Vol. ends: Dec.

Aud: Ac.

A smaller-than-digest size condenses into its 16 pages descriptions of the studies which this group undertakes and publishes. The Conference Board exists for two purposes. First, to conduct studies in any field of business or economics which is deemed to prove helpful for those in a position to guide the economy by making decisions and establishing policy. Its second purpose is the presentation of conferences and courses of study which will enable members of the top echelon of business and industry to explore topics of current importance to business and the economy. Some conference topics are of national character, some international in scope. Subjects range from sales management to industry's current pollution control costs, and from consumer attitudes and buying plans to the handling of protest at annual (corporation) meetings. Each issue contains a resume of one article from *The Record,* another publication of this group, giving enough data about the article to enable the reader to ascertain its value for him. In general, this serves to isolate and identify many of the problems and concerns of business, and to suggest at least one source (a study, or article in *The Record)* where some in-depth consideration of the problem may be found. Libraries serving business executives and institutions training them, if they are not members, should take steps to tap this source of material. (A.S.)

Focus. 1929. 1 or 2/yr. free. Ralph I. Fiester. Bausch & Lomb, 619 St. Paul St., Rochester, N.Y. 14602. Illus. Circ: 70,000. Sample. Vol. ends: Fall.

Aud: Ga.

Published to explain and promote the use of Bausch & Lomb scientific optical instruments and to promote interest in scientific investigation and research on several levels. Each issue contains two articles, of four to eight pages and fairly substantial content. Topics covered include a wide range of science and technology, and much of the material is presented on a level useful in secondary school teaching. Predictions of the impact of new technologies on such things as the office or library of the future are occasionally included. Articles are all signed, and contributors represent science teachers, laboratory personnel, and others interested in scientific research throughout the country. "For Your Information," a regular feature of about three pages, describes and suggests uses of B & L instruments. Another feature, of four to five pages, "Techniques" by Germain Crossman of the company's laboratory staff, suggests procedures and techniques and helpful tips for persons involved in the teaching of sci-

ence and in scientific laboratory work in general. The small size (6 by 9 in.), neat format, adequate illustrations and minimal advertising contribute to its value as a general scientific periodical. (A.S.)

Ford Truck Times. 1952. q. free. Henry J. Zaleski. Ford Division of Ford Marketing Corp., Dearborn, Mich. 48100. Ed. Offices: 420 Lexington Ave., New York, N.Y. 10017. Illus. Circ: 3,000,000 +. Sample. Vol. ends: Fall.

Aud: Ga, Hs.

"Provides helpful information to all truck owners, whether they drive Fords or trucks of any other make." Articles on a variety of travel, sports, adventure and general topics all include some tie-in with Ford trucks. Also given are excellent studies of driving and safety procedures for truckers. Good advice for campers is accompanied by information on models of Ford trucks and truck-mounted campers. The spring issue is sometimes almost completely devoted to recreational living and not only suggests places to see, but also outlines procedures to follow in planning, packing the camper, etc., to cut down on headaches after starting out. Each issue includes about 12 two to three page articles in its 32 pages, and all are signed except the Ford model promotional pieces. Good quality color photos illustrate all articles. Will be of use in the school or public library, mainly to those who own and use trucks of various sizes for business, and to that growing number who use trucks with or without camper bodies for pleasure. (A.S.)

Form & Function. 1965. q. free. Richard W. Bracker. United States Gypsum Co., 101 South Wacker Dr., Chicago, Ill. 60601. Illus. Circ: 120,000. Sample. Vol. ends: no. 4 (Fall).

Aud: Ga, Ac.

A "United States Gypsum publication serving the construction industry." Its 16–24 pages feature developments in the building materials field that affect design and structural systems of buildings. Descriptive studies include outstanding examples of school and college buildings, libraries, theaters, churches, public buildings and multiple-unit housing. In addition to an explanation of the steps in planning the facility for its specific purpose and the factors taken into consideration such as limitations of site, etc., most articles include some specifications and detailed descriptions of the construction features where such products as plaster and gypsum panels and acoustical and insulating materials were used. Potentials of some of this company's other products, i.e., roofing systems, adhesives and the new expanded metal webbing also are stressed. Short pieces give architects and engineers instructions for some specifics of construction where these products are used. Photos are exceptionally good, and drawings and diagrams also are used to good advantage. Subject matter will be of interest to school administrators, developers, and youth selecting a career, as well as to architects, engineers, and builders for whom *Form & Function* is primarily intended. (A.S.)

Free; the newsletter that brings you the "who's who" of free offers. 1971. bi-m. $2. Gail McNeil. Free Publns. Inc., Box 1053, Flushing, N.Y. 11352. Adv. Sample.

Aud: Ga, Ac, Hs, Ejh.

A four-page newsletter which briefly lists everything which is free, or almost free. It notes such items as a clothiers' catalog for stout men, pamphlets on everything from water to Indians, magazines, and even samples from tobacco to coffee. Full addresses and ordering information are given. Most of the material is of little value to libraries, but considering the modest price, it is well worth the investment. Not only will everyone from children to adults be interested, but it may help the library with a slim budget. Not essential, just a lot of fun. (B.K.)

The Freeman. 1950. m. free (available on request, donations invited, $5 yr). Paul L. Poirot. Foundation for Economic Education, Inc., Irvington-on-Hudson, N.Y. 10533. Illus., index. Circ: 50,000. Sample. Vol. ends: Dec. Microform: UM.

Indexed: PAIS. *Bk. rev:* 1 or 2, 1,000+ words. *Aud:* Ga, Ac.

Published for the purpose of expounding this organization's principles, stated as being: "to combat the prevailing trend toward state intervention in human affairs. F.E.E.'s method is to study and explain the alternatives to intervention: [that is] the free market, private property, limited government concepts, and the moral and spiritual principles on which this country was founded." The procedure is further outlined: "replacing interventionist notions with the freedom philosophy—the only possible antidote to an expanding socialism—involves . . . proper educational methods." Substantial articles explore in depth such subjects as poverty, violence, and protectionism, among others, and writing level assumes some background in the basic principles of sociology and economics. Of the signed articles, many are by officers and some of the trustees of F.E.E., most of whom hold positions of importance in a variety of industries and educational institutions. Although digest size, with few illustrations, this is not primarily a digest. A very few articles are excerpted from book-length works. Book reviews in each issue, some upwards of 1,000 words, evaluate one to two new books whose points of view are in agreement with the principles espoused by F.E.E. This should be used in public, college, and other libraries where a segment of the clientele is in need of this material, and where comparative political theory is studied. (A.S.)

French News. See Europe and Middle East/English Language General Section.

Friends. 1938. m. free. Alexander Suczek. Ceco Publishing Co., 17390 W. Eight Mile Rd., Southfield, Mich. 48075. (Subscriptions through courtesy of Chevrolet dealers.) Illus. Circ: 2,500,000. Sample. Vol. ends: Dec.

Aud: Ga, Hs.

Published for owners of Chevrolet autos, with subscriptions provided by local dealers. Its purpose is to provide picture articles, including a major travel article suggesting points of interest to be visited by automobile (Chevrolet, that is) in every issue. In addition to suggesting places of natural scenic beauty, *Friends* reports many annual celebrations, festivals, and other happenings, well worth visiting. Good advice is given on when to go and what to look for, and what the tourist should know about the background of the event. Subject matter is usually American, with only occasional articles on foreign subjects, and the range of topics includes sports, fashions, human interest, art, music, and theater, along with travel. Excellent quality color photography and some black and white photos are used for illustration, as well as some commercial art and maps. Writing style is designed to be compact, factual, and geared to the general reading public. A letters page and a photography page featuring contributions by readers are regular features. Two to three pages of advertising of various Chevrolet auto models and trucks are included. Its usefulness in a school library, in addition to general interest reading, would be for the travel articles which include some background material on American history and traditions, and for some material on the arts, sciences, education and crafts. (A.S.)

Frontier. 1937. s-a. free. Milton E. Nelson. IIT Research Institute, 10 W. 35th St., Chicago, Ill. 60616. Illus. Circ: 25,000. Sample. Vol. ends: Dec.

Aud: Ac.

"IIT Research Institute is an independent, contract research organization serving industry and government. Through *Frontier* magazine, it disseminates information on significant topics in the R & D field. Articles reflect the many interest areas of the staff, whose activities cover nearly all of the physical and biological sciences and their related technologies." The magazine consists of 26–30 pages of descriptions of research findings, and an occasional theoretical article on the research taxonomy, such as a very fine presentation of "Research—Innovation—Their Relationship," which appeared in a recent issue. Presentations are technical and assume a fairly extensive background knowledge of the field of specialty. Articles are signed, and qualifications of contributors are summarized at the end of the article. Authors are, of course, research experts. High quality format is in keeping with the content. Pictorial projections of the text are accomplished by clear, well-presented diagrams and some photos. For specialized libraries serving engineers and engineering students. Useful also for the study of research techniques. (A.S.)

Global Courrier. 1955. m. free. Miss Helen Laverty. Japan Air Lines, 655 Fifth Ave., New York, N.Y. 10022. Illus. Circ: 37,500. Sample. Vol. ends: Dec.

Aud: Ga, Hs.

Concentrating on places served by Japan Air Lines, articles and short news items help to inform the tourist of some of the lesser-known, as well as the much-visited attractions, and report schedules of coming events of potential interest to the traveler. Some of the longer pieces, of up to 1,200 words, include essential historical and other background information which help to make a visit more meaningful. In addition to Japan, this airline makes connections for all of the Far East and Australia, Asia, Europe and America. Many facets of Japanese culture, and customs uniquely Japanese are brought out in the travel articles. Longer articles are signed, many by members of the staff, and are generally written in first person travelogue form. Illustrations consist of photos, well chosen for their interest and subject matter. Libraries will find some of the geographical material of value, and patrons expecting to travel in Japan and other areas of the Far East will find helpful information here. (A.S.)

The Grace Log. 1918. q. free. John A. Murray. W. R. Grace & Co., 3 Hanover Square, New York, N.Y. 10004. Illus. Circ: 90,000. Sample. Vol. ends: Winter.

Aud: Ga, Ac, Hs. *Jv:* V.

W. R. Grace & Co. is an "international industrial concern with interests in chemicals, consumer products and services, and natural resources." Material in the magazine, while general in appeal, reflects the very wide spectrum of interests of this company, and a small amount of it is promotional in tone. Subjects of the 1,000–1,400 word articles cover many facets of business and economics, manufacturing processes, research and planning, and new developments related to the company's products and interests. Concerns of modern living are included, often without product tie-in, and range from outdoor recreation to one of the pet concerns of J. Peter Grace, Chairman and chief executive officer, that of libraries. "News of Grace" includes brief items relating to company changes and expansion, and personalities prominent in the company operations. Illustrations are of excellent quality, mostly in color, and especially noteworthy are some of the photos showing industrial processes. The policy of the magazine indicates that the libraries and schools on their list are a major consideration in editorial planning, and much of the material presented would most certainly be useful, especially in secondary school libraries. (A.S.)

Hercules Mixer. 1919. q. free. Cliff McGoon. Hercules Inc., Wilmington, Del. 19899. Illus. Circ: 30,000. Sample. Vol. ends: no. 4 (Fall).

Aud: Ga, Hs.

Tying in material with the wide range of products manufactured and marketed by Hercules has resulted in one of the very good general interest magazines available among the current industrial offerings. Emphasis is on the ways in which the products of this company are applied, combined, or otherwise used in a tremendous number of items which affect the everyday lives of most people. Products include chemicals of many types and for many purposes, a wide range of synthetics, explosives, and fibers and films. Some exceptionally good articles give descriptions of complete manufacturing facilities, including discussion of the product, steps in manufacturing and marketing, reason for selection of the manufacturing site, relationship to raw materials and potential market, and the installation itself, including equipment and storage facilities. Subject matter for many interesting articles is found in accounts of outside activities of Hercules employees, unusual vacations, fascinating hobbies and recreations, or social service projects. Economic data and other business information, training programs, and ecological topics help to round out the subject areas presented. Quality of photos used for illustration varies from good to superb, the latter category being applicable to the travel photos used with articles discussing foreign countries in which Hercules has operations. Many data are presented in the form of graphs, which in addition serve as excellent examples of this kind of illustration. This should be useful quite generally. (A.S.)

The Humble Way. 1945. q. free. Downs Matthews. Humble Oil and Refining Co., P.O. Box 2180, Houston, Tex. 77001. Illus. Circ: 150,000. Sample. Vol. ends: 4th q.

Indexed: PAIS. *Aud:* Ga.

A high quality offering of another of the major oil companies achieves a wide variety of subject matter with and without direct connection to the company's operations. Six substantial articles per issue choose such subjects as oil exploration and ancillary material on the land and water areas affected. A favorite subject seems to be the natural history of marshes, shore areas and other regions of unique natural beauty and geologic importance. Other articles are, occasionally, somewhat philosophical studies of environmental influences on man, and accounts of minority races and the attempts being made to encourage and preserve their cultural heritage while improving their economic status. Signed articles are credited to well-qualified authors and staff writers, with authors' backgrounds often noted. Excellent overall design, fine quality illustrations consisting of professional color photos and original artwork by competent illustrators. An excellent general interest magazine for almost all libraries. (A.S.)

Hyster Space. 1949. varies, 2 to 4/yr. free. Dennis G. Bitton. Hyster Company, P.O. Box 2902, Portland, Oreg. 97208. Illus. Circ: 65,000 Sample. Vol. numbers not used.

Aud: Ga, Hs.

Claiming to be ". . . designed to mail directly to potential and existing customers for Hyster industrial trucks," this magazine includes items which are written with this purpose in mind, making it primarily a sales tool. Its 16–20 pages show examples of the many models of this company's machines at work on the various types of jobs they are designed to do. Builders, shippers and warehouse operators, road builders and others with heavy loads to be lifted and positioned neatly and efficiently should get some ideas on the newest methods. Photos, an integral part of the presentation, are conceived to show these vehicles at work, and are well reproduced. Overall design is excellent for its purpose, and there is some evidence of experimental methods of photography, although no information on the process(es) used. From this, and others of the same genre, the interested nonspecialist can pick up a wealth of information on the current trends in shipping and cargo handling, such as "containerization." Youth interested in shipping and/or large vehicle operation, as a hobby or as a possible career, should find this fascinating. (A.S.)

Idaho Wildlife Review. 1948. bi-m. free. Milton T. Williams. Idaho Fish and Game Dept., 600 S. Walnut St., Boise, Idaho 83707. Illus. Circ: 29,000. Sample. Vol. ends: May/June.

Aud: Ga, Hs.

Stating as its purpose, "Dedicated to conservation, wise use and management of wildlife resources in Idaho," this 16-page magazine for both the sportsman and the conservationist includes well-written, authoritative information of interest to both, Wildlife studies, species and habitat descriptions, activities of state and national conservation agencies and of private sportsmen's groups constitute the bulk of the articles. The position of the hunter and fisherman in relation to the control of wildlife population is carefully considered and this "thumb of man on the balance of nature" is accepted as a sometimes desirable factor along with other controls. Although limited, of course, to activities and conditions in Idaho, the material is not limited in interest, and much of it is applicable to other states and regions. Useful in school and public libraries for material on wildlife management and the current ecological crisis. (A.S.)

Ideas for Better Living. 1945. m. free. James H. Mc-Gavran. Savings & Loan Publns., 1755 Northwest Blvd.,

Columbus, Ohio 43212. Illus., adv. Circ: 400,000+. Sample. Vols. vary with each individual local edition. *Bk. rev:* 15–16, 30 words avg. *Aud:* Ga, Hs.

Distributed through savings and loan associations in most major cities throughout the country. Requests for subscriptions, however, should be directed to the editor at the above address. Planned mainly for home owners or prospective builders of individual homes, each issue devotes several pages to new ideas in furniture, built-ins, new building materials being used with success and new concepts in home and neighborhood planning, all presented to help the home buyer make a wise and satisfying investment. House plans, usually four per issue, with sketches and capsule description, give the essential features. (Plans and specifications are available from sponsoring banks.) Two regular features are worth noting. A page of recipes is planned around a special occasion, often with serving suggestions. A single page "Bookshelf" in each issue lists new books in four categories, fiction, nonfiction, mysteries and juveniles, with a sentence annotation for each. Advertising on the insides of both covers calls attention to businesses in the immediate vicinity of the sponsoring bank. Should be useful in public libraries serving areas where there is individual housing, for beginning home-making classes, and anywhere there is need for a variety of house plans for consideration. The 16-page format is adequate, with a single color added to the black and white illustrations on some pages. (A.S.)

Industrial Gerontology. See Aging Section.

Inland Now. 1942. q. free. Van Lesley. Inland Steel Co., 30 W. Monroe St., Chicago, Ill. 60603. Illus. Circ: 45,000. Sample. Vol. ends: no. 4.

Aud: Ga, Hs.

In addition to the employees, for whom it is published, *Inland Now* will be of interest to those seeking information on the steel and housing industries, and on industrial management. In-depth articles, with clear, well-chosen photos, tell the complete story of some of the many facets of the steel and housing industries. Characteristics of those successful in management and operation of a large, diversified business are included within sketches of individuals prominent in this company's operations. Industrial planning, steelmaking developments, and quality control are also discussed, relative to the steel industry, but with implications for any other industry of similar size. In the area of housing, articles deal with the company's full spectrum of building activity, from mobile homes and single-family dwellings to large-scale urban renewal projects. Comments by the president, the chairman of the board or other top officers on the economy in general and its effect on steel, housing and related industries, reflect the viewpoint of top-level management. The 24–28 pages per issue, of well-written material, will be useful where the overall picture of a large, diversified industry is needed. Illustrations are black and white photos in generous quantity, providing excellent pictorial material on steelmaking and the shelter industry. (A.S.)

International Harvester Farm. 1915. q. free. J. B. Mann, Editorial Supervisor. International Harvester Co., 401 N. Michigan Ave. Chicago, Ill. 60611. Illus. Circ: 1,000,000. Sample. Vol. ends: Fall.

Aud: Ga, Hs.

Published "to help make farm life easier and more profitable," by showing uses of this company's tractors and other farm equipment. Articles show optimum use of many types of tractor-mounted planters, harvesters, etc., emphasizing their efficiency in the specialized jobs they have been designed to do. Accounts of farm operation, some of unique situations where ingenuity has played a large part in the success of the operation, are centered around the farmers who do the planning and make decisions. All serve as examples of the use of IH equipment. Other subjects covered, all with a view to better farm and machinery management, include news and comments on federal farm programs, information on desirable new crop strains and their potential uses, special services for farmers such as specialized local weather reporting for agriculture, and a few purely seasonal short pieces. A recent feature is a page on safety giving timely advice on ways to make fieldwork safer. Accounts are fairly short, factual and well organized, and credited mainly to the magazine staff and research personnel of IH. Most illustrations are in color and many show equipment in use. Only an occasional cover is a rural art shot. Useful where additional material on farming, on the practical level, is needed. (A.S.)

International Police Academy Review. See Criminology Section.

J M Action. 1930. q. free. Edward R. LiPuma. Johns-Manville Corp., 22 E. 40th St., New York, N.Y. 10016. Illus. Circ: 50,000. Sample. Vol. ends: Fall.

Aud: Ga.

Asbestos products, mainly roofing and pipe, form the company tie-in for most of the material in this 30 + page compact. Coverage is world-wide, showing uses of these products in new building developments in some of the emerging nations, and in cities of the United States and Canada. Emphasis is on progress, examples showing how existing conditions are being improved, and how a new life-style is being developed through the use of improved building materials to provide better housing. Additional products whose use is described include such other building materials as decorative and acoustical wall and ceiling panels, insulating materials for many industrial uses, chemicals for agriculture, and a recently developed antipollution "fence" for containment and elimination of floating oil

spills. All staff-written articles are directed to the general reader. Illustrations are mainly black and white photos showing installation of products. Will have some use where additional material on these types of building materials is needed. (A.S.)

JSAC Grapevine. See Religion/Counterculture Section.

Journal of Nursing Education. See Medical Sciences/Nursing Section.

Kaiser News. 1946. irreg. free (small handling charge for bulk orders). Don Fabun. Kaiser Aluminum & Chemical Corp., 300 Lakeside Dr. KB 765, Oakland, Calif. 94604. Illus. Circ: 120,000 initial press run, several issues to 500,000. Sample. Vol. ends irregularly, depending on series.

Aud: Ga, Ac, Hs. *Jv:* V.

A truly outstanding offering, published by Kaiser "as a kind of exploration of significant subjects for its friends throughout the world." From the selection of subjects for "exploration," the challenging ideas presented in the essays which make up each issue, and the competent literary style, to the unified concept of design and appropriate illustrations, this rates as a cut above the large number of house magazines which we consider close to the top in fine quality. Evaluation is being made on examination of a series of six issues entitled "The Markets of Change," recently published, in which each issue explores an individual topic as part of the larger subject, based on the thesis that "the inputs of technology are rapidly changing our value systems." Writing, attributed to the editor, shows an excellent command of the subject matter and professional expertise in the medium of presentation. The conversational tone of writing, rather than resulting in a casual presentation, is actually carefully calculated to be stimulating. It is further enhanced by the copious use of quotations from a wide variety of authors' books and magazine articles, all fully documented. Written for what we like to call "the informed generalist," there is an assumption of somewhat above average education and background in vocabulary and familiarity with concepts incorporated in the development of ideas. Original illustrations are obviously the work of top-level professional artists and represent some innovative approaches to complement the mind-stretching nature of the subject matter. New techniques are employed by the magazine's art director, and others, to produce photos of outstanding beauty and contemporary mood. Drawings from museums and other collected sources are reprinted. Fidelity of reproduction is in keeping with the high quality of the total format. A valuable addition to any library serving adults who enjoy and appreciate the challenge of stimulating ideas on topics of urgent current concern. (A.S.)

Kansas. See Travel/State and Regional Section.

The Lamp. 1918. q. free. Jack Long. Standard Oil Co. (New Jersey), 30 Rockefeller Plaza, Room 1626, New York, N.Y. 10020. Illus. Circ: 800,000. Sample. Vol. ends: Winter.

Indexed: Self-indexed, every three years, available on request. *Aud:* Ga, Hs.

While "published primarily for shareholders and employees . . ." and centered around material relating to the oil industry, this has a reader interest much wider than this segment of the public. Its international scope has much to offer to the field of education. Its chief concern is information and interpretation of the company and its business, and various facets of company operation are included. For instance, its computer system and a training program for tanker sea captains each make an interesting article. Others, in about equal number, are a valuable source of information on some aspects of modern life in many parts of the world. Emphasis is on human resources, especially training programs, etc., being undertaken. Also included are unusual travel articles, performances or celebrations of unusual interest, historical items in the field of transportation, and accomplishments of modern engineering. "Panorama," a regular feature with a two-page spread, reports interesting short items, both technical and nontechnical. Each issue contains an editorial written by the chairman of the board, explaining or commenting on some aspect of company policy. Articles are generally substantial, all are well written, and most are signed. The table of contents always appears on the outside back cover, with a short paragraph of explanation of the article, a note about the author if not a staff member, and a few additional illustrations. Its excellent illustrations consist of colored photographs of remarkable quality, some paintings and sketches by qualified illustrators, art reproductions and a few charts. (A.S.)

Light Magazine. 1928. s-a. free. Ted R. Carmack. Braille Inst. of America, Inc., 741 N. Vermont Ave., Los Angeles, Calif. 90029. Illus. Circ: 75,000. Sample. Vol. ends: Autumn.

Aud: Ga, Ac, Hs.

The Institute is a "nonprofit California corporation established for the purpose of furthering the educational, social and economic advancement of blind people without regard to race, color or creed." Each issue is comprised of 24 pages of generously illustrated staff-written accounts of types of training available and programs being carried on for cultural as well as economic betterment. Interesting also are such subjects as experiences arranged for blind persons, examples being a visit to an art exhibit designed for tactile exploration, athletic programs for the blind, and music lessons for blind children. One page in each issue out-lines this institute's free educational services to the blind of all ages. For any library where there is need for information on methods of teaching the blind and types of programs available to them, and schools on all levels offering sociology courses will want to include this as supplementary material on this integral part of social service work. (A.S.)

Llewellyn. See Occult and Witchcraft Section.

The Locomotive. 1867. q. free. John R. Eklund. The Hartford Steam Boiler Inspection and Insurance Co., 56 Prospect St., Hartford, Conn. 06102. Illus. Circ: 58,000. Sample. Vol. ends: Winter.

Indexed: Self-indexed with the bound vol. which includes two years. *Aud:* Ga, Ac.

Claiming the distinction of being "the country's oldest company magazine published continuously under the same name," this is intended primarily for owners and operators of boilers and power equipment. The name, of course, dates back to the era when the steam locomotive was a most widely used form of steam boiler. Material now being published covers a wide range of industrial boiler usage, as well as other steam and power equipment. Since the parent company is an insuring body, material is presented with a view to increasing the safe operation of this type of installation. This is done by descriptions of accidents which have occurred, together with an analysis of causes, and by suggesting safety measures and trouble warnings to look for. Safety principles expounded in some of the articles are applicable to any type of industry, and an occasional article is purely theoretical. Most of the material requires a knowledge of the basic operational principles, and vocabulary used assumes some background in the field. Authors of signed articles are engineers on the company staff. Occasionally an article is reprinted from another specialized journal. Useful mainly to those engaged in, or studying for a career in boiler operation, for maintenance personnel, the technically inclined layman, or steam boiler buff. (A.S.)

Lykes Fleet Flashes. 1933. m. free. Larry Guerin. Lykes Bros. Steamship Co., Inc., P. O. Box 53068, New Orleans, La. 70150. Illus. Circ: 12,000. Sample. Vol. ends: Dec.

Aud: Ga, Hs.

An excellent general interest offering by the operator of a major fleet of cargo vessels serving shipping in the Gulf of Mexico, and between the southeastern U.S. and major ports of the world. Subject matter in the articles, of varying length, has some relation to shipping. Lykes operations, new ships, and innovations in design are presented along with interesting types of cargo carried, as diverse as amusement park rides and fertilizer. Each issue includes one substantial article on a major port of the world, with emphasis on its shipping facilities, berthing, warehouse storage, lifting equipment, etc., and also includes some historical information on its importance as a port. A column, "Along the Cargo Lanes . . . ," introduces the prospective freighter passenger to a port or city of interest, pointing out the usual and some out-of-the-way sights to see when touring the area. Black and white photos illustrate all articles, and show Lykes ships in major ports of the world, good shots of various stages of ship building and details of operation, as well as photos of many Lykes personnel. May be useful from junior high up for some interesting accounts of shipping by water as supplementary curriculum material, as a means of showing the large force of personnel necessary to keep a fleet in operation, and for that small but select group of confirmed freighter passengers, as well as the dry-land sailors in every community. (A.S.)

MSU Business Topics. See Business/General Section.

Marathon World. 1965. q. free. Joe Callanan. Marathon Oil Co., 539 S. Main St., Findlay, Ohio 45840. Illus., index. Circ: 85,000. Sample. Vol. ends: no. 4.

Aud: Ga, Ac, Hs. *Jv:* V.

A quality magazine whose purpose seems to be the creation of an image of Marathon Oil Co. as a major producer, refiner, and marketer, with a mature viewpoint on the position of industry in present society. The selection of topics, level of presentation, and general design do much to accomplish this purpose. Each issue includes six to eight articles covering a variety of topics calculated to interest the general reader. Included is material relating to the expansion of the oil industry, geographical material emphasizing industrial expansion and its impact on an area, historical items concerning the area of the north central and southeastern states which comprise the Marathon marketing area, often an article on driving or driver training, and, of course, this industry's efforts to combat pollution. An occasional reference is made to technical and engineering research being carried on by American Petroleum Institute in the field of oil spill cleanup, etc. Writing by members of a competent staff and others is generally of a professional level, and presentation is largely nontechnical. Length of articles varies with the subject matter, from a 1,500-word treatise on progress being made in automobile design to reduce pollutant emissions, to a 350-word shortie on Cincinnati's new Riverfront Stadium on the Ohio, and from 2,000 words on Anchorage, Alaska, to 150 words on the new Ohio Historical Center at Columbus. The pleasing overall design includes cover art especially created and tied in with one of the articles. Some articles are illustrated with artwork which has been especially commissioned, and where color photos are used, they are of excellent quality. Artists are drawn from successful illustrators, and the art director and his staff are credited with the remainder of the fine illustrative

material. This should be well received by readers of public libraries, and will be useful in secondary schools. (A.S.)

Metropolitan Life Insurance Company Statistical Bulletin. See Health Section.

Michigan Business Review. See Business/General Section.

Microcard Bulletin, Microcosm, and Micropublisher. See *Microform Review* in Books and Book Reviews Section.

Mother's Manual. See Children/About Children Section.

Mothers-To-Be. See Children/About Children Section.

The Motorcycle Enthusiast in Action. 1926. m. free to factory-registered owners of Harley-Davidson vehicles, to libraries on request, others $1.00. T. C. Bolfert. Harley-Davidson Motor Co., Inc., 3700 W. Juneau, Milwaukee, Wis. 53201. Illus. Circ: 110,000. Sample. Vol. ends: Dec.

Aud: Ga, Hs.

The *Enthusiast* is devoted specifically to motorcycles and motor scooters built by Harley-Davidson, and published for the age-group dedicated to motorcycling as a sport or means of transportation. News of all categories of motorcycle racing and championships, and of some of the racing personalities, is featured, and accounts for the bulk of the material in each issue. One or two feature articles in each issue describe trips or tours taken by motorcycle in the U. S. or abroad. Engineering and manufacturing of the various models made by this company are also occasional subjects, as are other uses of motorcycles, such as police work. Photos, including many action shots, are of good quality. The oversize (11½ by 14½ in.) double-folded format is a little awkward for library use, but not prohibitive. This will be well received by the population of secondary schools, where a student's first "wheels" are likely to be a motorcycle. (A.S.)

NATO Letter. See Political Science Section.

Negro Book Club Newsletter. See Blacks Section.

Negro Braille Magazine. See Blacks Section.

Norelco Reporter. 1953. 2 to 4/yr. free. R. N. Rose. Philips Electronic Instruments, 750 S. Fulton Ave., Mt. Vernon, N.Y. 10050. Illus. Circ: 12,000. Sample. Vol. ends: no. 2 to no. 4.

Aud: Ac, Ga. *Jv:* V.

A specialized magazine, produced by the manufacturer of "Instrumentation for research, materials control and production automation," for users and potential users of electron microscopes and related tools of microanalysis, x-ray diffraction equipment, other x-ray devices, and electronic inspection and measuring instruments. Articles, five to eight per issue, consist of accounts of the uses of these instruments for the many types of investigation for which they have been designed, in medical, industrial and pure research. Substantial, detailed material is written for graduate engineers engaged in the research which utilizes microscopic investigation in all its current sophisticated diversity. Presentation assumes this background. Contributors, fully credited, are research scientists of this and other large industrial concerns and personnel of leading U. S. universities and their related research institutes. Illustrations are fine quality, well-reproduced photos of microscopic enlargements, pictures of various pieces of equipment, and diagrams which further clarify the presentations. This will be useful for the libraries serving scientists engaged in these types of research, and the executives responsible for planning and administering research programs for industry, the government, medical and other research institutes. (A.S.)

O-I Outlook. 1961. m. free. Dick Roberts. Owens-Illinois, Inc., P.O. Box 1035, Toledo, Ohio, 43601. Illus. Circ: 42,000. Sample. Vol. ends: Dec.

Aud: Ga, Hs.

While published primarily for employees, this 8–12-page newsletter reports activities on all levels of company operation. Status of the company's standing and explanations of decisions regarding company policy are reported to employees and others interested. Efforts of this company to encourage recycling of glass waste, as well as programs to combat all types of pollution, are highlighted. New installations, uses of O-I glass products, and accounts of some of the unusual individual orders filled, such as a giant telescope mirror blank, are reported along with employee news. Safety programs are sometimes stressed, and participation in civic projects is recognized. Especially noteworthy is a special edition recently published, entitled "We Have to Care," telling what the company is doing to protect the environment, listing its accomplishments, and taking a look at some unsolved problems. Tabloid-size four-column format employs a journalistic style and news-type photos. Will be useful where material on the glass industry and on the management of a large manufacturing concern will be helpful. (A.S.)

Occasional Papers. See Library Periodicals Section.

Off Center. See Library Periodicals Section.

Oil; Lifestream of Progress. 1951. q. free. Peter A. Kozack. Caltex Petroleum Corp., 380 Madison Ave., New York, N.Y. 10017. Illus. Circ: 50,000. Sample. Vol. ends: Fourth quarter.

Aud: Ga, Hs.

Caltex Petroleum Corporation, with interests throughout most of the eastern hemisphere, uses its excellent 24-page magazine to help interpret the role of petroleum in the modern world. Articles cover a wide variety of topics within the general areas of international industry and trade, communications and unusual tourist attractions, and events of international interest. There is some emphasis on the Far East in the selection of topics. Especially valuable for their content and pictures are the articles on what modern engineering is doing to help modernize underdeveloped areas. While there is generally a company tie-in, it is done tastefully and unobtrusively. Editorial tone is uncritical, and stresses achievement and long range planning. Articles are unsigned, and credit for good writing must go to the fine editorial staff. Each of the four articles is profusely illustrated with very good photos and sketches, and maps and charts are used where pertinent. Each article, listed on the contents page (page 1), is briefly summarized following its title in bold type, and an explanation of the cover photograph is given on the same page. It is indicated that 90 percent of the circulation is directed to more than sixty countries throughout the eastern hemisphere, and is designed to reach opinion leader audiences. (A.S.)

Olin Magazine. 1967. 3/yr. free. Walter H. Frommer. Olin Corp., 460 Park Ave., New York, N.Y. 10022. Illus. Circ: 55,000–60,000. Sample. Vol. ends: Oct. (no. 3).

Aud: Ga, Hs.

At the rate of one article to describe the operation of one of its subsidiary plants, the testing and developing of a new product, or an ancillary production based on the use of something supplied by Olin, in six–eight articles per issue, *Olin Magazine* will be assured of fresh subject matter indefinitely. As possibilities for subjects, add the related use of some Olin product as one ingredient or component of manufacture, and possibilities are limitless. Products range from chemicals, plastics, paper and wood products, to sporting arms and ammunition and outdoor sports equipment, from energy systems, fastenings and tools, to packaging machinery, with one subsidiary division engaged in developing and building residential communities and business properties. Olin's Winchester Adventures, a travel service, offers trips to six continents, including camera safaris in Africa and skin diving in the Bahamas. In addition, topics are drawn from several other fields in which Olin feels an interest, such as concerns which tend to improve the quality of life, civic pride, ecology, education, the fight against crime, etc. Announcement of books published by Winchester Press is included, with brief descriptions. Quality of color reproductions used for illustration is outstanding, complementing the fine format in general. An excellent source of general interest material for all libraries except the specialized. (A.S.)

Opportunity. 1971. 10/yr. free. Herschel Cribb. Office of Public Affairs, Office of Economic Opportunity, 1200 19th St., N. W., Washington, D.C. 20506. Illus. Circ: 70,000. Sample. Vol. ends: Dec.

Aud: Ga, Hs.

Programs being carried on for, and/or by, the poor constitute the bulk of the material in this Office of Economic Opportunity vehicle. Accounts cover, in some detail, specific projects designed to raise standards, mostly economic, with a few covering cultural aspects where they represent an improvement in the outlook, or self-image, of low-income economic or racial minority groups. Topics include, among others, actual "poverty" programs, educational innovations which are having some success in this field, legal aid for the poor, and health and dental care services and ways in which they are being carried to the poor. Some material is presented according to the various groups for whom it is intended, such as migrants, the low-income aged, the inner-city poor, those in rural areas of poverty, etc. OEO programs and projects in various areas are reported, and range from helping convicts to attend college while still serving time, to the administration of Atlanta's extensive program. Of great interest also are the economic success stories showing ways in which unique local talents have been organized and marketed, such as the sewing and handicraft industries of Appalachia being translated into high fashion throughout the country, and into good income for a formerly unemployed segment. Credit is given, often, to dedicated individuals or small independent groups who have had the compassion to see a need and the determination to enact a program to administer to it, often against formidable odds. All articles are several pages in length, are fairly comprehensive, and are written on a general interest level. Some, but not all, are signed, and an occasional article is reprinted from a regional news source or established periodical of national scope. It is nicely composed, with appropriate illustrations. Will be useful in public libraries, and in those serving institutions which offer sociology courses on any level. (A.S.)

The Orange Disc. 1933. bi-m. free. R. D. Lagenkamp. Gulf Oil Corp., Gulf Bldg., Pittsburgh, Pa. 15230. Illus. Circ: 240,000. Sample. Vol. ends: July/Aug.

Aud: Ga, Hs.

The company's petroleum interests in many parts of the world provide the subject matter for the majority of the articles in each issue. Pictorial essays of some of the large refineries and transshipment terminals of the world are especially well done. Other geographic material is presented as a study for one city, region, etc., with perceptive descriptions of its economy and culture as well. Photos accompanying these articles are outstanding, with many panoramic aerial views used, all in color. Some touristic material, without company tie-in, covers subjects as widely separated as historic houses in the United States, an art fair in Ireland, and ski racing in Scandinavia. The concern of the directors of the corporation for education is reflected in articles stating views on current educational policy or reporting special programs devised to raise the standards of the underprivileged. Imaginative, fine quality cover art amounts to a photo "essay" on a specific theme for each issue, and makes an inviting introduction. Written for the secondary school to adult reader, this will be useful where additional general interest material is needed, and will be notable for its format wherever used. (A.S.)

Our Sun. 1920. q. free. Charles E. Petty. Sun Oil Co., Corporate Public Relations, 1608 Walnut St., Philadelphia, Pa. 19103. Illus. Circ: 85,000. Sample. Vol. ends: Winter.

Aud: Ga, Hs.

A high quality offering of one of the major petroleum companies, this provides some worthwhile material. Each issue highlights a special theme on its cover and in three or more separate articles related to the topic. A few recent choices: "The Coming Energy Crunch," "Alaska, the Great Land," and "Special Issue on the Environment" serve to indicate the range of subject matter. Topics are related to Sun Oil's operations in many locations throughout the world, and usually provide supplemental geographic or other general interest material. Single articles fill out the six to eight per issue, on subjects related to transportation, agriculture, and a variety of others related in some way to a special use of petroleum products. Like most major oil companies, Sun uses this organ to try to explain the perspective which the oil industry has accepted, between the conservation of wildlife and other natural resources, and the tapping of the earth's crust for that natural resource so much in demand, petroleum. Well-written articles are complemented generously by fine quality photos, some of which deserve to be judged as prize-winning examples of color photography in both composition and technique. (A.S.)

Outdoors; the magazine of outdoor recreation. 1958. m. Lee Cullimore. Outdoors, Inc., Outdoors Bldg., Columbia, Mo. 65201. Illus. Sample. Vol. ends: May.

Aud: Ga, Hs.

The subtitle, indicates the purpose of this popularly written magazine. The eight–nine articles of each issue are intended to promote outdoor recreational activities connected mainly with boating, and to a lesser extent, snowmobiling. Subjects covered include places suitable for boating vacations and recreation, accounts of particular excursions, reports of fishing conditions and/or prospects, and some attention to recreational parks and isolated seashore areas. Usually there are also articles on wildlife resources, suggesting areas where some may be enjoyed, and also some species studies on a general rather than a specialized scientific level. Some articles refer to Mercury Outboard motors, although emphasis on models is minimal. Signed articles, many from contributors outside the magazine staff, will appeal to the general reader who may have found an interest in these two types of outdoor recreation. Well arranged for a pleasing overall effect, it is also illustrated with many very good black and white photos. Subscriptions and samples may be available to school and public libraries through the courtesy of local Mercury Outboard dealers. (A.S.)

Oxycat. 1968. q. free. J. Merle Smith. Oxy-Catalyst, Inc., West Chester, Pa. 19380. Illus. Circ: 4,000. Sample. Vol. ends: Fall.

Aud: Ga, Hs.

The subtitle, *Environmental Control News*, indicates the purpose and content of this four-page newsletter. Articles in journalistic style tell how this company's devices are helping to solve pollution problems related to sewage treatment fumes, waste from solvents used in industrial processes, and exhaust fumes from automotive engines, to name a few. Editorial comment is offered also, on federal and other regulations relating to pollution abatement, with straightforward discussion of the implications for industries involved. Presentation assumes an interest and a minimal amount of technical background in this field. Photos used help to show the company's products in operation. This will be of interest primarily to industrial executives concerned with the decision-making level of implementing pollution control, and to those making a study of the subject. (A.S.)

Petroleum Today. 1959. 3/yr. free. Robert L. Feuquay, Jr. Amer. Petroleum Inst., 1801 K St., N.W., Washington, D.C. 20006. Illus., index. Circ: 110,000. Sample. Vol. ends: Fall.

Indexed: PAIS. *Aud:* Ga, Hs.

"Published by the Institute's Committee on Public Affairs as a contribution to public understanding of the petroleum industry." Its policy further claims to avoid the "highly technical or promotional aspect," which it does. Material is presented, naturally, from the management viewpoint of the industry. Signed, very well written articles cover topics of general interest on all phases of petroleum and related products and activities. A wide variety is achieved within these limitations, including such aspects as exploration, experimentation and research, background material on localities, related products, operations, and personalities. Recent issues have included excellent articles on wildlife and other natural resources, and a responsible

viewpoint is evident toward the preservation of ecological balance, while supplying the world's need for oil. Length of articles varies, as does relative amount of text to number of illustrations, but all articles are nicely illustrated in black and white and in color, with drawings and sketches, and some beautiful examples of artistic color photography. (A.S.)

Philnews. 1937. m. free. Gene Hill. Phillips Petroleum Co., 4th Fl., Phillips Bldg., Bartlesville, Okla. 74003. Illus. Circ: 38,000. Sample. Vol. ends: Dec.

Aud: Ga.

The offering of a "major integrated oil company engaged in virtually every phase of the petroleum industry and in many petrochemical activities." Articles, some reprinted from other sources, include as subjects some of the many phases of petroleum exploration, refining and distribution, and related material such as plastics and synthetic fibers. Phillips has oil and gas exploration interests in 21 countries. Other products which are petroleum derivatives are described in articles which explain their use in specific instances. Outside activities of some Phillips employees, such as police volunteers in Kansas City, make interesting reading. Employee news accounts for several pages in each issue. Many good black and white photos enhance the presentation of general-interest-level material on the petroleum industry. The 32-page, 6 by 8½ in. format is adequate for its purpose, while less pretentious than some of the other oil company offerings. Will be useful where such supplementary material is needed. (A.S.)

Pool 'N Patio. See Interior Design Section.

Power From Oil. 1967. q. free. D. A. Burack. Metropolitan Petroleum Co., 380 Madison Ave., New York, N.Y. 10017. Illus. Circ: 20,000. Sample. Vol. ends: Summer.

Aud: Ga, Hs.

Not as pretentious as some other house offerings, yet this has enough to commend its 12 pages as an additional source of material on some commercial means of pollution control. Fairly short articles, illustrated with photos and/or diagrams, will be useful in secondary schools to bring to the attention of students studying means of pollution control concise accounts of some specific procedures now being used to combat oil spills, stack emissions, etc. Some simplified technical material on various phases of oil-fired boiler operation is included in most issues, the emphasis being on explanation of the mechanics and definition of terms, hopefully to improve the performance of such installations. The remainder of the material presented is almost completely concerned with new developments in the search for new oil sources, and its transportation by various means. Published by a company serving the northeastern states and Canada, its offering is geared primarily to industry and institutions using fuel oil for heating. This stands as an example of a growing company attempting to take a "responsible, professional approach" to the economics of its field, the distribution of industrial fuels, heating oils, and chemical conditioners. (A.S.)

Power Parade. 1948. q. free. E. J. Baldwin. Detroit Diesel Allison Div., General Motors Corp., 13400 W. Outer Dr., Detroit, Mich. 48228. Illus. Circ: 245,000. Sample. Vol. ends: Dec.

Aud: Ga, Hs.

"A magazine for the information and entertainment of users of heavy-duty power," its interest extends beyond "users," to those concerned with related industry, to students of industry and social studies, and to young people faced with the selection of a career. Material is chiefly application of case histories of equipment using GM diesel engines that perform outstanding or interesting work. New products, road building, major construction projects, and marine use of diesel power are frequent subjects. Mining and quarrying, truck and bus transportation, standby power systems, irrigation for agriculture, tug and other workboat operation, as well as pleasure craft sailing, illustrate some of the many other uses for this energy source. Staff-written articles run from one to six pages in length and highlight the performance and desirability of various GM diesel engine models. Value of the material is increased by profuse full-color illustrations of exceptionally high quality. Diagrams and maps are occasionally added to further illustrate the subject matter. High quality paper and pleasing typeface are other good features. (A.S.)

Prisoner's Rights Newsletter. See Criminology Section.

RCA Broadcast News. 1932. q. free. P. A. Greenmeyer. RCA Corp., Broadcast Div., Camden, N.J. 08102. Illus. Circ: 8,000. Sample. Vol. ends: Fall.

Aud: Ga, Ac, Hs. *Jv:* V.

As the name indicates, content of the eight to ten articles per issue centers around all aspects of the technical side, and around some of the business of programming, of television broadcasting. This company's products are shown in operation and discussed in articles of substantial length. Cameras, transmitters, controls, etc., are also described, with the necessary technical information, in "Products in the News," comprising about four full pages of each issue. Interesting information on television stations outside the United States is often included. Presentation assumes some technical background in the field. High quality format consists of good layout, pleasing type, and fine quality photos, many in color, in an average 48 pages. This will be of use in school and public libraries where there is some interest in technical aspects of television

broadcasting, and in technical schools where this is included in the curriculum. (A.S.)

Redbook's Young Mother. See Children/About Children Section.

Rockwell Standard News. 1932. q. free. William Toderan. North American Rockwell Corp., Clifford at Bagley, Detroit, Mich. 48231. Illus. Circ: 66,000. Sample. Vol. ends: Winter.

Aud: Ga, Hs, Ac.

This ". . . strives to present interesting, informative and timely articles describing the activities of our customers, particularly as they pertain to the use of Automotive Group products," which include such components as axles, automative and industrial brakes, gear drive assemblies and transmissions, springs, bumpers, extruded and molded plastics, hub caps, wheel covers, torsion bars, universal joints and assemblies. Customers mentioned in the publishing statement include operators of medium to heavy trucks, and activities described make interesting reading of accounts of successful trucking companies and the means by which they conduct their operations and solve some of the problems encountered. Accounts of individual instances of noteworthy transportation and hauling feats also will have appeal to those interested in trucking, from the youth who would like to consider this as a vocation, on up. There is also material on some categories of auto racing, some recreational activities and sports, and automotive history. An occasional presentation shows the new auto models of a brand which uses this company's parts and gives some technical information on them. Editorial comment by officials of this group of North American Rockwell Corporation is presented from the managerial point of view and explains company plans and policy. Articles are well written, adequately illustrated, and thorough in their presentation, often including historical background, and must be credited to the editorial staff. (A.S.)

Rotorways. 1969. q. free. Martin C. Reisch. Bell Helicopter Co., P.O. Box 482, Fort Worth, Tex. 76101. Illus. Circ: 28,000 (controlled). Sample. Vol. ends: no. 4 (July).

Aud: Ga, Hs.

One of the leading manufacturers of helicopters does a nice job of bringing together a composite picture of helicopter use for the general reader, and for the potential user. All articles are reprinted, by permission, from other sources, and represent a diversity of viewpoints and of style of presentation. Nine or ten articles comprising each issue cover the amazing span of uses which helicopters are serving. Subjects cover the many diverse phases of industry from personnel transportation to the moving of heavy objects, to otherwise inaccessible places. Helicopter use is shown as a regular part of municipal fire and police services: as ambulance service, safety patrol, and unusual rescues in remote areas. Other uses such as air sampling, new recreational uses, the military services, and new agricultural functions may prove surprising to the general reader. Photos and artwork used for illustration vary in quality depending on the original source from which they are reprinted, but are generally good. Covers all feature outstanding color photos of helicopters in use. A useful reference feature, not usually found in house magazines, is the addition of a subject heading to each entry in the table of contents. (A.S.)

SCL News. 1967 (replacing *Atlantic Coast Line News,* 1920). bi-m. free. F. Leon Joyner. Seaboard Coast Line Railroad Co., 500 W. Water St., Jacksonville, Fl. 32202. Illus. Circ: ca. 26,000. Sample. Vol. ends: Nov./Dec.

Aud: Ga, Hs.

The publishing statement, ". . . a source of information about the Company, and in appreciation for the loyalty, cooperation and performance of all whose efforts contribute to just pride in the services rendered to its customers and to the public by the railroad," sets the tone of this 20-page offering. Adequate space is given to reports of federal legislation and programs affecting railroads, which are described, together with comments on implications. Other accounts, some largely pictorial, cover notable train runs, railroad management, and customer service operations. Reports of "Industrial Developments" in the area served by this railroad list manufacturers' new or expanded facilities. Copious short reports of news events relating to this carrier and to railroads generally keep the interested reader up to date. Employee news, safety awards and other honors, and news relating to employment status account for several pages in each issue. Staff-written articles are generally journalistic in style. Speeches, where used as articles, are fully credited. The format is adequate with many news-type photos. Useful where there is an interest in railroads and a need for condensed reports of legislation regarding them. (A.S.)

San Francisco Business. 1965. m. free. Thomas O. Caylor. Greater San Francisco Chamber of Commerce, 400 Montgomery St., San Francisco, Calif. 94104. Illus. adv. Circ: 12,000. Sample. Vol. ends: Dec. 1.

Aud: Ga, Ac, Hs. *Jv:* V.

Ranks as one of the best chamber publications in the nation, and serves as the vehicle "to promote the legitimate interests and to voice the joint concerns of a highly diverse and complex business community . . .," which is the stated purpose of the Greater San Francisco Chamber of Commerce. Its articles "tell the business community story, and speak to the business community of common problems," by analyzing issues,

pointing out the business stake in these issues, and advocating a business position on them. Material focuses on "the broader interaction of business, government and the community-at-large . . ." by debating the broader government actions that affect business. Concerns range from world trade to downtown traffic, and from aviation to middle-income housing. Most material appears to be the work of staff writers, and the claim that all issues have been carefully researched seems to be justified. "The City," a one-page column in each issue, features the perceptive analysis of principles involved in issues of current importance as viewed by members of the editorial board. The statement that it "is read by key opinion makers of the community—editors, elected officials, union business agents, business leaders, and others," indicates its intended readership. Quality format includes high-grade paper, well-reproduced photos and the use of graphs for illustration. Some advertising is included. This should have appeal to the concerned general reader, and may serve as a point of comparison for chambers of other cities confronted by similar problems, and as a model both for chamber action, and for a vehicle for presenting it. (A.S.)

Scenic South. See Travel/State and Regional Section.

Scholarly Books in America. See Books and Book Reviews Section.

School Product News. 1962. m. free to schools and colleges, not to public libraries. J. Arlen Marsh. School Product News, 614 Superior Ave. West, Cleveland, Ohio 44113. Illus., adv. Circ: 80,000. Sample. Vol. ends: Dec.

Aud: Ga, Ac.

"The . . . magazine serving administrators in public, private, sectarian, higher education, and independent school systems," provides a service in presenting information on the whole gamut of products pertinent to equipping, servicing and administering a school. Product information is given in short items under one of several sections covering instructional hardware, software and supplies, such sections being arranged with no particular continuity, and sharing all pages about equally with advertising. Included in these sections are audiovisual equipment and storage facilities, playground equipment, furniture and floor coverings, secretarial and teaching supplies, food service needs and building and maintenance equipment and supplies. New sections, such as one on environmental education, are added or dropped according to need and availability of materials. Information is clear and concise, factual rather than evaluative, but does not include prices. Readers' service cards included in each issue will secure further information for the interested administrator. A few short articles report the installation and/or use of certain products or equipment at a particular school, giving details of the item used. A book review section is included in some issues, evaluating, in staff-written reviews, one to several books related to some technical aspect of education or intended for student use. The magazine is oversize and a little hard to store, but will be a welcome addition where concise material on new products is needed. (A.S.)

Service. See Consumer Services Section.

Seventy Six. 1921. bi-m. free. Peter Craigmoe. Union Oil Co., Box 7600, Los Angeles, Calif. 90054. Illus. Circ: 50,000. Sample. Vol. ends: Nov./Dec.

Aud: Ga, Hs.

A wide range of subject matter calculated to interest the general reader is combined into an attractive 48 pages. Each issue includes up to 15 or more articles, usually with several on a related theme, or highlighting the same geographic area. The location of some of Union's drilling and refining operations determines the selection of some subjects. Indonesia, Korea and other parts of the Far East, as well as the Gulf Coast and other localities in the United States are examples. Places in this country with some touristic attraction are often included, and short articles occasionally describe celebrations and seasonal events as well. Some emphasis is placed on the petroleum refining industry, with articles on the functioning of specific installations, and on the related petrochemical products being manufactured by Union, often with details of their uses. Nicely composed and imaginatively illustrated, this will be useful where additional general-interest reading material is needed. (A.S.)

Sikorsky News. 1944. m. free. Fred Hartman. Sikorsky Aircraft, Stratford, Conn. 06602. Illus. Circ: 17,000. Sample. Vol. ends: Dec.

Aud: Ga, Hs.

Tabloid-type newspaper which will be useful where there is more than the average amount of interest in helicopters and those who make and fly them. The range of subjects covers such areas as research, flight records, armed forces use of helicopters, uses and performance of new Sikorsky models, and some unusual tasks accomplished by helicopters. Employee news is included in each issue, as well as accounts of company-sponsored employee activities, and of interesting hobbies and accomplishments of individuals on the staff. Journalistic style is in keeping with the tabloid format, the standard newsprint used, and the black and white photos which have been selected for their news contribution. (A.S.)

Singer Light. 1931. bi-m. free. Jim Kleckner. The Singer Co., 30 Rockefeller Plaza, New York, N.Y. 10020. Illus. Circ: 85,000. Sample. Vol. ends: Dec.

Aud: Ga.

Singer, long a leader in the field of sewing machines, uses *Light* to feature some of its other products and those of subsidiaries it now controls, as well as home sewing machines. Interesting material is related to its other electronic and home appliances, a line of sophisticated photographic equipment, visual education aids, Friden Dev. computers and programmed business systems and a line of household furniture. Accounts of interesting events with some relation to the Singer line here and in Europe provide the material for some of the articles, while others are concerned with product applications. Recent issues, for instance, discussed the possibilities of a new low-light-level camera system for night surveillance by police, and the career of Enoch Light, musical personality, whose records are available at Singer stores. Fashion and sewing contests, awards and instruction programs are subjects frequently presented. Listed as an employee magazine, presentation is geared to general interest, with a generally thorough treatment of the subjects selected. Format is small size, 60+ pages, illustrations adequate, with some employee news and several pages of product review aimed at potential customers. (A.S.)

Skyline. 1941. q. free. L. B. Taylor, Jr. North American Rockwell, 5th and Wood Sts., Pittsburgh, Pa. 15222. Illus. Circ: 35,000. Sample. Vol. ends: no. 4.

Aud: Ga, Ac, Hs.

Concentrating on the scientific and technical aspects of the national aeronautics and aerospace programs, *Skyline* ranks as one of the leading house magazines devoted to coverage of these areas. Articles related to current developments in the space program make up the bulk of the 48 pages. Other articles emphasize pure research, scientific technique, development of new products, and research in areas only loosely related to the aerospace endeavor. Interesting also are applications of North American Rockwell's space age technology to other areas, including sophisticated consumer products and services, and to the solving of such problems as water supply, environmental pollution, etc. There is some evidence of the corporation's acceptance of a social responsibility toward the nation's work force, as shown by projects in the field of education for minority, and other, groups. Length of articles varies from 4–12 pages, all are well illustrated with black and white photos and a few drawings, and a very few articles presented are largely pictorial. Most articles are signed, some by members of the staff, and all seem to be completely authoritative. Writing style is geared to the adult reader interested in this field, and in some of the more technical pieces, vocabulary used assumes some scientific background on the part of the reader. Company tie-in is minimal, and *Skyline* makes a good contribution to the current information available in the aerospace field. (A.S.)

South African Panorama. 1956. m. free (to libraries). Mr. Johan Olivier. Dept. of Information, Private Bag 152, Pretoria, South Africa. U.S. Address: Director, Information Service of South Africa, 655 Madison Ave., New York, N.Y. 10021. Illus. Circ: 265,000 (international), 35,000 (U.S.A.). Sample. Vol. ends: Dec.

Aud: Ga, Ac, Hs. *Jv:* V.

Describing itself as "chiefly a magazine about people for people," this shows the wide diversity represented by the economic, cultural and recreational pursuits of the Republic of South Africa. General interest articles encompass agriculture and mining, shipping and construction, fur farming, the fashion industry, medicine, sports, and natural scenic beauty, among other topics, and serve to show to the outside world as well as to the populace, the accomplishments of the country since becoming a republic in 1961. Excellent material on local artists and their work is included in almost every issue, and is an important asset of the magazine. There appears to be some emphasis in the presentation toward the segment of the white population descended from the early settlers, who are known as Afrikaners. Much of the material depicts the rich and unique heritage of this vigorous and proud people. An occasional article describes educational, medical or cultural projects carried on for or by the "Cape Coloured." Cover art of excellent quality alternates color photos of the country's industries and agriculture with photos or prints depicting the strikingly beautiful flora and fauna of the area. This does an honest job of showing this facet of South Africa, and can be very useful where this point of view is recognized and balanced by other material. (A.S.)

South African Scope. 1958. bi-m. free. Editor: Sr. Officers of the Information Service of South Africa. Information Service of South Africa, 655 Madison Ave., New York, N.Y. 10021. Illus. Circ: 25,000. Sample. Vol. ends: Nov./Dec.

Indexed: PAIS. *Aud:* Ga, Hs.

In 12 pages of generously illustrated short journalistic articles, the presentation concentrates on the people of this nation of many population groups. Emphasis is placed on cultural and recreational activities of the white, black and other races. Subjects range from a critique of the first all-South African ballet to a tour of Johannesburg's "Greenwich Village," and from Bantu radio broadcasting to the popular national sport of canoe racing. Sufficient background information is incorporated to explain any facets of life which might not be familiar to western readers, with only an occasional word which is strange or has a different connotation to American readers. Somewhat less pretentious in scope and format than *South African Panorama*, this can help to round out the picture of the life of the people of that nation, as it gives somewhat more at-

tention to the Bantu population. Pleasing format with fine quality paper and well-chosen black and white photos, clearly reproduced. (A.S.)

Southern Pacific Bulletin. 1913. m. 10/yr. free. Robert G. Ottman. Southern Pacific Transportation Co., One Market St., Rm. 975, San Francisco, Calif. 94105. Illus. Circ: 80,000. Sample. Vol. ends: Dec.

Aud: Ga.

Subject matter in this popularly written offering is chiefly concerned with this railroad and the subsidiary Southern Pacific pipe line. Subjects for articles range from ways in which Southern Pacific's programs and research projects are carrying out the company's concern for ecology to new devices for better and safer shipping by rail, and from the current campaign for support of ASTRO (America's Sound Transportation Review Organization) to the labratory maintained for service to this railroad and its customers, solving problems of maintenance as well as those of shipping techniques and quality. A few shorter articles cover unusual freight cargoes, items about out-of-the-ordinary activities of employees on and off the job, and prizes, awards for safety, etc. Adequate format with some illustrative material in the form of cartoons, as well as good black and white photos. Three to four pages of each 16-page issue are devoted to employee news. Useful as an additional source of material on the present status of railroads, written on a popular level. (A.S.)

Stechert-Hafner Book News. See Books and Book Reviews Section.

Steinway News. 1935. q. free (libraries and music departments of colleges and conservatories). John H. Steinway. Steinway and Sons, Steinway Place, Long Island City, N.Y. 11105. Illus. Circ: 18,000. Sample. Vol. ends: Fall.

Aud: Ac.

Edited mainly for sales organizations and their customers throughout the country, this eight-page leaflet presents numerous short news items which accompany photos of recent events in the world of concert music and popular entertainers. Not intended to be a directory of artists and schedules, yet it includes much information on the appearances and other activities of musical personalities throughout the world. There is some emphasis, of course, on artists' preference for Steinway instruments and their association with this firm, and the Steinway piano is shown as the choice of musicians and music educators. The journalistic style is well complemented by the good quality photos, printed in sepia tone, and the cover is usually a full-page picture of a current musician, or reproduction of a portrait of one of the greats of classical music. Will be of interest where there is serious interest in music and where music courses are offered. (A.S.)

Surveyor. 1967. q. Controlled circ. Michael J. Robinson. Amer. Bureau of Shipping, 45 Broad St., New York, N.Y. 10004. Illus. Circ: 12,500. No samples, but individual issues available upon request. Vol. ends: Nov.

Indexed: PAIS. *Aud:* Ga, Ac, Hs. *Jv:* V.

Although the publishing body is American, coverage in this beautifully illustrated 32-page magazine is international. Photo essays move from historical material to current activities in world marine commerce with a wealth of material on modern shipbuilding and cargo handling. Uses of the ocean for other than shipping purposes are often covered. A recent issue, for example, included an article on aquaculture, or systematic farming of the sea, and one of the possibilities of pumping offshore oil from pressurized production systems on the sea floor. Most of the material is substantial but nontechnical, easily within the grasp of the interested layman and the high school or college student. The black and white illustrations are particularly useful where there is a need for material on ships, shipbuilding and navigation. (A.S.)

Synergy. See Library Periodicals Section.

Tech Notes. 1961. bi-m. free. David B. Katz. The Singer Co. Kearfott Div., 1150 McBride Ave., Little Falls, N.J. 07424. Illus. Circ: 11,000. Sample. Vol. ends: Nov./Dec.

Aud: Ac.

This is "intended to inform its readers about products and progress at Kearfott," by demonstrating the applications, mainly aerospace, of a wide range of electronic control systems. These include gyroscopes, computers, fluidics, guidance systems, and related electronic modules. Emphasis is placed on the capabilities of multipurpose basic modules, usable in various combinations. Progress is demonstrated by an occasional article which compares a present system with its various forerunners. "Research at Kearfott," a six-issue series currently being offered, gives a short account of some type of research being carried on, or of the facilities set up for use of the research staff. Presentations are on a level which will be of interest to physics students with a lively interest in their subject. Material will be most appreciated by those who have completed at least a two-year technical college course in physics and electronics, or have equivalent background. Articles are fairly short and are generously illustrated with clear photos, good diagrams and sketches. High quality paper, artistic layout and good overall design contribute to the pleasing format. Should be useful in libraries serving schools and colleges where a substantial curriculum in physics is offered. (A.S.)

Technical Education News. 1941. 3/yr. free to libraries in two-year colleges and technical institutes, some in business and government organizations. Armond Irwin. McGraw-Hill Book Co., 330 W. 42nd St., New York, N.Y. 10036. Illus. Circ: 30,000. Sample. Vol. ends: Oct./Nov.

Indexed: Self-indexed with bound sets, every two years. (Back issues available in bound sets: Vols. 25–26, Oct. 1965–May 1967, $3.50; Vols. 27–28, Oct. 1967–Oct/Nov 1969, $4.50.) *Aud:* Ac. *Bk rev:* 8–12 per issue, avg. 50–100 words.

Published "for administrators and teachers in the field of technical and vocational education and for those working with training programs in business, industry, and the government." Substantial articles discuss subjects related to curriculum, including both reports of new courses offered and the need for new courses to train technicians for newly developing fields, prospects of employment of technicians, and trends in general and professional attitudes toward, and status of, the subprofessional worker. All are documented where pertinent, and many take on added clarity by the presentation of well-arranged tabulated information. Writers of major articles are persons in positions of importance in the colleges and other institutions offering this training: presidents, directors, and consultants, as well as professors and instructors. Shorter items cover well the news of new courses offered, new degrees with important particulars noted, grants and fellowships available and awarded, status of course accreditation, etc. Book reviews, 8–12 per issue, give "brief descriptions of the new and forthcoming books from McGraw-Hill Book Co. that will be of interest to . . . technical and vocational educators. All books are categorized by a subject heading . . ." Descriptions also include the level of intended use, assumed prerequisite training, and usefulness toward meeting standards of technical achievement, if any. Other teaching aids available from this company are often described. For libraries which qualify, under the limited circulation policy, this will be a valuable asset to the professional holdings. (A.S.)

Telephone Review. 1910. 6/yr. free. Edward Oxford. New York Telephone, 140 West St., Rm. 1300, New York, N.Y. 10007. Illus. Circ: 120,000. Sample. Vol. ends: varies.

Aud: Ga, Ac, Hs. *Jv:* V.

"Its purpose is to inform, persuade, and recognize telephone employees in matters significant in the world of communications." Each issue usually presents one theme, in text and pictures, showing the possibilities of this medium of reaching and persuading a selected readership, and "the magazine aims, in the main, to be people-oriented." Emphasis is on the accomplishments of employees, working as a team for New York Telephone, and on the importance of each individual. From time to time, in single-theme issues, the magazine deals with such matters as pride in craftsmanship, individuality, change, quality, or other abstract subjects selected to instill pride and satisfaction in work well done. Recognition is further achieved by heavy pictorial emphasis on employees at their jobs. The format alone would recommend the magazine as an example of an extremely well-designed and coordinated presentation of a single theme or issue. Page layout, typeface and illustrations all contribute to the dynamic as well as aesthetically pleasing makeup. Subject matter deals with issues with which this company is concerned, within the framework of its stated purpose. With the need for communication being one of the urgent concerns of our present society, this can be of great use to educators perceptive enough to relate its material to their instructional goals. Essentially an adult publication, the magazine may be useful for secondary schools, and public libraries needing additional material in the field may want to add it to their offerings. (A.S.)

Tennessee Valley Perspective. 1970. q. free. J. Worth Wilkerson. Tennessee Valley Authority, Knoxville, Tenn. 37902. Illus. Circ: 5,000 external + TVA employees and retirees. Sample. Vol. ends: Summer.

Aud: Ga, Hs.

A new offering which is "designed to report and intrepret the changing nature of the Tennessee Valley Region—the region's uniqueness, vitality, strengths, and problems, and to help create a common awareness for its needs and opportunities." Its tone in general serves to show how change, brought about by TVA's diverse resource development activities, has helped increase economic opportunities to this area, covering parts of Tennessee and six adjoining states. Subjects for articles center around camping and other recreational activities, agriculture, emphasizing new and successful crops, and the unique beauty of the region. Variety is achieved in length of articles, which range from a 300-word picture essay on fall on the TVA lakes, to a 3,500-word description of life on the river as seen by the pilot of a large river towboat. Very nicely illustrated, with some color photos qualifying as real art shots, and generally excellent format. Will be of interest to show the geography and the economic of a developing region, with parallels for other areas facing problems of raising the standards of living by economic expansion. (A.S.)

The Texaco Star. 1913. q. free. Warren W. Jones. Texaco, Inc., 135 E. 42nd St., New York, N.Y. 10017. Illus. Circ: 380,000. Sample. Vol. ends: no. 4.

Aud: Ga, Hs.

The worldwide scope of Texaco enterprises is shown by descriptive articles about many countries and localities, and other subjects pertinent to the operation of a major petroleum corporation. A feature article in some issues consists of up to 10–12 pages of descrip- tion and superb color photos, plus maps, of a single country or area, with some description of Texaco operations there. The search for oil reserves, some of the problems encountered, processes used in refining, lesser-known uses of petroleum or applications of Texaco products, and accounts of some research ventures are reported, together with the company's part in them. While references to Texaco are made in most articles, they are factual, and unobtrusive. In connection with the stated policy—"Texaco is committed to a continual upgrading of its pollution abatement equipment and procedures"—nearly every issue includes some information on the implementation of this policy. Each issue includes a "Survey" section which reports upper-level personnel promotions and accomplishments, and short news items about the company's operations. The 28 pages of excellent-quality format include superior photographic covers. Useful for its excellent pictures and supplementary geographic material, sidelights on all phases of the petroleum industry, and specific instances of air and water pollution control, for the general reader. (A.S.)

The Totem. 1958. m. free. Margaret E. Felt. Washington State Dept. of Natural Resources, P.O. Box 168, Olympia, Wash. 98504. Illus. Circ: 10,700 + 2,000–5,000 depending upon subject. Sample. Vol. ends: Dec.

Aud: Ga, Hs.

An eight-page newsletter reporting the activities of the various branches of the Department of Natural Resources for Washington State. In a recent issue the Commissioner expressed the function of this department as "working together to bring industry, government, environmentalists, and the general public together in order that we may constructively solve the many serious conflicts over the use of our natural resources." Items covered show the broad spectrum of concerns of the department, which include protection of wildlife and of watersheds and streams, preservation of environmental areas for ecological study purposes and of unique areas and historic sites, forestry practices and fire control, recreation developments and beautification, and an extensive program of environmental education. An interesting current project under study is the exploratory work being done on the feasibility of geothermal power for the area. Reporting is factual, usually brief, and very well illustrated with black and white photos. This should be useful in other states in the Northwest as well as Washington, for its current reporting of what is being done there, and in some libraries elsewhere that are concerned with providing environmental conservation material for areas other than their own. (A.S.)

Transmission. 1951. q. free. Gordon Bacon. Northern Natural Gas Co., 2223 Dodge St., Omaha, Nebr. 68102. Illus. Circ: 34,000. Sample. Vol. ends: Dec.

Aud: Ga.

A general interest magazine published by Northern Natural Gas Co. and its subsidiaries "in the interest of the areas they serve." Articles of local interest are largely confined to this geographical area, the Northern Plains states, and stress economic and civic problems and progress. Industrial activity of natural gas distributing, as well as other manufacturing, account for a few of the articles, all staff written. Education, civic improvement, agriculture and geography of the region, and sports and entertainment are also included among the popularly written, profusely illustrated articles. While specifically confined to an eight-state area served by the company, the examples of progress and accomplishment and of civic enterprise may be of interest to communities outside this area, which are faced with similar problems. (A.S.)

Tune In. See Health/Counterculture Section.

US Steel News. 1936. bi-m. free. Arthur J. Beiler. U.S. Steel Corp., 600 Grant St., Rm. 5519, Pittsburgh, Pa. 15230. Illus. Circ: 270,000. Sample. Vol. ends: Nov./ Dec.

Indexed: Self-indexed separately, available on request only. *Aud:* Ga, Hs.

This producer of steel and of other products including coal, coke, chemicals, plastic, cement, and fertilizer, uses its *News* to tell the story of the parent company and of some of its subsidiaries such as American Bridge Division, and of its engineering and consulting services. Articles relating to the functioning of the company show the emphasis on research and on employee relations, including working conditions and benefits, on concern for the environment, and many unusual as well as conventional uses of steel. Interesting facets of company operation, such as payroll processing, help in an understanding of business management. Implications of pending and enacted legislation are presented. Length of articles varies from a substantial 2,000 words in a recent issue on findings of U.S. Steel's research on moon rocks, done with the company's high voltage microscope and other research equipment, to a short 450 words on readying one's car for winter. Presented for the general reader, as indicated by the wide range of topics covered, this may be useful also for showing some aspects of the functioning of a large corporation. Pleasing and adequate format with mostly black and white photos for illustration. (A.S.)

Unscheduled Events. See Sociology/General Section.

Urban Renewal and Low Income Housing. 1965. q. free. Miss Nancy E. Davies. Central Mortgage and Housing Corp., Head Office, Ottawa, Ont., Canada K1A OP7. Illus. Circ: 4,000. Samples. Vol. ends: no. 4. *Aud:* Ga, Ac, Hs.

The title is an indication of the scope and purpose of this Canadian offering. Public housing, under federal and/or provincial sponsorship, and urban renewal projects which have required the relocation of low-income groups, form the subjects of the majority of articles. The accounts of projects for extensive rebuilding of the center areas of some of Canada's older cities, either completed or contemplated, will be surprising to readers who have not had occasion to assess this area of Canada's progress recently. Also treated are topics such as the effects of relocation on families, some of the ethnic groups involved, reports of conferences on housing and urban planning, and projects in the area of family services which are being conducted. Especially interesting are accounts of the "practice house," where mothers who have, or are soon to move into recently completed public housing are taught skills and graces which will help to raise the standards of these families. Several pages of each issue are devoted to capsule news reports, "As Seen by the Press," wherein grants for renewal projects and for studies are reported by province. All articles are published in both English and French, on facing pages, with photo captions in both languages also. Illustrations consist of black and white photos and a few city maps or diagrams, all of good quality. This will be of interest to individuals or groups concerned with city planning, and to sociologists studying its effects, as well as to those needing material on the current Canadian scene. Because of its popular style, it may also have some usefulness as a French-language periodical where this is needed. (A.S.)

Venezuela Up-to-Date. 1949. q. free. Francisco J. Lara. Embassy of Venezuela, Inst. of Information and Culture, 2437 California St. N.W., Washington, D.C. 20008. Illus. Circ: 41,000. Sample. Vol. ends: no 12.

Indexed: Indexed in issue 12, at end of 3 yr. period. *Aud:* Ga, Hs.

Published "as a public service . . . to bring you important business, industrial, economic and cultural developments in Venezuela." Reports of industrial expansion supply the topics for many of the articles, both long and short. In most cases, emphasis is on progress made and goals which Venezuela hopes to achieve. Space is usually given to the President of the country, or some other high-placed official, who expresses his views, together with a discussion of conditions and aspirations for future accomplishments. Outside the political and economic spheres, reports are included on such cultural topics as history and historical celebrations, archeological finds and their implications, preservation of endangered species of wildlife, and some tourism suggestions, among others. Each issue includes, under "Venezuela Oil News," a listing of daily average production of each of the petroleum companies operating there, over a span of the preceding six months. In 16 pages of pleasing type arranged in double columns, with illustrations consisting mainly of good, though small, black and white photos, this assumes a format in keeping with its purpose. Will be useful in connection with courses in economic geography where South America is included, and for the general reader interested in Latin America. (A.S.)

Virginia Highway Bulletin. 1934. m. free. Floyd H. Mihill. Virginia Dept. of Highways, 1221 E. Broad St., Richmond, Va. 23219. Illus. Circ: 13,000. Sample. Vol. ends: Dec.

Aud: Ga, Hs.

Gives a picture for one state that is largely typical of many states which currently find themselves caught up in a huge, nationwide program of road building. The reader is given an insight into some of the problems of highway planning, the officials involved, and some basic principles of engineering of highways which might not be obvious to the highway user. Progress reports, with excellent photos for illustration, are included on some of the many arterials and super-highways now under construction in the state. Each issue contains an article of one or two pages on some aspect of safe driving, stressing human factors such as drinking, and external factors such as weather. Some related material is also included, such as the Department's concern for archeological finds and wildlife habitat, and occasionally some seasonal material of general interest. Length of articles runs up to 1,000 words, some are signed, others staff written, and all are well composed. Purely personal news of department personnel and their families fills about one third of the magazine's 36 pages. The format is small size (6 by 9 in.) with high quality paper and well-designed covers. (A.S.)

WE. 1949. m. 10/yr. free. Alan Newman. Western Electric Co., 195 Broadway, New York, N.Y. 10007. Illus. Circ: 235,000. Sample. Vol. ends: Dec.

Aud: Ga, Hs, Ac.

A sampling of the themes of three recent issues serves to illustrate the editorial viewpoint: "The world we seek to save," "The growth of the individual," and "College and the corporation." Drawing on a capable staff and outside writers, such issues seek to explore, in several articles, points of view which help to establish corporation policy, and to report related programs, activities, and research. In addition, most issues include articles on communications, a few with historical approach, some with direct company tie-in. Substantial, signed articles will be of interest to the general reader, and in many cases will present both facts and a viewpoint helpful to students working on topics included in the wide gamut of those covered. Liberally illustrated with fine quality color and black and white illustrations. Color photos on covers are artistic and imaginative. No employee news as such, but each issue devotes two pages to the accomplishments of several employees, and to news briefs concerning

communications on a broad scale. Published as an employee magazine, subscriptions will be supplied to libraries which feel this may be of interest to their patrons. (A.S.)

WRL News. See Peace Section.

Ward's Bulletin. 1962 (current series). m. Oct. to May, 8/yr. free. George Clement. Ward's Natural Science Establishment, Inc., P.O. Box 1712, Rochester, N.Y. 14603. Illus. Circ: 80,000. Sample. Vol. ends: May.

Aud: Ac, Hs.

One major article, several columns, and news of new products being presented by the company, concentrate a large amount of information into this eight-page leaflet primarily intended for college and secondary school science teachers. An article of up to 2,000 words, written by a company staff expert or by an educator or scientist, usually covers the natural history, geology, and/or customs of some relatively remote or little-known area of the world. "Teacher Workshop Notes" reports seminars and workshops for science teachers which have been held, and summarizes their achievements, and also publishes letters of comment and announcement on such programs of interest to science educators. "Geo-Topics," a signed column, discusses some phase of geology, usually relative to a specific geographical area. Publications and other teaching aids are described, potential uses explained, and prices listed. Small but excellent black and white photos illustrate all material. (A.S.)

Washington Wildlife. 1933. q. free. Tom Knight. Washington State Game Dept., 600 North Capitol Way, Olympia, Wash. 98501. Illus. Circ: 19,000. Sample. Vol. ends: Winter.

Aud: Ga.

The official magazine of the Washington State Game Dept., which is a public service agency designed to protect, perpetuate, and enhance wildlife through regulations and sound continuing programs, and to provide the maximum amount of wildlife-oriented recreation for the people of the state. Species and habitat studies, information on status of endangered species, the ecology of specific areas and the effects of various pollutants are presented on the level of the general reader and wildlife enthusiast. The magazines also serves as an instrument for bringing to the attention of sportsmen and interested citizens any questionable land use proposals being considered, with a discussion of the implications. Seasonal forecasts for sportsmen indicate hunting or fishing prospects by countries and regions for the entire state, prior to the opening of the hunting or fishing seasons. The generally fine format includes some excellent wildlife photographic studies, in black and white or two tone, on excellent quality dull paper. Will be of interest to students and devotees of wildlife and ecology everywhere, and to sportsmen considering the prospects of hunting or fishing in Washington State. (A.S.)

Weyerhaeuser World. 1969. m. free. Harry Shook. Weyerhaeuser Co., Tacoma, Wash. 98401. Illus. Circ: 50,000. Sample. Vol. ends: Dec.

Aud: Ga, Hs.

As of July 1969, this new monthly replaces *Weyerhaeuser Magazine,* and while it is published primarily for employees, a library subscription is well worth asking for. Choice of topics for the five to six articles in each issue of the new magazine seems to have broadened slightly, but most are still related to the lumber industry, its role in conservation of natural resources, antipollution measures, and reforestation and wood usage. A favorable impression has been created by several recent issues featuring articles dealing with student attitudes and student unrest. One showed how Weyerhaeuser personnel handled such things as a boycott of its company's recruiters, on the grounds that the company's South African operations were exploiting the black population of that country. All in all, it gives very good coverage of this large company's awareness of current problems, and of the means it is using to surmount some of those which the lumber and paper industries have been accused of causing. The size, a whopping 12 by 18½ in., is a good advertisement for its high-grade paper, a Weyerhaeuser product, but may cause display and storage problems in libraries. Well written and nicely illustrated. (A.S.)

Worldwide Marketing Horizons. 1960. bi-m. free. Alex. V. Roe. Pan American World Airways, Inc., 200 Park Ave., New York, N.Y. 10017. Illus. Circ: 205,000 (seven languages). Sample. Vol. ends: Nov./Dec.

Aud: Ga.

The main section of each issue consists of approximately 450 listings submitted by buyers and sellers around the world, seeking suppliers, outlets, representatives, wholesalers and agents, and exporters and importers for their products. Listed by continent and by country, essentials of the product are given with contacts to be arranged by Pan Am on written request. (The fee is $10 for each 25-word, or less, listing in each issue.) Two articles complete the content of each issue, with subjects relating to world trade or industry in a specific country. Writing is thorough and factual. A few good, though small, black and white photos illustrate the articles. Will be of interest in a business community where the large number of listings will serve their intended purpose, and where trends of world trade are watched. (A.S.)

GAMES

Bridge World. 1929. m. $8. Edgar Kaplan, 39 W. 94th St., New York, N.Y. 10025. Illus., adv. Circ: 16,500.

Bk. rev: Various number, length. *Aud:* Sa, Ga.

The top magazine for the serious bridge player. *Bridge World* stresses the finer points of the game's techniques, rather than the activities and personalities of bridge society. Because of this, it is better for library collections than *Contract Bridge Bulletin.*

Chess Life & Review. 1933. m. $8.50. Burt Hochberg. U. S. Chess Federation, 479 Broadway, Newburgh, N.Y. 12550. Illus., index, adv. Circ: 28,000. Sample. Vol. ends: Dec.

Aud: Ac, Ga, Hs, Ejh.

Subtitled, The World's Largest Chess Magazine, this has wide appeal for just about anyone, regardless of age or experience, who is interested in the game. It covers both tournament and correspondence chess, presenting international, regional, and interstate activities. Authorities discuss outstanding games, diagrammed plays, chess problems, and opening strategy. Correspondents are located in the 50 states, the District of Columbia, and throughout the world. Contains game and tournament reports and ratings, names of new postal players and prize winners, and tournament announcements for coming events in the United States. A good basic addition for any type of library.

Chess Player. 1971. m. $15. 12 Burton Ave., Carlton, Nottingham, England. Illus.

Aud: Ac, Ga, Hs.

The chess magazine for the man or woman who looks at the game as a game. Although there are some news items, it primarily consists of some 100 games per issue. These are annotated, and moves are recorded in pictorial algebraic notations. Selected games represent historical and current favorites. For example, in the first number there were all the games played in the international tournament at Netanya, Israel, plus selections of games from several other tournaments. There are some photographs, the typography is excellent, and the format suitable for anyone who wants to replay chess games. A first choice.

Contract Bridge Bulletin. m. Membership (Nonmembers $3). Steven Becker. American Contract Bridge League, 125 Greenwich Ave., Greenwich, Conn. 06830. Illus., index, adv. Circ: 140,000. Sample. Vol. ends: Dec.

Bk. rev: 2, ½–1 page, signed. *Aud:* Ga.

Approximating *The Bridge World* in physical dimensions but averaging 24 pages longer, this is the most widely distributed bridge magazine in the world because it is the official publication of the American Contract Bridge League. As such, it stresses the activities of the organization, featuring articles on results of major championships, club organization, procedural matters, and other activities throughout the United States. It contains many pictures of members. Information on the game itself is limited to a few articles in a regular "Masterpointers" Department.

Gambling Illustrated. 1965. m. $10. H. R. David. President Publns., Drawer AG, Beverly Hills, Calif. 90213. Illus., adv. Circ: 100,000.

Aud: Ga.

Dedicated to the proposition that gambling is more a matter of mathematical "money management" than chance. This includes 10 to 12 articles directed to the serious $2 better. The whole is illustrated, and balanced with advertisements. The tone is popular, yet serious. It is well documented with facts rather than conjecture, and there is a refreshing honesty of approach. If the letters to the editor are any indication, it is a magazine which is faithfully read by every type of gambler from those who follow the horses to card players. It would be a good choice for any library where there is a gambler within betting distance.

IFA News. 1968. q. $2. Goldy Norton, P.O. Box 38428, Los Angeles, Calif. 90038. Illus. Circ: 10,000. Sample.

Aud: Ac, Ga, Hs.

Once in a while a magazine ought to be purely for fun. One such is the International Frisbee Association *News. News* reports activities on campuses having IFA Chapters, offers information on starting new chapters. Technical articles on how to improve one's Frisbee-throwing skill are included, as are human interest photos and stories. The IFA itself is responsible for setting Frisbee tournament standards, prints a proficiency manual, and holds an annual tournament to which delegates from college chapters are sent. IFA membership in 1971 hit 60,000. Lifetime membership in IFA is now $1.00 and includes a personalized parchment certificate, membership card, a proficiency manual, and a copy of latest newsletter. Any librarian looking for inexpensive but interesting publications to add to the magazine rack might well consider this publication because of potential student interest.

100 Easy Crosswords. 1956. m. $4. Charlton Publications, Division St., Derby, Conn. 06518. Adv. Combined Circ. of all titles listed here: 600,000. Sample.

Aud: Ga, Hs, Ejh.

While not the most likely library acquisition, this is one of the more innovative. In some 65 pages the publisher offers 100 puzzles complete with answers and a "special vocabulary" section which gives definitions and words often found in crossword puzzles. The reader is expected to fill in the puzzle. Granted, this makes it a one-time shot for the library, but with a little imagination and ingenuity it might be used at least 100 times. The puzzles are relatively easy, and serve as a pleasant way of not only passing time, but enlarging the vocabulary of students and adults. Even if the library chooses not to buy it, it

might be recommended to those who never get enough of crosswords, or who tear them out of the local newspapers.

The publisher also offers seven other similar magazines with 60 to 100 crossword puzzles. Several include articles slanted towards history, science, etc., which are tied in with the puzzles. The format is the same for all, including the "special vocabulary section," and all range from the simple to the moderately difficult. *Fast'N Easy Crosswords* is a monthly, but the others are bi-monthly and are called: *Jiffy Crosswords, 99 Simple Crosswords, Snappy Crosswords, Veri-Best Crosswords, Everybody's Crosswords* and *10-Minute Crosswords.* Any library seriously considering these might write for samples.

Simulation and Games. See Political Science Section.

Strategy and Tactics. See Military Section.

GARDENING

Basic Periodicals

Ga: *Flower and Garden, Plants and Gardens, Home Garden and Flower Grower;* Jc & Ac: *Horticulture, Horticultural Research, Plants and Gardens, Baileya.*

Cessations

Popular Gardening and *Living Outdoors.*

American Fern Journal. 1910. q. $5.50. D. B. Lellinger. American Fern Soc., Inc., Dept. of Botany, Field Museum, Chicago, Ill. 60605. Illus., index, adv. Circ: 950. Sample. Vol. ends: Dec.

Indexed: BioAb. *Bk. rev:* 1–2, 2–3 paragraphs, signed. *Aud:* Ac, Ga.

While primarily a botanical journal, this will be of considerable interest to the amateur botanist and gardener. The articles tend to be both scientific and semipopular, deal with all aspects of ferns. Anyone interested enough to read a journal of this type will have no trouble understanding the text. An offbeat item for garden collections—and, of course, for many academic libraries.

American Rock Garden Society Bulletin. 1943. q. Membership $5. Albert M. Sutton. R. W. Redfield, Sec., Box 26, Closter, N.J. 07624. Index, adv. Circ: 1,800. Vol. ends: Oct.

Aud: Ga.

Designed for the rock garden enthusiast, but is valuable for the person interested in wild flowers. Usually there are about four, two to five page articles concerning plants in their natural rock environments or about rock gardening. Contributors are experienced gardeners and horticulturists.

American Rose Magazine. 1933. m. Membership (Nonmembers $4.50). Harold S. Goldstein. American Rose Soc., Inc., 4048 Roselea Pl., Columbus, Ohio 43214. Illus., index, adv. Circ: 16,000. Vol. ends: Dec.–every 2 yrs.

Bk. rev: 2, 50–100 words. *Aud:* Ga.

Articles cover such diverse topics as history of particular types of roses, research on rose diseases and new varieties, famous rose gardens, exhibitions, care of cut roses, and arrangement and practical gardening advice for rose growers in various parts of the United States. Frequently articles are written by amateurs about their work with roses. Rose growing in foreign countries is occasionally discussed. For both beginners and experts.

Baileya; a quarterly journal of horticultural taxonomy. 1953. q. $5. William J. Dress. Bailey Hortorium, Cornell Univ., Ithaca, N.Y. 14850. Illus., index. Circ: 700. Sample. Vol. ends: Winter.

Indexed: BioAb. *Bk. rev:* 1–5, 40 lines, signed. *Aud:* Ac, Ga.

Although primarily for the professional botanist, this has a given amount of charm and interest for the layman. It includes notes and short scientific papers on all cultivated plants, "especially to their identification, nomenclature, classification and history in cultivation." Most articles are accompanied by line drawings and photographs. This is an overlooked item for dedicated plant lovers, and one well worth bringing to their attention. Send for a sample, and find out.

Fairchild Tropical Garden Bulletin. 1945. q. $3. John Popenoe, 10901 Old Cutler Rd., Miami, Fla. 33156. Illus.

Aud: Ga.

Mainly a news bulletin for the tropical garden enthusiast. Contains information concerning tropical plants and gardens not usually found in other garden publications. Ordinarily, there is one three or four page article on a particular garden or group of plants found in a tropical setting.

Flower and Garden (Eastern, Mid-America and Western editions). 1957. m. $3. Rachel Snyder. Mid-American Publishing Corp., 4251 Pennsylvania Ave., Kansas City, Mo. 64111. Illus., index, adv. Circ: 610,000. Sample. Vol. ends: Dec.

Bk. rev: 3, notes. *Aud:* Ga.

A general how-to-do-it approach to gardening for the average layman. It is particularly suited for the man or woman who wants questions about flowers, lawns, shrubs, and plants answered in an easy nontechnical manner. The writing is authoritative, yet well within the grasp of anyone with a high school education. The many photographs, charts, and illustrative matter substantially add to the attractiveness of the magazine. There are a number of departments, including 15 regional reports, garden club news, questions and answers, etc. A basic gardening magazine.

Garden Journal (Formerly: *Garden Journal of the New York Botanical Garden*). 1951. bi-m. Membership (Nonmembers $5). Mary E. O'Brien. New York Botanical Garden, Bronx, N.Y. 10458. Illus., index, adv. Circ: 5,000. Sample. Vol. ends: Dec. Microform: UM.

Indexed: BioAg. *Bk. rev:* 10, 500 words, signed. *Aud:* Ga, Ac, Hs. *Jv:* V.

Although the circulation of this outstanding garden-botanical magazine is considerably less than many others in this category, it is one of the best. Articles, in a nontechnical language, cover such diverse subjects as famous gardens, historical aspects of plant use, conservation, ecology, and plant growth. The occasional how-to-do-it material about cuttings and grafting is for the advanced gardener, and some of the articles are well-suited for students of elementary botany. The contributors are professional gardeners, writers, and professors of horticulture. Regular features include Plant Clinic, Plant Identification, Book Reviews, and News, Notes, and Comments. The format of *Garden Journal* is more attractive than most other garden periodical and no distasteful advertising appears.

Garden News. 1958. w. $8. Tony Ireson. Garden News Ltd., Newspaper House, Broadway, Peterborough, England. Illus., adv. Circ: 81,000.

Aud: Ga.

Aimed primarily at the experienced British gardener, the 24 to 32 pages, presented in newspaper format, offer news concerning shows, garden societies, flowers, house plants, vegetables, fruit growing, and much practical gardening advice. Whether British or not, a person interested in new varieties of flowers and plants will find this coverage of the latest horticultural developments an excellent alerting device. Landscaping, greenhouses, and historical research involving plants and gardens are also frequently discussed. Regular features include questions and answers for English gardeners, and classified advertisements and gardening positions. While a good addition for libraries, the English emphasis limits it primarily to large collections.

Home Garden and Flower Grower. 1914. 9/yr. $5.40. William L. Meachem. Flower Grower Publishing, Inc., 235 E. 45th St., New York, N.Y. 10017. Illus., adv. Circ: 450,000. Sample. Vol. ends: Nov/Dec. Microform: UM.

Indexed: BioAb, BioAg, RG. *Aud:* Ga. *Jv:* V.

One of the best all-around gardening magazines for any library, this is primarily for homeowners in every area of the United States. The eight or nine short articles offer in nontechnical language how-to-do-it information for gardening and landscaping. Frequently, house plants are discussed as well as fruits and vegetables, and the latest in garden equipment. The emphasis is on decorative gardening and landscape design but conservation and ecological gardening written from the gardener's point of view are considered. Regular features include "Garden Events" and "Question Box" in which readers' questions are answered by an expert. The color photographs are excellent.

Horticultural Research; a journal for the publication of scientific work on horticulture. 1961. s-a. $7.50. Scottish Academic Press, 25 Peath St., Edinburgh, EDH3, 5DW, Scotland. Illus., index. Circ: 700. Sample. Vol. ends: Nov.

Indexed: BioAb, BioAg. *Bk. rev:* 2–3, lengthy, signed. *Aud:* Ac.

Aimed at advanced researchers and specialists. Seven to nine "research papers and research reviews on subjects connected with horticultural plants and practices" from all parts of the world are published in each issue. The general research concerns such subjects as plant breeding, genetics, plant physiology, plant pathology, and soil science, all as related to horticulture. Only for larger academic and public library collections.

Horticulture. 1904. m. $7.00. Edwin F. Steffek. Mass. Horticultural Soc., Horticultural Hall, 300 Massachusetts Ave., Boston, Mass. 02115. Illus., index, adv. Circ: 148,000. Sample. Vol. ends: Dec. Microform: UM.

Excellent color photographs coupled with a wide range of information about gardening and flora in all parts of the world make this an outstanding publication. Material is semipopular and by recognized authorities. It can be recommended for any enthusiastic gardening fan. (The fact that it is indexed in *Readers' Guide* helps too.) Librarians might check out local horticultural societies for equally good publications.

House Beautiful. See Interior Design Section.

House and Garden. See Interior Design Section.

The National Gardener. 1930. bi-m. $1.50. Ms. W. V. Donnan. National Council of State Garden Clubs, Inc. 4401 Magnolia Ave., St. Louis, Mo. 63110. Illus., adv. Circ: 40,000.

Bk. rev: 2, one-half page, signed. *Aud:* Ga.

Published primarily for news about state garden clubs. The 12 or 13 brief articles describe various civic projects such as beautification and conservation schemes. International projects are sometimes included. Although not a how-to-do-it magazine, there are occasional articles dealing with flower arranging and related activities. Useful, but way down the list for most libraries.

Organic Gardening and Farming. See Counterculture/ Alternative Living Section.

Plants and Gardens. 1945. q. Membership (Nonmembers $4). Frederick McGourty, Jr. Brooklyn Botanic Garden, 1000 Washington Ave., Brooklyn, N.Y. 11225. Illus. Circ: 12,500. Sample. Vol. ends: Winter.

Indexed: BioAb, BioAg. *Bk. rev:* Notes (35/yr.). *Aud:* Ga, Ac. *Jv:* V.

Aimed chiefly at the intelligent or more experienced gardener. Three of the four annual issues are written as comprehensive handbooks on particular topics. For example, "weed control," "orchids," "garden pests," "rock gardens," etc., have been done. The information in the 10 or 11 four or five page articles is practical and detailed. Often many pages of useful, easy to consult charts are presented. Research reports and suggestions concerning equipment and reading matter are included. The pamphlet and book suggestions are not always annotated but the reader is told where they are available. The contributors are university professors, entomologists, pathologists, writers of garden books, and horticulturists. The year-end issue (Winter) is done in *Reader's Digest* style, and includes the 10 to 15 articles judged by the editor to be the most significant gardening (or horticultural) articles published during the year in other periodicals.

Sunset. See Interior Design Section.

GENEALOGY AND HERALDRY

Basic Periodicals

Ga: *The Genealogical Helper;* Jc & Ac: *New England Historical and Genealogical Register, The Genealogists' Magazine, Pennsylvania Genealogical Magazine, American Genealogist.*

Introduction

Although there are myriads of genealogical magazines of all sizes and standards addressed to scholars, genealogists, and family searchers, there are few journals devoted to heraldry. Perhaps the explanation is simply that heraldry is more of a science than genealogy, and it is more difficult to write an article without fault. Whatever the reason, only two on heraldry are considered worthy of inclusion, where 19 on genealogy reach the standard necessary for inclusion. Even here the editors of the two heraldry journals failed to reply to my questionnaire so that certain details may well be out of date. But the addresses are accurate and no doubt enquiries will eventually elicit the desired information.

The method of selection had two phases. First the list of periodicals listed in the *Genealogical Periodical Annual Index* was scanned and the editor (George Ely Russell) questioned on the excellence of certain choices. It so happened that without exception the fine collection at the Maryland Historical Society held all those finally considered, and from there all sets were examined for trends and general content. Thus the final review took everything into account and a balanced review was the result. No doubt a few worthy magazines have been missed, but future editions will include them. (P.W.F.)

The American Genealogist. 1922. q. $7. Dr. George E. McCracken, 1232 39th St., Des Moines, Iowa 50311. Circ: 1,000. Vol. ends: Oct. Microform: UM.

Aud: Sa. *Jv:* V.

The magazine started in 1922 as *New Haven Genealogical Magazine,* and later became the *American Genealogist,* and throughout has set a high standard. Dr. McCracken has a formidable list of contributing editors, and although most are Fellows of the American Society of Genealogists, the top genealogical society in America, the magazine is not the official organ of the society. There are no advertisements; the few book reviews are critical and good; the articles are scholarly and footnoted. There are family records, ancestral tables, and queries. The annual index is very good and the volume usually contains about 300 pages. Until 1970 Donald Lines Jacobus (died 1970) was consulting editor, ensuring that the magazine was of top value. Jacobus was meticulous and severely critical. The journal is intended for the more scholarly genealogists. Although offset from typescript the text is very readable. (P.W.F.)

The Armorial. 1959. a. $5. Lt. Col. R. Gayre. Gayre and Nigg, 1 Darnaway St., Edinburgh 3, Scotland. Adv. Circ: 1,750. Vol. ends: Dec.

Aud: Sa, Ac.

The Armorial is an international journal of heraldry, genealogy, and related subjects. Originally it advertised that articles in foreign languages would have summaries but lately there have been no foreign-language articles. The articles are by recognized authorities, and there are few lists. The heraldry is frequently in color and special attention is given to ecclesiastical and civic heraldry. There are few reviews but all are authoritative. There are also charts and an adequate index. It is worldwide in its coverage. Originally a quarterly it has been sporadic in its appearances, but late in 1970 it was announced that an annual volume would be published in December 1970. This volume has not been seen by the editor, and so the above remarks concern the volumes from 1959 to 1969. (P.W.F.)

The Coat of Arms. 1950. q. $4. Lornie Leete-Hodge, 28 Museum St., London, WC1, England. Adv. Circ: 2,000. Vol. ends: July. Reprint: Johnson.

Indexed: BritHum. *Aud:* Sa.

As in the case of most heraldry journals, *Coat of Arms* is small, and averages 200–300 pages a volume. Originally a quarterly it has recently run into editorial difficulties and for some time its appearance has been sporadic. In the Fall of 1971 it announced that the difficulties had ended and that soon publication will be regular. Illustrations and articles are excellent—with J. P. Brooke-Little as former editor and an advisor its excellence is guaranteed. The book reviews are few but very good and critical. The correspondence is one of its best features; all letters are scholarly and informative. It is an international journal of top standard. (P.W.F.)

The Connecticut Nutmegger. 1968. q. $6. Herbert A. Hotchkiss. Connecticut Soc. of Genealogists, Inc., 16 Royal Oak Drive, West Hartford, Conn. 06107. Adv. Circ: 1,500. Sample. Vol. ends: Mar.

Aud: Sa.

This little magazine (it measures only 5½ × 8 inches) is packed with Connecticut information. Each number has about 150 pages so that when the volume ends there are no fewer than 600 pages of high standard transcripts, records, marriages, family histories, census records, and news of the Society's doings. There are no book reviews. It is offset from typescript, professionally edited and produced. The Society is highly organized and it is unlikely that many questions remain unanswered. (P.W.F.)

The Detroit Society of Genealogical Research Magazine. 1937. q. $5 Membership. Mrs. Eva Murrell Harmison. Detroit Society for Genealogical Research, c/o Burton History Collection, Detroit Public Library, Detroit, Mich. 48202. Circ: 1,000. Sample. Vol. ends: Summer.

Aud: Sa.

In spite of its title the Detroit Society publishes Michigan material with a considerable amount of material referring to other states, and it should be considered a national magazine. The articles are good, and much of the magazine concerns family records, census lists, marriage, Bible records, and a full report of the Society's meetings. Once a year the Burton Historical Collection, Detroit Public Library, gives its accession list for publication, and because so many books have been acquired it forms a useful bibliography. Book reviews are not over critical and are not long; the index is not very full and more could be done. The annual membership is only $5, so the magazine is a good buy. It is offset from typescript but completely readable, and although it is not as professionally produced as the *National Genealogical Society Quarterly* for example, it is every bit as professional. (P.W.F.)

French Canadian and Acadian Genealogical Review. 1968. q. $15. Roland-J. Auger, Case Postale 845,

Haute-Ville, Que. 4, Canada. Adv. Circ: 1,000. Vol. ends: Winter.

Aud: Sa, Ac. *Jv:* V.

This is one of the most beautiful journals imaginable. It has a color cover and often there are color illustrations in the text. It is well printed and there is an air of scholarly attention in every line. Each volume has about 300 pages and it contains well-footnoted articles, family genealogies in full, considerable coverage of Canadian archives, and studies of demography, Occasionally there are articles slightly off genealogy, e.g., early French-Canadian furniture and Ebenezer Parkman's diary. There are fewer lists than articles and with the exhaustive footnotes it qualifies as a historical magazine. The index is only fair, and it does not match those for some other journals listed here. Unfortunately, with such an ambitious, expensively produced magazine having a limited sale, the editor continually has difficulty in making ends meet. (P.W.F.)

Gateway to the West. 1967. q. $6. Anita Short and Ruth Bowers, Rural Rt. 1, Arcanum, Ohio 45304. Adv. Circ: 950. Vol. ends: Oct.

Aud: Sa.

Since this is a commercial venture the editors are able to devote every inch of space to source material, a query section, and a few book reviews. The area covered is Ohio but the reviews (or rather announcements and brief descriptions) have no restriction. In the source records are the usual wills, vital records, Bible records, inscriptions, census lists, etc. Each volume averages 200 pages and there is a fine annual index in addition. It is mimeographed but it has a smart businesslike appearance and is almost entirely free of typographical errors, unusual in this kind of magazine. (P.W.F.)

The Genealogical Helper. 1947. $7. bi-m. (varies). George Everton, Jr. Everton Publishers Inc., 526 N. Main St., Logan, Utah 84321. Adv. Circ: 22,000. Sample. Vol. ends: Dec.

Aud: Ga, Sa, Ac.

This magazine is published especially for those who wish to do their own general research. There are few articles, and it could not be described as particularly scholarly. Yet it fulfills a want, and is widely read, mostly by amateur genealogists. Advertisements are very useful and helpful; book reviews are numerous and assist would-be buyers without bias; they are not too penetrating or critical but never misleading. Special issues contain a directory of genealogists, genealogists' exchange (surnames sought), a directory of genealogical societies, libraries and professionals, and family associations and their leaders. In short, this magazine answers almost any question for the searcher—except the actual research itself. Anyone beginning family

searching must have this magazine. It is a family concern, run by Latter-Day Saints, and undoubtedly is bought heavily by Mormons, but genealogy is international and undenominational, and almost anyone will derive considerable interest and assistance from its pages—about 500 a volume. (P.W.F.)

The Genealogists' Magazine. 1925. q. $5. Lornie Leete-Hodge. Soc. of Genealogists, 37 Harrington Gardens, London, SW 7, England. Adv. Circ: 4,000. Sample. Vol. ends: every 4 yrs.

Indexed: BritHum. *Aud:* Sa, Ac. *Jv:* V.

This is the official journal of the Society of Genealogists, London, and although it has hundreds of American members the content is highly British. Each issue has about 70 pages and the composition is similar: excellent scholarly articles, footnoted pedigrees, queries, wills, and various lists, membership lists, minutes of Society, and additions to the Society library—the last mentioned is in itself a fine bibliography of genealogy and heraldry. The book reviews are long and highly critical. Each volume has about 16 numbers (covering 4 years), and since the index to persons and places is not made until the volume is complete, readers must wade through many pages when searching for a specific name. Nevertheless it ranks in the top two or three best magazines. It is free to members. For the scholarly genealogist. (P.W.F.)

Irish Ancestor. 1969. bi-a. $6.25. Rosemary ffolliott. Pirton House, Sydenham Villas, Dundrum, Dublin 14, Ireland. Illus., adv. Circ: 1,100. Sample. Vol. ends: Fall.

Aud: Sa, Ac.

The chief intention of this magazine is to collect and publish original source material and items of interest concerning Irish genealogy, biography, and domestic history. The 1972 volume is increasing coverage by including a considerable amount of history, costume, and architecture. The articles are scholarly; there are also tombstone inscriptions, tax lists, Christian names in Ireland, and testamentary records. There are many book reviews, most reviewed by Miss ffolliott excellently and critically. All concern Irish genealogy and history. (P.W.F.)

Kentucky Ancestors. 1965. q. $5. Mrs. William Fitzgerald. Kentucky Historical Society, Old State House, Box H, Frankfort, Ky., 40601. Circ: 10,000. Sample. Vol. ends: April.

Aud: Sa.

One of the better state magazines. The Kentucky Historical Society issues a historical magazine (*Kentucky Historical Register*) but it sensibly realizes that many of its members are genealogists (as is the case with almost every American historical society), and it issues a separate magazine for its genealogically inclined members—would that other historical societies paid more attention to their membership. It is a sound magazine for the researcher; there are few articles, but each number includes vital statistics, court, Bible, cementery and other records, book reviews, and queries, all relating to Kentucky. The reviews are not penetrating but eminently sensible. The text is offset from typescript and is easily readable. Altogether a distinguished magazine for the researcher. (P.W.F.)

The Maryland and Delaware Genealogist. 1959. q. $6 ($2 single issue.) Raymond B. and Sara Beth Clark, Box 352, St. Michaels, Md. 21663. Sample. Circ: 500. Vol. ends: Oct.

Aud: Sa.

There are few articles in this magazine, the prime emphasis being on source records. Lists abound—baptisms, inventories, wills, and family lineages. The Editor's page is newsworthy and the queries are well arranged. Naturally Maryland gets a larger share than Delaware, but this is expected. The annual index is good. The book reviews are critical and very useful for readers. (P.W.F.)

National Genealogical Society Quarterly. 1912. q. $8. George Ely Russell. National Genealogical Soc., 1921 Sunderland Place, N.W., Washington, D.C. 20036. Adv. Circ: 3,000. Sample. Vol. ends: Dec.

Aud: Sa, Ac.

This quarterly publishes unpublished American source materials with emphasis on areas of earlier settlements. The articles are often reprinted as pamphlets and the reviews by Milton Rubincam rank as the best in the field. Most books of any size are reviewed critically and severely. There are also abstracts from lists, and an accession list of books received in the Society. The standard is extremely high throughout, and as a bonus there is one very good index a year, with frequent consolidations. (P.W.F.)

New England Historical and Genealogical Register. 1847. q. $10. New England Historic Genealogical Soc., 101 Newbury St., Boston, Mass. 02116. Adv. Circ: 4,500. Sample. Vol. ends: Oct. Microform: G. Reprint: Carrollton.

Aud: Ga, Ac. *Jv:* V.

This, the doyen of genealogical magazines, has been published continuously for well over 100 years—by the end of 1971 over 500 numbers will have been issued. The articles are excellent, annotated, and authentic. There are lists of deeds, marriage records, family records, and other vital statistics. The list of recent books (gifts only) is useful, and the list of genealogies in preparation is valuable to the author. A roll of arms is published sporadically. Unfortunately no book is reviewed. True, the editor sometimes notes a book, but this is unsatisfactory. Even though the information is almost entirely devoted to New England the magazine remains one of the most widely read, and with the great Gilbert Doane as editor, the magazine's high standard is assured. (P.W.F.)

The New York Genealogical and Biographical Record. 1870. q. $10. William R. White and Kenn Stryker-Rodda. New York Genealogical and Biographical Soc., 122 E. 58th St., New York, N.Y. 10022. Adv. Circ: 1,200. Sample. Vol. ends: Oct. Microform: MF.

Aud: Sa, Ac.

The *Record* is the publication of the Society, and a cursory glance at the officers convinces the genealogist that everything the *Record* contains will be scholarly and authentic. There are articles with footnotes, family records, newspaper extracts, baptism and other lists, and a genealogical exchange and lists of books received by the Society. While there are more lists than articles, the standard of the *Record* is not impaired. Almost every item deals with New York, but since the reviews are so well written and so critical (the work of Dr. Kenn Stryker-Rodda), and since so many New Yorkers moved West, the magazine should be in all libraries where genealogists foregather. (P.W.F.)

Ohio Records and Pioneer Families. 1960. q. $6. Ohio Genealogical Soc., Rte. 1, Box 332 b, Ashland, Ohio 44805. Circ: 1,100. Vol. ends: Sept.

Aud: Sa.

Esther Weygandt Powell, an eminent genealogist, founded this journal and ran it for ten years. Now it has four editors and the same high quality is being maintained. There are few articles, but information for the researcher is full, authoritative, and expertly done. There are tax lists, pioneer family information, settlers, census records, family history, and queries. Almost everything is confined to Ohio. The book reviews are few and not particularly critical or penetrating. The annual surname index is comprehensive. Although offset from typescript it is very readable. One hundred fifty to 200 pages per year. (P.W.F.)

The Ontario Register. 1968. q. $7. Thomas B. Wilson. 38 Swan St., Lambertville, N.J. 08530. Circ: 1,000. Sample. Vol. ends: Oct.

Aud: Sa.

The fact that the editor lives in New Jersey inevitably means that a few New Jersey articles get in, but the magazine is primarily for those researching in Ontario. Each volume contains about 300 pages. Articles are few, but the lists—cemetery, marriage, militia, etc. are excellent. The annual index is superb. There are no advertisements and few reviews: the magazine is unpretentious but is clearly vital to researchers with Ontarion backgrounds. Although offset from typescript the text is very readable. (P.W.F.)

The Pennsylvania Genealogical Magazine. 1859. q. $5. Hannah Benner Roach. The Genealogical Soc. of Pennsylvania, 1300 Locust St., Philadelphia, Pa. 19107. Circ: 1,300. Vol. ends: March.

Aud: Sa, Ac. *Jv:* V.

The magazine began as *Publications of the Genealogical Society of Pennsylvania* in 1895 and continued for 15 volumes until 1947 when it changed to the present title. It is one of the very best genealogical magazines, well printed and tastefully arranged, using good type. The articles are scholarly and all have copious and authoritative footnotes. There are also family lists, pension rolls, Bible records, and general records. Almost all the magazine is devoted to Pennsylvania, and especially Pennsylvania–German genealogies. The book reviews are not restricted to Pennsylvania; all are excellent, as is the index which completes each volume of approximately 300 pages. The Society is housed in the Historical Society of Pennsylvania in Philadelphia, and with the harmony which prevails, articles are easy to come by, but are scrutinized carefully by the Publications Committee; thus the magazine maintains a high level of scholarship. (P.W.F.)

Tree Talks. 1961. q. $8. Robert V. Moyer. Central New York Genealogical Society, Box 104, Colvin Station, Syracuse, N.Y. 13205. Circ: 800. Vol. ends: Dec.

Aud: Sa.

Only New York State material is published, and this is restricted to upstate—nothing on New York City is attempted, and therefore the magazine is complementary to the *New York Genealogical and Biographical Record.* There are few articles, but the wills, vital records, society reports and talks and queries are above average. Editorial comment, queries, maps, immigration and naturalization details, and military and pension abstracts are also excellent. There are no book reviews, and the few book notes are not very penetrating or critical. In addition to the 200 to 250 pages annually there is a very fine index—subject and name—of about 100 pages a volume, costing an extra $3. The pagination presents an unusual but helpful arrangement. As in other journals, most lists are continued from number to number, and "serials" may concern as many as a dozen different subjects. There is an annual query issue, *Cousin Huntin',* free to members. *Tree Talks* has running pagination and separate cumulative pagination for the various "serials," thus with its three holes for looseleaf binding the owner can collate in any way desired. The magazine is offset from typescript and is easy to read. (P.W.F.)

The Virginia Genealogist. 1957. q. $10 ($3 single issue). John Frederick Dorman. Box 4883, Washington, D.C. 20008. Circ: 1,000. Vol. ends: Oct./Dec.

Aud: Sa.

Mr. Dorman, a renowned professional Virginia genealogist, produces this journal unaided. There are about 300 pages a year and of course every page (except reviews) concerns Virginia. There are details of Virginia families, tax and other lists and queries. Book reviews, mostly with a Virginia slant, are many and careful. There is a good annual index. Its format is offset typescript and it is easy to read. (P.W.F.)

GENERAL MAGAZINES

Basic Periodicals

MIDDLE TO HIGH INTELLECTUAL INTERESTS. (Note: the descriptor "intellectual interests" is meant only as a guide to reading levels, not to taste, social, or educational achievement. It is used, however, to label somewhat accurately the audience the editors of the magazines have in mind.) Hs: *New Yorker, Noonmark;* Ga: *New Yorker, Atlantic, Center Magazine;* Jc: *New Yorker, Atlantic, Center Magazine, Saturday Review;* Ac: *New Yorker, New York, Atlantic, Center Magazine, Saturday Review, Harper's.*

MIDDLE TO LOW INTELLECTUAL INTERESTS. Hs: *Ideals, Saturday Evening Post, Exploring;* Ga: *Reader's Digest, Intellectual Digest, Ideals, Saturday Evening Post.*

Basic Abstracts and Indexes

Readers' Guide to Periodical Literature, British Humanities Index, Canadian Periodical Index, Catholic Periodical and Literature Index.

Cessations

Look, Expanse: an annotated guide to magazines.

Introduction

(Note: this section includes only magazines which do not fit well into subject categories. However, all the magazines listed in the following tables are annotated somewhere in this volume.)

With the exception of *Reader's Digest* and *Life,* there is no general magazine left in America. We have all become too specialized, and now turn to the television or the movies for sharing a general program of entertainment or information.

What does this mean for libraries? Well, if the generalist is dead, he has been replaced with a large audience of specialists for any given title. And they may range from the homemaker who reads *Good Housekeeping* to the rake who reads *Playboy.* Another type of specialist cannot be measured quantitatively, i.e., in terms of circulation. He or she is the selective reader who turns to a given magazine for more than relaxation and entertainment.

So it comes to two major audiences for the specialized, relatively high circulation magazine. The first is the popular reader. The second, for lack of a better descriptor, is the intellectual. With these two extremes in mind the librarian may make up a basic list of magazines. And to assist, here are two tests—the first objective, the second highly subjective. The first measures what the average reader reads; the second what the intellectual reads.

Hopefully, a combination of lists will help the librarian build a general collection.

Building a General Collection in Terms of Popularity

The librarian who is truly aiming at the general public is advised to consider the list carefully. This—comics, true confessions, religious magazines, etc.,—is what America reads.

For better or for worse, *Readers' Guide* indexes about half them. Why one is chosen over another for indexing is an intangible factor.

Most Popular Magazines Ranked by 1970 Circulation

RANK	PERIODICAL	INDEXED RG	CIRCULATION (IN THOUSANDS)
1	*Reader's Digest*	yes	17,900
2	*TV Guide*	no	15,884
3	*Life*	yes	8,638
4	Marvel Comic Group (Some 23 titles)	no	8,445
5	*McCalls*	yes	8,440
6	*Woman's Day*	no	8,697
7	*Look* (ceased)	yes	8,440
8	*Better Homes & Gardens*	yes	7,914
9	*Family Circle*	no	7,836
10	Archie Comic Group (Some 12 titles)	no	7,050
11	*National Geographic*	yes	7,086
12	*Ladies Home Journal*	yes	7,025
13	Harvey Comic Group (Some 30 titles)	no	6,678
14	National Comics Group (Some 80 titles)	no	6,500
15	*Good Housekeeping*	yes	5,840
16	*Playboy*	no	5,743
17	Charlton Comics (Some 36 titles)		
18	*Redbook*		
19	Scholastic Magazines	yes	4,594
20	Gold Key Comics (Some 50 titles)	no	4,480
21	Time	yes	4,324
22	American Home	yes	3,676
23	American Legion	no	2,663
24	Newsweek	yes	2,597
25	Farm Journal	yes	2,499
26	True Story	no	2,484
27	Boy's Life	yes	2,258
28	Parents' Magazine	yes	2,115
29	True	no	2,089
30	Sports Illustrated	yes	2,031
31	National Enquirer	no	2,006

RANK	PERIODICAL	INDEXED RG	CIRCULATION (IN THOUSANDS)
32	*U.S. News & World Report*	yes	1,889
33	*Outdoor Life*	yes	1,767
34	*Field & Stream*	yes	1,667
35	*Popular Mechanics*	yes	1,666
36	*Popular Science Monthly*	yes	1,642
37	*VFW Magazine*	no	1,578
38	*Workbasket*	no	1,550
39	*Elks Magazine*	no	1,527
40	*Mechanix Illustrated*	yes	1,500
41	*Seventeen*	yes	1,489
42	*Glamour*	no	1,475
43	*Photoplay*	no	1,449
44	*Sports Afield*	no	1,424
45	*Sport*	no	1,365
46	*Scouting*	yes	1,342
47	*Today's Education*	yes	1,330
48	*Cosmopolitan*	no	1,325
49	*Argosy*	no	1,311
50	*TV Radio Mirror*	no	1,239
51	*Ebony*	yes	1,224
52	*Newstime*	no	1,219
53	*Esquire*	yes	1,200
54	*Grit*	no	1,180
55	*Progressive Farmer*	no	1,161
56	*Holiday*	yes	1,109
57	*Columbia*	no	1,053
58	*House & Garden*	yes	1,042
59	*Successful Farming*	yes	1,020
60	*Sunset*	yes	972
61	*Signature*	no	963
62	*Ingenue*	no	960
63	*Co-ed*	yes	885
64	*Modern Screen*	no	885
65	*Nation's Business*	yes	865
66	*American Girl*	no	854
67	*House Beautiful*	yes	833
68	*Hot Rod*	yes	819
69	*Teen*	no	780
70	*Modern Romances*	no	765
71	*Simplicity Fashion Magazine*	no	721
72	*Presbyterian Life*	no	706
73	*Business Week*	yes	677
74	*Mademoiselle*	yes	671
75	*Southern Living*	no	670
76	*Lady's Circle*	no	653
77	*Motor Trend*	yes	652
78	*Lion*	no	634
79	*Forbes*	yes	627
80	*Saturday Review*	yes	620
81	*Flower & Garden Magazine*	no	619
82	*Car & Driver*	no	591
83	*Fortune*	yes	568
84	*Popular Photography*	yes	545
85	*Lutheran*	no	542

Another approach to determining the most popular magazines was offered by Leon Garry in his *Media Industry Newsletter* (June 15, 1972). He asked: "Of all the . . . magazines you read regularly or just occasionally, which one do you most look forward to reading?" The result was hardly surprising. Among those people polled across America *Reader's Digest* was the most popular magazine (11% of all respondents ranked it first). Close behind with 10% was *Time*. Following up were *Good Housekeeping* (7%), *Playboy* (6%) and *Life* (6%). Finally, in descending order of readership (5%–1%) were *Better Homes & Gardens, Ladies' Home Journal, McCall's, National Geographic, Newsweek, Sports Illustrated, Redbook, Family Circle, Esquire, Field and Stream, Outdoor Life, Woman's Day, Business Week,* and *Fortune.*

Building a Collection in Terms of What High School Students Read

A suggestive study indicates that too frequently the notions of *would* and *should* are generations apart. Here, for example, is a listing of magazines preferred by high school students as contrasted with those ordered by librarians. (James R. Squire, "Student Reading and the High School Library," *School Libraries,* Summer 1967, Chart 6, pp. 15–16.)

Fifteen Most Popular Magazines among Students Compared to School Library Holdings

RANK IN POPULARITY		NO. TIMES RANKED FIRST	TOTAL NO. OF TIMES MENTIONED	% OF LIBRARIES WITH PERIOD-ICAL
1	Life	4,117	7,455	92
2	Post (ceased)	1,743	4,700	93
3	Time	1,602	3,212	95
4	Look (ceased)	1,356	4,291	79
5	Seventeen	892	1,988	80
6	Reader's Digest	632	1,877	98
7	Newsweek	577	1,616	97
8	McCalls	302	1,039	55
9	Sports Illustrated	297	850	90
10	National Geographic	285	855	96
11	Hot Rod	321	398	48
12	Sports	169	333	25
13	Ingenue	120	338	12
14	Ladies Home Journal	111	589	73
15	Playboy	106	264	0

Building a General Collection in Terms of Intellectual Interests

A 1970 poll of editors and professors to determine which magazines they read, discussed, and considered "the most influential among intellectuals" revealed that popularity is not the only key to selection.

Of the 36 journals selected only four—*Newsweek,*

Time, U.S. News & World Report, Esquire—appear on the most popular list of magazines ranked by circulation.

Again, *Readers' Guide* indexes only about one half of the titles. (The most notable omission is the top choice *New York Review of Books,* and the most understandable is *Evergreen Review.*)

In order of preference, intellectuals read the following journals. Note that "since 20 percent of the total number of possible selections are journals added to the list or blanks, the top 8 journals actually constitute 69 percent of the selection of 36 journals included." (Data from Charles Kadushin, Julia Hover, and Monique Tichy, "How and Where to Find Intellectual Elite in the United States," *Public Opinion Quarterly,* Spring 1971, pp. 1–18.)

Cumulative Percentage of Total Number of Times Journals Were Selected

	JOURNAL	SELECTIONS NO.	SELECTIONS %	CUMU-LATIVE %
1.	N.Y. Review of Books	306	13.9	13.9
2.	New Republic	173	7.9	21.8
3.	Commentary	129	5.9	27.7
4.	N.Y. Times Book Review	108	4.9	32.6
5.	New Yorker	105	4.8	37.4
6.	Saturday Review	85	3.9	41.3
7.	Partisan Review	79	3.6	44.9
8.	Harper's	78	3.5	48.4
9.	Nation	60	2.7	51.1
10.	Atlantic	58	2.6	53.7
11.	Newsweek	52	2.4	56.1
12.	Daedalus	48	2.2	58.3
13.	Ramparts	46	2.1	60.4
14.	Yale Review	38	1.7	62.1
15.	Dissent	35	1.6	63.7
16.	Time	34	1.5	65.2
17.	Kenyon Review (ceased)	33	1.5	66.7
18.	Reporter (ceased)	32	1.5	68.2
19.	American Scholar	28	1.3	69.5
20.	Hudson Review	25	1.1	70.6
21.	Village Voice	25	1.1	71.7
22.	Progressive	23	1.0	72.7
23.	Sewanee Review	20	0.9	73.6
24.	National Review	16	0.7	74.3
25.	Paris Review	16	0.7	75.0
26.	Esquire	15	0.7	75.7
27.	Evergreen Review	14	0.6	76.3
28.	Commonweal	13	0.6	76.9
29.	New American Review	13	0.6	77.5
30.	U.S. News & World Report	13	0.6	78.1

| JOURNAL | SELECTIONS | | CUMU- |
	NO.	%	LATIVE %
31. *Journal of Politics*	11	0.5	78.6
32. *Columbia Journalism Review*	7	0.3	78.9
33. *Antioch Review*	6	0.3	79.2
34. *Southern Review*	6	0.3	79.5
35. *Science and Society*	5	0.2	79.7
36. *Guardian*	4	0.2	79.9
37. Journals written-in	191	8.7	88.6
38. Blank	255	11.6	100.2

The American Legion Magazine. 1919. m. $2. Robert B. Pitkin. James F. O'Neil, 1345 Ave. of the Americas, New York, N.Y. 10019. Illus., adv. Circ: 2,700,000. Sample. Vol. ends: June and Dec.

Aud: Ga.

While veterans' affairs and problems are stressed, this is much closer to a general interest magazine than the title suggests. Each issue contains four or more articles on such things as buying a home or an automobile. While middle-of-the-road to conservative in editorial matters, the magazine features opposing views on major issues and tends to represent a broad section of public opinion. The writing is never exciting, but the circulation indicates more than a passing interest by many members of the Legion.

✓**American Scholar; a quarterly for the independent thinker.** 1932. q. $5. Hiram Haydn. United Chapters of Phi Beta Kappa, 1811 Q St., N.W., Washington, D.C. 20009. Illus., index, adv. Circ: 47,000. Sample. Vol. ends: Autumn. Microform: UM.

Indexed: PAIS, RG, SSHum. *Bk. rev:* 15–16, notes to essays, signed. *Aud:* Ac, Ga. *Jv:* V.

An excellent review of long standing, this is directed to the intelligent reader. It offers the frank opinions of such critics as Alfred Kazin, Jacques Barzun, R. Buckminster Fuller, and Anthony Burgess. Topics range from social issues to the arts. In his column, "The Despairing Optimist," Rene Dubos has offered his opinion on such subjects as ecology, the art of living, and the human zoo. On occasion an issue is given to a single subject, i.e., crime and punishment in America. There are book reviews and running commentary on arts and letters. A required item for the thinking man and woman in both public and academic libraries.

✓**Atlantic Monthly.** 1857. m. $10.50. Robert Manning. Atlantic Monthly Co., 8 Arlington St., Boston, Mass. 02116. Illus., adv. Circ: 325,000. Sample. Microform: UM.

Indexed: AbrRG, RG. *Bk. rev:* 5–10, lengthy, 10–20 notes. *Aud:* Ac, Ga, Hs. *Jv:* V.

With the ouster of Willie Morris at *Harper's, Atlantic* has taken on a new interest. The new *Harper's* is not the same, and its primary rival is stepping in to take over. One of the best and oldest of the general interest review magazines, this presents informative and entertaining articles by accepted authorities, stories and poetry by both established writers and talented newcomers. Regular features include "Reports & Comment," candid studies of important political activities and other foreign and domestic developments; "Life & Letters," short essays on people and performers in the fields of art, music, literature, film, travel, dance, and gourmet cooking. Articles, sometimes commissioned, explore controversial political and social questions, scientific and technical innovations, and the whole range of the arts. Quality literature and literary criticism earn a place for *The Atlantic* in the lists of literary magazines.

Audience. 1968. bi-m. $24. Geoffrey Ward. Hill Publishing Co., Sears Crescent, City Hall Plaza, Boston, Mass. 02138. Illus. Circ: 45,000 Sample. Vol ends: Nov./Dec.

Aud: Ga, Ac.

Serving as a chronicle of American taste, this is both a general magazine for the casual reader and an ongoing document of cultural activities for the specialist. Culture is interpreted in its broadest sense, i.e., there have been well-written articles on such items as Hallmark cards, a hobo convention, Mattel toys, a symphony percussionist, USIA films, a circus, the TV rating process, etc. Just about every aspect of the current scene is covered, usually by first rate observers such as William Stafford, Nelson Algren, and Isaac Singer. Using the hardbound approach of *American Heritage,* the content appeal of a *Harper's* or *Atlantic,* and the graphic talents of the Push Pin Studios (Milton Glaser and Seymour Chwast), this is an impressive effort. The high price is probably necessary to cover the 112 pages which do not rely on advertising. It is too bad, though, that it couldn't have been a little less extravagant in terms of layout—which is to start an argument on whether content is more important than format. Here the two are about equally matched, although content is so good as to not really need the frosting. An honest effort which most libraries should consider.

Avant Garde. 1967. q. $10. Ralph Ginzburg. Avant Garde Media, Inc., 110 W. 40th St., New York, N.Y. 10018. Illus., adv. Circ: 250,000.

Aud: Ga. *Jv:* C.

After five years this pseudo-little-art-political magazine continues to stagger on. A hodgepodge of colored plates, poetry, fiction, and various degrees of "shock" material, it seems to have never established any definite character or reason for existence. It is no better—indeed, now seems worse, than the first time it was analyzed here. Libraries can avoid without missing anything.

Blackwood's Magazine. 1817. m. $9. G. D. Blackwood. Blackwood & Sons, Ltd., 46 George St., Edinburgh, 2, Scotland. Adv. Circ: 15,364. Microform: UM.

Bk. rev: 5, 250 words. *Aud:* Ga, Ac. *Jv:* C.

Material is somewhat equally divided between insipid short stories and articles on travel and literary personalities. There is a section of comment on international affairs which is the best part of the magazine, but this 10 to 15 page section hardly justifies a subscription. Libraries taking the magazine will wish to continue, but a last choice for all others.

Canadian Forum. 1920. m. $5.35. Abraham Rotstein. Canadian Forum Ltd., 56 Esplanade, Toronto, Ont. Canada. Illus., index, adv. Circ: 3,400. Sample. Vol. ends: April.

Indexed: CanI. *Bk. rev:* 10, ½–full page, signed. *Aud:* Ga, Ac.

Somewhat like a Canadian version of *Harper's* and *Atlantic,* this is an austere "independent journal of opinion and the arts." Some of the writing is the best in Canada, and at one time or another it has published just about every distinguished Canadian writer. Articles move from the social to the political, and there are usually poems, short stories, and reports on the arts, i.e., again along the line of the *Harper's* or *Atlantic* approach. It is tending to become a bit more national, certainly more militant. There are excellent book reviews. While not the most exciting magazine in Canada, one of the more intellectual and more interesting.

Center Magazine. 1967. bi-m. Membership. $15. John Cogley. Center for the Study of Democratic Institutions, Box 4068, Santa Barbara, Calif. 93103. Illus. Circ: 100,000. Sample. Vol. ends: Nov./Dec.

Aud: Ga, Ac, Hs. *Jv:* V.

Gaining in influence, circulation, and importance, this general approach to world events can be recommended even more highly than in the first edition. Each issue covers various national and international questions which are of ultimate concern to us all, but of particular concern to the scholars who work at the Center. These vary from reports on current economic issues to long range diplomatic and political considerations of the United States and other world powers. The material, in other words, touches on almost anything which a general "thinking man or woman's" magazine would consider. The style of writing is lucid, presupposes no particular specialized knowledge. Contributors are well known scholars and public figures. The approach is objective, liberal, and sometimes controversial. An invaluable reference aid for any library, including high schools.

Columbia Forum; a quarterly journal of fact and opinion. 1957. q. $6.50. Erik Wensberg, 612 W. 114th St., New York, N.Y. 10025. Illus. Circ: 10,000. Vol. ends: No. 4.

Indexed: PAIS. *Bk. rev:* Occasional essay, signed. *Aud:* Ga, Ac.

Beginning with the Winter 1971 issue this free magazine became an independent subscription journal. What was once an excellent alumni publication is now an even better general magazine of literature, poetry, the arts, social sciences, etc. The 60 or so pages follow the format of the older magazine, but now there is more material. For example, the Winter 1971 number led off with an article by Christopher Lasch on the development of class rule in America, an essay on women's liberation by Carolyn G. Heilbrun, a report on the biological ecology task force, a perceptive article on modern Germany, etc. There is some poetry, the regular departments, and criticism. The style of writing is semipopular, although aimed for the better educated reader. Under its new banner, the magazine moves right up with the established reviews and quarterlies. It should be considered by most libraries. If no longer free, it is well worth the subscription price.

Coronet. 1936. m. $5. Claire Safran. Coronet Communications Inc., 315 Park Ave. S., New York, N.Y. 10010. Illus., adv. Circ: 345,000.

Aud: Ga.

Another version of the *Reader's Digest.* Even the format is familiar. Each issue contains articles, stories, pictures, cartoons, and a book condensation. There is more interest here in entertainment, less in politics than in *RD.* It is inexpensive enough entertainment, particularly for readers with little imagination. Might be welcomed into libraries where there is an outreach effort. Note: The magazine is due for a slight modification. As of mid–1972 it is to turn more to women, i.e. it "will change its editorial direction to become a woman's psychological service magazine that will cater to the blue collar middle-American women," the publisher announced.

Cosmopolitan. See Women's Magazines/General Section.

Country Life. 1897. w. $36. George Newnes Ltd., Tower House, Southampton St., London WC 2, England. Microform: UM.

Indexed: BritHum. *Aud:* Ga.

An expensive magazine with an expensive approach to existence. Articles, pictures, departments, and, most of all, the advertising are put together for one reason: to show how nice it is to have the money necessary to live the good, country life. Here, of course, the country life is the English countryside with castles, mansions, antiques, culture, etc. It is all harmless enough fun, although the subscription price is high for most libraries. Larger libraries may want it because there are some fair to good articles on historical and cultural matters.

Daedalus. 1955. q. $7.50. Stephen R. Grawbard. American Academy of Arts and Sciences, 7 Linden St., Harvard Univ., Cambridge, Mass. 02138. Illus., index. Circ: 70,000. Sample. Vol. ends: Fall.

Indexed: BioAb, ChemAb, PAIS, PsyAb, SSHum, SciAb. *Bk. rev:* 2–3, length varies, signed. *Aud:* Ac, Ga, Hs. *Jv:* V.

Concentrating on one particular social, political, or literary topic, each issue offers a current report on an aspect of American life. Contributors are leaders in the area covered, and normally there is a brief introductory essay with some 15 to 20 supporting articles. (Librarians who recognize the approach of *Library Trends* will find the same general monographic method here.) A run of *Daedalus* is equivalent to an updating service of texts and full length book studies found on the shelves. Many libraries and individuals tend to bind the copies and catalog them in the subject area. In view of its authority, the frequency of comment on an issue by the American press, and the topical nature of its coverage, this should be found in all libraries.

Eagle Magazine. 1911. m. $1. Arthur S. Ehrmann. Fraternal Order of Eagles, 2401 W. Wisconsin Ave., Milwaukee, Wis. 53233. Illus., adv. Circ: 742,000.

Aud: Ga.

A working man's fraternal order, the Eagles reflects the so-called blue collar and lower income American's interests. In addition to a tremendous amount of fraternal news (more so than in most magazines of this type), there are articles on patriotism, the home, retirement, travel, the outdoors, sports—and some social and political matters. The style of writing is fair, the contents interesting to a member of the order, and the overall impression one of a magazine which is probably a trifle more conservative and parochial than the other fraternal magazines.

Elks Magazine. 1922. Membership (Nonmembers $2). Ed. bd. Benevolent and Protective Order of Elks of the United States of America, 425 Diversey Parkway, Chicago, Ill. 60614. Illus., adv. Circ: 1,505,500.

Aud: Ga.

Here the target audience is the relatively affluent businessman, living in a small to medium-sized town. The editor pictures him as being middle-of-the-road to conservative, involved in his own sense of importance as a businessman, and mildly interested in history, hobbies, and humor. The articles are so geared. Aside from business (how-to-do-it and why I am a success type predominate) the primary interest seems to be sports, from baseball to hunting and fishing. Some fiction, passable photographs, and, of course, news of

the Elks and their activities—in fact, one third or more of every issue is given to organizational material. A not overly exciting magazine, but a well read one, and can be recommended for most libraries—even those without an Elks club about. (Note: not for the Black community. The Elks have long waged a battle to keep Blacks out of their organization.)

Encounter. 1953. m. $14. Nigel Dennis and Melvin J. Lasky. British Publns., Inc., 11–03 46th Ave., Long Island City, N.Y. 1101. Subs. to: 25 Haymarket St., London, England. Circ: 25,000. Vol. ends: Dec. Microform: UM.

Indexed: BritHum, PAIS, SSHum. *Bk. rev:* 2–5, 3–5 pages, signed. *Aud:* Ga, Ac, Hs. *Jv:* V.

A famous British magazine which is somewhat similar in purpose to *Harper's, Atlantic* and other general literary magazines. Although contributors are representatives of some of the world's leading scholars, the tone is not academic. Emphasis is on wit, style, and a sense of proportion between the ivory tower and the marketplace. Articles cover a wide field, from social and political studies to literary and philosophical considerations. There are excellent theatre, film, and book reviews. The writers presuppose a better than average educated audience with a liberal viewpoint. From its beginnings it was one of the more influential international periodicals. An important general magazine for all types of libraries.

Esquire. 1933. m. $8.50. Harold Hayes. 488 Madison Ave., New York, N.Y. 10022. Illus., index, adv. Circ: 1,200,000.

Indexed: RG. *Bk. rev:* Various number, length, signed. *Aud:* Ga. *Jv:* V.

No longer the oversized magazine of the 1960s, *Esquire* is now in a normal format with an imaginative approach to the general magazine scene. Although for men, its wide range of articles, fiction, and departments interest as many women. It is most noteworthy for special features which tend to trace trends in everything from the American campus to politics and the social-literary scene. The specials are made up of speculative editorial matter usually surrounded by satirical photographs, and cartoons which owe much to an extremely creative art director. The stories by the familiars, e.g., Styron, Updike, Nabokov (to name those who appeared in one issue) are good to excellent. The articles are timely, often include interviews and discussions. Malcolm Muggeridge writes first rate book reviews and there are film and record reviews, among others. There is no "girlie" material, except in a satirical way. The one real concession to the average male is the emphasis on clothing and the advertising. Otherwise it can (and should) be read by women as well. A first choice for a general reading collection.

Exploring. 1971. bi-a. $2. Robert E. Hood. Magazine Division of the Boy Scouts of America, North Brunswick, N. J. 08902. Illus. Sample.

Aud: Hs.

The teenage girl on the cover of this 50-page colorfully illustrated magazine indicates it is not *Boy's Life.* And while the sponsor is the same, emphasis is on the boy-girl syndrome. Aside from the factual material, there is a certain blandness about the focus. (An article on Blacks is nice, but meaningless.) On the positive side, the articles are written by and for young people, are matter-of-fact, free of righteous hints, and the illustrations and layout are good. The price is o.k., too. Librarians trying to find something for the 14 to 17 age group will be delighted with this latest addition.

Grit. See Newspapers/Special Interest Section.

Harper's. 1850. m. $8.50. Robert Shnayerson. 2 Park Ave., New York, N.Y. 10016. Illus., index, adv. Circ: 35,000. Microform: UM.

Indexed: AbrRG, RG. *Bk. rev:* 5–10, 250–750 words, signed. *Aud:* Ac, Ga, Hs.

Under the editorship of Willie Morris the oldest of America's general cultural magazines proved a booming success. It was innovative, imaginative, and leading the field in its advocacy of personalized journalism. Then in 1971 Morris retired in a quarrel with management over, among other things, Norman Mailer's use of dirty words. Mailer called the resignation "the most depressing event in American letters in many a year." Not quite. The hiring of a former Time–Life man, Robert Shnayerson, as editor may have been an even bigger disaster. By 1972 the magazine lacked life, seemed to be drifting aimlessly, looking for a reason or a cause. The stories lack the fire they had under Morris, and the whole thing now looks like a replay of the 1890s. Sad. Still, perhaps it will once more improve. In the meantime no library with a subscription should cancel, but there is no reason to begin one either. Try the *Atlantic.*

Ideals. 1944. bi-m. $7.95. Lorraine Obst, 11315 Watertown Plank Rd., Milwaukee, Wis. 53226. Illus.

Aud: Ga, Hs, Ejh.

The publisher's blurb pretty well sums up the editorial purpose: "It is clean, wholesome, old fashioned; American ideals, homey philosophy, poetry, art, music, inspiration, neighborliness, things many of us may have overlooked during these busy days." She will not reveal circulation figures, but in view of its long life it seems to be doing pretty well. The approach is not for the reader of *The New York Times,* but may have appeal for the *Reader's Digest* group. Aside from that, it is particularly good for the abundant illustrations both in color and black and white. The pictures follow the theme of the magazine which is based on the seasons,

e.g., a single issue is given over to Spring, Summer, Fall, Winter, Easter, and Christmas. Useful for secondary schools, and elementary teachers will find the seasonal apsects of the magazine helpful for filling in discussions.

Illustrated London News. 1842. m. James Bishop. Illustrated London News & Sketch Ltd., 100 Grays Inn Rd., London WC1X, 8AP England. Illus., index, adv. Circ: 60,000. Sample. Vol. ends: Dec. Microform: UM.

Indexed: BritHum. *Bk. rev:* 6, 600 words, signed. *Aud:* Ga, Ac.

In May 1971, this traditional weekly went monthly and in so doing changed its editorial policy. Whereas the old weekly put considerable emphasis on English social life, the new approach is to give "a considered view, with pictures of the most significant of world events." And while it remains firmly British in outlook, the view is wide enough to have appeal for anyone who is involved in the world's varied cultural activities. The film, theatre, and book reviews remain good to excellent. The net result of the change is a much improved general magazine, at least for American readers, and it can now be recommended for all collections.

Intellectual Digest. 1971. m. $10. Martin L. Gross. Communications/Research/Machines Inc. Subs. to: P.O. Box 2986, Boulder, Colo. 80302. Illus., adv. Sample. Vol. ends: Aug.

Bk. rev: 5–10 books reviewed in a single essay on a given subject. *Aud:* Ga, Ac, Hs. *Jv:* C.

From the folks who brought you *Psychology Today* comes a similar package with a new twist. Articles, apparently run in full, are lifted from such liberal voices as *Commonwealth, Modern Occasions, The New Republic,* and *The New Yorker*—to name only four of the some 200 magazines with which the publisher claims he deals. The "digest" bit applies primarily to books, and there are usually excerpts from three different titles. The neat use of "intellectual" is an apparent effort to kill the stigma of digests as so ably represented by *Reader's Digest.* The target audience, it is felt, is one that might shy at having the *Reader's Digest* in the home, but would welcome "intellectual" fare. Some issues aside, it comes down to a commercial ripoff. The *Reader's Digest* by any other name is still the *Reader's Digest.*

Kiwanis Magazine. 1917. $2.50. Dennis Moore. Kiwanis International, 101 E. Erie St., Chicago, Ill. 60611. Illus., adv. Circ: 270,000.

Aud: Ga.

One of the three devoted to local, international, and benevolent activities. (The other two are *Lion* and *Rotarian. Lion* seems to be at the bottom, *Kiwanis* in the middle and *Rotarian* at the top, i.e., this is the order of affluence and education of an average member. It is not, obviously, a measure of their worth to a library.) The average issue includes some good to excellent articles on social matters, local government, and business. There is the usual club material, some humor, and photographs. The level of writing is high for this type of magazine, and the reporting is accurate and unbiased. Membership regulations make this so because the club at the local level is limited to two members from any business or profession. The result is a true cross section of interests in most communities. Given this type of membership, the magazine is more lively than its rivals. If a choice is to be made between it and the other two, and all things are equal, it would be first.

Liberty; the nostalgia magazine. 1971. q. $3. Martty Simmons. Twenty First Century Communications, 635 Madison Ave., New York, N.Y. 10022. Illus., adv. Circ: 240,000.

Aud: Ga.

This is a nostalgia trip via a reprint; nothing new or current here. Reprinting articles from *Liberty* magazine (1924–1950), the publisher offers the good old days of the 1920s, thirties, and forties. *Liberty*, it will be recalled, was one of a number of successful large circulation general magazines in America. Much of the material, then as now, was on a level somewhat below that found in the old *Colliers* or the *Saturday Evening Post*. It did shine in terms of short stories (dutifully headed with the amount of time it should take a reader to complete), and many of these by MacKinlay Kantor, H.G. Wells, and lesser knowns are republished. The magazine is reprinted from photographic plates of the original magazine pages. The only thing new are the advertisements. As the publisher commented: "There's no typesetting, no royalties, or author's fees." And the price has gone from 5 cents to 75 cents. It is fun—but only for the oldsters.

Lion Magazine. 1918. m. $1.50. Albert D. Geller. International Assn. of Lions Clubs, York and Cermak Roads, Oak Brook, Ill. 60521. Illus., index, adv. Circ: 635,000.

Aud: Ga.

Most of the average issue is given over to news about the Lions, an international organization somewhat similar in intent to the Rotarians. Only about one third of each issue is devoted to articles (usually concerned with travel, personalities, humor, and the usual how-I-did-it improvement type). The editor steers a course between extremes—political or social—and the magazine can be read and enjoyed by almost any man regardless of his social or political persuasions. There tends to be a good deal of optimistic "go get 'em" type material, nicely balanced with pleas for help for those lacking the Lions' drive and

abilities. A general magazine for most men, even those who are not involved with the sponsoring organization.

The Listener and British Broadcasting Corporation Television Review. 1929. w. $11. K. F. C. Miller. British Broadcasting Corp., Broadcasting House, London W1A, England. Illus., index, adv. Circ: 40,000. Sample. Vol. ends: June and Dece.

Indexed: BritHum. *Bk. rev:* 7, 10,000 words, signed. *Aud:* Ga, Ac, Hs.

Although this is the printed voice of the British Broadcasting Corporation, it is much wider in scope and purpose than the sponsor would indicate. It does publish a number of talks from BBC's "third program," but the subject approach is purposefully less limited. Articles cover such diverse topics as the probable end of the world, the current concerns of philosophy, Jane Fonda, George Orwell, Stockhausen, and leek-growing. Editorially, it takes a middle-of-the-road approach, but the book, film, television, and radio reviews are refreshingly candid and critical. The tone is definitely intellectual, the writing style superb, and the whole an extremely worthwhile general weekly for almost any type of library, from senior high school up.

London Magazine. 1954. 1961 (new series). bi-m. $10. Alan Ross, 30 Thurloe Place, London SW7, England. Illus., index, adv. Circ: 5,500. Sample. Vol. ends: Feb./March.

Indexed: BritHum. *Bk. rev:* 8, 200 words, signed. *Aud:* Ac, Ga.

Something on the order of the familiar American review format, this English magazine devotes a high proportion of its content to poems, stories, pictures, and drawings. New writers as well as established ones are featured, and it maintains an excellent level of poetry. The special editorial aim is to discuss individual writers and painters out of season, and to keep literary contact with Europe, Africa, America, and the Commonwealth. Regular features are the sections on Theater, Cinema, Music, Art, Architecture, Poetry, and also Reminiscences. Book reviews are of scholarly works, poetry, and fiction. A first choice in academic libraries over *Contemporary Review,* but for public libraries it would probably have less appeal than the other English magazine.

Maclean's Magazine; Canada's national magazine. 1905. m. $3.50. Peter C. Newman. Maclean-Hunter Ltd. 481 Univ. Ave., Toronto 101, Ont., Canada. Illus., index, adv. Circ: 750,000.

Indexed: CanI. *Bk. rev:* 3–4, 180 words, signed. *Aud:* Ga.

Anyone looking for *The Saturday Evening Post* (old variety, not the quarterly) and *Colliers* is advised to turn to *Maclean's*—one of the few really general magazines left in North America. It is constantly rumored the magazine is going under, but it seems to survive on the same formula that made the *Post* famous. The difference is that the articles and fiction praise the Canadian way. While at one time I recommended this for American libraries, that is no longer the case. There are too many better Canadian magazines around, e.g., the old standby *Saturday Night*, the newer, more exciting *Last Post* or *Mysterious East*. In Canada, though, *Maclean's* seems to be a necessity.

The firm also issues a French-Canadian edition at the same price, but the content is somewhat different: *Magazine Maclean* (1961. m. $3.50. Jean Sisto. Maclean-Hunter, 2055 Peel St., Montreal 110, Canana. Illus., index, adv. Circ: 177,000.) This is no better than the parent, but the French text and numerous illustrations give it a place in any general French language collection.

New York Magazine. 1968. w. $8. Clay Felker. 207 E. 32nd St., New York, N.Y. 10016. Illus., index, adv. Circ: 245,000.

Aud: Ga, Ac, Hs. *Jv:* V.

While this started out as a "city" magazine, i.e., one devoted exclusively to activities in New York, it has become considerably more. It is now considered a serious rival to *The New Yorker*. Although not so broad in scope (or in advertising lineage) as the older magazine, the level of writing is just as sophisticated, often considerably more lively and timely. It is directed to upper middle class Americans, with a college education and better jobs—i.e., the same audience as the *New Yorker*. Unlike its rival, it is short on fiction, longer on meaningful articles about science, politics, personalities, art, business—just about any subject of interest to readers. A good deal of the material is specifically for the New York City or area resident, but an equal amount can be profitably enjoyed by the reader in mid-America and on the west coast. A good general magazine for most libraries, and a required item in high school, public, and academic libraries on the east coast.

New Yorker. 1925. w. $12. William Shawn. New Yorker Magazine, Inc. 25 W. 43rd St., New York, N.Y. 10036. Illus., index, adv. Circ: 465,000.

Indexed: MusicI, RG. *Bk. rev:* Essay, 10–20 notes of 50–100 words, signed. *Aud:* Ga, Ac, Hs. *Jv:* V.

The general magazine of the better educated, possibly more sophisticated American. The format and approach have not changed since the previous evaluation. The usual complaint is still heard, i.e. "I grow tired of the same thing week in week out." This is the "Talk of the Town," which has become increasingly political and, as might be expected, liberal; one or two short stories; a profile or article which later may develop into a book; and theatre, music, film, and book reviews. The film reviews by Pauline Kael and Penelope Gilliatt are among the best available. There is a New York group of writers and poets, and while a few of them, from John Updike to Sylvia T. Warner, are repeats, the editor does, on occasion, attempt to introduce some new talent. And, of course, there are the cartoons, which reflect the foibles of the upper American middle classes. Most people either hate or love the magazine, though some readers skim it indifferently. Be that as it may, it is a required general magazine for any library where there is a white middle class clientele. It may bore others, totally.

Noonmark. 1967. irreg. $1.75/issue. Charles Trueheart. Phillips Exeter Academy, Exeter, N.H., 03833. Illus. Sample.

Aud: Hs.

The objective of *Noonmark* is "to provide a medium through which young people can communicate freely and openly." The basis of the term "communication" for this magazine is "a search for human warmth, a search for the capacity to sympathize and empathize." The magazine which terms itself "a magazine for the creative arts in secondary schools" fulfills its mission and makes a contribution to life. It should be a part of all libraries. (L.G.)

Playboy. See Men's Magazines Section.

Reader's Digest. 1922. m. $4. Dewitt and Lila Wallace. Reader's Digest Assn., Pleasantville, N.Y. 10570. Illus., adv. Circ: 17,900,000

Indexed: AbrRg, RG. *Aud:* Ga. *Jv:* C.

Grows progressively more simplistic and more popular, which seems to prove Mencken's theory that you can never go wrong underestimating people's intelligence and good taste. Well, if 17 million Americans—not to mention millions of Europeans, Latin Americans, Asians, and, for all I know, Laplanders—want it, let us not argue. I would feel guilty about introducing it to innocent school children. As for the librarians who insist on indexing it in *Readers' Guide*, they are more innocent than the kids.

Rotarian. 1911. m. $2.50. Karl K. Krueger. Rotary International, 1600 Ridge Ave., Evanston, Ill. 60201. Illus., adv. Circ: 478,000.

Aud: Ga.

Rotary is the leading business-oriented fraternal organization in the United States (as contrasted with the Kiwanis who take in all community interests). The result is a magazine for the better-than-average educated and affluent American man. The articles are well written, tend to concentrate on international affairs and travel. There is the same flavor of good companionship, "go-get-'em" optimism and helpfulness to the less fortunate as found in *Lion* magazine, but here it is a trifle more sophisticated. About one third or more of every issue is given to club business. Not the most exciting of the magazines in this category, but one of the more widely read.

Saturday Evening Post. 1971. q. $4. Beurt SerVaas. Curtis Publishing Co., 1100 Waterway Blvd., Indianapolis, Ind. 46202. Illus., adv.

Aud: Ga. *Jv:* C.

Resurrected as a quarterly in early 1971, the better-left-dead-and-buried *Post* has emerged as a magazine for "middle America." The notion is to tell us all about the good life, and forget the world. The 160-page formula is a dream of those who tried to save the *Post* years ago. It appears as a mild nightmare. The stories, five or six per issue, are insipid; the articles are right out of the Sunday supplement, and the cartoons from an age long gone. A few reprints of older material are at least honest. It is hard to imagine who will buy this—particulary at $1 an issue. Television is too much closer and cheaper for the audience the *Post* envisions. Not recommended for any library. If you want a straightforward middle, silent, and not-too-smart American magazine stick to the *Reader's Digest*, the much better *Yankee,* or the unadulterated nostalgia in *Liberty*.

Saturday Review. 1924. m. $12. John J. Veronis and Nicholas H. Charney. Saturday Review Inc., 380 Madison Ave., New York, N.Y. 10017. Illus., index, adv. Circ: 600,000.

Indexed: AbrRG. MusicI, RG. *Aud:* Ga, Hs, Ac.

New ownership, new editors, and a new approach. *SR*, no longer influenced by the personality of Norman Cousins, who was editor for 29 years, is now headed up by John Veronis and Nick Charney. Cousins sold the magazine to the two former owners and creators of *Psychology Today* in 1971. Following announcements of new editorial plans, he resigned.

Saturday Review is now four monthly magazines. Confusing? Yes. This magazine is now in a period of transition, to say the least. Each week the company publishes an issue focusing on either education, science, society, or the arts. Readers interested in only one of the four subjects can subscribe to *Saturday Review of Science*, for example, and receive it monthly. The price for a year's subscription to one of the four is $12; to receive all four, one each week on a rotating basis, the rate is $24. However, if you are now a subscriber to *SR*, and renew your subscription before January 1, 1973, you will receive the four new monthlies, one each week, for $12.

One of the major differences between the new magazines and the old *SR* will be the editorial slant. Where Cousins' policies veered toward the Left, Veronis and Charney are trying to build circulation, and their editorial policies promise to be on a wider and less controversial political base.

Meanwhile, Cousins is bringing out a new magazine of his own—one to challenge *Saturday Review*. It is called *World: a review of ideas, creative arts and the human condition.* (1972. bi-w. $12. Norman Cousins. World, The Dag Hammerskjold Plaza, New York, N.Y. 10017). It is modeled after the old *Saturday Review,* and by April of 1972 it was reported to have 100,000 committed subscribers. It is, obviously, a magazine to watch.

Scouting Magazine. 1913. 7/yr. $1. Walter Babson. Boy Scouts of America, New Brunswick, N.J. 08903. Illus., index, adv. Circ: 1,400,000.

Bk. rev: Notes. *Aud:* Ga.

Not for the boys (and young girls) but for their parents, leaders, and interested adults who support the cub packs, Boy Scout troops and explorer units. The magazine's primary purpose is to tell the adult how to conduct meetings, lead the scouts into the woods, and keep up with the interests of the young. The articles are common sense, practical, and realistic. Interspersed are regular departments, personality sketches, humor, and photographic stories. The magazine is heavy on how-to-do-it in terms of leading a successful Scouting troop. Some effort is made to understand basic psychology of individuals, although most of this is aimed at an average situation or so called average boy. A rather different, somewhat interesting magazine whose low price accounts for its high circulation (right up with *Boy's Life*).

Signature; the Diner's Club magazine. 1954. m. $3.98. Ken Gouldthorpe, 660 Madison Ave., New York, N.Y. 10021. Illus., adv. Circ: 950,000. Sample.

Bk. rev: Notes. *Aud:* Ga.

A high circulation, general magazine which is the brain child of the famous Diner's Club. While it is directed to the "urban affluent, traveled and young businessman," the publisher of late has noticed the Women's Liberation Movement, and the journal is recognizing women too. Most of the articles deal with all aspects of a general world: travel, personalities, sports, and business. It is heaviest on the good life, i.e., entertainment, food, and drink—but some weight is given to relatively noncontroversial social issues. Past issues, for example, have included rather good articles on pollution and environment. The writing is professional, as are the format and the illustrations. A light, pleasing, and not overly intellectual approach to the world. It should be better known in libraries, particularly as it probably can be had for the asking from the publisher.

TV Guide. 1953. w. $7. Merrill Panitt. Triangle Publns., Inc., 250 King of Prussia Rd., Radnor, Pa. 19088. Illus., adv. Circ: 16,291,000. Sample. Vol. ends: Dec. 31.

Bk. rev: 1, 500 words, signed. *Aud:* Ac, Ga.

The largest-selling weekly magazine in America, this is directed to the general television viewer. It is made up of two parts: national and regional. The national editorial section carries about six 1,000 to 2,500 word articles by both staff members and well-known contributors. New York and Hollywood sections give brief items about performers and forthcoming programs. Complete program listings are given in the program section, which sometimes covers a large geographical area. There are 81 regional editions each week. Also included here are a critical column on the week's TV movies by Judith Crist, television criticism by Cleveland Amory, a report on network doings, and a page of readers' letters. Over the years it has moved from an unsophisticated listing to a magazine that is relatively critical. Its daily purpose is best suited to the home, but a run of the magazine will prove a valuable reference and research aid in the years to come. Larger academic and public libraries certainly should consider it for its long range research aspects.

TV Radio Mirror. 1933. m. $5. Lawrence B. Thomas. Macfadden-Bartell, 205 East 42nd St., New York, N.Y. 10017. Illus., adv. Circ: 1,115,000.

Aud: Ga, Hs.

This is not the same item as *TV Guide.* It is, rather, a confessional type magazine for young women. The terms "tv" and "radio" are dropped into the title to indicate the magazine will feature personalities found on talk and variety shows as well as the stars of standard television programs. Most of the push is to offer a counter to *Photoplay* and *Motion Picture Magazine,* both Macfadden-Bartell titles; but the counter is more of the same, i.e., personal stories about television stars. The articles, which are well illustrated with photographs, are of varying length but all are in simple, direct language. The magazine owes its success to careful editing with less of an eye on the sensational, more on the folksy and glamorous aspects of the star's personal and family life. Aside from the questionable importance of most of the so-called celebrities, or the details of their lives, the magazine is harmless enough. It is, in fact, one of the best of its genre and can be recommended to a library trying to do something about remedial reading, or bringing relevance to an essentially non-reading community. Then, too, it has some importance for the social historian. A run of it, along with *TV Guide,* would seem essential for any popular culture collection.

Town and Country. 1846. m. $10. Anthony Mazzola. Hearst Corp. 250 W. 55th St., New York, N.Y. 10019. Illus., index; adv. Circ: 117,000. Microform: UM.

Bk. rev: Various number, length. *Aud:* Ga.

Somewhat the American equivalent of the English *Country Life*—and just about as valuable for libraries. The main interest is in the glories of social life, and assisting the reader to weave his or her own fantasies by studying the activities of richer, more beautiful, obviously happier people in the pages of the magazine. They wind their ways through countryside and kitchen, from one art event and musical concert to another party and tea. Some of the photographs are fascinating, and the copy is right out of *Alice in Wonderland.* Harmless, in fact pleasant, but hardly a necessary item for the library.

GEOGRAPHY

Basic Periodicals

Ejh: *National Geographic School Bulletin;* Hs: *National Geographic, Focus;* Ga: *National Geographic, Focus;* Jc: *Association of American Geographers. Annals, Canadian Geographic Journal, Focus, Geographical Journal, National Geographic.*

Library and Teaching Aids

Journal of Geography, National Geographic School Bulletin.

Basic Abstracts and Indexes

Geographical Abstracts.

Annales de Geographie. See Europe and Middle East/French Language Section.

Antarctic Journal of the United States. 1966. bi-m. $3.50. K. G. Sandved. National Science Foundation. Subs. to: Supt. of Documents, U.S. Govt. Printing Office, Washington, D.C. 20402. Illus. Vol. ends: Dec.

Indexed: BioAb. *Aud:* Ac.

Issued by the National Science Foundation, with the assistance of the Department of Defense, this government periodical covers, with short factual articles, developments, problems, and research at the various U.S. installations in the Antarctic. Articles are scholarly, many with extensive references. The activities of the sites are also included. There are no book reviews, but publications dealing with the area are noted. Of interest to geology as well as geography collections. (D.D.)

Arctic. 1948. q. Membership $10. Mrs. Anna Monson. Arctic Inst. of North America, 3458 Redpath St., Montreal 25, Que., Canada. Illus., adv. Circ: 3,000. Microform: UM. Reprint: Johnson.

Indexed: BioAb, CanI, ChemAb. *Bk. rev:* 3–5, 350–1,000 words, signed. *Aud:* Ac.

Features scientific papers on subjects related to the Arctic, the Subarctic, and Antarctica, contributed by specialists in both the natural and social sciences. The main papers are abstracted in English, French, and

Russian. Also contains reports, notes, news items, and commentaries of more general interest on the exploration or study of the polar regions. A scholarly journal for only the large academic library.

Arctic and Alpine Research. 1969. q. $20 (Individuals $12, students $8). Kathleen Salzberg. Inst. of Arctic and Alpine Research, Univ. of Colorado, Boulder, Colo. 80302. Illus., index. Circ: 750. Sample. Vol ends: Fall. Refereed.

Indexed: BioAb, GeoAb. *Bk. rev:* 4, 1,000 words, signed. *Aud:* Ac.

Scientific papers deal with all aspects of the arctic and alpine environment. Covers a number of areas from Alaska and Canada to Colorado and Iceland. Articles presuppose knowledge of major sciences, e.g., "Nocturnal arthropods in the alpine tundra of Colorado," or "A conceptual model for alpine slope process study." Only for large, rather specialized collections.

√*Association of American Geographers. Annals.* 1911. q. $16. John F. Hart. Assn. of Amer. Geographers, General Office, 1146 16th St., N.W., Washington, D.C. 20036. Illus., index. Circ: 8,500. Microform: PMC. Reprint: Kraus.

Indexed: BioAb, SSHum. *Bk. rev:* 2–4, lengthy, signed. *Aud:* Ga, Ac. *Jv:* V.

A general, scholarly approach by professional geographers on any geographical subject—human, historical, economic, cultural, etc. Each article is extensively footnoted and illustrated with maps, photographs, tables, graphs, and charts. Material ranges from the technical to the semipopular, and while most articles presuppose more than passing knowledge of the field, the magazine's excellent illustrations can be appreciated by almost everyone. (See also *Professional Geographer.*) Abstracts of papers presented at annual meetings of the Association are given. Each issue has a review article which covers several studies on a particular subject. Symposia which are beyond the normal coverage of the journal are covered in special issues. This is the basic journal in the field for all academic and junior college libraries, as well as large public libraries.

√*Canadian Geographer/Geographe Canadien.* 1951. q. $15. John Britton. Univ. of Toronto Press, Front Campus, Univ. of Toronto, Toronto 5, Ont., Canada. Illus. Circ: 850.

Bk. rev: 4–6, 25–1,400 words, signed. *Aud:* Ac.

Dedicated to the advancement of geographical knowledge and to the dissemination of information on the geographical resources and people of Canada. Scholarly articles, written by experts in the field, and dealing mainly with Canadian geography, are followed by extensive bibliographies. Charts, maps, and black and white pictures are used, when necessary, to elucidate the text of the articles. The journal is bilingual and abstracts of the articles are given in both English and French. For all Canadian academic libraries and for large American collections.

Canadian Geographical Journal. 1930. m. $8. William J. Megill. Royal Canadian Geographical Soc., 488 Wilbrod St., Ottawa 2, Ont., Canada. Illus., adv. Circ: 22,500. Microform: UM. Reprint: Carrollton Press.

Indexed: CanI, PAIS, SSHum. *Bk. rev:* 2–3, 200–600 words, signed. *Aud:* Ga, Hs, Ac.

A popularly written magazine, the Canadian counterpart of *National Geographic.* Most of the articles cover different areas, peoples, and natural resources of Canada. However, in each issue there is always one article about a foreign land. All material is written by guest experts. The cover has an attractive color picture, but other illustrations are black and white. Once a year there is a report on the annual meeting of the Royal Canadian Geographical Society. Anyone who enjoys the American cousin to this publication will thank the librarian for bringing it to his or her attention.

Cartographic Journal. 1964. s-a. $7. A. D. Jones. British Cartographic Society, Sales and Distribution, 9 Kenilworth Close, Boreham Wood, Herts, England. Illus., adv. Vol. ends: Dec.

Bk. rev: 4–7, 500–800 words, signed. *Aud:* Ac.

The official publication of the British Cartographic Society, this journal thoroughly covers the field. The articles, many with maps, deal with technical aspects of cartography. In addition, short articles deal with general news of the field. Longer articles are abstracted. Maps as well as books are reviewed, and most issues contain a listing of recent maps and atlases, as well as recent literature. Valuable, if not essential, for any college offering advanced courses in geography. (D.D.)

√*Current Geographical Publications; additions to the research catalogue of the American Geographical Society.* 1938. m. (Sept.–June). $10. Amer. Geographical Soc., Broadway and 156th St., New York, N.Y. 10032. Circ: 1,200. Microform: UM. Reprint: Kraus.

Aud: Ac.

A straight listing by title of new books, pamphlets, and journals added to the collection of the American Geographical Society. It is divided into general titles and those in given areas of study. A basic checklist for large libraries, but of limited value for smaller collections.

√*Economic Geography.* 1925. q. $9. Gerald Kalaska. Clark Univ., Worcester, Mass. 01610. Illus., index. Circ: 4,900. Microform: UM. Reprint: Johnson.

Indexed: BioAb, PAIS, SSHum. *Bk. rev:* 8, 300–1,300 words, signed. *Aud:* Ac, Ga.

A journal for geographers, economists, businessmen, and others interested in the intelligent utilization of the world's resources. It is the only magazine of its type in English, and one of the few geographical journals comprising so many fields. Articles, written by experts, are devoted to economic and urban geography. Maps, tables, graphs, and occasional black and white pictures are used to illustrate the text. The book reviews vary in length, but are uniformly excellent. A basic magazine for larger collections, and one worth considering for most business and/or political science and history departments.

Die Erde. See Europe and Middle East/German Language Section.

Erdkunde. See Europe and Middle East/German Language Section.

Explorers Journal. 1921. q. Membership (Nonmembers $6). Elliott Roberts. Explorers Club, 46 E. 70th St., New York, N.Y. 10021. Illus. index, adv. Circ: 2,200. Sample. Vol. ends: Dec.

Bk. rev: 12–15, 300 words, signed. *Aud:* Ac, Ga, Hs.

A nice combination of the scholarly with the popular, this covers exploration throughout the world. Here "exploration" is used in its broadest sense, which means the articles may be as involved with anthropology and archaeology as with daring expeditions into little known areas for mapping or in search of natural resources. Short, critical book reviews, and some illustrations are included. A good general geographical and "adventure" magazine for both the special and the popular reading collection.

Focus; presenting a brief, readable, up-to-date survey of a country, region or resource, helpful in understanding current world events. 1950. m. (Sept.–June). $3.50. Alice Taylor. Amer. Geographical Soc., Broadway and 156th St., New York, N.Y. 10032. Circ: 17,000. Microform: UM, MF.

Indexed: RG. *Aud:* Ga, Ejh, Hs, Ac.

A twelve-page report that concentrates on one country or region in each issue, giving information about the peoples and their customs, the agricultural and mineral resources, and the industry and trade. It is written by an expert on the particular country, usually a professor of geography, in language that can be understood at the junior high school level. There are always several maps, black and white photographs, and an annotated bibliography. Although relatively elementary in style, the material is precise and it may be used to advantage in basic social studies in universities and junior colleges. Public libraries will find it helpful as an excellent reference source.

Geographical Journal. 1893. q. $15.50. L. P. Kirwan. Royal Geographical Soc., 1 Kensington Gore, London SW 7, England. Illus., index, adv. Circ: 9,500. Microform: UM. Reprint: Carrollton Press.

Indexed: BritHum, SSHum. *Bk. rev:* Numerous, length varies. *Aud:* Ac, Ga. *Jv:* V.

The world's leading scholarly geographical journal, particularly noteworthy for its original maps and material on exploration. Articles, with extensive bibliographies, include original papers presented at Society meetings and usually cover exploration and physical geography, with material on allied sciences. There are charts and maps to elucidate the text, but very few illustrations. A substantial part is devoted to reviews of geographical books, atlases, and a number of travel books of general interest. The reviews alone are well worth a subscription by any library which has more than a passing interest in the subject. Summary issues, devoted to various subjects such as the state of exploring, and maps give it added value for research in depth. Given a choice between this and the *Annals of the Association of American Geographers,* the English entry would come first. And while primarily for academic and junior college collections, it will be of value in medium to large-sized public libraries.

Geographical Magazine. 1935. m. $10.50. Derek Weber, 128 Long Acre, London, WC2E 9QH, England. Illus., adv. Circ: 69,000. Vol. ends: Sept. Microform: UM.

Indexed: BritHum, PAIS. *Bk. rev:* 8–10, 300–350 words, signed. *Aud:* Ga, Hs, Ac.

A popular British geographical magazine, with articles of interest to the general reader. Emphasis is on Britain and Commonwealth areas. Includes two sections of interest: a "Travel guide," with news notes from throughout the world, and "News and reviews" dealing more with geographical news. The book reviews are included in this section. Should be considered by any library wanting a popular geographical magazine with a different orientation. (D.D.)

Geographical Review. 1916. q. $17.50. Wilma B. Fairchild. Amer. Geographical Soc., Broadway and 156th St., New York, N.Y. 10032. Illus., index, Circ: 6,700. Vol. ends: Oct. Microform: UM, Canner, PMC. Reprint: Carrollton Press.

Indexed: PAIS, SSHum. *Bk. rev:* 10–12, 800–900 words, signed. *Aud:* Ac.

Scholarly articles cover the whole spectrum of geography, from the historical to current exploration. All material is extensively footnoted and illustrated with black and white pictures, maps, and charts. The book reviews (including new maps and atlases) are of the same scholarly, critical nature as those found in the *Geographical Journal.* The "Geographical Record" feature serves as a review medium for new journals, reports, monographs, and news about personalities and events in the field. In terms of reviews, more valuable than the *Annals of the Association of American Geographers,* and for this reason may be preferred by some libraries. Otherwise, the latter journal is somewhat more extensive in its coverage. Both are needed for medium to large-sized academic and junior college collections.

Geography. 1901. q. $7.50. Geographical Association. Subs. to: G. Philip and Sons, Ltd., Victoria Road, London, NW 10, England. Adv. Circ: 10,600. Vol. ends: Nov. Reprint: Johnson.

Indexed: BritEdI. *Bk. rev:* 40–60, 250–300 words, signed. *Aud:* Ac.

Issued by the British Geographical Association, with an emphasis on the teaching of geography. Articles are scholarly, with abstracts for most. While most articles deal with the teaching of geography, some more general articles do appear. Most of the books reviewed are British or Commonwealth. Of interest mainly to teacher training institutions and comprehensive collections. (D.D.)

Journal of Geography. 1897. m. $12. Harm J. de Blij. National Council for Geographic Education, Rm. 1226, 111 W. Washington St., Chicago, Ill. 60602. Illus., index, adv. Circ: 7,300. Microform: UM. Reprint: Kraus.

Indexed: CIJE, EdI, PAIS. *Bk. rev:* 5, 300–800 words, signed. *Aud:* Ejh, Hs, Ac.

The official organ of the National Council for Geographic Education is directed at teachers of elementary and high school geography. It emphasizes methods of teaching geography, suggesting techniques and audiovisual aids, but also contains some professional articles. Written by teachers in the field, the articles are generally brief, with footnotes and occasionally a bibliography. Regular features include a section in which the editor answers questions sent in by teachers, and a preview of films available for teaching geography. For all school and school of education libraries.

The Journal of Tropical Geography. 1953. s-a. $5. Ooi Jin Bee. Dept. of Geography, University of Singapore, Singapore, 10. Illus: maps and diagrams. Reprint: Johnson.

Aud: Ac.

Published jointly by the Departments of Geography of the University of Malaya and University of Singapore, this is one of the leading East Asian geographical journals. Articles are with few exceptions regional in coverage, but contributed by scholars from throughout the world. Typography and paper quality are excellent. Book reviews are not included. This title should be considered by all with Asian area studies, or by those with comprehensive collections. (D.D.)

National Geographic Magazine. 1888. m. Membership (Nonmembers $9). Gilbert M. Grosvenor. National Geographic Soc., 17th and M Sts., N.W., Washington, D.C. 20036. Illus., index, adv. Circ: 6,800,000. Microform: PMC.

Indexed: AbrRG, RG. *Aud:* Ga, Ejh, Hs, Ac. *Jv:* V.

Few magazines serve so many audiences and purposes as this old standby. It can be enjoyed by the elementary school child as well as by the professional geographer. Its reference value is particularly high, and it is one of the few magazines which should be in every library. In each issue, five or six clearly written articles, profusely illustrated with color photographs, tell of interesting people, places, customs, activities, animals, and plant life. Staff writers, contributors, and scientists range all over the world. Scientists often write about discoveries, such as the fossils of earliest known man, made with National Geographic support. Maps help the reader understand the text's geography; larger, supplemental maps are world-famous. As one critic put it, this is "a voyeur's dream . . . for gazing on all sorts of exotic delights." No more need be said.

National Geographic School Bulletin. 1922. w. (during sch. yr.) $2.25. Ralph Gray. National Geographic Soc., 17th and M Sts., N.W., Washington, D.C. 20036. Circ: 430,000.

Indexed: IChildMag. *Aud:* Ejh.

Geared for elementary and junior high students who want to read as well as look, this is a pocket-sized version of the monthly parent magazine. Written in a simplified style, it boasts a number of small maps and illustrations, and prepares the reader for a subscription to the *National Geographic.* There are a number of features, and the whole is in a tasteful format of some 10 to 20 pages. While it hardly replaces the larger work, it can be used by children who wish to follow text as much as pictures. A useful, inexpensive addition for almost all school and public libraries.

Norsk Geografisk Tidsskrift. 1926. q. $7.50. Aadel Brun Tschudi. Geografisk Institutt, Universitetet i Oslo, Blindern, Oslo 3, Norway. Subs. to: P.O. Box 142, Boston, Mass. 02113.

Bk. rev: 3–10, 200–400 words, signed. *Aud:* Ac.

This Norwegian journal publishes articles, notes, and reviews in English, the Scandinavian languages, and sometimes French. Articles deal both with research from throughout the world and with regional problems. An English language abstract appears with each article. In addition, all diagrams and photographs have both English and Norwegian captions. A journal for comprehensive collections or European studies programs with an emphasis on geography. (D.D.)

North. See Government Magazines/United States Section.

Professional Geographer. N.S. 1949. bi-m. $8. H. F. Raup. Subs. to Allen Press, Inc, 1041 New Hampshire St., Lawrence, Kans. 66044. Illus., adv. Circ: 6,800. Reprint: Johnson.

Bk. rev: 30, 150–500 words, signed. *Aud:* Ac.

A publication of the Association of American Geographers, this magazine includes short scholarly articles covering most aspects of geography. Maps, charts, and tables are used throughout. The short book reviews are exhaustive and, while not always critical, serve as a check list for libraries. From time to time the publication carries lists of recent geography dissertations and theses. Primarily, as the title suggests, for the teacher at the university level. Only for large collections.

Revista Geographica. See Latin American and Chicano/Spanish Language Section.

La Revue de Geographie de Montreal. See Europe and Middle East/French Language Section.

Scottish Geographical Magazine. 1885. 3/yr. $4. Alfred Jefferies. Royal Scottish Geographical Soc., 10 Randolph Crescent, Edinburgh 3, Scotland. Illus., adv. Circ: 4,000. Microform: UM.

Indexed: BioAb, BritHum. *Bk. rev:* 8–9, 250–800 words, signed. *Aud:* Ac.

An example of the numerous geographical magazines primarily devoted to a single nation. One article in each issue deals with a foreign country. There are many maps and some black and white photographs. News of meetings and lecture programs of the Royal Scottish Geographical Society is reported. As almost every nation issues its own geographical review (usually, to be sure, with some attention given to broader problems), colleges and universities may wish to subscribe to those which will not only meet the needs of the geography department, but complement other areas such as history and political science.

Societa Geographica Italiana. See Europe and Middle East/Italian Language Section.

The South African Geographical Journal. 1917. a. $4.25. P.O. Box 31201, Braamfontein, Transvaal, South Africa. Illus., adv.

Bk. rev: 4–10, 300 words, signed. *Aud:* Ac.

The official publication of the South African Geographical Society, this journal is regional in outlook, with most of the articles concerned with both physical and economic geography in South Africa and adjoining areas. Most articles are in English; articles in Afrikaans have an English language abstract. Should be considered by schools desiring a comprehensive collection. (D.D.)

Soviet Geography. See USSR and East Europe/English Language General Section.

GOVERNMENT MAGAZINES

Basic Periodicals

GUIDES AND INDEXES. All libraries: *Congressional Digest*; Ac: *CIS/Index, Congressional Quarterly Service.*

UNITED STATES. Hs: *Monthly Labor Review;* Ga: *Monthly Labor Review, Occupational Outlook Quarterly;* Jc: *American Education, Dept. of State Bulletin, Monthly Labor Review;* Ac: *American Education, Dept. of State Bulletin, Monthly Labor Review, HSMHA Health Reports, Federal Probation.*

UNITED NATIONS AND SELECTED FOREIGN. All libraries: *UNESCO Courier, U.N. Monthly Chronicle.*

Basic Abstracts and Indexes

Public Affairs Information Service. CIS Index, Monthly Catalog of U.S. Government Publications.

Introduction

The number of annotations in this section represents a twofold increase over the previous edition. Yet it is obvious that but a fraction of the total output in government periodical publishing is covered. Over one thousand periodical and serial publications of the United States government are listed in the February issue of the *Monthly Catalog* alone. Acknowledging the inadequacies of coverage, I hope that what is presented will be of some utility to the person seeking elusive information buried in the pages of these official publications of governments.

For United States government magazines, I have included in the basic bibliographic data the following symbols:

° – for sale by Superintendent of Documents, U.S. Government Printing Office, Washington, D.C. 20402

• – sent to depository libraries

SDC – Superintendent of Documents number; cite number when ordering.

Where distribution is made by the issuing agency, the full address is given in the bibliographic citation.

I have tried to cover thoroughly the information contained in the regular or recurring features of each periodical. Often this material is precisely the needle in the haystack that the patient researcher needs. All of us regret, I am sure, the poor access to the contents of government magazines in general. For example, fewer than half of United Nations and specialized agency periodicals are listed in *Ulrich's International Periodicals Directory,* and fewer still appear in indexing or abstracting services. In preparing this section, I have found very useful Jean Andriot's *Guide to Popular U.S. Publications* (Documents Index, 1960).

My thanks to several colleagues, from Newfoundland to California, whose kind suggestions have been most helpful. My graduate assistant, Pamela Beninati, deserves special mention for her aid in this effort. The shortcomings, alas, are solely mine. (J.M.)

Guides and Indexes

CIS/Index: Congressional Information Service/Index to Publications of the United States Congress. 1970.

m. $80–$400 (service basis). Congressional Information Service, 500 Montgomery Bldg., Washington, D.C. 20014. Index. Circ: 1,000.

Aud: Ac, Sa.

Opens up the contents of all 400,000 plus pages of hearings, reports, committee prints, and other documents produced yearly by the U.S. Congress. The extensive index utilizes every conceivable access point—from witness names and affiliations to the numbers and popular names of pending bills. Subject cross-references are numerous and helpful. And a pleasant surprise for abstract journals—the type is easy to look at. The journal's straightforward system of organizing Congressional documents by committee lends itself to ready use as a rapid classification scheme. It is, in fact, a comprehensive catalog, an analytic index, an announcement service, and a shelf list, all in one. This easy-to-use service will be welcomed by librarians, students, and the public alike. The CIS/Index has all the attributes of a basic reference resource of major value—it will be indispensable to every library with a U.S. documents collection, and is strongly recommended for any reference or research facility with a stake in current public issues. (J.M.)

Congressional Digest. 1921. 10/yr. $12.50. John E. Shields, 3231 P St., N.W., Washington, D.C. 20007. Index. Vol. ends: Dec. Microform: Available from publisher.

Indexed: PAIS, RG. *Aud:* Ga, Ac, Hs. *Jv:* V.

A monthly commercial magazine, which considers a current national topic in depth. The style is famous. First there is an objective description of the topic, which is followed by pro and con arguments, usually in the form of partisan speeches, debates, and testimony given in Congress. Those quoted are both authoritative and in the "middle" of the discussion. Its total effect is both lively and informative. A short "Month in Congress" gives a brief news summary of the previous month's activities in the legislature. As this magazine is useful for both the specialist and the generalist, it has wide use in any type of library. It certainly should be given priority in school libraries, from junior high up, where debate or current history is a consideration. Not to be confused with the *Congressional Record.*

Congressional Quarterly Service. Weekly Report. 1945. w. $144 (Includes bound almanac). Richard N. Billings. Congressional Quarterly, Inc., 1735 K St., N.W., Washington, D.C. 20006. Illus., index. Circ: 5,000. Sample. Vol. ends: Dec. Microform: UM.

Indexed: PAIS. *Aud:* Ga, Ac, Hs. *Jv:* V.

An overview of the weekly activities in Congress, and, as such, an invaluable aid for any library. The service is expensive, yet well worth the money. It offers a concise, accurate, easy-to-use method of keeping up with government activities. There is a 90-day

and annual index, as well as a weekly index. One drawback, however, is that there is no cumulative index before the 90 days. Each 60 to 70 page issue features summary articles; activities on bills before the Senate and the house; committee actions; a record of how the congressmen voted; and reports on what will be coming up in the weeks and months ahead. The reporting is objective, usually offering comments from the record, and the service is fairly easy to use, at least for reference librarians. Those unable to purchase the weekly service should consider the annual *CQ Almanac* which is both an index and a summary volume of congressional activities.

Consumer Price Index. See Consumer Services Section.

Current American Government. 1970. s-a. $6. Robert A. Diamond. Congressional Quarterly, 1735 K Street, N.W., Washington, D.C. 20006.

Aud: Ac, Ga.

Issues appear in the spring and fall of each year and are designed to demonstrate the interplay of forces that obtain in our political system. Action and reaction characterize the relations among the three branches of the federal establishment, and this periodical illumines the struggle by highlighting the salient events of the times. It is a judicious rearrangement of materials that have been compiled by the indefatigable CQ researchers. Of value to students of government and politics, it is also useful as background and reference for librarians working in these areas. Contents are largely paralleled in both issues, following a logical structure. Thus there are sections on the Presidency, Congress (both internal organization and substantive issues), the Federal Judiciary, Lobbies, and Federal–State Relations. Summarized and analyzed are the significant problems covering the reporting period. The Spring 1971 issue covered crime, the war, legislative reform, the economy—under the rubric of Congress; the Fall 1971 publication covers the administration's efforts for an all-volunteer armed force as Congress sees and deals with it.

Similarly, the section on the Presidency discusses the thrust of the chief executive as chief legislator. The Judiciary section contains analytic commentary on its relationship to the executive and the legislative branches. This dynamic enables us to see the tripartite tension working. It is one of the several methods that makes CQ publications so readable and informative. As a reference source, this semi-annual periodical is useful. Included in one or the other issue are biographies of the Supreme Court Justices and Cabinet Members; a superb account of the legislative process—bill to law; a glossary of Congressional terms; major bills passed by the ninety-second Congress to date of publication; a host of tables of valuable ready reference information (little gems such as a list of the 25 largest foundations with assets). Useful to student, layman, scholars, and to librarians, this is highly recommended for all libraries.

From the State Capitals. General Bulletin. 1946. m. $30. Ralph W. Ernest. Bethune Jones, 321 Sunset Ave., Asbury Park, N.J.

Aud: Ac; Ga.

One of 38 reports issued by this firm. It is the most general in that it covers current materials on such things as prospective legislation, administrative and judicial action, public works, taxes, etc., at both the state and local level. The mimeographed digest is primarily intended for those involved with public management and planning. However, it is an invaluable reference aid for any library dealing in legislative and legal matters. It is accurate, timely, and presents material in a concise manner. Libraries involved with urban and state problems are advised to contact the publisher for his complete list which covers topics from airport construction and financing to school construction, urban transit, and bus transportation. An invaluable service; well worth the price.

National Journal. 1969. w. $200 (Individuals $450). Cliff Sessions. Center of Political Research, 1730 M St., N.W., Washington D.C. 20036. Illus., index.

Indexed: PAIS. *Aud:* Ga, Ac.

An extraordinarily useful tool for students of political affairs, and for reference and documents librarians who need to keep abreast of events in the federal establishment. Each weekly issue contains: four to five well researched and lucidly written reports on current topics that shape federal policy, and a "Weekly Briefing" section, a checklist of significant actions by and concerning the federal establishment. This section is useful in that it follows the organization of government, containing news of the executive; departmental and agency notes; news from the independent agencies; and brief accounts of Congressional and Judiciary action with no direct impact on the executive branch, and political developments. Following this current awareness service, there is a section on the voting records of Congressmen and Senators on bills of importance. The weekly issues contain personal name, private organization, and geographic indexes. The quarterly cumulative indexes provide six different access routes to the material contained in the *National Journal*. The reports are listed by broad subject approach; there is an exhaustive personal name index; a private organization listing includes associations, law firms, lobby groups, corporations, universities, etc.; the index for government organizations includes international bodies and quasi-governmental units; the geographic index covers cities, states, congressional districts, foreign countries; and there is a comprehensive subject index to the entire contents of the issues. (J.M.)

Nuclear Science Abstracts. See Abstracts and Indexes Section.

Scientific and Technical Aerospace Reports. See Abstracts and Indexes Section.

U.S. Government Research and Development Reports. See *Government Reports Announcements* in Abstracts and Indexes Section.

United States

Aging. 1951. bi-m. (m., Jan., Apr., May, Aug.). $2.50. Olivia W. Coulter. ° · SDC: HE 17.309. Illus., adv. Circ: 21,000. Vol. ends: Dec. Microform: UM.

Indexed: RG, PAIS, AbSocWk. *Bk. rev:* Various number, length. *Aud:* Ga, Ac.

As a youngster entering its third decade of publication, this attractive magazine contains much useful information for the senior citizen. Though perhaps not so good as some of the many magazines commercially published for this large minority group, it at least does not have a saccharine title. It is also valuable as a supplement to other geriatrically oriented publications in its emphasis on the role of government concern for the welfare of the elderly. Topics are brief (one to two pages) and include such items as senior citizen centers, news on the social security front, low-cost meals for the elderly, Congressional hearings on the problems of the aging, services by and for senior citizens.

Among the regular features are: "Conference Calendar"—dates of conventions, institutes, conferences, associations, educational extension workshops and courses, projections of which are usually six months in advance of convocation; "News of State Agencies" —information culled from various state departments of aging, including programs, publications, statistics, and upbeat news of successful senior citizen accomplishments; "News of Federal Agencies"—primary emphasis is on reporting of provisions of federal legislation, including grants, administered by AoA and other agencies; "Publications"—annotations of government publications and commercial monographs and magazines, arranged by broad subject categories. This is an especially worthwhile feature, in that articles in other journals (both government and commercial) of interest to the elderly are analyzed, with information on availability of reprints and discounts for quantity orders. (J.M.)

Agricultural Economic Research. See Agriculture Section.

Agricultural Science Review. See Agriculture Section.

Airforce Driver Magazine. See Automobiles/General Section.

American Education. 1965. m. (10/yr.), bi-m. (Jan./Feb., Aug./Sept.). $4.50. William A. Horn, Walter Wood. ° · SDC: HE 5.75. Illus., index. Vol. ends: Dec. Microform: UM. Reprint: AN.

Indexed: EdI, PAIS, RG. *Bk. rev:* Number varies, brief. *Aud:* Ga, Ac, Hs.

A lively and interesting journal that replaced *School Life* and *Higher Education* on the theory that education is of a piece, not fragmented. Accordingly, the publication covers preschool to adult education, and includes new research and demonstration projects, major education legislation, school and college bond data, grants, loans, contracts, and fellowships. Each issue contains half a dozen or so articles on some contemporary problem or issue in education. Authors are knowledgeable layman as well as professional educationists. The style is generally popular. Sample articles include topics such as consumer education, open classroom experiments, curriculum development, drugs in the classroom, summer reading programs, and performance contracting. All articles are signed. Regular features include: "Federal Funds"—a listing of Office of Education–administered programs and activities; "Statistic of the Month"—a monthly review of a research report available from ERIC; "Recent Publications"—a briefly annotated checklist of documents available either from OE or from SUDOCS; and a chatty section of relatively trivial commentary called "Kaleidoscope."

Views of the authors do not necessarily reflect official policy; however, the content is directed to a general audience to explain the work of OE in an attractive and readable manner. Recommended for academic, public, and high school libraries. (J.M.)

Annual Report of the Librarian of Congress. See Library Periodicals Section.

Arms Control and Disarmament. 1964. q. $2.50 ° · SDC: LC 2.10. Index. Vol. ends: Fall. Microform: UM.

Indexed: PAIS. *Aud:* Ga, Ac.

Prepared by the Arms Control and Disarmament Bibliography Section of the Library of Congress, with the support of the Arms Control and Disarmament Agency, this publication attempts to bring under bibliographic control a large and growing body of literature in this important area. Each quarterly issue contains abstracts and annotations of current literature in the English, French, and German languages, as well as abstracts and annotations of current literature in all languages published in English translation. Author and subject indexes appear in the first three numbers of each volume, with the fourth number containing a cumulation. The title of each foreign language entry is preceded by its English translation in brackets. For Library of Congress patrons, locations are shown by call numbers for cataloged items and by symbols for uncataloged items and materials held by custodial units of the Library. Each issue contains a list of these symbols. Matters of fact and opinions of the authors of items abstracted do not necessarily coincide with Library of Congress or Arms Control and Disarmament Agency official policy. Sources surveyed include trade books, monographs, selected government publications, documents of national and international organizations and societies, and about 1,200 periodicals. The literature cited has usually been published in the three months preceding the month in which an issue is sent to press. Related topics like weapons development and world political factors are chosen; excluded are articles in newspapers and the reporting of day-to-day events in news magazines. Since the bibliography is compiled from a survey of the literature received by LC that is likely to be available in the larger research and public libraries, this publication is a valuable access tool for those institutions. (J.M.)

Average Monthly Weather Outlook. 1946. s-m. $3.50. ° · SDC: C 55.109 Charts. Vol. ends: Dec./mid Jan. issue.

Aud: Ac, Ga.

As Andriot says, this four-page publication is not "a specific forecast in the usual meteorological sense, but instead is an estimate of the rainfall and temperature for the next thirty days." It is also a resume of the average rainfall and temperature for the preceding month. Because any 30-day forecast is fraught with hazards, the publication is best adapted to the uses of business concerns with wide sectional or national interests, or to concerns which have a consistent month-to-month use for weather information.

Issued by the Extended Forecast Division, National Weather Service, the predictive value of this bulletin is modestly successful, due to extensive research over the past decade and the advent of weather satellites. Charts include temperature, precipitation, and predicted air flow patterns for a major part of the Northern Hemisphere. For each preceding month, a table of about 130 reporting stations (from Albany, N.Y. to Yuma, Ariz., including Honolulu and Anchorage) gives norms and class limits for temperature and precipitation. A final table, covering the same reporting stations, shows expected heating degree days, the base being 65 degrees Fahrenheit. For large research libraries and special collections. (J.M.)

BNDD Bulletin. 1968. bi-m. free. Frankie S. Braxton. · SDC: J24.3. Bureau of Narcotics and Dangerous Drugs, U.S. Dept. of Justice, 1405 I St., N.W., Washington, D.C. 20537. Illus.

Aud: Ga, Ac, Hs.

This publication is written for chiefs of police, other enforcement agencies such as state criminal investigation units, the National Park police, Indian reservations, drug abuse commissions and committees, and college and high school guidance counselors and teachers. It provides information on the activities of the Bureau of Narcotics and Dangerous Drugs, which was created in April 1968 by combining the Bureau of Drug Abuse Control and the Federal Bureau of Narcotics. With a slim, twenty-page "newsletter" format, the publication features: "Legal Corner"—an analytic summary of the salient aspects of new legislation on drug abuse, prevention and control; "Notable Cases'"—news items of arrests involving drug activities, arranged by cities in the United States and abroad; occasional brief reviews of government and commercial publications on the drug problem; and useful announcements on antidrug visual aids for schools, information from the National Clearinghouse for Drug Abuse, and the like. School libraries need not feel overwhelmed with literature on this problem by adding this modest bulletin to their collection. Also useful for academic and public libraries. (J.M.)

Business Conditions Digest. See Business/General Section.

Business Service Checklist. 1946. w. $2.50. Evelyn M. Farmer. ° • SDC: C 1.24: Charts.

Aud: Ga, Ac.

The chief value to librarians is that of an ordering guide. It lists, according to *Price List* 36, "news releases, books, pamphlets, reports and other materials of interest to business and industry which are published by the Department of Commerce and Defense agencies." Addresses, National Technical Information Service publications, bulletins, and the like are arranged by broad headings (e.g., Economic Affairs, Science and Technology, Domestic and International Business) and further subdivided by Commerce Department agencies. Especially useful are listings of periodical issues which note titles of articles.

Regular features include "Key Business Indicators"—a concise chart giving the latest statistics on personal income, gross national product, business inventories, consumer price index, balance of payments, etc. As a handy guide to Department of Commerce publications and important business indicators, this four-page newsletter far exceeds its size in value. Mandatory for business service collections and libraries, and useful for university and public libraries. All series except press releases, according to Andriot, "are cumulated in the annual supplements to *Department of Commerce Publications, A Catalog and Index.*" (J.M.)

Children. 1954. bi-m. $2. Judith Reed. ° • SDC: HE 21.9. Illus., index. Circ: 30,000. Vol. ends: Nov./Dec. Microform: UM.

Indexed: EdI, IMed, PAIS. *Bk. rev:* 4–5, 300 words, signed. *Aud:* Ga, Ac, Hs.

Subtitled "An Interdisciplinary Journal for the Professions Serving Children," the purpose of the magazine is to provide "a means of communication between them on the needs of children, on methods of meeting these needs, and on successes and failures in the applications of programs and techniques of care" (Andriot).

Approximately six to seven signed articles, with authors' credentials given, cover problems of day care centers, adoptions, sensitivity training, play programs,

drug use, state and local services, health and welfare laws, and the like. Articles are well written; easy to read. Teenage problems are included as well as the problems of tiny tots. Regular departments include: "Book Notes"—brief unsigned reviews of predominately nongovernment publications on various pertinent subjects; "Here and There"—a potpourri of news items on conferences and activities on problems of retardation, child development, etc., occasionally containing a roundup of federal legislation that will affect the health and welfare of children; "In the Journals"—useful summaries of articles in various government and commercial publications on topics relevant to the editorial interests of the magazine. It is disappointing that this magazine is not outstanding. It could be. However, it is useful for high school, college, and public libraries. (J.M.)

Civil Rights Digest. 1968. q. 35¢/copy. Wallace W. Johnson. ° • SDC: CR 1.12. Illus. Vol. ends: Fall.

Indexed: PAIS. *Bk. rev:* Various number, length. *Aud:* Ga, Ac, Hs.

Published by the Commission on Civil Rights as part of its clearinghouse responsibilities, this magazine is intended to stimulate ideas and interest in the various current issues concerning civil rights. The articles do not necessarily reflect Commission policy. Each issue consists of approximately six to eight articles of medium length on virtually every aspect of minority problems. Topics include third world studies, bilingual education, ethnic neighborhoods, minorities in sensitive jobs (e.g., police), and the larger issues of employment, voting, covert and overt prejudice, and so forth. Articles are signed, well written, and the coverage seems fairly balanced among Chicano, Indian, and Black problems. Regular features include a section titled "Reading and Viewing," which consists of annotations on relevant books, studies and reports, and films. The account of films is particularly useful, lucid, and comprehensive. "Book Reviews" contain thorough criticism, with reviews signed and the credentials of the reviewer given.

Of the many pamphlets and publications concerning the general subject of civil rights, few are as well packaged or as informative as this quarterly. Recommended for public, academic, and high school libraries. (J.M.)

Civil Service Journal. 1959. q. $1. Bacil B. Warren. ° • SDC: CS 1.66. Illus. Vol. ends Apr./June.

Aud: Ga, Ac.

When the magazine first appeared in 1959, its announced purpose was "better communication with our working publics. While primary distribution will be to the Government's key management and personnel people, we hope by variety of content and informal presentation to make each issue useful also to many other groups." Over the last decade, the quarterly has fulfilled this editorial intent reasonably well.

About four or five signed articles per issue focus attention on important developments in the federal civil service. Various aspects of federal employment are discussed, such as job evaluation and pay, executive positions in civil service, on-the-job training, retirement systems, the four-day work week, and so forth. Articles are written primarily by employees in the Civil Service Commission, with an occasional article by an authority in state and local government or in private business. Among the regular features are: "Legal Decisions"—a summary of court cases involving civil service employees and their constitutional rights; "Spotlight on Labor Relations"—accounts of various bargaining positions in the yet not wholly defined area of labor-management relations in public service; "Recruiters Roundup"—notes on career field opportunities, federal service examinations, summer employment, minority opportunities, etc.; "Employment Focus" —various graphs and charts showing some statistical breakdown by age, sex, occupation, etc., of the federal civil service, with explanatory text. The publication serves a useful purpose in keeping one informed on the activities, plans, and programs of close to three million employees. For large university and public library collections. (J.M.)

Commerce Today. 1970. bi-w. $20. Richard Evans ° SDC: C 1.58. Illus. Vol. ends: Apr. Microform: UM.

Indexed: BusI. *Bk. rev:* 30–50, approx. 50 words long.
Aud: Ga, Ac.

This magazine supersedes *International Commerce* and is "a news review of the Commerce Department's activity affecting private enterprise. Reports on domestic business, economic affairs, overseas trade (includes foreign sales leads), scientific research, applied technology, and authoritative comment on current national and international business problems." (*Price List* 36) There are approximately four to five lead articles in each issue on various developments in business and technology: problems of environment, urban development, exports, balance of payments, and the like. Regular departments include: "Domestic Business Report;" "Science and Technology Report;" "International Commerce"—which purports to do for businessmen in this country what the publication *Foreign Trade* (q.v.) does for Canadian traders; "Economic Highlights"—a one-page report prepared by the Assistant Secretary for Economic Affairs based upon the latest economic indicators, text supplemented by a graphic presentation; "How Commerce Serves You"—a one page summary of the services that specific Commerce Department units provide; "New Publications"—brief annotations of documents, including National Technical Information Service reports on government sponsored research; "Calendar for World Traders"—location and dates of international trade meetings.

Attractive, glossy format with many excellent photographs, this publication is recommended for business collections, and for university and larger public libraries. (J.M.)

Congressional Record. 1873. daily (when Congress is in session). $45. ° • SDC: X/a. Index. Vol. ends conclusion each session. Microform: UM.

Aud: Ga, Ac.

What can one say of this enterprise, except that truth is stranger and infinitely more bizarre than fiction? As it is known today, the *CR* began with the Forty-third Congress, first session, on March 4, 1873. Until then, the proceedings and debates of the Congress were published under various names: *Annals of the Congress of the United States* (1789–1824); *Register of Debates in Congress* (1824–1837); and *Congressional Globe* (1833–1873), its first five volumes overlapping the *Register of Debates.*

The *CR* consists of four sections: the proceedings of the Senate, the proceedings of the House, the Extensions of Remarks, containing matter not a part of the spoken debates and proceedings, and the Daily Digest of activity in the Congress. There are three editions of the *CR.* The daily edition reports each day's proceedings on the succeeding day. The "green-back," or biweekly, edition is an assemblage of the copies of the daily edition; bound with the fortnightly index, it is available to Members only (plus the Library of Congress and the Public Documents Library). The permanent bound edition consists of the text of the debates and proceedings and the Daily Digest, revised, rearranged, and printed without a break. Thus its pagination, which is continuous throughout the session, differs from that of the daily edition. Therefore, in checking a citation in the *CR,* one must first ascertain which edition is referred to. In addition to the difference in pagination, there may be variations in the text of the proceedings arising from a Member's privilege of revising his remarks or the right of either chamber to expunge from the permanent edition material which appeared in the daily edition. Accordingly, the daily edition assumes for the library serving students and researchers in the field a significance beyond the unique content. The section called Extensions of Remarks regularly contains material not germane to legislation under debate, but which a Member wishes to have printed. Until the Ninetieth Congress, second session, this section was called the Appendix. Separately paged, it formed a part of both the daily and the permanent editions from the Seventy-fifth Congress, first session, through the Eighty-third Congress, second session. Beginning with the Seventy-seventh Congress, first session, each page number was preceded by the designation "A" (now "E"), but with the Eighty-fourth Congress, first session, the Appendix pages were *omitted* from the permanent edition. The Index, however, to the permanent edition cited references to Appendix material which then could only be found in the daily edition. Materials considered germane to legislation were inserted in the permanent edition at the point where the legislation was under discussion. This outrageous tinkering made the search process more difficult than was necessary; fortunately, beginning with the Ninetieth Congress, second session, the Extensions of Remarks reappears in the permanent edition.

Another change made at the beginning of the Ninetieth Congress, second session, was the inclusion of an alphabetical listing on the last page of Members whose extended remarks appear in that issue, with page references. In substance, then, the *CR* is perhaps a "verbatim report" of the debates and proceedings, but the twin Congressional privileges of revision and extension provide the qualifying phrase.

The Daily Digest includes "Highlights" of the legislative day, chamber action which summarizes bills introduced, measures passed, quorum calls, bills signed by the President, committee meetings, recorded votes, and a schedule of events for the next day including time and location of committee meetings. The biweekly Index consists of two parts: an index to the proceedings including material in the Extensions of Remarks, and a History of Bills and Resolutions. The Index is weak in subject approach. Furthermore, biweekly indexes do not cumulate. The History lists only those bills which have been reported out of committee or have progressed beyond that point. Bill number references *are* cumulative, however, so that you can trace the history of a bill in page references to its introduction, committee report, debate, amendment(s), and enactment or defeat. The full text of bills and resolutions introduced are not always published, House and Senate Rules allowing for variations. In addition, though much of the real work on bills is done in committee, only a brief summary of committee activities appears in the Daily Digest. Names of witnesses testifying are given, however, in this section.

CR contains recurring features of some ready reference value, such as a list of Members with State and party affiliation; standing committees with Members' names; U.S. judicial circuits with Justices assigned and territory embraced; the various appellate courts and judges, official reporters of debates—names and home addresses; Supreme Court Justices and (for the mischievously inclined) their home addresses; and the several laws and rules for publication of the *CR*.

It must be noted that the *CR* is not the official record of the proceedings, that function having been designated for the House and Senate *Journals* by Constitutional fiat. The latter do not include the debates but are more convenient to use than the voluminous *CR* if proceedings information alone is needed. Like so many government publications, the *CR* is *sui generis* and cannot be evaluated save against a Platonic ideal

of a journal to match our Republic. Non-depository libraries ought to examine closely their needs to see if this is a valuable addition to the collection; the price is not exorbitant considering the extraordinary amount of information and the central importance of the *Record*. It need also be said that the Extensions of Remarks, like its vestigial predecessor, is an account of inestimable value for the historian and folklorist. (J.M.)

Consumer Alert. See Consumer Services Section.

Current Wage Developments. 1948. $4.50. SDC: L 2.44. Charts. U.S. Dept. of Labor, Bureau of Labor Statistics, Washington, D.C. 20212.

Aud: Ga, Ac.

Prior to July 1971, this magazine was distributed free to interested individuals and institutions, but effective that month (issue No. 282), it was placed on subscription. For over two decades the publication presented summaries of collective bargaining settlements, along with periodic statistical summaries. With the new policy, the information reported has been expanded to present a broader coverage of employee compensation.

The contents are divided into three sections. Section I presents a two to three page narrative account of important developments in the bargaining process in selected industries, including stabilization committee rulings, cash readjustment allowances, etc. Following that are tabular and statistical data on selected wage and benefit changes for the *second* month prior to publication. Data are arranged according to industry product: food, tobacco, lumber and furniture, paper, chemicals, metalworking, transportation, construction, etc. This section includes a useful list of the commonly used abbreviations of selected national and international unions. The next section includes statistics on compensation changes, seasonally adjusted. Since July 1971, additional detail is provided on changes in average hourly earnings adjusted to exclude the effects of interindustry employment shifts and overtime premiums. Previously available only for manufacturing, the data now are compiled for the total private nonfarm sector and separately for each industry division. Excluded still are the effects of overtime for manufacturing establishments. In addition this section now includes a table containing separate data on annual rates of change in wages over the life of contracts negotiated in bargaining units with and without cost-of-living escalator provisions. A final section covers major wage developments, cumulated quarterly. This summary is confined to production and related workers in manufacturing and to nonsupervisory employees in nomanufacturing industries. A short narration and explanation of methodology precedes the tables. Of principal value to business libraries, it is also recommended for university and large public library collections. (J.M.)

Dept. of State Bulletin. 1939. w. $16. ° •
SDC: S1.3. Illus., index, adv. Circ: 7,600. Vol. ends:
June and Dec. Microform: PMC.

Indexed: PAIS, RG. *Aud:* Ga, Ac, Hs.

The official weekly record of United States foreign
policy, this magazine "provides information on the
development of foreign relations, operations of the
State Department, statements by the President and
Secretary of State, and special articles on international
affairs." *(Price List* 36) In addition to the special articles on various aspects of international affairs and
Department functions, the *Bulletin* includes Presidential reports to Congress on foreign policy, and the
lengthier addresses (e.g., the "State of the World")
may occupy an entire issue, preempting even the regular features. Regular and recurring features have a
high information content for reference and readers'
service: "Treaty Information" is a weekly supplement
on current treaty actions and updates the annual *Treaties in Force;* included are executive agreements, bilateral and multilateral, as well as treaties and protocol
proclamations. "Checklist of Department of State
Press Releases" consists of selected press releases of
the White House, Secretary of State, and U.S. Mission
to the United Nations. "Publications" are of Department of State documents, available from SUDOCS or
the agency. "Congressional Documents Relating to
Foreign Policy" include brief, annotated publications
such as the elusive Senate Executive Reports and
Documents and committee prints. "United Nations
Documents: A Selected Bibliography" consists of processed documents as well as U.N. publications available from the Sales Section. There is a "Calendar of
International Conferences," a schedule of meetings in
which the U.S. Government expects to participate—
projected ahead about three months.

Though naturally a mirror of the Establishment, the
magazine is a necessary supplement to collections in
this field and provides the student and scholar another
bias to the biases of the pompously prestigious *Foreign
Affairs* and the lively, iconoclastic *Foreign Policy.*
Necessary also for high school collections and smaller
public libraries serving the high school student due in
large part to the egregious amount of homework assignments requiring its perusal. (J.M.)

Earthquake Information Bulletin. 1967. bi-m. $1.50.
Jerry L. Cottman ° • SDC: C 55.410. Illus. Vol. ends:
Nov./Dec.

Aud: Ga, Ac, Hs.

Prepared by the National Earthquake Information
Center, the bulletin provides current information on
earthquakes and seismological activities of interest to
both general and specialized readers. First published
in March 1967, its objective was to translate into understandable terms the techniques used in investigating and describing earthquakes and related phenome-

na, and to present the results of past and continuing
studies in seismology. From the beginning, the editors
wanted to bridge the gap between the technical reports of the seismologist and the need of the layman
for earth science information he can understand and
use. Today's *Bulletin* continues "to operate in that
uncrowded region between the technical journal and
the popular press," according to the editor's preface.
Two aspects of seismology have dominated the *Bulletin* from its inception: the search for basic understanding of the origin of the earth and the processes which
shape—and shake—it, and the practical matter of discovering ways to alleviate the effects of strong earthquakes. Plans for forthcoming issues, according to the
editor's preface in the January/February 1971 *Bulletin,* include a long, serious look at highly seismic California, efforts to reduce earthquake hazard in the
densely populated cities and suburbs, and analyses of
new computer-centered techniques for canvassing and
handling earthquake intensity data.

The issues contain from six to seven signed articles,
written by authorities in the field of seismology. To
preserve the editorial double theme, the articles are
scholarly yet popularly written. Topics include "Je-
suits in Seismology," some international aspects of
seismology, earthquake histories of various states and,
of course, emphasis on California and Alaska. Regular
features include: "Meetings"—listings of earth science
symposia, annual association meetings, national and
international conventions; "Publications"—includes
films as well as monographs, the latter being available
from the Superintendent of Documents; "Seismology
for the Classroom"—a practical lesson in a different
aspect of earthquake detection and measurement, with
accompanying diagrams, charts, and graphs. A useful
recurring department gives an account of earthquake
activity in the world, with fatality statistics, a useful
ready reference source. Highly recommended for college, public, and high school libraries. (J.M.)

Economic Indicators. 1948. m. $3. ° • SDC: Y4. Ec 7:
Charts. Microform: UM.

Aud: Ga, Ac.

Prepared for the Joint Economic Committee by the
Council of Economic Advisers, this publication is a
veritable treasure-trove of statistical information. According to Andriot, it "presents in chart and tabular
form statistics collected by various Government agencies on total output, income and spending; employment, unemployment and wages; production and business activity; prices; currency, credit and security
markets; and Federal finance." Also included are useful data on the balance of international payments, new
housing starts, corporate profits, and the like. Footnotes include agency where data were obtained. As a
convenient source of information on the state of the
economy, this monthly is indispensable for business
service libraries or collections, and should be included

in holdings of university and metropolitan public libraries. (J.M.)

Employment and Earnings. 1954. m. $10. Joseph M. Finerty. ° · SDC: L 2.41/2. Illus. Vol. ends: Dec. Microform: UM.

Indexed: PAIS. *Aud:* Ga, Ac.

Containing a minimum of written material and a maximum of tabular and statistical material, this publication "presents the most current information available on trends and levels of employment, hours of work, earnings and labor turnover. It gives not only overall trends, but also shows developments in particular industries in the States, and in local metropolitan areas." *(Price List* 36)

Each issue contains a three-page written summary of employment and unemployment developments for the preceding month. Occasional issues contain additional brief written reports on some aspect of the job scene. Regular departments include: "Technical Note"—a written explanation of the methodology used in compiling the statistics, a very useful feature for social scientists and economists. Special features are highlighted on the cover, such as an analysis of seasonally adjusted labor force statistics, a tabular summary of compensation trends, and the like. Recommended for larger academic and public library collections and for special libraries catering to interested clientele. (J.M.)

Employment Service Review. See *Manpower.*

F.A.A. Aviation News. 1962. m. $2. Lewis D. Gelfan. ° SDC: TD 4.9: Charts. Illus., adv. Circ: 69,000. Vol. ends: Apr. Microform: UM.

Aud: Ac, Ga, Hs.

This attractive magazine keeps us informed of the Federal Aviation Agency's role in the development of a National Aviation System. Though primarily designed to "promote understanding and cooperation with FAA safety programs," the publication also carries articles on various aspects of commercial aviation.

Each issue runs to about 15 pages, and contains about half a dozen unsigned articles. Examples of recent contents include an account of National Aeronautics and Space Administration research seeking a more stable light plane; women professionals in flight service; a series of articles on maintenance problems of general aviation aircraft; nostalgia (old flying circus stunt pilots and other glories); and VFR ceilings in control zones. The style is casual, readable, for the layman aficianado. Recurring features include: An alternating series entitled either "Famous Flyers" or "Famous Flights" (the former honors such sterling performers as the Farman brothers, as well-known in Europe as Orville and Wilbur were in the United States; the latter column recounts famous firsts, such as the inauguration of transatlantic jet service; "Pilot

Briefs"—news notes of interest to pilots, concerning especially FAA safety regulations and notices; "News Log"—announcements of activities such as flight instructor refresher courses, safety awards in general aviation, notices of public hearings; "Flight Forum"—one page devoted to readers' comments, with editorial rejoinders. (J.M.)

FBI Law Enforcement Bulletin. See Criminology and Law Enforcement Section.

FDA Papers. See Consumer Services Section.

Family Economic Review. See Consumer Services Section.

Farm Index. 1962. m. $2. Audrey Ames Cook. ° · SDC: A 93.33. Illus., index, adv. Circ: 23,000. Vol. ends: Dec.

Bk. rev: Various number, length. *Aud:* Ga, Ac, Hs.

According to Andriot, this journal's purpose is "to provide in non-technical language the results of the Economic Research Service's broad research program. Articles are grouped according to the special interests of farming, rural life, marketing, consumer news, and the foreign market." Articles on the above general areas are based on ERS research and on studies carried out in cooperation with State agricultural experiment stations. Primarily written by staffers of the various divisions within ERS, the articles are eminently readable and present the results of ERS activities in layman's terms. Regular departments in each issue include: "Agricultural Outlook"—news notes on current topics of interest to the farm community, including a "foreign spotlight" section on agricultural activities of various countries; "Recent Publications"—briefly annotated listing of publications issued by ERS and cooperatively by the State universities; "Economic Trends"—a table showing the latest figures for forty-five leading agricultural indexes such as prices, farm income, GNP, land values, and wages.

Though scarcely in the class of *Farm Journal* or *Farm Quarterly,* this twenty-page monthly is useful as an awareness source of USDE activities. (J.M.)

Federal Probation. 1936. q. free. Victor H. Evjen. SDC: Ju 10.8. Administrative Office of the U.S. Courts, Supreme Court Bldg., Washington, D.C. 20544. Illus., index, adv. Circ: 27,000. Vol. ends: Dec. Microform: UM. Reprint: Kraus.

Indexed: LegPer. *Aud:* Ga, Ac. *Jv:* V.

Subtitled "A Journal of Correctional Philosophy and Practice," this excellent publication is edited by the Probation Division of the Administrative Office of the U.S. Courts in Washington, D.C., and is published by the Administrative Office in cooperation with the Bureau of Prisons of the Justice Department. Its purpose is "to present constructively worthwhile points of view relating to all phases of preventive and correctional activities in delinquency and crime." (Publisher's statement)

There are about 10 to 12 signed articles. Authors' credentials given—the writers are experts in the field of criminal justice. A representative selection of authors includes probation authorities, college professors, policemen, parole board officials, etc. Since the opinions of the authors do not necessarily reflect the official editorial position, one cannot blame the sad state of our prison system on the far reaching views expressed. The articles are uniformly well written and reflect a judicious admixture of both the practical and theoretical aspects of probation. Among the regular departments are: "Legislation"—an analysis of significant bills and laws relating to all aspects of law enforcement and control; "Review of Professional Periodicals"—an outstanding feature which reviews significant articles in selected journals both scholarly and popular—foreign periodicals are included and the scope includes such fields as social work, correctional education, orthopsychiatry, law, and psychology—reviewers' credentials given; "Your Bookshelf on Review" —as above, the reviewers' qualifications are given, and the quality of reviewing is high; books on many subjects —psychology, delinquency, adult education, transactional analysis—given careful attention; "News from the Field"—news briefs on any and all items related to probation; "It Has Come to Our Attention"—a melange of items about people in the field, activities of government and private institutions, films, etc.

It is perhaps fitting that this journal is printed at the U.S. Penitentiary, Marion, Illinois, by inmates in a rehabilitation program. (J.M.)

Federal Register. 1936. Daily except Sun., Mon. and day following Federal holiday. $25. ° • SDC: GS4.107. Index. Vol. ends: Dec. 31st. Microform: PMC, AM, P. *Aud:* Ga, Ac.

For its direct impact on the individual and corporate body politic, this document is probably the most significant existing publication issued by the U.S. Government. Its specificity is pursuant to statutory law and its regulations have general applicability and legal effect. The contents include full text of Presidential proclamations and executive orders; rules and regulations of the various agencies; a section called "Proposed Rule Making," which consists of notifications of new rules proposed by administrative agencies pursuant to legislative intent; "Notices"—decisions of federal agencies affecting individuals and corporate bodies; and a "Cumulative List of Parts Affected," a numerical guide to the titles and sections of the *Code of Federal Regulations* affected by amendments published to date. On May 1, 1971, the publication changed cover design, printing the title sideways, and instituted a section called "Highlights of This Issue." The size remained the same. There is a subject index to the

daily issues, published separately in monthly, quarterly and annual cumulations. Entries are arranged primarily by issuing agency, with significant but broad subjects interfiled alphabetically.

Its companion, the *Code of Federal Regulations,* must be mentioned. Also available to depositories (Item 572) and for sale by the Superintendent of Documents ($175 per annum), the CFR codifies all executive and administrative rules and regulations first published in the *FR;* these are the "laws" in force, analogous to the relationship between the *U.S. Code* and the *Statutes at Large.* A *List of CFR Sections Affected* is part of the subscription to the *FR.* It serves as a codification guide designed to lead users of the *CFR* to amendatory decisions published in the *FR.* The guide cumulates monthly, and a finding aid at the end of each issue lists the page numbers with the date of publication in the *FR.* The size of the *List* suggests that it be shelved with current *CFR* volumes. *CFR* subscription includes a special *Supplement to Title 3, the President.* Because *Title 3* of the *CFR* consists only of references to Presidential documents cited, the full text is published only in the *FR* and in this series of supplements; at this writing compilations have been published covering the years 1938 to 1965.

Both publications are absolutely indispensable to academic libraries, larger public libraries, and special collections where clients have a need to know. (J.M.)

Federal Reserve Bulletin. 1915. m. $6. SDC: FR1. 3: Charts. Federal Reserve System Bd. of Governors, Div. of Admin. Services, Washington, D.C. 20551. Index, adv. Circ: 26,500. Vol. ends: Dec. Microform: UM, PMC. Reprint: Kraus.

Indexed: CurrCont, BusI, JEconLit, PAIS. *Aud:* Ga, Ac. *Jv:* V.

Libraries with large economic and banking holdings are not likely to be without this publication, which "presents articles of general and special interest, policy and other official statements issued by the (Federal Reserve) Board, and statistical information relating to domestic financial and business developments and to international financial developments." (Andriot)

Regular features include: "National Summary of Business Conditions"—brief coverage of industrial production, employment, retail sales, agriculture, wholesale and consumer prices, bank credit, deposits and reserves, and security markets; "Financial and Business Statistics"—includes a guide to tabular presentation and statistical releases, with latest *Bulletin* reference, also international statistics with an index to the statistical tables; "Federal Reserve Board Publications"—useful listing of documents not available from the Superintendent of Documents. Each issue notes policy actions taken by the Federal Open Market Committee at each meeting. These are released approximately 90 days after the date of the meeting. The records have been published regularly in the *Bulletin* since the July 1967 issue in the form in which they appear in the Board's Annual Reports. In addition, the Board's legal department publishes in this magazine statutes and the regulations and decisions of the Board, pursuant to law. For specialized collections. (J.M.)

Finance and Development. See Business Section.

HSMHA Health Reports. 1970. m. $8.50. Marion K. Priest. ° • SDC: HE 20.2010/2. Illus., index, adv. Circ.: 13,000. Vol. ends: Dec. Microform: UM.

Indexed: BioAb, ChemAb, IMed, PAIS. *Aud:* Ga, Ac. *Jv:* V.

This publication supersedes the old familiar *Public Health Reports;* it is a journal with a new look, a new name, and a new mission. Typographically, the new look is more modern, a bit bolder; the magazine was completely redesigned from cover to cover. The new name resulted from major reorganizational changes within the Department of Health, Education and Welfare during 1969 and 1970. Formerly published in the Office of the Surgeon General, the journal is now issued by the Health Services and Mental Health Administration, hence the name. It is also the official organ for this unit. The new mission arises from organizational changes; more scientific papers concerned with the delivery of health services and with the many facets of health care will be published. The magazine purports to be "a medium of communication with health practitioners, and not just an archivistic publication. In short, we plan to carry feature articles in addition to the scientific papers. We want to report the 'now' happenings in the health field as well as to document the successes or failures of the studies and projects of the past—even though the past may be only 2 to 5 years ago." (Ed. note)

Because the fields of health and community service are changing rapidly, the emphasis in this publication is upon new ideas, new programs, new projects, even when they are still relatively experimental in nature. Though solid, scientific achievement—the documented paper—is not slighted, the shibboleth clearly is "relevance." Features include about three to four articles, signed and by authorities in the field, on a myriad of subjects: superstitions related to health, training of mental health counselors, critical review of health insurance, and so on. Other regular departments are: "Programs, Practices, People"—a gaggle of items of interest to workers in the public health field; "Technical Reports"—the "journal" portion—consisting of scientific papers of technical interest, strictly research to balance the popular features. Glossy color and black and white photographs reinforce the new image. The journal is aimed at practicing public health officials, community health practitioners, faculty and students in college where the health disciplines are taught, and workers in research institutions, hospitals, and community health organizations. Libraries that support these special groups, and large public libraries, should subscribe to keep abreast of government activities in this vital area. (J.M.)

HUD Challenge. 1969. m. $6. Tacy Cook. ° • SDC: HH 1.36. Illus. Circ: 17,000. Sample. Vol. ends: Dec.

Indexed: PAIS, PHRA. *Bk. rev:* Various number, length. *Aud:* Ga, Ac.

Published monthly by the Office of Public Affairs of the U.S. Department of Housing and Urban Development, this magazine serves as a forum for the exchange of ideas and innovations between HUD staff members throughout the country, HUD-related agencies, institutions, businesses, and the concerned public. The official Departmental magazine, it provides a medium for discussing policies, programs, projects, and new directions.

Generally each issue is organized thematically. Examples include an issue on finance, devoted to ways housing and community development can be supported by innovative economic techniques; an international issue that surveyed housing programs in other nations and discussed forms of local government most capable of solving urban problems; a legislation and budget issue; and a recapitulation of HUD-FHA sponsored programs. There are approximately eight articles in each issue, usually signed, and written largely by HUD staffers with occasional contributions by leading union or industrial figures.

Written in a style suitable for the layman, the magazine carries special features. Included among these are: "Looking Ahead"—a one-page column devoted to recently launched programs or programs in the planning stage of more than routine interest; "Editor's Notebook"—a page of brief news squibs such as notices of appointments, awards, HUD regulations, urban workshops, research projects, and the like; "In-print"—a medium-length review of a commercially published monograph on urban affairs, plus brief annotations of commercial and government publications; "Lines and Numbers"—a brief analysis of some aspect of housing, such as mobile homes, budget outlays, or census of housing highlights, accompanied by statistics in tabular form.

Though without the editorial freedom of magazines like *Urban Affairs Quarterly,* it is a useful publication for college and university libraries as well as urban public libraries. (J.M.)

Housing and Urban Development Trends. 1968. q. free. SDC: HH 1.14; Charts. U.S. Dept. of Housing and Urban Development, Washington, D.C. 20410. Vol. ends: Dec.

Indexed: PAIS. *Aud:* Ga, Ac.

Begun in 1968 as a monthly, the journal is now published quarterly. The purpose of the publication has not changed, however, and still provides current information on housing production and financing, as well as programs and activities of the Department.

The magazine consists of some twenty-five tables of statistical data without any redeeming narrative to explicate the figures. Tabular information is divided into five parts, comprising production of housing units including new housing starts, mobile home shipments, housing completions, and the housing market; construction expenditures; prices, costs and employment hours and earnings in the industry; mortgage credit; and HUD programs such as FHA mortgage and loan insurance, rent supplements, college housing, and urban renewal projects. Sources of statistics other than HUD are shown; they include the Census Bureau, Veterans Administration, Labor Statistics Bureau, and Federal Home Loan Bank Board.

Entitled *Housing Statistics* prior to 1968, annual data are still issued separately in a supplement (H1.14/2: yr.). Recommended for business collections and academic and larger public libraries. (J.M.)

International Commerce. See *Commerce Today.*

International Monetary Fund Staff Papers. See Business/Banking and Finance Section.

Labor Development Abroad. See Labor and Industrial Relations Section.

Library of Congress Information Bulletin. See Library Periodicals Section.

Manpower. 1969. m. $5.50. Ellis Rottman. ° • SDC: L 1.39/9. Illus. Vol. ends: Dec.

Indexed: PAIS, Recent Publications on Government Problems. *Bk. rev:* Various number, length. *Aud:* Ga, Ac, Hs.

The official monthly journal of the Labor Department's Manpower Administration, this publication supercedes *Employment Service Review* and *Unemployment Insurance Review.* Although it is the official organ, expressions of opinion in the articles do not necessarily represent the views of the Labor Department.

Price List 36 states that the magazine is "designed for officials in industry, labor, and government who need authoritative information on what is being done about employment and why, where, how and for whom it is being done." Each issue contains about six to eight articles on subjects such as teacher training, black employment, day care centers, career guidance, job safety, etc. The wide-ranging topics are casually presented, readable, layman-oriented. Recurring and regular features include: "News and Notes"—brief squibs on news items relevant to the manpower situation; "R & D Reports"—a listing, with a few brief annotations, of recently received reports compiled under research contracts granted by the Manpower

Administration, most available for purchase from the National Technical Information Service, where order number is cited; "Statistics"—data on the total number of persons participating in various programs under the Manpower and Training Act as of a specific period of time; "Publications"—an annotated listing of documents issued by the Manpower Administration and the Bureau of Labor Statistics on manpower and related matters.

With an attractive format and many photographs, this is a useful magazine for university and public libraries, as well as for high school libraries. (J.M.)

Military Law Review. See Law Section.

Monthly Checklist of State Publications. 1910. m. $8. ° • SDC: LC 30.9. Index. Vol. ends: Dec. Microform: MF.

Aud: Ga, Ac.

With the exception of the *Annual Report, Librarian of Congress* and the Copyright Office issuances, this is the oldest serial publication of LC. It is a record of state documents issued during the previous five years which have been received by the Library of Congress. Precluded from the list are college and university catalogs, slip laws, and certain state university press documents that are official publications of the academic body. Included are territorial publications, documents of associations of state officials, information of interstate organizations, and the publications of societies and institutions at the state level. The majority of entries are on a current or three-to-five-months-after publication basis, although random sampling of key reports in states reveals gaps in the citations of publications. A good index to the entire listing is produced, but only annually. Periodicals issued by state agencies are listed in the June and December issues.

As an ordering tool, the publication is of limited value; there still remains inadequate control over the publications of state agencies. Though its usefulness is circumscribed accordingly, it can serve as a checklist for keeping aware of certain state publications in a field of interest. (J.M.)

Monthly Labor Review. 1915. m. $9. Herbert C. Morton. ° • SDC: L 2.6: Charts. Index, adv. Circ: 13,000. Vol. ends: Dec. Microform: P, UM, MF, PMC.

Indexed: BusI, PAIS, RG. *Bk. rev:* Various number, length. *Aud:* Ga, Ac, Hs. *Jv:* V.

Proudly claiming to be "the oldest and most authoritative Government research journal in the fields of economics and the social sciences," the publication is also the official organ of the Bureau of Labor Statistics, that indefatigable agency of figure-manipulators who shape and slice, with their decimals and percentages, our collective national destiny. It serves, as *Price List* 36 tells us, as "the medium through which the Labor Department publishes its regular monthly reports on such subjects as trends of employment and payrolls, hourly and weekly earnings, weekly working hours, collective agreements, industrial accidents, industrial disputes, and many others."

Issues contain approximately six to ten articles written by Labor Department employees and some nongovernment persons. All are experts in their field; the articles are unfailingly interesting and informative, signed, with credentials of the authors given. Not all articles represent necessarily the establishment position or editorial opinion. Of the many regular features there are included: "Foreign Labor Briefs"—pithy analyses of events abroad such as Poland's wage system, British labor troubles, social security in Latin America, and the like; "Significant Decisions in Labor Cases"—National Labor Relations Board rulings having an impact on labor-management relations; "Current Labor Statistics"—some thirty pages of statistics on over thirty categories of data covering employment, labor turnover, hours and earnings, prices and productivity, etc. There is also a monthly listing of collective bargaining agreements scheduled to expire the month following the date of issue; gives name and location of company, industry, union, and number of workers—a very useful reference source. An excellent book review section graces the magazine; reviews are signed and reviewers' credentials given.

The publication ranks with the best in its field, and should be subscribed to by virtually all libraries. (J.M.)

Monthly Weather Review. See Atmospheric Sciences Section.

Mosaic. 1970. q. $2.50. Jack Kratchman. ° • SDR: NS 1.29. Illus. Vol. ends: Fall.

Bk. rev: Various number, length. *Aud:* Ga, Ac, Hs.

The publication was founded to further communication among the many parties who are affected by and who influence the course of National Science Foundation programs. The name is symbolic of the nature of scientific effort, its reliance on many individual contributions to knowledge coming together to form patterns of science theory. In the developing mosaic of science, the quarterly is intended for two-way communication: articles from NSF staff as well as from members of the academic science and education community are included.

There are an average of three to five articles per issue, and the topics are eclectic: oceanography, philosophy of science, teaching science in the schools, climatology, astronomy, ecological problems, etc. Usually featured in each issue is an interview with a prominent scientist. The scope of the publication is interdisciplinary and the tone humanistic; articles are well written but do not obfuscate. There is a refreshing absence of technical jargon. Regular departments include: "Publications of the National Science Foundation"—several brief, annotated reports processed for printing by NSF and available from the Superintendent of Documents; "Data Highlights"—interesting statistical briefs on the number of scientists in government, immigration of engineers, trends in graduate enrollment in science and engineering, and other ready reference data; "NSF News"—notices of appointments, reorganization, NSF priorities. This feature is sometimes called "NSF Notes" and also contains important information affecting NSF activities, such as budget requests. A useful and objective document, this publication is enthusiastically recommended for academic, public, and high school collections. (J.M.)

North. See Indians (American) Section.

Occupational Outlook Quarterly. 1957. q. $1.50. Melvin Fountain. ° • SDC: L 2.70/4: Charts. Illus., index, adv. Circ: 9,500. Vol. ends: Winter.

Indexed: PAIS. *Bk. rev:* 5–10, 50–100 words. *Aud:* Ga, Ac, Hs.

This valuable publication supplements the information in the annual *Occupational Outlook Handbook,* one of the finest information sources in the redoubtable Bureau of Labor Statistics *Bulletin* series. It "contains current information on employment trends and outlook, based primarily on the continuous research and statistical programs of the BLS." *(Price List 36)*

Each issue contains anywhere from six to eleven articles on employment opportunities. These are of consistently high interest and readability, and the prognostications in the various professions and occupations are more accurate than in the *Handbook,* whose clairvoyance does not always penetrate into a President's mind and an uncertain future. Required reading for guidance counselors is the annual report on college graduates' prospects in the market place. Each year in late March the BLS regional office staff members interview a cross section of college placement officials for clues to the job situation for June college graduates. The result is an authoritative report. Among the regular features are: "Counseling Aids"—brief annotations of books, films, leaflets, etc., published by commercial firms and government agencies on career guidance subjects; "Recent Publications on Manpower"—contains information similar to the above. All high school, college, and public libraries should subscribe. (J.M.)

Our Public Lands. 1951. q. $1. Ed Parker. ° • SDC: I 53.12. Illus. Vol. ends: Fall.

Aud: Ga, Ac, Hs.

This quarterly is the official publication of the Bureau of Land Management, Interior Department. *Price List* 36 describes it as featuring "all news about the 460-million acre public domain such as: how to buy public lands, where to hunt and fish, new laws and regulations, scenic and natural areas, new camping sites, conservation highlights, Alaskan opportunities, and ancient ruins."

Consisting of about 23 pages per issue, it usually contains seven to nine short articles. Signed, they are written primarily by BLM staffers but sometimes by guest writers who are authorities in conservation. Articles are popularly written and cover such topics as natural history, erosion, environmental clean-up projects, wildfire detection, minerals exploration, and livestock range management. Among the regular features are: "Highlights"—brief news notes on Interior regulatory activities, personnel appointments, and internal housekeeping information of the bureau; "Public Sale Bulletin Board"—a compilation of the most up-to-date information possible on upcoming sales of public lands by land offices of the BLM, arranged alphabetically by states, with a brief description of the site and per-acre prices if appraised. This service is extremely useful for your interested public library patron. (J.M.)

Performance. 1950. m. free. Susan Bliss. • SDC: PrEx 1.10/3. President's Committee on Employment of the Handicapped, 7131 Dept. of Labor Bldg., Washington, D.C. 20210. Illus. Vol. ends: June.

Aud: Ga, Ac, Hs.

This slim publication is described (inside front cover) as "a nationally distributed magazine designed to report progress in the nationwide program to provide employment opportunities for all handicapped workers; to keep Governors' and Community Committees informed of new promotional and educational ideas and activities, and to provide all readers with up-to-date general information concerning latest developments in the fields of rehabilitation and placement of the disabled."

Averaging seventeen to twenty pages per issue, it usually contains from four to six articles on the various problems of the handicapped: jobs, education, favorable legislation, etc. Articles are signed and written in a simple style for the layman. A regular feature is "The Chairman's Column," a two to three page editorial opinion on a subject relevant to problems of the disabled. The author is chairman of the President's Committee on Employment of the Handicapped. Despite its less than scintillating performance, this magazine is free and is useful for providing limited insight into government plans and policies regarding the handicapped. (J.M.)

Pesticides Monitoring Journal. 1967. q. $1.75. Sylvia R. O'Rear. Environmental Protection Agency, 4770 Buford Hwy., Bldg. 29, Chamblee, Ga. 30341. Subs. to: Supt. of Docs., U.S. Govt. Printing Office, Washington, D.C. 20402. Illus. Vol. ends: no. 4. Refereed.

Indexed: ChemAb. *Aud:* Sa, Ac.

This publication is basically a technical journal directed at the scientific community investigating pesticide residues in water, soil, estuaries, food, fish, and wildlife. Although it does not serve as a vehicle for the publication of basic research on pesticides, it functions as a clearinghouse for data and evaluative reports on the subject. Important enough to be supported by academic libraries interested in this area of pollution.

Printing and Publishing. 1958. q. $1. William F. Lefquist. • SDC: C 41.18. Illus. Vol. ends: Oct.

Indexed: PAIS. *Aud:* Ga, Ac.

This brief publication consists of approximately five to six short articles on various aspects of the printing and publishing industry. Subjects covered include international book trade data, book industry trends, outlooks in the printing and publishing industries, analysis of various printing establishments in foreign countries, photo engraving, imports and exports. Regular features include a section called "Statistical Series," consisting of five series of data on U.S. exports and imports of printed matter, arranged by types of printed matter and by principal markets and suppliers. Also included are quarterly and annual averages of selected statistics on printing, publishing, and allied industries. Of primary value for the student or expert in the economics of the industry; recommended for large university and public library collections. (J.M.)

Prison Service Journal. 1960. q. 15¢ Mark S. Winston. H.M.S.O., 49 High Holborn, London, WC1, England.

Bk. rev: 5–10, 250–1,000 words. *Aud:* Ga, Ac.

Though not in the same league with its American cousin, *Federal Probation* (q.v.), this magazine is nevertheless useful as a guide to the theory and practice of British penology. Issued by the Home Office, Prison Department, the journal provides an opportunity for contributors to comment upon and discuss any topic relevant to the functions of the Prison Service and the areas in which it operates. Freedom of editorial opinion exists.

Beginning with the January 1971 issue the size and format of the publication changed, but the quantity of reading material remained at the previous level. Articles are written by politicians, prison officers, university professors, psychiatric social workers, and occasionally even prisoners. Articles are signed, and contributors' credentials given. It is written in a semischolarly style, accessible to the educated layman. Regular features include: "Reviews"—excellent coverage of current books and very useful reviews of articles from leading journals; "The Media and the Message"—formerly titled "Prison Problems and the Mass Media," devoted to informal and chatty comments on the reportage of crime, police, prisons, etc., by magazines, radio/TV, and those intrepid British newspapers. (J.M.)

Problems of Communism. 1952. bi-m. $3. Theodore Frankel. ° • SDC: IA 1.8. Illus., index. Vol. ends: Nov./Dec. Microform: C, UM. Reprint: Johnson.

Indexed: PAIS, SSHum. *Bk. rev:* Various number, length. *Aud:* Ga, Ac. *Jv:* V.

The publisher tells us that opinions expressed by contributors to this journal do not necessarily reflect the views or policies of the U.S. Information Agency, under whose aegis this document is prepared and is-sued. Its purpose is to provide analyses and significant background information on various aspects of world communism today. Both the theoretical and political aspects of communism are explored and, as expected, emphasis is placed upon the aims and policies of the Soviet Union and the People's Republic of China.

Articles number approximately four to six in each issue. They are written by distinguished scholars and authorities in the field, and the credentials of the con-tributors are given. The articles are consistently of a high level of competence, and the editorial freedom permits some variance from establishment dogma. Regular features include: "Reviews in Brief"—rather lengthy reviews, excellently written, which follow the main reviewing section; and "Notes and Views"—a section consisting of letters and an occasional "letter essay" of article length on a relevant topic. Outstand-ing is the main book review section, wherein three to five books are reviewed at length. The in-depth re-views are by authorities such as A. Doak Barnett and Richard M. Pfeffer. (J.M.)

Prologue. See History/American and Canadian Section.

Public Health Reports. See *HSMHA Health Reports.*

Public Roads. 1918. bi-m. $2. Harry C. Secrest. ° • SDC: TD 2.109: Charts. Illus., index, adv. Circ: 7,500. Vol. ends: Dec. Microform: UM.

Indexed: ASTI, ChemAb, EngI, Recent Publications on Government Problems. *Aud:* Ga, Ac.

The purpose of this bimonthly is "to acquaint high-way engineers and others interested in highway mat-ters with the results of the (Bureau of Public Roads') research in highway planning, design, construction, finance, highway use, and in a wide variety of mate-rials for use in road construction." (Andriot) Subtitled "A Journal of Highway Research," this magazine con-tains from two to four articles per issue, signed and with the authors' credentials given. The articles are technical in nature, with graphs, tables, and other sta-tistical data accompanying the text. Some articles, however, e.g., those on personnel management and travel, can be appreciated by the informed layman. Departments that recur regularly include: "Digest of Recent Research and Development Results"; "New Publications"—brief, annotated listing of Federal Highway Administration documents; and "Publica-tions of the Federal Highway Administration"—a list-ing, without annotations, of documents.

This is a useful publication of broad coverage to supplement such excellent journals as *Behavioral Re-search in Highway Safety,* which emphasize the hu-man factor primarily. For university, special, and large public libraries with collections in this discipline. (J.M.)

Quarterly Journal of the Librarian of Congress. See Library Periodicals Section.

Reclamation Era. 1908. q. $1.50. Gordon J. Forsyth. ° • SDC: I 27.5. Illus., index, adv. Circ: 6,000. Vol. ends: Nov.

Indexed: BibAg. *Aud:* Ga, Ac, Hs.

Subtitled "A Water Review Quarterly," this publi-cation "presents articles on various phases of land re-clamation, covering such subjects as irrigation, crops, pasturing and land recovery." *(Price List* 36) Approxi-mately six articles per issue cover these and other germane topics. The articles are written simply and are easily understood at layman and high school level. Little more than a newsletter, the publication none-theless has a glossy format, with attractive photo-graphs and illustrations. Regular departments include: "Water Quiz"—a feature that consists of four or five multiple-choice questions, a schoolboy's diversion with answers in a box below, printed upside down; "Fifty Years Ago in Our Magazine"—a photoreproduction of a page from an issue of the magazine published half a century ago, of visual nostalgic interest; "News Notes"—brief items of interest to readers; and "Major Recent Contract Awards"—which includes the specification number, project and award date, descrip-tion of the work, contractor's name and address, and cost of contract to the taxpayer. (J.M.)

Rehabilitation Record. 1960. bi-m. $3. Ron Bourgea. ° • SDC: HE 17.109: Charts. Vol. ends: Nov./Dec.

Indexed: IMed, Recent Publications on Government Problems. *Bk. rev:* Various number, length. *Aud:* Ga, Ac.

Superior to *Performance* (q.v.), this professional bimonthly of the Rehabilitation Services Administration "publishes articles by leading authorities in their fields about significant new ideas and techniques being used to rehabilitate handicapped men and women." *(Price List* 36) It contains approximately nine to eleven arti-cles in each issue by leading experts in the public and private spheres of rehabilitation and related fields. Andriot cites the purpose of the magazine as dissemi-nating "basic information on new projects and findings in vocational rehabilitation to people who are provid-ing such services and to those working directly with handicapped audiences." Despite its special audience, the information presented is not so technical that the informed layman cannot benefit. Regular departments include: "Across the Desk"—brief news notes on items such as announcements of seminars, correspondence courses, hiking, and the ubiquitous upbeat story; "New Publications"—briefly annotated announcements of books, proceedings, manuals, etc., largely commercially published with very few documents listed; "Films on Rehab"—a very useful annotated list of films and film-strips on various rehabilitation problems; "Project Reports"—unannotated listing of technical studies issuing from university and research centers. (J.M.)

Research in Education. See Abstracts and Indexes Section.

Service. See Consumer Services Section.

Smithsonian. See History/American and Canadian Section.

Social Security Bulletin. 1938. m. $4. ° · SDC: HE 3.3: Charts. Index. Vol. ends: Dec. Microform: UM.

Indexed: BibAg, BusI, PAIS, Recent Publications on Government Problems. *Aud:* Ga, Ac.

The official monthly publication of the Social Security Administration, this bulletin reports current data on the operations of the SSA and the results of research and analysis pertinent to the social security program. Usually there are no more than two signed articles. Topics cover the large range of problems the SSA is empowered to deal with: medicare, private health insurance, social welfare, retirement, disability insurance, benefits, etc. Articles are carefully and thoroughly written, well documented, and employ sophisticated methodological techniques. Statements in the articles do not, however, necessarily reflect official Administration policy.

Among the regular features are: "Social Security in Review"—highlights of Presidential messages on some aspect of social security, and current monthly data on Old-Age, Survivors, Disability and Health Insurance (OASDHI) benefits; "Notes and Brief Reports"—analysis and accompanying data on social security coverage of state and local government employees, workmen's compensation payments and costs, and the like. Also included in this section are reports on social security developments abroad. Occasionally recent publications of SSA are listed, with brief annotations. (J.M.)

Soil Conservation. 1935. m. $2. Ben O. Osborn. ° · SDC: A 57.9. Illus., index. Vol. ends: July.

Indexed: BibAg, BioAg. *Bk. rev:* Various number, length. *Aud:* Ga, Ac, Hs.

Running to about twenty pages per issue, this is the official magazine of the Soil Conservation Service, an agency of the Department of Agriculture. Approximately 8 to 12 short articles cover subjects such as cattle farming, contour strip-cropping, watershed programs, gully control, and other SCS activities at the local and district level. Written mostly in the popular vein, the articles are signed and largely composed by local agency conservationists. There are some technical articles, but they can be comprehended by the informed layman. Regular features include: "Conservation in Action"—a roundup, by states, of soil conservation activities of more than routine interest; "Meetings"—a listing of conferences, associations, symposia, youth science fairs, and the like; "Review"—short reviews of government and commercial publications in this field; "New Publications"—brief annotations of recent government documents. Each issue contains a

one-page editorial by the administrator of the SCS. (J.M.)

Survey of Current Business. 1921. m. $9. Lora S. Collins. ° · SDC: C 43.8: Charts. Illus., adv. Circ: 15,000. Vol. ends: Dec. Microform: UM. Reprint: Johnson.

Indexed: BusI, PAIS, Recent Publications on Government Problems. *Aud:* Ga, Ac.

Issued by the Office of Business Economics of the Commerce Department, the purpose of this journal is "to disseminate significant economic indicators for business use, including analytical findings of the OBE as well as over 2,500 statistical series originating from both public and private sources." (Andriot)

Section I is titled "The Business Situation," a narrative exposition of business trends, outlook, and other features relevant to the business world. Articles are signed. A useful feature is a boxed abstract of the summary of each special analysis. The summaries are complemented by charts and tables. The second section, "Current Business Statistics," consists of forty pages of statistical data. While there is duplication of information with *Economic Indicators* (q.v.) and other government statistics sources, the series is comprehensive and updates, when necessary, the data published in the previous edition of *Business Statistics,* the biennial supplement to this magazine. Recentness is further accomplished by a weekly release, "Business Statistics," which supplements the monthly data. A useful subject index to this regular feature is found on the inside back cover, arranged by general business indicators and specific industry data such as chemicals, lumber, metals, textiles, etc. (J.M.)

Treasury Bulletin. 1939. m. $13.50. ° · SDC: T 1.3. Illus, index.

Aud: Ga, Ac.

A monthly synopsis of Treasury Department activities, the purpose of this bulletin is "to extend knowledge of the public finances, monetary developments and activities of the Treasury Department by making information available in a more compact and usable form. The data contained in this publication supplement or recapitulate that contained in the daily treasury statements and other publications and press releases." (Andriot)

Each issue contains an introductory article under the rubric "Treasury Financing Operations," consisting of a two to three page account of reported tenders received for various treasury bills. Domestic and foreign series are included, as are eurodollar series subscriptions. Following are brief written explanatory summaries of the statistical data reported; these include federal fiscal operations, federal obligations, monetary statistics, the federal debt, U.S. savings bonds and notes, ownership of federal securities, international financial statistics, and so forth. A cumulative table of contents covers the yearly contents of the periodical. Valuable for large university and public library collections, and indispensable for specialized business service collections and libraries. (JM.)

Unemployment Insurance Review. See *Manpower.*

Weekly Compilation of Presidential Documents. 1965. w. $9. ° · SDC: GS 4.114. Index. Vol. ends: last wk. Dec. Microform: UM.

Indexed: PAIS. *Aud:* Ga, Ac. *Jv:* V.

Authority to publish this compilation is included in the Federal Register Act (49 *Stat.* 500, as amended), under regulations prescribed by the Administrative Committee of the Federal Register and approved by the President (1 CFR, pt. 32). In *Price List* 36 a detailed account of content and scope is given: "makes available transcripts of the President's news conferences, messages to Congress, public speeches and statements, and other presidential materials released by the White House up to 5 p.m. each Friday. . . . It includes an index of contents and a cumulative index. Other finding aids include lists of laws approved by the President and of nominations submitted to the Senate, and a checklist of White House releases."

As does the *Federal Register* (q.v.), this daily publishes the full text of Presidential executive orders and proclamations. Useful for ready reference is the arrangement of acts approved by the President: date of approval, bill number, public law number, and title of act are given. The section titled "Digest of Other White House Announcements" lists items of general interest which were announced to the press during the period covered by a particular issue but which are not carried elsewhere in the issue. "Nominations Submitted to the Senate" does not include promotions of members of the uniformed services, nominations to the Service Academies, or nominations of Foreign Service officers. The full text of Presidential messages to Congress is useful for libraries which do not receive the published documents of the Serial Set. (J.M.)

Welfare in Review. 1963. bi-m. $1.75. Catherine P. Williams. ° · SDC: HE 17.9: Charts. Index. Vol. ends: Nov./Dec.

Bk. rev: Various number, length. *Aud:* Ga, Ac.

Price List 36 notes that this bimonthly "contains research articles and program and operating statistical data covering the various programs of the Welfare Administration, such as old-age assistance, aid to families with dependent children, child welfare and maternal and child health services, and juvenile delinquency demonstration projects, etc." To make this research and statistical information available, there are signed articles written by experts within HEW and outside of government. Authors' credentials are given, and the articles are written in a style that interested laymen may understand.

Regular features include: "New Publications"—a listing of both government and nongovernment publications germane to the field, briefly annotated (occasionally one reviewed at length); "Public Assistance Statistics"—information, with accompanying statistical data, on recipients of welfare payments, broken down into categories such as old age, blind, disabled, families with dependent children, and the like (statistics based on reports compiled by the National Center for Social Statistics of the Social and Rehabilitation Service, HEW); "Research Notes"—detailed accounts of research in progress and recently completed studies on problems in the field of welfare, useful for guidelines in determining bases for potential legislation in this controversial area, especially in studies on aid to dependent children.

The features alone give this publication a useful reference value, in an area of such highly charged political and social import. (J.M.)

United Nations and Selected Foreign.

Bibliography, Documentation Terminology. See Bibliography Section.

Bulletin of the International Bureau of Education. See *Educational Documentation and Information.*

CERES: FAO Review. 1968. bi-m. $5. Andras Biro. UNIPUB, Inc., Box 433, New York, N.Y. 10016. Illus., charts, index, adv., Circ: 40,000. Sample. Vol. ends: Nov/Dec.

Indexed: PAIS. *Bk. rev:* 3–5, 500–750 words, signed. *Aud:* Ga, Ac.

With separate editions published in English, French, and Spanish, this illustrated magazine discourses on multiple aspects of agricultural, economic, and social development throughout the world. Opinions expressed by the contributors are not necessarily those of the Food and Agriculture Organization or of the editors.

There are about seven to nine signed articles per issue, with credentials of authors given. The contributors are international scholars and specialists in their field. Articles cover a wide range of subjects—investment trends and opportunities, interviews with prominent officials in decision-making capacities, technology and "third world" problems, pesticides, the ubiquitous ecology crisis, wildlife, etc. Though articles are scholarly in content, they are not written in the stilted jargon of the pedant. Some issues are devoted to a special topic, such as world unemployment, environmental deterioration, and foreign aid. Regular departments include: "World Report"—a summary section of items relevant to FAO activities, divided by country with a special section on problems and policies that cross national boundaries; "Opinion"—excerpts from addresses, radio/TV interviews, editorials, with quotable quotes of prominent personalities; "Commodities"—an analytical article in each issue on a specific topic, such as world meat production, dairy stocks, oilcakes, etc.; "Forum"—letters and comments from readers; and book reviews. (J.M.)

Copyright Bulletin. 1967. q. $3. Marie-Claude Dock. U.N. UNESCO, Place de Fontenoy 75, Paris 7e, France. Subs. to: UNIPUB, Box 433, New York, N.Y. 10016. Sample. Vol. ends: No. 4.

Aud: Ac.

Contains up-to-date documentation on developments, meetings, and bibliographies for the specialist in the field of international copyright. Regular sections cover publications received and professional news and information. Important documents are frequently reproduced in their entirety. These topics have appeared in recent issues: Report of the International Convention for the Protection of Performers, Producers of Phonograms, and Broadcasting Organizations; comparative studies of copyright law—right of performance and right of reproduction; and an article on unauthorized distribution of communications satellite signals.

Educational Documentation and Information (Formerly: **Bulletin of the International Bureau of Education.**) 1926. q. $8. UNESCO, Place de Fontenoy 75, Paris 7e, France. Subs. to: UNIPUB, Box 433, New York, N.Y. 10016. Sample. Vol. ends: No. 4.

Aud: Ac.

Primarily for those working in educational documentation, either in national centers or in training and research institutions. Each issue is devoted to a specific theme developed in a comprehensive introduction and documented in an annotated bibliography. A newly designed format with the 1971 issues makes for more enjoyable reading. Reader commentary is welcomed. There topics have appeared: financing of education; National Education Documentation Retrieval System of the United States (ERIC); social background of students and their prospects of success at school; vocational and educational guidance; design of adaptive and self-instructional systems; organization of special education.

External Affairs. See Political Science Section.

Food and Agricultural Legislation. 1952. bi-a. $2.50. Food and Agricultural Organization, Via delle Terme di Caracalla, 10100 Rome, Italy. Subs. to: UNIPUB, Box 433, New York, N.Y. 10016. Sample. Vol. ends: Dec.

Aud: Ac.

Contains a selection of food and agricultural laws and regulations of international significance. Included is current legislation for these agricultural areas: plant production and protection; animal production and protection; land and water use; financial laws affecting agriculture; agricultural cooperation; technical aspects of rural development; trade in agricultural products and requisites; forestry; fisheries; wildlife; the human environment. Specific legislation is documented for: inspection, reporting, and control of pests and diseases; manufacture and use of pesticides; stock breeding; soil conservation; water pollution control; farm prices; subsidies; foreign investments; cooperatives and other forms of association; national parks and nature reserves. Preference is given to legislation on agrarian reform and to food laws. Separate editions appear in English, Spanish, and French.

Foreign Trade (Canada). See Business/General Section.

Impact of Science on Society. 1950. q. $4. Bruno Friedman. UNIPUB, Box 433, New York, N.Y. 10016. Illus. Microform: UM. Vol. ends: Oct./Dec.

Aud: Ga, Ac.

Published in three editions—English, French, and Spanish—this journal is an extremely lively and readable publication which ranges over vast terrain exploring the often-troubled relationship between science and society and articulating aspects of that relationship. Every issue has about eight signed articles (credentials of the contributors are given in footnotes), devoted to a single theme. In fact, the theme may carry over into more than one issue, depending upon reader response or editorial intent. For example, *Impact* explored the matter of the alienation of science from society in three issues, one dealing with science and humor, the next with the way in which the nonscientist warily views science, a third giving scientists the chance to criticize their critics. Other topics surveyed in issues include quality vs. quantity in scientific research; women in the age of science and technology; the "ignorance explosion." Articles range from very scholarly to playfully reminiscent and subjective. They are uniformly excellent and provocative. (J.M.)

International Social Science Journal. 1949. q. $7. Peter Lengyel. UNIPUB, Box 433, New York, N.Y. 10016. Charts. Microform: UM. Reprint: Kraus.

Indexed: PAIS, PsyAb, SSHum. *Aud:* Ga, Ac. *Jv:* V.

Each issue of this journal presents an authoritative international conspectus of recent scholarship on an important topic. Signed, scholarly articles written by distinguished personages in their fields are usually revised versions of papers originally submitted at various interdisciplinary symposia organized by Unesco under the auspices of a government or learned society. Opinions expressed are those of the authors, not necessarily reflecting the views of Unesco.

Issues are devoted to a broad topic, such as trends in legal learning, social research, the sociology of science, public administration, controlling the human environment, etc. The purpose of the magazine is "to make this periodical into a forum of debate not only on intellectual matters, on the state of the art in various disciplines, or in emerging areas of interdisciplinary concern, but also on all those organizational or institutional questions which lie behind the production of these intellectual results." (Ed. note.) That these large mandated goals are admirably met is testimony to the quality of the magazine. Features include: an annual descriptive listing of new periodicals received by Unesco's Social Science Documentation Centre—full bibliographic information and a concise annotation are given; a list of forthcoming international conferences, often projected four to six years ahead (information on locations and dates uneven); a list of documents and publications (briefly annotated) of the United Nations and specialized agencies of more than routine interest, arranged by broad subjects (population, health, food, etc.); books received by the Centre are listed without annotation.

Also published in French under the title *Revue Internationale des Sciences Sociales*, the journal ranks with the best of its kind in the field. (J.M.)

International Trade Forum. 1965. bi-m. $3. Bruce Bendow. Intl. Trade Center, UNCIAD/GATT, Palais des Nations, 1211 Geneva 10, Switzerland. Subs. to: UNIPUB, Box 433, New York, N.Y. 10016. Sample. Vol. ends: Dec.

Bk. rev: 10, 160 words. *Aud:* Ac.

Published as part of a program of assistance to developing countries in promoting their exports. It focuses attention on export market opportunities, makes export marketing and promotion techniques better known, and draws attention to organizations that can assist in export promotion. Departments include coverage of Center news, and a commercial policy chronicle. Separate editions in English, French, and Spanish.

Journal of World History. 1953. q. $18. Guy S. Metraux. Sponsored by UNESCO, Editions de la Baconniere, Neuchatel, France. Subs. to: UNIPUB, Box 433, New York, N.Y. 10016. Sample. Vol. ends: No. 4.

Aud: Ac.

An interdisciplinary publication for history, philosophy, and social science collections, this contains new research, new interpretations, new bibliographies, and newly available translations of historical materials. Its scope encompasses: cross-cultural influences on regional, national, and local life; channels for cultural contact; history of ideas; growth and role of institutions in cultural life; cultural creativity; cultural approach to history and civilization. Special issues have been devoted to social life and social values of the Jewish people, and to society, sciences, and technology in Japan.

Labour Gazette. See Labor and Industrial Relations Section.

Monthly Bulletin of Agricultural Economics and Statistics. 1952. m. $6. R. D. Narain. Food and Agricultural Organization, Via delle Terme di Caracalla, 10100 Rome, Italy. Subs. to: UNIPUB, Box 433, New York, N.Y. 10016. Sample. Vol. ends: Dec.

Aud: Ac.

This periodical contains important reports and articles on world food and agricultural conditions with analysis of factors influencing them. Every issue presents up-to-date statistical data by commodity, country, region, and continent on production, trade, and prices. Data are compiled in tabular form and are easy to read. Twice a year, there are comparative tables of monthly average producer, wholesale, export, and import prices for selected commodities. A regular section of notes on individual commodities also appears—covering production, trade, stocks, consumption, prices, and related factors influencing the market situation. Recent articles focus on: pattern and potential of Asian agricultural trade; risks in agriculture and insurance coverage; economic problems and price policies for high-yielding varieties of cereals; size and efficiency of agricultural investment in selected developing countries; agricultural institutions for integrated rural development.

Monthly Bulletin of Statistics. 1947. m. $25. U.N. Statistical Office. U.N. Sales Section, New York, N.Y. 10017. Charts, index. Vol. ends: Dec. Microform: UM.

Aud: Ac, Ga.

To discover that Ireland's daily per capita consumption of calories is 3,450, that the Swedish population, per capita, has more TV sets than the United States, that Russia leads the world in books published yearly, and that Taiwan's denizens see 66 movies a year on the average is to peruse the data of that sterling compilation, the *U.N. Statistical Yearbook.* This journal updates the *Yearbook.* Published in bilingual English/French test, it provides monthly statistics on 70 subjects from over 200 countries and territories, together with special tables illustrating important economic developments. Quarterly data for significant world and regional aggregates are also prepared regularly for the bulletin.

Except where otherwise stated in the footnotes of the tables, the statistics are obtained from official sources in the countries. In addition, the following specialized agencies and intergovernmental bodies furnish data for the tables: Food and Agriculture Organization, International Civil Aviation Organization, International Labour Office, International Monetary Fund, Secretariat of the Rubber Study Group (London) and the International Tin Council (London). Areas covered include population, manpower, forestry, construction, mining, and wages and prices. Special tables include industrial production, mining and manufacturing, world trade and transport. (J.M.)

Museum. 1948. q. $10. Grace L. McCann Morley, Georges Henri Riviere. UNIPUB, Box 433, New York, N.Y. 10016. Illus., charts, index, adv. Circ: 3,600. Microform: UM.

Indexed: ArtI, ChemAb. *Aud:* Ga, Ac.

A successor to *Mouseion*, this magazine is published in Paris and serves as a quarterly survey of activities and means of research in the field of museography. It is primarily for those professionally interested in the running of museums, but can be useful for others interested in museums and in display techniques. The magazine contains bilingual English/French texts, with summaries in Russian and Spanish.

There are anywhere from three to nine signed articles. The contributors are generally distinguished museologists, educators, research specialists. Basic biographical data on them are given in the section at the end of each issue called "Contributors." The contents of the issues are often organized around a theme; recent examples of this include museums and computer technology, and public attitudes toward modern art. Regular features include "Museum Notes"—descriptive and analytic articles on various prominent museums, with worldwide coverage. Entirely on art paper, with superb photographs, this publication is a handsome addition to the collections of larger academic and public libraries. (J.M.)

Prospects in Education. 1969. q. $3.50. Unesco, Place de Fontenoy 75, Paris 7e, France. Subs. to: UNIPUB, Box 433, New York, N.Y. 10016. Illus., adv. Circ: 10,000. Sample. Vol. ends: No. 4.

Bk. rev: 3, 500 words, signed. *Aud:* Ac, Hs, Ejh.

Intended to provide educators in Unesco's member states with "articles and information from world-wide sources, sources rarely available at the national level." It is focused on the ten first years of schooling, covering basic problems in educational planning, administration, teaching methods, psychology, and solutions of concrete situations. Every issue is devoted to a special topic, e.g., Rural Education, Educational Systems and Structures, etc., reminiscent of Unesco's defunct *Education Abstracts*. Articles are not under copyright, they may freely be adapted and reproduced. The presentation of the periodical is well designed. *(Note:* in early 1972 the publisher informed readers there would be a format change, and possibly a change in title. Price and frequency will remain unchanged.)

Revue Internationale des Sciences Sociales. See *International Social Science Journal*.

Survey of British and Commonwealth Affairs. See Political Science Section.

U.N. Monthly Chronicle. 1964. m. (10/yr.), bi-m (Aug./Sept.) $9.50. UNIPUB, Box 433, New York, N.Y. 10016. Index, adv. Circ: 12,000. Vol. ends: Dec. Microform: UM.

Indexed: RG. *Bk. rev:* Various number, length. *Aud:* Ga, Ac, Hs. *Jv:* V.

The purpose of the magazine is to advance public understanding of the work of the United Nations by providing an objective, comprehensive, and documented account of the organization's activities as well as information on its related agencies. The publication fulfills its editorial intent admirably.

The journal divides, like Gaul, into three main parts. First there is a section titled "Record of the Month," which includes the categories of politics and security, economics and society, human rights, administration and budget, and legal. Under these rubrics, information is given on General Assembly decisions, actions, resolutions, and vote totals (not, however, broken down by member nation); meetings and debates of the Security Council, including voting record, with abstentions, by name of member; budget estimates, appropriations, committee actions; and a listing of Conventions and Agreements that were ratified, acceded to, or accepted. Next, the article portion includes addresses by the Secretary-General; special committee reports on recent, urgent topics; commemorative remarks, e g., the 25th anniversary of the founding of UNICEF; and reports of specific global problems such as marine pollution. Articles are signed and written by authorities in the area of interest. The concluding section, "Notes of the Month," consists of brief notices of personnel changes and the like; a selected list of documents arranged by category (political, security, etc.) and then by nation: and a listing of selected publications and official records. (J.M.)

UNESCO Bulletin for Libraries. See Library Periodicals Section.

UNESCO Chronicle. 1955. m. (10/yr.) bi-m. (Aug./Sept.) $3. Louis Cheissoux. UNIPUB, Box 433, New York, N.Y. 10016. Vol. ends: Dec.

Indexed: PAIS. *Bk. rev:* Various number, length. *Aud:* Ga, Ac.

Published in Arabic, English, French, and Spanish, the articles in this publication are informative accounts of worldwide activities engaged in by Unesco through its several offices. They consist of official reports from the agency on its plans and accomplishments as well as editorial commentary on the several aspects of its programs. Examples of concerns include educational aid for refugees, advances in educational technology, critical review of Unesco programs. The theme running through the articles is that of clarifying the major objectives of Unesco: contributing to world peace, insuring social and industrial development, and promoting human rights.

Regular and recurring features include: "News of the Secretariat"—notices of appointments and other activities of the Director-General's office, educational policies and programs, scientific activity, trends in the social sciences and humanities, developments in the communication arts (print and non-print); publications—brief annotated list of works in English published by Unesco and not reviewed elsewhere in the magazine; personnel changes in the permanent delegations and national commissions, and brief news items of commission activities arranged alphabetically by member nation; news of activities of various international organizations such as IFTC, ICSW, IFPH, and the like; a provisional calendar of conferences and meetings projected one to two months in advance. (J.M.)

✓ *UNESCO Courier.* 1948. m. (10/yr.) bi-m. (Aug./Sept.) $5. Sandy Koffler. UNIPUB, Box 433, New York, N.Y. 10016. Illus., index. Circ: 12,000. Vol. ends: Dec. Microform: UM.

Indexed: CurrCont, RG. *Bk. rev:* 8–10, length varies. *Aud:* Ga, Ac, Hs. *Jv:* V.

Subtitled "A Window Open on the World," this superior publication is issued in 12 editions: English, French, Spanish, Russian, German, Arabic, Japanese, Italian, Hindi, Tamil, Hebrew, and Persian. Each issue is devoted to a particular theme, and about eight articles explore various aspects of the topic. Articles are signed and the contributors are generally distinguished in their fields. The opinions of the contributors do not necessarily represent those of Unesco or of the editor.

Multiple use of the magazine is one of its great features. It contains material of special interest to teachers of science, history, geography, art, and music, with illustrations that may be cut out and used in class as visual aids. The various language editions are useful for teachers of foreign languages. There is an international correspondence column which provides a link with teachers in other countries. Examples of topics that have been explored include "TV—the New Tom-Tom," "The General Public Judges Modern Art," "Cultural Policy—A Modern Dilemma," "The Student of Tomorrow," and "Spin-Off—The Fruit of Space Research."

Many illustrations of striking quality grace the pages of this magazine. Regular departments include: "Bookshelf"—a listing of roughly eight to ten recent publications from Unesco and commercial sources; "Unesco Newsroom"—short news items on events that Unesco is directly or indirectly interested in; "Treasures of World Art"—each issue contains, on the inside front cover, a reproduction of an outstanding artifact, painting or other *objet d' art*, with an accompanying explanation of its significance and relation to art history. It should be noted that the magazine was one of the first publications to present to the world the great art of ancient African civilizations. (JM.)

WHO Chronicle. 1947. m. $4. WHO Publns., American Public Health Assn. Inc., 1015 18th St., N.W.,

Washington, D.C. 20036. Illus., index, adv. Circ: 10,300. Vol. ends: Dec. Microform: UM.

Indexed: BioAb, IMed. *Bk. rev:* 5–10, 100–250 words. *Aud:* Ga, Ac.

Published by the World Health Organization for the medical and public health professions, the journal provides a monthly record of the principal health activities undertaken in various countries with WHO assistance. Editions are published in Chinese, English, French, Russian, and Spanish. From five to seven articles each issue, usually but not always signed, are authoritative but not esoteric. Topics covered include health problems that can be satisfactorily solved only through the cooperation of many countries, for example eradication or control of communicable diseases, pesticide standards, disseminating epidemiological information, etc. Regular features include: "Notes and News"—brief items on WHO programs, activities, meetings, decisions; "Review of WHO Publications"; "People and Places"—personnel appointments, reassignments, and the like. Occasionally an issue will be devoted entirely to a specific topic, e.g., nutrition. (J.M.)

World Health. 1947. m. $5. F. J. Tomiche. World Health Org., American Public Health Assn., 1015 Eighteenth St., N.W., Washington, D.C. 20036. Illus., index. Circ: 160,000. Vol. ends: Dec.

Indexed: PAIS. *Aud:* Ga, Ac, Hs.

With an attractive format and many illustrations, this magazine is a commendable addition to most library collections. It appears in English, French, German, Hindi, Japanese, Portuguese, Russian, and Spanish. The problems it is concerned with, like those aired in *WHO Chronicle* (q.v.), are international in scope and require for their solution cooperative, interdisciplinary efforts. There are anywhere from five to nine articles in each issue. Articles are well written and eschew professional jargon. They are signed and the contributors include hospital directors and public relations experts as well as physicians. Most issues are concerned with a broad topic. Examples include hospitals, their activities and problems; diabetes—history of discoveries and advances in treatment; activities of WHO; and the inevitable issue devoted to air pollution and health. There has even been a piquant issue on medical proverbs. A regular feature is titled "Around the World" and consists of a miscellany of notes of interest to the field of health. (J.M.)

HEALTH

See also Medical Sciences Section.

Basic Periodicals

GENERAL. Hs: *Today's Health, Life & Health;* Ga:

Today's Health, Family Health, Fitness for Living; Jc: *Today's Health, Fitness for Living, Medical Aspects of Human Sexuality, Life & Health;* Ac: *Today's Health, Medical Aspects of Human Sexuality, American Journal of Public Health, Canadian Journal of Public Health, Life & Health.*

COUNTERCULTURE. Ga, Jc, Ac: *Health Right News, Health Pac Bulletin, The Layman Speaks.*

DRUGS. Hs: *Journal of Drug Issues, Stash Capsule;* Ga: *Journal of Drug Issues, Contemporary Drug Problems,* Jc & Ac: *Journal of Drug Issues, Stash Capsule, Grassroots, Journal of Psychedelic Drugs.*

Library and Teaching Aids

Drug and Drug Abuse Education Newsletter, Grassroots.

Basic Abstracts and Indexes

Index Medicus, Cumulative Index to Nursing Literature.

General

Accent on Living. 1956. q. $2.50. Raymond C. Cheever. Accent on Living, Inc., P.O. Box 726, Bloomington, Ill. Illus., adv. Circ: 7,500. Vol. ends: Winter. Sample.

Aud: Ga, Hs.

Uplift, news, and humor for the handicapped. The purpose and scope are summaried in the charter. "*Accent on Living* is a national magazine dedicated to serving all handicapped people, their families and their friends, regardless of race, religion or creed. *Accent* is an authorative clearing house for problems confronting handicapped people. *Accent* is edited and published with the firm belief that each person gains invaluable experience and knowledge as the result of a physical handicap. *Accent* believes in the complete dignity and respect of all persons. . . ."

Issues regularly feature an editorial, an interesting and rather extensive letters section, and numerous short articles by and about people who overcame handicaps or learned to live with them. A wide assortment of aids and appliances for the handicapped are advertised, and an effort is made by the publisher to include only those sold and manufactured by reputable companies. That in itself is worth the price of a subscription. The tone is inspirational and the journal is suitable for public and school libraries. (F.A.)

American College Health Association Journal. 1952. 5/yr. Membership (Nonmembers $15). Ralph W. Alexander. American College Health Assn., 2807 Central St., Evanston, Ill. 60201. Index, adv. Circ: 2,200. Sample. Vol. ends: June.

Indexed: ChemAb, IMed. *Bk. rev:* 1–2, length varies, signed. *Aud:* Ac.

A specialized journal, yet annotated here because it deals directly with health in college communities, and the practice of medicine in college and university health services. Also, the journal covers current topics, e.g., the February 1972 issue featured articles on environment, and in language any layman would appreciate. Contributors are doctors and specialists. A necessary title for the college or university library.

American Industrial Hygiene Association Journal. 1940. m. $20. Dohrman Byers. Heffernan Press, 35 New St., Worcester, Mass. 01605. Illus., adv. Circ: 3,000. Sample. Vol. ends: Dec.

Aud: Ac.

The safety or lack of safety found in any type of industrial situation is discussed here by experts. Some 12 articles move from the threat of mercury in the air at university facilities to the chemical composition of the coal miner's lung. While all of this is primarily for the man or woman involved directly with industrial hygiene, it has an added dimension for anyone interested in ecology and environment. The analytical reports, to be sure, are technical, but the message is clear enough—and it is spelled out with no ifs or buts. For example, it is questionable that the average layman realizes there is a threat of radioactivity in given types of gypsum building materials. This is one of those rare specialized journals which should be called to the attention of nonspecialists involved with the nation's health.

American Journal of Public Health. 1911. m. $20. George Rosen. American Public Health Assn., 1015. 18th St., N.W., Washington, D.C. 20036. Illus., index, adv. Circ: 30,000. Microform: UM.

Indexed: BioAb, ChemAb, IMed, PAIS. *Bk. rev:* 5–10, 100–500 words, signed. *Aud:* Ac, Ga.

The official publication of the American Public Health Association. It covers the entire public health field from environmental considerations to psychology. Articles are written by and for doctors and administrators, but unlike many medical journals a good deal of the material is within the grasp of the better educated layman—particularly that part dealing with the socioeconomic issues. With the growing interest in public health and methods, this is an important edition for larger collections.

Archives of Environmental Health. 1954. m. $12. John S. Chapman. American Medical Assn., 535 N. Dearborn St., Chicago, Ill. 60610. Illus., index, adv. Circ: 9,000. Sample. Vol. ends: June and Dec.

400/MAGAZINES FOR LIBRARIES

Indexed: ASTI, BioAb, ChemAb, IMed, PsyAb. *Bk. rev:* 1, 500 words, signed. *Aud:* Ac, Ga.

Noise, impure air, effects of continuous exposure to other harmful environmental dangers—all are discussed in medical terms in this journal. An average 75-page illustrated number includes eight to ten articles. Most deal with hazards of the work environment; some have wider scope. The language is complex, yet the summaries and abstracts are clear enough to the intelligent layman. A basic journal in the field of environmental health, and more particularly as it relates to industry. Should be in large academic and public libraries.

Archives of Sexual Behavior. 1971. q. $26. R. Green. Plenum Publishing Corp., 227 West 17th St., New York, N.Y. 10011.

Bk. rev: 3–5, 500 words, signed. *Aud:* Ac.

Can sex be dull? Well, from a layman's viewpoint the answer is a resounding yes—at least if this journal *is* any example of the research in the field. Articles, which touch on everything from neurosis to nymphomania, are carefully documented, represent original studies, and are so technical as to be quite beyond anyone but the experimental researcher. Only for special collections in medicine and psychiatry.

Best's Review; Life/Health Insurance Edition. 1899. m. $5. John C. Burridge. A. M. Best Co., Park Ave., Morristown, N.J. 07960. Illus., index, adv. Circ: 41,200. Vol. ends: Apr.

Indexed: BusI. *Bk. rev:* Various number, short. *Aud:* Ac.

Edited and written with the management of life and health insurance, companies and their salesmen in mind, this will be of interest to those involved in life insurance trends such as stock analysts and insurance professors. It covers both problems and developments within the life/health field. Statistics are given with accompanying comments. The marketing of life and health polities is touched upon. Another section deals with the physical set-up of insurance offices. The journal also has legal advice, new directors, plans, policies, and publications. *Best's* has an index which selectively lists periodical articles which might be of interest to the management or salesmen of insurance firms. This is a specialists' magazines for larger libraries. A similar review is available which covers liability insurance.

Better Nutrition. 1938. m. Free. Anthony Lord. Syndicate Magazines, Inc., 25 W. 45th St., New York, N.Y. 10036. Illus., adv. Circ: 250,000.

Bk. rev: Notes. *Aud:* Ga.

A give-away health food magazine which is made up almost entirely of advertising. There are some articles on the benefits of natural foods and what is wrong with the foods sold in most markets. Regular depart-

ments consider questions by readers about nutrition, recipes, diet, etc. As it is free, and seems reliable enough, it should be considered by many libraries. A sample copy will indicate if you can use.

Blue Cross Reports. See Free Magazines Section.

Blue Print for Health. See Free Magazines Section.

Canadian Journal of Public Health. 1909. bi-m. $10. John Keays. Canadian Public Health Assn., 1255 Yonge St., Toronto 7, Canada. Illus., index, adv. Circ: 5,000. Sample. Vol. ends: Dec.

Indexed: BioAb, IMed. *Bk. rev:* 8, 250 words, signed. *Aud:* Ac.

Provides all disciplines in the public health field "with scientific and other reports and articles of professional interest." An average 100-page issue includes 10 to 12 articles, a number of editorials, and notes and features about events and people. A small part—two or three articles—is in French. Topics vary from the health needs of Eskimos and the effects of urbanization to "the use of dictating equipment by public health nurses." Most of the material would be applicable anywhere. A basic journal for Canadian academic and special libraries, and should be in larger American collections.

Eugenics Quarterly. See *Social Biology.*

Family Health. 1969. m. $4. William H. White, 1271 Ave. of the Americas, New York, N.Y. 10020. Illus., index; adv. Circ: 1,029,000. Sample.

Bk. rev: Various number, length. *Aud:* Ac, Ga, Hs.

A general health magazine which has the largest circulation of any in this genre. Articles cover all aspects of health, are written in a popular fashion, and are backed by physicians and psychologists. The editor has no ax to grind, i.e., nothing here depends upon the reader's diet or exercise habits, his religion, or his age. (Nor is the magazine supported by an organization such as AMA's *Today's Health.*) The articles and features sometimes are a bit too breezy, but the information apparently is accurate enough, and when there is doubt, the author says so. It is written for all ages and situations. Regular articles consider aging, nutrition, food, child care, new developments in medical science, etc. Among the many departments are: "Ask The Doctor," "Product News," and "Month in Medicine." The material tends to be topical, i.e., health plans, birth control, legalized abortion, drug control, etc. have been discussed. There is a considerable amount of advertising, but the publisher will not accept tobacco or alcohol advertisements. One of the best general, easy to understand family health magazines—and at a low price.

Fitness for Living. 1967. Bi-m. $4.50. Robert Bahr. Rodale Press, Inc., 33 Minor St., Emmaus, Pa. 18049. Illus., adv. Circ: 200,000. Vol. ends: Nov./Dec. Sample.

Aud: Ga, Hs.

For the hypochondriacal health faddist. The major emphasis of this title is on diet and exercise for health. Written in a nontechnical, easy to digest style, articles discuss various exercise programs and techniques, examine exercise equipment, and explain facts about food and nutrition. A recent issue placed heavy emphasis on bicycle riding and also included such items as "Isometrics for a Beautiful Face," and "From New York to Los Angeles by Canoe." A letter department and brief summaries of health news and advice are regular features. (F.A.)

Good Health; the family health magazine. 1902. bi-m. $2.64. R. D. Vine. Stanborough Press, Ltd., Alma Park, Grantham, Lincolnshire, England. Illus., adv. Circ: 35,000. Vol. ends: Nov./Dec. Sample.

Aud: Ga.

"Written mainly by doctors, nurses, and dietitians, *Good Health* is dedicated to the concept that health of body, mind, and soul are vitally linked; and that natural health is to be preferred above artificial health as a means of maintaining life at its longest, fullest, and most useful. Our aim: A sound mind in a sound body." As with many of these journals, health is intimately linked to nutrition. The editor is a vegetarian and his influence is felt throughout the text, as demonstrated by a recent article in which Scriptures are quoted as a part of the author's admonitions against the consumption of pork or pork products. Numerous signed articles, departments for news and advice, and occasional religious exhortations are the regular bill of fare. Most appropriate for the home or church library. (F.A.)

HSMHA Health Reports. See Government Magazines/United States Section.

Health. 1955. m. $1. George W. Northup. American Osteopathic Assn., 212 E. Ohio St., Chicago, Ill. 60611. Illus., index, adv. Circ: 23,000. Sample.

Aud: Ga.

Although the publication of the American Osteopathic Association, this is a general health magazine for the layman. It features four to five articles on all aspects of health and medicine. The material is accurate and documented, and all of it is written for the interested layman, not for the professional. Some regular departments and features explain the benefits and the problems of being an osteopath, but this is minor. Considering its low, low price and its many useful articles, it should be considered by almost any library.

Health and Strength. 1892. m. $6. George Greenwood & Oscar Heidenstam. Health & Strength Publishing Co., Ltd., Halton House, 20/33 Holborn, London EC 1, England. Illus., adv. Circ: 10,000. Vol. ends: Dec. Sample.

Aud: Ga, Hs, Ac.

British beefcake. An official publication of the National Amateur Bodybuilders' Association, this journal is dedicated to promoting body building via weight training and diet. Although the lavish layout of muscle builder photographs might incline one to assume that the journal is only appropriate for those intent upon muscle competitions, the text is accessible to the average guy who is interested in body building and exercise but who has no intention of entering a Mr. Universe contest. Brief, but informative, signed articles explain various muscle and body building routines, explore diet problems and needs, and describe people and events concerned with body building. It should be noted that there is a distinction between body building and weight lifting; the former is aesthetic, the latter athletic. Recommended for school and academic libraries. (F.A.)

Healthways; magazine digest. 1946. m. (combining June/July, Nov./Dec.). $2.50. Louise Brownson. American Chiropractic Assoc., Inc., 2200 Grand Avenue, Des Moines, Iowa 50312. Illus., adv. Circ: 180,000. Vol. ends: Nov./Dec. Sample.

Aud: Ga, Ejh, Hs.

What *Today's Health* is to the American Medical Association, this journal is to the American Chiropractic Association. Issues contain brief, popular articles about nutrition, exercise, and posture. Emphasis, as would be expected, is away from drugs and surgery and towards basically "natural" methods of prophylactic and therapeutic medicine. Examples of recent articles include "Posture and Personality," "Prenatal Spinal Care," "Chiropractic Aids Visual Function," and "Corrective Shoulder Exercises." Regular features include "Reflections," an editorial section; "Science Survey," news about medicine; "Lifelines," humor and health; and "Food Features," recipes. Its nontechnical language and easy vocabulary make this journal suitable for school libraries. (F.A.)

Inquiry. 1963. q. $4. to libs. James E. Veney, Ph.D. Blue Cross Assn., 840 N. Lake Shore Dr., Chicago, Ill. 60611. Index. Circ: 5,000. Vol. ends: Dec. Sample.

Bk. rev.: 2–3, 350–1,000 words. *Aud:* Ac.

With the subtitle, "A Journal of Medical Care Organization, Provision and Financing," this qualifies as a professional journal for those engaged in the planning and administration of health care services. Its average length of 72 pages includes four or five articles, and occasionally a series in the form of a symposium, representing the work of well-prepared and qualified writers in this field, including results of research grants, with some material being reprints of papers presented at professional association meetings. Subjects included cover such topics as health insurance and its economic effects, trends in delivery of health services, desirability of planning health care services on various levels from neighborhood to more comprehensive systems, and some theoretical topics such as social responsibility for health care. References and notes for each article are extensive and complete, and writing is, of course, on the professional level. Book reviews of specialized publications range from 350 to 1,000 words or more, and occasionally two opposing views of one book, by two reviewers, are presented together. This will be useful in large public libraries and specialized libraries serving the health care specialists and others of the medical profession. (A.S.)

Journal of Health, Physical Education, Recreation. See Sports/Physical Education and School Sports.

Journal of School Health. See Medical Sciences/General Section.

Let's Live. 1933. m. $6. Norman W. Bassett. Oxford Industries, Inc., 444 N. Larchmond Blvd., Los Angeles, Calif. 90004. Illus., adv. Circ: 37,988. Vol. ends: Dec. Sample.

Bk. rev: 3, 600 words. *Aud:* Ga.

Health through nutrition. The title page has the following caveat: "When any troublesome condition persists or in case of uncertainty, it is suggested that one obtain the professional advice of the family doctor." In spite of or because of this warning, little mention is made of medicine in the text. In fact, it is implicit that one can live a healthy life without recourse to medications or physicians if he will only watch his diet and eat the proper foods. Endorsements of various diets, vitamins, and organic food products, as well as a morbid fascination with the body's metabolism, constitute the bulk of the signed articles and regular monthly features. There are departments for recipes, astrology, physical fitness, questions and answers, and more. While there does not appear to be anything actually harmful in the advice given in the journal, most of the claims made for diets and food preparations seem to be overly optimistic. Should only be considered for library collections when there is patron demand. (F.A.)

Life and Health; the national health journal. 1885. m. $6. J. DeWitt Fox. Review and Herald Publishing Assn., 6856 Eastern Ave, N.W., Washington, D.C. 20012. Illus., adv. Circ: 123,384. Vol. ends: Dec. Sample.

Indexed: CINL. *Aud:* Ga, Hs.

This title, the official journal of the Home Health Education Service, ranks in quality below *Today's Health* but above most other popular health titles. Articles and features are written or edited by specialists, and an attempt is made to present factual information in an interesting and readable style without sensationalism. The title page states that it is "a family magazine featuring religious health information," but there

is a minimum of religion and a maximum of health between the covers. In its 87th year of publication.

Medical Aspects of Human Sexuality. 1967. m. $20. Leonard H. Gross. Hospital Publns., Inc., 18 East 48th St., New York, N.Y. 10017. Illus., adv. Circ: 190,000. Vol. ends: Dec.

Aud: Ga, Ac. *Jv:* V.

"*Medical Aspects of Human Sexuality* will provide authoritative information on sexual problems that affect many patients. This clinical information will enable the physician to deal more effectively with a broad array of such problems, and it will be supplemented by pertinent current data from sociology, psychology, and other behavioral sciences. . . . As a scientific journal, it is not designed to promulgate any particular point of view. Our distinguished Consulting Editors represent a wide variety of opinions, but they do share one conviction: that sex-related problems are the proper concern of every physician, and that the importance of these problems deserves a responsible and authoritative journal. . . ." A Statement of Purpose, Vol. 1, No. 1.

Although written for the physician, this excellent journal can be appreciated and understood by the educated generalist. Regular features, in addition to the signed articles, include roundtable and panel discussions of topics likely to interest and inform the physician and a section to which physicians may address questions for replies. Articles are generally accompanied by reproductions of paintings and works of art, and there are occasional cartoons. Too many advertisements undermine this graphically superior journal. (F.A.)

Metropolitan Life Insurance Company. Statistical Bulletin. 1969. m. Free. 1 Madison Ave., New York, N.Y. 10010. Illus., index. Vol. ends: Dec.

Indexed: BusI, CurrCont. *Aud:* Ac, Ga.

This bulletin is for life insurance brokers and salesmen, but it is a bit different. The figures are liberally scattered among explanatory articles. In 1971 editors covered such subjects as mortality from kidney diseases, cancer survival, longevity of cabinet officers, etc. Belongs on the shelf of any academic or public library.

National Tuberculosis Bulletin. See Free Magazines Section.

Organic Gardening and Farming. See Counterculture/Alternative Living Section.

Prevention; the magazine for better health. 1950. m. $5.85. Rodale Press, Inc., 33 E. Minor St., Emmaus, Pa. 18049. Illus., index, adv. Circ: 702,289. Vol. ends: Dec. Sample.

Aud: Ga, Hs.

A frustrating, uneven, sometimes informative, but

often naive journal which focuses primarily on the relationship of nutrition to health. The majority of articles and advertisements clearly emphasize a bias against processed foods and food additives. Regular departments include "Mailbag," which has the singular distinction of reproducing the correspondent's signature, and a variety of informational and advisory columns. Until his recent death, during the taping of the Dick Cavett show, J. I. Rodale edited *Prevention*. For an interesting profile of the man and his publications see Wade Greene, "J. I. Rodale—Guru of the Organic Food Cult," *The New York Times Magazine*, June 6, 1971, pp. 30–31. (F.A.)

Sexology; educational facts for adults. 1933. m. $5. M. Harvey Gernsback. Sexology Corp., 200 Park Ave. S., New York, N.Y. 10003. Illus., adv. Circ: 110,000. Vol. ends: July. Sample.

Aud: Ga, Hs, Ac.

Few sex journals written for a general audience are informative; rather, their sole raison d'etre is titillation and exploitation. This journal is one of the few that treats sex popularly, with a minimum of sensation and a respectable level of information. Although not as sophisticated or attractive as *Medical Aspects of Human Sexuality* or *Sexual Behavior*, the journal does provide candid and sometimes expert articles on sex, ranging from "How Diabetes Affects Pregnancy," to "Men Who Seek Sex Thrills in Crowds." Regular departments include Sex in the News, Science Notes, Sex Scene, and Editor's Scrapbook, all of which review current events. There is also a monthly movie review and an extensive "Your Personal Questions Answered" column. Many appropriate diagrams and photographs are provided; however, there are also photographs of lovers embracing, which tend, at times, to lower the overall tone of the journal. A good selection for libraries supporting sex education curricula. (F.A.)

Sexual Behavior. 1971. m. $10. Leonard Gross. Interpersonal Publns. Inc., 299 Park Ave., New York, N.Y. 10017. Subs. to: Subscription Dept., 1225 Portland Place, Boulder, Colo. 80302. Illus., adv. Circ: 175,000. Sample. Microform: UM.

Aud: Ga, Hs, Ac.

Written and edited for the generalist, this journal is an attractive compendium of articles, information, and photographs for those seeking sexual enlightenment. Much like *Psychology Today* in format and layout, it has not yet achieved the same degree of sophistication. Most of the text is comprised of articles by MDs and PhDs, and the June 1971 issue included such items as "Adolescents and the Sexual Revolution," "The Stripteaser," and "Sexual Ideas in the Films of D. H. Lawrence." Regular features are Photohumor, Answers to Questions, Photoanalysis (a pictorial survey of a sexual topic), and Graffiti of the Month—"use erogenous zone numbers." (F.A.)

Social Biology (Formerly *Eugenics Quarterly*). 1953. q. $16 (Individuals $14). Richard H. Osborne. Univ. of Chicago Press, 5801 Ellis Avenue, Chicago, Ill. 60637. Index, adv. Circ: 1,235. Sample. Vol. ends: Dec. Refereed. Microform: UM.

Indexed: BioAb, CurrCont, IMed, PAIS, PsyAb. *Bk. rev:* 10–14, 1,200 words, signed. *Aud:* Ac.

Issued by the American Eugenics Society "to further knowledge of the biological and sociocultural forces affecting human populations." Articles cover family planning, genetic counseling, sex predetermination, interfaith marriage trends in the United States, interracial marriage, etc. Departments include brief reports, communications, behavior genetics, book reviews, and periodical abstracts. While clearly a specialized publication, it will be extremely useful for those concerned with genetics, sociology, reproduction, and social issues.

Strength and Health. 1933. m. $7.50. Bob Hoffman. Strength and Health Publishing Co., P.O. Box 1707, York, Pa. Illus., adv. Circ: 65,000. Vol. ends: Dec. Sample.

Aud: Ga, Hs, Ac.

Similar to, but more comprehensive than, the British *Health and Strength*, this journal surveys the world of competitive body building and weight lifting with some attention to their effects on athletics in general. The content ranges from the usual nutrition articles to personal profiles to descriptions of lifts and lifting techniques. There are numerous regular departments and the "Weight Lifting News" section is particularly noteworthy for its thorough listing of coming events. A somewhat alarming feature of the magazine is the ubiquitous Bob Hoffman, who is present as editor-in-chief and publisher, editorializer, feature writer, and mass advertiser. Advertising is almost totally for products sold by Hoffman, effectively making this a house organ. In spite of this serious distraction, the title is informative, respected, and recommended for libraries supporting physical education programs. (F.A.)

Today's Health. 1923. m. $5. David Sendler. Amer. Medical Assn., 535 N. Dearborn St., Chicago, Ill. 60610. Illus., index, adv. Circ: 650,000. Sample. Vol. ends: Dec. Microform: UM.

Indexed: AbrRG, BioAb, PAIS, RG. *Aud:* Ga, Ac, Hs, Ejh.

One of the more popular general health magazines, this is sponsored by the American Medical Association. In rather lengthy, well-illustrated articles it discusses the latest medical developments and treatment of major diseases, and considers topics of interest to almost anyone, e.g., nutrition, recreation, child development, ecology. Despite or because of the sponsor (it depends on your point of view), the material is objective; often includes controversial issues fairly presented. The editor reports there is an increasing emphasis "on coming up with fresh insights for improving the way people interact, health angles on major news events and personalities, and well-documented pieces crusading for better, healthier living." He seems to be right. In fact, the whole magazine is improving. It can be recommended for all libraries.

WHO Chronicle. See Government Magazines/United Nations and Selected Foreign Section.

Weight Watchers Magazine. 1968. m. $5. Matty Simmons. Twenty-first Century Communications Inc., 635, Madison Ave., New York, N.Y. 10022. Illus., index; adv. Circ: 560,000. Vol. ends: Dec.

Aud: Ga.

The publisher claims this is the only monthly magazine of its kind, although both men's and women's magazines usually features articles on the subject. Be that as it may, the target audience is primarily women; the object is to show them how to eat properly, not necessarily how to exercise. There are weight watcher recipes, articles on the mental and physical problems related to obesity, success stories, fashions aimed at those who are losing or who have lost weight, and related women's features. The editor points out, that this is for a general audience, and the average reader "is in middle and low-middle income brackets."

World Chronicle. See Government Magazines/United Nations and Selected Foreign Section.

NUDIST MAGAZINES. Social nudism, in the words of the American Sunbathing Association, means "improved health, physically, psychologically, and spiritually . . ." It also maintains that "true modesty is not related to the wearing of clothes" (*Encyclopedia of Associations,* 5th ed., Vol. 1, p. 941.) The Association has published a number of pamphlets on the subject. Titles range from "Some Facts about Nudism" through "A Father Speaks of Nudism," and "A Mother Speaks of Nudism" (who needs SIECUS?), to "The Bible and Nudism." One to five copies, free, from the Association, and in quantities of 200 or more, ½¢ each.

In spite of its disclaimer, the movement is profoundly religious (but then, isn't all of life really religious?). Their god is the naked human body, and the peace, serenity, and inner comfort that flow from time spent in a nudist resort comes in my opinion, from concentrated worship. As might be expected there are orthodox, conservative, and liberal elements; and nudist clubs fall in somewhere along the line.

Obtaining nudist periodicals for review is difficult if you do not want to spend much money. Finding titles truly representative of social nudism is even more difficult. The standard periodical directories are no help. I am indebted to Mrs. Rebecca Dixon, Librarian, Institute for Sex Research, Indiana University, for her list to get me started. Most nudist magazines on news dealers shelves are what Mrs. Dixon calls "pseudo-nudist."

Health and Efficiency. 20/yr. $10. Plant News Ltd., 43 Shoe Lane, London, EC4, England.

Modern Sunbathing Quarterly. 2/yr. $9. 8150 Central Park Ave., Skokie, Ill. 60076.

Nudism Today. 6/yr. 6 E. Main St., Mays Landing, N.J.

How much nudist writing is honest, and how much is good copy? These have provocative articles proposing nudism from several perspectives. Stark-naked illustrations, but for the faint-hearted, genitalia are air-brushed away. Caveat: nudists propagandize with the best. I am reliably told that nudist parks are not elysian fields populated by shapely naked women with bikini marks. Anyone brave enough to pioneer could well start with these titles. (J.M.)

Solus. $2.50 a copy. Box 66, Mays Landing, N.J. 08330.

Official journal of Solarians International, a hetero-orthodox nudist group that apparently cannot agree with the usual, no singles, no alcohol, no staring, clothes-on-when-dancing strictures of conventional nudism. No air-brush. It reports that nudist leaders calculate that over 3,000,000 Americans hold pro-nudist views and actually practice nudism in their daily lives. Take with a full container of Morton's. The fifth edition of the *Encyclopedia of Associations* reports 14,000 members in the two largest U.S. nudist groups. (J.M.)

Sun Tours. 4/yr. $3 a copy. Box 370, Baldwin Park, Calif. 91706.

Carries the National Nudist Council's seal of approval. Reports on international nudist activities and prints fetching pictures of mom, dad, kids and baby having fun in the altogether. The family that undresses together, stays together; let's hear it for Gesell. No airbrush and some photos suitable for lessons in the external anatomy of the female urogenital system. Not for the DAR. (J.M.)

Other "official" nudist publications that can be obtained only with a subscription: *American Sunbather* (1967. 2/yr. $9. Box 6026, Broadway Station, Long Island City, N.Y. 11106.); *Sunshine and Health* (1933. bi-m. $12.50. Church Publications, Whitehouse, Ohio.); *Sun Lore* (1964. m. $12.50. National Nudist Council, R-B-229, Whitehouse, Ohio.).

There is a host of so-called publications that are really "girlie" magazines taking advantage of recent

Supreme Court decisions. There is no air-brushing, and the intent (by commonsense judgment) is obviously scatological. Such titles are *Teenage Nudist, True Nudist, Live Naked, Nude Living, Nudist Field Trip, Mondo Naked.* (J.M.)

Counterculture

Health-Pac Bulletin. 1968. m. $7 (Students $5). Ed. collective. Health Policy Advisory Center, 17 Murray St., New York, N.Y. 10007. Sample. Vol. ends: Dec.

Aud: Ga, Ac, Hs.

The leader in the movement to strip the witch doctor of his magic, to bring medicine back to the people. *New York Magazine* called the Health Policy Advisory Center "the think tank of the movement where seven men and women bring out the monthly newsletter, and recently completed *The American Health Empire* (Vintage Books, 1970), an assessment of the country's health system." The November 1971 issue of 12 pages featured three factual, objective stories of funding medical education, prison hospitals, and the fight to keep neighborhoods intact when a hospital threatens to move in. The authors are clearly identified, as are the sources. The whole is readable, creditable, and something quite new for the average reader who may be digging all of his or her medical facts out of the AMA's *Today's Health.* The Bulletin takes a strong stand in favor of women having considerably more to say about their own health and the health of their kids—particularly since medicine is dominated by men. When not publishing, the group provides "technical assistance to insurgent groups interested in creating a more accountable health system."

Health Rights News. 1967. m. $3. Laura Green, John Linstead. Medical Committee for Human Rights, 710 S. Marshfield, Chicago, Ill. 60612. Illus. Sample. Vol. ends: Winter.

Bk. rev: 3–5, 500–1,000 words, signed. *Aud:* Ga, Ac. *Jv:* V.

A refreshing voice of liberal thought in the otherwise tradition-bound medical profession, this 20 to 30 page tabloid newspaper/magazine will come as a revelation to both laymen and doctors. Made up of physicians, nurses, technicians and consumers who think medicine needs a new outlook, the Medical Committee for Human Rights is dedicated to "topple hospitals from the pinnacle of the health system and end racial, sexual and economic injustice in medical care." The paper's articles and features are involved with such areas as support of a national health insurance program, liberal organizing of all involved with medicine, promotion of health reforms, and working for legislative changes such as abolition of health professional licensure laws. The articles and shorter pieces are nontechnical, well written, and topical, e.g., "Ever Wonder Why

Hospitals Put Up with Students?" or "Women Doctors: Too Little Too Late," and "Milton Berle Plays the Prison." The information is of interest to anyone who is likely to get involved with a doctor before he or she reaches the funeral parlor. Librarians will find it most useful for book reviews, bibliographies, directories and other types of reference information. All in all a fascinating effort, and one well worth supporting.

In the September 1971 issue a bibliography of the politics of health care appeared (sample copies available). The following periodicals were listed: *For the People's Health* (No price or frequency given). Health Revolutionary Unity Movement, 352 Willis Ave., Bronx, N.Y. *Health Law Newsletter* (No price or frequency given). National Legal Program on Health Programs of the Poor, 2477 Law School, 405 Hilgard Ave., Los Angeles, Calif.

The Layman Speaks; a homeopathic digest. 1947. m. $6. Arthur B. Green. American Foundation for Homeopathy, Inc., 2726 Quebec St., N.W., Washington, D.C. 20008. Index, adv. Circ: 1,800. Sample.

Bk. rev: Various number, length. *Aud:* Ac, Ga.

Although this homeopathic foundation is international and has been busy since the nineteenth century, it is not that well known among laymen. Probably the best single explanation of the group's fundamental convictions is outlined by Nicholas von Hoffman in the *Washington Post* (Jan. 5, 1970). He notes the organization is "alternately denounced and ignored . . . (although) out and out quackery is less often alleged because homeopathic physicians are ordinary doctors, who go to the standard medical schools." The journalist points out that the member doctors differ from the regular brand in that they are slow to use drugs or the knife, are more concerned with the individual's particular problems and have a healthy respect for the patient's life. "And if they can't cure you, they may be less likely to kill you." Mixing common sense, scientific knowledge and a bit of psychology in their journal, the foundation discusses everything from arthritis and cancer to "the worst medicine for colds." The 30 or so pages are quite within the grasp of the average adult and require no medical background. In a word, this is not only completely on the up-and-up, but will be of considerable value to many laymen seeking sound advice.

Organic Gardening and Farming. See Counterculture/Alternative Living Section.

Drugs

The Attack on Narcotic Addiction. See Free Magazines Section.

Contemporary Drug Problems: a law quarterly. 1971. q. $24 (Individuals $20). Laurence London. Federal

Legal Publns., Inc., 95 Morton St., New York, N.Y. 10014. Illus., index, adv. Sample. Vol. ends: Fall.

Bk. rev: 2–4, 3 pages, signed. *Aud:* Ac, Ga, Hs. *Jv:* V.

Although primarily a legal look at drugs, and edited by practicing attorneys, this is of considerable value to anyone involved with the problem, i.e., students, doctors, psychologists, pharmacologists, administrators, teachers, and, last but not least, parents. Each 200 to 250 page issue is geared for the informed reader and is quite free of legal jargon. Authoritative articles examine such things as the semantic problems of drugs, i.e., information on how to critically evaluate what you are told or read about drugs, regulating and controlling marijuana, heroin use among college students, student legal rights in drug arrest and prosecution, etc. There are also panel discussions offering pros and cons of current arguments in the field, and a bibliography of books and articles (an invaluable aid for the library). Given this objective, sane treatment of drugs, the journal offers an extraordinary vehicle for understanding a difficult problem. Highly recommended for any library (including high schools with counselors and interested teachers).

Drugs and Drug Abuse Education Newsletter. 1970. m. $30. Thomas Seay. Scope Publns., Inc., 474 National Press Bldg., Washington, D.C. 20004. Sample.

Aud: Ac, Ga.

An 8-page monthly newsletter which reports in a concise fashion on various federal and state bills regarding drugs, foundation activities, personalities, etc. In that this is a concise, topical report it is useful. The reporting is objective and apparently accurate. The major fault—an inflated price.

This organization publishes a newsletter for alcoholism: *Alcoholism and Alchohol Education* (1971. m. $33). The format and size are the same, as is the approach. A third entry is: *Mental Health Scope* (1967. bi-w. $40). All of the eight to ten page newsletters do have one particularly valuable feature for libraries; they report, if only briefly, on new publications covering the various interests of the newsletters.

Grassroots. 1970. m. $95. Peter G. Hammond. National Coordinating Council on Drug Education, Suite 212, 1211 Connecticut Ave., N.W., Washington, D.C. 20036. Illus. Circ: 700.

Aud: Ac, Ga, Hs, Ejh.

A basic reference source on all aspects of drugs, their use and abuse. The looseleaf service comes with an extensive bibliography and material which is added to by monthly supplements. Material on legislative and legal actions and changes in drug laws, film and book evaluations, reports of research, and some 20 other subject categories of drug information. (Marijuana and alcohol are treated separately.) The information is impartial, objective, and accurate. In view of the expense and scope, it is primarily of use in larger, metropolitan public and academic libraries.

The National Coordinating Council is an impartial, fact-finding group which is apparently free of any moral hang-ups about drugs. (As a private, nonprofit group, it has representatives from over 100 wide-ranging national organizations—from the National Association for Mental Health to the Boy Scouts.) It recognizes that drugs are being misused, and simply asks what a community or an individual can do about the problem. It tries to give answers, not only in the rather expensive *Grassroots,* but in a number of other publications. One is *Drug Education Report* (m., $18). This is a monthly newsletter on the latest developments in drug abuse education, treatment and enforcement, including reviews and recommendations of materials and programs. Although a bit brief on facts, it is long on ideas, and suited for just about any library, regardless of size or type. Another is *Drug Education Bibliography* ($5). An extensive listing of primarily educational materials to be used with all types and ages. Of equal benefit is the *Drug Education Directory* ($5), which lists the Council's 124 members and indicates what publications, films, etc., they issue.

Journal of Alcohol and Drug Education. 1955. 3/yr. $4. Robert D. Russell. North American Assn. of Alcohol Programs, 3500 N. Logan, Lansing, Mich. 48914. Illus. Circ: 2,000. Sample. Vol. ends: Winter.

Bk. rev: 1–2, length varies. *Aud:* Ac, Hs.

Primarily for teachers at the high school and college level. Offers in some 36 to 40 pages "a forum for various educational philosophies and for differing points of view . . . though the primary focus is on education about alcohol, there is a continuing secondary focus on education about . . . drugs and narotics." The articles are short, and represent actual research and study. For example, one report concludes: "Overstatements on the dangers of marihuana may serve to discredit the spokesman and reduce his general effectiveness as a resource to his students." Other opinions are stated too. An objective, down to earth approach to drink and drugs.

Journal of Drug Issues. 1971. q. $15 (Individuals $10). Richard L. Rachin, Box 4021, Tallahassee, Fla. 32303. Illus., index. Sample. Vol. ends: Oct.

Bk. rev: Various number, length. *Aud:* Ac, Ga, Hs. *Jv:* V.

With an editorial board of professors, lawyers, doctors, psychologists and those working closely with the drug issues of our times, this can be recommended as one of the more honest approaches to drugs. "The Journal advocates a reasoned, unemotional, and no 'sacred cow' examination of drug matters." A full and free expression of pertinent views and ideas, with which the editor may or may not agree is guaranteed.

JDI tells it like it is. Each 100 or so page issue begins with editorials which are really reports on the current scene, e.g., notes on the drug problems in Vietnam, government aid (or lack of it) for treatment, and on combatting panic by law officials. The articles are by experts who range from physicians to lawyers. They consistently write at a level which can be understood by an interested layman or, for that matter, an intelligent teenager. The journal aims to clarify problems from management of drug abuse to methods of treatment, and to explore viable alternatives to imprisonment for drug possession. Each issue tends to center on a given topic with pro and con arguments. Again, it should be stressed that there is little emotion, although strong convictions. All in all the best single journal in this field for both the expert and the layman. Highly recommended for any library.

Journal of Psychedelic Drugs. 1968. bi-a. $7. David E. Smith. Subs. to: 638 Pleasant Street, Beloit, Wis. 53511. Illus., adv.

Bk. rev: 4–6, essay length, signed; notes. *Aud:* Ga, Ac, Hs. *Jv:* V.

Co-sponsored by the Haight-Ashbury Free Medical Clinic and the Student Association for the Study of Hallucinogens (STASH), this is the opposite approach to *Listen.* The well-documented 110-page journal is dedicated to "the dissemination of unbiased and valid information about psychoactive drugs and their use." While *Listen's* contributors believe all unprescribed drug use bad (and include alcohol and cigarettes), another set of doctors, teachers, and students who write for this journal ask for a "critical attitude towards scientific pronouncements in this area." The viewpoint is decidedly more liberal and objective, although it should be noted that this journal's experts are as opposed to drug abuse as *Listen.* The reader—regardless of age or experience—who is uptight about drugs, who has an emotional, gut reaction to the subject, will find this enlightening. It will prove too technical for young people—*Stash Capsule* is better for younger readers—but it will have a definite place in any library where drug abuse is treated objectively and intellectually. The journal can be easily read, and as a whole the presentations tend to be fairly good. The fall number is devoted to a single topic, the spring issue to more heterogeneous collections of critical and speculative review articles. Highly recommended for most public and academic libraries, as well as more advanced high school collections; and should be regular reading for anyone involved with the various facets of drugs and their abuse.

Listen; a journal of better living. 1947. m. $5. Francis A. Soper. Pacific Press Publishing Assn., 1350 Villa St., Mountain View, Calif. 94040. Illus., index, adv. Circ: 100,000. Sample.

Aud: Ga, Hs.

Claiming to provide "a vigorous, positive educational approach to the problems arising out of the use of tobacco, alcohol, and narcotics," emphasis in recent issues has been primarily on the uses and abuses of marijuana, LSD, and "speed." The text is primarily first-person narrative, with individuals describing their problems with drugs and alcohol and their efforts to overcome their addictions or habituations. There are also signed articles by laymen and specialists who examine drug usage and research. A montly "Listen News" section reviews current events about the drug culture, including alcoholism, and governmental research and activity concerned with drugs. The layout and design of the journal are attractive, the contents relatively interesting, and it is recommended primarily for high school libraries. (F.A.)

Medical Letter on Drugs and Therapeutics. 1959. bi-w. $14.50 (Residents, interns, students $7.50). Harold Aaron. Drug and Therapeutic Information, Inc., 56 Harrison St., New Rochelle, N.Y. Index. Circ: 50,000. Microform: UM.

Indexed: IMed. *Aud:* Ga, Ac.

A nonprofit organization sponsors this newsletter whose purpose is to give unbiased information on new and old drugs. While written primarily for physicians, it can be understood by the informed layman. It is particularly valuable for the direct, no nonsense reports on drugs which are often sold over the counter or advertised in the media, e.g., a report in the *Letter* dampened a craze for Vitamin E—the physicians reporting it had little or no value. In a society becoming more consumer-conscious, and one concerned with medical practices, the *Letter* can be recommended for most libraries.

Psychedelic Review. 1963. q. $7.50. Robert Mogar. 4034 20th St., San Francisco, Calif. 94114. Illus., index, adv. Circ: 20,000.

Indexed: PsyAb. *Bk. rev:* 6–10, 200–1,000 words, signed. *Aud:* Ac, Ga. *Jv:* V.

A major effort to bring attention to the proper use of drugs in "all forms of consciousness-expanding activity." Among the contributing editors are Timothy Leary, Alan Watts, and Ralph Metzner. All have an MD or a PhD after their names—which at least signifies more than passing reflection on the use of drugs. As one critic properly puts it: "The review is the place to look if you are seriously interested in drug usage, drug effects, drug theories and drug oriented art and poetry." There was some discussion of discontinuing the effort, but it continues and the 92-page eleventh issue is typical with articles on the world of spirits, the use of pot in controlling alcoholism, the use of LSD as a preparation for death, and a discussion on "The Radicalization of Timothy Leary." There are notes, book reviews, editorials, and some rather interesting line drawings. Most of the material is well within the understanding of the layman. Recommended as one of the basic journals in a highly controversial field.

✓ *Quarterly Journal of Studies on Alcohol.* 1940. q. $15. Mark Keller. Rutgers Center of Alcohol Studies, New Brunswick, N.J. 08903. Illus., index, adv. Circ: 2,700. Vol. ends: Dec. Refereed.

Indexed: SocAb, BioAb, ChemAb, CurrCont, IMed, PsyAb. *Bk. rev:* Various number, length. *Aud:* Ac, Ga, Jv: V.

Both journal and abstracting service. The first section includes original articles—several of monographic length—on various aspects of alcoholism. The second section contains abstracts of over 600 articles published in scientific journals and books. Coverage is international. In the December issue there is an annual subject-author index. The basic journal in this field, and recommended for any library interested in the subject.

The Center also issues *Alcoholism Treatment Digest* which is "in effect a syndicated news service, sold on subscription to state and provincial alcoholism programs for use in their publications. It is not available for library subscription."

Stash Capsule. 1968. bi-m. $5. Jim Gamage. Student Assn. for the Study of Hallucinogens, 638 Pleasant St., Beloit, Wis. 53511. Illus., adv. Circ: 5,000. Sample. Vol. ends: 5th issue.

Bk. rev: 1, 250 words, signed. *Aud:* Ac, Ga, Hs.

The publisher of this four-page newsletter is a group "solely controlled by students, the majority of whom have had extensive involvement in, or contact with, drug use." Their purpose is to give unbaised and valid information about psychoactive drugs and their use. As a nonprofit and tax exempt educational organization, STASH has gained national prominence for its objective, valid reports on drugs. The newsletter contains short articles by the Association staff and consultants, abstracts of current research, and announcements of activities and publication. As a means of keeping up with developments in this area, it is excellent—particularly for those working with students from high school through college. The professional, realistic approach will be most welcome by students, too. One of the best such sources available. See also *Journal of Psychedelic Drugs.*

Tune In; drug abuse news for broadcasters—about broadcasting. m. Free. SDC: Pr Ex 13.11. Dept. of Health, Education and Welfare. Public Health Service, National Clearinghouse for Drug Abuse Information, 5454 Wisconsin Ave., Chevy Chase, Md. 20015. Circ: 5,600.

Aud: Ac, Ga, Hs, Ejh.

A seven to ten page newsletter which reviews films, audio tapes, recordings, scripts, and other materials suitable for use by radio and television in combatting drug abuse. Vital information is given (distributor, cost, running time, etc.) followed by "observations of the reviewers," and "suggestions for use." The observations and suggestions are objective, often critical. According to the publisher: "The reviews . . . are the work of an independent panel representing a broad range of professions and opinions related to drugs and drug use. These reviews thus represent neither an endorsement nor a criticism of the materials by the Federal government." Be that as it may, they are excellent, and will be of considerable help not only to broadcasters, but to libraries with an active interest in the subject. Highly recommended for all libraries.

HISTORY

Basic Periodicals

GENERAL. Ejh: *History Today;* Hs: *History Today, Horizon;* Ga: *History Today, Horizon, Mankind;* Jc: *Historian, History and Theory, History Today, Horizon;* Ac: *Historian, History, History and Theory, History Today, Horizon.*

AMERICAN AND CANADIAN. Ejh: *American Heritage* (illustrations); Hs: *American Heritage, The Beaver;* Ga: *American Heritage, American History Illustrated;* Jc: *American Historical Review, Canadian Historical Review, American Heritage;* Ac: *American Historical Review, Canadian Historical Review, Prologue, American Heritage, American History Illustrated.*

STATES AND PROVINCES. Ejh: *Badger History, Gopher Historian, Illinois History, Texas Historian, The Yorker.* All other libraries: regional and state historical journals as needed for the public and/or to support the curriculum.

Basic Abstracts and Indexes

America: History and Life, Historical Abstracts.

Cessations

The American West Review, History Studies.

General

African Historical Studies. See Africa Section.

Agricultural History. See Agriculture Section.

American Journal of Legal History. See Law Section.

Business History Review. See Business/General Section.

Catholic Historical Review. 1915. q. $10. Robert Trisco. Catholic Univ. of America Press, Washington, D.C. 20017. Illus., index, adv. Circ: 2,280. Vol. ends: Jan. Microform: UM. Reprint: Kraus.

Indexed: CathI, HistAb, SSHum. *Bk. rev:* Various number, length. *Aud:* Ga, Ac.

The official publication of the Catholic Historical Association. Emphasis is on Catholic Church history, although it is of interest to both the general historian and the non-Catholic religious student. There are some five articles per issue, which are international in scope and period. The book reviews are excellent, and often cover material not found elsewhere. For all religious and large historical collections.

Central European History. See Europe and Middle East/English Language General Section.

English Historical Review. 1886. q. $12. J. M. Wallace-Hadrill & J. M. Roberts. Longmans, Green & Co., Ltd., 48 Grosvenor St., London W1, England. Adv. Circ: 3,000. Vol. ends: Oct. Microform: Canner. Reprint: Johnson.

Indexed: BritHum, HistAb, SSHum. *Bk. rev:* Numerous, one page, signed. *Aud:* Ac. *Jv:* V.

Deals with history of all periods, with some emphasis on British studies. It usually contains four or five scholarly articles and shorter notes and documents. An invaluable book selection tool, for approximately half of each issue is devoted to one page book reviews. A valuable feature is its annotated list of periodical articles on European history which appear annually in the July issue. This is a basic journal for the university and junior college library, as well as for the layman with more than a passing interest in history.

French Historical Studies. See Europe and Middle East/English Language General Section.

Frontier Times. See Men's Magazines Section.

Hispanic American Historical Review. See Latin American and Chicano/English Language General Section.

Historian; a journal of history. 1938. q. $6. William D. Metz. Phi Alpha Theta National Honor Society in History, D. B. Hoffman, 2812 Livingston St., Allentown, Pa. 18104. Index, adv. Circ: 8,500. Vol. ends: Aug.

Indexed: HistAb, SSHum. *Bk. rev:* 60–70, 400–500 words, signed. *Aud:* Ac.

Each issue contains five to six articles covering the entire field of history and excludes no period or time. It is one of the best scholarly, general historical journals available. The writing style is consistently high, although at times a bit too deep, and articles are accepted from students, teachers, and interested laymen.

News of the Society is included. Its large number of book reviews makes it particularly valuable. This quarterly is of considerable value to the university library, as well as large public libraries.

Historical Journal. 1958. q. $15.50. F. H. Hinsley. Cambridge University Press, 32 E. 57th Street, New York, N.Y. 10022. Index, adv. Circ: 1,550. Vol. ends: Dec.

Indexed: BritHum, HistAb. *Bk. rev:* 8–10, lengthy, signed. *Aud:* Ac.

A publication of the Cambridge Historical Society and the successor to the *Cambridge Historical Journal* (1923–1957), each issue features six to eight long, well-documented articles and two to three review pieces. Social and political issues of England and Europe are the primary concern, and the authors span almost the whole time period from the Middle Ages to the present. The book reviews are usually in essay form and may include several related titles. As this journal is oriented towards the professional historian, it is only recommended for large academic libraries. (R.S.)

Historical Studies. 1940. $6.50. N. D. McLachlan. School of History, Univ. of Melbourne, Parkville, Victoria 3052, Australia. Index, adv. Circ: 1,500. Vol. ends: Oct. Reprint: Kraus.

Indexed: BritHum, HistAb, PAIS. *Bk. rev:* 15–20, 1–2 pages, signed. *Aud:* Ac.

Formerly *Historical Studies: Australia and New Zealand*, which presupposes an interest in those two countries, this journal now covers all aspects of history, although there is a decided emphasis on British and Australian history. (New Zealand affairs are now explored in the *New Zealand Journal of History, c.f.*) The bulk of the articles are on the nineteenth and twentieth centuries, especially American and European history. The magazine also includes news of professional interest as well as a list of recently completed research. As Australia has increasingly received recognition in so many areas, the book reviews are especially important as a source for published historical research emanating from this continent. The journal is a specialized work which is recommended for larger libraries.

Historische Zeitschrift. See Europe and Middle East/German Language Section.

History, the Journal of the Historical Association. 1912. 3/yr. Membership (Nonmembers $4.50). R. H. C. Davis. Historical Assn., 59a Kensington Park Rd., London SE 11, England. Index, adv. Circ: 9,500. Vol. ends: Oct. Reprint: Dawson.

Indexed: BritEdI, BritHum, HistAb, SSHum. *Bk. rev:* 80–90, lengthy, signed. *Aud:* Ac.

Deals with all aspects of history, but concentrates

on the European scene. There are usually five to six scholarly articles. The primary value for librarians is the book review section, which is arranged by subject and makes up most of the journal. Reviews are long, critical and particularly helpful for their wide coverage. It should be considered by any library with a particular interest in history; but, in America, the same type of specialized book review service is available in the *Historian*.

History and Theory; studies in the philosophy of history. 1960. 3/yr. (and Beihefte). $7.50. George H. Nadel. Wesleyan Univ. Press, Wesleyan Sta., Middletown, Conn. 06457. Illus., index. Circ: 2,600. Microform: UM.

Indexed: HistAb, SSHum, PhilosI. *Bk. rev:* 6–9, lengthy, signed. *Aud:* Ac.

Primarily concerned with the philosophy of history and historiography. The editorial committee, which is international in scope, includes such prominent scholars as Raymond Aron, Isaiah Berlin, and Sidney Hook. There are three to five scholarly monographs and six to nine book review essays. One Beihefte is issued per year, which tends to be bibliographical in nature or devoted to a particular topic, such as "Bibliography of Works in the Philosophy of History," "On Method in the History of Religions," and "Studies in Quantitative History and the Logic of the Social Sciences," which also reflects something of the interdisciplinary nature of this journal. This is an example of a highly specialized kind of historical journal which is excellent for its purposes, but should be limited to large academic collections.

History Today. 1951. m. $10.50. Peter Quennell and Alan Hodge. 388–389 Strand, London WC2R OLT, England. Index, illus., adv. Circ: 32,907. Vol. ends: Dec.

Indexed: BritHum, HistAb, SSHum. *Bk. rev:* Various number, length. *Aud:* Ga, Ejh, Ac. *Jv:* V.

One of the few historical magazines geared for the general reader and beginning student. Each issue contains some six to seven illustrated articles, written in a semipopular style by professional historians. All periods and places are covered, although the emphasis is on the English-speaking nations. The book reviews are good to excellent. Students from senior high through college will find that the "Notes for Further Reading" at the end of each article are helpful guides in preparing papers. While *American Heritage* and *Horizon* are preferable, if only for their illustrations, *History Today* is a good second or third choice—in fact, where budget problems might prohibit the other two quite costly magazines, *History Today* would be a very satisfactory first choice.

Horizon. 1958. q. $20.00 Joseph J. Thorndike. American Heritage Publishing Co., Inc., 551 Fifth Ave. New

York, N.Y., 10017. Illus., index. Circ: 160,000. Vol. ends: Sept.

Indexed: HistAb, RG. *Aud:* Ga, Ejh, Ac.

The first cousin to *American Heritage*, this has a similar hard cover and glossy format. It is replete with striking colored photographs and drawings, and is to be looked at as much as read. Although its primary target is world history, it is much broader in scope. A typical issue may consider all subjects related to the humanities from literature and art to archaeology and the performing arts. The articles are prepared by authorities, and are styled to be read with a minimum of effort. Some accuse it, as *American Heritage*, of a quasi-scholarly approach, but this is only to say it is not for the professional historian. It is for the high school and college student and for most adults who do not require footnotes with their history.

Indian Historian. See Indians (American) Section.

Industrial Archaeology, the Journal of the History of Industry and Technology (Formerly: *The Journal of Industrial Archaeology*). 1964. q. $7.40. John Butt. David & Charles, S. Devon House, Newton Abbott, Devon, England. Illus., index, adv. Vol. ends: Nov.

Indexed: BritHum, HistAb. *Bk. rev:* 8–10, 300–500 words, signed. *Aud:* Ga, Ac.

Each issue contains six to eight articles on various aspects of industrial history and technology—mining, engineering, transportation, factories, textiles, etc., with numerous illustrations, explanatory drawings, and graphs. Although there is a decidedly British slant, North American subjects are included. A regular feature is the "Annual Review of Literature on Industrial Archaeology and Industrial History," which selectively lists outstanding articles and books in the field. Although many of the articles are written by academicians, the layman and specialist in the field of technology are also represented. This journal should be included in the subscription lists of most university libraries, as well as larger public libraries. (R.S.)

International Journal of Middle East Studies. See Europe and Middle East/English Language General Section.

Irish Historical Studies. 1938. s-a. $3.60. T. W. Moody and T. D. Williams. Dublin University Press, Ltd., Trinity College, Dublin 2, Ireland. Index, adv. Vol. ends: Sept.

Indexed: BritHum. *Bk. rev:* 15–20, 1–2 pages, signed. *Aud:* Ac.

A joint publication of the Irish Historical Society and the Ulster Society for Irish Historical Studies which contains five to six articles on all aspects of Irish history and civilization. Regular features include "Writings on Irish History," the annual report of the Irish Committee of Historical Sciences, and the annual report from the American Committee for Irish Studies. As Irish affairs form such an important aspect of British studies, this journal is especially recommended for research libraries. (R.S.)

Journal of African History. See Africa Section.

Journal of Asian History. See China and Asia/Asia Section.

The Journal of British Studies. 1961. s-a. $6. Bernard Semmel, Box 1315, Trinity College, Hartford, Conn. 06106. Adv. Vol. ends: May.

Indexed: HistAb. *Aud:* Ac.

Published under the auspices of the Conference on British Studies, an affiliate of the American Historical Association, this journal is concerned with all aspects of British History and culture, including the colonial experience. The editorial board includes the major historians in British studies, both American and Canadian, especially Jack H. Hexter, Hermann Ausubel, Lacey Baldwin Smith, and Bertie Wilkinson, among others. This scholarly journal is especially recommended for university libraries. (R.S.)

Journal of Contemporary History. 1966. q. $8.50. Walter Laqueur & George L. Mosse. Weidenfeld & Nicholson, 5 Winsley St., London W1, England. Index. Vol. ends: Oct. Microform: UM.

Indexed: AbEnSt, HistAb. *Aud:* Ac.

This British journal is dedicated to the promotion of "research mainly in twentieth-century European history." The 12 to 15 articles are written by scholars and normally have a central focus. A separate insert, of particular value to librarians, is the "Quarterly Select List of Accessions of the Wiener Library"— divided by subject and country, this gives a full bibliographic description for each book. Limiting itself to the twentieth century, and then to Europe, this journal is of less general use than *Journal of Modern History,* which has a much wider scope. Conversely, the emphais on special topics of general interest make it a required item in larger libraries and in many high school professional collections.

Journal of Economic History. See Economics Section.

Journal of European Studies. See Europe and Middle East/English Language General Section.

Journal of Industrial Archaeology. See *Industrial Archaeology.*

The Journal of Interdisciplinary History. 1970. q. $10. Robert I. Rotberg and Theodore K. Rabb. M.I.T. Press, 28 Carleton Street, Cambridge, Mass. 02142. Index, adv.

Indexed: AmerH, HistAb. *Bk. rev:* 10–15, both review articles (8–10 pages) and short reviews (2–3 pages), signed. *Aud:* Ac.

Usually includes four to six substantive articles per issue, often methodological in nature. Makes available to the historian techniques outside his field both cultural and scientific, especially economics, sociology, history of science, linguistics, data processing, psychology, and statistics. This publication of the M.I.T. School of Humanities and Social Sciences has an outstanding editorial board comprising Bernard Bailyn and Hugh R. Trevor-Roper, among others. It is a journal geared to the needs of the professional historian and is recommended for university libraries. (R.S.)

Journal of Mexican American History. See Latin American and Chicano/English Language General Section.

Journal of Modern History. 1929. q. $8. William H. McNeil. Univ. of Chicago Press, 5750 Ellis Ave., Chicago, Ill. 60637. Index, adv. Circ: 3,550. Vol. ends: Dec. Microform: UM.

Indexed: HistAb, SSHum. *Bk. rev:* Numerous, signed. *Aud:* Ac.

Emphasis is on scholarly articles covering European history from the Renaissance to the present. Here it differs from the English *Journal of Contemporary History,* which deals only with twentieth-century history. Contributors are among the world's leading historians, and the magazine has reached an honored place in its field. All philosophical approaches to history are represented, and each article is thoroughly documented. Important documents are often published, in full or in part, with critical comments. The book reviews are excellent, and cover thoroughly the scope of the journal's interest. A required magazine for all medium to large-sized historical collections.

Journal of Negro History. See Blacks Section.

Journal of Pacific History. 1966. a. Aus. $4.50. J. W. Davidson and H. E. Maude. Australian National Univ., P.O. Box 4, Canberra, ACT 2600, Australia. Adv.

Indexed: HistAb. *Bk. rev:* 12–14, 700–800 words, signed. *Aud:* Ac.

Emphasizing the Pacific Islands, this journal deals with the political, economic, religious, and cultural history; archaeology, prehistory, and ethnohistory; and with contemporary government and political development. Each volume usually contains some seven to eight articles, a manuscript section which makes available unpublished manuscripts and a survey of an archival repository containing source material on this area of the world, as well as the 12 to 14 book reviews.

Journal of Social History. 1967. q. $10. Peter N. Stearns. Univ. of California Press, Berkeley, Calif. 94720. Index, adv. Circ: 1,000. Vol. ends: June. Microform: UM.

Indexed: HistAb, SocAb. *Bk. rev:* 5–6, lengthy, signed.

Articles are of a scholarly nature, interdisciplinarian, and geared to fill the need for a bridge between political and social historians, e.g., social history, sociological history, trends in American social history. Authors tend to be specialists writing with varying degrees of clarity and thought. A few of the entries are quite understandable to the layman, but most require at least some academic background.

Journal of Southeast Asian Studies. See China and Asia/Asia Section.

Journal of the History of Ideas. See Cultural-Social Studies Section.

Journal of World History. See Cultural-Social Studies Section.

Labor History. See Labor and Industrial Relations Section.

London University. Institute of Historical Research. Bulletin. 1923. s-a. $55. A. G. Dickens. Univ. of London, Senate House, London WC1E 7HU, England. Index, adv. Vol. ends: Nov. Reprint: Dawson.

Indexed: BritHum, HistAb. *Aud:* Ac.

Features articles on medieval and modern history, as well as shorter notes often accompanied by documents. As it is one of the few journals which prints documents, reference value is particularly high. Other regular features include news of professional interest, and an historical manuscript section which includes manuscript accessions at the British Museum, and "Migrations," which lists manuscripts which have recently been offered for sale by booksellers and auctioneers. It is recommended for large academic libraries.

Mankind; the magazine of popular history. 1967. bi-m. $6. Raymond F. Locke, 8060 Melrose Ave., Los Angeles, Calif. 90046. Illus., index, adv. Circ: 180,000. Sample.

Bk. rev: 5–6, 100–250 words. *Aud:* Ga, Hs.

A semipopular treatment of world history, this is written for the average layman. Emphasis is as much on illustrations (many in color) as lively, easy to read articles. This has improved considerably over the past four years, and while no match for the British counterpart, *History,* it should be considered by most libraries. The very lack of documentation, the emphasis on journalistic style may attract the disinterested reader. Should be of particular interest to high schools.

Military Affairs. See Military Section.

Negro History Bulletin. See Blacks Section.

New Zealand Journal of History. 1967. s-a. $5. Keith Sinclair. History Dept., Univ. of Auckland, Private Bag, Auckland, New Zealand. Illus., index, adv. Circ: 900. Vol. ends: Oct.

Indexed: HistAb. *Bk. rev:* 6–9, 1–3 pages, signed. *Aud:* Ac.

Although the emphasis is on New Zealand and, to a lesser extent, Australia, the scope of this journal touches upon all aspects of world history as seen through the eyes of New Zealand scholars. Pacific affairs bulk large in these pages, particularly wherein they touch upon South Africa, India, China, and Southeast Asia. The book reviews are strong on commonwealth studies, while a special feature is an annual article on theses completed and work in progress. J. C. Beaglehole, a scholar with a worldwide reputation in his area of specialization, serves on the editorial board. This is a specialized journal which is recommended for academic libraries with strong history collections. (R.S.)

Past and Present; a journal of historical studies. 1952. q. $9. T. H. Aston. Business Manager, 43A Queen St., Oxford, England. Index, adv. Circ: 4,500. Vol. ends: Nov.

Indexed: BritHum, HistAb. *Bk. rev:* Occasional, lengthy. *Aud:* Ga, Ac.

A lively, readable, often controversial journal which covers a broad spectrum of historical studies, but with special emphasis on British studies. It is "primarily concerned with social, economic, and cultural changes and their causes and consequences," and is written for the layman as well as the specialist without losing its scholarly flavor. There is an occasional long book review. This publication is especially recommended for public and junior college libraries as well as university and research collections.

Revue d'Histoire Moderne. See Europe and Middle East/French Language Section.

Revue Historique. See Europe and Middle East/French Language Section.

Rivista storica Italiana. See Europe and Middle East/Italian Language Section.

Scottish Historical Review. 1903. s-a. $6. DER Watt. Aberdeen Univ. Press, Ltd., Farmers Hall, Aberdeen, Scotland. Illus., index, adv. Vol. ends: Oct.

Indexed: BritHum. *Bk. rev:* 15–20, 1–4 pages, signed. *Aud:* Ac.

A publication of the Company of Scottish History which covers all aspects of Scottish history, including archaeology. Special departments include an annual list of periodical articles on Scottish history and descriptive articles on archival sources, such as "The Vatican Archives: a report on pre-reformation Scottish material" and "Records in the Danish Archives." This is a more specialized journal which is of interest to the academic community or areas with a large Scottish population. (R.S.)

American and Canadian

American Chronicle; a magazine of history. 1972. m. $8. Henry Eason, Box 6268, Savannah, Ga. 31405. Illus., index, adv.

Indexed: AmerH. *Bk. rev:* 5–7, 250 words, signed. *Aud:* Ga, Ac.

A general approach to American history in a pleasing, if not outstanding, format. The first issue included 11 articles, a reprint of an historical document, and several book reviews. Each of the pieces was illustrated with photographs, and the center article on Winslow Homer included four-color reproductions of his paintings. There was a photographic essay on Charleston. The editor will touch on all aspects of American History. What is different about this magazine is that the publisher presupposes the reader has a background in history, but is not a professional historian. "We are answering the demand of an increasingly large knowledgeable public which shies away from the esoteric as it does from the popular." Well, that is a nice road to follow, but as most of the authors are professors of history, it doesn't quite come off. There are, to be sure, no footnotes, but the writing style is no better or no worse than in most historical journals. The idea is interesting, though, and hopefully the editor can make it succeed. Meanwhile in view of the modest subscription price and the general approach suggested by the first issue, it can be recommended for medium to large-sized public and academic libraries. It's too dry for high school students.

American Heritage; the magazine of history. 1954. bi-m. $20. Oliver Jenson. American Heritage Publishing Co., Inc. 551 Fifth Ave., New York, N.Y. 10017. Illus., index. Circ: 350,000. Vol. ends: Oct. Microform: UM.

Indexed: AbrRG, AmerH, HistAb, RG. *Bk. rev:* 2, 1,500 words, signed. *Aud:* Ga, Hs, Ejh, Ac. *Jv:* V.

An outstanding historical journal which has succeeded in presenting scholarly material at a popular level. Articles are often written by outstanding authorities in the field of American history and cover every conceivable aspect of American history from major to minor events and personalities. It is particularly noteworthy for the attention it gives to social, educational, and cultural trends in America's past. If one article is concerned with a major military figure or battle, another may turn to a little-known artist, teacher, writer, or inventor who helped to change the course of history. From time to time, an entire issue is given over to a period, state, or important series of events. There is no advertising, which accounts in part for the relatively high price. The magazine's primary attraction for adults and young people alike is the handsome format and the numerous illustrations and photographs, many in color. The hard-covered periodical is often catalogued and shelved by librarians as a book. The "package" is expensive, but worthwhile for any library from junior high school up.

The American Historical Review. 1895. 5/yr. $20 (Students $10.00). R. K. Webb. American Historical Assn., 400 A Street, S.E., Washington, D.C. 20003. Index., adv. Circ: 25,000. Vol. ends: Dec. Microform: UM. Reprint: Kraus.

Indexed: AmerH, HistAb, RG. *Bk. rev:* Approx. half the journal, lengthy, signed. *Aud:* Ga, Ac. *Jv:* V.

The official organ of the American Historical Association, this is valuable both for its scholarly articles and its extensive book reviews. Contributions, representing original research, are usually some 6,000 to 10,000 words long, and may move from a study of the right wing in America to a monograph on some aspect of communism. The style is better than most journals of this type, although the writers presuppose some basic knowledge of historiography on the part of the reader. The 150 to 200 reviews are arranged according to period and area of historical interest, thus making them an invaluable book selection aid for libraries. Major articles, monographs, and documents are classified in much the same manner. Should be in every scholarly library, and in larger high school libraries.

American History Illustrated. 1966. 10/yr. $10 (ed. rate $8.50). Robert Fowler, Box 1831, Harrisburg, Pa. 17105. Illus., index, adv. Circ: 46,000.

Indexed: AmerH, HistAb. *Bk. rev:* 4–8, ½ page, signed. *Aud:* Ga, Hs, Ejh, Ac.

The contributions are devoted to all phases of American history, from prehistoric creatures who once inhabited this continent to events as recent as the Korean War. The articles are written by historians or actual participants in the events described. One of the strong points of the magazine is the excellent use it makes of photographs and illustrations to document its articles. It would be a second choice after its sister-type magazine, *American Heritage.*

American Jewish Historical Quarterly. 1893. q. $15. Nathan M. Kaganoff. Amer. Jewish Historical Soc., 2 Thornton Rd., Waltham, Mass. 02154. Illus., index, adv. Circ: 3,100. Vol. ends: June. Reprint: Kraus.

Indexed: AmerH, HistAb. *Bk. rev:* 7–10, 1–2 pages, signed. *Aud:* Ac, Ga.

Features two to three scholarly articles on some aspect of Judaism in the United States. There are notes and comments which are somewhat shorter articles on more esoteric aspects of the settlement and history of Jews in America. Although only for the largest libraries, it will be welcome in any library where there is a large Jewish audience.

American Neptune; a quarterly journal of maritime history. 1941. q. $12.50. Philip C. F. Smith, Managing

Ed. Peabody Museum, E. India Marine Hall, Salem, Mass. 01970. Illus., index, adv. Circ: 1,000. Vol. ends: Oct.

Indexed: AmerH, HistAb. *Bk. rev:* 5–9, ½–2 pages, signed. *Aud:* Ga, Ac.

Each issue contains four to five articles dealing with all aspects and periods of maritime history—voyages, discovery, trade, art, folklore, cartography, early technology, and naval history. There is a decidedly American emphasis. Each year a special pictorial supplement depicts, by means of old engravings and early photographs, many of the social aspects of life in port and at sea. Its distinguished editorial board includes Vernon D. Tate, Walter Muir Whitehill, and Samuel Eliot Morison. This journal, which spans the Renaissance through the nineteenth century, is recommended for the layman as well as the scholar. (R.S.)

The American West. 1964. 6/yr. $9. Donald E. Bower. Amer. West Publishing Co., 599 College Avenue, Palo Alto, Calif. 94306. Illus., adv. Circ: 30,000. Vol. ends: Nov.

Indexed: AmerHist, HistAb, SSHum. *Bk. rev:* Notes. *Aud:* Ga, Hs, Ac.

The magazine of the Western History Association describes itself as "a magazine devoted to the story of the Great West, past and present." While strong on historical scholarship, it is designed for the general reader as well as the specialist. It is particularly attentive to the value of pictorial history. There are eight or nine well-illustrated articles in each issue. They range from literary criticism and historical narrative to the subject of conservation. Authors represent a broad spectrum of professions and interests. One of the few scholarly magazines which is suitable for the nonspecialist adult or teenage reader, and will be welcome in most public and school libraries, as well as college and junior college collections.

The Beaver; a magazine of the North. 1920. q. $3. Malvina Bolus. Hudson's Bay Co., Hudson's Bay House, Winnipeg 1, Man., Canada. Illus., index Vol. ends: Dec.

Indexed: CanI, HistAb, IChildMags. *Bk. rev:* 6–8, one page, signed. *Aud:* Ga, Hs, Ac.

Somewhat similar in editorial approach to Canadian history as *American Heritage* is to American history. Although considerably more modest in size, the style of writing is similar, and the illustrations are carefully selected to augment all of the articles. Authors are historians and scholars, but gear their material to a lay audience. Articles are concerned with the Canadian Western Frontier, the fur trade, exploration, and Indian and Eskimo life. While this magazine is often recommended for elementary grades, the reading level is well beyond the average grade school child. Its primary value for the child is the illustrations and use by the teacher in the classroom. Conversely, it is an excellent choice for senior high. A required item in Canadian libraries and a good second for most American libraries.

Canadian Historical Review. 1920. q. $11. R. Craig Brown. Univ. of Toronto Press, Toronto, Ont., Canada. Index, adv. Circ: 3,700. Vol. ends: Dec.

Indexed: CanI, HistAb, SSHum. *Bk. rev:* 20–25, 1–2 pages, signed. *Aud:* Ga, Ac. *Jv:* V.

Concentrates on Canadian history, with special emphasis on political history and foreign relations. Each issue features three or four scholarly monographs written by professional historians. The book reviews cover, selectively, all fields of history, and are lengthy and evaluative. A regular feature is several pages listing recent publications relating to Canada. Both the scope and the nature of the book reviews make this a required journal in history departments and large libraries. Text is in English and French. It will be a necessary purchase for all types of Canadian libraries, even high school libraries.

Canadian Journal of History/Annales Canadiennes d'Histoire. 1966. s-a. $3.50. Ivo N. Lambi, Box 384, Sub Post Office No. 6, Saskatoon, Saskatchewan, Canada. Circ: 600. Vol. ends: Sept. Microform:. UM.

Indexed: HistAb, AmerH. *Bk. rev:* 1 essay, notes. *Aud:* Ac.

This journal is concerned with all aspects of history and its Advisory Board includes such notable American and Canadian scholars as Wallace K. Ferguson, Bertie Wilkinson, and John B. Wolf. The four to five well-documented articles cover all periods and countries; most are in English, one or two in French. There is usually a review article on one or more books, and then some 25 to 30 shorter notices of other general historical works. As many of the titles are issued abroad, this is an excellent checklist for the large history library.

The Canadian Review of American Studies. 1969. s-a. $5 (Individuals $3). Robert L. White. York Univ., Downsview, Ont., Canada. Index, adv. Circ: 500.

Indexed: AmerH, HistAb. *Bk. rev:* Various number, length. *Aud:* Ac.

The official publication of the Canadian Association for American Studies. Includes original articles in history and literature and review essays designed to foster understanding of the past and present culture of the United States as well as cultural relations between Canada and the United States. Recommended in view of the increasingly sensitive nature of its subject matter. (N.H.)

Civil War History; a journal of the middle period. 1955. q. John T. Hubbell. Kent State Univ. Press, 380

E. Lorain St., Oberlin, Ohio 44074. Index, adv. Circ: 1,800. Sample. Vol. ends: Dec. Reprint: Johnson.

Indexed: AmerH, HistAb. *Bk. rev:* 10–15, one page, signed. *Aud:* Ga, Ac.

Devoted to scholarly articles dealing with the American Civil War and Reconstruction, this considers all aspects and views of a popular reading period in history. Its editorial board is composed of eminent authorities on the Civil War such as T. Harry Williams and Robert. T. Johannsen. Each issue contains four or five articles, with occasional review articles and bibliographic information. There are critical book reviews and a regular feature is one or two pages of book notes. Only for large collections.

Civil War Times Illustrated. 1962. 10/yr. $10. Robert H. Fowler. Historical Times, Inc., 206 Hanover St., Gettysburg, Pa. 17325. Illus., index, adv. Circ: 24,000.

Indexed: AmerH, HistAb. *Bk. rev:* 4–5, 250–300 words, signed. *Aud:* Ga, Ejh. *Jv:* C.

Another special-period historical journal with emphasis on authentic photographs and illustrations. The articles are written by historians or are narratives of actual participants in the war, and concern all phases of the conflict. Considerable coverage is given to biographies of leading figures in the war. A semipopular historical magazine, this is particularly suited to the layman. But as is the case with the more scholarly *Civil War History*, it can only be recommended for large libraries, or where there is a particular interest in the subject.

Daughters of the American Revolution Magazine. 1892. 10/yr. $3. Mary Rose Hall. National Soc. Daughters of the Amer. Revolution, 1776 D St., N.W., Washington, D.C. 20006. Illus., index, adv. Circ: 50,000.

Aud: Ga.

The voice of the DAR, this is interesting for the viewpoint, usually conservative, and the few historical articles, which are not necessarily limited to the period of the American Revolution. The magazine makes frequent use of pictures and illustrations. A large part is given to official news of the DAR and is primarily of interest to communities with large DAR chapters. It is not recommended for most libraries.

Inland Seas; quarterly journal of the Great Lakes Historical Society. 1945. q. $7.50. Janet Coe Sanborn, Great Lakes Historical Soc., 480 Main St., Vermilion, Ohio 44089. Illus., adv. Circ: 1,500. Vol. ends: Dec.

Indexed: HistAb. *Bk. rev:* 6–8, ½–1 page, signed. *Aud:* Ga, Ac.

Inland Seas is the vehicle by which the Great Lakes Historical Society promotes interest in the discovery and preservation of materials relating to the Great Lakes and the Great Lakes region of the United States and Canada. The seven to eight articles in each issue cover all aspects of the history, geography, geology, commerce, and folklore of the Great Lakes, including shipping, racing, ship building, settlements, company histories, iconography, etc. Its contents are of interest to the layman and the scholar. Special features make known to the reader the various research and archival resources which are available at the Society's museum and elsewhere. The journal is especially recommended for large libraries and for public libraries with an interest in the inland waterways and the Great Lakes region. (R.S.)

Journal of American History (Formerly: *Mississippi Valley Historical Review*). 1914. q. $8 (Students $4). Martin Ridge. Organization of Amer. Historians, 112 N. Bryan St., Bloomington, Ind. 47401. Index, adv. Circ: 12,500. Vol. ends: March. Microform: UM. Reprint: Kraus.

Indexed: AmerH, HistAb, SSHum. *Bk. rev:* 75–120, ½–one page, signed. *Aud:* Ga, Ac.

One of the best American historical journals, and of particular value to the librarian, since over half of each issue is devoted to extensive book reviews. The scope is almost entirely American, and articles move from historical theory to biographical sketches. The writing is scholarly and primarily for the professional historian or student of history. Included are sections devoted to news on appointments, promotions, grants, aids, and other items about the Organization of American Historians. A basic journal for any medium to large-sized historical collection.

Journal of American Studies. 1967. 3/yr. $12.50. Dennis Welland. Cambridge Univ. Press, 32 E. 57th St., New York, N.Y. 10022. Index, adv. Circ: 1,500.

Indexed: AmerH, HistAb. *Bk. rev:* 15–20, 500–1,000 words, signed. *Aud:* Ac.

This publication of the British Association for American Studies "aims to promote the study of the history, institutions, literature and culture of the United States." Articles of an interdisciplinary nature are welcomed as are comparative studies of American and other cultures. There are three to four long reviews and the shorter notices consider both historical and literary publications. Useful for both the scholar and student of American history and literature, not to mention the individual who seeks the British viewpoint in these areas.

Smithsonian. 1970. m. $10. Edward K. Thompson. Subs. to: 420 Lexington Ave., New York, N.Y. 10017. Illus., adv.

Bk. rev: 4–5, 300–400 words, signed. *Aud:* Ga, Ejh, Ac.

A lively, readable, well-illustrated journal which should appeal to a broad spectrum of readers from junior high school through adult levels. It belongs in all classes of libraries, for the eight to ten articles include all those areas in which the Smithsonian Institution excels—archaeology, anthropology, oceanography, natural science, and art, as well as history—and should draw a wide public audience. There is an expressed and timely interest in man in relation to his environment and thus there are numerous articles on conservation, environmental quality, and historic preservation. This stimulating magazine makes the services of the Smithsonian Institution available on a nationwide basis. (R.S.)

William and Mary Quarterly; a magazine of early American history. 1892. q. $5. Thad W. Tate. Inst. of Early American History and Culture, Box 220, Williamsburg, Va. 23185. Illus., index, adv. Circ: 4,000. Vol. ends: Oct. Microform: UM.

Indexed: AmerH, HistAb, SSHum. *Bk. rev:* 15–25, lengthy, signed. *Aud:* Ac.

One of the earliest magazines devoted to the notion of culture as an important aspect of history, this is a scholarly approach to the American scene before 1815. Articles range from biographies to bibliographies, and many border on literary essays. The book reviews are broad in scope, critical, and quite reliable for both the historian and the teacher of comparative literature.

States and Provinces

Alabama Review; a journal of Alabama history. 1948. q. $5. Malcolm C. McMillan. Dept. of History, Auburn Univ., Auburn, Ala. Subs. to: Univ. of Alabama Press, Drawer 2877, University, Ala. 35486. Index. Circ: 1,924. Vol. ends: Oct.

Indexed: AmerH. *Bk. rev:* 4–5, 500–1,000 words, signed. *Aud:* Ac.

A general historical review. Most of the material is by professors, although from time to time there are articles by nonprofessionals. The magazine is well edited, but because of its scope is of limited use except to large comprehensive collections, or for libraries in Alabama and surrounding states.

In this same area: *Alabama Historical Quarterly.* (1930. q. Milo B. Howard. Alabama State Dept. of Archives and History, 624 Washington Ave., Montgomery, Ala. 36104. Illus., index. Circ: 1,000.)

The Alaska Journal; history and arts of the north-quarterly. 1971. q. $8. R. N. DeArmond. Alaska Northwest Publishing Co., Box 1271, Juneau, Alaska 99801. Illus. Circ: 8,000. Sample. Vol. ends: Winter.

Indexed: AmerH. *Bk. rev:* 4–8, 200 words, signed. *Aud:* Ga, Ac, Hs.

A handsome 64-page magazine which stresses both history and native Alaskan art. Articles are primarily written by laymen, and, interestingly enough, by al-

most as many women as men. The result is a fast-paced, easily read magazine which is a far cry from the normal academic type of historical journal. Let it be added that the articles appear authoritative, and while sometimes folksy, are always informative. There are numerous black and white illustrations, plus color photos with many of the pieces on art. Can be recommended for the library where there is an interest in Alaska, from the high school to the academic. And it should be a definite part of a meaningful art collection.

Alberta Historical Review. 1953. q. Membership. (Nonmembers $4). Hugh A. Dempsey. Historical Soc. of Alberta, Box 4035, Station C, Calgary, Alta., Canada. Illus. Circ: 2,000. Sample. Vol. ends: Autumn.

Indexed: AmerH. *Bk. rev:* 8, 300 words, signed. *Aud:* Ac, Ga.

Limited to the exploits and activities of Alberta pioneers, this journal has broad interest because of those activities. Many of the pioneers were involved in the fur trade, cattle raising, or a type of frontier politics that makes for good western flicks. And, too, there were the Indians, friendly and otherwise. The sum total is a 30-page or so journal with well-documented articles by well-read historians, but with one difference—most of the material is easy to read. Thanks to the style and content, it will have appeal for laymen as well as professional historians.

Mr. Dempsey is also editor of *Glenbow* (1968. 6/yr. Membership. $2. Glenbow Alberta Inst., 902, 11 Ave. SW, Calgary 3, Alta. Illus. Circ: 2,000. Sample.) This is an 8-page newsletter which reports on holdings of the Alberta Institute, a combination art gallery and historical museum.

Annals of Iowa. 1863. q. $1. Linda K. Thomson. Iowa State Dept. of History and Archives, Historical Building, Des Moines, Iowa 50319. Illus., index. Circ: 1,800. Vol. ends: Spring. Refereed.

Indexed: AmerH. *Bk. rev:* 3, ½ to 1 page. *Aud:* Ac, Ga, Hs.

An 80-page journal which, surprisingly enough, has held to the same price and size since 1892. Its purpose remains pretty much the same, too. Through articles and documents it attempts to cover the state and "homes in on specific facts which otherwise may have gone unnoticed, unrecorded, and lost to posterity." The style of writing is a bit uneven, but it is well within the understanding of a high school student. A good investment in local history for any library in Iowa, or surrounding areas. Otherwise, only for large academic libraries.

Annals of Wyoming. 1923. s-a. Membership (Nonmembers $4). Katherine Halverson. Wyoming State Historical Soc., State Office Bldg., Cheyenne, Wyo. 82001. Illus., index. Circ: 1,500.

Indexed: AmerH, HistAb. *Bk. rev:* 10–15, 250–500 words, signed. *Aud:* Ga, Ac.

Usually four to six articles on all aspects of Wyoming history, and the American Indians of the territory. This latter aspect gives the 160-page, well-produced and ably edited journal a definite value for even those not particularly interested in Wyoming history. There are usually some outstanding photographs, and good book reviews. The contributors are about evenly divided between professional historians and laymen. The style of writing is passable. One of the better state history journals.

Arizona and the West: a quarterly journal of history. 1959. q. $5. Harwood P. Hinton. Univ. of Arizona Press, Univ. of Arizona, Tucson, Ariz. 85271. Illus., index. Circ: 1,400. Sample. Vol. ends: Winter. Refereed.

Indexed: AmerH. *Bk. rev:* 20, 600 words, signed. *Aud:* Ac, Ga, Hs. *Jv:* V.

Covering the vast region west of the Mississippi river, this will be of considerable value to any professional western historian, or laymen involved with the more scholarly aspects of Indians and cowboys. A typical 120-page, well-printed and illustrated issue does have one or two of its four or five articles centered in Arizona or the Southwest, but others will discuss more general issues and topics. Articles manage to be both lucid and imaginative. Little of the content will be beyond the average involved layman, or, for that matter, interested high school student. A bonus for librarians: the excellent book reviews which often consider titles not found in standard media. One of the best of the regional historical magazines, this should be found in any medium to large collection, and might prove a real bonus for general collections where there is any interest in the West.

Arkansas Historical Quarterly. 1941. q. Membership $4. Walter L. Brown. History Dept., Univ. of Arkansas, Fayetteville, Ark. 72701. Illus., index. Circ: 1,700. Sample. Vol. ends: Winter.

Indexed: AmerH. *Bk. rev:* 2, 450 words, signed. *Aud:* Ac, Ga.

A well-edited state historical journal which concentrates almost entirely upon the history of Arkansas. A typical issue features four to five articles, news and notes on the Arkansas Historical Association, and book reviews. Articles, generally by historians, run from the highly specialized to the general—and in every number there seems to be something for almost everyone, i.e., layman to expert. Useful for all Arkansas, and many larger libraries both north and south.

Badger History. 1948. q. (during school yr.). $4. Howard W. Kanetzke. Wisconsin State Historical Soc., 816 State St., Madison, Wis. 53706. Illus. Circ: 25,000.

Indexed: IChildMag. *Aud:* Ejh.

While devoted primarily to Wisconsin history, this is useful in other states because the subject matter is concerned with general topics, e.g., pioneers, Indians, early trade, buildings, etc. Each issue is extremely well illustrated and runs some 60 or 70 pages. The material is of general enough interest to warrant consideration by many public and school libraries. The writing style is simple, yet never insulting. And while written particularly for fourth grade readers, the content is both meaningful and interesting—even for the older reader. One of several local historical magazines indexed by *Subject Index to Children's Magazines,* and both because of indexing and scope, of more than purely local interest. (See also *Gopher Historian, Illinois History, Junior Historian* and *The Yorker.*

California Historical Quarterly, the journal of the California Historical Society. 1922. q. $15. Roger R. Olmsted, 2090 Jackson St., San Francisco, Calif. 94109. Illus., index, adv. Circ: 4,500. Reprint: Johnson.

Indexed: AmerH, HistAb. *Bk. rev:* 10–15, 250–750 words, signed. *Aud:* Ga, Ac.

Features five or six articles, both by scholars and amateur historians, on California history. Many of the pieces are illustrated and they range from the story of printing or a personality, to economic and political issues. The book reviews usually concentrate solely on works relating to California or the West. The journal is particularly well printed, and a required item in all California libraries, and in larger historical collections.

There are two other very good west coast historical journals of note, both of which follow the same general pattern, i.e., concentration on a local area with a nod now and then to larger issues and national events. These are *Oregon Historical Quarterly* and the *Pacific Northwest Quarterly.*

Gopher Historian; the junior historical magazine of Minnesota. 1946. 3/yr. $2. A. H. Poatgieter. Minnesota Historical Soc., Historical Building, St. Paul, Minn. 55101. Illus., index. Circ: 5,000.

Indexed: IChildMag. *Aud:* Ejh.

Similar in purpose and scope to other state historical magazines for children, this is somewhat better than most in that it has good to excellent pictures. Many of the articles, while centered on Minnesota subjects, are applicable to other parts of the country, e.g., forests, Indians, conservation, etc. Primarily for those between 10 and 12 years of age.

Illinois History; a magazine for young people. 1957. m. (Oct.–May). $1.25 (Free to libraries and schools in Ill.). Olive S. Foster. Old State Capitol, Springfield, Ill. 62706. Illus., index.

Indexed: IChildMag. *Aud:* Ejh.

While written by specialists for an age group between 7 and 12, contents are above average for magazines of this type. In fact, the information is basic to any understanding of either Illinois or much Midwest history. Normally, a given issue is turned over to a single historical theme with a number of well-illustrated articles. Regular features include puzzles, contributions from students, and a brief section on additional reading. It will be of limited value outside of the Midwest, but there it should be found in every elementary, junior high, and not a few senior high school libraries.

Illinois State Historical Society. Journal. 1908. q. Membership. $5. Ellen M. Whitney. Illinois State Historical Soc., Springfield, Ill. 62706. Illus., index. Circ: 3,800.

Indexed: AmerH, HistAb. *Bk. rev:* 20–25, 250–1,000 words, signed. *Aud:* Ac, Ga.

Features numerous photographs and line drawings. The average 100-page issue is quite handsome. Particularly useful to libraries because of the book reviews which cover not only Illinois but much of the midwest, and national topics as well. Four to five articles per issue. The writing, primarily by historians, is somewhat better than average for this type of journal. A useful acquisition for all medium to large-sized history collections. See also the society's magazine for children, *Illinois History*.

Journal of Southern History. 1935. q. $7 (Students $4). Sanford W. Higginbotham. Southern Historical Assn., Tulane University, New Orleans, La. 70118. Index., adv. Circ: 4,300. Vol. ends: Nov.

Indexed: AmerH, HistAb, SSHum. *Bk. rev:* 50, one page, signed. *Aud:* Ac.

One of the basic American historical journals, this is a requirement in any library where there is more than a cursory history collection. A nonpartisan magazine that concentrates on the history of the southern United States, this usually contains three or four scholarly monographs by leading historians, many of whom are not from the region. In addition, it lists book notes and prints historical news and notices. The book reviews are more general in scope, and often make up a good one quarter or one half of the journal. They are long, critical, and required reading for any library with even a modest history collection. There are frequent bibliographic notes ranging from library acquisitions to detailed lists of materials in given areas of Southern history.

Journal of the West. 1962. q. $9. Lorrin L. Morrison and Carroll S. Morrison, 1915 S. Western Ave., Los Angeles, Calif. 90018. Illus., index, adv. Circ: 4,000. Vol. ends: Oct.

Indexed: AmerH, HistAb, SSHum. *Bk. rev:* 30–50, one page, signed. *Aud:* Ga, Ac.

Devoted to the history and geography of the American West. The editors welcome articles dealing with such related fields as anthropology and archaeology. Every issue has some ten scholarly articles written by historians or experts in other disciplines. The articles frequently contain maps and illustrations. An outstanding feature is the book review section, which is comprehensive, lengthy, and covers the whole of American western history and geography. While a good addition to most libraries, it would be a second choice after *The American West*. Larger libraries should automatically subscribe.

Junior Historian. See *Texas Historian*.

Kansas Historical Quarterly. 1931. q. Membership. $5. Nyle H. Miller. Kansas State Historical Soc., 120 W. Tenth St., Topeka, Kans. 66612. Illus., index. Circ: 2,700.

Indexed: AmerH. *Aud:* Ac, Ga.

One of the more memorable features of this journal is the attention paid to publishing original diaries, memoirs, letters, and documents heretofore locked away in archives. A good example: "Roughing It on her Kansas claim: the diary of Abbie Bright, 1870–1871." In addition there are usually three to four articles, usually by professional historians, notes, and a running bibliography: "Kansas history as published in the press." An average 100-page issue is well worth the modest price, and should be in all medium to large-sized history collections.

Maryland Historian. 1970. s-a. $2. Raymond W. Smock. Univ. of Maryland, History Dept., College Park, Md. 20742. Illus.

Bk. rev: 2–3 essays, length varies. *Aud:* Ac.

A general history magazine which is exceptionally literate, and, in some cases, downright entertaining, e.g., Avery Craven's article "Some Historians I Have Known," in the Spring 1970 number. Articles, by both students and professors, cover all of world history. There are two or three review essays, and an average 90-page issue is a good balance of scholarship and careful editing. (Not to be confused with the Maryland Historical Society's *Maryland Historical Magazine*, which is a state journal.)

Mid-America; an historical review. 1918. q. $3. John V. Mentag. Loyola University, 6525 Sheridan Rd., Chicago, Ill. 60626. Illus., index. Circ: 700. Vol. ends: Oct. Microform: UM.

Indexed: AmerH, CathI, HistAb. *Bk. rev:* 15–20, 200 words, signed. *Aud:* Ac.

In some 80 to 100 pages authors consider various aspects of American history, usually as it is concerned with the late nineteenth and early twentieth centuries. The 1970–1971 volume averaged four to five long articles per issue, and these varied from a survey of

American populism by Karel Bicha to a study of La-Folette and the Russians. Most of the material is well written, represents original scholarship, and tends to be the work of a representative group of professors from campuses throughout the United States. The fact that the journal is published by The Institute of Jesuit History has little or no effect on its editorial policy. Can be recommended as one of the better general American history magazines for medium to large collections.

Mississippi Valley Historical Review. See *Journal of American History.*

Montana, the Magazine of Western History. 1951. q. $6. Vivian A. Paladin. Montana Historical Soc., 225 N. Roberts, Helena, Mont. 59601. Illus., index, adv. Circ: 14,000. Vol. ends: Oct.

Indexed: AmerH, HistAb. *Bk. rev:* 15–20, 500–1,000 words, signed. *Aud:* Ga, Ac.

Emphasis is on Montana and bordering states, but the subject matter is diverse: ranching, mining, homesteading, Indians, fur trade, etc. The five or six well-written, well-documented articles are supported by an excellent format, including a number of photographs and illustrations. The book reviews are good to excellent, but as in many magazines of this type they tend to lag months behind publication date. A useful magazine for almost any library.

New England Quarterly; an historical review of New England life and letters. 1928. q. $8. Herbert Brown. Hubbard Hall, Bowdoin College, Brunswick, Maine 04011. Index. Circ: 1,900. Vol. ends: Dec.

Indexed: AmerH, HistAb, SSHum. *Bk. rev:* 15–20, lengthy, signed. *Aud:* Ac.

Devoted to the history and culture of New England, with emphasis on literary history. Among its editors are such distinguished scholars as Samuel Eliot Morison, Oscar Handlin and Bernard Bailyn. There are usually four or five scholarly articles, a section on memoranda and documents. The book reviews are critical and cover all aspects of New England. As this covers such a wide range of interests, it can be subscribed to by many libraries as much for its literary as its historical value. While the main appeal will be to New England libraries, the material is usually of value to anyone interested in American culture and life.

New York Historical Society Quarterly. 1917. q. Membership (Nonmembers $10). Kathleen A. Luhrs. N.Y. Historical Soc., 170 Central Park W., New York, N.Y. 10024. Illus., index. Circ: 1,850.

Indexed: AmerH. *Bk. rev:* 10–15, 200–1,000 words, signed. *Aud:* Ac.

Primarily features two to three long, detailed, and usually scholarly articles on some aspect of New York City history. (Note: This journal is about the city, al-though New York state and surrounding areas are often the subject of articles. Also, the book reviews are concerned with wider historical interests.) The 100 or so pages are handsomely printed, and there are usually a number of photographs and illustrations. The style of writing varies, although here an interest in the history of New York will carry any reader over the rougher spots.

New York History. 1919. q. Membership. $7.50. Wendell Tripp. N.Y. State Historical Assn., Cooperstown, N.Y. 13326. Illus., index.

Indexed: AmerH. *Bk. rev:* 10–15, 200–500 words, signed. *Aud:* Ac.

Features four to five long, scholarly articles. This journal covers all aspects of New York state history from politics and printers to ethnic groups and social mobility. It is quite strong on bibliographic information, and a good source for data on New York publications. The book reviews, too, are fine. The format is good, and the illustrations adequate. A basic journal for the area in and around New York state, but after that only for large, academic libraries.

North Dakota History; a journal of the Northern plains. 1945. q. $5. James E. Sperry. State Historical Soc. of North Dakota, Liberty Mutual Building, Bismarck, N.D. 58501. Illus. Circ: 1,500. Microform: UM.

Indexed: AmerH, HistAb. *Bk. rev:* Various number, length. *Aud:* Ac, Ga.

Covers history, anthropology, and all aspects of the plains Indians. There are usually three to four articles with original documents, diaries etc. Most material is written by professional historians. On occasion there is a double number devoted to reprinting in full an important document, e.g., the winter/spring 1971 issue of 188 pages was primarily an Indian girl's story. (This particular issue, by the way, is a reprint of a book first published in 1921. It is of considerable interest to historians, but will be enjoyed by high school students as well.)

Ohio History. 1887. q. Membership (Nonmembers $6). Helen M. Thurston. Ohio Historical Soc., Columbus, Ohio 43211. Illus., index.

Indexed: AmerH, HistAb. *Bk. rev:* 6–10, 250–1,500 words, signed. *Aud:* Ga, Ac.

Noteworthy for its excellent format. A usual 80-page issue features many photographs and line drawings. There are some four to five articles per number, and good book reviews. Material is primarily for and by professional historians. There is considerable interest in Ohio politics, as well as bibliographic articles on everything from archaeology to fiction.

Oregon Historical Quarterly. 1900. $7.50. Thomas Vaughan. Oregon Historical Soc., 1230 S.W. Park Ave., Portland, Ore. 97205. Illus., index. Circ: 3,400.

Indexed: AmerH. *Bk. rev:* 15–20, 250–500 words, signed. *Aud:* Ac, Ga.

The basic quarterly for western history, and, of course, for the Pacific Northwest. An average 100-page issue features two to three articles, documents, news of the society, and excellent book reviews. Most material is original, based on careful research. The writing is fair to good, most often by professional historians. A required item in all western libraries, and for most medium to large-sized history collections everywhere.

Pacific Historical Review. 1932. q. $5. Norris Hundley. Univ. of California Press, Berkeley, Calif. 94720. Index., adv. Circ: 2,000. Vol. ends: Nov. Microform: UM.

Indexed: AmerH, HistAb, SSHum. *Bk. rev:* 6–10, one page, signed. *Aud:* Ac.

This publication of the Pacific Coast Branch of the American Historical Association is "devoted to the history of American expansionism to the Pacific and beyond, and to the post-frontier developments of the twentieth century West." The journal also solicits contributions on methodology and philosophical trends. This is a required item in western libraries and in larger academic historical collections.

Pacific Northwest Quarterly. 1906. q. $5. Robert E. Burke. Univ. of Washington, Parrington Hall, Seattle, Wash. 98105. Illus., index.

Indexed: AmerH. *Bk. rev:* 6–10, 250–500 words, signed. *Aud:* Ac.

Despite its name, primarily involved with Washington state history. Some of the three to four articles are of a wider scope—particularly those dealing with early exploring, fur trading, etc. Most entries are from professional historians, and the editing is quite superior. The 30-page format is just passable, and while it is one of the oldest of the historical journals it remains the slightest in terms of quantity—one hastens to add, though, not quality. Good book reviews.

The Palimpsest. 1920. m. 50¢ per copy. William J. Petersen. State Historical Soc. of Iowa, Iowa City, Iowa 52240. Illus., index. Circ: 10,500. Vol. ends: Dec.

Indexed: AmerH, HistAb. *Aud:* Ga, Ac.

A somewhat different approach to local history by the State Historical Society of Iowa. Each issue is entirely devoted to covering one aspect of Iowa's history: the biography of a pioneer, the story of a college or railroad. It treat such diversified subjects as Indians, government and politics and social and cultural history. Photos and illustrations enliven the articles. A useful addition for not only Iowan, but all Midwestern, medium to large-sized academic libraries.

Pennsylvania History. 1933. q. Membership (Nonmembers $8). William G. Shade. Pennsylvania Historical Assn. Subs. to: Phillip E. Stebbins, Dept. of History, Pennsylvania State Univ., University Park, Pa. 16802. Circ: 1,400.

Indexed: AmerH. *Bk. rev:* 15–20, 250–500 words, signed. *Aud:* Ac.

A useful, although not overly exciting journal which features four to five long, detailed, and sometimes dull historical articles on Pennsylvania history. Here history is taken to mean anything from bibliography and work being done in the field to studies of politicians and Indians. Book reviews take up about one quarter of each 160-page plus issue. Required, of course, in and around Pennsylvania, but thereafter only for large academic libraries.

Prologue: the Journal of the National Archives. 1969. 2/yr. $5. Herman J. Viola. National Archives Bldg., General Services Admin., Washington, D.C. 20408. Illus., adv. Circ: 5,000. Vol. ends: Nov.

Indexed: AmerH, HistAb. *Bk. rev:* 10–12, 200–300 words. *Aud:* Ga, Ejh, Ac.

Prologue is an attempt to bridge the gap between the archivist and the academician by transmitting the types of material available in the National Archives that await scholarly exploration. It also reports on new publications and recent accessions. The five to six articles often deal with such diverse subjects as relationships between the Federal government and the researcher, or archival techniques. The articles are well written and often illustrated. The audience is wider than the specialist as is evidenced by more popularly oriented articles such as "Franklin D. Roosevelt, Collector." In this respect, this journal can be recommended for large public libraries as well as college and university collections. (R.S.)

Rhode Island History. 1942. q. Membership (Nonmembers $5). Joel A. Cohen. Rhode Island Historical Soc., 52 Power St., Providence, R.I. 02906. Illus., index. Circ: 2,700.

Indexed: AmerH. *Aud:* Ac, Ga.

Differs from most regional historical journals in that it is slight in size (averages between 30 and 40 pages), but, more important, depends upon two or three well-illustrated monographic articles. For example, the Winter 1972 issue featured "Facts in the case of H. P. Lovecraft," and "Social Turmoil and Governmental Reform in Providence, 1820–1832." Each article is accompanied by numerous photographs and drawings. The layout is remarkably good, and the total effect is one more of a popular than an esoteric journal. And yet the work is scholarly, original, and well written.

All in all an unusual approach which should have wide appeal.

Texas Historian (Formerly: *Junior Historian*). 1941. 5/yr. (Sept.–May). $2. Joe B. Frantz. Texas State Historical Assn., Box 8059, University Station, Univ. of Texas, Austin, Tex. 78712. Illus. Circ: 2,500.

Indexed: IChildMag.

"Designed to put its major emphasis on youthful inquiries into the way of life in the various Texas communities and fostering the most sound American patriotism of which we have any knowledge." Strictly a history magazine, it carries no advertising, but some pictures and reports of local chapters. Articles are well written, informative, and especially interesting to those who live in the Southwest or are students of that area.

Vermont History. 1930. q. Membership $5. John Duffy. Vermont Historical Soc., Montpelier, Vt. 05602. Illus., index. Circ: 3,200.

Indexed: AmerH. *Bk. rev:* 5–7, 200 words, signed. *Aud:* Ac.

Considers all aspects of Vermont history in a neat, well-printed 80 to 100 page journal. Contributors range from professors and museum directors to newspapermen. The seven to eight articles discuss everything from Vermont's opposition to the War of 1812 to "Two unrecorded printings of Fanny Hill." All articles are dutifully footnoted, and the style is fair to excellent. While primarily involved with Vermont, the magazine does publish articles "pertaining to northern New England and surrounding regions." A better than average regional history magazine which should be considered by all in the area, and by larger libraries everywhere.

Virginia Cavalcade. 1951. q. $2. Edward F. Heite. Virginia State Library, Richmond, Va. 23219. Illus. Circ: 17,000.

Indexed: AmerH, HistAb. *Aud:* Ga, Ac.

Devoted to all periods of Virginia history, and biographical articles on Virginia-born historical figures. Articles are accompanied by numerous illustrations in black and white and color. Historical documents frequently are reproduced. As a historical magazine from one of the oldest regions in the United States, much of the material has more than local interest. A necessary addition for large academic libraries.

Virginia Magazine of History and Biography. 1893. q. $6. William M. E. Rachal. Virginia Historical Soc., Box 7311, Richmond, Va. 23221. Illus., index. Circ: 3,000. Microform: UM.

Indexed: AmerH. *Bk. rev:* 15–20, 200–500 words, signed. *Aud:* Ac.

Such articles as "Sir Peyton Skipwith and the Byrd Land," and "Whither the Comparative History of Slavery" typify what is found in these 120 or so pages. There are usually five to seven articles which tend to concentrate on early Virginia history and personalities. The writing is sometimes a bit precious, but it is accurate and well documented. The book reviews are good, take up about one eighth of each number. Not an overly exciting magazine, but of considerable value to a historian of the South, and, as such, should be in all larger Southern libraries.

Western Historical Quarterly. 1970. q. $9. Leonard J. Arrington and S. George Ellsworth. Utah State Univ., Logan, Utah 84321. Illus., index, adv. Circ: 3,000. Sample. Vol. ends: Oct.

Indexed: AmerH, HistAb. *Bk. rev:* 15, 500 words, signed. *Aud:* Ac, Ga.

Sponsored by the Western History Association, this shows evidence of experience and expertise in its composition and authorship. Concentrating on "the westward movement from coast to coast, frontiers of occupation and settlement, the borderlands of Mexico, the westward movement in Canada and Alaska, with special attention given to the trans-Mississippi West, both nineteenth and twentieth century," the quarterly contains signed book reviews, new book annotations, and a subject bibliography of articles appearing in other journals. Special section Sources and Literature of Western American History includes: list of dissertations in the field (each July issue), a list of state histories and bibliographies, and profiles of great libraries and collections. Conservatively designed and printed on quality stock, the contents hold a general reader's interest without sacrificing scholarship. A worthy addition to casual and research collections of Western Americana. (R.S.)

The Yorker. 1942. bi-m. (Sept.–June). $2. Milo V. Stewart. New York State Historical Assn., Cooperstown, N.Y. 13326. Illus. Circ: 11,000.

Indexed: IChildMag. *Aud:* Ejh, Hs.

Student-written articles which are commendable for their high quality of writing and for their accurate and imaginative presentation of New York State's history. The articles, averaging 3,000 words or more, appear to be well researched, but are not documented. Most of them represent awards given by the Association to students in writing competitions held annually. Illustrations consist of old prints, documents, maps, portraits, etc., in black and white, sometimes with the addition of one color. Reports of the activities of "Yorker" chapters, conventions, trips, projects, and other activities are included in each issue. A useful addition for most eastern school libraries. Of limited value to others.

HOBBIES

See also Sports, Games, Gardening, etc.

Basic Periodicals

Almost every hobby has a magazine; some outstanding ones are listed here.

ANTIQUES & COLLECTING. *Antique Trader, Hobbies, Spinning Wheel.*

ARTS & CRAFTS. *Craft Horizons, Popular Science, Popular Mechanics.*

NUMISMATICS. *Coins (U.S.), Coin World.*

PHILATELY. *Linn's Weekly.*

MODELS. *Scale Models, Airfix, Air Enthusiast.*

Antiques and Collecting

The American Life: collectors quarterly. 1962. m. $7. G. L. Freeman. Century House, Watkins Glen, N.Y. 14891. Illus. Circ: 1,000. Sample.

Aud: Ga, Ac. *Jv:* C.

This is as much a literary mystery and curiosity as it is an oddity among periodicals on collecting. It is published by the American Life Foundation (whose background could not be checked) in a format similar to *American Heritage,* but with considerably less control of style, format, and academic and bibliographic accoutrements. Articles have appeared on the widest and strangest variety of subjects imaginable, e.g., "Funerary Art," an odd collection of information and illustrations on coffins, embalming equipment, proper funeral dress, and so on. The stated purpose has varied considerably since the early volumes though it purports to be "a permanent record of the big and small issues in collection that rise and fall with the times." Value is elusive, but seems to be as much for searchers of curiosities of Americana as for the collector. It is a fascinating title that may be useful to inclusive Americana historical collections. It is of dubious reference value for the general library. Should be inspected before subscribing. (G.L.)

Antique Airplane Association News. 1953. bi-m. $6. Robert L. Taylor. Antique Airplane Assn., Box H, Ottumwa, Iowa, 52501. Illus., index, adv. Circ: 3,000. Sample. Vol. ends: July/Aug.

Bk. rev: Various number, length. *Aud:* Ga, Hs.

Concerned primarily with "fly-ins." The emphasis is more on the performance of antique planes than their restoration. It includes reports of "fly-ins," a calendar of "fly-ins," news of various events and activities and chapter and club news. There are many small photographs of the different restored airplanes which attend the "fly-ins." Since this is an official association publication in a specialized area, it is recommended only if

there is a very large active group within the library's clientele. (F.B.)

Antique Automobile. 1947. bi-m. $6.50. William Bomgardner. Antique Automobile Club of Amer., Inc., 501 W. Governor Road, Hershey, Pa., 17033. Illus., index, adv. Circ: 27,000. Vol. ends: Nov./Dec.

Bk. rev: Various number, length. *Aud:* Ga, Hs.

Primarily devoted to reporting winners and showing pictures of show class winners at various competitions of the Antique Automobile Club of America. Some issues feature the history of a particular automobile manufacturer or restoration. Other articles note the going market price for antique cars, and there is information about the club and its activities and members. The magazine provides a good place to advertise and exchange cars, parts, and information. It has reasonably good reference value for the history of various cars with minimal value on restoration and mechanical repair information. A useful, although not necessary, magazine for both the adult and the high school student, not to mention a few college professors and their students. Because its scope is wider than that of *Horseless Carriage Gazette,* prefer this one for buying where needed. (F.B.)

The Antique Dealer and Collectors Guide. 1946. m. $21. Alison Brand. City Magazines, Aldwych House, 81 Aldwych, London WC 2, England. Illus., adv. Circ: 28,000. Sample. Vol. ends: Dec.

Aud: Ga, Ac.

This English periodical is one of the best on fine European antiques. About half of each issue consists of display advertisements which are educational in themselves. The remainder includes articles on ceramics, nineteenth century wax dolls, Scottish silver, and so on. In addition there are several departments which include "Round the Sales" (descriptions of recent auctions), book reviews or short lists, and "Collectors Scrapbook" (news items), among others. A short section of classified and small advertisements is also included. A beautiful publication, and of use to libraries that serve patrons who are interested in extremely fine antiques, historical societies, and importers. However, its subscription price and overseas publication location are definite disadvantages. Should be considered in academic libraries because the colored and black and white photographs increase its long term historical value. (G.L.)

Antique Monthly (Formerly: *Antique Quarterly*). 1967. m. $6. Gray D. Boone, Drawer 2, Tuscaloosa, Ala. 35401. Illus., adv. Circ: 67,000. Sample. Vol. ends: Nov.

Bk. rev: 12–15, 200–250 words. *Aud:* Ga, Ac.

The newspaper format limits the long range value of what could be called the American counterpart of

The Antique Dealer and Collector's Guide. Each issue consists of three sections which include numerous good color and black and white photographs, many full and half page advertisements, articles on auctions (past and forthcoming), "Upcoming Shows," classified advertisements, "Antique Furniture Forum" (questions and answers of readers, with illustrations), and a considerable number of book reviews. Articles tend to be on historical aspects, value of antiques, and museum acquisitions. This makes the title of particular value to historical societies and museums, and for libraries where there are serious antique collectors. Keep in mind its newspaper format. (G.L.)

Antique Motor News & Atlantic Auto Advertiser. 1961. m. $3. Walter R. Drew, 5406 Village Rd., Suite 6, Long Beach, Calif. 90808. Illus., adv. Circ: 6,000. Sample. Vol. ends: Dec.

Aud: Ga, Hs.

The content is simple and apparently constant: an article about the restored car pictured on the front cover, a second one dealing with social aspects—usually a fashion of the time the car was in style, a calendar of events, and several reprints of old car advertisements. The display and classified sections give the necessary information on where to buy, to help one restore a car. The restoration article in each issue is good and if there is a demand for this type of publication, its low price would make it a choice if *Horseless Carriage Gazette* or *Antique Automobile* could not be afforded. (F.B.)

The Antique Trader. 1957. w. $5. A. Babka. The Antique Trader, P.O. Box 1050, Dubuque, Iowa 52001. Illus., adv. Circ: 93,000. Sample. Vol. ends: Dec. 31.

Aud: Ga, Ac. *Jv:* V.

It calls itself "America's largest advertiser for antique dealers and collectors." This is to the collector what the *Wall Street Journal* is to the businessman and *Books in Print* is to the librarian. It consists entirely (about 60 pages) of advertisement, both classified and display. Advertisements are included from throughout the United States. A special section on antique shows and auctions is included in each weekly issue. There are numerous advertisements for books but no reviews. Of value in a library for collectors to compare current prices of collectables and popular antiques, but primarily for individuals who wish to capitalize on current trends in collecting. (G.L.)

The Antiques Journal. 1946. m. $6. John Mebane. Babka Publishing Co., Inc., Box 1046, Dubuque, Iowa 52001. Illus., adv. Circ: 32,500. Sample. Vol. ends: Dec.

Bk. rev: 8–12, 75–200 words. *Aud:* Ga, Ac.

Articles are mostly on nineteenth century collectables. The variety of topics is far ranging: earrings to

snuff boxes, political novelties to early American tea-kettles, bottles to gold scales. Many book advertisements and "New Books" column are of value to the acquisitions librarian. Advertisements, which make up about half of each issue, describe the most popular semiprecious collectables of current interest. Good for a public library serving the general collector. It complements *Spinning Wheel* very nicely. (G.L.)

Antiques Magazine. 1922. m. $16. Alice Winchester. Straight Enterprises, 551 Fifth Ave., New York, N.Y. 10017. Illus., adv. Circ: 65,000. Microform: UM.

Indexed: RG. *Bk. rev:* Various number, length. *Aud:* Ga, Ac.

One of the most popular general antique magazines, made even more so because it is indexed in *Reader's Guide.* All types of antiques are covered, but there is an emphasis on furniture and furnishings. Other articles deal with painting, prints, architecture, glass, ceramics, textiles, etc. Usually each issue features a piece on the history of some aspect of collecting. Regular departments include news of exhibitions, museum acquisitions, notes on collectors, and a various number of book reviews. This is not for the amateur with a limited budget. It is for the expert and semi-expert, and of primary interest in libraries for its social and historical value.

Apollo. See Art Section.

Auction. See Art Section.

Burlington Magazine. See Art Section.

The Canadian Journal of Arms Collecting. 1963. q. $4. James Gooding. Museum Restoration Service, Box 2037, Station D, Ottawa, Ont., Canada. Illus., adv. Circ: 1,500. Sample. Vol. ends: No. 4.

Bk. rev: Occasional. *Aud:* Ga.

Intended solely for the collector. There are no articles about shooting, hunting, or protection which are found in most arms journals. Well-documented articles give the history and description of various kinds of arms, e.g., guns, swords, bayonets, from all eras. Good, detailed photographs accompany descriptions. A regular feature is a calendar of gun shows in the United States and Canada. The book reviews are detailed and discriminating enough to aid in book selection in this subject area. One drawback (though slight since there are only three or four articles in each issue) is a lack of a table of contents. Recommended only if there are arms collectors or curious patrons. (C.F.)

The Classic Car. 1952. q. $10. William S. Jackson. Classic Car Club of Amer., Box 443, Madison, N.J. 07940. Illus., index; adv. Circ: 4,000. Sample. Vol. ends: Dec.

Bk. rev: 4–5, 100 words. *Aud:* Ga, Hs.

A publication of the Classic Car Club of America which ". . . seeks to further the restoration and preservation of distinctive motor cars produced in the period from 1925 to 1942. . . ." The magazine is as distinctive as its subject matter. There are excellent quality photographs accompanying the several articles, good book reviews, and a calendar of events. Though this is a quality publication, its subject matter limits subscription appeal except in large libraries. (F.B.)

Collectors News. 1960. m. $4. Mary E. Croker. Spokesman Press, 608 8th St., Grundy Center, Iowa 50638. Illus., adv. Circ: 30,500. Sample. Vol. ends: Apr.

Bk. rev: Occasional. *Aud:* Ga, Ac.

People apparently collect as wide a variety of "stuff" as can be imagined—doorknobs, cigar bands, comic books, license plates, calendars, Coca Cola curios, railroad tickets, duck decoys, fruit jars, post cards, insulators, and of course, bottles. Similar to *Antique Trader* but deals mostly with oddities such as the above instead of "antiques." A general index by department for classified advertisements, which compose about ninety percent of each issue, a few short articles on various collectables, some display advertisements, and numerous book advertisements make up each monthly issue. A section of advertisements for antique sales and auctions is also included. Of most interest as a subscription for the private collector, but might be of value in the public library. (G.L.)

Connoisseur. See Art Section.

Hobbies; the magazine for collectors. 1931. m. $5. Pearl Ann Reeder. Lightner Publishing Corp., 1006 S. Michigan Ave., Chicago, Ill. 60605. Illus., adv. Circ: 46,000. Vol. ends: Feb.

Indexed: MusicI, RG. *Bk. rev:* 10–12, 150–250 words. *Aud:* Ga, Ac, Hs. *Jv:* V.

A standard "magazine for collectors." Consists mostly of the various departments which appear regularly: "Historical Records," "Dollology," "Mechanical Banks," "Old Glass and China," "Metals," "On Time," "Button Collecting," "Stamps," "Numismatics," "History in Books," "Minituria," "Playing cards," "Old Prints," "Paintings," "Maps," "At the Sign of the Crest," "Post Cards," "Indian Relics," "Book Reviews," "Gems and Minerals," "Firearms," "Natural History," and "Autographs," as well as others from time to time. Display and classified advertisements comprise about two thirds of each issue; totally dominate the departmental and informational articles. Of use in all libraries that serve collectors, but should be supplemented by one or more titles that describe collectables and antiques in a more systematic manner, for example *Spinning Wheel.* (G.L.)

Horseless Carriage Gazette. 1937. bi-m. $7. W. Everett Miller. Horseless Carriage Club of Amer., 9031 E. Florence Ave., Downey, Calif. 90240. Illus., adv. Circ: 10,000. Sample. Vol. ends: Nov./Dec.

Aud: Ga, Hs.

Since this limits itself to cars of 1915 and before, its major distinction is its extremely fine color photographs. In addition, each issue has a centerfold color illustration usually accompanied by a short article. There is a fashion piece in each issue, making sure the ladies and gentlemen dress to fit their cars. In addition, there are the more common features: an identification column, restoration hints, and a calendar of events. Buy in preference to *Antique Automobile* only where there is a greater than usual historical interest in the early car period, or for its excellent illustrations. See also comments for *Antique Automobile.* (F.B.)

Live Steam. 1966. m. $5.50. William C. Fitt, P.O. Box 286, Cadillac, Mich. 49601. Illus., index, adv. Circ: 4,500. Sample. Vol. ends: Dec.

Aud: Ga, Hs.

Although steam power is rapidly giving way to diesel, gas, atomic, and even electric power, there are fans about who keep the last alive. They are the readers of this approximately 20-page hobby magazine which takes in all aspects of collecting and operating steam launches, locomotives, farm and construction tools —both fullsize and miniature. It has vocational interest, too. Students involved with drafting, pattern making, foundry and machine work will find much of interest, right down to detailed diagrams of a Southern Railway System locomotive. The magazine, for example, is reprinting ICS (International Correspondence School—Scranton, Pa.) courses on the steam locomotive. The series began with the April 1971 issue and will continue until the full series of 24 courses is completed. Reference material is included which is not available in any other source since it was originally offered only to ICS students and not distributed in book form.

Militaria. 1968. bi-m. $4.25. Odegard/Deeter. DO Enterprises, Box 6384, Los Angeles, Calif. 90055. Illus., index, adv. Circ: 2,000. Sample. Vol. ends: No. 6.

Bk. rev: 2, 50–150 words. *Aud:* Ga.

Presents general information about the minutia of the military: uniforms, guns, daggers, grenades, awards, insignias. Includes short, superficial articles on military history, principally twentieth century. There are many illustrations including photographs of outstanding collectors' items in a regular column, "Collector's Corner." For those few libraries who have a sizable number of military buffs as patrons this may be the best purchase because of its appeal to many kinds of collectors. (C.F.)

Military Collector and Historian. 1949. q. Membership. Henry I. Shaw, Jr. The Company of Military Historians, 8514 Oakford Dr., Springfield, Va. 22150. Illus., index, adv. Circ: 2,000. Sample. Vol. ends: Winter.

Bk. rev: 5–8, 50–150 words. *Aud:* Ga.

The articles in this official organ of the Company of Military Historians are well documented and considerably more specific and informative than those in *Militaria*. In fact, they are probably too specific to be useful in most libraries. The principal content is military history with one rather lengthy column devoted to collectors' information. The illustrations are commendable, especially the drawings of uniforms. The reviews are detailed enough to be valuable for selection in this subject area. Some issues include loose sheets of "The Company Bulletin Board," primarily personal want and sale advertisements. (C.F.)

National Antiques Review; the monthly guide to antique values. 1969. m. $6. George Michael, Box 619, Portland, Maine 04104. Illus., index, adv. Circ: 16,000. Sample. Vol. ends: June.

Bk. rev: Number varies, 50–100 words. *Aud:* Ga, Ac.

Early eastern Americana and European pieces sold at auction are the most frequently dealt with topics. The subtitle, "Monthly Guide to Antique Values," refers to the several articles on major auctions held during the previous month. Two to three informational pieces ranging from Portland Glass to Moravian pottery and ship carvings are included in each issue. "The Bell Ringer," a directory of upcoming auctions and shows; "Auction of the Month," a description of items and prices of major pieces sold; and "Bookmark," a review of new books, are regular columns. Display advertisements are mostly for eastern dealers. The fine quality and format make this of value to all libraries serving collectors of fine antiques. Conversely, its scope limits value. It should be considered as a secondary selection by libraries subscribing to antiques publications. (G.L.)

Old Stuff. 1971. bi-m. $3. John Rupnow. Johnson Hill's Press, Inc., 1233 Janesville Ave., Fort Atkinson, Wis. 53538. Illus., adv.

Aud: Ga.

"About old things everybody loves," this is a 42-page pocket-sized magazine loaded with information of value to antique collectors and those in quest of trivia. "Jumping about from one old thing to another older, gripping each subject for a quick squeeze to get at the essential . . . that, we believe, is *Old Stuff.*" That fairly well sums up the short pieces, notes, and quotes which cover: pawn shop golden balls, toby jugs, colophons, pebble pubs, lead soldiers, axminister carpets, railroads, walking around London etc., etc.— all of this, and only part way through a single issue. Apparently the editor writes the whole thing, or is responsible for quotes lifted from other texts. If the reader has a computer approach to existence, he or she is apt to blow a fuse. Others will thoroughly enjoy. An excellent item for browsing—and, one supposes, for reference desks once it is properly indexed.

Spinning Wheel: the national magazine about antiques. 1945. 10/yr. $6. Albert Christian Revi. Everybody's Press Inc., Exchange Place, Hanover, Pa. 17331. Illus., index, adv. Circ: 27,500. Sample. Vol. ends: Dec.

Bk. rev: 3–6, length varies. *Aud:* Ga, Ac, Hs. *Jv:* V.

This is particularly useful for beginning antique buffs. The most significant fact is that each issue contains about ten feature articles on an extremely wide range of antiques and collectables. In no other antiques magazine are there so many related subjects, e.g., "Tea and its Accoutrements," "Decorated Tools Reflect Traditional and Cultural Values," etc. Book reviews and advertisements for books on antiques are numerous. Departments which include a calendar of antique shows, letters, and "Who Knows?" may be particularly helpful to active collectors. A classified advertisement section is included in each monthly issue. Display advertisements compose about one quarter of each issue of this periodical which is similar in most aspects to *The Antiques Journal* (which complements it nicely). It may be of special interest to potential collectors who may need ideas and help in selecting a new collectable, certainly a fine choice for any library that has *Hobbies* and wants another, complementary magazine. (G.L.)

Trading Post. 1937. q. $7. W. E. Goodman, Jr. American Soc. of Military Insignia Collectors, 744 Warfield Ave., Oakland, Calif. 94610. Illus., index, adv. Circ: 1,350. Vol. ends: Oct./Dec.

Aud: Ga. *Jv:* C.

A journal for an esoteric group. It is filled with history, description, and drawings of military insignia, supplying the store of information a collector must gradually build up. Included are buying, trading, and selling advertisements which would be useful to the collector. Few libraries will have enough interested patrons to justify purchase. (C.F.)

Western Collector; pioneer for today's collector. 1963. m. $6. Joseph Weiss, 511 Harrison, San Francisco, Calif. 94105. Illus., adv. Circ: 15,000. Sample. Vol. ends: Dec.

Bk. rev: 2–4, 75–150 words. *Aud:* Ga. *Jv:* C.

The title should not deceive. The publishers desire this to be as much a national magazine as any other in the field. On the other hand, as the title suggests, it does deal with "collectables," i.e., items of interest because of their production rate rather than intrinsic artistic merit, e.g., carnival glass, depression glass, bottles, etc. Each issue has two to five illustrated articles devoted to one collectable or type of collectable, e.g., "little things" plus two or three articles on miscellaneous subjects. Several departments including "All about Avons" and "Bottle Buff's Calendar" are standard features. A calendar of antique shows and sales upcoming in California makes this of most use to Californians; still, does not lessen the value for those who want to fill in background information for their gathering of the latest in collectables. (G.L.)

Arts and Crafts

Ceramic Arts & Crafts. 1955. m. $6. Lois Scott. Scott Advertising & Publishing Co., 30595 W. 8 Mile Rd., Livonia, Mich. 48152. Illus., adv. Circ: 56,000. Sample. Vol. ends: Aug.

Aud: Ga.

This is one of the "this is how I did it" craft magazines. It tells the reader specifically what paints to use on greenware ceramic pieces which are bought by mold name, brushes to use, firing temperature, etc. Each article is written in the same format: brief introduction, then Step 1, Step 2, etc., a list of materials needed, and the author's address for further inquiries. One of the few features not in this vein is the list of upcoming shows. Where there is a demand for this type of magazine, *Popular Ceramics* would be preferred. (F.B.)

Ceramics Monthly. 1953. m. (except July and Aug.). $6. Thomas Sellers. Professional Publns., Inc., 1609 Northwest Blvd., Columbus, Ohio 43212. Illus., adv. Circ: 20,000. Sample. Vol. ends: Dec. Microform: UM.

Indexed: ArtI, RG. *Aud:* Ga, Ac, Hs.

A popular magazine for craftsmen engaged in the making of pottery. Practical articles clearly explain, with text and photographs, how to do everything in ceramics from the wedging of the clay to the final decoration of the pottery. Many types of ceramic products are discussed as well as the methods used in making them. The regular features include: "Answers to Questions"—CM staff answers questions from those with technical problems; "CeramActivities"—lists award winners and exhibitions; "Suggestions"—shares discoveries of other craftsmen to improve techniques, "Summer Workshops" (spring issues), "Intinerary"—where to go and where to show, and Biennial Ceramic Film and Slide Issue. Almost every issue has an article on a glaze—gives recipes with some background information. Each issue also has an article on enameling. As is true with most hobby magazines, this one can be recommended only where there is an interest in the subject, or where the school curriculum includes the subject. (F.B.)

Craft Horizons. 1941. bi-m. $10. Rose Slivka. American Crafts Council, 44 West 53rd St., New York, N.Y. 10019. Illus., adv. Circ: 31,000. Sample. Vol. ends: Dec. Microform: UM.

Indexed: ArtI, RG. *Bk. rev:* 2–3, 200–500 words. *Aud:* Ga, Ac, Hs. *Jv:* V.

A magazine for the craftsman, artist, teacher, and buyer interested in ceramics, weaving, metal and wood working, jewelry, glass, mosaics, and enameling. Articles cover the wide range of handicrafts, exhibitions, and market places. A new feature inaugurated in 1971 discusses "The burgeoning field of art film, as well as the art and craft of film itself, including all techniques using the medium—both cinematic and still." Biographical sketches of famous artists are included. Contributors are themselves practicing craftsmen and/or teachers in leading schools and universities. High quality paper, a pleasing layout, liberal use of artistic color, and black and white photography combine to make this a beautiful magazine. It is useful for both the layman and the student of design and crafts. As the one general handicraft magazine, it should be found in all types of libraries, from high schools to universities. (F.B.)

Craftsman: L'Artisan. 1968. 2/yr. $10. 14–16 Elgin St., Ottawa, Ont., Canada. Illus., adv. Circ: 1,000. Sample. ($1.50).

Bk. rev: 6–8, notes. *Aud:* Ga, Ac.

Primarily reports on activities, exhibits, and individual artists who make up the Canadian arts and crafts world. Reference value is heightened by the regular feature, "Competitions and exhibitions" and news notes from the provinces. The articles are short, uncomplicated, and written by subject experts, e.g., a nicely illustrated piece on rollprinting by a teacher of jewelry design is featured in the issue reviewed. Some 24 pages, it is nicely laid out with numerous black and white photographs. Should be of interest to all arts and crafts collections, and for larger art libraries.

The Craftsman; serving leather craftsmen. 1956. bi-m. $3.50. A. G. Belcher. Leather Craftsman, Inc., Box 1386, Forth Worth, Tex. 76101. Illus., index, adv. Circ: 25,000. Sample. Vol. ends: Sept./Oct.

Bk. rev: Occasional. *Aud:* Ga, Hs.

Geared as much for the teacher of arts and crafts as for the layman or the youngster, this gives detailed "how-to-do-it" information on making everything from a belt to a western saddle. The text is explicit and well illustrated. From an aesthetic viewpoint many of the design suggestions are highly questionable, but, then, this is not for the artist. It is for the dedicated leather craftsman who likes to read about shows, personalities, and other related hobbies. Teachers will find the information useful, and the magazine should be in larger hobby and crafts collections in both school and public libraries. (F.B.)

Creative Crafts. 1967. bi-m. $3. Sybil Harp. Model Craftsman Publishing Corp., 31 Arch St., Ramsey, N.J. 07446. Illus., index, adv. Circ: 100,000. Vol. ends: Every other Dec.

Bk. rev: Occasional. *Aud:* Ga, Hs.

Among the many features of this magazine are its

column interviewing a particular craftsman, a column giving information about new craft materials, a question and answer column, a list of craft events, and an evaluation of new craft kits on the market. In addition, there are six or so articles on different crafts, ranging from such unusual ones as collecting spider webs to put on wood and tie-dyeing eggs to more common activities such as silk-screening and macrame. Directions are general but adequate—room is left for the imagination to add interesting touches. Photographs with each article show the finished item and some of the steps involved. It would be an excellent choice for an all-purpose "this-is-how" crafts magazine. (F.B.)

The Family Handyman; the do-it-yourself magazine. 1950. 9/yr. $5. Morton Waters. Universal Publishing & Distributing Corp., 235 E. 45th St., New York, N.Y. 10017. Illus., index, adv. Circ: 500,000.

Aud: Ga, Hs.

This popular do-it-yourself magazine for homeowners covers practical suggestions for remodeling homes, fabricating built-in furniture and accessories, hints on gardening and decorating. Detailed building plans accompany articles on storage units and furniture to make in the home workshop. There are many advertisements for tools and building materials. Year's index in each issue is a convenience for readers who are looking for a solution to a specific problem. The best magazine of its kind, suitable for public libraries and, possibly, useful to schools with shop courses.

Flying Chips. 1932. bi-m. $1.75. James W. King. Rockwell Mfg. Co., 550 N. Lexington Ave., Pittsburgh, Pa. 15208. Illus., adv. Circ: 30,000. Sample. Vol. ends: Nov./Dec.

Aud: Ga, Hs.

Published by a leading manufacturer of power tools, this claims to be "written and edited for the home shop owner." School wood shop programs may find plans useful for all but their beginning courses. Each issue includes plans for four to six pieces of furniture and other items of wood. Directions include a bill of materials for the piece, perspective drawing or photo, scale plans from all necessary angles, and description of each step in building. Other pages feature descriptions of power tools, tips for tool care, and construction crafting details. The level of presentation assumes some skill and aptitude with power tools, although a few items presented could be handled by the novice. Heavy paper and punching for three-ring binder make a suitable format for use in the home or school workshop. (F.B.)

Gems and Minerals. 1937. m. $4.50. D. F. MacLachlan, Box 808, Mentone, Calif. 92359. Illus., adv. Circ: 38,000. Sample.

Bk. rev: Occasional. *Aud:* Ga, Hs.

Less sophisticated in its presentation than *Lapidary Journal, Gems and Minerals* nevertheless has something to offer. Its content differs from the former mainly in emphasis, since it also has book reviews, calendar listings, where to rock hound, and one or two "how-to-do-it" projects. There are fewer news reports but more information on new products. Some articles emphasize the geological aspect, for example "Interesting Facts About Geysers" (July 1971), and "Iowa's Ancient Bison" (June 1971). Where appropriate, articles are documented, e.g., "Salt Mine Pseudomorphs" in the June 1971 issue. Where more than one title in this area would be appropriate, it supplements *Lapidary Journal* nicely. (F.B.)

Good Housekeeping Needlecraft. 1968. s-a. $3. Vera P. Guild. Hearst Corp., 959 Eighth Ave., New York, N.Y. 10019. Subs. to: International Circulation Dist., 250 West 55th St., New York, N.Y. Illus., index, adv. Circ: 1,600,000. Sample.

Bk. rev: Notes. *Aud:* Ga, Hs.

Almost indistinguishable from *McCall's Needlework & Crafts.* Both have instructions on basic needlework stitches—mostly embroidery, crochet, and knitting—with instructions on how to care for such items. While *McCall's* has the basic stitch and care instructions scattered throughout, *Good Housekeeping Needlecraft* puts them together. The only distinction between the two, other than actual patterns, is that *Good Housekeeping Needlecraft* is younger and less sophisticated in the styles it chooses. Both, however, are excellent and the choice would lie with pattern preference. Though most women would probably want the magazine at home where they could consult it regularly, if a choice has to be made, this reviewer would suggest examining copies of both this title and *McCall's Needlework and Crafts* which can be found in almost all needlework departments and at newsstands. (F.B.)

Handweaver and Craftsman. 1950. bi-m. $6. Patric Donahue. Handweaver and Craftsman, 220 Fifth Ave., New York, N.Y., 10001. Illus., adv. Circ: 20,000. Microform: UM.

Indexed: ArtI. *Bk. rev:* 6–9, 50–150 words. *Aud:* Ga, Ac, Hs.

Appealing to both the expert and the amateur, this is devoted to handweaving and stitchery. Articles range from how-to-do-it to the history of the art. Good black and white illustration, news of exhibitions, fairs, and conferences. The advertisements, which cover everything from equipment and materials to instructional classes, are helpful. A good addition for any library where there is an interest in the subject. (F.B.)

Lapidary Journal. 1947. m. $5.75. Pansy D. Kraus, Box 2369, San Diego, Calif. 92112. Illus., adv. Circ: 54,000. Sample. Vol. ends: March.

Bk. rev: Various number, length. *Aud:* Ga, Hs.

For the rockhound patron this publication provides good articles, often with color illustrations, ranging from descriptions of specific stones to tours of mines to how to do a project. There are many short articles reprinted from local club publications, classified advertisements, news reports, book reviews on occasion, and calendar of events. About half of each issue is display advertising. In addition, there is an annual buyers' issue (April) listing clubs, shops both alphabetically by name and by geographical location, and a products list, while the June issue for 1971 gave the guide to fee-collecting areas. Recommended if there is a demand. (F.B.)

McCall's Needlework & Crafts. 1919. s-a. $5/2 yrs. Eleanor Spencer. McCall Pattern Co., 230 Park Ave., New York, N.Y. 10017. Illus., adv. Circ: 2,500,000. Vol. ends: Fall/Winter.

Bk. rev: 5–10, 25–50 words. *Aud:* Ga, Hs.

This title is older, and offers more information, but has essentially the same content as *Good Housekeeping Needlecraft.* Instructions are detailed, and with good illustrations. It has a section in each issue of "Nostalgia" telling how to make something which was popular decades ago. There is a section devoted specifically to items children can make which *Good Housekeeping Needlecraft* does not have. Other than these two major features, and its appeal to older and more sophisticated styles, both titles are about equal in scope and quality. (F.B.)

Mechanix Illustrated. 1928. m. $4. Robert G. Beason. Fawcett Publns., Inc., Fawcett Bldg., Greenwich, Conn. 06830. Illus., adv. Circ: 1,588,000. Vol. ends: Dec. Microform: UM.

Indexed: RG. *Aud:* Ga, Hs.

Written primarily for the amateur handyman and mechanically inclined teenager. Features articles of about 2,000 words on the latest developments in automobiles, aviation, inventions, and other mechanical and scientific areas. Largest portion of magazine's content is devoted to cars, followed by home improvements, sports and recreation, hobbies, and other forms of transportation. Special areas covered at times include money management for the family, advice on careers and advancement, health and medicine, photography, electronics. Some photographs are in color but most are in black and white. Diagrams and drawings are helpful additions. It is sometimes difficult to tell the differences among this, *Popular Mechanics,* and *Popular Science Monthly.* The latter two have the advantage of age and a somewhat better format, but on the whole the material covered is almost identical, as is the approach and reading level. While final decision on which one to subscribe to is a matter of personal preference (most libraries carry them all), this compiler suggests *Popular Science, Popular Mechanics* and *Mechanix Illustrated,* in that order. (F.B.)

Pack-O-Fun. 1951. m. (Sept.–June). $5. Edna Clapper. Clapper Publishing Co., 14 Main St., Park Ridge, Ill. 60068. Illus., adv. Circ: 24,000. Sample. Vol. ends: June.

Bk. rev: Occasional. *Aud:* Ga, Ejh, Hs.

"The only scrapcraft magazine," as it bills itself, is full of quick craft projects. Most items can be made with odds and ends or throw-aways and a little glue and paint. Specific, detailed information is given for each. Several columns give ideas on what to do with throw-aways, e.g., what to do with the foam containers used to hold packaged meat. In addition, there is a "Handy Hints" column where subscribers write in and tell what to do with a particular item. The writing style is simple and each issue includes sections on pen pals, children's activities, and stunts and games. Therefore, teachers and parents will also find it useful. It can be considered as an ecology magazine (How to use throw-aways), a crafts magazine, and a children's magazine. Because of its wide range, it would be especially useful in smaller public libraries and elementary school libraries. (F.B.)

Popular Ceramics. 1949. m. $7.50. Wiliam Geisler. Popular Ceramics Publns., Inc., 6011 Santa Monica Bldv., Los Angeles, Calif. 90038. Illus., index, adv. Circ: 50,000. Sample. Vol. ends: July.

Bk. rev: Occasional. *Aud:* Ga, Hs.

Similar to *Ceramic Arts & Crafts,* this title is preferable since it includes more than step-by-step instructions on how to paint molded greenware. A series on teaching ceramics to children, with hints on possible solutions to problems connected with this, and another on molds and slip casting were featured in the issues examined. Occasionally there is a book review and a regular column alerts readers to new products. A question and answer column and a show calendar add to the usefulness of this title. Other features parallel those of *Ceramic Arts & Crafts.* (F.B.)

Popular Mechanics. 1902. m. $5. Robert P. Crossley. Hearst Magazines, 224 W. 57th St., New York, N.Y. 10019. Subs. to: Box 646, New York, N.Y. 10019. Illus., adv. Circ: 1,666,450. Microform: UM.

Indexed: AbrRG, IChildMag, RG. *Aud:* Ac, Ga, Hs, Ejh.

A "how-to-do-it" magazine which popularizes science and mechanics for all age levels. Emphasis is on practical application rather than theory. Filled with amply illustrated articles on: automobiles and driving, science and inventions, environment, shop and craft, electronics, radio and TV, home and yard, photography, boating, and outdoor recreation. Contains many easy-to-follow directions for numerous useful projects such as sewing centers, patios, sailboards, etc. Tips are given on the care of automobiles, driving, and how to build, repair, and use equipment. There are occasional picture stories where the illustrations tell the story with little reliance on text. Approximately 14 pages of classified advertising appear each month. Editions are available in Australia, Brazil, the Caribbean, Denmark, France, Mexico, and Sweden. See concluding comments for *Mechanix Illustrated.* (F.B.)

Popular Science Monthly. 1872. m. $6. Hubert P. Luckett. Popular Science Publishing Co., 355 Lexington Ave., New York, N.Y. 10017. Subs. to: Popular Science Sub. Dept., Box 2871, Boulder, Colo. 80302. Illus., adv. Circ: 1,706,000. Vol. ends: Dec. Microform: UM.

Indexed: AbrRG, RG. *Aud:* Ac, Ga, Hs, Ejh. *Jv:* V.

Articles are written in simple language for the enjoyment of the weekend mechanic and hobby fan. It is divided into sections representing his (or her) varied interests: "Car and Driving," "Science and Invention," "Space and Aviation," "Home and Shop," "Electronics," "Boating," "Photography," and "What's New Digest; a Picture Roundup of New Products and Developments." In addition there are many special feature articles. Neither too general nor too technical for the average hobbyist. Illustrations and diagrams are plentiful and ingeniously simplified. Possibly there is more emphasis here on science than in its two competitors, *Popular Mechanics* and *Mechanix Illustrated,* but the difference is not great. On the whole, the editorial style, illustrations, and general treatment of material is somewhat better than either of the others, and for that reason it is preferred by this compiler. However, they are all so close that a conclusion as to merit can only be relative. See concluding comments in entry for *Mechanix Illustrated.* (F.B.)

Shuttle, Spindle & Dye Pot. 1969. q. Membership $5. Garnette Johnson. Handweavers Guild of Amer., 339 N. Steele Rd., West Hartford, Conn. 06117. Illus., adv. Sample.

Aud: Ga, Hs.

Directed primarily to those interested in handweaving, spinning, and dyeing, this 36 to 44 page magazine is a labor of love. Contributors receive no payment but as members of the sponsoring Guild seem to enjoy swapping tips, ideas, and chatty information about members. The material on how-to-do-it makes up about two thirds of each number, and it all looks official enough. There is some good historical material, too. Nicely illustrated. Should be of as much interest to teachers as to laymen.

Simplicity Fashion Magazine. 1949. 3/yr. $2. Alma Cunningham. Simplicity Pattern Co., 200 Madison Ave., New York, N.Y. 10016. Illus. Circ: 800,000.

Aud: Ga, Hs.

Features detailed and easy to follow patterns for women and children's clothing. The whole is sup-

ported by how-to-do-it type articles, new product information, and other features which have appeal for the woman who sews her own clothing. While this lacks the overall appeal of the *McCall's* entry, it does have a wide following among readers, and is particularly good for the beginner. The same firm issues the *Simplicity Home Catalog* (1967. s-a. $1.35) which offers some 500 garment patterns which include boys' and mens' clothes.

Textile Crafts. 1969. q. $5. Earl Bagby, Box 3216, Los Angeles, Calif. 90028. Illus., index, adv. Circ: 1,000. Sample. Vol. ends: Spring.

Bk. rev: 2–4, 50–150 words. *Aud:* Ga, Ac, Hs.

A potential contender for *Handweaver & Craftsman's* position, this young magazine offers articles primarily on weaving—"So you want to spin," "Weave by yourself, for yourself." Macramé, "Macramé Body Necklace"; embroidery, "Creative Stitch Textures"; and general themes, "Art schools in England," "Collecting Yesterday's Sewing Tools," are included along with a calendar of events. It is not a polished publication but has good clear illustrations, usually drawn, and large enough to see all the details. It is on the way up, and one to watch. (F.B.)

Weekend Projects; a countrywide build-it book. 1971. q. $1 per copy. Countrywide Publns. Inc., 222 Park Ave. S., New York, N.Y. 10003.

Aud: Ga.

A beginning handyman's dream, this magazine gives careful building instructions for over fifty projects that can be built in a single weekend. Each project description includes an isometric drawing of the finished piece, detailed drawings, dimensions, a complete list of materials needed, and building instructions. The paper and binding are not of especially good quality, but this magazine should be popular with the build-it crowd. It is aimed mainly at the man who enjoys building things but either has just begun carpentering or cannot think up his own designs. It is definitely not for the experienced cabinetmaker. (J.M.)

The Workbasket and Home Arts Magazine. 1935. m. $1.50. Mary Ida Sullivan. Modern Handcraft, Inc., 4251 Pennsylvania Ave., Kansas City, Mo. 64111. Illus., adv. Circ: 1,500,000. Vol. ends: Dec.

Bk. rev: Occasional. *Aud:* Ga, Hs.

As its title signifies, this contains a hodgepodge of different types of activities, which range from needlework, including tatting, to cooking and gardening, with particular emphasis on crocheting and knitting. It is keyed for the woman who is looking for practical help, not advice or suggestions on how to improve the world. Because of its frequency and low cost, it could be a contender for the position held by *McCall's Needlework & Crafts* and *Good Housekeeping Needlecraft.*

However, patterns are definitely not trend setters (as opposed to the range from trend setters to matronly fashions in the latter two). This will be a deciding factor in selection. Seems especially appropriate for small libraries where its small cost and wide range of features cover a lot of territory. For the same reason, it would be a good choice for the home economics section of the smaller high school library. (F.B.)

Workbench. 1957. bi-m. $2. Modern Handcrafts Inc., 4251 Pennsylvania Ave., Kansas City, Mo. 42111. Illus., adv. Circ: 350,000.

Aud: Ga, Hs.

This is for the do-it-yourself fan who wishes illustrated, explicit instructions on how to build everything from a bird house to an addition to the family mansion. There are numerous tips on home improvement, often tied in with the advertisements. The writing and the illustrations are pleasant, clear and quite understandable for the high school student interested in crafts and carpentry. A good second choice after *The Family Handyman.*

Numismatics

Coin World; the weekly newspaper of the entire numismatic field. 1960. w. $6. Margo Russell. Sidney Printing & Publishing Co., 119 E. Court St., Sidney, Ohio 45365. Illus., adv. Circ: 133,000. Sample. Vol. ends: Dec.

Bk. rev: Various number, length. *Aud:* Ga, Hs. *Jv:* V.

No longer the coin collectors' only weekly newspaper, this remains the patriarch. Being twice as large as *Numismatic News Weekly,* it offers more general coverage of numismatic activities. In addition, there are more classified and display advertisements and more space is given to Canadian activities. Valuable reference material appears, e.g., lists of American Merchant Tokens by state and the in-depth reports on specific coins in the "Collector's Clearinghouse" column. Mint reports and trends lists keep readers abreast of current additions and alert to changes. Preferable to *Numismatic News Weekly* because of its wider coverage, it is a basic addition to any library where there are more than a few collectors. (F.B.)

Coinage. 1964. m. $7. James L. Miller. Behn-Miller Publishers, 16250 Ventura Blvd., Encino, Calif. 91316. Illus., adv. Circ: 140,000.

Aud: Ga, Hs.

This title is primarily an armchair numismatist's approach. It is composed almost completely of very general articles on coins, medals, and currency, and occasionally an interesting facet of foreign issues (e.g., "The Coin That Failed; the 'Ugly' Churchill Crown."). Its most outstanding feature is "Current Coin Prices; Quick Guide to National Trends." While there are

more articles than in the somewhat similar *Coins* (U.S.), the reference value of the latter is so much greater that *Coinage* can only be considered as an extra selection. (F.B.)

Coins. 1964. m. $5.16. Heather Salter. Link House Publns., Ltd., Link House, Dingwall Ave., Croydon, CR9 2TA, England. Illus., index, adv. Circ: 15,000. Sample. Vol. ends: Dec.

Bk. rev: 3–4, 75–200 words. *Aud:* Ga.

Not to be confused with the U.S. publication by the same name, the British *Coins* is also a well-rounded publication in its field. It is one of the first choices for a foreign coin magazine. Naturally it gives major emphasis to Great Britain, but covers, with substantial articles, specific coins from other countries. It has a calendar of events for Great Britain; book reviews, including useful foreign-language ones; a question and answer column (all in statement form); Royal Mint report; articles on paper money as well as coins; and market trends (British). Recommended if there is a large clientele of British numismatic collectors. (F.B.)

Coins. 1962. m. $5. Clifford Mishler. Krause Publns., Inc., Iola, Wis. 54945. Illus., adv. Circ: 97,000. Sample. Vol. ends: Dec.

Bk. rev: 3–4, 100 words. *Aud:* Ga, Hs. *Jv:* V.

As a general, broad in scope, numismatic publication, there is little distinction between the quality of *Coins* and *Coin World.* Personal preference is the deciding factor. *Coins* is published less frequently (monthly as opposed to weekly), it has more information for beginners (a question and answer column and a beginners' page), several book reviews, and a currency exchange. On the other hand, it does not cover paper money, has less "news," and, as noted, is published less frequently than *Coin World.* Otherwise the content of the two is essentially the same. *Coins* seems of more use to the amateur and beginning collector while *Coin World* is more suited to the individual who wants to keep up with the news regularly. (F.B.)

Journal of Numismatic Fine Arts. 1971. q. $6. Joel Malter, Box 777, 16661 Ventura Blvd., Suite 518, Encino, Calif. 91316. Illus., adv. Circ: 12,500. Vol. ends: Dec.

Aud: Ga.

A new publication which concerns itself primarily with ancient and Middle Age coins and artifacts. There are two to three well-written articles with illustrations. Approximately half of the publication is an illustrated catalog of coins and artifacts for sale. At present this seems to be in the more ephemeral class for most libraries, those emphasizing the periods covered excepted, but it is one to keep an eye on, for it has the potential of becoming a substantial periodical. (F.B.)

The Medal Collector. 1950. m. $10. Fred Von Allendorfer. Sidney Printing and Publishing Co., Box 150, Sidney, Ohio 45365. Illus., adv. Circ: 850. Sample. Vol. ends: Dec.

Aud: Ga.

The "Official publication of the Orders and Medals Society of America," this deals with a specific subject or area each month, e.g., "Medals and Decorations of the Republic of India." A short bibliography and scattered photographs accompanied the articles, a total of 50 *Reader's Digest*-size pages. This made up the complete issue examined with the exception of two full-page advertisements. Ask for sample copies before making a decision. (F.B.)

Numismatic Literature. 1947. s-a. $4. Marion T. Brady. American Numismatic Soc., Broadway between 155th and 156th Sts., New York, N.Y. 10032. Vol. ends: Sept.

Aud: Ga, Ac.

The preface to this title accurately describes and indicates its purpose: ". . . a semiannual survey of current publications in or related to numismatics, with abstracts of their contents. . . . Abstracts are numbered consecutively within each issue. . . . Most entries are grouped under broad cultural, geographical or typological sections. . . . At the end of each section is a list of numbered cross references to abstracts with related material in other sections. Author and subject indexes are published at the back of each issue. The author index does not include references to the reviews, which are themselves alphabetically arranged by author. The hoard list is a separate list of abstracts in which reference is made to coin hoards." An excellent reference tool, but useful only in a very large library with a serious numismatic clientele, or in a special library. (F.B.)

Numismatic News Weekly. 1952. w. $5. Clifford Mishler. Krause Publns., Inc., Iola, Wis. 54945. Illus., adv. Circ: 50,000. Sample. Vol. ends: Dec.

Bk. rev: Occasional. *Aud:* Ga, Hs.

The major difference between this weekly and *Coin World* (other than size, and therefore amount of coverage) is that *Numismatic News Weekly* is primarily composed of columns—therefore it appears to be more than just a news weekly. Some of the columns: "Coin Clinic," a question and answer column; "Coinformation," aimed at the beginner; "Commonwealth of Coins"; "Exonumia Corner"; "Fakes and Fakers"; "Lore of Numismatics"; "Odd Corner"; and bimonthly, "Telequotes . . . an authoritative price supplement . . . updated . . . in the regular weekly issues." This, as the other Krause publications, is better suited to amateur and beginning collectors. Therefore, best for large libraries, where there are professional collectors, or where a weekly publication is preferable and the budget will not allow more than one periodical in this area. Otherwise, *Coin World*, supplemented with one or more of the monthly magazines, is preferable. (F.B.)

Numismatic Scrapbook Magazine. 1935. m. $5. Russell Rulau. Sidney Printing & Publishing Co., 119 E. Court St., Box 150, Sidney, Ohio 45365. Illus., adv. Circ: 11,000. Sample. Vol. ends: Dec.

Bk. rev: Occasional. *Aud:* Ga. *Jv:* C.

This title is now published by the same company that puts out *Coin World*, but at present it lacks any outstanding quality. Most of the current news, mint reports, news issues, and token and medal announcements are already in *Coin World. Coins,* a competitor, is a broader and better feature publication. The strong point of this title is in its research articles, e.g., "Numismatics of Alabama," some of which are continued over a period of several months. An inadequate table of content is sometimes frustrating. Only for larger public libraries. (F.B.)

The Numismatist. 1888. m. $7.50. Edward C. Rochette. American Numismatic Assn., Box 2366, Colorado Springs, Colo. 80901. Illus., index, adv. Circ: 27,000. Sample. Vol. ends: Dec.

Bk. rev: 3–5, 100–200 words. *Aud:* Ga.

The most scholarly publication in the numismatic field. As the official voice of the American Numismatic Association it publishes official news (which is prominent), information about domestic and foreign coins, ancient coins, tokens and medals, fakes, and book reviews. Some articles include bibliographies. The calendar of events is extensive, and advertisements abound. Like the official publication of almost any group, this is likely to be received by serious collectors who would belong to the Association. Therefore, it should be considered only as a supplementary title. (F.B.)

Paper Money. 1961. q. $5. Barbara R. Mueller. The Society of Paper Money Collectors, P.O. Box 858, Anderson, S.C. 29621. Illus., adv. Circ: 2,500. Sample. Vol. ends: Dec.

Bk. rev: Notes. *Aud:* Ga.

Several short, one-page articles and three or four longer, usually footnoted ones, make up this publication. With its glossy paper and good illustrations, it is an attractive publication, and suitable where there is any demand for this topic. (F.B.)

TAMS Journal. 1961. bi-m. $5. Virginia Culver, Box 96, Thiensville, Wis. 53092. Illus., index, adv. Circ: 1,200. Sample. Vol. ends: Dec.

Bk. rev: Notes. *Aud:* Ga.

This is the official organ of the Token and Medal Society. About three articles per issue are written by members and give the history of a specific token or medal. A few advertisements announce new medals, but numismatic magazines seem to cover this area equally well, if not better. The major advantage of this publications is its historical treatment and listing of tokens and medals. One disadvantage is that there is no table of contents, although there is a yearly index. One of the titles which serious collectors would probably already have because of Society membership. (F.B.)

Philately

American Philatelist; journal of the American Philatelic Society. 1887. m. $8. James M. Chemi. American Philatelic Soc., Box 800, State College, Pa. 16801. Illus., adv. Circ: 25,000. Sample 50¢. Vol. ends: Dec.

Bk. rev: Various number, length. *Aud:* Ga.

Furnishes authoritative articles on the many phases of philately as well as news of interest to Society members. Worldwide in coverage, several articles in each issue deal with countries other than the United States, e.g., "Japan: Plate Varieties on Cherry Blossom Stamped Envelopes" by Lois M. Evans, June 1971. Of special merit is the "Black Blot Assessments" column which advises readers as to which stamps may have questionable market value. Other departmental features such as a new issues listing, news notes, and a calendar of exhibitions and conventions round out this publication. Those who have a serious interest in philately probably belong to this organization and would receive membership copies. Therefore, should be considered a supplementary title in this field. (F.B.)

Linn's Weekly Stamp News. 1928. w. $5. William T. Amos. Sidney Printing & Publishing Co., 119 E. Court St., Box 150, Sidney, Ohio 45365. Illus., adv. Circ: 72,000. Sample. Vol. ends: Dec.

Bk. rev: Occasional. *Aud:* Ga, Hs. *Jv:* V.

This weekly newspaper covers the international stamp world more thoroughly than any other stamp periodical. It is among those with the highest circulation, and is an old standby for avid collectors. Frequent publication keeps philatelists informed of the latest issues and happenings in the stamp world. Many regular columns discuss geographic areas (e.g., "Canadian Comment" by Gorden Vaughn) or specific aspects of philately (e.g., "Precancel News" by Kenneth Gierhart), and at regular intervals the entire issue is devoted to various societies of specialist collectors (e.g., Flag Cancel Society). Both the display and classified advertisements, about 70 percent of each issue, are important for collectors who take a serious interest in purchase, or wish to compare prices. In view of the frequency and the reputation, should be in any library where stamps are a factor. See also *Stamps.* (F.B.)

Mekeel's Weekly Stamp News. 1891. w. $2. George F. Stilphen. Severn-Wylie-Jewett Co., Box 1660, Portland, Maine 04104. Illus., adv. Circ: 14,200. Sample. Vol. ends: Dec. and June.

Bk. rev: Occasional. *Aud:* Ga, Hs.

Less than half the price of *Linn's Weekly Stamp News,* this title also covers less than half of its competitor's material. It has a good question and answer column, announcements of new issues, both domestic and foreign, and a few articles. It does not have the extensive advertisements of *Linn's,* or cover anything else as extensively. Where cost is a serious consideration, this might be preferred to *Linn's Weekly Stamp News,* otherwise, *Linn's* is the better. (F.B.)

Minkus Stamp Journal. 1966. q. $3. Belmont Faries. Minkus Stamp Journal, Inc., 116 W. 32nd St., New York, N.Y. 10001. Illus., adv. Circ: 30,000. Sample. Vol. ends: Oct.

Aud: Ga, Hs.

This quarterly supplement to the Minkus stamp catalogs is similar in nature to *Scott's Monthly Stamp Journal* but they are not interchangeable since each supplements a different catalog. There are usually two articles of from five to eight pages concerning the history of a stamp, along with several interesting columns such as "Philatelic Quiz," "Designs that Didn't Make it," and "Why I like Stamp Collecting" (Ayn Rand told why in No. 2 for 1971). There is full purchase information for all stamps advertised, which is convenient for those not near stamp shops. The articles are so well written that this is probably the only philatelic magazine that non-philatelists will enjoy reading. Several full color pages of various stamps, good organization, low price, and interesting articles make this an attractive extra choice. (F.B.)

Scott's Monthly Stamp Journal. 1920. m. (except July-Aug.). $5. William Wylie Scott Publishing Co., 604 Fifth Ave., New York, N.Y. 10020. Illus., adv. Circ: 26,000. Sample. Vol. ends: Feb.

Aud: Ga, Hs.

The main purpose of this journal is to update *Scott's Catalogues.* In addition to the new issues section, there are usually three to four articles of one to three pages, concerning some aspect of philately. An editorial column, "It's Worth Mentioning," furnishes odds and ends of interest to stamp collectors, ranging from stamp errors to news of collectors. Each issue features a section of topical listings, and news about a particular stamp, why it was issued and something about the designer. Illustrations include photocopies of stamps, cartoons, and photographs, all in black and white. There is no table of contents to the articles and they are interspersed with the catalog listings, a slight aggravation which can be avoided, as shown by the *Minkus Stamp Journal.* Some articles may interest the general public but the journal is, by and large, intended to serve the serious philatelist. Its subscription value lies in its being a supplement to the Scott catalogs. (F.B.)

Stamp Magazine. 1934. m. $6. Arthur Blair. Link House Publns., Ltd., Link House, Dingwall Ave., Croydon CR9, 2TA, England. Illus., index, adv. Circ: 40,000. Sample. Vol. ends: Dec.

Bk. rev: 10, 100 words, signed. *Aud:* Ga, Ac, Hs, Ejh.

Approximately three quarters of this international stamp magazine is given over to advertising, primarily, although not exclusively, from Britain. There are some 10 to 12 short informative articles and a number of regular departments, e.g., Covers, Postmarks, New Books, etc. A center pink spread of some ten pages illustrates, with necessary details, the "British Commonwealth New Issues" and "Foreign Countries New Issues." This is a regular supplement. The emphasis on advertising is normal for this type of magazine, and the articles seem to be written for both the amateur and the expert. Recommended where there is a strong interest in the subject. (An annual 120-page *Stamp Year Book* is available from the same firm for approximately $1.50. This is a magazine which is an excellent source of data on the year's past activities in collecting.)

Stamps. 1932. w. $3.90. Mrs. C. N. Downs. H. L. Lindquist Publns., Inc., 153 Waverly Pl., New York, N.Y. 10014. Illus., adv. Circ: 32,000. Sample. Vol. ends: Dec., March, June, Sept.

Bk. rev: Various number, length. *Aud:* Ga, Hs.

This is another of the weekly stamp publications but in magazine format as opposed to the newspaper format of *Linn's, Mekeel's,* and *Western Stamp Collector.* Its major emphasis is its features, the most outstanding being "U.S. Precancels," "Philatelic Literature Reviews," "New Issues and Discoveries," and "Stamp Market Tips," the latter two also giving a good bit of coverage to foreign stamps. A calendar of events and approaching sales is useful to serious collectors. The "Trading Post" column is aimed at the beginning stamp collector. Various stamp associations' news is covered also. It lacks a table of contents, its coverage is slightly less than *Linn's,* but its size is physically much less cumbersome. It certainly should be considered for its format, small cost, and comparative coverage. A possible choice in place of *Linn's* in some instances, or an additional choice in others. (F.B.)

Western Stamp Collector. 1931. s-w. $4. Kenneth A. Wood. Van Dahl Publns., Box 10, Albany, Ore. 97321. Illus., adv. Circ: 28,000. Sample. Vol. ends: July 20.

Aud: Ga, Hs.

A newspaper of some 12 to 28 pages which covers the whole of the world of stamps but places emphasis on the issue of the United States, United Nations and Canada. Short articles are primarily concerned with current issues, though some present historical background, e.g., "Britain's First George V Stamps." The general writing style can be appreciated by anyone from the expert to the beginning collector in grade school. While not so large or extensive in coverage as *Linn's Weekly Stamp News,* this has the advantage of more frequent publication. (F.B.)

Models

Aero Modeller. 1935. m. $6. P. S. Richardson. Argus Press, Ltd., 12–18 Paul St., London EC 2, England. Subs. to: Aero Modeller, Eastern News Distributors, Inc., 155 W. 15th St., New York, N.Y. 10011. Illus., adv. Circ: 32,000

Aud: Ga, Ejh.

A small-format magazine about flying aircraft models. Gas and rubber power, and free flight receive approximately equal attention. All the latest products and flying meets are covered, and each issue includes a tear-out full-size set of plans. Because of its British bias, this should be purchased only after similar American magazines, such as *Flying Models, Model Airplane News,* and *American Aircraft Modeler.* (J.C.)

Air Classics. 1963. bi-m. $5.50. Ed Schnepf. Challenge Publns., Inc., 7950 Deering Ave., Canoga Park, Calif. 91304. Illus., adv. Vol. ends: Nov./Dec.

Bk. rev: 3–4, 100–250 words. *Aud:* Ga.

An illustrated, popular view of the history of aviation. Glossy paper and beautiful, often rare, photos (some in color) provide visual excitement. The text of the articles is, thankfully, short, as the editors often strain for a novel point of view where none is required. Books are carelessly reviewed. To be added to collections after *Air Enthusiast,* but better suited to American Libraries than *Airview* or *Koku-Fan.* (J.C.)

Air Enthusiast. 1971. m. $10. Gordon Swanborough. Air Enthusiast, De Worde House, 283 Lonsdale Rd., London SW 13, England. Illus., adv. Vol. ends: May.

Aud: Ga, Ac. *Jv:* V.

The best single aviation magazine for adults. Well illustrated, scholarly articles by internationally known aviation writers cover international aviation history and news. Monthly features include articles about World War II aircraft which contain cutaway plans or three-views; histories of the air forces of the world, with a page of color side views; and a modeling column which reviews the latest kits and includes detailed color schemes. The eye-catching format makes it enjoyable to those with even a small interest in aviation. (J.C.).

Airfix Magazine. 1958. m. $6.50. Chris Ellis. Surridge Dawson and Co. (Productions) Ltd., Publishing Dept., 136/142 New Kent Rd., London SE 1, England. Illus., adv. Circ: 32,000. Vol. ends: Aug.

Bk. rev: Various number, length. *Aud:* Ga, Hs. *Jv:* V.

Airfix is one of the leading plastic model manufacturers in the world. And while most of the articles deal with models produced by Airfix, this is by no means a major limitation. Articles cover plastic models of all types: aircraft, boats, AFV's, trains, cars, and military miniatures. They include such subjects as kit modifications, historical background of prototypes, and color and markings information. Regularly featured are book reviews, kit reviews (of other manufacturers' as well as Airfix's), scale plans, and photos of models and prototypes sent in by readers. This is useful to beginning and advanced modelers, and a good supplement to *Scale Models.* Superior, for experienced modelers, to *Scale Modeler.* (J.C.)

The Airview. 1948. m. Kantosha Co., Ltd., Kojun Bldg., 601, 6–4, Ginaz; Tokyo, Japan. Illus., adv.

Aud: Ga.

A Japanese language aviation history and news magazine. Truly international in scope—articles on Japanese aircraft do not predominate. While most modelers will find the text hard if not impossible to read, the over fifty pages of photographs in each issue more than make up for the language barrier. Photos sometimes have captions in English. An important feature for modelers is a gatefold color side, or three-view of a famous aircraft. (Query publisher for price–it tends to vary.) (J.C.)

American Aircraft Modeler. 1928. m. $7.50. Edward C. Sweeny, Jr., Potomac Aviation Publns., Inc., 733 15th St., N.W., Washington, D.C. 20005. Illus., adv. Circ: 80,000. Vol. ends: June.

Indexed: IChildMag. *Aud:* Ga, Hs, Ejh.

Concerns the construction and safe use of flying aircraft models. A typical issue puts considerable emphasis on radio control. It is well illustrated with black and white photos and some plans of scale and nonscale models. There is little choice between this and *Model Airplane News* and *Flying Models.* (J.C.)

Camouflage Air Journal. 1966. bi-m. 35 Fr. Paul Camelio. Camouflage Air Club, Marine Blanche, K 13 Marseilles 14, France. Illus. Vol. ends: Dec./Jan.

Aud: Ga, Hs.

One of the more difficult aspects of aircraft modeling is determining exactly in which color or colors the original prototype was painted. This small French language publication contains material written by enthusiasts on various aspects of camouflage. Articles consider the color schemes of the aircraft of a particular nationality during a given period, or the different finishes sported by one type during its operational career. Illustrations include photos, line drawings, and tone paintings of side and three-views. For the specialized modeler. (J.C.)

Car Model. 1961. m. $7.20. R. N. McLeod. OLR Publishing, 1301 E. McDowell, Phoenix, Ariz. 85006. Illus., adv. Circ: 168,000. Vol. ends: July.

Aud: Hs, Ejh.

One of the more poorly produced modeling magazines. It has blurry photos and is printed on pulp paper. Nevertheless, it serves the model car enthusiast by encouraging reader-submitted photos, and including many how-to-do articles. It includes new product and kit reviews, plus columns and question and answer features on model trucking, radio control, customizing, and racing in several scales. Primarily for the beginning modeler. (J.C.)

Flight Plan. 1970. bi-m. $4. Jim Maas. Flight Plan, 84 Willett St., 5A, Albany, N.Y. 12210. Illus.

Bk. rev: Various number, length. *Aud:* Ga.

This amateur publication is the journal of the Northeastern New York Chapter of the International Plastic Modelers Society. It is aimed at a highly specialized group of advanced modelers, and is heavily weighted in content towards World War II aircraft and armor. Articles center on the perfectability of kits, the modifications involved in reproducing specific variants of a given prototype, and the research and application of accurate color schemes. Detailed plans abound, and most articles include bibliographies. A useful supplement to less specialized magazines, if interest in your area warrants it. (J.C.)

Flying Models. 1927. m. $5. Don McGovern. Harold H. Carstens, 31 Arch St., Ramsey, N.J. 07446. Illus., adv.

Aud: Ga, Hs.

A magazine for teenagers and adults interested in designing and constructing flying model airplanes. It contains plans and articles about modeling and flying techniques. All types of airplanes are covered—radio control, control line, free flight, and helicopters. Monthly columns include a news report on the hobby and industry, and a question and answer clinic. A slightly more adult approach than *Model Airplane News* or *American Aircaft Modeler* makes this a choice for libraries with an older modeling clientele. (J.C.)

The I.P.M.S. Magazine. 1963. m. $8.50 (included in a joint subscription to *I.P.M.S.-U.S.A. Quarterly Magazine*). Malcolm Scott. The Intl. Plastic Modellers Soc., 230 Green Lane, Norbury, London SW 16, 3 BL, England. Illus., adv.

Bk. re: Various number, length. *Aud:* Ga.

This small-format amateur publication has spawned a host of offsprings. It treats plastic modeling from a specialist's point of view. Articles are concerned with modifying, super-detailing, and painting plastic kits so they become exact scale replicas rather than approximations of their prototypes. Coverage is mostly World War I and II aircraft and AFV's, although the Indochina conflict has recently become a popular period for modeling subjects. Of interest mainly to advanced modelers. (J.C.)

International Plastic Modelers Society. United States Quarterly Magazine. 1966. q. $8.50. John R. Beaman. Intl. Plastic Modelers Soc.-U.S.A., Box 163, Ben Franklin Sta., Washington, D.C. 20044. Illus. Vol. ends: Dec.

Aud: Ga.

An amateur publication concerned with all phases of scale plastic modeling. Contents include kit reviews, articles on modifying or correcting kits, scratch building plans, color information, and historical background of prototypes. Heavily weighted in favor of World War II aircraft and armor. Many photos, line drawings, and tone paintings. Generally, only the more experienced modeler will be interested. Buy it as a specialized supplement to others. (J.C.)

The Koku-Fan. 1951. m. Bunrin-do Co. Ltd., No. 55, 1-chome, Jinbo-cho, Kanda, Chiyoda-ku, Tokyo, Japan. Illus., adv. Vol. ends: Dec.

Aud: Ga.

This Japanese publication covers aviation history and news, and scale and non-scale aircraft modeling. The first half is printed on glossy paper and consists of black and white and some color photos of historical and present day aircraft. Each picture is briefly identified in English followed by a lengthier Japanese caption. The second half is Japanese text on pulp paper with a few illustrations. While the text is useless for most American modelers, the photos, diagrams, and plans more than make the magazine worthwhile for both beginning and advanced modelers as a supplement to *Air Enthusiast* and *Air Classics.* (Query publisher for price—tends to vary.) (J.C.)

Military Modelling. 1971. m. $6. Alec Gee. Argus Press Ltd., 12–18 Paul Street, London, EC2, England. Subs. to: Eastern News Distributors, Inc., 155 W. 15th St., New York, N.Y. 10011. Illus., adv. Vol. ends: Dec.

Bk. rev: 5–10, 300–600 words. *Aud:* Ga.

Despite its small format, this is successful in covering the field of military modeling. It includes military miniatures, model fighting vehicles, and war game figures, in all the popular scales in metal and plastic. Articles cover kit and figure reviews and conversion; historical background of weapons, uniforms, and campaigns; and war game rules. Two most important columns review the latest products and books. At least one scale vehicle plan is included each month. (J.C.)

Model Airplane News. 1929. m. $6. Arthur F. Scroeder. Air Age, Inc., 1 N. Broadway, White Plains, N.Y. 10601. Illus., adv. Circ: 75,000. Vol. ends: Dec.

Aud: Ga, Hs, Ejh.

Detailed charts, diagrams, and illustrated how-to articles make this an excellent guide for constructing scale and nonscale flying model airplanes. A separate section treats radio control. New products are re-

viewed each month, and model flying meets are given extensive coverage. Suits the needs of both junior and more advanced modelers. (J.C.)

Model Car Science. 1962. m. $5. Raymond E. Hoy. Delta Magazines, Inc., 131 Barrington Pl., Los Angeles, Calif. 90049. Illus., adv. Circ: 152,000.

Aud: Ga, Hs, Ejh.

A general model magazine for both the beginner and the advanced student. How-to-do-it articles cover all aspects of modeling, not just cars. Airplanes, boats, trains, rockets and similar subjects are considered. There are articles on full scale and model car racing and radio controlled models. Well illustrated, and the style is basic enough for anyone from junior high up. (J.C.)

Model Railroader. 1934. m. $7. Willard V. Anderson. Kalmbach Publishing Co., 1027 N. 7th St., Milwaukee, Wis. 52233. Illus., adv.

Aud: Ga, Hs, Ejh.

A good magazine for the model railroad fan, regardless of age. Illustrated articles aim at both the beginner and advanced modeler. Instructions are frequently given as to how to build, buy, or dream about a particular train or layout. There is news of others bitten by the bug, as well as anecdotes. Most libraries that buy this will also want *Railroad Model Craftsman.* (J.C.)

Model Rocketry. 1968. m. $7. George J. Flynn. Model Rocketry, Inc., Box 214, Astor St. Sta., Boston, Mass. 02123. Illus., adv. Circ: 15,000. Vol. ends: Oct.

Aud: Ga, Hs, Ejh.

Covers the design, construction, and flight of model rockets, both scale and nonscale. This magazine, like the rapidly growing hobby, is very competition oriented. New products are reviewed in each issue, and articles cover the scientific and technical aspects of the hobby, as well as reporting the highlights of the latest meets. Suitable for junior as well as advanced model rocketeers. Well illustrated, with plans and black and white photos. (J.C.)

R/C Modeler. 1963. m. $7.50. Don Dewey. R/C Modeler Corp., 171 W. Sierra Madre Blvd., Sierra Madre, Calif. 91024. Illus., adv. Vol. ends: Dec.

Aud: Ga.

The best single source for news of the latest products, techniques, and goings-on in the world of radio control enthusiasts. Dependable kit and electronics reviews combined with detailed pictorial coverage of state and national competitions will make this popular with all ages. The accent is on the experienced modeler, however, and some knowledge of the hobby is assumed of the reader. (J.C.)

Radio Control Models and Electronics. 1960. m. $6. Tony Dowdeswell. Argus Press Ltd., 12–18 Paul Street, London, EC 2, England. Subs. to: Radio Control Models & Electronics, Eastern News Distributors, Inc., 155 W. 15th St., New York, N.Y. 10011. Illus., adv. Vol. ends: Dec.

Aud: Ga.

A British-oriented view of the radio control scene. Powered and glider aircraft, as well as yachts and cars, are covered. This hobby consists of using a radio transmitter to actuate remote controls in the model which enables it to duplicate in minature the maneuvers of its full-size prototype. New electronic products and kits are reviewed monthly, and each issue contains plans, illustrated how-to articles, and coverage of recent British club meetings and competitions. A worthwhile addition if there is interest in your area, but less valuable than *RC Modeler.* (J.C.)

Railroad Magazine. 1906. m. $6. Freeman Hubbard. Popular Publns., Inc., 205 E. 42nd St., New York, N.Y. 10017. Illus., adv. Circ: 30,000. Vol. ends: Apr.

Aud: Ga.

A more popular look at railroads and railroadiana than *Trains.* Articles deal with railroads and their equipment, and are heavily illustrated. Fiction is often included, as are columns on such topics as diesels, transit, steam, model railroading, pen pals, and railroad questions and answers. (J.C.)

Railroad Model Craftsman. 1933. m. $6. Harold H. Carstens. Model Craftsman Publishing Corp., 31 Arch St., Ramsey, N.J. 07446. Illus., adv. Circ: 50,000. Vol. ends: May

Aud: Ga, Hs, Ejh.

Fully the equal of its competitor *Model Railroader,* this will appeal to both junior and advanced modelers. Illustrated features include how-to articles on constructing and detailing engines, rolling stock, scenery and buildings. Each issue contains scale plans and some color. A question and answer column appears each month, as do reviews of the latest models and equipment. (J.C.)

Scale Modeler. 1965. m. $11. Ed Schnepf. Challenge Publns., Inc., 7950 Deering Ave., Canoga Park, Calif. 91304. Illus., adv.

Bk. rev: 2–5, 100–200 words, unsigned. *Aud:* Ga, Hs, Ejh. *Jv:* C.

Not to be confused with the excellent *Scale Models,* this is a beautiful, padded, and shallow magazine. Devoted to all aspects of scale modeling, but weighted heavily with World War II aircraft and vehicles, it is well illustrated, including some color. New books and products are viewed in each issue. The editor's gung-ho style combined with the exciting layout provides a good introduction to the hobby for younger modelers, but more experienced hands may be irritated by the lack of scale plans, the use of many photos where a few would suffice, and the consistent misunderstanding of critical letters to the editor. (J.C.)

Scale Models. 1970. m. $6. R. G. Moulton. Argus Press Ltd., 12–18 Paul Street, London EC 2, England. Subs. to: Scale Models, Eastern News Distributors, Inc., 155 W. 15th St., New York, N.Y. 10011. Illus., adv. Vol. ends: Dec.

Bk. rev: 4–8, 300–600 words. *Aud:* Ga, Hs. *Jv:* V.

Despite its British bias, the best general scale modeling magazine. Deals with the construction and finishing of model aircraft, military vehicles, cars, and boats, with aircraft predominating. Although not so well illustrated as most model magazines, the text is usually the result of research, and often breaks new ground. Lengthy, scholarly book reviews and kit reviews keep the modeler informed about what is worth buying rather than just what is available. Included each month is a five-view scale aircraft plan, usually to 1/72nd scale, the most popular collectors' scale. (J.C.)

Sea Classics. 1968. bi-m. $6.50. Jim Scheetz. Challenge Publns., Inc., 7950 Deering Ave., Canoga Park, Calif. 91304. Illus., adv. Vol. ends: Nov./Dec.

Bk. rev: 2–4, 100–200 words, unsigned. *Aud:* Hs, Ga.

A popular, heavily illustrated history of ships and sailors, from the Phoenicians to modern aircraft carriers. Text is on a secondary school level, but libraries serving adults should consider adding it to their collections on the basis of the photos and illustrations alone. While indifferently captioned, they are well-chosen and clearly reproduced, and each issue contains a few in color. A monthly column of rave book reviews keeps the reader up to date. (J.C.)

Tankette. 1965. bi-m. $4.25. M. A. Hundleby. Miniature Armored Fighting Vehicles Assn., c/o G. E. Williams, 15 Berwick Ave., Heaton Meresey, Stockport, Chesire, SK4 3AA, England. Illus. Vol. ends: Aug./Sept.

Bk. rev: 4–10, 50–150 words. *Aud:* Ga, Ac.

An amateur modeling publication, *Tankette* publishes the results of original scholarship by enthusiasts. It includes the history of the armored fighting vehicle, kit reviews, and how-to articles on increasing the scale accuracy of existing kits or modifying them to create replicas of different prototypes. Since the AFV modeler has a less wide range of commercial kits to choose from than other modelers, many articles contain scale plans for scratch building. For the specialist. (J.C.)

Trains. 1940. m. $9. Daniel P. Morgan. Kalmbach Publishing Co., 1027 N. 7th Street, Milwaukee, Wis. 53233. Illus., adv. Circ: 51,000. Vol. ends: Oct.

Aud: Ga.

Railroad history and news for the adult train enthusiast. Articles deal with specific engines of various types, including diesel, electric, and steam, the sentimental favorite. Histories of railroad lines are also covered. Scope is generally American, but an occasional foreign article is included. Because of better photo reproduction and pleasing format, this is a first choice over *Railroad Magazine* for adults. (J.C.)

HOME ECONOMICS

See also Consumer Services Section.

Basic Periodicals

Journal of Home Economics.

American Dietetic Association. Journal. 1925. m. $10. Dorothea F. Turner. The Assn., 620 N. Michigan Ave., Chicago, Ill. Illus., index, adv. Circ: 27,335. Vol. ends: June and Dec. Refereed.

Indexed: BioAb, BioAg, ChemAb, IMed, NutrAb, PsyAb. *Bk. rev:* 3–4, 200–300 words, signed. *Aud:* Ac.

Although primarily written for the professional dietician there is much here to interest the better educated layman. Along with everyone else, the Association is involved with nutrition and diet, and a number of the articles concern such things as "Chemical residues in foods," "Minerals in preschool children's diets," and "Nutrition and the Pill." Written by doctors and dieticians, the articles are well documented, usually not too technical, and often of enough general interest to warrant a look by anyone interested in ecology, environment, and health. In addition to the papers, there is material on education, training, and administration, and news of the Association. One invaluable feature is "Current Literature," an abstracting service which covers about 50 magazines in the same and related fields. The abstracts can be revealing for anyone who is at all concerned with diet and health. All in all, a valuable journal which is probably overlooked by everyone but the experts.

Canadian Home Economics Journal. 1940. q. $5. Margaret C. Smith. Canadian Home Economics Assn., 151 Slater St., 901 Burnside Bldg., Ottawa, Ont. Canada. Illus., adv. Circ: 1,200. Sample. Vol. ends: Oct.

Bk. rev: 4–6, 250–500 words, signed. *Aud:* Ac, Ga.

A journal for professionals, although much of the material will interest any homemaker or consumer. For example, the 40-page October 1971 issue had an article on the worldwide consumer movement and changes in textiles. Also included are the usual professional reports, notes, messages, etc. "The editorial staff consists of members of the Association who are in the Toronto area. As we all have full time positions, our work on the journal is volunteer and we are all amateurs in this effort." Perhaps, but the result is readable; and the material, primarily from members, is topical. A required item for Canadian libraries, and of value for larger American collections.

Co-ed. 1956. 10/yr. $2.40. Margaret Hauser. Scholastic Magazines Inc., 50 W. 44th St., New York, N.Y. 10036. Illus., index, adv. Circ: 1,000,000. Sample.

Indexed: IChildMag. *Aud:* Hs, Ejh.

A Scholastic product for the girl in a home economics class at the junior or senior high level. Heavy on advertising, strong on the image of the woman as homemaker and consumer. Short, well-illustrated articles on fashion, food, finance, furnishings, and even fiction. While this kind of thing was good enough in its time, it is no longer satisfactory to more progressive educators. Conversely, it does serve a purpose in that the advice is solid and most emphasis is on the practical aspects of living—granted, without much thought. It is primarily a classroom aid. If the library is interested, it should save time and money by simply subscribing to *Forecast for Home Economics*, which includes *Co-ed* bound in. (See Education/Educational Aids Section for other Scholastic publications.)

Cookbooks Only. 1970. q. $1. Jain Kelly. Cookbooks Only, Inc., 1727 Second Ave., New York, N.Y. 10028. Illus. Circ: 1,000. Vol. ends: Fall.

Bk. rev: 3, 2 pages, signed. *Aud:* Ga.

A combination of a dealer's catalog and general information of interest to collectors. Background articles are witty, informative, and downright amazing, e.g., an item on "How to Cook Husbands." Reviews of new reprint items, and a listing of what the store has for sale. Also lists out-of-print cookbooks requested or offered by readers. Anyone involved with the stove will thoroughly enjoy.

Forecast for Home Economics. 1952. 9/yr. $6. Eleanor Adams. Scholastic Magazines Inc., 50 W. 44th St., New York, N.Y. 10036. Illus., index, adv. Circ: 75,000. Sample. Vol. ends: May/June. Microform: UM.

Indexed: EdI. *Bk. rev:* 9, 75 words. *Aud:* Hs, Ejh.

A 32 or so page teacher addition to the regular edition of *Co-ed.* The latter home economics magazine for junior and senior high school students is bound into every issue of *Forecast.* There are usually about a dozen short articles for the teacher and these cover such items as teaching methods, food and nutrition, clothing, home furnishings, etc. Although a bit conservative in its view of women, it is a good enough teaching aid. Outside of the classroom, a library might simply take *Forecast* and save the price of *Co-ed* which is included in *Forecast* anyway. (See Education/Educational Aids Section for other Scholastic publications.)

Gourmet. See Wine Magazines Section.

Journal of Home Economics. 1909. m. $12. Helen Pundt, 2010 Massachusetts Ave., N.W., Washington, D.C. 20036. Illus., index, adv. Circ: 52,995. Vol. ends: Dec.

Indexed: BioAb, ChemAb, EdI, PAIS. *Bk. rev:* 3–7, 250 words, signed. *Aud:* Ac, Hs. *Jv:* V.

Stresses new trends in home economic curricula at both the secondary and college level. The 6 to 11 articles, often based on research, offer newest developments in family relations and child development, family economics—home management, housing, furnishings and equipment, food and nutrition, institutions administration, and textiles and clothing. Notes on booklets, bulletins, and films are informative, not critical. A publication of major importance for anyone concerned with home economy in education, business, extension, health and welfare, and homemaking.

What's New in Home Economics. 1936. 8/yr. (Sept.–June) $8. Donna N. Creasy. R. H. Donnelley and Dun & Bradstreet, 466 Lexington Ave., New York, N.Y. 10017. Illus., index, adv. Circ. 60,000. Sample. Vol. ends: Nov./Dec.

Bk. rev: Notes. *Aud:* Ga, Hs.

A magazine for the home economics teacher, primarily at the high school and college level. Included are short articles on foods and nutrition, textiles and clothing, equipment around the house, teaching techniques, and regular departments. Authors tend to be teachers, and the material is of the how-to-do-it variety, i.e., practical and of interest to any man or woman who enjoys the home. Some attention is given to family living and consumer education. There is little about the *new* woman. There are reports from the American Home Economics Association. Heavy on advertising. Note: this is a controlled circulation magazine which means about one half the circulation is free. Most home economists are receiving free.

HORSES

Basic Periodicals

Ejh: *American Horseman;* Hs: *American Horseman, Horse & Rider;* Ga: *Horse Lover's Magazine, American Horseman, Horse & Rider, Western Horseman.*

Note: these magazines are primarily concerned with the horse as a pet, i.e., for riding. Readers seeking information on racing might begin with *The Blood Horse.*

Basic Indexes and Abstracts

Horseman's Abstracts.

American Horseman. 1970. bi-m. $4.50. Countrywide Publns. Inc., 222 Park Ave. S., New York, N.Y. 10003. Illus., adv. Circ: 90,000. Sample.

Aud: Ga, Hs, Ejh.

One of the new horse magazines, and one of the best because of its effort to concentrate almost entirely on problems of the general horse owner (child to adult). Emphasis is on how-to-do-it type articles from equipment and health of the horse, to the best breed to purchase for a given situation. It is nicely illustrated, and written in a style for the beginner and amateur as much as for the expert. As it seems to cover all aspects of horsemanship, it can be recommended for most general collections. Quite suitable too, for academic libraries where this type of sport is a concern. See also *Horse & Rider.*

Appaloosa News. 1946. m. $5. Don Walker. Appaloosa Horse Club Inc., Box 403, Moscow, Idaho 83843. Illus., adv. Circ: 23,000. Sample.

Indexed: HorsAb. *Aud:* Ga, Hs.

This is one of a number of magazines devoted to a particular breed of horse, and they all follow pretty much the same procedure. There are regular articles on care, riding, training, and developments in equipment. Some issues have historical background on the breed. A regular feature—one of several—is "Kids' Korral" which gives information of interest to children and teenagers. Because of the location of the organization, it is a magazine of special interest to western libraries.

Arabian Horse World. 1960. m. $7. Jay Shuler, 2650 E. Bayshore, Palo Alto, Calif. 94303. Illus., adv. Circ: 17,000. Sample. Vol. ends: Sept.

Indexed: HorsAb. *Aud:* Ga.

This is for the serious horse owner, i.e., one who takes owning an Arabian as a full time avocation. Articles are often by readers, point up the problems and joys of the horse, particularly as related to shows. There are numerous illustrations (many in color) which are as often submitted by the readers and advertisers as provided by the editor. In fact, the photographs are a major aspect of the 200-page magazine, and while the text will be of limited interest to youngsters, there is no denying an enterprising librarian might judiciously clip the illustrations for young horse lovers.

An equally good entry is *The Arabian Horse News* (1948. 10/yr. $6. Thomas Y. Funston; Box 1009, Boulder, Colo. 80302. Illus., adv. Circ: 13,000. Sample). This is well illustrated, too, but there is more emphasis on general horsemanship. If a library prefers a magazine with a somewhat wider scope, i.e., other than just Arabian horses, this would be preferable.

The Blood Horse. 1916. w. $20. Kent Hollingsworth. Thoroughbred Owners and Breeders' Assn., 1736 Alexandria Dr., P.O. Box 4038, Lexington, Ky. 40504. Illus., index, adv. Circ: 12,000.

Indexed: HorsAb. *Aud:* Ga.

Primarily a horse racing and horse breeding magazine, and, as such, for the dedicated adult. It is by the way of a "bible" for anyone who gives full time to the art of raising and racing horses. The articles are primarily concerned with major races, care and training, and pedigrees. There are numerous statistics which take up a good one third of each issue. While few general libraries will consider, it is a basic for specialized collection.

Chronicle of the Horse. 1937. w. $13. Alexander Mackay-Smith, Middleburg, Va. 22117. Illus., adv. Circ: 15,260. Sample. Vol. ends: Aug.

Indexed: HorsAb. *Aud:* Ga, Hs.

Primarily a news magazine of horses and racing. Each issue carries regular departments with roundups of both national and international events—racing, stud farms, hunting, horse shows, etc. A good part of the magazine is given over to the last area with a subdivision "Young Entry," which includes information on horse shows for teenagers and younger children. Full data is given from the names of owners and winning horses to precise technical information on each of the entries. As the official publication of some seven equestrian organizations, this deserves a place in any library where the sport is a serious matter. It is not for the casual horse lover or average high school student.

Dressage. 1971. m. $10. Ivan I. Bezugloff, Jr. EDA Corp., Box 2460, Cleveland, Ohio 44112. Illus., adv. Circ: 1,500. Sample. Vol. ends: June and Dec.

Bk. rev: 1–2, 150 words, signed. *Aud:* Ga.

The title is defined by *Webster's* as: "Guidance of a mount through a set of maneuvers without perceptible use of the hand, reins, legs, etc." The editor notes that his magazine is "dedicated to better equitation (English style) and especially to competitive dressage on national and international level. Includes: technical articles on riding and training of horses; reports on dressage activities in the United States and abroad (shows, clinics, etc.); profiles of riders, trainers, horses; organizational news; and announcements of rules by both the American Horse Show Association and the Federation Equestre International. About 95% of its readers are women. Authors contributing to the publication are both Americans and foreigners. Some articles are translated from German and French publications (Authorized translations only.)" Send for a sample.

Hoof Beats. 1933. m. $6. Eugene F. Fairbanks. U.S. Trotting Assn., 750 Michigan Ave., Columbus, Ohio 43215. Illus., adv. Circ: 40,000.

Indexed: HorsAb. *Aud:* Ga.

An official journal for those who participate in—and watch—harness racing. Each issue is given to articles on all aspects of the sport from breeding news to items concerned with training, trotting and pacing horses. There are a number of regular departments and features which report on the Association and its members. A specialized magazine for those involved in the sport.

Weekly reports on racing, statistics on winners, etc. will be found in: *The Harness Horse* (1935. w. $14. Bowman A. Brown. Telegraph Press, Box 1831, Harrisburg, Pa. 17105. Illus., adv. Circ: 13,000). A good part of each issue is devoted to race results, news of stables, sales, and hints on the health and care of the horse. It has fair to good illustrations. Some general articles, but primarily for the expert.

The Horse Lover's Magazine. 1936. bi-m. $3. Dennis Luptak. All Breeds Publns., Box 914, El Cerrito, Calif. 94530. Illus., adv. Circ: 150,000. Microform: UM.

Indexed: HorsAb. *Aud:* Ga, Hs.

A general magazine which covers news of anything related to horses. It also discusses ranching hobbies and sports, all written by experts in a popular style. A typical issue will include a biography of a horseman, tips on care, roping, care of stables, 4-H national horse competitions, and various articles on horses in all parts of the world. The magazine is well illustrated and will have strong appeal for anyone who is remotely interested in horses and riding.

Horse & Rider. 1962. m. $5. Ray Rich. Gallant Publishing Co., 116 E. Badillo St., Covina, Calif, 91722. Illus., adv. Circ: 107,000. Sample.

Indexed: HorsAb. *Aud:* Ga, Hs.

Another of the general horse magazines for the family with a single horse. The articles touch on all aspects of the sport, and give useful information on training, care, and even styles in western clothing. The writing is popular, well within the grasp of the interested teenager. A minimum of racing type articles are included, and the photographs and illustrations are good. Between this and the newer entry, *American Horseman*, the latter seems a bit broader in scope. A librarian trying to choose between the two had best send for sample copies. They seem fairly well matched.

Horseman; the magazine of western riding. 1956. m. $6. Bob Gray. Cordovan Corp., 5314 Bingle Rd., Houston, Tex. 77018. Illus., adv. Circ: 154,000.

Indexed: HorsAb. *Aud:* Ga, Hs.

Articles, photographs, and features consider all horses which can be classified as western, i.e., from Arabians to pleasure and rodeo horses. Contributors tend to be those with experience in breeding, riding, and competition. Emphasis is on the how-to-do-it approach to everything from riding to how to train a horse for a show. There is some historical material, and departments which include "Club & Posse" events.

This is a good general magazine for the amateur and expert alike. Quite suitable for high schools, although a bit too involved for lower grades.

Horseman's Journal. 1949. m. $5.50. Tony Chamblin, 425- 13th St., N.W., Suite 1038, Washington, D.C. 20004. Illus., adv. Circ: 27,000.

Indexed: HorsAb. *Aud:* Ga.

An official publication of the Horsemen's Benevolent and Protective Association, this is primarily for trainers and owners of thoroughbred race horses. It is not a general magazine, although the articles, illustrations, and features will have appeal for the racing fan. There is as much in this magazine about major personalities in the business as about the horses. Stretching it a bit, it might be considered a fair biographical source for specialized situations.

The Horsetrader. 1960. m. $4. Jerry Goldberg, 4131 Erie St., Willoughby, Ohio 44094. Illus., adv. Circ: 28,000. Sample.

Aud: Ga.

Entirely a classified and display advertising medium. If you have a horse to sell, or want to buy, this is the best source. It also lists equipment for sale, and announces meetings, shows, sales, rodeos, etc. While a doubtful addition for a library, it will be of considerable interest to any horselover.

The Quarter Horse Journal. 1948. m. $5. Roy Davis. American Quarter Horse Assn., 2900 W. 10th, Amarillo, Tex. 79102. Illus., adv. Circ: 50,000. Sample.

Indexed: HorsAb. *Aud:* Ga.

An official publication of the American Quarter Horse Association, this stresses association news from activities of young people to sale and race results. It is primarily for the man in the business of raising horses, not for the amateur.

Saddle and Bridle. 1928. m. $10. W. H. Thompson, 8011 Clayton Rd., St. Louis, Mo. 63117. Illus., adv. Circ: 6,000. Sample.

Indexed: HorsAb. *Aud:* Ga.

Devoted entirely to the show horse, this is given over to articles about people and horses, news of shows and show results. Coverage is national, and the content is for the serious horse owner.

Thoroughbred Record. 1875. w. $20. William Robertson. Record Publishing Co., Box 580, 904 N. Broadway, Lexington, Ky. 40501. Illus., adv. Circ: 12,000.

Aud: Ga.

As the *Blood Horse*, this is published in Lexington, Kentucky, and serves pretty much the same audience, i.e., the racing fan. There is considerable technical material on breeding, pedigrees, and statistics dealing with all aspects of the sport. General articles include interviews, profiles of personalities, and a number of photographs and illustrations. Along with *Blood Horse*, the basic publication in the field.

Western Horseman. 1936. m. $5. Dick Spencer. Western Horseman, Inc., 3850 N. Nevada Ave., Colorado Springs, Colo. 80901. Illus., adv. Circ: 224,872. Sample. Vol. ends: Dec.

Indexed: HorsAb. *Aud:* Ga, Hs.

Devoted to the training, breeding, handling, and care of stock horses, i.e., every breed from an Arabian and Palomino to a Quarter Horse and Morgan. The majority of short, illustrated articles cover the type of material of interest to the private horse owner. Regular features include activities at shows, rodeos, and sales. Special articles and departments are geared for young readers, and even those who have difficulty with the text will find the illustrations (and even the advertisements) fascinating. One of of the best general horse magazines for most libraries where there is a demand—and where isn't there?

HUMOR

Basic Periodicals

Ejh: Mad Magazine; Hs: *Mad Magazine, National Lampoon;* Ga: *National Lampoon, Private Eye;* Jc: *The Realist, Private Eye, Oz;* Ac: *The Realist, Private Eye, Oz, Punch, Subterranean Sociology Newsletter, Journal of Irreproducible Results.*

Canard. See Europe and Middle East/French Language Section.

Dublin Opinion: the national humorous journal of Ireland. 1922. m. $7. Gordon Clark. Dublin Opinion Ltd., 193 Pearse St., Dublin, L, Ireland. Illus., index, adv. Circ: 12,000.

Aud: Ac, Ga.

The Irish equivalent of *Punch*, with humorous articles, cartoons, verse, and even quotes from other magazines. It is not well enough known in this country, and seems to be having difficulty in spreading a smile in Ireland. Still, a most useful title where humor is required, and one which would be appreciated—hopefully—where there is an Irish or Irish loving group of library users.

Fits Magazine. 1971. q. $2. Collective. Fits, 4672 18th St., San Francisco, Calif. 94114. Illus. Sample.

Aud: Ac, Ga.

A satirical little magazine with the format of a comic and the outlook of a wicked, energetic underground newspaper. An average 60-page issue strikes hard at the war, the phony society, and even comics themselves. Contributions range from prose pieces and poetry to line drawings, to downright porno comics. But it is not all fun and games. There are some serious, straight stories on the political scene, e.g., "International harvesters—hacking the cane in Cuba." It is an unorganized, sometimes successful effort to blast the establishment via humor and hard hitting pornography. It does not always come off, but the spirit is bright, fascinating, and (if you are not offended by the shock treatment), fairly meaningful. Librarians should examine. America has too few satirical magazines, and this is, at the least, a great effort. P.S. The young people who are putting this out are perfectly sincere in trying to use humor to stir consciousness.

Harvard Lampoon. 1876. irreg.; 4–6 yr. $3. James H. Siegelman, 44 Bow St., Cambridge, Mass. 02138. Illus., adv. Circ: 6,000. Sample. Vol. ends: Jan.

Aud: Ga, Ac, Hs.

The mother, father, sister, and cousin of the *National Lampoon* advise you to take a look at the beginnings of it all. Now almost a century old, the Harvard based *Lampoon* continues to be the best of its type. While directed to Harvard students and alumni, it can be appreciated by anyone who has at least touched on a college or university campus. Of particular note is the one issue a year given to spoofing a mass circulation magazine: the entire number is put out in the format of the magazine, right down to departments and pictures. The major difference between the original and the imitation is the content, which is a take-off not only on the magazine but on its readers as well. (Everyone is waiting to see what they do with the *National Lampoon,* which was started by former staffers on the Harvard magazine.) Should be in every academic library, and the special numbers should find their way into all public and school libraries.

Journal of Irreproducible Results. 1955. 4/yr. $2. Alexander Kohn. Soc. for Basic Irreproducible Research, Box 234, Chicago Heights, Ill. 60411. Illus., Index, adv. Circ: 10,000. Sample, Vol. ends: No. 4. Refereed.

Aud: Ga, Ac, Hs.

A journal made up of impossible jargon, even more impossible theories, and a grand sense that the universe, or those who interpret it via science, is quite mad. Here scientists mock their self-righteousness, statistics, and very goals. For example, why does so much glassware disappear in science labs. The editor concocted a theory, (and an article) "The Kinetics of Inactivation of Glassware" to answer the question. The journal appeals to all of the sciences, e.g., D. D. Jackson provided a brief history of scholarly publishing, and two scientists at the University of California Medical Center provided a formula for mastering the confusion explosion. Some of it is a bit heavy, but on the whole it soars. A fine wit and humor magazine to balance off the thousands of scientific journals in any

library. And most useful too, for brighter high school students. There is one danger: the denser scientists who think and write like much of what the journal satirizes may take it seriously.

Krokodil. See USSR and East Europe/Slavic Language Section.

Mad. 1953. 8/yr. $7 for 19 issues. William M. Gaines. Albert B. Feldstein. E. C. Publns., Inc., 485 Madison Ave., New York, N.Y. 10022. Comic strips photos. Circ: 1,900,000.

Aud: Ga, Ac, Hs, Ejh. *Jv:* V.

In its constant harassment of the establishment, the culture, and the "American way," this has become the overground/underground satirical magazine of our times. Its importance in raising questions of values and standards cannot be underestimated—particularly as it is all done in a free and easy way which belies its basic purpose. Depending solely on subscriptions (there are no advertisements), the editors have built a loyal, devoted, and ever-growing audience. Although uneven in quality, *Mad* usually has one or two feature strip cartoon stories per issue which are little gems, usually those which satirize radio, television, or the movies. Artist Mort Drucker, perhaps the leading caricaturist in America today, has developed a style which is unmistakably *Mad's* and as recognizable as Alfred E. ("What—me worry?") Neuman himself. While its satirical point is often blunt, *Mad* at its best can be, and often is, uproariously funny. For a periodicals browsing collection serving readers of junior high school age and upwards.

Monocle. See *Antioch Review* in Literary Reviews Section.

National Lampoon. 1970. m. $5.95. Douglas C. Kenney. Twentieth Century Publishing Co., 635 Madison Ave., New York, N.Y. 10022. Illus., adv. Circ: 164,000. Sample.

Aud: Ac, Ga, Hs.

Somehow this offshoot of the *Harvard Lampoon* and *Mad* never found itself. Each month the editor turns to a specific theme for satire. In addition, there are regular columns and features not related to the central theme. While a national humor magazine is badly needed, some two years from its first issue, one can say with some confidence this is not that magazine. It seems tied to sophomoric concepts of humor, exploited years ago by *Mad.* Once in a while it does hit, but just barely, e.g., the September 1971 issue is given to a rough ride through the land of children's literature and magazines. Such treasures as an attack on *My Weekly Reader* and a rundown on horror toys gives anyone pause, if not a laugh. The problem seems to be the editor (s) really does not want to offend anyone, certainly does not want to challenge anyone's imagination or intellect. The humor is spelled out all too clearly. Even so, most libraries would do well to subscribe. It is about the only humor magazine we have, and acceptable to almost everyone. High schools should subscribe, but will not. Most teenagers will read it at the newsstands, or take it home along with all the other magazines the high school did not take this year.

Oz. 1967. m. $6. Collective. Oz Publns. Ltd., 52 Princedale Rd., London, SW 11, England. Illus., adv. Circ: 40,000. Sample. Microform: B&H.

Bk. rev: Various number, length. *Aud:* Ac, Ga.

Following the longest trial for obscenity in the history of England (summer of 1971), *Oz* gained worldwide attention, not to mention a jail sentence (later commuted) for its editors. The 48 to 60 page newspaper-type magazine found itself in court for language and illustrations put together in a special issue devoted to teenage interests. The court found those "interests" a bit difficult to take. In America there is not anything quite like *Oz*, although the underground papers of four or five years back come close, and some of the editorial content of the *Other Scenes Realist* is similar. But *Oz* is distinctively its own. Nothing is sacred from sex to politics, everything is up for sardonic grabs, and the editors tend to concentrate on problems which are an embarassment for the establishment. Some of the cartoons, drawings, and illustrations will leave non-British readers confused, but taken on the whole, the language employed in type or drawing is universal. It is bound to shock, or bring a chuckle—nothing in between. The 1961 trial cut back some of the more "outrageous" work, but the magazine remains required for liberal, large, and ego secure libraries.

Private Eye. 1961. bi-w. $8.40. Richard Ingrams. Pressdram Ltd., 34 Greek St., London W1, England. Illus., adv. Circ: 70,000. Sample.

Aud: Ac, Ga. *Jv:* V.

A devastating English wit and humor magazine. There is nothing quite like it in the United States—a comparison might be made between a crossing of *Mad* and the *Realist*, but the only way to appreciate *Private Eye* is to get a sample copy. The language and the cartoons are mildly shocking, and downright dangerous for politicans, whom it often attacks. The approach is ironic, belligerent. Favorite targets include royalty, the prime minister, and foreigners. Articles, stories, cartoons, and various features bring the reader face to face with some of the wittiest writing now coming out of England. If at one time it was considered an underground paper, it is now 10 years old, is published regularly, and has a growing circulation. Only the format (newsprint) gives an indication of its beginnings. It is now the leading English humor magazine. (*Punch*

is of another generation, or, at best, offers another approach.) This is recommended for just about any library where wit and humor are important. Americans will have little difficulty in understanding—particularly as Americans are sometimes a target.

Punch. 1841. w. $17.50. William Davis. Punch Publns. Ltd., 23–27 Tudor St., London EC 4Y OBD, England. Illus., index, adv. Circ: 120,000. Microform: B&H, UM.

Bk. rev: 10–12, 300–500 words, signed. *Aud:* Ac, Ga.

"Punch goes Playboy" proclaimed a headline on the cover of the early November 1971 *Punch*. And inside? A centerfold featured an artist's concept of Big Bunny Hugh Hefner. In the same issue were putdowns of New York intellectuals, in particular Norman Podhoretz, editor of *Commentary*. So it goes, but it goes a bit differently now that *Punch* has a new outlook. The outlook has changed from time to time since 1841. The format and approach remain the same, i.e., articles and cartoons poke fun at the British customs and manners. The difference now—most of the jokes are well within the grasp of the average American reader. A bit more sophisticated than most American humor (*The New Yorker* aside), but still a good bet in larger libraries, or smaller ones with a witty clientele.

The Realist. 1958. irreg. 6 issues $3. Paul Krassner, 595 Broadway, New York, N.Y. 10012. Illus. Circ: 150,000. Microform: B&H.

Indexed: API. *Aud:* Ac, Ga.

The primary question about Paul Krassner's satirical dig is its publication schedule. Although the masthead claims it is "published every other month by a non-profit corporation," no. 89 appeared in February 1971 and no. 90 showed up in November. In between there was a supplement to the *Last Whole Earth Catalog* (also called No. 90 and given a March/April publication date). Well, in any case, there is every indication that Krassner will go on forever, despite the fact that he is being sued by The Church of Scientology, makes fast trips to Europe and Mexico, and boasts three addresses. His magazine/paper (it now runs to some 55 pages, is printed on a newsprint of an even sadder quality than that used by *New Republic* and *Nation*) has become a legend in its time. Not many libraries subscribe, primarily because he features such items as "Martha Mitchell Uses Vaginal Deodorant" in the masthead, and proceeds to follow up with a serious enough Ken Kesey interview. This admixture of what is common in the *Ladies Home Journal* with material out of the political underground leaves many reader wondering what it is all about. Fortunately, many more (and hopefully a few librarians, by now) recognize that Krassner is one of the few first-rate wits we have left in America. He is rightfully compared with Lenny Bruce and H. L. Mencken, although never with

Richard Nixon or Billy Graham. The introduction to his magazine/paper seems necessary because it is unique. For those who do not know it, No. 90 is typical. In addition to material noted, there are comments by Krassner; an interview with Leslie Bacon (19, and not reading *Seventeen*); a nice exposé called "My Affair With Tricia Nixon;" a piece on communes; the parts that were left out of the *Magic Christian;* a script from "The Great American Dream Machine," etc., etc., etc. About half of it leaves the reader laughing at his own foibles and those of his fellowmen; the other half makes any sensitive person a bit ill, at least if war and politics do turn some people off. Sex is used as a weapon. It may not please some, but Krassner is not a clean fighter. Most libraries will find it too candid, which is too bad. Still, those with courage and faith in people (150,000 readers do subscribe), will subscribe to *The Realist.* I would like to see it in some high schools, too; but this may be asking too much. It is almost as bad as suggesting the high school library drop *Readers' Digest.*

Subterranean Sociology Newsletter. 1966. 3/yr. $3. Marcello Truzzi. Dept. of Sociology, New College, Sarasota, Fla. 33578. Circ: 600.

Bk. rev: 2, 1,000 words, signed. *Aud:* Ac.

"Reflects the idiosyncratic biases and personality of its editor." This is against pomposity and rejects seriousness about sociology. Truzzi argues that sociology at present lacks a "common data language," and "has no philosophically valid explanatory theory (since no true laws have been discovered yet) and is too often ritualistically involved in presenting the appearance of a developed science through a facade of a statistical and methodological rigor which belies its real contributions to knowledge, and . . . takes itself far too seriously." This light-hearted publication includes such articles as "The Ice Cube: A Sociological Analysis," "An All Purpose Form Letter For the Busy Sociologist," "How to Succeed in Sociology Without Really Trying." Departments include "Editorial Rantings; Announcements and Correspondence; Unfunded Research; Unpublished Materials of Interest in Irregular Sources; TSSN Lyrical Interlude; Student Quotes; Fuzzy Insights and Random Observations, and Unnoticed Classics." A charming spoof on the pomposity of many "learned journals," a pleasure to read, and a source of unusual highly specialized information.

INDIANS (AMERICAN)

Basic Periodicals

Ejh: *Weewish Tree;* Hs: *Akwesasne Notes, Amerindian;* Ga: *Akwesasne Notes, Amerindian, Indian Historian;* Jc, Ac: *Akwesasne Notes, American Indigena, Indian Historian, Indian Affairs, North.*

Library and Teaching Aids

Journal of American Indian Education.

General

Akwesasne Notes. 1969. m. (except Feb., Aug. and Nov.). $5 (plus contributions). Rarihokwats. Wesleyan Univ., Indian Studies Program, Middletown, Conn. Subs. to: Akwesasne Notes, Mohawk Nation via Rooseveltown, N.Y. 13683. Illus., adv. Circ: 21,000. Sample. Vol. ends: Dec. Microform: B&H.

Bk. rev: 4–6, 250 words. *Aud:* Ac, Ga, Hs. *Jv:* V.

Early numbers are out of print (but available on microfilm) which supports the impression that this is the single best ongoing report of American Indian life. It should have a considerably wider circulation than it now enjoys. The 44 to 50 page tabloid newspaper covers all aspects of Indian affairs from culture and art to politics and literature. The emphasis, though, is on a reasonable request for equal rights for Indians. (While issued out of New York, the editor takes on the problems of his brothers and sisters throughout the United States, including Alaska and Hawaii.) The touch of the Wesleyan University Advisors can be found in the frequent articles pointing out biases against the Indian in textbooks, films, television, and even civil service examinations. But what makes this paper unique is its wide coverage, total commitment, and diversity of interests. The illustrations, photographs, and even posters are as good as the lucid prose. Some particularly valuable features for libraries include: "Resources," a full page review and listing of books and paperbacks concerned with American Indians; "Indian Press," both a listing and a lifting of quotes from other Indian newspapers/and periodicals; and notes and commentataries on legal matters involving Indians. Aside from the news there are frequent historical articles, poetry, and touches of prose. And the letters to the editors from both Indians and other Americans are worth the price of admission. The whole is professional, impressive, and should be in every library from high school through university. (The subscription price is a contribution, and it can be less, one supposes, if your library is that hard up.)

America Indigena. 1940. q. $6. Inter-American Indian Inst., Nionos Heroes 139, Mexico 7, DF. Illus., index. Circ: 3,000. Sample. Vol. ends: Oct.

Indexed: HistAb, LatAm. *Bk. rev:* 6, 1–2 pages, signed. *Aud:* Ac.

A combination of technical and semipopular articles on the Indians in the Americas, particularly in Latin America. There is equal emphasis between current day activities and difficulties of the Indians, and the historical and anthropological aspects of the tribes. Two useful features: an annual listing of dissertations in cultural and social anthropology dealing with Indian life, and the *Indianist Yearbook* (December issue) which is concerned with Indian community development.

American Indian Law Newsletter. 1968. bi-w. $14. Joseph B. Sabatini. American Indian Law Center, Univ. of New Mexico School of Law, Albuquerque, N. Mex. 87106. Index. Circ: 530. Sample.

Aud: Ac.

A brief newsletter which reports on cases pending and decided which have anything to do with American Indians. It covers Congressional action in Indian affairs and reviews legislation, bills passed and pending. There are also official statements released by Indian and government leaders. An essential item in larger collections.

Americans Before Columbus. 1970. m. $5. 3102 Central S.E., Albuquerque, N. Mex. 87106.

Aud: Ga.

A type of underground newspaper, and one of the best of its kind. Carries news of Indian student protests, actions, and law suits, as well as articles, editorials, and other material directed to young, militant Indians. Not as complete or as informative as *Akwesasne Notes.*

The Amerindian; American Indian review. 1952. bi-m. $4. Marion E. Gridley, 1263 W. Pratt Blvd., Chicago, Ill. 60623. Illus., adv. Circ: 1,800. Sample. Vol. ends: July/Aug.

Bk. rev: 10–12, 50 words. *Aud:* Ga, Hs.

An eight-page news bulletin about all American Indians. The editor "seeks to present the Indian people with human dignity and in terms of accomplishment and endeavor." The nonprofit organization's efforts include brief articles about people, events, legislation, etc. The reporting is objective, represents primarily the work of the editor who has published 17 books on Indian subjects. (In 1971 she received a certificate of commendation from President Nixon "in recognition of exceptional service to others.") What this bulletin lacks in length it makes up for in substance. Particularly useful for all libraries because of the numerous, short, critical reviews of books about Indians.

Blue Cloud Quarterly. 1954. q. $1. Benet Tvedten. Blue Cloud Abbey, Marvin, S. Dak. 57251. Illus. Circ: 11,000. Sample.

Aud: Ga, Hs, Ejh.

A little magazine which centers around the American Indian. Published at a Benedictine Monastery, it demonstrates careful attention to format, and one of the really fine things about each issue is the illustrations. There are no religious overtones. The journal has covered such things as the Indian songs of Buffy

Sainte-Marie (with photographs from the Smithsonian), myths and legends of the plains Indians, and poems by students at the Institute of American Indian Arts in Sante Fe. An imaginative, inexpensive, and first rate addition for all libraries, regardless of size or type.

The Drum. 1966. w. $15 (Within the territory $10). T. Butters, Box 1069, Inuvik, Northwest Territory, Canada. Illus., adv. Circ: 1,200.

Aud: Ga.

An eight-page tabloid newspaper which is primarily a weekly report on events in the northern communities of Canada, Inuvik and Yellowknive. Oil seems to be the principal concern, followed by news about local residents. The Eskimo population is considered, but in no special way, and by no stretch of the imagination can this be considered a voice of the Eskimo or Indian. It is more—it is a voice for the whole population. And while of limited interest to anyone outside of the Territory, it is listed here to dispel the idea that it is solely an Eskimo newspaper—a notion that pops up from time to time in bibliographies.

The Indian. m. $3. American Indian Leadership Council, Rt. 3, Box 9, Rapid City, S. Dak. 57701. Sample.

Aud: Ga.

One of the better newspapers published by and for Indians. An average 12-page issue features news of interest to Indians in the Dakota area, but goes beyond that to include items of national interest. Features stories on all aspects of the Indian's social, political, economic, and artistic life. And while primarily a newspaper, it does include some poetry and prose.

Indian Affairs. 1922. q. Membership (Contributions $10 to $100, Students $5). Mary G. Byler. Assn. on Amer. Indian Affairs, 432 Park Ave. S., New York, N.Y. 10016. Illus. Circ: 55,000.

Aud: Ac, Ga, Hs.

A four to six page newsletter published by a nonprofit group dedicated to helping the American Indian. Short articles discuss current events of interest to Indians and Eskimos, e.g., native land rights in Alaska, restoration of Blue Lake to the people of Taos Pueblo, etc. Each issue also has a listing of AIAA grants to students. Membership is open to anyone interested, and includes people from every walk of life and every age group. A basic report for the library with a collection in Indian life and history.

Indian Eskimo Association of Canada. Bulletin. 1960. 5/yr. $3. Dianne MacKay. Indian-Eskimo Assn. of Canada, 277 Victoria St., Toronto, 2, Canada.

Aud: Ac, Ga.

The bulletin reports on various activities of the Association and tends to run to the technical and the financial. However, let it be noted that the Association publishes a number of pamphlets and other items which are invaluable to teachers and students. (Send for the free publications list which is revised annually.)

Indian Historian. 1964. q. $6. Jeannette Henry. American Indian Historical Soc., Inc., 1451 Masonic Ave., San Francisco, Calif. 94117. Index. Circ: 16,233.

Bk. rev: Various number, length. *Aud:* Ac, Ga, Hs.

The official publication of the American Indian Historical Society, this is edited by American Indian scholars and native historians. The title is perhaps misleading in that there is as much emphasis on contemporary events and problems as on history, and in that it is aimed at the concerned layman as well as the specialist. Areas covered, in addition to history, are anthropology, education, current affairs and issues, politics, psychology, and the arts. Each issue (of about 60 pages) contains approximately a dozen articles, most of which are followed by a bibliography, sometimes quite an extensive one. A poetry section usually contains the work of contemporary poets, although some space is devoted to English translations of older Indian poetry. Film reviews appear occasionally. An attractive feature is the cover (front and back) displaying sometimes appropriate photographs, sometimes reproductions of Indian drawings and paintings. If the budget allows only one American Indian magazine, this should be it. See the Society's *Weewish Tree*—a new magazine for younger children.

Indian Record. 1938. bi-m. $2. Rev. G. Laviolette. Oblate Fathers, 1301 Wellington Crescent, Winnipeg, 9, Man., Canada. Illus., index. Sample.

Bk. rev: Various number, length. *Aud:* Ga.

A brief report on various activities of both the local and national Indians. It has some importance because of the attention given to historical material and Indian culture. Primarily, however, for larger Canadian libraries.

Indian Truth. 1924. q. $5. Indian Rights Assn., 1505 Race St., Philadelphia, Pa. 19102. Illus. Sample.

Aud: Ga, Ac.

One of the oldest organizations working for the rights of the American Indians. Membership is primarily non-Indian, and there is almost as much interest in the Indian's culture and history as in his social and political welfare. It is an important publication for those who are working for Indian improvement, and it should be in larger collections.

Journal of American Indian Education. 1961. 3/yr. (Oct., Jan. and May). $3.50. George A. Gill. Center for Indian Education, Arizona State Univ., Tempe, Ariz. 85281. Sample.

Bk. rev: Various number, length. *Aud:* Ac, Hs, Ejh.

The only magazine devoted entirely to the education of the American Indian. It considers all levels from elementary through university. The articles are by Indians and non-Indians, but all represent careful thought and attention to the needs of youth. There is a minimum of jargon, a maximum of how-to-do-it. Should be found in any collection where there is the slightest involvement with education of Indians.

Masterkey. See Anthropology Section.

Mustang Review. 1965. s-a. $2. Karl Edd, 212 S. Broadway, Denver, Colo. 80209. Illus. Circ: 800.

Aud: Ga.

A small Indian poetry magazine for the man or woman who likes straight, easy to understand poetry. "Emphasis is on regional grass roots poetry of the Imagist type. We like Hart Crane and Carl Sandburg." And anyone who enjoys Sandburg (although possibly not the more difficult Crane) will appreciate the entries in this pocket sized magazine. Some line drawings.

North. 1954. bi-m. $3. Jane Pequegnat. Information Canada, 171 Slater St., Ottawa, Canada. Illus., adv. Circ: 5,000. Vol. ends: Nov./Dec.

Indexed: CanI. *Bk. rev:* 2–3, 150–250 words. *Aud:* Ga, Ac, Hs.

Published every second month by the Department of Indian Affairs and Northern Development, Ottawa, the publication is a journal of information and opinion. Views expressed are not necessarily those of the Department.

About ten articles, signed and with authors' credentials, grace each issue of this attractive magazine. The authors are freelance writers, historians, staffers for other Canadian journals, research scholars, and the like. The scope includes the many aspects of life and activity in this beautiful and forbidding territory; sample articles include "flying banks" that service arctic communities; health care in the eastern arctic; snowmobiles that are replacing dog teams; archeological discoveries in northern Newfoundland and on Baffin Island of significant historical import. The contributions are generally lucidly written and invariably interesting. Of excellence are photostories on various topics—routes, mountains, villages—and the photography is splended.

Recurring features include: "The North in Review"—two or three briefly noted books on pertinent subjects, such as Eskimos; "Face of the North"—a photograph of some scene of natural beauty, like Alexandra Falls in the Northwest Territories.

Recommended for academic, public, and high school libraries. (J.M.)

Northian. 1964. q. $5. Jerry Hammersmith. Soc. for Indian and Northern Education, Univ. of Saskatchewan, Saskatoon, Sask., Canada. Illus. Circ: 900.

Bk. rev: Various number, length. *Aud:* Ac, Hs, Ejh.

Aimed at "teachers in Indian, Eskimo, and northern schools and contains articles for all persons interested in the north" primarily Canada. (But a large proportion of its contents are applicable to Alaska.) Relevant, also, for those concerned with the education of Indian (and other) children in other areas of the United States, for the topics treated include such areas as the cultural relevance of textbooks. This magazine has encountered hard times. The format changed from printed magazine (vol. 7, no. 3, Summer 1970) to mimeograph (vol. 7, no. 4). Each issue ranges from 30 to 50 pages and contains seven to nine articles. Regular features include book reviews (mainly textbooks), poems, and letters. Although photographs disappeared with the printed format, attractive drawings continue in the processed issues. Essential for school libraries in the relevant areas, and for college libraries there with an interest in producing potential teachers.

Our Native Land. 1964. m. $1. Elizabeth Samson. Canadian Broadcasting Corp., Box 500, Terminal A, Toronto, 116, Ont., Canada. Circ: 1,350. Sample.

Aud: Ac, Ga, Hs.

A two to four page mimeographed newsletter which is the basis of a Canadian broadcast by the same name. Short news items report on activities of Canadian Indians, particularly in eastern and central Canada; give short biographical sketches; and from time to time note legal and government decisions which are of importance to Indians. While of limited use to most U.S. libraries, it should be a required item north of the border—and, too, it indicates the type of thing which a local library might carry out with cooperation from interested parties.

Plains Anthropologist. See Anthropology Section.

Weewish Tree; a magazine of Indian America for young people. 1971. 6/during school yr. $6.50. Jeannette Henry. American Indian Historical Soc., 1451 Masonic Ave., San Francisco, Calif. 94117. Illus., index. Circ: 10,000. Sample. Vol. ends: Nov.

Bk. rev: 1-2, notes, signed. *Aud:* Ejh. *Jv:* V.

The editors claim this is a first. This is hard to believe, but apparently it is truly the first magazine for children devoted entirely to Indians. The 40-page, illustrated, pocket-sized magazine by and about American Indians is "useful for young people from the age of six to sixteen." Most of the material is illustrated with line drawings which are excellent when they employ traditional Indian symbols, and awful when they tend to be cute. Fortunately, most depend on the former formula. There are eight to ten articles, stories, and poems. The legends, games, how-to-do-it crafts, etc., are from all tribes, and are handled in a direct and usually interesting fashion. Most material is for an older child's reading level, although of interest to those in early grades. The editors recognize this, suggest reading it aloud to younger children. In addition to the articles there are book reviews, and a "Weewish dictionary" which lists some dozen words used in the magazine. The material is authentic, well written, and particularly useful for the Indian child seeking some kind of image of himself. And, of course, it will offer much for the non-Indian child as well. An important publication by the founders of the adult *Indian Historian.*

Wloptoonakun; the good word. 1971. bi-a. $1. Georgetta Stonefish Ryan. Bleb Press, Box 322, Times Square Sta., New York, N.Y. 10036. Circ: 500. Sample. Vol. ends: Winter.

Aud: Ga, Ac, Hs.

A small, mimeographed, poetry magazine which is different in that the contributors are almost completely limited to American Indians and Eskimos—or those closely associated with them. The poetry is of more interest for what it has to say about a little-understood modern group of Americans, than for the style. (Objectively, one might find fault with the lack of polish—but no one who ever read William Carlos Williams can fault the poetry for lack of feeling.) All in all, a fascinating approach, and one which should be of considerable value to any reader. A good choice for high schools, too.

NEWSPAPERS AND BULLETINS. There are a number of newspapers, bulletins, and tabloids published by and for American Indians. Most of these are modestly priced—many are free to libraries. Aside from those annotated in the main section, here are others with information that is sketchy, but hopefully enough for the interested librarian. (Samples will usually be sent by the publisher.)

American Indian News. 5 Tudor City Pl., New York, N.Y. 10017.

American Indian Student Assn. Newsletter. 1314 Social Science Tower, Univ. of Minnesota, Minneapolis, Minn. 55455.

Chanta Anupa (Choctaw Times). 1725 Linden, Nashville, Tenn. 37212.

Chemehuevi Newsletter. 2804 W. Ave. 31, Los Angeles, Calif. 90065.

Cherokee One Feather. Box 501, Cherokee, N.C. 28719.

Cherokee Nation News. 1968. w. Oklahoma residents $3.50; others $4. Sue Thompson. Cherokee Nation of Oklahoma, Cherokee Industrial Site, Box 119, Tahlequeh, Okla. 74464.

Columbia River and Yakima News. Box 5, Cooks, Washington.

Indian Free Press. N'Amerind Friendship Centre, 613 Wellington St., London, 12, Ont., Canada.

Indian Reporter. m. $1. 3254 Orange St., Riverside, Calif. 92501.

An offset local paper which reports on activities of the California Indians, particularly in southern California. Of limited interest.

Indian Sportsman. 1971. bi-m. San Jose Indian Athletic Assn., 90 S. Second St., San Jose, Calif. 95113.

A newsletter covering all areas of Indian sports, including rodeos.

Kenomadiwin News. Box 402, Thunder Bay F., Ont., Canada.

Maine Indian Newsletter. m. $2. 42 Liberty St., Gardiner, Maine.

A mimeographed journal of some 19 to 30 pages with news and historical items on Indians living in and around Maine.

Many Smokes. 1966. q. $2. Sun Bear, Box 5895, Reno, Nev. 89503. Illus., adv. Circ: 5,300.

A local paper of some 18 to 25 pages, but it enjoys a national reputation. Considerable emphasis on historical material.

Navajo Times. w. $5. Windown Rock, Ariz. 86515.

Published by the Navajo council, and, as such, the official paper of the Tribe. Averages some 36 pages of local and national news.

Nishnawbe News. Room 214, Kaye Hall, Northern Mich. Univ., Marquette, Mich. 49855.

Northwest Indian News. 1900 Boren Ave., Seattle, Wash. 98101.

Northwest Indian Times. Box 2772, Spokane, Wash. 99220.

Papago Indian News. m. $1. Papago Indians, Sells, Ariz.

Powwow Trails. 10/yr. $4. Box 258, South Plainfield, N.J. 07080.

An arts and crafts magazine with how-to-do-it information on construction of various Indian items. Suitable for young people.

Rainbow People (Supersedes *Cherokee Examiner*). 1969. bi-m. $3. N. Magowan, Box 164, John Day, Ore. 97845.

A nicely edited newspaper/magazine which reports primarily on local Indian activities, but does include some illustrated articles on history, crafts, and culture.

River Times. 1971. Fairbanks Native Community Center, 102 Lacey, Fairbanks, Alaska 99701.

Rough Rock News. Rough Rock Demonstration School. Chinle, Ariz.

Sentinel. 1968. irreg. $3. National Congress of Amer. Indians. 1346 Connecticut Ave., N.W., Washington, D.C. 20036.

A mimeographed newsletter which reports on activities of the Congress—an organization dedicated to fighting for the rights of the American Indians.

Siksika. 1971. Box 125, Gleichen, Alta., Canada.

A 10-page mimeographed newsletter of the Blackfoot Reserve. Articles, fiction, announcements, etc.

Sota Eva Ye Yapi. Sisseton, S. Dak.

Southern Ute Drum. Ignacio, Colo. 81137.

Sun Trails. 1971. Supo. 20929. Univ. of Arizona, Tucson, Ariz.

A literary quarterly which is a vehicle for creative expression of the American Indian people, particularly Indian students.

Tundra Times. w. $8. Box 1287, Fairbanks, Alaska 99701.

An 8 to 16 page weekly newspaper which fights for the rights of the Eskimo, Indian, and Alaska natives. Important to all for reporting current activities in Alaska.

Wardrums. American Indian Cultural Workshop, 1165 Broadway, New York, N.Y.

Warpath, irreg. $5. Box 26149, San Francisco, Calif. 94126.

The voice of the United Native Americans, a militant Indian group. Carries strong articles on Indian rights. Some material on culture and arts.

Yakima Nation Review. Box 632. Toppenish, Wash. 98948.

INTERIOR DESIGN

Basic Periodicals

Hs: *House and Garden;* Ga: *House Beautiful, House and Garden.*

Apartment Ideas; the magazine of better apartment living. 1969. q. $3. Meredith Corp., 1716 Locust St., Meredith Bldg., Des Moines, Iowa 50303.

Aud: Ga.

While there are some parts of this magazine that will be of value only to apartment dwellers, much of it will be of general interest. Many of the decorating ideas are specifically for apartments (including one room apartments) but some are relevant to any decorating area. Decorating, however, is only one of the aspects of apartment life covered. Others are crafts, travel, savvy shopping, food and entertaining, apartment information (general information for apartment life), and the regular feature, Library of Planning Ideas (booklets to send for). The decorating ideas and the additional features place the magazine well above average interest. (J.M.)

Better Homes and Gardens. 1922. m. $4. (Regionally edited for nine different areas of the country.) James Autry. Meredith Corp., 1716 Locust St., Des Moines, Iowa 50336. Illus., adv. Circ: 7,777,777. Sample.

Indexed: AbrRG, RG. *Aud:* Ga, Hs.

Catering to America's middle class home and family way of life, "this is a home and family service encyclopedia of ideas and advice for better living." To help families plan activities, staff contributors offer step-by-step easily understandable information in such areas as food, decorating, building, gardening, travel, creative sewing and crafts, money management, and family health. The whole is attractively illustrated; the advice is generally sound. Circulation is primarily among American women who may not have yet caught up with the Women's Liberation movement (the editor is a man). Be that as it may, a practical addition for almost any public or high school library.

Budget Decorating. 1964. q. $3. Maco Publishing Co., 800 Second Ave., New York, N.Y. 10017. Circ: 200,000.

Aud: Ga.

The word "budget" in the title would tend to imply that the decorating ideas within the magazine are inexpensive. However, to quote the magazine itself, "'budget' is a noun as well as an adjective. A budget is a guideline and it doesn't always mean inexpensive. We try to show you value for your money, not just a great deal for your money." Instructions for a few do-it-yourself ideas, recipes, and where to write for information on featured merchandise are included. About one half of the photographs are in black and white, the others in color. The major drawback: no prices are given for items shown in the articles. (J.M.)

House Beautiful. 1896. m. $7. Wallace Guenther. Hearst Corp., 717 Fifth Ave., New York, N.Y. 10022. Illus., adv. Circ: 862,227.

Indexed: RG. *Aud:* Ga.

A close competitor for the same audience as *House and Garden*, this is designed for those who can afford and enjoy the "good life." Colorfully illustrated articles supply ideas concerning designing and building new homes, remodeling old ones, decorating in the modern and traditional styles. Landscaping, gardening, home furnishings and accessories, gourmet cooking, menu planning, travel, and entertainment are all discussed. Ideas and plans offered are seldom original; usually they are copies of work done for some famous celebrity or wealthy personality. The magazine is noted for its extensive offering of purchasing sources and prices of unusual items. Similar to *House and Garden*, and the choice between the two is a matter of personal preference.

House Beautiful's Decorating for Brides and Young Marrieds. 1968. s-a. $1.35 per no. Hearst Magazines Division, 717 Fifth Ave., New York, N.Y. 10022.

Aud: Ga.

Similar to *House Beautiful* in format, this is a large glossy magazine consisting mainly of photographs. (A fair number of the photographs are, in fact, directly from *House Beautiful*.) The magazine is thicker, with less advertising than most of the decorating magazines. Only one thing sets this apart: it is aimed at the newly married. There is a regular feature "Your Bridal Bookshelf," a bibliography of free or inexpensive booklets from a variety of companies specializing in everything related to decorating. Some attempt is made to scale down the typical decorating extravaganzas to apart-

ment size and modest pocketbook, but one gets the feeling that for most young marrieds this will be strictly a "wish-book" and of little practical value. (J.M.)

House and Garden. 1901. m. $7. Mary Jane Pool. Conde Nast Publns., Inc., 420 Lexington Ave., New York, N.Y. 10017. Illus., index, adv. Circ: 1,375,000. Microform: UM.

Indexed: RG. *Aud:* Ga, Hs.

A guide to the ultimate in luxurious living in which the decorating arts predominate. Beautiful photographs, artistically presented, should inspire students and general readers. Articles feature analysis of homes by leading architects and decorators. The editorial policy dictates that ideas for homes and hobbies fit the personality. A few pages are devoted to music and travel and each issue features a cookbook section. Suggestions are directed toward those with a cultivated interest in fine homes, furnishings and decor. Although geared for upper income groups, the magazine has a value for any reader with imagination and the ability to adapt expensive ideas to a modest home or checkbook.

Interior Design. 1932. m. $9. Sherman Emery. Whitney Communications Corp, Interior Design Div., 150 E. 58th St., New York, N.Y. 10022. Illus,, adv. Circ: 30,000.

Indexed: ArtI. *Bk. rev:* 2–4, 250–500 words. *Aud:* Sa, Ac.

Primarily a trade journal for both professional residential and contract interior decorators, the articles are keyed more towards business than aesthetics. The editors presuppose an educated audience which is interested in source of supply, and current trends in everything from antiques to floor covering. For all large academic and special libraries.

Interiors. 1888. m. $9. Olga Gueft. Whitney Publns., Inc., 130 E. 59th St., New York, N.Y. 10022. Illus., adv. Circ: 30,000. Microform: UM.

Indexed: ArtI. *Bk. rev:* 5–6, brief, signed. *Aud:* Sa, Ac.

"Published for the Interior Designers Group which includes: interior designers, architects, and industrial designers, who offer interior designing services, and the interior decorating departments of retail stores." Each issue is devoted to a special topic, and excellent black and white plates illustrate the articles. There are brief news notes of what designers are doing, forthcoming exhibitions and competitions, and a large advertising section of products used for interiors. Primarily for the professional architect and designer, but useful for graduate students.

One Thousand and One Decorating Ideas. 1941. q. (English edition); s-a. (Spanish edition). 75¢ per copy.

Conso Publishing Co., 149 Fifth Ave., New York, N.Y. 10010. Circ: 1,000,000.

Aud: Ga.

Individual decorating ideas predominate, rather than large integrated systems. There are few schemes for an entire room. Instead, there are many small ideas concentrating on one restricted area or piece of furniture. The "Shoppers Guide" gives the addresses of the manufacturers of the featured items and also gives approximate prices. Most photographs are in color. There is a large do-it-yourself section covering both home decorating and crafts. Available also in a Spanish edition. (J.M.)

Pool 'N Patio. 1961. s-a. free. Fay Coupe. General Publns. Ltd., 3923 W. 6th St., Los Angeles, Calif. 90005. Circ: 150,000.

Aud: Ga.

A free publication edited for pool owners in all parts of the country, not just California. The average issue features articles on how to care for the pool, landscaping methods of enlarging an existing facility or planning for a new one, types of entertainment and parties to build around a pool, and usually one or two items on water safety. There is nonevaluative advice on new products. Meant to be distributed by pool dealers, the magazine has considerable value and interest for libraries where the outdoor sport is popular. As it is free, all public libraries should try it, and certainly many pool owners will be grateful to learn about the magazine.

Sunset; the magazine of western living. 1898. m. $3 to western states and Hawaii; others $5. Proctor Mellquist. Lane Magazine & Book Co., Menlo Park, Calif. 94025. Illus., adv. Circ: 1,026,000.

Indexed: RG. *Aud:* Ga.

Primarily a western states version of *Better Homes and Gardens* and *Good Housekeeping.* The editors carefully combine all aspects of white, middle class living interests into their well produced magazine, filled with advertising. Gardens, travel, home, cooking, family relationships, good humor bits, personalities, how-to-do-it, etc., etc., etc.—and all at a relatively sophisticated level. We are all in this land of honey together, so let us make the most of it. The material is clear, well written, and usually nicely illustrated. The magazine is a help for someone who is trying to make his or her home a life's career. And it has a given charm for the apartment dweller, too. All in all, harmless, sometimes helpful, and certainly pleasant. One wonders why it is indexed in *Readers' Guide* since the magazine is essentially a regional item, of limited interest to anyone living in mid-America or on the East coast.

JOURNALISM AND WRITING

See also Communications & Media Section.

Basic Periodicals

JOURNALISM. Ga: *Editor & Publisher;* Jc: *Journalism Quarterly, Editor & Publisher;* Ac: *Journalism Quarterly, Editor & Publisher, Nieman Reports, Quill.*

JOURNALISM REVIEWS. Hs: *Columbia Journalism Review;* Ga: *Columbia Journalism Review;* local or regional journalism review. Jc & Ac: *Columbia Journalism Review, Chicago Journalism Review;* local or regional journalism review.

Library and Teaching Aids

Quill & Scroll, Scholastic Editor.

Cessations

Writer's Forum.

Journalism

American Press; the monthly feature magazine for newspaper management. 1882. m. $5. C. O. Schlaver. American Press Magazine Inc., 651 Council Hill Rd., Dundee, Ill. 60118. Illus., adv. Circ: 13,600. Sample. Vol. ends: Dec.

Aud: Ac, Ga.

"The nation's only independent journal for the entire newspaper management," useful in journalism departments of colleges and universities. "Newspaper Production," a special interest section, is applicable to the smaller publishers. It includes two or three articles plus columns on "Offset and Photomechanics" and "Look at Letterpress." "Suburban Publisher" is a person-to-person account of one publisher's improvement or success story. Among the other departments are "Tools of the Trade," a survey of newspaper production equipment, and regular stories on newspaper operations.

Catholic Journalist. 1945. m. $3. James A. Doyle. Catholic Press Assn., 432 Park Ave. S., New York, N.Y. 10016. Illus., adv. Circ: 2,500.

Index: CathI. *Bk. rev:* 5–10, notes to 250 words. *Aud:* Ga, Ac.

Serving the editors and publishers of a large segment of the journalism world, *Catholic Journalist* emphasizes material which will help the key executive make a profitable thing of his enterprise. In a sense, then, this is a combination of *Editor & Publisher* and *Advertising Age.* The emphasis is on current news about publishing markets, how-to-do-it, and there is little of a scholarly or, for that matter, crusading nature. It is primarily a trade journal. Although the material is keyed to Catholic publications, much of it is applicable to all newspapers and magazines. The editor comments: "Suggest you cancel this listing. We still publish, but not for librarians." We disagree, but let each library determine its own policy regarding this useful publication.

Columbia Scholastic Press Advisers Association. Bulletin. 1941. q. $4. James F. Paschal, Box 11, Central Mail Room, Columbia Univ., New York, N.Y. 10027. Illus. Circ: 2,000. Sample. Vol. ends: Winter.

Bk. rev: Various number, length. *Aud:* Hs, Ejh.

Primarily for secondary school and some elementary school teachers who teach journalism and direct the activities of the school newspaper, magazine, and yearbook. A number of practical articles give advice, solve problems, suggest methods of improvement, both in the publications and in methods of teaching. Examples are usually cited, and case histories are common. Larger problems of censorship, the role of the school newspaper, etc., are considered. A basic teaching aid for all school libraries.

Editor & Publisher—The Fourth Estate; spot news and features about newspapers, advertisers & agencies. (Annual numbers: *International Year Book; Market Guide*). 1884. w. $10. Jerome Walker. Editor & Publisher Co., 850 Third Ave., New York, N.Y. 10022. Illus., adv. Circ: 25,627. Sample. Vol. ends: Dec. Microform: B&H.

Indexed: BusI. *Bk. rev:* 1, ½ page. *Aud:* Ac, Ga.

The newspaperman's trade journal, this weekly reports on all aspects of journalism from reporting to advertising. The behind-the-scenes stories of newspapers and personalities make it of value to both journalism students and informed laymen. Background stories about reporters and photographers and articles on the sometimes difficult task of getting the news are well written. Editorials are short, pointed, and directed toward the improvement of newspapers and the reduction of abuses both by and of them. Regular features cover various areas: layout and design, advertising, circulation, printing equipment, photography, syndicated features. As both a trade and a professional journal, it is a required item in any journalism/advertising collection. The less specialized collection will turn first to the *Columbia Journalism Review* or *Journalism Quarterly.*

Journalism Quarterly; devoted to research in journalism and mass communications. 1924. q. $10. Edwin Emery, Sch. of Journalism, 111 Murphy Hall, Univ. of Minnesota, Minneapolis, Minn. 55455. Illus., index, adv. Circ: 4,000. Sample. Vol. ends: Winter. Refereed. Microform: UM.

Indexed: PAIS, PsyAb. *Bk. rev:* 30–40, length varies, signed. *Aud:* A, Ga. *Jv:* V.

The oldest single effort to analytically examine the national and international media, this set the pattern of a number of related reviews and newsletters which only recently have taken up the same concern. It differs from the current reports in that there is more emphasis on scholarship and long range studies than on topical issues. Articles are devoted to almost every aspect of communication from women's magazines to public opinion polls. Each of the contributions is well documented, normally written in a fashion intelligible to any educated layman. There are, to be sure, pragmatic contributions on how to do this or that well, but the emphasis is on research. The full book reviews are excellent, the best single source of information on new publications in every aspect of communications. In addition, there are selected bibliographies of articles, book lists, and summaries of major doctoral and master's theses. Research in progress, methods of teaching journalism, statistics on enrollment, etc., are included. In view of its broad field of interest, this is a magazine which should be found in all medium to large-sized public and academic libraries.

Nieman Reports. 1947. q. $5. Dwight E. Sargent. Soc. of Nieman Fellows, 48 Trowbridge, Cambridge, Mass. 02138. Circ: 2,500.

Bk. rev: Various number, length. *Aud:* Ac, Ga.

A liberal, working journalist's point of view is reflected here. Nieman Fellows are selected for a year at Harvard on the basis of their education and achievements. Only a few are chosen each year, and the *Nieman Reports* represents the writings of both present and past Fellows. Every topic of interest to a journalist is covered, from propaganda and politics to the reporting of the arts and bathing beauty contests. The book reviews are some of the best available and, this side of *Journalism Quarterly*, offer the widest, fullest selection for the librarian or journalist. Another feature which makes it particularly useful for reference is the republishing of major statements on the press by national and international leaders.

Quill; a magazine for journalists. 1912. m. $5. Charles Long. Sigma Delta Chi, 35 E. Wacker Dr., Chicago, Ill. 60601. Illus., index, adv. Circ: 23,000. Sample. Vol. ends: Dec. Microform: UM.

Bk. rev: 10, 300 words, signed. *Aud:* Ac.

The publication of the professional journalism society, Sigma Delta Chi, this features news of the organization and its members. It has wider interest in that there are frequently articles on the ethics of the press, censorship, biographies, advertising, radio, television, photography, and free lance writing, as well as newspaper and magazine work. Emphasis is on the philosophy that journalism is a profession, not simply a trade.

Quill and Scroll. 1926. q. $2.50. Lester G. Benz. Quill & Scroll Corp., School of Journalism, Univ. of Iowa,

Iowa City, Iowa 52240. Illus., adv. Circ: 31,750. Vol. ends: Apr./May.

Bk. rev: 8–12, notes, signed. *Aud:* Hs, Ejh.

A two-part magazine. The first consists of articles on how to improve the high school and junior high newspaper, annual, and other publications. The second section consists of news, biographies, and reports of events about school newspapers throughout the country. There is considerable emphasis on the ethics of journalism. The editor reports that journalism advisers in schools "consider *Quill and Scroll* as the top magazine in our field." No argument. Somewhat similar in approach, although far from as popular, is *Scholastic Editor.*

Scholastic Editor; graphics/communications. 1921. m. $5.75. Kristi Hawkinson. 18 Journalism Bldg., Univ. of Minnesota, Minneapolis, Minn. 55455. Illus., adv. Circ: 3,500. Sample. Vol. ends: May.

Aud: Ac, Hs, Ejh.

A how-to-do-it magazine for editors and teachers who have anything to do with school publications. Articles, usually derived from personal experience or the training of experts, tell how to put together newspapers, yearbooks, and magazines; give tips on how to succeed as a journalist or editor, methods of writing, markets, and the like. While this processed magazine includes information at the college level, the primary emphasis is on the high school student effort. One of the best for journalism classes. See also *Quill and Scroll.*

Journalism Reviews

In the past few years the reporters, writers, and creative men and women in communications have called for a more socially responsive voice in the affairs of newspapers—and television, radio, and film. Their views are best expressed in the journalism reviews. The reviews are of particular interest to the informed layman because they often tell the real story behind the story, cut through the self-imposed censorship. At least one or two should be found in most libraries—and as their numbers grow each year, this is not difficult. Usually there is at least one such review in the immediate or regional area.

Chicago Journalism Review. 1968. m. $5. Ron Dorfman. Assn. of Working Press, Inc., 11 E. Hubbard, Chicago, Ill. 60611. Illus. Circ: 9,000. Sample. Vol. ends: Dec.

Aud: Ac, Ga, Hs. *Jv:* V.

Having grown from 6 to 24 pages, and from a newspaper to a regular magazine format, this is one of the more influential and important of the journalism reviews, i.e., it ranks with *Columbia Journalism Review.* The purpose is to critically evaluate the media, not only in Chicago, but in surrounding areas. (Some articles have touched on journalism in Europe, Asia, and South America, not to mention Philadelphia.) Contributors include hundreds of reporters for local newspapers, and broadcasters, as well as working members of such national newspapers and magazines as *Time, Newsweek, The New York Times, Variety,* and others. Editorial assistant Bob Kamman says: "Our assumption is that the mistakes, omissions and distortions of the mass media are not going to be reported by those who make them, so a new kind of publication—a journalism review—is necessary. Eighty percent of our subscribers are not involved in the profession; rather, they're just newspaper reading, TV-watching people who want or need to be well-informed." A first choice for the Midwest, and second only to the Columbia publication for all libraries.

Columbia Journalism Review. 1962. bi-m. $9. Alfred Balk. Grad. Sch. of Journalism, Columbia Univ., New York, N.Y. 10027. Illus., index. Circ: 15,000. Sample. Vol. ends: March/Apr. Refereed.

Indexed: PAIS. *Bk. rev:* 3, 500 words, signed. *Aud:* Ac, Ga, Hs. *Jv:* V.

The first college-based journalism review, and the basic journalism magazine which should be found in all libraries. Articles deal with all aspects of the profession from reporting to broadcasting, and are for working members of the press, students, and laymen. It is particularly outstanding for review articles of specific magazines and newspapers. The style of writing is well within the range of the senior high school student and layman, and, more important, the crusading objective reports should be of interest to anyone who picks up a daily newspaper or a magazine. From time to time this bimonthly has taken on the "giants," and it features ongoing material on the failures of the press to accurately report given news stories. Since its inception it has become the conscience of the working press. In a word, a major magazine for most libraries, not simply journalism collections. (Note: beginning in late 1971 the editors began to carry excerpts from the other major journalism reviews. Sometimes these are in the form of a special insert. Still another reason for making this the first and most important choice in the area.)

IPI Report (International Press Institute). 1952. m. $6. Richard Peel. IPI, Munstergasse 9, 8001 Zurich, Switzerland. Illus., index, adv. Circ: 2,000. Sample. Vol ends: Apr.

Bk. rev: 1–2, 150 words, signed. *Aud:* Ac, Ga.

Published by the International Press Institute, composed of "leading journalists throughout the world," *IPI Report* can fairly claim to be the newspaperman's international "voice" and perhaps the most energetic and effective champion of press freedom anywhere. In addition to feature articles on sundry aspects of journalism (e.g., newspapers in school curricula and whether the mass media encourage violence), it exhaustively records the "toils of the press," both east and west, from Johannesburg to Prague to Saigon and Athens. Moreover, every January issue includes an "annual review of press freedom." An essential item for journalism collections, and a good bet—especially because of its global coverage (though it tends to minimize the "toils" undergone by unorthodox and "underground" presses)—for all libraries anxious to document the current censorial scene. But low budget operations should get the *Newsletter on Intellectual Freedom* first. (S.B.)

✓ *(More.)* 1971. m. $7.50. Richard Pollak. Rosebud Associates, Box 2971, Grand Central Station, New York, N.Y. 10017. Illus., adv.

Aud: Ga, Ac, Hs. *Jv:* V.

A critical review of New York City's media, although by 1972 the editor was including a look at the national scene. For example, the January 1972 issue featured an article on the *Washington Post* and a series on fair play on the air and the printed page. Among the writers are Nat Hentoff, Bill Greeley, and Edwin Diamond. There are usually a number of editorials, short reports, and notes on the media. The style is snappy, informative and of interest to anyone who looks behind the front page or the television screen. And the 20-page tabloid differs from others in that it includes advertising. Because of its scope, the paper ranks along with the more substantial Columbia University entry, a first choice for libraries.

Philadelphia Journalism Review. 1971. m. $5. Ed. bd. 1001 Chestnut St., Room 915, Philadelphia, Pa. 19107. Illus., adv. Circ: 3,000. Sample. Vol. ends: Dec.

Aud: Ac, Ga.

Primarily involved with careful analysis of three Philadelphia newspapers (*Inquirer, Bulletin* and *Daily News*), but from time to time features stories on the nation's press. The critical analyses are written by working members of the local journalism fraternity, professors, and freelancers. The 16 pages are nicely put together, well written, and of vast interest to anyone who is involved with journalism—which is just about all newspaper readers with more than an Alice-in-Wonderland view of the press. One of the better reviews, and of considerable worth for all large collections, not to mention all libraries in the greater Philadelphia area—including high schools.

Public Press News Network. 1971. $.15 per issue. Seth Siegelaub, P.O. Box 424, New York, N.Y. 10013.

Another critical analysis of the press. This four page bulletin proposes an alternate New York daily newspaper, outlines what is required, and in so doing makes it of interest for anyone involved with journalism. A modest price for major effort.

The Review of Southern California Journalism. 1970. $2.50. Jimmie D. Davis. Journalism Dept., California State College, Long Beach, Calif. 90804. Illus. Sample.

Aud: Ac, Ga, Hs.

Differs from most of the genre in that it is edited by students and teachers of journalism. Still, about one half of the 16-page issue is the work of reporters, e.g., "Why journalists are tools of the establishment," by Steve Roberts, the Los Angeles Bureau Chief of *The New York Times*. Given the sponsorship of a journalism school and the local Sigma Delta Chi chapter, the review is more involved with youth than others of its kind. Considerable attention is given to problems of college journalists, often overlooked in the other reviews. The push towards everything from pornography to action politics has tended to turn off some of the professionals, but it is precisely this attitude which gives the review an important place. It speaks the language of the young, not necessarily the crusty language of the reporter at work. Hence, a good bet for academic libraries, and a number of advanced high schools.

St. Louis Journalism Review. 1970. bi-m. $3. Ed. bd. of working journalists. Focus/Midwest Publishing Co., Box 3086, St. Louis, Mo., 63130. Illus., adv. Circ: 4,000. Sample. Vol. ends: No. 6.

Aud: Ac, Ga.

A 16-page tabloid designed to review the news media in St. Louis, and by so doing cast a light on reporting and journalism everywhere else. (While limited to the greater St. Louis area, the problems presented are universal, i.e., it points out that coverage of police, city elections, race, education, etc., often is less than perfect.) Written by local journalists, the no punch commentary is the type of reporting which should be of considerable assistance to any serious reader, not only those living in St. Louis.

The Unsatisfied Man; a review of Colorado journalism. 1970. m. $6. Colorado Media Project, Inc., Box 18470, Denver, Colo., 80218. Illus., index. Circ: 1,000. Sample. Vol. ends: Aug.

Aud: Ac, Ga.

One of the best written, certainly one of the wittiest of the journalism reviews. In 16 pages, the working reporters whack away at all aspects of the media in Colorado—the favorite targets being *The Denver Post* (Tweedledum) and *The Rocky Mountain News* (Tweedledee). They are not afraid to print criticism on their own review, e.g., an article in the August 1971 issue is a less than flattering summation of the review's projects as seen by a nonmember Colorado reporter.

This tendency to give both sides of an argument gives it a special place, and with its perceptive editorials, biting letters, and other features it can be recommended as tops for its type.

Writing and Communications

Canadian Author and Bookman. 1923. q. Membership (Nonmembers $2.50). Mary Dawe. Canadian Authors' Assn., Yorkville Public Library, 22 Yorkville Ave., Toronto, 185, Ont., Canada. Illus., adv. Circ: 1,600. Sample. Vol. ends: Fall.

Indexed: CanI. *Bk. rev:* 6, 250 words, signed. *Aud:* Ga, Ac, Hs.

The writer's magazine is the official organ of the Canadian Authors' Association. It incorporates the functions of literary magazine and gossip sheet with that of craft organ. Small and informal in format, the magazine offers articles on Canadian authors, Canadian literary trends, and literary and publishing history, as well as advice on writing and submitting manuscripts, and information on markets, contests, and prizes. Poetry and purely literary pieces, often by new authors, are featured.

Journal of Business Communication. 1963. s-a. Membership (Nonmembers $2.50). George H. Douglas. Univ. of Illinois, Urbana, Ill. 61801. Illus. Circ: 1,100.

Bk. rev: Various number, length. *Aud:* Ac.

The editors say they seek "articles on research results, theoretical or philosophical approaches to business communication, and techniques of wide applicability." Published by the American Business Communication Association, the journal emphasizes improvements in the teaching of business communication and examples of the practical application of communication techniques in business rather than communication theory. Most articles are 7 to 17 pages in length and are written by professors in business departments of colleges and universities around the U.S. Some articles are written by practitioners in business and industry. The book review section has a heavy emphasis on textbooks used in business report writing, but some attention is also given to books on the more general aspects of communication. (R.C.)

Journal of Technical Writing and Communication. 1971. q. $25. Jay R. Gould. Baywood Publishing Co., 1 Northwest Dr., Farmingdale, N.Y. 11735.

Aud: Ac, Ga.

A new, professional journal addressed to technical writers, editors, and communication specialists, it presents original papers by worldwide authorities on the subject—papers from industry, commerce, government, and universities. The first issue has articles from a great variety of sources, including authors in government and business, as well as academia. The journal integrates the graphic arts with technical communication and investigates interfacing disciplines. It presents techniques and research in laboratory and research reports, business and financial reports, teaching, operation and service manuals, advertising copywriting, sales promotion, audiovisual presentations, correspondence, film scripts, library services, educational TV, and technical illustrating. Unlike the *Journal of Communication* (See Communications and Media Section), it gives more attention to international authors and international aspects of the subject. (R.C.)

Technical Communications. 1960, bi-m. Membership. $12. A. Stanley Higgins. Soc. for Technical Communication, 1010 Vermont Ave., N. W., Suite 421, Washington, D.C. 20005. Circ: 5,000.

Bk. rev: 3-4, essays, signed. *Aud:* Ac, Ga.

The official journal of the Society for Technical Communication (formerly the Society of Technical Writers and Publishers) publishes articles for writers, editors, graphic designers, and other practitioners in technological fields. The emphasis is on practical applications of communications techniques, not on theory. Articles stress methods of improving the style and clarity of writing and design of illustrations, instituting cost savings, or boosting sales. Authors are generally practitioners in the field, though academic specialists also contribute. (R.C.)

The Writer. 1887. m. $7. A. S. Burack, 8 Arlington St., Boston, Mass. 02116. Index, adv. Circ: 43,000. Sample.

Indexed: RG. *Aud:* Ga.

See annotation for *Writer's Digest.*

Writer's Digest. 1919. m. $4. Kirk Polking. Richard Rosenthal, 22 E. 12th St., Cincinnati, Ohio 45210. Illus., index, adv. Circ: 75,000. Sample.

Indexed: RG. *Aud:* Ga.

If *The Writer* claims it is "the oldest magazine for literary workers," the *Writer's Digest* can boast it is "the nation's best selling" magazine of its type. (It does have a circulation about one third higher than its rival.) Aside from these fine differences and prices there is little to tell them apart. Both are geared to the aspirations of the would-be writer, whether he be a short story writer or television and film addict. Both give tips, ideas, and other bits of advice on how to make it. Both offer articles by prominent writers on their experiences in breaking into print. And both devote a part of each issue to annotated sources, i.e., markets where particular types of material may be sold. The *Writer's Digest* issues an annual *Writer's Market* which details some 4,000 places to sell; *The Writer* has its *The Writer's Handbook* which includes chapters on writing instruction and over 2,000 markets.

Why both are indexed in *Readers' Guide*, or for that matter either, is a puzzle. Be that as it may, only larger libraries with aspiring writers as clients need both. As to which is better, I would ask those who use—and be prepared for an argument.

LABOR AND INDUSTRIAL RELATIONS

Basic Periodicals

Hs: *American Labor;* Ga: *American Labor, Monthly Labor Review;* Jc: *Monthly Labor Review, American Labor, Issues in Industrial Society;* Ac: *Monthly Labor Review, American Labor, Industrial and Labor Relations Review, International Labor Review, Issues in Industrial Society, Labor History.*

Basic Abstracts and Indexes

Public Affairs Information Service

American Federationist. 1894. m. $2. George Meany. AFL-CIO, 815 16th St. N.W., Washington, D.C. 20006. Illus. Circ: 140,000. Sample. Vol. ends: Dec.

Indexed: PAIS. *Bk. rev:* 2–4, 1–2 pages. *Aud:* Ga, Ac, Hs.

The magazine for the working man. As the official voice of the trade unionists, Meany and his associates discuss in depth many of the problems facing the nation and labor. Their analyses and solutions represent labor's viewpoint. Thematically, the journal cries for labor's fair share in terms of buying power versus the cost of living. As America's economic face changes, it calls for the charting of new courses and the manipulation of trends to make more of the finer things of life accessible to more people. Although a journal of opinion, the materials dealing with economics, research, and education are prepared in cooperation with the staff of the Department of Research and the Department of Education. Its articles are vivid, full of colorful illustrations, and easily read graphs and charts. All 25 pages will interest any audience that detests private greed at public expense. (G.M.)

American Labor; the magazine of labor news. 1968. m. $10. Jay Victor. Master Communications, Inc., 444 Madison Ave., New York, N.Y. 10022. Illus., adv.

Aud: Ac, Ga, Hs.

Format and approach are somewhat similar to such business-oriented publications as *U.S. News and World Report,* but the orientation is definitely labor. The usual issue features five to eight articles on current items in the news, a profile of a personality, and regular departments. These latter, staccato-like features make it of particular value to the reference librarian. The writing style is good to excellent, the illustrations pertinent, and on the whole the authors are objective within their given direction. Deserves a place in almost all libraries.

American Teacher. See Education/General Section.

British Journal of Industrial Relations. 1963. 3/yr. $9. B. C. Roberts. London School of Econ. and Pol. Sci., Houghton St., Aldych, London WC2, England. Illus., adv. Circ: 1,500.

Indexed: PAIS. *Bk. rev:* 15–20, short, signed. *Aud:* Ac.

The rates will increase on this journal to an overseas subscription of six pounds a year, but the investment is worth the price. This is a scholarly, theoretical British journal primarily for those involved in the academic side of labor and industrial relations, as well as with labor and management leaders. Articles are written by faculty members of British universities, as well as some by Americans, Canadians, and Australians. "Chronicle" includes a statistical section about the business and labor picture in the United Kingdom and a listing of events such as strikes and government economic policy. Sections cover a four-month period which does not match most other statistical summaries which are published on a quarterly basis. For the specialized collection. (N.E.)

Bulletin of Labour Statistics. 1965. q. $5.50. International Labour Office. Publns., Sales Service, Geneva, 22, Switzerland.

Indexed: PAIS. *Aud:* Ac, Ga.

The quarterly supplement to the annual data presented in the *Year Book of Labour Statistics.* Containing international data on world wide employment, unemployment, wages, hours of work, and consumer prices, this is the best of its type. Information received between quarters is brought out in a trilingual *Supplement* issued eight times a year. The tables are retrospective for ten years, wherever possible, thus providing a time series for the researcher. This statistical record is invaluable to the library with any sort of business or economic interests. (N.E.)

CU Voice. See Library Periodicals Section.

Challenge Desafio. See Latin American and Chicano/Chicano Section.

Changing Education. See Education/General Section.

Civil Service Journal. See Government Magazines/United States Section.

Current Wage Developments. See Government Magazines/United States Section.

Employment and Earnings. See Government Magazines/United States Section.

The Federal Labor-Management Consultant. 1971. bi-w. free. David S. Dickinson. Office of Labor-Management Relations, U.S. Civil Service Commission, Room 7508, 1900 E St., N.W., Washington, D.C. 20415.

Aud: Ac.

This title began with the issue for June 11, 1971. If this four-page publication continues or expands, its features *The Arbitration Roundtable* and *The Federal Relations Council* will assist in providing background information and precedents for a number of civil service matters involving evaluation, promotion, grievance procedures, supervisor-employee relations, and other personnel actions. This is only one of a series of "information systems engineered by the Labor Department and the Civil Service Commission" serving as an information base for federal labor-management relations. The growing area of civil service labor problems indicates this may be a good choice for many collections which service labor and attempt to assist in finding answers relating to problem fields in labor relations. The value of this title will depend on success, its continued existence, and awareness by area specialists who need the information it contains. (N.E.)

ILR Research. See *Issues in Industrial Society.*

Industrial and Labor Relations Review. 1947. q. $8. Robert H. Ferguson, New York State School of Industrial and Labor Relations, Cornell University, Ithaca, N.Y. 14850. Illus., index, adv. Circ: 4,400. Microform: UM. Reprint: Kraus.

Indexed: BusI, PAIS. *Aud:* Ac.

This interdisciplinary journal in the field of industrial and labor relations publishes articles covering such topics as personnel administration, industrial sociology and psychology, labor economics, labor history, and labor law. Approximately six articles appear in each issue, most being written by university faculty members. Every number has a section on research, and occasionally there is a "Discussions" section, where current topics of interest are considered by leading experts, with a symposium section with essays written by top people. Issues include an extensive bibliography of new books arranged by subject. The section on book reviews is impressive, including about twenty which are fairly long and seem to review the book and not talk about the subject. Many of the articles are on foreign problems, especially ones which affect the domestic economy. Research notes cover work in progress and other matters of interest to subject specialists. (N.E.)

Industrial Relations; a journal of economy and society. 1961. 3/yr. $6. Raymond E. Miles, Institute of Industrial Relations, University of Calif., Berkeley, Calif. 94720. Illus., index, adv. Circ: 2,500.

Indexed: PAIS. *Aud:* Ac.

An interdisciplinary approach to the social, political, legal, and economic aspects of employment, labor relations, and personnel management. The predominantly theoretical slant results from its contributions being made from university faculty members. Each issue contains a symposium on a special industrial relations problem of general interest and four or five 20-page articles. Typical symposium subjects have been: British Incomes Policy, Manpower Projections, Labor Education, and Work and Leisure in Modern Society. Some issues include a Complementary Collection which is a brief group of articles on a unified subject; and Comment and Criticism consisting of just what the title says—reaction from others. The broad approach and highly literate quality of the contributors makes the journal of general business interest and especially good for students. (N.E.)

Industrial Relations Law Digest. 1964. q. $20. Benjamin Werne. Bureau of Industrial Relations, Univ. of Michigan, 703 Haven St., Ann Arbor, Mich. 48104. Circ: 900. Sample. Vol. ends: Apr.

Aud: Ac.

Two features, "Case Comments" and "Bibliography" make this journal a bible of current affairs for the practicing expert. The latter feature is a precis of current articles which pertain to industrial relations. The material is not quite of the book review nature, and the choice is subjective, but the issuing body, Michigan's Bureau of Industrial Relations, lends an air of real authority to the choice. Articles included are condensed from other sources, but the condensation is excellent. Issues at times are devoted to a single topic, e.g., the strike ban. Articles like "The NLRB and the Unit Clarification Petition," "Picket Line Observance," and "Coordinated Bargaining Tactics of Unions" are devoted to current topics. These are generally breezy, pointed, and have an uncluttered air. Excellent for the busy person who needs a rapid but accurate overview. (N.E.)

International Labour Review. 1921. m. $7.25. International Labour Office, Geneva, Switzerland. Dist. by: ILO, 917 15th Street, N.W., Washington, D.C. 20005. Index, adv. Circ: 7,500. Microform: UM.

Indexed: PAIS, SSHum. *Bk. rev:* 15, 100 words, signed. *Aud:* Ac.

Addressed particularly to students of social policy, whether in government, universities, or industries. Published in either English, French, or Spanish, the articles cover many aspects of international labor. Current information about meetings of labor organizations is given. There are short book reviews, and an extensive book list called Bibliography. Recent issues have included Automation Abstracts, a feature which may well split off into a separate publication. The need exists. The status of the issuing body lends authority to this journal which actually does what its title says without necessarily taking a stand. Neutrality and even reporting make it a tool for all sides of an issue. Excellent for the comparative picture. (N.E.)

Issues in Industrial Society. 1969. 3/yr. $5. Wayne Hodges, New York State School of Industrial and Labor Relations, Cornell University, Ithaca, N.Y. 14850.

Aud: Ga, Ac. *Jv:* V.

Replaces *ILR Research.* Emphasis on contemporary problems covering a wide range of interest results in a rather broad scope. Each issue is devoted to a single topic with a general background and information essay being written by the editorial staff. This is followed by half a dozen essays or articles written by individual experts called on for each issue. The first three issues were devoted to: Business, Labor, and Jobs in the Ghetto; Political Activities of Unions and Company Managers; and New Applications of Collective Bargaining.

The format is text-bookish and a bit grey, but the writing style and general level are both excellent. Issues contain letters to the editors and these are a fascinating form of reaction. Each issue contains an "Information Item" which is an annotated bibliography of books and articles relating to the topic of the issue. Broad and sweeping, and a contemporary, up-to-date summary of each topic, issues could easily be treated as monographs on the separate topics. Generally excellent and for most collections. (N.E.)

The Journal of Industrial Relations. 1959. q. $5. Kingsley M. Laffer, School of Industrial Relations, Dept. of Econ., Univ. of Sidney, Sidney, Australia. Vol. ends: Dec.

Aud: Ac.

Official journal of the Industrial Relations Society of Australia which is a federation of the industrial relations societies of New South Wales, South Australia, Queensland, Victoria, and Western Australia. These bring together representatives of management, trade unions, government services and professions, and specialists in the various academic disciplines concerned with industrial relations. The purpose of the federation is the development of an integrated approach to industrial relations. While representative of a different country's impact on labor and industrial relations, the journal includes articles such as "Labor-management Relations in the Metalworking Industries of Three Countries" which describes and analyzes relations in England, Israel, and Australia and makes comparisons to the United States. This type of treatment, as well as a scholarly standard, make the journal quite valuable. Such regular articles as "Decisions Affecting Industrial Relations" and a selected list of books relating to the areas covered in the magazine provide current information needed by the expert. (N.E.)

Labor Developments Abroad. 1955. m. $2.75. Florence S. James, Sup. of Documents, U.S. Govt. Printing Office, Washington, D.C. 20402; or regional offices of the Bureau of Labor Statistics, Division of Foreign Labor Conditions. Vol. ends: Dec.

Aud: Ga, Ac.

Prepared by the Division of Foreign Labor Conditions of the Bureau of Labor Statistics, the journal presents information and research on recent labor developments in foreign countries. Primary resources are reports from American Foreign Service Posts, foreign government publications, the foreign press, and experts on international labor developments. Without an ax to grind, the journal presents an even, neutral picture, sometimes comparing foreign situations to American ones but more often leaving comparisons and contrasts to the reader. It generally discusses one or two countries from broad areas like U.S.S.R. and Western Europe, Near East and South Asia and the Pacific, American Republics, and Africa. Not all areas are treated in every issue. Each issue has two U.S. Department of State tables: Indexes of Living Costs Abroad (excluding quarters), and Living Quarters Allowances. Several special-emphasis articles are followed by pithy, almost telegraphic statements from countries covered, including Iron Curtain - countries. Not overpowering, but highly useful if truncated information. Footnotes and bibliographies lead elsewhere. (N.E.)

Labor History. 1960. 3/yr. $7.50. Milton Cantor. Tamiment Institute, 7 E. 15th St., New York, N.Y. 10003. Adv. Circ: 1,400. Microform: UM. Reprint: Johnson.

Bk. rev: 10, 100 words, signed. *Aud:* Ac.

Those interested in the history and development of the labor movement will find this well-written journal invaluable. Emphasis is international, and on both past and contemporary labor studies and social history. In addition to an average of six articles per issue, there are often bibliographies of periodical articles and books. As one of the few journals that devotes itself exclusively to labor history, it should be a major consideration for history, business, and economics libraries. Because of the general tone and quality and the tendency to cover topics which have wide impact, this should be considered for collections which deal with American studies and cultural programs in general. (N.E.)

Labor Law Journal. 1949. m. $20. Allen E. Schechier. Commerce Clearing House, 4025 W. Peterson Ave., Chicago, Ill. 60646. Vol. ends: Dec.

Aud: Ac.

The publisher says this journal "will contain a continuing survey of important legislative, administrative and judicial developments and signed articles on subjects pertaining to legal problems in the labor field." Articles are on legal remedies, court decisions, job discrimination, and other contemporary and historical issues. There are regular features devoted to labor relations and arbitration. Articles on legal issues often contain extensive citations to law, often to CCH legal services. The quality and unbiased nature of CCH publications is reflected in the usefulness of this journal. Of high value as a beginning source and as a summary of trends in the field. (N.E.)

Labour Gazette. 1900. m. $3 (Outside of Canada $5) Jack E. Nugent. Canada Dept. of Labour, 340 Laurier Ave., W., Ottawa, Canada K1A 0J2. Illus., index. Circ: 15,790. Sample. Vol. ends: Dec.

Bk. rev: 1, 800 words. *Aud:* Ga.

The Canadian equivalent of the U.S. *Monthly Labor Review*. It is an official government publication which is published "for the purpose of disseminating accurate statistical and other information relating to the conditions of labour and the labour market. In recent years it has concentrated on reporting events and developments in industrial relations." There are usually three or four nontechnical articles on various aspects of labor, and then departments which range from statistics to legal decisions. In addition to book reviews, it has a useful bibliography, "Publications in the Library," listing recent acquisitions under broad subject headings. A major magazine for labor collections, and a required one for all medium to large-sized Canadian libraries.

Malcriado. See Latin American and Chicano/Chicano Section.

Manpower. See Government Magazines/United States Section.

The Miner's Voice. 1969. m. $5. Don Stillman, P.O. Box 255, Morgantown, W.Va. 26505. Illus., adv. Circ: 40,000. Sample.

Aud: Ac, Ga.

A grassroots tabloid newspaper of some eight to ten pages which is directed to change. The editor says the purpose of his effort is "to inform miners and others living in coal producing areas about health and safety conditions in the mines, the exploitation of Appalachia by the coal and oil monopolies, the destruction of the environment by strip miners, and the failure of the current leadership of the United Mine Workers." Of equal interest to environmentalists and those involved with labor.

Monthly Labor Review. See Government Magazines/United States Section.

Panorama; the magazine of the International Labour Office. 1964. bi-m. free. International Labour Office, Geneva 22, Switzerland. Subs. to: 917 15th St., N.W., Washington, D.C. 20005. Illus. Circ: 40,000.

Aud: Ac, Hs.

An international labor magazine. The purpose of the publishing organization, first founded in 1919 and now associated with the United Nations, "is to raise standards by building up a code of international law and practice." It is quite well done. The ILO was awarded the Nobel Peace Prize in 1969. The 32 to 40 pages have a professional format, offer five to six feature stories which are nontechnical and well within the grasp of the average reader. The material is tied to labor, but would be useful in any social studies situation. One of the best "freebies" of them all.

LATIN AMERICAN AND CHICANO

Basic Periodicals

ENGLISH LANGUAGE GENERAL. Ejh: *Américas* (OAS); Hs: *Américas* (OAS); Ga: *Américas* (OAS), *Mexican World;* Jr: *Latin American Research Review, Latin America, Américas;* Ac: *Latin American Research Review, Latin America, Américas, Journal of Inter-American Studies, Caribbean Studies, Journal of Mexican-American History.*

CHICANO. Hs: *Aztlán, Chicano Student Movement;* Ga: *Aztlán, El Grito, LaRaza;* Jc&Ac: *Aztlán, El Grito, LaRaza, Chicano Student Movement, Challenge Desafío.*

SPANISH LANGUAGE. Hs: *Mundo Hispanico, Temas;* Ga: *Hispano Americano, Mundo Hispanico, Artes de Mexico, Temas;* Jc: *Cuadernos Americanos, Hispano Americano, Mundo Hispanico;* Ac: *Cuadernos Americanos, Cuadernos Hispanoamericanos, Sur, Hispano Americano, Mundo Hispanico.*

Library and Teaching Aids

Inter-American Review of Bibliography, Commentarios Bibliograficos.

Basic Abstracts and Indexes

Index to Latin American Periodicals.

English Language General

Américas. 1949. m. $6. G. de Zendegui. Organization of American States, Dept. of Cultural Affairs, Washington, D.C. 20006. Illus., index. Circ: 110,000. Sample. Vol. ends: Dec. Microform: UM.

Indexed: LatAm, MLA, PAIS, RG. *Bk. rev:* 6–10, 250–750 words/notes. *Aud:* Ga, Hs.

A cultural approach to Latin America via some 50 illustrated pages which celebrate the best in business, art, music, literature, and architecture. The format is pleasing, the articles simple enough to be understood by a high school student. Bits of it are good enough, and the book reviews tend to bring to libraries titles otherwise overlooked. It avoids controversy, finds even the much-debated Kennedy Center without fault. Hardly the place to turn for an objective report on

Latin American politics, but what it does, it does well enough and it nicely augments the *National Geographic* on the one hand and the literary reviews on the other. A good general magazine for the average public library. Available also in Spanish.

The Americas; a quarterly review of inter-American cultural history. 1944. q. $6. Antonine S. Tibesar, OFM, Box 34440, Washington, D.C. 20034. Index. Circ: 1,200. Sample. Vol. ends: Apr. Refereed.

Indexed: HistAb, SSHum. *Bk. rev:* 10–15, approx. one page, signed. *Aud:* Ac, Ga.

Published by the Academy of American Franciscan History, this journal is devoted to the history of Latin America, with emphasis on cultural history. The period covered is from the beginning of European colonization until the twentieth century. Bibliographic and cultural news of interest to its readers is contained in a regular feature called "Inter-American Notes." While this is a limited circulation, scholarly journal, it does cover an area which is difficult to find in English, especially without political or economic bias. The religious sponsorship is rarely reflected in the articles and, on the whole, the magazine is quite objective. Should be considered by any library, from medium-size public to academic, where an intelligent coverage of this area would be appreciated. See also *Hispanic American Historical Review* and *Americas* (O.A.S.)

Bim. 1957. s-a. $3. Ed. bd. Woodville, Chelsea Rd., St. Michael, Barbados, W. Indies. Illus., adv. Circ: 750.

Bk. rev: various number, length. *Aud:* Ac.

A West Indian literary magazine containing mainly short stories and poems. Some of the works are delightful, but they are surprisingly uninnovative in style, form, and content. Although there are frequent black subjects, the race of the contributor is not obvious. One does get some glimpse of the native West Indian and the society in which he lives. *Bim* would be suitable for the large academic library. (J.G.)

Brazillian Bulletin. See Free Magazines Section.

Bulletin of Hispanic Studies. 1923. q. $6. Geoffrey Ribbans. Liverpool Univ. Press, 123 Grove St., Liverpool, 7AF, England. Illus., index, adv. Circ: 1,500. Sample. Vol ends: Oct. Refereed. Reprint: Kraus.

Indexed: BritHum. *Bk. rev:* 10–11, 600 words, signed. *Aud:* Ac.

Mainly concerned with studies of Spanish, Portuguese, and Latin American literature. Reviews cover books on history, politics, and social conditions, as well as language and literature. Special features are occasional "Notes" and "Memoirs." A semiannual "Review of Reviews" abstracts reviews printed in other significant journals in the field. Text is in English and Spanish, occasionally Catalan and Portuguese.

Caribbean Quarterly. 1949. q. $3. R. M. Nettleford. Dept. of Extra-Mural Studies, Univ. of the West Indies, Mona, Kingston 7, Jamaica. Circ. 1,000. Vol. ends: Dec.

Indexed: HistAb, LatAm. *Bk. rev:* 2–5, 650–5,000 words, signed. *Aud:* Ga, Ac.

This review is published in English and features two to six main articles in each issue which deal with a wide variety of subjects in the social sciences and humanities as they relate to the Caribbean. Representative titles from recent issues will indicate the scope of the publication: "West Indian Prose Fiction in the Sixties: a Survey," "The Yoruba Ancestor Cult in Gasparillo," "A Model Approach to the Understanding of the Transportation Network of Trinidad, W.I.," "History, Fable and Myth in the Caribbean and Guianas," and "Education for Jamaica's Needs." Poetry and short stories also are published. This is one of the leading reviews of the Caribbean and certainly should be included in any academic or public library where an interest in that part of the world exists. (N.H.)

Caribbean Studies. 1961. q. $6. Sybil Lewis. The Institute of Caribbean Studies, Univ. of Puerto Rico, Box B M, Univ. Station, Rio Piedras, Puerto Rico 00931. Circ: 1,500. Vol. ends: Jan.

Indexed: HistAb, LatAm. *Bk. rev:* 6–7, 500–2,500 words, signed. *Aud:* Ga, Ac.

A typical issue of this journal consists of from three to five main articles covering such diverse topics in the social sciences and humanities as the following articles selected from one issue indicate: "The American Image in British West Indian Literature," "Company Towns in the Caribbean: a Preliminary Analysis of Christianburg-Wismar-MacKenzie," and "The Oil Industry in the Economy of Trinidad." The editors state that the only fields excluded from this publication are the natural sciences. One of the most valuable features of each issue is the "Current Bibliography" which lists books, pamphlets, and articles concerning the Caribbean. As the consultants for this section correctly point out, the currency of this bibliography is particularly important because in this area of the world local publications are often soon out of print. Other features of this journal also include the publication of occasional important research surveys and review articles which give full commentary on major publications or authors. The geographic area, "the Caribbean," is defined by the editors as including "all of the Antilles, the three Guianas, British Honduras, and the offshore islands and Caribbean coastal zones of Venezuela, Colombia, Central America and Mexico." The periodical is published mainly in English with occasional articles in French and Spanish. A cumulative index for volumes 1 to 10 has recently been published. (N.H.)

Comentarios Bibliograficos Americanos. 1968. 5/yr. Price on request. Eduardo Darino. CBA Editores, Casilla de Correo 1677, Montevideo, Uruguay. Illus., index, adv. Circ: 20,000. Sample. Vol. ends: Dec.

Aud: Ga, Ac, Hs.

A 100 page photo-offset illustrated bilingual (Spanish/English) critical review of 300 to 500 Latin American books. Most 300 to 500 word signed reviews are in English, but some of the essays are in Spanish. The reviews cover primarily new titles, i.e., one month to a year after publication, and afford the best running record available. New magazines are noted too. The editor reports that "CBA draws on a roster of more than 300 university specialists and newspapermen to review and select books and to prepare articles, essays and interviews on bibliographical subjects." Also, the press puts out a yearbook which is a compilation of reviews. Both the magazine and the yearbook have author, title, and subject indexes. The editor notes the enormity of the task: "Our topics: lots of information, honest criticism, show to the world the new L.A. books. Now to publish a magazine that covers all the countries—with such mail as L. Americas has!—is really hard work."

Hispanic American Historical Review. 1918. q. $8 (Student $4). Stanley R. Ross. Duke Univ. Press, Box 6697, College Station, Durham, N.C. Index, adv. Circ: 2,400. Vol. ends: Nov. Reprint: Kraus.

Indexed: HistAb, LatAm, SSHum. *Bk. rev:* 50, lengthy or 400–500 words, signed. *Aud:* Ac.

Published in cooperation with the Conference on Latin American History of the American Historical Association, this journal is devoted to Latin American history, particularly the seventeenth to the nineteenth centuries. Each issue contains four or five scholarly articles, with some emphasis on politics and government. There is an extensive book review section, comprising some fifty percent of each issue, in which the reviews are classified by subject and period. Among the journal's regular features are sections on professional news and dissertations. It is nicely complemented by the somewhat broader scope of *Américas*, but of the two, this one is more valuable for its book reviews. The library with a special interest in this area would be wise to subscribe to both journals.

Hispanic Review. 1933. q. $9.50. Arnold G. Reichenberger, Russell P. Sebold. Romance Languages Dept., Univ. of Pennsylvania, Philadelphia, Pa. 19104. Circ: 1,300. Sample. Vol. ends: Oct. Microform: UM. Reprint: Johnson.

Indexed: MLA, SSHum. *Aud:* Ac.

An esoteric, scholarly journal, with text frequently in Spanish, devoted to research in the Hispanic languages and literatures. Published by the University of Pennsylvania, the emphasis is on literature. Includes a

"Varia" section with shorter articles. The book review section has substantial critical reviews of interest to scholars.

Inter-American Music Bulletin. 1957. 6/yr. free. Pan-American Union, Dept. of Cultural Affairs, Music Div., Washington, D. C. 20006. Illus. Circ: 3,000.

Indexed: MusicI. *Aud:* Ga, Ac.

The *Bulletin* is published to "complement the more extensive *Boletin Inter Americano de Musica* published by the section in Spanish. It is intended to acquaint English language readers with the music and composers of the Western Hemisphere, musical activities in Central and South America, and activities and movements in contemporary music in America and Europe." Most issues are devoted to one paper and range from 6 to 28 pages.

Inter-American Review of Bibliography/Revista Inter-Americana de Bibliografia. 1951. q. $3. Armando Correia Pacheco. Organization of American States, General Secretariat, Washington, D.C. 20006. Illus., index, adv. Circ: 3,000. Sample. Microform: UM. Reprint: Johnson.

Indexed: HistAb. *Bk. rev:* 12–15, 300–1,500 words, signed. *Aud:* Ac.

With articles and reviews in both English and Spanish (some, too, in Portuguese and French), the journal requires a bilingual facility. There are usually one or two main articles on some aspect of Latin American culture, literature, personality, etc.; a review article; and then book reviews which take up from one quarter to one third of each issue. This is followed by a specialized bibliography in a given subject area, and notes and news divided by various countries. The journal is indispensable for anyone attempting to keep up with the current Latin American publishing scene. It has become rather specialized, and is recommended only for larger collections or those with considerable interest in Latin America. (N.H.)

Jamaica Journal. 1967. q. $4. Alex Gradussov. Inst. of Jamaica, 12–16 East St., Kingston, Jamaica, West Indies. Illus. Circ: 5,000. Sample. Vol. ends: Dec.

Bk. rev: 3,000 words, signed. *Aud:* Ga, Ac, Hs.

Covers a particularly wide field—history, science, art, literature, and music. The glossy, oversized 80 pages are nicely illustrated, and the pictures will be suitable for use in schools and public libraries where there is little enough material from this area of other than the travel bureau variety. The level of writing is high, and while the magazine is obviously tailored to make Jamaica look its best, the material seems to give a well-balanced picture of the country. Hardly required, but in view of its low price, format, and generally intelligent presentation, should be welcomed for both recreational and reference purposes in larger public, academic, and some high school libraries.

Journal of Inter-American Studies. 1959. q. $15 (Individuals $10; Full-time students $8). John P. Harrison. Sage Publications, 275 S. Beverly Dr., Beverly Hills, Calif. 90212. Illus., index, adv. Circ: 4,000. Sample. Vol. ends: Nov. Refereed.

Indexed: LatAm, HistAb, PAIS, SSHum, PHRA. *Bk. rev:* 1–2, 2–3 pages. *Aud:* Ac.

Published for the Center for Advanced International Studies at the University of Miami, this consists of some five to eight articles on various aspects of Latin American politics, social conflicts, and economics. Authors are prominent American scholars, as well as scholars from various Latin American universities. Material is published in the language of the author, although most articles are in English. The journal tends to be relatively objective.

Journal of Latin American Studies. 1969. s-a. $8.50. Harold Blakesmore and Clifford T. Smith. Cambridge Univ. Press, 32 E. 57th. St., New York, N.Y. 10022. Index. Circ: 1,200. Sample. Vol. ends: Nov.

Indexed: HistAb. *Bk. rev:* 6–14, 700–2,000 words, signed. *Aud:* Ga, Ac.

A scholarly journal published under the sponsorship of the Centers of Institutes of Latin American Studies of the following universities: Cambridge, Glasgow, Liverpool, London, and Oxford. The editors state "the scope of the journal is the study of Latin America from the standpoint of the social sciences, including anthropology, archaeology, economics, geography, history, international relations, politics, sociology, etc. . . ." Along with other articles, issues contain a "Review Article," which gives in-depth analysis of the leading literature available on a specific topic. Examples are: "Industrialization in Brazil" and "Artists, Intellectuals and Revolution: Recent Books on Mexico." The articles in English, and the emphasis on other English language publications in the field make this of value to the many who have an interest in Latin America but not the ability to work with materials in Spanish. (N.H.)

Journal of Mexican American History. 1970. s-a (Fall and Spring). $8.64. Joseph Peter Navarro, P.O. Box 13861, Santa Barbara, Calif. 93107. Vol. ends: spring.

Bk. rev: 3–4; 500 words, signed. *Aud:* Ac.

The journal warns readers that it will publish independently of the scholastic establishment's traditional views and sentiments—to tell it like it was, historically speaking. While patently rebel in his approach to Mexican-American history, the editor welcomes all contributions in the subject area. Standards of objectivity and documentation are upheld. Initial issues are bibliographically strong, containing a "weeded" second edition of *Mexican-American History: A Critical Selective Bibliography* and a selected bibliography of U.S. theses and dissertations on historical aspects of Mexican-Americans. Both consist of eighteen pages and are valuable for research and collection building. Produced by mimeo from typed copy, its is recommended for minority studies and American history collections. (J.W.)

Journal of Mexican American Studies. 1970. q. $5.50. Daniel J. Gomez. Mexican-American Documentation and Educational Research Institute, 1229 E. Cypress St., Anaheim, Calif. 92805. Sample. Vol. ends: Summer.

Aud: Ga, Hs, Ac.

Dedicated to finding solutions to the minority group's socio-economic problems and offering a balanced selection of articles for students of Mexican-American affairs. The broad scope of material is concentrated in the social sciences: current affairs, ethnic history, sociology, psychology, and educational practices. Interviews and profiles of public figures connected with Mexican-American interests are included. Subjects receive substantial, documented treatment with authors briefly identified. Some Spanish is used, although usually as simultaneous translation of English text. Cleanly produced from typed mimeo copy. Recommended for college and minority studies collections. (J.W.)

Latin America. 1967. w. $60 (airmail, student rate $30). John Rettie, Christopher Roper, Jo Beresford. Latin American Newsletters, Ltd., 7th. floor, 69 Cannon Street, London EC4N 5AB, England. Circ: 2,000. Sample. Vol. ends: Dec 31.

Aud: Ga, Ac. *Jv:* V.

An eight-page airmail newsletter, this English-language publication features reporting and analysis of important developments on the political and economic scene in Latin America, and incidentally devotes a notable amount of its coverage to the Caribbean. The editors accurately state that the publication "Is designed for those who need to know what is happening in that part of the world, but who find most newspaper and magazine coverage inadequate and the specialist banking and academic reviews insufficiently up to date. *Latin America* receives extensive daily newscast by radio teletype from all the main cities in the area, to ensure topicality and first-hand information." A publication such as this one also derives some of its value from being able to publish and develop material which is given scant if any coverage in Latin American periodicals because of government censorship. A typical issue consists of several articles between 400 and 2,000 words and the regular features "Business Briefs" and "News in Brief" which contain many items in capsule form. The publication prepares a quarterly index. This is a most useful publication which many libraries would find well worth the subscription price. (N.H.)

Latin America Report. 1963. m. $10. Paul D. Bethel. Citizens Committee for a Free Cuba, 1009 Huntington Bldg., 168 S. E. First St., Miami, Fla. 33131. Illus. Circ: 20,000. Sample. Vol. ends: Dec.

Aud: Ac.

A four-page, politically conservative, illustrated newsletter which reports primarily on Castro's Cuba, but includes information on other Latin American countries. The three to four short articles and notes are expressly geared to indicate (1) Communists are infiltrating Latin America; (2) the Castro experiment is a failure; and (3) an effort should be made to free Cuba from Castro. Issues include such stories as: "Chile's Rush to Marxism," "Castro Agent Tells How Cuba Brainwashes U.S. Students, Reporters," and "Change of Cuba Policy—Near Revolt in Cuba." How much of this is factual, how much is opinion, and how much is just plain wishful thinking, the reader will have to determine for himself. The newsletter represents a legitimate point of view and should be included in larger academic collections, and in public libraries serving a Latin American-oriented clientele.

Latin American Research Review; a journal for the communication of research among individuals and institutions concerned with studies in Latin America. 1965. a. $13 (Institutions $25). Thomas F. McGann. Latin American Studies Assn. Subs. to: L.A.R.R., Sid Richardson Hall, Univ. of Texas, Austin, Tex. 78712. Illus., index, adv. Circ: 3,000. Microform: UM.

Indexed: LatAm, PAIS. *Aud:* Ac, Ga. *Jv:* V.

The basic guide to research in Latin American studies. It is difficult to imagine anyone working in this area who is not familiar with this journal's impressive coverage. A normal issue is divided into several parts; "Topic Reviews," which consist of four to five articles on research in everything from literary studies to taxes; "Reports," trends in research and sources; "Current Research Inventory," which makes up the heart of the journal and includes, by university and then subject, all post-doctoral research reported; news on libraries and archives; "Forum," a discussion of current questions. The research reports are divided geographically by areas of the United States, so that over a period of a year every major university is considered. A geographical index locates material by Latin American country. Libraries will find the 10 to 12 pages in each issue given to archives and libraries particularly useful, as this consists of short notes on 100 or more books, journals, monographs, etc., concerning Latin America. An absolute must for any library where there is the slightest interest in Latin American affairs.

Latin American Theatre Review; a journal devoted to the theatre and drama of Spanish and Portuguese America. 1967. s-a. $5.00 (Individuals $3). Fredric M. Litto and George W. Woodyard. Center of Latin American Studies, The Univ. of Kansas, Lawrence, Kans. 66044. Circ: 1,000. Sample. Vol. ends: Spring. Refereed.

Indexed: PMLA. *Bk. rev:* 2–4, 500–1,000 words, signed. *Aud:* Ga, Ac.

After reading a few issues of this publication one should feel he really knows what is what with Latin American theater. The editors state they "are particularly desirous of receiving articles which are historical, critical, or bibliographic in nature. Especially welcome will be histories of theatre activity in a particular city, of a single performing company, or of a theatre institution; critical assessments of the works of an individual playwright or a theatrical movement; studies of the accomplishments of a certain actor, director, designer, or other contributor to Latin American theatre. . . ." Articles are published in English, Portuguese, or Spanish. An abstract of each leading article is presented in English. Regular features include reviews of Latin American "Theatre Seasons and Festivals," "Play Reports and Synopses," "Works in Progress," "Plays in Performance" (in the U.S.), "Visiting Theatre Personnel," and "Conferences and Lectures." This is an excellent review for any academic library which collects material on either the theater or Latin American literature. It also should be included in large public library theater collections. (N.H.)

The Luso-Brazilian Review. 1964. s-a. $8 (Individuals $5). Lloyd Kasten. Univ. of Wisconsin Press, Box 1379, Madison, Wis. 53701. Index. Circ: 565.

Indexed: LatAm, PMLA. *Bk. rev:* 1–5, 900–2,700 words, signed. *Aud:* Ga, Ac.

A scholarly journal covering diverse aspects of the language, literature, history, and social sciences of the Portuguese-speaking world from Portugal and Brazil to the Portuguese possessions, both present and former, in Africa and Asia. Most issues contain a useful subject bibliography such as Brazil: Political Science; Brazilian Literature: History and Criticism; Portugal: Fine Arts and Geography. Articles are published in English and Portuguese, with emphasis on Portuguese. Since, as the periodical claims, it is "America's only scholarly journal devoted exclusively to the study of the Portuguese-speaking world" it deserves a place in academic libraries, large public libraries and any other libraries where an interest in this frequently neglected area of world studies exists. A cumulative index is published every two years. (N.H.)

Maguey: a bridge between worlds. 1968. q. $5. Jed Linde and Maria Esther Manni, P.O. Box 385, El Cerrito, Calif. 94530. Illus. Circ: 1,500. Sample.

Aud: Ac, Hs.

Bilingual (Spanish/English) and thick. In most cases, the Spanish language poems have English translations. A few poems are translated from several other languages. For Spanish-speaking people it offers some of the best American poetry and prose, and for the English-speaking, superior translations of the best of Latin American writers. Any library, public, high school, or academic, having a Spanish community of any size should subscribe. Also any library truly serious about little magazines.

Mexican World; the voice of Latin America. 1966. m. $4. James O. Niess. Graphic Service, Inc., 2617 E. Hennepin Ave., Minneapolis, Minn. 55413. Circ. 3,200 Sample. Vol. ends: Sept.

Aud: Ga.

This publication is designed for those interested in Mexico as a country in which to travel, study, and/or retire. It is not the place to look for articles of great depth but it does a good job of reporting on such items as new retirement communities and campsites. Each issue features several articles on different cities and areas of the country. These articles seem to be written for the most part by tourists and while their quality varies, many of them are excellent. Unfortunately one can find occasional stereotypes mentioned which could be offensive to Mexican people. One can also fault the publication for a certain carelessness in spelling ("seniorita," sic.). In addition, while the magazine is in English, many Spanish names and other words are used and the publication more often ignores accent marks than includes them. One of the regular features of the periodical is a column on the economy of Mexico which gives helpful information to those who are interested in living in Mexico or buying property there in addition to covering other economic developments in the country. Another valuable feature, the "News Briefs" section, includes items on new highways, trains, air fares, parks, etc. Would be of interest to the public library which maintains a travel collection or which is located in an area close to Mexico where interest in a travel publication concerning the country would be high. (N.H.)

NACLA Newsletter. 1967. 10/yr. $10 (Individuals $5). North American Congress on Latin America, Box 57, Cathedral Station, New York, N.Y. 10025. Circ: 1,600. Sample. Microform: B&H.

Indexed: API. *Bk. rev:* Notes, sometimes longer. *Aud:* Ac, Ga.

A 16 to 20 page newsletter which covers operations and activities in Latin America, more particularly those carried on officially or otherwise by the U.S. Government. For example, the editors have reported on investments in Latin America, the CIA, ties with the Pentagon, and how all these involvements have affected governments and people. The staff is made up of a group of experts whose politics are liberal, whose mission it is to bring attention to the needs of the people to the south. And while politics is a major con-

cern, the letter, also, touches on social and cultural activities. One of the best specific sources for an area rarely adequately covered in American libraries. The NACLA offers other services and publications. (It has issued a number of special reports on various Latin American countries, and has a student's handbook to help the researchers determine how involved his or her school is with the government.) The group should be contacted by libraries interested in developing meaningful Latin American and/or Spanish language collections.

The Pan American Review. 1970. s-a. $3.50. Seth Wade. Funch Press, 1100 West Samano, Edinburg, Tex. 78539. Illus.

Aud: Ga, Ac, Hs.

Well printed, academic in tone, this is a solid effort to cover Pan American literature. The high level of ability is indicated by translations by Robert Bly, articles by Hugh Fox. The Latin American poetry seems a cut above the American selections. This is probably the culling effect of translations: you do not bother to translate something unless it says something to you. Perhaps the American poetry will improve as this becomes better known. It reprints from other magazines liberally while it seeks to develop its own contributors. This is not a first selection yet, but will likely grow in importance. Certainly to be considered, especially by academic libraries, or others interested in a cosmopolitan collections. (D.D.)

Sevacou: a journal of the Caribbean artists movement. 1970. q. $4.50. Ed. bd. Box 170, Mona Kingston 7, Jamaica, W. Indies. Adv. Sample.

Aud: Ga, Ac, Hs.

The purpose of this literary magazine is to "present the works of creative writers, examine and assess the significance of artistic expression through slavery with a view to recognizing lost traditions, and to help towards the recognition of the Caribbean as a meaningful cultural entity." A typical issue covers a number of topics from "The Negro and the English Language in the West Indies" to "C.L.R. James on the Black Jacobin Revolution in San Domingo." The style and approach are suited to the student, and because of its rather important purpose it should be a major item for larger university and college libraries—not to mention public and school libraries in black communities.

Venezuela Up-to-date. See Free Magazines Section.

Chicano

Aztlán; Chicano journal of the social sciences and the arts. 1970. irreg. $3 per issue; standing orders accepted. Juan Gomez-Q and Roberto Sifuentes. Chicano Cultural Center, University of Calif., 405 Hilgard, Los Angeles, Calif. 90024. Circ: 1,000.

Aud: Ga, Ac. *Jv:* V.

This handsome journal is both written and edited by Chicano members of academic communities and sponsored by UCLA's Chicano Cultural Center. The Center's goal is to serve as coordinator between Chicano people and institutions of higher education in seeking solutions to problems of the barrios. In promotion of this goal, *Aztlán,* which the editors hope to accelerate in frequency of publication to quarterly in the future, will be a source for the general public as well as the teacher. Authors handle relevant topics with analytical skill while avoiding the dry prose of disciplinary jargon. Carefully documented articles cover a variety of subjects including historical, political, economic, social, literary, and educational aspects of Chicano culture. A small portion of the text is in Spanish. Essential for minority studies collections, academic and public libraries with Mexican-American constituents. (J.W.)

Challenge-Desafio. 1964. m. $2. Progressive Labor Party, Box 808, Brooklyn, N.Y. 11201. Illus. Circ: 20,000. Sample.

Aud: Ac, Ga.

A 40 to 50 page English and Spanish tabloid, this is "dedicated to the U.S. working class, and the working class of the entire world." Its purpose is to inform sympathizers on two levels: first, as to current events which are working for or against the revolution of the working class; and second, editorials and letters are printed which support a basic Marxist-Leninist philosophy "in which working people collectively own the factories and farms: society of socialism." The first 15 to 20 pages are in Spanish and feature material of interest to Spanish-speaking peoples locked into ghettoes. The remainder is in English. Sometimes, although not often, repeating some of the Spanish material. And while published in New York, the scope is both national and international. See also *Progressive Labor* (News and Opinion Magazines/Radical Left Section).

Chicano Student Movement. 1968. bi-m. $2.50. Box 31322, Los Angeles, Calif. 90031. Illus.

Aud: Ac, Ga, Hs.

An eight to ten page tabloid newspaper directed to those participating in the Mexican-American student movement. While primarily concerned with activities in southern California, it does report on Chicano movements elsewhere. The tone is militant, the reporting heavy, the message strong. Some poetry, fiction, photographs, etc., but this is in no way a typical underground newspaper.

Con Safos. 1968. irreg. (2 or 3 issues per year). $2.50 for 4 issues. Arturo Flores. Con Safos, Inc., P.O. Box 31085, Los Angeles, Calif. 90031. Illus.

Aud: Ga, Hs, Ac.

From amidst the spirit of revolution which pervades the barrios, this publication strives to develop literary and aesthetic art forms which will give expression to the Mexican-American people and reflect their life in the barrios. Holding to its intent to be a literary magazine, although not excluding socio-political essays, it argues that while journalistic writing is timely and stirring, creative literature can formulate a cultural basis for change and speed the advent of a social order free from oppression and discrimination. The prose and poetry is almost entirely in English with some parallel text in English/Spanish. It is well written and edited by Chicanos who take their inspiration from personal experience and observation. Drawings, cartoons, and photographs lend graphic, emotional appeal to the writing. Regular features include an editorial, readers' letters, and a glossary of idiomatic words and phrases from Calé, the argot of the Chicano. Handsomely printed, it is probably your best source for authentic insight into the barrios. Deserves the widest circulation in Mexican-American communities and in collections devoted to their study. (J.W.)

Entrelíneas. 1971. m. $5. Andrew P. Gutíerrez, Marciano Morales, Francisco H. Ruiz, Oscar Jorge Vigliano. P.O. Box 2566, Kansas City, Mo. 64142. Illus., index, adv. Sample. Vol. ends: Dec.

Bk. rev: 1, 200 words, signed. *Aud:* Ga, Hs, Ac.

Published through sponsorship of Penn Valley Community College Community Services, this is designed to articulate the Mexican-American drive for recognition, provide mutual understanding of identity, and enlighten those unfamiliar with Mexican-American culture. Regular departments include editorial comment, cultural study, book review, language study, poetry, and letters. A significant portion of the text is in parallel English/Spanish. On the whole, it presents positive aspects of Mexican-American life and thought. Constructive criticism is the approach. Should be particularly useful to schools and public libraries. (J.W.)

Forumeer. 1954. m. $5. E. David Sierra. American GI Forum of the U.S., 127 Graham Ave., no. 3, San Jose, Calif. 95110. Illus. Circ: 6,500. Sample. Vol. ends: Dec.

Aud: Ga. *Jv:* C.

Official publication of the American GI Forum, an independent veterans' family organization dedicated to the welfare of Mexican-Americans. This four-page, outspoken tabloid newsletter reports ethnic achievements, discriminatory incidents and information for veterans in addition to chapter news of the organization. It is written in summary style with headlines and photos which reflect the growing interest and participation of Mexican-Americans in civic affairs. It deserves a place in libraries serving Mexican-American communities. (J.W.)

El Grito: a journal of contemporary Mexican-American thought. 1967. q. $5. Octavio I. Romano-V. and Andres Ybarra. Quinto Sol Publns. Inc., P.O. Box 9275, Berkeley, Calif. 94709. Illus. Circ: 6,000. Sample. Vol. ends: Summer.

Bk. rev: Number varies, 200–400 words, signed. *Aud:* Ga, Hs, Ac. *Jv:* V.

A 75-page, nicely illustrated pocket-sized magazine mostly in English; some Spanish. Emphasis is divided among fiction, poetry, social research, and commentary. Occasionally there is a small, well-printed portfolio of a Mexican-American artist's work. The primary purpose is to acquaint readers with the talents, not to mention the socio-economic problems of Mexican-Americans in the United States. The tone is liberal, yet objective. The overall quality is quite high, and the total picture is one with which more Americans—particularly those living in California and the Southwest—should be familiar. For medium to large-sized libraries with an interest in social science, Mexican-American culture and the liberal arts. (J.W.)

El Grito del Norte. 1968. bi-m $4. Elizabeth Martinez and Jose Madril. El Grito del Norte, Inc., P.O. Box 466, Fairview Station, Espanola, N. Mex. 87532. Illus. Sample.

Indexed: API. *Aud:* Ga, Ac.

A militant newsprint tabloid prominent in the struggle for social justice and economic opportunities for Mexican-Americans. It is representative of Chicano youth's thinking in its coverage of protests, strikes, police actions, trials, and celebrations of the Chicano lifestyle. Background of Chicano people and the movement are subjects treated. There is some fiction and poetry. Compelling use is made of drawings and photography. Many of the articles and news stories carry a by-line. Portions of the text are in Spanish. Letters are regularly included. Written with conviction, spirit, and pride. For all Chicano collections. (J.W.)

Gráfica; la primera revista en Español de los Estados Unidos. 1947. bi-m. $4.50 for 12 issues. Armando del Moral. Orbe Publns. Inc., 705 N. Windsor Blvd., Hollywood, Calif. 90038. Illus, adv. Circ: 18,000. Sample.

Aud: Ga. *Jv:* C.

Advertising itself as a family magazine for the Spanish-speaking people in the United States, it is entirely in Spanish. Contents have something for everyone, although not in each issue. The wide range of articles includes personality features on the famous, successful, or holders of positions of leadership, on social functions, and occasionally on art, literature, cultural history and genealogy—all directly related to the Hispanic

world. Lacks both table of contents and index. Tone is conservative; no social commentary here. Emphasis is on entertainment. Useful to libraries with Spanish-speaking patrons. (J.W.)

Malcriado/Voice of the Farm Worker. 1964. bi-w. $3.50. Ed. Bd. United Farm Workers Organizing Committee, AFL-CIO, Box 130, Delano, Calif. 93215. Illus., adv. Circ: 18,000.

Bk. rev: Notes. *Aud:* Ga, Ac.

The voice of the United Farm Workers, this is a 16-page tabloid published in both English and Spanish. The purpose of the paper is to encourage the organization of the workers, to point out the wrongs in the system, and to give current news about strikes, benefits, harassment by owners and police, etc. It is one of the more informative in terms of what is going on with the average farm worker. A must in any agricultural area, and certainly a basic paper for larger social studies libraries.

Palante; Latin revolutionary news service. 1969. s-m. $5.75. Pablo Guzman. Young Lords Party, Latin Revolutionary News Service, 202 East 117th St., New York, N.Y. 10035. Illus.

Aud: Ac, Ga, Hs.

A revolutionary tabloid of some 28 pages which is published in both English and Spanish and carries the message of the Young Lords Party—a Puerto Rican militant group fighting for better living conditions in America, and New York in particular. In both content and approach it seems modeled after the better known, longer established Black Panther. The editors are for the "Liberation" of Puerto Rico from America, and call for revolution. An education program is constantly carried on in this area, e.g., an article "What is Class?" The writers ask readers not to serve in the army, and consider the police enemies. The writing is polemic, and a bit amateurish. The format is fair to good. But the message is there, and understandable enough. A good paper for any Spanish-speaking community not dominated by the establishment.

La Raza. 1970. irreg. (3–6 issues per year). $10 for 12 issues. Collective ed. group. El Barrio Communications Project, P.O. Box 31004, Los Angeles, Calif. 90031. Illus. Sample.

Aud: Ga, Ac. *Jv:* V.

Superseding a newsprint tabloid of the same title, this is a bilingual, militant organ of the Mexican-American movement for equality, justice, and an end to discrimination. Written from strong convictions, it contains numerous photos of Chicano activities, protests, and marches. A good source for portrayal of life in the barrios. Police actions and judicial proceedings concerning Chicanos also receive attention. Editorials and readers' letters are regular features. Articles are centered on Chicano culture and social commentary, and sometimes include poetry inspired by social conditions and experiences. Although amateurishly edited, it conveys a verve of ethnic pride other magazines might envy. No minority studies or Chicano collection can afford to omit. (J.W.)

Regeneración. 1970. 9–10 issues per year. $5. Francisca Flores, P.O. Box 54624, Los Angeles, Calif. 90054. Illus. Circ: 3,000.

Bk. rev: occasional, 500 words, signed. *Aud:* Ga, Hs.

An almost monthly newsmagazine which supersedes the newsletter, *Carta Editorial.* The interests of the Mexican-American movement "La Causa," to end discrimination and injustice, are central to its contents. In addition to summarized news and restrained editorial comment, letters and poetry are included. Some issues are devoted to a single topic such as women's self-determination and their contribution to the movement. It is attractively produced on colored paper with text in English except for an occasional poem in Spanish. Libraries with Mexican-American readers will find it of interest. (J.W.)

La Voz del Pueblo. 1970. m. $3.50. Centro Calitlan, Box 737, Hayward, Calif. 94543. Illus., adv. Sample.

Aud: Ga, Ac.

An important newspaper (in both Spanish and English) for Chicano studies. It has broadened its coverage since its beginnings. It has featured interviews with persons outstanding in Chicano and Mexican culture (e.g. Carlos Fuentes, Octavio Paz, Reies Lopez Tijerina). There is a concerted effort on the editor's part to provide an outlet for the intellectually inclined within the Chicano movement, although news coverage is still included. (K.R.)

Spanish Language

Artes de Mexico. 1953. m. $40. José Losada Tomé. Amores 262, Mexico 12, D.F., Mexico.

Indexed: LatAm. *Aud:* Hs, Ga, Ac.

A beautiful magazine with each issue devoted to one of the arts of Mexico which could be anything from Mexican silver work, Mexican dances, Mexican costumes and textiles to the bullfight in Mexico or Mexican cooking. Other issues are devoted to a Mexican museum or city. The illustrations in both black and white and color are outstanding. The articles, all in Spanish, are published with abbreviated translations in English and French and occasionally in German. A truly outstanding periodical with a great deal of browsing appeal in addition to giving full treatment to the subject being analyzed. Note: The magazine regularly publishes a list of back issues which are still available with a list of the titles and their prices. This could be an excellent way to obtain a good collection of material on Mexican art. (N.H.)

Blanco y Negro. 1891. w. $22.85. Guillermo Luca de Tena. Prensa Espanola, Serrano 61, Madrid, 6, Spain. Illus., adv.

Bk. rev: Notes. *Aud:* Ga, Ac.

A weekly featuring sports, world affairs, the arts. It has many color photos, essays. There is little, if any, discussion of Spanish politics, as might be expected. Somewhat cultural in orientation, but not too difficult to read. Similar to *Time.* (K.R.)

Boy y Lucha; el mundo del ring. 1951. w. $.25 per copy. Arturo Torres Yanez and Manuel Guerrero. Prensa Especializada S.A., Tenayuca No. 55, 5 Piso, Mexico 13, D.F./Mexico, Illus.

Aud: Ga.

Cheap format, poor but numerous photos. This is devoted to boxing and wrestling. Popular prose, such as *Rod and Gun, Sports Afield.* (K.R.)

Claudia (Mexico). 1965. m. $7.80. Vicente Leñero. Editorial Mex-Abril, S.A., Av. Morelos No. 16–40, Piso, Mexico 1, D.F., Mexico. Circ: 120,000.

Bk. rev: Notes. *Aud:* Ga, Hs.

This woman's magazine will be useful to public libraries and perhaps to high school libraries trying to meet the requests of Spanish-speaking women for a popular periodical. The emphasis of the publication is on fashions, but many articles also appear on cooking, family life, and entertainment. Short stories also are published. Recently the magazine has started to include a separate supplement designed for men, *Claudia, señor,* which features articles on sports, male fashions, etc. Different editions of *Claudia* are published in Argentina and Brazil, and while the Mexican publication is recommended because of its price, any library desiring to meet the special interests of patrons from either of the other countries might wish to subscribe to one of the following: *Claudia* (Argentina). 1957. m. $18 to $45. Editorial Abril S.A.I.C.I.F. y A., Avda. Leandro N. Alem 896, Buenos Aires, Argentina; *Claudia* (Brazil). 1961. m. $20.40. Editora Abril Ltda., Av. Otaviano A. de Lima 800, Sao Paulo, Brazil. Circ: 150,000. (N.H.)

Confidencias; la revista que busca su felicidad. 1943. w. $12. Clemente Cruzado. Editorial Confidencias, S.A., Ave. Juarez 64–511, Mexico 1 D.F., Mexico. Illus., adv. Circ: 100,000.

Aud: Ga.

The Mexican equivalent to *True Story.* "The magazine which looks for your happiness," it contains popular romances. Extremely popular with the ladies. (K.R.)

Cuadernos Americanos: la revista del nuevo mundo. 1942. bi-m. $13.50. Jesus Silva Herzog. Avenda Coyoacan 1035, Apdo. Postal 965, Mexico 12, D.F., Mexico. Index.

Indexed: LatAm, PMLA. *Bk. rev:* 4–8, 250–1,200 words, signed. *Aud:* Ga, Ac. *Jv:* V.

In one of Latin America's most respected reviews, readers will find articles concerning contemporary social problems, history, and literature. It is an excellent place for the student of Latin American affairs or literature to look for serious treatment of the topics of the greatest interest or importance. The journal is a vehicle for some of the continent's most prominent intellectuals, including Alfonso Reyes and Victor Raul Haya de la Torre. While the review does concern itself primarily with Latin American topics, occasional articles on Spain or international affairs (the United States and Vietnam) do appear. Articles on other than Latin American literature also are published from time to time. The journal is published entirely in Spanish and it prepares its own annual index. It should have a place in any basic collection on Latin America. (N.H.)

Cuadernos Hispanoamericanos; revista mensual de cultura Hispanica. 1948. m. $10. Jose Antonio Maravall. Instituto de Cultura Hispanica. Adva. de los Reyes Catolicos S-N, (Ciudad Universitaria), Madrid 3, Spain. Circ: 2,000.

Indexed: LatAm, PMLA. *Bk. rev:* 7–14, 900–3,500 words, signed. *Aud:* Ga, Ac. *Jv:* V.

A leading intellectual review which publishes original literature, literary criticism, articles on art, music, and the social sciences. There seems to be more material published concerning the arts than the social sciences. One interesting feature of this review is that the address of the author is given at the end of the article so if one has a comment one can write or wire direct. All of the articles are published in Spanish and they tend to be footnoted. An index is published at the end of each volume. Basic to any collection on the Hispanic world, that is, it covers both Spain and Latin America and occasionally includes material such as Spanish culture in Africa. (N.H.)

Goya; revista de arte. 1954. bi-m. $10. José Camón Aznar. Fundación Lazaro Galdiano, Serrano 122, Madrid, Spain. Sample. Vol. ends: Nov./Dec.

Indexed: ArtI. *Bk. rev:* 4–5, 225–1,300 words, signed. *Aud:* Ha, Ga, Ac.

Each issue contains between four and six articles on art history or criticism. Emphasis is on the art and artists of Spain, although most numbers contain at least one article on a foreign artist, school of art or exposition. Published in Spanish, with a brief summary in English of each of the leading articles. In each number there are several "Crónica," always one from Paris and Madrid, and usually one from Barcelona, Brussels, New York, or Tokyo. This feature describes the leading exhibitions taking place in the museums and galleries of that city. Another section, "Noticias de Arte," contains brief notes ón exhibits often in cities not covered by the more thorough reporting of the "crónicas." Although the periodical bears the name of the great Spanish painter Goya, and though articles are published on his art (some issues have been completely devoted to his work), it should be made clear that this is not a specialized journal. Its name honors "the painter who, rooted in tradition, opened the newest ways and the boldest techniques and inspirations of modern art." (N.H.)

El Hispanoamericano. w. $3. 630 Ninth St., Sacramento, Calif. 95825.

A Spanish-language paper for the Sacramento area. It focuses on local problems and the social scene. Á "straight" paper. (K.R.)

Hispano Americano; semanario de la vida y la verdad. 1946. w. $12. Ovidio Gondi, Barcelona 32, Mexico 6, D.F., Mexico.

Bk. rev: 5–11, 150–900 words, signed. *Aud:* Hs, Ga, Ac.

A leading Mexican news magazine with the familiar *Time* format. Various sections are devoted to national news, Mexican economics, news of the capital and the provinces, and the texts of the speeches of the president of the republic. While over half of the space is given to Mexican affairs, there is a section called "America de Polo a Polo" which gives coverage of United States, Canadian, and Latin American news from countries other than Mexico. Then there are the columns devoted to sports, art, cinema, theater, and books. The latter includes a list of bestsellers in Mexico City. The publication, while written for Spanish-speaking adults, is suitable for students with a good grasp of the language. It is appropriate for senior high schools, public libraries, and colleges.

It should be mentioned that this magazine circulates under the name *Hispano Americano* only in the United States and Puerto Rico. In the rest of Latin America, and the world for that matter, it is called *Tiempo*, and the contents of both editions are identical. When *Time* magazine objected to the use of the name *Tiempo* in 1946, the magazine began to publish a North American edition under the name *Hispano Americano*. (N.H.)

Manchete. 1950. w. $65.00 airmail. Bloch Editores S.A., Rua do Russell 804, Rio de Janeiro, Brazil. Subs. to: M&Z Representatives, 112 Ferry Street, Newark, N. J. 07105. Circ: 230,000. Sample. Vol. ends: last Dec. issue.

Aud: Ga, Ac.

An attractive news magazine with a *Life* format, *Manchete* will assist the large academic or public library in obtaining news of Brazil as it is popularly presented to the Brazilian people. This is one of several excellent reviews from the largest country in

Latin America and it is unfortunate that their publication in Portuguese reduces their usefulness to libraries in the United States even more severely than foreign journals published in French, German, or Spanish. One must also keep in mind when subscribing to a journal such as *Manchete* that in addition to interesting articles on education in Brazil or the Church in Latin America, one will find a fairly generous portion of articles devoted to beauty contests, movies, and their stars and other entertainers, in addition to items of international news of interest to Brazilians. For the library with an interest in Brazil, however, this would be a valuable addition to the collection. (N.H.)

Meridiano; sintesis de la prensa mundial al gusto Espanol. 1942. m. $4. Ediciones Joker, San Leonardo 12, Madrid 8, Spain. Illus., adv.

Aud: Ga, Ac, Hs.

A combination of *Atlas* and the *Readers' Digest,* this reprints articles from newspapers and magazines throughout the world. The selection, however, is short on controversy, and long on noncontroversial material in the arts, literature, and social sciences. In view of the base of publication, it is understandably (though not forgivably) reactionary. Nevertheless, it is a good cross section of the world's press, particularly the Spanish press (what there is of it), and is a useful magazine for the advanced, high school Spanish student or for those who want to brush up on their Spanish.

Mexico (City) Universidad Nacional. Revista. 1946. m. $8. Jorge Alberto Manrique. Universidad Nacional Autonoma de Mexico, Torre de la Rectoria, 10 Piso, Ciudad Universitaria, Mexico 20, D.F., Mexico.

Indexed: LatAm. *Bk. rev:* 2–6, 500–1,500 words, signed. *Aud:* Ga, Ac.

Easily one of the best Latin American university reviews published, this beautifully illustrated periodical contains poetry, short stories, and short plays as well as literary criticism and articles concerning philosophy and the social sciences. Articles often include short bibliographies. There is an interesting section, "Critica," which consists of reviews of books, the dance, the theatre, cinema and the plastic arts. Often an issue is devoted to one particular topic such as "La Novela Latinoamericana." Occasionally one is devoted to an individual such as Arturo Rosenbleuth (1900–1970), an eminent Mexican scientist. The appearance of the review is extremely attractive and some of Latin America's leading writers and scholars publish here. (N.H.)

Mundo Hispanico. 1948. m. $8. D. Francisco Leal Insua. Av Reyes Catolicos, C.U. Madrid 3, Spain. Illus., index, adv.

Bk. rev: Notes. *Aud:* Ac, Ga, Hs.

A *Life* approach to activities not only in Spain, but in all Spanish-speaking countries. It covers aspects of culture, art, literature, history, education, science, and activities of leading personalities. There is little political material. The text is relatively simple, and while the whole is geared for the Spanish-speaking adult, it can be used for both beginners and advanced students in Spanish. There are excellent black and white and color photographs.

Nueva Narrativa Hispanoamericana. 1971. s-a. $10 (Teachers $8; Students $6). Helmy Giacoman. Adelphi Univ., Garden City, N.Y.

Bk. rev: 14, 450–2,500 words, signed. *Aud:* Ac.

A promising new scholarly journal devoted exclusively to the study of Latin American narrative literature of the past thirty years. The entire publication is written in Spanish. Studies on such leading authors as Carlos Fuentes, Alejo Carpentier, and Gabriel García Márquez appeared in the first issue. Should be subscribed to by any academic library where an interest in Latin American literature exists. (N.H.)

Primera Plana; la revista de noticias de mayor circulación. 1962. w. $35. Victoria I. S. Dalle Nogare, Editorial Primera Plana, Peru 367, Pisos 10, 12, and 13, Buenos Aires, Argentina. Circ: 70,000.

Bk. rev: 3–4, 400–1,000 words. *Aud:* Ga, Ac.

Primera Plana is considered by many to be Argentina's leading news magazine. It devotes a great deal of its attention to covering the Argentine political scene and has run afoul of the government for its reporting. It was banned in 1969 and for several weeks was not able to publish, and when permitted to resume, had to change its title to *Periscopio* for several months before being able to take the name *Primera Plana* again. The publication has a reputation for giving a more realistic appraisal of Argentine political and social life than one tends to find in many other periodicals. It also gives coverage to important events in the rest of Latin America. The following are among the regular features of the magazine: the Country (Argentine news), Business and Economics, Modern Life, and the World. There are also columns on the arts, books, and sports. The first page features a brief summary of the leading articles and the most important pieces bear the authors' signatures. Needless to say, the entire publication is in Spanish. (N.H.)

Revista de Estudios Hispanicos. 1967. 3/yr. $6. Enrique Ruiz-Fornells. Univ. of Alabama Press, Drawer 2877, University, Ala. 35486. Index. Circ: 400. Vol. ends: Oct. Refereed.

Indexed: MLA. *Bk. rev:* 4, 1½ pages, signed. *Aud:* Ac.

Primarily for the scholar involved in aspects of Spanish literature and linguistics. Essays cover various schools of writing and individual writers. The scope for the Hispanic world is anywhere that Spanish is a language. Only for large, specialized collections.

Revista Geografica. 1941. s-a. $3. Nilo Bernades. Comissão de Geografia do Instituto Panamericano de Geografia e Historia, Av. Franklin Roosevelt, 39 S. 1414, Rio de Janeiro, GB-Brazil. Illus.

Bk. rev: 20–25, 150–300 words, signed. *Aud:* Ac.

Issued by a specialized agency of the Organization of American States, this South American publication publishes most articles in English or Spanish. Abstracts are provided in the other language. Subject matter is regional; most articles deal in some respect with Latin America. Economic and social geography is stressed. This magazine would be valuable to schools in Latin American area studies or to schools with comprehensive geographical collections. (D.D.)

Revista Iberoamericana; organo del Instituto Internacional de Literatura Iberoamericana. 1938. q. $8. Alfredo A. Roggiano. Mrs. Gloria J. Ward, 1617 C.L., Univ. of Pittsburgh, Pittsburgh, Pa. 15213. Circ: 970. Vol. ends: Oct./Dec.

Indexed: LatAm, PMLA. *Bk. rev:* 10–13, 450–3,000 words, signed. *Aud:* Ga, Ac.

"The Instituto Internacional de Literatura Iberoamericana was organized in 1938 in order to advance the study of Iberoamerican Literature and to promote cultural relations among the peoples of the Americas. To this end, the Institute publishes the *Revista Iberoamericana.* . . ." Over the past years complete issues have been devoted to the following prominent men of Latin American letters: Miguel Angel Asturias, César Vallejo, and Octavio Paz. Each of these issues consists of from 11 to 21 excellent studies of the figure including a valuable bibliography. Numbers not devoted to one individual contain approximately four to seven articles on leading Latin American writers or topics. Examples include: "Realidad y mitos latinoamericanos en el surrealismo francés" and "Unidad estructural en Alejo Carpentier." There is also a "Notas" section consisting of three or four brief items. All articles are in Spanish except for occasional ones in Portuguese. Basic to any collection on Latin American literature. (N.H.)

Revista de Occidente. 1923. m. $12. José Ortega Spottorno, Barbara de Braganza, 12, Madrid 4, Spain. Index. Circ: 10,000.

Indexed: PMLA. *Bk. rev:* 2–9, 350–2,500 words signed. *Aud:* Ga, Ac.

One of Spain's most prestigious scholarly reviews, this was founded in 1923 by José Ortega y Gasset. While there is an emphasis on Spanish literary topics, the journal is not limited to Spanish literature or to literature at all for that matter. One issue was devoted primarily to German literature and other numbers have featured articles on the following diverse intellectual topics: "Literatura Hispanoamericana," "Tres Poetas Españoles," "Biologiay Población," and "La España Siglo XIX." Thus, the social sciences are represented, too. The magazine publishes an index every three months covering that period. This is a leading review which should be in all academic libraries and large public libraries with an interest in Spain. (N.H.)

Siempre. w. $26.20. Editorial Siempre, Mexico. Subs. to: Nacional Distribuidora, 311 S. Broadway, Los Angeles, Calif. 90013. Illus., adv.

Aud: Ga.

Emphasis on Mexican material. It has a current events format, similar to *Life,* but with fewer photos. Easy to moderately difficult text. (K.R.)

Sucesos. w. $.40 per issue. Ed. bd. Suceso para Todos, Calzada de Tacubaya 103 (Esquina Con Juan Excutia), Mexico 18, D.F., Mexico. Illus., adv.

Aud: Ga, Ac.

Weekly news magazine subtitled "for everyone." The approximate equivalent of *Time,* but emphasizing Mexico and written on an easier level. (K.R.)

Sur. 1931. bi-m. $10. Victoria Ocampo. Revista Sur, Viamonte 494, 8°/ piso, Buenos Aires, Argentina. Circ: 5,000. Vol. ends: Dec.

Indexed: LatAm, PMLA. *Bk. rev:* 15–18, 200–2,000 words, signed. *Aud:* Ga, Ac. *Jv:* V.

With the issue No. 325 of this leading Argentine journal, the founder, Victoria Ocampo, one of the outstanding women of Latin American letters, announced that the review would have a new format. Instead of appearing six times a year, a triple number would be published twice a year. So far no such issue has arrived and while one fears for the existence of the publication, it still seems too soon to give up hope. If, in fact, this magazine has ceased after forty years, it will be the end of one of Latin America's finest reviews. Occasionally an issue has been devoted to one topic, the latest being "Joven Literatura Norteamericana," but the usual number is composed of two to four articles of literary criticism or commentary, an original story or two, and some poetry. Then there is a "Crónicas y Notas" section which includes the book reviews and interesting notes on art, music, and the cinema. Many of the great authors and scholars of Latin America such as Octavio Paz, Emmanual Carballo, Emir Rodríguez Monegal, and Enrique Anderson Imbert publish here and some such as Jorge Luis Borges and Eduardo Mallea serve on the editorial committee. Any institution with an interest in Latin American literature would not be without this periodical if it can still be obtained. (N.H.)

Temas. 1950. m. $6. José de la Vega. Club Familiar, Inc., 1560 Broadway, New York, N.Y. 10036. Illus., adv. Circ: 80,000. Sample.

Aud: Ga, Hs.

An illustrated, family magazine in Spanish focusing on the interests of Puerto Rican Americans. Large format and extensive use of photography suggest a Spanish language version of *Look*. Newsmakers of Puerto Rican background, entertainment personalitis, and national events receive maximum coverage. Regular features include fashions, sports, cooking, horoscope, cartoons, puzzles, and a letters column. Light reading level with emphasis on noncontroversial topics. Recommended for all public libraries with Puerto Rican readers. (J.W.)

Tiempo. See *Hispano Americano.*

Todo. 1933. m. $5. Enrique S. Ledesma. Editorial Salcedo, S.A., Calle de Hamburgo 36, Colonia Juarez, Mexico 6, D.F. Mexico. Illus.

Aud: Ga.

A news magazine with regular features (movies, gossip, etc.). Emphasis is on Mexican and world news. There are many black and white photos, whose quality is just fair. Poor paper-stock. On a level between *Life* and *Modern Screen.* (K.R.)

Vanidades Continental. 1961. bi-w. $14. Editorial America, S.A., Panama, Rep. of Panama. Subs. to: Saral Publns., Inc., 605 Third Ave., Suite 1616, New York, N.Y. 10016. Illus., adv. Circ: 405,000 (combined).

Aud: Ga.

This and *Claudia* are the two most popular general women's magazines in Latin America. As with *Claudia, Vanidades* is distributed in a number of countries, but primarily with the same basic features—the changes coming in advertising and local copy. Most American libraries will probably want the Mexican edition which is somewhat less expensive and enjoys the largest circulation of the group. It covers much the same material found in such American magazines as *Women's Day* and *Good Housekeeping,* i.e., emphasis is on the house and home and everything that implies: health, beauty, child care, romance, interior decoration, etc. There is usually a fair to good full-length novel by a Spanish novelist and short stories. It enjoys a tremendous popularity, and would be the woman's magazine to get for a general Spanish language collection. It would not—repeat—would not be the Spanish language magazine for the woman activist. Here one might consider the more involved Chicano magazines.

American Magazines in Spanish Editions

Lion en Espanol. 1944. bi-m. $1.50. Fidel V. Torres. International Assn. of Lions Clubs, 209 N. Michigan Ave., Chicago, Ill. 60601. Circ: 61,471.

Edited for Spanish-speaking members of Lions clubs. Primarily same content as *Lion.*

Mecanica Popular. 1947. m. $5. Felipe Rasco. Editorial America, S.A. 2180 S.W. 12th Ave., Miami, Fla. 33129. Illus., adv. Circ: 160,000.

The same format and contents as the English language *Popular Mechanics.*

Reader's Digest, Selecciones del. m. $3.97. Pablo Morales. S.A. de C.V., Paseo de la Reforma 116–12vo Piso, Mexico 6 D.F., Mexico. Illus., adv. Circ: 1,000,000. (400,000 in Mexico).

The same dreary content in Spanish. An even more discouraging thought—it is the largest circulating magazine in all Latin America.

Revista Rotaria. 1933. m. $3.75. Juan E. Milla, 1600 Ridge Ave., Evanston, Ill. 60201. Illus., index, adv. Circ: 46,000.

The Spanish edition, with only minor changes, of the *Rotarian.*

LAW

See also Criminology and Law Enforcement Section.

Basic Periodicals

Ga: *Law and Contemporary Problems, Journal of Urban Law, Trial;* Jc: *Law and Contemporary Problems, Law and Society Review;* Ac: *American Bar Association Journal, International Legal Materials, American Journal of International Law, Harvard Law Review, Columbia Journal of Law and Social Problems.*

Library and Teaching Aids

American Business Law Journal, Current Publications in Legal and Related Fields.

Basic Abstracts and Indexes

Index to Legal Periodicals, Abstracts on Criminology and Penology, Public Affairs Information Service.

American Bar Association Journal. 1915. m. Membership (Nonmembers $5). Richard Allen. Amer. Bar Assn., 1155 E. 60th St., Chicago, Ill. 60637. Illus. Circ: 154,000. Microform: UM.

Indexed: LegPer, PAIS. *Bk. rev:* 5–10, length varies, signed. *Aud:* Ac, Sa.

Directed to the practicing lawyer, this features sections on "Recent Supreme Court Decisions," "What's New in the Law," "Tax Notes," and abstracts of periodical articles, all of these geared to keeping the lawyer up to date. Contributions come from a wide range of professionals; lawyers, district attorneys, judges, insurance experts, and law librarians.

American Business Law Journal. 1921. 3/yr. Membership (Nonmembers $6.50). Gaylord A. Jentz. Univ. of

Texas, College of Bus. Admin., Austin, Tex. 78712. Adv. Circ: 1,000. Sample. Vol. ends: Winter. Microform: UM.

Indexed: LegPer. *Bk. rev:* 4, 2 pages, signed. *Aud:* Ac, Hs.

One of the few legal journals devoted to business law for the teacher. Articles, by professors of law and business, cover primarily those topics likely to be taken up in business law courses. Although written for the academic situation, many of the articles might be used by teachers of business law at the high school level. At any rate, high school teachers will profit from the book reviews. A typical issue covers news of the American Business Law Association, features three or four articles, and then finishes with comments, notes, and case digests.

American Journal of International Law. 1907. q. Membership (Nonmembers $30). R. R. Baxter. Amer. Soc. of Intl. Law, 2223 Massachusetts Ave., N.W., Washington, D.C. 20008. Illus., index, adv. Circ: 7,500. Microform: UM. Reprint: Johnson.

Indexed: LegPer, PAIS, SSHum. *Bk. rev:* 10–15, 600 words, signed. *Aud:*Ac.

A scholarly yet readable journal on international law which is of value to anyone concerned with current worldwide problems in political science, economics and, or course, law. The book reviews are well written and include a number of foreign publications. Of special importance are the sections devoted to publications of the United Nations, the United States, judicial decisions involving international law, and the contemporary practice of the United States in international legal matters.

American Journal of Legal History. 1957. q. $7.50. Erwin C. Surrency. Temple Univ. School of Law, 1715 N. Broad St., Philadelphia, Pa. 19122. Circ: 800.

Indexed: LegPer. *Bk. rev:* 2–3, 500–1,500 words. *Aud:* Sa, Ac.

The only journal in the English language which deals exclusively with legal history. As such it deserves a wider audience than lawyers, and should be in most large history collections. Articles cover every aspect of the law and the peripheral interests such as publishing, social aspects, literary works, personalities, and the like. The style varies, but is usually scholarly, and most of the articles are well documented.

✓ ***Antitrust Bulletin; journal of American and foreign antitrust and trade regulations.*** 1955. q. $33. James M. Glabault. Federal Legal Publns., Inc., 95 Morton St., New York, N.Y. 10014. Index, adv. Sample. Vol. ends: Winter.

Indexed: LegPer, PAIS. *Bk. rev:* 3–4, 2–4 pages, signed. *Aud:* Ac, Sa.

A specialized technical journal edited for experts interested in economics and antitrust matters. Current cases or specific issues are discussed. The periodical is strictly for the use of directly involved lawyers and economists, though very advanced students in the field will find it useful. (M.S.)

Antitrust Law & Economics Review. 1967. q. $25. Thomas M. Hiura. Antitrust Law & Economics Review, Inc., 6830 Elm St., McLean, Va. 22101. Illus. Vol. ends: Summer.

Bk. rev: various number, length. *Aud:* Ac, Sa.

While primarily a law journal, this has some value for the interested economist, businessman and legislator. The articles and documents make available the findings of economists in the field of industrial organization, i.e., antitrust activities. A specialized journal for larger collections. (M.S.)

Boston University Law Review. 1921. q. $5. Valerie C. Epps. Boston Univ. School of Law, 765 Commonwealth Ave., Boston, Mass. 02215. Index, adv. Circ: 5,100. Sample. Vol. ends: Fall.

Indexed: LegPer, PAIS. *Bk. rev:* 1–3, essays. *Aud:* Ac.

A substantial review which is noted for the high quality of its articles and case comments. A typical issue runs to almost 150 pages, features two or three topical articles, notes, comments, and book reviews. The writing varies, but generally the editing is such that the material is clear, if not always sparkling. Basic for any medium to large-sized law collection.

Columbia Journal of Law and Social Problems. 1965. 3/yr. Box 7, Columbia Univ. School of Law, 435 W. 116 St., New York, N.Y. 10027. Index. Circ: 3,000. Sample. Vol. ends: Sept.

Indexed: LegPer. *Aud:* Ac.

Broad areas of social concern as affected by the law are investigated in this publication by students of the Columbia Law School. Issues have included articles on school prayer, campus confrontation, fair election procedures and the UMW, cigarette advertising and the public health, problems of commuters, "Federal Narcotics Presumptions after Leary," integration, truth in packing, merit systems of examination, etc. For coverage of social problems and the law, this is one of the reviews to consider. Other titles including *Law and Contemporary Problems* and the *Yale Review of Law and Social Action* may be identified from the journals listed in the *Index to Legal Periodicals.* (M.S.)

Columbia Law Review. 1901. m. (Nov.–June). $12.50. Columbia Law Students, 435 W. 116th St., New York, N.Y. 10027. Index, adv.

Indexed: LegPer, PAIS. *Bk. rev:* 4–6, 350–750 words, signed. *Aud:* Ac.

Following the classic design of a review journal, there are two to three articles on current problems of interest, notes and comments which are really short articles, and a few highly topical book reviews. The whole is written by both professors and lawyers, and much of the material in the notes section is of interest to those in related areas, e.g., articles on developments in censorship, advertising, proposed constitutional changes, and the like. Law librarians consider this a must for any legal collection, and it has wider use in universities and colleges with strong political science departments.

Columbia Survey of Human Rights Law. 1967. bi-a. Donald R. Davis, Box 54, 435 W. 116th St., New York, N.Y. 10027. Index, adv. Circ: 500. Vol. ends: Fall.

Bk. rev: 4, 8 pages, signed. *Aud:* Ac, Sa.

Averaging some 200 pages, this is a student-edited journal devoted to civil liberties and urban problems. Primarily for the legal field, this is of value to anyone involved with civil rights. For example, the January 1971 number featured articles on state remedies for racial imbalance in education, an article on Indian tribal laws, and a study of conspiracy. Welfare, jury service, and problems of search and seizure are among the topics considered. While the style presupposes some knowledge of law, the articles are lively, well documented, certainly timely. Among the better review journals, and of broader interest than usual.

Criminal Law Bulletin. 1964. m. $24. Neil Fabrikant. Criminal Law Bulletin Inc., Hanover Lamont Corp., 89 Beach St., Boston, Mass. 02111.

Indexed: LegPer. *Aud:* Ac, Sa.

While written for lawyers and students, there is much here of interest to laymen dealing in areas of controversy. There is a full section given over to "Recent Decisions" which have wide effects in civic affairs. A "Criminal Law Bulletin Quiz" presents one or two model cases with suggestions as to where answers may be found.

Current Publications in Legal and Related Fields. 1952. m. (except June, July and Sept.). $20. Betty Wilkins. Fred B. Rothman & Co., 57 Leuning St., S. Hackensack, N.J. 07606. Index. Circ: 500. Sample. Vol. ends: Dec.

Aud: Ac, Sa.

A current awareness tool for acquisitions librarians by members of the American Association of Law Libraries. It is a bibliography of books, pamphlets, documents, and some news and magazine articles. Arrangement is alphabetical by authors, and there is an annual cumulation and subject index. Full bibliographic information is given to each item as well as an occasional reference to a review. (M.S.)

Harvard Law Review. 1887. 8/yr. (Nov.–June). $12.50. Harvard Law Review Assn., Grannett House, Cambridge, Mass. 02138. Index, adv. Circ: 11,000.

Indexed: LegPer, PAIS. *Bk. rev:* 2–3, 1,000–2,000, 400 words, signed. *Aud:* Ac. *Jv:* V.

Besides being *the* scholarly publication for lawyers, this periodical covers legal aspects of problems of general interest to social scientists. Articles appeal to political scientists, sociologists, and historians. The one or two main articles are highly literate and usually exhaustive studies of almost monographic length and quality. Every university and many colleges should have it available for faculty and students.

International and Comparative Law Quarterly. 1952. q. $15. K. R. Simmons. British Inst. of Intl. and Comparative Law, 32 Furnival St., London, EC 4A 1JN, England. Circ: 3,000. Vol. ends: Oct.

Indexed: LegPer. *Bk. rev:* 15–20, 500–1,500 words. *Aud:* Ac.

Articles deal with broad matters of international law, such as diplomatic protection, or specific problems in individual nations. Its scope is more technical and limited than the *American Journal of International Law,* but it does contain a useful section of comments on current legal developments. As a library source, it is mainly useful for providing supplementary readings in current international law. (M.S.)

International Legal Materials. 1962. bi-m. Membership $15 (Nonmembers $35). Marilou M. Righini. Intl. Legal Materials, 2223 Massachusetts Ave., N.W., Washington, D.C. 20008. Index. Circ: 1,125. Vol. ends: Nov.

Indexed: PAIS. *Aud:* Ac. *Jv:* V.

Designed to provide up-to-date information on legal aspects of international affairs, this does not contain articles, but rather presents the text of current documents. Its value lies in its currency, and in the wide scope of the sources included. International law is to be interpreted broadly here; the items selected for inclusion are those of substantial interest to a large number of scholars and lawyers. Technical subjects of a highly specialized nature are excluded. Some material is reprinted from other sources currently available (e.g., *The Department of State Bulletin*), but these usually concern important policy situations, and it is useful to have them concentrated in one place. Among the documents to be found are judicial decisions, treaties and agreements, legislation, and the statements of foreign leaders. Major U.N. material is also included. (M.S.)

Israel Law Review. 1966. q. $12. S. Ginossar. Israel Law Review Assn., c/o Faculty of Law, Hebrew Univ., Jerusalem, Israel. Circ: 1,500.

Indexed: IJewAr. *Bk. rev:* 1–4, lengthy, signed. *Aud:* Ac.

Scholarly review published under the auspices of the Faculty of Law of the Hebrew University of Jerusalem. Gives a good overview of the research interests of the Faculties of Law of Israel Universities and the legislative problems of the State of Israel. The contents are made up of five to six scholarly articles, authoritative comments on key judgments, critical assessments of significant laws, a digest of recent Israeli cases and book reviews. Articles cover purely legal matters—"The need for corroboration of accomplice testimony," legal aspects of other disciplines—"Legal problems of medical advance," history of law and Jewish law—"Purchase of the Cave of Machpelah," and international law, such as the legal aspects of the Israeli-Arab conflict—"The Six-day war and the right of self-defence." Contributors are mainly the academic staff of the Hebrew University, but staff of other Israeli universities, scholars from abroad, magistrates and prominent lawyers are also represented. (R.T.)

Journal of the American Trial Lawyers Association. 1946. Every 2 years. $25. Thomas F. Lambert, Jr. The Assn., 20 Garden St., Cambridge, Mass. 02138. Index. Circ: 34,000.

Aud: Ac, Sa.

By the same publisher of the semipopular *Trial*, this appears about every two years in a bound volume of some 800 pages. It covers the latest developments in the law, and the "essential background information necessary for the preparation of briefs and memoranda." Although technically a journal, it is more like a law reference book. Only for large legal collections.

The Journal of Criminal Law, Criminology and Police Science. 1910. q. $15. Fred C. Imbau. Williams & Wilkins Co., 428 E. Preston St., Baltimore, Md. 21202. Illus., index. Circ: 3,400. Microform: UM.

Indexed: ChemAb, LegPer, PAIS, PsyAb. *Bk. rev:* 5–6, 1,000–2,500 words, signed. *Aud:* Ac, Ga.

An interdisciplinary journal of use to students, lawyers, criminologists, and police officers. Emphasis is on court procedure, legal administration of evidence, and protection of civil liberties. Abstracts of recent cases are of interest to the trial attorney. In a second section, the police science field is covered. The articles reflect the necessary cooperation required in modern criminal justice. Issued by the Northwestern University School of Law, this is one of the best journals in the field and a first choice for larger collections.

Journal of Law and Economics. 1958. s-a. $7. Univ. of Chicago Law School, Univ. of Chicago Press, 5750 S. Ellis Ave., Chicago, Ill. 60637. Circ: 750.

Indexed: HistAb, JEconLit, LegPer. *Aud:* Ac.

A journal of equal interest to economists, lawyers, and students of business. The nine to twelve articles, written primarily by faculty, emphasize the legal aspects of national economic issues. Each piece is well documented, interpretive, and of considerable value for the specialist.

Journal of Legal Education. 1948. q. $12.50. Eugene F. Mooney. Univ. of Kentucky, School of Law Assn., Lexington, Ky. 40506. Circ: 5,000.

Indexed: LegPer. *Bk. rev:* 4–5, 500–1,000 words. *Aud:* Ac.

As the title implies, this is primarily for the law teacher, and is edited by professional legal educators. The articles are both specific and general, dealing with the problems of a law education and the process of law. A journal which is received as a matter of course by any university with a law program.

Journal of Urban Law. (Formerly: ***University of Detroit Law Review***). 1916. q. $6. Journal of Urban Law, Univ. of Detroit, 651 East Jefferson Ave., Detroit, Mich. 48226. Circ: 1,625. Sample. Vol. ends: Summer. Refereed.

Indexed: CathI, CIJE, LegPer. *Bk. rev:* 1, 1,500 words, signed. *Aud:* Ac, Ga.

Covers a wide range of material on matters of public policy, usually on the state or municipal level. Formerly the *University of Detroit Law Review*, it is now specializing in the urban field, and as a result has greatly increased its readership potential. Articles range from the technical and legal to those of a more general, public interest. Some subjects covered: urban riots (a special issue), planning and zoning, public housing, the elected representation of minorities, and environmental legislation. Special features are "legal comments" and "recent decisions." A law school journal, it follows the practice of student editorship with articles solicited from leading professional authorities. It differs from other journals of this type, however, in the emphasis placed on urban policy matters. It is recommended for any library going beyond a surface and general coverage of the environmental and social situation of our cities. (M.S.)

Labor Law Journal. See Labor and Industrial Relations Section.

Law and Contemporary Problems. 1933. q. $10. Clark C. Havighurst. Duke Univ. School of Law, Duke Station, Durham, N.C. 27706. Illus., adv. Circ: 1,850. Microform: UM.

Indexed: LegPer, PAIS, SSHum. *Aud:* Ga, Ac. *Jv:* V.

While technically a law periodical this is actually a series of symposia on contemporary problems. Each issue covers a specific subject, e.g., "Antipoverty Programs," "Privacy." Contributors tend to be economists, sociologists, and philosophy professors as well as law experts. This is a must for college and university libraries and of importance to public libraries.

Law and Society Review. 1967. q. Membership. $15. Samuel Krislov. Sage Publns., 275 Beverly Dr., S. Beverly Hills, Calif. 90212.

Indexed: LegPer. *Bk. rev:* 4–5, 7–8 pages, signed. *Aud:* Ac.

Differs from most law journals in that the editors attempt to stress the relationship between law and the social sciences. Issues have covered school segregation as seen from a lawyer's viewpoint and the same question as viewed by a sociologist, political scientist, and educator. Other topics have touched on such varied subjects as speeding laws, witchcraft, and population control. Special bibliographies.

Michigan Law Review. 1902. m. (Nov.–June). $12.50. Michigan Law Review Assn., Ann Arbor, Mich. 48108. Index, adv. Circ: 3,000.

Indexed: LegPer, PAIS. *Bk. rev:* 5, 4–8 pages, signed. *Aud:* Sa, Ac.

One of the basic law review journals, useful not only in law collections, but in libraries which have a strong interest in political science, economics, and government. Each issue features scholarly articles, often in the form of a symposium, on all aspects of law and society. In addition to detailed book reviews there is a "Periodical Index," which arranges, by subject, articles from other major law reviews.

Military Law Review. 1957. q. $2.50. Supt. of Documents, U.S. Govt. Printing Office, Washington, D.C. 20402. Refereed.

Indexed: LegPer, PAIS. *Aud:* Sa, Ac.

Concentrates on the narrow field of military law, which is no longer esoteric because it affects millions of draftable young men, servicemen, and veterans. The articles, though generally of a technical character, cover a number of subjects of wider interest. Some articles have been on the procedural rights of the accused, draft abuse, and religion, conscience, and military discipline. Features include recent developments and books received. Although it is a Department of Defense publication, it does not push any particular governmental policies. Despite the appeal of the subject, this is not an easy journal for the typical reader. (M.S.)

New York University Journal of International Law and Politics. 1968. 3/yr. $6. Paul A. Mapes. New York Univ. School of Law, 40 Washington Square S., New York, N.Y. 10003. Adv. Circ: 1,000. Sample. Vol. ends: Winter. Refereed.

Indexed: LegPer. *Bk. rev:* 2, 2,000–4,000 words, signed.

A good journal for the specialized collection, this does not have the scope, prominence, or volume of the *American Journal of International Law.* There have been articles on peace in Palestine, the European convention on human rights, and the U.N. Security Council. Some emphasis is placed on regulatory matters and international trade. It belongs in all law schools, and in any collection with a strong interest in international law. Unless this is included in one of the more readily available indexes, other libraries will want to consider carefully before purchase. (M.S.)

Trial. 1964. bi-m. $5. Richard S. Jacobson. American Trial Lawyers Assn., 20 Garden St., Cambridge, Mass. 02138. Illus., adv. Circ: 75,000. Sample. Vol. ends: Dec.

Indexed: LegPer. *Bk. rev:* 2–3, 500 words, signed. *Aud:* Ga, Sa, Ac, Hs.

A small but useful magazine, this periodical is subtitled "the only news magazine for lawyers." Employing a modern format, the various issues take up some matter of public debate and give the varied and divergent viewpoints that are held by leading national authorities. Written on a popular level, it may be helpful to those students writing papers or planning debates. Recommended for all libraries.

University of Detroit Law Review. See *Journal of Urban Law.*

Yale Law Journal. 1891. 8/yr. (m. Nov.–Jan.; Mar–July). $12.50. Yale Law Journal Co., Inc. 401-A Yale Station, New Haven, Conn. 06520. Illus., index, adv. Circ: 4,000. Microform: UM. Reprint: Fred B. Rothman Co.

Indexed: LegPer, PAIS. *Bk. rev:* 3–4, 2,300 words, signed. *Aud:* Ac.

A basic legal journal. It is also of some value to social scientists and scholars. Long articles (sometimes 100 pages) are devoted to topics of general interest. It has an excellent policy of occasionally having more than one reviewer report on the same book. Book reviews are long and complete and often include general-interest titles.

Yale Review of Law and Social Action. 1970. q. $9. Yale Law School, Box 87, New Haven, Conn. 06520. Illus., index, adv. Circ: 1,400. Sample. Vol. ends: Spring. Refereed.

Bk. rev: 2, 3,000 words, signed. *Aud:* Ac.

Another of the journals linking social problems and the law, this will interest students of sociology, social work, and related areas. "For too long, legal issues have been defined and discussed in terms of academic doctrine rather than strategies for social change. *Law and Social Action* is an attempt to go beyond the narrowness of such an approach to present forms of legal scholarship and journalism which focus on programmatic solutions to social problems . . . and . . . will serve as a forum in which practicing professionals, activists, community leaders, and scholars can share their insights and experience. . . ." Articles concern police and universities, rent strikes, poverty, revolutionaries, zoning, law reform, and activist legal service. (M.S.)

LIBRARY PERIODICALS

See also Bibliography and Books and Book Reviews Sections.

Basic Periodicals

In all cases the recommendations are for librarians, not for the general reading public. Furthermore, they are the more general titles within the specialized field.

Ejh: School Library Journal, Top of the News, School Media Quarterly; Hs: *School Library Journal, Top of the News, School Media Quarterly;* Ga: *Library Journal, American Libraries, Wilson Library Bulletin;* Jc: *Library Journal, College & Research Libraries, American Libraries, Library Trends;* Ac: *Library Journal, College & Research Libraries, American Libraries, Canadian Library Journal, Harvard Library Bulletin, Journal of Documentation, Library Trends.*

COUNTERCULTURE. *Synergy, CU Voice, Sipapu, Liberated Librarian, Library Journal, American Libraries,* and *Wilson Library Bulletin* whose editors are all part of the counterculture movement.

Basic Abstracts and Indexes

Library Literature, Library and Information Science Abstracts, CALL.

Cessations

Cornell Library Journal, MLA Quarterly, NELA Newsletter, North County Libraries, New York Public Library. Bulletin (see annotation), *New Jersey Librarians for Social Responsibilities.*

ALA Bulletin. See *American Libraries.*

APLA Bulletin. 1936. q. Membership. $8 (Individuals $5). Susan Whiteside. Subs. to: W. Patridge, Pine Hill Divinity Hall Library, Halifax, Nova Scotia. Illus., adv. Circ: 400. Sample. Vol. ends: Dec.

Indexed: CanI, LibLit, LibSciAb. *Aud:* Ac, Ga.

The official publication of the Atlantic Provinces Library Association, comprising Nova Scotia, New Brunswick, Prince Edward Island, Newfoundland. Emphasis is on activities of librarians in this area, but the articles tend to touch on material of interest to all librarians, regardless of location. The level of writing is high for this type of journal, the articles above average, and the editor includes items of value to all types of librarians. Some material in French.

ASLIB Proceedings. 1949. m. Membership (Nonmembers $24.20). Michael J. Tilleard. Assn. of Special Libraries and Information Bureaus, 3 Belgrave Sq., London SW 1, England. Illus., index, adv. Circ: 3,600. Sample. Vol. ends: Dec.

Indexed: LibLit, LibSciAb. *Bk. rev:* 4, 400 words. *Aud:* Ac, Ga.

The English counterpart of the American *Special Libraries.* As the official organ of the Association, it usually features two to three long, often illustrated articles on computers, documentation, indexing, and bibliographic control. The style of writing is good to excellent, the contributors among the leaders in the field. Of particular value to Americans is the regular feature "Current Awareness List," an annotated listing of books, pamphlets and articles of three to five pages.

Administrator's Digest. 1965. m. $15.80. Robert S. Alvarez, Box 993, S. San Francisco, Calif., 94080. Sample. Vol. ends: Dec. Microform: UM.

Aud: Ac, Sa, Hs.

A newsletter which contains about 60 brief items on school and library administration. The pieces are excerpted by the editor from publications which the average reader is not apt to scan. The emphasis is on "new ideas," and the newsletter serves to alert as much to inform. The price is a bit steep, but where the budget allows it is a useful item for larger libraries.

Advanced Technology/Libraries. 1972. 10/yr. $28. Frances G. Spigai. Becker & Hayes, Inc. (a subsidiary of John Wiley & Sons), 11661 San Vincente Blvd. Suite 907, Los Angeles, Calif. 90049. Sample.

Bk. rev: 8–12, notes. *Aud:* Ac, Ga.

Is 80 pages worth $28 a year? That is the basic question any economy-minded librarian must ask about this new newsletter. The price is not unusual, e.g., *Information Retrieval and Library Automation Letter* costs $24; and the older, more general *Knowledge Industry Report* sells for $60. Apparently there is going to be a run of this kind of thing. But this title is not worth the 30 cents per page cost to the library, at least not until *AT/L* (as it calls itself) improves considerably. Its purpose is to report on applications of technology to libraries, e.g., CATV, computers, facsimile transmission. The first issue consisted of a full page telling the reader about the subject, some six pages of "go get 'em and hurrah" concerning benefits to libraries of systems analysis, and another page of really good book reviews. The trouble is that, except for the first page, nothing was either timely or particularly new. Perhaps it will improve with time. Meanwhile, send for a sample before sending in the full subscription price.

Africana Library Journal. See *Africa Section.*

The American Archivist. 1938. q. $15. Edward Weldon. National Archives and Records Service, Washington, D.C. 20408. Adv. Circ: 2,500. Vol. ends: No. 4. Reprint: Johnson.

Indexed: LibLit, LibSciAb, PAIS. *Bk. rev:* 10–12, 150–700 words, signed. *Aud:* Ac.

One of the few literary, technical magazines in the library science field, this is indispensable for anyone dealing with any aspect of archives. Two or three of the four annual issues are usually turned over to special areas, e.g., automation in archives and manuscript collections archives of the arts. Other numbers feature six to ten articles on every aspect of archival librarianship from cataloging to collecting. The journal has an extensive bibliography of current works of interest to the archivist While of limited interest to the generalist, it has high reference value for both the librarian and historian.

American Documentation. See *American Society for Information Science. Journal.*

American Libraries (Formerly: **ALA Bulletin**). 1907. m. Members only. Gerald R. Shields. Amer. Library Assn., 50 E. Huron St., Chicago, Ill. 60611. Illus., index, adv. Circ: 35,000. Sample. Vol. ends: Dec. Microform: UM.

Indexed: CurrCont, EdI, LibLit, RG. *Bk. rev:* 20, notes. *Aud:* Ac, Ga, Hs, Ejh. *Jv:* V.

What was once the rather dull, pedestrian voice of the American Library Association has become a first rate magazine—a magazine which is required reading by any librarian, regardless of type or size of library. Under its editor, the format, content, and purpose of the journal have changed from simply reporting on ALA activities to leading the profession into viable new activities. Each issue features four to five thoughtful articles on everything from little magazines to operational procedures for a small school library. But the primary emphasis is on change—whether that change be in philosophy, administration, or collection purposes. (There are, to be sure, counter arguments for the old ways, which are dutifully given their day in the columns, too.) The activities of the Association are reported in full, and there are a number of departments from the activities of the Intellectual Freedom Committee to classified advertisements. In the last edition it was noted that "librarians tend to be hard on their own, and while in some ways this is commendable, let it be said that the *Bulletin* is no worse, and in fact, is better in many ways than a good number of other official association voices." The comment still stands, with the addition that it is the best single general library professional magazine about, right up there and fighting for attention with the traditional two, i.e., the *Library Journal* and *Wilson Library Bulletin*. You have to be a member of ALA to subscribe, and the best argument for joining now seems to be Mr. Shields' magazine.

American Library Association. 50 E. Huron St., Chicago, Ill. 60611.

The ALA publishes 26 different serials. The following is a complete list as of early 1972. Those which are annotated in the main section are given by title only. All are available from ALA; (°) indicates available only with membership, and not by subscription.

Adult Services. 1959. q. (°) Adult Services Division. *American Libraries.*

ALA Washington Newsletter. 1950. m. $5. Circ: 1,800.

AHIL Quarterly. 1960. q. (°) Assn. of Hospital and Institution Libraries. Circ: 1,800. Indexed: LibLit.

Armed Forces Librarians. Newsletter. (°) Circ: 200.

Booklist.

Choice.

College & Research Libraries.

Exhibit. 1955. q. (°) Exhibits Round Table. Circ: 200.

Journal of Library Automation.

Junior Members Round Table. 1967. q. (°) Circ: 700.

LED Newsletter. 1971. q. (°) Library Education Div.

Leads. 1960. q. (°) International Relations Round Table.

Libraries in International Development. Newsletter. 1968. m. $5.50. International Relations Office.

Library Resources and Technical Services.

Library Technology Reports.

Newsletter on Intellectual Freedom.

PLA Newsletter. 1961. 3/yr. (°) Public Library Assn. Circ: 13,000.

President's Newsletter. 1961. q. (°) Assn. of State Library Agencies.

Public Library Trustee. 1961. q. (°) American Library Trustee Assn.

Public Relations Reporter.

RQ.

Recruitment Newsletter. 1958. q. Free. Office for Recruitment.

SORT. 1964. q. (°) Staff Organizations Round Table.

School Media Quarterly.

Top of the News.

American Society for Information Science. Journal (JASIS) (Formerly: **American Documentation**).1950. bi-m. Membership (Nonmembers $35). Arthur W. Elias, 1140 Connecticut Ave., N.W., Washington, D.C. 20036. Illus., index, adv. Circ: 5,500. Sample. Vol. ends: Nov./Dec. Refereed. Microform: UM, MF. Reprint: Kraus.

Indexed: ChemAb, CurrCont, EngI, LibLit, LibSciAb, SCI. *Bk. rev:* 2–4, ½ column, signed. *Aud:* Ac.

The scholarly American journal devoted to documentation, broader in scope than the *Journal of Library Automation*, narrower in view than the English *Journal of Documentation*. The 10 to 15 articles are technical, written by subject experts and librarians, and presuppose considerable background in the field. The style varies, but the journal's primary value is that it encourages exploratory research and philosophical queries considerably above the intellectual level of most magazines of this type. An absolute necessity for the large library, the library school, and the specialist.

Annals of Library Science and Documentation. 1954. q. $3. B. Guha. Indian Natl. Scientific Documentation Centre (INSDOC), Hillside Rd., New Delhi, 12, India. Illus., index. Circ: 500. Sample. Vol. ends: Dec.

Indexed: LibLit, LibSciAb, *Bk. rev:* 1–3, 1 page, signed. *Aud:* Ac.

While published in India, the magazine is generally international in scope. According to the editor, the journal publishes original material "in the field of library classification, cataloging, bibliographic organization, documentation techniques, bibliographic standardization etc." The style of writing is fair to excellent. An interesting, even valuable addition for larger schools of library science.

Annual Report of the Librarian of Congress. 1866. a. Free to libraries (others should write to the Supt. of Documents, U.S. Govt. Printing Office for prices). Sarah L. Wallace. Library of Congress, Central Services Div., Washington, D.C. 20540. Illus., adv. Circ: 4,300. (300 paid).

Aud: Ac, Ga.

A summary of Library of Congress activities over the previous fiscal year. Covers all departments and areas, all new developments, in fact, anything which has a bearing upon present Library practices. It is becoming increasingly important as LC slowly assumes more and more leadership in centralized cataloging, reference service, and the like. And while a good part of it is routine and dull, there are enough important facts and data to make it a reference point for librarians. Well indexed.

The Assistant Librarian. 1898. m. Membership (Nonmembers $4.80). Bob Usherwood. Assn. of Assistant Librarians, Central Library, Ronford RM1, 3AR, England. Illus., index, adv. Circ: 12,500. Sample. Vol. ends: Dec.

Indexed: LibLit, LibSciAb. *Bk. rev:* 3, 500 words, signed. *Aud:* Ac, Ga.

The official journal of the Association, a division of the English Library Association. The format is somewhat confusing, the contents a potpourri of ideas, suggestions, and gripes by the younger members of the English library profession. It is a delight to read, primarily because unlike many similar American publications it takes a dim view of the establishment, is quick to chastise, and even quicker to shatter sacred ideas and notions. It should be required for all younger American librarians, and not a few older ones.

Association Canadienne Des Bibliothecaires De Langue Francaise. Bulletin. 1955. q. $7. Gisele Hogue. The Assn., 360 rue Le Moyne, Montreal, 125, Que., Canada. Illus., index, adv. Circ: 1,400. Sample. Vol. ends: Dec.

Indexed: CanI, LibLit, LibSciAb. *Bk. rev:* 5, 1 page, signed. *Aud:* Sa.

The publication of the French language side of the Canadian Library Association, although with no direct connection to the Association. The 60 or so page journal is professionally edited, features six to eight articles, book reviews, and news of the organization. All articles are in French. The bibliographies are in the language of the author. The material is good to excellent, the writing style seems at least adequate, and the magazine offers another sound approach to librarianship. It quite obviously is of limited use in non-French reading libraries, but for those who command the language it is a first choice.

Australian Academic and Research Libraries. 1970. q. $A6 (Individuals $A4). D. H. Borchardt. LaTrobe Univ., Bundora, Victoria, Australia 3083. Illus., index, adv. Circ: 300. Vol. ends: Dec. Refereed.

Bk. rev: 2–3, 500–700 words, signed. *Aud:* Ac.

The official journal of the University and College Libraries Section of the Library Association of Australia. Replaces the Section's earlier *News Sheet.* Most of the material is of interest to Australian libraries, but there is enough of a broader scope to give it decided interest for North American academic libraries. (N.H.)

Australian Library Journal. 1951. m. Membership (Nonmembers $13.50). W. L. Brown. Library Assn. of Australia, 32 Belvoir St., Surry Hills, NSW 2010, Australia. Illus., index, adv. Circ: 6,200. Sample. Vol. ends: Dec.

Indexed: LibLit, LibSciAb, PAIS. *Bk. rev:* Various number, length, signed. *Aud:* Sa.

The official organ of the Library Association of Australia. Somewhat like its British counterparts, it is lively, informative, and of considerable interest to librarians, both in and outside of Australia. The articles consider all aspects of the art, not simply what is applicable to the Australian scene. Includes the usual news items, book reviews, correspondence, etc. What is unusual is the above average style of writing and the amount of new information one can find in an average issue. Highly recommended for larger libraries, and for all library schools.

Bay State Librarian. 1910. q. $3. Robert E. Cain. Massachusetts Library Assn., Box 7, Nahant, Mass. 01908. Circ: 2,000.

Aud: Sa.

An eight-page newsletter which is better printed and edited than many of the much larger state publications. There is at least one long article—and it is normally an article which will be enjoyed by anyone. The editor has carried off the impossible: boiled down the news to essentials, and carefully selected material for the harried and over burdened reader. Well worth the modest price.

Bodleian Library Record. 1938. irreg. (Usually once or twice a year). $1.50 per issue. Bodleian Library, Oxford, Oxi, 3BG., England. Illus., index. Circ: 2,000. Sample. Vol. ends: Every 6 issues.

Indexed: LibSciAb. *Aud:* Ac.

Somewhat along the same lines as the *Harvard Library Bulletin* and other major American library/bibliographic journals. About one quarter of this 50-page journal is devoted to news and notes about the Bodleian Library; the remainder consists of four to five articles of bibliographic and historical interest. The whole is scholarly, documented, and of primary value to the subject expert. This is one of a number of library-based magazines which go considerably beyond being public relations vehicles, and are actually contributions to the scholarship of bibliography. In American adademic and public library collections they fill an important role —primarily as adjuncts to the two basic bibliographic journals, *Bibliographical Society of America. Papers* and the English *The Library.*

Bookmark. 1949. bi-m. $1.50. New York State Library, Albany, N.Y. 12224. Circ: 5,000.

Indexed: LibLit, PAIS. *Aud:* Ac, Sa, Ga, Hs.

One of the more useful state library publications. Usually features one or two bibliographies—often annotated—on current issues, a list of state publications, and articles on the New York State system and its various libraries. As New York State has one of the more advanced networks and reference services, the three to four articles are often of considerably more than local interest. In view of the modest price, the 32-page offset magazine should be found in most libraries.

British Columbia Library Quarterly. 1937. Membership (Nonmembers $5). Bryan L. Bacon and Madi Stainsby, British Columbia Library Assn., 2425 Macdonald St., Vancouver, 8, B.C. Illus., index, adv. Circ: 650. Sample. Vol. ends: Apr. Microform: UM.

Indexed: CanI, LibLit, LibSciAb. *Bk. rev:* 5–8, 200–500 words, signed. *Aud:* Sa.

A superior local publication, this 40-page periodical includes two to three articles on Canadian libraries, literature, and history. The signed book reviews offer an excellent source of information on Canada. Typographically, it is one of the best of its kind. A required item for all Canadian libraries, certainly for most large American collections.

CU Voice. 1965. irreg. Free. Allan Covici, Univ. Federation of Librarians, AFT 1795 (AFL/CIO) Berkeley Campus, Univ. of California. Subs. to: Box 997, Berkeley, Calif. 94701. Circ: 1,000.

Aud: Ac, Ga.

An 8-page newsletter issued by the American Federation of Teachers (AFL-CIO) Local 1795 to bring news of union organizing to members and would-be members of the organization. Of more than passing interest because it is: well edited and includes items

of value to those outside of the California system; normally has one or two longer articles on issues confronting anyone involved with the library-union movement, and is satirically militant. In view of the interest, pro and con, in the movement towards unions, it should appeal to both camps.

California Librarian. 1939. q. Membership (Nonmembers $8). Morris Polan, 717 K Street, Sacramento, Calif. 95814. Illus., index, adv. Circ: 4,200. Sample. Vol. ends: Oct.

Indexed: LibLit, LibSciAb. *Aud:* Ac, Ga.

Among the best of the state/regional library association magazines, this can be recommended for any basic collection. While a given amount of each issue is given over to parochial news items, the majority of the five to six articles are of interest to any bibliographer or librarian. The writers are much above average and deal with everything from book collecting and printing to common problems and solutions in library administration. The format is outstanding. The California Association of Schools also publishes an excellent journal, *California School Libraries* (1929. q. $3), and a monthly newsletter which is not available to nonmember subscribers.

Canadian Library Journal (Formerly: *Canadian Library*). 1944. bi-m. Membership (Nonmembers $10). Canadian Library Assn., 151 Sparks St., Ottawa KIP 5E3, Ont., Canada. Illus., adv. Circ: 5,000. Sample. Vol. ends: Nov./Dec. Microform: UM.

Indexed: CanI, LibLit, LibSciAb. *Bk. rev:* 13, 300–400 words, signed. *Aud:* Ac, Ga.

Last time around this was compared favorably with what was then the *ALA Bulletin* (now *American Libraries*). It is still fairly good, but by early 1972 it was between editors and lacked some of the fire and fervor of earlier issues. It covers the activities of the Canadian Library Association, still publishes the standard articles on all aspects of librarianship from jobs to bibliographies. It has an enlarged book review section which is rather good. There is no question that what it does, it does well. The trouble is that for a national journal it lacks some sense of identity, even of direction. Hopefully, given a full-time editor this will change. Until then American libraries can skip, although it will be useful in library schools and in larger libraries where attention is given to Canadian affairs. It still is a first choice for all Canadian libraries.

Catholic Library World. 1929. m. (Sept.–May). Membership (Nonmembers $6). Jane F. Hindman. Catholic Library Assn., 461 W. Lancaster Ave., Haverford, Pa. 19041. Illus., index, adv. Circ: 4,000. Sample. Vol. ends: June. Refereed. Microform: UM.

Indexed: CathI, LibLit, LibSciAb. *Bk. rev:* 50–100, 40–50 words. *Aud:* Ga, Ejh, Hs.

For the majority of readers this serves two distinct purposes: (1) it is the voice of the Catholic Library

Association, and, as such, presents news, articles and views on Catholic libraries from elementary through college level; (2) a book selection and bibliographic aid. The first purpose is well enough met, and, in the past two or three years, with a bit more enthusiasm and vitality than before. (It may be the current crisis in Catholic education is seeping down to the libraries, too.) Still, the reviews and the bibliographies are of more real importance. For example, in the October 1971 issue there was a selective annotated list of philosophy (read religion, too) titles for 1970–1971; a "bibliography on sex for youth," a well balanced and carefully annotated selection; a long, detailed review of an encyclopedia; reviews of professional reading; and the standard list: "books for young adults," and "books for school libraries." Impressive enough for the modest price.

Colby Library Quarterly. 1943. q. $3. Richard Cary. Colby College Library, Waterville, Maine 04901. Illus., index. Circ: 650. Sample. Vol. ends: every 3rd yr. Microform: UM.

Indexed: AbEnSt. *Aud:* Ac.

A bibliographical approach to Maine authors, historians, and others "who are well represented by special collections in the Colby College Library." An average 40 to 60 page pocket-sized issue includes three or four articles familiar to anyone who reads literary criticism and bibliographic journals, e.g., "The uncollected short stories of Sarah Orne Jewett," "The morality of consciousness in Henry James," etc. It employs satisfactory format, some illustrations. A required item for larger literature collections.

College and Research Libraries. 1939. bi-m. Membership (Nonmembers $10). Richard M. Dougherty. Assn. of College & Research Libraries, Amer. Library Assn., 50 E. Huron St., Chicago, Ill. 60611. Circ: 14,000. Sample. Vol. ends: Nov. Microform: UM. Reprint: Kraus.

Indexed: CurrCont, LibLit, LibSciAb, PAIS. *Bk. rev:* 5–10, 500–1,500 words, signed. *Aud:* Ac. *Jv:* V.

In many ways the best of the American Library Association publications, this is professionally edited and contains articles and features not only of interest to college and university librarians, but to anyone dealing with problems of bibliography, cataloging, acquisitions, and the whole range of professional librarianship. The articles tend to be uniformly good, usually thought provoking, and often controversial. There is a minimum of repetition, a maximum of new insights into old problems. Regular features include excellent book reviews, additions to the current edition of *Guide to Reference Books* (ALA), notes on new magazines, and news items on individuals and events. A monthly newsletter, *News,* is included in the subscription and this keeps the reader abreast of meetings, changes in personnel, and general current topics not covered in the regular publication. Useful for all college and university and many public and special libraries.

Columbia Library Columns. 1951. 3/yr. $6. Dallas Pratt. Friends of Columbia Libraries, 535 W. 114th St., New York, N.Y. 10027. Illus. index. Circ: 1,000. Vol. ends: May.

Indexed: LibLit. *Aud:* Ac.

A bibliographic-literary pocket-sized magazine which publishes articles of a high quality. Most material, of course, deals with collection at the Columbia libraries—but their collections are varied enough to call for articles on Allen Ginsberg and Jack Kerouac in one issue, and on "Timothy Cole—master engraver" in another. The format is excellent, and the illustrations suitable. Some short notes from the sponsoring group are included. A first rate bibliographical magazine for larger collections, and a nice addition to any librarian's personal subscription file.

Courier. 1958. q. Membership. $15 (Institutions $25). Arsine Schmavonian. Syracuse Univ. Library Associates, Syracuse Univ., Syracuse, N.Y. 13210. Illus. Circ: 1,100. Vol. ends: No. 4, July.

Aud: Ac.

A handsome pocket-sized 56-page journal which features five to six bibliographic articles, usually based upon materials found in the Syracuse University Library. The material is as diverse as the library collection, moving from Russian theatre to Shaker furniture and Nevil Shute. The writing style is much more relaxed than in similar journals. A casual reader will enjoy this as much as a dedicated bibliographer. In fact, it is one of the few of the genre which might be read cover to cover with delight. And the photographs and drawings help things along considerably.

Drexel Library Quarterly. 1965. q. $10. Mary E. Stillman. Grad. School of Library Science, Drexel Inst. of Technology, Philadelphia, Pa. 19104. Circ: 1,000. Vol. ends: Dec. Microform: UM.

Indexed: LibLit, LibSciAb, PAIS. *Bk. rev:* 5, 2 pages, signed. *Aud:* Ac.

"Devoted to examining contemporary aspects and problems of American library and information science. Each issue treats a single topic and attempts to provide a comprehensive survey of subjects not treated in depth elsewhere in professional literature; they might be characterized as mini-books." There are critical reviews of professional literature and other titles pertaining to librarianship. A required item for all large libraries and smaller libraries might check individual numbers for subjects of particular interest to their situation.

Florida Libraries. 1949. q. Membership (Nonmembers $2). Ms. Lu Alice Sands. Florida State Library, Tallahassee, Fla. 32304. Illus., index. Circ: 1,500.

Indexed: LibLit, LibSciAb. *Bk. rev:* Notes. *Aud:* Sa.

On the cover of one 45-page issue: "The 72 model from bustle to hotpants," and duly illustrated with two women librarians. The approach is typical of content. The magazine swerves between light humor and personal notes and rather well written, quite serious articles on the profession. Probably two or three of the five articles in each number will interest those outside of Florida—and this high average accounts for its popularity. One of the best state publications, certainly one of the best edited.

Georgia Librarian. 1964. s-a. Membership. (Nonmembers $5). Ms. Grace Hightower. Georgia Library Assn., Box 176, Decatur, Ga. 30031.

Aud: Sa.

Typical of many state library association publications, this offset 56-page bulletin is concerned solely with reporting on activities of the association and its members. Aside from a speech or special paper, there are no articles. Outside of Georgia of no value, but inside the state it is extremely useful.

Harvard Library Bulletin. 1947. q. $15. Edwin E. Williams. Harvard Univ. Press, 79 Garden St., Cambridge, Mass. 02138. Illus., index. Circ: 1,700. Sample. Vol. ends: Oct. Reprint: Johnson.

Indexed: LibLit. *Aud:* Ac. *Jv:* V.

Interested in the history of Victorian music halls? Perhaps the relationship of Robert Symour and Charles Dickens will be more fascinating. Whether it be history, biography, literature, or any aspect of the human condition, the reader will find it within these 100 pages. The focal point, to be sure, is an aspect of bibliography, something to do with material one finds in the Harvard Library. The six to ten articles are by men and women involved with both major and minor points in the fields of their particular interests. Take all of this, give it the careful editing of Mr. Williams, add a few illustrations, and the reader comes up with one of the best bibliographic magazines now available.

Huntington Library Quarterly; a journal for the history and interpretation of English and American civilization. 1937. q. $7.50. John M. Steadman, Huntington Library and Art Gallery, San Marion, Calif. 91108. Illus., index. Circ: 1,300. Microform: UM. Reprint: Kraus.

Indexed: AbEnSt. *Aud:* Ac.

A general journal of scholarship. Articles concentrate on American history and English literature. Most of the material is drawn from the Huntington Library collection—one of the best in the world. The articles are well documented, and tend to be relatively esoteric. There are the usual notes on the library and its

acquisitions. Ranks among the top ten such publications in America.

IPLO Quarterly. 1958. q. Membership. (Nonmembers $10). J. P. Wilkinson. Inst. of Professional Librarians of Ontario, 17 Inkerman St., Toronto, 5, Ont., Canada. Illus., index, adv.

Aud: Ac, Ga.

A pocket-sized (some 50 pages) library magazine which deserves more attention. The format, approach, and editing are quite professional and the magazine is put together with imagination and taste—not to mention a sense of humor. Articles touch on all aspects of bibliography and library science, are in no way limited to provincial items. An outstanding article for example: R. H. Blackburns' "Of Mice and Lions and Battleships and Interlibrary Things," an entirely new approach to interlibrary loan. There are, to be sure, the usual notes of interest to membership. For larger American collections, and most libraries in Canada.

Idaho Librarian. 1945. q. Membership (Nonmembers $5). Stanley A. Shepard. Idaho Library Assn., 1121 S. 4th Ave., Pocatello, Idaho 83201. Illus., index. Circ: 1,000.

Indexed: LibLit. *Aud:* Sa.

Usually features one or two brief articles. The remaining space is given to news of Idaho libraries and librarians and official Association notices. Adequate format and editing, but of limited value outside of the state.

Illinois Libraries. 1919. m. Free. Ms. Irma Bostian. Illinois State Library, Springfield, Ill. 62706. Circ: 8,000. Microform: UM.

Indexed: LibLit, LibSciAb. *Aud:* Sa.

A state library publication which is concerned with spreading news about libraries and librarians, laws, legislation (pending and passed), and other activities. Each 100-page (or more) issue tends to concentrate on a given subject, e.g., systems, state laws, etc. The presentation is always fulsome, and informative. Unfortunately, most of the material has limited application outside of Illinois. What it does, though, it does well, and it can be considered a model of sorts for other state libraries faced with problems of communicating.

Information—News/Sources/Profiles. 1969. bi-m. $25. Leonard Cohan. Science Associates, 23 E. 24th St., New York, N.Y. 10010. Illus.

Indexed: InfSciAb, LibSciAb. *Aud:* Sa, Ac.

A briefing service for those involved deeply with documentation and automation. Each 64 or so page issue includes short news items and sections on education, meetings, grants, sources of information, and profiles of individuals and libraries. It is rather a grab bag with some logic for the reader who has the time to go through the whole issue. It is difficult to say how much is helpful, how much repetitious. Also, the magazine is for the expert or near expert, not the librarian with a casual understanding of automation and documentation. On the plus side it does serve as a current-awareness journal and the reports seem accurate and authoritative enough. The price is high, although probably no higher than other efforts in this field. A useful but not necessary item for large academic and special libraries.

Information Retrieval and Library Automation Letter. See Communications and Media Section.

Iowa Library Quarterly. 1901. q. Free. Florence Stiles. Iowa State Traveling Library, Historical Bldg., Des Moines, Iowa 50319. Index. Circ: 14,000. Microform: UM.

Indexed: LibLit. *Aud:* Sa.

A 12 to 30 page chatty newsletter on activities of libraries and librarians in Iowa. Most material is too local to be of value to anyone outside of the state.

✓ ***JOLA Technical Communications.*** See *Journal of Library Automation.*

John Rylands Library. Bulletin. 1902. bi-a. $6.80. F. Taylor. The Library, Manchester, M3, 3EHI, England. Illus. Circ: 1,200. Vol. ends: Spring.

Aud: Ac.

Averaging some 500 pages a year, the *Bulletin* is more a collection of monographs than the usual journal or bulletin. Most material deals with the finer elements of English literature and bibliography. On occasion there are monographs on history and linguistics. The scholarship is close to perfect, and the writing style is passable. A basic journal for larger literature and bibliographic collections, but it will be of limited value for others.

The Journal of Documentation; devoted to the recording, organization and dissemination of special knowledge. 1945. q. Membership (Nonmembers $24). H. Coblans. Assn. of Special Libraries and Information Bureaus, 3 Belgrave Sq., London SW1, England. Circ: 3,200. Sample. Vol. ends: Dec. Reprint: Johnson, Kraus.

Indexed: LibLit, LibSciAb. *Bk. rev:* 12–15, 1 to 2 pages, signed. *Aud:* Ac, Ga. *Jv:* V.

This continues to hold the first place among journals in this field for clarity with authority, good writing with style, and solid information easy to digest. Which is to say, in a field filled with what Mason calls the "great gas bubble," this is a breath of fresh air. The authors manage to reduce technical material on documentation to a level where the average librarian understands it. All aspects of documentation are covered, "including translations, abstracts, indexes, and other

bibliographic aids." Although published in England, contributors and articles are international in scope, and in no way limited to an English audience. The book reviews are good to excellent. Each issue also includes a review article under the general heading of "Progress in Documentation," analyzing the current position in one particular subject area. An absolute must for any library interested in the subject.

Journal of Education for Librarianship. 1960. q. $8. Norm Horrocks, Library School, Dalhousie Univ., Halifax, Nova Scotia. Circ: 1,500.

Indexed: LibLit, LibSciAb. *Aud:* Sa.

The voice of the Association of American Library Schools, i.e., the women and men who teach in library schools both here and in Canada. The five to six articles touch on all aspects of the educational process for would-be librarians. The winter number is a directory of teachers and schools. A specialized magazine for a specialized audience.

✓ ***Journal of Library Automation.*** 1968. q. $10. Alvin L. Goldwyn. American Library Assn., 50 East Huron St., Chicago, Ill. 60611. llus., index, adv. Circ: 6,000. Vol. ends: Dec.

Indexed: LibLit, LibSciAb. *Bk. rev:* 6–10, 300 words, signed. *Aud:* Ac.

The journal of the Information Science and Automation Division, ALA, this usually features three or four articles on some technical aspect of how automation can be or is used in libraries. Most of the material tends to be on the technical side, although from time to time there are general, historical, and overview articles well within the grasp of the average reader. The writers normally are librarians, and while the style is not always pleasing it is at least clear. Primarily a journal for the technician and advanced student.

The Division, also, issues: ***JOLA Technical Communications.*** 1969. m. $5 (Available in combination with the *Journal* at $15). John P. McGowan. An eight-page offset newsletter which reports on projects, seminars, personnel, institutes, etc. Matters of major importance are usually treated later, at more length, in the *Journal.*

Journal of Library History; philosophy and comparative librarianship. 1966. q. $12. Harold Goldstein. Library School, Florida State Univ., Tallahassee, Fla. 32306. Illus., adv. Circ: 1,155. Sample. Vol. ends: Oct.

Indexed: HistAb, LibLit. *Bk. rev:* 4–5, 500–1,500 words, signed. *Aud:* Ac, Ga. *Jv:* V.

Presents the librarian, bibliophile, and interested layman with richly detailed articles on the history of librarianship, publishing, and books. It is international in scope, including articles on its chosen subjects from and about any area on earth. "Oral History" provides transcripts of interviews with leaders in librarianship and library history. Each issue reviews four or five titles concerned with library history. Indicates that librarianship can be significant and intellectually stimulating.

Journal of Typographic Research. See *Visible Language.*

Kansas Library Bulletin. 1932. q. Free. Cass Peterson. State House, Topeka, Kans. 66612. Circ: 4,000.

Indexed: LibLit. *Aud:* Sa.

A publication of the Kansas state library, this is different because of the emphasis on photographs and a professional editing job. About one to two articles of national interest are included. Stress is on Kansas personnel and libraries. Covers public and school libraries, with emphasis on the latter. Fine for Kansas, but only for larger libraries outside of the state.

Kentucky Library Association. Bulletin. 1936. q. Membership (Nonmembers $6). Jean Wiggins. Subs. to: Tom Sutherland, 555 Washington St., Paducah, Ky. 42001.

Indexed: LibLit. *Aud:* Sa.

Over the years this has improved considerably and a 40 to 50 page issue is now professionally put together. It usually has one or two long articles and a number of short pieces on activities of the KLA and its members. At least one of the longer articles is of interest to those beyond the Kentucky state line. A good, basic library journal for border and southern states, and for all larger libraries.

✓ *LJ/SLJ Hotline.* 1971. w. $50. Karl Nyren. R. R. Bowker Co., 1180 Ave. of the Americas, New York, N.Y. 10036.

Aud: Sa.

A six-page newsletter which gives fast reports on such things as funding, legislation, appointments, and general news items. The major question: Is such a newsletter necessary for librarians—particularly at $50? The answer: No. It does serve some purpose in its speed, but most of the material is available almost as quickly in the same publisher's *Library Journal,* and in considerable more detail. The editing is extremely capable, but the notion of a "hotline" in an essentially "cool," slow moving profession simply does not jive with reality. Conversely, those who take exception to the notion that library news is not "cool", but rather "hot," have an ideal vehicle here. The basic proposition has to be worked out before either accepting or rejecting *Hotline.*

Law Library Journal. 1908. q. C. E. Bolden. American Assn. of Law Libraries, Washington State Law Library, Olympia, Wash. 98501. Illus., index, adv. Circ: 1,250.

Indexed: LegPer, LibLit, LibSciAb. *Bk. rev:* Various number, length. *Aud:* Sa.

Covers all aspects of law librarianship, and usually in both a lively and informative style. The articles are general enough to be of interest to even the library with a small collection of legal materials. Beyond that, of course, it serves the needs of law librarians who are its staunch supporters. There are frequent bibliographies on subjects of more than passing interest to both law and non-law librarians.

✓ *Learning Today: an educational magazine of library-college thought* (Formerly: *Library College Journal*). 1968. 8/yr. $10. Howard Clayton. Library-College Associates, Inc., Box 956, Norman, Okla. 73069. Illus., adv. Circ: 2,500. Sample. Vol. ends: Dec.

Indexed: CIJE, CurrCont, LibLit, LibSciAb. *Bk. rev:* 3, 600 words, signed. *Aud:* Ac, Hs, Ejh.

A journal with five to six articles that have one thing in common—the theory that a library is an active (not a passive) element in the teaching process. In order to make the library important, the authors show how librarians have turned the library into a learning and resource center. For example, "The Librarian—Tutor in an Innovative College Experiment" is typical. In addition there are a number of departments, news features, personnel reports, etc. With a change in title in late 1972, the journal changed its scope. Before it limited itself to college libraries, now "in line with the name change, the journal will begin to include a generous amount of material concerning education at the elementary and secondary levels." The writing is sometimes more enthusiastic than practical, but no one can fault the authors for lack of drive or imagination. As such this is an important journal for all libraries and schools of education.

Liberated Librarian. Newsletter. 1969. 6/yr. Donation. Ms. Linda Katz and Ms. Julie Babcock. c/o Ms. Katz, Apt. 1708E, 2200 Benjamin Franklin Pkwy., Philadelphia, Pa. 19130. Illus. Circ: 250.

Bk. rev: 2–3, notes. *Aud:* Sa.

A three to four page mimeographed newsletter which includes editorials, comments, and information on all aspects of the "now" generation of librarians. This means reports on anti-war activities, film, politics, magazines, and the good yet tired ALA. No set price, but it is well worth the few dollars the librarian might care to send the two fellow librarians who are so diligently putting this out. If you want a sample copy, send 25¢ to cover postage. It is well worth it—at least if you are tuned-in to the liberated side of librarianship.

The Library Association Record. 1899. m. $20. E. Dudley. 7 Ridgmount St., London WC1E 7AE, England. Circ: 19,500. Sample. Vol. ends: Dec. Microform: UM.

Indexed: LibLit, LibSciAb. *Bk. rev:* 5, 600 words, signed. *Aud:* Ac.

The British equivalent of *American Libraries*. As the official journal of the Library Association, it includes the usual articles on news of the organization, personalities, meetings, and the like. The writing tends to be pedestrian and the journal suffers a bit from being an official publication. (The *Assistant Librarian* stands in marked contrast to its senior partner.) Articles cover all aspects of the field and there are a number of items of international interest. American librarians may learn from the experiences and ideas put forth by their English cousins. A basic journal for library school collections, and useful for academic and possibly public librarians who think it necessary to read more than the American professional magazines.

Library Chronicle of the University of Texas at Austin. 1944. irreg. Request. Warren Roberts. Univ. of Texas Library, Austin, Tex. 78712. Illus., index. Circ: 1,500.

Indexed: LibLit, LibSciAb.

A handsome bibliographic magazine which follows the format and the approach of *Harvard Library Bulletin*. There is a cavalier disregard for bibliographic information about this journal—price, frequency, etc.—but the content makes it worthwhile. In some 75 to 80 pages there are six to ten articles on various collections at the University of Texas, or material based on research in those collections. Herman Liebert may write on "Bibliography Old and New" and there probably will be a short piece on a prominent Texas collector. Some news notes are included. A truly interesting and well-edited journal which should be in all larger library and literary collections.

Library College Journal. See *Learning Today*.

✓***Library of Congress Information Bulletin.*** 1942. w. $5. SDC: LC 1.18. Library of Congress, Card Div., Bldg. 159, Navy Yard Annex, Washington, D.C. 20541. Illus. Vol. ends: Dec.

Indexed: LibLit, LibSciAbs. *Bk. rev:* Various number, length. *Aud:* Ga, Ac.

As the title suggests, this newsletter is replete with information and although some of the content is of intramural interest only, there remains a great deal of information useful to all librarians. Categories which recur with regularity include: "Acquisition Notes"—announcements of original documents of well- and lesser-known figures of American history, with a description of the content and scope of the gift; "Events in the Offing"—a schedule of forthcoming concerts, lectures, dramatizations, etc., held at LC; "Exhibits"—LC's outstanding series of photographic, painting, and manuscript exhibitions; "News in the Library World"—a potpourri of events, meetings, and the like; "Publications"—notices of accession lists, cataloging service *Bulletins*, MARC format series, and the many other LC documents. Also included are lists of vacant positions; announcements of new appointments, retirements, promotions; resumés of annual reports of the various divisions; and on occasion a review of the contents of the *Quarterly Journal*. Featured from time to time are items from the Superintendent of Documents and from the GPO. Well worth a few minutes browsing once a week. (J.M.)

Library Counselor. 1945. q. $4. Alberta DeNio. Colorado State Dept. of Social Services, Library, 1575 Sherman St., Denver, Colo. 80203.

Aud: Ac, Ga, Hs.

A mimeographed quarterly which serves a distinct purpose: each 40 or so page issue is given to a thorough, usually annotated bibliography of some subject of interest to social workers and those dealing in sociology and related subject fields. Past numbers, for example, have been bibliographies on: day care centers, minority groups, youth, public welfare, adoption, etc. The material is from both magazines and books. Arrangement varies from issue to issue, but it is adequate and there are good indexes. A vital, often overlooked item which will be useful for any student or library.

Library History. 1967. s-a. $3.50. P. A. Hoare. Library History Group, Library Assn., 7 Ridgmount St., London, WC1E 7AE, England. Subs. to: Kennet Beeches, 54 George Lane, Marlborough, Wits, England. Illus., index. Circ: 1,500.

Indexed: HistAb, LibLit, LibSciAb. *Bk. rev:* 5–7, 250–1,000 words, signed. *Aud:* Ac, Sa.

The English equivalent, although on a smaller scale, of the *Journal of Library History*. But if the size is not as impressive—usually about 45 pages in a pocket-sized format—the writing is excellent, and in the best British tradition. There are usually one or two long, scholarly articles on some aspect of the English library scene, followed by review articles and book reviews. The whole is engrossing, intelligent, and most useful for the bibliographer and historian. A good bet for any library.

✓***Library Journal.*** 1876. s-m. (Sept.–June); m. (July–Aug.). $15. John N. Berry III. R. R. Bowker Co., 1180 Ave. of the Americas, New York, N.Y. 10036. Illus., index, adv. Circ: 36,000. Microform: MF, UM.

Indexed: LibLit, LibSciAb, PAIS, RG. *Bk. rev:* 200–250, 125 words, signed. *Aud:* Ac, Ga, Hs, Ejh. *Jv:* V.

The oldest of U.S. library periodicals, this is a multipurpose journal running the gamut of library activities. (Bound in once a month is *School Library Journal*; see annotation, this section.) Articles frequently speak of controversy, as do the forthright editorials. A principal feature is the review section, which provides about two hundred reviews per issue, arranged by subject. Ten to twenty record reviews are provided in each issue. Other features include: a large News section providing coverage of the library and publishing worlds; Magazines, introducing the reader to new serials; a Checklist of free or inexpensive items of interest to the librarian; a buyer's guide to new equipment for use in libraries; a Calendar of upcoming events of importance, and a lively Letters to the Editor department. Each year there are a number of special issues, e.g., foreign libraries, equipment, lists of forthcoming titles in various subject areas or formats (paperbacks).

Library News Bulletin. 1932. q. Free. Charles A. Symon. Washington State Library, Olympia, Wash. 98501. Illus., Circ: 2,800.

Indexed: LibLit. *Aud:* Sa.

A processed 90 to 100 page report on activities of not only the Washington State library, but of libraries and librarians throughout the state. Most items are short—one to two pages. There is considerable news of the Washington Library Association. In its thorough coverage of state activities it has no peer. No one, or no event, seems to be overlooked. Conversely, it is of limited value for anyone living outside the Washington State sphere of influence.

The Library Quarterly; a journal of investigation and discussion in the field of library science. 1931. q. $8. Howard W. Winger. Univ. of Chicago Press, 5801 Ellis Ave., Chicago, Ill 60637. Circ: 3,800. Sample. Vol. ends: Oct. Microform: UM.

Indexed: LibLit, LibSciAb, PAIS. *Bk. rev:* 10–15, 500–1,500 words, signed. *Aud:* Ac, Ga.

This long-standing quarterly concentrates on research and investigation. There are usually three to four articles per issue, and one number a year is given to the proceedings of the annual Graduate Library School conference. The critical reviews by librarians are excellent. Sometimes the writing is a bit pedestrian, but the content is usually thought provoking. A must for anyone who sees librarianship as a profession.

Library Research News. 1969. q. $5. McMaster Univ., Mills Memorial Library, Hamilton, Ont., Canada. Illus., index.

Aud: Sa, Ac, Ga.

An 18 to 32 page report on activities and holdings of the McMaster University library. While the genre is hardly unusual, what makes it distinctive is the attention to format (good to excellent) and the scholarly bibliographies. For example, the February 1971 issue is given completely to "A catalogue of the literary papers of John Colombo and working archives of the Tamarack Review." The bibliography, compiled by J. David Morrow, is a salute to Colombo, "undoubtedly one of the most active people in Canadian literature." Other issues have dealt with the library's rare map collection and unpublished manuscripts in many

areas. A useful research aid for large academic and some public libraries.

Library Resources and Technical Services. 1957. q. Membership (Nonmembers $8). Robert Wedgeworth. Resources and Technical Services Div., Amer. Library Assn., 50 E. Huron St., Chicago, Ill. 60611. Index, adv. Circ: 12,000. Sample. Vol. ends: Fall. Microform: UM.

Indexed: LibLit, LibSciAb. *Bk. rev:* 6, 600 words, signed. *Aud:* Ga, Ac.

Concerned primarily with technical services—acquisitions, serials, but particularly cataloging and classification—this is one of the better ALA divisional publications. Articles are well documented, and there is a nice balance between the pragmatic how-to-do-it type and the scholarly research approach. There is a limited amount of jargon, but at times the writers go off the deep end of the catalog by stating problems in terms which are hardly understandable to anyone but the expert. Fortunately, this does not happen often. A required item for the technical services section of any library, and certainly for all library school students.

Library Technology Reports; evaluative information on library systems, equipment and supplies. 1965. bi-m. $100. Robert J. Shaw. American Library Assn., 50 E. Huron, Chicago, Ill. 60611. Illus., index.

Indexed: LibLit. *Aud:* Ac, Ga, Ejh, Hs.

The looseleaf reports are a type of consumer warning system for librarians and those purchasing library material. The members of the library technology program are on the staff of the American Library Association, but usually supervise, rather than run tests on materials. Studies have included everything from shelving and projection equipment to the testing of microform readers. A note in *American Libraries* (April 1972, p. 391) indicates the scope of these individual reports: "With the publication in the March issue of *Library Technology Reports* on two additional chairs tests, LTP's evaluation program for chairs suitable for general seating in libraries is concluded. The program, supported by a grant of $62,750 . . . was started late in 1967. A total of fifty chairs . . . have been evaluated." Notebooks and tabs are provided for the filing of the reports and there is a cumulative index and a table of contents. These make for easy use.

A librarian may purchase reports on a single item, e.g., *Library Technology Reports: Portfolio Series.* These contain all material on the subject published in the *Reports* as of date of purchase. Each portfolio sells for $35, covers everything from card catalog cabinets and electric erasers to steel shelving.

Library Trends. 1952. q. $8. Herbert Goldhor. Univ. of Illinois Grad. School of Library Science, Urbana, Ill. 61801. Subs. to: Univ. of Illinois Press, Subscription Dept., Urbana, Ill. 61801. Circ: 4,200. Vol. ends: Apr.

Indexed: LibLit, LibSciAb, PAIS. *Aud:* Ac, Ga. *Jv:* V.

Now in its twentieth year, this is the leading monographic series in library science. Usually with seven to ten specially written articles, and an introduction by the guest editor, each quarterly number is an in-depth study. Subject matter touches on all aspects of the art from censorship to administration and bibliography. All articles are by experts, documented, and normally well written. Coverage of the topic varies with the editor and with the contributors, but on the whole it is complete. The main advantage of *Library Trends* is that it serves as a vehicle for updating and reviewing material usually found only in sometimes dated texts or scattered periodical articles. Individual issues are frequently used as texts in library schools, and librarians find the journal useful for both practical and theoretical approaches to common problems. A required item for any library.

Library World. See *New Library World.*

Libri: international library review. 1951. q. $20.82. Palle Birkelund. Munksgaard, A/S, 35 Norre Sogade DK 1370, Copenhagen, Denmark. Illus., index, adv. Circ: 1,350. Sample. Vol. ends: No. 4.

Indexed: LibLit. *Bk. rev:* 5–10, 100–1,500 words, signed. *Aud:* Ac.

Published as the official organ of the International Federation of Library Associations (IFLA), this features original, well-documented studies on all aspects of libraries and bibliography. There are usually four or five articles per issue, and while the style is not brilliant, the material is usually original, the thought speculative, and the overall impression one of scholarship. The book reviews, which run from mere notes to essays, cover the entire field of international library work. There are the usual news items and announcements. Conveniently published in English, French, or German editions.

Michigan Librarian. 1935. q. Membership. (Nonmembers $4). Ms. H. F. Pletz. Michigan Library Assn. 226 W. Washtenaw, Lansing, Mich. 48933. Illus., adv. Circ: 1,800.

Indexed: LibLit. *Aud:* Sa.

With a format the size of *American Libraries*—although the pages are hardly as numerous—this is among the top ten local library magazines in the country. The editor has a definite touch for layout (a considerable number of good photographs are found in each issue) and choice of materials. There are usually three to five articles, and while not all of them are of equal quality, at least one is of value to the librarian outside of the Michigan system. The other half of the magazine is given over to Association news, personnel notes, and regular departments. An average 46-page issue is well worth the modest subscription price, and it should be considered by large libraries, certainly by all libraries in and around Michigan.

Microdoc. 1962. q. Membership (Nonmembers $12). W. D. Linton. Microfilm Assn. of Great Britain, 109 Kingsway, London WC 2B 6PU, England. Illus., index, adv. Circ: 500. Microform: Publisher.

Indexed: LibLit, LibSciAb. *Aud:* Sa.

A pocket-sized quarterly of some 30 pages which is about equally divided between reporting on activities of the British sponsoring group and publishing reports and short articles on microform. The contributions are technical, meant for the professional, not the layman. Still, with a little background the interested reader can follow the material. The price is too high, though, for anyone this side of the largest academic or highly specialized library.

An equally interesting, equally technical magazine in this same area from England is: *NRCD Bulletin.* 1967. q. $18. B. J. S. Williams. National Reprographic Centre for Documentation, Hatfield Polytechnic, Hatfield, Hertforshire, England. Illus., index. *Indexed:* LibSciAb.

Micrographic Weekly. 1970. w. $55. (Individuals $75). Arthur E. Gardner. Technical Information Inc., 6331 Hollywood Blvd., Los Angeles, Calif. 90028.

Aud: Sa.

The newsletter of the microform world, and while extremely high priced for only 8 pages or so a week, it is worth the subscription price. Each issue reports on current activities in short, newsletter fashion. The editor writes well, knows of what he speaks, and presents the information with a flair which makes it good, clear reading even for the nonexpert. Much of the material is suitable for libraries, and the librarian with a stake in microform might make it a practice to read it each week. (A good addition, too, for business collections where there is an interest in investing and higher management processes.)

In this same field, there are a number of other publications (see *Microdoc,* for one). Some any library might consider:

Journal of Micrographics. 1966. q. Membership. P. R. Poulin. National Microfilm Assn., 8728 Colesville Rd., Silver Spring, Md. 20910. Illus., index, adv. Circ: 5,500. Sample.

Micro News Bulletin. 1966. m. This is included with a subscription to the *Journal of Micrographics.*

Microform Review. See Books and Book Reviews Section.

Microfilm Newsletter; a monthly report for business executives who use or market microfilm services and equipment. 1969. $35. Box 2154, Grand Central Station, New York, N.Y. 10017.

Micrographics News & Views. 1970. bi-w. $95. Wilbur C. Myers, 916 Silver Spur Rd., Suite 306, Rolling Hills Estates, Calif. 90274.

Minnesota Libraries. 1904. q. free. Hannis S. Smith. Minnesota State Dept. of Education, Library Div., 117

University Ave., St. Paul, Minn. 55101. Index. Circ: 2,000.

Indexed: LibLit, LibSciAb. *Aud:* Sa.

Usually contains one or two articles of national interest, but more emphasis is on local material, news of the Department of Education, and libraries and personnel. A normal issue runs to 28 pages. A necessary addition for libraries in Minnesota, but only for larger libraries elsewhere.

Mountain Plains Library Association Quarterly. 1956. q. Membership (Nonmembers $2). Wichita Public Library, Wichita, Kans. 67202. Illus., adv.

Indexed: LibLit. *Aud:* Sa.

Members of the Mountain Plains Library Association include librarians and laymen from Kansas, Nebraska, North and South Dakota, Wyoming, Colorado, Utah, and Nevada. A considerable amount of each 28 to 36 page issue is given to Association events and personalities. There are usually two or three short general articles. The format is fair, and while the whole is of value to the Association membership, it is not a library journal for most libraries outside of the area.

Mousaion. 1955. 6 to 8/yr. Exchange. H. J. de Vleeschawer. Univ. of South Africa, 181 East Ave., Pretoria, S. Africa. Illus. Circ: 400. Microform: UM.

Indexed: LibLit, LibSciAb. *Aud:* Sa, Ac.

Somewhat similar in purpose to the University of Illinois *Occasional Papers.* Each number concentrates on research in a given area of librarianship, and if involved enough, may continue for several issues. While prepared for working librarians, the pamphlet-like magazine is often used in library schools. Much of the material is esoteric, at least in terms of American students.

New Jersey Libraries; a news and opinion letter. 1966. q. Arthur Curley, Ilse Moon and Kenneth Yamashita. Montclair Public Library, 50 S. Fullerton Ave., Montclair, N.J., 07042.

Indexed: LibLit. *Aud:* Sa.

A 20 to 25 page offset association newsletter which differs from most in that it is downright militant. It is, in fact, a voice of the library counterculture movement. (Note the editors—all rather well known for somewhat different approaches to libraries and librarians.) An example of what is meant will be found in the December 1971 issue where there is a full examination of the pros and cons of supporting the ALA Washington office. When not controversial, the magazine includes short notes on members and libraries, bibliographies, and notes on aspects of the library world. The format is not outstanding, but the content is first rate. Recommended for all New Jersey libraries, and for library schools everywhere.

New Library World (Formerly: *Library World*). 1898. m. $12. Clive Bingley, 16 Pembridge Rd., London W 11, England. Illus., index, adv.

Indexed: LibLit, LibSciAb. *Bk. rev:* 4–5, 250–500 words, signed. *Aud:* Sa.

The closest thing the British have to either *Library Journal* or *Wilson Library Bulletin,* but not as ambitious as either. A typical oversized 20-page issue features comments and news briefs on English libraries and librarians; one or two articles, short pieces and some excellent book reviews. Most of the material is concerned with British libraries, although there is some stress on comparative librarianship and questions of international interest. The style of writing is good, the material informative, and the whole approach of interest. Still, the subscription price for American librarians puts it out of reach, and it is a long way down the list on these shores. A first choice, though, in its home territory.

New York Public Library. Bulletin. 1897. 10/yr. $7.50. David Erdman. New York Public Library, Fifth Ave. and 42nd St., New York, N.Y. 10018. Illus., index. Circ: 1,800.

Indexed: AbEnSt, BibI, BioI, PAIS, PMLA. *Aud:* Ac. *Jv:* V.

Note: January 1, 1972 the publisher announced that the *Bulletin* would be suspended for six months. In the hopes that it will be continued when money is again available, an annotation is included here. Libraries should inquire before subscribing.

A major library publication which is considered to be a leader in the field of bibliography. Articles, by the world's best scholars, cover all aspects of literature from history to the novel. It is particularly useful for the numerous bibliographies, check lists, and notes. Format is outstanding. An absolute necessity for all academic libraries and, certainly, for library schools.

Newberry Library Bulletin. 1944. 2–4/yr. Free to qualified personnel. James M. Wells. The Newberry Library, 60 W. Walton St., Chicago, Ill. 60610. Illus., index. Circ: 3,000. Sample. Vol. ends: 8–10th issue.

Aud: Ac.

A vital journal, particularly for the serious student of English and history. For example, the July 1971 issue is devoted to Sherwood Anderson, features seven articles on his life and his work, ends with a "Checklist of Sherwood Anderson Studies." There are several superb, original photographs. This, of course, is only one example of what is to be found in one of the major basic bibliographic-library magazines. It is particularly useful for information on the humanities, typography and, on occasion, Americana. The articles are by the staff, or by scholars who have used the facilities of the library. Of interest to bibliographers in all medium to large-sized libraries.

Newsletter on Intellectual Freedom. See Civil Liberties Section.

Occasional Papers. 1949. irreg. free. Herbert Goldhor. Univ. of Illinois, Grad. School of Library Science, Urbana, Ill. 61801. Circ: 2,000.

Indexed: LibLit, LibSciAb. *Aud:* Sa, Ac.

Usually a mimeographed report of some 20 to 30 pages, this irregular series deals with all aspects of librarianship from studies of reference to censorship. The series was founded to issue papers which normally might not be published elsewhere because of specialization, length, or detail. Individual issues are of extreme value for an overview of a given area. Librarians should certainly ask to be put on the free list, although some issues are sold at a nominal cost.

Off Center. 1971. m. free. Vi Roisum. Univ. of Wisconsin Center System Libraries, 3111 State St., Madison, Wis. 53706.

Aud: Ac, Ga, Hs.

The 10-page mimeographed newsletter devotes notes to the best that has appeared in a variety of magazines from *The New Yorker* and *Media Methods* to *Vermont Life* and *Washington Monthly.* The annotations are discursive, personalized, witty, and informative. One issue ends with a short essay on women's liberation and some short critical notes. The publisher says about 400 copies are now being distributed, but if demand increases (and it should) a small subscription price will be asked. Send for a free copy today, if only for your own enlightenment. (Incidentally, the editor's approach and style is as winning as it is literate. Who says librarians can't write?)

Ohio Library Association. Bulletin. 1930. q. Membership. Robert H. Donahugh. Publns. Office, 40 S. Third St., Columbus, Ohio 43215. Illus., index, adv.

Indexed: LibLit.

Boasts one of the best formats of any of the state or regional library magazines. It usually includes two to three articles which often go beyond local interest, and can be recommended for a wider audience. The editor displays a true appreciation of his work, and the selection of materials often matches the excellent layout. An average number goes to 30 or so pages. Basic item for larger collections.

Oklahoma Librarian. 1950. q. Membership (Nonmembers $10). Vicki Withers. Subs. to: Oklahoma State Univ. Library, Stillwater, Okla. 74074. Illus., index. Circ: 1,000.

Indexed: LibLit. *Aud:* Sa.

Most of the material pertains only to Oklahoma, but usually one or two longer articles have wider appeal. An average 36-page issue is nicely produced and well edited. Basically, though, only for Oklahoma

libraries—the subscription price, for one thing, makes it prohibitive for others.

Ontario Library Review. 1916. q. $3. Irma McDonough. Provincial Library Service, 14th Floor, Mowat Block, Queen's Park, Toronto 182, Ont., Canada. Illus., index. Circ: 6,300. Sample. Vol. ends: Dec.

Indexed: CanI, LibLit, LibSciAb. *Bk. rev:* 3–4, 300–500 words, signed. *Aud:* Ac, Ga.

Probably Canada's best library magazine. It has a professional format of some 54 to 60 pages, includes both general articles on librarianship and specific reports for Ontario librarians. The December 1971 issue, for example, included an article on recordings (plus an inserted 33 rpm flexidisc record), another on library service for the blind, a piece on school libraries, and a self-explanatory question: "Where in hell are the books we ordered?" Most of the writing is jargon free, and fairly entertaining. It is almost always informative. Among regular features are: reviews of both adult and children's books, personnel notes, statistics, etc. The magazine is sent free to Ontario libraries. It is well worth a subscription by American libraries, and should be required in library schools.

PLA Bulletin. 1945. bi-m. $5. Hilda M. Reitzel. Pennsylvania Library Assn. Subs. to: Nancy L. Blundon, Room 506, 200 S. Craig St., Pittsburgh, Pa. 15213. Illus., index, adv. Circ: 3,000. Microform: UM.

Indexed: LibLit, LibSciAb. *Aud:* Sa.

Usually has three to four rather substantial, often original articles. It includes the usual association news and departments. Thanks to the contributors the magazine has use both inside and outside of Pennsylvania, and it can be recommended for larger library collections anywhere. Good editing.

PNLA Quarterly. 1936. q. Membership (Nonmembers $5). Richard E. Moore. Southern Oregon College Library, Ashland, Ore. 97520. Illus., index, adv. Circ: 1,300. Sample. Vol. ends: Summer.

Indexed: LibLit, LibSciAb. *Bk. rev:* 2–3, 250–500 words, signed. *Aud:* Ac, Ga, Hs, Ejh. *Jv:* V.

The official voice of the Pacific Northwest Library Association, which includes Washington, Oregon, Idaho, Montana, and British Columbia. An average 64-page issue features four or five articles on librarianship at all levels, written by practicing librarians. The material tends to be considerably better written and livelier than that found in most official publications, and is broad enough in scope to interest any librarian. Of particular value to the bibliographer and historian is the ongoing "Checklist of Books and Pamphlets Relating to the Pacific Northwest." This is comprehensive, scholarly, and in many ways a model of its kind for regional bibliography. One of the few library magazines which can be recommended for any medium to large-sized library.

Princeton University Library Chronicle. 1939. 3/yr. $7.50. Mina R. Bryan. Friends of the Library, Princeton Univ. Library, Princeton, N.J. 08540. Illus., index. Circ: 1,600. Sample. Vol. ends: Spring. Microform: UM. Reprint: Johnson, Abrahams.

Indexed: LibLit. *Aud:* Sa, Ac.

Another of the handsome library publications which are a joy to bibliographers and book collectors. Each 60 to 75 page issue features two or three long bibliographic articles, e.g., "Giovanni Battista Pieranesi . . ." or "Charles Reade versus The Round Table." The writing is scholarly yet lucid, free of jargon, and of interest to those involved with any aspect of culture. There are library notes, news, and information on the Friends of the Princeton Library. The whole is well documented, illustrated, and nicely printed.

Public Relations Reporter; a library public relations newsletter. 1962. m. $8. Public Relations Office, Amer. Library Assn., 50 E. Huron St., Chicago, Ill. 60611.

Aud: Ga.

Notes and short articles on all aspects of public relations work in libraries. Most of the material is practical advice based upon experience of librarians. Some news and notes on the activities of the office.

Quarterly Journal of the Library of Congress. 1943. q. $3.50. Sarah L. Wallace. Library of Congress, Washington, D.C. 20540. Dist. by: Supt. of Documents, U.S. Govt. Printing Office, Washington, D.C. 20402. Illus., index. Circ: 3,000. Sample. Vol. ends: Oct. Microform: UM.

Indexed: LibLit, MLA. *Aud:* Ga, Ac.

This is a "best buy" for any library or interested student from the standpoint of price and content. The 100-page magazine not only is beautifully designed and illustrated, but covers a variety of interests as reflected by the activities of the Library of Congress. The articles by scholars and members of the LC staff touch on every base from education and motion pictures to biography and music. Certain issues are given over in part to a particular field, e.g., modern poetry, Africana, American Revolution. Each issue concludes with an annotated listing of "Some Recent Publications of the Library of Congress," a valued checklist for any librarian. Although primarily for the specialist, the informed laymen will enjoy being introduced to this journal, and considering its low price it should be in most libraries.

RQ. 1960. Membership (Nonmembers $10). Bill Katz. ALA Reference Services Div., 50 E. Huron St., Chicago, Ill. 60611. Index, adv. Circ: 7,000. Sample. Vol. ends: Summer. Microform: UM.

Indexed: LibLit, LibSciAb. *Bk. rev:* 40–60, signed. *Aud:* Sa, Ac, Ga. *Jv:* V.

Published to reverse the reference process. *RQ* tries to provide answers instead of asking questions. Each issue features five to six articles, often one or two bibliographies, shorter notes "from the field," book reviews, and columns on government documents, research in reference, difficult questions, etc. Over the years the many contributing editors have made it particularly useful as an accurate, purposefully opinionated source of reviews of reference books and government documents. The style is kept as simple and direct as is possible when dealing with reference people who are constantly asking, "Yes, but what's the question?" Thanks to the contributors, it can be recommended for all libraries where there is a question about anything. (R.Q.)

School Libraries. See *School Media Quarterly.*

School Library Journal. 1954. m. $10. Lillian N. Gerhardt. R. R. Bowker Co., 1180 Ave. of the Americas, New York, N.Y. 10036. Illus., index, adv. Circ: 35,000. Sample. Vol. ends: Dec.

Indexed: LibLit, LibSciAb. *Bk. rev:* numerous, 150 words, signed. *Aud:* Sa. *Jv:* V.

The best of the magazines devoted to work with children and teen-agers in libraries. The staff, from the editor to the heads of various departments, are professional, and as knowledgeable as they are literate. Articles cover all aspects of work with young people, but the magazine has gained a deserved reputation for publishing material (both from librarians and from staffers) which leads, rather than follows, the movements and surges in the library field. There are usually four to five excellent, well-written articles per issue, a number of departments (news, professional reading, recordings, screenings, etc.), and first-rate book reviews. The reviews in themselves make the magazine a must for any library. They are equal to, and often superior to, those found in other sources. Thanks to its professional staff and its long, adventuresome life in the field, *School Library Journal* is the magazine for all school and public libraries. (Note: it is included also as part of the *Library Journal.*)

School Media Quarterly (Formerly: *School Libraries*). 1951. q. Membership (Single copies $2). Mary Frances Johnson. Amer. Assn. of School Librarians, 50 E. Huron St., Chicago, Ill. 60611. Illus., index, adv. Circ: 12,000. Sample. Vol. ends: Summer.

Indexed: LibLit, LibSciAb. *Bk. rev:* 5, 200–300 words, signed. *Aud:* Ejh, Hs.

Since the past edition of this book, this magazine has a new editor and, fortunately, a new outlook. What was once evaluated as a rather pedestrian journal has become innovative, even exciting. There are four or five articles, usually by practicing librarians, a number of departments, book reviews, and, of course, news of the Association. The articles are deeply involved with change in the elementary and high school library. And they are important. Along with *School Library Journal* and *Top of the News*, this is a must for school libraries.

Signal. 1970. 3/yr. $5. Nancy Chambers. Thimble Press, Stroud, Glos. GL6, 7LW, England.

Aud: Ac, Sa.

Signal is a fairly new journal which will be published three times a year, January, May and September, "without benefit of advertising revenue or any organizational support." The editor states that it "is being published to provide a voice for writers whose ideas about, and interests in, children's books cannot be contained in brief reviews and articles, or in periodicals whose purposes are basically pragmatic or educational." Although the articles are concerned primarily with British poets, authors, and illustrators, there is no indication that this national emphasis will continue as a matter of editorial policy. The informative, scholarly presentations in this unique journal should be of interest to anyone concerned with children's literature, and particularly of value to students and teachers. (L.O.)

Sipapu. 1970. bi-a. $2. Noel Peattie, Rt. 1, Box 216, Winters, Calif. 95694. Illus. Circ: 200. Sample. Vol. ends: July.

Aud: Ac, Ga.

A 12-page "newsletter for librarians, scholars, editors and others concerned with ethnic studies, the counter-culture, and the underground press," which is to say this is a roaring good effort to make librarians aware of the changes around them and the need to build collections which reflect that change. The issue examined discusses underground newspapers, gives helpful bibliographic information, and suggests ways "bold young librarians" may subvert some of the budget money for the Third World people's interests. The editor claims he has heard from over one hundred libraries who want copies, but where are the other seven or so thousand?

South Dakota Library Bulletin. 1914. q. Free. Mercedes B. MacKay. State Library Commission, 322 S. Fort St., Pierre, S.D. 29211. Circ: 1,500.

Indexed: LibLit. *Aud:* Sa.

A voice of a government body, and as such far from exciting, but solid enough in its information about South Dakota library activities. It is strong on one essential point: excellent bibliographies, e.g., "Environmental science—a bibliography for school libraries." As it is free to South Dakota libraries—and apparently to others for the asking—it is recommended for the really outstanding bibliographies. The rest is pretty much routine.

Southeastern Librarian. 1950. q. Membership (Non-members $6). Jerrold Orne. Box 1032, Decatur, Ga.

30030. Illus., index, adv. Circ: 2,300. Sample. Vol. ends: Winter.

Indexed: LibLit, LibSciAb. *Bk. rev:* 1, 1,000 words, signed. *Aud:* Ac, Ga.

The voice of the Southeastern Library Association, covering Alabama, Florida, Georgia, Kentucky, Mississippi, North Carolina, South Carolina, Tennessee, and Virginia. Content is about evenly divided among four to five articles on librarianship and features, news notes, reports from the various state memberships, bibliographies, and the annual proceedings of the Association. The articles are much above average, and cover such subjects as integration, faculty-library relationships, special collections, and other topics of interest to librarians in any part of the country or world. Bibliographies and author profiles give it an added dimension. Should be found in all southern libraries, and in larger libraries and library schools.

Special Libraries. 1910. m. $22.40. Janet D. Bailey. Special Libraries Assn., 235 Park Ave. S., New York, N.Y. 10003. Illus., index, adv. Circ: 9,400. Sample. Vol. ends: Dec. Microform: UM. Reprint: Kraus.

Indexed: BusI, HistAb, InfSciAb, LibLit, LibSciAb, PAIS, SCI. *Bk. rev:* 20–30, 40 words. *Aud:* Ac, Ga.

While this is directed to special libraries, it is of equal interest to many librarians in public and academic libraries. The five to six articles cover every aspect of the art from indexing and automation to administration and bibliographic control. The contributors, usually working librarians, write in a nontechnical way, can be easily understood by the average reader. News of the Association, as well as up-to-date information on developments in library and information science makes up about one half of every issue. There are brief reviews, too. In the last edition this was ranked low. A new editor, a new approach, have made this a considerably better journal, and it can now be recommended.

Synergy. 1967. bi-m. Free. Celeste West. BARC (Bay Area Reference Center), San Francisco Public Library, Civic Center, San Francisco, Calif. 94102. Sample.

Indexed: API, LibLit. *Aud:* Sa, Ga, Ac, Hs, Ejh. *Jv:* V.

Hands down (or is it up?), the best little magazine in the library world! Under the imaginative editorship of Celeste West, each issue considers another facet of the human condition. The approach is essentially twofold. First there is an introductory piece or two on the importance of the subject (and this will range from witches and the occult to the American family and the women's liberation movement). After the introductory remarks come detailed articles with bibliographies, which are guides to librarians trying to build collections and services in the area of the topic considered. Most of the writing is by staff members, i.e., those who work for BARC or the San Francisco Public Library. They are remarkably literate. Usually, too, there are outstanding illustrations and drawings. Footnotes to the main features include "Unanswered questions somebody asked us"—questions put to the BARC reference staff, usually with answers; plus assorted shorter items on just about anything of interest to the staff. A typical 44-page issue is a joy to read—and one of the few professional magazines (in any profession) that can be read for pleasure as well as for information. No library or librarian should be without *Synergy*.

Tennessee Librarian. 1948. q. Membership (Nonmembers $4). Paul Murphy. Tennessee Library Assn. Joint Univ. Libraries, Nashville, Tenn. 37203. Illus., index, adv. Circ: 1,600.

Indexed: LibLit. *Aud:* Sa.

Primarily concerned with Tennessee matters, this 36-page journal is heavy on Association business and personalities. There are usually three or four brief articles, and most of these are involved with the details of the profession, e.g., "Jobs, the current market for librarians." Well edited and produced.

Texas Library Journal. 1924. q. Membership (Nonmembers $8). Mary Pound. Texas Library Assn. Box 7763, University Station, Austin, Tex. 78712. Illus., index, adv. Circ: 3,200.

Indexed: LibLit. *Aud:* Sa.

A well produced, ably edited journal which often has material of more than local interest. There are usually five to six articles of varying length and importance, and of these about one half concern national or regional problems. The contributors tend to be local librarians. There is usually a bit of humor with each issue, and it is refreshing to report that even the business meetings (dutifully reported along with other Association news) are sometimes treated less solemnly than funeral proceedings. A good magazine for almost any library in the southwest.

Top of the News. 1942. q. Membership. Mary Jane Anderson. American Library Assn., Children's Services Div. and Young Adult Services Div., 50 E. Huron St., Chicago, Ill. 60611. Illus., adv. Circ: 13,500. Sample. Vol. ends: June.

Indexed: LibLit, LibSciAb. *Bk. rev:* 25, 30–50 words, signed. *Aud:* Ejh, Hs, Ac, Ga. *Jv:* V.

This and *School Library Journal* are the best general magazines covering the field of school librarianship from the elementary through high school scene. It has improved with the years, and while the writing is uneven, the overall feeling is of dedication with a dash of realism, and a larger dash of cynicism about instant cures for anything. Most of the authors are practicing librarians who know of what they speak. One of the best features for readers of this compilation is the magazine column which gives succinct, usually critical reviews of newer magazines. On occasion a group effort is launched, e.g., cycle magazines, which evaluates a number of similar titles. The short book reviews are equally good.

UNESCO Bulletin for Libraries. 1947. bi-m. $4. Unesco Publications Center, P.O. Box 433, New York, N.Y. 10016. Illus., index, adv. Circ: 1,600 (in U.S.). Vol. ends: Nov./Dec. Microform: UM.

Indexed: CIJE, CurrCont, LibLit, LibSciAb, PAIS. *Bk. rev:* Various number, length. *Aud:* Ga, Ac, Hs. *Jv:* V.

Each issue contains approximately six to eight articles written by librarians, archivists, researchers and educators from all countries. Topics covered include world information system analysis, responsibilities of library associations, current trends in library research in various countries, documentation, automation, book selection, and the like. Emphasis is on Unesco's role in international library cooperation, cultural agreements, copyright, microreproduction, and bibliographic control and access. Regular features include: "Book Review"—one or two rather lengthy critical reviews of important monographs in librarianship; "New Publications"—over 40 briefly annotated publications, both government and commercial, on a variety of topics; "News and Information"—notes on annual conferences in the library world, specific libraries, technical journals, research grants, and the like; "Exchange, Publications Wanted, Free Distribution"—a very useful feature in which libraries that have publications available for exchange send details to the *Bulletin* editor and the information is published; libraries needing publications may also advertise their wants. Also noted are publications that the *Bulletin* has for free distribution. (J.M.)

The Unabashed Librarian; a letter for innovators. 1971. q. $10. Marvin H. Scilken, G.P.O., Box 2631, New York, N.Y. 10001. Illus.

Aud: Ac.

Each issue of this new venture is about 32 mimeographed pages of practical ideas, e.g., information on subject headings, types of books most often stolen, or "some thoughts on weeding." Granted, the author/editor writes well, gets to the point, and does not waste any time with theory. In fact, his style is refreshing after most library literature, and his notions of saving time and nerves are good enough. Since the first review of the magazine in *LJ*, it has improved enough to warrant a qualified recommendation; but because of the price, send for a sample first.

Vermont Libraries. 1970. m. Free. Jim Igoe and Kathleen Nelson. Vermont Dept. of Libraries, Montpelier, Vt. 05602. Illus. Circ: 2,000.

Indexed: LibLit. *Aud:* Sa.

One of the few new state library publications—this

one sponsored by the Vermont Department of Libraries, the Vermont Library Association, and the Vermont Library Trustees Association. An average 25-page issue is involved with news of Vermont library activities, has few articles, and is primarily a device for spreading official information. Some useful bibliographies, but use is pretty well limited to Vermont libraries.

Virginia Librarian. 1953. q. $5. Dean Burgess. Virginia Library Assn., 5 Commander Drive, Hampton, Va. 23366. Illus. Circ: 1,250.

Aud: Sa.

Usually one original, long article and two or three shorter pieces highlight each issue. The material is primarily, although not exclusively, of interest only to Virginia librarians. Much of it consists of reports of meetings, activities of the Association, and personnel news. Adequate editing and format.

✓***Visible Language*** (Formerly: ***Journal of Typographic Research***). 1967. q. $11.. Gerald E. Wrolstad. Cleveland Museum of Art, Cleveland, Ohio, 44106. Illus., index, adv. Circ: 1,600.

Indexed: AbEnSt, PsyAb, SCI. *Aud:* Ac, Sa.

"Why would a magazine with a great name like *The Journal of Typographic Research* decide to change it? . . . It no longer adequately describes the research efforts in the field of the major concern of this journal." And so begins a lengthy explanation of the scope and purpose of the journal in the Winter 1971 issue. It will still be of most interest to analytical bibliographers and typographers, not to mention some English and art teachers and linguists. Articles are involved with calligraphy, type design, and computer printouts. The presentations are semitechnical, although usually within the capacities of a graduate student in library science, linguistics, art, etc. As the best single journal in this field (whatever the parameters of the field may be), it is highly recommended for art, typography, and linguistic library collections—and, of course, library schools.

✓***Wilson Library Bulletin.*** 1914. m. (Sept.–June). $9. William R. Eshelman. H. W. Wilson Co., 950 University Ave., Bronx, N.Y., 10452. Illus., index, adv. Circ: 38,000. Sample. Vol. ends: June. Microform: B&H, UM.

Indexed: CurrCont, HistAb, LibLit. LibSciAb. *Bk. rev:* 20, 100 words, signed. *Aud:* Ejh, Hs, Ac, Ga. *Jv:* V.

Along with *Library Journal*, the only national library magazine published by an independent publisher. It shows. Under the Eshelman editorship the magazine has grown in its importance to all types of libraries. Each issue is usually given to a single topic from sex education for children to survey articles on the state of the literature in everything from art to

zoology. The writing style is professional, lively, informative, and quite often controversial. There are many departments, including excellent reference book reviews and government document surveys. The makeup from the cover to the last page is as imaginative as are the contents.

Wisconsin Library Bulletin. 1905. bi-m. $2. William C. Kahal, State Supt., Dept. of Public Instruction, 126 Langdon St., Madison, Wis. 53702. Illus., index. Circ: 4,000.

Indexed: LibLit. *Aud:* Sa.

Features five to six articles, usually around a center theme such as "new concepts in audiovisual service." Contributions are short, tend to be overviews rather then original research. A number of features cover all types of libraries. Good, if uninspired, content. Primarily only for Wisconsin libraries.

Yale University Library Gazette. 1926. q. $6. Donald C. Gallup. Yale Univ. Library, New Haven, Conn. 06520. Illus., index. Circ: 1,400. Vol. ends: Apr.

Indexed: LibLit. *Aud:* Ac.

While the primary emphasis of this journal is on the resources of the Yale library, it has much wider application for the student of history and bibliography. The four to five articles, written for the most part by faculty and librarians at Yale, are universal in interest. Usually there are a number of excellent illustrations. The concluding "Recent Acquisitions," a descriptive listing of some six to eight pages, highlights important new manuscripts, books, broadsides, and the like acquired by the library. A must for the serious bibliographer and all library schools.

Library Newsletters

As a means of communication, staff associations may issue a newsletter to the library staff, to other library staff associations, to university faculty, and in some cases to the community. This relatively new means of communication within and among library staff members both professional and nonprofessional serves to formalize (by writing down) a large part of the grapevine which flourishes up and down the library corridors. The newsletter serves as a forum for discussing and reporting staff concerns and a means of presenting ideas and complaints. Many report the activities of the staff association, dates of local, state, and national conferences, and summaries of conference results written by staff members who attended. New programs of the library are reported, and changes in current programs are often outlined. New ideas in librarianship can be noted either through notes on research reports, a short bibliography, or reviews of pertinent articles. Recent notable acquisitions such as reference titles, rare books, or outstanding gifts are another possible inclusion. Necessary to formalizing the details of the grapevine is a section on who is engaged, who had twins, and who went to the Bahamas. Finally, a staff association newsletter can be used to inject a bit of humor into the library day by recording the funny thing that happened on the way to the reference desk.

What follows is a select listing of newsletters. Most are issued monthly, although some appear quarterly or on an irregular basis. All are free on request. For further comments, see *RQ*, Summer, 1970, p. 310. (A.P.)

PUBLIC LIBRARY STAFF NEWSLETTERS

Ad Lib. Indianapolis, Marion Co. (Ind.) Public Library. New programs, staff news—personal and personnel.

Ad Lib. Kern Co. Library (Shafter, Calif.) Staff Assn. Staff association news, staff news—personal and personnel.

As We Are. San Bernardino (Calif.) Public Library. New administrative procedures programs, staff news—personal and personnel.

The Booktruck. Milwaukee (Wis.) Public Library System. Report on extension of library service, defines administrative position on pornography, staff news—personal and personnel.

Branching Out. Baltimore (Md.) Co. Public Library. Current library activities, reports on meetings attended, library use statistics, ALA conference report, public library law amendments pending, staff news—personal and personnel—humor.

Dialog (a unique newsletter not really for staff). Tuxedo Park (N.Y.) Public Library. A community communication "featuring local news events to come and reviews of recent books," library programs and services, essay by local artist on his art, community affairs.

Echo. Cuyahoga County (Ohio) Public Library. Staff association news including annual report, staff poetry, staff news—personal and personnel—humor.

Fresno Free Library Intercom. Fresno (Calif.) Free Library. Reports of workshops, staff news—personal and personnel.

Happenings. Fort Worth (Tex.) Public Library. Staff news—personal and personnel.

The Interpreter. Buffalo and Erie Co. (N.Y.) Public Library. Staff news—personal and personnel. A nonstaff association publication of the library, the *Buffalo and Erie County Public Library Bulletin,* covers library programs, circulation statistics, administrative information and national library news. The two publications appear to supplement one another.

The Listening Post. Madison (Wis.) Public Library. Library board activities, library programs, bibliography of new professional material, staff news—personal and personnel.

Muncie Public Library Wire. Muncie (Ind.) Public Library. New library services, concern about state library legislation, staff news—personal and personnel—recipes.

News and Views. Cleveland (Ohio) Public Library. Formal request for further study of salary needs, grievance procedure, activities of and reports on state and association meetings.

Nor'Easter. N. Suburban Library System, Morton Grove, Ill. ALA meeting reports, notices of meetings and programs, staff news—personal and personnel.

Our Private Letter. Orlando (Fla.) Public Library. Staff news—personal and personnel—library services, and programs.

Outline. Dallas (Tex.) Public Library. Notices of library exhibits, meetings, branch activities, administrative information, editorial comment on libraries, reviews of periodical articles, staff news—personal and personnel.

Pilot Light. Jacksonville (Fla.) Public Library. Programs and schedules, staff news—personal and personnel—reports of state and county library meetings.

PLSB Newsletter. Public Library Services Branch, Oklahoma City, Okla. Staff news—personal and personnel—interesting facts.

Staff Association News. Free Library of Philadelphia (Pa.). Staff news—personal and personnel—suggested readings—annotated.

Staff Association News. Providence (R.I.) Public Library. Staff news—personal and personnel—results of poll to see "which two books to take to a desert island," bibliography of articles of library interest in nonlibrary literature.

Staff Bulletin. Public Library of Youngstown and Mahoning Co. (Ohio). Information on and in periodicals, administrative changes, staff news—personal and personnel—our library in history.

Staff Bulletin. Vigo County Public Library, Terre Haute, Ind. Administrative activities, list of most circulated books, circulation figures, staff news—personal and personnel.

Staff Lookout. Denver (Colo.) Public Library. Library programs and dates, staff information.

Staff News. Chicago (Ill.) Public Library. In-depth biographies of board members, profile of other libraries in Chicago, Board of Trustees report, stands on issues.

Staff News Bulletin. Evansville and Vandenburgh County (Ohio) Public Library. Publications of the EPL, review of ALA conference, staff news—personal and personnel.

Staff Notes. Cincinnati and Hamilton County (Ohio) Public Library. Staff news—personal and personnel—literary efforts.

Staff Reporter. Akron (Ohio) Public Library. Staff association news, staff news—personal and personnel.

Staff Reporter. Enoch Pratt Free Library, Baltimore, Md. Extensive report on an aspect of library service, film review, staff news—personal and personnel.

The Tasket. Hammond (Ind.) Public Library. Library calendar, gossip and humor.

Teaneck Points of Reference. Teaneck (N.J.) Public Library. Staff news, humor, book reviews. Personalized reporting by editor Allan Angoff.

COLLEGE AND UNIVERSITY STAFF ASSOCIATION NEWSLETTERS

Call Number. Univ. of Illinois at Chicago Circle. Humor, bibliographies, staff news, questions and answers.

Corner Quotes from Milner Library. Illinois State Univ. Library (Normal). Humor, attendance records.

The Green Pyle Leaf. Princeton Univ. "Concentrates on the news of the library system with particular emphasis on staff news. There will be one article every month on a special library or collection and provides for periodic feature articles where they seem appropriate."

Hue and Cry: A News Letter of Librarianese. Univ. of California at Riverside. Purposes of and arguments for a staff association, reports of meetings with administration concerning status of librarians, acquisitions of note, positions and stands on matters of library concern.

Kresge Kaleidoscope. Kresge Library, Oakland Univ., Rochester, Minn. Editorials with social comment, technical services reports, in-depth review of reference books, staff news—personal and personnel.

Library Link. William R. Perkins Library, Duke Univ., Durham, N.C. Articles on specific collections, information on a special library, in-depth reviews, reports on conferences, staff news—personal and personnel.

Library Staff News. San Diego (Calif.) State College. Reports on library activities and services, long report on ALA Conferences, staff news—personal and personnel—staff association news.

News and Views. Brigham Young Univ., Library Staff Assn., Provo, Utah. Administrative information, summary of R. Downs Survey of the University Library, bibliography on library unions, conference notes and notices, important acquisitions, library school curriculum information, continuing information on acquisition of Mormoniana.

News from the Library. Brooklyn College, Brooklyn, N.Y. Rose Sellers, editor, brings humor, bits of information, staff news, and astonishing trivia to all readers.

Northeastern Library News. Northeastern Univ., Evanston, Ill. Each issue explores one or two current issues in depth; staff news.

Oberlin Library Newsletter. Oberlin, Ohio. Reports on library conferences and special institutes.

Purdue Pulse. Purdue Univ. Library, Lafayette, Ind. Conference reports on such meetings as International Congress of Medical Librarianship in Amsterdam; report on Center for Research Libraries services; report on the microfilming of catalog cards; staff news—personal and personnel.

Quarto. Milton S. Eisenhower Library, Johns Hopkins Univ., Baltimore, Md. Notices of meetings, staff news—personal and personnel.

Schedule and Report. University Library, Univ. of California, Santa Barbara, Calif. New programs scheduled, staff news—personal and personnel—news from other UC campuses, extended reviews of publications, and national news of importance to California universities.

Staff Association Bulletin. University of Texas, Austin, Texas. Reports of meetings; report on heavy use of Latin American collection; summary of report on the library; results of a questionnaire concerning views on collective bargaining.

Staff Newsletter. Catholic Univ. of America Libraries, Washington, D.C. Information on Middle States evaluation policy; projects of the library; library exhibits; listing of library science research papers; reports on special conferences; information on reorganization of various divisions; some important acquisitions.

Tracings. University of Windsor, Windsor, Ontario, Canada. Reports on conferences, reports on travel, staff news—personal and personnel.

University of Michigan Librarian. Univ. of Michigan, Ann Arbor, Michigan. Notes about the library school, microfilming of the catalog, notes on shared cataloging, professional meeting notices.

State Library Association Publications

Almost all state library associations issue a publication, and they are listed here on a state by state basis. Major state periodicals that are indexed are also included. (School library association publications are listed separately.) Reference is also made to the regional periodicals, all of which are annotated in the main listing.

With some notable exceptions, content is rather parochial, limited to immediate interests of the state association—personal notes, business activities, meetings, etc. For purposes of purchase, all libraries within a state will want their own association publication, plus the regional magazine.

Alabama Library Assn., 4265 Amherst St., Montgomery, Ala. 36111. *Alabama Librarian.* 1949. q. Membership (Nonmembers $3.00). Luther E. Lee. Illus, adv. Circ: 750. *Indexed:* LibLit, LibSciAb. Bk. rev.

Arizona State Library Assn., Arizona State Univ. Library, Tucson, Ariz. 85721. *Arizona Librarian.* 1940. q. Membership (Nonmembers $5). Kenneth Slack. Adv. Circ: 850. *Indexed:* LibLit. Bk. rev.

Arkansas Library Assn. and Arkansas Library Commission, 506½ Center St., Little Rock, Ark. 72201. *Arkansas Libraries.* 1944. q. Membership. LaNell Compton. Illus. Circ: 809. *Indexed:* LibLit. Available in microform. Bk. rev.

California Library Assn., 717 K St., Sacramento, Calif. 95814. *California Librarian.* 1939. q. Membership (Nonmembers $10). Don Kunitz. Illus., index, adv, bk rev., cum. index. Circ: 4,500. *Indexed:* LibLit, LibSciAb, JofDoc.

California State Library, Box 2037, Sacramento, Calif. 95809. *News Notes of California Libraries.* 1906. q. Price not given. John W. Cully. Bibl., charts, illus., stat. Circ: 1,800. *Indexed:* LibLit, LibSciAb.

Colorado Library Assn., College and Univ. Section, Univ. of Denver Libraries, Boulder, Colo. 80302. *Colorado Academic Library.* 1963. q. Membership (Nonmembers $3). Carol Cushman and Joe Mapes.

Connecticut Library Assn., c/o Bridgeport Public Library, Bridgeport, Conn. 06603. *Connecticut Libraries* (Formerly: *C.L.A. News and Views*). Vol. 12, 1970. q. $5. Meredith Bloss. Circ: controlled. *Indexed:* LibLit.

Delaware Library Assn., Dept. of Public Instruction, Dover, Del. 19401. *Delaware Library Association. Bulletin.* 1946. Free. Helen Bennett.

District of Columbia. No library association publication.

Florida Library Assn., 3018 N.W. First Ave., Gainesville, Fla. 32601. *Florida Libraries.* 1949. q. Membership (Nonmembers $5, single issues $2). Mrs. Virginia Reif. Illus., adv. Circ: 1,400. *Indexed:* LibLit, LibSciAb. Bk. rev. (See also *Southeastern Librarian.*)

Georgia Library Assn., Box 176, Decatur, Ga. 30031. *Georgia Librarian* 1964. s-a. Membership. Grace Hightower. (See also *Southeastern Librarian.*)

Hawaii Library Assn., Box 4441, Honolulu, Hawaii 96813. *Hawaii Library Association Journal.* 1944. s-a. Linda Engelberg. Charts, illus. Circ: 600. *Indexed:* LibLit, LibSciAb.

Idaho State Library, 615 Fulton St., Boise, Idaho 83706. *Idaho Librarian.* 1945. q. Membership (Nonmembers $3). Bibl., illus., index. Circ: 1,000. *Indexed:* LibLit.

Illinois Library Assn., 326 S. 7th St., Springfield, Ill. 62701. *ILA Reporter.* 4/yr. Free. Mrs. Sella Morrison. Illus. Circ: 4,900.

Illinois State Library, Springfield, Ill. 62706. *Illinois Libraries.* 1919. m. Free. Irma Bostian. Illus. Circ: 8,000. *Indexed:* LibLit. Bk. rev.

Indiana Library Assn., Ball State Univ., Muncie, Ind., 47306. *Focus on Indiana Libraries.* 1947. q. Membership (Nonmembers $4). Larry DeVos. Illus., index, adv. Circ: 1,400. *Indexed:* LibLit.

Iowa State Travelling Library, Historical Bldg., Des Moines, Iowa 50319. *Iowa Library Quarterly.* 1901. q. Florence Stiles. Bibl., cum. index every 5 yrs. Circ: 14,000. *Indexed:* LibLit.

State Libraries of Kansas, Statehouse. 3rd Floor. Topeka, Kans. 66612. *Kansas Library Bulletin.* 1932. q. Free. Virginia Manley. Circ: 4,000. *Indexed:* LibLit.

Kentucky Library Assn., Morehead State Univ., Box 1272, Morehead, Ky. 40351. *Kentucky Library Association. Bulletin.* 1936. q. $6. Jean Wiggins. Illus., adv. Circ: 1,000 (controlled). *Indexed:* LibLit.

Louisiana Library Assn., PAR Council, Inc., Commerce Bldg., Baton Rouge, La. 70802. *Louisiana Library Association Bulletin.* 1937. q. Membership (Nonmembers $3). Mrs. Jackie Ducote. Illus., index, adv. Circ: 1,300. *Indexed:* LibLit. Bk. rev.

Maine Library Assn. Lithgow Public Library. Augusta, Maine 04330. *Maine Library Association: Newsletter* (Formerly: *Bulletin*). Vol. 31, 1970. 4/yr. Membership (Nonmembers $2). *Indexed:* LibLit.

Maryland Library Assn. and the Educational Media Assn. of Maryland, 115 W. Franklin St., Baltimore, Md. 21201. *Maryland Libraries.* 1932. q. Membership (Nonmembers $4). Mrs. Estelle Gutberlet. *Indexed:* LibLit. Bk. rev.

Massachusetts Library Assn., P.O. Box 7, Nahant, Mass. 01908. *Bay State Librarian.* 1911. q. Membership (Nonmembers $3). Robert E. Cain. Adv. Circ: 2,000. *Indexed:* LibLit.

Michigan Library Assn., 226 W. Washtenaw, Lansing, Mich. 48933. *Michigan Librarian.* 1935. 4/yr. Membership (Nonmembers $4). Mrs. H. F. Pletz. Adv. Circ: 1,725. *Indexed:* LibLit.

Minnesota State Dept. of Education, Library Div. 117 University Ave. St. Paul, Minn. 55101. *Minnesota Libraries.* 1904. q. Free to libraries in Minn. and on exchange to out of state and foreign libraries. Hannis S. Smith. Statistics. Index at end of vol. (3 yrs.). Circ: 1,968. *Indexed:* LibLit, LibSciAb. Bk. rev.

Mississippi Library Assn. and Mississippi Library Commission, 405 State Office Bldg., Jackson, Miss. 39201. *Mississippi Library News.* 1953. q. Free to public libraries in Miss., $5 to individuals and institutions. Mrs. C. C. Clark. Adv. Circ: 1,500. *Indexed:* LibLit. (See also *Southeastern Librarian.*)

Missouri Library Assn., 10 S. Seventh St. Columbia, Mo. 65201. *MLA Newsletter* (supersedes *MLA Quarterly*). 1970. 6/yr. Membership (Nonmembers $3). Nancy Doyle. Bibl., illus. Circ: 2,000. *Indexed:* LibLit.

Montana. No library association publication.

Nebraska. No library association publication. (See *Mountain Plains Library Quarterly.*)

Nevada Library Assn., State Library, Carson City, Nev. 89701. *Nevada Libraries.* 1964. q. Membership (Nonmembers $2). Barbara Mauseth. Adv. (See also *Mountain Plains Library Quarterly.*)

New Hampshire Library Assn., Woodbury Memorial Library, 9 Bell Hill Rd., Bedford, N.H. 03102. *Newsletter.* 1940. 3/yr. Free. Doris Peck. (See also *North Country Libraries.*)

New Jersey Library Assn., 800 Rathway Avenue, Woodbridge, N.J. 07095. *New Jersey Libraries.* 1966. q. Membership (Nonmembers $1). Jack Fishman. Illus., adv. *Indexed:* LibLit. Bk. rev.

New Mexico Library Assn. and State Library, P.O. Box 4141, University Park, N.M. 88001. *New Mexico Libraries.* 1932. q. Christine L. Buder. Circ: 559. *Indexed:* LibLit. Bk. rev.

New York Library Assn., Box 521, Woodside, N.Y. 11377. *NYLA Bulletin.* 1953. bi-m. $3. Mrs. R. K. Baum. Illus., adv. *Indexed:* LibLit, PAIS.

New York State Library, N.Y. State Education Dept., Albany, N.Y. 12224. *The Bookmark.* 1949. m. (Oct.–July). $1.50. R. Edwin Berry. Circ: 5,000. *Indexed:* LibLit. PAIS. Bk. rev.

North Carolina Library Assn., Dept. of Library Science, Appalachian State Univ., Boone, N.C. 28607. *North Carolina Libraries.* 1942. q. Membership (Nonmembers $3). Mell Busbin. Circ: 2,000. *Indexed:* LibLit, LibSciAb. Bk. rev. (See also *Southeastern Librarian.*)

North Dakota. No publication. (See *Mountain Plains Library Quarterly.*)

Ohio Library Assn., Publns. Office, Rm. 409, 40 S. Third St., Columbus, Ohio 43215. *Ohio Library Association Bulletin.* 1937. q. Free to members. Robert H. Donahugh. *Indexed:* LibLit.

Oklahoma Library Assn., Chicasaw Library System, 22 Broadlawn Village, Ardmore, Okla. 73401. *Oklahoma Librarian.* 1950. q. Membership (Nonmembers $3). Billee Day. Illus., adv. Circ: 774. *Indexed:* LibLit.

Oregon Library Assn., 1631 E. 24th Ave. Eugene, Ore. 97403. *Oregon Library News.* 1954. q. Membership (Nonmembers $1). Katherine G. Eaton. Circ: controlled. (See also *PNLA Quarterly.*)

Pennsylvania Library Assn., 200 S. Craig St., Pittsburgh, Pa. 15213. *Pennsylvania Library Association Bulletin.* 1945. bi-m. Membership (Nonmembers $5). Hilda Reitzel. Illus., adv. Circ: 3,700. *Indexed:* LibLit, LibSciAb.

Rhode Island. No publication. (See *NELA Newsletter.*)

South Carolina Library Assn., Box 11322 Columbia, S.C. 29211. *South Carolina Librarian.* 1956. s-a. Membership (Nonmembers $1) Lester Duncan. Illus. Circ: 900. *Indexed:* LibLit. Bk. rev. (See also *Southeastern Librarian.*)

South Dakota State Library Commission, 322 S. Fort St., Pierre, S.D. 57501. *South Dakota Library Bulletin.* 1914. q. Free to S.D. libraries. Mercedes B. Mackay. Circ: 1,500. *Indexed:* LibLit. (See also *Mountain Plains Library Quarterly.*)

Tennessee Library Assn., Joint Univ. Libraries, Nashville, Tenn. 37203. *Tennessee Librarian.* 1948. q. $2. Paul Murphy. Illus., adv. Circ: 1,600. *Indexed:* LibLit. (See also *Southeastern Librarian.*)

Texas Library Assn., Box 7763, Univ. Station, Austin, Tex. 78712. *Texas Library Journal.* 1924. q. Membership (Nonmembers $5). Mary Pound. Illus., adv. Circ: 3,200. *Indexed:* LibLit.

Texas Library and Historical Commission, Box 12927, Capitol Station, Austin, Tex. 78711. *Texas Libraries.* 1906. q. Free to Texas libraries. Millicent Huff. Circ: 1,950. *Indexed:* LibLit.

Utah Library Assn., 2150 S. 2nd West, Salt Lake City, Utah 84115. *Utah Libraries.* 1957. s-a. Membership (Nonmembers $2). Carol Oaks. Illus., adv. Circ: 650. *Indexed:* LibLit. Bk. rev. (See also *Mountain Plains Library Quarterly.*)

Vermont Department of Libraries, Montpelier, Vermont 05602. *Vermont Libraries,* 1970. m. Free. *Indexed:* LibLit.

Virginia Library Assn., 5 Commander Dr., Hampton, Va. 23366. *Virginia Librarian.* 1954. q. Membership (Nonmembers $1). Dean Burgess. Circ: 1,250. *Indexed:* LibLit, LibSciAb. Bk. rev. (See also *Southeastern Librarian.*)

Washington. No publication. (See *PNLA Quarterly.*)

Washington State Library, Olympia, Wash. 98501. *Library News Bulletin.* 1932. q. Free to Washington libraries. Charles A. Symon. Circ: 2,800. *Indexed:* LibLit. Bk. rev.

West Virginia Library Assn., West Virginia Univ., Morgantown, W.Va. 26506. *West Virginia Libraries.* 1948. q. $2.50. Lois Murphy. Circ: 525. *Indexed:* LibLit. Bk. rev.

Wisconsin Library Assn., Public Library, Madison, Wis. 53703. *President's Newsletter.* bi-m. Free. Bernard Schwab.

Wisconsin State Dept. of Public Instruction, Div. for Library Services, Madison, Wis. 53702. *Wisconsin Li-*

brary Bulletin. 1905. bi-m. $2. William C. Kahl. Illus. Circ: 4,000. *Indexed:* LibLit. Bk. rev.

Wyoming Library Assn., Wyoming State Library and Supreme Court Bldg., Cheyenne, Wyo. 82001. *Wyoming Library Roundup.* 1945. q. Membership (Nonmembers $3). Fay Simonse. Circ: 750. *Indexed:* LibLit. Bk. rev. (See also *Mountain Plains Library Quarterly.*)

State School Library Association Publications

There are few adequate publications from state school library associations (or, for that matter, from state departments of education). The only indexed magazine is *California School Libraries,* and it is by and large the best of the group. Conversely almost all the publications are free, and for this reason certainly worth trying. The following is an unannotated state-by-state list. Most of the bulletins, newsletters, and periodicals concentrate on local affairs, but a number do carry articles, from time to time, of interest to all school librarians. School libraries within a state issuing such a work will want to subscribe, and many school librarians should subscribe to publications in adjoining states.

Alabama Dept. of Education, Montgomery, Ala. 36104. *School Library Bulletin.* 1946. s-a. Free.

Alaska, Arizona: No publication.

Arkansas Dept. of Education, Little Rock, Ark. 72207. *Library Bulletin.* 1967. q. Free. Bk. rev.

California Assn. of School Librarians, Box 1277 Burlingame, Calif. 94010. *California School Libraries.* 1929. q. Membership (Nonmembers $5). Robert R. Carter. Illus., adv. Circ: 1,800. *Indexed:* LibLit.

Colorado. No publication.

Connecticut School Library Assn., Early Jr. High School Library, Wallingford, Conn. 06492. *Connecticut School Library Association Newsletter.* 1963. 5/yr. Free. Robert O'Neill. Circ: 450. Bk. rev.

Delaware, District of Columbia: No publication.

Florida Assn. of School Libraries, 1410 N.W. Second Ave., Miami, Fla. 33132. *Bookcase.* 1958. Free. Gus Adams. Bk. rev.

Georgia, Hawaii, Idaho: No publication.

Illinois Assn. of School Librarians, 1823 C. Valley Rd., Champaign, Ill. 61820. *IASL News for You.* 1948. q. Free. Cora Thomassen.

Indiana School Librarians Assn., N. Central High School Library, 1801 E. 86th St., Indianapolis, Ind. 46240. *Hoosier School Libraries.* 1962. q. Membership (Nonmembers $2). W. Duane Johnson. Illus., adv. Circ: 825. Bk. rev.

Iowa Assn. of School Librarians. Franklin Jr. High School, Des Moines, Iowa 58510. *Library Lines.* 1961. 3/yr. Free. Alice Darling.

Kansas Assn. of School Librarians, 965 Lexington St., Wichita, Kans. 65218. *Kansas Association of School Librarians. Newsletter.* 1952. 3/yr. Free. Aileen Watkins. Adv. Bk. rev.

Kentucky Assn. of School Librarians, 4027 St. Germaine Ct., Louisville, Ky. 40207. *Kentucky Association of School Librarians. Bulletin.* 1965. s-a. $2. Eleanor Koon. Adv.

Louisiana. No publication.

Maine School Library Assn., 78 Hill St., Orono, Maine 04473. *Maine School Library Association Bulletin.* 1939. q. $1. John Burnham, Adv. Bk. rev.

Maryland State Dept. of Education, 301 W. Preston St., Baltimore, Md. 21210. *Library Newsletter.* 1964. q. Free. Nettie Taylor.

Massachusetts. No publication.

Michigan Assn. of School Librarians, 401 S. Fourth St., Ann Arbor, Mich. 48103. *Forward.* 1951. s-a. Membership (Nonmembers $2). Illus. Connie Lamont.

Minnesota, Mississippi, Missouri, Montana, Nebraska, Nevada, New Hampshire: No publication.

New Jersey School of Library Councils Assn., Plainfield High School, Plainfield, N.J. 07060. *Library Council—ER.* 1954. q. Free. John Cordner.

New Mexico. No publication.

New York Board of Education, 110 Livingston St., Brooklyn, N.Y. 11201. *School Library Bulletin.* 1908. m. Free. Helen Sattley.

North Carolina Dept. of Public Instruction, Raleigh, N.C. 27602. *Educational Media Bulletin.* 1950. 3/yr. Free.

North Dakota. No publication.

Ohio Assn. of School Librarians, 5721 Seaman Rd. Oregon, Ohio 43616. *Ohio Association of School Librarians. Bulletin.* 1955. $3. Flora Benton. Adv. Bk. rev.

Oklahoma, Oregon: No publication.

Pennsylvania Dept. of Public Instruction, Harrisburg, Pa. 17126. *Instructional Materials Intercom.* 1964. q. Free.

Rhode Island. No publication.

South Carolina State Dept. of Education, 810 Rutledge Rd., Columbia, S.C. 29201. *S.C. State Dept of Education—Office of General Education Media Services. Newsletter.* 1946. 3/yr. Free.

South Dakota, Tennessee, Texas, Utah, Vermont: No publication.

Virginia Education Assn., School Librarians Dept., Richmond, Va. 23219. *Librachat.* 1952. s-a. Free.

Washington State Assn. of School Librarians, 18605–104th St. N.E., Bothell, Wash. 98011. *Library Leads.* 1951. q. $3. Helen Bumgardner. Adv.

West Virginia, Wisconsin, Wyoming: No publication.

LINGUISTICS AND PHILOLOGY

Basic Periodicals

Ga: *ETC;* Jc: *ETC, Modern Language Journal;* Ac: *Modern Language Journal, ETC, Linguistics, Language, Journal of Linguistics.*

Library and Teaching Aids
Language Learning.

Basic Abstracts and Indexes

Language and Language Behavior Abstracts, Language Teaching Abstracts.

American Journal of Philology. 1880. q. $15. George Luck. Johns Hopkins Press, Baltimore, Md. 21218. Index, adv. Circ: 1,350. Sample. Vol. ends: Oct. Microform: UM.

Indexed: SSHum. *Bk. rev:* 15, 1,000 words, signed. *Aud:* Ac.

"Original contributions in the field of Greco-Roman antiquity, especially in the areas of philology, literature, history, and philosophy." Articles are generally interpretive, with analyses of literary works, historical documents, and inscriptions—all involving close examination of original texts, corruptions, and new discoveries. Of primary interest to the classical scholar. See also *Classical Philology.*

Anthropological Linguistics. See Anthropology Section.

Anthropos. See Anthropology Section.

Archivum Linguisticum; a review of comparative philology and general linguistics. 1949. a. $8. I. F. Campbell and T. F. Mitchell. Scolar Press Ltd., 20 Main St., Menston, Yorkshire, U.K.

Bk. rev: 3–4, 500–1,500 words, signed. *Aud:* Ac.

An annual of some 165 pages which is basic in the field of linguistics, and difficult to understand unless one is blessed with considerable background in the area. Each of the six to eight articles is a monograph; deals with such things as "The German Strong Verb" or "The Design of Rules for DET." The majority of the authors are professors at English universities, and while an occasional foreign language article is accepted,

it is the exception rather than the rule. For large collections only.

Astrado Prouvencalo. See Europe and Middle East/ French Language Section.

The Canadian Journal of Linguistics. Revue Canadienne de Linguistique. 1954. s-a. $6. E. N. Burstynsky. Univ. of Toronto Press, Univ. of Toronto, Toronto 5, Canada. Circ: 750.

Bk. rev: Various number, length. *Aud:* Ac.

About two thirds of each issue is devoted to scholarly essays (two to four each issue) on specific items in the linguistic field. The remaining third is devoted to reviews and an annual report of the Canadian Linguistic Association. Although manuscripts in English or French are welcomed, French text has appeared recently only in the reviews and Association reports. Subject matter is not limited to these two languages, but does seem mainly confined to Indo-European languages, either contemporary or historical. An occasional feature is the updating of a Canadian bibliography of linguistics, first begun in 1955, added to annually for several years, and now supplemented at irregular intervals. The material is for the student and the scholar; the layman is not going to make much of most of it.

Canadian Modern Language Review. 1944. q. $6. G. A. Klinck. Ontario Modern Language Teachers' Assn., 34 Butternut St., Toronto 6, Canada. Illus., adv. Circ: 1,600. Sample. Vol. ends: June.

Bk. rev: 12–15, 500 words, signed. *Aud:* Ac.

A basic journal of information on teaching for elementary and secondary teachers of modern languages. Articles cover business of the Association—usually a minimum of the total—and various aspects of the profession from content analysis to methodology. Particularly valuable for the short notes on books—dictionaries, readers, guides, and literature suitable for classroom use, or for the further education of the teacher. The reviews are grouped by language. Articles appear in English, French, Italian, German, Russian, and Spanish. While primarily of value to Canadians, the reviews often cover material not mentioned in American professional journals.

Classical Philology; devoted to research in the languages, literature, history and life of classical antiquity. 1906. q. $8. Richard T. Bruere. Univ. of Chicago Press, 5750 Ellis Ave., Chicago, Ill. 60637. Illus., index, adv. Circ: 1,400. Sample. Microform: Princeton, UM. Reprint: Johnson.

Indexed: SSHum. *Bk. rev:* 20, lengthy, signed. *Aud:* Ac.

A scholarly approach to classical language for the serious student and professor. Articles cover all aspects of the ancient world, but usually in such a technical fashion as to leave a layman gasping. Supplements the *American Journal of Philology*.

Current Slang; a quarterly glossary of slang expressions presently in use. 1966. q. $1. Stephen H. Dill. Dept. of English, Univ. of South Dakota, Vermillion, S.D. 57069. Circ: 700. Sample.

Aud: Ac.

An annual 16 to 20 page publication which attempts to keep up with developments in the slang employed by various groups in our society, e.g., the armed forces, American poor whites, Midwesterners, laboring men, etc. The term or word is given, followed by a definition. Some of the words and phrases will shock, but the majority are simple slang. A solid way of keeping that current dictionary updated.

ETC; a review of general semantics. 1943. q. $4. Thomas Weiss. Intl. Soc. for General Semantics, Box 2469, San Francisco, Calif. 94126. Illus., index, adv. Circ: 7,000. Sample. Vol. ends: Dec. Microform: UM.

Indexed: PsyAb. *Bk. rev:* 5, 500 words, signed, notes. *Aud:* Ac, Ga. *Jv:* V.

The study of how language and symbols influence behavior is not limited in this journal to technical articles. An effort is made to expand the material to take in almost every form of communication from the television commercial to the slang employed by workingmen. Covering, as it does, art, the social sciences, science, and literature, the scope is wide enough to encourage even the most reluctant reader. Style is semipopular and always interesting. Poetry and line drawings are regularly included. A bibliography on general semantics appears irregularly.

English Language Notes. 1963. q. $4. Charles L. Proudfit. Univ. of Colorado, 1100 Univ. Ave., Boulder, Colo. 80302. Index. Circ: 1,000. Vol. ends: June.

Bk. rev: 10, 1,400 words, signed. *Aud:* Ac.

An expansion of the "notes" sections appearing in most philology journals, *English Language Notes* is a scholarly and specialized journal presenting the results of historical and textual research in English and American languages and literatures. Articles are brief and informative, covering incidents in authors' lives, literary sources and parallels, word usage, and corrupt texts. Contributors generally cite newly discovered documentary evidence—original manuscripts and historical documents. "The Romantic Movement: A Selective and Critical Bibliography" appears annually as a supplement to the September issue. Useful in larger academic libraries, but teachers of literature and English at almost any level will find here much of value.

English Studies; a journal of English language and literature. 1919. bi-m. $13. R. Derolez. Swets en Zeit-linger, Keizergracht 471, Amsterdam, Netherlands. Index, adv. Circ: 2,000.

Indexed: SSHum. *Bk. rev:* 9–12, 900 words, signed. *Aud:* Ac.

A Dutch journal devoted to English language and literature, including American English. It covers all periods and forms of English writing and speech, with a highly readable presentation appealing to undergraduates as well as scholars. Featured are long articles of original criticism, and linguistic analysis of early and modern English. The book reviews are highly critical, and considered among the best in the field. The June and August issues feature two annual bibliographic essays: "Current Literature" in prose, poetry, and drama, and "Current Literature" in criticism and biography.

FI/Forum Italicum. See Europe and Middle East/ Italian Language Section.

Foundations of Language: international journal of language and philosophy. 1965. q. $26.25. D. Reidel Publishing Co., Box 17, Dordrecht, Netherlands. Index.

Indexed: MLA, PhilosI, SciAb. *Bk. rev:* 6–15, signed. *Aud:* Ac.

Each issue of about 150 pages contains six or eight original articles, and one to three "Discussions," which are explications or (sometimes rather heated) refutations of other works. Articles and discussions are well documented, and the language is quite technical. At the back of each issue are short notices including brief, half-page reviews of recent books and journal articles. Suitable for university and special libraries. (S.G.)

International Journal of American Linguistics. 1917. q. $8. C. F. Voegelin. (Linguistic Soc. of Amer.: American Anthropological Assn.) Indiana Univ., Bloomington, Ind. 47401. Index. Circ: 2,375. Vol. ends: Oct.

Indexed: SSHum. *Bk. rev:* 2–4, 2 pages, signed. *Aud:* Ac.

Publishes results of research in North American Indian languages. Articles include scholarly and field research, general and theoretical material, and descriptive linguistics and classification of languages. Intended for a select audience of specialists in North American language, culture, and anthropology.

Journal of English and Germanic Philology. 1897. q. $7.50. Ed. bd. Univ. of Illinois Press, Urbana, Ill. 61801. Index. Circ: 1,800. Sample. Vol. ends: Oct.

Indexed: CurrCont, SSHum. *Bk. rev:* 35–40, 250–1,000 words, signed. *Aud:* Ac.

Includes the study of German, English, and Scandinavian languages and literature. The wide range of articles touches on every conceivable interest. There is an annual "Anglo-German Literary Bibliography" in the July issue. A scholarly journal, and only for large academic collections.

Journal of Linguistics. 1965. s-a. $8. F. R. Palmer. Cambridge Univ. Press, 32 E. 57th St., New York, N.Y. 10022. Adv. Circ: 2,181.

Indexed: MLA. *Bk. rev:* 6, 5–10 pages, signed. *Aud:* Ac.

"Concerned with all branches of linguistics (including phonetics). Preference is given to articles of general theoretical interest." An issue contains between four and eight articles written by scholars in the field and supported by notes and bibliographies. The language varies with the writer, but is usually understandable to the educated layman. (S.G.)

Journal of Psycholinguistic Research. 1971. q. $28. R. W. Rieber. Plenum Publishing Corp., 227 W. 17th St., New York, N.Y. 10011. Illus., index. Sample.

Aud: Ac.

The publisher claims this is "the first scientific periodical to bring together consistently high quality papers from the several disciplines engaged in psycholinguistic research." The 113-page issue examined includes such articles as Peter Fingestern's "Symbolism and Reality," not to mention Eric H. Lennebert's "Of Language Knowledge, Apes, and Brains." These evidence the journal's efforts to publish papers in the theoretical and experimental fields of speech, language, and the communicative process. An interesting notion, but only for the expert or advanced student. Others will be beyond normal depths.

Language. 1925. q. $8. (Nonmembers $16). Wm. Bright. Linguistic Soc. of Amer., Rm. 800, 1717 Mass. Ave., N.W., Washington, D.C. 20036. Illus., index. Circ: 4,500.

Indexed: PsyAb. *Aud:* Ac.

Devoted to the study of grammar of all languages, including some rather obscure ones. Articles are extensively documented, very technical, and obviously written by experts. Mainly for the university or special library. (A monograph series is included in the price for the journal, but special publications of the society are not.) (S.G.)

Language Learning, journal of applied linguistics. 1948. bi-a. $5 (Individuals $3). H. Douglas Brown, 2001 N. Univ. Bldg., Univ. of Michigan, Ann Arbor, Mich. 48104. Index. Circ: 3,000. Sample. Vol. ends: Dec. Microform: UM.

Indexed: EdI. *Bk. rev:* 2–3, 2,000 words, signed. *Aud:* Ac, Hs.

The main focus is on problems of language acquisition with emphasis on theoretical and practical aspects of second-language learning and teaching. Articles are either observational, descriptive, or experimental in nature. Generally eight to ten articles of medium length appear in each issue. Regular features are announcements, brief reviews of bibliographies in the field, and a list of new publications. Of interest to all college and university language instructors, and of some, though limited, value to high school teachers.

Language Sciences. 1968. 5/yr. $3.50. Kathleen Fenton. Research Center for the Language Sciences, Indiana Univ., 516 E. 6th St., Bloomington, Ind. 47401. Index, adv. Circ: 2,200.

Indexed: CIJE. *Bk. rev:* Various number, length. *Aud:* Ac.

Indiana University's interest and influence in the fields of psycholinguistics, sociolinguistics, formal languages, applied linguistics, animal communication, and stylistics is covered in scholarly articles. Many are understandable to the educated layman. Charts and diagrams are included where needed. Issues vary from 44 to 56 pages, and contributors are about evenly divided between IU faculty and outside scholars. Brief notes on conferences and publications are spread throughout. Suitable for academic libraries, special libraries in the field, and for individuals teaching or researching in linguistics and philology. Not much practical help for those teaching languages below college level. (F.B.)

Language and Speech. 1958. q. $27. D. B. Fry. Robert Draper Ltd., Kerbihan House, 85 Udney Pk. Rd., Teddington, Middlesex, England. Index. Circ: 900. Sample. Vol. ends: No. 4.

Indexed: PsyAb. *Aud:* Ac.

A British journal whose four to six articles cover such things as: transmission, perception, and patterns of speech; the relation between linguistics and psychology; social factors; and cognitive activities. Also includes reports on problems of mechanical translation and mechanical speech recognition, language statistics, and abnormalities of language and speech. Four to six articles appear in each issue. While a technical journal, it will have some appeal for more seriously involved teachers of speech and anyone interested in linguistics.

Lingua; international review of general linguistics. 1947. 6/yr. $34. A. Reichling. North-Holland Publishing Co., Box 3489, Amsterdam, Netherlands. Illus., index, adv. Circ: 950. Sample. Vol. ends: 4th issue. Refereed.

Bk. rev: 5–8, 600 words, signed. *Aud:* Ac.

A general linguistics journal, presenting "such studies as are likely to be of interest to any linguist, whatever his own specialization." Tends to be a forum of opinion, presenting new approaches, critical articles, and rebuttals of previously published work. The text is in English, French, and German. Regular features are:

"Publications Received"—a bulletin of new titles and reprints; a special section of review articles, featuring long and critical reviews of important new books; and state of the art reports.

Linguistics; an international review. 1963. m. $30. Mouton & Co., Herderstraat 5, The Hague, Netherlands. Illus., index, adv. Circ: 1,500.

Bk. rev: 6, 1,000 words, signed. *Aud:* Ac.

Offers scholarly studies in descriptive, historical, structural, and applied linguistics, as well as theoretical articles of a more general interest. Articles are rather long and monographic, often with charts. The text is in English, French, and German. The occasional supplement, "Linguistic Abstracts," contains short, informative abstracts of books, articles, and dissertations.

Modern Language Journal. 1916. m. (Oct.–May). $5. Charles King. George Banta Co., Curtis Reed Plaza, Menasha, Wis. 54952. Illus., index, adv. Circ: 10,000. Microform: UM.

Indexed: EdI. *Bk. rev:* 25, 750 words, signed. *Aud:* Ac, Hs, Ejh. *Jv:* V.

Published by the National Federation of Modern Language Teachers Associations, and is "devoted primarily to methods, pedagogical research, and to topics of professional interest to all language teachers" from the elementary to graduate levels. Articles are usually case studies in teaching materials, methods, and effects; the most recent issues focus on studies of the audio-lingual method. Linguistic analysis, critical discussions, theory, and occasional articles of literary interest also appear. Among the regular features are review essays, abstracts of articles from related periodicals, professional news, academic reports, "Books Received," an annual list of doctoral degrees awarded, and a directory of state, county, and city foreign language supervisors. A basic journal for any school or academic library.

Modern Language Quarterly. 1940. q. $6. William Matchett. Univ. of Washington, Parrington Hall, Seattle, Wash. 98195. Index, adv. Circ: 1,850. Vol. ends: Dec. Reprint: Johnson.

Indexed: SSHum. *Bk. rev:* 8, 2,000 words, signed. *Aud:* Ac.

Presents seven to ten critical studies of literary works and forms in the American, English, Germanic, and Romance languages. Contributors are primarily American, Canadian, and British. Articles focus on the use of language and form in literary works. Well written and nontechnical, the journal has an attractive format. Among the regular features are a comparative review of several recent books on a single topic and a listing of new books.

Modern Language Review. 1905. q. $20. C. P. Brand. Modern Humanities Research Assn., King's College, Strand, London WC2R 2LS, England. Adv. Circ: 2,500. Vol. ends: Oct. Reprint: Dawson.

Indexed: BritHum, SSHum. *Bk. rev:* 60, 450 words, signed. *Aud:* Ac. *Jv:* V.

Publishes "original articles . . . on language and literature, embodying the results of research and criticism" for the advanced researcher in the English, Germanic, Romance, and Slavonic languages. A majority of the contributions deal with historical, textual, linguistic, and critical approaches to literature. Occasional linguistic studies appear. Approximately one quarter to one half of the journal is devoted to critical book reviews.

Modern Philology. 1903. q. $8. Arthur Friedman. Univ. of Chicago Press, 5801 Ellis Ave., Chicago, Ill. 60637. Index; adv. Circ: 1,500. Sample. Vol. ends: Oct. Microform: Canner, Princeton, UM. Reprint: Johnson.

Indexed: SSHum. *Bk. rev:* 15–20, 1,200 words, signed. *Aud:* Ac.

The journal's main emphasis is on research into literary sources, literary indebtedness, comparative studies, historical criticism, and textual studies. All articles are well documented. English literature receives the most attention, with studies of Romance and Germanic works appearing occasionally. American and Canadian scholars contribute the three to five monographic articles which appear in each issue. A regular feature is a "Notes and Documents" section of short reports on the dating of works, attribution, newly discovered manuscripts, and clarifications of facts in an author's life.

Philological Quarterly. 1922. q. $7.50. Curt A. Zimansky. Dept. of Publications, Univ. of Iowa, Iowa City, Iowa 52240. Circ: 2,400. Vol. ends: Oct. Microform: UM.

Indexed: SSHum. *Bk. rev:* 2, lengthy, signed. *Aud:* Ac.

A journal devoted to scholarly investigation of the classical modern languages and literatures. Studies of English literature, especially the neoclassic period, predominate. The journal's primary concern is with investigation into textual and historical problems in the interpretation of literary works. A department for brief notes on sources, newly discovered texts, dating and authenticity of texts is included. An important bibliography, "The Eighteenth Century," appears annually in the July issue. It includes reviews of almost all books on English neoclassicism (usually 30 or more, maximum length 1,000 words). The writing is not as technical as that in most philology journals, and the content is interesting to all students of literature.

Romance Notes. 1972. q. $8. George B. Daniel. Dept. of Romance Languages, Univ. of North Carolina,

Chapel Hill, N.C. 27514. Index. Circ: 700. Sample. Vol. ends: Spring.

Aud: Ac.

A scholarly journal devoted to signed, short essays concerned with the various Romance languages and literatures. Each issue contains 30 to 40 "Notes," covering the field in breadth as much as in depth. The contributors are U.S. scholars, with a few Canadian and an occasional continental scholar also contributing. The text is in English, French, Italian, and Spanish.

Romance Philology. 1947. q. $10. Yakov Malkiel. Univ. of California Press, Berkeley, Calif. 94720. Adv. Circ: 1,200. Microform: UM. Reprint: AMS.

Indexed: SSHum. *Bk. rev:* 12–20, 800 words, signed. *Aud:* Sa, Ac.

Concerned with all phases of early Romance literature and Romance linguistics. Special interest is with the formative period of the Romance languages, from late antiquity to the early Renaissance. Contributions are written in French, Spanish, Portuguese, Italian, and German. Linguistic studies are both descriptive and theoretical, with structural and lexicological studies predominating. Literary research includes textual, interpretive, and bibliographic studies, with emphasis always on the analysis of original texts and source material.

Scandinavian Studies. 1911. q. $15. Geo. C. Schoolfield. Allen Press, Lawrence, Kans. 66044. Index, adv. Circ: 1,000.

Indexed: MLA, SSHum. *Bk. rev:* extensive, 3 pages, signed. *Aud:* Ac.

Publishes the results of scholarly research on "philology and linguistic problems of the Scandinavian languages" and on the literature and cultural history of Scandinavia. There are four to eight articles, and "News and Notes" records information on conferences, educational programs, grants, and research in progress. The journal is particularly useful as a source of bibliographic information for the field because of book reviews and a section entitled "News of Periodical Literature." There is an "Annual American-Scandinavian Bibliography" in the May or August issue. (S.G.)

Studies in Philology. 1906. 5/yr. $10. Ernest William Talbert. Univ. of North Carolina Press, Box 510, Chapel Hill, N.C. 27514. Illus., index, adv. Circ: 1,900. Sample. Vol. ends: Dec. Microform: UM.

Indexed: SSHum. *Aud:* Ac.

Presents textual and historical research in the classical and modern languages and literatures. It is intended for the scholar and prepared under the auspices of the graduate faculty of the language and literature departments of the University of North Carolina. All forms and periods of literature are covered. Articles are long, averaging 5,000 words, and include: analysis of poetic language—imagery, structure, etymology; examination of newly discovered texts and original manuscripts; historical studies. The December issue contains a texts and studies number.

Word. 1945. 3/yr. $10 (Students $7.50). International Linguistics Assn. Subs. to: James Macris, Dept. of English, Clark Univ., Worcester, Mass. 01619. Illus., index.

Bk. rev: 10, 4,000 words, signed. *Aud:* Sa, Ac.

Articles are divided equally among research, theory and history, and original studies. Fields of coverage include descriptive linguistics, all phases of structural analysis, and mentalistic or formal linguistics, which emphasizes the relationship between language and psychology.

LITERARY REVIEWS

See also Counterculture, Little Magazines, and News and Opinion Magazines Sections.

Basic Periodicals

Hs: *Antioch Review;* Ga: *Antioch Review, Voyages, Partisan Review;* Jc: *Antioch Review, Tri-Quarterly, Voyages, Partisan Review;* Ac: *Antioch Review, Tri-Quarterly, Voyages, Massachusetts Review, Modern Occasions, Partisan Review.*

Basic Abstracts and Indexes

Abstracts of English Studies, American Literature Abstracts, Index to Commonwealth Little Magazines, Index to Little Magazines, MLA International Bibliography.

Cessations

Kenyon Review, Midway, New Mexico Quarterly.

Agenda. 1959. $5. William Cookson, 5 Cranbourne Court, Albert Bridge Rd., London SW 11, England. Circ: 2,000.

Indexed: ICLM. *Bk. rev:* 6–8, 300–1,000 words, signed. *Aud:* Ga, Ac.

An established better magazine of new poetry and literary criticism. The poetry tends to the traditional, but is the best of the school, both British and American. Literary criticism is strong: textbook examples examining contemporary poetry in an intelligent, interesting, and interested way. Directed towards the intelligent adult.

Antaeus. 1970. q. $8. Daniel Helpern. Goea Society. Subs. to: D. Be Boer, 188 High St., Nutley, N.J. 07110

Aud: Ga, Ac.

Published in Tangier, Morocco, this outstanding, 140-page literary magazine's consulting editor is Paul Bowles. Among the contributors are just about every famous writer in the business from Lawrence Durrell and Tennessee Williams to W. H. Auden and Stephen Spender. In fact, the list of contributing poets, playwrights, prose writers, and essayists is a who's who of modern international writing. The issue examined includes fiction from Joyce Carol Oates, Heirich Boll, and William Burroughs and an interview with Edouard Roditi, "the oldest American expatriate in Paris." The poetry is as outstanding as the prose, and the whole such an unusual assemblage of first rate talent to dictate a place in any library where literature is important. Highly recommended for all large, and not a few medium sized libraries.

Antioch Review. 1941. q. $6. Lawrence Grauman. The Review, Box 148, Yellow Springs, Ohio, 45387. Illus., index, adv. Circ: 5,000. Vol. ends: No. 4. Microform: UM. Reprint: AMS.

Indexed: AbEnSt, HistAb, PAIS, SocAb, SSHum. *Bk. rev:* 18–20, 100–200 words, signed. *Aud:* Ac, Ga, Hs. *Jv:* V.

The most readable of the numerous reviews. In many ways, too, it is the most entertaining and informative. Under a new editor and a new policy the magazine has become increasingly more general in its outlook, purposefully geared for the intelligent layman, not the cloistered professor. An average 150-page issue features a series of articles on a specific theme, e.g., "The rediscovery of cultural pluralism," "Theatre as politics." But there are diverse articles on social, political, and literary themes; plus poetry, plus short reviews, plus some fiction, plus some first rate comments by James Aronson on the passing scene. In 1970 the magazine "absorbed" *Monocle,* a sometime publication of wit and humor. As a result, each issue of the *Review* tends to include a special *Monocle* feature, e.g., Ed Koren's "It can't happen here"—a series of satirical drawings on the American way. There is little or no precious type of writing, literary criticism, or in-fighting. It is closer to the old *Harper's* than to, say, the *Partisan Review.* A first-rate review which should have a wide, appreciative audience.

California Quarterly; a journal of literature, reviews & translations. 1971. q. $4. Alan Wald. Dept. of English, Sproul Hall 310, Univ. of California, Davis, Calif. 95616. Illus.

Aud: Ac.

The same stuff of the typical little magazine, although here a quarterly, university based, and boasting an editorial board of scholars. The issue examined, 85 neat pages, included: a Karl Shapiro translation of Catullus; a translation of seven Choco Indian stories (by far the best thing in the issue); some good poetry (Bernice Ames, Larry Rubin); and fair to so-so short stories. A few "names," a few students. It all makes for a good balance, although a somewhat indifferent magazine. Which is not precisely a criticism, but it makes one wonder if another magazine of this type is needed. A good translation medium, yes, another general literary magazine, no.

Cambridge Quarterly. 1965. q. $5. Ed. bd. New Hayes, Huntingdon Rd., Cambridge, England. Circ: 2,000.

Indexed: BritHum. *Bk. rev:* 4, long features, signed. *Aud:* Ac.

A somewhat idiosyncratic English literary magazine, published, distributed, and often written by the editorial board. The articles range over literature, art, music, movies, and sometimes get into politics, values, and so forth. In addition to two to four articles and the book reviews, there is usually some interesting and articulate correspondence.

Cambridge Review; a journal of university life and thought. 1879. 6/yr. $5. I. R. Wright. Barrie and Jenkins Ltd., 2 Clements Inn, London WC2A 2EP, England. Index. Circ: 1,200.

Indexed: IBZ.

A university magazine which is important because it sometimes is the first to print material which later appears in book form, e.g., Noam Chomsky's annual set of Cambridge lectures in honor of Bertrand Russell (1971), published as *The Russell Lectures* (1972) by Pantheon. There are the usual notes and articles of primary interest to students and faculty of Cambridge. It is considerably narrower in scope (and size) than the *Cambridge Quarterly.* If a choice is to be made, the *Quarterly* would come first.

The Carleton Miscellany. 1960. bi-a. $3. Wayne Carver. Carleton College, Northfield, Minn. 55057. Index. Circ: 1,000. Vol. ends: 2nd issue. Microform: UM.

Indexed: LMags. *Bk. rev:* 6, 1,500 words, signed. *Aud:* Ac.

Not a literary criticism magazine, but rather a journal given to essays which deal with literature in cultural, social, and historical contexts. In fact, the editor reports: "We use very few articles that I would call literary criticism. We don't want a merely close reading of literary texts." The editor attempts to treat the material as informally as possible, and the magazine is strong on satire. Given this direction, it is among the college-based literary magazines which many students —and teachers—enjoy reading. A good bet for the general collection.

Carolina Quarterly. 1949. 3/yr. $3. Junius Grimes. Univ. of North Carolina, Box 1117, Chapel Hill, N.C. 27514. Illus., adv. Circ: 1,800. Sample. Vol. ends: Fall.

Indexed: LMags. *Bk. rev:* 2, 2 pages, signed. *Aud:* Ac.

"A national literary review, which just happens to be based in Chapel Hill," the editor explains. He adds: "We try to encourage younger and/or experimental writers, feeling that established people don't need the outlet nearly as badly as the younger people." All of this is true. In fact, four stories which earlier appeared in the quarterly have been published as books, and several have found their way into national anthologies. And while the level of writing is uneven, nothing is really poor. There is a nice balance between poetry and fiction, book reviews and some critical essays. A good bet for any library with an interest in new writers.

The Chicago Review. 1946. q. $3.50. Judith S. Ruskamp. Univ. of Chicago, Faculty Exchange Box C., Chicago, Ill. 60637. Illus., index, adv. Circ: 3,000. Sample. Vol. ends: 4th issue.

Indexed: LMags, SSHum. *Bk. rev:* Number varies, 2–15 pages, signed. *Aud:* Ac, Ga.

A high quality literary review which is equally divided between fiction, poetry, notes on the arts, and literary criticism. Stories are longer than in many other little magazines and show better development. Poetry is usually traditional and workmanlike. Critical articles, which are sound without pendantry and not limited to the work of contemporary writers, make the magazine of value to the student of literature as well as to the intelligent layman.

Colorado Quarterly. 1952. q. $4. Paul J. Carter. Hellems 134, Univ. of Colorado, Boulder, Colo. 80302. Illus., index. Circ: 850. Sample.

Indexed: LMags. *Aud:* Ac, Ga.

A general approach to the current scene with articles, short prose pieces and poetry by teachers and graduate students featured. The Autumn 1971 issue, for example, began with Edwin Newman's "Television news and effect on public affairs," and included essays on student radicals, the new "kulchur," and western scholarship. Also, a short story, numerous poems, and a translation of Pushkin's three folk tales. It is pretty much the mixture associated with many university-based quarterlies, some of it good, some of it not so good, and most of it provocative for the casual reader. A modest enough price for some 150 pages of current thought.

Colorado State Review. See *Trans Pacific.*

Confrontation; a literary journal of Long Island University. 1968. s-a. $1. Martin Tucker. Long Island Univ., English Dept., Brooklyn, N.Y. 11201.

Bk. rev: 1–2, essays, signed. *Aud:* Ac.

Drawing from faculty and students of the university, as well as younger critics and poets in the New York

area, the editor puts together an 80-page literary magazine which is worth reading. Some of the fiction is weak, and not all of the poetry comes off, but the criticism seems first rate. For example, a piece by a Brazilian editor, "Will the Women's Lib Move South?" is well worth the modest price for a single issue. Hardly an essential item, but one of the better university publications.

The Critical Quarterly. 1959. q. $4. C. B. Cox and A. E. Dyson. Oxford Univ. Press, Press Rd., London, NW 10, England. Index, adv. Circ: 5,000.

Indexed: BritHum. *Bk. rev:* 3–4, 1–3 pages, signed. *Aud:* Ac.

An English literary quarterly which features new poetry and criticism of both American and British authors. Poets have included Auden, Hecht, Stead, and Wain. There is an annual poetry supplement which highlights modern contributors. The society also issues *The Critical Survey,* which is included in the subscriptions. Issued twice a year, the latter is a review of new novels and poetry, and is particularly useful to teachers, as it includes material on the teaching of literature at all grade levels.

Dalhousie Review. 1921. q. $4. A. R. Bevan. Dalhousie Univ. Press Ltd., Halifax, Nova Scotia, Canada. Index, adv. Circ: 1,100. Vol. ends: Winter.

Indexed: CanI, PAIS. *Bk. rev:* 12, 700 words, signed. *Aud:* Ac.

One of Canada's leading reviews, this is a general magazine which touches on all aspects of Canadian social, cultural, and political life. Contributors tend to be scholars, but write in a fashion which is pleasing, sometimes humorous, and usually perceptive. Each quarterly issue is a nice balance of material on current concerns, criticism and history, some poetry and fiction. The book reviews are excellent.

The DeKalb Literary Arts Journal; the magazine of literature and the arts of DeKalb college. 1966. q. $5. Mel McKee. DeKalb College, 555 Indian Creek Dr., Clarkston, Ga. 30021.

Aud: Ga, Ac.

One of the better regional magazines. Features special issues, such as American Poets, Atlanta Poets, the Creative Woman. Academic, featuring competence rather than brilliance. Each issue will have one or two well-known names, but the emphasis is on Georgia and the South. Thoroughly professional and respectable. (D.D.)

Delta. 1953. 3/yr. $3.00. 12 Hardwick St., Cambridge, CB3, 9JA, England. Circ: 1,000.

Indexed: AbEnSt, BritHum. *Bk. rev:* 2–5, lengthy, signed. *Aud:* Ac.

Publishes original articles, fiction, poetry, and a considerable amount of literary criticism. Considered to be one of the better small circulation English literary reviews, the primary emphasis is on new or little-published novelists. Not to be confused with the Dutch-based *Delta*.

Delta; a review of arts, life and thought in the Netherlands. 1958. q. $5.50. Hans van Marle. Delta Intl. Publn. Foundation, J. J. Viottastraat 41, Amsterdam 1007, The Netherlands. Illus., index. Circ: 6,000. Sample. Vol. ends: Winter.

Indexed: PAIS. *Bk. rev:* 2–3, length varies. *Aud:* Ac, Ga, Hs.

One of the best known literary reviews in Europe. (Not to be confused with the English *Delta*.) As the subtitle suggests, the editorial policy is broad. Articles are written primarily by Europeans. About one half of the issue is given over to the Netherlands, the remainder to European concerns. The tone is objective, even a bit conservative. As it is in English, it is recommended for any library where some effort is given to broaden the horizons of readers.

Epoch. 1947. 3/yr. $3. Baxter Hathaway, Walter Slatoff. Cornell Univ., 251 Goldwin Smith Hall, Ithaca, N.Y. 14850. Illus., index, adv. Circ: 1,100. Sample. Vol. ends: Spring.

Indexed: LMags. *Aud:* Ac, Ga, Hs.

A superior university literary magazine which in some 100 pages devotes itself to publication of new fiction and verse. The entries are divided about equally between poetry and prose. And while newness is evident, many of the authors are new only to the magazine, having published elsewhere with considerable success, e.g., Alvin Greenberg, Donald Gropman, Danny Rendleman, to name a few. The level of selection is high, so high in fact, that unlike many experimental vehicles, the degree of excellence is surprising. The short stories are quite up to anything found in better known, higher circulation magazines. Consequently, it can be enjoyed by just about anyone who has some taste in fiction and poetry. A good choice for any public or academic library—and it can be suggested for many high schools as well.

Event. 1971. 3/yr. $3.50. David Evanier. Bouglad College, 426 Columbia St., New Westminister, B.C., Canada.

Aud: Ac, Ga.

Featuring six to seven short stories, or excerpts from novels, this college-based literary magazine is unusual in that the emphasis is primarily on fiction, and while two or three contributors are students, about one half are tried and published authors, e.g., Cynthia Ozick, Robert Grant, and poet Harvey Shapiro. The level of professionalism is as high as the quality of the 88-page format. Should be of interest to the short story-oriented

layman, hence, highly recommended for general reading collections.

Evergreen Review. 1957. m. $9. Barney Rosset. Evergreen Review, Inc., 80 Univ. Place, New York, N.Y. 10003. Illus., index, adv. Circ: 125,000. Microform: UM.

Indexed: LMags. *Aud:* Ga.

(Note: In mid 1972 there were reports this magazine would cease publishing, or go to a different publishing schedule. Librarians should check with the publishers before subscribing.)

Over the years this has become familiar to librarians as the cause of many censorship cases. It seems to attract the censorious minds like no other magazine. The interesting thing is that it is considerably less deserving of a censor's pained expression than, say, *Playboy* (which the censor reads at home) or the journals his wife reads, e.g., *Cosmpolitan*, not to mention *Ladies' Home Journal*. At one time the Grove Press special could boast some of the best writing in America. No more. It recently has suffered a lack of direction and purpose. It is no longer the leading "big little" magazine which is both a literary review and a purveyor of the "Underground" to Everyman. There are still some interesting writers, e.g., Nat Hentoff, and some passable photo features, but on the whole it is pretty slim going. It is not really worth the fight, or for that matter, worth the annual subscription price. Librarians (not to mention censors) looking for a suitable substitute might consider *The Realist*, any one of the underground newspapers, a good number of the little magazines, etc. The trouble, of course, is that none of them has the reputation or the circulation of the *Evergreen Review*.

The Falcon. 1970. bi-a. $2. Mansfield State College, Mansfield, Pa. 16933. Illus. Circ: 1,500. Sample.

Aud: Ac.

Reaching for poets and prose writers from college campuses throughout the United States—and a few from outside the ivory tower—the editors come up with a 95-page neatly printed magazine. The first issue is about evenly balanced between fiction and poetry, but a short interview with Robert Boles on Jack Kerouac's last years takes the spotlight. The short stories, particularly an entry by William Joyce, are good to excellent; the poetry a bit weaker. All in all a solid enough effort which deserves support from most college libraries.

The Fiddlehead. 1949. q. $4.50 (Canada: $3.75). Robert Gibbs, Dept. of English, Univ. of New Brunswick, Fredericton, N.B., Canada. Illus., adv. Circ: 600.

Indexed: CanI. *Bk. rev:* 10–15, 750 words, signed. *Aud:* Ac, Ga.

Primarily concerned with publishing the poetry and

prose of promising Canadian writers, this average college-supported magazine has welcomed contributions from such well known writers as Joyce Carol Oates, Hugh Hood, Margaret Atwood, John Metcalf, Alden Nowlan, and Raymond Souser. As a staff member points out, most of these familiar names were "published in our magazine years before their reputations had become nationally and internationally established." The record is impressive, and it is one of a handful of Canadian literary magazines that has both a long history and a distinguished record. American libraries will find it useful for perceptive book reviews of titles rarely noted elsewhere.

Four Quarters. 1951. q. $2. John F. Keenan. La Salle College, Philadelphia, Pa. 19141.

Indexed: LMag. *Aud:* Ac, Ga.

As ambitious in neither size nor format as many other university and college sponsored literary magazines, this makes up for it by an unusually wide author net. Contributors are from many places, not only La-Salle. They may or may not be Catholics; famous (Thomas Kinsella, Richard Lattimore, Philip O'Connor) or just beginners. The prose and poetry are of an exceptionally high quality. No wonder it has gone through 20 years. A good bet for college and some high school libraries.

The Georgia Review; a southern journal of literature, history, and ideas. 1947. q. $3. James Colvert. Univ. of Georgia Press, Athens, Ga. 30601. Index, adv. Circ: 1,800.

Indexed: AbEnSt, HistAb. *Bk. rev:* Various number, length. *Aud:* Ac.

A general review with emphasis on southern or Georgian interests. A typical issue includes four to five articles; a definition of cultural values in antebellum Virginia, an interview with Walker Percy, a portrait of the redneck, and a defense of Flannery O'Connor. Some poetry, fiction and book reviews are included. The style of writing is fair to good, the subject matter of enough interest to be of value to larger academic and public libraries—particularly those in the South.

Green River Review. 1968. bi-a. $2.50. Raymond Tyner and Emil Ahnell. Green River Press, Box 594, Owensboro, Ky. 42301. Illus., index. Circ: 500.

Bk. rev: 3–5, 350 words, signed. *Aud:* Ac.

A regional literary/little magazine which features Kentucky and southern poets and short story writers, e.g., Wendell Berry and Jesse Stuart. There is some literary criticism. The division is about even between student and professional writers, and the whole is tastefully produced and edited. Should be in all Kentucky, and larger university, libraries.

The Hudson Review. 1948. q. $6. Frederick Morgan. The Hudson Review, Inc., 65 E. 55th St., New York,

N.Y. 10022. Illus., index, adv. Circ: 3,500. Sample. Vol. ends: Winter. Microform: UM. Reprint: AMS.

Indexed: SSHum. *Bk. rev:* 50, length varies, signed. *Aud:* Ga, Ac. *Jv:* V.

An outstanding literary periodical with perceptive coverage of cultural life in the United States and abroad. Well-known writers and scholars contribute articles on criticism, aesthetics, and literary topics. It has regular coverage of the British scene, and stimulating articles on architecture, art, ballet, film, music, and theater. Original fiction and poetry are of the highest quality. Book reviews are excellent, substantial, and critical. An unusually large number of poetry books are reviewed regularly in Poetry Chronicle. There are frequent illustrations. Ranks favorably among the top dozen relatively long standing literary magazines in this country, and should be a serious consideration for libraries.

Intro. 1968. a. $2.95. Walton Beacham and R. V. Cassill. Univ. Press of Virginia, Charlottesville, Va. 22903.

Aud: Ga, Ac, Hs.

An annual dedicated to the publishing of poetry and short stories by young writers—most of whom are enrolled in a university or college. The first three numbers were put out by Bantam Books, but with number four, the honor shifted to the University Press of Virginia. *Intro 4* (issued in mid 1972) consists of 207 pages, divided by university or college and by short story or poem. Over 100 different writers are represented in the collection supervised by the Associated Writing Programs, an organization that links various creative writing classes in the country. In the middle of what the editors call " a poetry boom," the collection is a welcome filter—which is to say the choices are good, the collection representative of some of the best young writers in America. The annual should be found in all universities and colleges, and in larger public and high school libraries.

The Journals of Pierre Menard. 1968. bi-a. $6. Peter Hoy and Anthony Rudolf, 97 Holywell St., Oxford, England. Illus. Circ: 250.

Aud: Ac.

Tellingly named after the hero of Borges' first story, who "dedicated his conscience and nightly studies to the repetition of a pre-existing book in a foreign tongue," this duplicated magazine, at present produced in limited editions of 250, is devoted entirely to translation and the theory of translation. It is venturesome, imaginative, resourcefully and intelligently edited. The now-rare first issue is devoted to Michael Hamburger's translations of Goethe and Hölderlin, not all of which were done especially for this magazine. Subscribers to four or more issues get (free) *The Notebooks of Pierre Menard*, a miscellany of excellent pieces too short to include in *The Journals*. Uncommitted to any "school" of translation, this magazine aims to be a disinterested medium for dialogue and exploration into the theory and practice of viable translation. Clearly a serious and deeply committed magazine, *The Journals of Pierre Menard* is indispensable for all academic libraries.

Kansas Quarterly. 1958. q. $7.50. Harold W. Schneider. The Univ. Press of Kansas, 366 Watson Library, Lawson, Kans. 66044.

Aud: Ga, Ac.

A literary review which pays particular attention to the talents of regional writers in mid-America. Emphasis is on creative poetry and prose. A small part of each number is given to critical essays. The whole is nicely printed and well edited. While not an essential magazine for anyone this side of the Kansas borders, it should be welcomed by larger academic libraries seeking publications representative of less well-known literary directions in America.

Landfall; a New Zealand quarterly. 1947. q. NZ $4. Robin Dudding, Caxton Press, 119 Victoria St., Christchurch, New Zealand. Illus., index, adv. Circ: 1,850.

Indexed: BritHum. *Bk. rev:* Various number, length. *Aud:* Ac, Ga.

A quarterly devoted to New Zealand literature. Contains articles, book reviews, poetry, and illustrations by New Zealand artists. For 25 years *Landfall* has provided a vehicle for work by new and established New Zealand writers and artists. (N.H.)

Literary Sketches. 1960. m. $1.50. Mary Lewis Chapman, P.O. Box 711, Williamsburg, Va. 23185. Illus., adv. Circ: 1,000. Sample. Vol. ends: Dec.

Bk. rev: 1–3, short, signed. *Aud:* Ac, Ga.

This "magazine of interviews, reviews, and memorabilia" in very few pages usually includes a three or four page article on some writer or historical literary personage, letters to the editor, a column of informational tidbits and comments, and a few advertisements not likely to be seen elsewhere. A bargain for any library, worthwhile in content, but slight in size. Produced as a hobby by Mrs. Chapman, who found that the literary "gossip" type of material in which she was so interested did not often reach print, so she began publishing a vehicle herself.

The Malahat Review. 1967. q. $5. John Peter and Robin Skelton. Univ. of Victoria, Victoria, B.C., Canada. Illus. Circ: 1,000. Sample. Vol. ends: Oct.

Bk. rev: 12, 500 words, signed. *Aud:* Ac, Ga.

This thick Canadian journal correctly styles itself as "international": its list of contributors includes writers from Canada, the United Kingdom, continental Europe, America, Latin America, Asia, the Middle East, and Australia. Included are short fiction, drama, literary criticism, line drawings, photos, and photos of art. Poetry worksheets, drama, and original letters and

journals are announced as a special interest of the review. For the student and general reader, it should also be considered a basic choice for larger Canadian libraries.

Massachusetts Review. 1959. q. $7. Jules Chametzky and John H. Hicks. Massachusetts Review, Inc., Univ. of Massachusetts, Amherst, Mass. 01002. Illus., index, adv. Circ: 2,000. Vol. ends: Fall.

Indexed: AbEnSt, LMags, SSHum. *Bk. rev:* 6, 2,500 words, signed. *Aud:* Ac, Ga. *Jv:* V.

This looks literally as good as its contents. (The illustrations are superb.) Not only is it one of the best-printed reviews available, it features fine articles on social issues, fiction, poetry, literature criticism; i.e., the mixture familiar enough to anyone who bothers to read the many reviews. It ranks with the four or five best, particularly in terms of its contributors who are some of the outstanding names in the arts. The book reviews, by the way, will alert a librarian to titles sometimes overlooked in the popular media—titles which run the full range of the magazine's interests.

Meanjin Quarterly; a magazine of literature, art and discussion. 1940. q. $5. Clement B. Christesen. Univ. of Melbourne, Parkville, Victoria 3052, Australia. Index.

Indexed: AusPAIS. *Bk. rev:* Various number, length. *Aud:* Ac.

A review of arts and letters in Australia. Includes poetry, political and literary articles, and excerpts from novels. Begun in 1940 as a vehicle for Queensland poets, it has now become Australia's leading literary journal. (N.H.)

The Mediterranean Review. 1970. q. $5. Robert DeMaria. The Review, Orient, N. Y. 11957. Illus., adv. Circ: 5,000. Sample.

Aud: Ac.

In some 80 pages, the Mallorca-based editors focus on "new literature not only from the Mediterranean area, but also from the rest of the world." In a typical issue, criticism of Robert Graves and Nikos Kazantzakis, the latter by Colin Wilson, is balanced by poetry from Graves, Galway Kinnell (who translates Yvan Goll), Neruda, and a stellar group of younger poets. The fiction pieces are a bit less exciting, although good enough. A superior format. The magazine will have particular interest for lovers of the Mallorca scene, but is of value to anyone involved with literature. Much above average, and recommended for just about all college and university libraries.

Michigan Quarterly Review. 1960. $6. Radcliff Squires, 3032 Rackham Bldg., Univ. of Michigan, Admin. Bldg., Ann Arbor, Mich. 48104. Illus., index, adv. Circ: 2,000. Sample. Vol. ends: Fall. Refereed.

Indexed: AbEnSt, CurrCont, MLA, PAIS. *Bk. rev:* 10–12, 1 page, signed. *Aud:* Ac, Ga. *Jv:* V.

Features an excellent format and articles of both topical and literary interest. The writing is skillful, well within the grasp of the average educated layman who seeks an overview of current thought in the humanities and social sciences. Some fiction is included, and a good deal of excellent poetry. In addition to the regular book reviews, there is generally one longer essay-type article on a current work. Among the top three or four in its class, and a first choice for medium to large-sized libraries.

Midwest Quarterly; a journal of contemporary thought. 1959. q. $2.50. Rebecca Patterson. Kansas State College, Pittsburg, Kans. 66762. Index. Circ: 1,000. Sample. Vol. ends: Oct. Microform: UM.

Indexed: PAIS, SSHum. *Bk. rev:* 2, 2–3 pages, signed. *Aud:* Ac.

A college based literary-social-political review which features some 10 to 12 articles per issue, along with poetry and book reviews. The material is written by teachers and students, is purposefully in a semipopular style, and will have some appeal for the better educated layman. It usually includes one or two really outstanding pieces per issue. A magazine libraries in the immediate area will want to take; should also be found in larger collections.

The Minnesota Review. 1960. bi-a. $5. C.W. Truesdale. New Rivers Press, Box 578, Cathedral Station, New York, N.Y. 10025. Illus. Circ: 1,000. Sample.

Indexed: LMags. *Bk. rev:* 2–4, 2–4 pages, signed. *Aud:* Ac.

More of a little magazine than the traditional college-based literary review, this puts considerable emphasis on modern poetry. About 50 pages out of every 130-page issue is given to original poetry and translations. The essays are usually on literary-cultural matters, and there are two or three stories. The book reviews are of particular interest because they tend to concentrate on publications of the little, or lesser-known, presses. There are special supplements from time to time. A good, considerably different type of review for academic libraries.

Modern Occasions. 1970. q. $5. Philip Rahv, 5A Bigelow St., Cambridge, Mass. 02139. Index, adv.

Bk. rev: 6–10 essays, signed. *Aud:* Ac, Ga.

Resembles the approach of the *Partisan Review,* i.e., strong leanings towards literature, liberal social criticism, and back biting. The similarity (both in content and format) is no accident—the editor at one time headed *Partisan Review.* The so called "spirited debate with the current literary and political scene" consists of editorials by Rahv, two or three stories or excerpts from novels, interviews, five or six articles,

poems, and excellent book reviews. Contributors represent the "eastern literary establishment," i.e., Rahv, Roth, Styron, X. J. Coleman, Bellow, Mary McCarthy, etc. A fascinating magazine which will be read, quoted, and fought over in most intellectual circles. It may, though, have little or no meaning for the average reader whose level of tolerance in this area usually does not reach beyond the *Atlantic.* A must for all academic and larger public library collections.

Monocle. See *Antioch Review.*

Mundus Artium; a journal of international literature and arts. 1957. 3/yr. $4. Rainer Schulte. Dept. of English, Ohio Univ., Athens, Ohio 45701. Illus., adv. Circ: 2,000. Sample.

Bk. rev: 5–7, 250–500 words, signed. *Aud:* Ac, Ga.

An excellent magazine for both the scholar and the layman. In addition to criticism, it publishes stories, poems, and essays (all in translation) of major world writers. One 124-page issue, devoted to Latin American fiction, begins with two shorts by Borges, and includes Carlos Fuentes, Hernandez, and 12 other writers who might otherwise not come to the attention of the average reader. Not all numbers, to be sure, are quite that interesting, but on balance it is much above the topical esoteric literary journal.

New American Review. 1967. 3/yr. $6.50 for 4 nos. Theodore Solotaroff. Simon & Schuster, 630 Fifth Ave., New York, N.Y. 10020.

Aud: Ga, Ac.

A book/magazine, and one of the few outlets for major new writing with wide national distribution. The paperback approach is not new, but this particular series seems to have been one of the more successful, certainly one of the longer lived. The trouble is, as some critics now point out, that it has grown too old. What was once a vehicle for new writing seems to be repetitious, stylistic, and, many times, just plain boring. The editor's taste is too well known now to offer many surprises. On the positive side, it does have some major new and older writers, does offer bits of penetrating and startling works. It should be found in all medium to large-sized collections. Hopefully, some others will take up the book/magazine format and offer other new approaches.

New Letters (Formerly: *The University Review*). 1932. q. $6. David Ray. Univ. of Missouri, Kansas City, Mo. 64110. Index, adv. Circ: 700.

Indexed: LMags, SSHum. *Aud:* Ac, Ga, Hs.

In some 175 to 200 pages, the editors bring together "the work of new and distinguished writers," thus "providing a medium for the best imaginative writing available." The claim is borne out by a typical issue which features work by such well-known writers as: Joyce Carol Oates, Richard Hugo, David Ignatow,

Robert Bly, Tom Raworth, Anselm Hollo, and Harvey Swados. The result is a superior collection of prose and poetry which is almost a roll call of international authors. From time to time single numbers are given to a single theme or topic, e.g., the Winter 1971 issue is devoted to the work of Richard Wright. Unfortunately, this magazine does not enjoy the circulation it so richly deserves. Hopefully all libraries with meaningful collections in fiction and poetry will enter a subscription. A required item for larger academic and public libraries.

The North American Review. 1815. q. $6. Robley Wilson, Jr. Univ. of Northern Iowa, Cedar Falls, Iowa 50613. Illus., index, adv. Circ: 3,100. Sample. Vol. ends: Winter. Microfilm: UM.

Indexed: LMags, SSHum, HistAb. *Bk. rev:* 10, 1,500 words, signed. *Aud:* Ga, Ac.

The original *North American Review* was founded in 1815 and flourished until 1941. It was revived in 1963. Despite the discontinuity in its publishing history, the editor claims the present day magazine "is what it was during its happier days: a literate reflection of the current American scene—political, social, historical, literary." He seems to be right. An average well printed and edited 80-page issue features one to five articles, poetry, and four to five short stories. Aside from the book reviews there are a number of departments which cover everything from theatre to politics. Usually one or more of the short stories is chosen for the "Best American Short Stories" collection of the year, several of the poems have received awards, and the staff members are equally distinguished. The result is an exceptionally well-rounded general review which will appeal to the same audience as *Harper's* or *Atlantic.* There is something refreshing about it, and hopefully librarians will at least send for a sample copy to find out for themselves.

Overland. 1954. q. $5. S. Murray-Smith, Box 98A, GPO., Melbourne, Australia. Illus., index, adv. Circ: 3,500. Vol. ends: No. 8.

Bk. rev: 6-8, 1,500 words, signed. *Aud:* Ac, Ga.

This Australian magazine of literary and social commentary is valuable to librarians on two counts: first, it includes excellent book reviews, primarily of works of Australian poets and novelists not covered in standard media; second, the articles, poems, and stories are of an exceptionally high quality, and give readers an insight into Australian life. For the timid, there is little here to offend anyone. Given this professional approach and high literary standard, it affords the library a first-class means of broadening the scope of its collection to include a meaningful magazine from outside of the United States. While most of the material is aimed at the sophisticated adult, it should have appeal for advanced high school students as well.

The Paris Review. 1952. q. $4. George A. Plimpton, 45-39 171st Place, Flushing, N.Y. 11358. Illus., adv. Circ: 19,000. Microform: UM. Reprint: Johnson.

Indexed: LMags, SSHum. *Aud:* Ga, Ac.

Once a "little," this is now an established literary magazine whose formula is getting a bit tiresome. Its primary claim to fame is its founder, George Plimpton, and its interviews with prominent authors. The interviews have been published in book form, and the techniques are as much of interest as the content. This review publishes new poetry and fiction. It is a good magazine with a mixed bag of excellent literary material. For the general adult reader as well as the college student and advanced high school student.

Partisan Review. 1934. q. $5.50. William Phillips. Rutgers Univ., 191 College Ave., New Brunswick, N.J. 08903. Illus., index; adv. Circ: 8,500. Sample. Vol. ends: Fall. Microform: UM. Reprint: AMS.

Indexed: SSHum. *Bk. rev:* 3-5, 1,500 words, signed. *Aud:* Ac, Ga, Hs. *Jv:* V.

Despite ups and downs, in and out of favor with America's activist intellectuals, this remains one of the most influential literary reviews in America or anywhere else. It is a controversial testing ground for new political, social, artistic, and literary ideas. Writers from Susan Sontag to Leslie Fiedler represent the best America has to offer in challenging thought, although admittedly at a semipopular rather than detailed scholarly level. The editor delights in an intellectual or political cause celebre. Creative criticism of current literature, and occasionally art and theater, is included. From time to time there are excellent interviews. The fiction and poetry are outstanding, book reviews are equally divided between literary topics and politics. There are frequent stimulating symposia or exchanges on the American political and social scenes, and a lively letters-to-the-editor section. As the leading voices for the avant-garde in the United States and abroad, contributors are a more select group than those writing for other leading reviews. Should be in every medium to large-sized library, and in most senior high school libraries.

Pembroke Magazine. 1971. irreg. $2. ea. Norman MacLeod. Pembroke State Univ., Pembroke, N.C. 28372. Illus., adv.

Aud: Ac.

Sending a review copy, a member of this magazine's editorial board commented: "Our institution used to be an Indian Normal School, and we still have a 20 per cent Indian enrollment"—in itself of no great importance, but the interest is reflected in the neatly printed 56-page poetry magazine. There are the usual and not so usual contributors, e.g., Hugh MacDiarmid, Guy Owen, Howard McCord, and some other "regulars." But the greatest number of contributors are students, among whom are Indians and Chicanos. The third issue of the magazine (December 1971) is given to Amerindian work, "some black poetry and a fair collection of poems by West Indian poets. Some Chicano poetry, too." There are brief book reviews and art work. All in all one of the more interesting and rewarding of the small university publications.

The Phoenix. 1970. q. $7. James Cooney. Morning Star Press, West Whately, RFD Haydenville, Mass. 01039. Illus., index. Circ: 3,400. Sample. Vol. ends: Every 4 issues.

Bk. rev: Various number, length. *Aud:* Ac, Ga. *Jv:* V.

This carefully edited, beautifully printed 200-plus-page magazine defies categorization, can as easily be termed a little magazine as a literary-political journal. It ran from 1938 to 1940, was started again by its editor in 1970. The whole is printed, bound, and published at the editor's home, and it is as much a typographical joy as a vechicle for first-rate material. The editor explains its purpose: "We resume from where we left off—opposing war, rejecting violence as a way to freedom, welcoming voices of affirmation, intercession and reconciliation. We are receptive to reports from the demonic underworld of irrational consciousness where the healing alchemy of reconciliations must transpire." A typical issue introduces new writers, translations, literature, poetry, and just about anything which the editor thinks will further the cause he so nobly follows. The level of the contributions is professional, much above the average in style and content. Highly recommended for public and academic libraries.

Note: The editor will send free copies "to libraries of all struggling groups that can't afford to subscribe such as migratory workers, free universities, war resisters, etc."

Prairie Schooner. 1927. q. $3. Bernice Slote. Nebraska Hall 215, Univ. of Nebraska, Lincoln, Neb. 68508. Index, adv. Circ: 1,500.

Bk. rev: 6–8, 1–3 pages, signed. *Aud:* Sa, Ac.

A general literary review magazine of some standing which publishes nonacademic material. Each issue usually features one or two articles of general interest, but concentrates on short stories, poetry, and literary essays. The amount of poetry is impressive, and the reviews frequently concentrate in this area. Contributors tend to be teachers from all parts of the country. One of the better general reviews for libraries with a large literary collection.

Prism International; a journal of contemporary writing. 1959. 3/yr. $5. Jacob Zilber. Univ. of British Columbia, Creative Writing Dept., Vancouver 8, B.C., Canada. Illus., adv. Circ: 1,000. Sample. Vol. ends: Spring. Refereed.

Aud: Ga, Ac.

One of Canada's major literary magazines, divided evenly between fiction and poetry (with occasional critical essays), with the prose usually illustrated. Although it originates in British Columbia, contributors are not necessarily limited to Canada, and there are always a number of translations. Conversely, every effort is made to give Canadian writers a platform, and through the years it has published almost every new voice. The format is as pleasing as the content. A necessary purchase for all medium to large-sized Canadian libraries and most American academic libraries, along with the equally fine *Malahat Review.*

Prose. 1970. bi-a. $3. Coburn Britton. Prose Publishers Inc., 6 St. Luke's Place, New York, N.Y. 10014. Subs. to: Horizon Press, 156 Fifth Ave., New York, N.Y. 10010. Sample.

Aud: Ac, Ga.

A journal which makes literature an exciting, living, and provocative thought process. Free of any association with traditional footnoted, badly constructed, and even dull approaches to the living word, the 160 or so page magazine proves that good criticism can be done by and about even better writers. Among its contributors have been such distinguished writers and scholars as W. H. Auden, Edward Dahlbert, Anthony Burgess, Richard Howard, Allen Tate, Glenway Wescott, Sanche de Gramont, Kay Boyle, Djuna Barnes, and Margaret Anderson. Almost all of the critics are working poets, novelists, historians, and essay writers, and, as the names indicate, have done well with their share of Pulitzer prizes. They discuss everything from "Miss Toklas' American Cake" to "The Function of Neurosis." The result is a journal which should have wide appeal among literate readers, particularly those who subscribe to the notion that literature is not the province of morticians. Highly recommended for all academic and larger public libraries.

Quarterly Review of Literature. 1943. s-a. $5 for 2 double no's. Theodore Weiss, 26 Haslet Ave., Princeton, N.J. 08540. Index, adv. Circ: 2,000.

Indexed: LMags. *Aud:* Ga, Ac.

An international literary magazine of modern creative work, this is one of the leaders in presenting significant writers, from Nobel Prize winners to lively newcomers. Publishes poetry, short stories, plays, and novellas. Features unpublished or little-known work of older American writers, and distinguished writers' translations from Dutch, German, Italian, French, Japanese, Greek, and Spanish, of new and older writers. It has considerably wider interest than most of the literary journals in this section, and because it stresses the work of the artist rather than the critic, can be enjoyed by any sophisticated adult reader. Hence, it should be found in many medium to larger-sized public libraries, as well as in all academic collections. (It should be emphasized that despite the title, this is not a quarterly but a semiannual anthology. The double issues, usually one in poetry and another in fiction, are an editorial nicety which allows retention of the title.)

Queen's Quarterly. 1893. q. $6. J. K. McSweeney. McGill's Queen's Univ. Press., 130 Lower Albert St., Kingston, Ont., Canada. Circ: 2,000. Vol. ends: No. 4.

Indexed: CanI, MLA, PAIS. *Bk. rev:* Notes, 25–40; essays, 200–400 words, signed. *Aud:* Ac.

One of Canada's oldest university-based literary journals of opinion. In close to 200 pages, the editor carries his readers from poetry and original prose to articles on the social sciences and humanities. About one quarter of every issue is given to two or three essay reviews of books, plus shorter notes. These cover titles from both Candian and American publishers. The writing is by some of Canada's better known scholars and authors, but is more academic and literary than political or controversial. It is a far cry, for example, from other Candian journals of opinion; probably closer in spirit to the better-than-average college or university-based American literary quarterly. The fiction, however, is outstanding. The attitude of the editor is quite pro-Canada. A solid choice for larger Candian and American collections.

The Review. 1962. q. $3.50. Ian Hamilton, 72 Westbourne Terrace, London W2, England.

Indexed: BritHum. *Aud:* Ac.

A pocket-sized, well-printed English magazine of some 70 pages which has gained a place as one of the more outstanding of its type. It is primarily concerned with poetry and criticism. The writing is almost at an academic level, and is considerably more astute than that found in the traditional little magazine. This is balanced by a telling wit and a degree of humor. A first choice for libraries and individuals, particularly those concerned with modern poetry.

St. Andrew's Review. 1970. s-a. $3.50. Ronald H. Bayes. St. Andrews Presbyterian College, Laurinburg, N.C. 28352. Illus., adv. Circ: 1,000.

Bk. rev: 5–6, 250–500 words, signed. *Aud:* Ac.

A combination literary and social review which features essays, fiction, poetry, graphics, etc. A typical issue had a long essay in verse by Bucky Fuller, an appreciation of him by Gene Fowler, a story by Guy Owen, and a number of lesser known though sometimes talented poets. The approach is familiar enough, distinguished by relatively good editing and make-up. It is hard to be either critical or excited, and it is one of those magazines which probably fits only into larger periodical collections.

Sewanee Review. 1892. q. $7. Andrew Lytle. Univ. of the South, Seqanee, Tenn. 37375. Circ: 4,000. Sample. Vol. ends: Autumn. Microform: UM. Reprint: Kraus.

Indexed: SSHum. *Bk. rev:* 12, grouped, 3,000 words, signed. *Aud:* Ga, Ac. *Jv:* V.

The oldest literary review magazine in the United States, yet remarkably up-to-date and often ahead of the times. Issues contain original fiction and poetry, and, in the Arts and Letters section, book review essays, occasional correspondence, and review articles covering recent criticism on a single literary figure. Essays vary in length from 2,000 to 10,000 words and deal predominantly with literature and literary criticism. Contributors are international scholars and writers in English. However, the editor reports he "seeks out young and gifted (and yet unpublished or little-published) talents and gives space to these in nearly every issue. Special attention, but not exclusive, is given to the South. The editorial policy is an allegiance to the humane tradition in learning and letters, with stern opposition to the debasement and perversion of words, and with vigilant care for language and style in not necessarily great but sound literature." Primarily for larger academic collections, but public libraries subscribing to the basic reviews will want to consider.

South Atlantic Quarterly. 1902. q. $6. William B. Hamilton, Duke Univ. Press, 6697 College Station, Durham, N.C. 27708. Adv. Circ: 1,285. Sample. Vol. ends: Autumn. Refereed.

Indexed: PAIS, SSHum. *Bk. rev:* Various number, length, signed. *Aud:* Ac.

A general literary magazine which covers public affairs, history, social studies, the arts, etc. It boasts that it is the second oldest review in the United States—the *Sewanee Review* (1892) being the first. Many of the contributors are from the South, and the emphasis is on southern affairs, although not exclusively. Articles tend to be scholarly, yet maintain a style which can be appreciated by any educated adult. Should be found in most southern libraries, and in the larger college and university collections nationally.

South Dakota Review. 1963. q. $4. John R. Milton. Univ. of South Dakota, Vermillion, S.D. 57069. Illus., index. Circ: 1,000. Vol. ends: Winter. Microform: UM.

Indexed: AbEnSt, LMags. *Bk. rev:* Occasional. *Aud:* Ac.

The place of publication has little or nothing to do with content, which is primarily poetry and short stories. Authors come from every part of the country. Most are campus oriented, many are students and teachers, but just as many are well known in their own rights in the little magazine scene. Thanks to careful editing, the level of the poetry and particularly the fiction is quite high. On occasion there is an article on some aspect of the culture, and the Spring 1971 issue featured conversations with four western American novelists. The whole is impressive, much above and beyond the average regional or campus-bound magazine. (Note: it is modest in size, rarely running over 100 pages.)

✓ **The Southern Review.** 1965. (Old series: 1935–1942). q. $5. Donald E. Stanford and Lewis P. Simpson. Louisiana State Univ. Subs. to: B. DeBoer, 188 High St., Nutley, N.J. 07100. Index, adv. Circ: 3,500. Sample. Vol. ends: Autumn.

Indexed: LMags. *Bk. rev:* 5, 2,000 words, signed. *Aud:* Ac, Ga. *Jv:* V.

At the modest price, this may well be a "best buy" among university-based reviews. An average issue runs from 250 to 300 well-printed pages. There are outstanding articles on literary criticism, but the editors have achieved an above-average magazine by featuring superior short stories and poetry. Among fiction contributors have been Isaac Singer, Joyce Carol Oates, and Nadine Gordimer. Usually one or two issues a year are devoted to a single subject, e.g., Summer 1971 consisted of a study in depth of Wallace Stevens. The magazine has tended to move away from southern topics and writers; now features material from the United States and abroad. The book reviews are essay length and particularly fine. The balance is excellent—something for almost anyone interested in any aspect of the current literary scene. While this is a required first choice in academic and large public libraries, it should be given serious consideration for smaller libraries and for advanced high schools.

✓ **Southwest Review.** 1915. q. $4. Margaret L. Hartley. Southern Methodist Univ. Press, Dallas, Tex. 75222. Index, adv. Circ: 1,000. Sample. Vol. ends: Autumn.

Indexed: LMags. *Bk. rev:* 10, 900 words, signed. *Aud:* Ac.

Primarily a literary magazine that issues articles by scholars on modern American writing and authors. Some short fiction, poetry, and critical articles on the social scene are also featured. Although neither regional in content nor in contributors, a given amount of emphasis is on the Southwest. A good magazine for libraries in the area, but a second choice for other medium to large-sized collections.

Spectrum; the Richmond tri-annual review. 1965. s-a. $2. Richard J. McCann. Virginia Commonwealth Univ., 916 W. Franklin St., Richmond, Va. 23220. Illus., adv. Circ: 1,200.

Bk. rev: 3–4, 500 words. *Aud:* Ac.

Unlike many university literary reviews, this one is heavy on art, features a dozen or so reproductions, some in color. Add to that a couple of short stories, some rather good verse and literary criticism and you have the typical review. Somehow, though, it strikes one as better than most because emphasis is placed on avant-garde writing, and the focus is as much with the future as the past. The style is usually fresh, and in 60 pages it has more than the average amount of imaginative literature. In fact, it could pass as a much above average little magazine.

Stand; quarterly of the arts. 1952. q. $3. Jon Silkin, Lorna Tracy. 58 Queens Rd., Newcastle on Tyne, NE 2 2PR, England. Illus., index, adv. Circ: 4,000. Sample. Vol. ends: 4th issue.

Indexed: ICLM. *Bk. rev:* 10–12, length varies, signed. *Aud:* Ac, Ga, Hs. *Jv:* V.

One of England's best, liveliest, and truly imaginative little magazines. The editor is a prominent English poet; the assistant editor, a former American librarian. It regularly features poems, fiction, essays on social and political issues, and grouped book reviews, primarily of poetry issued by little presses. (The reviews, by the way, are essential for any library trying to build a meaningful modern poetry collection.) Contributions are balanced geographically between the London scene and the wider spectrum of England. They all tend to be professionals, although from time to time the magazine does publish "firsts." The magazine's twofold aim is: (1) to be a platform for young British and North American writers, placing their work side by side; and (2) to publish in translation the best in contemporary writing from elsewhere in the world. Given this wide scope, and much above average format and selection, this is a basic little magazine for any library.

Tamarack Review. 1956. q. $4. Robert Weaver, Box 159. Postal Station K, Toronto, Ont., Canada. Adv. Circ: 2,000. Sample. Vol. ends: Summer.

Indexed: CanI. *Bk. rev:* 4–5, 1,200 words, signed. *Aud:* Ga, Ac.

Following the pattern of the traditional review, the editors feature material "almost entirely by Canadian writers." It is now one of the longest lived and best Canadian literary magazines. There is a nice balance of fiction, poetry, and critical reviews, and the level is usually quite high. It is a required item in almost all Canadian libraries—there simply are not enough first class Canadian literary magazines to warrant its exclusion—and should be in larger American academic and public libraries.

✓ **Texas Quarterly.** 1958. q. $4. Harry R. Ransom. Univ. of Texas, Box 7517, Univ. Station, Austin, Tex 78712. Illus., index. Circ: 4,000.

Indexed: PAIS, SSHum. *Aud:* Ga, Ac. *Jv:* V.

Drawing heavily upon holdings of the University of Texas Library, yet calling for contributions on an international scale, this is an impressive literary review. Both in format and size it measures up to its state of origin. Thanks in part to a relatively high payment for authors, it boasts excellent writers who, while being scholars, are still able to express themselves in terms understandable to any well-educated reader. Coverage is general, yet concentrates on literature and the humanities. Social criticism centers around the area of origin, and there are frequent articles on American-Mexican relationships. The whole is balanced with one or two short stories, some poetry, and a few illustrations. A major magazine for medium to large literature and social science collections.

Transatlantic Review. 1959. q. $3. J. F. McCrindle, 33 Ennismore Gardens, London SW7, England. Amer. subs. to: Box 3348, Grand Central Station, New York, N.Y. 10017. Illus., index, adv. Circ: 3,000. Sample.

Indexed: LMags. *Aud:* Ac, Ga.

In format and approach much like the *Paris Review.* It, too, appeals to audiences both in America and Europe, features articles from both sides of the Atlantic, usually has an interview with a literary figure, and includes fiction and poetry. It differs from the *Paris Review* in that there is considerably more fiction, and little or no social and political criticism. Among the contributors in one issue: Nobel Prize winner S. Y. Agnon; William Sansom, James Baldwin, Peter Barnes, Sol Yurick, Joyce Carol Oates, and Theodor Fontane. A run of this magazine represents a valuable collection of modern writing from all parts of the world, not just the United States and England. It is a bit less pretentious than the *Paris Review*, and these days considerably better edited. One of the basic reviews for modern literature collections.

TransPacific (Formerly: **Colorado State Review).** 1966. q. $4. Nicholas Irome. Antioch College, Yellow Springs, Ohio 45387. Illus. Circ: 1,000. Sample. Vol. ends: No. 8.

Indexed: LMags. *Aud:* Ac, Ga.

A 60-page, nicely printed, usually well illustrated little poetry and prose magazine. Its scope is international, and it has featured work from Europe, the United States, and Eastern countries. The editor notes: "Usually 50 to 70 percent is new American writing, and the other 30 to 40 percent translations—most often from non-Western countries." Thanks to this wide scope, careful editing, and a good choice of contributors, this can be recommended as one of the better, truly international little magazines. (It is independent, and in no way affiliated with Antioch College. The editor explains: "that's merely an address.")

Tri-Quarterly. 1964. 3/yr. Charles Newman. Northwestern Univ. Subs. to: B. DeBoer, 188 High St., Nutley, N.J. 07110. Illus., index, adv. Circ: 5,000. Sample.

Indexed: AbEnSt. *Bk. rev:* Various number, length. *Aud:* Ac, Ga. *Jv:* V.

As the editor tends to concentrate on a given subject for every number, each 400 or so page issue of this outstanding review is almost a book. The "new novel," trends in modern poetry and translations, changes in literary criticism—all have been considered. The essays are balanced by poetry and prose. Contributors range from little-known experts to some of the best-known names in the literary world, e.g., George Steiner, Joyce Carol Oates, Michel Butor, John Hawkes. The thrust is towards the modern, but the judicious editing assures that the content is always at a high intellectual and imaginative level. Many of the articles are nicely documented. Format, illustrations and the like are first rate; and there are some occasional supplements. Along with *Southern Review*, a first choice for medium to large-sized libraries.

University of Denver Quarterly. 1966. q. $4. Burton Feldman. Univ. of Denver, Denver, Colo. 80210. Index, adv. Circ: 1,000. Sample. Vol. ends: Winter.

Indexed: MLA. *Bk. rev:* 10–20, length varies, signed. *Aud:* Ac.

A general literary magazine with essays on modern literature and culture, poetry, fiction, reviews, and occasional letters from abroad. The Summer 1971 issue includes a short story, a long poem, an essay on Nietzsche, a memoir, and several book reviews. Aside from the essay, the 90 pages were adequate, relatively bland. But the piece on Nietzcshe was first rate, and if the Denver quarterly follows the normal pattern, this kind of average is to be expected. As a quarterly it is not better or no worse than the average; should be in larger collections.

University of Toronto Quarterly; a Canadian journal of the humanities. 1931. q. $8. W. F. Blissett. Univ. of Toronto Press, Toronto 5, Ont., Canada. Index. Circ: 1,400. Vol. ends: July. Refereed.

Indexed: CanI, RG. *Bk. rev:* 3, 500 words, signed. *Aud:* Ac.

A Canadian literary periodical with three issues devoted to approximately six scholarly articles on English, American, French, and German literature. The July bibliographic issue has one or two critical articles, but the rest is given to long review articles on the past year's work in Canadian literature including poetry, fiction, humanities, social studies, "livres en francais," and publications in other languages (chiefly Icelandic, Ukrainian, and German). Contributors are Canadian, English, and American scholars. A basic purchase for all medium to large-sized Canadian public and academic libraries, but only for large American university collection.

The University Review. See *New Letters.*

Virginia Quarterly Review; a national journal of literature and discussion. 1925. q. $5. Charlotte Kohler. Univ. of Virginia, 1 W. Range, Charlottesville, Va. 22903. Subs. to: B. DeBoer, 188 High St., Nutley, N.J. 07110. Index, adv. Microform: UM.

Indexed: PAIS, SSHum. *Bk. rev:* 70–90, 100–300 words. *Aud:* Ga, Ac.

Along with the *Sewanee Review* and the *Southern Review,* one of the three basic literary magazines published in the South. It is less parochial than *Southern Review,* more popular in style and content than *Sewanee.* Differences aside, it covers much the same general area as its competitors—literature, social sciences, politics, art, etc. Particularly valuable for all libraries because of the short notes on current books (preceded by several critical essays), and a section, "List of Reprints and New Editions." The reviews are as broad in scope as the magazine, i.e., fiction, history, poetry, etc. Because of its somewhat broader scope, it would be slightly ahead of *Southern Review* for library purchase, yet not up to *Sewanee.* Southern public and academic libraries will want all three, others may choose in the order suggested here.

Voyages, a national literary magazine. 1967. q. $6. William Claire, Box 4862, Washington, D.C. 20008. Illus. Circ: 2,500.

Indexed: AbEnSt. *Aud:* Ac. *Jv:* V.

Not only pays its contributors, but probably does so at higher rates than other little magazines. It has fiction, poetry, art, excerpts, reviews, criticism, and features two selected poets each issue. A solid and attractive magazine for anyone interested in literature and the arts. (D.D.)

West Coast Review, a quarterly magazine of the arts. 1965. q. $6. Frederick Candelaria. Simon Fraser Univ., Burnaby 2, B.C., Canada. Illus., index, adv. Circ: 600. Sample. Vol. ends: April.

Indexed: LMags. *Bk. rev:* 10–15, lengthy, signed. *Aud:* Ga, Ac.

Outstanding in many ways. It is academic to a degree, but short stories are superior, poetry good. Music, photographs, and drawings are included. A special feature is the bibliographies: recent issues have short biographies and extended bibliographies on Earle Birney and Gunter Grass. Book reviews are scholarly, covering Canadian belle lettres, university presses, and the alternative press. This should be a first choice for serious collections. (D.D.)

Works, a quarterly of writing. 1967. q. $4. John Hopper and Richard Brotherson. AMS Press, Inc., 56 E. 13th St., New York, N.Y. 10003. Illus. Circ: 3,500.

Indexed: AbEnSt. *Bk. rev:* 2–3, lengthy, signed. *Aud:* Ga, Ac.

A thick and sturdy magazine of fiction, poetry, articles, art, criticism, reviews—in essence, everything. It pays its contributors; is best at introducing new or relatively unknown writers. A short critical essay will be followed by a meaningful sampling of their work, making this a must for English departments and graduate schools. Also has the better-known writers. Good social commentary and book reviews. Almost a pure literary quarterly. (D.D.)

The Yale Review. 1911. q. $6. J. E. Palmer. Yale Univ., 28 Hillhouse Ave., New Haven, Conn. 06520. Index, adv. Circ: 7,000. Vol. ends: Summer. Microform: UM.

Indexed: AbEnSt, PAIS, RG. *Bk. rev:* 9, 1,500 words, signed; notes. *Aud:* Ac, Ga.

As one of the few university reviews indexed in *Readers' Guide,* this is to be found in most libraries. It deserves that place but let it be suggested there may be other equally good choices for general reading purposes. Given that warning, there is no quarrel with the magazine, itself. It features articles for the intelligent layman—not only the expert—in almost all fields from politics and economics to the arts. There are short stories, poems, film, record, and book reviews. The style of writing is as lively as the selection policy of the editor. (The articles are noteworthy for the lack of footnotes, bibliographies, and the like.) And while it is quarterly, the articles usually are right in line with current debates.

LITERATURE

Basic Periodicals

GENERAL. Ga: *American Literature, Canadian Literature;* Jc: *PMLA, American Literature, Journal of Modern Literature;* Ac: *PMLA, American Literature, Journal of Modern Literature, Literature and Ideology, Speculum, Modern Fiction Studies.*

Library and Teaching Aids
Review of English Studies.

Basic Abstracts and Indexes
Abstracts of English Studies, American Literature Abstracts, MLA International Bibliography.

General

American Literary Realism, 1870–1910. 1967. q. $3. Clayton L. Eichelberger. Dept. of English, Univ. of Texas, Arlington, Tex. 76010. Index. Circ: 600. Sample. Vol. ends: Fall. Refereed.

Indexed: AbEnSt, AmerLitAb, MLA. *Bk. rev:* 3–5, 500 words, signed. *Aud:* Ac.

The purpose of this bibliographic journal is to "emphasize the compilation and publication of comprehensive annotated bibliographies of secondary comment on those literary figures of the designated period." Some 15 to 20 authors are covered in each 100-page or so issue. A valuable reference aid for any large library.

American Literature; a journal of literary history, criticism and bibliography. 1929. q. $7. Arlin Turner. Duke Univ. Press, 6697 College Sta., Durham, N.C. 27708. Index, adv. Circ: 5,900. Sample. Vol. ends: Jan. Refereed. Microform: UM. Reprint: Kraus.

Indexed: AbEnSt, AmerLitAb, MLA. *Bk. rev:* 15–30, 750 words, signed. *Aud:* Ac, Ga. *Jv:* V.

Sponsored by the American Literature Section of the Modern Language Association (MLA), this is a scholarly journal, with research articles on the history, criticism, and bibliography of American literature. Contains both substantial, critical book reviews, and annotated listings of recent books not reviewed. Special features are research in progress, a listing of dissertations completed and in progress and other projects underway, and an index to articles on American literature appearing in current periodicals, with short annotations. While a basic journal for any academic library, it should interest secondary school English teachers and may be a suitable publication for larger professional collections in high schools.

American Notes & Queries. 1962. 10/yr. (Sept.–June). $6.50. Lee Ash, 31 Alden Rd., New Haven, Conn. 06515. Circ: 1,000. Sample.

Indexed: AbEnSt. *Bk. rev:* 10–15, length varies, signed. *Aud:* Ac.

Somewhat similar to its British counterpart—*Notes and Queries*—and normally made up of several well-defined sections: Three to four short items on literature; queries, and replies to questions regarding research and esoteric bibliographic problems; the editor's comments and readings; reviews of recent foreign reference books by Lawrence Thompson, and shorter book notes. The whole is usually 16 pages, and while small in format it is large in the amount of help it renders to students of literature. A necessary reference aid—and just good reading—for any academic library where there is serious interest in literary research and bibliography.

Australian Literary Studies. 1963. s-a. Aus. $4.50. L. T. Hergenhan. Univ. of Tasmania, Dept. of English, Box 252c, GPO, Hobart, Tasmania, Australia. Adv. Circ: 1,300.

Indexed: AbEnSt, PAIS. *Bk. rev:* 3–5, 250–500 words, signed. *Aud:* Ac.

Usually three to four articles on Australian writers and literature are included with a bibliographic article, e.g., "Price Warung: Some Bibliographical Details and a Checklist of Stories." In addition to reviews of books in the area (published worldwide) there are bibliographic notes. Useful in larger academic American libraries not only for the wide scope, but for the "Annual Bibliography of Studies In Australian Literature," which usually appears in the May number, and the "Research In Progress In Australian Literature." The bibliography includes a general section and one devoted to works by and about individual authors.

Ball State University Forum. 1960. q. $3. Frances and Merrill Rippy. Ball State Univ., Muncie, Ind. 47306. Illus., index, adv. Circ: 1,500. Sample. Vol. ends: Autumn.

Indexed: AbEnSt, MLA. *Aud:* Ac.

A general literature journal of 80 pages, with some six to seven articles, poems, and translations. The emphasis is on literary criticism, e.g., "A metaphoric approach to reading Milton," or "The Imagery of Pericles." Articles are by English professors from many universities and colleges. The material is shorter than that found in most such journals, and, as a result, a bit easier to follow. "Of its four issues per year *Forum* will generally devote one to British literature and one to American literature. A third issue will feature creative writing, and a fourth will be eclectic." The magazine is carefully edited, shows more than average imagination. A basic item for larger collections.

Canadian Literature/ Litterature Canadienne; a quarterly of criticism and review. 1959. q. $5.50. George Woodcock. Univ. of British Columbia, Vancouver, B.C., Canada. Illus., index, adv. Circ: 2,000. Vol. ends: Spring.

Indexed: CanI. *Bk. rev:* 15, 1,000 words, signed. *Aud:* Ac. *Jv:* V.

Stresses the traditional as well as the modern. Special issues, for example, have discussed explorers as writers, the Federation of Letters, and early Canadian journals. It includes essays in English and French on new and established Canadian writers, discussions of the writer's problems, autobiographical essays by Canadian writers, and studies of past and present trends in Canadian literature. There are unobtrusive editorials on Canadian literature or some phase of the Canadian publishing industry. Contributors include distinguished Canadian scholars and authors and also important foreign critics. In addition to the "Books in Review" section each issue also contains three to five longer critical analyses in the "Review Articles" section, averaging 1,000 to 2,000 words in length. Books reviewed are Canadian books in the fields of poetry, fiction, drama, criticism, biography, history, and belles lettres. Special features are the "Chronicle" section, with its "Letters from London," "Montreal," "Vancouver," etc., reporting on the current scene in these cities, and an annual checklist of the past year's Canadian literature, appearing in the April issue. It is the standard unannotated source in this field. (See also *University of Toronto Quarterly* in Literary Reviews section). A necessary purchase for all Canadian academic and larger public libraries, and certainly should be found in most American junior college libraries and university libraries.

Comparative Literature. 1949. q. $4.50. Chandler B. Beall. Univ. of Oregon Books, Eugene, Ore. 97403. Index. Circ: 2,500. Sample. Refereed. Microform: UM.

Indexed: SSHum. *Bk. rev:* 6–15, lengthy, signed. *Aud:* Ac.

Long, critical articles, averaging 6,000 words, deal with the "manifold relations of literatures," covering theory of literature, literary movements, themes, genres, periods, and authors—from the earliest times to the present. International themes and the tracing of influences from the literature of one country to another are also presented. Of interest to all advanced students of general literature.

Comparative Literature Studies. 1963. q. $7.50. A. Owen Aldridge. Univ. of Illinois Press, Univ. of Illinois, Urbana, Ill. 61801. Index, adv. Circ: 1,000. Vol. ends: Dec. Refereed.

Indexed: AbEnSt. *Bk. rev:* 8–13, 1,000 words, signed. *Aud:* Ac, Ga.

As the title implies, the journal focuses on literary influences. That is to say, the influence of one author on another, foreign influences on English literature, similar literary movements compared in different countries, etc. The articles are well documented and are on a scholarly level. The journal features English-language writing, but French, German, Italian, and Spanish language contributions are also in evidence. An abstract in English precedes every article, whatever its language. There are extensive reviews of books in the field. Recommended for academic and large public libraries. (H.D.)

Contemporary Literature. 1960. q. $5.50. L. S. Dembo. Journals Dept., Univ. of Wisconsin Press, Box 1379, Madison, Wis. 53701. Index, adv. Circ: 2,000. Sample. Refereed. Microform: UM.

Indexed: MLA, SSHum. *Bk. rev:* 4–6, 1,000 words, signed. *Aud:* Ac.

Devoted to studies of all areas of Anglo-American and continental literature—poetry, fiction, drama, and criticism—chiefly, but not exclusively, since the second World War. The journal features well-written, original, critical articles and reviews, ranging in coverage from analyses of writers—both the established and the little known—to explications, essays on poetry, critical theory and practice, and continental literature. Generally six to eight articles appear in each issue, averaging 5,000 words each. Frequently issues revolve around a central theme. Two basic bibliographies are issued annually: "Criticism: A Review," and "Poetry." The former is an essay on criticism and books of criticism about American and British authors; the latter, compiled by Samuel French Morse, evaluates 20 to 30 major English and American books of contemporary poetry. Useful in all academic libraries, and should be considered by larger public libraries.

Criticism; a quarterly for literature and the arts. 1959. q. $8. Wayne State Univ. Press, 5980 Cass Ave., Detroit, Mich. 48202. Index. Circ: 1,000. Sample. Vol. ends: Fall. Refereed.

Indexed: AbEnSt, MLA, SSHum. *Bk. rev:* 6–8, 1,000 words, signed. *Aud:* Ac, Hs.

Devoted to the study of literature and the fields of fine art and music. It includes evaluation and explication of artists and their works; examines the arts and literatures of all periods and nations, either individually or in their interrelationships, and critical theory regarding them. Contributors are U.S. and foreign scholars. Formal aesthetics and more technical studies in philology and linguistics are not included. Book review section has critical and authoritative reviews of vital books in the humanities. An excellent purchase for academic and some high school libraries.

Critique: **Studies in Modern Fiction.** 1956. 3/yr. $2.50. James Dean Young. Dept. of English. Georgia Inst. of Technology, Atlanta, Ga. 30332. Index. Circ: 1,300. Refereed.

Indexed: AbEnSt, AmerLitAb, SSHum. *Bk. rev:* 2–3, 3–4 pages, signed. *Aud:* Ac.

Covers both English and American modern fiction, and is particularly useful for extended coverage of a single author, e.g., Iris Murdoch and a checklist of her works. The tone is scholarly, yet not overly academic. The style is considerably better than many other literary magazines of this type.

Delos; a journal on and of translation. 1968. irreg. $7.50 for 6 nos. D. S. Carne-Ross, Natl. Translation Center, 2621 Speedway, Austin, Tex. 78705. Illus.

Bk. rev: 5–7, 500–2,000 words, signed. *Aud:* Ac.

A beautifully produced 250-page journal devoted to translations and the problems of translators. Experiences of translators are documented, and the book reviews touch on various translations of Russian, German, and classical poetry and prose. The whole is impressive yet a trifle uneven; while some parts are easy enough to read, others are bogged down in academic style. A major magazine for all literature and language collections in most public and academic libraries.

Diacritics, a review of contemporary criticism. 1971. 2/yr. $5. Dept. of Romance Studies, Cornell Univ., Ithaca, N.Y. 14850.

Aud: Ac.

The long essays published in this journal are actually literary reviews and reviews of reviews. Under the guise of literature they serve to discuss "fundamental human concerns," like sociology, psychology, philosophy, anthropology, and other issues embedded in literary works. Many of the articles are translations from European journals. Also in translation are presented several interviews with contemporary authors, among others Levy-Strauss, Sarduy, Grass. The layout and typography is tastefully designed. The whole publication is a fine piece for the intellectual gourmet and literary scholar. (P.V.)

Eighteenth Century Studies. 1967. q. $7. Robert H. Hopkins and Arthur E. McGuinness. Univ. of California Press. Periodicals Dept., 2223 Fulton St., Berkeley, Calif. 94720. Illus. Circ: 1,400. Sample. Vol. ends: Summer. Refereed.

Bk. rev: 8, 1,500 words, signed. *Aud:* Ac.

Employing somewhat the same approach as *Renaissance Quarterly,* this is a general magazine which uses literature as a base and explores, as well, art, intellectual history, painting, and music. The only limitation is that each article must have some bearing on the eighteenth century. Particularly useful in medium-sized libraries where it is not possible to subscribe to many literature magazines and it is desirable to touch a number of academic bases.

English Literary History/E.L.H. 1934. q. $10 (Individuals $8). Earl R. Wasserman. Johns Hopkins Press, Baltimore, Md. 21218. Illus., index. Circ: 1,880. Sample. Vol. ends: Dec. Reprint: Kraus, Johnson.

Indexed: SSHum. *Aud:* Ac.

Articles are restricted to criticism or aesthetics and are concerned mainly with English literature; only occasionally with American literature. No biographical, bibliographic or source studies are included unless they relate to textual study or criticism. There are from seven to nine articles of moderate length in each issue. Primarily for large academic libraries.

English Literary Renaissance. 1971. 3/yr. $15 (Individuals $10). Arthur F. Kinney. Dept. of English, Univ. of Massachusetts, Amherst, Mass. 01002.

Aud: Ac.

One of the best looking new magazines because it is designed and printed by the Stinehour Press, and Leonard Baskin and John Benson gave typographical advice. However, the 96 pages of content is standard enough for a learned journal. Here the emphasis is on "publication of texts, studies, and bibliographies on the literary achievement of Tudor and early Stuart England." The first issue had articles on Skelton, a reconstructed text of "The Nutbrown Maid," and material on *The Winter's Tale* and *Paradise Lost.* It winds up with an annotated list of recent studies on Skelton. The editor notes that a forthcoming double issue will contain "the texts of two Sidney letters never before published, and an annotated bibliography of Sidney scholarship for the past 27 years." A good choice for larger libraries.

English Literature in Transition, 1880–1920. 1957. irreg. $2.50. Helmut E. Gerber. Dept. of English, Ari-

zona State Univ., Tempe, Ariz. 85281. Circ: 800. Sample. Vol. ends: Dec. Refereed. Reprint: Kraus.

Indexed: AbEnSt, MLA. *Aud:* Ac.

Concentrates on the fusing genres and categories of the late Victorian and early modern periods. *ELT* includes articles on aesthetics, literary history, all varieties of criticism, and "appreciations" of minor figures. Articles vary in length from issue-long bibliographies to short notes. A major concern is the publishing of bibliographies of primary works, of abstracts of writings about some 100 authors of the period, and manuscript location lists. Since 1964 "Special Series" on individual authors and topics have appeared irregularly as a bonus to subscribers.

Essays in Criticism; a quarterly journal of literary criticism. 1951. q. $6. F. W. Bateson, Stephen Well, Christopher Ricks. Brill, Aylesbury, Bucks, England. Index. Circ: 2,200.

Bk. rev: 3–6, 2,500 words, signed. *Aud:* Ac.

Editorial policy is concerned with avoiding the mechanization of literary scholarship. Emphasis is on continental literatures rather than on American. International contributors provide articles on all aspects of literary criticism and individual authors. Preference is given to articles arising from earlier discussion in the journal. A regular feature is "Critical Forum," devoted to similar discussions but in a shorter, "Letters-to-the-Editor" format. The book reviews are classics of their type—long scholarly articles similar to *The Times Literary Supplement* in style and depth.

Explicator. 1942. 10/yr. $3. J. Edwin Whitesell. The Explicator, Virginia Commonwealth Univ., 901 W. Franklin St., Richmond, Va. 23220. Index. Circ: 2,500. Vol. ends: June. Refereed. Microform: UM. Reprint: Kraus.

Indexed: MLA. *Aud:* Ac.

A scholarly publication devoted exclusively to *explication de texte* of English, American, and continental literature. The literature under discussion is reprinted whenever it is short enough. Entries are generally short, concise signed notes, but occasionally somewhat longer articles. Comments and queries are included. Footnotes are incorporated in the body of the article. Contributors are American and foreign scholars. Bibliographic issue in June includes a checklist of the past year's explication of British and American writings. List includes "items of unquestioned explicatory merit and substance, but it has omitted nothing merely because it is brief or its subject . . . of doubtful literary importance." A basic journal for all types of academic libraries.

The Journal of Commonwealth Literature. 1965. bi-a. $7.90. Arthur Ravenscroft, Oxford Univ. Press, Press Rd., Neasden, London NW 10, England. Index. Circ: 1,200.

Indexed: AbEnSt, ICLM. *Bk. rev:* Various number, length, signed. *Aud:* Ac.

Although it has been said that there is no such thing as a "Commonwealth literature," this magazine provides a much-needed forum for "scholars throughout the world about creative writing in English from all Commonwealth countries except Great Britain." Contents encompass critical scholarly articles and reviews, together with bibliographies of Commonwealth countries (for the previous year) contributed by respected and mostly well-known scholars. Subscriptions should be held by any library with an English language and literature collection.

Journal of Modern Literature. 1970. 5/yr. $8. Maurice Beebe, 1904 N. Park Mall, Temple Univ., Philadelphia, Pa. 19122. Illus., index. Circ: 1,600. Sample. Vol. ends: June. Refereed.

Bk. rev: 8–9, 600–800 words, signed. *Aud:* Ac, Ga. *Jv:* V.

An excellent publication featuring solid articles on major literary figures as well as extensive book reviews. There is an annual review number which surveys in more than 330 pages critical scholarship on modern literature published from 1970 on. The format is appealing, with large black and white illustrations and easy-to-read type on heavy paper. The content seems consistently substantial, dealing with important currents and figures in modern literature. In the issues examined, there was no lapse of content into the trivial or purely experimental. The *Journal* incorporates special coverage of important professional events in twentieth century literature. One issue contained an interview with Durrenmatt and a report from the second International James Joyce Symposium; another, given to William Carlos Williams, featured an extensive checklist of writings about the poet. In all, it seems an interesting, informative publication. Recommended for all academic and large public libraries. (H.D.)

Journal of Narrative Technique. 1971. 3/yr. $3. George Perkins. Dept. of English, Eastern Michigan Univ., Ypsilanti, Mich. 48197.

Aud: Ac.

A specialized approach to criticism and English, i.e., four to five articles and notes are involved with the narrative elements in literature. "Subject matter may be drawn from all periods and all literary genres." Papers concern "characterization, style, biographical background, historical influences, etc." An important journal in this area, one of the few of its kind, and a liberal break from tradition. Finally, note the editorial consultants: K. J. Fielding, Northrop Frye, Hoover Jordan, Joyce Carol Oates, Ronald Paulson, Henry Nash Smith, and Brian Wicker.

Literature & Ideology. 1969. q. $3. Natl. Publns. Center, Box 727, Adelaide Station, Toronto 1, Canada.

Indexed: API. *Aud:* Ac.

The journal is "sponsored by the Necessity for Change Institute of Ideological Studies, Dublin and Montreal, as part of the worldwide struggle against imperialism. The Institute wishes to encourage progressive intellectuals to participate . . . in the discussion and analysis of the political and social role of literature, art and criticism." Each 50 to 100 page issue features seven to ten articles on every topic from a Marxist study of American literature to "Social Relations in Modern American Poetry." The authors' names are given, but they are not otherwise identified. The number examined is impressive in that the writing is good, the arguments cogent, and the conclusions logical—i.e., if the reader happens to subscribe to the basic theory of the Institute. Regardless of political faith, the journal is interesting for a viewpoint rarely found in traditional literary journals. It could be used by most college and university teachers when an effort is made to dramatically examine literature in a political fashion.

Literature and Psychology; a quarterly journal of literature criticism as informed by depth psychology. 1950. q. $8. Morton Kaplan. Dept. of English, Fairleigh Dickinson Univ., Teaneck, N.J. 07666. Index. Circ: 1,000. Sample. Vol. ends: Dec. Refereed. Microform: UM.

Indexed: AbEnSt, MLA. *Bk. rev:* 1–5, 750–1,000 words, signed. *Aud:* Ac.

An innovative interdisciplinary journal whose purpose is to apply the techniques of depth psychology to literary analysis and criticism, while trying to "not do violence to the peculiar life and character of the text." It has a practice of self-criticism and conscious change. An established yet absorbing experiment in interdisciplinary applications.

Modern Fiction Studies; a critical quarterly devoted to criticism, scholarship and bibliography of American, English, and European fiction since about 1880. 1955. q. $5. William P. Stafford. Purdue Univ., Dept. of English, Lafayette, Ind. 47907. Circ: 4,000. Sample. Vol. ends: Winter. Refereed. Microform: UM. Reprint: Kraus.

Indexed: MLA; SSHum. *Bk. rev:* 20–25, 500 words. *Aud:* Ac.

Each issue contains six to eight signed scholarly articles of from 2,500 to 7,000 words. Works of fiction, writers, or problems in fictional technique are covered in two of the four issues. The other two are devoted to a series of articles on an individual novelist, followed by a checklist of criticism by the editor. Book reviews appear in the "Newsletter" section of the two issues not devoted to individual novelists. They cover primarily American and British, and occasionally continental, fiction and special subjects. Useful in almost any type or size academic library, and in high schools with advanced literature programs. See also *Nineteenth-Century Fiction.*

Modern Language Notes/MLN. 1886. bi-m. $15. Elias Rivers. The Johns Hopkins Press, Baltimore, Md. 21218. Index, adv. Circ: 1,890. Sample. Vol. ends: Dec. Microform: UM. Reprint: Johnson.

Indexed: SSHum. *Bk. rev:* 10–12, 600 words, signed. *Aud:* Ac.

Publishes articles of literary criticism and discussions of problems in criticism of comparative literature. Each volume contains six issues devoted, in order of publication, to Italian, Spanish, German, French, again German, and comparative literature. All types and periods of the national literature are considered. Articles are generally original and critical. There is an emphasis on critical theory, and the history and problems of criticism. Occasionally the results of textual research are presented. Generally four to six articles appear in each issue, averaging 6,000 words each. Review articles and a section of short notes presenting literary research and linguistics also appear. Only for large collections.

New Literary History. 1969. $8. 3/yr. Ralph Cohen. Wilson Hall, Univ. of Virginia, Charlottesville, Va. 22903. Illus., index. Circ: 1,200. Sample. Vol. ends: Spring. Refereed.

Indexed: AbEnSt. *Aud:* Ac.

This journal features "articles on theory of literature . . . articles from other disciplines that help interpret or define the problems of literary history and articles on the rationale and function of literary history in the college and university." The focus is upon English and American literature and, as stated in the preface, articles on other disciplines are accepted. Therefore, the scope is quite wide, allowing the journal to treat such topics as form, philosophy of time, and style, along with its narrower coverage of literary history. Recommended for academic libraries. (H.D.)

Nineteenth-Century Fiction. 1945. q. $6. G. B. Tennyson. Univ. of California Press, Berkeley, Calif. 94720. Index. Circ: 2,600. Sample. Vol. ends: March. Refereed. Reprint: AMS.

Indexed: HistAb, MLA; SSHum. *Bk. rev:* 3–10, 1,200 words. *Aud:* Ac.

Covers English and American fiction of the entire nineteenth century. The critical and bibliographic studies cover both major and minor figures. The reviewing section occasionally prints "notes" or spirited discussions following from the reviews. The book reviews are specialized and critical. An obvious consideration for any academic library where nineteenth

century studies are a strong consideration in the curriculum.

Notes and Queries; for readers and writers, collectors and librarians. 1849. m. $10.50. J. C. Maxwell and E. G. Stanley. Oxford Univ. Press, Ely House, 37 Dover St., London, WI, England. Index. Circ: 1,750. Vol. ends: Dec. Microform: UM.

Indexed: BritHum, SSHum. *Bk. rev:* 6–16, 800 words. *Aud:* Sa, Ac.

Contains information on source materials, bibliographic data. English genealogy and heraldry, lexicography, textual emendations, literary parallels, etc., are included. Each month's issue is devoted to a particular literary period, which is announced in advance in the "Memorabilia" section. Queries about literary and historical subjects are also included, with answers appearing in later issues. *American Notes & Queries* employs the same approach, only with more emphasis on queries from the United States. Both magazines provide excellent means of tracing an elusive quotation or bit of information. While both are written primarily for the scholar, the reference desk of any medium to large-sized academic or public library should be aware of these publications.

Novel: A Forum on Fiction. 1967. 3/yr. $4.50. Edward Bloom. Box 1984, Brown Univ., Providence, R.I. 02912. Index. Circ: 1,500. Sample. Vol. ends: Spring. Refereed.

Bk. rev: 6–10 joint reviews; 6–15, 1,000 words; notes; signed. *Aud:* Ac, Hs.

Opposed to the usual pedantic dullness of literary studies, this concentrates on presenting six to eight articles on all aspects of fiction—primarily by popular scholars such as Carlos Baker and Leslie Fielder. The reviews are divided into two sections: the first built around a common theme, e.g., "Three Americans" and "Visions and Epistles," and the second around perceptive notes on recent fiction. All libraries will find the reviews helpful, and imaginative teachers will discover much here to spark a dull class. One of the few literary journals which can be used for high schools, and should be found in most professional collections.

PMLA. 1884. 6/yr. Membership (Libraries $25). William David Schaefer. Modern Language Assn. of America, 62 Fifth Ave., New York, N.Y. 10011. Index, adv. Circ: 34,000. Sample. Vol. ends: Nov. Refereed. Microform: UM. Reprint: Kraus.

Indexed: SSHum. *Aud:* Ac. Jv: V.

As the journal of the MLA, *PMLA* presents "the most distinguished contemporary scholarship and criticism in the modern languages and literatures." Unmatched in scholarship and authority, its articles serve researchers and teachers of literature. The journal is issued quarterly with two added numbers. Each regular issue contains from 15 to 20 articles with professional news and notes and a section of critical comment. More than one critic has accused it of being exceedingly dull, particularly as emphasis is on esoteric literary and critical matters of interest only to the most dedicated scholar. Its large circulation seems more due to the sponsor than the content, and the bibliographic data more than the style. The two yearly supplements contain the directory and the program. Both feature articles and addresses on language education. No large library can afford to be without a subscription.

Papers on Language and Literature; a quarterly journal. 1965. q. $7. Nicholas Joost. Southern Illinois Univ., Edwardsville, Ill. 62025. Circ: 1,000. Sample. Vol. ends: Fall. Refereed.

Indexed: MLA. *Bk. rev:* 1–6, 800 words. *Aud:* Ac.

Deals with English, American, and the various European literatures. Literary history, analysis, stylistics, and evaluation, as well as original materials relating to belles lettres—letters, journals, notebooks, and similar documents. While five to six papers of substantial length fill each issue, a section of brief notes also appears. Special features include review essays, which appear in alternate issues and are devoted to an individual writer. Occasional supplements feature a series of papers on an individual writer or subject. Only for large libraries.

Recovering Literature. 1972. 3/yr. $4.50. Ed. bd., 7343 Draper Ave., LaJolla, Calif. 92037.

Aud: Ac.

What makes this journal, which is devoted mainly to the publication of literary criticism, different from other literary magazines is the nature of its assumptions about literature. As the opening article, "Recovering Fiction," programmatically explains, the prevalent approach to literature assumes, usually tacitly, some form of idealism as the basis of its aesthetic. The editors offer an approach based on an anti-idealistic, specifically a "contextualist" basis, in the sense given it by the aesthetic theorist, Stephen C. Pepper. (F.D.)

Renaissance Quarterly. 1948. q. $16. Elizabeth S. Donno. Renaissance Soc. of America, 1161 Amsterdam Ave., New York, N.Y. 10027. Index, adv. Circ: 3,200. Vol. ends: Winter.

Indexed: ArtI. *Bk. rev:* 25, 650 words, signed. *Aud:* Ac.

A general magazine, limited only to some aspect of Renaissance study. Scholarly articles range from art and music to literature and history. Most of the writing touches on more than one area, and emphasis is on the synthesis of a theory or ideas about a particular period, place, or personality. There are extensive book reviews in each issue, and a bibliography of publications in the field, arranged by subject. In view of its wide interests, it is a must for medium to large-sized academic libraries.

Review of English Studies; a quarterly journal of English literature and the English language. 1925. q. $7.25. J. B. Bamborough. Oxford Univ. Press, Ely House, 37 Dover St., London, W1, England. Index, adv. Circ: 2,400. Sample.

Indexed: BritHum, SSHum. *Bk. rev:* 25–35, 1,000 words, signed. *Aud:* Ac.

A journal which concentrates on detailed and critical reviews. Many of the books are from British presses, but at least one third are scholarly publications from the United States. A few continental titles appear. Each issue contains a "Summary of Periodical Literature" listing the contents of various journals in English literature and philology. Alternate issues contain a "List of Publications Received." Literature of all periods is covered in 3,000 to 4,500 word signed, scholarly articles. While primarily for larger libraries, the reviews may make it worthwhile for smaller libraries where there is a particular need for detailed work in this area.

Review of National Literatures. 1970. s-a. $4. Anne Paolucci. St. John's Univ. Press, St. John's University, Perboyre Hall, Jamaica, N.Y. 11432. Circ: 600. Sample. Vol. ends: Fall. Refereed.

Aud: Ac.

An extremely substantial publication with reverence for the distinctions between literatures. No attempt is made to feature writings of an international or antinational character, adhering to the principle that only diversity reflects the infinite variety of the human mind. Each issue treats a particular theme, or national culture. For instance, one issue is concerned solely with "Hegel in Comparative Literature," another with Machiavelli. Special editors are brought in when the topics become highly specialized, thereby insuring a competent presentation. Recommended for academic and large public libraries with adequate literature collections. (H.D.)

Saint Louis Quarterly. See *Saint Louis University Research Journal.*

Saint Louis University Research Journal (Formerly: *Saint Louis Quarterly*). 1970. q. $9. Cecilia G. Muller. St. Louis Univ., Baguio City B-202, Philippines. Illus., adv. Circ: 1,500. Sample.

Indexed: MLA. *Bk. rev:* 10, 200 words, signed. *Aud:* Ac.

A Catholic university literary magazine of more than passing interest because it publishes outstanding material by both Filipino lay and religious writers. Emphasis is on research in literature, philosophy, language, history, and a limited amount of theology. Book reviews are perceptive, and cover all aspects of literature, history, and education. The level of writing is uniformly high.

Speculum; a journal of medieval studies. 1926. q. Membership (Nonmembers $18). Paul J. Meyvaert. Medieval Academy of Amer., 1430 Massachusetts Ave., Cambridge, Mass. 02138. Index, adv. Circ: 5,300. Sample. Refereed. Vol. ends: Oct. Microform: UM.

Indexed: ArtI, SSHum. *Bk. rev:* 30–40, lengthy, signed. *Aud:* Ac, Ga. *Jv:* V.

An interdisciplinary approach to history, art, music, literature, in fact, anything within a medieval scholar's interest. Emphasis is on literature and linguistics. Each issue contains several monographs, and all of these are of a uniformly high quality. The subject matter may be a trifle esoteric for the general reader, but frequently the writing style is as brilliant as the scholarship. Possibly of more importance to the librarian is the feature *Bibliography of American Periodical Literature.* Under various names, this has appeared in the journal since 1934. It consists of a classified arrangement of articles on medieval subjects from journals published in North America. There are also extensive book reviews and a regular listing of books received. A basic magazine for the academic or large public library.

Studies in English Literature 1500–1900. 1961. q. $8 (Individuals $6). Carroll Camden. Rice Univ., Houston, Tex. 77001. Index. Circ: 1,500. Sample. Vol. ends: Autumn. Refereed. Microform: UM. Reprint: Johnson.

Indexed: MLA, SSHum. *Bk. rev:* 25, 6,000 words, signed. *Aud:* Ac.

A scholarly journal with each seasonal issue devoted to a particular period and genre of English literature: "Nondramatic Prose and Poetry of the English Renaissance" (Winter); "Elizabethan and Jacobean Drama" (Spring); "Restoration and Eighteenth Century" (Summer); "Nineteenth Century" (Autumn). There are 10 to 12 articles of moderate length, which present the results of historical research, are concerned with matters of interpretation, and offer conclusions which involve scholarly criticism. Each number contains a review covering the significant scholarship of the year in the area of the issue's concentration. While primarily for the advanced scholar, the bibliographic feature gives it an added dimension for all teachers from the junior college to the university level.

Studies in the Literary Imagination. 1968. irreg. free. Paul G. Blount. Dept. of English, Georgia State Univ., Atlanta, Ga. 30303. Circ: 3,500. Sample. Vol. ends: March.

Aud: Ac.

A scholarly journal devoted to literature with slight emphasis on the manifestations of the literary imagination, not only in writing itself, but in other media. For instance, one article is on "Bacon's Use of Theatrical Imagery." However, no real attempt is made to ad-

here to this very specialized goal. In the two issues examined, both were devoted to a single author. The content is substantial and well documented. Recommended for academic libraries with adequate literature collections. (H.D.)

Studies in Romanticism. 1961. q. $6.50. W. H. Stevenson, 236 Bay State Rd., Boston, Mass. 02115. Index. Circ: 1,200. Sample. Vol. ends: Nov. Refereed.

Indexed: AbEnSt, MLA, SSHum. *Aud:* Ac.

Published by the Graduate School of the Boston University, the subject matter is more specific than its name implies. Its first concern is English literature of the period, and its second is poetry, particularly that of Byron and Shelley. Each issue has three to five long scholarly articles on Romantic literature and thought. A degree of familiarity is required to read it intelligently.

Studies in Short Fiction. 1963. q. $8. Frank L. Hoskins. Newberry College, Newberry, S.C. 29108. Index. Circ: 1,045. Sample. Vol. ends: Dec. Refereed.

Indexed: AbEnSt, MLA. *Bk. rev:* 12, 350 words, signed. *Aud:* Ac, Hs.

Devoted to filling a major gap left by the standard journals of literature, which are preoccupied with the longer-established forms of writing. Each issue has several long articles, frequently showing a special concern with the history of the short story, but not ignoring contemporary contributions to the form. Book reviews include coverage of recent anthologies and collections. Can be used to supplement high school English courses.

Sub-Stance. 1971. 3/yr. $4. Michel Pierssens. Dept. of French and Italian, Univ. of Wisconsin, 618 Van Hise, Madison, Wis. 53706.

Aud: Ac.

A loosely structured but highly disciplined journal of inquiry, interpretation, and criticism. Among the questions considered are: "Qu'est-ce que la litterature?" "What is criticism?" "To what extent is literature political?" Editors and contributors attempt to determine the extent to which methods of inquiry from other disciplines—especially the social sciences—can be applied to literary problems. According to the "Presentation" to the first issue, *Sub-Stance* will stress a collective approach to literary study, even though views of individual contributors may be quite divergent. "A dialectical approach . . . fundamental in formulating, testing, and correcting ideas . . ." is also emphasized, and importance is given to the recognition of ". . . the theoretical bases of . . . approaches to literature. . . ." Among the articles are critical pieces on Marcel Proust, Max Jacob, and Stendhal by faculty members Jonathan Botelho, Sydney Levy, and William J. Berg and an analysis of Francis Ponge's work by doctoral student

Stephani Smith. Readers should find Editor Michel Pierssens' *Commentaire* on French literary periodicals especially interesting and informative. (H.W.)

Symposium; a quarterly journal in modern foreign literatures. 1946. q. $6. J. H. Matthews. Syracuse Univ. Press, Box 87, Univ. Station, Syracuse, N.Y. 13210. Adv. Circ: 750. Reprint: Kraus.

Indexed: SSHum. *Bk. rev:* 2–5, 1,200 words, signed. *Aud:* Ac.

A scholarly journal devoted primarily to modern foreign literature. The five to eight articles, of moderate length, are generally written by American scholars. Dramatists, novelists, and poets are covered in the articles. Many of the substantial reviews, some of them remarkably thorough, are written by members of the editorial board. An occasional review of critical writings about one author appears in the "Book Review" section. An annual feature, usually in the Fall issue, is the bibliography "Relations of Literature and Science: Selected Bibliography for——." Text is mainly in English but includes French, German, and Spanish; less often, Portuguese, Italian, Russian, Modern Greek, and Arabic. Useful for both literature and foreign language collections in large academic libraries.

Texas Studies in Literature and Languages; a journal of the humanities. 1911. q. $8. Ernest J. Lovell, Jr. Univ. of Texas, Austin, Tex. 78712. Index. Circ: 800. Refereed. Reprint: Johnson.

Aud: Ac.

A scholarly journal featuring articles on the humanities. Emphasis is on English and American literature, language, philosophy, and fine arts. A few articles consider continental literature and social studies. The eight to ten articles may be critical, textual, bibliographic, or explicative. Contributors are international. Somewhat esoteric, and only for the large academic library.

Tulane Studies in English. 1949. a. $3. English Dept., Tulane Univ., New Orleans, La. 70118.

Aud: Ac.

Studies in English and American literature from Beowulf to contemporary. Articles are primarily by the Tulane faculty, a bit esoteric, yet of value to the professor or the graduate student. One of the best for medium to large-sized English collections, and required for larger, graduate programs.

Twentieth Century Literature; a scholarly and critical journal. 1955. q. $4. Fallon Evans. IHC Press, 2021 N. Western Ave., Los Angeles, Calif. 90027. Index, adv. Circ: 1,750. Refereed.

Indexed: SSHum. *Aud:* Ac.

Covers twentieth century authors of all nations, particularly those out of favor or overlooked by the tradi-

tional literary journal. Scholarly articles examine essays, novels, poetry, and all forms of literature. Its "Current Bibliography" is an abstract of periodical articles on twentieth century literature that have appeared in American, British, and European journals. Due to its frequency, it nicely augments the annual MLA *Bibliography*, and is useful for its relative currency. A major journal for any large academic or specialized literature collection in this field.

Victorian Studies; a journal of the humanities, arts and sciences. 1957. q. $12 (Individuals $7). Martha Vicinus. Ballantine Hall, Indiana Univ., Bloomington, Ind. 47401. Illus., index, adv. Circ: 3,100. Vol. ends: June.

Indexed: AbEnSt, SSHum. *Bk. rev:* 16–20, essays and notes, signed. *Aud:* Ac.

Covers all aspects of the so-called Victorian age (1830–1914) in terms of literature, social activities, and political and scientific achievements. For example, one issue was devoted to "The Victorian Woman," included five articles by scholars who discussed the governess, the debate over women by Ruskin and Mill, and feminine stereotypes. The book reviews cover as many topics as the articles, and are among the best published in this field. One issue a year is dedicated to an annual bibliography, prepared by a committee of the Victorian Literature Group of the Modern Language Association. Typographically, the 130-page journal is superior. An impressive scholarly effort, on all counts. Recommended for almost any medium to large-sized academic collection.

Author Newsletters and Journals

The academic biographical newsletters (and some journals) listed in this section constitute a special kind of "little" magazine in English and American literary periodicals. The present list concentrates on authors and periods in English and American literature. These newsletter/journals ordinarily do not exist long enough to have been reprinted or indexed in standard sources. Indeed, when they become large enough and circulation increases, they drop the newsletter designation and become full-fledged journals—and some of those journals are included here. Yet often the most current information about seminars, special studies, and bibliography is contained in these small periodicals. Back issues may be obtained, when available, by writing directly to editors. (E.W.)

Blackmore Studies. 1969. s-a. Membership $5. Blackmore Soc., 24 Linhope St., London NW1, England. Illus. index, adv. Circ: 600.

Bk. rev: Notes and essays, signed. *Aud:* Ac.

Covers all aspects of the life and times of Richard D. Blackmore (1825–1900). Articles tend to be scholarly, a trifle dull.

Blake Newsletter. 1966. q. $3. Morton D. Paley. Dept. of English, Univ. of California, Berkeley, Calif. 94704. Illus., index. Vol. ends: July

Bk. rev: 1–3, 500 words. *Aud:* Ac.

This is a mimeographed periodical of about 30 pages giving coverage to special William Blake studies, seminars, dissertations in progress, and also printing briefer articles and reviews of interest to Blake scholars. Primarily for genuine Blake readers. (E.W.)

Blake Studies. 1968. s-a. $5. Kay Parkhurst Easson and Roger R. Easson. Illinois State Univ., Dept. of English, Normal, Ill. 61761. Illus., index. Circ: 700. Microform: UM.

Indexed: AbEnSt. *Bk. rev:* Various number, length. *Aud:* Ac.

Unlike the *Blake Newsletter,* this is a rather substantial effort to publish articles by and about William Blake, his work and his times. The journal includes numerous long pieces and excellent book reviews. It would be a first choice, but anyone who is involved with Blake should take both.

Browning Newsletter. 1968. s-a. $3. Warner Barnes. Armstrong Browning Library, Box 6336, Baylor Univ., Waco, Tex. 76706. Circ: 350.

Bk. rev: 3, 600 words, signed. *Aud:* Ac. *Jv:* V.

Because of the importance of the Brownings, most libraries would find these typical issues containing a wide range of useful material. The journal attempts, as the editors say, "to include a review of the year's research for Robert and Elizabeth Barrett Browning, book reviews of all books concerning the Brownings and their circle, research in progress, notes and queries, unpublished letters, poems, desiderata, checklists of acquisitions of research materials by libraries throughout the world, announcements of library exhibits, catalogues, speeches, symposiums, and the like." In the strictest sense, this is a major journal, but still carries the title of *Newsletter.* Carefully compiled, attractive item. (E.W.)

Cabellian; a journal of the second American Renaissance. 1968. s-a. $7. Julius Rothman. James Branch Cabell Soc., 75 Noble St., Lynbrook, N.Y. 11563. Illus., index. Circ: 300. Microform: UM.

Indexed: MLA. *Bk. rev:* 2–3, length varies, signed. *Aud:* Ac.

Includes both short and long articles on all aspects of James B. Cabell's life, works, and times. Articles tend to be esoteric, deal with critical and biographical points. Some bibliographies. (E.W.)

Carleton Newsletter. 1970. q. Inquire. Eileen S. Ibarra, Logic Dept., Univ. of Florida, Gainesville, Fla.

Bk. rev: Occasional, brief. *Aud:* Ac. *Jv:* C.

Largely esoteric material relating to the Irish writer, William Carleton. (E.W.)

The Chaucer Review. 1966. q. $7.50. Robert W. Frank, Jr. Pennsylvania State Univ. Press, 215 Wagner Bldg., University Park, Pa. 16802. Index, adv. Circ: 1,100. Sample. Vol. ends: Spring. Refereed.

Indexed: MLA. *Aud:* Ac. *Jv:* V.

"A journal of medieval studies and literary criticism . . . published with the cooperation of the Chaucer group of the Modern Language Association." In scholarly fashion, the publication concerns itself with Chaucer in his proper historical context. Therefore, it treats medieval studies in literature as well as its narrower objective of Chaucer study. There is a yearly report (bibliography) on Chaucer. The contributors to this report, as well as the authors of the main articles, are usually Americans though information submitted by others is not excluded. For academic libraries and large public libraries. (H.D.)

Conradiana. 1967. 3/yr. $4. Daniel E. Lees. Texas Tech. Univ., Box 4229, Lubbock, Tex. 79409. Illus., index, adv. Circ: 700. Vol. ends: Sept. Refereed. Microform: UM.

Indexed: AbEnSt. *Bk. rev:* 3, 2 pages, signed. *Aud:* Ac.

A substantial journal, not a newsletter. This covers all aspects of Joseph Conrad's life and times and works. A good deal of the material appears to be much more lively, and even more controversial, than that found in many journals of this type. Good reviews, and numerous notes and queries.

Crane Newsletter. 1966. 4/yr. $3. Joseph Katz. Dept. of English, Univ. of South Carolina, Columbia, S.C.

Bk. rev: Number varies, brief. *Aud:* Ac.

A particularly useful little journal because of constant use of original Stephen Crane facsimiles. Editor has extensive collection of Crane materials some of which he reprints in each issue. (E.W.)

Dickens Studies Newsletter. 1970. q. Robert Partlow. Southern Illinois Univ., Dept. of English, Carbondale, Ill. 62901.

Indexed: AbEnSt. *Bk. rev:* 3–4, length varies, signed. *Aud:* Ac.

Somewhat more serious and more involved with criticism than the older, better-known *Dickensian.* It is useful because of frequent notes on activities, personalities, new works, studies, etc. in the field of Dickens. If this develops, it will better serve graduate students (although not common readers) than *Dickensian.* (E.W.)

Dickensian. 1905. 3/yr. $6.75. Leslie C. Staples. Dickens Fellowship, 48 Doughty St., London WC1, England. Illus., index, adv. Circ: 2,250.

Aud: Ga, Ac.

The longest-established journal devoted to an English novelist, this literary magazine is the best of its type. The *Dickensian* boasts substantial issues of estimable quality, and while contributors in the past years have been scholars, there is an indication that more amateur Dickens fans will be involved.

Emily Dickinson Bulletin. 1968. q. $5. Frederick L. Morey, 4508 38th St., Brentwood, Md. 20722.

Bk. rev: Various number, length. *Aud:* Ac.

Covers all aspects of Emily Dickinson's work and life. Articles may be from two to ten pages; are usually by teachers and graduate students. The writing style is a bit livelier than that found in other bulletins and newsletters of this type. Again, though, its primary value is to keep the Dickinson scholar alerted to activities in the field.

Dreiser Newsletter. 1970. bi-a. $2.50/four issues. John Brady. English Dept., Indiana State Univ., Terre Haute, Ind. 47809.

Aud: Ac.

A general newsletter which usually has one essay-length book review. The spring issue includes an annual checklist of William Dreiser scholarship. (E.W.) (E.W.)

✓**Emerson Society Quarterly; journal of the American Renaissance.** 1955. q. $13. Kenneth W. Cameron. Emerson Soc., Drawer 1080, Hartford, Conn. 06101. Illus., index.

Indexed: AbEnSt, MLA. *Bk. rev:* Essays, signed. *Aud:* Ac.

Although much of the material in the journal has direct reference to Emerson, it also includes articles and notes on his contemporaries, e.g., Thoreau and the Concord School. Beyond that, it is a literary journal with long, sometimes tedious and not particularly clarifying reports on everything from transcendentalism to the romantic movement. Only for larger collections.

Anales Galdosianos. 1966. a. $6. Rodolfo Cardona. Dept. of Spanish and Portuguese. Univ. of Texas, Austin, Tex. 78712. Illus., index. Circ: 600.

Bk. rev: Various number, length. *Aud:* Ac.

A 150 or so page annual with articles in both Spanish and English. The editor sums up the scope and purpose: "Devoted to articles, book reviews, documents and bibliography on and about the life and works of the 19th century Spanish novelist Benito Pérez Galdós. We also publish texts and documents related to the intellectual history of Galdós' Spain (1840–1920), and beginning with the 1969 issue we have published an exhaustive bibliography confined to work and notices on and about Galdós."

Gissing Newsletter. 1965. q. $3. Pierre Coustillas, C. C. Kohler, 141 High St., Dorking, Surrey, England. Circ: 180.

Aud: Ac. *Jv:* C.

This newsletter is very brief and prints only items pertaining to George Gissing. Attractive format, however. (E.W.)

Hopkins Research Bulletin. 1970. a. $1. Hopkins Secretariate, 114 Mount St., London WLY 6AH, England.

Aud: Ac.

A 26-page newsletter which includes news of research, bibliographic items, and short notes, pertaining to G. M. Hopkins. (E.W.)

Robinson Jeffers Newsletter. 1960. q. $4. Robert J. Brophy. Occidental College Library, 1600 Campus Rd., Los Angeles, Calif. 90041.

Aud: Ac.

Averaging some 10 to 15 offset pages, the newsletter is primarily made up of brief notes, news of meetings and personalities, reports on acquisitions, etc. Books, articles, and monographs on Robinson Jeffers are duly reviewed. The whole is professionally edited and nicely put together. Librarian Tryus Harmsen says that backfiles of the newsletter are available to libraries for $25.

Johnsonian Newsletter. 1940. m. $2.50. J. L. Clifford. Philosophy Hall, Columbia Univ., New York, N.Y. 10027. Index. Circ: 1,100. Reprint: Johnson.

Aud: Ac.

Prints notes, new books notices, and bibliographic items about both eighteenth century studies and Johnson. The first so-called newsletter printed in the United States and still one of the most ably done. *New Rambler* is another item in the field, but it is published in England.

New Rambler. 1941. s-a. Membership (Nonmembers $3.50). James H. Leicester. Johnson Soc. of London, Broadmead, Eynsford Rd., Farningham, Kent, England. Illus., index, adv. Circ: 350.

Indexed: AbEnSt. *Bk. rev:* Essays and notes, signed. *Aud:* Ac.

This is similar to the American publication, differs only in that the material tends to be a trifle more popular—at least is presented with considerably more humor.

✓**James Joyce Quarterly.** 1963. q. $5. Thomas F. Staley. Univ. of Tulsa, Tulsa, Okla. 74104. Illus., index, adv. Circ: 900. Vol. ends: Summer. Refereed.

Indexed: AbEnSt. *Bk. rev:* 2–6, 1,500 words, signed. *Aud:* Ac.

In addition to its main purpose of reporting Joyce research and criticism, certain issues are regularly devoted to Samuel Beckett and Sean O'Casey. Current information on what is happening professionally in Joycean circles is included in each issue, as well as signed book reviews. The journal also seeks to make available worthwhile foreign contributions on Joyce through translation. Not a large periodical, but competent. Recommended for university collections. (H.D.)

A somewhat more limited approach to Joyce is offered in the *A Wake Newslitter* (1962. 6/yr. $3. Clive Hart and Fritz Senn. Dept. of English, Univ. of Dundee, Dundee DD1 4HN, Scotland. Circ: 550. Sample. Vol. ends: Dec.). The 12-page "newslitter" is principally concerned with exegesis of Joyce's *Finnegans Wake*. From time to time it publishes notes and articles on Joyce's other works.

Kipling Journal. 1927. q. $3.50. L. Green. Kipling Soc., 18 Northumberland Ave., London, WC2, England. Illus., index. Circ: 900.

Bk. rev: Notes. *Aud:* Ga, Ac.

Although large in neither format nor content, the material here is quite readable. There is more emphasis on Kipling than on scholarly research and criticism. In fact, a good part of it can be read with interest by anyone who simply enjoys Kipling. (E.W.)

D. H. Lawrence Review. 1968. 3/yr. $3. James C. Cowan and Foster Park. Univ. of Arkansas, Box 1799, Fayetteville, Ark. 72701.

Indexed: AbEnSt. *Bk. rev:* Notes and essays, signed. *Aud:* Ac.

A combination of notes and queries and serious journal. It publishes a few long critical articles on Lawrence, but most of the material is shorter. Content is particularly involved with criticism and news of Lawrence studies, books, monographs, etc. Hence, it is an excellent method of keeping up with Lawrence works.

Lewis Newsletter. 1969. Irreg. $1. James Lundquist. St. Cloud State College, St. Cloud, Minn.

Bk. rev: Number varies, brief. *Aud:* Ac. *Jv:* C.

Because the journal is very small and thoroughly devoted to Sinclair Lewis minutia, it is recommended for most graduate libraries only. Well written, useful material, however. (E.W.)

London Newsletter. 1967. 3/yr. $2.50. Hensley C. Woodbridge. Southern Illinois Univ., Carbondale, Ill. 62901. Circ: 120.

Bk. rev: Various number, length. *Aud:* Ac, Hs.

Primarily a journal of Jack London criticism, this periodical also prints a current Jesse Stuart bibliography. In very recent years academic interest in London has swelled. A good deal of original material—unpublished letters, notes and other London items—is published here. Since London remains a popular writer for juvenile and adolescent studies, this newsletter may be particularly useful in some high school libraries. (E.W.)

Markham Review. 1968. 3/yr. Free. Joseph W. Slade. Horrmann Library, Wagner College, Staten Island, N.Y. 10301.

Indexed: AbEnSt. *Bk. rev:* Essays and notes, signed. *Aud:* Ac.

Dedicated to historical and critical material on Edwin Markham and authors of his period, i.e., 1865–1940. Primarily for scholars. (Check the "free"; by the time this is published the journal may have a charge.)

Menckeniana. 1962. q. $2. Betty Adler. Enoch Pratt Free Library, Baltimore, Md. 21210.

Indexed: AbEnSt, MLA. *Bk. rev:* Notes and essays, various length, signed. *Aud:* Ac.

A general quarterly which deals with all aspects of H. L. Mencken and his world. The material ranges from the scholarly to the popular, from the literary to the historical. Nicely edited, and can be enjoyed by anyone interested in Mencken and his times.

Mill News Letter. 1965. s-a. Free. John M. Robson. Univ. of Toronto Press, Toronto, 5, Ont. Canada.

Indexed: AbEnSt. *Bk. rev:* Notes. *Aud:* Ac.

A free newsletter of material about John Stuart Mill and friends. Articles are short, and the primary value of the letter is to keep scholars up to date on new items published about Mill, scholarship in the field, and bibliographies.

Milton Quarterly. 1966. q. $4. Roy C. Flannagan. English Dept., Ohio Univ., Athens, Ohio 45701. Illus., index. Circ: 900. Sample. Vol. ends: Dec.

Aud: Ac.

A handsome 26-page newsletter which includes two to three major articles on John Milton by such scholars as William Parker, Irene Damuel and Joseph Summers. Aside from the articles, the magazine is useful for libraries because it: (1) reviews current books in the subject area; (2) abstracts major articles from periodicals; (3) on occasion includes a bibliography on some aspect of Milton. An invaluable research aid.

(Nin) Under the Sign of Pisces: Anais Nin and Her Circle. 1970. q. $2. Publns. Committee, The Ohio State Univ. Libraries, 1858 Neil Ave., Columbus, Ohio 43210.

Aud: Ac.

This contains articles on Anais Nin, her work, and her "circle," which includes Henry Miller, Antonin Artaud, Lawrence Durrell, Otto Rank, and many others. It reports all kinds of news relating to her, such as notes and tips on new things coming out, pertinent films, interviews, old editions, hard to find articles, exhibits, and reviews. A very exciting and essential newsletter to Anais Nin followers, and particularly important for academic libraries where research on her and the others is likely to be done. (M.P.W.)

Poe Newsletter. 1968. 2–3/yr. $2.50. G. R. Thompson. Washington State Univ., Pullman, Wash. 99163. Circ: 1,000.

Indexed: AbEnSt. *Bk. rev:* Number varies, brief. *Aud:* Ac, Hs.

Because of the inclusion of Edgar Allan Poe in most high school American literature units, this journal may have special appeal to high school libraries as well as to college and university collections. Carefully edited, scholarly production. (E.W.)

Russell: the journal of the Bertrand Russell archives. 1971. q. $2. Bertrand Russell Archives, McMaster Univ. Library, Hamilton, Ont., Canada.

Aud: Ac.

Much of what Russell wrote and a good deal of related material has now, through the purchase of his library and papers by Will Ready of McMaster, been made available to scholars and the general public alike. (Ready, of course, is a man of letters himself, obviously also a collector of genius.) The purpose of the 12 to 16 page journal, according to its editor, is primarily bibliographic, as the putting in order of the collection—a task that will evidently require years of attention—is to be reported in detail. It is suggested, however, that articles will appear before long that deal with Russell himself and with his contribution to the civilization of the day. There are, as a matter of fact, a couple of very short articles of this sort in the first issue. (P.G.)

Shakespeare Newsletter. 1951. 6/yr. (Sept.–May). $2. Louis Marder. Dept. of English, Univ. of Illinois at Chicago Circle, Chicago, Ill. 60680. Index, adv. Circ: 1,800. Sample. Reprint: Johnson.

Bk. rev: Various number, length. *Aud:* Ac.

Contains reports on conferences and current productions; international coverage, with special emphasis on writings of English and German Shakespearean scholars; short articles on Shakespeare and related drama, history, social life, etc.; brief biographies of Shakespearean scholars; reprints, digests, and reviews of journal articles and book reviews; a list of books received; and queries. Advertising is plentiful and provides information on forthcoming books, etc.

Shakespeare Quarterly. 1950. q. Membership (Nonmembers $10). James G. McManaway. Shakespeare Assn. of Amer., Inc., Box 2653, Grand Central Sta., New York, N.Y. 10017. Illus., index. Circ: 2,500. Vol. ends: Autumn. Reprint: AMS.

Indexed: SSHum. *Bk. rev:* 6–12, 600 words, signed. *Aud:* Sa, Ac.

Generally contains six to eight critical articles by Shakespearean scholars, and is one of the few scholarly journals with illustrations. Articles are concerned with all phases of Shakespeare's life and work. Reviews of

festivals and the London and New York State productions are an annual feature. The Renaissance period in general is covered in the book reviews. "Queries and Notes" also appear. Only for large libraries.

Shakespearean Research and Opportunities. 1955. a. $6 (Individuals $3.) W. R. Elton. Grad. Center of the City Univ. of New York, 33 W. 42nd St., New York, N.Y. 10036. Index. Sample.

Bk. rev: 1, 8 pages, signed. *Aud:* Ac.

This publication is designed for the real Shakespearean *engagé*, and had originally two main functions: reporting the annual MLA conference "Opportunities for Research in Shakespearean Studies," and compiling the annual international "Work in Progress." It also includes topics of direct relevance to Shakespeare, such as artistic and intellectual contexts, special bibliographies, and checklists. A unique feature is the annual annotated selective bibliography "Shakespeare and Renaissance Intellectual Contexts." This has run to over 80 printed pages, and includes all areas of Renaissance interest. It embraces books, articles, and dissertations in all western languages. The journal is thus of primary use to any student of Renaissance thought and culture. The bibliography allows a quick scanning of materials in almost all fields; it also includes a list of themes, *topoi*, emblems, etc., as well as research tools which have appeared during the year. The aim is thus maximum utility for the working Renaissance and Shakespearean student and critic.

Shaw Review. 1951. 3/yr. $5. Stanley Weintraub. Pennsylvania State Univ. Press, University Park, Pa., 16802. Illus., index. Circ: 600. Microform: UM.

Indexed: AbEnSt. *Bk. rev:* Various number, length, signed. *Aud:* Ac.

A substantial effort to keep up with studies about the life, times, and work of Bernard Shaw. The journal generally succeeds. It is particularly useful for its reviews and bibliographies. The articles are fair, range over a wide field.

Spenser Newsletter. 1970. 3/yr. $2 (If invoiced, $3). Elizabeth Bieman, David Kaula. Dept. of English, Univ. of Western Ontario, London 72, Ont., Canada.

Bk. rev: 6–8, 100–200 words, signed. *Aud:* Ac.

Endorsed by the Renaissance Society of America, this is a well-written and edited newsletter which is of invaluable aid to students of Edmund Spenser, as well as those studying in the same period of English literature. (E.W.)

Steinbeck Quarterly. 1968. 4/yr. $6. T. Hayashi. John Steinbeck Soc., English Dept., Ball State Univ., Muncie, Ind. 47304. Index. Circ: 200.

Bk. rev: Various number, length, signed. *Aud:* Ac.

A good deal of material in what was once a newsletter but has graduated to a journal is involved with Steinbeck, the man and his works. There has been an effort to keep the material concise and meaningful. Particularly valuable to librarians: an annual bibliographic issue on Steinbeck and related areas and subjects.

Stevens Newsletter. 1969. s-a. $4/2 yr. W. T. Ford. Northwestern Univ. Library, Evanston, Ill. 60201. Illus. Circ: 300.

Indexed: AbEnSt, MLA. *Bk. rev:* Notes. *Aud:* Ac.

Considers the life, time, and works of Wallace Stevens. Primary interest, though, is with the poet and his work. Bibliographies are published annually. Too academic for anyone but the scholar. (E.W.)

Thoreau Journal Quarterly. 1969. q. $3. Mary P. Sherwood. Thoreau Fellowship, Box 551, Old Town, Maine 04468. Illus.

Indexed: AbEnSt. *Aud:* Ac, Ga.

A popular approach to Thoreau and his ideas. Short articles and notes, as well as original material on everything from conservation to Emerson.

Thoreau Society Bulletin: devoted to the life and writing of Henry David Thoreau. 1941. q. Membership (Nonmembers $2). Walter Harding. Thoreau Soc., Inc., State Univ. College, Geneseo, N.Y. 14454. Illus. Circ: 1,000. Microform: UM.

Indexed: AbEnSt. *Bk. rev:* Various number, length. *Aud:* Ac, Ga.

Primarily concerned with short reports on Thoreau. Some criticism is induced, and there is a minimum of footnotes and scholarship per se. The writing style is lively, usually interesting, and the *Bulletin* is almost as much for the layman as for the student. The *Thoreau Journal Quarterly* gives an even more folksy approach.

✓*Mark Twain Journal.* 1936. s-a. $3. Cyril Clemens. Kirkwood, Mo. 63122. Illus., index, adv.

Aud: Ac, Ga.

A nice combination of the popular with the scholarly. An average issue features both critical and biographical articles. It seems meant more for the layman than the scholar, but both will enjoy it.

Waugh Newsletter. 1966. q. $2.50. P. A. Doyle. Dept. of English, Nassau Community College, Garden City, N.Y. 11530.

Aud: Ac.

Recommended only for graduate collections because of limited specialists' interest for students of Evelyn Waugh. Solicits brief notes and news items. (E.W.)

✓*Walt Whitman Review.* 1955. q. $4. William White and Charles E. Feinberg. Wayne State Univ. Press, 5980 Cass, Detroit, Mich. 48202. Illus., index. Circ: 500.

Bk. rev: 3–4, 250–1,000 words, signed. *Aud:* Ac.

Brief notes, articles, and reviews about Whitman. The tone is scholarly, yet the style of writing is relaxed enough that the *Review* can be enjoyed by the interested layman. Considerable biographical and bibliographic material.

LITTLE MAGAZINES

See also Counterculture, Literary Reviews, and Poetry Sections.

Basic Periodicals

Hs: *The Smith, Spero;* Ga: *The Smith, December, Lillabulero;* Jc: *The Smith, December, Spero, Lillabulero;* Ac: *The Smith, December, Spero, Lillabulero, Quixote, Ghost Dance.*

Basic Abstracts and Indexes

Index to Little Magazines, Index To Commonwealth Little Magazines.

Cessations

Kauri, Manhattan Review, Outsider, Some/Thing, Trace, Fishpaste.

Introduction

There is no completely satisfactory definition of a little magazine. Traditionally any magazine which is mimeographed, less than 1,500 circulation, open to all comers, is issued irregularly, and is on a hazardous financial footing is a little magazine. Much of this applies to other types of magazines, yet "littles" are unique in that they pioneer new forms of writing, give inexperienced or unknown writers an opportunity to publish, and, most important, establish standards of taste based on the editor's individual aesthetics rather than what the general public or the advertiser wants. Finally, readers tend to be confined to that famous group under 30 years of age, or to elders interested enough in the newest forms of expression to push through a rugged and dangerous underbrush containing prejudices that prick, opinions that slash the unwary, along with the splattering at times with the flavor of bad taste, in order to seek the gems which can be found no place else.

Little magazines die rapidly and regularly, or, once successful, they change to literary reviews and find that death called respectability. Success may be defined as a thousand or so subscribers, and someone other than the editor paying the bills. Keep in mind that most of these editors are sincere enough to put their money behind their opinions.

Given these generalizations, the exceptions may be

noted. A few have large circulations; an increasing number are going offset; many set severe standards for acceptance, and even pay authors moderate amounts; some regularly meet publishing schedules; and almost all will inevitably include poetry or prose by an older literary figure who for one reason or another has yet to be welcomed into the literary establishment.

The difficulty of categorization or definition best explains the typical little magazine. It is an adventure in thought—an adventure not all readers will enjoy, but one which they should at least be aware of. While many devote enormous effort to proclaim the lunatic workings of society, they are also publishing now the next generation of the literary establishment and are shaping the techniques and forms which will prevail through the next 10 to 20 years. They are published for the young, that obstreperous and ungrateful group not satisfied (as they should be, by rights) with *Reader's Digest* or *Life*.

There are thousands of little magazines, most being on the fringes of colleges and universities. There are many active centers of the movement, such as Cleveland, Buffalo, or Berkeley, as well as the traditional centers in New York City and San Francisco. All of them are good, in that they represent their editor's judgment. And all of them are national, given the revolution in communication. This list has attempted to cover all types, qualities, and degrees of little magazines, and every school of writing. A loose, argumentative panel of younger writers have made suggestions, which were sometimes followed.

It should be noted that many of the little magazines are recommended for high schools. Few—very few—high schools subscribe, which is a pity. Part of the little magazine's natural audience is the brighter, more imaginative high school student. This audience will inevitably be served, whether in the high school library or elsewhere. Their librarians should be more aware.

Little magazines are labors of love. Among their editors is an ill-founded belief that if their individual magazines were seen as the powerful literary forces they are, thousands of libraries would subscribe. This is not true, but should be. No medium or large-sized library should be without a representative collection. Against this I have found very few libraries (even academic) having good holdings in this field.

This list cannot include all little magazines, or even all of the "better" little magazines. I have tried to avoid the narrowly political or the rigidly committed special-purpose, be it ecology or Woman's Liberation, which are covered elsewhere. Several newer magazines have been included in the belief and hope that they will have staying power. To the editors of magazines which I missed, my apologies. You are all valuable, you are all important. (D.D.)

Ed. note: What follows is somewhat more than Mr. Dorrance's list, but those curious to know the little magazines he thinks of importance will find his initials after each of his annotations.

Abyss. 1966. bi-m. $5. Gerard Dombrowski and Lionel Cabral, PO Box C, Sommerville, Maine 02143. Illus. Circ: 2,000.

Aud: Ga, Ac.

Literature in any form, broadened to consider "life in any form," even to the mystical. There is a wide range of material, covering the spectrum of current literature. Dombrowski also publishes significant books, important even if not generally known. Has interest in Zen, earth culture. (D.D.)

Action. bi-m. $3. Shirley Burghard, 610½ E. Division St., Syracuse, N.Y. Sample.

Aud: Ac, Ga.

A collection of essays and poems by and for mental patients. The editor is a registered nurse who sees the proper use of art, creative writing, dance, music, and poetry as a way of reaching the mentally ill. Her purpose seems valid enough and is explained in what appears to be the first issue. Send for a sample.

Afterbirth. 1970. $2/copy. Dist. by: Goliards Press, P.O. Box 1292, Bellingham, Wash. 98225.

Aud: Ga, Hs, Ac.

There is no indication whether or not this beautifully executed 54-page magazine will be continued or not, but it represents one of the best student efforts I have seen in a long time. Under the supervision of Jerry Burns of the Goliards Press, the students of Fairhaven College near Seattle have contributed photographs, art, poetry, and fiction to make up an attractive package. The printing ranks it with collector's items. Content, as might be expected, is a trifle uneven, at times sophomoric. Still, there is enough good material to make it worth the modest price. Librarians should get in contact with Burns, who issues little magazines and broadsides. He is one of the more active West Coast publishers and printers, and will be glad to send you a list of his offerings. It will be well worth the effort. (P.S. He does answer his mail.)

Aldebaran Reviw. 1968. irreg. $10. John Oliver Simon, 2209 California, Berkeley, Calif. 94703. Illus. Circ: 500.

Aud: Ga, Ac.

Interested in anything real, but adds direly, "If you don't know what you're doing keep your ——hands off it." A very tense magazine which hopes to upset much of the public. "Almost every poet I take seriously is strung out in an impossible mental position trying to keep up . . . watch out for verbs that move both ways at once." Radical, but serious, and will enliven any collection. (D.D.)

Ambit; a quarterly of poems, short stories, drawings and criticism. 1959. q. $2. 17 Priory Gardens, London N6, England. Illus., adv. Circ: 1,250.

Indexed: ICLM. *Bk. rev:* 5–10, length varies, signed. *Aud:* Ga, Ac.

Among the best known avant-garde English magazines, *Ambit* is devoted to original material: poems, short stories, groups of drawings. It resembles the American "little" more than most English smallpress magazines and should prove popular with young people who wish to find out about the new literature across the water.

Ann Arbor Review. 1967. irreg. $3. Fred Wolven, 2118 Arlene, Ann Arbor, Mich. 48103. Illus. Circ: 500.

Bk. rev: various number, length. *Aud:* Ga, Ac.

One of the leading of the semiacademic magazines. The poetry tends to be intellectual, somewhat dry, sometimes humorous in an academic way. This review has fiction, including works in progress, and reviews of small press books. Well represents a significant aspect of the literary scene. (D.D.)

Ante. 1964. q. $3.50. Vera Hickman. Echo Press, P.O. Box 29915, Los Angeles, Calif. 90029. Illus. Circ: 1,000.

Aud: Ga, Ac, Hs. *Jv:* V.

One of the few of the littles to attempt to pay its contributors, *Ante* maintains a very high level both in its fiction and its poetry. It features really good short stories. The poetry is good, somewhat traditional. Occasional book reviews and critical essays are included. Well produced, a thoroughly professional magazine. (D.D.)

Aspects. 1964. irreg. $1/5 issues. Jerry Paul Simpson, P.O. Box 3125, Eugene, Ore. 97403. Illus. Circ: 500.

Bk. rev: various number, length. *Aud:* Ga, Ac.

An extremist magazine, but with a degree of responsibility: it does more than simply shout. Independent and sharp, it also happens to publish the best experimental short fiction around. Mimeographed and angry, and proud of both. (D.D.)

Assembly. 1970. a. $2.50. Richard Kostelanetz, Mike Metz and Henry Korn. Assembling Press, Box 1967, Brooklyn, N.Y. 11202. Illus. Circ: 1,000.

Aud: Ac.

Editors compile this 100 or so page magazine by asking contributors to submit 1,000 copies of up to four 8½ by 11 inch pages of "Anything you want to include—printed at their own expense. No manuscript was refused so names and views expressed herein are not the responsibility of Assembling Press or the editors." The result is a mess of visuals, poetry, photographs. Some of it is passable to good, but the lack of organization or structure leaves it more as an item of interest to a psychologist than to a reader. Sure, it is an effort at concrete construction, but it ends in a heap.

Athanor. 1971. q. $5. Douglas Calhoun and George Butterick, 60 N. St., LeRoy, N.Y. 14482. Illus.

Bk. rev: 3–4, 200 words, signed. *Aud:* Ac.

A little magazine of some 70 pages which features interviews, poetry, prose, reviews, and essays. The format is just passable, but the contributors are among the best, e.g., Ted Enslin, Cid Corman, Larry Eigner. It is carefully edited. Recommended as basic for large magazine collections.

Avalanche. 1966. q. $2. Richard Krech, 2315a Russell St., Berkeley, Calif. 94702. Illus., adv. Circ: 1,000.

Aud: Ac, Hs.

Left-of-center to radical, publishing the best of advanced poetry. Communication is there, with or without discipline. This represents the counterculture almost to respectability. It will publish interviews with pop heroes, photographs, and art representing newest techniques to, possibly, shock and garble. For students, and those wishing to understand or live with students. (D.D.)

Boss. 1966. s-a. $2. Reginald Gay, Box 370, Madison Sq. Station, New York, N.Y. 10010. Illus.

Aud: Ga, Ac.

Advanced, and interested in a wide range of materials coverings all of the arts. Poetry, essays, interviews, photographs cover the theater, happenings, sculpture, whatever. It is briskly avant-garde, and well produced. Interesting and lively reflection of the New York scene. (D.D.)

Center. 1970. irreg. $5/4 issues. Carol Berge, Box 698, Woodstock, N.Y. 12498.

Aud: Ac.

Dedicated to nonform prose, which is what you get. There is much chaos in the manner of William Burroughs or the later Joyce, most of it mercifully short. Some of it is humorous, some confusing, but it will give you an insight into the state of experimental writing. Required for serious collections or schools with strong writing courses. (D.D.)

Chelsea; a magazine for poetry, plays, stories and translations. 1958. q. $3.50. Sonia Raiziss and Alfedo de Palchi, Box 242, Old Chelsea Station, New York, N.Y. 10011. Illus. Circ: 1,000.

Indexed: LMags. *Bk. rev:* Occasional, 500 words, signed. *Aud:* Ga, Ac. *Jv:* V.

One of the older magazines but still retaining its vitality, in part through guest editors and special issues. It pays attention to the European scene, as well as both traditional and experimental American poetry, and maintains a very high standard. Fiction is average to good, and essays, criticism, and interviews are also included. Preferred by writers. (D.D.)

City Lights Journal. 1963. irreg. $2.50. Lawrence Ferlinghetti. City Lights Books, 261 Columbus Ave., San Francisco, Calif. 94111. Illus.

Aud: Ga, Ac, Hs. *Jv:* V.

This appears once or twice a year, as the editor pleases. The San Francisco school, plus its international disciples, possibly is the most important school currently operating. The level of writing is high, the editing excellent. This is one of the magazines which make reputations. Paperback format, should be treated as the continuing anthology it is. (D.D.)

Contempora. 1969. bi-m. $3. Paul G. Putney. Contempora Inc., P.O. Box 673, Atlanta, Ga. 30301. Illus., adv. Circ: 1,000. Sample. Vol. ends: 6th issue.

Bk. rev: 10–12, 250–500 words, signed. *Aud:* Ac.

Combining photographs, essays, short stories, reviews, music, and poetry, the whole package is in the best tradition of the literary magazine. In some 50 well-printed pages it presents a cross section of modern culture. There is a long essay on the cinema in each issue. Generally, there is also an interview with a literary or arts figure. It is a trifle uneven; most of the short stories turned me off—but there is enough quality to make it worthy of consideration by larger libraries.

December; a magazine of arts and opinion. 1957. irreg. $6/4 issues. Curt Johnson, Box 274, Western Springs, Ill. 60558. Illus. Circ: 2,000.

Indexed: AbEnSt, LMags. *Aud:* Ga, Ac, Hs. *Jv:* V.

Another of the few which feature high quality prose. Extensive illustrated film reviews are a regular, and important, feature. It excerpts novels from the underground and little presses. The poetry is good but not its strongest point. Editor has strong and expressed opinions on the state and quality of American life. Title is suitable for high schools. Preferred by writers. (D.D.)

Dramatika. 1967. s-a. $3. John Pyros, Box 1965, University, Ala. 35486. Illus.

Aud: Ga, Ac.

Mimeographed, 60 to 80 pages an issue, devoted to dramatic arts; it includes happenings, the free-wheeling, and improvisations. The plays frequently involved physical danger to the cast, leading me to believe they are closet dramas, often rough in form and language, and show a sincere belief in the absurd. This journal tries to publish "the good and the true: unfearing and unfavoring—bearing malice to no one." The editor plans to discontinue publication after its tenth issue, in the fall of 1972. Any library with an interest in ad-

vanced theater should subscribe—should even seek back issues. (D.D.)

Dust. 1964. q. $3.50. W. M. DePew and Len Fulton. Dustbooks, 5218 Scottwood Rd., Paradise, Calif. 95969. Illus. Circ: 1,500.

Indexed: LMags. *Bk. rev:* Various number, length. *Aud:* Ga, Ac, Hs.

Alternative and experimental, for the underground public. Graphics and photos are above average. It expresses counter culture well while staying suitable for high schools. One of the offshoots of Len Fulton's genius, a significant figure on the scene. (D.D.)

Exit. 1965. bi-m. $3 (Students $2). Martin J. Martin, GPO Box 1812, New York, N.Y. 10001.

Aud: Ga, Ac.

A combination literary, left-of-center, 30 to 40 page contribution from freethought enthusiasts. The few stories and poems are relatively good; the articles on everything from drugs and sex to civil rights are familiar and well-intentioned efforts. Probably of more general value is the free newsletter coming with a subscription to *Exit.* This is *Index Repartee,* "opinion and discourse in the open-letter tradition—no subject or topic excluded." Issued ten times a year, the four to six page mimeographed communication has covered everything from scientific morality to the contributions of Robert Ingersoll. The emphasis here is definitely lack of belief in dogma. From time to time the editor also includes copies of other magazines which champion the same cause. More than worth the price for the more involved college student.

Folio. 1964. 3/yr. $3. Adele Sophie de la Barre, Box 31111, Birmingham, Ala. 35222. Circ: 700.

Aud: Ga, Ac, Hs.

A very good example of a local literary magazine, with a sprinkling of nationally known contributors. Good, civilized, not necessarily outstanding poetry and short fiction are included. Few cities have anything comparable. (D.D.)

Free Lance. 1950. s-a. $2. Casper Jordan and Russell Atkins, 6005 Grand Ave., Cleveland, Ohio 44104. Circ: 500.

Aud: Ga, Ac.

Representing the Cleveland scene, which was one of the most interesting and vital groups of the sixties. Poetry tends to be imagist, concrete, surreal, and prose is at times far-out. The late d.a. Levey influenced format and mood. Antiestablishment and sometimes bitter. (D.D.)

Ghost Dance; the international quarterly of experimental poetry. 1968. q. $2.50. Hugh Fox. University College, Dept. of American Thought and Language,

Michigan State Univ., E. Lansing, Mich. 38823. Illus. Circ: 600.

Aud: Ga, Ac. *Jv:* V.

One of the most exciting, interesting magazines around. It demonstrates printing itself as an art form. Format is loose, an "anything-goes" attitude. In many instances, the illustration is the poem, the poem is illustration. Concrete, found, dadaist—this is one of the best expressions of freedom of form (not to say explosion, in many instances). Content is truly international; the editor is an authority on Latin American poetry. Circulation is deliberately low—it is printed in the basement of the Fox home, with the editor turning the wheels. Color is well used. For those libraries interested in new adventures, and for those interested in the graphic arts. (D.D.)

Grande Ronde Review. 1964. q. $6. Benn Hiatt; 907 River Way, Folsom, Calif. 95630. Illus. Circ: 600.

Bk. rev: Notes. *Aud:* Ac, Ga.

A long-lived little which by 1972 found success and spirit enough to go from an irregular to a quarterly schedule. The editor offers 164 pages of poetry, fiction, and reviews, plus a variety of articles. No. 14, for example, included a section dedicated to the poet Al Masarik—a bibliography, and selections from his three books. The press work is not all it might be, but this gives the material a certain frenetic setting which seems quite all right. One thing—it is highly imaginative and individualized. The magazine is not likely to be confused with others in this field. Recommended for medium and large-sized libraries.

Heirs. 1967. q. $3.50. Thomas Welsh, 657 Mission St., Rm. 205, San Francisco, Calif. 94105. Illus.

Aud: Ac.

Most of the poets, short story writers, artists, and photographers who contribute to this 70-page little magazine are under 30 years of age, relatively unknown, and with varying degrees of talent. For example, Kathleen Raybin is one of the more gifted, probably about the same age as the University of California student-editor, and representative enough of the contributors. One subscribes to this kind of magazine for the off chance of meeting a Raybin, which may be reason enough.

The Honest Ulsterman. 1968. bi-m. $6. Michael Foley and Frank Ormsby. Ulsterman Publns., 56 Univ. St., Belfast, Northern Ireland. Sample. Vol. ends: Nov./Dec.

Bk. rev: 2, 1½ pages, signed. *Aud:* Ac, Ga, Hs. *Jv:* V.

With no apologies for being regional and no reason to apologize when a region can produce poets as good as Seamus Heaney, John Montague, and James Simmons, *The Honest Ulsterman,* subtitled "monthly handbook for a revolution," contains no recipes for petrol bombs. In 1968, when Jimmy Simmons began

this magazine, his view was that "literature starts and finishes with men talking to men, and the most important thing for a man talking to men is to be honest." A magazine with aims as serious as this could be a dull scene. In fact, this is a consistently delightful one. In addition to the unusually high average of genuinely good poetry per issue, it is flexible enough and has room enough for whatever the editors think is lively, whether it comes out of the correspondence file or from the desk of a professional writer. (L.T.)

IQ. 1964. s-a. $10/4 nos. Richard Grossinger, 370 Michell Rd., Cape Elizabeth, Maine 04107. Illus. Circ: 1,200.

Aud: Ga, Ac.

One of the strangest of the little magazines. Each issue is tightly thematic, with some emphasis/interest on occult and science fiction. The steadiness of the editor's vision makes this an off-beat artistic success. It is not a general magazine, but a classic example of creative editing. All serious collections should have the complete run, and general collections should certainly have examples. (D.D.)

Illuminations. 1965. s-a. $4. Norman and Hadassah Moser, Box 5341, Coronado Station, Santa Fe, N.M. 87501. Illus., adv. Circ: 1,000.

Bk. rev: various number, length. *Aud:* Ga, Ac.

Originally a large magazine of poetry, articles, art, fiction, comment, with excellent production values, this has evolved into a series of books, each shaped by the editorial judgment of its very sharp editors. It features the more established writers as well as the unknowns. Size will vary. Expect almost anything: a good middle-ground selection. (D.D.)

Ingluvin. 1970. q. $3. Seymour Mayne and Kenneth Hertz. Ingluvin Publns. 5355 Walkley Ave., No. 41, Montreal 265, Que., Canada. Illus. Circ: 3,000.

Bk. rev: 500–1,500 words, signed. *Aud:* Ga, Ac. *Jv:* V.

A new, brash Canadian magazine, vigorously pro-Canada. Poetry and illustrations are fair to good; prose good to excellent. Content is leavened by humor. Critical essays may provide a continuing knowledgeable look at both the Canadian literary establishment and its antiestablishment. Its format varies, being usually small and untidy. A very lively addition to the scene. (D.D.)

The Lamp in the Spine. 1971. 3/yr. $3. Patricia Hampl and James Moore, Box 242, Iowa City, Iowa 52240. Illus.

Bk. rev: 1–3, 250–500 words, signed. *Aud:* Ac, Ga.

A fat (65 to 96 pages), ably produced and carefully edited little magazine from the place where all good writers either go or visit. The scope, though, is hardly limited to Iowa. The first three issues examined give primary emphasis to original poetry—and the traditional "contributors notes" indicate most entries are from younger, lesser-known poets. There are a few "regulars" such as Robert Bly, Greg Kuzma, Wendell Berry, Lyn Lifshin—and even Pablo Neruda—but the real interest is with the new names. There are some interviews, stories, and essays as well as poems. This is one of the more fascinating new little magazines, and apparently one with staying power. Well worth a subscription.

Lillabulero. 1966. irreg. $2/yr. Russell Banks and William Matthews. Lillabulero Press, Krums Corner Rd., RD 3, Ithaca, N.Y. 14850. Circ: 1,000. Sample.

Bk. rev: 3, 4–5 pages, signed. *Aud:* Ac. *Jv:* V.

One of the leaders in the field, with good poetry, an occasional fair-to-good short story, first rate articles and criticism. Some special issues maintain its activist standing. Format is professional. The Press publishes chapbooks and miscellaneous productions of various sorts. Preferred by writers. (D.D.)

The Little Magazine (Formerly: ***The Quest***). 1965. q. $4. David G. Hartwell and Thomas T. Beeler, Box 207, Cathedral Station, New York, N.Y. 10025. Illus., index. Circ: 1,000. Sample.

Bk. rev: 3, 750 words, signed. *Aud:* Ac.

Under a new banner, this boasts a new format, a new approach, but the same good editors. The 64-page issue examined notes that one reason for a change of title is that: "there are seven quests in the world . . . everything from a travel magazine to a semiannual organ of a national association for the physical education of college women." Well, the present collection of poetry and prose is a far cry from a gymnasium. If anything, the magazine is much improved, and is recommended as one of the better littles.

Madrona. 1971. q. $4. J. K. Osborne and Vassilis Zambaras. Gemini Press, 502 12th Ave. E., Seattle, Wash. 98102. Illus.

Aud: Ac.

Seattle is rapidly becoming an important center for little magazines. From the looks of the first two issues, one of the more impressive is this 34 to 40 page offset magazine. Among contributors are David Ignatow, Clayton Eshleman, Robert Bly, Mark Strand, W. S. Merwin, Denise Levertov, etc.; but these "names" are nicely balanced by others who are teachers, editors, or students, and not so well known. Still they write exceptionally well, and this bespeaks much above average editing. The drive is towards socially significant poetry and art. Forthcoming issues will be given to a Roethke tribute, translations from the Third World, and essays, photographs, and criticism. A little magazine with a much above average outlook.

Maitreya. 1971. bi-a. $6.50/4 issues. Sather Gate, Box 4336, Berkeley, Calif. 94704. Illus.

Aud: Ga, Ac.

Dedicated to poetry and prose which celebrate meditation, nature, and in a broader sense the ritual of learning about oneself. Significantly, the first article in the second issue is entitled "Who Am I?" the answer suggesting an interest and a background in yoga and the finer aspects of Buddhism and Zen. The 25 or so other contributions in the handsomely printed and illustrated magazine are within much the same scope. The authors write for the nonexpert and layman, and the magazine will be welcomed by many readers, particularly those under 30, who are looking for new ways to change their life styles.

Man Root. 1969. irreg. $3.50/4 issues. Box 982, South San Francisco, Calif. 94080.

Some from California, some such names as Richard Tagett, Nanon Valaoritis, and Jean Cocteau, not to mention Jacques Prevert. Which is to say, if all the contributors are not from San Francisco, they would feel at home there, and this free, easy, and sometimes hedonistic approach shows in its poems. It is light on social issues, heavy on the personal; has a bit of prose, a few drawings. Adds up to a fairly good magazine.

Monday Morning Wash. 1972. irreg. $3.50/4 issues. Tom Montag, 2629 N. Bremen, Milwaukee, Wis. 53212.

Aud: Ac.

Poetry, essays, fiction, letters, reviews. It is highly personal, thick (60 plus full-sized pages) with attempt at intercommunication with contributors, and will have several selections by the same author. First issue features a long, absorbing letter by Dean Phelps on the state of fiction and the modern literary scene. There are guest editors for special issues. This journal is serious, and represents the little magazine as a cultural force. Monday Morning Press also publishes a series of very attractive broadsides, including the Wisconsin Poets series, at $3.00 for 12 issues. (D.D.)

Moving On. 1968. q. $3. George Hoyt, P.O. Box 624, Mendocino, Calif. 95460. Illus.

Aud: Ga, Ac.

"A magazine celebrating the extraordinary ordinary." This is a small, slim celebration of the earth, gentle and personal. It reprints short pieces on the movement, and has news notes; is interesting, if specialized. Not a first choice, but certainly to be considered, particularly with the current interest in the alternative culture. (D.D.)

Mulch. 1970. bi-a. $1.75. David Glotzer, Basil King, Harry Lewis, P.O. Box 455, Cooper Station, New York, N.Y. 10003. Illus., adv.

Bk. rev: 5–6, 750–1,600 words, signed. *Aud:* Ac.

A pocket-sized, 125-page magazine whose editor promised poetry, reviews, interviews, and articles covering a wide field of interest from history to the social sciences. The late Paul Blackburn and Ted Enslin are among the poets in the first issue, and there is a story by Cynthia Lasky and a filmscript by Milton Ginsberg.

New Collage. 1970. 3/yr. $3. A. McA. Miller, P.O. Box 1898, Sarasota, Fla. 33578. Illus.

Aud: Ga, Ac.

New and interesting example of essentially undergraduate writing. Format is good, poetry medium to good, illustrations superior. Representative of the substantial middle-ground in little magazines. (D.D.)

The New Renaissance. 1970. q. $5.50. Louise T. Reynolds, 9 Heath Rd., Arlington, Mass. 02184. Illus.

Bk. rev: 1–2, essays, signed. *Aud:* Ac.

Although cast on the format of a traditional little magazine, this 70-page journal seeks wider fields of interest than poetry and fiction. The lead article in one issue, for example, is a documented report on water pollution. This is followed by an analysis of the art of Nicholas Solovioff, several short stories, and poems and sketches. While the majority of authors are not well known, they write with skill and objectivity rarely associated with the traditional little magazine genre. As the editor says, "We try to publish original and honest writing, whether traditional or progressive —writing which has something to say." Indeed they do, and this is a refreshing contribution to what sometimes tends to become a rather esoteric, dull field.

The Open Cell. 1969. bi-m. $5/15 issues (Individuals $3). Milton Loventhal, P.O. Box 52, Berkeley, Calif., 94701. Illus., index. Circ: 1,000. Sample. Vol. ends: 20th issue.

Aud: Ga, Ac, Hs. *Jv:* V.

This is authentically a voice of the "people." Nothing censored, free and unconventional, it has reached beyond, with considerable success, the aims of too many of the recent "free" publications. Its contents are almost entirely by unknowns. *The Open Cell* has not restricted itself to any particular style or form. Essay, poetry, short story, pohotographs, and art, all varied, are scattered throughout. All are worthwhile and some excellent. *The Open Cell* has received considerable attention and praise in the Bay Area. KPFA's dramatic critic, Eleanor Sully, praised it for its quality, singular purity of purpose, and lack of flamboyancy. It may prove to be a binder's nightmare. It is now four large pages, 18-by-11 inches. The first numbers have become collector's items already. It is a publication for all libraries with an interest in a voice of the now generation.

Overland. 1954. q. $2. S. Murray Smith, G.P.O. Box 98a, Melbourne, Australia 3001. Illus., index, adv. Circ: 4,000.

Indexed: Aust. PAIS *Bk. rev:* 7–10, 750–1,500 words, signed. *Aud:* Ga, Ac.

This is among Australia's leading literary magazines, and an average 50-page issue is devoted to prose, poetry, and features which stress the liberal aspects of Australian politics. It attempts to combine writing by well-known Australian writers with new work by young people. The whole is professional, well edited, and a major contribution to the genre. According to contributing editor and librarian Barrett Reid, its importance is recognized by no less a figure than Robert Graves who claims: "There is a higher standard of good writing in *Overland* than in any other small magazines which I have looked at for many years, which includes England and the States." A review of two issues indicates this evaluation is correct. It should be in every major American library. Footnote: another argument for its inclusion is suggested by Mr. Reid: "It is usual for Australian academic and research libraries to subscribe to many U.S. literary periodicals such as *Poetry, Hudson Review,* even *Evergreen* when the Customs allows it in. It would be nice for some of your more outgoing libraries to help redress the balance in cultural trade." Enough said.

Part Time Publicity. 1971. irreg. $1 ea. Martin Wasserman, Haddock Pond, Fort Ann, N.Y. 12827.

Aud: Ac.

Reading little magazines can become discouraging, but once in a while all the wasted time is made worthwhile by a real discovery. Here is such a title, at least in issue no. 2 (Fall 1971). The lead item in the 35-page mimeographed magazine of poetry and prose is an article on David Smith, the sculptor, by a woman (Jean Rikhoff) who knew him well enough to be a friend. The memory piece is well written, revealing of the man, and something the reader is not likely to find anywhere else. The rest of the issue contains uneven poetry and prose.

Paunch. 1968. 3/yr. $4 (Students $2.50). Arthur Efron, 123 Woodward Ave., Buffalo, N.Y. 14214. Circ: 400.

Indexed: AbEnSt. *Aud:* Sa, Ac.

Named after Sancho Panza and "his notable gut," this differs from most little magazines in that the orientation is more literary, and the editor seeks material within the scope of Romantic criticism "in the radical sense defined . . .; the work of Alex Comfort, Paul Goodman, Wilhelm Reich, Norman O. Brown, Herbert Marcuse, A. S. Neill, and even John Dewey." This adds up to a much above-average base for criticism, poetry, and prose, as well as special issues. Contributors are primarily from academic circles, but having their day off to say what they really think. This demonstrates that literary criticism need not be dull. A good addition for all academic collections. (D.D.)

Penumbra. 1967. s-a. $1 ea. Charles Haseloff, Box 1501, New York, N.Y. 10001.

Aud: Ga, Ac.

Small, pocket-sized, interesting; also somewhat obscure. Design is well above average, poetry tends to follow e.e. cummings and Ezra Pound. Overall effect at times is that of affectation, but a sense of humor lurks somewhere in the editorial office. Specialized and distinctive. (D.D.)

Phalanx. 1969. 3/yr. $1.50. Martin Pumphrey and Raymond Donovan. The Palatinate Office, Dunelm House, Durham City, County Durham, England.

This magazine is amazing. It is almost unfair to include it in a batch of struggling little magazines that do not know where their next shekel is coming from. Produced by two lads in their early twenties and with some money from the Northern Arts Association, sumptuous is the descriptive word for *Phalanx* Each issue has a Big Theme. The Big Theme for no. 2 is Violence and it is dealt with not only through poetry, fiction, drawings, a photograph, but in articles by sociologists, stage directors and publishers, film makers and psychiatrists—some of them, like Peter Brook, with international credentials and reputations. This rather trendy interdisciplinary approach could make one a bit suspicious of the magazine's real objectives. Yet for all its glamour and pizazz one concludes that it does aim to be a serious publication within the little magazine scene. *Phalanx* is the bargain of the decade. Or perhaps, its most beautiful ephemera. (L.T.)

Pyramid. 1968. q. $5. Ottone M. Riccio. Hellric Pubns., 32 Waverly St., Belmont, Mass. 02178. Illus. Circ: 500.

Aud: Ac.

A nicely edited little magazine which is strong on good poetry, a bit weaker on prose. An average 80-page issue contains just enough good, new poetry to warrant consideration by any library. There are, too, some first rate bits of criticism. One of the more imaginative, certainly one of the most interesting of the littles.

Quartet; a magazine of the arts. 1962. q. $3. Richard H. Costa, 1119 Neal Pickett Dr., College Station, Tex. 77840. Illus. Circ: 1,000. Sample. Vol. ends: Every 8th issue.

Bk. rev: 4–5, 600 words, signed. *Aud:* Ac, Ga.

A general little magazine of the arts which covers music, literature, films, photography, etc. There are some fair to good short stories, poems, and prose. The book reviews are quite above average. This is a highly personalized little arts magazine which is interesting

for its broad approach. A good addition for general collections.

The Quest. See *The Little Magazine.*

Quixote. 1965. 6/yr. $10.50. Morris Edelson, 1040 Spaight St., Madison, Wis. 53703. Illus. Circ: 1,000.

Aud: Ga, Ac. *Jv:* V.

Considered to be a little magazine editor's little magazine—at least by the devoted. Contributors of poetry, prose, reviews, etc., are a "who's who" of the little magazine world. An average issue will be offset, run to some 100 pages, and appear to be thrown together. Actually, some thought does go into the selection, if not the printing. The result is: (1) delightful, if you happen to like Edelson; (2) frightful, if you seek order in the chaos. At any rate, an important little magazine because, in addition to publishing Americans, the editor has issued special numbers devoted to translations of major world figures. Note: the editor tends to move a bit, and if you have trouble getting a subscription, keep trying. It is worth the effort.

Red Clay Reader. 1964. a. $5. Charleen Whisnant, Rte. 2, Sharon Hills Rd., Charlotte, N.C. 28210. Illus. Circ: 4,000.

Aud: Ga, Ac.

Featuring a regular hard binding and issued annually, this is more of an anthology than a magazine. It modestly calls itself "one of the most important literary magazines in America," which it is not, but it does deserve kudos for the excellent format, the concentration on Southern writers—well known and otherwise—and an imaginative editorial policy which concentrates on off-beat material, from essays to poetry. Not essential, yet useful in larger literary collections and for many Southern public and academic libraries.

Samphire 7. 1968. q. $1.50. Michael Butler, 45 Westfields, Catshill/Bromsgrove, England. Illus. Circ: 600. Sample. Vol. ends: Winter.

Bk. rev: 2, 200 words, signed. *Aud:* Ac.

In *Samphire* 7, the work of Ida Affleck Graves and Don Mager stands out. There is also recent work by better-known poets like Lee Harwood, Wes Magee, and Omar (Son of Ezra) Pound. *Samphire* is attractively produced in offset with a nice heavy cover around its rather slender and austere self (24 pages including minimal notes on new contributors). The Arts Council of Great Britain has given this magazine a grant, which suggests that it will be with us for a bit. I at least have a good deal of faith in Michael Butler, judging by what he wrote on his page of commentary about the nature and function of the little magazine, and by what, in the realm of available new poetry, he and his co-editor choose to print. *Samphire's* emphasis is clearly on poetry and perhaps ought to be exclusively there, since the single example of fiction in *Samphire 7* is quite appallingly awful. This is a magazine for the comprehensive periodicals collection, obviously, but it ought to be seriously considered by other libraries willing to give little magazines from England a chance. The poetry is good and the price is right. (L.T.)

Second Aeon. 1967. q. $4. Peter Finch, 3 Maplewood Court, Maplewood Ave., Llandaff North, Cardiff CF4 2NB, Wales. Illus., adv. Circ: 1,500.

Aud: Ac, Ga. *Jv:* V.

A handsome, well-printed little magazine from Wales which has a feature to delight the little press fan: a running commentary on "the small press scene." There are some 15 pages of notes, carefully arranged by country, on little presses. The guide is particularly useful as it is timely and gives full bibliographic information, plus a short descriptive and evaluative annotation. (The editor is working with University of California in that he sends extra copies of the little magazines to that library for its collection.) Aside from this welcome feature, the other 100 or so pages are given to poetry, prose, photographs, interviews, and a variety of materials which rank this magazine among the best. Contributors are international, several from America, Yugoslovia, and other points. The editor exercises a strong selection faculty, and the result is a little magazine which can be recommended to anyone. A real joy for the dedicated or casual reader.

Second Coming. 1972. s-a. $2.50. Allan Winans, 118 Laidly St., San Francisco, Calif. 94131.

Aud: Ac.

An offset 48-page poetry and prose magazine with all the professionals present and accounted for, e.g., Doug Blazek, Jeff Woodward, Don Dorrance, Hugh Fox, Lyn Lifshin, Ottone M. Riccio, and others. An interesting point: most of the poets are editors in their own right. This reviewer is not overly familiar with Winans, but he is a good poet who is less successful with Henry Miller–type yarns. The others score fair to excellent. All in all a little poetry magazine which deserves to make it.

The Smith. 1964. q. $4. Harry Smith and Lloyd Van Brunt. Subs. to: Horizon Press, 156 Fifth Ave., New York, N.Y. 10010. Illus. Circ: 2,500. Sample. Vol. ends: Dec.

Bk. rev: 2,500 words, signed. *Aud:* Ga, Ac. *Jv:* V.

One of the most important and influential on the little magazine scene. It is also one of the few that attempts to pay contributors. "*The Smith* is the enemy of civilization itself, combatting the repressive institutions and the petty specialties. It is the more general magazine, seeking to forge order of great magnitude." And, to a surprising degree, it succeeds. It publishes the well known and established as well as newcomers. A very wide range of material, beautifully edited and

produced. Preferred by writers. See also *Newsletter on the State of the Culture.* (D.D.)

South and West, an international literary quarterly. 1962. q. $4. Sue Abbott Boyd, 2601 S. Phoenix, Fort Smith, Ark. 72901. Illus. Circ: 750.

Bk. rev: Various number, length. *Aud:* Ga, Ac, Hs.

The voice of the central South, but not parochial. This is a very important regional influence, yet can stand equal with many better-known national magazines. It has short fiction, good poetry. Also articles, criticism, interviews, interesting art. (D.D.)

Southern California Lit Scene. bi-m. $5. William J. Robson, PO Box 5429, Long Beach, Calif. 90805.

Aud: Ac.

Poetry, interviews, essays on the Southern California scene, all ably edited and professionally put together. Of particular interest in the second and third issues is an interview with *Trace* editor James B. May who with his 1972/1973 number stopped publishing one of the longest-lived little magazines in America.

Spero. 1963. s-a. $4. Douglas and Kathleen Casement, RFD 1, Dumont, Maine 04932. Illus. Circ: 1,000.

Aud: Ga, Ac, Hs. *Jv:* V.

The better-known poets contributing during the sixties represent the best of that time. There is short fiction by writers such as Henry Roth and William Sayers, as well as part of a Burroughs novel. Add to this quality excellent illustrations, including woodcuts and silk-screens, and you have a little magazine as a whole work of art. Some of the poetry has been printed with pouchbooks—independent small volumes contained within the cover flap. This title should be one of the first to be considered. For young adult and adult readers who want the best of contemporary American literature, with printing as an art thrown in. (D.D.)

Suenos. 1970. irreg. $.75/issue. B. Tokerud, 54 Sunkist Lane, Los Altos, Calif. 94022.

Aud: Ac, Ga.

The editor, who spends half the year in Mexico, has put together a 30-page art and poetry magazine which features work in both Spanish and English. The graphics share the same international flavor. While no *Maguey*, it is a pleasant addition to a field where there are too few good magazines.

Sumac. 1969. irreg. $5. Dan Gerber. Sumac Press, Box 29, Fremont, Mich. 49412. Illus., adv.

Bk. rev: 5–7, 750–1,000 words, signed, notes. *Aud:* Ac, Ga.

This 160-page "active anthology" is one of the best little magazines now being published. It is heavy on verse, with some fiction and a good book review section. The whole is professionally edited, and a fine balance is struck between the younger avant-garde poets and the older members of the faculty. For example, one issue featured George Oppen and Paul Zweig, a story by Sherwood Anderson, and a critical essay on William Carlos Williams. The make-up is excellent, and there are numerous graphics. By the end of 1971 the magazine had gone to a tentative annual schedule and the press began publishing books. The magazine itself seems a thing of the past, although the annual anthology apparently will incorporate the same features found in *Sumac*. For details write the editor.

Suppository: A Magazine of Contemplation. 1970. q. $3. Eustache Trevache, Box 14469, Santa Barbara, Calif., 93107.

Aud: Ac.

An offset little magazine of 40 pages whose subtitle is a bit deceptive. "Contemplation" is meant as the satirical expose of what some think is wrong with dogmatic thought. It is distinctive, though, for a couple of reasons: contributors range from Borneo and Baghdad to Portland, Oregon; the graphics are highly imaginative. One article, on the beginnings of the Provo movement, is documented, well written, and of importance to anyone involved with the history of radicals. Much above average, and a good item for larger college collections, not to mention individual readers.

Tlaloc. 1964. irreg. $1/6 issues. Cavan McCarthy, BCM/CAVAN, London WC1, England. Circ: 500.

Bk. rev: 2–3, 500 words, signed. *Aud:* Ac, Hs.

"Concerned with experimental & concrete poetry, news and reviews. Unsolicited mss of traditional poetry are not wanted and return is not guaranteed." Mimeographed, at times a hodge-podge, it has excellent reviews of new volumes of poetry. This is an international magazine, and frequently great fun. Also publishes news of the British small press scene under the little LOC-sheets. (D.D.)

Tracks and Tamarisk. 1967. 3/yr. $1.50. Neil Powell. Dept. of English, Univ. of Warwick, Coventry CV4 7AL, England.

Aud: Ac.

This splendidly produced magazine has been handsome from the beginning, but production is not the whole show so it is pleasant to be able to say that the content is equally excellent. Now no longer an official publication of the University of Warwick, it has grown by at least ten pages from its initial issue and has recently incorporated another literary magazine, *Tamarisk*, but this is still the rangy, no-nonsense magazine *Tracks* set out to be in 1967. Powell's firm hand and astute judgment have much to do with the magazine's uncompromising quality, its searching and sometimes downright waspish reviews. Penetrating critical articles are a strength at exactly the point where many little magazines are weakest. In addition to short fiction and pieces on films, drama, the fine arts, and music, *Tracks* commendably gives most of its poets enough space for several poems and so more accurately represents the direction of their current work. Very definitely an *English* magazine, *Tracks* reflects currents in contemporary English letters. (L.T.)

Tuatara. 1969. 3/yr. $3.50/4 issues. Mike Doyle, 759 Helvetin Cres., Victoria, B.C., Canada. Circ: 500. Sample.

Bk. rev: various number, length, signed. *Aud:* Ac.

Measuring 5½-by-8½ inches, this 48-page magazine is nicely designed and well printed. The editorial policy is equally excellent. Features work by Cid Corman, Allen DeLoach, and a dozen or so lesser-known but equally impressive younger poets.

Unicorn. 1967. irreg. $2/4 nos. Karen Rockow, 1153 E. 26th St., Brooklyn, N.Y. 11210. Circ: 500.

Aud: Ga, Ac.

Brightly intellectual, more for amusement than pretension. Interest in Tolkien, Dorothy L. Sayers, Celtic legends abounds. Illustrations are a high point, with first rate line drawings good enough to be framed. It published a thoroughly competent selective bibliography of Dorothy L. Sayers, both detective fiction and serious work. Probably a marginal choice, but it will lighten serious collections. One of the few with a well-developed sense of humor. (D.D.)

Unicorn Journal. 1967. s-a. $4 (Hardbound $8). Teo Savory. Unicorn Press, 317 E. de la Guerra, Santa Barbara, Calif. 93101. Illus. Circ: 2,500.

Aud: Ga, Ac. *Jv:* V.

Probably one of the best printed little magazines now available, and with content quality to match. It will print art works that are genuine art, concrete poetry, serious avant-garde material, poetry and prose. The emphasis, naturally, is on poetry published by Unicorn Press, which supports the magazine. As one of the major poetry publishers in the United States, this press is becoming very important both for original work and translations. Their journal adds another dimension, and should be in all medium to large-sized public and academic libraries. (Each issue is available in hardbound, which would be the best buy for most libraries.) (D.D.)

Unspeakable Visions of the Individual. 1971. 3/yr. $4.50. Arthur W. Knight, Box 439, California, Penn., 15419. Illus.

Aud: Ac.

A 32 to 40 page little magazine of short stories and poetry. The issue examined has a terrible format—but the editor says this is to change. Work by Ferlinghetti, Irving Shulman, a short poem by Norman Mailer, and a fine poem by Harry Smith are among the contents. The trouble is that one Sidney Bernard takes up most of the issue with poems and prose—and it is good reporting, but not much more than found every week in the *Village Voice*. So, the magazine has its ups and downs, but it is never dull. A good item for larger collections.

Vagabond. 1966. irreg. (3–4/yr.) $3/4 nos. J. Bennet, Jr. Vagabond Press, Box 2114, Redwood City, Calif. 94064. Illus.

Aud: Ac.

A 42-page mimeographed little magazine with long staying powers. Although the editor moves around a bit, he always manages to get out an issue or two a year, and sometimes even four. The magazine includes interviews (no. 12, for example, has a fascinating talk with Adolph Bruenn, a San Francisco north beach personality and eccentric), poetry, and some first-class line drawings by local artists. The fiction is not so good, but it is imaginative enough. A highly personal type of magazine which will interest anyone who is really into this scene.

Vibration. 1969. bi-m. Norm and Don Freeman, PO Box 08152, Cleveland, Ohio 44108.

Aud: Ac.

This one is printed, not mimeographed, but the 12 tight pages follow the 9-by-11 inch format. It is the reporting medium of activities in the Black Cleveland community, but includes poetry, politics, and reviews. It is considerably more subtle than most magazines of this type, and a real find for large Black collections.

Western World Review. 1965. q. $2. Robert E. Sagehorn. Western World Press, Box 2714, Culver City, Calif. 90230. Illus. Circ: 500. Sample. Vol. ends: no. 4.

Bk. rev: Number varies, essays and notes, signed. *Aud:* Ac.

In some 40 or so offset pages, the editor gathers together a variety of material from the literary to the political, from the original to reprint. Issues examined indicate this is primarily a reviewing medium, particularly of lesser-known political titles of both the left and the right. The reviews are unique in that most employ lengthy quotes from the book. (And the reviews of off-beat titles offer librarians another useful guide to the land of dissident titles.) It is the notion of its editor that "it is neither left or right or young or old"; it is, in fact, unique. Well, it is a real review, with a highly personalized touch. Some will like it, others will not, but it is certainly worth the small price.

Zeitgeist. 1965. irreg. $3.50/4 issues. Gary Groat. Zeitgeist Inc., Saugatuck, Mich. 49453. Illus., adv. Circ: 1,000. Sample.

Aud: Ac, Ga.

Measuring 4-by-7 inches, this small, pocket-sized, little magazine features poetry, fiction, drama, and critical essays in its 90 illustrated pages. Emphasis is on poetry, and most contributors are beginners (editor says "though a majority of our writers are usually not beginners; in other issues we have published original work by Corso, Algren, Turco, Piercy, etc."). The stylistic level is fair to good, but excellent in terms of a voice for revolutionary, bright, and highly imaginative new writers.

News and Sources of Little Magazines

Little magazines, not always easy to come by for examination, may be purchased in a number of bookstores. Among the best:

Asphodel Book Shop, Box 05006, Cleveland, Ohio. 44105.

Gotham Book Mart, 41 W. 47th St., New York, N.Y. 10036.

John B. Nomland, 404 S. Benton Way, Los Angeles, Calif. 94107.

Phoenix Bookshop, 18 Cornelia St., New York, N.Y. 10014.

The Tenth Muse, 983 Wisconsin St., San Francisco, Calif. 94107

Two excellent methods of keeping up with the little magazine file will be found in two magazines: *COSMEP Newsletter* and *Small Press Review.*

COSMEP Newsletter. 1969. m. $7.50. Richard Morris, Box 703, San Francisco, Calif. 94101. Circ: 800. Sample.

Aud: Ac, Ga, Hs.

The newsletter of the *Committee of Small Magazine Editors & Publishers*, an association of little magazines and small independent literary presses. While it is published primarily for members (membership is $15 and includes the *Newsletter*), it should be of value to libraries that maintain collections of little magazines or small press poetry publications. The *COSMEP Newsletter* regularly prints news notes and articles on small press publishing and reprints work of special interest that has appeared in member publications. It has occasionally also run such items as an exchange of letters between Robert Bly and George Plimpton on "censorship" in Plimpton's *American Literary Anthology,* an annual collection of the best articles from literary magazines.

Small Press Review. 1967. q. $3.50. Len Fulton. Dustbooks, 5218 Scottwood Rd., Paradise, Calif. 95969. Illus., adv. Circ: 2,000.

Bk. rev: various number, length. *Jv:* V.

The trade journal for the small press, little magazine scene, which also updates the *Annual Directory of Little Magazines.* A basic bibliographic tool, and of use to the same people needing the *Newsletter on the State of the Culture* (see Cultural-Social Studies Section). Has very sharp review essays by insiders. Anyone with a serious interest in the field should subscribe to both this and the *Newsletter,* for both sides of the same coin. (D.D.)

MATHEMATICS

Basic Periodicals

Ejh: *Arithmetic Teacher;* Hs: *Mathematics Teacher, Mathematics Student Journal* (see also Undergraduate and High School Periodicals in this section); Ga: *Journal of Recreational Mathematics;* Jc: *Mathematics Magazine, Mathematics Teacher, Mathematical Gazette* (see also Undergraduate and High School Periodicals in this section); Ac: *American Mathematical Monthly, Mathematics Magazine, SIAM Review,* and selected publications of the American Mathematical Society, depending on the needs of the institution.

Basic Abstracts and Indexes

Mathematical Reviews

Introduction

The periodicals in this section can roughly be classified into three main groups: research journals for academic libraries; periodicals embracing all aspects of mathematics education and teaching; and a few publications aimed at students (see, in particular, entry under Undergraduate Periodicals in this section). Clearly, the choice of research journals has been severely limited, mostly to publications of U.S. societies. Were one to supply even a modest list for academic libraries, one would naturally include such renowned foreign publications as *Mathematische Annalen, Mathematische Nachrichten,* and *Mathematische Zeitschrift,* representing some important German journals; the French *Journal Mathematiques Pures et Appliquées* and the *Bulletin de la Société Mathematique de France;* the Swiss publication *Commentarii Mathematicii Helvetecii; Acta Mathematica,* representing Scandinavian research in mathematics; a large body of East European journals and Japanese periodicals; as well as the high quality publications of some of our universities, such as *Illinois Journal of Mathematics, Michigan Mathematical Journal,* and the like. Specialized research publications, representing the subfields of mathematics, e.g., *Journal of Algebra, Journal of Combinatorial Theory, Topology,* etc., although excellent journals for academic libraries, have, of necessity, been excluded. Some selections have been added here, however, of journals representing studies in applied mathematics, and those applicable to computer mathematics.

Advances in Mathematics. 1967. bi-m. $52. Gian-Carlo Rota. Academic Press, Inc., 111 Fifth Ave.,

New York, N.Y. 10003. Index. Sample. Vol. ends: 2v./yr. Refereed.

Indexed: MathR, SCI. *Aud:* Sa, Ac.

The intent of this publication is to provide expository papers in any branch of pure and applied mathematics and, thus, to be of general interest to a wide number of mathematicians. Long, review-type papers may survey a field, discuss current theories, and include historical background. One paper, frequently over 150 pages in length, may comprise an entire issue. Since the scope is broad, the papers authoritative, and the nature of the publication expository, the journal is worth the attention of academic libraries with active math faculties, and is certainly required for research collections.

American Journal of Mathematics. 1878. q. $18. W. L. Chow. Johns Hopkins Press, Baltimore, Md. 21218. Index. Circ: 1,240. Vol. ends: no. 4. Refereed. Microform: UM. Reprint: Johnson.

Indexed: MathR, SCI. *Aud:* Sa, Ac.

Founded by Johns Hopkins University, and now produced also under the auspices of the American Mathematical Society, the publication has the distinction of being the oldest math journal published in the United States. Today, it still puts out authoritative and high quality papers dedicated to all areas of mathematical research, and represents a prestigious addition to any good mathematics collection.

American Mathematical Monthly. 1894. 10/yr. $18. Harley Flanders. Mathematical Assn. of America, 1225 Connecticut Ave., N.W., Washington, D.C. 20036. Index., adv. Circ: 22,000. Vol. ends: no. 10 (Dec.). Refereed. Reprint: Johnson.

Indexed: MathR, SCI. *Bk. rev:* 10–15, 200–500 words, signed. *Aud:* Sa, Ac.

The official journal of the Mathematical Association of America is dedicated purely to undergraduate mathematics. As such, it emphasizes expository papers which survey pertinent mathematical fields relevant to college-level instruction. Several interesting departments are also included in each issue. "Mathematical Notes" reports brief "mathematical pearls," or new proofs for old. From a pedagogical standpoint, "Classroom Notes" gives short, one to two page articles on appropriate proofs for undergraduate use; "Research Problems" introduce those which can be undertaken on a college level; and "Mathematical Education" deals with novel or controversial approaches to instruction. User participation is elicited through a "Problems and Solutions" section, on both elementary and advanced levels. Good features for librarians are the book reviews, and the brief "Telegraphic Reviews," which indicate the level of the publication. A fine, undergraduate journal for every type of academic library, junior college through university. (Note: the

MMA also publishes another excellent undergraduate periodical, *Mathematics Magazine,* listed below.)

American Mathematical Society. P.O. Box 6248, Providence, R. I.

The American Mathematical Society, one of the world's most distinguished organizations in the field, and also one of the chief publishers of the mathematics literature, including material in translation, has a number of high-quality journals similar enough in title to cause confusion.

Bulletin. 1894. bi-m. $12. Ed. bd. Index. Circ: 15,000. Sample. Vol. ends: no. 6. Refereed.

Indexed: MathR, SCI. *Bk. rev:* 1–2, 500–700 words, signed. *Aud:* Sa, Ac.

Considered the official organ of the Society. In addition to the usual reports and announcements of meetings, the *Bulletin* publishes long, expository articles which are usually addresses which have been presented before the Society. An important section of the journal is "Research Announcements," short research reports on mathematical studies in progress. Generally, these reports have to be communicated via a member of the AMS' prestigious Council. All areas of pure and applied mathematics are within the scope of this journal.

Proceedings. 1950. m. $100. Ed. bd. Index. Circ: 5,800. Sample. Vol. ends: 5v./yr. Refereed.

Indexed: MathR, SCI. *Aud:* Sa, Ac.

Dedicated entirely to research papers of moderate length in all fields of pure and applied mathematics. Subjects covered include algebra and algebraic number theory; modern or classical analysis; algebraic geometry; set theory and general topology; algebraic topology; applied mathematics and related fields of analysis; probability and statistics; logic and set theory.

Transactions. 1900. m. $180. Ed. bd. Index. Circ: 2,000. Sample. Vol. ends: 12v./yr. Refereed. Reprint: Johnson.

Indexed: EngI, MathR, SCI. *Aud:* Sa, Ac.

Papers published in the *Transactions* are longer than those appearing in the *Proceedings.* The same topics are covered, namely, analysis and applied mathematics; algebra and number theory; statistics and probability; geometry and abstract analysis; topology; mathematical logic and foundations.

Memoirs. 1950. irreg. Price varies. Ed. bd.

Indexed: MathR, SCI. *Aud:* Sa, Ac.

Each issue of the *Memoirs,* which can be purchased separately, consists of one long research tract, frequently of monographic length. Studies often represent part of a PhD dissertation.

Notices. 1953, 8/yr. $10. Everett Pitcher and Gordon L. Walker. Index. Circ: 16,000. Sample. Vol. ends: Dec.

The general news organ of the Society. Issues announce programs of forthcoming meetings; activities of other associations; news of the profession, including salary schedules; ratings of graduate programs; employment trends; personalia.

All of the above research publications are authoritative, high quality journals and most good, research-oriented mathematics collections will subscribe to the entire series, or as many as they can afford. The AMS is also the publisher of *Mathematics of Computation, Soviet Mathematics—Doklady* (English translation), and *Contents of Contemporary Mathematical Journals and New Publications* (see below). Newest in their long list of Russian translations are the two journals *Mathematics of the USSR—Izvestija* (cover-to-cover translations of *Izvestija Akademii Nauk SSSR Serija Mate-maticeskaja*) and *Mathematics of the USSR—Sbornik* (cover-to-cover translation of *Matematiceskii Sbornik* (New Series).

American Statistical Association. Journal. 1888. q. $25. Robert Ferber. 806 15th St., N.W., Washington, D.C. 20005. Index. Vol. ends: No. 4. Refereed.

Indexed: BPI, BioAb, PsyAb, MathR, SCI. *Bk. rev:* 17, 350 words, signed. Aud: Sa, Ac.

One of the most prominent US journals in this field. Research papers on theory, methodology, and application. Topics ranging from applications in science and engineering to social statistics, covering demographic studies to biometrics, and business and economics statistics. Belongs in most good academic collections.

Also from this association, a nonspecialist, less technical publication, *American Statistician* (5/yr. $25), and *Technometrics* (q. $25), a specialized statistical journal for the physical and engineering sciences.

Annals of Mathematics. 1884. bi-m. $18. Ed. bd. Box 231, Princeton, N.J. 08540. Index. Circ: 2,000. Vol. ends: no. 6. Refereed. Microform: UM. Reprint: Kraus.

Indexed: MathR, SCI. *Aud:* Sa, Ac.

An old and well-known mathematical research journal produced under the auspices of Princeton University and the Institute for Advanced Study. High-quality theoretical papers report on all areas of pure mathematics. Studies frequently represent comprehensive works and may range from 40 to 50 pages in length. Although too sophisticated for the small academic library, the scholarly publication belongs in every research collection of reasonable size.

Arithmetic Teacher. 1954. m. (Oct.–May). $10. Ed. bd. National Council of Teachers of Mathematics, 1201 16th St., N.W., Washington, D.C. 20036. Illus., index, adv. Circ: 44,000. Vol. ends: Dec. Refereed. Microform: UM. Reprint: AMS.

Indexed: EdI. *Bk. rev:* 3, 250–500 words, signed. *Aud:* Sa, Ac.

The National Council of Teachers of Mathematics is one of the main organizations in the United States interested in promoting the quality of math teaching at the elementary through college levels. *Arithmetic Teacher,* geared toward elementary school teachers, features articles discussing critical appraisals of new teaching methods, means of motivation in teaching, experiences in the elementary classroom, and other topics of interest to teachers. Some research results are also reported, although most of the research papers appear in the latest publication of the Society, *Journal for Research in Mathematics Education,* listed below. Regular departments, such as "Ideas," promote exchange of teaching experiences. Book reviews, coded to provide the level of sophistication, fall into two categories: reviews for teachers, and books for pupils. The scope of the publication is broad and should be of interest, as well as an informative and stimulating medium, to every elementary math teacher. A first-choice selection for every academic library connected with teacher education programs. Secondary school math teachers will find their interests equally met by the NACT's publication, *Mathematics Teacher,* also listed below.

Canadian Journal of Mathematics. 1949. bi-m. $18. K. Murasugi and J. H. H. Chalk. Univ. of Toronto Press, Toronto, Ontario, Canada. Circ: 1,450. Sample. Vol. ends: no. 6. Refereed.

Indexed: MathR. *Aud:* Sa, Ac.

Published for the Canadian Mathematical Congress. Largely reflecting the current research interests in Canadian universities and institutions, the journal puts out quality papers in all fields of pure and applied mathematics. Text is both in French and English. Contributions from Canadian mathematicians are given priority. A good journal appropriate for academic libraries. (Note: See also *Canadian Mathematical Bulletin,* for the expository publication and official organ of the Canadian Mathematical Congress.)

Canadian Mathematical Bulletin. 1958. 5/yr. $15. R. Bercov. Canadian Mathematical Congress, 985 Sherbrooke St., W., Montreal, Canada. Index, adv. Circ: 1,600. Vol. ends: No. 5. Refereed.

Indexed: MathR. *Bk. rev:* 10–12, 300 words, signed. *Aud:* Sa, Ac.

The journal acts as the official organ of the Canadian Mathematical Congress. As such it is not simply a research journal (although some short reports do appear) but is largely dedicated to expository works, biographical notes on mathematicians, and announcements of the Congress. Contributions from Canadian mathematicians are given first priority. A large portion of each issue is dedicated to book reviews. Canadian libraries will certainly need it for trends of news of mathematical research in that country. Appropriate for any undergraduate collection. (See also *Canadian Journal of Mathematics.*)

Communications on Pure and Applied Mathematics. 1948. bi-m. $30. Fritz John. Wiley-Interscience, Inc., 605 Third Ave., New York, N.Y. 10016. Index. Sample. Vol. ends: No. 6. Refereed. Reprint: Kraus.

Indexed: MathR, SCI. *Aud:* Sa, Ac.

Published for the Courant Institute of Mathematical Sciences, of New York University, the journal consists of research papers in the fields of applied mathematics, mathematical physics, and mathematical analysis. Contributions are primarily from the Institute or are solicited under its auspices from other authors. Many of the papers are outgrowths of technical papers, sponsored under government research contracts. Although the publication may be too specialized or sophisticated for small college collections, it is an authoritative and distinguished journal in its field for any research library.

Contents of Contemporary Mathematical Journals and New Publications. 1969. 26/yr. $24. Gordon L. Walker. Amer. Mathematical Soc., P.O. Box 6248, Providence, R.I. 02904. Circ: 2,400. Sample. Vol. ends: No. 26.

Since 1972 the *Contents,* formerly providing tables of contents of about 250 of the world's most important math journals, has incorporated *New Publications,* issued previously as a separate periodical of the American Mathematical Society. The scope of *Contents* now consists of recent and forthcoming publication announcements, including books, journals, reprints, and microforms. Expansion of tables of contents of a number of math journals has also been effected, particularly in the area of applied mathematics.

Duke Mathematical Journal. 1935. q. $18. J. R. Schoenfield. Duke Univ. Press, College Station, Box 6697. Durham, N.C. 27708. Index. Circ: 1,500. Vol. ends: no. 4. Refereed. Microform: Academic Archives.

Indexed: MathR, SCI. *Aud:* Sa, Ac.

A solid, general mathematics journal publishing research-type papers in both pure and applied mathematics. The popularity of this journal in academic libraries is well deserved, since it concentrates on papers not so esoteric as to be inappropriate for the generalist mathematician, and not too long or sophisticated to require the attention of the specialist and the research tract. Recommended for academic libraries.

Fibonacci Quarterly. 1963. q. $6. Brother U. Alfred. St. Mary's College, Calif. 94575. Index. Circ: 900. Sample. Vol. ends: no. 4. Refereed.

Indexed: MathR. *Aud:* Sa, Ac.

The official publication of the Fibonacci Association, "devoted to the study of integers with special properties." Though relatively specialized and definitely inaccessible to the layman with little mathematical background, the publication, the elementary half of it, at any rate, is directed to a nonspecialist (high-school ability) audience. Contributions are encouraged from math students and teachers, special sections include problems at an elementary level, and other sections pose problems appropriate for class work. At the other end of the spectrum, advanced problems in *Fibonacci* could be considered on a senior undergraduate or graduate level. A typical issue has 10 to 15 articles, and a number of problems and proofs submitted by readers. A good undergraduate periodical for any type of academic collection.

Indiana University Mathematics Journal. 1952. m. $30. Ed. bd. Dept. of Mathematics, Indiana Univ., Bloomington, Ind. Index. Vol. ends: no. 12. Refereed.

Indexed: EngI, MathR, SCI. *Aud:* Sa, Ac.

Until 1957 the journal carried the title *Journal of Rational Mechanics and Analysis,* when it changed to *Journal of Mathematics and Mechanics.* Since 1970, it has once again changed title to the present one, reflecting a general editorial policy of somewhat broader scope. Concentration in this journal is still on applied mathematics and mechanics. An important and authoritative research publication, particularly for university libraries supporting research in the engineering sciences.

Institute of Mathematics and Its Application. Journal. 1965. bi-m. $54. F. A. Goldsworthy and L. Fox. Academic Press, 111 Fifth Ave., New York, N.Y. 10003. Index. Sample. Vol. ends: no. 3 (2v./yr). Refereed.

Indexed: MathR. *Aud:* Sa, Ac.

Concerned with the applications of mathematical models to describe phenomena in the physical and biological sciences, and engineering, the journal has wide applicability. Studies center around such fields as applied statistics, optimization techniques, linear and nonlinear programming, and in large part, numerical analysis. A research journal for university collections concentrating on applied mathematics.

International Journal of Computer Mathematics. 1964. q. $53.50. Randall Rustin. Gordon and Breach, 150 Fifth Ave., New York, N.Y. 10011. Index. Sample. Refereed.

Indexed: MathR. *Aud:* Sa, Ac.

Commencing in 1972, the journal is splintering into two parts. Section A is dedicated to research papers on programming languages, both on theory and methodology. Topics include the fields of formal languages, automata, computational problems, and algorithms. Section B is concerned with mathematics of an applied nature, ancillary to, yet not necessarily connected with, computer work, such as numerical analysis, operations research, econometrics, and applied mathematics. More exclusively dedicated to the mathematics of computers than the American Mathematical Society's *Mathematics of Computation,* the journal is valuable particularly to mathematically oriented groups in the computing sciences, as well as other mathematicians.

Journal of Mathematical Physics. See Physics Section.

Journal of Recreational Mathematics. 1968. q. $10. J. S. Madachy. Greenwood Periodicals, Inc., 51 Riverside Ave., Westport, Conn. 06880. Illus., index. Sample. Vol. ends: no. 4. Refereed.

Bk. rev: 3, 300 words, signed. *Aud:* Sa, Ac, Ga, Hs.

For that portion of the population which delights in mathematical tricks, puzzles, games, mindteasers, curiosa, etc., this publication will be a welcome addition. Feature articles and a problems section include such topics as magic designs, geometric diversions, chess problems, and the like. And for that portion of the world which trembles at the mere thought of number manipulation, the periodical is also interesting by way of historical notes, articles on the relationship of math to other fields, etc. The value of recreational mathematics, as the editor expresses it, is to "stimulate an interest in math and in education," and indeed, a periodical of this sort will find wide audiences in public, high school, and undergraduate libraries. The tone is chatty, and the typography is large and clear. Highly recommended.

Journal for Research in Mathematics Education. 1970. q. $6. David C. Johnson. National Council of Teachers of Mathematics, 1201 16th St., N.W., Washington, D.C. 20036. Illus., index. Vol. ends: no. 4. Refereed.

Aud: Sa, Ac, Ejh and Hs (teachers).

The latest in the publications effort of the National Council of Teachers of Mathematics, concerned with teaching mathematics at all levels. (See also *Arithmetic Teacher* and *Mathematics Teacher.*) Papers report on experimental research in the classroom, and other scholarly studies from elementary levels through undergraduate mathematics. Although some balance between levels is struck in each issue, the preponderance would appear to lean toward elementary school research. Departments include a "Forum for Researchers," an opportunity to provide rejoinders on work published in the *Journal,* and other commentaries. An important publication for any institution concerned with teacher education; particularly necessary for those in which any type of research is conducted.

Two other journals also concerned with research in mathematics education are worth serious consideration. *Educational Studies in Mathematics* (D. Reidel Publishing Co., Holland) and *International Journal of Mathematical Education* (Wiley, England). Both are international publications and carry the user beyond the boundaries of U.S. teaching methods. Recommended.

London Mathematical Society, Burlington House, Piccadilly, London W1V ONL, England.

The London Mathematical Society, founded in 1865, is one of the prominent associations carried over from the nineteenth century, and one dedicated to the "promotion and extension of mathematical knowledge." Three journals characterize its endeavors: its *Bulletin, Journal,* and *Proceedings,* described below. In addition, it sponsors a translation journal, *Russian Mathematical Surveys,* also listed below. Although academic libraries may well look first to the publications of the American Mathematical Society, all the output of this organization are first-rate journals for good mathematics collections.

Bulletin. 1969. 3/yr. J. E. Reeve. C. F. Hodgson & Son, Ltd., 50 Holloway Rd., London, N7 8JL, England. Index. Vol. ends: no. 3. Refereed.

Indexed: MathR, SCI. *Bk. rev:* 7–8, 500 words, signed. *Aud:* Sa, Ac.

After a century of publishing high-quality mathematical contributions, the Society produced its latest journal, the *Bulletin,* to speed up the dissemination process for short reports of less than five pages. All areas of pure and applied mathematics are covered, including algebra, number theory, classical analysis, applied mathematics, analytic topology, set theory, logic, functional analysis, geometry, and geometric topology. In addition to short works, occasional, longish expository or survey papers also appear, as well as a few news briefs and announcements.

Journal. 1926. 8/yr. $64. R. F. Churchhouse. C. F. Hodgson & Son, Ltd., 50 Holloway Rd., London N7 8JL, England. Index. Vol. ends: no. 4 (2v./yr.). Refereed. Reprint: Dawson.

Indexed: MathR, SCI. *Aud:* Sa, Ac.

Research contributions to its *Journal* are limited to papers of less than ten pages. As with the *Bulletin,* all fields of pure and applied mathematics are covered, namely, real and complex analysis; abstract and functional analysis; differential equations; topology, geometry and related areas; logic; probability and statistics; algebra; number theory. Recommended for any mathematical research collection.

Proceedings. 1865. 2v./yr. 8/yr. £13/v. A. W. Ingleton. Oxford Univ. Press, Ely House, 37 Dover St., London, England. Index. Vol. ends: no. 4 (2v./yr.). Refereed. Reprint: Dawson.

Indexed: MathR, SCI. *Aud:* Sa, Ac.

Now in its third series, the publication was the first journal issued by the Society in the mid-nineteenth century. Through the years, it has chronicled not only the research efforts of a distinguished body of mathematicians, but has added to the annals of mathematical history many of the classic papers in the field. Today, all areas of mathematics are covered, i.e., real and complex analysis, abstract and functional analysis, differential equations, topology, geometry, logic, algebra, number theory, combinatorial theory, and probability and statistics. Papers are longer than those appearing in the *Journal,* namely more than ten pages, and represent comprehensive and authoritative studies.

Mathematical Gazette. 1894. 4/yr. $8.40. E. A. Maxwell. G. Bell and Sons, Ltd., York House, Portugal St., London, England. Index, adv. Vol. ends: no. 4. Refereed. Microform: UM. Reprint: Johnson.

Indexed: MathR. *Bk. rev* 50, 200–500 words, signed. *Aud:* Sa, Ac, Ejh, and Hs (teachers).

Published by the Mathematical Association, an "association of teachers and students of elementary mathematics," in the United Kingdom. Although primarily concerned with mathematics education and teaching in the English classroom, the publication should not be overlooked by U.S. libraries. The variety of expository papers, ranging from elementary to more advanced mathematics, the creative approaches described in teaching methods, and the interesting general articles make the journal a splendid choice for mathematics collections. A large and comprehensive book review section provides a good checklist for foreign publications. Certainly all academic libraries supporting mathematics education programs should have it.

Note: during the year 1971–72, another publication has emerged from the Mathematical Association. *Mathematics in School* (bi-m; Longman Group Journals Division, 5 Bentinck St., London W1M 5RN) is primarily focusing on teaching methods for elementary teachers of children from 7 to 16 years. The publication will attempt to be more of a discussion forum and sharing of techniques, rather than to publish the expository papers and research which appear in the *Mathematical Gazette.*

Mathematical Reviews. See Abstracts and Indexes Section.

Mathematics of Computation. 1943. q. $20. Eugene Isaacson. Amer. Mathematical Soc., Box 6248, Providence, R.I. 02904. Index. Circ: 3,200. Sample. Vol. ends: no. 4. Refereed. Microform: Microcard Ed.

Indexed: MathR, SciAb. *Bk. rev:* 8–10, 500–700 words, signed. *Aud:* Sa, Ac.

An outgrowth of the National Research Council's *Mathematical Tables and Other Aids to Computation,* started in 1943. The purpose of the present journal is to act as a "clearinghouse" for computational tools, by publishing papers in such areas as numerical analysis, theory of high speed electronic computers, math tables, and other aids. In the past decade, these tools have been greatly enhanced by the use of computers. A good portion of each issue is dedicated to critical reviews of books and unpublished math tables. The American Mathematical Society retains a repository of unpublished mathematical tables (described in this journal) which can be purchased by researchers. Another interesting feature is a pocket microfiche containing supplementary data or tables to papers appearing in that issue. Useful and necessary for any research mathematics collection, or for any science library interested in these mathematical aids.

Mathematics Magazine. 1926. bi-m. $4. Gerhard N. Wollan. Mathematical Assn. of America, 1225 Connecticut Ave., N.W., Washington, D.C. 20036. Index. Circ: 6,000. Vol. ends: no. 6. Refereed. Microform: UM.

Indexed: MathR. *Bk. rev:* 2–3, 300–500 words, signed. *Aud:* Sa, Ac, Hs (teachers).

An excellent general mathematics magazine. Catering to varying levels of sophistication and interest in undergraduate mathematics, the periodical should be equally useful to faculty (both college and secondary school level), students, and professionals. Papers and short notes are largely expository, and include fresh insights into familiar problems, as well as some original work. Some general articles are published, which range from the pedagogical—discussions of mathematics curricula, and the like—to the historical and philosophical. A problems and solutions section ensures a wide audience by posing problems from the elementary to more advanced levels. Highly recommended for all academic collections.

The Mathematics Teacher. 1908. m. (Oct.–May). $10. Ed. bd. National Council of Teachers of Mathematics, 1201 16th St., N.W., Washington, D.C. 20036. Illus., index. Circ: 52,000. Vol. ends: Dec. Refereed. Microform: UM. Reprint: AMS.

Indexed: EdI, MathR. *Bk. rev:* 4–10, 350–800 words, signed. *Aud:* Sa, Ac, Hs (teachers).

Aimed at math teachers of secondary through junior college education levels, the periodical is one of the oldest in this country concerned with improvement of the mathematics curriculum. Well-chosen, short articles, spanning these levels, discuss such topics as instructional problems, gaining interest in the classroom, usage of computer technology in teaching, methodologies of instruction, and related topics. A section on new products, programs, and publications discusses available instructional materials; book reviews contain codes to indicate the level of text. A first-choice se-

lection for secondary school teachers, high school libraries, and academic collections, particularly those supporting teacher education programs. Needs for elementary school teachers are best matched by *Arithmetic Teacher*. Articles relating to research in mathematics education are usually diverted to the NCTM's newest periodical, *Journal for Research in Mathematics Education*.

Pacific Journal of Mathematics. 1951. m. $32. Ed. bd. Richard Arens. c/o Dept. of Mathematics, Univ. of California, Los Angeles, Calif. 90024. Index. Circ: 1,400. Vol. ends: Dec. Refereed.

Indexed: MathR, SCI. *Aud:* Sa, Ac.

A general mathematical journal publishing research papers in both pure and applied math. The supporting institutions of this publication include a number of western U.S. and Canadian universities, and some Japanese universities or research establishments. Contributions in large part come from faculty of these organizations, but are not restricted to these groups by any means. For academic libraries.

Quarterly of Applied Mathematics. 1943. q. $15. W. F. Freiberger. Box 1885, Brown Univ., Providence, R.I. 02912. Index. Circ: 2,000. Sample. Vol. ends: no. 4. Refereed.

Indexed: EngI, MathR, SciAb, SCI. *Bk. rev:* 4, 300–500 words, signed. *Aud:* Sa, Ac.

The emphasis in this scholarly journal is on research papers which stress the applications of mathematics to all areas of engineering. Titles such as "Wave Equation on a Surface," or "Plate and Shell Aerodynamics" are typical. A good and authoritative applied mathematics journal for university libraries, particularly those supporting engineering curricula.

Quarterly Journal of Mathematics. 1930. q. 130s. E. C. Thompson. Oxford Univ. Press, Ely House, Dover St., London, England. Illus., index. Circ: 1,450. Sample. Vol. ends: no. 4. Refereed. Microform: UM. Reprint: Dawson.

Indexed: MathR, SCI. *Aud:* Sa, Ac.

Known as the Oxford Series, the publication was formed by the merger of the well-known *Quarterly Journal of Pure and Applied Mathematics* (1857–1927) and the *Messenger of Mathematics*. Today, it continues the tradition set by these journals and still maintains a high-quality reputation as one of the world's leading publications in pure and applied mathematics. Emphasis is more on the pure research than on applied papers. Contributors represent an international body of distinguished mathematicians. An excellent research journal for good mathematics collections.

Russian Mathematical Surveys. 6/yr. $69. K. A. Hirsch. Macmillan Journals, Ltd., 4 Little Essex St.,

London, England. Index. Circ: 678. Sample. Vol. ends: no. 6. Refereed. Reprint: Dawson.

Indexed: MathR. *Aud:* Sa, Ac.

Published for the London Mathematical Society, the journal is a cover-to-cover translation of *Uspekhi Matematicheskoi Nauk*, a leading Russian mathematical review journal. Available in translation since vol. 15, 1960, the periodical is dedicated to survey-type papers in both pure and applied mathematics. Reviews are comprehensive and authoritative works, and serve as a good point of departure for an indication of the direction of mathematical research in the USSR. Lengthy bibliographies are also valuable for leads into the Russian literature. Useful for both theoretician and applied mathematician, the journal is, understandably, not a first-choice selection for the small, academic library. Research collections, however, should find this publication, and several other translations of Russian journals (e.g., *Soviet Mathematics*) valuable for rounding out math holdings.

SIAM Review. 1959. q: $14. Ed bd. Society for Industrial and Applied Mathematics, 33 S. 17th St., Philadelphia, Pa. 19103. Illus., adv. Circ: 5,000.

Indexed: MathR, SCI. *Bk. rev:* 5–6, 300–500 words, signed. *Aud:* Jc, Ac, Sa.

The journal covers the broad field of applied mathematics comprising expository papers, survey articles on new research, and essays on general interest topics for the profession, such as historical reports, reviews of pedagogical techniques, and discussions of mathematical curricula. Short research notes on mathematical techniques are also published. Features include a "Problems and Solution" section, and news and notices.

The Society for Industrial and Applied Mathematics, devoted to promoting the application of mathematics to science and industry, sponsors other more specialized research publications:

SIAM Journal on Applied Mathematics. 1953. 8/yr. $36. Circ: 5,500. *Indexed:* ChemAb, EngI, MathR, SCI.

SIAM Journal on Control. 1963. q. $27. Circ: 1,100. *Indexed:* MathR, SCI.

SIAM Journal on Computing, 1972. q. $27.

SIAM Journal on Mathematical Analysis. 1970. q. $27.

SIAM Journal on Numerical Analysis. 1964. q. $14. Circ: 1,300. *Indexed:* MathR.

Theory of Probability and its Applications. 1956. q. $52. (Translation of the Russian *Teoriya Veroyatnostei ee Primeniya.*)

School Science and Mathematics. See Science/General Section.

Scripta Mathematica. 1933. q. $4. A. Gelbart. Yeshiva Univ., Amsterdam Ave. & 186th St., New York, N.Y. 10033. Illus., index. Reprint: AMS Press.

Indexed: MathR, SCI. *Bk. rev:* 40, 150–500 words, signed. *Aud:* Jc, Ac, Sa.

(Note: This journal has appeared infrequently in the past two years and its future is uncertain.)

Although originally devoted to the "philosophy, history and expository treatment of mathematics," including such entertainments as mathematical curiosa, the periodical has, in the last several years, concerned itself with research papers of varying levels of sophistication. Well-written expository papers often supply historical and biographical material, which make fascinating reading. The book review section, easily representing about one-quarter of each issue, emphasizes the exotic, drawing attention to many foreign mathematical works not generally found in the average U.S. library, thus punctuating the international scope of the journal. A rather large section on "Books and Pamphlets Received," Supplies brief annotations. In spite of *Scripta's* erratic publishing history, beginning collections would do well to collect back volumes.

Soviet Mathematics-Doklady. 1960. bi-m. $90. S. H. Gould. Amer. Mathematical Soc., Box 6248, Providence, R.I. 02904. Index. Circ: 975. Sample. Vol. ends: Nov./Dec. Refereed.

Indexed: MathR. *Aud:* Sa, Ac.

Prominent among Russian translations is *Soviet Mathematics-Doklady*, which comprises the whole pure mathematics section of *Doklady Akademii Nauk SSSR*. Since the *Doklady* (proceedings of the National Academy of Sciences USSR) are issued three times each month, with six issues making one volume, each issue of this journal equals one volume of *Doklady*. Generally, research reports cover all fields of pure mathematics and are very short in length. The time lag for translations is about six months, the standard for scholarly translations. Important for large mathematical collections of university libraries. (See also *Russian Mathematical Surveys.*)

Studies in Applied Mathematics. 1922. q. $12. Ed. bd. MIT Press, Cambridge, Mass. 02139. Index. Circ: 1,700. Sample. Vol. ends: no. 4, (Dec.). Refereed. Reprint: Johnson.

Indexed: ASTI, ChemAb, EngI, MathR, SCI. *Aud:* Sa, Ac.

Until 1970, the publication was known as *Journal of Mathematics and Physics*. The research papers in this journal emerge from or are invited by the Applied Mathematics Group of Massachusetts Institute of Technology. Studies reflect mathematics as applied to the physical sciences, and topics include works on mechanics. An authoritative and important research journal, particularly for university collections supporting physics and engineering research.

U.S. National Bureau of Standards. Journal of Research. Section B: Mathematical Sciences. See Science/General Section.

Undergraduate and High School Periodicals

There are a number of publications, modest in scope, format, and price, which are concerned with high school or undergraduate mathematics and more importantly, which are directed toward, or encourage publication by students. Many are the news organs of mathematics clubs, honor societies, or schools. The ones included in this section comprise only a random selection of the number available. High school and junior college libraries with enthusiastic math classes would be well advised to supplement their collections with a few titles; see *Fibonacci Quarterly* and *Journal of Recreational Mathematics,* for examples.

Delta Epsilon. 1960. irreg. Free. Dept. of Mathematics, Carleton College, Northfield, Minn. 55057.

Bk. rev: 1, 250 words, signed. *Aud:* Jc, Ac, Sa.

Issued by the students and faculty at Carleton, the publication is devoted to undergraduate mathematics: expository papers, unusual solutions to familiar problems, problem proposals and solutions. The tone is informal—as is the format (about 8–10 multilithed, stapled pages)—and the editors also supply some news of mathematics colloquia, research in progress, and a few alumni notes. Contributions from students include book reviews; reviewers are conscientious, critical, and highly articulate—more so than some who review in the more sophisticated journals.

Journal of Undergraduate Mathematics. 1969. s-a. $5. Dept. of Mathematics, Guilford College, Greensboro, N.C. 27410.

A newcomer to this field, the magazine concentrates on expository papers. Also included is a periodic feature "Proposals for Research." Contributions are solely by undergraduates. Nicely produced, well-designed issues are from typescript.

Mathematical Log. 1957. 3/yr. $1. Josephine & Richard V. Andree. Mu Alpha Theta, Dept. of Mathematics, Univ. of Oklahoma, Norman, Okla. 73069. Illus. Circ: 18,000.

Mu Alpha Theta, the National High School and Junior College Mathematics Club, supplies a good bit of educational and diversional material in its 4-page news organ. As well as notes on its meetings and chapters, it publishes short essays and problems contributed by educators and members, and occasionally reprints problems from other publications. Includes discussions on educational and employment opportunities for students. (Copies are circulated, in quantity, without charge, to chapters of this society.)

Mathematics Student Journal. 1954. q. $2. National Council of Teachers of Mathematics, 1201 16th St., N.W., Washington, D.C. 20036. Illus. Circ: 50,000.

Geared for students from the 7th through 12th grade, this periodical provides a variety of instructional and recreational material for this age group. Features include both math projects and a problems section, to which students are invited to send both queries and solutions.

Pentagon. 1940. s-a. $1.50. Mathematics Dept., Central Michigan Univ., Mt. Pleasant, Mich. 48858.

The publication of Kappa Mu Epsilon, the national mathematics honor society which boasts a membership of 29,400. Generally, the expository papers appearing here are award-winning papers by undergraduates from contests established by KME. Issues also carry a problem-solution section, book reviews, and news of the organization.

Pi Mu Epsilon. 1949. s-a. Membership (Nonmembers $2). K. Loewen. Dept. of Mathematics, Univ. of Oklahoma, Norman, Okla. 73069. Illus. Circ: 4,000.

The publication, which is the official journal of the honorary mathematical fraternity, Pi Mu Epsilon, supports the expressions of mathematical inclination and creativity by undergraduates, as well as faculty or professionals. Features range from expository papers to general interest articles on such topics as the etymology of mathematical terms, historical reviews, addresses presented before meetings of the organizations, etc. Departments include a "Problems and Answers" section designed for both intermediate and more advanced levels, and a section on recommended undergraduate research projects.

Washington State University. Mathematics Notes. 1958. q. Free. Dept. of Mathematics, Washington State Univ., Pullman, Wash. 99163.

Bk. rev: Occasional. *Aud:* Jc, Ac, Sa.

This small publication contains a variety of interesting material for readers at the high school level and up. The main article may consist of a short historical essay or biographical note on some mathematician, a review of famous and familiar problems, or a discussion of some events of professional interest. A section on problems and solutions is included, and, occasionally, a book review.

MEDICAL SCIENCES

See also Health Section.

Basic Periodicals

GENERAL. Ejh: *Journal of School Health;* Hs: *Journal of School Health;* Ga: *New England Journal of Medicine, Journal of School Health;* Jc & Ac: *New England Journal of Medicine, Lancet, Medical World News, Social Science and Medicine, British Medical Journal.*

NURSING. The magazines listed are all for specialized situations, or for the professional nurse.

Basic Abstracts and Indexes

Index Medicus, Psychological Abstracts, Cumulative Index to Nursing Literature, International Nursing Index, Medical Socioeconomic Research Sources.

Introduction

Hospital librarians wishing to develop or strengthen their journal resources have recourse to a number of excellent guides which can assist them in selecting appropriate titles. Some of the best of these guides are nicely summarized in "Listmanship," *Bulletin of the Medical Library Association*, Oct. 1969, p. 401. Alfred Brandon's "Selected List of Books and Journals for the Small Medical Library," *Bulletin of the Medical Library Association*, Apr. 1971, pp. 266–85, printed in its fourth revision, is also highly recommended. (F.A.)

General

American Journal of Clinical Hypnosis. 1958. q. Membership (Nonmembers $8). William E. Edmonston, Jr. Amer. Soc. of Clinical Hypnosis, Mt. Royal and Guilford Aves., Baltimore, Md. 21202. Subs. to: 800 Washington Ave. S.E., Minneapolis, Minn. 55414. Illus., index. Circ: 3,300. Sample. Vol. ends: April. Refereed.

Indexed: IMed, PsyAb. *Bk. rev:* 5, 1–2 pages, signed. *Aud:* Sa.

Along with the *International Journal of Clinical and Experimental Hypnosis,* this is the leading psychological journal in the field. The sponsoring organization is made up of psychologists and physicians. Authors are practicing in the field or teachers of psychology and psychiatry. All of which adds up to eight or ten articles supported by research and clinical experience, not guess work and mysticism. Most of the material is technical, e.g., "Two attempts to replicate the Parish-Lundy-Leibowitz experiment on hypnotic age regression." Still, it is useful to librarians and laymen for the occasional nontechnical piece and for the book reviews which cover a wide variety of titles related to hypnosis. There is also a section: "abstracts of current literature." For larger academic and public libraries.

American Journal of Medicine. 1946. m. $18. A. B. Gutman. R. H. Donnelley Corp., 466 Lexington Ave., New York, N.Y. 10017. Illus., index, adv. Circ: 27,000. Microform: UM.

Indexed: BioAb, ChemAb, IMed. *Aud:* Sa.

Covers developments in all fields of medicine, but internal medicine particularly. Sections include clinical studies, review papers, clinicopathologic conferences, and case reports. Editorial comments are written on controversial subjects. Significant symposia are published in the May and November issues.

American Medical Association. Journal. 1848. w. $23. H. H. Hussey. American Medical Assn., 535 N. Dearborn St., Chicago, Ill. 60610. Illus., index, adv. Circ: 240,000.

Indexed: BioAb, ChemAb, IMed, PAIS. *Bk. rev:* 6–10, 200 words, signed. *Aud:* Sa.

Better known as *JAMA*, the American Medical Association's *Journal* is edited for all physicians. Its particular importance is the publishing of articles and reports on current research and clinical studies. Its least important function, and often the most debatable, is its conservative stand on some socio-economic issues. There are the usual number of special departments and features. The style is a bit stuffy, the articles jargon-prone, and the whole not exactly the type of reading for recreation. Suffering from a large circulation with a mass audience it cannot do the job of less general magazines such as the *New England Journal of Medicine.*

Annals of Internal Medicine. 1922. m. $15. Edward J. Huth. Amer. College of Physicians, 4200 Pine St., Philadelphia, Pa. 19104. Illus., index, adv. Circ: 53,000. Sample. Vol. ends: June and Dec. Refereed. Microform: UM.

Indexed: BioAb, ChemAb, IMed, SCI. *Bk. rev:* 25, 250–600 words, signed. *Aud:* Sa.

Includes original articles, case reports, and reviews of current research interest, and covers the "broad field of internal medicine and allied sciences." Special articles of a general or review nature are frequently included. Editorial notes, medical news, questions and answers on particular aspects of internal medicine, and letters and comments are also regular features. Book reviews are short but good.

British Medical Journal. 1832. w. $36. Martin Ware. C. G. A. Parker, B. M. A. House, Tavistock Sq., London WC1H 9 JR, England. Illus., index, adv. Circ: 86,000. Sample. Vol. ends: March, June, Sept., Dec. Microform: UM.

Indexed: BioAb, ChemAb, IMed, SCI. *Bk. rev:* 7–8, 250–300 words, signed. *Aud:* Ac, Sa. *Jv:* V.

An international journal published by the British Medical Association. It contains papers of original research, commentaries on recent advances in medicine and related fields, articles on medical practice and clinical studies, news and correspondence. Along with *Lancet*, the leading journal of its type out of England, and a basic one for even the smallest medical collection. It is often quoted, and its papers represent some of the most advanced and original thinking now being published.

Bulletin of the History of Medicine. 1933. bi-m. $8 (Nonmembers $12). Lloyd G. Stevenson. Johns Hopkins Press, Baltimore, Md. 21218. Illus., adv. Circ: 1,993. Vol. ends: Nov./Dec.

Indexed: BioAB, IMed. *Bk. rev:* number varies, 200–2,000 words. *Aud:* Ga, Ac.

This journal, published jointly by the American Association for the History of Medicine and the Johns Hopkins Institute of the History of Medicine, is recognized as outstanding in its field. Scholarly articles by authorities are the emphasis of each issue. Regularly featured are "Notes and Comments," "Medico-Historical News and Activities," and "Contributors to this Number." The "Book Reviews" department is quite extensive. Although not so formidable as the technical titles in medicine, the arcane nature of the subject matter will appeal to a limited readership.

Two other fine journals should be mentioned. The first of these, *Journal of the History of Medicine and Allied Sciences* (1946. q. $15. Journal of the History of Medicine and Allied Sciences, Inc., Dept. of the History of Science and Medicine, Yale Univ., New Haven, Conn. Circ: 850) is perhaps the closest rival to the *Bulletin.* The other title, this time British, is *Medical History* (1956. q. $12. The Wellcome Institute of the History of Medicine, 183 Euston Road, London, NW1, England. Circ: 1,100). All three titles are similar in format and have like departments. They are highly recommended for libraries which emphasize medicine and biology in their collections. (F.A.)

China's Medicine. See China and Asia/China Section.

Hypnosis Quarterly. 1954. q. $6. Harry Arons, 60 Vose Ave., S. Orange, N.J. 07079. Illus., adv. Circ: 3,500. Sample. Vol. ends: Winter.

Bk. rev: 2, 250–500 words, signed. *Aud:* Ga, Ac.

Of the five journals in this field listed in the fourteenth edition of *Ulrich's,* this comes the closest to being semipopular. Even at that it is not for the average layman or high school student who wants to practice the noble art. Articles are easy enough to read, require no special background, but they do require an interest in the serious practice of hypnotism. Articles are by practitioners in the various areas of application —medical, dental, psychological. According to the editor, the primary purpose of this journal is to establish hypno-technicians as a worthy art ancillary to medicine, dentistry, and psychology. Hypno-technicians are trained lay hypnotists who work on therapeutic problems under the appropriate professional supervision. Recommended only for special situations, but if you think the situation is at hand, send for a sample copy and make your own decision.

International Journal of Psychobiology. 1970. q. $20. Samuel A. Corson. Plenum Publishing Corp., 227 W. 17th St., New York, N.Y. 10011. Illus., adv. Circ: 500. Sample.

Aud: Sa.

"Designed to present the most current information on the biophysical, biochemical, and neuroendocrine mechanism underlying the development of integrated adaptive reactions to psychoenvironmental changes." The publisher's description adds up to a scholarly journal for experts. The 100 or so pages is definitely not for anyone else.

Journal of School Health. 1927. m. (10 issues Sept.–June) Membership $15. Delbert Oberteuffer. Amer. School Health Assn., 107 S. Depeyster St., Kent, Ohio 44240. Illus., index, adv. Circ: 15,000. Sample. Vol. ends: Dec. Refereed.

Indexed: EdI, IMed. *Aud:* Hs, Ejh.

A journal for professionals concerned with the health of the student, kindergarten through college. School doctors, dentists, eye specialists, psychologists, educators, administrators, nurses, sociologists, and pharmacists will find a wide variety of articles on problems and programs concerned with the child and young adult in school. The journal also serves as the official repository of the annual reports of the study committees of the American School Health Association. It is one of the best single sources of information for personnel responsible for the health of the school child and the programs developed for him.

Lancet. 1823. w. $18.50. Ian Douglas Wilson. Lancet Ltd., 7 Adam St., London WC2, England. Subs. to: Little, Brown & Co., 34 Beacon St., Boston, Mass. 02106. Illus., adv. Circ: 45,000. Sample. Vol. ends: June and Dec. Refereed.

Indexed: BioAb, ChemAb, IMed, SCI. *Bk. rev:* 8, 225 words, signed. *Aud:* Ac, Ga. *Jv:* V.

This and the *New England Journal of Medicine* are by and large the most famous, most often quoted medical journals in the western world. *Lancet* is often the first to publish articles which are quoted in the world's press. And while the material is primarily technical, it can be understood by any well-educated layman. (It is no accident that this is among the regular reading items of mystery writer Georges Simenon.) The journal publishes articles dealing with medical postulates, methods, results, and discussions. An "Annotation Section" presents brief discussions of topics which deal with the relationship between medicine and the current problems of mankind. Editorial pages are informative, unbiased, and occasionally witty. One of the few medical journals which can be recommended for both public and academic libraries.

Medical Economics. 1923. bi-w. Free to doctors (Others $25). Cragin Lewis. Litton Publns., Oradell, N.J. 07649. Illus., index, adv. Circ: 194,000. Microform: UM.

Indexed: PAIS. *Aud:* Sa.

The oldest of a number of free (i.e., controlled circulation) medical magazines directed at doctors to promote ethical drugs via advertising. In order to get doctors to look at the advertisements, the publisher has to give him something he really wants to read. In this case it is articles on art, geography, history, literature, and sports. A good deal of the material, though, advises the doctor how to invest his money, how to save on taxes, etc. The interested layman will find much information here about why medical fees are so high. The magazine is sent only to doctors who request it, and it is free. Apparently an interested library should not have too much difficulty getting it. See also *Medical World News, Modern Medicine.* (One nice thing about all of them is that they are readable—in fact must be, if they are going to survive. And this is hardly a requirement for most other medical journals.)

Listed below are other magazines of this same genre, i.e., free to doctors for the express purpose of promoting drug advertisements.

MD; Medical News Magazine. 1957. m. Free to doctors (Others $12). Felix Marti-Ibanez. M.D. Publns., Inc., 30 E. 60th St., New York, N.Y. 10022. Illus., index, adv. Circ: 180,000.

A general news magazine with more emphasis on the arts and literature than its competitors. It is published in four editions, each with different advertising. One edition is in Spanish.

Physician's Management. 1961. m. Free to doctors (Others $10). Robert M. Hendrickson. Byrum Publns., 636 Church St., Evanston, Ill. 60201. Illus., index, adv. Circ: 175,000.

Total emphasis here is on the dollar. Experts tell the doctor about the management of his practice and finances, relationships with the patients and the community. Personal finance and investment considered.

RX Sports and Travel; the recreation and leisure magazine for physicians. 1966. bi-m. Free to doctors (Others $6.50). Tommy D. Harris. RX Golf and Travel Inc., 200 S. Main, Hillsboro, Ill. 62049. Illus., adv. Circ: 225,000.

Differs from the others in this genre in that it limits the amount of drug advertising, and includes advertisements for other items of interest to physicians from real estate to Rolls Royces. In between are articles on sports and travel.

Medical World News. 1960. w. Free to doctors (Others $15). Morris Fishbein. McGraw-Hill, Inc., 299 Park Ave., New York, N.Y. 10017. Illus., adv. Circ: 248,825. Vol. ends: Dec. Sample.

Indexed: BioAb. *Aud:* Ga, Ac.

As the title implies, a journal concerned with events, issues, and technical data of general interest to the medical practitioner. Each number is designed to alert the physician to any information which might affect his practice or increase his knowledge of trends in medicine, whether it be the certification of a new drug or legislation pending in Congress. The broad scope of the journal is indicated by two particular sections: "Focus on the News," and "Doctor's Business." Each issue has a special-interest article which treats a newsworthy topic with more than usual depth. Highly recommended for the library with a medical oriented clientele. (F.A.)

Modern Medicine; journal of diagnosis and treatment. 1933. bi-w. Free to doctors (Others $25). Irvine H. Page. Modern Medicine Publns., 4015 W. 65th St., Minneapolis, Minn. 55435. Illus., adv. Circ: 210,000. *Aud:* Sa.

A professionally written magazine which supports itself on advertising, not subscriptions. Nevertheless, of this genre it is one of the best because it sticks to medicine. A good part of each issue is given to abstracts of the more popular and useful articles from the world's medical literature. Some original articles, discussions, and a number of departments are included. Thanks to the good style and the abstracts, this, along with *Medical World News*, should be found in all medical collections. (F.A.)

New England Journal of Medicine. 1812. w. $15. Franz J. Ingelfinger. Massachusetts Medical Soc., 10 Shattuck St., Boston, Mass. 02115. Illus., index, adv. Circ: 126,000. Vol. ends: June and Dec. Refereed. Microform: UM.

Indexed: BioAb, IMed, SCI. *Bk. rev:* Various number, length, signed. *Aud:* Ac, Ga. *Jv:* V.

Probably the medical journal most often quoted in the popular press. Findings reported here on a weekly basis are many times concerned with basic health problems which affect just about everyone, e.g., current research on cancer and heart problems to statistical data on the nation's progress in health. While issued by the Massachusetts Medical Society, the scope is considerably broader than the interests of the Society. The weekly includes both original research papers (about four to five per issue), a review paper covering recent medical advances, some short case studies, and case records of the Massachusetts General Hospital. Brief editorials on medical topics and technical correspondence are also included. While the material is technical, it is of enough general interest to warrant inclusion in a public or academic library with a medium to large-sized collection of general health magazines.

Private Practice. 1969. m. Free to doctors (Others $7.50). Marvin H. Edwards. Congress of County Medical Societies (CCMS) Publishing Co., 1029 United

Founders Tower, Oklahoma City, Okla. 73116. Illus., index, adv. Circ: 65,000.

Aud: Ac, Ga.

The rightist socioeconomic publication of the medical set, and, as such, a natural foil for such magazines as *Health-Pac.* It has an advantage over its liberal counterpart, though. The publishers give it away. And while many laymen consider the American Medical Association at best conservative, the publishers of *Private Practice* think they are liberals. "Why? Because association policies and actions are dominated by educators and researchers." The articles and editorials point out how the country is going socialist or communist, or. . . . The writers are opposed to anything but private medicine. An interesting viewpoint, and one which should be found in the library where there are more liberal journals.

Social Science and Medicine. 1967. bi-m. $40. J. McEwan. Pergamon Press, Fairview Park, Elmsford, N.Y. 10523.

Bk. rev: 15–20, essays and notes. *Aud:* Ac.

An international journal which publishes papers on the interrelationship between medicine and the social sciences. Articles are in English, French, German, or Spanish, depending upon the nationality of the author. Extensive book reviews, proceedings, and monograph supplements. An interesting idea, but the price is too high for all but the largest special library.

Nursing

American Journal of Nursing. m. $8. Thelma M. Schoor. Amer. Journal of Nursing Co., 10 Columbus Circle, New York, N.Y. 10019. Illus., index, adv. Circ: 286,000. Vol. ends: Dec.

Indexed: IMed. *Bk. rev:* 6, 300 words, signed. *Aud:* Ac, Sa.

Ranging from material concerned with the highly specialized to the highly topical, this official magazine of the American Nurses' Association is geared toward both student and professional. Fifteen or so articles in each issue include contributions by nursing and allied medical and health specialists on new techniques or equipment, articles on professionalism, case studies or clinical reports, and short pieces on patient-nurse relations. An extensive news section touches on every aspect of nursing—education, legislation, service, professional practice—and special departments provide as good a current awareness program on research and nursing trends as any periodical in the field. Of particular note are "Drug Data," listing information on new pharmaceuticals, and "Medical Highlights," digesting new findings from the medical journals. Recommended for any library supporting a nursing program or any collection concerned with this aspect of health practice.

Canadian Nurse. 1905. m. $5. Virginia A. Lindabury. Canadian Nurses' Assn., 50 The Driveway, Ottawa 4, Ont., Canada. Illus., index, adv. Circ: 74,000. Sample. Vol. ends: Dec. Microform: UM.

Indexed: IMed. *Bk. rev:* 4, 250–500 words, signed. *Aud:* Ac.

Worldwide in scope, this periodical is available in both English and French language editions. The objective editorials deal with current topics and aim at stimulating interest in the profession's problem areas. The articles range from technical to popular; some have bibliographies. Featured departments are the recent additions to the CNA's library accession list, new products, and occasional research abstracts.

Journal of Nursing Education. 1962. q. Free. Mary A. Murray. McGraw-Hill, 330 W. 42nd St., New York, N.Y. 10036. Illus., index, adv. Circ: 10,000.

Indexed: CINL, IMed. *Aud:* Ac.

Short two to three page reports on various aspects and developments in nursing education. This is primarily for the teacher of nurses. As it is free, and as it is accurate and timely, it should be in all libraries with a nursing education program.

Journal of Practical Nursing. 1953. m. $6. Nancy Bass Lutzke. National Assn. for Practical Nurse Education and Service, 1465 Broadway, New York, N.Y. 10036. Illus., index, adv. Circ: 43,000. Sample. Vol. ends: Dec.

Bk. rev: 2, 400 words, signed. *Aud:* Ac, Sa.

Although primarily directed toward the licensed practical nurse, contains information which should be valuable to nursing students or the nursing profession at large. Authoritative, technical articles, by leading medical specialists, review current progress or practices in the medical sciences and represent excellent tutorials; current trends in continuing education for practical nurses, or professional attitudes are featured regularly; and informally written articles, contributed by LPNs, on nursing experiences, practical nursing notes and the like, are also included. Useful departments are: "Modern Medications," which reviews new drugs; "Health Highlights," which gives thumbnail reports on current medical news; and "A Look at Legislation," which deals with legislation affecting the profession. A good choice for vocational schools with medical technology programs.

Modern Nursing Home. 1947. m. $12. Robert M. Cunningham, Jr. McGraw-Hill, 230 W. Monroe St., Chicago, Ill. 60606. Illus., index. adv. Circ: 23,000. Sample.

Aud: Ac, Ga.

This is similar to its competitor, *Nursing Homes,* although neither publisher would admit as much. If a library takes one it might as well take the other. Both, let it be repeated, are controlled circulation, i.e., free to the select audiences the publisher is trying to reach via advertising which pays for the magazine.

The Nursing Clinics of North America. 1966. q. $12 (Students $10). Helen L. Dietz. W. B. Saunders Co., W. Washington Sq., Philadelphia, Pa. 19105. Illus., index. Vol. ends: Dec.

Indexed: CINL, IntNurI. *Aud:* Ac. *Jv.* V.

Issues contain two symposia on topics of interest to the nursing profession. The symposia, all of which have guest editors, focus on significant health-care problems and examine them from the appropriate social, psychological, and practical aspects. Recent symposia have been concerned with "The Nurse in Community Mental Health," "The Patient with Trauma," "The Ambulatory Patient," and "Administration on the Patient's Behalf." Articles are signed and "Contributors" lists the academic credentials of the authors. A "Special Features" section has one or two articles, generally with a practical emphasis. All issues of this case-bound journal have an excellent index, annually cumulated in December. (F.A.)

Nursing Forum. 1961. q. $7.50. Alice R. Clarke. Nursing Publns. Inc., Box 218, Hillsdale, N.J. 07642. Illus., index, adv. Circ: 6,000.

Indexed: CINL, IMed. *Bk. rev:* Various number, length. *Aud:* Sa.

A down-to-earth journal for the working nurse and the teacher. Material is purposefully written for the administrator or the leader who wants to keep up with activities in all areas of nursing from psychology to clinical medicine. Most of the material is original, in depth, and free of jargon. In fact, the articles tend to be better written than in many other journals of this type. A first choice for schools and for larger medical collections.

Nursing Homes. 1950. m. $10. Cogswell House, Inc., 222 Wisconsin Ave., Lake Forest, Ill. 60045. Illus., index, adv. Circ: 20,000. Sample.

Bk. rev: Various number, length. *Aud:* Ac, Sa.

A controlled circulation (i.e., free) magazine which is the official publication of the American Nursing Home Association. The purpose of the publication is to share with all nursing home workers the information that will encourage the highest standard of patient care. A variety of articles on the professional interests of nursing home owners, administrators, and staffs are found in the issues. An account of the legislative and federal administrative developments on the Medicare program, on the legal situations applicable to nursing homes; and other editorial pages are devoted to forum discussions. It has a book review section and colorful pictures are included. Recommended reading to the people who are associated with nursing home administration. (See also *Modern Nursing Home.*)

Nursing Mirror and Midwives Journal. 1886. w. $16.25. Yvonne Cross. IPC Specialist and Professional Press, Ltd. Subs. to: Subscription Manager, 40 Bowling Green Lane, London EC1, England. Illus., adv. Circ: 68,742. Vol. ends: Dec.

Indexed: CINL, IntNurI. *Bk. rev.* 6, 60–250 words, initialed. *Aud:* Sa, Ac.

Similar in many respects to *Nursing Times,* this journal has the subjective advantage of a more pleasing layout and more relaxed format. In addition to a weekly summary of news of interest to nurses, there are regular departments for letters, questions and answers, and editorial comments. Signed articles of general interest ("Healthier Future for Nepal's Children") and articles more technical in nature ("Surgical Conditions of the Head and Neck") are regularly featured. There is a huge classified section which would be of only passing interest to most American readers. Hospital and medical libraries could profit most from this title. (F.A.)

Nursing Outlook. 1953. m. $8. Edith P. Lewis. Amer. Journal of Nursing Co., 10 Columbus Circle, New York, N.Y. 10019. Illus., index, adv. Circ: 32,954. Sample. Vol. ends: Dec. Microform: UM.

Indexed: IMed, IntNurI, PsyAb. *Bk. rev:* 4–6, 250–300 words, signed. *Aud:* Sa.

Contains articles of interest to nurses, members of allied professions, and lay persons on the subjects of nursing service administration and community health nursing. The articles are presented in a broad context that underlines the increasingly important responsibilities of nursing in the delivery of health care. As the official publication of the National League for Nursing, it reports the programs and activities of the League's services and departments.

Nursing Research. 1952. bi-m. $15. Lucille E. Notter. Amer. Journal of Nursing Co., 10 Columbus Circle, New York, N.Y. 10019. Illus., index, adv. Circ: 7,500. Vol. ends: Nov./Dec. Refereed. Microform: UM.

Indexed: IMed, IntNurI, PsyAb. *Bk. rev:* 2–3, 500–1,000 words, signed. *Aud:* Sa.

Sponsored by the National League for Nursing and the American Nurse's Association, the publication stresses original research activities undertaken by the profession. Articles report on studies of nursing education, professional attitudes, experimental studies on nursing procedures, and clinical studies on nursing practices. Many of the papers are portions of doctoral and master's theses. Selected abstracts of the literature are featured regularly.

Nursing Times. 1905. w. $12.20. MacMillians Journals, Ltd., Bruner Road, Basingstroke, Hants, England. Illus., adv. Circ: 32,976. Vol. ends: Dec.

Indexed: CINL, IMed; IntNurI. *Bk. rev:* 1–3, 400–600 words, signed. *Aud:* Sa.

A comprehensive weekly reviewing events of interest to British nurses. In addition to the straight news coverage, there are brief signed articles potentially accessible to the nonspecialist, human interest stories concerned with nursing and medicine, and a letters section. Fully half of the journal is taken up by an exhaustive classified section. (F.A.)

RN Magazine; national magazine for nurses. 1937. m. $6. Richard F. Newcomb. Litton Publns., Oradell, N.J. 07649. Illus., index, adv. Circ: 230,000. Microform: UM.

Indexed: CINL. *Aud:* Sa, Ac.

By the same publisher who brings the doctor *Medical Economics*, and with about the same purpose in mind. According to the publisher, "Besides the regular paid subscribers, *RN Magazine* is sent free each year to some 35,000 senior nursing students, by personal request only." The articles are well written, accurate, and timely. They cover all aspects of the profession. The approach is clever, and the material is authentic. Much of it will interest the layman who is interested in medicine, but wishes to avoid the jargon. A first class semipopular magazine for nurses. In addition to the regular 100-page library edition, there is a special edition for intensive care, coronary care nurses; and another for operating room and emergency room nurses.

MEN'S MAGAZINES

Basic Periodicals

Hs: *True* Ga: *True, Argosy, Playboy;* Jc & Ac: *Playboy, Penthouse.*

Cessations

Dare.

Introduction

If women's magazines exploit the body consumer, so do the so-called men's magazines. They are a bit more crass, though. This accounts in part for the failure of their acceptance in libraries—or, for that matter, the stamp of index approval of any single one of them by *Readers' Guide.*

By "crass" is meant the stereotype of the man in quest of hi-fidelity in his sex life, his work, and his fantasies as an adventurer or sportsman. Few of the magazines assume he is less then James Bond. He will have it no other way.

"He," to be sure, refers to the young man in high school and the eternal youth fan. "He" is neither overly bright nor imaginative. "He," in fact, makes up a good part of the nonreading public.

Then, too, there is another "he." This is the chap who can take or leave the magazines, thumbs through them pretty much for the same reason a woman (who should know better) enjoys the women's magazines—i.e., for relaxation and fun.

Regardless of content, motive, or explanation for lack of the titles in libraries, they should be there. This seems particularly true at the high school level. After all, not every young man thinks the beginning and end of magazines is *Hot Rod* or *Popular Mechanics*. And if the library is not quite up to *Playboy*, there are other better magazines which will meet at least some of the fantasies realized via the *Playboy* syndrome.

See also titles in the Fiction Section—particularly the science fiction. Do not overlook the reliable comics, especially the underground variety.

Finally, please try to remember that men need liberating too. Not all of them identify with the so-called man's magazine. A good number will be quite happy with the general magazine, or the literary review, not to mention the automobile magazines. (P.S. Women, too, will enjoy many of the stereotyped men's magazines. Men have no corner on love of adventure, cars, or fantasy.)

Adam; the man's home companion. 1956. m. $.75 a copy. Merrill Miller. Publishers Service Inc., 8060 Melrose Ave., Los Angeles, Calif. 90046. Circ: 500,000.

Aud: Ga.

One of the better-known combination girlie-current-concern men's magazines. It is somewhat on the level of *Modern Man* and *Knight*, better than the former, not quite up to the latter, and somewhere in that great grey area of newsstand material which is so well known to anyone who browses. (*Adam* is by the same publisher as *Knight*.) The primary audience is the young man who is looking for information on sex, usually hidden in articles and stories, and identity in terms of what to think about current events and affairs. He obviously is not overly sophisticated, yet is not the average, and wants something more than the girls who do parade from page to page. The editors afford him a painless kind of education. Not for libraries, but an interesting item, nevertheless.

American Legion. See General Magazines Section.

Argosy. 1882. m. $5. Henry Steeger. Popular Publns., Inc., 205 E. 42nd St., New York, N.Y. 10017. Illus., adv. Circ: 1,311,000.

Aud: Ga, Hs.

A pre–*Playboy/Penthouse* view of the male. The target audience is the high school teenager and young man with a simplistic yet somehow refreshing view of existence. Here the editors and writers see him as transfixed by sports, hunting, fishing, and jumping in and out of automobiles. He has little or no time for women—unless, of course, they are Moms, good cooks, or fill in as background in an occasional travel piece. Some time he can give to culture, politics, and social issues, but not too much. Here pleasure is the last frontier of the western and adventure movie. It is all carried out with vim, vigour, and no little skill by professional writers and illustrators. And as life somehow never quite measures up to expectation, *Argosy* is one of the few men's magazines which puts great stress on short stories and excerpts from novels. The fiction is good to excellent, at least in terms of the genre. There is violence, of sorts, in both articles and fiction, but it is well enough controlled. There are no pinups, no Anglo-Saxon expressions of anger or lust, little or no mention of sex. It is a magazine for the graduate Boy Scout who may not be too bright or too imaginative, but gets a kick out of John Wayne's view of existence. Harmless, fun for over a million readers, and why is it not found in most libraries? The only real answer to that one might be: "Readers prefer *True*"—the only competitor *Argosy* has these days.

Cavalier. 1951. m. $9. Douglas Allen. Allen-Dugent Publishing, 236 East 46th St., New York, N.Y. 10017. Subs. to: Kable News Co., 777 Third Ave., New York, N.Y. 10017. Illus., index, adv. Circ: 225,000. Sample. Vol. ends: Dec.

Bk. rev: 1, 2 pages, signed. *Aud:* Ga.

One of the better, more successful men's magazines, this does have girls, but at a considerably more realistic level than found in *Playboy*. With that out of the way, the magazine can be recommended for a general collection on several counts: the articles are by well-known journalists; there is a three-page Deadbone comics (in color) by Vaughn Bode, one of the country's top underground cartoonists; music reviews by Lenny Kaye, selected by *Esquire* as one of the 100 most important people in Rock in 1971; monthly articles by Dale Remington, a CBS special assignment reporter; and even a column on cooking by Donald Kramer. Sure, men subscribe or buy it on the newsstands for the girls, but a good many more enjoy the text—material which stresses, believe it or not, the cultural as well as the practical aspects of being a man in America today. (Members of Women's Liberation will take exception to all of this—which is fine; but librarians who take exception because they do not like the girlie pictures are simply not with the 1946 scene—nor probably is their library.)

Elks. See General Magazines Section.

Esquire. See General Magazines Section.

Frontier Times. 1958. bi-m. $4. Pat Wagner. J. A. Small, Box 3338, Austin, Tex. 78704. Illus., index, adv. Circ: 141,000. Sample.

Bk. rev: Notes. *Aud:* Ga, Hs.

A popular man's magazine which features factual, authentic stories of the Old West. Photographs and illustrations of the period are used to give greater authenticity to the material. The articles are popularly written rather than scholarly, but every effort is made to present the facts as they happened. The articles deal with Indians, outlaws, lost gold, and many other facets of Western history. On occasion there are features on Mexico and Alaska and some modern looks at ghost towns, mining camps, and other points which may interest the tourist. An above average "Western" type magazine which will appeal to adults and teen-agers. It should be found in collections where there is any effort to lure the reader normally "turned off" by more scholarly history magazines. This is one of three popular history magazines on the West published by J. A. Small—see also *Old West* and *True West*.

Future Magazine. 1938. m. $2. Jim Lamb. The United States Jaycees, Boulder Park, Box 7, Tulsa, Okla. 74102. Illus., adv. Circ: 245,000.

Aud: Ga.

Although a publication of the well-known Jaycees, this comes close to being a general magazine for young men (i.e., those from about 21 to 36). There are no pinups, but there are some well-written articles on everything from drug abuse to the counterculture and how it affects business. The editors shy clear of controversy, although press for generally acceptable matters such as conservation and environment, better schools, etc. Only about one third of every number is given over to the Jaycees. A good magazine for the average young businessman.

Generation; the magazine of young executives. 1969. m. $9. Robert Tamarkin. Generation Inc., 444 North LaSalle St., Chicago, Ill. 60610. Illus., adv. Circ: 65,000. Sample.

Bk. rev: Various number, length. *Aud:* Ac, Ga.

While important parts of the general format of *Generation* are the up-to-date, concise, and well written departments under titles such as "Business Directions," "The Economic Pulse," "Taxes and Your Income," "Generation International," and "Personal Investments," the core of the magazine is the several articles which highlight trends affecting the young executive's personal as well as business career. These information pieces, which deal with contemporary issues, set the magazine apart from the general business interest magazine. A typical article, "The Agony of the Divorced Executive," presented a straightforward, honest accounting of a personal situation which can affect a man's relationships in the business world. Another, "Portrait of the Businessman as a Gorgon," dealt with the fictional faces of the businessman as rendered by writers in today's novels. *Generation* reflects the accomplishments and new attitudes of young businessmen by presenting personal case histories of successful young executives. (M.E.)

Gentlemen's Quarterly. 1957. 8/yr. $8. Jack Haber. Esquire Inc., 488 Madison Ave., New York, N.Y. 10022. Illus., adv. Circ: 200,000. Sample. Vol. ends: Winter.

Aud: Ga.

A man's high fashion magazine, this is unique in that it is the only consumer-oriented fashion periodical in the United States devoted solely to masculine interests. It is probably read as much by apparel manufacturers and dealers as the general public. A typical issue may touch on what color shirt to wear to the six button double-breasted styling, in addition to current fashion availabilities. Not for every library, or every reader, but it has more than passing interest for the fashion-aware man as well as the woman who helps him purchase his clothes.

His; magazine of inter-varsity fellowship. 1941. m. $4.50. Inter-Varsity Christian Fellowship, 5206 Main St., Donners Grove, Ill. 60515. Illus., index. Circ: 30,000. Sample.

Bk. rev: Various number, length. *Aud:* Ga, Hs.

An old magazine with a new format and an ageless message. It is a general magazine for the young Christian male on campus. Sex, culture, drugs, campus unrest, education, politics, the new technology and its implications are regularly discussed in the approximately six to eight two-page feature articles in each issue. Each article is, in effect, an instruction in the application of the Christian faith to campus life, but even with this in mind, the reader is not subjected to sermonizing. Most articles are authored by members of the Inter-Varsity Christian Fellowship, many of whom are college faculty members. Articles have dealt with a critical evaluation of the philosophy of Marcuse, a young man's first two months in the Army, and suggestions on living with sex. Regular departments include an editorial statement, letters to the editor, record and book reviews, and a new department which features excerpts from the great Christian writers of the past. Personal experiences and human interest stories are regularly featured. The magazine has very attractive art illustrations which make it even more appealing to the campus crowd. *His* would appeal to the young man on campus and in some cases to high school students. (M.E.)

Kiwanis. See General Magazines Section.

Knight; the magazine for the adult male. bi-m. $6. Jared Rutter. Publishers Service Inc., 8060 Melrose Ave., Los Angeles, Calif. 90046. Illus., adv. Circ: 275,000.

Aud: Ga.

While this is a bit stronger on pin-ups than *Cava-*

lier, the level of its articles and particularly its fiction is the same. The editor often features new writers, and a number of their efforts will have strong appeal to younger adults. Science fiction is also stressed. There are the usual number of features on the good life, e.g., sports cars, dining out, dress, personalities. Again, not to be confused with the run-of-the-mill girlie magazine.

Modern Man. 1950. m. $7.50. Publishers' Development Corp., 8150 N. Central Park Ave., Skokie, Ill. 60076. Illus., adv. Circ: 115,000.

Aud: Ga. Jv: C.

The girlie magazine is nowhere better represented than in *Modern Man.* There are just enough good (sometimes surprisingly good) articles on sports, adventure, and sex to keep it this side of the porno parade. Some of the photo features, in fact, have touched on current events from the war in Vietnam to concern over the environment. Yet the pervading interest of its readers is not the literary material. The visual, which is sometimes a bit bizarre in terms of physical proportions, is what attracts them. The magazine is mentioned not as a library consideration, but only in terms of contrast with such relatively harmless items as *Playboy, Cavalier,* and *Penthouse.* In contrast, *Modern Man* is to these magazines what *Pravda* is to the *Reader's Digest*—the only thing they have in common is newsprint.

Montana Lawman's Gunsmoke Gazette. 1971. bi-m. $3. Charles B. Wolfe. Governors Crime Commission and Montana Law Enforcement Academy, Butte, Mont.

Aud: Ac, Ga.

The *Gazette* is a tabloid newspaper format of approximately 20 pages in length. According to the editor's statement in the first issue "the Gazette is for the general practitioner in criminal justice. Police, courts and corrections share equal billing, side by side." Generally six or seven feature articles are provided with the content equally divided between training, educational, and general interest material for the layman. Articles are either staff written or authored by professionals in the criminal justice and allied fields. An attempt is made to strike a balance between professional interests and matters fascinating to any detective story fan. There are abstracts of articles from the popular press and reprints of articles from magazines such as *Crime Control Digest, Psychology Today,* and *Law and Order.* Several historical articles and an editorial or two from the early press of Montana add color and historical perspective. The *Gazette's* general appearance is that of a newspaper out of the "old west"; this western flavor is captured by the attractive illustrations and the lettering used at the head of each column. General appeal would be to men from high school up. (M.E.)

Old West. 1964. q. $2. Pat Wagner. Joe A. Small, Box 3338, Austin, Tex. 78704. Illus., adv. Circ: 150,000. Sample.

Bk. rev: Notes. *Aud:* Ga, Hs.

An above-average "western" for the historically inclined reader who desires more fact than fiction and is devoted to popular stories concerning western history. Frequent use is made of authentic photos, and the subject matter touches such varied facets of western life as ghost towns, lost treasure, Indians, and descriptions of colorful frontier characters. Among the contributors are the noted western writers J. Frank Dobie and S. Omar Barker. Each issue carries a reprint of a rare book that is costly or not available to the average reader. While a trifle more serious than *Frontier Times*, it is of the same genre and should be considered by high school and public libraries that feel a need for such material.

Penthouse. 1965. m. $10. Bob Guccione. Penthouse Intl. Ltd., 1560 Broadway, New York, N.Y. 10036. Illus., adv. Circ: 800,000. Sample.

Aud: Ga.

The British equivalent of *Playboy*, but with some interesting differences. A few years ago, i.e. around 1969, the English publisher brought his magazine to America. It has since enjoyed increased circulation, and the English firm is out to catch up with and pass *Playboy*. The method is to one-up, or one-better Hefner's enfant. There are the usual stories and articles, but there is more emphasis on humor. The primary features, to be sure, are the girls who seem a bit plumper than the *Playboy* variety, and are noticeable in that pubic hairs are more freely displayed. This "daring" step forward (or backward) has increased circulation almost as much as the writing, which is first rate, and as good as anything found in *Playboy*. The English bias at one time showed, but the magazine is by now almost an entirely American product. (Some material is published in both the American and English editions, but they are really two separate magazines.) In addition to stories and articles there are the regular features for young men, i.e., the target group of 18–30: food, fashion, grooming, films, theatre, recordings, etc. The magazine, this side of the photos, seems a bit more sophisticated than *Playboy*, at least considerably less serious. It is an affront to all women, but a joy to some men. One suspects no library that passed up *Playboy* will jump to take this one either, but for the daring, for the libraries with an eye on the men's interests, it can be recommended.

Playboy. 1953. m. $10. Hugh Hefner. Playboy Enterprises, Inc. 919 N. Michigan Ave., Chicago, Ill. 60611. Illus., index, adv. Circ: 5,935,000.

Bk. rev: Various number, length, signed. *Aud:* Ga, Hs.

A good general magazine which has appeal for both men and women. Articles are timely, often involved with current social and political issues. There are first rate, long, and intensive interviews with controversial public figures. The fiction, from Bellow to Wodehouse, is sometimes better known for its author than for its quality, but at least an effort is made to acquaint readers with "name" writers. The cartoons are a bit excessive sexually, yet entertaining and witty. The regular departments include book reviews, food and drink, record reviews, films, etc. Each fat issue is even more so for the numerous advertisements. Editorially the magazine is interested in "today's" world and concerns. Little is taboo, and controversy is as welcome as in any radical left or right wing journal. The factual material is carefully documented and much of what is found here could be safely used in any research or reference paper by a high school or undergraduate student. It adds up to a worthwhile magazine for some six million readers. Yet, it is rarely found in libraries. The reason, of course: bare barbie dolls.

Real West. 1957. m. $5. Pat Masulli. Charlton Publns., Inc. Charlton Bldg., Derby, Conn. 06418. Illus., adv. Circ: 130,000. Sample.

Aud: Ga, Hs, Ac.

Primarily an illustrated approach to western history, and in this particular differs from such magazines as *Frontier Times* and *True West*. A good number of relatively rare, and some heretofore unpublished photographs are used. This, along with articles which are documented, gives it a place in larger academic libraries as well as in general reading collections. The style is popular, the material moves from the Indians to the badmen. Some of the photos may shock, but then that was life in the real West.

Rotarian. See General Magazines Section.

Saga. 1951. m. $6. Martin M. Singer. McFadden-Bartell, 333 Johnson Ave., Brooklyn, N.Y. 11206. Illus., adv. Circ: 225,000. Sample. Vol. ends: Dec.

Aud: Ga, Hs.

Along with *True* and *Argosy*, one of the more popular general men's magazines. An average 100-page issue is for the high school student and the man with a high school education or less. (Some college graduates will enjoy, too, but the level of writing is intentionally geared for a relatively unsophisticated reading audience.) A typical well-illustrated issue includes a dozen articles, most of which stress current events and affairs. Lately, too, the magazine has taken on a social consciousness, e.g., "President Nixon's VA medicine is killing our veterans." But most of the material involves adventure, space travel, science, and man against nature. There is some biographical material about personalities in the news. Usually one or two pages of a pin-up gal, but clothed, if a bit exposed. Most of the photographs and line drawings are vivid, yet no more shocking than those found in a daily newspaper. The advertising is primarily concerned with building the body. A perfectly acceptable, harmless magazine for public and high school libraries. But send for sample, and see for yourself.

True. 1937. m. $7. Mark Penzer. Fawcett Publns., Inc., 1515 Broadway, N.Y., N.Y. 10036. Illus., adv. Circ: 1,600,000.

Bk. rev: Notes. *Aud:* Ga, Hs. *Jv:* V.

The best of the general men's magazines. The only close comparison is *Argosy*. The two differ in that *True* is directed to a better educated, more sophisticated, more ambitious audience of older men. They enjoy the *Argosy* adventure trip, but they also realize that life is more than a sporting affair with dreams. A balance is achieved by giving readers sports, adventure, and automobiles; and adding the important articles and features on careers, marriage, health, finance and, to a lesser degree, political and social issues. There are interviews with major figures in the news and entertainment world, and a number of departments which are informative and well written. The magazine is short on fiction, and while a woman in a bathing suit may appear occasionally, sex is played down more than in most standard, general women's magazines. During the past years the magazine has improved, particularly in terms of its layout which is now quite good. There are fine to excellent photographs and illustrations. A solid magazine for most high schools, public libraries, and not a few general reading collections in universities and colleges.

True Detective. 1924. m. $4. A. P. Govoni. Macfadden Bartell Publishing Corp. 205 E. 42nd St., New York, N.Y. 10017. Illus., adv. Circ: 168,000.

Aud: Ga.

One of three detective/crime magazines issued by Macfadden-Bartell. The other two (with approximately the same basic approach and circulation) are: *Master Detective* and *Official Detective*. Followers of the genre say there is a difference among these, but to the casual reader they seem pretty much the same. Most of the drive is towards posed or press photographs—the bloodier the better—and detailed step-by-step detective work. The cops always come out looking good, and the "bad guys" just as evil. Most of the material is based upon true cases, but one suspects that aside from the skeleton of truth the whole is fleshed out as much by the author's imagination as by the facts. Most of the stories follow a chronological pattern of crime, to solution, to jail. The motives are, at best, simplistic; but the solutions are often complex, even confusing. A somewhat different type of reader —usually a man, less sophisticated and less educated than average—prefers this type of reading. Few take it seriously, yet find the factual approach considerably

more satisfactory than work done by fictional characters. Libraries may not normally consider any of these —or half a dozen other titles by different publishers— but they are good to keep in mind when the library is seriously trying to reach out for certain types of nonusers.

True West. 1953. bi-m. $4. Pat Wagner. J. A. Small, Box 3338, Austin, Tex. 78704. Illus., index, adv. Circ: 169,000. Sample.

Aud: Ga, Hs.

A popular man's magazine, this features authentic nonfiction stories dealing with all facets of the Old West. Such colorful figures as famous lawmen, outlaws, and Indians are among the subjects featured. The well-known Western writer, Walt Coburn, is a frequent contributor, and on the whole the level of writing is good to excellent. The approach is similar to that of the publisher's other magazines, *Frontier Times* and *Old West*, and one or all would be equally good for most libraries.

Zane Grey Western Magazine. 1969. m. $7. Cylvia Kleinman. Renown Publns., 56 West 45th St., New York, N.Y. 10036. Illus., adv. Sample.

Aud: Ga, Hs.

An effort to immortalize Zane Grey and to publish stories by and about the great master of western fiction. "This year of 1972 marks an important and thrilling milestone for *Zane Grey Western Magazine*," the editor notes. "It marks the centennial of Zane Grey's birth." A typical issue opens with a story by Grey, is followed by six to ten true articles on the West—including a piece on some aspect of Grey and his activities—and four to five short Western stories. The writing style is simple, straightforward, and easily grasped by a teen-ager. The material seems truthful enough, although in part is greatly exaggerated. There are the usual strong man advertisements, although nothing here should offend even the most fastidious. A good light addition for a popular reading room catering to young men and older men who think that way.

MILITARY MAGAZINES

See also Peace Section.

Basic Periodicals

Ga: *Strategy & Tactics;* Jc&Ac: *Strategy & Tactics, Military Affairs, Infantry.*

Basic Abstracts and Indexes

Air University Library Index on Military Periodicals, Abstracts of Military Bibliography.

Air Force Times. see *Army Times* in Newspapers/ Special Interest Section.

Armed Forces Comptroller. 1954. q. Membership (Nonmembers $5). F. I Bowie, Amer. Soc. of Military Comptrollers, Box 368. Arlington, Va. 22210. Illus. Circ: 3,000. Sample. Vol. ends: Fall. Microform: UM.

Aud: Ac, Ga.

With attention being given to military waste and budget disasters, this professional journal of the American Society of Military Comptrollers has given appeal. It presents justification for spending and overspending. Most of the material is well within the understanding of the layman, at least one interested in business. It is listed here because it offers a source rarely noted in writings in this area. And lest anyone think it does not represent the military viewpoint, let it be noted that in order to submit a manuscript: (Spring 1971, p. 2) "1. Write the article and get it approved by your supervisor. 2. Have the article cleared for publication by your local Information Office. 3. After clearance, mail the article to the editor."

Armed Forces Journal. 1863. w. $12. J. D. Hessman. Army and Navy Journal, Inc., 1710 Connecticut Ave., N.W., Washington, D.C. 20009. Illus., adv. Circ: 21,000.

Indexed: AirUnLibI. *Bk. rev:* Notes. *Aud:* Sa.

A type of *U.S. News and World Report–Business Week* for people in and out of the armed forces who are as much concerned with government and finance as with war. The weekly reports are both objective and subjective. They are objective in that they report accurately on what is going on in Congress, the promotion and personal activities of key personnel, and the various developments in weapons. Conversely, they are subjective in that the whole tone is, understandably, almost paranoid when it comes to military and a larger and larger defense (or war) system. While meant primarily for men and women in the armed forces, there is much here of interest to any involved layman. Note the age of this magazine—it is good, in fact quite good for what it does.

Army. 1950. m. $7.50. L. James Binder. Assn. of the United States Army, 1529 18th St., N.W., Washington, D.C. 20036. Illus., index, adv. Circ: 105,000.

Indexed: AirUnLibI. *Bk. rev:* Various number, length. *Aud:* Sa.

Editorially prepared for both the members of the armed forces and for anyone involved indirectly with the army, i.e. defense workers, engineers, military buffs, etc. Most of the material is made up of the army, weaponry, battles, and personalities. There is considerable emphasis on military tactics to protect the United States from possible attack. The make-up is professional, the approach biased in favor of more military spending, and the tone relatively sophisticated. A first choice for many libraries who have to decide on one or two army magazines.

Army Digest. See *Soldiers.*

Army Times. See Newspapers/Special Interest Section.

Infantry. 1921. bi-m. $5.95. Lt. Col. Edward M. Bradford. Birmingham Publishing Co., 130 S. 19th St., Birmingham, Ala. 35233. Illus., index, adv. Circ: 15,000. Sample. Vol. ends: Nov./Dec.

Indexed: AirUnLibI. *Bk. rev:* 5, 90 words. *Aud:* Ga, Hs.

Written for and by the professional infantryman, this is a superior magazine of its type. The average 72-page issue is nicely edited, well written, and clearly illustrated. Articles cover every aspect of a soldier's life from what to do in an ambush to financial planning for a family. The editor says this "provides current doctrinal information on infantry organization, weapons, equipment, tactics and techniques." The key word is "doctrinal," for this is a professional magazine with a definite and understandable point of view. As such it will not have wide appeal among those who would just as soon forget the Army, but for anyone seriously interested in the Army as a career it will be most welcome. The material is accurate and usually candid. A publication of the Fort Benning Infantry School, it is supported solely by subscriptions, not Army funds. Depending on viewpoint, a possible addition for public and some senior high school libraries.

P.S. Revolutionaries might learn a few things from the pros.

Military Affairs, the journal of military history, including theory and technology. 1937. q. Membership $7.50 (Institutions $9). Robin Higham. Dept. of History, Kansas State Univ., Manhattan, Kans. 66502. Illus., index, adv. Circ: 2,000. Vol. ends: Dec. Reprint: Kraus.

Indexed: AmerH, HistAb. *Bk. rev:* 40–50, 250–300 words, signed.

This publication of the American Military Institute is a scholarly journal which concentrates on detailed articles by both professional historians and members of the armed forces. Emphasis tends to be on American military, but the magazine is international in scope. All branches of the armed forces are considered and most of the material is well documented. There are numerous historical journals in this area, but this is the standard American publication. Features include news of interest to military historians; "Museum Perspectives," which lists various exhibitions; and occasional lists of journal articles.

Military Law Review. See Law Section.

Military Review. 1922. m. $4. Col. Donald J. Delaney. U.S. Army Command and General Staff College, Fort

Leavenworth, Kans. 66027. Illus., index, adv. Circ: 22,000.

Indexed: AirUnLibI, PAIS. *Bk. rev:* Various number, length. *Aud:* Sa.

A general military journal at a relatively high level of sophistication. It is more involved with tactics than with politics, more interested in strategy and the higher levels of military command than with government spending. The articles presuppose some background in training to fight everything from small guerilla operations to full-scale wars. The writing is professional, precise, and documented. It is no accident that the journal is available in Spanish and Portuguese—it is a favored item among the Latin American military (and those, by the by, who are trying to overthrow the military). A basic magazine for collections in this area.

Navy Times. See *Army Times* in Newspapers/Special Interest Section.

Soldiers (Formerly: *Army Digest*). 1946. m. $9.50 stateside and A.P.O. addresses, $12.00 foreign. Col. Lane Carlson, WAC. *Soldiers* Magazine, Cameron Station, Alexandria, Va. 22314. Illus., index. Circ: 250,000. Vol. ends: Dec.

Indexed: AirUnLibI. *Aud:* Ga.

Soldiers is the U. S. Army's official magazine, whose mission is "to provide timely, factual information . . . on policies, plans, operations and technical developments of the Dept. of the Army to the Active Army, Army National Guard, Army Reserve, and Dept. of the Army Civilian employees." It also conveys views of the Secretary of Army and the Chief of Staff on topics of professional interest to Army members and assists in achieving information objectives of the Army. All of which pretty well sets the tone, interest level, and content of the (average) 20 articles and features in each 64-page issue. Coverage includes Army personal affairs, recreation and sports, benefits available to service personnel and their dependents, accounts of exploits, problems related to current social issues, professional endeavors, and some historical material often in a humorous vein. Authors are fully credited for their contributions and include a large representation of NCOs along with commissioned officers, civilians, and the regular magazine staff. Knowledge of Army terminology, abbreviations, and acronyms, as well as jargon in current use, is assumed. Some humor and one piece of "cheesecake" of the pin-up variety is included. For young men who may be interested in their forthcoming service careers and for adult general readers, with more interest for men than for women. (H.S.)

Soviet Military Review. See USSR and East Europe/English Language General Section.

Strategy & Tactics. 1966. bi-m. $10. Simulations Publns. Inc., Rm. 309, 34 E. 23rd St., New York, N.Y. 10010. Illus.

Bk. rev: Notes. *Aud:* Ga.

Both a magazine and a game, this consists of a 32 to 40 page issue and a ready-to-play war game with a playing surface and die-cut playing pieces. The magazine features articles on the game, as well as historical pieces on famous battles, e.g., some in Vietnam, tactical combat in Russia during World War II, and the war in the Pacific. Primarily for the individual rather than the library, this appeals to the man or woman who likes his fighting in the atmosphere of peace and quiet. The inclusion of the game would make it a first class headache for even the most devoted librarian. Aside from that, who needs a magazine like this? Just pick up today's paper.

U.S. Naval Institute Proceedings. 1873. m. $8.50. Robert P. Brewer. U.S. Naval Inst., Annapolis, Md. 21402. Illus., index, adv. Circ: 68,000.

Indexed: AirUnLibI, PAIS. *Bk. rev:* Various number, length. *Aud:* Sa.

Along with the *Armed Forces Journal*, one of the older, basic journals in this field. The *Proceedings* is for men and women of the Navy, Coast Guard, Marines and the general maritime services. Most of the material is noncontroversial, deals with aspects of weapons, tactics, and personnel. The articles may be monographic in length. They are well documented and authoritative. The journal includes a number of departments from a historical pictorial section to excellent book reviews. The magazine has some following among laymen and landsmen who are deeply interested in navy history and affairs.

MOTION PICTURES

See also Communications and Media Section.

Basic Periodicals

GENERAL. Hs: *Take One;* Ga: *Film Quarterly, Film Comment, Film Culture;* Jc: *Take One, Film Comment, Film Culture, Film Quarterly;* Ac: *Film Comment, Cineaste, Film Culture, Film Quarterly, Take One, Sight & Sound.*

FOREIGN LANGUAGE. Ga: *Cahiers du Cinema;* Jc & Ac: *Cahiers du Cinema, Positif.*

REVIEWS. Ejh: *Film News;* Hs: *Filmfacts, Film News;* Ga: *Filmfacts, Landers Film Review, Film News;* Jc & Ac: *Filmfacts, Monthly Film Bulletin.*

Library and Teaching Aids

Film Library Quarterly, American Film Institute. Report, Education Newsletter.

Cessations

Audio Visual Media, Montage, Moviegoer.

Abstracts and Indexes

There are several indexes to film reviews, but no index to film magazines per se. *Readers' Guide* indexes only *Film Quarterly*. The need for such an index has been obvious, and in 1973 R. R. Bowker will publish the international index being prepared by the Documentation Commission of the International Federation of Film Archives (FIAF). The Commission is already indexing 57 international film periodicals, including these US publications: *American Cinematographer, Cineaste, Film Comment, Film Culture, Film Heritage, Film Quarterly, Film Society Review, Filmmakers Newsletter, Films in Review* and *Inter/View*. Entries are prepared by member archives in the cooperating countries, then sent to the Danish Film Museum in Copenhagen where the information is duplicated onto standard film cards which are then sent to the member archives. Participating US and Canadian archives are the American Film Institute, Department of Theater Arts UCLA, Canadian Film Archives Ottawa, Library of Congress, and the Museum of Modern Art. Current periodicals are being indexed as they are published, but back issues and additional titles will be included in the future. It is intended to publish the index in book form at the end of each year.

Meanwhile another index is in the planning stages. Information on this second index may be obtained by writing Professor Vincent Aceto, Library School, State University of New York, Albany, N.Y.

General

American Film Institute. Report. Education Newsletter. 1970. 8/yr. Membership. $10. Sali Ann Kriegsman. American Film Inst., 1815 H St. N.W. Washington, D.C. 20006. Illus. Circ: 10,000. Sample. Vol. ends: No. 8.

Bk. Rev: 1, 600 words, signed. *Aud:* Ac, Hs.

Established "to preserve the heritage and advance the art" of the film, the nonprofit American Film Institute issues two magazines which are invaluable to the teacher and student of film. A magazine and a newsletter are included under a single cover, with the report taking some 14 pages, the newsletter another four. The letter gives news of grants, workshops and opportunities for film teachers. The report is more like a standard film magazine, has featured short articles on various directors, studios and individual films. Some news on educational television, too. A pretty steep price for a magazine although the price includes membership. A basic publication for the film teacher from high school on up.

✓***Audiovisual Instruction.*** See Communications and Media Section.

Billboard. See Newspapers/Special Interest Section.

Camera People; a biweekly journal of film, video and still photography. 1971. bi-w. $5. Sally Harris. Our-

gang Graphics, 372 Main St., Watertown, Mass. 02172. Illus., adv. Sample.

Aud: Ac, Ga, Hs.

A 12 to 16 page tabloid newspaper which covers all aspects of the film, but is particularly strong on still photography and motion pictures. Articles are short. There are excellent still shots by a number of different, younger photographers, e.g., four pages of an issue given completely to photos of boxers and poets. A useful double-page listing of current shows and films in the greater Boston area is included. Some brief material on audiovisual equipment.

Canyon Cinema News. 1966. 6–8/yr. $3/6 nos. Box 637 Sausalito, Calif. 94956. Illus., adv. Circ: 500.

Aud: Ac, Ga.

Somewhat the equivalent of *Filmmakers Newsletter* and *Making Films in New York*, but a smaller edition of both for west coast film makers and fans. (In format, it is a little newsletter.) Most of the material is concerned with the experimental film, film festivals, individual producers and directors, and some feature on excellent reviews of the avant-garde and underground film. A required, unfortunately too little-known item, for libraries where there is the slightest interest in doing it yourself and making it with the new film movement.

Cineaste. 1967. q. $3. Gary Crowdus. Cineaste Magazine, 144 Bleecker St., New York, N.Y. 10012. Illus., index, adv. Circ: 3,000. Sample. Vol. ends: Spring.

Bk. rev: 4, 1,000 words, signed. *Aud:* Ac, Ga. *Jv:* V.

The editor describes his 48 to 60 page offset magazine as devoted to "cinema engagé—a cinema engaged in the movement of social change." Strongly influenced by the activist philosophy of Godard, the average issue is a far cry from the traditional. It usually consists of four or five articles; film, magazine, and book reviews, and special reports. (Librarians trying to keep up with new film magazines should subscribe regardless of what they may think about the editorial philosophy—the section reviewing film magazines is the best going.) During the past couple of years the editorial policy change has meant a distinctive policy. As the editor puts it: "We feature material on political films and film makers—issues have included interviews with Costa-Gavras, Glauber Rocha, Fernando Solanas, Jorge Sanjines, Jean-Louis Bertucelli; articles on 'toward a third cinema,' and 'revolutionary cinema—Italian style.'"

Cinema. 1964. 3/yr. $5. Paul Schrader. Jach M. Hanson, 9667 Wilshire Blvd., Beverly Hills, Calif. 90212. Illus., adv. Circ: 3,000. Sample. Vol. ends: no. 3.

Bk. rev: Various number, length. *Aud:* Ac, Ga.

At one time this promoted the Hollywood commercial film. No more. It now presents the director as hero, and the emphasis is on film as an art form. The style of writing is good, the coverage international, and the approach quite original. For example, in the Spring 1971 issue there is a reprint of a long-forgotten monograph on John Ford by Lindsay Anderson, an analysis of Rossellini, a piece on new forms of television, and an article on the Japanese director Kenjii Mizoguchi. Besides all of this, the 56 pages include good book reviews and notes on film magazines. The format is outstanding, at least in terms of liberal use of photographs. But the typography employs san serif type of a size much too small for extended reading comfort. Comparatively speaking, it is somewhat like *Film Comment*. A good choice for serious film buffs.

Cinema Journal. 1961. s-a. $4. Richard MacCann. Soc. for Cinema Studies, c/o Gerald Noxon, 21 Maple Ave., Bridgewater, Mass. 02324. Circ: 200. Sample.

Bk. rev: Various number, length. *Aud:* Ac, Hs.

Primarily for the student of the film. The 50 to 60 page journal features reprints, e.g., H. L. Mencken's "On Hollywood," current technological advances in film and cassettes, film and book reviews. Most of the material is submitted by members of the Society for Cinema Studies—a group worth inquiring about. Its members include some of the better teachers of the film in this country. Deserves much wider support than the circulation indicates. See also *Cinema Studies*.

Cinema Studies. 1967. a. $2. Gerald Noxon. Experiment Press, 21 Maple Ave., Bridgewater, Mass. 02324. Illus. Circ: 200.

Aud: Ac.

An annual by the publisher of *Cinema Journal*. Intended for film students and scholars at the university level, with a cross-disciplinary approach. Literary and pictorial arts are compared with film arts. For example, one issue featured a monograph on mathematics, music, and film. A good purchase for the large, specialized collection in both film and art.

Classic Film Collector (Formerly: **Eight MM Collector**). 1962. q. $4. Samuel K. Rubin, 734 Philadelphia St., Indiana, Pa. 15701. Illus., index, adv. Circ: 1,600. Vol. ends: Winter.

Bk. rev: 15–20, 100 words, signed. *Aud:* Ac, Ga.

A grab bag of information, facts, fancy, and fun which will hold the attention of anyone involved with film. A normal tabloid newspaper issue runs to a full 64 pages, covers the stars, producers, and directors of the silent film and beginning of talkies. It is edited for the film buff historian and, equally, for the man or woman who simply enjoys the nostalgia of Hollywood. Of value to libraries because of extensive bibliographies, reviews of 8mm films and film rental services, authentic biographical articles and background on films, and, last but not least, classified advertisements which indicate sources of just about everything from books and magazines to equipment. The whole is illus-

trated with photographs and line drawings. The newspaper make-up encourages browsing. All in all it is a real joy. Articles are by film lovers, not necessarily scholars. The writing is lucid, often chatty, but always informative. Deserves wider support.

Count Dracula Society Quarterly; devoted to the serious study of horror films & Gothic literature. 1967. q. Membership (Nonmembers $2.50). Gordon R. Guy, Gothick Gateway, 22 Canterbury St., East Hartford, Conn. 06118. Illus.

Bk. rev: Notes and essays, signed. *Aud:* Ga, Ac.

An offset newsletter, review medium, and journal, all combined in one package. It will be of considerable interest to anyone who delights in Gothic and horror films, but only at a relatively serious level. Articles range over the whole of Gothic literature, not just films. There are good-to-excellent book and film reviews.

Eight MM Collector. See *Classic Film Collector*.

Eight MM Magazine. See *Film Making Magazine*.

Film. 1952. q. $1.50. Peter Cargin. British Federation of Film Societies, 81 Dean St., London W1, England. Subs. to: 21 Larchwood Rd., St. John's Working, Surrey, England. Illus., adv. Circ: 10,000. Sample. Vol. ends: Summer.

Bk. rev: 10–12, 350 words, signed. *Aud:* Ac, Ga.

A generalist approach to the film, with short articles, reviews, notes, and biographical sketches. Nicely illustrated. The Spring 1971 issue had articles on Bernardo Bertolucci, the national film threatre, Hollywood, the Negro in the contemporary cinema, French television, South America, etc. An average 36-page issue gives the reader a concise, factual, and always readable approach to development in films as seen from England. In view of the general coverage, low price, and intelligent overview it is suitable for larger collections.

Film Comment. 1962. q. $6. Richard Corliss and Austin Lamont. Film Comment Publishing Co., 100 Walnut Pl., Brookline, Mass. 02146. Illus., adv. Circ: 5,000. Sample. Vol. ends: Winter.

Bk. rev: 6, 1,000 words, signed. *Aud:* Ac, Ga, Hs. *Jv:* V.

The focus is the cultural and historical consciousness of the film. The style is scholarly, yet never stuffy; material is imaginative, yet never wild; and, finally, the editors exercise complete control over what is the best of the thinking man or woman's film magazines. Along with such basics as *Film Quarterly, Film Culture* and *Sight and Sound, Film Comment* is a primary magazine in the field. In an average 80-page, well-illustrated issue topics will range widely. Past issues have considered: Roger Corman's career, the films of Orson Welles, underground films, anthropological films, and interviews with directors. Recent special issues have been on the Hollywood Screenwriter (Winter 1970/1971), Masters of the Mise-en-scène: Murnau, Welles, Ophuls (Summer 1971). Nationally known critics like Stanley Kauffman and Andrew Sarris contribute articles. Added value for librarians is the book review section, which may run to six full pages. For all libraries, from high school through academic, where there is the slightest interest in film.

Film Culture. 1955. q. (irreg.). $4. Jonas Mekas, Box 1499, New York, N.Y. 10001. Illus., index. Circ: 2,000. Sample.

Bk. rev: Various number, essays and notes. *Aud:* Ac, Ga, Hs. *Jv:* V.

The major "little magazine" of the film world in America, and a required item for any collection. The editor is Jonas Mekas, leading exponent of the independent or underground film. (He is a regular contributor to the *Village Voice,* and his column is one of the best now going.) The format shifts from time to time. As of late 1971 it is pocket-sized with some 100 pages, illustrated. Among the contributors are Mekas, Gergory Markopoulos, Michael Snow, and just about every major figure in experimental films. Usually one or two lengthy, intelligent, and imaginative interviews with directors from Rossellini to Stan Brakhage. The writing style is nontechnical, wonderfully free of jargon, and a joy to anyone who takes film seriously. The Film-Makers' Cooperative, which handles distribution, plays an important part by reporting their news and latest developments to this magazine. In addition, there is coverage of film festivals and critical notes. In a special New York Film Festival issue, there were transcripts from film symposia. Each year the magazine presents the "Independent Film Award" to a film maker for an original American contribution. There is a bibliographic listing of books received in each issue, which may include 20 to 30 or more items.

Film Heritage. 1965. q. $2. F. Anthony Macklin. Univ. of Dayton. Film Heritage, Box 652, Univ. of Dayton, Dayton, Ohio 45409. Illus., index, adv. Circ: 2,000. Sample. Vol. ends: Summer.

Bk. rev: 1–2, 1,000 words, signed. *Aud:* Ga, Ac.

One of the few university-sponsored film magazines, the format looks like a version of *Film Quarterly* from the University of California. The contributors tend to be students and teachers, usually write scholarly articles on directors, schools of film, and popular culture. No film reviews per se. The articles are perceptive, often argumentative. A good choice for larger academic collections.

The Film Journal. 1971. q. $3.50. Thomas R. Atkins, 121 Varick St., New York, N.Y. 10013. Illus., adv. Sample.

Bk. rev: 5–6 notes, length varies, signed. *Aud:* Ac, Ga. *Jv:* C.

All that looks great is not necessarily legitimate, and while only one issue has been examined (it first came out in Spring 1971), judgement is pretty negative. In format it is glamorous—some 80 oversized pages, most filled with photographs. The copy, such as it is, seems pretty weak—although one article on Fred Wiseman by John Graham is first rate. Apparently the whole thing is for the young film maker and the teacher. The editorial statement of purpose reads: the magazine will feature "original documents and critical evaluations that will be useful to scholars, teachers, students or anyone seriously interested in film." Hopefully it will improve. Before subscribing send for a sample.

Film Library Quarterly. 1967. Membership (Nonmembers $8). William Sloan. Film Library Information Council, 17 W. 60th St., New York, N.Y. 10023. Illus., index, adv.

Bk. rev: 2–3, 100 words, signed. *Aud:* Ac, Ga, Hs, Ejh.

Sponsored by the Film Library Information Council (FLIC—no pun intended) as a vehicle for information on 16mm films used in public and academic library circles. However, it has appeal for school librarians, too. A typical 48-page pocket-sized issue features articles on films and film makers (primarily of experimental, educational, and documentary films), tips on how to use films with the community, reviews of new films, and news of the organization. Interviews are included too. The format and editing are excellent, and this is considerably above what one has come to expect from library organizations. The frank appraisals, the various critical film and book reviews, and the imaginative style recommend this for all libraries.

Film Making Magazine (Incorporating: **Eight MM Magazine**). 1960. m. $10.25. Russell Roworth. Haymarket Press, Ltd., Gillow House, 5 Winsley St., Oxford Circus, London, W1., England. Illus., adv. Circ: 23,000.

Aud: Ga, Hs.

An English how-to publication aimed at the home moviemaker. Typical articles deal with: beat those indoor sound problems, easy lip synchronization, filming a love scene, macro cameras analysed, film cements tested. There are test reports on various makes of film, cameras, and projectors plus tips on camera care; also three to four film reviews, 75 to 100 words, signed. Unfortunately, most of the equipment is British and some of the material is not applicable to American situations. Still, as one of the few magazines which concentrates on 8mm films, it is a necessary addition in any library where there is a film program or young film makers.

Film Quarterly. 1958. q. $6. Ernest Callenbach. Univ. of California Press, Berkeley, Calif. 94720. Illus., index, adv. Circ: 7,000. Sample. Vol. ends: June. Microform: UM.

Indexed: ArtI, RG, SSHum. *Bk. rev:* Various number, length (notes to 5,000 words), signed. *Aud:* Ac, Ga, Hs. *Jv:* V.

Probably the best known film magazine in libraries (it's the only one indexed in *Readers' Guide),* this has a well-earned reputation for its cool, scholarly analysis of the film world. Each issue opens with two or three long articles concerned with trends, history, or biographical aspects of motion picture productions. Recent articles have included: "Toward a Non-Bourgeois Camera Style," and "The Unloved One—Crisis at the American Film Institute." There is usually an interview with a director. Perhaps the best section of the magazine is the long reviews of films—reviews which touch on almost every aspect of the art from plot and performance to camera work and direction. This is followed by "short notices," for films of only passing interest. The book reviews and notes manage to select titles of interest to any library. All in all this ranks high for scholarship, a bit lower for liveliness, and can be recommended as a basic title. Hopefully, librarians will subscribe to a good many other film magazines, and not rely entirely on the *Readers' Guide's* mysterious selection policy.

Film Society Review. 1965. m. (Sept.–May). $5. William A. Starr. American Federation of Film Societies, 144 Bleecker St., New York, N.Y. 10012. Illus., index, adv. Circ: 2,000. Sample.

Bk. rev: 1–2, 750–1,000 words, signed. *Aud:* Ac, Ga.

Considerably more is offered here than films. Each 50-page issue includes overviews of television, the press, the international film and television scene, and general commentary. In addition, there are two or three feature articles on directors, films, and the history of cinema. Good book reviews are included. The writers are serious students of the film, and many are instructors at colleges and universities. The tone is liberal to radical, anti-education establishment, and in 1971, at least, at war with the American Film Institute. Despite the academic backdrop, or perhaps because of it, the writing style is relaxed, informative, and often perceptive. A nice addition for the intellectual's library of the film, and a required item for large collections. (In the first edition this was suggested for elementary and secondary schools. No longer true. It is now primarily for academic libraries, although it certainly should be on the subscription list of advanced high schools.)

The AFFS also issues *Film Society Bulletin.* m. (Sept.–June). Membership $10. which is an invaluable aid to anyone planning a film program or involved with teaching. Each monthly issue includes news on festivals, courses, and jobs, a handy listing of new film catalogs. One must be a member of the Society to receive the *Bulletin,* but it is well worth the $10.

Film World. 5/yr. $4. T. M. Ramachandran. Film World Intl., Bombay-54 AS, India. Illus., adv. Sample. Vol. ends: Feb.

Aud: Ga, Ac.

A truly international film magazine. Although published in India, the average 50 to 60 page issue covers news and events of the worldwide film industry. Single issues are devoted to work in a particular country, e.g., "Accent on France," "Accent on Japan." Critics from the countries spotlighted discuss all aspects of their craft. Marcel Martin, Claude Beylie, Louis Malle, for example, are featured in the French number. Regular features include filmographies, notes on film festivals, and reader comments. The prize, though, is the 120 to 140 page annual number which apparently focuses on a single country. Volume 5, no. 4 (1970) includes some 30 articles by Indians on Indian films and directors. The style is clear, the articles in English, and the presentation geared as much for the layman as the expert. Unfortunately, the paper is not all it might be (although the binding is firm enough) and as a result the photographs, which are numerous, lack definition. But this is a minor criticism of a good magazine. Recommended for larger film collections.

Filmmakers Newsletter. 1967. m. $5. Suni Mallow and H. Whitney Bailey, 41 Union Sq. W., New York, N.Y. 10003. Illus., adv. Circ: 10,000. Sample. Vol. ends: Oct.

Bk. rev: Occasional, notes. *Aud:* Ac, Ga.

A 66 to 70 page illustrated magazine which is a clearing house "for all and any information pertaining to film making working in 16 and 8." Articles cover film news in every state, not just New York; technological developments in equipment; hints on problems of making and selling independent films; as well as pieces on the art and the history of the film. There are usually four or five major articles, followed by the numerous departments, including details on various film festivals. In addition to regular departments, each issue features an in-depth study of some topic related to film making, e.g., dance and film; computer-made films; anthropology and film. The teaching of the film, new techniques for maximum use of equipment, and a realistic approach to the whole problem of the individual in the system make this a unique and useful magazine. It seems particularly suited for the college or university with film courses where it might be required reading.

Filmograph. 1970. q. $7. Murray Summers, 7926 Ashboro Dr., Alexandria, Va. 22309. Illus., adv. Circ: 500. Sample.

Aud: Ac, Ga.

One of the better film buff magazines. It is devoted to all aspects of the film, current and past. Articles and briefer notes on films and books run from the nostalgic to the current. The level of writing is semipopular. The tone is love—love with the flicks. And it is nicely printed and illustrated. Send for a sample.

✓ *Films and Filming.* 1954. m. $8.50. Robin Bean. Hanson Books, Artillery Mansions, 75 Victoria St., London SWIH, OJO, England. Illus., adv. Circ: 30,000. Sample. Vol. ends: Sept.

Aud: Ga, Ac, Hs.

Heavy on stills from current flicks, this is as much a joy to look at as to read. Emphasis is on the relatively popular, fiction film—which by English standards means the mass motion pictures and those associated with art houses in America. And while published in England, the coverage includes much of what is currently taking place in the European film world. Each issue discusses several general topics, e.g., violence in movies, the choice of titles for a box-office hit, current trends in erotic films, etc. More important to the average moviegoer are the excellent reviews (by David Austen, Raymond Durgnat, Michael Armstrong, to name a few), which make up a good part of every number. A fine magazine for high school libraries, although some of the illustrations from current films may frighten the more modest librarians.

Inter/View: Andy Warhol's film magazine. 1969. m. $3.50. Glenn O'Brien. Inter/View, 33 Union Sq. W., New York, N.Y. 10003. Illus., adv. Circ: 40,000. Sample. Vol. ends: No. 12.

Bk. rev: 2, length varies, signed. *Aud:* Ac, Ga.

A 40-page tabloid, loaded with full and half-page photographs of Warhol favorites. It is short on analysis, long on interviews. For example, in the August 1971 issue there were two to three page interviews with James Taylor and Monte Hellman, Natividad Abascal, David Gumpilil, John Frankenheimer, and Paul Jabara. If the names are not all familiar, it is only that Warhol, or more likely his partner, Paul Morrissey, is as much a showman as film maker and publisher. The well-endowed Natividad Abascal had a small part in *Bananas,* an even shorter interview, and five pages of photographs in a bathing suit, no more—no less. Conversely, the talk with Frankenheimer was perceptive and, at times, downright fascinating. In between are rather good film reviews and reports on this and that event or personality. Much of the information is as refreshing as the tongue-in-cheek writing. A matter of personal taste, but a good item for more imaginative academic libraries.

Kaleidoscope. 1965. 3/yr. $2. Don Shay and Ray Cabana, Jr., 95 Dearborn St., East Longmeadow, Mass. 01028. Illus. Circ: 1,000.

Aud: Ga, Ac.

An American "little magazine" of the film. It has highly personalized studies of directors, stars, and various types of films. Many photographs are used. This is a well-organized, thoughtfully put together journal, which will appeal to the intellectual flick fan, and deserves support by larger public and academic libraries.

Making Films in New York. 1967. bi-m. $4. Boone Mancall, 49 W. 45th St., New York, N.Y. 10036. Illus., adv. Circ: 8,500. Sample. Vol. ends: Dec.

Aud: Ga, Ac.

Devoted almost exclusively to New York and eastern film makers. However, has more than passing interest for anyone seriously involved with the making of films. A typical issue not only covers the current New York scene, but features relatively technical articles on how to make films, equipment, distribution, and the like. It assumes some basic knowledge of the field, but can be used effectively by anyone this side of amateur status.

✓ *Marquee.* 1968. $6. Andrew Corsini. Theatre Historical Soc., P.O. Box 4445, Washington, D.C. 20017. Illus.

Aud: Ga, Ac.

Dedicated to preserving the history and the spirit of the old motion picture palaces, these 16 pages of love feature articles and photos on every aspect of movie theatre lore from advertisements to architects, from models to marquees, from box office to switchboard. "The theatres of Milwaukee," for example, is the primary subject of a typical issue which is heavy on photographs and brief descriptive notes. Regular features include briefs about other theatres, letters, and an occasional book review. Nostalgia fans, architectural historians, and flick bugs will relish every page.

Movie. 1962. q. $4. Ian Cameron. Movie Magazine Ltd., 3 Cort St., London W1 England. Illus. Circ: 6,500. Microform: UM.

Aud: Ga, Ac.

Roughly the equivalent—if there can be such a thing—in England of France's *Cahiers du Cinema,* although, lacking, to a great extent, the political bias. It is the major English exponent of the "auteur school" of film criticism. Each issue contains five to ten highly critical, lengthy reviews which often analyze each film sequence by sequence, thus providing the reader with insight into the cinematic and theatrical devices and techniques employed by various directors. Each film chosen for review is usually examined in the context of the director's artistic development, and a review will often embark on a critical discussion of a director's other works. Brief reviews of films appearing at various international film festivals are also provided as are still photographs from the films discussed in the major reviews and interviews. Noteworthy are the long and probing interviews with directors of international stature often conducted on location—a 1971 issue, for example, contained interviews with Claude Chabrol and Arthur Penn. (W.D.)

New Cinema Review. 1970. 10/yr. (Sept.–June). $4. Box 34, New York, N.Y. 10012. Illus.

Bk. rev: Various number, length. *Aud:* Ac.

By the same publishers as *Filmmaker's Newsletter.* It is almost entirely devoted to reviews and interviews with members of the underground, avant-garde film. Much of the material is reprinted from other magazines and newspapers. The reviews are excellent, in fact some of the best now coming out of New York. A useful feature, found also in *Filmmaker's Newsletter,* is a calendar of where various films will be showing and film makers will be speaking. The scope is national. A required item for college and university libraries where there is an interest in the underground flick.

Prologue Film Series. 1969. q. $4. Joshua Freedman and Louis Phillips. Prologue Press, 515 E. 78th St., New York, N.Y. 10021. Illus. Circ: 200.

Aud: Ac, Ga.

A unique, valuable service which is too little known. The editors bring together reprints of articles difficult to find, generally lost to historians, or no longer readily available in most libraries. The articles trace all aspects of the early film. Should be in all larger film collections.

Show; the magazine of films and the arts. 1970. m. $8. Ann Guerin. H & R Publns., Inc., 866 United Nations Plaza, New York, N.Y. 10017. Illus., adv.

Aud: Ga, Jv: C.

An upgraded version of the familiar fan magazine, e.g., *Photoplay* or *Modern Screen.* The approach is a trifle more sophisticated, but by any other name the content is the same. Illustrated feature articles on stars, directors, and films dominate. Some material on television and the theatre is included. But the basic approach is the same as the fan magazines. There is nothing wrong with that, except that it is too general to appeal to any particular group, a trifle too advanced for the happy fan magazine reader, much too cute for the intellectual movie goer. Libraries would do well to leave it alone—at least until such time as it improves.

Sight And Sound: the international film quarterly. 1932. q. $5. Penelope Houston. British Film Inst., 81 Dean St., London WIV AA, England. Subs. to: Eastern News, 155 W. 15th St., New York, N.Y. 10001. Illus., index; adv. Circ: 32,000.

Indexed: ArtI, BritHum. *Bk. rev:* 1–2, essays, signed. *Aud:* Ac, Ga. *Jv:* V.

Along with *Cahiers du Cinema* in France and *Film Comment* and *Film Culture* in America this is one of the basic, most frequently quoted film magazines. It is also one of the more combative. Under the editorship of Penelope Houston it offers articles and reviews which are distinctly intellectual, imaginative, and original. In fact, of all the film magazines it probably has the most to offer—there are numerous articles, both on current and retrospective matters; reviews, features, and some fascinating letters. In addition to the editor, the writers are among the leaders in this field. The format of the oversized 50 to 75 page magazine is excellent. Illustrations, photographs, and typography fit together. It is somewhat wider in scope than Ian Cameron's *Movie,* although the latter is an excellent English magazine too. The difference between the two is primarily a point of view. Cameron stresses the director more than Houston.

Sightlines. See Communications and Media Section.

Silent Picture. 1968. q. $3. Anthony Slide, 613 Harrow Rd., London W 10, England. Illus., adv. Circ: 1,500.

Bk. rev: Various number, length. *Aud:* Ac, Ga.

Devoted exclusively to a study of the silent film era, this is one of the few periodicals of its type. It contains filmographies, film reviews, biographies, interviews, as well as still photographs of silent movie "greats" and classic film scenes. Entire issues are sometimes devoted to an examination of a single silent film personality and his art. Approximately a quarter to a half of the five to ten articles per issue are provided by the editor, Anthony Slide, with the remainder coming from interested readers and contributors. The regular "Correspondence" section provides a forum for the exchange of information among its worldwide readers and occasionally includes a letter from an interested and not-to-be-forgotten silent film personality. (W.D.)

Soviet Film. 1957. m. $5. Armen Medvedev. V/O Sovexportfilm 14, Kalashny Pereulok, Moscow K-9, U.S.S.R. Illus., index; adv. Sample. Vol. ends: Dec.

Aud: Ga, Ac.

Coverage is focused upon the current Soviet film-making scene, particularly the documentary and feature film. There are interviews with major Soviet directors, leading film stars, and cameramen. Articles appear regularly dealing with topical problems facing the Soviet cinema, its history, film industries of the Union Republics, debuts of young film makers. Features entitled "Masters" are devoted to prominent film makers of past and present. Eminent scientists, writers, military and public leaders contribute answers to "Films in Your Life" questionnaire. A feature entitled "On the Way to the Screen" describes the shooting of an up-and-coming film. The format is handsome, and there are numerous photographs, sometimes in color, throughout a typical 45-page issue. Propaganda is limited to boosting Soviet films, and the only advertising is to promote film exports. A fascinating magazine not only for the serious film student, but for anyone interested in Soviet culture. Should be in all academic, and larger public, libraries. (Besides the English edition, available in Russian, German, French, Spanish, and Arabic.)

Take One. 1966. bi-m. $3/2 yrs. Peter Lebensold, Box 1778, Station B, Montreal, 110, Canada. Illus., adv. Circ: 20,000. Sample. Vol. ends: No. 12.

Bk. rev: 2–4, 500–750 words, signed. *Aud:* Ac, Ga, Hs. *Jv:* V.

What started out as a Canadian film magazine for the film buff and the film maker has turned into an international success. Since the last review, *Take One's* circulation has skyrocketed, and it is assuming a position among film magazines somewhat equivalent to *Rolling Stone* for music and *This Magazine is About Schools* for education. In a word, the editor and writers have something to say. The 40 or so pages look somewhat like an illustrated version of *Nation* or *The New Republic,* but are legible enough. The tone is "folksy" in that almost everything of interest to the film fan is discussed. But there is a definite structure, too. It usually includes five or six articles on the major directors, e.g., "Fritz Lang on Godard & Comtemp," reviews of current films (both feature and experimental), and letters reporting on activities about films from Chicago to Budapest. It is written for the young men or women who go only to "X" or "R" films and avoid the "G" ratings. The style is lively, imaginative and challenging. This will have most appeal for students from high school through college, not to mention the dedicated film librarian. It is easy reading at a low, low price. A basic title, particularly for the school and academic library.

✓*Variety.* See Newspapers/Special Interest Section.

Views & Reviews Magazine. 1969. q. $3.60. Ruth Tuska. Jon Tuska, Box 4115, Milwaukee, Wis. 53210. Illus., index, adv. Circ: 5,000. Sample. Vol. ends: May.

Bk. rev: 2–3, 2 pages, signed. *Aud:* Ac, Ga.

The format is on the order of *Film Quarterly.* The number of pages runs from 72 to 84, and there are numerous illustrations. As for the purpose of the magazine, its editor best explains: "*Views & Reviews Magazine* is devoted to the popular, that is to say reproduced arts. We cover films, phonograph records, popular literature, and the reproduced visual arts. Our emphasis on the Western motion picture is dictated by our concern for the condition of the negatives, most all of which are in jeopardy at this time. We are also covering the films of Mae West, the "Falcon" series of detective films, and such classics as *Grand Hotel* will be treated to extended cinematographs. Detective fiction in literature as well as on celluloid has been a continuing interest. Science fiction is to get similar treatment in the near future. We tend to cover

the popular arts by genre rather than by media, by popular emotional constellation rather than by the 'isms, personalities, and chronologies which are used as crutches by many critics. Our cinematographs, filmographies and career studies are as fine as we can make them but *Views & Reviews* goes beyond these, driving to fundamental appreciation and understanding of art and aesthetics. But then we are artists on an alien ground, and tired of hearing aesthetics reduced to word games." This is somewhat lengthy, but in previous efforts to describe this worthwhile magazine I have apparently failed to do it properly. This time around I have given the editor a chance. At any rate, it can be recommended for medium-sized to larger collections. I like it.

Fan Magazines

Fame: personalities in movies & tv world. 1933. a. $3. Martin Quigley, Jr. Quigley Publishing Co., 1270 Sixth Ave., New York, N.Y. Illus., adv. Circ: 7,000.

Aud: Ga. *Jv:* C.

Issued in May of each year, this annual is primarily a listing of Hollywood and television stars. Included are a considerable number of photographs; little copy. It is mentioned here again because a run of the issues is an excellent source of sometimes difficult-to-find biographical information. Besides that, a good deal of fun for the casual reader and Hollywood fan.

Film Fan Monthly. 1961. m. $4.25. Leonard Matlin; 77 Grayson Pl., Teaneck, N.J. 07666. Illus., adv.

Bk. rev: 3–5, 150 words. *Aud:* Ga, *Jv:* C.

A nostalgic, historical magazine of some 15 to 20 pages, dedicated to stars, present and past. It includes interviews, filmographies, profiles, shorts on 8mm and 16mm home movies. Primarily for the film historian.

Modern Screen. 1939. m. $5. Joan Thursh. Dell Publishing Co., 750 Third Ave., New York, N.Y. 10017. Illus., adv. Circ: 885,000.

Aud: Ga, Hs. *Jv:* C.

After *Photoplay* (1,500,000 readers), *Modern Screen* is the biggest drawing card of the scores of fan magazines. The formula is directed to young women (18 to 30) who are working in menial taks or are housewives and long for the glamor promised in *Modern Screen.* Most of the heavily photographed magazine is made up of short, easy-to-read articles and interviews with movie stars, TV and show personalities, and the like. Regular departments cover such things as hair styling and film reviews. The tone is gossip, the promise is a vicarious thrill, and the total is harmless—if you think this type of reading is used for nothing more than escape from the dreary world. The escape hatch, some would argue, is a trap, but this is beyond the interests of the average reader. Of limited use as film history; of more use to lure nonreaders to the library. The same publisher also brings out: *Screen Stories* (1929. m. $5. Circ: 154,000); *TV Radio Talk* (1967. m. $5. Circ: 229,000); and, of course, *Modern Romances*, which is somewhat out of the movie group.

Motion Picture Magazine. 1911. m. $2.25. Alice Schoninger. Macfadden-Bartell, 205 E. 42nd St., New York, N.Y. 10017. Illus., adv. Circ: 460,000.

Aud: Ga, Hs.

Directed to young women who identify romantically, not aesthetically, with the "stars" of present and past flicks. Now that the Hollywood star is fading, the magazine is turning more and more to television and music stars. There is a good deal of the *True Story* approach here, with material which is long on sentiment and sensation, short on fact and reality. It is well illustrated with closeups of the stars and their romantic entanglements. The magazine of late is getting a bit more sensational and the gossip seems to be reaching new (low) levels. Its readership, generally, is not up to that of the other Macfadden-Bartell film entry, *Photoplay*, but it is sometimes difficult to tell them apart. This is a good title, as is any in this group, for the library trying to attract nonreaders. Its historical interest is not as great as *Photoplay* or *Modern Screen*.

Movie Life. 1937. m. $6. Pat deJager. Ideal Publishing, 295 Madison Ave., New York, N.Y. 10017. Illus., adv. Circ: 192,000.

Aud: Ga, Jv: C.

The most typical movie fan magazine of them all in that the whole purpose is to give readers the private life story of a movie or television star. There are numerous photographs, and some regular departments which touch on fashions, reviews, and beauty tips. Compared to the other fan magazines in this section, it has nothing more working for it than that it offers still another title for the avid reader. It has no historical reality, and even less social significance. It is important, though, for the joy or lack of grief it brings several thousand readers.

In this same unadulterated soap opera approach to films and television personalities, there are countless titles. It is difficult to differentiate one from the other. Some, to be sure, use more bizarre come-on headlines or pictures, but all come down to the same basic formula of making nonfiction more exciting than fiction. Among some favored titles—in terms of circulation—are three others from the publisher of *Movie Life: TV Star Parade* (1951. m. $6. Circ: 185,000); *Movie Stars* (1940. m. $6. Circ: 195,000); and *Intimate Story* and *Personal Romances* which are more closely allied with the "true" love group, but vary little from the movie magazines. The only thing that seems changed is the name; the game is the same.

Other publisher entries: KMR Publications, 21 W.

26th St., New York, N.Y.: *Movieland and TV Time* (m. 1943. Circ: 170,000). Sterling Publishing Co., Inc. 315 Park Ave. S., New York, N.Y. 10010.: *Movie Mirror, Photo Screen, TV and Movie Screen.*

Movieland and TV Times. 1943. m. $4.20. Lillian Smith. KMR Publns., 21 W. 26th St., New York, N.Y. 10010. Illus., index, adv. Circ: 150,000. Vol. ends: Dec.

Aud: Ga.

Differs from others of the genre, in that there is more emphasis on photographs than in most. Otherwise, this can be taken two ways. The primary reader is the one who is going to take the numerous photographs of motion picture and television stars (both close-ups and on set) in a fairly personal, emphatic way. The secondary reader is the student of films and television who looks to this, and magazines something like it, for a running record of what constitutes truly popular culture. The editing is clever, and everything from the layout and the photographs to the interviews, reports, and gossip items is guaranteed to hold the attention of the primary audience, i.e., relatively unsophisticated teen-agers and adults. It seems important, though, for the photos. Meanwhile, the magazine serves as a record for an expanding, ongoing, and always fascinating culture.

Photoplay. 1911. m. $5. Bernadette Carrozza. Macfadden-Bartell, 205 E. 42nd St., New York, N.Y. 10017. Illus., adv. Circ: 1,500,000.

Aud: Ga.

The big circulation title among the movie-fan group and one of the oldest to capitalize on some young woman's desire to dream and identify with Hollywood celebrities. As with its other titles *(Motion Picture Magazine* and *TV Radio Mirror),* Macfadden-Bartell has gone over more to plastic personalities. The formula remains constant. None of the articles requires more than a minimal grasp of English to understand. All are heavily reinforced with photographs of the stars. The magazine is put together as dream material, but for the film historian it does have value in tracing the fate of popular films and actors. It can be justified for a library because it is culturally significant, or, more likely, as being important for the library trying to attract the woman nonreader.

Screen Facts; the magazine of Hollywood. 1963. bi-m. $7. Alan G. Barbour, 123–140 83rd Ave., Kew Gardens, N.Y. 11415. Illus., adv. Circ: 3,000.

Aud: Ga.

Somewhat the same approach as *Film Fan Monthly* and others of the genre dedicated to the old Hollywood flicks and stars. It is a bit more sophisticated than most, and tends to trace persons and movements in some detail. Scholarly, and primarily for the historian and serious film fan.

Foreign Language

Avant Scene du Cinema. 1961. m. $10. 27 r. St. Andre des Arts, Paris 6, France. Subs. to: R. A. Reagan, Box 215, Cathedral Station, New York, N.Y. 10025. Illus. Sample.

Aud: Ga, Ac. *Jv:* V.

Each issue contains the script, usually in full, of a current film, e.g., the number examined had Louis Malle's *Zazie dans le Metro.* There is some short introductory material on the director and a photo supplement of one or two other films. Past issues have included scripts for such films as *Citizen Kane, L'enfant sauvage, Z,* and *Persona.* All are in French, with accompanying photographs. Presupposing a knowledge of French on the part of the reader, this is a major film magazine which should be in every large collection. The scripts are invaluable for the film student.

BN (Bianco E Nero); studi sul cinema e lo spettacolo. 1940. m. $15. Giacomo Gambetti, Via Tuscolana 1524, 00173 Rome, Italy. Illus., index, adv.

Bk. rev: Various number, length. *Aud:* Ac.

A scholarly overview of the film by one of Italy's oldest film magazines. Each issue is devoted to a particular school, country, film maker, etc. For example, the April 1971 number includes a lengthy survey of the Bulgarian cinema, a short piece by director Pier Pasolini on Chaplin, detailed shooting script of Istvan Gaal's *Magasiskola,* some 14 pages of film reviews, and book reviews and notes. The content, which may run to 150 pages or so, is as impressive for its length as its approach, and of all the Italian journals on the film, this is probably the best for the serious student. Requires a good knowledge of Italian.

Cahiers du Cinema. 1951. $16.55. Jean-Louis Comolli and Jean Narboni. Les editions de l'Etoile, 39, rue Coquilliere, Paris le, France. Illus., adv. Circ: 16,000; 5,000 abroad. Sample.

Aud: Ga, Ac. *Jv:* V.

The best-known French-language motion picture magazine. This title made an international reputation by its strong stand on the director as the primary mover in film making. Since 1969 it has become increasingly politicized, and most of the criticism is now from the viewpoint of whether or not a film is political in terms of content and/or direction. Every film, the editors believe, can be so categorized. (An English translation of the new editorial policy will be found in the Spring 1971 issue of *Screen.*) The editor writes: "This is a critical review whose main purpose is the treatment of Cinema (and audio-visual matters in general) in a theoretical and historical manner. The review consists essentially of film criticism, interviews with film directors, historical and theoretical articles about films." Even those unfamiliar with French will profit from the numerous illustrations. Useful, too, as a reference aid as it rates films, discusses film journals and books from time to time, and devotes particular issues to a given type of film or director.

The obvious political bias should be kept in mind, although should not hold anyone back from a subscription. Quite the contrary. If anything, the magazine becomes even more critical in the search for meaning in film. The wedding of political thought and aesthetics concerns a good number of directors and viewers. *Cahiers* offers all sides of the ongoing argument. (An English version of much the same approach can be found in *Cineaste*—a magazine which grows in importance.)

Cine Cubano. 1961. m. $5. Alfredo Guevara, 1155 Calle 23, Vedado, Havana, Cuba. Illus. Circ: 30,000. Sample.

A Spanish-language magazine of film as revolution. It averages 75 to 120 pages and features a wide variety of material, not just Cuban films and film makers. Remarkable for its wide cultural interests, and not only one of the better Latin American film magazines, one of the world's best. Unlike others of its type, it is published at the heart of the Latin American revolution. Short, analytical articles give excellent, if sometimes biased, reviews of Latin American and Spanish language films. The interviews and biographical sketches of directors are superb. Some historical material, but the emphasis is on today and the struggle of peoples to free themselves from tradition. The whole is carefully edited, and while the format is professional, it suffers a bit from poor paper. A minor criticism for a major film magazine. Should be in all medium to large-sized academic libraries.

Cineforum; rivista di cultura, cinematografica. 1960. m. $10. Giovan B. Cavallaro. Federazione Italiana Cineforum, Casella Postale 414, 30100 Venice, Italy. Illus. Circ: 5,000.

Aud: Ac.

The Italian-language rough equivalent to *Film Comment,* i.e., an intellectual's approach to the European film in general and the Italian scene in particular. An average 72-page issue includes interviews, critical articles, and film reviews. It is notable for frequent detailed scripts of movies, as well as background material on how a particular film was shot. There is more interest in the techniques of film production than in most magazines of this type. Requires an excellent knowledge of Italian. No English summaries.

Cinema Nuovo. 1947. bi-m. $10. Guido Aristarco. Capo Santa Chiara 6, 16146 Genova, Italy. Illus., index, adv.

Bk. rev: Various number, length. *Aud:* Ac.

A combative leftist Italian-language journal which features long, detailed, and argumentative articles on various films and directors. The orientation is towards politics and abstract philosophy. The approach is somewhat similar to what is found in the better English language film magazines such as *Sight and Sound* or *Film Quarterly*. Each issue includes three or four articles, reviews of films, and a number of critical reviews of books. Some articles (and book reviews) consider television and theatre—in fact, almost anything in the media which has some politically meaningful point of departure for discussion. More academic than *Cineforum*, although certainly more readable and down to earth than *Ikon*. Along with *Cineforum*, one of two or three basic Italian film magazines for the academic library.

Etudes Cinematographiques. 1960. 3–4/yr. $8/10 nos. Michel Esteve and Georges Albert Astre. Lettres Modernes, 73 rue du Cardinal-Lemoine, Paris (5e), France. Illus.

Aud: Ac.

Primarily monographs. Individual issues are devoted to studies of directors and/or film schools. A collection of the magazine represents a virtual history of the film. Some back issues, as a consequence, are a bit hard to come by, and are expensive. Subjects have been Bunuel, Antonioni, Resnais, Welles, Westerns, surrealism, theatre and film, etc. Authors are among some of the best critics and historians in Europe. Requires an excellent command of French.

Filmkritik. 1957. m. $10. Wilhelm Roth and Harald Greve. Filmkritiker Kooperative, Ainmillerstr. 7, Munich, W. Germany. Illus., adv.

Bk. rev: 1–2, 500 words, signed. *Aud:* Ac.

A general German film magazine which is roughly equivalent in format and intent to the American *Film Quarterly* and *Film Comment*. A good half of each issue is given to signed, sometimes rather long critical remarks about specific films. The remainder is made up of articles and interviews. The material is at a philosophical, theoretical level which is a trifle pedantic. Requires a solid knowledge of German.

Filmrutan. 1958. q. $4. Rolf Lindfors. Sveriges Foeranade Filmstudios (SFF), Kingsgatan 65, S-11122 Stockholm, Sweden. Illus., adv.

Bk. rev: Various number, length. *Aud:* Ac.

A Swedish-language general film magazine, noted for its attention to political and avant-garde films. A typical issue, for example, includes a summary article on Latin American revolutionary films; the American "Spagetti-western"; a directory of film studios, book stores, distributors, etc. in England; an inteview with Costa Gavras; and short notes on international film events. The format is handsome, the style of writing—if the reader grasps Swedish—is down to earth, nontechnical, and quite readable. A good addition for larger academic collections.

Ikon; cinema, televisione, iconografia. 1947. q. $5.90. Igiacomo C. Pellegrini. Instituto "Agostino Gemelli," Corso Monforte 33, Milan, Italy. Illus., index. Sample.

Aud: Ac.

International theoretical coverage of the film. There are usually three or four articles. The text is in French or Italian, and the material is unlike most film journals in that it is highly theoretical and technical, as well as philosophical. For example, here are two titles translated into English: "The Film as an Element in the Dynamics of Aggressiveness," and "A Note on Intermodal Phenomena, with an annotated bibliography." Needless to add, a good knowledge of Italian and French is needed. There are no English summaries. The magazine will have limited appeal for the average film buff, but will be of value to the educator.

Kosmorama. 1954. bi-m. Kr. 40. Danske Filmmuseum, Store Sondervoldstraede, 1419 Copenhagen K, Denmark. Illus., index.

Bk. rev: 5–7, 500–1,000 words, signed. *Aud:* Ac.

A nicely illustrated 50 to 60 page general Danish language film magazine which covers the whole world of motion pictures. In an early 1971 issue, for example, there were two views of Truffaut, including an interview; a lengthy critique of Buneul's *Tristana;* a portrait of Carlos Diegues; a detailed and critical article on the cassette revolution; letters to the editor, which constitute an ongoing debate; book reviews and film reviews. Considered to be the leading Danish film magazine, and of value to the serious student.

Positif; revue de cinema. m. $15/12 nos. Eric Losfeld. Editions Le Terrain Vague, 14–16 rue de Verneuil, 75 Paris (6e), France. Illus., index, adv.

Aud: Ac. *Jv:* V.

Now that *Cahiers du Cinema* has gone almost completely political, many critics think *Positif* gives a better, more balanced report of French cinema in particular and world cinema in general. The pocket-sized magazine of 80 to 100 pages boasts some of the best film critics in Europe. Of equal interest are the interviews, articles on various directors, studies of film makers and films, and regular reviews of current films. The whole is well illustrated, and the format is excellent. A good knowledge of French is required, although in the interviews it is possible to get by without too much difficulty. Between this and *Cahiers du Cinema*, or other French film magazines, *Positif* would be a better choice for the general film collection, although it is difficult to imagine a library in America taking one without the other.

Professional

Action: the magazine of the Directors Guild of America. 1966. bi-m. $4. Bob Thomas, 7950 Sunset Blvd., Hollywood, Calif. 90046. Illus., adv. Circ: 8,200. Sample. Vol. ends: Nov./Dec.

Bk. rev: 4, 250 words, signed. *Aud:* Ac, Sa.

Directed to professional and aspiring directors and their assistants with articles by and about them. A regular feature is the "News of the Guild." Typical articles cover such topics as TV telecast of the election year, a film maker's report on the Arab-Israeli War, an article by Gregory Peck on the purposes of the American Film Institute, and special reports on the exchange visits of American and Russian directors. Helpful for the industrial and professional slant to movies.

American Cinematographer. 1919. m. $7. Herb A. Lightman. American Soc. of Cinematographers, Inc., 1782 Orange Dr., Hollywood, Calif. 90028. Illus., index, adv. Circ: 14,000. Sample. Vol. ends: Dec. Microform: UM.

Bk. rev: 1, 500 words, signed. *Aud:* Ac, Sa.

Thanks to its nontechnical language and jargon-free approach, this trade journal is of interest to professional cameramen, and of some value to students of the film. Granted, much of the equipment discussed is economically beyond a beginner, but the suggestions as to movie making are within the grasp of anyone. Besides, it affords room for dreams. Typical articles deal with the latest in equipment advances and explain examples of special effects. Includes interviews with top cameramen.

Business Screen, the visual communications magazine. 1938. m. $6. Bob Seymour. Harcourt Brace Jovanovich, 1 E. First St., Duluth, Minn. 55802. Illus., adv. Circ: 16,500.

Aud: Sa, Ac.

As the title implies, gives the business side of films, audiovisual, television, etc. It is valuable primarily for its regular features: Newsreel, short notes on current events and trends in the fields; Audiovisual calendar, commentaries by a number of experts everything from labor to new books; a list of meetings and seminars; and a buyer's guide which lists new equipment. There are usually two or three articles on various aspects of business and film of interest to anyone actively engaged in working in audiovisual communications. The basic business magazine of the field.

Canadian Film Digest. 1971. m. $8.50 (Can. $5). Dan Krendel. Film Publns. of Canada Ltd., 175 Bloor St. E., Toronto 5, Ont., Canada. Illus., adv. Circ: 5,000. Sample.

Aud: Ac, Sa.

The publisher describes this as a "trade paper for the Canadian motion picture industry." It includes articles on production, both domestic and international; news concerning individuals in various aspects of the industry, worldwide. It also contains stories on film festivals. Regular features are: "Our Business" by N. A. Taylor, an editorial, the Canadian Production Scene, and the International Production Scene. Only for large collections, as a supplement for such papers as *Billboard* and *Variety.*

Film Français—Cinematographie Française. 1918. w. $24. Maurice Bessy, 28 rue Bayard, Paris (8e), France. Illus., adv. Circ: 7,200.

Aud: Sa, Ac.

A French trade journal something on the order of *Variety* and *Billboard.* The target audience is the theatre owner. It lists new films, news of the cinema, productions, films currently being shown, etc. Only for large, special collections.

Film and Television Daily. 1918. 5/wk. $25. Gene Arneel. Wid's Films and Film Folk Inc., 1600 Broadway, New York, N.Y. 10019. Illus., adv.

Aud: Sa, Ac.

Augments and supplements such standards as *Variety* and *Billboard.* The daily 15 to 20 page paper covers the business and personality side of motion pictures and television. Producers, directors, actors, and executives are the primary audience. Only for large special collections.

The Hollywood Reporter. 1930. d. $30. Paul S. Clark. Tichi Wilkerson Miles, 6715 Sunset Blvd., Los Angeles, Calif. 90028. Illus., index, adv. Circ: 15,000. Sample. Vol. ends: Dec. 31.

Bk. rev: 4-5, 200 words, signed (once a week). *Aud:* Sa, Ac.

A business daily of 22 to 30 pages (printed on slick stock) which reports news of interest to anyone involved in motion pictures, television, and to a lesser degree the theatre and popular music. Features include: Rambling reporter, a gossip column of sorts on all aspects of the film from stars to dollars; Broadway Ballyhoo which covers the New York scene; stock market reports; news of artists and agents; and Feature Film Production, a running account of what films are being produced, as well as Television Film Production which does the same thing for TV. It all ends with classified advertisements. Sandwiched in between are feature stories and news items for those who follow the movies and television. The style is somewhat along the line of *Variety,* and it is just about as informative. While primarily for the active participant in entertainment, it has a given amount of fascination for laymen. A required item in larger motion picture, television collections.

International Photographer; the magazine of motion picture arts and sciences. 1928. m. $2.50. Herbert Aller. Intl. Photographers, 7715 Sunset Blvd., Hollywood, Calif. 90046. Illus., adv. Circ: 3,500. Sample. Vol. ends: Dec.

Aud: Sa, Ac.

A 20-page, well-illustrated, oversized trade journal for members of the International Alliance of Theatrical State Employees and Moving Picture Machine Operators of the United States and Canada, Local 659. Regular columns chronicle what films are being produced, and give accurate data on new equipment. There are usually two or three feature stories about films, film making and television—particulary the future of videocassettes. While the magazine is pretty slim, the low, low price and the good articles make it a "sleeper." Libraries with medium to large-sized collections in motion pictures and television should subscribe.

Motion Picture Herald. 1907. bi-w. $5. Richard E. Gertner. Quigley Publishing Co., 1270 Sixth Ave., New York, N.Y. 10020. Illus., adv. Circ: 10,000.

Bk. rev: Various number, length. *Aud:* Ac, Sa.

A trade journal directed to movie theater owners. Regular features are: brief descriptive reviews of recent releases; reports on new products and recent promotional stunts and techniques; and general business news from the world of producers, distributors, and exhibitors. It occasionally includes longer, more in-depth articles on such topics as new trends and developments in film production and the debate over the classified ratings of films. Of possible reference value are the regular "Film Buyers Rating," which provides an index of the success of films based on their performance in theaters and the "Release Chart and Review Index," which lists among other things the release date, the ratings, and the classification of most major feature films currently on the motion picture circuit. (W.D.)

Producers Guild of America. Journal. 1953. q. Membership. Inquire. Lou Greenspan. The Guild, 141 El Camino Dr., Beverly Hills, Calif. 90212. Sample. Vol. ends: Dec.

Bk. rev: 10–15, 350–700 words, signed. *Aud:* Ac, Sa.

A pocket-sized 40 or so page approach to a subject of interest to producers and film makers. For example, the September 1971 issue has ten articles and an editorial on the film rating system. Arguments, pro and con, are presented by critics and those involved in the industry. The book reviews, usually by the editor, cover all aspects of the film and are sharp and critical. A well-balanced, unusually candid approach to films and film making. A good addition for medium to large-sized collections.

SMPTE Journal. 1916. m. Membership (Nonmembers $26). Victor H. Allen. Soc. of Motion Picture and Television Engineers, 9 E. 41st St., New York, N.Y. 11017. Illus., adv. Circ: 10,000. Sample. Vol. ends: Dec.

Indexed: ASTI, ComAb, EngI, PhAb. *Bk. rev:* 3, 500 words, signed. *Aud:* Ac, Sa.

Directed to its membership, the purpose of this well-written periodical is to keep its specialist membership abreast of current technological advances and education in the varied but related fields of motion pictures, TV, instrumentation, and high-speed photography. Articles cover scientific investigations into applications to the audiovisual field, recommended practices, SMPTE Technical Conferences, and a variety of technical problems. Appraisal of the latest equipment is also covered, e.g., "A New 16mm Sound News Camera." There are sections dealing with the current literature; books, booklets, and brochures; abstracts of papers from other journals; new products and developments; employment service; and the journals available/wanted section, which provides a useful service for the librarian seeking to sell or buy out-of-print journals (this title or others are an a/v nature). There is also a calendar of meetings. A technical, well-indexed journal for large library collections. It is not for the average film buff or even film historian.

Reviews

There are a number of magazines which specialize in motion picture reviews—both feature and educational. These are listed here.

In the Dec. 11, 1969 *Village Voice* (p. 54), Jonas Mekas asked and answered a question about film critics, and it seems worth reprinting here.

"Where can one read about cinema? Cinema that interests me, this is, the independently made film, the avant-garde film, the underground film? I will give the main sources:

(1) This column; (2) P. Adams Sitney's column in *Changes*; (3) *Film Culture Magazine*; (4) *Film-Makers' Newsletter*; (5) *New Cinema Review*; (6) *Canyon Cinema News*; (7) *Interview*. . . ."

More prominent sources of reviews in nonfilm magazines are: Canby, Vincent, *New York Times*; Crist, Judith, *New York Magazine*; Kael, Pauline, *New Yorker*; Mekas, Jonas, *Village Voice*; Rock, Gail, *Women's Wear Daily*; Sarris, Andrew, *Village Voice*; Simon, John, *New Leader*; Wolf, William, *Cue*; Zimmerman, Paul D., *Newsweek*.

Film Information. 1970. m. $6. James M. Wall and Beatrice M. Rothenbuecher. Broadcasting and Film Commission, Natl. Council of Churches, Box 500, Manhattanville Station, New York, N.Y. 10027. Illus., index. Circ: 5,000. Sample. Vol. ends: Dec.

Aud: Ac, Ga, Hs.

A major film reviewing service which in six to eight pages reviews 300 or so major feature films each year.

The 150 to 300 word descriptive and evaluative reviews are by staff, ministers, editors, and audiovisual experts. Considering the sponsor, the commentaries are surprisingly liberal—in fact, a careful check of four issues indicates that the moral aspects of film are considerably less important than the artistic and aesthetic aspects. All types of movies are examined from the art film to the western documentary. Unless the reader is a bigot there is no quarrel with the reviews, often first rate, always perceptive, and artistically honest. Among the first choices for feature film reviewing.

Film News; the international review of AV material and equipment. 1939. bi-m. $6. Rohama Lee. Film News Co., 250 W. 57th St., New York, N.Y. 10019. Illus., adv. Circ: 10,500. Sample. Vol. ends: Dec.

Bk. rev: 12–15, 75 words, signed. *Aud:* Ga, Hs, Ejh.

Primarily a review medium of film, filmstrips, and educational television for primary and secondary schools. It has some applicability for public libraries, too. There are usually three to six articles on the history and use of film in the school and community. But the real value of the 40-page magazine is the "Preview and Reviews" section, which presents signed, critical reviews of both new and older films. Aside from the editor, reviewers represent all aspects of education from audiovisual experts to teachers and librarians. Films are often grouped by topic, e.g., About Blackness or Buried Treasures—long-forgotten films. There is information on equipment, notes on new films not reviewed, and other material which makes this a good source for teachers, librarians, and community group leaders. The magazine is well known and equally well accepted by librarians, owes much of its success to its energetic editor who freely admits her magazine should be "supplemented or augmented by such specifically critique magazines as *Film Comment* or *Film Quarterly*." Meanwhile, in terms of educational film reviews, this is the leader in its field.

Film Review Index. 1970. q. $30. Wesley A. Doak and William J. Speed. Audio-Visual Associates, Box 324, Monterey Park, Calif. 91754.

Aud: Hs, Ejh, Ga. *Jv:* C.

A 32-page offset looseleaf index to reviews for some 600 to 700 16mm educational and informational films (not features) per quarter. Arrangement is by title. There is no subject approach. There is an annual cumulation. The course of the review, as well as the name of the reviewer, is given. Some 30 educational and media journals are tapped from *Booklist* and *Landers Film Reviews* to *Sightlines*. Interestingly enough, only one review is usually cited per film—interesting because many of the films are reviewed more than once, and it would be this comparison that would make the index truly valuable. One wonders how the indexing is carried out. At any rate, the price is much too high for the average library, and until the index improves it cannot be recommended. The money might be better employed to purchase standard review magazines.

Filmfacts. 1958. bi-m. $25. Ernest Parmentier. Amer. Film Inst., Box 213, Village Station, New York, N.Y. 10014. Illus., index. Sample.

Aud: Ac, Ga, Hs. *Jv:* V.

The basic film review service for all libraries, this differs from most in that it concentrates on feature films. It is somewhat like a film version of the *Book Review Digest*. The looseleaf publication focuses primarily on motion pictures released in major or art houses. For each of the 10 to 15 films selected there is a full listing of production credits, a synopsis, a critique, and a critical consensus which lists the number of favorable, mixed, and negative reviews. The critique section contains brief pertinent quotes from various reviews and is usually followed by extended excerpts from several of these reviews representing varying degrees of critical acceptance. Selected for excerpts are such established review sources as *Time, New York Times, Saturday Review, Village Voice, Variety, New Yorker,* etc. Coverage is fairly widespread including films appealing to the tastes of a wide range of moviegoers. A typical issue, for example, included such diverse films as Rohmer's *Claire's knee, How to Frame a Figg,* with Don Knotts; *Beast of Blood,* John Wayne's latest Western; and the lesser-known *Wanda,* by Barbara Loden. An annual looseleaf binder with index is included.

Films in Review. 1950. m. (Oct.–May); bi-m. (Jun./July; Aug./Sept.). $7.50. Henry Hart. Natl. Bd. of Review of Motion Pictures, Inc., 210 E. 68th St., New York, N.Y. 10021. Illus., index, adv. Circ: 6,500. Sample. Vol. ends: Dec.

Bk. rev: 4–5, 300 words, signed. *Aud:* Ga.

The National Board of Review of Motion Pictures which sponsors this 6-by-7-inch 75-page magazine states it is "an independent non-profit organization of public spirited citizens founded in 1909 to represent the interests of the motion picture public." A typical issue includes two or three articles on films and personalities, several regular features, including films on television, and some 10 to 15 capsule film reviews. The whole tone is moderate and nostalgic, particularly the latter. Much is made of the "good old Holywood" days. Interesting in part, but way down the list for most libraries.

Landers Film Reviews: the information guide to 16mm films. 1956. 9/yr. $35. Bertha Landers. Landers Associates, Box 69760, Los Angeles, Calif. 90069. Index. Circ: 3,000. Sample. Vol. ends: May.

Aud: Ga, Hs, Ejh.

The *Kirkus* of the 16 mm educational film world. Follows the format of the familiar book reviewing service, i.e., the monthly issues are published in looseleaf form; the reviews are critical and cover documentaries and educational films for elementary and high schools. Much of the material, to be sure, is useful for adults at the public and college or university level, but here one would be urged to consult other film and educational review magazines. An average issue reviews some 75 films, includes notes on film festivals, and information on multi-media materials. The 150-word reviews clearly state the purpose and scope of the film, tend to be liberal, thoughtful, and perceptive in terms of how the film might be used, and with what type of audience. Reviews are timely, both in choice of release date and the topics considered. There is full bibliographic information for each film, and monthly and annual cumulated subject-title indexes. Recommended for all schools, and many public libraries. See also *Film News*, a similar approach.

Monthly Film Bulletin. 1934. m. $4.75. Jan Dawson. British Film Inst., 81 Dean St., London WIV GAA, England. Index. Circ: 10,000. Sample.

Aud: Ga, Ac, Hs.

Somewhat similar in approach and format to the American *Filmfacts,* the British Film Institute's 16 to 20 page monthly service reviews some 60 to 75 films per issue. Each notice of 250 to 750 words is signed. Reviews are both descriptive and critical, and the criticism is often much sharper than that found in American magazines. The issue closes with what six critics think of the month's 18 to 20 best feature films. Each number, also, includes a feature "Checklist" which gives a short biographical sketch of a director and lists his films chronologically by title. And as in *Filmfacts,* full information is given for each film, i.e., distributor, cast, length of film, etc. (The major differences between the two: The *Bulletin* offers only brief synopses and short reviews, not quotes from other review media; the *Bulletin* does include, from time to time, short notices of educational and documentary films.) An excellent backup for *Filmfacts* and a required item in any library where current reviews are important. (It should be noted that this publisher also issues *Sight and Sound*).

MUSIC

See also Communications and Media Section.

Basic Periodicals

GENERAL. Ejh: *Guitar Player;* Hs: *High Fidelity;* Ga: *High Fidelity, Stereo Review,* Jc & Ac: *High Fidelity, Stereo Review, Source, Journal of Music Theory, Musical Quarterly.*

COUNTERCULTURE: *Folk, Rock and Jazz.* Ejh: *Creem, Sing Out;* Hs: *Rolling Stone, Creem, Sing Out;* Ga; *Rolling Stone;* Jc & Ac: *Rolling Stone, Crawdaddy, Creem.*

RECORD/TAPE REVIEWS. All libraries: *American Record Guide;* Jc & Ac: *American Record Guide, Music Library Assn. Notes, Gramophone.*

Library and Teaching Aids

Music Educator's Journal, American Music Teacher, School Musician.

Basic Abstracts and Indexes

Music Index, RILM Abstracts of Music Literature.

Cessations

Choral and Organ Guide, Electronic Music Review, Music.

General

Acta Musicologica. 1928. q. Membership (Nonmembers, $11.60). Hellmut Federhofer. Barenreiter-Verlag, Neuweilerstr. 15, CH 400 Basel 15, Switzerland. Illus.

Indexed: MusicI. *Aud:* Ac.

The official journal of the Société Internationale de Musicologie. It publishes erudite articles, which often include valuable bibliographies. Papers are presented in the language of the author's choice (text is in English, French and German). Considered the standard international musicological journal. Only for large academic libraries.

African Music. See Africa Section.

American Choral Review. 1958. q. Participating membership $7.50. Alfred Mann. American Choral Foundation, Inc., Assn. of Choral Conductors, 130 W. 56th St., New York, N.Y. 10019. Illus., adv. Circ: 2,000. Sample. Vol. ends: Oct.

Indexed: MusicI. *Bk. rev:* 1–2, 1,000–2,000 words, signed. *Aud:* Ac, Hs.

Published for composers, conductors, musicologists, and students of choral music, this usually runs to 56 pages, with three to four major articles dealing with choral music and related subjects. There are numerous musical examples. In addition to regular book reviews, there are record reviews, lists of recent scores, and feature columns: Choral Conductors Forum, Choral Music in the Curriculum, Choral Music in the Liturgy, and Choral Performances, The style presupposes a knowledge of the field, but the material discussed is of great value to any serious student or teacher of choral music.

The American Harp Journal. 1967. bi-a. $6 (Membership $8). Gail Barber. American Harp Soc.,

Inc., 6224 Louisville Dr., Lubbock, Tex. 79413. Illus., index; adv. Circ: 2,000. Sample. Vol. ends: Fall.

Bk. rev: Various number, length. *Aud:* Ga, Ac.

Periodicals designed to serve the needs and interests of amateur and professional musicians in their activities as performers, students, and teachers usually follow a similar plan. So it is with the journal of the American Harp Society. There are interesting and timely articles about the instrument, its music, its history, and its performers. There are reviews of new music editions and new books. Regular features include "People and Places" (news of activities of professional harpists), "Concert Calendar" (listings of up-coming concerts, with information on dates and programs), and "Chapter Reports" (information on the far-flung activities of the numerous local chapters of the Society). A must for music school libraries and large public libraries. (G.S.)

✓*American Music Teacher.* 1951. bi-m. Membership. (Nonmembers $4). Frank S. Stillings. Music Teachers Natl. Assn., 1831 Carew Tower, Cincinnati, Ohio 45202. Illus., adv. Circ: 15,000. Sample. Vol. ends: June/July. *Microform: UM.*

Indexed: EdI, MusicI. *Bk. rev:* 5, 150 words, signed. *Aud:* Ac, Hs.

Features articles on and reviews of keyboard, vocal, organ, and string music. The Association represents many private and studio teachers as well as secondary school and college music faculties. Articles are geared to assist the teacher. Occasional bibliographies add to the magazine's reference value. Because of its emphasis on individual teaching, this nicely augments the basic journal in the field of music education, *Music Educator's Journal.* Both would be advisable for secondary school and college music teachers, as well as libraries serving them. However, both stress the how-to-do-it approach, as contrasted with the more scholarly *Journal of Research in Music Education.* In elementary through secondary schools, the *Music Educator's Journal* would be a first choice, followed by *American Music Teacher.* Academic libraries of any size or type will wish to take all three, although *American Music Teacher* would be last on the list.

The American Recorder. 1960. q. $3.50 John Kock. The American Recorder Soc., 12 Stuyvesant Oval, New York, N.Y. 10009. Illus., index, adv. Circ: 3,000. Sample. Vol. ends: Winter.

Indexed: MusicI. *Bk. rev:* Various number, length. *Aud:* Ac, Ga, Hs.

In this case, the "recorder" is not the electrical device for recording and reproducing sound on disc or tape, but a musical instrument. It is an end-blown flute, traditionally made of wood (but lately made of wood or plastic) and coming in various sizes from a jumbo double-bass recorder to a sopranino "mini" re-corder. It is one of the most popular musical instruments for the amateur musician whose tastes run to the classics. It has had a considerable vogue in the United States since the late 1940s and today is even taught in some elementary and grade schools. There are few recorder players who would not find the *American Recorder* an indispensable guide to their instrument and its music. To the non-recorder player, some of the material in the *American Recorder* may seem technical (since it presupposes a knowledge of the rudiments of musical notation), but in fact none of it is at all esoteric to amateur recorder players. They are a hardy and dedicated lot and pursue their avocation with a zeal verging on fanaticism. Regular features in this modest journal (it runs to 35 or 40 pages an issue) include reviews of new recorder music, reviews of recordings of recorder music, and reviews of books of interest to the recorder player. Each issue contains two to four articles, e.g., "The Requirements of a Good Bell-Keyed Recorder," "Improving the Tone of Plastic Recorders," "The Three Ages of Recorder Players and How to Recognize Them." Any library of any type that can number at least ten recorder players among its clientele would not want to be without the *American Recorder.* (G.S.)

The Amica. 1963. m. Membership. $10. Virginia Billings. 1428 Liberty St., El Cerrito, Calif. 94530. Illus., index, adv. Circ: 400. Sample. Vol ends: Dec.

Aud: Ac, Ga.

A mimeographed, 22-page bulletin concerned with player and reproducing pianos, such as Ampico, Duo-Art Welte-Mignon. Some attention is given to orchestrations, nickelodeons, and 88-note rolls. Anita Nickels, who sent us a copy, points out that at least two libraries, Stanford and the University of Indiana have collections in this area. Primarily, though, it is a publication for the individual and will be welcomed by many who cherish an old player piano.

Audio. 1947. m. $5. George W. Tillett. North American Publishing Co., 134 N. 13th St., Philadelphia, Pa. 19107. Illus., index; adv. Circ: 72,000. Sample. Vol. ends: Dec.

Indexed: ASTI, MusicI, EngI. *Aud:* Ga, Ac, Hs.

Primarily for the enthusiast who thinks as much, if not more, of his equipment than what is played. This well-edited magazine carries numerous articles and features on equipment, recordings, tapes, etc. The analytical reviews of new stereo and video products are honest and unusually dependable. There are one or two articles on the theory of sound, and these are geared for both the expert and the amateur who may wish to learn about fundamentals. There are three record review sections—classical, popular, and jazz—and from time to time information on the making of recordings. *Audio* differs from its two main competitors, *Stereo Review* and *High Fidelity,* in that equipment is more important than the music which is emphasized in the other two magazines. Next to these two, it will be a second choice among general music magazines for any small to medium-sized library, and an automatic necessity in all larger libraries.

Audio Record Review. See *Hi-Fi News & Record Review.*

Billboard. See Newspapers/Special Interest Section.

Brass and Woodwind Quarterly; devoted to articles, research studies, bibliographies and reviews concerning wind instruments and their music. 1957. q. $6.50. Mary Rasmussen, Box 111, Durham, N.H. 03824. Illus., index, adv. Circ: 1,000.

Indexed: MusicI. *Aud:* Ac, Hs, Ejh.

Long articles on brass and woodwind instruments, their history, music, performance, practice, etc. It includes frequent bibliographies on musical instruments, performance practice, and music for wind instruments. Worthwhile for both the serious student and the teacher of music from the elementary grades through college and university.

Choral Journal. 1959. m. (Sept.–May). $4. R. Wayne Hugoboom. American Choral Directors Assn., Box 17736, Tampa, Fla. 33612. Illus., adv. Circ: 4,500. Sample. Vol. ends: May. Refereed.

Bk. rev: 1, 250 words, signed. *Aud:* Ac, Hs.

A 25-page journal published for high school and college choir directors, with some information of interest to church groups. Progressive and liberal in its outlook, the sponsoring Association seeks new approaches and methods. This is reflected in the short articles, news items, and comments. Most of the material is of a rather high level "how-to-do-it," and quite practical for anyone interested in choral work. Although short on book reviews, it usually has two to four pages of critical record notes, and this feature gives it importance for any large music library.

Clavier; a magazine for pianists and organists. 1962. 9/yr. $6. Dorothy Packard. Instrumentalist Co., 1418 Lake St., Evanston, Ill. 60201. Illus., index, adv. Circ: 20,000. Sample. Vol. ends: Dec.

Indexed: MusicI. *Bk. rev:* 3, 150–200 words. *Aud:* Ac, Hs.

The leading journal of piano and organ for advanced students and teachers. Articles include interviews with concert performers, "suggestions for improving keyboard technique, analytical discussion of the literature, and teaching methods." There is a regular review of materials for teachers by grades, descriptions of new products, and reviews of records, piano and organ music, and books. An interesting feature is the complete piece or pieces of music in each issue, together with a lesson on interpretation.

In this same field, *Piano Quarterly* (1952. q. $6. Box 3881, Grand Central Station, New York, N.Y. 10017) is directed almost exclusively to the teacher. It is particularly useful as it lists pieces of music and books by grades. *Clavier* would be a first choice, but for elementary piano teaching, the *Piano Quarterly* is somewhat better.

Connchord. See Free Magazines Section.

Current Musicology. 1965. s-a. $7 (Individuals $5). L. M. Griffel and M. R. Griffel. Columbia Univ., Dept of Music, New York, N.Y. 10027. Illus., adv. Circ: 1,100.

Indexed: MusicI. *Aud:* Ac.

Edited by the graduate students and published by the Department of Music of Columbia University, this is directed to other graduate students and faculty members. It contains reports on curricula, seminars, meetings; bibliographies; well-documented articles dealing with musical subjects in depth. A special feature is a dissertation review section which covers all areas of musical study, mostly in American universities. Illustrations are confined mainly to musical examples or musical instruments. Only for large academic libraries.

Diapason; devoted to the organ and the interests of organists. 1909. m. $4. Robert Schuneman. Diapason, Inc., 434 S. Wabash Ave., Chicago, Ill. 60605. Illus., adv. Circ: 10,000.

Indexed: MusicI. *Bk. rev:* 2, 500–1,000 words, signed. *Aud:* Ac.

For the professional organist and student. It is international in scope, and the "over all style is newsy with organists' appointments, academic achievements, obituaries, etc. forming the staple." There are usually two to three articles and reviews of church music conferences, books, organ music, choral music, and recordings. Numerous illustrations, about fifty percent advertising, and a large 13-x-9-inch format.

Ethnomusicology. 1955. 3/yr. Membership. $15 (Student $7.50). Norma McLeod. Wesleyan Univ. Press, Middletown, Conn. 06457. Illus., index. Circ: 1,500. Sample. Vol. ends: Sept.

Indexed: MusicI. *Bk. rev:* 3–10, 2 pages, signed. *Aud:* Ac.

The official journal of the Society for Ethnomusicology presents scholarly articles and book, film, and record reviews on folk and tribal music, jazz, non-western art music, dance, and the social-psychological basis of music in world cultures. All aspects of the subject, both national and international, are considered. It is particularly helpful in libraries for the extensive bibliographies and the book review section, which often features opposing views. Serious students of folk and primitive music will enjoy.

Guitar Player Magazine. 1967. 8/yr. $5. Jim Crockett, 348 N. Santa Cruz Ave., Los Gatos, Calif. 95030. Illus., adv. Circ: 55,000. Sample. Vol. ends: Dec.

Bk. rev: 8, 60–80 words, signed. *Aud:* Ga, Hs, Ejh.

The basic how-to-do-it magazine for guitar players from the youngest to the oldest. Since the previous edition this has grown in size and importance; now includes more material. But the format and approach are much the same, i.e., articles on folk and popular music, general information on instruments and playing, tunes and topics, book reviews, etc. This is for the popular, not the classical guitar. A good purchase for just about any library where there is an interest in folk music and the guitar.

Guitar Review. 1946. irreg. (app. 3/yr.). $8/3 issues. Vladimir Bobri. Soc. of the Classic Guitar. 409 E. 50th St., New York, N.Y. 10022. Illus., adv. Circ: 3,000. Sample. Vol. ends: no. 3.

Bk. rev: Various number, length. *Aud:* Ac, Hs, Ga.

Given the great popularity of the classic guitar in the United States, this publication should find a large audience. The field is the classic guitar—its history, music, construction, and technique; pop, jazz, folk, country and western, and electric guitar are not covered. Each issue is pure delight for each is a masterpiece of magazine production. There are beautiful illustrations and line drawings of various members of the guitar family, extensive musical examples, and each issue contains a number of previously unpublished compositions. Some of the recent issues have had articles on "Guitar Construction from A to Z," "Ukrainian Music and its Cultural Heritage," and "A Historical Perspective of the Guitar Duo." Regular features include "The Guitar on Discs" and "New Music in Print." Librarians will find it a good source for reviews of new music and recordings. All contributions are scholarly and this seems to be *the* major outlet for any material on any aspect of the classic guitar. A must for large public and academic libraries, but also a possibility for many medium-sized public and school libraries which number guitar enthusiasts among their users. (G.S.)

Harrison Tape Catalog. See *Schwann Record & Tape Guide.*

Hi-Fi News & Record Review (Incorporating: *Audio Record Review*). 1956. m. $7. John Grabble. Link House, Dignwall Ave., Croydon, Surrey Cr9 2TA, England. Illus., index, adv. Circ: 45,000.

Indexed: BritTechI. *Bk. rev:* Various number, length. *Aud:* Ac, Ga.

A combination of news about hi-fi equipment and record reviews, and in this respect similar to the American *High Fidelity.* With the incorporating of the old *Audio Record Review,* the 80 to 100 page magazine now includes some of best record reviews in England, or, for that matter, anywhere. Reviews cover all types of music from classical to pop. The remainder of the magazine is given to new products, the usual reports on music and musicians and equipment. Well edited. A good magazine for larger music collections.

Hi-Fi/Stereo Review. See *Stereo Review.*

High Fidelity. 1951. m. $7.95. Leonard Marcus. Billboard Publishing Co., 165 W. 46th St., New York, N.Y. 10036. Illus., index, adv. Circ: 214,000. Microform: UM.

Indexed: AbrRG, MusicI, RG. *Aud:* Ga, Ac, Hs. *Jv:* V.

Along with *Stereo Review,* one of the two general magazines for the informed hi-fi enthusiast and record buyer. It includes articles about music and musicians written by musicians or journalists who contribute outspoken and controversial comments on the recording scene. Audio equipment reports based on laboratory tests give the latest information on home entertainment electronics, and new trends are given coverage, as evidenced by the newly added section on video equipment for amateurs. The section devoted to critical reviews of recordings is afforded considerable space, and while classical records receive the greatest attention, folk, jazz, and pop music have received wider coverage of late. Published in several regional editions as well as in a "Musical America" edition ($14/yr.). The "Musical America" edition carries 32 extra pages which cover current music performances, music centers, and performing artists for those with a special interest in "live" as well as recorded music.

The Hill and Dale News. 1961. bi-m. $3. City of London Phonograph and Gramophone Soc., Seal Hollow Rd., Sevenoaks, Kent, England. Illus., adv. Circ: 600.

The *News* is written by and for the collector of acoustical records, phonographs, and related items. Content is furnished entirely by Society members, who use the *News* as a medium for exchange of experiences, information, and opinion. Membership accompanies subscription.

The Hymn. 1949. q. Membership $6.50. William W. Reid. Hymn Soc. of Amer., 474 Riverside Drive, New York, N.Y. 10027. Illus., index. Circ: 2,200. Sample. Vol. ends: Oct.

Indexed: MusicI. *Bk. rev:* 3–5, 250 words, signed. *Aud:* Ac, Ga.

The major English-language journal devoted to the study of hymns, ancient and modern. There are articles about specific hymns, types of hymns, about hymn writers, hymn poets, and discussions of the use of hymns in the church service. Included in every issue are texts of selected hymns discussed in the articles. The historical material is not overburdened with weighty scholarship, for *The Hymn* is oriented to practicing church musicians. Included are many fascinating historical items (e.g., a bibliography of "More American Temperance Song-Books," an article on shape-note hymnals), along with practical and timely discussions of current issues related to the use of hymns in the service. (G.S.)

Instrumentalist; a magazine for school and college band and orchestra directors, teacher-training specialists in music education, and instrumental teachers. 1946. m. (except July). $7. T. Rohner. Instrumentalist Co., 1418 Lake St., Evanston, Ill. 60204. Illus., index., adv. Circ: 16,500. Vol. ends: June. Microform: UM.

Indexed: MusicI. *Bk. rev:* 5, notes. *Aud:* Ac, Hs.

Deals chiefly with technical problems of teaching and playing the various band and orchestra instruments. (No coverage is given to piano, organ, and other instruments for which instruction is not generally provided in public schools.) Articles treat the specific problems encountered by string, woodwind, brass, and percussion instrumentalists, and deal with a wide variety of subjects including bibliographic material, special projects in music schools, and legislation. An important aspect is the annotated new music reviews meant to furnish school directors with reliable and expert guidance. An obvious selection for any school library where the band is an important consideration.

International Piano Library Bulletin. 1967. q. Membership $10. Gregor Benko. Intl. Piano Library, 215 W. 91st St., New York, N.Y. 10024. Illus. Circ: 1,000. Vol. ends: Winter.

Aud: Ac.

This is a quality publication which no serious music library should be without. The International Piano Library itself is an attempt to build a unique research collection of books, records, manuscripts, and all relevant material on the piano, pianists, and their music; and the *Bulletin* is a natural ougrowth of the library. Subscription entitles one to purchase scarce piano re-recordings "not sold or otherwise made available commercially." This is no record-of-the-month club come-on: titles issued so far are truly valuable, otherwise unobtainable recordings acquired by the IPL. The *IPL Bulletin* examined was completely devoted to the life and works of John Field, influential but obscure nineteenth century pianist. Included was a discography and facsimile reproductions of Field's *Serenade* and *Preludio.* An authoritative reference tool in music libraries. (G.S.)

Journal of Church Music. 1959. m. (except Aug.). $4.75. Robert A. Camburn. Fortress Press, 2900 Queen Lane, Philadelphia, Pa. 19129. Illus., adv. Circ: 4,200. Sample. Vol. ends: Dec. Microform: Academic Archives, Raleigh, N.C.

Indexed: MusicI. *Bk. rev:* 2, 100–200 words, signed. *Aud:* Ac.

The purpose "is to help those engaged in the music program to raise the standards of church music so that it adds to the total service." This is accomplished via articles on organ and choral techniques, hymns, and local church activities. Three or four complete anthems are reprinted in each issue. Special issues list suggested music for organ and adult and youth choirs, suggestions on wedding music, and planning the music program. There are an average of three articles per issue, 16 pages of text, 15 pages of music; illustrations. A specialized music magazine for a specialized audience.

Journal of Music Theory. 1957. s-a. $6. David Beach. Yale School of Music, New Haven, Conn. 06520. Illus., index. Circ: 1,400. Reprint: Johnson.

Indexed: MusicI, RILM. *Bk. rev:* Numerous, long and critical. *Aud:* Ac.

A forum for research papers devoted to contemporary and historical theory. Important bibliographies appear, as do extensive, critical book reviews. Of great reference value for music students, scholars, and teachers, but only for large collections.

Journal of Music Therapy. 1964. q. $5. Jo Ann Euper. Natl. Assn. for Music Therapy, Inc., P.O. Box 610, Lawrence, Kans. 66044. Illus., index. Circ: 1,700. Sample. Vol. ends: Dec.

Bk. rev: 5, 150–250 words, signed. *Aud:* Ac.

No doubt the incidence of withdrawal, insanity, and schizophrenia, which is already of monumental proportions, would be a national disaster if it were not for the theraputic affects of music. However, the controlled use of music as therapy in an institutional setting is a relatively new discipline. It is practiced in a surprisingly wide variety of settings, including clinics, settlement houses, hospitals, nursery schools, detention centers, neighborhood mobilization programs, and in recreational centers for the aged. And, since music therapists have not developed an esoteric mumbo-jumbo to discuss their work and make it incomprehensible to the layman, their articles will reach more people than you might think. Their *Journal* can be read and used by the nonspecialist. Some typical articles: "Music Therapy in a Decentralized Hospital," "Music Therapy—Its Function in Supporting the Rehabilitation of the Handicapped." Recommended especially to anyone (amateur or professional) who is involved in any of the programs mentioned above, including librarians. (G.S.)

Journal of Research in Music Education. 1953. q. Membership (Nonprofit institutions $8). Allen P. Britton. Soc. for Research in Music Education, Music Educators Natl. Conference, N.E.A. Bldg. 1201 16th St., N.W., Washington, D.C. 20036. Illus., index Circ: 9,000. Sample. Vol. ends: Winter. Microform: UM.

Indexed: EdI, MusicI. *Bk. rev:* 3–8, 200–1,000 words, signed. *Aud:* Ac, Hs.

Research efforts, pertinent in any way to music instruction, are published in this official journal. Efforts range from studies on professional standing—"The Professional Role and Status of Music Educators in the United States"—and changing curriculum ideas to more technical studies and bibliographies. Libraries supporting any research efforts in music education should have this periodical.

Keyboard. See *Modern Keyboard Review.*

Keyboard Jr. 1943. m. (Oct.–May). 80¢ Keyboard Jr. Publns., 1346 Chapel St., New Haven, Conn. 06511.

Indexed: IChildMag. *Aud:* Ejh, Hs.

An eight-page music appreciation bulletin for use in music classes for junior and senior high and possibly some advanced elementary grade students. Each issue features a one or two page illustrated article on a composer, musician, piece of music, orchestra, or type of composition. The writing style is surprisingly adult —musically ignorant adults might find much of interest here, too. Although small in size, the contents are impressive. The format of unbound pages will prove a librarian's nightmare. The same publisher also issues *Young Keyboard* (1946. m. 80¢), which is similarly indexed and follows the same format and style, although it is somewhat more simply written for ages four to six. One of the few music magazines which can be used in classroom situations with children, and if not in the school library, certainly should be brought to the attention of teachers.

Modern Keyboard Review (Formerly: *Keyboard).* 1969. bi-m. $4. Ernest Tamminga. William Irwin, 436 Via Media, Palos Verdes Estates, Calif. 90274. Illus., adv. Circ: 9,450. Sample. Vol. ends: Nov./Dec.

Aud: Hs, Ejh.

Subtitled "the magazine for modern contemporary, popular organists, pianists and accordionists," this is primarily for the teacher of music from elementary through adult. Such articles as "Group Instruction, from the Student's Viewpoint," and "Can Piano Improvisation and Modern Jazz Be Taught?" indicate the purpose of the 24-page issue. A useful feature: "Keyboard Reviews" of graded new and standard music solos and methods. News of members, activities of OPTA, and a complete organ and piano solo round out each issue. As a specialized voice, this has merit, and will be welcomed by piano and organ teachers, particularly at the junior high and high school level. (Not to be confused with *Keybaord Jr.*—a bulletin for junior and senior high by another publisher.)

Music Educators Journal. 1914. m. (except June, July and Aug.). $4. Malcolm E. Bessom. Music Educators Natl. Conference, 1201 16th St., N.W. Washington,

D.C. 20036. Illus., adv. Circ: 70,000. Sample. Vol. ends: May. Microform: UM. Reprint: Kraus.

Indexed: EdI, MusicI. *Bk. rev:* 4–8, 550 words, signed. *Aud:* Ac, Hs, Ejh.

The leading music education journal, it represents music education from grade school through university level. Articles range from philosophy to practical teaching suggestions, to news of current music activities and developments, research, awards, and competitions. Special features are a part of some issues, e.g., "The Tanglewood Symposium—Music in American Society." One issue a year is devoted to a single special topic, such as electronic music, technology in music teaching, and urban music education. Sketches illustrate many articles and there is good photo coverage. A basic acquisition for all school professional collections.

Music Journal; educational music magazine. 1943. m. (Sept.–June). $9. Robert Cumming. Music Journal Inc., 1776 Broadway, New York, N.Y. 10019. Illus., adv. Circ: 23,000. Sample. Vol. ends: Dec. Microform: UM.

Indexed: EdI, MusicI. *Bk. rev:* 5–6, 150 words, signed. *Aud:* Ga, Ac, Hs.

One of the best single sources for an overview of contemporary music by outstanding authorities in all fields of music. Often highly controversial articles appear, which provide the music educator, the student, or the general music lover with a knowledge of current thinking on a wide variety of musical topics. Editorials range from polite essays to information about legislation affecting musicians. In addition to announcements and accounts of recent musical happenings, critical reviews by identified writers cover books, records, and music. Highly regarded in music circles, this is useful where there is a growing interest in music and a need is felt to purchase additional magazines in the field.

Music and Letters. 1920. q. $6. J. A. Westrup. Music & Letters, Ltd., 44 Conduit St., London, W1R, ODE, England. Illus., index, adv. Microform: UM.

Indexed: BritHum, MusicI. *Bk. rev:* Various number, length. *Aud:* Ac.

A British music journal with international coverage of classical music and musicians. It is known for scholarship and intelligence in dealing with the complexities of music, past and present. Learned dissertations on styles, contributions by outstanding musicians, and subjects of historical significance are included. An important part is the critical reviews of books and new music. While the emphasis is British, it is widely circulated in the United States, and should be in all medium to large-sized academic libraries.

Music and Musicians. 1952. m. $8.50. Tom Sutcliffe. Hansom Books Ltd., Artillery Mansions, 75 Victoria St., London SW1, England. Illus., adv. Circ: 8,500.

Indexed: MusicI. *Bk. rev:* 5–10, 200 words, notes. *Aud:* Ga, Ac.

Covers music and musicians on an international scale, and is particularly useful for reports on the European scene. A typical issue covers current peformers, performances, musical style (both modern and traditional), and a calendar of events. The reviews of musical performances are objective, always fair, and tend to be critical. Book reviews are a minor part of each issue, but Americans will find the survey of current recordings of special value, as emphasis is on English and European releases. The format is noteworthy, primarily because there is extensive use of illustrations and photographs. Even the nonmusician will find much here of interest, and it is a good, general magazine for medium to large-sized music collections.

The Music Review. 1940. q. $14. Geoffrey Sharp. W. Heffer & Sons Ltd., 104 Hills Rd., Cambridge, England. Illus., index, adv. Circ: 1,000. Microform: UM.

Indexed: BritHum, MusicI, RILM. *Bk. rev:* 6–10, lengthy, signed. *Aud:* Ac.

Serves as a vehicle for five to six musicological papers, and furnishes exhaustive, critical reviews of books, records, and music. The reviews, by identified and competent reviewers, include foreign books and records. Many consider *The Music Review* to be the British parallel to the *Musical Quarterly* in America. Necessary in a college or university with a strong music program but of little interest to the lay person.

Musical Analysis. 1972. s-a. $1. James Siddons, Box 7652 NT Station, Denton, Tex. 76203. Illus., adv.

Bk. rev: Notes. *Aud:* Ac, Ga.

A little offset music magazine of some 22 pages, this replaces the editor-publisher's *Musical Happenings.* The primary interest of the first issue is not the two articles on classical music, but the biographies to two little-known black artists. Be that as it may, the editor plans a scholarly journal which, "while still maintaining a meaningful depth, bridges the gap between pure biography and pure theory." The price is low enough to warrant a subscription by any library with a medium to large-sized music collection.

Musical Newsletter. 1971. q. $10. Patrick J. Smith, Box 250, Lenox Hill Station, New York, N.Y. 10021. Illus., index. Circ: 250. Sample. Vol. ends: Oct.

Indexed: MusicI. *Aud:* Ac.

The "newsletter" in the title is deceptive, for this quarterly does not report on recent music news; and though the price is high for a quarterly which runs to only 23 pages an issue, it is a needed addition to the periodical literature on music. It is for the very knowledgeable music amateur and professional "who would like to know more about the field of music than the pap and circumstance that he is all too often fed."

The field covered is largely classical music and its scope may be judged by a sampling of articles from Volume I: "The Music of Berlioz," by Edward T. Cone; "A Comparison of Music Editions: Beethoven Scores," by David Hamilton; "How Should Handel's Oratorios Be Staged," by Winton Dean. It is not for the person who has only a marginal interest in music. (G.S.)

Musical Opinion; educational journal. 1877. m. $4.50. Laurence Swinyard. Musical Opinion Ltd., 87 Wellington St., Juton, Beds., England. Illus., adv. Circ: 8,000.

Indexed: MusicI. *Bk. rev:* 4–6, 1,000 words, signed. *Aud:* Sa, Ac.

Limited to classical music with particular emphasis on detailed record reviews and briefer notice of music scores. The book reviews are excellent. Although published in England, the magazine tends to discuss music from the continent as much as London. It includes a special section for organ enthusiasts. For larger music collections.

The Musical Quarterly. 1915. q. $9. Paul H. Lang. G. Schirmer, Inc., 609 Fifth Ave., New York, N.Y. 10017. Illus., adv. Circ: 5,616. Microform: UM.

Indexed: MusicI, RILM, SSHum. *Bk. rev:* 2–4, 2–8 pages, signed. *Aud:* Ac, Ga. *Jv:* V.

A basic journal in all medium to large-sized music collections, this strives to be "a mirror of the world's best musical thought," and serves as a vehicle for the publication of research efforts in the field of serious music. Music students will find it indispensable. A section of about 25 pages covers events in the United States as well as on the international scene. Signed critical book reviews thoroughly explore scholarly books on music, and a quarterly booklist, which is not annotated, covers international publications. Record reviews report in depth on the musical and technical aspects of classical offerings and useful bibliographies are included. Generous use of musical examples as well as charts and photos are useful features. For all academic and larger public libraries.

The Musical Times. 1844. m. $7, Stanley Sadie. Novell & Co., Ltd. 27 Soho Sq., London, W1, England. Illus., index, adv. Circ: 12,000.

Indexed: BritHum, MusicI, RILM. *Bk. rev:* 10–12, 700 words, signed. *Aud:* Ac, Hs.

A general British music magazine, this is written for both the student and the teacher. There are some five long articles per issue on music, musicians, concerts, instruments, and education. Most of the writing is of a semischolarly nature, representing original research. Features include: short news stories; book, record, new music, and concert reviews; a diary of London musical events, and a special section on church and organ music. Approximately one half of the 96 to 104 page magazine is turned over to advertising. This is somewhat the equivalent of the old *Musical America,* and as one of the best general music magazines published anywhere, should be in all medium to large-sized music collections.

Opera News. 1936. irreg. (during opera season); m. (rest of the year). $10. Frank Merkling. Metropolitan Opera Guild, 1865 Broadway, New York, N.Y. 10023. Illus., index, adv. Circ: 80,000. Sample. Vol. ends: June. Microform: UM.

Indexed: MusicI, RG. *Bk. rev:* 3, 250–300 words, signed. *Aud:* Ga, Ac, Hs, Ejh.

During the Metropolitan Opera season, issues deal with the opera that is currently being performed, and include the plot, cast, and historical notes as well as photographs of characters and staging. Monthly issues are more likely to probe history and personalities involved in opera and to feature important companies outside New York. Signed reports of 250 to 1000 words from various music centers in the United States and abroad are a regular feature. The principal periodical devoted to opera in the United States, and should be in most libraries.

Percussionist And Percussive Notes. 1963. q. Membership $8 (Students $5). Neal Fluegel. Percussive Arts Soc., 130 Carol Drive, Terre Haute, Ind. 47805. Illus., index. Circ: 2,500. Sample. Vol. ends: Summer.

Indexed: MusicI. *Bk. rev:* Notes, signed. *Aud:* Ac, Ga, Hs.

The Percussive Arts Society aims "to raise the level of musical percussion performance and teaching; to expand understanding of needs and responsibilities of percussion students, teachers, and performers; and to promote greater communication between all areas of the percussion arts." Students and teachers of percussion instruments at the high school and college level will find much practical material here (ranging from the niceties of producing a snare drum roll to the problems of performing the timpani part of Stravinsky's *Rite of Spring*). Besides providing analyses of performance problems generally, there are discussions of individual percussion instruments and details of specific pieces. Each issue includes an annotated checklist of new percussion music. Members of the Society also receive *Percussive Notes* (three issues per academic year), which is more oriented to students and also includes news of Society activities, up-coming percussion recitals, a "matter lesson" for students, news of new products and new published music. Indispensable to the teacher and student of the percussive arts. (G.S.)

Perspectives of New Music. 1962. s-a. $6. Benjamin Boretz. Princeton Univ. Press, Box 231, Princeton, N.J. 08540. Illus., index, adv.

Indexed: MusicI. *Bk. rev:* 2–4, 1–8 pages, signed. *Aud:* Ac.

A scholarly journal for teachers and students of music. It provides scholarly studies of the new and innovative in serious music, the contributions of various composers to this music, and includes detailed book reviews. Since it is the only periodical in the United States that emphasizes new music styles exclusively, its reference value is high for those interested in modern music trends. Research efforts in specialized areas serve the needs of advanced students. Only for large collections.

The School Musician, Director and Teacher. 1929. m. (Sept.–June). $5. Forrest L. McAllister. 4 E. Clinton St., Joliet, Ill. 60431. Illus., index, adv. Circ: 15,000. Sample. Vol. ends: Aug.

Indexed: CIJE, EdI, MusicI. *Aud:* Ejh, Hs.

This is written by and for public school music educators, instrumental and vocal. It is a practical tool devoted to methods of teaching and is chock full of how-to-do-it articles for the band and choral director. It is also the official organ of the American School Band Association, Phi Beta Mu, the National Band Directors Fraternity, the Woman Band Directors National Association, the International Music Honor Society, and the National Catholic Bandmasters Association. Regular features include a roundup of news of interest to school music educators, evaluations of new products, columns on teaching specific instruments (wind, percussion, and strings), and a very extensive review section devoted to new band music. Also, each of the many organizations mentioned have short sections of news. This is probably indispensable to educators and is needed in most high school libraries, but is not in any way oriented to the general public. (G.S.)

Schwann Record & Tape Guide. 1949. m. $8.50. W. Schwann Inc., 137 Newbury St., Boston, Mass. 02116. Adv. Circ: 85,000.

Aud: Ga, Ac, Hs, Ejh.

The *Books in Print* and *American Book Publishing Record* of the recording and tape business. Each issue lists some 45,000 items from 800 firms. The month's 600 to 800 new releases are incorporated into the main list and in the "new release" section. Full buying information is given for each item, i.e., label, catalog number, performers, and manufacturer's list prices. An absolutely necessary item for any library involved in the constant purchase of records or tapes—and of considerable help as a reference aid when working with the public.

Another useful item in this field is the *Harrison Tape Catalog* (1955. bi-m. $3.50. M. & N. Harrison, Inc., 274 Madison Ave., New York, N.Y. 10016). This lists all available tapes and is considerably more comprehensive than Schwann. It does not include recordings. Both are needed by most libraries.

Soul. See Blacks Section.

Soundings. 1972. q. $7. Peter Garland and John Bischoff, 15102 Polk St., Slymar, Calif. 91342. Illus., index.

Bk. rev: 1–2, 200 words, signed. *Aud:* Ac.

Another version of *Source*, although this is a less expensive package. Still, the intent is relatively the same. The editors sum it up: "*Source*, the only good magazine out, is too expensive. . . . Also, its avant garde posture seems less important now than it may have been in 1967. . . . Too much attention has been focused on machines to the detriment of the social and physical ground of music." And with that the editors, duly inspired by Dick Higgins (founder of Something Else Press), give the readers some 80 pages of diversion and information. There are almost 20 different items from criticism to songs and compositions. James Tenney's Choreogram, for example, is "for any number of players, using any instrument or sound sources." The offset printing is not sensational, but clear enough and the 8×11-inch format fits the program of the editors. A worthwhile magazine for any library involved in music of the avant-garde, and absolutely required for *Source* subscribers.

Source; music of the avant garde. 1967. s-a. $13 (Student $11). Stanley G. Lunetta and Arthur Woodbury. Composer/Performer Edition, 2101 22nd St., Sacramento, Calif. 95818. Illus., adv. Circ: 2,000.

Aud: Ac, Ga. *Jv:* V.

The magazine of the musical avant-garde—different in every respect from any music magazine about. For example, the Fall 1971 issue contains a visual-aural composition, the visual part of which is provided by a set of abstract color photographs and the aural part by a stereo record. The format is equally unconventional, but in terms of sheer form and grace, it is without match. (Which is to say, it is well worth the subscription price.) A marvelous find for anyone who is seriously involved with innovative music, and it should be introduced to the same group who "digs" everyone from John Cage to Ionesco. A must for larger and more imaginative collections.

Steinway News. See Free Magazines Section.

Stereo Review (Formerly: *Hi-Fi/Stereo Review*). 1958. m. $7. William Anderson. Ziff Davis Publishing Co., 1 Park Ave., New York, N.Y. 10016. Illus., index, adv. Circ: 300,000. Sample. Microform: UM.

Indexed: MusicI. *Aud:* Ga, Ac, Hs. *Jv:* V.

A popular, useful guide to equipment and recordings for the beginner as well as the knowledgeable user. General articles on music are included, all well illustrated. Test reports and reports on new products adequately cover equipment without allowing this aspect to dominate the magazine. Occasional surveys give a comprehensive view of available equipment. There are a number of special issues given to detailed reports on tape recordings and loudspeakers. But equipment is not all. The musicological articles weigh equally. The most important aspect of this periodical is the reviews of all types of recordings, both discs and tapes. Those recordings deemed outstanding (performance, recording, and stereo quality) are indicated. If circulation is any indication, this is considerably more popular than *High Fidelity*. Actually, it is a matter of personal opinion as to which is "best" or "better." Libraries should take both. If it comes to a choice between the two, *Stereo Review* would be first.

Tempo; a quarterly review of modern music. 1939. q. $3.50. Colin Mason. Boosey & Hawkes Music Publishers, Ltd., 295 Regent St., London W1, England. Subs. to: Boosey & Hawkes, Oceanside, N.Y. Illus., adv.

Indexed: MusicI. *Bk. rev:* 4–6, 750 words, signed. *Aud:* Ga, Ac.

Devoted entirely to twentieth century music, this 30 to 40 page English quarterly features articles on modern music, or on certain aspects of a particular composer's work. Regular features include perceptive reviews of first performances (in England), grouped record reviews, and book reviews. Illustrations, usually of ballet or opera, are included, and music examples. The articles are well written and, while for the serious student of music, are within the grasp of the interested layman. In view of its coverage and low price, a good periodical for medium to large-sized libraries.

Variety. See Newspapers/Special Interest Section.

The World of Music. 1959. q. $8. John Evarts. B. Schott's Söhne, D-65 Mainz, Weihergarten, P.O.B 36 40, West Germany. Illus., index, adv. Circ: 2,000. Sample.

Indexed: MusicI. *Bk. rev:* 2–3, 500 words, signed. *Aud:* Ac, Ga, Hs, Ejh.

This is the journal of the International Music Council (UNESCO) and is published in association with the International Institute for Comparative Music Studies. Its international orientation is reflected in its truly magnificent coverage of the worlds of music which are far off the mainstream of western classical music. Fortunately, it is trilingual (English, French, German—with each item published in each of the three languages), and though the English translations are a bit shaky at times, no one really interested in what music is all about can afford to miss it. Where else can you regularly find articles about the music of India, Greece, Africa, the Middle and the Far East? The articles are all written by experts, but they are largely nontechnical and are obviously directed to a nonprofessional audience of music lovers. The world of twentieth century western music is not neglected as is reflected in titles of some recent articles: "The Business Partnership Between Composer and Publisher," "Will There be any Instrumentalists in the Year 2000?", and "Electronic Music and the Composer's Future." There are some valuable regular features: an "Information" roundup of worldwide musical events, a directory of first performances, and selected book and record reviews. The photographs cover the world and some are downright exotic. There is nothing to which the *World of Music* can be compared; it is unique and it is essential for large public and academic libraries. But by no means is it too esoteric for medium-sized school and public libraries. (G.S.)

Counterculture: Folk, Rock, and Jazz

Bluegrass Unlimited. 1966. m. $5. Richard Spottswood, Box 111, Burke, Va. 22015. Illus., adv. Circ: 5,250. Sample.

Aud: Ac, Hs, Ga.

To connoisseurs of U.S. music, the word "bluegrass" means the style of country string band music developed in the 1930s by Bill Monroe and his Bluegrass Boys, one of the legends of country and western music. The style grew up with the so-called "race records" during the early days of radio and commercial recording. Lester Flatt and Earl Scruggs are exponents of the style, and the theme music to the movie *Bonnie and Clyde* is an example of bluegrass with a virtuoso touch characteristic of recent developments in the genre. This little magazine is a rallying point for anyone interested in bluegrass or country music. *Bluegrass Unlimited* tends to be "traditional" in that it is interested in the old-time bluegrass (i.e., the recent Nashville country and western music is not covered in any detail). The approach is quite popular (not scholarly like the *JEMF Quarterly*) and practical. There are some good articles about the music, its instruments, and groups such as the Stanley Brothers, the Lilly Brothers, and the Country Gentlemen. Extensive coverage is given to the surprisingly large number of annual Bluegrass, country music, and "old-time fiddlers'" conventions and festivals—in fact, this is one of the best sources for keeping track of these annual U.S. musical events. Each issue also includes a listing of "Bluegrass in the Clubs," which lists what bands are playing where and when; also a separate list consisting of a "Personal Appearance Calendar," which reports on up-coming concerts. The record reviews bring to country and western music the special background and knowledge needed for this type of music (and it is an area which is not reviewed in most standard review sources). The emphasis, then, is on the documentation of the current bluegrass scene, and no other source covers the field as well. *Bluegrass Unlimited* is for li-

braries serving rural America, or urban America where there is a general orientation in the direction of Grand Old Opry. Also, academic libraries with a remote interest in the music of the United States, and any library serving young people who are enthusiastic about the traditional, living music of the United States. (G.S.)

Blues Unlimited. 1950. m. $8. Simon Napier and Mike Leadbitter, 38a Sackville Rd., Bexhill-on-Sea, Sussex, England. Illus., index, adv. Circ: 1,500.

Bk. rev: Various number, length. *Aud:* Ga, Ac.

One of a number of British magazines devoted to jazz and the blues (see also *Jazz Journal*). It features excellent record reviews, and well-thought out and documented articles on all aspects of the blues. The articles, of course, are not limited to British interests, and the whole is truly international. The journal has excellent photographs. *Jazz Journal* would be preferable, but for larger collections this would come in a close second. Others, further down the list, but useful: *Blues World* (1965. irreg. $3/4 nos. Bob Groom, 22 Manor Crescent, Kinutsford, Cheshire, England.); *Jazz & Blues* (1955. m. $8.50. Hanover Books Ltd., 4 Mill Rd., London W1, England. Note: Formerly: *Jazz Monthly*).

Changes. 1969. bi-w. $9. Jack Banning, Box 631, Cooper Station, New York, N.Y. 10003. Illus., adv. Microform: B&H.

Bk. rev: 3–4, 500–750 words, signed. *Aud:* Ac, Ga, Hs.

A magazine/newspaper (the familiar *Rolling Stone* format) which is primarily dedicated to covering the popular music scene, but includes important sections on political commentary, the arts, film, and books. There is some fiction. And whereas the music scene is covered in numerous other magazines of this type (*Rolling Stone, Creem, Crawdaddy,* etc.), what makes this distinct is the material on films and the satirical political commentary. The critical writing is much above average, and it should be noted that a good number of the writers are women—in fact, the publisher is Susan Graham. A 32-page issue in late 1971 included an interview with film maker Dalton Trumbo; notes on the Living Theatre; a critical essay on Bob Dylan; and a brilliant political commentary, "America on Trial," by Peter Stafford; record and book reviews; and an article on Furry Lewis. There is some advertising, and good illustrations. A first rate magazine/newspaper of the modern arts for public, academic and, hopefully, a few high school collections.

Country Sky. 1971. m. $6. Tony Goldstein, 280 S. Beverly Dr., Beverly Hills, Calif. 90024. Illus., adv. Circ: 100,000. Sample. Vol. ends: Dec.

Aud: Hs, Ga.

We have long needed a magazine like *Country Sky*

to cover the U.S. country music scene in a style more general than *Bluegrass,* more current than the *JEMF Quarterly,* and less commercial than some of the country pop magazines. In its early issues this is what *Country Sky* seems to be trying to do. It is lively and well written and covers the current state of country and western music and selected historical (but timely) aspects of this basic U.S. genre. An early issue had a fine piece on the once-famous white country artist, J. E. Mainer, an intriguing article on "Prisons & Country Music," and an interview-type article on Loretta Lynn. There are extensive record reviews, editorials, and generous news from Nashville, the capitol of country and western music. It looks, then, to be a fine blend of the new and the traditional, and libraries needing only one such music magazine will find this to be their best bet; if one more is needed, the *JEMF Quarterly* would nicely supplement *Country sky.* (G.S.)

Crawdaddy. 1967. m. bi-w. $10. Raeanne Rubenstein. Superstar Productions, Inc., 232 Madison Ave. New York, N.Y. 10016. Illus., adv. Circ: 100,000. Sample. Microform: B&H.

Bk. rev: 1–2, 500 words, signed. *Aud:* Ac, Ga, Hs.

Crawdaddy began about the same time as *Rolling Stone.* For a bit both went along covering the monthly modern music scene, but by 1971 *Crawdaddy* was a bi-weekly and with a new editor and approach. It seems more carefully written and edited than *Rolling Stone,* certainly tighter in scope and presentation. There is more content too. The issue examined included book, film, and theatre reviews, as well as shorter pieces on politics and satirical shorts. But the coup (August 29, 1971) was almost a whole section on Yoko, her art and her philosophy. There are, to be sure, the usual interviews and shorter pieces on music stars. Still not *Rolling Stone's* equal it surpasses it in terms of wider coverage. As a general magazine of the arts, it rivals *Changes.* It is a good choice for almost any collection serving younger readers.

Creem. 1969. m. $6. David Marsh. Creem Magazine Inc., Box 202, Walled Lake, Mich. 48088. Illus., adv. Circ: 120,000. Sample. Vol. ends: Apr.

Bk. rev: 3–5, 500–1,000 words, signed. *Aud:* Ejh, Hs, Ga, Ac. *Jv:* V.

Originally this started out as another type of *Rolling Stone,* but is developing its own character. It continues to put primary emphasis on the current pop music scene, e.g., the February 1972 issue features Bob Dylan and his times, but other elements are beginning to creep into an average 80 to 100 page issue. There are now film reviews, sports, and increasing attention to what younger people are thinking in terms of social and political issues. The new editor will carry it beyond music. He says as much: "There is occasional, growing more frequent, coverage of political events,

generally seen in a radical left light." Meanwhile, the criticism is good to excellent, features such names as Craig Karpel from *Esquire,* Greil Marcus, formerly of *Rolling Stone,* Ed Ward from *Stone,* and Robert Christgau of *Village Voice.* The magazine is particularly good in its reviews of current popular albums—the reviewers are hard hitting, critical, and analytical. An interesting addition for any popular music culture collection.

Down Beat. 1934. bi-w. $8. Dan Morgenstern. Maher Publns., Inc., 222 W. Adams St., Chicago, Ill. 60606. Illus., index, adv. Circ: 85,000. Vol. ends: 2nd no. Dec. Microform: UM.

Indexed: MusicI. *Bk. rev:* 2–3, 300–600 words, signed, critical. *Aud:* Ga, Ac, Hs.

Jazz musicians and fans in 142 countries read *Down Beat,* the top magazine for current coverage of the personalities, the music, the scenes, and the recordings in the jazz world. There is liberal discussion as to the influence of various persons or groups. Of reference value are the many types of discerning reviews (books, recordings, concerts), some of which are not found elsewhere. A famous music magazine which should enjoy wide support by almost every type of library.

Hit Parader. m. $5. Ian Dove. Charlton Publns., Inc., Charlton Bldg., Derby, Conn. 06418. Illus., adv.

Aud: Ga, Hs, Ac.

Hit Parader is always oriented to "the scene" but the view is largely adulatory or, at best, non-critical. Some of the articles read like publicity agents' press releases. It is, nevertheless, an indispensable index to the most popular features of mass pop and rock music. The serious rock critic would say it is "commercial," and it is, but so is the "scene" which it covers. A long back run of *Hit Parader* (along with some other publications of the Charlton group) is an indispensable resource for the study of the history of music in American popular culture—it is also a resource found in very few U.S. libraries. As a current source, it will appeal to the more unsophisticated teen-agers and teeny-boppers who have not yet graduated to *Rolling Stone* territory. A major feature is "Parade of Hit Songs," which contains complete texts of around two dozen current "hits." A recent issue would contain a lead article about "the scene" (e.g., "Hard Rock Versus Soft Rock"), biographies of individuals (e.g., John Lennon, Jethro Tull, Rod Stewart), articles about groups (e.g., Moody Blues, Traffic, Sly and the Family Stones), and question-answer type interviews with current rock celebrities. There is an abudance of photographs. A good item for high school libraries, public libraries that serve teen-agers, and college libraries interested in the music or sociology of youth culture. For reference librarians, a good source for song texts which are usually difficult to find. (G.S.)

JEMF Quarterly. 1965. q. $7.50 (Individuals $5). Norm Cohen. John Edwards Memorial Foundation, Folklore and Mythology Center, Univ. of California, Los Angeles, Calif. 90024. Illus., index. Circ: 600. Sample. Vol. ends: Winter.

Bk. rev: 1–2, notes. *Aud:* Ac, Ga, Hs.

The *JEMF Quarterly* is unique, for it is devoted exclusively to the study of U.S. country and western music. The archives of the Foundation are built around the collection amassed by the Australian collector, John Edwards, and are devoted to furthering "the serious study and public recognition of those forms of American folk music disseminated by commercial media such as print, sound recordings, films, radio and television." In other words, the *Quarterly* is devoted to styles of music identified as "country," "country and western," "old time," "bluegrass," "mountain," "cowboy," etc., including race records, soul, rock—i.e., the entire field of U.S. regional popular and folk music. No one interested in these areas should be denied access to it. There are other magazines in country and western music (e.g., *Country Sky, Bluegrass*), but they are more oriented to the current scene and lack the solid historical perspective of *JEMF Quarterly.* But scholarship is not incompatible with interest and style, and the writers for *JEMF Quarterly* will surely find a large audience among amateurs and collectors of U.S. music. Here they will find, for example, "A Preliminary Vernon Dalhart Discography," "The Great Allen Brothers Search," and "The WLS National Barn Dance Story." Regular features include Archie Green's "Commercial Music Graphies," "Bibliographic Notes of Interest," and notes on "Work in Progress." (G.S.)

Jazz Journal. 1948. m. $7.50. Sinclair Trail. Novello & Co., 27 Soho Sq., London, W12, England. Illus., adv. Circ: 12,000.

Indexed: MusicI. *Bk. rev:* 2–3, 250–300 words. *Aud:* Ga, Ac, Hs.

There are more than a dozen magazines devoted entirely to jazz. Half are published abroad, and while opinion differs, the English *Jazz Journal* is considered by many to be the best of the group. It has wide use in America because of its international coverage, the excellent black and while illustrations, and, most important, the extensive record reviews. The editors make an effort to cover all jazz recordings—regardless of point of issue—of the previous month.

Jazz & Pop. 1962. m. $6. Janice Coughlan. Jazz Press, Inc., 1841 Broadway, New York, N.Y. 10023. Illus., index, adv. Sample.

Indexed: MusicI. *Aud:* Hs.

This is a jazz-oriented magazine aimed at the high school audience. It could be categorized as a "Junior Downbeat," for it emphasises jazz, touching only lightly on rock and folk music. It is quite conservative (editorially, textually, and graphically) when compared to the real swingers in the youth music field. *Jazz & Pop* is more interested in music as music than it is in the flamboyant and intransigent rock sub-cultures. It is difficult not to think of white, middle-class, affluent, rosy-cheeked, suburban, American "youngsters" browsing through the pages of *Jazz & Pop.* A sampling of recent articles: "Poco Power" (the story of a new music group—"nothing less than wonderful"), the story of "Fanny," an all-girl rock quartet ("folk music was just too tame"); and "George Martin" (who "looks back to the Beatles and forward with Seatrain"). All of this is completely harmless. There are some surprises, such as an interview with Ravi Shankar and a regular column by Nat Hentoff. Within its somewhat limited conception of jazz and rock music, this is a respectable item which should find a large audience among the users of high school libraries. (G.S.)

Kord. 1970. q. $2. Eric Kriss, Box 531, Northampton, Mass. 01060. Illus., adv. Sample.

Indexed: API. *Aud:* Ac, Ga.

A "little magazine" of the music world. In some 32 offset pages, the editor includes basic, often original material on the world of the folksong and the blues. For example, in one number there is an interview with Bee Houston, prison songs from San Quentin, an article on "rhythmic thinking and independence," and record reviews. The latter feature, which usually includes one third of each issue, is particularly valuable because the reviews touch on recordings seldom noted in standard, better-known services. Another interesting touch: reviews of catalogs of various record companies which feature blues and/or folk and country music. A modest price for a valuable item.

Living Blues. 1970. bi-m. $3. Jim and Amy O'Neal. Living Blues Publns., Box 11303, Chicago, Ill. 60611. Illus., adv. Circ: 3,000. Sample. Vol. ends: Winter.

Bk. rev: 2, ½ page, signed. *Aud:* Ac, Ga, Hs.

A "little magazine" of music (one of a growing number in this genre), devoted to all aspects of the blues. Articles and interviews have examined such musicians and composers as: Buddy Guy, Lonnie Johnson, Robert Pete Williams, Samy Myers, Bobo Jenkins, Bobby Bland, Hound Dog Taylor, etc. And the editors report on blues festivals, instruct in basic techniques, and generally breathe love and life into the form. There are frequent discographies, and each issue features reviews of blues made on LP and 45-speed records. Usually 15 to 30 photographs per 40 to 48 page issue. An excellent addition for any library where there is the slightest interest in the subject.

Melody Maker. 1926. w. $9.50. Ray Coleman. Longacre Press Ltd., 161 Fleet St., London EC 4, England. Illus. index, adv. Circ: 155,000.

Indexed: Music I. *Aud:* Ga.

Somewhat the British equivalent of *Rolling Stone.* Still, it has been around a few more years, and it has a personality and character all its own. An average 56 page issue covers the British pop scene, but spreads out to include most of what is going on in Europe and America. In fact, its particular claim to fame is its international coverage: news, views, articles, interviews, charts of what is hot or running cold, pictures, and just about all the other bits that make it a fast-selling paper in England. Some outstanding critics, too. Not a necessary item for libraries, but a most welcome one where popular music is a craze.

Rock. 1970. bi-w. $4. Larry Marshak. Rock, 166 Lexington Ave., New York, N.Y. 10016. Illus., index.
Bk. rev: Various number, length. *Aud:* Ejh, Hs, Ga.

Follows the *Rolling Stone* tabloid format, but there the similarity ends. It is more involved with serious criticism of modern rock music and musicians. There tend to be short reviews of concerts and news items, followed by feature stories which touch on all aspects of the business. For example, the March 27, 1972 32-page issue had a fine story on how record album covers are censored, an appreciation of Kris Kristofferson, and a long excerpt of a new book on the history of radio. The record reviews by various staff members are good to excellent. The format is acceptable, although not sensational, and the whole approach seems better suited for younger readers than the better known *Rolling Stone.* The library that takes the *Stone* should also consider.

Rolling Stone. 1967. bi-w. $10. Jann Wenner. Straight Arrow Publishers, Inc., 625 Third St., San Francisco, Calif. 94107. Illus., index, adv. Circ: 250,000. Sample. Vol. ends: every 15 issues.
Bk. rev: 2, ¾ page, signed. *Aud:* Ac, Ga, Hs. *Jv:* V.

The basic music magazine of the counterculture. Still, some four years after its founding, it is rapidly taking on the image of the establishment. The editor has moved into other fields, including books, and the advertising and circulation have grown to a point where it is no longer considered the "little" magazine of modern music. But philosophy of success aside, the tabloid newspaper owes its following to factual reporting about the music scene; interviews with media freaks from established personalities such as Bob Dylan to lesser-known music writers and musicians; excellent record reviews of both singles and albums; and a winning format—the magazine is put together as a tabloid newspaper with numerous illustrations and photographs. No follower of music, from the beginning reader to the culture vulture of the academic circle, would be without his or her issue. Should be in every library.

Its primary competitor is *Creem,* and for librarians who must decide between the two (it would be better to take both), let Ellen Willis, the popular-rock music critic of *The New Yorker* help. In the February 26, 1972 issue she compared the two: "*Creem* . . . is not put out by fresh kids who have never heard of Little Richard and could care less, but by—and largely for—fifties and sixties rockheads. Unlike *Rolling Stone,* which is a bastion of San Francisco countercultural 'rock and art' orthodoxy, *Creem* is committed to a Pop aesthetic; it speaks to fans who consciously value rock as an expression of urban teen-age culture and identify with a tradition whose first law is novelty." But the Willis separation is too easy. Actually, both have wide appeal to anyone who digs rock, pop, and all forms of modern music.

Sing Out. 1950. bi-m. $5. Rob Heder and Bob Norman. 33 W. 60th St., New York, N.Y. 10023. Illus., adv. Circ: 15,000. Sample. Vol. ends: no. 6. Microform: UM.
Indexed: MusicI. *Aud:* Ga, Hs, Ejh.

Although the folk music craze comes and goes, it never dies, and this is probably the best single magazine for anyone interested in "singing out." It features interviews with singers, song writers, teachers; articles on the guitar, banjo, and autoharp; news and notes on what is happening on the scene; and articles which cover every aspect of folk from traditional to contemporary. Regular columns include: Pete Seeger's "Johnny Appleseed," Mike Cooney's "General Delivery," record reviews, and news of folk festivals. It has added attraction for the player in that each number contains 10 to 15 folk songs, right down to words, music, and guitar chords. A first choice for any music-minded high school or junior high library, and worthwhile in medium to large-sized music collections anywhere.

Song Hits Magazine. 1942. m. $3.50. Patrick Masulli. Charlton Publns., Inc., Charlton Bldg., Derby, Conn. 06418. Illus., adv.
Aud: Ga, Hs, Ac.

Any library that is lucky enough to have a back run of this has a slice of Americana. Academic libraries have not taken much interest in this area, but with the growing interest in courses in "popular culture" many of them are going to find they lack basic source material. But the purpose of *Song Hits* is to publish the lyrics of current songs in the various fields of popular music, and for this reason it has a massive following, especially among teen-agers. Each issue has at least one article about some current "star" or group. The songs are arranged in these broad areas: pop songs, soul songs, country songs. Each issue runs to around fifty pages (on woodpulp paper) and contains the lyrics to sixty or more songs. There seems to be nothing else quite like it; another Charlton publication, *Hit Parad-*

er, comes closest, but does not attempt the broad coverage of lyrics found in *Song Hits*. (G.S.)

Storyville. 1965. bi-m. $2.80 (surface mail), $5. (airmail). Laurie Wright. Storyville Publns. & Co., 63, Orford Road, London E17 9NJ, England. Illus., adv. Circ: 1,750. Sample. Vol. ends: Aug.

Bk. rev: Number varies, 300–700 words, signed. *Aud:* Ac, Ga.

In the mythology of U.S. popular music, the Storyville section of New Orleans has long been considered "the birthplace of jazz." Hence the title of this little jazz magazine from England. Its interests are classic jazz and blues (i.e., earlier forms of jazz, largely predating the rise of the big "swing" bands). Its modest size (forty or fifty pages an issue) is deceptive, for it is always packed with a wealth of valuable and original historical and discographical jazz research. A typical issue might contain a biography of Ma Rainey (the legendary blues singer), an "oral-history" type article providing original source material on one of the black bands which worked the midwestern circuit out of Omaha or Kansas City in the heyday of the road bands in the 1920s and 1930s, and at least one authoritative discography. Regular features are "The Junkshoppers" column (a section for collectors of 78 rpm discs) and thorough review coverage of LP reissues of classic jazz and blues. Storyville Publications is now the publisher of the most comprehensive and basic of all jazz record reference books, Brian Rust's *Jazz Records: 1897–1942*, and additions, corrections, and changes in Rust's work will be published in *Storyville*. Libraries interested in U.S. music cannot do without this title. If you must choose between this and Albert McCarthy's *Jazz & Blues*, you have a problem. McCarthy is a jazz classicist, but his periodical has a much wider coverage (more on white bands, swing bands, the current scene, and more record reviews) than *Storyville*. (G.S.)

Record and Tape Reviews

American Record Guide. 1934. m. $6. James Lyons. American Record Guide, Box 319, Radio City Station, New York, N.Y. 10019. Illus., adv. Circ: 44,000. Sample. Vol. ends: Aug.

Indexed: MusicI, RG. *Bk. rev:* 1–3, see below. *Aud:* Ga, Ac, Hs, Ejh. *Jv:* V.

The best single review medium for recordings and tapes. As the oldest of its kind in the field, it aims for "encyclopedic, unbiased coverage of classical recordings by critics qualified to compare all new releases with all competitive versions." One major artist's work is studied each month, and there are separate columns devoted to rock, folk, pop, *and* jazz. "Sound Ideas," an equipment review by Larry Zide, is the only concession to the hardware aspect. The rest is devoted to such features as discographies and serious reviews of

music and drama recordings. Sometimes one recording is compared with another, and two reviewers will often present opposing views on the same recording. The May "anniversary issue" is particularly noteworthy for the extensive book reviews—up to 100 pages covering close to 50 titles issued in the previous months. This feature makes it a useful added check for the general library that may not be specializing in music titles, but wants an annual survey of the "best" and "better" items. The whole has vast reference value for any type of library, particularly where recordings are an important part of the collection.

Audio Record Review. See *Hi-Fi News and Record Review*. Music/General Section.

Gramophone. 1923. m. $6.50. Anthony Pollard. General Gramaphone Publns. Inc., 177 Kenton Rd., Kenton, Middlesex HA3 OHA, England. Circ: 73,000. Microform: UM.

Indexed: MusicI. *Aud:* Ga, Ac.

Contains long, critical reviews of the monthly output of classical recordings in the United Kingdom. There are also two or three articles on music and audio equipment. An extremely useful review medium for any library which has more than a moderate-sized record collection.

Hi-Fi News and Record Review. See Music/General Section.

Matrix. 1954. bi-m. $1.50. George Hulme, 7 Aynsley Road, Shelton, Stoke-On-Trent, Staffordshire ST 4 2RA, England. Adv. Circ: 500. Sample.

Indexed: MusicI. *Bk. rev:* Various number, length. *Aud:* Ac.

In the field of discographical research (i.e., the retrospective, systematic "bibliography" of recorded sound), *Matrix* has achieved a longevity which is quite unusual considering the low survival rate of this type of magazine. It can best be compared to its U.S. counterpart, *Record Research*, for both periodicals cover essentially the same field: the commercial 78 rpm discs produced prior to the rise of the LP. And, like *Record Research*, this one covers jazz, blues, and other commercial discs, but not the field of classical music. Since the field is so vast, there is room for two periodicals in this area, and there is little duplication. Libraries interested in professional competence in U.S. discographical research can get both, considering the modest prices. If only one is needed, the choice would fall to the domestic production. The contributors to *Matrix* are some of the best discographers in the business (a surprisingly large number of them are residents of England). There are discographies of individuals and groups. Another approach, important in historical discography, is the listing of the output of specific "labels" (i.e., specific recording companies), and there are a few short articles. (G.S.)

Music Library Association. Notes. 1943. q. $15. Frank C. Campbell. Music Library Assn., Inc. 104 W. Huron St., Rm. 329, Ann Arbor, Mich. 48108. Illus., index, adv. Circ: 3,650. Sample. Vol. ends: June.

Indexed: LibLit, MusicI. *Bk. rev:* 20–25, 600–1,600 words, signed. *Aud:* Ac, Ga, Hs. *Jv:* V.

One may not always agree with either the record or the book evaluations, but this remains one of the best single sources for both. Furthermore, it is an invaluable index, a type of *Book Review Digest,* for recordings (tape included). Usually some 19 periodicals are checked, and reviews of well over 200 different recordings are noted. This is the primary use of *Notes* for the average library, but there are also three or four articles, some business and association news, etc. A basic guide for all libraries. (G.S.)

Musica. 1946. bi-m. $7.50. Wolfram Schwinger, 3500 Kassel-Wilhelmshöhe, Heinrich-Schütz Allee 35, West Germany. Adv.

Indexed: MusicI. *Bk. rev:* Various number, length. *Aud:* Ac.

The subtitle of this standard German guide to European classical music gives a fair idea of its extensive scope: "Essays, Portraits, Reports, Books, Music, Records." It is "the complete music lover." The emphasis is on the current classical scene (performers, composers, opera, soloists, and concert music). There is nothing to which it can be compared in the United States. Each issue has one or two major articles, and then follow the detailed reports on the European scene. A major feature is the care given to world premieres, and though the standard repertory is given excellent coverage, there is a happy tendency to report on new music and new trends. The *Berichte* ("Reports") provide news from as far afield as Buenos Aires, Budapest, London, Hamburg, and Berlin. It is thorough, accurate, and indispensable. There is only one catch: it is all in German. In any case, a basic source for academic libraries (especially those serving graduate music schools) and large public libraries. (G.S.)

Record Research; the magazine of record statistics and information. 1955. 7–8 issues/yr. $3/12 issues. Leon Kunstadt and Bob Colton, 65 Grand Ave., Brooklyn, N.Y. 11205. Illus. Sample.

Indexed: MusicI. *Bk. rev:* Various number, length. *Aud:* Ac, Ga.

Record Research has been the hardiest of all U.S. discographical research periodicals. A pioneer in the discography of U.S. popular, folk, country and western, and jazz music, it has mined areas which have been almost completely neglected by academic scholars. It is basically a periodical for the private collector and discographer of 78 rpm discs, but this is an area where more librarians should offer reference services. The coverage is catholic and includes discogra-phies of such diverse artists as Tex Ritter, Zez Confrey, and A. A. Rolfe—indeed, any artists active during the era of the 78 rpm disc may turn up in the pages of *Record Research.* It is a modest publication, each issue generally running to around sixteen pages, and of these anywhere from six to ten are devoted to long lists of old 78 rpm discs which are up for auction. The whole area covered by *Record Research* has too long remained outside of the scope of most library activities, and if librarians are ever going to become as competent in discography as they are in bibliography, more of them will need to subscribe to this one. Some librarians who take this to be an area of serious concern will also want to consider the British counterpart of *Record Research: Matrix.* (G.S.)

Recorded Sound. 1961. q. Membership. $6. Patrick Saul. British Inst. of Recorded Sound, 29 Exhibition Rd., London SW 7, England. Index. Sample. Vol. ends: Oct.

Indexed: MusicI. *Bk. rev:* 8, 200 words, signed. *Aud:* Ac.

The British Institute of Recorded Sound is becoming one of the world's major national archives of recorded sound; and its journal, which reflects the broad interests of the Institute, reaches a level of editorial, discographical, and scholarly excellence which is unmatched by any other discographical journal in its area of interest. Although the interests of the Institute are quite broad, the journal has emphasized the discography of classical music in its historical aspects. Besides some of the finest discographical studies available anywhere, it includes very good articles (always original and important) on performers and composers. Recent issues have included articles on the great twentieth century Polish composer Karol Szymanowski, the French composer Francis Poulenc, the conductor Victor de Sabata, and the harpsichordist Violet Gordon Woodhouse. This is the aristocrat of the discographical journals and will reach a broad spectrum of library users who are interested in classical music. But the field is "historical discography" and reviews of current LPs are not included. (G.S.)

NEWS AND OPINION MAGAZINES

See also General Magazines, Literary Reviews, Counterculture, and Newspapers Sections.

Basic Periodicals

GENERAL. Ejh: *Life;* Hs: *Newsweek, Life, Current;* Ga: *Newsweek, Life, Time, Schism, U.S. News & World Report;* Jc: *Newsweek, Schism, Time, Life, U.S. News & World Report;* Ac: *Newsweek, Schism, U.S. News & World Report, Time, Current, Life.*

POLITICAL OPINION REVIEWS. Hs: *New Republic;* Ga: *New Republic, National Review, Ramparts;* Jc: *New Republic, National Review, Nation, Ramparts;* Ac: *New Republic, National Review, Nation, Washington Monthly, Dissent, Bulletin of the Atomic Scientists, Ramparts.*

RADICAL RIGHT. Ga, Jc & Ac: *American Opinion, Freeman, Cross and the Flag.*

RADICAL LEFT. Ga, Jc & Ac: *Monthly Review, Progressive Labor, International Socialist Review*

Basic Abstracts and Indexes

Alternate Press Index, Public Affairs Information Service, Readers' Guide to Periodical Literature, Social Science & Humanities Index.

Cessations

I. F. Stone's Weekly (See *New York Review of Books*), CAW, *Leviathan, Dan Smoot Report.*

General

Atlantic Advocate. 1909. M. $5. John Braddock. Univ. Press of New Brunswick Ltd., Fredericton, N.B., Canada. Illus., index, adv. Circ: 22,000.

Indexed: CanI. *Aud:* Ga, Ac.

General interest magazine emphasizing articles by or about the Atlantic provinces of Canada—Nova Scotia, New Brunswick, and Prince Edward Island. In addition to news and features on the Atlantic Provinces it includes original fiction, poetry, and book reviews. The appeal is wider than its geographical setting. (N.H.)

Atlas; a window on the world. 1961. m. $10. Malcolm Muir. World Press Co., 1180 Ave. of the Amer., New York, N.Y. 10036. Illus., index. Circ: 105,000.

Indexed: PAIS, SSHum. *Bk. rev:* 5–6, 300–500 words, signed. *Aud:* Ga, Ac, Hs.

An intelligent man's approach to the world's events. Each issue includes English translations—in part or in full—of material which has appeared in the world's press, i.e., both newspapers and magazines. The material, ranging from the cultural to the political, is selected by the editors to reinforce or back current interests in the United States. Thanks to judicious choices and careful translations, the magazine is particularly useful for students doing papers (high school though college) or for the professional person trying to keep up with world opinion. Cartoons and illustrations are reproduced, too. This side of subscribing to international magazines and newspapers, *Atlas* provides the best and fastest way of getting a necessary overview.

Current. 1960. m. $10 (Students, teachers $7.50). Grant S. McClelan. Goddard Publns., Inc., Plainfield, Vt. 05667. Illus., index. Circ: 12,000. Sample.

Indexed: RG, ABC PolSci, HistAb. *Aud:* Ga, Ac, Hs. *Jv:* V.

Primarily a reprint magazine, but of a considerably higher order than the familiar *Reader's Digest.* A definite effort is made to give two or more points of view; articles are taken in full from major newspapers, magazines, and journals; and the result of a 65-page issue is a balanced, thoughtful appraisal of current events. Usually there are six to seven major topics with two to four articles under each subject, i.e., "Has America Gone Awry," "The Computer and Society," "Protecting Our Lands," etc. The editorial board believes it a supplementary educational tool in three areas: (1) advanced high school courses; (2) college course work on contemporary American political, social, and economic issues; and (3) adult educational work. A 12-month breakdown of articles by section topics supports the editor's view of this audience. Domestic issues and American politics received the most attention, followed closely by foreign affairs. In one year some 74 different sources were tapped. There is no better approach for public, school, and university and college libraries. If not subscribing, send for a sample issue.

Current History. See Political Science Section..

Current World Leaders; biography and news. 1957. bi-m. $7.50. Marshall R. Crawshaw. Box 2238-D, Pasadena, Calif. 91005. Index. Circ: 5,000. Sample. Vol. ends: Dec. Microform: UM.

Bk. rev: 2, ½ page. *Aud:* Ga, Ac, Hs.

An invaluable aid for (a) keeping up-to-date information that is normally found in an almanac or yearbook; (b) current information on world officials; and (c) a running commentary on major events which have taken place throughout the world. A normal issue consists of individual or group biographies of leaders arranged by country; documents; current names of individuals in cabinets, parliaments, and other official positions; and running shorter items of interest. There is also a necrology and calendar for forthcoming events. While this is in the form of a pocketbook magazine, it is really a basic reference aid. It is augmented by the *Current World Leader Almanac,* a triannual which is another $7.50, or may be taken in conjunction with the magazine for $12. The *Almanac* gives a country-by-country listing of all major officials, as well as major United Nations' officials. Highly recommended for just about any reference situation.

Editorial Research Reports. 1923. w. $108. William B. Dickinson, Jr. Congressional Quarterly Inc., 1735 K St., N.W., Washington, D.C. 20006. Illus., index. Circ: 2,200. Vol. ends: Dec.

Indexed: PAIS. *Aud:* Ga, Ac.

A 20-page, 6,000-word weekly report on an item currently in the news, this is more a standard reference aid than a magazine. The unsigned studies are by subject experts, and range from the Supreme Court controversy to the black revolution, and from synthetic foods to Arab guerrillas. The editors outline the material on the first page, dividing it into three units: (1) a background discussion and how the topic has developed over the past week or month; (2) more background; (3) arguments pro and con, if there is a disagreement, and what might be done to settle the debate. There are semiannual bound volumes which include interim briefs. The latter is a single daily sheet which updates the initial report and is bound in with the six-month volume. A title and subject index ties all parts together. The whole can be readily understood by the average adult or high school student. It serves as an excellent springboard for 'debate, class papers, talks, and the like.

The Federalist. See Political Science Section.

Global Dialogue. 1968. m. $8. E. Weinfeld. Global Dialogue Publns. Inc., 11 Fifth Ave., Pelham, N.Y. 10803. Circ: 1,400. Sample. Vol. ends: Dec.

Bk. rev: 2, 1 page, signed. *Aud:* Ac, Hs.

A pocket-sized, 30-page, advertising-free magazine which reports on current political and social activities on a world-wide basis. A given amount of each issue is turned over to a central theme, e.g., the population explosion, the Catholic Church and birth control, or Nigeria. Articles are relatively objective, and by authorities who may or may not be identified by position. The tone is definitely intellectual and liberal. The editor claims that the majority of readers of the short articles are college students, more particularly those involved with debate on a formal or informal level. However, high school debating groups will find the magazine equally useful, and it is well worth the rather steep price.

Headline Series. 1935. 5/yr. $5. Norman Jacobs. Foreign Policy Assn., 345 E. 46th St., New York, N.Y. 10017. Illus., adv. Circ: 15,000.

Indexed: PAIS, SSHum. *Aud:* Ga, Ac, Hs.

Actually not a magazine, but a booklet that has high reference value for both the adult and student from senior high up. Issued by the nonpartisan Foreign Policy Association, each issue concentrates on a significant international relationship in the current news. Includes basic background on the subject, a discussion guide, and suggested reading. The magazine is prepared by experts who show a remarkable objectivity in presenting both sides of controversial topics. Maps and charts assist the reader to find his way. A basic work for any high school or college, and for

laymen who are preparing talks or leading discussion groups.

Life. 1936. w. $7.75. Thomas Griffith. Time Inc., Time & Life Bldg., Rockefeller Center, New York, N.Y. 10020. Illus., index, adv.

Indexed: AbrRG, RG. *Aud:* Ga, Ac, Hs.

Many claim this to be the last truly general mass magazine in America. Now that *Look, Colliers, Saturday Evening Post, et al.* are historical items, *Life* is the only magazine offering a little something to everyone. How long it will continue is a matter of conjecture. Ostensibly it is the pictorial side of its sister, *Time,* but while it does follow the weekly news to a given extent, it primarily uses the news as a point of departure for entertainment. The photographs are no longer great, or even outstanding. The articles rarely reveal much more than gut emotion, and the overall editorial policy is confusing. Since the death of its founder, Henry Luce, the editors have swung off the road leading to the Right, and often come to the Left. But they are never really that predictable. Still, as an American tradition, *Life* can no more be left out of the library than *Playboy* can be left out of the barbershop. It is not an important magazine; it is simply a well-known one.

Maxwell Review. 1964. bi-a. $4. R. G. Snyder and David Allor. Maxwell School of Citizenship and Public Affairs. Syracuse, N.Y. 13210. Illus., index. Microform: UM.

Indexed: PAIS. *Bk. rev:* 3–4, essay group, signed. *Aud:* Ac.

A student-edited journal of scholarship, opinion, and criticism in the social sciences. Most of the contributors are faculty, students, and alumni of the Maxwell School at Syracuse University. An average 130-page offset issue centers on a given theme, e.g., "The Political Economy of New York," "South Asia," or "Perspectives on Social Conflict." There are then eight to ten articles on the subject. Articles vary in style and depth, but all are at least carefully researched, and seem accurate enough. The magazine includes book reviews and a list of "current research projects of senior graduate students and faculty of the Maxwell School." The journal is of enough general interest to warrant careful consideration for purchase by academic and larger public libraries.

Newsweek. 1933. w. $14. Osborn Elliott. Newsweek, Inc. 444 Madison Ave., New York, N.Y. 10022. Illus., index, adv. Circ: 2,600,000. Microform: Newsweek, UM.

Indexed: AbrRG, RG. *Bk. rev:* 5–8, 300–1,000 words, signed. *Aud:* Ga, Ac, Hs.

The differences between this and *Time,* are rapidly becoming nil. When *Time* was under the right wing of its founder, Henry Luce, the editorial policy was predictable. The death of Luce meant the freedom of *Time* editors, at least in part, to catch up with the twentieth century. Since then, both magazines have tended to swing further and further away from featuring personalities to spotlighting issues; i.e., instead of an article on this year's beauty queen or husband killer, the magazine(s) examine the role of women in the feminist movement, politics, the home, etc. A rock musician might have once made the cover of either magazine, but he or she is now more likely to be replaced by a detailed story on the problems and future of youth. Aside from the issues, even the *Time* and *Newsweek* styles are becoming more and more alike. At one period *Time* could be distinguished from *Newsweek* by the fact that its rapid adjective-loaded sentences were not only nonobjective, but downright biased.

New York Review of Books. See Books and Book Reviews Section.

Politics and Society. See Political Science Section.

Schism, A Journal of Divergent American Opinion. 1969. q. $7.50. Donald L. Rice. Schism Publishing Co., 1109 W. Vine St., Mt. Vernon, Ohio 43050. Adv. Circ: 1,500. Sample. Vol. ends: Fall. Microform: UM.

Aud: Ac, Ga, Hs. *Jv:* V.

Librarians who claim they can't possibly take more than a few of the radical Left or Right periodicals will welcome this approach to digests. Drawing upon both conservative and radical magazines, and a few left and right of center, the editors reprint major articles, editorials, and even short comments. Titles vary from *Jewish Currents* to *The Torch,* "a publication of the conservative club of Grove City College." Subjects range from comments on "why students rise against hippies" to an article supporting GI opposition to the Vietnam war. Approximately 25 different magazines are clearly identified with a statement of policy, subscription information, and address at the head of each article or comment—an added bibliographic feature which is extremely useful. The editors apparently strive to strike a balance between viewpoints, but one suspects their basic sympathies are with the liberals. At any rate, this journal can be recommended highly, particularly for smaller and medium-sized libraries which now totally lack representative right- and left-wing magazines.

Science and Society. See Political Science Section.

Time; the weekly newsmagazine. 1923. w. $10. Henry A. Grunwald. Time Inc., Time & Life Bldg., 1271 Ave. of the Amer., New York, N.Y. 10020. Subs. to: Time Inc., 540 N. Michigan Ave., Chicago, Ill. 60611. Illus., index, adv. Circ: 4,250,000. Microform: UM, MC.

Indexed: AbrRG, RG. *Bk. rev:* 5–10, 100–1,000 words, signed. *Aud:* Ac, Ga, Hs.

This now has excellent film and music reviews. The news and features have picked up a bit since my last evaluation, and in many ways it is no longer the brainchild of the late Henry Luce, which is an improvement. It is difficult to tell it apart from *Newsweek,* but I prefer the latter. (See comments for *Newsweek,* and let it go at that.)

For someone honestly trying to keep up with the world's activities on a weekly basis, a much better approach is to be found through either (1) the *New York Times* Sunday edition, especially "The Week in Review," its news magazine, or (2) the weekly *National Observer.* Anyone who reads one or both of these consistently soon comes to realize that both *Time* and *Newsweek* seem to read both papers as well. Why not read the original?

U.S. News & World Report. 1933. w. $12. David Lawrence. U.S. News & World Report, Inc., John H. Sweet, 2300 N St., N.W., Washington, D.C. 20037. Illus., index, adv. Circ: 1,875,000. Sample. Vol. ends: June and Dec. Microform: UM.

Indexed: AbrRg, PAIS, RG. *Aud:* Ga.

A much-quoted large-circulation general news magazine. Although its circulation is not as great as that of *Time* (4,250,000) or *Newsweek* (2,600,000), it is right up there with both in terms of readership. The difference in "popularity" is due to the more general coverage by *Time* and *Newsweek* (both include sports, theater, medicine, etc., whereas *U.S. News* sticks to the national and international hard news). All three, however, are middle of the road to conservative. I quote from a letter from John H. Sweet, president of *U.S. News,* who objects to my calling his magazine "obviously conservative" (a viewpoint I still hold): "We certainly are not an obviously conservative magazine. I know of no publication that strives harder to tell it like it is. Many of our stories are reworked by the editors as many as four and five times to launder out the faintest aroma of bias." He also says that the well-known conservative editor David Lawrence "does not guide (and often does not even know) the subject matter in the main news section. . . . He has never, to my knowledge, suggested a sequence of stories or a so-called angle for approaching a subject."

Mr. Sweet admits "objective news is . . . an ideal goal, and reaching it requires a lot of thoughtful work and a high degree of skill. I think we do extremely well in approaching it." Well, there is no question that the interviews—usually with important public figures about equally important issues—are as objective as the personality being questioned will allow. And the news coverage is good to excellent in terms of timeliness, style of writing, and intelligence. In fact, it is in many ways superior to the magazine's two chief rivals, *Time* and *Newsweek.* But the librarian should be aware of the argument between myself and Mr. Sweet, not to mention others. I contend that his magazine is business oriented, primarily conservative, and not always objective. He counters: "It becomes possible that some readers who are accustomed to left-slanted or liberal approaches to events might conclude that we express an opposite viewpoint. Not true."

The magazine should be found in all libraries because it does represent an honest viewpoint on the world—and whether you agree with that viewpoint or not, it is worth considering.

Vital Speeches of the Day. 1934. m. $10. Thoms F. Daly III. City News Publishing Co., Box 606, Southold, N.Y. 11971. Index. Circ: 18,000. Sample. Microform: UM.

Indexed: RG. *Aud:* Ga, Ac, Hs.

Nothing changes with this magazine, and it remains a convenient source of speeches on every topic of the day. They are selected to give a balanced approach to the week's news and activities, to show two or more sides of any controversial issue. Some are a bit esoteric or downright boring, yet ring with authenticity perhaps for this very reason. The reading level—which isn't overly complimentary to some of our speakers—is generally at the junior high school range in terms of vocabulary, and too often in terms of ideas. Emphasis is on Americans, and all of the 10 to 15 speeches are published in full, or in excerpts (which is noted). Three words that appear on the cover of the magazine sum up its philosophy nicely: "Impartial–Constructive —and Authentic." A useful addition for most libraries.

World Federalist. See Political Science Section.

The World Today. 1945. m. $10. Margaret Cornell. Oxford Univ. Press, Ely House, Dover St., London W1, England. Index, adv. Circ: 5,000. Microform: UM. Reprint: Dawson.

Indexed: PAIS, SSHum. *Aud:* Ga, Ac, Hs.

Designed to keep the reader informed on current world problems. The four to five short articles are by authorities, yet are written in a style well within the understanding of the layman. A section entitled "Notes of the Month" continues the magazine's policy of presenting only the facts without expressing any particular viewpoint. Authoritative and scholarly, this can be used as well by scholars as by the interested general public for keeping up to date in foreign affairs. An excellent source for librarians in answering questions which require factual and very current information.

Political Opinion Reviews

ADA World. 1947. m. Membership (Nonmembers $5). Stina Santiestevan. Amer. for Democratic Action, 1424 16th St., N.W., Washington, D.C. 20036. Illus. Circ: 40,000. Sample. Vol. ends: Dec.

Bk. rev: 1–4, 500–1,000 words, signed. *Aud:* Ac, Ga.

The official publication of one of the oldest and most respected liberal organizations. The 16-page tabloid features three to five articles per issue, news items, an editorial, and a number of regular features. Through legislative and political action and education, ADA supports liberal foreign and political policies. In view of its major links with the Democratic party, it should be found in most medium-to-large libraries. The "other side of the aisle" is ably represented by the *Ripon Forum.*

Bulletin of the Atomic Scientists; a journal of science and public affairs. 1945. m. (Sept.–June). $8.50. Eugene Rabinowitch, Ed.-in-Chief. Educational Foundation for Nuclear Science, 1020–24 E. 58th St., Chicago, Ill. 60637. Illus., index, adv. Circ: 250,000. Sample. Vol. ends: Dec. Microform: UM.

Indexed: BioAb, PAIS, PsyAb, RG. *Bk. rev:* 2, 1,000 words, signed. *Aud:* Ga, Ac. *Jv:* V.

Despite its title, this is a general magazine directed toward the intelligent layman who believes there is a bridge between Snow's "two cultures." This offers such a bridge, and its subtitle indicates the wide scope. In a recent issue international affairs, disarmament, problems of world agriculture, racial questions, economic planning, and the relationship of the growth of science and technology to environment and institutions are discussed. All articles are by experts, written in an intelligible manner, and decidedly liberal. None require a scientific background, and all show the close relationships among science, the humanities, and politics. An ideal magazine for the scientist or humanist who seeks to understand the other's thinking. Suited for most high schools.

Canadian Dimension. 1963. 8/yr. $5. P.O. Box 1413, Winnepeg, 1, Man., Canada. Illus., adv. Circ: 7,500 Sample. Vol. ends: 8th issue.

Bk. rev: 3–4, 1,400–2,000 words, signed. *Aud:* Ac, Ga.

Winnipeg may not actually have been the birthplace of the New Democratic Party (NDP), or Co-operative Commonwealth Federation (CCF), as the Canadian socialist party used to be called, but it has nurtured quite a few prominent socialists and even from time to time sends a few to Parliament. This publication bills itself with true Winnipeg verve as the "largest magazine of political and social comment in Canada" and as the "only magazine of its kind available on Canadian affairs." Both statements contain some truth. It is large as such publications go, and it treats its material from a stance farther to the left than do all but the most febrile of the species. It is not likely, however, to supplant *Saturday Night* and *Canadian Forum*, both of which are devoted to a discussion of public affairs. What can be said for the new publication is that it combines elements of both older ones in a way that makes for fine, if somewhat cranky, reading. (The magazine editor observes: "Of course, I cannot agree that *Dimension* is "cranky." Any critical journal will sound cranky to those who are essentially content.") (P.L.)

Christian Century; an ecumenical weekly. 1884. w. $8.50. Kyle Haselden. Christian Century Foundation, 407 S. Dearborn St., Chicago, Ill 60605. Adv. Circ: 40,000. Microform: UM.

Indexed: RG. *Bk. rev:* 10–12, 200–900 words, signed. *Aud:* Ga, Ac. *Jv:* V.

A nondenominational Protestant weekly similar in purpose to *Commentary* (Jewish) and *Commonweal* (Catholic); i.e., it is more a liberal, general literary/political magazine than a religious periodical. Although its writers are among the leading theological thinkers in the world, the scope of the magazine is broad. It covers foreign policy, the arts, literature, social problems, and general news. The book reviews cover religious works, but are just as apt to discuss any current novel or nonfiction title. The editorial policy is definitely liberal. Probably the best summary of the magazine was made by John Cogley in the *New York Times* (Aug. 15, 1965, p.E5): "It is steadfastly urbane, highly respected and, cutting across denominational lines as it does, is probably the most influential of all protestant publications." A first choice for any library.

Commentary; journal of significant thought and opinion on contemporary issues. 1945. m. $10. Norman Podhoretz. Amer. Jewish Committee, 165 E. 56th St., New York, N.Y. 10022. Index, adv. Circ: 60,000. Sample. Vol. ends: June & Dec.

Index: PAIS, RG. *Bk. rev:* 5, essay length, signed. *Aud:* Ga, Ac.

Ideologically, this has switched from a hesitant champion of the New Left to a relatively conservative magazine. As Peter Steinfels pointed out in *Commonweal*, Podhoretz seems to be in the vanguard of a movement heretofore represented by the *Public Interest*. The chief target is the New Left. Let it be quickly noted that "conservatism" here has nothing to do with the *National Review* syndrome, but is rather a reaction against intellectual radicalism. Aside from this new twist, the magazine remains pretty much as before. Articles cover the whole general range of current interests, from politics, literature, and social issues to sex and art. All are extremely well written, usually by prestigious writers. The strong editorial hand of Podhoretz gives this a distinctive character, and it is a basic magazine for any library which caters to an educated public.

Commonweal. 1924. w. $14. James O'Gara. Commonweal Publishing Co., Inc., 232 Madison Ave., New York, N.Y. 10016. Illus., index, adv. Circ: 30,000. Sample. Vol. ends: March & Sept. Microform: UM.

Indexed: CathI, RG. *Bk. rev:* 6–8, 1,000 words, signed. *Aud:* Ga, Ac, Hs.

Independently edited by laymen for the better-educated Catholic and non-Catholic, this reports on current affairs and events relating to the Catholic church. Sometimes the relationship is a bit tenuous, at least from the viewpoint of more conservative church members and particularly as regards the editors' liberal ideas in the social and political fields. There are usually three to five articles by eminent scholars and lay experts, editorials, briefer comments, and regular departments. The book reviews tend to concentrate on religious titles, but this is interpreted broadly to include many related areas. Film reviews are excellent. The writing style is excellent; the coverage nicely augments what is found in general magazines of news and comment; and the overall impression is one of a much above average publication. Should be in almost all libraries, certainly in those serving a Catholic community.

Contemporary Review. 1866. m. $13.50. Rosalind Wade. Contemporary Review Ltd., 37 Union St., London SE1, England. Illus. Sample. Vol. ends: June & Dec.

Indexed: BritHum, SSHum. *Bk. rev:* 12, 500 words, signed. *Aud:* Ac, Ga.

A famous hundred-year-old British magazine which features a collection of commentaries on today's world happenings and on events of the past. It is written in a forthright manner, but emphasis is on material which will appeal to the educated and literary. The journal divides its entries between home and international politics, literature, arts, history, and a literary supplement. Books are reviewed in an authoritative style. The overall tone is independent, slightly left of center. It is an ideal magazine for public libraries and universities.

Dissent. 1954. q. $6. Irving Howe. Dissent Publishing Co., 509 Fifth Ave., New York, N.Y. 10017. Index, adv. Circ: 10,000. Microform: UM. Reprint: Kraus.

Bk. rev: Various number, length. *Aud:* Ac, Ga, Hs. *Jv:* V.

The major political-literary-social journal of the radical New Left. Under the capable editorship of Howe the magazine has attracted major writers and thinkers. Its editorial board and contributors claim Norman Mailer, Bayard Rustin, Michael Harrington, Lionel Abel, Erich Fromm, Paul Goodman, Harold Rosenberg, Paul Jacobs, and others. In the comparison of contents between liberal magazines, it is to the left of *Partisan Review* and *Modern Occasions*, and slightly to the right of *Liberation* and *Social Policy*. Beginning in 1972 the magazine changed from a bimonthly to a quarterly, increased the size of each issue, and revised the format. The Winter 1972 issue was devoted to a single theme, "The World of the Blue Collar Worker," and in some 31 articles, covering 304 pages, gave portraits of trade union locals, "descriptions of internal union relations between black and white workers, considered the problems of blue collar cities, the feelings of young workers." The issue is particularly important because it states a basic position of many liberals, i.e., "any radical reconstruction of American society must start with the premise that workers and their institutions form a crucial force for social action." *Dissent* is a crucial force in the ongoing debate between radicals, conservatives, and middle-of-the-road Americans. As such, it is of major importance for any library including those of more advanced high schools.

FOCUS/Midwest. 1962. bi-m. $4. Charles L. Klotzer. P.O. Box 3086, St. Louis, Mo. 63130. Illus., index, adv. Circ: 6,000. Sample. Vol. ends: Nov./Dec.

Index: PAIS, INeg, API. *Aud:* Ga, Ac.

A 28-page independent news magazine which is strong on exploring controversial issues; i.e., the annual index reveals articles on politics, poverty, education, voting records, and analysis of right-wing activities. The writers represent a wide cross section, from attorneys and public officials to journalists and teachers. The writing here is as good as, if not sometimes better than, that found in better-known national magazines. Although the focus is on the Midwest, the articles are wide enough in scope to be of value to almost anyone involved in the current social, political, and cultural scene. Some short stories and poems are included. As a type of *Nation* or *New Republic* for the Midwest, it should be in every library in that area, and certainly should be seriously considered by larger academic and public libraries everywhere. See also *St. Louis Journalism Review* by the same publisher.

Human Events. 1944. w. $15. Thomas W. Winter. Human Events, Inc., 422 First St., S.E., Washington, D.C. Illus., index, adv. Circ: 90,000. Sample. Vol. ends: Dec. 25. Microform: UM. Reprint: Johnson.

Bk. rev: 50, various length/yr. *Aud:* Ac, Ga.

One of the best conservative voices, this tabloid newspaper "looks at events through eyes that are biased in favor of limited constitutional government, local self government, private enterprise, and individual freedom." Within the scope of the editorial purpose, the editors and contributors manage to come up with a relatively objective, usually factual report on the week's activities in government and the social sciences. The tone is considerably more moderate than that usually associated with this type of magazine, which in this respect comes close to The *National Review* for balanced coverage. Conversely, it does support the traditional right-wing causes, from our Vietnam policy to continuing concern over Communist activities both here and abroad. After the *Re-*

view, a basic choice in this area for public and academic libraries.

Ideas; a journal of conservative thought. 1968. q. $6. Michael S. Kogan. Jewish Soc. of Amer., Inc., 28–13 Steinway St., Long Island City, N.Y. 11103. Adv. Circ: 7,500. Sample. Vol. ends: No. 4.

Bk. rev: 2–3, 650 words, signed. *Aud:* Ac, Ga.

A thinking man's approach to conservative political and social thought, which is to say there is more appeal to common sense here than to gut emotion. Although about one half of six or seven articles are involved with some aspect of Jews and Judaism, the remainder is given over to more general topics. Authors all share a conservative base, i.e., the editorials set the tone: support of President Nixon, the FBI, continuation of the draft, and the official position on Israel. The approach, though, is moderate, well reasoned, and of obvious appeal to the type of reader who finds the *National Review* to his or her liking. Some of the contributors, many of whom are professors, regularly write for the *National Review* and other conservative journals. Although the obvious appeal of *Ideas* is for the conservative Jewish reader, it will be of equal interest to more intellectually minded conservatives of all faiths.

The Intercollegiate Review; a journal of scholarship and opinion. 1964. q. Membership (Nonmembers $5). Wayne H. Valis. Subs. to: E. Victor Milione, 14 S. Bryn Mawr Ave., Bryn Mawr, Pa. 19010. Illus., index. Circ: 32,000. Sample. Vol. ends: Summer.

Bk. rev: 10, 1 page, signed. *Aud:* Ac, Ga. *Jv:* V.

One of the few scholarly journals devoted to the conservative political–social ethic, and a far cry from the less subtle efforts of such magazines as *American Opinion* or the *National Review*. A typical 75-page issue includes five or six articles, ranging over everything from foreign policy to the welfare state. The material is normally documented and written by professors—in fact, the editorial advisory board is almost exclusively made up of teachers. Although the writing style is far from lively, it is informative, and within the clearly stated purposes and biases of the editors, offers an objective platform for the conservative viewpoint. It is not, by the way, radical right. As one of the more intelligent approaches to conservatism, this should be found in all academic and larger public libraries.

LID News Bulletin. 1960. q. Membership (Nonmembers $2). League for Industrial Democracy, 112 E. 19th St., New York, N.Y. 10003. Circ: 3,000.

Bk. rev: Various number, length. *Aud:* Ac, Ga.

A liberal publication of an organization founded in 1905 for the purpose of protecting democracy via more education in the fields of economics, politics, and culture. Although the organization is a nonprofit and tax-exempt one, it tends to promulgate material which follows the leanings of the Democratic Left, i.e., the thinking of such men as the late Norman Thomas, Bayard Rustin, and Irving Howe. In recent years it has maintained a neutral position in the tug of war between the "conservative" Left and the "movement" Left, uniting with both only on major issues such as opposition to the Vietnam war. The format is an 8 to 16 page newsletter with short news notes and one or two articles in depth on various current matters, ranging from Ralph's Nader's findings to employment and the Nixon economic program. A good liberal, middle-of-the-road report for libraries with a limited income, or a desire to avoid extremes.

Last Post. 1970. 8/yr. $4. Collective. Box 98, Station G, Montreal, Que., Canada. Illus., adv. Circ: 10,000.

Bk. rev: Various number, length. *Aud:* Ac, Ga, Hs.

Somewhat the Canadian equivalent of *Ramparts.* The editorial content is fiercely to the left, muckracking, and involved with the Canadian political scene. Writers, for the most part, come from the Canadian newspapers and networks. Canadian novelist Mordecai Richlet calls it "easily the best" of the relatively new Canadian magazines. He notes "it surfaces again and again with lively and necessary pieces, about the role of the 'Time lobby' in Canada or hockey as big business." And the editors have whacked away at American investments, Canadian arms exports, personalities, etc. There are cartoons, some book reviews, and features which give it an important part in any Canadian and larger American magazine collection.

Liberation; an independent monthly. 1956. 11/yr. $7. Collective ed. bd. Liberation, 339 Lafayette St., New York, N.Y. 10012. Illus., index. Circ: 9,000. Sample. Vol. ends: Feb.

Index: API, PAIS. *Bk. rev:* Various number, length, signed. *Aud:* Ac, Ga. *Jv:* V.

A major voice of the liberal-to-leftist position which is noteworthy for its stand that a new concept of the governed and the government is needed. Emphasis is on nonviolence and change. The contributors are lined up solidly against the establishment which seeks to control and direct society. And while a number of the writers might be characterized as champions of the traditional New Left, an equal number refuse any handy political label. What results is a solid, general political magazine which presents numerous viewpoints. Edited and produced by a working collective, the monthly has frequent articles by such well-known liberals as Noam Chomsky, Norm Frucker, David Dellinger, Andre Gorz, Barbara Deming, and Doug Dowd. Over the years this voice has gained a place of major respect, even among its foes, and can be considered a basic title in any collection which swerves from the middle of the road.

Majority Report. 1970. m. $3. Marvin B. Jones. Box 2321, Washington, D. C. 20013. Illus., adv.

Aud: Ac, Ga.

A 20-page tabloid dedicated to bringing about change in America. The main coverage is of the House of Representatives and what it does or does not do in such areas as welfare, consumer protection, and women's rights. This paper has both spot news and columns of opinion. Most of it is written by the editor, but the issue examined has material by Rep. Paul McCloskey (out to beat Nixon in 1972) and Shirley Chisholm. Politically the paper represents an independent point of view, is liberal, and hopes for support from the grass roots of America. As a lobby for "peace, black women's liberation, low income, environmental and student groups," it is a success. It deserves support from libraries.

Modern Age. 1957. q. $4. David S. Collier. Foundation for Foreign Affairs, Inc., 743 N. Wabash Ave., Chicago, Ill. 60611. Index, adv. Circ: 6,600. Sample. Vol. ends: Fall.

Index: CathI, HistAb, PAIS. *Bk. rev:* 10, 2,500 words, signed. *Aud:* Ac, Ga.

A scholarly journal which enjoys a reputation as a rigorous champion of the conservative position. The writing, primarily by college professors, is a bit uneven. Among contributors are such names as Mario Pei, Francis Russell, Wolfe Mays, and Thomas Molnar. The essays cover all aspects of the modern scene. Of primary interest to librarians is the second one third to one half, which is given over to book reviews. The comments are noteworthy because they represent a point of view rarely found in the general press. And while better-known titles in the humanities and social sciences are evaluated, so are lesser-known works. The reviews, coupled with the extensive indexing, make this a primary journal for any library wishing to represent the more rational conservative position.

Mysterious East. 1969. m. $5.50. Robert Campbell and ed. bd. Rubber Duck Press Inc. Box 1172, Fredericton, N. B., Canada. Illus., adv. Circ: 10,000. Sample. Microform: B & H.

Bk. rev: 2–3, various length, signed. *Aud:* Ga, Ac.

Somewhat equivalent to the American journalism reviews and the city magazines rolled into one. This is a 36 to 40 page satirical, hard-hitting rebuttal to news coverage of the Maritime provinces by the local and Canadian national press. Each issue begins with short comments and editorials, which are followed by articles on all aspects of Canadian culture and politics. For example, one issue examined included articles on the problems of the French–English culture, nationalism, and interviews with a local politico, as well as shorter articles on everything from education to ecology. What strikes the reader as above average is the level of writing and the nice balance of material. There seems to be something to interest anyone living in eastern Canada. Although of limited interest to most Americans, it should be found in all Canadian libraries.

✓ *The Nation.* 1965. w. $10. Carey McWilliams. Nation Co., 333 Ave. of the Americas, New York, N.Y. 10014. Illus., index, adv. Circ: 30,000. Sample. Vol. ends: July 30 & Dec. 31. Microform: UM.

Indexed: PAIS, RG. *Bk. rev:* 4–6, 1,000–1,500 words, signed. *Aud:* Ga, Ac, Hs. *Jv:* V.

Well-documented articles concerned with foreign affairs, education, law, domestic policies, disarmament, etc., are presented with clarity and simplicity. Important events and significant undertakings are discussed in its pages sometimes long before they appear in other news media. Its list of outstanding contributors has included Henry and William James, H. L. Mencken, Carl Van Doren, Harold Laski, Bernard Fall, Fred J. Cook, Robert Sherrill, and Alexander Werth. Its scholarly appraisal of the theater, the arts, and literature contributes to its position of respect. Almost devoid of advertising, the magazine depends on contributions and subscriptions for its support.

✓ *National Review; a journal of fact and opinion.* 1955. bi-w. $12. William F. Buckley, Jr. William A. Rushev, 150 E. 35th St., New York, N.Y. 10016. Illus., index, adv. Circ: 120,000. Sample. Vol. ends: Dec. 31. Microform: UM.

Indexed: RG. *Bk. rev:* 5–8, 800 words, notes, signed. *Aud:* Ga, Ac, Hs. *Jv:* V.

The intellectual voice of conversatism in America, this is the outspoken critic of most liberal or progressive ideas. In coverage and scope it is somewhat similar to the *New Republic* and the *Nation*. Here the analogy ends. First and foremost, it is the child of its editor William Buckley, a controversial editor who has brought a degree of respectability to the conservative school. No friend of either the reactionary right wing or the progressive left wing, he blasts both with a telling wit and a style which is sometimes flippant, sometimes penetrating. The flag of bias is not only evident, it is flown with pride. Among contributors are Russell Kirk, James Burnham, Hugh Kenner, and Will Herberg. All are representative of a depth of thought and opinion rarely associated with the popular notion of conservatism. Except for the *National Review*, the conservatives have failed to produce a major journal of news or politicital commentary. Christopher Lasch gives one possible reason why there are a dozen liberal magazines to only one *National Review*. There are so few, he notes, because, "the opinions represented by the *National Review* are not dissenting opinions at all, but opinions which are readily endorsed, in whole or in part, by the mass media and, on at least one recent occasion by one of the major political parties" (*New York Times Magazine*, July 18, 1965, p. 33). Librarians and readers may no more agree with the *National Review* than they do with the *New Republic*, but because of its intellectual approach, this magazine should be in every library, from senior high school to academic.

New Individualist Review; a journal of classical liberal thought. 1961. q. $3. J. M. Cobb. Individualist Review, Ida Noyes Hall, Univ. of Chicago, Chicago, Ill. 60637. Adv. Circ: 6,000.

Indexed: PAIS. *Bk. rev:* 2, 500–1,000 words, signed. *Aud:* Ac.

This is an independent journal "of classical liberal thought." The purpose of the review, as stated in a preface, is to stimulate or encourage the exploration of important problems from a viewpoint characterized by a concern with individual liberty. It generally sides favorably with the concepts of private property, personal liberty, the rule of law, and strict limits on the power of government. More of a viewpoint magazine, the articles are not extensive. Articles have included the topics of Marxism and alienation (by David Levy), economic and social aspects of free tuition, Rhodesia, and conscription and the volunteer army.

✓ *New Leader; a bi-weekly of news and opinion.* 1927. bi-w. $10. Myron Kolatch. Amer. Labor Conference on Intl. Affairs, 212 Fifth Ave., New York, N.Y. 10010. Illus., adv.

Indexed: PAIS. *Bk. rev:* Various number, length. *Aud:* Ga, Ac.

A moderately liberal magazine of opinion which has somewhat the same political–social leanings as the *New Republic* and the *Nation*, yet is somewhat closer to a center position than either. The editor and the contributors frequently chastise both the left and the right wing, maintaining a staunchly independent policy on national and international affairs. The literary and fine arts reviews are excellent, often taking quite a different tack from that found in many regular reviewing services. A second choice for high school, college, and public libraries.

✓ *New Left Review.* 1957. bi-m. $7.50. Perry Anderson. 7 Carlisle St., London, England. Subs. to: B. DeBoer, 188 High St., Nutley, N.J. 07110. Adv.

Index: API, BritHum, PAIS. *Aud:* Ac, Ga.

A sounding board for English and European intellectuals. It is considerably more to the left than the *New Statesman*, yet has been highly critical of Soviet- or Chinese-oriented Communism. The particular value of the journal for Americans is that its articles give an intelligent, highly topical view of leftist issues which are of interest to those who follow the New Left in the United States. A normal number consists of two or three articles, poems, literary criticism, art and music criticism, documents, and short essays or discussions. From time to time a single issue is given over to a theme.

New Politics; a journal of socialist thought. 1961. q. $3.50. Julius Jacobson. New Politics Publishing Co., 507 Fifth Ave., New York, N.Y. 10017. Index, adv. Circ: 5,000. Sample. Vol. ends: No. 4.

Bk. rev: 2, 2–10 pages, signed. *Aud:* Ac, Ga.

An objective, liberal, and lucid political quarterly which is carefully read by many informed people who have little or no sympathy with socialism. Its sponsors include James Baldwin, Saul Bellow, Erich Fromm, Herbert Gold, Nat Hentoff, Paul Jacobs, Kenneth Rexroth, and many other liberals of all shades and varieties. During the past decade it has offered readers the pros and cons of almost every political, social, and economic issue facing America and the world. For example, late in 1971 one issue contained an article on President Nixon's economic program, a study of the miner's union, an exchange between Albert Shanker and Herbert Hill, a report on Cuba, a letter from London, and similar items. The style is clear, and the authors are authorities ranging from teachers and attorneys to politicians and writers. All in all, an excellent choice for medium-to-large academic and public libraries.

The New Republic; a journal of politics and the arts. 1914. w. $12. Gilbert A. Harrison. 1244 19th St., N.W., Washington, D.C. 20036. Subs. to: New Republic, Subscription Dept., 381 W. Center St., Marion, Ohio 43302. Illus., index, adv. Circ: 150,000. Vol ends: July and Dec. Microform: UM.

Indexed: RG. *Bk. rev:* 3–5, 1,500 words, signed. *Aud:* Ga, Ac, Hs. *Jv:* V.

Along with the *Nation*, whose format it resembles, this is the best-known American liberal magazine. It deserves its popularity. The weekly issues consider all aspects of current American and international events, and in the past few years have been giving added emphasis to critical film, theater, and book reviews. A good deal of space is given to domestic questions, particularly those relating to education and the problems of minority groups. The editorials are generally critical of the Nixon administration, particularly its policies of war and moneys spent on war items. The general tone is liberal, the style lucid, the total effect one of a hard-hitting editorial policy aimed at reform at any level. It differs from the *Nation* in that it is somewhat more vocal in its criticism, even a trifle more to the left. However, this is a subjective opinon which is of little importance. In any library both magazines should be mandatory for the collection.

New Statesman; an independent political and literary review. 1913. w. $15. Richard Crossman. Statesman &

Nation Publishing Co., 10 Great Turnstile, London WC1V, 7HJ, England. Illus., index, adv. Circ: 84,978. Microform: UM.

Indexed: BritHum, SSHum. *Bk. rev:* 15–20, 500–2,000 words, signed. *Aud:* Ac, Ga, Hs.

A hard-hitting liberal journal of political and social criticism which has a well-earned reputation for satire. The signed articles begin with England, move out within four to five pages to news of the world, and then feature half a dozen shorter items on culture. Regular features include the London diary—notes on English politics; letters to the editor (often as good as those found in the *Times Literary Supplement*); and book, film, and theater reviews. The writers are among the best in England. Often compared to the *New Republic* and the *Nation*, but when you get right down to it, there is only one *New Statesman*, and it should be found in all libraries. (Tabloid, newspaper format similar to the *Listener, New Society*, etc.)

Point of View. 1968. bi-w. $10. (Individuals $5). Roldo Bartimole, 2150 Rexwood Rd., Cleveland, Ohio 44118. Illus. Circ: 850. Sample. Vol. ends: May 30.

Aud: Ga, Ac.

A type of I.F. Stone approach at the local level, in this case Cleveland and Ohio. The primary drive is in the direction of civil rights, but there is a consistent examination of all aspects of local government, the press, officials, and even the wisdom of supporting the United Torch campaign. The editor-owner-staff is a former *Wall Street Journal* reporter, and the approach is professional. Only four short pages, but well written, researched, and worth the price. Should be in every library near or around Cleveland.

Progressive. 1909. m. $9. Morris H. Rubin. Progressive, Inc., 408 W. Gorham, Madison, Wis. 53703. Illus., index, adv. Circ: 40,000.

Indexed: PAIS. *Bk. rev:* 5–7, 1,000 words, signed. *Aud:* Ga, Ac.

One of the oldest liberal independent magazines in America, founded in 1909 by the late Senator R. M. LaFollette, Sr., as a voice for his then advanced political views. The editor is concerned with national and world affairs, and contributors are correspondents on the scene or prominent educators who are specialists in a given field. The writing is authoritative, calm, and objective. There are some ten pages of editorials, regular columns, and fascinating letters to the editor. The book reviews are excellent and range from politics to works on the social sciences and fine arts. All in all, this impressive magazine of opinion should be found in most libraries, and in a good number of libraries as a supplement to the better-known *Nation* and the *New Republic*.

The Public Interest. 1965. q. $7.50. Irving Kristol and Daniel Bell. Subs. to: Basic Books, 404 Park Ave.

South, New York, N.Y. 10016. Circ: 10,000. Sample. Vol. ends: Fall.

Bk. rev: 1–2, 3,000 words, signed. *Aud:* Ac, Ga.

The leading journal of the so-called new liberal conservatism. As one writer puts it, this group largely accepts the present structure of U.S. society "and strives for limited change within what they consider to be the narrow room for maneuver." They are not, let it be noted, traditional conservatives in the sense of Buckley's group. (Right along side it is *Commentary*, which often supports its policies.) Kristol, for example, takes an elitist view of censorship, believing that it is, to a degree, a necessity. Be that as it may, the five to six articles, by such scholars and public figures as Daniel Moynihan, Jacques Barzun, Charles Reich, and of course, editors Bell and Kristol, make this important for anyone trying to puzzle out the meaning of current developments in America. Some issues are given over to a single topic, e.g., "Capitalism Today," (Fall, 1970), and a symposium on pornography (Winter, 1971). A controversial, basically conservative contribution which should be in all medium-to-large libraries.

The Public Life; a biweekly journal of politics. 1968. bi-w. $6. H. R. Shapiro, 174 Fifth Ave., New York, N.Y. 10003. Circ: 3,000.

Aud: Ga, Ac.

The editors describe themselves "as the first Jeffersonians since the Populists in 1890." The style is candid, intelligent, and a major step toward a definition of new politics with the terms of humanistic goals. The four-page newsletter is dedicated to more self-government for Americans, considerably less centralization of power. A typical issue features two long articles, boxed quotes, and a short editorial. Since the editors are grinding no accepted political party's axe, they can swing their own individual hatchet.

✓*Ramparts.* 1962. m. $8.50. Ed. bd. Ramparts Magazine Inc., 2054 University Ave., Berkeley, Calif. 94704. Illus., adv. index. Circ: 125,000.

Indexed: RG. *Aud:* Hs, Ac, Ga. *Jv:* V.

With a circulation way ahead of *Nation*, yet lagging behind *New Republic*, this one-time rebel of the Left now stands pretty well between its two older relatives. The fire and daring of the earlier days have given way to more banked fires, less sensationalism, and considerably more interest in staying alive as a viable voice of the movement. But it is still lively enough. Articles move from discussions of big business to underground medicine, to "sickle cell and the pill," to comments on strategy for the Left. *Ramparts* definitely is of more interest to younger activists than the two older mags. (As such, it should be a first choice over both in a high school or college.) It even has a regular section called "Counter/Culture/Counter Culture" which considers recordings, sports, travel etc. The layout, too, is supe-

rior to its rivals, and each issue has a limited number of illustrated articles. Basic for most libraries.

Ripon Forum. m. $10 (Students $5). Evelyn F. Ellis and George Gilder. The Ripon Society, Inc., 14a Eliot St., Cambridge, Mass. 02138. Index. Circ: 3,000. Sample.

Aud: Ac, Ga.

A 24-page magazine which reports on the activities of Congress, the government, and events at large in reference to views held by the "liberal wing" of the Republican party. The Ripon Society is "a Republican research and policy organization whose members are young business, academic and professional men." In some respects it is the Republican counter of the Democrats' Americans for Democratic Action. Each number opens with a series of hard-hitting, literate editorials; goes on to several articles and assessments of Congress and the cabinet, e.g., "The Achievements of George Romney," "Ripon Ratings: The 91st Congress"; and concludes with short notes and letters. Some indication of the philosophy of the group can be given in the rating of Congressmen. The Society named Senators Goodell, Javits, and Percy for a Ripon position. Voting the other way, at least on most issues, are Senators Goldwater and Murphy. Some readers will feel the magazine is not liberal enough, others will say it is too liberal; but regardless, it is a required magazine for any library where there is the slightest interest in national politics.

Saturday Night; Canada's leading magazine of comment and opinion. 1887. m. $2.50. Robert Fulford. Second Century Canada Publns. Ltd., 52 St. Clair Ave., E., Toronto 7, Canada. Illus., adv. Circ: 100,000. Sample. Vol. ends: Dec.

Indexed: CanI, PAIS. *Bk. rev:* 5, 500 words, signed. *Aud:* Ac, Ga, Hs.

One of the few large-circulation magazines in Canada, and next to *Macleans* probably the closest thing Canada has to a general magazine. It is somewhat like a mixture of *Time*, *Newsweek*, and *U.S. News*, but more intellectual than any of these. Writers comment on contemporary social and cultural affairs in a Canadian context. The contributors analyze Canadian politics at the federal and provincial levels and describe the important personalities and ideas in these governments. Since 1968 there has been a particular emphasis on Canada's relationship with the U.S., and *Saturday Night's* pages have increasingly reflected Canadians' discomfort in this relationship. Most of the leading writers and journalists of Canada contribute to the magazine. A basic addition for all Canadian high school, public, and academic collections, it should be considered by the same type libraries in America. Although this is the oldest and most prestigious of the Canadian news magazines, a library should also consider other more liberal, controversial magazines, such as the *Mysterious East* or *Last Post.*

✓ *Science for the People.* 1969. bi-m. $3. Ed. bd. 9 Walden St., Jamaica Plain, Mass. 02130. Illus. Circ: 6,000. Sample. Vol. ends: Jan.

Bk. rev: Various number, length, signed. *Aud:* Ga, Ac, Hs.

An approach somewhat similar to *Bulletin of the Atomic Scientists*, but with a more urgent, crusading tone. In some 40 pages, those who are disenchanted with the no-no political attitude of such groups as the American Association for the Advancement of Science and the National Science Teachers Association speak out for more direct social involvement by scientists. Emphasis is on local action, volunteers, and a critical view of everything from the ABM to birth control. Articles are hard hitting, usually documented well enough, and geared to getting members out of the lab and into the world. The founders are opposed to activities of scientists with police, military, and intelligence, and to universities involved with war contracts. The whole is written in a style which any layman can understand. As a move against the military–scientific complex, this is a required item. Should be most useful in high schools and colleges where teachers are making an effort to train socially conscious scientists.

Social Action. 1935. m. (Sept.–May). $3.50. Huber F. Klemme. Council for Christian Social Action, United Church of Christ, 289 Park Ave. S., New York, N.Y. 10010. Illus. Circ: 6,000. Sample. Vol. ends: May.

Bk. rev: Notes. *Aud:* Ac, Ga, Hs.

A liberal, balanced approach to issues which face anyone dedicated to some form of social action. Usually each 40-page pocket-sized number is given over to a single question or problem, e.g., the March 1971 number discussed the pros and cons of abortion with viewpoints from a doctor, pastor, ethicist, and young woman. In October, "A Health Program for the 70's" led off with an article by Edward Kennedy and included arguments for and against health insurance. The sponsor makes views of the United Church of Christ clear in editorials, but in no way tampers with the articles, which as often as not are at odds with the official viewpoint. This gives it a particular position: while working from a Christian base, the material is so well written and nicely balanced that it could be used by almost anyone discussing the problems considered. In fact, it is an ideal acquisition for high schools and colleges where term papers and debate are the order of the day. Librarians who may wonder about the sponsor are advised to send for a sample copy. But it should not be overlooked. It will be a tremendous help in almost any library.

✓ *Social Policy.* 1970. bi-m. $8. Frank Riessman. Intl. Arts & Sciences Press, 901 N Broadway, White Plains,

N.Y. 10603. Illus., adv. Circ: 11,000. Sample. Vol. ends: March/April.

Bk. rev: Essay, signed. *Aud:* Ga, Ac. *Jv:* V.

Boasting supporters such as Noam Chomsky, Peter Edelman, Charles Hamilton, Roy Innis, Kenneth Keniston, and Rhody McCoy, this is a radical approach to social action and community control. It is in the same battlefield as *Liberation*, a bit farther out in left field than *Dissent*, and considerably more radical than such standard journals as *Partisan Review* and *Modern Occasions*. It is concerned with "the politics of the human services—community control, welfare rights, education, health care and the anti-service character of the welfare state." It demonstrates how the presently constituted human service institutions—in welfare, education, health, and mental health, corrections, and urban planning—frequently work against those they presume to serve. Articles cover current topics, such as national health insurance, organizing a community around health, advocacy planning, community control, the hard-core unemployed, black education, student activism, black studies, welfare rights, community mental health, and organizing paraprofessionals. Departments include "From the Movements, Black Angle; New Directions in the Human Service; Book Review, In Response." General libraries will wish to add it to their collections and academic libraries will be compelled to meet the demand for it.

✓ *Spectator.* 1828. w. $18. George Gale. Spectator Ltd., 99 Gower St., London WCIE 6AE, England. Illus., index, adv. Circ: 25,000. Sample. Vol. ends: June & Dec. Microform: UM.

Indexed: BritHum. *Bk. rev:* 7–10, 500–1,500 words, notes, signed. *Aud:* Ac, Ga.

An independent political and cultural approach to things English. The 35 to 40 pages are on oversize newsprint, a cross between the *Nation* and the *New Statesman*, but always itself. Editorials, general comments, political commentary, and feature articles of one or two pages on everything from medicine to politics make up the first half. The second part is noted for its excellent book reviews and its essays on the arts, television, etc. A fine crossword puzzle ends it all. Coverage tends to be primarily English and European. Some larger issues are considered. Contributors range from Kingsley Amis and W. H. Auden to lesser knowns, but all are first-rate writers. An excellent general source of information on English political and cultural events.

The Spokesman (Incorporating *The London Bulletin*). 1970. 9/yr. $9. Ken Coates. Bertrand Russell Peace Foundation, 45 Gamble St., Forest Road W., Nottingham NG7, 4Et, England. Illus., adv. Circ: 10,000 Sample. Vol. ends: Dec.

Bk. rev: 4, 1000 words, signed. *Aud:* Ac.

One of Bertrand Russell's last acts was to found this monthly magazine, which in 1970 incorporated *The London Bulletin*. Raymond Williams, a contributing editor, explains its purpose is "to carry news of the struggle against imperialism, to carry analyses of it, to carry reports from its leaders as they emerge." Earlier issues have included articles on war crimes, the Cambodian struggle, economic reports on England and other countries, and pieces by and about Russell. The tone is obviously to the left, but in the best radition of Russell in that the articles are factual and quite objective. One may not agree with the conclusions, yet there can be no argument with the precision of presentation. It is an effort to bring rigorous intellectual work to important world issues, and regardless of its English base and its point of view, it must be respected and read by anyone who is at all concerned with a more meaningful, peaceful world. An important addition to any collection of "establishment" news reporting, journal or magazine.

Twentieth Century. 1887. q. $7. Twentieth Century Magazine Ltd., Staple Inn Bldg., S., 335 High Holborn, London WC1, England. Illus., index, adv. Microform: UM.

Indexed: BritHum, SSHum. *Bk. rev:* 5, 300–500 words, signed. *Aud:* Ga, Ac.

A general, somewhat conservative, news and literary magazine which offers a direct look at different aspects of contemporary life from economics and politics to literature and art. Although published in Britain, the comments and reviews can be appreciated by the American reader. A major topic is covered, along with three or four smaller articles, in each issue. The book reviews are often lengthy and usually contain a bit of that infamous British satire. Not a required magazine for most collections, but a useful and enjoyable one for larger libraries.

The Washington Monthly. 1969. m. $10. Charles Peters. Washington Monthly Co., 1150 Connecticut Ave., N.W., Washington, D.C. 20036. Illus., index, adv. Circ: 23,000. Microform: UM.

Bk. rev: Various number, notes. *Aud:* Ga, Ac, Hs. *Jv:* V.

With the death of *I. F. Stone's Weekly* and *Hard Times,* this is about the only general muckracking magazine left in Washington, D.C. Somewhat like a toned-down version of Buckley's *National Review* on the Right and *Ramparts* on the Left, the 65-page *Washington Monthly* tries to walk the line of objective, hard-hitting reporting. Although ideologically to the Left, it has struck out at both Left and Right, won a Polk award for a series on Army surveillance of civilians. It is particularly good at indicating to the average citizen how he or she can make the government more responsive. The writers, who are just as likely to be government workers as professional reporters, have zeroed in on all the sacred cows from the Senate to the press. The material is well documented, objective, and reliable. In late 1971, for example, various issues included: the new Nader report; Agribusiness, overkill on the farm; the screwing of the average man, every day in every way you get taken; Senator Kennedy's tragedy in Bengal; and material from Joseph Lash's book on the Roosevelts. Regular features include Political Book Notes, a crossword puzzle, and letters. Of all the news magazines now being published it is one of the very best, should have the widest appeal for all groups, all political persuasions. A first choice for libraries.

Radical Right

American Dialog. 1964. q. $6.50. Joseph North. Dialogue Publns., 130 E. 16th St., New York, N.Y. 10003. Illus., adv. Circ: 8,000. Sample. Vol. ends: Fall.

Bk. rev: 4–8, 1,000–2,000 words, signed. *Aud:* Ac, Ga.

A general magazine which views the cultural scene from the Marxist viewpoint. The primary policy is stated briefly by the editor: "We know that sane politics are indispensable to healthy art and no wall can be erected between them." Among its sponsors are Linus Pauling, Pete Seeger, Pablo Neruda, and the late Bertrand Russell. The ten or so articles cover everything from art and literature (including some poetry) to music and social issues. An average 40-page number is well balanced, always literate, usually original, and objective within the limitations set forth by the sponsors. Although it is difficult to imagine a conservative enjoying the contents, it should have wide appeal for the moderate and liberal who are seeking an essentially interesting, often controversial, view of the arts.

American Mercury/Washington Observer. 1924. q. (American Mercury); s-m. except March, June, Sept. & Dec. (*Washington Observer.*) $10. LaVonne D. Furr. Box 1306, Torrance, Calif. Illus., index, adv. Circ: 10,000. Microform: UM. Reprint: Johnson.

Bk. rev: 1–2, 400–1,500 words, signed. *Aud:* Ga.

An early proponent of the American flag sticker, the notion of white racial supremacy, and the need for defeating the Communists in Vietnam. The frankly radical Right *Reader's Digest* format finds William Buckley's *National Review* a trifle too liberal. The *Washington Observer* is a newsletter which is free to subscribers, and it appears semimonthly. (There is no lower rate for taking just the *American Mercury.*) The magazine has little to recommend it, and is in no way either an original or a unique voice for the radical Right. (Note: it has absolutely nothing in common with the magazine founded by H. L. Mencken.)

American Opinion; a conservative review. 1958. 11/yr. $10. Robert Welch. Robert Welch, Inc., 395 Concord Ave., Belmont, Mass. 02178. Illus., index, adv. Circ: 32,000. Sample. Microform: UM.

Indexed: PAIS. *Bk. rev:* 5–10, 250–500 words, signed. *Aud:* Ga, Ac.

Robert Welch, founder of the John Birch Society, still claims this is not the official organ for that group, but merely reflects Birch ideas. The radical Right Birchers, less sticky about the whole thing, freely admit it is "their magazine." The pocket-sized, well-printed magazine is nicely edited and cleverly put together. The articles are by professionals, and usually direct right jabs at civil rights, sex education, the ever-present communists, etc. The style is deceptively casual or, if called for, scholarly. In the more scholarly pieces there is "documentation" of a less than factual nature, but it all looks official enough for its readers. The book reviews are equally good, touching on titles rarely found reviewed elsewhere. This is a basic radical right-wing magazine for any library trying to create a balanced collection. See also the *Review of the News.*

Christian Beacon. 1936. w. $3. Carl McIntire. Christian Beacon, 756 Haddon Ave., Collingswood, N.J. 08108. Illus. Circ: 125,000. Sample. Vol. ends: Feb.

Bk. rev: 6, 75 words, signed. *Aud:* Ga, Ac.

A familiar voice, particularly on radio, Rev. Carl McIntire represents a fundamentalist viewpoint of the world. Both the radio program and the eight-page tabloid newspaper preach the theme: Save America—stop communism. For example, a November 4, 1971, issue, has a lead story: "Red China U.N. Victory Advances Anti-God Forces," and notes elsewhere that "The spirit of anti-God and anti-Christ has fully captured the U.N." Furthermore, McIntire attacks political liberalism, socialism, peace marchers, and just about anything or anyone he feels is not in line with his basic assumptions. The paper's "News and Notes" ends with a weekly Bible school lesson, short book reviews, and usually a sermon by McIntire. One of the more extremist radical Right newspapers, it is important because it sounds the convictions of at least some Americans.

Christian Crusade Weekly. 1948. w. $2. Billy James Hargis. Christian Crusade, Box 977, Tulsa, Okla. 74102. Illus., index. Circ: 155,000. Sample. Vol. ends: Nov. 14.

Aud: Ga, Ac.

Probably best known for his Washington marches to support the Vietnam war, the editor's eight-page newspaper echoes the theme "for Christ against communism." It is definitely to the radical Right with a strong fundamentalist approach to everything from education to politics. Such stories as "Forced Bussing

. . . Immoral and Un-American," and "ACC Students and Choir Conduct Tent Revival at State Fair," or "The Suicide of a Nation—Ours," indicate the kind of material found in a typical issue. A good deal of the writing is by the editor, who is lucid, if not always objective. Advertisements tend to push material sold by the sponsoring group. Only for larger collections.

Christian Economics. 1948. m. $3. H. Edward Rowe. Christian Freedom Foundation Inc., 7960 Crescent Ave., Buena Park, Calif. 90620. Illus., index. Circ: 33,500. Sample. Vol. ends: Dec.

Bk. rev: 4, 250 words, signed. *Aud:* Ga.

A tabloid dedicated to "the cause of human freedom, self government and economic well being, to be achieved by loyalty to the moral law of God and a better understanding of economic problems and finance." Although the editor does not confine himself to economics, most of the sword in one hand (the paper is pro-Vietnam war) and the Bible in the other, is directed to the dollar. The moral enemy is the ubiquitous, although not well-defined, communist. The communist can be found anywhere near economic difficulties, or where there is a decline in "law and order" and moral rigor. An interesting viewpoint which might be considered in Bible belt territory, it will be of limited interest to economists.

The Citizen. 1955. m. $4. W. J. Simmons & Medford Evans. 254 E. Griffith St., Jackson, Miss. 39202. Illus., adv. Circ: 40,000. Microform: UM.

Aud: Ga.

Supported by the Citizens Councils of America—a group dedicated to segregation and the candidacy of George Wallace. Compared to such papers as the *Cross and the Flag* or *White Power* this is relatively moderate. It believes in restoration of white supremacy via the courts. The writers are convinced the Black is inferior, but wish to protect him from overt acts of violence. The format is passable, and each 24 to 36 page magazine includes a number of articles on all aspects of the conservative racist position. As a voice of a definite position the magazine has some importance for libraries, particularly those with large research collections, or serving whites who support the racist attitudes of the editors. (The co-editor, Medford Evans, is also associated with the John Birch *American Opinion.*)

Cross and the Flag. 1942. m. $2. Gerald L. K. Smith. Box 27895, Los Angeles, Calif. 90027. Circ: 35,000.

Aud: Ga.

The voice of the radical Right hero Gerald L. K. Smith, this paper is supported by his Christian Nationalist Crusade (not to be confused with the anticommunist *Christian Crusade,* published by Billy James Hargis). An average 36 to 40 page issue features one or two articles, and a number of features and short news items. The reporting is simplistic, obviously based more upon sentiment than fact. Still, it has considerable merit for the dreams it shares with its readers—nightmares to most, as the founder is a rampant antiblack, antisemitic, antidemocratic eccentric. Interestingly enough, this is one of four favored magazines of regular readers of the John Birch *American Opinion*. Because of its popularity and definitive viewpoint, a good periodical for larger balanced collections.

Efficacy. See *Objectivist.*

Freedom. 1955. q. $5. Willis E. Stone, 6413 Franklin Ave., Los Angeles, Calif. 90028. Illus., adv. Circ: 14,000. Sample. Vol. ends: Winter.

Bk. rev: 1, 400 words, signed. *Aud:* Ac, Ga.

Primarily a conservative voice to push through the publisher's pet project, the Liberty Amendment. This would take the government out of any form of business and prevent Congress from levying income and estate taxes. The Amendment has won approval by a number of states, is sometimes an argument for eliminating revenue sharing by adopting it instead of the federal–local financial plan. A usual 30-page issue includes speeches and articles by those who support the Amendment, comments on other economic legislation, and shorter notes on everything from student radicals to the Supreme Court. As this is basically a one-issue magazine, it is not representative of most conservative thought. What it does, however, it does well, and should have some appeal for economists and others interested in taxation.

✓ *The Freeman; a monthly journal of ideas on liberty.* 1950. m. Request. Paul L. Poirot. Foundation for Economic Education, Inc., Irvington-on-Hudson, N.Y. 10533. Illus. Circ: 50,000. Sample. Vol. ends: Dec.

Indexed: PAIS. *Bk. rev:* 2–3, 1,500 words. *Aud:* Ga, Ac.

Committed to the market economy and private property. Contributors argue for unrestricted trade and travel, support individual decision making instead of "government compulsion," claim that "price wars" result from "strikes and other forms of violence" rather than "open competition," and protest "interventionism," whether in the guise of Medicare, protective tariffs, or municipal garbage collection. Unlike some conservatives, *Freeman* writers do not deny that poverty exists, but maintain that it is a personal problem best treated by open competition in the market, supplemented by private charity.

Liberty Letter. 1960. m. $2. Doug Clee, 300 Independence Ave., S.E., Washington, D.C. 20003. Circ: 195,000.

Bk. rev: 2–3, 300 words, signed. *Aud:* Ga.

A four-page newsletter representing the opinions and feelings of a registered lobbying group in Washington, the Liberty Lobby. The name is a euphemism for a radical Right group. Of course the publisher doesn't see it that way, and his version of liberty is found in the pages of the newsletter. Specific legislation is discussed, and here the letter is useful for pinpointing pending bills which the radical Right either approves or disapproves. Editorials exhort the faithful to write their congressmen, and there is a scorecard of heros and villains in Congress. Its interesting point of view is doubly so because of the frequency of the publication and its interest in national legislation. Should be in all larger collections, and brought to the attention of anyone dealing with the finer points of government.

Manion Forum. 1955. w. $10. Dean Clarence Manion. The Manion Forum, St. Joseph Bank Bldg., South Bend, Ind. 46601. Index. Circ: 15,000. Sample. Vol. ends: Dec. 31. Microform: UM.

Aud: Ac, Ga.

A four-page newsletter which is primarily a transcript of the highlights of the publisher's weekly radio interview with a fellow conservative. The tone is mild and in no way representative of more radical conservative positions. (Broadcast tapes are also available for $3.75 each.) In October, 1971, the former dean of the University of Notre Dame Law School interviewed (1) Eugene Lyons, senior editor of *Reader's Digest:* "Today there is a kind of undifferential nihilism, an addiction to pornography, drugs, dynamite, destruction, chaos as an end in itself"; (2) Daniel Lyons, editor of the National Catholic *Twin Circle*, who reported on a trip to Latin America, describing the Latin American priests as "anti-imperialist, and, unfortunately, this includes some of our fellow countrymen." Depending on the reader or listener's viewpoint, the interviews are objective, or biased in favor of the conservative position. At any rate, they are rarely dull. A somewhat high price for most libraries, but interesting enough.

Objectivist. 1962. m. $8. Ayn Rand. Objectivist, Inc., 201 E. 34th St., New York, N.Y. 10016. Index. Circ: 21.

Aud: Ac.

A libertarian (i.e., laissez-faire, conservative) magazine edited by the author Ayn Rand. An average 16 to 20 page issue features two or three articles on objectivism, short news items, and events of interest to those who follow the Rand thinking. At one time Rand was pretty well a rage, but no longer. While the magazine has unquestionable value as an expression of a valid viewpoint, it is no longer of wide general interest. Only for larger academic libraries.

Another libertarian magazine is:

Efficacy. (1970. bi-m. $3. Robert Bakhaus. Box 1747,

Harlington, Texas 78550. Illus., adv. Circ: 600. Sample. Vol. ends: Nov.) The pocket-sized 20-page magazine, according to the editor, "is concerned with defining as concisely as possible the essential ideas, innovations and organizational aspects *evolving* from the Objectivist (Rand), Libertarian (von Mises) subcultural influences." A typical issue includes short fiction, clippings from papers, short book reviews, and items on taxation and free trade.

The Review of the News. 1967. w. $10. Scott Stanley, Jr. Correction, Please, Inc., 395 Concord Ave., Belmont, Mass. 02178. Illus., adv. Sample.

Aud: Ga, Ac.

A weekly, sister publication to the John Birch Society's *American Opinion*. (No indication is given in the masthead, other than the address, that the two are related.) There is no mystery concerning its purpose, which is to give a summary of news events of interest to conservatives. The 44-page pocket-sized magazine is professionally edited, and the short news items (which occupy a good half of each number) are presented in a straight-forward objective style. In fact, the language is less slanted than that often found in general news magazines. The rest of each issue is made up of editorials and one or two studies in depth of an event or personality—which, to say the least, indicated the publisher's views. Aside from reluctance to admit connection with the John Birch Society—a position held, too, for *American Opinion*—the magazine can be recommended as a better than average current conservative news source.

Through to Victory. 11/yr. $2. Paul C. Neipp, 731 N. Sanders, Ridgecrest, Calif. 93555. Illus., adv.

Aud: Ga.

A tabloid newspaper which claims it represents the conservative Lutheran laymen for Christ and country. The drift is the same as that of most radical Right publications, i.e., win the war in Vietnam, check the communists, pull out of the United Nations, etc. It differs from most in that Rev. Neipp does, from time to time, offer theological articles of interest to his brand of Lutheran. He also has a snappy style which is supported by great slogans. In some ways this is one of the best radical Right tabloids, primarily because the editor and his writers are never dull. An interesting, although hardly essential, addition.

White Power; the newspaper of white revolution. 1967. m. $3. William Striker. National Socialist White Peoples Party, 2507 N. Franklin Rd., Arlington, Va. 22205. Illus., adv. Circ: 25,000. Sample.

Anti-Semitic, anti-Black, opposed to almost everything, this is published by the National Socialists, i.e., the Nazi party in America. An average eight-page issue is filled with opinion and news on how the Blacks,

Jews, and liberals (including Nixon and George Wallace) and ruining the country. The viewpoint is definitely on the lunatic fringe, the writers seeming to have some kind of hangup with virility. If one can stand off from the editorial content, and consider the frank opinions are representative of some small part of American thinking, the paper has a given amount of interest—even value for the sociologist and psychologist. For this reason, it should be seriously considered by large academic libraries.

Radical Left

The Daily World (Formerly: **The Worker**). 1922. d. (5 days/wk. and weekend magazine). $15 (Weekend magazine $5). The Daily World, 205 W. 19th St., New York, N.Y. 10011. Illus., adv. Circ: 17,000 (Magazine, 37,000). Sample.

Aud: Ga, Ac.

After ten years as the weekly *Worker*, this again became a daily in 1968, continues as the official voice of the American Communist party. An average 12-page tabloid number is much like any newspaper in format and approach. There are the usual front page headlines, editorials, letters to the editor, regular columns, and sports. The editor points out that the paper "specializes in labor, black liberation, peace and youth news." The weekend 12-page magazine, *World Magazine*, contains longer articles and book reviews, not to mention a crossword puzzle. The writing is professional, considerably less flamboyant than that found in many standard tabloids, such as the *Daily News*, and the whole is a valuable source of a distinct viewpoint. It should be in all larger academic and many public libraries. See also *The People's World*.

Guardian; independent radical newsweekly. 1948. w. $10 (Students $5). Cooperative. Weekly Guardian Associates, Inc., 32 W. 22 St., New York, N.Y. 10010. Illus., index, adv. Circ: 35,000. Sample. Microform: B & H.

Indexed: API. *Bk. rev:* 1–2, essays, signed. *Aud:* Ga, Ac. *Jv:* V.

The basic voice of the independent radical movement in the United States, and as such, a major paper for almost any library. One of the earliest expressions on the New Left, which by 1968 had turned to a "clear-cut Marxist orientation." The tabloid newspaper of some 16 to 24 pages had a strong influence on the beginnings of the underground press, and remains today germinal to that movement. It is an excellent weekly newspaper, at least in terms of format (neat, easy to read); content (nonobjective, but clear, accurate, and highly personalized in an intellectual manner); and purpose (purely political). The reporting usually represents original effort and rarely depends on wire services. The first few pages are given over to short news items and feature stories; these are followed by editorials, letters, interviews, and more features. There are some perceptive film reviews, a regular Ac/Dc department which reports on culture and the press, often with quotes; and an occasional book review. The scope is international. This would be a first choice for any library trying to get a well-balanced, accurate, and meaningful voice from the "movement."

Independent Socialist. See *Worker's Power.*

Intercontinental Press. 1963. w. $15. Joseph Hansen, Intercontinental Press, Box 116, Village Station, New York, N.Y. 10014. Illus., index. Circ: 5,500. Sample. Vol. ends: Dec. 20.

Bk. rev: 1, 1,200 words, signed. *Aud:* Ac, Ga.

Committed to the political philosophy of Trotsky, a typical 24-page weekly issue concerns itself with such matters as antiwar demonstrations, an analysis of President Nixon's economic policies, a study of the "Mexican Left," and reports from the world around on activities of interest to the political or social activist. The newspaper/magazine is carefully edited, the material usually written by the editor or taken from the world's press. Despite the obvious bias, the reports are accurate, well written, and of considerable help to anyone trying to keep up with national and international politics and movements. There is little or none of the "hysteria" often associated with this type of publication. It can be recommended for larger public and academic libraries, particularly the latter, where there is an imaginative political–social science program.

International Socialist Review; the Marxist theoretical magazine of American socialism. 1934. m. $5. Les Evans. Intl. Socialist Review Publishing Assoc., 14 Charles Lane, New York, N.Y. 10014. Illus., index, adv. Circ: 8,000. Sample. Vol. ends: Dec. Microform: UM.

Indexed: API. *Bk. rev:* 1, essay, signed. *Aud:* Ac, Ga.

The editor explains the purpose and scope of his magazine: "It's a magazine of Marxism written by Marxists. Our aspiration is not to remain one of the many small journals of the American left. We see a place for a popular socialist magazine that can at the same time provide informed commentary on current trends in economy and philosophy while relating to the issues and demands of today's multiplying movements for social change." A well-printed and well-made-up 48-page issue pretty well carries out this desire. It is not a typical small political magazine. It is a general Marxist voice directed to alienated groups. In addition to articles, there are short news items and regular features which include items on labor, women, Blacks, and the antiwar movement. The reporters tend to cover current topics in depth, i.e., the Attica prison

riots are given a new dimension in an outstanding series of articles. The editors and writers endorse revolution, but the Communist party is a frequent object of criticism. In a word, the viewpoint is unique, militant, and, depending on the reader's attitudes, revealing. It is also extremely well edited, and of all the radical Left magazines (specific political policy aside) it is among the most representative of an important attitude in America. See also *The Militant.*

The Militant; a socialist newsweekly. 1934. w. $6. Les Evans. Intl. Socialist Review Publishing Assoc., 14 Charles Lane, New York, N.Y. 10014. Illus., index, adv. Circ: 8,200. Sample. Vol. ends: Dec.

Indexed: API. *Bk. rev:* 3, 900 words, signed. *Aud:* Ac, Ga.

The newspaper side of the Socialist Workers party. The magazine, by the same publisher, is *International Socialist Review.* The editorial policy is similar, the major difference being that the weekly 24-page tabloid makes an effort to keep readers advised of the previous week's news. About one half of the paper is turned over to short news stories, the other to features, editorials, and reviews. The liberal use of photographs adds to the liveliness of the makeup. Objectivity of reporting, though, is not a strong point. The writers are biased, make no bones about it, and the result is a side to the news rarely found in the conventional press. Considering the low price, the viewpoint, and the professional nature of it all, the paper should have appeal for the library trying to give all sides of current world events.

Monthly Review; an independent socialist magazine. 1949. m. (bi-m. July–Aug.). $7. Paul M. Sweezy and Harry Magdoff. Monthly Review Inc., 116 W. 14th St., New York, N.Y. 10011. Index, adv. Circ: 11,500. Sample. Vol. ends: April.

Indexed: API, PAIS. *Bk. rev:* 2, 6 pages, signed. *Aud:* Ac, Ga.

The intellectual's major Marxist magazine, and the most important of the group. Describes itself as "an independent magazine devoted to analyzing, from a socialist point of view, the most significant trends in domestic and foreign affairs." It should be stressed that it is Marxist, not communist. As the editors point out: "We analyze; we don't publish inspirational articles. Furthermore . . . our authors and editorials have been fraternally critical of some of Castro's innovations." The articles analyze all aspects of economics and politics from a Marxist-Leninist position. They are as apt to be critical of the Soviet Union and China as the United States, and take a strong position against imperialism, racial discrimination, and unfair labor practices wherever they are found. The writing is much above average; the message is clear, yet often debated; and the overall policy seems to be to hold up issues for discussion and let the truth win. An important magazine for almost any library.

People's World. 1938. w. $7. (Students $5). Carl Bloice. Pacific Publishing Foundation, Inc., 81 Clementina St., San Francisco, Calif. 94105. Illus., adv. Circ: 8,500. Sample. Vol. ends: Dec. 31.

Indexed: API. *Bk. rev:* 1, 500 words, signed. *Aud:* Ac, Ga.

The West Coast counterpart of the *Daily World,* this is a tabloid, radical newsweekly which speaks for a combination of communists and, according to the editor, "non-Communists of the Left." Usually carries several in-depth articles on politics, the Black Power movement, labor, foreign affairs, antiwar activities, and Mexican-American activities. Two of its 12 pages are devoted to book and film reviews, with occasional reviews of music, theater, and the graphic arts. The editor reports that "its purpose is to help create a viable, mass political movement on the Left," and its goal, "the socialist reconstruction of American society." While representative of communistic viewpoints, it is not necessarily a communist newspaper.

√*Political Affairs; theoretical journal of the Communist Party, U.S.A.* 1922. m. Hy Lumer. Affairs Publishers Inc., 23 W. 26th St., New York, N.Y. 10010. Index. Circ: 7,500. Sample.

Index: PAIS. *Aud:* Ac, Ga.

A carefully edited, 65 to 100 page intelligent approach to American and world politics as seen through the eyes of those sympathetic to Marxist thought and analysis. Each issue begins with an editorial comment on some current event, features eight to ten articles, and ends with "Communication," which are letters and brief notes. Among the regulars are Gus Hall, James West, and Herbert Aptheker. One of the more objective Communist party publications, this is suitable for any library trying to give that party a voice in its collection.

Progressive Labor. 1962. bi-m. $2.50. Milton Rosen. Box 808, Brooklyn, N.Y. 11201. Illus., adv. Circ: 16,000. Sample.

Aud: Ac, Ga.

A major voice of the Marxist–Leninist labor movement, this is an 80 to 100 page magazine which features articles on all aspects of current society, social and economic problems, and the current trends in politics, government, etc. The magazine is militant, generally well written, and gives an accurate picture of one group's concerns and its solutions to American difficulties.

Socialist Revolution. 1970. bi-m. $6. Collective. Agenda Publishing Co., 1445 Stockton St., San Francisco, Calif. 94107. Illus., index, adv. Circ: 5000. Sample. Vol. ends: Dec.

Bk. rev: 1, 4 pages, signed. *Aud:* Ac, Ga.

One of the best ongoing reports of the philosophy and activities of the Socialist movement (not limited solely to Socialist party doctrine), this 150-page journal should be a basic part of any political science or social science collection. It differs from most dissident magazines in that every effort is made to support argument with documentation and cold reason. The hypothesis may be questionable for some readers, but there is no argument with the methodology. For example, in one issue James Weinstein asked "Can a Historian Be a Socialist Revolutionary?" and in the following number Staughton Lynd replied with another viewpoint. Many of the articles are involved with the Women's Liberation movement, student activities, and problems besetting leftist intellectuals. The scope is worldwide, the authors authoritative. It all adds up to lively, intellectual reading which should have appeal for any activist, regardless of background or age.

Young Socialist—The Organizer (Formerly: *Young Socialist*). 1971. bi-w. $2.50. Rich Finkel. Young Socialist Alliance, Box 471, Cooper Station, New York, N.Y. 10003. Illus. Circ: 10,000. Sample.

Aud: Hs, Ac.

The publication of the youth wing of the Socialist Workers party (see also *The Militant* and *International Socialist Review*). It has taken the form of an underground newspaper, but remains essentially the same in purpose as its predecessor, the *Young Socialist*. It includes columns of interest to younger readers, and tries to pick up news items directly affecting the young. It is not as well edited as the other two publications, but has its place in schools where an effort is made to show more than one side of a given issue.

Weekly People; official organ of the Socialist Labor party. 1891. w. $3. John H. Timm. Socialist Labor Party, 116 Nassau St., Brooklyn, N.Y. 11201. Illus. Circ: 10,000. Sample. Vol. ends: March.

Bk. rev: Various number, length. *Aud:* Ac, Ga.

Of all the radical newspapers, this is probably the most familiar to the average American, who has seen it on newsstands and street corners for a good many years. In fact, the editor claims the six to eight page grey paper is the oldest radical publication in the world. The newsprint may be even dimmer than that of the *New York Times*, but the contents are lively enough: feature articles, reviews, editorials, news notes on Socialist activities in particular areas, and classified advertisements. Politically, it is pure Marxist, i.e., the editor and writers believe that both the Chinese and the Russians have gone astray, that the day has yet to dawn when true Marxism will reign (by which they mean total control of industry by government). The change is to be brought about by peaceful means—a major condition is that change will be evolutionary through education of the workers. The reporting is timely, intelligent, and always thoughtful. One may not agree with some or all of the philosophy behind the paper, but as a representative of an important leftist element it is hard to beat.

The Worker. See *Daily World.*

Workers' Power (Formerly: *Independent Socialist).* 1967. bi-w. $3.50. Kit Lyons. Intl. Socialist Publishing Co., 14131 Woodward, Highland Pk., Mich. 48203. Illus. Circ: 5,000. Sample. Vol. ends: Dec.

Indexed: API. *Bk. rev:* 1, 500–1,000 words, signed. *Aud:* Ac, Ga.

A 16-page tabloid newspaper which is noteworthy in terms of format: art, photographs, and layout are exceptional for this type of approach. The paper is aggressively Marxist, but undoctrinaire; committed to "collective ownership and democratic control of the economy" achieved by "revolution from below"; opposed to Washington, but equally to Moscow and Peking. The paper functions as a conduit for the thought of the I.S. and of the fraternal "International Socialism" group in Britain. Not a large group, the I.S. (then the Independent Socialist Club) was nevertheless the most influential force in creating the Peace and Freedom Party in 1968. Since 1969 the I.S. has increasingly concentrated on influencing the rank-and-file union members' upsurge in work places, and has helped in forming opposition groups in the telephone employees', teamsters', teachers', and other unions. *Workers' Power* is a source of hard-to-get information on grass-roots militancy among workers, as well as students and minorities, and on international struggles against Washington and the "bureaucratic-collectivist" communist states.

World Marxist Review; problems of peace and socialism. 1958. m. $5. Imported Publns., 1730 W. Arcade Pl., Chicago, Ill. 60612. Vol. ends: Dec. Microform: UM.

Bk. rev: 2–3, 600–1,000 words, signed. *Aud:* Ac.

This is the American edition of *Problems of Peace and Socialism,* published in Prague. It is a leading theoretical journal of the communist movement from an international standpoint. It contains programs, party decisions, and articles on the parties of specific countries. One feature, "In Brief," lists the current activities of Marxist parties, country by country.

NEWSPAPERS

Basic Newspapers

All libraries: The city or town newspaper, the state and/or regional newspaper, and the *New York Times.*

U.S. NATIONAL. Ga: *Christian Science Monitor, National Observer, Amsterdam News;* Jc & Ac: *Washington Post, Chicago Tribune, Los Angeles Times, Amsterdam News, Christian Science Monitor, National Observer.*

INTERNATIONAL. Ga: The *Guardian;* Jc & Ac: The *Guardian,* the *Times, Neue Zurcher Zeitung,* and what is needed to support curriculum and what is possible within the language capabilities of the students and faculty.

SPECIAL INTEREST. Ga: *Wall Street Journal;* Jc & Ac: *Wall Street Journal, Black Panther, etc.*

Basic Abstracts and Indexes

All libraries: *New York Times Index.*

U. S. National

Amsterdam News. 1909. w. $12. Clarence B. Jones. The News, 2340 Eighth Ave., New York, N.Y. 10027. Circ: 100,000.

Aud: Ac, Hs, Ga. *Jv:* V.

America's leading black newspaper. Aside from *Muhammad Speaks,* it enjoys the largest circulation of any of the nation's some 175 black newspapers. Since 1970 the newspaper has changed dramatically in content and format. Under new owners the conservative tone has become more liberal. There is now an aggressive effort to report news of interest to Blacks. (For example, in order to identify more closely with the black liberation movement, the paper is now printed in red and green, colors popularized by the late Marcus Garvey.) Most of the weekly news concerns the greater New York area, but this is gradually changing. The editor hopes to make it into a national black newspaper, and there have been special supplements on black writing, theater, etc., which may just pull it off. Meanwhile, the paper changes monthly, and it is well worth watching. Should be found in libraries serving a black community, and where possible, in other medium-to-large public and academic libraries.

The Atlanta Constitution. d. $39.10. Atlanta Newspapers, Inc. 10 Forsyth St., N.W., Atlanta, Ga. 30302. Circ: 209,000.

Aud: Ga, Hs, Ac.

Considered by many to be the leading newspaper of the southern and southeastern portion of the country, this paper has for years followed a liberal tone in editorials. It includes both conservative and liberal columnists, black and white. Essential for all Georgia libraries, and should be considered by others as a regional newspaper. (D.D.)

Chicago Daily Defender. 1956. daily & weekend edition. $17.50. Robert S. Abbott Publishing Co., 2406

S. Michigan Ave., Chicago, Illinois. 60616. Circ: 22,000. Microform: University of Chicago Library.

Aud: Ga, Hs, Ac.

One of the country's leading black newspapers. Orientation is toward black newsmakers throughout the country, with an emphasis on the Chicago area. Daily and weekend edition includes columns and editorials, and the weekend edition includes a feature section, "Flair," with emphasis on society and religion. Both editions should be purchased by schools or libraries with Chicago-area interests; others should consider the weekend edition. (D.D.) (Ed. note: The owner/publisher of the *Defender* is John H. Sengstacke. He also controls several other newspapers which follow the Chicago pattern, and are better choices for libraries in the areas. They are: *New Pittsburgh Courier, Ohio Courier, Philadelphia Courier, Georgia Courier, Florida Courier, Shreveport Sun, Memphis Tri-State Defender,* and the *Detroit Michigan Chronicle.* The chain, which has the largest combined circulation of any black newspaper group, has been accused of being more interested in profit than in changing condition of the black community. Most of the papers are conservative.)

✓ *Chicago Tribune.* 1847. d. $40 (Higher in some areas). 435 N. Michigan Ave., Chicago, Ill. 60611. Circ: 768,000. Microform: Mp.

Indexed: Newspaper index. *Aud:* Ga, Hs, Ac.

This paper has been labeled "the conservative voice of the Middlewest." Coverage of regional, national, and international news is extensive, through use of their own reporters plus the usual news services. The Sunday edition includes *Book World,* a reviewing magazine, and a color magazine, as well as features aimed at the traveler. Highly valuable for midwestern libraries; an example of a regional newspaper for others. (Note: Thanks to a falling away of some city circulation, the editors in 1971 introduced some liberal elements into the paper, e.g., "Perspective," an editorial page feature that offers middle-of-the-road to left-wing opinion.)

✓ *The Christian Science Monitor.* 1908. d. (Except Sunday and holidays). $30. The Christian Science Publishing Soc., 1 Norway St., Boston, Mass. 02115. Circ: 260,000.

Indexed: Self-index. *Aud:* Ga, Hs, Ac.

Next to the *New York Times* this comes as close as any newspaper in the United States to being a national paper. John Hughes, who became editor in late 1971, puts more emphasis on immediacy and editorial policies which reach out for the poor, Blacks, and other minority groups. The paper is now going after younger readers, and the result is a fresher, more meaningful newspaper. Although issued by the Christian Science Society, it is remarkably free of any religious overtones. A single paper is given over to church news and opinion. Aside from this, the paper is world famous for its objectivity and thoroughness. The writing is objective enough to recommend that this paper be read by persons who want to get a new and valuable perspective on events they may be following in detail elsewhere. A third basic newspaper for all sizes and types of libraries.

Denver Post. 1892. d. $30. P.O. Box 1709, Denver, Colo. 80201. Circ: 255,000. Microform: Mp.

Aud: Ga, Hs, Ac.

Self-billed as the "Voice of the Rocky Mountain Empire," a motto it consistently strives to live up to. Regional coverage is its strongest point. The Sunday edition includes several feature sections and an attractive magazine, "Empire." Should be available in all Intermountain libraries, and considered by others for its coverage of that portion of the West. (D.D.)

Los Angeles Times. 1881. d. $78. Times Mirror Co., Times Mirror Sq., Los Angeles, Calif. 90053. Circ: 966,000. Microform: Mp.

Indexed: Newspaper index. *Aud:* Ga, Ac.

Now the best newspaper on the West Coast, having replaced the San Francisco *Chronicle* in that position. In terms of other national newspapers, the *L. A. Times* remains a trifle conservative, though in the past few years it has taken on more of a middle-of-the-road attitude. While it is predominantly the voice of southern California, it speaks for the state in its coverage of political and social matters. A necessary addition for most California libraries, and larger academic and public libraries.

National Enquirer. 1926. w. $6. Nat Chrzan. Best Medium Publishing Co., 600 South East Coast Ave., Lantana, Fla. 33460. Illus., adv. Circ: 1,952,000.

Aud: Ga.

The middle- and lower-class American's counter to the *Village Voice.* (It enjoys a considerable vogue, too, among *Voice* readers.) A tabloid newspaper which has been around considerably longer than most, the *Enquirer* is by way of a national institution. Its weekly reports cover all aspects of American sex life, crime, violence, politics, motion picture personalities, and just about anything or anyone who can be worked into a sensational headline or news story. The writing is up to anything found in the *Daily News* or, for that matter, the *New York Times.* (The *Enquirer* seems to print all the news that the *Times* thinks is not fit to print, or the *News* would consider too outrageous.) The reporters, or more precisely rewrite men and women, understand the language and how to work the most out of even the slimmest bit of material. Still, it is more than a capsule news report; it includes puzzles, cartoons, features, and a good number of photographs. In fact, just about any really good story, whether it concerns a medical breakthrough or the breakup of a marriage, is accompanied by an explicit photograph. It all adds up to the cliché that fact is stranger than fiction, particularly when helped a bit. Consider, though, the size of the readership before putting it down completely. Not up to the *Reader's Digest*—a close competitor of sorts—but quite beyond most magazines.

The National Observer. 1962. w. $7. Dow Jones & Co., Inc., 11501 Columbia Pike, Silver Spring, Md. 20910. Circ: 524,000. Microform: Mp.

Indexed: Self-index. *Bk. rev:* 5–10, 300–500 words. *Aud:* Ga, Ac.

A weekly newspaper, run by the publisher of the *Wall Street Journal.* Contains summaries of important national and international news events and stories chosen for wide popular interest, all written in a popularized style. Topics include consumer news, science, education, civil rights, business, politics. Editorials have a conservative cast. This sort of *Time* magazine in newspaper form is often read by those too lazy to read a good daily newspaper. It does contain a great deal of information, and can be read with much profit; but the desire to please sometimes results in a certain simplicity and lack of perceptive when history becomes unpleasant. When it comes to reporting U.S. foreign policy, the paper does not match "The Week in Review" of the Sunday *New York Times.* Despite its weaknesses, it has a definite advantage over *Time* in that at least the style is straightforward and there is no confusing the conservative editorial bias. Small to medium-sized libraries would do well to take this, but only after a subscription to the Sunday *New York Times* and *Newsweek.*

New York Daily News. 1919. q. $22. Floyd Barger. News Syndicate, 220 E. 42nd St., New York, N.Y. 10017. Illus., adv. Circ: 2,200,000 (Sunday: 2,300,000). *Aud:* Ga.

The largest-circulation newspaper in America. Its other claim to fame is that it is the pioneer of the picture tabloid form; it is best known for short sensational stories, fast action pictures, and columnists who are more involved with gossip than news. Traditionally it has been conservative to middle of the road in political tone, strong on sports and entertainment. But things change, and in the past few years the paper has taken on a look of respectability, shifted to a more liberal position, and downplayed the senational—at least in terms of what it was ten years or so ago. (A television or Hollywood personality periodically dominates a front page, but hard news is now more likely to be there.) Lately, the *News* has become a newspaper: it is carrying news in the form of real information, background, and interpretation;

and it is particularly good in its coverage of New York City. Although not a choice for many libraries outside of New York, it is worth mentioning here because of its large circulation and because it proves papers can change.

The New York Times. 1951. d. $95. The N.Y. Times Co., 229 W. 43rd St., New York, N.Y. 10036. Illus., index, adv. Circ: 882,897 (Sunday: 1,480,500). Vol. ends: Sept. 17.

Indexed: Self-index. *Bk. rev:* Daily and Sunday edition. *Aud:* Ga, Ac, Hs. *Jv:* V.

The closest thing to a national paper available to the United States, the *Times* rightfully claims it "is a newspaper of objectivity." Time was when objectivity was taken for granted as a newspaper's goal, if not always an attained goal. "But we live in a time of commitment and advocacy when 'tell it like it is' really means 'tell it like I say it is' or 'tell it as I want it to be,'" the *Times's* Managing Editor, A. M. Rosenthal, once wrote. "For precisely that reason, it is more important than ever that *The Times* keeps objectivity in its news columns as its number one, bedrock principle."

Complete news coverage makes this the most useful newspaper in any size or type of library. It is the only one which prints verbatim the texts of important speeches, statements, and proceedings of news conferences and peace talks. Articles frequently appear which summarize and analyze topics in the news, and sometimes a long article will give a general report on an area, which will not have been called for by an immediate crisis.

Each issue contains news of cultural events, a book review (Christopher Lehmann-Haupt); a film review (Vincent Canby); a theatre column by Clive Barnes or Walter Kerr; an exceptional editorial page which includes columns by James Reston, Tom Wicker, and Russell Baker; a sports section; and a comprehensive business section. In short, for those who would know what is going on in the world, this paper is indispensable. It can only be supplemented.

SUNDAY EDITION. The Sunday edition has the same merits as the daily *Times,* but it is probably the heaviest newspaper published anywhere. It is swollen by separate sections devoted to the news, Arts and Leisure, Business and Finance, Real Estate, Resorts and Travel, Sports, Classified Advertisements, and three sections of particular note: "The Week in Review," The "New York Times Book Review," and the "New York Times Magazine." "The Week in Review" contains convenient, well-written summaries of the week's events on all important news fronts, as well as articles on education, law, medicine, science, and religion; editorials; and listings of librarian and teacher job openings. The "Book Review" section is well known to all who read or deal with books; in addition to the many book reviews, it contains the famed Best Seller List. The "Magazine" (see Sunday Magazine Supplements), usually rather thick, contains long articles on all subjects, written by prominent persons, and a good crossword puzzle. Libraries which cannot afford the daily and Sunday edition should at least subscribe to the Sunday issue ($49 a year). It is a must for almost any type library.

St. Louis Post-Dispatch. 1878. d. $62. Pulitzer Publishing Co., 1113 Franklin Ave., St. Louis, Mo. 63101. Circ: 326,000. Microform: MCA.

Aud: Ac, Hs, Ga.

Always named among the top ten best-edited newspapers in this country, the *Post-Dispatch* provides excellent news reports in a pleasant, precise format. A daily section called "Editorials—News Analysis and Interpretation" contains a few special news articles and some really good editorial writing, critical and perceptive. There are also syndicated columns by Tom Wicker, Joseph Kraft, and Joseph Alsop. This significant paper has a place in any large newspaper collection, and certainly would be a third choice for libraries within the region.

The Village Voice. 1955. w. $7. The Village Voice, Inc., Sheridan Square, New York, N.Y. 10014. Circ: 142,000.

Aud: Ga, Ac, Hs.

This began as an underground newspaper, but today is one of the more respected journals of opinion and the arts in the country. Although it purports to be the voice of the Bohemian element in Greenwich Village, New York, its scope is much greater, its interests more national and international. It has a particular fascination for the young because it is among the first to report on new activities in the arts, music, theater, and politics. Conversely, the really rebellious young have given it up for the more outspoken, usually less literate, underground newspapers. (In fact, the *East Village Other* began as a countervoice to the *Village Voice.*) Distinctly liberal in tone, the articles are geared for a sophisticated, well-educated audience. Writers include critics Pete Hammill, Nat Hentoff, Jonas Mekas, and Andrew Sarris. There are fascinating cartoonists (Jules Feiffer, for one), photographs, and an extremely entertaining classified advertisement section. Those in and around New York value the up-to-date weekly report on current activities, particularly senior high school libraries. On the other hand, it is not the type of newspaper which should be introduced into a rockbound conservative community.

The Washington Post. 1877. d. $60. Washington Post Co., 1515 L St., N.W., Washington, D.C. 20005. Circ: 500,000. Microform: MP.

Indexed: Newspaper index. *Aud:* Ga, Ac, Hs.

Next to the *New York Times*, one of the most widely influential and quoted newspapers in the United States. Features excellent hard-hitting analytical columns by Nicholas Von Hoffman and Maxine Cheshire. The work of Richard Harwood in revealing the truth about politics is also noteworthy. Liberal in tone, it offers complete news coverage of the Washington scene, frequently breaking stories before any other news service. It is usually one of two or three papers read by the President and every congressman. In terms of choice it would follow the *New York Times* and a local newspaper. Recommended for all types and sizes of libraries.

SUNDAY MAGAZINE SUPPLEMENTS. With the death of the familiar *This Week*, there are now only three national Sunday newspaper supplements: *Parade*, *Family Weekly*, and *Tuesday*, the latter directed to black audiences. In addition, there are a number of well-known newspaper supplements which, thanks to a large Sunday circulation, reach a good number of Americans. These are found in the *Los Angeles Times*, *Chicago Tribune*, and *New York Times*, with stops in between for almost every state in the union that has its own large Sunday newspaper.

Precisely how effective or how widely read any of these are—this side of the *New York Times* supplement, which is the only real magazine among them—is always a fascinating question. See Norman Hill's "The Last of the Red Hot Supplements" in *Saturday Review* (Dec. 12, 1970, p. 56). None of them need be found in a library unless incidentally a part of a subscription to a regular newspaper. None is worth retaining.

Family Weekly. 1953. w. Mort Persky. Family Weekly Inc., 641 Lexington Ave., New York, N.Y. 10022. Circ: 8,000,000.

Distributed to 261 newspapers in smaller towns and communities throughout America. The contents feature short articles and picture features on famous individuals, anecdotes, and personal experiences. Quality is poor. Entertainment is high.

Parade. w. W. J. Reynolds. 733 Third Ave., New York, N.Y. 10017. Circ: 16,875,000.

Distributed to 96 newspapers in larger cities in America; hence the circulation, which is double that of its closest competitor, *Family Weekly*. It is difficult to tell the two apart on the basis of content. But the style of writing and the photographs seem a bit better in *Parade*.

Tuesday. 1965. m. W. Leonard Evans, Jr. Tuesday Publns. Inc. 180 N. Michigan Ave., Chicago, Ill. 60601. Circ: 2,500,000.

This, and *Tuesday at Home*, by the same publisher, reaches Blacks who read some 20 metropolitan newspapers. The papers are not black newspapers. Material is aimed directly at the black reader, and while commendable for recognizing a long-neglected audience, the content isn't much better than either *Parade* or *Family Weekly*.

New York Times Magazine. 1896. w. N.Y. Times Co., 229 W. 43rd St., New York, N.Y. 10036. Circ: 1,500,000.

Although indexed in both the *Readers' Guide* and the abridged version, the magazine must be taken as part of the regular Sunday *Times*. (It cannot be subscribed to separately.) Of all the national and local supplements, it comes the closest to being an honest magazine. There are usually four or five articles by both staffers and leading national and international writers; a number of features, including fashions and architecture; and some of the more interesting advertising in any magazine. (The reputation for women's undergarments being advertised in a manner to shame *Playboy* has fairly well been lost.) Each 100-page or so issue is as substantial in its content as in format, and it is a required item in all libraries.

Variations on the theme of the *New York Times* will be found in the "Chicago Tribune Magazine," the *Los Angeles Times* "Home Magazine," the *Washington Post's* "Potomac Magazine," and countless others. None, however, is as important as the "Times Magazine," and all can be skipped unless the library happens to be located in the distribution area.

International

ABC. 1903. d. $34.10. Serrano 61, Madrid, Spain. Circ: 220,000.

Aud: Ac.

A tabloid Spanish-language newspaper which resembles in format and approach the *New York Daily News*. Aside from that, though, the two newspapers have nothing in common. After the picture magazine section—which usually makes up the first few pages—come the news and the features. The latter make the paper famous and sought after by Spanish-speaking people outside of Spain. Almost all of Spain's intellectual elite write, or have written, for *ABC*, and a daily or Sunday issue may read like a newspaper version of the *New York Review of Books* and the *Partisan Review*. There is excellent music, art, film, and theater criticism. Obviously, the political news is shaded by the regime, and is unreliable. However, the stringent press laws of Spain have little effect on the features, and this alone makes the paper well worth considering where there is a Spanish-speaking population—of, let it be added, fairly high educational achievement. It is not a popular approach. See also *Excelsior*.

Corriere della Sera. 1876. d. $67. Solferino 28, 20100 Milan, Italy. Circ: 600,000. Microform: UM.

Aud: Ac, Ga.

One of the leading Italian newspapers, and considered by many to be the best published in Italy today. Although it is published in Milan, the commercial center of Italy, it is national in scope, covering all of Italy. Uses a modern style of typography, with photographs and advertisements on most pages. Includes extensive sports and arts coverage. A weekly air mail edition is also available, and might serve for many libraries. The daily edition, however, should be obtained by all libraries serving a large Italian-American population. (D.D.)

Excelsior. 1916. d. $40. Cia Editorial. S.C.L., Paseo de la Reforma 18, Mexico DF, Mexico.

Aud: Ga, Ac.

One of the leading Spanish-language newspapers of the world. Covers Latin-American news through a network of reporters, and the rest of the world through the wire services. Includes editorials and columns, with extensive sports coverage—including U.S. baseball. "Society" and "Features" are included in separate sections. Would be of value to Spanish-language classes, and should be considered by libraries with a sizable Spanish-speaking population. See *La Nacion* for further information. (D.D.)

Le Figaro. 1826. d. $49. ($149.50/air). 14 Rond-Point, Champs-Elysées, Paris. Circ: 40,000. Microform: ACRPP.

Aud: Ga, Ac.

An exceptionally well-written, lively, and for the most part, politically conservative French newspaper. Its average 32-page format follows closely the usual American pattern, complete with advertising. Like its competitor *Le Monde*, it tends to emphasize political affairs, but coverage is not so critical. Conversely, it does cover the world and France in depth, giving special attention to the arts, literature, and education. There is more emphasis here on information, less on *Le Monde's* main mission of intellectual opinion. Hence, of the two, the average reader is apt to find more on current news events in *Le Figaro*, particularly those considered less important by its primary competitor. Thanks to the intentionally direct, clear writing it is a good choice for all general newspaper collections, and may be used with advanced French students in high schools.

The Guardian. 1821. d. (except Sunday). $38. ($146/air). 3 Cross St., Manchester, Eng. Circ: 303,000. Microform: UM.

Aud: Ga, Ac, *Jv:* V.

The intellectuals' newspaper in England, and to a degree in the United States, where many readers primarily know the *Guardian Weekly* (which includes major articles and features from the daily edition). The editorial policies are independent and liberal. Daily issues devote a good deal of space to foreign affairs, and boast correspondents in almost every major country. The American representative is Alistair Cooke. British news reflects the interest in both international affairs and the arts. The columnists cover much of the material found in the weekly edition, music, book reviews, art, political commentary, and the like. Also appearing regularly are sports, television, radio, and women's news and crossword puzzles. In view of its high level of writing, its consistent policy of calling for political and social reforms, and its many outstanding writers, it should be a first choice (along with the *Times* of London) for all academic libraries and for larger public libraries.

Guardian Weekly. 1919. w. $12 ($19.50 air edition). John Perkin. 164 Deansgate, Manchester, England. Subs. to: 20 E. 53rd St., New York, N.Y. 10022. Illus. adv. Circ: 25,000 in U.S. and Canada. Sample. Microform: UM.

Bk. rev: 5–6, 1–2 columns, signed. *Aud:* Ga, Ac. *Jv:* V

This, along with the daily *Guardian*, enjoys the position of being one of England's two leading newspapers. (The *Times* comes first, or second, depending on your view of things.) It should not be confused with the daily edition. The 24-page airmail, thin-paper format includes both new material and items from the daily. Coverage is international in scope, the viewpoint is liberal-British, and the editorials prove that literate opinion need not be dull or pedantic. It is of value for two basic reasons: it alerts Americans to current news sometimes overlooked, underplayed, or slanted in a different fashion in the American Press; and it keeps the reader advised of developments in England in books, politics, art, music, humor—to name a few of the regular features. The whole has the flavor of a somewhat modified cross between the "New York Times Magazine" and the back section of *Newsweek*. It excels them both in its brilliant style. Advertisements claim it is the magazine for "lively minds," and this is true whether those minds be in the community served by a public, college, or university library. Larger libraries will also wish to subscribe to the daily edition. (Note: as of late 1971 the English language edition of *Le Monde* ceased, and was incorporated into the *Guardian*. How long this will continue is a matter of speculation.)

Izvestiia (News). 1917. d. $4.80. Presidium of the Supreme Council of the USSR, Pushkinskaia Pl. 5, Moscow, USSR. Circ: 8,500,000.

Aud: Ac.

This large-format, six-page daily boasts the largest circulation in the USSR. Its emphasis is on the coverage of foreign news. In a regular column, titled "Panorama zarubezhnykh sobytii" (Panorama of Foreign Events) highlights of the news from the capitals of the world are presented in the version of the official Soviet news agency, TASS. The front page focuses on activities of the Communist party, reports on the technical achievements of the Soviet worker, and features large photos of machinery and people at work in various places. Local news from the outlying regions of the Soviet Union are written up by special correspondents, whose stories add a homey touch to this important paper. All articles are signed. Short paragraphs cover the field of sports. Television and radio program schedules, together with the weather forecast, make up the rest of the paper. There are no advertisements. Photos, of good quality with explicit captions, are used throughout the six pages and relieve the crowded appearance produced by small type and seven to eight columns on a page. A useful addition to the newspaper collection of the larger public library and the academic library. (E.L.)

Jen-min Jih-pao (People's Daily). 1948. d. $9. Peking, People's Republic of China. Subs. to: China Books & Periodicals, 2929 24th St., San Francisco, Calif. 94110. Circ: 2,000,000.

Aud: Ac.

The leading mainland China newspaper. Legend has it that the paper was first put together in the caves of Yenan province. Be as it may, it has been the official voice of the Communist party since 1948. It is exclusively the main line for the particular propaganda line put down by the government. It is just as likely to carry essays on the glories of work as the daily news, and in this respect it may be closer to a magazine than a daily newspaper. The six to eight pages require a fundamental knowledge of Chinese. As the major China paper, it is a must in any library where there are readers familiar with the language. (Note: The circulation figure is an educated guess by China watchers. Also, the paper's name is sometimes transcribed phonetically into *Renmin Ribao*.)

The Jerusalem Post. 1932. d. (Except Saturday). IL 175 (IL 521/air). Ted Lurie. The Palestine Post Ltd., 9 Rehov Hahavatzlet, P.O.B. 81, Jerusalem, Israel. Illus., adv. Circ: 27,000 (Friday: 37,000). Microform: Jewish Natl. and Univ. Library, Reprographic Service.

Indexed: Index of Articles on Jewish Studies, Middle East Record. *Bk. rev:* (Friday), 3–5, lengthy, signed. *Aud:* Ga, Hs, Ac.

Compared to some foreign or even to some Israeli newspapers, the *Jerusalem Post* is a modest (eight to twelve pages) daily. It is, however, a valuable source of information on events happening in or connected with Israel and on the Israeli point of view on foreign affairs, the Israeli–Arab conflict, etc. It is of use to the general reader as well as to researchers not familiar with Hebrew, the official language of the State of Israel. It was established in 1932 as the English organ of the Jewish Labor party as well as the Zionist institutions. Its main purpose was to keep members of the British administration informed on current events in the country. With the establishment of the State, its objectives changed; it now serves immigrants who have not mastered Hebrew, tourists, foreign representatives, and Christian communities. Like every Israeli newspaper, it devotes much space to foreign affairs and especially to the Middle East. Domestic news also receives wide coverage. News coverage is objective; editorials present the viewpoint of official circles on foreign policy. Although nominally independent, the paper is known to be connected to the ruling Labor Party. Readers' letters reflect Israeli public opinion. On domestic matters the Anglo-Saxon spirit of independence prevails. The enlarged Friday issue features a junior page with contributions by high school pupils. There is also a modestly illustrated weekend magazine, which publishes articles on actual issues, cultural events, and theater, as well as book reviews.

Smaller libraries may be interested in the *Jerusalem Post Weekly*, the overseas edition published every Tuesday on thin paper. It contains highlights of the news and features as well as the editorial columns that appeared during the preceding six days. ($21. Subs. to: The Jerusalem Post Weekly, 104E. 40th St., Suite 506, New York, N.Y. 10016. Circ: 31,000. (R.T.)

Le Monde. 1944. d. $77. ($220 airmail). Jacques Fauvet. 5 rue des Italiens, Paris 9e, France. Circ: 300,000. Microform: ACRPP.

Indexed: Self-index. *Aud:* Ac.

A highly respected French newspaper. Quoted throughout the world, its sedate, handsomely printed pages contain complete, detailed reporting and analysis of news in France, followed by news from the rest of the world, arranged geographically. Editorials and commentaries are scattered throughout the paper. It has a reputation for being liberal/independent, and thus freely critical, when need be, of any government or policy. It covers financial and business news, sports, television, theater, and films, and contains a classified section. It sometimes contains transcripts of important speeches (from the peace talks in Paris, e.g.). This, or other foreign-language newspapers, are useful in all medium-to-large libraries, but serve a particular purpose in the libraries of high schools where a foreign language is taught. Although there are a number of foreign-language papers published and written in the United States specifically for classroom use, they fail to serve the same purpose as the newspaper from the country itself. (The English-language weekly edition, which ceased publication in July 1971, became part of the *Guardian Weekly* later that year.)

La Nación. 1960. w. $11.90 (Intl. air edition). Dr. Bartolomé Mitre. San Martin 344, Buenos Aires, Argentina. Sample. Vol. ends: Dec.

Aud: Hs, Ga, Ac.

One of the excellent daily newspapers from Buenos Aires, *La Nación* publishes a weekly air mail edition. For reasons of economy and promptness of receipt, most libraries wishing Latin-American newspaper coverage will want to begin here. Each of these weekly issues consists of a selection of the news items of the previous week. While news of Argentina predominates, approximately one page of each eight-page issue is devoted to news of the other Latin-American countries. Usually one quarter of the space is given over to business news, and the arts and sporting events are also covered.

Many other fine Latin-American daily newspapers are available; hence, the choice will be made by the academic library on the basis of the programs taught and faculty interest, and by the public library on the basis of community interest. Some Latin-American newspapers with excellent reputations include *La Prensa* (Buenos Aires, Argentina), *Excélsior* (Mexico, D.F., Mexico), and *O Estado de S. Paulo* (São Paulo, Brazil). For Spain one could recommend the daily *ABC* or its weekly air mail edition (*ABC*. Edición semanal aérea. 1949. w. $12.95. Prensa Española, S.A., Serrano 61, Madrid, Spain.) (N.H.)

Neue Zurcher Zeitung. 1780. d. $31.00. Fred Luchsinger. Falkenstrasse 11, Zurich, Switzerland. Illus., index, adv. Circ: 92,000. Vol. ends: Dec.

Aud: Ga, Ac. *Jv:* V.

Although published in Switzerland, this is the world's leading German language newspaper. In any survey it usually ranks from first to fifth among the world's best newspapers. The judgment is based on a unique approach—it shuns typical reporting, putting particular emphasis on analyses in essay-type stories. The writers, based in every major world city, give purposefully analytical treatment to political and economic developments. Currency is not as important as background and accuracy. Objectivity is sought after in gathering facts, and the newspaper tends to take a middle-of-the-road stand on questions which require some type of editorial position. It is just as apt, in one day, to come down as hard on anti-Communists as on Communists, but it leans toward a relatively conservative line. An average tabloid-size issue of 40 to 60 pages devotes a good part of its space to international news and finance. At least one page in each issue is given over to literature and art. A basic—in fact, many consider it *the* basic—newspaper for the library where there is a strong interest in political science and economics.

La Opinion. d. (Except Sunday). $24. 1436 S. Main St., Los Angeles, Calif. 90015.

The Spanish-language daily newspaper of Los Angeles, this has national and international coverage.

Another California Spanish-language newspaper is *La Prensa* (w. $2. 2973 Sacramento St., Berkeley, Calif. 94702). News of local interest in Spanish for residents of northern California's East Bay. Formerly *La Prensa Libre*. (K.R.)

Pravda (Truth). 1912. d. $5.40. Organ of the Central Committee of the Communist Party of the Soviet Union. Ul. "Pravdy," 24, Moscow, A-47, USSR.

Aud: Ac, Ga.

The second-largest Russian newspaper with a large staff of foreign correspondents and many editions in major cities of the USSR. As the official publication of the Communist party of the Soviet Union, its contents reflect the party line throughout. The texts of official reports, speeches of government officials, and announcements of the various party committees are printed in full. National news and activities of the Party in all parts of the Soviet Union take up the greater part of the paper. Foreign news is covered in a regular column on the last page under the heading *Mir segodnia* ("The World Today"). Next to it, a commentator in a column called *Kolonka commentatora* ("The Corner of the Commentator") discusses a particular news item in great detail. The special heading and heavier print draw the reader's attention, indicating the importance of the issue under discussion. Usually, a large political cartoon, frequently directed against the United States, is a regular feature of this page. Articles on the cultural aspects of Soviet life, including poems and literary criticism, also reflect the viewpoint of the Party. Television, radio, and theater programs and schedules are given, as well as the weather. Illustrations include a variety of photos, as well as some drawings of good quality. An occasional satirical story represents the lighter side of life in the Soviet Union. Recommended for the larger public library and the academic library as the official voice of the Communist party. (E.L.)

La Prensa. See *La Opinion.*

Sunday Times. w. $41.60. ($85/air). 200 Grey's Inn Rd., London, England. Circ: 1,501,000.

Indexed: Self-index. *Aud:* Ga, Ac.

The *Sunday Times* comes closer to our *National Observer* in that it is more a summary of the week's news than another daily paper which happens to fall on Sunday. It is part of the *Times* group, but independent editorially of the daily *Times.* (The Association is something like the Luce chain of command; i.e., *Time, Life, Fortune* are all owned by the same company, but have different editorial staffs and approaches. Other members of the Associated Times Newspapers are the *Times Educational Supplement* and the *Times Literary Supplement.*) Again, the *Sunday Times* is not near the size of the Sunday *New York Times,* but is noteworthy

for its summary of theater, art, music, etc. Many of its feature writers make up the elite of the English writing corps. There is also a *Sunday Times Magazine,* which is fair to good; it includes stories on all aspects of English life. Libraries that cannot afford the daily *Times* might look into taking the *Sunday Times.*

In addition to the *Sunday Times* and the weekly *Guardian,* Britain's two other leading international newspapers, which many consider at least equal to the *Times* and the *Guardian,* are the *Observer* and the *Daily Telegraph.* Both often make journalist's lists of the world's best, and should be considered by larger American libraries.

The Times. 1785. d. (Except Sunday). $86. ($152/air). Printing House Square, London EC4, England. Subs. to: 201 E. 42nd St., New York, N.Y. 10017. Circ: 400,000. Microform: Self-filmed.

Indexed: Self-index. *Aud:* Ga, Ac. *Jv:* V.

The best known of all the British newspapers. The daily edition differs considerably from American counterparts, particularly from the *New York Times,* in that there is less advertising, and therefore less bulk. The *Times* tends to cover national and European matters in detail, is not so involved with American events. There are excellent sections on theater, books, films, stocks, television, etc. The tone is relatively conservative, yet objective. It contrasts with the majority of English newspapers, which, to say the least, are sensational in both content and makeup. A basic newspaper for any library which is involved with more than the local scene.

Die Welt. 1946. d. $50. Axel Springer, 36 Kaiser-Wilhelm Str., Hamburg 2, Germany.

Aud: Ga, Ac.

One of the major publications of Axel Springer, who is often accused of holding a virtual monopoly over the German middle-class press. News coverage is more comprehensive than in most European papers. The writing style is clear, and the whole comes close to the average well-edited American newspaper. With a circulation of over a million, it tends to be conservative in its approach and during the student revolts of 1968 came under heavy fire from the Left. Nevertheless, it enjoys a good reputation for its international coverage of politics, economics, and business. The 20 to 30 page daily boasts more pictures, certainly a more lively layout, than any other European newspaper. The large circulation is due to its wide coverage, and its focus on international issues gives it a special place abroad; it is also welcomed by many for stories on everything from sports and automobiles to stars and education. *Die Welt,* therefore, serves a real need for the average reader. It can be recommended, too, for advanced high school German classes, although teachers should point out its political attitudes.

Special Interest

See also News and Opinion Magazines/Political Opinion Reviews.

Advertising Age; the national newspaper of marketing. 1930. w. $10. J. J. Graham. Advertising Publns., Inc., 740 N. Rush St., Chicago, Ill. 60611. Illus., adv. Circ: 66,000. Sample. Vol. ends: Dec. Microform: UM.

Indexed: BusI, PsyAb. *Bk. rev:* 8–10, short. *Aud:* Ac, Ga.

The title of this excellent weekly paper is a bit deceptive; it is more than advertising. A typical issue includes articles, data, and briefs on all aspects of the nation's business. More importantly, it has considerable information on trends in television, broadcasting, newspapers, and other media. All that is recent and upcoming in the field of national sales and advertising and international news is presented. Personnel shifts, account changes, important rating figures, new products, and convention news are given through regular columns. There is often coverage of controversial subjects, interviews, and speeches, which makes the paper useful for students. During the year, six to eight large topical issues concentrate on a single subject, such as "Market Data" or "Leading Advertisers."

Army Times. 1940. w. $12. Tony March. Circ: 205,000. *Air Force Times.* 1947. w. $10. Ed Gates. Circ: 186,000. *Navy Times: Marine Corps, Navy, Coast Guard.* 1951. w. $12. John Slinkman. Circ: 116,631. All published by Army Times Publishing Co., 475 Schools St., S.W., Washington, D.C. 20024. Illus., index, adv. Microform: UM.

Aud: Ga.

The three basic, weekly tabloid newspapers by and for armed forces personnel and their families. (There's even a biweekly colored supplement, *Family,* which corresponds to the familiar *Parade.*) Although each of the papers has a separate editorial staff and policy, they basically approach news and events in the same way: emphasis is on noncontroversial, factual material. Where controversy does arise, the papers, quite naturally, come down on the side of the armed forces. And, by the by, from time to time they can be critical of such things as army housing, the PX system, salaries, etc. The papers make an effort to report on the nitty gritty of the military life, and all three are excellent sources of information for laymen as well as armed force personnel. There is, for example, no better place to get a rundown on the military budget and what it means to the average man or woman in the field. The writing is good, the style a bit flamboyant, yet generally accurate. Each is obviously an important part of any library serving the military forces. (There is a U.S., Pacific, and European edition of each.)

Barron's National Business and Financial Weekly. 1921. w. $21. Robert Bleiberg. Dow Jones & Co., Inc., 200 Burnett Rd., Chicopee, Mass. 01021. Adv. Circ: 237,946. Microform: NYPL.

Indexed: BusI. *Aud:* Ga, Ac.

This newspaper publication of Dow Jones (which also publishes the *Wall Street Journal*) has a decidedly conservative tone. Every issue contains a long laissez-faire editorial—against government regulation, proarmament, anti-Communist, and antiriot—the sometimes evangelical tone of which may lessen its validity for those used to a more rational tone from conservative writers. It contains objective articles on specific businesses or industries—e.g., merchandising, oil, electronics—which spell out the financial ups and downs of each. There is much business advertising, investment information, a book review of interest to financiers, a Wall Street section ("Up and Down Wall Street"), and a statistical section with weekly national and international market data. Political viewpoint aside, this is one of the basic business newspapers which should be taken by larger libraries. (R.B.)

Billboard; the international music-record newsweekly. 1894. w. $35. Leo Zhito. Billboard Publishing Co., 165 W. 46th St., New York, N.Y. 10006. Illus., adv. Circ: 33,000. Microform: UM.

Indexed: MusicI. *Aud:* Ac, Ga, Hs.

A newspaper for the businessman and advertiser concerned with publishing, recording, and selling music. Its value to laymen lies in its comprehensive coverage. It is the best single source of information on new albums, tapes, performers, and pop music. There are sections on country, gospel, and classical music; musical instruments; audio retailing; machines; and radio and TV programs. The writing style is similar to that of *Variety.* Although of limited value to smaller libraries, it is a must in larger public and academic libraries. High school librarians with a little extra money and imagination might try it for a season, too. It is bound to be a hit.

The Black Panther. Intercommunal News Service (Formerly: *The Black Panther*). 1964. s-m. $7.50. Huey P. Newton. Ministry of Information, Black Panther Party, Box 2976, Custom House, San Francisco, Calif. 94126. Illus. Circ: 100,000.

Indexed: API. *Aud:* Ac, Ga. *Jv:* V.

A 24-page tabloid newspaper which represents the voice of the strongest and most controversial black militant group in America. Despite divisions and splits among the leaders, e.g., the Eldridge Cleaver–Huey Newton controversy, the leadership is still dedicated to militant, political change. And the newspaper continues to enjoy a wide readership among Blacks, not to mention whites who do not necessarily agree with all policies and statements of the party. A typical issue focuses on methods of "Combatting American Fascism" via illustrated opinion articles from officials and correspondents throughout the country. This emphasis on revolutionary journalism, coupled with cartoons and illustrations, makes it more a magazine than a typical newspaper. The magazine/newspaper is well edited, has a good format, and is filled with information simply not found elsewhere; e.g., the September 4, 1971, issue was given over to a full discussion of the George Jackson slaying. The unfiltered, admittedly biased view makes this an absolute requirement in any library serving Blacks and politically oriented whites.

The Commercial and Financial Chronicle. 1839. s-w. $95. George J. Morrissey. William B. Dana Co., 25 Park Pl., New York, N.Y. 10007. Illus., index, adv. Circ: 10,000. Microform: UM.

Indexed: BusI. *Aud:* Ga, Ac.

This newspaper is for those interested in business, economics, and the international monetary system; it is definitely for a more specialized audience than that of the *Wall Street Journal.* A general news and advertising issue comes out every Thursday, and a complete statistical issue, containing market quotation records, securities, mutual funds, corporation news, bank clearings, state and city bond proposals, and the like, appears every Monday. Articles in the Thursday issue, written by professors of economics, corporation executives, and government economists, are long, theoretical, and deal with current problems. Noteworthy among Thursday's regular features are "Washington and You"; "The Security I Like Best," a weekly forum in which a group of experts in the field give reasons for favoring a particular security; calendar of "Coming Events in the Investment Field"; and "Dealer-Broker Investment Literature and Recommendations," listing materials available for the asking. Front-page articles in recent issues include "The New Dimensions of the OTC Market" and "The Commonwealth of Puerto Rico". (R.B.)

Grit. 1882. w. $7. Kenneth D. Rhone. Grit Publishing Co., 208 W. 3rd St., Williamsport, Pa., 17701. Illus., adv. Circ: 1,300,000. Sample. Vol. ends: Dec. 12.

Aud: Ga.

Although this has a tabloid newspaper format, it is a general magazine. (*Grit* was somewhat ahead, to say the least, of such tabloid newspaper/magazine formats as *Rolling Stone.*) The magazine "is edited for small town families," and has succeeded in attracting a large audience. No other weekly has quite that low price. No other weekly offers so much for everyone—features on food, fashion, and beauty hints for women; articles on sports, fishing, and hunting for the men; and a scattering of departments which range from a weekly sermon to comics. It is written for the relatively conservative American, and while long on family items is short on controversial material. (There is, however, an ongoing concern with the environment and the government of small towns—a definite plus.) One reader says it reminds her of the *Saturday Evening Post* and *Colliers* in the 1930s. And although in the last edition this was considered a last purchase, second thought and more familiarity with the publication leads to a more charitable conclusion—if your library is in a small town and the average reader is looking more for entertainment and information than enlightenment and well-rounded reports, it probably would be among the firsts for consideration. Larger libraries need not bother.

Maine Times; Maine environmental weekly. 1968. w. $10. John N. Cole, 13 Main St., Topsham, Maine 04086. Illus., adv. Circ: 13,000 Sample. Vol. ends: Sept.

Bk. rev: 1–2, 300–2,000 words, signed. *Aud:* Ga, Ac, Hs.

In tabloid newspaper format, a major portion of each issue is devoted to in-depth studies of environmental and related problems that directly affect Maine; e.g., the destruction of an 1,800-acre lake by effluent from an egg farm, a successful summer natural history course for children in Milbridge, problems in distribution of surplus foods in one county, the protection of offshore island birdlife, and the need for governmental controls over coastal development are featured in a recent issue. Also included are news briefs about specific pollution problems, letters to the editor, editorials, and critical reviews of drama, music, movies, etc., in the state. Although it is obviously devoted entirely to Maine problems, similar situations exist throughout the nation; hence, it can be recommended for all libraries concentrating on building environmental collections.

Muhammad Speaks. 1960. w. $10.40. Muhammads Mosque No. 2, 436 E. 79th St., Chicago, Ill. 60619. Illus., index, adv. Circ: 530,000. Sample.

The voice of Elijah Muhammad and the Black Muslims. Since its founding it has become more radical, more news oriented. A typical tabloid 32-page issue (which is often sold on the streets by the faithful) opens with news in brief and articles on current events (prison reform, police, and racial matters are usually found here), moves to reporting events in cities from Chicago and Detroit to the west coast, and turns over the last half or quarter to features such as "What Islam Has Done for Me." There is usually a long piece by Elijah Muhammad. The essentially puritanical outlook of the faithful shades every story. The "cesspool of modern living" is a favored subject. Nonviolence is stressed, too, as is the belief that God will take care of evil. It is a required item in any black community where there are any followers of the faith, and should be in all large academic and public libraries—not only for readers, but for its value as a view of ongoing black culture.

Romano Drom; Gypsy newspaper. q. $1.50. Jeremy Sandford and Ruth Templeton. 66a Deodar Rd., London SW15, England.

Aud: Ac.

"The Gypsy calls the whole world his home," says Kirsten Cubitt, "and finds it inhospitable" (*Times*, Feb. 2, 1972, p. 8). Despite centuries-long depredations, reaching their most terrible pitch in the Nazi destruction of some half-million Romanies, today's "traveller"—according to the Romani Institute—"has nearly 10 million brothers." A few *gaujos*, like Jean-Paul Clebert, Cubitt, and contributors to the June 1971 *Race Today*, have written sympathetically about the Gypsies' history, lifeways, and current plight. Most people, however—in Cubitt's words—"treat them with a heady mixture of petty persecution, contempt, and a kind of savage envy" (reflected in the Library of Congress subject scheme's callous, myth-strengthening cross-reference from "Rogues and vagabonds"). Other Anglophile vehicles may now deal less fictitiously and patronizingly with actual Gypsies, but none, not even the venerable Gypsy Lore Society *Journal*, could possibly compete with *Romano Drom* as a wholly authentic, prideful, and aggressive organ of contemporary Romanies themselves. As one woman who earlier "left the road" declares in a letter: "I was delighted that someone had the courage to speak out publicly about the unjust treatment of Gypsies. I felt like going down on my knees and thanking God that they were spoken of as human beings for a change." All subscription profits from the tabloid-format, photo-illustrated *Drom* "go back to Gypsies." The paper itself concentrates heavily, but not exclusively, on the British scene; issue no. 5, e.g., carries a two-page spread on last year's World Romani Congress, as well as letters from as far afield as Quebec and New Zealand. Additional features range from Romani-authored verse to publication notes and addresses of active Gypsy organizations. Nearly everyone harbors an interest in Gypsies, even if rooted in foolishly romantic or jealously malign fancies about what they were and are. Libraries investing in a subscription to *Romano Drom* would effectively respond to that widespread interest with a publication that faithfully conveys the vigorous spirit, cultural richness, and latter-day travails of a large and significant people. (S.B.)

Variety. 1905. w. $20. Abel Green. Variety, Inc., 154 W. 46th St., New York, N.Y. 10036. Illus., adv. Sample. Vol. ends: 13th issue.

Indexed: MusicI. *Aud:* Ga, Ac.

This is the official newspaper of show business, complete with clever headlines. The language is peculiar to the magazine, which echoes the language used in the entertainment field. Sections on movies, radio and television, music and records, and even vaudeville are included, along with news of the theater world. In addition to general news items of the stage, the "legitimate" section contains reviews of on-and-off-Broadway shows and shows abroad, information on casting, the amount of money grossed each week by Broadway and road shows, and where touring shows are playing. *Variety* is a necessity in large public and college libraries for its complete coverage of all areas of the entertainment world. It might even create interest in high schools with the top records of the week—both singles and albums. (C.B.)

The Wall Street Journal. 1889. d. (Except Saturday and Sunday). $35. Fred Taylor. Dow Jones & Co., Inc., 30 Broad St., New York, N.Y. 10004. Index, adv. Circ: 1,261,568. Microform: UM.

Indexed: PAIS. *Bk. rev:* 3/wk., signed. *Aud:* Ga, Ac. *Jv:* V.

The *Wall Street Journal* offers to the alert reader considerably more than a complete report on today's business. As it must report facts, not opinion or biases, its business news coverage is the best anywhere. Every issue contains three lengthy front-page articles about business news and news that affects business in its widest possible form. The editorial page contains some conservative opinion, another large article on almost any subject, and signed book and drama reviews, which are quite good. The more general news articles throughout the paper, on legislation being considered in Congress, for example, are recommended to everyone. About half of an average issue is devoted to advertising. This newspaper, geared to the world of business, is free of the cant and ravings often found in local less sophisticated journals. It should be a basic choice for public and academic libraries. Sample copies, too, should be available in high school libraries. (R.B.)

The Wall Street Transcript. 1963. w. $240/yr. Richard A. Holman. Wall St. Reports and Intelligence Bulletin, Inc. 54 Wall St., New York, N.Y. 10005. Microform: UM.

Aud: Ac, Ga.

Three quarters of the space in "the world's most expensive newspaper" is occupied by reprints of (1) company studies, industry surveys, and other reports issued by brokerage houses, and (2) presentations by company executives to meetings of security analysts. Business libraries which subscribe are spared the difficult job of maintaining files of brokerage house recommendations, except for those of the few brokers whose releases are excluded (e.g., Spencer Trask) and those issued exclusively to institutional clients. Original material which occupies the remaining space includes (1) the highly readable transcripts of weekly discussions, by editor Holman and a group of leading analysts, of a "hot" investment area (e.g., investing in the mobile home industry), and (2) a "Connoisseur Corner" concerned with investments in things rather than paper (e.g., French wines). It is well indexed. Libraries able to subscribe find copies are well worn by the end of the week. (R.B.)

Women's Wear Daily. 1910. 5/wk. $30. Fairchild Publns., Inc., 7 E. 12th St., New York, N.Y. 10003. Illus., adv. Circ: 85,000.

Aud: Ga, Ac.

The gossipy trade sheet of the retail fashion industry. Originally known and read only by retailers, it has apparently become the *Variety* of the fashion world; if one cares what the "beautiful people" are wearing and how much they paid for it, one has to keep up with *Women's Wear Daily.* In a field which depends so much on the whim and caprice of the elite—those who can afford to center their lives around their wardrobe—it is not surprising that the trade paper be whimsical and capricious, not to mention sometimes vicious and arbitrary. From the point of view of retailers, *WWD* fulfills its function of appraising changing fashions and buying trends, and reporting on practices of successful retailers, as well as presenting other pertinent news. The "extras" include a gossip column; one or two pages of theater, film, and arts reviews; and a general preoccupation with money and status. (M.M.)

Newspaper Indexes

California News Index. 1970. bi-w. Service. Subs. on request. Center for Calif. Public Affairs, 226 W. Foothill Blvd., Claremont, Calif. 91711.

Aud: Ac, Ga.

A six to ten page index of articles appearing in California newspapers which deal with California government and politics, business, social issues, educational affairs, travel, history, personalities, etc. The twice-monthly index covers these newspapers: *Los Angeles Times, Sacramento Bee, San Francisco Chronicle, San Francisco Examiner, San Diego Union, San Jose Mercury.* It also indexes in part seven magazines: *California Journal, Los Angeles Magazine, San Francisco Magazine, San Diego Magazine, Sunset, Westways,* and *Cry California.* The major problem is that the index touches only the high spots, concentrates primarily on political and social issues. Arrangement is by some 30 broad subject headings. But it is better than nothing, and with time may expand. Well worth a subscription (inquire as to price) for larger libraries, and all California libraries.

Christian Science Monitor Index. 1960. m. with annual cum. $20. Univ. Microfilms, 300 N. Zeeb Rd., Ann Arbor, Mich. 48106.

A useful index, with page citations for all four editions. It is not as detailed as the indexes for the *New York Times* or the London *Times.* Approach must be by subject; no authors are provided. (D.D.)

National Observer Index. 1969. a. $18. Dow Jones & Co., Inc., P.O. Box 300, Princeton, N.J. 08540.

A comprehensive index for this newspaper. Orientation is to the specific subject of the article. (D.D.)

New York Times Index. 1851. s-m. $87.50; annual cum. $87.50; combined $150. N.Y. Times, Times Sq., New York. 10036.

Not only does this index the *Times,* but for each major entry there is a short summary of content. Hence, it is a valued reference tool even without the newspaper. (D.D.)

Newspaper Index. 1972. m. with annual cum. $785. ($275/section). Bell & Howell Co., Old Mansfield Rd., Wooster, Ohio 44691.

A new service that indexes the *Chicago Tribune, Los Angeles Times, New Orleans Times-Picayune,* and *Washington Post.* It is available as separate sections or for all four papers in a combined edition. The arrangement is by subject, with separate listing of the names of people included in the indexed newspapers for that period. Essential for libraries that subscribe to the newspapers. (D.D.)

The Times (London). 1906. bi-m. $73. The Times, Printing House Sq., London EC4, England.

Not as detailed as the *New York Times Index,* but there are as many specific references. The relative infrequency of appearance works against this as an immediate reference tool, but it is excellent for retrospective researches.

Wall Street Journal Index. m. $75; annual cum. $75; combined $125. Dow Jones Books, P.O. Box 300, Princeton, N.J. 08540.

Particularly suited for business collections, but as there are numerous feature and general news stories in the paper, the index is also an invaluable reference tool. Index is for the eastern edition, possibly a handicap in other areas. (D.D.)

OCEANOGRAPHY

Basic Periodicals

Hs: *Sea Frontiers* (See also *Oceanus*); Ga: *Sea Frontiers, Oceans;* Ac: *Deep-Sea Research and Oceanographic Abstracts, Limnology and Oceanography, Journal of Physical Oceanography, Journal of Marine Research, Marine Biology, Marine Chemistry, Marine Geology.* (Note: First-choice for Ocean Engineering collections would be *Marine Technology Society. Journal, Ocean Engineering,* and *Ocean Industry.*

Basic Abstracts and Indexes
Oceanic Abstracts

Introduction

In the first edition, selected journals relating to oceanography were incorporated in the section on Earth Sciences. An entire section is now dedicated to this discipline for a number of reasons. Oceanography has rightly been called "the last frontier on Earth available for exploration." This concept has been abetted by massive programs supported by the Federal Government, including the establishment of the National Oceanic and Atmospheric Administration, the Sea-Grant program, etc. In academic institutions, including many inland universities, traditional courses of study are being supplanted by curricula in oceanography and ocean engineering. Even elementary school earth science classes focus far more on the oceans than a decade ago. The following is a representative sampling of the literature available on the marine sciences, including biological and physical oceanography, and ocean engineering. Some of the periodicals will be of interest to public and school libraries.

Academy of Sciences of the USSR. Oceanology. 1965. bi-m. $75. Ed. bd. Amer. Geophysical Union, 2100 Pennsylvania Ave., N.W., Washington, D. C. 20037. Illus., index. Circ: 350. Vol. ends: no. 6. Refereed. *Aud:* Sa, Ac.

Supersedes *Soviet Oceanography,* which also covered an English translation of *Trudy Marne Hydrophysical Institute.* The present journal is a cover-to-cover English translation of the oceanology section of *Doklady,* the well-known *Proceedings of the Academy of Sciences of the USSR.* This journal is the vehicle through which the best oceanographic research is reported from Russia. All aspects of oceanography are covered, including biological and physical oceanography, methodology and instrumentation, and information about new oceanographic ships and cruises. Most research collections will need it, although the journal will hardly be a first-choice selection for small, academic libraries. Unlike other translations of sections of *Doklady,* however (e.g., those of Consultants Bureau), there is no correlation between Russian pagination and English pages of the translation, nor any indication of the time lag in translation, which is a real inconvenience for reference librarians.

Aquatic Sciences and Fisheries Abstracts. See Abstracts and Indexes Section.

✓ *Biological Bulletin.* See Biological Sciences Section.

Deep-Sea Research and Oceanographic Abstracts. 1953. m. $85. Mary Sears and Mary Swallow. Pergamon Pr., Maxwell House, Fairview Pk., Elmsford, N.Y. 10523. Illus., index. Sample. Vol. ends: No. 12. Refereed. Microform: Maxwell. Reprint: Maxwell.

Indexed: BioAb, ChemAb, Met&GeoAb, SCI. *Bk. rev:* 1–2, 500 words, signed. *Aud:* Sa, Ac.

The journal was originally conceived by the Joint Commission on Oceanography of the International Council of Scientific Union as a medium for drawing together related studies on the deep sea. Research papers consider various facets of the field and report on morphology and stratigraphy of the sea floor; properties of sediments; the fauna which inhabit the deep sea; and the organisms, processes, and instrumentation important to it. Issued along with the journal proper is its bimonthly supplement, *Deep-Sea Research Oceanographic Abstracts and Oceanographic Bibliography Section.* Abstracts are provided in all phases of physical, biological, and chemical oceanography, submarine geology, etc. The journal, along with its bibliographic supplement, is an authoritative and primary one for every oceanography collection.

Journal of Hydronautics. 1967. q. $12. John P. Breslin. Amer. Inst. of Aeronautics and Astronautics, 1290 Ave. of the Americas, New York, N. Y. 10019. Illus., index. Circ: 2,200. Sample. Vol. ends: no. 4 (Oct.). Refereed.

Indexed: IntAe, SCI. *Aud:* Sa, Ac.

A technical journal dedicated to the science and engineering of "all types of marine craft, installations, and instrumentation devised to explore the oceans of the world." Primarily concerned with the hydromechanics of propulsion and the methods for mobility of marine vessels and submersibles, the publication is a good, representative journal for indicating one type of study undertaken under the broad heading "ocean engineering." Some papers deal with environmental characteristics of the oceans, e.g., currents, acoustical properties, and the like. The AIAA sponsors several other journals in aeronautics and astronautics, also concerned with problems of propulsion and guidance of craft through air and space, as well as the oceans. For technical collections.

Journal of Marine Research. 1937. 3/yr. $15. Yngve H. Olsen. Rm. 129, Osborn Memorial Lab., Yale Univ., New Haven, Conn. 06520. Illus., index. Circ: 1,300. Sample. Vol. ends: no. 3. Refereed.

Indexed: BioAb, ChemAb, Met&GeoAb, SciAb, SCI. *Aud:* Sa, Ac.

Published by the Sears Foundation for Marine Research, the journal is dedicated to research papers covering all aspects of oceanographic work, including biological, chemical, geological, and physical oceanography. In addition to full-length original articles, a small section in each issue contains short reports on "tools of oceanography." Discussions of previously published papers are also included. An important and authoritative journal for oceanography collections.

Journal of Physical Oceanography. 1971. q. $20. Robert O. Reid. Amer. Meteorological Soc., 45 Beacon St., Boston, Mass. 02108. Illus., index. Vol. ends: no. 4. Refereed.

Indexed: OceanAb., Met&GeoAb. *Aud:* Sa, Ac.

The newest in the long line of publications put out by the American Meteorological Society is concerned largely with the "physics and chemistry of the ocean, and of the processes operating at its boundaries." Concentrating, thus, on the air-sea interface, the topics of the research articles range from studies of internal waves in the deep ocean, through oceanic upwelling off the coasts of continents. An authoritative research journal combining elements of both physical oceanography and atmospheric sciences. For academic libraries.

Limnology and Oceanography. 1956. bi-m. $20. Yvette H. Edmondson. Allen Press, Lawrence, Kans. 66044. Illus., index. Circ: 3,400. Vol. ends: no. 6 (Nov.). Refereed.

Indexed: BioAb, ChemAb, Met&GeoAb, SCI. *Bk. rev:* 4, 200 words, signed. *Aud:* Sa, Ac.

In this official journal of the American Society of Limnology and Oceanography, research papers and short notes are concerned with biological and physical studies of lakes and oceans. Included in the physical reports are investigations in the area of marine geology as well as physical oceanography. The main portion of the journal concentrates on biological oceanography, in particular algae, plankton, chemistry of marine organisms, and the like. An authoritative research journal for oceanography collections.

Marine Biology. 1968. $38.50/v. O. Kinne. Springer-Verlag, 175 Fifth Ave., New York, N. Y. 10010. Illus., index, adv. Sample. Vol. ends: no. 4. Refereed.

Indexed: SCI. *Bk. rev:* Occasional, signed. *Aud:* Sa, Ac.

A scholarly and authoritative publication contributing to the literature of the zoology, botany, and microbiology of marine fauna and flora. Topics under discussion within this framework are such areas as ecological dynamics (including use of the resources of the sea, biological oceanography, water pollution); experimental ecology and physiology (e.g., effects of environmental factors on organisms); molecular biology and biochemistry as related to marine life; biogeography or distribution of marine organisms. For both oceanography collections and good collections in the biological sciences.

Marine Chemistry. 1972. q. $27. K. E. Chave. Elsevier Publishing Co., Box 211, Amsterdam, The Netherlands. Illus., index. Sample. Vol. ends: no. 4. Refereed.

Aud: Sa, Ac.

The latest in a long line of Elsevier publications dedicated to research on the marine environment and the geological sciences. This specialized journal concentrates on chemical aspects of the oceans, as well as other approaches to aquatic chemistry, including studies on instrumentation. Although it is too early to tell the focus of this new journal, the publication nonetheless promises to be an authoritative source of information for oceanographic collections. A well-known group of scientists heads the first editorial board.

Marine Geology. 1964. 10/yr. (2v./yr.) $15./v. L. M. J. U. Van Straaten and D. A. McManus. Elsevier Publishing Co., Box 211, Amsterdam, The Netherlands. Illus., index. Sample. Vol. ends: no. 5 (2v./yr.). Refereed.

Indexed: SCI. *Aud:* Sa, Ac.

A specialty publication concentrating on research papers on marine geology, geochemistry, and geophysics. Subjects carry over into all three fields and include studies on marine sediments, investigations of the sea floor, and research on ocean structures. Good geological collections will need this authoritative publication, as will oceanography collections. An even more specialized international journal along these same lines is *Marine Geophysical Researches* (D. Reidel), which is concerned with the analysis of marine structures by geophysics, sedimentary dynamics, etc.

Marine Pollution Bulletin. 1970. m. $11.17. R. B. Clark. Macmillan Journals, Ltd., Little Essex St., London, England. Illus., adv. Circ: 1,200. Sample. Vol. ends: no. 12. Refereed.

Aud: Sa, Ac.

Capitalizing on the current environmental crisis, the publication not only offers news and commentary on the agents polluting the world's lakes, estuaries, seas, and oceans, but also includes short, 1,000-word research-styled reports, including management of the resources of the oceans, as well as the dangers to marine life. Topics under recent discussion have covered oil spills, pesticides in the sea, and pollution of European waters. Each issue of about 16 pages contains two or three research reports. Nonspecialist reviews are fully within the grasp of students and interested laymen. An international publication of interest to both environmental and oceanography collections. Recommended.

Marine Technology. 1964. q. $8. Ed. bd. Soc. of Naval Architects and Marine Engineers, 74 Trinity Pl., New York, N. Y. 10006. Illus., index. Circ: 9,000. Sample. Vol. ends: no. 4. Refereed.

Indexed: OceanAb. *Aud:* Sa, Ac.

The focus in this technical journal is on ship design, shipbuilding, and ship-operating systems. While not immediately considered a part of ocean engineering, there are enough areas in naval architecture intimately related to it (e.g., design of submersibles to support ocean engineering, or reliability and maintaining of shipboard systems), which would make the publication a mandatory extension for ocean engineering collections. About seven to eight technical articles appear in each issue, as well as brief notices of the Society and news of its membership. (Note: other publications of SNAME include *Journal of Ship Research*, and their *Transactions*, issued annually).

Marine Technology Society. Journal. 1966. bi-m. $15. Thomas P. Meloy. Marine Technology Soc., 1730 M St., N.W., Washington, D.C. 20036. Illus., index, adv. Circ: 5,000. Vol. ends: no. 6 (Nov./Dec.). Refereed. Microform: MTS.

Indexed: Ocean Ab. *Bk. rev:* 8–10, 300 words, signed. *Aud:* Sa, Ac.

Formerly called *Journal of Ocean Technology*, the publication is the official journal of the MTS, an international organization dedicated to the advancement of studies of any aspect of the ocean: scientific, engineering, legal, resource, economic, as well as to the facilities and equipment designed to enhance these studies. The above statement about the aims of the Society does, in fact, characterize the contents of its *Journal*. Papers and short, technical notes discuss anything from a technical work on the ocean environment to surveys of manned submersibles, reviews of ocean dumping, and analyses of the law of the sea. Also included are regular monthly departments which comment on activities of interest to the profession at large, as well as to the membership. Drawing upon the expertise and subject specialties of scientists, engineers, social scientists, and legal authorities, the journal is a basic one for an interdisciplinary publication on the ocean environment. Recommended for all ocean engineering and oceanography collections.

Meerestechnik/Marine Technology. 1970. bi-m. Dieter Volk. VDI-Verlag GmbH, Dusseldorf, Germany. Subs. to: Peter Peregrinus, Ltd., P.O. Box 8, Southgate House, Stevenage, Herts, England. Illus., index, adv. Sample. Vol. ends: no. 6. Refereed.

Indexed: OceanAb. *Bk. rev:* 3, 150 words, unsigned. *Aud:* Sa, Ac.

Published for the Verein Deutscher Ingenieure, the technical journal is concerned with all aspects of ocean engineering: vehicles operating on the sea floor, equipment for marine engineering, marine geology study of sediments, design of propellers, and related topics. The usual reports from industry, and new products and services are also included. An interesting facet of this periodical is that it is a bilingual edition. Both German and English text run in parallel columns. A few paragraphs are not translated, e.g., selected book reviews, but by then, all users will have brushed up on their German. The publication is an international one, and contributions are not restricted to German studies. A valuable technical journal for ocean engineering and oceanography collections.

Ocean Engineering. 1968. bi-m. $40. Alan A. Johnson. Pergamon Press, Maxwell House, Fairview Pk., Elmsford, N.Y. 10523. Illus., index. Sample. Vol. ends: no. 6. Refereed. Microform: MR. Reprint: MR.

Indexed: OceanAb, EngI. *Aud:* Sa, Ac.

A scholarly research journal presently focusing its attention on such fields as engineering, design, and construction of submersibles or other structures on the ocean bottom; engineering properties of materials for such vehicles; stress analysis of underwater structures; soil mechanics; power and propulsion systems to propel these vehicles; and other studies appropriate to a young field whose boundaries are not as yet clearly defined. It is an interdisciplinary research journal which embraces elements of civil, materials, and mechanical engineering within its scope. For any engineering collection interested in this field.

Ocean Industry. 1966. m. $12 (Educational $6). Controlled circulation. Donald M. Taylor. Gulf Publishing Co., Box 2608, Houston, Tex. 77001. Illus., index, adv. Circ: 31,000. Sample. Vol. ends: no. 12. Microform: UM.

Indexed: OceanAb. *Bk. rev:* 3–4, 200 words, signed. *Aud:* Sa, Ac.

A trade journal specializing in "ocean/marine operations." Offshore drilling, subsea petroleum systems, supporting equipment such as diving rigs, gas and oil explorations, are all within its purview. Compared to the business-oriented *Offshore*, this trade journal is geared to the technical man, ocean engineer, diver, etc. World weather reports, and sea states for selected offshore areas are also monthly features. Main articles are usually contributed by specialists. The drift of the publication, of course, centers around the news developments, and new products and equipment. For any technical library fostering interest in this area.

Oceanic Abstracts. See Abstracts and Indexes Section.

Oceans. 1969. 6/yr. $12. Don Greame Kelley. Oceans Magazine, 125 Independence Dr., Menlo Pk., Calif. Illus. Sample. Vol. ends: no. 6.

Bk. rev: 4–5, 150 words, signed. *Aud:* Sa, Ga, Ac, Hs.

One of the newest publications "interpreting marine science for the layman." Each issue of this handsomely produced magazine can also be purchased in hard binding, a justly deserved treatment awarded to some magnificent underwater color photography. Blending biographical and geographical material with marine biology, economics with sea lore, and seagoing sculpture with underwater technology, the magazine is aimed at a general public. Some issues are dedicated to an examination of a section of the world in exhaustive detail. Articles are contributed both by scientific authorities and free lance writers, from underwater archaeologist to adventurer. The level of writing is nonspecialist and lucid; glossaries are also maintained for the uninitiated. The tone of the magazine is less concerned with the technical and instructional aspects, and more concerned with capturing the splendor of the sea, in large part through tone poems of good photography. A beautiful publication for any library which can afford it.

Oceanus. 1952. q. Free to qualified libraries and organizations. Jan Hahn. Woods Hole Oceanographic Institution, Woods Hole, Mass. 02543. Illus., index. Circ: 5,000. Sample. Vol. ends: no. 4.

Indexed: Met&GeoAb. *Aud:* Sa, Ac, Ga, Hs.

There are a few publications, available gratis, which are products of academic or oceanographic institutions, giving enough of the full flavor of oceanographic research to deserve notice by the interested librarian, student, or layman. *Oceanus,* from Woods Hole, is one of the best in this category. Short, one to two page feature articles describe, in popularly written style, the various types of research carried out in oceanographic cruises: geophysical studies, sedimentology, geochemistry, marine biology, and related types of research. Selected issues also carry book reviews, or checklists, screening the best of the breed for popular material in oceanography, as well as the more technical literature. Nicely illustrated contributions are all from the scientists at WHOI. Recommended for any type of library.

Offshore. 1954. m. $5. Controlled circulation. Robert G. Burke. Petroleum Publishing Co., Box 66909, Houston, Tex. 77006. Illus., index, adv. Circ: 11,000. Sample. Vol. ends: no. 12. Microform: UM.

Indexed: OceanAb. *Aud:* Sa, Ac.

Subtitled "the journal of ocean business," the major focus of this trade journal (one of the many publications produced by the Petroleum Publishing Co.) is on offshore technology: gas and oil discoveries, offshore drilling, deepwater rigs, floating platform construction, underwater devices, and other marine constructions. With emphasis less on the technical and more on the business aspect, the magazine includes sales and marketing information, international news, statistical data (e.g., number of rigs under construction), imports-exports, etc. It is the most useful U.S. trade journal concerned with offshore services. Professionals in the field will need it for the news bits, as will ocean engineering collections and other technical libraries interested in this field.

Offshore Technology. 1969. 4/yr. Scientific Surveys, 4 Burkes Parade, Beaconsfield, Bucks, England. Illus. Sample.

Indexed: OceanAb. *Aud:* Sa, Ac.

A British-based technical magazine "devoted to underwater exploration and engineering." Issues cover news, events, developments in drilling, diving, production, techniques, and services which supply the basis for work in ocean engineering and offshore exploration. Less a trade journal than a survey-type service, the magazine culls both technical, economic, and marketing information, with emphasis on the United Kingdom and Europe, as well as the United States. Ocean engineering collections will want it, as will any type of technical library active in the field. (Note: the same publisher puts out *Offshore Europe,* which concentrates more on international marketing studies.)

Sea Frontiers. 1954. 6/yr. $7.50. F. G. Walton Smith. Intl. Oceanographic Foundation, 10 Rickenbacker Causeway, Virginia Key, Miami, Fla. 33149. Illus., index. Circ: 70,000. Vol. ends: no. 6.

Indexed: BioAb, Met&GeoAb, RG. *Bk. rev:* 9–12, 200 words, signed. *Aud:* Sa, Ac, Ga, Ejh, Hs.

Excellently illustrated with some good color photography, the magazine still remains the best popular periodical for interpretations and "extension of human knowledge of oceans," including the science of the sea, its technologies in ocean exploration, and its exploitation for economic resources. Articles are generally contributed by experts, yet the level of sophistication of the magazine has been toned down to serve the interests of the general public as well as the student. A good book review section also separates the technical text from the popular works. Accompanying each issue is the insert, "Sea Secrets," an educational service (mailed to schools at cost) in the form of a question-answer aid about aspects of oceanography. One of the few authoritative, yet popular magazines in this dramatically growing area of science, and a first choice for any type of library.

Undersea Technology. 1960. m. $10. Controlled circulation. Larry L. Booda. Compass Publns., Inc., Suite 1000, 1117 N. 19th St., Arlington, Va. 22209. Illus., index, adv. Circ: 30,000. Sample. Vol. ends: Dec. Microform: UM.

Indexed: EngI, OceanAb. *Aud:* Sa, Ac.

With the assimilation of *Oceanology International Offshore Technology,* the magazine has now emerged as one of the chief U.S. trade journals in its field. The thrust of the periodical is in ocean engineering, including such areas as undersea defense, underwater exploration, undersea construction, drilling, and ocean mining. Some issues center around one theme, e.g., underwater photography. Useful feature articles, most of them contributed by the editorial staff, are written in nonspecialist language, so as to be intelligible to the interested layman. Reports of trends from government, industry, academia, and new products, exhibits, etc., ferret out the significant news developments for the professional concerned with marine science. This is a good information source for ocean engineering and oceanography collections. The budget-minded librarian, however, might try to obtain it through controlled circulation, rather than spend the subscription price on a slim, 40-page trade journal. (Note: the publishers also put out *UST Washington Letter of Oceanography*, recently incorporating the weekly *SEAS*, aimed at a business clientele.)

Underwater Journal and Information Bulletin. 1969. bi-m. $56. A. C. Hawkins. IPC Science and Technology Press, Ltd., IPC House, 32 High St., Guildford, Surrey, England. Illus., index, adv. Circ: 900. U.S. Subs. to: 300 E. 42nd St., New York, N.Y. 10017. Sample. Vol. ends: no. 6. Refereed.

Indexed: OceanAb. *Bk. rev:* 5–6, 350 words, signed. *Aud:* Sa, Ac.

Formed by the marriage of *Underwater Science and Technology Journal* and *Underwater Science and Technology Information Bulletin,* the publication, under the above title, is still issued in two parts, with a bipartite purpose also. Its *Journal* contains a few technical articles and nonspecialist review papers concerned with any aspect of the undersea environment, including research, engineering, education, industry and government news, supported by general news commentaries. A good department is the patent review, which provides, in one evaluative essay, recent technological advances in equipment and instrumentation. The second part of the publication, *Information Bulletin,* is a quick, classified index to recent literature in the field. Some of the subject breakdowns are worth repeating here to indicate the scope of the publication: marine biology, geology, geophysics, hydrology, oceanography, diving, surface vessels and submersibles, pollution, navigation, communications. A well-organized technological and review publication, a far cut above the trade journals, for oceanography and ocean engineering collections.

OCCULT AND WITCHCRAFT

See also Parapsychology Section.

Ambix. 1937. 3/yr. $7.80. W. A. Smeaton. Univ. College, Dept. of History & Philosophy of Science, London WC1E 6BT, England. Illus., index.

Indexed: ChemAb. *Bk. rev:* Various number, length. *Aud:* Ac, Ga.

Published by the Society for the Study of Alchemy and Early Chemistry, this is both a historical and a technical chemical journal. An average issue (there are three numbers a year, which cumulate into a single volume) includes scholarly articles on the social, scientific, and philosophical aspects of alchemy, as well as scientific studies of early chemical experiments. It requires knowledge of chemistry to understand, but

here and there are articles and parts of articles which will be understood by the dedicated amateur alchemist. (No. Barbara, no one has yet come up with the formula for the philosopher's stone.)

Green Egg. 1966. 8/yr. $5. Tim Zell. Church of All Worlds, Box 2953, St. Louis, Mo. 63130. Illus., adv. Circ: 800. Sample.

Aud: Ga.

One of the few magazines around on witchcraft, and for that reason a nice addition to any well-rounded collection. A mimeographed 40-page periodical, it is the official voice of a group professing belief in neopaganism and witchcraft. The magazine is dedicated to spreading the word. (The group's "call letters" are CAW, which should not be confused with the now defunct magazine by the same name which was the organ for the Students for a Democratic Society.) The issue examined (vol. 4, no. 43) included an article on the Aegean goddess Themis, a list of neopagan religious organizations, with common themes explained; an article on mortality and immortality by editor Tim Zell; something on the science of power; a long piece on witchcraft; a note on the principles and practice of operational magic, etc. The whole is on various colored sheets, but is clear enough typographically. I'm not so sure about the message. Several pages of letters point up that no one is sure about anything. As one of the few magazines on witchcraft—at least it seems to be tangentially so involved—it is worth examining. Send for a sample copy.

Korythalia. 1967. 13/yr. $5. Richard J. Stanewick. Feraferia, Inc., Box 691, Altadena, Calif. 91001. Circ: 50.

Aud: Ga.

A six-page mimeographed neopagan newsletter which is typical enough of the genre, yet untypical in that the circulation is low (or the editor more honest than most) and the writing skillful. Mr. Stanewick explains: "Korythalia is the newsletter of Feraferia, a neo-Pagan religious fellowship devoted to nature and Goddess worship and to the lyrical unification of ecology, mythology and sacrament." The copy he sent begins with an article, or question: "Do Goddesses and Gods Exist?"; turns to two pages of incantations; includes a chapter on "Notes towards an Ethnography of the Hesperides"; and finishes up with some thoughts by the editor and a full-page calendar. A natural kind of publication for the younger mystics and a few older ones, too. By the way, the editor is serious. This definitely is not a put-on.

Llewellyn. 1971. free. Ron Wright. Llewellyn Publns., Box 3383-LL1, St. Paul, Minn. 55101.

Aud: Ga. *Bk. rev:* 5 pages.

Although this is primarily a publisher's catalog (Llewellyn publications pushes everything from zodiac medallions to books on astrology), it will be of considerable interest to any library which recognizes the growing impact of the occult. Some 34 of the 50 pages are given over to articles. This single issue is centered around witchcraft. There are an interview with America's witch queen, five pages of book reviews (primarily a retrospective bibliography on witchcraft with many titles from other than the Llewellyn press), and a piece on the tarot. The authors write well, take their material seriously, and the whole has a definite impact, even for the nonbeliever.

Magic and Spells Quarterly. 1970. q. $6. Kirk Stiles. Box 1478, Hollywood, Fla. 33022. Illus. Circ: 300. Vol. ends: No. 4.

Aud: Ga, Hs, Ejh.

Although $6 seems pretty steep for a ten-page newsletter, it just may be worth it to magic fans. The issue examined included an illustrated article on "two card reverse"; a string trick; fun with dice; a bit of explained ESP, etc. The writing is clear, and the line drawings help to overcome any difficulties. The tricks seem interesting, yet simple enough for youngsters and beginning adults. And the whole has a nice feeling of fun and good will which is often lacking in more serious efforts. Despite the price, recommended for any library where there is an interest in magic.

The Occult Trade Journal; the business magazine for occult/metaphysics. 1971. m. $10. R. C. H. Parker. 15 Library Pl., Danbury, Conn. 06810. Illus., adv. Sample.

Bk. rev: 5–6, 250 words, signed. *Aud:* Ga.

If you take the occult seriously, this is equivalent to a catalog for plastic Jesus. It is a 22-page mimeographed key to business and success for "the thousands of dealers who sell astrological products and books, tarot cards, occult gift items and metaphysical supplies." The first issue (October 1971) was badly mimeographed, difficult to read, and offered at a stiff price. Still, the reader who is curious about, or believes in, the occult will find something there to overcome the bad printing job. Take, for example, an article on sales trends of tarot cards: "We have not yet peaked and the Tarot market is not yet saturated." Then come several book reviews, a short piece on the American Society of Dowsers, news items, and notes on lectures, library displays, shows, media, conferences, etc. If this were selling for about one tenth its price, or were five times as large, or were a giveaway, I'd suggest it. (On the other hand, the publisher says he's getting better equipment, so by the time this appears he may have improved. Send for a sample.)

Witchcraft & Sorcery; the modern magazine of weird tales (Formerly: *Coven 13*). 1971. bi-m. $3. Fantasy Publishing Co., 1855 W. Main St., Alhambra, Calif. 91801. Illus., adv.

Aud: Ga, Hs.

Some well-illustrated (monsters, giants, witches) 65 pulp pages feature original short stories, a long novelette, a bit of verse, and a number of items guaranteed to please the mystery show fan. It's all adult enough, although junior high kids might enjoy it, too. Limited on violence and sex, but long on suspense and the mystery of the strange, the weird. There is a rather good article on the fiction of H. P. Lovecraft, as well as shorter reviews. The prose will not win prizes, but is no worse than in many other magazines in the library. A harmless enough item to liven up a collection where there is a call for this type of material.

Witches International Craft Associates (WICA) Newsletter. 1970. 10/yr. $4. Leo L. Martello. Suite 1B, 153 W. 80th St., New York, N.Y. 10024. Illus., adv. Circ: 2,600.

Bk. rev: 3–4, 250–1,000 words, signed. *Aud:* Ga.

A processed publication of "one of the world's oldest religions, and probably one of the most persecuted minority religious groups." The 8 to 16 page newsletter is a serious matter for its publisher-editor. Articles, notes, and reviews all indicate as much. Still, it has a given fascination for the dabbler in the occult. The editor, who is in the best position to describe his unusual publication, claims his publication is "by witches, for witches, and those interested, concerned with witchcraft as the Old Religion, highly specialized. It aims to educate the public as to the truth of witchcraft as opposed to the sensationalized nonsense published in tabloid press. Primarily a religion, its worship consists of the pre-Christian Horned God and the Goddess. It is not satanism or black magic. . . . Witches don't believe in the devil." (Samples will be sent to libraries, but there is a $1 "service charge.")

The same organization publishes an annual magazine, *Witchcraft; the voice of the old religion.* (1971. $1.12/issue). The first issue had material and articles on all aspects of the art from herbs and spells to biographical sketches of prominent witches.

OCCUPATIONS AND EMPLOYMENT

Basic Periodicals

Hs: *Vocations for Social Change, American Vocational Journal;* Ga: *Vocations for Social Change, American Vocational Journal, Equal Opportunity;* Jc & Ac: *American Educational Journal, Vocations for Social Change, Equal Opportunity, American Journal of Occupational Therapy.*

Library and Teaching Aids

Occupational Outlook Quarterly.

Basic Abstracts and Indexes

Abstracts of Research, and related materials in vocational and technical education.

Cessations

Careers Today, Moderator.

American Journal of Occupational Therapy. 1956. 8/yr. Membership (Nonmembers $12.50). Cordelia Myers. Amer. Occupational Therapy Assn., 251 Park Ave. S., New York, N.Y. 10010. Illus., index, adv. Circ: 14,000. Sample. Vol. ends: Dec.

Indexed: AbVoc, CurrCont, IMed, PsyAb. *Bk. rev:* 5–10, 250–750 words, signed. *Aud:* Ac.

A technical magazine for the professional occupational therapist. An average 60 to 75 page issue contains 8 to 12 articles, short news reports, and organizational notes. Includes new approaches and techniques of practice, development of theory, research and educational activities, and professional trends. Material regarding new medical findings in any areas which would have treatment implications for occupational therapy is also included. Only for special collections.

American Vocational Journal. 1926. m. (Sept.–May). Membership (Nonmembers $4). Lowell A. Burkett. Amer. Vocational Assn., Inc., 1510 H St., N.W., Washington, D.C. 20005. Illus., adv. Circ: 50,000. Sample. Vol. ends: Dec. Microform: UM.

Indexed: AbVoc, EdI. *Bk. rev:* Various number, length. *Aud:* Ac, Hs. *Rv:* H. *Jv:* V.

A magazine of vocational-technical education issued by the American Vocational Association. The six to eight articles are directed to both administrators and teachers and guidance counselors, and include data useful not only for the vocational counselor, but also for teachers of business, distributive education, economics, industrial arts, health occupations, agriculture, and trades. Material tends to be as theoretical as practical, and there is considerable emphasis on research—a regular feature is a 10 to 20 page report on various research papers submitted by members and chapters. Other features include notes on books, a report of Washington activities, new equipment and aids to teaching, and news of the organization. A first choice for individuals and libraries dealing in this area.

Black Careers. See Blacks Section.

Careers in Business. 1952. a. $2.20. Career Publns., 685 Madison Ave., New York, N.Y. Illus., adv. *Aud:* Ac.

An annual which is primarily directed to college seniors. This publication indicates specific fields of business hiring. It is a directory of those hiring, interview schedules, etc. A bit dated after publication—about

October 1 of each year—but useful for general background information.

Careers for the Technician (1971. a. free) and *Careers in Technology* (1952. a. $2.20) are published by the same firm. Again, articles are descriptions of careers for the college graduate and/or those graduating from two-year or technical schools. Both publications show current needs and trends.

Equal Opportunity. 1969. a. $3.75. Equal Opportunity Publns., Inc., Box 202, Centerport, N.Y. 11721. Illus., adv. Circ: 12,500.

Aud: Ac, Ga.

A "tell it like it is" approach to opportunities in executive and high-echelon jobs for Blacks (and other minority groups). Interracially operated and staffed, the annual is primarily for the college student and graduate, although it has some appeal for the high school advisor as well. The primary purpose is to convince Blacks and members of other minorities that opportunities do exist, particularly for those with a college degree. Articles are written by and about prominent Blacks and others. The information is fairly free of "inspiration" and is realistic about what a young man or woman may expect. Although it is an annual, the magazine format and the importance of the effort should make it a required item in most libraries. (Note: There is considerable advertising, but this is one case when the ads help: They offer information and opportunities to potential job seekers.)

International Rehabilitation Review. 1949. q. $10. (Subscribing membership). Norman Acton and Charles Kalisky. Intl. Rehabilitation Review, 219 E. 44th St., New York, N.Y. 10017. Illus. Circ: 15,000 in English, Spanish, French, and Japanese. Vol. ends: Fourth quarter. Sample.

Aud: Ga, Ac.

Adopting the premise that "man's effort to organize the resources of society for the welfare of all is a major feature of the 20th century," the 43 affiliated and 45 associate member organizations which comprise Rehabilitation International maintain that the "development of organized services for those with special problems such as physical and mental disability is one principal result of that effort." Articles reflect the need for efficient evaluation, training, and placement in suitable employment of the disabled, and report such activities in countries throughout the world, with particular emphasis on programs in individual countries, specific disabilities, and descriptions of facilities. In addition to the major articles, each issue brings the reader up to date with news of research, rehabilitation workers, and a calendar of events. Copy is divided between well-developed articles by international experts in rehabilitation and staff-written reports. The 24-page format includes black and white photographic illustrations that are well related to the text. Will be useful in any community where rehabilitation work is well organized, or needs to be developed. (A.S.)

New Generation. 1919. q. $3. Leonard Mayhew. National Committee on Employment of Youth of the National Child Labor Committee, 145 E. 32nd St., New York, N.Y. 10016. Illus., index. Circ: 5,500. Sample. Vol. ends: Fall. Microform: UM.

Indexed: PAIS. *Aud:* Ac, Hs.

A modest pamphlet-sized periodical devoted to improving the employment possibilities for young people. Each issue is concerned with a specific topic, such as "Office of Economic Opportunity" or "The State of Integration versus Segregation." The topic is followed by a dialogue by the authors who have contributed to the issue. For guidance counselors, teachers, and community workers, as well as interested businessmen and union leaders.

Occupational Outlook Quarterly. See Government Magazines/United States Section.

Performance. See Government Magazines/United States Section.

Rehabilitation Record. See Government Magazines/United States Section.

Training in Business and Industry. 1964. m. $10. Wallace Hanson. Training Magazine, 33 W. 60th St., New York, N.Y. 10023. Illus., adv. Circ: 40,000. Microform: UM. Vol. ends: Dec.

Bk. rev: Avg. 7, 50 words (in Jan., Apr., July, and Oct. issues). *Aud:* Sa.

A specialized magazine designed to serve those responsible for employee training. Feature articles are concerned primarily with methodology, and cover many types of training for employees on all levels of proficiency and experience, as well as plant indoctrination for new employees. The five to eight articles in each issue concentrate on methods which have proved successful, and represent the suggestions and conclusions of persons actively engaged in this work. Several departments in each issue include news of products, materials, and services, a calendar of conventions and other meetings of interest to trainers, a listing of free literature related to employee training, audiovisual training, and an interesting column of Notes from a Training Director. The issue commencing each quarter includes a page of short book reviews of new titles with annotations recommending them. Adequate format, with black and white photos and copious advertising which, along with the readers' service cards, is a service to those using the magazine. For large public libraries, and for libraries serving institutions of advanced business management. (A.S.)

Vocational Guidance Quarterly. 1952. q. $8. Daniel Sinick. National Vocational Guidance Assn., 1607 New Hampshire Ave., N.W., Washington, D.C. 20009. Illus., index, adv. Circ: 14,000.

Indexed: CIJE, EdI. *Bk. rev:* 10–12, various length. *Aud:* Ac, Hs.

A basic quarterly for the vocational guidance expert at the university and high school level. Reports on latest methods of vocational guidance, problems, trends, and developments in the literature are presented. Good reviews of books, films, film strips, recordings, etc.

Vocations for Social Change. 1967. bi-m. $10. Ed. bd. Box 13, Canyon, Calif. 94516. Or c/o Emmaus House, 241 E. 116th St., New York, N.Y. 10029. Illus. Circ: 15,000. Sample.

Indexed: API. AbVoc. *Aud:* Ga, Ac, Hs. *Jv:* V.

A primary voice of the counterculture, this should be a required item in any library. It has grown from a mimeographed newsletter to a 64-page magazine, but the policy remains the same, viz., "to encourage formation of new jobs which implement values more humane than those our present structure reinforces." Issued by a nonprofit organization, it lists some 150 employers from the Alabama Committee for Freedom and Peace to the Washington Free Press. Employment opportunities range from architects and writers to librarians and political organizers. Full data are given for each position, along with what is provided in terms of salary and/or meals and housing without salary. Most organizations listed are out to change or improve the world. There are jobs for anyone (regardless of background or education) who is eager to help. There are a number of articles which discuss all aspects of the society and its relationship to employment. Of equal interest to librarians are the frequent bibliographies, which touch on aspects of the counterculture. This is not only an occupational magazine, it is a true voice of leadership for those trying to reshape our society in a meaningful way.

Who's Hiring Who. 1959. a. $3.25. Human Resources Press, 1629 K St., N.W., Washington, D.C. 20007. Illus., adv. Circ; 53,000.

Aud: Hs, Ga.

An annual which can be used by advisors and graduates at all levels, from high school through college. (The magazine has a quarterly system of updating information, so that although it is an annual, updated printings occur when there is a change in the job market.) Information includes general articles on resumes, interviews, personality traits, etc. More important is the "Job Directory," which covers some 2,000 occupations, shows hiring patterns, and indicates what each employer requires. This annual is useful to advisors in that the listings show education requirements, pay levels, benefits, etc. One of the better of its type, and although its annual status does limit its use, the updating is of some help.

PARAPSYCHOLOGY

Basic Periodicals

Hs: Fate; Ga: Fate; Jc & Ac: American Society for Psychical Research Journal, ESP Research Associates Foundation News Letter.

American Society for Psychical Research. Journal.
1907. q. Membership $15 (Students $10/2 yr.). $3/no. Laura A. Dale. ASPR, 5 W. 73rd St., New York, N.Y. 10023. Illus., index. Circ: 2,000. Sample. Vol. ends: Oct. Microform: UM.

Bk. rev: 1, 2–5 pages, signed. *Aud:* Ac, Ga. *Jv:* V.

The 100 or so page journal of the first American organization of its type (founded in 1885), whose purpose is to "advance the understanding of phenomena alleged to be paranormal: telepathy, clairvoyance, precognition, psychokinesis and related occurrences." The nonprofit group's journal has published William James, Henri Bergson, and Henry Sidgwick. The four or five articles report activities of the group, investigations of ESP, and parapsychological phenomena. Contributors vary from scientists to laymen, but generally write in a style which is understandable to either skeptic or believer. Most of the evidence, as might be expected, comes down on the side of the believer. Of the numerous magazines and journals in this field, this is the best for the scholar and/or serious investigator.

Creative Intelligence. 1971. q. $1. Anthony Campbell. 2 Bishopswood Rd., London N6, England. Subs. to: Students' Intl. Meditation Soc., 1015 Gayley Ave., Los Angeles, Calif. 90024. Sample.

Aud: Ga.

A magazine dedicated to the proposition that meditation will improve man and society. "Not intended as a learned journal, nor as a cultural magazine of the usual kind. . . . Articles should be written for the intelligent general reader." The seven entries in the initial issue are, as the editor promises, fairly easy to understand and challenging. Most contributors are professors, but free of the professional jargon, and the magazine builds nicely on both explanatory and research-type articles. It is definitely a serious, well-thought-out effort to bring information to laymen. It is not, repeat, not a cultist approach. Should be of interest to any larger public or academic library.

ESP Research Associates Foundation. News Letter.
1964. bi-m. Membership $15. Harold Sherman. 1750 Tower Bldg., Little Rock, Ark. 72201.

Aud: Ga.

The six to twelve page newsletter reports on the activities of the foundation "for exploration of the origin and nature of man's sixth sense," i.e., extrasensory perception. Its editor and founder, Harold Sherman,

notes that the "Foundation has been recognized by Internal Revenue Service as a non-profit organization." In addition to the newsletter there are a variety of books and pamphlets available, including Mr. Sherman's numerous works, e.g., *How to Foresee and Control Your Future, How to Make ESP Work for You.* Apparently there is no way for a library to get the newsletter without a membership, including an "ESP kit which contains instructions for sending and receiving thoughts and suggested visualizing and meditative techniques." The Foundation has faithful followers. Some 700 men and women "came from over 40 states and parts of Canada" for a meeting in 1971—a meeting at which the guest speaker was Jeane Dixon. The newsletter simply isn't worth $15 to a library, but the organization might be brought to the attention of anyone interested in the subject.

Fate. 1948. m. $4.50. Mary Margaret Fuller. Clark Publishing Co., Highland House, Highland Park, Ill. 60035. Illus., adv. Circ: 120,000. Sample. Vol. ends: Dec.

Bk. rev: 5–6, 400 words, signed. *Aud:* Ga, Ac, Hs.

One of the best-known and most popular parapsychological magazines. It offers a pocket-sized 146-page approach to "true stories of the strange and unknown." There are usually four or five stories, as many articles, and a great number of features. The advertising moves around from "over 100 ready to use mystic chants for money, power and love" to classified ads for ouija boards. The level of writing varies from relative sophistication and wit to sophomoric fiction. (The articles and features are considerably better than the stories.) But let the editor speak: "The parapsychological fields we cover vary widely: ESP, ghosts and hauntings, reincarnation, altered states of consciousness, sorcery, divination, possession, witchcraft, Fortean phenomena, UFOs, monsters such as the Loch Ness monster, abominable snowmen, werewolves, vampires; biographies and autobiographies of personalities in the psychic or occult fields; and mysteries in archaeology. In short we are interested in all the mysteries of the world—both physical and mental. Our purpose is to evaluate and disseminate the important work being done in parapsychology plus an overview of the history of the subject—all this with the underlying intent that our readers shall understand that science does not accurately describe the world we live in." Depending on your view of such things, this is a most welcome or less than welcome addition. I like it, and think it might spark more than one collection.

Journal of Parapsychology. 1937. q. $8. L. E. Rhine and D. H. Pope. Parapsychology Pr., Box 6847, College Sta., Durham, N.C. 27708. Illus., index. Circ: 1,200. Sample. Vol. ends: Dec. Refereed. Reprint: Johnson.

Indexed: PsyAb. *Bk. rev:* 2, 1,000 words, signed. *Aud:* Ac. *Jv:* V.

The basic journal in the field. It is devoted primarily to "the original publication of experimental results and other research findings in extrasensory perception and psychokinesis." Articles are by scientists, usually based on strict controls, and must measure up to the rigorous standards imposed by the Foundation for Research on the Nature of Man, the sponsor of the *Journal.* There are usually four or five articles, sometimes an interview, essay-length book reviews, and some ten pages of abstracts of major articles which have appeared elsewhere. The normal 60 to 80 page issue ends with a glossary of terms. Anyone deeply involved with the subject will have no trouble understanding the material, but the amateur had best try a less rigorous approach. As the major voice for publishing research from universities and other scientific centers, this should be in any medium-to-large academic, and possibly public, library collection.

Parapsychology Review (Formerly: ***Newsletter of the Parapsychology Foundation 1957-1969***). 1970. bi-m. $4. Betty Shapin and Allen Angoff. Parapsychology Foundation, 29 W. 57th St., New York, N.Y. 10019. Illus. Circ: 2,500. Sample.

Bk. rev: 5–11, 500–2,000 words, signed. *Aud:* Ga, Ac.

A 24 to 28 page newsletter which usually includes three to four articles, announcements of events and people, and book reviews or brief notes, it is published in support of the Parapsychology Foundation, whose aims are outlined in a pamphlet sent free upon request from the publisher. Articles center on such material as "ESP in England," "Parapsychology in the Mass Media," "Dowsing," and other subjects of psychical interest. The tone is serious and scientific, the format professional. Librarian Carolyn Wilson reports heavy use of it in their library by college students. No matter how you view it, a fascinating subject.

PEACE

Basic Periodicals

Hs: *Fellowship;* Ga: *Fellowship, Win Magazine;* Jc & Ac: *Fellowship, Win Magazine, War/Peace Report.*

Basic Abstracts and Indexes

Alternate Press Index, Arms Control and Disarmament, Peace Research Abstracts.

✓***Arms Control and Disarmament.*** See Government Magazines/United States Section.

Bulletin of Peace Proposals. 1970. q. $10. Mark Thee. Intl. Peace Research Inst., Box 307, Blindear, Oslo 3, Norway. Subs. to: Box 142, Boston, Mass. 02113.

Indexed: PAIS. *Aud:* Ac, Ga, Hs. *Jv:* V.

Edited in Oslo, printed in English, this is an impres-

sive effort to summarize articles, books, and reports which have anything to do with promoting activities for peace. In about 100 pages, the editor sums up 50 to 60 items in a uniform fashion, i.e., background on the author, date of publication, form and place, reference (where the article was discussed), and the content summary. The table of contents is a virtual index, and there is an annual subject and author index in the fourth number. Coverage is international; in addition to the long abstracts, there are usually two articles on some aspect of peace. It is difficult to imagine a better reference work for libraries, particularly if augmented by the same publisher's *Journal of Peace Research* (1970. q. $6). The abstracts, which run one or more pages, are so thorough that it is often not necessary to consult the original work abstracted. Consequently, the modest price virtually gives a small library a basic reference tool for all but research-oriented questions on peace. It should serve admirably for laymen and students from high school on up who are preparing papers on some aspect of the subject. Highly recommended.

EPF Newsletter. See Religion and Theology/Counterculture Section.

Fellowship. 1934. m. $5. James S. Best. Fellowship, Box 271, Nyack, N.Y. 10960. Illus., index, adv. Circ: 19,000. Sample.

Indexed: PAIS, ArmC. *Bk. rev:* 6–8, 300 words, signed. *Aud:* Ac, Ga, Hs. *Jv:* V.

A peace magazine, published by the Fellowship of Reconciliation—"men and women of all faiths who have recognized the essential unity of mankind and have joined to explore the power of love and truth for resolving human conflict." Members "identify with those of every nation, race, and religion who are victims of injustice and exploitation." Among those supporting the movement are Daniel Berrigan, Erich Fromm, Alfred Hassler, and representatives of religious affiliates, including the Baptist Fellowship for Peace and the Catholic Peace Fellowship. Four issues a year are from 24 to 32 pages long; the remainder are 8 pages long. Articles cover all aspects of the world and national scene related to peace and fellowship, such as "Environment and World Consciousness," "One World, the Third World and Revolution," and "New Peace Initiatives." They are written by experts for the layman. In addition, there are shorter news items, editorials, book reviews, and notes. An invaluable, objective source of information in this area, the magazine can be recommended for any library.

✓***Journal of Conflict Resolution; for research related to war and peace.*** 1957. q. $15. Elizabeth Converse and Clinton E. Fink. Center for Research on Conflict Resolution, Univ. of Mich., Ann Arbor, Mich. 48104. Illus., adv. Circ: 1,900. Microform: UM.

Indexed: PAIS, PsyAb. SSHum. *Bk. rev:* 2–3, several pages, signed. *Aud:* Ac.

Conflict here stands for war, and the sponsoring group publishes articles which consider problems relating to war and to peace. Authors cover a wide spectrum of interests, from political science and economics to literature and art. The five to six scholarly articles touch on historical implications of war in all parts of the world. Concerned, as well, with the effects of communication, the magazine should have wide appeal to any serious student of psychology, history, or sociology.

Peace News. 1936. w. $9.50 ($11.50 airmail). Howard Clark, Ian Dougall, Roger Moody, and Paul Wesley. 5 Caledonian Rd., Kings Cross, London N1 9PY, England. Illus., adv. Circ: 5,000. Sample. Vol. ends: Dec.

Indexed: API. *Aud:* Ga, Ac.

An international weekly newspaper with information on radical nonviolence and pacifism in theory and practice; analyses of oppressions; news of actions and strategies for radical social change on all levels; delineation of nonviolent models for society; reviews, letters, diary of coming events. Staffers and contributors are mainly English. The scope, however, is international. Because of its weekly publishing schedule, this is one of the best current guides to the peace movement. It is a must in any library where there is concern over the world peace movement. And considering the relatively low price, it can be recommended for small to medium-sized libraries.

The Peacemaker. 1948. Every 3 weeks. $3. Ernest R. Bromley. Peacemaker Movement, 10208 Sylvan Ave. (Gano), Cincinnati, Ohio 45241. Circ: 4,000. Vol. ends: Dec. Sample.

Indexed: API. *Aud:* Ac, Ga, Hs.

As the sponsoring group and title suggest, this eight-page newsletter is dedicated to a philosophy of nonviolence as a viable method of gaining peace. The group was organized in 1948 "for the purpose of developing a movement of disciplined and revolutionary pacifist activity." Members call for Peacemaker-type communities, nonviolent social and economic revolution, and mutual sharing. Among their many activities have been opposition to the war and active support for those who choose prison instead of the draft. Other action has been against discrimination, for civil rights, and "witnessing against bombs, missiles and tests." A regular feature of almost every issue is a list of names of those who have been imprisoned for their convictions.

Reporter for Conscience' Sake. 1942. m. $2.50. Richard Malishchak. National Interreligious Service Bd. for Conscientious Objectors, 550 Washington Bldg., 15th and New York Ave., N.W., Washington, D.C. 20005. Circ: 4,000. Sample. Vol. ends: Dec.

Indexed: API. *Aud:* Ac, Hs.

A four to eight page newsletter published for the information of conscientious objectors and their counselors. The sponsoring group is an organization founded during World War II and supported by over 40 religious and ethical groups. Articles touch on every matter of concern to a CO or anyone involved with the situation: law and regulations affecting conscientious objectors; procedures available to them; their experiences in the processes of classification and alternate service assignments; court cases; and general news about matters of peace, war, and conscience. The whole is objective, certainly of considerable interest to any young man who may have questions concerning the draft law. Should be of particular value in any library serving youth, particularly high schools.

Sane World. 1961. m. $3. Sanford Gottlieb. Sane, Inc., 318 Massachusetts Ave., N.E., Washington, D.C. 20002. Illus., adv. Circ: 30,000. Sample. Vol. ends: Dec.

Indexed: ArmC. *Bk. rev:* 1, essay, signed. *Aud:* Ga, Ac, Hs.

A four to eight page newsletter issued by the best-known peace group in America. Each issue features news on both national and international affairs which take the United States closer to or out of war. Aside from the basic editorial policy, the material is nonpartisan and objective and attracts writers and readers from every walk of life.

Survival. 1959. m. $7.50. Kenneth Hunt. Inst. for Strategic Studies, 18 Adam St., London WC2, England. Illus., index, adv. Circ: 5,000.

Indexed: ArmC. *Bk. rev:* Various number, length. *Aud:* Ac, Ga.

The publisher of this fascinating journal is international in its membership. According to a story in the *New York Times* (Dec. 27, 1971, p. 11), "Basically it is concerned with strategic questions, not simply in the military sense, but with the moral and political implications of the existence and use of armed force." Articles, based on original research among member nations' files, deal with objective methods of measuring economic, political, and social strengths and weaknesses. Implications for a country's ultimate welfare are examined. (Along with considerable emphasis on arms control, there are a number of translated articles from the Soviet Union and economic Chinese publications, although neither nation is a member.) Each year the Institute publishes "The Military Balance," an annual report on the world's nuclear and strategic forces. This is an accurate intelligence report. The magazine should be in all medium and large collections, and brought to the attention of readers who are in any way involved with disarmament and the political and social sciences.

Training in Nonviolence; WRI bulletin. 1970. q. $1.50. War Resisters Intl., 3 Caledonian Rd., London N1, England.

Aud: Ac, Ga.

In some 14 mimeographed pages, the contributors discuss war-resistant activities throughout the world. (By 1971 there was an equal interest in ecology campaigns, as well.) The lead article touches on some aspect of nonviolent action training; it is followed by short reports. International and aligned with no political group, the sponsoring organization offers objective, supportive material for anyone involved in bringing about social change through nonviolent means.

WRL News. 1948. bi-m. free. Jim Peck. War Resisters League, 339 Lafayette St., New York, N.Y. 10012. Illus., index. Circ: 14,000. Sample. Vol. ends: Dec.

Aud: Ac, Ga, Hs.

A four to six page newsletter put out by the War Resisters League, an international pacifist organization which supports nonviolent protest to war and social abuses. Supports tax resistance to help end war, and analyzes parties and individuals in terms of their commitment to peace. The WRL defines its membership as holding "a wide variety of religious, philosophical, and political beliefs. Our views of how to change society and work effectively to end war differ from one person to another. The absence of a narrow political program in the League encourages the widest experimentation with the theories and practices on nonviolence." There are short articles on various aspects of the peace and news items.

War/Peace Report. 1961. 10/yr. $5. Richard Hudson. Center for War/Peace Studies, 218 E. 18th St., New York, N.Y. 10003. Illus., index, adv. Circ: 6,000. Sample. Vol. ends: No. 10.

Indexed: PAIS. *Bk. rev:* 3, 1,500 words, signed, also notes. *Aud:* Ga, Ac, Hs.

A 24 to 30 page magazine published by the Center for War/Peace Studies, a program of the New York Friends Group. Its editor sums up its purpose as a platform for "reports on world crisis areas and analysis of the long-term problems of achieving peace. It also serves as a forum for the airing of various views on foreign policy and international affairs." The whole is objective, authoritative, and has featured such outstanding writers as Hans J. Morgenthau, Herbert F. York, Mark Van Doren, Erich Fromm, Norman Cousins, and Juan Bosch. In addition to short reviews, it carries one or two essay reviews in each issue. There are short reports, too, on organizational activities relating to world peace. An excellent magazine with a definite point of view which deserves a place in most libraries.

Win Magazine. 1965. s-m. $5. Maris Cakars. War Resisters League, 339 Lafayette St., New York, N.Y.

10012. Subs. to: Box 547, Rifton, N.Y. 12471. Illus., adv. Circ: 8,000. Sample. Vol. ends: Dec. 15.

Indexed: API. *Bk. rev:* 3, 2,500 words, signed. *Aud:* Ac, Ga, Hs. *Jv:* V.

A radical-pacifist magazine written for and by the front-line activists of the peace and nonviolent movement in America. Produced by the 45-year-old WRL, and hostile to "bureaucratic statism," each issue fuses analysis of national and world affairs with *engagé* poetry, accounts of civil disobedience and imprisonment, news of deserters and draft resisters, and appraisals of the "now scene," from rock music to offbeat cinema. The League also issues a free, bimonthly bulletin, *WRL News.*

PETS

See also Horses Section.

Basic Periodicals

Ejh: *Animals;* Hs: *Animals;* Ga: *Animals, National Humane Review.*

Cessations

Pet Life

American Field; the sportsman's newspaper of America. 1874. w. $9. William F. Brown. Amer. Field Publishing Co., 222 W. Adams St., Chicago, Ill. 60606. Illus., adv. Circ: 15,000. Vol. ends: Dec.

Bk. rev: 2–3, 150 words. *Aud:* Ga. *Rv:* M. *Jv:* B.

Devoted exclusively to pointing dogs and their sporting activities, this is not a magazine for the average dog lover. Special departments cover game and shooting, fish and fishing, natural history, travel, kennel, field trials, breeding, and everything else pertaining to canine interests. Excellent black and white photographs of winners in various competitions accompany many of the reports and articles.

American Pigeon Journal; devoted to all branches of pigeon raising—fancy, utility and racing. 1912. m. $3. Frank H. Hollman. Amer. Pigeon Journal Co., Warrenton, Mo. Illus., adv. Circ: 10,000.

Bk. rev: 20–25, 30–50 words. *Aud:* Ga, Hs.

Includes illustrations, and some rather fascinating advertising for those involved with pigeons. Articles, a few of which are reprints from other less specialized magazines, cover every aspect of the field: breeding, organizations, shows, and displays. Of interest to adults and high school students who see more in a pigeon that a bothersome park pedestrian.

Animals (Formerly: *Our Dumb Animals*). 1868. m. $3. William Mallard. Mass. Soc. for the Prevention of Cruelty to Animals, 180 Longwood Ave., Boston, Mass. 02115. Illus. Circ: 20,000. Sample.

Aud: Ga, Hs, Ejh.

This attractive sixteen-page publication has at least twelve articles per issue that are well written and signed by interested contributors and staff members. The message from the president speaks out for legislative action against man's inhumanity to animals. It has two regular features: Law Enforcement, devoted to current legislation, and a two-page section devoted to Boys and Girls. From time to time, articles are submitted by John C. Macfarlane under his old byline "As I See It." Will interest all animal lovers, and because of its reasonable price and excellent animal coverage, it is useful for a high school library. (P.M.)

Aquarium. 1932. m. $5. Ed. bd. Pet Books Inc., 87 Route 17, Maywood, N.J. 07607. Illus., index, adv. Circ: 50,000.

Indexed: BioAb. *Bk. rev:* 1–2, 150 words, signed. *Aud:* Ga, Hs.

Published for both the hobbyist and the dealer, this covers all aspects of aquarium life. Considerable emphasis on how to purchase and care for fish, as well as for other types of aquatic life. Numerous columns and features, and a number of longer feature articles. A good part of the material is relatively technical, but it will be of interest to anyone who takes the hobby seriously, and is quite suited for teen-agers as well as adults.

Aquarium Hobbyist. 1971. m. $8. Joan A. Johnson. Forge Assn. Publns., Inc. 1075 Post Rd., Riverside, Conn. 06873. Illus., index, adv. Circ: 10,000. Sample. Vol. ends: Sept.

Bk. rev: 3–5, 100 words. *Aud:* Ga, Hs, Ejh.

In 60 or so pages, this pocket-sized report on aquariums and fish features seven or eight short articles by experts on every aspect of the hobby. Each article is illustrated, often with brilliant color plates. Apparently every facet is covered, from photography and breeding to a calendar of shows. Both fresh and salt-water species are considered, and the editor notes she makes "a strong plea for conservation of endangered aquatic species." Differs from the older *Aquarium* in that there is nothing here for the retail dealer. Advertising (so far) is minimal. The makeup is good, and the style will appeal to just about any age or level of sophistication in the aquarium world.

Cat Fancy Magazine. 1966. bi-m. $4.50. Leslie S. Smith, 641 Lexington Ave., New York, N.Y. 10022. Illus., adv. Circ: 128,360. Sample.

Bk. rev: Various number, length. *Aud:* Ga, Hs, Ejh.

Eight departments explore the doings of cats under such headings as Editorial, Litter Box, Show Scene, Curious Cat, Cat Fancy Gallery, and What's New Pussy Cat. Articles deal with such things as litter pans, cats of Thailand, and the benefits of voluntarily regis-

tering your cat. The centerfold contains a color print of the Play Cat and/or Cats of the Month. (P.M.)

Cats Magazine. 1945. m. $6.50. Jean Amelia Laux. Raymond D. Smith, 2900 Jefferson Ave., Washington, Pa. 15301. Illus., index, adv. Circ: 40,000. Sample. Vol. ends: Dec.

Bk. rev: 3, 500 words, signed. *Aud:* Ga, Hs, Ejh.

Approximately half of the magazine is devoted to cat shows and advertisements of interest to the owners of show cats. The editorial column brings current topics, including humane issues, to the attention of all cat owners. There are usually five or six signed articles or short stories in each issue. Regular features include poetry, letters and photographs from subscribers, the staff veterinarian's responses to general health questions, the show calendar, and "Aunty and Arabella" (a comic strip). Will appeal to any cat owner, regardless of age.

Dog Fancy. 1970. bi-m. $4.50. Leslie S. Smith. Pet Magazine, Inc., 641 Lexington Ave., New York, N.Y. 10022. Illus., adv. Circ: 75,000. Sample.

Bk. rev: Various number, length. *Aud:* Ga, Hs, Ejh.

The format of this magazine is remarkably like *Cat Fancy Magazine* mainly because the editor and publisher are the same. Eight departments report on the doings of dogs under such headings as Dog Fancy Gallery, Puppouri, Tell Me Why, What's New. The signed feature articles deal with such topics as Following the Hounds, Amb & U Pet, Dog Buyers' Dilemma. Like *Cat Fancy Magazine* the centerfold contains a color print of a dog(s). (P.M.)

Dog World. 1916. m. $10. Helen Nowicki. Dog World Magazine, 10060 W. Roosevelt Rd., Westchester, Ill. 60153. Illus., adv. Circ: 56,709. Vol. ends: Dec.

Bk. rev: 1–2, 200 words. *Aud:* Ga, Hs.

The aim of the world's largest dog magazine is to disseminate pertinent information to those interested in purebred dogs. The articles are written so that they can be readily understood by the informed layman who has some knowledge of dog shows, standards, and breeding. The magazine also carries more specialized and scientific articles. It is heavy on advertisements by breeders of various breeds of dogs. The material tends to be a bit too complex for the less than enthusiastic adult or teen-ager, but it can be recommended for larger public and high school collections.

Dogs; the magazine for everyone who enjoys them. bi-m. $6. Marjorie Farmsworth. Countrywide Publns., Inc., 222 Park Ave. S., New York, N.Y. 10003. Illus., adv. Circ: 105,000. Sample.

Bk. rev: Various number, length. *Aud:* Gs, Hs, Ejh.

As the title implies, this magazine concerns itself exclusively with dogs of all breeds. Eleven regular features include both A Word from the Editor and Legislation Alert, as well as the staff veterinarian's replies to general dog questions, science abstracts of interest to dog readers, helpful suggestions, dogs' bookshelf, and breeders' market. Special articles give advice on housebreaking a puppy, how a dog owner can prevent antidog-pollution ordinances from being passed by simply cleaning up after his dog, and articles dealing with the care of special breeds. Black and white photographs are generously provided throughout the magazine. It will appeal to almost anyone regardless of age. (P.M.)

Dogs Illustrated/1971. a. $1.25. Larry Mueller. Special Interest Publns., Holt, Rinehart & Winston, Inc., 383 Madison Ave., New York, N.Y. 10017.

Bk. rev: Various number, length. *Aud:* Ga, Hs, Ejh.

This 128-page annual is published by *Field and Stream.* The thirteen unsigned articles deal with small house dogs and large hunting dogs. The potential owner is given helpful hints on how to select and train a dog, proper diet, first aid, breeding, and how to care for him when he grows old. (P.M.)

International Turtle and Tortoise Society Journal. 1966. 5/yr. $7.50. 8847 de Haviland Ave., Los Angeles, Calif. 90045. Illus., index, adv. Circ: 4,000. Sample. Vol. ends: Nov./Dec.

Aud: Ga, Sh, Ejh.

Photographs, scholarly but easily followed articles, and obvious enthusiasm point the way to a hobby. Suitable for both adults and children, and useful in those libraries catering to a large contingent of animal enthusiasts.

National Humane Review. 1913. bi-m. $1.50. Eileen Schoen. Amer. Humane Assn., Box 1266, Denver, Colo. 80201. Illus., index, adv. Circ: 18,500. Sample. Vol. ends: Nov./Dec.

Bk. rev: 3–4, 100 words, signed. *Aud:* Ga, Ejh, Hs.

Now that ecology and conservation have become of importance to the average citizen, this magazine takes on a new dimension. While still primarily concerned with protection of animals, its scope has been broadened to include articles on every aspect of wildlife conservation, such as "Is This Farewell to the Bluebird of Happiness?" Subjects in a single issue may range from cats and dogs to alligators. There is less emphasis now on membership activities. The articles are lively, relatively simple to read, and broad enough in scope to involve almost any pet fancier. A good bet for general reading in libraries from the junior high level through the public library.

Our Dumb Animals. See *Animals.*

Pet Shop Management. 1947. m. $7.50. Victor W. Hinze. Pet Shop Management, Inc., Box 6109, Duluth, Minn. 55806. Illus., adv. Circ: 10,000.

Aud: Sa.

A magazine with considerably wider appeal than might at first be suspected. A good number of dollar-making tips are noted in each issue, but there are other articles on dog ownership, ticks, hamsters, etc. *The Annual Directory of Pets and Supplies* sells for $1. Note: The magazine is free, i.e., controlled circulation for the majority, and may be free for libraries. Inquire.

Pure Bred Dogs, American Kennel Gazette. 1889. m. $8. Amer. Kennel Club, 51 Madison Ave., New York, N.Y. 10010. Illus., adv. Circ: 17,500.

Aud: Sa.

A professional journal for those who breed dogs and take an active part in shows. It consists primarily of detailed news of Club activities and breed clubs throughout the United States, and includes features on obedience and field trials. Photographs and data on winners will interest younger dog lovers, but on the whole this is not for the amateur or child.

PHILOSOPHY

Basic Periodicals

Ga; *Philosophy & Public Affairs, Philosophy of Science;* Jc: *Philosophy & Public Affairs, Philosophy of Science, Philosophy;* Ac: *IPQ, Philosophy East & West, Philosophy, Philosophy and Phenomenological Research, Philosophy & Public Affairs, Philosophy of Science.*

Library and Teaching Aids

Philosophical Books

Basic Abstracts and Indexes

Philosopher's Index, Repertoire Bibliographique de la Philosophie

American Philosophical Quarterly. 1964. q. $8 (Institutions $14). Nicholas Rescher, Dept. of Philosophy, Univ. of Pittsburg, Pittsburgh, Pa. 15213. Circ: 1,200. Vol. ends: Oct.

Indexed: PhilosI, RepBibPhil. *Aud:* Ac.

Only self-sufficient articles are published—no book reviews, news items, or discussion notes. The papers are consequently somewhat longer than ordinary. Much logic and linguistic analysis are included: hence, this journal is not for the fainthearted. For large philosophy collections. (J.A.)

American Philosophical Society Proceedings. See Science Section.

Analysis. 1933. bi-m. $4. Peter Winch. Basil Blackwell, 49 Broad St., Oxford, England. Circ: 1,200. Vol. ends: June.

Indexed: PhilosI, RepBibPhil, BritHum. *Aud:* Ac.

A scholarly journal demanding at least an elementary knowledge of mathematical logic as well as a familiarity with the rhetoric of British analysis and the "ordinary language" schools of philosophy. Articles, by professional philosophers, are very specific, closely reasoned, and in the nature of contributions to the solution of a problem rather than broad statements of a philosophy. One of the most valuable periodicals (along with *Mind* and the *Australasian Journal*) to students of the field of contemporary British and American empiricism. (J.A.)

Australasian Journal of Philosophy. 1923. 3/yr. $5 G. N. Nerlich. Philosophy Dept., Univ. of Sydney, N.S.W., Australia. Index. Circ: 1,100. Sample. Vol. ends: Dec. Reprint: Kraus.

Indexed: PhilosI, RepBibPhil. *Bk. rev:* 8, 2 pages, signed. *Aud:* Ac.

One of the leading periodicals of contemporary academic empiricism. The dominant concerns have been with language, logic, and moral philosophy. The techniques of logic have been subordinated to those of explanation of a philosophical argument and do not present an insuperable barrier to those with a non-technical philosophical background. Generally for the academic audience, but can be enjoyed by the layman with some background in contemporary philosophy. (J.A.)

British Journal of Aesthetics. 1960. q. $7.50. Harold Osborne. Thames & Hudson Ltd., 30 Bloomsbury St., London WC1, England. Index, adv. Vol. ends: Autumn.

Indexed: PhilosI, RepBibPhil, BritHum, ArtInd. *Bk. rev:* 5–10, 200–2,000 words, signed. *Aud:* Ga, Ac.

The official organ of the British Society of Aesthetics, which is concerned with theoretical study of the arts from many standpoints. Most contributors are philosophers, but some are associated more directly with the arts. This is the most significant of the few English-language periodicals devoted exclusively to aesthetics. Well written and produced; recommended for medium and large public and academic libraries. (J.A.)

British Journal for the Philosophy of Science. 1950. q. $9.50. Prof. I. Lakatos. Cambridge Univ. Press, 32 E. 57th St., New York, N.Y. 10022. Index, adv. Circ: 1,600. Sample. Vol. ends: Nov. Reprint: Kraus.

Indexed: PhilosI, BritHum, PsyAb, RepBibPhil. *Bk. rev:* 10, 2–6 pages, signed. *Aud:* Ac, Ga.

The official journal of the British Society for the Philosophy of Science. Highly technical papers by philosophers and scientists deal with such topics as language, scientific "laws," mathematical theory, probability, space, and time. Audience is limited to those with some background in science and mathematics.

Along with its American counterpart, *Philosophy of Science,* this is a must for academic libraries supporting philosophy programs, and highly desirable for large public libraries. (J.A.)

Dialogue; Canadian Philosophical Review; Revue Canadienne de Philosophie. 1962. q. $10 (Libraries $12). Venant Cauchy and Martyn Estall. Queen's Univ., Kingston, Ont., Canada. Index, adv. Circ: 1,500. Sample to college libraries. Vol. ends: Dec.

Indexed: PhilI, RepBibPhil. *Bk. rev:* 20–25; 1,200 words, signed. *Aud:* Ac.

Published for the Canadian Philosophical Association, with articles in French or English, this journal deals with all aspects and periods of philosophy. Though its subject matter gives *Dialogue* a wide audience among readers of philosophical literature, the fact that fully half of its articles are in French makes it less useful for small libraries. (J.A.)

Diogenes; an international review of philosophy and humanistic studies. 1953. q. $6. Roger Caillois. Mario Casalini Ltd., 4 Via Leopardi, Florence, Italy. Index, adv. Circ: 1,8000.

Indexed: PAIS. *Bk. rev:* 1–2, lengthy, signed. *Aud:* Ac.

Published by the International Council for Philosophy and Humanistic Studies, under the auspices of UNESCO. Articles are written in English, French, Spanish, and the language of the authors. Scholars treat philosophy, politics, geopolitics, history, and economics at the theoretical level. The style is lively. Regular features include one or two lengthy book reviews, recent happenings and discoveries in the field of the humanities, and articles on "current events."

Ethics; an international journal of social, political, and legal philosophy. 1890. q. $8. Charles Wegener and Warner Wick. Univ. of Chicago Press, 5801 Ellis Ave., Chicago, Ill. 60637. Adv. Circ: 1,700. Microform: UM. Reprint: Johnson.

Indexed: PhilosI, RepBibPhil, SSHum. *Bk. rev:* 1–2, 2 pages, signed. *Aud:* Ga, Ac.

Specializes in ethical theory, social science, and jurisprudence. Contributors have included social scientists and psychologists as well as philosophers and jurists. This journal would be of value to both the specialist and the intelligent, well-read adult interested in social philosophy. Recommended for academic and larger public libraries. (J.A.)

Foundations of Language. See Linguistics Section.

History and Theory. See History/General Section.

IPQ, International Philosophical Quarterly. 1961. q. $8. Norris Clarke, S. J. Fordham Univ. Press, Bronx, N.Y. 10458. Index, adv. Circ: 1,900. Sample. Vol. ends: Dec.

Indexed: PhilosI, SSHum, CathI, RepBibPhil. *Bk. rev:* 4, 2 pages, signed. *Aud:* Ga, Ac. *Jv:* V.

IPQ is coedited at Fordham University and Berchmans Philosophicum in Belgium. Its primary goal is to encourage vital contemporary expression—creative, critical, and historical—in the intercultural tradition of theistic, spiritualist, and personalist humanism, but without further restriction of school within these broad perspectives. Oriental philosophy receives its share of attention, as do Marxism, existentialism, phenomenology, American philosophy, and Wittgensteinian analysis—to name some recent high spots. Besides the usual five or six long articles, there is a section called Contemporary Currents, usually with several selections, which is devoted to recent trends. Interesting, solid, and alive, *IPQ* belongs in all philosophy collections. (J.A.)

✓ *Journal of Aesthetics and Art Criticism.* See Cultural-Social Studies Section.

✓ *Journal of the History of Ideas.* See Cultural-Social Studies Section.

✓ *Journal of the History of Philosophy.* 1963. q. $7 (Institutions $8.50). Richard H. Popkin, Dept. of Philosophy, Univ. of California, La Jolla, Calif. 92037. Index, adv. Circ: 1,800. Sample. Vol. ends: Oct. Refereed. Microform: UM.

Indexed: PhilosI, RepBibPhil. *Bk. rev:* 15–20, 2 pages, signed. *Aud:* Ac.

An international journal which publishes notes, articles, reviews, and discussions about the history of western philosophy, broadly conceived. Though most articles are in English, material in other major western languages is included. As the title implies, most articles are critical and interpretive, rather than expositions of the authors' original thought. Solid and well produced—recommended for academic collections. (J.A.)

✓ *The Journal of Philosophy.* 1904. s-m. $9. 720 Philosophy Hall, Columbia Univ., New York, N.Y. 10027. Index, adv. Circ: 4,500. Sample. Vol. ends: Dec.

Indexed: PhilosI, SSHum, RepBibPhil. *Bk. rev:* Occasional, lengthy, signed. *Aud:* Ac.

The most widely circulated journal of academic philosophy published in the United States. Logical analysis, linguistic philosophy, and philosophy of science are emphasized. Historical articles on philosophers or systems tend to be explications of concepts in relation to current thinking. Not for the uninitiated; recommended for large philosophy collections. (J.A.)

The Journal of Symbolic Logic. 1936. q. $20. Alfons Borgers. Assn. for Symbolic Logic, Box 6248, Providence, R.I. 02904. Index, adv. Circ: 3,500. Sample. Vol. ends: Dec. Refereed.

Indexed: PhilI, SSHum, RepBibPhil. *Bk. rev:* Over 50, 400 words, signed. *Aud:* Ac.

Contains original technical papers in the field of symbolic logic, expository papers in this field, philosophical papers which bear upon this field or make use of its methods, and studies in the history of logic in which modern technical developments are taken into account. The Reviews section contains not only critiques of books, but also reviews of recently published articles. Audience restricted to persons with advanced knowledge of logic and mathematics. (J.A.)

Man and World. 1968. q. $9.50 (Institutions $15.00). John Anderson, Joseph Kockelmans, and Calvin Schrag. Martinus Nijhoff, 9–11 Lange Vourhout, The Hague, Netherlands. Index. Circ: 500. Vol. ends: Nov.

Indexed: PhilosI, RepBibPhil. *Bk. rev:* 2–3, various length, signed. *Aud:* Ac.

Articles are in English, French, German, Spanish, or Italian. Those not in English are accompanied by an abstract in English. Definitely not slanted toward linguistic analysis, logic, or philosophy of science, this appears to be primarily a forum for humanist-existentialist thinkers. There is a helpful Chronicle section dedicated to news about the profession, including announcements concerning journals. For large philosophy collections. (J.A.)

✓ *Mind; a quarterly review of psychology and philosophy.* 1876. q. $4. Gilbert Ryle. Basil Blackwell, 49 Broad St., Oxford, England. Adv.

Indexed: BritHum, PhilI, RepBibPhil. *Bk. rev:* 3–6, 2,000 words, signed. *Aud:* Ac.

Devoted to all aspects of philosophy, although discussions of "ordinary language" and the logic of ethical discourse occupy much space at present. There are papers of historical interest as well as discussions of current philosophical problems. Despite the subtitle, it's now a purely philosophical journal. The book reviews are few, but among the best published in any philosophical periodical. One of the most prestigious journals in the field, it should be included in all academic libraries which support significant course work in philosophy. (J.A.)

✓ *The Monist.* 1890. q. $6 (Institutions $8). Eugene Freeman. Open Ct. Publishing Co., Box 402, LaSalle, Ill. 61301. Index, adv. Circ: 1,000. Sample. Vol. ends: Oct. Reprint: Kraus.

Indexed: PhilI, RepBibPhil. *Aud:* Ac, Ga. *Jv:* V.

More general in character than most philosophical journals, and one of the most interesting to the nonspecialist. Each issue is devoted to a particular topic set by the editorial board. Recent topics include democracy, Spinoza, proofs for God's existence, civil disobedience, and nineteenth-century British philosophy. Papers attempt to explore the current status of the issues posed, or to analyze the work of philosophers who have dealt significantly with these issues. An interesting feature is the Author's Abstracts of Recent Books section, in which about a dozen books are summarized in abstracts of about 100 to 200 words. One of the first philosophy journals for any academic or public library to consider. (J.A.)

New Scholasticism. See Religion and Theology/Denominational Section.

Noûs. 1967. q. $8. H. Castaneda. Indiana Univ., Ballantine 703, Philosophy Dept., Bloomington, Ind. 47401. Index. Circ: 800. Vol. ends: Nov. Refereed.

Indexed: PhilosI, RepBibPhil. *Bk. rev:* About 4 critical studies/yr., 20 pages, signed. *Aud:* Ac.

No particular point of view, but includes much logic and metaphysics which is highly technical reading. Occasionally, symposia and surveys of work recently done on special topics are published. A well-respected journal, it is suggested for libraries building large philosophy collections. (J.A.)

The Personalist. 1920. q. $5. John Hospers. School of Philosophy, Univ. of Southern Calif., Los Angeles, Calif. 90007. Index, adv. Sample. Vol. ends: Autumn.

Indexed: PhilosI, RepBibPhil. *Bk. rev:* Occasional, 5–7 pages, signed. *Aud:* Ac.

Publishes relatively short articles in all areas of philosophy. As is the case with most other general philosophy journals, most articles are critical or interpretive; a small percentage present the original philosophy of the authors. Comparable in scope and difficulty to *Dialogue,* this journal is recommended for academic libraries. (J.A.)

Philosophical Books. 1960. 3/yr. $2.40. J. Kemp. Leicester Univ. Press, Leicester, England. Adv. Circ: 700. Vol ends: Oct. *Aud:* Ac.

A review medium for current books in philosophy. All articles are signed and truly critical; i.e., they investigate and comment upon a book's argument carefully and in detail. The average length of a review is from 750 to 1,500 words, and each issue reviews more than a dozen recently published works. Since the number of philosophical books published during a year so far exceeds the less than 50 reviewed in this journal, balance must be difficult to achieve. Understandably, books in languages other than English are excluded. However, the almost total absence of books on oriental philosophy, phenomenology, and existentialism is less understandable. For larger collections. (J.A.)

Philosophical Quarterly. 1950. q. $4. G. P. Henderson. Queen's College, Dundee, Scotland. Index, adv. Circ: 1,300. Microform: UM. Reprint: Swets.

Indexed: BritHum, PhilosI, RepBibPhil. *Bk. rev:* 16–20, 900 words, signed. *Aud:* Ac.

A scholarly journal demanding a knowledge of the language of modern philosophy. Although some papers are historical and expository, the emphasis is upon progress toward the solution of problems which interest professional philosophers. Although its difficulty seems to restrict this journal's readership, the review section will be of interest to librarians and bibliographers because of its extent and quality. (J.A.)

The Philosophical Review. 1892. q. $3 (Institutions $6). Sage School of Philosophy, Cornell Univ., 218 Golden Smith Hall, Cornell Univ., Ithaca, N.Y. 14850. Adv. Circ: 4,000. Sample. Vol. ends: Oct.

Indexed: PhilosI, SSHum, RepBibPhil. *Bk. rev:* 10; 1,000 words, signed. *Aud:* Ac.

A general philosophical periodical of high quality and reputation. Reflects current interests of the professional philosophical academy; heavy emphasis on linguistic philosophy and logical analysis. Contains five or six articles per issue, and like most other periodicals in this field, appeals primarily to the specialist. (J.A.)

Philosophical Studies. 1950. 6/yr. $3. Wilfred Sellars and Herbert Feigl. Univ. of Minn. Press, 2037 University Ave. S.E., Minneapolis, Minn. 55455. Circ: 1,000. Sample. Vol. ends: Dec.

Indexed: PhilosI, CathI, RepBibPhil. *Aud:* Ac.

Papers in this journal tend to be shorter than those in most other philosophical periodicals. They are usually addressed to the solution of a specific, limited problem. Many are in the form of statement and counterstatement—short installments in the philosophical dialogue centered about a specific issue. Since the papers presuppose a detailed knowledge of and interest in the techniques of mathematical logic, the journal's greatest value is to the professional and academic audience. (J.A.)

Philosophy. 1931. q. $6. H. B. Acton. Macmillan Journals Ltd., London, England. Circ: 2,800. Reprint: Johnson, AMS.

Indexed: BritHum, PhilosI, PsyAb, RePBibPhil. *Bk. rev:* 8–12, 1,000 words, signed. *Aud:* Ga, Ac. *Jv:* V.

One of the few British philosophy journals not given over to the technical jargon of linguistic philosophy and logic. Most of the articles are concerned with problems of current interest, but some deal with philosophy from a historical standpoint. In addition to the regular book reviews, there are occasional lengthy review articles. A journal of professional caliber, written by professional philosophers but of interest to the educated layman as well as students of philosophy, it is generally recommended. (J.A.)

Philosophy East and West. 1951. q. $6. Eliot Deutsch. Univ. of Hawaii Press, 535 Ward Ave., Honolulu, Hawaii 96814. Index, adv. Circ: 1,250. Sample. Vol. ends: Oct. Refereed. Reprint: Johnson..

Indexed: PhilI, RepBibPhil. *Bk. rev:* 8, 500 words. *Aud:* Ac, Ga. *Jv:* V.

The most valuable periodical published in English on Asian philosophy. Attempts to illuminate, in a comparative manner, the distinctive characteristics of the various philosophical traditions in the East and West. It is particularly concerned with comparative areas of methodology, metaphysics, ethics, aesthetics, and social philosophy. Since widespread American awareness of and interest in oriental philosophy is relatively recent, this comparative approach is particularly helpful to the nonspecialist. All periods, from ancient through contemporary, receive attention. Original philosophy which arises out of intercultural synthesis, as well as historical–critical articles, are included. For all libraries attempting even a minimum philosophy collection. (J.A.)

Philosophy and Phenomenological Research. 1940. q. $7.50 (Libraries and Institutions $9). Marvin Farber. State Univ. of N. Y. at Buffalo, Buffalo, N.Y. 14226. Index, adv. Sample. Vol. ends: June. Refereed.

Indexed: Philos I, RepBibPhil. *Bk. rev:* 15–18, 300–600 words, signed. *Aud:* Ac, Ga. *Jv:* V.

This journal is the official organ of the International Phenomenological Society, and is one of the most readable periodicals published in the field of philosophy. Each issue contains about eight articles in sufficiently nontechnical language and style to appeal to the layman who is reasonably well read in philosophy. Subjects covered are quite varied: skepticism, fatalism, aesthetics, social relations, ethics, metaphysics, to name a few. The point of view, of course, tends to be that of the phenomenologists, an important contemporary school of thinkers. Recommended for academic libraries and larger public libraries. (J.A.)

Philosophy & Public Affairs. 1971. q. $10 (Individuals $7.50). Marshall Cohen. Princeton Univ. Press, Princeton, N.J. 08540. Index, adv. Sample. Vol. ends: Summer.

Bk. rev: Various number, length. *Aud:* Ac, Ga. *Jv:* V.

A philosophy magazine designed "to fill the need for a periodical in which philosophers with different viewpoints and philosophically inclined writers from various disciplines (law to sociology) can bring their distinctive methods to bear on problems that concern everyone." The first issue includes five long, not always easy-to-grasp articles. Abortion, at least in its philosophical aspects, is discussed in two contributions, and the morals of the second World War and the Nuremberg trials make up two more. Primarily concerned with political philosophy and the practical life, the journal offers an interesting change from the usual approach. But until it is a few more issues away, it is difficult to tell how successful it will be. Smaller libraries might send for a sample before ordering, al-

though all larger libraries will want it because it is out there and doing something a bit differently.

Philosophy and Rhetoric. 1968. q. $7. Henry W. Johnstone, Jr. Pa. State Univ. Press, 215 Wagner Bldg., University Park, Pa. 16802. Index, adv. Circ: 750. Vol. ends: Fall.

Indexed: PhilosI, RepBibPhil. *Bk. rev:* 4–5, 3 pages, signed. *Aud:* Ac.

Concerns itself with rhetoric as a philosophical concept; its nature, scope, and limits; its value; its relationship to other human activities. Articles have been contributed by specialists in speech and communications, as well as by professional philosophers. The subject matter of this journal should not be confused with philosophy of *language*, a wider field which has occupied the attention of contemporary philosophers for some time. Valuable to libraries supporting advanced programs in philosophy or speech. (J.A.)

Philosophy of Science. 1934. q. $10 (Nonmembers $15). Richard S. Rudner. Dept. of Philosophy, Mich. State Univ., East Lansing, Mich. 48823. Index, adv. Circ: 2,800. Sample. Vol. ends: Dec. Refereed.

Indexed: PhilosI, RepBibPhil, SCI, SSHum. *Bk. rev:* 4, 1,000 words, signed. *Aud:* Ac, Ga.

The official journal of the Philosophy of Science Association, and, along with the *British Journal for the Philosophy of Science*, one of the two most important English-language periodicals dealing with this specialty. Though some articles might seem more scientific than philosophical, there are many contributions dealing with knowledge, scientific method, causality, and other subjects of more general philosophical interest. Both original thought and historical–critical articles are included. Some background in philosophy and science should enable the nonspecialist to profit from acquaintance with this journal. For all academic libraries supporting philosophy programs, and large public libraries. (J.A.)

Philosophy Today. 1957. q. $5. Robert F. Lechner. Messenger Press, Carthagena Sta., Celina, Ohio 45822. Index, adv. Circ: 1,400. Vol. ends: Winter.

Aud: Ac.

"Directed to the interests of scholars and teachers within the Christian tradition." But the gospel is according to St. Martin Heidegger, not St. Thomas Aquinas. A very readable journal of existentialism and phenomenology, recommended for academic and larger public libraries. (J.A.)

Phronesis; a journal for ancient philosophy. (Text in English, French, German, and Latin.) 1955. s-a. $7.50. David Furley. Royal Van Gorcum Ltd., Assen, The Netherlands. Adv. Circ: 800. Vol ends: No. 2.

Indexed: PhilosI, RepBibPhil. *Aud:* Ac.

One of the few journals devoted exclusively to ancient Western philosophy. Emphasis is naturally on Plato and Aristotle, though some articles on pre-Socratic and Roman thought have appeared in recent volumes. Each issue averages about six articles, most of which are in English. Though specialized, it has a place in any library with more than a minimal philosophy collection. (J.A.)

Process Studies. 1971. q. $6 (Institutions $7). Lewis S. Ford and John B. Cobb, Jr. 1325 N. College Ave., Claremont, Calif. 91711. Index, adv. Sample. Vol. ends: Winter. Refereed.

Bk. rev: 3, 3 pages, signed. *Aud:* Ac.

This new periodical has a rather narrow focus: the thought of Whitehead and his philosophical kin, who view reality more as "process" than fact—more as "becoming" than "being." The need for such a journal can be measured by the recent growth of literature devoted to process philosophy. It is the intent of the editors to include essays applying Whitehead's conceptuality in many fields, such as literary criticism, physics, political science, and theology, as well as philosophy. Abstracts of relevant articles, as well as a bibliography of secondary literature on Whitehead (to be updated annually), will be published on a regular basis. Though *Process Studies* may be too specialized for small libraries, it will probably be well received by the philosophical community, and should find a place in moderately ambitious philosophy collections. (J.A.)

Ratio. 1957. s-a. $4.30. Stephan Korner. Basil Blackwell, Broad. St., Oxford, England. Index, adv. Circ: 650. Sample. Vol. ends: Dec.

Indexed: PhilosI, RepBibPhil, BritHum. *Bk. rev:* Various numbers, length, signed.

Deals with all branches of pure and applied philosophy, from a rational (as opposed to a skeptical or intuitive) point of view. The articles are highly technical, rather short, and directed to specialists. For large philosophy collections. (J.A.)

Review of Existential Psychology. See Psychology Section.

Review of Metaphysics. 1947. q. $6 (Students $4, institutions $10). Richard J. Bernstein. Philosophical Education Soc., Inc., 214 Lyman Beecher Hall, Haverford College, Haverford, Pa. 19041. Circ: 3,400. Microform: UM. Reprint: AMS.

Indexed: PhilosI. *Bk. rev:* 50–75, 160 words, signed. *Aud:* Ac.

This eclectic journal of philosophy does not limit its contributors to a particular metaphysical school. The only unifying bond between articles is philosophical relevance and technical competence. While there are occasional historical essays, most articles investigate a topic of current concern to contemporary philoso-

phers. The papers submitted are quite technical, but there is not the obsession with logic, the foundations of mathematics, and the philosophy of science which is so common in English-language journals of similar professional caliber. Of great interest to students, librarians, and bibliographers will be the Books Received—Summary and Comments section, which contains short critical reviews of new books (comments prepared by members of the staff), and the section Current Periodical Articles—Philosophical Periodicals, which abstracts some 60 to 75 journal articles. For the professional audience. (J.A.)

Revue Philosophique de Louvain. See Europe and Middle East/French Language Section.

Southern Journal of Philosophy. 1963. q. $6. (Institutions $8). Carrol R. Bowman, Gene G. James, and William B. Barton. Dept. of Philosophy, Memphis State Univ., Memphis, Tenn. 38111. Index, Adv. Circ: 700. Sample. Vol. ends: Winter.

Indexed: PhilosI, RepBibPhil. *Bk. rev:* Various number, length, signed. *Aud:* Ac.

Not confined to any particular set of issues or problems, nor to any particular orientation, but often publishes issues devoted to a special topic or philosopher. More readable than the more specialized journals, although the double-column format and narrow margins are no help in this respect. Should have a wide audience, particularly among colleges and universities with strong philosophy departments. (J.A.)

Soviet Studies in Philosophy. See USSR and East Europe/English Language General Section.

Studies in Soviet Thought. See USSR and East Europe/English Language General Section.

Synthèse. 1936. q. $13.50. Rudel Publishing Co., Box 17, Dordrecht, Netherlands. Circ: 1,500.

Indexed: PhilosI. *Bk. rev:* 3–5, 1,500 words, signed. *Aud:* Ac.

A very sophisticated journal of scientific epistemology and methodology, it concerns itself almost exclusively with logic, truth and meaning, linguistic usage, and language games. Advanced knowledge of science and mathematics is presupposed. For libraries supporting major programs in philosophy or mathematics. (J.A.)

Theoria; a Swedish journal of philosophy. 1935. 3/yr. Skr. 30K. Segerberg and G. Hermerén. Gleerups, Oresundsvagen 1, 222 38 Lund, Sweden. Adv. Circ: 500. Sample. Vol. ends: No. 3. Refereed.

Indexed: PhilosI, RepBibPhil. *Aud:* Ac.

Scope includes all fields of analytic philosophy. Most articles are in English; some are in French and German. All are highly technical, and require knowledge of symbolic logic, as well as familiarity with the specialized language of the field. For large philosophy or mathematics collections. (J.A.)

Thought. See Religion and Theology/Denominational Section.

PHOTOGRAPHY

Basic Periodicals

Ejh: *Popular Photography;* Hs: *Popular Photography;* Ga: *Popular Photography, Modern Photography, Camera;* Jc: *Camera, Aperture, Modern Photography;* Ac: *Camera, Aperture, Modern Photography, Professional Photographer.*

Basic Abstracts and Indexes

Photographic Abstracts, Abstracts Photographic Science.

Cessations

U.S. Camera and Travel Magazine.

Aperture. 1952. q. $14. Minor White. Aperture, Inc., Elm St., Millerton, N.Y. 12546. Illus., index, adv. Circ: 4,500. Sample. Vol. ends: no. 4. Microform: UM.

Indexed: ArtI. *Bk. rev:* 3–5, 103 pages, signed. *Aud:* Ga, Ac, Hs. *Jv:* V.

The leading American photography journal for the student of photography as an art. Serious examples of artistic photography are sometimes accompanied by essays, comments, poetry. Format varies from a complete issue devoted to the works, chronology, and bibliography of one photographer (e.g., Jerry N. Uelsmann: "An Aperture Monograph," vol. 15, no. 4, 1971) to issues containing portfolios of lesser-known photographers. The photographic works presented range from avantgarde to classical. Articles avoid detailed technical processes and stress the artistic merits of photography. Usually, some 50 or more black and white (and sometimes color) photographs are reproduced in each issue. This, along with *Camera,* represents one of the few photographic magazines which treats the subject as an art form, and should be in all academic libraries and many public and school collections.

Bolex Reporter. 1950. s-a. $2. Walter Braun. Paillard, Inc., 1900 Lower Rd., Linden, N.J. 07036. Illus. Circ: 50,000. Sample. Vol. ends: No. 2.

Aud: Ga.

For any amateur moviemaker, whether using super 8 or 16 mm equipment, this offering presents subject matter centered around the techniques of moving picture making, stressing (of course) the desirability of using Bolex equipment. Specific instructions for techniques of photographing, as well as suggestions for selection of material and good ideas on the composition of the total amateur movie, are given. In one re-

cent issue, a series of five contributors recounted their experiences with moviemaking in as many parts of the world. These narratives included descriptions of points of interest, as well as of the adventure of filming them. Fine quality reproductions of excellent full-color single shots serve as illustrations; pictures of the equipment, where it is discussed, are also shown. This is worth the nominal cost for school and public libraries where additional material on photography is needed. It is possible that local dealers may provide complimentary subscriptions to their local libraries, in the interest of developing more interest in amateur moviemaking, thus increasing the demand for Bolex equipment. (A.S.)

British Journal of Photography. 1854. w. $22. Geoffrey Crawley. Henry Greenwood, 24 Wellington St., London WC2, England. Illus., adv., diag. Circ: 11,800. Sample. Vol. ends: Dec.

Indexed: ChemAb, PhAb. *Bk. rev:* Notes and abstracts. *Aud:* Ac.

This British weekly, published on good paper, is intended for all concerned with photography or any of its applications, but it is primarily an organ for professionals. It is international in scope, useful in American libraries. Articles on the press, industrial, medical, scientific, and industrial cinematographic fields, as well as news of interest to photographers, appear regularly. There are good equipment and material test reports. A portfolio of a photographer's work is a usual feature (e.g., "My Best Six by Maurice Rowe" by Leslie Sansom, Nov. 3, 1967—examples of *Motor* magazine cover photos). The Technical and Scientific Digest gives an up-to-date report on current new books, periodicals, photographic tools, and techniques. There are regular reports from Japan and West Germany. Because of its scope and frequency it is an excellent basic photography journal for larger collections.

Camera. 1922. m. $18. Allen Porter. C. J. Bucher Ltd., Lucerne, Switzerland. Illus., index, adv. Circ: 3,700. Sample. Vol. ends: Dec. Microform: UM.

Indexed: ArtI, PhAb. *Aud:* Ga, Ac, Hs. *Jv:* V.

Like *Aperture* and *Infinity,* this concentrates on the work of photographers, not the how-to-do-it aspect. Each issue is a portfolio of outstanding photographs, usually centered around a given theme and representing five to eight masters of the art. Reproductions are in black and white and in color. They are uniformly excellent. The issue ends with brief notes on new equipment, and there is some information on the photographers and their work represented in the given number. International in scope and reputation, this would be a first choice in any library where photography is viewed as an art form.

Camera 35. 1957. bi-m. $6. Jim Hughes. U.S. Camera Publishing Co., 132 W. 31st St., New York, N.Y. 10001. Illus., adv. Circ: 100,000.

Aud: Ga.

Devoted exclusively to the 35 mm camera. Material is prepared by experts and ranges from how-to-do-it articles to more sophisticated reports on photographers and their work. Particularly useful for the accurate, unbiased test reports of cameras and lenses. Many good-to-excellent black and white photographs and usually at least eight pages of color shots. About one third of each issue is given over to advertising. A third or fourth choice for collections in public libraries.

Industrial and Commercial Photographer. 1961. m. $9.50. George H. Wilkinson. Distinctive Publns., 230 Vauxhall Bridge Rd., London SW1, England. Illus., index, adv. Circ: 6,000. Sample. Vol. ends: Dec.

Indexed: PhAb. *Bk. rev:* 2, 400 words, signed. *Aud:* Ac, Sa.

A professional photography magazine for the man or woman working in commercial studios and industrial in-plant departments. An excellent graphic arts supplement is published six times a year. There is also a strong bimonthly section on industrial cinema. Most of the magazine deals with the work of individual photographers, and gives the advanced student reports on new equipment. About one half of every issue is advertising.

Industrial Photography; the magazine that advances technical progress. 1952. m. $8. Arthur H. Rosien. United Business Publns., Inc., 200 Madison Ave., New York, N.Y. 10016. Illus., adv. Circ: 33,400.

Indexed: ASTI, PhAb. *Aud:* Sa.

Controlled circulation puts this periodical into the hands of working photographers. In it they find articles which stress photography as "a major force in explaining man to man." Some articles are fully documented studies, whereas others are primarily staff reports. Each issue usually focuses on a particular topic and is fully illustrated. A valuable reference issue in December lists photographic books and provides a categorized and annotated guide to bulletins designed to give readers information about photographic equipment, material, and services.

Infinity; the magazine of photo journalism. 1952. m. $9.75. John Trevor. Amer. Soc. of Magazine Photographers, Inc., 60 E. 42nd St., New York, N.Y. 10017. Illus., index., adv. Circ: 7,000.

Indexed: AbPhoto. *Bk. rev:* 1–5, 500 words, signed. *Aud:* Ac, Ga.

Primarily a showcase for outstanding photography. Somewhat on the line of *Aperture* and *Camera,* this gives more attention to the "practical" aspects of the art. Little how-to-do-it material is presented, but some articles touch on technical developments. Emphasis is on the work of the individual photographer, and the color and black and white reproductions are excellent.

Camera and *Aperture* would be first choices for the art collection; *Infinity* is slimmer in content.

The Journal of Photographic Science. 1953. bi-m. Membership (Nonmembers $12.60). R. J. Cox. Royal Photographic Soc. of Great Britain, 14 S. Andley St., London W14 50P, England. Illus., index, adv.

Indexed: BritTech, ChemAb, PhAb. *Bk. rev:* Occasional. *Aud:* Sa.

Stresses scientific and technical photography. Scholarly papers read at the Society's meetings as well as important contributions by others are issued. Book reviews, news and reports of meetings, new equipment, and correspondence are included on a irregular basis.

Leica Photography. 1932. Irreg. 2–4/yr. Free. Ed. bd. E. Leitz, Inc., Rockleigh, N.J. 07647. Illus. Circ: 50,000.

Aud: Ga, Hs.

A camera company house organ (free to Leica owners, and presumably to interested libraries). This is typical of magazines issued for a specific type of camera. It is, however, vastly superior to many of its younger cousins. Included are technical, practical, and inspirational articles. Picture spreads by professionals or proficient amateurs are atttractively presented on good paper. While especially useful for owners of Leica cameras, it has application for others interested in photography.

✓***Modern Photography.*** 1937. m. $7. Julia Scully. Herbert Keppler, 165 W. 46th St., New York, N.Y. 10036. Illus., index, adv. Circ: 370,000. Vol. ends: Dec.

Indexed: ASTI, ChemAb, RG. *Bk. rev:* 5, 200–500 words, signed. *Aud:* Ga, Ac, Hs. *Jv:* V.

Along with *Popular Photography,* one of the two basic photo magazines for general collections. It is more specialized than its rival, tends to emphasize technical aspects of photography and equipment. (Particularly valuable is the annual guide to the top 45 cameras, which is similar to the *Consumer Report* approach.) The writing is good to excellent, usually well within the grasp of the average reader. Top photographers often present new ideas on composition and techniques. If a choice has to be made between the two general photographic magazines, this would be first in academic libraries, a probable second in the average public library.

Officiel de la Photographie. See Europe and Middle East/French Language Section.

P.S.A. Journal. 1935. m. $5. Robert L. McIntyre. Photographic Soc. of Amer., 2005 Walnut St., Philadelphia, Pa. Illus., index, adv. Circ: 12,979. Vol. ends: Dec. Microform: UM.

Indexed: ChemAb. AbPhoto. *Bk. rev:* 2–3, 100–800 words, signed. *Aud:* Ac, Sa.

A technical journal for the professional photographer, and the dedicated amateur. As a publication of the Photographic Society of America it carries news of society activities, accurate information on new products, a calendar of events, and a good correspondence column. The several articles stress photography as an art form, yet are readily within the grasp of the average interested layman. Reference value: A "Who's Who" appears in May, identifying personalities in the various areas of photography.

Photographic Business and Product News. 1964. m. $4. R. Maschke. Photographic Product News, Inc., 250 Fulton Ave., Hempstead, N.Y. 11550. Illus., adv. Circ: 30,000. Sample. Vol. ends: Dec.

Bk. rev: 2, ½ page, signed. *Aud:* Sa.

Primarily for the commercial, portrait, or journalism photographer, this features ways of improving business methods as well as photographic techniques. Of some value to the layman because of the objective analysis of new equipment.

Photographic Science and Engineering. 1957. bi-m. Membership (Nonmembers $25). D. R. White. Soc. of Photographic Scientists & Engineers, 1330 Massachusetts Ave., N.W., Washington, D.C. 20005. Illus. Circ: 3,500.

Indexed: EngI, PhAb, AbPhoto. *Bk. rev:* 2, 200 words, signed. *Aud:* Sa.

Features six to eight articles of a relatively high technical level on the application of photography to science and engineering. In addition to the good-to-fine photographic illustrations, there are regular departments which cover new products, meetings, and biographies and obituaries. Probably the best magazine of its type in the United States. The Society also issues *Image Technology* (formerly *SPSE News*), a bimonthly newsletter, and *Abstracts of Photographic Science and Engineering.*

Photon Ciné Review. See Europe and Middle East/French Language Section.

✓ ***Popular Photography.*** 1937. m. $7. Ken Poll. Ziff Davis Publishing Co., 1 Park Ave., New York, N.Y. 10016. Subs. to: Popular Photography, Circulation Dept., Portland Pl., Boulder, Colo. 80311. Illus., adv. Circ: 545,000. Microform: UM.

Indexed: ChemAb, RG. *Bk. rev:* Notes. *Aud:* Ga, Hs. *Jv:* V.

One of two general photography magazines (see also *Modern Photography*), and a first choice for public and school libraries. Why? It is less technical than its rival, more geared to the beginner, and less affluent. Articles stress technique, and buying advice considers the average reader. Contributions cover every phase of photography and include many practical hints. The examples of photography by outstanding photographers,

including eight pages in full color, are an inspiration. The hobbyist who takes photography seriously will find it indispensable.

Professional Photographer. 1907. m. $7.50. Fred Schmidt. Professional Photographers of Amer. Inc., 1090 Executive Way, Des Plaines, Ill. 60018. Illus., index, adv. Circ: 20,000. Sample. Vol. ends: Dec.

Bk. rev: 2–3, 100 words. *Aud:* Sa.

This claims to be "the oldest professional photographic publication in the Western Hemisphere." Illustrated articles for the portrait, commercial, and industrial photographer are geared to help him "become a better business man, a better technician." About half is technical, the rest tips. Somewhat similar to *Photographic Business and Product News* and only for large public libraries.

PHYSICS

Basic Periodicals:

Hs: *Physics Today, Physics Teacher;* Ga: *Physics Today;* Jc: *American Journal of Physics, Physics Today, Physics Teacher;* Ac: *American Journal of Physics.* (Note: Several others should be considered "basic," depending on the makeup of the library and the institution which it serves. See annotations.)

Basic Abstracts and Indexes

Science Abstracts, Section A: Physics Abstracts.

Introduction

In the main, the journals covered in this section are authoritative research publications sponsored by some outstanding scientific societies; papers included therein have generally been subjected to review by specialists prior to publication and represent high-quality studies. Titles have been limited largely to U.S. and English publications representing general physics journals; a few journals emphasizing applications of physical principles; some foreign titles of historical prominence; and selected periodicals applicable to physics educators, students, and interested laymen. In the case of specialized journals, titles were chosen that represent interdisciplinary publications having applicability to many sciences; specialized journals concerned solely with the subfields of physics have, of necessity, been excluded. Of course the selection represents a mere fragment of the titles commonly found in academic libraries supporting research interests. Most academic libraries would probably subscribe to many of the prestigious publications of the American Institute of Physics, and to many excellent foreign journals such as *Journal of the Physical Society of Japan, Helvetica Physica Acta, Nuovo Cimento, Annales de Physique, Progress of Theoretical Physics,*

Zeitschrift für Physik, as well as to a wide variety of specialized journals.

Academy of Sciences of the USSR. Bulletin. 1954. m. $310. Eugene Brunner. Columbia Technical Translations, 5 Vermont Ave., White Plains, N.Y. 10606. Illus., index. Sample. Vol. ends: No. 12. Refereed.

Indexed: ChemAb, EngI, SciAb. *Aud:* Sa, Ac.

The publications output of the prestigious Academy of Sciences (USSR) is well known to science librarians, and a number of its journals are available in translation (see also the *Soviet Physics* series put out by the American Institute of Physics). This *Bulletin*, a cover-to-cover translation of *Izvestiya Akademii Nauk SSR, Seriya Fizicheskaya*, has significance to research libraries, since it publishes the entire proceedings of selected physics conferences held in the USSR. Symposia range over a broad number of subjects, and topics covered in recent issues have included spectroscopy, laser physics, nuclear magnetic resonance, nuclear physics, solid state, etc. Its price is higher than most translation journals, however, and thus it will probably be available only to large research libraries.

Acoustical Society of America. Journal. 1929. m. $45. R. Bruce Lindsay. Amer. Inst. of Physics, 335 E. 45th St., New York, N.Y. 10017. Illus., index. Circ: 7,000. Sample. Vol. ends: June/Dec. Refereed. Microform: UM.

Indexed: BioAb, ChemAb, EngI, MathR, Meteor&GeoastAb, PsyAb, SciAb, SCI. *Bk. rev:* 1–2, 400–700 words, signed. *Aud:* Sa, Ac.

With applications to both biological and physical sciences, the publication is an important acquisition for research libraries. Issued in two parts monthly, Part 1 is dedicated to general acoustics papers, including architectural acoustics, instruments and apparatus, noise, and signal processing. Also incorporated in Part 1 are Society and technical news, programs of meetings, and useful bibliographic aids, discussed below. Part 2 alternates, monthly, between research papers in the physical sciences (e.g., ultrasonics, mechanical vibrations and shock, underwater sound), and the biological disciplines (e.g., physiological and psychological acoustics, speech, music and musical instruments). Of particular interest to librarians are two continuing bibliographies in Part 1: References to Contemporary Papers cites current literature; and Review of Acoustical patents provides abstracts of newly released patents. Because of its wide scope, the periodical, one of the world's leading acoustics journals, is a noteworthy addition to a university collection.

Another publication put out by the American Institute of Physics is *Soviet Physics-Acoustics* ($35/yr.), a cover-to-cover translation of the prominent USSR research journal, *Akusticheskii Zhurnal*. Similarly, specialized collections supporting accoustical research will also find need for *Acoustica* (S. Hirzel Verlag,

$21.45/vol.), sponsored by three major European organizations: Acoustics Group of the Physical Society of London, Acousticiens de Langue Française, and Deutsche Physikalische Gesellschaft. Smaller academic collections will find their needs well served by the *Acoustical Society Journal*, however.

Advances in Physics. 1952. bi-m. $64.40. B. R. Coles. Taylor & Francis, Ltd., 10–14 Macklin St., London WC2B 5ND, England. Sample. Vol. ends: no. 6. Refereed. Microform: Taylor & Francis.

Indexed: BritTech, ChemAb, EngI, MathR, MetAb, SciAb, SCI. *Aud:* Sa, Ac.

Originally issued as a supplement to *Philosophical Magazine* (see below), the journal serves as a critical reviewing medium for theoretical and experimental work in all areas of physics, including applied mechanics. Emphasis is on the specialized review paper in a fairly narrow field, however, rather than on the broad surveys offered by such journals as *Reports on Progress in Physics*. Studies tend to be extremely long, frequently extending over 150 pages; bibliographies are correspondingly lengthy. The publication is an important one for physics research collections, since it acts more or less as the midpoint between the appearance of original research and the publication of the specialized monograph. For university libraries.

American Journal of Physics. 1933. m. $22. Forrest I. Boley. Amer. Inst. of Physics, Inc., 335 E. 45th St., New York, N.Y. 10017. Illus., index, adv. Circ: 13,000. Sample. Vol. ends: Dec. Refereed. Microform: UM.

Indexed: ASTI, ChemAb, EngI, MathR, MetAb, SciAb, SCI. *Bk. rev:* 9–10, 350–600 words, signed. *Aud:* Sa, Ac.

Geared toward college and university professors, the official publication of the American Association of Physics Teachers deserves a place in any type of academic library supporting physics curricula. The journal ranges over the entire field of physics—classical mechanics through nuclear physics—and emphasizes three types of papers: expository articles; historical/philosophical works; or unique instructional methods in the classroom or laboratory. In recent years attention has also been given to use of the computer with respect to the field. On occasion, abstracts of meetings of the Association appear, as well as news announcements and personalia. Book reviews are excellent; films and other audiovisual material are also reviewed. The diversity of subject matter, often on a nonspecialist level, makes this fine publication accessible to students as well. Highly recommended as a first choice for any type of academic library. (For another good publication of the American Association of Physics Teachers, see *Physics Teacher*, listed below.)

American Physical Society. Bulletin. 1956. 13/yr. $16. W. W. Havens. Amer. Physical Soc., 335 E. 45th St.,

New York, N.Y. 10017. Index. Circ: 30,000. Sample. Vol. ends: Dec.

Indexed: BioAb, ChemAb, SciAb. *Aud:* Sa, Ac.

The official *Bulletin* contains the abstracts of papers presented at meetings of the Society. (Usually no written text of these papers is available.) The importance of such a publication to a research collection is that it gives access to information which may never appear in print, or is scheduled for publication months later. Also included in each issue are news of the divisions of the APS, programs of forthcoming meetings, and a cumulative author index. Year-end indexes are also published. A valuable alerting medium for physicists and university libraries.

Annalen der Physik. 1790. Irreg. 2 vol./yr. (4 nos./vol.) $18.94/vol. G. Richter and W. Walcher. Johann Ambrosius Barth, Salomonstr. 188, 701 Leipzig, E. Germany. Illus., index. Circ: 2,100. Refereed. Microform: UM, PMC, McA, Maxwell. Reprint: Johnson.

Indexed: ChemAb, EngI, MathR, MetAb, SciAb, SCI. *Aud:* Sa, Ac.

One of the venerable old journals, left over from the eighteenth century, which gave us some of the world's greatest contributions to physics. By now, every library owning the 1905 and 1916 original volumes, containing Einstein's early contributions on general relativity, has safely deposited them in the rare book room. Today, the journal is still a distinctive, international general physics journal, publishing both theoretical and experimental papers. Libraries owning the complete run, from volume one on, definitely have a prestige item. For university collections.

Annals of Physics. 1957. m. (6 vol./yr). $28/vol. Philip M. Morse. Academic Press, Inc., 111 Fifth Ave., New York, N.Y. 10003. Index. Sample. Refereed.

Indexed: ChemAb, EngI, MathR, MetAb, SciAb, SCI. *Aud:* Sa, Ac.

Theoretical and scholarly, the publication chronicles the basic research work considered highly significant in terms of today's trends in fundamental physics. Papers do contain enough historical or background information, however, so that its readership can extend beyond a specialist group. Recommended as a general physics journal for university collections.

Applied Optics. 1962. m. $45. J. N. Howard. Amer. Inst. of Physics, 335 E. 45th St., New York, N.Y. 10017. Illus., index, adv. Circ: 10,000. Sample. Vol. ends: Dec. Refereed.

Indexed: EngI, MetAb, SciAb, SCI. *Bk. rev:* 7, 250 words, signed. *Aud:* Sa, Ac.

Sponsored by the Optical Society of America, the journal is concerned with "applications of facts, principles, and methods of optics." (More fundamental studies are reported in the Society's other research journal, *Journal of the Optical Society,* listed below.) All areas of optics are covered: physics, instrumentation, materials, lenses, lasers, and, more recently, information processing through optics. In addition to full-length papers, the journal also releases "rapid communications," short research reports given preferential publication. Frequently, papers may center around a specific theme. Some review, historical, or tutorial papers also appear from time to time. A large part of the periodical is also given over to several departments, including news, personalia, meeting reports, research briefs, and patent abstracts. Recommended for any research library dealing with the field.

A Russian counterpart, *Soviet Journal of Optical Technology* (translation of *Optiko-Mekhanicheskaya Promyshlennost*), also published by the American Institute of Physics, is valuable for research collections, as well.

Applied Physics Letters. See *Journal of Applied Physics.*

Astrophysical Journal. See Astronomy Section for this title and others in the field of astrophysics.

Bell System Technical Journal. See Electrical Engineering Section.

Canadian Journal of Physics. 1929. s-m. $40. R. R. Haering. National Research Council of Canada, Ottawa 7, Canada. Illus., index. Circ: 2,500. Sample. Vol. ends: Dec. Refereed. Microform: PMC.

Indexed: BioAb, ChemAb, EngI, MathR, MetAb, Meteor&GeoastAb, NuclSciAb, SciAb, SCI. *Aud:* Sa, Ac.

Part of the Canadian Journals of Research group, sponsored by NRC-Canada, the main research establishment for that country. The publication is a good, general physics journal representing all branches of the field. Research articles, plus short notes, appear under such topics as atoms, molecules; atoms, nuclei, and particles in matter; fluids, thermodynamics; solids; nuclei; elementary particles and fields. Contributions are mainly from, but not restricted to, Canadian universities and laboratories. A distinguished editorial board counts, among its members Dr. G. Herzberg, recent Nobel laureate. An established and authoritative research publication for university libraries.

Comments on Modern Physics. 1967. $157.50 for all five parts. Gordon & Breach Science Publishers, 440 Park Ave. S., New York, N.Y. 10011. Sample. Microform: Gordon & Breach.

Indexed: ChemAb, SciAb, SCI. *Aud:* Sa, Ac.

A new genre of scientific journal has taken hold in the last few years, namely, the review journal which offers critiques of current research and developments based on papers appearing in the literature. Briefly, the *Comments* series have, for each specialty journal listed below, a regular panel of authoritative and elite "correspondents," who write short commentaries, and may include discussions of their own research. Available to date in six sections, the journals not only provide excellent tutorials for students, but also serve professionals who seek to enrich their scope beyond their immediate specialty. The coverage of each publication (representing the major areas of physics) is self evident from its title. Editorial boards are represented by active and distinguished specialists. One or all of the *Comments* are highly recommended for academic libraries with strong undergraduate programs in physics. Listed below are details on the series, each of which may be purchased separately.

Part A: *Comments on Nuclear & Particle Physics.* 1967. bi-m. $35 (Individuals $11). J. Schiffer and J. Sandweiss.

Part B: *Comments on Solid State Physics.* 1968. bi-m. $35 (Individuals $11). E. Burstein and R. Smoluchowski.

Part C: *Comments on Astrophysics and Space Physics.* For annotation see Astronomy Section.

Part D: *Comments on Atomic and Molecular Physics.* 1969. bi-m. $35 (Individuals $11). Benjamin Bederson and E. Gerjnoy.

Part E: *Comments on Plasma Physics and Controlled Fusion.* 1971. bi-m. $35 (Individuals $11). Burton D. Fried.

Comments and Communications in Statistical Physics. 1972. bi-m. $35. P. Resibois and Joel L. Lebowitz. Newest in the series. Follows the formats of other *Comments,* but also includes short papers on statistical physics.

(Note: The publishers have also started another complementary series, *Comments on Earth Sciences,* the first of which, *Geophysics,* should also be of interest to physics libraries. See Earth Sciences Section for annotation.)

Contemporary Physics. 1959. m. $35.65. G. R. Noakes. Taylor & Francis, Red Lion Ct., Fleet St., London, England. Illus., index, adv. Circ: 2,000. Sample. Vol. ends: Dec. Refereed.

Indexed: EngI, MetAb, SciAb, SCI. *Bk. rev:* 20, 200 words, signed. *Aud:* Sa, Ac, Sh.

For both nonspecialists and students (advanced senior high through undergraduate), the periodical supplies interpretive survey-type articles contributed by known authorities. Broadly encompassing not only the major fields of physics, but also new technologies utilizing physical principles, its scope passes far beyond the limits of the discipline. Language is kept relatively unsophisticated, to best serve its audience, but some technical knowledge is necessary. About three to four articles appear in each issue; some issues also carry essay-type book reviews which further act as tutorials

in particular fields. Highly recommended for undergraduate collections, including junior colleges, and even for some sophisticated senior high school libraries.

Current Papers in Physics. See *Science Abstracts, Part A, Physics Abstracts,* in Abstracts and Indexes Section.

Current Physics Information. The American Institute of Physics, AIP, and its 26 member societies and affiliates, represent not only the U.S. physics community in its broadest sense, but also one of the most important scientific organizations in the world. In 1972 a new approach to the literature was set forth by AIP through the reformatting of information into a variety of media. Stated simply, *Current Physics Information,* CPI, the name of the service, consists of the following. Seventy core journals, considered the most prominent in the field by a tally of U.S. physicists, have been selected for input to the system. (For details see H. W. Koch, "Current Physics Information," *Science,* vol. 174, pp. 918–922, Nov. 26, 1971.) The main elements of the system produce these outputs.

Searchable Physics Information Notes, SPIN, a monthly computer tape service, represents the heart of the system. SPIN tapes, sold on a lease basis since 1971 for $2,500, contain not only bibliographic citation and abstracts extracted from the 70 core journals, and their classification descriptors, but also the reference cited in the source article (a feature unique to this tape service).

Current Physics Advance Abstracts, CPAA (m., $40 for each part; $15 to members) at present limited to the 34 AIP-produced journals, publishes monthly abstracts of papers accepted for publication. Abstracts are thus issued two to four months prior to the appearance of the original paper in the journal literature. To accommodate the needs of individual subscribers, CPAA is issued in the following three parts: (a) *solid state;* (b) *nuclei and particles* (includes astrophysics, plasma physics, nuclear physics); and (c) *atoms and waves* (incl. acoustical, chemical, optical physics, geophysics, and fluids).

Current Physics Titles, CPT (m., $25 for each section; $10 to members), computer-composed from the SPIN tapes, also appears monthly in three sections: *solid state, nuclei and particles,* and *atoms and waves.* Issues contain complete bibliographic citation of titles arranged under classified headings taken from 65 of the core journals.

Current Physics Microform, issued monthly in 16mm microfilm cartridges (and leased annually for $2,850) contains every paper included in the 34 AIP-produced journals published that month. Eventually, it will include all 70 *Current Physics* core journals. CPM cartridge and frame numbers appear on the SPIN tapes and on *Current Physics Titles,* to provide easy accessibility to the full text from these alerting tools.

Additional applications, such as the production of

"user journals," as well as a stepping-up of frequency of publication, are anticipated in the next few years.

Admittedly, the full scope of an abstracting service such as *Physics Abstracts* (see section on *Abstracts and Indexes*) and other INSPEC publications is not here. Nonetheless, the AIP rightly points out that nearly fifty percent of the world's significant physics literature is embraced through the *Current Physics* journals. Certainly, those of timely importance to U.S. physicists are in this count. Since this is the first operational year of CIP, it will be interesting to note how developments continue. Surely all physics libraries, at one time or other, will want to purchase portions of CPI.

Faraday Transactions. See *Chemical Society. Journal. Faraday Transactions* Chemistry Section.

Foundations of Physics. 1970. q. $35. H. Margenau and W. Yourgrau. Plenum Publishing Corp. 227 W. 17th St., New York, N.Y. 10011. Illus., index. Sample. Vol. ends: No. 4. Sample. Refereed.

Headed by a prominent editorial board, this journal explores problems concerned with the philosophical bases of theories in physics. Topics covered include relativity, quantum mechanics, field theory, time and space, problems of symmetry. The papers stress fundamental and speculative problems motivating modern physics and offer approaches to other sciences, including chemistry and biology. As such the journal is unique since the majority of physics journals are specialized. A valuable publication particularly for undergraduate collections.

Franklin Institute. Journal. See Science/General Section.

IBM Journal of Research and Development. See Science/General Section.

Journal of Applied Physics. 1931. m. $52. Frank E. Myers. Amer. Inst. of Physics, 335 E. 45th St., New York, N.Y. 10017. Illus., index. Circ: 10,000. Sample. Vol. ends: Dec. Refereed. Microform: UM. Reprint: Johnson.

Indexed: ASTI, ChemAb, EngI, MathR, MetAb, SciAb, SCI. *Aud:* Sa, Ac.

Veering away from the highly theoretical, the journal concentrates on research papers stressing the applications of physics to engineering, other physical sciences, or industry. Within its scope are studies on solid state, optics, magnetism, spectroscopy, etc. Both full-length articles and brief communications are published, but important short reports appear in a sister publication, *Applied Physics Letters* (s-m. $25, Gilbert J. Perlow). The *Letters,* sharing the same subject interests and operating under the same rigorous editorial policies as the *Journal,* provide the vehicle for disseminating reports on the latest developments in ongoing research. Both journals are major ones in physics and

necessary for all research collections. (Note: The British counterpart in the field is the excellent *Journal of Physics D: Applied Physics,* listed below.)

Journal of Atmospheric and Terrestrial Physics. See Atmospheric Sciences Section.

Journal of Chemical Physics. 1931. s-m. $105. J. W. Stout. Amer. Inst. of Physics, 335 E. 45th St., New York, N.Y. 10017. Illus., index. Circ: 6,300. Sample. Vol. ends: Dec. Refereed. Microform: UM. Reprint: Johnson.

Indexed: BioAb, ChemAb, EngI, MathR, MetAb, SciAb, SCI. *Aud:* Sa, Ac.

The purpose of this excellent research publication is to "bridge a gap between journals of physics and journals of chemistry." As such, theoretical papers report on valence, quantum theory, statistical mechanics, intermolecular forces, spectroscopy, etc. A sophisticated and primary publication for chemical and physics research collections in university libraries.

Active research collections will also be interested in North-Holland's *Chemical Physics Letters,* which publishes reports describing research of a preliminary nature.

Journal of Computational Physics. 1966. bi-m. $60. Ed.bd. Academic Press, Inc., 111 Fifth Ave., New York, N.Y. 10003. Illus., index. Sample. Vol. ends: Dec. *Aud:* Sa, Ac.

The specialty journal has limited appeal beyond a narrow circle of researchers in the field. Yet some publications, admittedly special, are useful for their reports on tools or techniques widely employed in the physical sciences. This journal concerns itself with problems of manipulating large quantities of data, and their solutions, by either computers or mathematical methods. A good complementary choice for collections supporting physics research.

(Note: In the same vein is North Holland's *Computer Physics Communications,* a periodical given over to descriptions of computer programs written for physics problems.)

Journal of Geophysical Research. For this title and other geophysical journals, see Earth Sciences Section.

Journal of Mathematical Physics. 1960. m. $45. Morton Hamermesh. Amer. Inst. of Physics, 335 E. 45th St., New York, N.Y. 10017. Illus., index. Circ: 3,000. Sample. Vol. ends: Dec. Microform: UM.

Indexed: MathR, MetAb, SciAb, SCI. *Aud:* Sa, Ac.

The line between theoretical physics and mathematics is finely drawn. (Moreover, the same group which was responsible for classical physics also developed classical math.) The aim of this research journal is to publish physics papers containing a high degree of mathematics, or math papers appropriate to applications in physics. Topics covered include math problems related to quantum theory of fields, statistical mechanics, theory of graphs, math questions regarding elementary particles, etc. Although too sophisticated for undergraduates, the publication is important for university collections supporting research in theoretical physics.

Another high-quality research publication in the same field is Springer-Verlag's *Communications in Mathematical Physics,* also designed to relate theoretical physics with modern mathematics.

Journal of the Mechanics and Physics of Solids. 1952. bi-m. $60. H. G. Hopkins. Pergamon Press, Inc., Maxwell House, Fairview Park, Elmsford, N.Y. 10523. Illus., index. Sample. Vol. ends: no. 6. Refereed. Microform: Maxwell. Reprint: Maxwell.

Indexed: ChemAb, EngI, MathR, MetAb, SciAb, SCI. *Bk. rev:* Occasional, 500 words, signed. *Aud:* Sa, Ac.

Another research journal dedicated to studies of the properties and structures of solids. With particular emphasis on applied mechanics and the properties of constructional materials, the periodical has significance to materials scientists, engineers, and applied mathematicians, as well as physicists. For research libraries.

Journal of Physical and Chemical Reference Data. 1972. q. $60. (AIP members $20) David R. Lide. Amer. Chemical Soc. and Amer. Inst. of Physics. Subs. to: Amer. Chemical Soc., 1155 16th St., N.W., Washington, D.C. 20036. Index. Sample. Vol. ends: No. 4.

Indexed: ChemAb. *Aud:* Sa, Ac.

For many years critical reviews, evaluations, and compilations of data in all segments of the physical sciences have been prepared by the U.S. National Bureau of Standards' National Standard Reference Data System. Beginning in 1972, under joint publication with two prominent technical societies and coordination with the NSRDS, these data of physical properties have been collected in one research journal. Input is provided by various data analysis centers (governmental, industrial, and university) supported by NBS. A journal of this type, with such high reference value, should be an absolute necessity for any library supporting research in the physical sciences.

Journal of Physical Chemistry. See Chemistry Section.

Journal of Physics. $459 for all six parts. Inst. Physics and the Physical Soc., 47 Belgrave Sq., London SW1, England, Subs. to: Amer. Inst. of Physics, 335 East 45th St., New York, N.Y. 10017. Illus., index. Sample. Refereed. Microform: UM. Reprint: Selected sections available from Dawson.

Aud: Sa, Ac.

In 1968 the Physical Society, London, and the Institute of Physics merged their various and prominent research journals into six sections of one common publication under the generic title *Journal of Physics.* Delineated below are the special characteristics and bibliographic details of these sections, each of which may be purchased separately. Both the prominence of the sponsoring organizations and the high quality of the publications make them excellent and important journals for any research collection.

Journal of Physics A: General Physics. 1874. m. $64.80. R. G. Chambers. Circ: 2,500.
Indexed: ChemAb, EngI, MathR, MetAb, SciAb, SCI.

Journal of Physics B: Atomic and Molecular Physics. 1874. m. $118.80. M. J. Seaton. Circ: 2,500.
Indexed: Chem Ab, EngI, MathR, MetAb, SciAb, SCI.

Journal of Physics C: Solid State Physics. 1874. 18/yr. $108. A. B. Lidiard. Circ: 2,500.
Indexed: ChemAb, EngI, MathR, MetAb, SciAb, SCI.

Sections A through C were continuations of the prestigious *Proceedings of the Physical Society* (London), one of the foremost scientific societies of the nineteenth century. Research papers today have been separated according to subjects indicated by the titles. Topics discussed vary from (Section A) mathematical physics, general relativity, field theory, nuclear physics, and high-energy physics to (Section B) studies of atoms formed into molecules, nature of intermolecular forces, etc., and (Section C) solid state physics. This series, plus the AIP's choice *Physical Review* (see below) would be integral parts of any research collection.

Journal of Physics D: Applied Physics. 1950. m. $75.60. A. J. Forty. Circ: 3,000.

Indexed: BritTech, ChemAb, EngI, MetAb, SciAb, SCI.

A carry-over of the original *British Journal of Applied Physics.* Comparable in scope to the U.S. *Journal of Applied Physics,* its papers on applied research concentrate on such fields as fluids, plasmas, gas discharges, structure and mechanical properties of solids, electrical and magnetic properties of solids, spectroscopy, and optical properties of solids. Occasionally, books are reviewed. A particularly important journal for physics collections with applied interests.

Journal of Physics E: Scientific Instruments. 1922. m. $43.20. J. Ring. Circ: 5,300.

Indexed: ASTI, BioAb, BritTech, ChemAb, EngI, SciAb, SCI.

Continuation of *Journal of Scientific Instruments.* (For a corollary publication see *Review of Scientific Instruments,* listed below.) The scope of this journal extends over instrumentation related to the physical sciences, their apparatus, techniques, and design and research. Review papers and research articles are included, as well as book reviews.

Journal of Physics F: Metal Physics. 1971. bi-m. $36. Issued first as a supplement to *Journal of Physics*

C: Solid State, the publication has achieved status as a journal in its own right. Its main concern is research on the physics of the solid state as studied on metals. The journal should have a wide audience among metallurgists and materials scientists, as well as physicists.

Journal of Physics and Chemistry of Solids. 1956. m. $160. Harvey Brooks. Pergamon Press, Inc., Maxwell House, Fairview Park, Elmsford, N.Y. 10523. Illus., index. Sample. Vol. ends: Dec. Refereed. Microform: Maxwell. Reprint: Maxwell.

Indexed: ChemAb, SciAb, SCI. *Aud:* Sa, Ac.

Prominent among the international publications in the solid state sciences is this authoritative journal concerned with research on every aspect of physical and chemical properties of solids. Papers explore areas such as the electronic structure of solids, excitation of solids, and statistical mechanics of condensed systems. A supplementary periodical containing short reports (formerly carried in the *Journal*) is *Solid State Communications* (s-m., $75, Elias Burstein). Included in the *Communications* are abstracts of papers to be published in the *Journal,* and a calendar of solid state events. Of interest to chemists and specialists in solid state electronics, as well as physicists, the journals are important ones for libraries supporting research in these fields.

Nuclear Physics. 1956. w. $26.80/vol. L. Rosenfeld. North-Holland Publishing Co., Box 211, Amsterdam, Netherlands. Illus., index. Sample. Refereed.

Indexed: ChemAb, MathR, MetAb, SciAb, SCI. *Bk. rev:* Occasional, 400–600 words, signed. *Aud:* Sa, Ac.

A publication dedicated to research on "fundamental constituents of matter." In 1967 the journal inaugurated two separate series. Part A (w.) is given over to nuclear physics proper, including nuclear structure, nuclear reactions, electromagnetic radiation, etc. Part B (s-m.) concentrates on quantum field theory and study of fundamental particles. The journal is one of the most important in the field of nuclear physics. Though too sophisticated for small academic libraries, it is a basic one for university collections.

(Note: The American Institute of Physics publishes a research journal in the same field. *Soviet Journal of Nuclear Physics* is a cover-to-cover translation of the prominent Russian *Yadernaya Fizika.*)

Optical Society of America. Journal. 1917. m. $40. David L. MacAdam. Amer. Inst. of Physics, 335 E. 45th St., New York, N.Y. 10017. Illus., index. Circ: 9,600. Sample. Vol. ends: Dec. Refereed. Reprint: Johnson.

Indexed: BioAb, ChemAb, EngI, MathR, PsyAb, SciAb, SCI. *Bk. rev:* 5, 300 words, signed. *Aud:* Sa, Ac.

The official journal of the Society has relevance to many fields, as witnessed by the abstracting services which index the publication. Papers are concerned with research studies on "optical phenomena, principles, or methods," and cover areas such as physiological and medical optics and color vision, as well as those fields embodied by physical principles. Theoretical work is stressed; papers involving applications of optical principles appear in the Society's other journal, *Applied Optics,* listed above. Included in many issues are news of the profession and personalia, as well as reports and minutes of meetings of the Society. An excellent research journal with wide applications for any academic library supporting interest in optics research.

For university libraries heavily involved in the field, there are a number of other fine research journals available. Two others also sponsored by the American Institute of Physics are translations of leading Russian publications: *Optics and Spectroscopy* (a translation of *Optika i Spektroskopiya) and Soviet Journal of Optical Technology* (Optiko-Mekhanicheskaya Promyshlennost). *Optica Acta* (published by Taylor & Francis) is an international journal also concentrating on principles of optics. And *Optics Communications* (North-Holland) specializes in the short paper reporting ongoing research. All would be necessary for good research collections.

Philosophical Magazine. 1798. m. $115.28. Nevill Mott. Taylor & Francis, Ltd., 10–14 Mackline St., London WC2B 5NX, England. Illus., index. Circ: 2,500. Sample. Vol. ends: 2v./year. Refereed. Microform: Taylor & Francis, Maxwell, MF, PMC. Reprint: Dawson.

Indexed: ChemAb, EngI, MathR, MetAb, SciAb, SCI. *Bk. rev:* Occasional, 300–500 words, signed. *Aud:* Sa, Ac.

The lengthy history of *Phil. Mag.* began with its first series at the end of the eighteenth century. At a time when the scientific periodical was beginning to flower, its original intent was to "comprehend the various branches of science, the liberal and fine arts, agriculture, manufactures and commerce." Following a series of changes and title alterations, the publication later became a general physics journal, concerned with both theoretical and experimental papers. Currently, its issues are dedicated largely to research on solid state physics. Prominent for its historical significance, the journal is still a fine research publication for university libraries.

Physical Review. 1893. 72/yr. $240 for all parts. S. A. Goudsmit. Amer. Inst. of Physics (for Amer. Physical Soc.), 335 E. 45th St., New York, N.Y. 10003. Illus., index. Circ: 6,500. Sample. Refereed. Microform: UM. Reprint: Johnson.

Indexed: ChemAb, EngI, MathR, SciAb, SCI. *Aud:* Sa, Ac.

Easily, this is one of the most important and distinctive research journals in the world's physics literature. Moreover, in *Chemical Abstracts'* list of the 1,000 most frequently cited journals, *Phys. Rev.* stands first. Careful refereeing by leading authorities has assured the high caliber of the journal. With the proliferation of the literature, the publication, now in its third series, has fragmented into four parts, with various periodicities, prices, and editors, as indicated below. Each part may be subscribed to separately.

Physical Review A, General Physics (m. $40, C. L. Sneed) is devoted to atomic and molecular physics, fluids, thermodynamics, plasmas.

Physical Review B, Solid State (s-m., $80, P. D. Adams) publishes, on the first of the month, papers on atoms in matter; Mossbauer effect, electrons and ion emission; range and energy loss; magnetic impurities, ferroelectrics, spectra of solids; and on the fifteenth, papers on metals, semiconductors, and insulators.

Physical Review C, Nuclear Physics (m., $40, P. D. Adams). Dedicated to research work in nuclear properties, reactions.

Physical Review D, Particles & Fields (s-m., $80, S. Pasternak). Given over on the first of the month to high-energy physics and particles and fields; and on the fifteenth to quantum mechanics, scattering theory, general relativity, and some astrophysics.

Research libraries and university collections will undoubtedly need all four parts. Small academic libraries would find the publication too sophisticated (and too costly), but might subscribe to one or more parts, depending on the interest of their faculty. (Note: A cumulative index is also available for all six parts, semiannually for $9). See below its sister publication, *Physical Review Letters.*

Physical Review Letters. 1958. w. $50. S. A. Goudsmit and G. L. Trigg. Amer. Inst. of Physics, 335 E. 45th St., New York, N.Y. 10003. Illus., index. Circ: 12,000. Sample. Vol. ends: Dec. Refereed. Microform: UM.

Indexed: ChemAb, EngI, MathR, SciAb, SCI. *Aud:* Sa, Ac.

Considered the cream of the physics literature, probably because it turns away fifty percent of the manuscripts submitted. Its editors emphasize, however, that its high rejection rate is not necessarily because of quality, but because the criteria of brevity and novelty in short communications are rarely met. The publication is one of the first letters-type journals, originally issued as a complementary periodical to *Physical Review,* to describe research of a preliminary nature and significant value, in a one to two page report. Topics covered include atoms, molecules, plasmas, fluids, thermodynamics, solids, nuclei, elementary particles, and fields. Breakthroughs in physics research in the United States are likely to be reported here first. Necessary for every research collection.

Physics Bulletin. 1950. m. $24. Cecil Pedersen. Inst. of Physics, 47 Belgrave Sq., London SW1X 80QZ, England; U.S. orders to Amer. Inst. of Physics, 335 E. 45th St., New York, N.Y. 10017. Illus., index. Sample. Vol. ends: Dec.

Bk. rev: 14, 200–300 words, signed. *Aud:* Sa, Ga, Ac.

As *Physics Today* voices the news of the American Institute of Physics, *Physics Bulletin* is the general, nonspecialist publication of the Institute of Physics, London. Articles review important physics developments, comment on government policy, discuss physics education, and supply general professional news, including reports of recent scientific meetings. Academic libraries will find its nonspecialist highlights and interpretations of newly explored physical principles useful, particularly for undergraduate tutorials. Research librarians will also welcome book reviews and regular listings of PhD theses available in the United Kingdom. A large portion of the periodical is directed to news for the professional, with a slant, however, toward activities in Great Britain. Public libraries and small academic institutions will find their interests served well enough by *Physics Today.*

Physics Letters. 1962. w. $84. Ed. bd. North-Holland Publishing Co., Box 211, Amsterdam, The Netherlands. Illus., index. Sample. Refereed.

Indexed: MathR, SciAb. *Aud:* Sa, Ac.

In the last 15 years the letters-type journal has come to the forefront as the mechanism for disseminating short reports on research in progress. Issued now weekly, this international journal is also put out in two sections. *Part A* (edited by: ter Haar, Low, Wienecke, and Volger) concentrates on general, atomic, and solid state physics. *Part B* (edited by: G. Brown, Endt, Hamilton, Gatto, and Squires) is given over to theoretical and experimental nuclear physics, high-energy physics, and elementary particles. The one to two page reports may appear in English, French, or German. A subscription to the full *Physics Letters* includes copies of *Physics Reports* (vol. 1, no. 1, 1971), a review-type journal publishing survey papers on current interest topics. (Note: Each may be subscribed to separately.) All of the foregoing are important for research collections, because they highlight the mainstream of European (and U.S.) physics. A prominent editorial board, scattered geographically, assures an international balance and the high quality of the papers. For university libraries.

Physics Reports. See *Physics Letters.*

Physics Teacher. 1963. 9/yr. $8. Clifford E. Swartz and Lester G. Paldy. Amer. Assn. of Physics Teachers. Amer. Inst. of Physics, 335 E. 45th St., New York, N.Y. 10017. Illus., index, adv. Circ: 8,500. Sample. Vol. ends: Dec. Refereed. Microform: UM.

Indexed: EducI, SCI. *Bk. rev:* 7, 150–300 words, signed. *Aud:* Sa, Ac, Ht.

Another publication of the American Association of Physics Teachers. (See also *American Journal of Physics.*) Addressed to "all those who teach introductory physics" at high school, junior college, or undergraduate level, the periodical is particularly commendable to high school teachers. Three to four features in each issue blend authoritative essays on current topics in physics and interviews with scientists with current trends in science education, evaluation of curricula, and other problems of the educator. Regularly published are brief communications on classroom techniques, lab demonstrations, new equipment, tips on improving apparatus, etc. The book review section periodically includes reviews of films and other audiovisual material. Highly recommended for any library supporting physics instruction at a beginning level.

Physics Today. 1948. m. $9. Harold L. Davis. Amer. Inst. of Physics, 335 E. 45th St., New York, N.Y. 10017. Illus., index, adv. Circ: 50,000. Sample. Vol. ends: Dec. Refereed. Microform: UM.

Indexed: ASTI, ChemAb, EngI, RG, SciAb, SCI. *Bk. rev:* 5–6, 500–700 words, signed. *Aud:* Sa, Ga, Hs, Ac. *Jv:* V.

Informative, interpretive, and authoritative, the periodical is a fine choice for a generalized treatment of physics at any level (layman, student, professional). Well-written articles by specialists review physics research, its applications to other fields, its philosophy and history, trends in education, government, or industry, and problems of the profession. Features may be scholarly and technical, or informal and nontechnical, depending on the subject matter. The special departments of the magazine serve as a news medium for physicists: detailed reports of technical meetings, activities of the American Physical Society, personalia, calendars. A good book review section and checklist of new books provides a fertile area for librarians selecting physics titles. Highly recommended for any public or high school, as well as academic, library, that would like to acquire more than a general science periodical.

RCA Review. See Electrical Engineering Section.

Reports on Progress in Physics. 1934. m. $57.60. Inst. of Physics, 47 Belgrave Sq., London SW1, England; Subs. to (U.S.): Amer. Inst. of Physics, 335 E. 45th St., New York, N.Y. 10017. Illus., index. Sample. Vol. ends: Dec. Refereed.

Indexed: SciAb. *Aud:* Sa, Ac.

Issued for many years as an annual volume, the publication stepped up to monthly periodicity to provide timely and authoritative review articles in all branches of physics. Applied physics is well represented, and its scope includes astrophysics and geo-

physics. Far too sophisticated for the layman, the journal is still addressed to nonspecialists, although a background in physics is required. Articles, varying between 30 and 60 pages, contain enough historical material and key references to serve as tutorials for advanced or graduate students. As is typical of most review journals, contributions are invited by the editors. Compared to a publication such as *Advances in Physics,* these *Reports* are less specialized. Most academic libraries supporting research programs will need this journal in combination with the distinguished *Reviews of Modern Physics* (see below), for excellent, critical overviews of ongoing research. Small libraries on slim budgets would probably settle first on *Reviews of Modern Physics,* however.

Review of Physics in Technology. 1970. 3/yr. $12. L. R. G. Treloar. Inst. of Physics, 47 Belgrave Sq., London SW1, England; Subs. to (U.S.): Amer. Inst. of Physics, 335 E. 45th St., New York, N.Y. 10017. Illus., index. Sample. Vol. ends: No. 3. Refereed.

Indexed: SciAb. *Bk. rev:* 10, 300–500 words, signed. *Aud:* Sa, Ac.

The bulk of material in this review journal consists of articles reprinted from *Journal of Physics D: Applied Physics.* Well-known authorities, generally through invitation of the editors, present the state of art in fields where physics has close association with new technologies, e.g., materials research, applications of cryogenics, luminescence. About three long papers appear in each issue. Announcements of forthcoming conferences, courses, etc., are also published. A solid survey journal for nonspecialists needing digests of the literature in applied physics, or for technical libraries not requiring the full output of theoretical material provided by other well-established research journals.

Review of Scientific Instruments. 1930. m. $22. J. B. H. Kuper. Amer. Inst. of Physics, 335 E. 45th St., New York, N.Y. 10017. Illus., index, adv. Circ: 9,500. Sample. Vol. ends: Dec. Refereed. Microform: UM; Canner. Reprint: Johnson.

Indexed: BioAb, ChemAb, EngI, MathR, SciAb, SCI. *Bk. rev:* Occasional, 300–500 words, signed. *Aud:* Sa, Ac.

Emphasis in this publication is on any type of scientific instrumentation applicable primarily to the physical sciences, and to a much lesser degree, the life sciences. Papers and review articles discuss research in instrumentation, as well as new apparatus, novel techniques, or components related to apparatus. Separate sections on new materials, components, and equipment in each issue describe new products as reported by their manufacturers' literature. This is a valuable and necessary publication for most libraries supporting research in physics. Large academic libraries will need both this and its British counterpart, *Journal of Phys-*

ics E: Scientific Instruments, published by the Institute of Physics, London.

Reviews of Modern Physics. 1929. q. $12. L. M. Branscomb. Amer. Inst. of Physics, 335 E. 45th St., New York, N.Y. 10017. Illus., index. Circ: 11,500. Sample. Vol. ends: Oct. Refereed. Microform: UM; Canner. Reprint: Johnson.

Indexed: BioAb, ChemAb, EngI, MathR, SciAb, SCI. *Aud:* Sa, Ac.

Scholarly and critical, the journal publishes excellent review reports on current research problems in all the major branches of physics. Included within its subject range are plasma physics; statistical mechanics; quantum electronics; electron, atomic, and molecular physics; high-energy physics; particles and fields; nuclear physics; solid state physics; and astrophysics. Authoritative articles by well-known specialists, often invited by the editors, range from 10 to 50 pages in length; bibliographies are generally comprehensive. The publication furnishes a thorough review of background material to both professionals and advanced physics students, and provides the specialist with an accurate account of the current state of research in his field. Considering the cost of most scientific journals, and the still modest subscription price of this periodical, the *Reviews* are one of the outstanding publications recommended for any university library. (See also *Advances in Physics* for more specialized reviews, and *Reports on Progress in Physics*, for survey articles, including reviews in applied physics.)

Royal Society. Proceedings. Series A: Mathematical and Physical Sciences. See Science/General Section.

Soviet Physics-JETP. 1955. $105. Ed. bd. Amer. Inst. of Physics, 335 E. 45th St., New York, N.Y. 10017. Illus., index. Circ: 1,500. Sample. Vol. ends: June/Dec. Refereed.

Indexed: ChemAb, EngI, MathR, SciAb, SCI. *Aud:* Sa, Ac.

The periodical, a leading Russian journal, is a full translation of *Zhurnal Eksperimental'noi I Teoreticheskoi Fiziki (Journal of Experimental and Theoretical Physics of the USSR)*. Similar in nature to *Physical Review*, it publishes significant research papers in all areas of fundamental and experimental physics—general, atomic, and molecular through solid state and nuclear. Reports represent full-length studies. Shorter papers, or important preliminary communications, appear semimonthly in a sister journal, *JETP Letters* ($40), a translation of *JETP Pis'ma v Redaktsiyn*, and somewhat a counterpart to *Physical Review Letters*.

Two other authoritative, comprehensive physics journals also published by the American Institute of Physics are *Soviet Physics-Doklady* and *Soviet Physics-Uspekhi*. The widely known *Doklady* represent translations of cumulated short research reports of the

Proceedings of the Academy of Sciences USSR (see Science/General Section). *Uspekhi (Advances in the Physical Sciences of the Academy of Sciences USSR)* provides translations of review papers comparable to those published in *Reviews of Modern Physics*. Of course, the American Institute of Physics puts out nine other journals in translation. The foregoing were arbitrarily selected as representative of high-quality general physics publications for research libraries. For the record, the remaining AIP translation journals are *Soviet Astronomy AJ* (See Astronomy Section), *Soviet J. of Nuclear Physics*, *Soviet Physics-Acoustics*, *Soviet Physics-Crystallography*, *Soviet Physics-Semiconductors*, *Soviet Physics-Solid State*, *Soviet Physics-Technical Physics*, *Soviet J. of Optical Technology*, Optics and Spectroscopy.

U.S. National Bureau of Standards. Journal of Research. Section A: Physics and Chemistry. See Science/General Section.

POETRY

Basic Periodicals

LITTLE MAGAZINE GENRE. Hs: *Seventies;* Ga: *Seventies, Kayak;* Jc: *Seventies, Kayak, New: American and Canadian Poetry;* Ac: *Seventies, Kayak, New: American and Canadian Poetry, Wormwood Review, Intrepid, Field.*

TRADITIONAL ACADEMIC. Hs: *Poetry;* Ga: *Poetry, New York Quarterly;* Jc: *Poetry, New York Quarterly, Modern Poetry in Translation;* Ac: *Poetry, New York Quarterly, Beloit Poetry Journal, Poetry Northwest, Modern Poetry in Translation, Alcheringa.*

Basic Abstracts and Indexes

Index to Little Magazines, Index to Commonwealth Little Magazines.

Cessations

Caterpillar, El Corno Emplumado.

Introduction

An attempt has been made to include representatives of all aspects, schools, and movements of the chaotic poetry scene. Final decisions were influenced by the recommendations of a volunteer panel of poets. The consensus was forced from a series of contradictory lists: each poet had his preferred outlet, with little or no agreement among them. Some newer magazines have been included, on the basis of uniqueness or the compiler's evaluation of their long-term worth. Some attention has been paid to whether the magazines print long poems, or excerpts from longer works. Also, magazines which print a definitive sampling of a single poet have been given preference. In selecting from this list, you should consider that magazines such as *Prairie Schooner* are defined as literary quarterlies, or academic magazines, while being first-class outlets for poets. (Don Dorrance)

Ed. note: what follows is somewhat more than Mr. Dorrance's list, but those curious to know his choices will find Mr. Dorrance's initials after his choices.

Little Magazine Genre

Amphora. 1970. q. $5. Thomas Head. 14 Guy Pl., San Francisco, Calif. 94105.

Aud: Ac

A modest, offset pocket-sized unnumbered 40-page poetry magazine with first-rate contributors, viz., Diane di Prima, Denise Levertov, Larry Eigner, David and Maria Gitlin, Ron Silliman, etc. And there are some relative unknowns, too. The overall quality is high. No particular school or governing principle of selection prevails. The unpretentious effort may have some appeal.

Angel Hair. 1966. irreg. $5/4 issues. Lewis Warsh and Anne Waldman, Box 257, Peter Stuyvesant St., New York, N.Y. 10009. Circ: 700. Vol. ends: No. 6. Reprint: Kraus.

Aud: Ac, Ga.

A highly thought of poetry magazine which had brought out only six issues as of early 1972. The publishers now tend to concentrate on books of poetry, but from time to time do return to the magazine. It is well worth the wait. Features in past numbers: John Wieners, Frank O'Hara, Joe Brainard, Robert Creeley, Gerard Malanga, etc.

Another Poetry Magazine. 1971. 3/yr. $2.50. Dale and Margery Zieroth, 32 Marchmount Rd., Toronto 4, Ont., Canada.

Aud: Ac.

A nicely printed 70-page poetry magazine which is more than "another" such because it stresses Canadian poets, primarily those around Toronto. The contributors are generally young and speak to the problems of youth, but usually with a considerably greater degree of skill and feeling than is generally associated with the counterculture. It's not all good. It's not all bad. And much gives pause.

Apple. 1967. irreg. $3.50/4 issues. David Cutty. Box 2271, Springfield, Ill. 62705. Circ: 600.

Bk. rev: 1, 3–5 pages, signed. *Aud:* Ac, Ga, Hs. *Jv:* V.

A carefully edited, equally well-printed magazine. Each issue features a critical essay or book review, and some 15 to 20 poets. Contributors tend to be relatively well known, like Wendell Berry, Greg Kuzma, Lyn Lifshin, Robert Bly, and William Matthews. Thanks to

the superior choices, this is one of the best of the little poetry magazines now being published.

Ark River Review. 1971. q. $2. Jonathan Katz, A. G. Sobin, and Arthur Vogelsang. 1410 W. Murdock, Wichita, Kans. 67203. Illus.

Aud: Ac.

Primarily a vehicle for midwest poets; i.e., the majority represented in early issues are students or teachers from Kansas and Iowa. Some, to be sure, are from the two coasts (New York and Oregon). The editors call their 48-page offset a "literary quarterly," which means it is balanced between poetry and prose, with the emphasis on poetry. Some notes and reviews. It is uneven in quality, although there is enough good, original material to warrant a subscription by libraries in the area, and by larger libraries anywhere.

Atom Mind. 1968. q. $2. Gregory Smith. Box 827, Syracuse, N.Y. 13201. Circ: 500.

Aud: Ga, Ac,

"All aimed toward the free and not-so-free-youth," this may irritate, but it communicates to its audience. Preferred by poets. (D.D.)

Audit/Poetry. 1960. 3/yr. $3 (Libraries $3.50). George Butterick and Albert Glover. 180 Winspeare Ave., Buffalo, N.Y. 14215. Circ: 1,000.

Aud: Ga, Ac,

Publishes modern American poetry, often of those deserving attention from a lay audience, yet well known only in poetry circles. Occasionally a single issue is given over to the work of one poet. The selection is careful, the editing superior, and the letterpress format good. (D.D.)

Bardic Echoes. 1959. q. $2. Clarence L. Weaver. 1036 Emerald Ave., N.E., Grand Rapids, Mich. 49503. Circ: 375.

Bk. rev: 10–15, 50 words, signed. *Aud:* Hs.

Small, mimeographed, issued by a cultural group interested in poetry and music. A nice amateur magazine, this is suitable for libraries needing a poetry magazine which will never shock or irritate. At the same time, it does represent a substantial public. (D.D.)

Beyond Baroque. 1968. bi-a. $3.50. George Drury Smith, Bayrock Press, 1639 Washington Blvd., Venice, Calif. 90291. Illus., adv. Circ: 1,800. Sample.

Bk. rev: 3, 100 words. *Aud:* Ac, Ga, Hs.

A widely advertised little magazine which has improved considerably since the first issue. Content is uneven, but of interest because the editor is inclined to publish a good number of little-known poets, i.e. "New Venice Poets," and "Naissance—Prose and Poetry for the 70s." The poems tend to be better than the prose. Should be of particular interest to younger poets, from high school through college.

Bleb. 1970. 3/yr. $1.50. George Ryan. Box 322, Times Sq. Sta., New York, N.Y. 10036.

Aud: Ac, Ga.

A 30 to 40 page mimeographed little poetry magazine which normally features 15 to 20 poets. The whole is highly experimental, and the works range from the structured to the free, from the excellent to the poor. In a word, a grab bag for the adventuresome, but not for the reader looking for better-known well-accepted poets. See also *Wloptoonakun*, by the same publisher in Indians section.

Bones. 1967. Irreg. 2–3/yr. $1 each. Katherine Greef and Terence Anderson. 319 W. 100th St., Apt. 5, New York, N.Y. 10025. Circ.: 500.

Aud: Ga, Ac.

Lively, at times outrageous, this 80-odd-page mimeographed magazine has a wide range of experimental poetry, with some prose and prose-poems. Much of it is confused, but some is striking. An introduction to the various ways, opinions, and general formlessness of the younger writers. (D.D.)

Buddhist 3rd Class Junkmail Oracle. irreg. 15¢/issue. Steve Ferguson, c/o The Asphodel, 306 W. Superior Ave., Cleveland, Ohio. 44113.

Aud: Ga, Ac.

A tabloid newspaper, completely irreverent but relevant to its scene. Cut up and concrete poetry, collage, reviews, cartoons, and whatever the editor happens to stumble on is included. For the street people, perhaps, but honest in its attempt "to communicate in this universe." (D.D.)

Consumption. 1967. q. $2. Paul Hunter and others. 539½ N.E. Ravenna Blvd., Seattle, Washington. Illus. Circ: 500.

Aud: Ga, Ac.

Small and honest, "No dogs or dogmas." Well represents the northwest. The illustrations are a big plus. Almost a general magazine featuring poetry of a high level. (D.D.)

Corduroy. 1968. irreg. $2/2 issues. Richard Immersi. Corduroy Publns., 406 Highland Ave., Newark, N.J. 07104. Circ: 400. Sample. Vol. ends: No. 4.

Bk. rev: 5, notes. *Aud:* Ga, Hs.

An offset 34-page poetry magazine which is primarily a vehicle for unknown writers. The contributions tend to be a trifle sophomoric, but here and there a really fascinating item appears. In view of the editorial policy, the magazine must be evaluated in terms of an honest effort to give writers an opportu-nity to find publication. Should have appeal for younger readers.

Crazy Horse. 1969. q. $4. Thomas McGrath, S.W. Minn. State College, Marshall, Minn. 56258.

Aud: Ac.

This is an example of what a little money and support mean to a poetry magazine. Nicely printed, it comes to 40 pages and one issue included an interview with Galway Kinnel, poetry by Stafford, Hollo, Novak, and a dozen other lesser-known, although just as competent, poets. McGrath is a professional editor who really knows how to put a magazine together.

Cronopios. 1969. Irreg. $3.50/4 issues. James Stephens, 815 E. Johnson, Apt. 4, Madison Wis. 53703.

One 86-page bilingual issue features translations by Robert Bly, Daisy Aldan, and a number of others. The whole is a genuine experience, and serves to introduce a first-rate talent to many Americans. Previous issues have celebrated the work of several important younger American poets. The mimeo format is pleasing, the editing good, and the bits of criticism quite above average. An intelligent and worthwhile addition to the mainstream of little magazines.

The Dragonfly. 1969. q. $2.50 Duane Ackerson. Box 147, Idaho State Univ., Pocatello, Idaho 83201. Illus. Circ: 350. Vol. ends: Winter.

Bk. rev: 4, essay, signed. *Aud:* Ac.

The editor says the purpose of his magazine is to publish "poetry, reviews and controversy, and poetry in translation." There have been special issues such as "A Prose Poem Anthology." Among the contributors are Robert Bly, James Tate, John Hains, William Stafford, Charles Simic, Bill Matthews—a stellar group which makes this one of the better university-based poetry magazines.

Dryad. 1968. q. $2.75. Merrill Leffler and Neil Lehrman. Box 1656, Washington, D.C. 20013. Circ: 850.

Aud: Ga, Ac.

Well produced and edited, with a wide range of material. This magazine will publish long poems and excerpts, and appreciates craftsmanship. It also allows a sense of humor. One of the better of the more recent magazines. (D.D.)

Earthjoy. 1971. s-a. $1. Jim Jordon, 2219 Colony Ct., Ft. Wayne, Ind. 46805.

Aud: Ac.

Measuring 5½ by 5½ inches before it folds out, this will be hard to keep track of, but the local poetry is better than average, certainly of considerable interest to any library within distance of Ft. Wayne. Philip Dacey and Dick Lourie are about the only ones I recognized, but the dozen or so other poets run the usual range from pretty bad to excellent. A grab bag of joy.

Epos, the work of American and British poets. 1949. q. $2. Will Tullos and Evelyn Thorne. Crescent City, Fla. 32012. Circ: 500.

Indexed: LMags. *Aud:* Ga, Ac.

Poetry only. Important in part for its longevity: this open-minded publication, characterized by attention to quality, gives a good spectrum of poetry in English over the past 20 (and more) years. Not as well known as it should be. (D.D.)

Erratica. 1971. irreg. 4 issues. $2. Don Dorrance, 2101 E. Newberry Blvd., Milwaukee, Wis., 53211. Illus.

Subtitled a Magazine of Literature, this is the work of librarian and little-press critic, Don Dorrance. The five by eight inch 40-page journal is mimeographed and illustrated with material "stolen from various sources." There are short stories, and the rest is poetry. Most of the names won't ring the recognition bell. Still, the content is impressive, and it seems particularly strong on command of language and form.

Extensions. 1969. Irreg. $4/4 issues. S. Lavrian and J. Neugroschel. Box 383, Cathedral St. Sta., New York, N.Y. Illus. Circ: 3,000. Sample.

Aud: Ac, Ga.

The editors note: "We intend to devote as much space as possible to experimental and foreign writing," and this 96-page, well-printed issue features several such items. Emphasis, however, is on young American poets, from such familiars as Allen Kapland and John Perreault to Stanley Cooperman and Steve Katz. A good number are New Yorkers; the themes and style are good, if not revolutionary. Also included are plays, stories, and essays. Above average little magazine.

Field. 1969. s-a. $3. David P. Young. Rice Hall, Oberlin College, Oberlin, Ohio 44074.

Aud: Ga, Ac. *Jv:* V.

Relatively new, college-based, but not of the academic mold. Thick (75 to 110 pages) and growing, this magazine has reached a high level in a very short time. Libraries interested in poetry should try for a complete run. (D.D.)

First Issue. 1969. 3/yr. $3.25 Bill Wertheim, 503 W. 122nd St., New York, N.Y. 10027.

Aud: Ac.

Well over 50 neat pages, and publishing half again as many poets, this magazine has made a point of printing younger poets, especially students from the New York City school system. The sometimes earnest, sometimes imaginative, work of students is balanced by established poets such as Berrigan, di Prima, and the late Paul Blackburn. No background is given for the writers, so unless one recognizes a name, the game is to differentiate the teenagers from the pros. Not always easy.

Goliards. 1964. s-a. $3. Jerry Burns. Goliards Press, Box 703, San Francisco, Calif. 94101. Illus. Circ: 1,000.

Aud: Ga, Ac, Hs.

"Crafted ecstasy swings," and this is a magazine which is wildy uneven, always interesting, and fun to read. Each 120 to 150 page issue offers a wide sampling of younger poets. Although many of the contributors will never be heard of again, germinal works occur often enough to make this exciting. Some bias toward the occult. (D.D.)

The Greenfield Review. 1970. q. $3. Joseph Bruchac. Greenfield Center, N.Y. 12833. Circ: 750. Sample. Vol. ends: Winter.

Bk. rev: 3–4, various length, signed. *Aud:* Ac.

A professional-type little magazine whose careful editor brings the reader the best in both new and more established poets. Averaging 45 to 50 pages, it has a good format. The contributors range from Robert Bly and James Wright to Peter Wild and Clarence Major. The style is as varied as the poets, usually satisfying just about anyone's taste. From time to time there are special issues, such as one on modern African poetry. A well-rounded poetry magazine for most colleges and universities.

Haiku Magazine. q. $4. William J. Higginson. Box 2702, Paterson, N.J. 07509.

Bk. rev: Notes. *Aud:* Ga, Ac, Hs.

As the title indicates, this is turned over to poets and poems which follow the haiku form and its numerous variants. There are comments on the craft of haiku, short book reviews, and a limited amount of prose. The 40-page offset magazine is carefully edited, can be recommended for most poetry collections, and certainly should be part of any magazine list where a teacher is involved with haiku. The editor suggests other titles of this same category; what follows is from his Spring 1971 issue.

Haiku Byways. q. $2.50. Gerry Loose, 14 Frognal, London, NW3, England: Haiku, senryu, Zen poems and sayings, haibun, sketches, and translations. 30 pages, letterpress and offset.

Haiku Highlights. bi-m. $3. Jean Calkins, Box 15, Kanona, N.Y. 14856. Haiku, senryu, articles, a section of "other short poems," and bimonthly contests. 40–45 pages, mimeo.

Haiku West. bi-a. $2. Leroy Kanterman. c/o Japan Soc., Inc., 333 E. 47th St., New York, N.Y. 10017.

Janus & SCTH. 2. $2.50. Rhoda de Long Jewell. 5905 Sherman, Downers Grove, Ill. 60515. General poetry; about half of each issue devoted to the sonnet, cinquain, tanka, and haiku. 35 pp. letterpress.

Modern Haiku. 2. $4. Kay Titus Mormino. 414 N. Orange Dr., Los Angeles, Calif. 90036. Haiku, sneryu, articles, reviews, and drawings. 48 pp. offset.

Hanging Loose. 1966. q. $3.50. Robert Hershon and others. 301 Hicks St., Brooklyn, N.Y. 11201.

Indexed: LMags. *Aud:* Ga, Ac, Hs.

Another strange format to bedevil librarians, *Hanging Loose* is an envelope with 60 to 70 unbound pages. At least the numerical sequence is maintained. It will print a set by an author, and is not afraid of longer poems. Contributors tend to be teachers or students, making much of the material both advanced and undergraduate. Every other issue features three to four high school poets. A potpourri, and always interesting. (D.D.)

Hearse. 1967. Irreg. $3.50/4 issues. E. V. Griffith, 3118 K St., Eureka, Calif. 95501.

Aud: Ac.

A considerably better than average voice for poets closely identified with little magazines, i.e., Enslin, William Matthews, Russell Banks, Ron Schreiber, Lyn Lifshim, Doug Blazek, and Charles Bukowski. Even Hayden Carruth, former editor of *Poetry*, is heard from, and the overall quality is exceptionally high for a little poetry magazine.

Ho-Gung Poetry. 1970. Irreg. $2/4 issues. Don Montgomery. Don's Printing, 1455 N. 27th St., Milwaukee, Wis. 53208. Illus.

Aud: Ga, Ac.

The Milwaukee circle. This small, roughly illustrated magazine presents a wide range of poetry, from good to fairly bad. Selection is dependent on the amount of beer available during the prepublication party. At the same time, no magazine, regardless of rating, will be more enjoyable. This reflects free spirits generally having a ball. (D.D.)

Hyperion. 1967. q. $3. Judith Hogan and Paul Foreman. 2311-C Woolsey St., Berkeley, Calif. 94705. Circ: 500.

Aud: Ga, Ac.

Pocket-sized 48-page magazine, somewhat academic. Excellent translations, sometimes with dual text, are featured. It will have three to four poems by the same author, and publishes long poems. Its small size enables it to keep its standards high. (D.D.)

Intrepid. 1964. 3/yr. $3. Allen De Loach. Box 1423, Buffalo, N.Y. 14214. Circ: 750.

Aud: Ga, Ac. *Jv:* V.

Committed to the new, nonestablishment, and nonacademic, this is one of the magazines publishing the best of the young writers. It should be one of the first purchases in the field. It is mimeographed, and thick. The main effort has gone into the quality of the material rather than format. Letters are of special interest. (D.D.)

Invisible City. 1971. Irreg. $2/3 issues. Paul Vangelisiti and John McBride. Red Hill Press, 6 San Gabriel Dr., Fairfax, Calif. 94930.

Aud: Ga, Ac.

One of the more interesting of the newer publications. Its format is that of a tabloid newspaper, with several selections by each of 10 to 12 poets or translators in an issue. It tends to be far out, showing both the best and the worst, and publishes "whenever enough material is available," favoring the prolific. (D.D.)

Journal of Black Poetry. See Blacks Section.

Kayak. 1964. q. $3. George Hitchcock. 2808 Laguna St., San Francisco, Calif. 94123. Illus. Circ: 1,000. Reprint: Johnson.

Indexed: LMags. *Bk. rev:* 2-5, 1,500 words, signed. *Aud:* Ga, Ac, Hs. *Jv:* V.

Publishing "the best poets now working in the United States and Canada," with a bias toward imagist, surrealist, and political poetry. Reviews are good, and the articles are an important part of the literary scene. Probably the best-known west coast magazine. (D.D.)

Litmus. 1966. Irreg. $3/6 issues. Charles Potts. 15 S. Third St. E., Suite 2, Salt Lake City, Utah, 84111. Circ: 450.

Aud: Ga, Ac.

Definitely the counterculture. A tabloid paper that strenuously goes in for mind-blowing, it prints very long and unshaped poems which lead to bad temper, and jangled nerves. Yet it represents an important segment of our continuing culture. (D.D.)

The Little Square Review. 1966. Irreg. $2/4 issues. John Ridland. 1940 Mission Ridge Rd., Santa Barbara, Calif. 93103. Illus. Circ: 2,000. Sample.

Aud: Ga, Ac.

Measuring six by six inches, the handsome format explains the name. There is nothing "square" about the poets in an average 36-page well-printed issue. Particularly noteworthy is the editor's policy of limiting a number to three or four poets, giving them full opportunity of expression. And from time to time there are special numbers; e.g., the Spring–Summer 1968 issue is given over to poetry of the American Indians. Contributors have included Walter Clark, Robert Peters, Edwin Fussell, Barry Spacks, and Robert Brandts.

Magazine. 1963. a. $1. Kirby Congdon. Box 35, New York, N.Y. 10014.

Aud: Ga, Ac, Hs.

Large mimeo, going for quantity. Always interesting, nonacademic, experimental. Its almost "anything goes" approach guarantees a number of failures, but the good poems wouldn't be found elsewhere. Preferred by poets. (D.D.)

Mele; international poetry letter. 1965. q. $4. Stefan Baciu and Jose L. Varela Ibarra. Dept. of European Languages, Univ. of Hawaii, Honolulu, Hawaii 96822. Circ: 500.

Aud: Ga, Ac.

One of the few magazines anywhere that offers to accept submissions in any language. Attempts to find "young American poetry with passion and guts to blend with the Asian, African, European and Latin-American poetry we publish." It is actively cross-cultural, as might be imagined, including some transliterated Hawaiian poetry. As this becomes better known it could, and should, increase in importance. One of the magazines which determine if a collection is really first rate. (D.D.)

Mojo Navigator(e) 1970. q. $3.50. John Jacob. 1615 Ferndale, Ann Arbor, Mich. 48104. Illus. Sample.

Aud: Ac, Ga, Hs.

A 40-page offset little poetry magazine which makes it all (i.e., the search for something interesting among the products of the now-established mimeograph "revolution") worthwhile. The editor, no mean poet himself, puts out a deceptively simple-looking magazine without benefit of anything but the poetry. And the selection is tight, solid, and well worth a subscription. Poets run from Allen Ginsberg, Michael McClure, D. r. Wagner, and Lyn Lifshin to David and Maria Gitlin, Arthur Knight, and Dick Lourie. The editor scatters informative notes on new magazines, books, and news throughout the pages. A first-class effort.

Monument in Canto and Essays. 1968. a. 3yrs./$2.75. Victor Myers. Rte. 10, Columbia, Mo. 65201. Illus., index, adv. Circ: 500. Sample.

Aud: Ac.

Calls itself "one of the good, honest little magazines." It's all of that, and in 50 well-printed pages features cantos by such veterans of the underground as Doug Blazek, Peter Wild, and John Tagliabue. More professional and polished than most publications of this type.

New: American and Canadian Poetry. 1966. 3/yr. $2.50. John Grill. RD 3, Trumansburg, N.Y., 14886. Circ: 1,000. Sample. Vol. ends: Dec.

Bk. rev: 5, 350 words, signed. *Aud:* Ga, Ac, Hs. *Jv:* V.

One of the best, longest-lived of the little poetry magazines. It is particularly useful for libraries because the editor prints poetry from both sides of the border and tries to publish for all schools—university, underground, regional, etc. The average 40 to 50 page issue is good, the short criticism excellent, and the choice of poets imaginative. Poets such as Lyn Lif-

shin, Alvin Greenberg, and Emmett Jarrett demonstrate an approach to poetry that catches the dreams and frustrations of most of us. Others tend to be equally excellent.

Northeast. 1962. bi-a. $6. John Judson. Northeast/Juniper Books, 1310 Shorewood Dr., La Crosse, Wis. 54601. Illus., index. Circ: 500.

Bk. rev: 2–4, 2 pages, signed.

An offset poetry magazine, edited by a poet who includes in the subscription price two chapbooks. Each of the Juniper books is devoted entirely to the work of a single poet; e.g., with the Summer 1971 issue of the magazine, George Hitchcock's (of *Kayak* fame) "The Rococo Eye" was also part of the mailing. Poets, in either the magazine or the chapbooks, have included the editor, Lisel Mueller, Felix Pollak, John Knoepfle, Dave Etter, and others. Everything is at a highly professional level, and reviews of other little poetry titles are refreshingly critical. This is much above the average approach to poetry and poets, and can be recommended for larger academic and public library collections.

Patterns. 1970. irreg. (3–4/yr.). $3.50/4 issues. Vera Raynor. 2 Whaleback Waddy, Denville, N.J. 07834. Illus.

Aud: Ac, Ga.

One of the few poetry magazines edited by "a member of the Family of Woman (human beings, collectively speaking)." The pocket-sized, offset, 42-page magazine reflects the editor's wish to publish poetry of and for "the free-thinkers, visionaries, spiritual miners—those whose poetry is grounded in awareness of self and the world around oneself." Well, the world looks fairly bright from a reader's viewpoint. Of the 15 to 20 contributors in each issue, about one third are good to first rate. The rest go up and down the scale, but the average is quite exceptional for a little poetry magazine. I particularly enjoy the well-structured and highly imaginative work of the editor.

Pebble. 1968. irreg. (2–3/yr.). $3.50/4 issues. Greg Kuzma. The Best Cellar Press, 1031 Charleston St., Lincoln, Nebr. 68508. Illus. Circ: 400. Sample.

Bk. rev: 1–2, 800 words, signed. *Aud:* Ac, Ga.

Improving with each issue, *Pebble* is a nicely edited, well-printed little magazine of poetry. The editor-poet has an above average appreciation of quality. The result is 40 or so pages of good-to-excellent verse. And while much of it may be by poets new to the average reader, there are a number of regulars to the little magazine scene, including Duane Ackerson, Barry Targan, Lyn Lifshin, Harold Witt, and even Joyce Carol Oates in the Winter 1970 number. (Where does she get the time to write such fine verse and prose? These days her name is as familiar to the literary and little magazine scene as it ever was—which is to say success has not spoiled Joyce Carol.) Meanwhile, Mr. Kuzma is offering a number of pamphlet series from the same press, again well printed, carefully edited, and by some first-rate people. Any library involved or interested in poetry should send for a sample copy, and more information on the pamphlets. It is well worth the small effort.

Poet and Critic. 1965. 3/yr. $3. Richard Gustafson. Iowa State Univ. Press, Press Bldg., Ames, Iowa. 50010. Illus. Circ: 500.

Indexed: AbEnSt. *Bk. rev:* 4–8, 250 words, signed. *Aud:* Ga, Ac, Jc.

Academic, but at its best. Somewhat round robin, it has everyone commenting on everyone else's work. This is a pleasantly produced magazine with good illustrations. Almost an example of a good, standard creative writing class in action. (D.D.)

Poetry Australia. 1964. bi-m. $6. Grace Perry. S. Head Press, 350 Lyons Rd., Five Dock, Sidney, N.S.W., Australia. Circ: 3,000.

Indexed: ICLM. *Bk. rev:* 3–5, grouped, 200 words, signed. *Aud:* Ac.

Not only Australian, but international poetry. The poetry is not outstanding, but a good spectrum. European, Africa, and North American poetry is reviewed. One of the more useful titles for an international flavor. (D.D.)

Poetry Eastwest. 1969. irreg. $2/issue. Syed Amanuddin, Box 391, Sumter, S.C. 29150.

Aud: Ac.

Tends to concentrate on translations and has featured poetry from India, Brazil, and Australia. This usually consists of about 36 printed pages. The contributors are fair to good, but except for a few translations, the appeal is probably more to dedicated poets than laymen.

Poetry Review. 1964. q. $2. Duane Locke. Univ. of Tampa, Tampa, Fla. 33606. Circ: 500.

Aud: Ga, Ac.

Somewhat academic but open to all types. This has consistently published good poetry, well balanced between schools and streams. (D.D.)

Poets. 1967. a. $1.75. Harper Sq. Press, 5649 S. Harper Ave., Chicago, Ill. 60637.

Aud: Ga, Ac.

Comes out once a year and is usually organized around a theme, i.e., the last of the three so far is concerned with "levitations." This section consists of poems and photographs of paintings and sculpture "having to do with mechanically accomplished, spiritual or fanciful levitations." The second section is sim-

ply headed Observations and brings together poets "on matters of concern to the poets." The some 50 contributors are from all walks of life, but more are students and teachers who have been published from time to time in many little magazines. The quality is exceptionally high, and the whole serves as a good annual introduction to some of our better younger writers. The format is excellent, although the book size (4 by 11 inches) makes it a bit awkward to shelve.

Poor Old Tired Horse. 1961. irreg. $3. Ian Hamilton Finlay. Wild Hawthorn Press, Stonypath, Dunsyre, Lanark, Scotland. Illus. Circ: 1,000.

Indexed: ComLMags. *Aud:* Ga, Ac, Hs.

The poem as thing: concrete poetry, found poetry, or whatever. Lots of fun, it will make sense to a part of the public. It represents a good first-round choice for high school libraries. Illustrations and format are first rate. (D.D.)

Priapus. 1962. 3/yr. $2. John Cotton, 37 Lombardy Dr., Berkhamsted, Hertfordshire, England. Illus. Circ: 350. Sample. Vol. ends: Winter.

Bk. rev: 6, 600 words, signed. *Aud:* Ac.

A colorfully illustrated, mimeographed magazine which has consistently published some of the best poetry in England—note, if you will, the founding date. In the past ten years it has featured Ted Walker, Rigby Graham (an illustrator), Philip Hosbaum, etc. A modest-priced publication with major implications.

Quetzal. 1971. 3/yr. $4. Randall Ackley, Box 696, Pembroke, N.C. 28372.

Aud: Ac.

This differs from most poetry magazines because it puts strong emphasis on the American Indian, Tibetan, and medieval themes—a mixed bag tied together by the mystical reality which seems to fascinate the poets: Howard McCord, Stanley Noyes, Peter Wild, and Gene Frumkin, to name a few. The magazine is oblong in size, offset, with some illustrations, and fairly well edited.

Runcible Spoon. 1966. irreg. D. r. Wagner and Barbara O'Connelly. Box 4622, Sacramento, Calif. 95825. Circ: 500.

Aud: Ga, Ac.

Interesting, at time far out, this magazine is inbred to a degree, as an expression of D. r. Wagner and his friends. Fortunately, it is a very alert, interesting circle, forming an important literary movement of their own. Marked at times by genuine wit. (D.D.)

Salt Lick. 1969. s-a. $2. James Haining. 721 St. Paul St., Baltimore, Md. 21202. Illus., adv. Circ: 1,000. Sample. Vol. ends: Spring.

Bk. rev: 2, 2 pages, signed. *Aud:* Ac, Ga.

Primarily a poetry magazine with bits of prose, essays, book reviews, and notes on the passing scene. Beginning in late 1971, the editor adopted a policy of turning over his 25 to 50 pages to no more than a half dozen poets. "Hopefully, there will be 10 to 15 poems per poet with a statement or essay on verse, so readers will know what he or she thinks he is, or is not doing." Poets include Michael Lally, David Search, William Hart, Lyn Lifshin, Barbara Drake, and Robert Trammell, among others. A professional job, and well worth the modest price.

Search for Tomorrow. 1970. irreg. $4/yr. George Mattingly, 530 N. Clinton, Iowa City, Iowa 52240. Illus.

Aud: Ac.

Each of the poems in this well-printed little magazine is accompanied by a drawing, sketch, or photograph. Most tip off the reader to the expected mood, if not precise subject matter, which seems a notch more imaginative than many because the editor, who presumably arranged for the art, has given concrete poetry another dimension, or is it definition? Rather than arrange the words in some graphic form, he sticks to the old process and superimposes an image on the poem. *Kayak* is by far the most successful innovator in this field, but editor Mattingly has a touch all his own. Seems equally of value to those studying art and graphics as those carried away by poetry.

The Seventies. 1958. irreg. $3/4 issues. Robert Bly. Odin House, Madison, Minn. 56256. Circ: 2,000.

Indexed: LMags. *Aud:* Ga, Ac, Hs. *Jv:* V.

The best poetry magazine published and edited by one man in the United States, it consistently reflects the best in modern poetry. Its editor is highly regarded by younger poets and has done much to encourage their efforts. Equally important, he has issued the original texts and translations of leading European and South American poets. Long essays on aspects of American poetry are disguised as book reviews. In all aspects, excellence shines through. Acquisitions librarians will be made nervous, however, by his highly erratic publishing schedule. This should be one of the first purchases for all libraries from senior high school to the most academic. (D.D.)

The Small Pond; magazine of literature. 1964. 3/yr. $2.50. Napoleon St. Cyr. 10 Overland Drive, Stratford, Conn. 06597. Illus. Sample.

Aud: Ac, Ga.

Although this has been around much longer than most little poetry magazines, it is not as well known as it might be, particularly to libraries. With plaudits from such poets as May Sarton, James Merrill, and Walter Lowenfels, it can be considered a much above average effort. Averaging some 40 neat offset pages, it features a dozen or so poets, short essays, fiction, and

brief reviews. A run of this magazine may prove important when some of the poets gain in age and reputation. In view of its impressive editing, not to mention the businesslike approach to subscriptions and publishing dates, this can be recommended for library poetry collections.

Solstice. 1965. 3/yr. Brian Morse and Steve Bradshaw. 21a Silver St., Cambridge, England. Circ: 4,000.

Indexed: ICLM. *Aud:* Ga, Ac, Hs.

Solstice now enjoys one of the largest circulations of any small literary magazine in the United Kingdom (or, for that matter, the United States). Many of the poets published appear here for the first time, while a good representation of established poets is also printed. Has printed supplements presenting new poets of the United States and Latin America. (D.D.)

Spring Rain. 1971. Karen and John Sollid, Box 15319, Wedgwood Sta., Seattle, Wash. 98115. Sample.

Aud: Ac.

Coming out of Seattle, the title is no surprise. What is unusual is that fact that the 34-page magazine is handset by the editors, and the whole run off on their own press. The typography is functional, and the eight poets are primarily teachers and students from the Seattle area. Both a joy to read and to look at, this is a far cry from the normal mimeographed little, and it has enjoyed a favorable reception. The editors explained that Karen is teaching English in a local high school, and John, when not operating the press, is a watercolorist. Space doesn't permit quoting John's interesting letter, but a bit of it indicates man and wife can work well together on little magazines: "The cost of the press is borne wholly by Karen. She works and I do the setting of type . . . the writing of business letters and that sort of thing. She and I edit together and she writes to poets. We have this arrangement so that we can afford to continue our collections in spite of the low volume and the slight return." It all seems more than worth a library's support, although if in doubt, write for a free sample copy.

Steelhead. 1971. q. $3.50. The editors. Box 3082, Duluth, Minn. 55803.

Aud: Ac.

A new 40-page little offset poetry magazine whose editors are "interested in all types of quality, contemporary poetry and translations." The contributors include the heavies Robert Bly, Philip Haskell, and David Ignatow; plus some well knowns—Eduardo Escobar, Toma Transtromer, and Adam Mickiewicz—in translations. Others are lesser knowns. The quality of poetry is high. No particular school, and a broad selection of types appears. A good choice for larger poetry collections, and for all libraries in the greater Minnesota area where support of the arts is a foregone conclusion.

Steppenwolf. 1965. a. $2. Philip Boatright and Jean Shannon. Box 55045, Omaha, Nebr. 68155.

Aud: Ga, Ac.

With admirable restraint, the editors limit themselves to one issue per year. Little-known but highly talented poets account for most of the well-printed journal. Editoral judgment is first rate. Will print longer poems, translations. (D.D.)

Stone. 1967. bi-a. $2. Mike Chervenak, Harry Cording, and Richard Jorgensen. 26 Dublin Rd., Pennington, N.J. Illus.

Aud: Ac.

An 80-page little poetry magazine with a new dimension. Editor Chervenak explains: "The Stone is also available—live and in person. This is a program of down home multi-media poetry read both unaccompanied and accompanied by acoustic guitars, flute or piano; songs, art, and experiments with sound." The eight man group has performed in Leslie Fiedler's backyard (a command performance with Allen Ginsberg) and in more conventional university settings. Some notion of the poetry is found in the magazine, but Mike has the last word: "In one section, we do things like 'spin music' in which five or six readers read different groupings of words at the same time while a single microphone passed around focuses on a single voice." Any library interested in multimedia and poetry experiments would do well to (a) subscribe to Mike's mag; and (b) write him asking about a performance. We guarantee that no one will fall asleep, either reading the magazine or attending the show.

Two Feet of Poetry. 1970. irreg. 60¢ each. Barry Targan. Dept. of English, Skidmore College, Saratoga Springs, N.Y. 12866.

Aud: Ga, Ac.

Quite literally, this is two feet of poetry, i.e., an eight-inch-wide broadside which is two feet long. Usually four or five poets are represented, and their poetry is set off by pleasant woodcuts and engravings. The whole is nicely printed, and it makes an interesting kind of poster. Larger libraries will want it as a permanent part of their collections because the poets are first rate. Smaller libraries might simply hang it up and let readers enjoy the spirit of the thing. From time to time he publishes separates such as "To avery thinnesse beate," a portfolio of poems by various poets. Write the publisher for more information. (He is reliable and replies promptly.)

West Coast Poetry Review. 1971. q. $5. W. M. Ransom. Box 149, Virginia City, Nev. 89440.

Indexed: LMags. *Bk. rev:* 3, 500 words, signed. *Aud:* Ac.

Nevada isn't quite the west coast, but no matter, the poetry here is hardly limited to the western part

of the divide either. For every westerner, like Mark McCloskey and Joan Kuban (Alaska), there is an easterner, like Nancy Davies and Jack Driscoll (both from Massachusetts). The quality of the poetry in the well-printed 42-page magazine is high, particularly since a great number of contributors have published before. Few are as well known as a Richard Wilbur (who translates here the work of Yevgeni Yevtushenko), but they are all unique in their various approaches. Another feature is good reviews. The editor reports, for example, an upcoming review of Galway Kinnell's *The Book of Nightmares* by Robert Baty. A much better than average little poetry mag, and one that should have a long, and hopefully prosperous, life. A solid bet for all libraries.

Westigan Review. 1969. q. $2. John Knapp II. Chemistry Dept., Western Mich. College, Kalamazoo, Mich. 49001.

Bk. rev: 2–3, 250 words, signed. *Aud:* Ga, Ac.

Small, select, and somewhat academic, this is redeemed by very good taste. It will provide good coverage for better midwestern poets, but editorial board mechanism may make it somewhat conservative. Most of the poems are short. (D.D.)

The Windless Orchard. 1970. q. $3.75. Robert Novak. 6718 Baytree Dr., Ft. Wayne, Ind. 46825. Illus. Circ: 500. Sample.

Bk. rev: 2, 600 words, signed. *Aud:* Ac, Ga.

A pleasing combination of photographs and poetry. Its calm, thoughtful approach has included little-known poets as well as poetry by W. H. Auden. Although a trifle uneven, it is certainly interesting enough, and has promise of real development.

Wormwood Review. 1959. q. $3.50. Marvin Malone. Wormwood Review Press, Boxes 101 and 111, Storrs, Conn. 06268. Illus. Circ: 600.

Bk. rev: Various number, length. *Aud:* Ga, Ac. *Jv:* V.

An outstanding magazine whose aim is to "reflect the temper and depth of the human scene." The poems it prints are, almost without exception, good. In fact, there is little about the magazine that isn't first rate. It maintains a consistent freshness, and even at times humor. A useful addendum is the continuing bibliography of little magazines and other items of interest to poets and their readers. This bibliography is a prime selection tool, giving short but solid annotations that rate from "highly recommended" to "totally panned and damned." A first-choice magazine, preferred by poets. (D.D.)

Zahir. 1970. bi-a. $2. Diane Kruchkow. English Dept., Univ. of New Hampshire, Durham, N.H. 03824.

Aud: Ac.

Although this opened with University support, it's

now on its own, and joins the ranks of true, highly personalized little poetry magazines. The 48-page product is well printed; the content is an up and down affair. Poets are relative beginners, a few have published in other little mags, and almost all are students, in reality or at heart. There are the usual better-known names, from Larry Eigner to Ted Enslin. All in all, typical enough of a genuine effort which is exciting, risky, and well worth the modest price.

Traditional Academic

Alcheringa. 1970. bi-a. $2.50/issue. Jerome Rothenberg and Dennis Tedlock. 600 W. 163 St., New York, N.Y. 10032. Subs. to: Book People, 2940 7th St., Berkeley, Calif. 94310. Illus. Circ: 2,000.

Aud: Ac, Ga. *Jv:* V.

Of equal interest to the poet, anthropologist, and linguist, this is a semipopular magazine of English translations of tribal poetry. Although directed to the layman, and relatively free of jargon and technical language, it assumes an interest and "loving respect" for the world's tribal past and present. The second issue included an insert recording of an oral translation of Navajo horse songs arranged for four voices; a preconquest Mayan drama; African praise poems; and a technical discussion of linguistic aspects of retranslating American Indian texts. They plan issues on South American and Papuan tribal poetry, interviews, picture poems, and a variety of material which takes in the tribal culture of the world. It has something for all, and can be highly recommended.

The Beloit Poetry Journal. 1950. q. $2. Robert Glauber and others. Box 2, Beloit, Wis. 53511. Circ: 1,100.

Indexed: LMags. *Bk. rev:* Notes. *Aud:* Ga, Ac, Hs. *Jv:* V.

"It is the function of a little poetry magazine to print good poetry and to discover new poets." This has been long established and highly respected as an outlet for the young, the experimental, and the unknown. Sometimes uneven, it does apply critical standards and is one of the important showcases. Some issues contain Books in Brief, reviewing up to eight books of current poetry. Will issue chapbooks on one poet or subject. Academic libraries should have a complete run. Preferred by poets. (D.D.)

Choice; a magazine of poetry and photographs. 1961. irreg. $6.50/4 issues. John Logan and others. Box 4858, Chicago, Ill. 60680. Distr. by: Follett Publishing Co., 1010 W. Washington Blvd., Chicago, Ill. 60607. Illus., index. Circ: 2,000.

Aud: Ga, Ac, Hs.

Averaging between 120 and 160 pages, well printed and nicely designed, featuring established poets, this is a good general magazine. Each issue includes 50 to 60 poets, some well known and others just beginning to establish themselves. An excellent, somewhat conservative, survey, it is essential for serious collections of poetry, and a good choice for high schools. (D.D.)

Concerning Poetry. 1968. bi-a. $3. L. L. Lee. English Dept., Western Wash. State College, Bellingham, Wash. 98225. Adv. Circ: 400. Vol. ends: Fall.

Bk. rev: 4, 750 words, signed. *Aud:* Ac.

This journal has introduced a twist that is more or less its own—a bearing-down on explication. Its primary purpose, then, is to print "knowledgeable, intelligent, and clear articles which will help [people] to read poetry better." Each issue contains two or three such articles, and notes on points of explication, reviews of books of poetry and books on poetry, and a section of original poems. So far there have been a couple of articles on the nature of poetry—one by Lewis Turco—and others on the poetry of Browning, Yeats, and Williams. The articles are about what might be expected; the poems, on the other hand, are of exceptional quality. Such poets as Allen Ginsberg, James Tate, and X. J. Kennedy have been represented. The journal's greatest coup to date: a remarkable collection, in its first issue, of five poems by William Stafford.

Counter/Measures; a magazine of rime, meter and song. 1972. a. $2. X. J. Kennedy. Box 431, Bedford, Mass. 01730.

Bk. rev: 15, 250–400 words, signed. *Aud:* Ac, Ga.

An annual, and as such really a 116-page paperback collection of poets, both famous and not so, who share one thing: they all write in rime or meter. The editor, of course, is the famous, and in this same category are such as W. D. Snodgrass, Anthony Hecht, J. V. Cunningham, Richard Eberhart, etc. It comes to about 40 poets with one to two poems for each. But there is a plus: eight song lyrics (Kennedy has a thing about popular songwriting; he explains it in his essay, which is downright fascinating); four translations; an essay on poetry by Kennedy (in which he explains why he is holding contributors to poems written in meter, or in rime, or in both; no free verse for him or this magazine); and some first-rate book reviews by the same gentleman. The whole is nicely printed and bound by Furbush-Roberts of Bangor, Maine. (I don't really know them, but they do deserve credit.) The collection is much above average, and can be safely and wisely purchased by just about any library looking for a current cross section of famous and not so famous American poets. Unless, of course, you happen to disagree with Kennedy's notions about the joys of meter and rime.

Hiram Poetry Review. 1966. s-a. $2. Hale Chatfield. English Dept., Hiram College, Hiram, Ohio 44234. Index. Circ: 500. Sample.

Indexed: LMags. *Bk. rev:* Various number, length. *Aud:* Ac.

A small college-based poetry magazine whose editor works on the assumption "that there are too many poetry magazines, and they are generally too thick." Well, in less than 30 pages the editor includes work by from 8 to 12 poets, usually only one poem for each. The level of quality is high, the poets primarily teachers and students who represent no distinct school. Some witty editorial comments and book reviews, too.

Modern Poetry in Translation. 1965. $5. Ted Hughes and Daniel Weissbort. 10 Compayne Gardens, London NW6, England. Circ: 5,000.

Indexed: ComLMags. *Aud:* Ac, Ga. *Jv:* V.

There are a number of poetry magazines which feature translations, but this is by far the most important. Although issued in England, it has international support, and deserves the attention of larger academic and public libraries in the United States. Published as a tabloid, an average 25 to 30 page number concentrates on modern French, Scandinavian, and German works. Translations by Muriel Rukeyser, Anselm Hollo, Michael Hamburger, and Edward Lucie-Smith are printed. Editor Hughes insists on a literal word-by-word translation, and as only the English version is given, it is difficult to judge the merits of the case. Still, the magazine has no competitors, and it is a major influence on many poets.

The New York Quarterly. 1970. q. $7. William Packard. Subs. to: Pocket Books/Ace, 1120 Ave. of the Amer., New York, N.Y. 10036. Illus., adv. Circ: 8,000.

Aud: Ac, Ga, Hs. *Jv:* V.

One of the best general poetry magazines published in America today. In addition to featuring New York-centered poetry, the editors have a distinctive approach of value to teachers, students, and the laymen. They are concerned with the craft of writing poetry. There are interviews with poets, worksheets showing the progress of a poem from inception to finished work, data on workshops and grants, a calendar of poetry readings, and essays on techniques of the poet. In addition to contributions from some of the leading established and new poets, the magazine has run features on the poetry of ethnic minorities, e.g., Puerto Ricans, Chinese poets in New York, Afro-Americans, Yiddish poets, and the contemporary American Indian. The wide scope of this unique poetry magazine will make it a required subscription for any library, from high school through university, where poetry is a consideration in the curriculum.

Poetry. 1912. m. $12. Daryl Hine. 1228 N. Dearborn Pkwy., Chicago, Ill. 60610. Circ: 9,000. Reprint: AMS.

Indexed: RG. *Bk. rev:* 1–16, grouped, signed. *Aud:* Ga, Ac, Hs. *Rv:* H. *Jv:* V.

The most respected magazine of poetry in the United States (or for that matter, anywhere), it is outstanding for experimental and important new poetry. It publishes the work of the complete range of significant poets, from the youngest and least known to the best established. Essays on poetry and excellent critical reviews of books of and about poetry are included. Other special features are Books Received, notices of poetry prizes, and News Notes, which contains dates of poetry readings and announcements of new periodicals that are beginning publication. T. S. Eliot once remarked that "*Poetry* has had imitators, but has so far survived them all. It is an American institution." Should be in every library from senior high on up.

Poetry Northwest. 1959. q. $3.50. David Wagoner. Parrington Hall, Univ. of Washington, Seattle, Wash. 98105. Circ: 1,500.

Indexed: LMags. *Bk. rev:* Occasional. *Aud:* Ga, Ac, Jc.

This is one of the more impressive regional poetry magazines, comparable with *Poetry* (Chicago). It gained fame under the editorship of Carolyn Kizer and has continued an impressive record under Wagoner's sure hand. It has continued to display a remarkable power for discovering new, worthwhile poets. Outstanding art work by Northwest artists and photographers is included. A good magazine for all libraries.

Southern Poetry Review. 1958. 3/yr. $3. Guy Owen, Thomas N. Walters, and Michael Reynolds. Dept. of English, North Carolina State Univ., Raleigh, N.C. 27607. Circ: 800. Sample.

Bk. rev: 1, 1000 words, signed. *Aud:* Ac, Ga.

One of the longest-lived little poetry magazines. The reasons for its vitality are quality; meeting subscriptions with a magazine, not a promise; and a conviction on the part of the editors that they and their contributors have something worth saying. Unfortunately, the small circulation indicates that the good word has not spread far; which is the library's and the reader's loss. Among the contributors, surely represented by at least one volume on most library shelves, are A. R. Ammonds, Wendell Berry, Charles Bukowski, Hayden Carruth, John Ciardi, Edward Field, X. J. Kennedy, Howard Nemerov, and on down the alphabet of distinguished names. There are, to be sure, lesser-known poets, but what they have here is among their best work. All in all, a really fine poetry magazine which hopefully will win more support from readers and librarians.

Victorian Poetry. 1963. q. $6. John F. Stasny. 129 Armstrong Hall, W. Virginia Univ., Morgantown, W. Va. 26506. Index. Circ: 1,300. Sample. Vol. ends: Winter. Refereed.

Bk. rev: 2–5, essay length, signed. *Aud:* Ac.

Devoted to criticism of Victorian poetry, and requires some knowledge of the author or work being discussed. Each issue has five to eight articles of some length, and several shorter articles. The former are devoted to extended discussions, whereas the latter are more often concerned with the presentation of esoteric items of scholarship. Some of the book reviews are delightful, all of them excellent. An annual review, "The Year's Work in Victorian Poetry," appears in the summer issue.

POLITICAL SCIENCE

Basic Periodicals

Hs: *Current History;* Ga: *Current History, Foreign Affairs;* Jc: *American Academy of Political and Social Sciences. Annals, Foreign Affairs, Current History;* Ac: *American Political Science Review, American Academy of Political and Social Sciences. Annals, Foreign Affairs, International Development Review, Orbis, World Politics.*

Library and Teaching Aids

Intercom, Perspective, Political Science Quarterly.

Basic Abstracts and Indexes

ABC Political Science, America: History and Life, Current Contents, Public Affairs Information Service, International Political Science Abstracts.

Cessations

Foreign Policy Briefs, International Conciliation.

AUFS Reports. 1952. 60/yr. $35. Janet Gregory. Amer. Univ. Field Staff, Box 150, Hanover, N.H. 03755. Illus., index. Circ: 2300. Sample.

Aud: Ac.

Short (10 to 20 page) offset reports on various aspects of world developments, these are written by American University Field Staff employees. The reports are objective, cover all aspects of world affairs, and are of interest to anyone deeply involved with the social, political, or economic trends of various countries. The supporting group is made up of various American universities and is a nonprofit organization.

American Academy of Political & Social Science. Annals. 1889. bi-m. Membership $12 (Cloth ed. $16). Richard D. Lambert. The Academy, 3937 Chestnut St., Philadelphia, Pa. 19104. Index, adv. Circ: 25,000. Vol. ends: Nov. Microform: UM. Reprint: Kraus.

Indexed: AmerH, CurrCont, PAIS, RG. *Bk. rev:* 80–90, 1 page, signed. *Aud:* Ac. *Jv:* V.

Covering most of the major political and social issues of our times, the *Annals* has a long-established

policy of devoting each number to a given topic and then presenting all sides of the topic. Authors are experts, often more scholarly than fascinating, more detailed than lucid. The magazine, which due to its length of some 250 to 300 pages is really a monograph, has considerable value for the researcher and may be of limited interest to advanced high school students and teachers, but generally it is much too academic for the average teen-ager. For libraries it has an added value: there are extensive book reviews, classified by broad subjects and covering every major title in the area of political and social sciences. Many, however, are late in terms of original publishing date. All in all reliable, although too scholarly for the general user.

American Political Science Review. 1906. q. Membership. $35. Austin Ranney. Amer. Political Science Assn., 1527 New Hampshire Ave., N.W., Washington, D.C. 20036. Illus., index., adv. Circ: 20,000. Sample. Microform: UM.

Indexed: PAIS, SSHum. *Bk. rev:* 60–80, 1,000–1,500 words, signed. *Aud:* Ac, Ga. *Jv:* V.

The basic political science journal, as much because it presents original articles as because it is the voice of the influential American Political Science Association. It covers government, administration, public law, international relations, and political theory. It is of primary value to libraries because of the extensive, detailed, and usually critical book reviews. While the audience for the magazine is the graduate student and teacher, it has some value for the layman. The articles are not the most fascinating in terms of style, but they are authoritative, usually ahead of what is to be found in other places. Although it will have greatest use in academic libraries, the book reviews make it worth considering for larger public library collections. Included in the membership, which brings libraries the *Review,* is a newsletter, the *PS Newsjournal* which apparently cannot be subscribed to separately.

PS Newsjournal (1968. q. Walter E. Beach. Illus., adv. Sample. Vol. ends: Fall.) is virtually a postscript to the Association's *Review.* It has information on professional developments, research and study support, and professional as well as Association activities. One issue a year is devoted to a preliminary program description of the annual meeting. Each issue has a limited number of articles about the discipline and the profession.

Asia. See China and Asia/Asia Section.

Asian Quarterly. See China and Asia/Asia Section.

The Atlantic Community Quarterly. 1963. q. $5. Theodore C. Achilles and Richard Wallace. Atlantic Council of the U.S., Inc., 1616 H St., N.W., Washington, D.C. 20006. Adv., index. Circ: 4,500. Sample. Vol. ends: Winter. Microform: UM.

Indexed: HistAb, AmerH, SSHum. *Aud:* Ga, Ac.

Provides useful coverage of chiefly Western European affairs, and U.S. policies with regard to the Atlantic alliance. Articles cover matters of broad international scope, such as the political integration of Europe; in some instances, they zero in on the internal affairs of a particular nation. The material is on a scholarly level, with emphasis on current political developments, rather than their historical background. Source material, in the way of important documents, is provided in each issue, which may be useful for those libraries which cannot subscribe to foreign document series. A short "Atlantic Bibliography" is given at the end.

The Black Politician. See Blacks Section.

Black Politics. See Blacks Section.

British Journal of Political Science. 1971. q. $19.50. Brian Barry. Cambridge Univ. Press, 32 E. 57th St., New York, N.Y. 10022. Adv.

Aud: Ac.

This scholarly journal is aimed primarily at the academic community. Topics range from matters of local English interest to broader international affairs. While some of the articles tend to be empirical, others (such as an essay on "Politics in Kenya") may be more suitable for the generalist. It does not have the diversity of approaches or topics that may be found in the *American Political Science Review.* Recommended for libraries with larger political science collections.

Canadian Journal of Political Science. 1968. q. $12. John Meisel. Canadian Political Science Assn., Univ. of Toronto Press, Toronto 181, Ont., Canada. Circ: 3,000. *Indexed:* IntPolSci, CanI, PAIS, SSHum. *Bk. rev:* 20-25, 250-750 words, signed. *Aud:* Sa, Ac. *Rv:* H. *Jv:* B.

Publishes general articles on political science in both French and English. A given number of the five to six articles deal with Canadian problems, but the journal is in no way limited to that country. There are excellent book reviews, covering titles not often found in many similar American publications. A required item for all large collections, and for medium-to-large Canadian libraries.

China Quarterly. See China and Asia/China Section.

Comparative Political Studies. 1968. q. $18 (Individuals $12; students $9). Sage Publns., Inc., 275 S. Beverly Dr., Beverly Hills, Calif. 90212. Illus., adv. Circ: 3,000. Sample. Vol. ends: Jan. Refereed.

Indexed: ABCPolSci. *Aud:* Ac.

Men of science are usually tempted to use mathematical formulas in sizing up social events. This publication devotes its pages mainly to such theories and statistical approaches to politics, but also provides some valuable empirical research articles. The scope is international. Well-documented scholarly papers, research notes, and an annotated bibliography make every issue an interesting companion to the researcher of political topics. Recommended for academic and research libraries.

Comparative Politics. 1968. q. $12 (Individuals $8). Ed. committee. City Univ. of N.Y., Grad. Center, 33 W. 42nd St., New York, N.Y. 10036. Illus., index, adv. Circ: 2,000. Sample. Vol. ends: July.

Bk. rev: 10-15, essays, signed. *Aud:* Ac.

According to the editors, the purpose here is to publish articles and book reviews "devoted to comparative analysis of political institutions and behavior." There are usually four to five pieces, shorter "research notes," and the book reviews. Material is for the and by the professor of political science. The scope is international. The language, while technical, is well within the understanding of the interested student. A better than average magazine for medium-to-large academic collections.

Congressional Record. See Government Magazines/United States Section.

Current Digest of the Soviet Press. See USSR and East Europe/English Language Section.

Current History; the monthly magazine of world affairs. 1922. m. $9.50. Carol L. Thompson. Current History, Inc., 1822 Ludlow St., Philadelphia, Pa. 19103. Illus., index. Circ: 28,000. Microform: UM.

Indexed: AbrRG, PAIS, RG. *Bk. rev:* 10-20, 200-500 words. *Aud:* Ga, Ac, Hs. *Jv:* V.

One of the best history and international events review magazines now available for the nonspecialist. A concerned effort is made to present material in a popular style, but it is usually prepared by noted historians and scholars. The result is an authoritative overview in language that can be grasped by both the high school and college student. Each issue is devoted to a specific area or topic, with about six to ten individual articles on different aspects. There are maps, current documents and speeches (which often can be found in no other source), and book reviews. A magazine for every library.

Department of State Bulletin. See Government Magazines/United States Section.

EMK. 1969. q. $3. James Spada. 101 Chester Ave., Staten Island, N.Y. 10312. Illus. Circ: 1,000. Sample. Vol. ends: Winter. Microform: UM.

Bk. rev: 6, 1,000 words, signed. *Aud:* Ga, Ac.

A partisan magazine which reports on the life and times of Sen. Edward Kennedy. Of broader interest, though, because it takes in articles of interest to any citizen, i.e., 18-year-olds voting, volunteer army, and health insurance. Book reviews, too, are broader in scope. The 20 to 30 pages should be of interest to any liberal.

External Affairs. 1948. m. $2. Dept. of External Affairs, Information Canada, 171 Slater St., Ottawa, Canada. Illus., index, adv. Circ: 4,261. Vol. ends: Dec.

Indexed: CanI, PAIS. *Aud:* Ga, Ac.

This journal is issued monthly in English and French by the Department of External Affairs, Ottawa. It provides information on Canada's foreign relations and reports the current work and activities of the Department.

Approximately four or five articles in each issue cover various aspects of external relations. Written for the student of foreign policy, they are literate and clear, and may be profitably read by the informed layman. Sample topics that have appeared include coverage of the Prime Minister's Asian tour early in 1971, the Department's deep involvement in international scientific diplomacy, official participation of Canada in trade, industrial and cultural happenings abroad, and a series of articles describing the work of the legal divisions of the Department. Generous coverage is given of Canada's efforts in the United Nations in political, educational, scientific, and cultural areas. Usually the articles are unsigned; occasionally signed articles are by counsellors or other officials.

Recurring features include External Affairs in Parliament, statements in the House of Commons by the Secretary of State for External Affairs, policy toward the United Nations, and the like; Conferences, a listing of projected conferences of international organizations, with locations and dates; Treaty Information, current action on agreements, protocols, exchanges of notes, acts, amendments, conventions (as in the *Department of State Bulletin,* q.v.) bilateral and multilateral; Appointments, Transfers and Resignations in the Department of External Affairs.

Recommended for academic and large public library collections. (J.M.)

The Federalist. 1951. 10/yr. Membership (Nonmembers $2). World Federalists, USA. 2029 K St., N.W., Washington, D.C. 20006. Illus. Circ: 18,000.

Bk. rev: Notes. *Aud:* Ac, Ga, Hs.

A six to ten page newsletter which reports on activities of the United World Federalists in the United States; a "voluntary, non-partisan political action organization dedicated to creating a limited world federal government." The organization leads fights for cutting back on military spending, universal membership in the United Nations, international peace, etc. See also *World Federalist.*

Federal Register. See Government Magazines/United States Section.

Foreign Affairs. 1922. q. $10. William Bundy. Council on Foreign Relations, Inc., 58 E. 68th St., New York, N.Y. 10021. Adv. Circ: 70,000. Microform: UM. Reprint: Kraus.

Indexed: PAIS, RG. *Bk. rev:* Extensive notes. *Aud:* Ga, Ac.

The most prestigious of the political science journals, and often one of the most controversial. The 1971 appointment of Bundy caused a furor. Kenneth Galbraith in *New York* (Nov. 15, 1971) put it this way: "Although the establishment has lost stature, it is not disposed to introspection. It has just elected Mr. William Bundy, the civilian most responsible for the Vietnam policy, to be editor of *Foreign Affairs,* a highly unreadable journal which, for many years, has served as its official voice." A thick issue is indeed a formidable affair, and most of the scholarly articles are too much even for the scholars. Still it continues to enjoy a reputation based upon weight and name. Topics include social and political issues, economics, and in fact, any aspect of international affairs which would be of interest to the alert layman or student. Fifteen 20 to 30 page articles written by the great scholars and journalists of the day make *Foreign Affairs* the prestige journal for political scientists. Along with the brief but critical book reviews, there are sections on source materials and biographical sketches of the contributors. It is too involved for the average student or layman, but would be a first choice for academic libraries.

Government and Opposition; a journal of comparative politics. 1965. q. $14. Ghita Ionescu. Government and Opposition Ltd., London School of Economics and Political Science, Houghton St., London WC2, Eng. Johns Hopkins Press, Baltimore, Md. 21218. Index, adv. Vol. ends: Autumn.

Bk. rev: 5, 2,000–5,000 words, signed. *Aud:* Ac.

An advanced theoretical journal, this periodical concentrates on the forces that confront government organization and bureaucracy. Some recent articles have covered political toleration, the Albanian political experience, and forces in Colombia. It is published by the London School of Economics and Political Science. (M.S)

Intercom. 1959. bi-m. $6. Charles Bloomstein. Center for War-Peace Studies, 218 E. 18th St., New York, N.Y. 10003. Illus. Circ: 16,000. Microform: UM. Reprint: Johnson.

Indexed: PAIS. *Bk. rev:* 50–60, 50–100 words, unsigned. *Aud:* Ga, Ac, Hs.

Offers information on new books, pamphlets, films, etc, on world affairs. Suggestions for curricular resources and teaching projects suitable from senior high school through the first years of college or university are offered. Each issue focuses upon one major current area or subject of interest, followed by an up-to-date bibliography. The reporting is objective and nonpartisan. A valuable aid to social studies teachers and leaders of adult discussion groups.

International Affairs. 1922. q. $10. Wendy Hinde. Royal Inst. of Intl. Affairs, Chatham House, St. James Sq., London SW1, England. Index, adv. Circ: 6,000. Sample. Vol. ends: Oct. Reprint: Dawson.

Indexed: BritHum, PAIS, SSHum. *Bk. rev:* 135, 700 words, signed. *Aud:* Ac, Ga.

Contains articles analyzing current topics—political, economics, and social—of broad international interest. There is an extensive book section, divided by subject matter, reviewing a wide selection of British and foreign publications on international affairs; and a list of books reviewed. The journal is circulated among members of the RIIA, embassies, and university and college libraries all over the world.

International Development Review. 1959. q. Membership (Libraries $9). Andrew E. Rice. Soc. for Intl. Development, 1346 Connecticut Ave., N.W., Washington, D.C. 20036. Index, adv. Circ: 7,000. Sample. Reprint: Johnson, Abrahams.

Indexed: PAIS. *Bk. rev:* 5, 500 words, signed. *Aud:* Ac.

A well-written, readable journal devoted to the economic development of the emerging nations. Articles are practical, documented, and usually in English. Those in French or Spanish have English abstracts. News of the United Nations, film reviews, and short, perceptive book reviews round out the average issue. Valuable magazine for difficult-to-find information on smaller nations. (M.S.)

International Organization. 1947. q. $10. Alfred O. Hero. World Peace Foundation, 40 Mt. Vernon St., Boston, Mass. 02108. Illus., index, adv. Circ: 2,600.

Indexed: PAIS, SSHum. *Bk. rev:* 2, 500 words, signed. *Aud:* Ac, Ga.

Contains short articles on subjects of broad international scope, such as the history of the League of Nations, the cold war, the future of the United Nations, and the principle of nonintervention. A special feature is Notes on Theory and Method, which gives information on ongoing projects using empirical data. A selected bibliography is also provided in each issue. (M.S.)

International Political Science Abstracts. 1951. $9. S. Hurtig. Basil Blackwell & Mott Ltd., 108 Cowley Rd., Oxford OX4 1JF, England. Circ: 1,492.

Edited by the International Political Science Association and the International Studies Conference. Abstracts run to about 150 words, and are usually six months to one year behind the date of periodical publication. They are arranged by classified method with author and subject index. Some 150 journals from various countries are covered. Invaluable for most libraries dealing in this area.

Interplay. 1967. m. $10. Anthony Hartely. Welkin Corp., 200 W. 57th St., New York, N.Y. 10019. Illus., adv. Circ: 30,000.

Bk. rev: 2–4, 1,000–1,500 words, signed. *Aud:* Ga, Sc, Hs.

A journal of opinion that explores the economic, political, and social aspects of Europe and America. Although the magazine has an international editorial staff, the focus is Europe. The tone is intellectual, the style relatively popular, the viewpoint objective, although on the liberal side. Among the usual features are biographic sketches of leaders, an economic newsletter, and a limited number of in-depth book reviews. Quite within the grasp of senior high school students.

The Journal of Development Studies. 1964. q. $12.50. Donal Cruise O'Brien and Michael Lipton. Subs. to: Frank Cass Ltd., 67 Great Russell St., London WC1B, 3BT, England.

Bk. rev: 12–16, essay, signed. *Aud:* Ac.

Primarily involved with the economics of development, but includes related articles on politics and social issues. The six to eight articles in the 100 or so pages are written by and for experts; examples are "An Application of the Stone Model to the Turkish Financial Accounts" and "The Statistics of Birth Rate Determinants." Although English based, the scope is international. Only for large, special collections. (M.S.)

Journal of International Affairs. 1947. s-a. $4.50. James D. Grant. 420 W. 118th St., New York, N.Y. 10027. Index, adv. Circ: 3,500. Vol. ends: Spring. Microform: UM. Reprint: Johnson.

Indexed: ABCPolSci, PAIS, SSHum. *Bk. rev:* Numerous, various length, signed. *Aud:* Ac.

The primary use to libraries (and to scholars) of this journal is found in the book reviews, which make up a good half of each issue. They are subdivided under 16 subject headings (including an occasional heading, New Periodicals). Descriptive and critical, they manage to cover all major titles issued here and abroad. In addition, there are usually four or five long articles which are timely (e.g., "European Unification in the Seventies") scholarly, well written, and only for the initiated.

The Journal of Politics. 1939. q. $10. (Individual $8). Southern Political Science Assn., Peabody Hall, Univ. of Florida, Gainesville, Fla. 32603. Illus., index, adv. Circ: 3,900. Vol. ends: Nov. Microform: UM. Reprint: AMS.

Indexed: ABCPolSci, AmerH, HistAb, PAIS, SSHum. *Bk. rev:* 10, 2 pages, signed, and 40 notes. *Aud:* Ac.

"Publishes the results of the latest research in all aspects of political science." Articles are balanced between international politics and American political research. There is no regional bias or emphasis. Excellent book reviews are included. News and Notes lists appointments, promotions, and obituaries of the Association. Only for large collections, but because of the sponsor may be of wider interest in the southern states.

Latin American Research Review. See Latin American and Chicano/English Language General Section.

Midwest Journal of Political Science. 1957. q. Membership (Nonmembers $10). Malcolm E. Jewell. Wayne State Univ. Press, 5980 Cass Ave., Detroit, Mich. 48202. Adv. Circ: 2,400. Vol. ends: Nov. Refereed. Microform: UM. Reprint: Kraus.

Indexed: PAIS. *Bk. rev:* 15, 1,500 words, signed. *Aud:* Ac.

A general review of political science. While there are articles dealing with the Midwest, the major emphasis is on American government and politics. A high reference value and its readability make this a valuable addition to academic libraries, particularly those in the Midwest.

NATO Letter. 1953. bi-m. Free. Gerald Van Rossum. North Atlantic Treaty Organization, 1110 Brussels, Belgium. Subs. to: Distribution Services Staff, Office of Media Services, Dept. of State, Washington, D.C. 20520. Illus. Circ: 150,000.

Aud: Ejh, Hs, Ac. *Jv:* C.

More in a newsletter tradition, this publication contains information about current happenings in the Atlantic community, NATO military affairs, and problems of general international concern, such as the rule of law, pollution, and economic conditions. It also reprints the text of important policy statements, contains a bibliography, and is well illustrated. (M.S.)

✓*Orbis; a quarterly journal of world affairs.* 1957. q. $7.50. William R. Kinter. Univ. of Pennsylvania, Foreign Policy Research Inst., 3508 Market St., Suite 350, Philadelphia, Pa. 19104. Illus., index, adv. Circ: 3,000. Sample. Vol. ends: Winter. Microform: UM. Reprint: Kraus.

Indexed: ABCPolSci, AmerH, CurrCont, PAIS, SSHum. *Bk. rev:* 4, 1,500 words, signed. *Aud:* Ac, Ga.

One of the larger (close to 300 pages) political science journals, it features 10 to 15 articles by leading experts. Most are relatively easy to read, and usually timely enough, e.g., "New China Policy," "Vietnam and U.S. Diplomacy." An effort is made to appeal to both the scholar and the educated layman, and the journal often succeeds—at least it is as informative and as well edited as the better-known *Foreign Affairs.* For larger academic and public libraries.

Parliamentary Affairs; devoted to all aspects of parliamentary democracy. 1947. q. $7.20. Ann Dewar.

Hansard Society for Parliamentary Government, 162 Buckingham Palace Road, London SW1, England. Adv. Circ: 2,000. Vol. ends: Fall.

Indexed: BritHum, PAIS. *Bk. rev:* 3, 500 words, signed. *Aud:* Ac.

Covers the whole field of British government and politics (including constitutional matters, Parliament, government administration and elections), but also has a fair amount on foreign countries, including the United States. Over a recent one-year period there were nine articles on the British government, three on the United States, and one each for five other countries. Authoritative and scholarly, the journal can be recommended for most colleges with courses in comparative government. (M.S.)

✓*Perspective.* 1972. m. $15 (Individuals $10). Cornelius W. Vahle and Theodore L. Stoddard. Operations & Policy Research Inc., 4000 Albermarle St. N.W., Washington, D.C. 20016. Sample.

Aud: Ac.

A 20-page review of books on government, politics, and international affairs. Coverage is international, moving from the United States to Europe, Asia, and Africa. (Most titles, however, are published in the United States.) The 250 to 400 word reviews are primarily by university professors, and are set up to appear within 60 days after publication date. The writing is clear, and usually more descriptive than critical. While the more basic titles are now being reviewed elsewhere, the publisher is unquestionably correct when he says that of the 600 books published in this area every year, "many of them are not reviewed in the scholarly journals for months or years after publication, and a substantial number are never reviewed at all." Arrangement is by broad subject areas, and there is an author index. There is no indication of a cumulative subject index, but the author index will be cumulated annually. The pilot issue indicates this will be a valuable service for large public and academic libraries. Much too specialized (and expensive) for smaller libraries.

Policy Sciences; policy analysis, systems approaches and decision making. 1970. q. $17. E. S. Quade. Amer. Elsevier Publishing Co., Inc., 52 Vanderbilt Ave., New York, N.Y. 10017. Illus., adv. Refereed.

Indexed: EconAb, IntAb, InAb, IntPolSciAb, SciAb. *Bk. rev:* 3, 600 words. *Aud:* Ac.

Edited by Edward S. Quade of the Rand Corporation, who sums up the purpose of the journal as an effort to publish papers which will "augment, by scientific decision methods and the behavioral sciences, the process that humans use in making judgments and taking decisions." The first 165 pages list ten contributions to identify the aims and processes of policy procedure. There are three book reviews. A good deal will interest any socially involved nonexpert. For example, a Rand Corporation specialist methodically justifies government support of medical aid for the poor. It's a cold-blooded analysis which tends to assess moral necessity in terms of "health as an investment." Probably this kind of thing is needed, but it seems to do more to support Lewis Mumford's challenge to "The Megamachine" (see the *New Yorker*, Oct. 10, 1970, and subsequent issues) than anything else recently. The new journal will nevertheless find a place in larger university and special libraries.

Politeia. 1971. 4/yr. Membership. Amer. Assn. of Political Consultants, 1028 Connecticut Ave., Washington, D.C. 20036.

Bk. rev: Various number, length. *Aud:* Ac, Ga.

This political quarterly was launched with the intention of being bipartisan and informative. The issues are kept in pretty fair balance. The articles embrace politics in all its forms and stages. Constitution, religion, civil rights, polls, campaigning, mass media, and other topics are discussed. Articles are directed to activists and only to a lesser degree to academics. A sophisticated book review section is included. Being intelligent, neutral, and yet interesting, this publication deserves a place in academic institutions and large public libraries. (P.V.)

Political Events Calendar. 1972. bi-w. (19/yr.). $35. Holt Information System, Holt, Rinehart & Winston, 383 Madison Ave., New York, N.Y. 10017.

Aud: Ac, Ga, Sa.

A 12 to 18 page newsletter which gives advance reports on activities of major political figures in campaigns for Congress and the presidency. The calendar comes out about every two weeks. It is arranged chronologically with brief notes for each of the days. The February 16 to February 29, 1972, issue includes such information (for Feb. 16) as "Vice President Spiro Agnew addresses the American Association of School Administrators at Convention Hall in Atlantic City, New Jersey." Skip to February 26 and the user finds this was the "First day of two-day meetings of the New Democratic Coalition North East Regional Conference at Public School 6 in New York." There are similar telegraphic briefs for each day. The average is eight to ten items a day, although on Saturdays the number of entries tends to double. According to the publisher, the idea began at CBS in 1964. Until 1972 it was "for the sole use of the CBS News staff." But given the subscription price, the publisher will send it to any individual or library who is interested in the daily schedules of the politicos. The work of compiling the schedule, though, continues to be the task of CBS. What happens when the November 1972 elections are over, when political events cool off a bit? Ms. Phyllis B. Steckler at Holt reports: "CBS News prepares these reports continuously, in general election

years on a semimonthy basis, and in off years on a monthly basis. In off years, they cover significant mayoralty, congressional, and special elections, as well as the activities of all the potentially important candidates on a national level. We are offering a serial service, on a ongoing basis. We're accepting two- and three-year subscriptions at the 1972 rate, at least for the time being." A useful although somewhat esoteric reference aid for larger libraries.

Political Quarterly. 1930. q. $7.20. William A. Robson. Political Quarterly Publishing Co., 49 Park Lane, London W1, England. Index., adv. Circ: 2,500.

Indexed: BritHum, IBZ, PAIS, SSHum. *Bk. rev:* 10–12, 100 words, signed. *Aud:* Ac.

Covers general political science subjects and public administration both in England and abroad. Contributors are leading scholars from all countries. A typical 200 or so page issue includes excellent book reviews and long, often detailed studies of interest to the teacher, advanced student, and intelligent layman. A nice addition for the library that takes *Parliamentary Affairs.*

Political Science Quarterly. 1886. q. Membership $15 (Students $9). Sigmund Diamond. The Academy of Political Science, Columbia Univ., 420 W. 118th St., New York, N.Y. 10027. Adv. Circ: 11,000. Sample. Vol. ends: Dec. Microform: UM. Reprint: Kraus.

Indexed: ABCPolSci, HistAb, PAIS, SSHum. *Bk. rev:* 50, 1 page, signed. *Aud:* Ac.

Although each issue includes four or five articles, the primary purpose here is to offer the political scientist book reviews. The one-page or longer reviews account for one half of the contents. The drawback: most of the books were published one or even three years ago. In the September 1971 issue, nine of the 60 reviews were of books issued in 1970, the remainder were for titles primarily released in 1969, with a few in 1968. Aside from the time factor, they are consistently critical, evaluative, and reliable. The articles, which tend to concentrate on America and American foreign policy, are equally excellent. It all adds up to a basic journal for any medium-to-large political science collection. The journal is edited for the Academy of Political Science, which also issues *Academy of Political Science Proceedings.*

Political Studies. 1953. q. $10. R. Ridley. Oxford Univ. Press, Press Rd., Neasden, London NW10, England. Index., adv. Circ: 1,900. Sample. Microform: UM. Reprint: Dawson.

Indexed: BritHum, PAIS, SSHum. *Bk. rev:* 150, 500–700 words, signed. *Aud:* Ac.

A 140 to 160 page British political science journal whose chief value to American librarians is the extensive book review section. All major political science titles published in England and abroad are reviewed in both a descriptive and a critical fashion. The editor takes political science to mean a broad view of almost every activity of man, from sociology and law to philosophy and psychology. Hence, articles are international and interdisciplinarian, often quite beyond the scope of the average political science journal. A must for academic and some larger public libraries.

Politics and Society. 1970. q. $15 (Individuals $10). Ira Katznelson. Geron-X, Inc., Publishers, Box 1108, Los Altos, Calif. 94022. Adv. Vol. ends: Aug. Refereed.

Bk. rev: 2, 5,000–6,000 words, signed. *Aud:* Ac.

The stated purpose of this journal is to provide an "alternative" forum dealing with important political concerns and avoiding an obsession with techniques. Having disclaimed the lengthy tabulation of data, it seeks instead to transcend "the sterile behavioral–antibehavioral debate," and examine rather "some outrageous hypotheses." In spite of this salvo, the journal has a definite ability to handle controversial arguments in a scholarly way. The articles show both quality and substance. A recent article was "The Vocation of Radical Intellectuals." (M.S.)

Polity. 1968. q. Membership $10 (Nonmembers $9). Loren P. Beth. Polity, Thompson Hall, Univ. of Mass., Amherst, Mass. 01002. Illus., adv. Circ: 1,150. Sample. Vol. ends: Summer.

Bk. rev: 4, 2,500–3,000 words, signed. *Aud:* Ac.

The origins and objectives of this political science magazine are considered in the first few pages of the first issue. William C. Havard, a member of the editorial board, deserves credit for outlining the hazards and joys of starting any new scholarly journal. Librarians and students might read his words carefully before suggesting another magazine. There are four articles and three extensive book reviews, and while none is calculated to thrill the nonexpert, the quality and style do credit to the sponsoring organization. All respectable political science collections will want it, particularly as the scope seems to be international and coverage will include almost all aspects of the discipline. The format is much above average. (M.S.)

Problems of Communism. See Government Magazines/ United States Section.

The Review of Politics. 1939. q. $5. M. A. Fitzsimmons. Box B, Notre Dame, Ind. 46556. Index, adv. Circ: 2,600. Vol. ends: Oct. Microform: UM. Reprint: Kraus.

Indexed: ABCPolSci, CathI, SSHum. *Bk. rev:* 8–18, 600 words, signed. *Aud:* Ac.

The primary focus here is on the philosophical and deeper historical meaning of current events. Authors are acknowledged experts, but manage to write in a style well within the grasp of the better-educated layman. Among contributors have been Paul Eldel-

berg, Lord Bowden, Rodney J. Morrison, and David Spitz. Articles range from a discussion of current morality in America to "Apartheid and International Monetary Reform." Published by a Catholic University, the journal does reflect the basic concerns of the Catholic church. However, scholarship and objectivity are the ruling factors; hence, it can be recommended for any medium-to-large academic library.

The Round Table. 1910. $8. Robert Jackson. All Souls College, Oxford. Round Table Ltd., 18 Northumberland Ave., London WC1, England. Index. Circ: 1,800. Sample. Vol. ends: No. 4. Microform: UM.

Indexed: PAIS, SSHum. *Aud:* Ga, Ac.

The *RT* is the Commonwealth's Journal of International Affairs. It publishes articles on all subjects of contemporary concern to members of the Commonwealth of Nations of any race and on every continent. British entry into the European Communities has brought with it an extension of the *RT's* interest in European subjects. The short articles, about current and significant problems make this journal as valuable to the general reader as to the scholar.

Science and Society; an independent journal of Marxism. 1936. q. $6. Ed. bd. Science and Soc., 30 E. 20th St., New York, N.Y. 10003. Adv. Circ: 3,000. Sample. Vol. ends: Winter. Microform: UM.

Indexed: AmerH, HistAb, PAIS, SSHum. *Bk. rev:* 8, 1,200 words, signed. *Aud:* Ac.

A scholarly journal which represents the Marxist viewpoint of history and political science. Approximately one half of each 120-page pocket-sized issue is turned over to reviews of books. These are of some importance because the reviews represent a point of view rarely found in standard journals. The articles tend to trace the historical aspects of Marxism and socialism: "Historians and American Socialism, 1900–1920," or "Communism in California, 1919–1924." A limited amount of material is involved with the arts. There is little or no comment on current events, and the majority of writers take the long, detached view of the Marxist philosophy and how it has worked (not how it presently works). Authors tend to be professors, and the tone is cool, academic, and at times even a bit dull. Removing Marxism to the academic stage takes a good part of its glamor away, but does give it a perspective rarely found in the daily journals and papers.

Simulation and Games, an international journal of theory, design and research. 1970. q. $15 (Individuals $10). Michael Inbar. Sage Publns., 275 S. Beverly Dr., Beverly Hills, Calif. 90212. Illus., adv.

Bk. rev: 1–2, 500–600 words, signed. *Aud:* Ac.

This highly specialized journal includes articles on computer simulation, gaming, and teaching the techniques of simulation. The articles relate the techniques of gaming to the political and social fields. A simulation review section has notes on the latest developments in the field, often with an unbiased, critical review of recently designed models.

Social and Economic Studies. 1953. q. $5.60. A. McIntyre, Inst. of Social and Economic Research, Univ. of the West Indies, Mona, Jamaica, B.W.I. Index, adv. Circ: 1,750. Vol. ends: Dec. Refereed.

Indexed: PAIS, PsyAb. *Aud:* Ac.

Issued by the Institute of Social and Economic Research of the University of the West Indies, this journal reports on work related to the Institute and includes other material on the social, economic, and political problems of economically underdeveloped territories, and of general interest. Issues cover such topics as savings and foreign trade, a macroeconomic model of Jamaica, analysis of discriminatory credit in Chile, "Socio-Economic Status and Family Planning Knowledge . . . in Pakistan," "Assimilation of West Indians in Vancouver," and reform of the public services. The scope is limited to economic and sociological studies and underdeveloped and developing areas. Its scholarly orientation will interest students and scholars. (M.S.)

Stanford Journal of Internation Studies. 1966. a. $5. Stanford School of Law, Stanford, Calif. 94305.

Aud: Ac, Ga.

A product of interdisciplinary thinking, designed to contribute to a broad-based approach to international problems. Each annual issue is devoted to a single theme. Topics dealt with in past volumes include foreign intervention in civil strife (1968), ocean resources (1969), telecommunications (1970), development (1971), and arms control (1972). Articles are contributed by faculty, students, and professionals working in the problem area. Of considerable help to any student of the area, it will be welcomed by those seeking background material for papers or debate—not to mention, of course, the interested layman who can turn to the journal for a well-rounded discussion of a particular problem.

✓ ***State Government.*** 1930. q. $7. Robert H. Weber. Council of State Govts., Iron Works Pike, Lexington, Ky. 40505. Illus., index. Circ: 8,500. Sample. Vol. ends: Autumn. Microform: UM. Reprint: Kraus.

Indexed: PAIS. *Aud:* Ga, Ac, Jc, Sh. *Rv:* H.

Renewed awareness about the problems of states, from financing to pollution control, gives this magazine added importance. It is one of the few to treat state government objectively. Because of the many aspects covered—governmental, political, economic, and social—it should be of interest to a large public. This popular approach does not reduce the authority

or value of the articles. Governors, legislators, and political science professors are among the many fine contributors. Easy to read, short articles make it useful for the high school as well as college libraries.

✓ ***Studies in Comparative International Development.*** 1966. m. $12 (Individuals $8). Irving Louis Horowitz. Sage Publns., Inc., 275 S. Beverly Dr., Beverly Hills, Calif. 90212. Illus. Circ: 1,000 Vol. ends: Dec., every other yr. Refereed.

Indexed: SSHum, SocAb. *Aud:* Ac.

Provides monographic material concerning the political, social, and economic aspects of developing countries. The monographic pamphlets are organized under a continuing series of subject areas, such as "Military Sociology" or "Managerial Versus Cooperative Decision Making in Israel." The publication "Marginality and Revolution in Latin America: 1809–1969" was in a series on political sociology. Other subject areas include political economy and rural sociology.

This series can be compared with the *AUFS Reports*. The two series complement one another because *Studies in Comparative International Development* tends to concern itself more with Latin America, while the *AUFS Reports* spread over a much wider area and provide less concentration on Latin America. (M.S.)

Survey, a journal of East & West Studies. q. $8. Leopold Labedz. Ilford House, 133 Oxford St., London W1, England. Circ: 6,500.

Indexed: AbEnSt, PAIS, MLA. *Bk. rev:* 2–5, lengthy, signed. *Aud:* Ac.

Topics cover a broad range, including history, politics, economics, and literature, and are not limited geographically. Articles deal with Russia, Eastern Europe, Indonesia, Latin America, and the United States. As of 1971, this journal was published by Oxford University Press, although still under the sponsorship of the International Association for Cultural Freedom and Stanford University. To aid in long-term planning, an International Advisory Board was formed whose members are from universities and institutes in various countries throughout the world.

Survey of British and Commonwealth Affairs. 1955. s-m. $8.70. British Information Services, H.M.S.O., London, England. Index, charts. Vol. ends: Dec.

Aud: Ga, Ac.

Produced for British Information Service, this journal reports on the activities and posture of the government as it is involved in all aspects of domestic and international conduct.

Sections are divided into broad areas of governmental responsibility: administration, defense, economic and scientific, social and cultural. The reports cover domestic and commonwealth activities, examples being Fiji independence, central government reorganization, overseas aid, investment abroad, entertainment, and the arts. Material in the magazine reflects the official view of the party in office.

A special section entitled Documentation lists some 40 official British documents with some annotations. Price and how to order are included. It is useful as a checklist for libraries selectively buying British documents.

As an authoritative guide to activities of the British government, this is an informative journal and is recommended for academic and public libraries. (J.M.)

Weekly Compilation of Presidential Documents. See Government Magazines/United States Section.

Western Political Quarterly. 1948. q. $6. Ellsworth E. Weaver. Inst. of Govt., Univ. of Utah, Salt Lake City, Utah 84112. Adv. Microform: UM.

Indexed: PAIS, SSHum. *Bk. rev:* 30–40, 500 words, signed. *Aud:* Sa, Ac. *Rv:* H. *Jv:* B.

The official journal of the Western Political Science, Pacific Science Associations, this discusses many international problems as well as local political problems. Excellent for research on western United States political problems. Book reviews follow the scope of the magazine, concentrating on general works, but including many of immediate interest to western scholars.

World Federalist. 1968. 6/yr. $3. Ernie Regehr. World Assn. of World Federalists, 63 Spark St., 6th fl., Ottawa, Canada K1P5A6. Illus., adv. Circ: 8,000. Sample. Vol. ends: No. 10.

Bk. rev: 1, 250–500 words, signed. *Aud:* Ac, Ga, Hs.

An 18 to 20 page magazine dedicated to the notion that the world should and can unite into a loose federalism. The idea is hardly new, but in recent years the organization has launched a wider campaign which seeks for cooperation between nations in such areas as environmental pollution, population, resources, and economic developments. Hence, while individual readers may not subscribe to the underlying philosophy of the group, it is difficult to argue with the fallout. There are usually three to four articles, news notes, editorials, fascinating letters, and reports from the United Nations. Among contributors are some of the world's leading scholars and authorities on political science (e.g., Arnold J. Toynbee). The scope is international, the message important.

World Politics. 1948. q. $9.00. Ed bd. Princeton Univ. Press, Princeton, N.J. 08540. Adv. Circ: 4,400. Sample. Vol. ends: July. Refereed. Microform: UM. Reprint: Johnson.

Indexed: ABCPolSci, HistAb, PAIS, SSHum. *Bk. rev:* 2, 5,000 words, signed. *Aud:* Ac, Ga. *Rv:* H. *Jv:* B.

Deals primarily with problems in international rela-

tions. The articles, by famous scholars, tend to stress concepts and theory. A review section incorporates a series of book reviews under a single topic. A must for larger libraries, and should be checked regularly by librarians for the books reviewed.

PSYCHOLOGY

Basic Periodicals

Hs: *Mental Hygiene, Psychology Today;* Ga: *Mental Hygiene, American Imago, Psychology Today;* Jc: *Mental Hygiene, American Imago, Psychology Today;* Ac: *British Journal of Psychiatry,* American Psychological Association journals as needed.

COUNTERCULTURE. *Radical Therapist.*

Library and Teaching Aids

Contemporary Psychology, Journal of Counseling Psychology, Psychology in the Schools.

Basic Abstracts and Indexes

Psychological Abstracts, Index Medicus, Biological Abstracts.

Cessations

Perceptual Cognitive Development.

Acta Psychologica; European journal of psychology. 1935. m. $18. D. A. Vroon. North-Holland Publishing Co., Box 3489, Amsterdam, The Netherlands. Illus., index, adv. Circ: 900. Sample. Vol. ends: Dec. Refereed.

Indexed: PsyAb. *Aud:* Ac.

The editor explains the purpose and scope of this specialized journal "devoted to the publication of psychonomic studies. Psychonomics is defined—rather loosely—as the field of psychological research that is fundamental rather than applied, oriented towards quantitative models rather than verbal theories. Psychonomics implies more than experimental psychology, since it overlaps considerably with various other fields, such as biophysics, physiology, neurology, systems analysis and computer sciences."

American Imago; a psychoanalytic journal for culture, science and the arts. 1939. q. $10. Harry Slochower. Assn. for Applied Psychoanalysis, Inc., 46 E. 73rd St., New York, N.Y. 10002. Subs. to: Wayne State Univ. Press, 5980 Cass Ave., Detroit, Mich. 48202. Illus., index. Circ: 1,500. Sample. Vol. ends: Winter. Microform: UM. Reprint: Kraus.

Indexed: PsyAb, RG. *Bk. rev:* 2–3, 500 words, signed. *Aud:* Ac, Ga. *Jv:* V.

While neither as general as *Psychology Today,* nor

as geared for a mass audience, this excellent journal should enjoy a much higher circulation. It will have appeal for the better-educated, more imaginative readers of *Psychology Today,* and it is too bad it is not brought to the attention of more readers via public and academic libraries. It applies the nonmedical principles of psychoanalysis to all phases of the arts and culture. Selected issues deal with a specific topic or individual, and cover the subject with six to eight lengthy, well-documented articles. Also included are signed, critical theater and film reviews. It is not an essential magazine for most libraries, but should be in all larger collections.

American Journal of Mental Deficiency. 1876. bi-m. $36 (Individuals $18). H. Carl Haywood. Amer. Assn. on Mental Deficiency, 5201 Connecticut Ave., N.W., Washington, D.C. 20015. Subs. to: 49 Sheridan Ave., Albany, N.Y. 12210. Adv. Circ: 11,000. Sample. Vol. ends: Nov. Refereed.

Indexed: CurrCont, EdI, IMed, PsyAb, SCI. *Bk. rev:* 10, 250–500 words, signed. *Aud:* Ac.

The basic journal in the field of mental retardation. Publishes original, scientific articles from "the several disciplines dealing with mental retardation. In general the *Journal* emphasizes an objective, scientific, experimental and theoretical approach. The direction is mainly toward pure rather than applied research." The result is a technical journal of primary value to doctors and other experts.

An approach for those working on a day-to-day basis with retardation is the second journal published by the Association:

Mental Retardation. 1963. bi-m. $7. Sue A. Warren. Illus., index, adv. Circ: 11,000. Sample. Vol. ends: Dec.

Indexed: PsyAb. *Bk. rev:* 15, 100 words, signed. *Aud:* Ac, Ga, Hs.

In addition to covering news of the Association and its members, a typical 50 to 60 page issue features 10 to 12 articles on all aspects of the situation. Most of the material is written in a semipopular way, and is well within the grasp of the student and better-educated layman. The editor tries to "include essays on critical issues and problems, case studies, program descriptions, new approaches in methodology etc." This is a first choice for the general to specialized collection at the public and academic level, and of some use in high schools dealing with mental retardation. (Note: Membership in the organization brings both journals at a reduced rate. Libraries should inquire.)

American Journal of Psychiatry. 1844. m. $12. Francis J. Braceland. Amer. Psychiatric Assn., 1700 18th St. N.W., Washington, D.C. 20009. Illus., adv. Circ: 25,000. Vol. ends: June. Microform: UM. Reprint: Johnson.

Indexed: BioAb, ChemAb, IMed, PsyAb. *Bk. rev:* 14, 500 words, signed. *Aud:* Ac.

While a professional journal for practicing psychiatrists, the 140 to 160 pages often include material of value to students of the behavioral sciences. Articles represent original research or viewpoints and cover all aspects of the profession, from practical problems facing psychiatrists to diagnosis, case histories, and psychiatric education. There are numerous, long book reviews, clinical notes (which often concentrate on the use of drugs), and reports of the official action of the association.

American Journal of Psychology. 1887. q. $10. Lloyd G. Humphreys. Psychology Bldg., Univ. of Illinois, Champaign, Ill. 61820. Circ: 3,000. Sample. Vol. ends: Dec. Refereed. Microform: UM.

Indexed: PsyAb. *Bk. rev:* 5–15, ½–3 pages, signed. *Aud:* Ac.

The emphasis is on reports of original research in general experimental psychology. There are usually about 12 scholarly articles, which may be somewhat longer than those in the journals of the American Psychological Association. Only for larger academic collections.

American Journal of Psychotherapy. 1946. q. $16. Stanley Lesse. Assn. for the Advancement of Psychotherapy, 15 W. 81st St., New York, N.Y. 10024. Illus., index, adv. Circ: 3,500. Sample. Vol. ends: Oct. Reprint: Abrahams, Johnson.

Indexed: IMed, PsyAb. *Bk. rev:* 10–12, 1–3 pages, signed. *Aud:* Ac.

The official organ of the Association. There are usually 10 to 12 articles, about 12 pages long, with extensive bibliographies, as well as case reports on specific problems of patients. One section contains abstracts of current articles in other psychology journals, arranged by subject. There is also a section of abstracts from foreign countries.

American Psychological Association. *American Psychologist* (1946. m. $10); *APA Monitor* (m. $3); *Contemporary Psychology* (1956. m. $10); *Developmental Psychology* (bi-m. $10); *Journal of Abnormal Psychology* (1965. bi-m. $10); *Journal of Applied Psychology* (1917. bi-m. $10); *Journal of Comparative and Physiological Psychology* (1908. bi-m. $20); *Journal of Consulting Psychology* (1937. bi-m. $10); *Journal of Counseling Psychology* (1954. m. $10); *Journal of Educational Psychology* (1910. bi-m. $10); *Journal of Experimental Psychology* (1916. m. $20); *Journal of Personality and Social Psychology* (1965. m. $30); *Professional Psychology* (2. $10); *Psychological Bulletin* (1904. m. $20); *Psychological Review* (1894. bi-m. $10). American Psychological Assn., 1200 17th St., N.W., Washington, D.C. 20036.

The basic journals in support of graduate study in psychology, all published by the American Psychological Association, which also issues *Psychological Abstracts* (where all of the above are indexed), and a number of other bibliographic aids. The titles of the journals are self-explanatory, and each is for a particular area. They have several things in common. All articles are prepared for the psychologist or advanced student of the subject. Most are illustrated with charts and diagrams. Few have book reviews. They are authoritative, usually highly technical, and quite beyond the interests and special talents of the average layman. Conversely, each is apt to carry an article or two of interest to students of related fields, such as education, political science, and journalism. Most findings of more than specialized interest inevitably find their way into one of these semipopular journals. Hence, what remains is a basic set of authoritative periodicals for serious research purposes. All of these titles belong in large academic libraries and in many public libraries where research is important. With the possible exception of the *Contemporary Psychology, Journal of Counseling Psychology, Journal of Educational Psychology, Journal of Applied Psychology, Journal of Personality,* and *Contemporary Psychology,* none is required for the average public or junior college library.

Archives of General Psychiatry. 1959. m. $12. Daniel X. Freedman. Amer. Medical Assn., 535 N. Dearborn St., Chicago, Ill. 60610. Illus., index, adv. Circ: 22,000. Sample. Vol. ends: June and Dec.

Indexed: BioAb, IMed, PsyAb. *Bk. rev:* 1–3, ½ page, signed. *Aud:* Ac.

One of the major professional journals in psychiatry, and, as such, only for the expert and advanced student. The articles are documented, technical, and usually require a considerable background to understand. The editor reports, "Our purpose is to cover the scope of relevant, original research in general psychiatry—biological, psychoanalytic, biomedical and clinical—so that our readership can have soundly critiqued, authoritative, up to date touch with practical and theoretical development in psychiatry through original contributions and occasional reviews."

Association for the Study of Perception Journal. 1966. s-a. $12. Joseph R. Ellis. ASP, Box 744, DeKalb, Ill., 60115. Index. Circ: 650, Sample. Vol. ends: Fall.

Bk. rev: 1–2, 6 pages, signed. *Aud:* Ac.

The primary purpose of the association is to study perceptual limitations and disseminate educational information relative to perception. When this journal began, there were some 90 members representing nine states. The present membership expresses varied perceptual interests, including perception in reading, listening, and color; perception and personality; perceptually handicapped; and perception and kinetics. The journal has as its purposes the stimulation of thought and interest in the area of perception and the dissemination of information about perception. Of interest only to academic or medical libraries.

Australian Journal of Psychology. 1948. 3/yr. $9.50. Ronald Taft. Australian Psychological Soc., Natl. Science Centre, 191 Royal Parade, Parville, Victoria 3052, Australia. Index. Circ: 3,000. Sample. Vol. ends: Dec. Refereed. Microform: UM.

Indexed: BioAb, PAIS, PsyAb. *Bk. rev:* 9, 500 words, signed. *Aud:* Ac.

The major Australian journal in the field. Articles are scholarly, technical, and often of monographic length. Most of them are universal enough to warrant attention by psychologists and students living outside of Australia. Theoretical, experimental, and survey contributions are included.

Behavior Therapy. 1970. q. $35. Cyril M. Franks. Academic Press, Inc., 111 Fifth Ave., New York, N.Y. 10003.

Bk. rev: Extensive, lengthy, signed. *Aud:* Ac.

An interdisciplinary journal, published by the Association for the Advancement of Behavior Therapy, written by professionals in the behaviorist field for other specialists. Publishes results of original research of an experimental or clinical nature which contribute to the theory or practice of behavior therapy or techniques in the field. There are generally 10 to 12 articles, varying in length from 5 to 20 pages with lengthy references, plus substantial book and film reviews (as well as briefly noted books), conference proceedings, news, and notes on reprints and other available materials and training programs. Should be in all college and university libraries. (B.B.)

Behavioral Science. 1956. bi-m. $30 (Individuals $15). James Miller. Mental Health Research Inst., Univ. of Mich., Ann Arbor, Mich. 48104. Adv. Circ: 5,000. Sample. Vol. ends: Nov. Refereed.

Indexed: BioAb, IMed, MathR, PsyAb. *Bk. rev:* 1–2, 1 page, signed. *Aud:* Ac.

Contains five to ten well-documented articles on general theories and research in the problems of behavior. A section in each issue is devoted to the use of computers in behavioral science. The book reviews are on books in the field and are critical and comprehensive. While primarily for the professional, the emphasis on communication makes it of some importance for the general student.

Behaviour Research and Therapy. 1963. q. $40. Prof. J. J. Eysenck. Pergamon Press, Maxwell House, Fairview Pk., Elmsford, New York 10523.

Indexed: PsyAb. *Aud:* Ac.

An international multidisciplinary journal, which is

interested in applying modern learning theories in order to control maladaptive behavior and improve learning effectiveness. Contains from 8 to 15 articles, written by specialists and dealing mainly with the use of deconditioning, aversion therapy, methods of desensitization, learning machines, operant conditioning, and behavior therapy. Thus, it cuts across many fields and would be of great interest to psychiatry, education, clinical psychology, social work, etc. (B.B.)

Biological Psychiatry. 1969. q. $21. Joseph Wortis. Plenum Publishing Corp., 227 W. 17th St., New York, N.Y. 10011. Illus., index. Sample.

Indexed: CurrCont. *Aud:* Ac.

In some 100 pages covers the whole range of psychiatric research. Usually 10 to 12 scholarly articles, brief reports, clinical comments, and news and notes. An official journal of the Society of Biological Psychiatry, this is only for the professional and advanced student.

British Journal of Psychiatry. 1853. m. $42. Eliot Slater. Royal College of Psychiatrists. Subs. to: Headley Brothers, Ltd., Ashford, Kent, England. Illus., index, adv. Circ: 7,000. Sample. Vol. ends: Dec. Refereed.

Indexed: BioAb, ChemAb, IMed, PsyAb. *Bk. rev:* 20, 150–100 words, signed. *Aud:* Ac. *Jv:* V.

One of the world's oldest journals in this field (first appeared as *The Asylum Journal*, two years later as the *Journal of Mental Science*). It is also one of the world's leading journals, and is often quoted by the press. Contributions are not limited to psychiatry, but include material on sociology, anthropology, and other related subjects. Although most of the articles are as technical as they are authoritative, they are well written, generally free of excessive jargon. Thanks to its wide scope, its fine editing, and its topical material, this is a basic journal for all collections.

British Journal of Psychology. 1904. q. $25. W. Sluckin. British Psychological Soc., Cambridge Univ. Press, 32 E. 57th St., New York, N.Y. 10022. Circ: 3,300. Sample. Vol. ends: Nov. Refereed.

Indexed: BioAb, BritHum, IMed, PsyAb. *Bk. rev:* 30–90, notes or lengthy, signed. *Aud:* Ac.

Published by the British Psychological Society, this is the English equivalent of the *American Journal of Psychology*. It is particularly valuable for its extensive book review section, which covers publications in German as well as English. Emphasis is on general psychology, experimental psychology and methods of testing for and measuring psychological variants. A basic work in larger collections.

Canadian Journal of Behavioral Science/ Revue Canadienne des Sciences du Comportement. 1969. q. $20. James Inglis. Canadian Psychological Assn., 1390

Sherbrooke St. W., Montreal, Que., Canada. Illus., adv. Circ: 1,100. Sample. Vol. ends: No. 4. Refereed.

Indexed: PsyAb. *Aud:* Ac.

Articles published in either English or French, with short summaries in the alternate language. Papers in the applied areas of psychology and both research and theoretical articles in the areas of social, personality, abnormal, educational, developmental, and child psychology are published. The material is technical, for the psychologist and advanced student.

Canadian Journal of Psychology /Revue Canadienne de Psychologie. 1947. q. $10. Canadian Psychological Assn., 1390 Sherbrooke St. W., Montreal PG 109, Canada. Illus., index, adv. Circ: 2,100. Sample.

Indexed: IMed, PsyAb. *Aud:* Ac.

The Canadian equivalent of the *American Journal of Psychology*, i.e., a highly technical journal for the specialist. It includes experimental and theoretical articles in all fields of psychology. Articles appear in both English and French, and an abstract is translated into French (or into English for papers submitted in French) and printed at the end of the article.

Canadian Psychologist. 1951. q. $11, membership (Nonmembers $7). David Gibson, Univ. of Calgary, Alberta. Subs. to: Canadian Psychological Assn., 1390 Sherbrooke St. W., Montreal PG 109, Canada. Circ: 2,000. Sample. Vol. ends: Oct. Refereed.

Indexed: PsyAb. *Bk. rev:* 2, 2 pages, signed. *Aud:* Ac.

A publication of a group somewhat equivalent to the American Psychological Association. Material is written by and for psychologists and is international in scope, although it more often reports on activities of Canadians. It includes original research and theoretical articles, and a valuable feature, Abstracts of Research, again closely related to work in Canada. News and official papers of the Association make up the remainder of the journal. The organization also issues the *Canadian Journal of Psychology* and *Canadian Journal of Behavioral Science*. Invaluable in large academic libraries where there are active departments of psychology.

Cognitive Psychology. 1970. q. $25. Walter Reitman. Academic Press, Inc., 111 Fifth Ave., New York, N.Y. 10003.

Aud: Ac.

Highly technical, very detailed papers dealing with original research on memory, language processing, problem solving, and thinking. This journal is about 100 pages long, and includes from five to seven articles (with many references) designed for the specialist. For academic libraries only. (B.B.)

Community Mental Health Journal. 1965. q. $20. Sheldon R. Roen. Behavioral Publns., Inc., 2852 Broadway, New York, N.Y. 10025. Index, adv. Circ: 4,000. Sample. Vol. ends: Nov. Refereed.

Indexed: BioAb, IMed, PsyAb, SocAb. *Bk. rev:* 2, 1,000 words, signed. *Aud:* Ac.

This is "devoted to emergent approaches in mental health research, theory, and practice as they relate to community, broadly defined. Mental health is seen as more or less congruent with the general concept of social well-being." Articles concern such topics as community mental health, urban relocation, art, law enforcement, mentally retarded children, industrial psychiatry, disruptive children, and paraprofessionals in community mental health. Regular listings of publications received, book reviews, film reviews, and classified ads appear. This journal is of value to those in helping professions concerned with mental health and the community: psychiatrists, public health practitioners, community psychiatrists, social workers, and psychologists, among others.

Comparative Group Studies. 1970. q. $15 (Professionals $10; students $7.50). William Fawcett Hill. Sage Publns., Inc., 275 S. Beverly Dr., Beverly Hills, Calif. 90212. Illus., index, adv. Circ: 1,000. Sample. Vol. ends: Nov. Refereed.

Bk. rev: 2, 500–700 words, signed. *Aud:* Ac.

"An international and interdisciplinary journal presenting research and theory about all types of small groups including but not limited to therapy and treatment groups. It is the long-term goal of CGS to encourage the development of a comparative social science of group work." Departments include News Notes and Bibliography, each with its own editor. Articles concern prediction of psychotherapeutic change, group dynamics with children, group conformity, semantics, group counseling, and marathon group sessions. The May 1971 issue, for example, is entirely concerned with the theme of "Mathematical Models of Small Groups." For any collection on group psychotherapy, T groups, social group work, or small group behavior, this journal should not be overlooked.

Contemporary Psychology; a journal of reviews. 1956. m. $10. Gardner Lindzey. Amer. Psychological Assn., Inc., 1200 17th St., N.W., Washington, D.C. 20036. Circ: 10,500. Reprint: Abrahams. Microform: UM.

Indexed: PsyAb. *Bk. rev:* Entire issue. *Aud:* Sa, Ac.

Composed entirely of long, signed, critical reviews of current books, films, and other instructional media in the field of psychology. There are no articles other than an editorial message. The film and instructional media review section is usually three or four pages long. Basic for librarians who need a substantial collection of books in psychology.

Corrective Psychiatry and Journal of Social Therapy. 1958. q. $10. Nathan K. Rickles and Clyde V. Martin.

Martin Psychiatric Research Foundation, Box 8371, Prairie Village, Kans. 66208.

Aud: Ac.

Dedicated to dissemination of "information on the origin, nature and treatment of antisocial behavior," this 64-page journal is a "forum for progressive techniques" in psychiatric therapy. The well-documented articles move from military psychiatric facilities to motivations for murder and check forging. Although written for the expert, the interested layman will not be put off by the style, which is remarkably free of jargon and, in part, fascinating. The material covers a wide number of situations and for that reason will be of value to libraries with medium-to-large psychology and social science collections.

Educational and Psychological Measurement; devoted to the development and application of measures of individual differences. 1941. q. $10. Box 6907, College Sta., Durham, N.C. 27708.

Indexed: EdI, PsyAb. *Bk. rev:* Various number, length. *Aud:* Sa, Ac.

Primarily a technical magazine on testing for the psychologist and counselor. Averaging some 7 to 12 scholarly articles an issue, contributors cover the use of tests in education, government, and industry. Particularly useful for full descriptions of new testing programs.

Existential Psychiatry. 1966. q. $10. Jordan Scher. Amer. Ontoanalytic Assn., Suite 310, 8 S. Michigan Ave., Chicago, Ill. 60603. Illus., index, adv. Circ: 5,000.

Indexed: IMed, PsyAb. *Bk. rev:* Various number, length. *Aud:* Sa, Ac.

Speaks to the specialist but also carries interesting nontechnical essays on psychology, sociology, theology, philosophy, literature, and the arts for the educated general audience. The ethical values of existentialism are always stressed over the medical aspects of psychiatry. Signed critical book reviews, some of them quite lengthy, are included.

Foreign Psychiatry. 1972. q. $50 (Individuals $15). Jules Angst and Nathan Kline. Intl. Arts & Sciences Press, 901 N. Broadway, White Plains, N.Y. 10603.

Aud: Ac.

Another of what is rapidly becoming a massive assult on foreign-language magazines and journals by International Arts & Sciences Press, or more exactly, their translators. This time around it is psychiatry, and the translations represent the best of what the editors think is found in Japanese, Russian, French, German, and Spanish journals. In the first issue of this service there are six highly technical articles, most of which appeared in 1970. Although unquestionably of value for the graduate student and psychiatrist, is it worth

$50 to an institution? The price is within what the publisher asks for his similar efforts. It is a matter of need rather than worth. The value is there. Does your library have the need?

Group Psychotherapy and Psychodrama. 1947. q. $12. J. L. Moreno. Beacon House, Inc., Box 311, Beacon, N.Y. 12508. Index, adv. Circ: 1,250. Sample. Refereed.

Indexed: PsyAb. *Aud:* Ac.

Issued as official organ of the American Society of Group Psychotherapy and Psychodrama. Issues have included articles on "Is God a Single Person . . .?"; the generation gap; techniques in psychodrama; sociodrama; use of media in teaching; role playing; psychodrama crisis intervention; and sociometry. An occasional contribution appears in German. It includes a section on announcements of meetings, events, etc. This is a journal for practitioners, and the academic libraries supporting their training.

Human Relations; a journal of studies toward the integration of the social sciences. 1957. bi-m. $18. Eric L. Trist. Plenum Publishing Corp., 227 W. 17th St., New York, N.Y. 10011. Adv. Circ: 2,100. Microform: UM.

Indexed: BritHum, SSHum, PAIS, PsyAb. *Aud:* Ac.

International in scope, with three editorial committees (Europe, Britain, and the United States). It is increasingly concerned with social problems and "identification of conditions which will render decision making more apposite and social action more effective." There are, on an average, seven articles per issue, which are either reports on research proposals carried out by the author or extensive monographs based on thorough and extensive reading and rethinking of theory and procedural design. The articles are primarily devoted to the psychological and sociological aspects of group process, systems, and interpersonal relations and interactions. Of value to psychologists and social scientists.

Individual Psychologist. 1963. s-a. $2. Manford Sonstegard and Ed Stormer. W. Va. Univ., FT 504, Morgantown, W. Va. Index. Circ: 800.

Indexed: PsyAb. *Bk. rev:* Notes, signed. *Aud:* Ac, Ga.

One of a growing number of Adlerian journals. (The first of these was *International Journal of Individual Psychology,* which ceased publication many years ago.) The West Virginia magazine includes articles, notes, and features of interest to anyone who follows the Adler cult of individual psychology. It is as much for the interested layman as for the expert, and will be welcomed by anyone who follows Adler's work.

International Journal of Mental Health. 1972. q. $20 (Individuals $10). Martin Gittelman. Intl. Arts & Sciences Press, Inc., 901 N. Broadway, White Plains, N.Y. 10603. Illus., adv. Sample. Vol. ends: Spring.

Aud: Ac.

"The policy of the journal will be to publish in-depth reports on a single topic in each issue." By way of a monograph, the first 230-page double number is devoted to genetics and mental disorders. The 12 reports on original research are primarily for the psychologist or psychiatrist working in the field of mental health. Only for large, specialized collections.

The Israel Annals of Psychiatry and Related Disciplines. 1963. q. $8. H. Z. Winnik. Jerusalem Academic Press, Box 2390, Jerusalem, Israel. Illus., adv. Circ: 1,000. Sample.

Indexed: PsyAb. *Bk. rev:* 4–6, lengthy, signed. *Aud:* Ac.

This journal publishes articles by Israeli and foreign scholars on psychiatric theory and practice. The related disciplines include clinical psychology, psychiatric social work, cultural anthropology, and applied sociology. This magazine is of interest to psychiatrists as well as to behavioral scientists. Many articles are devoted to mental health and to the sociological problems caused by political and social conditions in Israel and the cultural diversity of Israeli society. Typical articles featured are "Behavioral Individuality in Kibbutz Children," "Ethnic Characteristics of Psychiatric Symptomatology," and "Psychological Comparative Study of the Samaritan Community." The Current Events section reports briefly on lectures, local and international meetings, and activities of Israeli associations. (R.T.)

Journal of Applied Behavior Analysis. 1968. q. $16 (Individuals $8). Todd R. Risley. Dept. of Human Development, Univ. of Kans., Lawrence, Kans. 66044. Illus., adv. Circ: 5,500. Vol. ends: Winter.

Indexed: BioAb, ChemAb, IMed, PsyAb. *Aud:* Ac.

Published by the Society for the Experimental Analysis of Behavior, this is "primarily for the original publication of reports of experimental research involving applications of the analysis of behavior to problems of social importance." Each 75 to 100 page issue contains eight to ten articles of a technical nature, e.g., "Training Generative Verb Usage . . . ," and "Modification of Preschool Isolate Behavior." Numerous illustrations and graphs, and reports on ongoing research are included. Valuable for psychology, social sciences, and education schools, particularly at the graduate level. See also *Journal of the Experimental Analysis of Behavior.*

Journal of Applied Behavioral Science. 1965. bi-m. $15. Matthew B. Miles. Inst. for Applied Behavioral Science, associated with NEA, 1201 16th St., N.W., Washington, D.C. 20036. Adv. Circ: 7,000. Sample. Vol. ends: Nov./Dec. Refereed.

Indexed: AbSocWk, SocAb. *Bk. rev:* Bibliographic essay. *Aud:* Ac.

Behavioral science intervention is the scope of this publication, which has made editors of many specialists in small group and organizational research. Articles concern organizational behavior and change, management training, group dynamics, social psychology, action groups, and self awareness, among other topics. The articles are followed by comments from other specialists. A bibliographic essay appears in most issues as a book review, covering an average of five titles per issue. All interested in training groups (read "sensitivity training") will welcome this journal. Collections concerned with sociology, social work, psychology, and organizational behavior should subscribe.

Journal of Applied Psychology. 1917. bi-m. $10. Ewin A. Fleishman. Amer. Psychological Assn., Inc., 1200 17th St., N.W., Washington, D.C. 20036. Adv. Circ: 6,200. Vol. ends: Dec. Microform: UM. Reprint: Johnson.

Indexed: BioAb, PsyAb. *Aud:* Ac.

For people interested "in the following broad areas: personnel selection and training; criterion development; job attitudes; group influences; motivation; communication; organizational behavior . . ." Each issue contains about 25 short articles. Subject matter is wide enough to appeal to both the psychologist and the expert in business practices, and personnel.

Journal of Counseling Psychology. 1954. m. $10. Frances P. Robinson. Amer. Psychological Assn., Inc., 1200 17th St., N.W., Washington, D.C. 20036. Circ: 3,100.

Indexed: EdI, PsyAb. *Bk. rev:* Various number, length. *Aud:* Sa, Ac, Hs, Ejh.

A particularly useful journal for the college or school counselor and others working with personnel. Emphasis is on original research and reports, both practical and theoretical, in the field. Particularly good for regular analysis of other research papers. The 15 to 18 articles per issue cover well the whole spectrum of interests of counselors at almost any level. In view of its reliability, authority, and overview of the field, a first choice in medium-to-large schools where there are counselors or psychologists on the staff.

Journal of the Experimental Analysis of Behavior. 1958. bi-m. $16 (Individuals $8). Stanley S. Pliskoff. Subs. to: Psychology Dept., Indiana Univ., Bloomington, Ind. 47401. Illus., adv. Circ: 3,600. Vol. ends: Winter.

Indexed: BioAb, ChemAb, IMed, PsyAb. *Bk. rev:* 1–2, essay length. *Aud:* Ac.

"Primarily for the original publication of experiments relevant to the behavior of individual organisms," this is published by the Society for the Experimental Analysis of Behavior. Some 12 to 14 articles, technical notes, and essay-length book reviews make up the 130 to 150 page journal. Charts illustrate most of the material, which is even more technical than that in its sister publication, *Journal of Applied Behavior Analysis.* Primarily for graduate study in psychology.

Journal of Health and Social Behavior (Formerly: *Journal of Health and Human Behavior).* 1960. q. $10. Howard E. Freeman. Amer. Sociological Assn., 1722 N. St., N.W., Washington, D.C. 20036. Adv. Circ: 2,700. Vol. ends: Dec. Refereed.

Indexed: IMed, PsyAb. *Bk. rev:* 6, 1,200 words, signed. *Aud:* Ac.

The relationship between health and the social and behavioral sciences is commented on and explored. Among authors are psychiatrists, sociologists, psychologists, psychophysiological researchers, and students of environmental studies, organizations, business administration, etc. Articles concern such topics as community mental health; smoking; drug use; medical care; health care; deviant behavior; characteristics, attitudes, and behavior of physicians; and the relationship between socialization and medical care utilization. This is a specialized journal for scholars and practitioners concerned with health and social behavior.

Journal of Personality and Social Psychology. 1965. m. $30. William McGuire, Amer. Psychological Assn., Inc., 1200 17th St., N.W., Washington, D.C. 20036. Microform: UM.

Indexed: PsyAb. *Aud:* Sa, Ac.

Covers recent research on a wide range of subjects, such as personality dynamics and group process. Contributors are from all segments of the fields of psychology and sociology, though there is predominance of social psychologists. Only for the college or university library.

Journal of Social Issues. 1944. q. $7. Bertram H. Raven. Soc. for the Psychological Study of Social Issues, Box 1248, Ann Arbor, Mich. 48106. Illus., adv. Circ: 7,500. Microform: UM. Reprint: Kraus.

Indexed: BioAb, PsyAb, SSHum. *Aud:* Ac, Ga.

Seeks to bring theory and practice into focus on human problems of the group, community, and nation. The goal is to communicate scientific findings in a nontechnical manner without the sacrifice of professional standards. Each issue has a guest editor and about seven articles on different aspects of a single topic, such as bilingualism or cultural change in small communities. Extensive bibliographies accompany each article. In the back of the issue are perforated pages of three-by-five cards, giving full bibliographic citations and annotations of the articles. Because of the interdisciplinary and nontechnical approach and analysis of current social issues, the journal would be of value to most libraries, including high schools.

Journal of Verbal Learning and Verbal Behavior. 1962. bi-m. $35. Endel Tulving. Academic Press, Inc., 111 Fifth Ave., New York, N.Y. 10003.

Indexed: PsyAb. *Aud:* Sa.

Concentrates on highly specialized work in the fields of psychology and social psychology. There are anywhere from 20 to 50 articles varying in length from 2 to 20 pages. Author and subject indexes are issued annually. For experts only.

Mental Health. See *Mind and Mental Health.*

Mental Hygiene. 1917. q. $10. Henry A. Davidson. The National Assn. for Mental Health, 10 Columbus Circle, New York, N.Y. 10019. Circ: 5,000. Microform: UM.

Indexed: BioAb, IMed, PAIS, PsyAb, RG. *Bk. rev:* Various number, length, signed. *Aud:* Ga, Sa, Ac, Hs. *Rv:* H. *Jv:* V.

One of the few psychology-directed magazines suitable for laymen and students. All articles are prepared by experts, but are written in a style which can be understood by the average educated reader. Emphasis is on reporting new developments in mental health; it is probably of most interest for the authoritative articles on prevention and treatment of various types of mental problems. Social workers and teachers will find much of assistance in understanding given types of personalities, both adult and child, that they encounter in their work. The book reviews vary in length and number, covering all important titles in the field and related areas; and there are reports of major surveys and other briefer works. A limited amount of space is turned over to activities of the sponsoring agency. For all types of libraries, regardless of size.

Mind and Mental Health (Formerly: *Mental Health*). 1940. q. $3. John Payne. National Assn. for Mental Health, Maurice Graig House, 39 Queen Anne St., London W1, England. Illus., index, adv. Circ: 7,000. Sample. Vol. ends: Winter. Microform: UM.

Indexed: PAIS, PsyAb. *Bk. rev:* 10, 300 words, signed. *Aud:* Ga, Ac. *Jv:* V.

A popular 50-plus-page nicely made-up magazine which offers a wide variety of articles on all aspects of mental health, in terms any layman can understand. The magazine considers "mental health" to mean almost anything which deals with human relations. Although it is the voice of the British National Association for Mental Health, most of the material has universal application; e.g., the Summer 1971 issue featured the problem of overcrowding in cities; the pros and cons of abortion; and a fascinating article on images of insanity in films. There are excellent photographs and good book, theater, and film reviews. It is a considerably less slick version of *Psychology Today* for the English; and in many ways it is more convincing and appealing than the American entry. One of the best of its type, it is highly recommended for all medium-to-large public and academic libraries.

Omega; international journal for the psychological study of dying, death, bereavement, suicide and other lethal behaviors. 1970. q. $20. Richard A. Kalish. Greenwood Periodicals Inc., 51 Riverside Ave., Westport, Conn. 06880. Illus., index, adv. Circ: 500. Sample.

Indexed: IMed, PsyAb. *Aud:* Ac, Ga.

The psychological study of dying is now coming to the attention not only of the specialist, but of the popular press as well. A number of articles appeared on the subject in 1972, and it has become of increased interest to laymen and expert alike. This is the only journal exclusively dedicated to publishing reports and articles on the subject. Although the main emphasis is on the psychological and medical aspects of death, the editors are reaching out into all related areas, from the law and ministry to public health and even funeral directors. Then, too, there are articles on how death and dying have been reflected in the arts. About one half to three quarters of the articles are too technical for the passing reader, but the remainder will give him or her something to consider.

Personality; an international journal. 1970. q. $12. Robert A. C. Stewart. Plenum Publishing Corp, 227 W. 17th St., New York, N.Y. 10011.

Indexed: PsyAb. *Aud:* Ac.

Personality research and theory are considered in seven or eight articles by international experts. Most of it is technical, but such articles as "Bunnies and Baskets: A Temporal Analysis of Children's Drawings before and after Easter," (Autumn 1971) gives it an added dimension for the involved nonexpert. (The size of the bunny drawings diminishes after Easter—at least according to this experiment.) Contributors are divided between the United States and Canada, and often seem to be talking as much to themselves as to the reader.

Personnel Psychology. 1948. q. $12. Frederick Kuder. Box 6965, College Sta., Durham, N.C. 27708. Index. Sample. Vol. ends: Winter.

Indexed: BusI, PsyAb. *Bk. rev:* 12–15, 100–500 words, signed. *Aud:* Ac.

Written for and primarily by industrial psychologists, this has wider application than most psychological journals. Articles are useful for anyone doing counseling work, or directly involved with personnel at almost any level of business or in a professional capacity. Teachers may find much of value here, too. While the articles are technical and presuppose at least a basic knowledge of psychology, they touch on problems common in everyday life. In addition to the book reviews, there are surveys of the current literature on personnel psychology. A useful journal for medium-to-large libraries.

Professional Psychology. 1969. q. $10. Donald Freedheim. Amer. Psychological Assn., Inc., 1200 17th St. N.W., Washington, D.C. 20036. Circ: 6,000.

Indexed: PsyAb. *Aud:* Ac, Ga.

Published by the American Psychological Association, and devoted to the promotion of human welfare. Emphasizes the psychologist's social action role, as well as his professional obligations. Many articles deal with mental health in the community, and clinics. There are generally 10 to 14 short articles which are well written and in a style which can be understood by any educated layman. The lead article is often a symposium with comments on different aspects of a certain topical issue. There are many special features: Teaching Tips, The Federal Scene, Issues and Opportunities in Internship Training, problems of private practice, industrial and organizational psychology, and lengthy reviews, often written by two different people, on books, films, new tests, and educational techniques. Of interest to students, educators, practitioners, and researchers in the field, as well as the interested layman. (B.B.)

Psychoanalytic Quarterly. 1932. q. $15. Jacob A. Arlow. Psychoanalytic Inc., 57 W. 57th St., New York, N.Y. 10019. Adv. Circ: 4,200. Vol. ends: Oct.

Indexed: IMed, PsyAb. *Bk. rev:* 15, 2–3 pages, signed. *Aud:* Ac.

A professional journal for psychoanalysts and psychiatrists. There are generally five to seven fairly long articles (10 to 30 pages), most with extensive bibliographies. Many articles are case studies or collections of similar cases. Of some interest to students and adults, but not necessary to a general collection.

Psychology; a journal of human behavior. 1964. q. $6. John A. Blazer. Box 6495, Sta. C, Savannah, Ga. 31405. Circ: 4,000.

Indexed: PsyAb. *Aud:* Ac.

Devoted to basic research, theory, and techniques in the general field of psychology, with emphasis on human behavior. It contains about ten articles in 80 pages, each fairly concise, written by psychologists and related specialists. Material covers such fields as home environment; students; alcohol addiction; and race riots; articles are written in a language that the educated person with a background in psychology can easily understand. Should be in all college and university libraries. (B.B.)

Psychology in the Schools. 1964. q. $20. G. B. Fuller. Clinical Psychology Publishing Co., Inc., 4 Conant Sq., Brandon, Vt. 05733. Adv. Circ: 2,000. Vol. ends: Oct.

Bk. rev: 4, 1 page, signed. *Aud:* Ejs, Hs, Ac.

A semipopular journal of psychology aimed primarily at teachers from elementary school through college. Articles are by both educators and professional psychologists and include a wide variety of material on interpretation, methodology, and research. This would also be useful for counselors. Not a necessity, but a worthwhile addition for larger collections.

Psychology Today. 1967. m. $12. George Harris. John Suhler, 1330 Camino del Mar, Del Mar, Calif. 92014. Illus., index, adv. Circ: 600,000. Vol. ends: April.

Bk. rev: 4, 1 page, signed. *Aud:* Ac, Ga, Hs.

One of the most successful specialized magazines of the 1960s, this promises to do as well in the decade ahead. (*Intellectual Digest,* another effort by the same firm, is on shakier ground.) As the title implies, the emphasis is on interpreting psychology in terms any educated layman can understand. The type of material handled often makes national news, e.g., the early publication of parts of the Skinner book, *Beyond Freedom and Dignity,* and a story debunking the notion that athletics make better citizens. Some may object that the reduction of serious study to "what does it mean to me" is not the ideal end for research, but this is to miss the point. The magazine is interested in and involved with all aspects of the world as seen through the filter of reputable psychologists, sociologists, and related experts. It brings otherwise esoteric journal material to the attention of a considerably wider audience. Recommended for all libraries, including more advanced high schools.

Psychotherapy. 1963. q. $10. Eugene T. Gendlin. Dept. of Psychology, Univ. of Chicago, 5848 University Ave., Chicago, Ill. 60637. Circ: 3,000.

Bk. rev: Various number, length. *Aud:* Ac.

Primarily for practicing psychotherapists. Practice-relevant articles are very short, omit the lengthy introductions and conclusions of most scientific articles, and concentrate on the actual study, or case report. Emphasis is on new, controversial ideas which may help other practitioners. There are summaries of research being done, and comments on articles. (B.B.)

Psychotherapy & Social Science Review. 1967. m. $9. Jane Lassner. 59 Fourth Ave., New York, N.Y. 10003. Illus. Circ: 38,000. Vol. ends: Dec.

Aud: Ga, Ac. *Jv:* V.

A 32-page illustrated review which calls upon leading social scientists, psychologists, and psychiatrists to write long essay-type reviews of major new publications. Contributors have included Paul Goodman, Ernest van den Haag, Edward Glover, and Karl Menninger. Some 10 to 12 current books, usually about a central theme (children and youth, community action, personality, etc.) are noted in each issue. Other issues are more diversified, some even resorting to articles on a given subject. Somewhat like the *New York Review of Books* (only in magazine format) in that books examined are simply springboards for learned essays. Many of the titles are not mentioned or thoroughly reviewed elsewhere. The style is semipopular, the titles selected of interest to both the specialist and the layman. The end result is both a review and a social commentary on a subject of vital interest. The nice combination of authority with a pleasing, informative approach makes this an excellent item for all medium-to-large public and academic libraries. It also should be in most professional high school collections.

Radical Therapist. 1970. 9/yr. $6. Radical Therapist, 23 Hancock St., Somerville, Mass. 02144. Illus. Circ: 5,000. Sample. Vol. ends: Aug.

Bk. rev: 2–3, various length, signed. *Aud:* Ac, Ga.

A new radical look at psychology and how it does or does not affect our society and the individual. It all comes in a 24-page tabloid newspaper. (It was first published in magazine format, but "collating 6,000 or more issues by hand was becoming too much work.) So what is it? It is the voice of a radical group exploring such topics as Male Supremacy in Freud, with a three-page scholarly, documented article. One issue included shorter pieces on various aspects of psychology and psychiatry; four long, detailed and fascinating statements on how to survive psychotherapy; a piece on military psychiatry, plus book reviews and shorter essays. The writers are experts and are as involved with the psychiatric profession as with the social revolution. *Radical Therapist* has a topical message which will be vastly interesting to anyone involved with revolution, women's liberation, ecology/environment, etc. The authors show how people can use psychology and psychiatry instead of being taken by psychological techniques employed by big business and/or big government. There are tips, for example, on how to effectively employ psychological methods in the field of social work, and how to practice psychology on the establishment in order to achieve change. It is not, though, for the uptight, would be patient. An unusual approach in line with other avenues now being opened up by radical medical groups. See also in the Health/Counterculture section, *Health-Pac Bulletin.*

Rehabilitation Record. 1960. bi-m. $3. Vocational Rehabilitation Admin. Subs. to: Supt. of Documents, U.S. Govt. Printing Office, Washington, D. C. 20402. Illus. Circ: 8,000.

Indexed: IMed. *Bk. rev:* Notes. *Aud:* Sa, Ac.

A standard-sized glossy magazine prepared by a government agency to report significant opinions, programs, and techniques in the field of rehabilitation of disabled persons. Each article of the usual ten is about 1,500 words long and is illustrated and signed. The magazine also covers research, and training programs

for professionals. Of use to guidance departments as well as to those who work in the field of rehabilitation.

The School Psychology Digest. 1972. q. Membership (Nonmembers $10). John Guidubaldi. National Assn. of School Psychologists. Subs. to: *The Digest*, 311 Education Bldg., Kent State Univ., Kent, Ohio 44242. Adv.

Bk. rev: 1–2, 250 words signed. *Aud:* Sa.

A 42-page pocket-sized magazine which "is the new official quarterly publication of the National Association of School Psychologists." The organization has 2,000 members who will receive the digest as part of their membership. (Libraries might try to get a free copy from the school psychologist. The price is a bit steep for nonmembers.) Aside from price, though, the magazine is quite good. It includes three original articles, four condensed pieces from other magazines, abstracts, and book reviews. According to the editor, "The ultimate goal of the *Digest* is to help the profession of school psychology to resolve its identity crisis and achieve its true potential." I'm not sure publishing is always the answer to fixing oneself in the universe, but along the way it will assist teachers and parents to realize that the school psychologist (if he or she is really into the scene) can be of considerable help.

Spring. 1962. q. $4.25. James Hillman. Spring Publns., Suite 306, 130 E. 39th St., New York, N.Y.

Aud: Ac.

Subtitled "an annual of archetypal psychology and Jungian thought," this is really a collection of essays in 220 well-printed pages. The 1970 number was dedicated to the late Franz Riklin and featured a timely paper of his, "The Crisis of Middle Life." The remainder of the volume is in three parts: new papers and translations; excerpts from works in progress; and Jungiana. The some dozen contributors represent international scholarship. The whole is in English. The essays are primarily for the professional but the subject matter is rarely beyond the layman who has the slightest interest in Jung. A note indicates that back issues which contain long excerpts from Jung's seminars in English are available at rather modest prices.

RADIO, TELEVISION, AND ELECTRONICS

See also Communications and Media Section.

Basic Periodicals

Ejh: *Electronics Illustrated, QST;* Hs: *Popular Electronics, QST;* Ga: *Popular Electronics, Electronics World, Seventy-Three;* Jc: *Electronics World, Electronic Engineer, Popular Electronics;* Ac: *IEEE Transactions on Broadcasting, Electronic Engineer, Electronics World, Seventy-Three.*

Basic Abstracts and Indexes

Engineering Index, Applied Science and Technology Index.

The Bell System Technical Journal. 1922. 10/yr. $10. G. E. Schindler. Amer. Telephone and Telegraph Co., Treasury Dept., Rm. 2312C, 195 Broadway, New York, N.Y. 10007. Illus. Circ: 14,000. Vol. ends: Dec.

Indexed: ChemAb, EngI, MetAbs, PsyAb, SciAb. *Aud:* Ac, Sa.

This is essentially an in-house journal for engineers of the Bell System. It contains many derivations, and while a technically oriented publication, about two thirds is applicable to radio, television, and electronics. The other third is about AT&T activities. A short scientific biography is included for every contributer. All types of electromagnetic communication are covered, from power supplies to antennas, from audio frequencies to super-high frequencies. A magazine which belongs in every electronics library whether on the university or the industrial level. (W.H.)

CQ; the radio amateurs' journal. 1945. m. $6. R. A. Ross. Cowan Publishing Corp., 14 Vanderventer Ave., Port Washington, N.Y. 11050. Illus., adv. Circ: 98,000. Vol. ends: Dec.

Aud: Ga, Hs.

Somewhat the same in approach and scope as *QST,* this concentrates on "ham" radio and related fields. Equipment reports and instruction for construction of electronics projects by the amateur, i.e., receivers, antennas, transmitters, and accessories, are accurate and useful. *CQ* and *QST* cover much the same ground, but although their audiences overlap, their articles do not duplicate each other. Like a number of specialized magazines, selection is more a matter of personal bias than objective judgment. Some will prefer *QST* because it is one of the oldest of its type in the field; others will turn to *CQ* for a given feature. Librarians should either subscribe to both, or try one after the other. Both are suitable for anyone involved in the subject, from junior high students to senior citizens. (F.L.)

Canadian Electronics Engineering. m. $12. C. S. Hand. Maclean-Hunter Ltd., 481 University Ave., Toronto 101, Canada. Illus., adv. Circ: 11, 213.

Indexed: EngI. *Bk. rev:* Notes. *Aud:* Ac, Sa.

Canadian Electronics Engineering contains about five articles on topics of interest to salesmen working the Canadian electronics market. It also would be of interest to anyone who wished to be kept up to date on Canadian electronics. It has the usual industry news, communication news, a business reading, new products and literature, people and new contracts. This is not an engineer's magazine, despite the title. *CEE* has an annual directory and buyer's guide which provides most of the reason for the magazine's existence. This directory is Canadian in the main but does have sections on the rest of the world. The publication is for the generalist interested in Canadian electronics or for the browsing room of university or special libraries. The annual directory is invaluable to both. (F.L.)

Collins Signal. See Free Magazines Section.

Electronic Engineer (Formerly: *Electronic Industries*). 1942. m. $12. Alberto Socolovsky. Chilton Co., 56th and Chestnut Sts., Philadelphia, Pa. 19139. Illus., adv. Circ: 80,000. Vol ends: Dec. Microform: UM.

Indexed: ASTI, SciAb, EngI. *Aud:* Sa, Ac.

An engineering magazine with an emphasis on computers. It has a regular department, Data Communications, which is of interest to those working with computerized information systems, notably telemetry, telegraphy, and facsimile. Articles on telecommunications may be anything from nationwide TV systems to techniques of sending back information from deep space. A technical magazine written for electronic engineers, it reports forthcoming meetings, new products, results of laboratory studies, and news events of the electronic industry. Similar to *Electronics World,* but since it has fewer articles and more advertisements, makes heavy use of reader service cards, and is more specialized, this would be the second choice for most libraries. (F.L.)

Electronic Technician. 1953. m. $6. Phillip B. Dahlen. Harcourt Brace Jovanovich Publns., Inc., 1 E. 1st St., Duluth, Minn. 55802. Illus., adv. Circ: 85,000. Vol. ends: June and Dec.

Bk. rev: 4, 180 words, unsigned. *Aud:* Sa. *Jv:* V.

Most radio-TV magazines are either too elementary for the average TV serviceman or aimed at the engineer in industry. On about the same level as *Electronics World, Electronic Technician* differs in that every article deals in some way with servicing electronic equipment, mostly TV sets. It deals with the problems of the electronic serviceman and seeks to make his work easier, whether it be replacing a VHF tuner in a Japanese TV, servicing an auto tape deck, or improving customer relations. Although this is a narrow audience, it is one that public libraries are just beginning to cultivate. This magazine claims to have the world's largest circulation among those read by radio and TV service- and salesmen. A special feature of each issue is a complete set of manufacturer's circuit diagrams for five new sets. In separate departments are reports on test equipment; surveys of new products, instruments, and merchandise of special interest; and a technical digest containing hints for efficient and effective servicing. A specialist's magazine recommended for large public libraries, it will also be appreciated in any town large enough to support a TV repair shop. (F.L.)

Electronics Digest. 1967. bi-m. $2.50. William M. Palmer. Electronics Digest Periodicals, Inc., 2615 W. 7th St., Ft. Worth, Tex. 76107. Illus., adv. Circ: 38,000. Vol. ends: May/June.

Aud: Ga, Hs. *Jv:* C.

Articles on technological achievements made possible through the use of electronics. There is some emphasis on ecology. Typical articles portray applications of electronics as used to monitor heart patients, claim minerals from the sea, or measure air pollution concentrations. Biographical sketches of inventors and business pioneers in electronics also appear. Occasionally, construction projects for building working replicas of extinct radio receivers are featured. Although not essential, *Electronics Digest* is a nontechnical magazine of potential interest to anyone who uses the high school or public library. (F.L.)

Electronics Illustrated. 1958. bi-m. $3. Robert G. Beason. Fawcett Publns. Inc., 67 W. 44th St., New York, N.Y. 10036. Illus., adv. Circ: 305,000. Vol. ends: Nov. Microform: UM.

Bk. rev: Occasional. *Aud:* Ga, Ejh, Hs.

A popular magazine for electronic hobbyists of all ages. Articles survey a broad area of electronics with emphasis on shortwave listening, new products, and equipment available in kit form. The primary value of the magazine for younger readers is that it gives detailed step-by-step instructions for constructing such items as shortwave radios, hi-fi sets, and less technical radio equipment. The articles are nontechnical and well illustrated. Should be a source of instruction for the teenager and casual reading for the adult. (F.L.)

Electronics World. 1919. m. $7. William Stocklin. Ziff Davis Publishing Co., 1 Park Ave., New York, N.Y. 10016. Illus., adv. Circ: 176,000. Vol. ends: June and Dec. Microform: UM.

Indexed: ChemAb, RG. *Bk. rev:* 6–7, 150 words, unsigned. *Aud:* Ga, Ac. *Jv:* V.

Unlike *Electronics Illustrated* and *Popular Electronics,* this is primarily for the expert in electronics. It is for adults who have some basic knowledge of circuit design and are seeking information on technical advances, new products and equipment, and changes in personnel in various plants and government-sponsored activities. Articles contain recent developments in electronics, from analog computers to lab tests of stereo equipment, and are presented in detailed technical language. Although this magazine is popular with engineers, it would be a second choice to *Popular Electronics* in all but the larger libraries serving a specialized group of readers. (F.L.)

Elementary Electronics. 1963. bi-m. $4. Julien M. Sienkiewicz. Science & Mechanics Publishing Co., A subsidiary of Davis Publns., Inc., 229 Park Ave. S., New York, N.Y. 10003 Illus., adv. Circ: 100,000. Vol. ends: Jan./Feb.

Aud: Ga, Hs, Ejh.

A magazine for young enthusiasts of electricity and electronics, brief lessons in various phases providing, such as understanding transformers, theory and applications of batteries, or tips on the care of tools. Construction articles written with a minimum of technical jargon include easy-to-follow diagrams of projects that serve to stimulate and educate the reader. Articles are generally less ambitious than those in *Electronics Illustrated,* but place greater emphasis on teaching fundamentals. Occasionally there are pieces on shortwave radio. Although not an essential item, a useful hobby magazine to be read and enjoyed from the junior high level and up. (F.L.)

Ham Radio. 1968. m. $6. James R. Fisk. Communications Technology, Inc., Greenville, N.H. 03048. Illus., adv. Circ: 35,000. Microform: UM.

Aud: Ga.

An amateur radio magazine which is somewhat more technical than either of the two standards, *CQ* and *QST.* Designed for a more selective audience than *Seventy-Three,* it presupposes a basic knowledge of electronics and an ability to read the many useful technical diagrams which illustrate each of the 10 to 12 articles. One issue, for example, featured such items as "Strip-Line Kilowatt for 432 MHz" and "Thermoelectric Power Supplies." There are several departments, including appraisals of new equipment and products. It will be of primary value to the adult, serious student of the subject. Definitely not a high school magazine, at least at the average level. (F.L.)

IEEE Transactions on Broadcast and Television Receivers. 1952. q. $18. Chester W. Sall. Inst. of Electrical and Electronics Engineers, Inc., 345 E. 47th St. New York, N.Y. 10017. Illus. Vol. ends: Nov.

Indexed: ASTI, ChemAb, Ei, MathR, SciAb. *Aud:* Ac, Sa.

Serves as an outlet for papers bringing technical developments to the attention of engineers and supervisors of the broadcast and television receiver industry. It is the mouthpiece of the organization within the framework of the Institute of Electrical and Electronic Engineers whose members maintain a professional interest in broadcast and television receivers. It is of interest to those readers with some knowledge of electronics who wish to keep up with new developments in the industry. Articles present the results of research and development affecting the radio and television industry, including new theories, designs, applications, and products. They are written by engineers of the leading firms producing radio and television equipment and contain extensive biographical information. Contains tentative programs of forthcoming conferences on broadcast and television receivers. (F.L.)

IEEE Transactions on Broadcasting. 1952. q. $18. Robert M. Morris. Inst. of Electrical and Electronics Engineers, Inc., 345 E. 47th St., New York, N.Y. 10017. Illus. Vol. ends: Dec.

Indexed: ASTI, ChemAb, EngI, MathR, SciAb. *Aud:* Ac, Sa. *Jv:* V.

Directed toward engineers engaged in research and development in the field of broadcasting. Articles often serve to disseminate papers delivered at the IEEE's Annual Broadcasting Symposium. All articles represent high-level research in radio and television transmitting and receiving phenomena. Articles are well abstracted, sometimes highly mathematical, and generally list many references. Devoted exclusively to research papers, this would be of interest to academic libraries supporting an electrical engineering program or the occasional large public library that is called upon to support research in this area. (F.L.)

International Journal of Electronics; theoretical and experimental. 1965. m. $73.50. J. Thomson. Taylor & Francis Ltd., 10–14 Macklin St., London, England. Illus., adv. Vol. ends: June and Dec. Refereed.

Aud: Ac, Sa.

Tries to cover all of electronics, but concentrates on very high frequencies and above. There is very little advertising. It contains a valuable series of research notes which could be useful, if checked on a regular basis. For the specialist. (W.H.)

Laser Journal. 1969. m. $20. G. Gronau. A. Z. Publishing Corp., 825 S. Barrington Ave., Los Angeles, Calif. 90049. Illus., adv. Circ: 10,927. Vol. ends: Nov./Dec.

Aud: Ac, Sa.

The *Laser Journal* is the official publication of the Laser Industry Association, and covers all uses of lasers, from medical to military. The articles are short and few in number. It is written for the salesman rather than the engineer. The purpose is to inform and educate the users of lasers and to keep them up to date on the latest developments in the field, mainly through its advertising, which takes up at least two thirds of the magazine. It also has sections on industry news, new literature, and new products. Should be in every academic library and special library with a clientele interested in lasers or super-high frequencies. (W.H.)

Microwave Journal. 1958. m. (s-m. in March). $25 (Free to qualified persons including university libraries). Theodore S. Saad. Horizon House, 610 Washington St., Dedham, Mass. 02026. Illus., adv. Circ: 46,000. Refereed.

Indexed: EngI, SciAb. *Aud:* Ac, Sa.

Appeals to military microwave engineers, and includes everything from very high frequencies through light frequencies. It has industry, financial, personnel, and new products sections, a guest editorial, and many derivations and charts to aid the engineer. About two thirds is advertising. Covers much the same ground as the IEEE publications but not as completely, nor is it as technical. In March it is semimonthly with the publication of the *Microwave Engineers Buyers Guide.* It often suggests what the IEEE should be doing and occasionally throws orchids at them. Since it is free to university libraries and any other qualified person, it is suggested this be on the list of any university or special library which has work going on in this field. (W.H.)

Philips Technical Review. 1936. m. $10. J. W. Miltenburg. Research Laboratories of N. V. Philips' Gloeilampenfabriekan, Box 76, Eindhoven, Netherlands. Illus. Vol. ends: Dec.

Indexed: ChemAb, EngI, MetAb, PsyAb, SciAb. *Aud:* Ac, Sa.

A medium of publication for employees of the N. V. Philips' laboratories. The articles tend to be nonspecialized, with the general scientist or technician in mind. They cover all fields of electronics, with some interdisciplinary forays into the chemical or physical backgrounds of the electronic principle being discussed. In 1971 it covered such varied fields as transistors, antennas, ferrites, and delay lines. This deserves to be both in the browsing room and on the regular reading list of any library with electronics patrons. (W.H.)

Popular Electronics. 1954. m. $6. Milton S. Snitzer. Ziff-Davis Publishing Co., 1 Park Ave., New York, N.Y. 10016. Illus., adv. Circ: 380,000. Vol. ends: Dec. Microform: UM.

Indexed: RG. *Bk. rev:* 6–8, 175–200 words, signed. *Aud:* Ga, Hs. *Jv:* V.

This is for the amateur, but for a more learned one than envisioned by *Electronics Illustrated.* The features and articles presuppose some knowledge of the fundamentals of electronics and an interest in the way things work. *Popular Electronics* is comprehensive in scope and features articles on such subjects as citizens band radio, home stereo sets, solid state electronics, ham radio, careers in the field, and new products. Although not for serious hams or engineers, a typical issue may feature items ranging from how to make a toy that whistles like a bird, to an article explaining operational amplifier theory. The construction projects contain detailed diagrams, text, and photos to ensure successful results. Much advertising. (F.L.)

QST. 1915. m. Membership (Nonmembers $7.50). John Huntoon. Amer. Radio Relay League, Inc., 225 Main St., Newington, Conn. 06111. Illus., adv. Circ: 105,000. Vol. ends: Dec. Microform: UM.

Indexed: ASTI, SciAb. *Bk. rev:* 6/year, 150 words, signed. *Aud:* Ga, Hs, Ac. *Jv:* V.

The oldest radio magazine devoted entirely to the interests of the ham, it is also the most authoritative, as it acts as the official bulletin of the organized activities of the largest amateur organization in the world, the American Radio Relay League. Contains information on special activities and contests that are held to promote skill in operating a station. Although most articles are technical, they contain useful information for the novice as well as the expert. The writers cover all aspects of ham radio operating and present amateur news gathered from every section of the country about individuals, their stations, and their activities. Will be welcomed by all adults and students with more than a passing interest in ham radio. (F.L.)

RCA Broadcast News. See Free Magazines Section.

The Radio Constructor. 1947. m. $6. Proprietors and Publishers, Data Publns., Ltd., 57 Maida Vale, London, W9 ISN, England. Illus., index, adv. Circ: 31,500. Vol. ends: July.

Bk. rev: Various number, 200 words. *Aud:* Ga, Ac.

A good general magazine reflecting the present practices of the British amateur and shortwave listener. It covers the field well, although there are few articles on the very high frequencies. It has Now Hear These, a shortwave listener's corner; News and Comment, QSX, another shortwave listener's corner; In Your Work-shop; and Current Schedules of commercial stations. It also runs continuing articles, such as Understanding Basic Principles of Radio. This magazine is for the shortwave listener, the novice amateur radio operator, and anyone who is interested in electronics. Definitely to be bought when your library has all four American magazines. (W.H.)

Radio-Electronics. 1929. m. $7. Larry Steckler. Gernsback Publns., Inc., 200 Park Ave. S., New York, N.Y. 10003. Illus., adv. Circ: 158,000. Vol. ends: Dec. Microform: UM.

Indexed: ASTI, RG. *Bk. rev:* 4, 50 words. *Aud:* Ga, Hs, Ac.

Of interest to students, technicians, servicemen, do-it-yourself buffs, and all others with ideas in electronics; the magazine keeps a good balance between practical articles for building new equipment (with an occasional evaluation by the editorial staff), servicing and repair of home appliances, and tutorials on new technological advances or refreshers on basic physical principles and mathematical tools. Articles are popularly written; easily comprehensible. Departments include news briefs; Technotes, tips for the trade; Service Clinic, data on servicing radio and TV receivers; Noteworthy Circuits, information on novel circuitry as gleaned from other technical periodicals; and information on recent equipment and literature. (F.L.)

S Nine Two way Radio. 1969. m. $5. Thomas Kneitel. Cowan Publishing Corp., 14 Vanderventer Ave., Port Washington, New York, N.Y. 10032. Illus., adv. Circ: 50,000. Vol. ends: Dec.

Aud: Ga, Hs.

Of interest to anyone involved in citizens' band (CB) radio. *S Nine* covers many aspects of CB radio transmitting and receiving, from enforcement of FCC rules to how to make a quad-beam antenna. There is less emphasis on theory than on discussion of new products and the activities of CB clubs and their members. That CB radio could spawn its own periodical and support it with such a high circulation is noteworthy, but the magazine does not contain anything of interest to the serious student of radio–electronics. If you have an active CB club in the neighborhood you may want to try this one, but it is not at all essential. (F.L.)

Seventy-Three; amateur radio. 1960. m. (Jan.-Dec.). $6. Wayne Green. 73 Inc., Peterborough, N.H. 03458. Illus., adv. Circ: 65,000. Vol. ends: Dec. Microform: UM.

Bk. rev: 1–2/issue, 100–200 words. *Aud:* Ga, Hs, Ac. *Jv:* V.

A magazine about ham radio similar to *CQ* but devotes more space to equipment and less to readership activities. It describes ham radio, and how one may take part, in a popularized manner which appeals to those for whom the hobby is still new, and who are not specialists in electronics. Articles are on such subjects as elementary theory, tips on passing radio license exams, building simple transmitters, and guidelines for buying equipment. Other material is presented in newspaper format and titled "Amateur Radio News Page." This contains articles like new FCC regulations affecting hams, newsworthy events and inventions, new products, a lengthy editorial, news of social events and contests, results of American Radio Relay League board meetings, awards, book reviews, and letters to the editor. Each issue is given an area of emphasis. One month it may be devoted to mobile ham radio, the next, antennas. Although *QST* is probably the standard and most essential amateur radio magazine, there are many hams who turn to *Seventy-Three* first, as can be seen by the large number of subscriptions. The articles are written in an interesting manner with provocative editorials and are of value to all hams. Because of its popular following, *Seventy-Three* should be tried by all libraries where there is an interest in amateur radio. (F.L.)

Solid State Electronics; an international journal. 1960. m. $80. W. Crawford Dunlap. Pergamon Press, Maxwell House, Fairview Park, Elmsford N.Y. 10523; and Headington Hill Hall, Oxford, England. Index, adv. Refereed.

Indexed: ChemAb, EngI, MetAb, SciAb. *Aud:* Ac, Sa.

Good coverage of the solid state field, but only if the reader thinks of it as consisting only of transistors, which is bending the facts a little. It does have derivations and very few advertisements. Articles are primarily in English with abstracts in German and French. Anyone with an interest in semiconductors, and this includes almost everyone with an interest in electronics, will enjoy this magazine. (W.H.)

Tech Notes. See Free Magazines Section.

Telephone Review. See Free Magazines Section.

Television/Radio Age (Formerly: *Television Age*). 1953. bi-w. $9. Alfred Jaffe. Television Editorial Corp., 34 N. Crystal St., E. Stroudsburg, Pa. 18301. Illus., adv. Circ: 15,000.

Aud: Ac, Sa.

A general magazine for radio and television engineers, which has about six articles of three pages each on varied timely topics. It has regular features, including a business barometer; communications; inside the FCC; and people, places, and things happening in the radio television industry. Should be of interest to special academic and business libraries. (W.H.)

RELIGION

See also Children/Religious Magazines for the Child Section.

Basic Periodicals

GENERAL. Ga; *Journal of Ecumenical Studies;* Jc: *Journal of Ecumenical Studies;* Ac: *Interpretation, Journal of Ecumenical Studies, Journal of Church and State, Religious Education, Harvard Theological Review.*

SECULAR. All libraries: *The Humanist, Church & State.*

COUNTERCULTURE. All libraries: *Katallagete* (Protestant); *National Catholic Reporter; Catonsville Roadrunner.*

Basic Abstracts and Indexes

Index to Religious Periodical Literature, Religious and Theological Abstracts, Catholic Periodical and Literature Index.

Cessations

Ave Maria, Best Sermons, Church Quarterly, Concurrence, Hibbert Journal, Intercollegian, Jubilee, Motive.

General

Christian Century. See News and Opinion Magazines/ Political Opinion Reviews.

Christian Scholar. See *Soundings.*

Church History. 1888. q. $10. Ed. bd. Amer. Soc. of Church History, 305 E. Country Club Lane, Wallingford, Pa. 19086. Index, adv. Circ: 2,740. Sample. Vol. ends: Dec.

Indexed: RelAb, SSHum. *Bk. rev:* 70, 150–250 words, signed. *Aud:* Ac.

A nondenominational, scholarly journal which considers all aspects of church history. Contributors and editors are representative of the nation's leading theological seminaries and schools—University of Chicago, Harvard, Union Theological Seminary, etc. In addition to the book reviews and shorter book notes, there is a regular section on Dissertation Abstracts, business news of the organization, and general information on religion in America and abroad. A basic journal for any medium-to-large academic library.

Commentary. See News and Opinion Magazines/ Political Opinion Reviews.

Commonweal. See News and Opinion Magazines/ Political Opinion Reviews.

Context. 1972. bi-w. $16.50. Martin E. Marty. Thomas More Assn., 180 N. Wabash Ave., Chicago, Ill. 60601.

Aud: Ac.

A six-page biweekly newsletter which is a commentary on "the interaction of religion and culture" by Martin E. Marty, a member of the University of Chicago Divinity School faculty. The letters tend to be timely and chatty, are divided into six or seven sections, and cover topics of interest to those involved with the intellectual side of religion. No particular bias is evident, and the editor praises and whacks all faiths with pleasant regularity. He draws the ideas for most of his material from new books and articles he has scanned. Will appeal to anyone who appreciates I. F. Stone, or understands the importance of Alexander Solzhenitsyn—two individuals quoted in a single newsletter. The price, by the way, is about right.

Harvard Theological Review. 1908. q. $8. Krister Stendhal. Harvard Univ. Press, 79 Garden St., Cambridge, Mass. 02138. Circ: 1,600. Sample. Vol. ends: Oct. Reprint: Kraus.

Indexed: RelAb, SSHum. *Aud:* Ac.

Covers a wide number of areas, from church history and Biblical studies to the philosophy of religion and science. Contributors are international, with a number of them drawn from Harvard. The articles are generally quite within the grasp of the well-educated reader. It is one of the best journals in the field. This nondenominational publication of the Harvard Divinity School is particularly valuable for the student and educated layman.

History of Religions; an international journal for comparative historical studies. 1961. q. $8. Mircea Eliade, Joseph Katagawa, and Charles Long. Univ. of Chicago Press, 5801 S. Ellis, Chicago, Ill. 60637. Index, adv. Circ: 1,615. Sample. Vol. ends: May. Refereed. Microform: UM.

Indexed: AbFolkSt, HistAb, RelAb, RelPer. *Bk. rev:* 3, 2 pages, signed. *Aud:* Ac. *Jv:* V.

Given a high rating and a required place in most libraries because of its particular value to the general collection. Not only does it explore all facets and faiths of religious history, but in so doing it offers material of value to the graduate student or professor in many related fields, from folklore to theology and sociology. It deserves a wider circulation, although admittedly it is not always easy to read. The articles are on a high level of scholarship and are sometimes virtually inaccessible without background, but this is eventually a corollary to its excellence. There are about four rather long articles per issue. There are no other features. Excellent for college and university libraries, and necessary for any basic collection on religion.

Ideas. See News and Opinion Magazines/Political Opinion Reviews.

Interpretation; a journal of bible and theology. 1947. q. $6. James L. Mays. Union Theological Seminary, 3401 Brook Rd., Richmond, Va. 23227. Index, adv. Circ: 7,000. Sample. Vol. ends: Oct.

Indexed: RelAb, RelPer. *Bk. rev:* 18, various length, signed. *Aud:* Ac.

A scholarly theological journal whose contributors and readers are primarily teachers and students. Although this is based in Virginia, the authors are from a number of countries and parts of the United States. In fact, it is one of the more international journals in this field. Articles are objective, interdenominational, and usually well documented. The style tends to be a bit difficult. Subject matter ranges from biblical interpretation to current questions in theology. Excellent and extensive book reviews.

Journal of the American Academy of Religion (Formerly: *Journal of Bible and Religion*). 1967. q. $15. Ray L. Hart. Wilson College, Chambersburg, Pa. 17201. Index, adv. Circ: 4,700. Sample. Vol. ends: No. 4. Refereed.

Indexed: RelAb, RelPer. *Bk. rev:* 30, 1–4 pages, signed. *Aud:* Ac.

A professional journal covering the field of religion studies, including the history of religions, biblical studies, theology, the history and philosophy of religion, history of Judaism, and other topics. Particularly valuable for the comprehensive and critical book reviews.

Journal of Church and State. 1959. q. $5. James E. Wood and J. M. Dawson. Journal of Church and State, Box 380, Baylor Univ., Waco, Texas 76703. Adv. Circ: 1,500. Sample.

Indexed: RelPer, PAIS, HistAb, AmerH, RelTheolAbs. *Bk. rev:* 15–20, 600–1,000 words, signed. *Aud:* Ac.

Covers the relationship between church and religious life within the larger context of social patterns as reflected in governmental and political affairs. Articles have appeared on the ethical aspects of limited war, Jewish–Christian relations, and church schools and public funds. The periodical is independent in its views and does not take a denominational stand. It also contains articles concerning some rather minor historical and theological disputes, which tends to limit its readership.

Journal of Ecumenical Studies. 1964. q. $8. Leonard Swidler. Temple Univ. Press, Philadelphia, Pa. 19122. Index, adv. Circ: 3,500. Sample. Vol. ends: Fall.

Indexed: RelAb, RelPer. *Bk. rev:* 30, 800 words, signed. *Aud:* Ga, Ac. *Jv:* V.

In a 1971 survey conducted by the Centro Pro Unione in Rome of the 185 ecumenical institutes and centers throughout the world, *JES* was judged the single most important ecumenical publication. It is often technical, always scholarly, yet designed for the general reader. Each article is preceded by a précis, and is supplemented with a special study guide, which is well constructed. Articles generally include many footnotes, often of help to the layman. The articles cover a wide range of subjects and are contributed by scholars. The book reviews are excellent. There are about 1,000 abstracts yearly of relevant articles from 600 journals around the world. Current news notes, which cover meetings, studies, and significant events, also appear. Needed in any college, university, and public library.

Journal of Religion. 1882. q. $8. Nathan A. Scott and Schubert M. Ogden. Univ. of Chicago Press, 5801 Ellis Ave., Chicago, Ill. 60637. Index, adv. Circ: 2,000. Vol. ends: Oct. Refereed. Microform: UM.

Indexed: SSHum. *Bk. rev:* 5, 8–25 pages, signed. *Aud:* Ac.

A scholarly approach to all aspects of religious and theological thought. The articles tend to be technical and are primarily for the student and teacher of theology. There are excellent book reviews and notes of new publications. In that the journal is totally removed from any religious creed, it is one of the best for a general collection where there is any consideration of the social, philosophical, or historical implications of religion. In the past edition this was compared to the British *Hibbert Journal*. Not fair, says a critic who notes that "the British have such a peculiar theological mentality" that the comparison is not welcome. Comment withdrawn.

Journal of Religious Thought. 1943. s-a. $3. S. L. Gandy. Howard Univ., Washington, D. C. 20001. Illus., adv. Circ: 400. Microform: UM.

Indexed: RelAb, RelPer, INeg. *Bk. rev:* 5–6, 200–400 words, signed. *Aud:* Sa, Ac.

Not specifically black-oriented, but published by a black university. The scholarly articles deal with abstract theological as well as more practical approaches to modern-day human problems. Some issues contain editorial comment on recent events. Only for large collections.

Journal for the Scientific Study of Religion. 1961. q. $15 (Students $8). Benton Johnson. Soc. for the Scientific Study of Religion, Univ. of Conn., Box U68A, Storrs, Conn. 06268. Index. Circ: 3,000. Vol. ends: Winter. Microform: UM.

Indexed: RelPer. *Bk. rev:* 6–20, various length, signed. *Aud:* Ac.

An objective, scientific view of what is admittedly a nonscientific subject area. The contributors meet the challenge by offering articles on aspects of sociology, psychology, bibliography, etc., which tend to build a scientific support for religious study and speculation. Each of the disciplines has a section, along with sections on history and theory. The book reviews cover nearly everything relevant and are as well done as the rest of the journal. Excellent for any college or university library.

Religion in Communist Dominated Areas (RCDA). 1962. m. $10. Blahoslav S. Hruby. Research Center for Religion and Human Rights in Closed Societies, Ltd., 475 Riverside Dr., Suite 452, New York, N.Y. 10027. Illus., index. Circ: 3,000. Sample. Vol. ends: Dec.

Aud: Ac.

This fairly large offset publication makes available what it calls "authentic information" on the attitudes and practices of Communist parties with respect to the life, work, and vital concerns of Christians, Jews, and peoples of other religions in all Communist-dominated countries. *RCDA* publishes English translations of articles and news items from the Communist newspapers and periodicals, and transcripts of Communist broadcasts concerning religion, antireligious propaganda, and related subjects. Also, it prints translations of articles from the religious press and pays special attention to the violation of religious freedom and human rights in the USSR and other Communist countries. In recent years it published translations from the underground religious press and appeals of Christians, Jews, and other groups harassed and persecuted for their religious faith or their national or political dissent. For the past ten years *RCDA* has been published by the National Council of Churches in the United States. On January 1, 1972, it became a publication of Research Center for Religion and Human Rights in Closed Societies, Ltd.

Religious Education. 1906. bi-m. $12.50. Randolph C. Miller. Religious Education Assn., 545 W. 111th St., New York, N.Y. 10025. Circ: 4,500. Sample. Vol. ends: No. 6. Microform: UM.

Indexed: CathI, EdI, IJewPer, PsyAb, RelAb. *Bk. rev:* 8, various length, signed. *Aud:* Ac, Hs, Ejh.

The basic journal for religious education. It is basic because it is one of the few which is objective and representative of all points of view. Authorities, who usually write fairly well, report on the teaching of religion as it is involved with the curriculum from the elementary and secondary schools through the universities. There are often special symposia on various aspects of religion and society and on problems besetting the teacher of religion at every level, although emphasis is on colleges and universities. A useful feature is the abstracts of doctoral dissertations in the field. The magazine is useful for the nontheologically oriented library in that many articles and frequent special issues touch on topics of interest to anyone remotely involved with today's changing society. One of the few religion-oriented magazines that can be recommended in just about any educational situation.

Religious Studies. 1965. q. $13.50. H. D. Lewis. Cambridge Univ. Press, 32 E. 57th St., New York, N.Y. 10022. Index. Sample. Vol. ends: Dec.

Indexed: RelPer. *Bk. rev:* Review articles, 6, 500–1500 words, signed. *Aud:* Ac.

Provides space, time, and continuity for the discussion of modern religious concepts and questions. It has, naturally, a strong theological and philosophical bent, but it devotes considerable space to historical and comparative religious studies, and to the sociology and psychology of religion. The editor welcomes answers to articles, and symposia presenting differing views of questions are frequent, as in a special section on the ontological argument for the existence of God.

Respond. 1967. Irreg. $5. Laymen's League of the Unitarian Universalist Assn., 25 Beacon St., Boston, Mass. 02108. Illus. Circ: 4,000.

Aud: Ga.

"The purpose of this magazine is to share events, ideas, concerns that are of significance to the liberal religious community." While the orientation reflects the sponsor—Unitarian—the appeal is general enough to remove it almost entirely from any religious affiliation. An average 50-page issue includes poetry, black and white photographs, and articles on issues of current interest. The writing is scholarly, yet styled for the reader of average education.

Review of Metaphysics. See Philosophy Section.

Social Action. See News and Opinion Magazines/Political Opinion Reviews.

Soundings; an interdisciplinary journal (Supersedes *Christian Scholar*). 1968. q. $9. Sallie TeSelle. Soc. for

Religion in Higher Education, 400 Prospect St., New Haven, Conn. 06511. Adv. Circ: 2,000. Microform: UM.

Indexed: EdI, RelAb. *Aud:* Ac.

A literary/religious magazine which encourages articles on all aspects of the moral and ethical questions faced by individuals in our society. The implications of ethics and religion for an average life are carefully considered. The editor attempts to publish interdisciplinarian studies and articles representive of all fields, from mathematics and chemistry to poetry and literature. An interesting, challenging magazine for anyone involved in religious education and study.

Theological Studies. 1940. q. $7. Walter J. Burghardt. Soc. of Jesus in the U. S., 475 Riverside Dr., New York, N.Y. 10027. Index, adv. Circ: 5,863. Sample. Vol. ends: Dec.

Indexed: CathI, RelPer. *Bk. rev:* 50, 750 words, signed. *Aud:* Ac.

Devoted to theological matters in general. Its tone is formal but by no means formidable. Articles deal with such matters as sin and grace, moral considerations in decision making, and present-day agnosticism. Ecumenism occupies quite a bit of space. The numerous critical reviews give it an important place in the selection process.

Zygon; journal of religion and science. 1966. q. $12 (Individuals $9). Ralph W. Burhoe. Univ. of Chicago Press, 5801 Ellis Ave., Chicago, Ill. 60637. Index, adv. Circ: 1,500. Sample. Vol. ends: Dec. Refereed. Microform: UM.

Indexed: RelPer. *Bk. rev:* 4, 1 page, signed. *Aud:* Ac.

Another religious journal from the University of Chicago (see also *Journal of Religion* and *History of Religions*). This expresses two major purposes: to analyze scientifically the nature of religion; and to bring scientific knowledge into positive relation to theology. Subjects of special concern are relativism, evolution, and scientific studies of the nature of man. The motivation is more theological than scientific but it is relevant and enlightening. (See also *Journal for the Scientific Study of Religion.*)

JESUS MOVEMENT. For those teen-agers who have joined the Jesus Movement—whose target date for saturating the United States with the gospel of Jesus Christ is 1976 (for the world the target date is 1980); whose mark of identity is total belief in a supernatural Jesus Christ, not just a marvelous man who lived 2,000 years ago, but a living God who is both Savior and Judge, the ruler of human destinies; whose lives revolve around the necessity for an intense personal relationship with that Jesus and the belief that such a relationship should condition every human life—and who would not be interested in the run-of-the-mill teen-age journal, the following magazines are suggested. These

magazines are filled with character-building articles; general tips for teen-agers; beauty hints; reviews of movies, records, and books, and lengthy discussions on topics of current interest (drugs, women's liberation, ecology, etc.). The outlook stressed in these magazines might help balance a library's teen-age collection. (J.G.)

Accent on Youth. 1970. m. $3.75. Methodist Publishing House, 201 Eighth Ave. S., Nashville, Tenn. 37202. Illus.

For high school students, a delightful magazine, very well rounded.

Action for Young Teens. 1968. m. $3.75. Amer. Baptist Bd. of Education and Publns. Valley Forge, Pa. 19481. Illus.

A worthwhile magazine which would have wide appeal for teen-agers (ages 12 to 18).

Alive for Young Teens. 1969. m. $4. Youth Dept. of the Local Church Curriculum Div., Christian Bd. of Publn., Box 179, 2640 Pine Blvd., St. Louis, Mo. 63166. Illus. Circ: 24,000.

Geared to the young teen-ager of the seventh and eighth grades, this is an alive publication with lots of sparkle.

Campus Life. 1943. m. $5. Harold Myra. Youth for Christ Intl., Box 419, Wheaton, Ill. 60187. Illus., adv. Circ: 60,000. Sample. Vol. ends: Dec.

A professionally edited magazine addressed "primarily to the junior and senior in high school, although kids as early as junior high and as late as college read our magazine." The typical well-illustrated 80-page issue includes features (usually on sports figures), short bits of fiction, and excerpts from books with a religious subject.

Etc. 1970. m. $2.50. Paul Miller. Nazarene Publishing House, 2923 Troost Ave., Kansas City, Mo. 64109. Illus.

A magazine in newspaper format for the older teen-ager, this provides good reading on current topics.

Insight. 1970. w. $8.95. Don Yost. Review and Herald Publishing Assn. 6856 Eastern Ave., N.W., Washington, D. C. 20012. Illus.

More narrow in scope than the other magazines listed, but a good one for basic principles.

Young Ambassador. 1946. m. $3. Ruth Johnson Jay. Good News Broadcasting Assn., Inc., Box 82808, Lincoln, Nebr. 68501. Illus., index. Circ: 90,000. Sample. Vol. ends: Dec.

Advertised as a back-to-the-Bible magazine for youth (ages 12 to 20). Interdenominational stories, articles, and special departments are all faith centered, with lessons for positive Christian living. Puzzles, quizzes, and song of the month are regular features.

Denominations

America; national Catholic weekly review. 1909. w. $10. Donald R. Campion. Amer. Press, 106 W. 56th St., New York, N.Y. 10019. Illus., index, adv. Circ:

55,000. Sample. Vol. ends: June and Dec. Microform: UM.

Indexed: AbrRG, CathI, RG. *Bk. rev:* 5–7, 500 words, signed. *Aud:* Ga, Ac. *Jv:* V.

A Roman Catholic weekly directed at the better-educated, more sophisticated reader. The editor concentrates on political and social events, but there is a broad variety of topics—national, international, educational, social, political. Articles are written by outstanding Catholics, usually lay persons. The editorial policy represents the liberal Catholic viewpoint in regard to such topics as birth control, education, and civil rights. In addition to weekly book reviews, there is a semiannual cumulation of book reviews and a good film review section.

Somewhat similar, if comparisons are in order, to the position of the *New Republic* in relation to the *Nation, America* would be compared to the other Catholic weekly, *Commonweal.* Both are liberal, intelligent, and controversial. How do they differ? *Commonweal* is a bit more general, certainly more to the left. *America* tends to concentrate heavily on basic Catholic issues, and its editorials are middle of the road to liberal. Given its editorial policy, *America* draws upon a larger audience than *Commonweal;* its circulation is a good one half more than that of its rival. Why are both indexed in *Readers' Guide,* but only *America* included in the abridged version as well?

American Judaism. See *Dimensions in American Judaism.*

Awake. 1919. s-m. $1.50. Watchtower Bible & Tract Soc. of N.Y., Inc., 117 Adams St., Brooklyn, N.Y. 11201. Illus., index. Circ: 7,175,000. Sample. Vol. ends: Dec.

Aud: Ga.

By way of a magazine of current opinion on a variety of secular topics, this is an intelligent, politically-free organ for Jehovah's Christian witnesses. It has a much wider scope than most people suspect. The editors examine fields of interest to everyone. For example, in late 1971, various issues were given over to "Relief from Today's Pressures"—a study of what causes misery, and "Earth's Future—Garbage Dump or Garden Home?"—a direct discussion of ecology. Other numbers are a bit more diverse, but usually contain articles for adults and children on everything from health and nature to reports on major social issues. Each 32-page newsprint copy ends with short news notes. There are, to be sure, articles directly reflecting the beliefs of the sponsoring group, but these are rarely objectionable to a nonbeliever. The folksy, yet accurate, style obviously accounts for the large circulation. It is probably of questionable use in a library, but librarians should be aware of any magazine that commands this many readers.

Awake should not be confused with the purely propagation-of-the-faith magazine of a similar format, issued by the same group, *Watchtower* (1879. s-m. $1). The latter enjoys an equally high circulation, but is primarily concerned with religious questions.

The Catholic Biblical Quarterly. 1939. q. Membership (Nonmembers $10). Catholic Biblical Assn. of Amer., Catholic Univ. of Amer., Washington, D.C. 20017. Illus., index, adv. Circ: 3,600. Sample. Vol. ends: Oct. Microform: UM. Reprint: AMS.

Indexed: CathI, RelAb, RelPer. *Bk. rev:* 35, 500–600 words, signed. *Aud:* Ac.

Publishes articles of a scientific and scholarly nature in scripture and in related fields (e.g., archeology, textual criticism, literary criticism, hermeneutics, Near Eastern history). There is nothing ponderous or old-fashioned about the scholarship of *CBQ*. It is widely used and highly respected in all circles of scriptural scholarship, Catholic and non-Catholic, American or European. Many of the articles are contributed by non-Catholic scholars. An extensive book review section is included, as well as a brief column of Biblical News.

Catholic Digest. 1936. m. $4. Kenneth Ryan. Catholic Publishing Center of the College of St. Thomas, Box 3090, St. Paul, Minn. 55165. Illus., adv. Circ: 625,000. Sample. Microform: UM.

Indexed: CathI. *Aud:* Ga.

A family-type magazine which is somewhat the equivalent of *Presbyterian Life,* but aimed directly at Catholics. As the title suggests, it lifts the "best" material from other publications—magazines, books, newspapers—which are not necessarily Catholic. The level of choice is relatively high, but the magazine avoids most controversial or sophisticated, challenging matters. It favors features on travel, hobbies, sports, health, education, and the like. Approximately one quarter is given over to religious affairs. A solid, pedestrian magazine for the less intellectually motivated Catholic community.

Catholic World. See *New Catholic World.*

Christian Herald. 1878. m. $6. Ford Stewart. Christian Herald Assn., 27 E. 39th St., New York, N.Y. 10016. Illus., adv. Circ: 300,000. Sample. Vol. ends: Dec.

Bk. rev: 8, 50–100 words, signed. *Aud:* Ga.

An interdenominational Protestant family magazine, this features six to eight major articles on current events, news, and general-interest religious and ethical questions. It includes daily devotional features and an editorial essay. Both photos and drawings are used, and the overall makeup is professional and appealing. As one of the oldest Christian magazines, it boasts a middle-of-the-road, yet realistic, approach to both religion and events. It should be in most medium-to-large libraries where religious material of this type is needed.

Christian News from Israel. 1949. q. $3. Yona Malachy. Ministry of Religious Affairs, Dept. for Information to Christians, 23 Shlomo Hamelech, Box 1167, Jerusalem, Israel. Illus., adv. Circ: 9,000. Sample.

Indexed: IJewAr. *Bk. rev:* 2–4, lengthy, signed. *Aud:* Ga, Ac.

Issued by the Department for Information to Christians of the Israeli Ministry of Religious Affairs, this presents news about non-Jewish communities in Israel and articles of interest to them. In the Chronicle of Events, the journal lists information about visits, celebrations, new buildings, appointments, and the relations of Christian communities with Israeli authorities and with foreign bodies. The articles deal with current problems of interest to the Christian communities ("Status of Jerusalem"), Biblical scholarship ("The Easter Cycle in the Light of Biblical Typology"), and archaeology ("St. Peter's House in Capernaum Rediscovered"). The articles are written by clerics and scholars of all faiths. *Christian News from Israel* is also published in French and Spanish. (R.T.)

Christianity and Crisis; a Christian journal of opinion. 1941. bi-w. $7. Wayne Cowan. 537 W. 12th St., New York, N.Y. 10027. Illus., index, adv. Circ: 11,500. Sample. Vol. ends: Jan. Microform: UM.

Indexed: RelPer. *Aud:* Ac, Ga. *Jv:* V.

One of the most respected Protestant periodicals. As the editor notes, it "explores the implications of Christian faith for the modern world and interprets the significance of 'secular' events for our Christian witness." The articles are clearly written in language an educated layman can understand, and usually number two or three in each issue. Many of the journal's editors are leaders in the Protestant church and the ecumenical movement, and the influence of the magazine goes beyond its subscribers. It should be found in any library where there is active interest in the full range of religious opinion.

Christianity Today. 1956. bi-w. $6. Harold Lindsell. 1014 Washington Blvd., Washington, D.C. 20005. Illus., index, adv. Circ: 130,000. Sample. Vol. ends: Sept. Microform: UM.

Indexed: PAIS, RG, RelAb, RelPer. *Bk. rev:* 5, 700 words, signed, and notes. *Aud:* Ga.

The basic conservative magazine for the Protestant. Material is staff written, highly readable, and precise. The editor submits the following description—which is accurate and fair enough: "A trans-denominational Protestant magazine which is for conservatives and evangelicals what *The Christian Century* is for liberals and those committed to the ecumenical movement.

Generally considered the most articulate, significant, and intellectual magazine of its type. Attempts comprehensive news and book coverage of the whole religious scene along with articles, editorials and columns on contemporary theological and ethical issues. Affirms Biblical authority but not in a hyper-literal way. To offer readers a balanced fare, should be in any library which receives the *Century*." Agreed!

Columbia; America's largest Catholic family magazine. 1921. m. $2. Elmer Von Feldt. Knights of Columbus, Columbus Plaza, New Haven, Conn. 06507. Illus., index, adv. Circ: 1,150,000.

Indexed: CathI. *Bk. rev:* Notes. *Aud:* Ga.

A middle-of-the-road to conservative approach to day-by-day activities of the average Catholic family. There is considerable emphasis, though, on the interests of the man who is more than likely to be a member of the sponsoring group, the Knights of Columbus. The editing is good; the material (which may run from a rather sentimental family story to a hard-hitting article on Catholic education) fair, and the level of interest for most readers high. Articles and regular departments deal with books, music, television, movies, and even legislative matters. The format is passable. The large circulation (all of which represents actual payments) indicates the magazine has wide acceptance among Catholic families. As such it should be considered by Catholic schools and libraries serving Catholics.

Critic; a Catholic review of books and the arts. 1942. bi-m. $6. Joel Wells, Thomas More Assn., 180 N. Wabash Ave., Chicago, Ill. 60601. Illus., adv. Circ: 31,000. Microform: UM.

Indexed: CathI. *Bk. rev:* 8–10, 900–1,700 words, signed. *Aud:* Ga, Ac. *Jv:* V.

One of the few liberal Catholic magazines that seems to have been able to weather economic storms. And it comes on stronger than ever. In both format and content it is an outstanding example of how some members of the church are attempting to find relevancy for themselves and their brothers and sisters. Although addressed to liberal Catholics, it has much broader social and cultural appeal. There are usually six to seven articles, a photo story, cartoons, and many illustrations. Writers are among the leading intellectuals (both Catholic and non-Catholic) from the United States and abroad. The book review section, which includes both long and short statements, is considered by many to be one of the best general sources for objective comments on new religious works. Now that *Jubilee* is no more, the *Critic* has a clear field. It is recommended for both the lay and religious collection, and if a Catholic magazine is to be chosen for its general interest, this is the one. (*America* and *Commonweal*, to be sure, but they serve different purposes.)

Dialogue; a journal of Mormon thought. 1965. q. $9. Robert A. Rees. Dialogue Foundation, 900 Hilgard Ave., Los Angeles, Calif. 90024. Circ: 5,000.

Aud: Ac.

Describes Mormon culture and the relating of the Mormon experience to everyday life. It is, as its editors say, a journal in which an exchange of opinion is invited on any subject with a bearing on Mormonism. A matter of note is that although *Dialogue* in general puts forward the Mormon viewpoint, it does so with an impartiality that must sometimes seem perilously close to apostasy to conservative-minded Latter-Day Saints. *Dialogue's* editors are determined to show that Mormonism can break out of the solemn stereotype it has acquired for itself over the years. In both content and presentation, this magazine is of enviably high quality.

Dimension; journal of pastoral concern. 1969. 3/yr. $5. Henry B. Degnan. St. Charles Seminary, Overbrook, Philadelphia, Pa. 19151. Index, adv. Circ: 900. Sample. Vol. ends: Winter.

Aud: Ac, Ga.

A Catholic journal which appeals to Protestant theological libraries, as well. Some issues are given over to special subjects, i.e., marriage and the church; but the average 64-page number is more general. Articles range from "The Priesthood and Professional Administration," to "The New Rite for Infant Baptism." The policy is to "avoid unrealistic idealism . . . and a polemicism destructive of the Church." Articles are well written, scholarly, and usually documented. For large theological collections.

Dimensions in American Judaism (Formerly: *American Judaism*). 1966. 2. $3. Myrna Pollak. Union of American-Hebrew Congregations, 838 Fifth Ave., New York, N.Y. 10021. Illus., adv. Circ: 227,000. Microform: UM.

Bk. rev: Various number, length. *Aud:* Ga.

A middle-of-the-road publication which features above average articles on all aspects of Judaism. There are good book reviews, and reports on art and drama. Although this in no way compares with the more intellectual, more universal *Commentary*, it has wide appeal for the average family. A must for any library serving a Jewish community.

Ecumenist. 1962. bi-m. Free. Gregory Baum and Kevin Lynch. Paulist Press, 304 W. 58th St., New York, N.Y. 10019. Circ: 22,000.

Bk. rev: 2, 200 words. *Aud:* Ac.

A Catholic journal for promoting Christian unity, this is broader in scope than the title implies. As the editor explains: "Since the ecumenical movement in the Christian Churches now focuses on social-religious issues—race, poverty, war, etc.—, it concerns itself with these." There are frequent articles on the Jewish–Christian dialogue, some ecumenical news notes, and all important documentation in the field. This last feature, coupled with the fact the magazine is free, makes it a highly desirable reference item for many libraries. In this same area, the World Council of Churches issues two good magazines: *Ecumenical Review* (1948. q. $6. 150 route de Ferney, 1211 Geneva 20, Switzerland) and the *Ecumenical Courier* (1941. q. Contributions. 475 Riverside Dr., New York, N.Y. 10027). Neither has quite the Catholic emphasis of the *Ecumenist*, but they are equally broad in coverage and interests.

Jewish Currents. 1946. m. (Sept.–June). $5. Morris U. Schappes. Jewish Currents Inc., 22 E. 17th St., Suite 601, New York, N.Y. 10003. Illus., index, adv. Circ: 4,500. Sample. Vol. ends: Dec.

Indexed: API. *Bk. rev:* 2–3, 1,000–1,200 words, signed. *Aud:* Ac, Ga.

Very much the work of its editor, this is an independent, liberal magazine geared for the Jewish community. Its 50 or so pocket-sized pages tend to stress politics: "The Middle East Crisis: Who is Responsible," the role of the Jew in the community: "Jewish Values and Social Crisis," as well as historical pieces, and some poetry. Regular features include: "Inside the Jewish Community," "Parent's Corner," and "The Editor's Diary." Topics of other than purely Jewish interest are considered too, e.g., the Attica prison riots, racial inequalities, and drug addiction. The style is lively, the material current, and the viewpoints original. A good choice for any library serving a Jewish clientele.

Jewish Spectator. 1935. m. $6. Trude Weiss-Rosmarin, 250 W. 57th St., New York, N.Y. 10019. Adv. Circ: 19,000. Sample. Vol. ends: Dec.

Bk. rev: 6, 1,000 words. *Aud:* Ac, Ga.

Unlike the better-known *Commentary*, this 32-page magazine is turned over almost entirely to problems and questions besetting Jews, e.g., "Blacks, Jews, and Violence," "How Not to Fight Anti-Semitism," and "Non-Jewish Jews." The articles are direct, well written, and of interest to both the Jew and the Gentile. Obviously, a consideration for the library serving any size Jewish community.

Lutheran; news magazine of the Lutheran Church in America. 1963. s-m. $3. G. Elson Ruff, 2900 Queen Lane, Philadelphia, Pa. 19129. Illus, index, adv. Circ: 570,000.

Bk. rev: Various number, length. *Aud:* Ga.

One of the major circulation general religious magazines, *Lutheran* has an attractive format and a professional approach to material. The articles are popularly written, and while not overly sophisticated, are nevertheless factual and based upon research rather than opinion. The magazine reports not only on the activities of the Lutheran Church, but on all major religious activities here and abroad. There are a number of profiles of prominent Lutherans and other Christians, and some articles on social issues. While the amount of controversy is limited, the magazine is a reliable source of one point of view on major religious issues. Not a choice for most libraries, but of importance because of its large following.

Midstream; a monthly Jewish review. 1955. m. $7. Shlomo Katz. Theodor Herzl Foundation, 515 Park Ave., New York, N.Y. 10024. Illus., index, adv. Circ: 11,000. Sample. Vol. ends: Dec.

Bk. rev: 4, 1,500–2,000 words, signed. *Aud:* Ac, Ga.

A Zionist publication devoted to "a questioning of the Jewish status quo, and a steady confrontation of the problems of Jewish existence." The emphasis is on the social-cultural scene. Although supported by the Theodor Herzl Foundation, the review is not an official organ of the foundation. In fact, it welcomes a wide range of thought and controversy. A typical 80-page issue includes five or six articles, poetry and sometimes fiction, interviews, and book reviews. Articles range from such things as the "Jewish Predicament in the Soviet Union," to an exchange between the editor and James Baldwin on Angela Davis. The orientation is scholarly, and the topics of primary concern to Jews. It will be of limited interest to others.

New Catholic World (Formerly: **Catholic World**). 1865. bi-m. $4.50. Robert Heyer. The World, 1865 Broadway, New York, N.Y. 10023. Subs. to: 400 Sette Dr., Paramus, N.J. 07652. Illus., index, adv. Circ: 15,000. Sample. Vol. ends: Nov./Dec. Microform: UM.

Indexed: CathI, RG. *Bk. rev:* 10, 250–500 words, signed. *Aud:* Ac, Ga.

"With the January/February 1972 issue we offer our readers the New Catholic World." So, one of the oldest religious journals of opinion moved in 1972 from a monthly to a bi-monthly. And it switched editorial policy from a general approach to a thematic one, e.g., the first issue focused on "Religious Education." Under the direction of the Paulist Fathers, the new journal is vitally concerned with "the real religious questions that people are asking and what can be said about them." In the education issue, for example, both sides of the problem of religious education are argued, such as the ultimate fate of Catholic Schools, as well as problems faced by those who support a pluralistic educational system. While every effort is made to make the magazine of interest to all Christians, the primary focus remains Catholic.

New Scholasticism. 1926. q. $8. John A. Oesterle. Amer. Catholic Philosophical Assn., Catholic Univ. of America, Washington, D.C. 20017. Circ: 2,500. Microform: UM. Reprint: Johnson.

Indexed: CathI, PhilosI, PsyAb. *Bk. rev:* 10, 1,200 words, signed. *Aud:* Sa, Ac, Jc.

A journal of wide philosophic interest. Articles, by professional philosophers, are concerned with the clarification and solution of contemporary issues as well as historical investigation of the philosophic systems of former metaphysicians. Since the articles are well written and usually nontechnical, this periodical can be enjoyed by the educated layman as well as the college student working in the field of philosophy. Of special interest to those concerned with the progress of Roman Catholic neorealism.

One Church. 1947. bi-m. $4. Rev. Photius Donahue. Patriarchate of Moscow in the United States. 15 E. 97th St., New York, N.Y. 10029. Illus., index, adv. Circ: 1,200. Sample.

Index: RelPer. *Bk. rev:* 2–3, 500 words, signed. *Aud:* Ac.

Admittedly, this 50-page, well-printed journal is fairly esoteric—primarily directed to the Russian Orthodox Church members—but it serves as an example of a number of such periodicals which are often overlooked by librarians. In that it fairly represents a point of view not often found in other magazines, it deserves a place in any large religious collection. Along with other better denominational publications, it also has some place in the public and college library serving communities of like persuasion.

The Orthodox Word. 1969. bi-m. $4. Eugene Rose and Gleb Podmoshensky. Orthodox Christian Books & Icons, Platina, Calif. 96076. Illus., index. Circ: 1,500.

Indexed: RelPer. *Aud:* Ga.

A voice of the Holy Orthodox Church, primarily in accordance with the Russian tradition, this is a hand-printed 40-page little magazine. "Little" is used advisedly, because as in the literary genre, it represents a minority group with what they believe to be an important message. A normal issue includes four or five articles, as well as a four-page insert of a translation of "The spiritual instructions to laymen and monks." The format is good, the contents of interest to those of the faith and to younger people exploring the area of religious belief.

The Plain Truth. 1934. m. Free. A. A. Ferdig. Ambassador College, Box 111, Pasadena, Calif. 91109. Circ: 2,000,000.

Aud: Ga.

According to the publisher this is a nonsubsidized "world news magazine not controlled by any commercial powers, interests, organizations or forces." However, it is issued from Ambassador College, which places considerable emphasis on Biblical fundamentalism. It is a good example of a religious voice which takes free swings at Communism, Fascism and, to a degree, Western decadence. Again, according to the editor, the *Plain Truth* "speaks authoritatively—certainly—spiritually. These are opposite approaches to knowledge—opposite goals. Its articles on news, education and social, religious, or scientific issues, bring into focus the real issues facing the world today." A fascinating case of a dedicated religious group which gives an interesting view of world affairs.

Presbyterian Life. 1948. m. $3.50. Robert J. Cadigan. United Presbyterian Church, Witherspoon Bldg., Philadelphia, Pa. 19107. Illus., index, adv. Circ: 610,000. Sample.

Bk. rev: 2, 800 words, signed. *Aud:* Ga.

Claiming to be the "nation's largest church affairs magazine," this is family centered. It appeals to the group not touched by more sophisticated magazines such as *Christian Century*. Nevertheless, the content and the style are unpretentious and the format quite professional. It covers topics usually covered by a general magazine: current events, history, music, recreation, home, literature, and, of course, theology. It avoids emotionalism, features semipopular writers, and is middle-of-the-road in social and political affairs. While published specifically for Presbyterians, it will appeal to most Protestants.

Religious Education; a platform for the free discussion of issues in the field of religion and their bearing on education. 1906. bi-m. $12.50 (Members, free). R. C. Miller. Religious Education Assn., 545 W. 111th St., New York, N.Y. 10025. Index, adv. Circ: 5,000. Microform: UM. Reprint: AMS.

Indexed: CIJE, EdI, CathI, PsyAb, RelAb. *Bk. rev:* Various number, length. *Aud:* Ac, Hs, Ejh.

As the subtitle suggests, this is a nondenominational approach to all problems in religious education, at all levels from elementary school through graduate studies. Articles represent many viewpoints and faiths and cover the teaching of religion, history, and various aspects of religion and society. What it comes down to is an interdisciplinary journal which has appeal to any teacher or educator. (Although it touches all grades, most emphasis is at the university and college level.) A useful feature: abstracts of doctoral disserations in the field.

Response; a contemporary Jewish review. 1967. q. $5 (Students, $4). Bill Novak, Brandeis Univ., 415 South St., Waltham, Mass. 02154. Illus. Circ: 5,000.

Aud: Ac, Ga, Hs.

Edited by a group of young Jews at Brandeis University, this is a literary, political, social, and a somewhat religious quarterly of 130 or so pages. The drive is toward a new, viable way of life for the young, and most numbers are concerned with questions about the arts, from film and theater, to poetry and fiction, to a special issue (Winter 1970–71) devoted to a frank discussion of traditional Jewish belief as understood and applied by today's young. This is very much an ethnic magazine, with primary concern for the Jewish way of life. Because of what must seem revolutionary approaches to older Jews, it is controversial. Should be in any library serving a Jewish population, but will be of some interest to all youth.

Theology Digest. 1953. q. $5. Gerald Van Ackern. St. Louis Univ., School of Divinity, St. Louis, Mo. 63103. Index, adv. Circ: 9,860. Sample. Vol. ends: no. 4. Microform: UM.

Indexed: CathI. *Bk. rev:* 300, 75 words, signed. *Aud:* Ga, Ac.

A Catholic journal directed to well-educated people, both clergy and laity, who are interested in following international trends in scripture study, theology, and religious education. Most of the digested articles come from abroad—Germany, France, Holland, Spain, and so forth—and represent the more significant scriptural, theological, and religious studies of our times. Each issue also carries an annotated book survey which tries to include *all* of the important religious books published in the United States, whether Catholic or non-Catholic. For the nonreligiously oriented student as well, the magazine has much to offer. A good publication for all medium to large libraries seeking a cross section of current religious writings.

Thought. 1926. q. $8.00. Joseph E. O'Neill. Fordham Univ. Press. 441 E. Fordham Rd., Bronx, N.Y. 10458. Illus., index, adv. Circ: 2,300. Sample. Vol. ends: Winter. Reprint: AMS. Microform: UM.

Indexed: CathI, PhilosI, SSHum. *Bk. rev:* 24–30, 600 words, signed. *Aud:* Ga, Ac.

An eclectic Catholic journal of the humanities, this covers the fields of literary criticism, current political affairs, and history. The papers are scholarly, but eminently readable. The numerous, recent book reviews are from a wide variety of fields such as literature, the arts, theology, religion, philosophy, and history. Division of the reviews into subject sections facilitates use. Because of its many articles relating to such subjects as Catholic reform, religion and secular life, and ecumenism, *Thought* should prove of special interest to educated laymen of all faiths.

The Upper Room. 1935. bi-m. $1.50. Wilson O. Weldon, 1908 Grand Ave., Nashville, Tenn. 37203. Illus. Circ: 2,600,000. Sample.

Aud: Ga.

Enjoying the single largest circulation of any Protestant interdenominational, evangelical religious publication in the United States, this is also published in 39 languages with 47 editions. Quite rightfully it claims to be "Interracial, interdenominational, and international." The scope and purpose is direct—for each day of the month there is an appropriate scripture reading suggested, a scripture verse, and a meditation and prayer. Advertising is limited to only those devotional books published by *The Upper Room* devotional department. *The Upper Room* should offend no one and certainly would be of value to the average reader who may have only a passing interest in either theology or religion, but who seeks comfort from the Bible. Particularly suited for the elderly and the not over sophisticated reader.

Watchtower. See *Awake.*

World Order. 1966. q. $3.50. Ed. bd. 112 Linden Ave., Wilmette, Ill. 60091. Circ: 4,000.

Aud: Ga.

The voice of the Baha'i faith, a combination of religion, philosophy, and humanism which has captured the imagination of many. The magazine has a message, presents it in an intelligent fashion, and leaves it to the reader to reach his own decisions.

Secular

The American Rationalist; an independent journal of news and views for all rationalists, humanists, freethinkers. 1956. bi-m. $4.50. Walter Hoops. 5437 Enright, St. Louis, Mo. 63112. Illus., adv. Circ: 1,000. Sample. Vol. ends: March/April.

Bk. rev: 4–5, 250–500 words, signed. *Aud:* Ac, Ga.

"I would have a man virtuous without heaven and hell." This quote is carried on the cover of each issue, and Pierre Charron's statement pretty well sums up the purpose and content of an average 20-page number. Such articles as "Why I am not a Christian" (Bertrand Russell), "An Atheist Response," and "Students, Wars and Superstitious Beliefs," indicate the editor's primary concern with a rational, nonreligious view of the world. The writing is clear, the style lucid, the argument cogent. In addition, there are letters and short notes about various activities of humanists, freethinkers and rationalists, not to mention responses from those with opposing ideas. A well-rounded, nicely balanced magazine which should be considered for any library where all viewpoints are eagerly sought.

American Report; review of religion and American power. 1970. w. $7. Robert Lecky. Astoria Press, Inc., 435 Hudson St., New York, N.Y. 10014. Illus. Sample.

Aud: Ac, Ga.

An eight-page tabloid newspaper issued by "Clergy and Laymen Concerned," a group fighting war, social injustice, and racial intolerance. Writers represent all denominations and faiths, but no political persuasion.

The brief reports, letters, and articles are written by laymen, clergy, and professional reporters. The weekly schedule allows for a given amount of timeliness, and the items suggest an approach to the news not found in many American newspapers. One of the better, more objective, liberal religiously oriented dissident papers.

Church & State. 1947. m. $5. (Students, $1.50). C. Stanley Lowell. Americans United, 8120 Fenton St., Silver Spring, Md., 20910. Illus. index. Circ: 104,000. Sample. Vol. ends: Dec.

Bk. rev: 2, 500 words. *Aud:* Ac, Ga.

Dedicated to the proposition that state and church should be separate, the editor and contributors report on any event, legislation, or activity which may threaten the separation. The result is a lively 24-page magazine made up primarily of short news items, and one or two general articles. The group stands for taxing churches, spreading the word about birth control, eliminating support of church schools, etc. Readers who are in basic agreement or are neutral will find little objection to anything here, but others will howl. At any rate, the information is accurate, and of considerable help for situations where material is needed on a growing controversial subject.

Freethinker; the secular humanist weekly. 1881. w. $6.25. William McIlroy, G. W. Foote & Co. Ltd., 103 Borough High Street, London, SE1, England. Illus. index. Sample. Vol. ends: Dec.

Bk. rev: 2–3, 1,000 words, signed. *Aud:* Ac, Ga.

Libraries which wish to represent a counter view to traditional religion—as represented by such terms as "humanist," "agnostic," "secular," or "freethought" —should consider this 90-year-old magazine. (The two best known in this field are *The Humanist*, published under the same title in America and England, but two distinct magazines.) Compared to the others, which have become relatively glossy, almost general interest productions (which is not, however, to put them down), the *Freethinker*, in eight rarely illustrated, letterpress pages, concentrates steadfastly on traditional, yet continuingly relevant secular concerns, and does so with much wit and might. Well nourished on Voltaire, Tom Paine, Ingersol, and Bertrand Russell, contributors tend to be libertarian as well as rationalist. Recognizing the massive ecological and social challenges facing mankind, they seek "to direct attention away from dogma and hysteria . . . towards a concerned and reasoned approach based on the best available knowledge." No surprise, then, that they come down hard on every major and minor religion, metaphysics, and all other supernatural-rooted creeds or worldviews, regarding them as intellect-trussers, barriers to rational debate and action. They are no less severe with Victorian morality and Bible-spawned inhibitions such as personal liberty and relationships with elitists, narrow-minded canons of taste and conduct. (S.B.)

The Humanist; a journal of humanist and ethical concern. 1941. bi-m. $6. Paul Kurtz. The Humanist, 923 Kensington Ave., Buffalo, N.Y. 14215. Illus. adv. Circ: 28,000. Sample. Vol. ends: Nov./Dec.

Bk. rev: 3–4, 1,000 words, signed. *Aud:* Ac, Ga.

A substantial, 50-page magazine which "attempts to serve as a bridge between theoretical philosophical discussions and the practical applications of humanism to ethical and social problems." Alternate issues zero in on a central theme, one which is of interest to almost any reader, regardless of his or her feeling about humanism. Writing on "Psychology and Humanism," are such regular contributors as Sidney Hook, Noam Chomsky, Julius Novick, Corliss Lamont, and others. Leslie Fiedler, Jacques Barzun, and A. H. Maslow were among those commenting on the question "Does the University Have a Future?" in another issue. Given this type of contributor, the magazine offers an unusually high quality of reading matter for the educated layman as well as the professional. One might disagree with the humanist viewpoint, but no one can take exception to the intellectual, well-reasoned approach to today's questions which the editor so successfully considers. It all adds up to an excellent general magazine for most libraries.

Progressive World. 1945. m. $4.50. Catherine Sears. United Secularists of America, 377 Vernon St., Oakland, Calif. 94610. Circ: 2,000. Sample. Vol. ends: Feb.

Aud: Ac, Ga.

A pocket-sized, 50-page magazine whose purpose is to: "uphold the right of every person to freedom of thought, of inquiry, and of expression . . . to advance science rather than religious tradition. . . ." There are no political overtones: "our organization in non-partisan, and stands for the full Constitutional and civil rights of all citizens." Editorials, about three or five short articles, letters, and news notes make up each issue. The writers discuss everything from organized religion to economics and social problems, and usually with a given amount of objectivity, not to mention conviction. The writing style is a trifle uneven, but there is a nice balance of humor. The total impression is of a magazine particularly suited for the average free thinker who may want emotional support, rather than the somewhat more involved intellectual exercises found in such titles as *The Humanist* or *The American Rationalist.*

Counterculture

The Catholic Agitator. 1971. m. 50¢/10 mos. Ammom Hennacy House of Hospitality, 605 N. Cummings St., Los Angeles, Calif. 90033. Illus. Sample.

Aud: Ac, Ga.

A 12-page newspaper issued by a Catholic Worker community, this joins the ranks of activist Catholic magazines and papers. The sponsoring organization's masthead indicates its purpose, i.e., it gives draft counseling and sanctuary, offers information on tax resistance, and calls for ending the war and feeding the poor—radical, indeed. The paper is professionally put together, considers subjects of interest to anyone involved with change, Catholic or not. The issue examined was primarily devoted to testimony of Vietnam Veterans Against the War. In view of the modest price, it can be suggested for libraries not frightened by the censor.

Catholic Worker. 1939. m. (Sept.–June, bi-m.). 25¢. Dorothy Day, 36 E. First Street, New York, N.Y. 10003. Illus. Circ: 85,000. Sample.

Indexed: API, CathI. *Aud:* Ga, Ac.

An 8-page tabloid newspaper which preaches a peaceful revolution of Christian communism akin to many conceptions of the early church. It is not supported by the Church, but is the voice of a radical political offshoot of the Church. It is anti-Vietnam, problack, and has a long history of interest in migrant workers' problems. It is often interesting and has frequent striking woodcuts. However, it has little detail that is not available from many other sources. Its major interest is as an example of a particular genre of political/moral thought.

The Catonsville Roadrunner. 1969. m. $5. Janette Hammender. 138 Mayall Rd., London, SE24, England. Illus. index, adv. Circ: 3,000. Sample.

Bk. rev: 1, ½–1 page, signed. *Aud:* Ga, Ac.

Subtitled "Monthly Jesus Show" and "Revolutionary Christian Monthly," this is a nondenominational approach to changes in religion, and while published in England, it should have wide appeal anywhere. The average issue is primarily devoted to short news items about radical Christianity throughout the world; there are also a long sermon-article, plenty of discussion and polemics, and good cartoons.

EPF Newsletter. 6/yr. Free. Episcopal Peace Fellowship. 300 Ninth Ave., New York, N.Y. 10001. Illus. Circ: 4,000.

Aud: Ac, Ga.

A four to eight page tabloid which reports on activities of the Episcopal-based peace effort. Articles discuss past and pending actions, review the status of "Episcopal prisoners of conscience," i.e., those in jail for refusing induction, and consider various aspects of draft resistance. Of value to anyone who is sympathetic with the peace movement.

JSAC Grapevine. 1969. 10/yr. Free. Trudi Klijn. 475 Riverside Dr., Rm. 1700A, New York, N.Y. 10027. Illus. Circ: 10,500. Vol. ends: May.

Aud: Ac, Ga.

A four to six page newsletter published by a coalition of the "national mission" agencies of the major Protestant denominations. Each number is devoted to a given topic, e.g., "Gay Liberation and the Church," "Public Education in Trouble," "A New Area for Mission Investment Policies." The latter examines holdings of major Protestant churches and how those holdings are helping the war effort, or assisting to sustain racial inequality. (Among favorite companies of church groups are IBM, General Motors, General Electric, Standard Oil NJ.) Of particular help to librarians is a closing feature, "Some Resources," which lists books, pamphlets, and even individuals to contact about the issue discussed. The tone is liberal, the information appears accurate, and the whole is another dimension to the role of religion in social and political dissent.

Katallagete; Be Reconciled; journal of the committee of southern churchmen. 1965. q. $5 (Individuals, $2). Committee of Southern Churchmen, Inc., Box 12044, Nashville, Tenn. 37212. Illus. Circ: 10,000. Sample. Vol. ends: no. 4.

Aud: Ac, Ga, Hs.

Fighting against institutionalized religion, the Protestant sponsors come out for a liberal South. "We suggest that the real cop-outs today may be those who worship in zeal and dedication their institutions." The Winter 1971 issue featured an article by Robert Sherrill on freedom of the press, and in previous numbers Christopher Lasch, Julius Lester, and Walker Percy have appeared. The 36 to 60 page well-printed, often illustrated magazine isn't going to have appeal for the followers of Billy Graham—who is attacked with scripture in one issue—but it will have wide appeal for the liberal intellectual, religious or not, southern or not. It is a bit of a sleeper which deserves much wider attention. The social and moral issues are considered more important than any dogma, and the editor and contributors are first rate minds working for meaningful change.

National Catholic Reporter. 1964. w. $12. Donald J. Thorman. National Catholic Reporter Publishing Co., P.O. Box 281, Kansas City, Mo. 64141. Illus., adv. Circ: 50,000. Sample. Vol. ends: Oct.

Bk. rev: 4, 600 words, signed. *Aud:* Ga, Ac. *Jv:* V.

One of the most lively, controversial Catholic magazines, in newspaper format, and often referred to as a newspaper. Edited by Catholic laymen (it has no official connection with the Church), the appeal is to the educated readers of almost any faith. Coverage is by no means completely religiously oriented, and articles and stories move from civil rights and Vietnam to humor and cartoons by Jules Feiffer. As a public forum for radical views on birth control, priestly celiba-

cy, and other church issues, the magazine has earned a place for itself among all those attempting to reform society in general, and the Church in particular. Articles are by staff members, leading laymen, and church leaders from all faiths. The style is semipopular, similar to what is associated with such lay journals as the *New Republic* or *The Nation.* It has an added value for libraries—a page or more of book reviews in each issue. The short reviews cover about 40 percent religious books, 60 percent general titles. There are also lists of titles and news about publishing. An outstanding religious, socially oriented magazine for most general and academic collections.

SCIENCE

Basic Periodicals

Hs: *Scientific American, Natural History, Science News* (see also *School Science and Mathematics* in Education Section); Ga: *Scientific American, Natural History, Science News;* Jc: *Scientific American, Science, Nature;* Ac: *Scientific American, Nature, Science, Endeavor, American Scientist, New Scientist.*

Introduction

Grouped in this section are publications which encompass more than one branch of science or technology. Periodicals range from scholarly journals, which publish research accounts and reviews in both the physical and biological sciences, to some very popular magazines, which interpret the latest developments in these areas.

The Fall 1968 issue of *RQ* contained a basic list of 37 nonspecialist periodicals interpreting scientific progress to laymen. Many of these titles which are still in print appear in this section and in the other more specialized chapters of this book.

Academie des Sciences; comptes rendus hebdomadaires des seances. 1835. w. $400. Gauthier Villars, 55 Quai des Grands Augustins, Paris, France. Illus., index. Circ: 3,100. Vol. ends: irreg. Refereed. Microform: PMC, MF.

Indexed: BioAb, ChemAb, EngI, IMed, MathR, Met& GeoAb, SciAb, SCI. *Aud:* Sa, Ac.

Comptes Rendus, an outgrowth of earlier publications of the famed Academy of Sciences of Paris, established in 1666, is one of the pioneers of the scholarly, general science journals. Its influence on the early development of science should not be minimized. Today, all branches of the physical and natural sciences are represented by fairly short research reports. The journal is issued in three parts, each of which may be purchased separately. *Sections A and B* (one part) include papers on pure and applied mathematics, and celestial mechanics, as well as the mathematics of physics, geography, and navigation. Theoretical and experimental studies in physics also comprise astrophysics and geophysics. *Section C* covers the chemical sciences (analytical, inorganic, organic and physical). *Section D* is dedicated to all branches of the biological sciences, medicine, geology, paleontology, and mineralogy. Very short notices and news of the Academy are also reported. An important journal for large, academic libraries or for collections with strong research interests.

Akademiya Nauk SSSR. Doklady. 1933. 36/yr. $115.20. A. I. Oparin. Podsosenski Per. 21, Moscow K-62, USSR. Illus., index. Circ: 5,500. Vol. ends: 6v./yr. Refereed.

Indexed: BioAb, ChemAb, MathR, MetAb, Met& GeoAb, PsyAb, SciAb. *Aud:* Sa, Ac.

The *Doklady* are the Proceedings of the Academy of Sciences of the USSR, the most prestigious scientific organization in the Soviet Union. Issued three times each month, every 10 days, *Doklady* publishes in every branch of science supported by the Academy, including the mathematical, physical, and natural sciences. Papers, in Russian, are generally short (three to four pages) and are, as a rule, important reports of research which may subsequently be amplified in other specialized journals, such as in a number of their *Izvestiya* (Bulletins). Studies are of high quality and widely cited. (In a recent study done by *Chemical Abstracts*, *Doklady* ranked fifth in the 1,000 most frequently cited journals covered by *CA.*) Tables of contents of each issue are available in English translation. Of course, only large academic libraries will subscribe to the original. However, several professional societies and commercial outfits have provided translations of selected sections of *Doklady* (e.g., *Doklady Physical Chemistry, Doklady Botanical Sciences*) and undoubtedly many university libraries or research-oriented institutions will subscribe to these translations, depending on their specialized needs.

American Philosophical Society. Proceedings. 1838. bi-m. $5. George W. Corner. Amer. Philosophical Soc., 104 S. 5th St., Philadelphia, Pa. 19106. Circ: 1,200. Microform: Canner, UM. Reprint: Kraus.

Indexed: BioAb, ChemAb. *Aud:* Ac, Ga. *Jv:* V.

Despite the title and sponsor, this comes closer to being a general interest magazine than a specialist's journal. Articles cover every aspect of philosophy and the humanities, but always in its widest context. Hence, there will be contributions ranging from a discussion of current scientific ethical problems to social history. And while the writing is scholarly, it is written with a touch of style familiar to readers of such publications as *Scientific American* and *The American Scholar*. The magazine deserves a much wider audience, and should be found in more stimulating general

reading collections in all academic libraries and large public library collections.

The American Philosophical Society also publishes *Transactions of the American Philosophical Society* (5–10 yr. $15), which follows the same general approach, yet tends to limit itself to a single monograph of interest. Sometimes the subjects are a bit esoteric, but because there are enough of wider appeal, it too deserves attention by the same libraries which would consider the *Proceedings*. (B.K.)

American Scientist. 1912. bi-m. $9. Caryl Haskins. 155 Whitney Ave., New Haven, Conn. 06510. Illus., index, adv. Circ: 130,000. Sample. Vol. ends: no. 6. Refereed.

Indexed: ASTI, BioAb, ChemAb, EngI, IMed, PsyAb, SCI. *Bk. rev:* 50–100, 300 words, signed. *Aud:* Sa, Ac.

Published jointly by Sigma Xi, the national honorary science fraternity, and RESA (Scientific Research Society of America), its industrial affiliate, the journal is an excellent, broad-based, general science periodical. Articles run the gamut of the physical, natural, and behavioral sciences, from engineering and the applied sciences to the philosophy and history of science. Papers generally represent reviews or views of recently developed research of wide interest. Titles such as "Conservation Comes of Age," and "Scientists and their Dreams," are typical. Contributors are all leading authorities of the scientific community; frequently articles may be reprints by distinguished scholars of addresses presented at national meetings of the Society or other noteworthy organizations. The lengthy book review section includes some of the best, most authoritative reviews available to librarians. In addition, a long list of "Books Received for Review," representing a wide selection of publishers, can serve as a good checklist for new material. Brief news of Sigma Xi and RESA are also included. The periodical belongs in every academic library, as well as large public libraries.

Applied Science and Technology Index. See Abstracts and Indexes Section.

British Journal for the Philosophy of Science. See Philosophy Section.

Bulletin of the Atomic Scientists. See News and Opinion Magazines/Political Opinion Reviews Section.

Endeavour. 1942. 3/yr. Free. T. I. Williams. Imperial Chemical Industries, Ltd., Millbank, London, SW1, England. Illus., index. Sample. Vol. ends: no. 3. Refereed.

Indexed: BioAb, BritTechI, ChemAb, EngI, PsyAb, SciAb, SCI. *Bk. rev:* 20, 200 words, signed. *Aud:* Sa, Ga, Ac, Hs.

The producers of this fine, company-sponsored periodical intend to record and "review the progress of science," and indeed, they have achieved just this over the past 30 years. They count some 30 Nobel Laureates among their distinguished contributors; they cover all the sciences, including the behavioral; and their articles are geared to nearly every type of audience in terms of interest and level of sophistication. Essays may be historical or biographical, may survey an entire field, or may simply be limited to a highly specialized research review. A good balance between the different disciplines is maintained in each issue. Articles are fairly short and often elegantly illustrated, frequently with colored plates. Subjects are selected on the basis of timeliness and importance in today's research; moreover, the scope is not limited to British science. The publication is also published in French, Spanish, and German editions. Highly recommended for all libraries.

Experientia. 1945. m. $48.80. Ed. bd. Birkhauser Verlag, 4010 Basel, Elisabethenstrasse 19, Switzerland. Illus., index, adv. Sample. Vol. ends: no. 12. Refereed.

Indexed: BioAb, ChemAb, SciAb, MetAb, SCI. *Aud:* Sa, Ac.

An international research journal of "pure and applied science." Noted for its short reports, the periodical, although purportedly a general science journal, is almost exclusively dedicated to the biological sciences. Papers discuss areas of biochemistry and biophysics, physiology, pharmacology, anatomy, embryology, immunology, endocrinology, genetics, and microbiology. Text may be in English, French, German, Italian, Russian, or Spanish; translated abstracts are provided. Special supplements, issued from time to time, and sold separately, are an important feature of this journal. For academic libraries with a strong biological orientation.

Franklin Institute. Journal. 1826. m. $50. M. A. Pomerantz. Franklin Inst. Subs. to: Pergamon Pr., Maxwell House, Fairview Pk., Elmsford, N.Y. 10523. Illus., index. Circ: 3,200. Sample. Vol. ends: Dec. Refereed. Microform: MR, PMC, MF. Reprint: Kraus, MR.

Indexed: ASTI, BioAb, ChemAb, EngI, MathR, SciAb, SCI. *Bk. rev:* 10, 350 words, signed. *Aud:* Sa, Ac.

Formerly *The Franklin Journal*, this is the second oldest general science journal published in the U.S. The research papers and short communications in this periodical "devoted to science and the mechanic arts" span the entire spectrum of physical sciences, although the focus is on the engineering sciences. A well-known, prestigious, and authoritative journal, particularly for engineering collections.

Government Reports Announcement. See Abstracts and Indexes Section.

IBM Journal of Research and Development. 1957. bi-m. $7.50. R. J. Joenk. Intl. Business Machines Corp.,

Armonk, N.Y. 10504. Illus., index. Sample. Vol. ends: no. 6 (Nov.). Refereed. Microform: UM.

Indexed: BioAb, ChemAb, EngI, MathR, PsyAb, SciAb, SCI. *Aud:* Sa, Ac.

Sponsor of some of the world's important basic and applied research, the IBM Corporation produces its own journal to describe a part of the original work performed by their scientists and engineers. Included within the scope of the periodical have been papers on chemistry, physics, mathematics, engineering, the computing sciences, psychological reports, and applications to the biological sciences. Papers frequently center around a specific topic or one product of the firm. Contributions include both lengthy research papers and a few one to two-page communications. Titles of articles by IBM authors appearing elsewhere in the literature are also included, as are lists of recent IBM patents. Particularly valuable for any collection in the computing sciences, the journal is recommended for every academic library.

ISIS. 1913. q. $12. Robert P. Multhauf. History of Science Soc. Subs. to: NLAP Co., 11420 Old Baltimore Pike, Beltsville, Md. 20705. Illus., index. Circ: 2,000. Vol. ends: no. 4 (Dec.). Refereed. Microform: Canner, UM. Reprint: Johnson.

Indexed: BioAb, ChemAb, EngI, HistAb, MathR, SSHum. *Bk. rev:* 6, 300–500 words, signed. *Aud:* Sa, Ac.

Founded by the eminent science historian, George Sarton. Long essays and short, two to three-page research notes represent authoritative, scholarly studies on any aspect of the history of science and "its cultural influences." There are no particular limitations in terms of era, or special point of view covered, and studies range from prehistory to the contemporary scene. All branches of the physical and natural sciences and technology are explored; also included are works on institutions, instruments, etc. The publication is the official journal of the learned History of Science Society, and a section of each issue is also given to accounts of research in progress, acquisition of manuscripts, news, notes, and correspondence. Excellent book reviews take up a good portion of each issue as well. An important, separate "Critical Bibliography," part of the subscription price, is also issued annually. The leading journal in this field for any academic library. (See also *Technology and Culture*, for the history of technology.)

There are a number of other journals also dealing with the history of science, which are authoritative and valuable additions for academic collections: *Annals of Science*, which deals with history since the Renaissance; *British Journal for the History of Science*, a publication of the British Society for the History of Science, and *Studies in History and Philosophy of Science*, recently published by Macmillan.

Journal of College Science Teaching. 1971. q. $10. Leo Schubert. National Science Teachers Assn., 1201 16th St., N.W., Washington, D.C. 20036. Illus., index, adv. Sample. Vol. ends: April. Refereed.

Bk. rev: 5, 100–400 words, signed. *Aud:* Sa, Ac.

Publishers also of *Science Teacher,* the National Science Teachers Association now focus their interest on the college scene. From a review of the first volume, it would seem to be a valuable medium for drawing together articles hitherto published in discipline-oriented specialty journals. The main emphasis in the publication is on teaching and on the first two years of college, for nonscience majors in particular. Feature articles, including some invited papers, not only stress enrichment in the classroom and laboratory, but approach relevant historical and philosophical problems as well. Multidisciplinary, the journal is concerned with all the sciences; pertinent abstracts from papers appearing in the chemical, geological, and biological literature on this subject are included. National and legislative news, laboratory innovations, and new products and equipment, are all treated in separate departments. An important journal for any academic library concerned with the quality of its undergraduate education.

Journal of Irreproducible Results. See Humor Section.

Journal of Research in Science Teaching. 1963. q. $10. O. Roger Anderson. John Wiley & Sons, 605 Third Ave., New York, N.Y. 10016. Illus., index. Sample. Vol. ends: No. 4. Refereed.

Bk. rev: 2, 500 words, signed. *Aud:* Sa, Ac.

Sponsored by two organizations dedicated to improving education programs for science teachers, namely the National Association for Research in Science Teaching, and the Association for the Education of Teachers in Science. The journal serves as a forum for papers concerned with research investigations on teaching strategy, effectiveness of science teachers, characteristics of science students, etc. Many of the articles are based on authors' doctoral dissertations. All levels of education are considered, elementary through college and all branches of science and mathematics are covered. Since its orientation is based on research, a publication such as *School Science and Mathematics* offers the teacher more day-to-day classroom help. However, academic libraries concerned with teacher education programs will probably need it.

Minerva; a review of science learning and policy. 1962. $5. q. Edward Shils. 135 Oxford St., London W.1. Adv. Circ: 1,700. Vol. ends: No. 4.

Indexed: PAIS. *Bk. rev:* 2–3 long review articles, signed. *Aud:* Sa, Ac, Jc.

A solidly based attempt to provide discussion and debate on topics relevant to the theory and practice of the application of knowledge. It has some of the best intellectual backing of any journal. *Minerva's* concerns are many, ranging from education and the concerned academic community to underdeveloped countries and the implications of government sponsorship of research. Each issue has 3–8 articles, sections on various documents and reports, correspondence, and a chronicle of relevant current events. Mandatory for college and university libraries; and excellent for public libraries.

Mosaic. 1970. q. $2.50. Bruce Abell. Supt. of Documents, U.S. Govt. Printing Office, Washington, D.C. 20550. Illus. Vol. ends: no. 4.

Aud: Sa, Ga, Ac.

Publicizes the research being conducted under the sponsorship of the National Science Foundation. Written in popular language, the periodical explores themes of wide interest to a general audience, particularly those embracing current problems of our society (e.g., the State University of New York at Stony Brook and its garbage disposal program; Cornell's Science, Technology, and Society seminars). Articles concentrate on personalities, and the tone is chatty and informal. Also included are a few NSF notes, and the breakdown of the NSF budget. For any library interested in NSF efforts.

National Academy of Sciences. Proceedings. 1915. m. $35. Jerold A. Last. National Academy of Sciences, 2101 Constitution Ave., N.W., Washington, D.C. 20418. Illus., index. Circ: 8,600. Vol. ends: Dec. Refereed. Microform: UM, Canner, PMC. Reprint: Johnson.

Indexed: BioAb, ChemAb, EngI, IMed, MathR, MetAb, SciAb, SCI. *Aud:* Sa, Ac.

The most prestigious U.S. organization to which a scientist can be elected is our National Academy of Sciences. Their *Proceedings* does not fully reflect the scope of this august group, however. Although purportedly containing papers in all the sciences, only a small representation from the physical sciences (astronomy, chemistry, mathematics, and physics) appears in each issue, and the major portion of the journal is devoted to the biological sciences. Within the realm of the biological sciences, the immunologists and molecular biologists have virtually taken over. Contributions to the journal can only be made by, or through, a member of the Academy. Thus, papers submitted by members are not refereed, although submissions by nonmembers undergo the appropriate scrutiny. An authoritative publication and a very prominent one for the biological sciences.

Natural History (Incorporating *Nature Magazine*). 1900. m. (Oct.-May); bi-m. (June-Sept.). $8. Alfred Meyer. Amer. Museum of Natural History, 79th St. &

Central Park West, New York, N.Y. 10024. Illus., adv. Circ: 190,000. Vol. ends: No. 4. Microform: UM.

Indexed: BioAb, RG. *Bk. rev:* 1 essay, 1,000 words, signed; 1–2, 200 words, signed. *Aud:* Ga, Hs, Ac, Jc. *Jv:* V.

Issued by the American Museum of Natural History, this is a popular approach to conservation, anthropology, geography, astronomy—in fact, almost anything of interest to the nature lover. Although the style is semi-popular, the articles are authoritative, and are written by experts who have the facility for being as lucid as they are intelligent. Outstanding photographs give this added value for lower grades. An exceptional magazine for almost all libraries.

Nature. 1869. w. $48. (all 3 editions, Mon., Wed., and Fri., $108). J. Maddox. Macmillan Journals, Ltd., Little Essex St., London WC2R 3LF, England. Illus., index, adv. Sample. Circ: 16,000. Refereed. Microform: UM, MF, PMC. Reprint: Johnson.

Indexed: BioAb, BritTech, ChemAb, EngI, IMed, MathR, Met&GeoAb, PsyAb, SciAb, SCI. *Bk. rev:* 10–15, 300–500 words, signed. *Aud:* Sa, Ac. *Jv:* V.

For over a century, this outstanding British weekly has provided news, views, short essays, and reviews by leading scientists, along with brief reports on original research. With its centennial, the journal became three distinct publications, produced on a Monday–Wednesday–Friday basis. *Nature* (Friday) is the original journal, well-known to all science librarians. It represents every branch of science. International coverage of timely developments is interspersed with interesting editorial comments, some of which discuss social, economic, or political conditions. Signed articles vary in levels of technicality from general to highly specialized reviews of important scientific endeavors. Also included in each issue are the important "Letters to the Editor" which are short research studies. In addition to good book reviews, a classified checklist of recent scientific publications is included regularly.

Nature New Biology (Wednesday) is dedicated exclusively to research reports in the biological sciences, along with a page or two of news bits and a small book review section. *Nature Physical Science* (Monday) carries short research studies on physics, chemistry, geology, meteorology, etc. Although small academic libraries may not be interested in the more specialized Monday and Wednesday sections, certainly all academic institutions ought to have the excellent base journal (Friday). Highly recommended.

New Scientist. 1956. w. $29.25. New Science Publns., 128 Long Acre, London WC2E 9QH, England. Illus., index, adv. Circ: 72,000. Sample. Vol. ends: no. 52. Microform: UM.

Indexed: BioAb, BritTech, MetAb. *Aud:* Sa, Ac, Ga.

The intent of this weekly is to provide "lively news presentation with authoritative comment in the world of science." With the absorption of *Science Journal,* its issues are now somewhat fuller. The liveliness is still there, supplied by crisp editorial comment and interpretive news coverage. (Statements on U.S. policies are either provocative or amusing, depending on one's point of view.) The world of science and technology is well represented by short articles (one to two pages), written by both staff and specialists. All the sciences and technologies are reviewed; international news emerges from academia, as well as industry; language is always on a layman's level. The magazine also includes a few puzzles, and feedback from readers. The frills in this periodical are not in the format nor in the illustrations, but in the prose. Highly recommended for any library which wants to add another science magazine with a British flavor; and certainly, every academic library should carry it.

New York Academy of Sciences. Transactions. 1881. 8/yr. $20. L. Motz. N.Y. Academy of Sciences. 2 E. 63 St., New York, N.Y. 10021. Illus., index. Vol. ends: No. 8. Refereed.

Indexed: BioAb, ChemAb, MathR, SciAb, SCI. *Aud:* Sa, Ac.

The academy has long been dedicated to the advancement of scientific research. Within the scope of its publications are not only the physical, biological, chemical, engineering, environmental, geological, and medical sciences, but the behavioral sciences as well. Since 1971 its *Transactions* has become a refereed journal covering research papers in the above fields. Another prominent serial is its *Annals* (1877. irreg.) which largely contains papers presented at symposia organized by the Academy. Both publications are recommended for academic collections supporting research. The Academy also puts out a nonspecialist interdisciplinary publication, The *Sciences* (1961. $5.), carrying short articles and selected news.

Oceans. 1969. bi-m. $12. Don G. Kelley. Oceans Magazine Co., 125 Independence Dr., Menlo Park, Calif. 94025. Illus., index, adv. Circ: 21,000. Sample. Vol. ends: Nov./Dec.

Bk. rev: 5, notes. *Aud:* Ga, Ac, Hs. *Jv:* V.

Illustrated with color and black-and-white plates, drawings and photographs, this is a handsome 80 to 100 page look at every aspect of life in and around the world's oceans. It is an independent magazine, not associated with any organization or group, and seems more intent upon presenting authentic material than winning advertisers. The editorial stance is oriented toward environmental issues, and usually one or two articles touch on some aspect of saving the seas. Other pieces, all written in a style well within the grasp of teen-agers and interested laymen, range from historical surveys to studies of sea animals. Regular departments include a Washington Report, answers to questions about the sea, and even a glossary of terms. The whole is a professional, winning package which should be a required item in any library from high school on up. Highly recommended. (B.K.)

Philosophy of Science. See Philosophy Section.

Royal Society. Philosophical Transactions. 1665. irreg. The Royal Society, 6 Carlton House Terrace, London, SW1Y 5AG, England. Illus., index. Sample. Refereed. Microform: MF. Reprint: Johnson, Kraus.

Indexed: ChemAb, EngI, MathR, SciAb, SCI (Series A); BioAb, ChemAb, SCI (Series B). *Aud:* Sa, Ac.

The prominence of the Royal Society and its contributors has been well described in the literature. (See, for example, Hartley, Sir Harold, ed. *The Royal Society: Origins and Founders.* Royal Society, 1960.) As one of the oldest, extant, scientific societies devoted to "improving Natural Knowledge," its publications have chronicled the advances of science through the centuries. Its first-issued journal, *Philosophical Transactions,* is now available in two series: *Series A: Mathematical and Physical Sciences* ($37) and *Series B: Biological Sciences.* ($37). Each issue of the *Transactions* is devoted to a single monograph-length research paper which represents a definitive and authoritative study. Experimental details and tabular material are exhaustive.

Other noteworthy publications of the Royal Society are its *Notes and Records,* which publishes essays on history of science and biographical sketches; its *Biographical Memoirs,* and the *Year Book.* (See also *Royal Society, Proceedings,* below.)

Royal Society. Proceedings. 1854. irreg. $16/v. The Royal Society, 6 Carlton House Terrace, London SW1Y 5AG, England. Illus., index. Sample. Circ: 3,000. Refereed. Microform: MF. Reprint: Dawson.

Indexed: ChemAb, EngI, MathR, Met&GeoAb, SciAb, SCI (Series A); BioAb, ChemAb, IMed, SCI (Series B).

As with its sister publication, *Philosophical Transactions,* the *Proceedings* are issued in two series. *Series A: Mathematical and Physical Sciences* includes all aspects of these fields, and also carries studies in the engineering sciences. *Series B: Biological Sciences* is dedicated solely to reports on the biological sciences, many papers of which are theoretical. Generally, research papers published in the *Proceedings* do not exceed 24 pages, longer research tracts appearing in *Phil. Trans.* Both series are high quality and authoritative publications for research collections.

Science. 1880. w. $12. P. H. Abelson. Amer. Assn. for the Advancement of Science, 1515 Mass. Ave., N.W., Washington, D.C. 20005. Illus., index, adv. Circ: 155,514. Sample. Vol. ends: 4v./yr. Refereed. Microform: UM.

Indexed: BioAb, ChemAb, EngI, IMed, Met&GeoAb, PsyAb, RG, SciAb, SCI. *Bk. rev:* 10, 300 words, signed. *Aud:* Sa, Ac, Ga, Hs.

Serving as a "forum for the presentation of important issues related to the advancement of science," the periodical is a splendid choice for a combination of technical articles and general essays. Features review developments in all the sciences—physical, biological, and behavioral—some with a higher degree of technicality than others, and contributions are usually by distinguished specialists. An important section is that devoted to short reports of original research, much of which, in recent years, falls within the scope of the biological sciences. Departments give thorough coverage: "News and Comment" screens events of the week and airs opinions, particularly on legislation and politics affecting the sciences. Detailed digests of important conferences and a calendar of events cover both national and international symposia. Book reviews and checklists are comprehensive; the longer, essay-reviews, in particular, are excellent. Also issued annually is a "Guide to Scientific Instruments," which serves not only as a buyers' guide, but as a reference tool on new equipment. Every academic library should have it. Small public and school libraries, taking material selectively from *Reader's Guide,* may find the technical treatment too sophisticated for their needs. Generally, however, highly recommended for every type of library.

Science Digest. 1937. m. $5. R. F. Dempewolff. Hearst Corp., 959 Eighth Ave., New York, N.Y. 10019. Illus., adv. Circ: 150,000. Vol. ends: No. 12.

Indexed: AbrRG, RG. *Bk. rev:* 2, 250–350 words, signed. *Aud:* Ga, Ejh, Hs.

A popularization of science, this magazine covers an A–Z range of subjects in short, easy-to-read articles. The emphasis is usually on the sensational—flashy covers, catchy titles—but the articles are not necessarily sensational from a scientific standpoint. A large part of the material is reprints, book condensations, or toned-down digests of technical papers. Contributors are frequently well-known authors. However, there are a number of better publications, *Natural History* for one, which serve the same purpose. Yet the popular appeal is there, and one assumes it serves a purpose in public libraries.

Science Education. 1916. q. $12. N. E. Bingham. Wiley-Interscience Co., 605 Third Ave., New York, N.Y. 10016. Illus., index. Circ: 2,000. Sample. Vol. ends: No. 4. Refereed.

Indexed: EdI. *Bk. rev:* 7–8, 400 words, signed. *Aud:* Sa, Ac.

Though more scholarly than *School Science and Mathematics,* and less extensive in its coverage of elementary and secondary school studies, this publication explores research on curriculum development, teacher training, and other facets of education in the sciences—elementary through college. The major emphasis is for the teacher education program, yet enough articles and informative programs would be interesting to science faculty in colleges. An authoritative and quality publication in science education.

Science and Government Report. 1971. s-m. $25. Daniel S. Greenberg, Box 21123, Washington, D.C. Sample. Vol. ends: Dec.

Aud: Sa, Ac, Ga.

Long a veteran of the Washington scene, Daniel S. Greenberg has produced a 4–6 page newsletter offering comment and review of the Federal Government's science policies. Domestic, international, industrial, and educational news is covered. Heading the list are accounts of the National Science Foundation's activities, as well as gossip about other fund-giving organizations. The brief notes do not simply report hearsay, but are backed by pertinent facts and statistics. Contrary to the maddening practice of some newsletters, *S&GR* documents its sources with full references. Well-written and witty reporting gives honest overviews both of Washington personalities and politics, and a hard look at some of our more sacrosanct institutions. An "In Print" section selects government publications of special interest. Highly recommended, particularly for any person or institution supported by research grants, and for academic libraries.

Science News. 1922. w. $7.50. Kendrick Frazier. Subs. to: 231 W. Center St., Marion, Ohio. Illus., index, adv. Circ: 120,000. Sample. Microform: UM, MF.

Indexed: AbrRG, RG, EngI. *Bk. rev:* Several, 35–40 words, unsigned. *Aud:* Ga, Ejh, Hs, Ac.

Celebrating its fiftieth year, the publication has offered popularizations of scientific developments since its original introduction as *Science News Letter.* Currently, the periodical concentrates on short announcements and interpretations of scientific developments for the week, as gleaned from research journals, symposia, interviews, etc. All fields of science are covered, including aerospace, behavioral, biological, earth, engineering, environmental, medical, and physical sciences. Contributions are mostly written by staff editors. Facts are well documented, and the prose is readable and appropriately illustrated. Reviews of books and films are descriptive, rather than critical; new equipment, products, etc., are also announced. Recommended for any type of library seeking quick, popularized, international news coverage in science and technology. Two indexes per year facilitate fact finding.

Science for the People. See News and Opinion Magazines/Political Opinion Reviews Section.

Science Progress. 1894. q. $20. D. Lewis and J. M. Ziman. Blackwell Scientific Publns., Ltd., 5 Alfred St., Oxford OX1 4HB, England. Illus., index, adv. Circ: 2,000. Sample. Vol. ends: No. 4. Microform: UM, MF.

Indexed: BioAb, BritTech, ChemAb, SciAb. *Bk. rev:* 12, 2,000 words, signed.

The journal presupposes some scientific background, and is directed toward professionals (albeit nonspecialists) and the advanced undergraduate. All areas—physical through biological sciences—are explored. About five or six review articles in each issue are contributed by specialists in their respective fields; reviews usually contain a good bit of historical background and lengthy bibliographies. Subject matter in each issue is quite diversified. A valuable book review section selects the most prominent—or popular—books for review in each field. The journal is a good, authoritative nonspecialist publication for academic libraries.

Scientific American. 1845. m. $10. Dennis Flanagan. Scientific American, 415 Madison Ave., New York, N.Y. 10017. Illus., index, adv. Circ: 425,081. Sample. Vol. ends: Dec. Refereed. Microform: UM, MF, PMC, B&H.

Indexed: ASTI, BioAb, ChemAb, AbrRG, IMed, MathR, MetAb, PsyAb, RG, SciAb, SCI. *Bk. rev:* 1, 3,000 words, signed; short reviews, 10, 250–500 words, unsigned. *Aud:* Ejh, Hs, Ac, Ga, Sa.

Surely the periodical needs little introduction to the library world, for the magazine has been interpreting scientific and technological advances and theories to laymen for well over 125 years. It is by far the best general science publication available. Articles vary in sophistication, and experts have stated that some of the more cogent reviews in their own fields have been published here. The general reader, however, will always to able to find material written on his level and directed toward his interests, ranging from research in prehistory to the latest developments in space explorations. The quality is high and the contributors are distinguished specialists from both academia and industry. Each issue contains a carefully balanced selection from the physical, life, and behavioral sciences; and many articles are beautifully illustrated. Special departments such as mathematical games and home-style experiments invite reader participation. Also, a review section briefly reports on research developments gleaned from the more specialized journals. An excellent feature is the main book review, which frequently serves as a tutorial essay in itself. In an age when the lack of communication between specialist and laymen is decried, the magazine belongs in every library.

Soviet Science Review. 1970. bi-m. $37.50. Zdenek Novak. IPC Science and Technology Business Press, Ltd., 32 High St., Guildford, Surrey, England. Illus., index. Circ: 2,000. Sample. Vol. ends: no. 6. Refereed.

Aud: Sa, Ac, Ga.

Produced in cooperation with the Novosti Press Agency (USSR) and the Academy of Sciences of the USSR, as well as the Deutsche Verlags Anstalt, Stuttgart. The magazine, a *Scientific American* type, is a popularized treatment of scientific endeavors emanating from the USSR. The publication is not a translation of a Russian journal; rather, it has been prepared exclusively for a Western audience. All branches of the physical, biological, behavioral, and engineering sciences are covered. A recent issue carried articles extending from archaeological studies, through medicine, physics, atomic power, and water pollution, to marine biology. A few abstracts of significant literature are also included. The two to three-page articles are authored by prominent Russian scientists, and a distinguished editorial advisory board is headed by Nobel Laureate Semyonov. With Soviet science having achieved such prominence since Sputnik, academic libraries with good science collections would be well advised to add this title to their holdings.

Technology and Culture. See Engineering and Technology Section.

Technology Review. 1899. 9/yr. (Nov.–July). $9. J. I. Matthill. Alumni Assn., Mass. Inst. of Technology, Cambridge, Mass. 02139. Illus., index, adv. Circ: 44,000. Sample. Vol. ends: no. 9.

Indexed: ChemAb. *Bk. rev:* 2–5, 500 words, signed. *Aud:* Ga, Sa, Ac, Hs.

One would hope that the periodical enjoys a wider circulation than in the homes of M.I.T. alumni. Its emphasis is on reviewing current technological and scientific advances and their impact on our culture: in art, education, government, history, industry, philosophy, politics, etc. Feature articles, usually written on a layman's level, are supplied by alumni or faculty. The contributors are distinguished, the contents interesting, the graphic work dramatic, the format good, and the quality high. Special departments cover trends in government, science, news of the Institute, math puzzles, and other features. Mention should be made, too, of the well-written book reviews, which are not necessarily restricted to science. Of course, issues also carry alumni notes. Recommended for larger libraries, public and academic alike.

U.S. National Bureau of Standards. Journal of Research. 1928. Supt. of Documents, Govt. Printing Office, Washington, D.C. 20402. Illus., index. Circ: 4,000. Refereed. Microform: UM, MF, PMC.

Indexed: ASTI, BioAb, ChemAb, EngI, SciAb, SCI. *Aud:* Sa, Ac.

The National Bureau of Standards is dedicated to the "applications of the physical and engineering sciences to the advancement of technology in industry and commerce." Its excellent *Journal of Research,* available in three parts and identified below, publishes the reports of research of their scientists and engineers in the various NBS laboratories, including their Institute for Basic Research, Institute for Materials Research, Center for Radiation Research, and Center for Computer Sciences. The entire series, or portions thereof, should be a necessary acquisition for most university libraries or other research-oriented collections. Other noteworthy publications of the NBS include their *Technical News Bulletin,* which reports briefly on the current research programs and activities of the entire NBS, and *NBS Publications Newsletter,* which provides librarians with a good checklist of available and forthcoming literature from this prolific organization. Their newest journal, cosponsored with the American Institute of Physics and the American Chemical Society, is *Journal of Physical and Chemical Reference Data* (see Physics Section).

Section A: *Physics and Chemistry.* 1959. 6/yr. $9.50. C. W. Beckett.

Covers basic and applied research in most branches of physics and chemistry.

Section B: *Mathematical Sciences.* 1959. q. $5. Morris Newman.

"Presents studies designed mainly for the mathematician and the theoretical physicist." Studies include pure mathematics, mathematical physics, numerical analysis, and programs for digital computers.

Section C: *Engineering and Instrumentation.* q. $5. Martin Greenspan.

"Reports research and development of interest chiefly to the engineer and the applied scientist." Studies cover all aspects of instrumentation and measurement.

SOCIOLOGY

See also Cultural-Social Studies Section.

Basic Periodicals

GENERAL. Hs: *Society;* Ga; *Society, Journal of Social Issues;* Jc: *Society, Journal of Social Issues, American Sociological Review;* Ac: *American Sociological Review, American Behavioral Science, Society, Journal of Social Issues, Social Problems, Race Today.*

SOCIAL SERVICE AND WELFARE. Ga: *Public Welfare, Social Security Bulletin;* Ac&Jc: *Public Welfare, Social Security Bulletin, Social Work.*

COUNTERCULTURE. *Welfare Fighter.*

Basic Abstracts and Indexes

Sociological Abstracts, Social Science and Humanities Index, Abstracts for Social Workers.

Acta Sociologica; Scandinavian review of sociology.
1955. q. $15.75. Erik Allardt. Munksgaard, 35 Nörre
Sögade, D.K. 1370, Copenhagen K, Denmark. Index,
adv. Refereed.

Indexed: PAIS. *Bk. rev:* 6, 500 words, signed. *Aud:* Ac.

Issued by Scandinavian Sociological Association.
The text is either in English, French, or German. This
is an international journal of extremely high interest.
Articles concern such things as: differential rates of
change and road accidents, rating news media, attitudes on the functioning of institutions, changes in sex
roles, Marxist class theory, and residential relocation
and voting behavior. University libraries will wish to
include this journal in their holdings. (M.W.)

American Behavioral Scientist. 1957. bi-m. $18
(Individuals $12, Students $9). Sage Publns., Inc., 275
S. Beverly Dr., Beverly Hills, Calif. 90212. Illus., index, adv. Circ: 3,000. Sample. Vol. ends: July. Microform: UM.

Indexed: PsyAb, PAIS, SocAb. *Bk. rev:* 200, 50-75
words. *Aud:* Ac. *Jv:* V.

Each issue is devoted to a single topic on the methods and techniques of social research. There are usually eight to ten short articles following an introduction by a guest editor. The authors are specialists in
research and clinical work. Topics studied have included: advances in information retrieval in the social
sciences, multinational comparisons of social research,
overviews of the relations of environment and behavior, communication and behavior, and interdisciplinary relationships in political science. The "New Studies Section" is a guide to recent publications in the
social and behavioral sciences. The magazine's staff
periodically checks over 360 journals and lists and
annotates about 200 new books, pamphlets, and articles on sociology, psychology, and other behavioral
sciences. This feature makes it of considerable value
for bibliographers. Frequent articles on communication give it a particular importance for all related
fields.

American Catholic Sociological Review. See *Sociological Analysis.*

American Journal of Sociology. 1895. bi-m. $15. Ar-
nold Anderson. Univ. of Chicago Press, 5801 Ellis
Ave., Chicago, Ill. 60637. Illus., adv. Circ: 1,950. Microform: UM. Reprint: Johnson.

Indexed: CurrCont, SSHum, SocAb. *Bk. rev:* 24-30,
400-700 words, signed. *Aud:* Ac. *Jv:* V.

A professional and scholarly coverage of advanced
thinking and empirical research in the various areas of
sociology and social psychology. Most of the articles
are a result of field work and research on specific social problems. The signed, evaluative book reviews
and the bibliographic listing of current books received

(averaging 200-300 titles) provide means for keeping
abreast with the latest and best American and foreign
titles available in sociology and related areas. A valuable feature is the yearly listing of newly begun dissertations and completed PhDs in sociology. Valuable for
all academic and larger public libraries.

*American Sociological Review; official journal of the
American Sociological Association.* 1936. bi-m. Mem-
bership, $20 (Individuals $15). James F. Short. Amer.
Sociological Assn., Executive Office, 1722 N. St. N.W.,
Washington, D.C. 20036. Illus., adv. Circ: 20,000. Vol.
ends: Dec. Microform: UM. Reprint: Johnson.

Indexed: AbSocWk, PAIS, PsyAb, SSHum, SocAb. *Bk.
rev:* 30-50, 800-1,200 words, signed. *Aud:* Ac. *Jv:* V.

Similar to the *American Journal of Sociology* in its
presentation includes research articles on theory and
methodology, case studies and field work in all
branches of sociology along with the official reports
and proceedings of the association. Language tends to
be technical and theoretical, frequently involving the
use of formulas and other symbolic means of representing relationships. There are usually ten studies per
issue; each is from 15 to 20 pages in length. The "Review Symposium" presents three reviews on a significant new work in the field. Primarily of interest to
professionals in the field, it is also useful to advanced
students.

American Sociologist. 1965. q. Membership (Institutions $10). Harold W. Pfautz. Amer. Sociological Assn.,
Executive Office, 1722 N St. N.W., Washington, D.C.
20036. Illus., adv. Circ: 14,000. Microform: UM.

Aud: Ac.

Unlike its sister publication, the *American Sociological Review,* this tends to be more of a professional
journal for the membership. Commencing with the
August 1971 issue, *American Sociologist* contains "articles concerning the discipline and the ASA Official
Reports and Proceedings." An informal newsletter to
be issued ten times a year and sent to members will
carry employment bulletins and personals. Scholarly
articles concerning the field continue to appear and
reviews are included.

*Archives Européenes de Sociologie/European Journal
of Sociology.* 1960. s-a. $5. Librarie Plon, 8 rue Garan-
cière, Paris 6e, France. Index, adv. Refereed.

Aud: Ac. *Jv:* V.

Publishes scholarly articles in French, German, and
English on aspects of sociology. Occasional issues carry
articles on a single theme, i.e., "Stimulation in Sociology," including one on "The Use of Electronic Computers in the Study of Social Organizations." Scholars in
various fields contribute in their areas of expertise.
Authors have included Raymond Aron, Reinhard Ben-
dix, Asa Briggs, Amitai Etzioni, Ernest Gellner, Sey-

mour Martin Lipset, Robert K. Merton, and Arnold Rose. "Notes Critiques" are brief statements about previously published articles. A journal of impeccable scholarship which will be referred to in university libraries. (M.W.)

Australian & New Zealand Journal of Sociology. 1965. s-a. $6. F. Lancaster Jones. Australian National Univ., Box 4, Canberra 2600, Australia. Index, adv. Circ: 1,250. Vol. ends: Nov. Refereed.

Indexed: CurrCont, SocAb. *Bk. rev:* 15–20, 500 words, signed. *Aud:* Ac.

The journal has two main objectives. First, to reflect what is going on in sociology in Australia and New Zealand and to tell the rest of the world about it. Second, it aims to serve as an outlet for scholarly contributions by Australian and New Zealand sociologists as well as for articles by overseas scholars writing about Australia. The articles all deal with theory and methodology as well as major social issues. Special features of the *Journal* include reports from various departments of sociology as well as individuals engaged in sociological research. From time to time, publishers report on research trends in a specific aspect of the social structure.

British Journal of Sociology. 1950. q. $8.30. Terence Morris. Routledge & Kegan Paul, Ltd., 68–74 Carter Lane, London, EC4 VsEL, England. Illus., index, adv. Microform: UM.

Indexed: BritHum, BritEJI, PAIS, PsyAb, SSHum. *Bk. rev:* 20–40, 500–600 words, signed. *Aud:* Ac.

Sponsored by the London School of Economics and Political Science, this journal presents scholarly articles ranging over the fields of theoretical and applied sociology. The editors state that there is no attempt to favor any "school center, country, or variety of sociology," and an effort is made to represent fairly social anthropology, social administration, and several relevant areas of history, philosophy, and social psychology. Occasionally, in addition to the regular book reviews, there is a six to nine page review of material on a specific subject such as suicide, race relations in the United States, or alcoholism. Reviews provide greater coverage of British and European publications than do comparable American journals. Of primary value to sociologists and graduate students.

Cameo Newsletter. See Free Magazines Section.

Canadian Review of Sociology and Anthropology. 1964. q. $12. Lynn McDonald. Canadian Sociology and Anthropology Assn., Box 878, Montreal, Canada. Index, adv. Circ: 1,300. Vol. ends: Nov. Refereed.

Bk. rev: 3, various number, length. signed. *Aud:* Ac.

Primarily for and by Canadian scholars in the fields of anthropology and sociology. Most of the articles are concerned with Canada and Canadian society. The

book review section supplements and complements the "review coverage in other journals by reviewing works of Canadian interest, and especially works that are unlikely to receive wide distribution, such as reports etc." For all medium to large Canadian libraries, but only for large American collections.

Civilisations. 1951. q. $9 (Students $6). International Institute of Differing Civilizations, 11 bd. de Waterloo, 1000 Brussels, Belgium. Index.

Indexed: SocAb. *Bk. rev:* 8, 600 words, signed. *Aud:* Ga, Ac.

An international journal broadly concerned with anthropology, sociology, community development, and social change. The social sciences in general are stressed within its frame of reference. The IIDC studies the problems of varying peoples and attempts to promote relations, understanding, and knowledge through study and publications. *Civilisations* includes material on development in differing areas in articles in either English or French and a résumé in the language not used in the text. It includes biographical information on contributors, editorials, "Communiqué," document(s), bibliography, and "Books Received." (M.W.)

Community. See Blacks Section.

Current Sociology/Sociologie Contemporaine. 1959. 3/yr. $7.50. Mouton & Co., 5 Herderstraat, The Hague, Netherlands. Circ: 1,200. Reprint: Johnson, Kraus.

Indexed: PAIS. *Aud:* Ac.

A publication of the International Sociological Association. This is primarily a lengthy, annotated bibliography of material in a given subject area. Each issue, concentrating on a particular subject of interest, is preceded by a "Trend Report" on the topic and/or several papers of related interest. The main text is in both English and French; the annotations, a combination. Coverage is international, and a run of the periodical gives the individual or library one of the best single sources of information on all major subjects related to sociology, e.g., demography, underdeveloped nations, human organizations, social issues, etc. A basic work for any library or student seriously interested in sociology.

The Family Coordinator; journal of education, counseling, and services. 1952. q. Membership $10. William C. Nichols, Jr. National Council on Family Relations, 1219 University Ave., S.W., Minneapolis, Minn. 55414. Illus., index, adv. Circ: 6,100.

Indexed: SocAb. *Bk. rev:* 19, 375 words, signed. *Aud:* Ga, Ac.

A professional journal for counselors, psychologists, and teachers on problems of marriage and the family. The articles are written by experts and well documented. While much of the material will be of only professional interest, a few articles touch on problems of concern to the layman: birth control, sex education, divorce, and teen-age sex. A few advanced high school students may find the publication of value, but for the most part it is only for larger academic and public libraries.

Family Process. 1962. q. $10. Donald A. Bloch. Nathan W. Ackerman Family Inst., 149 E. 78th St., New York, N.Y. 10021. Index, adv. Circ: 2,700. Sample. Refereed. Vol. ends: Dec.

Indexed: AbSocWk, PsyAb, SocAb. *Bk. rev:* various number, long. *Aud:* Ac.

Sponsored by the Nathan W. Ackerman Family Institute of New York and the Mental Research Institute of Palo Alto, Calif. This is "a multidisciplinary journal of family study research and treatment. . . ." Its scope includes ". . . the broad area of family studies with particular emphasis on family mental health and family psychotherapy." Articles concern such things as early marriage, the child in family therapy, "The Easy Rider Syndrome: A Pattern of Hetero- and Homosexual Relationship in a Heroin Addict Population," "Nonverbal Communication and Marital Satisfaction," etc. Features include correspondence, books, and abstracts. An average of 24 abstracts of current books and articles appear in each issue. While this journal may not appeal to the average reader it will interest specialists, educators, and students.

Impact of Science on Society. See Government Magazines/United States Section.

International Journal of Comparative Sociology. 1960. q. Approx. $16. K. Ishwaran. E. J. Brill Publishers, Leiden, The Netherlands. Adv. Vol. ends: Dec.

Indexed: SSHum. *Bk. rev:* 15, 500–700 words, signed. *Aud:* Ac.

Coverage of world-wide research and developments in sociology. The primary aim is "the furtherance of pure research in the field." The scholarly studies describe and interpret social situations with comparisons to other countries. The evaluative and descriptive reviews submitted by scholars from all over the world provide a sampling of new materials in the field from non-Western areas. Occasionally an entire issue is devoted to a single topic, which draws information from differing cultures. For example, there have been presentations on the relationship between politics and social change, and kinship and geographic mobility. Primarily for the scholar and advanced students interested in an international and comparative view of sociology.

International Migration Review. 1964. q. $12. Silvan M. Tomasi. Center of Migration Studies, 209 Flagg Place, Staten Island, N.Y. 10304. Circ: 2,000. Microform: UM.

Indexed: AmerH, HistAb, PAIS, SocAb. *Bk. rev:* various number, length. *Aud:* Ac.

A scientific journal of international scope, studying sociological, demographic, historical, and legislative aspects of migration movements. Included are papers by specialists, statistics on migration trends, and book reviews covering an unusually high number of titles. Primarily of use to sociologists and other social scientists concerned with this subject. (M.W.)

International Social Science Journal. See Government Magazines/United Nations Section.

Interracial Review. See Blacks Section.

The Jewish Journal of Sociology. 1959. s-a. $4. Morris Freedman. The Jewish Journal of Sociology, 55 New Cavendish Street, London W1M 8BT, England. Index, adv.

Indexed: PAIS, PsyAb. *Bk. rev:* 8, 1,250 words, signed. *Aud:* Ga, Ac.

"Published on behalf of the World Jewish Congress by William Heinemann Ltd," this is a scholarly journal. Articles are concerned with Jewish political voting patterns, intermarriage and conversion, the sabbath and television in Israel, adoption in Israel, curriculum for national education in Israel, social values of Israeli students, Jewish community relations in the United States, financing Jewish community activities, authority in the Jewish community, and Jewish demography. Features include book reviews, a chronicle of events, list of books received, and notes on contributors. Articles are less historical and more in the field of sociology than those in *Jewish Social Studies* (see below). This will be of considerable interest to those concerned with Jewish affairs and the social sciences. Articles are mainly written by academics. (M.W.)

Jewish Social Studies. 1939. q. $15. Perry M. Goldman. Conference on Jewish Social Studies, 2929 Broadway, New York, N.Y. 10025. Index. Circ: 1,250. Refereed. Vol. ends: Oct.

Indexed: SSHum. *Bk. rev:* 10, 1,000 words, signed. *Aud:* Ga, Ac.

"A quarterly journal devoted to contemporary and historical aspects of Jewish Life. . . ." This journal has articles on Jewish immigrants in Argentina from 1881 to 1892, "Roosevelt, Russian Persecution of Jews and American Public Opinion," German-Zionist relations in 1917, and on Jewish intermarriage. Departments include book reviews, books received, communications and notes on contributors. All academic institutions and larger libraries interested in Jewish social and historical studies should consider it for subscription. (M.W.)

Journal of Human Relations. See Blacks Section.

Journal of Human Resources; Education, Manpower, and Welfare Policies. 1965. q. $16 ($8 to individuals). Robert Lampman. Univ. of Wisconsin Press, Box 1379, Madison, Wis. 53701. Index, adv. Circ: 1,800. Sample. Refereed. Vol. ends: Fall.

Bk. rev: 6, 800 words, signed. *Aud:* Ac.

Under auspices of the Industrial Relations Research Institute, the Center for Studies in Vocational and Technical Education, and the Institute for Research on Poverty of the University of Wisconsin, this journal ". . . gives primary emphasis to the role of education and training, at home and abroad, in enhancing productive skills, employment opportunities and income. It includes articles on more general manpower, health and welfare policies, as they relate to the labor market and to economic and social development." Articles treat such things as an examination of school funding by race and status, income distribution, and the allocation of resources to health. Of interest to those concerned with social welfare, education, and manpower economics. (M.W.)

Journal of Leisure Research. 1969. q. $10. Carolton S. Van Doren. National Recreation and Park Assn., 1700 Pennsylvania Ave. N.W., Washington, D.C. 20006. Illus., index, adv. Vol. ends: Fall.

Bk. rev: 1, 350 words, signed. *Aud:* Ac.

This journal tries, through definition, investigation, and interdisciplinary research, to identify the problems of leisure and, through dissemination of investigations and findings, and description of their practical applications, to lead towards their solution. Approaches used may be historical or philosophical, and may concern sociology, psychology, planning, design, law, or administration. An interchange between the social and natural sciences is hoped for. Articles discuss residence location in recreational areas, demands on parks and beaches, definition of "leisure activity," and "A Thesaurus of Keywords for Indexing and Retrieval of Recreation Literature." Departments include research notes, communications, and books received. Should interest all libraries with scholarly collections on leisure and recreation plus many more concerned with the social and behavioral sciences. (M.W.)

Journal of Marriage and the Family. 1938. q. $12. Carlfried B. Broderick. National Council on Family Relations, 1219 Univ. Ave. S.E., Minneapolis, Minn. 55414. Illus., adv. Circ: 7,500. Vol. ends: Nov. Microform: UM. Reprint: Kraus.

Indexed: PsyAb, SSHum. *Bk. rev:* 8-10, 900-1,000 words, signed. *Aud:* Ac.

A medium for the presentation of original theory, research, interpretation, and critical discussion on material related to marriage and the family. It is sponsored by the National Council on Family Relations, which seeks to bring together the leaders in research, teaching, and professional service in this field so as to advance cultural values secured through family relations. Most of the 20 articles per issue are theoretical proposals or reports of research dealing with particular areas of marriage and family relations and are from four to ten pages in length. A regular feature is the "International Department," with three to four articles submitted from overseas. Included also is a book review section. Occasionally, an entire issue is devoted to a single topic, such as the American adolescent, the poverty family, and family planning. Of value in larger libraries or in specialized sociology, social work, family life, and health collections, this will be of primary interest to scholars, college students, and instructors in the above areas.

Journal of Social Issues. 1945. q. $15 (Individuals $9). Bertram H. Raven. Soc. for the Psychological Study of Social Issues, Box 1248, Ann Arbor, Mich. 48106. Illus., index, adv. Circ: 6,500. Sample. Vol. ends: Dec. Reprint: Kraus. Microform: UM.

Indexed: BioAb, PsyAb, SSHum. *Aud:* Hs, Ga. *Jv:* V.

An analysis of current social issues which should have wide appeal for both the layman and the expert. Thanks to a general lucidity, plus a lack of jargon, the problems discussed can be understood by anyone. The editor's goal, to communicate scientific findings in a nontechnical manner, is achieved. Each issue has a guest editor and eight articles on different aspects of a single topic, like bilingualism or cultural change in small communities. Authors are professors or specialists in the field. Extensive bibliographies accompany each article. In the back of each issue are perforated pages of three-by-five cards giving a full bibliographic citation and an annotation of the articles appearing. Because of the interdisciplinary and nontechnical approach and analysis of current social issues, the journal would be of value to most libraries—including high schools.

Light Magazine. See Free Magazines Section.

Neighbors. See Urban Studies Section.

New Society. 1962. w. $12. Paul Barker. New Science Publns., 128 Long Acre, London WC2, England. Illus., index, adv.

Bk. rev: 15-20, 350-1500 words, signed. *Aud:* Ac.

A tabloid British version of the American *Society* (formerly *Trans-Action*) which seeks to bring social and cultural levels to the informed laymen in language he or she can understand and appreciate. A typical issue, for example, begins with an editorial, short news items and then a number of articles by both lay and professional people. Most of the material is geared for the British reader, although will be of value to any American sociologist or teacher. Conversely, the shorter news and feature items will fascinate anyone involved with popular culture, and the book reviews are some of the best going, e.g., Albert Hunt's summary of five titles of American rock n' roll. About 15 out of every 45 pages are devoted to display and classified advertising for social and government workers. (M.W.)

Opportunity. See Free Magazines Section.

Pacific Sociological Review. 1958. q. $15. John MacGregor. Sage Publns., Inc., 275 So. Beverly Dr., Beverly Hills, Calif. 90212. Illus., adv. Circ: 1,200. Vol. ends: Oct.

Indexed: AbSocWk, HistAb, SocAb. *Aud:* Ac.

Devoted to the publication of research, theory, and methodology in sociology. An average of seven articles per issue range from 6 to 14 pages in length and are generally submitted from the Washington–Oregon–California area.

Public Choice. 1966. q. $7 (Hardback $11). Center for Public Choice, Virginia Polytechnic Inst. and State Univ., Blacksburg, Va. 24061.

Bk. rev: 3, 300–600 words, signed. *Aud:* Ac. *Jv:* C.

Covers decision making in government, the economic market, and by the public. It places stress on a mathematical and statistical approach to evaluating mass trends. Articles have included the topics of politics and economic development, and ideology, public approval and government behavior. Recommended only for those research collections with a strong interest in the newer methods of data handling, for the fields of political science and sociology. The printing is below average. (M.W.)

Race; a journal of race and group relations. 1959. q. $9.50. Simon Abbott. Oxford Univ. Press, Ely House, 37 Dover St., London W10, England. Circ: 1,300. Vol. ends: Apr.

Indexed: PsyAb, SocAb. *Bk. rev:* Extensive essays. *Aud:* Ga, Ac.

The journal of the Institute of Race Relations of London. Discusses matters of race in generally learned tones, but manages without effort to be readable as well as informative. Each rather bulky issue contains half a dozen full-scale articles on such divergent matters as the genesis of segregation, intermarriage, immigration to Great Britain, and Negro higher education. About half the available space is devoted to signed book reviews.

Race Relations Reporter. See Blacks Section.

Race Today. 1967. m. $6. Institute of Race Relations. Research Publns. Services Ltd., Victoria Hall, E. Greenwich, London, SE10, England.

Bk. rev: Various number, length. *Aud:* Ga, Ac. *Jv:* V.

The subject of race relations is not only of mounting (if not paramount) interest to governments and laymen alike in much of the world—most notably East and South Africa, Britain, Switzerland, North America, Southeast Asia, the Caribbean, and Latin America—but has also become a bona fide subdiscipline within sociology, already manifest in solid studies by Pierre L. van den Berghe, Michael Banton, John Rex, and S. Zubaida, among others. London's Institute of Race Relations, founded in 1958 to "initiate policy research and coordinate information" on how racial groups interact and how "relations between the peoples of mankind" might be improved, publishes two invaluable journals in this field. *Race*, for a specialized audience, belongs in all academic and Ethnic Studies collections. The second, *Race Today*, may surely interest specialists, but its topical contents, attractively designed, photo-studded format, and forthright (yet not simplistic) prose make it ideal for general readers. In fact, it is probably unequaled as a popular, authoritative source of global data and views on immigration, communal conflicts, discrimination; it has reported on conversations with "Soledad Sister" Penny Jackson. Short notes on research concerning "Racial self-esteem" and "Teaching race," and reviews of books dealing with both migration and South African "resettlement" schemes have also been included. (S.B.)

Revue Française du Sociologie. See Europe and Middle East/French Language Section.

Rural Sociology. 1936. q. $12 (Free to members). Frederick C. Fliegel. Howard M. Sauer, Rural Sociological Soc., South Dakota State Univ., Brookings, S. Dak. 47006. Illus., adv. Circ: 2,600. Vol. ends: Dec. Microform: UM. Reprint: Johnson.

Indexed: AbSocWk, HistAb, PAIS, PHRA, PsyAb, SCI, SocAb. *Aud:* Ac.

Covers all aspects of rural life in the United States and other countries—including the economic, cultural, social, and demographic components. Articles have dealt with migration and settlement patterns; educational and occupational aspirations and achievements; social characteristics of rural peoples and areas; the adoption of agricultural practices; and the relations of rural and urban areas and peoples. The authors are associated with departments of sociology and are concerned with rural sociology, rural education, or agricultural economics. The "Bulletin Index" is a topical list of new bulletins currently available, and there is a regular listing of recent theses and dissertations on rural sociology. With renewed interest in "back to the land" movements, this may prove of greater value to large sociology and agriculture collections than ever before.

Social Forces; a scientific medium of social study and interpretation. 1922. q. $7.50. Richard L. Simpson. Univ. of North Carolina Press, Box 510, Chapel Hill.

N.C. 27514. Illus., index, adv. Circ: 3,500 Vol. ends: June. Microform: UM. Reprint: Johnson.

Indexed: PAIS, PsyAb, SSHum, SocAb. *Bk. rev:* 40–50, 400–800 words, signed. *Aud:* Ga, Ac.

Brief, scholarly articles report research over the entire range of theoretical and applied sociology. Related subjects include the family, social psychology, regionalism, public opinion, and population. Emphasis is placed on the motivation and reasons behind social action, developments, and mobility. The theoretical studies have included the relating of social mobility and such matters as job satisfaction, occupational groups and reasons for participation in community activities, and the relations of educational expectations and parents' occupations. Of value to most libraries because it concerns the social forces behind the behavior of the average individual.

Social Problems. 1953. q. $15. David Gold. Soc. for the Study of Social Problems, Exec. Off. 1316½ Mishawaka Ave., South Bend, Ind. 46615. Illus. adv. Circ: 4,300. Vol. ends: Spring. Microform: UM. Reprint: Johnson.

Indexed: PAIS, PsyAb, SSHum, SocAb. *Aud:* Ga, Ac.

Research articles present current data on a full range of social problems. Studies deal with such topics as deviant behavior, comparisons of role behavior, and the differences in activities and occupational pursuits between the sexes. A regular feature is the "Revue Essay," which provides an overview of information on a particular subject. Since much of the material is clearly presented, college students and informed laymen as well as professionals will find it to be valuable. For all college and university libraries, and many public libraries.

Social Research; an international quarterly of political and social science. 1934. q. $10. Arien Mack. Graduate Faculty of Political and Social Science, New School for Social Research, 65 Fifth Ave., New York, N.Y. 10011. Adv. Circ: 1,800. Vol. ends: Winter. Microform: UM. Reprint: Kraus.

Indexed: PAIS SSHum, *Bk. rev:* 6, 800–1,500 words. *Aud:* Ga, Ac.

Features articles by economists, philosophers, political scientists, sociologists, and psychologists. The presentations analyze and interpret theories and ideas in the social sciences. Concerned with the philosophy, theory, and content of the social sciences in contemporary society, this journal contains interpretations of philosophical schools and important figures in the field. Because of its clear, brief presentation, this journal is of value to most libraries, and necessary in college and university collections.

Social Science Information. bi-m. $18. Mouton & Co., Box 1132, The Hague, Netherlands. Adv. Circ: 1,500.

Aud: Ac.

Issued by the International Social Science Council, this carries articles concerning theory and research in the social sciences. Departments include inventories and bibliographies providing information on studies in the social sciences; new periodicals; social science methodology; and activities of organizations. International contributors include scholars from New York, Chicago, Paris, Zurich, Geneva, Cambridge (Mass.), and London. Text in English and French. For international coverage, a useful journal for university libraries. (M.W.)

Society (Formerly: *Trans-Action; social science and modern society*). 1963. m. (Combined issues July–Aug., Nov.–Dec.) $9.75. Irving L. Horowitz. Box A, Rutgers–The State University, New Brunswick, N.J. 08903. Illus., adv. Circ: 75,000. Microform: B&H.

Indexed: CurrCont, RG. *Aud:* Hs, Ga, Ac. *Jv:* V.

This is a forerunner of the approach of *Psychology Today.* One of the few sociologically oriented periodicals for all general collections. It is written for the layman by sociologists, case workers, and nationally famous social scientists. It publishes diverse views on subjects of public interest in the fields of government, labor, education, medicine, housing, welfare, law, religion, race relations, social service, and politics. Having undergone a number of editorial changes since the previous edition of this book, the magazine today is better then ever, even more geared for the average interested layman. Unfortunately, it does not have the same advertising advantages of *Psychology Today,* but, it is equally as good. Particularly useful for high schools and public libraries, and invaluable in any academic library.

Society and Leisure; bulletin for sociology of leisure, education and culture. 1969. q. Přemysl Maydl. European Centre for Leisure and Education, Prague 1, Jilská 1, Czechoslovakia. Circ: 800.

Bk. rev: Various number, length. *Aud:* Ac.

A joint effort of Unesco and the Czechoslovak Academy of Sciences. An early article indicates some uncertainty as to the status of the bulletin. The dozen articles from European sociologists indicate that the affluent society is not limited to America. Most propose solutions to the much heralded leisure which no one seems quite certain how to handle. The Socialist countries have distinct social-political considerations, but the English-translated articles from other sections of Europe run the whole spectrum from television and film to leisure time studies. Primarily for the academic library. (M.W.)

Sociological Analysis (Formerly: *American Catholic Sociological Review*). 1940. q. $8. Dr. Rovert Hassenger. Bro. Eugene Janson, The Assn. for the Sociology of Religion, 1403 N. St. Mary's St., San Antonio, Tex.

78215. Index, adv. Circ: 1,200. Sample. Refereed. Vol. ends: Winter.

Indexed: CathI, SocAb. *Bk. rev:* various number, 2,500–3,000 words, signed. *Aud:* Ac.

Concerned with "religion and values." Articles in the Spring 1971 issue: "Phenomenology and Socialization," "Inter-Ethnic Marriage. . . ." "Catholic Attitudes Towards Nuclear War," church attendance among Catholic mates, attitudes towards race, dogmatism, and "Local Congregations and Social Chance." For specialized collections ranging from sociology through religion. (M.W.)

Sociological Inquiry. 1930. q. $6. Andrew Effrat. Ontario Inst. for Studies in Education, Univ. of Toronto, 252 Bloor St. W., Toronto 5, Ont., Canada. Adv. Circ: 5,500. Sample. Refereed. Vol. ends: Nov./Dec.

Indexed: ABCPolSci, AbSocWk, SocAb. *Bk. rev:* 2–3, 250 words, signed. *Aud:* Ac.

Journal of the National Sociology Honor Society, Alpha Kappa Delta, this publication tries "to implement the scientific aims of the Alpha Kappa Delta by communicating and reviewing developments of sociological interest in the service of faculty, investigators, and students alike." It wishes to "include all professional manuscripts which, in the eyes of the staff, constitute sound and significant contributions to knowledge in our discipline." Individual issues relate to an overall editorial theme. For Spring 1971 the theme was "Sensitivity Training: Approaches and Applications," and the distinguished small groups scholar, A. Paul Hare, edited the issue. Other issues have concerned "The Craft of Sociology," "Innovations in Theory and Method," and "Some Radical Perspectives in Sociology." Lack of special features permits the single theme approach, a unique quality of this journal. Review symposia provide various viewpoints on books reviewed. A solid, scholarly journal for all academic libraries and larger public libraries. (M.W.)

Sociological Quarterly. 1960. q. $7. Robert W. Habenstein. Secretary, The Sociological Quarterly, 1004 Elm St., Columbia, Mo. 65201. Index, adv. Circ: 2,180.

Indexed: SSHum. *Bk. rev:* 8–12, 500–700 words, signed. *Aud:* Ga, Ac.

Issued by the Midwest Sociological Society, this emphasizes the theoretical significance of research in the general field of sociology. Articles deal with trends in social thought or an analysis of the ideas and contributions of an individual practitioner. Other studies concern the impact of automation on status, and the relationship between education and social station. Of use in most academic libraries and may provide material for the layman as well.

Sociological Review. 1908. q. $10. W. M. Williams. The Univ. of Keele, Staffordshire, England. Illus., adv.

Circ: 1,500. Microform: UM. Reprint: Kraus.

Indexed: BritHum, PsyAb, SSHum. *Bk. rev:* 20–30, 900–1,200 words, signed. *Aud:* Ac.

A British journal presenting articles on a wide range of topics, along with short notes on sociological research, and critical comments on previous articles. Occasionally pieces summarize work in a special area, e.g., the role of education in national development, or the positivist movement and the development of English sociology. The book reviews emphasize British publications. For larger academic collections.

Sociology. 1966. 3/yr. $9.50. John H. Goldthorpe. Oxford Univ. Press, 37 Dover St., London W1, England. Circ: 1,750.

Bk. rev: various number, length, signed. *Aud:* Ac.

This is the official journal of the British Sociological Association, highly specialized, and of value to American libraries as much for its articles as for its book reviews. There are usually four to five documented contributions—varying in one issue from a study of toys to one on compositors. This is only for large, specialized collections.

Sociology and Social Research: an international journal. 1916. $6. Martin H. Neumeyer. Univ. of Southern California, Los Angeles, Calif. 90007. Index. Circ: 2,000. Microform: UM. Reprint: Johnson.

Indexed: HistAb, PAIS, PsychAb, SSHum, SocAb. *Bk. rev:* 10–15, 500 words, signed. *Aud:* Ac.

The results of recent research on special aspects of current sociological problems are presented along with occasional theoretical articles. Coverage is international, with studies conducted in such countries as New Zealand, South Africa, Iraq, as well as in the United States. Each issue includes historical surveys, articles on sociologists, on research in, for example, juvenile delinquency, and attitude surveys.

Sociometry; a journal of research in social psychology. 1937. q. $9 (Institutions $11). Karl W. Backman. Amer. Sociological Assn. 1722 N. St. N.W., Washington, D.C. 20036. Illus., index, adv. Circ: 2,650. Microform: UM.

Indexed: PAIS, PsyAb. *Aud:* Ac.

Particularly concerned with research which will provide a theoretical structure for the field of social psychology. Research is generally clearly focused, well designed, and competently executed. The topics studied included interaction and socialization in connection with social conformity and attitude change; the development of similarities between observers and models, and the relation of religious behavior to personality.

Subterranean Sociology Newsletter. See Humor Section.

Trans-Action. See *Society.*

Unscheduled Events. 1967. q. free. Barbara J. Tootle. Disaster Research Center, Ohio State Univ., 127–129 W. Tenth Ave., Columbus, Ohio 43201. Illus. Circ: 600. Vol. ends: Winter.

Bk. rev: notes. *Aud:* Ac.

Unscheduled Events could mean many sorts of happenings, but in this context it spells disaster, of all kinds, both natural and man induced. A sketchy newsletter, for current information only, it is good for pinpointing research of a sociological nature, and could well be used in a reference or vertical file. It also announces new books on such popular events as riots and disorder. It is a controlled circulation magazine; "We print fewer than one thousand copies and wish to limit the circulation to those truly concerned with this area. The publication is available to university libraries within the limit of our publishing total." (M.W.)

Social Service and Welfare

Public Welfare. 1943. q. $8. Malvin Morton. Amer. Public Welfare Assn., 1313 E. 60th St., Chicago, Ill. 60637. Illus., adv. Circ: 13,000.

Indexed: AbSocWk, PAIS, PHRA. *Bk. rev:* 4–5, 600–800 words, signed. *Aud:* Ga, Ac. *Jv:* V.

Devotes attention to public welfare programs, dependent children, the aged, dependent families, administration, staff training, and general welfare. Articles are written by the staff and directors of welfare programs at federal, state and local levels, faculty members of schools of social work, and civic leaders. The 8 to 11 articles are based on the author's personal, "on-the-job" experiences. Regular features include notes which list many publications of national organizations and publishers; and summaries of national and regional activities. While admittedly a specialized publication, the interest in its field is so great that few libraries can afford to do without it.

Smith College Studies in Social Work. 1930. 3/yr. $8. Roger R. Miller. Smith College School for Social Work, Northampton, Mass. 01060. Circ: 1,600.

Indexed: ABSocWK, PAIS, PsyAb. *Aud:* Ac.

Approximately half of each issue is devoted to reports of investigations based on master's theses and doctoral dissertations submitted to the Smith College School. A number of papers presented by leading scholars and practitioners in the fields of social welfare and mental health, including social work, psychiatry, and sociology are also included. Of primary interest to libraries concerned with social welfare and mental health.

Social Casework. 1920. m. (except Aug. and Sept.). $9. Margaret M. Mangold. Family Service Assn. of America, 44 E. 23rd St., New York, N.Y. 10010. Adv. Circ: 17,500. Microform: UM. Reprint: Kraus.

Indexed: AbSocWk, AmerH, CurrCont, PsyAb, SSHum. *Bk. rev:* 2–6, 800–1,200 words, signed. *Aud:* Ga, Ac.

Written for the social workers, this journal pays particular attention to new approaches and techniques for helping children and adults with problems concerning interpersonal relations and social functioning. Authors are the directors of public and voluntary welfare agencies and their professional staffs, plus faculty members of social welfare schools. Articles deal with the role of the social workers in such settings as family courts and marriage counselling, and with the training of paraprofessionals, and relate to practical rather than theoretical experience. There are occasional editorial notes and reader comments. An important periodical for larger public libraries, professional collections, and most college and university libraries.

Social Security Bulletin. See Government Magazines/ United States Section.

Social Service Review. 1917. q. $8. Rachel B. Marks. Univ. of Chicago Press, 5801 Ellis Ave., Chicago, Ill 60637. Illus., adv. Circ: 3,657. Microform: Canner, UM.

Indexed: AbSocWk, PAIS, PsyAb, SSHum. *Bk. rev:* 15–20, 800–1,200 words, signed. *Aud:* Ac.

Emphasis is on original research and there are both specialized articles and presentations which "deal more broadly with social issues and problems." Specialized research reports and general articles deal with issues widely applicable in the field of social work, such as an historical survey of American thought on poverty, the role of voluntary agencies in social work, educating the social worker, interagency coordination, and bureaucratic and professional orientation patterns in social casework. There is a yearly abstracting of PhD dissertations completed in social work (September issue) and a listing of those in progress. The "Notes and Comments" section offers briefer items on current developments in the field. A scholarly journal supplementing, rather than duplicating, others in the field. All colleges with social work programs will wish to subscribe.

Social Work. 1956. q. $10. Editors: Alvin L. Schorr and Beatrice Saunders. National Assn. of Social Workers, 2 Park Ave., New York, N.Y. 10016. Illus., index, adv. Circ: 57,000. Vol. ends: Oct. Microform: UM.

Indexed: AbSocWk, PAIS, PsyAb. *Bk. rev:* 10–15, 300 words, signed. *Aud:* Ac. *Jv:* V.

"A professional journal committed to improving practice and extending knowledge in the field of social welfare." Editors welcome manuscripts which "yield new insights into established practices, evaluate new techniques and research, examine current social problems or bring serious critical analysis to bear on problems of the profession itself." Authors discuss such social problems as poverty, illegitimacy, chronic illness, methods and techniques used in intervention, and the rationale and ideology underlying social work and its specific programs. Regular features include "Points & Viewpoints," which extends the discussion of controversial matters from previous issues, and "Comments on Currents," which deals with current trends such as the guaranteed annual income and poverty legislation. Of value to specialized collections in social welfare.

Social Worker. 1933. q. $4. Anthony Gray. Canadian Assn. of Social Workers, 55 Parkdale Ave., Suite 400, Ottawa, Ont. K1Y 1E5, Canada. Index. Circ: 4,500. Sample. Vol. ends: Nov.

Indexed: AbSocWk, PsyAb. *Bk. rev:* 5–6, 1 page, signed. *Aud:* Ac.

The Canadian equivalent of the American *Social Work.* It covers pretty much the same material as in the American magazine, but from a Canadian viewpoint, some articles in French. The basic Canadian magazine in this field.

Welfare Fighter. 1967. m. $10. Wilbur Colom. National Welfare Rights Organization, 1419 H St. N.W., Washington, D.C. 20005. Illus., index, adv. Circ: 40,000. Sample. Vol. ends: Dec.

Aud: Ga, Ac.

A paper for people who want to know about welfare. Edited chiefly by Blacks, it has dealt with "Appalachian People March," "Chart of the Four Welfare Bills Before Congress," "Farmworkers Boycott Safeway Food Stores." Such is the stuff of this 16 to 24 page tabloid newspaper. Published by a national nonpartisan organization. It is the voice of the poor and those attempting to help them. But there is nothing here of the hat in hand approach. It is a cry for welfare reform. The cry is militant, based upon real need, and the fact that in a land of plenty children are starving. Its primary function for the nonmember is to clear up some of the mystery and misconceptions regarding welfare. The writing is good to excellent; the coverage usually not found in standard sources. One added bonus: the major stories are published in Spanish, too.

Welfare World. 1971. q. $3. Linda L. Cummins. Venture Media Inc., 4444 Rice St., Suite 229, Lihue, Kauai, Hawaii 96766. Illus., adv. Circ: 100,000.

Aud: Ga.

A popular magazine aimed at not only those on welfare, but the aged and others who are unable to work. The primary purpose is to inform; i.e., there are articles on all aspects of welfare from how to get along on a limited diet to how to hire an attorney. A secondary purpose is to entertain, and there are numerous short pieces on everything from diet and beauty tips to movie and record reviews. A useful magazine for almost anyone with a fixed income, and if it isn't precisely high on intellectual content, it is useful in terms of accurate information. The Hawaii base has some, but relatively little, influence over editorial content. Most of the material is as meaningful for someone in Kansas as in Hawaii.

Welfare in Review. See Government Magazines/ United States Section.

SPORTS

Basic Periodicals

GENERAL. Ejh: *Sports;* Hs: *Sports Illustrated, Sports;* Ga: *Sports Illustrated, Sports, Sports Afield;* Jc and Ac: *Sports Illustrated.*

BOATS AND BOATING. Hs: *Motorboating and Sailing;* Ga: *Motorboating and Sailing, Boating.*

FISHING, HUNTING, AND GUNS. Ejh: *Field and Stream;* Hs: *Outdoor Life;* Ga: *Outdoor Life, Field and Stream, American Rifleman.*

PHYSICAL EDUCATION AND SCHOOL SPORTS. Ga: *Olympic Review;* Jc and Ac: *Journal of Health, Physical Education, Recreation.*

Basic Abstracts and Indexes

Boating Abstracts (ceased).

General

Archery World. 1952. bi-m. $3. Glenn Helgeland. Market Communications Inc., 534 N. Broadway, Milwaukee, Wis. 53202. Illus., adv. Circ: 60,000. Sample. Vol. ends: Oct.-Nov.

Bk. rev: 2, 150–200 words, signed. *Aud:* Hs, Ga, Ac.

The official publication of the National Archery Association of the United States, this is the best of two or three magazines in the field. It contains articles on hunting, major tournaments and interviews with famous bowmen. There are how-to-do-it features and book reviews which offer news of titles rarely found in most journals. Suitable for the backyard amateur or the professional, and a good bet for schools where archery is part of the physical education program. See also *Bow and Arrow.*

Baseball Digest. 1942. m. $5. John Kuenster. Century Publishing Co., 1020 Church St., Evanston, Ill. 60201. Illus., adv. Circ: 150,000. Sample. Vol. ends: Dec.

Aud: Ejh, Hs, Ga.

The editor claims this is the only monthly magazine devoted to baseball "and read by those from 8 to 92." He seems to be right, and because of that it can be recommended for any library where there is an on-going interest in the subject. Emphasis is on the major leagues, but there is occasional coverage of amateur leagues, i.e. little league, Babe Ruth, etc. There are photos, player profiles, statistics, and even puzzles and games. The material is written by leading sports writers, primarily from newspapers, and the style will please anyone. See also *Football Digest.* Neither may be essential, but both will enliven any general reading collection.

Bike World. 1972. bi-m. $3. Bob Anderson. Box 366, Mountain View, Calif. 94040. Illus., index, adv. Sample.

Aud: Ga.

A popular bike magazine which is directed to both the expert and the amateur. The editor reports it is ". . . a magazine for active riders written by active riders. We are going to discuss training, cover technical information, coming events and cycling highlights. Profiles on riders, accounts of tours, new ideas, etc." One issue included a fascinating article on an early bike manufacturer; one on touring Utah on bikes; an illustrated piece on what makes a bike go, or fail to go; training articles and reports on events etc. All in all one of the more impressive efforts, and of particular interest to the bike health fan. Send for a sample copy. See also *Runner's World* and *International Cycle Sport.* (See also Automobiles/Motorcycles section.)

Black Belt Magazine. 1960. m. $5.75. Anthony De Leonardis. Black Belt, Inc., 5650 W. Washington Blvd., Los Angeles, Calif. Illus., adv. Circ: 100,000.

Bk. rev: 1–2, 500 words, signed. *Aud:* Hs, Ga.

Primarily devoted to judo, karate, kung fu, etc. Informative and well-illustrated articles feature the art of self defense and cover the history of the martial arts. Personalities, tournaments, and techniques are highlighted. Young boys and adults make up the audience for this magazine. The material is presented in an intelligent fashion, and can be recommended for most school and public libraries. Librarians who dread violence in any magazine are advised that all the violence here is presented in terms of a sport leading to healthy body building.

Black Sports. See Blacks Section.

Bow and Arrow. 1963. bi-m. $3.50. Charles Tyler. Gallant Publishing Co., 130 Olinda Village, Brea, Calif. 92621. Illus., adv. Circ: 89,000. Sample. Vol. ends: Mar./Apr.

Bk. rev: 1, 250 words, signed. *Aud:* Hs, Ga.

Although a somewhat more popular approach than *Archery World,* this magazine takes a similar approach. There are a considerable number of illustrations, advertisements, and tips on new products. One of the most useful features is the testing of new equip-ment done in the field; the results appear to be quite objective. A handy guide for both the coach and the serious archer. Articles range from the use of the bow in war to backyard target practice. Some historical emphasis. For both the beginner and the expert, useful in high schools as well as public libraries.

Bowling Magazine. 1934. m. $3. Stephen K. James. Amer. Bowling Congress, Inc., 1572 E. Capital Dr., Milwaukee, Wis. 53211. Illus., adv. Circ: 125,000.

Aud: Ga.

This official publication of the American Bowling Congress stresses membership news, items regarding events and personalities, and new legislation and equipment. A given amount of space is turned over to detailed tournament results. There is a strong editorial bias favoring the sport as a legitimate expression of Americanism. Little how-to-do-it type material. Primarily for the dedicated bowler.

Caves and Karst; research in speleology. 1959. bi-m. $3.25. A. Lange. Cave Research Associates, 3842 Brookdale Blvd., Castro Valley, Calif. 94546. Illus., index. Circ: 325. Vol. ends: Nov/Dec. Refereed.

Aud: Ac, Sa.

An eight to ten page pocket-sized magazine published by a nonprofit group dedicated to "further study and preservation of natural caves." It usually has one or two detailed articles. Of particular value to cave lovers is the column "from the current literature" which briefly annotates articles and books—selection is world wide. A serious, journal for the expert and would-be expert. It is too technical for general collections. See also *NSS News.*

The Compass. See Free Magazines Section.

Football Digest. 1971. 10/yr. $3. Norman Jacobs. Century Publishing Co., 1020 Church St., Evanston, Ill. 60201. Illus., adv. Circ: 100,000. Sample. Vol. ends: Aug.

Aud: Ejh, Hs, Ga.

This is on the same order as the publisher's *Baseball Digest,* i.e., it covers professional football (and, only occasionally, the amateur scene). There are the usual statistics, players profiles, pictures, and general articles on the sport. The journalistic style will appeal to any fan, regardless of age. A good item for most libraries. (Incidentally, the publisher mails free copies to high school and university coaches. If you cannot afford the magazine you might hit up the coach for his copy. The same procedure applies to *Baseball Digest.*)

Golf Digest. 1950. m. $7.50. Richard Aultman. Golf Digest, Inc., 88 Scribner Ave., Norwalk, Conn. 06856. Illus., adv. Circ: 535,000. Vol. ends: Dec.

Bk. rev: 2, 250 words, signed. *Aud:* Hs, Ga.

Written and edited for the beginning and professional golfer. Detailed and thorough instruction in good golfing principles and techniques from professionals such as Snead, Nelson, and Casper. Informative articles highlight profiles of promising and established golfing personalities, interesting and unusual golfing situations and feats, records, predictions, and biographies. Includes "Golf Information Directory," information on televised matches, vacation tips, and a complete guide to courses that can be played. Liberal use of charts, diagrams, and photographs (black-and-white; color) throughout. Owned and published by the *New York Times.*

Golf Magazine. 1959. m. $7.95. John Fry. Universal Publishing and Distributing Corp., 235 E. 45th St., New York, N.Y. 10017. Illus., adv. Circ: 481,000.

Aud: Ga.

One of the basic golf magazines for the dedicated fan. Among the contributors: Gene Sarazen and Oscar Fraley. Offers tips and suggestions for handling all types of golfing situations and difficulties. Answers questions on techniques, tactics, and rules of the game. Spotlights the latest in golfing attire, tournaments, and equipment. Golf vacation guide included. Between this and *Golf Digest* the decision is simply a matter of personal preference. Librarians might try them both, or one after the other.

Golf World. 1960. m. $7. Keith Mackie. Golf World Ltd., Golf House, South Rd., Brighton BN1 6SY, England. Illus., adv. Circ: 50,000.

Aud: Ga.

Primarily involved with the British golf scene, but does include information and articles on international events. Useful, too, for simplified instructions and biographical sketches. Hardly a required item in American libraries, but one worth considering where the game is a phobia.

International Cycle Sport. 1968. m. $10. John Wilcockson. Kennedy Brothers, Yorkshire, England. Subs. to: 3570 Warrensville Center Rd., Shaker Heights, Ohio 44122. Illus., index, adv. Sample.

Aud: Hs, Ga.

A 40-page, profusely illustrated magazine devoted almost exclusively to bike riding contests in Europe. (Note: this is bicycles, not motorcycles.) The European emphasis is underlined by a *Washington Post* piece published in the November 1971 issue: "In spite of the Americans' current desire to buy almost every available bicycle on the market, the interest in racing them or watching races is slight at the present time. . . . The fact that a man is a jogger doesn't necessarily mean he enjoys track meets." Still, there may be enough American bike fans about who share the rest of the world's fascination with the sport. All the races,

records, personalities, and events are dutifully listed here. The well-written articles require no special knowledge of the sport. The advertisements will fascinate anyone interested in bikes. All-in-all, an interesting consideration for any general collection.

Lykes Fleet Flashes. See Free Magazines Section.

NSS News. 1942. m. $6. Ron A. Bridgeman. National Speleological Soc., 2318 N. Kenmore St., Arlington, Va. 22201. Illus., index, adv. Circ: 3,800.

Bk. rev: 2–3, 500 words. *Aud:* Hs, Ga, Ac.

Primarily a news and notes approach to speleology (the study of caves), a sport which is as scientific as it is exciting. In some 20 to 30 illustrated pages the editor presents one or two short articles, letters, book reviews and activities of various regional groups—not just those in Virginia. The audience for this type of thing tends to be a well-informed group; it should have particular appeal for better educated, somewhat sophisticated readers. Which is to say, it will go as well in academic and high school libraries, as in public libraries.

Outdoors. See Free Magazines Section.

The Ring; world's official boxing magazine. 1922. m. $6. Nat Loubet. The Ring, Inc., 120 W. 31st., New York, N.Y. 10019. Illus., adv. Circ: 100,000. Sample. Vol. ends: Jan.

Bk. rev: 1,500 words. *Aud:* Ga.

Featured articles, fully illustrated with photographs and drawings, cover the whole boxing universe. Ring fight reports from all parts of the world, boxing personalities present and past, and news of interest to the boxing world are included. The deliberate inclusion of some articles by editors and boxing notables is designed to evoke controversy and interest. Contains world rating of various fighters and tips on fighters of promise. Appeal limited to those interested in boxing.

Runner's World. 1965. bi-m. $3. Joe Henderson. Bob Anderson, Box 366, Mountain View, Calif. 94040. Illus., index, adv. Circ: 8,000. Sample. Vol. ends: Nov.

Aud: Ga.

A 56-page illustrated magazine for amateur and expert, man and woman, child and oldster—in fact, for anyone interested in running for fun and life or for the sport and the winner's circle. Most emphasis, though, is on the amateur who is running to keep himself or herself in good health. The tone is set by a nice combination of experienced editing and "folksy" touches which bring all readers into one magic track. The only requirement for interest and membership is a desire for fun. There are usually three or four articles, e.g., a coach's story on track, a piece on the effects of running, and a nine-page feature on crosscountry running, plus numerous departments which report on running/walking events, track records, medical hints, letters, etc. The whole is authoritative, quite sane for this type of magazine, and one of the best available for anyone who enjoys the idea of running for health. It would be a first choice in its category, and suitable for any size or kind of library. See also *Bike World*. (Note: The publisher has a series of pamphlets on running which are issued each month, e.g., *Running After Forty, New Views of Speed Training*. They are illustrated, vary from 24 to 36 pages, and sell for various prices. The series, i.e., an annual subscription for 12 pamphlets, is $12. They are well worth considering, and interested librarians might write for a sample and the complete catalog.)

Skating. 1923. m. $3.50. Karen MacDonald. United States Figure Skating Assn., 178 Tremont St., Boston, Mass. 02111. Illus., index, adv. Circ: 22,000. Sample. Vol. ends: June.

Aud: Hs, Ga.

Geared to the competitive and the recreational skater of all ages. Profiles of skating personalities, meet results, and technical articles are included. There are tips for beginners and tips on figure, dance, and freestyle skating, appropriately illustrated. It spotlights ice show reviews and itineraries. A section of the magazine is devoted to the Association-affiliated skater; it includes lists of tests passed in the United States. Of its type the best magazine available, and a good addition for all kinds of libraries.

Ski. 1935. 8/yr. $5. John Fry. Universal Publishing and Distributing Corp., 235 E. 45th St., New York, N.Y. 10017. Illus., adv. Circ: 365,000. Sample.

Aud: Ga.

Editors claim this is "world's leading ski magazine." Informative articles, lavishly illustrated, spotlight activities throughout the ski world. Contains "where to go and where to stay" information here and abroad. Expert advice and instruction from nationally and internationally famous masters. Profiles of famous ski personalities and great moments in racing. Offers winter driving tips, up-to-date equipment ideas for skiers on the slopes or in competition. Appeal limited to those in middle or upper middle income brackets, but for skiers of all ages and expertise.

Skiing. 1947. 7/yr (Sept.–Mar.). $4. Doug Pfeiffer. Ziff Davis Publishing Co., 1 Park Ave., New York, N.Y. 10016. Illus., adv. Circ: 450,000.

Bk. rev: notes. *Aud:* Ejh, Hs, Ga.

Of the 15 to 20 skiing magazines published here and abroad, this is the most popular, i.e., at least in terms of circulation and advertising. It puts strong emphasis on equipment and how-to-do–type information, with the usual articles on resorts, competitions, and feature stories. A regional section gives specific ski data on

conditions in the East, Midwest, and the Far West. Illustrations, which are numerous, are good to excellent. A first choice for the high school and public library. (In the previous edition, it was pointed out that this appeals to the less affluent. Not so, says the editor—which may be a plus or minus, depending on how you look at it. Both this and *Ski* push the fact they have strong appeal for those in the higher income brackets. At any rate, the sport as envisioned by either magazine is not for the poor.)

Skin Diver Magazine. 1951. m. $7.50. Paul J. Tzimoulis. Petersen Publishing Co., 8490 Sunset Blvd., Los Angeles, Calif., 90069. Illus., adv. Circ: 100,000. Sample. Vol. ends: Dec.

Bk. rev: 8, short notes. *Aud:* Hs, Ga.

An action packed magazine devoted to skin diving and the whole underwater world. Excellent articles range the broad spectrum from ocean science to spear fishing, travel, and boats. Famous ship wrecks, sunken treasure, diving techniques, and true life experiences stimulate the reader's interest and imagination. Brilliantly illustrated with full color and black-and-white photographs. The Diver's Directory serves the local and traveling diver. Suggestions and tips on "where to go" and "what to do" for the diving enthusiast included. Should delight the teen-ager as well as the adult audience.

Softball Illustrated. 1967. $3. Don Sarno and Milton Stark. P.O. Box 1081, Whittier, Calif. 90603. Circ: 10,000.

Aud: Hs, Ga.

Covers all aspects of softball: activities of the industrial leagues, how to organize children's teams, how to improve a woman's game, even a section entitled "National Tournament Review." Should be particularly useful to urban libraries in areas where there are several teams, or in high schools and colleges where the game is played regularly.

Sport. 1946. m. $6. Al Silverman. MacFadden-Bartell, 205 E. 42nd St., New York, N.Y. 10017. Illus., index, adv. Circ: 1,365,000. Sample. Vol. ends: Dec.

Bk. rev: 2, 250 words, signed. *Aud:* Ejh, Hs, Ga. *Jv:* V.

Since our last edition, the circulation has almost doubled and this continues to be one of the most popular general sporting magazines published. Emphasis is on the "fan" approach to sports, and the fair to good illustrated articles feature what this or that baseball player or football star thinks about the game. The writing style is in the tradition of sports journalism. Articles are heavy on the "stars," light on intellectual content. Each issue is balanced by special features and news of current sporting events. It differs radically from its competitor *Sports Illustrated.* The format is not as good, and it stresses the nitty gritty of the sporting life. It pays little or no attention to the gentlemanly aspects. As such it offends the sensitive, disturbs the dedicated sportsman, and is a constant joy for teen-agers and less sophisticated adults. A good bet to lure the nonreader to the library; first choice for junior high and high school libraries.

The Sporting News; the nation's oldest sports publication. 1886. w. $12. Lowell Reidenbaugh. The Sporting News, 1212 N. Lindbergh Blvd., St. Louis, Mo. 63166.

Aud: Ga.

This informative, entertaining, easy-to-read newspaper is America's oldest national sports weekly. Interesting and exciting articles cover baseball, basketball, golf, soccer, and other sports in season. Special departments include both professional and collegiate football. Filled with statistics, stories, gossip, and action photographs (black-and-white; color) that capture and hold the reader's interest. Capsule treatment of sporting news of yesteryear. For sports fans of all ages, although the format and relatively high price dictate inclusion only in larger collections, or where there is a particularly strong interest in the subject.

Sports Afield. 1888. m. $4. Lamar Underwood. Hearst Publishing Corp., 250 W. 55th St. New York, N.Y. 10019. Illus., index, adv. Circ: 1,424,000. Vol. ends: Dec. Sample.

Bk. rev: 1–4, 150–300 words. *Aud:* Hs, Ga.

Takes in all types of activities from conservation to camping. It is particularly good for down-to-earth tips on outdoor living. The style is simple, direct, and easily understood by the high school student. It is extensively illustrated, but the photographs are only poor to good. The more sophisticated fisherman or hunter probably would put this somewhere behind *Outdoor Life* and *Field and Stream.* But the differences are few, and a choice among the three is more a matter of personal bias than objective judgment. A library might try one after the other for a number of years. (P.B.)

Sports Digest. 1971. m. $3.50. Douglas A. Lang. Sports Digest, Box 3429, Miami, Fla. 33101. Illus., adv.

Aud: Hs, Ga. *Jv:* C.

Primarily a vehicle for advertising, this pocket-sized magazine is made up of two parts. There are 30 pages from the Florida base which includes general articles on both spectator and participating sports. Then there is a 30-page insert from the Westchester, N.Y., area which is devoted to the local scene. For every line of copy there are four lines of advertising. Can be overlooked by all libraries.

Sports Illustrated. 1954. w. $12. Andre Laguerre. Time. Inc., Time-Life Bldg., New York, N.Y. 10020. Illus., index, adv. Circ: 2,200,000. Sample. Vol. ends: Dec. 21. Microform: UM.

Indexed: AbrRG, RG. *Bk. rev:* 1, 1–2 columns, signed. *Aud:* Ejh, Hs, Ga, Ac. *Jv:* V.

America's best-known general sports magazine, this is the Time/Life approach to the "wide world of sports." Covers the usual spectator sports (baseball, basketball, boxing, football), and features lengthy articles (2,000–5,000 words) on mountain climbing, big game hunts, horse racing, boating, and major sports personalities. Lists sports records, "backs" and "players of the week," and reports timely news of current interest to the sporting world. Primarily staff written, but articles have also been commissioned from major literary figures. Extensive use is made of brilliant paintings, black-and-white and color photography. And while the level of writing is a bit difficult for anyone in an elementary school, the illustrations and statistical data give it a place even here, certainly in junior high schools. Even readers with a limited interest in sports will find something of interest here. Should be in all libraries.

Surfer Magazine. 1960. bi-m. $5. Steve Pezman. P.O. Box 1028, Dana Point, Calif. 92629. Illus., adv. Circ: 100,000. Sample. Vol. ends: Feb.

Aud: Ejh, Hs, Ga.

One of the best magazines devoted to surfing. Particularly good for the how-to-do-it articles and where to go for the best surf. This latter feature makes it a type of travel magazine, and the well illustrated articles—many in color—on the waters of France, South America and the eastern and western United States (to mention a few spots covered) give it some appeal for nonswimmers. Good cartoons, but the limited fiction is a bit weak. A good bet for any school or public library where there is interest in the sport.

Surveyor. See Free Magazines Section.

Swimming World. m. $7.50. Albert Schoenfield. 12618 Killion St., North Hollywood, Calif. 91607. Illus., adv. Circ: 18,000. Sample. Vol. ends: Dec.

Bk. rev: 3, notes. *Aud:* Hs, Ga, Ac.

Geared for dedicated swimmers and coaches, this is the official magazine of the American Swimming Coaches Association, the National Interscholastic Swimming Coaches Association and the College Swimming Coaches Association. A great deal of space is devoted to naming conference dates and record holders, all Americans, national champions, and Olympic summaries. One or two articles per issue stress diving, swimming, body building (conditioning) or stroke techniques and are written by coaches of universities and colleges. Individual champions and record holders are interviewed and photographed. Prolific advertising devoted entirely to the related field—anything from wheat germ to diving boards. For the competitive swimmer, diver, and water polo player; and for high school libraries.

Tennis. 1965. m. $5. P.O. Box 5, Ravina Station, Highland Park, Ill. 60039. Illus., adv. Circ: 15,000.

Aud: Hs, Ac.

One of two official publications of the United States Professional Lawn Association, this differs from *Tennis U.S.A.* in that it includes all racquet sports, e.g., tennis, badminton, table tennis and squash. The articles and news items are directed to both the professional and the young amateur. The mixture of how-to-do-it material with fashions, cartoons and personalities is a little too diverse for the serious tennis player, but has appeal for youngsters. There are the usual calendar of tournaments, results of national and regional matches, products reports and even a gift guide. No substitute for either *Tennis U.S.A.* or *World Tennis*, and a third choice in most libraries.

Tennis: National Magazine of the Racquet Sports. 1965. m. $5. Asher J. Birnbaum. Tennis Features, Box 805, Highland Park, Ill. 60035. Circ: 70,000.

Aud: Hs, Ga, Ac.

Despite the fact that this is the official monthly publication of the United States Professional Tennis Association, the swinging side of tennis is presented here as well as reports of tournament results. Although tennis is the primary field of coverage, squash, table tennis, paddle ball, platform tennis, and badminton are included. Guides for technique improvement written by professionals, such as "Pro Stroke Guide," and a series on "How to coach your own child," will be of interest to the practitioner. A health column, travel news, fashion news, and articles on the lighter side of tennis provide a good variety. Action photos are found throughout the magazine, including the "Picture of the month." Tennis fans will be pleased to find this publication in the public or school library. (M.A.)

Tennis U.S.A. 1937. m. $4. Hal Steeger. Popular Publns., Inc., 205 E. 42nd St., New York, N.Y. 10017. Illus., adv. Circ: 30,000. Sample. Vol. ends: Dec.

Aud: Hs, Ac.

Primarily for tennis coaches and serious players, this is the official publication of the United States Lawn Tennis Association. Emphasis is on how to promote, teach and to an extent, play the game. Particularly useful in reference because it gives full reports on national and international tournaments, many supported by the Association. Features include court and equipment reports, profiles of national champions, news of the organization, and rule changes. Differs from *World Tennis* in that it concentrates on amateur efforts, while the other tennis magazine considers professional play equally important. Of the two, *Tennis U.S.A.* will be of more direct benefit to teachers and players from high school through college, while the *World Tennis* will have greater appeal for fans of all ages.

The Woman Bowler. 1936. m. (except May and July). $2. Charles W. Westlake. Woman's Intl. Bowling Congress, Inc., 1225 Dublin Rd., Columbus, Ohio 43212. Illus., adv. Circ: 125,000. Sample.

Aud: Ga.

Details activities and events involving women bowlers, and includes some discussion of rules and regulations pertinent to the sport. Outstanding games and performances are spotlighted along with leading prize winners and personalities in various tournaments. Photographs, color and black-and-white, are widely used throughout and bowling fashion news and equipment are featured.

World Tennis. 1953. m. $6. Gladys M. Heldman. World Tennis Magazine, 8100 Westglen, Houston, Tex. 77042. Illus., adv. Circ: 80,000. Sample. Vol. ends: May.

Aud: Hs, Ga.

Features eight to ten instruction articles monthly and the tennis lessons are accompanied by action photographs, diagrams. Some picture stories on personalities and matches are included. Articles are written by well-known professionals. Features: tennis news from around the world; lists the world ranking of outstanding tennis stars; happenings of "25 years ago"; answers questions posed by correspondents; tips on tennis fashions; detailed results of tournaments; and equipment evaluation. Probably the best tennis magazine for the general collection. See also *Tennis U.S.A.*

Boats and Boating

American White Water. 1955. q. Membership (Nonmembers $3.50) Iris Sindelar. George Larsen, Box 1584, San Bruno, Calif. 94066. Illus., index, adv. Circ: 2,000. Sample. Vol. ends: winter.

Indexed: BoAb. *Bk. rev:* Occasional. *Aud:* Ga, Ac.

There are few American periodicals dealing specifically with canoeing and although this magazine is written for whitewater kayak enthusiasts there is much of interest to the general canoeist. While the technique articles are of whitewater interest only the magazine carries others on canoe touring, wilderness camping, free rivers and conservation of unspoiled areas. The book reviews are frequently evaluations of canoeing guides for all areas of the United States. A magazine to be considered by any library serving a clientele interested in kayaking or canoe touring. Another canoe possibility is *Canoeing Magazine* (25 Featherbed Lane, Croydon CRO9AE, England). (M.B.)

Boating. 1956. m. $7. M. H. Farnham. Ziff Davis Pub. Co., 1 Park Ave., New York, N.Y. 10016. Illus., adv. Circ: 200,000. Sample. Vol. ends: Dec. Microform: UM.

Indexed: BoAb. *Bk. rev:* 3, 1 column, signed. *Aud:* Hs, Ga, Ac.

A general interest boating magazine of particular value to the beginning boatman and the boat owner of moderate means. The design section evaluates plans of power and sail craft, including some low priced smaller boats. A good choice for almost any library and a second choice for libraries which have already committed themselves to *Motor Boating and Sailing* or *Yachting*. (M.B.)

Classic Boat Monthly. 1971. m. $5. David Kasanof. 108 Germonds Rd., New York, N.Y. 10956. Illus. Circ: 500. Sample. Vol. ends: Dec.

Bk. rev: 1–2, 200 words. *Aud:* Ga.

An eight-page newsletter which a fan says is well worth the $5 subscription price. The purpose of the illustrated letter is to spread the word about both classic sail and power boats. The material is written by the editor, is accurate, folksy and full of love for the craft. A couple of short articles, several news notes, and some classifieds. Short, but to the point. Interested librarians should send for a sample.

Family Houseboating. 1968. bi-m. $4. Art Rouse. Trailer Life Publishing Co., 1048 Riverside Dr., North Hollywood, Calif. 91602. Illus., index, adv. Sample. Vol. ends: Dec.

Aud: Ga.

This magazine, for both owners and renters of houseboats, contains articles about recreational houseboating as well as full time living aboard. The cruising articles describe both domestic and foreign cruises and would be interesting even to a nonboater. Original designs submitted by readers are evaluated together with plans for commercially available craft. A directory of rental operators is published and revised periodically. *Family Houseboating* is another title recommended in the last revision of the *Whole Earth Catalog.* Not a first choice but would be a good alternate for public libraries in areas where houseboats are popular. (M.B.)

Lake Michigan Sailing. See *Sailing.*

Lakeland Boating. 1946. 10/yr. $5. David R. Kitz. Parkken Publns., Box 523, Ann Arbor, Mich. 48107. Illus., adv. Circ: 25,000. Sample. Vol. ends: Nov./Dec.

Indexed: BoAb. *Aud:* Ga.

A magazine for the Great Lakes and upper Mississippi area. Regional boating news, interesting cruises and evaluations of new designs are regular features. Articles are short, in popular style, illustrated and aimed at the practical side of boating, e.g., "How to buy a used trailer" in the April 1971 issue. A high percentage of advertising versus content but a good second or third choice for public libraries in the area covered. (M.B.)

Motor Boating and Sailing (Formerly: ***Motor Boating***). 1908. m. $7. Peter R. Smith. Hearst Corp., 224 W. 57th St., New York, N.Y. 10017. Illus., adv. Circ: 110,000. Sample. Vol. ends: Dec. Microform: UM.

Indexed: BoAb, RG. *Bk. rev:* 3, signed. *Aud:* Hs, Ga, Ac. *Jv:* V.

Possibly the best overall boating magazine. While the title might indicate more articles of interest to the power-boatman there is much material for the sailor, and also a section on watersports which covers fishing, scuba diving, and other aquatic sports. Articles are lengthy and informative. Book reviews, averaging 100–200 words, are evaluative and include titles of interest to fishermen and travelers. Detailed evaluation of designs and new boats, narrative articles, a calendar of forthcoming events and descriptions of new products are included as regular departments. Its wide scope and authoritative information make *Motor Boating and Sailing* an excellent choice for almost any library. (M.B.)

National Fisherman. 1903. m. (plus, yearbook). $5. David R. Getschell. Journal Publns., 21 Elm St., Camden, Maine. 04843. Illus., index, adv. Circ: 43,000. Sample. Vol. ends: Apr.

Bk. rev: 2, 100–300 words. *Aud:* Ga, Ac.

The trade journal of the fishing industry, but it has more comprehensive boating information than the title would indicate. Besides news and information on the fishing industry there are articles on maritime history, boat builders and seafood recipes. The journal is amply illustrated with photographs and drawings. The May 1971 issue had a 16-page annotated supplement of books relating to fishing, sailing, navigation, and other marine interests. *National Fisherman* is one of the few periodicals included in the final revision of the *Whole Earth Catalog*, and it would be a title valuable to the fisherman, the marine historian and the average reader of boating magazines and books. A disadvantage from a library point of view is that the journal is a tabloid printed on newsprint but this fact should not stand in the way of at least a trial subscription. An excellent value for any library needing nautical information. (M.B.)

One-Design and Offshore Yachtsman. 1962. m. $8. Bruce Kirby. 154 E. St., Rm. 610, Chicago, Ill. 60611. Dist. by: Eastern News Co., 155 W. 15th St., N.Y. Illus., adv. Circ: 55,000. Sample. Vol. ends: Dec.

Indexed: BoAb. *Aud:* Ga, Ac.

A specialized magazine for the serious sailboat racer in organized classes from sailfish to ocean racers. Articles feature various classes, items of racing equipment and evaluations of major races. Regular departments include discussions of racing tactics, lengthy analyses of designs and news of worldwide races as well as U.S. intercollegiate racing results. Good format with ample illustrations, diagrams and tables. One issue each year is an illustrated catalog of available sailboat classes with specifications, prices and the address of the class information officer if there is one. Not a first choice for the general library but should be considered by public libraries in areas where sailboat racing is popular and in academic libraries whose institutions offer sailing programs or compete in intercollegiate racing. (M.B.)

Rudder. 1890. m. $7. Stuart James. Fawcett Publns., Fawcett Bldg., Greenwich, Conn. 06830. Illus., adv. Circ: 120,000. Sample. Vol. ends: Dec.

Indexed: BoAb. *Aud:* Ga.

Another general boating magazine, with articles of interest to the sailor and power boatman. A regular feature is question and answer columns on boat maintenance, boat design, engines, electronics, and cruising. Although seemingly aimed at the "little boat owner" *Rudder* would probably not be a first choice for the library; *Motor Boating and Sailing* would be better for technical information and *Boating* is a better general second choice. (M.B.)

Sail. 1970. m. $8. Murray L. Davis. Inst. for Advancement of Sailing, 38 Commercial Wharf, Boston, Mass. 02110. Illus., adv. Circ: 75,000.

Bk. rev: notes. *Aud:* Hs, Ga, Ac.

The Road and Track of the sailing world. This does for the sailor what the leading automobile mag does for the serious car buff. Both cater to dreams, and fancies, yet give practical advice on technical matters. While the magazine is written for the man or woman who can afford a sail boat, it is, also, down to earth in advice and the recognition one can have as much fun with a small catamaran as with a racing cruiser. The style of writing in *Sail* is excellent, the illustrations and charts as good, and the editorial comments leave *Road and Track* behind. Why? Well, dedicated to getting along primarily without engines, *Sail* is pushing environment and preservation of our waters. The editorials are persuasive. Published in Boston, most of what is said is applicable to any part of the world, inland seas as well as oceans. In fact, there are a number of world wide historical articles. All in all an excellent magazine for the sailing fanatic of any age.

Sailing; the beauty of sail (Formerly: *Lake Michigan Sailing).* 1966. m. $5. William F. Schanen. Port Publns., Inc., 125 E. Main St., Port Washington, Wis. 53074. Illus., adv. Circ: 12,000.

Bk. rev: 3–4, 150 words. *Aud:* Ga. *Jv:* C.

Strong on oversized photos—the magazine measures 16 by 11 inches—bits of supporting copy, and a good deal of advertising. And while fun to look at, it is not much for the serious fan. A third or fourth choice for libraries, although for only $5 the sailing fan does get a tremendous amount of visuals in 50 to 60 pages.

Sea Classics. 1968. bi-m. $6.50. Challenge Publns., Inc., 7950 Deering Ave., Canoga Park, Calif. 91304. Illus.

Aud: Hs, Ga.

A handsome pictorial chronicle of seafaring all over the world. It explores the sea and attempts to satisfy the timeless interest of the ageless saga of ships and men, in war and peace. Features interesting and informative documented articles on ships of all kinds, as well as stories of adventure connected with them. Each article is colorfully illustrated with excellent photographs, drawings, color paintings, cutaways, and profiles. One article detailed the story of "hell ships" —those prison ships used from the American Revolution to the California Gold Rush days; another dealt with the construction of the Panama Canal. Authors present both the historical perspective and contemporary stories of seafaring. Mainly written for popular consumption, this would fit best into a public and high school library and for recreational reading in a college library. For the general male reader from high school on up. (M.E.)

Sea and Pacific Motor Boat. 1904. m. $7. Robert E. Walters. Miller Freeman Publns., P.O. Box 20227, Long Beach, Calif. 90801. Illus., index, adv. Circ: 56,000. Sample. Vol. ends: Dec. Microform: UM.

Indexed: BoAb. *Bk. rev:* 5, various lengths. *Aud:* Ga.

The regional boating magazine for the western United States and Canada, covering yacht club activities, race results and forthcoming events of nautical interest. Articles are short and generally of regional interest; a good second or third choice for western public libraries. (M.B.)

Skipper. 1947. m. $8. H. K. Rigg. 2nd St. at Spa Creek, Annapolis, Md. 21404. Illus., adv. Circ: 38,000.

Indexed: BoAb. *Bk. rev:* 3–7, 150–300 words, signed. *Aud:* Ga.

Articles of interest to boatmen (both power and sail), manufacturers of boating equipment, and designers. Fresh, well written narratives, approximately 75 percent by free lance contributors, cover topics pertaining to the sea and sailing. Good nautical fiction and true adventure stories are sometimes included. Special departments given over to news, notes and comments from around the world. All articles are well illustrated with excellent photographs. The addition of fiction and the relatively popular style make this particularly suited for those who may or may not have a boat. (M.B.)

Watersport. 1967. q. Membership $5. A. W. Limburgh. Boat Owners Council of America, 534 N. Broadway, Milwaukee, Wis. 53202. Illus.

Aud: Ga. *Jv:* C.

Although this title was recommended in the first edition of *Magazines*, recent issues seem to indicate that it is more of a general interest magazine similar to those distributed by credit card companies and various airlines. Written for popular consumption, the articles are interesting and colorfully illustrated but short on factual information. No technical information. An interesting time-passer but not an essential boating magazine. (M.B.)

Yachting. 1907. m. $8.50. William W. Robinson. Yachting Publishing Co., 50 W. 44th St., New York, N.Y. 10036. Illus., index, adv. Circ: 122,000. Sample. Vol. ends: June, Dec. Microform: UM.

Indexed: BoAb, RG. *Bk. rev:* 4, 250 words, signed. *Aud:* Ga, Ac.

Experienced boatmen will find *Yachting* an interesting and informative publication. Articles are lengthy, authoritative and technical accompanied by useful photographs, diagrams and charts. Although *Yachting* is indexed in *Reader's Guide* it would be a second or third choice for libraries which need advanced boating information. (M.B.)

Fishing, Hunting, and Guns

The American Rifleman. 1885. m. $7.50. Ashley Halsey, Jr. National Rifle Assn. of America, 1600 Rhode Island Ave. N.W., Washington, D.C. 20036. Illus., index, adv. Circ: 1,021,000. Vol. ends: Dec. Sample.

Bk. rev: 1–4, 300–500 words, signed. *Aud:* Hs, Ga, Ac. *Jv:* V.

The *American Rifleman* has one essential reference function for *any* library which receives calls for information on gun control legislation, for it includes a monthly report on *all* state and federal laws, proposed or passed, as well as expanded articles on significant legislation. Articles are usually on the technical, historical, or how-to-do-it aspects of shooting and hunting. Close-up photography is excellent. The factual, journalistic style of presentation will discourage all but the most interested readers of any age group. However, this is still the best general gun magazine for public libraries, followed by *Sporting Times* and *Guns.* In high school libraries where there is a need for a gun magazine, *Sporting Times* should be the first choice. (P.B.)

Angling Times. 1953. w. $7.80. Jack Thorndike. East Midland Press, Ltd., Newspaper House, Broadway, Peterborough, England. Illus., index, adv. Circ: 147,090. Vol. ends: June. Samples.

Bk. rev: 1–4, 750–1,000 words. *Aud:* Ga, Ac.

An informative and well-illustrated publication devoted to the sport of angling with rod and line in Great Britain and Ireland. Latest equipment and methods for capturing freshwater, sea or game fish are covered in detail. Advocates intelligent and responsible use of public and private waters. Provides answering service for reader's queries and clues to good fishing around the coast. Features the "Kingfisher Page" for young anglers under 16. Newspaper format. The publisher also issues two other related journals: *Trout and*

Salmon and *Fishing.* Both are excellent sources of information for the fishing enthusiast. (P.B.)

Field and Stream. 1895. m. 2vol./yr. $5. Clare Conley. Holt, Rinehart & Winston, Inc., 383 Madison Ave., New York, N.Y. 10017. Illus., adv. Circ: 1,650,000. Sample.

Indexed: AbrG, RG. *Bk. rev:* various number, length. *Aud:* Ejh, Hs, Ga, Ac.

One of the major American outdoor sporting magazines, this puts primary emphasis on "where to go" and "how to do it." It has appeal for all men and boys who enjoy hunting, fishing, and boating. The editors have a strong commitment to conservation, which is reflected in many of the articles and illustrations. One or two personal accounts of hunting and fishing experiences are usually included. The advertisements are informative and geared to the specialized audience. This side of an all-girl's school (and it might be enjoyed there), this is a required magazine in almost any type of library from the junior high to the public library. (P.B.)

Fur-Fish-Game (Harding's Magazine). 1904. $3.50. A. R. Harding. Harding Publishing Co., 2878 E. Main St., Columbus, Ohio. 43209. Illus., index. Circ: 135,000. *Aud:* Hs, Ga.

Few magazines have existed as quietly and successfully as *Fur-Fish-Game. Fur-Fish-Game* stresses hunting and conservation rather than guns and shooting, hence it is more useful than *Shooting Times* where libraries wish to place heavy emphasis in these areas. Libraries on low periodicals budgets and those in rural areas where hunting, fishing, trapping, and conservation are ways of life should not be without this fine and inexpensive magazine with its very fine photographs and, incidentally, one of the most comprehensive subject-related advertising sections to be found anywhere. (P.B.)

Gun Report; dedicated to the interests of gun enthusiasts everywhere. 1955. m. $6. Kenneth W. Liggett. World-Wide Gun Report, Inc., Box 111, Aledo, Ill. 61231. Illus., index, adv. Circ: 8,324. Vol. ends: May. Sample.

Aud: Ga.

The official publication of the Florida Gun Collectors Association and the Vermillion Trail Historical Arms Association this is a "must" for the gun and cartridge collector. News and articles of interest are written by experts in the field. Historical material is liberally illustrated. Important features are the "Antique Arm Prices" and the "Collectors Cartridge Prices," which are derived from reports of bonafide sales at collectors' meetings and from recent catalogs. Handsome photographs in black and white, charts, and diagrams throughout. Although this is, technically speaking, a "regional" magazine, its value as a source of information in its field of competence is unquestionably national in importance. (P.B.)

Gun Talk. 1961. Membership (Nonmembers $5) John Harold. Saskatchewan Gun Collectors Assn., Box 1334, Regina, Saskatchewan, Canada. Illus., index, adv. Circ: 240. Vol. ends: Dec.

Bk. rev: 1, 50 words. *Aud:* Ga. *Jv:* C.

An amateur effort which is primarily of value to members of the sponsoring organization. It is a potpourri of personal anecdotes, folks, wisdom and humor. There is rather superficial information about fake, real and ideal guns; condensations from books; and even an article on the sex appeal of Adolph Hitler. While not recommended, it is included here as an example of many such local publications. Some, to be sure are better; others worse, but before ordering material of this type the wise librarian will check out a sample copy. (C.F.)

Gun Week. 1966. w. $5. John Amos. Sidney Printing and Publishing Co., Box 150, Sidney, Ohio 45365. Illus., index, adv. Circ: 35,000. Sample. Vol. ends: Dec.

Aud: Ga.

A 20-page tabloid newspaper which is of considerable value for anyone who wants to keep up with current news in the gun and shooting world. Articles deal with trophy matches, new guns and equipment, the use of arms, personalities, and legislation and court cases which will affect the gun fan. Some attention is given to conservation and hunting, collecting, and the history of arms. Editorially, the paper is opposed to most legislation limiting gun ownership; but, on the other hand, takes a strong stand for stringent measures to protect the environment. Although not the most objective or well-written journal of this type, it is superior to most in its wide and timely reporting. (C.F.)

Guns (Formerly: **Guns Magazine**). 1955. m. $7.50. J. Rakusan. Publishers' Development Corp., 8150 N. Central Park Ave., Skokie, Ill. 60076. Illus., adv. Circ: 132,250. Vol. ends: Dec.

Bk. rev: 3–5, 50–300 words, signed. *Aud:* Ga.

Informative articles on modern and antique guns, ballistics, technology, patents, and how-to material related to guns and shooting. Special departments are devoted to guns and the law, answering queries from correspondents, gun collecting, gunsmithing tips, and the guns market. Useful, but not always critical book reviews. Liberal use of handsome color photographs along with regular pictures in black and white. This is a more popular, general approach than *Gun Report*, and probably would be first choice in most libraries, although the latter has a higher reference value for pricing guns. (P.B.)

Guns & Ammo. 1958. m. $7.50. Tom Siatos. Peterson Publishing Co., 5959 Hollywood Blvd., Los Angeles, Calif. 90028. Illus., index, adv. Circ: 250,000. Sample. Vol. ends: Dec. Microform: UM.

Bk. rev: 3–5, 400–700 words, signed. *Aud:* Ga.

This is the "glamour" gun publication, catering to the off-beat, do-it-yourself, esoterica of shooting and hunting. G & A can serve one valued reference function as the purveyor of a series of accurate, well-written and illustrated articles on historical arms and arms collecting. Thus G & A, backfiles included, can be an excellent substitute for assembling an expensive collection of books on guns. Many articles border on the sensational, and the gun legislation controversy is much more objectively handled by other magazines. Note: this now incorporates *Guns & Hunting* which, since the last edition, is no longer published as a separate magazine. (P.B.)

Guns & Game. 1963. bi-m. $4.50. Theodore Hecht. Stanley Publns., Inc., 261 Fifth Ave., New York, N.Y. 10016. Illus.

Aud: Hs, Ga.

The title of this magazine hits the nail on the head as to the subject area covered, and the issues observed seem to balance and blend the two subjects well. Although *Guns & Game* is one of the least-known titles in this field, several veteran, highly respected writers appear regularly. Photographs are good but suffer from low grade paper. Still, if one required a blend of the two subjects, this title, for content, ought to rank second only to *Fur-Fish-Game*, with *Shooting Times*, because of its pro gun imbalance, coming in third. (P.B.)

Guns Review. 1958. m. $9. G. H. Brown. Ravenhill Publishing Co., Ltd., Standard House, Rowhill St., London EC2, England. Illus., index, adv. Circ: 13,000. Sample. Vol. ends: Dec.

Bk. rev: Occasionally. *Aud:* Ga.

The greatest asset of this official journal of the British Sporting Rifle Club is its broad scope. Some of the topics covered are the history of various weapons and the people and firms connected with them; the design development, care and maintenance of weapons; hunting tips and anecdotes; calendars and news of shooting meets and arms exhibitions. For libraries with a limited collection in this area this would be a good choice although its British slant offsets its advantages to some extent. (C.F.)

The Handloader. 1965. bi-m. Neal Knox. Dave Wolfe Publishing Co., Box 3030, Prescott, Ariz. 86301. Illus., index, adv. Circ: 34,000. Vol. ends: Nov./Dec.

Bk. rev: 1–2, 200–300 words, signed. *Aud:* Ga.

For the uninitiated, the title of this nicely illustrated magazine represents a hobby—the filling of your own cartridges for eventual use in hunting or target practice. Graphs, equations, and diagrams accompany articles on the intricacies and the intrigue of handloading. Various components of cartridges, bullets, shot pellets, wads, powder, cases, and primers are compared. Velocity and accuracy of various cartridges are discussed along with description and history. Instruction in the technique of handloading is given. With the exception of a regular column, "Reviewing the Basics," articles are quite technical. (C.F.)

National Fisherman. See Boats and Boating Section.

Outdoor Life. 1898. m. $6. William E. Rae. Popular Science Publishing Co., Inc., 355 Lexington Ave., New York, N.Y. 10017. Illus., adv. Circ: 1,789,000. Sample. Vol. ends: Dec. Microform: UM.

Indexed: RG. *Aud:* Ejh, Hs, Ga, Ac. *Jv:* V.

A magazine similar to *Field and Stream,* equally geared to hunting and fishing. The 11 to 15 articles, 3,000 to 4,000 words long, usually detail real life adventures and experiences of hunters and fishermen. Information on conservation, game laws, and regulations is included, as well as practical tips on sporting equipment. The articles are by staff specialists and nonstaff contributors. Stories are illustrated with drawings and photographs. In addition, regular departments are devoted to boating, archery, fresh and saltwater fishing, camping, dogs, woodcraft, and firearms. The type of articles featured, the quality of the illustrations, and the novelty of the items advertised make this an appealing magazine for all age levels. Between this and *Field and Stream,* the latter probably will be favored in junior high schools for a somewhat similar approach. But at the adult and senior high level, *Outdoor Life* has a slight edge. (P.B.)

The Rifle Magazine. 1969. bi-m. $9. Neal Knox. Wolfe Publishing Co., Box 3030, Prescott, Arizona. 86301. Illus., index. Sample.

Aud: Ac, Ga.

Though a recent publication, this expensive magazine gives full value as the official publication of the National Bench Rest Shooters' Association. Its signed articles are authoritative products of the top precision target shooters in the country. Some technical terms will confuse the amateur but by and large this is resorted to only when necessary. While this magazine ranks high in reference and judgment value, it is hard to recommend it for any libraries but those with a partronage highly interested in this subject area, and such a situation would seldom occur. *The American Rifleman* frequently touches on the same subject material one finds in *The Rifle Magazine,* yet offers more to the general audience and is therefore a better and cheaper acquisition. Within its limited and specialized area of interest, however, *The Rifle Magazine* has no equal, journalistically speaking. (P.B.)

Rod & Gun in Canada; the outdoor man's magazine. 1899. m. $4. Harry A. Wilsie. Rod and Gun Publishing Corp., 1219 Hotel de Ville, Montreal, Que., Canada. Illus., adv. Circ: 44,000. Sample. Vol. ends: Dec.

Indexed: CanI. *Aud:* Hs, Ga.

Devoted primarily to hunting and fishing in Canada. Strong emphasis is placed on conservation of wildlife and natural resources. Principles of wildlife management are stressed, and personal accounts of real life adventures related. Safety suggestions and tips, including first aid, are given prominent attention. Canadian libraries should make this a first choice in the field, and large American collections might want it after subscribing to the main American magazines. (P.B.)

Salt Water Sportsman. 1939. m. $5. Frank Woolner. Salt Water Sportsman, Inc., 10 High St., Boston, Mass. 02110. Illus., adv. Circ: 75,000. Sample. Vol. ends: Dec.

Aud: Ga.

Written and edited for salt water fishing and fishermen, this features factual articles on tackle, boats, boating, marine biology, and related subjects. Liberal use of photographs. The magazine attempts to keep the public informed about environmental issues affecting salt water anglers and the outdoor recreational field. Obviously, of interest only to libraries on either coast, or in the gulf region.

Shooting Times. 1882. w. $20. P. B. Brown. Burlington Publishing Co. Ltd., Braywick House, Braywick Rd., Maidenhead, Berks, England. Illus., adv. Circ: 30,000. Sample. Vol. ends: Dec.

Bk. rev: 3, 300 words, signed. *Aud:* Ga.

The official organ of two of the best-known shooting clubs: Wildfowlers Association of Great Britain and the Clay Pigeon Shooting Association. Primarily a publication for shooters and fishermen. Long articles, well illustrated with photographs in black and white, cover fishing, clay pigeon shooting, guns, gun dogs, and wildfowling. Illustrations on various types of weapons and birds. Some personal narratives included. (P.B.)

Shooting Times. 1959. m. $5.85. Alex Bartimo. Peoria Journal Star, Inc., News Plaza, Peoria, Ill. 61601. Illus., adv. Circ: 116,000. Sample. Vol. ends: Dec.

Bk. rev: 2-4, 100 words, signed. *Aud:* Hs, Ga.

A magazine which has established national circulation only in recent years, *Shooting Times* may not be familiar to many libraries which could use it. The title is misleading, as the magazine emphasizes shooting as it is involved with the allied fields of hunting, camping, and conservation, and it thus becomes an excellent magazine for high school libraries that do not need the reference value of *The American Rifleman,* nor the sensational approach of *Guns & Ammo.* Articles are aimed at discussing and solving the problems of the average hunter, target shooter, or conservation-minded sportsman. Quality of photographs varies, but otherwise it is the "best buy" of the gun magazines. Not to be confused with the older, English periodical by the same name. (P.B.)

Physical Education and School Sports

Amateur Athlete. 1929. m. Membership (Nonmembers $7). Rita Cooper. Amateur Athletic Union of the U.S.A., Review Publishing Co., 1100 Waterway Blvd., Indianapolis, Ind. 46202. Illus., adv. Circ: 12,000.

Aud: Hs, Ac.

A reporting medium for amateur sports, and particularly useful for detailed accounts of the Olympic games. A scoreboard tallies results in a variety of sports from swimming to skating. A number of articles on changes in rules and regulations, medical considerations, and individual games. Much of the basic material is covered in other sporting magazines, but this is a handy type reference tool for larger collections.

Athletic Journal. 1921. m. (Sept.-June). $4. M. M. Arns. Athletic Journal Publishing Co., 1719 Howart St., Evanston, Ill. 60602. Illus., index, adv. Circ: 32,000. Sample. Vol. ends: June.

Indexed: EdI. *Bk. rev:* 15–20 notes. *Aud:* Hs, Ac.

Covers the broad spectrum of high school and college sports and appeals to the coach, player and nonplayer alike. Well-written articles are by high school and college coaches and physical education specialists. Various experiments and theories for the development, training and conditioning of high school and college athletes are treated. Special departments devoted to coaching clinics and new ideas in equipment and products. There are numerous photographs, charts, drawings, etc. The editor claims his journal "has several times as many pictures as any other magazine in its field." More emphasis is placed upon physical education in *Scholastic Coach*, but in many ways the two are similar. (One important difference, though—*Scholastic Coach* is distributed free to most high schools and colleges. Not so, the *Athletic Journal*.)

CAHPER Journal. 1933. bi-m. Membership (Libraries $10). Noreen V. Oakey. Canadian Assn. for Health, Physical Education, and Recreation, 333 River Rd., Vanier City, Ontario, KIL, Canada. Illus., adv. Circ: 2,500. Sample. Refereed.

Indexed: CanEdI. *Bk. rev:* 4, ½ page, signed. *Aud:* Ejh, Hs.

A journal for teachers of physical education in the primary and secondary Canadian schools. Includes within its 45 pages material "on any aspect of health, physical, outdoor, safety and driver education; athletics and recreation." Articles tend to the practical, how-to-do-it type, but some are given over to the theoretical. Although many of the tips would be useful elsewhere, the journal is primarily for Canadian schools. Note: The Association has a number of inexpensive monographs and books available on all aspects of coaching and physical education. Interested librarians might send for the list.

Coach & Athlete; magazine for coaches, players, trainers, officials. 1938. m. (Aug.–June). $4. Dwight Keith, Jr. Coach & Athlete, Inc., 1421 Mayson St., N.E., Atlanta, Ga. 30324. Illus., adv. Circ: 18,500 Sample. Vol. ends: June.

Indexed: EdI, CIJE. *Aud:* Hs, Ac.

The official publication of some 20 associations from the Arizona High School Coaches Association to the National Junior College Athletic Association. It is primarily geared for the professional high school or college coach, and includes articles by and for them on various technical aspects of every sport from baseball to wrestling. Features such as a profile of the college of the month and news on various regional activities will make the magazine of some interest to sports fans. A limited number of nonspecialized articles broadens the potential audience. However, for most libraries it will be of value to those directly involved with coaching or training. As many of the associations it represents are in the southern and southeastern United States, it will be of special interest to libraries in those areas.

Coaching Clinic. 1963. m. (special issues Apr. and Oct.). $24. Budd Theobald. Prentice-Hall, Inc., Englewood Cliffs, N.J. 07632. Illus. Circ: 5,000. Sample. Vol. ends: Dec.

Aud: Hs.

A pocket-sized 32-page magazine devoted to coaches in all sports from football and baseball to track and swimming. Even lacrosse, wrestling, and golf are included. The 12 to 16 articles are by coaches in high schools, and they outline (usually with charts) various moves. According to an advertisement, the magazine is to insure "Victory on the field. The prime purpose of the program is to help coaches field winning teams." Other goals include "setting an example," "handling the administrative end," and "building strong personal relationships." The writing is good, the material topical, and, if the circulation is any indication, the advice is solid enough. Still, with tight budgets, what school library can afford $24, particularly when *Coach & Athlete* comes in at a considerably lower price. But, in case the funds are there, this is a good periodical for the coach. Send for a sample copy.

Journal of Health, Physical Education, Recreation. 1930. 9/yr. Membership (Nonmembers $25). Nancy Rosenberg. Amer. Assn. for Health, Physical Education, and Recreation, 1201 16th St. N.W., Washington, D.C. 20036. Illus., index, adv. Circ: 45,000. Sample. Vol. ends: Nov./Dec. Refereed. Microform: UM.

Indexed: EdI. *Aud:* Ejh, Hs, Ac.

The basic journal for teachers at all levels involved with physical education, athletics, and dance. The 96-page magazine regularly includes some 10 to 15 major articles dealing with theory and practice of physical education and related areas; a series of specialized columns including such topics as history, kinesiology, international affairs, intramural sports, audiovisual aids, rules for games; and advertising. Special materials are presented for college students majoring in physical education. Recent features include: the lesser known Olympic sports, dance in elementary schools, innovative programs in secondary school physical education, and leisure today.

Journal of Leisure Research. See Sociology Section.

Letterman; the magazine for high school athletes. 1970. m. (during school year). $2 (Students $1). Paul Nyberg. Letterman Publns., Inc., Box 804, 330 Naperville Rd., Wheaton, Ill. 60187. Illus., adv. Circ: 510,000. Sample. Vol. ends: Dec.

Bk. rev: 2–3, short. *Aud:* Hs.

Similar in size and in format to *Sports Illustrated*, this new national magazine is written and edited for the high school athlete. Regular articles include features on individual athletes and teams, "how-to" articles, regular training column, Gallery, a question and answer column and interviews with pro athletes. National in coverage and in circulation, *Letterman* is the authority on high school sports records, events, top performers, and techniques. The editor says: "sign-up-rosters for free subs. are available to coaches of any interscholastic sport. No other use will be made of the mailing list." School libraries should consider this as one of the best of its type, particularly at the low price.

Mademoiselle Gymnast. 1966. q. $3. Barbara and Glenn Sundby. Sundby Publns., 410 Broadway, Santa Monica, Calif. 90406. Illus., adv. Circ: 4,400.

Bk. rev: notes. *Aud:* Hs, Ac.

Specifically geared for the instructor in women's gymnastics (high school and adult), this features articles on the importance of programs, methodology, and world-wide activities in the field. The articles are illustrated with photographs, sketches, and diagrams, which are particularly good for teaching purposes. Features include news of workshops and clinics, association activities, and short book reviews and notices. Attention is given to participants, and anyone actively interested in the sport will enjoy the magazine almost as much as the teacher. See also *Modern Gymnast*.

Modern Gymnast. 1957. 10/yr. $6. Glenn Sundby. Sundby Publns., 410 Broadway, Santa Monica, Calif. 90406. Illus., adv. Circ: 9,500.

Aud: Hs, Ac.

Covers all aspects of amateur gymnastics. About three-quarters of every issue is given over to complete reports on national, Canadian and international events. The other quarters include regular features which cover developments in gymnastics for teachers and students alike. Emphasis is primarily on men's activities, from high school through the university. A fundamental purchase for any high school or university where gymnastics are a concern. Large public libraries may also wish to consider.

Olympic Review/Revue Olympique. 1894. m. $10. Monique Berlioux. International Olympic Committee, Chateau de Vidy, 1007 Lausanne, Switzerland. Illus., index. Circ: 5,000. Sample. Vol. ends: Dec.

Aud: Ga, Ac.

Published in both an English and a French edition, includes five to six nonpartisan articles on all facets of the Olympics. About one-quarter of the 56-page magazine is turned over to official information, news, brief notes on publications, and personalities. During the Olympic games a given number of issues are devoted to the results, and in considerably more detail than found in most publications—hence, its high reference value. A few illustrations. As the official organ of the International Olympic Committee, it occupies a unique place, and should be considered by larger public and academic libraries.

Research Quarterly. 1930. q. Membership (Nonmembers $15). John C. Mitchum. Amer. Assn. for Health, Physical Education and Recreation, 1201 16th St. N.W., Washington, D.C. 20036. Illus., index, adv. Circ: 15,000. Sample. Vol. ends: Dec. Refereed.

Indexed: EdI, PsyAb. *Aud:* Hs, Ac.

Devoted to research concerning various aspects of physical education, health, and recreation. In general, articles deal with such subjects as "Estimation of maximal oxygen intake from submaximal work parameters," and "Internal-external control and social reinforcement effects on motor performance," of interest primarily to research workers in these areas. However, other articles such as "Effect of shoe type and cleat length on incidence and severity of knee injuries among high school football players," or "Effects of physical education on fitness and motor development of trainable mentally retarded children," would be of help to teachers and coaches. The periodical also carries occasional historical studies, e.g., "Home front, battle field, and sport during the Civil War." Of value for both high school and academic teacher collections.

Scholastic Coach. 1931. m. (Sept-June). $4. Herman L. Masin. Scholastic Magazines, 50 W. 44th St., New York, N.Y. 10036. Illus., index, adv. Circ: 36,000.

Indexed: EdI. *Bk. rev:* 5–6, 200 words. *Aud:* Ac, Hs.

The target audience is coaches in high schools, junior colleges and colleges. The purpose is to give up-to-date, reliable information on coaching practices, as well as material on physical education, conditioning, first aid, etc. The January issue emphasizes equipment, and the April and May numbers feature coaching schools. Some book and equipment reviews. A fair, although not outstanding approach. About half the circulation is free to coaches, so librarians might try to get a helping hand from the playing field. (See also Scholastic Magazines in Education section.)

Track & Field News. 1948. m. $6. Bert Nelson. P.O. Box 296, Los Altos, Calif. 94022. Illus., index, adv. Circ: 16,000. Sample. Vol. ends: Jan.

Bk. rev: 5–10, 100–250 words. *Aud:* Hs, Ga, Ac.

The basic track magazine for coaches and participants. Coverage is international, with a special report from Europe. Sections devoted to records and events in major high school competitions. Filled with statistics, data, current news, photos, and a number of columns. Recommended for high school and academic libraries where the sport is important.

THEATER

Basic Periodicals

Ejh: *Plays;* Hs: *Performance, Drama Review;* Ga: *Performance, Drama Review, Plays and Players;* Jc: *Performance, Drama Review, Scripts;* Ac: *Performance, Drama Review, Scripts, Modern International Drama.*

Library and Teaching Aids

Creative Drama, Dramatics, Educational Theatre Journal.

Cessations

Drama Critique, Drama Survey, Religious Theatre, World Theatre.

After Dark; the magazine of entertainment (Formerly: *Ballroom Dance Magazine*). 1968. m. $8. William Como. Danad Publishing Co., Inc., 10 Columbus Circle, N.Y., N.Y. 10019. Illus., adv. Circ: 118,733. Sample. Vol. ends: Dec.

Bk. rev: 5, various length, signed. *Aud:* Ga.

Written for the layman interested in theater, opera, television, films, dance, rock, and fashion. Besides the regular monthly articles covering these various aspects of the entertainment world, there are special indepth feature stories of performers and performances accompanied by photographs. The magazine provides a comprehensive guide not only to the New York entertainment world, but covers the national and the international scenes as well. A nice combination of education and enjoyment.

Avant Scene du Theatre. See Europe and Middle East/French Language Section.

Ballroom Dance Magazine. See *After Dark.*

Billboard. Newspapers/Special Interest Section.

Black Theatre. See Blacks Section.

Comparative Drama. 1967. q. $3.50. Clifford Davidson. Dept. of English, Western Michigan Univ., Kalamazoo, Mich. 49001. Illus. Circ: 600. Vol. ends: winter.

Indexed: AbEnSt. *Aud:* Ac.

A scholarly journal, featuring from four to six articles which stress both the international and the interdisciplinary scope of drama. The articles are well documented and a few are illustrated. *Comparative Drama* would be useful for both literature and drama history collections. (C.B.)

Concerned Theatre Japan. 1970. q. $10. Hikari-cho 2–13–25, Kokubunjishi, Tokyo, 185.

Aud: Ac.

Somewhat in the tradition of the American *Drama Review,* the Japanese entry differs in that emphasis is on Oriental theater, not international drama. But in terms of format, size, and approach it comes close to its American counterpart. All in English, a typical issue features nine entries from a photo essay and interview to a famous short story, and a contemporary play. While a bit esoteric, the photographs and examples of current Japanese thought give it value for almost anyone. Certainly a major inclusion for medium to large college libraries.

Creative Drama. 1950. s-a. $1. Miriam Cameron. Educational Drama Assn, 1 Hawthorndene Rd., Hayes, Bromley, BR2 7DZ, Kent, England. Illus., adv. Circ: 3,000. Sample.

Aud: Ejh, Hs, Ac.

The publication of the British Educational Drama Association is written for teachers of English, speech, and drama or anyone who is interested in involving children and young people in the performing arts. The articles discuss the link that drama may provide for children in helping them adjust to life. Written by contributors in all parts of the world, emphasis is also given to the use of drama in helping emotionally disturbed children. Drama is considered not as a literary form but as a method of teaching and learning. (C.B.)

Critical Digest. 1958. w. $25. Ted Kraus. Critical Digest, GPO Box 2403, N.Y., N.Y. 10001. Sample. Vol. ends: April 1.

Aud: Ac. *Jv:* C.

A four-page weekly newsletter which includes regular features on the theater such as: "This Week in NYC," "NYC Calendar," a page of digests of reviews on the current theater, and a page of controversial pros and cons on various aspects of theater. The publisher says its purpose is to "keep theatre educators, fans, professionals fully informed of the NYC theatre scene and of stimulating theatre information from throughout the world." Well, it may do all this, but the Sunday edition of *The New York Times* offers a fuller, more satisfactory treatment, as do most theater magazines at considerably lower prices.

Cue. 1935. $8.50. w. Stanley Newman. Cue Publishing Co., 20 W. 43rd St., New York, New York, 10036. Illus., adv. Circ: 300,000. Sample. Vol. ends: Dec. 31.

Aud: Ga, Ac.

A complete weekly magazine guide on what to see and do in New York City. There are usually two or three short articles on New York-related subjects. The rest of each issue is devoted to news, listings, and reviews of theatre, movies, television, FM radio, records, restaurants, night clubs, shopping, children's entertainment, concerts, art exhibitions, and museums in the New York City vicinity. A special issue on shopping is published annually. A useful feature of *Cue* is the citing of prices for diverse activities along with addresses and other pertinent information. This is certainly the magazine for any public or college library in the northeastern area with clientele who still take advantage of what New York City has to offer. (C.B.)

Drama; the quarterly drama review. 1919. q. $3. Walter Lucas. British Drama League, 9 Fitzroy Sq., London W1, England. Illus., index, adv. Circ: 7,000. Sample. Microform: UM.

Indexed: AbEnSt. BritHum. *Bk rev:* Numerous, various length, signed. *Aud:* Ga, Ac.

This British review considers all aspects of theater including stage management, theater history, important actors, and playwrights. Coverage is evaluative as well as informative. At least one article per issue takes the unpopular side of a controversy. Often as much as a quarter of the periodical is devoted to book reviews. These are some of the best in any drama magazine, short, critical, and frequently humorous. Required for medium to large theater collections.

✓*Drama Review* (Formerly: *TDR*). 1956. q. $6. Michael Kirby and Paul Ryan. New York Univ., 32 Washington Pl., N.Y., N.Y. 10003. Illus., index, adv. Circ: 20,000. Sample. Microform: UM.

Indexed: AbEnSt, MLA, SSHum. *Bk. rev:* various number, length. *Aud:* Ac, Ga. *Jv:* V.

Despite the loss of the editor and most of the top staff to another theater mag *(Performance) Drama Review* carries on. And rumor to the contrary, the editor insists it will continue for a good time to come. Little seems to have changed, and it remains one of the best radical and experimental drama magazines about. Within its 180 to 200 well illustrated pages, it covers every aspect of the 20th-century theater. Normally a single issue is given over to a major topic, e.g. European theater, acting, directing etc. Contributors range from playwrights and actors to directors and teachers. Almost every major writer on the theater has appeared at one time or another. Many short plays (a number translated from various languages) are included in full. Emphasis is definitely on the international avant-garde, intellectual side of drama, and it is the voice of what has come to be known as the Off-Broadway theater. It definitely is not for the lover of musical comedies and traditional dramas. In view of the concentration on given areas, a run of the magazine offers the best single source of a history of the theater in our time. Should be found in almost every type of library where drama and the fine arts have any importance.

Drama and Theatre (Formerly: *First Stage*). 1961–62. q. $4.50. Henry F. Salerno. Dept. of English, State Univ. College, Fredonia, N.Y. 14063. Circ: 1,500. Vol. ends: summer.

Index: AbEnSt. *Aud:* Ac.

Publishes three to five new plays by American and foreign authors. The plays are short, usually one act, and are not truly experimental works. They appear to be chosen more for artistic and literary merit than for their commercial value. Each issue also features an interview with a theatrical personality and two or three articles on contemporary theater around the world. This would certainly be useful in medium to large academic libraries. (C.B.)

✓*Dramatics; devoted to the advancement of dramatics in secondary schools.* 1929. m. (Oct.–May). $5. R. Glenn Webb. International Thespian Soc., College Hill Sta., Box E, Cincinnati, Ohio. 45224. Illus., adv. Circ: 50,000. Sample. Vol. ends: May.

Bk. rev: 4–6, 200–500 words. *Aud:* Hs, Ac.

Published by the International Thespian Society which is "devoted to the advancement of Theatre Arts in the secondary school," *Dramatics* might also be useful for college theater groups. Four or five illustrated articles on staging, designing, theater personalities, and specific types of plays are included in each issue. Monthly features include "On Stage," photographs of high school productions, "Call Board," reviews of high school productions and "Technicalities," a how-to-do-it column on any aspect of theater production. A necessity for high school theater groups. (C.B.)

Educational Theatre Journal. 1949. q. Membership (nonmembers $14.50). David Schall. Amer. Education Theatre Assn., 1317 F St. N.W., Washington, D.C. 20004. Illus., adv. Circ: 6,000. Vol. ends: Dec. Microform: UM.

Indexed: EdI, SSHum. *Bk. rev:* 4–6, 500–1,000 words, signed. *Aud:* Ac. Jv: V.

A journal of contemporary scholarship and criticism in theater arts for both drama students and teachers. The articles cover historical aspects of drama, playwrights, drama criticism, design and technical developments, and acting and production techniques. Regular features include "Theatre in Review" which reviews college and university productions as well as those of professional companies around the world, and "Books Received," a subject bibliography of new plays, histories, and textbooks. A valuable asset for academic theater collections. (C.B.)

First Stage. See *Drama and Theatre.*

Janus. 1971. bi-a. $3/2 yrs. Pat Garczynski. Janus, 128 12th Ave., Seaside Park, N.J. 08752. Illus. Sample.
Aud: Ac, Hs.

Considering the modest price and the purpose—to give new playwrights a hearing—this should be supported by any library where drama is important. The magazine features three to five original plays, has some reviews and newsnotes on the theater. The 32 glossy pages are adequately printed (type is a bit small, yet what do you expect for the price?). One issue included work of E. Amadon Toney, Charles Ghigna, Ranson Jeffery, and Paul Dexter. The plays are uneven, but the Jeffery piece is certainly provocative, and the others demonstrate a tremendous potential. Primarily for college students and adults. Imaginative high school drama teachers will appreciate looking over a copy. (C.B.)

Latin American Theatre Review. See Latin American and Chicano/English Language General Section.

Modern Drama. 1958. q. $4. A. C. Edwards. Univ. of Kansas, Lawrence, Kans. 66044. Circ: 2,300. Vol. ends: Feb. Sample.

Indexed: SSHum. *Bk. rev:* 6–8, 500–1,000 words, signed. *Aud:* Ac.

Ten to 12 well documented articles, written by recognized scholars make *Modern Drama* an excellent journal for the study of drama as literature. The scope is international and includes interviews with notables in the field, discussions of playwrights and plays, and state of the art reports. Suitable for medium to large academic collections. (C.B.)

Modern International Drama: magazine of contemporary international drama in translation. 1967. s-a. $4.50. George E. Wellwarth and Anthony Pasquariello. Max Reinhardt Archive, State Univ. of New York, Binghamton, N.Y. 13901. Adv. Circ: 950. Sample. Vol. ends: Spring.

Aud: Ac. Jv: V.

A journal with the purpose of making "the best modern foreign theatre available to American readers and producers." Two or three plays are published in each issue with no attempt at a representative cross section of the country of origin. Recent issues include works from Spain, Germany, and Finland. A brief note about the author, the translator, and play is included along with information on performing rights. The translations are simply that, not adaptations or transliterations. Since it is extremely difficult for foreign plays to be published in the United States, this represents a breakthrough for anyone interested in international drama. An excellent choice for large academic libraries and drama collections. Also good for students and teachers of literature. (C.B.)

New Theatre Magazine. 1959. 3/yr. $3. John Adler and Michael Bath, Tim Applebee. Dept. of Drama, Univ. of Bristol, Park Row, Bristol, BS1 5 LT, England. Illus, adv. Circ: 1,300. Sample. Vol. ends: Oct.

Bk. rev: 7–10, 1,000 words. *Aud:* Ac.

With the evolution of a new policy, *New Theatre Magazine* now devotes an entire issue to one theme related to the theory and practice of modern drama. Recent subjects covered include problems of playwrights, street theater, and drama and young people. Although it has a distinct British tone, it would be a good companion to the American *Players Magazine.* (C.B.)

New York Theatre Critics Reviews. 1940. 30/year. $40. Joan Marlowe and Betty Blake. New York Theatre Critics Reviews, 4 Park Ave., Suite 21D, N.Y., N.Y. 10016. Sample. Vol. ends with 30th issue.

Aud: Ga, Ac.

This compilation is more valuable as a reference tool than as a periodical. It publishes the complete Broadway theater reviews from the *Daily News, Wall Street Journal,* WABC-TV, *New York Post, Women's Wear Daily,* CBS-TV, *Time, Newsweek,* and WNBC-TV. For anyone wanting to compare the reviews of a certain play, on or Off-Broadway, here they all are in a neat, compact form. There is no need to run from newspaper to magazine to newspaper getting varying views. The price may be high but one must remember that the television reviews are literally unavailable after they are read, and the four newspaper subscriptions would cost far more than the price of the service. Certainly necessary for any library with a theater-going clientele or one with a large drama collection. (C.B.)

Performance; a quarterly of new ideas and live work.
1971. q. $7 (Combined with *Scripts*, $11.). Erika
Munk. Joseph Papp, N.Y. Shakespeare Festival Public
Theatre, 425 Lafayette St., N.Y., N.Y. 10003. Illus.,
adv. Sample.

Aud: Ac, Ga. *Jv:* V.

The editors and staff of *Performance* are the same
people who until May 1971, put out *Drama Review*.
The publisher is Joe Papp of the lively, interesting
Off-Broadway New York Public Theatre. The result is
another form of the much praised *Drama Review*,
right down to the format, size, and approach. For
example, the first issue centers around "Growing Out
of the Sixties," and includes articles by Jan Kott, Peter
Brook, Ed Bullins, Richard Gilman on playwriting,
collectives, films, critics, etc. Other issues, like the
Drama Review, build around a single topic, e.g. Sexuality and Performance, Theatre After the Revolution,
Popular Entertainment, etc. This complements *Drama
Review* as the single most important American magazine now being published in the theater. See also,
Scripts.

**Performing Arts Review; the journal of management
& law of the arts.** 1969. q. $10. Joseph Taubman. Law
Arts Publishers Inc., 453 Greenwich St., N.Y., N.Y.
10013. Illus. adv.

Bk. rev: 2–3, essay length. *Aud:* Ac. *Jv:* V.

What does it take to finance a symphony orchestra?
How do financial patterns govern the movies? Are
budget cutbacks of the arts in college a threat and
weapon against dissent? How can you get a large industry to support theater? And so it goes, countless
questions about dollars and cents which determine and
shape the arts. All of these are covered in this 100 to
160 page journal, usually by experts who are looking
at financial problems from the viewpoint of the lawyer, businessman, or, just as often, the artist. It is a
singularly important approach which is touched on in
other magazines, but is the center of focus in this two
year old journal. There is a nice balance between the
nuts and bolts approach and such things as interviews,
poetry, book reviews and literary comment. Contributors are experts who are as deliberate and straight
forward as commentators in the *Wall Street Journal*.
Not only is this an important contribution to the arts
library but it is invaluable for the social sciences and
the business and law collection. Highly recommended.

Playbill; the magazine for theatre goers. 1884. m. $4.
Leo Lerman. Amer. Theatre Press, 579 Fifth Ave.,
N.Y., N.Y. 10017. Illus., adv. Circ: 1,716,000.

Aud: Ga.

This is the small magazine the theater goer often

receives as he tries to find his seat. Established in
1884, it is a combination of information about the
show at hand and advertising. Editorally it supplies
the synopsis and/or scenes and/or musical numbers of
a particular play, as well as biographical sketches of
the cast. A number of articles relevant to the understanding and enjoyment of theater are included. The
publisher reports that for $20.00 libraries will receive
the publication "for every Broadway opening."

Players Magazine. 1924. bi-m. $5. Byron Schaeffer.
National Collegiate Players, University Theatre,
Northern Illinois Univ., DeKalb, Ill. 60115. Illus., adv.
Circ: 6,000. Sample. Vol. ends: Aug.-Sept.

Bk. rev: 3–4, 500 words, signed. *Aud:* Ac.

The publication of the National Collegiate Players,
this includes three or four articles which discuss teaching methods and stage techniques. A listing of college
theater productions and "The New Play: Premieres in
America" are annual features. Each month an interview with a director of a theater is published with a
data sheet about the theater staff and performances.
Players rarely treats drama as a literary form and includes only the activities of educational groups. Of
interest to students and teachers at collegiate theaters.
(C.B.)

Plays; the drama magazine for young people. 1941.
m. (Oct.–May). $8. A. S. Burack. Plays, Inc., 8 Arlington St., Boston, Mass. 02116. Adv. Circ: 26,000. Sample.
Vol. ends: May. Microform: UM.

Indexed: IChildMags, RG. *Bk. rev:* 3–4, 125 words.
Aud: Ejh.

Features eight to ten plays per issue designated for
lower, middle grades, junior, and senior high. Most are
original, unimaginative one act plays which may be
performed in less than a hour. A few plays represent
adaptations of better known classics. There are often
skits or puppet programs. For each play production
notes are included (number and sex of characters, costumes, time, and properties). The only advantage of
the magazine is that the work is within the abilities of
the actors and teachers and the themes are traditional
and always acceptable for middle and lower grades.
However, its use in junior and senior high school is
questionable. Today's high school youth is sophisticated enough to reject such things. Moreover, there
are still some excellent Broadway plays which could
be produced with greater pleasure and success by high
school groups. It should be noted that *Plays* is a classroom aid and is not likely to be a magazine read for
pleasure. An acceptable purchase for elementary and
middle schools. (C.B.)

Plays and Players. 1953. m. $9.75. Peter Roberts.
Hansom Books, Artillery Mansions, 75 Victoria St.,
London SW1, England. Illus., adv. Circ: 16,000. Sample. Vol. ends: Sept.

Bk. rev: Occasional, signed. *Aud:* Ga, Ac.

This is a British publication with no comparable U.S. counterpart. It presents a comprehensive coverage of the London theater scene with complete reviews of current productions. There are also reviews of other European and New York productions. The reviews are not scholarly but are well written and illustrated with black-and-white photographs. Regular features include the complete text of at least one new play which has been produced recently, a list of current London plays, news and notes of the theater, articles about playwrights or actors, and columns on both British television and radio drama. *Plays and Players* provides excellent coverage of the English theater and is recommended for all medium to large libraries. (C.B.)

Scripts; a monthly of plays and theater pieces. 1971. 10/yr. $7.50. Erika Munk. Joseph Papp, N.Y. Shakespeare Festival Public Theatre, 425 Lafayette St., N.Y., N.Y. 10003. Illus., adv. Sample.

Aud: Ac, Ga, Hs. *Jv:* V.

A collection of complete plays for the director, performer and producer. "We are going to publish texts which have been done already, so they will be easily available to directors in a usable form. . . . We also plan to publish American and foreign radio plays, filmscripts, TV plays and documentaries, music pieces, dance scenarios." The magazine deserves support. Its publisher is the unpredictable and imaginative New York producer and director who has given Off-Broadway a new dimension. The issues examined averaged about 100 pages and included the award winning *The Basic Training of Pavlo Hummel*, Adrienne Kennedy's *Sun*, and numerous other plays and productions. Scripts encompass a wide range of styles and subject matter, yet all are professional, socially involved. The typography is fair to good and the make-up clear. Need for such a magazine has existed for a long time, and hopefully this meets that need. See also, *Performance*, a second new magazine by the same publisher.

TDR. See *Drama Review.*

Theatre Crafts. 1967. bi-m. $5. C. Ray Smith. Rodale Press, Emmaus, Pa. 18049. Illus., adv. Circ: 35,000. Sample. Microform: UM.

Bk. rev: Notes. *Aud:* Ac, Ga, Hs.

By the same people who plug organic gardening and clean living through diet and exercise, *Theatre Crafts* is of little importance other than to stress it is an honest, practical magazine for just about anyone involved with some aspect of what goes on behind the scenes at the theater. Articles are for the pro or amateur who is responsible for lighting, costumes, billboards, and advertising, etc. There are usually three or four articles, news about personalities, some notes on

books, and record reviews. While not for the general public, it will be of much use for anyone involved with theater production at any level from high school to Off-Broadway.

Theatre Design and Technology. 1965. q. $12. Fordham Korper. U.S. Inst. for Theatre Technology, 245 W. 52nd St., N.Y., N.Y. 10019. Illus., adv. Circ: 1,350. Sample.

Bk. rev: 4–6, 1,000 words, signed. *Aud:* Ac.

This is the journal of the United States Institute for Theatre Technology and contains articles on the construction of new theaters, new technical developments, stage design, lighting, sound, and administration. The October issue is devoted entirely to the annual USITT conference. There are usually at least two bibliographies in each issue, the continuing, "Recent Publications on Theatre Architecture," and annotated bibliographies on such subjects as lighting for the arena stage or theater design and technology in the dance. An excellent choice for all drama collections. (C.B.)

Theatre Notebook. 1946. q. 30s. Sybil Rosenfeld, Bamber Gascoigne and George Speaight. Soc. for Theatre Research, 77 Kinnerton St., London, SW1, England. Illus., adv. Vol. ends: Summer.

Bk. rev: 5–7, 300–500 words, signed. *Aud:* Ac.

A specialized scholarly journal for those interested in the history of the British theater. The four to five well researched and tastefully illustrated articles cover all aspects of theatrical history including architecture, playwrights, costuming, and staging. Regular features include "Notes and Queries," and "Books Received." A necessary item for theater history collections. (C.B.)

Theatre Research/Recherches Theatrales. 1958. 3/yr. $4. J. F. Arnott. Intl. Federation for Theatre Research, 14 Woronzow Rd., London NW8, England. Illus., adv. Circ: 1,500. Vol. ends: no. 3.

Bk. rev: 7–9, 500 words, signed. *Aud:* Ac.

Directed toward a specific audience this publication includes theatrical research from Europe and the United States. The five to seven articles deal with actors, playwrights, theaters, and designers. They are written by scholars of drama or professional writers and are documented as well as illustrated. One or two of the articles are in French. Papers from the International Congress on Theatre Research are also included. Good for large academic libraries. (C.B.)

Theatre Survey. 1960. s-a. $4. Attilio Favorini and George E. Bogusch. Amer. Society for Theatre Research, Dept. of Speech and Theatre Arts, Univ. of Pittsburg, Pittsburg, Pa. 15213. Illus. Circ: 750. Vol. ends: Nov. Sample.

Aud: Ac.

A journal of theater history published by the American Society for Theatre Research. The five or six scholarly articles of each issue deal with historical aspects of European theater as well as that of the United States. In addition to articles on technical aspects, playwrights and plays, biographies of great actors of the past are published regularly. Recommended for collections which support theater history courses. (C.B.)

Variety. See Newspapers/Special Interest Section.

Yale Theatre. 1968. 3/yr. $5.50. John Hay. Box 2040, Yale Sta., New Haven, Conn. 06520. Illus., adv. Circ: 4,000. Vol. ends: Spring. Microform: UM.

Aud: Ac, Ga.

Published by the students at the Yale School of Drama, and based on the School's activities, this is not the parochial journal its title might suggest. A wide ranging, beautifully designed periodical, its "true focus is contemporary American theatre. It wants to foster a way of thinking about this theatre that refuses received mythologies and practices which dwindle the heart and numb the imagination." Highly relevant for theater collections.

TRAVEL AND REGIONAL MAGAZINES

Basic Periodicals

GENERAL TRAVEL. Hs: *Travel;* Ga: *Holiday, Travel, Travel & Leisure;* Jc & Ac: *Holiday, Travel & Leisure, Travel.*

REGIONAL. Ejh: *Arizona Highways;* Hs: *Arizona Highways, Colorado Magazine;* Ga: *Arizona Highways, Colorado Magazine, Down East;* Jc & Ac: Regional as needed. All libraries: First and foremost the regional magazine of the area, or surrounding area. *Arizona Highways* for children and some high schools because of the illustrations and because it is indexed. But it is no better than many of this genre.

Cessations

Venture

General Travel

Bon Voyage. 1969. bi-m. $2. Jane Rosenthal. Bon Voyage, Div. of the Pillsbury Co., 4700 Bellview, Kansas City, Mo. 64112. Illus., adv. Circ: 60,000. Sample. Vol. ends: Nov./Dec.

Bk. rev: 5–7, 500 words. *Aud:* Ga.

With less than 25 pages every two months, *Bon Voyage* "for the discerning traveler," may be the only magazine that one can read completely before the next issue arrives! The four or five feature articles of each issue, illustrated with many color photographs, deal with modes of travel as well as specific places. The monthly column "Travel Spectrum" reveals all types of tidbits for the traveler from a listing of elegant European shops to suggestions for a bon voyage party. For people with travelmania this is well worth the subscription price! (C.B.)

Discovery Magazine. 1961. q. $2. David L. Watt. Allstate Enterprises, Inc., Allstate Plaza, Northbrook, Ill. 60062. Illus., adv. Circ: 750,000. Sample. Vol. ends: Autumn. Microform: UM.

Bk. rev: 10–12, 50–100 words. *Aud:* Ga, Ejh, Hs.

One of the better house organ type magazines written for the United States motorist by the Allstate Motor Club. Articles deal with automobile safety, tourist attractions, and national parks and are illustrated with photographs, many in color. Monthly features include "Events of the Season," a calendar of events by region, "Touring with the Editors," information on a variety of guidebooks and tourists brochures and where and how to get them, and "Food for the Traveler," recipes from well-known restaurants in the United States. A good magazine for the person who wants to discover America. (C.B.)

Dodge News. See Free Magazines Section.

Friends. See Free Magazines Section.

Global Courier. See Free Magazines Section.

Holiday. 1946. m. (except Dec./Jan., May/June, July/Aug.). $7. Cory SerVaas. Holiday Publishing Co., 1100 Waterway Blvd., Indianapolis, Ind. 46202. Illus., adv. Circ: 1,000,000. Sample. Microform: UM. Vol. ends: Nov.

Indexed: AbrRG, RG. *Aud:* Ga, Hs, Ac.

With a new editor and a smaller size (from *Life* size to *Time* size), *Holiday* has slipped from its place as "the" travel magazine. A slash in staff may help make a profit but quality has suffered. Although it is still profusely illustrated with beautiful color photographs many are advertisements for Holiday tours. Often one wades through 16 pages of advertising before getting to the regular articles. They still describe the history, climate, people, cuisine and tourist attractions of famous and little known places around the world, but they are not written by the eminent contributors of previous issues. Nevertheless, there is a sophistication in the choice of material used. Regular features still include Rex Reed's movie reviews, travel and beauty care, and the *Holiday* travel handbook which gives concise travel information, including monthly weather listings for places mentioned in the main articles. New innovations include "Places and Faces," pictures and captions of the jet set on the go, and "Speaking of Holiday," a travel editorial often written by a guest contributor. With the demise of *Venture, Holiday* remains as one of the two or three general travel magazines and is still needed in library travel collections. Perhaps time will fade the image of the old *Holiday*, and hopefully, the new *Holiday* will improve. (C.B.)

Holiday Inn Magazine for Travelers. 1959. m. $2.50. Lois Ray Crowe. Holiday Inns, Inc., 3791 Lamar Ave., Memphis, Tenn. 38118. Illus., adv. Circ: 800,000. Sample. Vol. ends: Dec.

Aud: Ga, Hs.

A somewhat promotional travel magazine presenting almost every type of tourist or recreational attraction in the U.S., and throughout those parts of the world served by Holiday Inns. Calculated to tempt the traveler, articles range from the beautiful and the picturesque in scenery to unusual night spots such as Munich's Yellow Submarine; and from recreational sports, especially fishing in all types of settings, to the famous and the lesser-known regional celebrations, seasonal events, and contests. A recent issue reported bona fide bath tub racing in the waters surrounding Vancouver Island, British Columbia! Regular features in each issue include a calendar of scheduled events to interest travelers in all parts of the U.S., some areas of Canada, and a few farther afield. Humor pages and a recipe section divulging the secrets of some Holiday Inn chefs for their regional specialties also appear regularly. Popular level reporting, some excellent photographic illustrations, and broad coverage recommend this as an additional source for travel material and general interest reading. (A.S.)

Mainliner. 1957. m. $4. Tom Cavanaugh. United Air Lines, Box 66100, Chicago, Ill. 60666. Illus., adv. Sample. Circ: 1,265,000. Vol. ends: Dec.

Aud: Ga.

"For the 27 million travelers who fly the friendly skies of United," *Mainliner* provides a general interest magazine with emphasis on travel and on celebrities and interesting personalities. Material is well selected and copiously and colorfully illustrated. Travel subjects are usually related to areas served by this airline, and include some unusual spots. Signed articles vary in length from two to five pages including illustrations, and are written for the general adult reader. Six to eight pages of advertising present auxiliary services such as auto rentals, hotel accommodations, etc. Library usefulness, in addition to its general interest matter, will be for the travel articles and excellent illustrations. (A.S.)

Mexico This Month. 1955. m. $4. Anita Brenner, Altenas 42–601, Mexico, D. F. Mexico. Illus., adv. Circ: 30,000

Aud: Ga, Ha, Ejh.

An English language, Mexico-oriented magazine di-

rected to the prospective tourist and businessman, this is a notch above the average chamber of commerce approach. Its publisher editor seems to produce most of the contents, and writes in a lively, candid style. Emphasis is on the arts, literature, culture, customs, and, in fact, anything which is likely to involve the tourist. There is some discussion of current affairs, and a given number will feature an aspect of the Mexican social situation. However, there is little or no questioning about the Mexican political system. The middle-of-the-road approach is understandable in a publication of this type, and given this understanding it is suitable for most school libraries and public libraries—particularly the latter, as it methodically lists events of interest to the tourist. The illustrations are good, but the quality of paper and the format are dull.

Negro Traveller and Conventioneer. See Blacks Section.

Official Airline Guide Quick Reference North American Edition. s-m. $45. Reuben H. Donnelley Corp., 200 Clearwater Drive, Oak Brook, Ill. 60521. Adv. Circ: 130,000.

Aud: Ga.

This is the guide to clock schedules of planes operating on the North American continent and in the Caribbean. It also includes car rental, credit and helicopter information. Almost every travel agent or local airline desk will have this journal; and since it is expensive, should be considered only by large reference libraries.

Pacific Islands Monthly. 1930. m. $10. Stuart Inder. Pacific Publns., Box 3408, GPO, Sydney, Australia. Illus., index., adv. Circ: 11,000. Sample.

Bk. rev: Various number, length. *Aud:* Ga.

It doesn't take a trip to the Pacific Islands to enjoy this one—it can be enjoyed in a chair. Many of the subscribers are that variety of traveler. A typical issue runs to some 150 pages, will be loaded with advertising, photographs and articles. The latter include such items as news on the Gilbert Islands government, a sketch of a Polynesian princess, how to make Palm Toddy, and what's going on around Fiji. But it isn't a travel magazine per se, and that's its real charm. It serves as a news media for the Pacific Islands, includes views of residents on just about every conceivable topic. Send for a sample (you should expect to pay for postage). Not an absolute necessity, but a wonderful added treat for any library.

Travel. 1901. m. Malcolm McTear Davis. $6. Travel Magazine Inc., Travel Bldg., Floral Park, N.Y. 11001. Illus., adv. Circ: 500,000. Samples. Vol. ends: Dec.

Indexed: RG. *Bk. rev:* 1,500 words. *Aud:* Ga, Hs, Ac. *Jv:* V.

Now that *Holiday* has reduced its size, it may have

more competition from *Travel*. With the subtitle, "the Magazine that Roams the Globe," *Travel* does just that but not with the sophistication that *Holiday* employs. Compared with *Holiday*, *Travel* is down to earth and contains a greater amount of news and practical information on traveling. Each issue features articles on more than one foreign country and on two or three areas or cities of the United States, all illustrated with colored photographs. Monthly features include news of new hotels, a listing of new shows on Broadway, a review of a current Broadway show, tours of the month, and a camera column. "Travel Digest" gives concise news bulletins from around the travel world, and "Roaming the Globe" contains notes from *Travel* correspondents on what to see and do in their particular area. Perhaps this would be a first choice for high school libraries and/or those libraries that do not care about the status of the jet set. (C.B.)

Travel and Camera. See *Travel and Leisure.*

Travel and Leisure. 1971. bi-m. $6. Caskie Stinnett. U.S. Camera Publishing Co., 132 W. 31st St., N.Y., N.Y. 10001. Illus., adv.

Aud: Ga, Hs, Ac. *Jv:* V.

A bright spot in the travel magazine field is *Travel and Leisure,* formerly *Travel and Camera.* Published by a subsidiary of American Express, many of its readers are American Express Card members and the benefits of the company are advertised throughout. Each issue emphasizes the growth of the leisure class in the United States and describes what may occupy the time of this class. Since the editor-in-chief is a former *Holiday* editor, *Travel and Leisure* is copying ideas, but at this point they seem to be doing an excellent job. However, it may be a year or two before a consistent style is evolved. Written for people who can afford the good life, tastefully illustrated articles center around fashion, food, great destinations, life styles, and sports, all with a travel emphasis. Articles are written by such notables as Claire Booth Luce, Heywood Hale Broun, and Art Buchwald. Contributing editors are Temple Fielding, Eugenia Sheppard, and Red Smith. For the experienced, affluent traveler, or even those who live vicariously, this might be preferred over *Holiday.* It still does not equal *Travel* in practical information for the vacationer. (C.B.)

Travelers' Directory. See Counterculture/Alternative Living Section.

State and Regional

Alaska; the magazine of life on the last frontier (Formerly: *Alaska Sportsman).* 1935. m. $7. Bob Henning. Alaska Northwest Publishing Co., Box 1271, Juneau, Alaska 99801. Illus., adv. Circ: 132,000. Sample. Vol. ends: Dec.

Bk. rev: 3 to 5, 100–400 words. *Aud:* Ga, Hs.

A general magazine devoted to the glories of life in Alaska, The Yukon, British Columbia, and the North Pacific. Factual articles on history, hunting and fishing, scenic trails, and current happenings provide rich sources of information for those interested. There are true adventures but no fiction. It is illustrated by photographs, many in color. Although the magazine's appeal is primarily to the general adult, it has value for the high school student.

American Motorist. 1909. m. $2. Glenn T. Lashley. American Automobile Association, 1712 G St. N.W., Washington, D.C. 20006. Illus., adv. Circ: 231,000. Sample.

Aud: Ga, Hs.

The basic magazine of the American Automobile Association. It has national coverage, is included for the most part as a free item in membership in the AAA. (Libraries might wish to pay, but it generally can be had for the asking.) While of primary interest to the motorist, it will be of some value to any traveller. It has articles not only on cars and motoring, but on travel in all parts of North America and, lately, in Europe. The articles are well written, the photographs good, and the format professional. Editorial policy tends to justify activities of the automobile and highway industries, but lately even this is changing to more interest in environment and safety. Other AAA magazines with independent editorial policies are representative of local, regional and state travel. All are fair to good in terms of editorial matter, and most feature photographs and drawings. As of 1972 some 45 states and all of the major Canadian provinces had such magazines, although in many areas they are little more then bulletins. The better titles, in terms of being useful for travel and tour information, are listed below. The majority are regular-sized magazines of various lengths (running from 16 to as much as 60 pages). All publishers will send libraries free samples.

Motorland (California–Nevada). 1917. bi-m. $2. California State Automobile Assn., 150 Van Ness Ave., San Francisco, Calif. 94101. Illus., adv. Circ: 750,000.

Maryland Motorist. 1910. bi-m. $1. Automobile Club of Maryland, 1401 Mt. Royal Ave., Baltimore, Md. 21217. Illus., adv. Circ: 68,000.

Motor News (Michigan). 1917. m. $3. Automobile Club of Michigan, 150 Bagley Ave., Detroit, Mich. 48226. Illus., adv. Circ: 607,000.

Minnesota AAA Motorist. 1914. m. $1. Minnesota State Automobile Assn., 7 Travelers Trail, Burnsville, Minn. 55378. Illus., adv. Circ: 223,000.

Driving (New Jersey). 1969. bi-m. $2.75. New Jersey Auto Club, 1 Hanover Rd. Florham Park, N.J. Illus., adv. Circ: 32,000.

New York Motorist. 1926. m. 50¢. Automobile Club of New York, AAA Building, 28 E. 78th St., N.Y., N.Y. 10021. Illus., adv. Circ: 400,000.

Ohio Motorist. 1909. m. $2. Ohio Motorist Publishing

Co., 6000 S. Marginal Rd., Cleveland, Ohio 44103. Illus., adv. Circ: 135,000.

Motour (Ohio). 1923. m. $1. Cincinnati Automobile Club, Central Parkway and Race St., Cincinnati, Ohio 45202. Illus., adv. Circ: 75,000.

Keystone Motorist (Pennsylvania). 1911. m. $1. Keystone Automobile Club, 2040 Market St., Philadelphia, Pa. 19103. Illus., adv. Circ: 173,000.

Washington Motorist. 1915. m. $1. Automobile Club of Washington, 330 6th Ave., Seattle, Wash. 98109. Illus., adv. Circ: 100,000.

Wisconsin AAA Motor News. 1937. m. $1. American Automobile Assn., Wisconsin Division, Box 33, 433 W. Washington Ave., Madison, Wis. 53701. Illus., adv. Circ: 180,000.

Arizona Highways. 1925. m. $5. Raymond Carlson. W. A. Krueger Co., 2802 West Palm Lane, Phoenix, Ariz. 85009. Illus. Circ: 400,000. Sample. Vol. ends: Dec.

Indexed: IChildMag, RG. *Aud:* Ga, Ejh, Hs.

The promotion of Arizona and the Southwest as a tourist attraction is the aim of this regional magazine. The many beautiful color photographs of this scenic area account for its wide use in schools. Each issue is devoted entirely to some aspect or area of life in Arizona past or present. The articles are well written and recently have emphasized conservation of natural resources. Certainly a first choice for any library in the area and for school and public libraries where illustrations are as important as text. See also other regional magazines such as *Colorado Magazine* and *Maryland Magazine.* (C.B.)

Atlantic Advocate. 1909. m. $5. John Braddock. Univ. Press of New Brunswick Ltd., Federicton, N.B., Canada. Illus., index, adv. Circ: 22,000.

Indexed: CanI. *Aud:* Ga.

Primarily for Canadians, this covers interests and activities in the maritime provinces. Each issue includes popular short articles on personalities, events, business, travel, and even some politics. There is a limited amount of fiction, humor etc. The tone is middle of the road. The editing is good and the magazine serves its purpose well enough. It is by way of a regional magazine, is good, and should be in all Canadian maritime libraries. Of limited value to others.

The Automobilist. See *Away.*

Away (Formerly: *The Automobilist)* 1917. q. $1. Gerard J. Gagnon. ALA Auto & Travel Club, 1047 Commonwealth Ave., Boston, Mass. 02215. Illus., adv. Circ: 220,000. Sample. Vol. ends: winter.

Bk. rev: irreg. *Aud:* Ga, Hs. *Jv:* C.

The magazine is published for members of the Automobile Legal Association, and may provide better coverage of the New England area than the American Automobile Association. Scenic spots, pertinent state and federal legislation, and a regular question and answer column are all typical fare, while motels and resorts in the area regularly advertise in the magazine. ALA appointed garages are listed in the back of each issue. *Away* would find use only in libraries in the region. (H.B.)

Beautiful British Columbia Magazine. 1959. q. $2. B. H. Atkins and B. J. Pauls. Province of British Columbia, Minister of Travel Industry. 1019 Wharf St., Victoria, B.C. Illus. Circ: 250,000.

Aud: Ga.

A handsome, nicely produced travel and general culture magazine. The photographs and drawings, often in full color, supplement a variety of articles on the arts, crafts, history, travel and personalities. It is edited for an intelligent reader, and while trying to sell the beauties of British Columbia, it never insults. In view of the low price and interest in this part of the world, a solid addition for almost any library near B.C., or with readers involved with western Canada.

Carolina Highways. 1949. m. Free. Jesse A. Rutledge. S.C. Highway Dept., Drawer 191, Columbia, S.C. 20202. Illus., index. Circ: 7,200. Vol. ends: Dec.

Aud: Ac.

Some 32 pages are given over to highways and highway safety. There is little on the natural beauties or on travel in North Carolina. Its purpose is "to inform the Highway Department's employees and others to whom it is distributed of the Department's activities in the fields of highway construction, planning, maintenance, traffic law enforcement, administration, motor vehicle and driver matters, promotions, retirements, deaths and other matters in which the Department is involved." As such, interest is fairly well limited to state residents and to those dealing directly with traffic safety and problems. See also *Sandlapper Magazine.*

Colorado Magazine. 1965. bi-m. $5. David Sumner. Colorado Magazine Inc., 7190 W. 14th Ave., Denver, Colo. 80215. Illus. adv. Circ: 145,000. Sample. Vol. ends: May–June.

Aud: Ga, Ejh, Hs.

Colorado Magazine is one of the top regional magazines and compares favorably with *Arizona Highways,* although it emphasizes activities for the sportsman and conservationist as well as the traveler. Of the six or seven illustrated articles, a series of three or four in each issue are on a single subject, such as fishing, skiing, the wilderness, etc. Other articles deal with the history, art, flora and fauna of Colorado, New Mexico, Utah, and Wyoming. Monthly features include a beautiful color portfolio of scenic photography, educational, sporting, and cultural events in the region, and a section on recommended restaurants. *Colorado Magazine* would be useful for school libraries in the Rocky Mountain West as well as for anyone interested in the beauty, history, and preservation of a fascinating area of the United States. (C.B.)

The Commonwealth. 1934. m. $4. J. S. Wamsley. Virginia State Chamber of Commerce, 611 E. Franklin, Richmond, Va. 23219. Illus., index, adv. Circ: 12,000.

Indexed: PAIS. *Aud:* Ga.

A general travel, historical, business, cultural magazine which attempts to put Virginia's best foot forward. It rarely stumbles, but it does shuffle a bit. If there isn't much excitement, at least the makeup and format is good, the photographs fair, and the writing acceptable. There are special numbers, such as the one devoted to travel in Virginia, and features and interviews. A must for any library in or around Virginia, and because of the historical interest of the state, it might be considered by more distant libraries.

Culture Vivante. 1966. q. $2. Claude Paulette. Cultural Affairs Dept., Hôtel du Government, Québec, Canada. Illus. Circ: 12,500 Sample. Vol. ends: Dec.

Aud: Ga, Ac, Hs.

An extraordinarily handsome publication, issued at cost (and perhaps less), in order to bring attention to the new look that Quebec has acquired during the past half dozen years or so. Most issues are made up of articles on a variety of subjects, all of course dealing in one way or another with Quebec. Occasional issues, however, are given over entirely to a single subject, as for instance *joual* and the language as it ought to be spoken and the work of the *Conservatoire de Musique et d'Art Dramatique*. The entire publication is in French, but this should not stop libraries from buying it. It is both a bargain and a fine source of information on matters of general culture in *La Belle Province*. (P.G.)

Desert Magazine. 1937. m. $5. Jack Pepper. Desert Magazine, Palm Desert, Calif. 92260. Illus., adv. Circ: 49,000. Sample. Vol. ends: Dec.

Bk. rev: 2–3, 200–300 words. *Aud:* Ga, Hs.

A magazine devoted to the west, emphasizing the desert area (primarily California, Colorado and Arizona). In addition to articles on travel in the western states, one or two articles of each issue are devoted to historical subjects. It is not as attractive as *Arizona Highways* but does include color photographs and maps. The advertisements, pertaining to tourist attractions, motels, restaurants, etc., are often as useful as the text. A second choice, after *Arizona Highways*, for western libraries or schools and those with courses related to this section of the United States. (G.B.)

Down East. 1954. 10/yr. $5.50. Duane Doolittle. Bayview St., Camden, Maine 04843. Illus., adv. Circ: 75,000. Vol. ends: July.

Bk. rev: 4–5, various length, signed. *Aud:* Ga.

A good travel-history-scenic magazine which is edited as much for the nonresident as for the Maine native; a good format, with many photographs, some in color. Subjects touch all aspects of life in Maine from sports and camping to the historical and current personalities. Some fiction, poetry, humor and a good amount of filler make it as much fun to browse in as to read. While off on another tack than the tabloid *Maine Times*, it is pleasant and relaxing enough. The environmentally minded, however, will prefer the *Times* (see Newspapers/Special Interest Section).

Georgia Magazine. 1957. m. $5. Ann E. Lewis. Box 1047, Decatur, Ga. 30031. Illus, index, adv. Circ: 12,000.

Bk. rev: Notes. *Aud:* Ga.

A somewhat better than average approach to the combination history-travel-literature-business syndrome. The well illustrated magazine is nicely edited, and has a folksy personalized touch. Special numbers consider the state of business and travel possibilities. More apt to be appreciated by natives than visitors, but should be considered by libraries in adjoining states as well.

Iowan; Iowa's own magazine. 1952. q. $8. David E. Archie. Box 130, Shenandoah, Iowa 51601. Illus. index. Circ: 9,000.

Bk. rev: various number, length. *Aud:* Ga.

A report to natives on the glories of the state, i.e. most of the material is involved with business, boosting Iowa and various personalities. Some history is included. The editing is fair to good, the writing and format adequate. Of limited interest to any library outside of Iowa.

Kansas. 1945. q. Free. Frances L. Smith. Kansas Economic Development Commission, State Office Bldg., Topeka, Kans. 66612. Illus.

Aud: Ga, Hs, Ejh.

"While other areas of America battle to save forests and lakes, Kansas has been building forests and lakes." And this attractively illustrated and written chamber of commerce approach to Kansas tells why and how. The bid for tourists, industry and understanding is handled nicely. The many photographs, usually in color, are suitable for all ages. Considering it is free, certainly worth a look.

Maryland Magazine. 1968. q. $3. Margaret E. Daugherty. Division of Economic Development, State Office Building, Room 407, Annapolis, Md. 21401. Illus. Circ: 14,000. Sample. Vol. ends: summer.

Aud: Ga, Ejh, Hs.

This is certainly one of the best state published magazines which has appeared in the last decade.

Produced on heavy paper and the size of *Life* or *Look*, it has many artistic full color photographs which make it well worth the subscription price. No advertisements detract from the beautiful photographs. With six to eight articles the history, happenings, flora and fauna of Maryland are explained. Every issue contains portraits of famous Marylanders from a lady seafood packer to a Potomac pilot. A calendar of events for the state is also included. Certainly an excellent choice for Delmarvian residents and schools which have units on this area. (C.B.)

Mississippi News and Views. 1939. bi-m. $3.50 Floyd Mobley, Jr. Mississippi First Assn. Inc., Box 5301, Jackson, Miss. 39216. Illus., adv. Circ: 12,800.

Bk. rev: 1–2, 200 words. *Aud:* Ga, Hs.

The editor describes his 30-page magazine accurately noting that it "is published by a private firm for the purpose of promoting business, industry and tourist attractions in the State of Mississippi. It features people, places, events and historical articles. It utilizes photographs, drawings and feature stories, primarily by professionals. Its editorial scope is restricted to people, places, events and articles concerning these in Mississippi, as Mississippi relates to them, or as they relate to Mississippi." Suitable for any public or high school collection.

Nevada Highways and Parks. 1964. q. $2. Donald L. Bowers. Nevada State Highway Dept., Stewart St., Carson City, Nev. Illus., adv. Circ: 80,000. Sample. Vol. ends: Winter.

Aud: Ga, Hs, Ejh.

Another regional magazine, this one published by the growing state of Nevada. Excellent for tourists, the diversity of the state is discussed in five or six articles, all illustrated with maps and color photographs. A regular feature is "Showsville U.S.A." which lists the schedule of performances at the major resorts in Lake Tahoe, Reno, and Las Vegas. Well worth the subscription price for citizens of Nevada and the surrounding territory. (C.B.)

New Hampshire Profiles. 1951. m. $7. Peter E. Randall. 3 Sheafe St., Portsmouth, N.H. 03801. Illus., adv. Circ: 19,000. Sample. Vol. ends: Dec.

Bk. rev: 4–6, notes, signed. *Aud:* Ga, Hs, Ejh.

A handsome, close to 100-page lure for anyone living in or near a city and who longs to get out there and live. The abundant real estate advertising indicates considerable interest in New Hampshire, and the magazine is as much geared to the out-of-stater as the local residents. It follows the normal format, although here there is more emphasis on photography. About fifty percent of the editorial content is photographic, often in color, and the work of people who enjoy the out of doors. Usually five to six general articles, and a

number of departments concerning restaurants, real estate, hotels, etc. Thanks to the photography and the down to earth stories about history and the land, the magazine can be used in almost any library, for almost any age group. One of the best of its kind.

New Mexico Magazine. 1923. bi-m. $3.25. Walter Briggs. New Mexico Dept. of Development, 113 Washington Ave., Santa Fe, N.M. 87501. Illus., adv. Circ: 100,000.

Bk. rev: 10, 100–200 words, signed. *Aud:* Ga.

Railroads, cowboys, nature, animals, history, and just plain fun—it's all in this nicely edited, well illustrated effort to sell the benefits of travel and life in New Mexico. There are usually five to seven articles with beautifully colored illustrations and photographs. And there are a number of departments from book reviews to a list of activities in the state. The articles are by professional writers, popular but well enough supported by documentation. There is a minimum of chamber of commerce type material. One of the better state magazines and, while the editor is not interested in sending out samples, the price is low enough for risking a year. (If you are cautious, individual copies are 60 cents.)

Oklahoma Today. 1956. q. $2.50. Bill Curchardt. Will Rogers Memorial Bldg., Okla. 73105. Illus. Circ: 42,000.

Aud: Ga.

For anyone living outside of Oklahoma, where this magazine has its chief appeal, here is some interesting, often fascinating photography. The landscape, Indians, industry, personalities, etc., are handled with skill, and the photographs are well worth the modest price. In addition to that there are the usual booster type articles, features, and personality sketches. A better than average regional magazine for those living in the southwest.

Outdoor West Virginia. See *Wonderful West Virginia.*

Sandlapper; the magazine of South Carolina. 1968. 10/yr. $9. Delmar L. Roberts. Robert P. Wilkins, Sandlapper Press Inc., Box 1668, Columbia, S.C. 29202. Illus., index, adv. Circ: 25,000.

Bk. rev: Various number, length. *Aud:* Ga.

With a handsome format and a professional approach to photography, this is one of the better state magazines. It ranks right up there with the Colorado and Maryland entries. As a general state magazine, it includes features and articles on the arts, travel, personalities, history, hobbies, sports etc. There are regular features, including a book review section and a listing of cultural events. The magazine is printed in full color, includes many beautiful photographs and illustrations. Thanks to its more than average eye appeal it can be recommended for high schools and elementary schools. The students will dig the photographs.

Still another magazine from South Carolina is *South Carolina Magazine* (1937. m. $4. Sidney L. Wise, Box 89, Columbia, S.C. 29202. Illus., index, adv. Circ: 5,000). Considerably less modest than *Sandlapper,* but within the scope of its editorial policy quite good. Here more emphasis is on South Carolina history and historical figures. The format is not as good but the articles are quite acceptable. Send for a sample.

Scenic South. 1944. q. Free. Robert B. Montgomery. Chevron Oil Co., Box 1446, Louisville, Ky. 40201. Illus. Circ: 350,000.

Aud: Ga.

Consisting completely of captioned photographs in black-and-white, with color photos on both covers, this little magazine features 20 pages of interesting views of some lesser known attractions for the sightseer in the deep South. All places are of either scenic or historical note, and short descriptions contain a surprising amount of information on history, significance, and related personages, and details of viewing times, etc., for visitors. Views are grouped by geographic area, although one issue usually includes several localities. In addition to pleasant perusing, this has some usefulness as illustrative material on Southern history and ante-bellum architecture and furnishings, as well as in whetting the interest of the traveler.

Southern Living. 1966. m. $4. Gary E. McCalla. Progressive Farmer Co., Box 523, 821 N. 19th St., Birmingham, Ala. 35201. Illus., adv. Circ: 750,000. Vol. ends: Dec.

Bk. rev: 1, 250 words. *Aud:* Ga.

Somewhat the southern equivalent of the north's *Yankee* or the west's *Sunset;* it is a general regional magazine. The editors concentrate on four to five main articles which touch on travel, fashion, housing, history, etc. There are then special Departments on travel and recreation, foods and entertaining, homes and buildings, crafts, and gardening. An average 100-page issue is fairly well edited, nicely illustrated and written for the average white Southern layman. As the editor points out, the magazine is "published for the modern urban and suburban family of the South." Apparently, though, this does not include Blacks. In the January 1972 issue not one Black can be found. It is heavy on advertising, light on controversy. Unfortunately, the publisher will not send samples. A good enough addition for most southern libraries.

Vermont Life. 1946. q. $3.50. Walter R. Hard Jr. Vermont Life Magazine, 61 Elm St., Montpelier, Vt. 05602. Illus. Circ: 129,000. Vol. ends: summer.

Aud: Ga, Hs.

A well edited magazine describing Vermont as the good place to live. Articles are concise, well written, and cover the usual topics, e.g. personalities, history, sights, travel, business. Some good to excellent color and black-and-white photographs. A good bet for almost any library in Vermont or the eastern states.

Wisconsin Trails. 1960. q. $6. Mrs. Jill Dean. Wisconsin Tales and Trails, Inc., 6120 Univ. Ave., Madison, Wis. 53705. Illus. Circ: 18,000. Sample. Vol. ends: winter.

Aud: Ga, Ejh, Hs.

Another regional magazine with a format similar to that of *Arizona Highways* or *Maryland Magazine.* Printed on heavy paper, the photographic quality is almost equal to that of *Maryland Magazine.* The four or five articles of each issue tell of events and personalities, both current and historical, of the state. Although written for adults it will have appeal for elementary libraries because of the illustrations. Fully as useful as other regional magazines and certainly better for libraries in the Wisconsin area. (C.B.)

Wonderful West Virginia (Formerly: *Outdoor West Virginia).* 1936. m. $2. Ed Johnson. West Virginia Dept. of Natural Resources, State Capitol, Charleston, W. Va. 25305. Illus. Circ: 39,500. Sample.

Aud: Ga, Hs.

A 30 to 50 pager highlighting the natural resources of West Virginia. Numerous illustrations (many in color) complement the eight to ten articles which range from historical material to articles on wildlife. There is the usual chamber of commerce theme, but it is not dominant. Anyone involved with the out-of-doors (hunting and fishing or environment) will find this pleasant, relaxing reading.

Yankee. 1935. m. $4. Judson D. Hale. C. R. Trowbridge, Yankee Inc., Dublin, N.H. 03444. Illus., index, adv. Circ: 450,000. Sample. Vol. ends: Dec. Microform: UM.

Aud: Ga, Hs.

With the ecology drive on full blast, the exit from the city encouraged, and the dream of country bliss, this old standby has garnered new friends. While a general New England Magazine, the content has wide appeal; note, for example, the circulation. Since the death of its editor Robb Sagendorph, it has taken on a bit more of the modern tone. There are still the fiction, poetry, food, travel and historical articles, but there is new emphasis on finding other approaches to existence, approaches which have particular appeal to city residents. It is well illustrated with photographs, many in color, and there is a monthly double-page print of a typical New England scene. The classified advertisement section, "Trading Post," and the "Shopper's Guide" offer useful aid for anyone interested in antiques and crafts. A diversion for public or school libraries looking for something a bit different.

URBAN STUDIES

Basic Periodicals

Hs: *City;* Ga: *City, Urban and Social Change Review, Nation's Cities;* Jc: *City, Nation's Cities, Journal of Regional Science;* Ac: *City, Urban and Social Change Review, Journal of Regional Science, Nation's Cities, American Institute of Planners Journal.*

Basic Abstracts and Indexes

Ekistic Index, Poverty and Human Relations Abstracts. In addition many of the other general and specific abstracts and indexes in the social sciences and sciences contain material relevant to urban studies. *Urban and Social Change Review* and several other journals listed here present, from an interdisciplinary point of view, current guides to the literature, abstracts, reviews, and lists of current journal issue contents. *The Council of Planning Librarians. Exchange Bibliographies* (1958. irreg. prices vary. Mrs. Mary Vance, Box 229, Monticello, Ill. 61856) produces from 60 to 80 excellent bibliographies per year on a wide variety of subjects of interest to both planners and urban affairs collections.

Introduction

The continual urbanization of our society and the dissatisfaction people express with the cities in which they live have stimulated a great deal of research and discussion on urban problems. The "urban problem" is not one but many problems. These include transportation, poverty, education, public services, housing, community development, race relations, public utilities, and many aspects of environmental quality. Virtually every discipline has something to say about one or another urban problem. However, there is a growing body of writing which recognizes that urban problems do not respect traditional disciplinary lines and can best be investigated and solved by an interdisciplinary approach. As yet there is no discipline of "urbanology."

This section attempts only to include those periodicals which deal with urban problems in an interdisciplinary framework. For the most part, they are broadly based in the social sciences with a strong input of planning, management and policy. In addition to magazines which cover the general urban scene, titles are included which take three basic approaches to urban problems: city government, regional or community development, and planning. Also included are periodicals dealing with such specific urban problems as public housing, transportation, urban law, public utilities, human problems and poverty, and urban environmental quality. (M.D.)

American City Magazine. 1909. m. $15. William S. Foster. Buttenheim Publishing Corp., Berkshire Com-

mon, Pittsfield, Mass. 01201. Illus., index, adv. Circ: 32,000. Samples. Vol. ends: Dec. Microform: UM.

Indexed: CurrCont, EngI, PAIS, RG. *Bk. rev:* 2–3, 300 words, unsigned. *Aud:* Sa, Ga, Ac.

One of the most useful municipal government publications. *American City Magazine* deals with the management and engineering of local government services. The areas covered are divided into the following: administration, street construction and maintenance, sewage disposal, traffic and transportation, refuse disposal, public safety, parks and recreation, water supply, planning, airports, air pollution, and new products. It emphasizes individual site planning and specific results of projects. In all cases the point of view is problem oriented and pragmatic. This is supported by an extremely popular style and a large amount of special product advertising (50 percent of each issue). It is the best popular level magazine on local government services but neglects the financial aspects of local government management. Of primary interest to libraries specializing in municipal management but also of value to anyone interested in new municipal services. (M.D.)

American County Government. 1936. m. $10. Bernard F. Hillenbrand. National Assn. of Counties, 1001 Connecticut Ave. N.W., Washington, D.C. 20036. Illus., index, adv. Circ: 18,000.

Indexed: PAIS. *Aud:* Ac, Ga, Sa.

Discusses common political and economic problems of county government in a semipopular style. The relatively short articles usually pinpoint a specific situation and explain what decision should or should not have been made. Experiences of personnel from the elected officials to the appointed county planners are highlighted. Rapid urbanization, crime and delinquency, new equipment, finance, legal problems, and even civil defense make up a good part of the material covered in each issue. While written for the official, there is enough here of general interest to warrant consideration in any medium to large public or academic library where there is emphasis on government and political science.

American Institute of Planners. Journal. 1935. bi-m. $10. David R. Godschalk. Amer. Institute of Planners, 917 15th St. N.W., Washington, D.C. 20005. Illus., adv. Circ: 12,000. Vol. ends: Nov. Microform: UM. Reprint: Kraus-Thomson.

Indexed: AmerH, ArtI, CIJE, CurrCont, EKI, HistAb, PAIS. *Bk. rev:* 5–10, 1,000 words, signed. *Aud:* Sa, Ga, Ac. *Jv:* V.

A scholarly journal concerning city planning, emphasizing solutions to social problems of urban areas. *AIP Journal* contains well-written articles by city planners, architects, social scientists and other experts in the field. The book reviews cover relevant scholarly works. "Periodical Literature in Urban Studies" is a regular current awareness feature. Oriented towards professionals and students in the planning fields but contains much material of general interest. The best planning journal available. (M.D.)

American Society of Civil Engineers. Urban Planning and Development Division. Journal. 1964. 1–3 issues per year. $6. William L. Grecco. Amer. Society of Civil Engineers, 2500 S. State St., Ann Arbor, Mich. 48104. Illus., index. Microform: UM.

Indexed: ASTI, ChemAb, EngI. *Aud:* Ac, Sa.

The journal contains articles dealing with all aspects of urban planning with special emphasis on the engineering point of view. That is, the articles deal with design goals and parameters and with ways to design physical systems. Little attention is paid to problems of the social impact and desirabiliy of alternative projects. The articles are generally readable and informative. A listing of articles in this journal is found in *Civil Engineering* and articles can be ordered individually if this journal is not available. Because there is greater emphasis on physical planning than is contained in *American Institute of Planners. Journal,* the two supplement each other. For university and large public libraries. (M.D.)

City; magazine of urban life and environment. 1967. bi-m. $10. Donald Canty. National Urban Coalition, 2100 M St., N.W., Washington, D.C. 20037. Illus., adv. Circ: 50,000. Sample. Vol. ends: Nov./Dec. Microform: UM. Reprint: Annemarie Schnase, Reprint Dept., 120 Brown Rd., Box 119, Scarsdale, N.Y. 10583.

Indexed: PAIS. *Bk. rev:* 6, 1,500 words, signed. *Aud:* Ejh, Hs, Ga, Ac. *Jv:* V.

The first choice for most libraries, *City* is published by the National Urban Coalition. It attempts to be an independent voice to "increase . . . national discussion of urban issues" and is "dedicated to the Coalition's goals of improving urban life and environment." The 60- to 70-page magazine covers all fields of urban interest—congressional action, housing, manpower programs, city planning and government, social environment of cities, etc. Most articles are prepared by staff members, or experts on urban planning. All are authoritative, liberal, and extremely well written. Its content is intentionally geared for laymen and students and it has a highly attractive format. An especially useful feature is "Chronicle of Urban Events and Ideas." Because of its broad content and approach it is of more value to general libraries than the municipal government oriented publications such as *American City Magazine* and *Nation's Cities. City* is the only popular level magazine currently available which deals with all aspects of the urban scene. (M.D.)

Ekistics; Reviews on the problems and science of human settlements. 1955. m. $12. J. Tyrwhitt and G. Bell. Athens Center of Ekistics of the Athens Techno-

logical Organization, Box 471, Athens, Greece. Illus., index. Circ: 4,000. Sample. Vols. end: July and Dec. Microform: UM.

Indexed: CurrCont, EKI, GeoAb. *Aud:* Ac, Sa.

Contains lengthy, detailed abstracts of academic and general articles from a variety of sources, and is accompanied by appropriate graphs and charts. The articles deal with the broadest range of topics of interest to the urbanologist. An easy but sophisticated source of information which is useful to public libraries and high schools. Valuable even though it contains no original work with the exception of occasional interviews. (M.D.)

Environment and Planning; international journal of urban and regional research. 1969. q. $13.50. (institutions $27). A. G. Wilson. Pion, Ltd., 207 Brondesbury Park, London, NW 25 JN, England. Illus., index. Sample. Vol. ends: Winter. Refereed.

Indexed: EKI. *Bk. rev:* 8–10, 800 words, signed. *Aud:* Sa, Ac.

This journal deals mainly with techniques of model building for comprehensive urban planning, with evaluations of models which have been built, as well as empirical studies providing information useful to comprehensive planning efforts. The writings are most often technical and contain a relatively large amount of mathematics. Content is more practical than the *Journal of Regional Science* and more theoretical than the *Journal of the American Institute of Planners.* It should be noted that "environmental" is used to mean all aspects of human existence beyond the individual, rather than the more specific meaning of man's effects on the quality of the earth's natural resources, a more common use of the term. For libraries specializing in urban planning and academic libraries. (M.D.)

HUD Challenge. See Government Magazines/United States Section.

Housing and Urban Development. See Government Magazines/United States Section.

Institute of Human Sciences Review. See *Urban and Social Change Review.*

Journal of Housing. 1944. 11 per yr. $8. Dorothy Gazzolo. National Association of Housing and Redevelopment Officials, Watergate Building, 2600 Virginia Ave., NW, Washington, D.C. 20037. Illus, index, adv. Circ: 15,000. Sample. Vol. ends: Dec. Reprint: Johnson.

Indexed: AbSocWk, PAIS. *Bk. rev:* 9–12, 300 words, *Aud:* Hs, Ga, Ac.

The official organ of the issuing association, this deals with various aspects of public housing including project design, project management, and planning for future needs. Some articles deal with these subjects from a philosophical point of view while others follow a practical approach. Presents the opinions of local public housing officials as contrasted with the views of federal officials expressed in *HUD Challenge*. It has various special features including news items, book reviews and job listings. For academic and public libraries. (M.D.)

Journal of Regional Science. 1958. 3 per year. $12. Walter Izard and Benjamin H. Stevens. Regional Science Research Institute, G.P.O. Box 8776. Philadelphia, Pa. 19101. Illus., index, adv. Circ: 2,700. Vol. ends: Dec. Refereed. Microform: UM.

Indexed: EkI. *Bk. rev:* 8, 1,000 words, signed. *Aud:* Ga, Ac. *Jv:* V.

Published in cooperation with the Department of Regional Science of the Wharton School of the University of Pennsylvania, *Journal of Regional Science* is one of the most significant academic journals dealing with urban and regional affairs. It concentrates on highly theoretical and empirical subjects in the study of urban and regional development. Most contributors are economists but the subject matter is of major interest to planners as well, covering research and studies on the structure, function, and operation of regions from an economic, social, and political standpoint. For college and university libraries and urban public libraries. (M.D.)

Journal of Urban Law. See Law Section.

Land Economics; a quarterly journal devoted to the study of economic and social institutions. 1925. q. $15. Mary Amend Lescohier. Social Science Building, Univ. of Wisconsin, Madison, Wis. 53706. Illus., index, adv. Circ: 3,600. Sample. Vol. ends: Nov. Refereed. Microform: UM. Reprint: Kraus.

Indexed: BusI. PAIS. *Aud:* Ga, Ac.

Land Economics is one of the oldest and best known scholarly economics journals. "It reflects the growing emphasis on planning and the wise use of urban and rural land to meet the needs of an expanding population. Housing, air and water use, and land reform are within its scope. It views land economics as economics in the broadest sense with particular emphasis on public action to achieve the best use of resources in the public interest." In spite of the above planning statement, it is an economics journal rather than a planning journal. *Land Economics* was the first journal in economics to emphasize the importance of institutional structure and locational factors in the allocation of resources. This realization has led it to publish articles on current and alternative structures and interpretations of the results in terms of what is best for society. An excellent journal with many articles less technically written than those in the *American Economic Review*. Consequently, it is very useful to public as well as university libraries. (M.D.)

National Civic Review (Formerly: *National Municipal Review*). 1911. m. (Sept.-July). $7.50. William N. Cassella, Jr. National Municipal League, 47 E. 68th St., N.Y., N.Y. 10021. Illus., index, adv. Circ: 6,200. Sample. Vol. ends: Dec. Microform: UM.

Indexed: ABCPolSci, BusI, LegPer, PAIS. *Bk. rev:* 1–3, 500–700 words, signed. *Aud:* Hs, Ga, Ac. *Jv:* V.

Intended for civic leaders, public officials, and students of state and local government and intergovernmental relations. Each issue contains three or four articles concerning problems of state and local government with emphasis on definition of problems, proposed solutions, and action taken. The articles are written by prominent academicians, practitioners, and political leaders giving their insights and perspectives on urban problems and proposed government action. All articles are written in a highly readable and popular style. More than half of each number is devoted to "News in Review" with significant developments reported in: "City, State and Nation," "Representation," "Metropolitan Areas," "Taxation and Finance," "Citizen Action," "Researcher's Digest," and "Books in Review." A detailed annual index is published which makes this a basic reference source on the chronology of state and local government reform and reorganization which is widely cited in textbooks. Very useful to public libraries as well as specialists. (M.D.)

National Municipal Review. See *National Civic Review.*

Nation's Cities. 1963. m. $6. Patrick Healy. National League of Cities, 1612 K St. N.W., Washington, D.C. 20006. Illus., index, adv. Circ: 58,000. Sample. Vol. ends: Dec. Microform: UM, MF.

Indexed: ABCPolSci, CurrCont, ManI, PAIS. *Bk. rev:* Notes. *Aud:* Hs, Ga, Ac. *Jv:* V.

Nation's Cities is devoted to city government. As the official organ of the National League of Cities, it deals more directly with broad policy issues rather than the pragmatic departmental management issues covered in *American City Magazine*. However, advice on such practical matters as preparing for a municipal bond issue, surveying low cost housing, and methodology for providing slum clearance, health care, and recreational facilities is included. The tone tends to be both knowledgeable and pro-government, with articles prepared by experts in the fields being discussed. Regular departments include news from Washington, traffic, public relations, an employment clearinghouse, and municipal news. In view of its broad scope, it would be a first choice in all library collections where there is any interest in municipal government.

Neighbors 1971. bi-m. $5 (12 issues). National Neighbors, 5 Longford St., Philadelphia, Pa. 19136. Sample. *Aud:* Ga, Ac.

A six- to eight-page newsletter "that reports on events of interest to interracial neighborhoods, particularly on action to achieve open housing in fact as well as in law." The nonprofit organization reports, usually in a paragraph or two, laws, events, meetings, and actions which either support or destroy efforts to integrate neighborhoods. Coverage is national, tends to concentrate on activities in the northern cities. Reporting is objective and factual. Both a useful reference tool and a supportive publication for groups attempting to take the bias out of housing. Recommended for all libraries, but send for a sample copy and judge for yourself.

The New Atlantis; an international journal of urban and regional studies. 1969. s-a. $10. Paolo Ceccarelli. Marsilio Editori, Piazza de Gasperi 41, 35100 Padova, Italy. Subs. to: Sage Publn, 275 S. Beverly Dr., Beverly Hills, Calif. 90212. Illus., adv. Vol. ends: winter.

Aud: Ac.

Edited in Italy, with articles—all in English—written by international experts, each 200-page issue is by way of a monograph. Single topics are considered, e.g., Minorities in European Cities, Comparative Research on Community Decision Making, etc. Most material concerning Europe will be of interest to the professional urban planner and teacher.

Parking. 1952. q. Membership (libraries $6). Norene Dann Martin. National Parking Assn., Inc., 1101 17th St. N.W., Washington, D.C. 20036. Illus., adv. Circ: 6,500. Sample. Vol. ends: Oct.

Indexed: PAIS. *Aud:* Sa.

Parking is a current awareness magazine for the parking structure construction industry. The subject matter is extremely narrow. However, the innovative ideas contained make it of interest to anyone concerned with the problem of where to put the large volume of cars which travel into downtown areas each day. Of use primarily for libraries specializing in municipal management and engineering. (M.D.)

Planning; a newsletter of the American Society of Planning Officials. 1934. m. (Feb.-Mar. combined). $15. Virginia Curtis. Amer. Society of Planning Officials, 1313 East 60th St., Chicago, Ill. 60637. Illus., index. Circ: 10,000. Vol. ends: Dec.

Bk. rev: 4–5, 600–650 words, signed. *Aud:* Sa, Ac.

While subtitled a newsletter and intended for ASPO members, *Planning* is useful to anyone interested in community development and planning. Each issue contains several articles of varying length which interpret the effects of such news items as court decisions and agency reorganization as they affect the practicing planner. In addition one or more signed articles discuss subjects of interest to planners. The broad range of subjects covered, the clear writing style, and

the excellent literature review also give it general library appeal. (M.D.)

Public Administration Review. 1940. bi-m. $25. Dwight Waldo. Amer. Soc. for Public Admin., 1225 Connecticut Ave., N.W., Washington, D.C. 20036. Illus., index, adv. Circ: 12,500. Sample. Vol. ends: Nov.-Dec. Microform: UM. Reprint: Kraus.

Indexed: CIJE, PAIS, SSHum. *Bk. rev:* Essays, notes, signed. *Aud:* Ac.

Designed for the teacher and student, with a nod to the man or woman working in the field. An average issue of 100 pages includes a symposium on some current event of interest, e.g. "The Crisis in Health Care: Problems of Public Administration," or "The American City Manager." Five to six experts speak to the subject, give pros and cons of any argument. This is followed by two or three articles, then book reviews and professional notes. The whole is highly professional, a bit academic, but certainly of interest to any student of the urban community and its problems. Considering its wide scope, it is basic in this field.

Public Management. 1919. m. $6. David S. Arnold. International City Management Assn., 1140 Connecticut Ave., N.W., Washington, D.C. 20036. Illus. adv. Circ: 16,000. Sample. Vol. ends: Dec. Microform: UM. Reprint: Kraus.

Indexed: BusI, PAIS. *Bk. rev:* 1–2, 900 words, signed, 5–10 notes. *Aud:* Ga, Ac.

As the official publication of the International City Management Association, *Public Management* has as its primary purpose service to the urban government administrator. While each issue focuses on one central topic, a wide range of management issues are covered. It parallels *Nation's Cities* in subject matter but with relatively more emphasis on personnel management. It also contains special features with brief reports of developments in cities. The frequent contributions by professional and political leaders make it a useful addition to a general library collection.

Public Works. 1896. m. $7. E. B. Rodie, Public Works Journal Corp., 200 S. Broad St., Ridgewood, N.J. 07450. Illus., index, adv. Circ: 28,800. Samples. Vol. ends: Dec. Microform: UM.

Indexed: ASTI, ChemAb, Engl. *Bk. rev:* 8, 180 words, unsigned. *Aud:* Ga, Sa, Ac.

Public Works is intended for civil engineers who specialize in the design, construction, and operation of locally provided public services. Among the areas covered are water supply, sewage disposal, refuse disposal, streets, and recreation facilities. Articles are written both by academicians and practicing public works engineers and managers. The emphasis is practical and innovative solutions to typical public works problems are presented in a popular nontechnical style. Because of its practical point of view and subject matter, it is appropriate for public and high school libraries as well as academic libraries. (M.D.)

Regional Studies, Journal of the Regional Studies Association. 1967. q. $20. Peter Hall. Pergamon Press, Inc., Maxwell House, Fairview Park, Elmsford, N.Y. 10523. Illus., index. Vol. ends: Dec.

Indexed: EKI, PAIS. *Bk. rev:* 5–10, 1,000–1,500 words, signed. *Aud:* Sa, Ac.

A scholarly, international journal which covers a broad spectrum of issues but concentrates on economic aspects of urban and regional development. The contents tend to be theoretical and/or empirical. While oriented toward the British experience, it contains much of interest to Americans. Abstracts in English, German, French, and Russian. Mainly for college and university collections. (M.D.)

Royal Town Planning Institute. Journal (Formerly: *Town Planning Institute. Journal.)* 1914. 10 per year. $7.50. Mark Pritchard. Royal Town Planning Inst., 26 Portland Place, London W1N4BE, England. Illus., index, adv. Circ: 9,000. Vol. ends: Dec.

Indexed: EKI, PAIS. *Bk. rev:* 8, 750 words, signed. *Aud:* Sa, Ac.

This journal gives the reader insights into the British viewpoint and methods of urban and regional planning. Since the British use planning more extensively in the control of urban development (as in their unique concept of "new towns"), the articles are of interest as a contrast to American journals. The format generally employs the case-study approach. With highly readable articles this journal would be a good choice to provide an awareness of the British experience. For inclusion in large urban public and academic collections. (M.D.)

San Francisco Business. See Free Magazines Section.

Town Planning Institute. Journal. See *Royal Town Planning Institute. Journal.*

Traffic Quarterly. 1947. q. Free. Wilbur S. Smith. Eno Foundation for Transportation, Inc., Box 55, Saugatuck Station, Westport Conn. 06880. Illus., index. Circ: 5,400 Vol. ends: Oct.

Indexed: ASTI, EKI, EngI, PAIS. *Aud:* Sa, Ac.

A specialized academic journal dealing with all aspects of transportation planning, design, operation, innovation and regulation. However, many articles deal with intra-urban movements and methods of movements of people and goods, an important aspect of urban problems. For the transportation specialist and college and university collections. (M.D.)

Traffic World; a working tool for traffic and transportation men. 1907. w. $48. J. C. Scheleen. Traffic Service Corp., Washington Bldg., Washington, D.C.

20005. Illus., index, adv. Circ: 11,500. Microform: UM. *Aud:* Ac, Sa.

Directed to transportation managers in the manufacturing industries, and to water, motor, rail, and air carriers. Articles give world-wide coverage to all aspects relating to the movement of goods. Regular features include ICC decisions, applications, petitions and hearings; FAB News; Maritime Commission News; Court News; international transportation; legislative news; statistics, etc. There are some black-and-white pictures and many advertisements. While a specialized trade journal, the scope is wide enough to warrant consideration in many medium to large public and academic libraries.

Urban Affairs Quarterly. 1965. q. $10 (Institutions $15). Peter Bouxsein. Sage Publn., Inc., 275 South Beverly Drive, Beverly Hills, Calif. 90212. Illus., index, adv. Circ: 2,500 Sample. Vol. ends: June. Refereed.

Indexed: EKI, PAIS, SocAb. *Bk. rev:* 1–2, 300–500 words, signed, notes. *Aud:* Ga, Ac.

An omnibus journal of city problems, with a more academic approach than *City.* It has excellent credentials, being sponsored by the City University of New York. Each issue has five to eight long articles, often devoted to different views of a single topic such as race relations or urban renewal. The number of subjects covered in a span of just a few issues is quite large: poverty, law enforcement, urban renewal, education, interest groups, urban planning, finance, and politics. A worthwhile addition to any college or university library and to urban public libraries. (M.D.)

Urban Crisis Monitor. 1967. w. $4.35. Urban Research Corp. 5464 South Shore Dr., Chicago, Ill. 60615. Sample.

Indexed: PAIS. *Aud:* Ac.

A weekly 40- to 60-page service which provides objective, summary reports on developments "in urban education, employment, housing, politics, race relations, law, welfare" etc. Most issues close with a special section of editorial opinions from the Black press. There is an annual, cumulative index, but apparently no monthly or quarterly approach. Users can call on the firm's data bank for print outs of information required. The *Monitor* is one of many services offered by the firm, and in view of its price, interested librarians should write for more information and sample copies. It seems solid enough, certainly is needed, and should prove of real value to larger and special libraries. (M.D.)

Urban Land; news and trends in land development. 1942. m. (July/Aug. combined). Membership $10. Robert E. Boley. Urban Land Inst., 1200 18th St., N.W., Washington, D.C. 20036. Illus., index. Circ: 5,200. Vol. ends: Dec. Microform: UM.

Indexed: PAIS. *Bk. rev:* 3, 1,000 words, signed (varies). *Aud:* Sa, Ac.

Devoted to news items and articles on urban and suburban real estate development such as the revival of downtown shopping centers, slum clearance, population trends, and parking problems. There are usually one or two long article in this 15- to 20-page newsletter. Articles and research reports are written for the layman and are usually concerned with research supported by the Urban Land Institute. For both general and specialized collections. (M.D.)

Urban Renewal. See Free Magazines Section.

Urban and Social Change Review (Formerly: *Institute of Human Sciences Review.)* 1967. s-a. (Fall and Spring) $4. (Institutions $6). David Horton Smith. Inst. of Human Sciences, McGuinn Hall, Boston College, Chestnut Hill, Mass. 02167. Illus. Circ: 4,500. Vol. ends: Spring.

Indexed: ABCPolSci, AbSocWk, CurrCont, EconAb, GeoAb, HistAb, PHRA, SocAb, TransAb. *Bk. rev:* Varies, unsigned. *Aud:* Hs, Ga, Ac. *Jv:* V.

Each issue contains several "theme articles." Most are written in a popular style. Recent topics included new towns and urban policy, participatory democracy, and urban transportation. There are other articles in each issue and "Urban Science and Action Dialog" (brief comments, notes and letters to the editor). Half of each issue is devoted to "Urban Information Clearinghouse," which covers published and unpublished source material. In addition to extensive book notes and reviews of bibliographies, government publications and reference tools, it includes reviews of such hard to find materials as data banks and retrieval systems, research in progress, simulation games, mathematical models, conferences, degree programs, audiovisual materials and goals and programs of professional associations, foundations, research centers, and public and private organizations. An inclusive list of journals, newsletters, annuals and indexing and abstracting tools has been published as part of the journal and each issue continues to update this bibliography. An inclusive guide to the literature in an interdisciplinary area. A useful magazine for any library, unfortunately published only semiannually. (M.D.)

✓*Urban Studies.* 1964. 3/yr. $7.50. G. C. Cameron (Amer. Advisory Ed: Anthony H. Pascal). Longman Group Ltd., 5 Bentinck St., London W1M 5RN, England. Dist. by: Sage Publns., 275 South Beverly St., Beverly Hills, Calif. 90212. Illus., index, adv. Circ: 4,000. Sample. Vol. ends: Oct. Refereed.

Indexed: EKI. *Bk. rev:* 10–15, 1,000 words, signed. *Aud:* Ac.

An academic journal devoted to all aspects of urban affairs. Articles are written by sociologists, political scientists, economists, geographers, urban historians, and experts in public administration. Although recent issues have given particular emphasis to economic topics, *Urban Studies* still represents a wide range of subject and geographical content. Published in Great Britain for the University of Glasgow but with an American advisory editor and numerous American contributors. Contains about four long articles, several brief notes and comments and extensive book reviews and book notes. (M.D.)

USSR AND EAST EUROPE

Basic Periodicals

ENGLISH LANGUAGE. Hs: *Sputnik;* Ga; *Sputnik;* Ga: *Sputnik, Soviet Life;* Jc: *Chronicle of Current Events, Current Digest Soviet Press, Slavic Review;* Ac: *Chronicle of Current Events, Moscow News, Slavic Review, Sputnik, Soviet Life, East Europe, Polish Perspective.*

LIBRARY AND TEACHING AIDS
ABSEES, *Kritika, Recenzija, Soviet Education.*

SLAVIC LANGUAGE. All libraries where Slavic is a concern or interest: *Krokodil, Novyi Mir.*

Note: Libraries interested in subscribing to a limited number of these magazines or newspapers, or wishing to purchase sample copies are advised to write Four Continent Book Corp., 156 Fifth Ave., N.Y., N.Y. 10010.

English Language

ABSEES: Soviet and East European Abstracts Series. 1950. q. $12 (joint subscription with *Soviet Studies* $18). Vladimir V. Kusin. Inst. of Soviet and East European Studies, Univ. of Glasgow, W.2, Scotland.

Aud: Ac. *Jv:* V.

Each issue, of over 250 pages, consists entirely of abstracts of newspaper and periodical articles and books appearing in the U.S.S.R. and East Europe (Albania, Bulgaria, Czechoslovakia, East Germany, Hungary, Poland, Rumania, and Yugoslavia). Abstracts are in English, average 180 words long for articles and 500 for books. Most abstracts appear from two months to a year after original publication. Arrangement is by two broad subject headings, Social and Economic, under each country. Within the major headings, articles are listed by narrower subject, such as arts, education, foreign relations. An "Information Bulletin" appears in the January and July issues, listing vacancies and staff changes in British universities, articles and research projects in preparation and completed, post graduate theses started and completed, and future visits of foreign scholars and of U.K. scholars to USSR and Eastern Europe. This is an excellent and reasonably priced publication. (E.L.)

California Slavic Studies. 1960. irreg. Inquire. N.V. Riasanovsky and Gleb Struve. Univ. of California Press, Berkeley, Calif.

Aud: Ac.

Written by and for scholars, each volume of these studies presents six to eight thoroughly researched and annotated articles on Russian literature, linguistics, and history. Contributors are not identified but their erudition is evident. In journals examined literary and linguistic topics outnumbered those pertaining to history. Whereas the *Canadian Slavonic Papers* are useful for both, undergraduate and graduate students, the *California Slavic Studies* appear more suited for the advanced student. (E.L.)

Canadian-American Slavic Studies/Revue Canadienne-Americaine d'études slaves (Formerly: *Canadian Slavic Studies*). 1967. q. $10. Charles Schlacks, Jr. Center for Intl. Studies, G7A Social Science Bldg., Univ. of Pittsburgh, Pittsburgh, Pa. 15213. Illus., index, adv. Circ: 1,100. Sample. Vol. ends: winter.

Indexed: HistAb. *Bk. rev:* 20–25, 2 pages, signed. *Aud:* Ac.

A "forum for debate and reflection on the affairs of the Soviet Union and Eastern Europe." A bilingual format with articles contributed from North America, Western Europe and Eastern Europe. The editor points out: "Distinctive features include frequent contributions from East European scholars, heavy advertising by East European publishing houses and academies of sciences, and an interest in publishing serializations, documents and translations." A basic journal for any medium to large university with a slavic studies program.

Canadian Slavic Studies. See *Canadian-American Slavic Studies.*

Canadian Slavonic Papers/Revue Canadienne des Slavistes. 1956. q. $10. John Strong. Carleton Univ. Ottawa 1, Canada.

Indexed: HistAb, MLA, PAIS. *Bk. rev:* 8–10, various length. *Aud:* Ac.

A scholarly literary-linguistic and socio-historical journal, distinguished by contributions of more than esoteric interest, this publication should be useful in all areas of Russian studies. The book reviews consider works by Soviet and other authors. Major events in Soviet literature are sometimes honored by special issues, devoted to one subject or a personality. Most articles are in English with brief resume in French. Occasionally, this is reversed. (E.L.)

A Chronicle of Current Events. 1968. bi-m. $10. Amnesty International Publns., Turnagain Lane, Farringdon Street, London, E.C. 4, England.

Aud: Ga, Ac, Hs. *Jv:* V.

"A journal of the Soviet Civil Rights Movement translated from the typewritten Russian originals, produced in Moscow and circulated in samizdat." (The "samizdat," of course, are the by now famous typewritten or handwritten or mimeographed copies of underground publications circulated by hand among Russians. The samizdat include many publications banned in the USSR, but sold in the West, e.g. the novels of Nobel prize winner Solzhenitsyn.) This slim (23 pages) unpretentious booklet prints "factual information on political trials, political prisoners, labour camps and current samizdat (underground) publications circulating in the U.S.S.R." An issue examined included: open letters to Soviet government agencies, signed by different individuals, among them the writer Solzhenitsyn and members of the Committee for Human Rights; short reports on a psychiatric hospital; regional political protest movements; an article on the Jewish emigration issue; investigation of a trial; and short paragraphs on underground publications. Footnotes by the English publisher refer to books and newspaper articles in the western press. Recommended not so much for its news value as for the insight into a civil rights movement's activities in a Communist country. (E.L. & L.H.)

Current Digest of the Soviet Press. 1949. w. $250 (Low budget libraries and two year colleges $75; secondary schools $25; faculty and students of subscribing institutions $25). Leo Gruliow. American Assn. for the Advancement of Slavic Studies, 2043 Millikin Rd., Ohio State Univ., Columbus, Ohio 43210. Illus., index. Circ: 1,300. Sample. Vol. ends: no. 52.

Indexed: PAIS. *Aud:* Ac, Ga, Hs. *Jv:* V.

The weekly basic source of material in English translated from the Soviet press. Approximately one-third of the daily national newspapers, *Pravda* and *Izvestiia*, are translated and the contents listing of each is given in full. In addition, selections are taken from some 60 other newspapers and magazines. Where articles are abridged, this is noted, and full bibliographic details are given for each item. The Association for Slavic Studies is nonpartisan, refrains from comments on works translated, and affords the American student an excellent cross section of Soviet opinion. If libraries cannot afford this service, they should bring it to the attention of any serious student who is relying on *Problems of Communism* or even *Soviet Life* for a picture of Russia today. The *Current Digest* has an index of the same name which is published quarterly as a supplement. Up until 1972 the cost made it prohibitive for all but the largest academic and public libraries. Thanks to reduced rates for various size and type libraries it is now well within the means of any library. As such it is highly recommended. However, see *Reprints from the Soviet Press* also.

East Europe; a monthly review of East European Affairs. 1952. m. $10. Herman Singer. Robert Speller & Sons Publishers, Inc., 10 E. 23rd St., N.Y., N.Y. 10010. Illus., adv. Circ: 20,000. Sample. Vol. ends: Dec.

Indexed: AmerH, PAIS. *Aud:* Ac.

A scholarly journal whose scope has been broadened in the past two years to include not only East Europe but "advances of Soviet and China into Middle East and a study of U.S.–Soviet relations." The overlap gives the 48-page journal added value. The four to five articles per issue are factually authoritative, and lately the evaluation is objective but still somewhat biased. There are two other sections: English translations of excerpts from articles appearing in East European journals and newspapers, and short notes on current developments. A few articles are devoted to outstanding literary figures. Best for the graduate student and scholar. Undergraduates and advanced high school students might use this for background material, but *Survey* is better suited for most.

East European Quarterly. 1967. q. $10. Stephen Fischer-Galati. Univ. of Colorado. Regent Hall, Boulder, Colo. 80302. Adv. Circ: 750. Sample. Vol. ends: Jan.

Indexed: HistAb. *Bk. rev:* 6, 1,000 words, signed. *Aud:* Ac.

Focuses attention on the history, politics, economics and personalities of the Baltic, Adriatic, Aegean and Black Sea areas. Usually four to five scholarly papers in English from American, Russian, Hungarian and East European universities. Book reviews cover publications from Europe and the United States. The whole is for the scholar, and primarily for large academic libraries.

Eastern European Economics; a journal of translations from Bulgaria, Czechoslovakia, East Germany, Hungary, Poland, Rumania and Yugoslavia. 1962. q. $60 (Individuals $15). Helen M. Kramer. Intl. Arts and Sciences Press, Inc., 901 N. Broadway, White Plains, N.Y. 10603. Illus., index, adv. Sample. Vol. ends: Summer.

Indexed: PAIS. *Aud:* Sa, Ac.

Includes "selected articles from scholarly journals of Eastern Europe in English translations." There are usually four to five translations from the Eastern European press. It is of invaluable assistance for research in this area.

Foreign Trade. m. $12. V. T. Zoloyev. U.S.S.R. Ministry of Foreign Trade, 4 Pudovkin St., Moscow G-285, U.S.S.R.

Aud: Ac.

An English language journal that covers: foreign trade developments and reprints of foreign trade agreements; international exhibits and trade fairs; foreign exchange; analyses of other economic systems; legal aspects of trade relations; and results of recent trade conferences. Some articles cover the subject superficially. Approximately one-sixth of the publication is devoted to full-page advertisements of items available for export. The Soviet point of view is valuable and the economic information is useful. This periodical also appears in Russian, French, Spanish, and German. A supplement—the annual statistical survey of the foreign trade of the USSR—is available for an additional $1.80. (E.L.)

Indiana Slavic Studies. 1956. irreg. Price—inquire. Walter N. Vickery & Wm. B. Edgerton. Indiana Univ., Bloomington, Ind. 47401.

Indexed: MLA, PAIS. *Aud:* Ac.

Part of the Indiana University *Slavic and East European Series.* Volume 1 appeared in 1956 as a collection of studies by members of Indiana University faculty. Subsequent volumes contain contributions by scholars from other American universities, translations from abroad, reprints of reports read before learned societies and excerpts from books in preparation. Includes well annotated essays on Slavic literature, religion, folklore, linguistics, history and government. Some articles contain many valuable bibliographies in special fields. (E.L.)

International Affairs. (USSR); a monthly journal of political analysis. 1955. m. $3.50. I. L. Melamed. 14 Gorokhovsky Pereulok, Moscow K-64, USSR.

Indexed: PAIS. *Bk. rev:* 3–6, 800–1,800 words. signed. *Aud:* Ac.

Published by *Izvestiia* in Russian, English, and French, this journal provides a platform for discussion of international events in Russian terms. Economics and politics are of chief concern. Although the propaganda provided in most of the articles is academic in tone, its quantity can become overwhelming. However, the Soviet viewpoint (on Berlin, the UN, the Voice of America) is fascinating and useful. Recent attention has focused on Africa and Asia, and this provides a different picture from what is offered in standard western sources. Contributors are rarely identified except by name alone. (I.L.)

International Journal of Slavic Linguistics and Poetics. 1959. irreg. $8/ea. D. S. Worth. Dept. of Slavic Languages, Univ. of Calif., Los Angeles, Calif. 90024. Illus., adv. Circ: 550.

Bk. rev: 6–10, 2,500 words, signed. *Aud:* Ac.

Considers structural or descriptive analyses of the Slavic languages during all periods of development. Features discussions of Slavic contributions to linguistic science and studies in applied linguistics, especially dialects. Literary studies are usually textual and linguistic. The text is in English, French, German, and all Slavic languages.

Kritika; a review of current Soviet books on Russian history. 1964. 3/yr. $5 (individuals $2). Richard Pipes. 1737 Cambridge St., Cambridge, Mass. 02138. Circ: 350.

Indexed: HistAb. *Aud:* Ac. *Jv:* V.

The best ongoing review of current Russian history titles. Each 55- to 70-page issue contains five to six lengthy reviews of books published in the Soviet Union. Reviewers are members of the Russian Research Center of Harvard University, and they have an obvious expertise in the language which enables them to interpret the semantic complexities of literary Russian in the context of history. Supporting their critical analysis of the work and evaluation of the Russian perspective with bibliographical references and footnotes as well as translated paragraphs from the work in question, the reviewers provide a scientific, but stimulating text. In selecting books they consider the various periods of Russian history. Some issues focus on one single theme, as for example, on books about the Russian revolution of 1917, at the time of the 50th anniversary. In addition to books dealing with historical events works about famous Russians, i.e. the theater director Meierhold are also reviewed with equal attention to detail. *Kritika* is recommended for research and academic libraries as a valuable source of research material for the student of Russian history and culture. (E.L.)

Moscow News. 1956. q. $5. V. A. Lomko. Union of Soviet Societies for Friendship and Cultural Relations with Foreign Countries. Izvestiia, 16/2 Gorky St., Moscow, USSR. Dist. by: Four Continents Book Corp., 156 Fifth Ave., N.Y., N.Y. 10010. Illus., adv.

Bk. rev: various number, length. *Aud:* Ac, Ga, Hs. *Jv:* V.

Published by the same progressive union as *Kultura i zhizn*, this is a 16-page English-language tabloid (also available in French, Spanish, and Arabic). The editors seek to project an image of a peace-loving Soviet Union, concentrate on the exchange of international visits between heads of state of foreign countries and its own. The general layout with its large type headlines, variety of illustrations as well as diversity of coverage is reminiscent of the American *Daily News.* The special feature "Round-up of Soviet Press" brings reprints from newspapers in the other republics and from the official Soviet news agency Tass. Local news is covered in special columns "Moscow and Muscovites," and "Kaleidoscope." The theater and film programs appear in "What's on next week." A stamp corner, quiz program, the weather and Intourist news

are some of the other features. The letters to the editor column serves as a platform for indoctrination and propaganda. Some of the political articles are written to refute statements about Soviet politics in the international press. A whole page is reserved for the teaching of Russian. *Moscow News* is one of the few papers to run advertisements. These are well designed, large sized, illustrated announcements of service or a technical product available in USSR. Sport occupies an entire page with a special column "Headlines and highlights" for special events. Some issues include a supplement comprising reprints of official speeches or lengthy articles on the recent history of USSR. Recommended for public, high school and academic libraries as a useful source of government issued news in English on the Soviet Union. (E.L.)

Polish Perspectives, monthly review. 1958. m. $5.50. Stefan Arski. Wydawnictwo Wspolczesne RSW PRASA, Wiejska 12, Warsaw, Poland. Illus., adv.

Bk. rev: 3, 500–1,500 words, signed. *Aud:* Ac. *Jv:* V.

The tone of this English-language review is sophisticated and intelligent. Emphasis is on economic topics, but each issue also carries information on the arts, history, and other aspects of Polish life. Although the party line has influence, its ideas are more implied than stated. Judging by several articles, authors are free to criticize aspects of economic policy. Five to seven major articles appear in each issue, along with the following regular sections: the press in review; economy and life; art and science. In addition to book reviews, there is a section on new publications. These are chiefly works in Polish. The original title, and its English translation is given, plus annotations in English. The scope and coverage of this publication is impressive. It will have appeal for the intelligent general reader as well as for the specialist. French and German editions, also. (E.L.)

Polish Review. 1956. q. $8. Ludwik Krzyzanowski. Polish Institute of Arts and Sciences in America, 59 E. 66th St., N.Y., N.Y. 10021.

Indexed: AbEnSt, MLA, PAIS. *Bk. rev:* 3, 500–3,000 words, signed. *Aud:* Ac.

Contributors to this journal of Polish Studies are primarily of Polish extraction. Subject coverage is wide ranging, determined by the interest and talents of the contributor. Polish education, economics, language changes, art and history have been recent topics. The letters to the editor section in each issue produces strongly worded replies to articles and comments on Polish life. A long bibliography section is featured, citing "materials written in English and items by Polish authors." Notes of events and awards involving Polish immigrants and of lectures relating to polish studies are always listed. (E.L.)

Recenzija; A review of Soviet Ukrainian Scholarly Publications. 1971. bi-a. $5 (individuals $3). Harvard Univ., 1737 Cambridge St., Room 208, Cambridge, Mass., 02138.

Aud: Ac.

An 80-page, offset, journal which reviews current books, and some periodicals, in lengthy subject oriented essays. The reviewers cover all aspects of Soviet Ukrainian interest, but the primary emphasis is on scholarly works. Although the whole is in English, the reference is primarily to Russian-language titles. A useful bibliographical guide for academic libraries. (E.L.)

Reprints from the Soviet Press. 1965. bi-w. $25. Jean Karsavina. Compass Publns., Inc., Box 568 Peter Stuyvesant Sta., N.Y., N.Y. 10009. Circ: 1,500. Sample. Vol. ends: June and Dec.

Aud: Ac.

Entirely in English, this small magazine translates and reprints material from a number of Russian and other Communist sources. There are articles by Soviet leaders, texts of official announcements, etc. It is highly selective in what it includes, however, with an international audience in mind. It does not have as wide a range or coverage as found in the *Current Digest of the Soviet Press.* On the other hand, where the *Digest* prints excerpts, the present magazine may include the full text of some article or pronouncement. It is a good source for following the policy positions of the USSR. (E.L.)

The Russian Review; an American quarterly devoted to Russia past and present. 1941. q. $9.00. Dmitri Von Mohrenschildt. Russian Review, Inc., Hoover Institution, Stanford, Calif. 94305. Indexed, adv. Circ: 1,850. Sample. Vol. ends: no. 4. Microform: UM.

Indexed: HistAb, PAIS, SSHum. *Bk. rev:* 25–30, 250–500 words, signed. *Aud:* Ac.

One of the most prestigious Slavic journals published in America. According to an editorial note, its purpose is "to interpret the real aims and aspirations of the Russian people, as distinguished from and contrasted with Soviet Communism, and to advance general knowledge of Russian culture, history and civilization." This journal, which began at the time of the Russian entry into World War II, has among its contributors such people as George Kennan, Alexander Kerensky, Vladimir Nabokov, and Alexandra Tolstoy. Although much space is given over to political and historical discussion, consideration of general cultural matters is frequent. The critical, short book reviews are a particular help to any library trying to build in this area. Of considerable importance to university and large public libraries. (A 30-year cumulative index, 1941–1971, became available early in 1972 for $7.50.)

Slavic Review; American quarterly of Soviet and East European Studies. 1941. q. $15. Donald W. Treadgold. Amer. Assn. for the Advancement of Slavic Studies. Thomson Hall, Univ. of Washington, Seattle, Wash. 98105. Subs. to: Amer. Assn. for the Advancement of Slavic Studies, 190 W. 19th Ave., Ohio State Univ., Columbus, Ohio. 43210. Illus., index, adv. Circ: 3,700. Vol. ends: Dec. Refereed. Microform: UM. Reprint: Johnson.

Indexed: PAIS, SSHum. *Bk. rev:* 75, one page, signed. *Aud:* Ac. *Jv:* V.

A basic journal which examines matters of interest to Slavicists of every stripe. Although the tone is learned (footnotes burgeon), readability is, on the whole, high. Each issue contains: some half-dozen major articles; a section of notes and comments, in which shorter articles appear; a forum, presenting opinions on journal articles, and a large review section. Each has also Letters-to-the-Editor and News-of-the-Profession columns. Inclusion is eclectic. Attention has been given to such subjects as problems of the Russian soldier in 1917, Norman influences on Kievan law, sociology in Eastern Europe, and Solzhenitsyn's recent novels. (E.L.)

Slavonic and East European Review. 1922. q. $13.50. F. L. Carsten. School of Slavonic and East European Studies, Univ. of London, Malet St., London, England. Subs. to: Cambridge Univ. Press, 32 E. 57th St., N.Y., N.Y. 10022. Index, adv. Circ: 1,300. Sample. Vol. ends: Oct.

Indexed: BritHum, HistAb, SSHum. *Bk. rev:* Various number, 500–800 words, signed. *Aud:* Ac.

Devoted to both the social sciences and humanities. Articles deal with history, literature, philosophy, and social commentary. The detailed, critical reviews cover all aspects of Slavonic studies. A basic journal for academic and junior college libraries with appropriate curricula.

Social Sciences; USSR Academy of Sciences. 1970. q. $10. I. R. Grigulevich. 33/12 Arbat, Moscow, USSR.

Bk. rev: 12, 1,000–2,400 words, signed. *Aud:* Ac.

Each issue centers around a theme in the social sciences: history and history journals, economic sciences, problems of the developing countries, demography. New methods in the social sciences receive special emphasis. Books selected for review cover the whole area of the social sciences, but a majority of them relate to the USSR or to the Soviet philosophy. Special features include a list of Soviet journal reviews of foreign books in the social sciences and a list of books translated into Russian and published in the USSR. Articles for each issue are long, academic, and sometimes turgid in style. Unlike many Soviet journals, this one provides a paragraph of background information about each author. The journal appears in English,

French, and Spanish. It is sponsored by the Department of Social Sciences, Presidium of the USSR Academy of Sciences. (E.L.)

Soviet Anthropology and Archaeology; a journal of translations. 1962. q. $60. (individuals $15). Stephen Dunn. Intl. Arts & Sciences Press, 901 N. Broadway, White Plains, N.Y. 10603. Illus., index, adv. Circ: 1,000. Sample. Vol. ends: spring.

Aud: Ac.

One of 15 translation journals from Soviet publications issued by this press, the format follows a set pattern. Articles are translated in full, usually from six to eight Soviet journals are considered, and the time lapse between publication of the journal and translation is six to 18 months. Translations are reliable, and the selection is particularly good. The high price makes it prohibitive for most libraries, but it deserves a place in any large collection.

Soviet Education; selected articles from Soviet education journals in English translation. 1958. m. $95. (individuals $25). Harold J. Noah and Beatrice Beach. Intl. Arts and Sciences Press, 901 N. Broadway, White Plains, N.Y. 10603.

Indexed: EdI, CIJE, PAIS. *Aud:* Ac, Hs, Ejh.

Unabridged articles translated from basic Soviet education journals and government documents. Each issue focuses on a theme, such as rural education, economics of education, programmed instruction, etc. Articles run about six months behind their original publication date, although this varies considerably because they are selected on a theme basis. Although the reader may occasionally have to struggle through quantities of simplistic propagandist rhetoric, this journal provides information and data available nowhere else and frequently of high quality. (E.L.)

Soviet Geography: Review and Translation. 1960. m. (Sept.–June). $35. Theodore Shabad. Amer. Geographical Soc., Broadway & 156th, N.Y., N.Y. 10032. Circ: 900. Microform: UM.

Indexed: PAIS. *Aud:* Ac.

Despite the title, this is an American publication. Includes: (1) English translations of current Soviet research in geography taken from the principal Russian geographic journals; (2) brief abstracts preceding each article; (3) tables of contents of the current issues of the Russian journals. Readers are invited to suggest articles of general interest for translation. News notes on geographic changes in the Soviet Union are provided. Special issues are devoted to translations of the legend matter and text of important Soviet atlases and to a directory of Soviet geographers. Occasional review articles by American scholars summarize Soviet work in a particular field of geography. Obviously, only for the large academic collection, although it may be useful in smaller schools where Soviet studies are emphasized.

Soviet Life. 1956. m. $3.95. Oleg P. Benyukh. Embassy of the Soviet Union in the USA, 18th St. N.W. Washington, D.C. Illus. Circ: 62,000.

Indexed: MusicI, PAIS. *Aud:* Hs, Ga, Ac.

Published as the Russian counterpart to *America* by reciprocal agreement between the two governments. Glossy in makeup, with many photos of excellent quality, it follows the style of the American *Life* in bringing personalities and topical issues to the reader. Contributions include well-written pieces on everyday life, science, art, literature, education, sport, nature, etc. Many are signed by well-known Soviet citizens and specialists connected with academies and universities. Aimed specifically at the American reader, the family type magazine projects the image of a people enjoying the good life in a Communist society. Admitting the existence of universal problems concerning youth, health, ecology, etc., the writers find they can deal with them best through the ideology of socialism. Keeping in mind its propaganda quality the American reader will find the *Soviet Life* informative and entertaining. Recommended for public, high school, and academic libraries. (E.L.)

Soviet Literature. 1932. m. $4.50. Savva Dangulev. Writers Union of the USSR, 1/7 Kutuzovsky Prospect, Moscow, 121248, USSR. Illus.

Indexed: MLA. *Bk. rev:* 2–3, lengthy. *Aud:* Ac, Ga.

Official organ of the Writers Union, published originally in Russian and translated into English, German, Polish and Spanish. In the tradition of government publications, the magazine leans heavily on Marxist-Lenin ideology, apparent in editorials as well as in the reports of socio-political activities of Soviet writers. Features poetry and fiction: discussion of literary trends and movements; works of classical authors; and literary criticism of foreign writers translated into Russian. Some articles on art, theater, ballet and science. Adding measurably to the attraction of the journal are the many excellent color reproductions of paintings by Soviet artists. Their landscapes and city views project a vivid and cheerful image of the country. Good layout, handy format, excellent print and paper, and contributors such as Vosnesensky and Evtushenko make *Soviet Literature* a worthwhile choice for academic and large public libraries. (E.L.)

Soviet Military Review. 1965. m. $7. Anatoly Korkeshkin. 2, Marshal Biryuzov St., Moscow 123298, U.S.S.R.

Bk. rev: 1–2, 300–1,800 words. *Aud:* Ac.

This heavily illustrated monthly is published in English, French and Arabic. It emphasizes the glorious accomplishments of the Russian armed forces. Many articles honor individual achievements of officers, generally as examples of the highest in Soviet effort and ability. Each issue also contains 10 to 20 pages on combat training. There is at least one article on military history and one directly attacking the United States. The majority of the writers are Russian officers. Coverage is probably unique, but library value is limited, except for very large academic or for military libraries. (E.L.)

Soviet Studies. 1949. q. $10. Ed. Bd. Inst. of Soviet and East European Studies, Univ. of Glasgow, Glasgow W2, Scotland. Index, adv. Circ: 1,750. Sample. Vol. ends: Apr. Microform: UM. Reprint: Johnson, Abrahams.

Indexed: BritHum, PAIS, SSHum. *Bk. rev:* 15, 1,000 words, signed. *Aud:* Ac.

A scholarly journal, covering social sciences, as well as economics of the Soviet and East European nations. In each issue there is an extensive bibliography of books in the field. The *"Information Supplement"* (see last edition's annotation) has been discontinued. Its place has been taken by a separate *Soviet and East European Abstracts Series,* known as ABSEES. This appears quarterly, in the same months as *Soviet Studies,* i.e. July, October, January, and April. (E.L.)

Soviet Studies in Philosophy. 1962. q. $60 (Individuals associated with subscribing institutions $15). John Somerville. International Arts and Sciences Press, Inc., 901 N. Broadway, White Plains, N.Y. 10603. Index, adv. Sample. Vol. ends: Dec.

Indexed: PhilI, RepBibPhil. *Aud:* Ac.

Contains unabridged translations of articles from four Soviet philosophical journals; the articles are generally less than a year old. Besides discussions of Marxism and Leninism, recent issues have included articles on Hegel, logic, ethics, and philosophy of science. Useful to libraries supporting significant philosophy programs or Soviet area studies. (J.A.)

Soviet Studies in History; a journal of translations. 1962. q. $60 (Individuals $15). Paul Aron. International Arts and Sciences Press, 901 N. Broadway, White Plains, N.Y. 10603. Sample.

Aud: Ac.

English translations of articles from Soviet history journals, appearing about a year behind date of original publication. As in other IASP journals, selections are those "which best reflect developments in Soviet historiography and which are of most interest to those professionally concerned with this field." Each issue carries three or four lengthy articles, most with clearly stated Marxist bias. Writers are historians or military officers. The officers' ranks are given, but historians are identified only by name. (E.L.)

Soviet Union. Sovetskii soyuz. 1930. m. $4.50. N. M. Gribachev. Pravda Publishing House, ul. Moskvina 8., USSR. Ill.

Aud: Ga, Ac, Hs.

Another English-language monthly published by Pravda for distribution in foreign countries (translated into 19 languages.) Lavish illustrations, an attractive layout and generally bland survey type articles place this journal in the same class as *Soviet Life.* It offers information and entertainment for the whole family. Special attention is given to the development and growth of Soviet science, technology and industry. Many articles, written for the layman, are contributed by specialists. Sport, women's interests, humor, theater and film are represented in attractive fashion found in similar sophisticated magazines of the international press. The outstanding artwork and a lively style are the most remarkable features of this magazine, but it is not quite up to *Soviet Life.* In its Russian language version, students will find it a useful aid in addition to newspapers and textbooks. (E.L.)

Soviet Woman/Sovetskaia zhenshchina. 1945. m. $4.50. V. I. Fedotova. Soviet Women's Committee and the Central Council of Trade Unions of the USSR Moscow 22, Kuznetsky Most, USSR. Subs. to: Four Continent Book Corp., 156 Fifth Ave., New York, N.Y. Illus.

Bk. rev: Various number, length. *Aud:* Ac, Ga.

A testimonial to the triumph of "women's liberation" in the USSR this English-language magazine focuses on women in all aspects of the Soviet economy. Their accomplishments in science, technology, education, government, medicine, transportation, the arts, etc., constitute the main theme. This is in contrast to similar American publications which devote considerable space to the problems of women as working girls, wives, mothers, and homemakers. Articles varying in length from very short to 2 pages are signed by specialists, government officials, personalities from the literary world and special correspondents from outlying areas. Numerous illustrations, some in color, add to the entertainment value of this large glossy periodical. Special features include poetry and short stories by Soviet writers, as well as translations of stories from remote republics and other Slavic countries. Considerable attention is given to fashion in color and photos; a special column on new ideas in Soviet modes and patterns for sewing and knitting. Humorous items, short sketches and a children's page appear regularly. An entertaining and informative magazine for public libraries and secondary school libraries. Useful in the Russian version as an aid for language study. (E.L.)

Sport in the USSR. 1966. m. $3. Moscow K-31, ul. Mskvina, i., USSR. Illus.

Aud: Ga, Hs, Ejh.

One of the few sport magazines published in the Soviet Union. Issued in Russian, English, German, Hungarian and Spanish, this lacks the slickness and glossy makeup of other export periodicals. Trying to cover all types of sport the publishers have crammed a variety of articles into 32 pages. Numerous black-and-white photos, often of excellent action quality, chronicle achievements of Soviet athletes, sport events in the various republics, international competitions, and training programs. The Soviet Union's role in the Olympics is given wide coverage. The participation of women in national and international competitions receives special attention. Useful as a source of information on the development of sport in the USSR. In the Russian version the magazine is recommended as an aid in language instruction. (E.L.)

Sputnik. 1967. m. $5. N.I. Efimov. Sputnik Novosti Press, 2 Pushkin Sq., Moscow, USSR. Subs. to: Eastern News Distributors, Inc., 155 W. 15th St., New York, N.Y. 10011. Illus., index, adv.

Aud: Ga, Ac, Hs.

A somewhat more sophisticated approach than *Soviet Life*, this English language periodical has about the same format as *Reader's Digest* but closer to *Life* in the profusion and beauty of its illustrations and choice of subjects for picture stories. Condensations from 11,000 Soviet magazines and newspapers are signed by writers, scientists, military personnel, government officials, and personalities in sport, the arts and literature. Picture stories, memoirs, fashions, recipes and humor balance the more serious features on history, politics and economics which reflect the viewpoint of the press from which they are taken. Letters to the editor give an insight into Soviet life. A book condensation is a regular feature. Short stories also appear. Reproductions of Soviet paintings, or music, accompany articles on famous artists. Sport is covered extensively in pictures and interviews. The magazine carries some advertisements mainly for the Soviet Travel Agency Intourist and the Government Publishing House Mezhdunarodnaya Kniga in addition to announcements of international exhibitions. Designed for export this magazine offers interesting information on Soviet culture in readable and entertaining form. Secondary school libraries as well as public libraries should find *Sputnik* useful for broad if bland coverage of the USSR. (E.L.)

Studies in Soviet Thought. 1961. q. $16.95. Joseph M. Bocheński, Thomas J. Blakely, and Nikolous Lobkowicz. D. Reidel Publishing Co., Dordrecht, Holland. Index, adv. Vol. ends: Dec.

Indexed: PhilI, RepBibPhil. *Bk. rev:* 1–6; 600–122 words. *Aud:* Ac.

Published jointly by the Institute of East European

Studies and the University of Fribourg (Switzerland). the Russian Philosophical Studies Program at Boston College, and the Seminar for Political Theory and Philosophy at the University of Munich. Contains original articles, mostly in English, about contemporary Soviet philosophy, as well as philosophy of other communist countries. Also includes the *Bibliographie der Sovjetischen Philosophie*, which, prior to 1967, was published separately by the Institute of East European Studies at Fribourg. This bibliography aims at completeness, and should be of considerable value to specialists. Important for libraries supporting significant philosophy programs; essential for libraries supporting Soviet area studies. (J.A.)

Slavic Language

Iunost' (Youth.) 1955. m. $3.60. B. N. Polevoi. Pravda, ul. Pravdy 24, Moscow A-47, GSP, U.S.S.R. Illus. Circ: 2,000,000.

Aud: Hs, Ga.

A more serious and scholarly journal than *Smena*, this official Russian language organ of the Writers Union of U.S.S.R. is designed to educate young people rather than to entertain them. The great part of each 112 page issue includes poetry and fiction by young authors, often representing their first publication. The remainder features essays on literature, art, education and sociology. For humor, one finds satire, aphorisms and cartoons. Among the illustrations are reproductions of the works of contemporary Soviet artists, some of very good quality. In general, *Iunost'* lacks the visual appeal of *Smena* but surpasses it in depth, in both approach and writing. Like its sister publication it avoids controversial issues and generally submits to the political influence of their common publisher. (E.L.)

Krokodil (Crocodile) 1922. s-m. $6. M. G. Semenov. Pravda Publishing House, Bumazhny proezs, d. 14, Moscow, A-15, USSR. Illus. Circ: 5,750,000.

Aud: Ac, Ga, Hs. *Jv:* V.

The world's most famous satirical magazine. Issued by the publishers of *Pravda*, this weekly 16-page comic paper derives its perspective from the point of view of the official Communist party line. It carries cartoons, short articles, anecdotes, poems and special features in a humorous, witty and satirical vein. Much of the satire is directed towards the capitalistic world, and the United States appears to be the principal target of a tendentious acid treatment. A more benevolent humor is applied to the foibles and fallacies of the Russians. Some stories meant for them, however, carry a thinly disguised party message under a humorous treatment. Much of the situational humor can only be appreciated by the reader who is familiar with the local scene. The quality of the drawings is excellent and the general layout of text and cartoons is attractive and stimulating. There is a simple quality to most of the content which is reminiscent of the less sophisticated American comics. A good exponent of Russian humor, *Krokodil* belongs in high school, public, and academic libraries. For the teachers of Russian language it is recommended as a useful aid. (E.L.)

Kultura i zhizni' (Culture and Life). 1957. m. $2.50. B. S. Rzhanov. Union of Soviet Societies for Friendly and Cultural Relations with Foreign Countries, 13/15 Proezd' Sapunova, Moscow—Center, USSR. Illus.

Bk. rev: various number, length. *Aud:* Ac, Ga, Hs.

A more sophisticated version of *Soviet Life*, issued in English, French, Spanish, German, and Russian. Focuses on the cultural achievements and developments of the Soviet Union. Articles on the theater, opera, art, ballet, and music by officials of the cultural government agencies. Profiles of prominent artists in Moscow and stories on personalities in some of the other republics alternate with theoretical writings—some with political overtones. Cultural ties with foreign countries, are given extensive coverage; this reflects the publisher's philosophy of seeking a rapprochement with other countries through the exchange of and the meeting of artists. Recommended in the English version for public and academic libraries as a good information source on the general cultural scene of the Soviet Union. In the Russian version it represents a useful study aid for the advanced language student. (E.L.)

Literaturnaia Gazeta (Literature paper). 1929. w. $6. Alexander Chakovsky. Soyuz pisatelei USSR, Tsvetnoi bul'var 30, Moscow, 1–51, USSR. Illus. Circ: 1,000,000.

Bk. rev: various number, length. *Aud:* Ac, Ga, Hs.

The slogan "Workers of the world unite" is the masthead of this weekly newspaper of the Union of Soviet Writers, as it is for *Izvestiia* and *Pravda*. However, the party line point of view of *LG* is somewhat tempered by the artistic approach of literary journalism. Half of the paper is devoted to analysis, discussion and criticism of literature and the arts. Contributions of original poetry and prose from Soviet writers and occasional translations from foreign authors, including Americans, provide a varied picture of the literary scene. Articles on politics, science, law, international affairs and philosophy compose the other half, together with critiques on the theater, films, television and radio. Short satirical and humorous items including a liberal use of clever cartoons reveal the ability of the Soviets to poke fun at themselves and also exhibit their tendency to caricaturize the capitalistic world. Occasional short book reviews and some bibliographical material are included. Maintaining the large format of the other two papers, *Literaturnaia Gazeta*, with its photos, sketches, colored typography, mixed

lettering and attention drawing devices produces, however, a poster or broadside effect, especially on its front page. Style and variety of subjects combine to make this weekly a more readable representative of the Soviet Press than *Pravda* or *Izvestiia*. *LG* is frequently quoted in the international press and news service as the voice of the Soviet intelligentsia on many subjects besides literature. A must for academic libraries and recommended for the larger public libraries as well as high school libraries. (E.L.)

Muzikal'naia Zhizn (Musical Life). 1957. s-m. $8.40. V. A. Bely. "Sovetskii kompozitor," naberezhnaiz Morisa Toreza, d. 30, Moscow, ZH-35, USSR. Subs. to: Four Continent Book Corp., 156 Fifth Ave., N.Y., N.Y.; Illus., index. Circ: 115,000.

Bk. rev: various number, length. *Aud:* Ac.

A large illustrated glossy with very small print, this fortnightly magazine utilizes the format and features of the popular entertainment journal to bring the reader information on a special subject. Papers read at the Union of Soviet Composers are reprinted in shortened form. Regular features include articles about international music competitions, musical premieres, announcements of musical events, interviews with famous musical personalities, writeups of great singers and composers from the past, news of the music world abroad, a column on concerts and a music oriented crossword puzzle. New Soviet books on music are reviewed and short literary pieces with musical or theatrical themes appear. Several pages are devoted to reprint of music of Soviet songs. Length of articles varies from very short to several pages. All articles are signed and explanatory footnotes are used when necessary. Popular in format, but specialized in theme, this journal has limited appeal. Suitable for large city and academic libraries for readers fluent in the Russian language. (E.L.)

Nauka i zhizn' (Science and Life). 1934. m. $3.60. N. V. Vokhovitinov. Pravda, ul. Pravdy, 24, Moscow A-47, GSP, USSR. Illus. Circ: 3,000,000. Microform: B & H.

Indexed: BioAbs. *Aud:* Ga, Hs, Ac.

A popular science Russian language journal sponsored by the all union society "Znanie" (knowledge). In general, the subject and treatment is suited to the reader with a basic knowledge in science. The reader will have no difficulty following the text which is sufficiently illustrated with graphs, maps and photos. Endeavors to acquaint the general reader with the latest developments in science and technology. Articles are written by specialists, many from the Academy of Sciences and other official institutions. The journal introduces new products and processes, and has essays on archeology, history and linguistics. Of special interest to the American reader are two regular features:

the list of new scientific terms, and the etymological column on Slavic family names. Illustrations are plentiful, often in color, well placed and executed and include portraits, reproductions, facsimiles and many excellent photos. The print, regrettably, is hard on the eyes. Good comprehension of Russian required. (E.L. & L.H.)

Novyi Mir: literaturno-khudozhestvennyi i obschchestvenno-politicheskii zhurnal. 1933. m. $6.60. V. A. Kosolapov. Izvestiia Sovetov Deputatov Trudiashchikhsia SSSR, Pushkinskaia pl., d. 5, Moscow, k–6, USSR. Adv. Circ: 120,000. Microform: B&H.

Indexed: MLA. *Bk. rev:* 6–8, signed. *Aud:* Ac. *Jv:* V.

The best known, certainly the most often quoted Russian language literary magazine. It is an official publication of the Soviet Delegation of Workers of the Soviet Union and tends to fluctuate between liberalism and a strict party line. Specializing in literature, art, social science and politics, it includes poetry, short stories, novels (in continuations) by contemporary writers from all parts of the Union, and diaries and memoirs of military personnel. Lengthy analysis of international political issues is a regular feature. Each issue presents an indepth article on a single theme of socio-political or historical importance, e.g., the city. All articles are signed and some are documented by footnotes. Literary criticism concerns itself with the problems of contemporary Soviet literature. Book reviews are divided into two categories: literature and art; politics and science. The Party ideology is evident in most of the writings, and the style is reminiscent of other official publications (*Pravda, Literaturnaia Gazeta*). This together with the poor quality of paper and print and frequent double column arrangement makes the reading of *Novyi Mir* somewhat laborious. However, the academic librarian should add it to the collection because it represents the thinking and direction of Soviet intelligentsia. (E.L.)

Ogonek (The Flame). 1923. w. $8.40. A. V. Safronov. Pravda Publishing House, Ul, Pravdy 24, Moscow A–47, USSR. Illus. Circ: 2,000,000.

Bk. rev: various number, length. *Aud:* Ac, Ga.

This weekly publication of Pravda is a glossy magazine devoted to social, political, literary and artistic themes. Its emphasis is on national events and topics of current interest in Russia and the other federated republics of the USSR. Articles by special correspondents acquaint the Soviet citizen with the cultural, economic, scientific and political life of his fellow countrymen in Azerbeizhan, Uzbekeistan, Moldovia, etc. Poetry, short stories, serialized novels, interviews with party officials, book reviews, articles about the theater and film present a multifaceted picture of the entire country. Crossword puzzles and humorous items are included. The absence of a table of contents is noted with regret. The journal is enriched by many excellent photos (especially those of children) and there are good reproductions of the work of Soviet artists. The colors are not as bright as those in *Soviet Life,* neither does the print or quality of paper compare favorably with the other magazine which is designed for export. Nor does *Ogonek,* which is tailored to educate and entertain the Soviet citizen, provide a platform for discussion of the problems and ills of society. By ignoring these and concentrating in word and pictures on the advances and achievements of the Soviet Union only, the journal follows the dictates of the party line which is forever present in tone and content. The absence of a dissenting voice is characteristic for this magazine as it is for other publications of *Pravda.* The world outside is dealt with in a regular short column "Nash Vzgliad" (Our View) and exhibits the usual polemics against U.S. The reading of the journal requires a good command of the Russian language. The larger public libraries and the academic libraries will benefit most from it. (E.L.)

SSHA: ekonomika, politika, ideologiia. 1970. m. 60 kop. V. M. Berezhkov. Izd. "Nauka," ul. Gorkogo, 16/2, Moscow, USSR. Illus. Circ: 22,000.

Bk. rev: various number, length. *Aud:* Ac.

A Russian-language journal, devoted entirely to American politics, economics and ideology, and published by the Institute of U.S. Studies of the Academy of Sciences. Soviet scholars, journalists and public officials discuss, analyze and interpret the national and foreign policies of the U.S., e.g. relations with Latin America, the two party system, Mafia crimes, labor management problems, etc. The Russian reader, for whom this magazine is published, will find the criticism and accusations a familiar refrain. Of interest are the translations and condensed books of American authors. Herbert York's *Race to Oblivion* was one such selection, brought out in continuation. It is followed by a lengthy review. Books for reviewing are generally chosen for their socio-political subjects and controversial themes. These also include books by Russian writers. The journal includes profiles of some states. These are well written reports on the physical make-up. A "political vocabulary" interprets some American innovations, such as the Eurodollars. Since reading *SSHA* requires a fair knowledge of Russian and a special interest in Soviet politics it will be most useful to those in academic libraries. Some numbers are available in translation through the National Technical Information Service, Springfield, Va., 22151. (E.L.)

Smena (Rising Generation). 1924. bi-w. $3.60. A. D. Golubev. Pravda, Moscow, A–15, GSP, USSR. Bumazhnyi proezd, 14. Illus. Circ: 1,000,000. Microform: B & H.

Aud: Hs, Ga.

A slick, richly illustrated Russian-language glossy fortnightly devoted to the interests and problems of young people in the Soviet Union. Articles, oriented towards both sexes, center on sport, science, social issues, fashion and entertainment. The latter includes humorous items, crossword puzzles, music and cartoons. Among the regular features is a lengthy report on a profession or trade, with action pictures illustrating the fast moving text. Each issue gives in depth coverage to a special subject displayed over the entire front page, similar to the American *Life* or the *Soviet Life*. Poetry, stories, and serialized fiction also appear reflecting a world curiously free of controversial issues that trouble our youngsters. Sex, drugs, drop outs, sit-ins, confrontations or generation gap apparently do not occupy the thoughts of the Soviet teenagers whose minds are filled with patriotism and loyalty to the Komsomolsk. The appearance and behavior of the Soviet boys and girls impress one as an imitation of the American "bourgeois" jeunesse of the 1950s or middle 1960s. For a look at the world outside the Iron Curtain *Smena* prints enticing travelogs of the satellite nations or allies. The reports on the American youth, in contrast, repeat the cliches of gangsterism, racism, exploitation, etc., employing sensational photos for emphasis. Issued by the Central Kommittee of the Leninist Young Communist League of the Soviet Union, this magazine reflects all that is implied in the official status of its publisher. (E.L.)

Sovetskaya Muzyka (Soviet Music). 1935. m. $13.50. U.S. Korev. Sovetskii kimpozitor, ul. Ogareva, 13, Moscow, Center, GSP–3, USSR. Illus. Circ: 18,200. Microform: B&H.

Indexed: MusI. *Aud:* Ac.

This is an official organ of the Union of Soviet Composers and the Minister of Culture of the U.S.S.R. It covers all aspects of music and offers a panoramic view of the musical world of the Soviet Union. An average 160-page issue includes articles on music theory, research, education, critiques and analyses of new works and performances, biographies of famous composers, reprints of research papers read before the Union of Composers. Musical events and development in all parts of the Soviet Union as well as abroad are also included. Scholarly treatment, supported by ample bibliographies and examples. Black and white illustrations offer diversity of subjects but are poor in quality. Pleasant format and layout. A more serious journal than *Muzikal'naia Zhizn* providing a valuable and interesting source for the student of music. Requires good knowledge of Russian language. Recommended for academic libraries. (E.L.)

Teatr (Theater). 1939. m. $15. V. Lavrent'ev. Writers Union of the USSR and Ministry of Culture of the USSR. Kuznetskii most, 9/10, Moscow, K-31, USSR. Illus., adv. Microform: UM.

Aud: Ac.

An important Russian-language monthly containing a wealth of information on every aspect of the theater and stage in the Soviet Union, and in other countries. Detailed analyses and critical evaluation by specialists, cover: acting, direction, state design, costume, theory of the drama, and development and trends. Of particular interest to the American students of the theater are the stories on important directors and actors of the Soviet stage. The cultural and political role of the theater forms the basis for discussions of the national and foreign plays and productions. As an organ of a government agency *Theater* prints reports from the Writers Congresses and generally carries the official ideological message, both implicitly and explicitly. Liberally illustrated, this 192-page journal offers valuable source material for students of drama and the theater with a good command of Russian. (E.L.)

Ukraina (**Ukraine**). 1941. w. $6. V. G. Bol'shak. Radians'ka Ukraina, Brest-Litovskii Prospekt, 94, Kiev 47, USSR. Circ: 350,000.

Aud: Ga.

A popular illustrated Ukrainian-language weekly, published also in Russian. Concentrating on regional events and personalities, the journal covers the sociopolitical and general cultural aspects of Ukrainian life. Informative and entertaining, it covers: scientific and technological developments; art and literature; theater and film; poetry and fiction of contemporary Ukrainian authors; a special subject with full cover illustration; sport pages; and humorous stories, cartoons and crossword puzzles; numerous illustrations, including some fine art reproductions. Although of the same political cast as other Soviet publications this magazine refrains from anti-American attacks. (E.L.)

Voprosy Istorii KPSS (Problems of History of the CPSU). 1957. m. $14.50. Pravda, ul. Pravdy, 24, Moscow, A-47, GSP, USSR. Microform: B&H.

Bk. rev: Various number, length. *Aud:* Ac.

Russian-language organ of the Marx-Lenin Institute under the Central Committee of the Communist Party of the Soviet Union (CPSU), this is a scholarly journal specializing in the problems of the Party and the history of international labor movements. Soviet and foreign historiography is followed in articles contributed by scholars with particular attention to the "bourgeois ideology" point of view. Present activities and developments of the CPSU and its significance for the economic and industrial progress of the country are subjects of regular features. There are also reports on congresses and important party members. Propagation of the Party and teaching of its history are an integral part of the journal. Of particular interest to the foreign reader are the critical book reviews, bibliographies, and lists of doctorial dissertations. The content page appears in Chinese, German, French, and English at the end of each issue. (E.L.)

Voprosy Istorii (Problems of History). 1926. m. $20. V. G. Trukhanovskii. Pravda, ul. Pravdy, 24, Moscow, A-47, GSP, USSR. Circ: 30,000. Microform: B&H.

Bk. rev: Various number, length. *Aud:* Ac.

A scholarly Russian-language publication from the Department of History of the Academy of Sciences, the journal is also the voice of the Ministry of Special Education of the U.S.S.R. Well documented articles, surveys, and memoirs. There are reviews of Russian and foreign books and periodicals. A page of biographical information on the authors helps the reader to evaluate the material. Print and paper are not of the best quality. The last number in the year includes an index by author and category. Somewhat unusual in a scholarly journal of this type is the advertisement for car insurance on the back of one issue. Recommended for academic libraries. Major articles are summarized in English, French or Spanish at the back of the journal, and the contents are repeated in English, in compressed form. (E.L.)

Émigré Magazines

Grani; zhurnal literatury, iskusstva, nauki i obshchestvenno-politicheskoi mysli. 1946. q. $13.20. N. B. Tapasova. Possev Verlag, Frankfurt 3 Main 80, Flurscheideweg 15, West Germany. Illus., adv. Circ: 1,500.

Bk. rev: 6–8, various length. *Aud:* Ac.

An independent Russian émigré journal of some 270 pages published in West Germany, devoted to literature, art, science, philosophy, and socio-politics. Provides an outlet for contemporary, as well as early Soviet writers whose work is suppressed at home. Poetry and short stories, excerpts of novels, literary criticism and interpretation of the works of classic and modern Russian writers are featured. Memoirs and documentaries contributed by émigré authors reflect the anti-Communist feeling which characterizes the journal in general. Each issue prints an appeal to the "Russian intelligentsia" in the USSR to forward their unpublished manuscripts to the editor who promises to safeguard them and preserve the anonymity of the author. A list of new books by Russian and other authors is published, and there are announcements of forthcoming complete versions of works of Soviet authors that were subjected to cuts by censors in the USSR. *Grani* should prove a useful addition to the Russian collection of an academic library because of its literary quality and the access it provides to the works of dissident Soviet authors. (E.L.)

Kultura. 1947. m. $15. Jerzy Giedroyc. Institut Litteraire, 91, Av. de Poissy 78, Maisons-Lafitte, Paris, France. Index, adv. Circ: 5,500.

Indexed: HistAb. *Bk. rev:* Various number, length. *Aud:* Ga, Ac.

The Polish-language counterpart of the Russian *Grani*, this monthly represents the anti-Communist point of view of the Polish émigrés. Similar to *Grani*, it reflects the expatriates' continued interest in the cultural and political development of the homeland. Polish scholars and specialists contribute articles and essays on literature, art, and history. Political and international news is sent in by the journal's foreign correspondents in the world's capitals. Their comments and views arouse considerable attention at home. Short stories and poetry of contemporary Polish authors appear regularly. Book reviews focus on significant contemporary Slavic publications. Advertisements of books and series by the publisher of *Kultura* also appear in each issue. The format is small, the layout well designed, paper and print of good quality. Public libraries with a Polish reading public and academic libraries supporting a Slavic program will find this a useful acquisition. (E.L.)

Novoe Russkoe Slovo (New Russian Word). 1910. d. 15¢. Mark Weinbaum. 243 W. 56th St., N.Y., N.Y. 10019. Ill., adv. Circ: 25,800.

Bk. rev: Various number, length. *Aud:* Ac, Ga.

A Russian émigré four-page paper, which boasts distribution in 40 countries. A good representative of the Russian anti-Communist press in the United States, with characteristics of the small town newspaper, it is a bit right of center. Particular attention is lavished on the affairs of the Soviet Union whose domestic and foreign politics come under close scrutinization and severe criticism. The anti-Communist bias is obvious and shared by both reader and editor. American happenings and especially news of New York are covered in detail. The Sunday eight-page edition enlarges the scope by adding literary works and occasional reprints of materials from the Soviet press, e.g. articles on the theater, television, radio and film, as well as book reviews. There are announcements of émigré societies, church news and necrologies. Small newsy items about members of the Russian colony in various parts of the U.S. convey a homey touch. Recommended for public libraries who cater to the Russian emigree, but also useful to the students of Russian language in the high school and academic institutions. (E.L.)

Novyi Zhurnal (New Review) 1942. q. $15. Roman Gul'. New Review Inc., N.Y., N.Y. 10025. Adv. Circ: 1,200.

Indexed: MLA. *Bk. rev:* 4–10. *Aud:* Ac.

Published by Russian émigré scholars, this independent literary journal offers poetry and short stories of Soviet writers on either side of the Iron Curtain. It also includes documentaries and articles on current political and cultural topics. Memoirs of contemporaries of famous Russians—a typical Russian literary genre—are featured regularly. Literary criticism as well as lengthy analytical book reviews constitute an important part of this 300-page monthly. There are also obituaries of Russian émigré scholars which are valuable for their detailed biographical data and literary style. In each issue there is a list of new books by Russian authors and also works of other writers on Russian literature, politics, linguistics and history. Although *Novyi Zhurnal* is the product of anti-Soviet writers, it uses restraint throughout the content. Recommended for academic libraries for its literary value as well as for significant historical writings. Published in Russian, it requires considerable language facility. (E.L.)

Ukrainian Quarterly; a journal of East European and Asian Affairs. 1944. q. $7. Walter Dushnyck. Ukrainian Congress Comm., of Amer., Inc., 302 W. 13th St., N.Y., N.Y. 10014. Index., adv. Circ: 5,000.

Indexed: PAIS. *Bk. rev:* 6, 1,000–2,400 words, signed. *Aud:* Ac.

Each English-language issue contains four or five long articles on Ukrainian life, literature, communications, history, etc., plus numerous book reviews presented from the Ukrainian viewpoint. Includes, also, a "Chronicle of Current Events" in the Ukraine and among Ukrainians abroad; and a bibliography of "Ucrainica (sic) in American and foreign periodicals." Each entry in the bibliography has a 150 word annotation. This quarterly, like the *Ukrainian Review,* stresses the need for a free Ukraine (the rest of Eastern Europe and Asia receive little attention). Because of PAIS indexing, *UQ* has the edge on the *Ukrainian Review,* should a choice need to be made. (E.L.)

Ukrainian Review. 1954. q. $7. Vasyl Oreleckyj. Assn. of Ukrainians in Great Britian, Ltd., 49 Linden Gardens, London, W. 2, England.

Bk. rev: 2, 460–760 words, signed. *Aud:* Ac.

A typical émigré publication, similar to the American-based *Ukrainian Quarterly.* The review has liberation of the Ukraine as its objective, and at least one article in each issue refers to the expected revolt of the enslaved countries of Russia. The contributors (identified only by name, with occasional reference to university affiliation) are not impressed with the support the Ukrainian nationalist movement has received from the U.S. and other western countries. One author laid the blame for this on Russian émigrés who married into well-placed families in the United States and subsequently saw to it that the Russian viewpoint was the one presented. Authors are not necessarily anti-Communist, just anti-Russian. Each issue carries reports on persecution of Ukrainian nationalists in the USSR. Other articles cover history, literature, and émigré life. Each issue also provides a bibliography of books or articles relating to the Ukraine or Ukrainians. Of interest primarily to the specialist. (E.L.)

Vozrozhdenie (La Renaissance). m. $21. S. S. Obolensky. M. Serge Obolensky, Chemin de la Cote-du-Moulin, L'Etang-la-Ville, 78- France, C.C.P. 21148 15-Paris. Subs. to: Slavonic Bazaar, 31 Middle St., Bridgeport, Conn. 06603.

Aud: Ac, Ga.

An independent émigré Russian-language journal devoted to Russian literature, politics, and history of the past and present. Its editor-publisher aims to provide a forum "for fruitful discussion of divergent views on serious questions" of special interest to the Russian émigré. Concentrating on developments within the Soviet Union, various contributors from the anti-Communist camps take a critical close look at the cultural and political scene of their homeland. Of special interest to the student of literature are the interpretations of controversial authors; short stories by émigré writers; and critical book reviews of literary and historical publications by émigré writers. Articles on art and famous artists also appear. The attractive makeup, excellent paper and print add to the readability of this monthly which is recommended for the larger public library with a Russian émigré following and also for the academic library supporting a Russian program. (E.L.)

Znamiia Rossii (The Banner of Russia). 1945. m. $4. N. H. Chukhnov. 3544 Broadway, N.Y. 10031.

Bk. rev: Various number, length. *Aud:* Ga, Ac.

An organ of Independent Russian Monarchist thought this 16-page glossy journal is devoted to the cult of Czarist Russia. Editorials and individual articles consist of lengthy discussion of historical events and personalities of Russia's past. The articles are signed, some are reprints from other publications. Letters to the editor, announcements by émigré societies, and obituaries are some of the regular features. Literature and subjects of general interest are included. Reviews of Russian books and new periodicals selected from the anti-Communist point of view are well written and signed. Unlike another Russian émigré paper, *Novoe Russkoe Slovo,* this magazine does not identify with the United States in either culture or politics. A useful addition to a public library that wishes to satisfy the needs of a very special group of readers—the elderly Russian émigrés. (E.L.)

WINE MAGAZINES

All libraries (Ejh and Hs excepted, although teachers may be vitally interested): *Vintage, Amateur Winemaker, Grand Cru.*

Introduction

Wine is the miracle once declared unconstitutional in this country. But its glow survives all—the puritanism, elitism, immoderation, and fraud. Now there is a veritable flood of wine magazines, and Americans turn from the jolt of hard liquor toward the gentle delight of wine. Sante! (C.W.)

The Amateur Enologist. q. $2. Stanley F. Anderson, Box 2701, Vancouver 3, B.C. Illus., adv.

Bk. rev: 1-2, words. *Aud:* Ga.

For the amateur, home winemaker. Clear articles on the chemistry of fermentation, equipment, recipes, and new developments in the art. The editor is owner of the rapidly expanding "Wine-Art Sales Ltd." which stocks wine making supplies and equipment for Wine-Art franchise stores throughout Canada and the United States. The magazine carries articles by big names in the wine press, yet retains the unassuming homespun cheer of the true amateur. Even Letters to the Editor are dialogues not diatribes, and flow charts really do. A new column has been introduced, Vinicare, dealing with the relationship of wine, medicine, and viticulture. (C.W.)

The Amateur Winemaker. 1958. m. $4. C. J. J. Berry. North Croye, The Avenue, Andover, Hants, England Subs to: Semplex of USA, Box 12276, Minneapolis, Minn. 55412. Illus., adv. Circ: 18,000.

Aud: Ga.

Reflects the tradition of avid amateur winemaking in England, with news from the many local "winemaking circles," wine festivals, and tastings; active discussion from the readers; recipes; how-to articles; a column answering questions; a "Winemaker's Mart." Much copy focuses on nongrape or "folk wines" and beer making. The magazine has a British country squire's style which roots out the "codswallop," and simply celebrates the hobby with great zest. *Amateur Winemaker* publishes popular books of its collected recipes and winemaking instructions. (C.W.)

American Journal of Enology and Viticulture. 1954. q. $15. Klayton E. Nelson. Amer. Soc. of Enologists, Box 411, Davis, Calif. 95616. Illus., adv.

Indexed: BioAb, ChemAb. *Bk. rev:* 3-4, 100–200 words. *Aud:* Ac.

Scholarly journal publishing high-level research in chemistry of wine making and the art and science of viticulture. As well as book reviews, journal articles and studies are abstracted (distilled?). (C.W.)

California Wine Letter. 1948. bi-w. $25. Charles van Kriedt. Box 70, Mill Valley, Calif. 94941. Adv.

Bk. rev: Various number, length. *Aud:* Ga.

Styled the "independent wine industry news service," Charles van Kriedt's four-page typed newsletter includes biweekly trade statistics, as well as industry events on personnel, three dot journalism, and even the wife's wine tasting opinions and recipes. Refreshing change from the "grapevines," produced by committee. See also, *The Wineletter.* (C.W.)

Gourmet; the magazine of good living. 1941. m. $6. Justine Valenti. Gourmet, Inc., 777 Third Ave., N.Y., N.Y. 10017. Illus., index, adv. Circ: 600,000. Vol. ends: Dec. Microform: UM.

Aud: Ga, Ac.

Covers all aspects of fine food and wine. The emphasis is definitely on the reader who has the money to enjoy the best, or dreams about travel to fabulous restaurants. It is geared for those who wish to gain knowledge about what makes a fine wine, an exceptional dish, or tips on regional products. Although the publisher claims some 1,000 recipes are published each year, few of them are for the average housewife. All concentrate on the best in eating, usually equated with expense. Supporting articles plug the good life from travel to hunting and fishing. The whole is nicely illustrated, and will be a delight to either the man or the woman who sees the kitchen as an art gallery. Of some use for more imaginative high school and college and university home economics courses. Not a necessary item for libraries, but one sure to be enjoyed.

Grand Cru. 1971. bi-m. $4.50. Jane Claire Drews and Mary Elizabeth Sagartz. 6684 North Oliphant Ave., Chicago, Ill. 60631. Adv.

Aud: Ga., Ac. *Jv:* V.

Don't worry about the la-de-da title, of the three slicks for the wine consumer, *Grand Cru* is the warmest and most inviting (see also *Vintage, Wine World.*) It combines beauty, heartiness, and good humor for all kindred spirits of the wine. The editors are developing very good regular departments such as Philip Jackisch's sharp witted "Technical Wine Advisor," Arnold Landsman's candid evaluations of restaurant cellars in the Chicago area, and the irrepressible Angelo Pellegrini's heady celebration of the grape. There is also a regular *Grand Cru* menu feature by various chefs on how to prepare an *haute cuisine* feast. One issue contained a truly sane article on stocking a cellar; the requisite article has appeared on the "healing spirit" of wine; and a real surprise, wines of the Pacific Northwest. There are some deep drinking, detailed articles, far removed from facile wine chic. Advertisements are not intrusive. (C.W.)

The Purple Thumb. 1963. bi-m. $5.50. Sidney B. Taylor. Winepress Publishing Co., Box 2008, Van Nuys, Calif. 91405. Illus., adv.

Bk. rev: 2-3, 150–200 words. *Aud:* Ga.

A boldly, beautifully designed magazine, mainly for the amateur wine and beer maker, but also for the lover of wine lore, wisdom, and whimsey. In addition to how-to articles and recipes, there are articles on special wines, American grape varietals, cookery, wine and medicine, wine quotes, and a reader's wine forum. Fine layout, with fortuitous use of old prints and designs. (C.W.)

Robert Lawrence Balzer's Private Guide to Food and Wine. 1970. m. $12.50. Robert Lawrence Balzer. The Wine Press, Ltd. 682 El Rancho Road, Santa Barbara, Calif. 93103. Illus., index.

Bk. rev: Notes. *Aud:* Ga.

A unique personal newsletter by the dedicated, for the dedicated. Each month, in a blind tasting, expert Robert Balzer and an experienced panel rate a group of wines of a specific type—California Cabernet Sauvignon, sherry, French champagne, etc.—often proving price and prestige don't necessarily guarantee quality. The rest of the handsome 12-page newsletter includes an unusual "conversation piece" wine, Balzer's voluble notes on the art of wine tasting, a "memorable dining" menu, conversations with wine makers. Where *Vintage* is rather slick and imposing, Balzer's *Private Guide* is fun. A yearly index is provided. (C.W.)

Vineyard View. 1970. q. $2.50. Nancy Dorwart. Finger Lakes Wine Museum, Bully Hill Road, Hammondsport, N.Y. 14840. Illus.

Aud: Ga.

New York State-oriented 10-page newsletter on viticulture, wine making, and wine lore. Charming pen and ink drawings are done by the well-known winemaker, Walter Taylor. Possibly the most unstilted wine publication in existence: one issue included an essay from the grape picker's point of view. (C.W.)

Vintage. 1971. 10/yr. $15. Philip Seldon. Box 866. New York, N.Y. 10010. Illus., adv.

Bk. rev: notes. *Aud:* Ga, Ac. *Jv:* V.

Handsome, new magazine for the wine consumer in America. Articles on the classic foreign wines and vineyards plus regular features on "Great Cellars of America," California and eastern U.S. wine production, and the better U.S. wine merchants. A useful section is "Vintage Recommends," listing wines currently judged of exceptional value. Sizeable space is given to readers' comments and tasting notes; classified ads are available should one wish to buy, sell, or exchange wines. News coverage of the wine scene is good. The magazine, while slick, seems dedicated to increasing the consumer's knowledge and pleasure in wines and has editorially come out against the cant (and fraud) surrounding the gentle art. (C.W.)

The Wineletter. 1967. m. $6. Charles van Kriedt. Box 70, Mill Valley, Calif. 94941.

Bk. rev: Various number, length. *Aud:* Ga.

The first, and most individualistic, consumer wine periodical. On four typed pages Charles van Kriedt, again complete with three dot journalism and weird margin notes, addresses himself to folk of the wine cup (see also, *California Wineletter*). He provides winery information, covers tasting events, notes vinous references in the media, and reviews wine books. Included is a gourmet recipe by Phyllis van Kriedt. A best buy—if you can do without pretty trappings of most wine mags. (C.W.)

Wine Magazine. 1958. bi-m. $6. K. C. Bourke. Wine and Spirit Publications Ltd., Southbank House, Black Prince Road, Lambeth, London, S.E. 1, England. Subs to: Air and Sea Freight Inc., Box 1305, L.I.C. N.Y. 11101. Illus., adv. Circ: 15,000.

Bk. rev: 4, 75 words. *Aud:* Ga.

Elegance tinged with decadence. Lovingly discusses vintages, noble vineyards and their owners, makes cellar suggestions, includes articles on travel, entertaining, haut cuisine. U.S. wines politely ignored. A lamentable feature, which *Vintage* magazine is, even more lamentably, trying to copy, is a panel's excruciatingly meticulous evaluation of food and wine while dining in a posh restaurant. The Letters to the Editor are notable for the heights British style can attain on the fanatical subject of wine. (C.W.)

Wine Mine. 1959. s-a. 25¢ per copy. Anthony Hogg. Peter Dominic, Ltd., 12 York Gate, London NW 1 4PU, England. Illus., adv.

Aud: Ga.

In winedom, a collector's item magazine: bold art work, including charming old prints; witty, personal wine essays; light scholarship; sumptuous ads. *Wine Mine* is published by one of England's largest spirit and wine merchants, so almost half the magazine is a very detailed catalog of their assorted stock. (C.W.)

Wines and Vines. 1919. m. $7. ($12 with Directory). Philip Hiaring. 703 Market St., San Francisco, Calif. 94103. Illus., adv. Circ: 3,200.

Indexed: ChemAb. *Bk. rev:* 2–3, 150–250 words. *Aud:* Ga.

Trade magazine of the American wine industry and as pleasant as its product. Though full of facts and figures, being published for the commercial producer and merchandiser, its articles, even on technology, are highly readable and informative for the consumer. The emphasis, of course, is on current trends and developments, rather than remembered bottles. Coverage is largely, but by no means exclusively, California. There is a good question and answer column on amateur wine making by authority Julius Fessler. (C.W.)

Wine World. 1971. bi-m. $4.75. Robert O'Hara. 7555 Woodley Ave., Van Nuys, Calif. 91406. Adv.

Aud: Ga, Ac.

For the wine consumer, this magazine is published by the people who do *The Purple Thumb* for amateur wine makers. The same concern for the charm of lore, tradition, and history is shown. *Wine World* lives up to its name in discussing wines and vineyards from less widely publicized areas like Yugoslavia and New Zealand, as well as California and Europe. There is good current wine news reportage, a rather gimmicky "New Products" section, an instructive "How to Read a Wine Label" feature, a "Cooking with Wines" adventure, and a glossary of selected wine terms. No intrusive ads. A friendly, low-keyed, yet poshly illustrated invitation to the vine. (C.W.)

WOMEN AND TEEN-AGE MAGAZINES

See also Blacks and Latin American and Chicano sections for women's magazines in special interest or ethnic groups.

Basic Periodicals

GENERAL. Hs: *Glamour;* Ga: *Good Housekeeping, McCalls, Ladies Home Journal;* Ac and Jc: Only as needed, but approximately the same as for Ga. (Note: *The Media Industry Newsletter* (June 29, 1972) asked 1,200 women throughout the USA the following question: "Which one of the following women's magazines do you think is best? The percentage response on each of the seven magazines on *MIN's* list are as follows: *Good Housekeeping,* 33%; *Ladies' Home Journal,* 21%; *McCall's,* 13%; *Family Circle,* 10%; *Redbook,* 7%; *Woman's Day,* 7%; *Cosmopolitan,* 3%.")

WOMEN'S LIBERATION. Hs: *Ms;* Ga: *Women: A Journal of Liberation, Ms, Everywoman;* Jc: *Off Our Backs, Everywoman, Women: A Journal of Liberation, Ms;* Ac: *Off Our Backs, Everywoman, Women: A Journal of Liberation, Ms, Up from Under.*

TEEN-AGE (See also titles above). Ejh: *Seventeen;* Hs: *Seventeen, Ingenue;* Ga: *Seventeen, Ingenue.*

Basic Abstracts and Indexes *Readers' Guide to Periodical Literature. Women's Studies Abstracts.*

Cessations

TEEN-AGE. *American Red Cross Journal, Allied Youth, Datebook, Dig, In Magazine, PACE, Way Forum.*

Introduction

On the surface, women's magazines are quite harmless. Preoccupied as they are with the mundane (daily household or child-rearing tasks) and the ephemeral (cocktail parties and the latest fashions), they are rarely taken seriously. But the damage they may do to women can be very serious indeed. They project and reinforce society's expectations of women, adhering strictly to the limited roles in which women are granted jurisdiction, or at least a certain amount of leeway: mother, wife, career "girl," swinger. The common denominator in all these roles is men; because women's magazines, like the real world, stress that Man is Woman's *raison d'être.* (For this reason women's magazines are intrinsically propagandistic, as they do not encourage women to pursue interests of their own but only to pursue men.)

No matter what the apparent emphasis of the respective magazines (motherhood, the working world, etc.) it is to woman-as-consumer that they are all ultimately addressed. It is customary for advertising to dominate their pages, but the ads are only the message in its least diluted form. In "self-improvement" articles, in photographs of glamorous models, in displays of expensive home furnishings, the reader is presented with an image (an image dictated by commercial interests) and assured that she will achieve all the good things that go along with the image if she only spends a little money. Here, social expectations and commercial interests can hardly be separated. It is advantageous to those who run the cosmetics and fashion industries that women be "feminine" as society defines the word, and to be materialistic in pursuit of this goal.

Some of the glaring consistencies among women's magazines follow.

What-Women-Can-Do Syndrome. Women are treated like a specialized subgroup of people, like coin collectors, whose interests are narrow and well-defined. (But even coin collectors are assumed to have a life away from their specialty.) In controversial and important matters, What-Women-Can-Do usually consists of things like recycling glass bottles and urging one's husband to write *his* congressman.

Famous-Woman Syndrome. The models for women to emulate are not the adventurous, the creative, or the daring among us, but the rich dowagers and upper-class women who have married or given birth to some (adventurous, creative, or daring) man. Why else would Ladybird Johnson and Rose Kennedy be consistently among the ten most popular women in America?

Needlework Syndrome. To assuage the few homemakers who may want something more out of life, women's magazines are replete with sewing patterns, embroidery stitches, and instructions for macramé. The illusion to be maintained at all costs is that life at home can be fulfilling even to the most creative spirit; and needlework is harmless enough to keep the little woman from running off to a bohemian artists' colony.

The Liberated-Woman Syndrome. The higher the social or financial level of the reader, the more likely the magazine is to appeal to the "liberated woman" in her; liberation is, of course, defined to suit the interests of the cosmetics firms, jewelry stores, and male editors who run the magazine.

Even aside from content, the patronizing tone of most articles, the attitude of moral instruction, the view of the reader as passive, dependent, almost child-like, are perhaps the most offensive characteristics of women's magazines. This tendency can be partially explained by the fact that all the magazines are either edited or published by men.

Any library that subscribes matter-of-factly to these magazines (and most do) should re-evaluate the women they serve and order at least one or two of the publications of the women's liberation movement (also reviewed in this section). High school or conservative public libraries will find *Women: A Journal of Liberation* respectable in appearance and "scholarly" in content, though high school women might relate better to *Everywoman* or *Off Our Backs* (both tabloids), and libraries in working class communities would be better off with *Up from Under*. (M.M.)

General

Bride's Magazine. 1934. 8/Yr. $7. Barbara Donovan. Conde Nast Publns., Inc., 420 Lexington Ave., New York, N.Y. 10017. Subs. to: Box 1711, Des Moines, Iowa 50306. Illus., adv. Circ: 230,000. Vol. ends: Dec.
Aud: Ga.

Modern Bride. 1949. bi-m. $4. Robert W. Houseman. Ziff-Davis Publishing Co., 1 Park Ave., New York, N.Y. 10016. Illus., adv. Circ: 207,000.
Aud: Ga.

The bridal magazine is the quintessence of women's magazines, and it is here that American advertising has its finest hour. In the name of love ("If he loves you enough to get you a Spring Air Back Supporter mattress you've got it made"), all manner of paraphernalia is sold, and the young couple take their debt-ridden place in society. Nowhere is it more evident that advertising is what women's magazines are really about. Clearly 90 percent of the bridal magazines are straight advertising—props for the wedding itself, like rings, dresses, accessories; furnishings for the new home, especially mattresses, china, furniture, and kitchenware; exotic honeymoon trips; and of course a wealth of personal beauty products. Much of the small proportion of space not devoted directly to advertising is still used to sell the bride-to-be on elaborate wedding parties or other expensive accouterments of the ritual. The tiny percentage of remaining space is taken up by beauty tips, etiquette, practical directions for choosing a contraceptive or finding an apartment, and much spurious advice on how to make a marriage work. (The extent to which this depends on the bride's self-sacrifice is especially evident from one article that discusses the women's liberation movement only as it

benefits men!) There is no appreciable difference between *Modern Bride* and *Bride's Magazine*. (M.M)

Claudia. See Latin American and Chicano/Spanish Language Section.

Confidencias. See Latin American and Chicano/Spanish Language Section.

Cosmopolitan. 1901. m. $9. Helen Gurley Brown. Hearst Corp., 57th St. at Eighth Ave., N.Y., N.Y. 10019. Illus., adv. Circ: 1,406,000. Microform: UM.
Bk. rev: 4–5, short. *Aud:* Ga, Ac.

"That *Cosmopolitan* Girl" is the same old Miss Teen-age America in modern dress. Helen Gurley Brown and her staff would have us believe that the *Cosmo* reader is the ideal "liberated" woman, but in this case liberation is only skin-deep. The articles usually confuse liberation with "sexual freedom." *Cosmo* is aimed at the sophisticated big city working girl, but job discrimination is rarely if ever discussed. The work itself is not as important as the fact that a swinging career is *sexy* and will help you get a man (not for marriage necessarily, but for an exciting affair). Fashion, beauty, and sex instructions are the predominant features of the magazine. But despite its claims to sophisticated wickedness a la *Playboy*, *Cosmo* retains the traditional image of women. Femininity, with sexiness, is considered the ideal. Serious solutions to world problems are left up to the men, but there are some halfhearted attempts at keeping in touch with reality (ecology begins at home: incorporate bird cages and potted plants into your living room decor). Still, most libraries will probably want it, it certainly has a readership. (M.M.)

Elle. See European and Middle East/French Section.

Essence. See Blacks Section.

Family Circle. 1932. m. No subscriptions; back issues: 35¢. 488 Madison Ave., N.Y., N.Y. 10022. Illus., adv. Circ: 7,830,000.
Aud: Ga. *Jv:* C.

Family Circle is much like *Woman's Day*, its competitor at the supermarket checkout counter. Its recipes are down-to-earth and inexpensive, its decorating ideas useful for a family with few resources. But it contains more advertising than other women's magazines, little else of any substance and would not be a worthwhile addition to a library. (M.M.) (Ed. note: The magazine has been purchased by *The New York Times*. There may be editorial changes which will improve the publication.)

Glamour. 1939. m. $6. Conde Nast Publns., Inc., 420 Lexington Ave., N.Y., N.Y. 10017. Subs. to: Glamour, Box 5203, Boulder, Colo. 80302. Illus., adv. Circ: 1,500,000. Vol. ends: Aug. UM. Microform: UM.

Bk. rev: two, 500 words, signed. *Aud:* Ga, Ac, Hs.

Glamour sits on more than one side of more than one fence. It addresses itself, at various times, to college age (and younger) women, career women ("working girls"), young mothers, and women's liberationists. Although beauty and fashion occupy by far the greatest percentage of space, the three or four general articles each month touch on a number of subjects. One "diary" of a mother who decides to return to work is an obvious imitation of the popular "Diary of a Mad Housewife" and is sufficiently ambiguous that feminists and anti-feminists alike can see something in it. An article in which "A Young Lesbian Talks About Her Feelings" is, superficially, a plea for an understanding of homosexuality; but because the "young lesbian" in the article is in reality a bisexual who prefers men and is unhappy and confused in her gay lifestyle, the implication is that lesbians in general feel this way and would be better off as heterosexuals. (M.M.)

Good Housekeeping. 1895. m. $5. Wade H. Nichols. Hearst Corp., 959 8th Ave., N.Y., N.Y. 10019. Illus., adv. Circ: 6,000,000. Vol. ends: Dec. Microform: UM.

Indexed: AbrRG, RG. *Aud:* Ga, Hs. *Jv:* V.

"The Magazine America Lives By" is unabashedly directed at the middle-class housewife—fashions for every day, menus for the family rather than for dinner parties, and few articles of general (i.e., "non-womanly") concern. The emphasis—and greatest asset—of *Good Housekeeping* is on consumer facts and practical advice for keeping home and family intact. Much of the material consists of findings of the Good Housekeeping Institute, where products are tested and consumer research done. The Institute reports monthly on beauty products, appliances and home care, food, needlework, and textiles. (The findings of the Institute, however, have been called into question by various government commissions, who charge that the "seal of approval" is awarded only to those manufacturers who advertise in *Good Housekeeping.* The products tested are received directly from the manufacturer, whereas the Consumers' Union—a nonprofit testing laboratory, publishers of *Consumers Report*—buys its products on the open market and is not tied to advertisers in any way.) "The Better Way" gives further consumer advice, and other departments cover home building, decorating, diets and nutrition. Other regular features, in addition to patterns, fashions, and recipes, include "Keep Up with Medicine"; Dr. Joyce Brothers' "On Being a Woman"; humor by Erma Bombeck; and fiction, usually a short novel and three or four short stories. General articles are often on schools, children, or famous women. In the issues examined, articles on more "prestigious" subjects—pollution, the American Indian, and psychiatry—were written by men. The four top editors of *Good Housekeeping* are men, as are four of the ten

top directors and consultants of the Institute, and all the listed officials of the publisher, the Hearst Corporation. (M.M.)

Hairdo & Beauty. 1956. m. $5. Dell Publishing Co., Inc., 750 Third Ave., N.Y., N.Y. 10017. Illus., adv. Circ: 510,000.

Aud: Ga.

Although this is unique in being the only large circulation hairstyle magazine, several types of women won't like it at all—the Women's Liberation group, those who check out hair styles in other women's magazines, and those who are independent of this type of advice. Still, over one-half million women do read the magazine, so it has some appeal and might be considered by larger public libraries. Feature articles advise the women on the latest styles, include interviews with hairdo experts, and are strong on how-to-do-it at home items. Considerable advertising. (P.S. Lately the mag has included a department on men's hairstyles.)

Harper's Bazaar. 1867. m. $7. Nancy White. Hearst Corp., 717 Fifth Ave., N.Y., N.Y. 10022. Illus., adv. Circ: 445,000.

Aud: Ga, Ac.

Harper's Bazaar is a lightweight fashion magazine that lacks *Vogue's* intellectual pretense but substitutes nothing for it. The whole thing is fashion display and it includes short beauty tips that usually revolve around product promotion. Attention grabbing articles like, "Is What We Do in Our Own Beds Illegal?", bits on astrology and travel, trivial interviews with important people, and flagrantly irrelevant space-fillers (e.g. a two-page spread showing close-ups of Clint Eastwood and Marcello Mastroianni—the gimmick, one wears cologne, the other doesn't). If high fashion is your bag, *Harper's Bazaar* will show it to you; beyond that, its pure hype. (M.M.)

Lady's Circle Magazine. 1964. m. $3. Betty Etter. Lady's Circle, Inc., 21 W. 26th St., N.Y., N.Y. 10010. Illus., adv. Circ: 655,000.

Aud: Ga.

Edited for the stereotype version of housewives and mothers. Still, it sells well—check that circulation. What do women get for the price of a copy? Like *Family Circle* and *Woman's Day,* it is a supermarket item and readers pick it up for articles on homemaking, sewing, cooking, gardening, health, and baby care. The magazine is different from its rivals in that the editor rather wisely pushes the friendship bit, i.e. all the women are in this thing together, and let us share our joys or woes. Hence, a good number of the articles are the "how I did it variety," which seem to be as much concerned with managing a budget and a needle as with getting along with other family members. Valuable for useful hints on hobbies, crafts, and methods of making money at home. Not a necessary item for a library, but the librarian who considers the others in this field might be interested in this one too.

Ladies Home Journal. 1883. m. $4. John Mack Carter. Downe Publishing, Inc., 641 Lexington Ave., N.Y., N.Y. 10022. Illus., adv. Circ: 7,000,000. Vol. ends: Dec.

Indexed: AbrRg, RG. *Aud:* Ga, Ac.

Motherhood and apple pie are alive and well within the pages of the *Ladies Home Journal,* second highest in circulation among "the big three" women's magazines. Though the masthead proclaims, "Never Underestimate the Power of a Woman," it is clear from the lineup of editors and writers, and from the contents of the magazine, the man still sits on the throne and woman must operate her power base from somewhere else. In the *Journal,* as in the other women's magazines, woman is always secondary: articles tell how to cook food that *he* will like; how to make *him* happy in bed; how to handle the cooking, household duties, a full-time job, and at the same time keep *him* satisfied. The column "Can This Marriage Be Saved" is predicated on the assumption that the wife is almost always at fault. And if it's not the husband who needs attention, it's the children; mother is lost as an individual. Regular columnists are Bruno Bettleheim, Dr. Theodore Isaac Rubin, and Amy Vanderbilt. Fiction usually consists of two romance-type stories, and sometimes a "book bonus." Other features include the usual food, beauty, decorating, and patterns sections. A fascination with such famous women as Rose Kennedy and Princess Grace is evident. (M.M.)

McCall's. 1870. m. $3.95. Shana Alexander. McCall Publishing Co., 230 Park Ave., N.Y., N.Y. 10017. Subs. to: McCall's Subscription Dept., P.O. Box 986, Dayton, Ohio 45401. Illus., adv. Circ: 7,500,000. Vol. ends: Sept. Microform: UM.

Indexed: RG. *Aud:* Ga, Ac.

McCall's blows the theory that a female editor necessarily makes the difference between a good and a bad women's magazine. Being the only one of the "big three" (*Good Housekeeping* and *Ladies Home Journal*) with a woman as editor, it is also the worst of the three. Despite its new, smaller format, it seems to have deteriorated in quality, or at least not improved. A sensationalistic approach to some subjects ("The Two Women Who Broke Up the Beatles," which reads exactly like a fanzine article); a rehash of old attitudes about current controversies ("What Makes a Homosexual?"); and a desperate, cloying attempt to be hip (columns by Dr. David Reuben, Betty Friedan, and Dr. William A. Nolen; and "Right Now," a "monthly newsletter for women"—a weird mixture of women's liberation news and "human interest" or freak items) combine to make the new *McCall's* a very

strange animal indeed. Some articles that result from the magazine's sudden infatuation with controversy, are probably invaluable in educating *McCall's* particular audience ("From Adam's Rib to Women's Lib" discusses "religious myths that keep women in their place"). Unfortunately, they backslide—a fashion display in one issue pictured women failing at various sports with the caption, "Even if the sportswoman of the '70's isn't good at her game, she certainly tries to look it." However, the *Wall Street Journal* notes that in spite of the new image it is trying to project, half of the women who read *McCall's* and *Ladies Home Journal* are over 41, and only one in eight has finished college. Regular features include fiction, gardening, patterns, beauty, fashion, food, equipment (household appliances, etc.). (M.M.)

Mademoiselle. 1935. m. $6. Edith Raymond Locke. Conde Nast Publns., Inc. 420 Lexington Ave., N.Y., 10017. Subs. to: Box 5204, Boulder, Colo. 80302. Illus., adv. Circ: 641,000. Microform: UM.

Indexed: RG *Aud:* Ga, Ac, Hs.

Mademoiselle is one of the three most popular magazines for women who are still caught up in the feminine mystique. *Seventeen* is a competitor for approximately the same market but is read more by high school women; *Cosmopolitan's* appeal is to college women and working women in their twenties. All have about the same emphasis and areas of interest—fashion, beauty, and some version of female sexuality. *Mademoiselle* is relatively honest in its approach to women, at least in its articles, and seems to approve of the new trend toward liberation. However, the profusion of advertising, mostly for clothes and cosmetics, and its abundance of articles and features on self-adornment tell a different story. Yes, a woman should be independent, but to be sure you get your man, you'd better buy all those products that will make you look "natural" (or whatever the current look is). Besides fashion and beauty articles, each issue includes one or two short stories, a "hip" column by David Newman and Robert Benton, and some coverage of travel. A recent issue featured *Mademoiselle's* college guest editors and annual prize-winning photography, poetry, and fiction, along with back-to-college fall fashions. (M.M.)

Modern Bride. See *Bride's Magazine.*

Modern Romances. 1937. m. $5. Henry P. Malmgreen. Dell Publishing Co., 750 Third Ave., N.Y., N.Y. 10017. Illus., adv. Circ: 765,000.

Aud: Ga.

Unless you happen to be an avid reader, the mag's primary claim to fame is that it is second in circulation in the field of romance/confession titles. (*True Story,* of course, is way out in front of them all.) The material differs from *True Story* only in that it puts added emphasis on the confessional, is a trifle more sensational (and conversely, even more moral) than its rival. Most of it concerns first person yarns of fall and ultimate redemption. There are the usual departments from baby care to food and beauty helps. The advice column is remarkably sane. A woman here is envisioned as being a wife, not overly imaginative or well educated, and badly in need of reinforcement about her family life. The magazine does its best to reassure her that it could be worse.

New Lady. See Blacks Section.

Pageant. 1944. m. $6. Victoria Pellegrino. Macfadden-Bartell Corp. 205 E. 42nd St., N.Y., N.Y. 10017. Illus., adv. Circ: 500,000.

Bk. rev: 2, ½ page, signed. *Aud:* Ga, Hs.

Since the last edition, this magazine has changed editors and editorial policy. While still a general title, it is moving toward a woman audience and in the process is becoming considerably better. The format remains the same, i.e. digest size with numerous photographs. What has changed drastically is content. In the January 1972 issue, for example, there are articles by Pearl Buck, Adelle Davis, and Dr. Spock. Other issues have featured Bella Abzug, Gloria Steinem and pieces on prominent American leaders. The style of writing is good, the presentation accurate and nonsensational or nonsentimental, and the whole will have wide appeal for the average reader from high school on. While hardly an intellectual delight, it is considerably more sophisticated then *Coronet*, more honest then *Reader's Digest*. *Pageant* can be recommended for public libraries and high schools, especially for women readers who are just beginning to dig the women's liberation scene. And, to be sure, it still has some appeal for men.

Parents' Magazine and Better Family Living. 1926. m. $5.95. Dorothy Whyte Cotton. Parents' Magazine Enterprises, Inc., 52 Vanderbilt Ave., N.Y., N.Y. 10017. Illus., index, adv. Circ: 2,115,000. Microform: UM.

Indexed: AbrRG, PAIS, RG. *Bk. rev:* Notes, signed. *Aud:* Ga.

Although "parents" implies a father as well as a mother, the parent referred to in the title is just mother. The ad copy boasts that the readers are "3 million mothers with 7 million young children . . . just the women who are buying more of most of the nation's consumer products." The result is a woman's consumer-family magazine. In it women will find much valuable health, education, personality, and child discipline information, presented in an intelligent and authoritative fashion. Family and marital relationships are discussed. Finally, there are articles which encourage the parent and the child to take an active role in social matters. The eight to ten articles

are counterpointed by such features as Family Movie Guide, Family Quiz Guide, Family Clinic, and the like. A down-to-earth approach to the whole business of children and families, but not for the woman's liberation follower.

Redbook. 1904. m. $3.95. Sey Chassler, McCall Publishing Co., 230 Park Ave., N.Y., N.Y., 10017. Subs. to: P.O. Box 986, Dayton, Ohio 45401. Illus., adv. Circ: 4,800,000. Vol. ends: Oct. Microform: UM.

Indexed: RG. *Aud:* Ga, Hs.

As with most women's magazines, the five top editors of the "Magazine for Young Women" are men. This may be the reason that *Redbook*—no less than other, less prestigious publications—appeals more to the reader's (feminine) role aspirations than to her mind. Articles on children clearly predominate, with secondary emphasis on male-female relations, and token coverage of social issues. Columns by Margaret Mead and Dr. Benjamin Spock; features on food, beauty, fashion, sewing, and home furnishings; and a novel and four stories—most of which avoid the usual mawkishness of the women's market—are regularly included. *Redbook's* articles are generally well written, and issues raised by the new feminist movement are occasionally discussed; e.g., one article examined sex discrimination in children's books, and another, woman's changing role in marriage. But for claiming an audience of educated young women, it should do better. It may be that even a call to revolution would be absorbed by the magazine's overall impression of feminine docility. (Ed. note: *Redbook's New Home*, devoted to the woman of 18 to 35 during her first year of marriage, was scheduled for publication in 1972. It will carry articles on topics such as: one room home decorating, convenience foods, beauty aids and health and sex information.) (M.M.)

Simplicity Fashion Magazine. See Hobbies/Arts and Crafts Section.

Soviet Woman. See USSR and East Europe/English Language Section.

True Story. 1919 m. $6. 205 East 42nd St., N.Y., N.Y. 10017. Illus., adv. Circ: 2,500,000. Vol. ends: Jan.

Aud: Ga. *Jv:* C.

This classic true love romance magazine has changed some over the years. Articles on homemaking have been added: recipes, consumer columns, and fashion secrets accompany the traditional pulp fiction. But the stories are the same as ever—titillating headlines over a disappointingly mild and moralistic tale. Though the plots now incorporate such new dangers as marijuana and revolutionary bombers, the moral tone and values have not changed. If letters to the editor can be taken as any sort of gauge of reader opinion, the stories have a lesson to teach: that life is really wholesome and good, that God couldn't possibly be dead else what would we do, that love conquers everything from incest to impotence. This "Woman's Guide to Love and Marriage" teaches, above all else, that a woman's place is just where it always has been.

True to Life. 1970. 35¢ a copy. Marjorie Crow. Emory Univ. Family Planning Program, Box 26003, 80 Butler St., Atlanta, Ga. 30303. Illus. Circ: 10,000. Samples.

Aud: Ga.

Librarians concerned with dispensing vital information should send for this magazine, and see that women in their communities have access to it. It is a women's-health primer packaged in the format of a true romance magazine. Stories headed, "How I Spent My Summer Vacation—and Nearly Died Three Months Later!" and "I Had to Prove My Manhood—and My Wife Had to Pay the Price!" disguise valuable counsel in such matters as sex, marriage, and abortion. Elsewhere in the magazine, specific health information is available: "True to Life Wants to Know" is an advice column for married couples, to which readers are encouraged to furnish solutions; "We've Come a Long Way, Ladies" is a cartoon illustrated column of outdated beliefs about sex and pregnancy; and "Dr. Adams' Advice to Couples" answers readers' questions about birth control and other sex related problems. A special feature in the first issue shows exactly what is involved in having a pelvic examination. As *True to Life* is geared to pulp-magazine readers, its stories tend to mimic the patronizing, moralistic tone of *True Story,* and to support the same values (monogamy, female subservience, etc.)—it is not necessarily, or superficially, a feminist publication. But its goals are certainly worthwhile and it may be taking the most sensible step toward reaching to women who would not read *Off Our Backs* or even *Up from Under.* (M.M.)

Vogue. 1892. s-m (m. May, June, July, Dec.). $10. Diana Vreeland. Conde Nast Publns., Inc., 420 Lexington Ave., N.Y., N.Y. 10017. Illus., adv. Circ: 500,000 Microform: UM.

Indexed: RG. *Bk. rev:* Various number, length. *Aud:* Ga, Ac.

Vogue is the fashion magazine for women who have apparently unlimited money and leisure to spend on their appearance, and the education and high social ranking (or aspirations) to dabble elegantly in the arts. *Vogue* is high fashion (the latest from the Paris collection, the Rome collection, the New York collection, etc.), and high society (news and gossip of the beautiful people), mixed with an abundance of tips and articles on beauty care (the assumption being that the reader is already beautiful—and rich), and a dilettante's approach to film, books, theater, dance, and "controversy" (ever encroaching reality). All this is in

marked contrast to the slant of most other women's magazines. Here you'll find no cloying advice on how to get a man, no practical hints on homemaking or childrearing. *Vogue* is for women who already have their man/men and can afford to hire someone to take care of the cleaning and the children. Regular features: Fashion, Beauty and Health, Fashions in Living (avant-garde home decorating), Food Gazette (special recipes, often European), Horoscope, Men in Vogue (men's fashions), and "Vogue's Notebook" (what's new in high society). Reviews of books, films, dance performances, and art showings are fairly common, and sometimes writers or artists themselves are interviewed. At least one article in each issue skims the surface of a profound subject (e.g. sexuality or politics) and some are written by fairly prestigious writers, such as Alfred Kazin, John Lahr, and Arthur Schlesinger, Jr. Ads are almost all for cosmetics or expensive clothing, and they ocasionally capitalize on the new catchword "liberation." Curiously enough, though, elsewhere in the magazine the women's movement is rarely mentioned. (M.M.)

Woman's Day. 1937. m. 20¢/copy (library subs: $2.40 or $2 for school year). Geraldine E. Rhoads. Fawcett Publns. 67 W. 44th St., N.Y., N.Y. 10036. Illus., adv. Circ: 8,687,000. Vol. ends: Sept.

Aud: Ga, Hs.

This unpretentious homemakers' magazine, marketed in grocery stores along with its competitor *Family Circle,* has little coffee table appeal but can be useful if one is responsible for running a home on a tight budget. Although such "extras" as macramé jewelry, fancy hairdos, and crocheted earrings are not uncommon, the decided emphasis of *Woman's Day* is on money-saving ideas. Readers' money-saving tips; money-saving menus and recipes; "built-in money-savers" for houses; and suggestions for avoiding expensive repairs, disguising leftovers, and making your own furniture are examples of the slant of many articles. (Despite this well-meaning advice, however, the paradox of juxtaposing tips on saving money and ads beseeching the reader to spend it, cannot be overlooked.) Also featured are sections on food, home decorating and building, fashion, travel, health and medicine, "Woman at the Wheel," and children. This last is worthwhile if only for reprinting the parents' guide from *Sesame Street Magazine.* A higher than usual percentage of writers for *Woman's Day* are women, and two out of the three top editors are women but the publisher and all other listed officials of Fawcett Publications are men. (M.M.)

Women Today. 1971. bi-w. $15. Poppy Walker. Today Publications and News Service, National Press Bldg., Washington, D.C. 20004. Circ: 1,500.

Aud: Ac, Ga.

A four-to six-page newsletter "subscribed to by both a national and international audience of individual women and women's organizations." The presentation is in form of short, well written notes on issues of interest to women—particularly those who are activists in everything from women's liberation to consumer rights. The flavor is probably best indicated by some subjects in a single issue: Shirley Chisholm makes it official; IAWS (Intercollegiate Association of Women Students) invites women's groups to send representatives to national convention; Victory for the justice department in sex and race bias case; Feminists honor Susan B. Anthony; New thrust for American home economists association publications; Sassower scores archaic divorce laws. As a type of "Facts on File" for women, the treatment of material is objective, although often tongue in cheek and just below a slow boil. Material seems up-to-date and topical. As this comes out every two weeks, and as much of the coverage is not found elsewhere, the price seems reasonable enough. Recommended for most libraries.

Women's Wear Daily. See Newspapers/Special Interest Section.

Women's Liberation

Adams Rib. 1969. m. $7. Lucianne S. Goldberg. Pussycat League, 156 E. 52nd St., N.Y., N.Y. 10022. Circ: 10,000. Sample.

Aud: Ga, Ac.

To join the Pussycat League, the "first requirement is that you enjoy being a woman—and want to be treated as one." *Adam's Rib* is the newsletter of this organization, which is waging a "quiet crusade to keep women in their wonderfully special place, while at the same time easing some of the more jarring frustrations that keep them from being lovable women." The Pussycat League is "for abortion and divorce reforms and against the inequities in hiring and job advancement" but believes that "for the majority of women, life without some of the inequities—some of them absurd, some of them charming, some, indeed, infuriating—would not be very rewarding." A philosophy of kissing the hand that slaps you. The newsletter itself is insulting to the point of slander toward women's liberation leaders such as Ti-Grace Atkinson ("the Lesbian fringe's nomination for Playmate of the Month"), Betty Friedan, Germaine Greer, Bella Abzug, and the other "noisy militants." Short news items and collaborating statements by others who value femininity over personhood make up the bulk of the newsletter. Ephemera, certainly, but an indication of what the movement is up against. (M.M.)

Ain't I a Woman. 1970. Every 3 weeks. $20. AIAW Collective, P.O. Box 1169, Iowa City, Iowa. 52240. Illus., adv. Sample. Vol. ends: June.

Aud: Ga, Ac. *Jv:* V.

Spectre. 1971. bi-m. $1. Revolutionary Lesbians, P.O. Box 305, Ann Arbor, Mich. 48107. Illus. Circ: 1,000. Sample. Vol. ends: 6th issue.

Aud: Ga, Ac.

Both of these papers are published by angry gay women, and both use approximately the same free form approach to communicating their ideas. *Ain't I a Woman,* "a collective of . . . women functioning as a world-wide conspiracy of Radical Lesbians," takes its name from the famous statement by Sojourner Truth (". . . nobody ever helped me into carriages, or over mud puddles, or gives me a best place . . . And ain't I a woman?") Many of the recent issues have been concerned with the problems of a class in the women's movement and with such concepts as monogamy, machismo, and differences between the "old" and "new" gay woman. Articles are written from personal experience and often take the form of "dialogues," in which two or more writers alternate responses to each other. The women who publish *Spectre* have said repeatedly that what appears on the printed page is not sacrosanct. "*Spectre* is one way we have of talking to lots of people—it is also a way of working through things. It is not a journal of dogmatic pronouncements." Articles are extremely informal, more like letters between friends, and "criticism/self-criticism" often follows a controversial or misunderstood article in an earlier issue. *Spectre* women are separatists, antiimperialists, antiracists, revolutionaries as well as lesbians. Their goals are to eliminate class chauvinism, age chauvinism, and racism, as well as sexism. *Ain't I a Woman* is especially recommended, though either would provide a necessary gay voice. (M.M.)

Aphra. 1969. q. $3.50. Elizabeth Fisher. 4 Jones St., N.Y., N.Y. 10014. Illus. Sample. Vol. ends: fall.

Bk. rev: One to three. *Aud:* Ga, Ac, *Jv:* V.

Every good feminist writer who emerges from the current movement (or, simply, has been ignored until now) is certain to show up in *Aphra,* the best and most solid women's literary magazine around. It is distinguished from the traditionally avant-garde (male) "little magazine" by its high political as well as emotional content; that is, its awareness of womanhood as an experience largely unexplored except through men's eyes. Certainly many fine women writers have been heard in the past, but there have been few outlets for experimentation and few sources of encouragement for women. *Aphra* bolsters the movement and provides the needed outlet. Fiction, poetry, artwork, and literary and cultural criticism usually unite in each issue around a common theme, such as "the whore issue" and "woman as artist." Regularly featured is a section called "aphra-isms," which are "quotations, thoughts, overheard remarks, anything that counters the prevailing male tone with our hysterical perspective." (M.M.)

Battle Acts. 1970. bi-m. $3. Sue Davis, Laurie Fierstein, and Emily Hanlon. YAWF Women, 58 West 25th St., N.Y., N.Y. 10010. Illus.

Aud: Ga, Ac.

Women of a New Left organization called Youth Against War and Fascism publish this journal in the interests of radical, anti-imperialist politics. While *Battle Acts* deals with a wide variety of subjects, all of which relate to women, the effect is not of a feminist consciousness raising so much as a radical one. Most articles concern third world women or Black or working class women in America. One issue deals with prisoners' families, Cuban women, a Canadian Conference on Indochina attended by several Indochinese women, Nixon's statement against abortion contrasted with his imperialist policies, children jailed in "youth houses," migrant workers, child labor, illegitimate children of American GIs in Vietnam, waitresses' conditions, Mayday 1971 actions around the country, and the story of the Grimke sisters. In this journal women's oppression seems to be cited more as an example, a rallying point, than as a call to feminist revolution. The magazine is surprisingly undoctrinaire, i.e. not given to spurious rhetoric; accusations are backed up with specifics, and articles (most of which deal with personal situations rather than general conditions) are very well-written. (M.M.)

Earth's Daughters. 1971. q. $2.50/8 issues. Judith Kerman. 409 Richmond Ave., Buffalo, N.Y. 14222. Illus., adv. Circ: 1,000. Sample. Vol. ends: winter.

Bk. rev: Various number, length. *Aud:* Ga, Ac. *Jv:* V.

Matrix. 1970. 4 issues planned. $6.50. Idell. Box 46067, Los Angeles, Calif. 90046. Illus., adv.

Aud: Ga, Ac.

These two excellent feminist literary magazines do not have the scope of *Aphra* but are nonetheless important outlets for women's creative efforts, especially poetry. The first issue of *Earth's Daughters* (named for Emma Goldman, editor and founder of *Mother Earth*) is starkly impressive—each poem is printed on a separate white sheet, the cover folding into a packet to hold them all. The quality of the poetry is even higher than what appears in *Aphra,* and drawings by Ruth Geller, an Italian artist, round off the issue beautifully. *Matrix,* "for the She of the New Eon," has an uneven quality and a somewhat disconcerting mysticism: is "a magic mirror and a lodestone for all sexes." The editors planned only four issues and wish *Matrix* to be classified as an anthology rather than a magazine. Volume I is "mostly about the female/male spirit," and Volume II is "mostly about the female human . . . what she is & becomes & the secret trails to her heart." Both publications are recommended. (M.M.)

Everywoman. 1970. Every 3 weeks. $15. 1043B W. Washington Blvd., Venice, Calif. 90291. Illus., adv. Sample. Vol. ends: Dec.

Indexed: API. *Bk. rev:* Various number, length. *Aud:* Ga, Ac.

Everywoman is an eclectic newspaper of the women's liberation movement. Contents range from straight news items and analyses of the news to articles of theory, analysis, or criticism of the movement or the role of women in general. Although the viewpoint of the young ex-radical seems to predominate (as it does, for that matter, in the movement as a whole), no one ideology or group is exclusively represented. Articles have dealt with secretaries and other working women, day care, abortions, lesbians, Black women, male supremacy, the new left, pornography, women's history, and many other relevant concerns. Significant features in every issue include the "herstory" (as opposed to his-story) almanac for the period covered and a column called "Manglish," in which Varda One dissects the English language for examples of sexist grammar and usage. *Everywoman* is a good source for reviews of feminist books, and poetry is featured in every issue. (M.M.)

Goodbye to All That! 1970. s-m. $10. P.O. Box 3092, San Diego, Calif. 92103. Illus., adv. Circ: 6,000. Sample. Vol. ends: 26th issue.

Bk. rev: Occasional, half-page, unsigned. *Aud:* Ga, Ac.

Goodbye to All That!, written "from, to and for San Diego women," contains a little bit of everything but seems to be most concerned with international issues. Though no part of the movement is neglected, primary attention is given to Indochina (particularly Vietnamese and Laotian women) and to the struggles of Black and poor women and families in America. Not all articles deal exclusively with women; the politics are generally New Leftist. *Goodbye to All That!* could be described as a women's underground paper, rather than solely a feminist publication. (M.M.)

Journal of Female Liberation. 1968. irreg. $1 an issue. Cell 16, 16 Lexington St., Cambridge, Mass. Illus.

Indexed: API. *Aud:* Ga, Ac.

This is an exhaustive and exhausting journal, packed with articles on virtually every aspect of women's liberation and the female experience. Its tone is often strident, and its opinions are frequently based on a Marxian analysis of society: Man is the oppressor, Woman is the slave. Much of it may sound foreign to those not used to radical rhetoric, but most points raised are thoughtful and well taken. Articles tend to be written from a subjective point of view, and writers do not hesitate to show their passionate feelings. This unique contribution to the literature of women's liberation may convince skeptics of the real purposes of the movement. (M.M.)

The Ladder. 1956. bi-m. $7.50. Gene Damon. Box 5025, Washington Station, Reno, Nev. 89503. Illus., adv. Vol. ends: Sept.

Indexed: API. *Bk. rev:* Various number, length. *Aud:* Ga, Ac. *Jv:* V.

This publication, the oldest of today's feminist magazines (preceding the current movement by at least ten years), was published exclusively for lesbians until its August-September 1970 issue, when it declared itself to be "directed to ALL women seeking full human dignity." Though it is no longer affiliated with Daughters of Bilitis, it is still published by lesbians and deals most frequently with the problems and needs of lesbians. But now the editor and writers explicitly relate the oppression of lesbians to the oppression of heterosexual women, in hopes of forming a coherent and united feminist movement. *The Ladder's* claim that it is "the only women's magazine openly supporting Lesbians" is not quite accurate—*Ain't I a Woman,* for example, is published by a collective of "radical lesbians"—but it is certainly a unique publication. The discovery of love of women for each other is reflected in many current women's publications, but there is often a chasm between the "newly gay" and the women who have been lesbians all their lives—and as such have lived very different life-styles. *The Ladder* represents these women specifically but is attempting to bridge the many cultural differences between them and their newfound sisters. Articles cover such subjects as lesbian authors, the new women's movement, lesbians and the church, lifestyles, sex roles, and anything else that is relevant to lesbians or heterosexual women. A typical issue also includes an editorial, one or two short stories, poetry, one or more book reviews, a chronology of news items pertaining to women, and "Lesbiana," a bibliographical article by the editor. An absolutely essential addition to any collection. (M.M.)

Ms.; the new magazine for women. 1971. m. $9. Ed. bd. Subs. to: 370 Lexington Ave., N.Y., N.Y. 10017.

Aud: Ga, Ac, Hs. *Jv:* V.

In some ways *Ms.* is a revolutionary magazine. Even though it shows decided middle-class and heterosexual bias, it reaches a large audience with sufficiently radical content to be worth the inevitable prostitution required by any sort of mass market revolution. While there is a danger in this kind of approach, the women's movement is not yet taken seriously enough that advertisers would attempt to influence or censor articles; at the same time, women readers with any degree of openness will be jolted into recognition by the truths stated there.

In the preview issue of *Ms.* (bound within *New York* magazine, December 20, 1971) all the articles related directly to middle-class women (to encourage subscribers?). In one article, Gloria Steinem wrote on "Sisterhood," proclaiming that all women share a common oppression. But she made little concrete analysis of the meaning of women's liberation for nonmiddle-class women. An article by Vivian Gornick called "Why Women Fear Success" described the conflict women face between their need for human fulfillment and for "feminine" fulfillment and asserted that what we now call natural behavior for women is not natural at all, but merely normative.

The Spring 1972 issue included a very good, if tokenistic, article on lesbianism (this most central concern of the movement is accorded only one other brief mention in the entire issue); an interview on the subject of "Black Women and Feminism"; articles on welfare women and the failure of the sexual "revolution"; and a brief article signed by several well-known women who have had abortions. The best thing about *Ms.* is its diversity and, as noted above, its potential for bringing women into the real movement (as opposed to the media myth perpetrated by most women's magazines). It not only exposes uninitiated readers to women's culture, but furnishes fuel for those never-ending arguments with husbands and hostile males. Most of all, it helps women see themselves and each other as strong, righteous beings. (M.M.)

(Ed. note: The first full issue of *Ms.* appeared in July, 1972 and was notable for its downplaying of sexist advertising—the editors claim to be rejecting advertisements which insult women's intelligence—and for a wide divergence of viewpoints. The 138 pages offer something for just about anyone involved with the new image of women. The format, writing, and overall approach are professional. The total impression is of a magazine which is here to stay, and one which will make an impressive contribution. It should be found in every library.)

Matrix. See *Earth's Daughters.*

Mother. 1971. m. $3.50. R. G. Parker. Mother Publns., P.O. Box 8507, Stanford, Calif. 94305.

Bk. rev: Occasional. *Aud:* Ga.

Mother is a gay women's newspaper, written in the style of professional journalists and politically moderate rather than radical. Mother Publications also distributes news items about gay women through Gay Women's News Service to the straight press, radio stations, news services, the underground press, and libraries throughout the United States, Canada, and Europe. The paper is composed of news articles, an editorial, "legal notes," and occasional interviews, guest editorials, book reviews, and other items of interest to gay women. It is the best source of "straight" information about lesbians, similar in tone to *The Advocate* a male homosexual publication. *Mother* planned to change its name in February 1972. (M.M.)

Mother Lode. 1971. bi-m. $1. Mother Lode Collective, P.O. Box 40213, San Francisco, Calif. 94140. Illus., adv. Circ: 5,000. Vol. ends: Dec.

Aud: Ga, Ac.

Mother Lode is a large broadsheet—printed on both sides—containing women's testimony about personal life situations (always with the consciousness that "the personal is the political"). One issue relates experiences of women in prison, and another deals mainly with male/female relationships (e.g. "Why I Want a Wife" details the myriad privileges of husbands). An interesting paper, but not essential. (M.M.)

The New Feminist. 1970. irreg. $3. P.O. Box 597, Station A, Toronto 116, Ontario, Canada.

Aud: Ga, Ac.

This is a small mimeographed newsletter, written by only three women. While not achieving the scope of the larger women's publications, it nonetheless presents an interesting variety of material, with a strong feminist approach. The longest article in the issue examined refutes the findings of the Report of the Royal Commission on the Status of Women in Canada and of the National Ad Hoc Committee on the Status of Women, both generally considered to be "favorable" toward women. The other major article concerns consciousness-raising and includes a week-by-week suggested order of topics for consciousness-raising groups. Other, shorter, items attack male chauvinism and the charge that feminists have no sense of humor; the last two pages are given over to news items. (M.M.)

New Woman. 1970. m. $4.50. Margaret Harold. P.O. Box 24202, Fort Lauderdale, Fla. 33310. Illus., adv. Circ: 200,000. Vol. ends: May.

Aud: Ga, Ac. *Jv:* C.

From the first page, which is a brassiere ad, through the nude male centerfold and beyond, this magazine can be summed up in one hyphenated word: rip-off. It is even more audacious than *Cosmopolitan* in its slick, breezy attempt to represent today's liberated female —the "new woman." It claims to be "the only magazine dedicated to the elevation of the status and image of the thinking woman" and aims to cover the activities of "keen-minded, knowledgeable and influential females." The "new woman" rhapsodized in these pages is a swinger, a junior executive on the make, a potential government leader. And she most emphatically does not hate men! (The magazine is riddled with cosmetics ads to prove it.) The idea is that women can do all the things men do now, but with a soft feminine touch. The emphasis is on equal rights within the present system rather than a restructuring of power, and it's clear that in personal relationships at least, the man is still the aggressor and the woman her traditionally coy, flirty self. In other words, the "new woman" wants a bigger piece of the pie but is still willing to let the "new man" cut it. Regular departments include advice of all sorts: on legal rights, divorce, "non-sexist" child-rearing ("If the

nuclear family structure is to survive"—note the assumption—"radical changes must be made within it."), finance, sex, and housewifery. Other regular features include the "new woman" in marriage, politics, industry ("there's room at the top for women in banking today"), and travel, besides the usual fashion and beauty spread ("the new executive look"). Each issue will also include a feature article on a prototypical "new woman" and "new man." Articles in the first issue discuss motherhood, menopause, sex discrimination in universities, and "6 Untapped Fields for Women to Enter and Clean Up." (M.M.)

(Note: By mid-1972 there was a report that this magazine would soon cease publishing. The publisher denied it and claims a new publication schedule. Check before subscribing.)

NOW Acts. q. $3. National Organization of Women, National Headquarters, 1952 E. 73rd St., Chicago, Ill. 60649. Adv.

Aud: Ga, Ac. *Jv:* V.

NOW Acts is the substantial and informative newsletter of the National Organization of Women. Oriented toward action, especially legislative reform, *NOW Acts* reports on legal suits and cases and the fight against sex discrimination in education, the media, employment, religion, medicine, and other fields. Significant news items and statements by notable people (both for and against women's liberation) are quoted, as well as new studies and statistics pertaining to women's status. Some items are very short, and some are full-length reports on an important case or development. "Glib Lib (or what to say to a cliché)" is a regular column containing valuable statistics to use as rejoinders when someone makes a remark like, "Women are emotionally unstable." As a record of the current status of women and the attempts being made to change it, *NOW Acts* is an important addition to any collection. (M.M.)

Off Our Backs. 1970. m. $5. Collective. 1346 Connecticut Ave. N.W., Washington, D.C. 20036. Illus., adv. Circ: 10,000. Sample. Vol. ends: Sept. 1.

Indexed: API. *Bk. rev:* One one-page review per issue. *Aud:* Ga, Ac. *Jv:* V.

This is one of the best produced newspapers in the movement. Subtitled "a women's new journal," it combines straight news of women's actions, sex discrimination, and other movement concerns with special reports on women's problems (on women in other cultures or different classes) and articles on theory or reflection. Several issues have been thematic: women and imperialism and women and the church are two subjects that were covered thoroughly. It is almost impossible to characterize the paper's contents from issue to issue, because *OOB* simply covers it all— feminists in history, child care and children's liberation, abortion and medical care, the struggle of women in Palestine and Vietnam, class differences among U.S. women, lesbianism, communal living, women's liberation and the new left, etc., plus occasional fiction, lots of poetry, and good artwork. *OOB* is superior to both *Everywoman* and *Rat,* for its clear style, coherent presentations, and generally together feeling. (M.M.)

Rat. 1968. bi-w. $6. 241 E. 14th St., N.Y., N.Y. 10003. Illus., adv.

Indexed: API. *Aud:* Ga, Ac.

Rat has a singular history and serves as a rare and encouraging example to women who have found the New Left to be just as oppressive as straight society. Begun as a male-dominated underground paper, it was taken over in January 1970 by women who objected to its "flashy" reportage of the movement and its pornographic overtones. The paper is still in the hands of the women, and women's liberation is a primary (but not the sole) focus of the paper. (It has been criticized for not devoting itself exclusively to feminism.) Although most of the articles have a leftist orientation and often deal with so-called movement issues—the Palestinian resistance, U.S. imperialism, the war in Indochina, squatters and rent strikers in New York City, and problems of various ethnic groups—the emphasis is still on women: women in the movement, women on welfare, Puerto Rican and Black women; high school women; gay women. Much emphasis is placed on community organizing in the City, with top priority given to women's struggles. *Rat* is published by a collective of women, none of whom are paid for their work. (M.M.)

Second Wave. 1971. q. $3. Female Liberation, Box 303 Kenmore Sq. Sta., Boston, Mass. 02215. Illus., adv. Circ: 5,000. Vol. ends: winter.

Indexed: API. *Bk. rev:* 2, 500–1,000 words, signed. *Aud:* Ga, Ac.

Remembering the suffrage movement of a century ago, this publication was begun by "the second wave of feminists in an ongoing struggle." It is published, along with *Journal of Female Liberation,* by Female Liberation in Boston, one of the oldest groups in the movement. The *Second Wave,* "a magazine of the new feminism," is less heavily theoretical than its sister publication and features a completely different group of writers and editors. A variety of subjects is covered in the first issue, including Nixon's child care plan, social control and female emancipation, "the case for studied ugliness," lesbians in the movement, the Angela Davis case, and an interview with Myrna Lamb, feminist playwright. The tone throughout the magazine is militant and borders on a socialist emphasis rather than on a strictly feminist one. (Rumor has it that Female Liberation has been "infiltrated" by the Young Socialist Alliance/Socialist Workers Party.)

Poetry, film and book reviews, and some local and national news of interest to feminists are also included. The magazine is not highly recommended, in that neither its material nor its approach is particularly original. (M.M.)

Shrew. 1969. m. $2.50. Women's Liberation Workshop, 12–13 Little Newport St., London, W.C. 2, England. Illus. Circ: 3,000. Sample. Vol. ends: Dec.

Bk. rev: Occasional, various lengths, signed. *Aud:* Ga, Ac.

Shrew is the publication of the Women's Liberation Workshop, a collective made up of seven representatives of seven regional small (consciousness-raising/action) groups. Each month a different group puts *Shrew* together, usually collecting articles on a single theme (e.g. confrontation, the family). As such it is a good representative publication of the British women's liberation movement, which is shown here to have generally the same concerns as the American —abortion, working mothers, gay/straight relationships, the family, with a dual emphasis on objective conditions (such as sex discrimination) and personal feelings and social expectations. "The Women's Liberation Workshop questions women's role and redefines the possibilities. It seeks to bring women to a full awareness of the meaning of their inferior status and to devise methods to change it." *Shrew* is intended both as a forum for discussion within the movement and as a consciousness-raising journal for the general public. (M.M.)

Socialist Woman. 1969. bi-m. $1/5 issues. 16 Ella Rd., West Bridgford, Nottingham, England. Illus. Vol. ends: Dec.

Aud: Ga, Ac.

Socialist Woman addresses itself to the needs of women, especially in the working class, from the point of view of a socialist politics. The dual concerns of socialism and women's liberation are considered equally important, i.e. "female liberation can only occur under Socialism." Along with a class analysis of existing inequities ("female oppression is peculiarly intertwined with the organization of the Capitalist system"), *Socialist Woman* examines woman's "imprisoned psyche." Some articles are personal statements about women's lives, some are news reports of various women's actions (such as strikes and other union activities), and some are theoretical discussions of the movement and its directions. The magazine is interesting for its combined assault on capitalism and women's oppression and for its perspective on the British woman's situation. (M.M.)

Spectre. See *Ain't I a Woman.*

Up from Under. 1970. 5/yr. $5. Up from Under, Inc., 339 Lafayette St., N.Y., N.Y. 10012. Illus.

Indexed: API. *Aud:* Ga, Ac. *Jv:* V.

The most striking characteristic of *Up from Under,* a magazine "by, for, and about women," is that it seems to have suspended mere rhetoric about women's liberation and has gotten down to talking directly to women. An amazing diversity of subjects is covered—simple household repairs; explanations of the menstrual cycle and techniques of abortion; the everyday problems of working mothers, single women, women on welfare, middle-aged women, Black women; the origin of the family; women's place in a capitalistic society; child care; sex roles in marriage; the myths of femininity and romance; women's history, especially the history of working women and their struggles to unionize; the lives of Vietnamese women; besides fiction and poetry. Throughout the magazine the prose is simple without being condescending; the most complicated issues are set forth in a clear, readable style. The articles invariably reach directly into the lives of women—particularly working class women, who have been talked *about* in other publications but rarely *to.* Many articles are written by working class women themselves, with lapses in grammar but a great deal of dignity. The magazine is very well produced, with shiny covers, good white paper, and artful use of photographs, drawings, and woodcuts. *Up from Under* is published by a collective of women, none of whom receive salaries. (M.M.)

Voice of Women/La Voix des Femmes. National Newsletter. 1960. q. Moira Armour. 1554 Younge St., Toronto 195, Ontario, Canada. Illus. Circ: 3,000. Vol. ends: last issue of calendar year. Sample.

Bk. rev: 2, 100–200 words, signed. *Aud:* Ga, Ac.

Voice of Women/La Voix des Femmes is an organization similar in nature to our Women's Strike for Peace. Its members are not exclusively feminists, but are concerned with the issues of world peace, disarmament, and equal rights for women and racial minorities. Their greatest concern at this time is the war in Indochina, and at least as much space is given to this as to Canadian politics, the other predominating concern. In addition, Voice of Women supports the independence of Quebec, the right to abortion and sterilization, greater opportunities and services for youth, the right to dissent, and good relations with the People's Republic of China. VOW criticizes U.S. imperialism in Canada, exploitation of resources to the detriment of the environment, war toys, nuclear testing, chemical-biological warfare research, and any other activity that leads to war or the exploitation of the mass of people by the few. The newsletter contains internal news and resolutions, articles about VOW activities (such as their sponsoring of Laotian women to a Canadian Conference on Indochina), and general articles on problems such as nuclear warfare and industrial pollution, often reprinted from other sources. (M.M.)

Women: a journal of liberation. 1969. q. $4. 3028 Greenmount Ave., Baltimore, Md. 21218. Illus. Circ: 20,000. Vol. ends: summer.

Indexed: API. *Bk. rev:* occasional. *Aud:* Ga, Ac. *Jv:* V.

This militant and well produced journal is probably the most comprehensive publication of the movement. Each issue is built around a specific theme, such as "Innate Nature or Cultural Conditioning?," "Women in Revolution," "Women in the Arts," "How We Live and with Whom," "Women as Workers under Capitalism," and "The Power and Scope of the Women's Liberation Movement." *Women* presents a well documented critique of women's subjugation in this society and analyses and reports on current directions of the movement. Articles include a diversity of history, philosophy, and analysis of the subject. If you can afford only one righteous women's publication, make it this one. (M.M.)

Woman's World. 1971. bi-m. $2/6mos. Kathie Sarachild and Barbara Leon. P.O. Box 694, Stuyvesant Station, N.Y., N.Y. 10009. Illus., adv. Circ: 5,000. Sample. Vol. ends: Dec.

Bk. rev: One, 1,500 words, signed. *Aud:* Ga, Ac.

Women's Page. 1970. irreg. $2/6 mos. 1227 37th Ave., San Francisco, Calif. 94122. Illus.

Aud: Ga, Ac.

Woman's World and the *Women's Page* represent similar minority views within the feminist movement. Attacked by more moderate groups as "man-haters," "elitists," and "crazies," these women are interested in power for women and in the reality of the present male-dominated system. (In other words, "equality" for women demands a struggle and not simply a polite request.) Their prevailing slogan is, "This time we are going all the way!" The *Women's Page* resulted from a purge of sorts within the staff of the now defunct *It Ain't Me Babe;* among the founders is Laura X, best known for her founding of the Women's History Research Center in Berkeley. Writers for these papers espouse many views that conflict with those of other feminists, such as the idea that women are not so much "conditioned" into their role as forced into it by daily reality. They deny that men and women suffer equally under the burden of their sex roles and believe that the imbalance of power between the two sexes exists because men benefit from it. These are not your "nice" accommodating, shuffling, champions of "women's rights"; they're the boot stomping feminists your father warned you about. (M.M.)

Teen-Age

American Girl. 1917. m. $5. Patricia di Sernia, Girl Scouts of the USA, 830 Third Ave., N.Y., N.Y. 10022. Illus., adv. Circ: 1,000,000. Sample.

Indexed: IChildMag. *Bk. rev:* Varying. *Aud:* Ejh, Hs.

This magazine is written around a central theme each month for the preteen and teen girl who needs a broader outlook on life. It helps her develop personal skills, gives her an idea of the latest fashions and trends, and gives her an opportunity to express her ideas through writing. The magazine has limited advertising and stresses schools and camps for teenagers. Although a very popular magazine, it should be supplied through a personal subscription. (J.G.)

Calling All Girls. See *Young Miss.*

Charlie; a magazine for the adventurous generation. 1969. m. $6. Richard A. Desberg. Devon International, Ld. 360 Park Ave. S., N.Y., N.Y. 10010. Illus., adv.

Bk. rev: Occasionally. *Aud:* Hs, Ga.

As stated in the title, really for the adventurous teen-age girl generation. Contains the latest trends in fashion, music and footwear, several extensive interviews with celebrities, condensed books, poetry, movie and record reviews. A good magazine for the "now" generation. (J.G.)

Co-ed; for the lively ones. 1956. m (Sept.-May/June and Aug.). $2.40. Margaret Houser. Scholastic Magazines, 902 Sylvan Ave., Englewood Cliffs, N.J. 07632. Illus., adv. Circ: 1,000,000. Microfilm: UM.

Indexed: IChildMag *Bk. rev:* several. *Aud:* Hs. *Jv:* V.

A well written and designed magazine for the teen-age homemaker—specializes in fashion, sewing, crafts, grooming, foods, menus and finances. A good magazine for the more domesticated teen-ager: teaches how to do. Gives a good basic background for the mature years. Should be placed in a library to expose all girls to the responsible side of teen-age existence. (J.G.)

Fave. See *Tiger Beat Fave.*

Flip Magazine. 1964. m. $5. Valerie Berger. Youthway Corp., 405 Park Ave., N.Y., N.Y. 10022. Illus., adv. Circ: 300,000.

Aud: Ejh, Hs.

Primarily a fan magazine for the 12 to 17 year-old. (The publishers advertise that this magazine is for the young woman who is still too young for *Seventeen,* which may give the librarian some notion of the real target audience.) Emphasis is on the pop scene with interviews and profiles of recording stars, movie stars and television personalities. The reporting is accurate and candid, the writing a bit simple, but never insulting. Heavy on photographs, brilliant makeup and relevance for the young woman who wants to become part of the going, modern set. Quite a notch, by the way, above the average movie fan magazine, and the two genres should not be confused. *Flip* is written for the teen-ager, not for the older woman who dreams of those days. One of the better of this type. See also, *Tiger Beat Fave.*

For Teens Only. 1962. q. $2. Rena Adler. Reese Publishing Co., 235 Park Ave. S., N.Y., N.Y. 10003. Illus., adv.

Aud: Hs, Ejh. *Jv:* C.

The predominant theme is entertainment (movies and television and music), beauty, fashions, and "real life" situations. Although for the 12 to 16 year-old teen-age girl, the primary emphasis is how to get along without being different. Fiction moves from the usual love story to family life. Poor quality, and only acceptable where the library is running out of material for teen-agers who have reading problems.

Ingenue. 1959. $5. Joan Wym. Dell Publishing Co., Inc., 750 Third Ave., N.Y., N.Y. 10017. Illus., adv. Circ: 750,000. Sample. Vol. ends: Dec. Microform: UM.

Bk. rev: 2, 2 pages. *Aud:* Hs.

One of the more sophisticated approaches to the teen-age woman but still a long way from liberation. Articles which are above average in literate and informative presentation, touch on all interests: education, family, sports, sex, and in the past few years, social and political issues. Interesting teen-agers are highlighted in intelligent biographical sketches. Some fiction, but not up to the articles. About 50 percent advertising. A good magazine for a general high school or public library collection. The popular style of writing assumes an audience of girls in early teens, somewhat younger than that of *Mademoiselle,* and it is to the 14 to 17 age group that it has the strongest appeal.

Masterkey. See Anthropology Section.

Miss Chatelaine; fashion magazine for girls in their late teens and early twenties. 1964. 6/yr. $1.50. Mildred Istona. Maclean Hunter Publishing Co., 481 Univ. Way, Toronto, 2, Ontario, Canada. Illus., adv. Circ: 140,000.

Aud: Hs, Ga.

Issued by the same publisher that brings Canadians *Maclean's* and *Chatelaine,* this is a small fashion magazine for girls between 15 and 20 years of age. It is considerably less flamboyant than many similar American magazines, with a good half of it usually given over to colored photographs of fashions. The remainder is an average approach to life and problems via short stories by teenagers, articles about Canadians who have met success, and the usual short reviews of books, films and recording. An acceptable magazine for Canadian public and high school libraries.

Nineteen. 1968. m. $7.50. Margaret Koumi. IPC Magazines Ld., Tower House, Southampton St., London, WC2E9QX, England. Illus., adv. Circ: 200,000. Sample.

Aud: Hs, Ga.

A shiny formatted magazine which could be considered the British *Seventeen*. Fashions are vividly displayed in full-page advertisements. Beauty aids and tips are also impressively arranged. Several complete short stories, fashion articles, astrascopes, shopping guides and short articles on subjects of current interest, make this a sure bet for today's teenager looking for the British approach. (J.G.)

Plains Anthropologist. See Anthropology Section.

Seventeen. 1944. m. $6. Ray Robinson (nonservice) and Rosemary McMurtry (service). Triangle Publns., Inc., 250 King of Prussia Rd., Radnor, Pa. 19088. Illus., adv., index. Circ: 1,400,000. Sample. Vol. ends: Dec. Microform: UM.

Indexed: RG. *Bk. rev:* Notes. *Aud:* Hs, Ejh.

A dollar vision of the teen-age girl in America; a junior version of a combination *Glamour* and *Ladies Home Journal;* a salesman's delight. And it is all in an oversized, brilliantly illustrated and edited package for the young lady who wants to keep up with fashion, fads and food. There is little or nothing of the women's liberation movement. The primary social message of three representative issues (Sept.-Nov. 1971) as headlined on the covers: "Virginity, is it outmoded?" "John Wayne last of the father figures?"; "On The Road to Red China; I was a ping pong diplomat," "Russian Romantics: new ways with long hair," "My life and hard times with Nader's Raiders." The writing, which is sandwiched in between some 60 to 70 percent of advertising, is good to excellent. The format is colorful. It all adds up to a relaxing bit of nothing for the average teen-age (or early 20s) girl. Harmless, even beneficial if one believes in letting the mind go slack while trying to solve some of life's less pressing problems.

Teen, Young America's Fashion, Beauty and Entertainment Magazine. 1957. m. $5. Robert Macleod. Petersen Publishing Co., 8490 Sunset Blvd., Los Angeles, Calif. 90069. Illus., adv. Circ: 800,000.

Aud: Hs. *Jv:* V.

One of the best teen-age magazines on the market today. Has articles of importance to the teenager; fashion and beauty aids play an important part in the magazine. Colorful full-page advertisements point the teenager to items of interest to her age group. The interviews with teen celebrities and the short stories are appropriate. It features horoscopes, simple recipes and record reviews. A must for libraries. (J.G.)

Teen Times. 1945. q. $1.50. Future Homemakers of America, U.S. Office of Education, Washington, D.C. 20202. Illus.

Aud: Hs, Ejh.

Primarily for the 13 to 17 year-old girl who participates in the Future Homemakers of America pro-

grams. The 20- to 24-page magazine is geared to present news of the organization, groups and individuals. Some information of a practical nature, but this is basically a newsletter. Will interest FHA members, but few other teenagers.

Tiger Beat Fave (Formerly: *Fave*). 1965. m. $5. Ralph Benner. Laufer Co., 1800 N. Highland Ave., Los Angeles, Calif. 90028. Illus., adv. Circ: 180,000.

Aud: Ejh, Hs.

For the 12 to 16 year-old, with the emphasis on fanzine material, i.e. interviews, articles, and pictures of leaders in television, film, and records. There is a strong emphasis on photographs and a startling layout. (Some full page pictures of teen-age idols.) The reader only needs a limited vocabulary to understand the import of the material. Most of it is simple minded, but nonoffensive. Not up to the editorial treatment of *Flip*, but good enough as far as it goes.

You. 1971. m. $9. Diane Silver. Trend Magazines, Inc., 261 Fifth Ave., N.Y., N.Y. 10016. Illus., adv. Vol. ends: Apr.

Aud: Ga, Hs.

You proves that a little liberation is a dangerous thing. Not as overpowering and blatantly hypocritical as *New Woman*, it nonetheless coopts a vital movement and attempts to dissipate righteous female anger by granting certain concessions to the feminist cause. One article in the first issue briefly—and rather favorably—discusses several alternatives to marriage, including homosexual marriages and communal arrangements. Another condemns the makers of feminine deodorant sprays for trading on women's feelings of inferiority; yet another claims that fashion and beauty are not synonymous: "we are all beautiful." But *You* subverts a true feminist revolution by asserting that no major changes in the system of male domination are necessary: ". . . it is we women who have, for the most part, denied the existence of male-female equality." "This is not a time for militancy. . . . This is not a time to reject or blame men. . . . We have all been willing participants in the same game." That is, we have only ourselves to blame if we aren't "liberated." Articles deal not only with women's concerns (the Pill for men, women in politics, "How a Working Woman is Better Able to Love"), but with general areas of interest to young people, such as drugs and encounter groups. Art, music, films, theater, and advertising are reviewed. The point of view in most articles isn't exactly revolutionary but is certainly "liberal"—a surprise for a commercial magazine in the young-woman market. It would be easy to consider *You* an innocuous, low-key—even worthwhile—magazine for young women who now read *Seventeen* and *Mademoiselle*—but better that they read the real thing. (M.M.)

Young Miss (Formerly: *Calling All Girls*). 1953. m (except June and Aug.). $5.95. Rubie Saunders. Parent's Magazine Enterprises, Inc. Young Miss, Subscription Dept. Bergenfield, N.J. 07621. Illus., adv. Circ: 350,000.

Bk. rev: Several, short. *Aud:* Ejh, Hs.

A magazine for the early teen-ager. Its *Reader's Digest* format makes for easy reading, but the lack of vivid colors throughout the magazine detracts from the fashions displayed and the magazine as a whole. On the other hand, the contents: fiction, fashion and beauty tips, hints for maturing, simple recipes, fun and games, and helpful advice on dating, popularity and partyplanning make this a basic journal for the early teenager who needs subtle guidance. (J.G.)

BIBLIOGRAPHY

Grant T. Skelley
School of Librarianship, University of Washington

The following bibliography represents a substantial revision, updating and enlargement of the one which appeared in the first edition of *Magazines for Libraries* (1969). Most of the material listed here was published in 1968 or later, with the exception of certain earlier material which is either basic, or for which no suitable later substitute was found. Many worthwhile things that appeared in the first edition bibliography have been deleted in the interest of conserving space and fostering currency, and consultation of that edition is recommended.

Material was selected with the intention of (1) providing references to lists of magazines that may supplement those lists contained in the main section of this book, and (2) citing articles, books and other material that may be useful to one either working with magazines or just interested in them. Little about any single magazine is included, except for a small number of items deemed to have some general application.

Part I includes material of somewhat general nature, Part II material relating to specific subjects, specific audiences, or specific types of publications. The few entries without annotations represent material unavailable for the compiler to examine, and are included more or less on faith.

Entries are numbered, and are gathered under the following headings:

Part II. SPECIFIC SUBJECTS, AUDIENCES, TYPES

As the subjects heading here were compiled slightly before the main subjects, some are not in alphabetical order.

Part I. GENERAL WORKS

History and Background

1. Cort, David, "The Voices of the Magazines." In Neil Postman, et al., eds., *Language in America*, pp. 187–196. New York: Pegasus, 1969.

Discusses with some despair the varied roles of American magazines in either contributing to or reacting against contemporary "language pollution," which this book is all about.

2. Ford, James L. C. *Magazines for Millions: The Story of Specialized Publications.* Carbondale: Southern Illinois Univ. Press, 1969.

Analyzes and describes the various types of currently published American magazines and the way they operate. Covers the whole spectrum, with considerable information about many specific titles.

3. Kadushin, Charles, Julie Hover, and Monique Tichy, "How and Where to Find Intellectual Elite in the United States," *Public Opinion Quarterly* 35 (Spring 1971): 1–18.

The authors find that "the top [American] intellectual journals constitute the equivalent of an Oxbridge establishment." A sample of people identified as intellectuals were asked questions about 36 journals, the resultant data indicating that of 24 influential journals, there were eight "most influential": *New York Review of Books, New Republic, Commentary, New York Times Book Review, New Yorker, Saturday Review, Partisan Review,* and *Harper's.*

4. Mott, Frank Luther. *A History of American Magazines,* 5 vols. Cambridge: Harvard Univ. Press, 1930–1968.

The standard history of the American magazine from its beginning until 1930. A cumulative index to the entire five-volume set was issued in the concluding, posthumous volume, published in 1968.

5. Peterson, Theodore. *Magazines in the Twentieth Century,* 2nd ed. Urbana: Univ. of Illinois Press, 1964.

Takes up more or less where Mott left off, but concentrates primarily on consumer-type magazines. Explores the major economic and social implications of the mass magazine.

6. Tebbel, John. *The American Magazine: A Compact History.* New York: Hawthorne, 1969.

A readable, succinct, narrative history, unencumbered with footnotes. The author expresses his gratitude for the work of Mott and Peterson. A good introduction to the subject.

7. "What's Happened to Magazines?" *Antioch Review* 29 (Spring 1969).

Special issue on above theme. Articles are for the most part critical of what's happened.

8. Wolseley, Roland E. *Understanding Magazines,* 2nd ed. Ames: Iowa State Univ. Press, 1969.

"An overview of magazines in the United States—their history, functions, organization, types, responsibilities, problems, vocational opportunities, and future."

9. Wood, James P. *The Curtis Magazines.* New York: Ronald, 1971.

A journalistic treatment of the rise and fall of the publishing empire established by Cyrus H. K. Curtis, written by a knowledgeable former Curtis employee. Includes many insights about mass magazines in general.

10. Wood, James P. *Magazines in the United States,* 3rd ed. New York: Ronald, 1971.

"Attempts to show, from general magazines that were important in their time, and from important nationally circulated magazines of today, what magazines are and in what directions they exert their social and economic influence." Particularly examines changes in the magazine scene. Second edition was 1956.

Bibliographies

11. Harvard University Library. *Periodical Classes; Classified Listing by Call Number, Alphabetical Listing by Title.* Cambridge: the Library, 1968. (Widener Library Shelf-list No. 15)

There are 25,685 titles in two groups, one language-oriented, one subject-oriented. Since in the Widener scheme there are many subjects for which there is no separate periodical class number, this list represents about half the library's holdings. Nonetheless, especially because of the subject access, this is a valuable reference.

12. Magazine Advertising Bureau. *Sources of Consumer Magazine Information,* 2nd rev. ed. New York: Magazine Center, 1965.

From time to time the Bureau issues pamphlets and lists for anyone dealing with general, commercial magazines: the above, for instance, and a three-page mimeographed bibliography entitled *Magazines and Magazine Publishing—Bibliography,* published in October 1967. Specifically, the pamphlet listed here gives information on where to find data on circulation, readership, marketing, rates, costs, etc. While geared for the advertiser and professional journalist, still of great value for the librarian.

13. Price, Warren C., and Calder M. Pickett. *An Annotated Journalism Bibliography, 1958–1968.* Minneapolis: Univ. of Minnesota Press, 1970.

Mostly about newspapers, but has some material on magazines. Supplements the Price *Literature of Journalism,* 1959. U.S. and Canada.

14. Schacht, J. H. *A Bibliography for the Study of Magazines.* Urbana: Univ. of Illinois, College of Journalism, 1968.

The best general bibliography on magazines. Approximately 500 briefly annotated citations under 15 broad subject headings. Prepared primarily for a course in magazine editing, the bibliography includes basic articles of a general nature and many concerned with individual magazines.

Directories

Note: Included here are only directories of a general nature. Directories for periodicals in special subjects or areas are listed under the appropriate heading. A good source for directories of both kinds is the Public Affairs Information Service (PAIS) *Bulletin,* under "Directories—Periodicals."

15. *Ayer's Directory of Newspapers and Periodicals.* annual, 1880–. Philadelphia: N. W. Ayer & Son.

A standard guide found in most libraries, this is primarily a state-by-state, city-by-city listing of newspapers, but includes many magazines, major and minor. Useful for classified lists: religious, fraternal, trade, technical, etc. The British equivalent of this is *Willing's Press Guide* (1871–   ) which includes basic information on the press of the United Kingdom and Commonwealth.

16. Koltay, Emery, ed. *Irregular Serials and Annuals: An International Directory.* New York: R. R. Bowker, 1972.

A subject arrangement—with title and subject index—of some 18,000 serials and continuations. Useful for location of magazine supplements and annuals. Complete bibliographic information.

17. *Standard Periodical Directory.* annual, 1964–   , New York: Oxbridge.

Concentrates on American magazines. Listed by subject with full bibliographic details, and usually with a brief descriptive note. Title and subject guide.

18. *Standard Rate & Data Media Catalogs.* Skokie: Standard Rate & Data Service.

Two Standard publications are relevant here: *Business Publication Rates and Data* and *Consumer Magazine and Farm Publication Rates and Data.* While published primarily for advertisers seeking data on rates, format, circulation, etc., the service is useful for the capsule annotations which precede almost all listed magazine titles. The annotations are noncritical, but give an excellent summary of content. The firm publishes a number of other well-known services on television, spot radio rates, and newspapers, to name a few. Unfortunately, as all of the services are directed to advertisers and publishers, the vast number of scholarly and nonprofit journals are not usually listed.

19. *Ulrich's International Periodical Directory 1971/72,* 14th ed. 2 vols. New York: R. R. Bowker, 1971.

Covers over 50,000 magazines, here and abroad, in all fields of interest. Arranged alphabetically by subject, with a title index. Complete bibliographic details for each title. Particularly useful for libraries as it indicates in which index(es) or abstracting service(s) the listed magazine is noted. The basic guide to magazines for any library in the United States and abroad. Supplements keep the work updated between editions.

20. *Working Press of the Nation: Magazine Directory.* Vol. 2. annual, 1947–   , New York: National Research Bureau.

Primarily for advertisers and those actively engaged in the business. Still, the information is often useful to a librarian or a layman seeking unbiased data about a given publication. For purposes of content information, however, not as helpful as the *Standard Rate and Data Media Catalogs* (No. 18).

21. *Writers' and Artists' Year Book.* annual, 1906–   , London: Adam & Charles Black.

Contains both English and American magazines which publish material of interest to authors, i.e., fiction, articles, plays, cartoons, poetry, etc. Annotations indicate type of material the magazine uses. Often gives a truer picture of a magazine's interests than annotations in some other sources.

22. *Writer's Market.* annual, 1929–   . Cincinnati: Writer's Digest.

A market guide which lists close to 4,000 periodicals, with data on types of materials wanted for publication. Not only useful for free-lance writers, but an invaluable guide to the type of material magazine publishers are seeking. (See also No. 206.)

23. *The Writer's Handbook.* irreg. Boston: The Writer, Inc.

Published by *The Writer,* a competitor of *Writer's Digest.* Differs from the *Writer's Market* in that most emphasis (584pp.) is devoted to how to write, where to sell, etc. The remainder, some 200 pages, is given over to market information. Of the two, *Writer's Market* is preferable for up-to-date material on a broader scale; but the *Writer's Handbook* would be a first for general reading about the subject.

Union Lists

24. *British Union Catalogue of Periodicals.* 4 vols. London: Butterworth, 1955–1958.

The four basic volumes locate more than 140,000 titles in 440 British libraries. Quarterly and annual cumulations list magazines which began publication after January 1, 1960. The *World List of Scientific Periodicals* (No. 303) is continued in the *British Union Catalogue.*

25. Freitag, Ruth S. *Union Lists of Serials: a bibliography.* Washington: Library of Congress, 1964.

A geographical listing, by region and country, of around 1,200 union lists. Takes in separate lists and those published as parts of journals or books. A bit dated, but still useful. *New Serial Titles* (No. 26) lists some union lists.

26. *New Serial Titles.* 8/yr., 1961–   . Washington: Library of Congress, and New York: R. R. Bowker.

A continuation of the *Union List of Serials* (No. 27). Has various editions, cumulations, and supplements. Lists by title some 165,000 serials which began publishing January 1, 1950 or later. Shows over 6,000,000 locations, and records title changes, suspensions, etc. Supplemented by monthly and annual volumes. There is also a *Subject Index to New Serial Titles* (Ann Arbor: Pierian Press, 1968) with Dewey approach.

27. *Union List of Serials in Libraries of the United States and Canada,* 3rd ed. 5 vols. New York: H. W. Wilson, 1965.

An alphabetical listing of 156,499 serials held by 956 libraries in the United States and Canada. Complete bibliographic data. Particularly useful for beginning and ending dates of publication and changes in name. Covers through December 1949.

Guides

Note: There are a large number of guides—usually free to libraries—issued by various commercial agencies. The two listed here are representative, and the listing in no way constitutes an endorsement of the agencies by the compiler of this bibliography.

28. F. W. Faxon Library Subscription Agency. *The Faxon Librarians' Guide to Periodicals.* annual. Westwood: F. W. Faxon.

Alphabetical by title. One of the most complete commercial catalogs (over 40,000 titles). No annotations, but does include information on indexing.

29. Franklin Square-Mayfair Subscription Agency. *Periodical Handbook.* annual. Teaneck: Franklin Square.

Includes an alphabetical list of some 6,000 periodicals, a classified index, and then brief annotations for: general interest and farm publications, business and trade publications, and educational, medical and scientific periodicals. Annotations are noncritical. Bibliographic information includes price, frequency of self-indexing, editor's name, and sometimes indexing services.

Current Reviews

See also Children's and Teenage Magazines

30. *Bulletin of Bibliography.* 3/yr., 1900– .

Its subtitle is descriptive: "Births, deaths and magazine notes: a record of new titles, changed titles, deaths in the periodical world." Usually simple listing without annotations. Augments *New Serial Titles* (No. 26) for this kind of information.

31. *College and Research Libraries.* monthly, 1939– .

Has a biannual feature, usually in September and March, which includes brief critical annotations of 50 to 75 new magazines of particular value to academic and research libraries.

32. *Library Journal.* semimonthly, 1876– .

Since January 1, 1967, has carried a column, "Magazines," edited by Bill Katz, which covers recent magazine entries in all fields, but with stress upon those in the humanities, literature, and the social sciences. The 50 to 100-word annotations are by the editor and guest contributors. Signed.

33. *Library Resources and Technical Services.* quarterly, 1955– .

An annual feature is "A Survey of Serial Activities During ____," which concentrates primarily on bibliographic control, i.e., bibliographies, indexes, abstracts, etc. Little information on new magazines per se, yet invaluable for ancillary material.

34. *New Periodicals Report.* monthly, 1967– . Box 4406, New York, N.Y. 10017.

A four-page newsletter which briefly annotates some 15 or 20 new titles per month. While helpful—it has a cumulative index—most of the titles are covered in more depth, often more critically, in the standard review services.

35. *Stechert-Hafner Book News.* 9/yr., 1945– .

"Periodicals and other Serials" is a title listing, with full bibliographic information. No annotations, but useful as a check on new magazines, particularly in the sciences and foreign publications.

Evaluation; Management of Magazines in Libraries; Use Studies

36. Allen, Walter C., ed. *Serial Publications in Large Libraries.* Univ. of Illinois Graduate School of Library Science, Allerton Park Institute Publication No. 16. 1970. Available from Illini Union Bookstore, 715 S. Wright St., Champaign, Ill. 61820.

Eleven institute papers, concerning selection, acquisition, cataloging, and other aspects of serials.

37. Bates, Marcia J., *User Studies: A Review for Librarians and Information Scientists.* n.p., 1971. (ERIC Document 047 738)

A selective review covering 181 user studies from the standpoints of both the user and the library. Analyses of whole information systems and the methodology and philosophy of user studies are included. Some direct and indirect pertinence to use of periodicals. The studies are listed.

38. Brooks, B.C. "Obsolescence of Special Library Periodicals: Sampling errors and utility contours." *Journal of the American Society for Information Science* 21 (Sept.-Oct. 1970): 320–329.

Argues that discarding policies must vary with circumstances in each library, but suggests techniques that have general utility. A mathematical model is presented.

39. Brooks, B.C. "Optimum P Percent Library of Scientific Periodicals." *Nature* 232 (Aug. 13, 1971): 458–461.

Describes a quantitative method for determining the optimum percentage of periodicals for a library in a given field. Applies two empirical laws—Bradford's law of scatter and the negative exponential law of obsolescence.

This and the foregoing item are included as being representative of an approach to various problems of library management that seem to be susceptible to the application of the Bradford and related distributions. (See also No. 46.)

40. Burns, Robert W., Jr. *An Investigation into the Significance of Age as a Factor in Selecting an Optimum Circulation Period(s) for Serials.* Fort Collins: Colorado State Univ. Libraries, 1970. (ERIC Document 048 881)

Finds that heaviest use occurs in first five years, that use is inversely proportional to age, and that perhaps, beginning with the sixth year, short loan periods are no longer called for.

41. Claridge, P. R. P. "Microfiching of Periodicals from the User's Point of View." *Aslib Proceedings* 21 (Aug. 1969): 306–311.

A look at one library's experience with an increasingly valuable microform, including space comparisons with hard copy.

42. Clasquin, Frank F. "The Jobber's Side: Cost of Acquiring Periodicals." *RQ* 10 (Summer 1971): 328–330.

Another slant on a practical problem. (See also No. 52).

43. *Coombs, Donald J.* "Information Exchange; Serials: Free, Gift & Exchange Programs." *Wilson Library Bulletin* 45 (June 1971): 1010–1011.

Some practical suggestions about the vexed problem of "free," "gift," and "exchange" serials.

44. Coover, W. "User Needs and their Effect on Information Center Administration: A Review 1953/66." *Special Libraries* 60 (Sept. 1969): 446–456.

Details various techniques for determining user need, describes user and system interaction, and discusses administrative aspects.

45. Davinson, Donald E. *The Periodicals Collection: Its Purpose and Uses in Libraries.* London: Deutsch, 1969.

A reworking of his earlier *Periodicals* (2nd ed., 1964). This is a handbook, useful for students and librarians alike.

46. Goffman, William, and Thomas G. Morris. "Bradford's Law and Library Acquisitions." *Nature* 226 (June 6, 1970): 922–923.

Another application of Bradford's law (see No. 39) as an acquisitions aid, here utilizing periodical circulation data. A shortened version of this appears in T. Saracevic, ed. *Introduction to Information Science.* New York: R. R. Bowker, 1970, pp. 200–203, with the title "Bradford's Law Applied to the Maintenance of Library Collections."

47. Huff, William Howard. "Acquisition of Serial Publications." *Library Trends* 18 (Jan. 1970): 294–317.

Results of a survey of practices and problems connected with serials in 49 American research libraries, with observations on such matters as agents, exchange, foreign serials, etc.

48. Katz, Bill. *Magazine Selection: How to Build a Community-Oriented Collection.* New York: R. R. Bowker, 1971.

In the author's own words, "the purpose of this book is to suggest several approaches to magazine selection—approaches which may or may not be acceptable to all librarians. . . . Emphasis is on selection, not on the technical aspects of acquisition and record keeping. Also, the stress is primarily upon the general American magazine." In conclusion there is a summary and interpretation of the results of a 1969–1970 survey of public library practice. Definitely aimed at the public librarian, should be of value to anyone interested in magazines and their function, and to librarians wherever.

49. Paul, Huibert. "Serials: Chaos and Standardization." *Library Resources and Technical Services* 14 (Winter 1970): 19–30.

Proposes standardization of titles and other criteria, with enforcement through the U.S. Post Office, to help eliminate costly inefficiency.

50. Pound, Mary. "Serials: A Review of 1970." *Library Resources and Technical Services* 15 (Spring 1971): 143–149.

51. Pound, Mary. "A Serials Synopsis: 1969." *Library Resources and Technical Services* 14 (Spring 1970): 231–235.

This item and the one preceding it are examples of the annual reviews mentioned in No. 33.

52. Smith, Katherine R. "Serials Agents/Serials Librarians." *Library Resources and Technical Services* 14 (Winter 1970): 5–18.

Presents methods of choosing an agent for a particular library, and means of evaluating existing relationships between serials librarian and agent. (See also No. 42.)

53. Trueswell, Richard W. "Article Use and Its Relationship to Individual User Satisfaction." *College and Research Libraries* 31 (July 1970): 239–245.

One way of using use statistics to determine optimum journal holdings.

54. Williams, Gordon, et al. *Library Cost Models: Owning Versus Borrowing Serial Publications.* Washington: Office of Science Information, National Science Foundation, 1968.

Suggests that a journal which is used less frequently than four times per year can be more cheaply provided through interlibrary loan than through a paid subscription.

55. Zwemer, Raymond L. "Identification of Journal Characteristics Useful in Improving Input and Output of a Retrieval System." *Federation Proceedings* (Federation of American Societies for Experimental Biology) 29 (Sept. 1970): 1595–1604.

An assessment of criteria by which one might identify a journal of quality. Though based primarily upon analysis of biomedical journals, much of this is certainly applicable to serial publication in other fields. (See also Nos. 128, 223.)

Foreign

56. Feuereisen, Fritz. *Die Presse in Europa/The Press in Europe.* München-Pullach: Verlag Dokumentation; New York: R. R. Bowker, 1971.

57. Feuereisen, Fritz, and Ernst Schmacke. *Die Presse in Asien und Ozeanien.* München-Pullach: Verlag Dokumentation, 1968.

Both of these are handbooks primarily for advertisers. Newspapers (mostly) and magazines arranged by country, giving address, frequency, language, readership, size and other such information of interest to advertisers. In German and English.

58. "Foreign Literary Periodicals." in *Literary Market Place.* annual, 1940–. New York: R. R. Bowker.

Arranged by country. Taken from Ulrich (No. 19).

59. *Foreign Periodicals on Non-Literary Topics: French, German, Italian, Russian, Spanish.* Information Guide No. 3. London: Centre for Information on Language Teaching, 1969(?). (ERIC Document 039 790)

Principally a guide to bibliographies of foreign periodicals, but has a select list of journals.

60. Gidwani, N. N., and K. Navlani. *Indian Periodicals: An Annotated Guide.* Jaipur: N. N. Gidwani, 1969.

Claims to be "the most complete picture of the present Indian situation in the field of journal publishing in English." Two lists, one classified, one alphabetical by title, of over 5,000 titles. Some annotations.

61. Peterson, Agnes F. *Western Europe: A Survey of Holdings at the Hoover Institution on War, Revolution and Peace.* Stanford: The Institution, 1970.

Lists holdings of current and noncurrent periodicals and newspapers from the countries concerned.

62. *The Press in . . . Latin America . . . Africa . . . Asia.* 3 vols. New York: R. R. Bowker, 1968.

Although primarily a listing, by country, of newspapers, the three volumes are of interest to magazine-oriented librarians for one major reason. Each concludes with a section devoted to what magazines (and newspapers) are issued internationally, such as *Time, The Economist,* and *Fortune.* Entries include title, where issued, address, circulation, frequency, language, type of readers, format, printing method, price of advertising, and closing date for advertising. Similar information is given for all of the newspapers listed in the main body of the work—some 600 in Latin America, 365 in Africa, and 628 in Asia.

63. U.S. Library of Congress. *The USSR and Eastern Europe: Periodicals in Western Languages,* 3rd ed. Washington: The Library, 1967.

Selected list of around 700 titles *about* the USSR and Eastern Europe, mostly in English, French, and German. Annotated.

64. Vaughan, H. R. *Overseas Newspapers and Periodicals Guidebook,* 9th ed. 2 vols. London: Publishing and Distributing Company, 1969.

Volume 1, *Markets in Europe;* Volume 2, *Markets Outside Europe.* Like some of the others, this is aimed at advertisers, but useful for other information about the magazines covered.

65. Woodworth, David. *Guide to Current British Journals.* London: The Library Association, 1970.

Classified list. For the most part descriptions are based on publishers' replies to a questionnaire. Gives full publication details, plus indexing and "level of appeal" information. Over 2,800 titles included. Has index, and an appendix lists titles that include abstracts. Updates the 1962 publication with the same title by Mary Toase. (See also Nos. 74, 101, 104, 145, 146, 164, 196, 241, 249, 292, 294, 307.) See also Africa section.

Audiences

Who reads what, and why? This should be of primary concern to librarians, and there are a number of articles in this important subject area. None is listed here, as all major ones will be found in Schacht's bibliography (No. 14). An excellent index to such material is *Psychological Abstracts,* and as Schacht points out, "many journalism libraries have dozens of studies of audiences of individual magazines," usually conducted by professional services for the publisher. Certain aspects of "audience" analysis are represented in the use studies and other items cited elsewhere in this bibliography.

Ongoing research into audience reaction—at the commercial level—will be found in the standard advertising magazines such as *Media/Scope, Advertising Age,* and *Media Decisions.* The *Journalism Quarterly* and the *Columbia Journalism Review* are the two best sources of scholarly, well-researched articles on individual magazines and their audiences, and *Public Opinion Quarterly* is also an occasional source.

Economics of Publishing

66. *Media Industry Newsletter.* weekly, 1947–   , New York: Business Magazine.

Averaging six to eight pages, this presents information on editorial attitudes, advertising, and circulation of major magazine publishers. The material is in capsule form, and the total a refreshing insight into the magazine business as it is practiced, not as it is plugged.

67. *Report of the Task Group on the Economics of Primary Publishing.* Washington: National Academy of Sciences, 1970. (ERIC Document 041 187)

Considers the role of primary journals, production costs, library costs, financial policies, and numerous other aspects of the topic. Makes recommendations pertaining to the operation and financing of primary journals.

68. Welter, Rush. *Problems of Scholarly Publication in the Humanities and Social Sciences.* New York: American Council of Learned Societies, 1959.

A study which surveys some 75 learned journals. Basic problems are still much the same as they were when this work was published. (See also Nos. 202, 255, 301.)

Part II. SPECIFIC SUBJECTS, AUDIENCES, TYPES

Aeronautics and Space Science

69. *Aerospace Bibliography,* 5th ed. Washington: National Aerospace Education Council, 1970. (ERIC Document 040 882)

Part 4 is an annotated list of periodicals. Aimed at elementary and secondary teachers, and the general adult reader.

70. Hilburn, Paul. *Aerospace Science Education: A Curriculum Guide.* Juneau: Alaska State Department of Education, 1968. (ERIC Document 032 233)

Has an unannotated list of 18 aerospace periodicals.

71. U.S. Library of Congress. *Aeronautics and Space Serial Publications: A World List.* Washington: U.S. Government Printing Office, 1962.

An unannotated listing of 4,551 titles from 76 countries. Considerably dated, but basic and still available.

Africa

72. Berman, Sanford. "African Magazines for American Libraries," *Library Journal* 95 (Apr. 1, 1970): 1289–1293.

Selected, annotated bibliography of English-language titles which were produced wholly or mainly by Africans in Africa.

73. de Benko, Eugene, and Patricia L. Butts. *Research Sources for African Studies: A Checklist of Relevant Serial Publications Based on Library Collections at [Michigan State University].* East Lansing: African Studies Center, 1969.

Alphabetical listing of about 2,100 titles. Because it includes some kinds of materials excluded from the Library of Congress list (No. 78), will serve to supplement it, though containing approximately half as many entries. Subject index.

74. Feuereisen, Fritz, and Ernst Schmacke. *Africa: A Guide to Newspapers and Magazines.* New York: Africana Publishing Corp., 1970.

75. Feuereisen, Fritz, and Ernst Schmacke. *Die Presse in Afrika.* München-Pullach: Verlag Dokumentation, 1968.

Same information and arrangement as in Nos. 56, 57.

76. Maison des Sciences de l'Homme. *World List of Specialized Periodicals: African Studies.* Paris: Mouton, 1969.

Lists 492 titles concerned with Africa south of the Sahara, published there or elsewhere. Much less extensive than the Library of Congress list (No. 78).

77. "Periodicals and Magazines on African Literature." *Africana Library Journal* 1 (Fall 1970): 14–20.

Features what it calls major literary and cultural periodicals, and also cites general Africanist journals which frequently include creative writing from Africa and/or material about African literature. Annotated.

78. U.S. Library of Congress. *Sub-Saharan Africa: A Guide to Serials.* Washington: The Library, 1970.

"Publications relating to Africa south of the Sahara that are issued in Western languages or in African languages that use the Roman alphabet," regardless of where published. Even with its intentional exclusions (e.g. certain government publications), this list gives bibliographic information about 4,670 titles, with some brief annotations. Has subject index.

Blacks

79. Buckley, Richard D. "Negro Periodicals: Historical Notes and Suggestions for Use." *Social Education* 33 (Apr. 1969): 426–428.

80. Levi, Doris J., and Nerissa L. Milton. *Directory of Black Literary Magazines.* Washington: Negro Bibliography and Research Center, 1970.

Lists about 75 magazines, with nonevaluative annotations.

81. Schneider, Joyce B. *Selected List of Periodicals Relating to Negroes, with Holdings in the Libraries of Yale University.* Bibliography Series No. 2, New Haven: Yale Univ. Library, 1970.

Emphasis is on the Negro in the United States. Has many current titles, but will probably be of special use to libraries trying to build a historical collection in the subject.

Agriculture

82. Crane, Eva. "Where Bee Research is Published." *Bee World* 52 (1971): 27–32.

May not be of paramount importance to everyone, but has some broader application. A compilation of a core list of most productive journals for *Agricultural Abstracts.* Compares results with similar studies of *Physics Abstracts* and *Cardiovascular Serial Literature.*

83. Gill, W. R. "Locating Foreign Scientific Information." *Agricultural Engineering* 50 (Jan. 1969): 22–23.

How to conduct a search of foreign literature in the sciences, especially those related to agriculture. Nine indexes that most libraries have are described, plus several agencies from which one might obtain translations or learn if any particular item has been translated. A practical article, suggesting ways to fill the gap left when *Agricultural and Horticultural Engineering Abstracts* ceased publication (in 1967).

84. International Association of Agricultural Librarians and Documentalists. *Quarterly Bulletin.* 1956— .

Carries a list of new agricultural serials.

85. Littleton, Isaac T. "The Literature of Agricultural Economics: Its bibliographic organization and use." *Library Quarterly* 39 (Apr. 1969): 140–152.

An informative study of the bibliographic control in this field.

86. U.S. National Agricultural Library. *Serial Publications Indexed in Bibliography of Agriculture,* rev. ed. Washington: The Library, 1968.

87. von Frauendorfer, Sigmund. *Survey of Abstracting Services and Current Bibliographical Tools in Agriculture, Forestry, Fisheries, Nutrition, Veterinary Medicine and Related Subjects,* Munich: BLV Verlagsgesellschaft, 1969.

Besides a general narrative survey, has a list of 692 titles, with full bibliographic descriptions. Originally done for the Food and Agricultural Organization.

Indians (American)

88. *American Indians: An Annotated Bibliography of Selected Library Resources.* St. Paul: Univ. of Minnesota Library Institute for Minnesota Indians, 1970. (ERIC Document 040 004)

Sixteen titles of Indian-oriented periodicals annotated, with titles of 16 others considered to be excellent sources. Not restricted to Minnesota Indians. Grade level indicated.

89. Brown, Carol, and Celeste West. "A Bibliography of Indian Newspapers and Periodicals." *Synergy* No. 25 (Jan.-Feb. 1970): 4–10.

Annotated list of about 40 current publications, with "first purchase" recommendations.

90. Bush, Alfred L., and Robert S. Fraser. *American Indian Periodicals in the Princeton University Library: A Preliminary List.* Princeton: the Library, 1971. (ERIC Document 050 847)

Lists 271 periodicals published by and for American Indians, current and no longer published.

91. Price, John. *U.S. and Canadian Indian Periodicals.* Minneapolis: Training Center for Community Programs, Univ. of Minnesota, 1971. (ERIC Document 051 940)

Lists 113 newspapers and magazines, and gives publishers' addresses.

Anthropology

92. *International Bibliography of Social and Cultural Anthropology.* annual, 1955— . London: Stevens & Sons.

Includes periodical articles, and is a useful checklist for new titles.

Archaeology

93. *Antiquity.* quarterly, 1927— .

"New Archaeological Journals" is an occasional feature.

Architecture

94. Branch, Melville C. *Comprehensive Urban Planning: A Selective Annotated Bibliography with Related Materials.* Beverly Hills: Sage, 1970.

Pages 133–134 give a list of about 110 periodicals, with the number of times cited indicated for each. Could be a helpful selection guide.

95. Finrow, Jerry. "Current Information: Literature Surveys." *AIA Journal* 52 (Oct. 1969): 85–86.

The second column of what is planned to be a regular feature on research resources. Periodical information included.

96. Harvard University. *Catalogue of the Library of the Graduate School of Design.* 44 vols. Boston: G. K. Hall, 1968.

Of the approximately 1,700 periodicals listed, nearly 400 were current at time of publication. A complete list is found under "Periodicals."

97. Lawrence, Deloris. *Architecture, Building, and Engineering.* Washington: U.S. Air Force, 1970.

One of a series of basic bibliographies for Pacific air force base libraries. Has a selected list of periodicals in the fields named.

98. Roberts, Margaret. "Use of Periodicals in Architecture." *Construction Industry Information Group [CIIG] Bulletin* 1 (Jan. 1971): 7–12.

Surveys opinions of the role of the periodical in architecture, and reports recent findings that architects (like almost any other group) read a very small proportion of available journals.

99. Stephens, Suzanne. "Architectural Journalism Analyzed: Reflections on a Half-Century." *Progressive Architecture* 51 (June 1970): 132–39.

A state-of-the-art report. Some emphasis on the magazine in which the article appears, but attention is drawn to architectural journals in general. Discusses the role of the architectural journal, and what journalistic techniques are appropriate. (See also No. 184.)

Art

100. *Art Journal.* quarterly, 1941– .

Has a more or less regular feature, "Periodicals," with comments about both new and established journals.

101. *International Directory of Arts.* annual, 1952– . Berlin: Deutsche Zentraldruckeri.

Includes a list of art periodicals, arranged by country, usually with address but little other information.

Bibliography

102. Harvard University Library. *Bibliography and Bibliography Periodicals.* Widener Library Shelflist No. 7. Cambridge: Harvard Univ. Press, 1966.

An unannotated list of 19,586 titles which cover bibliography (interpreted in one of its wider senses). Other shelflists in this series also include periodicals in various subject areas, but are of limited use except as checklists.

103. Ulrich, Carolyn. *Books and Printing.* Woodstock: Rudge, 1943.

Although now quite dated, a still useful checklist for periodicals published between 1800 and 1942. Subject arrangement.

Biological Sciences

104. Abrams, Fred. "A Market Survey: Translations of Foreign Language Biomedical Periodicals." *RQ* 10 (Summer 1971): 321–324.

Reports the preferences of 43 medical school libraries for hypothesized cover-to-cover translations of 58 journals.

105. Gurtowski, C. Grace. *Selected Current Primary Serial Publications in the Biological Sciences.* Council on Biological Sciences Information Working Document No. 1. Bethesda: Federation of American Societies for Experimental Biology, 1970. (ERIC Document 045 342)

About 600 titles that are current, issued at least twice a year, covered by at least three major indexing and abstracting services. Titles are devoted mainly to the publication of original research. A "core" collection. Unannotated.

106. *List of Journals Indexed in Index Medicus.* Bethesda: National Library of Medicine, 1971.

Includes title, subject, and country lists of 2,199 journals.

107. "Listmanship: Recommended Lists of Journals for the Hospital Library." *Medical Library Association Bulletin* 57 (Oct. 1969): 401.

Editorial observations on the proliferation of select lists of journals, with conclusion that "the trick is not to make a list, but to find a way of making a selection of titles that will reflect the best of the present and will suggest the best of the future in this quicksilver field called science." (See also No. 110.)

108. Shilling, Charles W., and Mildred C. Benton. *Serials Relating to Biochemistry and Endocrinology: Their Identification and an Analysis of Their Characteristics.* BSCP Communique, 1965, 21. Washington: Biological Sciences Communication Project, George Washington Univ., 1965.

Dated, but useful.

109. Steere, William C., ed. *Information Handling in the Life Sciences.* Washington: Division of Biology and Agriculture, National Research Council, 1970. (ERIC Document 040 722)

A state-of-the-art report with information on users, informal transfer of information, primary publications, secondary services, and libraries. Some recommendations are made. Should be of interest to all concerned with information in this field, or in any science.

110. Timour, John A. "Selected Lists of Journals for the Small Medical Library: A Comparative Analysis." *Medical Library Association Bulletin* 59 (Jan. 1971): 87–93.

Describes the results of a survey and weighted summary of 12 major suggested journal subscription lists for hospital libraries. There are citations here for the 12. (See No. 107 for editorial comment about lists in general.)

111. Williams, Peter C. *Abbreviated Titles of Biological Journals,* 3rd ed. London: The Biological Council, 1968.

Culled from the *World List of Scientific Periodicals* (No. 302), with indications of the abbreviations recommended by the U.S.A. Standards Institute where these differ. No bibliographical information, just titles and abbreviations, arranged by title.

Blind. See Physically Handicapped.

Books and Book Reviews

112. Bowman, Lois Hassenauer. "A Study of Book Reviews in Popular Magazines for Young Adults." M.A. thesis, Catholic Univ. 1968.

113. Busha, Charles H. "An Evaluation of Four Book Review Media Commonly Used by Public Libraries. . . ." *South Carolina Librarian* 12 (Mar. 1968): 29–34.

A study of promptness of reviewing and how well the *Library Journal, New York Times Book Review, Saturday Review,* and *Booklist* meet the needs of librarians.

114. Gray, Richard A. *A Guide to Book Review Citations: A Bibliography of Sources.* Columbus: Ohio State Univ. Press, 1969.

Some of the sources are monographic, some are serials. Because of the subject arrangement, could be useful in selecting periodicals on a basis of their book reviewing scope.

115. Wall, C. Edward. "Book Reviewing Indexes." *RQ* 10 (Winter 1970): 140–142.

Comments about *Book Review Digest* and other index-type sources.

Business

116. Baker, Anthony. *Union List of Current Commercial Periodicals.* London: Library Association, 1968.

An alphabetical listing of 978 titles, with minimal bibliographic information. Covers economics, accounting, banking, insurance, management, commercial law, statistics, shipping, and general trade. International, but emphasis is on British periodicals.

117. Coman, Edwin T. *Sources of Business Information,* 2nd rev. ed. Berkeley: Univ. of California Press, 1964.

This standard guide to the literature includes a section on American and Canadian periodicals and business publications. Another useful general guide, although more dated than Coman, is Marian C. Manley's *Business Information* (New York: Harper, 1955).

118. Fink, Louis C. "Digesting Financial News." *Burroughs Clearing House* 54 (Mar. 1970): 30 ff.

Suggestions about how to keep up with the literature.

119. Forsythe, David P. *The Business Press in America, 1750–1865.* Philadelphia: Chilton, 1963.

A history of the growth and development of a major type of magazine which is only touched on lightly by other histories.

120. Frank, Nathalie D. Data Sources for Business and Market Analysis, 2nd ed. Metuchen: Scarecrow, 1969.

Especially strong on U.S. government publications in this field, it also lists many commercially published serials. Annotated.

121. Georgi, Charlotte. "How to Keep a Business Library Going: Lesson Number Two." *Library Journal* 93 (Mar. 1, 1968): 959–963.

A bibliography. Includes indexes, abstracts, journals, and newspapers. See also her "How to Start a Business Library in One Easy Lesson," *Library Journal* 90 (Mar. 1, 1965): 1058–1062.

122. Harvard University. Graduate School of Business Administration. Baker Library. *Current Journals in the Library,* 7th ed. Cambridge: The Library, 1969.

Has two parts, a title list and a subject list.

123. IAA World Directory of Marketing Communications Periodicals. New York: International Advertising Association, 1968.

This comes out every once in awhile, "as needed."

124. *U.S. Department of Commerce Periodicals to Aid Businessmen.* Washington: Government Printing Office, 1969.

Describes about 75 titles, grouped under broad headings such as "Population Statistics" and "Retail and Wholesale Trade." (See also No. 303.) See also Investments Section.

Chemistry

125. Barker, Dale B., "World's Chemical Literature Continues to Expand," *Chemical and Engineering News* v. 49 (July 12, 1971): pp. 37–40.

125a. *CAS Source Index Quarterly.* 1969– . Columbus: American Chemical Society.

One of the numerous publications of the Chemical Abstracts Service, this gives full bibliographic data and library locations for all sources cited in *Chemical Abstracts.* It cumulates annually into the *CAS Source Index.* This title supersedes *ACCESS,* which in turn superseded the *CA List of Periodicals* (1961–1967). The thoroughness of *CA* is deservedly famous, and a recent cumulation of sources—*ACCESS* for 1969—contained over 10,000 titles, most of which were serials.

126. *International Chemistry Directory, 1969/70.* annual, 1969–. New York: Benjamin.

Has a "journals" section, listing about 260 titles, with full bibliographic information.

127. Marquardt, D. N. *Guidelines and Suggested Title List for Undergraduate Chemistry Libraries.* Serial Publication No. 44. Stanford: Stanford Univ. Department of Chemistry, Advisory Council on College Chemistry, 1969. (ERIC Document 040 037)

Lists, with some comments, recommended journals, abstracts, and reviews.

128. Panton, D., and B. G. Reuben. "What do Chemists Read?" *Chemistry in Britain* 7 (Jan. 1971): 18–22.

As a model of an attempt to measure the usefulness of an academic library's journals, this report may be a guide to those seeking to do the same. The report suggests that, at least in chemistry, the library was not getting its money's worth.

128a. Reid, E. Emmet. *Invitation to Chemical Research.* Palisade, N.J.: Franklin Publishing Co., 1961.

Chicano

129. Kennedy, Diane. "Chicano Press." *Missouri Library Association Quarterly* 30 (Sept. 1969): 221–224.

Includes about 35 newspapers and magazines addressed to Spanish-speaking Americans.

130. Nogales, Luis G. *The Mexican American: A Selected and Annotated Bibliography.* Stanford: Center for Latin American Studies, Stanford University, 1971. (ERIC Document 050 865)

A list of 64 Chicano periodicals. This is a second edition, and a more comprehensive third edition is planned.

Urban Studies

131. McMurrey, Katherine M., and B. Shelton. "Regional Periodicals: Bane or Boon?" *Texas Libraries* 33 (Spring 1971): 25–30.

132. "Metropolitan Magazines," *Publisher's Weekly* 197 (Mar. 30, 1970): 36–37.

A review of selected "city" magazines.

Consumer Services

133. International Organization of Consumer Unions. *Consumers Directory 1971–72*. The Hague: IOCU, 1971.

A national listing of consumer groups with full information on publications, if any, issued by said groups. The IOCU is an international, nonprofit organization which has a membership in 32 countries.

134. U.S. Office of Consumer Affairs and N.Y. Public Library. *Consumer Education Bibliography*. Washington: Supt. of Documents, U. S. Govt. Printing Office, 1971.

An annotated review of over 4,000 books, pamphlets, periodical articles, audiovisual aids, and teacher materials relating to consumer interests and consumer education.

Dance

135. Belknap, Sara. Y. *Guide to Dance Periodicals*. New York: Scarecrow, 1948– .

An index to some 18 periodicals, which the compiler has taken back to 1931, and is slowly working through to the present. While an index and a bibliography, it serves as a selection guide, particularly for those magazines not indexed in *Music Index*.

Deaf. See Physically Handicapped.

Physically Handicapped

136. *American Annals of the Deaf.* 5/yr., 1847– . Washington: Gallaudet College.

Has an annual listing of "Periodicals for the Deaf."

137. *DSH Abstracts.* quarterly, 1960– . Washington: Deafness, Speech and Hearing Publishing Co.

For material on deafness, speech, and hearing the list of abstracted periodicals should be a good guide.

138. McIntyre, Keren H. *Bibliography on the Deaf and Hard of Hearing*. Los Angeles: Instructional Materials Center, Univ. of Southern California, 1968. (ERIC Document 040 524)

Includes a list of ten or so periodicals and other serials for or about the deaf.

139. "Periodicals Dealing with Rehabilitation and the Handicapped." In Edward W. Lowman and Judith L. Klinger. *Aids to Independent Living: Self-Help for the Handicapped*, pp. 742–748. New York: McGraw-Hill, 1969.

Gives subscription information on about 130 titles, most of which are completely devoted to, or frequently have articles on, rehabilitation. Should be about as comprehensive a list as most libraries would need.

140. U. S. Library of Congress. Division for the Blind and Physically Handicapped. *Magazines: Braille and Recorded*. Washington: The Library, 1968.

Underground Newspapers

Note: The literature on what are variously called "underground," "alternative," "dissident," "protest," and "radical" serial publications is fairly extensive. Items included here are principally those which have some bibliographic utility, though some interpretive pieces have been cited. For leads to more of the latter, see No. 154, below. See also under Little Magazines, a term which is sometimes associated with the type of publication listed here.

141. *Alternatives! Periodicals of the Counter Culture.* mimeo., free, 1971. Contact Richard Greene, Free Public Library of Woodbridge, 800 Rahway Ave., Woodbridge, N.J. 07095.

142. Cooper, John C. *The Turn Right*. Philadelphia: Westminster, 1970.

A selected, unannotated list of newspapers and periodicals, both rightist and leftist, is included in this study of a modern political phenomenon.

143. Douglas, John R. "Tribal Literature: Publications of the Counter Culture." *Wilson Library Bulletin* 45 (Dec. 1970): 364–371.

Recommended titles among those published by the "agrarian" (as opposed to urban) underground press. The unifying theme is concern for the use of natural resources.

144. Goldwater, Walter. *Radical Periodicals in America, 1890–1950*, 1st rev. ed. New Haven: Yale Univ. Press, 1966.

An annotated list of 321 radical periodicals, giving information on the groups which issued them. Especially good for the earlier period.

145. Kehde, Ned. "Hip Corporations and Anti-Establishment Press of the Left." *Missouri Library Association Quarterly* 30 (Sept. 1969): 197–220.

See annotation next item.

146. Kehde, Ned. "Hip Corporations, Minimal Journalism, Late Sensate Thrills, and Others: A Supplement." *Missouri Library Association Quarterly* 30 (Dec. 1969): 332–340.

Between them, this and item No. 145 by the same author provide subscription information and some description of around 800 "underground" titles published throughout the world. A fulsome enough list for almost anybody's needs.

147. Leibl, A. "Canada's Underground Press." *Canadian Library Journal* 27 (Jan. 1970): 18–19 ff.

Has an annotated list.

148. Lewis, Roger. "American Underground Press." *Assistant Librarian* 63 (Aug. 1970): 122–224.

Observations for an audience of British professional librarians.

149. Muller, Robert H., et al. *From Radical Left to Extreme Right: A Bibliography of Current Periodicals of Protest, Controversy, [etc.] . . .*, 2nd ed. Ann Arbor: Campus Publishers, 1970.

The best single guide now available to such magazines. Full bibliographic information, with annotations, for over 400 titles.

150. Politella, Dario. *Director of the College Student Press in America*, 2nd ed. New York: Oxbridge, 1970.

Perhaps not all "dissident," but perhaps not all "establishment" either. Arranged by state, then by institution, giving address, faculty adviser's name, and advertising information. Has indexes by newspapers, yearbooks, and magazines.

151. "Publications on the Right." *Synergy* Nos. 18–19 (June-July 1969): 5–25.

Points out that the sheer volume of rightist material outnumbers that of the Left, title-to-title, about 20 to 1, and comments on 54 "representative samples within the conservative/right-wing spectrum, emphasizing California publications."

152. Spencer, Michael J. "Why is Youth so Revolting Nowadays: The Underground and New Left Press." *Wilson Library Bulletin* 43 (Mar. 1969): 640–647.

A sympathetic interpretation of the whys and wherefores of the dissident press.

153. Tatko, Daniel, and Carol Brown. "The Underground and New Left Press." *Wilson Library Bulletin* 43 (Mar. 1969): 648–652.

Companion piece to No. 152 above. About 30 publications are described.

154. Whitmore, Harry E. "Confrontation: The Library and THOSE Magazines." *RQ* 10 (Summer 1971): 313–317.

Has an annotated bibliography of writings about the dissident press.

155. Young-Smith, Lorna R. "Indexing of Periodicals of the Underground and Left-Wing." M.A. thesis, Univ. of Chicago, 1970.

(See also Nos. 233, 266.) See also Little Magazines Section.

Earth Sciences

156. Craig, J. E. G. "Characteristics of Use of Geology Literature." *College and Research Libraries* 30 (May 1969): 230–236.

A citation analysis, the results of which could be helpful in making decisions about the library management of specific serials.

157. Harvey, Anthony P. "Recent Developments in Geological Documentation and Bibliography," in *Geoscience Information Society Proceedings*. Vol. 1, pp. 27–53. Washington: The Society, 1969.

Reviews significant developments according to type of publication, such as bibliographies, reviews, etc. Though the review is somewhat dated ("recent" being circa 1967) this is valuable for its comments and thorough coverage of the field.

158. *A Survey of Authors on the Publication Practices in Meteorology.* Baltimore: Johns Hopkins University, 1968. (ERIC Document 045 334)

An analysis of six journals. Approach is indicative of how one might appraise other journals, even in other fields.

Ecology. See Environmental Sciences.

Economics

159. Fletcher, John. *The Use of Economics Literature.* Handen: Archon, 1971.

A chapter on general economics periodicals rates them by importance.

160. Fundaburk, Emma L. *Reference Materials and Periodicals in Economics.* Vol. 1. Metuchen: Scarecrow, 1971.

Agricultural economics is covered in the first of what is planned to be five volumes. Others to cover general economics, business and industry in general, specific industries in mining and manufacturing, and specific industries in services. An international, alphabetical, unannotated list of periodicals. Subject index.

161. Harvard University Library. *Economics and Economic Periodicals.* Widener Shelflist No. 23–24. Cambridge: The Library, 1970.

162. Institut fur Weltwirtschaft (Institute for World Economics, Kiel). *Standortskartei der Periodika (Shelflist of Periodical Holdings).* 6 vols. Boston: G. K. Hall, 1968.

The outstanding collection of this noted research library is here represented by 82,500 cards. The meticulous cataloging (title changes, editors, etc.) makes it a superior source for bibliographic information. However, because of its arrangement (by type, then size, then by sequential arbitrary location numbers) it must be used in conjunction with one of the other parts of this library's catalog, such as the *Titelkatalog (Title Catalog)*, also issued in book form by Hall.

163. *International Bibliography of Economics.* annual, 1952–. London: Stevens & Son.

Affords one of the best methods of keeping abreast of new periodicals. International.

164. *Latin American Economic and Social Serials.* London: Clive Bingley, 1969.

Concentrates on current and recent serials, excluding titles known to have ceased publication before 1945. Arranged for the most part by geographic area, including journals published in the area, and those concerned with the area but published elsewhere. Has title index and index of sponsoring bodies.

165. Organization for Economic Co-Operation and Development. *Library Catalogue of Periodicals, 1967–1968.* Paris: The Organization, 1968.

Current periodicals received at the library as of August 1, 1968.

Education

166. AASL-TEPS Coordinating Committee for the Teachers' Library Project. *The Teachers' Library.* Washington: National Education Association, 1968.

Lists and annotates about 100 periodicals, many of which are outside the field of education.

167. Camp, William L. *Guide to Periodicals in Education.* Metuchen: Scarecrow, 1968.

A guide for educators who wish to submit articles to periodicals for publication. Some 449 nationally distributed education magazines are listed, with bibliographic information and data on the type of material required.

168. Columbia University. Teachers College Library. *Periodicals Currently Received.* New York: Columbia Univ., 1968.

A basic alphabetical listing, useful as a checklist for larger collections.

169. Dews, J. David, and John Michael Smethurst. *Union List of Periodicals in Institute of Education Libraries as of 31 July 1968.* Newcastle Upon Tyne: Oriel Press, 1968.

170. Diener, Thomas J., and David L. Tower. *An Annotated Guide to Periodical Literature: Higher Education.* Athens: Institute of Higher Education, Georgia Univ., 1969. (ERIC Document 038 941)

171. Educational Press Association of America. *America's Education Press.* biennial, 1926–. Syracuse: School of Journalism, Syracuse Univ.

Classified list of education publications issued in the United States. Also includes an international list in English, French, and Spanish.

172. Hartung, A. Bruce. *A Writer's Guide to Journals in Education.* Dallas, N.C.: Gaston College, 1970.

173. Hefferlin, JB [sic] Lon. *Information Services for Academic Administration.* San Francisco: Jossey-Bass, 1971.

Has a chapter on publications that includes an annotated list of magazines. Emphasis is on higher education.

174. Herner, Saul, et al. *Study of Periodicals and Serials in Education. Final Report.* Washington: Herner & Co., 1968. (ERIC Document 017 747)

Analyzes index coverage of a basic list of 357 English-language periodicals, over half of which are described as being wholly in the field of education.

175. Manheim, Theodore, et al. *Sources in Educational Research: A Selected and Annotated Bibliography.* Vol. 1. Detroit: Wayne State Univ. Press, 1969.

Covers general and subject-oriented works in ten parts, each having a selected annotated list of periodicals. Future volumes are intended to cover other areas, such as history of education, educational administration, etc.

176. Narin, Francis. *Analysis of Research Journals, and Related Research Structure, in Special Education. Final Report.* Chicago: Computer Horizons, 1971. (ERIC Document 050 505)

Citation analysis involving 118 journals in general education, special education, and psychology, with some conclusions about scatter.

177. National Education Association. *NEA Handbook.* annual, 1945–   . Washington: The Association.

Lists publications of the NEA and also includes a number of periodicals from its 50 or so departments and units. Also useful is the annual *NEA Publications Catalog.*

178. Thurmas, R. S. *Annotated Bibliography of Education Periodicals in the William Allen White Library.* Emporia: Kansas State Teachers College, 1960.

A good basic list. The annotations make it particularly helpful for the medium to large size library. (See also No. 303.)

Engineering and Technology

179. *Publications Indexed for Engineering.* New York: Engineering Index, 1971.

Lists 2, 246 professional and trade journals, proceedings, transactions, etc., with essential bibliographic information.

180. Semler, E. G. "What's Wrong with the Technical Press?" *Chartered Mechanical Engineer* 17 (Dec. 1970): 491–494, 504.

Discusses commercial prestige journals, controlled circulation journals, and institutional publications. Suggests solutions to their various inadequacies and problems. (See also Nos. 293, 294, 295.)

Environmental Sciences

181. Brown, Carol. "Ecophilia: Selected Bibliography of Periodicals," *Synergy* No. 26 (Mar. 1970): 20–26.

An annotated list.

182. Durrenberger, Robert W. *Environment and Man: A Bibliography.* Palo Alto: National Press Books, 1970.

Has a list of the journals cited in this 2,225-item bibliography.

183. Finrow, Jerry. "Periodicals in Environmental Design." *AIA Journal* 51 (May 1969): 90.

Eight "special interest" periodicals, described as either "behavioral" or "methodological," annotated and with ordering information. Limited to newsletters of fairly recent origin reporting "hard" research.

183a. McDonald, Rita, comp. *Guide to Literature on Environmental Sciences.* Washington: American Society for Engineering Education, 1970.

184. Moholy-Nagy, Sibylle. *Matrix of Man: An Illustrated History of Urban Environment.* New York: Praeger, 1968.

Includes a selected list of general and specialized journals that regularly contain city plans and other information relating to the present, past, and future of urban environment.

185. Oxford University. Commonwealth Forestry Institute Library. *List of Periodicals and Serials in the Library,* 3rd ed. Oxford: The Library, 1968.

International, arranged by country. About 3,000 serials of all kinds, with some 500 magazines listed in an alphabetical index.

186. Schwartz, Elizabeth. "Ecology, Conservation, Etc." *Library Journal* 96 (Oct. 15, 1971): 3304–3305.

In the "Magazines" department. A selected annotated list of publications dealing with the finer, often technical, points.

187. "Selected List of Periodicals." *Stechert-Hafner Book News* 26 (Nov.-Dec. 1971): 38–39.

A cross-section of current periodicals, about 100 titles, reflecting "man's growing concern for the dangers threatening the future survival of all species." Unannotated. (See also No. 143.)

French Language

188. Bowen, Willis H. "Selective Critical Bibliography of Interest to Students of French and Spanish." *Bulletin of Bibliography* 27 (Apr.-June 1970): 29–33 ff.

Annotated list of about 90 titles, some of general linguistic and literary scope, but with emphasis on French and Spanish.

189. Cruickshank, John. "Literary Magazines in French." (London) *Times Literary Supplement* 3504 (Apr. 24, 1969): 445–446.

A general survey, with specific reference to 15 journals.

190. Lavers, Annette. "French Literary Magazines." (London) *Times Literary Supplement* 3521 (Aug. 21, 1969): 936.

An account of new trends, with some analysis of eight individual journals.

Genealogy

191. Cappon, Lester J. *American Genealogical Periodicals: A Bibliography with a Chronological Finding-List.* New York: New York Public Library, 1964.

Has alphabetical, chronological, and geographic lists of magazines beginning publication during the period of 1845 to 1961. The compiler's introduction provides insight into some of the problems involved with the material of genealogy. A standard list.

Geography

192. Burkett, Jack, ed. *Concise Guide to the Literature of Geography.* London: Ealing Technical College, 1967.

Gives summaries of the types of periodical coverage in the field, with titles, frequencies, and brief descriptions relating each to the coverage as a whole.

193. Harris, Chauncey D. *Annotated World List of Selected Current Geographical Serials in English.* Chicago: Univ. of Chicago Department of Geography, 1964.

An annotated listing of 62 serials in English and 56 more in various other languages. Useful for both the general and the specialized library.

194. Harris, Chauncey D. *Bibliographies and Reference Works for Research in Geography.* Chicago: Univ. of Chicago Department of Geography, 1967.

Supplements Wright and Platt's basic guide *(Aids to Geographical Research,* New York: Columbia Univ., 1947). Does not list periodicals, but does list guides to periodicals.

195. "New Periodicals of Geographical Interest." *Geographical Review* 59 (Apr. 1969): 290–294; 60 (Jan. 1970): 129–132.

Two examples of a more or less annual review in the form of a bibliographic essay, conducted recently by Lym S. Mullins.

German Language

196. Bridgwater, Patrick. "Little Magazines in German." (London) *Times Literary Supplement* 3484 (Dec. 5, 1968): 1393; 3488 (Jan. 2, 1969): 18; 3514 (Jul. 3, 1969): 734.

Discusses a couple of dozen or so representatives of the "booming" European little magazine industry.

Government Magazines

Note: The annual listing in the February issue of the *Monthly Catalog* is still the basic source for current information about the majority of U.S. government serial publications.

197. Andriot, John L. *Guide to U.S. Government Serials and Periodicals.* annual, 1962– . MacLean, Va.: Documents Index.

The major guide to this intricate and often idiosyncratic world. Arranged by issuing agency, with title, subject, and agency indexes. Bibliographic information, plus many informative annotations. Early editions are useful for tracing title changes, etc.

198. British Museum. State Papers Room. *Checklist of British Official Serial Publications,* 4th ed. London: The Museum, 1970.

Gives title, issuing body, frequency. Includes information on changed and suspended titles.

199. Kapilow, Mildred. "FAO to WMO: Selected Intergovernmental Periodicals." *RQ* 9 (Summer 1970): 306–309.

An annotated list of periodicals issued by various specialized agencies of the UN and other intergovernmental organizations.

200. U. S. Department of Labor. *Daily Newspapers, General Periodicals and Official State (U.S.) Periodicals Received in the Department of Labor Library.* Washington: The Library, 1971.

Alphabetical list of some 800 titles. No information other than title, but could be helpful for identifying state publications. (See also Nos. 124, 263.)

History

201. Boehm, Erich H. *Historical Periodicals.* Santa Barbara: Clio, 1961.

The basic list of historical periodicals. Includes brief annotations for 4,500 titles, not only in history, but related areas as well. International in scope.

202. Hay, Denys. "Historical Periodical: Some Problems." *History* 54 (June 1969): 165–177.

Remarks addressed to the Historical Association (England), but applicable to the American scene. Gives historical background and enumerates contemporary problems, such as costs, timelag, and specialization.

203. Kirby, John L. *Guide to Historical Periodicals in the English Language.* Helps for Students of History No. 80. London: Historical Association, 1970.

204. Pasler, Margaret, and Rudolph Pasler. "Periodical Abstracting and Indexing: U.S. History." *RQ* 10 (Spring 1971): 232–236.

An assessment of the various available tools.

205. Perman, D. H. *Bibliography and the Historian.* Santa Barbara: Clio, 1968.

A report on the Belmont Conference on bibliographic control. Periodicals, indexes, and abstracts are discussed in the first chapter, and there is other information relating to serial publications in the field of history. (See also No. 233).

Free Magazines

206. *Gebbie House Magazine Directory.* triennial, 1952– Sioux City: Gebbie Directory.

The basic guide to house organs published in the United States. Alphabetical by title, with geographical index. Particularly useful for libraries with tight budgets since many of the titles are free or inexpensive.

207. Smith, Adeline M. "The House Organ: An Index to Free Magazines." *RQ* 10 (Summer 1971): 319–321.

Tips about the utility of house organs.

Abstracts and Indexes

208. Christianson, Elin B. "Variation of Editorial Material in Periodicals Indexed in *Readers Guide. ALA Bulletin* 62 (Feb. 1968): 173–182.

A detailed discussion of variations in editions of national magazines and the effect on indexing and reference work.

209. Clements, F. "Indexing of Periodicals: a Survey," *Indexer* 7 (Autumn 1970): 70–79.

The individual indexes to about 100 periodicals taken from the *British Technology Index* were examined to test their adherence or nonadherence to British Standards 3700 and 2509, which make recommendations for the *Preparation of Indexes* and for *Periodicals of Reference Value*, respectively. Results are given in summary form (no specific titles mentioned) but the method and criteria used could be profitably applied in judging the quality of any periodical's index.

210. Collison, Robert L. *Abstracts and Abstracting Services.* Santa Barbara: ABC-Clio, 1971.

A fine general survey of abstracts as abstracts, offering considerable background and information about their production. Has a substantial list of selected readings on the subject.

211. Kujoth, Jean S. *Subject Guide to Periodical Indexes and Review Indexes.* Metuchen: Scarecrow, 1969.

Two lists, one by topic or subject, the other alphabetical. The latter has detailed information, including some about contents, type of access, material covered, etc.

212. U.S. Library of Congress. *A Guide to the World's Abstracting and Indexing Services in Science and Technology.* Philadelphia: National Federation of Science Abstracting and Indexing Services, 1963.

A classified approach to 1,855 titles. Also an alphabetical arrangement with bibliographical information, and a country and subject index. This is updated by the various editions of *Ulrich's* (No. 19).

213. Winn, V. A. "A Case Study in the Problems of Information Processing in a Social Science Field: The OSTI-SEA Project." *Aslib Proceedings* 23 (Feb. 1971): 76–88.

While this article concerns the *Sociology of Education Abstracts* project, many of the difficulties and problems discussed are shared by other fields, and the study provides some useful insights. (See also Nos. 275, 295, 298.)

Investments

214. Burgess, Robert S. "Specialized Investment Services." *Library Journal* 95 (Mar. 1, 1970): 867–869.

A discussion of reference materials, with an annotated list of recommended services. Oriented to the public library.

215. Cheney, Harlan L. "How Good Are Subscription Investment Advising Services?" *Financial Executive* 37 (Nov. 1969): 30–35.

Report of a 12-year study concluding that some subscription investment advisory services are able to select stocks which offer better than average return on investment. No specific services are mentioned.

Italian Language

216. Singh, G. "Literary Magazines in Italian." (London) *Times Literary Supplement* 3519 (Aug. 7, 1969): 885.

Discusses eight titles, some published outside Italy. A previous article by the author on the same subject appeared in *TLS* 3483 (Nov. 28, 1958): 1349.

Library Periodicals

217. Foster, Donald L. "Magazines in the Library School." *Journal of Education for Librarianship* 9 (Fall 1968): 144–148.

Citation analysis to discover most frequently used foreign and international library science journals in five U. S. library periodicals. The study indicates a "reluctance or inability to use" these publications on the part of the contributors to the U. S. journals. Author suggests priorities for library collections of serials in librarianship.

218. International Federation for Documentation. *Library and Documentation Journals,* 3rd ed. The Hague: The Federation, 1968.

Complements Springman and Winckler, below (Nos. 222, 223.).

219. "Know your ALA . . . Publishing for the Profession." *AIA Bulletin* 63 (Apr. 1969): 503–505.

A list, with subscription information, of about 28 ALA serials.

220. Moon, Eric. "The Library Press." *Library Journal* 94 (Nov. 15, 1969): 4104–4109.

Articulate and pointed criticism of American library magazines by a former editor of *LJ*.

221. Prentice, Ann. "Grapevine + Hard Data + Duplicator = Staff Association Newsletter." *RQ* 9 (Summer 1970): 310–316.

Includes an annotated list of 45 public and academic library staff newsletters.

222. Springman, Mary, and Betty Brown. *The Directory of Library Periodicals.* Philadelphia: Drexel Press, 1967.

An alphabetical list by issuing agency with a title index. Probably required only for extremely specialized collections.

223. Winckler, Paul A. *Library Periodicals Directory.* Brookville: Graduate Library School of Long Island Univ., 1967.

A subject-arranged and annotated list of world-wide library science periodicals. Also includes sections on bibliography, books, and book selection. For most purposes, probably the best list in its field.

Linguistics

224. Pietrzyk, Alfred, and A. Hood Roberts. *An Inventory of Information Services in the Language Sciences.* Washington: Center for Applied Linguistics, 1969. (ERIC Document 043 868)

Succinct information about 84 information centers throughout the world, with descriptions of their publications. An updated listing is planned.

225. Rappaport, Miriam W. *Citation Patterns in Selected Core Journals for Linguistics.* Washington: Center for Applied Linguistics, 1971. (ERIC Document 047 322)

Surveys 12 journals over one year (1967), reporting, among other things, percentages of citations in various time periods, median date and median age of citations. Findings are compared with those of similar studies in other fields. (See also No. 188.)

Literature

226. Chandler, G. *How To Find Out About Literature.* Oxford: Pergamon, 1968.

Has one chapter on magazines, with comments about various abstracts, indexes, and journals.

227. Gerstenberger, Donna, and George Hendrick. *Third Directory of Periodicals Publishing Articles in English and American Literature and Language.* Chicago: Swallow, 1970.

Describes 547 periodicals, including information on their major fields of interest and on the preparation of copy for each. Has subject index.

228. Lavelle, John. "Facts of Journal Publishing, IV." *Publications of the Modern Language Association* 81 (Nov. 1966): 3–12.

A revealing survey of 145 American journals in the modern language field, with information about circulation, editorial problems, number of manuscripts involved, publication time lag, and much more. Parts I, II and III appeared in *PMLA* in December 1954, September 1957 and December 1961, respectively.

229. Whelan, Alice, and Robert Pierson. "Another Approach: Serial Bibliographies on Literature." *RQ* 8 (Spring 1969): 188–192.

A useful list of journals in the field of literature that regularly (or more or less regularly) include a bibliography of material in their particular areas.

230. Wilcox, Earl. "Academic Newsletters." *Choice* 7 (Dec. 1970): 1346–1348.

Specialist publications in American and English literary studies are discussed in general, and about 20 specific titles "which seem to have most value for college and university library collections" are listed, with some subscription information. (See also No. 58.)

Little Magazines

231. *Directory of Little Magazines.* annual, 1964–   . 5218 Scottwood Rd. Paradise, Calif. 95969: Dustbooks.

An alphabetical, annotated list, with full bibliographic description and notes on contents. Supplemented by the *Small Press Review* (No. 236). The same publisher also issues an annual *Directory of Small Magazine Press Editors and Publishers,* begun in 1970.

232. Fulton, Len. "Anima Rising; Little Magazines in the Sixties." *American Libraries* 2 (Jan. 1971): 25–47.

An informative survey of the sixties. The accompanying bibliography lists over 100 titles, and, while there is some overlap with Kehde (Nos. 145, 146), the annotations are much more extensive.

233. Gilbert, James B. *Writers and Partisans: A History of Literary Radicalism in America.* New York: Wiley, 1968.

"A history of assumptions about literature and the role of the intellectual seen through an important institution, the little magazine." There is some emphasis on the *Partisan Review,* but otherwise this is a thoroughgoing study of a whole milieu.

234. Hoffman, Frederick, J., and Caroline F. Ulrich. *The Little Magazine: A History and Bibliography.* Princeton: Princeton Univ. Press, 1946.

The standard history and bibliography of the little magazine in the United States, England, and Europe to 1945.

235. May, Derwent. "American Little Magazines." (London) *Times Literary Supplement* 3525 (Sept. 18, 1969): 1032.

Comments restricted to some of the more recently begun titles.

236. *Small Press Review.* irregular, 1967–   . Paradise, Calif.: Dustbooks.

This is more or less quarterly. Put out by the editor of the annual *Directory of Little Magazines* (No. 231), it is an attempt to give a running report on new little magazines and books issued by small presses. Coverage is international, and bibliographic information complete.

237. *The Something Else Newsletter.* irregular, 1966–   . New York: Something Else Press.

Normally runs to only four pages, but is an excellent medium for keeping up with the news of the avant-garde press.

Mathematics

238. Committee on the Undergraduate Program in Mathematics. *Basic Library List.* Berkeley, Calif.: CUPM, January, 1965.

238a. London University Library. *Union List of Periodicals on Mathematics and Allied Subjects in London Libraries,* 2nd ed. London: The Library, 1968.

Medicine. See Biological Sciences.

Mexican-American. See Chicano.

Motion Pictures

239. Aaronson, Charles S. *International Motion Picture Almanac.* annual, 1929–   . New York: Quigley.

Includes a section on periodicals, usually with brief annotations.

240. Brown, Carol. "Reel Mags." *Synergy* No. 27 (May–June 1970): 16–20.

Annotated list of U.S. publications, intended as a cross-section of the kinds of film periodicals available.

241. "Magazines." *Film Culture* Nos. 48–49 (Winter-Spring 1970): 86.

Lists magazines in its "Books Received" section. A likely source, especially for foreign titles.

242. Reilly, Adam. *Current Film Periodicals in English: An Annotated Bibliography.* [n.p.], 1970.

Compiled under the direction of William Sloan, Donnell Public Library, New York.

243. Schillaci, A. "Bibliography for Film Study," in A. Schillaci and John M. Culkin. *Films Deliver: Teaching Creatively with Film,* pp. 307–322. New York: Citation Press, 1970.

244. *World List of Film Periodicals and Serials,* 2nd ed. Brussels: Cinematheque de Belgique, 1960.

This list of 769 titles with brief annotations is still useful. Hopefully there will soon be a new edition as the number of periodicals in this field has grown substantially since 1960.

Music

245. Duckles, Vincent H. *Music Reference and Research Materials: An Annotated Bibliography,* 2nd ed. New York: Free Press, 1967.

Cites 29 lists of music periodicals, with the reminder that the most comprehensive is still that in *Grove's Dictionary of Music and Musicians,* 5th ed., 1954. The forthcoming 6th edition presumably will update this.

246. London University Library, *Union List of Periodicals in Music in the Libraries of the University and Some Other London Libraries.* London: The Library, 1969.

247. Watanabe, Ruth T. *Introduction to Music Research.* Englewood Cliffs: Prentice-Hall, 1967.

One chapter is an annotated list arranged by broad subject headings. Another useful list, for any type of library, is the author's "Current Periodicals for Music Libraries," *Notes* 23 (Dec. 1966): 225–235.

248. Weichlein, William J. *A Checklist of American Music Periodicals, 1850–1900.* Detroit: Information Coordinators, 1970.

Unannotated list of 309 titles which commenced publication during the period specified. Six extended into the twentieth century, and none is current. Two appendixes give chronological and geographic arrangements. Includes selected library locations. A good guide for the research collection.

Philosophy

249. Dennison, Anne T. "Philosophy Periodicals: An Annotated Select World List of Current Serial Publications." *International Library Review* 2 (Jul. 1970): 355–386.

Covers only about 100 of the serial publications in the field, but claims to include all the major U. S. and English titles. Besides general descriptions and subscription data, includes information about indexing, reprints, microforms, and special features.

250. U. S. Library of Congress. *Philosophical Periodicals.* Washington: The Library, 1952.

Although dated, this is still a basic world list of major periodicals in the field.

Photography

251. Hanson, Peter P. "Abstract Journals in Photography." *Sci-Tech News* 23 (Summer 1969): 38–39.

Concerned with technical rather than esthetic aspects. A list of 25 "most productive" nonabstracting journals is appended.

Physics

252. "Books and Journals, a Special Report." *Physics Today* 23 (Aug. 1970): 51–71.

Includes a list of about 40 periodicals in astronomy and physics beginning since 1968, with some comments about the pros and cons of journal mergers.

253. Cooper, Marianne, and Candace W. Thayer. *Primary Journal Literature of Physics.* New York: American Institute of Physics, 1969. (ERIC Document 038 996)

An analysis of the basic characteristics of 491 periodicals covered by *Physics Abstracts,* including sponsorship, language, frequency, coverage other than *Physics Abstracts,* etc.

254. Cooper, Marianne, and Edward Terry. *Secondary Services in Physics.* New York: American Institute of Physics, 1969. (ERIC Document 038 999)

The same sort of analysis as applied in No. 253, involving 69 services.

254a. Herschman, Arthur et. al. "New Information Program for AIP," *Physics Today* v. 22 (December 1969) pp. 29–32.

254b. "IPPS Revises Journals, AIP to be North American Agent," *Physics Today* v. 21 (Oct. 1968) p. 67.

254c. Koch, H. William. "Current Physics Information," *Science* v. 174 (Nov. 26, 1971) pp. 918–922.

255. Koch, H. William. *Economics of Primary Journals in Physics.* New York: American Institute of Physics, 1969. (ERIC Document 038 990)

Presents the basic economics of the present system of journal publishing, plus some preliminary considerations for new, more user-oriented journals. Has carry-over for publishing in other fields.

256. Koch, H. William. *The Role of the Primary Journal in Physics.* New York: American Institute of Physics, 1970. (ERIC Document 038 989)

A discussion of anticipated changes in science communication techniques.

Political Science

257. *ABC POL SCI.* 8/yr., 1969–   . Santa Barbara: ABC-Clio.

A regular December feature of this current awareness service is a list of journals cited during the year, in the form of an analysis of contents.

258. Brock, Clifton. *Literature of Political Science: A Guide for Students, Librarians and Teachers.* New York: R. R. Bowker, 1969.

A general guide to the literature, this has a chapter on indexes and abstracts in the field.

259. Finch, Eleanor H. "Student International Law Journals." *American Journal of International Law* 63 (Apr. 1969): 304–306.

Annotations and order information on five new student-edited journals. Updates similar lists published in this magazine in April 1965 and January 1966.

260. Harmon, Robert B. *Political Science: A Bibliographical Guide to the Literature, Supplement.* Metuchen: Scarecrow, 1968.

Original volume was published in 1965. Both contain annotated lists of selected periodicals in English.

261. *International Bibliography of Political Science.* annual, 1953– . Publisher varies.

Like the other UNESCO bibliographies in this series, a good place to check for new titles.

262. Mason, John Brown. *Research Resources: Annotated Guide to the Social Sciences: Vol. 1, International Relations and Recent History: Indexes, Abstracts and Periodicals.* Santa Barbara: ABC-Clio, 1968.

Describes over 400 periodicals, plus about 130 indexes and abstracts.

263. Mason, John Brown. *Research Resources: Annotated Guide to the Social Sciences, Vol. 2, Official Publications: U.S. Government, UN, International Organizations and Statistical Sources.* Santa Barbara: ABC-Clio, 1971.

Includes many serials, arranged by subject, with index. Orientation is to political science.

264. Merritt, Richard L., and Gloria Pyszka. *Student Political Scientist's Handbook.* Cambridge: Schenkman, 1969.

Has a selected annotated list of periodicals.

265. Stewart, June L. "Literature of Politics: A Citation Analysis." *International Library Review* 2 (Jul. 1970): 329–353.

A thoroughly done qualitative and quantitative examination of the literature of politics, with interesting implications about the utility of periodicals in the field.

266. Teodori, Massimo. *New Left: A Documentary History.* Indianapolis: Bobbs, 1969.

Includes a list of current and defunct periodicals, large and little, and indicates those considered to be "particularly important." About 90 titles. (See also No. 303.)

Psychology

267. Garvey, William D., and Belver C. Griffith. *Reports of the American Psychological Association's Project on Scientific Information Exchange in Psychology.* 2 vols. Washington: American Psychological Association, 1963–1965.

A landmark study, providing considerable information about the function of serials and their use in the information process.

268. Mannino, Fortune V. *Consultation in Mental Health and Related Fields: A Reference Guide.* Public Health Service Publication No. 1920. Chevy Chase: National Institute of Mental Health, 1969.

Essentially a guide to the literature in the relatively new field of mental health consultation, this work contains a list of journals consulted. Most are in the behavioral sciences or medicine.

269. Tompkins, Margaret, and Norma Shirley. *A Checklist of Serials in Psychology and Allied Fields.* New York: Whitson, 1969.

The compilers state that most of the information here is available elsewhere, but not in one volume. Includes subscription data, date of first issue, circulation, objectives, fields of interest, and related facts. Attempts to be comprehensive. Current publications only.

270. Woods, Joan B., et al. "Basic Psychiatric Literature: II, Articles and Article Sources. *Medical Library Association Bulletin* 56 (Oct. 1968): 404–427.

Results of a study of reading lists from 140 psychiatric training programs, with statistical analysis of serials in which recommended articles appeared. Part I of this study analyzed the recommended books on the reading lists.

Religion and Theology

271. *American Jewish Yearbook.* annual, 1900–. New York: American Jewish Committee.

Sometimes includes a section "Jewish Periodicals," arranged by state and province, with titles, address, editors' names, etc., for those publications known to be current and in existence at least one year or so.

272. *Associated Church Press Directory.* biennial. Chicago: Associated Church Press.

A roster of about 200 American Protestant and Orthodox periodicals, with typical directory-type information.

273. *Bibliography of Church and Synagogue Library Resources.* Bryn Mawr: Church and Synagogue Library Association, 1969. (ERIC Document 039 912)

Not a list of religious periodicals, but of titles that might be of help to those who operate church or synagogue libraries. Ten titles given.

274. *Catholic Press Directory.* annual, 1923–. New York: Catholic Press Association.

Lists U. S. and Canadian newspapers and magazines, with information designed primarily for the advertiser.

275. Diener, Ronald E. "Status of Indexing: Theological and Religious Periodicals." *RQ* 10 (Summer 1971): 324–328.

An evaluation of current bibliographic access, with some suggestions for improvement.

Children's and Teenage Magazines

Note: There has been much "recommending" in this reading area, and a plentitude of lists has resulted. Included here are only a few that are concerned solely or at least substantially with magazines, though some of the "Basic Book Collection for . . ." compilations do also include suggested subscriptions. Besides lists, there are some items about magazines in this area.

276. Carroll, Evelyn. "Magazines on Trial." *Top of the News* 25 (June 1969): 400–401.

The Magazine Evaluation Committee of the Young Adult Services Division of the American Library Association presents some criteria for selecting young adult magazines for school and public libraries.

277. *The Booklist.* bi-w, 1970–

"Periodicals for School Libraries" is an annotated listing of magazines which acts as an update and supplement to Scott's *Periodicals for School Libraries.* It is prepared by the same committee that worked with Scott, and appears at least twice a year in April and November. The reviews are good to excellent, and nicely supplement those found in *Top-of-the-News.*

278. Dobler, Lavinia G., and Muriel L. Fuller. *Dobler World Directory of Youth Periodicals*, 3rd ed. New York: Citation Press, 1970.

An international listing of 1,000 magazines. American magazines are arranged by subject; foreign magazines are grouped into (1) English-language and (2) non-English-language, by country. Gives reading level and sufficient ordering information.

279. Donaldson, Helen E. J. "A Selected List of Periodicals for Children's Libraries, Librarians and Teachers." *Ontario Library Review* 55 (June 1971): 109–121.

A well-balanced list, though in terms of provenance may have some emphasis on Canadian and British publications. Annotated.

280. Johnson, W. Duane. "The School Library Press: A Survey of State Association Periodicals." *School Libraries* 19 (Spring 1970): 21–25.

Description of a survey done by AASL Publications Committee which includes a list of state school library periodicals.

281. Scott, Marian H., ed. *Periodicals for School Libraries: A Guide to Magazines, Newspapers and Periodical Indexes.* Chicago: American Library Association, 1969.

An alphabetically arranged list of 429 magazines for grades K–12. Selection and annotation were done by an ALA committee. Basic data are given for each title, with indication of grade level. No judgment of relative quality is given, but this is often obvious from the annotations. The scope of the list is determined by the content of contemporary school curricula, so that many types of periodicals are excluded though their value is recognized by the compilers.

282. Sebesta, Sam L. "Magazines for Children." *Reading Teacher* 22 (Oct. 1968): 73–76.

The author is critical of modern magazines for children, and presents considerations he thinks must be made in promoting magazines in a reading program.

283. Smith, Adeline M. "Free and Inexpensive Magazines for Schools." *Library Journal* 96 (June 15, 1971): 2065–2066.

An annotated list of nine titles.

284. Suchara, Helen T., and Jane A. Romatowski. "Magazines and Newspapers for Children." *Childhood Education* 46 (May 1970): 443–447.

Prepared by the Among the Magazines Committee of the Association for Childhood Education International. Annotated list of magazines intended for children and adult magazines of value to children.

285. *Top-of-the-News,* q. 1967–   .

"Magazine evaluation" is an annotated listing of magazines suitable for young adults. Since 1971 the YASD Magazine Evaluation Committee, which prepares the annotations, has shifted from individual titles to groups, i.e. current listings of magazines on automobiles and motorcycles, sports, etc. The evaluations and annotations are excellent, of considerable value to any library serving both young people and adults.

286. Wright, Sylvia H. *Magazines Recommended for Use with Children, Grades K–12: A Comparative Survey of Six Basic Lists Compiled by Librarians and Educators,* 2nd ed. Teaneck: Franklin Square-Mayfair Subscription Agency, 1969. (ERIC Document 029 873)

An annotated list, with grade level and indexing data. Information as of Spring 1969. (See also No. 112.)

Science

287. Brookes, B. C. "The Growth, Utility, and Obsolescence of Scientific Periodical Literature." *Journal of Documentation* 26 (Dec. 1970): 282–294.

A technical consideration of the problems involved in attempts to measure rates of obsolescence. Some recently proposed methods are criticized, and lines of investigation proposed.

287a. Brown, W. S., Pierce, J. R. and Traub, J. F. "The Future of Scientific Journals." *Science* v. 158 (1967) p. 1153.

288. Committee on Scientific and Technical Communication of the National Academy of Sciences and National Academy of Engineering. *Scientific and Technical Communication, a Pressing National Problem and Recommendations for its Solution.* Washington: National Academy of Sciences, 1969.

An important document known familiarly as "The SAT-COM Report," this is an exhaustive study of the whole communication process. It includes thorough analyses of primary communications, access services, document availability, bibliographic control, and services for the user. A must for anyone seriously concerned with the information process.

289. *Current Serials Received by the National Lending Library—March 1971.* London: Her Majesty's Stationery Office, 1971.

Thirty-six thousand titles, published in over 100 countries, thought to be current and of use to practitioners in natural sciences, technologies, and social sciences. Because of the increasingly hazy lines between "disciplines," a good number of these titles are nominally in the humanities and social sciences.

290. *Directory of Canadian Scientific and Technical Periodicals: A Guide to Currently Published Titles,* 4th ed. Ottawa: National Science Library, 1969.

Classified unannotated list of 890 titles, with dates, frequency, price, editor, and where indexed. Periodicals in both English and French are included, and those with editions in both languages are so noted.

290a. Fallwell, William F. "Information Explosion Closer to Control." *Chemical and Engineering News* v. 49 (December 20, 1971) pp. 28, 33, 36.

291. Fowler, Maureen. *Guides to Scientific Periodicals.* London: The Library Association, 1966.

The best single guide to the vast number of specialized and general lists, directories, etc., in the field of scientific periodicals. Some 1,048 items are arranged by subject and briefly annotated.

291a. Grogan, Denis. *Science and Technology; an Introduction to the Literature.* London: Clive Bingley, 1970.

292. Harvard University Library. *Current Journals in the Sciences,* 4th ed. Cambridge: The Library, 1970.

An alphabetical list of 5,300 titles.

293. Herner, Saul. *Brief Guide to Sources of Scientific and Technical Information.* Washington: Information Resources Press, 1969.

In terms of periodical publications, this is especially strong on indexing and abstracting services.

293a. Herschman, A. "The Primary Journal: Past, Present, and Future." *J. Chemical Documentation* v. 10 (1970): p. 37.

294. Himmelsbach, Carl J., and Grace E. Boyd. *Guide to Scientific and Technical Journals in Translation.* New York: Special Libraries Association, 1968.

Gives ordering and other information about English translations.

295. Keenan, Stella. "Abstracting and Indexing Services in Science and Technology." in *Annual Review of Information Science and Technology.* Vol. 4. Chicago: Encyclopedia Britannica, 1969, 273–303.

Reviews developments noted in the literature during 1967 and 1968. A thorough, reliable, state-of-the-art presentation.

296. Kinkade, Robert G. *Desirable Characteristics of a Scientific Publication System.* Washington: American Psychological Association, 1970. (ERIC Document 038 995)

Six characteristics are evaluated: (1) prompt dissemination, (2) focused distribution, (3) diversity of content, (4) catalog of abstracts, (5) articles printed separately, and (6) low acceptance criteria.

297. Krondick, David A. *History of Scientific and Technical Periodicals.* New York: Scarecrow Press, 1962.

297a. Matarazzo, James M. "Scientific Journals." *Special Libraries* v. 63 (February 1972) pp. 53–58.

298. National Federation of Science Abstracting and Indexing Services. *Federation Member Service Descriptions, 1969–70.* Philadelphia: The Federation, 1969.

298a. Pritchard, Alan. *A Guide to Computer Literature.* London: Clive Bingley, 1969.

299. "Science Abstracting Services—Commercial, Institutional and Personal." *Library Trends* 16 (Jan. 1968).

Entire issue devoted to the subject. There have been developments since this was published, of course, but most of it is still pertinent, though individual articles vary considerably in level and specificity.

299a. "Science Libraries Face Budget Bind." *Chemical and Engineering News* v. 50 (March 6, 1972) pp. 22, 25.

299b. Virgo, Julie A. "The Review Article: its Characteristics and Problems." *Library Quarterly* v. 41 (October 1971) pp. 275–291.

300. Wood, James L. *A Review of the Availablility of Primary Scientific and Technical Documents within the United States,* 3 vols. Columbus: American Chemical Society, 1969. (ERIC Document 046 437–39)

A study of availability of materials indexed in *Chemical Abstracts* is given libraries and via interlibrary loan. Volume 1 has a statement of objectives and the results of the study. Volumes 2 and 3 contain background and supportive material.

301. Wooster, Harold. "The Future of Scientific Publishing—Or, What Will Scientists Be Doing for Brownie Points." *Journal of the Washington Academy of Sciences* 60 (June 1970): 41–45.

Somewhat after-dinner-speechish, but with worthwhile content. The author comments on the increasing number of scientific journals, and the problems this is causing. He considers use, obsolescence, and costs.

302. *World List of Scientific Periodicals,* 4th ed. 3 vols. London: Butterworth, 1963–1965.

A listing of more than 60,000 titles issued between 1900 and 1960. Arrangement is alphabetical by title. Kept up to date by separate annual publications of pertinent *British Union Catalogue of Periodicals* (No. 24) entries. (See also Nos. 39, 46, 55, 67, 212.)

Social Sciences

303. Goodman, Steven E. *Guide to Two Hundred Free Periodicals in the Social Sciences: Education, Business, Management, Government.* Donellen, N.J.: Education & Training Associates, 1970.

304. *International Social Science Journal.* quarterly, 1949– .

Has annual lists, international, with full annotations. The 1970 list appeared in 22 (no. 1, 1970): 129–140.

305. *Periodicals in the Social Sciences and Humanities Currently Received by Canadian Libraries,* 2 vols. Ottawa: National Library, 1968.

An interim compilation prior to publication of a full-scale union list. About 12,000 titles in an alphabetical arrangement.

306. Senn, Peter R., and Mary Senn. *A Short Guide to the Literature of the Social Sciences.* Social Science Education

Consortium, Publication 126. Boulder: The Consortium, 1968. (ERIC Document 039 159)

Has a selected, unannotated short title list of journals. Might be of use for a small library "basic" collection in the field.

307. Vesenyi, Paul E. *European Periodical Literature in the Social Sciences and the Humanities.* Metuchen: Scarecrow, 1969.

An analyzed list of indexes and abstracts, miscellaneous bibliographical directors and union lists. Emphasis on European tools.

308. White, Carl M. *Sources of Information in the Social Sciences.* Totowa: Bedminster Press, 1964.

The standard general guide in this field. Serves to introduce the reader to magazines in the following areas: social sciences in general, anthropology, business, education, history, political science, psychology, and sociology. A new edition is hoped for.

309. Wood, D. N., and C. A. Bower. "Use of Social Science Periodical Literature." *Journal of Documentation* 25 (June 1969): 108–122.

The results of a survey made at the National Lending Library (England). Includes a copy of the questionnaire used, a list of titles requested six or more times, and a list of abstracting and indexing services cited five or more times.

310. *World List of Social Science Periodicals,* 3rd ed. Paris: UNESCO, 1966.

Geographical arrangement, with indexes by title, institution, and subject, of scholarly periodicals currently published in 1963. Though obviously dated in terms of births and deaths, this remains a basic list.

Sociology

311. *International Bibliography of Sociology.* annual, 1957–   Publisher varies.

Like the other UNESCO bibliographies in this series, a good place to check for new titles.

312. Pease, John, and Joan Rytina. "Sociology Reference Periodicals." *Sociology and Social Research* 53 (Oct. 1968): 95–98.

Annotated list of ten bibliographic services, all of which are at least partly in English, and are not interdisciplinary. The compilers claim that the list includes every sociology reference periodical of this nature ever published.

313. "Selected List of Sociological Journals." In Erwin O. Smigel, ed., *Handbook on the Study of Social Problems,* pp. 408–412. Chicago: Rand McNally, 1971.

A list of 154 journals, current and noncurrent, whose contents are at least 30 percent in English. "Core journals" are indicated. There is also a list of secondary periodical publications "of value to researchers in sociology."

Space. See Aeronautics and Space Science.

Spanish Language

314. Bleznick, Donald W. "Guide to Journals in the Hispanic Field: Selected annotated List of Journals Central to the Study of Spanish and Spanish American Language and Literature." *Hispania* 52 (Nov. 1969): 723–737.

Seventy-seven journals, mostly current. Has a useful subject and area index.

315. Zubatsky, David S. "Bibliography of Cumulative Indexes to Hispanic American Language and Literary Reviews of the 19th and 20th Centuries." *Inter-American Review of Bibliography* 20 (Jan. 1970): 20–57.

(See also No. 188.) See also Chicano section.

Theater

316. Kottwinkel, James L., et al. "A Checklist of Current Theatre Arts Periodicals." *Theatre Documentation* 1 (Spring 1969): 3–36.

An unannotated list of about 275 theater and theater-related periodicals, with ample bibliographic information. International in scope.

317. Stratman, Carl J. *American Theatrical Periodicals, 1789–1967: A Bibliographical Guide.* Durham: Duke Univ. Press, 1970.

Chronological arrangement, with full bibliographic treatment, of nearly 800 journals. A helpful schematic of publication spans is provided. Gives library locations.

Women's Magazines

318. Kitchen, Paddy. "I Read Them Anyway." *New Statesman* 80 (Aug. 14, 1970): 169.

319. Magid, Nora L. "Heart, the Mind, the Pickled Okra: Women's Magazines in the Sixties." *North American Review* 7 (Winter 1970): 20–29.

320. Women's History Library (2325 Oak St., Berkeley, Calif.). *Syllabi and Bibliographies.* 1971.

One of a number of bibliographies issued by this leading Women's Liberation group—and a solid counter to most items about women's magazines.

INDEX

Mecanica Popular, 469
Mechanical Engineering, 286
MECHANICAL ENGINEERING, 284
Mechanix Illustrated, 428
The Medal Collector, 431
MEDIA, see COMMUNICATIONS AND MEDIA
Media Decisions, 194
Media Industry Newsletter, 194
Media & Methods, 194
Media Mix Newsletter, 195
Media/Scope, ceased
Medical Aspects of Human Sexuality, 402
Medical Dimensions, see MBA: the magazine of management education for the masters in business administration
Medical Economics, 545
Medical History, see Bulletin of the History of Medicine
Medical Letter on Drugs and Therapeutics, 407
MEDICAL SCIENCES, 543
Medical Socioeconomic Research Sources, 20
Medical World News, 546
The Mediterranean Review, 505
Meerestechnik/Marine Technology, 615
Mekeel's Weekly Stamp News, 432
Mele, 648
Melody Maker, 580
Memphis Tri-State Defender, see Chicago Daily Defender
Menckeniana, 523
MEN'S MAGAZINES, 549
Mental Health, see Mind and Mental Health
Mental Health Court Digest, see Civil Rights Court Digest
Mental Health Scope, see Drugs and Drug Abuse Education Newsletter
Mental Hygiene, 669
Mental Retardation, see American Journal of Mental Deficiency
Mercury, 75
Mergers & Acquisitions, 253
Meridiano, 467
Merkur, 315
Merry-Go-Round, see Vacation Fun
Messenger of Mathematics, see Quarterly Journal of Mathematics
Metallurgical Abstracts, see Metals Abstracts
Metals Abstracts, 20
Metals Abstracts Index, see Metals Abstracts
Meteorological and Geoastrophysical Abstracts, 20
Meteorological Magazine, 79

Metro, 318
Metropolitan Life Insurance Company. Statistical Bulletin, 402
Metropolitan Museum of Art. Bulletin, N.S., 68
Mexican World, 462
Mexico This Month, 722
Mexico (city) Universidad Nacional. Revista, 467
Miamian, 175
Michigan Business Review, 130
Michigan Law Review, 473
Michigan Librarian, 484, 493
Michigan Quarterly Review, 505
Micro News Bulletin, see Micrographic Weekly
MICROBIOLOGY, 101
Microbiology Abstracts, see Aquatic Sciences and Fisheries Abstracts
Microcard Bulletin, see Microform Review
Microcosm, see Microform Review
Microdoc, 484
Microfilm Newsletter, see Micrographic Weekly
Microform Review, 121
Micrographic Weekly, 484
Micrographics News and Views, see Micrographic Weekly
Micropublisher, see Microform Review
Microwave Engineers Buyers Guide, see Microwave Journal
Microwave Journal, 674
Mid-America, 418
Mid-Atlantic Graphic Arts Review, 69
The Middle East Journal, 307
Middle Eastern Affairs, 307
Middle Eastern Studies, 307
Midstream, 683
Midway, ceased
Midwest Folklore, see Folklore Institute. Journal
Midwest Journal of Political Science, 658
Midwest Quarterly, 506
Mike Shayne Mystery Magazine, 320
The Militant, 599
Militaria, 424
Military Affairs, the journal of military history, including Theory and Technology, 554
Military Collector and Historian, 424
Military Law Review, 473
MILITARY MAGAZINES, 553
Military Modelling, 435
Military Review, 554
Mill News Letter, 523
Milton Quarterly, 523
Milwaukee, 175

Mind, 628
Mind and Mental Health, 669
Mineral Digest, 248
Mineralogical Abstracts, see Mineralogical Magazine
Mineralogical Magazine, 248
Mineralogical Record, 248
MINERALOGY, see EARTH SCIENCES
The Miner's Voice, 457
Minerva, 690
Mini-Bike Guide, 85
Minkus Stamp Journal, 432
Minnesota AAA Motorist, see American Motorist
Minnesota Journal of Education, 265
Minnesota Libraries, 484, 493
The Minnesota Review, 506
Miss Chatelaine, 760
Mississippi Educational Advance, 265
Mississippi Library News, 493
Mississippi News and Views, 726
Mississippi Valley Historical Review, see Journal of American History
Mister Miracle, see The New Gods
Mobilia, 69
The Mobster Times, see Screw
Model Airplane News, 435
Model Car Science, 435
Model Railroader, 435
Model Rocketry, 435
MODELS (HANDICRAFT), see HOBBIES/MODELS
Moderator, ceased
Modern Age, 590
Modern Asian Studies, 172
Modern Bride, see Bride's Magazine
Modern Cycle Magazine, 85
Modern Drama, 718
Modern Fiction Studies, 516
Modern Geology, 248
Modern Gymnast, 715
Modern Haiku, see Haiku Magazine
Modern International Drama, 718
Modern Keyboard Review, 574
Modern Language Journal, 499
Modern Language Notes/MLN, 517
Modern Language Quarterly, 499
Modern Language Review 499
Modern Lithography, 142
Modern Man, 551
Modern Manufacturing, 142
Modern Maturity, 44
Modern Media Teacher, see K–Eight
Modern Medicine, 546
Modern Nursing Home, 547
Modern Occasions, 506
Modern Office Procedures, 131
Modern Philology, 499
Modern Photography, 633
Modern Poetry in Translation, 653